ELEMENTS OF
LITERATURE
ANNOTATED TEACHER'S EDITION

SIXTH COURSE

Literature of Britain

The Authors

Robert Anderson is a playwright, novelist, screen-writer, and teacher. His plays include *Tea and Sympathy; Silent Night, Lonely Night; You Know I Can't Hear You When the Water's Running;* and *I Never Sang for My Father.* His screenplays include *The Nun's Story* and *The Sand Pebbles.* Mr. Anderson has taught at the Writer's Workshop at the University of Iowa, the American Theatre Wing Professional Training Program, and the Salzburg Seminar in American Studies. He is a Past President of the Dramatists' Guild, Vice-President of the Authors' League of America, and a member of the Theater Hall of Fame. He makes his home in Connecticut and New York.

John Malcolm Brinnin, author of six volumes of poetry which have received many prizes and awards, is a member of the American Academy and Institute of Arts and Letters. He is also a critic of poetry and a biographer of poets and was for a number of years Director of New York's famous Poetry Center. His teaching career, begun at Vassar College, included long terms at the University of Connecticut and Boston University, where he succeeded Robert Lowell as professor of creative writing and contemporary letters. Mr. Brinnin has also written *Dylan Thomas in America: An Intimate Journal* and *Sextet: T. S. Eliot & Truman Capote & Others.* He divides his time between Duxbury, Massachusetts, and Key West, Florida.

John Leggett is a novelist, a biographer, and a teacher who went to the Writer's Workshop at the University of Iowa in the spring of 1969, expecting to teach for a single semester. In 1970 he assumed temporary charge of the program and was its Director for the next seventeen years. Mr. Leggett's novels include *Wilder Stone, The Gloucester*

Branch, Who Took the Gold Away, Gulliver House, and *Making Believe.* He is also the author of the highly acclaimed biography *Ross and Tom: Two American Tragedies.* His short fiction, articles, and reviews have appeared in *Harper's, Esquire, Mademoiselle, The Ladies Home Journal,* and the *Los Angeles Times.* A native New Yorker, Mr. Leggett now lives in San Francisco, where he is working on a biography of William Saroyan.

John Algeo is Professor of English at the University of Georgia at Athens. He is co-author with Thomas Pyles of *The Origins and Development of the English Language.*

Harley Henry is Associate Professor in the English Department of Macalester College in St. Paul, Minnesota. He teaches courses on the Romantic period, as well as in nineteenth-century American literature, the novel, and baseball fiction.

Donald Gray is Professor in the Department of English at Indiana University, Bloomington. Dr. Gray has written essays on Victorian poetry and culture and has been editor of *College English.*

David Adams Leeming is Professor of English at the University of Connecticut and the author of several books on mythology, including *Mythology: The Voyage of the Hero; Flights: Readings in Magic, Mysticism, Fantasy, and Myth;* and *The World of Myth.*

C. F. Main was for many years Professor of English at Rutgers University in New Brunswick, New Jersey. He is the editor of *Poems: Wadsworth Handbook and Anthology* and has written reviews and articles on sixteenth-, seventeenth-, and eighteenth-century literature.

ELEMENTS OF LITERATURE
ANNOTATED TEACHER'S EDITION

SIXTH COURSE

Literature of Britain

Holt, Rinehart and Winston, Inc.
Harcourt Brace Jovanovich, Inc.
Austin • Orlando • San Diego • Chicago • Dallas • Toronto

Tale,'' pp. 232–249; the ''Prologue,'' pp. 19–41, by Geoffrey Chaucer, and a passage from the Introduction by Nevill Coghill from *Chaucer: The Canterbury Tales*, translated by Nevill Coghill (Penguin Classics, Revised Edition, 1977). Copyright 1951 by Nevill Coghill; copyright © 1958, 1960, 1975, 1977 by Nevill Coghill. From *Bede: A History of the English Church and People* (Retitled: ''The Saxon Temples Are Destroyed'' and ''Caedmon''), translated by Leo Sherley-Price (Penguin Classics, Revised Edition, 1968). Copyright © 1955, 1968 by Leo Sherley-Price. **Peters Fraser & Dunlop Group Ltd.:** ''Naming of Parts'' from *A Map of Verona* by Henry Reed. Copyright 1947, 1975 by the Estate of Henry Reed. From *When the Going Was Good* by Evelyn Waugh. Copyright 1946, © 1976 by Peters Fraser & Dunlop Group Ltd. **S. G. Phillips:** From *Look Back in Anger* by John Osborne. Copyright © 1957 by Criterion Books, Inc. **Random House, Inc.:** ''Musée des Beaux Arts,'' ''As I Walked Out One Evening,'' and ''The Unknown Citizen'' from *W. H. Auden: Collected Poems*, edited by Edward Mendelson. Copyright 1940 and renewed © 1968 by W. H. Auden. From *Ulysses* by James Joyce. Copyright 1918 by James Joyce. From *The Letters and Journals of Katherine Mansfield*, edited by C. K. Stead. Copyright © 1977 by C. K. Stead. ''The Express'' from *Collected Poems 1928–1953* by Stephen Spender. Copyright 1934 and renewed © 1962 by Stephen Spender. From *The Thirties and After* by Stephen Spender. Copyright © 1978 by Stephen Spender. **Marian Reiner on behalf of Joan Daves:** From *An Only Child* by Frank O'Connor. Copyright © 1961 and renewed © 1989 by Frank O'Connor. **Rogers, Coleridge and White Ltd.:** ''The Wanderer'' from *The Anglo-Saxon World* by Kevin Crossley-Holland. Copyright © 1982 by Boydell and Brewer. **Russell & Volkening:** ''Katherine Mansfield's 'Miss Brill''' by Eudora Welty. Copyright 1949, © 1967 by Eudora Welty. **Russell & Volkening Inc. as agents for Nadine Gordimer:** ''The Soft Voice of the Serpent'' from *The Soft Voice of the Serpent* by Nadine Gordimer. Copyright © 1952 and renewed © 1980 by Nadine Gordimer. **Charles Scribner's Sons, an imprint of Macmillan Publishing Company:** From *My Early Life: A Roving Commission* by Winston Churchill. Copyright 1930 by Charles Scribner's Sons; copyright renewed © 1958 by Winston Churchill. **Simon & Schuster, Inc.:** ''No Witchcraft for Sale'' from *African Stories* by Doris Lessing. Copyright © 1951, 1953, 1954, 1957, 1958, 1962, 1963, 1964, 1965 by Doris Lessing. **The Society of Authors, as the Literary Representatives of the Estate of James**

Joyce: From ''Stephen Hero'' by James Joyce. **Stanford University Press:** From *Bernard Shaw: The Darker Side* by Arnold Silver. Published by Stanford University Press. **Nancy R. Sweeten:** From *The Ballad Book*, edited by MacEdward Leach. **Twayne Publishers, a division of G. K. Hall and Co., Boston:** From *Oscar Wilde* by Donald H. Ericksen. Copyright © 1977 by Twayne Publishers, a division of G. K. Hall and Co. **The University of Chicago Press:** From ''Sir Gawain and the Green Knight'' from *The Complete Works of the Gawain Poet*, translated by John Gardner. Copyright © 1965 by The University of Chicago Press. **University of Nebraska Press:** ''Riddle #32,'' ''Riddle #33,'' ''Riddle #47'' ''The Seafarer,'' and from the Introduction to *Poems from the Old English*, translated by Burton Raffel. Copyright © 1960, 1964 by the University of Nebraska Press. **University of Toronto Press:** ''The Flood Tide'' by E. J. Pratt from *E. J. Pratt: Complete Poems*, edited by Sandra Djwa and R. G. Moyles. Copyright 1945, © 1968 by E. J. Pratt. **Viking Penguin, a division of Penguin Books USA Inc.:** ''The Destructors'' from *Collected Stories* by Graham Greene. Copyright © 1972 by Graham Greene. Copyright 1930 and renewed © 1958 by The Viking Press, Inc. From *Finnegans Wake* by James Joyce. Copyright 1939 by James Joyce; copyright © 1967 by George Joyce and Lucia Joyce. From *My Brother's Keeper: James Joyce's Early Years* by Stanislaus Joyce. Copyright © 1958, 1986 by Nelly Joyce. ''Snake'' from *The Complete Poems of D. H. Lawrence*, collected and edited by Vivan de Sola Pinto and F. Warren Roberts. Copyright © 1964, 1971 by Angelo Ravagli and C. M. Weekley, Executors for the Estate of Frieda Lawrence Ravagli. ''The Rocking-Horse Winner'' from *The Complete Short Stories of D. H. Lawrence*. Copyright 1934 by Frieda Lawrence; copyright renewed © 1962 by Angelo Ravagli and C. M. Weekley, Executors of the Estate of Frieda Lawrence Ravagli. ''In the Shadow of War'' from *Stars of the New Curfew* by Ben Okri. Copyright © 1988 by Ben Okri. ''The Rear Guard'' from *Collected Poems* by Siegfried Sassoon. Copyright 1946 and renewed © 1974 by Siegfried Sassoon. **George Weidenfield & Nicolson Limited:** From *The Waterfall* by Margaret Drabble. Copyright © 1969 by Margaret Drabble. **Yale University Press:** From ''Heorot and the Guest-Hall of Eden: Symbolic Metaphor and the Design of *Beowulf*'' from *The Guest-Hall of Eden: Four Essays on the Design of Old English Poetry* by Alvin A. Lee. Copyright © 1972 by Yale University.

PICTURE CREDITS

Unit 1 p. 1: C.M. Dixon/Photoresources, London; p. 2: Adam Woolfitt/Woodfin Camp; p. 3: Patrick Ward/Wheeler Pictures; p. 5 top: Bridgeman Art Library, London; 5 bot.: Lee Boltin, Croton-on-Hudson, New York; p. 7: Farrell Grehan, Photo Researchers; p. 8 top: Bridgeman Art Library, London; p. 8 bot: Giraudon/Art Resource; p. 9: Adam Woolfitt/Woodfin Camp; p. 10: Lee Boltin, Croton-on-Hudson, New York; p. 11: photograph by Green Studio Ltd., Dublin; p. 12: Erich Lessing/Magnum; p. 13: Bettmann Archive; p. 15: C.M. Dixon/Photoresources, London; p. 22: Lee Boltin, Croton-on-Hudson, New York; p. 24: The Granger Collection, New York; pp. 25 and 31: Michael Holford, Essex; p. 33: Werner Forman Archive, London; p. 41: Lee Boltin, Croton-on-Hudson, New York; p. 42: Werner Forman Archive; p. 48: Linda Albrizio/Stock Market; p. 54: Art Resource; p. 57: Bridgeman Art Library, London; p. 59: Lee Boltin, Croton-on-Hudson, New York; p. 60: The Granger Collection, New York; p. 62: Art Resource; p. 63: Angelina Lax/Photo Researchers. **Unit 2** p. 67: Robert Harding Associates, London; p. 73: Bridgeman Art Library, London; p. 74: Robert Harding Associates, London; p. 81: The Granger Collection, New York; p. 106: Bridgeman Art Library, London; p. 114: Art Resource; p. 159: Max Polster Archive; p. 160 top: Art Resource. **Unit 3** p. 165: Bridgeman Art Library, London; pp. 166, 167 (t), 169: Art Resource; p. 172: Bridgeman Art Library, London; p. 174:

Robert Harding Associates, London; p. 175: Rebus, Inc.; p. 182: Robert Harding Associates, London; p. 185: Robert Harding Associates, London; p. 194: The Granger Collection, New York; p. 196: Art Resource; p. 198: The Granger Collection, New York; p. 204: The Bettmann Archive; p. 207: The Granger Collection, New York; pp. 212, 214, 215: Bridgeman Art Library, London; p. 217: Art Resource; p. 219: Bridgeman Art Library, London; pp. 220, 224: Robert Harding Associates, London; p. 225: Art Resource; p. 237 top: Bridgeman Art Library, London; p. 238: Robert Harding Associates, London; pp. 239, 241: The Granger Collection, New York; p. 242: C. Walter Hodges, *The Globe Restored*, © 1973 by W.W. Norton & Co. By arrangement with Coward, McCann & Geohegan, Inc.; p. 244: The Granger Collection, New York; p. 245: Robert Harding Associates, London; p. 246: C. Walter Hodges, *The Globe Restored*, © 1973 by W.W. Norton & Co. By arrangement with Coward, McCann & Geohegan, Inc.; p. 247: Robert Harding Associates, London; p. 249 (t): Art Resource, NY; p. 250: Adam Woolfitt/Woodfin Camp; pp. 253, 254, 264, 267, 287, 292, 318: The Billy Rose Theatre Collection, New York Public Library, Lincoln Center for the Performing Arts; pp. 259, 273, 276, 284, 295, 305, 325: Robert C. Ragsdale, Courtesy of Stratford Festival Archives, Canada; pp. 271, 316: Nat Karson Collection, The Billy Rose Theatre Collection, New York Public Library,

Lincoln Center for the Performing Arts; p. 330: Art Resource; p. 337: Kennedy Galleries, Inc., New York City; p. 338: Bridgeman Art Library, London; p. 345: The Bettmann Archive; p. 347: Art Resource, NY; pp. 348, 355: Bridgeman Art Library, London; p. 357: Art Resource, NY; pp. 358, 359: Art Resource; p. 360: Bridgeman Art Library, London; pp. 362, 374, 375: The Granger Collection, New York; p. 376: Robert Harding Associates, London; p. 380: The Granger Collection, New York; pp. 381, 384: Art Resource; p. 386: The Granger Collection, New York; p. 394: Rare Books and Manuscripts Division, The New York Picture Collection; p. 395 (t): Bridgeman Art Library, London; (b): The Granger Collection, New York; p. 396: Art Resource; p. 400: The British Library; pp. 401, 402: Art Resource; p. 405: New York Public Library, Picture Collection; pp. 407, 409: Art Resource; p. 412: Robert Harding Associates, London; p. 416: The Granger Collection, New York; p. 419: Adam Woolfitt/Woodfin Camp; p. 422: The Granger Collection, New York; p. 425: Art Resource, NY; pp. 431, 435: The Granger Collection, New York; p. 439: Robert Harding Associates, London; p. 441: Bridgeman Art Library, London. **Unit 4** p. 447: Art Resource; p. 448: Bridgeman Art Library, London; p. 449: The Bettmann Archive; p. 450: Bridgeman Art Library, London; p. 451: Robert Harding Associates, London; p. 456: Bridgeman Art Library, London; p. 458: The Granger Collection, New York; p. 460: Art Resource, NY; p. 463: Bridgeman Art Library, London; pp. 468, 469, 472, 473, 476, 477: Robert Harding Associates, London; p. 480: Bridgeman Art Library, London; p. 482: Sergio Larrain/Magnum; pp. 491, 494, 499, 500: The Granger Collection, New York; p. 503: Bettmann Archive; pp. 507, 517, The Granger Collection, New York; p. 518: Robert Harding Associates; p. 525: Bridgeman Art Library, London; p. 526: Bridgeman Art Library, London; p. 553: Art Resource, NY; pp. 556, 557: Robert Harding Associates, London; p. 565: Fotomas Index/Bridgeman Art Library, London; p. 570: Photo by Permission of the magazine "Antiques"; p. 573: Art Resource, NY; p. 575: Bridgeman Art Library, London; p. 577: Bettmann Archive; pp. 581, 582: The Granger Collection, New York; p. 583: New York Public Library, Rare Book Room; p. 591: The Granger Collection, New York; p. 594: Robert Harding Associates, London. **Unit 5** p. 599: The Bridgeman Art Library, London; p. 601: Bettmann Archive; p. 602: The Granger Collection, New York; p. 603: Snark International/Art Resource; p. 605: The Bridgeman Art Library, London; pp. 606, 607: Bettmann Archive; p. 610: Robert Harding Associates, London; pp. 611, 612: The Granger Collection, New York; p. 614: Giraudon/Art Resource; pp. 617, 619, 620, 624: The Granger Collection, New York; p. 627: Bridgeman/Art Resource; pp. 629, 631, 634: The Granger Collection, New York; p. 639: Scala/Art Resource; p. 642: Bridgeman/Art Resource; pp. 647, 650, 651: The Granger Collection, New York; p. 657: Bettmann Archive; p. 658: Snark/Art Resource, NY; p. 662: The Bettmann Archive; pp. 667, 670: The Granger Collection, New York; p. 674: The Bettmann Archive; p. 678: The Granger Collection, New York; p. 687: Bettmann Archive; p. 693: The Granger Collection, New York; p. 695: Robert Harding Associates, London; p. 696: The Granger Collection, New York; p. 699: Art Resource; p. 702: Scala/Art Resource; p. 707: The Granger Collection, New York; p. 713: Bildarchiv Foto Marburg/Art Resource; p. 716, 720: The Granger Collection, New York; pp. 723, 733: Bridgeman/Art Resource; p. 736: Bettmann Archive; p. 738: Scala/Art Resource; p. 741: The Granger Collection, New York; p. 744: Photofest; p. 748: New York Public Library. **Unit 6** p. 759, 760: The Granger Collection, New York; p. 761: Culver Pictures; p. 762: Bettmann Archive; pp. 763, 765: The Granger Collection, New York; p. 767: Photo Bob Rubic; p. 768: The Granger Collection, New York; p. 769: Max Polster Archive; pp. 772, 773: The Granger Collection, New York; pp. 774, 775: Photo Bob Rubic; p. 777: The Granger Collection, New York; p. 784: Art Resource, NY; pp. 789, 798: The Granger Collection, New York; p. 803: Art Resource, NY; p. 806: Scala/Art Resource; pp. 808, 810: The Granger Collection, New York; p. 811: The Bridgeman Art Library, London; p. 812: Art Resource, NY; pp. 819, 825: Bettmann Archive; p. 827: The Granger Collection, New York; p. 831: Art Resource, NY; p. 833: Culver Pictures; p. 840: Bettmann Archive; p. 843: Art Resource, NY; p. 845: The Granger Collection, New York; p. 849: Tate Gallery, London/Art Resource, New York; p. 856: New York Public Library, Photo Bob Rubic; p. 858: The Granger Collection, New York; p. 859: Culver Pictures; p. 868: The Granger Collection, New York; p. 869: The Billy Rose Theatre Collection, New York Public Library, Lincoln Center for the Performing Arts; pp. 870, 878, 884, 891, 895, 897, 900, 905: Vandamm Collection, The Billy Rose Theatre Collection, New York Public Library, Lincoln Center for the Performing Arts; p. 907: Robert Kristofik/The Image Bank; p. 908: Ivor Sharp/The Image Bank. **Unit 7** p. 915: Bridgeman Art Library, London; p. 916: Bridgeman Art Library, London; p. 918: Transition, No. 21, March 1932; p. 921: The Granger Collection, New York; p. 923: Art Resource, NY; p. 950: The Granger Collection, New York; p. 952: John Kelly/Image Bank; p. 956: The Granger Collection, New York; p. 959: Bridgeman Art Library, London; p. 966: Hans Neleman/Wheeler Pictures; p. 969: Sylvia Beach Collection, Princeton University Library; p. 971: The Bettmann Archive; pp. 975, 982: Bridgeman Art Library, London; p. 983: The Granger Collection, New York; p. 992: Elliott Erwitt/Magnum; p. 993: Patrick Ward/Wheeler Pictures; p. 995: Bridgeman Art Library, London; p. 1001: Elliott Erwitt/Magnum; p. 1002: A. DeAndrade/Magnum; p. 1005: Bruce Davidson/Magnum; p. 1010: Bettmann Archive; p. 1018-1019: The Bridgeman Art Library, London; p. 1021: Bettmann Archive; p. 1023: E. Sparks/Stock Market; p. 1028: Fay Godwin/Werner Forman Archive, London; p. 1033: AP/Wide World; p. 1040: © Andrew Douglas; p. 1042: G. Beutter/Magnum; p. 1043: G. Beutter/Magnum; p. 1045: Photo World/FPG International; p. 1046: John Bova/Photo Researchers; p. 1051: Dennis Stock/Magnum; p. 1055: Photo Trends; pp. 1058, 1059: Bruce Davidson/Magnum; p. 1064: AP/Wide World; p. 1067: © Alain Evrard/Photo Researchers; p. 1071: Bridgeman Art Library, London; p. 1072: Ross Madden/Black Star; p. 1073: Giraudon/Art Resource; p. 1074: Weidenfeld and Nicholson; p. 1075: Bridgeman Art Library; p. 1076: Picture Collection, New York Public Library; p. 1078: J.P. Laffont/Sygma; p. 1079: Bettmann Archive; p. 1082: Bettmann Archive; p. 1086: The Granger Collection, New York; p. 1087: Irish Tourist Office; p. 1089: Adam Woolfitt/Woodfin Camp; p. 1091: Art Wolfe/Image Bank; p. 1093: Bridgeman Art Library, London; p. 1094: Lee Boltin, Croton-on-Hudson, New York; p. 1096: Photo Researchers; p. 1102: Bettmann Archive; p. 1104: Archive Photos/Camera Press; p. 1108: Giraudon/Art Resource; p. 1112: Bridgeman Art Library, London; p. 1118: Dennis Stock/Magnum; p. 1123: © C. Herscovici/Artists Rights Society; p. 1124: Bridgeman Art Library, London; p. 1127: Adam Woolfitt/Woodfin Camp; p. 1128: Dorothy Seidman; p. 1132: Fay Godwin/Werner Forman Archive, London; p. 1134: Mark Godfrey; pp. 1138, 1140: Fay Godwin/Werner Forman Archive, London; p. 1142: Jerry Bauer; p. 1143: © Don Johnson: Photo/Nats; p. 1144: David Dennis/Tom Stack Associates; p. 1145: (left) © Greg Crisci: Photo/Nats; (right) © Marilyn Wood: Photo/Nats; p. 1146: Culver Pictures, Inc.; p. 1148–1149: Zoe Dominic; p. 1151: from *The Genius of Shaw*, edited by Michael Holroyd, New York, Holt, Rinehart and Winston, 1979; pp. 1154, 1163, 1170: Zoe Dominic; p. 1173: Van-
(continued on p. 1325)

For permission to reprint copyrighted material in the Annotated Teacher's Edition, grateful acknowledgment is made to the following sources:

George Braziller, Inc.: From *Celtic and Anglo-Saxon Painting: Book Illumination in the British Isles 600-800* by Carl Nordenfalk. Copyright © 1977 by Carl Nordenfalk. **Curtis Brown Ltd. on behalf of the Estate of Sir Winston Churchill:** From *The New World* by Winston S. Churchill. Copyright by The Estate of Sir Winston Churchill. **J. M. Dent & Sons, Ltd.:** From *Joseph Conrad: The Modern Imagination* by C. B. Cox. Copyright © 1974 by C. B. Cox. **Martin Gardner:** From *The Annotated Ancient Mariner*, with an Introduction and Notes by Martin Gardner. Copyright © 1965 by Martin Gardner. **Harcourt Brace Jovanovich, Inc.:** From "The Love Song of J. Alfred Prufrock" from *Collected Poems 1909-1962* by T. S. Eliot. Copyright 1936 by Harcourt Brace Jovanovich, Inc.; copyright © 1963 by T. S. Eliot. From "Edmund Spenser" by C. S. Lewis from *Major British Writers I.* Copyright © 1959 by Harcourt Brace Jovanovich, Inc. **Harvard University Press:** From *John Keats* by Walter Jackson Bate. Copyright © 1963 by the President and Fellows of Harvard College. **Holt, Rinehart and Winston, Inc.:** From *Understanding Poetry: An Anthology for College Students* by Cleanth Brooks. Copyright © 1950 by Holt, Rinehart and Winston, Inc.

CONTENTS
A Chronological Survey of British Literature

722   Robert Browning   798

THEME SIX: WAR AND THE DISINTEGRATION OF ORDER

THEME SEVEN: THE CRUELTY OF TIME

THEME EIGHT: THE WAY TO DUSTY DEATH

THEME NINE: SPIRITUALITY AND THE SOUL

"The best we can do when faced with the strange is to try to remain open to the new, to let it try to educate us and broaden our appreciation, rather than to reject it because it is strange and new."
—Robert Anderson, page 1219

INTEGRATING the LANGUAGE ARTS

UNIT 1: The Anglo-Saxons: The Emergent Period (450–1066)

Selection	Literary Elements	WRITING ABOUT LITERATURE Creative Response	Critical Response	Language and Style
UNIT INTRODUCTION	Old English Poetics Iamb Iambic Tetrameter Alliteration Caesura Kenning			
From **Beowulf** translated by Burton Raffel	Motivation Imagery Symbol Characterization Central Conflict Elegiac Mood Theme	Changing the Point of View	Analyzing a Character Analyzing the Epic	Kennings Alliteration
The Wanderer translated by Charles W. Kennedy	Elegiac Mood Caesura Imagery Tone Symbol	Imitating a Verse Style	Analyzing the Poem Comparing and Contrasting Translations	
The Seafarer translated by Burton Raffel	Metaphors Setting Characterization Atmosphere		Supporting an Opinion Comparing and Contrasting Poems	
Riddles translated by Burton Raffel	Personification Paradox	Writing a Riddle		
From **Ecclesiastical History of the English People** the Venerable Bede	Extended Simile Symbol Simile Metaphor	Imitating the Writer's Technique		*Language Skills:* Active and Passive Voice
THE ENGLISH LANGUAGE: OLD ENGLISH: WHERE ENGLISH CAME FROM				Proto-Indo-European Languages Indo-European Languages Latin Influence Norse Influence Old English Grammar Old English Alphabet/ Writing System
EXERCISES IN CRITICAL THINKING AND WRITING: ANALYZING A PASSAGE			Analyzing a Passage of *Beowulf*	
Word Analogies				*Word Analogies*

All entries refer to Pupil's Edition features *except* entries in italics, which are located in the Core Components Binder.

Elements of Literature, Sixth Course   **A21**

UNIT 2: The Middle Ages (1066–1485)

Selection	Literary Elements	WRITING ABOUT LITERATURE		Language and Style
		Creative Response	Critical Response	
UNIT INTRODUCTION	Romances			
The Three Ravens	Ballads Mood Tone Refrain			
Lord Randall	Meter Rhyme Incremental Repetition Refrain			
Get Up and Bar the Door	Repetition Plot Ironic Humor	Retelling a Ballad as a News Report Writing a Folk Ballad	Comparing Ballads	
THE ELEMENTS OF LITERATURE: BALLAD METER	Ballad Meter			
The Canterbury Tales Geoffrey Chaucer **The Prologue**	Vernacular Iambic Pentameter Couplet Rime Royal Characterization Satire Frame Story	Writing a Frame Story	Responding to a Critic Comparing and Contrasting Two Characters	Rhymes: Couplet, Half Rhyme, Approximate Rhyme
From **The Nun's Priest's Tale** Geoffrey Chaucer	Characterization Conflict Allusion Irony Moral	Continuing the Frame Story		
From **The Pardoner's Tale** Geoffrey Chaucer	Frame Story Personification Symbol Irony Satire Moral	Finishing the Frame Story	Comparing Storytellers Evaluating the Tales as Short Stories Analyzing Character	Imagery *Language Skills:* Revision Worksheet
From **Sir Gawain and the Green Knight** translated by John Gardner	Romance Quest Conflict Character Symbol Imagery Theme	Using a Different Point of View Displacing the Story	Analyzing a Romance	Alliteration Bob and Wheel

All entries refer to Pupil's Edition features *except* entries in italics, which are located in the Core Components Binder.

UNIT 2: The Middle Ages (continued)

Selection	Literary Elements	WRITING ABOUT LITERATURE		Language and Style
		Creative Response	Critical Response	
THE ELEMENTS OF LITERATURE: THE ROMANCE	Romance			
From **Le Morte Darthur** Sir Thomas Malory	Mood Setting Symbol Allusion Supernatural	Using Another Point of View	Writing a Research Report	Archaic Constructions and Context Clues
THE ENGLISH LANGUAGE: MIDDLE ENGLISH: THE LANGUAGE IN TRANSITION				Pronunciation Grammatical Changes Unstressed Vowel Sounds Gender Mood Plural Forms Case Endings French Influence Triumph of English French Loan Words
EXERCISES IN CRITICAL THINKING AND SPEAKING: EVALUATING LITERATURE IN GROUP DISCUSSION			Evaluating One of the Canterbury Tales (Group Discussion)	
Word Analogies				
				Word Analogies

> " **N**owadays there are few languages spoken upon Earth from which English has not borrowed, and even fewer that have not borrowed from it. That is another benefit of the Norman Conquest that William and his bullyboys could not have imagined or understood."
> —John Algeo, page 162

UNIT 3: The Renaissance (1485–1660)

Selection	Literary Elements	WRITING ABOUT LITERATURE		Language and Style
		Creative Response	Critical Response	
UNIT INTRODUCTION	Sonnet Pastoral Epithalamia Epigram Epitaph Song Air Madrigal Extended Metaphor Conceit Narrative Poetry Epic Renaissance Drama Miracle Play Mystery Play Morality Play Interludes Tragicomedy Renaissance Prose			Excesses of Renaissance Prose: Long Sentences, Lists, Allusions, Quotations, Latin Phrases and Sentences
Whoso List to Hunt Sir Thomas Wyatt	Conceit Symbol Extended Metaphor	Responding to the Poem		
They Flee from Me Sir Thomas Wyatt	Pun Tone	Responding to the Poem	Analyzing Diction	Diction
THE ELEMENTS OF LITERATURE: PETRARCHAN SONNETS	Sonnet Petrarchan Conceit Iambic Pentameter Octave Sestet Turn			Conceit
Love That Doth Reign Henry Howard, Earl of Surrey **The Long Love** Sir Thomas Wyatt	Metaphor Conceit	Creating a Petrarchan Conceit	Comparing and Contrasting Translations	
THE ELEMENTS OF LITERATURE: POETIC METER	Metrical Foot Iamb Trochee Anapest Dactyl Scansion Dimeter Trimeter Tetrameter Pentameter Hexameter Iambic Pentameter Spondee Caesura			

All entries refer to Pupil's Edition features *except* entries in italics, which are located in the Core Components Binder.

UNIT 3: The Renaissance (continued)

Selection	Literary Elements	WRITING ABOUT LITERATURE		Language and Style
		Creative Response	Critical Response	
Nature, That Washed Her Hands in Milk Sir Walter Raleigh	Personification	Creating Personification	Analyzing Variations in a Poem's Ending	
What Is Our Life? Sir Walter Raleigh	Metaphor Pun		Expressing an Opinion	
From The Faerie Queen Edmund Spenser	Epic Alexandrine Allegory Conflict Symbol Epic Simile	Creating Allegorical Characters	Translating Spenser	Spenser's Language: Alliteration; Spelling; Pronunciations; Archaic Words; Final "e" Sound
From Amoretti Edmund Spenser	Paradox		Comparing Poems	Multiple Meanings
The Nightingale Sir Philip Sydney	Setting		Responding to a Critical Remark	
From Astrophel and Stella Sir Phillip Sydney	Octave Hexameter Pentameter	Describing a Process	Analyzing Petrarchan Conventions	
Of Studies Sir Francis Bacon	Paradox	Imitating Style	Interpreting an Author's Bias	Parallel Structures Balanced Sentences
From The Essays: Axioms Sir Francis Bacon				
From Doctor Faustus Christopher Marlowe	Foreshadowing Soliloquy Iambic Pentameter Meter Theme	Showing Internal Conflict	Applying a Theme	Dialogue
The Passionate Shepherd to His Love Christopher Marlowe The Nymph's Reply to the Shepherd Sir Walter Raleigh	Pastoral Imagery Tone	Responding to the Poem	Analyzing Argument	
THE ENGLISH LANGUAGE: THE BIRTH OF MODERN ENGLISH				Grammatical Differences Between Middle and Modern English Inflected Ending The Great Vowel Shift Spelling The Spread of English Borrowed Words Classical Influences Standard English

UNIT 3: The Renaissance (continued)

Selection	Literary Elements	WRITING ABOUT LITERATURE		Language and Style
		Creative Response	Critical Response	
THE RENAISSANCE THEATER	Acts and Scenes Props and Effects			
The Tragedy of Macbeth William Shakespeare **Act I**	Conflict Characterization Irony			Blank Verse Iamb Pentameter
Act II	Foreshadowing Suspense Characterization Mood Imagery			
Act III	Character Setting Turning Point Imagery			
Act IV	Character Dumb Show Characterization Suspense Emotion			
Act V	Foreshadowing Internal Conflict External Conflict Themes Climax Resolution	Extending a Character Updating a Scene Changing the Outcome	Interpreting Characterization Analyzing a Character Evaluating Dramatic Effects Analyzing the Playwright's Intent Analyzing Irony Applying Logic Responding to a Critic	Soliloquy Asides Imagery Figurative Language Climax Metaphor Simile Personification *Language Skills:* *Revision Worksheet*
A COMMENT ON THE PLAY	Character Imagery Meter Blank Verse Tragedy and Society			
On the Knocking at the Gate in Macbeth Thomas de Quincey				
Sonnets	Sonnet Iambic Pentameter Quatrain Couplet Turn			
Sonnet 29 William Shakespeare	Turn Tone Simile			

All entries refer to Pupil's Edition features *except* entries in italics, which are located in the Core Components Binder.

UNIT 3: The Renaissance (continued)

Selection	Literary Elements	WRITING ABOUT LITERATURE		Language and Style
		Creative Response	Critical Response	
Sonnet 30 William Shakespeare	Turn Metaphor Tone			
Sonnet 71 William Shakespeare	Alliteration Mood Turn			
Sonnet 73 William Shakespeare	Metaphor Paraphrase Turn Imagery Tone			
Sonnet 116 William Shakespeare	Metaphor Personification Turn Mood Couplet			
Sonnet 130 William Shakespeare	Couplet	Writing a Parody	Comparing Poems Analyzing Poetic Technique	
Winter William Shakespeare	Imagery Attitude	Imitating the Writer's Technique		
Under the Green-wood Tree William Shakespeare	Imagery			
Blow, Blow, Thou Winter Wind William Shakespeare	Personification Paraphrase			
O Mistress Mine William Shakespeare	Stanza Song	Answering the Speaker		
Fear No More the Heat o' the Sun William Shakespeare	Theme Simile			
Full Fathom Five William Shakespeare	Imagery Alliteration			
THE ENGLISH LAN-GUAGE: SHAKE-SPEARE'S LANGUAGE				Pronunciation Grammar Pronouns Verb Endings Verb Forms Vocabulary
THE ELEMENTS OF LIT-ERATURE: METAPHYSI-CAL POETRY	Metaphysical Poetry Tone			Colloquial English
The Bait John Donne	Syntax Rhyme Meter Tone	Constructing a Con-ceit	Comparing Two Poems	Syntax
Song John Donne	Hyperbole Tone	Using Hyperbole		

UNIT 3: The Renaissance (continued)

Selection	Literary Elements	WRITING ABOUT LITERATURE		Language and Style
		Creative Response	Critical Response	
A Valediction: Forbidding Mourning John Donne	Simile Rhythm	Writing a Farewell	Analyzing Conceits	Conceits
Meditation 17 John Donne	Metaphor Main Idea Tone		Analyzing Metaphors	Context Clues
At the Round Earth's Imagined Corners John Donne	Octave Sestet			Sound Shifts
Death Be Not Proud John Donne	Paradox		Comparing Two Sonnets	
Batter My Heart John Donne	Simile Imagery Alliteration Paradox		Analyzing Rhythm and Sound Effects	
To Fool or Knave **To the Ghost of Martial** Ben Jonson	Epigrams			
On My First Son Ben Jonson	Irony Epitaph		Responding to a Theme	
To Celia **Still to Be Neat** Ben Jonson	Connotation	Responding to the Main Idea		
Delight in Disorder Robert Herrick	Oxymoron Message Tone	Writing a Parody	Comparing Poems	
To the Virgins, to Make Much of Time Robert Herrick	Imagery	Extending the Poem Answering the Poet		
Virtue George Herbert	Title Paraphrase			Figures of Speech
The Altar George Herbert	Metaphor	Writing a "Picture Poem"		
The Pulley George Herbert	Title		Supporting the Idea	Multiple Meanings
Out Upon It! **Why So Pale and Wan, Fond Lover?** Sir John Suckling	Tone Metaphor Simile			
To Lucasta Richard Lovelace	Paradox	Responding to the Speaker		
To Althea Richard Lovelace	Comparison Paradox		Relating the Poem to Current Events	

All entries refer to Pupil's Edition features *except* entries in italics, which are located in the Core Components Binder.

UNIT 3: The Renaissance (continued)

Selection	Literary Elements	WRITING ABOUT LITERATURE		Language and Style
		Creative Response	Critical Response	
The King James Bible (1611) From **Genesis**	Foreshadowing			
Psalms	Parallel Structure			
Psalms 8, 23, 24, and 137	Imagery Figurative Language Tone Parallel Structure		Comparing Another Translation	Reading Aloud (Repetition and Parallel Structures)
Jonah	Audience Lesson		Discussing the Theme	
The Parable of the Good Samaritan	Parable Irony			
The Retreat Henry Vaughan	Imagery Tone		Evaluating the Main Idea	
On His Blindness John Milton	Octave Sestet		Paraphrasing the Poem	Diction
On Shakespeare John Milton			Comparing Poems	
Paradise Lost (Introduction)	Epic Blank Verse			
From **Paradise Lost: The Temptation of Eve** John Milton	Metaphor Characterization	Extending the Narrative	Paraphrasing a Speech Researching Sources	Milton's Poetic Style: Epic Simile Syntax (Inversion; Missing Words) Blank Verse
To His Coy Mistress Andrew Marvell	Exaggeration Understatement	Writing a Response	Comparing and Contrasting Poems	
THE ENGLISH LANGUAGE: THE GROWTH OF MODERN ENGLISH				Grammar Dictionaries Ornate Style Euphemism Metaphysical Conceit Plain Style What Is Style? Types and Elements of Style: Sentence Length; Active vs. Passive Verbs; Direct vs. Qualified Statements; Noun- vs. Verb-Centeredness; Plain vs. Fancy Words
EXERCISES IN CRITICAL THINKING AND WRITING: ANALYZING A POET'S WORK			Analyzing Poems by One Poet (Using Primary and Secondary Sources)	
Word Analogies				*Word Analogies*

Selection	Literary Elements	WRITING ABOUT LITERATURE		Language and Style
		Creative Response	Critical Response	
UNIT INTRODUCTION	Neoclassicism Dramatic Unities Augustan Poetry Elegy Satire Epic Ode Pastoral Poetry Meter Rhyme Novel			
Shakespeare from **Of Dramatic Poesy: An Essay** John Dryden	Argumentation Opposing Viewpoints Generalization		Applying a Generalization	
From **Baucis and Philemon** John Dryden	Moral Symbol Comic Relief Theme Tone	Changing the Setting	Analyzing Characterization	
From **The Diary of Samuel Pepys** Samuel Pepys	Primary Source	Planning a Diary	Using a Primary Source	Eighteenth-Century Usage
From **Robinson Crusoe** Daniel Defoe	First-Person Point of View Characterization	Narrating a Different Outcome	Explaining Literary Appeal Analyzing a Character's Responses Comparing and Contrasting Two Treatments of Solitude	*Language Skills:* Homonyms
From **A Journal of the Plague Year** Daniel Defoe	Tone	Narrating from Primary Sources	Comparing and Contrasting Literary Works Supporting an Opinion	*Language Skills:* Run-on Sentences and Sentence Fragments
From **Gulliver's Travels** Jonathan Swift	Allegory Satire Parody Symbol Characterization Verbal Irony	Using First-Person Point of View Varying a Plot		*Language Skills:* Repetition and Wordiness
THE ELEMENTS OF LITERATURE: SATIRE	Satire Exaggeration Understatement Irony			
A Modest Proposal Jonathan Swift	Characterization Satire Purpose	Writing a Newspaper Editorial Responding to the Essay	Relating the Essay to Current Events	Diction Connotation

All entries refer to Pupil's Edition features *except* entries in italics, which are located in the **Core Components Binder.**

UNIT 4: The Restoration and the Eighteenth Century (continued)

Selection	Literary Elements	WRITING ABOUT LITERATURE		Language and Style
		Creative Response	Critical Response	
Heroic Couplets Alexander Pope	Couplet Aphorism Metrical Pattern			Pope's Poetics Antithesis
From **An Essay on Criticism** Alexander Pope	Rhythm	Creating Sounds		
From **An Essay on Man** Alexander Pope	Characterization	Writing an Illustration		
From **The Rape of the Lock** Alexander Pope	Satire Tone Irony Theme	Using the Mock-Heroic Style	Analyzing a Satire Comparing and Contrasting Epics	
THE ELEMENTS OF LITERATURE: WIT	Wit			
Artifices in Tragedy Joseph Addison	Tragedy Paradox Personal Essay Hyperbole Understatement		Describing Comic Devices	Satirical Techniques: Hyperbole Understatement Sarcasm Tone
Alexander Selkirk Sir Richard Steele	Characterization Theme		Examining a Conclusion	Precise Meanings
From **A Dictionary** Samuel Johnson	Tone	Writing Dictionary Definitions	Drawing Inferences	
Letter to Lord Chesterfield Samuel Johnson	Purpose Irony Tone	Replying to a Letter Paraphrasing a Letter	Identifying Satirical Elements	
From **The Preface to Shakespeare** Samuel Johnson	Tone		Analyzing a Character	
THE ELEMENTS OF LITERATURE: STYLE	Style			Johnson's Style: Latin-Based Words Parallel Sentences Exact Expressions Concise Statements Strong Metaphors
Elegy Written in a Country Churchyard Thomas Gray	Imagery Personification Stereotype Message	Writing an Epitaph Imitating the Writer's Technique	Comparing and Contrasting Poems	A Poetic Style Syntax
THE ELEMENTS OF LITERATURE: THE ELEGY	Elegy Pastoral Gothic Generalizations About Life and Death			
From **The Life of Samuel Johnson** James Boswell	Biography Characterization	Writing a Biographical Sketch	Writing an Explanation	

Selection	Literary Elements	WRITING ABOUT LITERATURE		Language and Style
		Creative Response	Critical Response	
From **The Pilgrim's Progress** John Bunyan	Allegory	Changing a Character Outlining an Allegory Recasting the Story		
THE ELEMENTS OF LITERATURE: ALLEGORY	Allegory Surface Story Submerged Story			
THE ENGLISH LANGUAGE: DECORUM AND ORDER				Changing Language Refining English Writing Rules Fixing English Dictionaries Changing Pronunciations Homophones Changing Grammar "Good" and "Bad" English Comparing Dictionary Entries Examining Recent Dictionary Entries Usage
EXERCISES IN CRITICAL THINKING AND WRITING: USING LOGICAL REASONING TO WRITE A PERSUASIVE ESSAY			Refuting a Generalization	Hasty Generalization Circular Reasoning
Word Analogies				*Word Analogies*

I n the eighteenth century "poems were not to sound like spontaneous and impromptu utterances, just as people were not to appear in public except in fancy dress. Those who could afford it adorned themselves with vast wigs, beribboned and bejeweled clothing, and red shoes with high heels. . . . Nothing was what we would call 'natural.' "

—C. F. Main, page 456

All entries refer to Pupil's Edition features *except* entries in italics, which are located in the Core Components Binder.

UNIT 5: The Romantic Period (1798–1832)

Selection	Literary Elements	WRITING ABOUT LITERATURE		Language and Style
		Creative Response	Critical Response	
UNIT INTRODUCTION	Lyric Poetry Imagination Narrative Poetry Novel			
To a Mouse Robert Burns	Tone Alliteration	Imitating the Writer's Technique	Responding to the Poem	Dialect
John Anderson, My Jo Robert Burns	Symbol	Changing the Point of View	Rewriting Dialect	Dialect
The Tyger William Blake	Imagery Symbol		Analyzing the Poem Comparing and Contrasting Two Versions of a Poem	
The Lamb William Blake	Speaker Symbol		Comparing and Contrasting Two Poems	
The Chimney Sweeper William Blake	Irony Tone			
The Chimney Sweeper William Blake	Irony Purpose	Writing a Narrative	Writing an Analysis	
London William Blake	Imagery Symbol	Writing a Description	Comparing Two Poems	Puns
Jerusalem William Blake	Tone Symbol Imagery		Comparing Visions	Diction Parallelism
Lines Composed a Few Miles Above Tintern Abbey William Wordsworth	Meter Run-on Line Theme Verse Paragraphs	Describing a Scene	Analyzing the Structure of a Poem	Verse Paragraphs Blank Verse Run-on Line
Strange Fits of Passion Have I Known She Dwelt Among the Untrodden Ways A Slumber Did My Spirit Seal William Wordsworth	Audience Figure of Speech Theme Imagery	Using Another Point of View	Analyzing Romantic Themes	
London, 1802 William Wordsworth	Metaphor Symbol	Writing an Apostrophe		
I Wandered Lonely as a Cloud William Wordsworth	Mood Personification	Creating a Simile	Comparing Poems Evaluating a Metaphor	
Composed upon Westminster Bridge William Wordsworth	Personification Mood Paradox	Imitating the Writer's Technique		
The Solitary Reaper William Wordsworth	Rhythm		Comparing Poems	

UNIT 5: The Romantic Period (continued)

| Selection | Literary Elements | WRITING ABOUT LITERATURE | | Language and Style |
		Creative Response	Critical Response	
THE ELEMENTS OF LITERATURE: ROMANTIC LYRICS	Sonnet Italian Sonnet Petrarchan Sonnet Shakespearean Sonnet Ode Apostrophe Meditative Poem Blank Verse			
Kubla Khan Samuel Taylor Coleridge	Imagery Rhyme Scheme Meter Alliteration Symbol	Completing the Poem	Analyzing the Poem	
This Lime-Tree Bower My Prison Samuel Taylor Coleridge	Paradox Tone	Writing a Description	Comparing Two Meditative Lyrics Supporting a Topic Statement	
The Rime of the Ancient Mariner Samuel Taylor Coleridge	Narrator Moral Imagery Sound Effects Simile Metaphor Personification Alliteration Assonance Internal Rhyme Ballad Stanza Meter	Extending the Poem	Analyzing Plot Identifying Allegory	Archaic Words
She Walks in Beauty George Gordon, Lord Byron	Simile			
So We'll Go No More A-Roving George Gordon, Lord Byron	Meter Rhyme Repetition Anapest Iambs Refrain		Analyzing Techniques	
The Destruction of Sennacherib George Gordon, Lord Byron	Simile Meter Anapest Rhythm		Analyzing Similes	

All entries refer to Pupil's Edition features *except* entries in italics, which are located in the Core Components Binder.

A34   Elements of Literature, Sixth Course

UNIT 5: The Romantic Period (continued)

Selection	Literary Elements	WRITING ABOUT LITERATURE		Language and Style
		Creative Response	Critical Response	
From **Don Juan, Canto II** George Gordon, Lord Byron	Cantos Setting Figures of Speech Simile Rhyme Scheme Alliteration Tone Satire	Continuing the Story	Comparing Epics	
From **Childe Harold's Pilgrimage** George Gordon, Lord Byron	Figure of Speech Rhyme Scheme Rhythm Irony	Writing an Apostrophe	Analyzing a Stanza Form	
Ode to the West Wind Percy Bysshe Shelley	Paradox Sonnet Turn		Analyzing Sound Effects	Terza Rima
THE ELEMENTS OF LITERATURE: APOSTROPHE	Extended Apostrophe			
To a Skylark Percy Bysshe Shelley	Simile		Comparing Poems	
England in 1819 Percy Bysshe Shelley	Figures of Speech Paradox			Connotations
Ozymandias Percy Bysshe Shelley	Narrative Frame Irony		Comparing and Contrasting Sonnets	
On First Looking into Chapman's Homer John Keats	Rhyme Scheme Simile	Writing Similes	Analyzing the Poem's Structure	
Bright Star, Would I Were Steadfast as Thou Art John Keats	Personification		Analyzing Figures of Speech	
When I Have Fears John Keats	Simile Tone	Answering the Speaker	Analyzing the Poem's Structure	
La Belle Dame Sans Merci John Keats	Imagery Meter	Setting a Ballad to Music Writing a Short Story		
Ode to a Nightingale John Keats	Setting Mood		Analyzing Symbolism Comparing and Contrasting Odes Comparing and Contrasting Poems	Imagery Synaesthesia
Ode on a Grecian Urn John Keats	Romantic	Imitating the Writer's Technique	Analyzing a Main Idea	

UNIT 5: The Romantic Period (continued)

Selection	Literary Elements	WRITING ABOUT LITERATURE		Language and Style
		Creative Response	Critical Response	
To Autumn John Keats	Personification Meter Rhyme Scheme Assonance Onomatopoeia	Writing a Description	Analyzing Poetic Techniques	
The Eve of St. Agnes John Keats	Setting Symbol	Creating and Staging a Dramatic Version	Comparing Stories Supporting a Statement	Imagery
Dream Children: A Reverie Charles Lamb	Essay Tone	Writing a Reverie		The Familiar Essay (Language, Sentences, Tone)
From **Frankenstein** Mary Wollstonecraft Shelley	Characterization Theme	Extending the Story	Identifying a Theme	*Language Skills:* Varying Sentence Length *Language Skills:* Making Revisions
From **The Journals** Dorothy Wordsworth	Figures of Speech Tone		Comparing the Journal to the Poem	*Language Skills:* Transitional Expressions
THE ENGLISH LANGUAGE: VARIETY IN LANGUAGE				Dialects Registers Vocabulary Regional Dialects Ethnic Dialects
EXERCISES IN CRITICAL THINKING AND WRITING: INTERPRETING POETRY			Explaining the Meaning of a Poem	
Word Analogies				*Word Analogies*

> " ' **B**liss was it in that dawn to be alive,' Wordsworth later wrote, 'but to be young was very heaven.' "
> —Donald Gray, page 601

All entries refer to Pupil's Edition features *except* entries in italics, which are located in the Core Components Binder.

UNIT 6: The Victorian Period (1832–1901)

Selection	Literary Elements	WRITING ABOUT LITERATURE		Language and Style
		Creative Response	Critical Response	
UNIT INTRODUCTION	Victorian vs. Romantic Literature			
London Streets Thomas Babington Macaulay	Tone Audience	Conducting an Interview	Presenting an Oral Report	*Language Skills:* Varying Sentence Structure
Tears, Idle Tears Alfred, Lord Tennyson	Imagery			
Now Sleeps the Crimson Petal Alfred, Lord Tennyson	Repetition Parallel Syntax Imagery	Setting the Lyric to Music	Analyzing Words and Images	Connotations
Break, Break, Break Alfred, Lord Tennyson	Atmosphere Tone Imagery		Analyzing the Poem's Structure	
Crossing the Bar Alfred, Lord Tennyson	Metaphor Rhythm	Writing a Letter	Comparing and Contrasting Imagery	
The Lady of Shalott Alfred, Lord Tennyson	Setting Rhythm Rhyme Scheme Foreshadowing Imagery	Filming the Poem	Analyzing the Ending	*Language Skills:* Nouns
The Eagle: A Fragment Alfred, Lord Tennyson	Setting Tercet	Extending the Poem Imitiating the Writer's Technique	Interpreting the Poem	
Ulysses Alfred, Lord Tennyson	Characterization	Extending the Poem	Comparing Heroes	
From **In Memoriam** Alfred, Lord Tennyson	Setting Rhyme Scheme		Writing an Essay	
My Last Duchess Robert Browning	Rhyme Rhythm Characterization Dramatic Monologue	Writing a Dramatic Monologue	Analyzing the Theme	
Porphyria's Lover Robert Browning	Dramatic Monologue Setting	Extending the Poem	Comparing and Contrasting Two Dramatic Monologues	
Meeting at Night and **Parting at Morning** Robert Browning	Rhythm	Extending the Poems Using Another Point of View		
Prospice Robert Browning	Imagery Attitude		Comparing and Contrasting Two Poets' Views	

Selection	Literary Elements	WRITING ABOUT LITERATURE		Language and Style
		Creative Response	Critical Response	
Sonnet 43 Elizabeth Barrett Browning	Rhythm	Extending the Poem	Analyzing Concrete and Abstract Words	Concrete and Abstract Words
Dover Beach Matthew Arnold	Setting Mood Allusion Metaphor Simile Rhyme Scheme Rhythm		Analyzing a Problem	
Requiescat Matthew Arnold	Metaphor Repetition Tone	Writing a Character Sketch	Contrasting Poems	
To Marguerite— Continued Matthew Arnold	Extended Metaphor Mood Connotation	Writing an Extended Metaphor	Comparing and Contrasting Two Poems	
The Blessed Damozel Dante Gabriel Rossetti	Mood Atmosphere	Illustrating the Poem	Analyzing the Poem	
A Birthday Christina Rossetti	Simile Imagery Subject Tone			
Spring and Fall Gerard Manley Hopkins	Alliteration Assonance		Writing a Paraphrase	
Felix Randal Gerard Manley Hopkins	Sonnet Onomatopoeia			
Pied Beauty Gerard Manley Hopkins	Imagery Theme Alliteration Antithesis Rhythm	Extending the Poem	Analyzing Diction	Diction
The Darkling Thrush Thomas Hardy	Setting Tone	Writing a Prediction	Comparing and Contrasting Two Poems	
Channel Firing Thomas Hardy	Irony Theme	Writing an Editorial	Analyzing Point of View	
The Convergence of the Twain Thomas Hardy	Title Main Idea	Writing a Commentary	Writing an Essay	
Ah, Are You Digging on My Grave? Thomas Hardy	Tone	Writing a Character Sketch	Analyzing Irony	*Language Skills:* Pronouns

All entries refer to Pupil's Edition features **except** entries in italics, which are located in the Core Components Binder.

UNIT 6: The Victorian Period (continued)

Selection	Literary Elements	WRITING ABOUT LITERATURE		Language and Style
		Creative Response	Critical Response	
When I Was One-and-Twenty A. E. Housman	Repetition Theme Tone Imagery			
The Night Is Freezing Fast A. E. Housman	Rhyme Scheme Extended Metaphor Theme Tone Imagery			Connotations
With Rue My Heart Is Laden A. E. Housman	Rhythm Rhyme Theme Tone Imagery	Imitating the Writer's Technique	Comparing and Contrasting Poems	Diction
On Moonlit Heath and Lonesome Bank A. E. Housman	Theme Tone Setting		Writing a Paraphrase Analyzing the Effects of Setting	
From **David Copperfield** Charles Dickens	Imagery Characterization Point of View	Predicting Outcomes	Analyzing Character	*Language Skills:* Participles and Participial Phrases
The Miracle of Purun Bhagat Rudyard Kipling	Title Theme	Writing a Story or a Personal Narrative	Supporting an Opinion	*Language Skills:* Prepositions and Prepositional Phrases
VICTORIAN DRAMA				
The Importance of Being Earnest (Introduction)	Farce			
The Importance of Being Earnest Oscar Wilde **Act One**	Obstacle Foreshadowing Tone Blocking Figure Motivation Epigram			
Act Two	Complications Reversal Satire Comic Motif Repetition			
Act Three	Irony Farce *Deus ex Machina* Tone Plot Disguise Mistaken Identity Mysterious Parentage Triangle of Boy-Girl-and-Obstinate Parent	Writing Epigrams Writing a Sequel	Writing an Analysis	Epigram Pun Paradox *Language Skills:* Diction

| Selection | Literary Elements | WRITING ABOUT LITERATURE | | Language and Style |
		Creative Response	Critical Response	
THE ENGLISH LANGUAGE: ONE LANGUAGE—MANY NATIONS				Spread of English Dialects of English Differences Between American English and British English: Vocabulary Pronunciation Spelling Grammar
EXERCISES IN CRITICAL THINKING AND WRITING: DEVELOPING AND SUPPORTING GENERALIZATIONS			Supporting Generalizations	
Word Analogies				*Word Analogies*

" **V**ictoria came to the throne in the first year of a depression that by 1842 had put a million and a half unemployed workers and their families (in a population of sixteen million in England and Wales) on some form of poor relief. Government commissions investigating working conditions learned of children mangled when they fell asleep at machines at the end of a twelve-hour working day. They discovered young girls and boys hauling sledges of coal through narrow mine tunnels, working shifts so long that in winter they saw the sun only on Sunday."

—Donald Gray, page 761

All entries refer to Pupil's Edition features *except* entries in italics, which are located in the Core Components Binder.

UNIT 7: The Twentieth Century

Selection	Literary Elements	WRITING ABOUT LITERATURE		Language and Style
		Creative Response	Critical Response	
UNIT INTRODUCTION	Experimentation in the Arts			
The Secret Sharer Joseph Conrad	Motivation Motif of the Double Symbolism Allusions Theme Point of View Atmosphere Mood Marginal Hero	Extending the Story Writing About a Secret Sharer	Analyzing a Theme Analyzing a Character Analyzing Imagery Interpreting the Ending	*Language Skills:* Verb Tenses *Language Skills:* Mechanics—Commas *Language Skills:* Revisions
Sredni Vashtar Hector Hugh Munro (Saki)	Direct Characterization Indirect Characterization Theme Situational Irony Dramatic Irony	Recasting the Story	Responding to a Critical Comment	*Language Skills:* Clauses
Araby James Joyce	Setting Atmosphere Connotation Theme Irony Tone Plot Character	Changing the Setting	Analyzing the Story Analyzing a Character Analyzing a Theme Comparing Characters	*Language Skills:* Pronoun–Antecedent Agreement *Language Skills:* Appositives and Appositive Phrases
THE ELEMENTS OF LITERATURE: IRONY	Verbal Irony Sarcasm Situational Irony Dramatic Irony			
From **A Portrait of the Artist as a Young Man** James Joyce	Point of View Free Association Tone Stream of Consciousness	Using the Stream-of-Consciousness Technique	Comparing and Contrasting Characters	
THE ELEMENTS OF LITERATURE: THE STREAM OF CONSCIOUSNESS	Stream of Consciousness Puns			
The Rocking-Horse Winner D. H. Lawrence	Character Symbolism Theme Tone Satire	Writing a New Resolution	Analyzing a Character Applying a Quotation to a Story Comparing and Contrasting Characters	*Language Skills:* Infinitives and Infinitive Phrases
Miss Brill Katherine Mansfield	Basic Situation Irony Symbolism Theme Ambiguity	Narrating What Happens Next	Analyzing Point of View	*Language Skills:* Subject-Verb Agreement *Language Skills:* Adverb Clauses

Selection	Literary Elements	WRITING ABOUT LITERATURE		Language and Style
		Creative Response	Critical Response	
THE ELEMENTS OF LITERATURE: THE MODERN SHORT STORY	Unified Effect Closure Trick Ending Realism Slice-of-Life Psychological Realism Irony Language Theme Imagery Symbol			Diction
The Demon Lover Elizabeth Bowen	Setting Mood Imagery Foreshadowing Omniscient Narrator Theme Dramatic Irony Flashback	Describing a Character Mixing Media	Comparing Literature	*Language Skills:* Parallel Sentence Structure
My Oedipus Complex Frank O'Connor	Narrator Conflict Irony Character Theme	Using a Different Point of View	Comparing and Contrasting Characters Responding to the Story	*Language Skills:* Ornate and Plain Style *Language Skills:* Punctuating Dialogue
The Destructors Graham Greene	Motivation Irony Connotations Theme	Using Another Point of View	Explaining Imagery	Slang *Language Skills:* Sentence Inversion
No Witchcraft for Sale Doris Lessing	Irony Theme	Extending a Character	Analyzing Conflict Analyzing Point of View	*Language Skills:* Verbs
The Soft Voice of the Serpent Nadine Gordimer	Protagonist Simile Title Theme	Using Similes in a Description	Analyzing a Character	*Language Skills:* Noun Clauses
B. Wordsworth V. S. Naipaul	Theme Contrast Setting Imagery Characterization	Writing a Character Sketch	Analyzing a Character	Vernacular *Language Skills:* The Narrative Paragraph
In the Shadow of War Ben Okri	Motivation Third-Person Limited Point of View	Using a Third-Person Limited Point of View	Analyzing a Symbol	*Language Skills:* Coherence—Using Spatial Order
The Death of the Moth Virginia Woolf	Essay Setting Tone Theme	Imagining a Different Environment	Analyzing the Writer's Discovery	*Language Skills:* Adjective Clauses

All entries refer to Pupil's Edition features *except* entries in italics, which are located in the Core Components Binder.

UNIT 7: The Twentieth Century (continued)

Selection	Literary Elements	WRITING ABOUT LITERATURE		Language and Style
		Creative Response	Critical Response	
A Child's Christmas in Wales Dylan Thomas	Tone Characterization Mood	Writing a Sensory Description	Analyzing the Writer's Style	*Language Skills:* Adjectives *Language Skills:* Semicolons and Colons
From **The Road to Wigan Pier** George Orwell	Tone Theme	Writing About a Social Problem	Analyzing a Writer's Technique	*Language Skills:* Adverbs *Language Skills:* Weak Words and Clichés
By Any Other Name Santha Rama Rau	Theme Characterization Conflict Anecdote	Persuading a Person	Describing Contrasts	*Language Skills:* The Descriptive Paragraph
TWENTIETH-CENTURY POETRY	Modernism French Symbolists French Poets			
Dulce et Decorum Est Wilfred Owen	Rhyme Scheme Half Rhyme Figure of Speech Metaphor Theme Tone		Writing an Essay Comparing and Contrasting Poems	
The Rear-Guard Siegfried Sassoon	Onomatopoeia Setting Irony		Comparing Two Poems ("Dulce et Decorum Est" and "The Rear-Guard")	
Feature: The Influence of T. S. Eliot John Malcolm Brinnin	"Modern Poetry"			*Language Skills:* Subordinate Clauses
Preludes T. S. Eliot	*Tone* *Irony* *Mood*	*Imitating the Writer's Technique*	*Analyzing an Image*	
The Hollow Men T. S. Eliot	*Imagery* *Setting* *Theme* *Alliteration* *Extended Metaphor* *Sound Devices*	*Writing a Character Sketch* *Responding to the Poet*	*Explaining the Poet's Viewpoint* *Analyzing an Image*	
The Lake Isle of Innisfree William Butler Yeats	Tone	Imitating the Writer's Technique	Comparing Poems	Assonance Alliteration
The Wild Swans at Coole William Butler Yeats	Symbolism Theme		Comparing Poems Analyzing a Poem	

Selection	Literary Elements	WRITING ABOUT LITERATURE		Language and Style
		Creative Response	Critical Response	
The Second Coming William Butler Yeats	Imagery Irony	Evaluating the Effect of a Poem	Comparing and Contrasting Two Works Commenting on Famous Lines	
Sailing to Byzantium William Butler Yeats	Imagery Theme Tone Symbol	Describing a Symbolic Setting	Comparing and Contrasting Two Poems Exploring a Symbol	
Still Falls the Rain Edith Sitwell	Rhyme Scheme Refrain Meter	Preparing a Choral Reading	Relating Technique to Theme	
Snake D. H. Lawrence	Internal Conflict Imagery Symbolism Allusions		Explaining an Allusion Comparing and Contrasting Two Poems	Free Verse Onomatopoeia Alliteration Repetition
Warning to Children Robert Graves	Repetition Theme Rhythm	Writing a Reply Imitating the Writer's Technique		
Not Waving but Drowning Stevie Smith	Title	Writing Verse	Explaining a Metaphor	
Musée des Beaux Arts W. H. Auden	Title Theme	Describing a Painting	Researching a Myth	
Song: As I Walked Out One Evening W. H. Auden	Metaphor Imagery Figures of Speech Reversals Irony Tone Sounds Metrics	Responding to the Poem		
The Unknown Citizen W. H. Auden	Tone Free Verse Theme	Shifting the Point of View Imitating the Writer's Technique	Analyzing Satire	
Prayer Before Birth Louis MacNeice	Point of View Simile Metaphor Epigraph Tone	Using a Different Point of View	Connecting Two Poems	Free Verse Rhyme Alliteration Onomatopoeia
The Express Stephen Spender	Simile Metaphor Alliteration Onomatopoeia	Imitating the Writer's Technique	Comparing and Contrasting Poems	Connotations
Naming of Parts Henry Reed	Setting Tone	Writing a Dialogue		Diction

All entries refer to Pupil's Edition features *except* entries in italics, which are located in the Core Components Binder.

UNIT 7: The Twentieth Century (continued)

Selection	Literary Elements	WRITING ABOUT LITERATURE		Language and Style
		Creative Response	Critical Response	
Fern Hill Dylan Thomas	Personification Paradox Rhythm Alliteration Onomatopoeia Theme	Imitating the Writer's Technique	Analyzing a Theme	Word Play (Puns) Cliché
A Refusal to Mourn the Death, by Fire, of a Child in London Dylan Thomas	Tone	Relating the Poem to Contemporary Experience	Paraphrasing the Poem	
Do Not Go Gentle into That Good Night Dylan Thomas	Pun Metaphor	Responding to the Speaker Writing a Villanelle		The Villanelle
Church Going Philip Larkin	Rhyme Scheme Title Tone		Writing a Character Sketch Comparing Two Poems	
The Virgins Derek Walcott	Irony Imagery		Supporting a Critical Statement	
Hawk Roosting Ted Hughes	Theme	Writing a Poem	Analyzing Theme	
Digging Seamus Heaney	Imagery Figures of Speech	Extending the Poem		
Mushrooms Margaret Atwood	Sensory Appeals Metaphor	Fitting Sounds to Meanings		
Pygmalion: A Romance in Five Acts Bernard Shaw **Preface** and **Act One**	Exposition Foreshadowing Character			Cockney Dialect
Act Two	Paradox Satire Characterization Conflict Resolution			
Act Three	Characterization Incongruity			
Act Four	Reversals Crisis			
Act Five and **Epilogue**				

| Selection | Literary Elements | WRITING ABOUT LITERATURE | | Language and Style |
		Creative Response	Critical Response	

THE PLAY AS A WHOLE	Protagonist
	Character Types
	Theme
	Satire
		Extending the Play
		Updating the Story
		Adapting Another
		    Myth to the Stage
			Analyzing Dialogue
			Analyzing Themes
			Analyzing an Adapta-
			  tion
			Responding to
			  Shaw's Women
			Responding to a
			  Critic
			Responding to
			  Shaw's Epilogue
				Language Skills:
				Varying Sentence Be-
				  ginnings; Mechan-
				  ics: End Punctua-
				  tion
				Language Skills:
				Revision

MODERN BRITISH DRAMA	New Subjects New Forms English Comedy Angry Young Men Theater of the Absurd Pinter Dialogue			
THE ENGLISH LAN-GUAGE: ENGLISH TODAY AND TOMORROW				New Words Loanwords Compound Words Affixes Shortenings Back-Formations Blends Shifted Words

EXERCISES IN CRITICAL THINKING AND WRITING: ANALYZING A WRITER'S STYLE			Analyzing a Writer's
			  Style
				Words
				Sentences
				Stylistic Devices
				  (Repetition, Paral-
				  lelism)

Word Analogies				*Word Analogies*

" 'Here I live in a society which is fundamentally out of joint. One can't but be politically concerned,' she has said, but she disclaims a political allegiance. 'I don't understand politics except in terms of what politics does to influence lives. What interests me is the infinite variety of effects apartheid has had on men and women.' "
—Nadine Gordimer, page 1028

All entries refer to Pupil's Edition features *except* entries in italics, which are located in the Core Components Binder.

Literature and Language

Selection	Literary Elements	WRITING ABOUT LITERATURE		Language and Style
		Creative Response	Critical Response	
Literature and Language: Using Pronouns and Antecedents Correctly (Laurie Lee)		Writing About a Childhood Memory Creating a Fantasy		Pronouns Antecedents
Literature and Language: Varying Sentences (William Manchester)			Varying Sentences	Sentence Lengths Independent Clauses Subordinate Clauses Simple, Compound, Complex, and Compound-Complex Sentences
Literature and Language: Using Subordinate Clauses Correctly (Margaret Atwood)		Narrating the Further Adventures of the Bat	Creating Subordinate Clauses	Subordinate Clauses Adjective Clause Adverb Clause Noun Clause
Literature and Language: Using Commas Correctly (Charles Dickens)			Editing a Passage to Modernize Punctuation	Commas (5 rules) Restrictive Clauses
Literature and Language: Using the Narrative Mode (Margaret Drabble)	Point of View Characterization Direct Statement of Meaning Order of Events Suspense	Writing a First-Person Narrative		Narration Topic Sentence Clincher Sentence
Literature and Language: Using the Expository Aim (Evelyn Waugh)	Description Persuasion	Writing an Expository Composition		The Writer's Purpose Sensory Language Emotional Language Thesis Statement
Literature and Language: Using the Persuasive Aim (Virginia Woolf)	Persuasion		Writing to Persuade Readers of the Opposite Opinion	Facts Opinions Interpretations of Facts Logical Reasoning Appeals to Emotion
Literature and Language: Choosing Words to Create a Tone (Emily Brontë)	Tone Parody Satire Setting Character	Describing a Landscape Writing a Parody		Diction Adjectives Adverbs Nouns Emotionally Charged Words

> "This language and this literature do not belong to one nation or to one people only, but are shared by many. English belongs to all those all over the world who speak and write it, who read its literature, and who treasure it. They are the ones who are its tomorrow."
>
> —John Algeo, page 1228

THE ANGLO-SAXONS
THE EMERGENT PERIOD
450–1066

Chessmen carved of walrus ivory (12th century).   British Museum.

UNIT ONE

A. HUMANITIES CONNECTION: DISCUSSING THE FINE ART
These Scandinavian warriors preparing for battle are really tiny chessmen carved from walrus tusks. They were found on the Isle of Lewis, which is in the Outer Hebrides off the coast of Scotland. The little cache of warriors was accidentally discovered by a farmer when his cow trod on the soft ground near a cliff by the sea, and the earth caved in. Peering inside, the amazed farmer saw a tiny army of fierce warriors staring at him from the darkness. Terrified that they were spirits from the Underworld, he left them where they were. But his wife was more canny, and less superstitious. She persuaded the farmer to dig up the little army and take it home. These chessmen (and women) can now be seen in the British Museum, along with many other treasures from England's rich past.

? What predictions can you make about the literature of this period, given the kind of image that opens the unit?

TEACHING ANGLO-SAXON LITERATURE

Because the language of the period—Old English—seems like a foreign language to our students, they usually approach the Anglo-Saxon period in British literature with no small amount of apprehension. The highly readable translations used in this unit should help not only to alleviate anxieties on that score but also to make readily accessible the unique perspectives on early life in Britain offered by Anglo-Saxon literature.

The history of these times is important, for these works are typical products of their age. Students should understand that the Anglo-Saxon period is characterized by the contributions of the major groups that invaded England during this time. These groups—the Angles, Saxons, and Danes—brought with them not only the desire to conquer but also the inevitable merging of their several cultures.

During the Anglo-Saxon period, literature reflected the juxtaposition of the church and the pagan world. In the most important work of the period, *Beowulf,* readers may easily discern these two divergent worlds. Much criticism regarding *Beowulf,* in fact, deals with Christian and pagan references in the epic. A preoccupation with ecclesiastical matters is evident in another seminal work of the period, Bede's *Ecclesiastical History.*

In reading Anglo-Saxon poetry, the dominant genre of the period, students should understand its three key characteristics: its tendency toward didacticism, its unique verse form, and its explanation of "epic" topics.

The excerpt from *Beowulf* is the only selection that will require more than a single class period for coverage. As with all poetry, this, and the other poetry selections in the unit, will be enhanced by oral interpretation. You might also want to reserve space in your class schedule for the fascinating source-and-analogue material presented under the Primary Sources heading at various points in the unit.

OBJECTIVES OF THE ANGLO-SAXON UNIT

1. To improve reading proficiency and expand vocabulary
2. To gain exposure to notable Anglo-Saxon poetry
3. To define and identify elements of poetry
4. To respond to poetry orally and in writing
5. To practice the following critical thinking and writing skills:
   a. Recognizing motive
   b. Identifying images and symbols
   c. Analyzing theme
   d. Comparing point of view
   e. Analyzing character

A. Responding to the Quotation

The most significant of the Anglo-Saxon works students will read in this unit is *Beowulf,* an epic that, like much Anglo-Saxon literature, is generally considered to be tragic in form and elegiac in tone. In his battles with Grendel and the dragon, Beowulf fights against the powers of darkness for a glory and a treasure that will live even after him. At the end of the epic, in fact, Beowulf states, "I sold my life / For this treasure, and I sold it well."

You might want students, at this point, to review the traditional definition of *tragedy* (see text pages 332 and 1272). Note that the fall of a despicable or very ordinary person is not, by this definition, a tragedy. What does it suggest about a people's world view that their literature is mainly tragic and elegiac? Do we view life elegiacally? Do we believe a sense of glory or fulfillment or happiness is within human grasp?

THE ANGLO-SAXONS
THE EMERGENT PERIOD
450–1066

by **David Adams Leeming**
and
John Malcolm Brinnin

> *There can be no tragedy in literature without a sense of glory or happiness or fulfilled ambition potentially within human grasp . . . .*
>
> —Alvin A. Lee

England is only part of a relatively small island that also includes Scotland and Wales. This small island has been invaded and settled many times: by an ancient people we call the Iberians, by the Celts, by the Romans, by the Angles and Saxons, and by the Normans. Whatever we think of as "English" today must owe something to each of these invaders.

Isolated from the European continent, rain-drenched, and often fogged in, but also green and dotted with thatched cottages, quaint stone churches, and mysterious megalithic ceremonial ruins, England seems made for elves, legends, and poets. Yet if this land of mystery, beauty, and melancholy weather has produced Stonehenge, Robin Hood, and Shakespeare, it has also produced the theory of gravity, the Industrial Revolution, radar, and penicillin. We tend to associate the English with their monarchy and their former Empire. But we should also remember that while most of the world suffered under various forms of tyranny, the English from the time of the Magna Carta (1215) were gradually creating a political system "by and for the people" that remains today a source of envy and inspiration for many nations.

Although it was against English rule that Americans rebelled in 1776, we in America would not be what we are today without English common law—with its emphasis on personal rights and freedom—English parliamentary government, English literature,

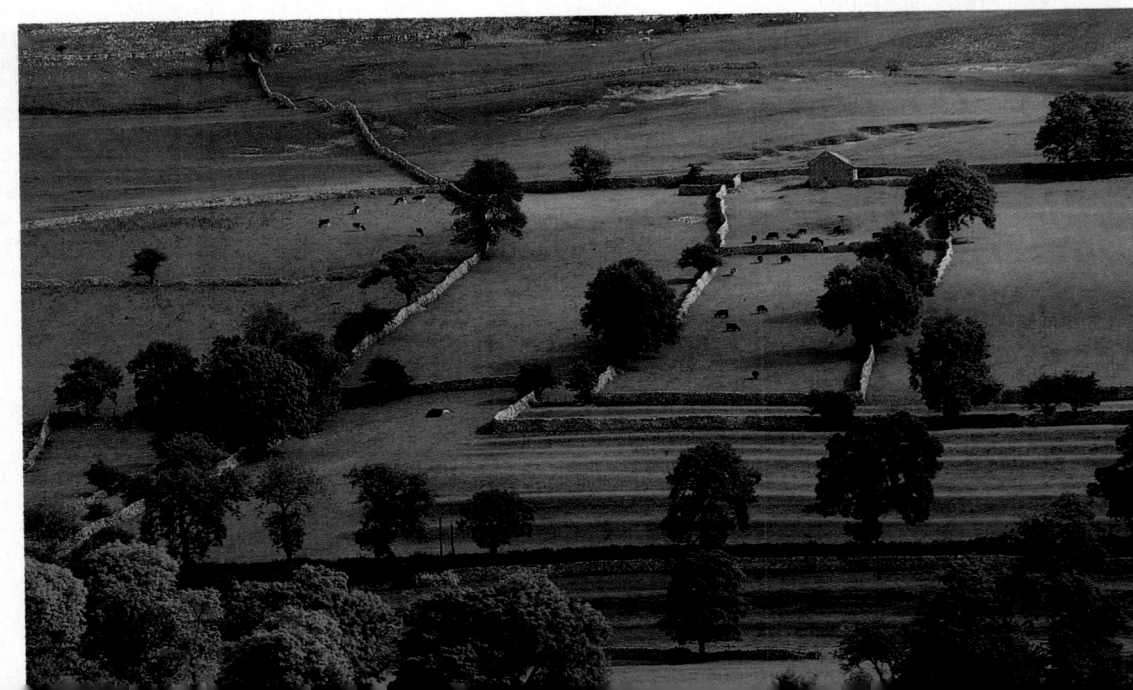

2

FOR FURTHER RESEARCH
Students may be interested in researching a group of British settlers not discussed in this introduction—the Iceni, who lived in what is now Norfolk. The Iceni are interesting because their queen, Boudica (sometimes misspelled Boadicea) led a bloody revolt against the Romans. In Dio Cassius's *Roman History,* Boudica is described as "very tall, the glance of her eye most fierce; her voice harsh. A great mass of the reddest hair fell down to her hips. . . . Her appearance was terrifying."

A. The Celts
From about 700 B.C., the Celts dominated most of what is now western and central Europe. Skilled craftsmen, they introduced the use of iron to the rest of Europe. They also had a highly developed religion, mythology, and legal system that specified the rights of the individual.

The language of the Celts was dominant in Britain until around the fifth century A.D. Welsh, Breton, and Gaelic are forms of the Celtic language that may still be heard in Wales, Scotland, and Ireland today.

B. About the Photograph
Using radiocarbon dating methods on charcoal taken from pits within the circle of stones, historians have postulated that Stonehenge was in use around 1848 B.C. The huge stones are a type found only in western Wales, three hundred miles away, so a great mystery is how the stones, some weighing more than eighty tons, were moved to their present location and arranged in their original positions. A stone marker east of an altar in the center was set to cast a shadow on the altar at dawn on the summer solstice, around June 21.

and the English language. The achievements of England have helped to define and shape our American experience since the birth of our republic. The statesman Winston Churchill once jokingly referred to the unique kinship of America and England when he spoke of two peoples on either side of the Atlantic Ocean "separated by a common language." The United States has, in its more than two centuries of existence as an independent nation, developed a great literature of its own and has fostered a distinctive culture, even a distinctive speech now recognized as "American English." But our American system of government, our language and literature, our whole culture, retain profound links to England. It is, of course, possible to disapprove of English ways and English policies both past and present, but to ignore England and its history and culture would be to ignore our own heritage.

The Celts and Their Religion

When Greek travelers visited what is now Great Britain in the fourth century B.C., they found an island settled by people closely related to the tall, blond Celtic warriors who had sacked Rome earlier, in 387 B.C. Among these island Celts was a group called Brythons or Britons, who left their permanent stamp in one of the names eventually adopted by the land they settled.

The religion of the Celts was evidently a form of **animism,** from the Latin word for "spirit." The Celts saw spirits everywhere—in rivers, trees, stones, ponds, fire, and thunder. These spirits or gods controlled all aspects of existence and they had to be constantly placated. It was the Druids who acted as priestly intermediaries between the gods and the people. Sometimes ritual dances were called for, sometimes human sacrifice. It is thought by some that Stonehenge—that enormous pile of megalithic stones on Salisbury Plain in Wiltshire—was used by the Druids for religious rites having to do with the lunar and solar cycles.

Of great importance to the old Celtic religion was the Mother Goddess, a fertility figure who appears in many forms in the Celtic sculpture. Nearly everything in life could be explained by the relationship of this goddess with her male counterpart in many forms, including the forms of warrior and craftsman. The Great Mother was primarily associated with nature; the male god was associated with the tribe and its particular culture. For life to be good, nature and society needed to be in proper balance. The ancient Celts, then, hoped that the marriage of the Great Mother and the Great Father could produce a world in perfect harmony.

The Romans: The Great Administrators

Beginning with a campaign led by Julius Caesar in 55 B.C. and culminating in one organized by the Emperor Claudius in the first century A.D., the Britons were conquered by the legions of Rome. Using the administrative genius that enabled them to hold domin-

B

A

The ruins of Stonehenge. The stones are about thirteen and a half feet high.

A. Humanities Connection: Discussing the Fine Art

There is evidence that the Romans were producing illuminated (ornately decorated) manuscripts before the birth of Christ, and the Anglo-Saxons as early as the middle of the seventh century.

❓ How does this page from an illuminated manuscript illustrate the savageness of the Viking attacks? (Perceptive students will note that in the top half of the illustration, the Britains seem to be holding their own against the Viking invaders, but that in the bottom half, the Britains, their faces masks of horror, are beaten and bloodied. Nothing in the history of the British people—certainly not the invasions of the Angles, Saxons, and Jutes—had prepared them for the savage and unremitting attacks of the Vikings. In settlements that could not pay sufficient tribute to the barbarians, every man, woman, and child was often slaughtered. As a basis for comparison, students might search for contemporary art that attempts to capture the barbarity of more recent past events.)

B. King Arthur

Students might want to read more about the "most heroic of Celtic leaders," King Arthur, perhaps in Sir Thomas Malory's treatment of the King Arthur legend in *Le Morte Darthur* (c. 1469), in Tennyson's *Idylls of the King* (1859–1885), or in T. H. White's *The Once and Future King* (1958).

C. King Alfred

King Alfred may be one king who truly deserves the appellation "the great." Not only may he have saved Wessex and England from the Danes, but he also helped to create a cohesive English society from small, fractious kingdoms, restored cities destroyed during the invasions, and revived an interest in learning and in the English language.

ion over much of the known world, the Romans provided the organization that prevented further serious invasions of Britain for several hundred years. During Roman rule, Christianity, which would later become a unifying force, gradually took hold under the leadership of missionaries from Europe, and the old Celtic religion began to vanish.

By 410 A.D., however, the Romans, with troubles at home, had essentially evacuated their troops from Britain. When the Roman legions withdrew, they did not leave a viable nation behind them. They left roads, walls, villas, and great public baths, but no central government. Never eager to overextend themselves, the Romans had been content to push warlike tribes that they could not assimilate to the west and north. Thus, Britain without Roman control was a country of separate clans who were now free to pursue their own interests without regard for the general welfare. The result was weakness and a series of successful invasions by non-Christian peoples from the Germanic regions of continental Europe in the mid-fifth century.

The Anglo-Saxons: From King Arthur to King Alfred

The invaders, Angles and Saxons from the Baltic shores of Germany and Jutes from the peninsula of Jutland in Denmark, drove the old Britons before them and eventually settled the greater part of Britain. The language of the Anglo-Saxons became the dominant language in a land which was to take another name from the Angles (Englalond, or England).

This is not to say that the latest newcomers had an easy time of it. The Celts put up a strong resistance before they retreated into Wales in the far West of the country. There, traces of their culture, especially their language, can still be found. One of the most heroic Celtic leaders was a man called Arthur, who developed in legend as the "once and future king."

At first, Anglo-Saxon England was no more politically unified than Celtic Britain had been. The country was divided into several independent principalities, each with its own "king." Occasionally, certain monarchs, such as Ethelbert I of Kent (560–616), achieved extraordinary power. But it was not until King Alfred of Wessex (871–899), also known as Alfred the Great, led the Anglo-Saxons against the invading Danes that England became in any true sense a nation.

The Danes were one of the Viking peoples who crossed the North Sea in the eighth and ninth centuries and eventually took over parts of northeast and central England, where Danish law (Danelaw) replaced that of the Anglo-Saxons. In 878, Alfred forced the Danes out of Wessex. His reign was the beginning of the shaky dominance of Wessex kings in the South of England, a dominance that lasted until the Anglo-Saxons themselves were overwhelmed by the last conqueror of England: William, Duke of Normandy, who landed his boats in England in 1066.

A Viking attack. From a manuscript (12th century).

© 1988 Pierpont Morgan Library, New York.

A. Humanities Connection: About the Fine Art

Throughout this unit, relics from the Sutton Hoo discovery are depicted (see text page 41). Made in the summer of 1939 near the Suffolk coast, the discovery consisted of the impression in the sands of a wooden ship ninety feet long that apparently had been the burial ship of Raedwald, king of East Anglia, who died in 624 or 625. In the center of the ship, close to where the king's body would have lain, were found a helmet, a richly ornate sword and shield, and other items that supposedly designated kingship.

The implications of the Sutton Hoo discovery are immense. For years, scholars had doubted that artisans of that time were capable of creating the magnificent treasures described in *Beowulf.* The Sutton Hoo find indicates clearly that these Anglo-Saxons were skilled artisans. Also, since many of the treasures—such as a Coptic bronze bowl from Egypt—were not of Anglo-Saxon origin, the Anglo-Saxons seemed to have carried on a much livelier and more extensive trade than was once believed.

A

Helmet fragment. Sutton Hoo Ship treasure (7th century).

British Museum.

The Reemergence of Christianity

It is possible that even King Alfred would have failed as a unifier had it not been for the gradual reemergence of Christianity among the Anglo-Saxons. This process was to a great extent due to the work of Irish and Continental missionaries, the most important of whom was probably St. Augustine (the second of that name), who converted King Ethelbert of Kent in 597, founded the cathedral at Canterbury, and became the first Archbishop of Canterbury, or leader of the Church in England. Augustine of Canterbury's mission, however, was not immediately or permanently successful, since the Anglo-Saxon religion was persistent. We are told, for instance, that Ethelbert converted his dependent, King Raedwald of East Anglia, to Christianity, but that Raedwald's wife clung to her old religion, to the extent that she had altars to the Anglo-Saxon gods placed side by side with the Christian altars.

It is interesting to note that Raedwald seems to have had some connection with a tribe from Swedish Jutland called Geatas or Geats. These were the people of *Beowulf* (page 14), the great Anglo-Saxon epic. As you will see, this epic combines elements of the Anglo-Saxon and Christian religions. It is also worth noting that among the most important archeological sites in England were the burial mounds of Sutton Hoo in the land of King Raedwald. These mounds, rich in both Christian and Anglo-Saxon treasures of gold, silver, and bronze—scepters, swords, shields, and rings—date from Raedwald's time. These artifacts cannot help but remind us of the great treasure-filled burial mound of King Beowulf.

B

Anglo-Saxon shoulder clasp, gold inlaid with garnet and glass. Sutton Hoo Ship treasure (7th century).

British Museum.

B. Primary Source

To St. Augustine and his followers, the Anglo-Saxons must have seemed the most untamed of savages. The Venerable Bede, however, reports on St. Augustine's reception by King Ethelbert: "Your words and promises are fair indeed; they are new and uncertain, and I cannot accept them and abandon the age-old beliefs that I have held together with the whole English nation. But since you have travelled far, and I can see that you are sincere in your desire to impart to us what you believe to be true and excellent, we will not harm you." King Ethelbert kept his word, and by the end of the eighth century, England was largely Christianized.

A. About the Jewel

The Latin inscription on the jewel means "Alfred had me made." Some scholars believe the piece to be the head of a book marker, a suitable relic from a man for whom learning and books were so important.

B. Wyrd

The word *wyrd* was used by the Anglo-Saxons to represent one's lot in life. Since the early Anglo-Saxons did not believe strongly in an afterlife, it was mostly through personal fame, attained through heroic action, that one lived on and thus resisted *wyrd*.

A

Gold and enamel jewel thought to have belonged to King Alfred (9th century).

Ashmolean Museum, Oxford.

B

A knight, from a chess set carved of walrus ivory (12th century).

British Museum.

Life in Anglo-Saxon England: Loyal Dependency

As the Sutton Hoo treasures indicate, the Anglo-Saxons were not barbarians, though they were frequently depicted that way. And craftsmanship was not their only talent. There were genuinely important Anglo-Saxon historians and scholars, such as the Venerable Bede (page 54) and King Alfred himself. And there were poets: the *Beowulf* poet, the monk Caedmon (whom we discover in Bede's history), and Cynewulf, once thought to be the author of "The Wanderer" (page 43) and "The Seafarer" (page 48).

Life for the Anglo-Saxons, however, was certainly not luxurious, and it was not dominated by scholarship and the arts. Warfare was the order of the day: war between principalities and between tribes, between clans (subdivisions of tribes), and between established settlers and new invaders. As *Beowulf* shows, law and order, at least in the early days, was the responsibility of the leader in any given group, whether family, clan, tribe, or kingdom. Fame and success, even survival, were achieved through loyalty to such a leader, especially during war, and success was measured in gifts from the leader. So it is that Beowulf "makes his name" and gains riches by defeating the monsters who try to destroy King Hrothgar.

This pattern of loyal dependency was basic to Anglo-Saxon life. It grew out of a need to protect the group from the terrors of an enemy-infested virgin wilderness—a wilderness that became particularly frightening during the long, inhospitable nights of winter. In most of England, the Anglo-Saxons tended to live close to their animals in single-family homesteads, wooden buildings that surrounded a communal court or chieftain's hall. This cluster of buildings was protected by a wooden stockade fence. Such an arrangement contributed to a sense of security, to the close relationship between leader and followers, and to the Anglo-Saxon tendency toward community discussion and rule by consensus.

The Anglo-Saxon Religion

The religion of the early Anglo-Saxons had come with them from Germany and had much in common with what we think of as Norse or Scandinavian mythology. The Anglo-Saxon deity named Thunor was essentially the same as Thor, the god of weather, and particularly of thunder and lightning. His sign was the hammer and possibly also the twisted cross we call the swastika, which is found on so many Anglo-Saxon gravestones. Thunor was a terrifying god, but he could also function as a protector, whose mother was the god Earth itself. (His name survives in *Thursday,* "Thor's day.")

As she did for the Celts, the earth mother took on many forms for the Anglo-Saxons. In fact, the goddess in her group form as the "mothers" was common to the Celts and the Anglo-Saxons. Not surprisingly, given what we know of the male-centered Anglo-Saxon social life, the female deity was concerned with childbearing and homemaking.

One of the most important Norse gods was Odin, the god who overcame death itself in order to learn the great mysteries contained in the runes, or religious inscriptions. As the god of death, poetry, and magic, Odin could help humans communicate with spirits. He was especially associated with burial rites and with ecstatic trances, important for both poetry and religious "mysteries." The Old English name for Odin was Woden (from which we have *Wednesday*, "Woden's day"). It is perhaps not surprising that this god of poetry and death would have been so important to a people who produced great poetry and who tended particularly toward the elegiac or mournful mood.

Still another significant figure in Anglo-Saxon mythology is the dragon. It seems always, as in *Beowulf*, to be the protector of a treasure. Some scholars suggest that the fiery dragon should be seen as both a personification of "death the devourer" and as the guardian of the grave mound, in which are laid not only a warrior's ashes but his treasure as well.

On the whole, the religion of the Anglo-Saxons seems to have been more concerned with ethics—with the "manly" virtues of bravery, loyalty, generosity, and friendship—than with the mystical aspects of reality. One historian, G. M. Trevelyan, in describing the Anglo-Saxon ethic, has even suggested that "the social standards of the modern English schoolboy come nearest to it."

A

A monk's cell on Skellig Michael, off the coast of Kerry, Ireland (7th or 8th century).

B

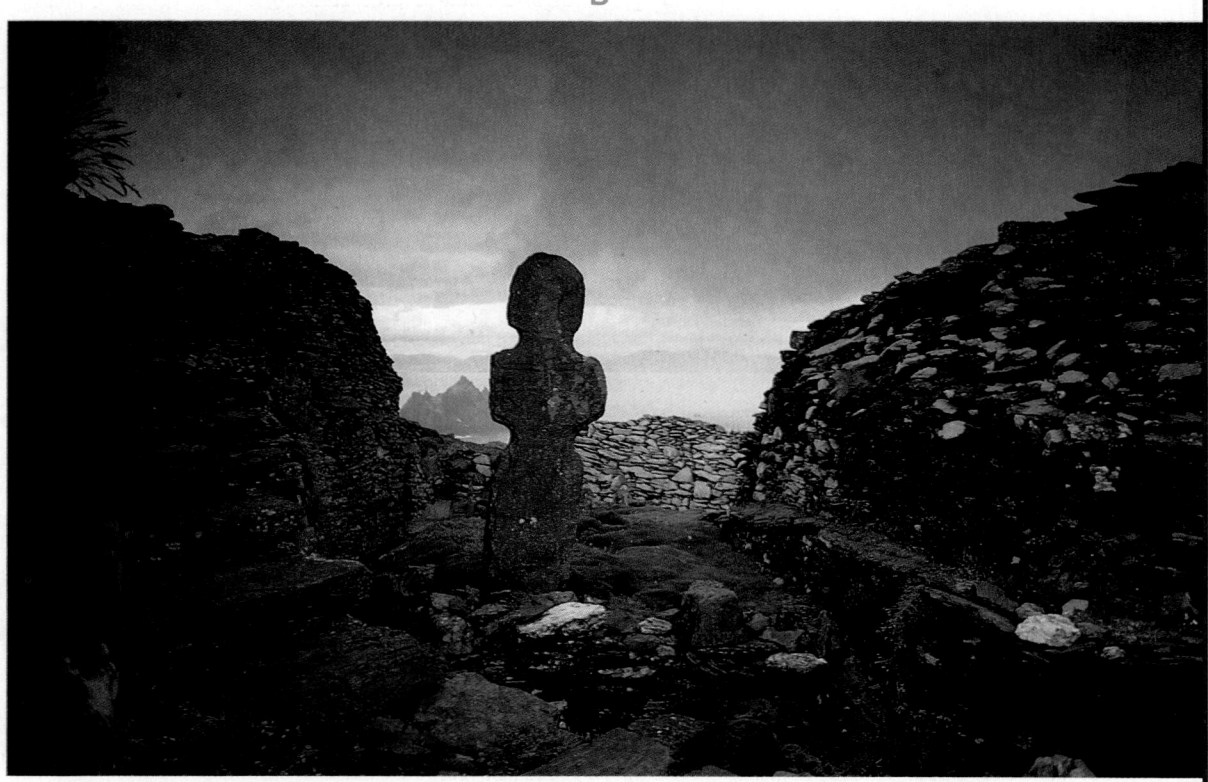

Since the beginning of recorded history, humans have had strong, dual emotional reactions to serpents. This could be accounted for by their power to do harm, or it could be because snakes occupy a position between the lower world and the upper one: They can live on top of the ground and below it. In fifteenth-century Europe, a serpent eating its tail symbolized the cyclical, positive nature of life. In China, dragons are benevolent tomb guardians. But in most Western myths, such as the myth of St. George, the dragon (*dra'kōn,* "serpent") symbolizes evil.

B. About the Photograph
Deserted now, of course, Skellig Michael can be visited by boat. The cells were cold, the rocks are often swept by rain and gales of wind from the Atlantic, and food was minimal.

A. The Bard

? The text points out the high esteem in which the bard (or scop) was held in Anglo-Saxon society. What is the role of the writer in our society today? (Students may suggest that among the roles are those of historian, entertainer, and teacher.)

B. Humanities Connection: About the Fine Art

The Bayeux Tapestry is a piece of embroidery, measuring 230 feet by 20 inches, that depicts more than seventy scenes of the Norman Conquest of England. Because of a complex political situation, explained on text page 68, many noblemen thought that William of Normandy, rather than Harold, the man depicted here being crowned king in January 1066, should have been acclaimed king. Astute students might notice, in fact, the beasts from Aesop's fables at the feet of King Harold (possibly the artist's comment on his selection). Other scenes in the tapestry depict William's preparation of a fleet of ships, his sailing from the coast of France and landing at Hastings, the battles between Harold and William, and the ensuing death of Harold. The tapestry remains today an important historical source for information about the Norman Conquest. It can be seen in the Town Hall of Bayeux, France.

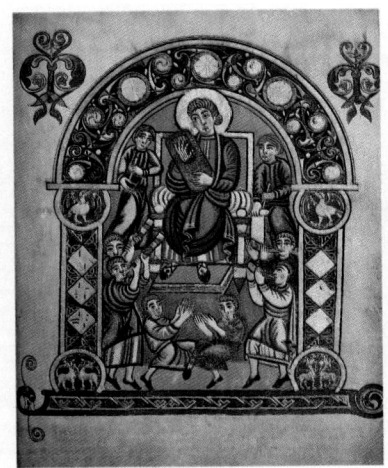

King David and musicians.

British Library.

Bards and Poets in Anglo-Saxon England

The Anglo-Saxon communal hall, besides offering shelter and a place for holding council meetings, also provided space and opportunity for entertainment. As in other parts of the ancient world (notably in Homeric Greece more than one thousand years earlier), entertainment was provided to a great extent by skilled storytellers or **bards,** such as this one described in *Beowulf:*

A

> . . . And sometimes a proud old soldier
> Who had heard songs of the ancient heroes
> And could sing them all through, story after story,
> Would weave a net of words for Beowulf's
> Victory, tying the knot of his verses
> Smoothly, swiftly, into place with a poet's
> Quick skill, singing his new song aloud
> While he shaped it, and the old songs as *well* . . .
>
> Lines 867–874

These bards (called *scops*) were in no way considered inferior to other warriors. To the Anglo-Saxons, creating poetry was as "manly" as fighting, hunting, farming, or loving. The poets sang to the accompaniment of a harp. As sources for their improvisational poetry, the storytellers had a rich supply of traditional heroic tales, narratives that reflected the ideals of a people constantly under threat of annihilation by war, disease, or old age. We are told of the king in *Beowulf:*

B

Coronation of Harold, King of England (11th century). French Bayeux Tapestry.

A. About the Photograph
Before Henry VIII dissolved the English monasteries in the early sixteenth century, there were twenty-eight abbeys, twenty-six priories, twenty-three convents, thirty friaries, and thirteen cells in Yorkshire alone. All are in ruins today.

B. Primary Source
In the preface to the *Consolation of Philosophy*, Alfred writes about himself: "What I set out to do was to virtuously and justly administer the authority given me. I desired the exercise of power so that my talents and my power might not be forgotten. But every natural gift and every capacity in us soon grows old and is forgotten if wisdom is not in it. Without wisdom no faculty can be fully brought out, for anything done unwisely cannot be accounted as skill. To be brief, I may say that it has always been my wish to live honourably, and after my death to leave to those who come after me my memory in good works."
❓ Is Alfred's philosophy of leadership applicable to our lives today? Why? (Students probably will consider wisdom to be an important leadership trait but may agree that it rarely is talked about as such.)

> . . . sometimes Hrothgar himself, with the harp
> In his lap, stroked its silvery strings
> And told wonderful stories, a brave king
> Reciting unhappy truths about good
> And evil—and sometimes he wove his stories
> On the mournful thread of old age, remembering
> Buried strength and the battles it had won.
> He would weep, the old king . . .
>
> Lines 2107–2114

Anglo-Saxon literature contains many works in this same elegiac, or mournful, strain; poems such as "The Wanderer" and "The Seafarer" (pages 43 and 48), for example, stress the transience of a life frequently identified with the cold and darkness of winter. For the non-Christian Anglo-Saxon, only fame and its reverberation in poetry could provide an enduring defense against death. Perhaps this is why the Anglo-Saxon bards, uniquely gifted with the skill to preserve fame in the collective memory, were such honored members of their society.

Monasteries and Anglo-Saxon Literature

In the death-shadowed world of the Anglo-Saxons, the poets or bards provided one element of hope: the possibility that heroic deeds might be enshrined in the collective memory. Another element of hope was supplied by Christianity. The strongholds of Christianity in this period, as in the later Middle Ages, were the monasteries, centers of faith and learning. Their cultural and spiritual influence existed right alongside the heroic ideals and traditions of the older Anglo-Saxon religion. In fact, the monasteries probably preserved some of the older traditions: in all likelihood, it was monks who wrote down (and reworked) the great works of popular literature such as *Beowulf* and "The Wanderer."

These works from the older oral tradition were composed in the vernacular, or the language of the people, a Germanic tongue that we now classify as Old English. But the principal works of learning in the monasteries were written in the language of the Church, which was Latin. The greatest of the Latin writers in Anglo-Saxon England was the Venerable Bede (673–735), a monk who had an international reputation as a scholar. Bede's *Ecclesiastical History of the English People* (731) provides us with our first major source about early English history.

Latin remained the language of "serious" study (as opposed to popular culture) until the time of King Alfred, who was responsible for the *Anglo-Saxon Chronicle* (892), a running history of England which began in the earliest days and was continued until 1154. Alfred made much use of Bede's work and had texts of his *Ecclesiastical History* translated into English. Partly because of King Alfred's efforts, Old English began to gain respect as a language of culture, and works such as the ones in this unit came to be recognized as the great works of literature that they are.

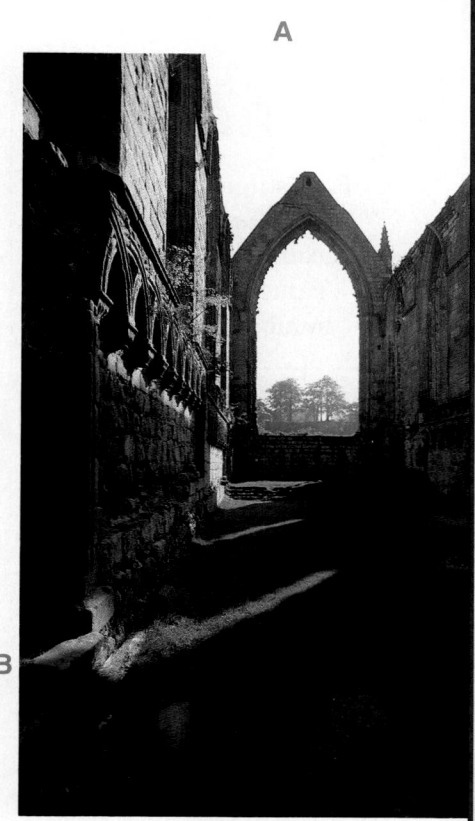

A

B

The ruins of Yorkshire Abbey.

1. King Alfred led the Anglo-Saxons against the invading Danes and helped to unify England.
2. The people of *Beowulf* are the Swedish tribe known as the Geats.
3. The Anglo-Saxon oral poet used descriptive compounds known as kennings.
4. The Anglo-Saxon poets who sang stories to the accompaniment of a harp were known as bards or scops.
5. The last conquerer of England was William, Duke of Normandy.

FOR FURTHER READING
STUDENTS
Michael Woods's *In Search of the Dark Ages* (1975) is an eminently readable account of the Anglo-Saxon period, with chapters on Boudica, King Arthur, and the Sutton Hoo "man."

A. The Recording
For more information on kennings and alliteration in Anglo-Saxon poetry, see Analyzing Language and Style, text page 40. At this point you might want to play for students a recording of *Beowulf* in Old English, available in many school and community libraries. You might also play the audiocassette recording of the battle of Grendel that accompanies Raffel's translation of the *Beowulf* selection in the text. Students can listen for the distinctive characteristics of Anglo-Saxon verse discussed here, and compare those sounds with Raffel's translation (which has not attempted to reproduce all the alliteration).

A fifteenth-century wooden harp.

> "**O**ld English poetics are more like a musical system, concerned with time rather than with the number of syllables."

Old English Poetics

Anglo-Saxon or Old English poetry was sung or recited aloud. As we discover from references in *Beowulf,* poetic recitation was usually accompanied by the harp. The purpose of accompaniment was certainly to provide a regular rhythm: A stroke of the harp would have been used, for instance, to maintain the beat during a breathing pulse of the minstrel-poet.

Besides the use of the harp, internal workings, or poetics, of Anglo-Saxon verse point to its oral aspect. From the time of Chaucer (1340?–1400), English poetry has traditionally derived its rhythm from the strict number and order of stressed and unstressed syllables in a line. Thus, for example, in the first line of Samuel Taylor Coleridge's ''Kubla Khan'' (written in 1816), there are eight syllables: Four unstressed syllables alternate with four stressed ones. We call such alternation of syllables an **iamb.** Four of these iambs in a line produce a poetic pattern called **iambic tetrameter:**

In Xánadú dĭd Kúblă Khán

But the rhythmical system in Old English poetry is markedly different. As many scholars have suggested, Old English poetics are more like a musical system, concerned with time rather than with the number of syllables. Thus, it is the regular amount of time between primary stresses or beats (rather than the number of syllables between them) that is important. The number of syllables in the individual lines of *Beowulf,* for example, varies; but each line always has four primary stresses:

Hróðgar máþelode, hélm Séyldinga
Hýrde ic þæt he ðone héalsbeah, Hýðge geséalde.

You can see that the second line contains many more syllables than the first; yet in both lines there are only four primary stresses or major beats. This regular repetition of four stresses may have made the improvisational poet's task easier (it aided memory); it certainly adds to the musical quality of the verse.

An outstanding feature of this poetry is its use of **alliteration,** or the repetition of consonant and vowel sounds at the beginning of words. In fact, Anglo-Saxon poetry is often called alliterative poetry: Instead of rhyme unifying the poem, we find the verse line divided into two halves, separated by a rhythmical pause or **caesura** and joined by the use of a repeated consonant or vowel sound in both halves of the line. Notice the alliterative use of *h* in the two lines above, and of *g* in this line:

God mid Geatum Grendles daeda

The Anglo-Saxon oral poet was also assisted by a store of ready-made descriptive compound words, or **kennings,** that evoke vivid images. In the *Iliad* and *Odyssey* (which are also the products of oral composition), Homer used something like kennings in such constructions as ''rosy-fingered dawn'' and ''the wine-dark sea.'' The *Beowulf* poet speaks of the sea as the ''whale-road'' and of ships as ''sea-stallions.''

TEACHERS
Translations of *Beowulf* with commentary on the text and on the Anglo-Saxons include:
Francis B. Gummere (1909)
William Ellery Leonard (1923)
D. H. Crawford (1926)
Charles W. Kennedy (1940)
Mary E. Waterhouse (1949)

Kevin Crossley-Holland (1968)
Howell D. Chickering, Jr. (1977)

Studies of *Beowulf* include:
Arthur G. Brodeur, *The Art of "Beowulf"* (1959)
Edward B. Irving, Jr., *A Reading of "Beowulf"* (1968)

Alvin A. Lee, *The Guest Hall of Eden* (1972)
Kenneth Sisam, *The Structure of "Beowulf"* (1965)
A useful bibliography for *Beowulf* translations and studies is Douglas D. Short's *"Beowulf" Scholarship: An Annotated Bibliography* (1980).

Finally, in *Beowulf,* as in the *Iliad* and the *Odyssey,* we find ready-made formulas used to describe particular activities, such as voyaging on the sea, greeting a stranger, eating a feast, receiving or giving riches. Repeating these formula descriptions word for word and line by line took some of the burden off the bard: he could sing them automatically while thinking ahead to the next part of his story.

The poetry of oral epic is thus a combination of traditional and inventive elements, and each public recitation or "performance" of a narrative probably differed to some degree from every other.

We now have available some excellent modern translations of Old English poetry. "Now indeed," says scholar Robert Creed about Burton Raffel's translations, "the exalted vision of the dead poet in his dead language can speak to us in the living language of a living poet: 'Oh wonderful miracle worked among men.'"

From *The Book of Kells* (8th century).

Trinity College, Dublin.

A. The Time Line
Have students use an encyclopedia o[r] other reference source to place th[e] following major events in science and the arts on the time line.

—Euclid publishes *The Elements of Geometry.* (c. 300 B.C.)

—Li Po writes poetry during China's "golden age of literature." (c. 701–762 A.D.)

—Chang Heng builds the world's first seismograph. (A.D. 132)

—Lady Murasaki writes the world's first significant novel, *The Tale of Genji.* (c. 970–1050 A.D.)

—The Greeks build the Pantheon, one of architecture's most influential buildings. (c. 118–125 A.D.)

300 B.C.–55 B.C.	A.D. 380–410	432–449	510–551
Celts called Brythons live in Britain, 300's B.C. Julius Caesar invades Britain, 55 B.C.	Christianity made official religion of Roman Empire, A.D. 380 Roman legions evacuate Britain, 410	Patrick converts the High King and Christianizes Ireland, 432 Angles and Saxons invade Britain, 449	King Arthur rules a Celtic tribe, 510 (?) Confucius born in China, 551

563	563–570	601–700	664–700's
Augustine converts Anglo-Saxon King Ethelbert of Kent and establishes monastery at Canterbury, 563	Monastery founded on island of Iona off Scottish coast by Irish monk Columba, 563 Muhammad born in Mecca, 570	Paulinus is first Roman missionary to arrive in northern England, 601 ***Beowulf* written down, 700 (?)**	Synod at Whitby Abbey unites British Christian Church with Roman Church, 664 *Book of Kells* produced in Ireland, 700's

618–711	731–787	800–878	900–1000
Golden Age of Tang Dynasty begins in China, 618 Muslims invade Spain, 711	**Bede writes *History of the English Church and People,* 731** Danes invade Britain and Viking invasions begin, 787	Decline of great Mayan civilization in Central America, 800 King Alfred forces Danes out of Wessex, 878	Height of Kingdom of Ghana in Africa, 900's **Lady Murasaki writes the world's first novel, *The Tale of Genjii,* in Japan, c. 1000**

A

You might want to discuss with students how scholars have determined some of the facts mentioned in this introductory material, such as the method and date of *Beowulf*'s composition. (The pool of formulaic diction, repeated with some variations throughout the poem, is the clue to its oral composition. Howell D. Chickering, Jr., a *Beowulf* scholar, comments

that "the bard would use familiar themes and phrases in his improvisations much as jazz musicians today combine riffs, tags, and other musical formulas when they improvise upon a tune." The earliest speculative date is based on the historical fact that Beowulf's liege lord, Higlac, was killed around 594. This, then, is the earliest possible date for the poem. Other historical data and data from the text

place it around the 700–750 date mentioned here.)

A. About the Caldron

The caldron shown here is a product of the highest period of Celtic culture, known as the La Tène culture. As is evident here, these Celts were particularly skilled in metalwork. Much of the art on the caldron depicts the mythology of the Celts. On an inner plate, for example, the figure wearing stag antlers represents the Lord of the Wild Beasts. The significance of many of the figures can only be guessed at. The caldron was used as a kind of kettle for holding warm water or drink.

Beowulf

Beowulf is to England what Homer's *Iliad* and *Odyssey* are to ancient Greece: It is the first great work of a national literature. *Beowulf* is the mythical and literary record of a formative stage of English civilization; it is also an epic of the heroic sources of English culture. As such, it uses a host of traditional motifs associated with heroic literature all over the world.

Like most early heroic literature, *Beowulf* is oral art. It was handed down, with changes, and embellishments, from one minstrel to another. The stories of *Beowulf,* like those of all oral epics, are traditional ones, familiar to the audiences who crowded around the harpist-bards in the communal halls at night. The tales in the *Beowulf* epic are the stories of dream and legend, of monsters and of god-fashioned weapons, of descents to the underworld and of fights with dragons, of the hero's quest and of a community threatened by the powers of evil.

Beowulf was composed in Old English, probably in Northumbria in northeast England, sometime between the years 700 and 750. The world it depicts, however, is much older, that of the early sixth century. Much of the material of the poem is based on early folk legends—some Celtic, some Scandinavian. Since the scenery describes the coast of Northumbria, not of Scandinavia, it has been assumed that the poet who wrote the version that has come down to us was Northumbrian. Given the Christian elements in the epic, this poet may also have been a monk.

A Celtic caldron, silver-plated (1st century B.C.).

Nationalmuseet, Copenhagen.

A

The only manuscript we have of *Beowulf* dates from the year 1000 and is now in the British Museum in London. Burned and stained, it was discovered in the eighteenth century: Somehow it had survived Henry VIII's destruction of the monasteries two hundred years earlier.

By the standards of Homer, whose epics run to nearly 15,000 lines, *Beowulf,* with approximately 3,200 lines, is relatively short. The epic tells the story of Beowulf (his name may mean "bear"), a Geat from Sweden who crosses the sea to Denmark in a quest to rescue King Hrothgar from the demonic monster Grendel. This epic hero, who emerges from the misty reaches of the English past, is a far-Northern mask of a national hero "type," who in other stories wears the mask of St. George or King Arthur. This hero-type is the dragon slayer, the representative of a beseiged community that stands in precarious unity against the satanic forces that lurk everywhere in the cold darkness. When Grendel appeared to the Anglo-Saxon listener, he was not viewed as a legend; he was the embodiment of an all-too-present reality.

A List of Characters and Places

Here are some of the important people, monsters, and places that appear in *Beowulf* or are mentioned in the story:

Beowulf: a Geat, son of Edgetho and nephew of Higlac, king of the Geats. Higlac is Beowulf's feudal lord, as well as his uncle.

Brecca: chief of a tribe called Brondings and a friend of Beowulf.

Grendel: a man-eating monster who lives at the bottom of a foul mere, or mountain lake. His name might be related to the old Norse *grindill,* meaning "storm," or *grenja,* "to bellow."

Herot: the golden guest-hall built by King Hrothgar, the Danish ruler. It was decorated with the antlers of stags; the name means "hart [stag] hall." Scholars think Herot might have been built near Lejre on the coast of Zealand, in Denmark.

Hrothgar: king of the Danes, builder of Herot. He had once befriended Beowulf's father. His father was called Healfdane (which probably means "half Dane"). Hrothgar's name might mean "glory spear" or "spear of triumph."

Unferth: one of Hrothgar's courtiers, who is reputed to be a skilled warrior. His sword, called Hrunting, is used by Beowulf in a later battle.

Welthow: Hrothgar's wife, queen of the Danes.

Wiglaf: a Geat warrior, one of Beowulf's select band, and the only one to help him in his final fight with the dragon. Wiglaf might be related to Beowulf.

Page from the *Beowulf* manuscript (c. 1000).

British Library.

A. Expansion

The *Beowulf* manuscript mentioned here is part of a volume, or codex, that also contains four other works in Old English: *The Passion of St. Christopher, The Wonders of East, Alexander's Letter to Aristotle,* and a fragment of *Judith. Beowulf* was composed about two hundred years before it was copied into this codex of five works.

Interestingly, Beowulf himself is the only character who appears only within the poem; every other character is found in earlier legends or in actual history. The Grendel character, for example, almost surely has his roots in the Old Norse stories of the *draugar,* or animated corpses, dead men of supernatural strength who walked at night spreading evil and terror. Often a *draugar* had a mother even more terrible than he, known as a *ketta,* or "she-cat."

1. BUILDING ON PRIOR KNOWLEDGE. Begin by reviewing with students relevant historical information from the introduction. During the time that *Beowulf* was composed, the Anglo-Saxons, their language, and their values dominated much of Britain. An Anglo-Saxon warrior's loyalty to his leader was one of the most important virtues, and a warrior's success was measured in the fame he won through battle and in gifts from his leader. Most Anglo-Saxons, who were non-Christians, believed that life was a constant struggle against oncoming darkness and that life was controlled by *wyrd*, or fate. The only way of defeating *wyrd* was to gain personal fame.

2. ESTABLISHING A PURPOSE. The original, complete *Beowulf* consists of 3,182 lines. A Modern English version of 842 lines, divided into twelve parts, is reprinted here. For some of those parts, an individual purpose for reading is suggested. Overall, you might begin by suggesting that, since the triumph of good over evil is the most pervasive theme of the epic, students read for characters, events, and images that reinforce that theme.

Part 1 Summary
Grendel, a monster existing in darkness and suffering, is introduced.

A. Imagery
? What imagery is associated with Grendel, making his evil nature apparent? What imagery is associated with Hrothgar's men? (Grendel lives in darkness and pain; he is associated with "monsters born of Cain" and with "a thousand forms of evil." Hrothgar's men, on the other hand, are associated with the imagery of the Creation as it is being sung by the poet in the hall.)

B. Allusions
? What is the poet alluding to in lines 5–13? (The Biblical story of the Creation. Some critics maintain that Herot symbolically represents Creation, the goodness of which is abhorrent to the evil Grendel. All Biblical allusions in *Beowulf* are from Genesis.)

C. Cain
See Primary Sources: The Mark of Cain, text page 30, for the Cain and Abel story.

Though the poetic form of the *Beowulf* story may seem foreign to you, the hero himself should seem very familiar. He embodies many virtues we still admire in the heroic "dragon-slayers" of today. Beowulf has superior physical prowess, he is supremely ethical, and he risks his own life to save the lives of those who are in mortal danger and cannot protect themselves.

The setting of the first part of the epic is Herot, a guest-hall or "mead-hall." (Mead is a fermented drink made from honey.) The hall had a central place in Anglo-Saxon society. Here the lord's warriors could feast, listen to the bard's stories, and sleep in safety.

You'll notice that Grendel is immediately identified as a spawn of Cain. In the Bible, Cain is the first murderer. His crime was fratricide—the murder of his own brother. For an account of Cain's murder of Abel and of the curse put on Cain's descendants, see page 30.

from Beowulf

Translated by Burton Raffel

The Monster Grendel

1

A A powerful monster, living down
In the darkness, growled in pain, impatient
As day after day the music rang
Loud in that hall, the harp's rejoicing
5 Call and the poet's clear songs, sung
Of the ancient beginnings of us all, recalling
The Almighty making the earth, shaping
These beautiful plains marked off by oceans,
B Then proudly setting the sun and moon
10 To glow across the land and light it;
The corners of the earth were made lovely with trees
And leaves, made quick with life, with each
Of the nations who now move on its face. And then
As now warriors sang of their pleasure:
15 So Hrothgar's men lived happy in his hall
Till the monster stirred, that demon, that fiend,
Grendel, who haunted the moors, the wild
Marshes, and made his home in a hell
Not hell but earth. He was spawned in that slime,
20 Conceived by a pair of those monsters born
C Of Cain, murderous creatures banished
By God, punished forever for the crime
Of Abel's death. The Almighty drove
Those demons out, and their exile was bitter,
25 Shut away from men; they split
Into a thousand forms of evil—spirits
And fiends, goblins, monsters, giants,
A brood forever opposing the Lord's
Will, and again and again defeated.

image of Grendel - darkness evil

creation allusion

Herot - goodness happiness

Biblical

defeat of evil

SUPPLEMENTARY SUPPORT MATERIALS

1. Vocabulary Activity Worksheet (*CCB*)
2. Review and Response Worksheets: Characterization; Kennings (*CCB*)
3. Selection Test (*CCB*)
4. Audiocassette recording

DEVELOPING VOCABULARY

The following words from the epic are tested in the Selection Test. (See also Vocabulary Activity Worksheet.)

moor	scabbard
reparation	hilt
mail	hoary
to purge	to unsheathe
reprisal	kinship

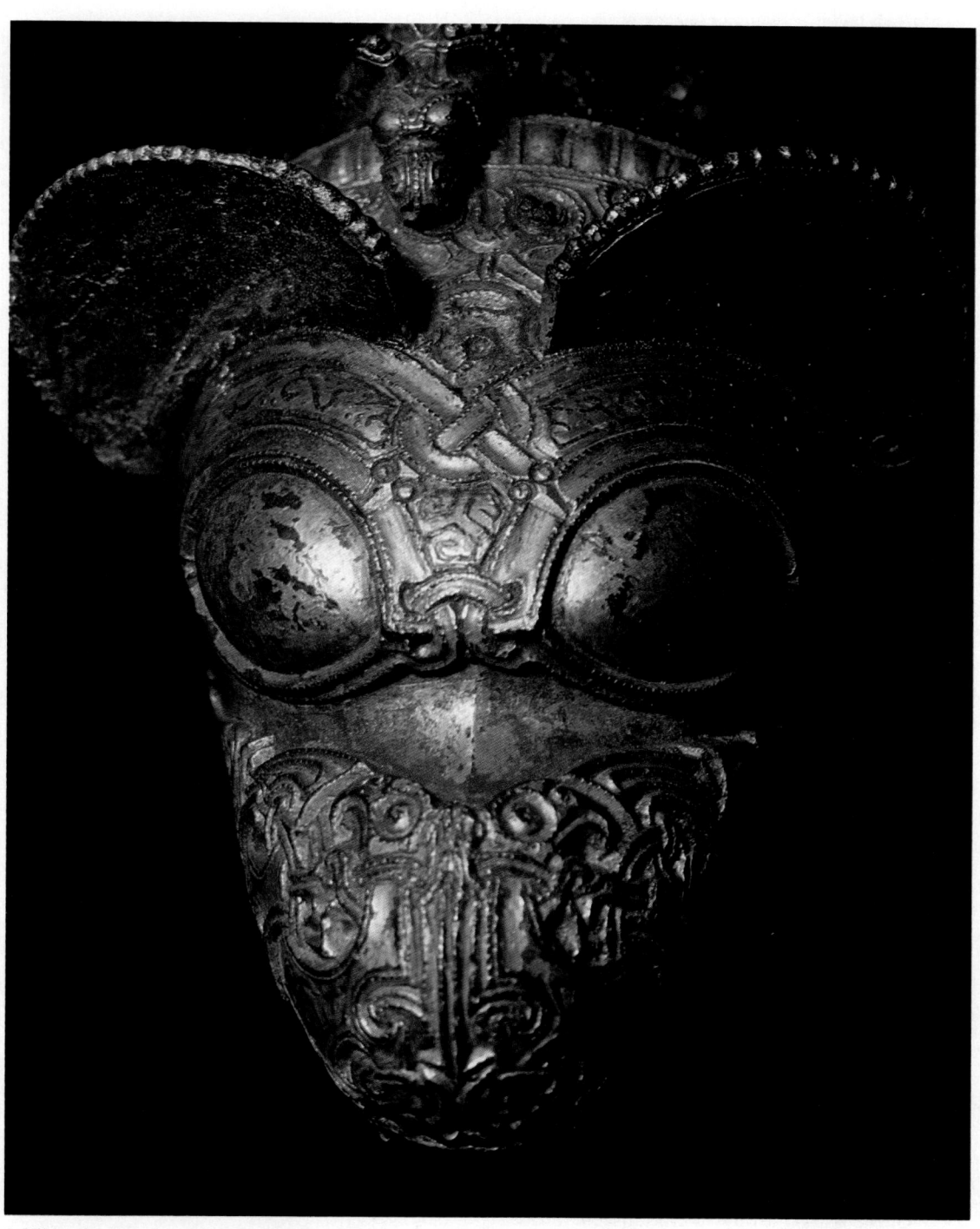

A Viking harness bow or a horse collar (detail). Gilt bronzework mounted on wood.

Under cover of darkness, Grendel goes to Herot, where he slaughters thirty sleeping men. His terrorism continues as Hrothgar's men seek safety in flight. Herot has now stood empty for twelve years as Hrothgar debates remedies with his councils, including sacrifice to the old pagan gods.

PREPARATION
ESTABLISHING A PURPOSE. You might suggest that students read Part 2 to answer this question: Why do none of Hrothgar's men challenge Grendel? (Answers will vary, but students should note that Grendel is depicted as a superhuman monster that no ordinary mortal could hope to defeat. Students will learn later, from Hrothgar [lines 214–219, text

pages 20–21], that the men did make some ineffectual attempts.)

A. Herot
Herot means "hart" or "stag," an animal that was a symbol of kingship to the Anglo-Saxons. A stag-topped scepter was uncovered in the Sutton Hoo mound.

B. Characterization
? What evidence is there that Grendel is a superhuman monster? (He is referred to as a "monster" with claws who lives in a lair. He is able to slaughter thirty men at once.)

C. Symbolism/Conflict
? What evidence is there that Grendel symbolizes evil and that the conflict is not only between men but also between good and evil? (Grendel, in lines 52–53, is motivated by a "lust for evil." When Grendel has managed to empty Herot, the poet says that "hate has triumphed." Hrothgar's men, Grendel's adversaries, on the other hand, are referred to in line 59 as "the righteous.")

2

30   Then, when darkness had dropped, Grendel
A Went up to Herot, wondering what the warriors
      Would do in that hall when their drinking was done.
      He found them sprawled in sleep, suspecting
      Nothing, their dreams undisturbed. The monster's
35   Thoughts were as quick as his greed or his claws:
      He slipped through the door and there in the silence
B Snatched up thirty men, smashed them
      Unknowing in their beds and ran out with their bodies,
      The blood dripping behind him, back
40   To his lair, delighted with his night's slaughter.
      At daybreak, with the sun's first light, they saw
      How well he had worked, and in that gray morning
      Broke their long feast with tears and laments
      For the dead. Hrothgar, their lord, sat joyless
45   In Herot, a mighty prince mourning
      The fate of his lost friends and companions,
      Knowing by its tracks that some demon had torn
      His followers apart. He wept, fearing
      The beginning might not be the end. And that night
50   Grendel came again, so set
      On murder that no crime could ever be enough,
      No savage assault quench his lust
      For evil. Then each warrior tried
C To escape him, searched for rest in different
55   Beds, as far from Herot as they could find,
      Seeing how Grendel hunted when they slept.
      Distance was safety; the only survivors
      Were those who fled him. Hate had triumphed.
      So Grendel ruled, fought with the righteous,
60   One against many, and won; so Herot
      Stood empty, and stayed deserted for years,
      Twelve winters of grief for Hrothgar, king
      Of the Danes, sorrow heaped at his door
      By hell-forged hands. His misery leaped
65   The seas, was told and sung in all
      Men's ears: how Grendel's hatred began,
      How the monster relished his savage war
      On the Danes, keeping the bloody feud
      Alive, seeking no peace, offering
70   No truce, accepting no settlement, no price
      In gold or land, and paying the living
      For one crime only with another. No one
      Waited for reparation from his plundering claws:
      That shadow of death hunted in the darkness,
75   Stalked Hrothgar's warriors, old
      And young, lying in waiting, hidden
      In mist, invisibly following them from the edge
      Of the marsh, always there, unseen.

[handwritten marginal notes: kills 30 men; Grendel superhuman monster strength; kings; Conflict — good vs. evil; man vs. monster; Evil triumphs — Hrothgar's men; 12 years; Grendel's story spread to other part of world; kenning]

16

Part 3 Summary
The news of Grendel's terror has reached Beowulf of the Geats, who is "greater and stronger than anyone anywhere in this world." With fourteen of his best men, Beowulf sails to Hrothgar's aid.

So mankind's enemy continued his crimes,
80   Killing as often as he could, coming
    Alone, bloodthirsty and horrible. Though he lived
    In Herot, when the night hid him, he never
A   Dared to touch king Hrothgar's glorious
    Throne, protected by God—God,
85   Whose love Grendel could not know. But Hrothgar's
    Heart was bent. The best and most noble
    Of his council debated remedies, sat
    In secret sessions, talking of the terror
    And wondering what the bravest of warriors could do.
90   And sometimes they sacrificed to the old stone gods,
    Made heathen vows, hoping for Hell's
B   Support, the Devil's guidance in driving
    Their affliction off. That was their way,
    And the heathen's only hope, Hell
95   Always in their hearts, knowing neither God
    Nor His passing as He walks through our world, the
      Lord
    Of Heaven and earth; their ears could not hear
    His praise nor know His glory. Let them
    Beware, those who are thrust into danger,
100 Clutched at by trouble, yet can carry no solace
    In their hearts, cannot hope to be better! Hail
    To those who will rise to God, drop off
    Their dead bodies and seek our Father's peace!

3

So the living sorrow of Healfdane's son°
105 Simmered, bitter and fresh, and no wisdom
    Or strength could break it: that agony hung
    On king and people alike, harsh
    And unending, violent and cruel, and evil.
C   In his far-off home Beowulf, Higlac's
110 Follower and the strongest of the Geats—greater
    And stronger than anyone anywhere in this world—
    Heard how Grendel filled nights with horror
    And quickly commanded a boat fitted out,
    Proclaiming that he'd go to that famous king,
115 Would sail across the sea to Hrothgar,
    Now when help was needed. None
    Of the wise ones regretted his going, much
    As he was loved by the Geats: the omens were good,
    And they urged the adventure on. So Beowulf
120 Chose the mightiest men he could find,
    The bravest and best of the Geats, fourteen
    In all, and led them down to their boat;
    He knew the sea, would point the prow
    Straight to that distant Danish shore.

104. **Healfdane's son:** Hrothgar.

A. Hrothgar's Throne
Scholars have made much of the fact that Hrothgar's throne is protected by God. Margaret Pepperdene notes that "the limit set upon Grendel's power is a promise of hope," an indication that God has not deserted the Danes.

B. Pagan and Christian Elements
The motivation for the Danes' reversion to "old pagan ways" is probably desperation and is an example of the pagan elements intermixed with the generally Christian atmosphere of the poem.

C. The Geats
The Geats lived in what is today southwestern Sweden. Higlac, king of the Geats and Beowulf's uncle, was killed in a raid on the Franks in 521. In the complete version, the Geats' defeat by the Swedes is forecast at the end of the poem.

A. Humanities Connection: Discussing the Fine Art

❓ How accurately does this stylized painting reflect what you already know about the Vikings and their invasions of England? (Although the ships of the Vikings were much larger, holding between forty and fifty men, they were deckless, as they are in this painting, and powered only by sail or oar. The prows of the ships were often decorated with elaborate animal images meant to protect the Vikings and frighten the enemy. Although the ships may have attacked in large numbers, one ship of sixty men was enough to wreak devastation on a small settlement.) Note that the warriors are barefooted.

Vikings sailing to England. From a manuscript (12th century).

© 1987 Pierpont Morgan Library, New York.

Part 4 Summary
Appearing before Hrothgar, Beowulf explains how his sense of duty has brought him to save the Danes. He boasts of his prowess in war and of other great exploits. Beowulf requests of Hrothgar that he be allowed to fight Grendel without using his sword.

PREPARATION
ESTABLISHING A PURPOSE. Have students read Part 4 and be prepared to write two or three sentences characterizing Beowulf.

Beowulf arrives in Denmark and is directed to Herot, the guest-hall of King Hrothgar. The king sends his thane Wulfgar to greet the visitors.

The Arrival of the Hero

4

125   Then Wulfgar went to the door and addressed
The waiting seafarers with soldier's words:
    "My lord, the great king of the Danes, commands me
To tell you that he knows of your noble birth
And that having come to him from over the open
130 Sea you have come bravely and are welcome.
Now go to him as you are, in your armor and helmets,
But leave your battle shields here, and your spears,
Let them lie waiting for the promises your words
May make."
            Beowulf arose, with his men
135 Around him, ordering a few to remain
With their weapons, leading the others quickly
Along under Herot's steep roof into Hrothgar's
Presence. Standing on that prince's own hearth,
Helmeted, the silvery metal of his mail shirt
140 Gleaming with a smith's high art, he greeted
The Danes' great lord:
                "Hail, Hrothgar!
Higlac is my cousin° and my king; the days
Of my youth have been filled with glory. Now Grendel's
Name has echoed in our land: sailors
145 Have brought us stories of Herot, the best
Of all mead-halls, deserted and useless when the moon
Hangs in skies the sun had lit,
Light and life fleeing together.
My people have said, the wisest, most knowing
150 And best of them, that my duty was to go to the Danes'
Great King. They have seen my strength for themselves,
Have watched me rise from the darkness of war,
Dripping with my enemies' blood. I drove
Five great giants into chains, chased
155 All of that race from the earth. I swam
In the blackness of night, hunting monsters
Out of the ocean, and killing them one
By one; death was my errand and the fate
They had earned. Now Grendel and I are called
160 Together, and I've come. Grant me, then,
Lord and protector of this noble place,
A single request! I have come so far,
Oh shelterer of warriors and your people's loved friend,
That this one favor you should not refuse me—
165 That I, alone and with the help of my men,
May purge all evil from this hall. I have heard,

142. **cousin:** meaning "relative." Higlac is Beowulf's uncle and feudal lord.

Beowulf's speech

Christian ref

will fight Grendel

A. Expansion
The "mail shirt" described here would have been composed of as many as twenty thousand small iron rings riveted or welded shut, creating a mesh-net effect. The shirt will later save Beowulf's life and thus prove the solidness of its construction.

B. Epic Poetry
You may wish to caution students against judging Beowulf by today's standards of modesty.
    Beowulf scholar F. Talbot Donaldson, for example, notes that modern readers often find this boasting offensive but that "Beowulf is not only demonstrating that he has chosen the heroic way of life, but is also choosing it, for when he invokes his former courage as pledge of his future courage, his boast becomes a vow." Students should also note that such boasting is a tradition of epic poetry.

Part 5 Summary
Responding to Beowulf's boast, Hrothgar relates how, as a new king, he had aided Beowulf's father and that one reason Beowulf has come is to repay that aid. He describes to Beowulf the horror of Grendel's assaults on Herot. A banquet in Beowulf's honor ends Part 5.

PREPARATION
ESTABLISHING A PURPOSE. Have students read Part 5 to learn why Hrothgar finds it necessary to remind Beowulf of the time he helped Beowulf's father.

A. Responding
❓ Why do you think Beowulf intends to fight Grendel without a sword? (Beowulf's stated reason is his concern for Higlac's opinion of him. Also, without weapons, Grendel and Beowulf will come into closer contact, thus pitting good against evil on a more elemental level. See question 10 on text page 30.)

B. Characterization
❓ How would you characterize Hrothgar? (Hrothgar was once a strong king and loyal to his allies, but now he seems old and weak. The death of his thanes at Grendel's hands has caused him great suffering, so he is considered a compassionate ruler.)

Too, that the monster's scorn of men
Is so great that he needs no weapons and fears none.
Nor will I. My lord Higlac
170   Might think less of me if I let my sword
Go where my feet were afraid to, if I hid
Behind some broad linden shield:° my hands
A Alone shall fight for me, struggle for life
Against the monster. God must decide
175   Who will be given to death's cold grip.
Grendel's plan, I think, will be
What it has been before, to invade this hall
And gorge his belly with our bodies. If he can,
If he can. And I think, if my time will have come,
180   There'll be nothing to mourn over, no corpse to prepare
For its grave: Grendel will carry our bloody
Flesh to the moors, crunch on our bones
And smear torn scraps of our skin on the walls
Of his den. No, I expect no Danes
185   Will fret about sewing our shrouds,° if he wins.
And if death does take me, send the hammered
Mail of my armor to Higlac, return
The inheritance I had from Hrethel,° and he
From Wayland.° Fate will unwind as it must!"

says he will fight with no weapon
religious ref
pagan

172. **linden shield:** shield made of wood of the linden tree.

185. **shrouds:** cloths used to wrap a body for burial.

188. **Hrethel:** Beowulf's grandfather, former king of the Geats.
189. **Wayland:** a smith celebrated for his wonderful workmanship in making swords and shirts of ringed metal (mail shirts).

5

190   Hrothgar replied, protector of the Danes:
"Beowulf, you've come to us in friendship, and
    because
Of the reception your father found at our court.
Edgetho had begun a bitter feud,
Killing Hathlaf, a Wulfing warrior:°
195   Your father's countrymen were afraid of war,
If he returned to his home, and they turned him away.
Then he traveled across the curving waves
To the land of the Danes. I was new to the throne,
Then, a young man ruling this wide
200   Kingdom and its golden city: Hergar,
My older brother, a far better man
Than I, had died and dying made me,
Second among Healfdane's sons, first
In this nation. I bought the end of Edgetho's
205   Quarrel, sent ancient treasures through the ocean's
Furrows to the Wulfings; your father swore
He'd keep that peace. My tongue grows heavy,
And my heart, when I try to tell you what Grendel
Has brought us, the damage he's done, here
210   In this hall. You see for yourself how much smaller
Our ranks have become, and can guess what we've lost
To his terror. Surely the Lord Almighty
Could stop his madness, smother his lust!
How many times have my men, glowing

194. **Wulfing warrior:** the Wulfings were a Germanic tribe. Hrothgar's queen might have been a Wulfing.

Christian ref

Unferth, one of the younger warriors, is angered by Beowulf's boasting and challenges Beowulf's claims. Beowulf responds to Unferth's challenge by describing how, swept apart from Brecca by a storm, he fought beasts of the sea with his naked sword.

Celtic bronze vessel. Sutton Hoo Ship treasure (7th century).

British Museum.

A. A. Humanities Connection: About the Fine Art
The rings on the rim of this vessel and the ornamented plates indicate that the vessel would have been hung. Its function, however, is uncertain. It may have been used in Celtic religious rites.

B. Characterization
❓ What is Unferth's motive for challenging Beowulf? (He is envious of anyone who claims to have greater fame and glory than his own. Scholars have commented that Beowulf's challenge by a retainer is a regular motif of heroic poetry. It allows the hero to show not only his self-assertiveness but also his restraint and courtesy.)

215   With courage drawn from too many cups
        Of ale, sworn to stay after dark
        And stem that horror with a sweep of their swords.
        And then, in the morning, this mead-hall glittering
        With new light would be drenched with blood, the
            benches
220   Stained red, the floors, all wet from that fiend's
        Savage assault—and my soldiers would be fewer
        Still, death taking more and more.
        But to table, Beowulf, a banquet in your honor:
        Let us toast your victories, and talk of the future.''
225   Then Hrothgar's men gave places to the Geats,
        Yielded benches to the brave visitors
        And led them to the feast. The keeper of the mead
        Came carrying out the carved flasks,
        And poured that bright sweetness. A poet
230   Sang, from time to time, in a clear
        Pure voice. Danes and visiting Geats
        Celebrated as one, drank and rejoiced.

Unferth's Challenge

6

B.   Unferth spoke, Ecglaf's son,
        Who sat at Hrothgar's feet, spoke harshly
235   And sharp (vexed by Beowulf's adventure,
        By their visitor's courage, and angry that anyone
        In Denmark or anywhere on earth had ever
        Acquired glory and fame greater
        Than his own):
                    "You're Beowulf, are you—the same
240   Boastful fool who fought a swimming
        Match with Brecca, both of you daring
        And young and proud, exploring the deepest

(Handwritten margin notes: "Hrothgar's men tried to fight but were unsuccessful." "Banquet in Beo's honor" "Unferth jealous of Beowulf")

A. Noting Details

? What is Unferth's version of Beowulf's swimming match with Beowulf's young friend Brecca? (Unferth claims that Beowulf and Brecca fought a swimming match that Brecca won.)

B. Expansion

Unferth is sometimes translated to mean "strife," and his father's name, *Ecglaf,* to mean "sword's legacy."

C. Alliteration

? What examples of alliteration do you find in this passage? (There are numerous examples, including lines 272–273: "Sword, prepared for whales or the swift / Sharp teeth and beaks of needlefish" and lines 288–290: "But fate let me / Find its heart with my sword, hack myself / Free.")

Seas, risking your lives for no reason
But the danger? All older and wiser heads warned you
245 Not to, but no one could check such pride.
With Brecca at your side you swam along
The sea-paths, your swift-moving hands pulling you
Over the ocean's face. Then winter
Churned through the water, the waves ran you
250 As they willed, and you struggled seven long nights
To survive. And at the end victory was his,
Not yours. The sea carried him close
To his home, to southern Norway, near
The land of the Brondings, where he ruled and was
        loved,
Where his treasure was piled and his strength
255   protected
His towns and his people. He'd promised to outswim
        you:
Bonstan's son° made that boast ring true.
You've been lucky in your battles, Beowulf, but I think
Your luck may change if you challenge Grendel,
260 Staying a whole night through in this hall,
Waiting where that fiercest of demons can find you."
    Beowulf answered, Edgetho's great son:
    "Ah! Unferth, my friend, your face
Is hot with ale, and your tongue has tried
265 To tell us about Brecca's doings. But the truth
Is simple: no man swims in the sea
As I can, no strength is a match for mine.
As boys, Brecca and I had boasted—
We were both too young to know better—that we'd risk
270 Our lives far out at sea, and so
We did. Each of us carried a naked
Sword, prepared for whales or the swift
Sharp teeth and beaks of needlefish.
He could never leave me behind, swim faster
275 Across the waves than I could, and I
Had chosen to remain close to his side.
I remained near him for five long nights,
Until a flood swept us apart;
The frozen sea surged around me,
280 It grew dark, the wind turned bitter, blowing
From the north, and the waves were savage. Creatures
Who sleep deep in the sea were stirred
Into life—and the iron hammered links
Of my mail shirt, these shining bits of metal
285 Woven across my breast, saved me
From death. A monster seized me, drew me
Swiftly toward the bottom, swimming with its claws
Tight in my flesh. But fate let me
Find its heart with my sword, hack myself
290 Free; I fought that beast's last battle,
Left it floating lifeless in the sea.

kenning

kenning

257. **Bonstan's son:** Brecca's father was Bonstan.

relates deeds

pagan

Anglo-Saxon gold buckle. Sutton Hoo Ship treasure (7th century).

British Museum.

Part 7 Summary
Using the metaphor of a feast, Beowulf describes how he defeated the sea monsters by filling their bellies with "no banquet-rich food" (his sword), slaughtered nine of these "sea-huge" monsters, and made the seas safe for sailors. Beowulf announces once again that no one can match him for courage in battle, especially Unferth, who has murdered his brothers and will suffer in hell for the sin. Welthow, Hrothgar's queen, greets the warriors, serves them mead, and salutes Beowulf. As night falls, Herot empties and Hrothgar wishes Beowulf well in his battle with Grendel.

7

"Other monsters crowded around me,
Continually attacking. I treated them politely,
Offering the edge of my razor-sharp sword.
295   But the feast, I think, did not please them, filled
Their evil bellies with no banquet-rich food,
Thrashing there at the bottom of the sea;
By morning they'd decided to sleep on the shore,
Lying on their backs, their blood spilled out
300   On the sand. Afterwards, sailors could cross
That sea-road and feel no fear; nothing
Would stop their passing. Then God's bright beacon
Appeared in the east, the water lay still,
And at last I could see the land, wind-swept
305   Cliff walls at the edge of the coast. Fate saves
A   The living when they drive away death by themselves!
Lucky or not, nine was the number
Of sea-huge monsters I killed. What man,
Anywhere under Heaven's high arch, has fought
310   In such darkness, endured more misery or been harder
Pressed? Yet I survived the sea, smashed
The monsters' hot jaws, swam home from my journey.
The swift-flowing waters swept me along
B   And I landed on Finnish soil. I've heard
315   No tales of you, Unferth, telling
Of such clashing terror, such contests in the night!
Brecca's battles were never so bold;
Neither he nor you can match me—and I mean
No boast, have announced no more than I know
To be true. And there's more: you murdered your
320   brothers,
Your own close kin. Words and bright wit
Won't help your soul; you'll suffer hell's fires,
Unferth, forever tormented. Ecglaf's
Proud son, if your hands were as hard, your heart
325   As fierce as you think it, no fool would dare
To raid your hall, ruin Herot
And oppress its prince, as Grendel has done.
But he's learned that terror is his alone,
Discovered he can come for your people with no fear
330   Of reprisal; he's found no fighting, here,
But only food, only delight.
He murders as he likes, with no mercy, gorges
And feasts on your flesh, and expects no trouble,
No quarrel from the quiet Danes. Now
335   The Geats will show him courage, soon
He can test his strength in battle. And when the sun
Comes up again, opening another
Bright day from the south, anyone in Denmark
May enter this hall: that evil will be gone!"
340   Hrothgar, gray-haired and brave, sat happily
Listening, the famous ring-giver sure,

[handwritten annotations:] kenning · kenning · theme · Unferth – function as foil. · Unferth murdered his kin – heinous act · religious · kenning

A. Theme
Another theme of *Beowulf* deals with self vs. fate (or *wyrd*).
❓ In what context does Beowulf mention fate as he describes his sea exploits? (Beowulf says that fate "saves / The living when they drive away death by themselves.")

B. Characterization
In literature, a character foil is one character who enhances another character through contrast.
❓ In what way is Unferth a foil to Beowulf? (Unferth is a spiteful, idle boaster who has committed the unpardonable sin of murdering his kinsmen. Beowulf, on the other hand, has defended those more helpless than he, actions that have brought him glory. Also, as Beowulf says at the end of the complete version of the poem, "I slew no kindred, sought no enemies, swore no false oaths." In all of these, Unferth stands in contrast.)

A. Expansion

Welthow exhibits the qualities of Anglo-Saxon women of the time, as they are described in what is known as the *Exeter Book Gnomes:* "A woman shall prosper, beloved among many her people, shall be cheerful, keep counsel, shall be generous with horses and treasure; at the mead-taking she shall always, everywhere, first greet the lord of nobles before the troop of retainers, place the first cup promptly in her lord's hand; and she shall know good counsel in housekeeping, for their mutual benefit."

B. Noting Details

❓ How does Beowulf's response to the queen exemplify the Anglo-Saxon code for warriors? (For an Anglo-Saxon warrior, life without "greatness and courage" is death.)

C. Personification

❓ How is the coming of night personified as the sun sets? (Night "covered the earth with its net"; "shapes of darkness moved black and silent / Through the world.")

At last, that Grendel could be killed; he believed
In Beowulf's bold strength and the firmness of his
    spirit.
  There was the sound of laughter, and the cheerful
    clanking
345 Of cups, and pleasant words. Then Welthow,
     Hrothgar's gold-ringed queen, greeted
A The warriors; a noble woman who knew
  What was right, she raised a flowing cup
  To Hrothgar first, holding it high
350 For the lord of the Danes to drink, wishing him
  Joy in that feast. The famous king
  Drank with pleasure and blessed their banquet.
  Then Welthow went from warrior to warrior,
  Pouring a portion from the jeweled cup
355 For each, till the bracelet-wearing queen
  Had carried the mead-cup among them and it was
     Beowulf's
  Turn to be served. She saluted the Geats'
  Great prince, thanked God for answering her prayers,
  For allowing her hands the happy duty
360 Of offering mead to a hero who would help
  Her afflicted people. He drank what she poured,
  Edgetho's brave son, then assured the Danish
  Queen that his heart was firm and his hands
  Ready:
     "When we crossed the sea, my comrades
365 And I, I already knew that all
  My purpose was this: to win the good will
B Of your people or die in battle, pressed
  In Grendel's fierce grip. Let me live in greatness
  And courage, or here in this hall welcome
370 My death!"
     Welthow was pleased with his words,
  His bright-tongued boasts; she carried them back
  To her lord, walked nobly across to his side.
    The feast went on, laughter and music
  And the brave words of warriors celebrating
375 Their delight. Then Hrothgar rose, Healfdane's
  Son, heavy with sleep; as soon
  As the sun had gone, he knew that Grendel
  Would come to Herot, would visit that hall
C When night had covered the earth with its net
380 And the shapes of darkness moved black and silent
  Through the world. Hrothgar's warriors rose with him.
    He went to Beowulf, embraced the Geats'
  Brave prince, wished him well, and hoped
  That Herot would be his to command. And then
385 He declared:
     "No one strange to this land
  Has ever been granted what I've given you,
  No one in all the years of my rule.

Two drinking horns. Sutton Hoo Ship treasure (7th century).

Beowulf's purpose

imagery of light

24

On this cloudy night, Grendel slides silently from his gruesome lair to Herot, intent on his usual savagery. After killing his first Geat, however, Grendel finds himself in Beowulf's grasp and knows at once that he has met his fate: "hell's captive caught in the arms / Of him who of all the men on earth / Was the strongest."

Make this best of all mead-halls yours, and then
Keep it free of evil, fight
390   With glory in your heart! Purge Herot
And your ship will sail home with its treasure-holds
        full.''

rewards for success

The feast ends. Beowulf and his men take the place of Hrothgar's followers and lie down to sleep in Herot. Beowulf, however, is wakeful, eager to meet his enemy.

The Battle with Grendel

8

A ⌈   Out from the marsh, from the foot of misty
  | Hills and bogs, bearing God's hatred,
  | Grendel came, hoping to kill
395 ⌊ Anyone he could trap on this trip to high Herot.
      He moved quickly through the cloudy night,
      Up from his swampland, sliding silently
      Toward that gold-shining hall. He had visited Hrothgar's
      Home before, knew the way—
400   But never, before nor after that night,
      Found Herot defended so firmly, his reception
      So harsh. He journeyed, forever joyless,
      Straight to the door, then snapped it open,
      Tore its iron fasteners with a touch
405   And rushed angrily over the threshold.
      He strode quickly across the inlaid
      Floor, snarling and fierce: his eyes
      Gleamed in the darkness, burned with a gruesome
      Light. Then he stopped, seeing the hall
410   Crowded with sleeping warriors, stuffed
      With rows of young soldiers resting together.
      And his heart laughed, he relished the sight,
      Intended to tear the life from those bodies
      By morning; the monster's mind was hot
415   With the thought of food and the feasting his belly
      Would soon know. But fate, that night, intended
      Grendel to gnaw the broken bones
      Of his last human supper. Human
      Eyes were watching his evil steps,
420   Waiting to see his swift hard claws.

suspense

imagery of Grendel

pagan
Beowulf is awake

C ⌈ Grendel snatched at the first Geat
  | He came to, ripped him apart, cut
  ⌊ His body to bits with powerful jaws,
      Drank the blood from his veins and bolted
425   Him down, hands and feet; death
      And Grendel's great teeth came together,
      Snapping life shut. Then he stepped to another
      Still body, clutched at Beowulf with his claws,

B

Gold ornament for a shield. Sutton Hoo Ship treasure (7th century).

British Museum.

A. Responding

More lines in this section are devoted to preparation for the battle than for the battle itself. Why do you think this is so? (To build suspense)

B. About the Shield

The Anglo-Saxon shield was probably made from the wood of a linden or other soft tree. The front of the shield was usually covered with leather and an iron boss was placed in the center of the shield.

C. Responding

Why do you think Beowulf allows Grendel to slaughter one of the Geats before he takes action against Grendel himself? (Answers will vary. Some scholars have suggested that Beowulf is taking time to formulate a plan of attack, just as Odysseus does when he escapes from the One-Eyed Cyclops, but not before the Cyclops has devoured some of his men.)

Literature and Language: Using Specific Verbs to Create a Tone

Share with students that the *Beowulf* poet creates his tone of fierceness largely through his use of specific, no-holds-barred verbs. In Beowulf's confrontation with Grendel, for instance, he uses the verbs *tore, bit, gulped, gobbled,* and *gorged* as Grendel devours the warrior next to Beowulf.

Have students work in pairs to rewrite the following sentences with specific verbs that create the same kind of tone. Later, have each pair of students exchange their sentences with another set of partners to compare and contrast their verb choices.

1. The monster waited for Gwelf and Gwenter in the depths of the sea.
2. As their ship drew near, it raised itself out of the water and took Gwenter by the neck.
3. With one swift movement it tore the hero in half and returned to the deep.
4. Pieces of Gwenter appeared in the waves as Gwelf cried out in horror.
5. But the monster returned and finished the rest of Gwenter as a warning to Gwelf.
6. Filled with rage and disgust, Gwelf shouted a new challenge to the monster.

A. Humanities Connection: Responding to the Fine Art

This bronze coin, which may have existed centuries before *Beowulf* was written, illustrates the widespread familiarity with the "warrior *vs.* monster" myth.

? How does the fight depicted here differ from that between Beowulf and Grendel? (The warrior on this coin is using a weapon.)

B. Kennings

? What kennings associate Grendel with evil? (He is referred to as "shepherd of evil, guardian of crime.")

A

Bronze coin showing a warrior killing a monster.

Statens Historiska Museer, Stockholm.

GraspED at a strong-hearted wakeful sleeper
430 —And was instantly seized himself, claws
Bent back as Beowulf leaned up on one arm.
B That shepherd of evil, guardian of crime,
Knew at once that nowhere on earth
Had he met a man whose hands were harder;
435 His mind was flooded with fear—but nothing
Could take his talons and himself from that tight

Beowulf's men attempt to come to their
lord's aid, but find that their weapons are
useless, and the battle is between Grendel and Beowulf. Embraced in mortal
combat, Beowulf rips off Grendel's arm
and hangs it from the rafters of Herot.
The wounded Grendel escapes to his lair
and waits to die.

Grendel is afraid

Hard grip. Grendel's one thought was to run
From Beowulf, flee back to his marsh and hide there:
This was a different Herot than the hall he had emptied.
440 But Higlac's follower remembered his final
Boast and, standing erect, stopped
The monster's flight, fastened those claws
In his fists till they cracked, clutched Grendel
Closer. The infamous killer fought
445 For his freedom, wanting no flesh but retreat,
Desiring nothing but escape; his claws
Had been caught, he was trapped. That trip to Herot
Was a miserable journey for the writhing monster!
　　The high hall rang, its roof boards swayed,
450 And Danes shook with terror. Down
A The aisles the battle swept, angry
And wild. Herot trembled, wonderfully
Built to withstand the blows, the struggling
Great bodies beating at its beautiful walls;
455 Shaped and fastened with iron, inside
And out, artfully worked, the building
Stood firm. Its benches rattled, fell
To the floor, gold-covered boards grating
As Grendel and Beowulf battled across them.
460 Hrothgar's wise men had fashioned Herot
To stand forever; only fire,
They had planned, could shatter what such skill had put
Together, swallow in hot flames such splendor
Of ivory and iron and wood. Suddenly
465 The sounds changed, the Danes started
In new terror, cowering in their beds as the terrible
Screams of the Almighty's enemy sang
In the darkness, the horrible shrieks of pain
And defeat, the tears torn out of Grendel's
470 Taut throat, hell's captive caught in the arms
Of him who of all the men on earth
Was the strongest.

description of Herot and fight

Grendel's screams

9

　　　That mighty protector of men
Meant to hold the monster till its life
Leaped out, knowing the fiend was no use
475 To anyone in Denmark. All of Beowulf's
B Band had jumped from their beds, ancestral
Swords raised and ready, determined
To protect their prince if they could. Their courage
Was great but all wasted: they could hack at Grendel
480 From every side, trying to open
A path for his evil soul, but their points
Could not hurt him, the sharpest and hardest iron
Could not scratch at his skin, for that sin-stained demon
Had bewitched all men's weapons, laid spells

Loyalty of Beowulf's men.

A. Theme
The description of
Herot in these
lines has been
confirmed by ar-
chaeological finds.
The building was
apparently built of
wood held together
with iron bands.
The highly gabled
roof was overlaid
with gold.

? The Danes lis-
tened to the
screams of the
battle within Herot.
Earlier in the epic,
the Danes heard
other songs in He-
rot. What were
these earlier
songs, and how do
they contrast with
the shrieks of pain
now being heard?
What purpose do
you think the con-
trast serves? (In
the first part of Be-
owulf, the Danes
hear scops sing
the songs of Cre-
ation. What they
listen to now may
be a battle for the
survival of Cre-
ation. The contrast
between the two
songs illustrates
once again the
theme of good vs.
evil.)

B. Responding
? How do the ac-
tions of Beo-
wulf's men uphold
the Anglo-Saxon
code of honor?
(They are prepared
to defend their lord
with their lives.)

Part 10 Summary
Warriors return to Herot to observe traces of Grendel's retreat and to rejoice at this defeat. The Danes retell stories of Beowulf's prowess.

PREPARATION
BUILDING ON PRIOR KNOWLEDGE. Many critics think that *Beowulf* may have been sung during three settings, one for each of the fights. As students finish Part 10, have them summarize Beowulf's arrival at Herot and his battle with Grendel. This will help students draw parallels with the two remaining fights.

A. Symbolism
What additional evidence is there that the fight between Grendel and Beowulf is symbolic of the war between good and evil? (Grendel is doomed to go "down to hell." In fighting Beowulf, the monster has learned "what it meant / To feud with Almighty God." It is also significant that Grendel's power leaves him as he grapples with Beowulf.)

B. Responding
Why do you think Beowulf hangs Grendel's arm from the rafters of Herot? (If Herot, with its shining gold roof, does represent Creation, or good, then this evil symbol has been placed in direct juxtaposition with sublime good. All can see that the evil has been rendered harmless.)

485	That blunted every mortal man's blade.
	And yet his time had come, his days
	Were over, his death near; down
	To hell he would go, swept groaning and helpless
A	To the waiting hands of still worse fiends.
490	Now he discovered—once the afflictor
	Of men, tormentor of their days—what it meant
	To feud with Almighty God: Grendel
	Saw that his strength was deserting him, his claws
	Bound fast, Higlac's brave follower tearing at
495	His hands. The monster's hatred rose higher,
	But his power had gone. He twisted in pain,
	And the bleeding sinews deep in his shoulder
	Snapped, muscle and bone split
	And broke. The battle was over, Beowulf
500	Had been granted new glory: Grendel escaped,
	But wounded as he was could flee to his den,
	His miserable hole at the bottom of the marsh,
	Only to die, to wait for the end
	Of all his days. And after that bloody
505	Combat the Danes laughed with delight.
	He who had come to them from across the sea,
	Bold and strong-minded, had driven affliction
	Off, purged Herot clean. He was happy,
	Now, with that night's fierce work; the Danes
	Had been served as he'd boasted he'd serve them;
510	Beowulf,
	A prince of the Geats, had killed Grendel,
	Ended the grief, the sorrow, the suffering
	Forced on Hrothgar's helpless people
	By a bloodthirsty fiend. No Dane doubted
515	The victory, for the proof, hanging high
B	From the rafters where Beowulf had hung it, was the monster's
	Arm, claw and shoulder and all.

10

	And then, in the morning, crowds surrounded
	Herot, warriors coming to that hall
520	From faraway lands, princes and leaders
	Of men hurrying to behold the monster's
	Great staggering tracks. They gaped with no sense
	Of sorrow, felt no regret for his suffering,
	Went tracing his bloody footprints, his beaten
525	And lonely flight, to the edge of the lake
	Where he'd dragged his corpselike way, doomed
	And already weary of his vanishing life.
	The water was bloody, steaming and boiling
	In horrible pounding waves, heat
530	Sucked from his magic veins; but the swirling
	Surf had covered his death, hidden

Christian ref.

Beowulf wins

evil has been rendered useless

Rejoice at Grendel's defeat

READING CHECK TEST
1. Grendel had been attacking Herot Hall for six months. (F)
2. Beowulf requests that Hrothgar allow him to fight Grendel without the use of any of his weapons. (T)
3. Beowulf states that no man is his match for strength. (T)

4. Hrothgar gives Beowulf command of Herot, promising him treasures if he succeeds in killing Grendel. (T)
5. When Grendel feels Beowulf's incredible strength, he is enraged and determined to kill Beowulf. (F)

Part 11 Summary
Beowulf is called upon once again to rescue the Danes, this time from Grendel's mother, who has attacked Herot and carried off Hrothgar's closest friend, along with Grendel's arm hanging from the rafters of Herot. Part 11 is devoted to a description of the terrible place where Grendel and his mother live.

Deep in murky darkness his miserable
End, as hell opened to receive him.
  Then old and young rejoiced, turned back
From that happy pilgrimage, mounted their hard-
  hooved
535 Horses, high-spirited stallions, and rode them
Slowly toward Herot again, retelling
Beowulf's bravery as they jogged along.
And over and over they swore that nowhere
540 On earth or under the spreading sky
Or between the seas, neither south nor north,
Was there a warrior worthier to rule over men.
(But no one meant Beowulf's praise to belittle
Hrothgar, their kind and gracious king!)

Grendel's monster mother, in grief for her son, next attacks Herot, and in her dripping claws carries off one man—Hrothgar's closest friend. The monster also carries off Grendel's arm, which Beowulf had hung high from the rafters. Beowulf is awakened and called for again. In one of the most famous verses in the epic, the old king describes where Grendel and his mother are said to live.

A

11

545 "They live in secret places, windy
Cliffs, wolf-dens where water pours
From the rocks, then runs underground, where mist
Steams like black clouds, and the groves of trees
Growing out over their lake are all covered
550 With frozen spray, and wind down snakelike
Roots that reach as far as the water
And help keep it dark. At night that lake
Burns like a torch. No one knows its bottom,
No wisdom reaches such depths. A deer,

B
555 Hunted through the woods by packs of hounds,
A stag with great horns, though driven through the
  forest
From faraway places, prefers to die
On those shores, refuses to save its life
In that water. It isn't far, nor is it
560 A pleasant spot! When the wind stirs
And storms, waves splash toward the sky,
As dark as the air, as black as the rain
That the heavens weep. Our only help,
Again, lies with you. Grendel's mother
565 Is hidden in her terrible home, in a place
You've not seen. Seek it, if you dare! Save us,
Once more, and again twisted gold,
Heaped-up ancient treasure, will reward you
For the battle you win!"

A. Grendel's Mere
Some scholars point out a close parallel between Grendel's mere and the vision of hell in Sermon 17 of the tenth-century *Bickling Homilies,* in which St. Paul visits Hell under the protection of St. Michael. The parallel is seen as evidence that the Anglo-Saxons would have equated Grendel's lair with the Christian hell.

B. Imagery
? What imagery in the description of Grendel's lair associates Grendel with death and darkness? (Images of blackness abound. The mist "Steams like black clouds" and the "snakelike / Roots" help to keep the water dark. When the wind stirs the waves, the waves are dark and black as they splash toward the sky. The deer and stag, who prefer to die on the shore rather than to attempt to save their lives by jumping into the lair, are also associated with death.)

Praise to Beowulf.

home of Grendel & his mother

reward for killing G. mother.

Identifying Details

1. Grendel was conceived by a pair of demons who were offspring of Cain.
2. Because of Grendel's murderous raids, the warriors of King Hrothgar are afraid to gather in their hall.
3. God protects Hrothgar's throne. Hrothgar's men make sacrifices and vows to the pagan gods.

4. To help the king.
   Beowulf and his men leave their shields and spears at the entrance.
5. Unferth calls him a boaster and charges that he was bested in the swimming match with Brecca.
   Beowulf says that he and Brecca were separated by a storm and that, afterwards, Beowulf slew nine sea-monsters.
6. After destroying one Geat, Grendel

tries to grasp Beowulf. The hero grips the monster and traps him. Beowulf mortally wounds the monster by tearing off his arm, and Grendel flees from the hall.

Interpreting Meanings

7. Herot is a bright hall, a place of drinking, singing, and feasting. Grendel lives in a cold, dark lake that is so forbidding that even hunted deer prefer to die on its

A. Expansion
Even before Christianity, killing one's kindred was considered a heinous act among Anglo-Saxon noblemen. *Wergild* ("man-payment") that was considered satisfactory recompense to the relatives of a slain man could not be made to one's own relatives. Death of kindred by kindred, then, could not be appeased.

B. Connections
In *Macbeth,* Shakespeare uses this code against killing one's kinsman to make Macbeth's murder of Duncan a particularly vile act. Duncan is not only Macbeth's king and guest; he is also his kinsman.

**Part 12
Summary**
Beowulf dives into the mere to confront Grendel's mother. Neither the sword, Hrunting, nor his helmet is protection for Beowulf as Grendel's mother tears and claws at him. Beowulf finds himself on his back, where the she-monster's dagger would have killed him had it not been for his mail shirt.

Responding to the Epic

Analyzing the Epic

Identifying Details

1. What does the poet tell us about Grendel's origins?
2. Why does Herot remain empty for twelve years?
3. Explain why Grendel does not touch King Hrothgar's throne. What means does Hrothgar resort to in his desperate effort to save his guest-hall?
4. What is Beowulf's **motive** for traveling to Hrothgar's country? What do he and his men do with their weapons when they arrive at Herot?
5. How is Beowulf taunted by the jealous Unferth? How does Beowulf reply to these taunts?
6. Describe what happens to Grendel when he raids Herot and finds Beowulf in charge.

Interpreting Meanings

7. In what specific ways does Herot contrast with the place where Grendel lives? What reasons can you propose for Grendel's hatred of Herot?

8. In lines 3–13, the poet describes the songs of the bard in Hrothgar's hall. How does the content of the songs contrast with Grendel and his world? (Could you say that the songs are about creation and that Grendel is associated with destruction?)
9. What significance can you see in the fact that Grendel attacks at night? What **images** describing Grendel might associate him with death or darkness?
10. Considering Grendel's origin and lair, what **symbolic** meaning might underlie the confrontation between Grendel and Hrothgar? What symbolism do you see in the uselessness of human weapons against Grendel?
11. Analyze the narrative function of the tale-within-a-tale about Beowulf's swimming match with Brecca. How does this story contribute to the **characterization** of Beowulf? How does it establish Beowulf's superiority to sea beasts and to the sea itself?
12. Does this account of Grendel and Beowulf have anything in common with fantasy or adventure movies today? Explain.

Primary Sources
The Mark of Cain

"And Adam knew Eve his wife; and she conceived, and bare Cain, and said, I have gotten a man from the Lord.

"And she again bare his brother Abel. And Abel was a keeper of sheep, but, Cain was a tiller of the ground.

"And in process of time it came to pass, that Cain brought of the fruit of the ground an offering unto the Lord.

"And Abel, he also brought of the firstlings of his flock and of the fat thereof. And the Lord had respect unto Abel and to his offering:

"But unto Cain and to his offering he had not respect. And Cain was very wroth, and his countenance fell.

"And the Lord said unto Cain, Why art thou wroth? And why is thy countenance fallen?

"If thou doest well, shalt thou not be accepted? and if thou doest not well, sin lieth at the door: and unto thee shall be his desire, and thou shalt rule over him.

A "And Cain talked with Abel his brother: and it came to pass, when they were in the field, that Cain rose up against Abel his brother, and slew him.

"And the Lord said unto Cain, Where is Abel thy brother? And he said, I know not: Am I my brother's keeper?

"And he said, What hast thou done? the voice of thy brother's blood crieth unto me from the ground.

"And now art thou cursed from the Earth, which hath opened her mouth to receive thy brother's blood from thy hand.

"When thou tillest the ground, it shall not henceforth yield unto thee her strength; a fugitive and a vagabond shalt thou be in the Earth.

"And Cain said unto the Lord, My punishment is greater than I can bear.

"Behold, thou hast driven me out this day from the face of the Earth; and from thy face shall I be hid; and I shall be a fugitive and a vagabond in the Earth; and it shall come to pass, that everyone that findeth me shall slay me.

"And the Lord said unto him, Therefore whosoever slayeth Cain, vengeance shall be taken on him sevenfold. And the Lord set a mark upon Cain, lest any finding him should kill him." B

—Genesis 4:1-15

shores rather than save their lives by plunging into its waters.

Herot represents order, light—even godliness. Grendel, God's enemy, would naturally hate such a symbol.

8. Most students will agree with the suggestion. In fact, the text of the poem specifically indicates that the bard's songs are about God's creation of the world (see lines 7–13).

9. The evil and destructive Grendel is consistently associated with death, destruction, and darkness: See especially lines 2, 18–19, 30, 49–50, 82, 112, 392–396, 547–548, and 562.

10. Students may suggest that the symbolic meaning is the universal struggle between light and dark, good and evil, life and death.

Student answers will vary. Some students may suggest that this motif symbolically indicates that the struggle is really on a spiritual level, rather than on a literal, physical level. In other words, the battle against Grendel is really a battle against the forces of evil.

11. The tale-within-a-tale foreshadows Beowulf's strength and courage. Although Beowulf does not boast about his victories, he is appropriately proud of them.

Beowulf's astonishing feats reveal his superiority to the sea and to the sea monsters. This superiority, in turn, foreshadows Beowulf's victory over Grendel, whose habitat is said to be the dark waters of the marshy lake.

12. Student answers will vary. Many students may suggest parallels with contemporary fantasy or adventure movies. Encourage students to elaborate on their answers in class.

Carrying the sword Hrunting, Beowulf goes to the lake where the monster's mother has her underwater lair. Then, fully armed, he makes a heroic dive to the depths of this watery Hell.

The Monster's Mother

12

570   He leaped into the lake, would not wait for anyone's
     Answer; the heaving water covered him
     Over. For hours he sank through the waves;
     At last he saw the mud of the bottom.
     And all at once the greedy she-wolf
575   Who'd ruled those waters for half a hundred
     Years discovered him, saw that a creature
     From above had come to explore the bottom
     Of her wet world. She welcomed him in her claws,
     Clutched at him savagely but could not harm him,
580   Tried to work her fingers through the tight
     Ring-woven mail on his breast, but tore
     And scratched in vain. Then she carried him, armor
     And sword and all, to her home; he struggled
     To free his weapon, and failed. The fight
585   Brought other monsters swimming to see
     Her catch, a host of sea beasts who beat at
     His mail shirt, stabbing with tusks and teeth
     As they followed along. Then he realized, suddenly,
     That she'd brought him into someone's battle hall,
590   And there the water's heat could not hurt him,
     Nor anything in the lake attack him through
     The building's high-arching roof. A brilliant
     Light burned all around him, the lake
     Itself like a fiery flame.
              Then he saw
595   The mighty water witch, and swung his sword,
     His ring-marked blade, straight at her head;
     The iron sang its fierce song,
     Sang Beowulf's strength. But her guest
     Discovered that no sword could slice her evil
600   Skin, that Hrunting could not hurt her, was useless
     Now when he needed it. They wrestled, she ripped
     And tore and clawed at him, bit holes in his helmet,
     And that too failed him; for the first time in years
     Of being worn to war it would earn no glory;
605   It was the last time anyone would wear it. But Beowulf
     Longed only for fame, leaped back
     Into battle. He tossed his sword aside,
     Angry; the steel-edged blade lay where
     He'd dropped it. If weapons were useless he'd use
610   His hands, the strength in his fingers. So fame
     Comes to the men who mean to win it
     And care about nothing else! He raised

Swedish sword (10th century).

Statens Historiska Museer, Stockholm.

As Beowulf seems to be getting the worse of the battle with Grendel's mother, he sees, hanging on the wall, a fabulous sword, so large that it could be used by no ordinary man. Beowulf uses the sword to decapitate Grendel's mother, and, still seeking revenge for Grendel's vicious attacks, also cuts off the head from Grendel's dead body.

PREPARATION

PREREADING JOURNAL. Have students write several sentences in their journals describing what they think the final battle between Beowulf and Grendel's mother will be like. Then have students read to discover if their descriptions are accurate.

A. Plot

? What saves Beowulf from being killed by Grendel's mother's dagger? (His chain mail shirt)

B. Christian Parallels

Much has been made of the brilliant light that shines (line 646) when Beowulf succeeds in killing Grendel's mother. Critics who see Christian parallels throughout the epic have commented that Beowulf's immersion into the lair is a kind of baptism by which he is washed clean of sins. The light, then, would indicate God's favor.

His arms and seized her by the shoulder; anger
Doubled his strength, he threw her to the floor.
615 She fell, Grendel's fierce mother, and the Geats'
Proud prince was ready to leap on her. But she rose
At once and repaid him with her clutching claws,
Wildly tearing at him. He was weary, that best
And strongest of soldiers; his feet stumbled
620 And in an instant she had him down, held helpless.
Squatting with her weight on his stomach, she drew
A dagger, brown with dried blood, and prepared

A To avenge her only son. But he was stretched
On his back, and her stabbing blade was blunted
625 By the woven mail shirt he wore on his chest.
The hammered links held; the point
Could not touch him. He'd have traveled to the bottom
of the earth,
Edgetho's son, and died there, if that shining
Woven metal had not helped—and Holy
630 God, who sent him victory, gave judgment
For truth and right, Ruler of the Heavens,
Once Beowulf was back on his feet and fighting.

13

Then he saw, hanging on the wall, a heavy
Sword, hammered by giants, strong
635 And blessed with their magic, the best of all weapons
But so massive that no ordinary man could lift
Its carved and decorated length. He drew it
From its scabbard, broke the chain on its hilt,
And then, savage, now, angry
640 And desperate, lifted it high over his head
And struck with all the strength he had left,
Caught her in the neck and cut it through,
Broke bones and all. Her body fell
To the floor, lifeless, the sword was wet
645 With her blood, and Beowulf rejoiced at the sight.

B The brilliant light shone, suddenly,
As though burning in that hall, and as bright as
Heaven's
Own candle, lit in the sky. He looked
At her home, then following along the wall
650 Went walking, his hands tight on the sword,
His heart still angry. He was hunting another
Dead monster, and took his weapon with him
For final revenge against Grendel's vicious
Attacks, his nighttime raids, over
655 And over, coming to Herot when Hrothgar's
Men slept, killing them in their beds,
Eating some on the spot, fifteen
Or more, and running to his loathsome moor
With another such sickening meal waiting

chain-mail saves him

Christian reference

alliteration

Kills Grendel's mother

kenning

Christian reference – cleansed of sin

A. About the Portal
In German legend, Siegfried kills a dragon and helps the king of Burgundy win his wife. Sigurd is the Norse counterpart to Siegfried.

A

The hero Sigurd battling the dragon. Detail of a carved portal of Hyllestad Stave-Church, Setesdal, Norway (12th century).

Universitetets, Oldsaksamling, Oslo.

660   In his pouch. But Beowulf repaid him for those visits,
Found him lying dead in his corner,
Armless, exactly as that fierce fighter
Had sent him out from Herot, then struck off
His head with a single swift blow. The body
665   Jerked for the last time, then lay still.

B C *Beowulf carries the head of Grendel to King Hrothgar and then returns gift-laden to the land of the Geats, where he succeeds to the throne. After fifty winters pass, Beowulf, now an old man, faces his final task: He must fight a dragon who, angry because a thief had stolen a jeweled cup from its hoard of gold, is laying waste to the Geats' land. Beowulf and eleven warriors are guided to the dragon's lair by the thief who stole the cup. For Beowulf, the price of this last victory will be great.*

B. Characterization
At this point in the poem, Beowulf has returned to the land of the Geats, where he has ruled as a wise and just king for fifty years.
? Why is Beowulf not content to rest on his laurels at this point rather than to fight, as an aged and weak king, a battle whose odds are against him?

C. Ulysses
At this point, you might want students to compare Beowulf with Ulysses, as he is portrayed in Lord Tennyson's poem of that name (see text page 791).
? Could the final lines of "Ulysses" also have been the thoughts of Beowulf at this point: "We are not now that strength which in old days / Moved earth and heaven, that which we are, we are, / One equal temper of heroic hearts, / Made weak by time and fate, but strong in will / To strive, to seek, to find, and not to yield"?

Beowulf 33

A. Characterization

Briefly describe Beowulf as he sets out for this final encounter. (Beowulf is calm, almost stoical, as he faces his final enemy—"My heart is firm, / My hands calm"—and he is "still brave, still strong" in spite of his age. In the midst of the battle, the "Great Prince stood firm, unmoving, prepared." Students should understand that in displaying these characteristics, Beowulf epitomizes the Anglo-Saxon code of valor and courage to the very end.)

B. Characterization

What do you think is Beowulf's motivation in going after the dragon's treasure hoard? (Students should remember that amassing treasure through war was seen as a sign of valor on the part of the leader.)

C. About the Shield

A Celtic chief supposedly threw this bronze shield into the River Thames as an offering to a river god. Some of the enamel designs may represent highly stylized animals believed to be endowed with magical properties.

Part 14 Summary

Beowulf announces his intention to battle the dragon and recover his treasure, this time using his shield and sword. The dragon's flames, however, melt the iron shield, and for the first time in his life, Beowulf finds fate against him. Sizing up the battle, all of Beowulf's men, except one, desert him.

PREPARATION

PREREADING JOURNAL. Have students write a few lines in their journals explaining why Beowulf undertakes this final encounter in spite of the odds against him. Once students have read Part 14, have them share their reasons.

The Final Battle

14

Then he said farewell to his followers,
Each in his turn, for the last time:
"I'd use no sword, no weapon, if this beast
Could be killed without it, crushed to death
670   Like Grendel, gripped in my hands and torn
Limb from limb. But his breath will be burning
Hot, poison will pour from his tongue.
I feel no shame, with shield and sword
And armor, against this monster: when he comes to me
675   I mean to stand, not run from his shooting
Flames, stand till fate decides
Which of us wins. My heart is firm,
My hands calm: I need no hot
Words. Wait for me close by, my friends.
680   We shall see, soon, who will survive
This bloody battle, stand when the fighting
Is done. No one else could do
What I mean to, here, no man but me
Could hope to defeat this monster. No one
685   Could try. And this dragon's treasure, his gold
And everything hidden in that tower, will be mine
Or war will sweep me to a bitter death!"
    Then Beowulf rose, still brave, still strong
And with his shield at his side, and a mail shirt on his
      breast,
690   Strode calmly, confidently, toward the tower, under
The rocky cliffs: no coward could have walked there!
And then he who'd endured dozens of desperate
Battles, who'd stood boldly while swords and shields
Clashed, the best of kings, saw
695   Huge stone arches and felt the heat
Of the dragon's breath, flooding down
Through the hidden entrance, too hot for anyone
To stand, a streaming current of fire
And smoke that blocked all passage. And the Geats'
700   Lord and leader, angry, lowered
His sword and roared out a battle cry,
A call so loud and clear that it reached through
The hoary rock, hung in the dragon's
Ear. The beast rose, angry,
705   Knowing a man had come—and then nothing
But war could have followed. Its breath came first.
A steaming cloud pouring from the stone,
Then the earth itself shook. Beowulf
Swung his shield into place, held it
710   In front of him, facing the entrance. The dragon
Coiled and uncoiled, its heart urging it
Into battle. Beowulf's ancient sword

Celtic bronze shield (1st century).

British Museum.

Part 15 Summary
Wiglaf, Beowulf's warrior, who remembers the kindness and treasures his kinsman and lord has given him, comes to Beowulf's aid.

PREPARATION

PREREADING JOURNAL. In a journal entry, have students describe the words Beowulf might have said to his followers who abandoned him during his fight with the dragon.

Was waiting, <u>unsheathed</u>, his sharp and gleaming
Blade. The beast came closer; both of them
715 Were ready, each set on slaughter. The <u>Geats'</u>
Great <u>prince</u> stood firm, unmoving, prepared   *kenning*
Behind his high shield, waiting in his shining
Armor. The monster came quickly toward him,
Pouring out fire and smoke, hurrying
720 To its fate. Flames beat at the iron   *shield melts*
Shield, and for a time it held, protected
Beowulf as he'd planned; then it began to melt,
And for the first time in his life that famous prince
Fought with fate against him, with glory
725 Denied him. He knew it, but he raised his sword
And struck at the dragon's scaly hide.   *blade breaks*
The ancient <u>blade broke</u>, bit into
The monster's skin, drew blood, but cracked
And failed him before it went deep enough, helped him
730 Less than he needed. The dragon leaped
With pain, thrashed and beat at him, spouting
Murderous flames, spreading them everywhere.   *kenning*
And the Geats' <u>ring-giver</u> did not boast of glorious
Victories in other wars: his weapon
735 Had failed him, deserted him, now when he needed it
Most, that excellent sword. Edgetho's
Famous son stared at death,   *faces death*
A Unwilling to leave this world, to exchange it   *knows he is going to die*
For a dwelling in some distant place—a journey
740 Into darkness that all men must make, as death
Ends their few brief hours on earth.
   Quickly, the dragon came at <u>him</u>, encouraged
As Beowulf fell back; its breath flared,
And he suffered, wrapped around in swirling
745 Flames—a king, before, but now
A beaten warrior. None of his comrades   *comrades desert him*
B Came to <u>him</u>, helped him, his brave and noble
Followers; they ran for their lives, fled
Deep in a wood. And <u>only one of them</u>
750 Remained, stood there, miserable, remembering,
As a good man must, what <u>kinship</u> should mean. . . .

15

   His name was <u>Wiglaf</u>, he was Wexstan's son   *alliteration*
And a good soldier; his family had been Swedish,
Once. Watching Beowulf, he could see
755 How his king was suffering, burning. Remembering   *alliteration*
Everything his lord and cousin had given him,
C Armor and gold and the great estates
Wexstan's family enjoyed, Wiglaf's
Mind was made up; he raised his yellow
760 Shield and drew his sword . . . .

A. Responding
? Would you agree or disagree with the following statement: In his battle with the dragon, Beowulf accepts with valor and virtue his *wyrd,* the inescapable destiny all men in this world must accept. (Most students will agree that although Beowulf is not happy at the thought of dying, his willingness to face the dragon—and to remain when his blade breaks—proves his valor and virtue.)

B. The Demise of the Anglo-Saxons
Some critics see the failure of Beowulf's men to come to Beowulf's aid as an ominous forecast of the demise of the Anglo-Saxons (see question 8 on text page 38).

C. Anglo-Saxon Code
All of Part 15 is an expression of the Anglo-Saxon code—the leader who rewards his loyal followers with riches and expects loyalty in return.

Part 16 Summary

As Beowulf lies dying, Wiglaf brings the dragon's treasure for him to see. Beowulf passes the leadership of the Geats to Wiglaf and gives him the golden necklace, his helmet, his mail shirt, and his rings. Beowulf also asks that the Geats build a funeral pyre that passing ships can see and thus remember Beowulf.

A. Responding

Earlier, when Beowulf fought Grendel, his men were eager to come to his aid. Why do you think they desert him now? (Answers will vary. Students should note, however, Wiglaf's words in lines 775–778. Just as people today may desert powerful people when they lose their positions of authority, so Beowulf's men may be deserting a king whose "strength and daring" no longer dazzle.)

And Wiglaf, his heart heavy, uttered
The kind of words his comrades deserved:
"I remember how we sat in the mead-hall, drinking
And boasting of how brave we'd be when Beowulf
765 Needed us, he who gave us these swords
And armor: all of us swore to repay him,
When the time came, kindness for kindness
—With our lives, if he needed them. He allowed us to
    join him,
Chose us from all his great army, thinking
770 Our boasting words had some weight, believing
Our promises, trusting our swords. He took us
For soldiers, for men. He meant to kill
This monster himself, our mighty king,
Fight this battle alone and unaided,
775 As in the days when his strength and daring dazzled
Men's eyes. But those days are over and gone
And now our lord must lean on younger
Arms. And we must go to him, while angry
Flames burn at his flesh, help
780 Our glorious king! By almighty God,
I'd rather burn myself than see
Flames swirling around my lord.
And who are we to carry home
Our shields before we've slain his enemy
785 And ours, to run back to our homes with Beowulf
So hard-pressed here? I swear that nothing
He ever did deserved an end
Like this, dying miserably and alone,
Butchered by this savage beast: we swore
790 That these swords and armor were each for us all!". . .

Together, Beowulf and the young Wiglaf kill the dragon, but the old king is fatally wounded. Beowulf, thinking of his people, asks to see the monster's treasure. Wiglaf enters the dragon's cave and finds a priceless hoard of jewels and gold.

16

Then Wiglaf went back, anxious
To return while Beowulf was alive, to bring him
Treasure they'd won together. He ran,
Hoping his wounded king, weak
795 And dying, had not left the world too soon.
Then he brought their treasure to Beowulf, and found
His famous king bloody, gasping
For breath. But Wiglaf sprinkled water
Over his lord, until the words
800 Deep in his breast broke through and were heard.
Beholding the treasure he spoke, haltingly:

READING CHECK TEST
1. Using his own ancestral sword, Beo-wulf kills Grendel's mother. (F)
2. Beowulf carries Grendel's head to King Hrothgar and returns home with many fine gifts. (T)
3. Beowulf becomes king of the Geats. (T)

4. After Beowulf's weapons fail him against the dragon, his men rush to help him, but he orders them away. (F)
5. Beowulf names Wiglaf as his succes-sor to the throne. (T)

CLOSURE
Have students explain the Anglo-Saxon code of loyalty and valor and how adher-ence to it is basic to *Beowulf*.

"For this, this gold, these jewels, I thank
Our Father in Heaven, Ruler of the Earth—
For all of this, that His grace has given me,
805   Allowed me to bring to my people while breath
Still came to my lips. I sold my life
For this treasure, and I sold it well. Take
What I leave, Wiglaf, lead my people,
Help them; my time is gone. Have
810   The brave Geats build me a tomb,
When the funeral flames have burned me, and build it
Here, at the water's edge, high
On this spit of land, so sailors can see
This tower, and remember my name, and call it
815   Beowulf's tower, and boats in the darkness
And mist, crossing the sea, will know it."
    Then that brave king gave the golden
Necklace from around his throat to Wiglaf,
Gave him his gold-covered helmet, and his rings,
820   And his mail shirt, and ordered him to use them well:
    "You're the last of all our far-flung family.
Fate has swept our race away,
Taken warriors in their strength and led them
To the death that was waiting. And now I follow them."
825   The old man's mouth was silent, spoke
No more, had said as much as it could;
He would sleep in the fire, soon. His soul
Left his flesh, flew to glory.

(handwritten marginalia: Christian references)

(handwritten marginalia: Choose Niglaf as successor)

(handwritten marginalia: Christian ref)

Swedish gold collar (6th century).

Statens Historiska Museer,
Stockholm.

Wiglaf berates the faithless warriors who had not gone to the aid of their king. With sorrow, the Geats then cremate the corpse of their greatest king. They place his ashes, along with all of the dragon's treasure, in a huge burial mound by the sea, where it can be seen by voyagers.

17

And then twelve of the bravest Geats
830   Rode their horses around the tower,
Telling their sorrow, telling stories
Of their dead king and his greatness, his glory,
Praising him for heroic deeds, for a life
As noble as his name. So should all men
835   Raise up words for their lords, warm
With love, when their shield and protector leaves
His body behind, sends his soul
On high. And so Beowulf's followers
Rode, mourning their beloved leader,
840   Crying that no better king had ever
Lived, no prince so mild, no man
So open to his people, so deserving of praise.

(handwritten marginalia: Relating tales of Beowulf's deeds)

A. The Symbolism of the Hoard
You might want to remind students of the importance of amassing treasure in the Anglo-Saxon code as a way of momentarily de-feating *wyrd*, or fate. Thus, when Beowulf's dying words are, "I sold my life / For this treasure," he is do-ing more than equating his life with material pos-sessions, as the same words might indicate today. Stu-dents should prob-ably be reminded once again that the entire action of this poem must be placed within the context of the An-glo-Saxon codes of conduct and val-ues rather than within the context of twentieth-centu-ry codes and val-ues.

B. Foreshadowing
Other than Beo-wulf's men's desertion of him, what might foretell the end of the Anglo-Saxons? (Lines 821–824, when Beowulf says to Wiglaf, "Fate has swept our race away," might be such a forecast.)

1. Beowulf finds that the sword, Hrunting, is useless against the monster, so he grapples with her with his bare hands. At one point, she pins him to the ground and tries to stab him with a dagger, but Beowulf is protected, both by his mail shirt and by supernatural aid. The hero then spies a heavy sword hanging on the wall. Even though the sword is massive, the hero manages to grasp and draw it, and with one stroke he mortally wounds Grendel's mother in the neck.

2. The only warrior to come to Beowulf's aid is Wiglaf, who pities Beowulf's suffering and honors his oaths of loyalty.

3. The funeral of Beowulf and the raising of his burial mound conclude the epic.

Interpreting Meanings

4. Among the images students may mention are the fiery lake, the claws of Grendel's mother, the invulnerability of the evil monster's skin, and the sudden shining of light when Grendel's mother is slain.

5. This fact might suggest that the dragon, who guards the treasure, is symbolic

A. Psychological Aspects of Personality
Students might need an explanation of the psychological terms used here. The *ego* is the conscious part of the personality, the part that deals with reality. The *id* is generally used to mean the part of the personality that fulfills basic, instinctual needs, such as those for food and sex. *Superego* is often used to mean one's conscience or set of values.

A Comment on the Epic

"*Beowulf* is a poem about hell's possession of middle-earth. Within its overall tragic structure, the joys of the golden dryht [here, the lord's guest hall] and the actions of good kings and heroes are presented as capable of a splendid but precarious realization; the dominant vision, however, is of the defeat of man in the kingdoms of this world by the powers of darkness. . . .

". . . *Beowulf* is not about an individual as such but about a man of archetypal proportions, whose significance, in the broadest and deepest sense, is social. The poem is an imaginative vision of two kinds of human society, one symbolized by the gold-hall and banqueting and characterized by generosity, loyalty, and love, the other by monsters of darkness and bloodshed who prey on the ordered, light-filled world man desires and clings to. Despite the lyric overtones to the poet's presentation of his theme (that brooding, melancholy reflectiveness that every reader recognizes), *Beowulf* is not about a complex, individual character whose interior mental processes lead plausibly to certain actions and relations with other people. Beowulf does not have an ego, despite his boasting, and certainly has no discernible id; he is publicly conceived, all superego and controlled by the divine favor he bears. We do not know why, psychologically, Unferth behaves so oddly or what Hrothulf is thinking at any point. We learn a little more about what goes on in the mind of Hrothgar or Welthow or the aged Beowulf (late in the poem) but only in terms of their functions in relation to God and to the kindred and dryht [lord] in whose social fabric their lives have meaning. They are all functionaries playing out their roles as long as wyrd [fate] permits, not images of real people but exemplars of human types. . . ."

—from *The Guest-Hall of Eden*, Alvin A. Lee

Responding to the Epic

Analyzing the Epic

Identifying Details

1. Describe how Beowulf manages to kill Grendel's mother.
2. Who comes to aid Beowulf in his final battle with the dragon? Why does he help Beowulf?
3. What sad scene concludes the epic?

Interpreting Meanings

4. What **images** suggest that the lair in which Grendel and his mother live is like Hell?
5. A hoarded treasure in Old English literature usually **symbolizes** spiritual death or damnation. How might this fact add significance to the hero's last fight with the dragon? What happens to the dragon's hoard?
6. Find details that describe the dragon in terms of a serpent. (Remember that a dragon *is* a kind of serpent.) What might the dragon **symbolize** as Beowulf's final foe?
7. Beowulf battles Grendel, Grendel's mother, and the dragon. But none of these battles could be called the **central conflict** of the epic, though each certainly relates to it. How would you state the central conflict in *Beowulf*? How is it resolved?

8. Given what you know about the structure of Anglo-Saxon society, explain what is especially ominous about the behavior of Beowulf's men during the final battle. What might this suggest about the future of the kingdom?
9. The epic closes on a somber, **elegiac** note—a note of mourning. What words and **images** contribute to this tone?
10. Great epic poetry generally embodies the attitudes and ideals of an entire culture. In what ways do you think *Beowulf* reveals the values of the Anglo-Saxon society? What universal **themes** does it also reveal?
11. How are these Anglo-Saxon values and heroic ideals both similar to, and different from, our own?

Writing About the Epic

A Creative Response

1. **Changing the Point of View.** In a book called *Grendel*, contemporary American writer John Gardner retells part of *Beowulf* from the point of view of the monster. Gardner's Grendel has contemporary psychological reasons for his demonic behavior. He had a lonely, confused childhood; he feels alienated from his mother; and he is infuriated by the heroic idealism of

of death and evil, perhaps even of the devil. It is significant that, even though Beowulf wants to give the captured treasure to the Geats, the treasure is finally buried, along with Beowulf's body.

6. Details describing the dragon as a serpent occur in lines 711 ("coiled and uncoiled") and 726 ("scaly hide").

As suggested above, the dragon may symbolize death or the devil.

7. The central conflict might be described as the struggle of good against evil. The conflict is resolved in favor of good, but at the price of the death of the hero.

8. Given that the structure of Anglo-Saxon society was built on loyalty to a king or protector, the men's failure to help Beowulf is especially ominous. This failure perhaps foreshadows the disintegration of the kingdom after Beowulf's death.

9. Among the words and images students may mention are the following: "telling their sorrow" (line 831), "mourning their beloved leader" (line 839), and "crying that no better king had ever lived" (lines 840–841). Students may also mention the somber implications of lines 834–837. Beowulf, who had been "their shield and protector," is now dead.

10. Student answers will vary. In general, students should mention instances from the epic that reveal the values of courage, loyalty, and strength (both physical and spiritual). The poem also clearly contains universal themes: Loyalty and self-sacrifice are admirable traits, good triumphs over evil (but at a painful cost), different members of society have obligations toward one another, and fame can be achieved through good deeds.

11. Students may find similarities in the way we continue to idealize strength and courage. Encourage students to consider the modern view of kinship and of the concept of *wyrd*.

Hrothgar and his people, seeing it as egotistic and self-deceptive. Read the following excerpt, in which Grendel tells his own version of one of his raids on Hrothgar's hall.

I sigh, sink into the silence, and cross it like wind. Behind my back, at the world's end, my pale slightly glowing fat mother sleeps on, old, sick at heart, in our dingy underground room. Life-bloated, baffled, long-suffering hag. Guilty, she imagines, of some unremembered, perhaps ancestral crime. (She must have some human in her.) Not that she thinks. Not that she dissects and ponders the dusty mechanical bits of her miserable life's curse. She clutches at me in her sleep as if to crush me. I break away. "Why are we here?" I used to ask her. "Why do we stand this putrid, stinking hole?" She trembles at my words. Her fat lips shake. "Don't ask!" her wiggling claws implore. (She never speaks.) "Don't ask!" It must be some terrible secret, I used to think. I'd give her a crafty squint. She'll tell me, in time, I thought. But she told me nothing. I waited on. That was before the old dragon, calm as winter, unveiled the truth. He was not a friend.

And so I come through trees and towns to the lights of Hrothgar's meadhall. I am no stranger here. A respected guest. Eleven years now and going on twelve I have come up this clean-mown central hill, dark shadow out of the woods below, and have knocked politely on the high oak door, bursting its hinges and sending the shock of my greeting inward like a cold blast out of a cave. "Grendel!" they squeak, and I smile like exploding spring. The old Shaper, a man I cannot help but admire, goes out the back window with his harp at a single bound, though blind as a bat. The drunkest of Hrothgar's thanes come reeling and clanking down from their well-hung beds, all shouting their meady, outrageous boasts, their heavy swords aswirl like eagles' wings. "Woe, woe, woe!" cries Hrothgar, hoary with winters, peeking in, wide-eyed, from his bedroom in back. His wife, looking in behind him, makes a scene. The thanes in the meadhall blow out the lights and cover the wide stone fireplace with shields. I laugh, crumple over; I can't help myself. In the darkness, I alone see clear as day. While they squeal and screech and bump into each other, I silently sack up my dead and withdraw to the woods. I eat and laugh and eat until I can barely walk, my chest hair matted with dribbled blood, and then the roosters on the hill crow, and dawn comes over the roofs of the houses, and all at once I am filled with gloom again.

"This is some punishment sent us," I hear them bawling from the hill.

My head aches. Morning nails my eyes.

"Some god is angry," I hear a woman keen. "The people of Scyld and Herogar and Hrothgar are mired in sin!"

My belly rumbles, sick on their sour meat. I crawl through bloodstained leaves to the eaves of the forest, and there peek out. The dogs fall silent at the edge of my spell, and where the king's hall surmounts the town, the blind old Shaper, harp clutched tight to his fragile chest, stares futilely down, straight at me. Otherwise nothing. Pigs root dully at the posts of a wooden fence. A rumple-horned ox lies chewing in dew and shade. A few men, lean, wearing animal skins, look up at the gables of the king's hall, or at the vultures circling casually beyond. Hrothgar says nothing, hoarfrost-bearded, his features cracked and crazed. Inside, I hear the people praying—whimpering, whining, mumbling, pleading—to their numerous sticks and stones. He doesn't go in. The king has lofty theories of his own.

"Theories," I whisper to the bloodstained ground. So the dragon once spoke. ("They'd map out roads through Hell with their crackpot theories!" I recall his laugh.)

Then the groaning and praying stop, and on the side of the hill the dirge-slow shoveling begins. . . .

—from *Grendel*, John Gardner

Write your own version of one episode from the portion of *Beowulf* you have read. Retell the story in the first person, from the point of view of one of the characters—perhaps Grendel, his mother, the dragon, Wiglaf, Unferth, Hrothgar, or Welthow.

A Critical Response

2. Analyzing a Character. In an essay, analyze the character of Grendel, based on what you've read of the epic here. Open with a statement of what you see as most important about Grendel. Before you write, gather your data by filling in a chart like the following. Quote passages directly from the epic to support your main points.

Images Describing Grendel		
Sin and Rebellion Against God	Darkness and Winter	Enmity Toward Humans
1. 2. etc.	1. 2. etc.	1. 2. etc.

3. Analyzing the Epic. Beowulf is thought to be an old Scandinavian story which was taken over by the Anglo-Saxons and eventually transcribed by English Christian monks. Scholars used to deplore what they saw as Christian elements grafted onto a basically "pagan'' story. But now many scholars believe Beowulf is basically a Christian story, and definitely the work of a Christian poet. In an essay, discuss the Christian and "pagan" elements in the epic. How prominent do you think each religious tradition is in the story?

Analyzing Language and Style

Kennings and Alliteration

The **kenning,** a specialized metaphor made of compound words, is unique to the Old Germanic languages, and is especially prominent in Old Norse and Anglo-Saxon literature. The earliest and simplest kennings are compound words formed of two common nouns: "sky-candle" for the sun, "battle-dew" for blood, and "whale-road" for the sea. Later, kennings grew more elaborate, and compound adjectives joined the compound nouns. A ship became a "foamy-throated ship," then a "foamy-throated sea-stallion," and finally a "foamy-throated stallion of the whale-road." Once a kenning had been coined, it was used by the singer-poets over and over again.

Scholars believe that kennings filled three needs for these early bards: (1) Old Norse and Anglo-Saxon poetry depended heavily on **alliteration,** or words that begin with the same sound, but neither language had a large vocabulary. Poets created the alliterative words they needed by combining existing words. (2) Because the poetry was oral, not written, and had to be memorized, bards valued ready-made phrases. Such phrases made finished poetry easier to remember, and they gave the bard time to think ahead when he was composing new poetry on the spot during a feast or ceremony. (3) The increasingly complex structure of the kennings must have satisfied the early Norse and Anglo-Saxon people's taste for elaboration, a taste apparent not only in their literature but also in their art and artifacts.

Jorge Luis Borges, a modern writer and scholar from Argentina, explains kennings in the following way:

> Kennings have a functional quality. Generally they define things by their use and tend to give life to inanimate objects, freely reversing the procedure with living subjects. And so the sword may be "the wolf of wounds"; the spear, "the corpse-dragon"; and the warrior, "the sword's tree." . . .
>
> Kennings . . . are, or seem to be, the result of a mental process that looks for an accidental likeness. They answer to no particular feeling. They are the outcome of a deliberate combining process, not of a sudden discovery of hidden affinities. Mere logic may justify them, not human sentiment. . . .
>
> Now and then, however, poetry may come to us through the kenning. So we read, in the Saxon riddle of the nightingale, *"eald aefenscop, eorlum bringe blisse in burhum"* ("old poet of the evening, I bring

to men happiness in their cities")—perhaps the selfsame song that John Keats heard some nine hundred years after in the garden of a London suburb.

—Jorge Luis Borges

In their original languages, kennings are almost always written as simple compounds, with no hyphens or spaces between the words. When kennings appear in translation, however, their form changes. Kennings in translation are often written as hyphenated compounds ("sky-candle," "foamy-throated"), as prepositional phrases ("wolf of wounds," "poet of the evening"), or as possessives ("the sword's tree"). Raffel's poem is not formulaic, but there are enough echoes of the old *scop's* techniques to remind us of how the story might have sounded in the original.

1. Look back over lines 233–391 from *Beowulf,* in which Unferth taunts Beowulf, Beowulf answers, and the feast begins. Locate at least two examples of kennings written as hyphenated compounds, two examples of kennings written as prepositional phrases, and two examples of kennings written as possessives.
2. To what does each kenning refer?
3. Which kennings define things by their use? Which ones seem poetic? Which seem merely logical?

In Anglo-Saxon poetry, **alliteration** is used in each half of a poetic line. In the first half of the line, two words alliterate; in the second half, one word alliterates with the other two. Many lines, however, have only two alliterative words, one in each half of the poetic line.

1. Look at the account of Beowulf's death (lines 791–828), and find some examples of alliteration there.
2. Can you find any lines from this section in which vowels, rather than consonants, are repeated?
3. Translators differ dramatically in how they rephrase the Old English to handle alliteration and the kennings. Here is a line from a translation done many years before the Raffel translation. How does it compare with the comparable lines (104–108) in Raffel's translation? Which translation sounds more modern? Which do you prefer to listen to?

> Thus boiled with care the breast of Hrothgar;
> Ceaselessly sorrowed the son of Healfdene,
> None of his chieftains might change his lot.
> Too fell was the foe that afflicted the people
> With wrongs unnumbered, and nightly horrors.
>
> —Translated by J. Duncan Spaeth

40   The Anglo-Saxons

Anglo-Saxon purse lid, gold with garnets and glass (7th century).

British Museum.

A

A. Humanities Connection: About the Fine Art
With intricate designs created through colored glass, the purse lid depicts birds and men between wolves. At this point in the development of Anglo-Saxon art, animals used in ornamentation usually had a religious or mythological connotation.

B. Expansion
For a commentary on the Sutton Hoo discovery, see the Humanities Connection annotation on page 5.

Primary Sources
The Treasure at Sutton Hoo

B

Scholar Robert Creed, in an afterword to Burton Raffel's translation of *Beowulf,* talks of the importance of the harps used by bards in their oral performances of an epic.

"These harps really existed. At the very moment that Professor John Pope was demonstrating how the harp was needed—at least at some of those vacant spaces marked with a primary stress (')—an Anglo-Saxon harp was being dug out of the earth and carefully reconstructed by archaeologists.

"This harp was found buried with the other treasures of a great king or noble warrior in the ship-grave at Sutton Hoo in Suffolk, England. The mound that covered the great ship and its wonderful freight was excavated as recently as the summer of 1939 and the harp and the other treasures placed on exhibition in the British Museum only within the last fifteen years.

"These 'ancient riches' had been 'left in the darkness'

of the grave for thirteen hundred years. No one knows exactly who the warrior or king was for whom these riches were buried. There was no trace of his body or his ashes beside the great store of his wealth. But his sword lay there, and his stag-tipped standard and a blunt and primitively carved object that may have been his royal scepter. His purse decorated with delicate and beautiful cloisonné [enamel] work and the coins that were in it, and his intricately wrought great gold buckle lay there. There lay his silver serving vessels brought from afar—a fitting treasure for a dragon to hoard, or for a royal funeral. . . .

"The wood of the Sutton Hoo harp, like the wood of the ship which held it, had rotted almost away. But enough of its shape remained to make it possible for the firm of Dolmetsch in England to build a new harp from its pattern."

—Robert P. Creed

1. BUILDING ON PRIOR KNOWLEDGE. The Anglo-Saxon reciprocal code of loyalty between the chieftain and his followers, with which students are familiar from *Beowulf,* is important in this poem. You might review with students that while the chieftain, or "gold-lord," received loyalty in the form of an available fighting force, the follower was repaid with protection, gifts, and the camaraderie of the mead-hall.

2. ESTABLISHING A PURPOSE. Many scholars believe the poem to be an archetypal expression of the effects of wandering, of a lack of "center," on the human spirit. Have students read to discover the effects of wandering on the speaker of the poem. Then have them decide whether or not they agree on the devastating effects of a lack of purpose in one's life.

3. PREREADING JOURNAL. Before they read, have students write about an experience in which they felt somewhat isolated and "adrift," such as entering a new school or visiting an unfamiliar place.

A. Humanities Connection: About the Fine Art
The Oseberg ship, unearthed in 1904, was the burial ship of Asa, a Viking queen who belies the passive role women are sometimes believed to have played at this time in history. Married against her will to a Norwegian king, Asa had her husband killed and ruled alone until her death in 850.

Accompanying Asa on her voyage to the afterlife was the body of a maidservant, priceless gold and gems that were stolen by looters, and such objects as sleds and wagons, so that Asa might enjoy travel in the afterlife as much as the Vikings enjoyed it in the present one.

The Wanderer

A

The **elegiac mood** is the dominant mood in Anglo-Saxon poetry. As we have seen, this tone of sadness and lamentation over the grimness and transience of earthly life is found in the heroic epic; it is also found in several Old English fragments and poems in which a bard laments the passing of better days and greater glories.

Among the most beautiful of the elegiac poems is "The Wanderer," a poignant work of 108 lines found in the so-called Exeter Book, a manuscript of miscellaneous Anglo-Saxon poems dating from around A.D. 940 and now preserved at Exeter Cathedral in England. Though the manuscript survived the raids and fires of the centuries, the Exeter Book had not been well cared for. There are signs that its cover had been used as a chopping board; its pages are marked by beer stains, and some have been partly burned. But today its "songs"—copied down by monks—are our chief source of Anglo-Saxon poetry.

The translation of "The Wanderer" that follows attempts to imitate the alliteration of the original Old English poem. Note the four-beat, two-part line with a **caesura** (pause) in the middle.

The poem is bracketed by an opening and a closing comment on the wanderer's situation. Some critics think that these comments were added by the Christian monk who copied the poem.

The background of this and other Anglo-Saxon poems is a grim life of struggle against the elements. The Anglo-Saxons were sea voyagers and the northern seas were then, as now, especially cruel. The aging wanderer in this poem, without the protection of his overlord, lacks a defining purpose in life. A sorrowful exile, he wanders over the seas looking for a new lord and dreaming of better days.

Prow of the Oseberg ship.

Viking Ships Museum, Bygdøy, Oslo.

SUPPLEMENTARY SUPPORT MATERIALS
1. Vocabulary Activity Worksheet (CCB)
2. Review and Response Worksheet:
Elegaic Mood (CCB)
3. Selection Test (CCB)

DEVELOPING VOCABULARY
The following words from the poem are
tested in the Selection Test. (See also
Vocabulary Activity Worksheet.)
bane   to molder
to ponder   to redress

"The Wanderer" is elaborately crafted, and is rich in alliteration and imagery. Modern readers, accustomed to the plainer style of today's literature, may find all this elaboration more of a barrier than a pleasure. One way around the barrier is to think of "The Wanderer" as a time capsule.

It is filled with details, such as the touching description of a warrior swearing loyalty to his lord, which can bring home to us the realities of Anglo-Saxon life. As you read, look for other details that reveal something about the lives of these people who shared your language so many centuries ago.

The Wanderer

Translated by **Charles W. Kennedy**

Oft to the wanderer,   weary of exile,
Cometh God's pity,   compassionate love,
Though woefully toiling   on wintry seas
With churning oar   in the icy wave,
5   Homeless and helpless   he fled from fate.
Thus saith the wanderer   mindful of misery,
Grievous disasters,   and death of kin:
     "Oft when the day broke,   oft at the dawning,
Lonely and wretched   I wailed my woe.
10   No man is living,   no comrade left,
To whom I dare fully   unlock my heart.
I have learned truly   the mark of a man
Is keeping his counsel   and locking his lips,
Let him think what he will!   For, woe of heart
15   Withstandeth not fate;   a failing spirit
Earneth no help.   Men eager for honor
Bury their sorrow   deep in the breast.
     "So have I also,   often in wretchedness
Fettered° my feelings,   far from my kin,
20   Homeless and hapless,°   since days of old,
When the dark earth   covered my dear lord's face,
And I sailed away   with sorrowful heart,
Over wintry seas,   seeking a gold-lord,
If far or near   lived one to befriend me
25   With gift in the mead-hall   and comfort for grief.
     "Who bears it, knows   what a bitter companion,
Shoulder to shoulder,   sorrow can be,
When friends are no more.   His fortune is exile.
Not gifts of fine gold;   a heart that is frozen,
Earth's winsomeness dead.   And he dreams of the hall-
30   men,
The dealing of treasure,   the days of his youth,
When his lord bade welcome   to wassail° and feast.
But gone is that gladness,   and never again
Shall come the loved counsel   of comrade and king.
35   "Even in slumber   his sorrow assaileth,
And, dreaming he claspeth   his dear lord again,
Head on knee, hand on knee,   loyally laying,

19. **fettered:** chained.
20. **hapless:** unfortunate.

32. **wassail:** a toast to one's health, or the revelry accompanying such toasts.

A. Point of View
At what point does the speaker's point of view change? Why do you think the speaker changes his point of view? (The point of view changes from first- to third-person at line 26, when the speaker begins to reminisce about the mead-hall. Some critics have asserted that the switch allows the speaker to cope better with the intense pain that the memory brings him.)

B. Symbolism
How does the speaker's life in the mead-hall contrast with his life now? What does this contrast symbolize? (Life in the mead-hall was one of "dealing of treasure" and "wassail and feast." The speaker's life now is one of "wintry seas." The contrast between the warmth and shining of the mead-hall and the "wintry" seas symbolizes the contrasting states of the "centered" human psyche and the isolated psyche.)

Remind students that although the amount of alliteration in "The Wanderer" might be a bit too much for contemporary readers, a little alliteration can enhance a message and add a natural rhythm to one's words.

Have students add a small amount of alliteration to each of the following sentences, being careful not to overdo it. Remind them that alliteration comes from a repetition of consonant *sounds* rather than from specific letters. Later, students may share their work in small groups.

1. I am a wanderer on the earth.
2. I set my back to the wind and travel where it pushes me.
3. No one knows where I'll be tomorrow.
4. I have no home, though once I lived in a town much like yours.
5. My old friends died; new ones were hard to find.
6. So one day I walked away, and this is where my journey has brought me.
7. Today I am old and weak.
8. Soon I will rest, and this weary body will be still once more.

A. Point of View
Note the speaker's return to first-person here.

B. Responding
In lines 59–65, the speaker gives advice about wisdom and courage. Why do you think he feels himself in a position to give advice to others? (In the play *Agamemnon,* Aeschylus writes, "Suffering brings knowledge." It may be that through his suffering the speaker feels that he, too, has gained knowledge.)

C. Anglo-Saxon Code
Lines 69–79 depict a ruined city that might represent the crumbling of the Anglo-Saxon code and way of life. You may want students to compare these lines with those of Wiglaf in *Beowulf* (lines 762–790, text page 36) when he chides his comrades for not coming to Beowulf's aid. Their action, too, might forecast the end of Anglo-Saxon society.

Pledging his liege°   as in days long past.
Then from his slumber   he starts lonely-hearted,
40   Beholding gray stretches   of tossing sea,
Seabirds bathing,   with wings outspread,
While hailstorms darken,   and driving snow.
Bitterer then   is the <u>bane</u> of his wretchedness,
The longing for loved one: his grief is renewed.
45   The forms of his kinsmen   take shape in the silence;
In rapture he greets them;   in gladness he scans
Old comrades remembered.   But they melt into air
With no word of greeting   to gladden his heart.
Then again surges   his sorrow upon him;
50   And grimly he spurs   his weary soul
Once more to the toil   of the tossing sea.

A   "No wonder therefore,   in all the world,
If a shadow darkens   upon my spirit
When I reflect   on the fates of men—
55   How one by one   proud warriors vanish
From the halls that knew them,   and day by day
All this earth ages   and droops unto death.
No man may know wisdom   till many a winter

B   Has been his portion.   A wise man is patient,
60   Not swift to anger,   nor hasty of speech,
Neither too weak,   nor too reckless, in war,
Neither fearful nor fain,   nor too wishful of wealth,
Nor too eager in vow—   ere he know the event.
A brave man must bide°   when he speaketh his boast
65   Until he know surely   the goal of his spirit.
"A wise man will <u>ponder</u>   how dread is that doom
When all this world's wealth   shall be scattered and
     waste
As now, over all,   through the regions of earth,

C   Walls stand rime-covered   and swept by the winds.
70   The battlements crumble,   the wine halls decay;
Joyless and silent   the heroes are sleeping
Where the proud host fell   by the wall they defended.
Some battle launched   on their long, last journey;
One a bird bore   o'er the billowing sea;
75   One the gray wolf slew;   one a grieving earl
Sadly gave   to the grave's embrace.
The warden of men   hath wasted this world
Till the sound of music   and revel is stilled,
And these giant-built structures   stand empty of life.
80   "He who shall muse   on these <u>moldering</u> ruins,
And deeply ponder   this darkling life,
Must brood on old legends   of battle and bloodshed,
And heavy the mood   that troubles his heart:
'Where now is the warrior?   Where is the warhorse?
85   Bestowal of treasure,   and sharing of feast?
Alas! the bright ale cup,   the byrny-clad° warrior,
The prince in his splendor   —those days are long sped
In the night of the past,   as if they never had been!'

38. **liege:** loyalty.

64. **bide:** wait.

86. **byrny-clad:** wearing a coat or shirt of mail.

1. The Wanderer left his homeland after his lord died, hoping to find a new lord to serve. (T)
2. The Wanderer states that a wise man is one who is patient. (T)
3. Because it is so painful to him, the Wanderer refuses to think about the past. (F)
4. The Wanderer is confident he will find a new lord and a new life as good as his last ones were. (F)
5. The Wanderer comments that the effects of fate make life fleeting. (T)

CLOSURE
Have students assume the viewpoint of the Wanderer and explain, in their own words, the feelings described in this poem.

Viking ship with sea monster, possibly a version of Jonah and the whale. From a manuscript (13th century).

Bodleian Library, Oxford.

A. About the Manuscript
The illumination of book manuscripts began in English monasteries with the conversion of the Anglo-Saxons to Christianity. The skill developed very quickly into a highly sophisticated art form. Anglo-Saxon art historian Carl Nordenfalk comments on the effects of the new Christian religion on Anglo-Saxon art: "The Christian missionaries had been taught to proceed with care. Far from lacking cultural resources of their own, the natives possessed a highly accomplished prehistoric art, which was chiefly decorative, and unlike their pagan idols, it was of no evident danger to the new faith. On the contrary, it could be put to a new use by the artisans now serving the Church as they once had served the pagan chieftains."

The page shown here, late in the development of illumination, is from a bestiary (collection of animal tales). The Jonah story is on text page 406.

A

ANALYZING THE POEM
Identifying Details
1. The Wanderer has learned that human beings who desire honor should veil their sorrow, for misfortune is inevitable in this life.
2. After the death of his liege-lord, the Wanderer left home and embarked on a voyage to find another king who would be willing to serve as his protector.

3. In lines 30–32, the Wanderer recalls memories of his youth, when he was happy in the hall with his lord and his companions.
4. The Wanderer describes the death of his lord, his own endless voyaging, the loss of his kin and friends, the decay of battlements and wine-halls, and the death of a proud host.

5. At lines 59–63, the Wanderer says that a wise man is patient, even-tempered, not hasty of speech, not greedy, and not eager to make vows that he may not be able to keep.

Interpreting Meanings
6. Students may mention wintry images in lines 3, 4, 23, 29, 40, 42, 51, 58, 69, 94, and 97.

A. Responding
❓ Various critics have maintained that the speaker of the poem has a pagan outlook and that the first and last six lines were added by a later, Christian poet. What evidence is there in the tone of the first and last six lines and the tone in the remainder of the poem to support this position? (In all but the first and last six lines, the poet despairs of any solace from God. These first and last comments speak of the comfort to be found in God.)

90 And now remains only,   for warriors' memorial,
A wall wondrous high   with serpent shapes carved.
Storms of ash spears   have smitten the earls,
Carnage of weapon,   and conquering fate.
   "Storms now batter   these ramparts of stone;
Blowing snow   and the blast of winter
95 Enfold the earth;   night shadows fall
Darkly lowering,   from the north driving
Ranging hail   in wrath upon men.
Wretchedness fills   the realm of earth,
And fate's decrees   transform the world.
100 Here wealth is fleeting,   friends are fleeting,
Man is fleeting,   maid is fleeting;
All the foundation of earth   shall fail!''
   Thus spake the sage   in solitude pondering.
A   Good man is he   who guardeth his faith.
105 He must never too quickly   unburden his breast
Of its sorrow, but eagerly   strive for redress;
And happy the man   who seeketh for mercy
From his heavenly Father,   our fortress and strength.

Responding to the Poem

Analyzing the Poem

Identifying Details

1. What has the Wanderer learned about sorrow and misfortune?
2. Why did the Wanderer leave his home and embark on this sea voyage?
3. What happier memories does the Wanderer recall?
4. What mournful events does he describe?
5. How does the Wanderer describe a wise man?

Interpreting Meanings

6. List all the wintry **images** created by the writer of "The Wanderer." How are these wintry images in the poem suited to the speaker's mood? Would you say that the speaker is a "wintry person"? Explain.
7. When the Wanderer says that no man may know wisdom "till many a winter has been his portion" (lines 58–59), what do you think he means? Who do you think is "the warden of men" (line 77)?
8. Would you describe the Wanderer's **tone** as resigned, ironic, bitter, or self-pitying? Explain.
9. Summarize the comments that frame the Wanderer's speech. Do you think they offer hope to the speaker? Explain.

10. What **symbolic** meaning do you think this wandering exile might have? Some critics have noted a connection between the Wanderer and Adam's exile from the Garden of Eden. Can you see the relationship?
11. In the modern world, is there any experience equivalent to the loss of an overlord's protection that might drive someone to an emotional state like the Wanderer's? Explain.

Writing About the Poem

A Creative Response

1. **Imitating a Verse Style.** Choose an object that has special meaning for you and write at least two lines about it, using the poetic techniques of Anglo-Saxon poetry. You might want to write in a serious tone, or you might want to create a humorous parody of the somber tone of "The Wanderer."

   Begin by writing down the name of the object you have chosen; then write three adjectives that describe the object and that **alliterate,** or begin with the same sound.

Example: topic—my favorite socks
            adjectives—soft, striped, size-eleven

The wintry images correspond to and reinforce the speaker's bleak mood.

Most students will agree that the Wanderer is a "wintry" person is the sense that he is melancholy and pessimistic; the speaker says that "No man may know wisdom till many a winter / Has been his portion" (lines 58–59).

7. He means that no man is truly wise until he has endured suffering.

The "warden of men" is probably God, who will bring the end of the world on the Last Day. This is the "doom" that is described in lines 66–79.

8. Student answers will vary. Most students will agree that the tone is more melancholy than bitter or harshly ironic.

9. In lines 1–7, the poet refers to "God's pity," which comes often to the Wanderer, even in his most melancholy mo-

ments. In the concluding comment at lines 103–108, the speaker says that men who guard their faith and trust in God's mercy are good. Both comments seem to offer hope to the speaker.

10. Students may suggest that one's journey through life could be described as a *wandering*. Encourage students to support their answers with details from the poem.

Students should see that both cases involve exile from a place of goodness and protection—banishment to a life filled with fear, violence, and the certainty of death.

11. Again, student answers will vary. Some students may suggest that the loss of a parent, a relative, a spouse, or even a job might produce a similarly anguished emotional state.

These will become the four stressed words in your first line. Join them with as many unstressed connecting words as you want. Remember to leave a pause—a **caesura**—between the second and third stressed syllables.

For the second line, compose a **kenning** that describes your topic. Remember that a kenning is a compound descriptive word that usually functions as a metaphor. For example, you might refer to a sock as a "foot-cradle," since it warms and protects your foot. After you have composed your kenning, choose three other important words that alliterate with it. These can be the stressed syllables in your second line. Continue in this manner for as many lines as you can. After you have finished, mark your stressed syllables.

A Critical Response

2. **Analyzing the Poem.** In a brief essay, refute or support the following interpretation of the meaning of "The Wanderer":

The Wanderer, like all men . . . , is an exile from Paradise, . . . and therefore overwhelmed with terror and hopelessness before the threat of nonbeing symbolized by the . . . sea and winter storms.

—from *The Guest-Hall of Eden,* Alvin A. Lee

Support your opinion by using quotations from "The Wanderer."

3. **Comparing and Contrasting Translations.** (A third translation, by Burton Raffel, follows under "Primary Sources.") Here is another translation of the opening lines of "The Wanderer."

The lonely wanderer prays often for compassion
And for mercy from Lord God; but for a long time
Destiny decrees that with a heavy heart he must dip
His oars into icy waters, working his passage over the
    sea.
He must follow the paths of exile. Fate is inexorable!
The wanderer's mind moved upon adversity
And savage slaughter and the ruin of kinsmen. He said,
"Time and again at the day's dawning
I must mourn all my afflictions alone. . . ."

—Translated by
Kevin Crossley-Holland

In an essay, compare and contrast the three translations. Consider (a) the degree to which each translator has attempted to imitate the original, and (b) the overall effect of each translation as a poem. Conclude your essay with your evaluation of each translation.

Primary Sources
The Original Language

Here is the opening of "The Wanderer" in Old English. Following these lines, Burton Raffel (whose translation of *Beowulf* is on page 14) has proposed a translation. Raffel's translation is "free." That is, he has not attempted to reproduce the alliteration and the poetic line of the original.

> Oft him anhaga are gebideð,
> metudes miltse, þeach þe he modcearig
> geond lagulade longe sceolde
> hreran mid hondum hrimcealde sae,
> wadan wraeclastas. Wyrd bið ful araed!
>
> Swa cwaeð eardstapa, earfeþa gemyndig,
> wraþra waelsleahta, winemaega hryre:
>
> "Oft ic sceolde ana uhtna gehwylce
> mine ceare cwiþan. . . ."

This lonely traveler longs for grace,
For the mercy of God; grief hangs on
His heart and follows the frost-cold foam
He cuts in the sea, sculling endlessly,
Aimlessly, in exile. Fate has opened
A single port: memory. He sees
His kinsmen slaughtered again, and cries:
   "I've drunk too many lonely dawns,
Gray with mourning. . . ."

PREPARATION
ESTABLISHING A PURPOSE. Have students read to compare and contrast the theme, atmosphere, and point of view of this poem and "The Wanderer."

SUPPLEMENTARY SUPPORT MATERIALS
1. Vocabulary Activity Worksheet (*CCB*)
2. Review and Response Worksheet: Metaphor (*CCB*)
3. Selection Test (*CCB*)

DEVELOPING VOCABULARY
The following words from the poem are tested in the Selection Test. (See also Vocabulary Activity Worksheet.)

tern	rancor
to admonish	to tarnish
ravenous	chaste

A. About the Photograph
The cliffs of Moher, depicted here, are located on the western coast of Ireland in County Clare. This area, once inhabited by the Celts, was also the site of a castle stronghold. (No enemy could scale these cliffs.) The ruins of the castle can still be seen today.

? Why do you think this photograph was chosen to illustrate "The Seafarer"? Use details from the poem to support your answer. (Answers will vary, but students should note how details in the first twenty-six lines of the poem seem to describe the appearance of these forbidding cliffs and the thundering ocean below: "smashing surf," "ice-cold sea," "roaring sea," "freezing waves," and so on. Students should also note the general desolation of the cliffs compared with the desolation of the Seafarer.)

"The Seafarer," like "The Wanderer," dates from before 950 and is preserved in the Exeter Book. Like "The Wanderer," the poem is about an exile cut off from human companionship. In this case, however, the poet assumes the voice of an old sailor reflecting on the way of life he has chosen.

Some critics regard "The Seafarer" as a sequel to "The Wanderer."

This translation dispenses with the conventional Anglo-Saxon split line, but it preserves the alliterative four-beat structure, as well as the power and grace of the original.

The Seafarer

Translated by **Burton Raffel**

A

1. The narrator claims that the tale he tells is true. (T)
2. The narrator states that he never feared the sea. (F)
3. Fate's three threats are illness, age, and poverty. (F)

4. The narrator states that the days of glory are gone. (T)
5. According to the narrator, man's goal is to get to Heaven. (T)

The Translation of Verse

"Verse translation is a minor art, but a unique one. The assignment is, by definition, almost impossible. A synthesis in one language, fused at high pressure into form and beauty and coherence, has to be taken apart and, with infinite care, rebuilt in a totally different mould.

". . . The translator's only hope is to re-create something roughly equivalent in the new language, something that is itself good poetry and that at the same time carries a reasonable measure of the force and flavor of the original. . . ."
—Burton Raffel

A. Responding

How would you characterize the Seafarer's experience on the ocean? (The experience has been one of hardship and desolation.)

B. Interpreting

Why does the Seafarer return to the ocean time after time? (He seems to feel a need to seek "foreigners' homes." He can't rest.)

C. Theme

Our universal need to experience the world is also an important theme in the *Odyssey* and, centuries later, in Tennyson's "Ulysses" (see text page 791). You might want students to compare the expression of this theme in these three works.

This tale is true, and mine. It tells
How the sea took me, swept me back
And forth in sorrow and fear and pain,
Showed me suffering in a hundred ships,
5 In a thousand ports, and in me. It tells
Of smashing surf when I sweated in the cold
Of an anxious watch, perched in the bow
As it dashed under cliffs. My feet were cast
In icy bands, bound with frost,
10 With frozen chains, and hardship groaned
Around my heart. Hunger tore
At my sea-weary soul. No man sheltered
On the quiet fairness of earth can feel
How wretched I was, drifting through winter
15 On an ice-cold sea, whirled in sorrow,
Alone in a world blown clear of love,
Hung with icicles. The hailstorms flew.
The only sound was the roaring sea,
The freezing waves. The song of the swan
20 Might serve for pleasure, the cry of the sea-fowl,
The death-noise of birds instead of laughter,
The mewing of gulls instead of mead.
Storms beat on the rocky cliffs and were echoed
By icy-feathered terns and the eagle's screams;
25 No kinsman could offer comfort there,
To a soul left drowning in desolation.
    And who could believe, knowing but
The passion of cities, swelled proud with wine
And no taste of misfortune, how often, how wearily,
30 I put myself back on the paths of the sea.
Night would blacken; it would snow from the north;
Frost bound the earth and hail would fall,
The coldest seeds. And how my heart
Would begin to beat, knowing once more
35 The salt waves tossing and the towering sea!
The time for journeys would come and my soul
Called me eagerly out, sent me over
The horizon, seeking foreigners' homes.
    But there isn't a man on earth so proud,
40 So born to greatness, so bold with his youth,
Grown so brave, or so graced by God,
That he feels no fear as the sails unfurl,
Wondering what Fate has willed and will do.
No harps ring in his heart, no rewards,
45 No passion for women, no worldly pleasures,
Nothing, only the ocean's heave;
But longing wraps itself around him.
Orchards blossom, the towns bloom,
Fields grow lovely as the world springs fresh,
50 And all these admonish that willing mind
Leaping to journeys, always set
In thoughts traveling on a quickening tide.

[handwritten annotations: "hardships of life at sea - cold"; "hunger"; "lonely"; "Feels need to be at sea, even though life is hard."; "all men are afraid at sea"; "pagan"; "universal need to experience the world"]

CLOSURE
Have students write two or three sentences expressing the speaker's philosophy about seafaring and his attitude toward God.

ANALYZING THE POEM
Identifying Details
1. In these lines, the speaker describes himself on watch on the bow of a ship in

a wintry sea.
2. Lines 27–29 imply that the speaker dislikes "the passion of cities, swelled proud with wine." Lines 33–38 and 58–64 suggest the speaker's love of journeys and adventures.
3. At lines 69–71, the speaker describes the three threats of fate as illness, age, and death from an enemy's sword.
4. The speaker says that the present is

a pale reflection of the past. Men have grown old and weak, and "all glory is tarnished."
5. The speaker praises the eternal God, creator of the earth.

A. Kenning
Note the popular kenning "whales' home" for sea.

B. Connections
These lines are referred to in question 4 and should be cited in answering the essay question, number 2. These sentiments are typical of people who feel they are living at the end of a heroic era; the response of the speaker here to the tawdriness of his age has strong parallels even in our own time, as the twentieth century draws to a close. A good comparison could also be made with Shelley's "Ozymandias" on text page 706, an ironic lament on the transience of glory. You might also refer to Tennyson's feelings of loss and bewilderment as the nineteenth century drew to a close. (See "Tears, Idle Tears," text page 779, and "Break, Break, Break," text page 781.) See also another spokesman for the Victorians, Matthew Arnold, in "Dover Beach," text page 813.

So summer's sentinel, the cuckoo, sings
In his murmuring voice, and our hearts mourn
55 As he urges. Who could understand,
In ignorant ease, what we others suffer
As the paths of exile stretch endlessly on?
    And yet my heart wanders away,
A My soul roams with the sea, the whales'
60 Home, wandering to the widest corners
Of the world, returning ravenous with desire,
Flying solitary, screaming, exciting me
To the open ocean, breaking oaths
On the curve of a wave.
                    Thus the joys of God
65 Are fervent with life, where life itself
Fades quickly into the earth. The wealth
Of the world neither reaches to Heaven nor remains.
No man has ever faced the dawn
Certain which of Fate's three threats
70 Would fall: illness, or age, or an enemy's
Sword, snatching the life from his soul.
The praise the living pour on the dead
Flowers from reputation: plant
An earthly life of profit reaped
75 Even from hatred and rancor, of bravery
Flung in the devil's face, and death
Can only bring you earthly praise
And a song to celebrate a place
With the angels, life eternally blessed
80 In the hosts of Heaven.
                    The days are gone
B When the kingdoms of earth flourished in glory;
Now there are no rulers, no emperors,
No givers of gold, as once there were,
When wonderful things were worked among them
85 And they lived in lordly magnificence.
Those powers have vanished, those pleasures are dead.
The weakest survives and the world continues,
Kept spinning by toil. All glory is tarnished.
The world's honor ages and shrinks,
90 Bent like the men who mold it. Their faces
Blanch as time advances, their beards
Wither and they mourn the memory of friends.
The sons of princes, sown in the dust.
The soul stripped of its flesh knows nothing
95 Of sweetness or sour, feels no pain,
Bends neither its hand nor its brain. A brother
Opens his palms and pours down gold
On his kinsman's grave, strewing his coffin
With treasures intended for Heaven, but nothing
100 Golden shakes the wrath of God
For a soul overflowing with sin, and nothing
Hidden on earth rises to Heaven.

elegaic lament of the past

Interpreting Meanings

6. "Home" here probably means heaven.
7. Answers will vary; many students may conclude that the seafarer is searching for "home"—a port where he can settle down or circumstances that will bring peace to his restless spirit.
8. Student answers will vary. Among the metaphors students may select are the following: "frozen chains" (line 10),

"whirled in sorrow" (line 15), "drowning in desolation" (line 26), "the coldest seeds" (line 33), "summer's sentinel" (line 53), "ravenous with desire" (line 61), "The praise the living pour on the dead / Flowers from reputation" (lines 72–73), "All glory is tarnished" (line 88), "a soul overflowing with sin" (line 101), "Death leaps at the fools who forget their God" (line 106). Make sure that students

relate each metaphor they select to setting, characterization, and atmosphere in context.
9. Fate is an inevitable force that seems bound up with human restlessness, anxiety, and the general decline of the world.

Fate was similarly regarded by the Wanderer as a force against which men are powerless to struggle.
10. Most students will agree that the sentiments—praise of the past, unhappiness at the decline of the present—may still be heard today.

We all fear God. He turns the earth,
He set it swinging firmly in space,
105   Gave life to the world and light to the sky.

Christian ideas

Death leaps at the fools who forget their God.
He who lives humbly has angels from Heaven
To carry him courage and strength and belief.
A man must conquer pride, not kill it,
110   Be firm with his fellows, chaste for himself,
Treat all the world as the world deserves,
With love or with hate but never with harm,
Though an enemy seek to scorch him in hell,
Or set the flames of a funeral pyre
115   Under his lord. Fate is stronger
And God mightier than any man's mind.
Our thoughts should turn to where our home is,

heaven

Consider the ways of coming there,
Then strive for sure permission for us
120   To rise to that eternal joy,
That life born in the love of God
And the hope of Heaven. Praise the Holy
Grace of Him who honored us,
Eternal, unchanging creator of earth. Amen.

Responding to the Poem

Analyzing the Poem

Identifying Details

1. In lines 5–26, what scene does the speaker describe?
2. What passages explain why the seafarer seeks the rigors of the sea rather than the delight of the land?
3. According to the speaker, what are the three "threats" of fate?
4. How does the speaker contrast the present state of the world with the past (lines 80–102)?
5. What prayer concludes the poem?

Interpreting Meanings

6. What meaning do you give to *home* in line 117?
7. What do you think the seafarer is searching for?
8. This short lyric is full of striking **metaphors**. Select three of these metaphors and explain what each contributes to the **setting, characterization,** and/or **atmosphere** in the poem.
9. What role does fate play in this poem? How was fate regarded by the Wanderer (page 43)?
10. Do you hear the sentiments in lines 87–90 still expressed by people today? Explain.

Writing About the Poem

A Critical Response

1. **Supporting an Opinion.** *The Wanderer is grimly resigned to his fate, but the Seafarer willingly renounces the easy but transitory pleasures of the land world.* In an essay, support or refute this statement. Justify your opinion by quoting directly from the poems.
2. **Comparing and Contrasting Poems.** In a brief essay, compare and contrast the Seafarer's feelings about the permanence of earthly delights with the sentiments expressed in the following poem:

Nothing Gold Can Stay

Nature's first green is gold,
Her hardest hue to hold.
Her early leaf's a flower;
But only so an hour.
Then leaf subsides to leaf.
So Eden sank to grief,
So dawn goes down to day.
Nothing gold can stay.

—Robert Frost

ESTABLISHING A PURPOSE. The purpose of reading these riddles is, of course, to solve them. The solution will come more easily to students if you tell them in advance that the riddles are metaphors and that they contain personification.

SUPPLEMENTARY SUPPORT MATERIALS
1. Review and Response Worksheet: Personification (*CCB*)
2. Selection Test (*CCB*)
3. Instructional Overhead Transparency

CLOSURE
Have students tell riddles of their own and try to solve those told by their classmates.

Critical Comment
In *A Feast of Creatures: Anglo-Saxon Riddle Songs*, Craig Williamson comments on the metaphoric nature of riddles: "The riddles are primitive flower and lyric seed. To us, they offer a world in which there is an eye (I) in every other, a charged world where as Walt Whitman says, there is 'God in every object.' "

A. Vocabulary
Use of the word *machine* in this context may give students difficulty if they associate a machine only with something that operates on electricity. You might remind students that the word was first applied to *any* apparatus used for doing work.

B. Metaphor/ Connections
Students should note that the basic metaphor of this riddle is that of a powerful woman. Compare this description with that of the iceberg hitting the *Titanic* in John Malcolm Brinnin's essay on text page 838.

Anglo-Saxon Riddles

The poetic riddle has always been a popular form. In the Anglo-Saxon period, riddles were "everyday" poetry. They were intellectual exercises that entertained by puzzling. As in most cultures, the Anglo-Saxon riddle could be slightly coarse; it usually described some household or farm object or some aspect of ordinary life. Ninety-five riddles are found in the Exeter Book. Some can be traced to Latin originals, and several were ascribed to the great northern poet Cynewulf.

The Anglo-Saxons must have whiled away many a long, dark, winter evening by repeating riddles like these and having friends guess the answers.

The elaborate construction of the riddles assured that answers could not be guessed quickly. The answer to each riddle is found on page 53.

Riddles

Translated by **Burton Raffel**

32

Our world is lovely in different ways,
Hung with beauty and works of hands.
A ⌐ I saw a strange machine, made
For motion, slide against the sand,
5 Shrieking as it went. It walked swiftly
On its only foot, this odd-shaped monster,
Traveled in an open country without
Seeing, without arms, or hands,
With many ribs, and its mouth in its middle.
10 Its work is useful, and welcome, for it loads
Its belly with food, and brings abundance
To men, to poor and to rich, paying
Its tribute year after year. Solve
This riddle, if you can, and unravel its name.

33

A creature came through the waves, beautiful
And strange, calling to shore, its voice
Loud and deep; its laughter froze
Men's blood; its sides were like sword-blades. It swam
5 Contemptuously along, slow and sluggish,
A bitter warrior and a thief, ripping
B Ships apart, and plundering. Like a witch
It wove spells—and knew its own nature, shouting:
"My mother is the fairest virgin of a race
10 Of noble virgins: she is my daughter
Grown great. All men know her, and me,
And know, everywhere on earth, with what joy
We will come to join them, to live on land!"

Craig Williamson has suggested that this riddle is a rather ironic comment on the end of the oral tradition with its eloquent poet and its replacement with the scribe and book.

ANALYZING THE RIDDLES
Identifying Details
1. Students should mention the following clues: "slide against the sand" (line 4, actually referring to the ship's being beached), "traveled in an open country" (line 7, actually referring to the ship sailing on the sea), "loads its belly with food" (lines 10–11, actually referring to the ship's cargoes).

2. Among the words that personify the speaker in this riddle are: "calling to shore" (line 2), "its voice loud and deep" (lines 2–3), "its laughter froze men's blood" (lines 3–4), "its sides were like sword-blades" (line 4), "it swam contemptuously" (lines 4–5), "A bitter warrior and a thief" (line 6), "plundering" (line 7), "It wove spells" (line 8), "shouting" (line 8). Students may also mention the quotation in lines 9–13, referring to the speaker's mother.
3. The speaker thinks that it is strange that a worm could eat words.

Interpreting Meanings
4. Students probably will agree that there is some deception, at least in the use of a metaphor.
5. Students may note that like the creature, icebergs move; they also may note that the ice in icebergs is considered very pure ("virgin").
6. Paradoxes occur in lines 1, 3, and 6.
7. Students will have their own opinions about which clues are most significant or misleading. Possibilities might include lines 4 and 9 in Riddle 32, lines 3 and 6–7 in Riddle 33, and lines 1 and 3 in Riddle 47.
8. Again student answers will vary. Possibilities might include crossword puzzles, games like "20 Questions" and Trivial Pursuit, acrostics, anagrams, and solving rebuses.

47

A
A worm ate words. I thought that wonderfully
Strange—a miracle—when they told me a crawling
Insect had swallowed noble songs,
A night-time thief had stolen writing
So famous, so weighty. But the bug was foolish
Still, though its belly was full of thought.

Answers: 32. a ship; 33. an iceberg; 47. a bookworm.

Responding to the Riddles

Analyzing the Riddles

Identifying Details

1. List all the clues given to describe the object in Riddle 32. What does each clue actually refer to?
2. What words **personify** the speaker in Riddle 33?
3. What does the speaker think is strange in Riddle 47?

Interpreting Meanings

4. Riddles usually open with a deliberate deception. Do you think these examples follow this pattern? Explain.
5. Can you explain the significance of the last five lines of Riddle 33?
6. What lines in Riddle 47 present a **paradox**—a seeming contradiction?
7. What clues are most significant in each riddle? Are any details too misleading? Explain.
8. Can you think of any forms of entertainment popular today that are similar to the Anglo-Saxon riddles?

Writing About the Riddles

A Creative Response

Writing a Riddle. Bookworms, icebergs, and ships must have been familiar sights to most Anglo-Saxons. Choose an object familiar to you and your classmates (perhaps a lightbulb, a soda can, a sneaker). Take a minute to observe or remember how the object *looks* and how it *functions*. Then let the object describe itself, using metaphors and personification as clues. Do not give the identity of the object away; see if you can guess one another's riddles. You can write in prose or in verse.

A. Expansion
Actually given by his parents to the Church as an "oblate," or offering, Bede, working alone in his austere world of monastery walls and church bells, became what historian R. W. Southern refers to as the "first scientific intellect among the Germanic peoples." Students might be interested to know that Bede gained his reputation through many of the same practices that they are asked to perform with their own work, such as validating sources and verifying generalizations.

Even if students have never read Bede, they are affected by him on a daily basis: It was Bede who introduced the term *anno Domini* ("in the year of our Lord") and the system of dating from the birth of Christ.

B. Humanities Connection: About the Fine Art
The great work of St. Jerome (c. 374–419) was a translation of the Hebrew and Greek Bible into Latin. This translation was known as the Vulgate text of the Bible and was the version in use by Roman Catholics for centuries. Jerome lived for many years as a recluse in the desert. He is frequently pictured with a lion lying at his feet. (According to legend, he removed a thorn from the lion's paw and so was saved from attack by the beast.) You can identify the saint by the nimbus around his head.

The Venerable Bede (673–735)

About A.D. 680, a gifted seven-year-old boy named Bede (Baeda) was placed by his parents under the care of the abbot of the great monastery of Jarrow in northeast England. As a center of learning, the monastery turned out to be the right place for this remarkable child. Bede was destined to become a monk whose scholarly brilliance would be famous throughout medieval Europe. He was later given the title "venerable" because of his reputation for wisdom and piety.

Bede was the author of forty respected and widely read books. He composed verse, biographies of the saints, theological commentaries, and most important, the *Ecclesiastical History of the English Church and People*. Written in Latin, and later translated into Old English by King Alfred, this great work remains our major source of facts about life in Anglo-Saxon England. It tells of early invasions and conquests of Britain, of the work of the early missionaries, of the founding of monasteries; it also recounts wonderful tales of miracles and of colorful figures in early English history.

Among Bede's stories of missionaries is one included here about the conversion of the powerful King Edwin of Northumbria by the holy Paulinus. Through Paulinus's efforts, the "pagan" cult of Woden was dramatically overthrown in Northumbria, and the Christian Church was substituted for it.

Perhaps the traditional favorite among the tales of Bede is the story of the saintly poet Caedmon, who died the same year that the young Bede came to Jarrow. Caedmon had lived in the nearby monastery of Whitby, which was led by St. Hilda from 658 to 680. Caedmon was uneducated but inspired. He used the old secular forms of poetry for his religious outpourings. The "Hymn of Caedmon to God the Father," as reported in Bede's *History*, is the earliest literary document in English. Perhaps it is significant that a prayer was to survive as the beginning of a national literature in which religion was to play such a significant role.

St. Jerome dictating to his scribes.

Convent of San Paolo Fuori LeMura, Rome.

PREPARATION

ESTABLISHING A PURPOSE. Have students think about the fact that the religious practices of the Anglo-Saxons disappeared forever when England was Christianized. Ask them to read this important account to learn just how this enormously significant conversion took place. Could anything like this happen today?

SUPPLEMENTARY SUPPORT MATERIALS
1. Vocabulary Activity Worksheet (*CCB*)
2. Review and Response Worksheet: Understanding Anglo-Saxon History (*CCB*)
3. Language Skills Worksheet: Active and Passive Voice (*CCB*)
4. Selection Test (*CCB*)

DEVELOPING VOCABULARY
The following words from the history are tested in the Selection Test. (See also Vocabulary Activity Worksheet.)

diligently — secular
to desecrate — abbess
idolatry — to render
to profane — auditor
to gird — to rebuke

FROM ECCLESIASTICAL HISTORY OF THE ENGLISH PEOPLE

A

As this part of the history opens, King Edwin has not yet become a Christian, though he has been talking to the Christian priest Paulinus and has abandoned worship of Woden. Coifi, Chief Priest of the old religion, has told the king that though he himself has been zealous in serving the old gods, they have not favored him. Therefore, Coifi suggests, they should all accept the new religion. In the history of England, this was a profoundly important moment.

The Saxon Temples Are Destroyed, A.D. 625

B

Another of the king's chief men signified his agreement with this prudent argument, and went on to say, "Your Majesty, when we compare the present life of man on earth with that time of which we have no knowledge, it seems to me like the swift flight of a single sparrow through the banqueting hall where you are sitting at dinner on a winter's day with your thanes and counselors. In the midst there is a comforting fire to warm the hall; outside, the storms of winter rain or snow are raging. This sparrow flies swiftly in through one door of the hall, and out through another. While he is inside, he is safe from the winter storms; but after a few moments of comfort, he vanishes from sight into the wintry world from which he came. Even so, man appears on earth for a little while; but of what went before this life or of what follows, we know nothing. Therefore, if this new teaching has brought any more certain knowledge, it seems only right that we should follow it." The other elders and counselors of the king, under God's guidance, gave similar advice.

Coifi then added that he wished to hear Paulinus's teaching about God in greater detail; and when, at the king's bidding, this had been given, he exclaimed: "I have long realized that there is nothing in our way of worship; for the more diligently I sought after truth in our religion, the less I found. I now publicly confess that this teaching clearly reveals truths that will afford us the blessings of life, salvation, and eternal happiness. Therefore, Your Majesty, I submit that the temples and altars that we have dedicated to no advantage be immediately desecrated and burned."

In short, the king granted blessed Paulinus full permission to preach, renounced idolatry, and professed his acceptance of the Faith of Christ. And when he asked the Chief Priest who should be the first to profane the altars and shrines of the idols, together with the enclosures that surrounded them, Coifi replied: "I will do this myself; for now that the true God has granted me knowledge, who more suitably than I can set a public example and destroy the idols that I worshiped in ignorance?" So he formally renounced his empty superstitions and asked the king to give him arms and a stallion—for hitherto it had not been lawful for the Chief Priest to carry arms or to ride anything but a mare—and, thus equipped, he set out to destroy the idols. Girded with a sword and with a spear in his hand, he mounted the king's stallion and rode up to the idols. When the crowd saw him, they thought he had gone mad; but without hesitation, as soon as he reached the temple, he cast into it the spear he carried and thus profaned it. Then, full of joy at his knowledge of the worship of the true God, he told his companions to set fire to the temple and its enclosures and destroy them. The site where the idols once stood is still shown, not far east of York, beyond the river Derwent, and is known today as Goodmanham. Here it was that the Chief Priest, inspired by the true God, desecrated and destroyed the altars that he had himself dedicated.

A. An Original Source
Students might be surprised at the lack of resistance to Christianity by King Edwin. The conversion of the Anglo-Saxons to Christianity was a smooth process, thanks in great part to the enlightened attitude of Church officials. That attitude is apparent in a letter, included by Bede in his *History*, in which Pope Gregory I directs the preservation of the pagan temples so that "the people, seeing that their temples are not destroyed, may abandon their error and, flocking more readily to their accustomed resorts, may come to know and adore the true God." In the same letter, Gregory comments that "it is certainly impossible to eradicate all errors from obstinate minds at one stroke, and whoever wishes to climb to a mountain top climbs gradually step by step, and not in one leap."

B. Extended Simile
This is the famous "sparrow" simile (see question 1 on text page 58).

READING CHECK TEST
1. Coifi, chief priest of the pagan religion, destroys pagan idols.
2. King Edwin's attitude toward Paulinus is one of cooperation, acceptance.
3. Caedmon receives his art of poetry as a gift from God.
4. Caedmon is in a stable when he first sings verses.
5. Caedmon turned all that he knew into verses.

CLOSURE
Have students "translate," in brief, one-paragraph summaries, each of these two excerpts from Bede. Have them suppose their audience is someone who has never read Bede.

A. Expansion
This section is typical of the legends of saints and tales of local traditions that Bede included in his *History*. The monastery mentioned here is in Northumbria.

B. Expansion
Caedmon is the first person known by name to have composed poetry in the English language.

C. Expansion
The reference here is to the proscription in Leviticus (11:26) against eating the flesh of animals with divided hoofs who do not chew their cuds. Such animals are called unclean. (The cow chews its cud, so it is clean.)

Caedmon

A In this monastery of Streanaeshalch lived a brother singularly gifted by God's grace. So skillful was he in composing religious and devotional songs that, when any passage of Scripture was explained to him by interpreters, he could quickly turn it into delightful and moving poetry in his own English tongue. These verses of his have stirred the hearts of many folk to despise the world and aspire to heavenly things. **B** Others after him tried to compose religious poems in English, but none could compare with him; for he did not acquire the art of poetry from men or through any human teacher but received it as a free gift from God. For this reason he could never compose any frivolous or profane verses; but only such as had a religious theme fell fittingly from his devout lips. He had followed a secular occupation until well advanced in years without ever learning anything about poetry. Indeed it sometimes happened at a feast that all the guests in turn would be invited to sing and entertain the company; then, when he saw the harp coming his way, he would get up from table and go home.

On one such occasion he had left the house in which the entertainment was being held and went out to the stable, where it was his duty that night to look after the beasts. There when the time came he settled down to sleep. Suddenly in a dream he saw a man standing beside him who called him by name. "Caedmon," he said, "sing me a song." "I don't know how to sing," he replied. "It is because I cannot sing that I left the feast and came here." The man who addressed him then said: "But you shall sing to me." "What should I sing about?" he replied. "Sing about the Creation of all things," the other answered. And Caedmon immediately began to sing verses in praise of God the Creator that he had never heard before, and their theme ran thus:

Praise we the Fashioner now of Heaven's
    fabric,
The majesty of his might and his mind's
    wisdom,
Work of the world-warden, worker of all
    wonders,
How he the Lord of Glory everlasting,
Wrought first for the race of men Heaven as a
    rooftree,
Then made he Middle Earth to be their mansion.

This is the general sense, but not the actual words that Caedmon sang in his dream; for verses, however masterly, cannot be translated literally from one language into another without losing much of their beauty and dignity. When Caedmon awoke, he remembered everything that he had sung in his dream, and soon added more verses in the same style to a song truly worthy of God.

Early in the morning he went to his superior the reeve,[1] and told him about this gift that he had received. The reeve took him before the abbess, who ordered him to give an account of his dream and repeat the verses in the presence of many learned men, so that a decision might be reached by common consent as to their quality and origin. All of them agreed that Caedmon's gift had been given him by our Lord. And they explained to him a passage of scriptural history or doctrine and asked him to render it into verse if he could. He promised to do this, and returned next morning with excellent verses as they had ordered him. The abbess was delighted that God had given such grace to the man, and advised him to abandon secular life and adopt the monastic state. And when she had admitted him into the Community as a brother, she ordered him to be instructed in the events of sacred history. **C** So Caedmon stored up in his memory all that he learned, and like one of the clean animals chewing the cud, turned it into such melodious verse that his delightful renderings turned his instructors into auditors. He sang of the creation of the world, the origin of the human race, and the whole story of Genesis. He sang of Israel's exodus from Egypt, the entry into the Promised Land, and many other events of scriptural history. He sang of the Lord's Incarnation, Passion, Resurrection, and Ascension into heaven, the coming of the Holy Spirit, and the teaching of the Apostles. He also made many poems on the terrors of the Last Judgement, the horrible pains of Hell, and the joys of the Kingdom of Heaven. In addition to these, he composed several others on the blessings and judgments of God, by which he sought to turn his hearers from delight in wickedness and to inspire them to love and do good. For Caedmon was a deeply religious man, who humbly submitted to regular discipline and hotly rebuked all who tried to follow another course. And so he crowned his life with a happy end.

---

1. **reeve:** the overseer of the monastery, the steward.

Analyzing the History
Identifying Facts

1. The terms of the comparison are, on the one hand, the brief life of human beings, and, on the other, the swift flight of a sparrow in and out of a warm banqueting hall in winter time. The simile might be paraphrased this way: A person's life is as fleeting as the flight of a single sparrow through a banqueting hall.

2. He recommends the acceptance of Paulinus's teachings because the practice of the pagan religion has failed to provide its followers with sure and certain truth.

He rides up to the temple, thrusts a spear into it, and then orders the people to burn the shrine.

3. Caedmon is a brother in the monastery at Streanaeshalch. His special gift is the composition of religious and devotional songs.

The gift came from God.

4. Caedmon's songs were on Biblical and devotional themes. Among his subjects were the Creation, the origin of the human race, the story of Genesis, the Exodus from Egypt and the entry into the Promised Land, the Lord's Incarna- *(Answers continue on next page.)*

Portrait of Saint Matthew from the Lindisfarne Gospels.

British Library.

A. Humanities Connection: Discussing the Fine Art
This page from the great treasure of English art called the *Lindisfarne Gospels*, created some time before 698, shows both the high degree of development of Hiberno[Irish]-Saxon art and the artist's reverence for his religious subject. The illumination shows the evangelist Matthew writing his gospel. The winged figure above the evangelist symbolizes the heralding of the good news of the Gospel. The man peering from behind the curtain could be Matthew's symbol, the man: Matthew's Gospels stress Jesus as the Messiah looked for in the Old Testament. The lettering above St. Matthew's symbol is Latin for "in the image of man," and that next to the symbol is Greek for "the holy." Matthew appears to have written his gospel for Greek-speaking Jews.

(Answers begin on previous page.)
tion, Passion, Resurrection, and Ascension, the coming of the Holy Spirit, the teaching of the Apostles, the terrors of the Last Judgment, the pains of Hell, and the joys of the Kingdom of Heaven.

Interpreting Meanings
5. The sparrow might be said to symbolize the vulnerability and fragility of human life.

The guest-hall may symbolize life on earth; the storms outside the hall may symbolize the dangers of the unknown, perhaps the unknown nature of existence after death in particular.

6. All three speakers view life as brief, dangerous, uncertain, and fraught with misfortunes.

7. Student answers will vary. Urge students to support their opinions.

Again, student answers will vary. Encourage students to supply illustrations from foreign cultures with which they are familiar.

8. Caedmon implicitly compares God the creator to a fashioner of fabric. He also compares heaven to a "roof-tree" and Middle Earth, where humans live, to a *(Answers continue in left-hand column.)*

(Continued from top.)
mansion.
9. Bede compares Caedmon to "one of the clean animals chewing the cud."
10. Students should point out that Caedmon, a humble, uneducated man, became the great "singer" or poet of the English people. The motif of the rise of a humble person to greatness is common.

Students will agree that the motif is often pointed out in American history; the lives of Presidents Abraham Lincoln and Harry Truman, among others, furnish examples.

Responding to the History

Analyzing the History

Identifying Facts

1. At the opening of the first extract, Bede reports a famous **extended simile** made by one of King Edwin's counselors. State the simile in your own words: What are the terms of the comparison?
2. Why does Coifi recommend that Paulinus's teachings be accepted? How does Coifi himself profane the Saxon temple?
3. Who is Caedmon, and what is his special gift? Where, according to Bede, did this gift come from?
4. What were some of the subjects of Caedmon's songs?

Interpreting Meanings

5. In the **extended simile** about the sparrow, what could the sparrow **symbolize?** What does the guest-hall symbolize, and the storms outside the hall?
6. How does this sparrow **simile** connect with the attitudes of the Wanderer (page 43) and the Seafarer (page 48)?
7. Does the **simile** about the sparrow seem valid for us today? That is, do many people agree that a human lifespan is a brief flash of warmth in an eternity of cold and darkness? Explain. How might such a belief affect a society's values?
8. Explain the **metaphors** Caedmon uses in his song to describe God and the act of creation.
9. What **simile,** drawn from ordinary rural life, describes Caedmon's creative process?
10. How does Caedmon's story illustrate the idea that lowly people can be exalted? Is this motif ever pointed out in histories today? Explain.

Writing About the History

A Creative Response

Imitating the Writer's Technique. In the short-short story that follows, the modern Argentine writer Jorge Luis Borges imagines what happened to the last living witness to the rites of the cult of Woden in England. Borges speculates that everyone carries memories of things no one else will ever see again or even care about. These memories, which die when we die, may be as impressive as the memory of a major battle in a war. Or they may be as commonplace as the memory of a familiar object in a desk drawer.

The Witness

In a stable which is almost in the shadow of the new stone church, a man with gray eyes and gray beard, lying amidst the odor of the animals, humbly seeks death as one would seek sleep. The day, faithful to vast and secret laws, is shifting and confusing the shadows inside the poor shelter; outside are the plowed fields and a ditch clogged with dead leaves and the tracks of a wolf in the black mud where the forests begin. The man sleeps and dreams, forgotten. He is awakened by the bells tolling the Angelus.[1] In the kingdoms of England the ringing of bells is now one of the customs of the evening, but this man, as a child, has seen the face of Woden, the divine horror and exultation, the crude wooden idol hung with Roman coins and heavy clothing, the sacrificing of horses, dogs, and prisoners. Before dawn he will die and with him will die, and never return, the last immediate images of these pagan rites; the world will be a little poorer when this Saxon has died.

Deeds which populate the dimensions of space and which reach their end when someone dies may cause us wonderment, but one thing, or an infinite number of things, dies in every final agony, unless there is a universal memory as the theosophists have conjectured. In time there was a day that extinguished the last eyes to see Christ; the battle of Junín and the love of Helen died with the death of man. What will die with me when I die, what pathetic or fragile form will the world lose? The voice of Macedonio Fernández, the image of a red horse in the vacant lot at Serrano and Charcas, a bar of sulfur in the drawer of a mahogany desk?

—Jorge Luis Borges,
translated by James E. Irby

As Borges did, imagine the last witness to some now-vanished practice. You may, for instance, imagine the very last person who heard a scop sing the *Beowulf* story, the last Greek who made sacrifices to Zeus, the last native American to live in the forests of what is now New York City. Describe the witness you have imagined. What has your witness seen, and what has it meant to him or her? Write one or two paragraphs.

---

1. **Angelus:** bells ringing three times a day calling people to prayer. The world *angelus* ("angel") is the Latin word used at the beginning of the prayer.

A. Origins and Development of English

This essay addresses the question of how a language spoken by a group of people living in an area near what is today the Asian U.S.S.R. more than 7,000 years ago became the language of *Beowulf* and, eventually, the English we speak today.

In this unit students have read about the events that influenced the English language. They know, for example, about the early Roman occupation of Britain, the invasions of the Angles and Saxons, the conversion of these people to Christianity, and the later invasions of the Vikings.

THE ENGLISH LANGUAGE
by John Algeo

We have biological ancestors, from whom we inherit the tint of our skin, the shape of our skulls, and everything about our bodies. We also have cultural ancestors, from whom we inherit the society in which we live and especially the language we speak. We in the United States have diverse biological ancestors—various types of Caucasian, Mongol, and Negroid peoples from whom we get our genes—but we all share a common cultural ancestry. Whether we or our ancestors came from Africa, China, Great Britain, Ireland, Italy, Japan, Germany, Poland, Siberia, or Yemen, we have all learned English, and thus acquired a common set of cultural ancestors. The language we speak embodies our shared cultural ancestry, so in studying English and its history, we learn about our past.

Out of the East: The Ancestor of English

Languages, like people, have histories. We cannot say when any language began, however, because the histories of all languages recede into the mists of early time. Written records of English have been preserved for about 1300 years. Before that time, progressively earlier forms of English were spoken on the island of Britain, in northern Europe, and eastward into what is now southern Russia. We have no direct records of the earliest ancestral form of English, but it was probably used by a people living near the Caspian Sea. We call their language *Proto-Indo-European* because at the beginning of recorded history varieties of it were spoken from India to Europe. (*Proto-* means the "first" or earliest form of the language we know about.)

The speakers of Proto-Indo-European were a vigorous sort who raised cattle, horses, and other animals. They were fighters, farmers, and herders who traveled in great four-wheeled carts and built fortresses on the hilltops surrounded by small villages. About seven thousand years ago they got the urge to travel and began spreading out. Some of them went down into what is now Turkey, others into Iran and India, while still others spread over most of Europe. Wherever they went, these migrating groups carried their language with them, although naturally it changed over the centuries and millennia. In various places it became the languages we now call Persian, Hindi, Armenian, Greek, Russian, Polish, Irish, Italian, French, Spanish, German, English, Norwegian, Dutch, Swedish, and a good many others. These descendant languages we call *Indo-European.*

Old English: Where English Came From

Scythian gold.

B. Origins of Human Language

Students might be interested in doing research to learn about the theories on the origins of human language. Linguist Noam Chomsky, for example, believes that language is an innate ability of human beings. On the other hand, psychologist B. F. Skinner believes that language was initially an imitation of sounds in the environment. An additional area of research is the work of the British judge Sir William Jones and the writer Jakob Grimm, who were the first to note similarities among Indo-European languages and to trace them back to a common origin.

C. Scythian Gold

The Scythians formed an ancient civilization in what is today the southern U.S.S.R. from the seventh century B.C. until the fourth century B.C. The Scythians would have spoken a variety of the Proto-Indo-European language discussed here.

A. The Jutes
Students might also be familiar with the Jutes, a Germanic people, probably from Frisia (today's Belgium), who invaded England along with the Angles and Saxons. Because they had less of an influence on English history and on the English language, they are not included here.

B. Responding
❓ Why did the Angles and Saxons migrate to, or invade, Britain? (The text implies a kind of wanderlust. The Angles were known to have been particularly barbarous, however, and the availability of plunder was probably also a reason.)

Insignia of the Roman civil governor in charge of the five British provinces. An early 15th century copy of a 4th century list.

Wanderlust: The Migrations

Speakers of Indo-European languages seem to have inherited a desire to travel. Eventually they wandered all over the Earth and were the first human beings to travel into space and reach the moon. The Indo-European speakers whose language is the ancestor of English lived in an area that is now southern Denmark and northern Germany. Called Angles and Saxons, they were part of a large group of Germanic peoples who lived over much of northern Europe. About the middle of the fifth century (the traditional date is A.D. 449), the Angles and Saxons migrated across the North Sea to the island of Britain and settled very happily in the green and fruitful land they found there.

The British Isles had already been inhabited by some distant cousins of the Angles and Saxons. They were the Britons, a Celtic people after whom the island was named, who also spoke an Indo-European language. The Britons had been conquered by the Roman Empire and annexed as one of its outlying provinces. The Romans were Indo-Europeans too, so all this jostling for space in the island was just one branch of the family trying to move in on another, rather like relatives from Chicago moving in with their kin in Florida for the winter.

By the time the Angles and Saxons invaded Britain, the Romans had already pulled out to defend their mother city of Rome against incursions by other Germanic tribes that were swarming over Europe. What the Angles and Saxons got from the Romans in Britain was mainly the Latin word *castra* ("camp"), which can be seen in the names of many English cities (*Chester, Chesterfield, Dorchester, Gloucester, Lancaster, Manchester, Winchester,* and *Worcester*). They found the cities that the Romans had built, with temples and waterworks and public baths. They moved into the cities and admired the great buildings, but they never learned to share the Roman passion for bathing.

Meeting the Neighbors

When the Angles and Saxons first arrived in Britain (which came to be called Englalond, England—the land of the Angles), they had very little to do with the Celts, whom they assimilated, killed, or drove into the west, where they survive today as the Welsh (an Anglo-Saxon word that means "foreigner"). But later they got better acquainted with other Celts when the Irish, called Scots then, who had been converted to Christianity during the Roman occupation of the island, sent missionaries to the Angles living in the north of Britain. About the same time, in 597, the Roman church sent St. Augustine to the southern part of Britain, also to do missionary work. Very quickly during the seventh century most of the English, as all of the Angles and Saxons came to be called, were converted to Christianity.

The conversion of the English was important because it brought them into the mainstream of European civilization, which the

Christian church represented during the Middle Ages. Although there is very little early Celtic influence on the English language—hardly more than a few place names, such as *London* and *Dover*—Latin, the language of the Christian church, has been enormously influential. Even before the Angles and Saxons came to Britain, while they were still living on the Continent, they had learned some Latin from Roman soldiers and merchants and had borrowed words like *mile, street, wall, wine, cheese, butter,* and *dish.* After the Anglo-Saxons settled in England and were converted, they borrowed a great many other Latin words that had to do with religion and learning; for example, *school, candle, altar, paper,* and *circle.*

A

After the English had settled into their new country and adopted their new religion, they in turn were invaded by some linguistic cousins—the Northmen or Vikings from Scandinavia. Beginning near the end of the eighth century, Viking bands invaded England, at first just pillaging in pirate raids, but later settling on the land. They were led by such memorably named worthies as Ivar the Boneless, son of Ragnar Shaggy-britches. It would be a mistake, however, to think of these Vikings as amusingly rough but lovable, like the comic-strip character Hagar the Horrible. They were fierce fighters and very nearly made England into another Scandinavian country. It was the English King Alfred the Great who defeated the Viking invaders and set about assimilating the Northmen into English life.

The influence of the Vikings' Norse language has been very great. Among the words borrowed are *get, give, hit, kick, law, sister, sky, take, window, they, their,* and *them.* These everyday words show the close contact between the English and the Vikings.

B

> " **V**iking bands were led by such memorably named worthies as Ivar the Boneless, son of Ragnar Shaggy-britches."

What Tongue Is This?

Despite the foreign influences, especially from Latin and Norse, the language of the early English, which we call Old English or sometimes Anglo-Saxon, was clearly a Germanic tongue. An example of their language is the following short piece—a text that most readers of this book will know in a modern form:

Fæder ūre, þū þe eart on heofonum, sī nama gehālgod. Tōbecume þīn rīce. Gewurðe þīn willa on eorðan swā swā on heofonum. Ūrne gedæghwāmlican hlāf syle ūs tō dæg. And forgyf ūs ūre gyltas, swā wē forgyfað ūrum gylltendum. And ne gelǣd þū ūs on costnunge, ac ālȳs ūs of yfele. Sōðlice.

This text is the Lord's Prayer from about the year 1000. There are many differences between this text and the prayer we know today. Words are different (*costnunge* instead of the later Latin borrowing *temptation*). Spellings and pronunciations are different (*nama*, pronounced "nah-mah," instead of the present-day *name*). Meanings are different (*hlāf* in the sense of "bread," which survives today as *loaf*). And grammar is different. Note the word order of *Fæder ūre* for *our Father;* and the word ending, or case inflection, *-um* in *on heofonum* ("in heaven").

> " **T**he language of the early English, which we call Old English or sometimes Anglo-Saxon, was clearly a Germanic tongue."

A. Responding

Why do you suppose that there was so little Celtic influence on the English language and so much Latin influence? (The Celts were driven by the Anglo-Saxons into the western and northern parts of the island, where their descendants still live today. The Christian Church, on the other hand, eventually permeated Anglo-Saxon life. Because the Church represented learning to these people, its language, Latin, was considered a "prestige" language. It was used for all forms of writing until King Alfred translated important books into English and encouraged the use of the native language.)

B. Expansion
Some language scholars believe that the most significant contribution of the Vikings was the simplification of the system of inflection used in Old English (see text page 62).

The Book of Kells, an illuminated Latin manuscript of the Gospels, richly and intricately ornamented, is the most remarkable of all the illuminated manuscripts of the Anglo-Saxon period. The chief characteristic of the illuminations is their intricate interlocking patterning of letters and borderwork. The figure here, based on a design of intertwining serpents, is from the borderwork. The figures on text pages 11 and 64 are initial letters of the text. *The Book of Kells*, named for a monastery in Kells, Ireland, was the work of Irish monks and can be seen today in Trinity College, Dublin. A statement made in the twelfth century about an illuminated manuscript, possibly *The Book of Kells* itself, still applies today as we rediscover its beauty: "Examine it carefully, and you will penetrate to the very shrine of art. You will make out intricacies so delicate and subtle, so concise and compact, so full of knots and links, with colors so fresh and vivid, that you might think all this was the work of an angel, not a man."

B. Expansion

Students who have studied Latin will be familiar with a language that uses inflected endings to show relationships among words.

Students are probably already familiar with changes in words through their study of etymology. This discussion makes the point that English, like other languages, also changes in syntax and in sound.

A

From *The Book of Kells* (8th century).

Trinity College, Dublin. Photograph by Green Studio, Ltd., Dublin.

Old English grammar was different from ours in a number of other ways. For example, all nouns were of one of three genders—masculine, feminine, or neuter—and the grammatical gender of a noun might have little to do with sex. Thus of three words for "woman," *hlǣfdige* was feminine, *wīf* was neuter, and *wīfmann* was masculine.

Adjectives had different forms depending on the gender, number, and case of the nouns they modified (*þaet tile wīf* but *se tila wīfmann,* both meaning "the good woman").

Whereas our verbs have two forms in the present tense (for example, *ride, rides*), Old English had four: *ic rīde* ("I ride"), *þū rīdest* ("you ride"), *hē rīdeþ* ("he rides"), and *wē rīdon* ("we ride").

B Like other Indo-European languages, Old English used endings on words to show how they relate to one another and how they are used in a sentence. For example, "The boy killed the dragon" might have been "Se cnapa slōh þone dracan," while "The dragon killed the boy" would have been "Se draca slōh þone cnapan." The words for *boy* and *dragon* change their forms, according to whether they are the subject or the object of the verb, and the word for *the* is different depending on the function of the word it modifies. Today word order shows the difference in grammar; Old English relied mainly on word form.

Read aloud, the Old English Lord's Prayer would sound even stranger than it looks in print, for the way we pronounce English has changed very greatly during the last thousand years. Old English had sounds that we have lost. One lost sound is the vowel they spelled *y,* which was an "ee" sound made with the lips protruded, as for a kiss—like the vowel in modern French *pur* or German *Tür.* In turn, we have added some sounds that Old English lacked, for example, the vowel of *toy* or the middle consonant of *vision.* Old and Modern English also differ in the way they combine sounds; for example, Old English could pronounce an *h* before various consonants, as in *hlāf,* whereas we do not. Old English words were generally stressed on the first syllable (except for certain prefixes), much like modern German.

Even as actually written down by Anglo-Saxon scribes, the Lord's Prayer would have looked considerably different from that printed on page 61, which uses mainly present-day letter shapes. Old English was written in a script called Insular, which the Anglo-Saxons learned from Celtic missionaries. It was a pleasant-looking, rounded style of writing, as the following sample shows:

Sepone peoc oema per ppide apilear · quircenpa man
na cheqie jajioo co oeoplep pillan · pahec peqpellepio
per cirqiep cempan ealle geofppuan · heopa lac pam
goum · Papepion onpam cuinp oeme aippaoonipe
cempan · peopenar quircenpa unpopliee onmooe · ep
pqrliee libbenoe eppen goep laqie · par geloiae pe

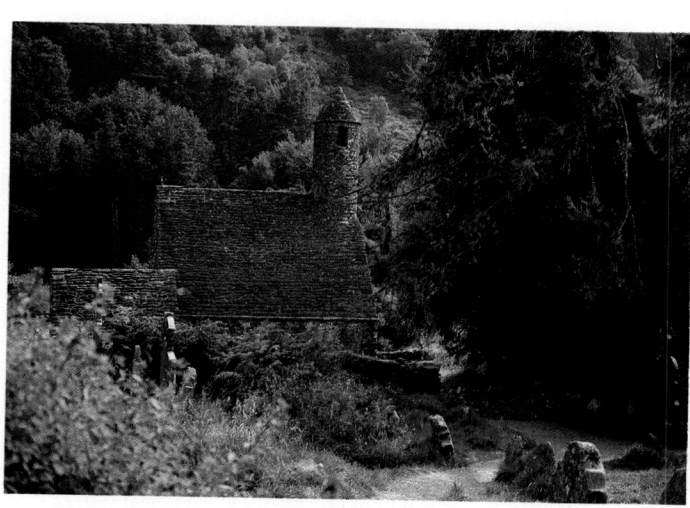

St. Kevin's Monastery,
Glendalough, Ireland
(6th century).

A

Occasionally, for special purposes, Old English writers used an altogether different alphabet, called the *futhorc,* or *runes,* which they had learned from their Germanic cousins while they still lived on the Continent. These runes were probably used by the very early pagan English for magic and for monuments. They were straight, angular letters that were used for carving on wood.

In fact, the Anglo-Saxons did not write in English a great deal. They liked to keep historical records and legal documents, and sometimes used English to do so. They translated the scriptures and wrote sermons in English. Occasionally a monk would write down some poetry, and in that way various Anglo-Saxon poems, including the epic *Beowulf,* have been preserved for us. But Old English mainly was oral. Because writing was important business, it was usually reserved for Latin.

The church was a powerful influence on Anglo-Saxon society and on the English language, especially through Latin, the church's language. Church services were conducted in Latin. Learned books were written in Latin, and education was conducted in Latin. Contact with other nations was made in Latin. To know Latin was to be learned; not to know Latin was to be illiterate. It is small wonder that Latin came to have a greater and more lasting influence on English than any other language did.

Old English would have sounded much more like German, Dutch, Norwegian, Swedish, or Danish than does Modern English. Indeed Old English was closer to the older forms of those other Germanic languages than their present-day forms are to one another. All languages change with time, and if two peoples who speak the same, or almost the same, language lose touch with one another or are in contact only rarely, their descendants several hundred years later will talk quite differently from one another. In time, they will come to speak distinct languages. No one knows exactly why languages drift off in various directions over time, but that they do so is undeniable.

"**C**hurch services
were conducted in Latin.
Learned books
were written in Latin,
and education
was conducted in Latin.
Contact
with other nations
was made in Latin.
To know Latin
was to be learned;
not to know Latin
was to be illiterate."

B

A. Expansion
St. Kevin's Monastery, established in the sixth century, was one of the great centers of learning in Europe. Its ruins, including a famous Norman tower, can be seen today in Wicklow.

B. Responding
Why is it that a common language spoken by two groups of people will change in different ways if those people are separated? (The groups' experiences are likely to be different, and it is these differences that can cause languages to change. When the English settlers first came to this country, for example, they incorporated into their language Native American words for food and animals they had not known in England—such as *raccoon* and *squash.*)

A. Humanities Connection: About the Fine Art

This illustration from *The Book of Kells* is the highly decorated initial letter of a line of print. It was not unusual for these letters to be decorated with animals and even human beings (see text pages 11 and 62).

A

From *The Book of Kells* (8th century).

Trinity College, Dublin. Photograph by Green Studio, Ltd., Dublin.

Our Anglo-Saxon Heritage

We have come a long way since Anglo-Saxon times—in technology, in society, and in language. But much of the Anglo-Saxons' language, Old English, is still evident in our language.

Although today we have borrowed words from most of the world's languages, our basic vocabulary comes to us from Old English. Words like *heart, foot, head, day, year, earth, father, mother, son, daughter, name, east, full, hound, tooth, eat, weave,* and *sew* are survivals of Old English words (*heorte, fōt, hēafod, dæg, gēar, eorþe, fæder, mōdor, sunu, dohtor, nama, ēast, full, hund, tōþ, etan, wefan,* and *siwan*). Indeed, all of those words come to us from Proto-Indo-European sources; thus, they have been part of our language for at least seven thousand years.

Our noun plural ending *s* and possessive ending *'s* (as in *hounds, hound's*) come to us from Old English (*hundas, hundes*). So do the endings we use to compare adjectives, as in *darker, darkest (deorcor, deorcost)*. The regular endings for the past tense and past participle of our verbs, as in *healed, has healed,* are from Old English (*hǣlde, hæfþ hǣled*), as are the vowel changes in verbs like *sing, sang, sung (singan, sang, sungen)*. In many other ways, our English is recognizably the same as the oldest English of which we have any record.

Although we have lost most of the endings that Old English words had, and have borrowed far more words than we have kept from Old English times, the heart of our speech is still the same. The preceding sentence consists entirely of words that have come to us from Old English, and its grammar would probably have been understood by an English speaker of the year 700. Despite its many changes, English has remained basically true to itself.

Analyzing Language

1. On a map of the world, locate the countries where the following Indo-European languages are spoken. Some languages are spoken in more than one country. English and Spanish, for example, are each the national language in many countries. (Consult an encyclopedia if you are in doubt about what countries have English and Spanish as their languages.) Can you identify at least three other languages that are used in more than one country?

English	Icelandic	Russian	Irish
German	Spanish	Polish	Albanian
Dutch	Portuguese	Czech	Greek
Danish	French	Serbo-Croatian	Iranian
Swedish	Italian	Bulgarian	Hindi
Norwegian	Romanian		

2. Four of the following are native words in Old English, four are Latin words borrowed into English very early (some while English speakers still lived on the Continent), and four are Scandinavian words borrowed as a result of the Norse invasions of England. Try to guess which words belong in each group. Then check your guesses by looking at the etymologies in a college or unabridged dictionary.

belt	horse	noon	rug
brother	house	pillow	skin
filly	night	pipe	until

3. The Anglo-Saxons sometimes used a form of writing called *futhorc* or *futhark* and also *runes*. The first six letters of that alphabet looked like this:

ᚠᚢᚦᛗᚱᛕ   or   ᚠᚢᚦᚠᚱᚲ

Look up the names of this writing system in a dictionary to find out where those names come from.

ANALYZING A PASSAGE

Writing Assignment

Write an essay of at least five paragraphs in which you analyze the elements of **plot** and **setting** in one of the numbered sections of *Beowulf*. In your essay, discuss also your emotional response to the passage.

Background

As a high school student, you are asked to move beyond simply recalling facts about the literature that you read. Instead, you are asked to use **critical thinking skills** to analyze and evaluate literature. You may be asked to perform the following operations:

1. **Analysis.** When you analyze a literary work, you focus on the elements of literature (plot, character, setting, imagery, tone, theme, and so forth). You discuss how each functions within the work of literature and how they all interact to create a whole. For example, you may be asked to discuss the character of Grendel and the imagery associated with him. You may also be asked to compare and contrast parts of a work (two battles, for example) or whole works (*Beowulf* and "The Wanderer").

2. **Evaluation.** When you evaluate a poem or story, you make a judgment about how good it is. You may be asked to tell which of two works you think is better, and why. To help make your judgments about a work's worth or value, you will rely on objective **criteria**, or standards, developed by literary critics and writers.

3. **Synthesis.** At this level, you may be asked to make a **generalization** about a work. For example, in what ways is *Beowulf* like other early works of British literature? You may also be asked to formulate or test a **hypothesis** (a theory) about a work of literature, finding specific evidence in the work to support the hypothesis.

Each of these critical thinking operations involves an **intellectual** response to a work of literature. On a different level, you cannot help but have emotional, or **affective**, responses, which are also worth examining.

1. Do you like or dislike the work? Do you find it exciting, boring, amusing, or intriguing? Can you give reasons to explain your response? You can like or dislike a work of literature as readily as you can a movie or television show. Literature, however, is sometimes not as accessible as movies or television because the language or the conventions of the genre may be unfamiliar to you. Try not to discount a work of literature for this reason. Instead, ask yourself how you would like the work if it were "translated" into a film or more contemporary story or poem.

2. Does the work relate to your personal experiences? Can you identify with any part of the work or with any character? For example, did you find yourself cheering Beowulf as he fights Grendel? Does Beowulf remind you of Superman or a modern movie hero?

3. How does the writer's use of language make you feel? Can you experience what the writer describes? For example, when Grendel comes "up from his swampland, sliding silently," can you visualize the movement of the slimy monster?

Prewriting

1. Choose the numbered passage of *Beowulf* that you found most interesting or exciting, and reread it carefully. Take notes on each of the following:

   a. Identify the number of the episode.
   b. Summarize what happens. What makes the episode exciting and suspenseful?
   c. Describe the setting of the episode and the mood the setting creates.
   d. Explain how the episode relates to the work as a whole. (Does it introduce the conflict? Is it the climax?)
   e. List some examples of particularly vivid language and imagery.
   f. Describe how you felt as you read the episode.

2. Because you are including your emotional response in your essay, at least part of the essay will use the first-person pronoun *I*. This does not mean that you are writing an informal essay. Unless your teacher directs otherwise, avoid the use of colloquialisms, contractions, and sentence fragments. Keep the **tone** of your essay serious.

Writing

You might want to use the following organization:

Paragraph 1: Identify the passage, and briefly place it in the context of the work. Then, in a **thesis statement**, tell

A. Expansion
Generally speaking, the older the literature, the more inaccessible it seems to students, usually because of archaic vocabulary and syntax. Although the translations in this unit were chosen because they capture the spirit of the literature and, at the same time, are highly readable, some students may still have difficulty. If so, you may want to concentrate on encouraging students to distill the "essence" of the literature and to "translate" it in their own minds to another medium or to a more contemporary work.

A. Expansion

In an interesting book review in the June 20, 1988, issue of *The New Yorker*, Terrence Rafferty analyzes two popular books of the "suspense" or "escape" variety against criteria for that particular genre, rather than against the criteria for judging "good" literature. Students might be interested in reading this review and in discussing why Rafferty criticizes these books. They might think of how their own favorite "suspense" or "escape" books would be received by Rafferty. Students might also be interested in making their own list of criteria for a favorite genre of their own.

Revising Essays

As students revise their essays, refer them to **Grammar, Usage, and Mechanics: A Reference Guide** at the back of their books.

why you chose this episode as the most exciting and suspenseful.

Paragraph 2: Briefly summarize the events of the episode, and describe the setting.

A **Paragraph 3:** Briefly analyze what makes this episode exciting and suspenseful. What details of setting help to create a mood, for example? Tell how the episode relates to the plot as a whole (state the conflict, climax, and resolution). Cite specific lines and phrases to support your points.

Paragraph 4: Discuss your emotional response to any aspect of the passage.

Paragraph 5: In your concluding paragraph, summarize your main ideas, and make a final comment on the passage.

In the following sample paragraph (Paragraph 4 in the essay), a reader discusses her emotional response to the language of the passage. Notice the use of specific details from the work.

> I found the language of this passage so vivid that I could imagine the year's greatest horror movie being created from its lines. To begin with, there is the sinister foreshadowing as Grendel moves toward the hall: "Up from his swampland, sliding silently." Hollywood has yet to paint so effective a scene of a monster gliding up from the sea to terrorize a sleeping town. Then, from the moment that Grendel approaches the hall, the action does not let down. I can see the enthralled movie audience as Grendel, in rapid succession, tears away the iron fasteners, rushes across the threshold, and strides across the floor. At this point, however, the movie might need some editing, for not even Stephen King has created a scene so gruesome as that in which Grendel rips apart and devours his victim.

Revising and Proofreading

For help in revising and proofreading your essay, see the section on **Writing About Literature** at the back of this book.

THE MIDDLE AGES
1066–1485

Romance of the Rose. From
a French manuscript (15th century).

British Museum.

UNIT TWO

ABOUT THE FINE ART

The *Romance of the Rose,* or *Roman de la Rose,* is a great French romance of the thirteenth century written in two parts. The first part, written by Guillaume de Lorris (c. 1240), is an allegory in which a young lover tries to win the Rose, a lady who is withheld from him by all the conventions of courtly love. This part of the romance expounds the glories of courtly love. In the second part (c. 1280), however, the author, Jean de Meun, refutes the doctrines of courtly love and describes love in the real world. This part takes a more cynical view of love between the sexes.

Chaucer greatly admired the *Romance of the Rose,* and his Wife of Bath is thought to resemble its character called the Crone. The Crone is an embittered old woman, however, and represents the last stage of the life of a greedy, self-centered woman; the Wife of Bath, on the other hand, is eternally optimistic and buoyant. Another allegorical character in the *Romance of the Rose,* False Semblance, might have inspired Chaucer's Pardoner.

TEACHING MEDIEVAL LITERATURE

In order for students to have a historical context for the literature of the Middle Ages, begin by reviewing with them the introductory material on pages 68–75 of their text. Be sure students understand why 1066 is traditionally used to reflect the start of the Medieval period. You may wish to have more able students consult history texts in order to understand thoroughly the sociopolitical climate of the age. Films focusing on the history of the period will help all classes:

(1) *A Lion in Winter* (1968), starring Peter O'Toole as an aging Henry II and Katharine Hepburn as Eleanor of Aquitaine.
(2) *Robin and Marion* (1976), starring Sean Connery as Robin Hood and Audrey Hepburn as Marion.
(3) *Becket* (1964), starring Peter O'Toole again as Henry II and Richard Burton as Thomas.
(4) *The Seventh Seal* (1957), Ingmar Bergman's famous story of the Black Death in medieval Sweden.
(5) *Monty Python and the Holy Grail* (1975), a British satire on the Arthurian legend.

To help students appreciate the monasteries' contributions to the age, you may wish to review material found in George Sampson's insightful *Concise Cambridge History of English* (1970).

You should consider devoting some time to the useful material contained in the two sections appearing under the heading "The Elements of Literature," one of which discusses ballad meter, the other the elements of the romance.

OBJECTIVES OF THE MEDIEVAL UNIT

1. To gain an overview of the Medieval period in English history
2. To understand the characteristics of the ballad
3. To understand the "frame story"
4. To understand the elements of the romance
5. To define and identify significant literary techniques
6. To interpret and respond to poetry, orally and in writing
7. To practice the following critical thinking and writing skills:
   a. Comparing ballads
   b. Responding to criticism
   c. Comparing and contrasting characters
   d. Comparing storytelling techniques
   e. Evaluating a short story
   f. Analyzing a character
   g. Analyzing a romance
   h. Writing a research report

SUPPLEMENTARY SUPPORT MATERIALS: UNIT TWO

1. Unit Introduction Test (*CCB*)
2. English Language Test (*CCB*)
3. Word Analogies Test (*CCB*)
4. Unit Review Test (*CCB*)

5. Critical Thinking and Writing Test (*CCB*)
6. Instructional Overhead Transparencies

A. Responding to the Quotation

The opening quotation from "The Prologue" to *The Canterbury Tales* applies literally to the pilgrims making their way to Canterbury. But the quotation also has a broader meaning, as William Blake observes: "Every age is Canterbury pilgrimage; we all pass on, each sustaining one or other of these characters; nor can a child be born who is not one of these characters of Chaucer."

For now, you may want students to discuss or to react in their journals to the idea that we are all pilgrims and that every age is a pilgrimage. (The idea comes up again on text page 584 in Unit Four with John Bunyan's *The Pilgrim's Progress.*) After students have read the selections from *The Canterbury Tales,* you may also want them to react to Blake's idea that every child born is "one of these characters of Chaucer."

THE MIDDLE AGES 1066–1485

by **David Adams Leeming**
and
John Malcolm Brinnin

The Norman Conquest

Norman warriors crossing the channel in 1066. From a French manuscript (11th century).

Bibliothèque Nationale, Paris.

> *. . . and pilgrymes were they alle*
>
> —Geoffrey Chaucer

In October 1066, a day-long battle that changed the course of history took place in England near Hastings, a town on the channel that divides England from France. There, Duke William from Normandy, in France, used superior military might and organization to defeat (and kill) King Harold of England, the last of the Anglo-Saxon kings. This victory began the Norman Conquest, an event which radically affected the development of English history, the English character, and the English language. Unlike the Romans, the Normans were never to withdraw from England.

Who was this William the Conqueror? He was the illegitimate son of the Duke of Normandy, who was in turn related to the English king called Edward the Confessor. The year the invasion would take place, Edward had died childless, and the succession to his throne fell into dispute. William said that the old king had promised it to him, but Harold had other ideas. Thus William sailed with an enormous army across the English Channel to seize what he thought was legally his.

William was an efficient and ruthless soldier, but he wished to rule the Anglo-Saxons, not to eliminate them. So it was that Anglo-Saxon culture survived under the Normans, and rather than a Norman, French-speaking England (and America) today, we find a culture and a language that subtly intermingles Norman and Anglo-Saxon elements. In fact, the joining of Norman administrative ability, Norman emphasis on law and order, and Norman cultural unity with the more democratic and artistic tendencies of the Anglo-Saxons might well add up to the national temperament that we think of today as typically British. *British* is a term, after all, that encompasses William Shakespeare and John Lennon, as well as Henry VIII and Field Marshall Montgomery (who led the British armies in World War II). *British* is a term perhaps best personified in those great administrator-eccentrics Queen Elizabeth I and Winston Churchill.

One of William's great administrative feats (in the days before computers or data banks) was the inventory of every piece of property in England—land, cattle, buildings—in a book called *The Domesday Book* (suggesting a comparison of William's judgment of men's financial worth with God's final judgment of their moral worth). For the first time in European history, people could be taxed based on what they owned.

Although the Normans did not eradicate Anglo-Saxon culture, the changes they brought to England should not be underestimated. William and many of his successors remained dukes of Normandy as well as kings of England, and the result was a powerful Anglo-Norman entity that brought England into the "mainstream" of European civilization in a way that it had not been before the conquest. For example, William divided the holdings of the fallen English landowners among his own followers. These men and their families brought to England not only the French language, but also a system of social arrangements that displaced the Nordic ones described in *Beowulf* and Bede's *History.* In short, feudalism as it was practiced on the continent, with all its autocratic and chivalric trappings, became the social system of England.

Feudalism and Knighthood

Feudalism was a caste system, a property system, a military system, and a system of social behavior. Ultimately, it was based on a religious concept of hierarchy, with God as the supreme overlord-landowner-general. In this sense, even a king held land as a vassal by "divine right." When a king was as powerful as William the Conqueror, he could stand firmly at the top of the feudal pyramid as the supreme lord of the land. He could appoint certain barons as his immediate vassals and place them in charge of certain portions of his land. In turn, the barons could appoint vassals of their own, and these vassals could appoint still lower vassals, all the way down to the landless knights and the serfs, who were not free to leave the land they tilled. Each vassal owed economic and/or military allegiance to his overlord.

The feudal system did not always work. When an overlord was weak, the pyramid tended to break down. A vassal, secure in a well-fortified castle, might choose not to honor his obligations to a weakened overlord. The result would be those battles between iron-clad knights around moated castles that we so readily associate with the Middle Ages.

An attack on a fortress. From a French manuscript (13th–14th century).

Bibliothèque Nationale, Paris.

A. The Oath of Fealty

A typical oath of fealty sworn by the vassal reflects this "religious concept of hierarchy": "By the Lord before whom this sanctuary is holy, I will to N. be true and faithful, and love all which he loves and shun all which he shuns, according to the laws of God and the order of the world. Nor will I ever with will or action, through word or deed, do anything which is unpleasing to him, on condition that he will perform everything as it was in our agreement when I submitted myself to him and chose his will."

The economic system of England, divided as it was into large manors, or fiefs, was dependent on the labor of the peasants. The widespread peasant revolutions during the fourteenth century showed the extent to which the peasants suffered under this system. John Ball, the priest who led the Peasants' Revolt in 1381, sounded the rallying cry: "Ay, ye good people, the matter goeth not well to pass in England, nor shall not do so till everything be common, and that there be no villeins [country folk] or gentlemen, but that we may all be united together and that the lords be no greater masters than we be. What have we deserved or why should we be kept thus in serfdom? We be all come from one father and one mother Adam and Eve."

A knight receiving a sword.

Durham Cathedral, Durham, England.

Off for a day of haying, a peasant pushes his wife to work in a wheelbarrow.

Bibliothèque Nationale, Paris.

Nevertheless, whatever its limitations, the feudal system did carry with it a sense of form and manners that permeated the life, art, and literature of the Middle Ages. This sense came to life most fully in the institution of knighthood and in the related practice, or code, of chivalry.

We cannot think of the medieval period without thinking of knights. Since the primary duty of a male above the serf class was a military obligation to his lord, boys were trained from an early age to become warriors. They were often trained in houses other than their own, so that the strictness of their training might be ensured. The culmination of this training was the "dubbing"—the tap on the shoulder with a sword that had originally been a hard, testing blow. In the dubbing ceremony the trainee became a knight; that is, he became a man with the title of "sir" and the full rights of the warrior caste. The institution of knighthood was firmly based in the feudal ideal of loyalty and was intricately related to a whole system of social codes, the breaking of any one of which would undermine the knight's position and the institution of knighthood itself. We see this clearly in a romance such as *Sir Gawain and the Green Knight* (page 133), when Sir Gawain feels honor-bound to accept a challenge that he believes will bring certain death.

The Woman's Place in Medieval Society

What of the woman's place in the feudal system? The peasant woman's life was predictable—childbearing, housework, and hard field work. For women of higher station there were household supervision and childbearing. A woman was always subservient to a male, whether husband, father, or brother. As she was not a soldier, she had no political rights in a system that was primarily military. Depending on the social standing of her husband or father, however, she commanded a certain respect, and in the chivalric system that developed in the eleventh and twelfth centuries, she became much more important than she had been before.

A

Chivalry and Courtly Love

Chivalry was a system of ideals and behavior codes that governed both knight and gentlewoman. It included such diverse aspects as the adherence to one's oath of loyalty to the overlord, the acceptance of certain rules of warfare (one did not, for example, attack an unarmed knight), and the adoration of a particular lady (not necessarily one's wife) for purposes of self-improvement. The idea that by revering and acting in the name of a lady the knight would become braver and better is an important element in that aspect of chivalry which is called **courtly love.**

Courtly love probably had its source in the religious cult of the Virgin Mary, and in its ideal form it was nonsexual. A knight might wear the colors of his lady in battle, he might glorify her in words and be inspired by her, but she was in every way "above him"; she remained, like the Virgin, inviolate on her pedestal. Naturally, such a concept provided built-in drama for poets and storytellers, since it flew in the face of human nature. In the King Arthur sagas, when Sir Lancelot and Queen Guinevere cross the boundary between courtly and physical love, the whole social system represented by Arthur's Round Table is destroyed.

The great contribution of chivalry was not only an improved, and even idealized, attitude toward women. Chivalry also gave rise to the form of literature known as the romance (see page 147). The greatest English example of the genre is *Sir Gawain and the Green Knight.* Though many other romances were told by wandering minstrels in England, most of them were the equivalents of dum-de-dum doggerel verse today.

While it is true that medieval society centered around the feudal castle, it is also true that an increasing number of people were living in the towns and cities which would eventually render the feudal system obsolete. The development of the city classes—lower, middle, and upper middle—is evident when we read the works of Geoffrey Chaucer (page 84). Not only do we find people there who make their livings outside the feudal system, but we also find a world whose horizons are defined not by any lord's manor but by such cities as London and Canterbury.

Most important, the emerging merchant class had its own tastes in the arts and the ability to pay for what it wanted, so that much of what we think of as medieval art is not aristocratic: It is middle class, and even "people's" art. The people of the cities were free; they were not tied to the land or to restrictive institutions such as knighthood and chivalry. The esthetic expression of their freedom is found in the ballads sung in alehouses and at firesides (page 77), in the mystery and miracle plays performed by the new guilds or craft unions, and even in the great cathedrals and municipal buildings that are synonymous with England to so many travelers today.

A

Knights of the Crusades. From a German manuscript (c. 12th century).

Universitätsbibliothek, Heidelberg.

The New City Classes

A. The Chivalric Code

In *The Middle Ages,* Morris Bishop describes how the system of chivalry influences us still: "In time the chivalric code was modified, but it has never died. It set a standard for upper-class behavior, especially in the Victorian era. Our esteem for sentimental love is a medieval relic. 'Women and children first' is a chivalric motto. When the *Titanic* sank and the gentlemen bowed the ladies into the lifeboats, they were 'verray parfit gentil' knights. We may still see on illumined screens the knight, with a change of clothing and locale. He has gone Western, but still he is the dexterous cavalier, vaulting to his saddle, the mighty fighter for virtue, ill educated but possessed of a salty wisdom, worshipful, faithful, and tongue-tied in the presence of good women."

Under Henry II, a
system of common
law was developed
that applied to all
of England and
that formed the ba-
sis for British com-
mon law today.
The conflict be-
tween Henry and
Becket developed
when Henry at-
tempted to bring
the Church under
this system. Before
this time, Church
courts dispensed
mild forms of jus-
tice for both clergy
and for learned
men who claimed
"benefit of cler-
gy"—perhaps they
sentenced defen-
dants to saying
prayers or going
on a pilgrimage.
   Details of this il-
lumination conform
to historical ac-
counts of Becket's
assassination.

B. Connections
T.S. Eliot's poetic
drama *Murder in
the Cathedral*
(1935) is a play
about the martyr-
dom of Becket.

The Great Happenings

To understand English literature from the period of King William to that of Henry VII (reigned 1485–1509), we must be aware not only of the feudal system imported from the continent, but of several specific events that radically influenced the course of English history and English life.

The Crusades

In Chaucer's *Canterbury Tales,* we meet a knight who has fought "heathens" along the Mediterranean Sea and in North Africa. The struggle against the Muslims in the fourteenth century was really an extension of an earlier phenomenon known as the Crusades—a series of wars waged in the eleventh, twelfth, and thirteenth centuries by Christian Europe against the followers of Muhammad, with Jerusalem and the Holy Land as the prize. The Crusades were a significant factor in medieval life. They began in 1096 (only thirty years after the Norman Conquest), and certain English kings—most notably Richard the Lion-Hearted (reigned 1189–1199) in the Third Crusade—played significant roles in them. The Europeans ultimately failed to hold Jerusalem, but they did benefit from contact with the higher civilization of the Middle East. It was that contact—with mathematics, astronomy, architecture, and crafts—that led to the richer, more varied life that we find in Chaucer, for instance, as opposed to the life portrayed by Bede or in *Beowulf.* If the Crusades produced Chaucer's fairly conventional knight, they were also at least indirectly responsible for his lively squire and elegant prioress.

The Martyrdom of Thomas à Becket

When Chaucer's pilgrims set out for Canterbury, their goal was to visit the shrine of Saint Thomas à Becket (c. 1118–1170), the "holy blissful martyr." Thomas was a Norman who had risen to great power as chancellor (prime minister) under his friend King Henry II (reigned 1154–1189). At this time, all Christians belonged to one church—the Church of Rome. This meant that King Henry was the vassal of the Pope, who was the head of the Church and the representative of God. By appointing the trusted Thomas as Archbishop of Canterbury, or head of the Church in England, Henry hoped to gain the upper hand in certain disputes between the Crown and the Roman Church. But, as archbishop, the independent and often combative Thomas took the part of the Pope against the king and certain of the English barons and bishops. In December 1170, in a particular rage against his old friend, Henry expressed a wish for the archbishop's death: "Will no one rid me of this meddlesome priest?" Four of his knights took the words literally and murdered Becket in the cathedral at Canterbury. The result of this rash deed was the cult of St. Thomas the Martyr, a popular reaction against the king, and a significant setback for the monarchy in its struggle with Rome for power in England.

A

Martyrdom of Thomas Becket. From
an English Psalter.   B

Walters Art Gallery, Baltimore.

Teachers and pupils from an illuminated manuscript (c. 1335-1340).

Bodleian Library, Oxford.

A

A

At its worst, this setback led to the kinds of liberties taken by several of the ecclesiastics in *The Canterbury Tales.* In the wake of its victory over the Crown, the Church unwittingly spawned corruption which the state was in no position to curtail, even if it had wished to. Thus Chaucer's Monk lives a life of luxury without regard for the poor, his Friar takes advantage of his position to pursue women and money, and his Summoner and his Pardoner blackmail people with threats of church courts and eternal damnation.

But the most positive effect of the medieval Church's power was the cultural unity it fostered. The Church continued to be the center of learning in the medieval period, just as it had in Anglo-Saxon days. Its language, Latin, was the international tongue of statesmen and educated people. Its leader, the Pope, was king of all kings, and his "kingdom" had no boundaries. The Church's monasteries were the libraries and publishers of the time. In short, the Church maintained a unified system of belief and symbol which transcended the conflicting national cultures of Europe.

The Magna Carta

The event in England that most clearly heralded a return to older, independent, democratic tendencies was the signing of the Magna Carta (the "Great Charter") by King John at Runnymede in 1215. John, who was vicious but pragmatic, was strongly backed by the Pope, but the English barons forced him to sign the document. The signing, then, was a defeat for central papal power. It is true, of course, that the Magna Carta was written by aristocrats for aristocrats; the barons had no interest in the rights of the common people. But in later years, the document they composed became the basis for English constitutional law in which such rights as trial by jury and legislative taxation were established.

A. Humanities Connection: About the Fine Art
Derek Brewer describes a typical schoolday during Chaucer's boyhood: "The schoolmaster was a clergyman, helped by an usher or two. He ruled with tongue and rod over a large but crowded room of up to a hundred and fifty boys of ages from seven to fourteen or older, at different stages of learning. . . . It was not easy to learn, since a lot of what was learned was singing the Latin church services, and such an 'open plan' arrangement was very noisy. . . . There was also a fair amount of restlessness, asking for permission to go to the privy and so forth. The master sat in a high chair and held the symbol of his office—not a book but a rod—in one hand. Boys sat on forms around and were called out one by one to read. Woe betide them if they could not!"

A. Humanities Connection: About the Fine Art

Historians have commented that it was in the Hundred Years' War that war became a business rather than a chivalrous undertaking. Note in this picture that hordes of well-ordered soldiers are using cannons and longbows to storm the castle walls. Gone is the hand-to-hand combat between knights.

B. Joan of Arc

Perhaps the best-known figure to come out of the Hundred Years' War is the illiterate French peasant girl known in English as Joan of Arc (1412–1431). Joan persuaded the King of France to allow her to lead the French armies to fight the English. For almost two years she was incredibly successful, until she was captured in Burgundy and sold to the English. Found guilty by an ecclesiastical court for crimes ranging from witchcraft to wearing men's clothes, Joan was burned to death by the English army. (You might recommend Bernard Shaw's play *Saint Joan* to advanced students.)

READING CHECK TEST

1. The Norman Conquest of 1066 radically altered the development of English history, character, and language. (T)
2. Feudalism was a caste system, a property system, a military system, and a system of social behavior. (T)
3. In the feudal system, a woman was considered equal to a man. (F)
4. The Magna Carta, signed in 1215, placed restrictions on democratic tendencies. (F)
5. One long-term result of the Black Death was freedom of the serfs, who were the last support of feudalism. (T)

A

Battle scene. Manuscript.

By courtesy of the Trustees of Sir John Soane's Museum, London.

The Hundred Years' War

War is a phenomenon we automatically associate with nationalism, but in the early Middle Ages there were no nations as we know them today. What might be called the first great national war was waged by England against France. Based on the old Anglo-Norman connection and the dubious claims of two English Kings—Edward III (reigned 1327–1377) and Henry V (reigned 1413–1422)—to the throne of France, the Hundred Years' War (1337–1453) was fought on the continent. This protracted war (which lasted 116 years) involved such colorful national heroes as the Black Prince, the most famous warrior in English history, who wore black armor and at the age of sixteen commanded a wing of his father's army.

Like the Crusades, the war caused a great deal of unrest and, for the English, was militarily unsuccessful. It was important, however, as a factor in the gradual development of a British national consciousness. After the Hundred Years' War, the English were no longer Anglo-Norman; they were more accurately represented by the green-clad yeoman with his longbow and arrows than by the chivalric knight in armor, a figure imported from the continent. The yeoman, or small landowner, formed the nucleus of the English armies in France and became a dominant force in the emerging, nonfeudal England. The yeoman's yard-long arrows,

B

FOR FURTHER READING
TEACHERS AND STUDENTS
A useful survey that balances treatment of the social, political, military, and economic systems with a discussion of daily life in the Middle Ages is Morris Bishop's *The Middle Ages* (1987).

To place the Middle Ages against the broader perspective of Western civiliza-tion, students might consult John McKay, Bennett Hill, and John Buckler's authoritative *A History of Western Society, 3rd Edition: Volume I: From Antiquity to the Enlightenment* (1987).

Derek Brewer's *Chaucer and His World* (1978) is a wonderfully readable and beautifully illustrated book that brings both the poet and his age to life.

Sigrid Undset's *Kristin Lavransdatter* (1929) is a novel in three volumes about the life of a young girl in Norway in the thirteenth and fourteenth centuries.

which could fly over the walls of castles and pierce even the armor of knights, brought about the demise of both castle and knight as symbols of significant military power. With the advent of the yeoman class, the modern democratic England was born. Within the new society that grew out of the ruins of feudalism, the old ideals of chivalry lived on only in stories, such as those by Sir Thomas Malory (page 150).

The Black Death

Another blow to feudalism, besides the growth of cities and the Hundred Years' War, was the Black Death, or bubonic plague, that struck England in 1348–1349. (Chaucer was then a child.) The disease, highly contagious and spread by fleas from infected rats, reduced the nation's population by a third. This caused a labor shortage and inevitably gave the lower classes more leverage than they had ever had against their overlords. One long-term result was the freedom of the serfs, which knocked out the last support of feudalism. By the time the marriage of King Henry VII in 1485 reconciled the warring Houses of York and Lancaster, the Middle Ages can be said to have ended in England. Henry, a strong king, was the first of the Tudor line that would lead to Elizabeth I. England's Renaissance was about to begin.

> " The disease, highly contagious and spread by fleas from infected rats, reduced the nation's population by a third."

A. Discussing the Time Line
Note that events do not simply occur in history and then disappear forever—their effects may last hundreds of years. During the Crusades, for example, Arabic medicine, with its sophisticated use of drugs derived from plants, was introduced to the West. It was through the Arabs, also, that Europe first learned the techniques of iron and silk manufacture that helped to industrialize entire countries. The influences of Gothic architecture, epitomized by the Cathedral of Notre Dame in Paris, are with us today, and students have only to look around them to see the effects of the printing press.

As a class or group project, you may want students to take other events from this time line and trace their effects through history.

1066	1086–1099	1100–1200	1215–1250
King Edward the Confessor dies without an heir, January 1066	Domesday Book, 1086	Cathedral of Notre Dame built in Paris, 1100's	Barons force King John to sign Magna Carta, 1215
	Crusades begin, 1096	Thomas à Becket murdered, 1170	English language has spread to upper classes, 1250
Duke of Normandy invades England, October 1066	Crusaders capture Jerusalem from the Turks, 1099	Chivalry flourishes in England, 1200–1400	

1270–1340's	1348–1370	1388–1399	1400–1500's
Crusades end, 1270	Boccaccio writes the *Decameron* in Italy, c. 1348	Entire Bible translated into English for first time, by John Wycliffe, 1388	Benin Kingdom in Africa, 1400's
Hundred Years' War with France begins, 1337	Black Death strikes England, 1348–1349		Inca Empire in South America, 1400's
Chaucer born, c. 1343	***Sir Gawain and the Green Knight* written, c. 1370**	King Richard II deposed, 1399	Iroquois League in North America, 1400's and 1500's

A

1400–1431	1450–1483	1471–1483	1485
Chaucer dies, 1400	First books produced from moveable type by Gutenberg, in Germany, 1450	**Malory dies, 1471**	***Le Morte Darthur* printed by Caxton, 1485**
Malory born, 1405		Printing press invented by Caxton, 1476	The first Tudor king, Henry VII, is crowned, 1485
Joan of Arc burned at the stake by the English in Rouen, France, May 30, 1431	Wars between the Houses of York and Lancaster, 1455–1485	Martin Luther born in Germany, 1483	

A. Expansion
Ballads (known as stall-ballads) continued to be sold in England and Scotland at local fairs well into the nineteenth century. They were sold by ballad singers, who would sing the latest ballads and sell copies of them for a penny apiece.

B. Humanities Connection: About the Fine Art
Song and music were very important in the Middle Ages. The small harp in this illustration might have served as an accompaniment for the ballad singers, although a commoner instrument would have been the psaltery, which was like our modern guitar. This scene is set in a wealthy household; these might be travelers at the table. It was not unusual for gentlemen and their ladies to ask for a night's lodging at a stranger's castle and to be received with courtesy and a merry feast.

BALLADS

A In the Middle Ages, ballads were the poetry of the common people. Much of the literature of Anglo-Norman and late medieval times was influenced by the courtly literature of France, but the ballads were passed down orally from generation to generation by ordinary people. The ballads as we know them today probably took their form in the fifteenth century, but they were not printed until three hundred years later, when Sir Thomas Percy, Sir Walter Scott, and others traveled around the British Isles and collected them from the people who still sang them.

The word *ballad* is originally derived from an Old French word meaning "dancing song." Though the English ballads' connection with dance has been lost, it is clear from their meter and their structure that the original ballads were composed to be sung to music. The most noticeable features of the ballads are simplicity and repetition—both characteristics of oral, improvisational, and formulaic poetry. Possibly, the narrative portion of the ballad would have been sung by an individual and the refrain would have been sung in response by the audience. All of this is guesswork, however; the origins of the English ballad are unknown.

The subject matter of the ballads is, predictably, popular. (Similar plots abound in today's soap operas, another form of mass entertainment.) There are ballads of domestic tragedy and false love, such as "Lord Randall" (page 78), or of true love, such as "The Three Ravens" (page 77). There are also simple comic songs based on the absurdities of domestic relationships, such as "Get Up and Bar the Door" (page 80). The supernatural elements so prominent in the ballads might have come from pre-Christian religions: The ethics of Christianity have little place in these old songs.

The meter of the old ballads is characterized by a strong, simple beat. The verse forms are relatively uncomplicated and have a primitive freshness that appeals to a general, rather than to an elitist, audience. Only later, in the era of so-called "literary ballads" (more sophisticated poems that artfully evoked the atmosphere of the originals),

B

Women entertaining. From the *Book of Hours,* French manuscript (16th century).

Bodleian Library, Oxford.

did the rhyme scheme *(abcb)* and meter (a quatrain in which lines of four stresses alternate with lines of three stresses) of the so-called "ballad stanza" become standard.

When the English, Scottish, Welsh, and Irish people left their homes to settle in America, these old ballads were part of their baggage. Today you can still hear echoes of many of the old folk stories sung in homes and in country music festivals all over the United States.

PREPARATION

1. **BUILDING ON PRIOR KNOWLEDGE.** See if students know anything about the sport of falcony; the hawks that guard this dead knight would be hawks he had trained. Note that falcony and the hunt in general are often linked to the "hunt" in a love affair. (See the illustrations on text pages 79 and 114.)

SUPPLEMENTARY SUPPORT MATERIALS

1. Review and Response Worksheet: Ballads (CCB)
2. Selection Test (CCB)

CLOSURE

Have students cite at least three traditional ballad features found in this song.

ANALYZING THE BALLAD
Identifying Details

1. They discuss where they will take their breakfast. One of the birds reports that a knight lies slain in a green field and that his hounds and his hawks protect him.
2. He is attended by such faithful hawks and hounds and by such a loyal mistress.

Not typical Ballad structure —   *Rhyme —*

Many people feel that this is one of the most powerful and moving of all the ballads. (Some modern versions have made the story humorous, perhaps because today we associate talking birds and supernatural transformations with children's television programs.) The refrain of the song uses words common in balladry; they are even used years later in Shakespeare's songs. Each pair of lines was meant to be repeated and sung with the <u>refrain</u>, as is done in the first verse. Do you agree that love and death are themes of this ballad? Do you detect any other themes?

The Three Ravens
Refrain — Lines 2,4, + 7

There were three ravens sat on a tree,
   Down a down, hay down, hay down,
There were three ravens sat on a tree,
   With a down,
5 There were three ravens sat on a tree,
They were as black as they might be,
   With a down, derry, derry, derry, down,
   down.

The one of them said to his mate,
"Where shall we our breakfast take?"

10 "Down in yonder green field   *Dead Knight*
There lies a knight slain under his shield.

"His hounds they lie down at his feet,   *Dogs to loyal to knight*
So well they can their master keep.

"His hawks they fly so eagerly,
15 There's no fowl dare him come nigh."

hawks remain loyal

(mistress) pregnant Doe

Down there comes a fallow° doe,
As great with young as she might go.

She lifted up his bloody head,   *kisses his wounds*
And kissed his wounds that were so red.

20 She got him up upon her back,   *carries Knight to a pit + buries him*
And carried him to earthen lake.°

She buried him before the prime;°
She was dead herself ere evensong time.   *she dies by evening*

God send every gentleman
25 Such hawks, such hounds, and such a
    lemman.°

---

16. **fallow:** reddish-brown.
21. **earthen lake:** a pit.
22. **prime:** morning hour for monastic prayer.
25. **lemman:** mistress.

mood — somber, melancholy — mentions death, ravens

tone — mournful admires the love between the knight + mistress

Responding to the Ballad

Analyzing the Ballad

Identifying Details

1. What do the ravens discuss in the poem?
2. According to the ballad, why is the fate of the dead knight enviable?

Interpreting Meanings

3. What elements of the supernatural are found in this ballad? Are such elements common in popular music today? What do you think the presence, or absence, of the supernatural indicates about the culture in which a song flourishes?
4. Who might the red deer be? What might be the significance of the fact that she is "great with young"?
5. Describe what you feel is the **mood** of this ballad. How would you say this mood is created?
6. What seems to be the **tone** of the ballad—the singer's attitude toward love and death? Is it an attitude common in popular music today?
7. The song's **refrain** is a series of nonsensical words. In music today, do you ever hear this type of nonsense "patter"?

Interpreting Meanings

3. The speaking ravens, the mistress in the form of a doe, and her mysterious death. Such supernatural motifs are found in the music and poetry of most cultures. At periods when the supernatural is absent, the society might be in a phase of irony or "anti-romance"; it might even be materialistic and "anti-spiritual."
4. <u>Perhaps the knight's lover.</u>
   Perhaps that the woman is pregnant with the knight's child.
5. Most students will agree that the mood of the ballad is somber and melancholic. The mood is created in a variety of ways: by the melancholy refrain, by the presence of the ravens, and by the overt references to death.
6. Mournful, admiring of the love between knight and mistress, awed. The attitude can probably be located in contemporary songs.
7. Answers will vary. Scat singing, in jazz, contains many examples.

ESTABLISHING A PURPOSE. Ask students to recall the most notable features of ballads: simplicity and repetition (text page 76, paragraph 2). Then recall with them the way the refrain is used and the subject matter of most ballads (paragraph 3). Have them read or listen to this song to note its classic ballad characteristics.

SUPPLEMENTARY SUPPORT MATERIALS
1. Review and Response Worksheet: Rhyme and Meter (*CCB*)
2. Selection Test (*CCB*)
3. Instructional Overhead Transparency

CLOSURE
In class discussion, have students summarize the ballad's plot.

ANALYZING THE BALLAD
Identifying Details
1. The speakers in the ballad are Lord Randall and his mother.
2. He has been hunting and has dined with his true love. His hounds have swelled and died, and now he is deathly ill, having been poisoned.
3. Each line has four strong beats. The same end words are used in each

A. Ballad Conventions
Whenever a character in a ballad asks someone to make his bed, or to make his bed narrow, you can predict that the person is preparing for death. (Perhaps the narrow bed stands for the narrow grave.)

B. Ballad Conventions
This question-and-answer format is frequently used in ballads. Notice how this heightens our suspense, as we learn, little by little, the facts of the story from the answers.

C. Inferring
? What inference do you have to make here? (That the dogs were fed the leftover eels and also died of poisoning)

Mood sad

Tone Disappointed

Stanzas – 4 lines
Beats – 4 beats in each line

Incremental Repetition
Repetition

This ballad is sung in different versions in several countries. The basic story of the song varies little, but Randall is variously known as Donald, Randolph, Ramsay, Ransome, and Durango. Sometimes his last meal consists of fish, sometimes snakes. Read the ballad aloud, using a male and a female voice. The dialect in this version is Scottish.

Lord Randall

"Oh where ha'e ye been, Lord Randall my son?   *> Mother*
O where ha'e ye been, my handsome young man?"

A "I ha'e been to the wild wood: mother, make my bed soon,   *> Son*
For I'm weary wi' hunting, and fain wald lie down."   *— Death - grave*

B
5 "Where gat ye your dinner, Lord Randall my son?   *> mother*
Where gat ye your dinner, my handsome young man?"
"I dined wi' my true love: mother, make my bed soon,   *Ate dinner w/ lover*
For I'm weary wi' hunting, and fain wald lie down."

"What gat ye to your dinner, Lord Randall my son?   *> mother*
10 What gat ye to your dinner, my handsome young man?"
"I gat eels boiled in broo°: mother, make my bed soon,
For I'm weary wi' hunting and fain wald lie down."

11. **broo**: broth.

C
"What became of your bloodhounds, Lord Randall my son?   *> mother*
What became of your bloodhounds, my handsome young man?"
15 "O they swelled and they died: mother, make my bed soon,
For I'm weary wi' hunting and fain wald lie down."

"O I fear ye are poisoned, Lord Randall my son!   *> mother   Climax*
O I fear ye are poisoned, my handsome young man!"
"O yes, I am poisoned: mother, make my bed soon,
20 For I'm sick at the heart, and I fain wald lie down."

Knight heartsick at the betrayal of his love

Responding to the Ballad

Analyzing the Ballad

Identifying Details

1. Who are the speakers in this ballad?
2. What has happened to Lord Randall?
3. How many strong **beats** do you hear in each line? What observation can you make about the **rhyme**?

Interpreting Meanings

4. This ballad provides a good example of **incremental repetition**—the repetition of lines with a new element introduced each time to advance the story until the climax is reached. At what point in this ballad did you discover what is wrong with Lord Randall? How would the incremental repetition increase the listener's suspense?
5. What line is repeated in the first four stanzas? How is this **refrain** echoed in the fifth stanza, and what is the emotional effect of this variation?
6. Typical of ballads, "Lord Randall" ends with only half the story told. Why do you suppose the young man's lover has poisoned him? What other questions regarding the plot are left unanswered?
7. Do any contemporary songs remind you of "Lord Randall," in subject matter, tone, or technique?

stanza. The words *son/soon* are slant or half rhymes. (*Man* and *down* may also be seen as half rhymes with *son/soon*.)

Interpreting Meanings

4. Line 17 makes Lord Randall's poisoning explicit.

The incremental repetition draws out the story and leads up to this climax slowly; note that Lord Randall's dinner and the death of his bloodhounds were mentioned in stanzas 2–4.

5. The last line of each stanza is repeated: "For I'm weary wi' hunting, and fain wald lie down."

The last line of the fifth stanza varies this line in its first half: Instead of "For I'm weary wi' hunting," Lord Randall says "For I'm sick at the heart." The emotional effect is horror as the knight conveys heartsickness at his betrayal.

6. Perhaps she is jealous or vengeful. Perhaps Lord Randall has deceived her or she is deceiving him. Perhaps she is after his money. Perhaps she is insane. Or, perhaps she didn't poison the eels at all, but someone else got into the broth.

Questions raised might include the identity of the "true love," the poison used, the whereabouts of the woman now, and the relationship of the mother to the plot as a whole. (Did she suspect the woman of treachery all along?)

7. Many popular songs sing of unrequited love and of domestic violence.

A. Humanities Connection: About the Fine Art

Falconry was a popular sport among noblemen in Europe during the Middle Ages. The red ribbon tied to this falcon's leg would be held by the knight to keep the bird from escaping while on the ground. Since the knight is feeding the bird a piece of meat, the hunt must be over, since the falcon would hunt well only when it's hungry. In the Middle Ages the falcon hunting its quarry (a small animal) was often a symbol of the knight "hunting" his love.

A

A knight and his lady feeding a falcon.
From a German manuscript (c. 14th century).

Universitätsbibliothek, Heidelberg.

1. The husband and the wife argue about who will get up and bar the door.

They say that they will keep silent, come what may; the first one to utter a word will have to get up and bar the door.

2. The husband is enraged at the fact that the visitors are going to kiss his wife and use hot broth to soften his beard and cut it off.

3. The phrase "bar the door" or a variation on it is repeated six times.

Interpreting Meanings

4. In the first stanza, the wife is boiling pudding for the Martinmas feast. In the seventh stanza, the two gentlemen who come in uninvited to the house eat the puddings. In the ninth stanza, one gentleman humorously advises the other to use the pudding broth to shave off the husband's beard.

5. The gentlemen's threats to kiss the wife and humiliate the husband by shaving off his beard are menacing and violent. You would expect the couple to save themselves from the intruders, but *(Answers continue in left-hand column.)*

(Continued from top.) they are stubborn. Ironically, the wife never does object to the gentlemen's rough behavior, not even to their threatened kiss. She is totally involved in the pact and too angry at her husband to be thwarted, even by threat of violence.

6. Answers will vary; encourage students to defend their responses.

Responding to the Ballad

Analyzing the Ballad

Identifying Details

1. What do the husband and wife argue about? What pact do they make?
2. What causes the husband to speak first?
3. This ballad does not have a repeated refrain, yet it does contain **repetition**. What phrase is repeated?

Interpreting Meanings

4. What prominent parts do puddings or sausages play in the **plot** of the story?
5. Explain how the poet combines hints of violence with **ironic humor** in this ballad.
6. As you read the ballad, did you find yourself siding with the husband or the wife? With neither?

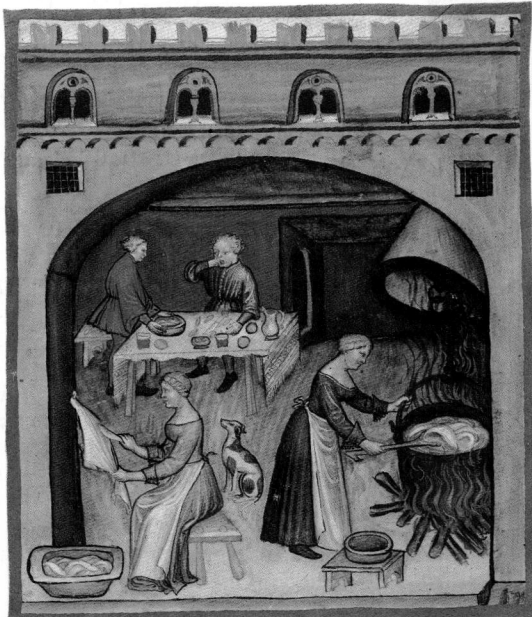

Preparing and cooking tripe. From an Italian manuscript (c. 1385).

Österreichische Nationalbibliothek Bildarchiv und Porträtsammlung, Vienna.

Writing About the Ballads

A Creative Response

1. **Retelling a Ballad as a News Report.** Take one of the basic situations in these ballads and retell it as a contemporary news story. Be sure to tell *what* happened, *where* and *when* it happened, *whom* it happened to, *why* it happened, and *how* it happened.
2. **Writing a Folk Ballad.** Experiment with writing a folk ballad in four-line stanzas on a subject of your choice. Remember that your ballad should tell a brief story, perhaps about some domestic tragedy. You might find a subject in the newspaper or on television. Try to use dialogue and incremental repetition.

A Critical Response

3. **Comparing Ballads.** In an essay of at least three paragraphs, compare and contrast these three ballads. Base your observations on some of the characteristics of the ballad form listed below. Conclude your essay with a comment giving your own response to the ballads.

    a. Supernatural events
    b. Sensational, sordid, or tragic subject matter
    c. Incremental repetition
    d. Refrain
    e. Rhyme scheme
    f. Omission of details
    g. Four and three beats to a line

The Elements of Literature

BALLAD METER

"Ballad rhythms and rhythmical patterns are intimately connected with ballad music; in fact, we now realize that ballad structure cannot be studied accurately without constant reference to the music. Phrases and lines that seem awkward and crude when read are usually effective and right when sung. One used to the conventional poetry of conscious art who turns to ballad poetry is bound to find it crude, childish, and irregular, for his experience with poetry leads him to try to read a ballad as he would conventional narrative poetry. But he finds that accents do not always fall where expected, that too many syllables often crowd a foot, that elisions[1] occur frequently, that stanzaic patterns change within a poem, that all the stresses are not of the same weight. However, the student of the ballad should never forget that ballads are texts of songs and that a line of verse sung to a melody and the same line spoken may produce quite different effects. Music adapts language to its needs by syncopating or resolving syllables, by shortening or lengthening syllables, by eliciting subtle connotations of sound. The result is that a stress falling on an unimportant word like an article or on the unaccented element in a word—each very awkward when read—can become effective or is at least unnoticed when sung. . . .

"Stress or accentuation is not as simple as some of the critics would lead us to believe. In general, ballad verse follows the iambic pattern, but the ballad poet, like any good poet, varies his pattern when it is effective to do so. Verses may begin on an accented syllable; constant use is made of the feminine ending—the unaccented syllable at the end of a line: caddie, laddie. Shifted accents likewise occur, usually, it would seem, as a result of conscious planning: 'And the truth tell thou me.' The placing of the accents is meaningful here, not accidental. The music that accompanies this line carries a rest between 'truth' and 'tell.' In reading the line one should likewise come to a full stop; the infelicity[2] of the two accents coming together is thus eliminated and the emphasis the author intended made manifest. Many instances of 'hovering' accent and 'wrenched' accent are felicitous enough when sung and can be made so in reading if one lets the text lead him rather than himself imposing strict usage on it. . . . And finally the modern

A musician. Detail from a German manuscript (c. 14th century).

Universitätsbibliothek, Heidelberg.

reader must not forget that many of the ballads are old and that their words may have different values from those of today. The final inflectional e had disappeared in pronunciation before most of the ballad texts were recorded, but it often influenced meter long after it had disappeared in pronunciation; in like manner the possessive often has the force of an extra syllable: 'I am your bairn's father.' "

—from *The Ballad Book*,
MacEdward Leach

Reread one of the three ballads, and then answer the following questions.

1. Do you find any lines which seem awkward and crude without music?
2. Can you imagine how music might shorten or lengthen certain syllables?
3. Do the lines of the ballad you have chosen follow an iambic pattern?
4. Do they begin on an accented syllable?
5. Do the lines have feminine endings (unaccented syllables at the end of a line)?
6. Are there any important shifts in accents, or should any words be pronounced with syllables that have disappeared today?

---

1. **elisions:** the omission or slurring over of a vowel or syllable, usually to preserve meter (as in "th' inevitable hour").
2. **infelicity:** quality of being unsuitable; unpleasantness.

A. **Connections**
Elisions and deliberate mispronunciations of words still occur today.
❓ What examples can you think of in songs that you know? (Answers will vary, but students first may think of songs that make use of dialect. Encourage them to think not only of the current Top 40 but to consider children's songs and theme songs for TV programs.)

B. **Humanities Connection: About the Fine Art**
The three-stringed fiddle at top left is known as a *rote*. The fiddle being played with a bow was called a *rubible*. Notice the woman dancing.

A. Pages at Court

It was not unusual for rich merchants' sons to find such places at court, where they would be apprentices to the manners and customs of courtly life.

B. Prisoners

Noble prisoners were regularly captured by both sides during the Hundred Years' War. Edward III's court included for a time King John of France and many of his nobles. They lived quite well while awaiting ransom, as Chaucer probably did also while a prisoner in France.

C. Humanities Connection: About the Fine Art

It is not known who commissioned this manuscript of *The Canterbury Tales,* but it was unusual to give such lavish treatment to a secular manuscript written in English at a time when the upper classes preferred French. The little figures that illustrate the pilgrims in the text are from this same manuscript.

Geoffrey Chaucer (c. 1343–1400)

Geoffrey Chaucer is often called the father of English poetry, and without question he was the greatest English poet of the Middle Ages.

The language spoken by ordinary people in Chaucer's England was the Anglo-Norman composite now called Middle English, which became the ancestor of modern English. But the languages of literature, science, diplomacy, and religion were still Latin and French. Before Chaucer, it was not fashionable for serious poets to compose in English. There were, it is true, the works in a northwestern dialect by the Gawain poet (page 132), and there were the poems attributed to Chaucer's older contemporary William Langland, of which the most important is *The Vision of Piers Plowman.* And, of course, there were the popular ballads.

But the poets who wrote these works lacked the social stature of Chaucer, who was a well-known government official who served under three kings—Edward III, Richard II, and Henry IV. By composing in the vernacular—the emerging standard English of London and the East Midlands—Chaucer lent respectability to the language that would develop into the medium for one of the world's greatest bodies of literature. In this sense, he was indeed the father of English poetry.

Not a great deal is known of Chaucer's life. He was born into a middle-class family in London in the early 1340's, not long after the beginning of the Hundred Years' War. We are told that his father was a merchant with sufficient means to provide his son with some education. The young Chaucer read a great deal and had some legal training. He became a page to an eminent family and received the finest training in good manners. As he advanced in his career he became attached to several noble patrons, especially to Edward III's fourth son, the powerful John of Gaunt, Duke of Lancaster, who was made famous by Shakespeare in his play *Richard II.*

We know, too, that Chaucer was captured in France during the Hundred Years' War and was important enough to have the king contribute to

A page from *The Canterbury Tales* with a picture of Chaucer. From The Ellesmere Manuscript (c. 1410).

The Huntington Library, San Marino, California.

his ransom; that he married and had several children; and that he was on several occasions sent to Europe as the king's ambassador. In 1367, he was awarded the first of several pensions for his services to the Crown. On April 23, 1374, he was granted the promise of a daily pitcher of wine. In 1385, he was appointed Justice of the Peace in the county of Kent, later becoming a member of Parliament. He continued to serve and to enjoy the king's protection even after the death of his great patron, John of Gaunt.

It seems clear that Chaucer was a relatively important government servant and that his work took precedence over his writing. Yet he wrote a great deal, and sometimes for personal advancement. In 1369, for example, he composed his first important poem, *The Book of the Duchess,* in memory of the wife of John of Gaunt, who had just died of the plague. But Chaucer's writing is just as clearly more than a passing fancy or an attempt at political advancement. Between 1374 and 1386 he managed, despite his responsibilities to his patron and his king, to create several great poems, including the *House of Fame,* the *Parliament of Fowls,* and his great love story, *Troylus and Criseyde.*

In 1373 and 1378 he traveled in Italy and was very likely influenced by the poems of Dante and Petrarch, and by the stories of Boccaccio. The connection between Boccaccio's *Decameron* (1348–1353) and Chaucer's *The Canterbury Tales* (1387–1400) is evident both in the framing device within which the characters tell their tales and in the plots of some of the tales themselves.

Most important, in 1387 Chaucer began *The Canterbury Tales,* a work he never completed, but which must be considered one of the very greatest works in the English language. *The Canterbury Tales* alone—perhaps even only the Prologue to the *Tales*—would be sufficient to place Chaucer in the company of Shakespeare and Milton.

What is so great about *The Canterbury Tales?* In part, their greatness must lie in Chaucer's language. But in another part, their greatness comes from the picture they have left us of an age that is now long past. "In all literature," writes Nevill Coghill, one of Chaucer's skilled translators, "there is nothing that touches or resembles the Prologue. It is the concise portrait of an entire nation, high and low, old and young, male and female, lay and clerical, learned and ignorant, rogue and righteous, land and sea, town and country, but without extremes. Apart from the stunning clarity, touched with nuance, of the characters presented, the most noticeable thing about them is their normality. They are the perennial progeny of men and women. Sharply individual, together they make a party."

We even have a portrait of Chaucer himself in *The Canterbury Tales.* After the Prioress tells her tale, the Host of the inn where the pilgrims had met calls upon Chaucer to tell his story, and then the Host comments on his appearance. The Host, a fat man himself, uses irony to make fun of Chaucer's own plumpness. (His words are left here in the original Middle English.)

> He in the waast[1] is shape as wel as I!
> This were a popet[2] in an arm t'enbrace
> For any wommwn, smal and fair of face.
> He semeth elvyssh by his contenaunce,
> For unto no wight dooth he daliaunce.[3]
>
> Lines 700–704

Chaucer used several metrical forms and some prose in *The Canterbury Tales,* but the dominant meter is based on ten syllables, with an unstressed syllable followed by a stressed syllable, which we call **iambic pentameter.** For example:

And bathèd every veyne in swich licour

When we read a line such as this, we experience a version of the meter that was to become the most popular metrical line in English. At a stroke, we have abandoned the old, alliterative world of the Anglo-Saxons and have entered the modern world of Shakespeare, Dryden, and Wordsworth.

Chaucer's favorite rhyme scheme in *The Canterbury Tales* was the **couplet.** The rhymed couplet in iambic pentameter would later be called the "heroic" or "closed" couplet, and would be refined by such neoclassical poets of the eighteenth century as Jonathan Swift and Alexander Pope. Another of Chaucer's favorite verse forms was the **rime royal** or Chaucerian stanza, a seven-line iambic pentameter stanza rhyming *ababbcc.*

Chaucer died on October 25, 1400, if we are to believe the date on his tombstone (which was erected in 1556 in Westminster Abbey by an admirer). Chaucer was the very first of those English writers who would be gathered into what we know today as the Poets' Corner. "The Father of English poetry," notes Nevill Coghill, "lies in his family vault."

---

1. **waast:** waist.
2. **popet:** doll.
3. **daliaunce:** small talk.

A. Expansion
Despite his travels abroad, Chaucer was a thoroughly southeastern Englishman. He refers seldom to northern and western England, and, when he does, the references are brief and not necessarily flattering. For example, Holderness, on the north coast near Hull, is a "mershy countree" notorious for its grasping friars in "The Summoner's Tale."

B. Expansion
Earlier tales, such as those in Boccaccio's *Decameron*, were always told by nobles.

C. Chaucer Biography
Marchette Chute's *Geoffrey Chaucer of England* (1946) is a lively, readable biography of Chaucer; it also brings the Middle Ages to vivid life.

A. The Geography

The pilgrim's way from London to Canterbury was originally a Roman road, known in early times as Watling Street. The pilgrims would average fifteen to twenty miles per day and probably make the entire journey in four days. (Today it would take three hours.) Though one can still travel on the road to Dover, it bears little resemblance to the rural road that passed through hayfields and forests in Chaucer's day. The pilgrims called the road a "slough." It was probably very muddy in April.

B. Expansion

Southwark was the starting point for pilgrimages not just to Canterbury but also to holy places all over England, such as Salisbury, Glastonbury, and Walsingham.

The Canterbury Tales themselves are told during a pilgrimage journey from London to the shrine of the martyr St. Thomas à Becket at Canterbury Cathedral, approximately seventy miles to the southeast. The tales begin with a General Prologue, the first lines of which establish the fact that this pilgrimage takes place in the spring, the archetypal time of new life and awakening. Seventy miles is a long journey by horseback along muddy tracks that would hardly pass as roads today. An inn was always a welcome oasis, even if it provided few luxuries. Our poet-pilgrim starts out at the Tabard Inn in Southwark, a borough in the south of London. There he meets twenty-nine other pilgrims also bound for Canterbury. It is the Host of the Tabard who suggests to the pilgrims, as they sit around the fire after dinner, that they exchange tales to while away the time along the way to Canterbury and back to London. As the Prologue progresses, we are introduced to the pilgrims, who represent many stations in life and who, taken together, form a brilliant picture of life in late medieval England. "The Nun's Priest's Tale" and "The Pardoner's Tale" are included here, along with the General Prologue.

As you read, pay attention to the ways Chaucer fits the substance of his tales to the nature of the characters who tell them.

Chaucer's Middle English is here rendered into modern English by the British scholar Nevill Coghill. As true to the spirit of Chaucer as this rendering is, the brave reader would do well to attempt at least bits of the *Tales* in the wonderfully musical original.

Chaucer's Canterbury Pilgrims by William Blake (1810). Engraving.

Brief Pronunciation Guide to Middle English

Vowels

a: *ah*, as in *father*.
ai, ay, ei, ey: a long *a*, as in *pay*.
au, aw: *ou*, as in *house*.
oo: *oh*, as in *oat*.
e: at times, like a long *a*, as in *mate*. When a double *e* is used, it is always long. *Eek* is pronounced āk.
e: at times, like a short *e*, as in *men*.

The final *e* in Middle English is a separate syllable sounded like a final *ah: soote* rhymes with *soda*. But when the final *e* precedes a word that starts with a vowel or an *h*, it is not sounded. In "droghte of March," the final *e* in *droghte* is silent.

Consonants

g: hard *g*, as in *go*, except before *e* or *i* (in words borrowed from French) where it is sounded like *zh*, as in *garage*. *Pilgrimage* rhymes with *garage*.
gh, ch: like the German *ch*, as in *nicht*. (These sounds are usually silent in modern English.) *Knight* is pronounced k·nicht′.
-tion, -cial: the *t* and *c* in such words are not blended with the *i* as they are in modern English (as in the words *condition* and *special*). The *i* is sounded as a separate syllable. *Special* would have three syllables and *condition* four: con·di·se·on′. (*C* has the sound of *s* when it comes before *i*.)

The great William Blake (1757–1827; see text page 617) painted a fresco of the Canterbury pilgrims showing their inner qualities as they journeyed through life. This engraving of the fresco was published in 1810. After students finish "The Prologue," see how many of the pilgrims they can identify.

Note that the inn is identified as "Henry Bailly's"; he was a real innkeeper in Southwark in Chaucer's day. A new inn supposedly built on the site of the old Tabard is pictured on text page 99.

A

The Huntington Library, San Marino, California.

Be sure to have students listen to the reading on the tape cassette of "The Prologue" in Middle English. The reading is outstanding.

PREPARATION

1. BUILDING ON PRIOR KNOWLEDGE. Less-advanced students may need help getting into the poem. Ask them to describe contemporary "pilgrimages," religious as well as secular. Think of pilgrimages to Lourdes and to Jerusalem. Or, think of tour groups meeting in an airport or bus depot as they set off for a trip to Europe or to Florida. Have them imagine the various "types" of people they might see in one of these tour groups. Imagine that they tell stories to amuse themselves as they travel.

2. ESTABLISHING A PURPOSE. As they read, suggest that students try to *visualize* each of Chaucer's very distinctive pilgrims: Here they can meet a whole cross-section of medieval society. How are these pilgrims like people we know today?

A. Meter and Rhyme Scheme

Note that the meter of "The Prologue" is iambic pentameter and that the rhyme scheme is in couplets. As students read aloud or follow the reading on the cassette, have them note that the lines are not all end-stopped: To get the sense, you often have to read on to the next line. This means that Chaucer uses "open couplets," a technique that prevents his verse from sounding singsong.

Tape recording

Here bygynneth the Book of the Tales of Caunterbury.

A
> Whan that Aprill with his shoures soote
> The droghte of March hath perced to the roote,
> And bathed every veyne in swich licour
> Of which vertu engendred is the flour;

5 Whan Zephirus eek with his sweete breeth
   Inspired hath in every holt and heeth
   The tendre croppes, and the yonge sonne
   Hath in the Ram his halve cours yronne,
   And smale foweles maken melodye,
10 That slepen al the nyght with open yë
   (So priketh hem nature in hir corages)—
   Thanne longen folk to goon on pilgrimages,
   And palmeres for to seken straunge strondes,
   To ferne halwes, kowthe in sondry londes;
15 And specially from every shires ende
   Of Engelond to Caunterbury they wende,
   The hooly blisful martir for to seke,
   That hem hath holpen whan that they were seeke.
      Bifil that in that seson on a day,
20 In Southwerk at the Tabard as I lay
   Redy to wenden on my pilgrymage
   To Caunterbury with ful devout corage,
   At nyght was come into that hostelrye
   Wel nyne and twenty in a compaignye,
25 Of sondry folk, by aventure yfalle
   In felaweshipe, and pilgrimes were they alle,
   That toward Caunterbury wolden ryde.
   The chambres and the stables weren wyde,
   And wel we weren esed atte beste.
30 And shortly, whan the sonne was to reste,
   So hadde I spoken with hem everichon
   That I was of hir felaweshipe anon,
   And made forward erly for to ryse,
   To take oure wey ther as I yow devyse.
35   But nathelees, whil I have tyme and space,
   Er that I ferther in this tale pace,
   Me thynketh it acordaunt to resoun
   To telle yow al the condicioun
   Of ech of hem, so as it semed me,
40 And whiche they weren, and of what degree,
   And eek in what array that they were inne;
   And at a knyght that wol I first bigynne.

3. PREREADING JOURNAL. Refer to writing assignment number 1 on text page 108, Writing a Frame Story. Before they read, have students take notes on the "situation" they might set their own pilgrims in: a bus station, an airport, a western dude ranch, a senior-citizen center. It must be some setting and purpose that will bring together a cross-section of twentieth-century American society.

SUPPLEMENTARY SUPPORT MATERIALS
1. Vocabulary Activity Worksheet (*CCB*)
2. Review and Response Worksheet: Characterization (*CCB*)
3. Selection Test (*CCB*)

DEVELOPING VOCABULARY
The following words from the poem are tested in the Selection Test. (See also Vocabulary Activity Worksheet.)

heath	penitent
hallowed	vintage
sundry	effigies
boorish	buffoon
burnished	prevarication

The Canterbury Tales

The Prologue

When in April the sweet showers fall
And pierce the drought of March to the root, and all
The veins are bathed in liquor of such power
As brings about the engendering of the flower,
5 When also Zephyrus° with his sweet breath
Exhales an air in every grove and heath
Upon the tender shoots, and the young sun
A His half-course in the sign of the *Ram* has run,°
And the small fowl are making melody
10 That sleep away the night with open eye
(So nature pricks them and their heart engages)
Then people long to go on pilgrimages
And palmers° long to seek the stranger strands
Of far-off saints, hallowed in sundry lands,
15 And specially, from every shire's end
In England, down to Canterbury they wend
B To seek the holy blissful martyr,° quick
To give his help to them when they were sick.
    It happened in that season that one day
20 In Southwark, at *The Tabard*, as I lay
Ready to go on pilgrimage and start
For Canterbury, most devout at heart,
At night there came into that hostelry
Some nine and twenty in a company
25 Of sundry folk happening then to fall
In fellowship, and they were pilgrims all
That toward Canterbury meant to ride.
The rooms and stables of the inn were wide;
They made us easy, all was of the best.
30 And shortly, when the sun had gone to rest,
By speaking to them all upon the trip
I soon was one of them in fellowship
And promised to rise early and take the way
To Canterbury, as you heard me say.
35   But nonetheless, while I have time and space,
Before my story takes a further pace,
It seems a reasonable thing to say
What their condition was, the full array
Of each of them, as it appeared to me
40 According to profession and degree,
And what apparel they were riding in;
And at a Knight I therefore will begin.
There was a *Knight*, a most distinguished man,
Who from the day on which he first began
45 To ride abroad had followed chivalry,
Truth, honor, generousness, and courtesy.
He had done nobly in his sovereign's war

[Handwritten annotations: Time – Spring; Description of spring; Birds singing; Pilgrimages; Destination; Believed St. could help sickness; Inn; Chaucer – narrator; 29 people all going to canterbury; Inn was comfortable; Visits w/ all decides to join them; Going to describe each character give impressions; Ideal Knight; ①]

5. **Zephyrus:** the west wind.

8. The ram is a sign of the zodiac. The date is around April 11.

13. **palmers:** people who had visited the Holy Land and wore two crossed palms to prove it.

17. **martyr:** St. Thomas à Becket was martyred at Canterbury, December 29, 1170.

The Knight. Detail from
The Ellesmere Manuscript.

The Huntington Library,
San Marino, California.

A. Syntax
Notice that the first sentence of the poem runs from line 1 to line 18, and that it opens with a long adverbial clause starting with "when." The main subjects and verbs are found in lines 12-17 ("Then people long to go on pilgrimages and palmers long to seek stranger strands [land]", and in England "they wend to seek the holy blissful martyr . . .")

B. Translation
? Compare lines 17-18 of this translation with the original Middle English lines on page 88. How has the translator preserved the rhyming couplet? (The modern translations for the Middle English end words do not rhyme exactly [*seek/sick*], so the translator has reworded the "modern" line.)

The Horses

Derek Brewer notes the status symbol of the horse in Chaucer's day:

"Means of transport were limited. The poor, both the actual and the professional, such as friars, walked. Most regular travelers rode, on horses good or bad. You judged a man by the horse he rode, as some people do nowadays by cars. Chaucer's Knight in *The Canterbury Tales* has good horses, though he himself is not flashy in dress. The Monk, on the other hand, is richly dressed and has many a fine horse in his stable—and we draw the appropriate conclusion that he has what in modern terms would be a very lush expense account, though vowed to poverty. The admirable Clerk, ideal university professor, does not go out for the money and rides a horse as lean as a rake. The equally ideal, humble, hardworking Plowman rides a poor mare. We are not told what the Plowman's brother, the Parson, rides, but in his remote parish where the houses are far apart he goes on foot, with a staff. Women normally rode on horseback and astride, though riding side-saddle began to come in during Chaucer's lifetime."

A. The Knight's Wars

The Knight's wars covered forty years and fell into three groups: (1) against the Moors at the west end of the Mediterranean, (2) against the Turks at the Mediterranean's east end, and (3) against Lithuanians and Tartars on the Russian border. (The Knight's enemies would be considered pagans or infidels—unbelievers in Christ.)

B. Characterization

How does the Knight's clothing reveal his character? (The Knight's dress suggests a plain, hard-fighting man. His clothes are simple, stained with blood or dirt, and worn from armor. His deeds speak for him; he has no need for fancy attire.) Contrast with the Squire, who follows.

C. Simile

What does this famous simile suggest about the Squire? (That he is young and "pretty" and bright—it's hard not to like someone who is compared to a flowery meadow.)

High opinion of the knight

And ridden into battle, no man more,
As well in Christian as in heathen places,
50 And ever honored for his noble graces.
   When we took Alexandria,° he was there.
He often sat at table in the chair
Of honor, above all nations, when in Prussia.
In Lithuania he had ridden, and Russia,
55 No Christian man so often, of his rank.
When, in Granada, Algeciras sank
Under assault, he had been there, and in
North Africa, raiding Benamarin;
In Anatolia he had been as well
60 And fought when Ayas and Attalia fell,
For all along the Mediterranean coast
He had embarked with many a noble host.
A In fifteen mortal battles he had been
And jousted for our faith at Tramissene
65 Thrice in the lists, and always killed his man.
This same distinguished knight had led the van
Once with the Bey of Balat, doing work
For him against another heathen Turk;
He was of sovereign value in all eyes.
70 And though so much distinguished, he was wise
And in his bearing modest as a maid.
He never yet a boorish thing had said
In all his life to any, come what might;
He was a true, a perfect gentle-knight.°
75   Speaking of his equipment, he possessed
B Fine horses, but he was not gaily dressed.
He wore a fustian° tunic stained and dark
With smudges where his armor had left mark;
Just home from service, he had joined our ranks
80 To do his pilgrimage and render thanks.
   He had his son with him, a fine young *Squire*,
A lover and cadet,° a lad of fire
With locks as curly as if they had been pressed.
He was some twenty years of age, I guessed.
85 In stature he was of a moderate length,
With wonderful agility and strength.
He'd seen some service with the cavalry
In Flanders and Artois and Picardy
And had done valiantly in little space
90 Of time, in hope to win his lady's grace.
C He was embroidered like a meadow bright
And full of freshest flowers, red and white.
Singing he was, or fluting all the day;
He was as fresh as is the month of May.
95 Short was his gown, the sleeves were long and wide;
He knew the way to sit a horse and ride.
He could make songs and poems and recite,
Knew how to joust and dance, to draw and write.
He loved so hotly that till dawn grew pale

All wars are religious wars — fought for faith

51. Alexandria: an Egyptian city captured by the Crusaders in 1365. Chaucer is indicating the knight's distinguished and extensive career in the next few lines.

honored man

Fought in many places
Egypt
Turkey
mediterranean
Africa
Russia

(Al´ ji sir əs)
(Ben a mar in)
(An´ ə tō li ə)
cities in Anatolia
Turkey

fought for Christianity
Turkish wars
→ front of an army
Governor of Turkish district

Represents old order of chivalry + knighthood

Clumsy, awkward

74. In Chaucer's day, *gentle* meant "well-bred and considerate."

wore battle clothes

77. fustian: coarse cloth made of cotton and linen.
82. cadet: soldier.

purpose of pilgrimage sincere
Student of military training

young immature

Vain
20 yrs old

(Ar·twä) N. France

Wants to impress the ladies.
Squire loves life
young

The Squire. Detail from The Ellesmere Manuscript.

The Huntington Library, San Marino, California.

Stays out all Night

[handwritten top margin: gently critical of Squire]

[handwritten: Servant of Knight — Squire will never be his fathers equal. only good enough to serve, not sit with. Squire uses knighthood for different means. Father is noble —]

[handwritten: Represents the new order of changing attitudes of young]

100 He slept as little as a nightingale.
    Courteous he was, lowly and serviceable,
    And carved to serve his father at the table.

③ A   There was a *Yeoman* with him at his side,
    No other servant; so he chose to ride.

105 This Yeoman wore a coat and hood of green,
    And peacock-feathered arrows, bright and keen
    And neatly sheathed, hung at his belt the while
    —For he could dress his gear in yeoman style,
    His arrows never drooped their feathers low—

110 And in his hand he bore a mighty bow.
    His head was like a nut, his face was brown.
    He knew the whole of woodcraft up and down.
    A saucy brace was on his arm to ward
    It from the bowstring, and a shield and sword

115 Hung at one side, and at the other slipped
    A jaunty dirk,° spear-sharp and well-equipped.

B   A medal of St. Christopher he wore
    Of shining silver on his breast, and bore
    A hunting horn, well slung and burnished clean,

120 That dangled from a baldrick° of bright green.
    He was a proper forester I guess.

④ C   There also was a *Nun*, a Prioress,
    Her way of smiling very simple and coy.

D   Her greatest oath was only "By St. Loy!"°

125 And she was known as Madam Eglantyne.
    And well she sang a service, with a fine
    Intoning through her nose, as was most seemly,
    And she spoke daintily in French, extremely,
    After the school of Stratford-atte-Bowe;°

130 French in the Paris style she did not know.
    At meat her manners were well taught withal;
    No morsel from her lips did she let fall,
    Nor dipped her fingers in the sauce too deep;
    But she could carry a morsel up and keep

135 The smallest drop from falling on her breast.
    For courtliness she had a special zest,
    And she would wipe her upper lip so clean
    That not a trace of grease was to be seen
    Upon the cup when she had drunk; to eat,

140 She reached a hand sedately for the meat.
    She certainly was very entertaining,
    Pleasant and friendly in her ways, and straining

E   To counterfeit a courtly kind of grace,
    A stately bearing fitting to her place,

145 And to seem dignified in all her dealings.
    As for her sympathies and tender feelings,
    She was so charitably solicitous
    She used to weep if she but saw a mouse
    Caught in a trap, if it were dead or bleeding.

150 And she had little dogs she would be feeding
    With roasted flesh, or milk, or fine white bread.

[handwritten annotations in margins: not a high opinion of Squire; Not equal to father — manservant of Knight; Physical description; Seriousness about character; meticulously dressed - neat - cares for appearance + equipment; Yeoman does not speak much so Chaucer bases his perceptions on the physical appearance; flirting - pretending; Ironic; Nun w/ such a name; Doesn't know Parisian French - poor French; Manners impeccable. Very concious of how she appears; Not something you would think of a nun. worked hard to appear courtly - fake; more concerned about animals than humans; kept dogs. feels them the finest food]

116. **dirk:** dagger.
120. **baldrick:** belt slung over the shoulder and chest to hold a sword.
124. **St. Loy:** St. Eligius, a saint known for his perfect manners.

129. **Stratford-atte-Bowe:** a Benedictine convent near London (where inferior French was spoken).

The Yeoman. Detail from The Ellesmere Manuscript.

The Huntington Library, San Marino, California.

F

The Prioress. Detail from The Ellesmere Manuscript.

The Huntington Library, San Marino, California.

A. Expansion
A yeoman (yō′mən) was at this time a manservant, above the rank of groom (the servant who tended horses).

B. Expansion
St. Christopher is the patron saint of travelers.

C. Expansion
A nun was a woman who lived in a convent and took vows of poverty, chastity, and obedience. A prioress was in charge of a group of nuns in a convent, or priory.

D. Irony
The Prioress's swearing by St. Loy is ironic because the saint was known for his refusal to swear.

E. Connotation
What is suggested by the word *counterfeit*? (That the Prioress is not sincere in her vows or piety)

F. About the Illustration
The Prioress rides sidesaddle and her horse is elaborately attired. Medieval art, while not very realistic in its treatment of human individuality, paid scrupulous attention to accurate and telling details that reveal the subject's social position, trade, and so on.

A. About the Illustration

Canterbury was a circular walled city, containing a cathedral, a number of churches, and friaries for Grey and Black friars. The cathedral was begun in Norman times and contains, among others, the tombs of Edward the Black Prince and Henry IV.

Today Canterbury is a large city and the seat of the Archbishop of Canterbury, the spiritual head of the Church of England.

A

CANTERBVRY.

1. Chriſts church.
2. ỷ market Place.
3. our Lady.
4. St. Andrewes.
5. St. Peter.
6. weſtgate church.
7. St. michel.
8. the caſtell.
9. our Lady.
10. St. george.
11. the freeres.
12. Alhalowes.

Plan of Canterbury in the 15th century.

British Museum.

Literature and Language: Using Specific Adjectives in a Description
Remind students that Chaucer describes his pilgrims in minute detail, using <u>specific adjectives</u> to give an exact picture of each one. For example, he describes the monk as *manly, fat,* and *personable,* wearing a robe trimmed with *fine gray* fur. These details <u>not only picture</u> the man but also <u>hint at his character.</u>

Have students attempt a description in the same vein. Though their work need not be in verse, students may wish to use the following model.

Kristin is a lovely girl, as tall
As many boys, and fair and blonde, with all
Her friends around her every hour and day.
She wears the brightest colors, never gray
Or black or violet because, says she,
The darker colors make her sad. Now see
How quick she is, with what athletic grace
She dunks a basketball or steals a base!
Her voice is clear and bright, and with sweet fire
She sings strong harmony in Sunday choir.

[handwritten top margin:] Chaucer completely ignores her religious or spiritual side, thereby emphasizing what the Prioress is to what she should be.

And bitterly she wept if one were dead
Or someone took a stick and made it smart;
She was all sentiment and tender heart.
155 Her veil was gathered in a seemly way,
Her nose was elegant, her eyes glass-gray;
Her mouth was very small, but soft and red,
A Her forehead, certainly, was fair of spread,
Almost a span across the brows, I own;
160 She was indeed by no means undergrown.
Her cloak, I noticed, had a graceful charm.
B She wore a coral trinket on her arm,
A set of beads, the gaudies tricked in green,°
Whence hung a golden brooch of brightest sheen
165 On which there first was graven a crowned A,
And lower, *Amor vincit omnia.*°
C Another *Nun,* the chaplain at her cell,
Was riding with her, and *three Priests* as well.
D A *Monk* there was, one of the finest sort
170 Who rode the country; hunting was his sport.
A manly man, to be an Abbot able;
Many a dainty horse he had in stable.
His bridle, when he rode, a man might hear
Jingling in a whistling wind as clear,
175 Aye, and as loud as does the chapel bell
Where my lord Monk was <u>Prior</u> of the cell.
The Rule of good St. Benet or St. Maur°
As old and strict he tended to <u>ignore;</u>
He let go by the things of yesterday
180 And took the modern world's more spacious way.
He did not rate that text at a plucked hen
Which says that hunters are not holy men
And that a monk uncloistered is a mere
Fish out of water, flapping on the pier,
185 That is to say a monk out of his cloister.
That was a text he held not worth an oyster;
And I agreed and said his views were sound;
Was he to study till his head went round
Poring over books in cloisters? Must he toil
190 As Austin° bade and till the very soil?
Was he to leave the world upon the shelf?
Let Austin have his labor to himself.
This Monk was therefore a good man to horse;
Grayhounds he had, as swift as birds, to course.
195 Hunting a hare or riding at a fence
Was all his fun, he spared for no expense.
I saw his sleeves were garnished at the hand
With fine gray fur, the finest in the land,
And on his hood, to fasten it at his chin
200 He had a wrought-gold cunningly fashioned pin;
Into a lover's knot it seemed to pass.
His head was bald and shone like looking-glass;
So did his face, as if it had been greased.

[handwritten annotations in left/center margins:]
physical description
intelligent / fair breeding
large woman
Irony - love charm / secular & spiritual
Jewelry
Love conquers all
4-7 other companions
loved hunting
owned horses
bells on bridle - fashionable
Head of a group of monks
Ignored vows / liked modern ways - secular ways
Cloistering was a rule of a monk's life / monk thinks this is ridiculous
— irony
Is he to give up everything
owned horses - accomplished rider
owned dogs
fancy clothes
gold pin - lover's knot

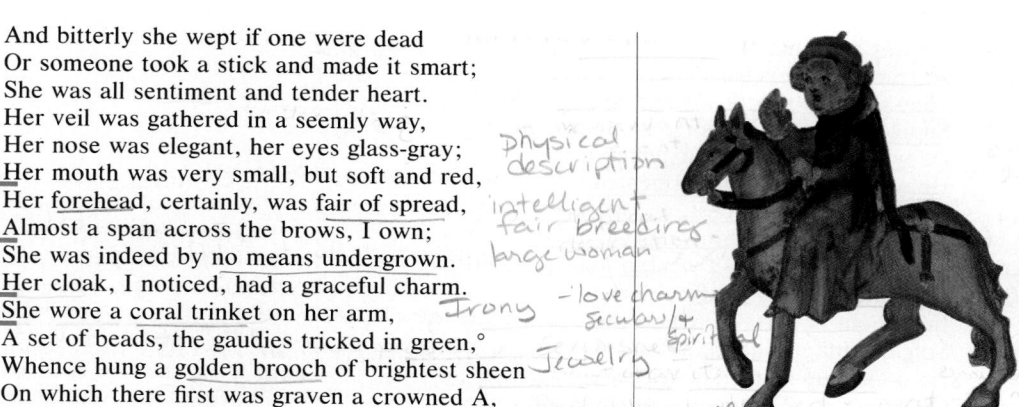

The Nun's Priest. Detail from The Ellesmere Manuscript.
The Huntington Library, San Marino, California.

163. Beads are rosaries, "prayer beads," and gauds are the large beads indicating where an Our Father is to be said.
166. *Amor vincit omnia:* Latin for "Love conquers all."
177. **St. Benet** (Benedict) **or St. Maur** (Maurice): St. Benedict founded several monasteries and wrote a famous Rule for monastic life. St. Maurice was a follower of Benedict.
190. **Austin:** St. Augustine, who was critical of lazy monks and suggested they do some hard manual labor.

A. Physiognomy
As pointed out on text page 131, Chaucer often used physical characteristics to indicate inner nature. A high forehead was a sign of intelligence and breeding.

B. Irony
Coral was considered a defense against wordly temptation and an earthly love charm—indication that the Prioress stands with one foot in the secular world and one in the spiritual.

C. The Nun's Priest
Here is the teller of the tale of Chanticleer and Pertelote (see text page 110). A *cell* is the nun's (plain) room.

D. The Monk
A monk is a member of a religious order, usually living under the vows of poverty, chastity, and obedience.

Handwritten notes at top:
Monk - cloistered, study, prayers
Friar - out in the world, minister to people, preaching, living only on what they could beg

A. The Friar

Friars (in the tradition of St. Francis of Assisi) were supposed to travel about preaching, living only on what they could beg, as a constant reminder of the simple life Christ had led.

B. Expansion

Absolution is the forgiveness of those sins confessed to a priest. A "pleasant absolution" means that the penance ("penalty," usually prayers or good works) assigned to the penitent were light. Note that the Friar's penances were light and given in return for a gift.

C. Physiognomy

A white neck was thought to be a sign of a loose or immoral person.

D. Character

Note that here is another way in which the Monk / Friar mocks the teachings of Christ, who set examples for His followers by associating with the poor and sick.

He was a fat and personable priest;
205 His prominent eyeballs never seemed to settle.
They glittered like the flames beneath a kettle;
Supple his boots, his horse in fine condition.
He was a prelate fit for exhibition,
He was not pale like a tormented soul.
210 He liked a fat swan best, and roasted whole.
His palfrey° was as brown as is a berry.
There was a *Friar,* a wanton° one and merry,
A Limiter,° a very festive fellow.
In all Four Orders° there was none so mellow.
215 So glib with gallant phrase and well-turned speech.
He'd fixed up many a marriage, giving each
Of his young women what he could afford her.
He was a noble pillar to his Order.
Highly beloved and intimate was he
220 With County folk within his boundary,
And city dames of honor and possessions;
For he was qualified to hear confessions,
Or so he said, with more than priestly scope
He had a special license from the Pope.
225 Sweetly he heard his penitents at shrift°
With pleasant absolution, for a gift.
He was an easy man in penance-giving
Where he could hope to make a decent living;
It's a sure sign whenever gifts are given
230 To a poor Order that a man's well shriven,°
And should he give enough he knew in verity
The penitent repented in sincerity.
For many a fellow is so hard of heart
He cannot weep, for all his inward smart.
235 Therefore instead of weeping and of prayer
One should give silver for a poor Friar's care.
He kept his tippet° stuffed with pins for curls,
And pocketknives, to give to pretty girls.
And certainly his voice was gay and sturdy,
240 For he sang well and played the hurdy-gurdy.
At sing-songs he was champion of the hour.
His neck was whiter than a lily flower
But strong enough to butt a bruiser down.
He knew the taverns well in every town
245 And every innkeeper and barmaid too
Better than lepers, beggars, and that crew,
For in so eminent a man as he
It was not fitting with the dignity
Of his position, dealing with a scum
250 Of wretched lepers; nothing good can come
Of dealings with the slum-and-gutter dwellers,
But only with the rich and victual-sellers.
But anywhere a profit might accrue
Courteous he was and lowly of service too.
255 Natural gifts like his were hard to match.

---

211. **palfrey:** horse.
212. **wanton:** here, jolly.
213. **Limiter:** a friar having the exclusive right to beg and preach within an assigned (limited) district.
214. **Four Orders:** The four orders of mendicant (beggar) friars are the Franciscans, the Dominicans, the Carmelites, and the Augustinians.
225. **shrift:** confession.
230. **well shriven:** well confessed, or forgiven of his sins.
237. **tippet:** hood or long sleeve (of his robe). Even today, they are often used as pockets by friars wearing the robe.

The Friar. Detail from The Ellesmere Manuscript.

The Huntington Library, San Marino, California.

Handwritten annotations:
high-ranking church official
good boots
what a monk should be
fixed marriages for women he got in trouble
— irony
familiar + well-known in the country + city - women of wealth
says he has special privileges from the pope
gave absolution for a fee
light penances given for a fee
one should pay the Friars for helping
gave gifts to girls
lutelike instrument played by cranking a wheel
sign of a loose or immoral person
enjoys the taverns
didn't like dealing w/ lepers + poor, no profit. Rich people you can get something from
The Monk should be associating w/ the poor
irony
got profit wherever he could

94

94 The Middle Ages

He was the finest beggar of his batch,
And, for his begging district, payed a rent;
His brethren did no poaching where he went.
For though a widow mightn't have a shoe,
260 So pleasant was his holy how-d'ye-do
He got his farthing from her just the same
Before he left, and so his income came
To more than he laid out. And how he romped,
Just like a puppy! He was ever prompt
265 To arbitrate disputes on settling days°
(For a small fee) in many helpful ways,
Not then appearing as your cloistered scholar
With threadbare habit hardly worth a dollar,
A But much more like a Doctor or a Pope.
270 Of double-worsted was the semi-cope
Upon his shoulders, and the swelling fold
About him, like a bell about its mold
When it is casting, rounded out his dress.
He lisped a little out of wantonness°
275 To make his English sweet upon his tongue.
When he had played his harp, or having sung,
His eyes would twinkle in his head as bright
As any star upon a frosty night.
B This worthy's name was Hubert, it appeared.
280 There was a *Merchant* with a forking beard
And motley° dress; high on his horse he sat,
Upon his head a Flemish beaver hat
And on his feet daintily buckled boots.
He told of his opinions and pursuits
285 In solemn tones, and how he never lost.
The sea should be kept free at any cost
(He thought) upon the Harwich–Holland range,
He was expert at currency exchange.
This estimable Merchant so had set
290 His wits to work, none knew he was in debt,
He was so stately in negotiation,
Loan, bargain, and commercial obligation.
He was an excellent fellow all the same;
To tell the truth I do not know his name.
295 An *Oxford Cleric*, still a student though,
One who had taken logic long ago,
Was there; his horse was thinner than a rake,
And he was not too fat, I undertake,
But had a hollow look, a sober stare;
300 The thread upon his overcoat was bare.
C He had found no preferment in the church
And he was too unworldly to make search
For secular employment. By his bed
He preferred having twenty books in red
305 And black, of Aristotle's philosophy,
To having fine clothes, fiddle, or psaltery.°
Though a philosopher, as I have told,

265. **settling days:** days on which disputes could be settled by independent negotiators out of court. Though friars often acted as the negotiators (and were paid for it), they were officially forbidden to do so.

274. **wantonness:** here, affectation.

281. **motley:** multi-colored.

The Clerk. Detail from
The Ellesmere Manuscript.
The Huntington Library,
San Marino, California.

306. **psaltery:** a stringed instrument.

[Handwritten margin notes:]
— Irony — good beggar
con man — talks well
Takes money from women who have no shoes
settle disputes for a fee
↓ appearance
↳ should be coarse + threadbare
ironic — not worthy Friar
Talkative
brags of success
Money is his only concern
Pretends to be successful even though he is in debt.
— like all other merchants where money is priority
thin — horse thin
serious man
not clergy of church — could not find employment elsewhere
Preferred spending time + money on books rather than clothes or extras

A. Irony
What is ironic about the Monk's dress? (It is not threadbare but like that worn by a Doctor of Laws or a Pope.) Note the simile comparing the great cloak to a bell setting into its mold.

The rule of the Order states that friars' "mantles must be of vile and coarse cloth" so that there would be a constant mortification of the body.

B. The Merchant
Many of Chaucer's characters are thought to be taken from real life. The Merchant was probably modeled on Gilbert Maghfield, who lent Chaucer money and whose Guild of Merchant Venturers did, in fact, set up a kind of safety patrol at the English Channel crossing.

C. The Cleric
In order to enter a university, medieval students had to become members of minor orders of the Church. But once out of the university, they had to seek secular employment.

A. Books
In 1374, twenty books would have cost a small fortune. Chaucer was a great book lover, in a time when books were scarce.

B. A Famous Line
This line is often quoted to describe outstanding teachers. In Middle English it reads, "And gladly wolde he lerne and gladly teche."

C. The Serjeant
In Chaucer's day, a serjeant at the law had practiced law with distinction for at least sixteen years.

D. Expansion
Parti-colored means "many colored." Such a coat would be a sign of affluence, since poor people would have coats dyed a single color. The silk belt is also a sign of affluence, because silk had to be imported from the East.

E. The Franklin
Customarily, medieval Britons ate two meals a day, a mid-morning dinner and an early evening supper. The Franklin ate, in addition, a "sop in wine," a mixture of wine, almond milk, ginger, sugar, cinnamon, cloves, and mace poured over the best quality bread ("cake").

[handwritten top margin: Critical because his only concern is w/ books. No other aspect to his life.]

He had not found the stone for making gold.°
A Whatever money from his friends he took
310 He spent on learning or another book
And prayed for them most earnestly, returning
Thanks to them thus for paying for his learning.
His only care was study, and indeed
He never spoke a word more than was need,
315 Formal at that, respectful in the extreme,
Short, to the point, and lofty in his theme,
The thought of moral virtue filled his speech
B And he would gladly learn, and gladly teach.
C A *Serjeant at the Law* who paid his calls,
320 Wary and wise, for clients at St. Paul's°
There also was, of noted excellence.
Discreet he was, a man to reverence,
Or so he seemed, his sayings were so wise.
He often had been Justice of Assize
325 By letters patent, and in full commission.°
His fame and learning and his high position
Had won him many a robe and many a fee.
There was no such conveyancer as he;
All was fee-simple to his strong digestion,
330 Not one conveyance could be called in question.
Nowhere there was so busy a man as he;
But was less busy than he seemed to be.
He knew of every judgment, case and crime
Recorded, ever since King William's time.
335 He could dictate defenses or draft deeds;
No one could pinch a comma from his screeds,°
And he knew every statute off by rote.
D He wore a homely parti-colored coat
340 Girt with a silken belt of pinstripe stuff;
Of his appearance I have said enough.
There was a *Franklin*° with him, it appeared;
White as a daisy petal was his beard.
A sanguine man, high-colored and benign,
E He loved a morning sop of cake in wine.
345 He lived for pleasure and had always done,
For he was Epicurus' very son,°
In whose opinion sensual delight
Was the one true felicity in sight.
As noted as St. Julian° was for bounty
350 He made his household free to all the County.
His bread, his ale were finest of the fine
And no one had a better stock of wine.
His house was never short of bake-meat pies,
Of fish and flesh, and these in such supplies
355 It positively snowed with meat and drink
And all the dainties that a man could think.
According to the seasons of the year
Changes of dish were ordered to appear.
He kept fat partridges in coops, beyond,

[handwritten right-margin notes near lines: twenty books would have cost a fortune; Only concern w/ study; only spoke when needed; quiet - reader; short, to the pt. - lofty; Virtuous speech; gladly learn + teach; lawyer practiced for 16 yrs at least; irony sarcastic; - circuit judge; greedy; one who draws up legal papers for the transfer of property; - appears busy, but really isn't; Knew the law; sign of wealth Rich; landowner; Traveling w/ sgt.; white beard; cheerful, happy; pleasure-seeker Goal of life was happiness; fine food + entertainment]

308. Alchemists at the time were searching for a stone that was supposed to turn ordinary metals into gold.

320. **St. Paul's:** a favorite place for lawyers to congregate when courts were closed.

325. Letters from the king permitted people to act as judges at the Assizes, court sessions held periodically.

336. **screeds:** long, tiresome writings.
341. *Franklin:* well-to-do landowner, but not of the nobility.
346. Epicurus was a philosopher of ancient Greece who taught that the goal of life is happiness. Most people came to think of Epicureans as pleasure-seekers.
349. **St. Julian:** patron saint of hospitality.

The Franklin. Detail from The Ellesmere Manuscript.

The Huntington Library, San Marino, California.

360   Many a bream and pike were in his pond.
    Woe to the cook whose sauces had no sting
    Or who was unprepared in anything!
    And in his hall a table stood arrayed
    And ready all day long, with places laid.
365   As Justice at the Sessions none stood higher;
    He often had been Member for the Shire.
    A dagger and a little purse of silk
    Hung at his girdle,° white as morning milk.
    As Sheriff he checked audit, every entry.
370   He was a model among landed gentry.
       A *Haberdasher*, a *Dyer*, a *Carpenter*,
    A *Weaver*, and a *Carpetmaker* were
    Among our ranks, all in the livery
A   Of one impressive guild-fraternity.
375   They were so trim and fresh their gear would pass
    For new. Their knives were not tricked out with brass
    But wrought with purest silver, which avouches
    A like display on girdles and on pouches.
B   Each seemed a worthy burgess, fit to grace
380   A guild-hall with a seat upon the dais.
    Their wisdom would have justified a plan
C   To make each one of them an alderman;
    They had the capital and revenue,
    Besides their wives declared it was their due.
385   And if they did not think so, then they ought;
    To be called *Madam* is a glorious thought,
    And so is going to church and being seen
    Having your mantle carried like a queen.
       They had a *Cook* with them who stood alone
390   For boiling chicken with a marrow bone,
    Sharp flavoring powder and a spice for savor.
    He could distinguish London ale by flavor,
    And he could roast and seethe and broil and fry,
    Make good thick soup and bake a tasty pie.
395   But what a pity—so it seemed to me,
    That he should have an ulcer on his knee.
    As for blancmange,° he made it with the best.
       There was a *Skipper* hailing from far west;
D   He came from Dartmouth, so I understood.
400   He rode a farmer's horse as best he could,
    In a woolen gown that reached his knee.
    A dagger on a lanyard° falling free
    Hung from his neck under his arm and down.
    The summer heat had tanned his color brown,
405   And certainly he was an excellent fellow.
    Many a draft of vintage, red and yellow,
    He'd drawn at Bordeaux, while the trader snored.
    The nicer rules of conscience he ignored.
    If, when he fought, the enemy vessel sank,
410   He sent his prisoners home; they walked the plank.
    As for his skill in reckoning his tides,

[Handwritten annotations:]

Perhaps entertains lavishly because these offices were elected offices

368. girdle: belt.

Irony

Guildsmen

14 - 18

trade association / union — powerful organization

neatly dressed

Each appeared a worthy citizen

all had plans to be aldermen

rich, wealthy

wives believe they should be aldermen — women wanted position

Traveling w/ Guildsmen

wonderful cook

Describes them as a group — All alike

Sore — undermines the thought of eating his food

unfortunate that he had an ulcer on his knee — skin disease — poor diet or hygiene, or by STD

19

20

The Cook. Detail from *The Ellesmere Manuscript.*

The Huntington Library, San Marino, California.

397. blancmange (blə·mänj′): French for "white food." In Chaucer's day this was a sweet dish containing diced chicken, milk, sugar, and almonds.

not a rider

carries knife

tan

irony

Dartmouth — known for its piracy + for the brutality of its sailors

402. lanyard: cord.

Stole wine w/ trader slept

no conscience

prisoners walked the plank

Sidebar:

A. Guilds
Guilds were early associations of tradesmen who taught their trades to others through a system of apprenticeship. The guilds acquired a great deal of power.

B. Vocabulary
A *burgess* was a citizen.

C. Vocabulary
An *alderman* was a senior member of a county or borough council.

D. The Skipper
Dartmouth, in Devonshire, was known for its piracy and for the brutality of its sailors, a fact that Chaucer's readers would have known.

E. About the Illustration
The illustration of the Cook shows him carrying a meat hook. The ulcer on his knee was caused by a skin disease associated with faulty diet and poor hygiene, or by a sexually transmitted disease.

A. Expansion
Natural Magic was different from Black Magic, or witchcraft.

B. Medieval Medicine
These effigies were small reproductions of the signs of the zodiac. They were placed on the diseased part of the body at the time when the sign of the zodiac was at its height.

C. Satire
How is Chaucer's depiction of the Doctor satirical? (The Doctor makes money from the drugs he prescribes for patients and profits from plagues.)

D. About the Illustration
The whip in the wife's hand symbolizes her control over men. There are only three women on this pilgrimage; the nun is never heard of again after line 167.

Currents and many another risk besides,
Moons, harbors, pilots, he had such dispatch
That none from Hull to Carthage was his match.
415   Hardy he was, prudent in undertaking;
His beard in many a tempest had its shaking,
And he knew all the havens as they were
From Gottland to the Cape of Finisterre,
And every creek in Brittany and Spain;
420   The barge he owned was called *The Maudelayne*.
       A *Doctor* too emerged as we proceeded;
No one alive could talk as well as he did
On points of medicine and of surgery,
For, being grounded in astronomy,
425   He watched his patient's favorable star
A   And, by his Natural Magic, knew what are
The lucky hours and planetary degrees
B   For making charms and magic effigies.
The cause of every malady you'd got
430   He knew, and whether dry, cold, moist or hot;°
He knew their seat, their humor and condition.
He was a perfect practicing physician.
These causes being known for what they were,
He gave the man his medicine then and there.
435   All his apothecaries in a tribe
Were ready with the drugs he would prescribe
And each made money from the other's guile;
They had been friendly for a goodish while.
He was well-versed in Aesculapius° too
440   And what Hippocrates and Rufus knew
And Dioscorides, now dead and gone,
Galen and Rhazes, Hali, Serapion,
Averroes, Avicenna, Constantine,
Scotch Bernard, John of Gaddesden, Gilbertine.
445   In his own diet he observed some measure;
There were no superfluities for pleasure,
Only digestives, nutritives and such.
He did not read the Bible very much.
In blood-red garments, slashed with bluish-gray
450   And lined with taffeta, he rode his way;
Yet he was rather close as to expenses
And kept the gold he won in pestilences.
C   Gold stimulates the heart, or so we're told.
He therefore had a special love of gold.
455   A worthy *woman* from beside *Bath* city
Was with us, somewhat deaf, which was a pity.
In making cloth she showed so great a bent
She bettered those of Ypres and of Ghent.°
In all the parish not a dame dared stir
460   Towards the altar steps in front of her,
And if indeed they did, so wrath was she
As to be quite put out of charity.
Her kerchiefs were of finely woven ground;

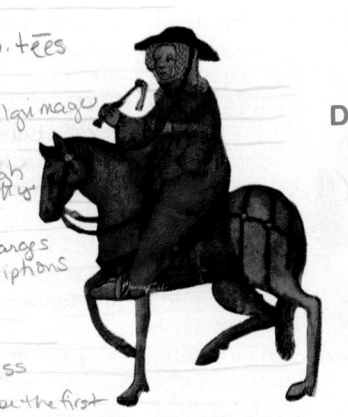

The Physician. Detail from *The Ellesmere Manuscript.*

The Huntington Library, San Marino, California.

430. dry . . . hot: people of the time believed the body was composed of certain proportions of earth (dryness), water (coldness), air (moisture), and fire (heat), and that an imbalance of these elements caused disease.

439. Aesculapius: this and the names that follow were early Greek, Roman, Middle Eastern, and medieval medical authorities. **458. Ypres** (ē′pr) and **Ghent:** Flemish centers of the wool trade.

The Wife of Bath. Detail from *The Ellesmere Manuscript.*

The Huntington Library, San Marino, California.

465   I dared have sworn they weighed a good ten pound,
      The ones she wore on Sunday, on her head.
      Her hose were of the finest scarlet red
      And gartered tight; her shoes were soft and new.
      Bold was her face, handsome, and red in hue.
470   She'd had five husbands, all at the church door,°
      Apart from other company in youth;
      No need just now to speak of that, forsooth.
A   ⌈ And she had thrice been to Jerusalem,
    | Seen many strange rivers and passed over them;
475 | She'd been to Rome and also to Boulogne,
    ⌊ St. James of Compostella and Cologne,
      And she was skilled in wandering by the way.
B   ⌈ She had gap-teeth, set widely, truth to say.
      Easily on an ambling horse she sat
480   Well wimpled° up, and on her head a hat

(handwritten annotations:)
Red hose – loose woman – Red – passionate
5 husbands – Traveling alone
Young men when she was young
Other sites of famous pilgrimages traveled a lot
– wanders – travels → travel far, bold, well suited for love
good horse woman

470. In Chaucer's day, the marriage ceremony was performed at the church door.

480. A wimple was a linen covering for the head and neck.

C

The old Tabard Inn, Southwark, England (1810). Engraving.

A. Pilgrim Centers
Jerusalem, Rome, Boulogne (in France), St. James of Compostella (in Spain), and Cologne (in Germany) were all famous pilgrimage centers.

B. The Gap-Teeth
A gap between a woman's two front teeth was thought to indicate that she would travel far. It also suggested that she was bold and especially suited for love.

C. The Wife of Bath
[?] What words or phrases would you use to describe the famous Wife of Bath? (Possible responses include: lusty, earthy, imposing, bold.) What sort of tale do you think she'd tell? (The tale is predictably bawdy and rather militantly feminist, but it ends by asserting fidelity in marriage.) Some critics think the much-married Wife is modeled on Chaucer's thrice-married paternal grandmother.

A. The Parson
In contrast to the other churchmen, the Parson is a good, simple, and pious man. Like the Clerk, he is poor, a quality Chaucer seems to equate with goodness.

B. Metaphors
The metaphors comparing the Priest to a shepherd and his parishioners to a flock of sheep derive from the Bible. Note Psalm 23 ("The Lord is my shepherd"); Isaiah 40:11; and John 10:14 (where Christ says, "I am the Good Shepherd"). Note the famous proverbs in lines 510 and 513–514. The soiled shepherd, of course, is soiled with sin (just as sheep are often soiled with their own excrement).

C. About the Illustration
Point out to students that the Parson's hands are crossed on his chest in a gesture of piety and submission to God's will.

As broad as is a buckler or a shield;
She had a flowing mantle that concealed
Large hips, her heels spurred sharply under that.
In company she liked to laugh and chat
485   And knew the remedies for love's mischances,
An art in which she knew the oldest dances.
A holy-minded man of good renown
There was, and poor, the *Parson* to a town,
Yet he was rich in holy thought and work.
490   He also was a learned man, a clerk,
Who truly knew Christ's gospel and would preach it
Devoutly to parishioners, and teach it.
Benign and wonderfully diligent,
And patient when adversity was sent
495   (For so he proved in great adversity)
He much disliked extorting tithe° or fee,
Nay rather he preferred beyond a doubt
Giving to poor parishioners round about
From his own goods and Easter offerings.
500   He found sufficiency in little things.
Wide was his parish, with houses far asunder,
Yet he neglected not in rain or thunder,
In sickness or in grief, to pay a call
On the remotest, whether great or small,
505   Upon his feet, and in his hand a stave.°
This noble example to his sheep he gave,
First following the word before he taught it,
And it was from the gospel he had caught it.
This little proverb he would add thereto
510   That if gold rust, what then will iron do?
For if a priest be foul in whom we trust
No wonder that a common man should rust;
And shame it is to see—let priests take stock—
A shitten shepherd and a snowy flock.
515   The true example that a priest should give
Is one of cleanness, how the sheep should live.
He did not set his benefice° to hire
And leave his sheep encumbered in the mire
Or run to London to earn easy bread
520   By singing masses for the wealthy dead,
Or find some Brotherhood and get enrolled.°
He stayed at home and watched over his fold
So that no wolf should make the sheep miscarry.
He was a shepherd and no mercenary.
525   Holy and virtuous he was, but then
Never contemptuous of sinful men,
Ever disdainful, never too proud or fine,
But was discreet in teaching and benign.
His business was to show a fair behavior
530   And draw men thus to Heaven and their Savior,
Unless indeed a man were obstinate;
And such, whether of high or low estate,

The Parson. Detail from
The Ellesmere Manuscript.

The Huntington Library,
San Marino, California.

496. **tithe:** people were tithed in those days, meaning they had to give ten percent of their income or produce to the church.
505. **stave:** staff.

517. **benefice:** duties.

521. He doesn't get a job as a paid chaplain to a guild.

He put to sharp rebuke to say the least.
I think there never was a better priest.
535 He sought no pomp or glory in his dealings,
No scrupulosity had spiced his feelings.
Christ and His Twelve Apostles and their lore
He taught, but followed it himself before.
    There was a *Plowman* with him there, his brother
540 Many a load of dung one time or other
He must have carted through the morning dew.
He was an honest worker, good and true,
Living in peace and perfect charity,
And, as the gospel bade him, so did he,
545 Loving God best with all his heart and mind
And then his neighbor as himself, repined
At no misfortune, slacked for no content,
For steadily about his work he went
To thrash his corn, to dig or to manure
550 Or make a ditch; and he would help the poor
For love of Christ and never take a penny
If he could help it, and, as prompt as any,
He paid his tithes in full when they were due
On what he owned, and on his earnings too.
555 He wore a tabard smock° and rode a mare.
    There was a *Reeve,*° also a *Miller,* there,
A College *Manciple*° from the Inns of Court
A papal *Pardoner* and, in close consort,
A Church-Court *Summoner,*° riding at a trot,
560 And finally myself—that was the lot.
    The *Miller* was a chap of sixteen stone,°
A great stout fellow big in brawn and bone.
He did well out of them, for he could go
And win the ram at any wrestling show.
565 Broad, knotty, and short-shouldered, he would boast
He could heave any door off hinge and post,
Or take a run and break it with his head.
His beard, like any sow or fox, was red
And broad as well, as though it were a spade;
570 And, at its very tip, his nose displayed
A wart on which there stood a tuft of hair
Red as the bristles in an old sow's ear.
His nostrils were as black as they were wide.
He had a sword and buckler at his side,
575 His mighty mouth was like a furnace door.
A wrangler and buffoon, he had a store
Of tavern stories, filthy in the main.
His was a master-hand at stealing grain.
He felt it with his thumb and thus he knew
580 Its quality and took three times his due—
A thumb of gold, by God, to gauge an oat!°
He wore a hood of blue and a white coat.
He liked to play his bagpipes up and down
And that was how he brought us out of town.

The Miller. Detail from
The Ellesmere Manuscript.

The Huntington Library,
San Marino, California.

555. **tabard smock:** short jacket.
556. **Reeve:** a serf who was the steward of his manor. He saw that the estate's work was done and that everything was accounted for.
557. **Manciple:** a minor employee whose principal duty was to purchase provisions for a college or law firm.
559. **Summoner:** a petty officer who summoned people to appear in church court.
561. **sixteen stone:** 224 pounds.

581. In other words, he pressed on the scale with his thumb to increase the weight.

A. The Plowman
Chaucer's picture of the lowly Plowman may refer to the earlier poem *Piers Plowman* by William Langland, in which the plowman is seen as an instrument of salvation to his community.
    Chaucer may be presenting in this Plowman a picture of peasants as he thought they should be, not as they were. At this time, peasants were generally ridiculed by writers, not held up for praise.

B. Allusion
In Luke 10:27, Christ cites the two great commandments: "Thou shalt love the Lord thy God with thy whole heart . . . ; and thy neighbor as thyself."

C. The Miller's Tale
Predictably, the Miller's tale is a ribald tale of seduction.

D. About the Illustration
Bagpipes were thought to represent lust and gluttony (the bag was like a stomach).

A. The Inns of Court

The Inns of Court, which still stand in London (the Inner Temple is one), were, in Chaucer's time, inhabited by university graduates taking up the practice of law. The Manciple was a purchasing agent for over thirty lawyers.

B. Expansion

"Wipe their eye" means to deceive them.

C. The Four Humors

People in Chaucer's time believed that four bodily humors (or "moistures") were the sources of disease and personality, somewhat as we think of glands and genes today. (1) Black bile was associated with depression and delusions. (2) Choler, or yellow bile, was associated with unkindness, wrath, instability, and pride. (3) Phlegm created sloth, obesity, short and crooked bodies, and hairless skin. (4) Too much blood made a person sensual. In an older person, it caused a heart attack.

D. Expansion

His hair was cut straight across the forehead (as priests' hair was). The style was a sign of servility.

purchasing agent – bought goods for university of law

A

585 The *Manciple* came from the Inner Temple;°
     All caterers might follow his example
     In buying victuals; he was never rash
     Whether he bought on credit or paid cash.
     He used to watch the market most precisely
590 And got in first, and so he did quite nicely.
     Now isn't it a marvel of God's grace
     That an illiterate fellow can outpace   *quite shrewd for having no formal education*
     The wisdom of a heap of learned men?
     His masters—he had more than thirty then—
595 All versed in the abstrusest legal knowledge,
     Could have produced a dozen from their College   *lawyers are smart + are being trained to be stewards + lawyers + yet this Manciple can deceive them*
     Fit to be stewards in land and rents and game
     To any Peer in England you could name,
     And show him how to live on what he had
600 Debt-free (unless of course the Peer were mad)
     Or be as frugal as he might desire,
     And they were fit to help about the Shire
     In any legal case there was to try;

B And yet this Manciple could wipe their eye.   *Manciple could deceive them*

585. **Inner Temple:** a place used by a society of lawyers.

The Manciple. Detail from The Ellesmere Manuscript.

The Huntington Library, San Marino, California.

C The *Reeve* was old and choleric° and thin;   *Superintendent of an estate*
605 His beard was shaven closely to the skin,
D His shorn hair came abruptly to a stop
     Above his ears, and he was docked on top   *sign of servility*
     Just like a priest in front; his legs were lean,   *Thin*
610 Like sticks they were, no calf was to be seen.
     He kept his bins and garners very trim;
     No auditor could gain a point on him.
     And he could judge by watching drought and rain
     The yield he might expect from seed and grain.
615 His master's sheep, his animals and hens,   *Runs estate*
     Pigs, horses, dairies, stores, and cattle pens
     Were wholly trusted to his government.
     And he was under contract to present   *does accounts*
     The accounts, right from his master's earliest years.
620 No one had ever caught him in arrears.
     No bailiff, serf, or herdsman dared to kick,   *No one tried to cheat him, because he knew*
     He knew their dodges, knew their every trick;   *him*
     Feared like the plague he was, by those beneath.   *People feared him*
     He had a lovely dwelling on a heath,   *lovely home*
625 Shadowed in green by trees above the sward.
     A better hand at bargains than his lord,   *rich*
     He had grown rich and had a store of treasure   *Better businessman than his master*
     Well tucked away, yet out it came to pleasure   *steals money from employer + uses that money to buy gifts for employer.*
     His lord with subtle loans or gifts of goods,
630 To earn his thanks and even coats and hoods.   *gives loans*
     When young he'd learnt a useful trade and still
     He was a carpenter of first-rate skill.   *carpenter*
     The stallion-cob he rode at a slow trot
     Was dapple-gray and bore the name of Scot.
635 He wore an overcoat of bluish shade
     And rather long; he had a rusty blade

605. **choleric:** having too much choler, or yellow bile, and thus bad-tempered.

The Reeve. Detail from The Ellesmere Manuscript.

The Huntington Library, San Marino, California.

Slung at his side. He came, as I heard tell,
From Norfolk, near a place called Baldeswell.
His coat was tucked under his belt and splayed.
640 He rode the hindmost of our cavalcade.

A There was a *Summoner* with us in the place
Who had a fire-red cherubinnish face,°
For he had carbuncles.° His eyes were narrow,
He was as hot and lecherous as a sparrow.
645 Black, scabby brows he had, and a thin beard.
Children were afraid when he appeared.
No quicksilver, lead ointments, tartar creams,
Boracic, no, nor brimstone, so it seems,
Could make a salve that had the power to bite,
650 Clean up or cure his whelks of knobby white
Or purge the pimples sitting on his cheeks.

B Garlic he loved, and onions too, and leeks,
And drinking strong red wine till all was hazy.
Then he would shout and jabber as if crazy,
655 And wouldn't speak a word except in Latin
When he was drunk, such tags as he was pat in;
He only had a few, say two or three,
That he had mugged up out of some decree;
No wonder, for he heard them every day.
660 And, as you know, a man can teach a jay
To call out "Walter" better than the Pope.
But had you tried to test his wits and grope
For more, you'd have found nothing in the bag.
Then "*Questio quid juris*"° was his tag.
665 He was a gentle varlet and a kind one,
No better fellow if you went to find one.

C He would allow—just for a quart of wine—
Any good lad to keep a concubine
A twelvemonth and dispense it altogether!
670 Yet he could pluck a finch to leave no feather:
And if he found some rascal with a maid
He would instruct him not to be afraid
In such a case of the Archdeacon's curse
(Unless the rascal's soul were in his purse)
675 For in his purse the punishment should be.
"Purse is the good Archdeacon's Hell," said he.
But well I know he lied in what he said;
A curse should put a guilty man in dread,
For curses kill, as shriving brings, salvation.
680 We should beware of excommunication.
Thus, as he pleased, the man could bring duress
On any young fellow in the diocese.
He knew their secrets, they did what he said.
He wore a garland set upon his head
685 Large as the hollybush upon a stake
Outside an alehouse, and he had a cake,
A round one, which it was his joke to wield
As if it were intended for a shield.

[Handwritten margin annotations, left of text:]
last rider
ugly man
Possibly venereal disease or leprosy
Skin disease
Like eating or drinking
Only spoke Latin when drunk
short familiar quotations
Sometimes falsely summon people
not intelligent
Irony
Bribes
for money he would get the offender off
lian & cheat
Summoner could blackmail anyone

[Handwritten margin annotations, top:]
Employee of Church courts - Presented people w/ summons for infractions of Church Law

[Printed notes in center column:]

642. Cherubins, or little angels, had red faces.
643. **carbuncles:** pus-filled skin inflammations, something like boils.

The Summoner. Detail from The Ellesmere Manuscript.

The Huntington Library, San Marino, California.

[Handwritten: gluttony; Perhaps not as bad as others like him]

664. "*Questio quid juris*": "I ask what point of the law [applies]." The Summoner uses this to stall and dodge the issue.

[Right margin side-notes:]

A. The Summoner
A summoner presented a person with a summons (like a subpoena) for some infraction of Church law.

B. Characterization
Some say that the Summoner suffered from a severe skin disease caused by gluttony, especially by eating and drinking these very foods listed as his favorites. Chaucer is again making a commentary about character in what seems to be a simple list of facts.

C. Expansion
Adultery was cause for excommunication, and the Summoner was to track down offenders and bring them to the Archdeacon for punishment. Note that money would get the offender off.

D. About the Illustration
The Summoner holds a writ of excommunication, which could cut off the receiver from the Church and from salvation. The Summoner himself is probably in more danger of losing his soul than anyone to whom he might be giving this writ!

A. The Pardoner

Chaucer may have modeled his Pardoner on a real pardoner from St. Mary Rouncival Hospital. The hospital went through a series of money scandals in the 1380's. *Gentle* means he was of the upper classes, not that his nature was gentle.

B. Characterization

Long hair was a violation of the rule that churchmen should be tonsured (short hair with a shaved spot on top). At once, an aspect of the Pardoner's character is revealed. In the passage that follows, note references to his effeminacy.

C. Relics

Relics were believed to be the remains (bones, hair, nails, garments, and so on) of a holy person. Saying a prayer with the relic in hand would bring the person an *indulgence*—a limited respite from the sufferings he or she would have to undergo in Purgatory before reaching Heaven. The pigs' bones in line 720 are passed off as the bones of a saint. Boccaccio presents a similarly unscrupulous cleric in his funny and satiric "Friar Onion" in the *Decameron*.

[handwritten top: Sold Pardons to people — proceeds supposed to go to church]

A
690
He and a gentle *Pardoner°* rode together, *[upper class]*
A bird from Charing Cross of the same feather,
Just back from visiting the Court of Rome.
He loudly sang "*Come hither, love, come home!*" *[sings love songs — dirty song]*
The Summoner sang deep seconds to this song,
No trumpet ever sounded half so strong.

695
B
This Pardoner had hair as yellow as wax, *[long hair forbidden in church]*
Hanging down smoothly like a hank of flax.
In driblets fell his locks behind his head
Down to his shoulders which they overspread;
Thinly they fell, like rattails, one by one.

700
He wore no hood upon his head, for fun; *[disheveled appearance]*
The hood inside his wallet had been stowed,
He aimed at riding in the latest mode; *[effeminate description]*
But for a little cap his head was bare
And he had bulging eyeballs, like a hare.

705
He'd sewed a holy relic on his cap;
His wallet lay before him on his lap,
Brimful of pardons come from Rome all hot.
He had the same small voice a goat has got.
His chin no beard had harbored, nor would harbor,

710
Smoother than ever chin was left by barber.
I judge he was a gelding, or a mare. *[gelding - castrated male] [mare - female horse]*
As to his trade, from Berwick down to Ware
There was no pardoner of equal grace, *[- Irony]*

C
For in his trunk he had a pillowcase *[Holy relics]*
715
Which he asserted was Our Lady's veil.
He said he had a gobbet of the sail
Saint Peter had the time when he made bold
To walk the waves, till Jesu Christ took hold.
He had a cross of metal set with stones
720
And, in a glass, a rubble of pigs' bones.
And with these relics, anytime he found
Some poor up-country parson to astound, *[Sold fake relics]*
On one short day, in money down, he drew
More than the parson in a month or two, *[& made lots of money]*
725
And by his flatteries and prevarication
Made monkeys of the priest and congregation.
But still to do him justice first and last
In church he was a noble ecclesiast. *[- Irony]*
How well he read a lesson or told a story!
730
But best of all he sang an Offertory, *[Sang offertory well because he knew he would get money]*
For well he knew that when that song was sung
He'd have to preach and tune his honey-tongue
And (well he could) win silver from the crowd.
That's why he sang so merrily and loud.
735
    Now I have told you shortly, in a clause,
The rank, the array, the number and the cause
Of our assembly in this company
In Southwark, at that high-class hostelry
Known as *The Tabard,* close beside *The Bell.*
740
And now the time has come for me to tell

689. *Pardoner:* Pardoners were minor members of the church who bought pardons for sinners and sold them. These were small strips of parchment with papal seals attached. They were sold as *indulgences* (pardons for sins), with the proceeds supposedly going to a religious house. Many pardoners were dishonest, and even loyal members of the church ridiculed them.

The Pardoner. Detail from The Ellesmere Manuscript.

The Huntington Library, San Marino, California.

How we behaved that evening; I'll begin
After we had alighted at the Inn,
Then I'll report our journey, stage by stage,
All the remainder of our pilgrimage.
745 But first I beg of you, in courtesy,
Not to condemn me as unmannerly
If I speak plainly and with no concealings
And give account of all their words and dealings.
Using their very phrases as they fell.
750 For certainly, as you all know so well,
He who repeats a tale after a man
Is bound to say, as nearly as he can,
Each single word, if he remembers it,
However rudely spoken or unfit,
755 Or else the tale he tells will be untrue,
A   The things invented and the phrases new.
He may not flinch although it were his brother,
If he says one word he must say the other.
And Christ Himself spoke broad in Holy Writ,
760 And as you know there's nothing there unfit,
And Plato says, for those with power to read,
"The word should be as cousin to the deed."
Further I beg you to forgive it me
If I neglect the order and degree
765 And what is due to rank in what I've planned.
I'm short of wit as you will understand.
    Our *Host* gave us great welcome; everyone
Was given a place and supper was begun.
He served the finest victuals you could think.
770 The wine was strong and we were glad to drink.
A very striking man our Host withal,
And fit to be a marshal in a hall.
His eyes were bright, his girth a little wide;
There is no finer burgess in Cheapside.°
775 Bold in his speech, yet wise and full of tact,
There was no manly attribute he lacked,
What's more he was a merry-hearted man.
After our meal he jokingly began
To talk of sport, and, among other things
780 After we'd settled up our reckonings,
He said as follows: "Truly, gentlemen,
You're very welcome and I can't think when
—Upon my word I'm telling you no lie—
I've seen a gathering here that looked so spry,
785 No, not this year, as in this tavern now.
I'd think you up some fun if I knew how.
And, as it happens, a thought has just occurred
And it will cost you nothing, on my word.
You're off to Canterbury—well, God speed!
790 Blessed St. Thomas answer to your need!
And I don't doubt, before the journey's done
You mean to while the time in tales and fun.

[handwritten margin notes:]
Apologizes for reporting exactly how people behave + speak

must tell it truthfully or the tale will be untrue

Big man
Admirable man
Cheerful

The Host. Detail from
The Ellesmere Manuscript.

The Huntington Library,
San Marino, California.

774. A burgess was a citizen; Cheapside is
a district in London.

A. Framework Device
❓ Who is really the author of these tales? Why do you think Chaucer says he is merely recording what other people have said? (Chaucer, of course, is the author of all the tales, but pretending that the pilgrims are telling their tales relieves him of a certain responsibility for their content, especially in the bawdier tales.)

Additional Writing Assignment
It is generally supposed that in describing the host, Chaucer is describing himself. Ask students to write a description of Chaucer's personality as well as his appearance, using evidence they find in "The Prologue."

What similari-
ties and differ-
ences do you see
in this depiction of
the pilgrims and
Blake's engraving
on text pages 86–
87? (Much of the
difference in color
and line is, of
course, due to dif-
ferences in medi-
um. Students
might also note the
somewhat more
ethereal figures in
the Blake engrav-
ing compared with
the earthiness in
this painting.) No-
tice the walled city
of Canterbury.

A

Indeed, there's little pleasure for your bones
Riding along and all as dumb as stones.
795   So let me then propose for your enjoyment,
Just as I said, a suitable employment.
And if my notion suits and you agree
And promise to submit yourselves to me
Playing your parts exactly as I say
800   Tomorrow as you ride along the way,
Then by my father's soul (and he is dead)
If you don't like it you can have my head!
Hold up your hands, and not another word."
      Well, our consent of course was not deferred,
805   It seemed not worth a serious debate;

Pilgrims leaving Canterbury.
From a manuscript.

British Library, London.

1. Why are the pilgrims going to Canterbury? To visit the shrine of St. Thomas à Becket
2. Name three of the pilgrims described by Chaucer.
3. What is the name of the inn in which they meet? The Tabard
4. What time of year is it? April
5. What does the host suggest? That each pilgrim tell two stories going and two returning and that the winner gets a free supper

We all agreed to it at any rate
And bade him issue what commands he would.
"My lords," he said, "now listen for your good,
And please don't treat my notion with disdain.
810 This is the point. I'll make it short and plain.
Each one of you shall help to make things slip
By telling two stories on the outward trip
A To Canterbury, that's what I intend,
And, on the homeward way to journey's end
815 Another two, tales from the days of old;
And then the man whose story is best told,
That is to say who gives the fullest measure
Of good morality and general pleasure,
He shall be given a supper, paid by all,
820 Here in this tavern, in this very hall,
When we come back again from Canterbury.
And in the hope to keep you bright and merry
I'll go along with you myself and ride
All at my own expense and serve as guide.
825 I'll be the judge, and those who won't obey
Shall pay for what we spend upon the way.
Now if you all agree to what you've heard
Tell me at once without another word,
And I will make arrangements early for it."
830 Of course we all agreed, in fact we swore it
Delightedly, and made entreaty too
That he should act as he proposed to do,
Become our Governor in short, and be
Judge of our tales and general referee,
835 And set the supper at a certain price.
We promised to be ruled by his advice
Come high, come low; unanimously thus
We set him up in judgment over us.
More wine was fetched, the business being done;
840 We drank it off and up went everyone
To bed without a moment of delay.
  Early next morning at the spring of day
Up rose our Host and roused us like a cock,
Gathering us together in a flock,
845 And off we rode at slightly faster pace
Than walking to St. Thomas' watering-place;
And there our Host drew up, began to ease
His horse, and said, "Now, listen if you please,
My lords! Remember what you promised me.
850 If evensong and matins will agree°
Let's see who shall be first to tell a tale.
And as I hope to drink good wine and ale
I'll be your judge. The rebel who disobeys,
However much the journey costs, he pays.
855 Now draw for cut and then we can depart;
The man who draws the shortest cut shall start.

Host proposes contest of storytelling
Sets up frame story

all agree to contest
Set price of supper

850. In other words, if you feel in the evening (at evensong) what you feel in the morning (at matins).

1. The pilgrims gather at the Tabard Inn in April to prepare for a pilgrimage to the shrine of St. Thomas à Becket, in Canterbury.
2. The Host proposes that each pilgrim should tell two tales on the journey from London to Canterbury, and two tales on the return journey. The pilgrim who tells the best tale, as judged by the Host, will get a free dinner at the Tabard Inn.
3. Pilgrims from the feudal system include the Knight, Squire, Yeoman, Franklin, Plowman, Reeve, and Miller. Pilgrims from the Church include the Prioress, the other Nun, the Nun's three Priests, the Monk, Friar, Cleric, Parson, Pardoner, and Summoner. Pilgrims from the city include the Merchant, Serjeant-at-the-law, Haberdasher, Dyer, Carpenter, Weaver, Carpetmaker, Cook, Skipper, Doctor, Wife of Bath, and the Manciple.
4. Chaucer will faithfully report what everyone said on the pilgrimage because he is obligated to tell the truth. On the other hand, his readers should not hold it against him if they find some stories ribald or offensive.

Responding to the Prologue

Analyzing the Prologue

Identifying Details

1. When, where, and for what purpose do the pilgrims gather?
2. What plan does the Host propose to the pilgrims?
3. Chaucer's pilgrims come from a cross-section of medieval society and they include three important groups. Categorize the pilgrims into those from the feudal system (related to the land); those from the Church; and those from the city (merchants and professionals).
4. What plea does Chaucer make to his readers concerning his own report about the pilgrimage?

Interpreting Meanings

5. Chaucer is a master at using physical details—eyes, hair, complexion, body type, clothing—to reveal **character.** Find at least three pilgrims whose inner natures are revealed by their outer appearances.
6. Clearly, Chaucer **satirizes** the Church of his time in the Prologue. Show how this is true by analyzing two characters connected with the Church. Where does Chaucer balance his satire by presenting a "good" churchman or woman?
7. Where does Chaucer **satirize** other aspects of his own society?
8. Which characters do you think Chaucer idealizes?
9. In describing the pilgrims, what has Chaucer revealed about his own personality, biases, and values?
10. Which of the pilgrims' professions or trades have survived in society today? Which of the character "types" presented here have contemporary equivalents?
11. What events in contemporary life could be compared to the pilgrimage to Canterbury? That is, when would people from all walks of life today travel together in large groups for a common purpose, whether that purpose is religious or not? How are these "journeys" similar to, and different from, the journey that Chaucer's pilgrims undertake?

Writing About the Prologue

A Creative Response

1. **Writing a Frame Story.** Begin your own frame story. (For more on the form, see page 130.) List six characters who will go on a journey. Decide what your "framework" will be: What has brought them all together? Who will your narrator be? (In *The Arabian Nights,* the stories are "framed" by the narrator, Scheherazade. She is beguiling her wicked husband with stories so that he will not kill her until she gets to the end; since each story leads into another, his suspense is always unsatisfied. In Boccaccio's *Decameron,* the stories are "framed" by the fact that a group of young people have fled to a country estate to escape the plague raging in the city. To pass the time, they tell stories.) Make notes of what your characters are like. What do they look like? How do they act? What are their jobs? In a prologue, introduce these characters. You may either write in prose or try your hand at rhymed couplets like Chaucer's. Devote at least six lines to each character, and save your work.

A Critical Response

2. **Responding to a Critic.** Read the following comment on Chaucer's General Prologue:

> The General Prologue to *The Canterbury Tales* of Geoffrey Chaucer stands at the threshold of the Anglo-American literary tradition. This is the earliest piece written in such language and embodying such concepts that later generations in the culture respond instinctively to it, respond with what Edmund Wilson called the "shock of recognition."
>
> —John H. Fisher

Do you agree that the characters in *The Canterbury Tales* have stood the test of time? In an essay of at least five paragraphs, using specific references to the General Prologue, explain what makes it possible (or impossible) to "respond instinctively" with a "shock of recognition" to the characters that Chaucer describes in the Prologue.

3. **Comparing and Contrasting Two Characters.** The Wife of Bath and the Prioress are the only two women described at any length in the Prologue. In an essay, compare and contrast these two travelers. Consider each of the following elements in Chaucer's characterizations:

a. Appearance and clothing
b. Manner and personality
c. Tastes
d. Social position
e. Life experiences

At the conclusion of your essay, tell whether or not you think their "types" are still found in contemporary life.

5. Possibilities include the Pardoner, Squire, Monk, Wife of Bath, and Miller.

6. Students could analyze the satiric descriptions of the Prioress, Monk, Friar, Pardoner, and Summoner.

Chaucer presents favorable pictures of the Oxford Cleric and the Parson (among the Church representatives).

7. Students' answers will vary. For ex-

ample, in the portrait of the Merchant, Chaucer seems to satirize "know-it-all" experts in business. In the portrait of the Franklin, Chaucer seems to be poking fun at the pleasure-loving habits of the lesser nobility. The portrait of the Doctor satirizes medical obscurantism and the greed of the profession for gold. Finally, the Miller is portrayed as a petty thief.

8. He idealizes the Knight, Cleric, and

Parson, and maybe the Squire.

9. In general, Chaucer reveals himself as worldly, keenly observant of the appearances and motives of others, even-tempered and good-natured, and intensely curious. He values honesty, simplicity, and genuine piety. He dislikes hypocrisy and corruption.

10. Surviving professions are those of plowman, prioress, nun, friar, merchant, monk, cook, and doctor.

The surviving "types" include everyone. We have Chaucer's pilgrims all around us: rogues, hypocrites, worldly clerics, shrewd businessmen, cheats, saints, good soldiers, playboys, book lovers, and so on.

11. Possibilities include religious pilgrimages, such as those to Lourdes (France), Knock (Ireland), and Mecca (Saudi Arabia).

Analyzing Language and Style

Rhymes

Chaucer's favorite rhyme was the **couplet.** (When he was growing old, he complained that his faculty of rhyming was leaving him, which may account for the reason he never finished *The Canterbury Tales.*) The translator of the tales used here (Nevill Coghill) followed Chaucer's rhyme scheme, though he did not always use Chaucer's own rhyming words.

1. Read aloud parts of the Prologue to see how the rhyming couplets animate the survey of the pilgrims. Find some rhymes here that are humorous.

2. Which couplets seem to use **half rhymes** (also called **approximate rhymes**)?

3. According to the rhymes in the original Prologue, (see page 88), how would the following words have been pronounced in Chaucer's day?

   a. flower   d. courage
   b. breath   e. condition
   c. eye

   What word is each of these words rhymed with?

4. Compare the couplets used in Coghill's translation of the first 42 lines of the Prologue with the couplets used in Chaucer's original. Then try to translate these original lines of the Prologue yourself, perhaps using more of Chaucer's original couplets. You might want to compare your version and Coghill's with this one:

> When April with his showers hath pierced the drought
> Of March with sweetness to the very root,
> And flooded every vein with liquid power
> That of its strength engendereth the flower;
> When Zephyr also with his fragrant breath
> Hath urged to life in every holt and heath . . .
>
> —Translated by F. N. Robinson

Pages from The Ellesmere Manuscript, showing the beginning of "The Clerk's Tale."

The Huntington Library, San Marino, California.

ESTABLISHING A PURPOSE. Contemporary cartoons are often based on a similar premise to that in "The Nun's Priest's Tale": One character tricks another through flattery. Ask students to watch for two such tricks in this story. (The fox tricks the cock, and then the cock tricks the fox.) Have them remember who is telling this story: one of the nun's priests.

(The tale is slightly abridged, omitting some long classical allusions. Ellipses indicate the omissions.)

SUPPLEMENTARY SUPPORT MATERIALS
1. Vocabulary Activity Worksheet (CCB)
2. Review and Response Worksheet: Allusion (CCB)
3. Selection Test (CCB)

DEVELOPING VOCABULARY
The following words from the tale are tested in the Selection Test. (See also Vocabulary Activity Worksheet.)

dale	timorous
repletion	superfluity
azure	manifest
paramour	iniquity
russet	emulate

A. Expansion
Chaucer probably read a Latin or French edition of Aesop's fables. (Chaucer's favorite Latin work was Ovid's *Metamorphoses*.)

B. Life Styles
In 1382, the Earl of Flanders took refuge from a mob in a cottage that might have been like this one. He described it as "only a small house, dirty and smoky and as black as jet: There was only in this place one poor chamber, over which was a sort of garret that was entered by means of a ladder of seven steps, where on a miserable bed, the children of this poor woman lay." At night, in a cottage like this, the chickens would roost in the sooty hall downstairs. Such peasant cottages could be seen in remote parts of the British Isles even recently.

C. Expansion
In other words, overeating never troubled her digestion. Her "physic" (laxative) was her temperate diet. Gout is a joint inflammation, usually in the foot.

A "The Nun's Priest's Tale" is an example of an animal fable, a form that originally stems from the ancient Greek tales of Aesop. Fables are short tales told to illustrate practical moral lessons. The rooster and the fox in "The Nun's Priest's Tale" are versions of Aesop's and Fontaine's well-known fox and crow, although the craftiness of the fox at the expense of the rooster is just a small part of the plot of this tale. As you read the tale, look for a moral lesson and think of what it reveals about the character of the priest. What sort of story would you predict he'd tell?

from The Nun's Priest's Tale

Once, long ago, there dwelt a poor old widow
In a small cottage, by a little meadow
Beside a grove and standing in a <u>dale</u>.
This widow-woman of whom I tell my tale
5   Since the sad day when last she was a wife
Had led a very patient, simple life.
Little she had in capital or rent,
But still, by making do with what God sent,
She kept herself and her two daughters going.
10 Three hefty sows—no more—were all her showing,
Three cows as well; there was a sheep called Molly.

B Sooty her hall, her kitchen melancholy,
And there she ate full many a slender meal;
There was no *sauce piquante*° to spice her veal,
15 No dainty morsel ever passed her throat,
According to her cloth she cut her coat.
<u>Repletion</u> never left her in disquiet
And all her physic was a temperate diet,
C Hard work for exercise and heart's content.
20 And rich man's gout did nothing to prevent
Her dancing, apoplexy struck her not;
She drank no wine, nor white nor red had got.
Her board was mostly served with white and black,
Milk and brown bread, in which she found no lack;
25 Broiled bacon or an egg or two were common,
She was in fact a sort of dairy-woman.
   She had a yard that was enclosed about
By a stockade and a dry ditch without,
In which she kept a cock called Chanticleer.
30 In all the land for crowing he'd no peer;
His voice was jollier than the organ blowing
In church on Sundays, he was great at crowing.
Far, far more regular than any clock
Or abbey bell the crowing of this cock.
35 The equinoctial wheel° and its position
At each ascent he knew by intuition;
At every hour—fifteen degrees of movement—
He crowed so well there could be no improvement.
His comb was redder than fine coral, tall
40 And battlemented like a castle wall,
His bill was black and shone as bright as jet,

14. *sauce piquante* (pē'känt'): spiced sauce. Spices were expensive delicacies in medieval England.

35. **equinoctial wheel:** in Chaucer's day people believed that a great circle in the heavens made a complete revolution every day so that fifteen degrees ascended every hour. They also believed that cocks crowed every hour.

A woman feeding chickens. From an Italian manuscript (c. 1385).

Österreichische Nationalbibliothek, Vienna.

Galli ꝯplo. ca. ꞇ fic. mi. Electo qui fuꞇ ꞇpate uocis. iniamtum patentiby colici ꝯfectuꞇ ai
fuꞇ uectes. s. coꞇi clisfati. ꞇ ꝛcipue cu falle cartamo polipodio. ꞇ caulib. innenes aꞇ cu
cacire incipiuꞇ ꞇ puꞇlle aꞇ ꝗ ouificeꞇ pnutrimito ꝯfecuꞇt. floeuiꞇtum uectes nocec ſtó.
Remó noeti fatigatioe aꞇ uꞇfectioe:. Quid griauꞇ uimeꞇis nutrimitum Lauꝺabile. Con-

A. Humanities Connection: About the Fine Art

This beautiful illumination of an ordinary domestic scene is interesting for many reasons. For one thing, it shows a scene taking place six hundred years ago that still takes place today. The chicken coop has changed, but the chickens haven't. Note in the Latin text that the writer has indicated an insertion in the last line. Even Latin scholars would be challenged in translating the text. The medieval script is different from ours in many ways, and often abbreviations were used for easily recognized words. See if your students of Latin can decipher any of this.

A

A. Expansion
Chanticleer's gorgeous colors—
gold, azure,
black—are the colors of Henry Bolingbroke, who was
involved in a quarrel with a man
named Mowbray
and his follower,
Nicholas Colfax,
known as "the
fox," in 1398.

B. Connections
"The Nun's Priest's
Tale," like "Get Up
and Bar the Door,"
is an example of
medieval satire
against women. As
they read on, have
students note ways
in which the outspoken Pertelote is
characterized.
Then have them
compare her to the
widow in this tale
and to the goodwife in "Get Up
and Bar the Door."
(The widow is
hardworking and
meek and keeps to
her subservient
role. Pertelote is
proud and sees
herself as equal to
her husband, as
does the goodwife.
However, the
goodwife wins in
her competition
with her husband;
what will happen to
Pertelote?)

A

> Like <u>azure</u> were his legs and they were set
> On azure toes with nails of lily white,
> Like burnished gold his feathers, flaming bright.

45   This gentlecock was master in some measure
Of seven hens, all there to do his pleasure.
They were his sisters and his <u>paramours</u>,
Colored like him in all particulars;

B

> She with the loveliest dyes upon her throat
50   > Was known as gracious Lady Pertelote.
Courteous she was, discreet and debonair,
Companionable too, and took such care
In her deportment, since she was seven days old
She held the heart of Chanticleer controlled,
55   Locked up securely in her every limb;
O such happiness his love to him!
And such a joy it was to hear them sing,
As when the glorious sun began to spring,
In sweet accord *My Love is far from land*
60   —For in those far off days I understand
All birds and animals could speak and sing.
   Now it befell, as dawn began to spring,
When Chanticleer and Pertelote and all
His wives were perched in this poor widow's hall
65   (Fair Pertelote was next him on the perch),
This Chanticleer began to groan and lurch
Like someone sorely troubled by a dream,
And Pertelote who heard him roar and scream
Was quite aghast and said, "O dearest heart,
70   What's ailing you? Why do you groan and start?
Fie, what a sleeper! What a noise to make!"
"Madam," he said, "I beg you not to take
Offense, but by the Lord I had a dream
So terrible just now I had to scream;
75   I still can feel my heart racing from fear.
God turn my dream to good and guard all here,
And keep my body out of durance vile!
I dreamt that roaming up and down a while
Within our yard I saw a kind of beast,
80   A sort of hound that tried or seemed at least
To try and seize me . . . would have killed me dead!
His color was a blend of yellow and red,
His ears and tail were tipped with sable fur
Unlike the rest; he was a <u>russet</u> cur.
85   Small was his snout, his eyes were glowing bright.
It was enough to make one die of fright.
That was no doubt what made me groan and swoon."
   "For shame," she said, "you <u>timorous</u> poltroon!°
Alas, what cowardice! By God above,
90   You've forfeited my heart and lost my love.
I cannot love a coward, come what may.
For certainly, whatever we may say,
All women long—and O that it might be!—

88. **poltroon:** coward.

For husbands tough, dependable and free,
95 Secret, discreet, no niggard, not a fool
That boasts and then will find his courage cool
At every trifling thing. By God above,
How dare you say for shame, and to your love,
That anything at all was to be feared?
100 Have you no manly heart to match your beard?
And can a dream reduce you to such terror?
Dreams are a vanity, God knows, pure error.
Dreams are engendered in the too-replete°
From vapors in the belly, which compete
105 With others, too abundant, swollen tight.

A   "No doubt the redness in your dream tonight
Comes from the superfluity and force
Of the red choler in your blood. Of course.
That is what puts a dreamer in the dread
110 Of crimsoned arrows, fires flaming red,
Of great red monsters making as to fight him,
And big red whelps and little ones to bite him;
Just so the black and melancholy vapors
Will set a sleeper shrieking, cutting capers
115 And swearing that black bears, black bulls as well,
Or blackest fiends are haling him to Hell.
And there are other vapors that I know
That on a sleeping man will work their woe,

B   But I'll pass on as lightly as I can.
120 "Take Cato° now, that was so wise a man,
Did he not say, 'Take no account of dreams'?
Now, sir," she said, "on flying from these beams,
For love of God do take some laxative;
Upon my soul that's the advice to give
125 For melancholy choler; let me urge
You free yourself from vapors with a purge.
And that you may have no excuse to tarry
By saying this town has no apothecary,
I shall myself instruct you and prescribe
130 Herbs that will cure all vapors of that tribe,
Herbs from our very farmyard! You will find
Their natural property is to unbind
And purge you well beneath and well above.
Now don't forget it, dear, for God's own love!
135 Your face is choleric and shows distension;
Be careful lest the sun in his ascension
Should catch you full of humors,° hot and many.
And if he does, my dear, I'll lay a penny
It means a bout of fever or a breath
140 Of tertian ague.° You may catch your death.
"Worms for a day or two I'll have to give
As a digestive, then your laxative.

C   Centaury, fumitory, caper-spurge
And hellebore will make a splendid purge;
145 And then there's laurel or the blackthorn berry,

103. **the too-replete:** the over-stuffed.

120. **Cato:** Roman statesman and orator, considered both ethical and wise, who opposed Julius Caesar.

137. **humors:** moods. The choleric humor was believed to be caused by yellow bile, which brought on irritability.

140. **tertian ague** (ā′gyo͞o): fever that increases every third day.

A. Medieval Medicine
According to the tenets of medieval medicine, Pertelote's diagnosis and suggested treatment are correct.

B. Allusion
Be sure students catch the humor in a chicken quoting Cato. Notice in the passage that follows how much the domineering Pertelote enjoys analyzing and prescribing treatments for her husband's choleric dream.

C. Character
Pertelote is relishing the idea of administering a laxative to Chanticleer.

? Lady Pertelote uses the names of various medicinal plants in this section. Does she remind you of any comic characters on TV? (Encourage students to name characters who recklessly offer advice about things they don't understand.)

A. Humanitites Connection: About the Fine Art
Tapestries were woven by noble ladies, and often, even when donated to a church, they contained scenes from popular ballads and myths. Tapestries both decorated and warmed the cold stone walls of castles and manors. One of the most famous of these tapestries is the Bayeux Tapestry (see the illustration on text page 8). Another famous tapestry is the series known as the Unicorn Tapestries, which can be seen in the Cloisters Museum in New York City.

B. Character
Note how Chanticleer cites Cato's lack of authority and attempts to overwhelm his opinionated Pertelote with his own superior knowledge.

C. Expansion
"Greatest author" is a play on the name of Valerius Maximus (*Maximus* means "greatest"), who is the probable source for this tale.

A

Offering of the Heart
(15th century). Arras Tapestry.

Musée Cluny, Paris.

Ground-ivy too that makes our yard so merry;
Peck them right up, my dear, and swallow whole.
Be happy, husband, by your father's soul!
Don't be afraid of dreams. I'll say no more.''

150   ''Madam,'' he said, ''I thank you for your lore,
But with regard to Cato all the same,
His wisdom has, no doubt, a certain fame,
B   But though he said that we should take no heed
Of dreams, by God, in ancient books I read

155   Of many a man of more authority
Than ever Cato was, believe you me,
Who say the very opposite is true
And prove their theories by experience too.
Dreams have quite often been significations

160   As well of triumphs as of tribulations
That people undergo in this our life.
This needs no argument at all, dear wife,
The proof is all too manifest indeed.

C   ''One of the greatest authors one can read

165   Says thus: There were two comrades once who went
On pilgrimage, sincere in their intent.
And as it happened they had reached a town
Where such a throng was milling up and down
And yet so scanty the accommodation,

170   They could not find themselves a habitation,
No, not a cottage that could lodge them both.

And so they separated, very loath,
Under constraint of this necessity
And each went off to find some hostelry,
175   And lodge whatever way his luck might fall.

A
"The first of them found refuge in a stall
Down in a yard with oxen and a plow.
His friend found lodging for himself somehow
Elsewhere, by accident or destiny,
180   Which governs all of us and equally.
"Now it so happened, long ere it was day,
This fellow had a dream, and as he lay
In bed it seemed he heard his comrade call,
'Help! I am lying in an ox's stall
185   And shall tonight be murdered as I lie.
Help me, dear brother, help or I shall die!
Come in all haste!' Such were the words he spoke;
The dreamer, lost in terror, then awoke.
But once awake he paid it no attention,
190   Turned over and dismissed it as invention,
It was a dream, he thought, a fantasy.
And twice he dreamt this dream successively.
"Yet a third time his comrade came again,
Or seemed to come, and said, 'I have been slain
195   Look, look! My wounds are bleeding wide and deep.
Rise early in the morning, break your sleep
And go to the west gate. You there shall see
A cart all loaded up with dung,' said he,
'And in that dung my body has been hidden.
200   Boldly arrest that cart as you are bidden.
It was my money that they killed me for.'

B
"He told him every detail, sighing sore,
And pitiful in feature, pale of hue.
This dream, believe me, Madam, turned out true;
205   For in the dawn, as soon as it was light,
He went to where his friend had spent the night
And when he came upon the cattle stall
He looked about him and began to call.
"The innkeeper, appearing thereupon,
210   Quickly gave answer, 'Sir, your friend has gone.
He left the town a little after dawn.'
The man began to feel suspicious, drawn
By memories of his dream—the western gate,
The dung-cart—off he went, he would not wait,
215   Towards the western entry. There he found,
Seemingly on its way to dung some ground,
A dung-cart loaded on the very plan
Described so closely by the murdered man.
So he began to shout courageously
220   For right and vengeance on the felony,
'My friend's been killed! There's been a foul attack,
He's in that cart and gaping on his back!

A. Connections

? What details in the tale on pages 114–116 are reminiscent of the account of Christ's birth? (No room at the inn, sleeping in a stable, a warning dream like the one had by the Magi)

B. Stories-Within-Stories

? How many storytellers are we listening to now? (Chaucer; the narrator of the whole Canterbury Tales; the Nun's Priest; Chanticleer; the comrade who had the dream)

A. Recalling

? Why did Chanticleer tell that story? (He had had a dream that a beast was trying to kill him.)

B. Taking Notes
You might note that this is the first example in the tale of someone using flattery to get his way. Have students keep track of other points at which this occurs, which character uses flattery on whom, and what the results are.

C. Expansion
In the original, "col-fox" is perhaps another reference to Nicholas Colfax.

Fetch the authorities, get the sheriff down
—Whosever job it is to run the town—
225   Help! My companion's murdered, sent to glory!'
    "What need I add to finish off the story?
People ran out and cast the cart to ground,
And in the middle of the dung they found
The murdered man. The corpse was fresh and new.
230   "O blessed God, that art so just and true,
Thus thou revealest murder! As we say,
'Murder will out.' We see it day by day.
Murder's a foul, abominable treason,
So loathsome to God's justice, to God's reason,
235   He will not suffer its concealment. True,
Things may lie hidden for a year or two,
A   But still 'Murder will out,' that's my conclusion. . . .

*Chanticleer offers several other examples of dreams that have
come true. He produces stories from the lives of the saints, from
the Old Testament, and from Greek mythology.*

    "And now, let's talk of fun and stop all this.
Dear Madam, as I hope for Heaven's bliss.
240   Of one thing God has sent me plenteous grace,
B   For when I see the beauty of your face,
That scarlet loveliness about your eyes,
All thought of terror and confusion dies.
For it's as certain as the Creed, I know,
245   *Mulier est hominis confusio*
(A Latin tag, dear Madam, meaning this:
'Woman is man's delight and all his bliss'°),
For when at night I feel your feathery side,
Although perforce I cannot take a ride
250   Because, alas, our perch was made too narrow,
Delight and solace fill me to the marrow
And I defy all visions and all dreams!''
    And with that word he flew down from the beams,
For it was day, and down his hens flew all,
255   And with a chuck he gave the troupe a call
For he had found a seed upon the floor.
Royal he was, he was afraid no more. . . .
Leave we this Chanticleer engaged on feeding
C   And pass to the adventure that was breeding. . . .
260   A coal-tipped fox of sly <u>iniquity</u>
That had been lurking round the grove for three
Long years, that very night burst through and passed
Stockade and hedge, as Providence forecast,
Into the yard where Chanticleer the Fair
265   Was wont, with all his ladies, to repair.
Still, in a bed of cabbages, he lay
Until about the middle of the day
Watching the cock and waiting for his cue,
As all these homicides so gladly do

247. The quotation really means "Woman is man's confusion." Chanticleer is taking advantage of Pertelote's ignorance of Latin.

270 That lie about in wait to murder men.
O false assassin, lurking in thy den!
O new Iscariot, new Ganelon!°
And O Greek Sinon,° thou whose treachery won
Troy town and brought it utterly to sorrow!
275 O Chanticleer, accursed be that morrow
That brought thee to the yard from thy high beams!
Thou hadst been warned, and truly, by thy dreams
That this would be a perilous day for thee.
     But that which God's foreknowledge can foresee
280 Must needs occur, as certain men of learning
Have said. Ask any scholar of discerning;
He'll say the Schools are filled with altercation
On this vexed matter of predestination . . .
     But I decline discussion of the matter;
285 My tale is of a cock and of the clatter
That came of following his wife's advice
To walk about his yard on the precise
Morning after the dream of which I told.
     O woman's counsel is so often cold!
290 A woman's counsel brought us first to woe,
Made Adam out of Paradise to go
Where he had been so merry, so well at ease.
But, for I know not whom it may displease
If I suggest that women are to blame,
295 Pass over that; I only speak in game.
Read the authorities to know about
What has been said of women; you'll find out.
These are the cock's words, and not mine, I'm giving;
I think no harm of any woman living.
300   Merrily in her dustbath in the sand
Lay Pertelote. Her sisters were at hand
Basking in sunlight. Chanticleer sang free,
More merrily than a mermaid in the sea . . .
And so it happened as he cast his eye
305 Toward the cabbage at a butterfly
It fell upon the fox there, lying low.
Gone was all inclination then to crow.
"Cok cok," he cried, giving a sudden start,
As one who feels a terror at his heart,
310 For natural instinct teaches beasts to flee
The moment they perceive an enemy,
Though they had never met with it before.
     This Chanticleer was shaken to the core
And would have fled. The fox was quick to say
315 However, "Sir! Whither so fast away?
Are you afraid of me, that am your friend?
A fiend, or worse, I should be, to intend
You harm, or practice villainy upon you;
Dear sir, I was not even spying on you!
320 Truly I came to do no other thing
Than just to lie and listen to you sing.

272. **Iscariot:** Judas Iscariot, who betrayed Jesus. **Ganelon:** the man who caused the hero Roland's death in the *Chanson de Roland.*
273. **Sinon:** the Greek whose lies persuaded the Trojans to take the wooden horse (full of enemy soldiers) into their city.

B. Characterization
? The Nun's Priest is not described in "The Prologue." What do you think this passage might reveal about his feelings for women? Note that he, like Chaucer in "The Prologue," denies responsibility for what he is saying: "These are the cock's words, and not mine." (Although he says that he thinks no harm of women, he points out that the Bible blames them for all our problems.)

C. Allegory
Lines 300–303 might remind readers of Eden before the Fall. "The Nun's Priest's Tale" is, in part, an allegory of the Fall: Chanticleer (Adam) listens to Pertelote (Eve) rather than to his better instincts and falls prey to Russel Fox (serpent, Devil).

D. Noting Details
Here is another example of a flatterer. Note how the fox is wily, like the serpent in Paradise.

A. Expansion
Boethius (c. 470–525) wrote the *Consolation of Philosophy*, one of Chaucer's favorite books. It held that the mind is superior to matter and included a long debate on free will and predestination.

B. Connections
The fox has traditionally been represented as a cunning trickster. Chaucer probably knew the medieval French *Roman de Renart* (thirteenth century). One of its tales is about a fox who captures a cock by praising his father's singing, then loses him when the cock persuades him to boast of his victory.

C. Noting Details
Note that flattery again "gets you anywhere," as Russel Fox flatters Chanticleer into his jaws.

D. Mock Heroism
The Nun's Priest continues his mock-heroic tone here with a comparison of Pertelote's grief (remember she is only a chicken) to that of royal and noble heroines of antiquity.

You have as merry a voice as God has given
To any angel in the courts of Heaven;
To that you add a musical sense as strong

A
325   As had Boethius who was skilled in song.
My Lord your Father (God receive his soul!),
Your mother too—how courtly, what control!—
Have honored my poor house, to my great ease;
And you, sir, too, I should be glad to please.
330   For, when it comes to singing, I'll say this
(Else may these eyes of mine be barred from bliss),

B
There never was a singer I would rather
Have heard at dawn than your respected father.
All that he sang came welling from his soul
335   And how he put his voice under control!
The pains he took to keep his eyes tight shut
In concentration—then the tiptoe strut,
The slender neck stretched out, the delicate beak!
No singer could approach him in technique . . .
340   Can you not emulate your sire and sing?''
     This Chanticleer began to beat a wing
As one incapable of smelling treason,
So wholly had this flattery ravished reason. . . .
     This Chanticleer stood high upon his toes,
345   He stretched his neck, his eyes began to close,
His beak to open; with his eyes shut tight
He then began to sing with all his might.

C
     Sir Russel Fox then leapt to the attack,
Grabbing his gorge he flung him o'er his back
350   And off he bore him to the woods, the brute,
And for the moment there was no pursuit.
     O Destiny that may not be evaded!
Alas that Chanticleer had so paraded!
Alas that he had flown down from the beams!
355   O that his wife took no account of dreams!
And on a Friday too to risk their necks!
O Venus, goddess of the joys of sex,
Since Chanticleer thy mysteries professed
And in thy service always did his best,
360   And more for pleasure than to multiply
His kind, on thine own day° is he to die? . . .

D
     Sure never such a cry or lamentation
Was made by ladies of high Trojan station,
When Ilium fell and Pyrrhus with his sword
365   Grabbed Priam by the beard, their king and lord,
And slew him there as the *Aeneid*° tells,
As what was uttered by those hens. Their yells
Surpassed them all in palpitating fear
When they beheld the rape of Chanticleer.
370   Dame Pertelote emitted sovereign shrieks
That echoed up in anguish to the peaks
Louder than those extorted from the wife
Of Hasdrubal,° when he had lost his life

361. **own day:** Friday was named for Frigga, Norse goddess of love, who corresponds to the Roman Venus.

366. *Aeneid:* Roman epic poem recounting the fall of Troy (Ilium) and the murder of King Priam. The Nun's Priest uses allusions to classical literature to create a mock-serious tone.

373. **Hasdrubal:** king of Carthage when Scipio conquered it in 146 B.C.

And Carthage all in flame and ashes lay.
375   She was so full of torment and dismay
That in the very flames she chose her part
And burnt to ashes with a steadfast heart.
O woeful hens, louder your shrieks and higher
Than those of Roman matrons when the fire
380   Consumed their husbands, senators of Rome,
When Nero° burnt their city and their home,
Beyond a doubt that Nero was their bale!
      Now let me turn again to tell my tale;
A   This blessed widow and her daughters two
385   Heard all these hens in clamor and halloo
And, rushing to the door at all this shrieking,
They saw the fox toward the covert° streaking
And, on his shoulder, Chanticleer stretched flat.
"Look, look!" they cried, "O mercy, look at that!
390   Ha! Ha! the fox!" and after him they ran,
And stick in hand ran many a serving man,
B   Ran Coll our dog, ran Talbot, Bran, and Shaggy,
And with a distaff in her hand ran Maggie,
Ran cow and calf and ran the very hogs
395   In terror at the barking of the dogs;

381. **Nero:** Roman emperor so oblivious to his civic duties that he was said to have fiddled while a fire destroyed Rome.

387. **covert:** thicket.

A woman chases a fox, from "The Nun's Priest's Tale." From a Flemish manuscript of *The Book of Hours* (14th century).

British Library, London.

A. Noting Details
Discuss the effect the entrance of the widow and her daughters makes at this point. (The realistic picture of the barnyard and the animals quickly punctures the artificial pomposity of the passage before, a juxtaposition that adds to the mock-heroic effect.)

B. Names
Notice the names that people give farm animals in Chaucer's day. (Are they all dogs?)

C. Humanities Connection: About the Fine Art
Many medieval manuscripts took the form of Books of Hours, which contained illustrations and texts appropriate for the seasons of the year. These books were perpetual calendars that helped people keep track of saints' days and other religious feasts. Perhaps the most famous and beautiful of these is the book made for the French Duc de Berry.

C

READING CHECK TEST
1. Who are the main characters in "The Nun's Priest's Tale"? Chanticleer, Pertelote, and Sir Russel Fox (two chickens and a fox)
2. What does Chanticleer dream? That a beast wanted to kill him
3. What does Pertelote think about the dream? That it was caused by indigestion
4. How does the fox catch Chanticleer? He praises his singing and asks for a song.

CLOSURE
Have one student summarize in a two- or three-sentence statement the moral lesson of this tale. Then have another student state at least one way in which that lesson is applicable today.

A. Noting Details
Make sure that students note the third and final use of flattery in "The Nun's Priest's Tale." As in the French tale of Renart, the cock now persuades the fox to brag about his victory and so escapes from the fox's jaws. (Some critics think this is a veiled reference to the Peasants' Revolt of 1381, and that this may be Chaucer's way of telling the peasants what he thought they should do.)

B. Character
The Nun's Priest speaks again, as he did in lines 289–299, in his role as a spiritual leader. After having told a hilarious tale, filled with references to pagan heroes, he piously wraps up with a Christian moral, invoking St. Paul's name to lend it weight.

The men and women shouted, ran and cursed,
They ran so hard they thought their hearts would burst,
They yelled like fiends in Hell, ducks left the water
Quacking and flapping as on point of slaughter,
400 Up flew the geese in terror over the trees,
Out of the hive came forth the swarm of bees; . . .
    And now, good people, pay attention all.
See how Dame Fortune quickly changes side
And robs her enemy of hope of pride!
405 This cock that lay upon the fox's back
In all his dread contrived to give a quack

A
410
And said, "Sir Fox, if I were you, as God's
My witness, I would round upon these clods
And shout, 'Turn back, you saucy bumpkins all!
A very pestilence upon you fall!
Now that I have in safety reached the wood
Do what you like, the cock is mine for good;
I'll eat him there in spite of every one.' "
    The fox replying, "Faith, it shall be done!"
415 Opened his mouth and spoke. The nimble bird,
Breaking away upon the uttered word,
Flew high into the treetops on the spot.
And when the fox perceived where he had got,
"Alas," he cried, "alas, my Chanticleer,
420 I've done you grievous wrong, indeed I fear
I must have frightened you; I grabbed too hard
When I caught hold and took you from the yard.
But, sir, I meant no harm, don't be offended,
Come down and I'll explain what I intended;
425 So help me God I'll tell the truth—on oath!"
"No," said the cock, "and curses on us both,
And first on me if I were such a dunce
As let you fool me oftener than once.
Never again, for all your flattering lies,
430 You'll coax a song to make me blink my eyes;
And as for those who blink when they should look,
God blot them from his everlasting Book!"
"Nay, rather," said the fox, "his plagues be flung
On all who chatter that should hold their tongue."
435   Lo, such it is not to be on your guard
Against the flatterers of the world, or yard,
And if you think my story is absurd,
A foolish trifle of a beast and bird,
A fable of a fox, a cock, a hen,
440 Take hold upon the moral, gentlemen.

B
445
    St. Paul himself, a saint of great discerning
Says that all things are written for our learning;
So take the grain and let the chaff be still.
And, gracious Father, if it be thy will
As saith my Savior, make us all good men,
And bring us to his heavenly bliss.
                                Amen

1. The three main characters are Chanticleer (the cock), Pertelote (the hen), and Russel Fox.

The conflict is that the fox wants to eat the chicken.

2. In Chanticleer's dream, a red and yellow beast tries to kill him.

Pertelote tells Chanticleer that he is a coward and that dreams are often caused by vapors in the belly. She will treat his conditions with various laxatives, including worms!

3. Chanticleer gives examples of dreams having import from classical mythology and from the Bible. He also tells a lengthy tale of two comrades on a pilgrimage, one of whom dreamed his friend was murdered (and he was).

4. Chanticleer persuades the fox to brag about his feat. When the fox opens his mouth, Chanticleer flies away.

Interpeting Meanings

5. Chanticleer: superstition, timidity, susceptibility to flattery, and pride.

Pertelote: practicality, level-headedness, bossiness.

6. We don't expect noble characters and themes of classical mythology to apply to chickens.

7. The Host describes the (celibate) priest as strong and good-looking enough to take care of more than seven wives.

In general, the story is wonderfully comical and satirical, and shows a wry understanding of human nature, a good deal of classical learning, and firsthand knowledge of the barnyard.

8. Lines 431–436 could stand as the moral. Or, we might say that pride and susceptibility to flattery can lead to disaster.

In general, students will probably agree that the story is not that serious but is told primarily for entertainment.

Words of the Host to the Nun's Priest

"Sir Priest," our Host remarked in merry tones,
"Blest be your breeches and your precious stones,
That was a merry tale of Chanticleer!
450   If you had only been a secular
You would have trodden a pretty fowl, no doubt,
Had you the heart, your muscles would hold out.
You look as if you needed hens, I mean,
Yes, more than seven. Seven times seventeen!
455   Just look what brawn he has, this gentle priest,
And what a neck! His chest's not of the least.
As for his eyes, they're like a sparrow hawk's,
And his complexion like a box of chalks;
He needs no dyes imported from the East
460   Or Portugal. Good luck to you, Sir Priest,
For telling a fine tale!" And saying thus
He turned, as you shall hear, to one of us.

Responding to the Tale

Analyzing the Tale

Identifying Details

1. Describe the three main **characters** in the tale. What is their problem, or **conflict**?

2. Describe Chanticleer's dream. How does the practical Pertelote respond to it?

3. What examples does Chanticleer give to support his view of dreams?

4. What trick does Chanticleer use to escape his captor?

Interpreting Meanings

5. What human characteristics are reflected in the portrait of Chanticleer? In the portrait of Lady Pertelote? How did you respond to these characterizations?

6. The Nun's Priest fills his tale with **allusions** to classical literature. Given the characters in his story, why are these classical allusions **ironic**?

7. How do the Host's comments reflect ironically on the teller of this tale? What do you think the tale reveals about the character of the Nun's Priest?

8. How would you state the **moral** in the tale of Chanticleer? Is the story serious, or is it told to poke fun at "the battle of the sexes"? Explain.

Writing About the Tale

A Creative Response

Continuing the Frame Story. Now that you have your characters for a frame story, begin to write two or three of their tales. Each character should tell one tale appropriate to his or her personality. Many of Chaucer's tales, like "The Nun's Priest's Tale," were translations or retellings of old stories. You may wish to have your characters retell old stories, too, perhaps legends or fables you have heard. Or you may want to give old stories new twists. Keep each tale short, and keep the tone of each tale consistent.

1. Building On Prior Knowledge. Review with the class what they know of the Pardoner from "The Prologue." (He is an unpleasant-looking man, rather effeminate, who buys and sells pardons and specializes in fake relics.)

2. Establishing A Purpose. As the headnote suggests, students should read to determine why Chaucer chose the Pardoner to tell this tale. The illustration on text page 123 might impel students to discover what happens to the three "rioters."

SUPPLEMENTARY SUPPORT MATERIALS
1. Vocabulary Activity Worksheet (*CCB*)
2. Review and Response Worksheet: Dramatic Irony (*CCB*)
3. Language Skills Worksheet: Revision Worksheet 1 (*CCB*)
4. Selection Test (*CCB*)
5. Audiocassette recording

A. Irony
Ask students to look for evidence of irony in the Pardoner's prologue to his tale. (The Pardoner indicates that he is aware of the irony in the fact that he preaches against the very vice he makes his living from. It is also ironic that, however guilty of avarice he is, he *can* bring others to repent of the same sin. Chaucer adds further to the irony by making this preacher drunk—perhaps the only time when he is capable of acknowledging his true character.)

B. Vocabulary
Avarice and *cupidity* are both from Latin. *Cupiditas* is Latin for "a strong desire, especially for money." Interestingly, it is related to the name of the god *Cupid* (*Cupido*), meaning "desire or passion," and is from an Indo-European base word meaning "to boil, smoke, or be disturbed." *Avarice*, from the Latin word *avere*, "to desire," means specifically "too great a desire for wealth."

As with the animal fable of the fox and the crow, the story in "The Pardoner's Tale" has roots that are old and widespread. Avarice (or greed) as the root of evil is a theme that appears in stories of many lands. Remember how Chaucer portrayed the Pardoner in the General Prologue. Then, as you read this tale, think about why Chaucer chose the Pardoner to tell it.

from The Pardoner's Tale

The Prologue

A
    "But let me briefly make my purpose plain;
I preach for nothing but for greed of gain
And use the same old text, as bold as brass,
Radix malorum est cupiditas.°
5 And thus I preach against the very vice
I make my living out of—avarice.

B
And yet however guilty of that sin
Myself, with others I have power to win
Them from it, I can bring them to repent;
10 But that is not my principal intent.
Covetousness is both the root and stuff
Of all I preach. That ought to be enough.
    "Well, then I give examples thick and fast
From bygone times, old stories from the past
15 A yokel mind loves stories from of old,
Being the kind it can repeat and hold.
What! Do you think, as long as I can preach
And get their silver for the things I teach,
That I will live in poverty, from choice?
20 That's not the counsel of my inner voice!
No! Let me preach and beg from kirk to kirk°
And never do an honest job of work,
No, nor make baskets, like St. Paul, to gain
A livelihood. I do not preach in vain.
25 Why copy the apostles? Why pretend?
I must have wool, cheese, wheat, and cash to spend,
Though it were given me by the poorest lad
Or poorest village widow, though she had
A string of starving children, all agape.
30 No, let me drink the liquor of the grape
And keep a jolly wench in every town!
    "But listen, gentlemen; to bring things down
To a conclusion, would you like a tale?
Now as I've drunk a draft of corn-ripe ale,
35 By God it stands to reason I can strike
On some good story that you all will like.
For though I am a wholly vicious man
Don't think I can't tell moral tales. I can!
Here's one I often preach when out for winning;
40 Now please be quiet. Here is the beginning."

4. *Radix . . . cupiditas:* "The love of money is the root of all evil" (1 Timothy 6:10).

21. kirk: church.

[Handwritten annotations:]
Pardoner acknowledges his own vice Preaches against what he himself does

has power to get others to repent

person living in rural area

conscience

Admits too corruption

Pardoner is drunk shows true self

DEVELOPING VOCABULARY
The following words from the tale are
tested in the Selection Test. (See also
Vocabulary Activity Worksheet.)

avarice	pallor
yokel	to prate
ribaldry	to tarry
adversary	absolution
wretched	pique

The three rioters living.
The three dead. From the psalter
of Bonne of Luxembourg
(late 13th C.).

The Metropolitan Museum of Art. The
Cloisters Collection, New York, 1969.
(69.86).

Description of youngsters

A. Humanities Connection: About the Fine Art
Medieval art often shows people faced with their own bodily corruption and skeletons as a reminder of their mortality.

B. Irony
Point out to students the fact that this gruesome moral tale is told by the drunken and corrupt Pardoner, which adds to its irony. ("The Pardoner's Tale" may have been set in Flanders because the Flemish, against whom the English had a strong bias in the fourteenth century, were notorious for their drinking and their greed.)

C. Vocabulary
A *knave* was a male servant. Later the word came to mean "rascal."

The Tale

In Flanders once there was a company
Of youngsters haunting vice and ribaldry,   *coarse king-of humor*
Riot and gambling, stews and public houses
Where each with harp, guitar, or lute carouses,
45   Dancing and dicing day and night, and bold
B   To eat and drink far more than they can hold,
Doing thereby the devil sacrifice
Within that devil's temple of cursed vice,
Abominable in superfluity,   *excess*
50   With oaths so damnable in blasphemy
That it's a grisly thing to hear them swear.
Our dear Lord's body they will rend and tear . . .

It's of three rioters I have to tell
Who long before the morning service bell
55   Were sitting in a tavern for a drink.
And as they sat, they heard the handbell clink
Before a coffin going to the grave;
C   One of them called the little tavern knave
And said "Go and find out at once—look spry!—

1st rioter

A. Connections

"The Pardoner's Tale" is set in the time of the Black Death. The theme of luxurious self-indulgence or riotous living in the face of death is also seen in Boccaccio's *Decameron* (1351–1353). Edgar Allan Poe (1809–1849) returns to this theme with a vengeance in his short story "The Masque of the Red Death."

B. Personification/Allegory

Be certain that students understand that death here is personified—treated as if it existed in the form of a real person. This device is seldom used today, but is essential to allegories (stories that use symbolic characters to express some truth about life).

C. Vocabulary

"God's arms" is a mild oath. Many medieval oaths invoked the parts of Christ's body. See line 52 on the previous page.

D. Irony

Note the amusing irony here.

E. Vocabulary

A *stile* is a step that allows people to cross over a wall.

60 Whose corpse is in that coffin passing by;
    And see you get the name correctly too."
    "Sir," said the boy, "no need, I promise you;
    Two hours before you came here I was told.
    He was a friend of yours in days of old,
65 And suddenly, last night, the man was slain,
    Upon his bench, face up, dead drunk again.
    There came a privy thief, they call him Death,
    Who kills us all round here, and in a breath
    He speared him through the heart, he never stirred.
70 And then Death went his way without a word.
    He's killed a thousand in the present plague,
    And, sir, it doesn't do to be too vague
    If you should meet him; you had best be wary.
    Be on your guard with such an adversary,
75 Be primed to meet him everywhere you go,
    That's what my mother said. It's all I know."
        The publican° joined in with, "By St. Mary,
    What the child says is right; you'd best be wary,
    This very year he killed, in a large village
80 A mile away, man, woman, serf at tillage,
    Page in the household, children—all there were.
    Yes, I imagine that he lives round there.
    It's well to be prepared in these alarms,
    He might do you dishonor." "Huh, God's arms!"
85 The rioter said, "Is he so fierce to meet?
    I'll search for him, by Jesus, street by street.
    God's blessed bones! I'll register a vow!
    Here, chaps! The three of us together now,
    Hold up your hands, like me, and we'll be brothers
90 In this affair, and each defend the others,
    And we will kill this traitor Death, I say!
    Away with him as he has made away
    With all our friends. God's dignity! Tonight!"
        They made their bargain, swore with appetite,
95 These three, to live and die for one another
    As brother-born might swear to his born brother.
    And up they started in their drunken rage
    And made toward this village which the page
    And publican had spoken of before.
100 Many and grisly were the oaths they swore,
    Tearing Christ's blessed body to a shred;°
    "If we can only catch him, Death is dead!"
        When they had gone not fully half a mile,
    Just as they were about to cross a stile,
105 They came upon a very poor old man
    Who humbly greeted them and thus began,
    "God look to you, my lords, and give you quiet!"
    To which the proudest of these men of riot
    Gave back the answer, "What, old fool? Give place!
110 Why are you all wrapped up except your face?
    Why live so long? Isn't it time to die?"

77. **publican:** tavern keeper (from "public house," a term for a bar or tavern still used in the British Isles).

101. Their oaths refer to "God's arms" and "God's blessed bones."

Irony – Men are killed by each other
They are going to kill Death
We know the rioters are going to kill each other even though
they don't
They actually do find Death

Irony – Old man wants to find death

The old, old fellow looked him in the eye
And said, "Because I never yet have found,
Though I have walked to India, searching round
115 Village and city on my pilgrimage,
One who would change his youth to have my age.
And so my age is mine and must be still
Upon me, for such time as God may will.

"Not even Death, alas, will take my life;
120 So, like a wretched prisoner at strife
Within himself, I walk alone and wait
About the earth, which is my mother's gate,
Knock-knocking with my staff from night to noon
And crying, 'Mother, open to me soon!
125 Look at me, mother, won't you let me in?
A See how I wither, flesh and blood and skin!
Alas! When will these bones be laid to rest?
Mother, I would exchange—for that were best—
The wardrobe in my chamber, standing there
130 So long, for yours! Aye, for a shirt of hair°
To wrap me in!' She has refused her grace,
Whence comes the pallor of my withered face.

"But it dishonored you when you began
To speak so roughly, sir, to an old man,
135 Unless he had injured you in word or deed.
It says in holy writ, as you may read,
'Thou shalt rise up before the hoary° head
And honor it.' And therefore be it said
'Do no more harm to an old man than you,
140 Being now young, would have another do
When you are old'—if you should live till then.
And so may God be with you, gentlemen,
For I must go whither I have to go."

"By God," the gambler said, "you shan't do so,
145 You don't get off so easy, by St. John!
I heard you mention, just a moment gone,
A certain traitor Death who singles out
And kills the fine young fellows hereabout.
And you're his spy, by God! You wait a bit.
150 Say where he is or you shall pay for it,
By God and by the Holy Sacrament!
I say you've joined together by consent
To kill us younger folk, you thieving swine!"

"Well, sirs," he said, "if it be your design
155 To find out Death, turn up this crooked way
B Toward that grove, I left him there today
Under a tree, and there you'll find him waiting.
He isn't one to hide for all your prating.
You see that oak? He won't be far to find.
160 And God protect you that redeemed mankind,
Aye, and amend you!" Thus that ancient man.

At once the three young rioters began
To run, and reached the tree, and there they found

Old Man
Symbol of wisdom
wants to impart wisdom to
young men, but they will not
take it.

Death will not take him

wanders the earth requesting to die

Young men are so blinded
by ease + self-indulgence
that they have no appreciation
of life + lose it

Death
house (earth)
surrounded by
a gate

130. shirt of hair: shirts woven with coarse horse's hairs were worn as penance. Here, the old man refers to one of these shirts used to wrap his body for burial.

Rebukes, scolds rioters for behavior

You should honor your elders

137. hoary: white.

foreshadowing

Accuses him of being Death's spy

Symbol – Death, Old Age
directs them to Death

Wisdom, Virtue – warns young
men, yet they do
not listen

A. Irony and Personification
Note the irony here. The old man is weary of life and would like to be rid of it, to find the ease of death. In contrast, the young men are so blinded by ease and self-indulgence that they have no appreciation of life and lose it to death.

Note that Death is personified as a mother whose house is surrounded by a gate (the earth).

B. The Old Man
The old man has caused much disagreement among critics. A number, George Lyman Kitteredge and Raymond Preston among them, believe the old man is himself Death. At the opposite extreme, W. J. B. Owen says the old man "is an old man and nothing more," giving as proof the fact that he is looking for Death himself. Ask students to consider the old man carefully and to draw their own conclusions as to what he might symbolize.

A. Vocabulary
A *florin* was a gold coin of Florence issued in 1252.

B. The Seven Deadly Sins
Avarice (or covetousness), to which the Pardoner has already admitted and to which the three young men succumb here, is one of the seven deadly sins: pride, avarice, lust, anger, gluttony, envy, and sloth. The commission of any of these sins would bring spiritual death to the sinner's soul and put him or her in danger of eternal damnation, unless the sinner confessed the sin and obtained a pardon (the very business the Pardoner is in). Thus, in succumbing to avarice, the young men have fallen into the Devil's hands.

C. Irony
Later you'll want to remind students that the young men believe it is *Fortune* who has left the money and not Death, whom they have forgotten in their greed.

A
165 A pile of golden florins on the ground,
      New-coined, eight bushels of them as they thought.
      No longer was it Death those fellows sought,
      For they were all so thrilled to see the sight,
B   The florins were so beautiful and bright,
170 That down they sat beside the precious pile.
      The wickedest spoke first after a while.
      "Brothers," he said, "you listen to what I say.
      I'm pretty sharp although I joke away.
C   It's clear that Fortune has bestowed this treasure
      To let us live in jollity and pleasure.
175 Light come, light go! We'll spend it as we ought.
      God's precious dignity! Who would have thought
      This morning was to be our lucky day?
          "If one could only get the gold away,
      Back to my house, or else to yours, perhaps—
180 For as you know, the gold is ours, chaps—
      We'd all be at the top of fortune, hey?
      But certainly it can't be done by day.
      People would call us robbers—a strong gang,
      So our own property would make us hang.
185 No, we must bring this treasure back by night
      Some prudent way, and keep it out of sight.
      And so as a solution I propose
      We draw for lots and see the way it goes,
      The one who draws the longest, lucky man,
190 Shall run to town as quickly as he can
      To fetch us bread and wine—but keep things dark—
      While two remain in hiding here to mark
      Our heap of treasure. If there's no delay,
      When night comes down we'll carry it away,
195 All three of us, wherever we have planned."
          He gathered lots and hid them in his hand
      Bidding them draw for where the luck should fall.
      It fell upon the youngest of them all,
      And off he ran at once toward the town.
200   As soon as he had gone the first sat down
      And thus began a parley with the other:
      "You know that you can trust me as a brother;
      Now let me tell you where your profit lies;
      You know our friend had gone to get supplies
205 And here's a lot of gold that is to be
      Divided equally amongst us three.
      Nevertheless, if I could shape things thus
      So that we shared it out—the two of us—
      Wouldn't you take it as a friendly turn?"
210   "But how?" the other said with some concern,
      "Because he knows the gold's with me and you;
      What can we tell him? What are we to do?"
          "Is it a bargain," said the first, "or no?
      For I can tell you in a word or so
215 What's to be done to bring the thing about."

[Handwritten margin notes: gold coins; Interest turned to gold; Irony – They believe Fortune left money not Death; Plan; Proposes only splitting wealth 2 ways; acting too much; laziness]

126   126 The Middle Ages

A "Trust me," the other said, "you needn't doubt
My word. I won't betray you, I'll be true."
   "Well," said his friend, "you see that we are two,
And two are twice as powerful as one.
220 Now look; when he comes back, get up in fun
To have a wrestle; then, as you attack,
I'll up and put my dagger through his back
While you and he are struggling, as in game;
Then draw your dagger too and do the same.
225 Then all this money will be ours to spend,
Divided equally of course, dear friend.
Then we can gratify our lusts and fill
The day with dicing at our own sweet will."
Thus these two miscreants° agreed to slay
230 The third and youngest, as you heard me say.
   The youngest, as he ran toward the town,
Kept turning over, rolling up and down
Within his heart the beauty of those bright
New florins, saying, "Lord, to think I might
235 Have all that treasure to myself alone!
Could there be anyone beneath the throne
Of God so happy as I then should be?"
   And so the Fiend, our common enemy,
Was given power to put it in his thought
240 That there was always poison to be bought,
And that with poison he could kill his friends.
B To men in such a state the Devil sends
Thoughts of this kind, and has a full permission
To lure them on to sorrow and perdition;°
245 For this young man was utterly content
To kill them both and never to repent.
   And on he ran, he had no thought to tarry,
Came to the town, found an apothecary
And said, "Sell me some poison if you will,
250 I have a lot of rats I want to kill
C And there's a polecat too about my yard
That takes my chickens and it hits me hard;
But I'll get even, as is only right,
With vermin that destroy a man by night."
255 The chemist answered, "I've a preparation
Which you shall have, and by my soul's salvation
If any living creature eat or drink
A mouthful, ere he has the time to think,
Though he took less than makes a grain of wheat,
260 You'll see him fall down dying at your feet;
Yes, die he must, and in so short a while
You'd hardly have the time to walk a mile,
The poison is so strong, you understand."
   This cursed fellow grabbed into his hand
265 The box of poison and away he ran
Into a neighboring street, and found a man
Who lent him three large bottles. He withdrew

229. **miscreants:** criminals (literally, "unbelievers").

244. **perdition:** damnation.

A. Irony
In the context of "The Pardoner's Tale," a more ironic phrase than this could hardly have been uttered by the young man.

B. Medieval Theology
Here the Pardoner is describing the consequences of sin. The young man has already fallen from a state of grace into a state of sin because of his drunkenness. As a result, God allows the Devil to lure him (and his fellows) further. According to this theology, God does not cause evil but allows human beings to be tempted by it.

C. Irony
What is ironic about the reason the young man gives for buying the poison? (He wants it for "vermin that destroy a man by night." Ironically, the "vermin" he intends to kill will indeed die, but not before destroying the young man himself.)

The bell carried by
Death is like the
bell plague victims
and lepers—both
carriers of death in
medieval eyes—
were supposed to
carry to warn oth-
ers of their ap-
proach.

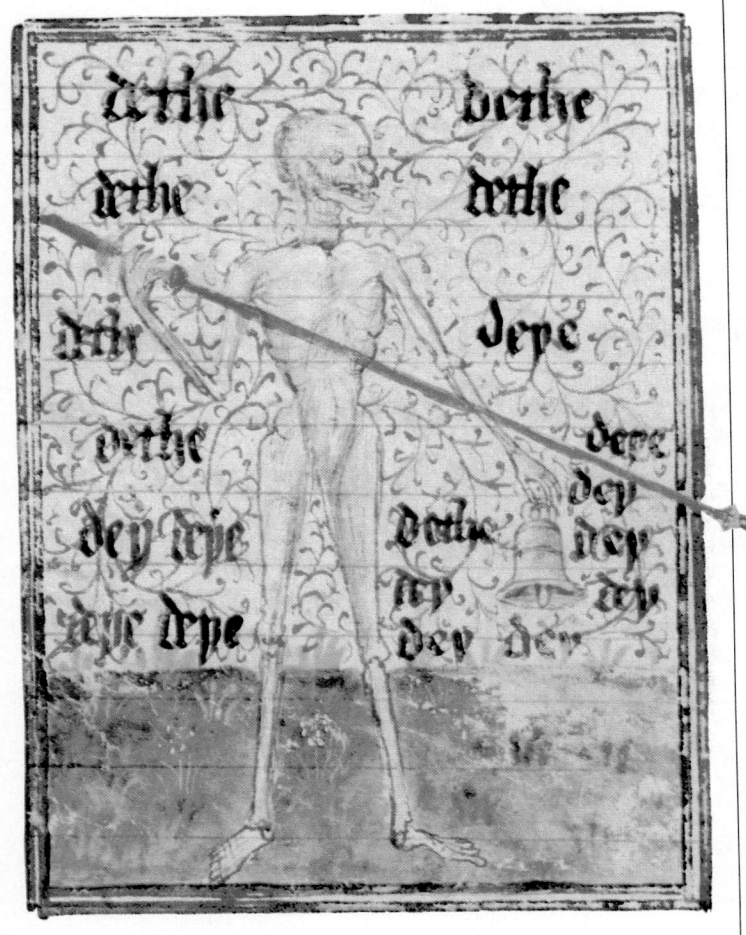

Death with his spear, from
"The Pardoner's Tale."

Bodleian Library, Oxford.

And deftly poured the poison into two.
He kept the third one clean, as well he might,
270   For his own drink, meaning to work all night
Stacking the gold and carrying it away.
And when this rioter, this devil's clay,
Had filled his bottles up with wine, all three,
Back to rejoin his comrades sauntered he.
275   Why make a sermon of it? Why waste breath?
Exactly in the way they'd planned his death
They fell on him and slew him, two to one.
Then said the first of them when this was done,
"Now for a drink. Sit down and let's be merry,
280   For later on there'll be the corpse to bury."
And, as it happened, reaching for a sup,
He took a bottle full of poison up

Kill young man (handwritten marginal note)

READING CHECK TEST

1. What is the Pardoner's text? Radix malorum est cupiditas
2. What vice does the Pardoner always preach against? Avarice
3. How does the Pardoner make his living? By avarice—by selling pardons and fake relics

4. Whom are the three rioters looking for? Death
5. How do they find what they are looking for? They kill one another in their efforts to get more gold.

CLOSURE
Have one student tell the class how this tale illustrates the moral Radix malorum est cupiditas. Then have another student explain how the Pardoner himself embodies the vice of "cupiditas."

And drank; and his companion, nothing loth,
Drank from it also, and they perished both.
285   There is, in Avicenna's° long relation
Concerning poison and its operation,
Trust me, no ghastlier section to transcend
What these two wretches suffered at their end.
Thus these two murderers received their due,
290   So did the treacherous young poisoner too.

     . . . One thing I should have mentioned in my tale,
Dear people. I've some relics in my bale
And pardons too, as full and fine, I hope,
As any in England, given me by the Pope.
295   If there be one among you that is willing
A To have my absolution for a shilling
Devoutly given, come! and do not harden
Your hearts but kneel in humbleness for pardon;
Or else, receive my pardon as we go.
300   You can renew it every town or so
Always provided that you still renew
Each time, and in good money, what is due.
It is an honor to you to have found
A pardoner with his credentials sound
305   Who can absolve you as you ply the spur
In any accident that may occur.
For instance—we are all at Fortune's beck—
Your horse may throw you down and break your neck.
What a security it is to all
310   To have me here among you and at call
With pardon for the lowly and the great
When soul leaves body for the future state!
And I advise our Host here to begin,
The most enveloped of you all in sin.
315   Come forward, Host, you shall be first to pay,
And kiss my holy relics right away.
Only a groat.° Come on, unbuckle your purse!"
    "No, no," said he, "not I, and may the curse
Of Christ descend upon me if I do! . . ."
320   The Pardoner said nothing, not a word;

He was so angry that he couldn't speak.
"Well," said our Host, "If you're for showing pique,
I'll joke no more, not with an angry man."
    The worthy Knight immediately began,
325   Seeing the fun was getting rather rough,
B And said, "No more, we've all had quite enough.
Now, Master Pardoner, perk up, look cheerly!
And you, Sir Host, whom I esteem so dearly,
I beg of you to kiss the Pardoner.
330   "Come, Pardoner, draw nearer, my dear sir.
Let's laugh again and keep the ball in play."
They kissed, and we continued on our way.

285. Avicenna: famous Arabic doctor, and author of a medical book with a chapter on poisons.

317. groat: silver coin worth four pence.

[Handwritten margin notes: "Irony" — "Both die from poison" — "Irony / Selling Pardons after telling Tale" — "Pardoner attempts to sell pardons to the pilgrims" — "What luck it is for you to have me here to sell you absolution" — "accuses the Host of being most sinful" — "Host angry" — "Knight intervenes stops fight"]

A. Irony
In an almost incredible turn, the Pardoner, who has admitted to using this tale to hoodwink ignorant peasants into buying pardons from him, suddenly attempts to sell pardons to the pilgrims themselves. Compounding his bad judgment, he tries to sell one to the Host (lines 313–317) by accusing him of being the greatest sinner of all. At the same time, he makes a sly reference to the traditional avarice of innkeepers by offering to sell a pardon for "only a groat"—hardly the way to make a sale. Nor is it surprising that the Host responds with wrath. Perhaps, for all his boasts, the Pardoner is not so successful as he pretends.

B. The Knight
The Knight appears here in a role that he takes frequently in The Canterbury Tales—as a superior who intervenes among his inferiors to invoke order.

A. Sir Gawain

Gawain (gä′win is the preferred pronunciation) was the eldest of four sons of King Lot of Orkney and Arthur's sister Morgawse. In the earliest versions of Arthurian legends, Gawain is foremost of Arthur's knights, the epitome of purity, courage, and courtesy. In late versions, notably Malory's, Gawain's character becomes harsher and more ruthless, and he is often a philanderer. He becomes the sworn enemy of Lancelot after Lancelot kills Gawain's brothers, and he dies in combat with Lancelot.

B. *Pearl*

Pearl is a lament for the poet's daughter, who died before she was two. In one part of the poem, the poet falls asleep in the garden where she is buried and dreams of his daughter grown into a beautiful young woman dressed in a white gown trimmed with pearls. She tells her father not to grieve for her because she has achieved a blessed state.

Sir Gawain and the Green Knight

A

One of the greatest works of medieval literature is the verse romance called *Sir Gawain and the Green Knight,* probably composed about 1370. The unknown author of this work, who wrote in a northwestern dialect of Middle English and in a consciously old-fashioned, or archaic, style, is known simply as the Gawain poet or the Pearl poet, because he is thought by many

B

to have also written *Pearl, Patience,* and *Purity,* three poems contained in the same manuscript with *Sir Gawain.* Whoever this poet was, he succeeded in transforming popular romance into great art.

Romances (see page 147) are narratives set in a world where the ordinary laws of nature are suspended, and where idealized heroes fight the forces of evil. The basic narrative pattern of the romance is the **quest,** in which a hero undertakes a perilous journey in search of something of great value.

Romances are often too incredible for modern readers, too lacking in the realistic details of life we have come to expect of literature. Yet in *Sir Gawain and the Green Knight,* we feel the gripping reality of sexual temptation and of life in the medieval castle. This poem is a controlled, unified narrative of great power that speaks to us still.

In *Gawain* we have the model of the chivalric hero whose character is being tested. On trial are the virtues of courage, fidelity, and sexual morality. This is a serious romance, not a frivolous one, whose purpose is clearly to teach a moral lesson. Yet the hero does not have unlimited powers. Gawain is a human being who, like all of us, is limited in his moral and physical strength.

This powerful and precise translation is by the American writer John Gardner (see page 38).

The Round Table at Winchester Castle (possibly 13th century). The table was probably painted like this during the reign of Henry VII: The Tudor rose and the Tudor colors of green and white are reminders that the royal family claimed descendancy from King Arthur. Malory believed Winchester was the site of Camelot.

ESTABLISHING A PURPOSE. The headnote sets a purpose for reading. You might tell advanced students that one interpretation of *Sir Gawain and the Green Knight* is that it is based in part on an ancient fertility myth. The Green Knight is said to represent fertility, and Sir Gawain (whose name means "bright-haired" in Welsh) represents the Welsh sun god Gwalch-mei, who travels through a wintry wasteland to restore fertility to the land.

SUPPLEMENTARY SUPPORT MATERIALS
1. Vocabulary Activity Worksheet (*CCB*)
2. Review and Response Worksheet: The Romance (*CCB*)
3. Selection Test (*CCB*)

DEVELOPING VOCABULARY
The following words from the romance are tested in the Selection Test. (See also Vocabulary Activity Worksheet.)

asunder	efficacious
retainer	staunch
baleful	reproof
to requite	to feint
churl	covetousness

Sir Gawain and the Green Knight was written toward the end of the Middle Ages, when the ideals of knightly conduct—courage, loyalty, and courtesy—were just beginning to erode. As you read the poem, look for clues to the author's attitude toward those ideals. Does he respect them? Ridicule them? See them as desirable but unattainable?

As *Sir Gawain and the Green Knight* opens, King Arthur and the Knights of the Round Table are feasting. Suddenly an enormous green stranger bursts in. King Arthur greets the Green Knight and asks him to state his business. The knight, after a few scornful words about the manliness of the knights of Arthur's court, says he only wishes to play a New Year's game. He challenges any knight there to agree to "exchange one blow for another" and he will give that knight his gisarme, his two-bladed ax. The stranger says he will stand for the first blow; the knight must agree to let the Green Knight have *his* turn in a year and a day. Gawain accepts the challenge—no other knight except Arthur himself has dared to.

A

Sir Gawain and the Green Knight

Part One

On the ground, the Green Knight got himself into
    position,
B His head bent forward a little, the bare flesh showing,
His long and lovely locks laid over his crown
So that any man there might note the naked neck.
5 Sir Gawain laid hold of the ax and he hefted it high,
His pivot foot thrown forward before him on the floor,
And then, swiftly, he slashed at the naked neck;
The sharp of the battleblade shattered asunder the bones
And sank through the shining fat and slit it in two,
10 And the bit of the bright steel buried itself in the ground.
The fair head fell from the neck to the floor of the hall
And the people all kicked it away as it came near their
    feet.
The blood splashed up from the body and glistened on
    the green,
But he never faltered or fell for all of that,
15 But swiftly he started forth upon stout shanks
And rushed to reach out, where the King's retainers
    stood,
Caught hold of the lovely head, and lifted it up,
And leaped to his steed and snatched up the reins of
    the bridle,
Stepped into stirrups of steel and, striding aloft,
20 He held his head by the hair, high, in his hand;
And the stranger sat there as steadily in his saddle
As a man entirely unharmed, although he was headless
    on his steed.
    He turned his trunk about,
    That baleful body that bled,
25   And many were faint with fright
    When all his say was said.

Comment from a Critic

In *The Monsters and the Critics and Other Essays,* J. R. R. Tolkien writes: "Behind our poem stalk the figures of elder myth, and through the lines are heard the echoes of ancient cults, beliefs, and symbols remote from the consciousness of an educated moralist (but also a poet) of the late fourteenth century. His story is not *about* those old things, but it receives part of its life, its vividness, its tension from them. That is the way with the greater fairy-stories—of which this is one."

A. Character
? What does Gawain's acceptance of the Green Knight's challenge tell us about his character? (He demonstrates humility, loyalty, and self-sacrifice.)

B. Alliteration
Be sure to have parts of the poem read aloud so students can enjoy the alliteration, which is sometimes exaggerated. See especially lines 23–26; see also text page 146.

This illustration is
from the original
manuscript of the
Pearl Poet's four
poems, all of which
are illustrated with
similar, rather primi-
tive drawings.

A

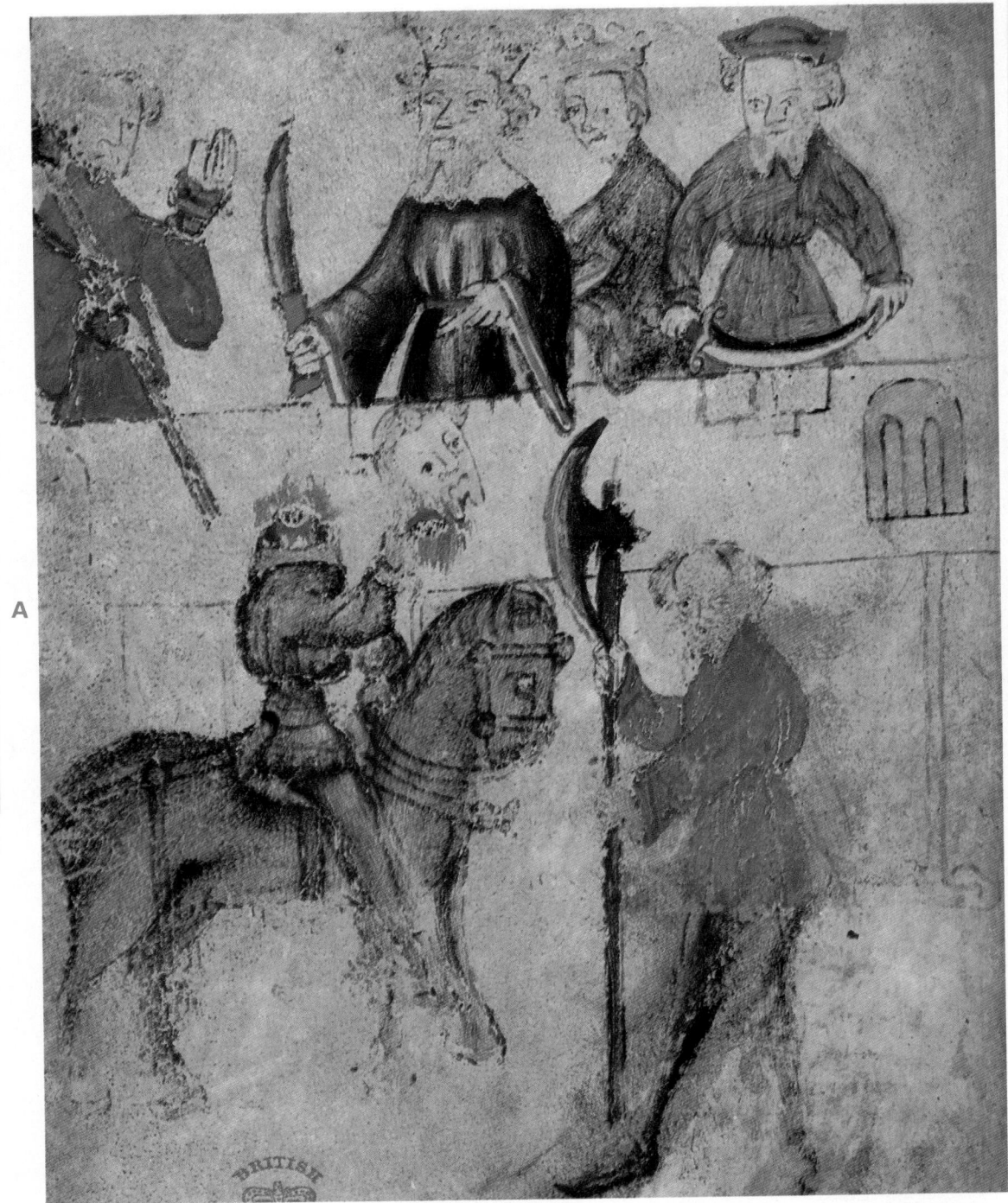

Sir Gawain strikes off the head of the Green Knight in King Arthur's
presence. From an English manuscript (c. 1390–1400).

The British Museum.

One of the characteristics of romances is that they often contain supernatural or magical events. Students may wonder why an ordinary mortal like Gawain would accept a challenge from the clearly superhuman Green Knight. The complete manuscript indicates that, although Gawain and Arthur's court might have harbored some suspicions because of the knight's extraordinary size and color, in fact, they took his challenge at face value as a foolhardy but not especially unusual engagement between two gentlemen. When the Green Knight's magic is evident, it becomes crucial for Gawain to obtain some magic himself if he is to survive—a major factor in the moral turning point of the tale.

He held his head in his hand up high before him,   **A**
Addressing the face to the dearest of all on the dais;
And the eyelids lifted wide, and the eyes looked out,
And the mouth said just this much, as you may now
30   hear:
"Look that you go, Sir Gawain, as good as your word,
And seek till you find me, as loyally, my friend,
As you've sworn in this hall to do, in the hearing of the
      knights.
Come to the Green Chapel, I charge you, and take
35 A stroke the same as you've given, for well you deserve
To be readily requited on New Year's morn.
Many men know me, the Knight of the Green Chapel;
Therefore if you seek to find me, you shall not fail.
Come or be counted a coward, as is fitting."
40 Then with a rough jerk he turned the reins
And haled away through the hall door, his head in his
      hand,
And fire of the flint flew out from the hooves of the foal.
To what kingdom he was carried no man there knew,
No more than they knew what country it was he came
      from. What then?
45   The King and Gawain there
      Laugh at the thing and grin;
      And yet, it was an affair
      Most marvelous to men.

The next year, just before Christmas, Gawain sets off to honor   **B**
his pledge. Through moors and forests and mountains he rides,
searching for the Green Knight. One day he comes upon the
most beautiful castle he has ever seen. The lord of the castle
welcomes him and promises to help him find the Green Knight.
But he urges Gawain first to rest a few days in the castle with
him and his lady.

Gawain's host then proposes an unusual "game." He will go
hunting each day. Whatever he wins in the hunt, he will give to
Gawain when he returns. In turn, Gawain must promise to give
the lord whatever he has won that day.

Twice the lord goes hunting, and each time the lord leaves the
castle, his wife secretly visits Gawain's room and tries to seduce
him. Though Gawain resists the lady and exchanges only inno-
cent kisses with her, he has become greatly alarmed. When the
host returns from his hunts and gives Gawain what he won that
day, Gawain, true to his promises, gives the host in return the
innocent kisses.

Now the Lord goes out to hunt for the third morning. Gawain
is in his room asleep, worried about many things.

From the depths of his mournful sleep Sir Gawain
      muttered,
50 A man who was suffering throngs of sorrowful thoughts
Of how Destiny would that day deal him his doom

Sir Gawain and the Green Knight 135

A. Expansion
The power of religion is invoked with Mary's name, so that we know she is watching over Gawain. The following stanzas show Gawain struggling with the competing claims of chivalry, in which the knight was to obey a lady's every command, and his religious obligation to reject adultery.

Note the alliteration in line 68.

B. Characterization
Gawain has a reputation for being a ladies' man, so his temptation is based on his weakness. If he meets the test, his character will be strengthened; if he fails, he will be doomed.

C. Characterization
❓ How does Gawain respond to the lady's demand for information about his love life? (He tells her he's pledged to no one, and won't be for a while, by which he implies that he will not be her lover, either.)

At the Green Chapel, where he dreamed he was facing
    the giant
Whose blow he must abide without further debate.
But soon our rosy knight had recovered his wits;
55 He struggled up out of his sleep and responded in haste.
The lovely lady came laughing sweetly,
Fell over his fair face and fondly kissed him;
Sir Gawain welcomed her worthily and with pleasure;
He found her so glorious, so attractively dressed,
60 So faultless in every feature, her colors so fine
Welling joy rushed up in his heart at once.
Their sweet and subtle smiles swept them upward like
    wings
And all that passed between them was music and bliss
    and delight.
    How sweet was now their state!
65   Their talk, how loving and light!
    But the danger might have been great
    Had Mary° not watched her knight!

A
For that priceless princess pressed our poor hero so hard
And drove him so close to the line that she left him no
    choice
But to take the full pleasure she offered or flatly refuse
70   her;
He feared for his name, lest men call him a common
    churl,
But he feared even more what evil might follow his fall
If he dared to betray his just duty as guest to his host.
B *God help me,* thought the knight, *I can't let it happen!*
75 With a loving little laugh he parried her lunges,
Those words of undying love she let fall from her lips.
Said the lady then, "It's surely a shameful thing
If you'll lie with a lady like this yet not love her at all—
The woman most broken-hearted in all the wide world!
80 Is there someone else? Some lady you love still more
To whom you've sworn your faith and so firmly fixed
Your heart that you can't break free? I can't believe it!
But tell me if it's so. I beg you—truly—
By all the loves in life, let me know, and hide nothing
    with guile."
85   The knight said, "By Saint John,"
C   And smooth was Gawain's smile,
    "I've pledged myself to none,
    Nor will I for awhile."

"Of all the words you might have said," said she,
90 "That's surely cruelest: But alas, I'm answered.
Kiss me kindly, then, and I'll go from you.
I'll mourn through life as one who loved too much."

67. **Mary:** the Virgin Mary, mother of Jesus. A cult of the Virgin was very strong among the knights.

She bent above him, sighing, and softly kissed him:
Then, drawing back once more, she said as she stood,
95   "But my love, since we must part, be kind to me:
Leave me some little remembrance—if only a glove—
To bring back fond memories sometimes and soften my
        sorrow."
"Truly," said he, "with all my heart I wish
I had here with me the handsomest treasure I own,
100   For surely you have deserved on so many occasions
A gift more fine than any gift I could give you;
But as to my giving some token of trifling value,
It would hardly suit your great honor to have from your
        knight

A

A glove as a treasured keepsake and gift from Gawain;
105   And I've come here on my errand to countries unknown
Without any attendants with treasures in their trunks;
It sadly grieves me, for love's sake, that it's so,
But every man must do what he must and not murmur
        or pine."
    "Ah no, my prince of all honors,"
110   Said she so fair and fine,
    "Though I get nothing of yours,
    You shall have something of mine."

She held toward him a ring of the yellowest gold
And, standing aloft on the band, a stone like a star
115   From which flew splendid beams like the light of the sun;
And mark you well, it was worth a rich king's ransom.
But right away he refused it, replying in haste,

B

"My lady gay, I can hardly take gifts at the moment;
Having nothing to give, I'd be wrong to take gifts in
        turn."
120   She implored him again, still more earnestly, but again
He refused it and swore on his knighthood that he could
        take nothing.
Grieved that he still would not take it, she told him then:
"If taking my ring would be wrong on account of its
        worth,
And being so much in my debt would be bothersome to
        you,
125   I'll give you merely this sash that's of slighter value."
She swiftly unfastened the sash that encircled her waist,
Tied around her fair tunic, inside her bright mantle;
It was made of green silk and was marked of gleaming
        gold
Embroidered along the edges, ingeniously stitched.
This too she held out to the knight, and she earnestly
130   begged him
To take it, trifling as it was, to remember her by.

C

But again he said no, there was nothing at all he could
        take,

A. Characteriza-
tion

How does Ga-
wain get out of
giving the lady a
gift? (He says he
has nothing worthy
of her.)

B. Characteriza-
tion

On what basis
does Gawain
refuse the lady's
ring? (He says it
would be wrong to
take such a valu-
able gift when he
has nothing to give
her.) Note his chiv-
alry and quickness
of mind.

C. Characteriza-
tion

How does Ga-
wain respond
initially to the
lady's offer of her
sash? (He again
says he can take
nothing from her.)

A. Characterization

? How does Gawain soothe the lady's possible anger at his refusal? (He pledges to be her humble knight.)

B. Turning Point
This is a turning point of the poem. Having resisted the obvious temptations of the Green Knight's lady, Gawain here succumbs to his own human will to live. He knows by now that the Green Knight has magic, and he is afraid that only magic can save him from death. Notice that, in lines 157–159, Gawain, compounding his fault, not only takes the scarf, but also betrays his host by not telling him he has it.

Neither treasure nor token, until such time as the Lord
Had granted him some end to his adventure.
135 "And therefore, I pray you, do not be displeased,
But give up, for I cannot grant it, however fair or right.
 I know your worth and price,
 And my debt's by no means slight;
 A   I swear through fire and ice
140 To be your humble knight."

"Do you lay aside this silk," said the lady then,
"Because it seems unworthy—as well it may?
Listen. Little as it is, it seems less in value,
But he who knew what charms are woven within it
145 Might place a better price on it, perchance.
For the man who goes to battle in this green lace,
As long as he keeps it looped around him,
No man under Heaven can hurt him, whoever may try,
For nothing on earth, however uncanny, can kill him."
The knight cast about in distress, and it came to his
150   heart
 This might be a treasure indeed when the time came to
     take
 B The blow he had bargained to suffer beside the Green
     Chapel.
 If the gift meant remaining alive, it might well be worth
     it;
So he listened in silence and suffered the lady to speak,
And she pressed the sash upon him and begged him to
155   take it,
And Gawain did, and she gave him the gift with great
     pleasure
And begged him, for her sake, to say not a word,
And to keep it hidden from her lord. And he said he
     would,
That except for themselves, this business would never
     be known to a man.
160   He thanked her earnestly,
     And boldly his heart now ran;
     And now a third time she
     Leaned down and kissed her man.

When the lord returns from the third hunt, he gives Gawain a fox, and Gawain in return gives him three kisses, but not the lady's sash. The next day is New Year's Day, when Gawain must rendezvous with the Green Knight. Snow and sleet fall that night, and howling winds pile up huge drifts of snow. Before dawn, Gawain dresses in burnished armor and a red velvet cloak, winding the lady's green sash around him twice. He leaves the castle with a servant to show him the way. The servant urges him not to keep his appointment, for he will surely die, but Gawain refuses.

Part Two

He put his spurs to Gringolet,° plunged down the path,
Shoved through the heavy thicket grown up by the
165   woods
And rode down the steep slope to the floor of the valley;
He looked around him then—a strange, wild place,
And not a sign of a chapel on any side
But only steep, high banks surrounding him,
170 And great, rough knots of rock and rugged crags
That scraped the passing clouds, as it seemed to him.
He heaved at the heavy reins to hold back his horse
A And squinted in every direction in search of the Chapel,
And still he saw nothing except—and this was strange—
175 A small green hill all alone, a sort of barrow,°
A low, smooth bulge on the bank of the brimming creek
That flowed from the foot of a waterfall,
And the water in the pool was bubbling as if it were
      boiling.
Sir Gawain urged Gringolet on till he came to the mound
180 And lightly dismounted and made the reins secure
On the great, thick limb of a gnarled and ancient tree;
Then he went up to the barrow and walked all around it,
Wondering in his wits what on earth it might be.
It had at each end and on either side an entrance,
185 And patches of grass were growing all over the thing,
And all the inside was hollow—an old, old cave
Or the cleft of some ancient crag, he couldn't tell which
      it was.
    "Whoo, Lord!" thought the knight,
    "Is *this* the fellow's place?
190   Here the Devil might
    Recite his midnight mass.

"Dear God," thought Gawain, "the place is deserted
      enough!
And it's ugly enough, all overgrown with weeds!
Well might it amuse that marvel of green
195 To do his devotions here, in his devilish way!
In my five senses I fear it's the Fiend himself
Who's brought me to meet him here to murder me.
May fire and fury befall this fiendish Chapel,
As cursed a kirk° as I ever yet came across!"
200 With his helmet on his head and his lance in hand
He leaped up onto the roof of the rock-walled room
And, high on that hill, he heard, from an echoing rock
Beyond the pool, on the hillside, a horrible noise.
Brrrack! It clattered in the cliffs as if to cleave them,
205 A sound like a grindstone grinding on a scythe!
Brrrack! It whirred and rattled like water on a mill
      wheel!

---

164. **Gringolet:** his horse.

175. **barrow:** a grave mound.

199. **kirk:** church.

A. Setting
In contrast to the comfort and ease of the Green Knight's castle, the site of his temptation, Gawain now enters a forsaken wilderness, the site of his trial.

❓ List the words and phrases that describe the dreadful place where Gawain will meet the Green Knight. (Heavy thicket; steep slope; strange wild place; not a sign of a chapel; steep, high banks; rough knots of rock and rugged crags; water in pool bubbling as if boiling; gnarled and ancient tree)

LITERATURE AND LANGUAGE: VARYING WORD ORDER IN SENTENCES
Point out that the poet of *Sir Gawain and the Green Knight* varied his word order to produce a flowing, readable story. Point out the varied structure in lines 213 through 235. (Refer students who wish to review sentence-builders to **Grammar, Usage, and Mechanics: A Reference Guide.**)

Have students work independently to vary the word order of the following sentences. Encourage them to share their improved sentences orally with the class.
1. Lady Jasmine knew how to wield an ax.
2. She struck the roots of the vine.
3. She brushed aside the fallen branches.
4. Then she saw a most wonderful sight.
5. A castle stood on a nearby mountain.
6. Its walls gleamed in the sun.
7. Lady Jasmine had never seen such a magnificent structure.
8. She picked up the ax.
9. She brushed off her robe.
10. Then she headed toward the mountain.

A. Irony
Is Gawain really "the Good"? (He is good in that he has resisted the lady's blandishments, but he might more appropriately be called "Sir Gawain Try-to-Be-Good," in that he has succumbed to the temptation to take the lady's scarf without telling her husband.)

B. Interpreting
What is the ax being sharpened for? (To cut off Gawain's head)

C. Irony
Has Gawain given up the right to be guarded by God in taking the lady's scarf? (Answers will vary.)

Brrrrack! It rushed and rang till your blood ran cold.
And then: "Oh God," thought Gawain, "it grinds, I think,
For me—a blade prepared for the blow I must take as my right!
210   God's will be done! But here!
He may well get his knight,
But still, no use in fear;
I won't fall dead of fright!"

And then Sir Gawain roared in a ringing voice,
"Where is the hero who swore he'd be here to meet me?
215   Sir Gawain the Good is come to the Green Chapel!
If any man would meet me, make it now,
For it's now or never, I've no wish to dawdle here long."
"Stay there!" called someone high above his head,
220   "I'll pay you promptly all that I promised before."
But still he went on with that whetting noise a while,
Turning again to his grinding before he'd come down.
At last, from a hole by a rock he came out into sight,
Came plunging out of his den with a terrible weapon,
225   A huge new Danish ax to deliver his blow with,
With a vicious swine of a bit bent back to the handle,
Filed to a razor's edge and four foot long,
Not one inch less by the length of that gleaming lace.
The great Green Knight was garbed as before.
230   Face, legs, hair, beard, all as before but for this:
That now he walked the world on his own two legs,
The ax handle striking the stone like a walking stave.
When the knight came down to the water he would not wade
But vaulted across on his ax, then with awful strides
235   Came fiercely over the field filled all around with snow.
Sir Gawain met him there
And bowed—but none too low!
Said the other, "I see, sweet sir,
You go where you say you'll go!

"Gawain," the Green Knight said, "may God be your
240   guard!
You're very welcome indeed, sir, here at my place;
You've timed your travel, my friend, as a true man should.
You recall the terms of the contract drawn up between us:
At this time a year ago you took your chances,
And I'm pledged now, this New Year, to make you my
245   payment.

A

Sir Gawain. From a French manuscript of *Lancelot du Lac* (14th C.).

© 1987 The Pierpont Morgan Library, New York City.

A. Humanities Connection: About the Fine Art
Medieval manuscripts often used the beginning letter of a book or chapter or page as the occasion for beautiful and elaborate decorations. This picture of Sir Gawain is placed in such a way in the center of the letter *O*.

B. Noting Details
What does Gawain resolve? (That he'll show no fear)

And here we are in this valley, all alone,
And no man here to part us, proceed as we may;
Heave off your helmet then, and have here your pay;
And debate no more with me than I did then
When you severed my head from my neck with a single
250   swipe.''
''Never fear,'' said Gawain, ''by God who gave
Me life, I'll raise no complaint at the grimness of it;
But take your single stroke, and I'll stand still
And allow you to work as you like and not oppose you
           here.''
255   He bowed toward the ground
 B   And let his skin show clear;
      However his heart might pound,
      He would not show his fear.

      Quickly then the man in the green made ready,
260   Grabbed up his keen-ground ax to strike Sir Gawain:
      With all the might in his body he bore it aloft

A. Noting Details

? What happens when the Green Knight brings his ax down the first time? (Gawain flinches.) What does this show us about Gawain's resolve not to show fear? (He cannot sustain it.)

B. Noting Details

? How does the Green Knight play on Sir Gawain's fear? (He taunts him with his reputation as fearless and points out that he, the Green Knight, did not flinch against Sir Gawain's blow.)

C. Characterization

? How does the poet point up the difference between the Green Knight's magical powers and Sir Gawain's lack of them? (Gawain says, "If my head falls to the stones, it cannot be restored.")

D. Noting Details

? Do you think the Green Knight is trying to wear Sir Gawain down? (First he taunts Sir Gawain with his lack of courage, then he stops his second blow, engaging in a war of nerves with Sir Gawain, who is standing there waiting to be killed.) Notice, as in fairy tales, the use of the number 3.

And sharply brought it down as if to slay him;
Had he made it fall with the force he first intended
He would have stretched out the strongest man on
    earth.
265   But Sir Gawain cast a side glance at the ax

A   As it glided down to give him his Kingdom Come,°
    And his shoulders jerked away from the iron a little,
    And the Green Knight caught the handle, holding it
        back,
    And mocked the prince with many a proud reproof:
    "*You* can't be Gawain," he said, "who's thought so
270   good,
    A man who's never been daunted on hill or dale!

B   For look how you flinch for fear before anything's felt!
    I never heard tell that Sir Gawain was ever a coward!
    I never moved a muscle when *you* came down;
275   In Arthur's hall I never so much as winced.
    My head fell off at my feet, yet I never flickered;
    But you! You tremble at heart before you're touched!
    I'm bound to be called a better man than you, then, my
        lord."
    Said Gawain, "I shied once:
280   No more. You have my word.

C   But if my head falls to the stones
    It cannot be restored.

    "But be brisk, man, by your faith, and come to the
        point!
    Deal out my doom if you can, and do it at once,
285   For I'll stand for one good stroke, and I'll start no more
    Until your ax has hit—and that I swear."
    "Here goes, then," said the other, and heaves it aloft

D   And stands there waiting, scowling like a madman;
    He swings down sharp, then suddenly stops again,
290   Holds back the ax with his hand before it can hurt.
    And Gawain stands there stirring not even a nerve;
    He stood there still as a stone or the stock of a tree
    That's wedged in rocky ground by a hundred roots.
    O, merrily then he spoke, the man in green:
295   "Good! You've got your heart back! Now I can hit you.
    May all that glory the good King Arthur gave you
    Prove efficacious now—if it ever can—
    And save your neck." In rage Sir Gawain shouted,
    "*Hit* me, hero! I'm right up to here with your threats!
300   Is it *you* that's the cringing coward after all?"
    "Whoo!" said the man in green, "he's wrathful, too!
    No pauses, then; I'll pay up my pledge at once, I vow!"
      He takes his stride to strike
      And lifts his lip and brow;
305   It's not a thing Gawain can like,
      For nothing can save him now!

266. **his Kingdom Come:** his afterlife.

He raises that ax up lightly and flashes it down,
And that blinding bit bites in at the knight's bare neck—
But hard as he hammered it down, it hurt him no more
310 Than to nick the nape of his neck, so it split the skin;
The sharp blade slit to the flesh through the shiny hide,
And red blood shot to his shoulders and spattered the
    ground.
And when Gawain saw his blood where it blinked in the
    snow
He sprang from the man with a leap to the length of a
    spear;
315 He snatched up his helmet swiftly and slapped it on,
Shifted his shield into place with a jerk of his shoulders,
And snapped his sword out faster than sight; said
    boldly—

A And, mortal born of his mother that he was,
There was never on earth a man so happy by half—
320 "No more strokes, my friend; you've had your swing!
I've stood one swipe of your ax without resistance;
If you offer me anymore, I'll repay you at once
With all the force and fire I've got—as you will see.
    I take one stroke, that's all,
325   For that was the compact we
    Arranged in Arthur's hall;
    But now, no more for me!"

The Green Knight remained where he stood, relaxing on
    his ax—
Settled the shaft on the rocks and leaned on the sharp
    end—
And studied the young man standing there, shoulders
330   hunched,
And considered that <u>staunch</u> and doughty° stance he
    took,
Undaunted yet, and in his heart he liked it;
And then he said merrily, with a mighty voice—
B With a roar like rushing wind he <u>reproved</u> the knight—
335 "Here, don't be such an ogre on your ground!
Nobody here has behaved with bad manners toward you
Or done a thing except as the contract said.
I owed you a stroke, and I've struck; consider yourself
Well paid. And now I release you from all further duties.
340 If I'd cared to hustle, it may be, perchance, that I might
Have hit somewhat harder, and then you might well be
    cross!
The first time I lifted my ax it was lighthearted sport,
I merely <u>feinted</u> and made no mark, as was right,
For you kept our pact of the first night with honor
345 And abided by your word and held yourself true to me,
Giving me all you owed as a good man should.
I feinted a second time, friend, for the morning

331. **doughty:** brave.

A. **Noting Details**

❓ How does the poet remind us again of Sir Gawain's humanness? (He calls Gawain "mortal born of mother." We also see Gawain's pride and temper breaking through after his humiliation by the Green Knight.)

B. **Simile**

This comparison of the Green Knight to a force of nature might support the idea that this story is related to an old fertility myth.

READING CHECK TEST
1. Why does Sir Gawain go to find the Green Knight? He accepted a challenge made by the Knight and must fulfill it.
2. How many times is Sir Gawain tempted by the lady? Three
3. What is the lady's husband's true identity? He is the Green Knight.

4. Does her husband know what his lady is doing? Yes
5. Why does Gawain keep the green sash? He wants the magic to save his life when he faces the Green Knight's sword.

CLOSURE
Name two panels of five students each. Have one group ask the other five questions about Sir Gawain and the Green Knight. They should try to cover plot, characters, setting, and moral lesson.

A. Noting Details
The Green Knight here reveals that the three strokes he took at Gawain correlate precisely with Gawain's earlier actions.
❓ Tell what each of the Green Knight's strokes is related to. (The first two strokes were feints because Gawain had kept his vow to give the Green Knight anything he won during the day. The first two days he spent in the castle, he was kissed by the Green Knight's wife and kissed the Green Knight in return. However, on the third day, Gawain kept the Green Knight's wife's scarf, thus breaking his vow. The Green Knight nicked Sir Gawain because he only "lacked a little" in loyalty, and had taken the scarf because he loved his life, not because of lust. See lines 363–364.)

A
350
You kissed my pretty wife twice and returned me the
    kisses;
And so for the first two days, mere feints, nothing more
    severe.
    A man who's true to his word,
    There's nothing he needs to fear;
    You failed me, though, on the third
    Exchange, so I've tapped you here.

355
"That sash you wear by your scabbard belongs to me;
My own wife gave it to you, as I ought to know.
I know, too, of your kisses and all your words
And my wife's advances, for I myself arranged them.
It was I who sent her to test you. I'm convinced
You're the finest man that ever walked this earth.
360
As a pearl is of greater price than dry white peas,
So Gawain indeed stands out above all other knights.
But you lacked a little, sir; you were less than loyal;
But since it was not for the sash itself or for lust
But because you loved your life, I blame you less."
365
Sir Gawain stood in a study a long, long while,
So miserable with disgrace that he wept within,
And all the blood of his chest went up to his face
And he shrank away in shame from the man's gentle
    words.
The first words Gawain could find to say were these:
370
"Cursed be cowardice and covetousness both,
Villainy and vice that destroy all virtue!"
He caught at the knots of the girdle and loosened them
And fiercely flung the sash at the Green Knight.
"There, there's my fault! The foul fiend vex it!
375
Foolish cowardice taught me, from fear of your stroke,
To bargain, covetous, and abandon my kind,
The selflessness and loyalty suitable in knights;
Here I stand, faulty, and false, much as I've feared them,
Both of them, untruth and treachery; may they see
    sorrow and care!
380
    I can't deny my guilt;
    My works shine none too fair!
    Give me your good will
    And henceforth I'll beware."

385
At that, the Green Knight laughed, saying graciously,
"Whatever harm I've had, I hold it amended
Since now you're confessed so clean, acknowledging
    sins
And bearing the plain penance of my point;
I consider you polished as white and as perfectly clean
As if you had never fallen since first you were born.
390
and I give you, sir, this gold-embroidered girdle,

144

144   The Middle Ages

1. To exchange one blow with another with the two-bladed ax. The Green Knight will suffer the first blow; in return, the challenger who strikes him must agree to withstand one blow from the Green Knight a year hence.
2. Sir Gawain agrees to meet the Green Knight at the Green Chapel, on the next New Year's Day.
3. Sir Gawain's conflict pits his loyalty to his host against the temptations offered by the host's wife, who seems eager to seduce Gawain.
4. He is silent about the magic sash that the lady has given him.
5. At the first stroke of the ax, Sir Gawain flinches slightly and the Green Knight holds back his ax. At the second stroke, Sir Gawain stands boldly, but the Green Knight stops again and holds back his ax. On the third stroke, the ax nicks the nape of Gawain's neck and wounds him slightly. The Green Knight then forgives Sir Gawain's lapses from the code of chivalry and gives him a gold-embroidered green girdle.
(Answers continue on next page.)

> For the cloth is as green as my gown. Sir Gawain, think
> On this when you go forth among great princes;
> Remember our struggle here; recall to your mind
> This rich token. Remember the Green Chapel.
> 395 And now, come on, let's both go back to my castle
> And finish the New Year's revels with feasting and joy,
>   not strife,
>   I beg you," said the lord,
>   And said, "As for my wife,
>   She'll be your friend, no more
> 400   A threat against your life."

Sir Gawain is tempted by the lady of the castle. From an English manuscript (c. 1400).

The British Museum.

A. The Ending

In the complete version, Gawain refuses the lady's friendship and speaks out against women in general who have tempted men through the ages. (He mentions Adam tempted by Eve, Solomon by many, and David by Bathsheba.)

The Green Knight then reveals to Sir Gawain that he himself is Sir Bercilak de Hautdesert and that he had been enchanted by Morgan le Fay, King Arthur's half-sister, who had set up the challenge to test Arthur's knights and frighten Queen Guinevere, whom Morgan le Fay viewed as a hated rival.

Gawain ever after wears the green sash as a reminder of his failing.

Honi soit qui mal y pense ends the tale: "Shame to whoever thinks evil of it." This is the motto of the Order of the Garter, a prestigious British order of modern "knights." The motto is also inscribed on the Royal Arms of Great Britain.

A

Interpreting Meanings

6. Most students will say the Green Knight.

7. Sir Gawain is a hero in that he is superbly handsome and courageous.

He displays such human qualities as susceptibility to passion, desire, lying, and fear.

8. He is able to carry his own head, to disguise himself as the lord of the castle, and then to reappear as the Green Knight.

Opinions will differ. He is not, however, presented as evil.

He might symbolize a natural force, or fertility, or the green world that is able to renew itself each year.

9. The color green may symbolize hope and renewal.

New Year's Day suggests a new beginning; Sir Gawain makes a more perfect renewal of his knightly code.

10. See the details in the two stanzas at the beginning of Part Two (lines 164–213). Especially note the boiling water and the grave mound.

The setting could symbolize Hell and Gawain's encounter with the forces of evil who want to destroy his soul.

Responding to the Romance

Analyzing the Romance

Identifying Details

1. What exactly is the Green Knight's challenge to King Arthur's court?
2. What is his agreement with Sir Gawain?
3. Describe the **conflict** Gawain faces in the castle.
4. How does Gawain break his promise to the lord?
5. Describe what happens when Gawain meets the Green Knight on New Year's Day.

Interpreting Meanings

6. Who would you say finally wins the conflict between Gawain and the Green Knight?
7. Discuss the **character** of Sir Gawain. How is he a superhuman romance hero? How is he also flawed, just as a real person may be flawed?
8. The figure of the Green Knight remains a puzzle to many critics. In what ways is he a "shape-changer," like so many characters in romances? Is he totally evil, or totally good, or somewhere in between? What might he **symbolize** in the narrative?
9. Explore the possible **symbolic** use of the color green in this work. (Green usually symbolizes hope; it is associated with the appearance of new life in the plant world.) Why do you think the meeting with the Green Knight takes place on New Year's Day?
10. What **images** make the setting of the confrontation seem demonic? Do you think there is any **symbolism** suggested by this setting? Explain.
11. Why might the lord's wife have had such power over Gawain?
12. How would you state the **theme** of this romance?
13. In romance literature, women are often represented as (a) maidens, (b) mothers, (c) temptresses, or (d) crones. How is the lady in this story characterized? Do these character roles for women still exist in fiction and movies today? Explain.
14. Compare the romantic triangle in this story—the two men and a woman—with romantic triangles in contemporary fiction or movies. Is Gawain's response credible?

Writing About the Romance

A Creative Response

1. **Using a Different Point of View.** While the lord of the mysterious castle is out hunting, his wife is at home on a hunt of her own. What might she have to say about the situation? In a brief narrative, written from the wife's point of view, describe her feelings about entrapping Gawain. How does she feel about Gawain? About her husband? Does she resent carrying out her wifely duty, or does she enjoy it?

2. **Displacing the Story.** When the elements of a romance story (or myth) are adapted to a more modern setting, we say that the story has been "displaced." In at least a paragraph, describe how this story of Gawain might be displaced into a contemporary novel or movie. Consider what would happen to the **plot**, **characterization**, and **theme** in the modernization.

A Critical Response

3. **Analyzing a Romance.** Read the material on the romance pattern (page 147). In a five-paragraph essay, discuss the Gawain story as a romance. Is the story different from a typical romance in any way? Consider these typical elements of a romance:

   a. An all-good hero   **d.** A test of the hero
   b. An evil enemy   **e.** Supernatural elements
   c. A quest   **f.** Good *vs.* evil

Analyzing Language and Style

The Bob and Wheel

Before the time of Chaucer, the dominant English verse form was alliterative. **Alliteration** is the repetition of initial sounds in the stressed syllables of words.

In order to achieve variety in the otherwise somewhat monotonous alliterative verse, the inventive Gawain poet broke the poem into stanza-like sections by making use of a technique we now refer to as **bob and wheel.** The "wheels" are groups of four short, alternatively rhymed lines. The bobs are lines, or "tags," which come before the wheels. The last word of the bob always rhymes with the second and fourth lines of the wheel. Consider the translated line at the end of section 16 of *Sir Gawain.* The bob and the wheel together bring the section to a tidy conclusion:

In joy they passed that day until darkness came in the land.	bob
And now think well, Sir Gawain,	*b*
Lest you from terror stand	*a*
Betrayer of the bargain	*b* wheel
That you have now in hand!	*a*

Reread the account of Gawain's last encounter with the Green Knight. Note at which points in the narrative the writer places the bob and wheel. What events or ideas are emphasized by the writer's use of this device?

11. Despite his distinction in so many other respects, Gawain's "besetting sin" may have been sensuality.

12. Student summaries of theme will differ. One statement might run as follows: To achieve nobility, human beings must rely on and constantly practice a number of virtues, especially courage, honesty, and self-denial.

13. The lady in the story is characterized principally as a temptress.

Most students will agree that they do. Think especially of movies and Westerns.

14. Gawain's response is certainly credible. A hero's or heroine's response to sexual temptation (adultery) would differ from era to era, depending on prevailing mores. Analyze current movies and TV shows.

The Elements of Literature

THE ROMANCE

There is one story and one story only
That will prove worth your telling,
Whether as learned bard or gifted child;
To it all lines or lesser gauds belong
That startle with their shining
Such common stories as they stray into.
—From "To Juan at the Winter Solstice,"
Robert Graves

A "The one story Robert Graves refers to is the romance, and we may wonder why he makes such a large claim for it. We can agree that elements of the romance narrative recur in a variety of stories in every age and culture. Beowulf, in an eighth-century Anglo-Saxon world, and Herman Melville's Ahab, in nineteenth-century America, are both variations of the questing romantic hero. . . . But this does not make the romance the only story worth telling; the narrative patterns of tragedy, comedy, and irony are as recurrent and as universal.

B "However, there may be other grounds on which Graves could rest his claim. Let us consider this typical romance narrative: A young knight, after a series of adventures in which he has proved his valor, encounters a dragon that has laid waste to the land. In a battle that lasts for three days, he finally kills the dragon. He then liberates the kingdom and marries the king's daughter. In later times he becomes the patron saint of the land. Whatever else we might say about this story, most of us would agree, first, that it has something of the supernatural or mysterious about it; second, that it has an old or archaic quality; and finally, that is has a simple, even inevitable, plot. It is a familiar tale whether or not we have read Spenser's more complex version in *The Faerie Queene.* These intuitions about the romance as a narrative that is essentially mysterious or supernatural in character, old in origin, and simple in structure can help us to discover why someone might claim for it a primary status among the narrative patterns.

"The mysterious and supernatural character of the romance suggests its resemblance to legend and myth. In romance narratives, as in the myths they often draw on, animals give warnings, dragons threaten, and princes inevitably rescue the beleaguered at the darkest moment. Events and characters come in sets of three, like Gawain's three temptations and the three harpooners in *Moby-Dick.* Havelok the Dane's life is threatened during his childhood as are the lives of legendary characters from Oedipus to Snow White. And when the romantic hero dies, he takes on the features of a god or, at least, is memorialized as someone more than human. His final union with the mysterious suggests the romance form's return to the realm of legend and myth, from which, we feel, it has never been too distant.

C "There are historical reasons for thinking of the romance as a primary form. The romance narrative most often dominates the earliest period in the literary history of a culture. It is the dominant form in Anglo-Saxon and medieval English literature. The same is true in American literary history. From the late eighteenth century when Joel Barlow wrote his ponderous epic about Columbus to the early nineteenth when Cooper wrote his Leatherstocking saga, poets and novelists turned to the romance pattern to fashion heroes and articulate ideals commensurate with the American adventure. Writers in later periods often testify to the archaic quality associated with the romance by setting their narratives in an earlier time when such forms were more frequent. In England Spenser did this with *The Faerie Queene,* as did John Keats with 'The Eve of Saint Agnes' and Sir Walter Scott with *Ivanhoe.*

"We may think of the romance pattern as simpler than the others because it is so familiar to us in children's literature and in movies, cartoons, comic strips, and television dramas. Much of the popularity of these forms lies in the simplicity of the questions they raise and the inevitability of their answers. Will good triumph over evil? Will the innocent young find protection? Will the skeptical elders be proved wrong? Such questions arise in the suspense we feel over whether the cavalry will arrive in time, whether Dorothy will find the Wizard of Oz, whether Godzilla will be destroyed, and whether the Little Engine That Could can. The romance pattern asks us to entertain these questions as if there were some doubt as to their answers and at the same time assures us that there is none. If we rewrite the conclusion of the story of Snow White so that the young prince visits her glass coffin in the forest, turns away with a shrug, and marries the wicked queen, even a child, however caught up he may be in the story, *knows* it must not end this way. Because of its simplicity, at least in its popular versions, its early place in literary history, and its affinity with legend and myth, we may think of the romance pattern as a primary imaginative form. There is some justice, then, in a poet's saying that to it all lesser things belong 'that startle with their shining / Such common stories as they stray into.' "
—Robert Foulke and Paul Smith

A. Expansion
Romance comes from the old French word *romanz,* which simply means "in the Roman language" (not in Latin). The most direct ancestor of the English romance is the French *roman,* a metrical narrative, the most famous of which is the *Roman de la Rose.* (See text page 67.)

B. Connections
You can relate this basic romance quest pattern to any number of other narratives, ancient and modern: The movie *Star Wars* is an excellent example from popular culture.

C. Connections
See *Le Morte Darthur,* text page 149.

Eugene Vinaver, editor of the Oxford University Press edition of the Winchester manuscript, suggests that Malory's picture of Arthur may be seen as a tribute to Henry V. He notes, for example, that Malory "makes Arthur's expedition against the Romans resemble Henry V's triumphant campaign in France," and that Arthur's "itinerary through France is altered so as to resemble the route followed by Henry."

A. Expansion

Until 1934, Caxton's was the only known version of *Le Morte Darthur*. In the summer of that year, a fifteenth-century manuscript of Malory's tales was discovered in the library of Winchester College. The manuscript was probably lost after it was first cataloged in 1839 because it was missing eight pages at the beginning and end. Though still a copy and not Malory's original, this manuscript was in many ways more complete and authentic than Caxton's. For example, the Winchester manuscript showed that Malory had originally written not a single book, as Caxton published it, but a series of separate romances.

Sir Thomas Malory (1405?–1471)

Sir Thomas Malory was a knight, an adventurer, a soldier in the Hundred Years' War, a member of Parliament, and one of England's finest and most enduring writers. He was born in Warwickshire shortly after Chaucer's death, and he died after spending some twenty years in prison, probably for supporting the losing side in the Wars of the Roses. It was in prison that he wrote his famous series of tales about King Arthur and the Round Table. This work, published in 1485 as *Le Morte Darthur* ("The Death of Arthur") by the first English printer, William Caxton, is to a great extent made up of translations of older English and Continental stories. But Malory's compilation has a beauty and artistic unity that make it one of the most popular prose works in English.

In a sense *Le Morte Darthur*, coming as it does at the end of the fifteenth century, serves as a literary end to, and a nostalgic summary of, the Middle Ages, with its castles, knights, feudal order, and chivalric traditions. The characters in the book are figures from an older medieval fairy tale; they were no longer real to Malory's audience, which was developing into a new class of tradesmen, leaving the old feudal system to die out. The King Arthur depicted by Malory almost certainly never existed, although a certain Arthur did lead the old Britons in their struggle against the Anglo-Saxon invaders during the sixth century. Using the Continental and Celtic legends, Malory mythically enlarged this Arthur until he became the very embodiment of British values and even a supposed ancestor of the English kings.

In Malory's mythic form, Arthur has the mysterious birth typical of the romance hero. His childhood initiation—the pulling of a magic sword from a rock—points to his kinship with such mythic and romance heroes as the Greek Theseus and the German Siegfried. His strange death, departure, and promised return also place him among other "once and future kings"—heroes who become emblematic representations of national or cultural visions.

If King Arthur, Merlin, Lancelot, Galahad, and Guinevere were, for the post-Chaucerian English, no longer historical figures, they were still powerful expressions of the chivalric ideals of the English past. Their spirit of adventure and their sense of a heroic destiny would be very much a part of the tumultuous Elizabethan age that was on the horizon.

These figures from England's feudal past will reappear in the nineteenth century, in Alfred Tennyson's group of narrative poems called *Idylls of the King*. Tennyson brought Arthur and his knights back at a time when the English nation needed a reminder of its heroic past and of its destiny. The Arthurian legend reappeared yet again in the twentieth century in a book called *The Once and Future King* (1958), by British writer T. H. White. Controversial as White's treatment is, the power of the Arthurian stories is evidenced by the fact that his book was a best seller and that in its musical form, called *Camelot*, it became a long-running Broadway hit.

PREPARATION

ESTABLISHING A PURPOSE. More than one critic has suggested that the Arthurian legend becomes strongest in societies that have a need for it. (Tennyson's retelling was popular in the late nineteenth century, when England needed a reminder of its glorious past.) Have students read to discover if the legend answers a need in American society today.

SUPPLEMENTARY SUPPORT MATERIALS
1. Vocabulary Activity Worksheet (*CCB*)
2. Review and Response Worksheet: Evaluating a Story (*CCB*)
3. Selection Test (*CCB*)

DEVELOPING VOCABULARY
The following terms from the story are tested in the Selection Test. (See also Vocabulary Activity Worksheet.)

fell on	untruly said of thee
host	spare not
full sore	lightly
doleful	fromward
whereof	into

FROM LE MORTE DARTHUR

King Arthur battling Mordred. From a manuscript (15th century).

Lambeth Palace Library, London.

A. Humanities Connection: Discussing the Fine Art
This illustration from the St. Albans Chronicle shows how, because men in armor were difficult to identify, their shields became important indicators of who was inside all that metal. Coats of arms were developed to display not only who the shield bearer was but also to show his family lineage.
? Who was Mordred, and why was he so important? (Mordred was Arthur's treacherous nephew and also his illegitimate son by his own sister, the evil necromancer Morgan le Fay. Mordred and Arthur killed each other in battle, as this selection narrates.)

Mordred's Story

Mordred was begotten by Arthur on his half-sister Morgan le Fay. When the sorcerer Merlin prophesied to Arthur that he would be slain by a child born on May Day, Arthur, unaware that he had a son (Mordred) born on that day, ordered that all children of nobility born on May Day be put out to sea on a ship. The ship was wrecked and all the babies perished—except Mordred, who was rescued. Students may recognize echoes of other events here, such as Moses's rescue from his bulrush boat and the slaying of the innocents in an attempt to kill the infant Jesus. As in Greek tragedies, this beginning (with Arthur's secret sin) sets the stage for the difficulties that will dog Arthur throughout his life. It also assures that his life will end in tragedy.

A. Connections

❓ What characteristic does Sir Gawain display here that he shows in *Sir Gawain and the Green Knight* (page 133)? (Sir Gawain appears here as a ladies' man, a characteristic that helped determine the form his temptation would take in the Green Knight's castle.)

In the early parts of Malory's story, Arthur persuades the knights in his kingdom to unite in the fellowship of the Round Table, dedicated to knighthood's code of chivalry and honor. For a while, Arthur's plan works, and justice prevails in his kingdom. But human frailties, including Arthur's own, gradually undermine the plan. The fellowship of the Round Table becomes corrupt and no longer holds the kingdom together. In this diseased state, the domain of Arthur is vulnerable to the evil forces personified in Sir Mordred, the king's own illegitimate son. Ultimately Arthur dies, but even in his death, we are reminded that his role is eternal.

What follows here is Malory's account of King Arthur's death, which comes at the end of *Le Morte Darthur*, and which gives the book its title.

So upon Trinity Sunday at night King Arthur dreamed a wonderful dream, and in his dream he seemed that he saw upon a chafflet[1] a chair, and the chair was fast to a wheel, and thereupon sat King Arthur in the richest cloth of gold that might be made. And the King thought there was under him, far from him, an hideous deep black water, and therein was all manner of serpents, and worms, and wild beasts, foul and horrible. And suddenly the King thought that the wheel turned upside down, and he fell among the serpents, and every beast took him by a limb. And then the King cried as he lay in his bed, "Help, help!"

And then knights, squires, and yeomen awaked the King, and then he was so amazed that he wist[2] not where he was. And then so he awaked until it was nigh day, and then he fell on slumbering again, not sleeping nor thoroughly waking. So the King seemed verily that there came Sir Gawain unto him with a number of fair ladies with him. So when King Arthur saw him, he said, "Welcome, my sister's son. I weened ye had been dead. And now I see thee on-live, much am I beholden unto Almighty Jesu. Ah, fair nephew and my sister's son, what been these ladies that hither be come with you?"

"Sir," said Sir Gawain, "all these be ladies for whom I have foughten for when I was man living. And all these are tho[3] that I did battle for in righteous quarrels, and God hath given them that grace, at their great prayer, because I did battle for them for their right, that they should bring me hither unto you. Thus much hath given me leave God, for to warn you of your death. For and ye fight as tomorn[4] with Sir Mordred, as ye both have assigned,[5] doubt ye not ye must be slain, and the most party of your people on both parties. And for the great grace and goodness that Almighty Jesu hath unto you, and for pity of you and many mo[6] other good men there shall be slain, God hath sent me to you of his special grace to give you warning that in no wise ye do battle as tomorn, but that ye take a treatise[7] for a month-day. And proffer you largely,[8] so that tomorn ye put in a delay. For within a month shall come Sir Lancelot with all his noble knights and rescue you worshipfully and slay Sir Mordred and all that ever will hold with him."

Then Sir Gawain and all the ladies vanished. And anon the King called upon his knights, squires, and yeomen, and charged them wightly[9] to fetch his noble lords and wise bishops unto him. And when they were come the King told them of his avision,[10] that Sir Gawain had told him and warned him that, and he fought on the morn, he should be slain. Then the King commanded Sir Lucan the Butler and his brother Sir Bedivere the Bold, with two bishops with them, and charged them in any wise to take a treatise for a month-day with Sir Mordred. "And spare not: Proffer him lands and goods as much as ye think reasonable."

So then they departed and came to Sir Mordred where he had a grim host of an hundred thousand, and there they entreated[11] Sir Mordred long time. And at the last Sir Mordred was agreed for to

---

1. **chafflet:** scaffold.
2. **wist:** knew.
3. **tho:** those.
4. **For . . . tomorn:** If you fight tomorrow.
5. **assigned:** decided.
6. **mo:** more.
7. **treatise:** treaty, truce.
8. **proffer you largely:** make generous offers.
9. **wightly:** quickly.
10. **avision:** dream.
11. **entreated:** dealt with.

have Cornwall and Kent by King Arthur's days, and after that, all England, after the days of King Arthur.

Then were they condescended[12] that King Arthur and Sir Mordred should meet betwixt both their hosts, and everich[13] of them should bring fourteen persons. And so they came with this word unto Arthur. Then said he, "I am glad that this is done," and so he went into the field.

And when King Arthur should depart, he warned all his host that, and they see any sword drawn, "Look ye come on fiercely and slay that traitor Sir Mordred, for I in no wise trust him." In like wise Sir Mordred warned his host that "And ye see any manner of sword drawn, look that ye come on fiercely, and so slay all that ever before you standeth, for in no wise I will not trust for this treatise." And in the same wise said Sir Mordred unto his host, "For I know well my father will be avenged upon me."

And so they met as their pointment[14] was and were agreed and accorded thoroughly. And wine was fetched and they drank together. Right so came an adder out of a little heath bush, and it stung a knight in the foot. And so when the knight felt him so stung, he looked down and saw the adder. And anon he drew his sword to slay the adder, and thought none other harm. And when the host on both parties saw that sword drawn, then they blew beams,[15] trumpets, and horns, and shouted grimly. And so both hosts dressed them[16] together. And King Arthur took his horse and said, "Alas, this unhappy day!" and so rode to his party, and Sir Mordred in like wise.

And never since was there never seen a more dolefuller battle in no Christian land, for there was but rushing and riding, foining[17] and striking; and many a grim word was there spoken of either to other, and many a deadly stroke. But ever King Arthur rode throughout the battle[18] of Sir Mordred many times and did full nobly, as a noble king should do, and at all times he fainted never. And Sir Mordred did his devoir[19] that day and put himself in great peril.

And thus they fought all the long day, and never stinted till the noble knights were laid to the cold earth. And ever they fought still till it was near night, and by then was there an hundred thousand laid dead upon the down. Then was King Arthur wood-wroth[20] out of measure when he saw his people so slain from him. And so he looked about him and could see no mo of all his host, and good knights left no mo on-live, but two knights; the t'one was Sir Lucan the Butler and [the other] his brother Sir Bedivere. And yet they were full sore wounded.

"Jesu, mercy," said the King, "where are all my noble knights become? Alas that ever I should see this doleful day! For now," said King Arthur, "I am come to mine end. But would to God," said he, "that I wist now where were that traitor Sir Mordred that has caused all this mischief."

Then King Arthur looked about and was ware where stood Sir Mordred leaning upon his sword among a great heap of dead men.

"Now give me my spear," said King Arthur unto Sir Lucan, "for yonder I have espied the traitor that all this woe hath wrought."

"Sir, let him be," said Sir Lucan, "for he is unhappy.[21] And if ye pass this unhappy day ye shall be right well revenged upon him. And, good lord, remember ye of your night's dream, and what the spirit of Sir Gawain told you tonight, and yet God of his great goodness hath preserved you hitherto. And for God's sake, my lord, leave off by this, for, blessed be God, ye have won the field: for yet we been here three on-live, and with Sir Mordred is not one on-live. And therefore if ye leave off now, this wicked day of destiny is past."

"Now, tide[22] me death, tide me life," said the King, "now I see him yonder alone, he shall never escape mine hands. For at a better avail[23] shall I never have him."

"God speed you well!" said Sir Bedivere.

Then the King got his spear in both his hands and ran toward Sir Mordred, crying and saying, "Traitor, now is thy deathday come!"

And when Sir Mordred saw King Arthur he ran

---

12. **condescended:** agreed.
13. **everich:** each.
14. **pointment:** arrangement.
15. **beams:** trumpets.
16. **dressed them:** prepared to come.
17. **foining:** lunging.
18. **battle:** battalion.
19. **devoir:** knightly duty.

20. **wood-wroth:** mad with rage.
21. **unhappy:** unlucky for you.
22. **tide:** betide.
23. **avail:** advantage.

A. Expansion
Although there is much debate about what Arthur's kingdom may have consisted of (if Arthur actually existed at all), he has always been associated with the south and west of England, especially Cornwall. By the twelfth century, Tintagel, a Cornish castle situated high on a rocky headland and narrowly connected to the mainland, had become Arthur's traditional birthplace.

B. Characterization
Recall for students the fact that Arthur in *Sir Gawain and the Green Knight* impetuously agreed to fight the Green Knight. Only Sir Gawain's intervention kept this from happening.
? What does this exchange between Sir Lucan and King Arthur tell us about Arthur's character? (He acts as he thinks he must without regard for the consequences. Despite Sir Lucan's reasoned argument, Arthur goes ahead to fight Mordred, thus fulfilling the tragic prophecy of his dream. Arthur has a sense of tragic inevitability.)

A. Noting Details
❓ Describe in your own words Sir Mordred's death and his last attack on King Arthur. (Arthur spears Mordred; Mordred in turn pushes his body along the spear until he reaches the hand guard so that he can get close enough to King Arthur to strike him with his sword. Mordred hits the King so hard that his sword pierces Arthur's helmet and his brain as well. Upon doing this, Mordred falls down dead.)

Arthur's last battle, the Battle of Camlann (14th century).

A

until him with his sword drawn in his hand, and there King Arthur smote Sir Mordred under the shield, with a foin of his spear, throughout the body more than a fathom.[24] And when Sir Mordred felt that he had his death's wound, he thrust himself with the might that he had up to the burr[25] of King Arthur's spear and right so he smote his father King Arthur with his sword holden in both his hands, upon the side of his head, that the sword pierced the helmet and the tay[26] of the brain. And therewith Sir Mordred dashed down stark dead to the earth.

And noble King Arthur fell in a swough[27] to the earth, and there he swooned oftentimes, and Sir Lucan and Sir Bedivere ofttimes heaved him up. And so, weakly betwixt them, they led him to a little chapel not far from the seaside, and when the King was there, him thought him reasonably eased. Then heard they people cry in the field. "Now go thou, Sir Lucan," said the King, "and

24. **fathom:** six feet.
25. **burr:** hand guard.
26. **tay:** edge.

27. **swough:** swoon.

152

Royal Library, The Hague.

A. Humanities Connection: Discussing the Fine Art

Note how the medieval illuminations often were drawn as a series of events, much as cartoons today. Note how this artist managed to suggest the furious activity of battle within a very small space. Look also at the expression on Arthur's face as he is drawn offstage.

For years, argument has raged over whether Arthur was a real king or chieftain. Convincing evidence comes from some medieval Easter Annals. These notes on major historical events were written alongside calculations to determine when Easter was to be celebrated each year. Two entries mention Arthur. The second entry, dated 539, reads, "The Battle of Camlann, in which Arthur and Mordred perished. And there was plague in Britain and Ireland." Malory places the Battle of Camlann on Salisbury Plain, the site of Stonehenge. (See the photograph on text page 3.)

do me to wit[28] what betokens that noise in the field."

So Sir Lucan departed, for he was grievously wounded in many places. And so as he yede[29] he saw and harkened by the moonlight how that pillers[30] and robbers were come into the field to pill and to rob many a full noble knight of brooches and bees[31] and of many a good ring and many a rich jewel. And who that were not dead all out

there they slew them for their harness and their riches. When Sir Lucan understood this work, he came to the King as soon as he might and told him all what he had heard and seen. "Therefore by my read,"[32] said Sir Lucan, "it is best that we bring you to some town."

"I would it were so," said the King, "but I may not stand, my head works[33] so. Ah, Sir Lancelot," said King Arthur, "this day have I sore missed

---

28. **do me to wit:** let me know.
29. **yede:** walked.
30. **pillers:** plunderers.
31. **bees:** bracelets.

32. **read:** advice.
33. **works:** aches.

READING CHECK TEST
1. Who kills King Arthur? Mordred, his illegitimate son
2. What does King Arthur tell Sir Bedivere to do? Throw his sword Excalibur into the lake
3. What does Sir Bedivere see in the lake? A hand rising to take the sword
4. What happens to Arthur? He is placed on a barge with three queens and goes to Avilion.
5. How is Arthur described in the inscription on his tomb? As the once and future king

CLOSURE
In class discussion, have students consider the symbolic significance of Arthur's tombstone inscription, "Here lies Arthur, the once and future king." Is the spirit of Arthur still invoked today?

A. Lancelot and Guinevere

Sir Lancelot is not present because his affair with Guinevere had been discovered by Arthur's sons Mordred and Agravaine. Lancelot fled, but when he heard that Guinevere was to be burned at the stake for her adultery, he came back to rescue her. In the ensuing fight, Lancelot unknowingly killed Gaheris and Gareth. Lancelot and Guinevere then fled to his castle, where they were attacked by Arthur and the other knights. After a lengthy seige, King Arthur obeyed a command from the Pope to take Guinevere back. Gawain, however, was determined to avenge his brothers' deaths, and he insisted that Arthur banish Lancelot. Arthur then followed Lancelot to France to make war on him. The evil Mordred was left as regent of England in his father's absence. Arthur returned to Britain to find Mordred's troops waiting for him. The Battle of Camlann was the result.

A ⌈thee. And alas that ever I was against thee, for now have I my death, wherefore Sir Gawain me warned in my dream."

Then Sir Lucan took up the King the t'one party[34] and Sir Bedivere the other party; and in the lifting up the King swooned and in the lifting Sir Lucan fell in a swoon that part of his guts fell out of his body, and therewith the noble knight's heart burst. And when the King awoke he beheld Sir Lucan how he lay foaming at the mouth and part of his guts lay at his feet.

"Alas," said the King, "this is to me a full heavy sight to see this noble duke so die for my sake, for he would have holpen me that had more need of help than I. Alas that he would not complain him for his heart was so set to help me. Now Jesu have mercy upon his soul."

Then Sir Bedivere wept for the death of his brother.

"Now leave this mourning and weeping, gentle knight," said the King, "for all this will not avail me. For wit thou well, and[35] I might live myself, the death of Sir Lucan would grieve me evermore. But my time passeth on fast," said the King. "Therefore," said King Arthur unto Sir Bedivere, "take thou here Excalibur[36] my good sword and go with it to yonder water's side; and when thou comest there I charge thee throw my sword in that water and come again and tell me what thou sawest there."

"My lord," said Sir Bedivere, "your commandment shall be done, and [I shall] lightly[37] bring you word again."

So Sir Bedivere departed. And by the way he beheld that noble sword, that the pommel and the haft was all precious stones. And then he said to himself, "If I throw this rich sword in the water, thereof shall never come good, but harm and loss." And then Sir Bedivere hid Excalibur under a tree. And so, as soon as he might, he came again unto the King and said he had been at the water and had thrown the sword into the water.

"What saw thou there?" said the King.

"Sir," he said, "I saw nothing but waves and winds."

"That is untruly said of thee," said the King.

"And therefore go thou lightly again and do my commandment; as thou art to me lief[38] and dear, spare not, but throw it in."

Then Sir Bedivere returned again and took the sword in his hand. And yet him thought sin and shame to throw away that noble sword. And so eft[39] he hid the sword and returned again and told the King that he had been at the water and done his commandment.

"What sawest thou there?" said the King.

"Sir," he said, "I saw nothing but waters and wap and waves wan."

"Ah, traitor unto me and untrue," said King Arthur, "now hast thou betrayed me twice. Who would have weened that thou that hast been to me so lief and dear, and thou art named a noble knight, and would betray me for the riches of this sword. But now go again lightly, for thy long tarrying putteth me in great jeopardy of my life, for I have taken cold. And but if thou do now as I bid thee, if ever I may see thee I shall slay thee mine own hands, for thou wouldest for my rich sword see me dead."

Then Sir Bedivere departed and went to the sword and lightly took it up, and so he went to the water's side; and there he bound the girdle about the hilts, and threw the sword as far into the water as he might. And there came an arm and a hand above the water and took it and clutched it, and shook it thrice and brandished; and then vanished away the hand with the sword into the water. So Sir Bedivere came again to the King and told him what he saw.

"Alas," said the King, "help me hence, for I dread me I have tarried overlong."

Then Sir Bedivere took the King upon his back and so went with him to that water's side. And when they were at the water's side, even fast by the bank hoved[40] a little barge with many fair ladies in it; and among them all was a queen; and all they had black hoods, and all they wept and shrieked when they saw King Arthur.

"Now put me into that barge," said the King; and so he did softly. And there received him three ladies with great mourning, and so they set them down. And in one of their laps King Arthur laid his head, and then the queen said, "Ah, my dear

---

34. **t'one party:** on one side.
35. **and:** if.
36. **Excalibur:** Arthur's sword, given him by the mysterious Lady of the Lake.
37. **lightly:** quickly.
38. **lief:** beloved.
39. **eft:** again.
40. **hoved:** waited.

ANALYZING THE STORY
Identifying Facts
1. He learns from Sir Gawain that if he fights with Sir Mordred they must both be slain.

Lucan advises the King not to attack Sir Mordred.
2. The soldiers' orders were not to draw swords until they saw the other side draw. Then an adder stings one of the

knights in the foot. When the host on both sides see the knight draw his sword to kill the adder, they begin to fight.
3. Arthur requests that Sir Bedivere throw the sword Excalibur into the lake.

Bedivere hesitates twice to comply with this request; finally, at the King's insistence, he casts the royal sword into the lake.
4. The final paragraph suggests that

King Arthur may one day return.

Interpreting Meanings
5. In general the mood is somber, elegiac, and mysterious.

The description of the mourning ladies in the barge, waiting to bear King Arthur to Avilion, especially reinforces this mood.
(Answers continue on next page.)

brother, why have ye tarried so long from me? Alas, this wound on your head hath caught overmuch cold." And anon they rowed <u>fromward</u> the land, and Sir Bedivere beheld all tho ladies go froward him.

Then Sir Bedivere cried and said, "Ah, my lord Arthur, what shall become of me, now ye go from me and leave me here alone among mine enemies?"

"Comfort thyself," said the King, "and do as well as thou mayest, for in me is no trust for to trust in. For I must <u>into</u> the vale of Avilion[41] to heal me of my grievous wound. And if thou hear nevermore of me, pray for my soul."

But ever the queen and ladies wept and shrieked that it was pity to hear. And as soon as Sir Bedivere had lost the sight of the barge he wept and wailed and so took[42] the forest, and went all that night. And in the morning he was ware betwixt two holts hoar[43] of a chapel and an hermitage. . . .

Thus of Arthur I find no more written in books that been authorized, neither more of the very

certainty of his death heard I never read, but thus was he led away in a ship wherein were three queens: that one was King Arthur's sister, Queen Morgan la Fée, the t'other was the Queen of North Wales, and the third was the Queen of the Waste Lands. . . .

Now more of the death of King Arthur could I never find but that these ladies brought him to his burials, and such one was buried there that the hermit bore witness that sometime was Bishop of Canterbury. But yet the hermit knew not in certain that he was verily the body of King Arthur, for this tale Sir Bedivere, a Knight of the Table Round, made it to be written. Yet some men say in many parts of England that King Arthur is not dead, but had by the will of our Lord Jesu into another place. And men say that he shall come again and he shall win the Holy Cross. Yet I will not say that it shall be so, but rather I will say, Here in this world he changed his life. And many men say that there is written upon his tomb this verse: *Hic iacet Arthurus, rex quondam, rexque futurus.*[44]

---

41. **Avilion:** a legendary island, sometimes identified with the earthly Paradise.
42. **took:** took to.
43. **holts hoar:** old thickets.

44. *Hic . . . futurus:* "Here lies Arthur, the once and future king."

Responding to the Story

Analyzing the Story

Identifying Facts

1. What does King Arthur learn in his dream on Trinity Sunday? What is Sir Lucan's advice to Arthur?
2. Explain what causes the battle to start.
3. As he is about to die, what does Arthur request of Sir Bedivere? How does Bedivere comply with this request?
4. What mysterious possibility is contained in the final paragraph?

Interpreting Meanings

5. In a word or phrase, sum up the atmosphere, or **mood,** of this story. How does Malory use details of **setting** to achieve that mood?
6. What Christian **symbolism** or **allusions** do you find in this excerpt? Consider the way the battle starts, Sir

Bedivere's responses to Arthur's dying request, and any other details. What might these Christian overtones signify about Arthur's role in British mythology?
7. In what ways do you think *Le Morte Darthur* reflects the dreams and values of the time during which it was written?
8. Near the end of the romance, Malory says of Arthur, "Here in this world he changed his life." Is such an accomplishment important in literature (and life) today?
9. What aspects of this story might appeal especially to people living in the last years of the twentieth century? Or do you think the story has little appeal to people today? Why?
10. List all the **supernatural** elements in this story. Do you recognize any of these elements as similar to those used in other romances (including contemporary movies, television stories, and science-fiction novels)?

6. The battle starts as a result of a serpent's bite or sting, perhaps an echo of the temptation of Adam and Eve in the Garden of Eden, where the Devil was disguised as a serpent; Sir Bedivere's denials of King Arthur's dying request echo Peter's denials of Christ in the New Testament; and the conclusion of the tale includes the possibility of King Arthur's resurrection. One may possibly conclude that King Arthur had a heroic, perhaps semidivine, place in British mythology as the hero who will one day return to save his people.

7. *Le Morte Darthur* certainly reflects the wish for a national savior. It also reflects values of obedience, loyalty, and acceptance of one's fate.

8. This great line can stand many interpretations. It certainly seems important in heroic stories throughout history.

9. Many students may observe that in the last years of the twentieth century we are especially eager to find hero-figures. Note the popularity of the musical *Camelot* and the best-selling status of T.H. White's *The Once and Future King*.

10. Among the supernatural elements *(Answers continue in left-hand column.)*

(Continued from top.)

are the following: King Arthur's prophetic dream, the appearance of the arm above the water that clasps the sword Excalibur, and the final scene of the three ladies in the barge.

Prophetic dreams are recurring motifs. Mysterious departures and rescues are also stock-in-trade of fantasies today. Answers will depend on what is currently popular in viewing and reading with the class.

Writing About the Story

A Creative Response

1. **Using Another Point of View.** Imagine that you are Sir Bedivere and that you are writing a letter to a far-off friend to describe the death of your liege-lord, King Arthur. Select one of the scenes from Malory's account and narrate it from Sir Bedivere's point of view. Let sir Bedivere describe his private thoughts about what he witnessed.

A Critical Response

2. **Writing a Research Report.** Write a research report on King Arthur as a figure in legend and literature. For your report, investigate at least one of the following topics.

   a. Continental and British sources for the Arthurian legend
   b. The historical figure of Arthur
   c. The cult of Glastonbury
   d. The use of the legend by later writers, especially by T. S. Eliot in his poem *The Waste Land*
   e. Jessie Weston's *From Ritual to Romance*

Analyzing Language and Style

Archaic Constructions and Context Clues

Archaic sentence constructions—those that are no longer used in contemporary standard English—mark Malory's style. Archaic words are also prominent in this story—words that have gone out of common use. Many words are footnoted in the story, but you will have to figure out many other archaic constructions and archaic words from context clues. How would you rephrase each of these statements from the first two paragraphs in contemporary English?

1. . . . in his dream he seemed that he saw . . .
2. . . . so he awaked until it was nigh day . . .
3. So the King seemed verily that there came Sir Gawain unto him . . .
4. "I weened ye had been dead."
5. "And now I see thee on-live . . ."
6. ". . . What been these ladies that hither be come with you?"

List at least five other archaic words or constructions from the story. Use some of these constructions in a paragraph of your own, to see how you can create an archaic flavor.

A Comment on the Legend
John Steinbeck on the Arthurian Legend

In 1976, American writer John Steinbeck's wife Elaine brought out a retelling of the Arthurian legends begun by her husband and left incomplete at his death. Here, in a portion of the preface to that book, Steinbeck talks about the influence of the legends on his childhood:

"Books were printed demons—the tongs and thumbscrews of outrageous persecution. And then, one day, an aunt gave me a book and fatuously ignored my resentment. I stared at the black print with hatred, and then, gradually, the pages opened and let me in. The magic happened. The Bible and Shakespeare and *Pilgrim's Progress* belonged to everyone. But this was mine— It was a cut version of the Caxton *Morte d'Arthur* of Thomas Malory. I loved the old spelling of the words—and the words no longer used. Perhaps a passionate love for the English language opened to me from this one book. I was delighted to find out paradoxes—that *cleave* means both to stick together and to cut apart; that *host* means both an enemy and a welcoming friend; that *king* and *gens* (people) stem from the same root. For a long time, I had a secret language—*yclept* and *hyght, wist*—and *accord* meaning peace, and *entente* meaning purpose, and *fyaunce* meaning promise. . . . But beyond the glorious and secret words—'And when the chylde is borne lete it be delyvered to me at yonder privy posterne uncrystened'—oddly enough I knew the words from whispering them to myself. The very strangeness of the language dyd me enchante, and vaulted me into an ancient scene.

"And in that scene were all the vices that ever were—and courage and sadness and frustration, but particularly gallantry—perhaps the only single quality of man that the West has invented. I think my sense of right and wrong, my feeling of noblesse oblige, and any thought I may have against the oppressor and for the oppressed came from this secret book. It did not outrage my sensibilities as nearly all the children's books did. It did not seem strange to me that Uther Pendragon wanted the wife of his vassal and took her by trickery. I was not frightened to find that there were evil knights, as well as noble ones. In my own town there were men who wore the clothes of virtue whom I knew to be bad. In pain or sorrow or confusion, I went back to my magic book. Children are violent and cruel—and good—and I was all of these—and all of these were in the secret book."

—John Steinbeck

THE ENGLISH LANGUAGE
by John Algeo

Although there are no hard and fast boundaries between one historical stage of our language and another, it is customary to divide the history of English into three large periods: Old English (before 1066), Middle English (1066–1485), and Modern English (1485 to the present). To be sure, all English speakers did not go to bed on the night of December 31, 1065, speaking Old English and wake up on the morning of January 1, 1066, saying, "Let's talk Middle English now!" Language change is slower and subtler than that. And speakers are seldom aware of the significance of changes happening in their own lifetimes.

Some important changes in pronunciation and grammar happened shortly before 1066, however. Then, in 1066, the Normans conquered England, eventually causing extensive changes in vocabulary. As a result, the pre-1066 language looks like a foreign tongue, but by the end of the Middle English period it was quite similar to the language we use today.

What Happened to the Endings? Pronunciation Changes That Produced Middle English

Old English, like the other Germanic languages, tended to pronounce words with a strong accent on the first syllable. In present-day English we still stress the first syllable in such two-syllable words as *census, legal, ribbon, valid,* and *weather;* in such three-syllable words as *algebra* and *innocent;* and in such four-syllable words as *admirable* and *nominative.* So too, the vowel in the first syllable of Old English words was said loudly, clearly, and distinctly, but the vowels in the other syllables tended to be rushed over. They consequently lost their distinctive sounds and began to be pronounced all alike. Unstressed vowels, especially those at the ends of words, were often reduced to schwa (ə)—the sound in the last syllable of our word *cola* or in the first syllable of *alone.*

We know that the unstressed vowel sounds were merging in late Old English because of the misspellings that begin to turn up in the manuscripts. Most speakers of Old English were undoubtedly illiterate, and most writing was done by scribes in monasteries. A scribe sat at his desk all day long, dipping his goose-quill pen into a pot of ink and tracing out letter shapes on parchment (sheets of writing material made from the skins of sheep or goats). Writing was reserved for important documents like sermons and legal records; it was not used for grocery lists or reminders to put out the cat. And the scribes were carefully trained.

Despite this training, however, about the year 1000 scribes began to have a great deal of trouble in remembering how the endings of words ought to be spelled. They had a hard time decid-

Middle English: The Language in Transition

A

B

Scriptorium in the tower of the monastery of Tavara, Spain. From a Spanish manuscript (13th C.).

© 1987 The Pierpont Morgan Library, New York City.

A. Expansion
You might want students to look back at the sample of Middle English on page 88. By comparing this excerpt from *The Canterbury Tales* with its "translation" on page 89, students will realize the extent to which Middle English is, indeed, similar to the English we use today.

B. Interpreting
How do we know that unstressed vowel sounds were merging in late Old English? (Because the increase in misspellings indicates that people no longer pronounced words with different endings differently—for example, *-as* and *-es, -on* and *-an.* All these are now pronounced as a schwa sound.)

A. Humanities Connection: About the Fine Art

For information on the Lindisfarne Gospels, see the Humanities Connection annotation, page 57.

A

Lindisfarne Gospels
(early 18th century).

British Museum.

ing whether to write *stanas* or *stanes* ("stones"), *comon* or *coman* ("they came"). This indecision shows that the scribes had ceased to pronounce the vowels of those endings differently from one another. These unstressed vowels had all fallen together as a schwa sound. Eventually the scribes gave up trying to spell the endings differently and just used the letter *e* to write the unstressed vowel: *stanes, comen.* When that happened, the language became what we call Middle English.

Endings and Order: Grammatical Changes That Produced Middle English

The change in the pronunciation and spelling of vowels not only changed the way English sounded, but also had some far-reaching effects on English grammar. Old English nouns had changed their endings to show their grammatical function. For example, the Old English word for "door" used as the subject of a sentence was *duru;* used as the direct object, the word was *dure.* The plural "doors" was *dura.* After the unstressed vowels had fallen together, all three forms became *dore,* with a schwa sound at the end.

Old English had depended on the vowels in the last syllables of words to help tell many things: They indicated whether an adjective's or noun's gender was masculine, feminine, or neuter; whether a verb was indicative (stating a fact) or subjunctive (stating a wish or an unreality); whether a noun was singular or plural; what function a noun filled in a sentence (subject or object); and so on. The loss of the vowel distinctions meant that English speakers had to find other ways of indicating those things, or they had to do without such information.

Effects on Gender. For gender, Middle English speakers decided to do without. And today almost no one is sorry that Middle English replaced grammatical gender with natural gender. Instead of talking about "the door . . . she," "the roof . . . he," and "the wife . . . it," we follow Middle English in using *he* for males, *she* for females, and *it* for things without sex.

Effects on Mood (Indicative vs. Subjunctive). For mood (the indicative-subjunctive distinction, as in "I am sure" versus "If I were sure"), Middle English speakers began to let the difference slip away. Today the subjunctive form survives only in a few of its former uses and only for verbs that have strikingly different forms for the two moods (*am* versus *were*). Today's speakers, including educated and well-spoken ones, are often uncertain about how to use the few surviving forms of the subjunctive. Probably those forms will follow the path of grammatical gender to extinction.

Effects on the Plural Forms. For number, Middle English came to rely on a few plural endings. Old English had many ways of marking the plural of a noun. A few of these survive in Modern English irregular plurals: *tooth/teeth, ox/oxen, child/children,* and *deer/deer* (in which the difference is not marked at all). Other Old English plural forms, such as *duru* ("door") versus *dura* ("doors") have not survived at all. In Old English, the ending *-as* was used

'Twas brillig, and the slithy toves
 Did gyre and gimble in the wabe;
All mimsy were the borogoves,
 And the mome raths outgrabe.

"Beware the Jabberwock, my son!
 The jaws that bite, the claws
 that catch!
Beware the Jubjub bird, and shun
 The frumious Bandersnatch!"

to form quite a large number of noun plurals. Middle English speakers stopped using many of these plurals, favoring instead the ending -es. Thus we have Old English *hund/hundas,* which became in Middle English *hound/houndes,* which became in Modern English *hound/hounds.* Over a period of time, Middle English came to use the -s ending for almost all nouns, as we still do today.

Effects on Case Endings. Instead of case endings to show the function of nouns in a sentence, Middle English came to rely on word order. English has long tended to put the subject of a sentence before, and the object after, the verb. That order, which seems so natural to us, is not used in all languages; and even in Old English it was much less frequent than it is today. As it does in Modern English, in Middle English "The knave slough [killed] the dragon" means something quite different from "The dragon slough the knave"; and that difference is signaled only by the order of the words.

Gender, mood, plurals, and case are only some of the grammatical concepts affected by the loss of the distinct vowels in unstressed syllables. Because Middle English could no longer rely upon distinct vowels in the final syllables of its words to signal various kinds of grammatical meaning, it gave up many of those meanings and found new ways of signaling the ones it kept. The result was that, whereas Old English was a highly inflected language—that is, it showed grammatical meanings and relations by word endings—Middle English was a more analytical language— that is, it showed meanings and relations by word order and by function words such as prepositions, auxiliary verbs, articles, and other particles.

Old English had a grammar more like that of Latin. Middle English had a grammar very much like the one we still use today. The difference is profound.

"*Period. New paragraph.*"

Drawing by Carl Rose; © 1950, 1978
The New Yorker Magazine, Inc.

B. Responding to the Cartoon
The humor in this cartoon arises from an *anachronism:* A modern office practice—dictating—is placed in the setting of a *scriptorium,* a room set aside in a medieval monastery for copying.
❓ How do we know that the kind of dictation in this cartoon did not actually go on in a scriptorium? (Punctuation and paragraph indentations were late developments in writing.)

Shortly after the unstressed vowels had come to be pronounced as schwas, a political event occurred which was to have far-reaching, long-lasting consequences for the English language. In 1066, William, Duke of Normandy, invaded England with an army of soldiers from France. He defeated the English defenders, led by King Harold, at the Battle of Hastings.

Under William the Conqueror (as he came to be called), French nobles took over the government of England, the French clergy assumed leading roles in the English church, and French became the language of government, law, education, and upper-class life. English continued to be spoken, of course, by most of the inhabitants of England: by servants, craftsmen, farmers, foresters—the sturdy yeomenry of the land. But French was the language of the rulers. England had once been in danger of becoming an outpost of Scandinavia. Now it seemed likely to become a province of France.

The two people—Vikings from Scandinavia and Normans from France—were in fact related. The Normans were, as their name

Uninvited Guests: The Norman Conquest and French in England

A. Expansion

Two hundred years after William's conquest, French was still so much spoken in places of power that Robert of Gloucester writes in the thirteenth century, "I ween that in all the world there is no country that holds not to her own speech, save England alone." Even in the fourteenth century, accounts of the sitting of Parliament were still recorded in French, and all the "best" poets continued to write in French.

Detail from the Bayeaux Tapestry (c. 1077).

Musée de l'Eveche. With special authorization of the city of Bayeaux.

Stained glass panels depicting the harvest of corn in August. From the Labors of the Months (15th C.).

Victoria and Albert Museum, London.

suggests, not really French, but rather people from the North (Normen), Scandinavians who had settled in the western regions of France. Having settled there, they gave up their original Scandinavian speech and acquired the language of their new home, although they never learned to speak it the way proper Frenchmen did. To the elegant speakers of Paris, the Normans always sounded strange, foreign, and provincial.

Thus the conquerors of Anglo-Saxon England were not refined emissaries of a higher civilization who brought culture to primitive England. On the contrary, they were a wild bunch, only a few generations removed from their piratical ancestors, who had acquired a veneer of civilization. The Norman Conquest was a near disaster for England. It drove the English language underground— out of use for prestigious social purposes by the ruling class— leaving it only on the tongues of the common people.

In the long run, however, the Conquest was probably a blessing for English. The language was left to itself, to develop and grow without interference by scholars or government officials, in the direction in which the merger of unstressed vowels had started it. The common folk of the early Middle English period were quite untroubled by traditions of spelling or preconceived notions of what their language ought to be like. So they spoke naturally—letting the vowels fall together and giving up the many grammatical endings of Old English, with no sense that they were losing anything of importance. And they were right.

The Battle of the Languages and the Triumph of English

For several hundred years, England was a bilingual country. French was spoken by the upper classes among themselves, it was used for the business of law courts and government, and it was used for literature. English was spoken by the lower classes for all the ordinary purposes of daily life—selling grain, buying dishes, scolding children, squabbling with neighbors, and loving the family. Latin was also being spoken in the church, but no one learned Latin for common use.

For a time no one could have said confidently whether French or English would win out as the national language of England. However, several factors eventually tipped the balance to English. Not least important was the fact that the bulk of the population spoke English. The Norman conquerors had not come as a wave of settlers to displace the English, but rather as a ruling group with a relatively small number of retainers to replace the native nobility, many of whom had been killed at the Battle of Hastings. The Norman nobility fit into the top of the existing social order; they had no need or desire to destroy that order. There was no effort to eradicate English or those who spoke it, so the life of the average yeoman continued much as it had before the Conquest.

Another factor that favored English was the gradual loss of contact between England and France. William the Conqueror was both King of England and Duke of Normandy, but his great-grandson, King John (who was something of a loser), lost control of Normandy. Later, England undertook the Hundred Years' War against France; the conflict naturally intensified a feeling of patriotism for things English, including the language, as against the foreign French.

During the centuries following the Conquest, the English language gradually reasserted its place in the national life. In the second half of the fourteenth century, about three hundred years after the Conquest, English had again become the primary language used for all purposes in England. This was symbolized by a bill passed in Parliament in 1362 requiring that all law cases be conducted in English instead of in French.

At that time there was no standard form of English, since English for so long had had no official or governmental use. Instead, people spoke the form of English found in their own native area. With the reestablishment of English as a language of government, however, the dialect of London (the capital city) quickly became a model to be followed, especially the variety used by the lawyers and law clerks for keeping court records.

In the fourteenth century, also, literature in English was revitalized. The common people had never been without their own literature: ballads and songs, tales and sermons. But for the most part it was common stuff to entertain ordinary people, about the equivalent of television comedies and soap operas today—effective but ephemeral entertainment. By the fourteenth century, however, first-rate literature was being written in English. Chaucer, one of the greatest writers of all time, was writing in the London dialect for the royal court. The anonymous author of *Sir Gawain and the Green Knight* was producing his courtly tale in a northwestern dialect for country gentry. As the language flowered, so did the literature, with the same exuberance and variety.

A

B

David playing his harp for Saul. From an English psalter (c. 1225).

© 1987 The Pierpont Morgan Library, New York City.

A. Expansion
Royal decrees in England and in France in 1224 made it illegal for anyone to hold land in both countries.

B. Humanities Connection: About the Fine Art
A *psalter* is a book of Psalms. Many of the Pilgrims brought a psalter to the New World with them as one of their few books. David is traditionally regarded as the author of the Psalms. According to 1 Samuel 16:14–23, David was able to cure King Saul of his melancholy by playing his harp.

Loan Words from French

Both a Borrower and a Lender Be

It may seem strange, but at the time the English language was replacing the French, English was borrowing words from French most intensely. But such borrowing was inevitable. For three hundred years, English citizens had used French to run the country, to operate the law courts, to order the army, to entertain the nobility, and to do a myriad of things characteristic of upper-class life. Because English had not been used for such purposes for three hundred years, English speakers had forgotten whatever technical words they had once had for governmental, legal, military, literary, and other such subjects. When they started to use English again to talk about those matters, they were literally at a loss for words. The simplest thing to do was to borrow the French terms. And that is just what sensible English speakers did.

English was flooded with French loan words during the Middle English period, the crest coming in the late fourteenth century.

> **"A**nimals on the hoof looked after by English-speaking workers were, and are still, called by native English names: *cow, hog, sheep, calf, deer.*"

Examples of the French influence are *baron, castle, chancellor, country, duke, government, noble, prince, royal, state; attorney, court, crime, judge, jury, prison; army, captain, corporal, lieutenant, sergeant, soldier; juggler, literature, magic, melody, poetry, sport.* Animals on the hoof looked after by English-speaking workers were, and are still, called by native English names: *cow, hog, sheep, calf, deer.* But when they were slaughtered and served up on the table as food, they were given the French names that the invading nobility gave them: *beef, pork, bacon, mutton, veal, venison.* Thus our vocabulary continues to echo the English-worker/French-ruler dichotomy of six hundred years ago.

The French influence on the English vocabulary has been very great, and has continued from the time of the Conquest until now. Even today, English borrows more words from French than from any other language. But the importance of the French loan words is even greater. Because so many words came into English from French in a relatively short space of time, English speakers became accustomed to absorbing foreign influences and to adapting words from other languages for their own use. We have been doing it ever since.

Since the fourteenth century, English has borrowed large numbers of words from many languages, and today our vocabulary is one of the most international and thus also one of the richest in the world. In turn, English has become a major source of loan words to other languages. Nowadays there are few languages spoken upon Earth from which English has not borrowed, and even fewer that have not borrowed from it. That is another benefit of the Norman Conquest that William and his bullyboys could not have imagined or understood.

Analyzing Language

1. Here is a Middle English version of the Lord's Prayer, from the Bible as translated by John Wycliffe and his followers in 1380.

   > Oure fadir that art in heuenes halowid be thi name, thi kyngdom come to, be thi wille don in erthe as in heuene, yeue to us this day oure breed ouir other substaunce, & foryeue to us oure dettis, as we foryeuen to oure dettouris, & lede us not in to temptacioun: but delyuer us from yuel, amen.

   Compare this version with the Old English text (page 61), which is about four hundred years older. What differences do you see in vocabulary, syntax (word order), and spelling? Does the Middle English version seem to be more like Old English or like the Modern English that we use today? Give several reasons to support your answer.

2. Many new words came into English during the Middle English period. Just before the definition of a word, *Webster's Ninth New Collegiate Dictionary* gives the date or century when the word was first recorded in use. Find that date or century for each of these words. Note the language from which each was borrowed.

army	gentleman	justice	royal
castle	guide	master	servant
chief	herb	roast	soldier

3. In each of the following groups, (a) one word was used in Old English, (b) one is a Middle English loan from French, and (c) one is a Modern English loan from French. Guess which origin each word has. Then check your guesses in a dictionary.

chair	table	automobile
chaise longue	tableau	(wheel) barrow
stool	tablet	car

gender	boutique	city
genre	shop	habitue
kin	store	town

EVALUATING LITERATURE IN GROUP DISCUSSION

Assignment

A In a small-group discussion, evaluate "The Pardoner's Tale" (or any other tale) from *The Canterbury Tales* by Geoffrey Chaucer.

Background

To **evaluate** a story, you make a judgment about its merits by examining elements such as plot, characterization, point of view, and theme. Consider the following questions:

Guidelines for Evaluating a Story

1. Is the **plot** believable and natural, or does it seem contrived? Does it rely too much on coincidence and chance?
2. Is the ending satisfying, or does it seem a cliché ending?
3. Is the story suspenseful? Is the writer's purpose simply to entertain with a "thriller," or does the plot involve complex issues and behavior?
4. Are the **characters** believable?
5. Are their **motivations** (the reasons for their actions) clear and believable? Do they behave consistently?
6. Do any of the characters develop or change during the course of the story?
7. What is the **point of view**? What are its advantages and disadvantages?
8. Is the point of view consistent? If not, does the writer have a good reason for switching the point of view?
9. Does the story have a **theme**? That is, does it communicate some meaningful insight into human nature or life?
10. Does the theme deal with an important aspect of life? Does it present a new idea or an accepted "truth"?
11. Does the theme seem believable? Does it relate to human life as I know it?

Preparing for the Discussion

1. Reread "The Pardoner's Tale" by Geoffrey Chaucer. Refer to the guidelines as you read, and take notes in response to the evaluation questions.
2. Prepare a series of 5" × 7" note cards to which you can easily refer during the discussion. Give each note card a heading, such as *Plot, Character, Point of View,* or *Theme*. On each card, cite an incident, a character, or a detail from the story that supports your opinion of how good (or bad) the story is. Here are two sample note cards:

Character

Three young men introduced as rioters who drink instead of go to church (lines 52–54).

Their characters further developed in disrespectful treatment of old man (lines 108–110).

Plot

Plot develops logically out of the rioters' character.

Ironic quest: They go to "kill this traitor Death" (line 91), and all three perish.

Conducting the Group Discussion

Follow these guidelines for conducting your discussion:

1. As your teacher directs, form groups of six to eight students.
2. If your teacher does not appoint group leaders, each group should quickly elect a leader. The leader's responsibility is to make sure that each member participates in the discussion and that everyone's ideas get a fair hearing.
3. Each group's task is to come to a **consensus** on an evaluation of "The Pardoner's Tale" (or any other of the tales you select to discuss). A consensus is a decision that every member of the group agrees to. (Juries must reach a consensus on the guilt or innocence of a person; a split vote is not acceptable.)
4. Members of your group are bound to have varying opinions about the story. Listen critically to what they say, and be prepared to express your own opinion

A. Extension
Students might have some difficulty understanding the difference between *evaluating* a story based on a set of criteria such as those presented on this page and *reviewing* a story by giving personal opinions. In preparation for this assignment, you might want to have students bring in film reviews from their local newspapers or from magazines such as *Time* or *Newsweek*. Have students share the reviews and note instances, if there are any, where the reviewers use criteria for evaluating films and where they simply give their opinions. Students might enjoy forming small groups to develop their own criteria for films. They can evaluate the same films reviewed in newspapers and magazines based on their own criteria.

about the story's worth. Make sure that you can back up your opinions by citing evidence from the story. (Use the Prewriting note cards you've prepared.)

5. When your group seems close to agreement, work together to draft a statement reflecting the group's evaluation of the story. Every member of the group must agree to this statement—if you are to reach a consensus. If your group cannot come to a consensus, it is the leader's responsibility to suggest changes in wording that will make the statement acceptable to everyone.

6. Compare your group's consensus statement with those of the other groups.

Evaluating the Discussion

Take a few minutes to talk about your group's discussion. Did you learn anything new from what other group members said? What can you do to improve your next discussion? What skills do you think an effective leader needs to have?

THE RENAISSANCE
1485–1660

Ladies and Gentlemen Dancing in a Sumptuous Interior by Paulus Vrendeman DeVries.

Christie's, London.

UNIT THREE

HUMANITIES CONNECTION: DISCUSSING THE FINE ART

Paulus DeVries (1567–1630?), a Flemish painter, continued his famous father's tradition of painting architectural scenes with figures.

However elegant this palatial Renaissance interior, we would probably find it uncomfortable today. Huge, drafty halls such as these were nearly impossible to heat, making several layers of clothing necessary. Garments could not be cleaned in those days—the soap, made from ashes and lye, was far too harsh. Little wonder that there was a brisk trade in perfumes!

? Describe the architectural details of this room. What is the painting's tone? (The musicians, dancing couples, and bright yellows and reds certainly lend cheer to the scene.)

TEACHING RENAISSANCE LITERATURE

Begin by writing the word *renaissance* on the chalkboard, and ask students to attempt to derive the word's meaning from its parts. The prefix *re-* (again) should be easy for them, and you might volunteer words that share the meaning of the root, such as *nativity* and *postnatal*. Ask what sorts of events students might associate with a rebirth. Then point out that this particular rebirth saw advances in the arts (with Michelangelo, Raphael, Leonardo da Vinci), in philosophy (with Erasmus), and, of course, in literature.

OBJECTIVES OF THE RENAISSANCE UNIT

1. To improve reading proficiency and expand vocabulary
2. To gain exposure to notable authors and works of the period
3. To define and identify significant literary techniques, including pun, tone, sonnet, meter, personification, metaphor, allegory, symbol, alliteration, epic simile, paradox, imagery, setting, parallel structure, foreshadowing, dialogue, theme, blank verse, suspense, mood, couplet, syntax, rhyme, hyperbole, conceit, irony, exaggeration, understatement, and figure of speech
4. To interpret and respond to nonfiction and poetry, orally and in writing, through analysis of their elements
5. To practice the following critical thinking and writing skills:

a. Comparing and contrasting poems, prose works, and authors
b. Responding to criticism
c. Analyzing effects of literary techniques
d. Evaluating a poem, play, or prose work
e. Analyzing a character
f. Writing a research report

FOR FURTHER READING
STUDENTS

Historical novels can give students a better grasp of all aspects of the times. An especially good choice, in terms also of Henry VIII's establishment of the English Church, is Margaret George's *The Autobiography of Henry VIII: With Notes by His Fool, Will Somers* (1986). For a look at the Reformation's effect on the abbeys and monasteries, try H. F. Prescott's compelling novel *Man on a Donkey* (1981 paperback). Advanced students might look into Antonia Fraser's prize-winning *Mary Queen of Scots* (1984 paperback).

SUPPLEMENTARY SUPPORT MATERIALS: UNIT THREE

1. Unit Introduction Test (*CCB*)
2. English Language Test (*CCB*)
3. Word Analogies Test (*CCB*)
4. Unit Review Test (*CCB*)

5. Critical Thinking and Writing Test (*CCB*)
6. Instructional Overhead Transparencies

A. About the Quotation

The quotation is from Sidney's *An Apology for Poetry* (see text page 215). Sidney compares the poet with the moral philosopher and the historian. The poet is their "monarch" (superior) because not only can he give precepts and examples, he can also affect people's feelings and actions. Poets can create "another nature," new and beautiful.

B. Humanities Connection: Discussing the Fine Art

Botticelli (c. 1444–1510) was one of the notable painters of the Italian Renaissance. One of his best-known paintings is *The Birth of Venus,* in the Uffizi in Florence. Here he depicts Saint Augustine (354–430), Bishop of Hippo (in today's Algeria), and a great writer and theologian. Note the bishop's miter (pointed hat) at the saint's right.

? Can you identify the objects in this study that suggest learning? (Books, globe, a clock) Compare the lush draperies and rich objects in this picture with the simple lines and background in the illuminations on text pages 54 and 57. Botticelli has put this fifth-century monk in the environment of a Renaissance prince.

THE RENAISSANCE 1485–1660

by **C. F. Main**

St. Augustine by Sandro Botticelli. Fresco.

Church of the Ognissanti, Florence.

> *Now therein of all sciences is our poet the monarch. For he doth not only show the way, but giveth so sweet a prospect into the way as will entice any man to enter it.*
>
> —Sir Philip Sidney

As the French philosopher Voltaire said, "The ancients did not know they were the ancients"; nor did the people of Europe living in the 1400's, 1500's, and 1600's know that they were living in the Renaissance. Voltaire's quip reminds us that historical periods—the Middle Ages, the Renaissance, the Romantic period—are historians' inventions, useful labels for complex phenomena. The Middle Ages did not end at 11:59 P.M. on a certain night in 1484, nor did the Renaissance begin at 12:01 A.M. the next morning. Instead, changes in people's values, beliefs, and behavior occurred gradually, and much that could be called "medieval" lingered on long after the period known as the Middle Ages was past. Historical periods cannot be rigidly separated from one another, but they can be distinguished.

The term *renaissance* itself is a French word meaning "rebirth," and it refers particularly to renewed interest in classical learning, the writings of ancient Greece and Rome. In the Middle Ages, people forgot the Greek language and debased the Latin; in the Renaissance people learned to read Greek once more and reformed the Latin that they read, wrote, and spoke. And some people became more curious about themselves and their world than people in general had been in the Middle Ages, so that gradually there was a rebirth or renewal of the human spirit. New energy seemed to be available for creating beautiful things and thinking new thoughts. Today we still call a strong, versatile, and productive human being a "Renaissance person."

The Italian Renaissance

The new energy and creativity were first observable in Italy, where the Renaissance began in the fourteenth century and lasted into the sixteenth. Just mentioning a few of the geniuses who flourished in this period—Boccaccio, Petrarch, Raphael, da Vinci, Galileo, Machiavelli, Michelangelo, Columbus—reminds us how remarkably rich this civilization was, and how much we owe to it. Many of the Popes and many of the rulers of the independent cities and states that then made up Italy were lavish patrons of artists, architects, and scholars, as well as collectors of ancient manuscripts, statues, and coins. Pope Nicholas V, for instance, founded a new Vatican library, which rapidly became the most impressive collection of its kind, and Pope Julian II commissioned Michelangelo to paint gigantic scenes from the Bible on the ceiling of the Vatican's

A. Humanities Connection: Discussing the Fine Art

This panel illustrates Genesis 1:6–7, the second day of creation. A detail can only suggest the splendor of the gigantic figures that cover the ceiling of the Sistine Chapel. The work took Michelangelo (1475–1564) four years to complete. Lying on his back on a scaffold, he had to keep in mind the entire scheme of his work, which moved from the creation of the world to the great Flood. The fresco form—the application of paint onto fresh plaster—created additional challenges. It required daily plastering of the exact area he expected to complete; the plaster had to be kept dry enough to adhere but wet enough to absorb the paint.

The detail here shows Michelangelo's virile, humanized idea of God (the central figure) and of the angels (the surrounding figures). In a characteristic Renaissance style, human beings and their creator are seen as members of the same species.

Today the Sistine ceiling is being cleaned of layers of grime, and for the first time in centuries people are able to see these monumental figures in the colors Michelangelo actually used. Michelangelo is considered the typical Renaissance man—he was a painter, sculptor (*David*, the *Pietà*), architect, and poet. You might recommend Irving Stone's fictionalized biography *The Agony and the Ecstasy* (1961).

B. Expansion

You may wish to refer students to the first two chapters of Genesis, with special attention to 1:26–29 and 2:19–23, to evaluate the degree to which the passages from the Bible inspired the words of Mirandola.

A

Sistine Chapel. Michelangelo's scenes represent the Creation, the fall of man and woman, the flood, and other subjects. His immense, bright figures are perfectly proportioned, and they suggest that individual human beings are noble and capable of perfection. This optimistic view of human nature was also expressed by many other Renaissance painters and writers, and especially by the philosopher Pico della Mirandola, who said the following in his speech entitled *On the Dignity of Humanity*:

God Separating Land from Sea by Michelangelo (1508–12). Fresco. Detail from the ceiling of the Sistine Chapel, St. Peter's, Rome.

> God made man and woman at the close of the creation, to know the laws of the universe, to love its beauty, and to admire its greatness. He bound his human creatures to no fixed place, to no prescribed form of work, and by no iron necessity, but gave them freedom to will and to love. "I have set thee," says the Creator, "in the midst of the world, that thou mayst the more easily behold and see all that is therein. I created thee a being neither heavenly nor earthly, neither mortal nor immortal only, that thou mightest be free to shape and to overcome thyself. Thou mayest sink into a beast or be born anew to the divine likeness. To thee alone is given a growth and a development depending on thine own free will."
>
> —Pico della Mirandola

B

John Milton, the last great figure of the English Renaissance, expressed the same view of the free will, potential greatness, and possible degradation of humanity.

Pico della Mirandola by Niccolo Florentino. Medal.

The British Museum.

Printing in the Renaissance

Have students consider the sheer hand labor involved in early publishing. (See the illustration below.) The printer had to place each tiny metal letter into a frame, attach the frame to the press, ink it, and print a page at a time. (See the pages drying on a clothesline below.) Furthermore, in Elizabethan England, the output of a press was tightly regulated, and printing a work without the approval of the Church could lead to severe punishment. Nonetheless, in the characteristic exuberance of the age, more than 26,000 items were published between 1475 and 1640.

Compare all this with today's technology that made it possible for Arthur C. Clarke to note at the end of his novel *2010: Odyssey Two,* "This book was written on an Archives III microcomputer with WordStar software and sent from Colombo [Sri Lanka] to New York on one five-inch diskette. Last-minute corrections were transmitted through the Padukka Earth Station and the Indian Ocean Intelsat V."

A. About the Illustration

A catechism (from the Greek *katechesis,* "to teach") is a question-and-answer book used for religious instruction. Popular since the late Middle Ages, catechisms gained in importance during the Reformation, when Martin Luther (see text page 172) stressed the religious education of children. (His own *Small Catechism* of 1529 is still a basic Lutheran text.)

Notice that, though the catechism is for English children, it is written in Latin.

B. Humanism

Some people today criticize "secular humanism."

How, on the basis of the words themselves, would you expect "*secular* humanism" to differ from this Renaissance concept of humanism? (It would not contain religious references or components.)

Title page of *Catechismus* (1573).

Folger Shakespeare Library, Washington, D.C.

Humanism

Writers like Pico and Milton were exponents of an intellectual movement known as humanism, a movement that attempted to derive from the Latin and Greek classics answers to such questions as, "What is a human being?" "What is a good life?" and "How does one lead a good life?" Of course the Christian religion already provided complete answers to these questions, answers that the Renaissance humanists readily accepted as true. Renaissance humanists could find no essential conflicts in the teachings of St. Paul, for instance, and an ancient Roman moralist like Cicero. They sought to harmonize two great sources of wisdom: the Bible and the classics. Their aim was to use the classics to strengthen, not discredit, religion.

The humanists' first task was to recover accurate copies of ancient writings, and their searches through dusty old collections in Italian monasteries turned up authors and works whose very existence had been forgotten. Their next task was to disseminate their findings, and so they became teachers, especially of the young men who would become the next generation's rulers—wise and virtuous rulers, they hoped. The humanist-teachers had their students read Latin and Greek books for their content, not just their language. From the Greek Plutarch, for instance, they would learn that the proper aim of life is to attain virtue, not success or

Printing Shop by Jan van der Straet (1580's). Engraving.

Folger Shakespeare Library, Washington, D.C.

money or fame, because virtue is the best possible human possession and the only source of true happiness. The aim of humanistic teaching, as Milton summarized it in his essay *Of Education,* was not to produce scholars but to fit their students to "perform justly, skillfully, and magnanimously all the duties, public and private, of peace and war."

Printing

The printing of books with movable type and presses began in the Renaissance, and it rapidly replaced the laborious reproduction of books by hand. The inventor of printing, a German named Johann Gutenberg (1400?–1468), was probably responsible for the first printed book, an immense Latin Bible produced at Mainz in Germany. From there the art and craft of printing spread to other cities in Germany, the Low Countries, and northern Italy, so that by 1500 inexpensive books were available throughout Western Europe. The most distinguished printing and publishing house was that of Aldus Manutius and his family, in Venice. They employed humanists to locate and prepare for printing accurate texts of all the most important works in Greek and Latin, and they issued these products of the new learning in beautifully printed editions.

In 1476 printing reached England, then regarded as an island remote from the centers of civilization. In that year William Caxton (1422?–1491), a merchant, diplomat, and writer who had been living in the Low Countries, set up a printing press in Westminster (now a part of London). In 1477 Caxton published *The Dictes or Sayings of the Philosophers,* an anthology of passages from classical works that he had translated. In all, Caxton's press issued about one hundred different titles, initiating a flood of print in English that is still increasing.

Erasmus and More

Desiderius Erasmus (1466?–1536), today perhaps the best known of all the Renaissance humanists, took full advantage of printing and the new international traffic in books. The son of a Dutch priest, Erasmus was given a good classical education by his rich relatives, and at twenty-two he became a monk. But with the permission of his bishop, he spent his life outside the cloister, first earning a degree at the University of Paris and then visiting other countries, including Italy, France, Germany, and England. He belonged, then, to all Europe. Because he wrote in Latin, he could address his many writings to all the educated people of Western Europe. Among his most famous books are *Adages,* a large and useful collection of proverbs and quotations; *Colloquies,* dialogues on contemporary life; and *The Handbook of a Christian Soldier,* a guide to the spiritual warfare of good against evil. Erasmus also published Bible commentaries as well as improved texts of the New Testament and the Church Fathers.

A

B

Erasmus von Rotterdam by Quentin Metsys. Oil.

Palazzo Barberini, Rome.

A. Responding

[?] From students' knowledge of history and from their reading of the unit introduction to this point, you might ask them why it is not surprising that Gutenberg chose to print the Bible first, rather than some other book. (It was the one book people would have been familiar with.) How do they account for the fact that, even today, the Bible (in a broad range of translations and editions) annually tops the best-seller lists? (Answers may include that the stories of the Bible are universally known, even by nonreligious people.)

B. Humanities Connection: About the Fine Art

Quentin Metsys (also spelled Massys, Matsys, or Messys, c. 1466–1530) was a Flemish painter known for his calm style of portraiture, with solid textures, and a background suited to his subject. This portrait is a good example. Everything about Erasmus—his attitude, clothing, activity, and environment—says "scholar."

A. Utopia

Book I of More's *Utopia* is a dialogue analyzing the social, economic, penal, and moral ills in England. Book II is a narrative describing Utopia (from Greek *ou,* "not," and *topos,* "place"), meaning (ironically) "Nowhere." In Utopia, poverty, crime, injustice, and other ills do not exist.

B. Sir Thomas More

In contrast to the rich and scandalously immoral Lorenzo de Medici, More lived a simple life and was a devoted and loving family man. (Defying custom, he taught his daughter Meg Latin; few women were given any kind of higher education in those days.) More is seen today as an example of the individual who places the dictates of his conscience over the pressures of political authority.

A

Headpiece from *Utopia* by Sir Thomas More (1516). Engraving.

> "**M**ore and Erasmus had much in common: They both loved life, laughter, and classical learning."

On his visits to England, Erasmus taught Greek at Cambridge University and became very friendly with a number of important people, among them a young lawyer named Thomas More (1478–1535). More and Erasmus had much in common: They both loved life, laughter, and classical learning, and they both were dedicated churchmen, though they were impatient with some of the Church's practices at that time. At More's suggestion, Erasmus wrote a satire on medieval ideas and attitudes that became his most popular book, *Encomium Moriae.* The classical title of this book contains a pun on More's name: it can be translated as "The Praise of More" or "The Praise of Folly." And it is an entirely ironical book; in it Erasmus pretends to praise various kinds of foolishness that he is really laughing at.

Like Erasmus, More wrote much in Latin—poems, controversial pamphlets, biographies, and his famous speculative treatise on human society called *Utopia* (1516). This book became immediately popular, and it has been repeatedly translated into English and many other languages. Hundreds of authors have imitated and parodied it, and it has given everybody a useful adjective for describing impractical social schemes: *utopian.* More himself was far from impractical; he held a number of important offices, rose to the very top of his profession, was knighted, and as Lord Chancellor became one of the realm's chief ministers. A man of wealth, versatility, and charm, More was the sober English equivalent of the great princes of Renaissance Italy such as the Florentine nobleman Lorenzo de Medici, known as "the Magnificent."

B

As a result of the conquests of Alexander the Great (356–323 B.C.), *koine* or "common" Greek became for many centuries the international language of Mediterranean regions and parts of Asia Minor and Africa. (Most of the New Testament was written in koine.) Koine was succeeded by Vulgar (or "common") Latin, carried throughout the Roman Empire by soldiers and colonists. In the Middle Ages, Latin yielded as the language of commerce to Lingua Franca ("language of the Franks," the Arabs' term for Western Europeans). Lingua Franca had an Italian base with a mixture of Spanish, French, Greek, and Arabic. Latin, however, flourished into the Renaissance as the language of the Church, universities, scholars, and writers. It was the language of diplomacy in Europe as late as the seventeenth century, and it remains today the official Vatican language. French next replaced Latin as the tongue of diplomacy. In the past century, French has been succeeded by the first truly *global* language—English. (See "One Language—Many Nations," text page 907.)

The English Renaissance

The Renaissance was well underway in England by the time Erasmus first visited More at his handsome estate outside London. By then at least two or three generations of English scholars had traveled to Italy, learned to admire and imitate classical Latin, and begun the study of classical Greek. England's Renaissance was more restrained and pious than Italy's: English humanists were less likely to become pleasure-loving pagans than Italy's, and they regarded classical learning more as a means for better understanding the Bible and leading a moral life than as an end in itself. England's Renaissance was also more bookish and much less productive of great works of art.

Besides More, other important English humanists include his teachers William Grocyn and Thomas Linacre, the former a profound student of the Greek New Testament, the latter an eminent physician and founder of the Royal College of Physicians. A third humanist, John Colet, made a great sensation when he returned from Italy in 1497. He lectured at Cambridge on the letters that St. Paul wrote in Greek—part of the New Testament—and he scandalized the older professors because he never once mentioned the ingenious Latin commentaries on those letters that had accumulated during the past four centuries. These three humanists, as well as two more of the next generation, Sir Thomas Elyot and Roger Ascham, had as their aim the spiritual, moral, and intellectual education of England's future leaders. Elyot's *The Book Named the Governor* (1531) argued that England's leaders needed a knowledge of ancient literature, history, and philosophy. And Ascham's *The Schoolmaster* (1570), according to Samuel Johnson (1709–1784), "contains the best advice that was ever given for the study of languages." Both Elyot and Ascham wrote in English, a sign of what was to come, when Latin would cease to be the language of all learned discourse.

Sir Thomas More by Hans Holbein the Younger. Oil.

© The Frick Collection, New York.

Establishment of the English Church

While the Renaissance was going on in Europe, there occurred in some countries another important series of events known as the Reformation. In England these two vast movements were intimately related, and their forces were felt by all English writers, and especially by the two greatest nondramatic poets of the period, Edmund Spenser and John Milton. Although the exact nature of the Reformation varied from country to country, there was one feature common to all Reformers: They repudiated the authority of the Pope and the Roman Catholic Church. In England, conflicts with the Papacy had occurred off and on over the centuries, but adjustments had always been made on both sides and an open break was avoided until the 1530's.

By then, a number of circumstances made such a break possible. Strong feelings of patriotism and national identity made the English people resent the financial burdens imposed on them by the Vatican—a foreign power in far-off Italy. Moreover, new religious ideas were coming into England from the Continent, espe-

A. Humanities Connection: Discussing the Portrait
Hans Holbein, the Younger (c. 1497–1543), was an outstanding German Renaissance artist who enjoyed a long friendship with Erasmus. Holbein eventually was named court painter to Henry VIII. He died of the plague in London at age forty-six.
? How can you tell that the subject of this portrait held an important post? (The seal of office worn on a chain around his neck)

B. Expansion
See the comment above on universal languages.

C. Expansion
Be sure students understand that up to this time, a large majority of Christians in Western Europe and England were members of the Roman Catholic Church, subject to the authority of the Pope (the Bishop of Rome) in matters of faith and morals.

A. Expansion
Pause at the end of this paragraph to clarify or summarize Henry's grievances against the Roman Catholic Church. Remind students of churchmen like the Pardoner who are satirized by Chaucer in *The Canterbury Tales* (see text page 104). The Church tacitly recognized many of these complaints by calling the Council of Trent (1545) to deal with the Protestant Reformation. By that time, however, internal reform was too late, and the Christian Church was broken up by the many "protestant" reformers.
❓ What do you think of Henry's reasoning? (It was self-serving rather than religious.)

B. Expansion
Note that "his [More's] church" means the Roman Catholic Church. Advanced students might read Robert Bolt's play *A Man for All Seasons* (1966 paperback), which dramatizes More's complex reasons for refusing to recognize Henry as head of the Church.

Queen Elizabeth I, from an illuminated manuscript (16th century).

Museum of London.

cially from Germany, where Martin Luther had founded a new kind of Christianity based on his understanding of the Bible rather than on the authoritative teaching of the Roman Catholic Church. And right at home in England humanists like More, Erasmus, and Colet were ridiculing what they called the superstitious use of relics as well as the ignorance and idleness of monks and the loose living of priests.

Matters came to a climax when Henry VIII, the second of the Tudor Kings, asked Pope Clement to declare that he was not properly married to his Spanish wife, Catherine of Aragon, because she had previously been wedded to his older brother Arthur, now dead. Henry had two motives for wanting to send Catherine back to Spain: First, although she had borne him a princess, she appeared to be incapable of giving him the male heir that he thought he must have. What is more, he was in love with, and wanted to marry, another woman, Anne Boleyn. The Pope was quite unable to grant Henry the annulment, even had he wanted to, because he was in the control of Queen Catherine's nephew and protector, Emperor Charles V, ruler of Spain, the Netherlands, and Germany. (Charles's armies had just sacked the city of Rome.) And so, upon receiving the Pope's refusal, Henry had himself declared head of the English Church in 1531. He then appointed a new Archbishop of Canterbury, who declared his marriage to Catherine invalid. He also confiscated all church revenues intended for Rome and sold all of England's rich monastic buildings and lands to his subjects. While the vast majority of his subjects agreed with Henry's changes in the church, some of them did not. The best known of all those who remained loyal to the Pope was Sir Thomas More, who, because he refused to recognize his friend Henry's religious supremacy, was beheaded at his friend's command. Four hundred years later (1935), his church declared him a saint.

At the very beginning of the English Church many were dissatisfied with it, for reasons just the opposite of More's. They felt that it was not reformed enough, that it was merely a compromise between Protestantism and Catholicism, as in some respects it was. These dissidents, who were soon to become known as Puritans, Baptists, Presbyterians, Dissenters, Nonconformists, and so on, wanted to get rid of many different things they called "Popish," such as the bishops, the prayer book, the priest's vestments, and even the bell on the church. Some of them said that religion was solely a matter between the individual and God. This idea, which is still frequently expressed, is directly traceable to the teachings of those Renaissance humanists who emphasized the freedom and autonomy of all human beings.

The Tudor Monarchs (1485–1603)

The five Tudor rulers are easy to remember: They consist of a grandfather, a father, and three children. The grandfather was Henry VII, a Welsh nobleman named Henry Tudor who seized the throne after England was totally exhausted by the long and bloody

A

An Allegory of the Tudor Succession:
The Family of Henry VIII,
British school (c. 1589–95). Oil.

Yale Center for British Art.
Paul Mellon Collection.

struggle of the Wars of the Roses. Henry VII was a shrewd, patient, and stingy man who restored peace and order to the kingdom; without these, there could never have been a cultural Renaissance.

His son Henry VIII (1509–1547) had, as everybody knows, six wives: Catherine of Aragon, Anne Boleyn, Jane Seymour, Anne of Cleves, Catherine Howard, and Catherine Parr. Their fates are summarized in a jingle: "Divorced, beheaded, died, divorced, beheaded, survived." Despite his messy home life, Henry VIII was very important. He created the Royal Navy, which effectively put a stop to foreign invasions of England and provided the means whereby this island kingdom eventually spread its political power, language, and literature all over the globe. Henry VIII himself deserves the title "Renaissance man." He wrote poetry and performed well on many different musical instruments; he was a champion athlete and a mighty hunter; he patronized the new humanistic learning; and he even wrote a learned book against Martin Luther. Although he broke the Pope's power in England, he never thought of himself as a Protestant. Coarse, dissolute, imperious, and brutal in his old age, he was, in Shakespeare's words, "every inch a king."

Henry VIII was survived by three children: Mary, daughter of Catherine of Aragon; Elizabeth, daughter of Anne Boleyn; and Edward, son of Jane Seymour. According to the laws of succession,

A. Humanities Connection: About the Fine Art

The seated monarch is Henry VIII. Henry hands a sword to the boy king, Edward VI. From the left comes Mary, linked to the Spanish King Philip II—the English always depicted the Spanish in melancholic black. At the far left is the god of war, Mars. At the right is Elizabeth I, who renounces Mary's sword and ushers in Peace and Plenty, at the far right. In contrast to the motherly queen (opposite), Elizabeth wears here a stiff, inverted-triangle bodice over a bell-shaped skirt. Her extremely white face (it's powdered) is surrounded by reddish hair and a large ruff. (In later years, a wig disguised her scanty hair, a result of smallpox.)

The Death of Mary Queen of Scots

Winston Churchill describes Mary's final moments in this passage from his history, *The New World:* "Mary had arrayed herself superbly for the final scene. As she disrobed for the headsman's act, her garments of black satin, removed by the weeping handmaids, revealed a bodice and petticoat of crimson velvet. One of her ladies handed her a pair of crimson sleeves, which she put on. Thus the unhappy Queen halted, for one last moment, standing blood-red from head to foot against the black background of the scaffold. There was a deathly hush throughout the hall. She knelt, and at the second stroke the final blow was delivered. The assembly had fulfilled its task. In death the majestic illusion was shattered. The head of an aging woman with false hair was held up by the executioner. A lapdog crept out from beneath the clothes of the bleeding trunk."

A. Expansion
"Virginia" comes by way of her sobriquet, "the *Virgin* Queen."

B. The Two Marys
Mary Stuart, Queen of Scots (1542–1587), was Elizabeth's cousin, She is not to be confused with "Bloody Mary," who was Mary Tudor (1516–1558), Elizabeth's half-sister. Though gentle personally, Mary Tudor acquired the nickname "Bloody" from the persecutions she endorsed against Protestants.

Mary Stuart was the daughter of Henry VIII's sister's son, James V. Her mother was French. Married to Francis II of France, Mary returned to Scotland in 1560, after her husband's death, to claim the throne of Scotland, which was still independent of England. Mary Stuart's ties to Spain are explained by religion: Spain and Mary Stuart were both Catholic. She was beheaded at Fotheringay on February 8, 1587.

> " **E**lizabeth I knew that her strength lay in her independence and her ability to play one suitor off against another."

Execution of Mary Queen of Scots (16th century). Drawing.

The National Gallery of Scotland, Edinburgh.

the son had to be crowned first, and so at age nine he became Edward VI (1547–1553). An intelligent but sickly boy, he ruled in name only while his relatives wielded the actual power. He died and was followed by his half-Spanish half-sister Mary (1553–1558), a devout, strong-willed woman determined to avenge the wrongs done to her mother and restore the Pope's power in England. Had she lived longer, and had she exercised better judgment, she might have undone all her father's accomplishments. But she burned at the stake about three hundred of her subjects, and then lost the support of her people entirely when she married Philip II, king of Spain, a country England was beginning to fear and hate. When Mary died, Elizabeth became Queen.

Elizabeth I (1558–1603) was one of the most brilliant and successful monarchs in history. She inherited a kingdom torn by fierce religious feuds, and her first task—like that of her grandfather—was to restore law and order. She reestablished the Church of England and again repudiated the Pope, who promptly excommunicated her. To keep Spain appeased, she pretended that she just might marry her widowed brother-in-law King Philip, who was the first of a long procession of eligible noblemen, both foreign and English, who wanted to wed her. But she resisted marriage her whole life (thereby giving the American colony Virginia its name) because she knew that her strength lay in her independence and her ability to play one suitor off against another. "I am your anointed Queen," she told a deputation from Parliament that urged her to marry. "I will never be by violence constrained to do anything. I thank God I am endued with such qualities that if I were turned out of the realm in my petticoat, I were able to live in any place in Christendom."

A truly heroic person, Elizabeth survived many plots against her life. Several of these were fomented in support of her cousin, Mary

1. The term *Renaissance* refers to a "rebirth" of interest in the writings of classical Greece and Rome.   (T)
2. New creativity in the arts first appeared in Italy.   (T)
3. Renaissance humanists rejected the Bible.   (F)

4. The invention of printing helped make the old classical texts more readily available.   (T)
5. Erasmus and More wrote exclusively in Latin.   (F)
6. In all countries where the Reformation occurred, a key element was rejec-

tion of the authority of the Pope.   (T)
7. Some people felt that Henry VIII's break with Rome did not go far enough to reform the English Church.   (T)
8. Henry VIII was a weak, inactive man of few talents.   (F)
9. The defeat of the Spanish Armada

An Engagement Between the
English Fleet and the
Spanish Armada. Oil.

National Maritime Museum, Greenwich,
England.

A. Humanities Connection: About the Fine Art

The Spanish Armada consisted of 130 ships and carried about 30,000 men. The Spanish ships were huge; they had to grapple enemy ships and send soldiers across the decks for hand combat. These lumbering galleons were severely battered by the guns of the smaller, more maneuverable English ships. (In the painting, a Spanish boat can be identified by its flag, which flies the papal coat of arms; see the long boat in front.) Many of the Spanish warships that survived the battle with the English were further battered by storms; only about half the original fleet limped home. Several of the ships were pounded to pieces, and five thousand Spanish sailors drowned off the west coast of Ireland. The English lost only about a hundred men and not a single ship.

Stuart, Queen of Scots. Mary was Elizabeth's heir because she too was a direct descendant of Henry VII. What is more, she was a Catholic deposed from her throne in Protestant Scotland and living as an exile in England. Elizabeth endured her and her plots for twenty years and then, a true daughter of her father, had Mary beheaded. King Philip used this act as an excuse to invade England, and he assembled a vast fleet of warships for that purpose: the famous Spanish Armada. In 1588, the Royal Navy, assisted greatly by the weather, destroyed the Armada and assured England's and all of Northern Europe's independence from the powerful Catholic countries of the Mediterranean. It was a great turning point in history and Elizabeth's finest moment.

What is the connection between these political events and English literature? With their own religious and national identity firmly established, the English started writing as they had never written before. After the defeat of the Armada, Elizabeth became a beloved symbol of peace, security, and prosperity to her subjects, and to scores of English authors she provided inspiration. They represented her mythologically in poetry, drama, and fiction—as Gloriana, Diana, the Faerie Queene, Cynthia. Literary works that did not directly represent her were dedicated to her because authors knew that she was a connoisseur of literature and a person of remarkably wide learning. From her earliest years she was tutored by humanists, so that she was fluent in Latin, Spanish, French, and Italian—all without ever leaving her island. Like her father, she was skilled in music, dancing, and religious controversy, and also vain, headstrong, and clever. But her reign far surpassed her father's in the production of literary works.

assured England's independence from the powerful Catholic countries of the Mediterranean. (T)

10. Elizabeth's long reign led to peace, prosperity, and a sense of national identity. (T)

A. About the Illustration

Students might notice the spelling of *songs, sonnets,* and *earl.* (The topic of spelling is also addressed on text page 237.) Before the age of full-fledged dictionaries, people wrote as they spoke. (Shakespeare's rhymes, for example, give many good clues about pronunciation.) Printers were the first to try to introduce consistency into spelling, but even so, the aristocracy in particular continued to spell as they spoke (*sartinly* for *certainly, byled* for *boiled*) well into the eighteenth century.

B. Vocabulary

What words are related to *pastoral*? (*Pasture, pastor*) Note how they are all connected to the idea of sheep and country life (a pastor is a guardian of a "flock").

Renaissance Poetry

SONGES AND SONETTES, written by the right honorable Lorde Henry Haward late Earle of Surrey, and other.

Apud Ricardum Tottel. Cum priuilegio ad imprimendum solum. ·1557·

Title page of *Tottel's Miscellany.* Engraving.

> "Any poets lacking education and knowledge of Latin (like John Taylor the Water Poet, a man who ran a boat service on the Thames) were treated as public jokes."

In 1557, the year before Elizabeth became Queen, a printer named Richard Tottel put out an important collection of poems entitled *Songs and Sonnets.* The best poems in this book, which is commonly called *Tottel's Miscellany,* had been written some years before by Sir Thomas Wyatt and by Henry Howard, the Earl of Surrey. Wyatt and Surrey were both inspired by the Italian humanist and poet Francis Petrarch, and they were responsible for introducing Petrarch into England. By 1595 or so, Petrarch had many followers busily producing love **sonnets** by the yard, many of them mediocre but some of them brilliant, especially some written by Sir Philip Sidney, Edmund Spenser, and William Shakespeare. Even John Donne, a Renaissance poet whose view of love was very different from Petrarch's, could not escape his influence. The Petrarchan vogue illustrates how conscious the poets of Renaissance England were of their predecessors, older poets who wrote not only in English but especially in Italian and Latin, and to some extent in Spanish, French, and Greek.

The century after *Tottel's Miscellany* was one of the greatest ages of English poetry; any attempt to summarize it or reduce it to formulas is bound to fail. Yet it did have certain characteristics that set it off from other great ages of English poetry. One of these was that Renaissance poets wrote with one eye on their subject and the other on what preceding poets had said about the subject. They aimed at making new poems that used the themes and forms of older poems. And so poets who wanted to treat love as something erotic and funny would not look to see how Petrarch did it because Petrarch idealized love; instead, they consulted the ancient Roman poet Ovid. Similarly, if they wanted to satirize and ridicule certain kinds of human behavior, they studied the techniques of ancient satirists like Horace and Juvenal.

Unless they also wrote plays, English poets could not expect to make much money from their writings. So for support they looked to aristocratic patrons, people with wealth and influence who would reward writers who dedicated their books to them. Consequently, most poetry and other literature in the Renaissance tended to be aristocratic in tone and, with very few exceptions, unconcerned with working people. When people of the working classes appeared, they were usually treated comically, and any poets lacking education and knowledge of Latin (like John Taylor the Water Poet, a man who ran a boat service on the Thames) were treated as public jokes. A kind of writing known as **pastoral** enabled poets and storytellers to portray leisured and educated people as though they were shepherds or other country dwellers. Marlowe's "The Passionate Shepherd to His Love" is a famous example of pastoral poetry. Poets who were themselves aristocrats, like Sir Philip Sidney and Sir Walter Raleigh, as well as poets like Donne who aspired to membership in the ruling classes, did not publish their works but gave them to their friends, who circulated them in manuscript.

Of course English poets drew on their personal experiences, but they depended on traditional ways of expressing those experiences. And they did not write just a poem; they wrote a particular kind of poem. As they wrote they were conscious of other poems of that

Humanities Connection: Renaissance
Music
You might play some Renaissance music
to allow students to hear these marvelous instruments pictured below. Look for
works by des Prés, Palestrina, Tallis,
Byrd, and Monteverdi. Madrigals are also
available in many recordings.

kind already written. There were **epithalamia** (wedding songs), **epi-grams** (brief poems sometimes praising but more often making fun of either real or fictitious people), **epitaphs** (brief poems on dead people), and **songs** (lyrics suitable for setting to music). Renaissance poets were particularly adept at writing songs of great beauty and charm; thousands of them survive, both **airs** for solos and elaborate **madrigals,** or part-songs for group singing. These songs expressed a great variety of moods and covered a great variety of subjects, from love to religion. Everybody was expected to sing, if anecdotes like the following from Henry Morley's *Plain and Easy Introduction to Music* (1597) can be trusted:

> Supper being ended, and music-books (according to the cus-tom) being brought to the tables, the mistress of the house presented me with a part, earnestly requesting me to sing. But when, after many excuses I protested unfainedly that I could not, every one began to wonder. Yea, some whispered to others, demanding how I was brought up.

A

With its high regard for skill in singing, the Renaissance produced some of the greatest lyric poets in the language; even relatively minor writers like John Lyly, Robert Greene, Thomas Nashe, John Dowland, Thomas Campion, Samuel Daniel, and Richard Crashaw each produced a handful of songs that rival those of such major poets as Sidney, Shakespeare, Donne, George Herbert, and Andrew Marvell.

Spinet lid (detail: Concert)
by F. Van Valchenborch.

Germanisches National Museum,
Nuremberg.

A. Music
The belief that an appreciation of music indicated character is affirmed by Shake-speare, whose Ju-lius Caesar says to Mark Antony, "I do not know the man I should avoid / So soon as that spare Cassius . . . . He loves no plays, / As thou dost, An-tony; he hears no music." (*Julius Caesar,* Act I, Scene 2, lines 200–204)

B. Humanities Connection: About the Fine Art
The *spinet* (the central instrument here) was a rela-tive of the harpsi-chord. (The huge chest here is not part of the spinet.) The four different sizes of *viol,* with frets and six strings, were the most important en-semble instru-ments of the sixteenth and sev-enteenth centuries. The larger *violas da gamba* ("knee viols") were bowed while held upright between the knees, and the smaller *violas da bracchio* ("arm viols") were tucked under the chin like the later violin.

B

Have students match the letter of the words and phrases below with their definitions, which follow.

a. Air
b. Conceit
c. Epic
d. Epigram
e. Epitaph
f. Epithalamium
g. Madrigal
h. Narrative poem
i. Pastoral poem
j. Sonnet

1. A long, elaborate narrative poem considered the highest kind of poetry (c)
2. A short poem written by Petrarch, an Italian (j)
3. A poem portraying leisured and educated people as if they were shepherds (i)

A. Humanities Connection: "Artificiality"

Just as *artificial* meant "skillful," so *curious* meant "elaborate or beautifully wrought." In horticulture, topiary (the trimming of shrubs into odd or intricate shapes) was popular, as were square gardens filled with intricate plots and paths. In music there was the elaborate contrapuntal madrigal; in painting, the miniature; in the decorative arts, delicate settings for jewels. A few enthusiasts went so far as to build their houses in the shape of an *E* in honor of the queen.

"*Artificial* was a term of approval and admiration."

A

HERO AND
LEANDER:

Begun by *Christopher Marloe*; and finished by George Chapman.

Vt Nectar, Ingenium.

At London
Printed by *Felix Kingston*, for *Paule Linley*, and are to be solde in Paules Church-yard, at the signe of the Blacke-beare.
1598.

Frontispiece of Christopher Marlowe's *Hero and Leander* (1598). Engraving.

Aside from the songs, many of which seem simple and sincere, most other Renaissance poems tend to be clever and elaborate, full of puns and other exuberant wordplay. *Artificial* was a term of approval and admiration; it was used to describe anything skillfully made, and poets were often referred to as "makers" and their works as their "doings." In the Renaissance all sorts of people wrote poetry, just as they do today, but their poems, unlike most of ours, are always in meter and, with very few exceptions, in rhyme. The notion that a poem should seem to be a natural outpouring of personal feeling in ordinary language was totally foreign to them. Instead, they thought of a poem as something made out of figurative language fitted into formal patterns. Some of their metaphors seem farfetched to us: as when human life was said to be a bowling alley, or two lovers were called a geometer's compass, or a young woman's beauty became the sun at noonday. **Extended metaphors** of this kind, bringing together things totally unlike each other, are called **conceits,** and they may distract us because we have been taught to visualize the images in poetry. Renaissance readers apparently did not try to picture conceits in their minds; instead, they admired them for their boldness and ingenuity. As time passed, the practice of writing conceits intensified and reached a peak in the followers of Donne.

Many more kinds of poetry were written in the Renaissance than today because people then used verse for purposes that are now served by prose. For instance, the verse letter was a recognized genre; sometimes it took the form of a discourse on a topic that would now be treated in an essay or an article. Poetry could be used to describe places, as in Michael Drayton's *Polyolbion* (1622), a sort of travel book about England and Wales. Poetry could also be used for instruction and edification, as in *The Divine Weeks* (1605), an entertaining paraphrase about the creation translated from French by Joshua Sylvester. Many **narrative poems** were written to satisfy people's need for fiction; there were few short stories at this time, no novels, and no magazines. Perhaps the most popular book of narrative poems, first published early in Elizabeth's reign and republished many times, was *The Mirror for Magistrates,* a collection of twenty sensational and disastrous stories in verse by various poets, showing how rich, proud, successful people can come to a bad end. Finally, a much less preachy sort of narrative poem must be mentioned: *Hero and Leander* (written in or before 1593) by Christopher Marlowe. This entertaining poem mingles the erotic and the ideal, mythology and philosophy, romantic and cynical views of love. Hero, oddly enough, is the name of the heroine.

In the Renaissance, and for long after, literary people agreed that the highest kind of poetry was **epic,** exemplified in England by *Beowulf,* as you have seen, and in classical antiquity by Homer's *Iliad* and *Odyssey* and Virgil's *Aeneid*. These long, elaborate narrative poems use traditional literary devices and are concerned with national heroes and supernatural beings, both good and bad. The Italian Renaissance produced two great epic poets, Tasso and Ariosto, and they—particularly Ariosto—provided precedents and

4. A brief poem about a dead person   (e)

5. A song to be sung in parts by a group   (g)

6. A lyric set to music   (a)

7. A wedding song   (f)

8. A poem telling a story   (h)

9. A bold, ingenious metaphor   (b)

10. A very brief poem either praising or making fun of a person   (d)

---

models for England's Spenser. Milton, England's other epic poet, was the last and in many ways the greatest of all the nondramatic poets of England's Renaissance. The view of humanity found in Spenser's and Milton's epics was the view of all the Renaissance humanists: Human beings are completely free agents possessing a power, known as Reason, that enables them first to distinguish between good and evil and then to choose the good and avoid the evil. Shakespeare's Hamlet sums up this view in these words:

> Sure he that made us with such large discourse,
> Looking before and after, gave us not
> That capability and godlike Reason
> To fust[1] in us unused.

A

1. **fust:** decay.

B *Renaissance Drama*

Shakespeare was far from being the only great dramatist in this age; even without him, the Renaissance would be the preeminent period of English drama. And even before the Renaissance the English had been writing and performing plays for several centuries.

The Forerunners

Some scholars believe that medieval drama evolved from church ceremonies such as the dialogue-songs performed at Easter Eve services. In these tiny playlets three women would appear at a door representing the tomb of Christ and guarded by an angel. The angel would ask, in Latin, "Whom do you seek?" and then he **C** would announce the Resurrection. From this obscure beginning, drama moved out of the churches and into the marketplaces of towns. There, in the 1300's and 1400's, various workmen's guilds cooperated in staging cycles of plays that dramatized the whole history of the human race as then understood: its creation by God, its fall through the wiles of Satan, its life in Old Testament times, its redemption by Christ, and its final judgment at the end of the world. Parts of four cycles of these plays have been preserved, and they are named after the towns where they probably originated: York, Chester, Coventry, and Wakefield. Gradually, the plays became less religious, and comedy was incorporated into them. The wife of Noah, for instance, makes a great fuss about entering the ark, and is carried kicking and screaming aboard. In another play about Christmas Eve, while the shepherds are watching their flocks by night a clownish thief steals a sheep and a rowdy scene takes place before the angel appears to tell the shepherds to go to Bethlehem and present gifts to the newborn Christ. This well-developed comic scene takes place in one of the best of the cyclical plays, *The Second Shepherds' Play* of the Wakefield cycle. It seems to harmonize perfectly with the biblical theme: an early example of English skill in mixing the comic with the serious in drama. The

> " **W**hile the shepherds are watching their flocks by night a clownish thief steals a sheep and a rowdy scene takes place."

A. The Power of Reason
You might refer students back to the words of Pico della Mirandola on text page 167 and have them talk about the use of reason to distinguish between good and evil, and then to choose good and avoid evil.

? Why do some people deliberately choose evil? (Answers may include that they are influenced by a variety of factors including temptation, greed, insensitivity to others.)

B. Expansion
The dramatic literature of the age is said to be its greatest cultural achievement. These next paragraphs ("The Forerunners") describe its roots. Encourage students to visualize the early plays performed in a setting like the one shown in the engraving at the top of text page 180.

C. Expansion
Also known as *Quem Quaeritis* ("Whom do you seek?" in Latin).

180

A. About the Illustration

The mystery play being enacted here is the trial of Jesus (standing, center) before Pontius Pilate (seated). High priests, wearing anachronistic bishops' miters, here present Jesus to the crowd. Note the types of people in the crowd and their behavior.

B. Expansion

A *miracle play* was based on a miracle that occurred in a saint's life. A *mystery play* was based on a Bible story. ("Mystery" refers to the spiritual mystery of human redemption.) A *morality play* was an allegory of some phase of human life: temptation, sin, the quest for salvation, death. An *interlude* (Latin, *inter-*, "between," and *ludus,* "play") was staged between the courses of a meal or between the acts of a longer play.

Mystery Play, Coventry. Engraving.

British Library.

A

First page of *Everyman* from the Britwell copy. Engraving.

Folger Shakespeare Library, Washington, D.C.

most notable serious play of the period just before the Renaissance is *Everyman,* based on a Dutch original. This is a morality play in which Death summons Everyman, who stands for exactly what his name indicates. Everyman asks his friends, who have such allegorical names as Goods, Kindred, Fellowship, Beauty, and Strength, to accompany him, but only Good Deeds stays with him to the end.

Several kinds of plays, then, were written and produced before the Renaissance: **miracle** and **mystery plays** based on the Bible and saints' legends; **moralities** that taught people how to live and die; and, starting in the early 1500's, a new kind called **interludes.** These were one-act plays, some of them indistinguishable from moralities, others rowdy and farcical. With the interludes the playwrights stop being anonymous. The best writer of comic interludes was John Heywood, grandfather of John Donne and a great favorite of Queen Mary. In Heywood's *Play of the Weather* (1533) everybody complains to Jupiter about the dreadful weather, but nobody agrees on the definition of *dreadful.* And in his *Four P's* (1545?) a pardoner, a palmer (or pilgrim), a 'pothecary (or druggist), and a peddler boast about their occupations; the palmer wins a prize for telling the biggest lie, and the pardoner describes a ludicrous trip that he took down to Hell. We can conclude that even before the new humanist learning came in, there were strong dramatic traditions that the great Renaissance playwrights knew about.

Mystery and *miracle plays* were acted by amateurs who belonged to trade guilds (a combination of club, trade union, and fraternal society). Each guild had a traditional play to perform. The story of Noah's Ark, for example, was done by the carpenters. *Moralities* and *interludes* were performed by semiprofessional traveling groups or by the servants of a lord in his own hall. By 1450 one professional group of actors was on tour, but because actors had no guild, they were considered to be of dubious character. By 1545, in fact, actors were legally named idle rogues unless they wore the livery (colors) of a specific nobleman. Technically, this made the actors the noble's servants, even though they earned their living by performing for the public.

Renaissance Dramatists

The humanistic influence was first felt in comedy. As early as 1533, a schoolmaster named Nicholas Udall wrote, for his students to perform, *Ralph Roister Doister,* in the manner of the Roman comic playwrights Plautus and Terence. This play, in which a clever young man encourages an absolute simpleton named Roister Doister to court a rich young woman, first exploited some funny character types and plot patterns that are still with us in our so-called situation comedies.

Some twenty years after this first comedy showing the influence of classical antiquity, there appeared the first tragedy of that kind, *Gorboduc,* by Thomas Norton and Thomas Sackville, Earl of Dorset. A declamatory play with nothing much actually happening on stage, this tragedy is full of long speeches describing bloody events—a prince kills his brother and is then killed by his mother—that took place in ancient Britain, at the court of King Gorboduc. The first syllable of this unfortunate monarch's name is not irrelevant to this play about him. Both in its gory subject matter and its windy style *Gorboduc* shows the strong influence of the Emperor Nero's tutor Seneca, the author of nine unperformable tragedies of blood and revenge that were much studied and imitated in Renaissance England.

While plays written before 1590 are, admittedly, mainly of historical interest, it is important to know that the great flowering of English drama in the 1590's and early 1600's had firm roots in the immediate past. Like the schoolmaster Udall, Shakespeare very early in his career turned to Plautus for his *Comedy of Errors;* he developed the tradition of the bloody revenge play in some of his greatest tragedies; and he used in all his plays the blank verse invented by Surrey and first used in a play by the authors of *Gorboduc.*

The dramatists of the 1590's may be divided into two groups: those who, like Marlowe, were university graduates and those who, like Shakespeare, were not. In the first group were Robert Greene and John Lyly. Greene, a colorful youth who died young, wrote among other works five plays, the best known being *Friar Bacon and Friar Bungay* (1594). The plays of Lyly are in prose—a novelty—and they provide the first examples in English of what became known as high comedy: witty, sophisticated dialogue rather than knockabout farce. Lyly's plays include *Endimion* (1591) and *The Woman in the Moon* (1594). Among the writers who attended neither Oxford nor Cambridge is Thomas Kyd, author of the thunderous and very popular *Spanish Tragedy* (1592?) in which a man becomes frantic and ferocious after he comes upon his dead son. Ben Jonson, another dramatist and poet who never studied in a university but was nevertheless a true humanist, probably acted in, and may well have made additions to, *The Spanish Tragedy.* Like Shakespeare, Jonson learned his craft and art in the theater itself: His apprentice work came in the sixteenth century, his masterpieces in the seventeenth.

After 1600 there appeared several new and important tragedy

A

"A clever young man encourages an absolute simpleton named Roister Doister to court a rich young woman."

B

Title page of Thomas Kyd's *The Spanish Tragedy* (1615). Engraving.

Folger Shakespeare Library, Washington, D.C.

A. Expansion
About the same time as Udall's comedy, a play with much knock-about horseplay was being enacted at Christ's College, Cambridge—*Gammer Gurton's Needle.* Such comedies introduced the stock character of the *miles gloriosus* (the cowardly, bragging soldier), whose type is fully realized in Shakespeare's Sir John Falstaff in the *Henry IV* plays.

B. Expansion
Remember that in the twentieth century writers also went to Terence and Plautus for the plot of the Broadway hit *A Funny Thing Happened on the Way to the Forum.*

Using the Time Line
Note that the time line reads from left to right and that it does not attempt to divide blocks of time evenly by decades. (History is not made in neat decades!) You can relate the writers' lives and literary events to the socio-historical background by asking questions like these:

? What was happening in Japan the year Shakespeare moved to London?

(The Kabuki theater was beginning.) What was happening in the New World when Shakespeare was producing *The Merchant of Venice?* (Sir Walter Raleigh was exploring the Orinold River.) What happened in America four years after Elizabeth was crowned? (Slave trade to America began.) What great Spanish work began to appear during the later part of Shakespeare's career? *(Don Quixote)*

Some students may enjoy using Bernard Grun's *The Timetables of History* (Simon and Schuster, 1963) to add to this timetable other events or trivia that interest them.

A. About the Illustration

The *masque* was an elaborate court entertainment. It combined a slight, often mythological or allegorical plot with plenty of music, dance, and splendid costumes. The actors included courtiers and even royalty. At the end of the play, the actors would doff their masks (masques) and choose dance partners from the audience. These elaborate spectacles used the finest talent of the day, including Ben Jonson (text page 374) for scripts, and architect Inigo Jones (1573–1652) for costumes and sets. Two masques are still known: one in Act IV of Shakespeare's *The Tempest,* and one in *Comus* by John Milton.

The Banqueting House at Whitehall and the Queen's House at Greenwich were designed by Inigo Jones and still stand today. Jones was later violently persecuted by the Puritans, who hated art as much as they hated kings.

A

Lady Masquer by Inigo Jones (c. 1610).

Victoria and Albert Museum, London.

writers, among them John Webster, whose *White Devil* (1608?) and *Duchess of Malfi* are both about splendid women whom their brothers, husbands, and lovers destroy. Cyril Tourneur was probably the author of *The Revenger's Tragedy* (1607) and *The Atheist's Tragedy* (1611), both subtle additions to the Senecan revenge tradition.

Turning to comedy, we find a bewildering variety of fine plays besides the famous ones by Shakespeare and Jonson. In the early years of the new century, a large number of satirical comedies were written and produced. The best one of these (not counting Shakespeare's *Measure for Measure* and *Troilus and Cressida*), John Marston's *The Malcontent* (1604), features a foul-mouthed, railing sort of hero—if he can be called a hero—and the whole play exposes the folly and viciousness of a Renaissance "court"—that is, the people surrounding a ruler and wielding political power. (All the English plays that specialized in cruel, outrageous behavior were set in Italy or Spain, where such things, every proper English person assumed, were routine.) A much less scandalous and perhaps more amusing play than *The Malcontent* is *A Trick to Catch the Old One* (1608) by Thomas Middleton; it satirizes English, not Italian, misbehavior. Philip Massinger completely rewrote Middleton's play and called it *A New Way to Pay Old Debts* (1626); this became one of the most popular comedies in all theater history.

1492–1498	1501–1503	1503–1516	1517
Columbus arrives in America, 1492 Da Vinci's *The Last Supper*, 1495–1498 Michelangelo's *Pietà*, 1498	Michelangelo's *David*, 1501 **Sir Thomas Wyatt 1503–1542 (poems first published in 1557)**	Da Vinci's *Mona Lisa*, 1503 Henry VIII crowned, 1509 **Thomas More's *Utopia*, 1516**	Luther posts his 95 theses on the door of church in Wittenberg, Germany, and starts Protestant Reformation, 1517

1556–1557	1558–1562	1564–1565	1574–1577
Suleiman's Mosque in Constantinople completed, 1556 Influenza epidemic kills thousands in Europe, 1557	Elizabeth I becomes Queen of England, 1558 Slave trade to America begins, 1562	**William Shakespeare and Christopher Marlowe born, 1564** Spaniards occupy Philippines and build Manila, 1565	**James Burbage receives license to open first theater in London, 1576** Sir Francis Drake begins voyage around the world, 1577

1596–1599	1600–1603	1605	1607–1609
Spenser completes *The Faerie Queene*, 1596 **Globe Theater built, 1599** **Shakespeare's *Julius Caesar, As You Like It,* and *Twelfth Night*, 1599**	**Shakespeare's *Hamlet* and *The Merry Wives of Windsor*, 1600** James I named King of England and Scotland, 1603	**Shakespeare's *King Lear* and *Macbeth*, 1605** **Cervantes publishes Part 1 of *Don Quixote*, 1605 (Part 2 published 1615)**	First permanent English settlement in New World (Jamestown), 1607 **John Milton born, 1608** **Shakespeare writes sonnets, 1609**

1. Shakespeare was the only great dramatist of this age.   (F)
2. Some scholars believe medieval drama evolved from church ceremonies.   (T)

3. Miracle and mystery plays were based on the Bible and stories of saints.   (T)
4. Tragedies of the sixteenth century tended toward gory dramas of revenge and intrigue.   (T)

5. Theaters were closed in 1642 because no one was interested in plays and attendance was very poor.   (F)

The kind of romantic play in which Shakespeare specialized, the sort of comedy that ends with the marriage of attractive lovers, was carried on by John Fletcher. For a short time Fletcher collaborated with Francis Beaumont. Then he went on by himself to have a long career in the theater, becoming the chief writer for the King's Men company of actors when Shakespeare retired in 1612. Fletcher was a prolific writer of both comedies and tragedies, and he even invented a new kind of play which he called **tragicomedy**: that is, the play ends happily as in comedy though the characters are involved in death-threatening circumstances as in tragedy. Fletcher's first tragicomedy was *The Faithfull Shepherdess*.

In 1642 Parliament, under the control of people who regarded plays and acting as wicked, shut down the London theaters. By then the golden years of English drama were over, and the only considerable talent that was stifled belonged to James Shirley. Even so, Shirley managed to write more plays than anybody else except Shakespeare and Fletcher before he was forced to stop. Some of his plays look forward to the new age when the theaters would reopen right after the restoration of King Charles II in 1660. Shirley's *Witty Fair One* (1628) and his *Lady of Pleasure* (1635) anticipate the worldly comedies of William Congreve (1670–1729) and William Wycherley (1640–1716), in which the behavior of the fashionable upper classes is put to the test of laughter.

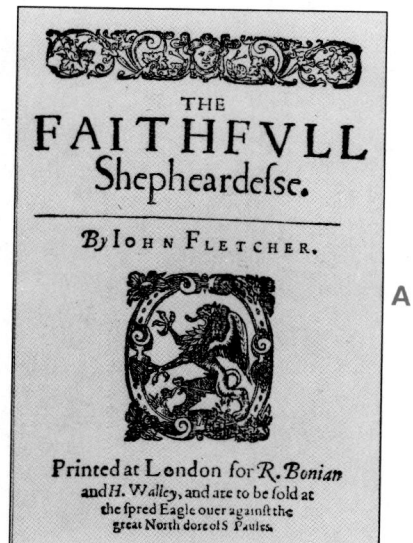

A

Title page of John Fletcher's *The Faithfull Shepherdess*. Engraving.

A. About the Illustration

John Fletcher (1579–1623) often wrote with Francis Beaumont (1584?–1616), and may also have collaborated with Shakespeare on *Henry VIII* and *Two Noble Kinsmen*. Fletcher-Beaumont plays were popular both in their own day and in the eighteenth century, but we would now generally find them overly contrived. Note the details telling where copies can be purchased.

1524–1531	1535–1543	1546–1547	1553–1558
Giovanni da Verrazano discovers New York Bay, 1524	Henry VIII beheads his friend Sir Thomas More, 1535	Michelangelo designs dome of St. Peter's Church in Rome, 1546	"Bloody" Mary Tudor reigns and attempts to restore Catholic authority in England, 1553–1558
Henry VIII names himself Supreme Head of the Church in England, 1531	Copernicus publishes his conclusions about the heliocentric theory, 1543	Henry VIII dies, 1547	Aztec dictionary published, 1555

1585–1586	1588	1592–1594	1595
Shakespeare moves to London, 1585	**Christopher Marlowe's *Doctor Faustus* performed, 1588**	**Shakespeare's *Richard III* and *The Comedy of Errors*, 1592**	Sir Walter Raleigh explores the Orinoco River in the New World, 1595
Beginning of Kabuki theater in Japan, 1586	British navy defeats Spanish Armada, 1588	**London theaters closed because of plague, 1593–1594**	**Shakespeare's *King John* and *The Merchant of Venice*, 1595**

1609–1611	1616–1642	1642–1658	1660
Donne's *Holy Sonnets* written, 1609–1611	**Shakespeare and Cervantes die, 1616**	**Puritans close theaters, 1642–1660**	**Milton begins *Paradise Lost*, 1660**
Shakespeare retires to Stratford, 1610	*Mayflower* sails for the New World, 1620	Charles I beheaded, 1649	Puritan Commonwealth ends, 1660
King James Bible completed, 1611	English Civil War 1642–1649	Cromwell establishes military dictatorship, 1653–1658	Monarchy restored, 1660

Galileo

Then, as now, new ideas sometimes met opposition, notably so in the case of Galileo Galilei (1564–1642), whose discoveries challenged the then official teachings of the Roman Catholic Church. Galileo's Copernican view—that the earth revolved around the sun, rather than the opposite—was denounced by the Church in 1616 as heresy because it contradicted the Bible and displaced man as the crown of God's creation and the center of the universe. Galileo was ordered not to spread his theory. In 1632, however, he published *Dialogue on Two Chief World Systems.* He was again summoned by the Church, and this time knelt to recant his views publicly. He is said, however, to have muttered on arising, *"Eppur si muove"* ("But still it [the earth] moves"). He spent the last eight years of his life under house arrest. (In 1979 the Church finally rescinded its condemnation of Galileo on the advice of Pope John Paul II.)

A. The "Great Chain of Being"

The concept of the "Great Chain of Being" assumed that God's infinite creativity is expressed in a universe that contains every possible form of life; that there is a graded continuity of species; and that there is a hierarchy in the arrangement of all things. (Just as there are stars of various magnitudes, so there were four classes in England: gentlemen, citizens, yeoman artificers, and laborers.)

Standing halfway between the angels (pure intelligence) and the beasts (pure sense or instinct), humanity held a precarious position. Since the soul was prisoner of the body, religious discipline was vital to human perfection.

Alexander Pope used the concept of the Great Chain of Being in *An Essay on Man* (text page 530).

Renaissance Prose

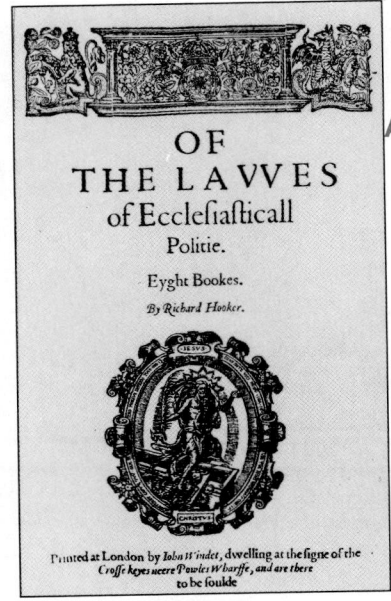

Title page of Richard Hooker's *The Laws of Ecclesiastical Polity.* Engraving.

Most Renaissance books, like most books in any age, especially since the invention of printing, are written in prose, and most Renaissance prose is argumentative. The printing press made it possible to carry on elaborate controversies, mainly religious. Only scholars read these books today, though a few of them do rise to the status of literature. For instance, *The Laws of Ecclesiastical Polity,* a tome with a forbidding title written by Richard Hooker in the 1590's, eloquently expresses the Renaissance view of humanity as centrally located in the Great Chain of Being, midway between God and the animals.

Of fiction there is also a considerable amount, mainly in the form of complicated romances about fighting and love; these satisfied their readers' desire for mystery, violence, passion, and even philosophical reflection. By far the best romance is Sidney's *Arcadia,* which his sister published after he was killed in war. A very influential book, it is still good reading. A much shorter work, and perhaps more suited to our taste today, is Thomas Nashe's *The Unfortunate Traveler* (1594), about a young *picaro,* or rascal, named Jack Wilton. Wilton wanders about Europe, observing hangings, rapes, murders, tortures. He hears Martin Luther preach, meets Erasmus and More, and becomes a page to the Earl of Surrey. This book is not a novel in the ways that the narratives of Daniel Defoe are, but it does anticipate elements of the novel as a literary genre. Two other romances, out of dozens that were published, deserve mention because Shakespeare made plays out of them: *Pandosto* (1588) by Robert Greene became *The Winter's Tale,* and *Rosalynde* (1590) by Thomas Lodge became *As You Like It.*

The Renaissance saw an enormous increase in writing about travel, exploration, and discovery. It was an age in which Europeans began to extend their boundaries and increase their knowledge of the earth and heavens. Columbus, sailing west, arrived at an unknown hemisphere; Amerigo Vespucci named it; Magellan sailed beyond it and circumnavigated the whole globe for the first time. Galileo saw Jupiter's satellites through his telescope, and thereby added evidence to support the new view of the cosmos promulgated by the Polish astronomer and mathematician Copernicus. These and many other discoveries, disseminated by the printing press, had an enormous impact on the imaginations of poets and dramatists. Milton, for instance, would never have expressed the vast cosmic distances of *Paradise Lost* without a knowledge of the new astronomy, nor would Shakespeare have imagined the exotic locales of *The Tempest* without the knowledge of faraway places.

The English themselves were relatively late addicts to the discovery craze, though Henry VII had dispatched John Cabot on a voyage across the North Atlantic. After Spain was so badly crippled in 1588, the English became active explorers and eventually successful colonizers. One of the great events of Elizabeth's reign came when she went aboard the *Golden Hind* and knighted Francis Drake for his successful trip around the world and the damages he had inflicted on Spanish shipping. Sir Walter Raleigh was a great builder of colonies—at least in his head. He dreamed of a vast empire that would put all of North and South America under the just rule of England in defiance of the Pope, who had recently divided up the whole new world between Spain and Portugal. And before the Renaissance was over, the English people had indeed begun to scatter themselves over the earth. Most of the earliest accounts of English discovery and exploration were collected and published by Richard Hakluyt in his *Principal Navigations, Voyages, and Discoveries of the English Nation* (1589–1600) and by Samuel Purchas in *Purchas His Pilgrims* (1625), both fascinating collections of tales of which more than half are true.

Renaissance prose is represented in this anthology by selections from Francis Bacon's *Essays* and by excerpts from the great King James Bible. Many other prose works might have been sampled, such as Robert Burton's *Anatomy of Melancholy* (1621) and Sir Thomas Browne's *Religio Medici* (*A Doctor's Religion,* 1642). The former, a great and large book, discusses all kinds of melancholia, or what we call depression, especially depression caused by love and religion. It is a vast compendium of anecdotes, quotations, and information. Stylistically it exhibits most of the excesses of Renaissance prose, such as enormously long sentences swollen with names, lists, allusions, quotations, and Latin phrases and sentences. Browne, a physician, wrote a poetic sort of prose that

B

A

The Great Harry (1546). From the Anthony Rolls manuscript.

Magdalene College, Cambridge.

C

Title page of *The Mariner's Mirror* (1588). Engraving.

Folger Shakespeare Library, Washington, D.C.

A. Expansion
The effects of this Spain-Portugal division are still evident: Spanish is the language of most of Latin America, while Portuguese is spoken in Brazil. The effect on trade is evident in James Clavell's best-selling novel, *Shōgun* (1975), in which an Englishman schemes to wrest from the Portuguese control of trade between China and Japan.

B. About the Illustration
The Great Harry was constructed by King Henry VII in 1488. Henry's interest in ships was continued by his son Henry VIII, whose use of the latest shipbuilding techniques led to the gunships that helped England defeat the Spanish Armada.

C. About the Illustration
Contrast this navigation handbook's elegant title page with those of the how-to books published today.

READING CHECK TEST (Text pages 184–186)

1. What invention made it possible for writers to carry on extensive public controversies? (The printing press)
2. What is a *picaro*? (A rascal)
3. Why were so many travel books written during this period? (Europeans were traveling all over the globe.)

4. What king succeeded Elizabeth to the English throne? (James VI of Scotland)
5. What work from this period is still considered the principal achievement in English prose of any era? (The King James Bible)

A. James I and VI
James VI was the only son of Mary Queen of Scots and her second husband, an English nobleman named Lord Darnly. When he succeeded his mother's cousin Elizabeth as sovereign of England *and* of Scotland, James was called King James I because he was the first James to rule the newly formed Great Britain. The reign of James is called the Jacobean period (*Jacobus* is the Latin form of James).

B. The Civil War
By the time Charles I came to the throne, the Puritans had risen to prominence and their Parliamentary Party had gained power. By 1642, England was embroiled in a civil war that pitted this Parliamentary Party, led by Oliver Cromwell, against the King's Party, or Royalists. By the war's end, Cromwell's men had the king killed.

Decline of the Renaissance

> " **H**e was a spendthrift where she had been thrifty, a thick-tongued and goggle-eyed male where she had been a glamorous and witty female."

A

B

many generations of readers have found delightful because the author himself is so delighted to be alive and capable of wondering about the mysteries of creation.

As for the King James Bible, it is still the principal achievement of English prose in any period and the one book that has most influenced English literature. Like most other Renaissance prose works, it contains much poetry. In the words that the ancient psalmist addresses to God, Renaissance humanists could find answers to their profoundest questions:

> When I consider thy heavens, the work of thy fingers,
> The moon, the stars, which thou hast ordained;
> What is man, that thou art mindful of him?
> And the son of man, that thou visitest him?
> For thou hast made him a little lower than the angels,
> And hast crowned him with glory and honor.
> Thou madest him to have dominion over the works of thy hands;
> Thou hast put all things under his feet.
>
> —Psalm 108

The two kings who ruled England during the last part of the Renaissance were James Stuart and his son Charles. As a second cousin of Queen Elizabeth, James VI of Scotland was necessarily her successor, but as James I of England (1603–1625) he lacked her consummate ability to resolve (or postpone) critical issues, especially religious and economic ones. He was a spendthrift where she had been thrifty, a thick-tongued and goggle-eyed male where she had been a glamorous and witty female, essentially a foreigner where she had been a complete Englishwoman. James I tried hard, wrote learned books in favor of the divine right of kings and against tobacco, patronized Shakespeare and Jonson, persuaded Donne to become a clergyman, sponsored a new translation of the Bible, and was in many respects an admirable man and a benevolent, peaceful ruler. Yet his relationships with many of his subjects, especially with pious, puritanically minded merchants, went from bad to worse, and the difficulties of his reign became the impossibilities of his son's. Charles I (1625–1649) turned out to be remote, autocratic, and self-destructive. Some of his most powerful subjects had him beheaded in 1649. When his sons returned to power eleven years later, the country had changed in many important ways.

Of course the Renaissance did not end in 1649, just as it did not begin at any one definite date. Its values, which were never held by everyone, gradually eroded, and its energies gradually unwound. The last great exemplar of the English Renaissance was John Milton, who lived on into an age in which educated people were becoming worldly in their outlook and scientific truths were just beginning to replace the revealed truths of religion.

Sir Thomas Wyatt (1503–1542)
Henry Howard, Earl of Surrey (1517–1547)

Wyatt and Surrey have much in common: they were courtiers of Henry VIII, they admired and imitated foreign—especially Italian—poetry, and they were literary innovators. Wyatt spent much of his life traveling abroad as an ambassador for King Henry. Twice Henry had him imprisoned on charges that were probably false, and twice Wyatt managed to regain his favor. Surrey was not so lucky. He was a brilliant soldier and both his parents were descended from English kings. Thus he had two qualifications for being a king himself. That did not endear him to the jealous Henry, who had him executed when he was only thirty years old.

Both Wyatt and Surrey helped to change the nature of English poetry, which up to their time was still essentially medieval in matter and manner, subject and form. Wyatt brought a new kind of poem, the love sonnet, to England from Italy. His English sonnets are adaptations of Italian sonnets. Surrey also wrote sonnets, and in his translation of parts of Virgil's *Aeneid* he used, for the first time in English, blank verse, which is unrhymed iambic pentameter. Because Shakespeare, Milton, Wordsworth, and many other later poets used blank verse, this poetic form now seems the most natural of all English meters.

Aside from their sonnets and Surrey's blank verse, both poets produced a variety of other kinds of works. But neither of these poets had any of his works printed and publicly distributed, except for one poem that Surrey wrote on Wyatt's death. They had no ambition to be known as "clerks," or learned men of letters, the sort of people who published books. As courtiers they were expected to compose songs and verses, just as they were expected to do bat-

Henry Howard, Earl of Surrey by W. Sertos (c. 1550). Oil.

National Portrait Gallery, London.

tle for their king, joust in tournaments, dance, and carry on intrigues with the ladies. And so they circulated their poems privately, in handwritten copies, amongst their friends. Not until ten years after Surrey's death did most of their poems appear in print. In 1557 an enterprising printer named Richard Tottel published an anthology called *Songs and Sonnets* containing ninety-seven of Wyatt's poems and forty of Surrey's. This book, now called *Tottel's Miscellany,* has a rather bad reputation today because Tottel "improved" the poems by changing their words so that they seemed smoother to his ears. To make certain that we read Wyatt's and Surrey's words, rather than Tottel's, scholars have searched out the handwritten copies of the poems that predate their publication.

A. Humanities Connection: About the Fine Art
Stories say that in his youth, Surrey's high spirits led him to wander the streets at night with Sir Thomas Wyatt's son, breaking the windows of sleeping citizens.

This painting by no means demonstrates the extravagant dress of the true Elizabethan "dandy" or "fop," but it does show that gentlemen dressed as elaborately as women did.

B. "Miscellanies"
In aristocratic circles, poems circulated and were copied by hand. They did not reach the public unless someone enterprising published a "miscellany." The most important such collection was *Tottel's Miscellany* (its title page is on text page 176), then known by Tottel's title, *Songs and Sonnets.* Shakespeare's character Master Slender (in *The Merry Wives of Windsor*) confirms this book's popularity when he remarks, "I had rather than forty shillings I had my book of Songs and Sonnets here."

Prepare students to find references in the poem to Anne Boleyn and Henry VIII.

SUPPLEMENTARY SUPPORT MATERIALS
1. Review and Response Worksheet: Petrarchan Sonnet (*CCB*)
2. Selection Test (*CCB*)

DEVELOPING VOCABULARY
The following words and expressions from the poem are tested in the Selection Test. (See also Vocabulary Activity Worksheet.)

whoso	where is
list	draw from

CLOSURE
Have one student explain to the class what *Noli me tangere* means and how it is used in this poem.

ANALYZING THE POEM
Identifying Details
1. He is weary and he thinks that the hind is unattainable.
2. He tells them that they will spend their time in vain.
3. The Latin phrase *Noli me tangere,* or "Don't touch me."

Interpreting Meanings
4. The hind is Anne Boleyn, and Caesar is King Henry VIII.
5. You are engaging in a futile endeavor.
   The phrase implies that the hunter has no chance of success.
6. A yearning or desire that is unattainable.

A. Irony
There is some irony in the image of Anne's "fair neck" in a diamond collar, since her neck was shortly to be severed from her body by the same "Caesar" who claims her here.
❓ What additional meanings can you find in the words on Anne's collar, given what eventually happened to her? (Caesar so owned her that he felt free to kill her.)

According to traditional gossip, this poem by Wyatt is about the attraction he felt for Anne Boleyn, a beautiful young woman at court. When he noticed that no less a person than King Henry was also attracted to Anne, he gave up the pursuit (as he says in line 1) to whoever else wanted to "hunt" her. No one knows whether this story is true or not, but Henry did make Anne the second of his six queens. Wyatt adapted the poem from an Italian sonnet by Petrarch. Wyatt also took from Petrarch's commentators the information in line 13 about Julius Caesar's tame deer, who wore collars saying in Latin "Don't touch me, I am Caesar's" so that hunters would not molest them.

Whoso List to Hunt

Whoso list° to hunt, I know where is an hind,°
But as for me, alas, I may no more.
The vain travail hath wearied me so sore
I am of them that farthest cometh behind.
5 Yet may I, by no means, my wearied mind
Draw from the deer, but as she fleeth afore,
Fainting I follow. I leave off therefore,
Since in a net I seek to hold the wind.

Whoso list her hunt, I put him out of doubt,°
10 As well as I, may spend his time in vain.
And graven with diamonds in letters plain
There is written, her fair neck round about,
"*Noli me tangere*,° for Caesar's I am,
And wild for to hold, though I seem tame."

1. **list:** desires. **hind:** a female deer (rhymes with *kind*).

9. **put him out of doubt:** assure him (that he).

13. *Noli me tangere* (Latin): "Don't touch me."

Responding to the Poem

Analyzing the Poem

Identifying Details
1. According to the speaker, why is he ending his hunt of the hind?
2. What advice does he give to potential hunters of this hind?
3. What does he say is written about the hind's neck?

Interpreting Meanings
4. Given the information in the headnote, tell who the hind is and who Caesar is.
5. When you try "in a net . . . to hold the wind" (line 8), what are you doing? What does this imply about the hunter's chances?

6. Whether the poem is autobiographical or not, it does describe an experience that is fairly common in life. What is that experience?

Writing About the Poem

A Creative Response
Responding to the Poem. What does this poem reveal about the position of women in Wyatt's time? What is your response to the phrase "I am Caesar's"? Write a paragraph from the point of view of the "hind" and give her response to the situation described in the poem.

A. Humanities Connection: About the Fine Art

Anne Boleyn (1507?–1536) was the second wife of Henry VIII (see jingle on text page 173) and the mother of Elizabeth I. (The Latin legend across the top of the painting reads, "Anna Bolina, uxor [wife] Henri-Octa [of Henry VIII].") On her mother's side she was related to the Howard family of the Earl of Surrey. After some time in France, Anne was introduced to the English court, where Henry began pursuing her. She held out for marriage, however, and Henry began attempts to dissolve his first marriage. He eventually declared himself head of the Church of England, which enabled his tame archbishop, Thomas Cranmer, to grant the annulment that the Pope could not grant. Henry then publicly married Anne (they had already married in secret because she was pregnant), but he was bitterly disappointed when she bore him a daughter. By the time Anne miscarried a son, Henry's attentions had turned to Jane Seymour. He freed himself from Anne by accusing her of adultery and incest—treason for a queen, argued Henry, since the king *is* the state. Anne was convicted and beheaded; her guilt has never been determined. Ten days after her execution Henry married Jane Seymour, who died in childbirth eighteen months later.

A

Anne Boleyn by an unknown artist. Oil.

National Portrait Gallery, London.

PREPARATION

ESTABLISHING A PURPOSE. Use the head-note to help students empathize with the speaker. A good purpose-setting question is number 4 on page 191.

DEVELOPING VOCABULARY
The following words and expressions from the poem are tested in the Selection Test. (See also Vocabulary Activity Worksheet.)
to take bread at my hand
broad waking
would fain know

A. Metaphor
Note that these lines contain words that compare women with a creature like a deer. (See the second writing assignment, Analyzing Diction, on page 191.)

B. Vocabulary
Broad means "fully."

C. Vocabulary
Newfangleness refers to the desire for novelty.

This is one of Wyatt's original poems about love. The speaker in this poem is a man who has apparently had relationships with several women—and one woman in particular—but now has no relationships with women at all. In the poem, he thinks about the experiences he has had. He seems unable to understand what has happened. "It wasn't a dream," he says. But what was it? And why is it over?

They Flee from Me

They flee from me that sometime° did me seek,
    With naked foot stalking° in my chamber.
I have seen them gentle, tame, and meek,
    That now are wild, and do not remember
5   That sometime they put themself in danger°
To take bread at my hand; and now they range
Busily seeking with a continual change.

Thanked be fortune, it hath been otherwise
    Twenty times better; but once, in special,
10   In thin array, after a pleasant guise,°
    When her loose gown from her shoulders did fall,
    And she me caught in her arms long and small,°
There with all sweetly did me kiss,
And softly said, "Dear heart, how like you this?"

15   It was no dream; I lay broad waking.
    But all is turned through my gentleness,°
Into a strange fashion of forsaking;
    And I have leave to go of her goodness,
    And she also to use newfangleness.°
20   But since that I so kindly am served,
I would fain know what she hath deserved.

1. **sometime:** once.
2. **stalking:** walking softly.

5. **in danger:** in my power.

10. **guise:** fashion of dressing.

12. **small:** slender.

16. **gentleness:** good manners.

19. **use newfangleness:** be unfaithful to me.

1. The contrast has to do with the women's behavior: In the past they were gentle and meek, but in the present they are wild and unpredictable.
2. The woman takes the initiative.
3. He blames himself, saying that "all is turned through my gentleness."
4. He wonders what the woman "hath deserved," namely, what has happened to her and whom she has met after she deserted him.

Interpreting Meanings
5. The speaker is obviously displeased with the way the woman has treated him. He doesn't think her behavior is at all kind, though it's typical.
6. Answers may vary, but students should recognize that the tone mingles nostalgia with bitterness.
7. Answers might include its universality, its imagery, its "modern" tone.

Responding to the Poem

Analyzing the Poem

Identifying Details

1. What contrast between the past and the present is emphasized in stanza 1?

2. In the encounter described in stanza 2, which lover takes the initiative?

3. In stanza 3, whom does the speaker blame for the break-up of the passionate affair with one special woman?

4. What does the speaker ask at the poem's end?

Interpreting Meanings

5. The word *kindly* (line 20) is probably a **pun** because it has two meanings: (a) "naturally, typically" and (b) "graciously, sweetly." Why might the word seem sarcastic as it is used here?

6. How would you describe the **tone** of the whole poem?

7. This poem was largely ignored before the twentieth century, but it is now highly regarded by people who like poetry. How would you account for its popularity?

Writing About the Poem

A Creative Response

1. Responding to the Poem. Suppose this speaker were directing his remarks to you. How would you respond to him? How would you answer his questions? Answer in a poem or a prose paragraph.

A Critical Response

2. Analyzing Diction. *The pronoun* they *in lines 1 and 6 certainly refers to women, but the poet presents these women as though they were small, shy creatures, perhaps deer.* Write a paragraph showing how specific words in the poem support this analysis of Wyatt's diction.

The Elements of Literature

PETRARCHAN SONNETS

A
Wyatt's and Surrey's **sonnets** are adaptations or translations of sonnets originally written in Italian by Francesco Petraca, known in English as Francis Petrarch (1304–1374). Petrarch addressed many love poems to a woman identified only as Laura, a proud woman of ideal virtue and beauty who, in the poems, remains totally indifferent to the poet. The poet-lover, an abject, humble figure, alternately burns with desire for the lady and freezes from her disdain of him. Here is how Wyatt describes this stressful condition:

I fear and hope, I burn and freeze like ice;
I fly above the world, yet can I not arise.

Although the love they express is hopeless, sonnets written in the Petrarchan manner are interesting for two reasons. First, they contain many ingenious and remarkable comparisons, which in time became known as **Petrarchan conceits.** Love is a baited hook, for instance, and being in love is like plowing water or sowing seed in sand.

And love itself is warfare—or a hunt, as we have seen in Wyatt's poem.

Petrarchan, or Italian, sonnets are also interesting for their strict structure to which the poet must conform. The ideas in the poem must be expressed in fourteen lines, no more and no less. In a good sonnet the poem never seems to be squeezed or stretched to fit the form. Moreover, each line of the sonnet has to consist of ten syllables: five unaccented ones alternating with five accented. This kind of meter is called **iambic pentameter;** it differs from blank verse only in being rhymed. Finally, the sonnet must be organized into two unequal parts: an **octave,** consisting of the first eight lines, and a **sestet,** consisting of the final six. In most Italian sonnets the octave describes a situation and the sestet describes a change in the situation. This change is called the **turn.** The turn signals a logical or emotional shift, or a new beginning. Sometimes the octave presents a problem and the sestet a solution, or the octave and the sestet present the same problem from two different points of view. Sometimes the problem of the octave is intensified in the sestet, and no solution is given. The possibilities are endless.

In "Whoso List to Hunt," find the line with the turn. Does the turn show a logical or an emotional shift?

PREPARATION

1. **ESTABLISHING A PURPOSE.** Use the headnote, and have students read to find the conceit that underlies the poems and to compare the translations.

2. **PREREADING JOURNAL.** As question 6 suggests, Petrarch's poem compares love with war. *Is* love a kind of warfare? Have students write their responses to this very old idea.

SUPPLEMENTARY SUPPORT MATERIALS

1. Vocabulary Activity Worksheet (*CCB*)
2. Review and Response Worksheet: The Petrarchan Conceit (*CCB*)
3. Selection Test (*CCB*)

DEVELOPING VOCABULARY

The following words from the poem are tested in the Selection Test. (See also Vocabulary Activity Worksheet.)

to reign	refrain
captive	converteth
clad	ire
oft	doth
banner	to lurk

A. Expansion
Surrey's importance as a poet is based on two facts. He was the first English poet to use blank verse (unrhymed iambic pentameter). Also, he not only continued the sonnet tradition in English begun by Wyatt but gave it the form now known as the "English" sonnet: three quatrains and a couplet, rhymed *abab, cdcd, efef, gg,* as in this translation.

B. Paraphrase
Note that these lines can be more readily understood in comparison to lines 5–8 in Wyatt's version. They might be paraphrased: She who taught me to love and suffer pain, who taught me to conceal my hopes and desires with modesty, changes from smiles to anger when she sees love in my face.

C. Syntax
The subject of the sentence is "She" (line 5), and the predicate is "taketh displeasure" (line 8).

D. Syntax
The "he" here is love.

Both of the following sonnets are translations of a sonnet by Petrarch: "Love That Doth Reign" is Surrey's translation; "The Long Love" is Wyatt's. In Petrarch's sonnet, the situation is the usual one: The poet loves a lady, but she will not permit him to declare his love. In "Whoso List to Hunt," Wyatt compares a woman with a hind. In the following poem, notice how the speaker describes his feeling of love. Love's banner (line 4) is usually taken as a conceit for the lover's blush.

A Love That Doth Reign

Love that doth <u>reign</u> and live within my thought,
And build his seat within my <u>captive</u> breast,
<u>Clad</u> in the arms wherein with me he fought,
Oft in my face he doth his <u>banner</u> rest.
5 But she that taught me° love and suffer pain,
My doubtful hope and eke° my hot desire
B With shamefast° look to shadow and <u>refrain</u>,
Her smiling grace <u>converteth</u> straight to <u>ire</u>.

And coward love then to the heart apace°
10 Taketh his flight, where he <u>doth lurk</u> and plain°
His purpose lost, and dare not show his face.
For my lord's guilt thus faultless bide° I pain.
Yet from my lord shall not my foot remove:°
Sweet is the death that taketh end by love.
—Henry Howard, Earl of Surrey

5. **taught me:** taught me to.

6. **eke:** also.

7. **shamefast:** modest.

9. **apace:** quickly.
10. **plain:** complain.

12. **bide:** endure.
13. **not my foot remove:** that is, I'll stand by him.

The Long Love

The long° love that in my thought doth harbor°
And in my heart doth keep his residence,
Into my face presseth with bold pretense°
And therein campeth, spreading his banner.
5 She that me learneth° to love and suffer
And wills that my trust and lust's negligence°
C Be reined by reason, shame,° and reverence
With his hardiness° taketh displeasure.

D Wherewithal unto the heart's forest he fleeth,
10 Leaving his enterprise with pain and cry,
And there him hideth, and not appeareth.
What may I do, when my master° feareth,
But in the field with him to live and die?
For good is the life ending faithfully.
—Sir Thomas Wyatt

1. **long:** long-standing. **harbor:** dwell.

3. **pretense:** claims.

5. **me learneth:** teaches me.
6. **lust's negligence:** the seemingly careless way I reveal my feelings for her.
7. **shame:** modesty.
8. **hardiness:** boldness.

12. **master:** that is, love.

CLOSURE
Have one student explain to the class
how Renaissance poets typically seem to
feel about love.

ANALYZING THE POEMS
Identifying Details
1. The lover's face blushes.
2. She urges him to be more moderate
and to conceal his hope and desire.

3. Love retreats to the lover's heart and
hides there.
4. The sweetness of dying for love and
for faithfulness.

Interpreting Meanings
5. Each translator compares love to a
master, or lord, in a military context.
   In Surrey's poem, such details include
the notion of love "reigning" (line 1), the

mentions of "arms" and "banner" (lines 3
and 4), and the idea that the lover will
stand by his lord (line 13). In Wyatt's
poem, military details include "campeth"
and "banner" (line 4), "enterprise" and
"master" (lines 10 and 12), and the
"field" (battlefield) (line 13).
6. Answers will vary. (In the conventions
of Renaissance poetry, the victor seems
to be the woman.)

Additional Writing
Assignment
You might have
students compare
these poems to
Keats's "La Belle
Dame Sans Merci"
on text page 712.

Responding to the Poems

Analyzing the Poems

Identifying Details

1. According to each translation, what happens to the lover's face (lines 1–4)?
2. According to lines 5–8 in each poem, how does the woman respond to the lover's feelings?
3. According to lines 9–12 in each poem, how does love respond to the woman's reactions?
4. According to the last two lines, what are the compensations of dying for love?

Interpreting Meanings

5. What **metaphor** does each translator use to characterize love? What specific details extend the metaphor in each poem?
6. If, according to the familiar **conceit**, love is warfare, who is more likely to be victor—the lover or the woman? What do you think of this notion?

Writing About the Poems

A Creative Response

1. **Creating a Petrarchan Conceit.** Complete the second part of each metaphor below to create a Petrarchan conceit. Remember, such a conceit is an ingenious comparison, such as "Love is a baited hook."

   a. Happiness is . . .
   b. Sorrow is . . .
   c. A blush is . . .
   d. Love is . . .

A Critical Response

2. **Comparing and Contrasting Translations.** In a brief essay, tell which translation you prefer and why.

The Elements of Literature

POETIC METER

The basic unit of poetic meter is the **metrical foot,** which is one stressed syllable and one or more unstressed syllables. Stressed syllables are usually indicated by ˊ and unstressed by �‿. The four kinds of of metrical feet are

1. **Iamb** (‿ˊ), as in irate
2. **Trochee** (ˊ‿), as in apple
3. **Anapest** (‿‿ˊ), as in insincere
4. **Dactyl** (ˊ‿‿), as in spatula

The analysis of poetic meter is called **scansion.** To scan a poem, you should first identify the kind of metrical foot used; then you should count the number of feet per line. A line with two feet (two iambs, two trochees, etc.) is written in **dimeter.** A line with three feet is written in **trimeter;** with four feet, **tetrameter;** with five feet, **pentameter;** with six feet, **hexameter.** (Few lines of poetry con-

tain more than six feet.) One line of **iambic pentameter,** then, would contain five iambs, as does the first line of Wyatt's "They Flee from Me":

They flee / from me / that some / time did / me seek

Poets may make use of two metrical devices to vary the meter of a line: the **spondee** (ˊˊ), or double stress; and the **caesura** (||), or pause.

Few poems are written in a meter that remains exactly regular throughout. The perception of meter may also vary from reader to reader, depending on which parts of phrases or sentences the reader thinks are most heavily stressed. Generally, however, readers can easily identify the dominant metrical pattern used in a poem.

You have seen that the first line of Wyatt's "They Flee from Me" shows regular iambic pentameter. Does the rest of the poem follow the same pattern? If not, where is the meter irregular?

Sir Thomas Wyatt and Henry Howard, Earl of Surrey 193

The son of a goldsmith, Nicholas Hilliard (1537–1619) was first trained as a jeweler. A self-taught painter, he became England's first true miniaturist and a court painter to Elizabeth I and James I. In this meticulous painting (about the size it is shown here), note how the circular ruff matches the circular frame. In the sixteenth century, aristocratic partners to arranged marriages often met before the wedding *only* by way of portraits like this one. The Victoria and Albert Museum in London has an extensive collection of exquisite miniatures.

B. Expansion

Whether or not Raleigh ever placed his expensive cloak in the mud for Queen Elizabeth to step on (ruining it—no dry cleaners), it is the kind of act that the charming Raleigh *would* have done for the queen. Raleigh's wit is revealed in his famous reply to Marlowe's "The Passionate Shepherd to His Love" (see text pages 232 and 234).

Sir Walter Raleigh (1552–1618)

Raleigh is one of the most colorful figures of a very colorful age. A handsome, expensively dressed, and probably arrogant man, at the peak of his success he was Queen Elizabeth's confidential secretary and captain of her guard. He fought brilliantly for England in France, Spain, Ireland, and America. He was passionately devoted to the cause of colonizing the New World, and to advertise its products he became one of the first bold Englishmen to smoke tobacco and grow potatoes.

In his rise to power Raleigh made many enemies, who saw their chance to destroy him when the Queen died. They poisoned King James's mind against him, and—on trumped-up evidence—he was convicted of treason. Raleigh was sentenced to death in 1603, though his execution was not carried out until 1618.

Imprisoned in the Tower of London during this long interval, he conducted chemical experiments and wrote a *History of the World* that runs from Adam and Eve to the establishment of the Roman Empire. He also dreamed of another expedition to Guiana, on the northern coast of South America; he had explored Guiana earlier in his life and believed it contained vast hoards of gold and jewels. In 1617, still under a death sentence, he was allowed to undertake his last voyage to Guiana. It turned out to be a disaster. The English obtained no treasure, and the Spanish killed many of Raleigh's men, including his beloved son. Very ill with fever, Raleigh sailed home to face a certain and shameful death. But according to the verdict of history, the shame is King James's, not Raleigh's. Raleigh was sacrificed to placate the Spanish, who were clamoring for his death as a condition for maintaining peaceful relations with England. The English, who hated and feared the Spanish, had not forgotten Raleigh when they deposed and beheaded James's son, King Charles I, in 1649.

A

Sir Walter Raleigh by Nicholas Hilliard (c. 1585). Miniature.

In his speech on the scaffold Raleigh described himself as "a seafaring man, a soldier, and a courtier." Although he did publish his *History,* he did not think of himself as a writer. He was carefree with his poems; only about thirty-five of them have survived, and they have been slowly assembled by literary researchers through the past four centuries. His most ambitious poem is *The Ocean to Cynthia,* one of the hundreds of literary works that Queen Elizabeth's subjects wrote to express their love and devotion. It survives only in fragments. This is unfortunate, because Raleigh's poems have considerable merit. They are powerful, outspoken, even blunt, and suffused with the courage of a man who was always ready to accept without self-pity whatever life might bring him. He could have been thinking of himself when he wrote in his *History,* "There is no man so assured of his honor, of his riches, health, or life, but that he may be deprived of either or all, the very next hour or day to come."

B

PREPARATION
ESTABLISHING A PURPOSE. Have students read the headnote and look for the personification of Nature, Love, and Time as they read the poem.

SUPPLEMENTARY SUPPORT MATERIALS
1. Vocabulary Activity Worksheet (*CCB*)
2. Review and Response Worksheet: Personification (*CCB*)
3. Selection Test (*CCB*)

DEVELOPING VOCABULARY
The following words from the poem are tested in the Selection Test. (See also Vocabulary Activity Worksheet.)
destiny   despise

This poem is Raleigh's contribution to a large body of poetry—from all countries and all ages—concerned with the passage of time and its effects on human life. The poem contains three *personifications* (of Nature, Time, and Love), in which abstract ideas are spoken of as if they were human.

Nature, That Washed Her Hands in Milk

A   Nature, that washed her hands in milk,
     And had forgot to dry them,
     Instead of earth took snow and silk,
     At Love's request to try them,
5   If she a mistress° could compose
B   To please Love's fancy out of those.

C   Her eyes he would should be of light,
     A violet breath, and lips of jelly;
     Her hair not black, nor overbright,
10   And of the softest down her belly;
     As for her inside° he'd have it
D   Only of wantonness and wit.

     At Love's entreaty such a one
     Nature made, but with her beauty
15   She hath framed a heart of stone;
     So as Love, by ill destiny,
     Must die for her whom Nature gave him,
     Because her darling would not save him.

E   But Time (which nature doth despise,
20   And rudely gives her love the lie,
     Makes hope a fool, and sorrow wise)
F   His hands do neither wash nor dry;
     But being made of steel and rust,
     Turns snow and silk and milk to dust.

25   The light, the belly, lips, and breath,
     He dims, discolors, and destroys;
     With those° he feeds but fills not death,°
     Which sometimes° were the food of joys.
     Yea, Time doth dull each lively wit,
30   And dries all wantonness with it.

     Oh, cruel Time! which takes in trust°
     Our youth, our joys, and all we have,
     And pays us but with age and dust;
     Who in the dark and silent grave
35   When we have wandered all our ways
     Shuts up the story of our days.

5. **mistress:** young woman.

11. **inside:** mind.

27. **those:** the "light, belly, lips." **fills not death:** Death is insatiable.
28. **sometimes:** formerly.

31. **trust:** custody.

A. Syntax
? Whom does "her" refer to? (The young woman)

B. Vocabulary
Fancy means "imagination" or "illusion" or "mental picture."

C. Syntax
? Who is "he"? (The lover)

D. Vocabulary
Wantonness is a poetic word meaning something like "friskiness" or "playfulness." You might have students look up its several other meanings.

E. Interpreting
? Why would nature despise time? (Time ruins all of nature's beautiful work.)

F. Syntax
? Whose hands? (Time's) What is the significance of steel and rust? (Steel is hard and inflexible; rust is a sign of decay and corrosion. Thus, time is uncaring and destructive.)

Write the words *Nature, Time,* and *Love* on the chalkboard, and have students as a group describe the "persona" each is given in the poem.

ANALYZING THE POEM
Identifying Details
1. Love asks Nature to make a beautiful woman, with eyes of light, violet breath, lips of jelly, hair neither black nor over-bright, belly of down, and mind of "wantonness and wit."
2. She has a heart of stone.
3. Love dies.
4. She turns to dust; her eyes, belly, lips, and breath grow dim, discolor, and are destroyed; her wit and wantonness grow dull and dry.

Interpreting Meanings
5. Nature is motherly and benign; Time is a cruel destroyer; Love is an entreating, passionate lover.
6. Snow and silk are fragile, soft, and destructible. Earth is lasting, heavy, fecund, etc.
7. See marginal note.

A. Humanities Connection: Discussing the Portrait

❓ Ask students to describe their first impressions of this famous portrait. (The dramatic colors; the look-alike sisters; the small variations in ruffs and jewelry; the babies that look like stiff, miniature adults)

B. Expansion
There are at least two motifs in this poem: the idea of the stony-hearted lover or femme fatale (recall Keats's "La Belle Dame Sans Merci," text page 712); and the idea of creating a perfect person (recall the myth of Pygmalion).

Additional Writing Assignment
Students might compare this poem with Shakespeare's "Fear No More the Heat o' the Sun" (text page 354) and Frost's "Nothing Gold Can Stay" (text page 51).

The Cholmondeley Sisters (17th century). Oil.   The Tate Gallery, London.

Responding to the Poem

Analyzing the Poem

Identifying Details

1. What exactly does Love request Nature to do? What are his explicit requests?
2. What defect does Love's mistress have?
3. What becomes of Love as a result?
4. What changes does Time make in the young woman?

Interpreting Meanings

5. What specific human attributes and actions **personify** Nature, Time, and Love? Do you think the personifications are appropriate?
6. Why is it significant that Nature composes the woman from snow and silk, rather than from the earth?
7. Does the story of Love's mistress remind you of any other stories, ancient or modern, that you have heard?

Writing About the Poem

A Creative Response

1. **Creating Personification.** Choose an emotion (love, hate, jealousy, despair) and personify it in the same way Raleigh does, by giving it appropriate human characteristics and actions.

A Critical Response

2. **Analyzing Variations in a Poem's Ending.** Just after Raleigh was beheaded, the last stanza of this poem was publicly circulated as a separate little poem, with a note saying that the lines had been written the night before his execution. Two lines were added to the stanza:

   And from which earth, and grave, and dust,
   The Lord will raise me up, I trust.

Write a paragraph explaining how these two lines alter the meaning of the whole poem.

BUILDING ON PRIOR KNOWLEDGE. Use the headnote to focus students' attention on the metaphor of life as a stage play. Although the context differs, another Shakespearean reference to life as a play occurs in *Macbeth,* Act V, Scene 5, lines 24–26; see the top of text page 324.

SUPPLEMENTARY SUPPORT MATERIALS
1. Vocabulary Activity Worksheet (*CCB*)
2. Review and Response Worksheet: Extended Metaphors (*CCB*)
3. Selection Test (*CCB*)

DEVELOPING VOCABULARY
The following words from the poem are tested in the Selection Test. (See also Vocabulary Activity Worksheet.)
judicious   amiss
mark   jest

A In 1612, this poem was set to music and published as a madrigal, or part-song, by Orlando Gibbons. When sung by several voices, it sounds something like a round, but much more complicated. The poem's comparison of life to a stage play, sometimes a comedy and sometimes a tragedy, occurs in ancient Greek literature and in many later writings, including Jaques's famous speech in Shakespeare's *As You Like It,* beginning "All the world's a stage, and all the men and women merely players."

What Is Our Life?

What is our life? A play of passion.
Our mirth, the music of division.°
Our mother's wombs the tiring houses° be,
Where we are dressed for this short comedy.
5 Heaven the judicious, sharp spectator is,
That sits and marks still° who doth act amiss.
Our graves that hide us from the searching sun
Are like drawn curtains when the play is done:
B Thus march we, playing, to our latest° rest;
10 Only we die in earnest. That's no jest!

C

2. **music of division:** rapid passages, resembling laughter; perhaps also the music played between the acts of a play.
3. **tiring houses:** dressing rooms.

6. **still:** continually.

9. **latest:** last.

A. Humanities Connection: Music
Orlando Gibbons (1583–1625) was an organist and composer who in 1619 served James I as court virginalist.

B. Puns
This line answers question 3.

C. Tone
? What is the speaker's tone? (Ironic, mocking)

ANALYZING THE POEM
Identifying Details
1. See lines 1, 2, 3, 5, 7–8, 9.
2. Death (line 10).

Interpreting Meanings
3. Line 9: *Playing* can mean "acting"; "amusing oneself."
4. Perhaps because human actions are trivial or insignificant in the grand scheme of things.
5. Answers will vary.

Responding to the Poem

Analyzing the Poem
Identifying Details
1. Identify all the **metaphors** used to describe life in terms of a drama.
2. Which aspect of life is *not* a comedy?

Interpreting Meanings
3. Where in the poem does Raleigh make a **pun** by using two common but different meanings of the word *play*?
4. Why do you think Raleigh calls life a "short comedy," and not a tragedy?
5. Do you think that people can bear their ups and downs better if they regard life as a performance or as an act? Is there any harm in regarding life as a play? Explain.

Writing About the Poem
A Critical Response
Expressing an Opinion. According to Horace Walpole, an eighteenth-century English writer, "This world is a comedy to those that think, a tragedy to those that feel." Write a paragraph telling whether you agree or disagree with this distinction.

Comment from a Critic
The contemporary medieval scholar C. S. Lewis writes about Spenser's ambiguous relationship with Ireland and its effect on his writing:

"He was coming to need that Irish life: the freedom, the informality, the old clothes, the hunting, farming, and fishing (he was proud of the superexcellent trout in his own river at Kilcolman). He may,
as a poet, have needed the very country. There is a real affinity between his *Faerie Queene,* a poem of quests and wanderings and inextinguishable desires, and Ireland itself—the soft, wet air, the loneliness, the muffed shapes of the hills, the heart-rending sunsets. It was of course a different Ireland from ours, an Ireland without potatoes, whitewashed cottages, or bottled stout: but it must already have been 'the land of longing.'

"*The Faerie Queene* should perhaps be regarded as the work of one who is turning into an Irishman. For Ireland shares with China the power of assimilating all her invaders. It is an old complaint that all who go there—Danes, Normans, English, Scotch, very Firbolgs—rapidly become 'more Irish than the Irish themselves.' With Spenser the process was

A. Expansion
You may wish to relate the unrest in Spenser's Ireland to the political situation in Northern Ireland today.

B. Expansion
The titles of Spenser's marriage songs come from the Greek word *thalamos,* "room" or "bridal chamber."

Edmund Spenser
(1552–1599)

Spenser—unlike such gentlemanly writers as Wyatt, Surrey, Sidney, and Raleigh—regarded himself primarily as a poet. Indeed, in the eighteenth and nineteenth centuries he became known as "the poet's poet" because so many young writers learned the art and craft of poetry by studying him. Spenser began publishing poetry about the time he graduated from the Merchant Taylors' School and went to Cambridge University, from which he received the B.A. and M.A. degrees. Upon leaving the university, he served as personal secretary to the Earl of Leicester, favorite of Queen Elizabeth. Leicester, a great patron of scholars and writers, surrounded himself with brilliant people, and in his household Spenser became acquainted with several poets, among them Sir Philip Sidney. He dedicated to Sidney his first book, *The Shepherds' Calendar* (1579). This is a set of twelve pastoral poems, one for each month, in a variety of meters, some of them experimental and all of them original and interesting. Literary historians have long recognized 1579 as the date when the great age of Elizabethan literature began.

In 1580, Spenser and his new wife went to Ireland in the service of the Lord Deputy of Ireland; except for two or three visits to England, he was to spend the rest of his life in that war-torn country. English troops had invaded and conquered Ireland, but the Irish did not regard themselves as conquered. They particularly resented people like Spenser, who was given an Irish castle and a vast estate in Kilcolman, a rather wild and remote place in County Cork. Thirty miles away, Sir Walter Raleigh was the proprietor of an even vaster estate than Spenser's. When Raleigh was in Ireland, the two poets met and discussed their works in progress: Raleigh's *The Ocean to Cynthia* and Spenser's *The Faerie Queene.* Raleigh was so impressed with the latter that he persuaded Spenser to accompany him to London in 1589, and there in the following year Books I–III of *The Faerie Queene* were published with this dedication: "To the Most Mighty and Magnificent Empress Elizabeth, by the Grace of God Queen of Eng-

land, France, and Ireland." The Queen, notoriously stingy, rewarded him with the unusually large pension of fifty pounds annually, and Spenser was generally recognized as the leading poet of the day. After publishing two more volumes of poems in 1591, he returned to Ireland.

There conditions remained very unsettled and dangerous, but Spenser managed to continue work on *The Faerie Queene* and other poems. His first wife having died, he courted and married Elizabeth Boyle, an Anglo-Irish lady living in Cork. His sonnet sequence *Amoretti* and his marriage hymn *Epithalamion* (both 1595) have often been read autobiographically as records of his intense devotion to his wife. In 1596, Books IV–VI of *The Faerie Queene* appeared, along with two other works: a set of philosophical poems called *Four Hymns* and another marriage song called *Prothalamion.*

As the century drew to a close, the Irish intensified their efforts to expel the English from their land. During one of their raids, Spenser's castle was burned and his infant son killed. Spenser himself took refuge in Cork City, and from there he went over to London, carrying messages to the government and some poems in perhaps beginning. It is true he hated the Irish and they him: but, as an Irishman myself, I take leave to doubt whether that is a very un-Irish trait. ('The Irish, sir,' said Dr. Johnson, 'are an honest people. They never speak well of one another.')"

manuscript. He died suddenly, in 1599, and was given a splendid funeral and burial in the part of Westminster Abbey that has become known as the "Poet's Corner." He lies near Chaucer, a poet who provided much of his inspiration.

Chaucer, Spenser, and Milton—these three have long been regarded as England's greatest nondramatic poets. Though the achievements of each have been questioned from time to time, all three have maintained their high reputations, despite changes in literary taste. Of the three, Spenser is perhaps the least highly regarded today. Our age does not itself produce long poems of very high quality, and Spenser's fame depends mainly on the enormously long *Faerie Queene,*

which despite its unfinished state runs about 33,000 lines. This poem is such a characteristic product of the Renaissance that some people find it has little to say to our own time. Moreover, Spenser's language is such a hybrid of Chaucerian and Elizabethan English that even when the work was brand new some purists objected to it. The dramatist and poet Ben Jonson, for instance, called it "no language." But Spenser's special language is just right for his subject matter, and all the objections to him are easily overlooked by readers who want to lose themselves in the glorious world of imagination. They will always love Spenser.

A. About the Engraving
Kilcolman had once been the seat of the Desmond family. By 1598, when the Irish rose under the leadership of Hugh O'Neill, the Earl of Tyrone, the castle was occupied by Spenser, who was regarded as a foreigner and a usurper. Ben Jonson reports that Spenser's third child, a baby son, died after the Irish set the castle on fire. By the end of 1598, Spenser had reached London, where some say he died of hunger.

This romantic engraving shows how Kilcolman looked in the nineteenth century. Only a few of the castle walls remain, along with an old gate and a thatched gate house. (Ruined castles like this one are common sights in Ireland even today.)

A

Ruins of Kilcolman Castle. Engraving.

1. BUILDING ON PRIOR KNOWLEDGE. Discuss briefly the motifs of romance fiction, which many students are already familiar with from the King Arthur stories, fairy tales, and even modern Westerns. (See text page 147.) These motifs include the quest, the perilous journey, the rescue, the good hero, the virtuous woman, the hag, the villain who often has supernatural powers, the dragon or monster who threatens a society, and the supernatural help received by the hero. You might write these motifs on the chalkboard and let students supply examples.

2. ESTABLISHING A PURPOSE. At first, students should read for pure enjoyment. C. S. Lewis's comment on the poem might spur them on and make the poem's archaic language seem less of a hurdle:

"It demands of us a child's love of marvels and dread of bogies, a child's thirst for adventures, . . . It is of course much more than a fairy tale, but unless we can enjoy it as a fairy tale first of all, we shall not really care for it."

"Translating" the Poem

You might devote one class period to translating into Modern English all thirty-six stanzas in the text *before* you assign any reading. Taking time to do so has several benefits: Students discover that they *can* handle Spenser's language; they practice language skills; and they enjoy being the "expert" on a passage.

Assign each student one or two stanzas, or assign groups as many stanzas as there are group members. (Because of internal references, the following stanzas should be translated together: 2–3, 7–9, 10–11, 21–23, 24–25, 26–28, 38–40, 42–43, 44–45, 46–47, 49–50.) The students' task is to rewrite the stanzas into paragraphs in standard word order and Modern English (no slang) that will be clear to their classmates. They are to produce clean copies (numbered as in the text). Assemble the translations in numerical order, and make copies for class reference.

The Faerie Queene

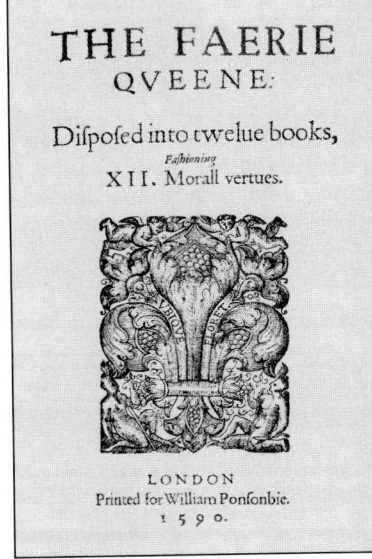

Frontispiece to *The Faerie Queene* (1590). Engraving.

New York Public Library, Rare Books and Manuscripts Division.

Because this poem is both complex and unfinished, and because some of the remarks that Spenser and his contemporaries made about it don't correspond to the parts we have, *The Faerie Queene* has always been the subject of controversy and discussion. Most commentators agree about what kind of poem it is: a romantic or chivalric **epic**, a kind of writing first brought to perfection in Renaissance Italy by Ariosto and Tasso. While *The Faerie Queene* shows the influence of Homer and Virgil, it is not written in the form of a classical epic. Instead, romantic epics like *The Faerie Queene* have an open form, with many characters and many different plots spreading out in all directions. Their marvels, knights, ladies, battles, tournaments, enchantments, dragons, giants, dwarfs, and demons are derived from such medieval romances of chivalry as the tales and poems about King Arthur. One can enjoy a romantic epic for its adventures alone, because there is always something exciting happening.

But its lively stories are only the surface of *The Faerie Queene*. By using what he called a "dark conceit," Spenser incorporated into his poem an immense amount of moral significance, philosophical thought, and political commentary. His moral or teaching purposes are particularly evident. In a letter addressed to Raleigh, he said that the leading characters in the twelve projected books were each supposed to embody a particular virtue or quality, and taken together all these virtues would characterize a truly noble person—that is, a person fully aware of what it means to be human. The first six books—all that Spenser completed—have heroes or heroines who exemplify holiness, temperance, chastity, friendship, justice, and courtesy. There is, therefore, much more to *The Faerie Queene* than there is to a fairy tale that a child might enjoy.

As it is used in this poem, the word *faerie* is nothing like our word *fairy*, which suggests a wee airy creature dancing among the flowers. Rather, *faerie* suggests beings who are heroic, grand, with superhuman powers bestowed on them by their own virtue and piety. The Faerie Queene herself is a remote and glorious monarch who does not even appear in the completed parts of the poem. She is Gloriana, an idealized portrait of Queen Elizabeth, and the realm that she rules over is at once the England that Spenser loved and a strange, imaginary country with a heroic past and a brilliant future.

The Faerie Queene, then, is an elaborate and exuberant poem that draws on works of art and literature dating from biblical times to Spenser's own century. It mixes and synthesizes classical mythology, Christian theology, Renaissance humanism, and Elizabethan politics. What holds all these varied ingredients together is the poet's compelling voice, going on and on and on, speaking a special poetic language, and endlessly weaving ingenious stanzas. Each of the stanzas has only three rhymes, and so among its other splendors *The Faerie Queene* is a tremendous feat of rhyming. The form of the stanzas is Spenser's own invention: nine iambic lines rhyming *ababbcbcc*, the last line (called an **alexandrine**) having an extra foot and thus making it iambic hexameter. The alexandrine often sums up a stanza and adds a final comment.

As they read, have students remember that the characters are allegorical. You might write on the chalkboard the characters' names and what they symbolize to help students keep track. (See the headnote.)

SUPPLEMENTARY SUPPORT MATERIALS
1. Vocabulary Activity Worksheet (CCB)
2. Review and Response Worksheet: Allegory (CCB)
3. Selection Test (CCB)

DEVELOPING VOCABULARY
The following words from the poem are tested in the Selection Test. (See also Vocabulary Activity Worksheet.)

nigh	mortall (mortal)
tyrannie (tyranny)	riven
steede (steed)	dolefull (doleful)
countenance	manifold
disdaine (disdain)	penaunce (penance)

Trying to experience this immense poem by reading a canto of it is like trying to experience the ocean by looking at a teacup of seawater. However, Canto VIII of Book I can be taken as representative of one aspect of *The Faerie Queene:* its delight in heroic violence and the gusto with which it describes ugliness. This rhyme opens the canto and sums up its action:

> Faire virgin to redeeme her deare
>   Brings Arthur to the fight:
> Who slayes the Gyant, wounds the beast,
>   And strips Duessa quight.

The "faire virgin" is Una, or Truth. She has been traveling with "her deare," a Knight called Redcrosse, but she has accidentally become separated from him. Without Una, Redcrosse has fallen into the coils of a beautiful but sinister woman called Duessa, or Falsehood. Duessa's boyfriend, a giant called Orgoglio (ôr·gō′lē·ō), or Pride, has thrown Redcrosse into his dungeon. Meantime, Redcrosse's Dwarf has run off to locate Una. As the canto opens, Una is bringing Prince Arthur and his Squire to rescue Redcrosse. (Reading aloud will make the language easier to understand.)

from The Faerie Queene

1

Aye me, how many perils doe enfold
  The righteous man, to make him daily fall?
Were not, that heavenly grace doth him uphold,
  And stedfast truth acquite° him out of all.
5 Her love is firme, her care continuall,
  So oft as he through his owne foolish pride,
  Or weaknesse is to sinfull bands° made thrall:°
  Else should this Redcrosse knight in bands have dyde,
For whose deliverance she this Prince doth thither guide.

4. **acquite:** acquit, set free.

7. **bands:** bonds. **thrall:** prisoner.

2

10 They sadly traveiled thus, untill they came
  Nigh to a castle builded strong and hie:
  Then cryde the Dwarfe, "lo yonder is the same,
  In which my Lord my liege doth luckless lie,
  Thrall to that Gyants hatefull tyrannie:
15 Therefore, deare Sir, your mightie powres assay."
  The noble knight alighted by and by°
  From loftie steede, and bad the Ladie stay,
To see what end of fight should him befall that day.

16. **by and by:** at once.

3

So with the Squire, th' admirer of his might,
20 He marchèd forth towards that castle wall;
  Whose gates he found fast shut, ne living wight°
  To ward° the same, nor answere commers call.
  Then tooke that Squire an horne of bugle small,
  Which hong adowne his side in twisted gold,
25 And tassels gay. Wyde wonders over all
  Of that same hornes great vertues weren told,
Which had approvèd° bene in uses manifold.

21. **wight:** person.
22. **ward:** guard.

27. **approvèd:** proved.

A. Syntax
In lines 5–9, "Her" and "She" refer to heavenly grace.

B. Vocabulary
Note the special use of *travail,* meaning "to journey" or "to travel." (How is travel a travail?) "They" is Una, Prince Arthur, the Squire, and Redcrosse's dwarf.

C. Alliteration
❓ What words alliterate here? (There are four.) Have students read the line aloud to enjoy the exaggerated sounds. "My Lord" is Redcrosse, held by the giant.

D. Vocabulary
Assay means "try." The "noble knight" is Prince Arthur.

E. Vocabulary
A "bugle" is a wild ox. The "wyde wonders" (marvelous tales) told about the horn in the next two stanzas connect it with the legendary horn of Roland and with the ram's horn of Joshua, used to tumble the walls of Jericho (Joshua 6:5).

F. Vocabulary
❓ Can you guess what *bene* means? ("Good")

Allegory
Allegorically, the battle described in stanzas 7–11 has been read as the conflict of Protestants with the Roman Catholic Church, or as the struggle of the Christian against evil, especially as personified in the Antichrist of the Book of Revelation. (But it's more fun to read it as a real battle between the Gyant and Prince Arthur.)

A. Vocabulary
Which homonym is meant here: *vain, vein,* or *vane? (Vein)* Which homonym is meant in line 34? *(Vain)*

B. Syntax
"The same" refers to the horn.

C. Vocabulary
"Geants" is "giant's." In lines 14 and 40, it's spelled "gyant."

D. Alliteration
Read these lines aloud to enjoy the alliteration of *s* and *d* sounds.

E. Allegory
Spenser may be comparing the evil Duessa to the whore of Babylon, described in Revelation 17:4–6. Babylon, "arrayed in purple and scarlet," sits upon a seven-headed beast holding a golden cup full of abominations and filth, "drunken with the blood of the saints."

F. Syntax
The "Peer" is Prince Arthur.

4

Was never wight, that heard that shrilling sound,
    But trembling feare did feele in every vaine;
30   Three miles it might be easie heard around,
    And Ecchoes three answerd it selfe againe:
    No false enchauntment, nor deceiptfull traine°
    Might once abide the terror of that blast,
    But presently° was voide and wholly vaine:°
35   No gate so strong, no locke so firme and fast,
But with that percing noise flew open quite, or brast.°

32. **traine:** trap.

34. **presently:** immediately.
vaine: powerless.

36. **brast:** burst.

5

The same before the Geants gate he blew,
    That all the castle quakèd from the ground,
    And every dore of freewill open flew.
40   The Gyant selfe dismaièd with that sownd,
    Where he with his Duessa dalliance fownd,°
    In hast came rushing forth from inner bowre,
    With staring countenance sterne, as one astownd,°
    And staggering steps, to weet,° what suddin stowre°
45 Had wrought that horror strange, and dared his dreaded
      powre.

41. **dalliance fownd:** found amorous pleasure.

43. **astownd:** astonished.

44. **weet:** know. **stowre:** uproar.

6

And after him the proud Duessa came,
    High mounted on her manyheaded beast,
    And every head with fyrie tongue did flame,
    And every head was crownèd on his creast,
    And bloudie mouthèd with late cruell feast.
50   That when the knight beheld, his mightie shild
    Upon his manly arme he soone addrest,°
    And at him fiercely flew, with courage fild,
And eger greedinesse° through every member thrild.

52. **addrest:** places.

54. **greedinesse:** longing.

7

55   Therewith the Gyant buckled him to fight,
    Inflamed with scornefull wrath and high disdaine,
    And lifting up his dreadfull club on hight,
    All armed with ragged snubbes° and knottie graine,
    Him thought at first encounter to have slaine.
60   But wise and warie was that noble Pere,°
    And lightly leaping from so monstrous main,°
    Did faire avoide the violence him nere;
It booted nought,° to thinke, such thunderbolts to beare.

58. **snubbes:** knobs.

60. **Pere:** Peer.
61. **main:** might.

63. **booted nought:** did not pay.

8

Ne shame he thought to shunne so hideous might:
65   The idle° stroke, enforcing furious way,
    Missing the marke of his misaymèd sight
    Did fall to ground, and with his heavie sway°

65. **idle:** ill-aimed.

67. **sway:** force.

So deepely dinted in the driven clay,
That three yardes deepe a furrow up did throw:
70   The sad earth wounded with so sore assay,°
  A Did grone full grievous underneath the blow,
And trembling with strange feare, did like an earthquake
    show.

9

  B As when almightie Jove in wrathfull mood,
    To wreake° the guilt of mortall sins is bent,
75   Hurles forth his thundring dart with deadly food,°
Enrold in flames, and smouldring dreriment,°
Through riven cloudes and molten firmament;°
  C The fierce threeforkèd engin° making way,
Both loftie towres and highest trees hath rent,
80   And all that might his angrie passage stay,
And shouting in the earth, casts up a mount of clay.

10

His boystrous° club, so buried in the ground,
He could not rearen up againe so light,°
But that the knight him at avantage found,
85   And whiles he strove his combred clubbe to quight°
  D Out of the earth, with blade all burning bright
  E He smote off his left arme, which like a blocke
Did fall to ground, deprived of native might;
    Large streames of bloud out of the trunckèd stocke
90   **F** Forth gushèd, like fresh water streame from riven rocke.

11

  G Dismaièd with so desperate deadly wound,
And eke impatient of unwonted paine,°
He loudly brayd with beastly yelling sound,
That all the fields rebellowèd againe;
95   As great a noyse, as when in Cymbrian plaine°
  H An heard of Bulles, whom kindly rage° doth sting,
Do for the milkie mothers want° complaine,
And fill the fields with troublous bellowing,
And neighbour woods around with hollow murmur ring.

  I *Duessa sends her dragon to attack the knight. The Squire de-*
fends the knight, but Duessa uses her magic to paralyze the
  J *Squire. The knight rescues the Squire and attacks the dragon,*
tearing its monstrous scalp down to its teeth. The giant Orgoglio
rescues Duessa as the dragon collapses beneath her. Her gar-
ments are stained with the dragon's filthy gore and the giant's
feet are wading in the monster's blood. The giant now turns to
the knight and, enraged with pain, deals him a forceful blow.

70. **assay:** blow.

74. **wreake:** punish.
75. **food:** feud.
76. **dreriment:** dreariness.
77. **firmament:** heavens.
78. **engin:** weapon.

82. **boystrous:** immense.
83. **light:** easily.

85. **quight:** release.

92. **eke . . . paine:** also suffering from un-accustomed pain.

95. **Cymbrian plaine:** a place in Denmark.
96. **kindly rage:** natural urge to procreate.
97. **milkie mothers want:** lack of cows.

A. Vocabulary
Grone is *groan.*

B. Simile
Jove's darts are thunderbolts.

C. Interpreting
The "threeforkèd engin" is Jove's tri-dent, a weapon usually associated with Neptune.

D. Alliteration
Note the almost humorous allitera-tion here.

E. Syntax
"He" is Arthur.

F. Allusion
Water flowed from a rock for Moses and the Israelites in Exodus 17:6.

G. Alliteration
Be sure to read aloud these exag-gerated allitera-tions.

H. Vocabulary/ Simile
Heard is *herd. Kindly* in this line refers to *kine,* "cat-tle." Note this ex-tended simile, in which the bray of the wounded giant is compared with the bellowing of a herd of bulls in heat.

I. Meaning
The Knight here is Prince Arthur.

J. Meaning
The dragon has many heads. Ar-thur kills one.

A. About the Woodcut

Walter Crane (1845–1915) was an English designer, illustrator, and painter best known for his illustrations for Nathaniel Hawthorne's *A Wonder Book* (1852), Grimm's *Fairy Tales,* and the works of Spenser. (Another illustration by Crane is on text page 713.)

❓ What typical dragon-slaying motifs can you spot in this drawing? (The

rearing horse, the fiery-breathed and winged dragon, the knight in armor, the spear) Compare this woodcut with the twelfth-century carving on text page 33.

Students might also do some research on dragons and on their recurring use in the West as symbols of destruction and evil. The word *dragon* is from the Greek word *drakōn,* meaning "serpent," so the medieval dragon traces its lineage back

to the serpents of the very oldest stories: Genesis, Medusa's snaky hair, the Python killed by Apollo at Delphi, and the Hydra killed by Hercules. Students might skip ahead to text page 1099 to D. H. Lawrence's poem about a snake.

B. Syntax
"He" is the wounded Gyant.

C. Meaning
Just when it looks as though Arthur has had it, the light blazing from his shield dazzles and blinds his opponent (stanzas 19 and 20). Questions 5 and 9 (text page 211) address the magical powers of the shield and their symbolism.

D. Rhythm
❓ To maintain the meter, how must *aier* be pronounced? (With two syllables)

Knight on Horseback Killing a Dragon by Walter Crane. Woodcut.

A

18

100   The force, which wont in two to be disperst,
B ⌈   In one alone left° hand he new unites,
         Which is through rage more strong than both were erst;
         With which his hideous club aloft he dites,°
         And at his foe with furious rigour smites,
105   That strongest Oake might seeme to overthrow:
         The stroke upon his shield so heavie lites,
C ⌈   That to the ground it doubleth him full low:
         What mortall wight could ever beare so monstrous blow?

101. **left:** remaining. (His left arm was cut off.)

103. **dites:** lifts.

19

         And in his fall his shield, that covered was,
110   Did loose his vele° by chaunce, and open flew:
         The light whereof, that heavens light did pas,°
D ⌈   Such blazing brightness through the aier threw,

110. **his vele:** its veil, covering.
111. **pas:** surpass.

A   That eye mote not the same endure to vew.
     Which when the Gyaunt spyde with staring eye,
115   He downe let fall his arme, and soft withdrew
     His weapon huge, that heavèd was on hye
     For to have slaine the man, that on the ground did lye.

20

     And eke the fruitfull-headed° beast, amazed
     At flashing beames of that sunshiny shield,
120   Became starke blind, and all his senses dazed,
     That downe he tumbled on the durtie field,
B   And seemed himselfe as conquerèd to yield.
     Whom when his maistresse proud perceived to fall,
     Whiles yet his feeble feet for faintnesse reeld,
125   Unto the Gyant loudly she gan call,
     "O helpe, Orgoglio, helpe, or else we perish all."

21

     At her so pitteous cry was much amooved
C   Her champion stout, and for to ayde his frend,
     Againe his wonted angry weapon prooved:°
130   But all in vaine: for he has read his end
     In that bright shield, and all their forces spend
     Themselves in vaine: for since that glauncing° sight,
     He hath no powre to hurt, nor to defend;
D   As where th' Almighties lightning brond does light,
135   It dimmes the dazèd eyen, and daunts the senses quight.

22

     Whom when the Prince, to battell new addrest,
     And threatning high his dreadfull stroke did see,
     His sparkling blade about his head he blest,°
E   And smote off quite his right leg by the knee,
140   That downe he tombled; as an aged tree,
     High growing on the top of rocky clift,
F   Whose hartstrings with keene steele nigh hewen be,
     The mightie trunck halfe rent, with ragged rift
     Doth roll adowne the rocks, and fall with fearefull drift.°

23

145   Or as a Castle rearèd high and round,
     By subtile engins and malitious slight°
     Is underminèd from the lowest ground,
G   And her foundation forst,° and feebled quight,
     At last downe falles, and with her heapèd hight
150   Her hastie ruine does more heavie make,
     And yields it selfe unto the victours might;
     Such was this Gyaunts fall, that seemed to shake
     The stedfast globe of earth, as it for feare did quake.

118. **fruitfull-headed:** many-headed.

129. **prooved:** tried.

132. **glauncing:** shining.

138. **blest:** waved.

144. **drift:** force.

146. **slight:** magical trickery.

148. **forst:** destroyed.

A. Paraphrase
A paraphrase of this line might read: That eye might not endure to view the same [the bright light].

B. Visualizing
Be sure students describe the mental picture created by this stanza, especially of the fainting dragon's feeble feet.

C. Meaning
Her "champion stout" is the Gyant.

D. Simile
What is the simile here? (The light from Arthur's shield is compared to the light from God's lightning brand.)

E. Syntax
Whose leg? (The Gyant's)

F. Simile
Identify the simile in lines 140–144. (The Gyant's fall is compared to the fall of an aged tree that has been cut in half and rolled down the cliff.)

G. Simile
The Gyant's fall is compared to the fall of a high castle that has had its foundation undermined. Pride can be dashed when it is undermined.

Parallels

Students should by now be recognizing the hero vs. villain, good woman vs. bad woman antitheses that are repeated today in many Westerns and melodramas. Fans of the *Star Wars* movies of the 1970's and 1980's may find parallels with the adventures of Luke Skywalker in the first movie (1977), including the hero's descent into a filthy pit (see stanza 39, text page 208). The pit might remind some students also of Beowulf's descent into the watery hell of Grendel's mother's lair.

? If you were casting a deliberately melodramatic filming of Spenser's story, which actors would you select for the various roles? Why?

A. Vocabulary
In lines 154 and 171, *pray* is *prey.*

B. Simile
Be sure students describe the visual image suggested by this comparison of the Gyant's emptied carcass with an emptied bladder. (Note that Pride is now emptied and shown to have nothing substantial or good inside it.)

C. Parallels
Consider the Biblical parallel of David beheading the giant Goliath (1 Samuel 17:49–51), another instance of goodness subduing the monster evil. You might also note the parallel with Beowulf and Grendel, another dragon-slayer story.

D. Expansion
See the golden cup in Copley's painting on the facing page, and the note on lines 47–50 on page 202.

E. Reference
The "royall Virgin" is Una.

24

A The knight then lightly leaping to the pray,
155   With mortall steele him smot againe so sore,
      That headlesse his unweldy bodie lay,
      All wallowd in his owne fowle bloudy gore,
      Which flowèd from his wounds in wondrous store.
      But soone as breath out of his breast did pas,
160   That huge great body, which the Gyaunt bore,
B   Was vanisht quite, and of that monstrous mas
      Was nothing left, but like an emptie bladder was.

25

C Whose grievous fall, when false Duessa spide,
D   Her golden cup she cast unto the ground,
165   And crownèd mitre° rudely threw aside;
      Such percing griefe her stubborne hart did wound,
      That she could not endure that dolefull stound,°
      But leaving all behind her, fled away:
      The light-foot Squire her quickly turnd around,
170   And by hard meanes enforcing her to stay,
   So brought unto his Lord, as his deservèd pray.

165. mitre: a crown with three peaks.

167. stound: sadness.

26

E The royall Virgin, which beheld from farre,
      In pensive plight, and sad perplexitie,
      The whole atchievement° of this doubtfull warre,
175   Came running fast to greet his victorie,
      With sober gladnesse, and myld modestie,
      And with sweet joyous cheare him thus bespake;
      "Faire braunch of nobless, flowre of chevalrie,
      That with your worth the world amazèd make,
180   How shall I quite° the paines, ye suffer for my sake?

174. atchievement: progress.

180. quite: repay.

27

   "And you° fresh bud of vertue springing fast,
      Whom these sad eyes saw nigh unto deaths dore,
      What hath poore Virgin for such perill past,
      Wherewith you to reward? Accept therefore
185   My simple selfe, and service evermore;
      And he that high does sit, and all things see
      With equall° eyes, their merits to restore,°
      Behold what ye this day have done for mee,
   And what I cannot quite, requite with usuree.°

181. you: that is, the Squire.

187. equall: impartial. **restore:** reward.

189. usuree: interest.

28

190   "But sith° the heavens, and your faire handeling°
      Have made you maister of the field this day,
      Your fortune maister eke with governing,°
      And well begun end all so well, I pray,
      Ne let that wicked woman scape away;

190. sith: since. **handeling:** behavior.

192. Your fortune . . . governing: Confirm your good fortune also by prudent conduct.

A. Humanities Connection:
Discussing the Fine Art
John Singleton Copley (1738–1815) gained a reputation from masterful portraits painted in Boston (where he was born), New York City, and Philadelphia. These portraits, which provide a graphic commentary on Copley's times, are noteworthy for their brilliance, clarity, and straightforward characterization. (One famous example is his *Paul Revere* in the Boston Museum of Fine Arts.) Copley moved to London in 1774 and remained there for the rest of his life, enjoying many honors and extending his repertoire to popular but less powerful historical and literary paintings.

❓ Compare the knight in this painting with those in the medieval paintings on text pages 134, 141, 149, and 152–153. Which rendering of the knight is more romantic and more idealized? Which illustrations do you prefer, and why? Who are the two women in Copley's painting? (Duessa with the cup and snake and Una in blue)

B. Allusion
For the source of "that scarlet whore," see note on lines 47–50, text page 202, and stanza 47, text page 210.

A

The Red Cross Knight by John Singleton Copley (ca. 1780). Oil.

195   For she it is, that did my Lord bethrall,°
        My dearest Lord, and deepe in dongeon lay,
        Where he his better dayes hath wasted all.
        O heare, how piteous he to you for ayd does call.''

                 29
B   Forthwith he gave in charge unto his Squire,
200   That scarlot whore to keepen carefully;
        Whiles he himselfe with greedie great desire
        Into the Castle entred forcibly,
        Where living creature none he did espye;
        Then gan he lowdly through the house to call:
205   But no man cared to answere to his crye.
        There raigned a solemne silence over all,
    Nor voice was heard, nor wight was seene in bowre° or hall.

195. **bethrall:** enslave.

207. **bowre:** private apartment.

A. Parallels
Some students
might recall Walter
de la Mare's poem
"The Listeners"
and see an intrigu-
ing similarity.

B. Clarification
Pause after stanza
38 to be sure stu-
dents can identify
the prisoner (Red-
crosse). (Refer
back to the head-
note if necessary.)
How long has Red-
crosse been im-
prisoned? (Line
222, three months)

C. Vocabulary
Fowle is *foul.*

D. Vocabulary
Fell means "dead-
ly."

E. Vocabulary
The word *annoy*
comes from the
same root as the
word *noisome,*
which means
"harmful" or "stink-
ing" (not "noisy,"
as many people
think).

F. Vocabulary
Corse is *corpse,*
an archaic usage
also found in
Shakespeare.

37

Through every rowme he sought, and every bowr,
　But no where could he find that wofull thrall:
210　At last he came unto an yron doore,
　That fast was lockt, but key found not at all
A　Emongst that bounch,° to open it withall;
　But in the same a little grate was pight,°
　Through which he sent his voyce, and lowd did call
215　With all his powre, to weet if living wight
Were housèd therewithin, whom he enlargen° might.

38

Therewith an hollow, dreary, murmuring voyce
　These piteous plaints and dolours did resound;
　"O who is that, which brings me happy choyce
220　Of death, that here lye dying every stound,°
B　Yet live perforce in balefull darkenesse bound?
　For now three Moones have changèd thrice their hew,°
　And have beene thrice hid underneath the ground,
　Since I the heavens chearefull face did vew,
225　O welcome thou, that doest of death bring tydings trew."

39

Which when that Champion heard, with percing point
　Of pity deare° his hart was thrillèd sore,
　And trembling horrour ran through every joynt,
C　For ruth° of gentle knight so fowle forlore:°
230　Which shaking off, he rent that yron dore,
D　With furious force, and indignation fell;
　Where entred in, his foot could find no flore,
　But all a deep descent, as darke as hell,
That breathèd ever forth a filthie banefull° smell.

40

235　But neither darkenesse fowle, nor filthy bands,
E　Nor noyous° smell his purpose could withhold,
　(Entire affection hateth nicer° hands)
　But that with constant zeale, and courage bold,
　After long paines and labours manifold,
240　He found the meanes that Prisoner up to reare;
　Whose feeble thighes, unhable to uphold
F　His pinèd° corse, him scarse to light could beare,
　A ruefull spectacle of death and ghastly drere.°

41

　His sad dull eyes deepe suncke in hollow pits,
245　Could not endure th' unwonted sunne to view;
　His bare thin cheekes for want of better bits,°
　And empty sides deceivèd of° their dew,°

212. **bounch:** a bunch of keys that Arthur took from an old man in the castle.
213. **pight:** placed.

216. **enlargen:** set free.

220. **stound:** moment.

222. **hew:** form.

227. **deare:** dire.

229. **ruth:** pity. **forlore:** lost.

234. **banefull:** poisonous.

236. **noyous:** noxious.
237. **nicer:** too fussy, difficult to please.

242. **pinèd:** wasted.
243. **drere:** dreariness.

246. **bits:** that is, of food.
247. **deceivèd of:** deprived of. **dew:** due.

READING CHECK TEST

1. The Redcrosse Knight is being held prisoner by an evil Giant.
2. Una, who symbolizes Truth, brings Prince Arthur to rescue the knight.
3. Duessa, who stands for Falsehood, rides a beast with many heads.

4. In battle with the Giant, the Prince first cuts off the Giant's left arm.
5. A blinding light comes from the Prince's shield when it is uncovered.
6. The Prince rescues the Redcrosse Knight, whom he finds inside the castle.

7. As punishment for Duessa, Una declares that they should remove her royal scarlet robe.

A
Could make a stony hart his hap to rew;
His rawbone armes, whose mighty brawnèd bowrs°
250 Were wont to rive° steele plates, and helmets hew,
Were cleane consumed, and all his vitall powres
Decayd, and all his flesh shronk up like withered flowres.

B
42
Whom when his Lady saw, to him she ran
With hasty joy: to see him made her glad,
255 And sad to view his visage pale and wan,
Who earst° in flowres of freshest youth was clad.
C Tho° when her well of teares she wasted had,
She said, "Ah dearest Lord, what evill starre
On you hath fround, and pourd his influence bad,
260 That of your selfe ye thus berobbèd arre,
And this misseeming hew° your manly looks doth marre?

43
"But welcome now my Lord, in wele or woe,
Whose presence I have lackt too long a day;
And fie on Fortune mine avowèd foe,
265 Whose wrathrull wreakes° them selves do now alay.°
And for these wrongs shall treble penaunce pay
Of treble good: good growes of evils priefe."°
The chearelesse man, whom sorrow did dismay,
Had no delight to treaten° of his griefe;
270 His long endurèd famine needed more reliefe.

44
"Faire Lady," then said that victorious knight,
"The things, that grievous were to do, or beare,
Them to renew,° I wote,° breeds no delight;
Best musicke breeds delight in loathing eare:
275 But th' onely good, that growes of passèd feare,
Is to be wise, and ware° of like ageín.
This dayes ensample hath this lesson deare
Deepe written in my heart with yron pen,
D That blisse may not abide in state of mortall men.

45
280 "Henceforth, sir knight, take to you wonted strength,
And maister these mishaps with patient might;
Loe! where your foe lyes stretcht in monstrous length,
and loe! that wicked woman in your sight,
The roote of all your care, and wretched plight,°
285 Now in your powre, to let her live, or dye."
E "To do her dye," quoth Una, "were despight,°
And shame t'avenge so weake an enimy;
But spoile° her of her scarlot robe, and let her fly."

249. **bowrs:** muscles.
250. **rive:** rip up.

256. **earst:** formerly.
257. **Tho:** then.

261. **hew:** appearance.

265. **wreakes:** revenges. **alay:** decrease.

267. **priefe:** experience.

269. **treaten:** talk.

273. **renew:** remember. **wote:** think.

276. **ware:** wary.

284. **plight:** condition.

286. **despight:** wrong.

288. **spoile:** deprive.

A. Vocabulary
Hap is "luck" or "fortune." *Rew* is "rue."

B. Imagery
Have students stop here and describe the remarkable appearance of Redcrosse.

C. Clarification
Almost all Elizabethans believed in astrology. Shakespeare, writing at about the same time as Spenser, writes of the "star-crossed lovers" Romeo and Juliet. Yet he also has Julius Caesar observe, "Men at some time are masters of their fates: / The fault, dear Brutus, is not in our stars, / But in ourselves . . ." (*Julius Caesar*, Act I, Scene 2, lines 138–140).

D. Moral
Pause after stanza 44 to clarify the moral the knight expounds.

E. Character
? Why, considering Una's character—she is Truth, remember—do you think she recommends releasing the evil Duessa—who is Falsehood? (Because of Una's sense of fair play; because countering with an evil deed would be wrong)

Have students (1) summarize the events described in this episode and (2) explain how Spenser uses allegory in this part of his poem.

ANALYZING THE POEM
Identifying Details
1. The horn inspires terrible fear; it can be heard for three miles; its sounds echo three times; it overcomes enchantments and magically opens gates and locks.
2. A dragon.
3. The giant tries to crush Prince Arthur with his massive club, but Arthur leaps aside and the stroke misses. The force of the blow creates a furrow three yards deep.
4. Using his left hand, the giant lifts his club and strikes the knight's shield. The force of the blow is so great that the knight falls to the ground.
5. Arthur's shield emits a light that causes the giant to drop his weapon and to become blind and paralyzed.
6. Mortal bliss is fleeting (line 279).

A. Vocabulary
Bad is "bade."

B. Imagery
The ugliness of this allegorical description of Falsehood exposed is addressed in question 10. Spenser would also have been aware of Revelations 17:16, "These shall hate the whore and shall make her desolate and naked." Artistic students might draw Duessa, or Falsehood, as she looks when she is stripped of her deceptive disguise. (Stanza 48 is omitted; Spenser's gusto can be offensive.)

C. Interpreting
Relate this detail about Duessa's "borrowed light" to the portrayal of the two women in Copley's painting, text page 207. (Duessa is lit only by Una's glow.) In what ways does falsehood "borrow light"? (It pretends to be truth.) Note that when falsehood is seen as it really is, it can cause no harm.

46

A So as she bad, that witch they disaraid,
290   And robd of royall robes, and purple pall,°
       And ornaments that richly were displaid;
       Ne spared they to strip her naked all.
       Then when they had despoild her tire and call,°
       Such as she was, their eyes might her behold,
295   That her misshapèd parts did them appall:
       A loathly, wrinckled hag, ill favoured, old,
Whose secret filth good manners biddeth not be told.

290. **pall:** mantle.

293. **tire and call:** attire and headgear.

47

   Her craftie head was altogether bald,
       And as in hate of honorable eld,°
300   Was overgrowne with scurfe and filthy scald;°
       Her teeth out of her rotten gummes were feld,°
B   And her sowre breath abhominably smeld;
       Her dried dugs,° like bladders lacking wind,
       Hong downe, and filthy matter from them weld;°
305   Her wrizled° skin as rough, as maple rind,°
So scabby was, that would have loathd all womankind.

299. **eld:** old age.
300. **scald:** scabs.
301. **feld:** fallen.

303. **dugs:** breasts.
304. **weld:** ran.
305. **wrizled:** wrinkled. **rind:** bark.

49

   Which when the knights beheld, amazd they were,
       And wondred at so fowle deformèd wight.
       "Such then," said Una, "as she seemeth here,
310   Such is the face of falshood, such the sight
C   Of fowle Duessa, when her borrowed light
       Is laid away, and counterfesaunce° knowne."
       Thus when they had the witch disrobèd quight,
       And her filthy feature° open showne,
315   They let her goe at will, and wander wayes unknowne.

312. **counterfesaunce:** hypocrisy.

314. **feature:** appearance.

50

   She, flying fast from heavens hated face,
       And from the world that her discovered wide,°
       Fled to the wastfull° wildernesse apace,
       From living eyes her open shame to hide,
320   And lurkt in rocks and caves long unespide.
       But that faire crew of knights, and Una faire,
       Did in that castle afterwards abide,
       To rest them selves, and weary powres repaire,
Where store they found of all that dainty was and rare.

317. **wide:** completely.
318. **wastfull:** desolate.

7. Student answers will vary. In general, Una represents truth, Duessa falsehood, Arthur courage, Orgoglio pride, the Squire loyalty, and the Redcrosse Knight holiness.

Students may cite numerous physical descriptions and other details that make each figure seem human.

Student answers will vary. Ask them to explain their opinions.

8. Arthur's magic seems divinely sanctioned.

9. Arthur's shield and its magical properties might symbolize the power of goodness to overwhelm evil.

10. Student answers will vary. By exposing Duessa (both literally and figuratively) as an allegorical representation of falsehood, she is shown to be the direct opposite of what she seems to be—ugly rather than beautiful.

11. Other examples of epic similes occur in lines 95–99, 140–144, and 145–153. The similes are supposed to please the reader with apt, extended comparisons.

Responding to the Poem

Analyzing the Poem

Identifying Details

1. What are the magical properties of the horn described in stanza 4?
2. In stanza 6, what is the "manyheaded beast"?
3. In your own words, describe the action in stanzas 7 and 8. What happens to Prince Arthur?
4. What is the action in stanza 18? Describe it in your own words.
5. What powers does Arthur's shield have?
6. What moral does Arthur deliver in stanza 44?

Interpreting Meanings

7. The characters Una, Duessa, Arthur, Orgoglio, the Squire, and Redcrosse play roles in this Canto. How is each one used as an **allegorical** figure to embody some abstract concept? How does each one also seem human? In what ways could people today identify with each of them?
8. In the **conflict** between the Giant and Duessa and Arthur and his squire, the contestants on both sides have supernatural, even magical, powers. What makes Arthur's magic more effective than the Giant's?
9. What do Arthur's shield and its magical properties **symbolize**?
10. The description of Duessa with her clothes off is full of grotesque details. What defense can you think of for this offensive language?
11. Stanza 9, which is devoted entirely to comparing the Giant's club with Jove's thunderbolt, is an example of an **epic simile**, in which the narrative stands still for a moment while the poet develops an elaborate comparison between something in the narrative and something entirely outside it (frequently an animal or other living creature). Find other examples of epic similes in the poem. What effect are they apparently supposed to have on the reader?

Writing About the Poem

A Creative Response

1. **Creating Allegorical Characters.** Convert four abstract concepts, such as goodness, evil, jealousy, and ambition, into characters. Name your characters and describe what they look like and how they think.

A Critical Response

2. **Translating Spenser.** Select at least four stanzas to translate into contemporary English. Standardize and modernize spellings, and replace archaic words with their contemporary equivalents. Maintain the rhyme scheme and rhythm of Spenser's lines.

Analyzing Language and Style

Spenser's Language

Spenser's epic is full of interesting sound devices and words. One device he uses frequently is **alliteration**—the repetition of the same or similar consonant sounds.

1. Find at least five good examples of alliteration in the poem. Say them aloud. Do they add to the pleasure of the poem? Can you find any examples that are almost humorously exaggerated?

Other aspects of Spenser's poem are interesting because they show how the English language has changed since his day.

2. For example, list at least ten words from the poem that are spelled differently today.
3. List another ten words that are pronounced differently. (You can tell from examining the word they rhyme with.)
4. List five words that are no longer used today. What contemporary words would be used in their places?
5. Were all the final e's on the words in this poem sounded? How can you tell?

Additional Writing Assignment (Challenging). Have students review the essay on Romance (text page 147) and write an essay comparing this excerpt from *The Faerie Queene* with the episodes from *Beowulf* and *Sir Gawain.* They should consider the nature of the quest, the characters (both human and nonhuman), the conflict, the settings, and supernatural elements.

DEVELOPING VOCABULARY
The following words from the poem are tested in the Selection Test. (See also Vocabulary Activity Worksheet.)

to entreat	strand
to allay	to immortalize
to augment	baser
to congeal	to eternize
to kindle	to subdue

A. Paradoxes
Have students re-state in their own words the fire/ice paradoxes in lines 2–4, 5–8, and 9–12.

B. Connections
Compare Sonnet 30 with "Fire and Ice" by the American poet Robert Frost.

C. Humanities Connection: Discussing the Portrait
Isaac Oliver (1556?–1617) followed Hilliard (see text page 194) as painter of miniatures for Elizabeth's court.
? How might the poem explain the flames? (The man is enflamed with love. Actually, this was a convention of the time: to show a man as a burning lover. Probably these miniatures were given to the women who inspired such passion.)

CLOSURE
Have one student explain to the class how lines 13–14 sum up the main idea of Sonnet 30.

Spenser's *Amoretti*, whose title means "little love poems," is one of the three best Elizabethan sonnet sequences, the other two being Sidney's and Shakespeare's. In eighty-nine sonnets Spenser records a man's (perhaps his own) courtship of a woman named Elizabeth (perhaps Elizabeth Boyle, whom he married). The sonnets cover a little more than a year in time, and as a whole they are more closely focused on the charms and virtues of the lady than on the man's frustrated feelings.

Sonnet 30, the first of our selections, shows Spenser using, in an original way, the Petrarchan convention of the burning man and the icy lady. In Sonnet 75, Spenser uses another convention, the so-called "eternizing conceit": the man argues that the woman should give in to him, because he will make her famous and even immortal by writing about her in his poems. But again Spenser gives this old notion a new twist.

The rhyme scheme of the *Amoretti* sonnets is original with Spenser: *abab bcbc cdcd ee*. Since it demands four words for two of the rhymes, only a clever rhymer can manage it.

from **Amoretti**

Sonnet 30

A

My love is like to ice, and I to fire:
How comes it then that this her cold so great
Is not dissolvèd through my so hot desire,
But harder grows the more I her <u>entreat</u>?
5 Or how comes it that my exceeding heat
Is not <u>allayed</u> by her heart-frozen cold,
But that I burn much more in boiling sweat,
And feel my flames <u>augmented</u> manifold?
What more miraculous thing may be told,
10 That fire, which all things melts, should harden ice,
And ice, which is <u>congealed</u> with senseless cold,
Should <u>kindle</u> fire by wonderful device?°

B
Such is the power of love in gentle mind,
That it can alter all the course of kind.°

12. **device:** trick.
14. **kind:** nature.

Portrait of a Man Against a Background of Flames by Isaac Oliver (ca. 1610). Oil.

Ham House, London.

1. If his love is like ice and he is like fire, how is it that the ice does not melt, but grows harder? And how is it that his heat is not allayed, but made warmer?
2. Love for his beloved.
3. The poem has two central paradoxes: ice "kindles" fire, and the fire makes ice colder and harder.

4. The woman tells the man that it is futile to write her name in the sand where it will be washed away by the tide. She says that she too will decay and die. The man responds that, on the contrary, she and their love will live eternally in his verses.

Interpreting Meanings
5. In line 14, Spenser says that love has

the power to alter the course of nature.
6. *Vain* can mean "proud and self-centered" and "futile."
7. Their love still lives because Spenser's poem is still read and admired.
8. Answers will vary. (Make sure students understand that the question refers to the sonnets, not the attitudes.)

Sonnet 75

A One day I wrote her name upon the <u>strand</u>,
   But came the waves and washèd it away:
   Again I wrote it with a second hand,
B But came the tide, and made my paines his pray.°
5 "Vaine man," said she, "that doest in vain assay,°
   A mortal thing so to <u>immortalize</u>,
   For I myself shall like to this decay,
   And eke my name be wipéd out likewise."
C "No so," quod° I, "let <u>baser</u> things devise°
10 To die in dust, but you shall live by fame:
   My verse your virtues rare shall <u>eternize</u>,
   And in the heavens write your glorious name.
   Where whenas death shall all the world <u>subdue</u>,
   Our love shall live, and later life renew."

---

4. **pray:** prey.
5. **assay:** try.
9. **quod:** quoth (said).   **devise:** plan.

A. Vocabulary
A *strand* is a beach.

B. Metaphor
? What is the tide compared to? (A ravening beast)

C. Vocabulary
Baser means "less pure, less refined" (as in baser metals).

CLOSURE
Ask a student to explain how Spenser uses the "eternizing conceit" in Sonnet 75.

Responding to the Poems

Analyzing the Poems

Identifying Details

1. What puzzles the speaker about ice and fire in Sonnet 30?
2. What kindles the man's fire?
3. What **paradoxes,** or seeming contradictions, can you find in Sonnet 30?
4. Summarize the conversation that takes place between the man and woman in Sonnet 75.

Interpreting Meanings

5. Many fire and ice poems are clever, but in Sonnet 30 Spenser also says something serious about love, as Shakespeare does in Sonnet 116. Explain how Spenser turns the conventional frustrations of the lover into a positive statement about the power of love.
6. What different meanings can the word *vain* have in Sonnet 75?
7. In what sense does the love of the two people in Sonnet 75 still live?
8. Some attitudes toward love and toward men and women have changed since these sonnets were written. Do you find them dated, or still pertinent?

Writing About the Poems

A Critical Response

Comparing Poems. In a brief essay, compare Sonnet 75 with this poem by a twentieth-century Canadian poet. Consider these elements of the poems: **message, imagery,** and **tone.** Which poem do you like better, and why?

The Flood-Tide

He paused a moment by the sea,
    Then stooped, and with a leisured hand
He wrote in casual tracery
    Her name upon the flux of sand.

5 The waves beat up and swiftly spun
    A silver web at every stride;
He watched their long, thin fingers run
    The letters back into the tide.

But she had written where the tide
10   Could never its gray waters fling;
She watched the longest wave subside
    Ere it could touch the lettering.

—E. J. Pratt

A. Humanities Connection:
Discussing the Portrait
Ask students to compare this portrait with those of Raleigh and Spenser (text pages 194 and 198).
❓ What do the portraits as a group suggest about the Renaissance ideals of manliness? (Males too—at least those associated with the court—dressed decoratively with lace and brocade; the men

appear physically fit [no obesity, for example]; neatly trimmed beards and mustaches were the norm; hair was medium in length.)

B. Sidney's Character
A traditional tale that reveals Sidney's character comes to us from his friend and biographer Fulke Greville. It is said that as he lay wounded and dying, Sidney gallantly gave his own water bottle to another soldier, saying, "Thy necessity is greater than mine."

C. Sonnet Sequence
Call students' attention to the definition of a sonnet sequence. This definition applies also to the sonnets of Shakespeare (text page 338).

Sir Philip Sidney (1554–1586)

By profession Sir Philip Sidney was a soldier and a statesman. Although he became the most admired of all English writers during the hundred years after his death, none of his works were published during his lifetime. When not involved in political and military life, he "slipt," as he said, "into the title of Poet." But few people knew that he was a writer at all until he was dead. Then people started saying that Sidney had modeled his life on the ideal gentleman as he was described by the Italian writer Castiglione, whose famous book about behavior, *The Courtier,* had recently been translated into English. Sidney had Castiglione's *sprezzatura*—the ability to do difficult things like riding a horse or writing a sonnet very well, though in a casual manner.

He was connected with many important people. His father was Sir Henry Sidney, for many years Lord Governor of Ireland. His uncle was Robert Dudley, Earl of Leicester, a handsome and talented man whom Queen Elizabeth loved passionately but never married. His wife Frances was the daughter of the great statesman Sir Francis Walsingham. His sister was Mary, Countess of Pembroke, a writer and a patron of many other writers. Sidney attended Oxford, but left without taking the degree that he had no need for. He went on a three-year grand tour of the Continent and met many famous people, including William the Silent, founder of the Dutch Republic. As a boy he probably first met Queen Elizabeth when his uncle Leicester put on a spectacular entertainment for her at Kenilworth. Elizabeth later made Sidney her cupbearer. But as an adult, Sidney was ill-equipped personally to cope with the intrigues of the court, and from a practical, financial point of view his life was something of a failure.

In 1585 Queen Elizabeth appointed Sidney governor of Flushing, an important English fortress in the Netherlands. This assignment delighted him because he had long sympathized with the Dutch in their struggle to remain independent of Spain. For almost a year, he distin-

Sir Philip Sidney attributed to John de Critz the Elder. Oil.

Hall i' th' Wood Museum, Bolten, Lancashire, England.

guished himself as a military tactician, and then, in November of 1586, he rashly led a band of six hundred English soldiers against forty-five hundred Spanish troops. Inevitably he was wounded; inevitably the wound became gangrenous, and he died just short of his thirty-second birthday. His body was brought back to England and given a hero's burial in St. Paul's Cathedral.

The English idolized Sidney, and held him up as the embodiment of perfect knighthood. His luster as a man is evident in his writings. Three of these remain important. First, the long chivalric-pastoral romance called *The Countess of Pembroke's Arcadia* (1590, 1593) is full of high adventure and deep moralizing; many literary historians regard it as the most important piece of English prose fiction before the eighteenth century. Second, a collection of poems entitled *Astrophel and Stella* (1591) consisting of 108 sonnets and 11 songs is the first of many Elizabethan sonnet sequences, or linked poems that, taken together, imply a story without lapsing into narrative. The publication of Sidney's sequence started an absolute frenzy of sonneteering in the 1590's. (The best sequences are written by Sidney himself, and by Edmund Spenser, Samuel Daniel, Michael Drayton, and William Shakespeare.) Finally, *An Apology for Poetry* (1595), also known as *The Defense of Poesy,* is the first substantial critical essay in English literature and a rousing defense of imaginative literature against its detractors, who were saying that poets lie. To this charge, Sidney replied that poets can't lie because they don't pretend to be giving factual information. "The poet nothing affirmeth," he argued.

Lady Sidney and Her Children by an unknown artist. Oil.

Penshurst House.

A. Expansion
The poet Samuel Daniel (1562?–1619) is primarily known as a tutor of the wealthy and a writer of masques for the court of Elizabeth. Michael Drayton (1563–1631) saw his first volume of poetry publicly burned but went on to publish popular verse.

A quotation from Sidney's *An Apology for Poetry* begins the unit (text page 166).

B. Humanities Connection: Discussing the Fine Art
Note that Lady Sidney's hands rest on her sons. **?** What can you deduce about how small children were dressed in the sixteenth century? (All children must have worn skirts; only the hat and sword suggest that the middle child is male.) How do both portraits convey the notion that children were simply miniature adults? (Height is the only way to guess their age.)

PREPARATION

1. BUILDING ON PRIOR KNOWLEDGE. See if students know anything about the nightingale (a small, homely bird not found in North America, known for its lush but sad song). Perhaps no other bird has inspired so many British poets. (See Keat's ode on text page 715.) Before students read the headnote, note that many cultures tell stories to explain

SUPPLEMENTARY SUPPORT MATERIALS

1. Vocabulary Activity Worksheet (*CCB*)
2. Review and Response Worksheet: Setting and Theme (*CCB*)
3. Selection Test (*CCB*)

DEVELOPING VOCABULARY

The following words from the poem are tested in the Selection Test. (See also Vocabulary Activity Worksheet.)

woes	anguish
bewailing	to languish
oppresseth	craving
prevailing	

A. Connections
Lines 1–4 are reminiscent of Chaucer's "Prologue" to *The Canterbury Tales* (text page 88). In April life springs anew, and "smale foweles maken melodye."

B. Personification
❓ What words in lines 1–4 personify earth? (It is proud; it wears new clothes.)

C. Puns
❓ How does the poet pun on the word *spring* in stanza 1? (In line 3 *spring* means "comes into being." In line 11 it means three things: the season; the bouncy feeling of yielding earth after winter ice has melted; and a sudden unexpected appearance, like a leaping forth.)

D. Interpreting
❓ Who has "too much"? (Philomela has too much of Thereus.) Lines 17–20 answer question 3 on page 217.

This poem is based on a grotesque and pathetic legend from Ovid's *Metamorphoses,* a collection of mythological stories in Latin verse. Tereus, King of Thrace, is married to Procne, by whom he has one son. Procne has a sister, Philomela, who quite innocently becomes the object of the king's lustfulness. With the lawless, might-is-right privilege of a king, Tereus imprisons his wife, rapes her sister, and cuts out the sister's tongue to prevent her from telling of his wickedness. Deprived of speech, Philomela tells her story on a piece of needlework she sends to her sister. Together, they plan gruesome revenge. One day when the king has gone hunting, they kill his son and make a meat pie of his flesh. They arrange to have the pie served when, hungry after a day of sport, Tereus takes his place at the royal table. When he learns of their revenge on him, the king decides to mur-

der both women. But as he pursues them, the gods miraculously intervene: Tereus is changed into a hoopoe, Procne into a swallow, Philomela into a nightingale.

As the centuries passed, the legend was embellished without obscuring the point that the nightingale's song was a symbol of suffering transformed into beauty. When it was noted that English nightingales would sing for only a brief time after they'd come back from their winter nesting places, some unknown observer came up with an explanation. The bird's plaintive song ("plaintful" in the poem), he decided, was produced when "she" deliberately pressed her breast against a sharp thorn in order to commemorate the pain and humiliation suffered at the hands of King Tereus.

The Nightingale

A The nightingale, as soon as April bringeth
Unto her rested sense a perfect waking,
B While late bare earth, proud of new clothing, springeth,
Sings out her <u>woes</u>, a thorn her songbook making,
5   And mournfully <u>bewailing</u>,
Her throat in tunes expresseth
What grief her breast <u>oppresseth</u>,
For Tereus' force on her chaste will <u>prevailing</u>.
   O Philomela fair, O take some gladness
10   That here is juster cause of plaintful sadness:
Thine earth now springs, mine fadeth;
Thy thorn, without, my thorn my heart invadeth.

C
Alas she hath no other cause of <u>anguish</u>
But Tereus' love, on her by strong hand wroken°
15 Wherein she suffring all her spirits' <u>languish</u>,
Full womanlike complains her will was broken.
   But I who daily <u>craving</u>,
Cannot have to content me,
Have more cause to lament me,
20 D Since wanting is more woe than too much having.
   O Philomela fair, O take some gladness,
That here is juster cause of plaintful sadness:
Thine earth now springs, mine fadeth;
Thy thorn without, my thorn my heart invadeth.

14. **wroken:** inflicted.

216

ANALYZING THE POEM
Identifying Details
1. The time of year—spring—is mentioned or alluded to in lines 1, 3, 11, and 23.
2. The nightingale is sad because of Thereus's violence to Philomela.
3. The speaker is worse off because of his frustrated love.

Interpreting Meanings
4. The setting, springtime, increases the poignancy of the complaint because spring is usually associated with joy, love, and renewal.
5. The first "thorn" refers to Thereus, the cause of anguish for the nightingale. The second thorn refers to the speaker's unhappiness, or possibly to the beloved, who does not requite his love.

6. Answers will vary. Encourage students to discuss their opinions.

Il Vecchio L'aria (detail) by Jan Brueghel the Elder. Oil.   Galleria Doria Pamphili, Rome.

CLOSURE
Have students write a brief paraphrase of the refrain to show that they understand it. Responses should be shared in class.

Additional Writing Assignments
1. Comparing Poems. Compare Sidney's treatment of a nightingale with Keats's (text page 715). Consider each poem's message, tone, and images.

2. Answering the Speaker. In a poem or prose paragraph, write the nightingale's answer to the lovelorn poet.

Responding to the Poem

Analyzing the Poem

Identifying Details

1. Locate three or more places in the poem where the time of year is mentioned.
2. The speaker explains in the first stanza what is making the nightingale sad. What is it?
3. According to the second stanza, who is worse off—the speaker or the nightingale? Why?

Interpreting Meanings

4. How might the **setting** increase the poignancy of the speaker's complaint?
5. Explain whether the first thorn in lines 12 and 24 has the same meaning as the second thorn in those two lines.
6. Do you agree that "wanting is more woe than too much having" (line 20)?

Writing About the Poem

A Critical Response

Responding to a Critical Remark. In one paragraph, agree or disagree with the following remark. Support your views with specific references to the poem.

Sidney's nightingale poem is of little value to readers today, especially American readers, most of whom have never heard, and probably never will hear, a nightingale sing. Moreover, Sidney makes a number of factual mistakes. Only the male nightingale actually sings, and he does so for mating purposes, not to lament his woes. He is probably happy rather than sad. A final objection to the poem is that the speaker doesn't say what is troubling him. Readers have to supply that information from their knowledge of the Petrarchan lover, a man who is always complaining about some woman's unkindness to him.

Establishing a Purpose. The headnote provides students with background on the poem and ends with a final question that will establish their purpose in reading. Students will find the poem easier to grasp if you examine the glosses together in class and then read the poem aloud.

Supplementary Support Materials
1. Vocabulary Activity Worksheet (*CCB*)
2. Review and Response Worksheet: Meter (*CCB*)
3. Selection Test (*CCB*)

Developing Vocabulary
The following words from the poem are tested in the Selection Test. (See also Vocabulary Activity Worksheet.)
leaves   throes
step-dame

A. Vocabulary
Leaves here means "pages."

B. Personification
How are Invention and Study personified? (Invention is the child of nature; study is the stepmother of invention—not the true mother.)

C. Metaphor
What "child" does the speaker want to give birth to? (A poem) What are his "throes"? (Labor pains)

D. Expansion
In ancient myth, the Muses were the nine daughters of Zeus and Mnemosyne. They presided over the arts of epic poetry, history, lyric poetry, music, tragedy, religious music, dance, comedy, and astronomy. Many writers today speak of having a muse who inspires them. (Relate to the words *musing, music,* and *museum.*)

Closure
Be sure students can recite from memory the poem's last line and explain what it means.

Sidney's *Astrophel and Stella* has two purposes: to praise Stella ("Star") and to explore and express the feelings of Astrophel ("Star Lover"). Sidney pays much more attention to the second purpose than to the first; compared with Petrarch's Laura, Stella is a rather dim figure.

Many readers have mistakenly assumed that Astrophel is Sidney himself, and, looking around for Stella, they long ago identified Penelope Devereaux, Lady Rich, a prominent person at Elizabeth's court. Several sonnets make puns on the name Rich, supporting the identification. Contemporary gossip, however, weakens the identification: Lady Rich apparently dispensed her favors freely, whereas Stella is a model of virtuous behavior. The best way to resolve this contradiction is to remember Sidney's insistence that poetry does not give factual information, biographical or otherwise.

In the following sonnet, Astrophel plans to express his love for Stella in poems that will make her love him in return. He imagines a pleasant sequence of events culminating in her favors. But how and what will he write? He studies other people's poems in the hope of finding inspiration in them for his own. But studying does not help. Why not?

from Astrophel and Stella

Loving in truth, and fain° in verse my love to show,
That the dear she° might take some pleasure of my pain:
Pleasure might cause her read,° reading might make her know,
Knowledge might pity win, and pity grace° obtain,
5   I sought fit words to paint the blackest face of woe,
Studying inventions° fine, her wits to entertain:
A Oft turning others' leaves, to see if thence would flow
Some fresh and fruitful showers upon my sun-burn'd° brain.
But words came halting° forth, wanting° Invention's stay,°
10 B Invention, Nature's child, fled step-dame Study's blows,
And others' feet still seemed but strangers in my way.
C Thus great with child to speak, and helpless in my throes,
Biting my truant° pen, beating myself for spite,
D "Fool," said my Muse to me, "look in thy heart and write."

1. **fain:** desiring.
2. **the dear she:** Stella.
3. **read:** that is, to read my poems.
4. **grace:** favor.
6. **inventions:** poems.
8. **sun-burn'd:** burned both by the "sun" of Stella's beauty and by the brilliance of other poets' work.
9. **halting:** limping. **wanting:** lacking. **stay:** prop, support.
13. **truant:** rebellious.

ANALYZING THE POEM
Identifying Details
1. The subject of the sentence is "I" (line 5).
2. The steps are pleasure, reading, knowledge, pity, and grace.
3. Astrophel hears his muse bidding him to look into his heart and write.

Interpreting Meanings
4. Poets have many "feet" because they have written metrical verses. We might use the term "meter."
5. Student answers will vary. This particular poem does seem to read in a more even, less choppy way than Wyatt's does. Some students may find that the longer line also encourages a slower reading.

6. The advice may work for some, but writer's block can be a very intractable problem.

Responding to the Poem

Analyzing the Poem

Identifying Details

1. The **octave**—the eight-line part of the sonnet—is a single sentence. What is its subject?
2. By what steps does Astrophel hope Stella will come to love him?
3. What does Astrophel decide to do when "studying" fails him?

Interpreting Meanings

4. In line 11, Astrophel complains that other poets' feet are always getting in the way of his own. In what sense of the word *feet* do poets have a great many feet? What is the term for a word like *feet* in this poem?
5. This sonnet is unusual in form because its lines have twelve syllables instead of the usual ten; that is, it is written in **hexameter** instead of **pentameter**. Do you think that having an even number of feet in each line makes the poem sound more balanced than a sonnet written in pentameter (Sir Thomas Wyatt's "They Flee from Me," for example)? What other effects does the longer line create?
6. The last line of the poem is famous. A poet has said that it "continues to echo through the history of literature and through every classroom where students are asked to write compositions." What do you think of this advice as a solution to the well-known problem of writer's block?

Writing About the Poem

A Creative Response

1. **Describing a Process.** What do you think of Astrophel's plan for making Stella fall in love with him? Think of the way you fall in love or the way you make friends. Is it anything like the steps Astrophel envisioned Stella going through? Write one or two paragraphs in which you outline the process by which you fall in love or make friends, pointing out resemblances your process has (or doesn't have) to Astrophel's ideas.

April: Lovers in a Garden (16th century). Flemish calendar.

The British Library.

A Critical Response

2. **Analyzing Petrarchan Conventions.** One very common explanation of the last line in the sonnet is based on the stock Petrarchan image of the loved one dwelling in the lover's heart. This occurs in thousands of Renaissance poems. In a paragraph, explain what the Muse's advice to Astrophel might mean in light of that image. How might the sonnet then be seen as an elaborate compliment to Stella?

A. Humanities Connection: Discussing the Illustration
Ask students to notice how the two lovers are set in the midst of a busy, burgeoning world. Note the blossoming trees, the nesting stork, the flowing water, the weeding or planting, the hawker, and the pet dog. The picture is full of conventional symbols pertaining to lovers: The trees are symbols of fertility, the enclosed garden of virginity, the water of purity, the birds of sexuality and motherhood.

? Why is it appropriate to illustrate April with lovers? (Spring is the time when young people traditionally fall in love.) How does this compare with calendar art today? (Answers will vary. Encourage students to think beyond swimsuit calendars to those that reproduce paintings or include photographs of nature.)

A. Expansion

Bacon aimed to write a gigantic compendium of knowledge but completed only the parts listed here. In *New Atlantis*, a small utopian fantasy, he described a "Solomon's House" devoted to scientific study and research. Bacon's concept was responsible for the chartering, more than thirty years after his death, of the Royal Society (1660). Although this sci-

entific academy was later satirized by Jonathan Swift in *Gulliver's Travels* (1726), it boasts a distinguished history and remains in existence today.

B. Humanities Connection: Discussing the Portrait

Have students compare this portrait with that of Sir Thomas More, an earlier Lord Chancellor, on text page 171.

? How had men's clothing changed in a hundred years? (More is less elaborately dressed; note Bacon's ruff and long hair and neatly trimmed Van Dyke. In fact, Bacon was passionate about elaborate display and loved luxury. More was just the opposite.)

C. The Essay Genre

Bacon made so little effort to follow the Montaigne pattern of leisurely self-revelation that his essays are sometimes said to be an original literary form, not imitated until Addison and Steele (text page 543). Some of Bacon's famous essays are "Of Truth," "Of Death," "Of Cunning," "Of Wisdom for a Man's Self," and "Of Suspicion."

Sir Francis Bacon (1561–1626)

From his earliest days, Francis Bacon knew that he was an important person. When he was about nine, Queen Elizabeth asked him how old he was, and he is said to have replied, "Two years younger than your Majesty's happy reign." A boy who speaks like this will go far, and Bacon went far. He rose in his chosen profession, the law, until he reached the very top and became Lord Keeper of the Great Seal and Lord Chancellor of England—offices that his father, Sir Nicholas Bacon, had also held. He was elevated to the peerage as Lord Verulam and Viscount St. Albans, and he amassed a large fortune, though he was sometimes arrested for debt because he lived grandly and extravagantly, like the Renaissance prince he was. At the height of his political career he was accused of taking bribes, tried by the House of Lords, found guilty, stripped of his honors, and banished to his country estate. He then devoted himself full time to his other career, that of a scientist-philosopher-intellectual-writer.

Bacon once wrote a now-famous letter to his uncle, Lord Burleigh, Elizabeth's Secretary of State, in which he said, "I have taken all knowledge to be my province." Of course he did not master all knowledge, but he did make important contributions to many different branches of knowledge: political science, economics, biology, physics, music, architecture, botany, constitutional law, industrial development, philosophy, religious thought, mythology, astronomy, chemistry, landscape gardening, literature. But he is most famous for his vision of humanity's future, a future in which knowledge would be based on verifiable experimentation, and science would be separate from theology. This hope for a perfectly rational world is eloquently expressed in *The Advancement of Learning* (1605) and *New Atlantis* (1626).

Because he was addressing a European audience and because he felt that English was an unstable, shifting language, Bacon wrote many of his works in Latin. Of these, perhaps the most important is *Novum Organum* (1620), or "new

Sir Francis Bacon by Paul van Somer. Oil.

Gorhambury Collection, St. Alban's, Hertfordshire, England.

organon." An organon (pronounced or′gan·on) is an instrument for discovering knowledge, and Bacon intended his new one to replace the old organon of Aristotle and his followers, whose philosophy had dominated Medieval and early Renaissance thinking about natural phenomena.

Bacon's best known literary works, the *Essays,* are intended to help young people get ahead in life. Bacon was the first Englishman to use the word *essay* to designate a brief discourse in prose. He took the word from a Frenchman, Montaigne (män·tān′). But, whereas Montaigne's delightful *essaies* are mainly about a fascinating person, Montaigne himself, Bacon writes instead of humanity in general. Bacon's *Essays* are highly polished, finished works, despite the paradoxical fact that the root meaning of the word *essay* is "trial" or "attempt." Bacon's collection of essays grew over the years: By 1597, he had written ten; by 1613, thirty-nine; and by 1625, fifty-eight.

ESTABLISHING A PURPOSE. Use the head-note to prepare students to look for Bacon's sober practicality.

SUPPLEMENTARY SUPPORT MATERIALS
1. Vocabulary Activity Worksheet (*CCB*)
2. Review and Response Worksheet: Parallel Structures (*CCB*)
3. Selection Test (*CCB*)

DEVELOPING VOCABULARY
The following words from the essay are tested in the Selection Test. (See also Vocabulary Activity Worksheet.)
discourse   to distill
affectation   cunning
diligence   rhetoric
deputy

Although known primarily as a philosopher of science, Bacon had embarked on a new career as a practicing scientist when death overtook him. One wintry day he descended from his carriage carrying a dead chicken, to freeze it in the snow and thereby test the preservative powers of cold. Today this seems like a painfully obvious thing to do, but nobody had tried it in a systematic way before 1626. Suddenly, in the midst of the experiment, Bacon took a chill. His servants carried him into nearby Arundel Castle. In poor health most of his life, Bacon died there of complications resulting from exposure.

In all his works, Bacon's aim was to make the world better. As the destroyer of old ways of thinking and the stimulator of new ones, Bacon has no equal. "If you seek Bacon's monument," someone has said, "look at the world about you."

OF STUDIES

This is one of the best known of Bacon's essays, and in its practicality it is representative of the collection as a whole. Though at the beginning Bacon says that reading and studying are delightful, throughout the essay he emphasizes their practical use.

William Harvey, who first told European people how their blood circulates through their bodies, said that Bacon—his contemporary—wrote "like a Lord Chancellor." No one expects a Lord Chancellor (who presides over both judicial and legislative areas of English government) to be whimsical or spontaneous, even when writing an essay. From a person with such an exalted title we expect practical wisdom, advice that will help us stay out of trouble and get ahead in life. Bacon's essays give us all that, and more.

A. Style
Bacon's use of parallelism and balanced sentences is evident in this opening statement. (See question 3 and the first writing assignment on the next page.) Additional examples of this style are Mark Antony's speech in *Julius Caesar* (Act III, Scene 2, lines 74–108); Lincoln's Gettysburg Address; and John F. Kennedy's 1961 Inaugural Address. Students may analyze and attempt to imitate the construction in those passages.

B. Vocabulary
Except means "unless."

C. Vocabulary
Contemn means "despise."

D. Vocabulary
A *deputy* is an assistant.

Studies serve for delight, for ornament, and for ability. Their chief use for delight is in privateness and retiring;[1] for ornament, is in discourse; and for ability, is in the judgment and disposition of business. For expert men can execute and perhaps judge of particulars, one by one; but the general counsels, and the plots and marshaling of affairs, come best from those that are learned. To spend too much time in studies is sloth;[2] to use them too much for ornament is affectation; to make judgment wholly by their rules is the humor[3] of a scholar. They perfect nature, and are perfected by experience; for natural abilities are like natural plants, that need proyning[4] by study; and studies themselves do give forth directions too much at large, except they be bounded in by experience. Crafty men contemn studies; simple men admire them; and wise men use them: For they teach not their own use; but that is a wisdom without them[5] and above them, won by observation. Read not to contradict and confute;[6] nor to believe and take for granted; nor to find talk and discourse; but to weigh and consider. Some books are to be tasted, others to be swallowed, and some few to be chewed and digested: That is, some books are to be read only in parts; others to be read, but not curiously;[7] and some few to be read wholly, and with diligence and attention. Some books also may be read by deputy, and extracts made of them by others; but

1. **privateness and retiring:** privacy and leisure.
2. **sloth:** laziness.
3. **humor:** whim.
4. **proyning:** pruning.

5. **without them:** separate from them, outside them.
6. **confute:** dispute.
7. **curiously:** carefully.

ANALYZING THE ESSAY
Identifying Facts
1. They help people form good counsel, weigh and consider matters, and improve their exactness.
2. A wandering wit (mathematics), an inability to distinguish differences (study of the schoolmen), and an inability to discuss matters thoroughly (study of lawyer's cases).

A. Vocabulary
Here, *meaner* means "more common."

B. Expansion
This conclusion (beginning with "Nay") was omitted from the first printing of the essay in 1597.

☐ Which way of ending the essay do you prefer? Why? (Students may feel that the longer version, and especially the last sentence, is a more satisfactory ending. You might explain that this material was probably left out by accident.)

CLOSURE
Ask each student for three examples of parallel structure—either from Bacon's essay, from a newspaper or magazine, or from a famous speech.

3. Examples students may mention include the sentences beginning: "To spend too much time in studies is sloth . . ."; "Crafty men contemn studies. . . ."; "Reading maketh a full man. . . ."

Interpreting Meanings
4. Bacon means that excessive studying, at the expense of the conduct of practical affairs in the world, exhibits a lazy na-

ture. Someone who studies too much is unwilling or unable to engage in the practical affairs of life.
5. Examples include sentences beginning: "So if a man's wit be wandering, . . ."; "If he be not apt to beat over matters, . . ."

A that would be only in the less important arguments, and the meaner sort of books; else distilled books are like common distilled waters,[8] flashy[9] things. Reading maketh a full man; conference[10] a ready man; and writing an exact man. And therefore, if a man write little, he had need have a great memory; if he confer little, he had need have a present wit;[11] and if he read little, he had need have much cunning, to seem to know that[12] he doth not. Histories make men wise; poets witty;[13] the mathematics subtile; natural philosophy deep; moral grave; logic and rhetoric able to contend. *Abeunt studia in mores.*[14] Nay, there is no stond[15]

B or impediment in the wit, but may be wrought[16] out by fit studies, like as diseases of the body may have appropriate exercises. Bowling is good for the stone and reins;[17] shooting for the lungs and breast; gentle walking for the stomach; riding for the head; and the like. So if a man's wit be wandering, let him study the mathematics; for a demonstration, if his wit be called away never so little, he must begin again: If his wit be not apt to distinguish or find differences, let him study the schoolmen;[18] for they are *cymini sectores:*[19] If he be not apt to beat over[20] matters, and to call one thing to prove and illustrate another, let him study the lawyers' cases: So every defect of the mind may have a special receipt.[21]

---

8. **distilled waters:** homemade concoctions.
9. **flashy:** superficial.
10. **conference:** conversation, discussion.
11. **present wit:** ability to think fast.
12. **that:** what.
13. **witty:** imaginative.
14. *Abeunt . . . mores:* Studies help form character.
15. **stond:** impediment.
16. **wrought:** worked.

17. **stone and reins:** kidney stones and the kidneys.
18. **schoolmen:** medieval philosophers.
19. *cymini sectores:* seed-splitters, i.e., hair-splitters.
20. **beat over:** discuss thoroughly.
21. **receipt:** remedy.

Responding to the Essay

Analyzing the Essay

Identifying Facts
1. What are some of the ways in which studies improve people's abilities?
2. What are some specific problems that studies can remedy? Which studies can remedy each problem?
3. Bacon's fondness for **parallel structure** and **balanced sentences** is apparent in "Of Studies." (For example: "Some books are to be tasted, others to be swallowed, and some few to be chewed and digested.") Find other examples of parallel structure and balance.

Interpreting Meanings
4. Bacon says that too much studying is laziness. Explain how this **paradox** can be true.
5. Bacon has the reputation of being a hard, ambitious man, and his essays are frequently said to be cynical and lacking in warmth. Find remarks in "Of Studies" that seem to support this view.

Writing About the Essay

A Creative Response
1. **Imitating Style.** Write a paragraph explaining how to do something or how something works. In your paragraph, mimic Bacon's style as closely as possible. Speak universally rather than personally (avoid *I* and *you*), and use **parallel structures** and **balanced sentences.** You might rewrite a factual paragraph from one of your textbooks to mimic Bacon's style.

A Critical Response
2. **Interpreting an Author's Bias.** Bacon maintains that a person who reads little needs to "have much cunning, to seem to know" what he actually doesn't know. Analyze this part of "Of Studies" to determine Bacon's attitude toward such a pretense. Does he speak strongly against it, or does he imply that it is not a serious failing? Explain your findings in a short composition.

SUPPLEMENTARY SUPPORT MATERIALS
1. Vocabulary Activity Worksheet (CCB)
2. Review and Response Worksheet: Parallel Structures (CCB)
3. Selection Test (CCB)

DEVELOPING VOCABULARY
The following words from the axioms are tested in the Selection Test. (See also Vocabulary Activity Worksheet.)
temperance   fortitude
adversity

EXTENDING THE LESSON
Students may wish to compare Bacon's aphorisms with the sayings of Benjamin Franklin or Mark Twain. Or, they may make their own compilation of that popular contemporary version of the axiom, the bumper-sticker slogan.

FROM THE *ESSAYS*: AXIOMS

Bacon's essays are written in a terse, compressed style that demands a reader's full attention. For the most part Bacon does not develop his ideas into paragraphs; he writes a sentence containing one idea, then follows it with a sentence containing another. Of course the sentences are all related to the topic of the essay, but they are related in different ways, and they could be rearranged without much damage to the whole. The effect is like a string of beads all the same size.

Many of the sentences contain nuggets of wisdom known as axioms or adages; like proverbs, axioms do not argue or explain, but merely make positive statements. What do the axioms in this selection suggest about Bacon's values?

Men fear death, as children fear to go in the dark; and as that natural fear in children is increased with tales, so is the other.

—''Of Death''

Revenge is a kind of wild justice, which the more man's nature runs to, the more ought Law to weed it out.

—''Of Revenge''

The virtue of prosperity is temperance; the virtue of adversity is fortitude.

—''Of Adversity''

A He that hath wife and children hath given hostages to fortune.

—''Of Marriage and the Single Life''

There was never proud man thought so absurdly well of himself as the lover doth of the person loved: and therefore it was well said, that it is impossible to love and be wise.

—''Of Love''

They that deny a God destroy man's nobility; for certainly man is of kin to the beasts by his body; and if he be not of kin to God by his spirit, he is a base and ignoble creature.

—''Of Atheism''

A principal fruit of friendship is the ease and discharge of the fullness and swellings of the heart.

—''Of Friendship''

A man's own observation, what he finds good of, and what he finds hurt of, is the best physic [i.e., medicine] to preserve health.

—''Of Regimen of Health''

As the baggage is to an army, so is riches to virtue. B
—''Of Riches''

No man prospers so suddenly as by others' errors.
—''Of Fortune''

There is no excellent beauty that hath not some strangeness in the proportion.
—''Of Beauty''

God Almighty first planted a garden, and indeed it is the purest of human pleasures.
—''Of Gardens''

Men in great place are thrice servants: servants of the sovereign or state, servants of fame, and servants of business.

—''Of Great Place''

It were better to have no opinion of God at all than such an opinion as is unworthy of Him.
—''Of Superstition''

A. Expansion
The complete opening sentence of Bacon's essay adds a comma and the words, "for they are impediments to great enterprises, either of virtue or mischief." Bacon's essay does not reveal that he was, in fact, married. He waited till the prudent age of forty-five, however, and never had children.

B. Parallels
⁉ How does this axiom compare with the one from the Bible: "It is easier for a camel to go through the eye of a needle than for a rich man to enter into the Kingdom of God" (Matthew 19:24)? (They are very similar. Baggage slows an army down and gets in the way of its work. Those who have lots of money find it more difficult to behave in a virtuous way.)

A. Background
Kyd was arrested first and tortured. He extricated himself by implicating Marlowe, an act that cost him both his reputation and his self-respect.

B. Expansion
If students refer to the time line on text pages 182–183, they'll see that Marlowe died in the first year that the London theaters were closed because of the plague. Many of Marlowe's smug contemporaries felt that Marlowe's death was a retribution from God for his sins as a free thinker.

Christopher Marlowe (1564–1593)

Marlowe belonged to the first generation of Elizabethan dramatists. His career ended about the time when Shakespeare's began, although he was only two months older than Shakespeare. The son of a shoemaker in Canterbury, Marlowe was apparently a brilliant student; he won scholarships to the King's School in Canterbury and then to Corpus Christi College, Cambridge. Such scholarships ordinarily were given only to boys who intended to become priests, and perhaps that was Marlowe's original plan. If so, he changed it rather dramatically: After earning his B.A. and M.A. degrees, he apparently became a spy. Elizabeth's government maintained an elaborate espionage system to keep track of Roman Catholics, especially those living in exile on the Continent. The man in charge of this system was the Secretary of State, Sir Francis Walsingham (Sidney's father-in-law). His name, as well as the names of others in the secret service, keeps cropping up in documents relating to Marlowe, but just what spying Marlowe did for the government remains uncertain.

It *is* certain that Marlowe had only six more years to live when, at twenty-three, he came down to London from Cambridge. During those years, he associated with a number of other recent university graduates living near the London theaters and supporting themselves by writing plays and pamphlets. The lives led by this group were not without excitement. Along with a poet named Thomas Watson, Marlowe got involved in a street fight, which ended with one man murdered and Marlowe and Watson in jail. Another brush with the law came when Marlowe's roommate, a fellow dramatist named Thomas Kyd, accused him of making scandalous, seditious, and atheistic speeches. Marlowe was arrested. A few days before the case was to be heard he went with some rather shady characters, who were apparently acquaintances of his, down the Thames to Eleanor Bull's tavern in Deptford. There the group had dinner around noon, walked and talked in a garden of the tavern all afternoon, and after supper in their room got into a fight over the bill. The record of the coroner's

Christopher Marlowe, French school (1585). Oil.

Corpus Christi College Collection, Cambridge University.

inquest, which an American scholar discovered not long ago, says that Marlowe died instantly from a two-inch dagger wound inflicted above the eye. The court acquitted the man who stabbed him on the grounds of self-defense, though it is very possible that all the testimony in this case was fabricated, and that Marlowe was assassinated for reasons yet to be discovered. Theories about Marlowe's life and death are abundant; there are even a few people today who believe that Marlowe wasn't murdered but lived on to write all of Shakespeare's plays for him.

Like many of the facts of Marlowe's life, the chronology of his works is hard to establish. While still at the university, he translated some love poems by Ovid, the Roman poet who had great influence on Medieval and Renaissance literature. When these were published, the Bishop of London declared them to be too sexy and had them burnt by the hangman. Among Marlowe's

A. Expansion

Marlowe's blank verse could be rolled so thunderously from the stage that Ben Jonson (text page 374) later characterized lines like those of Marlowe's *Tamburlaine* as "Marlowe's mighty line."

B. Humanities Connection: Relating the Fine Art to Music

Aeneas and Dido is one of the best-known works of Baron Pierre Narcisse Guérin (1774–1833), a French painter and teacher of the great French Romantic painter Eugène Delacroix. Relate this painting to Marlowe's play *Dido, Queen of Carthage,* and note how both works reveal the Renaissance interest in the old literature of Greece and Rome.

According to Roman legend, Dido, the founder and queen of Carthage in North Africa, received the shipwrecked Trojans led by Aeneas. Through the plotting of the goddess Venus, Dido and Aeneas fell in love, but the gods ordered Aeneas to abandon Dido and establish his own nation in Italy (he founded Rome). When Aeneas sailed off and left her, Dido killed herself with a sword and was cremated on a great funeral pyre visible to Aeneas far out to sea.

own nondramatic poems is *Hero and Leander,* a tale of ill-fated love elegantly and sensually told, but unfortunately incomplete. All of Marlowe's seven dramatic poems are tragedies, and they are often listed in this order: *Dido, Queen of Carthage* (with Thomas Nashe), *Tamburlaine* (in two parts), *The Jew of Malta, The Massacre of Paris, Edward II,* and *Doctor Faustus.* Marlowe's greatest tragic heroes have been called "overreachers": self-driven and power-hungry men who refuse to recognize either their limitations as human beings or their responsibilities to God and their fellow creatures. Tamburlaine seeks power through military conquest; Barrabas, through money; Faustus, through knowledge. They all want to be more than mere men, and only death can put an end to their monstrous ambitions. To express these grandiose themes, Marlowe created wild and soaring poetry, like nothing ever heard before on the stage. Although Marlowe did not write Shakespeare's plays, he showed Shakespeare what was possible in dramatic poetry.

A

The story of Aeneas and Dido is related in Virgil's epic the *Aeneid.* Students interested in music might be introduced to Henry Purcell's (1659–1695) great opera *Dido and Aeneas* (1689).

B

Aeneas and Dido, Queen of Carthage by P. N. Guérin.

Louvre, Paris.

1. BUILDING ON PRIOR KNOWLEDGE. Students may be familiar with the old story about a man who sells his soul to the devil from two American short stories: Washington Irving's "The Devil and Tom Walker" and Stephen Vincent Benét's "The Devil and Daniel Webster."

2. ESTABLISHING A PURPOSE. Stress the final paragraph of the headnote, and then refer to question 5 for a purpose-setting question.

SUPPLEMENTARY SUPPORT MATERIALS
1. Vocabulary Activity Worksheet (*CCB*)
2. Review and Response Worksheet: Blank Verse (*CCB*)
3. Selection Test (*CCB*)

DEVELOPING VOCABULARY
The following words from the play are tested in the Selection Test. (See also Vocabulary Activity Worksheet.)

to glut	execrable
to ransack	dross
servile	hapless
resolute	entrails
to abjure	incessant

A. The Faust Legend
Note that Marlowe's audience believed that when Faustus asked for the power of invisibility he was taking on an attribute of Satan.

The Faust legend has remained peculiarly relevant over the centuries. Perhaps the greatest embodiment of the legend is in Johann Wolfgang von Goethe's two-part poetic drama *Faust* (1808), in which Faust escapes in the end. Faust also appears in Thomas Mann's novel *Dr. Faustus* (1947) and in operas by Charles Gounoud (*Faust*, 1859) and Arrigo Boito (*Mefistofele*, 1868).

B. Humanities Connection: About the Engraving
This engraving (used on the title page of the play's sixth printing) shows Faustus standing in a circle of cabalistic symbols and holding a book on necromancy. The demon he has just summoned rises from hell to greet him.

FROM DOCTOR FAUSTUS

John Faust or Faustus (the first syllable rhymes with *house*) was a traveling German magician who died about 1540. After his death he became a legendary figure and the subject of various pamphlets that described his remarkable tricks—all attributed to a pact he had made with the Devil. Marlowe transformed this folklore figure into an ambitious professor at Wittenberg University who has mastered all the academic subjects—law, philosophy, theology, medicine—and now, as the play opens, is bored by all of them. His vast knowledge has not given him any real power in the world outside the University. To obtain further knowledge, for which he has an insatiable thirst, he has decided to sell his soul to the Devil. In a *soliloquy* (a solo speech) near the beginning of the play he enumerates the great projects he will undertake during the next twenty-four years, before the Devil claims his soul.

Marlowe's audience believed in Satan as firmly as they believed in God. If good people could worship and receive help from God, so could bad people devote themselves to the Devil and receive his assistance.

A

B

Doctor Faustus and Mephistophilis (1631). Engraving.

At this point in Act I, Dr. Faustus is becoming obsessed with the "world of profit and delight" he perceives as promised to masters of the occult. He has just rejected the Good Angel's advice to desist and has accepted the Bad Angel's urging to "go forward" to become "on earth, as Jove is in the sky, / Lord and commander of these elements."

Faust's seduction has a literary parallel in Adam and Eve's belief in the serpent who claimed that if they ate the forbidden fruit, they would become "as gods" (Genesis 3:5). Note that the forbidden tree is called the "Tree of *Knowledge* of Good and Evil" (Genesis 2:17).

A. Setting
Wittenberg in eastern Germany was famous for its university, where Dr. Faustus taught. Luther made the same city a center of the Protestant Reformation (see text pages 171–172). The Rhine does not flow near Wittenberg at all; if it circled the city, it would provide a perfect defense.

Faustus Gloats

Faustus. How am I <u>glutted</u> with conceit° of this!
   Shall I make spirits fetch me what I please,
   Resolve me of all ambiguities,°
   Perform what desperate enterprise I will?
5   I'll have them fly to India for gold,
   <u>Ransack</u> the ocean for orient° pearl,
   And search all corners of the new-found world
   For pleasant fruits and princely delicates.°
   I'll have them read me strange philosophy
10   And tell the secrets of all foreign kings;
   I'll have them wall all Germany with brass
A   And make swift Rhine circle fair Wittenberg.
   I'll have them fill the public schools° with silk
   Wherewith the students shall be bravely clad.
15   I'll levy soldiers with the coin they bring
   And chase the Prince of Parma° from our land
   And reign sole king of all the provinces.
   Yea, stranger engines for the brunt of war
B   Than was the fiery keel° at Antwerp's bridge
20   I'll make my <u>servile</u> spirits to invent.

1. **conceit:** imagination.

3. **ambiguities:** problems, puzzles.

6. **orient:** lustrous.

8. **delicates:** delicacies.

13. **public schools:** preparatory schools.

16. **Prince of Parma:** the leader of the Spanish forces occupying the Netherlands.

19. **fiery keel:** a burning ship used to destroy a blockade made of ships.

Faustus has inner conflicts and twinges of conscience after making his pact with the Devil. Throughout the play Marlowe represents these contrary feelings by showing a good angel quarreling with a bad angel over Faustus's soul. The point of these scenes is that repentance is always open to Faustus, however much he may feel that what he has done is unforgivable. He can always break his agreement with the Devil, but as the years pass it becomes progressively more difficult for him to do so. The audience would recognize that Faustus is gradually falling into the sinful state of despair, which prevents him from truly repenting.

B. Expansion
In 1585, the Netherlands sent a burning ship against a barrier on the Scheldt River erected by Parma to blockade the Belgian city of Antwerp. Parma is a city and region that is now a part of northern Italy; its prince was quite aggressive in Elizabethan times.

C. Plot Background
The excerpt that follows opens Act II. Earlier, in Act I, when Faustus asked Mephistophilis why he had been allowed to leave hell, the demon replied, "Why, this is hell, nor am I out of it." (In *Paradise Lost,* text page 420, John Milton repeated this idea: that hell accompanies the damned.) Nevertheless, Faustus continues to traffic with Mephistophilis.

C   ## The Conflict Within Faustus

[*Enter* FAUSTUS *in his study.*]

Faustus. Now Faustus must thou needs be damned,
   And canst thou not be saved.
   What boots it° then to think on God or heaven?
   Away with such vain fancies, and despair;
5   Despair in God, and trust in Beëlzebub.°
   Now go not backward; Faustus, be <u>resolute</u>.
   Why waver'st thou? Oh, something soundeth in mine
     ear:
   '<u>Abjure</u> this magic; turn to God again.'
   Ay, and Faustus will turn to God again!
10   To God? He loves thee not.
   The God thou serv'st is thine own appetite,

3. **what boots it:** what is the point.

5. **Beëlzebub:** one of the chief demons.

A. Names

The name *Mephistophilis* may mean either "not loving light" (Greek) or "destroyer and liar" (Hebrew).

B. Plot Background

Faustus uses the devil's tricks when in Act III Mephistophilis takes him to visit the Pope. The invisible Faustus so harasses the Pope during a meal that the Pope summons "bell, book, and candle; candle, book, and bell"—the traditional paraphernalia of exorcism—to get rid of the pesky spirit.

C. Visual Image

This famous Helen of Troy episode from Act V, Scene 1, alludes to the "topless towers" of Troy—towers so high they appear to extend infinitely into the heavens. The "thousand ships" are the ships the Greeks launched to sail to Troy to retrieve Helen.

Twentieth-century Irish poet William Butler Yeats wrote a famous poem alluding to Helen, "No Second Troy." Yeats, like many other poets, cast as Helen of Troy a beautiful woman (Maude Gonne) who had rejected him.

Wherein is fixed the love of Beëlzebub.
To him I'll build an altar and a church,
And offer lukewarm blood of new-born babes.

[*Enter the* TWO ANGELS.]

15   **Bad Angel.** Go forward, Faustus, in that famous art.°

      Good Angel. Sweet Faustus, leave that execrable art.

      Faustus. Contrition, prayer, repentance—what of these?

      Good Angel. Oh, they are means to bring thee unto heaven.

      Bad Angel. Rather illusions, fruits of lunacy,

20   That make men foolish that do use them most.

      Good Angel. Sweet Faustus, think of heaven and heavenly things.

      Bad Angel. No Faustus; think of honor and wealth.

[*Exeunt* ANGELS.]

      Faustus. Wealth? Why, the signory° of Emden° shall be mine.

A   When Mephistophilis° shall stand by me,

25   What power can hurt me? Faustus, thou art safe.

      Cast no more doubts. Mephistophilis, come

      And bring glad tidings from great Lucifer.°

      Is't not midnight? Come, Mephistophilis.

15. **art:** black magic.

23. **signory:** domain. **Emden:** a rich trading city.

24. **Mephistophilis:** a chief demon who is Faustus's constant companion.

27. **Lucifer:** the name, meaning "Light-bearer," by which Satan was known before he rebelled against God and was exiled from Heaven.

B *Before Faustus made his pact, he had grandiose projects and plans to benefit himself and his fellow countrymen. But as it turns out he cannot use the knowledge and power he obtains from the Devil for good purposes; the Devil shows him only how to do tricks and stunts, to make things materialize and disappear. With the help of Mephistophilis he flies to far-off places, but these journeys accomplish nothing, and over the years he becomes lazy, self-indulgent, and pleasure-loving. He finally asks Mephistophilis to produce Helen of Troy, whom a committee of Wittenberg scholars has pronounced the most beautiful woman who ever lived. (Marlowe assumed that everybody had heard of this gorgeous adventuress. When Paris, the Trojan prince, stole Helen away from her Greek husband Menelaus, it started the war described in Homer's* Iliad.*) And so Mephistophilis conjures up Helen. Whoever plays this role on the stage must be very attractive, but needs no acting skill, since she says nothing: only God can make a real person; the Devil makes dummies.*

C   **Helen of Troy**

      Faustus. Was this the face that launched a thousand ships

          And burnt the topless towers of Ilium?°

          Sweet Helen, make me immortal with a kiss.

[*She kisses him.*]

2. **Ilium:** Troy.

READING CHECK TEST
1. Faustus plans to use all his powers to benefit others. (F)
2. Faustus chiefly wants money. (F)
3. When Faustus sees Helen of Troy, he sees she is no longer beautiful. (F)

4. As his death nears, Faustus wishes he were an animal, since animals' souls die with them. (T)
5. As the clock strikes twelve, the Good Angel saves Faustus from Hell. (F)

CLOSURE
Have three students explain to the class the following: (1) Who was Dr. Faustus? (2) What famous words did he say when he saw Helen of Troy? (3) What debt did he pay for gaining all his knowledge?

A
    Her lips suck forth my soul. See where it flies!
5   Come, Helen, come, give me my soul again.
    Here will I dwell, for heaven is in these lips,
    And all is <u>dross</u> that is not Helena.
    I will be Paris, and for love of thee
    Instead of Troy shall Wittenberg be sacked;
10   And I will combat with weak Menelaus°
    And wear thy colors on my plumèd crest.
    Yea, I will wound Achilles° in the heel
    And then return to Helen for a kiss.
    Oh, thou art fairer than the evening's air,
15   Clad in the beauty of a thousand stars.
    Brighter art thou than flaming Jupiter
    When he appeared to <u>hapless</u> Semele.°

10. **Menelaus** (men′ə·lā′əs).

12. **Achilles** (ə·kil′ēz): the Greek hero of the *Iliad,* whom Paris wounds in his only vulnerable spot, the heel.

17. **Semele:** Semele's son by Jupiter (Zeus) was Dionysus.

B
Faustus Pays His Debt

[*The clock strikes eleven.*]

Faustus. Ah Faustus,
    Now hast thou but one bare hour to live,
    And then thou must be damned perpetually.
    Stand still, you ever-moving spheres of heaven,
5   That time may cease and midnight never come.
C   Fair nature's eye, rise, rise again, and make
    Perpetual day; or let this hour be but
    A year, a month, a week, a natural day,
    That Faustus may repent and save his soul.
10   *O lente, lente currite noctis equi!*°
    The stars move still; time runs; the clock will strike;
    The devil will come, and Faustus must be damned.
D   Oh, I'll leap up to my God! Who pulls me down?
    See, see, where Christ's blood° streams in the firmament!°
    One drop would save my soul, half a drop! Ah, my
15   Christ!

    Rend not my heart for naming of my Christ!
    Yet will I call on him. Oh, spare me, Lucifer!
    Where is it now? 'Tis gone. And see where God
    Stretcheth out his arm and bends his ireful brows.
20   Mountains and hills, come, come, and fall on me,
    And hide me from the heavy wrath of God.
    No, no!
    Then will I headlong run into the earth.
    Earth, gape! Oh no, it will not harbor me!
25   You stars that reigned at my nativity,°
    Whose influence hath allotted death and hell,
    Now draw up Faustus like a foggy mist
    Into the <u>entrails</u> of yon laboring cloud,
    That when you vomit forth into the air,

10. *"O lente . . . equi":* "Ye horses of the night, run slowly, Oh slowly!" This line is from one of Ovid's poems.

14. **Christ's blood:** shed on the cross, to save humanity from damnation. **firmament:** sky.

25. **nativity:** birth.

A. Interpreting
Marlowe's audience would have foreseen Faustus's damnation here. The sin of intercourse with a demonic spirit was considered so great an evil that the sinner could never repent.

B. Background
This episode occurs in Act V, Scene 3.

C. Metaphor
? What is "fair nature's eye"? (The sun)

D. Allusion
Edith Sitwell quotes this famous line in her poem "Still Falls the Rain" (see text page 1097).
? What visual image is suggested in the line? (Rising from the earth, an ascension to heaven)

1. He plans to order the spirits to search India for gold and ransack the ocean for pearls; search the world for delicacies; tell him the secrets of foreign kings; wall Germany with brass and make the Rhine circle Wittenberg; fill schools with silk; raise an army to chase the Prince of Parma from the land; and make himself king.

2. The good angel tells Faustus to think of heaven and heavenly things and to repent. The bad angel bids Faustus think of honor and wealth.

Faustus pledges allegiance to Mephistophilis, the devil.

3. He feels his soul being sucked out of his body.

4. First, he bids time stand still. Then he calls upon Christ. Finally, he tries to bargain with God, pleading that he be punished in hell for only a thousand years, not for eternity.

He curses himself and Lucifer.

Interpreting Meanings

5. Most students will probably agree that, while Faustus's projects described in "Faustus Gloats" may benefit others as well as himself, his projects are all

---

A. Resolution of the Plot

After Faustus exits with the devils, scholars come to check on his safety, "For such a dreadful night was never seen / Since first the world's creation did begin, / Such fearful shrieks and cries were never heard." They find Faustus dead, torn limb from limb, and realize that the shrieks were his. The closing lines of Marlowe's play are given in the second writing assignment on text page 231.

---

30   My limbs may issue from your smoky mouths,
       So that my soul may but ascend to heaven.

[The watch strikes.]

       Ah, half the hour is past; 'twill all be past anon.
       Oh, God,
       If thou wilt not have mercy on my soul,
35   Yet for Christ's sake, whose blood hath ransomed me,
       Impose some end to my <u>incessant</u> pain.
       Let Faustus live in hell a thousand years,
       A hundred thousand, and at last be saved.
       Oh, no end is limited to damnèd souls.
40   Why wert thou not a creature wanting soul?
       Or why is this immortal that thou hast?
       Ah, Pythagoras' *metempsychosis,*° were that true,
       This soul should fly from me and I be changed
       Into some brutish beast. All beasts are happy,
45   For, when they die
       Their souls are soon dissolved in elements,
       But mine must live still° to be plagued in hell.
       Cursed be the parents that engendered me!
       No, Faustus, curse thyself, curse Lucifer
50   That hath deprived thee of the joys of heaven.

[The clock strikes twelve.]

       Oh, it strikes, it strikes! Now, body, turn to air,
       Or Lucifer will bear thee quick° to hell.
       Oh, soul, be changed to little water-drops,
       And fall into the ocean, ne'er be found!

[Thunder, and enter the DEVILS.*]*

55   My God, my God, look not so fierce on me!
       Adders and serpents, let me breathe a while!
       Ugly hell, gape not! Come not, Lucifer!
  A I'll burn my books! Ah, Mephistophilis!
                      *[*FAUSTUS *and* DEVILS *Exeunt.]*

42. Pythagoras' *metempsychosis:* the doctrine of the transmigration of souls after death, taught by the Greek philosopher and mathematician Pythagoras.

47. still: forever.

52. quick: alive.

Responding to the Play

Analyzing the Play

Identifying Facts

1. What does Dr. Faustus plan to do with his new powers?
2. When the good angel and the bad angel vie for Faustus's soul, how does each attempt to persuade Faustus? To whom does Faustus finally pledge allegiance?
3. What happens when Faustus kisses Helen of Troy?

4. As Faustus waits for the devil to come fetch his soul, how does he try to escape his damnation? Whom does he blame for his predicament?

Interpreting Meanings

5. Does Faustus seek power and knowledge for admirable purposes? What evidence in the drama lets the audience infer Faustus's purposes?

materialistic.

The evidence includes the speech on pages 227–228, in which Faustus rejects God and says that he will worship Beëlzebub and the fact that Faust asks for Helen of Troy.

6. Paris's rape of Helen was the traditional cause of the tragic and bloody Trojan War. In light of this, the comparison foreshadows destruction for Faustus.

7. Students may point to lines 6, 10, 14, 15, 19, 20, 22, 24, 33, 42, 45, 56, 57, and 58. Encourage students to listen for how the metrical variations are related to the content of each line and to the speaker's emotions.

8. Answers will vary. Places where one might sympathize with him include the "Faustus Gloats" segment, in which he wishes for the power to do good (even

dressing students in silk) or when he faces damnation.

---

6. Faustus says to Helen of Troy, "I will be Paris." Considering the result of Paris's actions and of his relationship with Helen, what might that statement **foreshadow**?

7. Examine Faustus's final **soliloquy** for metrical irregularities—places where Marlowe has taken liberties with the **iambic pentameter** line. For example, the first line of the soliloquy consists only of the words "Ah Faustus"—one iamb, and a long silence where listeners would expect four more metrical feet. The silence communicates more effectively than words the gravity of Faustus's predicament. Find other examples in the soliloquy of striking irregularities in **meter**, and explain what you think their effects are.

8. Do you sympathize with Faustus at any point in the play? Explain why or why not.

Writing About the Play

A Creative Response

1. Showing Internal Conflict. Marlowe uses a good and a bad angel to show **internal conflict** in the character of Faustus. Write a **dialogue** similar to the scene in Faustus's study, in which you use two voices to illustrate a conflict within a character. For instance, you might create the character of a student trying to decide whether to spend the summer working or traveling. A practical yet dull voice could argue in favor of working, while a fun-loving yet impractical voice could argue in favor of travel. In the dialogue, give each voice a different speaking style and have each use a different method of reasoning.

A Critical Response

2. Applying a Theme. When the tragedy of Dr. Faustus is over, an actor called Chorus (commentator) comes forward and makes this speech:

[*Enter Chorus.*]

Chorus. Cut is the branch that might have grown full straight,
And burnèd is Apollo's laurel bough
That sometime grew within this learnèd man.
Faustus is gone. Regard his hellish fall,
Whose fiendful fortune may exhort the wise
Only to wonder at unlawful things,
Whose deepness doth entice such forward wits
To practice more than heavenly power permits.

The "laurel bough" is the classical symbol of wisdom and of intellectual and artistic accomplishment; Apollo is the god of these attributes. Marlowe puts the bough and the god together to suggest Faustus's great potential, now lost forever.

The Chorus's statement could be said to sum up the **theme** of the play. In an essay, state the play's theme in your own words. Then explain one way in which the theme and the play might be relevant for our time. (To help spark your thinking, consider what sort of person today might agree with the view of knowledge presented by the Chorus, and what sort of person might disagree.)

FOR FURTHER READING

STUDENTS
Students may compare the finality and despair of the tragic Faust legend with the lighter-hearted resolution of Stephen Vincent Benét's "The Devil and Daniel Webster" (1937). In this American short story, New Hampshire farmer Jabez Stone sells his soul to the devil in return for ten years of prosperity, but by means of the debating skills of Daniel Webster, he wins release from the bargain.

The English ballad "The Demon Lover" (text page 999) and Elizabeth Bowen's short story of the same title (text page 994) also deal with the theme of the devil's returning to collect his due.

1. ESTABLISHING A PURPOSE. Have students read writing assignment 2 on text page 234. If students are turned off by the very notion of shepherds and nymphs, ask them to read the poems as if the speakers were idealized farmers.

2. INTRODUCING THE POEMS. An effective way to dramatize these two poems is to have a male student read the shepherd's invitation and a female student read the nymph's reply.

DEVELOPING VOCABULARY
The following words from the poem are tested in the Selection Test. (See also Vocabulary Activity Worksheet.)

melodious	studs
posies	dumb
amber	wanton

This poem of Marlowe's belongs to two literary traditions. It is first of all a pastoral, from *pastor*, the Latin word for shepherd. Pastoral works, which may be poems, plays, or prose fictions, are set in an idealized countryside, and their characters are amusing blends of the naïve and the sophisticated. The poem also belongs to another poetic tradition in which a male speaker presents reasons why a female listener should surrender her charms to him. Marlowe's is perhaps the most famous pastoral work in English: Several composers have set it to music, and several poets have written answers or sequels to it. Sir Hugh Evans sings a bit of it in Shakespeare's *Merry Wives of Windsor*, Act III, Scene 1.

Marlowe never published the poem, but it appeared anonymously in two Elizabethan anthologies, and Izaak Walton identified it as Marlowe's in *The Compleat Angler*.

The Passionate Shepherd to His Love

Come live with me and be my love,
And we will all the pleasures prove°
That valleys, groves, hills, and fields,
Woods, or steepy mountain yields.

5   And we will sit upon the rocks,
Seeing the shepherds feed their flocks,
By shallow rivers, to whose falls
Melodious birds sing madrigals.°

And I will make thee beds of roses
10 And a thousand fragrant posies,
A cap of flowers, and a kirtle°
Embroidered all with leaves of myrtle;

A gown made of the finest wool,
Which from our pretty lambs we pull;
15 Fair linèd slippers for the cold,
With buckles of the purest gold;

A belt of straw and ivy buds,
With coral clasps and amber studs;
And if these pleasures may thee move,
20 Come live with me and be my love.

The shepherd swains° shall dance and sing
For thy delight each May morning;
If these delights thy mind may move,
Then live with me and be my love.

2. **prove:** experience.

8. **madrigals:** complicated songs for several voices.

11. **kirtle:** dress, gown, skirt.

21. **swains:** young boys.

A. Humanities Connection: Discussing the Art

Embroidery is so ancient an art that it is mentioned in the Hindu Vedas and the Book of Exodus in the Bible. Made with all kinds of fabrics, threads, and decorative objects, embroidery was used by the ancient Egyptians, Greeks, Romans, and Chinese. It was introduced into Europe via Byzantium after Crusaders returned with samples of Eastern fabrics. In Europe, sacred and ecclesiastical themes eventually gave way to secular subjects. As evident from some of the portraits in this unit, the Elizabethan period was justly famous for its household and costume embroidery.

❓ What details tell you that these are not realistic shepherds, but idealized ones in the pastoral tradition of poetry?

(See text page 176.) (The mythological figure of Cupid, the elegance of the shepherd and the woman—no muck on their feet, no common work clothes)

Shepherd and Shepherdess with Cupid in Pastoral Landscape (detail) (17th century). Embroidery.

The Metropolitan Museum of Art. New York. Gift of Irwin Untermyer. 1964. (64.101.1313).

A

ANALYZING THE POEMS
Identifying Details
1. The speaker envisions a life of care-free pleasure. The speaker will make his love beds of flowers, a cap of flowers, a gown embroidered with myrtle leaves, a gown of the finest wool, lined slippers with gold buckles, a belt of straw and ivy buds decorated with coral and amber. The couple will sit on rocks watching shepherds dance and sing.
2. The nymph points out that time reveals flaws in the idyllic vision: Winter replaces spring, rivers rage, flowers fade, rocks grow cold, birds stop singing, the pretty dress rots. She also implies that not every shepherd speaks the truth.

She would agree to be his love if youth and joy could last forever.

Interpreting Meanings
3. Marlowe's pastoral details include "melodious birds," gowns and slippers, dancing, and singing shepherds.
4. The nymph's tone is cynical, realistic, ironic, sarcastic.
5. You might suggest songs.

Most students will agree that an idyllic escape still has appeal.

A. Argument
❓ The nymph begins with two prerequisites for agreeing to the shepherd's request. What are they? (That all the world and love be young, that all shepherds be honest) Note that since these are clearly impossible, we know from the outset what her reply will be.

B. Imagery
Have students point out the imagery she uses to "prove" that everything changes for the worse.

Elizabethan London was a small place, and Raleigh's and Marlowe's paths must have crossed more than once. Here is Raleigh's reply to Marlowe's "Passionate Shepherd." Other poets, including John Donne and Robert Herrick, also replied to Marlowe. But Raleigh wrote the best answer. He put it into the mouth of a "nymph," or young woman. She, like her maker, has a strong character.

The Nymph's Reply to the Shepherd

A
If all the world and love were young,
And truth in every shepherd's tongue,
These pretty pleasures might me move
To live with thee and be thy love.

5   Time drives the flocks from field to fold,°
When rivers rage and rocks grow cold,
And Philomel° becometh <u>dumb</u>;
The rest complains of cares to come.

B
The flowers do fade, and <u>wanton</u> fields
10   To wayward winter reckoning yields.
A honey tongue, a heart of gall,°
Is fancy's spring, but sorrow's fall.

Thy gowns, thy shoes, thy beds of roses,
Thy cap, thy kirtle, and thy posies
15   Soon break, soon wither, soon forgotten;
In folly ripe, in reason rotten.

Thy belt of straw and ivy buds,
Thy coral clasps and amber studs,
All these in me no means can move
20   To come to thee and be thy love.

But could youth last and love still breed,
Had joys no date° nor age no need,
Then these delights my mind might move
To live with thee and be thy love.
                                   —Sir Walter Raleigh

5. **fold:** the building where sheep are housed in winter.
7. **Philomel:** the nightingale.
11. **gall:** a bitter substance.

22. **date:** end.

Responding to the Poems

Analyzing the Poems

Identifying Details

1. Describe the life that the shepherd envisions with his love. How will they be dressed? How will they spend their time?
2. In the nymph's reply, what flaws does she find with the shepherd's idyllic vision? Under what conditions would she agree to be his love?

Interpreting Meanings

3. In **pastoral** writing, the harsher realities of country life do not exist; there is no dirt, pain, or struggle, and there is certainly no ugliness or violence. Which details make Marlowe's poem distinctly pastoral?
4. What is the **tone** of the nymph's reply?

5. What modern kinds of writing about love are as idyllic as Marlowe's poem? Do you think the idea of an idyllic escape with a loved one still has a strong appeal?

Writing About the Poems

A Creative Response

1. **Responding to the Poem.** How would a modern young woman respond to the shepherd's invitation? Write a response in verse and give it a title.

A Critical Response

2. **Analyzing Argument.** Why does Raleigh's nymph refuse to be seduced by Marlowe's shepherd? Answer this question in two or three paragraphs.

THE ENGLISH LANGUAGE
by John Algeo

The Modern English period can be dated from 1485, when Henry VII, the first of the Tudor kings of England, came to the throne. The House of Tudor brought peace to the land, introduced the Reformation and Renaissance to England, helped to promote a pride in things English that led to an increased respect for the English language and its potentials, and began the spread of our language all over the world. Just ten years before, in 1475, William Caxton had printed the first book in English. That event might also be taken as marking the beginning of the Modern period, for printed books were to help unify and spread English and make the ability to read and write readily available to all English-speaking people.

The Language Changes That Made Modern English

When William Caxton printed the first books in English, he tried to make them look as much like handwritten manuscripts as he could. The shapes of the letters in his type font, the spellings he used, his choice of words and sentence structures, all suggested the manuscript writing of an earlier time. Because printing was a newfangled invention, Caxton wanted his printed books to look as much as possible like the manuscript books that people were familiar with. Yet despite his efforts, it is clear that the language of the late 1400's and early 1500's was a new form of English.

English during the first part of the Modern period, when it still resembled Middle English in some ways and had not yet reached the form that we recognize as our own, is known as "early Modern English." That term embraces English from about 1485 through the seventeenth century. The differences that set this early Modern English apart from older forms of the language are in grammar, pronunciation, and vocabulary. The latter two kinds of differences are most important.

The grammatical differences between Middle and Modern English were not very great. Middle English had already lost many of the inflections of Old English. The few that it retained and passed on to early Modern English are mainly ones we still have today: the plural ending -s and the possessive ending -'s for nouns; the comparative and superlative endings -er and -est for adjectives; and the verb endings for the past tense (-ed), past participle (-ed or -en), present participle (-ing), and the third-person singular of the present tense (-s). In place of -s, early Modern English also had an ending we no longer use, -eth, and in addition one for the second-person singular, -est (as in "he thinketh" and "thou think-est").

The Birth of Modern English

Bookbinding in the 15th century.

A. Expansion
When William Caxton (c. 1422–1491) set up his press at Westminster, he began a great communications revolution.

Until 1500 a total of 35,000 books were printed throughout Europe, mostly in Latin. But between 1500 and 1640, in England alone, more than 20,000 items were printed in English. Literacy rose accordingly; by 1600, nearly half the people in towns and cities had minimal literacy.

B. Discussing the Engraving
Note the way the men dress and their bookbinding tools displayed on the walls.

❓ What tasks are the men doing? (The man in the background is folding or arranging the printed sheets; the man in the foreground is binding them as books.)

A. Clarification
See the diagram below, which illustrates this paragraph.

B. Pronunciation
Read aloud the different pronunciations of "See the same old moon in the cloudy sky" (at the top of text page 237 also). Students who have studied modern French, Spanish, or German may notice (as mentioned in the middle of page 237) that the Middle English vowels are like those of these modern European languages.

C. Using the Diagram
Explain that the quotation marks indicate the earlier pronunciation of the modern word, which does *not* have quotation marks. Thus, "beet" is the old pronunciation for our word *bite;* "fate" is the old pronunciation for our word *feet,* etc.

A

B

C

" **If**
we could go back
to London in the time
of Chaucer by a
time-travel machine,
our first impression
would be
that some language
other than English
was being spoken."

There were, to be sure, some differences between the grammar of Middle and early Modern English, as there are between early Modern and present-day English, but those differences are not great.

Shifting Vowels

The greatest change between Middle and early Modern English was in the pronunciation of the "long" or tense vowels, illustrated by these words (given in their present-day spellings): *bite, feet, cane, mouse, boot, load.* In Middle English times, the vowel of these words had been pronounced as follows: *bite* like "beet," *feet* like "fate," *cane* like "khan" or "con," *mouse* like "moose," *boot* like "boat," and *load* like "laud" or "(out-)lawed." The sentence *See the same old moon in the cloudy sky* would have sounded in Middle English something like "Say the sahm awld moan in the cloody skee."

Obviously, Middle English sounded very different from the language we are used to, and the chief cause for its different sound is this difference in vowels. If we could go back to London in the time of Chaucer by a time-travel machine, our first impression would be that some language other than English was being spoken. After a while, however, we would probably get used to it and decide that it was English after all, although pronounced very oddly.

The change in vowel sounds may look haphazard, but in fact it is very regular and patterned. Each of the "long" or tense vowels came to be pronounced with the tongue a little higher in the mouth. The two that were originally highest turned into diphthongs (combinations of two vowels pronounced together). The accompanying diagram shows the "movement" of these vowels. The process by which the vowels were thus "raised" in their pronunciation is called the "Great Vowel Shift." It probably began in the late years of the fourteenth century, shortly before Chaucer's death, and was completed during the first years of the early Modern English period. (There was a seventh vowel that participated in the Great Vowel Shift, but it has been omitted from the discussion because of some special complications in its history.)

"beet"   "moose"

feet   *boot*

"fate"   "boat"

cane   *load*

"khan"   "laud"

bite   *mouse*

A. About the Engraving
Elizabethan London was a crammed, commercial, overgrown village. The city had grown from about 50,000 in Chaucer's time to almost 94,000 in 1563 and nearly 225,000 by 1605. Water taxis crowded the Thames River; royalty rode on gilded barges past criminals chained to the banks to be punished by the tides. The severed heads of executed criminals were mounted on London Bridge, the only bridge across the Thames.

No one knows why the Great Vowel Shift happened—many such big changes in language are inexplicable. However, something rather similar is going on in some varieties of English today. In New York City, Philadelphia, and various other places, especially in the middle part of the East Coast and westward from there, words like *bad, cab,* and *fan* are being pronounced with a "higher" and tenser vowel; they sound something like "behd," "kehb," "fehn." If that kind of change should become general again and extend to other words and other parts of the country, two hundred years from now people may be pronouncing *See the same old moon in the cloudy sky* something like "Sigh the seem oold moun in the clawdy skay." Stranger things have happened in the history of languages, and that change is no more improbable than the Great Vowel Shift was five hundred years ago.

Lagging Spelling

Ever since 1475, when books were first printed, we have had a tendency to keep our spelling unchanged, whatever happens to our pronunciation. Spelling has changed somewhat during the last six hundred years, but not nearly so much as pronunciation. As a consequence, our spelling tends to become further and further out of line with the way we say words. When Caxton started printing books, he used a spelling for English that was already old-fashioned then; and we have done comparatively little to modernize it since.

The Middle English spelling that Caxton adopted for writing early Modern English had used the five vowel letters more or less in the same way that they are still used in writing Spanish, French, or German. That is, *a* stood for the vowel sound in *spa,* *e* for that in *toupee,* *i* for that in *ski,* *o* for that in *so,* and *u* for that in *tutu.* In Caxton's post-Great Vowel Shift pronunciation, however, the sounds originally represented by the five vowel letters had become quite different. Because English adopted a pre-Great Vowel Shift spelling for post-Great Vowel Shift sounds, today we use the five vowel letters in a different way from that of other European languages.

Ever since English first began to be printed, people have worried about the failure of our spelling to match our pronunciation. Many proposals have been made to reform English spelling, ranging from simply omitting silent letters, as in *tho* for *though* and *thru* for *through,* to more thorough reforms: "Wun sistem uv spelling wood seek tu eeliminaet awl irregguelarity." There have been even more radical suggestions, such as abandoning the Latin alphabet altogether and adopting a new one. One example is called the Shaw alphabet, designed for a contest set up by the twentieth-century writer George Bernard Shaw in his will. An example of the Shaw alphabet is on the right.

Radical spelling reforms have no chance whatever of adoption; even modest reforms have very little, though our spelling lags far behind our pronunciation. English speakers have been remarkably faithful to the spellings that were decided upon during the early Modern English period. We seem unlikely to change them now.

London View Across the Thames from South Bank (detail) by Johann B. Homanns. Engraving.

The British Library.

From Bernard Shaw's *Androcles and the Lion.*

B. Spelling Reforms
Have students "translate" this: "One system of spelling would seek to eliminate all irregularity." Note that some words (*eliminate, irregularity*) are more complicated here than the way we spell them. Have students suggest other spelling reforms, or try to spell their names phonetically.

C. Shaw's Spelling
For a translation of this passage, see question 4 on text page 240.

At Tillsbury (or Tilbury Fort) near the mouth of the Thames, Queen Elizabeth reviewed the royal troops in 1588. All remnants of the defeated Spanish Armada had not yet limped home, and there were rumors that the Duke of Parma was plotting to invade England. The queen inspired her troops with these famous words: "I know I have the body but of a weak and feeble woman, but I have the heart and stomach of a king, and of a king of England too, and think foul scorn that Parma or Spain, or any prince of Europe should dare to invade the borders of my realm; to which, rather than any dishonor shall grow by me, I myself will take up arms. I myself will be your general, judge, and rewarder of every one of your virtues in the field."

Queen Elizabeth addressing the troops at Tillsbury (1588). Painting on wood.

St. Faith's Church, King's Lynn, England.

O Brave New World: The Spread of English and Foreign Influences

The reign of Queen Elizabeth I saw the beginning of the extension of English to the far corners of the world. The British established colonies in America—in a land they called Virginia after the Virgin Queen and later in New England and many other places. British sailors crisscrossed the seas. British merchants carried their wares abroad and brought back the produce of foreign shores. Exploration, settlement, and commerce all led to the borrowing by English of words from many other languages. And the kinds of contact English speakers had with other nations are reflected in the words we have borrowed.

English continued to borrow words from French, such as *bigot*, *bombast*, *duel*, *explore*, *jaunty*, *mustache*, *shock*, and *vogue*. From Italian we acquired *balcony*, *cameo*, *design*, *duo*, *fugue*, *grotto*, *portico*, *stanza*, *trill*, and *violin*; from Spanish or Portuguese, *alligator*, *apricot*, *banana*, *brocade*, *corral*, *hammock*, *renegade*, and *tobacco*; from Indian languages of Central America and the Caribbean, by way of Spanish, *avocado*, *cannibal*, *chocolate*, *maize*, *potato*, and *tomato*; from Dutch, *cruise*, *deck*, *freight*, *keel*, *skipper*, *smuggle*, *yacht*, and also *duffel*, *spool*, *knapsack*, *easel*, *etch*, and *landscape*.

As English speakers traveled through the continent of Europe, explored the New World, rounded the tip of Africa, and circumnavigated the globe, they had new experiences wherever they went, encountered new objects, and learned new words. The adventures of British explorers during the early Modern English period enriched our vocabulary immensely. Because they had an itch to travel, and scratched it vigorously, the English language has never been the same.

The New Learning: Classical Influences

While English was picking up words from languages abroad, it did not neglect the classical languages, Latin and Greek. Latin had been an important influence on English since the time before A.D. 449, when English speakers still lived on the Continent. But during the early Modern period, Latin and Greek became increasingly important. The literature, art, philosophy, history, and culture of Rome and Athens were taken as ideals during the Renaissance. All over Europe people turned away from the ornate, rambling, and heavenward-reaching style of Medieval art and began to look instead to the delicately proportioned, earth-hugging canons of classical art. Naturally, modern European languages, including English, also borrowed words from Latin and Greek.

Among many other words, English borrowed from Latin *abdomen*, *area*, *compensate*, *delirium*, *editor*, *gradual*, *imitate*, *janitor*, *medium*, *orbit*, *peninsula*, *quota*, *series*, *strict*, *superintendent*, *ultimate*, *urban*, and *urge*. From Greek, usually by way of Latin

The versatile Sir Walter Raleigh (text page 194) organized the first English-speaking colonies in the New World. In 1585, he commissioned the first colonizing mission, which included the artist and map maker John White, who later became the colony's first governor. (White's watercolors of animals and plants provide an excellent record of the area's natural history.) This colony ran into trouble with the Indians, however, and the colonists had to be rescued by Sir Francis Drake.

In July 1587, Raleigh sent another group of colonists to Roanoke Island, where they celebrated the birth of Virginia Dare (White's granddaughter), the first English child born in the New World. White sailed to England for supplies and took nearly four years to return (English ships were busy with the Spanish Armada). When White and his men landed in 1591, they found only silence; the colonists and their houses had vanished.

and sometimes other intermediate languages, came *aristocracy, barbarous, chaos, comedy, cycle, drama, epoch, history, mystery, rhythm, theory, tragedy,* and *zone.*

Classical influence extended also to spelling. English had many words that were ultimately from Latin, but which were borrowed directly from French long before. For example, Middle English had taken the word *dout* from Old French, although it was ultimately from Latin *dubitare* ("to waver"); similarly *dette* came also from Old French, ultimately from Latin *debitum* ("something owed"). The spellings of those words (*dout* and *dette*) suggested quite well the way they were then, and still are, pronounced. Renaissance scholars, however, with more sense of history than of reality, decided the words ought to be respelled to suggest the Latin originals from which they had ultimately come. So they stuck a *b* into each word to echo the *b*'s in Latin *dubitare* and *debitum.* And so English spelling, which had been archaic to begin with, became even less realistic.

In a similar way, scholars respelled *paum,* from Old French, as *palm* to make it look more like its ultimate Latin source, *palma.* Although generally no one tries to pronounce the *b*'s in *doubt* and *debt,* English speakers do now often pronounce the *l* in *palm,* although there is no longer any reason do to so. Thus Renaissance scholars not only introduced many Greek and Latin words into English, but they also complicated our spelling of some older ones and occasionally changed the way we pronounce such words.

The Rise of Standard English

Languages come in many varieties. A standard language is one variety that is used widely throughout a country and enjoys the respect of both those who use it and those who do not. It is typically the language of government and education, and is learned by everyone who aspires to a place of influence in national life. Old English was developing a standard language in the intervals between invasions by Norsemen and Normans, but its full development was cut short by the Conquest of 1066. Thereafter, since French was used as the language of government, no variety of English had the opportunity of developing into a standard. During the early Modern English period, however, such a standard did arise, and has existed ever since.

The early Modern English standard language was the result of several influences. The law clerks who recorded the proceedings of courts and who maintained the legal archives of England set a pattern of language use that others followed. Especially important was the usage of the Court of Chancery, presided over by the Lord High Chancellor of England; consequently, the widely used and prestigious form of early Modern English is sometimes called "Chancery Standard."

The introduction of the printing press, as already noted, helped to spread the new standard written language throughout England, making it available to all literate English speakers. Literacy was

A

Manuscript map of Raleigh's Virginia by John White (c. 1585). Drawing.

also increasing at this time. English people were reading the Book of Common Prayer (first published during the reign of Queen Elizabeth's brother and predecessor, King Edward VI) and the Authorized Version of the Bible (popularly known as the King James Bible because it was published during the reign of Elizabeth's successor, King James I). The phrases and rhythms of those two books, prayer book and Bible, were powerful influences in shaping the ideal of language to which English speakers looked during the Renaissance and for centuries after.

Analyzing Language

1. Renaissance English differs from ours in both vocabulary and grammar. Read the essay "Of Studies" by Sir Francis Bacon to find examples of these kinds of differences.

   a. What do the following words used in Bacon's essays mean?

humor	contemn	reins	wit
proyning	stond	receipt	physic

   b. How might we today say the ideas expressed by Bacon as follows?

   (1) . . . studies themselves do give forth directions too much at large, except they be bounded in by experience.

   (2) Reading maketh a full man. . . . And therefore, if a man . . . read little, he had need have much cunning, to seem to know that he doth not.

   (3) There was never proud man thought so absurdly well of himself as the lover doth of the person loved.

2. The fact that some words are pronounced in more than one way today is a sign that our language is still in the process of change. What pronunciations do you know for the following words? Look in a dictionary to see whether other pronunciations are listed.

brooch	garage	roof
creek	height	which

3. Although our spelling is more consistent than that of the Renaissance, some words still have more than one possible spelling. What other spellings can the following words have? If you do not know, look in a dictionary.

adviser	finicky	cozy
descendent	collectible	parakeet
cater-cornered	mama	

4. Using the following key, write the passage in the Shaw alphabet on page 237 in conventional spelling.

THE SHAW ALPHABET READING KEY
The letters are classified as Tall, Deep, Short, and Compound.
Beneath each letter is its full name; its *sound* is shown in **bold** type.

5. During the Renaissance, English borrowed words from many foreign languages. From what language does each of the following words come? Look up the words in a dictionary that gives etymologies.

balcony	catastrophe	scientific
brocade	landscape	volcano
canoe	mustache	

6. Like *debt*, *doubt*, and *palm*, some other words have also been respelled to show something about their etymology. In the following words, what letters are not pronounced? Look up the words in a dictionary with etymologies to find what it says about the histories of the words.

indict	receipt	subtle	victual

7. The standard English of the Renaissance was based on the language used by the government in law courts and was spread by the printing press. What influences affect the way we talk and write today?

PREPARATION
ESTABLISHING A PURPOSE. Build on your students' prior study of the Shakespearean theater. Assign this section as homework, and ask them to read and take notes with these questions in mind: What details did I already know? Which were new to me? Were any of my ideas changed by this introduction? Do any details puzzle me?

SUPPLEMENTARY SUPPORT MATERIALS
Test on Understanding the Renaissance Theater (CCB)

The Renaissance Theater

A

By the mid-sixteenth century, the art of drama in England was three centuries old, but the idea of housing it in a permanent building was new, and even after theaters had been built, plays were still regularly performed in improvised spaces when acting companies were touring the provinces or presenting their plays in the large houses of royalty and nobility.

In 1576, James Burbage, the father of Shakespeare's partner and fellow actor Richard Burbage, built the first public theater and called it, appropriately, the Theater. Shortly thereafter, a second playhouse called the Curtain was erected. Both of these were located in a northern suburb of London, where they would not affront the more staid and sober-minded residents of London proper. Then came the Rose, the Swan, the Fortune, the Globe, the Red Bull, and the Hope: an astonishing number of public theaters and far more than there were in any other capital city of Europe at that time.

The Globe

The Globe, of course, is the most famous of these because it was owned by the company which Shakespeare belonged to. It was built out of timbers salvaged from the Theater when the latter was demolished in 1599. These timbers were carted across London, rafted over the Thames, and reassembled on the Bankside, near a bear garden—not the most elegant of London suburbs. Since many of Shakespeare's plays received their first performances in the Globe, curiosity and speculation about this famous building have been common for the last two hundred years or more. Unfortunately, the plans for the Globe have not survived, though there still exist old panoramic drawings of London in which its exterior is pictured, and there is still considerable information available about some other theaters, including a sketch of the Swan's stage and the building contract for the Fortune. But the most important sources of information are the plays themselves, with their stage directions and other clues to the structure of the theater.

The Structure of the Globe

At the present time, most scholars accept as accurate the reconstruction of the Globe published by C. Walter Hodges, whose drawing appears on the next page. Notice that the theater in this drawing has three main parts: the building proper, the stage, and the tiring house (or "backstage" area), with the flag flying from its peak to indicate that there will be a performance today.

The theater building proper was a wooden structure three stories high surrounding a spacious inner yard open to the sky. It was probably a sixteen-sided polygon. Any structure with that many sides would appear circular, so it is not surprising that Shakespeare referred to the Globe as "this wooden O" in his play *Henry V*. There

B

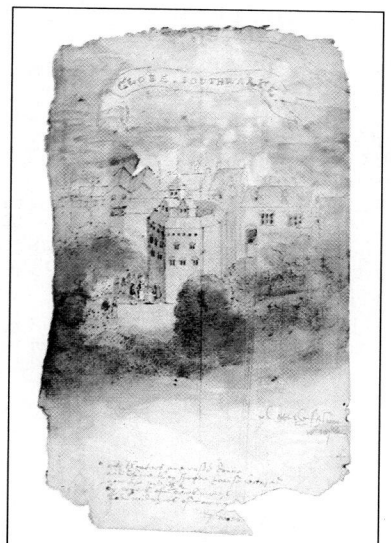

Globe Theater at Bankside (17th century). Watercolor.

A. The Theaters
Theaters built in the suburbs escaped the demands of profit-sharing innkeepers and the rancor of city authorities. The authorities claimed, with some justification, that the boisterous crowds gathered in innyards (especially on Sundays) occasioned a danger not just of "ungodliness" and licentiousness (all those rooms and secret places), but also of fire, riot, accident, crime, and the spread of plague. (Problems with crowds at rock concerts might be a contemporary parallel.)

B. About the Illustration
This watercolor is the only extant painting of the Globe done at firsthand. The painter, thought to be a traveler in London, is unknown. The banner reads, "Globe. Southwarke."

A. The Globe Fire
The fire in the Globe occurred in June 1613 during the first scenes of a new play by Shakespeare, _Henry VIII_ (see page 251). When drum and trumpet were sounded and cannon fired to herald the entrance of a royal party in the play, the linstock (the forked staff for holding a match) ignited the thatched roof of the theater. No one was injured, but it was fortunate that the theater sold beverages because when one man's breeches caught fire, the fire was quickly doused with "pottle" (bottled) ale. The company, however, lost not just the building, but also costumes, properties, and scripts.

The Globe was rebuilt in 1614 (it stood until pulled down to make room for residences in 1644), but the fire of 1613 marked the close of Shakespeare's London career. (See also text page 251, "The Last Years.")

In 1988, the 424th anniversary of Shakespeare's birth, a drive was begun to rebuild the Globe on a site just 200 yards from the old theater. (Marking the exact location of the old Globe is just a plaque on a brewery wall.)

B. The Plague
The London theaters were closed because of the plague from June 1592 to April 1594. This highly infectious disease, caused by _Pasteurella pestis_ and transmitted to humans by fleas from infected rats, is characterized by high fever, chills, delirium, and painful, festering enlargements of the lymph glands called "buboes" (hence, "bubonic plague"). Death could come in three or four days. The worst recorded epidemic, in the fourteenth century, is estimated to have killed up to three-quarters of the people in Asia and Europe in less than twenty years.

Globe Playhouse (c. 1599–1613). Reconstruction drawing by C. Walter Hodges.

A were probably only two entrances to the building, one for the public and one for the theater company. But there may well have been another public door used as an exit, because when the Globe burned down in 1613, the crowd all escaped the flames quickly and safely. General admission to the theater cost one penny; this entitled a spectator to be a groundling, which meant he or she could stand in the yard. Patrons paid a little more to mount up into the galleries, where there were seats and where there was a better view of the stage. The most expensive seats of all were chairs set right on the stage, along its two sides; people who wanted to be conspicuous rented them, and they must have been a great nuisance to the rest of the audience and the actors. A public theater could hold a surprisingly large number of spectators: three thousand according to two different contemporary accounts. The spectators must have been squeezed together, and so it is no wonder that the authorities always closed the theaters during epidemics of plague.

B

The stage jutted halfway out into the yard, so that the actors were in much closer contact with the audience than they are in modern theaters, most of which have picture-frame stages with

A. Repertory Theater

In Shakespeare's day, actors formed what we call repertory companies. Instead of signing up to perform a single play for a long run, they were members of an acting company that performed a number of different plays on consecutive days. These companies filled the roles of each play with members of their own group; they employed no outside actors.

(See text pages 251–252 on writing for such a company.)

The actors shared in the company profits, and boys were apprenticed as they would have been in a guild. Boys acted the women's roles until their voices changed, which accounts for the lack of older women's roles in the plays (too difficult) and the number of women characters who disguise themselves as men.

Many Shakespearean repertory groups exist today in the United States and other countries. The Shakespearean Festival at Ashland, Oregon, uses a Globe-like theater in its annual summer repertory performances. Minneapolis also has the Tyrone Guthrie Theater, designed in the Shakespearean manner, but with enclosed roof and modern lighting and machinery.

orchestra pit, proscenium arch, and front curtains. A picture-frame stage usually attempts to give the illusion of reality: its painted scenery represents the walls of a room or an outdoor vista, and the actors pretend that nobody is watching them perform, at least until it is time to take a bow. To be sure, theater designs have been changing since World War II, and people have again learned to enjoy plays "in the round," without elaborate realistic settings. Modern audiences are learning to accept what Renaissance audiences took for granted: that the theater cannot show "reality." Whatever happens on the stage is make-believe. Spectators at the Globe loved to see witches or devils emerge through the trapdoor in the stage, which everybody pretended led down to Hell, though everybody knew that it did not, just as everybody knew that the ceiling over part of the stage was not really the Heavens. This ceiling was painted with elaborate suns, moons, and stars, and it contained a trapdoor through which angels, gods, and spirits could be lowered on a wire and even flown over the other actors' heads. Such large, sensational effects as these were plentiful in the Renaissance theater. At the opposite extreme, every tiny nuance of an individual actor's performance could affect the audience, which was so very close to the stage. The actors were highly trained, and they could sing, dance, declaim, wrestle, fence, clown, roar, weep, and whisper. Unfortunately, none of this liveliness can be conveyed by the printed page; we must imagine all the activity on stage as we read.

The third structural element in this theater was the tiring house, a tall building that contained machinery and dressing rooms and that provided a two-story back wall for the stage. The drawing shows that this wall contained a gallery above and a curtained space below. The gallery had multiple purposes, depending on what play was being performed. Spectators could sit there, musicians could perform there, or parts of the play could be acted there. Many plays have stage directions indicating that some actors should appear on a level above the other actors—on balconies, towers, city walls, parapets, fortifications, hills, and the like. The curtained area below the gallery was used mainly for "discoveries" of things prepared in advance and temporarily kept hidden from the audience until the proper times for showing them. In Shakespeare's *Merchant of Venice,* for example, the curtain is drawn to reveal (or "discover") three small chests, in one of which is hidden the heroine's picture. Some modern accounts of Renaissance theaters refer to this curtained area as an "inner stage," but apparently it was too small, too shallow, and too far out of the sight of some spectators to be used as a performance space. If a performer were "discovered" behind the curtains, as Marlowe's Dr. Faustus is discovered in his study with his books, he would quickly move out onto the stage to be better seen and heard. Thrones, banquets, beds, writing desks, and so on could be pushed through the curtains onto the stage, and as soon as a large property of this sort appeared, the audience would know at once that the action was taking place indoors. When the action shifted to the outdoors, the property could be pulled back behind the curtain.

" **M** odern audiences are learning to accept what Renaissance audiences took for granted: that the theater cannot show 'reality.' "

A

A. About the Illustration

The engraving provides an especially clear view of the inner or curtained place at the back of the stage, the gallery for actors or musicians above this curtained alcove, and the sitting and standing space for the audience, which surrounded the stage. If students can imagine that the three tiers of balconies are like three tiers of rooms overlooking an innyard, they'll see the Globe's relationship to the inns of the day. (Today, many hotels are built around a similar open area called an atrium.)

Scenery

The people in the audience were quite prepared to use their imagination. When they saw actors carrying lanterns, they knew it was night, even though the sun was shining brightly overhead. Often, instead of seeing a scene, they heard it described, as when a character exclaims,

> But look, the morn in russet mantle clad
> Walks o'er the dew of yon high eastward hill.
>
> —from *Hamlet*,
> Act I, Scene 1

Shakespeare could not show a sunrise; instead of trying to, he wrote a speech inviting the audience to imagine one. When the stage had to become a forest, as in several of Shakespeare's comedies, there was no painted scenery trying (and usually failing) to look like real trees, bushes, flowers, and so on. Instead, a few bushes and small trees might be pushed onto the stage, and then the actors created the rest of the scenery by speaking poetry that

Reconstruction of the second Globe Theater. Engraving.

A

evoked images in the spectators' minds. In *As You Like It,* Rosalind simply looks around her and announces "Well, this is the Forest of Arden."

The great advantage of this theater was its speed and flexibility. The stage could be anywhere, and the play did not have to be interrupted while the sets were shifted. By listening to what was being said, the audience learned all that they needed to know about where the action was taking place at any given moment; they did not need to consult a printed program.

Act and Scene Divisions

Most of the act and scene divisions in Renaissance drama have been added by later editors, who have tried to adapt plays written for the old platform stage to the modern picture-frame stage. In this process, editors have badly damaged one play in particular, Shakespeare's *Antony and Cleopatra.* This play was published and republished for a hundred years after Shakespeare's death without any act and scene divisions at all. Then one editor cut it up into twenty-seven different scenes, and another into forty-four, thus better suiting the play to the picture-frame stage, or so they thought. But a stage manager would go mad trying to provide realistic scenery for this many different locales. Even a reader becomes confused and irritated trying to imagine all the different places where the characters are going according to the modern stage directions, which are of a kind that Shakespeare and his contemporaries never heard of. "Theirs was a drama of persons, not a drama of places," according to Gerald Bentley, one of our best theatrical historians.

Props and Effects

Some modern accounts have overemphasized the bareness of Renaissance theaters; actually, they were ornate rather than bare. Their interiors were painted brightly, there were many decorations, and the space at the rear of the stage could be covered with colorful tapestries or hangings. Costumes were rich, elaborate, and expensive. The manager-producer Philip Henslowe, whose account books preserve much important information about the early theater, once paid twenty pounds, then an enormous sum, for a single cloak for one of his actors to wear in a play. Henslowe's lists of theatrical properties mention, among other things, chariots, fountains, dragons, beds, tents, thrones, booths, wayside crosses. The audience enjoyed the processions—religious, royal, military—that occur in many plays. These would enter the stage from one door, pass over the stage, and then exit by the other door. A few quick costume changes in the tiring house, as the actors passed through, could double and triple the number of people in a procession. Pagentry, sound effects, music both vocal and instrumental—all these elements helped give the audience their money's worth of theatrical experience.

Torch-bearer as Oceania by Inigo Jones (1605). Watercolor.

Victoria and Albert Museum, London.

A. About the Illustration
See the annotation on Inigo Jones and the masque, text page 182. An Oceanid (ō·sē′ă·nĭd) was one of three thousand ocean nymphs in Greek mythology, daughters of Oceanus and Tethys. In Renaissance England, the queen of the sea was also called Oceania, and stood symbolically for Elizabeth.

B. Sound Effects
Like Shakespeare's other plays, *Macbeth* demands musical flourishes, trumpets, drums, "alarums" (clamor and martial sounds—clanking swords, galloping hoofs, shouting voices), cannons, and thunder. Available musical instruments included viols and virginals, the recorder (a flute-like instrument), the cornet (a trumpet-sounding cylinder of ivory or wood with finger holes like a recorder), the sackbut (trombone), and a double-reed instrument called the hautboy (hō′boi, ō′boi) or oboe.

READING CHECK TEST
(The Renaissance Theater)
1. Who built the first public theater in England—the Theater? (James Burbage)
2. In what theater were many of Shakespeare's plays first performed? (The Globe)
3. Why was Shakespeare's theater described as a "wooden O"? (It was probably a 16-sided polygon that looked circular.)
4. What was the "tiring house"? (A room that held stage machinery and dressing rooms)
5. What was the main use of the small curtained area at the back of the stage? (To "discover" hidden things or people)

A. About the Illustration
The drawing shows the movable booth stages used in innyards, halls, or bear-baiting arenas.

B. Indoor Acting
Many plays were performed at court by royal command, and the rewards in money and prestige were great. As noted on text page 249, Shakespeare may have written *The Merry Wives of Windsor* at the command of Queen Elizabeth, and he clearly wrote *Macbeth* with the Scottish interests of James I in mind.

C. Blackfriars
Burbage had earlier acquired the right to lease Blackfriars Hall (in a former Dominican priory); but moneyed neighbors refused to accept adult actors in their midst, so the hall was leased to a company of boy actors. By 1608 Shakespeare had a coat of arms and his company had acquired considerable status; the Council was happy to turn Blackfriars over to the now respectable adult professionals.

A

Stage in an Amphitheater (c. 1576). Reconstruction drawing by C. Walter Hodges.

Private Halls and Indoor Theaters

B

These, then, were the chief features of the public theaters that Renaissance dramatists had to keep in mind as they wrote their plays. In addition to these theaters, the acting companies also performed in two other kinds of spaces: in the great halls of castles and manor houses, and in certain indoor theaters in London (which are called indoor theaters to distinguish them from theaters like the Globe, which were only partly roofed over).

For performances in a great hall, a theater company must have had a portable booth stage, like the one shown here in the drawing of an amphitheater, a building where the usual entertainment was a bear being attacked by dogs. The bear pits were vile places, but the temporary stages set up in them could easily accommodate any play written for the public theater except for scenes requiring the use of Heavens overhanging the stage.

C

Something like this booth stage may also have been used in the private theaters like the Blackfriars, which Shakespeare's company, the King's Men, acquired in 1608. Although nothing is known about the physical features of the Blackfriars stage, we know that the building itself—a disused monastery—was entirely roofed over, unlike the Globe, where only part of the stage and part of the audience had the protection of a roof. One great advantage of Blackfriars was that the company could perform there in cold weather and, since artificial lighting always had to be used, at night. And so the King's Men could put on plays all during the year, with increased profits for the shareholders, among them Shakespeare.

PREPARATION
BUILDING ON PRIOR KNOWLEDGE/
ESTABLISHING A PURPOSE.   You may wish
to begin with a brainstorming session,
assigning two or three "scribes" to the
chalkboard. Ask for all phrases or generalizations the name "William Shakespeare" brings to mind (e.g., Anne Hathaway, Stratford, names of famous plays,
some famous lines, etc.). Then assign

students to read the biography and to
take notes on details the list on the
chalkboard omits or misrepresents. Follow the next day with a discussion that
supplements the students' notes as
necessary.

SUPPLEMENTARY SUPPORT MATERIALS
Test on Shakespeare Introduction
(CCB)

William Shakespeare (1564–1616)

Every literate person has heard of Shakespeare, the author of more than three dozen remarkable plays and more than 150 poems. Over the centuries, these literary works have made such a deep impression on the human race that all sorts of fancies, legends, and theories have been invented about their author. There are even those who say that somebody other than Shakespeare wrote the works that bear his name, although these deluded people cannot agree on who, among a dozen candidates, this other author actually was. Such speculation is based on the wrong assumption that little is known about Shakespeare's life; in fact, Shakespeare's life is better documented than the life of any other dramatist of the time except perhaps for Ben Jonson, a writer who seems almost modern in the way he publicized himself. Jonson was an honest, blunt, and outspoken man who knew Shakespeare well; for a time the two dramatists wrote for the same theatrical company, and Shakespeare even acted in Jonson's plays. Often niggardly in his judgments of other writers, Jonson published a poem praising Shakespeare, asserting that he was superior to all Greek, Roman, and English dramatists, and predicting that he would be "not of an age, but for all time." Jonson's judgment is now commonly accepted, and his prophecy has come true.

Shakespeare was born in Stratford-on-Avon, a historic and prosperous market town in Warwickshire, and was christened in the parish church there on April 26, 1564. His father was John Shakespeare, a merchant at one time active in the town government; his mother—born Mary Arden—came from a prominent family in the county. For seven years or so, William attended the Stratford Grammar School, where he obtained an excellent education in Latin, the Bible, and English composition. (The students had to write out English translations of Latin works and then turn them back into Latin.) After leaving school, he may have been apprenticed to a butcher, but because he shows in his plays very detailed knowledge of many different crafts and trades, speculators have proposed a number of

Flower Portrait of William Shakespeare, Anon. Oil.

Royal Shakespeare Theater, London.

different occupations that he could have followed. At eighteen, Shakespeare married Anne Hathaway, the twenty-seven-year-old daughter of a farmer living near Stratford. They had three children, a daughter named Susanna and a pair of twins named Hamnet and Judith. We don't know how the young Shakespeare supported his family, but according to tradition he taught school for a few years. The two daughters grew up and married; the son died when he was eleven.

How did Shakespeare first become interested in the theater? Presumably, by seeing plays. We know that traveling acting companies frequently visited Stratford, and we assume that he attended their performances and that he also went to the nearby city of Coventry where a famous cycle of religious plays was put on every year. But to be a dramatist, one had to be in London, where the theater was flourishing in the 1580's. Just when Shakespeare left his family and

A. About the Portrait

This "Flower" portrait (1609) might be the only surviving painting done of Shakespeare during his lifetime. (Mrs. Charles Flower donated it to the Shakespeare Memorial in the late nineteenth century.) The most widely reproduced of all pictures of Shakespeare has been the engraving on the title page of the First Folio, done by the London-born Flemish engraver Martin Droeshout in 1623. Another portrait with an old but now challenged claim to authenticity is the expertly executed Chandros oil. Like the Flower portrait, it shows a man with receding (though blacker) hair, but it adds a gold earring in the left ear and a beard. The church at Stratford contains a painted limestone bust of Shakespeare, possibly based on a death mask. The bust has been in place since 1623.

A. Greene's Attack

Here is Greene's full warning to his educated friends who wrote for the theater. (The italicized phrase is an allusion to lines from Shakespeare's *Henry VI.*) "There is an upstart crow, beautified with our feathers, that with his *tiger's heart wrapped in a player's hide* supposes he is as well able to bombast out a blank verse as the best of you, and being an absolute Johannes-factotem is in his own conceit the only Shake-scene in a country." Greene, a university graduate, was attacking a nonuniversity man, an actor who dared to write plays. The crow was often used as a symbol of a writer who pilfered from others. In *Pandosto* (1588), Greene provided a plot that Shakespeare developed more fully in *The Winter's Tale* (1610–1611).

Discuss the meaning of the caricature below in relation to the meanings of *conceit* (*conceipte*)—"idea," "fanciful metaphor," "excessive self-appreciation." Greene appears to be wrapped in a sack or blanket: wrapped in his own conceit.

B. Shakespeare's Poetry

During the plague of 1592–1594, when theaters were closed, Shakespeare's income probably came from his patron, for two verse narratives. The immensely popular *Venus and Adonis* (1593) went through six editions in nine years. Based on Ovid, it deals with Adonis's rejection of the goddess of love, his death, and the resultant disappearance of beauty from the world. Shakespeare's more conservative contemporaries objected to the poem's sensuality, however, and it may have been in response to this criticism that he wrote *The Rape of Lucrece* (1594), which praises the chaste Roman matron Lucretia.

Though Shakespeare was ranked as a top dramatist even in his own day, both he and his world expected enduring fame to come from his poems, not from his plays. Besides verse narratives and songs, Shakespeare wrote some 154 sonnets (see text page 338).

Greene in Conceipte. Caricature.

Folger Shakespeare Library.

A

moved to London (there is no evidence that his wife was ever in the city) is uncertain; scholars say that he arrived there in 1587 or 1588. It is certain that he was busy and successful in the London theater by 1592, when a fellow dramatist named Robert Greene attacked him in print and ridiculed a passage in his early play *Henry VI.* Greene, a down-and-out Cambridge graduate, warned other university men then writing plays to beware of this "upstart crow beautified with our feathers." Greene died of dissipation just as his ill-natured attack was being published, but a friend of his named Henry Chettle immediately apologized in print to Shakespeare and commended Shakespeare's acting and writing ability, and his personal honesty.

From 1592 on there is ample documentation of Shakespeare's life and works. We know where he lived in London, at least approximately when his plays were produced and printed, and even how he spent his money. From 1594 to his retirement about 1613 he was continuously a member of one company, which also included the great tragic actor Richard Burbage and the popular clown Will Kemp. Although actors and others connected with the theater had a very low status legally, in practice they enjoyed the patronage of noblemen and even royalty. It is a mistake to think of Shakespeare as an ob-

scure actor who somehow wrote great plays; he was well known even as a young man. He first became famous as the author of a best-seller, an erotic narrative poem called *Venus and Adonis* (1593). This poem, as well as a more serious one entitled *Lucrece* (1594), was dedicated to a rich and extravagant young nobleman, the Earl of Southampton. The dedication of *Lucrece* suggests that Shakespeare and his patron were on very friendly terms.

B

Shakespeare's Early Plays

Among Shakespeare's earliest plays are the following, with the generally but not universally accepted dates of their first performance: *Richard III* (1592–1593), a "chronicle" or history play about a deformed usurper who became king of England; *The Comedy of Errors* (1592–1593), a rowdy farce of mistaken identity based on a Latin play; *Titus Andronicus* (1593–1594), a blood-and-thunder tragedy full of rant and atrocities; *The Taming of the Shrew, The Two Gentlemen of Verona,* and *Love's Labor's Lost* (all 1593–1595), three agreeable comedies; and *Romeo and Juliet* (1594–1595), a poetic tragedy of ill-fated lovers. The extraordinary thing about these plays is not so much their immense variety—each one is quite different from all the others—but the fact that they are all regularly revived and performed on stages all over the world today.

By 1596 Shakespeare was beginning to prosper. He had his father apply to the Heralds' College for a coat of arms that the family could display, signifying that they were "gentlefolks." On Shakespeare's family crest a falcon is shown, shaking a spear. To support this claim to gentility, Shakespeare bought New Place, a handsome house and grounds in Stratford, a place so commodious and elegant that the Queen of England once stayed there after Shakespeare's daughter Susanna inherited it. Shakespeare also, in 1599, joined with a few other members of his company, now called the Lord Chamberlain's Men, to finance a new theater on the south side of the Thames—the famous Globe. The "honey-tongued Shakespeare," as he was called in a book about English literature published in 1598, was now earning money as a playwright, an actor, and a shareholder in a theater. By 1600 Shakespeare was regularly associating with members of the aristocracy, and six of his plays

The French painter Eugène Delacroix (1798–1863) and the English J. M. W. Turner were great nineteenth-century Romantic painters. Delacroix was a brilliant colorist whose later innovations anticipated Impressionism. Shown here is a scene from *Hamlet*. Hamlet (in black) and his friend Horatio have come upon men digging a grave for the drowned Ophelia. Here one of the diggers holds up a skull he has just unearthed; it is the skull of Yorick, the king's jester. Hamlet is about to say the famous speech starting, "Alas, poor Yorick! I knew him, Horatio . . . ."

A

Hamlet and Horatio by Eugene Delacroix. Oil.

Louvre, Paris.

had been given command performances at the court of Queen Elizabeth.

During the last years of Elizabeth I's reign Shakespeare completed his cycle of plays about England during the Wars of the Roses: *Richard II* (1595–1596), both parts of *Henry IV* (1597–1598), and *Henry V* (1599–1600). Also in this period he wrote the play most frequently studied in schools—*Julius Caesar* (1599–1600)—and the comedies that are most frequently performed today: *A Midsummer Night's Dream* (1595–1596), *The Merchant of Venice* (1596–1597), *Much Ado About Nothing* (1598–1599), *As You Like It* and *Twelfth Night* (1599–1600). And finally at this time he wrote or rewrote *Hamlet* (1600–1601), the tragedy that, of all his tragedies, has provoked the most varied and controversial interpretations from critics, scholars, and actors.

Shakespeare indeed prospered under Queen Elizabeth; according to an old tradition, she asked him to write *The Merry Wives of Windsor* (1600–1601) because she wanted to see the merry, fat old knight Sir John Falstaff (of the "Henry plays") in love.

He prospered even more under Elizabeth's successor, King James of Scotland. Fortunately for Shakespeare's company, as it turned out, James's royal entry into London in 1603 had to be postponed for several months because the plague was raging in the city. While waiting for the epidemic to subside, the royal court stayed in various palaces outside London. Shakespeare's company took advantage of this situation and, since the city theaters were closed, performed several plays for the court and the new king. Shakespeare's plays delighted James, for he loved literature and was starved for pleasure after the grim experience of ruling Scotland for many years. He immediately took the company under his patronage, renamed them the King's Men, gave them patents to perform anywhere in the realm, provided them with special clothing for state occasions, increased their salaries, and appointed their chief members, including Shakespeare, to be Grooms of the Royal Chamber. All this patronage brought such prosperity to Shakespeare that he was able to make some very profitable real estate investments in Stratford and London.

B

Shakespeare's signature from his will at Somerset House, London.

Shakespeare's "Tragic Period"

In the early years of the seventeenth century, while his financial affairs were flourishing and everything was apparently going very well for Shakespeare, he wrote his greatest tragedies: *Hamlet* (already mentioned), *Othello* (1604–

A. National Mood

Shakespeare's plays demonstrated box-office sensitivity by appealing to the national mood. The 1590's, ushered in by the Armada victory in 1588, were a time of elation and patriotic fervor. Shakespeare responded with youthfully optimistic comedies and with nationalistic histories. An affirmation of both life and national spirit shine through a speech he wrote for John of Gaunt in *Richard II* (1595–1596): "This other Eden, demiparadise, / This fortress built by Nature for herself / Against infection and the hand of war, / This happy breed of men, this little world, / This precious stone set in the silver sea. . . ."

But as 1600 neared, the mood of the country darkened. The queen was nearly seventy and childless; Ireland had inflicted a humiliating defeat on the English in the Ulster wars, which threatened to undo the whole Anglicization of Ireland; and religious strife was in the air. After 1600, Shakespeare wrote comedies and tragedies that never lose sight of the existence of evil.

B. About the Photograph

Hewlett Farm, now known as Anne Hathaway's Cottage, was really her father's house. When she married Will Shakespeare, Anne was living there with her widowed stepmother (her father's second wife), three half brothers, and a sister-in-law. The twenty-six-year-old Anne married the eighteen-year-old Will on November 28, 1582, and the couple most likely moved into Will's father's house on Henley Street. Shakespeare's mother probably welcomed Anne's help with her own youngest children. Will and Anne's daughter Susanna was born in May 1583 and their twins Hamnet and Judith in February 1585. It was not until May 1597 that Shakespeare could buy New Place, his own Stratford estate and the second-largest house in town.

1605), *King Lear* (1605–1606), *Macbeth* (1605–1606), and *Antony and Cleopatra* (1606–1607). Because these famous plays are so preoccupied with evil, violence, and death, some people feel that Shakespeare must have been very unhappy and depressed when he wrote them. Moveover, such people find even the comedies he wrote at this time more sour than sweet: *Troilus and Cressida* (1601–1602), *All's Well That Ends Well* (1602–1603), and *Measure for Measure* (1604–1605). And so, instead of paying tribute to Shakespeare's powerful imagination, which is everywhere evident, these people invent a "tragic period" in Shakespeare's biography, and they search for personal crises in his private life. When they cannot find these agonies, they invent them. To be sure, in 1607 an actor named Edward Shakespeare, who may well have been William's younger brother, died in London. But by 1607 Shakespeare's alleged "tragic period" was almost over!

It is quite wrong to assume a one-to-one correspondence between writers' biographies and their works, because writers must be allowed to imagine whatever they can. It is especially wrong in the case of a writer like Shakespeare, who did not write to express himself but to satisfy the patrons of the theater that he and his partners owned. Shakespeare must have repeatedly given the audience just what it wanted; otherwise, he could not have made so much money out of the theater. To insist that he had to experience and feel personally everything that he wrote about is absurd. He wrote about King Lear, who cursed his two monstrous daughters for treating him very badly; in contrast, what evidence there is suggests that he got along very well with his own two daughters. And so, instead of "tragic" we should think of the years 1600–1607 as glorious, because in them Shakespeare's productivity was at its peak. It seems very doubtful that a depressed person would write plays like these. In fact, they would make their creator feel exhilarated rather than sad.

A

B

Anne Hathaway's Cottage.

A. Shakespeare's Will

Shakespeare's will, revised in 1616 (see the illustration on text page 249), is famous for the bequest to his wife of his "second-best bed." But since the best bed would probably have been reserved for the couple inheriting the house, this was less an insult than a way of indicating Anne's continued right to the room in which the bed stood. She had a position now as a dowager in the house taken over by her daughter Susanna and son-in-law Dr. John Hall. She also had, by common law, what was called a widow's dower (one third of the income from her husband's estate).

Shakespeare had four grandchildren. His last descendant was a granddaughter, who died in 1670. At that point New Place, the large house that he had bought in 1597, was taken over by someone outside the family.

The Last Years

In 1612 Shakespeare decided that, having made a considerable sum from his plays and theatrical enterprises, he would retire to his handsome house in Stratford, a place he had never forgotten, though he seems to have kept his life there rather separate from his life in London. His retirement was not complete, for the records show that after he returned to Stratford he still took part in the management of the King's Men and their two theaters: the Globe, an octagonal building opened in 1599 and used for performances in good weather, and the Blackfriars, acquired in 1608 and used for indoor performances. Shakespeare's works in this period show no signs of diminished creativity, except that in some years he wrote one play instead of the customary two, and they continue to illustrate the great diversity of his genius. Among them are the tragedies *Timon of Athens* (1607–1608) and *Coriolanus* (1607–1608) and five plays that have been variously classified as comedies, romances, or tragicomedies: *Pericles* (1608–1609), *Cymbeline* (1609–1610), *The Winter's Tale* (1610–1611), *The Tempest* (1611–1612), and *The Two Noble Kinsmen* (1612–1613). His last English history play, *Henry VIII* (1613), contained a tribute to Queen Elizabeth—a somewhat tardy tribute, because, unlike most of the other poets of the day, Shakespeare did not praise her in print when she died in 1603. (Some scholars argue, on very little evidence, that he was an admirer of the Earl of Essex, a former intimate of Elizabeth whom she had beheaded for rebelliousness.) During the first performance of *Henry VIII*, in June of 1613, the firing of the cannon at the end of Act I set the Globe on fire (it had a thatched roof), and it burned to the ground. Only one casualty is recorded: a bottle of ale had to be poured on a man whose breeches were burning. Fortunately, the company had the Blackfriars in which to perform until the Globe could be rebuilt and reopened in 1614.

Shakespeare's last recorded visit to London, accompanied by his son-in-law Dr. John Hall, was in November 1614, though he may have gone down to the city afterward because he continued to own property there, including a building very near the Blackfriars Theater. Probably, though, he spent most of the last two years of his life at New Place, with his daughter Susanna Hall (and his granddaughter Elizabeth) living nearby. He died on April 23, 1616, and was buried under the floor of Stratford Church, with this epitaph warning posterity not to dig him up and transfer him to the graveyard outside the church—a common practice in those days when space was needed:

> Good friend, for Jesus' sake forbear
> To dig the bones enclosèd here!
> Blest be the man that spares these stones,
> And curst be he that moves my bones.

Shakespeare's Genius

What sort of man was Shakespeare? This is a very hard question to answer because he left no letters, diaries, or other private writings containing his personal views; instead, he left us plays, and in a good play the actors do not speak for the dramatist but for the characters they are impersonating. We cannot, then, say that Shakespeare approved of evil because he created murderers, or advocated religion because he created clergymen; we cannot say that he believed in fatalism because he created fatalists, or admired flattery because he created flatterers. All these would be naive, and contradictory, reactions to the plays. Shakespeare's characters represent such a vast range of human behavior and attitudes that they must be products of his careful observation and fertile imagination rather than extensions of himself. A critic named Desmond McCarthy once said that trying to identify Shakespeare the man in his plays is like looking at a very dim portrait under glass: The more you peer at it, the more you see only yourself.

One thing is certain: Shakespeare was a complete man of the theater who created works specifically for his own acting company and his own stage. He had, for instance, to provide good parts in every play for the principal performers in the company, including the comedians acting in tragedies. Since there were no actresses, he had to limit the number of female parts in his plays and create them in such a way that they could readily be taken by boys. For instance, although there are many fathers in the plays, there are very few mothers: while boys could be taught to flirt and play shy, acting maternally would be difficult for them. Several of Shakespeare's young women disguise themselves as young men early in Act I—an easy solution to

B. Women's Roles

According to the Signet edition of Shakespeare's works, the old Nurse in *Romeo and Juliet* might have been played by a man. The use of only male actors might be traced back to drama's origins in church ritual. In the earliest times, women played no role at all in the church liturgy, so they would never have participated in the old miracle and morality plays. It will be hard for today's students to realize that up until the 1960's churches were thoroughly male-dominated, even the most liberal Protestant churches in the United States.

READING CHECK TEST
(William Shakespeare)

1. When and where was Shakespeare born? (April 26, 1564, in Stratford-on-Avon)

2. What education did he have? (Seven years of grammar school, where he studied Latin, the Bible, and English composition)

3. Name Shakespeare's acting company. (The King's Men)

4. Name one Shakespearean play from each of these categories: a tragedy, a comedy, a play about English history. (Examples will vary.)

5. Why were young women characters often disguised as men? (Boys played all women's roles.)

A. About the Engraving

The English actress Sarah Kemble Siddons (1775–1831) was one of the all-time great Shakespearean actresses. Asked to describe her performance as Lady Macbeth, one viewer said, "Well, sir, I smelt blood! I swear that I smelt blood."

B. Piracy of Plays

Acting companies (not the writers) owned the plays written for them. After the advent of printing, the problem of piracy mushroomed as the public and rival companies clamored for copies of popular plays. (Compare with the piracy of videos today.) England's first copyright act was passed in 1710.

C. Quartos and Folios

Each sheet in a *quarto* is folded twice, making four leaves (eight pages), 7" × 9". A *folio* is a volume consisting of sheets folded once, each sheet making four pages, 8½" × 13".

A

Sarah Siddons, an English actress (1785). Engraving.

Harry R. Beard collection, The Theatre Museum, Victoria and Albert Museum, London.

the problem of boys playing girls' parts. Shakespeare also had to provide the words for songs because theatergoers expected singing in every play; furthermore, the songs had to be devised so that they would exhibit the talents of particular actors with good voices. Since many of the plays contain many characters, and since there were a limited number of actors in the company, Shakespeare had to arrange for doubling and even tripling of roles: that is, a single actor would have to perform more than one part. Since, of course, an actor could impersonate only one character at a time, Shakespeare had to plan his scenes carefully, so that nobody would

ever have to be onstage in two different roles at the same time. A careful study of the plays shows that Shakespeare handled all these technical problems of dramaturgy very masterfully.

Although the plays are primarily performance scripts, from earliest times the public has wanted to read them as well as see them staged. In every generation, people have felt that the plays contain so much wisdom, so much knowledge of human nature, so much remarkable poetry that they need to be pondered in private as well as enjoyed in public. Most readers have agreed with what the poet John Dryden said about Shakespeare's "soul": The man who wrote the plays may be elusive, but he was obviously a great genius whose lofty imagination is matched by his sympathy for all kinds of human behavior. Reading the plays, then, is a rewarding experience in itself; it is also an excellent preparation for seeing them performed on stage or on film.

B Shakespeare's contemporaries were so eager to read his plays that enterprising publishers did everything possible, including stealing them, to make them available. Of course the company generally tried to keep the plays unpublished because they did not want them performed by rival companies. **C** Even so, eighteen plays were published in small books called quartos before Shakespeare's partners collected them together and published them after his death. This collection, known as the "first folio" because of its large size, was published in 1623. Surviving copies of this folio are regarded as valuable treasures today. But, of course, the general reader need not consult any of the original texts of Shakespeare because his works never go out of print; they are always available in many different languages and many different formats. The plays that exist in two different versions (one in a quarto and one in the folio) have provided scholars with endless matter for speculation about what Shakespeare actually intended the correct text to be. Indeed, every aspect of Shakespeare has been, and continues to be, thoroughly studied and written about, by literary and historical scholars, by theater and film people, by experts in many fields, and by amateurs of every stripe. No wonder that he is mistakenly regarded as a great mystery.

SUPPLEMENTARY SUPPORT MATERIALS
1. Vocabulary Activity Worksheet (*CCB*)
2. Review and Response Worksheets: Conflict; Imagery; Characterization; Elements of the Play (*CCB*)
3. Language Skills Worksheet: Revision Worksheet 2 (*CCB*)
4. Selection Test (*CCB*)
5. Audiocassette recording

acbeth, as everyone knows, is a tragedy: a kind of play in which human actions have their inevitable consequences, in which the characters' bad deeds, errors, mistakes, and crimes are never forgiven or rectified. The characters in a comedy do not live under this iron law of cause and effect; they can do whatever they please so long as they amuse their audience, and at the end of the play the funny mess they have made is easily cleaned up. But in tragedy, an ill-judged action will remorselessly lead to a catastrophe, usually but not necessarily a death or multiple deaths. In *Macbeth,* a brave and intelligent man deliberately murders one of his fellow men—his friend, his kinsman, his guest, his king—and then he must immediately, as a consequence of his first murder, kill two other innocent men. After that, he cannot turn back from his evil course: It leads him to further appalling crimes and finally to disgrace, alienation, isolation, despair, violent death, and decapitation.

The Sources of the Play

Macbeth conforms with the general rule that Renaissance tragedies had to be about real people, men and women whose deeds are recorded in history. Renaissance comedies, on the other hand, concerned the imaginary doings of fictitious characters. Shakespeare took the main events of Macbeth's career as King of Scotland (1040–1057) from Raphael Holinshed's *Chronicles of England, Scotland, and Ireland,* the book that provided him with historical material for many of his plays. But there are striking differences between his account of Macbeth and Holinshed's. The historical Macbeth had a much more legitimate claim to King Duncan's throne than the tragic Macbeth did; the historical Macbeth gained the throne with the help of other noblemen dissatisfied with King Duncan, and he ruled rather successfully. In contrast, Shakespeare's Macbeth has no supporters except his wife, whose strong and ambitious nature Shakespeare develops from a brief statement in the history. The King Duncan in the play whose murder they plot is a revered old man who reminds Lady Macbeth of her father; Holinshed, on the other hand, shows Duncan as younger and more ineffectual as a ruler. And the reign of Macbeth and his wife (she is always known as Lady Macbeth even after she becomes Queen) brings nothing but violence and disaster to Scotland in the play. Altogether, Shakespeare made many changes in the story because he was much more interested in psychological truth than in historical fact.

A

Macbeth

A. Background: Sources and Themes

Had Shakespeare so chosen, he could have used additional information from Holinshed's *Chronicles* to justify a blood-feud of long standing. Macbeth's father and Lady Macbeth's grandfather, brother, and first husband had been treacherously killed by King Duncan's predecessor, yet Macbeth served Duncan loyally. Moreover, the crown of Scotland in the eleventh century did not automatically go to the King's son, but was open to election. As the King's cousin and a great general, Macbeth could therefore have been elected king with no action on his part.

Politics did not, however, interest Shakespeare, and dwelling on these details can distract students from the psychological focus of the play—a play in which evil is almost a protagonist in its own right.

A. Discussing the Photograph

Critic Northrop Frye notes in his book *On Shakespeare* (1986) that some of the best Shakespearean productions have been done as movies. This 1971 Polanski film is described by film critic Leonard Maltin as a "gripping, atmospheric, and extremely violent re-creation" of Shakespeare's tragedy.

? Ask students to study the illustration as a thing in itself, apart from what they know about the play. What time period is suggested by the clothing of the characters? (Long ago, medieval times) What relationship seems to exist between this man and woman? (The man appears to be looking for an answer or reaction the woman does not want to give.) What is their mood? How old do they seem to be? (in their twenties)

1. BUILDING ON PRIOR KNOWLEDGE. Unfortunately, students are all too familiar with the unscrupulous efforts of some powerful people to get more power. They also know from news stories and from history that some people who seem moral and responsible can, under pressure, turn into criminals, even murderers. You might review some instances of deadly ambition and analyze with students the pressures or motives or weaknesses that might turn an ethical person into a criminal.

2. ESTABLISHING A PURPOSE. This opening act introduces the main characters and reveals their "wants." The play will be driven by the characters taking action to get what they want. Direct students to

THE TRAGEDY OF MACBETH

A

The illustrations on pages 254, 264, 267, 287, 292, 318 are from a 1971 film directed by Roman Polanski. Those on pages 259, 273, 276, 284, 295, 305, 325 are from the 1983 Stratford Festival in Canada.

look for the main characters and note their wants as this act unfolds.

If at all possible, play Scenes 1 and 2 on one of the available recordings of the play. Have students follow in their texts and listen for information on two men, Banquo and Macbeth. Discuss the students' responses, and then take the two scenes line by line, speech by speech, using the glosses and side questions to clarify meaning and interpretation of character.

3. PREREADING JOURNAL. Call students' attention to the fact that the witches equivocate—they speak in paradoxes or doubletalk: "When the battle's lost and won" and "Fair is foul, and foul is fair." Have students copy the latter line and, in three or four sentences, record their first impression of what the line might mean. (This motif of equivocation is found throughout the play.)

Plot Summary
Scene 1. Three witches plan to meet Macbeth later in the day on the heath, after the battle. Note that we hear about Macbeth before we see him on stage.

Answer to margin question
Line 2. Menace can be conveyed by demeanor: hunched, hulking movements and sidelong glances. The witches can also use their voices to convey a sense of menace: cackling and weird, "unnatural" pitch and tones.

A. Expansion
A bit of trivia you may wish to share is that the historical Lady Macbeth's first name, as reported in the 1909 British Isles edition of *The Dictionary of National Biography*, was Gruach. It's little wonder that Shakespeare, if he knew it, chose not to use her first name.

Characters

Duncan, King of Scotland
Malcolm }
Donalbain } his sons
Macbeth ⎫
Banquo
Macduff
Lennox
Ross } noblemen of Scotland
Menteith
Angus
Caithness ⎭
Fleance, son to Banquo
Siward, Earl of Northumberland, general of the English forces
Young Siward, his son
Seyton, an officer attending on Macbeth

Son to Macduff
An English Doctor
A Scottish Doctor
A Porter
An Old Man
Three Murderers
Lady Macbeth ⎤ **A**
Lady Macduff
A Gentlewoman attending on Lady Macbeth
Hecate
Witches
Apparitions
Lords, Officers, Soldiers, Attendants, Messengers

Scene: Scotland; England

Act I Scene 1. *An open place.*

Thunder and lightning. Enter three WITCHES.

First Witch.
    When shall we three meet again?
    In thunder, lightning, or in rain?
Second Witch.
    When the hurlyburly's done,
    When the battle's lost and won.
Third Witch.
5   That will be ere the set of sun.
First Witch.
    Where the place?
Second Witch.   Upon the heath.
Third Witch.
    There to meet with Macbeth.
First Witch.
    I come, Graymalkin.°
Second Witch.
    Paddock° calls.
Third Witch.   Anon!°
All.
10   Fair is foul, and foul is fair.
    Hover through the fog and filthy air.   [*Exeunt.*]

[Handwritten annotations: "Mood is dark / foul / mysterious"; "Paradox"; "Meet Macbeth Before sunset"; "Paradox"]

2. *This scene, played against thunder and lightning, sets the mood of the play. The witches might have made their appearance through the trapdoors on the stage. Thunder would have been produced by rolling cannon balls in the area above the stage. How could these actresses (actors in Shakespeare's day) convey a sense of menace?*

8. Graymalkin: the witches' attendant, a cat.

9. Paddock: toad. **Anon!:** Soon!

Macbeth, Act I, Scene 1   **255**

255

Plot Summary
Scene 2. A captain reports to the Scottish king that Macbeth has killed the traitor Macdonwald in a battle against the Norwegians. The Norwegians, faced with the fury of the Scottish captains Banquo and Macbeth, ask for peace terms. The king decides to give the Thane of Cawdor's title to Macbeth; he condemns the present Cawdor to death.

Answers to margin questions
Line 7. The captain gasps from weakness but speaks urgently to convey the bravery of Banquo and Macbeth.
Line 23. Macbeth slashed Macdonwald open from stomach to jaws, beheaded him, and stuck the head on a column.
Line 35. The line is usually spoken ironically. It could be spoken admiringly.

B. Vocabulary
"Sergeant" means an officer—the captain of this scene. It is pronounced with three syllables.

C. Simile
? Explain the captain's simile. (It compares the fighters to two weary, struggling swimmers clinging to each other in exhaustion.)

D. Personification
? What is fortune personified as? (As a prostitute, a woman who sells her favors. A rebel's whore would be a camp-follower.) Note that Fortune appeared to be favoring the rebel Macdonwald.

E. Character
? How is Macbeth described here? (As a tremendously brave soldier) Valor is personified as a person, perhaps a woman, and Macbeth is one of her favorites.

F. Character
Students should realize that "cousin" here is meant literally, since Macbeth is a relative of the king.

Exposition — sets up situation in country

Scene 2. *A camp.*

A *Alarum within.° Enter* KING DUNCAN, MALCOLM, DONALBAIN, LENNOX, *with* ATTENDANTS, *meeting a bleeding* CAPTAIN.

King.
What bloody man is that? He can <u>report</u>,
As seemeth by his plight, of the revolt
The newest state.

Eldest son

B **Malcolm.**   This is the sergeant
Who like a good and hardy soldier fought
5   'Gainst my captivity. Hail, brave friend!
Say to the king the knowledge of the broil°
As thou didst leave it.

C **Captain.**   Doubtful it stood,
As two spent swimmers that do cling together
And choke their art.° The merciless <u>Macdonwald</u>—
10   Worthy to be a rebel for to that
The multiplying villainies of nature
Do swarm upon him—from the Western Isles°
Of kerns and gallowglasses° is supplied;

D And Fortune, on his damnèd quarrel smiling,
15   Showed like a rebel's whore: but all's too weak:
For brave Macbeth—well he deserves that name—

E Disdaining Fortune, with his brandished steel,
Which smoked with bloody execution,
Like valor's minion° carved out his passage
20   Till he faced the slave;
Which nev'r shook hands, nor bade farewell to him,
Till he <u>unseamed him from the nave to th' chops,°</u>
And fixed his head upon our battlements.

King.
F O valiant <u>cousin</u>! Worthy gentleman!
Captain.
25   As whence the sun 'gins his reflection°
Shipwracking storms and direful thunders break,
So from that spring whence comfort seemed to come
Discomfort swells. Mark, King of Scotland, mark:
No sooner justice had, with valor armed,
30   Compelled these skipping kerns to trust their heels
But the <u>Norweyan°</u> lord, surveying vantage
With furbished arms and new supplies of men,
Began a fresh assault.
King.   Dismayed not this
Our captains, <u>Macbeth and Banquo</u>?
Captain.   Yes;
35   As° sparrows eagles, or the hare the lion.
If I say sooth,° I must report they were
As cannons overcharged with double cracks;
So they <u>doubly</u> redoubled strokes upon the foe.
Except° they meant to bathe in reeking wounds,
40   Or memorize another Golgotha,°

Right margin printed notes:

Alarum within: trumpets offstage.

6. **broil:** quarrel.

? 7. *The captain is bloody and could be carried in or supported by others. How would he speak his lines?*
9. **choke their art:** hinder each other's ability to swim.

12. **Western Isles:** the Hebrides, off the Northwest coast of Scotland, and Ireland.

13. **kerns and gallowglasses:** lightly armed Irish soldiers and heavily armed soldiers.

19. **valor's minion:** valor's favorite.

22. **unseamed . . . chops:** split him from navel to jaws.
? 23. *Notice how this horrible action is described by a messenger, not shown on stage. What did Macbeth do to the rebellious Macdonwald?*
25. **'gins his reflection:** rises.

31. **Norweyan:** Norwegian.

35. **As:** No more than.
? 35. *This line can be delivered in several ways. How do you imagine the captain speaks it?*
36. **sooth:** truth.
39. **Except:** unless.
40. **memorize another Golgotha:** make the place as memorable as Golgotha, where Christ was crucified.

Handwritten margin annotations: report offstage action; Plays / Opens w/ blood imagery; Give report; rebel; Macbeth kills Macdonwald; relative of King; sunrise; Norwegian assault; Macbeth + Banquo redoubled their effort

Plot Summary
Scene 3. Macbeth and Banquo meet the three witches, who make three predictions: They call Macbeth Thane of Cawdor, they say Macbeth will be king, they say Banquo will beget kings but be none. Ross and Angus tell Macbeth he has in fact been made Thane of Cawdor. Macbeth takes the witches' prophecies seriously and has disturbing thoughts.

Answers to margin questions
Line 44. Answers will vary. Most will come to see Duncan as naive at reading character. Encourage students to think of alternate interpretations, justified by the text.
Line 67. He has given Macbeth the second title by which the witches hailed him. Duncan would probably sound delighted at the fine thing he is doing for Macbeth.

He could also say the line sadly and convey a sense of dramatic irony to the audience.

I cannot tell—
But I am faint; my gashes cry for help.
King.
So well thy words become thee as thy wounds;
They smack of honor both. Go get him surgeons.

                        [*Exit* CAPTAIN, *attended.*]

[*Enter* ROSS *and* ANGUS.]

A
   Who comes here?
45 **Malcolm.**   The Worthy Thane° of Ross.
Lennox.
What a haste looks through his eyes! So should he look
That seems to° speak things strange.
Ross.   God save the king!
King.
Whence cam'st thou, worthy thane?
Ross.   From Fife, great king;
Where the Norweyan banners flout the sky
50 And fan our people cold.
Norway himself,° with terrible numbers,
Assisted by that most disloyal traitor
B
The Thane of Cawdor, began a dismal conflict;
Till that Bellona's bridegroom,° lapped in proof,°
55 Confronted him with self-comparisons,°
Point against point, rebellious arm 'gainst arm,
Curbing his lavish° spirit: and, to conclude,
The victory fell on us.
King.   Great happiness!
Ross.   That now
Sweno, the Norway's king, craves composition;°
60 Nor would we deign him burial of his men
Till he disbursèd, at Saint Colme's Inch,°
Ten thousand dollars to our general use.
King.
No more that Thane of Cawdor shall deceive
Our bosom interest:° go pronounce his present° death,
65 And with his former title greet Macbeth.
Ross.
I'll see it done.
King.
C
What he hath lost, noble Macbeth hath won. [*Exeunt.*]

Scene 3. *A heath.*

Thunder. Enter the three WITCHES.

First Witch.
Where hast thou been, sister?
Second Witch.
Killing swine.

(margin annotations, handwritten:)
Sergeant is wounded
Blood imagery
Macbeth wins
truce
irony foreshadows
Impression of Macbeth thus far?

(margin questions and glosses:)

? **44.** *Duncan can be played in several ways: as a strong but aging king; as a frail old man; as a kind of foolish old man who doesn't understand what's going on. As the play goes on, decide how you interpret Duncan's character.*

45. Thane: Scottish title of nobility.

47. seems to: seems about to.

51. Norway himself: that is, the King of Norway.

54. Bellona's bridegroom: Bellona is the goddess of war. **lapped in proof:** clad in armor.
55. self-comparisons: countermovements.
57. lavish: insolent, rude.

59. composition: peace terms.

61. Saint Colme's Inch: island off the coast of Scotland.

64. bosom interest: heart's trust. **present:** immediate.

? **67.** *How has the king fulfilled part of the witches' prophecy, though he is unaware of it? How would you have him say these lines?*

A. The Title "Thane"
A thane was a Scottish feudal lord who held specific lands granted by the monarch and, in return, performed military service for the monarch.

B. Characterization
Note that the epithet "Bellona's bridegroom" further establishes Macbeth's military prowess.

C. Responding to Scenes 1 and 2
Pause at the end of Scene 2 to discuss response questions 1–4 and 10 on text pages 270–271. Then, if you have a recording, play it again, with students again following in the text.
   Students should now be able to read Scenes 3–7 as homework (through page 270). Have students read primarily for plot ("what happens") and for characterization. It will help if they write two- to three-sentence summaries of each scene for their own notes. Discuss students' summaries before listening to and analyzing Scenes 3–7 in class on the next day(s).

Answer to margin question
Line 38. Macbeth echoes the witches'
"Fair is foul, and foul is fair" (Scene 1,
line 10). Victory makes the day "fair."

A. The Witches
Lines 24–25 suggest limitations to the witches' powers: They can make a man's life miserable, but his life remains his own. Sylvan Barnet in the Signet Shakespeare suggests that the witches might show us that the play is set in a world in which "inhuman and inscrutable forces operate." This might signify that Macbeth is a tragic victim of mysterious forces well out of his control. (See the comment on text page 334.)

B. Interpreting
Weird derives from the Old English word *wyrd*, meaning "fate" or "destiny" (see page 6).
❓ What might this information add to your interpretation of the witches' influence over Macbeth? (They cast a spell giving them control of his destiny and depriving him of his own free will.)

Third Witch.
Sister, where thou?
First Witch.
A sailor's wife had chestnuts in her lap,
And mounched, and mounched, and mounched. "Give
5   me," quoth I.
"Aroint thee,° witch!" the rump-fed ronyon° cries.
Her husband's to Aleppo gone, master o' th' *Tiger:*
But in a sieve° I'll thither sail,
And, like a rat without a tail,
10   I'll do, I'll do, and I'll do.
Second Witch.
I'll give thee a wind.
First Witch.
Th' art kind.
Third Witch.
And I another.
First Witch.
I myself have all the other;
15   And the very ports they blow,°
All the quarters they know
I' th' shipman's card.°
I'll drain him dry as hay:
Sleep shall neither night nor day
20   Hang upon his penthouse lid;°
He shall live a man forbid:°
Weary sev'nights nine times nine
Shall he dwindle, peak,° and pine:
A ⌈ Though his bark cannot be lost,
25 ⌊ Yet it shall be tempest-tossed.
Look what I have.
Second Witch.
Show me, show me.
First Witch.
Here I have a pilot's thumb,
Wracked as homeward he did come.

[*Drum within.*]

Third Witch.
30   A drum, a drum!
Macbeth doth come.
All.
B ⌈ The weird sisters, hand in hand,
⌊ Posters° of the sea and land,
Thus do go about, about:
35   Thrice to thine, and thrice to mine,
And thrice again, to make up nine.
Peace! The charm's wound up.

[*Enter* MACBETH *and* BANQUO.]

Macbeth.
So foul and fair a day I have not seen.

6. **Aroint thee:** begone. **rump-fed ronyon:** fat-rumped, scabby creature.

8. Witches were believed to have the power to sail in sieves.

15. **ports they blow:** harbors they blow into.

17. **card:** compass.

20. **penthouse lid:** eyelid.
21. **forbid:** cursed.

23. **peak:** grow pale.

33. **Posters:** travelers.

❓ **38.** *What words is Macbeth echoing here? Why, given the weather, does Macbeth think the day is "fair"?*

A. Discussing the Photograph

No seventeenth-century person would have been able to dismiss the words of strange old women met on a lonely heath. This terror in the face of witchcraft is hard to convey to modern audiences, who sometimes laugh at the "weird sisters'" scenes in *Macbeth.* Modern directors have staged the witches' scenes and costumed them in many different ways.

In some productions the witches even (over) act like the baccantes in a Greek play—frenzied women drunk on Dionysian wine. How do you think a director should present the witches? (Answers will vary but may include creatures not entirely of this world.) In this photograph, what do you like or dislike about the casting and staging of the witches? (Answers will vary.) Are they true to details in the speeches? (The literal details are not as important as the overall impression the witches make.) What does the bluish background add to the atmosphere? (It adds to the mystery since the sky is light although it is night.) What could the animal head be for? Note the middle sister's left hand. (For some ritual they have already completed since one sister's hand is bloody)

A

"All hail, Macbeth! Hail to thee, Thane of Glamis!"

Banquo.

      How far is't called to Forres?° What are these

40   So withered, and so wild in their attire,

      That look not like th' inhabitants o' th' earth,

      And yet are on't? Live you, or are you aught

      That man may question? You seem to understand me,

      By each at once her choppy° fingers laying

45   Upon her skinny lips. You should° be women,

      And yet your beards forbid me to interpret

      That you are so.

39. Forres: a town in northeast Scotland, site of King Duncan's castle.

40. *What should Banquo do as he sees the witches? How should his voice change between the words* Forres *and* What?

44. choppy: chapped, sore.

45. should: must.

Macbeth, Act I, Scene 3 **259**

Line 51. Macbeth is startled and stares fearfully at the witches. In "Are ye fantastical," Banquo addresses the witches.
Line 61. Banquo asks the witches to foretell his future too, if they can.
Line 71. Macbeth is puzzled; eagerness and excitement may be creeping into his voice.
Stage direction. Banquo is more intrigued than disturbed. Macbeth is wildly curious to hear more.

A. Predicting Outcomes

What do you think this first prophecy could mean? (Macbeth will be king.)

B. Predicting Outcomes

Predict all the different situations that could fulfill these paradoxical prophecies. (Macbeth will have power but Banquo will be happier and his descendants will be kings.)

C. Interpreting

What do we know that Macbeth does not? (Duncan has ordered Cawdor's execution and given his title to Macbeth.) What does this speech reveal about Macbeth's ambition to be king at this point in the play? (He isn't thinking of it.)

D. Imagery and Mood

How does this image (of mineral or sulphur hot springs) contribute to the mood of the play? (It suggests mysterious forces at work; it might also suggest foulness, since sulphur has a strong, unpleasant odor.)

Macbeth.   Speak, if you can: what are you?
First Witch.
   All hail, Macbeth! Hail to thee, Thane of Glamis!
Second Witch.
   All hail, Macbeth! Hail to thee, Thane of Cawdor!
Third Witch.
50   All hail, Macbeth, that shalt be king hereafter!
Banquo.
   Good sir, why do you start, and seem to fear
   Things that do sound so fair? I' th' name of truth,
   Are ye fantastical, or that indeed
   Which outwardly ye show? My noble partner
55   You greet with present grace and great prediction
   Of noble having and of royal hope,
   That he seems rapt withal: to me you speak not.
   If you can look into the seeds of time,
   And say which grain will grow and which will not,
60   Speak then to me, who neither beg nor fear
   Your favors nor your hate.
First Witch. Hail!
Second Witch. Hail!
Third Witch. Hail!
First Witch.
65   Lesser than Macbeth, and greater.
Second Witch.
   Not so happy,° yet much happier.
Third Witch.
   Thou shalt get° kings, though thou be none.
   So all hail, Macbeth and Banquo!
First Witch.
   Banquo and Macbeth, all hail!
Macbeth.
70   Stay, you imperfect° speakers, tell me more:
   By Sinel's death I know I am Thane of Glamis;
   But how of Cawdor? The Thane of Cawdor lives,
   A prosperous gentleman; and to be king
   Stands not within the prospect of belief,
75   No more than to be Cawdor. Say from whence
   You owe this strange intelligence? Or why
   Upon this blasted heath you stop our way
   With such prophetic greeting? Speak, I charge you.

                    [WITCHES *vanish*.]

Banquo.
   The earth hath bubbles as the water has,
80   And these are of them. Whither are they vanished?
Macbeth.
   Into the air, and what seemed corporal° melted
   As breath into the wind. Would they had stayed!

---

51. *Banquo's words give a clue as to how Macbeth reacts to the witches. What is he doing? When Banquo asks, "Are ye fantastical," whom is he addressing?*

61. *What does Banquo ask the witches?*

66. happy: lucky.

67. get: beget.

70. imperfect: incomplete.
71. *Sinel is Macbeth's father. What do you think his tone is here? Is he over-eager? Or just casually curious?*

Stage direction. *The witches on Shakespeare's stage would have vanished through the trapdoor. Is Banquo, in his next speech, intrigued or disturbed? How does Macbeth feel?*

81. corporal: corporeal (bodily, physical).

Banquo.
Were such things here as we do speak about?
Or have we eaten on the insane root°
85 That takes the reason prisoner?
A **Macbeth.**
Your children shall be kings.
Banquo.   You shall be king.
Macbeth.
And Thane of Cawdor too. Went it not so?
Banquo.
To th' selfsame tune and words. Who's here?

[*Enter* ROSS *and* ANGUS.]

Ross.
The king hath happily received, Macbeth,
90 The news of thy success; and when he reads°
Thy personal venture in the rebels' fight,
His wonders and his praises do contend
Which should be thine or his. Silenced with that,
In viewing o'er the rest o' th' selfsame day,
95 He finds thee in the stout Norweyan ranks,
Nothing afeard of what thyself didst make,
Strange images of death.° As thick as tale
Came post with post,° and every one did bear
Thy praises in his kingdom's great defense,
And poured them down before him.
100 **Angus.**   We are sent
To give thee, from our royal master, thanks;
Only to herald thee into his sight,
Not pay thee.
Ross.
And for an earnest° of a greater honor,
105 He bade me, from him, call thee Thane of Cawdor;
In which addition,° hail, most worthy thane!
For it is thine.
Banquo.   What, can the devil speak true?
Macbeth.
B The Thane of Cawdor lives: why do you dress me
In borrowed robes?
Angus.   Who was the thane lives yet,
110 But under heavy judgment bears that life
Which he deserves to lose. Whether he was combined
With those of Norway, or did line° the rebel
With hidden help and vantage, or that with both
He labored in his country's wrack, I know not;
115 But treasons capital,° confessed and proved,
Have overthrown him.
C **Macbeth** [*aside*].   Glamis, and Thane of Cawdor:
The greatest is behind. (*To* ROSS *and* ANGUS.) Thanks
for your pains.

84. insane root: henbane, believed to cause insanity.

90. reads: considers.

97. Nothing . . . death: killing, and not being afraid of being killed.
98. post with post: messenger with a message.

104. earnest: pledge.

106. addition: title.

112. line: support.

115. capital: deserving death.

? 117. *"Behind" here means "to follow." How should this important aside be spoken? What is Macbeth's mood?*

A. Characterization

? Which man seems skeptical of the witches? (Banquo) Which seems to believe in them immediately? (Macbeth) What does this imply about each man's character? (Banquo is practical and down-to-earth; Macbeth may be superstitious.)

B. Imagery
In lines 108–109 Macbeth uses an image of clothing. Another clothing image comes on the next page, line 145. Some students may wish to trace such images throughout the play, analyzing them at the end for what they say about the man Macbeth or the play.

C. Interpreting

? What is "the greatest"? (Kingship)

Answers to margin questions
Line 126. Banquo sees the witches as tools of the devil and warns Macbeth that trusting them may prove ruinous.
Stage direction. Macbeth is down front, turned halfway or fully away from Banquo, Ross, and Angus, who converse quietly upstage. The "swelling act" may suggest the stately music that heralds a king's coming: Macbeth sees his new title as a sign of his coming kingship.
Line 137. Macbeth may be imagining murder as his way to the throne.
Line 142. Macbeth may be merely distracted or he may be ominously brooding and plotting. Encourage several interpretations.
Line 145. New honors are like new clothes that are not yet broken in. Yes—Banquo seems to have dismissed the witches; Macbeth has taken their words to heart.

A. Paraphrasing

How would you say these lines in your own words? (The powers of darkness tell us truths only to betray us later.)

B. Interpreting

Note that nothing has yet been said about *how* Macbeth will become king.

What do these lines suggest about a method he may already have been considering? (Murder of King Duncan)

C. Metaphors

Macbeth uses a time metaphor, perhaps of an hourglass, in lines 146–147; and a book metaphor in lines 150–152.

Is it valid to suggest that Macbeth is more imaginative than Banquo? (Yes) How would this trait contribute to his susceptibility to the witches? (He may be far more affected by imaginary or supernatural things.)

D. Responding to Scene 3

This scene is discussed in questions 5 and 11–14 on text pages 270–271.

(*Aside to* BANQUO.) Do you not hope your children
  shall be kings,
When those that gave the Thane of Cawdor to me
Promised no less to them?

120 **Banquo** (*aside to* MACBETH). That, trusted home,°
Might yet enkindle you unto the crown,°
Besides the Thane of Cawdor. But 'tis strange:
And oftentimes, to win us to our harm,
The instruments of darkness tell us truths,
125 Win us with honest trifles, to betray 's
In deepest consequence.
Cousins,° a word, I pray you.

Macbeth (*aside*).   Two truths are told,
As happy prologues to the swelling act
Of the imperial theme.—I thank you, gentlemen.—
130 (*Aside.*) This supernatural soliciting
Cannot be ill, cannot be good. If ill,
Why hath it given me earnest of success,
Commencing in a truth? I am Thane of Cawdor:
If good, why do I yield to that suggestion
135 Whose horrid image doth unfix my hair
And make my seated heart knock at my ribs,
Against the use of nature? Present fears
Are less than horrible imaginings.
My thought, whose murder yet is but fantastical,
140 Shakes so my single° state of man that function
Is smothered in surmise, and nothing is
But what is not.°

Banquo.   Look, how our partner's rapt.
Macbeth (*aside*). If chance will have me king, why,
  chance may crown me,
Without my stir.

Banquo.   New honors come upon him,
145 Like our strange° garments, cleave not to their mold
But with the aid of use.

Macbeth (*aside*).   Come what come may
Time and the hour runs through the roughest day.

Banquo.
Worthy Macbeth, we stay upon your leisure.

Macbeth.
Give me your favor.° My dull brain was wrought
150 With things forgotten. Kind gentlemen, your pains
Are registered where every day I turn
The leaf to read them. Let us toward the king.
(*Aside to* BANQUO.) Think upon what hath chanced,
  and at more time,
The interim having weighed it, let us speak
Our free hearts each to other.

155 **Banquo.**   Very gladly.
Macbeth.
Till then, enough. Come, friends.   [*Exeunt.*]

---

120. **trusted home:** trusted all the way.

121. **enkindle . . . crown:** arouse in you the ambition to become king.

126. *How does this speech show Banquo as part of the conscience of the play?*
127. **Cousins:** This word is used frequently by Shakespeare to mean "fellows" or "kindred friends" of some sort.

Stage direction. *When a character is delivering an aside, the director or the playwright must arrange for the others on stage to be involved in some way so that it would be natural for them not to notice the character delivering the aside. Where should Macbeth go on stage to deliver this important aside? What do you think he meant by the "swelling act" in the previous line? Where are Banquo, Angus, and Ross?*
137. *What do you suppose Macbeth is thinking of that makes his seated (fixed) heart knock at his ribs in an unnatural way?*
140. **single:** unaided, weak.

141. **nothing . . . not:** Nothing is real to me except my imaginings.
142. *What might Macbeth do as Banquo notices him brooding?*

145. **strange:** new.
145. *What does Banquo compare Macbeth and his new honors to? Is Banquo's mood different from Macbeth's?*

149. **favor:** pardon.

Handwritten annotations:
Warning — Witches are instruments of darkness win our confidence only to betray us.
Aside
Idea of murder crosses his mind
decides to take no action
Macbeth is more imaginative than Banquo more susceptible to witches
Asks Banquo that the speak about the witches later

Plot Summary

Scene 4. Duncan proclaims his son Malcolm heir to the throne. Macbeth exits to tell his wife that Duncan will spend the night with them. Macbeth speaks of his black desires when he hears that Duncan has bestowed the title on Malcolm.

Answers to margin questions

Line 8. The way he died was the finest, most courageous thing he ever did. (This idea might serve as a topic for students' journals: Can they apply it to actual life?)

Line 12. The irony is that we realize that just as Duncan failed to recognize Cawdor's treachery, he will not recognize Macbeth's dark thoughts. Duncan shows no awareness that people often mask their true selves.

Line 32. Many will see Macbeth as a "fake" or "phony." He may glower jealously, face turned aside, at Duncan's even warmer praise of Banquo.

Line 35. Duncan is wiping away tears.

Scene 4. *Forres. The palace.*

Flourish.° Enter KING DUNCAN, LENNOX, MALCOLM, DON-ALBAIN, *and* ATTENDANTS.

King.
Is execution done on Cawdor? Are not
Those in commission yet returned?

Malcolm.   My liege,
They are not yet come back. But I have spoke
With one that saw him die, who did report
5 That very frankly he confessed his treasons,
Implored your highness' pardon and set forth
A deep repentance: nothing in his life
Became him like the leaving it. He died
As one that had been studied in his death
10 To throw away the dearest thing he owed
As 'twere a careless trifle.

A **King.**   There's no art
To find the mind's construction in the face:
He was a gentleman on whom I built
An absolute trust.

[*Enter* MACBETH, BANQUO, ROSS, *and* ANGUS.]

                    O worthiest cousin!
15 The sin of my ingratitude even now
Was heavy on me: thou art so far before,
That swiftest wing of recompense is slow
To overtake thee. Would thou hadst less deserved,
That the proportion° both of thanks and payment
20 Might have been mine! Only I have left to say,
More is thy due than more than all can pay.

Macbeth.
The service and the loyalty I owe,
In doing it, pays itself.° Your highness' part
Is to receive our duties: and our duties
25 Are to your throne and state children and servants;
Which do but what they should, by doing every thing
Safe toward° your love and honor.

King.   Welcome hither.
I have begun to plant thee, and will labor
To make thee full of growing. Noble Banquo,
30 That hast no less deserved, nor must be known
B No less to have done so, let me enfold thee
And hold thee to my heart.

Banquo.   There if I grow,
The harvest is your own.

King.   My plenteous joys,
Wanton in fullness, seek to hide themselves
35 In drops of sorrow. Sons, kinsmen, thanes,
And you whose places are the nearest, know,
C We will establish our estate upon

Flourish: of trumpets.

Executed Cawdor

? 8. *What does this famous line mean: "nothing in his life / Became him like the leaving it"?*

Dramatic Irony

? 12. *What irony would you feel here? What does Duncan fail to realize about another face?*

– No way to judge a person's character by their face. Trusted Cawdor + Cawdor betrayed him.

Irony is that he is trusting Macbeth.

Irony — *Macbeth enters after these words*

Duncan thanks Macbeth

19. proportion: preponderance.

— *Irony*

23. pays itself: is its own reward.

It was my duty

27. safe toward: safeguarding.

Reward thee

Reward Banquo also

? 32. *You know Macbeth's thoughts. How do you feel about him as the king lavishes praise on him? Is the king's reception of Banquo even warmer? How might Macbeth react here?*

? 35. *There's a clue in this line that shows how moved the king is. What is the king doing at the words "drops of sorrow"?*

A. Interpreting
? Relate "Fair is foul, and foul is fair" to these lines. (A traitor can wear an honest face. Things are not always what they appear to be.)

B. Imagery
Duncan and Banquo use wholesome images of growing plants. Note the contrast with earlier images of death and blood (Scene 2, lines 1, 18, 22–23, 39–40, etc.)

C. The Royal "We"
Duncan uses the "royal we" to indicate that he is speaking as the whole state, not as an individual. The "royal we" is still used today by British royalty and by the pope. Shakespeare sometimes has a king switch from "we" to "I" to indicate a change in personality or fortunes.

A. Discussing the Photograph

? Does this Duncan match your image of him? Why or why not? (Answers will vary.) What does the scepter he is lifting symbolize? (Power, rule)

B. Titles

Students will know that Prince Charles, the male heir first in line to the throne of England, has the title "Prince of Wales." Duncan's naming his son "Prince of Cumberland" carried, for Scotland, the same significance.

C. Character

Lines 48–53 reveal Macbeth's true reaction to Duncan's news about his son.

? How does the contrast between the two speeches again illustrate that "Fair is foul, and foul is fair"? (Macbeth appears to be loyal to Duncan but he is not.) Which view of Macbeth does Duncan take as true? (See the next speech, lines 54–58.) (Duncan trusts Macbeth believing him to be good and true.)

D. Responding to Scene 4

Scene 4 is discussed in question 15 on text page 271.

Answers to margin questions
Line 43. Duncan is promising the crown to Malcolm, the older of his two sons.
Line 53. Macbeth speaks first of literal darkness in "Stars, hide your fires . . ." (line 50) and of the darkness of his heart in "Let not light see my black and deep desires . . ." (line 51).

A

*"We will establish our estate upon
Our eldest, Malcolm, . . ."*

B
    Our eldest, Malcolm, whom we name hereafter
    The Prince of Cumberland: which honor must
40   Not unaccompanied invest him only,
    But signs of nobleness, like stars, shall shine
    On all deservers. From hence to Inverness,°
    And bind us further to you.
Macbeth.
    The rest is labor, which is not used for you.°
45   I'll be myself the harbinger,° and make joyful
    The hearing of my wife with your approach;
    So, humbly take my leave.
King.   My worthy Cawdor!
Macbeth (*aside*). The Prince of Cumberland! That is a step
    On which I must fall down, or else o'erleap,
50   For in my way it lies. Stars, hide your fires;
C   Let not light see my black and deep desires:
    The eye wink at the hand;° yet let that be
    Which the eye fears, when it is done, to see.   [*Exit.*]
King.
    True, worthy Banquo; he is full so valiant,
55   And in his commendations° I am fed;
    It is a banquet to me. Let's after him,
    Whose care is gone before to bid us welcome.
D   It is a peerless kinsman.   [*Flourish. Exeunt.*]

[margin notes, handwritten:] makes Malcolm his heir
— Going to Macbeth's
Must get Malcolm out of the way
Doesn't want anyone to know what he is thinking

42. Inverness: Macbeth's castle.
? **43.** *Who is to inherit Duncan's crown?*

44. In other words, when rest is not used for you, it is labor.
45. harbinger: sign of something to come.

52. wink . . . hand: be blind to the hand's deed.
? **53.** *Where in this speech do we begin to hear Macbeth talk in terms of darkness?*

55. his commendations: praises of him.

Stage direction. Encourage several interpretations. She may be pacing, reading lines with varying emphasis, throwing her head back, laughing at some points, frowning at others, and so on.

Line 15. Lady Macbeth may literally "lay [the letter] to [her] heart": clutch it to her breast or tuck it in her dress. "Thou" and "thy" address the absent Macbeth. Student interpretations of the "milk of human kindness" will vary; perhaps it is the tenderness associated with mother's milk.

Line 28. The "golden round" is the king's crown.

Plot Summary
Scene 5. Lady Macbeth is introduced. Macbeth tells her about the witches' prophecies. A messenger tells her the king will visit there tonight. Lady Macbeth determines to murder Duncan.

Scene 5. *Inverness. Macbeth's castle.*

Enter Macbeth's wife, LADY MACBETH, *alone, with a letter.*

[handwritten: Soliloquy]

Lady Macbeth (*reads*). "They met me in the day of success; and I have learned by the perfect'st report they have more in them than mortal knowledge. When I
5   burned in desire to question them further, they made themselves air, into which they vanished. Whiles I stood rapt in the wonder of it, came missives from the king, who all-hailed me 'Thane of Cawdor'; by which title, before, these weird sisters saluted me, and re-
10   ferred me to the coming on of time, with 'Hail, king that shalt be!' This have I thought good to deliver thee, my dearest partner of greatness, that thou mightst not lose the dues of rejoicing, by being ignorant of what greatness is promised thee. Lay it to thy heart, and farewell."

15   Glamis thou art, and Cawdor, and shalt be
  What thou art promised. Yet do I fear thy nature;
  It is too full o' th' milk of human kindness
  To catch the nearest way. Thou wouldst be great,
  Art not without ambition, but without
20   The illness° should attend it. What thou wouldst highly,
  That wouldst thou holily; wouldst not play false,
  And yet wouldst wrongly win. Thou'dst have, great Glamis,
  That which cries, "Thus thou must do" if thou have it;
  And that which rather thou dost fear to do
25   Than wishest should be undone. Hie thee hither,
  That I may pour my spirits in thine ear,
  And chastise with the valor of my tongue
  All that impedes thee from the golden round
  Which fate and metaphysical° aid doth seem
30   To have thee crowned withal.

  [*Enter* MESSENGER.]

                        What is your tidings?
Messenger.
  The king comes here tonight.
Lady Macbeth.   Thou'rt mad to say it!
  Is not thy master with him, who, were't so,
  Would have informed for preparation?
Messenger.
  So please you, it is true. Our thane is coming.
35   One of my fellows had the speed of him,°
  Who, almost dead for breath, had scarcely more
  Than would make up his message.

Stage direction. *As you picture Lady Macbeth reading this letter, try to imagine what she would be doing on stage and what her mood would be, especially at the words "Thane of Cawdor."*

[handwritten: Letter from Macbeth]

[handwritten: What is their relationship like?]

[handwritten: Believes Macbeth is not courageous enough to take the crown]

15. *What does Lady Macbeth do with the letter? Whom is she addressing here with* thou *and* thy? *How would you explain "the milk of human kindness"?*

[handwritten: Ambitious, but don't have an evil nature]

20. illness: wickedness, evil nature.

[handwritten: The things you want require to do certain things to obtain it, things you are afraid to do, but once done you will not want it undone]

[handwritten: She will convince him]

[handwritten: crown]

28. *What do you guess the "golden round" is?*
29. metaphysical: supernatural.

[handwritten: Informed that the King is coming]

35. speed of him: had more speed than he did.

A. Character
The great Shakespearean actress Sarah Kemble Siddons (see text page 252), herself tall and strong, was able to project a Lady Macbeth who was fragile and delicate, yet able to dominate Macbeth by her intellect and beauty. Siddons delivered this speech with sudden energy on "Shalt be" (line 15) and a clear association of "my spirits" (line 26) with the supernatural beings she has read about in her husband's letter.

Line 38. The messenger was hoarse. The glossy black raven is a scavenger and is considered an omen of evil.
Line 54. In general, Lady Macbeth has petitioned that her finest (fairest) female qualities be converted to foulness.
Line 59. Macbeth's greeting suggests real passion. A director might have Macbeth and Lady Macbeth embrace and gaze deeply into each other's eyes.
Line 71. Macbeth may be astonished but curious at her fervor and intent.

A. Interpreting

Why does Lady Macbeth ask the spirits to "unsex" her? (Her feminine nature, she feels, would not allow her to accomplish what she is set to do. She will no longer create and nurture life; she will destroy it.)

B. Imagery

Students should be alert to the images of blood that will become more and more prominent.

C. Characterization

So far, who seems stronger in character—Lady Macbeth or Macbeth? (Certainly Lady Macbeth)

D. Interpreting

What does this line indicate? (Duncan will never see the light of tomorrow.)

E. Responding to Scene 5

See questions 6, 7, and 16 on text pages 270–271 for a discussion of this scene.

[handwritten: Who seems the stronger character?]

Lady Macbeth.   Give him tending;
He brings great news.

[*Exit* MESSENGER.]   *[handwritten: Bird of death]*

[handwritten: Soliloquy]

                    The raven himself is hoarse
That croaks the fatal entrance of Duncan
40   Under my battlements. Come, you spirits   *[handwritten: Calling spirits to unsex her, give her courage to kill Duncan]*
A   That tend on mortal° thoughts, unsex me here,
     And fill me, from the crown to the toe, top-full
B   Of direst cruelty! Make thick my blood,
     Stop up th' access and passage to remorse,
45   That no compunctious visitings of nature°
     Shake my fell° purpose, nor keep peace between
     Th' effect and it! Come to my woman's breasts,
     [handwritten: Take away all motherly instincts] And take my milk for gall,° you murd'ring ministers,°
     Wherever in your sightless° substances
50   You wait on nature's mischief! Come, thick night,
     And pall° thee in the dunnest° smoke of hell,
     [handwritten: Night will cover deed] That my keen knife see not the wound it makes,
C   Nor heaven peep through the blanket of the dark,
     To cry, "Hold, hold!"

[*Enter* MACBETH.]

                    Great Glamis! Worthy Cawdor!
55   Greater than both, by the all-hail hereafter!
     Thy letters have transported me beyond
     This ignorant present, and I feel now
     The future in the instant.
Macbeth.   My dearest love,
     Duncan comes here tonight.
Lady Macbeth.   And when goes hence?
Macbeth.
     Tomorrow, as he purposes.
60   **Lady Macbeth.**   O, never
D   Shall sun that morrow see!   *[handwritten: Duncan will never see the sunrise]*
     Your face, my thane, is as a book where men
     May read strange matters. To beguile the time,°
     Look like the time; bear welcome in your eye,
65   Your hand, your tongue: look like th' innocent flower,
     But be the serpent under't. He that's coming
     Must be provided for: and you shall put
     This night's great business into my dispatch;
     Which shall to all our nights and days to come
70   Give solely sovereign sway and masterdom.   *[handwritten: She will take care of details]*
Macbeth.
     We will speak further.
Lady Macbeth.   Only look up clear.°
     To alter favor ever is to fear.°
E   Leave all the rest to me.   [*Exeunt.*]

---

38. *Who is the raven she refers to as being hoarse? Why does she call him a "raven"?*

41. mortal: deadly.

45. nature: natural feeling of compassion.
46. fell: savage.

48. gall: a bitter substance; bile.
murd'ring ministers: agents of murder.
49. sightless: invisible.

51. pall: cover with a shroud, a burial cloth. **dunnest:** darkest.

54. *How has Lady Macbeth reinforced the witches' statement: "Fair is foul, and foul is fair . . ."?*

59. *Is their passion for each other as great as their passion for power? If you feel it is, how might a director illustrate it here?*

63. beguile the time: deceive people of the day.

[handwritten: Tells him to look kindly on Duncan – hide his thoughts. Be the serpent]

71. *How is Macbeth feeling?*

71. clear: undisturbed.
72. To alter . . . fear: To show an altered face is dangerous.

Answer to margin question
Line 9. This is a brief "pastoral" interlude in a play reeking with blood and evil. We feel the irony in Duncan's appreciation of the castle's beauty, for we know that treachery and evil really dwell there.

Lady Macbeth acts the part of a perfect hostess, whose words ring with sincerity.

Plot Summary
Scene 6. Duncan arrives at Macbeth's castle. We feel dramatic irony as Duncan comments on the pleasant air in Macbeth's home. Lady Macbeth graciously welcomes Duncan, even as she plots his murder.

CLOSURE ACT I
When they have finished reading Act I, instruct students to write on a piece of paper a brief description of what the main characters in this play want and what actions they plan to take to get it. How, by the end of this act, is each character affected by these plans? Compare responses in class.

A. Setting
According to Mark Van Doren, Scene 6 gives Macbeth's castle, through Duncan's words, the only "moment of serenity and fairness" it ever knows. See the questions on line 9 in the text.

Scene 6. *Before Macbeth's castle.*

Hautboys° and torches. Enter KING DUNCAN, MALCOLM, DONALBAIN, BANQUO, LENNOX, MACDUFF, ROSS, ANGUS, *and* ATTENDANTS.

A

King.
This castle hath a pleasant seat;° the air
Nimbly and sweetly recommends itself
Unto our gentle senses.

Banquo.   This guest of summer,
5   The temple-haunting martlet,° does approve°
By his loved masionry° that the heaven's breath
Smells wooingly here. No jutty,° frieze,
Buttress, nor coign of vantage,° but this bird
Hath made his pendent bed and procreant° cradle.
Where they most breed and haunt, I have observed
The air is delicate.

[*Enter* LADY MACBETH.]

Hautboys: oboes.

(handwritten notes in margin: seems pleasant home — irony — Duncan appreciates the castle — evil dwells there)

1. seat: situation, setting.

4. martlet: a bird that builds nests in churches. **approve:** prove.
5. masionry: nests (dwellings).
6. jutty: projection.
7. coign of vantage: advantageous corner (of the castle).
8. procreant: breeding.

9. *This scene contrasts strongly with the previous one. Again, what irony do you feel as Duncan admires the castle? How do you imagine Lady Macbeth acts as she now enters to greet her guests?*

B. About the Photograph
This photograph, taken during the filming of Polanski's movie, illustrates lines 10–30 on the next page. Notice the rough-hewn details of this castle, which suggest just the way a Scottish castle would probably have looked in the eleventh century.

What does the audience know about the inner tensions of this scene that the attendants shown in the photograph would not have known? (Others in the scene would take Lady Macbeth's greeting at face value and expect a good time; the audience knows treachery is to come). Can students find the modern onlooker?

"See, see, our honored hostess!"

B

Answers to margin questions

Line 31. Perhaps Duncan and Lady Macbeth, hands joined and raised, move offstage.

Line 1. Macbeth reasons that if the deci-sion has been made, it had best be en-acted quickly; in line 27, he acknowl-edges that his "vaulting ambition" moti-vates the murder. On the other hand, murder condemns a killer to Hell; the murder of Duncan may encourage others to kill the next king—Macbeth himself; he owes Duncan protection (not harm) as his relative, loyal subject, and host; Dun-can is a good king, whose murder will outrage the public.

Plot Summary

Scene 7. Macbeth speaks his first im-portant soliloquy, explaining that his vaulting ambition leads him to thoughts of murder. Lady Macbeth encourages her husband to commit the murder.

A. Characterization

As Mark Van Do-ren points out, Duncan's clear, open spirit is shown by the ease with which the word *love* comes to his lips (four times in this scene). Duncan's inner brightness is also symbolized in Act II, Scene 1, line 15, by the dia-mond he sends Lady Macbeth.

B. Comparing Characters

? Have students compare Lady Macbeth's polite responses to Dun-can to those of Macbeth in Scene 4, lines 44–47. Who is better at this sort of "diplo-macy"—Macbeth or his lady? (Lady Macbeth)

C. Responding to Scene 6

See questions 16 and 18 on text page 271.

King.   See, see, our honored hostess!
10   The love that follows us sometime is our trouble,
A   Which still we thank as love. Herein I teach you
      How you shall bid God 'ield° us for your pains
      And thank us for your trouble.
Lady Macbeth.   All our service
15   In every point twice done, and then done double,
      Were poor and single business to contend
B   Against those honors deep and broad wherewith
      Your majesty loads our house: for those of old,
      And the late dignities heaped up to them,
      We rest your hermits.°
20 **King.**   Where's the Thane of Cawdor?
      We coursed° him at the heels, and had a purpose
      To be his purveyor:° but he rides well,
      And his great love, sharp as his spur, hath holp him
      To his home before us. Fair and noble hostess,
      We are your guest tonight.
25 **Lady Macbeth.**   Your servants ever
      Have theirs, themselves, and what is theirs, in compt,°
      To make their audit at your highness' pleasure,
      Still° to return your own.
King.   Give me your hand.
      Conduct me to mine host: we love him highly,
30   And shall continue our graces toward him.
      By your leave, hostess.   [*Exeunt.*]
C

13. **'ield:** reward.

20. **We rest your hermits:** We'll remain de-pendents who will pray for you.

21. **coursed:** chased.
22. **purveyor:** advance man.

26. **in compt:** in trust.

28. **Still:** always.

? 31. *How do you imagine the scene ends?*

Scene 7. *Macbeth's castle.*

Hautboys. Torches. Enter a SEWER,° *and diverse* SER-VANTS *with dishes and service, and pass over the stage. Then enter* MACBETH.

Macbeth.
      If it were done when 'tis done, then 'twere well
      It were done quickly. If th' assassination
      Could trammel up the consequence, and catch,
      With his surcease,° success; that but this blow
5   Might be the be-all and the end-all—here,
      But here, upon this bank and shoal of time,
      We'd jump° the life to come. But in these cases
      We still have judgment here; that we but teach
      Bloody instructions, which, being taught, return
10   To plague th'inventor: this even-handed justice
      Commends° th' ingredients of our poisoned chalice
      To our own lips. He's here in double trust:
      First, as I am his kinsman and his subject,
      Strong both against the deed; then, as his host,
15   Who should against his murderer shut the door,

Sewer: butler.

? 1. *This is one of Shakespeare's great soliloquies, in which Macbeth voices his indecision and possibly his conscience. What are his conflicts?*

4. **surcease:** Duncan's death.

7. **jump:** risk. (Macbeth knows he will be condemned to Hell for the sin of murder.)

11. **Commends:** offers.

READING CHECK TEST (Act I)

1. What characters open the play? (Three witches)

2. In Scene 2, why does King Duncan give Macbeth a new title? (To reward Macbeth for his bravery)

3. What titles do the witches predict for Macbeth? (Thane of Cawdor and king)

4. What do the witches predict for Banquo? (That he will beget kings)

5. Whom does Duncan name as his successor? (Malcolm)

6. When we first meet Lady Macbeth, what is she doing? (Reading a letter)

7. What does she complain Macbeth lacks? (The inclination to do evil)

8. When she hears that Duncan plans to visit, what does Lady Macbeth resolve? (To kill the king)

9. In the final scene, what conflict do Lady Macbeth and Macbeth have? (Whether or not to kill Duncan)

10. Who seems more forceful and ambitious—Macbeth or his wife? (Lady Macbeth)

Not bear the knife myself. Besides, this Duncan
Hath borne his faculties° so meek, hath been
So clear° in his great office, that his virtues
Will plead like angels trumpet-tongued against
20 The deep damnation of his taking-off;°

A And pity, like a naked newborn babe,
Striding the blast, or heaven's cherubin horsed
Upon the sightless couriers° of the air,
Shall blow the horrid deed in every eye,
25 That° tears shall drown the wind. I have no spur

B To prick the sides of my intent, but only
Vaulting ambition, which o'erleaps itself
And falls on th' other—

[Enter LADY MACBETH.]

                  How now! What news?

Lady Macbeth.
  He has almost supped. Why have you left the chamber?

Macbeth.
  Hath he asked for me?

30 **Lady Macbeth.**   Know you not he has?

Macbeth.
  We will proceed no further in this business:
He hath honored me of late, and I have bought
Golden opinions from all sorts of people,
Which would be worn now in their newest gloss,
Not cast aside so soon.

35 **Lady Macbeth.**   Was the hope drunk
Wherein you dressed yourself? Hath it slept since?
And wakes it now, to look so green° and pale
At what it did so freely? From this time
Such I account thy love. Art thou afeard
40 To be the same in thine own act and valor
As thou art in desire? Wouldst thou have that
Which thou esteem'st the ornament of life,°
And live a coward in thine own esteem,
Letting "I dare not" wait upon° "I would,"
Like the poor cat i' th' adage?°

45 **Macbeth.**   Prithee, peace!
I dare do all that may become a man;
Who dares do more is none.

Lady Macbeth.   What beast was't then
That made you break this enterprise to me?
When you durst do it, then you were a man;
50 And to be more than what you were, you would
Be so much more the man. Nor time nor place
C Did then adhere,° and yet you would make both.
They have made themselves, and that their fitness now
Does unmake you. I have given suck, and know
55 How tender 'tis to love the babe that milks me:
I would, while it was smiling in my face,
Have plucked my nipple from his boneless gums,

17. **faculties:** powers.
18. **clear:** clean.

20. **taking-off:** murder.

23. **sightless couriers:** winds.

25. **That:** so that.

? 28. *Macbeth says he has no spur to prick the sides of his intent. Is that true?*

37. **green:** sickly.

42. **ornament of life:** the crown.

44. **wait upon:** follow.
45. **adage:** anecdote about a cat who wants fish but won't wet its paws.

52. **adhere:** suit.

[Handwritten annotations:] Cons / Pros / Kinsman loyal subj host good King who will be mourned / getting caught / Good King / Ambition / Needs some motivation / We will not kill Duncan. Based on opinion of others / Are you afraid? Coward? / I do what a man would do. To do more one is not a man / Appeals to his manhood Going back on his word

A. Personification

? Why is the first image of pity so appropriate? (It makes us feel the innocence, fragility, and might of pity.)

B. Metaphor

? What comparison is Macbeth using here? (He is comparing his intent to a horse that is spurred on by ambition. But his ambition, like an inept rider, often misjudges the horse and leaps so high he vaults to the horse's other side and falls.)

C. Characterization

In this shocking speech (continues on next page), Siddons's voice moved from great tenderness on "I have given suck" to fiendish cruelty on "plucked my nipple from his boneless gums."

? Why do you think we never hear about the Macbeths' children? (They are too involved with their actions and the aftermath.)

1. The witches plan to gather on the heath to meet Macbeth.
2. The Captain reports that Macbeth has distinguished himself in battle and has turned the tide of the conflict by slaying Macdonwald.
3. The Thane of Cawdor is a traitor who aided the Norwegian king.

4. He orders that the Thane of Cawdor be executed and gives his title to Macbeth.
5. The witches tell Macbeth he will be the Thane of Cawdor and then king. They tell Banquo he will not be king but will father a line of kings.
6. She ambitiously looks forward to her husband's becoming king but fears he may not be strong enough to do evil.

7. The speech that begins "The raven himself. . . ." reveals her plans to murder Duncan.
8. He hesitates to murder Duncan, who is a good king, a kinsman, and a guest. He also fears going to Hell and the people's reactions.
9. She tells him that he is a coward and then describes her murder plan.

Answers to margin questions

Line 54. She challenges Macbeth's manliness and makes murder sound easy. The statement connotes defiance.

Line 72. She plans to get Duncan's grooms so drunk they pass out; the Macbeths will kill Duncan and frame the servants.

Line 81. A pause and grim voice are one possibility. The tone could also be sadly defiant.

Line 82. The face is fair; the heart is foul.

A. Metaphor
Another reading of this line refers to the act of tuning a lute: tightening the screw until the string holds (sticks).

B. Interpreting
This famous speech could suggest admiration or sad horror.
❓ How would you speak it? (Answers will vary, but interpretations should be supported by interpretation of Macbeth's character.)

C. Responding to Scene 7
See questions 8, 9, and 17 below and on page 271.

And dashed the brains out, had I so sworn as you
Have done to this.
Macbeth.   If we should fail?   *Uncertain*
Lady Macbeth.   We fail?
60 **A** But° screw your courage to the sticking-place,°   *We won't fail*
And we'll not fail. When Duncan is asleep—
Whereto the rather shall his day's hard journey
Soundly invite him—his two chamberlains   *The plan*
Will I with wine and wassail° so convince,°   *Drug guards*
65 That memory, the warder of the brain,
Shall be a fume, and the receipt of reason
A limbeck only:° when in swinish sleep
Their drenchèd natures lie as in a death,
What cannot you and I perform upon
70 Th' unguarded Duncan, what not put upon
His spongy officers, who shall bear the guilt
Of our great quell?
Macbeth.   Bring forth men-children only;   *opinion of wife*
B For thy undaunted mettle should compose
Nothing but males. Will it not be received,
75 When we have marked with blood those sleepy two
Of his own chamber, and used their very daggers,
That they have done't?
Lady Macbeth.   Who dares receive it other,
As we shall make our griefs and clamor roar
Upon his death?   *Agrees to kill Duncan*
Macbeth.   I am settled, and bend up
80 Each corporal agent to this terrible feat.
Away, and mock the time° with fairest show:
C False face must hide what the false heart doth know.
                                    [*Exeunt.*]

Echo of Fair is foul Foul is fair

❓ **54.** *How does Lady Macbeth try to intimidate her husband in this speech? Watch what she says about herself in the next lines. There has been some question as to whether "We fail?" (line 59) should be a question. How does the meaning change if the line is spoken as a statement?*

60. But: only. **sticking-place:** a reference to the notch in a crossbow.

64. wassail: drinking. **convince:** overcome.

67. the receipt . . . only: The reasoning part of the brain would become like a **limbeck,** a still, distilling only confused thoughts.

❓ **72.** *"Quell" is murder. What are Lady Macbeth's plans?*

❓ **81.** *Should Macbeth pause here? How should these key words be spoken?*
81. mock the time: deceive the world.
❓ **82.** *How is this yet another echo of the witches' words in Scene 1?*

Responding to the Play

Analyzing Act I

Identifying Facts

1. In Scene 1, where do the witches plan to meet again, and why?
2. What news about Macbeth does the blood-stained Captain bring to the king in Scene 2?
3. What news does Ross bring about the Thane of Cawdor?
4. What does the king determine to do for Macbeth?
5. What do the witches tell Macbeth and Banquo in Scene 3?
6. In Scene 5, what is Lady Macbeth's response to her husband's letter with the news about his title and the witches' prophecy?
7. What speech tells you what Lady Macbeth plans to do to Duncan when he visits the castle?
8. What are Macbeth's misgivings in Scene 7?
9. What is his wife's response?

Interpreting Meanings

10. In the very first scene of a play, a dramatist must tell the audience what kind of play they are about to see. What does the brief opening scene of *Macbeth*

Interpreting Meanings

10. Scene 1 suggests a stormy, violent play in which supernatural elements play a part.

11. The fulfillment of part of the prophecy (that Macbeth will be Thane of Cawdor) occurs so swiftly that Macbeth is tempted to think that, if he took matters into his own hands, the rest of the prophecy will come true.

12. Although Banquo will be Macbeth's subject ("lesser"), he will be "greater" than Macbeth because many of his descendants will rule Scotland.

13. Macbeth seems to believe the witches' prophecies; Banquo is skeptical and wary.

Macbeth's reaction may suggest that he is credulous, superstitious, and ambitious.

14. Macbeth was always ambitious and always capable of murder even though he had not formulated exact plans to kill Duncan.

15. His inner conflict is between his ambition and his horror of any violence that he might commit against the king.

In scene 4, Duncan blocks Macbeth's path to royalty by naming Malcolm as heir to the throne. This tips the balance in Macbeth's mind in favor of violence.

16. Students may mention her violence, ruthlessness, ambition, and skill at dissembling.

17. Lady Macbeth is more single-minded and logical; Macbeth is more imaginative and sensitive. Lady Macbeth wins the argument.

18. The audience knows that the castle's outward calm conceals a plot to murder Duncan.

A

Costume design for the three witches by Nat Karson for the 1936 Works Progress Administration (WPA) Federal Theater Project production of *Macbeth*.

15. The most interesting part of any serious play is what goes on inside the characters' minds. What **conflict** rages in Macbeth after he hears the witches' prophecy? What effect do the events of Scene 4 have on the conflict?

16. We see Lady Macbeth alone for most of Scene 5, then with King Duncan and his party in Scene 6. What impressions do you have of her **character** by the end of Scene 6?

17. Describe the temperamental differences between Macbeth and his wife. Who is more single-minded and logical? Who is more imaginative and sensitive? Which one wins the argument?

18. What **irony** would the audience feel as they watch Duncan enter the castle and hear him praise its peacefulness?

Analyzing Language and Style

Blank Verse

Almost all of *Macbeth* is written in **blank verse,** or unrhymed iambic pentameter, a form of poetry that comes close to imitating the natural rhythms of English speech. An **iamb** is a metrical foot that has one unstressed syllable followed by one stressed syllable. (Each of the following is an iamb: *Macbeth, success, to win.*) **Pentameter** means that each line of verse has five feet, so one line of iambic pentameter has five iambs:

> **Banquo.** Good sir, why do you start, and seem to fear . . .

Some lines in *Macbeth* are irregular, with fewer feet or feet that are not iambs. The play even has a few prose passages, indicated by lines that are set full measure.

Blank verse, first used by Henry Howard, the Earl of Surrey, in his translation of Virgil's *Aeneid*, was the most popular verse form for sixteenth-century drama. John Milton was one of the first poets to use it in a long poem (*Paradise Lost*); and later poets, such as Wordsworth, Tennyson, Browning, and Eliot, continued to use blank verse.

1. Scan one speech by Macbeth and one by Lady Macbeth anywhere in Act I. What variations in iambic pentameter do you find?

2. Do the witches speak in blank verse? Why do you suppose Shakespeare wrote their speeches in this way?

3. Find one prose passage in Act I. Why is prose appropriate for this passage?

A. About the Illustration
Orson Welles's touring production of *Macbeth* was seen by some 100,000 people. Welles set the play in early nineteenth-century Haiti with an all-black cast, throbbing drums, and brilliantly colored tropical scenery and costumes. Macbeth wore canary yellow, emerald green, and shining top-boots; the ghost of Banquo was represented by a luminous death mask.

Encourage artistic students to design costumes for their production of *Macbeth*.

reveal about the play that will follow? How does the weather reflect the human passions revealed in the rest of the act?

11. The witches apparently recognize Macbeth as a man marked for success. Explain why their prophecy of Macbeth's coming greatness is actually a temptation to him.

12. Explain the seeming contradiction in the witches' greeting to Banquo in Scene 3: "Lesser than Macbeth, and greater." How is this true?

13. How do Banquo's reactions to the witches differ from Macbeth's? What does Macbeth's reaction suggest at once about his character?

14. One critic has said that the witches are "in some sense representative of potentialities within" Macbeth. Explain that statement. Is there any evidence that Macbeth has wanted to be king before?

ESTABLISHING A PURPOSE. Duncan is now a guest in Macbeth's castle. What events are now possible? Will the Macbeths actually kill him, or will they lose their will and let the opportunity pass? Why? What difficulties will face them if they go ahead?

DEVELOPING VOCABULARY
The following words from the play are tested in the Selection Test. (See also Vocabulary Activity Worksheet.)

to augment	multitudinous
to prate	rough
to knell	sacrilegious
mad	to steep
infirm	to entomb

Plot Summary
Scene 1. Macbeth comes upon Banquo and his son Fleance after midnight on their way to bed. They talk of the witches' predictions, and Macbeth again suggests a private talk with Banquo. After they leave, Macbeth sees a blood-covered dagger before him. The bell sounds, and Macbeth leaves to commit the murder.

Answers to margin questions
Stage direction. Fleance is Banquo's son. We remember, "Thou shalt get kings." We have no information about the Macbeths' children, except that Lady Macbeth refers to having nursed babies (Act I, Scene 7, lines 54–55).

Line 24. Ultimately Macbeth's motives are self-serving, although he may honestly value Banquo and seek his good will. He may even hope to enlist his aid, and in the next two lines misreads Banquo enough to suggest a bribe.

A. Setting
What clues in stage directions, in speeches, and in actions on this page would have alerted the Globe audience that the setting was a dark night? (Fleance carries a torch; Banquo says it is night and there are no stars; Fleance says it's past midnight.)

Act II

Scene 1. *Inverness. Court of Macbeth's castle.*

Enter BANQUO, *and* FLEANCE, *with a torch before him (on the way to bed).*

Banquo.
How goes the night, boy?
Fleance.
The moon is down; I have not heard the clock.
Banquo.
And she goes down at twelve.
Fleance.   I take't, 'tis later, sir.
Banquo.
Hold, take my sword. There's husbandry° in heaven.
Their candles are all out. Take thee that too.
A heavy summons° lies like lead upon me,
And yet I would not sleep. Merciful powers,
Restrain in me the cursèd thoughts that nature
Gives way to in repose!

[*Enter* MACBETH, *and a* SERVANT *with a torch.*]

                    Give me my sword!
10   Who's there?
Macbeth.
A friend.
Banquo.
What, sir, not yet at rest? The king's a-bed:
He hath been in unusual pleasure, and
Sent forth great largess to your offices:°
15   This diamond he greets your wife withal,
By the name of most kind hostess; and shut up°
In measureless content.
Macbeth.   Being unprepared,
Our will became the servant to defect,°
Which else should free have wrought.
Banquo.   All's well.
20   I dreamt last night of the three weird sisters:
To you they have showed some truth.
Macbeth.   I think not of them.
Yet, when we can entreat an hour to serve,
We would spend it in some words upon that business,
If you would grant the time.
Banquo.   At your kind'st leisure.
Macbeth.
25   If you shall cleave to my consent, when 'tis,°
It shall make honor for you.
Banquo.   So° I lose none
In seeking to <u>augment</u> it, but still keep
My bosom franchised° and allegiance clear,°
I shall be counseled.
Macbeth.   Good repose the while!

Stage direction. Who is Fleance? What would you remember of the witches' prophecy when you see him here? Do we know if Macbeth and his wife have any children?

4. **husbandry:** economizing.

6. **summons:** to sleep.

14. **offices:** servants.

16. **shut up:** concluded.

18. **to defect:** to insufficient preparations.

24. This is the second time Macbeth has suggested he and Banquo talk. Do you think he might want to confide in Banquo? Does he want to get Banquo on his side? How would you characterize his motives?
25. **cleave . . . 'tis:** join my cause, when the time comes.
26. **So:** provided that.
28. **franchised:** free (from guilt). **clear:** clean.

Answers to margin questions
Line 32. The bell signals the murder of Duncan.
Line 41. He draws his own dagger to compare it with the imaginary one. Some find the play more effective if Macbeth sees only the "dagger of the mind."

Banquo.

30   Thanks, sir. The like to you!

[*Exit* BANQUO, *with* FLEANCE.]

Macbeth.

Go bid thy mistress, when my drink is ready,
She strike upon the bell. Get thee to bed.

[*Exit* SERVANT.]

A

Is this a dagger which I see before me,
The handle toward my hand? Come, let me clutch thee.

35   I have thee not, and yet I see thee still.
Art thou not, fatal vision, sensible°
To feeling as to sight, or art thou but
A dagger of the mind, a false creation,
Proceeding from the heat-oppressèd brain?

40   I see thee yet, in form as palpable°
As this which now I draw.
Thou marshal'st me the way that I was going;

32. *What is to happen upon the ringing of the bell?*

36. sensible: perceptible to the senses.

40. palpable: obvious.

41. *What does Macbeth do at this moment? If you were directing the play, would you suspend a dagger in front of Macbeth during this speech? Why or why not?*

"*Is this a dagger which I see before me,*
The handle toward my hand?"

A. Soliloquy

This great soliloquy extends through line 64 on the next page. Line-by-line analysis or paraphrase (done individually or in groups) will give students insight into Macbeth's complex, tormented character. The glosses (see especially those on lines 41 and 64) will help students to see the organization of the soliloquy and to imagine Macbeth's actions. His thoughts are broken by the bell after line 61.

One Shakespearean critic, G. Wilson Knight, points out that Shakespeare made *Macbeth* a Christian drama depicting the conflict between grace and evil.

If one interprets the play in this way, how does Macbeth, in this soliloquy, reject grace and turn himself over to the powers of evil? (He sees an imaginary dagger covered with blood. He then commits himself to making an imaginary act of killing a real act.)

Macbeth, Act II, Scene 1   273

Answers to margin questions

Line 64. *Vision:* lines 33–41. *Call to action:* lines 42–61. *Leave taking:* lines 62–64. An audience would feel suspense and horror.

Line 3. An owl shrieks. The grooms are "them"; Macbeth is "he."

Line 13. Lady Macbeth should speak with some tenderness. If she is not feeling remorse, she at least shows a more vulnerable side of her character.

Plot Summary
Scene 2. Macbeth murders Duncan offstage. Lady Macbeth was unable to commit the murder because the sleeping Duncan reminded her of her father. Lady Macbeth seems calm yet thrilled with the murder; Macbeth is deeply troubled and seems dazed. He heard a voice crying, "Macbeth has murdered sleep." Macbeth has mistakenly taken the grooms' daggers from the room; Lady Macbeth places them beside the sleeping grooms, whom she smears with Duncan's blood.

A. Personification
❓ What is murder compared to? (A withered man who moves stealthily toward his victim)

B. Responding to Scene 1
See questions 1 and 2 on text page 284.

C. Characterization
Lines 12–13 reveal a tender side to Lady Macbeth we have not seen before.
❓ How are you visualizing Lady Macbeth? (English actor and producer William Poel saw her as about thirty-five with bright red hair, pink complexion, white hands and neck, bright red lips. Her head is erect, back straight, and shoulders squared; she moves with a slight swing.)

Many actresses have played Lady Macbeth. (See Ellen Terry on text page 330.) One of the more recent is Glenda Jackson, whose very aggressive portrayal might have matched Poel's description.

And such an instrument I was to use.
Mine eyes are made the fools o' th' other senses,
45 Or else worth all the rest. I see thee still;
And on thy blade and dudgeon° gouts of blood,
Which was not so before. There's no such thing.
It is the bloody business which informs°
Thus to mine eyes. Now o'er the one half-world
50 Nature seems dead, and wicked dreams abuse°
The curtained sleep; witchcraft celebrates
Pale Hecate's° offerings; and withered murder,
Alarumed° by his sentinel, the wolf,
Whose howl's his watch, thus with his stealthy pace,
55 With Tarquin's° ravishing strides, towards his design
Moves like a ghost. Thou sure and firm-set earth,
Hear not my steps, which way they walk, for fear
Thy very stones prate of my whereabout,
And take the present horror from the time,
60 Which now suits with it.° Whiles I threat, he lives:
Words to the heat of deeds too cold breath gives.

[*A bell rings.*]

I go, and it is done: the bell invites me.
Hear it not, Duncan, for it is a knell
That summons thee to heaven, or to hell.   [*Exit.*]

46. dudgeon: hilt.

48. informs: gives shape.

50. abuse: deceive.

52. Hecate: goddess of sorcery.
53. Alarumed: called to action.

55. Tarquin: an allusion to a Roman tyrant who raped a woman named Lucrece.

60. now suits with it: now seems suitable to it.

❓ **64.** *Trace in this soliloquy a vision; a call to action; and a leave taking. What should you be feeling as an audience as Macbeth exits?*

Scene 2. *Macbeth's castle.*

Enter LADY MACBETH.

Lady Macbeth.
That which hath made them drunk hath made me bold;
What hath quenched them hath given me fire. Hark!
  Peace!
It was the owl that shrieked, the fatal bellman,
Which gives the stern'st good-night.° He is about it.
5 The doors are open, and the surfeited grooms
Do mock their charge with snores. I have drugged their
  possets,°
That death and nature do contend about them,
Whether they live or die.
Macbeth (*within*).   Who's there? What, ho?
Lady Macbeth.
Alack, I am afraid they have awaked
10 And 'tis not done! Th' attempt and not the deed
Confounds° us. Hark! I laid their daggers ready;
He could not miss 'em. Had he not resembled
My father as he slept, I had done't.

[*Enter* MACBETH.]

          My husband!

❓ **3.** *What sound would you hear here? In this soliloquy, who are the "them" and who is "He"?*
4. stern'st good-night: The owl's call is supposed to portend death. The bellman was a person who rang a bell outside a condemned person's cell the night before his execution, to warn him to confess his sins.
6. possets: bedtime drinks.

11. Confounds: ruins.

❓ **13.** *How should Lady Macbeth say this last line, which reveals why the plans have changed? Do you think she is beginning to show remorse?*

274   274 The Renaissance

In this scene, Macbeth and Lady Macbeth are speaking in hushed, urgent whispers in a darkened castle. Macbeth begins to babble metaphysically about murdering sleep (lines 34–39), interrupted by his wife's abrupt "What do you mean?"

The image of sleep or sleeplessness is a powerful one that recurs throughout the play. Mark Van Doren points out that nothing could be more horrible than that Macbeth has murdered sleep, for in Shakespeare's plays, sleep "is ever the privilege of the good and the reward of the innocent. If it has been put to death, there is no goodness left. One of the witches knows how to torture sailors by keeping sleep from their penthouse lids [Act I, Scene 3, lines 19–20], but only Macbeth can murder sleep itself." The loss of sleep is the loss of hope; Macbeth's world is beginning to disintegrate.

Note reactions of characters to the dead.

Macbeth.
  I have done the deed. Didst thou not hear a noise?
Lady Macbeth.
15 I heard the owl scream and the crickets cry.
  Did not you speak?
Macbeth.   When?
Lady Macbeth.   Now.
Macbeth.   As I descended?
Lady Macbeth. Ay.
Macbeth. Hark!
  Who lies i' th' second chamber?
Lady Macbeth.   Donalbain.
20 **Macbeth.** This is a sorry sight.
Lady Macbeth.
  A foolish thought, to say a sorry sight.
Macbeth.
  There's one did laugh in's sleep, and one cried, "Murder!"
  That they did wake each other. I stood and heard them.
  But they did say their prayers, and addressed them
  Again to sleep.
25 **Lady Macbeth.**   There are two lodged together.
Macbeth.
  One cried, "God bless us!" and "Amen" the other,
  As they had seen me with these hangman's hands:
  List'ning their fear, I could not say, "Amen,"
  When they did say, "God bless us!"
Lady Macbeth.   Consider it not so deeply.
Macbeth.
30 But wherefore could not I pronounce "Amen"?
A I had most need of blessing, and "Amen"
  Stuck in my throat.
Lady Macbeth.   These deeds must not be thought
  After these ways; so, it will make us mad.
Macbeth.
  Methought I heard a voice cry "Sleep no more!
35 Macbeth does murder sleep"—the innocent sleep,
  Sleep that knits up the raveled sleave° of care,
B The death of each day's life, sore labor's bath,
  Balm of hurt minds, great nature's second course,°
  Chief nourisher in life's feast—
Lady Macbeth.   What do you mean?
Macbeth.
40 Still it cried, "Sleep no more!" to all the house:
  "Glamis hath murdered sleep, and therefore Cawdor
  Shall sleep no more: Macbeth shall sleep no more."
Lady Macbeth.
  Who was it that thus cried? Why, worthy thane,
  You do unbend your noble strength, to think
45 So brainsickly of things. Go get some water,
  And wash this filthy witness from your hand.
  Why did you bring these daggers from the place?

Macbeth very emotional Thinks he hears people yelling "Murder!"

Practical

Feels guilt + fears separation from God

Insist he not think of it - May disturb her also

? 33. *Is Lady Macbeth fighting for control here?*

Images of sleep - which gives rest MacBeth will never have sleep (rest) again Sleep = King. King nourishes the kingdom

36. raveled sleave: tangled thread.

38. second course: that is, sleep (the less substantial first course is food).

Vows he hears the voice announcing it to the house.

? 41. *Who else complained about sleep? In what way has Glamis "murdered sleep"?*

? 46. *What is the "filthy witness"? What actions are the couple engaged in here? In the next line Lady Macbeth discovers the daggers. Why is she so alarmed at seeing them in her husband's hands? How could Macbeth have been carrying them so they weren't visible before?*

You are hearing things
Practical
Why bring the daggers

A. Character
? What is already happening to Macbeth? (He feels guilt and fears separation from God.) Discuss how ironic it is that Macbeth feels the need of a blessing at this moment.

Answer to margin question
Line 33. "*Must not*" and "make *us* mad" suggest that she is also deeply troubled.

B. Metaphors
? Identify the metaphors that describe sleep. (A knitter who untangles threads; the death of each day; the bath that soothes the laborer; the ointment that heals hurt minds; food and nourishment)

Answers to margin questions
Line 41. Banquo could not sleep (Act II, Scene 1). See critic's comment, above.
Line 46. The "filthy witness" is Duncan's blood. Lady Macbeth is horrified that he has removed the daggers from the chamber. Macbeth may have had them in his belt or sleeves.

A. Discussing the Photograph

The caption identifies this scene from the Stratford (Canada) Festival production as illustrating lines 63 and 64 on the facing page.

❓ How well do you think the photograph captures the feelings of Macbeth and Lady Macbeth in this scene? (Answers will vary. Macbeth's hands are literally bloody because he performed the murders. Lady Macbeth's hands are also bloody because she urged him to do it. The emphasis on their hands is dramatically correct.) What details do or do not interpret the scene as you imagine it? (Students may discuss Lady Macbeth's dominant physical position, which reflects her dominance over her husband.)

"My hands are of your color, but I shame
To wear a heart so white."

Answers to margin questions
Line 55. She will smear his blood on the grooms.
Line 63. Her hands are bloody, but she moves confidently.
Line 71. He is lost in his own thoughts.
Stage direction. He might wish the bell could return him to a state of grace.
Stage direction. He would act the clown: He might stagger, fumble with the
gates or keys, pantomime the people he is imagining, put his hands over his ears, pretend to do his own knocking, forget what he's doing, and so on.

Plot Summary
Scene 3. A drunken porter responds to Macduff's and Lennox's knocking at the gate the next morning. Macbeth now appears calm. Macduff discovers Duncan's body while Lennox describes the unnatural occurrences during the night. Malcolm and Donalbain flee the country. Macbeth announces that he killed Duncan's grooms because they had murdered Duncan. Lady Macbeth faints.

They must lie there: go carry them, and smear
The sleepy grooms with blood.   *[Take them back]*

Macbeth.   I'll go no more.
50 I am afraid to think what I have done;   *[Afraid — refuses to return]*
Look on't again I dare not.

Lady Macbeth.   Infirm of purpose!
Give me the daggers. The sleeping and the dead   *[She takes the daggers]*
Are but as pictures. 'Tis the eye of childhood   *[Impatient — no reason to fear the dead]*
That fears a painted devil. If he do bleed,
55 I'll gild° the faces of the grooms withal.
A   For it must seem their guilt.   [*Exit. Knock within.*]

? 55. *What will Lady Macbeth do to the grooms if Duncan bleeds enough?*

Macbeth.   Whence is that knocking?
How is't with me, when every noise appalls me?
What hands are here? Ha! They pluck out mine eyes!   *[Allusion — all the water in ocean will not cleanse him of this deed. Duncan's blood w/ stain him & country]*
Will all great Neptune's ocean wash this blood
60 Clean from my hand? No; this my hand will rather
B   The multitudinous seas incarnadine,°
Making the green one red.

61. incarnadine: make red.

[*Enter* LADY MACBETH.]

Lady Macbeth.
My hands are of your color, but I shame   *[— Scolds him for his cowardice — feels no remorse]*
To wear a heart so white. (*Knock.*) I hear a knocking
65 At the south entry. Retire we to our chamber.   *[We need to wash & return to our chambers]*
A little water clears us of this deed:
How easy is it then! Your constancy
Hath left you unattended.° (*Knock.*) Hark! more knocking.
Get on your nightgown, lest occasion call us
70 And show us to be watchers.° Be not lost
So poorly in your thoughts.

? 63. *From this speech, what does Lady Macbeth look like?*

68. Your . . . unattended: Your firmness has deserted you.

70. watchers: that is, up late.

? 71. *What is Macbeth acting like?*

Macbeth.
To know my deed, 'twere best not know myself.

[*Knock.*]

Wake Duncan with thy knocking! I would thou couldst!   *[I would wake him if I could]*   [*Exeunt.*]

C
D

? Stage direction: *In the theater, this sharp, loud knocking is frightening. In the next line, what might Macbeth wish the knocking could awake in himself?*

Scene 3. *Macbeth's castle.*   *[Comic relief]*

Enter a PORTER. *Knocking within.*

Porter. Here's a knocking indeed! If a man were porter of hell gate, he should have old° turning the key. (*Knock*). Knock, knock, knock! Who's there, i' th' name of Beelzebub?° Here's a farmer, that hanged himself on th' expectation of plenty. Come in time!
5 Have napkins enow° about you; here you'll sweat for't. (*Knock.*) Knock, knock! Who's there, in th' other devil's name? Faith, here's an equivocator,° that could swear in both the scales against either scale;

? Stage direction. *Note that the porter is drunk. What would he be doing during this long speech while the knocking persists?*
2. have old: grow old.

4. Beelzebub: the Devil.

6. enow: enough.

8. equivocator: here, the porter means a Jesuit (who allegedly used false arguments in the zeal for souls).

A. Puns
Gild (to put gold leaf on) and *guilt* is a pun (gilt / guilt).

B. Imagery
Note that Macbeth's speech and Lady Macbeth's line 66 serve as contrasts. Macbeth knows the whole ocean cannot cleanse him of guilt for the murder; Lady Macbeth, in a more literal frame of mind, knows that only a bit of water will wash away the blood.

? What does Macbeth's speech in lines 60–62 suggest about the spreading effects of sin or evil? (Macbeth's guilt would pollute the entire ocean.)

C. Responding to Scene 2
See questions 3–5 and 12–13 on text page 284.

D. Planning to Teach Scene 3
See the commentary called "Macbeth's Porter" on text page 283 and Thomas De Quincey's essay "On the Knocking at the Gate in *Macbeth*" on text pages 335–337.

Castle is Hell —
Porter — porter to hell
references to hell

Prolongs the suspense.

Comic relief — relieve some of the tension of previous scene

A. The Porter
At the end of this scene, have students offer their own theories explaining its significance. Be sure they read the commentary "Macbeth's Porter" on text page 283.

? What explicit details in the porter's speech might support the idea that the castle is hell? ("Porter of hell gate," "Beelzebub," "here you'll sweat," "in th' other devil's name," "This place is too cold for hell. I'll devil-porter it no further," " . . . the primrose way to th' eternal bonfire")

Answer to margin question
Line 41. The king's men are about to discover Duncan's body and the bloodstained grooms.

10 who committed treason enough for God's sake, yet could not equivocate to heaven. O, come in, equivo-cator. (*Knock.*) Knock, knock, knock! Who's there? Faith, here's an English tailor come hither for stealing out of a French hose:° come in, tailor. Here you may
15 roast your goose.° (*Knock.*) Knock, knock; never at quiet! What are you? But this place is too cold for hell. I'll devil-porter it no further. I had thought to have let in some of all professions that go the primrose way to th' everlasting bonfire. (*Knock.*) Anon, anon!
20 (*Opens an entrance.*) I pray you, remember the porter.

14. French hose: tight-fitting stockings.
15. goose: an iron used by a tailor for pressing.

[*Enter* MACDUFF *and* LENNOX.]

Macduff.
  Was it so late, friend, ere you went to bed,
  That you do lie so late?
Porter. Faith, sir, we were carousing till the second cock:° and drink, sir, is a great provoker of three things.

23. second cock: about 3 A.M.

25 **Macduff.** What three things does drink especially pro-voke?
Porter. Marry, sir, nose-painting, sleep, and urine. Lech-ery, sir, it provokes and unprovokes; it provokes the desire, but it takes away the performance: therefore
30 much drink may be said to be an equivocator with lechery: it makes him and it mars him; it sets him on and it takes him off; it persuades him and disheartens him; makes him stand to and not stand to; in conclu-sion, equivocates him in a sleep, and giving him the
35 lie, leaves him.
Macduff. I believe drink gave thee the lie° last night.
Porter. That it did, sir, i' the very throat on me: but I requited him for his lie, and, I think, being too strong for him, though he took up my legs sometimes, yet I
40 made a shift to cast° him.
Macduff. Is thy master stirring?

36. gave thee the lie: a pun meaning "called you a liar" and "stretched you out, lying in bed."

40. cast: a pun meaning "to cast in plas-ter" and "to vomit" (cast out).
? **41.** *All the time this humorous bantering is going on, what do we know these king's men are about to discover?*

[*Enter* MACBETH.]

  Our knocking has awakened him; here he comes.
Lennox.
  Good morrow, noble sir.
Macbeth.   Good morrow, both.
Macduff.
  Is the king stirring, worthy thane?
Macbeth.   Not yet.
Macduff.

Duncan summoned him

45 He did command me to call timely° on him:
  I have almost slipped the hour.
Macbeth.   I'll bring you to him.
Macduff.
  I know this a joyful trouble to you;
  But yet 'tis one.

45. timely: early.

Answers to margin questions
Line 52. Macbeth must be feeling nearly sick with tension.
Line 59. "Unnatural" upsets in nature parallel the unnatural death of Duncan.
Line 60. The reference is to " 'Twas a rough night." Macbeth might speak as if simply agreeing with Lennox but with a sidelong glance at his wife. Or he might say it full of irony. Encourage students to

try out various interpretations for speaking this line.
Line 68. Macduff speaks of the king as a sacred building that it is a sacrilege to attack. His image suggests the concept of kings as divinely anointed.

Macbeth.
The labor we delight in physics° pain.
This is the door.

50 **Macduff.**   I'll make so bold to call,
For 'tis my limited service.°   [*Exit* MACDUFF.]

Lennox.
Goes the king hence today?

Macbeth.   He does: he did appoint so.

Lennox.
The night has been unruly. Where we lay,
Our chimneys were blown down, and, as they say,
55 Lamentings heard i' th' air, strange screams of death,
And prophesying with accents terrible
Of dire combustion and confused events
New hatched to th' woeful time: the obscure bird
Clamored the livelong night. Some say, the earth
60 Was feverous and did shake.

Macbeth.   'Twas a rough night.

Lennox.
My young remembrance cannot parallel
A fellow to it.

[*Enter* MACDUFF.]

Macduff.
O horror, horror, horror! Tongue nor heart
Cannot conceive nor name thee.

Macbeth and Lennox.   What's the matter?

Macduff.
65 Confusion now hath made his masterpiece.
Most sacrilegious murder hath broke ope
The Lord's anointed temple,° and stole thence
The life o' th' building.

Macbeth.   What is't you say? The life?

Lennox.
Mean you his majesty?

Macduff.
70 Approach the chamber, and destroy your sight
With a new Gorgon:° do not bid me speak;
See, and then speak yourselves. Awake, awake!

[*Exeunt* MACBETH *and* LENNOX.]

Ring the alarum bell. Murder and treason!
Banquo and Donalbain! Malcolm! Awake!
75 Shake off this downy sleep, death's counterfeit,
And look on death itself! Up, up, and see
The great doom's image! Malcolm! Banquo!
As from your graves rise up, and walk like sprites,
To countenance° this horror. Ring the bell.

[*Bell rings. Enter* LADY MACBETH.]

Lady Macbeth.
80 What's the business,

49. **physics:** cures.

51. **limited service:** appointed duty.

? 52. *How must Macbeth be feeling?*

Lennox talks about the troubled night
weather is bad
nature mirrors events of human society

? 59. *In Elizabethan times people often believed that Nature mirrored terrible things happening to human beings, especially to kings. How did this weather mirror what was happening to the king in Macbeth's castle?*

? 60. *A single line, but full of irony. How would Macbeth say it?*

> *Macduff discovers Duncan's body*

Life of the king is gone.

67. **Lord's anointed temple:** the body of the king.

? 68. *How would you explain Macduff's metaphors?*

Sight will turn you cold

71. **Gorgon:** a creature from Greek mythology whose face could turn an onlooker to stone.

Calls the Alarm

Image of sleep

79. **countenance:** be in keeping with.

A. Nature Symbolism
Recall the "Fair is foul, and foul is fair" of Act I, extending even to the weather. In Lennox's report we have another instance of nature mirroring events in human society. If students remember Shakespeare's *Julius Caesar,* they may recall the portents that prefigured tragedy for Caesar (Act I, Scene 3).

B. Imagery
Another comment on sleep; here it is associated with death.

Answers to margin questions

Line 87. She must play the part seriously, acting as a genuinely shocked hostess would.

Line 99. Lennox says that the groom "as it seemed, had done't." His words suggest that he is not completely satisfied.

A. Metaphor
Note Macbeth's metaphoric account and Macduff's straightforward language; they are both saying that the king is dead.

❓ To what is the king compared in Macbeth's speech? (A spring, the head of a river, a fountain)

B. Plot and Character
Note the shock Macbeth introduces here; in all the confusion he has managed to kill Duncan's servants, apparently without the slightest trace of guilt.

❓ What is happening to Macbeth? (He is becoming skilled in crime and in deception.)

C. Character
Shakespeare made his Macbeth more introspective and evil than Holinshed's competent warrior-king, and his Duncan is far more saintly. The contrast shows even in Macbeth's words here. His earlier images of blood have focused on sickening gore, but he sees the venerable Duncan as having "silver skin" and "golden blood."

That such a hideous trumpet calls to parley°
The sleepers of the house? Speak, speak!
Macduff.   O gentle lady,
'Tis not for you to hear what I can speak:
The repetition, in a woman's ear,
Would murder as it fell.

[*Enter* BANQUO.]

85   O Banquo, Banquo!
Our royal master's murdered.
Lady Macbeth.   Woe, alas!
What, in our house?
Banquo.   Too cruel anywhere.
Dear Duff, I prithee, contradict thyself,
And say it is not so.

[*Enter* MACBETH, LENNOX, *and* ROSS.]

Macbeth.
90   Had I but died an hour before this chance,
I had lived a blessèd time; for from this instant
There's nothing serious in mortality:°
All is but toys. Renown and grace is dead,
The wine of life is drawn, and the mere lees°
95   Is left this vault° to brag of.

[*Enter* MALCOLM *and* DONALBAIN.]

Donalbain.
What is amiss?
Macbeth.   You are, and do not know't.
The spring, the head, the fountain of your blood
Is stopped; the very source of it is stopped.
Macduff.
Your royal father's murdered.
Malcolm.   O, by whom?
Lennox.
100   Those of his chamber, as it seemed, had done't:
Their hands and faces were all badged° with blood;
So were their daggers, which unwiped we found
Upon their pillows. They stared, and were distracted.
No man's life was to be trusted with them.
Macbeth.
105   O, yet I do repent me of my fury,
That I did kill them.
Macduff.   Wherefore did you so?
Macbeth.
Who can be wise, amazed, temp'rate and furious,
Loyal and neutral, in a moment? No man.
The expedition° of my violent love
110   Outrun the pauser, reason. Here lay Duncan,
His silver skin laced with his golden blood,
And his gashed stabs looked like a breach in nature

81. **parley:** a conference of war.

❓ 87. *The emphasis on Lady Macbeth's gentleness and fairness when we know the foulness underneath might well merit a snicker from the audience: It might be expected to grow into a laugh when she says, "What, in our house?" These are difficult moments to act. How do you think Lady Macbeth should be behaving?*

92. **mortality:** life.

94. **lees:** dregs.

95. **vault:** a pun on "wine vault" and the "vault of heaven."

❓ 99. *Macbeth and Lady Macbeth might well look at each other at this moment. Does Lennox draw the conclusion they wanted him to draw: that the servants killed Duncan?*
101. **badged:** marked.

109. **expedition:** haste.

280

280   The Renaissance

READING CHECK TEST (Act II)

1. How does Duncan die? (Macbeth stabs him.)

2. Why doesn't Lady Macbeth do it? (The sleeping Duncan reminds her of her father.)

3. Who smears the blood on Duncan's servants? (Lady Macbeth)

4. Right after Duncan dies, Macbeth hears a voice cry out. What does it say Macbeth has murdered? (Sleep)

5. What two young men flee the castle in fear? (Duncan's sons Malcolm and Donalbain)

For ruin's wasteful entrance: there, the murderers,
Steeped in the colors of their trade, their daggers
115   Unmannerly breeched with gore. Who could refrain,°
That had a heart to love, and in that heart
Courage to make's love known?

A   **Lady Macbeth.**   Help me hence, ho!
Macduff.
    Look to the lady.
Malcolm (*aside to* DONALBAIN). Why do we hold our tongues,
120   That most may claim this argument for ours?°
Donalbain (*aside to* MALCOLM). What should be spoken here,
B   Where our fate, hid in an auger-hole,°
May rush, and seize us? Let's away:
Our tears are not yet brewed.
125   **Malcolm** (*aside to* DONALBAIN). Nor our strong sorrow
Upon the foot of motion.°
Banquo.   Look to the lady.

[LADY MACBETH *is carried out*.]

    And when we have our naked frailties hid,°
That suffer in exposure, let us meet
And question° this most bloody piece of work,
130   To know it further. Fears and scruples° shake us.
In the great hand of God I stand, and thence
Against the undivulged pretense° I fight
Of treasonous malice.
Macduff.   And so do I.
All.   So all.
Macbeth.
C   Let's briefly° put on manly readiness,
And meet i' th' hall together.
135   **All.**   Well contented.

[*Exeunt all but* MALCOLM *and* DONALBAIN.]

Malcolm.
    What will you do? Let's not consort with them.
To show an unfelt sorrow is an office°
Which the false man does easy. I'll to England.
Donalbain.
    To Ireland, I; our separated fortune
140   Shall keep us both the safer. Where we are
D   There's daggers in men's smiles; the near in blood,
The nearer bloody.
Malcolm.   This murderous shaft that's shot
Hath not yet lighted, and our safest way
Is to avoid the aim. Therefore to horse;
145   And let us not be dainty of° leave-taking,
But shift away. There's warrant° in that theft
Which steals itself° when there's no mercy left.

[*Exeunt*.]

E

---

115. **refrain:** check oneself.

[handwritten: faints (shock or distract?)]

[handwritten: They are danger.]

120. **That . . . ours:** who are the most concerned with this topic.

122. **auger-hole:** unsuspected place.

[handwritten: Need time to think about the consequences.]

126. **Our tears . . . motion:** We have not yet had time for tears nor to express our sorrows in action.

[handwritten: Let's get dressed + then meet back here to talk about it.]

127. **naked frailties hid:** poor bodies clothed.

129. **question:** discuss.
130. **scruples:** suspicions.

132. **undivulged pretense:** hidden purpose.

134. **briefly:** quickly.

137. **office:** function.

145. **dainty of:** fussy about.
146. **warrant:** justification.
147. **steals itself:** steals oneself away.

A. Interpreting

? Do you believe Lady Macbeth faints because of genuine shock or to distract attention from Macbeth? (She could be shocked: Killing the grooms was unnecessary, even stupid. She could also realize that Macbeth could give himself away if pressed too closely.)

B. Clarification
Be sure students understand that Malcolm and Donalbain are Duncan's young sons.

? Why would they be in danger? (They are in line for the throne.)

C. Clarification
Macbeth and his guests, still in nightclothes, need to get dressed ("manly readiness").

D. Metaphor
This famous statement relates to the "Fair is foul" theme.

E. Responding to Scene 3
See questions 6–9 and 14–17 on text page 284.

ANALYZING ACT II
Identifying Facts
1. Macbeth tells Banquo that if he supports him when the time comes, he will receive honors.

Banquo says that he will agree, provided that Macbeth does not ask him to do anything that will compromise a clear conscience.
2. Macbeth sees a dagger in the air that gradually grows red with blood. Details that foreshadow the action to come include the gouts of blood, the figurative description of "withered murder," and Macbeth's comments on the bell that summons Duncan "to heaven, or to hell."
3. Lady Macbeth hears the shriek of an owl and the cry of crickets.

Macbeth hears the laughter of one of the guards in his sleep and the cries of

A. Nature Symbolism
Relate the dialogue of the Old Man and Ross to Lennox's speech (lines 53–60, text page 279).
❓ How is the time setting again revealed, and what kind of day is it? (It's day but it's dark as night—the sun is in eclipse.)

B. Character
❓ Macduff appears to speak plainly. What happens to his meaning if you add a sarcastic or ironic tone to his voice? (He would be casting doubt upon Macbeth's interpretation of the facts and be accusing Macbeth of the king's murder.) Do you think he believes everything he reports, as in lines 25–27? (Probably not since he does not attend the coronation and fears Macbeth's kingship) Encourage several interpretations. Ask students to support their opinions with reasons.

Scene 4. *Outside Macbeth's castle.*

Enter ROSS *with an* OLD MAN.

Old Man.
  Threescore and ten I can remember well:
  Within the volume of which time I have seen
  Hours dreadful and things strange, but this sore° night
  Hath trifled former knowings.°

Ross.   Ha, good father,

5 Thou see'st the heavens, as troubled with man's act,
  Threatens his bloody stage. By th' clock 'tis day,
  And yet dark night strangles the traveling lamp:°
  Is't night's predominance,° or the day's shame,
  That darkness does the face of earth entomb,
  When living light should kiss it?

Old Man.   'Tis unnatural,

10 Even like the deed that's done. On Tuesday last
  A falcon, tow'ring in her pride of place,°
  Was by a mousing° owl hawked at and killed.

Ross.
  And Duncan's horses—a thing most strange and certain—

15 Beauteous and swift, the minions° of their race,
  Turned wild in nature, broke their stalls, flung out,°
  Contending 'gainst obedience, as they would make
  War with mankind.

Old Man.   'Tis said they eat° each other.

Ross.
  They did so, to th' amazement of mine eyes,
  That looked upon't.

[*Enter* MACDUFF.]

20   Here comes the good Macduff.
  How goes the world, sir, now?

Macduff.   Why, see you not?

Ross.
  Is't known who did this more than bloody deed?

Macduff.
  Those that Macbeth hath slain.

Ross.   Alas, the day!
  What good could they pretend?°

Macduff.   They were suborned:°

25 Malcolm and Donalbain, the king's two sons,
  Are stol'n away and fled, which puts upon them
  Suspicion of the deed.

Ross.   'Gainst nature still.
  Thriftless° ambition, that will ravin up°
  Thine own life's means!° Then 'tis most like

30 The sovereignty will fall upon Macbeth.

Macduff.
  He is already named,° and gone to Scone°
  To be invested.°

3. sore: grievous.
4. trifled former knowings: made trifles of former experiences.

7. traveling lamp: the sun.
8. predominance: astrological supremacy.

12. tow'ring . . . place: soaring at her summit.
13. mousing: normally mouse-eating.

15. minions: darlings.
16. flung out: lunged wildly.

18. eat: ate.

24. pretend: hope for. **suborned:** bribed.

28. Thriftless: wasteful. **ravin up:** greedily devour.
29. own life's means: parent.

31. named: elected. **Scone** (skoon).
32. invested: installed as king.

"Murder" and "God bless us." Then he thinks that he hears repeated cries that say, "Sleep no more."
4. She says that Duncan resembled her father as he slept.

She plants the daggers near the grooms and tells Macbeth to wash the blood from his hands and put on his nightgown.
5. He says that not even "great Nep-tune's ocean" can make his hands clean; rather, the blood on his hands will make the sea turn from green to red.
6. The porter is pretending that someone is knocking on the gate of hell.
7. Macduff has come because the king had commanded him to meet him at the castle early in the morning.
8. He says that he killed them out of fury at their "murder" of the king.
9. Malcolm decides to go to England, and Donalbain makes for Ireland.
10. Macduff says he suspects the king's sons because they have fled.

Interpreting Meanings
11. Answers may vary. Though Duncan's sons also voice their suspicions, the character who edges toward suspi-
(Answers continue on next page.)

Ross.   Where is Duncan's body?
Macduff.
   Carried to Colmekill,°   *Buried.*
   The sacred storehouse of his predecessors
   And guardian of their bones.
35 Ross.   Will you to Scone?
Macduff.
   No, cousin, I'll to Fife.
Ross.   Well, I will thither.
Macduff.

A ⌈ Well, may you see things well done there. Adieu,
   ⌊ Lest our old robes sit easier than our new!
Ross.
   Farewell, father.
Old Man.
40   God's benison° go with you, and with those
   That would make good of bad, and friends of foes!
                                   [*Exeunt omnes.*]
B

33. Colmekill: Iona Island, the ancient burying place of Scottish kings. (It was founded by St. Colm.)

Macduff refuses to go to Scone.

40. benison: blessing.

Macduff —
*   suspicious of*
*   Macbeth.*
foreshadows future
*   interaction between*
*   them.*

A. Imagery
? What is Macduff suggesting in this line about old and new "robes"? (This clothing image means that their new positions may not suit them as well as their old ones did.)

B. Responding to Scene 4
See questions 10–11 and 17 on text page 284.

CLOSURE
Have students describe the actions the characters have taken to get what they want, and the complications that have arisen (or that might possibly arise).

Macbeth's Porter

Why does Macbeth's comic porter, speaking a gross, drunken rigmarole, appear just at this point in the play, right after the murder of Duncan? Is this not a monstrous interruption?

One way to account for the scene is to remind ourselves that Shakespeare was writer in residence to a company of actors and therefore bound to provide parts for every member in every play—even a part for the chief comedian in a tragedy. But this is not a satisfactory explanation because it was not characteristic of Shakespeare merely to do what was expected of him as a professional writer; he always did something more, almost made a virtue out of theatrical necessity. And so, as a second explanation of the porter's scene, some critics have argued that it is designed to provide comic relief from the tense aftermath of Duncan's murder. But this also is not a convincing reason, because the scene actually increases tension rather than relieves it. As Macbeth and his wife stand whispering about the evil thing they have done, they—and the audience—are startled to hear a loud and totally unexpected knocking on the main gate of the castle. Even a hardened criminal would be startled by the coincidence of these events, and Macbeth and his wife are mere beginners in crime. While they hastily retreat into their bedroom, the porter (a word meaning door tender) shuffles on stage to answer the knocking at his leisure, thus prolonging the interval between the murder and its discovery and greatly increasing suspense, which is what makes drama interesting.

Theatergoers in Shakespeare's day were accustomed to comic porters; they were familiar figures in miracle plays, in which they kept the gates of hell. They were expected to be droll and at the same time sinister. "Who's there, in the name of Beelzebub?" asks Macbeth's porter, referring to one of the chief devils and implying that the castle is a place the devil occupies. And indeed it already has become hell, which is as much a state of mind as a particular place. Lady Macbeth has called for the "smoke of hell" in Act I and Macbeth has been unable to say "Amen" when one of Duncan's men cried, "God bless us" in Act II. To cut out the porter's scene, as many directors have done (and also many editors of school texts) is to weaken the fabric of the play.

See also Thomas DeQuincey's essay, "On the Knocking at the Gate in *Macbeth*," following the play.

(Answers begin on page 282.)

cion is Macduff. He asks why Macbeth murdered the grooms (Scene 2) and by Scene 4 says he will not attend Macbeth's coronation and expresses fears about his reign.

12. Lady Macbeth's reason is that the king resembles her father as he sleeps. Student answers will vary. Ask the students to explain their opinions in class.

13. Student answers will vary. Some students may argue that the murders become even more horrible if the audience is allowed to imagine them.

14. The speech can be interpreted in two ways. On the level of a hypocritical lament, it is intended to convey sorrow at the king's violent death and to avert suspicion from Macbeth. But Macbeth's words are ambiguous: They may be tak-

en to mean that, with the murder, he knows he has lost his true peace of mind, renown, and grace. Interpreted in this way, the speech reveals Macbeth's regret and guilt.

15. She probably wants her fainting spell to distract attention from Macbeth's elaborate explanation of why he killed the guards. She may also be sending him *(Answers continue in left-hand column.)*

(Continued from top.)
the message not to reveal too much information.

16. In their minds is the possibility that Macbeth, despite his professions of sorrow, has actually murdered the king. They hint about this possibility by indirectly referring to an "unfelt sorrow" and "daggers in men's smiles."

17. Shakespeare characterizes Macduff as direct, loyal, and perhaps a bit naive.

18. The mood of Act II is sinister and violent. Among the images that help to create this mood are Banquo's opening description of the starless night, the repeated references to blood, the dagger, Lennox's description of the storm, the shriek of the owl, and the porter's references to the gate of hell.

Responding to the Play

Analyzing Act II

Identifying Facts

1. In Scene 1, Macbeth asks Banquo to meet him later for "some words." What incentive does he offer Banquo? How does Banquo reply?
2. Describe the vision that Macbeth has at the end of Scene 1. What details **foreshadow** the action to come?
3. In Scene 2, as Macbeth kills Duncan, what does Lady Macbeth hear? What does Macbeth hear?
4. Why, according to Lady Macbeth, was she unable to kill Duncan herself? Which tasks related to the murder does she perform?
5. In Scene 2, Lady Macbeth sensibly suggests that Macbeth go wash the "filthy witness" from his hands after the murder. How does Macbeth respond?
6. In Scene 3, what is the porter pretending as he goes to open the gate?
7. Why has Macduff come?
8. What reason does Macbeth give for killing Duncan's two guards?
9. Where do Duncan's sons decide to go?
10. In Scene 4, whom does Macduff suspect of Duncan's murder?

Interpreting Meanings

11. Though Macbeth encounters no actual opposition until long after Duncan is murdered, Shakespeare must **foreshadow** some trouble for him and, to build up **suspense**, must start one character edging toward suspicion of Macbeth. Who is this character, and what inkling does he give of his dissatisfaction with Macbeth?
12. In Act I, Scene 7, Lady Macbeth seemed to be planning to murder Duncan herself. But at the last moment, in Act II, Scene 2, she is unable to wield her dagger. Consider the reason she gives, and decide what her actions and explanation reveal about her **character.**
13. Many people are killed onstage in Shakespeare's plays. Why, then, do you suppose he decided to have the murder of Duncan and his guards take place offstage?
14. In Scene 3, when Duncan's corpse is discovered, Macbeth utters a hypocritical lament beginning, "Had I but died. . . ." But is it really hypocritical? The critic A. C. Bradly argued that, although the speech is meant to be a lie, it actually contains "Macbeth's profoundest feelings." Explain this apparent contradiction. How does Macbeth feel about

Mervyn Blake as the Porter in the Stratford Festival, Canada, production (1983).

having murdered Duncan? What clues tell you how he feels?
15. Lady Macbeth's fainting spell, like everything else she has done so far, has a purpose. What message do you think she wants her fainting spell to convey?
16. Malcolm and Donalbain are little more than boys, yet they already know enough about life to keep their mouths shut. What is in their minds, but left unsaid? How do they hint about it to each other?
17. Macduff is an important character in the three remaining acts. Describe how Shakespeare **characterizes** Macduff in Scenes 3 and 4.
18. What would you say is the **mood** of Act II? What **images** and actions help to create this mood?

PREPARATION
ESTABLISHING A PURPOSE. Macbeth is now king; Lady Macbeth is now queen. They invite Banquo to a state banquet and inquire about his plans for the day. Considering the prophecies of the weird sisters, how might the Macbeths actually now feel about Banquo? Can their gracious words be trusted?

Plot Summary
Scene 1. Banquo reveals that he suspects Macbeth of having murdered Duncan and the grooms. Macbeth invites Banquo to a banquet that night and learns that Banquo and his son Fleance will be riding out. Macbeth arranges for the murder of Banquo and Fleance.

Act III   Scene 1. *Forres. The palace.*

Enter BANQUO.

Banquo.
    Thou hast it now: king, Cawdor, Glamis, all,
    As the weird women promised, and I fear
    Thou play'dst most foully for't. Yet it was said
    It should not stand° in thy posterity,
5   But that myself should be the root and father
    Of many kings. If there come truth from them—
    As upon thee, Macbeth, their speeches shine—
    Why, by the verities on thee made good,
    May they not be my oracles as well
10 And set me up in hope? But hush, no more!

    [*Sennet*° *sounded. Enter* MACBETH *as king,* LADY MAC-
    BETH, LENNOX, ROSS, LORDS, *and* ATTENDANTS.]

Macbeth.
    Here's our chief guest.
Lady Macbeth.   If he had been forgotten,
    It had been as a gap in our great feast,
    And all-thing° unbecoming.
Macbeth.
    Tonight we hold a solemn supper, sir,
    And I'll request your presence.
15 **Banquo.**   Let your highness
    Command upon me, to the which my duties
    Are with a most indissoluble tie
    Forever knit.
Macbeth.
    Ride you this afternoon?
Banquo.   Ay, my good lord.
Macbeth.
20 We should have else desired your good advice
    (Which still° hath been both grave and prosperous°)
    In this day's council; but we'll take tomorrow.
    Is't far you ride?
Banquo.
    As far, my lord, as will fill up the time
25 'Twixt this and supper. Go not my horse the better,°
    I must become a borrower of the night
    For a dark hour or twain.
Macbeth.   Fail not our feast.
Banquo.
    My lord, I will not.
Macbeth.
    We hear our bloody cousins are bestowed°
30 In England and in Ireland, not confessing
    Their cruel parricide, filling their hearers
    With strange invention. But of that tomorrow,
    When therewithal we shall have cause of state

4. stand: continue.

10. *What would you say Banquo's mood is? Is he envious or thoughtful and troubled?*
Sennet: trumpet.

13. all-thing: altogether.

21. still: always. **grave and prosperous:** weighty and profitable.

25. Go not my horse the better: Unless my horse goes faster than I expected.

29. are bestowed: have taken refuge.

[Handwritten annotations: "soliloquy"; "Banquo suspects Macbeth"; "Banquo is troubled + thoughtful wonders about the prophecies of his descendents being kings"; "Dinner = a banquet Request Banquo be there"; "Banquo leaving but will be back for supper"; "Malcolm Donaldbain"; "Tomorrow we will talk of what to do about Mal. + Don"]

Line 35. Macbeth asks if Banquo is going riding, how far, and whether Fleance is going. He would speak as casually as he could.

Line 42. Answers will vary. It soon becomes obvious that he has set up a secret meeting.

Line 63. "Barren scepter" and "unlineal hand" both refer to a throne inherited not by one's children but by a nonrelative. Macbeth worries that Banquo's "sons" will inherit Macbeth's throne.

Line 72. He is angry that he has endangered his soul with the foul sin of murder only to benefit another man's descendants.

Line 74. Answers will vary. After students have finished reading the scene, you might return to the question. Students may suggest that they are basically solid citizens who have been suborned by Macbeth.

A. "Father to a Line of Kings"
James VI of Scotland, shortly after assuming the English throne in 1603 as James I, gave his patronage to Shakespeare's company, which then became known as the King's Men. *Macbeth* is the Shakespearean play most clearly reflecting the company's special relationship with the king: James regarded the virtuous Banquo as his direct ancestor, and later in the play (Act IV, Scene I) the ghostly Banquo points to "a show of eight kings" as his descendants. (See text page 304.)

Craving us jointly.° Hie you to horse. Adieu,

35 Till you return at night. Goes Fleance with you?

Banquo.
Ay, my good lord: our time does call upon 's.

Macbeth.
I wish your horses swift and sure of foot,
And so I do commend you to their backs.
Farewell.   [*Exit* BANQUO.]

40 Let every man be master of his time
Till seven at night. To make society
The sweeter welcome, we will keep ourself
Till supper-time alone. While° then, God be with you!

[*Exeunt* LORDS *and all but* MACBETH *and a* SERVANT.]

Sirrah, a word with you: attend° those men

45 Our pleasure?

Attendant.
They are, my lord, without the palace gate.

Macbeth.
Bring them before us.   [*Exit* SERVANT.]
To be thus° is nothing, but° to be safely thus—
Our fears in Banquo stick deep,

50 And in his royalty of nature reigns that
Which would be feared. 'Tis much he dares;
And, to that dauntless temper of his mind,
He hath a wisdom that doth guide his valor
To act in safety. There is none but he

55 Whose being I do fear: and under him
My genius is rebuked,° as it is said
Mark Antony's was by Caesar. He chid the sisters,
When first they put the name of king upon me,
And bade them speak to him; then prophetlike

A
60 They hailed him father to a line of kings.
Upon my head they placed a fruitless crown
And put a barren scepter in my grip,
Thence to be wrenched with an unlineal hand,
No son of mine succeeding. If't be so,

65 For Banquo's issue have I filed° my mind;
For them the gracious Duncan have I murdered;
Put rancors° in the vessel of my peace
Only for them, and mine eternal jewel°
Given to the common enemy of man,°

70 To make them kings, the seeds of Banquo kings!
Rather than so, come, fate, into the list,°
And champion me to th' utterance!° Who's there?

[*Enter* SERVANT *and two* MURDERERS.]

Now go to the door, and stay there till we call.

[*Exit* SERVANT.]

Was it not yesterday we spoke together?

---

34. us jointly: our joint attention.

35. *Macbeth has asked three important questions in this scene. What are they? How do you think he would ask them?*

42. *Notice that Macbeth uses the "royal we"; that is, he speaks of himself as "we," as a representative of all the people. Why do you think he wants to be alone?*

43. While: until.
44. attend: await.

48. thus: king. **but:** unless.

56. genius is rebuked: guardian spirit is cowed.

63. *What is an "unlineal hand"? What is a "barren scepter"? What is eating at Macbeth now?*
65. filed: defiled, dirtied.

67. rancors: bitter enmity.
68. jewel: immortal soul.
69. common enemy of man: Satan.

71. list: battle.
72. champion me to th' utterance: fight against me till I give up.
72. *Why exactly is Macbeth so angry? What has he given up in order to make Banquo's sons kings?*
74. *What do you imagine the murderers would be like: the all-too-common "hit" men of contemporary movies? Or could they simply be officers who have a grudge against Banquo? (They have been portrayed in many ways.)*

[Handwritten annotations: "Everyone find something to do until supper"; "Soliloquy"; "Macbeth afraid, but more afraid not as afraid as in 1st or 2nd Act"; "Fears Banquo"; "Fears the prophesies"; "Banquo - wise to act cautiously"; "Fears only Banquo"; "Fears prophesies / Reason he fears Banquo"; "I have done all this for Banquo's benefit"; "Soul"; "Satan"]

Murderers.
    It was, so please your highness.

75 **Macbeth.**   Well then, now
    Have you considered of my speeches? Know
A   That it was he in the times past, which held you
    So under fortune,° which you thought had been
    Our innocent self: this I made good to you

80   In our last conference; passed in probation° with you,
    How you were borne in hand,° how crossed; the in-
      struments,°
    Who wrought with them, and all things else that might
    To half a soul° and to a notion° crazed
    Say, ''Thus did Banquo.''

First Murderer.   You made it known to us.
Macbeth.
85   I did so; and went further, which is now

Have you considered my proposal

Banquo kept you from good fortune

78. held you/So under fortune: kept you
from good fortune.

80. probation: review.

81. borne in hand: deceived. **instruments:**
tools.

83. half a soul: half a brain. **notion:** mind.

A. Reading Critically
Ask students to examine carefully what Macbeth says to the murderers here and on the next page and a half. Note that his speeches reveal his own tyranny and his attempts to deflect the blame.
❓ Who is "he" in line 77?
(Banquo)

B. About the Photograph
This still from the Polanski film illustrates lines 141–142 on text page 289, at the conclusion of Macbeth's meeting with his hired killers. Note that although these lines are cast in the *form* of direct address, Banquo is not present; the lines are a comment on the deal just concluded.

B

*"It is concluded: Banquo, thy soul's flight,
If it find heaven, must find it out tonight."*

Macbeth, Act III, Scene 1   287

Line 91. Macbeth is trying to convince the murderers that Banquo is to blame for all their troubles and that they are unmanly if they are not angry. His arguments are much like those that Lady Macbeth used on him.

Line 126. Macbeth argues that he must appear unblemished, needing to retain the good will of his and Banquo's friends, and for other "weighty reasons"—in other words, for reasons of state or for political reasons.

A. Simile

Have students paraphrase lines 92–101.

❓ What is the point of Macbeth's extended comparison of men and dogs? (He says, in effect, that the word *men* doesn't distinguish among the different types of men any more than the word *dog* distinguishes the different breeds of dogs he names. Men are more precisely described by their values and by their traits.)

B. Responding

❓ Do you find the murderers at all sympathetic here? (Student responses will vary. They blame their willingness to murder on past wrongs and misfortunes.)

[handwritten margin note, top] Convincing the men that Banquo is responsible for all their troubles if they are unmanly if they are not angry.

Our point of second meeting. Do you find
Your patience so predominant in your nature,
That you can let this go? Are you so gospeled,°
To pray for this good man and for his issue,
90   Whose heavy hand hath bowed you to the grave
And beggared yours forever?

First Murderer.   We are men, my liege.

Macbeth.

[handwritten: Metaphor / Similes]

Ay, in the catalogue ye go for° men;
As hounds and greyhounds, mongrels, spaniels, curs,
Shoughs, water-rugs° and demi-wolves, are clept° *called*
95   All by the name of dogs: the valued file°
A   Distinguishes the swift, the slow, the subtle,
The housekeeper, the hunter, every one
According to the gift which bounteous nature
Hath in him closed,° whereby he does receive
100 Particular addition, from the bill°
That writes them all alike: and so of men.
Now if you have a station in the file,
Not i' th' worst rank of manhood, say't,
And I will put that business in your bosoms
105 Whose execution takes your enemy off,
Grapples you to the heart and love of us,
Who wear our health but sickly in his life,°
Which in his death were perfect.

Second Murderer.   I am one, my liege,
Whom the vile blows and buffets of the world
110 Hath so incensed that I am reckless what
B   I do to spite the world.

First Murderer.   And I another
So weary with disasters, tugged with fortune,
That I would set° my life on any chance,
To mend it or be rid on't.

Macbeth.   Both of you
Know Banquo was your enemy.

115 **Both Murderers.**   True, my lord.

Macbeth.

So is he mine, and in such bloody distance°
That every minute of his being thrusts
Against my near'st of life:° and though I could
With barefaced power sweep him from my sight
120 And bid my will avouch° it, yet I must not,
For° certain friends that are both his and mine,
Whose loves I may not drop, but wail his fall
Who I myself struck down: and thence it is
That I to your assistance do make love,
125 Masking the business from the common eye
For sundry weighty reasons.

Second Murderer.   We shall, my lord,
Perform what you command us.

First Murderer.   Though our lives—

[handwritten margin note] He could kill Banquo himself, but others would question the action

88. gospeled: so meek from reading the Gospel (of Jesus).

❓ **91.** *What techniques is Macbeth using on the murderers? Does it remind you of the way Lady Macbeth goaded him into killing Duncan?*
92. go for: pass as.

94. Shoughs, water-rugs: shaggy dogs and long-haired water dogs. **clept:** called.
95. valued file: classification by valuable traits.

99. closed: enclosed.
100. bill: list.

[handwritten margin note] Word dog doesn't distinguish the different breeds of dogs. Word men doesn't distinguish between different types of men. Set yourselves apart as men & kill Banquo

107. who wear . . . life: who are "sick" while he (Banquo) still lives.

[handwritten margin note] Agree to Macbeth's proposal

113. set: risk.

116. distance: quarrel.

118. near'st of life: vital spot.

120. avouch: justify.
121. For: because of.

❓ **126.** *How is Macbeth justifying to the murderers the fact that he has to ask them to do the job of killing Banquo?*

Line 140. The murderers are to wait until Macbeth gives them the exact time for the ambush. Macbeth is cold and calculating. Lady Macbeth has no part in these arrangements.

Line 7. Finding that they must now live with fear and suspicion, Lady Macbeth is beginning to believe Duncan's murder was not worth it.

Line 12. Lady Macbeth can be seen as sympathetic, pleading, even gently cajoling in her attempts to restore Macbeth to reason.

Plot Summary
Scene 2. Lady Macbeth expresses her discontent in a brief soliloquy. She urges Macbeth to be fearless and more cheerful. He says he envies Duncan, who is at peace. Macbeth says that he fears Banquo and his children and that a dreadful deed will soon be accomplished. He tells Lady Macbeth nothing of his plans.

A. Clarification
Be sure students know that Fleance, Banquo's son, is to be killed also, so that the witches' prophecy for Banquo cannot be fulfilled.

B. Interpreting
How do these proposed murders differ from those Macbeth has already committed? (He is now hiring someone else to commit the crime.) Why might Macbeth have changed tactics? (Perhaps as king he is too publicly visible; perhaps people are so suspicious of him already that he must be careful. See also question 7 on page 300.)

C. Responding to Scene 1
See questions 1 and 7 on text page 300.

D. Metaphor
Be sure students understand that the "snake" is all that stands in the way of Macbeth's intention to be king and to pass the crown on to his sons (not Banquo's).

Macbeth.

Your spirits shine through you. Within this hour at
        most
I will advise you where to plant yourselves,
130   Acquaint you with the perfect spy° o' th' time,
The moment on't; for't must be done tonight,
And something° from the palace; always thought°
That I require a clearness:° and with him—
To leave no rubs° nor botches in the work—
135   Fleance his son, that keeps him company,
Whose absence is no less material to me
Than is his father's, must embrace the fate
Of that dark hour. Resolve yourselves apart:°
I'll come to you anon.

Murderers.   We are resolved, my lord.

Macbeth.
140   I'll call upon you straight. Abide within.
It is concluded: Banquo, thy soul's flight,
If it find heaven, must find it out tonight.   [*Exeunt*.]

130. **perfect spy:** exact information.

132. **something:** some distance.   **thought:** remembered.
133. **clearness:** He has to appear "clear," or clear of suspicion.
134. **rubs:** flaw.

Kill Banquo + Fleance Tonight — away from the palace

138. **apart:** alone (make up your minds by yourselves).

140. *What has Macbeth arranged with the murderers? What is his mood here? Does Lady Macbeth have any part in arranging these next murders?*

How do these proposed murders differ from those Macbeth has already committed?
hiring someone else
acting alone
not afraid
more ruthless
Change in character

Scene 2. *The palace.*

Enter LADY MACBETH *and a* SERVANT.

Lady Macbeth.
Is Banquo gone from court?

Servant.
Ay, madam, but returns again tonight.

Lady Macbeth.
Say to the king, I would attend his leisure
For a few words.

Servant.   Madam, I will.   [*Exit*.]

Lady Macbeth.   Nought's had, all's spent,
5   Where our desire is got without content:
'Tis safer to be that which we destroy
Than by destruction dwell in doubtful joy.

[*Enter* MACBETH.]

How now, my lord! Why do you keep alone,
Of sorriest fancies your companions making,
10   Using those thoughts which should indeed have died
With them they think on? Things without° all remedy
Should be without regard: what's done is done.

Macbeth.
We have scorched° the snake, not killed it:
She'll close° and be herself, whilst our poor malice°

Finding that they must now live in fear + suspicion, LM is beginning to believe Duncan's murder is not worth it

7. *What reversal of attitudes is taking place here?*

Don't seclude yourself + think of what you have done
Be more cheerful

11. **without:** beyond.
12. *This scene can be played in several ways. Is Lady Macbeth hostile to her husband, and angry with him? Or can she be shown to have some tenderness in this scene?*
13. **scorched:** slashed.
14. **close:** heal.   **malice:** enmity, hatred.

Line 26. Answers will vary. If one sees the Macbeths as still emotionally close or dependent, they may touch each other as one or the other moves about. But Lady Macbeth complains that he "keeps alone." If they are drifting apart, they may avoid the slightest touch.

Line 35. Lady Macbeth speaks with great urgency and fear. She is worried about Macbeth's state of mind and of the "sorriest fancies" that he dwells on.

A. Sleep Imagery

How well is Macbeth sleeping? (He is having nightmares.) What does he equate with death? (Peace and sleep) Is evil natural to Macbeth, or does he have an active conscience? (The latter) Note that he wishes to be with the dead.

B. Theme

Note that Lady Macbeth's words and Macbeth's reply restate the "Fair is foul, and foul is fair" motif.

C. Hecate

See the commentary on Hecate, text page 315.

D. Clarification

Questions 2 and 8 on text page 300 address Lady Macbeth's lack of involvement in every murder but Duncan's.

E. Word Choice

Notice that the word *thickens* suggests both the thickening of a plot and the thickening (congealing) of blood on the hands of Macbeth.

F. Responding to Scene 2

See questions 2, 8, and 9 on text page 300.

---

15   Remains in danger of her former tooth.
      But let the frame of things disjoint,° both the worlds°
         suffer,
      Ere we will eat our meal in fear, and sleep
      In the affliction of these terrible dreams   *having nightmares*
   A That shake us nightly: better be with the dead,   *wishes to be w/ the dead*
20   Whom we, to gain our peace, have sent to peace,
      Than on the torture of the mind to lie
      In restless ecstasy.° Duncan is in his grave;
      After life's fitful fever he sleeps well.
      Treason has done his worst: nor steel, nor poison,
25   Malice domestic,° foreign levy,° nothing,
      Can touch him further.
   Lady Macbeth.   Come on.
      Gentle my lord, sleek° o'er your rugged° looks;   *Be cheerful*
      Be bright and jovial among your guests tonight.
   Macbeth.
      So shall I, love; and so, I pray, be you:
30   Let your remembrance apply to Banquo;°
   B Present him eminence,° both with eye and tongue:
      Unsafe the while, that we must lave°
      Our honors in these flattering streams
      And make our faces vizards° to our hearts,
      Disguising what they are.   *worried about his state of mind*
35 **Lady Macbeth.**   You must leave this.
   Macbeth.
      O, full of scorpions is my mind, dear wife!
      Thou know'st that Banquo, and his Fleance, lives.
   Lady Macbeth.
      But in them nature's copy's° not eternal.
   Macbeth.
      There's comfort yet; they are assailable.
40   Then be thou jocund. Ere the bat hath flown
   C His cloistered flight, ere to black Hecate's summons
      The shard-borne° beetle with his drowsy hums
      Hath rung night's yawning peal, there shall be done   *hints that something is going to happen*
      A deed of dreadful note.
   Lady Macbeth.   What's to be done?
   D **Macbeth.**   *won't tell her — does not confide in her)*
45   Be innocent of the knowledge, dearest chuck,°
      Till thou applaud the deed. Come, seeling° night,
      Scarf up° the tender eye of pitiful day,
      And with thy bloody and invisible hand
      Cancel and tear to pieces that great bond
50   Which keeps me pale! Light thickens, and the crow
   E Makes wing to th' rooky° wood.
      Good things of day begin to droop and drowse,
      Whiles night's black agents to their preys do rouse.
      Thou marvel'st at my words: but hold thee still;
55   Things bad begun make strong themselves by ill:
      So, prithee, go with me.   [*Exeunt.*]
   F

Foul is fair motif.
Night coming

16. **frame of things disjoint:** universe collapse.   **worlds:** heaven and earth.

22. **ecstasy:** frenzy.

25. **Malice domestic:** domestic war (civil war).   **foreign levy:** exaction of tribute by a foreign country.

26. *What do you picture the couple doing in this scene? Are they sitting together? Are they close, or is there a distance between them?*
27. **sleek:** smooth.   **rugged:** furrowed.

30. That is, focus your thoughts on Banquo.
31. **eminence:** honors.
32. **lave:** wash.

34. **vizards:** masks.

35. *With what degree of urgency must Lady Macbeth say this line?*

38. **copy:** lease (they won't live forever).

42. **shard-borne:** carried on scaly wings.

45. **chuck:** chick (a term of endearment).
46. **seeling:** eye-closing; blinding.
47. **Scarf up:** blindfold.

51. **rooky:** full of rooks, or crows.

Answers to margin questions
Line 1. Answers will vary; see annotation A below.
Line 14. As they speak their next lines, the murderers would be blindly bumping into each other.
Line 21. Answers will vary. A good choice is to have the murderers move the body.
Line 22. So far Macbeth has acquired

Cawdor and the throne, and is free of open suspicion. Fleance's escape is his first clear failure. (See also questions 3 and 10, text page 300.)

Plot Summary
Scene 3. The murderers kill Banquo, but Fleance escapes.

3d Murderer

Scene 3. *Near the palace.*

Enter three MURDERERS.

First Murderer.
  But who bid thee join with us?
Third Murderer.   Macbeth.
Second Murderer.
  He needs not our mistrust; since he delivers
  Our offices and what we have to do
  To the direction just.°
First Murderer.   Then stand with us.
5   The west glimmers with some streaks of day.
  Now spurs the lated° traveler apace
  To gain the timely inn, and near approaches
  The subject of our watch.
Third Murderer.   Hark! I hear horses.
Banquo (*within*). Give us a light there, ho!
Second Murderer.   Then 'tis he. The rest
10   That are within the note of expectation°
  Already are i' th' court.
First Murderer.   His horses go about.
Third Murderer.
  Almost a mile: but he does usually—
  So all men do—from hence to th' palace gate
  Make it their walk.

[*Enter* BANQUO *and* FLEANCE, *with a torch.*]

Second Murderer.
  A light, a light!
Third Murderer. 'Tis he.
15 **First Murderer.**   Stand to't.
Banquo.
  It will be rain tonight.
First Murderer.   Let it come down.

[*They set upon* BANQUO.]

Banquo.
  O, treachery! Fly, good Fleance, fly, fly, fly!

                      [*Exit* FLEANCE.]

  Thou mayst revenge. O slave!   [*Dies.*]

Banquo dies

Third Murderer.
  Who did strike out the light?
First Murderer.   Was't not the way?°
Third Murderer.
20   There's but one down; the son is fled.
Second Murderer.
  We have lost best half of our affair.
First Murderer.
  Well, let's away and say how much is done.   [*Exeunt.*]

Fleance escapes

? **1.** *Who is the third murderer? (Much has been written about this. Macbeth himself is often mentioned as a possibility. Another is Seyton, an officer who is an attendant to Macbeth. How would you cast this murderer?)*

4. He needs . . . just: We need not mistrust him (the Third Murderer) since he describes our duties according to our exact directions.
6. lated: belated.

10. within . . . expectation: on the list of expected guests.

? **14.** *Fleance escapes because he drops the torch. What would the murderers be doing as the light goes out?*

19. way: that is, thing to do.
? **21.** *Disposal of bodies is always a problem for directors of Shakespeare's plays. How would you have Banquo's body carried off? By whom?*
? **22.** *This nonliterary scene, so necessary to the play, is often called its turning point or technical climax. What have been Macbeth's good fortunes so far?*

A. The Murderers
See the question here on line 1. Students might come up with another explanation, including the ways Shakespeare's plays were printed, to account for the third murderer. (With banquet guests already arriving [line 10], it seems unlikely that Macbeth himself could be the third man. Perhaps Shakespeare needed to give an actor a part. Or perhaps the number of murderers was consistent in some acting scripts of the play, but not in the one used for the First Folio.)

B. Turning Point
Emotional intensity has been and will be greater in other scenes, especially in the dramatically intense banquet scene (Scene 4). But students should note Fleance's escape; it is a turning point in the sense that now Macbeth's fortunes are turning for the worst. Unless he can kill Fleance, his crimes will benefit Banquo's lineage, not his.

Visualizing Scene 4

The critic G. Wilson Knight suggests this simple stage set:

Upstage

Stage Right

Stairs

Dais and thrones

Macbeth's table-chair

Table

Stage Left

Downstage

He suggests staging the scene (through page 297) as follows. You may wish to suggest the movements at appropriate times.

The scene begins with the Macbeths on their thrones, the guests at table. Macbeth goes to the stairs to speak aside to the murderers; he returns down right. The Ghost of Banquo first enters in a stately walk down the stairs. It takes Macbeth's chair at table. Lady Macbeth leads Macbeth downstage right to calm him. The Ghost exits behind the thrones. The Ghost next stalks directly to the dais and sits in Macbeth's throne, the place Macbeth most hates to associate with Banquo. Macbeth approaches the Ghost and banishes it; the Ghost again exits into upstage shadow. The guests go off both right and left; Macbeth sinks

A. Discussing the Photograph

Again from the Polanski film, this scene depicts the death of Banquo. Do students feel that it conveys more horror, or less, than the earlier offstage murders? Why? (Students might discuss whether or not the viewer's imagination is more powerful than any perceived act.) You might also ask them to comment on how a staged version would differ from the scene shown here. (No forest; perhaps a bare side or front corner of the stage)

A

"O, treachery! Fly, good Fleance, fly, fly, fly!"

292   The Renaissance

onto the dais, and Lady Macbeth kneels before him. Finally, they slowly and laboriously climb the stairs hand in hand, stopping halfway up for Macbeth's final lines.

Answer to margin question
Line 20. Macbeth would be angry and horrified that Fleance has escaped.

Plot Summary
Scene 4. The banquet is under way when a murderer calls Macbeth aside to tell him that Banquo is dead but Fleance has escaped. Macbeth alone among the guests sees Banquo's ghost. Lady Macbeth says her husband is ill and dismisses the guests. Macbeth will send for Macduff and visit the witches.

A. Vocabulary
Nonpareil
(non′pə·rel′)
means "a person without equal."

B. Metaphor
Who is the serpent (Banquo) and who the worm (Fleance)?

Scene 4. *The palace.*

Banquet prepared. Enter MACBETH, LADY MACBETH, ROSS, LENNOX, LORDS, *and* ATTENDANTS.

Macbeth.
You know your own degrees;° sit down:
At first and last, the hearty welcome.
Lords.
Thanks to your majesty.

welcoming guests

Macbeth.
Ourself will mingle with society°
5   And play the humble host.
Our hostess keeps her state,° but in best time
We will require° her welcome.
Lady Macbeth.
Pronounce it for me, sir, to all our friends,
For my heart speaks they are welcome.

[*Enter* FIRST MURDERER.]

Macbeth.
10   See, they encounter° thee with their hearts' thanks.
Both sides are even: here I'll sit i' th' midst:
Be large in mirth; anon we'll drink a measure°
The table round. (*Goes to* FIRST MURDERER.) There's blood upon thy face.
Murderer.
'Tis Banquo's then.
Macbeth.
15   'Tis better thee without than he within.°
Is he dispatched?
Murderer.   My lord, his throat is cut;
That I did for him.
Macbeth.   Thou art the best o' th' cutthroats.
Yet he's good that did the like for Fleance;
A If thou didst it, thou art the nonpareil.   *w/o equal*
Murderer.
20   Most royal sir, Fleance is 'scaped.
Macbeth (*aside*). Then comes my fit again: I had else been perfect,
Whole as the marble, founded° as the rock,
As broad and general as the casing° air:
But now I am cabined, cribbed,° confined, bound in
25   To saucy° doubts and fears.—But Banquo's safe?
Murderer.
Ay, my good lord: safe in a ditch he bides,
With twenty trenchèd° gashes on his head,
The least a death to nature.
Macbeth.   Thanks for that.
B (*Aside.*) There the grown serpent lies; the worm° that's fled

1. **degrees:** ranks.
2. *This crucial scene is often called the dramatic climax of the play; it is tremendously exciting when staged well. Notice where Macbeth's subjects become aware of his capacity for irrational behavior.*
4. **society:** the company.

6. **keeps her state:** remains seated in her chair of state.
7. **require:** request.

10. **encounter:** meet.

12. **measure:** goblet.

15. **thee . . . within:** outside you than inside him.

20. *How would Macbeth react to this line?*

22. **founded:** firmly based.
23. **broad . . . casing:** unconfined as the surrounding.
24. **cribbed:** penned up.
25. **saucy:** insolent.

Informed of Banquo's death + Fleance's escape

27. **trenchèd:** trenchlike.

29. **worm:** serpent.

Line 37. Lady Macbeth may be both alarmed at and disgusted by Macbeth's behavior.

Stage direction. Answers will vary. A good case can be made for either a ghost of Macbeth's mind only, or the same Banquo, but with bloody gashes on his head.

Line 46. Macbeth sees the Ghost of Banquo sitting in Macbeth's place at table.

Line 49. Macbeth speaks accusingly at his guests as if one of them is playing a cruel joke on him.

Line 51. The ghost is shaking its head at Macbeth. No one else sees the ghost. The guests should be alarmed, perhaps embarrassed by Macbeth's strange behavior.

Line 53. Even though Macbeth previously imagined a dagger, no specific illness has been mentioned. She is covering for him.

Line 58. She has pulled him away from the guests.

A. Interpreting

❓ What does this line mean? (Fleance has no power now, but he will have sons later.)

B. Interpreting

These words, revealing that Macbeth sees an apparition visible to no one else, are illustrated in the scene from the 1983 Stratford (Canada) Festival production, shown on the facing page. Note that it is still early in the banquet. Until he speaks these lines, Macbeth has appeared calm and been gracious to his guests.

[margin handwriting: Metaphor]

[handwriting: Fleance not as great a threat now because he young]

30

A Hath nature that in time will venom breed,
No teeth for th' present. Get thee gone. Tomorrow
We'll hear ourselves° again. [*Exit* FIRST MURDERER.]

Lady Macbeth.   My royal lord,
You do not give the cheer.° The feast is sold
That is not often vouched, while 'tis a-making,

35 'Tis given with welcome. To feed were best at home;°
From thence, the sauce to meat° is ceremony;
Meeting were bare without it.

[*Enter the* GHOST OF BANQUO, *and sits in* MACBETH's *place.*]

Macbeth.   Sweet remembrancer!°
Now good digestion wait on appetite,
And health on both!

Lennox.   May't please your highness sit.

Macbeth.

40 Here had we now our country's honor roofed,°
Were the graced person of our Banquo present—
Who may I rather challenge for unkindness
Than pity for mischance!°

Ross.   His absence, sir,
Lays blame upon his promise. Please't your highness

45 To grace us with your royal company?

Macbeth.
The table's full.

Lennox.   Here is a place reserved, sir.

Macbeth.
Where?

Lennox.
Here, my good lord. What is't that moves your highness?

Macbeth.
Which of you have done this?

Lords.   What, my good lord?

B **Macbeth.**
50 Thou canst not say I did it. Never shake
Thy gory locks at me.

Ross.
Gentlemen, rise, his highness is not well.

Lady Macbeth.
Sir, worthy friends. My lord is often thus,
And hath been from his youth. Pray you, keep seat.

55 The fit is momentary; upon a thought°
He will again be well. If much you note him,
You shall offend him and extend his passion.°
Feed, and regard him not.—Are you a man?

Macbeth.
Ay, and a bold one, that dare look on that
Which might appall the devil.

60 **Lady Macbeth** (*aside to* MACBETH). O proper stuff!
This is the very painting of your fear.

[margin handwriting: speaks to the ghost]
[handwriting: Macbeth sees Banquo's ghost]
[handwriting: addresses guests, tries to explain behaviour away]
[handwriting: scolds him]

---

32. hear ourselves: talk it over.

33. the cheer: a sense of cordiality.

35. The feast . . . home: The feast seems sold (not given) during which the host fails to welcome the guests. Mere eating is best done at home.
36. meat: food.

❓ **37.** *Lady Macbeth has summoned her husband to her area of the stage. What mood is she in?*

❓ **Stage direction.** *The ghost is crucial to this scene. From what you read here, should it be imagined? Or should it actually appear on stage? How should it look, if so? When does Macbeth see it?*
37. remembrancer: reminder.

40. our . . . roofed: our nobility under one roof.

43. Who . . . mischance: whom I hope I may reprove because he is unkind rather than pity because he has encountered an accident.

❓ **46.** *When Macbeth says this line, what does he see?*

❓ **49.** *How should Macbeth ask this question? Whom should he be talking to?*

❓ **51.** *According to Macbeth's speech here, what is the ghost doing? Does anyone else see the ghost? How should they be acting?*

❓ **53.** *Do you think this is true? Or is Lady Macbeth desperately trying to cover for her husband?*
55. upon a thought: as quick as a thought.

57. extend his passion: lengthen his fit.

❓ **58.** *Where do you think Lady Macbeth has taken her husband so that she can whisper this intimidating line?*

Answers to margin questions
Line 68. Banquo could be staring in a frightening way at Macbeth. He also might be jeering at him or using threatening gestures.
Line 70. Macbeth is pointing at the ghost, perhaps turning to Lady Macbeth for confirmation of what he sees. Students' ideas about the tone of line 70 will vary. Perhaps Macbeth speaks in a de-

spairing tone, or perhaps he speaks the line in a mock-offhand manner.

A. Character
Call students' attention to Lady Macbeth's resumption here of her earlier, goading role. Again, she taunts Macbeth for being womanly. Her goading this time has a different motive, however. Earlier, she urged Macbeth to kill; here, she seems more concerned about loss of face and, if the king is mad, what will become of their bloodily gained position. Remember, she does not see Banquo's ghost.

*"Thou canst not say I did it. Never shake
Thy gory locks at me."*

— this is your imagination

goading him as being womanly

A
65

This is the air-drawn dagger which, you said,
Led you to Duncan. O, these flaws° and starts,
Impostors to° true fear, would well become
A woman's story at a winter's fire,
Authorized° by her grandam. Shame itself!
Why do you make such faces? When all's done,
You look but on a stool.

Macbeth.   Prithee, see there!
Behold! Look! Lo! How say you?

70   Why, what care I? If thou canst nod, speak too.
If charnel houses° and our graves must send

speaks to ghost

63. **flaws:** gusts, outbursts.
64. **to:** compared with.

66. **Authorized:** vouched for.

? **68.** *What could the actor playing Banquo do here in mockery of Macbeth?*
? **70.** *What actions is Macbeth engaged in here? What is his tone?*
71. **charnel houses:** vaults containing bones.

Answers to margin questions
Line 75. Macbeth is talking to himself.
Line 85. Macbeth is trying to play an
apologetic, slightly embarrassed host.
Notice his strength in lines 84–92. He
has just been shaken to the core by Banquo's ghost, yet here he is able, at least
momentarily, to dismiss the nightmarish
vision and return to himself. It is an admirable strength.

Line 93. Macbeth is shouting at the
ghost, which stares accusingly at him.
Line 108. Macbeth is brave enough to
plant his feet firmly on the floor, though
he is shaking and is terrified. His mood
on "I am a man again" is relief.

A. Interpreting
Note that Lady
Macbeth questions
Macbeth's man-
hood once again.

Those that we bury back, our monuments
Shall be the maws of kites.°   [*Exit* GHOST.]

A **Lady Macbeth.**   What, quite unmanned in folly?
Macbeth.
If I stand here, I saw him.
Lady Macbeth.   Fie, for shame!
Macbeth.
75   Blood hath been shed ere now, i' th' olden time,
Ere humane statute purged the gentle weal;°
Ay, and since too, murders have been performed
Too terrible for the ear. The time has been
That, when the brains were out, the man would die,
80   And there an end; but now they rise again,
With twenty mortal murders on their crowns,°
And push us from our stools. This is more strange
Than such a murder is.
Lady Macbeth.   My worthy lord,
Your noble friends do lack you.
Macbeth.   I do forget.
85   Do not muse at me, my most worthy friends;
I have a strange infirmity, which is nothing
To those that know me. Come, love and health to all!
Then I'll sit down. Give me some wine, fill full.

[*Enter* GHOST.]

I drink to th' general joy o' th' whole table,
90   And to our dear friend Banquo, whom we miss;
Would he were here! To all and him we thirst,°
And all to all.°
Lords.   Our duties, and the pledge.
Macbeth.
Avaunt! and quit my sight! Let the earth hide thee!
Thy bones are marrowless, thy blood is cold;
95   Thou has no speculation° in those eyes
Which thou dost glare with.
Lady Macbeth.   Think of this, good peers,
But as a thing of custom; 'tis no other.
Only it spoils the pleasure of the time.
Macbeth.
What man dare, I dare.
100   Approach thou like the rugged Russian bear,
The armed rhinoceros, or th' Hyrcan° tiger;
Take any shape but that, and my firm nerves°
Shall never tremble. Or be alive again,
And dare me to the desert° with thy sword.
105   If trembling I inhabit then, protest me
The baby of a girl.° Hence, horrible shadow!
Unreal mock'ry, hence!

[*Exit* GHOST.]

Why, so: being gone,
I am a man again. Pray you, sit still.

72. **our . . . kites:** our tombs shall be the
bellies of rapacious birds.

? 75. *Whom is Macbeth talking to?*
76. **purged . . . weal:** that is, cleansed the
state and made it gentle.

81. **mortal . . . crowns:** deadly wounds on
their heads.

? 85. *What impression is Macbeth trying
to create?*

91. **thirst:** desire to drink.
92. **all to all:** everything to everybody, let
everybody drink to everybody.

? 93. *Whom is Macbeth talking to now?
According to this speech, what might
the ghost be doing?*
95. **speculation:** sight.

101. **Hyrcan:** of Hyrcania (near the Caspian Sea).
102. **nerves:** sinews.

104. **the desert:** a lonely place.

106. **If . . . girl:** If then I tremble, proclaim me a baby girl.

? 108. *How "brave" should Macbeth appear to be with all the "brave" talk in
these lines? What is his mood when he says
"I am a man again"?*

Answers to margin questions
Line 110. The other guests may speak in subdued whispers, glancing or gesturing toward Macbeth.
Line 117. "He grows worse and worse": Macbeth may be staring goggle-eyed or babbling; he is oblivious to his guests.
Line 122. The speech is often done slowly in a weary, resigned manner.
Line 127. Lady Macbeth is exhausted;

her fire is spent.
Line 140. Macbeth, too, is exhausted. (In line 138 he finds his bloody business "tedious"; in line 141 Lady Macbeth tells him he lacks "the season of all natures, sleep." For Macbeth, however, the murderer of sleep, even sleep brings no peace, as we have seen.)
Line 144. Lady Macbeth might shake her head in sorrow and dismay.

Lady Macbeth.
> You have displaced the mirth, broke the good meeting,
> With most admired° disorder.

110 **Macbeth.**   Can such things be,
> And overcome us° like a summer's cloud,
> Without our special wonder? You make me strange
> Even to the disposition that I owe,°
> When now I think you can behold such sights,
115 > And keep the natural ruby of your cheeks,
> When mine is blanched with fear.

Ross.   What sights, my lord?

Lady Macbeth.
> I pray you, speak not: he grows worse and worse;
> Question enrages him: at once, good night.
> Stand not upon the order of your going,°
> But go at once.

120 **Lennox.**   Good night; and better health
> Attend his majesty!

Lady Macbeth.   A kind good night to all!

                      [*Exeunt* LORDS.]

A **Macbeth.**
> It will have blood, they say: blood will have blood.
> Stones have been known to move and trees to speak;
> Augurs and understood relations° have
125 > By maggot-pies and choughs and rooks brought forth°
> The secret'st man of blood. What is the night?°

Lady Macbeth.
> Almost at odds with morning, which is which.

Macbeth.
> How say'st thou, that Macduff denies his person
> At our great bidding?

Lady Macbeth.   Did you send to him, sir?

Macbeth.
130 > I hear it by the way,° but I will send:
> There's not a one of them but in his house
> I keep a servant fee'd.° I will tomorrow,
> And betimes° I will, to the weird sisters:
> More shall they speak, for now I am bent° to know
135 > By the worst means the worst. For mine own good
> All causes° shall give way. I am in blood
> Stepped in so far that, should I wade no more,
> Returning were as tedious as go o'er.
> Strange things I have in head that will to hand,
140 > Which must be acted ere they may be scanned.°

B **Lady Macbeth.**
> You lack the season of all natures,° sleep.

Macbeth.
> Come, we'll to sleep. My strange and self-abuse°
> Is the initiate fear that wants hard use.°
> We are yet but young in deed.   [*Exeunt.*]

C

[Handwritten margin notes: "You have ruined the evening"; "Dismisses all"; "Important"; "Climax"; "Spies in Macduff's house"; "Strange ideas or plans I have that must be acted out before I can examine them"; "Inexperienced in murder"]

110. **admired:** amazing.
? 110. *Lady Macbeth and her husband converse in private again. What would the other guests be doing?*
111. **overcome us:** come over us.
113. **You . . . owe:** You make me wonder what my nature is.

? 117. *What clue here would tell the actor playing Macbeth how he is to be behaving?*
119. **Stand . . . going:** Do not insist on departing in your order of rank.

? 122. *Read this speech carefully and decide how Macbeth would deliver it: Slow? Fast? What is his mood?*
124. **Augurs . . . relations:** auguries (omens) and comprehended reports.
125. **By . . . forth:** by magpies, choughs, and rooks (telltale birds) revealed.
126. **What . . . night:** What time of night is it?
? 127. *Is the old fire still present in Lady Macbeth? Or is she suddenly tired and broken?*

130. **by the way:** incidentally.

132. **fee'd:** that is, paid to spy.
133. **betimes:** quickly.
134. **bent:** determined.

136. **causes:** considerations.

? 140. *Does the prospect of a new adventure animate Macbeth? Or is he spent and exhausted?*
140. **may be scanned:** can be examined.
141. **season . . . natures:** seasoning (preservative) of all living creatures.
142. **self-abuse:** delusion.
143. **initiate . . . use:** beginner's fear that lacks hardening practice.
? 144. *How might Lady Macbeth react to this last line?*

A. The "Blood" Speech
Macbeth's speech capsulizes several themes or images of the play—the blood in which everything is drenched, the punishment sure to follow capital crime, upheavals in Nature paralleling upheavals in human nature, and the foulness hidden behind a fair exterior.

B. Sleep Imagery
In line 138 Macbeth finds his bloody business "tedious"; in line 141 Lady Macbeth tells him he lacks "the season of all natures, sleep."
? You might ask students whether at this point even sleep can do much for Macbeth. If not, why not? (His own actions so sicken him that he has nightmares; he gets no peace even in sleep.)

C. Responding to Scene 4
See questions 4, 11, and 12 on text page 300, focusing especially on the appearance of the Ghost of Banquo.

1. Why is Macbeth so determined to have Fleance killed? (To avoid having Banquo's sons rule)
2. Whom do the murderers kill? (Banquo)
3. Who escapes? (Fleance)

4. What does Macbeth see at the banquet? (The Ghost of Banquo)
5. What are Macduff and Malcolm doing? (Raising an army to overthrow Macbeth)

Plot Summary
Scene 5. Hecate and the three witches meet, and Hecate berates them for leaving her out of their dealing with Macbeth.

A. The Hecate Scene

See the commentary "Hecate," text page 315. This is a scene that most scholars believe was inserted by someone else, perhaps Thomas Middleton. At this point you may wish simply to identify Hecate and give students the pronunciation of her name. Notice also the question in the text on the "sounds" of the scene. It differs markedly from the blank verse (unrhymed iambic pentameter) of the rest of the play; it is written, starting about line 4, in rhymed tetrameter couplets.

A

Scene 5. *A witches' haunt.*

Thunder. Enter the three WITCHES, *meeting* HECATE.

First Witch.
　　Why, how now, Hecate! you look angerly.
Hecate.
　　Have I not reason, beldams° as you are,
　　Saucy and overbold? How did you dare
　　To trade and traffic with Macbeth
5　　In riddles and affairs of death;
　　And I, the mistress of your charms,
　　The close contriver° of all harms,
　　Was never called to bear my part,
　　Or show the glory of our art?
10　　And, which is worse, all you have done
　　Hath been but for a wayward son,
　　Spiteful and wrathful; who, as others do,
　　Loves for his own ends, not for you.
　　But make amends now: get you gone,
15　　And at the pit of Acheron°
　　Meet me i' th' morning: thither he
　　Will come to know his destiny.
　　Your vessels and your spells provide,
　　Your charms and everything beside.
20　　I am for th' air; this night I'll spend
　　Unto a dismal and a fatal end:
　　Great business must be wrought ere noon.
　　Upon the corner of the moon
　　There hangs a vap'rous drop profound;°
25　　I'll catch it ere it come to ground:
　　And that distilled by magic sleights°
　　Shall raise such artificial sprites°
　　As by the strength of their illusion
　　Shall draw him on to his confusion.°
30　　He shall spurn fate, scorn death, and bear
　　His hopes 'bove wisdom, grace, and fear:
　　And you all know security°
　　Is mortals' chiefest enemy.

[*Music and a song.*]

　　Hark! I am called; my little spirit, see,
35　　Sits in a foggy cloud and stays for me.　　[*Exit.*]

[*Sing within,* "Come away, come away," *etc.*]

First Witch.
　　Come, let's make haste; she'll soon be back again.
　　　　　　　　　　　　　　　　　　[*Exeunt.*]

? Macbeth was published in the first folio in 1623, seven years after Shakespeare had died. Some people think that this scene was written by someone else because the play was short and needed fleshing out. After you read the scene, decide if you think it "sounds" like the rest of the play.

2. **beldams:** hags.

7. **close contriver:** secret inventor.

15. **Acheron:** river of Hades.

24. **profound:** heavy.

26. **sleights:** arts.
27. **artificial sprites:** spirits created by magic arts.
29. **confusion:** ruin.

32. **security:** overconfidence.

Plot Summary

Scene 6. A conversation in the palace brings us up-to-date. Lennox explains his suspicions of Macbeth and asks a lord where Macduff is now. The lord answers that Macduff is in England, raising an army against Macbeth. Macbeth, he reports, summoned Macduff, who refused to come.

ANALYZING ACT III
Identifying Facts

1. He knows that Macbeth played "most foully" to get the crown.

He will wait for the rest of the prophecies to come true.

2. Macbeth cannot endure the thought of Banquo's descendants succeeding him.

Lady Macbeth does not participate in these planned murders.

3. Fleance escapes the murderers.

4. Macbeth is terrified by Banquo's ghost.

Lady Macbeth tries in vain to reassure the guests. Privately, she reproaches Macbeth for his weakness.

5. They think he is a murderous tyrant.

6. Macduff has joined Malcolm in England to raise an army.

(Answers continue on next page.)

Answer to margin question
Line 24. Lennox has spoken with some irony or doubt in his voice on previous occasions, as in reporting the blood-smeared grooms (text page 280). These lines convey an irony better caught when the lines are read aloud. Read the speech aloud to the class, or coach a student to read it to express sarcasm.

A. Interpreting

? What is Macduff about to do? (To raise an army against Macbeth)

Scene 6. *The palace.*

Enter LENNOX *and another* LORD.

Lennox.
My former speeches have but hit your thoughts,°
Which can interpret farther. Only I say
Things have been strangely borne.° The gracious Duncan
Was pitied of Macbeth: marry, he was dead.
5 And the right-valiant Banquo walked too late;
Whom, you may say, if't please you, Fleance killed,
For Fleance fled. Men must not walk too late.
Who cannot want the thought,° how monstrous
It was for Malcolm and for Donalbain
10 To kill their gracious father? Damnèd fact!°
How it did grieve Macbeth! Did he not straight,
In pious rage, the two delinquents tear,
That were the slaves of drink and thralls° of sleep?
Was not that nobly done? Ay, and wisely too;
15 For 'twould have angered any heart alive
To hear the men deny't. So that I say
He has borne all things well: and I do think
That, had he Duncan's sons under his key—
As, an't° please heaven, he shall not—they should find
20 What 'twere to kill a father. So should Fleance.
But, peace! for from broad words,° and 'cause he failed
His presence at the tyrant's feast, I hear,
Macduff lives in disgrace. Sir, can you tell
Where he bestows himself?
Lord.   The son of Duncan,
25 From whom this tyrant holds the due of birth,°
Lives in the English court, and is received
Of the most pious Edward° with such grace
That the malevolence of fortune nothing
A Takes from his high respect.° Thither Macduff
30 Is gone to pray the holy king, upon his aid°
To wake Northumberland° and warlike Siward;°
That by the help of these, with Him above
To ratify the work, we may again
Give to our tables meat, sleep to our nights,
35 Free from our feasts and banquets bloody knives,
Do faithful homage and receive free° honors:
All which we pine for now. And this report
Hath so exasperate the king that he
Prepares for some attempt at war.
Lennox.   Sent he to Macduff?
Lord.
40 He did: and with an absolute "Sir, not I,"

This scene shows what Scotland is like under Macbeth

1. My . . . thoughts: My recent words have only coincided with what you have in your mind.
3. borne: managed.

Discontent + afraid

8. cannot . . . thought: can fail to think.

10. fact: evil deed.

13. thralls: slaves.

19. an't: if it.

21. for . . . words: because of frank talk.

? 24. *Lennox is sometimes called the "ironic" character of the play. Do you agree? What tone would he use in these lines?*
25. due of birth: birthright.
27. Edward: Edward the Confessor (reigned 1042–1066).

29. nothing . . . respect: does not diminish the high respect in which he is held.
30. upon his aid: to aid him (Malcolm).
31. To wake Northumberland: that is, to arouse the people in an English county near Scotland. **Siward:** Earl of Northumberland.

36. free: freely granted.

Interpreting Meanings

7. Perhaps Shakespeare meant to suggest how rapidly Macbeth's moral nature has deteriorated.

8. Macbeth and his wife have grown somewhat estranged and more formal.

Guilt and fear are the probable reasons for these changes.

9. The words suggest that the distinction between good and evil has at first been blurred and then completely erased in the hero's mind.

Remarks include: Act I, Scene 3, line 141, "nothing is but what is not"; Act II, Scene 1, line 36, "fatal vision." Also Macbeth's anguish at the sight of the ghost compels him again to question the distinction between illusion and reality.

10. Fleance's escape signifies that the witches' prophecies may come true because he is Banquo's son.

11. The appearance of Banquo might contribute to realism, while having nobody appear would emphasize Macbeth's inner conflicts and guilt.

12. It causes Macbeth to wonder if he is going mad.

Students may point to a number of scenes. (See the answer to question 9.)

A. Interpreting
In other words, you'll regret you wasted my time by asking that question.

Answer to margin question
Line 49. The lords have grown so suspicious about Duncan's death, Macbeth's motive for silencing the grooms, and his placing blame on those who have fled, that Malcolm and Macduff are working in England to raise an army against Macbeth.

CLOSURE
Have three students describe to the class the attack on Banquo and Fleance and why this could be the turning point.

A [The cloudy° messenger turns me his back,
And hums, as who should say, "You'll rue the time
That clogs° me with this answer."

Lennox. And that well might
Advise him to a caution, t' hold what distance
45 His wisdom can provide. Some holy angel
Fly to the court of England and unfold
His message ere he come, that a swift blessing
May soon return to this our suffering country
Under a hand accursed!

Lord. I'll send my prayers with him.
[*Exeunt.*]

41. **cloudy:** disturbed.

43. **clogs:** burdens.

49. *This is basically an "information" scene. Can you summarize what it tells you about the plot?*

Lords have grown suspicions about Duncan's death
Macbeth's motive for silencing grooms
placing blame on malcolm
Malc + Macduff in England raising army

Responding to the Play

Analyzing Act III

Identifying Facts

1. In the short soliloquy that opens Scene 1, what does Banquo reveal that he knows about Macbeth? What does he decide to do?
2. How and why does Macbeth arrange Banquo's murder? How is Lady Macbeth involved in the murder?
3. In Scene 3, who escapes the murderers?
4. Describe what happens in Scene 4 when Ross, Lennox, and the other lords invite Macbeth to share their table. What does Macbeth do? What does Lady Macbeth do?
5. By Scene 6, what opinion do Lennox and the other lords hold of Macbeth?
6. Macduff does not appear at all in Act III. Where is he, and why?

Interpreting Meanings

7. Why do you suppose Shakespeare did not have Macbeth kill Banquo with his own hands, as he killed Duncan and his two guards? What can you infer about Macbeth's changing **character** from seeing how readily he engages in this complex plan involving professional murderers?
8. The relationship between Macbeth and his wife has changed in several ways since they became rulers of Scotland. Describe some of these changes. What reasons can you suggest for these changes?
9. In Scene 2, Shakespeare helps the audience imagine the **setting** by having Macbeth say, "Light thickens, and the crow makes wing to the rooky wood." How can these remarks also be seen as a metaphorical commentary on the events of the play? Find other remarks of this sort that Shakespeare has Macbeth make, and explain how they function.
10. How is Fleance's escape a **turning point** in the play?
11. Nobody except Macbeth sees Banquo's ghost. In some productions of the play the ghost does not appear onstage; in others, it does. What is gained by having Banquo appear at the banquet, made up as a ghost? What is gained by having nobody actually appear to motivate Macbeth's terrified behavior?
12. How does the banquet scene blur the clear-cut and common-sense distinction that most of us make between the real and the imaginary? In what other scenes has this distinction also been blurred?

PREPARATION

ESTABLISHING A PURPOSE. Most students enjoy the caldron scene. In Shakespearean tragedies, the fourth act usually shows the hero's fortunes getting worse and worse. Have them look for what happens to Macbeth now. What could happen to save him? (Could anything? Should anything?)

Plot Summary

Scene 1. The act begins with the three witches chanting over a caldron. Macbeth enters, demanding to know the future. The witches show him three apparitions (an armed head, a bloody child, a child with a crown on its head). When Macbeth demands to learn more, the witches show him another apparition: Eight kings appear, including Banquo, who points to the kings as his descendants and holds a mirror indicating a continuation of his line. The witches vanish, and Lennox appears, telling Macbeth that Macduff has fled to England. As the scene ends, Macbeth is planning to murder Lady Macduff and her children.

Act IV   Scene 1. *A witches' haunt.*

Thunder. Enter the three WITCHES.

First Witch.
A
    Thrice the brinded° cat hath mewed.
Second Witch.
    Thrice and once the hedge-pig° whined.
Third Witch.
    Harpier° cries, 'Tis time, 'tis time.
First Witch.
    Round about the caldron go:
5   In the poisoned entrails throw.
    Toad, that under cold stone
    Days and nights has thirty-one
    Swelt'red venom sleeping got,°
    Boil thou first i' th' charmèd pot.
All.
10   Double, double, toil and trouble;
    Fire burn and caldron bubble.
Second Witch.
    Fillet° of a fenny° snake,
    In the caldron boil and bake;
    Eye of newt and toe of frog,
15   Wool of bat and tongue of dog,
    Adder's fork° and blindworm's° sting,
    Lizard's leg and howlet's° wing,
    For a charm of pow'rful trouble,
    Like a hell-broth boil and bubble.
All.
20   Double, double, toil and trouble;
    Fire burn and caldron bubble.
Third Witch.
    Scale of dragon, tooth of wolf,
    Witch's mummy,° maw and gulf°
    Of the ravined° salt-sea shark,
25   Root of hemlock digged i' th' dark,
    Liver of blaspheming Jew,
    Gall of goat, and slips of yew
    Slivered in the moon's eclipse,
    Nose of Turk and Tartar's lips,
30   Finger of birth-strangled babe
    Ditch-delivered by a drab,°
    Make the gruel thick and slab:°
    Add thereto a tiger's chaudron,°
    For th' ingredients of our caldron.
All.
35   Double, double, toil and trouble;
    Fire burn and caldron bubble.
Second Witch.
    Cool it with a baboon's blood,
    Then the charm is firm and good.
B

Making a spell of some sort

? Stage direction. *This scene usually begins in darkness. In Shakespeare's day, the caldron might have risen through the trapdoor. How would you have the witches act: Gleeful? Lamenting?*

1. **brinded:** brindled.
2. **hedge-pig:** hedgehog.

3. **Harpier:** an attendant spirit like Graymalkin and Paddock in Act I, Scene 1.

8. **Swelt'red . . . got:** venom sweated out while sleeping.

12. **Fillet:** slice.   **fenny:** from a swamp.

16. **fork:** forked tongue.   **blindworm:** a legless lizard.
17. **howlet:** owl.

23. **Witch's mummy:** mummified flesh of a witch.   **maw and gulf:** stomach and gullet.
24. **ravined:** ravenous.

31. **drab:** harlot.
32. **slab:** slimy.
33. **chaudron:** entrails.

Answer to margin question
Stage direction. Answers will vary, though gleeful is more likely.

A. Discussing the Details
Students might be upset or angered by some of the ingredients to follow, but unfortunately these details serve to illustrate the biases prevalent in Elizabethan England. Remember that *Macbeth* is a play about evil, and the witches are its embodiment.

B. A Creative Response
Students who enjoy the rhyme and meter of the witches' incantations might write a humorous contemporary parody, throwing into the pot things they particularly dislike, such as TV commercials, etc.

302

Scene sections: (1) caldron scene, page 301; (2) entrance of Hecate and Macbeth, page 302; (3) the three apparitions, page 303; (4) the show of eight kings, page 304; (5) the scene with Lennox and Macbeth, page 304.

Line 48. Macbeth is no longer awed by the witches. Totally contemptuous, he treats them like dirt.

A. Hecate
See the commentary on Hecate, text page 315.

B. Allusion
Science-fiction and fantasy writer Ray Bradbury (b. 1920) chose this line as the title of his novel published in 1962.

C. Character
Again, notice Macbeth's nerve in the face of the supernatural.

D. Interpreting
If this is read aloud, you might notice a similarity to E. E. Cummings's poem "what if a much of a which of a wind," which is also about doomsday.
? What various apocalyptic events does Macbeth mention here? (Winds destroy churches; the sea swallows ships; vegetation is destroyed; castles, palaces, and pyramids fall down; seeds are all destroyed.) Note that Macbeth reveals now that he cares for nothing but his own gain.

Line 61. The witches do appear to see Macbeth as a participant in evil.
Line 67. Answers will vary. They are tossing ingredients into the caldron, muttering and cackling to each other.

A *[Enter* HECATE *and the other three* WITCHES.*]*

Hecate.
 O, well done! I commend your pains;
40 And every one shall share i' th' gains:
 And now about the caldron sing,
 Like elves and fairies in a ring,
 Enchanting all that you put in.

[Music and a song: "Black spirits," *etc.]*

[Exeunt HECATE *and the other three* WITCHES.*]*

Second Witch.
B By the pricking of my thumbs,
45 Something wicked this way comes:
 Open, locks,
 Whoever knocks!

[Enter MACBETH.*]*

[handwritten: foreshadows Macbeth's entrance]

Macbeth.
C How now, you secret, black, and midnight hags!
 What is't you do?
All.   A deed without a name.
Macbeth.
50 I conjure you, by that which you profess,
 Howe'er you come to know it, answer me:
 Though you untie the winds and let them fight
 Against the churches; though the yesty° waves
 Confound° and swallow navigation up;
55 Though bladed corn be lodged° and trees blown down;
 Though castles topple on their warders' heads;
D Though palaces and pyramids do slope°
 Their heads to their foundations; though the treasure
 Of nature's germens° tumble all together,
60 Even till destruction sicken,° answer me
 To what I ask you.
First Witch.   Speak.
Second Witch.   Demand.
Third Witch.   We'll answer.
First Witch.
 Say, if th' hadst rather hear it from our mouths,
 Or from our masters?
Macbeth.   Call 'em, let me see 'em.
First Witch.
 Pour in sow's blood, that hath eaten
65 Her nine farrow,° grease that's sweaten°
 From the murderer's gibbet° throw
 Into the flame.
All.   Come, high or low,
 Thyself and office° deftly show!

[Thunder. FIRST APPARITION: *a helmeted head.]*

[handwritten: Macbeth treats witches contemptuously. He is not afraid]

[handwritten: Demands]

[handwritten: Doomsday]

[handwritten: Macbeth cares for nothing but his own gain]

[handwritten: Demands that they answer]

? *This exciting scene has five major sections, each with its own intensity. See if you can identify them when you're finished.*

? **48.** *How does Macbeth's attitude toward the witches vary from his earlier encounters with them?*

53. yesty: foamy.
54. Confound: destroy.
55. bladed . . . lodged: grain in the ear be beaten down.
57. slope: bend.
59. nature's germens: seeds of all life.
60. sicken: sicken at its own work.

? **61.** *These exchanges are spoken rapidly. Do the witches now see Macbeth as a participant in evil?*

65. farrow: young pigs. **sweaten:** sweated.
66. gibbet: gallows.
? **67.** *What are the witches doing all during this scene?*
68. office: function.

Answers to margin questions
Line 71. This might be Macduff, the Thane of Fife. He warns against Macduff.
Line 80. The bloody child prophesies that none of woman born can harm Macbeth. The child might be the son of Macduff, whom Macbeth is about to have killed, but students would not yet know this. The bloody child might also be Macduff himself.

Line 93. Macbeth (in his royal castle at Dunsinane) will not be defeated until Birnam Wood marches on Dunsinane. At this point Macbeth must feel exultant and unbeatable. Prophecies two and three seem to fly in the face of reason.

Macbeth.
   Tell me, thou unknown power—
First Witch.   He knows thy thought:
70   Hear his speech, but say thou nought.
First Apparition.
   Macbeth! Macbeth! Macbeth! Beware Macduff!
   Beware the Thane of Fife. Dismiss me: enough.

                [*He descends*.]

Macbeth.
   Whate'er thou art, for thy good caution thanks:
   Thou hast harped° my fear aright. But one word
     more—
First Witch.
75   He will not be commanded. Here's another,
   More potent than the first.

[*Thunder.* SECOND APPARITION: *a bloody child.*]

Second Apparition.
   Macbeth! Macbeth! Macbeth!
Macbeth.
   Had I three ears, I'd hear thee.
Second Apparition.
   Be bloody, bold, and resolute! Laugh to scorn
80   The pow'r of man, for none of woman born
   Shall harm Macbeth.   [*Descends*.]
Macbeth.
   Then live, Macduff: what need I fear of thee?
   But yet I'll make assurance double sure,
   And take a bond of fate.° Thou shalt not live;
85   That I may tell pale-hearted fear it lies,
   And sleep in spite of thunder.

[*Thunder.* THIRD APPARITION: *a child crowned, with a tree in his hand.*]

                What is this,
   That rises like the issue° of a king,
   And wears upon his baby-brow the round
   And top of sovereignty?°
All.   Listen, but speak not to't.
Third Apparition.
90   Be lion-mettled, proud, and take no care
   Who chafes, who frets, or where conspirers are:
   Macbeth shall never vanquished be until
   Great Birnam Wood to high Dunsinane Hill
   Shall come against him.   [*Descends*.]
Macbeth.   That will never be.
95   Who can impress° the forest, bid the tree
   Unfix his earth-bound root? Sweet bodements,° good!
   Rebellious dead, rise never, till the Wood
   Of Birnam rise, and our high-placed Macbeth
   Shall live the lease of nature,° pay his breath

Macduff's head

71. *Whose head is this, whose armor glows as the apparition holds it over the fire? What is his warning?*

74. harped: hit upon, struck the note of.

Macduff as child

Macduff at birth

80. *What does the bloody child prophesy? Who might this child be?*

Kill Macduff

84. take . . . fate: get a guarantee from fate (that is, he will kill Macduff and thus will compel fate to keep its word).

87. issue: offspring.

89. round . . . sovereignty: that is, crown.

Macbeth is excited takes prophesies at face value

93. *What does the third apparition prophesy? What must be Macbeth's mental state at this point?*

95. impress: conscript, draft.
96. bodements: prophecies.

99. lease of nature: natural lifespan.

A. The Apparitions and Their Prophecies
Several different answers are possible as to who might be represented by each of these three apparitions. Encourage students to defend their interpretations with information drawn from the play. It is important that students grasp the literal meaning of each prophecy in order that they later see how each is fulfilled. You might have them paraphrase each prophecy and check the paraphrases for accuracy before you move on.

Line 102. Macbeth is consumed by the need to know whether Banquo's descendants will inherit his throne; his tone might change from glee to anxiety.

Stage direction. Banquo smiles at Macbeth and gestures to show that the eight kings are his descendants (see lines 123–124).

Line 124. Banquo still has bloody gashes on his head. Macbeth must be angry and dismayed that, despite the three promising prophecies, Banquo will "win" in the end.

A. The Future
Note that the witches are not eager to reveal the future, but Macbeth insists.

B. The Kings
See question 11, text page 316, on the meaning of "a dumb show." See also "Father to a Line of Kings," page 286. G. Wilson Knight suggests that this scene be played "with deliberation and ceremony." He would have the kings pause as they pass Macbeth and then group themselves around a throne as if posing for a photograph, waiting for the Ghost of Banquo. Banquo actually seats himself in the throne to illustrate his truly royal spirit, as contrasted with the meanness of Macbeth.

C. Interpreting
The three balls (orbs) and scepters symbolize the kingdoms of England, Scotland, and Ireland, which became the United Kingdom in 1603 under James I.

To time and mortal custom.° Yet my heart
Throbs to know one thing. Tell me, if your art
Can tell so much: shall Banquo's issue ever
Reign in this kingdom?

All.   Seek to know no more.

Macbeth.
I will be satisfied.° Deny me this,
And an eternal curse fall on you! Let me know.
Why sinks that caldron? And what noise° is this?

[*Hautboys.*]

First Witch. Show!
Second Witch. Show!
Third Witch. Show!
All.
110   Show his eyes, and grieve his heart;
Come like shadows, so depart!

[*A show of eight* KINGS *and* BANQUO, *last* KING *with a glass° in his hand.*]

Macbeth.
Thou art too like the spirit of Banquo. Down!
Thy crown does sear mine eyelids. And thy hair,
Thou other gold-bound brow, is like the first.
A third is like the former. Filthy hags!
Why do you show me this? A fourth! Start,° eyes!
What, will the line stretch out to th' crack of doom?°
Another yet! A seventh! I'll see no more.
And yet the eighth° appears, who bears a glass
120   Which shows me many more; and some I see
That twofold balls and treble scepters° carry:
Horrible sight! Now I see 'tis true;
For the blood-boltered° Banquo smiles upon me,
And points at them for his.° What, is this so?

First Witch.
125   Ay, sir, all this is so. But why
Stands Macbeth thus amazedly?
Come, sisters, cheer we up his sprites,°
And show the best of our delights:
I'll charm the air to give a sound,
130   While you perform your antic round,°
That this great king may kindly say
Our duties did his welcome pay.

[*Music. The* WITCHES *dance, and vanish.*]

Macbeth.
Where are they? Gone? Let this pernicious hour
Stand aye accursèd in the calendar!
Come in, without there!

[*Enter* LENNOX.]

135   **Lennox.**   What's your grace's will?

100. **mortal custom:** natural death.

102. *What is Macbeth's mood? How might his tone change when he asks about Banquo's issue, or children?*

104. **satisfied:** that is, fully informed.

106. **noise:** music.

Stage direction. *A parade of eight Stuart kings passes before Macbeth. These are the kings of Banquo's line. The last king holds up a mirror (glass) to suggest an infinite number of descendants. Banquo appears last. According to the next speech, how does Banquo act toward Macbeth?*

116. **Start:** that is, from the sockets.
117. **crack of doom:** blast (of a trumpet) at Doomsday.
119. **eighth:** King James I of England (the present king).
121. **twofold . . . scepters:** coronation emblems.
123. **blood-boltered:** matted with blood.
124. *What does Banquo look like? What must be Macbeth's mental state now?*
124. **his:** his descendants.

127. **sprites:** spirits.

130. **antic round:** grotesque circular dance.

"I will be satisfied. Deny me this,
And an eternal curse fall on you!"

A

This photograph
from the 1983
Stratford (Canada)
Festival production
illustrates lines
104–105 on text
page 304.
? What elements
of the scene
match or expand
upon the way you
imagine the
scene? (Answers
will vary. Students
might imagine
witches with non-
human features.)
What would you do
differently in your
own production of
the play? (Answers
will vary. They
might use the color
red to imply hell.)
(See also the an-
notation on anoth-
er scene with the
witches, text page
259.) Note the
trapdoor that will
lower the caldron
and witches off the
stage, as if they
disappear into thin
air.

Line 136. Lennox's reappearance marks the sudden return of everyday reality and sanity. The intensity would lessen. In line 142 Lennox tells Macbeth that Macduff has fled to England.

Line 156. Macbeth has grown so evil that he can now order murder without a second thought. On his motive for killing Macduff's family, answers will vary.

Some students may observe that he has little reason beyond hatred for Macduff.
Stage direction. Answers will vary. See Comment from a Critic on next page.

Plot Summary
Scene 2. At Macduff's castle, Ross tells Lady Macduff that Macduff has gone to England. He leaves. As Lady Macduff and her young son talk, a messenger arrives and warns them to flee. Murderers arrive immediately and coldbloodedly kill first her son and then Lady Macduff.

A. Plot
By his flight to England, Macduff makes known his enmity to Macbeth. Note that Macbeth's crimes are becoming outrageously evil: Now he is ordering the slaughter of women and babies.

B. Responding to Scene 1
This scene is analyzed in questions 1–4 and 9–11 on text page 316.

C. Syntax
Who is "he"? (Her husband, who has gone to England to raise an army against Macbeth)

Macbeth.
  Saw you the weird sisters?
Lennox.   No, my lord.
Macbeth.
  Came they not by you?
Lennox.   No indeed, my lord.
Macbeth.
  Infected be the air whereon they ride,
  And damned all those that trust them! I did hear
  The galloping of horse.° Who was't came by?
140
Lennox.
  'Tis two or three, my lord, that bring you word
  Macduff is fled to England.
Macbeth.   Fled to England?
Lennox.
  Ay, my good lord.
Macbeth (*aside*). Time, thou anticipat'st ° my dread exploits.
145
  The flighty purpose never is o'ertook
  Unless the deed go with it.° From this moment
  The very firstlings of my heart° shall be
  The firstlings of my hand. And even now,
  To crown my thoughts with acts, be it thought and done;
150
A
  The castle of Macduff I will surprise;°
  Seize upon Fife; give to th' edge o' th' sword
  His wife, his babes, and all unfortunate souls
  That trace him in his line.° No boasting like a fool;
  This deed I'll do before this purpose cool:
155
  But no more sights!—Where are these gentlemen?
  Come, bring me where they are.   [*Exeunt.*]
B

136. *How would the mood on stage change as Lennox appears? What crucial information does he give Macbeth?*

140. horse: horses (or horsemen).

144. anticipat'st: foretold.

146. The flighty . . . it: The fleeting plan is never accomplished unless an action accompanies it.
147. firstlings . . . heart: that is, first thoughts, impulses.

150. surprise: attack suddenly.

153. trace . . . line: are of his lineage.
156. *By this speech, how does Macbeth show he has fallen ever deeper into evil? How different is Macbeth now from the reluctant murderer of the first part of the play? Why does Macbeth want to murder Macduff's children?*

Scene 2. *Macduff's castle.*

Enter Macduff's wife LADY MACDUFF, *her* SON, *and* ROSS.

C
Lady Macduff.
  What had he done, to make him fly the land?
Ross.
  You must have patience, madam.
Lady Macduff.   He had none:
  His flight was madness. When our actions do not,
  Our fears do make us traitors.
Ross.   You know not
5
  Whether it was his wisdom or his fear.
Lady Macduff.
  Wisdom! To leave his wife, to leave his babes,
  His mansion and his titles,° in a place
  From whence himself does fly? He loves us not;

Stage direction. *In many productions, the mood of this scene contrasts dramatically with the previous scenes of horror. How would you stage this domestic scene to suggest the vulnerability of Lady Macduff and her children?*

7. titles: possessions.

Answers to margin questions

Line 17. Ross might extend his hands as if pleading, or he might look over his shoulder to see if anyone is listening.

Line 29. Ross might kiss Lady Macduff's cheek and tousle the boy's hair. He may be about the same age as Lady Macduff, perhaps a little younger than Macduff himself.

Line 31. Consider the ideas of G. Wilson

Knight (at right). Have students cite lines to support their interpretation of Lady Macduff's manner.

---

10 He wants the natural touch:° for the poor wren,
The most diminutive of birds, will fight,
Her young ones in her nest, against the owl.
All is the fear and nothing is the love;
As little is the wisdom, where the flight
So runs against all reason.
Ross.   My dearest coz,°
15 I pray you, school° yourself. But, for your husband,
He is noble, wise, judicious, and best knows
The fits o' th' season.° I dare not speak much further:
But cruel are the times, when we are traitors
And do not know ourselves; when we hold rumor
20 From what we fear,° yet know not what we fear,
But float upon a wild and violent sea
Each way and move. I take my leave of you.
Shall not be long but I'll be here again.
Things at the worst will cease,° or else climb upward
25 To what they were before. My pretty cousin,
Blessing upon you!
Lady Macduff.
Fathered he is, and yet he's fatherless.
Ross.
I am so much a fool, should I stay longer,
It would be my disgrace° and your discomfort.
I take my leave at once.   [*Exit* ROSS.]
30 **Lady Macduff.**   Sirrah,° your father's dead:
And what will you do now? How will you live?
Son.
As birds do, mother.
Lady Macduff.   What, with worms and flies?
Son.
With what I get, I mean; and so do they.
Lady Macduff.
Poor bird! thou'dst never fear the net nor lime,°
35 The pitfall nor the gin.°
Son.
Why should I, mother? Poor birds they are not set for.
My father is not dead, for all your saying.
Lady Macduff.
Yes, he is dead: how wilt thou do for a father?
Son. Nay, how will you do for a husband?
40 **Lady Macduff.** Why, I can buy me twenty at any market.
Son. Then you'll buy 'em to sell° again.
Lady Macduff.
Thou speak'st with all thy wit, and yet, i' faith,
With wit enough for thee.°
Son.
Was my father a traitor, mother?
45 **Lady Macduff.** Ay, that he was.
Son. What is a traitor?
Lady Macduff. Why, one that swears and lies.°
Son. And be all traitors that do so?

toward — *he doesn't love her*

9. wants . . . touch: that is, lacks natural affection for his wife and children.

14. coz: cousin.
15. school: control.

17. *How could Ross show his fear in line 17?*
17. fits . . . season: disorders of the time.

20. hold . . . fear: believe rumors because we fear.

24. cease: cease worsening.

29. It . . . disgrace: that is, I would weep.
29. *In taking his leave, how would Ross show affection for Lady Macduff and her young son? Would you have Ross be younger or older than Lady Macduff?*
30. Sirrah: here an affectionate address to a child.
31. *How would you have Lady Macduff act in this scene? Frightened? Bitter? Loving? Resigned?*

Shows affection w/ son

34. lime: bird lime (smeared on branches to catch birds).
35. gin: trap.

41. sell: betray.

43. for thee: for a child.

47. swears and lies: takes an oath and breaks it.

Comment from a Critic

You might share with your students the following comment of G. Wilson Knight on this scene, and invite their reactions: "The murder of Lady Macduff can be best done before simple curtains. Generally it gets laughter. It is, however, not meant to hold any grandeur of action. Macbeth's exploits get less and less dignified and more mad. They are meant to. Duncan's murder was tragically grand; Banquo's melodramatic; and this is almost ludicrous. The producer must bring out its quality of ghoulish horror fearlessly and no one will laugh. He must avoid a lot of screams at the end."

Students might vigorously disagree that this pitiful scene could provoke laughter.

Macbeth, Act IV, Scene 2   307

307

Answers to margin questons

Line 71. Answers will vary. It is difficult to see how Lady Macbeth would have known of Macbeth's plans, although many students will agree that sending the messenger is appropriate to the reversal of character she has shown.

Line 77. Answers will vary. Lady Macduff might gather the boy in her arms, or try to shield him with her body. The boy might boldly confront the murderers, as suggested by what he says in line 81.

A. Responding

Macduff's small son is very wise and witty throughout this conversation.

❓ What do you think is the point of this conversation between mother and son? (Shakespeare gives us a bit of comic/witty relief, and establishing the mother and son as real characters makes their murders more horrible.)

B. Plot

❓ What's the point of having this messenger arrive to warn of danger? (It certainly increases suspense, for we hope the mother and son will escape.)

C. Responding to Scene 2

See questions 5 and 12–14 on text page 316.

Lady Macduff. Every one that does so is a traitor, and must be hanged.

50 **Son.** And must they all be hanged that swear and lie?

Lady Macduff. Every one.

Son. Who must hang them?

Lady Macduff. Why, the honest men.

A 55 **Son.** Then the liars and swearers are fools; for there are liars and swearers enow° to beat the honest men and hang up them.

Lady Macduff. Now, God help thee, poor monkey! But how wilt thou do for a father?

60 **Son.** If he were dead, you'd weep for him. If you would not, it were a good sign that I should quickly have a new father.

Lady Macduff. Poor prattler, how thou talk'st!

[*Enter a* MESSENGER.]

Messenger.
Bless you, fair dame! I am not to you known,
Though in your state of honor I am perfect.°
65 I doubt° some danger does approach you nearly:
If you will take a homely° man's advice,
B Be not found here; hence, with your little ones.
To fright you thus, methinks I am too savage;
To do worse to you were fell° cruelty,
70 Which is too nigh your person. Heaven preserve you!
I dare abide no longer.   [*Exit* MESSENGER.]

Lady Macduff.   Whither should I fly?
I have done no harm. But I remember now
I am in this earthly world, where to do harm
Is often laudable, to do good sometime
75 Accounted dangerous folly. Why then, alas,
Do I put up that womanly defense,
To say I have done no harm?—What are these faces?

[*Enter* MURDERERS.]

Murderer.
Where is your husband?

Lady Macduff.
I hope, in no place so unsanctified
Where such as thou mayst find him.

80 **Murderer.**   He's a traitor.

Son.
Thou li'st, thou shag-eared° villain!

Murderer.   What, you egg!

[*Stabbing him.*]

Young fry° of treachery!

Son.   He has killed me, mother:
Run away, I pray you!   [*Dies.*]

C   [*Exit* LADY MACDUFF, *crying* ''Murder!''
followed by MURDERERS.]

---

55. **enow:** enough.

64. **in . . . perfect:** I am fully informed of your honorable rank.
65. **doubt:** fear.
66. **homely:** plain.

69. **fell:** fierce.

❓ **71.** *Some readers think that this messenger has been sent by Lady Macbeth. Is there any support for this theory? Would it be within her character? What must Lady Macduff do when she hears this terrible message?*

❓ **77.** *What would Lady Macduff and her son do as they see the murderers enter the room?*

81. **shag-eared:** hairy-eared.

82. **fry:** spawn.

[handwritten annotations: "comic relief", "real people", "makes murder more horrible", "Increase suspense", "Kills son"]

308

Dramatic Purpose: Comment from a Critic

After the swift-moving action of previous scenes, students sometimes feel that this scene adds little to the story. Critic Mark Van Doren observes, however, that the scene does not interrupt the play; rather, "it is one of its essential parts, glancing forward as it does to a conclusion wherein Macduff can say, 'The time is free'

(Act V, Scene 8, line 55), and wherein Malcolm can promise . . . deeds of justice."

Ask students to recall how bloody and dangerous a place Macbeth's Scotland has become. From this scene, Van Doren says, students get a sense that there is "another country to the south where a good king works miracles with his touch." Stormy, chaotic Scotland is but a small part of a more peaceful, larger world.

Plot Summary
Scene 3. Macduff attempts to secure Malcolm's aid in fighting Macbeth, but Malcolm first tests Macduff's loyalty to Scotland. After Macduff proves his integrity, Malcolm tells him an army is ready to attack Macbeth. Ross then tells Macduff that his wife and children are murdered. Macduff prays to meet Macbeth in battle.

Answers to margin questions
Line 14. Neither Malcolm nor Macduff knows that Macbeth has already had Macduff's family killed.
Line 37. He may play it as if offended by Malcolm's words in lines 25–28 and demonstrating his own nobility.

A. Theme
Note the reiteration of the "Fair is foul" theme.

B. Irony
Note the dramatic irony we feel here: We know, though Macduff and Malcolm do not, that Macduff's wife and child are already murdered.

Scene 3. *England. Before the king's palace.*

Enter MALCOLM *and* MACDUFF.

Malcolm.
    Let us seek out some desolate shade, and there
    Weep our sad bosoms empty.
Macduff.   Let us rather
    Hold fast the mortal° sword, and like good men
    Bestride our down-fall'n birthdom.° Each new morn
5   New widows howl, new orphans cry, new sorrows
    Strike heaven on the face, that° it resounds
    As if it felt with Scotland and yelled out
    Like syllable of dolor.°
Malcolm.   What I believe, I'll wail;
    What know, believe; and what I can redress,
10 As I shall find the time to friend,° I will.
    What you have spoke, it may be so perchance.
    This tyrant, whose sole° name blisters our tongues,
    Was once thought honest:° you have loved him well;
    He hath not touched you yet. I am young; but something
15 You may deserve of him through me;° and wisdom°
    To offer up a weak, poor, innocent lamb
    T' appease an angry god.
Macduff.
    I am not treacherous.
Malcolm.   But Macbeth is.
    A good and virtuous nature may recoil
20 In° an imperial charge. But I shall crave your pardon;
    That which you are, my thoughts cannot transpose:°
    Angels are bright still, though the brightest° fell:
    Though all things foul would wear° the brows of grace,
    Yet grace must still look so.°
Macduff.   I have lost my hopes.
Malcolm.
25 Perchance even there where I did find my doubts.
    Why in that rawness° left you wife and child,
    Those precious motives, those strong knots of love,
    Without leave-taking? I pray you,
    Let not my jealousies° be your dishonors,
30 But mine own safeties. You may be rightly just°
    Whatever I shall think.
Macduff.   Bleed, bleed, poor country:
    Great tyranny, lay thou thy basis° sure,
    For goodness dare not check° thee: wear thou thy
        wrongs;
    The title is affeered.° Fare thee well, lord:
35 I would not be the villain that thou think'st
    For the whole space that's in the tyrant's grasp
    And the rich East to boot.
Malcolm.   Be not offended:
    I speak not as in absolute fear of you.

[margin glosses:]

3. **mortal:** deadly.

4. **Bestride . . . birthdom:** protectively stand over our native land.

6. **that:** so that.

8. **Like . . . dolor:** similar sound of grief.

10. **to friend:** friendly, propitious.

12. **sole:** very.
13. **honest:** good.

? 14. *What great irony would the audience feel upon hearing this line, given what has just taken place in the previous scene?*
15. **deserve . . . me:** that is, earn by betraying me to Macbeth. **wisdom:** it may be wise.

20. **recoil / In:** give way under.

21. **transpose:** transform.
22. **the brightest:** Lucifer, the angel who led the revolt of the angels and was thrown out of Heaven; Satan.
23. **would wear:** desire to wear.
24. **so:** like itself.

26. **rawness:** unprotected condition.

29. **jealousies:** suspicions.
30. **rightly just:** perfectly honorable.

32. **basis:** foundation.
33. **check:** restrain.

34. **affeered:** legally confirmed.

? 37. *This speech might present a problem for the actor playing Macduff because it does not clearly relate to what has gone before it. It seems "too grand" and philosophical at this point in the play. How would you have the actor deliver this speech?*

[handwritten margin notes:] Must fight for Scotland / Malcolm does not trust Macduff / Declares loyalty / a noble man may commit a wicked deed if commanded by the king / Despair / Why have you left your wife + children to come here / I am not traitorous but noble

Answers to margin questions
Line 57. Macduff says that no one is more evil than Macbeth, not even a devil from hell.
Line 66. In lines 60–66 Malcolm must convince Macduff that he is obsessed with women and must at the same time convince the audience that he is not—perhaps by side glances or by occasionally turning aside from Macduff as

he speaks.
Line 84. Malcolm must be convincing for Macduff yet let the audience know that all of these allegations about himself are false.

A. Malcolm's Test
If students do not seem to be catching on to the fact that Malcolm is assuming a pose in order to test Macduff, direct them to the three questions in the right-hand column. (Questions 7, 8, and 15 on text page 316 also focus on this testing.)

B. Clarification
Malcolm's first vice is lust. Notice Macduff's rationalization in lines 66–76.

C. Clarification
Malcolm's second vice is avarice (greed).

[Handwritten note:] Malcolm believes he has support at home & from England but IF I become King, the country will have more problems than it does now

I think our country sinks beneath the yoke;
It weeps, it bleeds, and each new day a gash
Is added to her wounds. I think withal°
There would be hands uplifted in my right;°
And here from gracious England° have I offer
Of goodly thousands: but, for° all this,
45 When I shall tread upon the tyrant's head,
Or wear it on my sword, yet my poor country
Shall have more vices than it had before,
More suffer, and more sundry ways than ever,
By him that shall succeed.

Macduff.   What should he be?
Malcolm.

[Handwritten note:] I have vices & will be a worse King

50 It is myself I mean, in whom I know
All the particulars° of vice so grafted°
That, when they shall be opened,° black Macbeth
Will seem as pure as snow, and the poor state
Esteem him as a lamb, being compared
With my confineless harms.°
55 **Macduff.**   Not in the legions
Of horrid hell can come a devil more damned
In evils to top Macbeth.

[Handwritten note:] No one is as evil as Macbeth

Malcolm.   I grant him bloody,
Luxurious,° avaricious, false, deceitful,
Sudden,° malicious, smacking of every sin

[Handwritten note:] Lust B

60 That has a name: but there's no bottom, none,
In my voluptuousness:° your wives, your daughters,
Your matrons and your maids, could not fill up
The cistern of my lust, and my desire
All continent° impediments would o'erbear,
65 That did oppose my will. Better Macbeth
Than such an one to reign.

Macduff.   Boundless intemperance
In nature° is a tyranny; it hath been
Th' untimely emptying of the happy throne,
And fall of many kings. But fear not yet

[Handwritten note:] Macduff says that there will be plenty of those women that are willing (has) & you manage (can secretly)

70 To take upon you what is yours: you may
Convey° your pleasures in a spacious plenty,
And yet seem cold, the time° you may so hoodwink.
We have willing dames enough. There cannot be
That vulture in you, to devour so many
75 As will to greatness dedicate themselves,
Finding it so inclined.

Malcolm.   With this there grows
In my most ill-composed affection° such

[Handwritten note:] Greed C Avarice

A stanchless° avarice that, were I king,
I should cut off the nobles for their lands,
80 Desire his jewels and this other's house:
And my more-having would be as a sauce
To make me hunger more, that I should forge
Quarrels unjust against the good and loyal,
Destroying them for wealth.

---

41. **withal:** moreover.
42. **in my right:** on behalf of my claim.
43. **England:** the King of England.
44. **for:** despite.

51. **particulars:** special kinds. **grafted:** engrafted.
52. **opened:** in bloom, that is, revealed.

55. **confineless harms:** unbounded evils.

? 57. *How has Macduff responded to this speech?*

58. **Luxurious:** lecherous.
59. **Sudden:** violent.

61. **voluptuousness:** lust.

64. **continent:** restraining.

? 66. *An actor is always more interesting when he can convey two ideas at once. What two ideas should the actor playing Malcolm convey from line 60 to the end of this speech?*
67. **In nature:** in man's nature.

71. **Convey:** secretly manage.
72. **time:** here, people.

77. **ill-composed affection:** evilly compounded character.
78. **stanchless:** never-ending.

? 84. *This series of speeches is an extension of Malcolm's elaborate testing of Macduff's loyalty and sincerity. What should Malcolm's behavior be like?*

Answer to margin question
Line 114. On this line Malcolm drops his
sinful, man-of-the-world air, and speaks
in his own normal, gentle manner. Macduff has proved that he is totally loyal to
his country.

Greed is more serious than lust, but there is plenty in Scotland for you

Macduff.   This avarice

85 Sticks deeper, grows with more pernicious root
    Than summer-seeming° lust, and it hath been
A   The sword of our slain kings.° Yet do not fear.
    Scotland hath foisons to fill up your will
    Of your mere own.° All these are portable,°
90 With other graces weighed.

Malcolm.
    But I have none: the king-becoming graces,
    As justice, verity, temp'rance, stableness,
    Bounty, perseverance, mercy, lowliness,
    Devotion, patience, courage, fortitude,
95 I have no relish of them, but abound
    In the division of each several crime,°
B   Acting in many ways. Nay, had I pow'r, I should
    Pour the sweet milk of concord into hell,
    Uproar° the universal peace, confound
    All unity on earth.

100 **Macduff.**   O Scotland, Scotland!
Malcolm.
    If such a one be fit to govern, speak:
    I am as I have spoken.
Macduff.   Fit to govern!
    No, not to live. O nation miserable!
    With an untitled° tyrant bloody-sceptered,
105 When shalt thou see thy wholesome days again,
    Since that the truest issue of thy throne
    By his own interdiction° stands accursed,
    And does blaspheme his breed?° Thy royal father
    Was a most sainted king: the queen that bore thee,
110 Oft'ner upon her knees than on her feet,
    Died° every day she lived. Fare thee well!
    These evils thou repeat'st upon thyself
    Hath banished me from Scotland. O my breast,
    Thy hope ends here!

Malcolm.   Macduff, this noble passion,
115 Child of integrity, hath from my soul
    Wiped the black scruples,° reconciled my thoughts
    To thy good truth and honor. Devilish Macbeth
    By many of these trains° hath sought to win me
    Into his power; and modest wisdom° plucks me
120 From over-credulous haste: but God above
    Deal between thee and me! For even now
    I put myself to° thy direction, and
    Unspeak mine own detraction;° here abjure
    The taints and blames I laid upon myself,
125 For° strangers to my nature. I am yet
    Unknown to woman, never was forsworn,
    Scarcely have coveted what was mine own,
    At no time broke my faith, would not betray
    The devil to his fellow, and delight
130 No less in truth than life. My first false speaking

86. **summer-seeming:** youthful, or transitory.
87. **sword . . . kings:** the cause of death
to our kings.
89. **foisons . . . own:** enough abundance
of your own to satisfy your covetousness.
portable: bearable.

Characteristics of a true king

96. **division . . . crime:** variations of each
kind of crime.

I would create chaos if I were king

99. **Uproar:** put into a tumult.

create war

You are the true king + you blaspheme your birth

104. **untitled:** having no right to the
throne.

You come from noble parents + will make a fine king

107. **interdiction:** curse, exclusion.
108. **breed:** ancestry.

111. **Died:** that is, prepared for heaven.

I believe in you enough that I have banished myself from my home

? 114. *How might the tone change here?
How has Macduff proved himself?*

116. **scruples:** suspicions.

You have convinced me of your loyalty

118. **trains:** plots.
119. **modest wisdom:** prudence.

122. **to:** under.
123. **detraction:** slander.

125. **For:** as.

Explains what he said earlier was a lie

A. Macduff's Rationalization
Note that Macduff is a political realist who can tolerate quite a number of imperfections in a king: He does not expect a saint. Yet even he places limits on the extent of a king's faults, as revealed in the lines that follow. Here he rationalizes Malcolm's confessed avarice (lines 76–84).

B. Clarification
Malcolm's third vice is his intention to make war and destroy all peace. Note Macduff's despair in the next line.

A. Interpreting
❓ What good news has Malcolm been holding back? (That ten thousand men under Siward are ready to march)

B. "The Evil"
See the commentary "The King's Evil," text page 315.

Was this upon myself. What I am truly,
Is thine and my poor country's to command:
Whither indeed, before thy here-approach,
Old Siward, with ten thousand warlike men,
135   Already at a point,° was setting forth.
Now we'll together, and the chance of goodness
Be like our warranted quarrel!° Why are you silent?
Macduff.
Such welcome and unwelcome things at once
'Tis hard to reconcile.

[Enter a DOCTOR.]

Malcolm.
140   Well, more anon. Comes the king forth, I pray you?
Doctor.
Ay, sir. There are a crew of wretched souls
That stay° his cure: their malady convinces
The great assay of art;° but at his touch,
Such sanctity hath heaven given his hand,
145   They presently amend.°
Malcolm.   I thank you, doctor.

[Exit DOCTOR.]

Macduff.
What's the disease he means?
Malcolm.   'Tis called the evil:°
A most miraculous work in this good king,
Which often since my here-remain in England
I have seen him do. How he solicits heaven,
150   Himself best knows: but strangely visited° people,
All swoll'n and ulcerous, pitiful to the eye,
The mere° despair of surgery, he cures,
Hanging a golden stamp° about their necks,
Put on with holy prayers: and 'tis spoken,
155   To the succeeding royalty he leaves
The healing benediction. With this strange virtue°
He hath a heavenly gift of prophecy,
And sundry blessings hang about his throne
That speak° him full of grace.

[Enter ROSS.]

Macduff.   See, who comes here?
Malcolm.
160   My countryman; but yet I know him not.
Macduff.
My ever gentle° cousin, welcome hither.
Malcolm.
I know him now: good God, betimes° remove
The means that makes us strangers!
Ross.   Sir, amen.

---

135. at a point: prepared.

137. the chance . . . quarrel: May our chance of success equal the justice of our cause.
❓ **137.** *Where should Malcolm pause in this line? Should he act puzzled, or matter-of-fact?*

142. stay: await.
143. convinces . . . art: that is, defies the efforts of medical science.
145. presently amend: immediately recover.

146. evil: scrofula, called "the king's evil" because it allegedly could be cured by the king's touch.

150. strangely visited: oddly afflicted.

152. mere: utter.
153. stamp: coin.

156. virtue: power.

159. speak: proclaim.

❓ **Stage direction:** *What should be Ross's rate of entrance?*

161. gentle: noble.

162. betimes: quickly.

(handwritten margin notes: "Old Siward has an army ready"; "King of England had healing powers"; "— Skin disease")

Answers to margin questions
Line 176. Ross would probably look away on "Each minute teems a new one," all too aware of the "newest grief" he must report.
Line 179. For Macduff, "peace" means that his family is well. For Ross it means the peace that comes in death.

Macduff.
A
Stands Scotland where it did?
Ross.   Alas, poor country!
165 Almost afraid to know itself! It cannot
Be called our mother but our grave, where nothing°
But who knows nothing is once seen to smile;
Where sighs and groans, and shrieks that rent the air,
Are made, not marked;° where violent sorrow seems
170 A modern ecstasy.° The dead man's knell
Is there scarce asked for who, and good men's lives
Expire before the flowers in their caps,
Dying or ere they sicken.
Macduff.   O, relation
Too nice,° and yet too true!
Malcolm.   What's the newest grief?
Ross.
175 That of an hour's age doth hiss the speaker;°
Each minute teems° a new one.
Macduff.   How does my wife?
Ross.
Why, well.
Macduff.   And all my children?
Ross.   Well too.
Macduff.
The tyrant has not battered at their peace?
Ross.
No; they were well at peace when I did leave 'em.
Macduff.
180 Be not a niggard of your speech: how goes't?
Ross.
When I came hither to transport the tidings,
Which I have heavily° borne, there ran a rumor
Of many worthy fellows that were out;°
Which was to my belief witnessed° the rather,
185 For that I saw the tyrant's power° afoot.
Now is the time of help. Your eye in Scotland
Would create soldiers, make our women fight,
To doff their dire distresses.
Malcolm.   Be't their comfort
We are coming thither. Gracious England hath
190 Lent us good Siward and ten thousand men;
An older and a better soldier none
That Christendom gives out.°
Ross.   Would I could answer
This comfort with the like! But I have words
That would° be howled out in the desert air,
Where hearing should not latch° them.
195 **Macduff.**   What concern they?
The general cause or is it a fee-grief
Due to some single breast?°

166. **nothing:** no one. *Country in turmoil*

169. **marked:** noticed. *People dying*
170. **modern ecstasy:** ordinary emotion.
Cannot keep track of Macbeth's victims

174. **relation/Too nice:** tale too accurate.

175. **That . . . speaker:** The report of the grief of an hour ago is hissed as stale news
? 176. *Does Ross look at Macduff on this line, or does he turn away?*
176. **teems:** gives birth to.
Asks about family

Irony
? 179. *What is the double meaning of this line?*

182. **heavily:** sadly.
183. **out:** up in arms. *Rebellion*
184. **witnessed:** attested.
185. **power:** army.

Siward + 10,000 men

192. **gives out:** reports.

194. **would:** should.
195. **latch:** catch.

197. **fee-grief . . . breast:** that is, a personal grief belonging to an individual.

Terrible news

A. Interpreting a Role
Have students read pages 313–314 as if they were Ross. Ross has come to England to tell a good friend, Macduff, that Macbeth has murdered his entire family. How would Ross feel? (Sad, upset, pained, vengeful) Why would it be hard for him to come directly to the point? (He knows how shocked and grieved Macduff will feel.) How, therefore, would students deliver Ross's lines? (Slowly, unwillingly, avoiding Macduff's eyes, then angrily and finally with fervor)

1. When the witches say, "Something wicked this way comes," they are referring to __Macbeth__ .

2. The second apparition says that Macbeth cannot be harmed by __a man born of woman__ .

3. The third apparition says that Macbeth will be vanquished when Birnam Wood __comes to Dunsinane Hill__ .

4. Lady Macduff and her children are murdered by __killers hired by Macbeth__ .

5. Malcolm tests Macduff's loyalty by pretending to have three __vices__ .

A. Interpreting
This line means, approximately, "And I had to be gone!" It conveys anger, sorrow, and perhaps even guilt.

Answers to margin questions
Line 203. Most students will recognize that Macduff has guessed at least part of the truth. It will show in his facial expression.
Line 211. Answers will vary. Intense feeling can be conveyed both in soft speech and in a near shout.
Line 216. Macduff's voice would drip with pain and scorn on "He," meaning Macbeth.
Line 220. Malcolm is urging Macduff to do something in retaliation. The remark seems more encouraging than critical.

Ross.   No mind that's honest
But in it shares some woe, though the main part
Pertains to you alone.   *Macduff*
Macduff.   If it be mine,
200   Keep it not from me, quickly let me have it.
Ross.
Let not your ears despise my tongue forever,
Which shall possess them with the heaviest sound
That ever yet they heard.
Macduff.   Humh! I guess at it.
Ross.
Your castle is surprised;° your wife and babes
205   Savagely slaughtered. To relate the manner,
Were, on the quarry° of these murdered deer,
To add the death of you.
Malcolm.   Merciful heaven!
What, man! Ne'er pull your hat upon your brows.
Give sorrow words. The grief that does not speak
210   Whispers the o'er-fraught heart,° and bids it break.
Macduff.
My children too?
Ross.   Wife, children, servants, all
That could be found.
A   **Macduff.**   And I must be from thence!
My wife killed too?
Ross.   I have said.
Malcolm.   Be comforted.
Let's make us med'cines of our great revenge,
215   To cure this deadly grief.
Macduff.
He has no children. All my pretty ones?
Did you say all? O hell-kite!° All?
What, all my pretty chickens and their dam°
At one fell swoop?
Malcolm.
Dispute° it like a man.   *Take it like a man*
220   **Macduff.**   I shall do so;
But I must also feel it as a man.
I cannot but remember such things were,
That were most precious to me. Did heaven look on,
And would not take their part? Sinful Macduff,
225   They were all struck for thee! Naught° that I am,
Not for their own demerits but for mine
Fell slaughter on their souls. Heaven rest them now!
Malcolm.
Be this the whetstone of your sword. Let grief
Convert to anger; blunt not the heart, enrage it.
Macduff.
230   O, I could play the woman with mine eyes,
And braggart with my tongue! But, gentle heavens,
Cut short all intermission;° front to front°

Do not hate me for telling

203. *Macduff's pain becomes visible. How should we see it?*

204. surprised: suddenly attacked.

206. quarry: heap of slaughtered game.

210. Whispers . . . heart: whispers to the overburdened heart.
211. *How full, or soft, a voice would you have Macduff use in this line?*

Everyone

Macduff can't believe it

216. *How would Macduff say this line: "He has no children"?*
217. hell-kite: hellish bird of prey.
218. dam: mother.

220. Dispute: counter.
220. *Is Malcolm being critical or encouraging here?*

Blames himself

225. Naught: wicked.

Convert grief to anger

232. intermission: interval. **front to front:** forehead to forehead (that is, face to face).

1. Students should mention the ingredients named on text page 301.

Their purpose is to summon Hecate and other witches to cast a spell.

2. The first apparition, an armed head, tells Macbeth to beware of Macduff. The second, a bloody child, tells Macbeth none of woman born shall harm him. The third, a crowned child, tells him that he will never be vanquished until Birnam Wood shall come to Dunsinane Hill.

3. Macbeth has come to learn if Banquo's descendants will ever gain the throne. The witches show him a procession of eight kings who are Banquo's descendants.

4. He plans to murder Macduff.

His plan is foiled because Macduff has fled to England.

5. He vows to murder Macduff's wife, young children, and relatives.

Murderers burst in on Lady Macduff and her son and kill them.

6. Each day brings new widows, new orphans, and new sorrows to Scotland.

7. He "confesses" that he is lustful, greedy, and would destroy peace.

(Answers continue on next page.)

Bring thou this fiend of Scotland and myself;
Within my sword's length set him. If he 'scape,
Heaven forgive him too!

235 **Malcolm.**   This time goes manly.
Come, go we to the king. Our power is ready;
Our lack is nothing but our leave.° Macbeth
Is ripe for shaking, and the pow'rs above
Put on their instruments.° Receive what cheer you may.
240 The night is long that never finds the day.   [*Exeunt.*]

237. Our lack . . . leave: We need only to take our leave.

239. Put . . . instruments: arm themselves.

See King of England + then to Scotland

A. Interpreting
Does this speech convey a sense of hope? (It could have two interpretations.)

B. Responding to Scene 3
Questions 6–8 and 15–16 on the next page discuss Scene 3.

CLOSURE
Students should be able to summarize the ways in which we sense that Macbeth's fortunes are now beginning to decline. (They should include the apparitions' prophecies; the significance of Banquo's ghost and the Stuart kings; the murder of Macduff's family and its probable consequences; the alliance of Malcolm and Macduff.)

C. The King's Evil
See Act IV, Scene 3, lines 141–159 on text page 312.

D. Hecate
See Macbeth's reference to Hecate in Act III, Scene 3, line 41 on text page 290 and Hecate's appearances on text pages 298 and 302.

The King's Evil

In Act IV, Scene 3, Malcolm and Macduff, exiled from Scotland, discuss the characteristics of a good king and praise King Edward, who has given them political asylum in England. Edward, a saintly monarch known to history as "the Confessor," had the gift of healing any of his subjects who suffered from an ailment known as the king's evil, a kind of scrofula or tuberculosis of the lymphatic glands and primarily a disease of children. Long before Shakespeare's time, the custom of being touched by the king was abandoned, but King James revived the practice and his successors continued it for a century or so. Scrofulous as a child, Samuel Johnson (Unit Four) was one of the last English people to receive the royal touch.

The conversation between Malcolm and Macduff not only compliments King James indirectly, but it also implicitly condemns Macbeth, a kingly killer rather than a healer of children. Edward cures evil; Macbeth *is* evil.

Hecate

Hecate (here pronounced in two syllables, with the accent on the first: hek'it) is a figure from Greek mythology, a queen of the night and protectress of witches and enchanters. She comes from books, unlike the witches, who were typical of the solitary and possibly deranged old women to be found in many isolated Scottish villages. Every theatergoer would find the witches believable, and every educated person would know that King James had written an important book called *Demonology,* asserting that witches "are channels through which the malignity of evil spirits might be visited upon human beings."

Most Shakespearean scholars believe that the scenes involving Hecate (Act III, Scene 5; Act IV, Scene 1) were written by somebody other than Shakespeare and introduced into *Macbeth* at some time before 1623, when the play was first printed. This other writer has never been positively identified, though some people think he was a contemporary of Shakespeare and a fellow writer for the King's Men called Thomas Middleton (d. 1627). Two songs, the first beginning with the words "Come away" (Act III, Scene 5) and the second with "Black spirits" (Act IV, Scene 1), were also added to the Hecate scenes, and these songs are indeed by Middleton, the complete texts of them occurring in his thriller *The Witch.*

And so the practice of adding things to *Macbeth* began very early, and it has continued throughout most of the play's long stage history. The supernatural elements seem to invite directors to devise spectacles and take liberties, especially with the witches, who have been flown on wires in some productions and whose parts have been taken by ballet dancers in others.

(Answers begin on previous page.)
8. Macduff rationalizes Malcolm's lust and greed, but responds to his warlike temperament by saying that Malcolm is unfit to live, much less to govern Scotland.

Interpreting Meanings

9. His situation has changed because he is unnerved by opposition and by the es-

cape of Fleance.

His character has changed: He has become corrupt and bloodthirsty.

10. Student answers will vary. (The witches caused direct changes by putting a spell on him, indirect by encouraging his ambition to be king.) Encourage them to discuss and defend their opinions.

11. The point is to stress to Macbeth that the witches' prophecy will come true:

Banquo's descendants will rule Scotland.

12. Lady Macduff is shown as tender, weak, and a bit hysterical; she has drawn the wrong conclusion about her husband. Her son is portrayed as witty and courageous.

13. Student answers will vary. Ask them to explain their opinions. The onstage *(Answers continue in left-hand column.)*

(Continued from top.)
violence reveals how evil Macbeth has become.

14. Lady Macduff thinks her husband is a traitor because he has abandoned his family. The murderer means Macduff is a traitor to the king.

Students will probably agree that Macduff is not a traitor in either sense.

15. Malcolm is cautious, skeptical, and prudent.

16. Student responses will vary. Students may suggest that Shakespeare builds suspense and emotion with the unsuspecting Lady Macduff and her son, with Malcolm's false "confessions" to Macduff, with Ross's telling Macduff his bad news.

Set design by Nat Karson for the 1936 WPA Federal Theater production of *Macbeth*.

Responding to the Play

Analyzing Act IV

Identifying Facts

1. What ingredients go into the witches' stew? What is the purpose of this vile concoction?
2. Describe the three apparitions Macbeth sees when he visits the witches. What does each apparition tell him?
3. What question has Macbeth come to ask the witches, and how do they answer?
4. Which nobleman does Macbeth plan to murder after talking with the witches? How is his plan foiled?
5. At the end of Scene 1, what does Macbeth vow? Describe the way his vow is carried out in Scene 2.
6. According to the conversation between Malcolm and Macduff in Scene 3, what has happened to Scotland during Macbeth's reign?
7. What does Malcolm "confess" about his own faults?
8. How does Macduff respond to Malcolm's "confessions"?

Interpreting Meanings

9. In this act Macbeth seeks out the witches, just as they took the initiative in approaching him in Act I. How has his situation changed since he last talked with them? How has his **character** changed?

10. Do you think the witches have caused any of these changes, directly or indirectly? Explain your reasons for thinking as you do.
11. In Scene 1, the eight kings appear in what was called in Shakespeare's day a **dumb show**—an interpolated brief scene in which nothing is said. What is the point of this particular dumb show?
12. In Scene 2, the lines spoken by Macduff's wife and son illustrate Shakespeare's great skill at **characterization.** Using only a few words, he brings the woman and the child to life, showing both faults and virtues in each. How would you describe Lady Macduff? How would you describe the boy?
13. The murder of Macduff's wife and small son is one of the most pitiful and shocking scenes in Shakespeare. Why do you suppose he decided to show it onstage, rather than just having it reported after it happens?
14. Both the murderer and Lady Macduff herself call Macduff a traitor. In what sense does each mean it? Do you think Macduff is a traitor, in either sense?
15. In Scene 3, Malcolm deliberately lies to Macduff. What does this behavior, and the reason for it, reveal about Malcolm?
16. Describe how you felt as you read Scene 3. How does Shakespeare build **suspense** and **emotions** in the scene?

Have students review the three prophecies given to Macbeth by the apparitions called forth by the weird sisters. Have them be alert for these events as this act unfolds. For example, they should note that this act opens in Dunsinane Castle (Birnam Wood is nearby); they should recall what Macbeth was told about this castle and its nearby wood.

They should also note that the conflicts between Macbeth and his rivals and between Macbeth and his conscience are about to be concluded. In what different ways could this play end?

Plot Summary
Scene 1. Lady Macbeth's lady-in-waiting and doctor discuss her sleepwalking. She enters, walking in her sleep. She rubs her hands repeatedly to get rid of the blood. From her speeches, the onlookers infer that the Macbeths murdered Duncan. The doctor will not speak of his suspicions.

Act V
Scene 1. *Dunsinane. In the castle.*

Enter a DOCTOR *of physic and a waiting-*GENTLEWOMAN.

Doctor. I have two nights watched with you, but can perceive no truth in your report. When was it she last walked?

Gentlewoman. Since his majesty went into the field, I have
5   seen her rise from her bed, throw her nightgown upon her, unlock her closet,° take forth paper, fold it, write upon't, read it, afterwards seal it, and again return to bed; yet all this while in a most fast sleep.

Doctor. A great perturbation in nature, to receive at once
10   the benefit of sleep and do the effects of watching!° In this slumb'ry agitation, besides her walking and other actual performances,° what, at any time, have you heard her say?

Gentlewoman. That, sir, which I will not report after her.
15 **Doctor.** You may to me, and 'tis most meet° you should.

Gentlewoman. Neither to you nor anyone, having no witness to confirm my speech.

A   [*Enter* LADY MACBETH *with a taper.*]

Lo you, here she comes! This is her very guise,° and upon my life, fast asleep! Observe her; stand close.°
20 **Doctor.** How came she by that light?

Gentlewoman. Why, it stood by her. She has light by her continually. 'Tis her command.

Doctor. You see, her eyes are open.

Gentlewoman. Ay, but their sense° are shut.
25 **Doctor.** What is it she does now? Look, how she rubs her hands.

Gentlewoman. It is an accustomed action with her, to seem thus washing her hands: I have known her continue in this a quarter of an hour.
30 **Lady Macbeth.** Yet here's a spot.

Doctor. Hark! She speaks. I will set down what comes from her, to satisfy° my remembrance the more strongly.

B **Lady Macbeth.** Out, damned spot! Out, I say! One: two:
35   why, then 'tis time to do't. Hell is murky. Fie, my lord, fie! A soldier, and afeard? What need we fear who knows it, when none can call our pow'r to accompt?° Yet who would have thought the old man to have had so much blood in him?
40 **Doctor.** Do you mark that?

Lady Macbeth. The Thane of Fife had a wife. Where is she now? What, will these hands ne'er be clean? No more o' that, my lord, no more o' that! You mar all with this starting.
45 **C** **Doctor.** Go to,° go to! You have known what you should not.

---

6. closet: chest.

10. effects of watching: deeds of one awake.

12. actual performances: deeds.

15. meet: suitable.

18. guise: custom.
19. close: hidden.

? **22.** *Why must Lady Macbeth have light by her continually?*

24. sense: powers of sight.

? **30.** *After setting down the taper on a table, what does Lady Macbeth do with her hands?*
32. satisfy: confirm.

37. to accompt: into account.

? **39.** *What does she think is still on her hands?*

? **41.** *Who is the Thane of Fife?*

45. Go to: an exclamation.

Handwritten notes:
Lady Macbeth Sleepwalking
afraid to repeat what she says
afraid of the dark
cannot bear the dark – associates it w/ murder
Refers to Duncan's blood
Lady Macduff
realizes / L. Mc. knows she shouldn't – things she shouldn't participated in the murder of Duncan

---

Answers to margin questions
Line 22. She cannot bear darkness, associating it with murder.
Line 30. Lady Macbeth studies her hands and rubs at invisible marks.
Line 39. The blood of Duncan
Line 41. Macduff

A. The Sleep-Walking Scene
Recall that Act IV ended with a couplet about the night being long that never finds the day. Recall also all the references to sleep we've had so far, especially Macbeth's cry, "Methought I heard a voice cry 'Sleep no more! Macbeth does murder sleep' " (Act II, Scene 2, lines 34–35).

B. Interpreting
Be sure students recognize the various events and people Lady Macbeth is referring to in this scene.

C. Interpreting
? What does the doctor realize? (Lady Macbeth must have participated in the murder of Duncan.)

Macbeth, Act V, Scene 1   317

Literature and Language: Using Commas To Separate Complex Ideas

Remind students that one use of the comma is to divide long sentences and complex ideas into parts, thus making each thought clear. Point out how the commas improve one's ability to understand lines 1–19 on the previous page of *Macbeth*.

Have students copy the following sentences and mark where they think the commas should go. (Remind them, however, to refer to **Grammar, Usage, and Mechanics: A Reference Guide** for the rules governing commas.) Then have them check their work by comparing their sentences in small groups.

1. Methinks sir that the enemy approaches for I hear the clamor of their passage.

2. Could it not my friend be simply the clatter of our troops' own armor?

3. Methinks not sir for unless I heard wrongly mine ears report their trumpets' blare as well.

4. Then go and make our armies set for battle as it is mine aim to meet them where we stand.

A. Discussing the Photograph

The caption for this scene from Polanski's movie is from lines 49–50 on the facing page. Contrast this famous line with Lady Macbeth's earlier in words in Act II, Scene 2: "A little water clears us of this deed."

❓ What has become of Lady Macbeth? (She has been driven out of her mind by sin and guilt.)

A

"Here's the smell of the blood still. All the perfumes of Arabia will not sweeten this little hand."

ESTABLISHING A PURPOSE. The rest of Act V, the denouement, is crammed with action in a series of seven short scenes. Have students approach the scenes not so much as sharply divided episodes, but as a series of quick, almost cinematic shots of nearly simultaneous events taking place in different areas. Ask them to imagine that they are directing a movie for these scenes. What camera shots would they use, how would they assemble the film, and what effects would they aim for? How could similar effects be achieved in a stage production? (There would be no sharp breaks between scenes; actors would be entering one section of the stage as actors in the previous scene exited by another route.)

Gentlewoman. She has spoke what she should not, I am sure of that. Heaven knows what she has known.

Lady Macbeth. Here's the smell of the blood still. All the
50 perfumes of Arabia will not sweeten this little hand. Oh, oh, oh!

Doctor. What a sigh is there! The heart is sorely charged.°

Gentlewoman. I would not have such a heart in my bosom for the dignity° of the whole body.

55 **Doctor.** Well, well, well—

Gentlewoman. Pray God it be, sir.

Doctor. This disease is beyond my practice.° Yet I have known those which have walked in their sleep who have died holily in their beds.

60 **Lady Macbeth.** Wash your hands; put on your nightgown; look not so pale! I tell you yet again, Banquo's buried. He cannot come out on's° grave.

Doctor. Even so?

Lady Macbeth. To bed, to bed! There's knocking at the
65 gate. Come, come, come, come, give me your hand! What's done cannot be undone. To bed, to bed, to bed!   [*Exit* LADY MACBETH.]

Doctor. Will she go now to bed?

Gentlewoman. Directly.

Doctor.
70 Foul whisp'rings are abroad. Unnatural deeds
Do breed unnatural troubles. Infected minds
To their deaf pillows will discharge their secrets.
More needs she the divine° than the physician.
God, God forgive us all! Look after her;
75 Remove from her the means of all annoyance,°
And still° keep eyes upon her. So good night,
My mind she has mated° and amazed my sight:
I think, but dare not speak.

Gentlewoman.   Good night, good doctor.
                                    [*Exeunt.*]

A   (*In danger if they speak*

Scene 2. *The country near Dunsinane.*

Drum and colors. Enter MENTEITH, CAITHNESS, ANGUS,
LENNOX, SOLDIERS.

Menteith.
The English pow'r° is near, led on by Malcolm,
His uncle Siward and the good Macduff.
Revenges burn in them; for their dear° causes
Would to the bleeding and the grim alarm°
Excite the mortified° man.
5 **Angus.**   Near Birnam Wood
Shall we well meet them; that way are they coming.
Caithness.
Who knows if Donalbain be with his brother?

49. *What action is suggested by this line?*

52. **charged:** burdened.

54. **dignity:** worth, rank.

57. **practice:** professional skill.

— Banquo

62. **on's:** of his.
62. *Whom does she think she is speaking to here?*

66. *Once again there is a sudden dramatic change. What echo from the past brings it about? How do you think Lady Macbeth leaves the stage?*

73. **divine:** priest.   — Needs priest not physician
75. **annoyance:** injury.   — Remove anything that she might harm herself w/
76. **still:** continuously.
77. **mated:** baffled.
78. *What do the doctor and gentlewoman know? Why won't they speak out?*

English army is near

1. **pow'r:** army.

3. **dear:** heartfelt.
4. **alarm:** call to arms.
5. **mortified:** half dead.
5. *Where have you heard about Birnam Wood before?*

Answers to margin questions
Line 49. Lady Macbeth is sniffing a "spot" on one hand.
Line 62. Lady Macbeth thinks she is speaking to Macbeth after the murder of Duncan.
Line 66. She thinks she hears knocking at the gate, as in Act II, Scene 2. She leaves the stage in frantic haste.
Line 78. The doctor and gentlewoman recognize the truth about Duncan's murder, but realize they would endanger their lives by speaking out.
Line 5. The third apparition (Act IV, Scene 1, lines 92 –94): "Macbeth shall never vanquished be until / Great Birnam Wood to high Dunsinane Hill / Shall come against him" (text page 303).

A. Responding to Scene 1
See questions 1, 9, and 10 on text page 332.

Plot Summary

Scene 2. In Birnam Wood, Malcolm, Macduff, and their forces gather. The Scottish lords discuss their plans and Macbeth's reported state of mind.

Scene 3. Inside his castle, Macbeth feels confident (because of the witches' prophecies) that he is invincible. A servant brings news of the approaching army.

Macbeth talks with Seyton, resolves to fight, and asks the doctor about Lady Macbeth.

Answer to margin question
Line 31. Lennox and other Scottish lords are marching toward Dunsinane. They report that English forces led by Malcolm, Siward, and Macduff are nearby.

A. Repeated Motifs
See Macbeth's own words, "The secret'st man of blood," line 126, text page 297; note also the clothing references on text pages 261 (lines 108–109) and 262 (line 145). Note the concluding simile.

B. Responding to Scene 2
Question 2 on Scene 2, text page 332, addresses the lords' opinion of Macbeth.

C. The Prophecies
Macbeth refers here to two prophecies from text page 303. You might ask students what the other one was, and whether they can yet predict how all three might figure in the denouement. (They should be aware that a grief-motivated Macduff will be formidable, but they may as yet see no solution to the two riddle-like warnings.)

Lennox.
For certain, sir, he is not. I have a file°
Of all the gentry: there is Siward's son,
10   And many unrough° youths that even now
Protest° their first of manhood.
Menteith.   What does the tyrant?
Caithness.
Great Dunsinane he strongly fortifies.
Some say he's mad; others, that lesser hate him,
Do call it valiant fury: but, for certain,
15   He cannot buckle his distempered° cause
Within the belt of rule.°
Angus.   Now does he feel
His secret murders sticking on his hands;
Now minutely revolts upbraid° his faith-breach.
Those he commands move only in command,
20   Nothing in love. Now does he feel his title
Hang loose about him, like a giant's robe
Upon a dwarfish thief.
Menteith.   Who then shall blame
His pestered° senses to recoil and start,
When all that is within him does condemn
Itself for being there?
25   **Caithness.**   Well, march we on,
To give obedience where 'tis truly owed.
Meet we the med'cine° of the sickly weal,°
And with him pour we, in our country's purge,
Each drop of us.°
Lennox.   Or so much as it needs
30   To dew° the sovereign° flower and drown the weeds.
Make we our march towards Birnam.
                              [*Exeunt, marching.*]

8. **file:** list.

10. **unrough:** beardless.
11. **Protest:** assert.

15. **distempered:** swollen by dropsy.
16. **rule:** self-control.

18. **minutely revolts upbraid:** rebellions every minute rebuke.

23. **pestered:** tormented.

27. **med'cine:** that is, Malcolm. **weal:** commonwealth.
29. **Each . . . us:** that is, every last drop of our blood.
30. **dew:** bedew, water (and thus make grow). **sovereign:** royal; also, remedial.
❓ 31. *The "falling action" of a Shakespearean play is usually swift. How does this scene show that the hero's enemies are now rallying to crush him? What group is shown in this scene?*

(handwritten margin notes: "People know he murdered Duncan"; "rebellions"; "Those that follow do so out of fear not loyalty"; "who blames him for being tortured"; "Going to join Malcolm's forces"; "Malcolm")

Scene 3. *Dunsinane. In the castle.*

Enter MACBETH, DOCTOR, *and* ATTENDANTS.

Macbeth.
Bring me no more reports; let them fly all!
Till Birnam Wood remove to Dunsinane
I cannot taint° with fear. What's the boy Malcolm?
Was he not born of woman? The spirits that know
5   All mortal consequences° have pronounced me thus:
"Fear not, Macbeth; no man that's born of woman
Shall e'er have power upon thee." Then fly, false thanes,
And mingle with the English epicures.
The mind I sway° by and the heart I bear
10   Shall never sag with doubt nor shake with fear.

[*Enter* SERVANT.]

3. **taint:** become infected.

5. **mortal consequences:** future human events.

9. **sway:** move.

(handwritten margin notes: "let them all desert"; "Confidence in prophesy"; "Angry / confident")

Answers to margin questions
Line 12. Macbeth is relying on the prophecy that "no man . . . born of woman" shall have power over him. (See lines 5–7 on the preceding page.)
Line 22. Macbeth is feeling resigned to whatever comes.
Line 37. The patient is Lady Macbeth.

Macbeth agitated

A The devil damn thee black, thou cream-faced loon!°
Where got'st thou that goose look?

Servant.
There is ten thousand—

Macbeth.   Geese, villain?

Servant.   Soldiers, sir.

Macbeth.
Go prick thy face and over-red° thy fear,
15 Thou lily-livered boy. What soldiers, patch?°
Death of° thy soul! Those linen° cheeks of thine
Are counselors to fear. What soldiers, whey-face?

Servant.
The English force, so please you.

Macbeth.
Take thy face hence.

[*Exit* SERVANT.]

                    Seyton!—I am sick at heart,
20 When I behold—Seyton, I say!—This push°   *attack*
Will cheer me ever, or disseat° me now.
B I have lived long enough. My way of life
Is fall'n into the sear,° the yellow leaf,
And that which should accompany old age,
25 As honor, love, obedience, troops of friends,
I must not look to have; but, in their stead,
Curses not loud but deep, mouth-honor, breath,
Which the poor heart would fain deny, and dare not.
Seyton!

[*Enter* SEYTON.]

Seyton.
What's your gracious pleasure?

30 **Macbeth.**   What news more?

Seyton.
All is confirmed, my lord, which was reported.

Macbeth.
I'll fight, till from my bones my flesh be hacked.
Give me my armor.

Seyton.   'Tis not needed yet.

Macbeth.
I'll put it on.
35 **C** Send out moe° horses, skirr° the country round.
Hang those that talk of fear. Give me mine armor.
How does your patient, doctor?   *Lady Macbeth*

D **Doctor.**   Not so sick, my lord,
As she is troubled with thick-coming fancies
That keep her from her rest.

Macbeth.   Cure her of that.
40 Canst thou not minister to a mind diseased,
Pluck from the memory a rooted sorrow,
Raze out° the written troubles of the brain,
And with some sweet oblivious° antidote

---

11. **loon:** fool.

12. *Macbeth is in an extreme state of agitation. Which of the witches' prophecies is he relying on? How would you stage his treatment of the servant, which follows?*

14. **over-red:** cover with red.
15. **patch:** fool.
16. **of:** upon. **linen:** pale.

20. **push:** effort.
21. **disseat:** unthrone (with wordplay on *cheer*, pronounced *chair*).
22. *What mood is Macbeth in now?*
23. **sear:** withered.

Macbeth looks on his life ready to die
All the benefits of old age are denied him
Resigned mood

35. **moe:** more. **skirr:** scour.

hang people who talk of fear
solution to all his problems— Kill

37. *Who is the doctor's patient?*

She is troubled — insane

42. **Raze out:** erase.
43. **oblivious:** causing forgetfulness.

A. Character
❓ What do you think of Macbeth from the way he treats this servant?

B. Imagery
See Shakespeare's "Sonnet 73," text page 344, for another use of seasonal metaphors.

C. Character
Note Macbeth's solution to all problems.
❓ What sort of man has he become? (Cruel, insensitive, carelessly "macho" in the face of danger)

D. Plot
At this point Lady Macbeth is alive but insane, her mind filled with "fancies"—horrid images.

Line 56. Some possibilities are disgust, irritation, self-pity, concern for Lady Macbeth, and whimsy.
Line 60. He seems to be shoring himself up with bravado based on the enigmatic words of the apparitions.
Line 5. Each soldier is to cut a leafy branch and carry it in front of him as camouflage.

Line 7. In this and later scenes Malcolm might march in the lead. By their manner others would show that they defer to and protect him.

Plot Summary
Scene 4. The troops have gathered to attack Macbeth. Malcolm orders the soldiers to carry branches from Birnam Wood as camouflage.

A. Imagery
Compare the metaphor of a land diseased with similar lines spoken by Caithness (lines 27–29, text page 320) and the power of a king to heal (text page 312). Macbeth, however, views his opposition as the scourge, and they see him as a plague.

Note the rhetorical devices in this speech that suggest that Macbeth is becoming a bit unhinged himself, perhaps panicky or hysterical.

B. The Prophecies
Students must visualize what is happening here in this important speech.

[?] As the camouflaged forces move on Dunsinane, how will they look to a watcher on the battlements of the castle? (The forest of Birnam Wood will appear to be moving toward Dunsinane.)

Cleanse the stuffed bosom of that perilous stuff
Which weighs upon the heart?

45 **Doctor.**   Therein the patient
Must minister to himself.

Macbeth.
Throw physic° to the dogs, I'll none of it.
Come, put mine armor on. Give me my staff.
50 Seyton, send out.—Doctor, the thanes fly from me.—
Come sir, dispatch.° If thou couldst, doctor, cast
The water° of my land, find her disease
And purge it to a sound and pristine health,
I would applaud thee to the very echo,
That should applaud again.—Pull't off, I say.—
55 What rhubarb, senna, or what purgative drug,
A Would scour these English hence? Hear'st thou of them?

Doctor.
Ay, my good lord; your royal preparation
Makes us hear something.

Macbeth.   Bring it° after me.
I will not be afraid of death and bane°
60 Till Birnam Forest come to Dunsinane.

Doctor (*aside*). Were I from Dunsinane away and clear,
Profit again should hardly draw me here.   [*Exeunt.*]

[handwritten margin notes: Macbeth becoming a bit unhinged loss of control panicky hysterical]

47. physic: medical science.

[handwritten: Patient must do it herself]

[handwritten: Putting on armour as he says this]

50. dispatch: hurry.
51. cast / The water: literally, analyze the urine.

[?] **56.** *Lines 47–56 contain almost a roller coaster of emotions. Can you cite some?*

58. it: the armor.
59. bane: destruction.

[?] **60.** *Is Macbeth truly courageous here? Or would you suggest that he is merely coasting on a kind of false bravery lent to him by the witches' prophecies?*

Scene 4. *Country near Birnam Wood.*

Drum and colors. Enter MALCOLM, SIWARD, MACDUFF, *Siward's son* YOUNG SIWARD, MENTEITH, CAITHNESS, ANGUS, *and* SOLDIERS, *marching.*

Malcolm.
Cousins, I hope the days are near at hand
That chambers will be safe.°

Menteith.   We doubt it nothing.°

Siward.
What wood is this before us?

Menteith.   The Wood of Birnam.

Malcolm.
Let every soldier hew him down a bough
And bear't before him. Thereby shall we shadow
5 The numbers of our host, and make discovery°
Err in report of us.

Soldiers.   It shall be done.

Siward.
We learn no other but° the confident tyrant
Keeps still in Dunsinane, and will endure°
Our setting down before't.

10 **Malcolm.**   'Tis his main hope,
For where there is advantage to be given°

[handwritten margin note: cutting bows to use as camouflage — B]

2. That . . . safe: that a man will be safe in his bedroom.   **nothing:** not at all.

[?] **5.** *Stop and describe what the soldiers are to do here; and why.*
6. discovery: Macbeth's scouts.
[?] **7.** *Malcolm seems to have more authority at this point in the play. Can you find specific instances where his new authority could be dramatized?*
8. no other but: nothing but that.
9. endure: allow.

11. advantage . . . given: afforded an opportunity.

Answer to margin question
Line 7. In contrast with Malcolm's calm forcefulness, Macbeth should act bitter and scornful and show a false bravery.

Plot Summary
Scene 5. In the castle, as Macbeth awaits the approaching army, an offstage cry is heard. Seyton enters with news that Lady Macbeth is dead. Macbeth delivers his famous soliloquy ("Tomorrow, and tomorrow, and tomorrow . . ."). A messenger brings news that Birnam Wood is approaching the castle.

[handwritten: Revolts against Macbeth]

Both more and less° have given him the revolt,
And none serve with him but constrainèd things
Whose hearts are absent too.

Macduff.   Let our just censures
15   Attend the true event,° and put we on
Industrious soldiership.

Siward.   The time approaches,
That will with due decision make us know
What we shall say we have and what we owe.°
Thoughts speculative their unsure hopes relate,
20   But certain issue strokes must arbitrate:°
Towards which advance the war.° [*Exeunt, marching.*]

12. more and less: high and low.

15. just . . . event: true judgment await the actual outcome.

18. owe: own. The contrast is between "what we shall say we have" and "what we shall really have."
20. certain . . . arbitrate: the definite outcome must be decided by battle.
21. war: army.

Scene 5. *Dunsinane. Within the castle.*

Enter MACBETH, SEYTON, *and* SOLDIERS, *with drum and colors.*

Macbeth.
Hang out our banners on the outward walls.
The cry is still "They come!" Our castle's strength
Will laugh a siege to scorn. Here let them lie
Till famine and the ague° eat them up.
5   Were they not forced° with those that should be ours,
We might have met them dareful,° beard to beard,
And beat them backward home.

[*A cry within of women.*]

             What is that noise?

Seyton.
It is the cry of women, my good lord.   [*Exit.*]
Macbeth.
I have almost forgot the taste of fears:
10   The time has been, my senses would have cooled
To hear a night-shriek, and my fell° of hair
Would at a dismal treatise° rouse and stir
As life were in't. I have supped full with horrors.
Direness, familiar to my slaughterous thoughts,
Cannot once start° me.

[*Enter* SEYTON.]

15   Wherefore was that cry?

Seyton.
The queen, my lord, is dead.
Macbeth.
She should° have died hereafter;
There would have been a time for such a word.°
Tomorrow, and tomorrow, and tomorrow
20   Creeps in this petty pace from day to day,
To the last syllable of recorded time;

[handwritten: confident — false bravery — bitter]
[handwritten: Instead of meeting in battle, Macbeth is making Malcolm seige the castle]

4. ague: fever.
5. forced: reinforced.
6. met them dareful: that is, met them on the battlefield boldly.
7. *Macbeth should contrast with Malcolm now. How should he be acting?*

[handwritten: He cannot feel fear anymore. He is so corrupt he cannot feel fear]

11. fell: pelt.
12. treatise: story.

15. start: startle.

[handwritten: feels nothing]

17. should: inevitably would.
18. word: message.

[handwritten: soliloquy]

A. Plot
Instead of meeting the army in battle, Macbeth plans to let the attackers lay seige to his castle. Note that the Scottish forces have joined with the English.

B. Character
Do you think the death of Lady Macbeth arouses little feeling in Macbeth? Or is he saying that if she had died later, he could have mourned her? (He seems to be saying he has experienced so much horror he can no longer feel anything.) How do you think Lady Macbeth died? (The traditional response is that she threw herself from the battlements.)

C. Soliloquy
This famous "Tomorrow" soliloquy is the source of several titles: Robert Frost's "Out Out—" and William Faulkner's *The Sound and the Fury* (narrated in part by the idiot boy Benjy).
   Compare the central metaphor (beginning line 24) to the metaphor in "All the world's a stage . . ." (*As You Like It,* Act II, Scene 7).

Line 28. Macbeth shows philosophical resignation to the shortness of life. Students may not agree with Macbeth, but will see that he is describing the general human condition.

Line 35. Macbeth is recalling the prophecy about Birnam Wood advancing on Dunsinane.

Line 52. Having seen the duplicity of one

prophecy, Macbeth is experiencing the inner fatigue of final despair. Realizing that it matters little whether he remains in the castle or goes out, he resolves to die fighting.

Plot Summary
Scene 6. Near the castle, Malcolm orders his troops to throw down their camouflage and to attack.

A. Plot
Macbeth realizes there might be double meanings in the apparitions' words. Can students yet predict a way Macbeth might meet a man *not* "born of woman"? (See also question 7 on text page 332.)

B. Responding to Scene 5
See questions 5–6 and 12 on text page 332.

[Handwritten notes: Life is a theatre, a play / resignation to the shortness of life]

[Handwritten notes: Life is merely endless repetition in which experiences of those before us cannot change the fate of those who follow / Life is nothing / Players that act & then are heard no more. / Allusion adding to nothing]

And all our yesterdays have lighted fools
The way to dusty death. Out, out, brief candle!
Life's but a walking shadow, a poor player
That struts and frets his hour upon the stage
25 And then is heard no more. It is a tale
Told by an idiot, full of sound and fury,
Signifying nothing.

[*Enter a* MESSENGER.]

Thou com'st to use thy tongue; thy story quickly!
Messenger.
30 Gracious my lord,
I should report that which I say I saw,
But know not how to do't.
Macbeth.   Well, say, sir.
Messenger.
As I did stand my watch upon the hill,
I looked toward Birnam, and anon, methought,
The wood began to move.
35 **Macbeth.**   Liar and slave!
Messenger.
Let me endure your wrath, if't be not so.
Within this three mile may you see it coming;
I say a moving grove.
Macbeth.   If thou speak'st false,
Upon the next tree shalt thou hang alive,
40 Till famine cling° thee. If thy speech be sooth,°
I care not if thou dost for me as much.

[Bracket marked A]
I pull in resolution,° and begin
To doubt° th' equivocation of the fiend
That lies like truth: "Fear not, till Birnam Wood
45 Do come to Dunsinane!" And now a wood
Comes toward Dunsinane. Arm, arm, and out!
If this which he avouches° does appear,
There is nor flying hence nor tarrying here.
I 'gin to be aweary of the sun,
50 And wish th' estate° o' th' world were now undone.
Ring the alarum bell! Blow wind, come wrack!
At least we'll die with harness° on our back. [*Exeunt.*]

[Handwritten notes beside lines: Realizes their may be double meanings in the prophesies]
[Handwritten: Wishes it were over & he were dead. despair]

28. *A scene that began in defiance changes with the great speech beginning "She should have died hereafter." What is Macbeth's new mood? Does Macbeth speak only for himself here, or for the general human condition?*

35. *What is Macbeth thinking of now?*

[Handwritten: Prophesy / Angered]

40. cling: wither. **sooth:** truth.

42. pull in resolution: restore confidence.
43. doubt: suspect.

47. avouches: asserts.

50. th' estate: the orderly condition.
52. *Macbeth ends the scene in a state of great emotion. How would you characterize his mental state?*
52. harness: armor.

B

Scene 6. *Dunsinane. Before the castle.*

Drum and colors. Enter MALCOLM, SIWARD, MACDUFF, *and their* ARMY, *with boughs.*

Malcolm.
Now near enough. Your leavy° screens throw down,
And show like those you are. You, worthy uncle,
Shall, with my cousin, your right noble son,
Lead our first battle.° Worthy Macduff and we°

1. leavy: leafy.

4. battle: battalion. **we:** Malcolm uses the royal "we."

A

"Make all our trumpets speak; give them all breath,
Those clamorous harbingers of blood and death."

A. Discussing the Photograph
Shown is the beginning of Scene 6. Macduff speaks the lines used as the caption (see bottom of page). Whom do students identify as Macduff? as Malcolm? Why? Have students imagine fighting a battle in the garments shown (the costumer's idea of eleventh-century soldiers' garb).
❓ How much protection would a man have? (Only that provided by his shield) On what would his safety and success depend? (His alertness and his skills with sword and shield)

5   Shall take upon's what else remains to do,
       According to our order.°

Siward.   Fare you well.
       Do we° but find the tyrant's power° tonight,
       Let us be beaten, if we cannot fight.

Macduff.
       Make all our trumpets speak; give them all breath,
10   Those clamorous harbingers of blood and death.
                      [*Exeunt. Alarums continued.*]

Attack begins

6. **order:** plan.

7. **Do we:** if we do.   **power:** forces.

Macbeth, Act V, Scene 6   325

325

Plot Summary
Scene 7. On the field, Macbeth kills Young Siward. Macbeth exits with Macduff hot in pursuit.

A. Imagery
The bear-baiting allusion would have been familiar to Shakespeare's audience. (See the gloss to the right.) In that bloody sport, the bear, however valiant, had no real chance. You might ask students what Macbeth's use of the image reveals about his state of mind. (He feels utterly trapped, in a world that becomes more and more enclosed, as the bear's chain limits its movements to a small circle.)

B. Siward's Fight
Young Siward is praised by Ross and by the older Siward in lines 39–53 on text page 328.

C. Motivation
Macbeth said earlier that "blood will have blood" (line 122, text page 297). Notice how directly the idea is borne out in Macduff's motivation.

Scene 7. *Another part of the field.*

Enter MACBETH.

feels trapped

A

Macbeth.
They have tied me to a stake; I cannot fly,
But bearlike I must fight the course.° What's he
That was not born of woman? Such a one
Am I to fear, or none.

still relies on prophesies

2. **course:** bout, round (he has in mind an attack of dogs or men upon a bear chained to a stake).

4. *What is Macbeth desperately clinging to now?*

[*Enter* YOUNG SIWARD.]

Young Siward.
What is thy name?
5   **Macbeth.**   Thou'lt be afraid to hear it.
Young Siward.
No; though thou call'st thyself a hotter name
Than any is in hell.
Macbeth.   My name's Macbeth.
Young Siward.
The devil himself could not pronounce a title
More hateful to mine ear.
Macbeth.   No, nor more fearful.
Young Siward.
10   Thou liest, abhorrèd tyrant; with my sword
I'll prove the lie thou speak'st.

B [*Fight, and* YOUNG SIWARD *slain.*]

Young Siward slain makes Macbeth confident

Macbeth.   Thou wast born of woman.
But swords I smile at, weapons laugh to scorn,
Brandished by man that's of a woman born.   [*Exit.*]

[*Alarums. Enter* MACDUFF.]

Macduff.
That way the noise is. Tyrant, show thy face!
15   If thou be'st slain and with no stroke of mine,
My wife and children's ghosts will haunt me still.
I cannot strike at wretched kerns,° whose arms
C   Are hired to bear their staves.° Either thou, Macbeth,
Or else my sword, with an unbattered edge,
20   I sheathe again undeeded.° There thou shouldst be;
By this great clatter, one of greatest note
Seems bruited.° Let me find him, Fortune!
And more I beg not.   [*Exit. Alarums.*]

If he is already dead his family will haunt him

Blood will have blood

17. **kerns:** foot soldiers (contemptuous).
18. **staves:** spears.

20. **undeeded:** that is, having done nothing.

22. **bruited:** reported.

[*Enter* MALCOLM *and* SIWARD.]

Siward.
This way, my lord. The castle's gently rend'red:°
25   The tyrant's people on both sides do fight;
The noble thanes do bravely in the war;

24. **gently rend'red:** surrendered without a struggle.

Scene 8. Macduff confronts Macbeth, who at first refuses to fight him, warning Macduff that "none born of woman" can harm him. Macduff explains that he was not born of woman but was "untimely ripped." Macbeth again refuses to fight, but Macduff goads him by vowing to place him in a cage and display him as a fallen tyrant. Their fight begins and con- tinues offstage. Ross reports to Siward that Young Siward has died bravely. Macduff returns with the head of Macbeth and acclaims Malcolm as king of Scotland. Malcolm promises to restore peace and order to Scotland.

Answer to margin question
Line 16. Macduff was not "of woman born" in the natural way, but was delivered by Caesarean section.

The day almost itself professes° yours,
And little is to do.

Malcolm.   We have met with foes
That strike beside us.°

Siward.   Enter, sir, the castle.
                    [*Exeunt. Alarum.*]

27. **itself professes:** declares itself.

We have met those that side w/ us

29. **That . . . us:** that is, who deliberately miss us as our comrades.

Enter the castle

Scene 8. *Another part of the field.*

Enter MACBETH.

Macbeth.
Why should I play the Roman fool, and die
On mine own sword? Whiles I see lives,° the gashes
Do better upon them.

Why should I kill myself

2. **Whiles . . . lives:** so long as I see living men.

[*Enter* MACDUFF.]

Macduff.   Turn, hell-hound, turn!
A [**Macbeth.**
Of all men else I have avoided thee.
5   But get thee back! My soul is too much charged°
With blood of thine already.

Possibly some remorse

5. **charged:** burdened.

Macduff.   I have no words:
My voice is in my sword, thou bloodier villain
Than terms can give thee out!°   [*Fight. Alarum.*]

Macbeth.   Thou losest labor:
As easy mayst thou the intrenchant° air
10   With thy keen sword impress° as make me bleed:
Let fall thy blade on vulnerable crests;°
I bear a charmèd life, which must not yield
To one of woman born.

8. **terms . . . out:** words can describe you.

9. **intrenchant:** incapable of being cut.

10. **impress:** make an impression on.

11. **vulnerable crests:** heads that can be wounded.

wasting time
fighting w/ him

Delivered by C-section

Macduff.   Despair° thy charm,
And let the angel° whom thou still has served
15   Tell thee, Macduff was from his mother's womb
Untimely ripped.

13. **Despair:** despair of.

14. **angel:** that is, fallen angel, fiend.

Macbeth.
Accursèd be that tongue that tells me so,
For it hath cowed my better part of man!°
And be these juggling fiends no more believed,
20   That palter° with us in a double sense;
That keep the word of promise to our ear,
And break it to our hope. I'll not fight with thee.

? 16. *What is the meaning of lines 15–16? How do they relate to the prophecy?*

courage begins to fail him

18. **better . . . man:** manly spirit.

Realizes the witches (or himself) betrayed him

20. **palter:** equivocate.

refuses to fight

B [**Macduff.**
Then yield thee, coward,
And live to be the show and gaze o' th' time:°
25   We'll have thee, as our rarer monsters° are,
Painted upon a pole,° and underwrit,
"Here may you see the tyrant."

Make fool of him

24. **gaze . . . time:** spectacle of the age.

25. **monsters:** freaks.

26. **Painted . . . pole:** pictured on a banner set by a showman's booth.

A. Motivation
? Does this show that Macbeth still has human feelings? (Macduff was a friend. Macbeth may be experiencing some remorse over the needless murder of his wife and child.)

B. Interpreting
Note that Macbeth says he will just give up, but Macduff goads him with a fate worse than death. Can students *see* the fate Macduff proposes?

Macbeth, Act V, Scene 8   327

Line 53. Malcolm exhibits great concern for each missing man and promises some posthumous honor for Young Siward. Old Siward, satisfied that his son died bravely, says that no further honor is necessary.

Stage direction. Macduff is relieved, jubilant, and nearly ecstatic.

A. Death of Macbeth

? Do you think Macbeth's determination to fight it out shows bravery? Or does he have other motivation? (Perhaps relief at fighting a physical enemy rather than abstract terror)

The death of Macbeth usually takes place offstage, perhaps to avoid having one more body to remove or to dramatize Macduff's reentry with Macbeth's head. The great Shakespearean actor David Garrick (1717–1779) felt it was beneath his dignity as an actor simply to "go off fighting" with Macduff, and therefore he introduced an onstage fight and death scene.

? Is this a good idea, or do you prefer to have Macbeth killed offstage? Why? (Offstage since we know Macbeth must die.)

B. Interpreting

These lines refer to Young Siward's fight with Macbeth in Scene 7. The "hurts before" (in the front of the body) indicate that he died fighting, not running away.

Macbeth.   I will not yield,
To kiss the ground before young Malcolm's feet,
And to be baited° with the rabble's curse.
30   Though Birnam Wood be come to Dunsinane,
And thou opposed, being of no woman born,
Yet I will try the last. Before my body
I throw my warlike shield. Lay on, Macduff;
And damned be him that first cries, "Hold, enough!"

[Exeunt, fighting. Alarums.]

A   *[Reenter fighting, and* MACBETH *slain. Exit* MACDUFF, *with* MACBETH. *Retreat and flourish.° Enter, with drum and colors,* MALCOLM, SIWARD, ROSS, THANES, *and* SOLDIERS.]

Malcolm.
35   I would the friends we miss were safe arrived.
Siward.
Some must go off;° and yet, by these I see,
So great a day as this is cheaply bought.
Malcolm.
Macduff is missing, and your noble son.
Ross.
Your son, my lord, has paid a soldier's debt:
40   He only lived but till he was a man;
The which no sooner had his prowess confirmed
In the unshrinking station° where he fought,
But like a man he died.
Siward.   Then he is dead?
B   **Ross.**
Ay, and brought off the field. Your cause of sorrow
45   Must not be measured by his worth, for then
It hath no end.
Siward.   Had he his hurts before?
Ross.
Ay, on the front.
Siward.   Why then, God's soldier be he!
Had I as many sons as I have hairs,
I would not wish them to a fairer death:
And so his knell is knolled.
50   **Malcolm.**   He's worth more sorrow,
And that I'll spend for him.
Siward.   He's worth no more:
They say he parted well and paid his score:°
And so God be with him! Here comes newer comfort.

[Enter MACDUFF *with Macbeth's head.]*

Macduff.
Hail, king! for so thou art: behold, where stands
55   Th' usurper's cursèd head. The time is free.°
I see thee compassed° with thy kingdom's pearl,
That speak my salutation in their minds,

29. **baited:** assailed (like a bear by dogs).

Stage direction: Retreat and flourish: Trumpet call to withdraw, and fanfare.

36. **go off:** die (theatrical metaphor).

42. **unshrinking station:** that is, place at which he stood firmly.

52. **parted . . . score:** departed well and settled his account.

? 53. *What character traits does Malcolm show in this scene? How is old Siward like a military man to the end?*

? **Stage direction:** *Macduff enters with Macbeth's head on a pole. A great shout goes up. What is Macduff's tone in the next speech?*

55. **The time is free:** The world is liberated.

56. **compassed:** surrounded.

Handwritten margin notes:
- Refuses to pledge loyalty to Malcolm. Does not want to be made a fool of
- Fight to the end
- Not many killed
- Young Siward dead
- Died fighting not running away
- Macbeth is dead

1. Lady Macbeth walks in her sleep and rubs her hands as if washing them. (T)

2. When Macbeth learns of the invading English soldiers, he tries to escape. (F)

3. The Doctor tells Malcolm that the Macbeths murdered Duncan. (F)

4. Birnam Wood comes to Dunsinane by means of a miracle. (F)

5. When he hears of Lady Macbeth's death, Macbeth reveals his hatred of her. (F)

6. When he learns that Birnam Wood seems to be moving toward Dunsinane, Macbeth begins to suspect that the witches have tricked him. (T)

7. Macbeth kills Young Siward. (T)

8. Macduff was taken "untimely" from his mother's womb. (T)

9. Macbeth chooses to fight Macduff to the death. (T)

10. Macduff hails Malcolm as king of Scotland. (T)

Whose voices I desire aloud with mine:
Hail, King of Scotland!

All.   Hail, King of Scotland!

[*Flourish.*]

Malcolm.

60   We shall not spend a large expense of time
Before we reckon with your several loves,°
And make us even with you. My thanes and kinsmen,
Henceforth be earls, the first that ever Scotland
A   In such an honor named. What's more to do,
65   Which would be planted newly with the time°—
As calling home our exiled friends abroad
That fled the snares of watchful tyranny,
Producing forth the cruel ministers°
Of this dead butcher and his fiendlike queen,
70   Who, as 'tis thought, by self and violent hands°
Took off her life—this, and what needful else
That calls upon us,° by the grace of Grace
We will perform in measure, time, and place:°
So thanks to all at once and to each one,
75   Whom we invite to see us crowned at Scone.

[*Flourish. Exeunt omnes.*]

[Handwritten annotations: "reward all" near line 60; "Gives title of earl" near line 63; "Image of New growth" near line 65; "thanks" near line 73; "Restoration of order and harmony" at bottom]

61. **reckon . . . loves:** reward the devotion of each of you.

65. **What's . . . time:** What else must be done that should be newly established in this age.
68. **ministers:** agents.
70. **self . . . hands:** her own violent hands.
72. **calls upon us:** demands my attention.
73. **in . . . place:** fittingly, at the appropriate time and place.

? 75. *Scone is a stone upon which the Scottish kings sat at their coronation. (It is now in Westminster Abbey in London, beneath the coronation chair of the English kings.) Scone is usually pronounced "scoon." How would you have the characters exit? Who would exit last?*

Soliloquies and Asides

Renaissance playwrights had two useful devices for revealing to an audience or reader a dramatic character's inmost thoughts and feelings: soliloquies and asides. A **soliloquy** is a meditative kind of speech in which a character, usually alone on the stage and pretending that the audience is not present, thinks out loud. Everybody understood that the speaker of a soliloquy tells the truth freely and openly, however discreditable that truth may **B** be. For instance, in his famous soliloquy beginning "To be or not to be," Shakespeare's Hamlet admits to the audience that he is thinking of committing suicide.

Asides are much shorter than soliloquies, but just as truthful. **Asides** are a character's private comments on what is happening at a given moment in a play. They are spoken out of the side of the mouth, so to speak, for the benefit of the audience; the other characters on stage pretend that they do not hear the asides. For example, Macbeth's asides in Act I, Scene 3, tell us that he cannot put the witches' prophecy out of his mind.

Macbeth's tragic decline can be best traced in his solo speeches—his asides and soliloquies. The most important of these, which are what make the play so interesting psychologically, occur as follows:

Act I, Scene 3, lines 130–42
Act I, Scene 4, lines 48–53
Act I, Scene 7, lines 1–28
Act II, Scene 1, lines 33–64
Act III, Scene 1, lines 48–72
Act IV, Scene 1, lines 144–56
Act V, Scene 3, lines 19–29
Act V, Scene 5, lines 9–15

The early soliloquies show Macbeth's indecision and his fierce inner conflict; then, after he succumbs to evil, they show the terror in his soul and his inability to recover his lost innocence. At times they even show that he is reconciled to his murderous career, especially after the second set of prophecies gives him a false sense of security. But finally the soliloquies show his despair and loss of feeling about, and interest in, life itself. All these changing states of mind are expressed in powerful images that help the audience share Macbeth's suffering. In contrast, we see Lady Macbeth mainly from the outside, though an attentive reader can find speeches in which she also reveals feelings. In *Macbeth* the inner spiritual catastrophe parallels the outer physical catastrophe.

A. Imagery
Notice Malcolm's use of the image of new growth. This planting image connects him with the venerable Duncan and the noble Banquo (see lines 28–33, text page 263). You might ask students how such imagery relates to G. Wilson Knight's observation that "the play moves from social and structural order through nightmare and blood to daylight sanity and a new harmony."

Answer to margin question
Line 75. Students may suggest that Malcolm be led off in triumph by his men with Macduff last, carrying the head of Macbeth. Or, to emphasize the resumption of order in the kingdom, the last to exit might be Malcolm.

B. Soliloquies and Asides
? Did you have these same reactions to Macbeth's soliloquies? (They show how he changes.) Why or why not? How do you feel about the man, Macbeth? How do you feel about Lady Macbeth? (Answers will vary.)

Macbeth, Act V, Scene 8   **329**

A. Using This Essay

Have students read this essay before they do any of the writing assignments on text pages 333–334. This first section on the characters of Macbeth and Lady Macbeth provides ideas for critical writing assignments 4, 5, 7, and 10. The section called "The Poetry" will also be helpful for essays on Macbeth and Lady Macbeth, and a look ahead to the watercolor

B. Humanities Connection: About the Fine Art

John Singer Sargent (1856–1925) was born in Italy of American parents, and educated in Italy, France, and Germany. By 1884, when he moved to London, he had established a reputation as a notable portrait painter.

Dame Ellen Terry (1848–1928) made her debut at eight in a production of Shakespeare's *The Winter's Tale.* Celebrated for her talent and charm, she carried on a long correspondence with George Bernard Shaw, who wrote *Captain Brassbound's Conversion* for her in 1899. In 1925, Ellen Terry was made Dame of the British Empire, the female equivalent to knighthood.

Although Sargent's portrait is not tied to specific lines in the play, the pose may symbolize Lady Macbeth's ambition (see Act I, Scene 5). Note "the golden round" referred to on text page 265, line 28.

on text page 337 may help students focus their own ideas about Lady Macbeth.

The section on imagery (text page 331) may help students with critical writing assignments 7 and 9 (text pages 333–334), which address the play's supernatural elements.

A A Comment on the Play
The Characters Macbeth and Lady Macbeth

B

Macbeth fascinates us because it shows, perhaps more clearly than any of Shakespeare's other tragedies, how a character can change as a result of what he does. Of course *Macbeth* also shows us that crime does not pay, but that smug cliché is not very relevant to the play if it means only that criminals will eventually be caught and punished. Macbeth is "caught" as soon as he understands what the witches in Act I, Scene 3 are saying to him, and his punishment, in the form of mental anguish, begins even before he commits any crimes. At the start of the play, the mere thought of committing a murder terrifies Macbeth, makes his hair stand on end and his heart knock at his ribs, although he is a veteran of many battles and no novice at carving up men with a sword. But it is one thing to fight openly, quite another to kill stealthily. His wife says her great warrior-husband is "full of the milk of human kindness," as though he were a mother. Shakespeare apparently wants us to think of him as a good man, by no means a "born criminal," and to feel sympathetic toward him even after he becomes a murderer. When Duncan's body is found, Macbeth does not feel excited by the prospect of becoming king; instead, he mutters to himself, "The wine of life is drawn." We never see him enjoying his kingly state; he is too terrified by what he is doing. "Full of scorpions is my mind," he says to his "dear wife." He lives in such constant terror that by the end of the play he is numb to all feeling—even to the death of his beloved wife. "A dead butcher," Malcolm calls him: an automatic killer.

Lady Macbeth's deterioration is different from her husband's but just as dramatic. Legally she is only an abettor or accomplice, never an actual murderer. But she is the first to decide that Duncan must die; Macbeth wavers right up to the last moment. After the first murders, she exerts immense self-control over herself, while he surrenders to his nerves. But it would be incorrect to think of her as an unfeminine monster or she-devil, because she does eventually crack under the strain. Malcolm might not have called her a "fiendlike queen" after her death had he known how much she suffered from pangs of conscience. Both Macbeth and his wife are moral beings who excite our pity rather than our contempt or disgust. We see what they do to their king and their country; but more than that, we see what they do to themselves.

But why do they commit their crimes? The customary answer to this question—that they are ambitious—is a superficial one because it leads only to another question: "Why are they so ambitious that they are willing to commit such crimes?" Ultimately, of course, these questions are unanswerable because evil is just as mysterious as it is real. Shakespeare makes no attempt to solve the mystery; instead, in *Macbeth,* he uses language to make it

Ellen Terry as Lady Macbeth by John Singer Sargent (1889). Oil.

National Portrait Gallery, London.

1. Have the class work together as a group to map out the play's plot, using Freitag's pyramid or a modification of it. They should be able to fill in all the points on the pyramid with corresponding plot events. Students should refer to the Handbook of Literary Terms (text page 1259) for definitions of terms.

2. Critic Northrop Frye says in *Fools of Time* (1967) that in Shakespeare's "social tragedies," the tragic action is based on three character groups: (1) the order figure, who is killed by (2) a rebel figure, or usurper, and avenged by (3) a nemesis figure, who restores the previous social order. Have students identify and discuss these three character groups in *Macbeth*.

even more mysterious. If we may speak of the "world" of a literary work, then it is possible to say that the world of *Macbeth* is permeated, from beginning to end, with mysterious and repulsive images of evil.

The Imagery in the Play

First of all, there are the witches. The play opens with the three of them performing their sinister rites and chanting "Fair is foul, and foul is fair." Surely this is not a true statement because fair and foul are opposites; the differences between them must not be blurred. Yet Macbeth's first speech also joins them, as though they were synonyms: "So foul and fair a day I have not seen." Macbeth's speech establishes a connection between himself and the witches, even before he meets them. And everybody in Shakespeare's audience would immediately recognize the witches as embodiments of evil—skinny, bearded hags in league with Satan himself. Several times later in the play they refer to themselves, or are referred to by others, as the "weird sisters"—*weird* not meaning freakish, though they certainly are that, but meaning maliciously and perversely supernatural, possessing harmful powers given them by evil spirits in the form of nasty pet animals such as old gray tomcats and toads. Although they injure people in every way they can, English and Scottish witches are not to be regarded as the Fates of Greek mythology whose baleful influence could not be resisted. Rather, they are tempters of a kind that Shakespeare's contemporaries believed they should always avoid and never listen to. One of the witches seems to foretell Macbeth's future merely by saying, "All hail, Macbeth, that shalt be king hereafter." After an inner struggle and under the influence of his wife's goading, Macbeth chooses to make "hereafter" happen immediately. Nowhere in the play do the witches *cause* Macbeth to make this wicked decision. Rather, he voluntarily surrenders himself, following a visionary dagger—a manifestation of his decision—that leads him into Duncan's bedroom. Having once given in to evil, Macbeth is thereafter in the control of evil forces that are stronger than his own moral sense.

Shakespeare expresses these evil forces in images of darkness, night, and blood. He has Macbeth's friend Banquo call the weird sisters "instruments of darkness," linking them to the thick gloom that pervades the whole play and provides a cover under which evil can do its work. Even in daylight Macbeth and his wife invoke the night. "Come, thick night," Lady Macbeth cries, as part of her prayer asking evil spirits to "unsex" her. Macbeth also calls for night to come, to blind "the tender eye of pitiful day," so that the professional killers he has hired can safely murder innocent Banquo and his son. By setting many of the violent scenes at night, and by making the nights in *Macbeth* "murky," full of "fog and filthy air," and pierced by the cries of owls, Shakespeare suppresses all the pleasant associations that night might

have, especially as the time for refreshing sleep. Just as he commits his first murder, Macbeth hears a horrible voice crying, "Macbeth does murder sleep"; thereafter, he becomes an insomniac and his wife a sleepwalker. Darkness, voices, ghosts, hallucinations—these are not in the play just to create a spooky atmosphere; they are used to express Macbeth's and his wife's surrender to evil and their subsequent despair.

Evil in *Macbeth* takes the form of violence and bloodshed. Right after the very short scene with the witches, which opens the play, a man covered with gashes appears before King Duncan, who asks his bodyguard, "What bloody man is that?" Between this scene and the final one, in which Macbeth's bleeding and "cursèd" head is displayed on a pike, human blood hardly stops running. Blood seems to be everywhere: on Duncan's skin, up over Macbeth's feet and legs, in Banquo's matted hair. Images of blood appeal not only to the readers' and audience's sense of sight but also to their sense of touch (Macbeth's bloody and "secret murders [are] sticking on his hands" in the last act), and even their sense of smell ("Here's the smell of the blood still" Lady Macbeth moans in Act V as she holds out her "little hand" which once held the bloody dagger Macbeth used to kill Duncan). Such imagery is, of course, repulsive, but it is designed to make us feel moral revulsion, not just physical disgust. Bloodshed leads only to more bloodshed, as Macbeth discovers when he sees Banquo's ghost in Act III, Scene 4: "Blood will have blood."

The Poetry

All this imagery reminds us that *Macbeth* is a poem as well as a play—a dramatic poem, of course, but sharing many of the characteristics of lyric poetry. The most obvious of these characteristics is **meter,** here the unrhymed iambic pentameter or **blank verse** that Shakespeare's predecessor Christopher Marlowe established as the appropriate medium for tragedy. Poetry is to tragedy as singing is to opera: It elevates, enhances, and increases the emotional impact of whatever experience is being communicated to the audience. Of course it is "unrealistic" to speak blank verse on the stage; Macbeth is quite unlike a murderous usurper in real life because he continually speaks not only in meter but in metaphor. But without the poetry there could be no tragedy because otherwise Shakespeare could not have expressed the dark night into which Macbeth's soul sinks, a spiritual night corresponding to the literal night in which so many bloody deeds occur. And a tragic poet is much more concerned with states of mind and feeling than with physical action. Macbeth shares with Shakespeare's other great tragic heroes—Hamlet, Lear, Othello—the ability to express in eloquent, moving language whatever he is feeling. One of the most famous speeches of this kind occurs when, near the end of his bloody career, Macbeth sums up what life now means to him:

1. She has a guilty conscience.
2. They think he is mad or cruelly violent because of guilt at his "secret murders."
3. She kills herself as the enemy approaches the castle.
4. Macbeth will let the enemy besiege his castle. He would have preferred to fight them face to face, but troops that

should have been his have joined the enemy.
5. He has forgotten how to be afraid because of all the horrors he has experienced.
6. He describes life as brief, dreary, and meaningless, using metaphors of a brief candle, an actor strutting briefly onstage, a tale told by an idiot.
7. Third apparition—Malcolm's troops

camouflage themselves with branches from Birnam Wood. Second apparition—Macduff reveals that he was "untimely ripped" from his mother's womb. First apparition—Macduff kills Macbeth.
8. He has been slain by Macduff and beheaded; Macduff displays his head.
(Answers continue in left-hand column.)

(Continued from top.)

Interpreting Meanings
9. Lady Macbeth's sleepwalking emphasizes the torment and pathos of her guilt and fulfills the voice's cry (in Act II, Scene 2) that Macbeth hath murdered sleep.
10. Examples include references to the washing of hands and putting on the nightgown (actions on the night of Duncan's murder); the Thane of Fife's wife (the murder of Lady Macduff); the burial of Banquo (Macbeth's behavior during the banquet); the knocking at the gate (the morning after Duncan's murder).
11. Answers may vary. Night and day may stand for tyranny and freedom, or enslavement and liberation. The remark foreshadows the outcome of the play because it hints that Macbeth will, in the end, be defeated.
12. Many students will suggest the "Tomorrow, and tomorrow, and tomorrow . . ." soliloquy. Have them explain their rea-
(Answers continue at top page 333.)

Tomorrow, and tomorrow, and tomorrow
Creeps in this petty pace from day to day,
To the last syllable of recorded time;
And all our yesterdays have lighted fools
The way to dusty death. Out, out, brief candle!
Life's but a walking shadow, a poor player
That struts and frets his hour upon the stage
And then is heard no more. It is a tale
Told by an idiot, full of sound and fury,
Signifying nothing.
                                    (Act V, Scene 5, lines 19–28)

The bitter nihilism of these metaphors suggests that Macbeth is already dead in spirit, although his body must undergo a last battle. By murdering Duncan, he has murdered more than sleep. He has destroyed himself.

Tragedy and Society

Macbeth has also ruined his country. Tragedy in classical antiquity and in the Renaissance—the two periods when it most flourished as an art form—always concerned people of rank and title, people with public responsibilities whose actions had dire consequences not only for themselves but for their country. In this play, Scotland, like its king, has been stabbed: "It weeps, it bleeds," says one of the noblemen in Act IV, "and each new day a gash / Is added to her wounds."

If he ever saw it, *Macbeth* must have pleased King James, the patron of Shakespeare's company; James had recently survived a conspiracy known to history and to all English people as the Gunpowder Plot, and so he was especially interested in attacks on kings. James always defended the idea that he ruled by divine right. Moreover, he was a Scot and a direct descendant of Banquo, to whom the third witch says, "Thou shalt get kings, though thou be none." For these reasons, scholars have for a long time thought of *Macbeth* as a play written for a command performance at court, though there is absolutely no proof that it was. James refused to sit through long plays, and this royal shortcoming has even been used to explain the fact that *Macbeth* is by far Shakespeare's shortest play. Its brevity, for whatever reason, is most effective; without the usual Shakespearean subplots, it moves relentlessly to its tragic conclusion. Macbeth and his wife risk all, gain nothing, lose everything.

Responding to the Play

Analyzing Act V

Identifying Facts

1. Why, according to the doctor, is Lady Macbeth walking in her sleep?
2. In Scene 2, what opinion of Macbeth do the Scottish lords now hold?
3. Describe how and when Lady Macbeth dies.
4. Describe Macbeth's plan for dealing with the attacking troops. He says that he would prefer to deal with the troops in a different way; why has he been forced to choose this plan instead?
5. In Scene 5, Macbeth describes changes in his own personality. What are those changes?
6. In the speech in Scene 5 that begins, "Tomorrow, and tomorrow, and tomorrow . . ." (lines 19–28), how does Macbeth describe life? What metaphors does he use?
7. In Act IV, Scene 1, the first three apparitions shown Macbeth by the witches all referred, in reverse chronological order, to events in Act V. Find the things in Act V that correspond with the three apparitions in Act IV.
8. At the end of the play, what has become of Macbeth?

Interpreting Meanings

9. Theatrically, the spectacle of Lady Macbeth walking in her sleep is one of the most striking scenes in the play. It is entirely Shakespeare's invention, not found or suggested in his source. Why do you suppose Shakespeare has her walk in her sleep? How is this scene related to the remarks that Macbeth makes about sleep in Act II, Scene 2, just after he kills Duncan?
10. In the sleepwalking scene, Lady Macbeth refers to many of her waking experiences. For example, the words "one; two" may refer to Act II, Scene 1, when she struck the bell signaling Macbeth to go kill Duncan. Find traces of other experiences in what she says in her sleep.
11. Malcolm, at the very end of Act IV, says "The night is long that never finds the day." In what metaphorical sense did he use the terms "night" and "day"? How does his remark **foreshadow** the outcome of the play?
12. Shakespeare gave most of his tragic heroes an impressive dying speech in which they say something significant about their life and death. He did not write such a speech for Macbeth. Which speech of Macbeth's do you think serves in the play as his

sons for choosing any speech.
13. Student answers will vary. Ask them to give reasons to support their opinions.

The Play as a Whole
Interpreting Meanings
1. Macbeth's internal conflicts include ambition *vs.* loyalty; honor *vs.* guilt; rationality *vs.* delusion; hope *vs.* despair; strength *vs.* weakness. His external conflicts include his conflicts with Banquo, the witches, Macduff, Malcolm, and (for a time) with his wife.
2. Student answers will vary. (Some may say justice triumphs in the end. Others will say he was the victim of a spell he could not control.) Ask students to explain and defend their opinions in class.
3. Student answers will vary. Many stu-dents will suggest that Macbeth's death is the climax. Some may say that the cli-max occurs when Macduff reveals that he was ripped from his mother's womb. This fulfills the third warning of the appa-ritions, and from this moment Macbeth knows that he is doomed.
4. Students may suggest that Macbeth's strengths include courage in battle, loyalty, ambition, imagination, and persuasive ability. The last three of these may also be said to work against him.
5. Student an-swers will vary. Ask them to be specific in compar-ing the figures.

dying speech? Why do you select this speech rather than some other one?

13. "Nothing in his life/Became him like the leaving it." Malcolm says this in Act I, Scene 4, about the ex-ecution of the traitorous Thane of Cawdor. Malcolm also says that this Thane of Cawdor threw away the dearest thing he owned. Might these two statements also apply to Macbeth? Explain.

The Play as a Whole

Interpreting Meanings

1. **Internal conflicts** rage within Macbeth, as well as **ex-ternal conflicts** with other characters. Explain some of the play's main conflicts, and trace their **resolution.**

2. One of the **themes** of *Macbeth* centers on evil, which Shakespeare saw as a force beyond human under-standing. Do you think Shakespeare also saw evil as stronger than the forces of good? To answer, consider the events and outcome of *Macbeth.* Explain your reasons for thinking as you do.

3. The last act of Macbeth contains the play's **climax**— the most emotional and suspenseful part of the ac-tion—the moment when the characters' conflict is finally resolved. Which part of Act V do you consider the climax? Explain.

4. One critic has observed that a part of Macbeth's trag-edy is the fact that many of his strengths are also his weaknesses. Explain this apparent contradiction. What are Macbeth's strengths? Which ones also work against him?

5. Think of a modern figure, real or fictional, whose downfall, like Macbeth's, came after an attempt to gain great power. How is this modern figure like Mac-beth, and how different? Do you think the modern figure would make a good tragic hero or heroine?

Writing About the Play

A Creative Response

1. **Extending a Character.** Banquo's son Fleance has a pivotal but small role in *Macbeth;* almost all we know about him is that he becomes the ancestor of the eight Stuart kings. Imagine what sort of person Fle-ance might be and how he might have been affected by the events of the play. Write a scene starring Fleance that takes place at some point after Ban-quo's death. Where does Fleance go? What does he do, think, and feel? Does anyone help him? Use stage directions to tell where and when your scene is set. Let Fleance's words and actions reveal what kind of person he is.

2. **Updating a Scene.** Rewrite the banquet scene (Act III, Scene 4), when Macbeth sees Banquo's ghost. In your revision, change the setting to a modern time and place, and let the characters speak in today's language. For example, Lady Macbeth might explain to the other banquet guests that Macbeth is suffering from stress or burnout. Describe your setting in your stage directions before you begin writing the scene. If you change characters to make them more modern (the Scottish lords might be cabinet members or board members, for example), provide a list of char-acters at the beginning of the scene.

3. **Changing the Outcome.** Think of a single event, at any time during the course of the play, that could have averted Macbeth's tragic end. Write three paragraphs in which you narrate the event, explain how it could have come about, and explain how it would affect the outcome of the play.

A Critical Response

4. **Interpreting Characterization.** The philosopher Aris-totle and many of his followers argued that a bad man cannot be the principal character of a tragedy. Although Shakespeare apparently was not much in-terested in Aristotle's or anyone else's theories, he does take pains to keep us from losing all sympathy for Macbeth and interest in him even though he becomes increasingly vicious. In an essay, discuss how Shakespeare accomplishes this feat. Consider what Macbeth does and says as well as what he does *not* do and say. (He does not, for example, blame the witches or his wife for what has happened to him.) In your essay, tell whether you were still in sympathy with Macbeth at the end of the play. If not, at what point did you lose sympathy for him?

5. **Analyzing a Character.** Lady Macbeth is sometimes regarded as a monster, ruthlessly ambitious and fiendishly cruel. What clues can you find in the play suggesting that Shakespeare did not want us to judge her so severely? In an essay, analyze her character based on what she does and says, what she seems to look like, what her husband thinks of her, what she thinks of him, and how she treats him. Consider, too, what her death reveals about her.

6. **Evaluating Dramatic Effects.** Sometime shortly after 1610, a playwright named William Davenant (who claimed to be a natural son of Shakespeare) added another sleepwalking scene to *Macbeth:* He had the ghost of Duncan chase Lady Macbeth about the stage. In a paragraph, discuss the ways in which such a scene might affect the play. How might it change the way audiences perceive Lady Macbeth's character? Might it make the other ghosts in the play seem any more or less real? What might the scene add to the play, and what might it take away?

7. **Analyzing the Playwright's Intent.** When Macbeth dis-covers how Macduff entered the world (Act V, Scene 8), he also discovers that the witches are "juggling fiends" who have given him a false sense of security.

Additional Writing Assignments

As a creative response to the play, suggest that students write a theater review as if they were a critic attending the opening night performance of *Macbeth*. Another possible assignment is an imaginary interview with the playwright. Those who choose to write the interview should have Shakespeare discuss *Macbeth* and tell where he got his ideas and characters, and how he feels about them.

Why do you think Shakespeare shows Macbeth taken in by their prophecies? What might Shakespeare be implying about Macbeth's character? About the witches' powers? Write your answer in a paragraph.

8. **Analyzing Irony.** "A little water clears us of this deed," says Lady Macbeth in Act II, Scene 2. Trace how, as the play progresses, this becomes an increasingly **ironic** statement. Present your findings in a brief essay.

9. **Applying Logic.** Living, as most of us do, in a rational and scientifically explainable world, we may find it hard to believe in supernatural intervention in human life as readily as Shakespeare's audience believed in it. Indeed, some of the supernatural phenomena—the fiends, ghosts, voices, visions—in *Macbeth* can be accounted for by common sense. For instance, the voice that tells Macbeth that he has murdered sleep could come from within his own disordered mind. And the witches telling him he will be king could be malicious and deranged old women who know that he is a great warrior and that the thanes are always squabbling over the Scottish throne. In a brief essay, discuss the supernatural elements in *Macbeth* from a rational, logical point of view. If you find events that could not have a logical explanation, discuss why they could not.

10. **Responding to a Critic.** In a brief essay, write your response to one of these critical comments about the characters of Macbeth and Lady Macbeth. You may agree with this critic or refute him, but be sure to support your response with evidence from the play.

> When one reads or sees *Macbeth,* one cannot help feeling that one is experiencing a re-creation or re-presentation of what a man is, in the present, even in the timeless.

> We may insist, on reflection, that Macbeth is a free agent who need not have yielded to the witches' hints; certainly he harbors within him what they present to our eye. Yet can we feel sure that he has not been ensnared: the charm has been wound up, and if he is the tyrant, viewed another way he is the victim of infernal tyranny.

> . . . if she [Lady Macbeth] here seems as black as the evil angel that prompts Mankind to illicit deeds in the old morality plays, she too reveals inner depths in the sleepwalking scene, when we see that like her husband she is troubled with thick-coming fancies that keep her from her rest.
>
> —Sylvan Barnet

Analyzing Language and Style

Imagery and Figurative Language

Macbeth's poetry is rich in **imagery** and **figurative language** that help to create atmosphere and reveal character and theme.

1. Throughout the play, Shakespeare uses powerful **images** to contrast the natural and unnatural, as in Lady Macbeth's speech in Act I, Scene 7:

   > . . . I have given suck, and know
   > How tender 'tis to love the babe that milks me;
   > I would, while it was smiling in my face,
   > Have plucked my nipple from his boneless gums,
   > And dashed the brains out, had I so sworn as you
   > Have done to this.

   a. What unnatural sounds and events are reported in Act II, Scenes 2–4? What mood do these **images** create?

   b. Examine the scenes in which the three witches appear. What would you say is the emotional effect of each scene? Besides the witches themselves, what unnatural **images** occur in these scenes?

2. Sleep and sleeplessness are mentioned throughout the play. Analyze the **figures of speech** in the following speeches:

   a. **First Witch.** . . . I'll drain him dry as hay:
   Sleep shall neither night nor day
   Hang upon his penthouse lid; . . . .
   > —Act I, Scene 3

   b. **Macbeth.** Methought I heard a voice cry "Sleep no more!
   Macbeth does murder sleep"—the innocent sleep,
   Sleep that knits up the raveled sleave of care,
   The death of each day's life, sore labor's bath,
   Balm of hurt minds, great nature's second course,
   Chief nourisher in life's feast—
   > —Act II, Scene 2

   c. Reread the sleepwalking scene in Act V, Scene 1. What does this scene reveal, and how does it build toward the play's **climax**? Why do you suppose Shakespeare does not use figurative language in this scene?

3. Choose one of the following **images,** and find three speeches (from different scenes in the play) in which the image occurs:

   blood   darkness   disease   planting

   Identify the **metaphors, similes,** and **personification** in each speech. Look back at the context of each speech (what happens just before and after): what is the emotional effect of each one?

1. ABOUT THE AUTHOR. The son of a wealthy merchant, Thomas De Quincey (1785–1859) was educated at Oxford. As an adult, he lived in the beautiful Lake District, where he befriended Wordsworth (text page 631) and Coleridge (text page 647) and supported their efforts to create a new kind of poetry. De Quincey is best known for this essay on *Macbeth* and for his *Confessions of an English Opium Eater* (1822), an account of his addiction to the drug he began taking for a stomach problem.

2. BUILDING ON PRIOR KNOWLEDGE. This essay, in De Quincey's usual discursive style, should be contrasted with the points made in the commentary on text page 283. Have students review Act II, Scenes 1–3 (especially the knocking at the gate, text page 277).

3. ESTABLISHING A PURPOSE. Have students read the first paragraph and state in their own words the question De Quincey poses. Then have them read the rest of the essay to find his answer.

ON THE KNOCKING AT THE GATE IN *MACBETH*

Thomas De Quincey

Charles Lamb, it is said, was at a literary dinner one evening and pointed to another man at the party. "Do you see that little man?" he whispered to his neighbor. "Well, though he is so little, he has written a thing about *Macbeth* better than anything I could write;—no—not better than anything I could write, but I could not write anything better."

The little man was Thomas De Quincey (1785–1859), an English essayist and critic.

From my boyish days I had always felt a great perplexity on one point in *Macbeth*. It was this: The knocking at the gate, which succeeds to the murder of Duncan, produced to my feelings an effect for which I never could account. The effect was, that it reflected back upon the murderer a peculiar awfulness and a depth of solemnity; yet, however obstinately I endeavored with my understanding to comprehend this, for many years I never could see *why* it should produce such an effect.

Here I pause for one moment, to exhort the reader never to pay any attention to his understanding, when it stands in opposition to any other faculty of his mind. The mere understanding, however useful and indispensable, is the meanest faculty in the human mind, and the most to be distrusted; and yet the great majority of people trust to nothing else, which may do for ordinary life, but not for philosophical purposes. Of this out of ten thousand instances that I might produce, I will cite one. Ask of any person whatsoever, who is not previously prepared for the demand by a knowledge of the perspective, to draw in the rudest way the commonest appearance which depends upon the laws of that science; as, for instance, to represent the effect of two walls standing at right angles to each other, or the appearance of the houses on each side of a street, as seen by a person looking down the street from one extremity. Now in all cases, unless the person has happened to observe in pictures how it is that artists produce these effects, he will be utterly unable to make the smallest approximation to it. Yet why? For he has actually seen the effect every day of his life. The reason is—that he allows his understanding to overrule his eyes. His understanding, which includes no intuitive knowledge of the laws of vision, can furnish him with no reason why a line which is known and can be proved to be a horizontal line, should not appear a horizontal line; a line that made any angle with the perpendicular, less than a right angle, would seem to him to indicate that his houses were all tumbling down together. Accordingly, he makes the line of his houses a horizontal line, and fails, of course, to produce the effect demanded. Here, then, is one instance out of many, in which not only the understanding is allowed to overrule the eyes, but where the understanding is positively allowed to obliterate the eyes, as it were; for not only does the man believe the evidence of his understanding in opposition to that of his eyes, but (what is monstrous!) the idiot is not aware that his eyes ever gave such evidence. He does not know that he has seen (and therefore *quoad* his consciousness has *not* seen) that which he *has* seen every day of his life.

But to return from this digression, my understanding could furnish no reason why the knocking at the gate in *Macbeth* should produce any effect, direct or reflected. In fact, my understanding said positively that it could *not* produce any effect. But I knew better; I felt that it did; and I waited and clung to the problem until further knowledge should enable me to solve it. At length, in 1812, Mr. Williams made his debut on the stage of Ratcliffe Highway, and executed those unparalleled murders which have procured for him such a brilliant and undying reputation. On which murders, by the way, I must observe, that in one respect they have had an ill effect, by making the connoisseur in murder very fastidious in his taste, and dissatisfied by anything that has been since

A. Responding

❓ Do you agree or disagree with De Quincey here? If understanding is not to be trusted, what is? (Intuition and vision)

B. Critical Thinking

Ask students to analyze the argument here.

❓ What idea is De Quincey trying to "prove"? What "evidence" does he give to support this idea? How convincing is the evidence? (Murder is the worst crime. Therefore we must feel the passion in the mind of the murderer so we can understand him. Because the murderer lives in a separate world, we must see the re-entry of the real world—in the case of Macbeth, symbolized by the knocking at the gate.)

C. Expansion

De Quincey alludes to an actual event. In December 1811 (not 1812, as De Quincey reports), a sailor named John Williams threw London into a panic by first murdering the Marr family and then, twelve days later, the Williamson family.

A. Clarification
In the Marr family murders, the knocking at the door was that of a maidservant returning from buying oysters for supper.

B. Allusion
The quote is from Shakespeare's *Measure for Measure,* Act II, Scene 1: "The sense of death is most in apprehension, / And the poor beetle, that we tread upon, / In corporal sufferance finds a pang as great / As when a giant dies."

C. Diction
De Quincey deplored the use of *sympathy* as a synonym for *pity.* He defined *sympathy* as "the act of reproducing in our minds the feelings of another, whether for hatred, indignation, love, pity, or approbation."

D. Analysis
❓ What is De Quincey's point in these two examples of a lady's fainting and a city after a funeral? (He's illustrating the suspension and resumption of time.)

done in that line. All other murders look pale by the deep crimson of his; and, as an amateur once said to me in a querulous tone, "There has been absolutely nothing *doing* since his time, or nothing that's worth speaking of." But this is wrong; for it is unreasonable to expect all men to be great artists, and born with the genius of Mr. Williams. Now it will be remembered, that in the first of these murders (that of the Marrs), the same incident (of a knocking at the door, soon after the work of extermination was complete) did actually occur, which the genius of Shakespeare has invented; and all good judges, and the most eminent dilettanti,[1] acknowledged the felicity of Shakespeare's suggestion, as soon as it was actually realized. Here, then, was a fresh proof that I was right in relying on my own feeling, in opposition to my understanding; and I again set myself to study the problem; at length I solved it to my own satisfaction, and my solution is this. Murder, in ordinary cases, where the sympathy is wholly directed to the case of the murdered person, is an incident of coarse and vulgar horror; and for this reason, that it flings the interest exclusively upon the natural but ignoble instinct by which we cleave to life; an instinct which, as being indispensable to the primal law of self-preservation, is the same in kind (though different in degree) amongst all living creatures: this instinct, therefore, because it annihilates all distinctions, and degrades the greatest of men to the level of "the poor beetle that we tread on," exhibits human nature in its most abject and humiliating attitude. Such an attitude would little suit the purposes of the poet. What then must he do? He must throw the interest on the murderer. Our sympathy must be with *him* (of course I mean a sympathy of comprehension, a sympathy by which we enter into his feelings, and are made to understand them, not a sympathy of pity or approbation). In the murdered person, all strife of thought, all flux and reflux of passion and of purpose, are crushed by one overwhelming panic; the fear of instant death smites him "with its petrific mace." But in the murderer, such a murderer as a poet will condescend to, there must be raging some great storm of passion—jealousy, ambition, vengeance, hatred—which will create a hell within him; and into this hell we are to look.

In *Macbeth,* for the sake of gratifying his own enormous and teeming faculty of creation, Shake-

1. **dilettanti:** those who follow the arts.

speare has introduced two murderers: and, as usual in his hands, they are remarkably discriminated: but, though in Macbeth the strife of mind is greater than in his wife, the tiger spirit not so awake, and his feelings caught chiefly by contagion from her, yet, as both were finally involved in the guilt of murder, the murderous mind of necessity is finally to be presumed in both. This was to be expressed; and on its own account, as well as to make it a more proportionable antagonist to the unoffending nature of their victim, "the gracious Duncan," and adequately to expound "the deep damnation of his taking off," this was to be expressed with peculiar energy. We were to be made to feel that the human nature, i.e., the divine nature of love and mercy, spread through the hearts of all creatures, and seldom utterly withdrawn from man—was gone, vanished, extinct; and that the fiendish nature had taken its place. And, as this effect is marvelously accomplished in the *dialogues* and *soliloquies* themselves, so it is finally consummated by the expedient under consideration; and it is to this that I now solicit the reader's attention. If the reader has ever witnessed a wife, daughter, or sister in a fainting fit, he may chance to have observed that the most affecting moment in such a spectacle is *that* in which a sigh and a stirring announce the recommencement of suspended life. Or, if the reader has ever been present in a vast metropolis, on the day when some great national idol was carried in funeral pomp to his grave, and chancing to walk near the course through which it passed, has felt powerfully in the silence and desertion of the streets, and in the stagnation of ordinary business, the deep interest which at that moment was possessing the heart of man—if all at once he should hear the deathlike stillness broken up by the sound of wheels rattling away from the scene, and making known that the transitory vision was dissolved, he will be aware that at no moment was his sense of the complete suspension and pause in ordinary human concerns so full and affecting, as at that moment when the suspension ceases, and the goings-on of human life are suddenly resumed. All action in any direction is best expounded, measured, and made apprehensible, by reaction. Now apply this to the case of *Macbeth.* Here, as I have said, the retiring of the human heart, and the entrance of the fiendish heart was to be expressed and made sensible. Another world has stepped in; and the murderers are

A. Humanities Connection: Responding to the Fine Art
Schussele's Lady Macbeth differs markedly from Sargent's painting of Ellen Terry on text page 330. Have students compare and contrast the two paintings and tell which one they prefer, and which one they feel is more powerful.

? What emotions does Lady Macbeth seem to be feeling in Schussele's painting? (Students may say horror, anguish, fear, surprise.) How has the artist conveyed these emotions? (Her facial expression, especially the eyes; the odd pose with her hands; the dramatic lighting) Do you think the artist has portrayed her before or after Duncan's murder? How can you tell? (Before, because the knife is not bloody)

Lady Macbeth by Christian Schussele (1864). Watercolor.

Kennedy Galleries, Inc., New York.

A

B. Responding

? What is De Quincey's main point? (That the knocking represents a return from the devil's world of Duncan's murder to the ordinary, everyday world) Do you agree or disagree with this interpretation of the scene? (Answers will vary but may mention that the scene also creates suspense.)

taken out of the region of human things, human purposes, human desires. They are transfigured: Lady Macbeth is "unsexed"; Macbeth has forgot that he was born of woman; both are conformed to the image of devils; and the world of devils is suddenly revealed. But how shall this be conveyed and made palpable? In order that a new world may step in, this world must for a time disappear. The murderers, and the murder must be insulated—cut off by an immeasurable gulf from the ordinary tide and succession of human affairs—locked up and sequestered in some deep recess; we must be made sensible that the world of ordinary life is suddenly arrested—laid asleep—tranced—racked into a dread armistice; time must be annihilated; relation to things without abolished; and all must pass self-withdrawn into a deep syncope[2] and suspension of earthly passion. Hence it is, that when the deed is done, when the work of darkness is perfect, then the world of

darkness passes away like a pageantry in the clouds: The knocking at the gate is heard; and it makes known audibly that the reaction has commenced; the human has made its reflux upon the fiendish; the pulses of life are beginning to beat again; and the reestablishment of the goings-on of the world in which we live first makes us profoundly sensible of the awful parenthesis that had suspended them.

B

O mighty poet! Thy works are not as those of other men, simply and merely great works of art; but are also like the phenomena of nature, like the sun and the sea, the stars and the flowers; like frost and snow, rain and dew, hailstorm and thunder, which are to be studied with entire submission of our own faculties, and in the perfect faith that in them there can be no too much or too little, nothing useless or inert—but that, the further we press in our discoveries, the more we shall see proofs of design and self-supporting arrangement where the careless eye had seen nothing but accident!

2. **syncope:** unconsciousness.

Thomas De Quincey 337

PREPARATION
1. BUILDING ON PRIOR KNOWLEDGE.
Shakespeare was an accomplished poet as well as a playwright, and the acknowledged master of the type of sonnet named for him. Review its characteristics (which students have already studied in the sonnets of Wyatt, Surrey, and Sidney) by referring to the diagram of Sonnet 18 on text page 339.

2. ESTABLISHING A PURPOSE. Discuss in class Sonnet 18 (text page 339) and its analysis. Help students to see how Shakespeare neatly fit his ideas into the complicated sonnet form.

Suggest that students approach each sonnet by first reading the headnote, then reading the poem aloud twice, then answering these questions: (1) What is the poem saying? (A brief paraphrase will be helpful.) (2) What figures of speech and imagery are important? (3) How do I respond (feelings, ideas, memories) to the poem?

3. READING THE POEMS ALOUD. Be sure to let students hear these sonnets read aloud by a good reader. Use the audio-cassette for Sonnets 30 and 73.

Sonnets

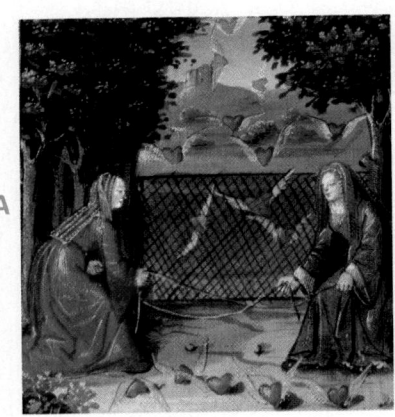

Emblems and Devices of Love
(detail) by Pierre Sala. Manuscript.

The British Library.

Had Shakespeare written no plays at all, he would still have an immense reputation as a poet, not so much for his long narrative poems on classical subjects, *Venus and Adonis* (1593) and *The Rape of Lucrece* (1594), as for his *Sonnets* (1609). There are altogether 154 sonnets, their speaker is male, and their chief subject is love.

On these three points everybody might agree, but beyond these three points, there is no agreement, only question:

Is the speaker of the sonnets a dramatic character invented by Shakespeare, like Romeo, Mercutio, or the Nurse, or is he the dramatist himself? The speaker does call himself Will a few times, and he does make puns on his name, but what evidence exists to prove that all the sonnets are spoken by this Will? If the sonnets are about the real man Shakespeare, then who are the real people behind the other characters mentioned in them: the beloved young man who may be the subject of many of the first 126 sonnets, or the beautiful and exciting dark-complexioned woman who may be the subject of some of the later sonnets? Who is the rival poet referred to in several sonnets? Are there only these four characters (speaker, fair young man, dark lady, other poet), or are there more?

Is the order of the sonnets in which they were published— probably without Shakespeare's consent—the correct one? Shouldn't they be rearranged to tell a more satisfactory story?

And who is the "Mr. W. H." mentioned in the 1609 publication as the "only begetter" of the sonnets? Is he the same person as the young man (or one of the young men), or is he someone else? And so on.

These and dozens of other questions about the sonnets have been asked and answered over and over again—but never to everybody's satisfaction. Instead of convincing answers to the questions, all we have are hundreds of conflicting theories.

Fortunately, these problems need not trouble us here, since we are not concerned with the whole sequence but only with individual sonnets. And about these sonnets there is indeed general agreement: They are among the supreme utterances in English. They say profound things about important human experiences, and they say them with great art.

The Sonnets' Form

Among their other admirable features, the sonnets show how well Shakespeare handled the difficult sonnet form, a fixed form into which all the words of the poem, and the ideas expressed by those words, must be fitted. Each sonnet has its formal organization established by the rules of the sonnet, which Shakespeare did not invent but inherited from Wyatt, Surrey, Sidney, and others. Each sonnet also has its logical organization—the appropriate placement of ideas within the sonnet form. How these two organizations are made to cooperate may be illustrated by a close analysis of the structure of Shakespeare's Sonnet 18:

SUPPLEMENTARY SUPPORT MATERIALS

1. Review and Response Worksheets: The Shakespearean Sonnet; Metaphor and Theme; Sound Effects; Imagery and Tone; Metaphor and Theme; Parody (*CCB*)

2. Selection Test (*CCB*)
3. Audiocassette recording

Logical organization			Formal organization
	Shall I compare thee to a summer's day?	*a*	
	Thou art more lovely and more temperate.	*b*	
	Rough winds do shake the darling buds of May,	*a*	First quatrain
	And summer's lease° hath all too short a date.°	*b*	
A question and tentative answers	Sometime too hot the eye of heaven shines,	*c*	
	And often is his gold complexion dimmed;	*d*	
	And every fair° from fair sometimes declines,	*c*	Second quatrain
	By chance, or nature's changing course, untrimmed.°	*d*	
The turn	But thy eternal summer shall not fade.	*e*	
	Nor lose possession of that fair thou ow'st,°	*f*	
A final answer	Nor shall Death brag thou wander'st in his shade	*e*	Third quatrain
	When in eternal lines to time thou grow'st.	*f*	
	So long as men can breathe or eyes can see,	*g*	Couplet
	So long lives this, and this gives life to thee.	*g*	

The sonnet's formal organization calls for fourteen **iambic pentameter lines** divided into three **quatrains** and a **couplet,** as indicated in the diagram. These are the fixed requirements of all sonnets of the kind known as English, or Shakespearean; Italian (or Petrarchan) sonnets are slightly different. The logical organization will vary, of course, from sonnet to sonnet. Here in Sonnet 18 it consists of a **question** followed by negative **answers:** The beloved "thee" addressed by the speaker does have some resemblances to a summer's day, but they are superficial. The summer's day has many shortcomings, and the first two quatrains concentrate on these rather than on the loved one.

Then comes the **turn,** a shift or change in the focus of the speaker's remarks. Here the speaker turns from examining the faulty summer's day and concentrates on the beloved. By the time he reaches the end of the third quatrain, the speaker has entirely abandoned the comparison of the opening question. Like most literary terms, the word *turn* is a metaphor; the speaker, figuratively speaking, is "turning" from one thing to another. In an Italian sonnet, the turn usually occurs after the eighth line, between the octave (lines 1–8) and the sestet (lines 9–14). In an English sonnet, the turn sometimes occurs late, after the end of the third quatrain. It could be argued that Sonnet 18 has such a second turn, since the final couplet summarizes and explains what has gone before. It says, perhaps with some exaggeration, that by being addressed in this poem, the beloved person has become immortal.

A

B

C

4. **lease:** allotted time. **date:** period. 7. **fair:** beauty. 8. **untrimmed:** deprived of beauty. 10. **ow'st:** ownest, possesseth.

A. Literary Terms
Students will need to be familiar with these boldfaced terms. Have them use the Handbook of Literary Terms (text page 1259) to review any unfamiliar terms.

B. Italian Sonnet Form
Have students turn to text pages 192 and 212 to review the characteristics of an Italian sonnet.

C. Journal Assignment
You might ask students to spend five minutes writing freely in their journals about their responses to Sonnet 18.

? How does this poem strike you? What do you think of the language and feelings expressed? Encourage students to do this kind of free response writing frequently. It not only helps them clarify their thoughts and feelings, but also gives them much-needed practice in expressing and supporting opinions.

PREREADING JOURNAL. Ask students to imagine that they could change places with anyone in the world. Who would you like to be, and why? What do you think you'd like best about your new life?

ANALYZING THE POEM
Identifying Details
1. Luck, material prospects, optimism,

A. Syntax
The long introductory clause ends with line 8. The sentence's main clause is "Haply I think on thee, and then my state . . . sings hymns. . . ."

B. Simile
The speaker compares himself thinking of his lover to a lark singing at dawn. Have students note the parallel and striking contrast in lines 3 and 12.

C. Diction
To appreciate Shakespeare's word choices, have students try to substitute other words for "beweep" (line 2), "deaf" (line 3), "sullen" (line 12), and "scorn" (line 14).

appearance, friends, talent, and power.
2. The turn occurs in line 10.
3. The remembrance of the beloved and the beloved's sweet love.

Interpreting Meanings
4. In line 10 the speaker's depressed, wretched tone changes to one of happiness.
    The lark simile adds a joyful, even ex-

alted note, for the bird rises from the "sullen earth" and "sings hymns at heaven's gate."
5. Answers will vary. The numerous complaints in lines 1–9 suggest the sheer weight of the speaker's unhappiness. The sudden "cure" makes "thy sweet love" seem bright, shining, and all-powerful.

Here the speaker describes how he rids himself of such ugly emotions as envy, self-pity, self-hatred, and the dismal certainty that everybody else is luckier than he is.

Like many of the sonnets, Sonnet 29 is actually a single sentence. What does the long introductory clause describe? What does the main part of the sentence describe?

Sonnet 29

When, in disgrace° with fortune and men's eyes,
I all alone beweep my outcast state,
And trouble deaf heaven with my bootless° cries,
And look upon myself and curse my fate,
5 Wishing me like to one more rich in hope,
    Featured like him, like him° with friends possessed,
A   Desiring this man's art,° and that man's scope,°
    With what I most enjoy contented least;
    Yet in these thoughts myself almost despising,
10 ⎡ Haply° I think on thee, and then my state,
B ⎢ Like to the lark° at break of day arising
   ⎣ From sullen° earth, sings hymns at heaven's gate;
       For thy sweet love remembered such wealth brings
       That then I scorn to change my state with kings.

C

1. **disgrace:** out of favor.

3. **bootless:** futile.

5–6. **one . . . him . . . him:** three different men whom the speaker envies.

7. **art:** literary ability. **scope:** power.

10. **haply:** by chance.
11. **lark:** the English skylark, whose beautiful song seems to rain down from the sky.
12. **sullen:** gloomy.

Responding to the Poem

Analyzing the Poem

Identifying Details
1. Name the traits of others that the speaker is envious of.
2. Which line carries the **turn** of the sonnet?
3. What remembrance changes the speaker's state of mind?

Interpreting Meanings
4. Show how the **turn** signals a change in the speaker's **tone.** What tone does the lark **simile** add to the poem?
5. What is the effect of devoting so many lines in the sonnet to the speaker's mental problems and so few to their cure?

1. Frustration of the speaker's hopes, his waste of time, the deaths of friends, the loss of love.
   Line 5 describes his weeping.
2. Thoughts of his "dear friend."
3. Line 13.

Interpreting Meanings
4. The related metaphors all involve financial terms: *canceled* (line 7), *expense* (line 8), *tell* (line 10), *account* (line 11), *pay* and *paid* (line 12), *losses* (line 14). The metaphors reinforce what the speaker is saying because they constitute, in effect, a single suppressed metaphor: The speaker's thought of his friend brings him a benefit that compensates for all his prior losses.
5. Most of the sonnet has a pessimistic, mournful tone.
6. Student answers may vary. In Sonnet 30, the speaker is depressed not because he envies other people (as in Sonnet 29), but because he is conscious of the losses he has endured in the passage of time.

Shakespeare's best sonnets are remarkable for their original, imaginative metaphors. Sonnet 30 begins with such a metaphor: Periods of quiet meditation are called *sessions*, as though they were court trials, when one's thoughts come to the bar of justice to hear their cases tried. Notice how line 2 continues the legal metaphor.

Sonnet 30

A   When to the sessions of sweet silent thought
B   I summon up remembrance of things past,
    I sigh the lack of many a thing I sought,
    And with old woes new wail° my dear time's waste.°
5   Then can I drown an eye (unused to flow)
    For precious friends hid in death's dateless° night,
    And weep afresh love's long since canceled woe,
    And moan th' expense° of many a vanished sight.°
    Then can I grieve at grievances foregone,
10   And heavily from woe to woe tell° o'er
    The sad account of fore° bemoanèd moan,
    Which I new pay as if not paid before.
      But if the while I think on thee, dear friend,
      All losses are restored and sorrows end.

C

4. **new wail:** again lament. **my . . . waste:** the damage that time has done to things dear to me.
6. **dateless:** endless.

8. **expense:** loss. **vanished sight:** such as the sight of dead friends.

10. **tell:** count.
11. **fore:** already.

A. Alliteration
Note the alliteration in line 1, and ask students to find other examples (lines 3, 6, 7, 9, 10, 11).

B. Allusion
The French novelist Marcel Proust (1871–1922) chose *Remembrance of Things Past* as the title of his sixteen-volume novel about memory and time.

C. Repetition
Find examples of repeated words in lines 8–12 ("moan," "fore," "grieve," "woe," "pay"). What is the effect of this repetition? (The repeated words "drum" the speaker's unhappiness and also create internal rhymes.)

USING THE AUDIOCASSETTE
Have students listen for the rich sound effects (alliteration, assonance, internal rhyme, end rhyme) as they listen to the recording.

Responding to the Poem

Analyzing the Poem

Identifying Details

1. What are the various grievances the speaker remembers when he starts thinking? What is he describing in line 5?
2. What thoughts cheer him up?
3. Where does the **turn** take place?

Interpreting Meanings

4. There are a number of related **metaphors** in lines 7–14. Identify them, and explain how they are related and how they reinforce what the speaker is saying.
5. Describe the **tone** of most of the sonnet.
6. Sonnet 30 is a companion to Sonnet 29, but differs from it in one important respect. What is that difference?

Identifying Details

1. (1) The speaker does not wish his memory to cause grief to his lover (lines 6–8). (2) The speaker does not want the "wise world" to mock him and his loved one after his death (lines 13–14).

2. Alliteration occurs in lines 2, 3, 4, 10, 12, 14.

Interpreting Meanings

3. Student answers will vary. Possible answers include: "surly sullen bell"; "vile world"; "But let your love even with my life decay."

4. The turn occurs in line 12.
   The speaker is bitter at the world and wants to protect his lover.

5. Answers will vary. Some may think that "vilest worms" (line 4), "compound-ed am with clay" (line 10), "decay" (line 12) are morbid ways of referring to death.

6. Answers will vary. Many will agree that *wise* is ironic here, given the speaker's evidently sincere emotion for his beloved. Ask students to support their opinions.

A. Personification
Note the emotions Shakespeare attributes to the funeral bell.

? What do the words *surly* and *sullen* connote? (Negative feelings of anger, unhappiness) What words might personify a wedding bell? (Answers might include *mellow* and *merry.*)

B. Repetition
We have already seen Shakespeare use this device—repeating a word within a line.

? What is its effect here? (*Vileness* is emphasized; it creates assonance, alliteration.) What do you think this line reveals about the speaker? (He is not content; he views the world bitterly.)

C. Rhyme
Note Shakespeare's use of approximate rhyme. Ask students to find other examples in Sonnet 29 (lines 6 and 8) and Sonnet 30 (lines 2 and 4, 9 and 11).

In several sonnets the speaker emphasizes the difference between his age and his beloved's: He is much older, and so presumably he will die first. This sonnet says, surprisingly, that after he dies, he does not want his loved one to remember him at all. "Forget me," he says, "as soon as you hear my funeral bell."

Sonnet 71

A
No longer mourn for me when I am dead
Than you shall hear the surly sullen bell
Give warning to the world that I am fled
B
From this vile world, with vilest worms to dwell.
5   Nay, if you read this line, remember not
The hand that writ it; for I love you so
That I in your sweet thoughts would be forgot
If thinking on me then should make you woe.
O, if, I say, you look upon this verse
10   When I, perhaps, compounded am with clay,
Do not so much as my poor name rehearse,
But let your love even with my life decay,
C
Lest the wise world should look into your moan
And mock you with me after I am gone.

Responding to the Poem

Analyzing the Poem

Identifying Details

1. The speaker gives two reasons for wanting his beloved to forget about him. What are they?

2. Where does the poet use **alliteration** to create sound effects?

Interpreting Meanings

3. List the descriptive words and phrases that you think make this poem powerful.

4. The shift in **mood** is more subtle than in the preceding sonnets. Where does the **turn** occur? What mood does the speaker shift into?

5. Support or refute this statement: *The speaker of the sonnet is somewhat morbid.* Give evidence from the sonnet.

6. Discuss this statement: *The speaker is using irony when he calls the world "wise" in line 13.*

A. Humanities Connection: Responding to the Fine Art

This painting is similar to other Renaissance portraits that attempt to represent a subject's entire life span.

? What elements of the painting can you easily decipher? (An angel blowing a trumpet offers Sir Henry a crown. Inside the church, he seems to be speaking to a large assembly of men. Below the writing table is his funeral procession with pallbearers carrying his coffin; others carry his coat of arms and other symbols of his power. In the upper right is Death with the hourglass symbolizing his lifespan). Which details are mysterious? (Next to Death the perhaps-weeping figure of Sir Henry sits on the floor beside a banquet table. Other details remain puzzling.)

As a class or in small groups, students may enjoy creating a fictionalized biography of this Renaissance gentleman in which they explain all of the painting's details.

A

The Life and Death of Sir Henry Unton (detail). Artist unknown (1580). Oil. National Portrait Gallery, London.

1. The three metaphors compare the speaker to a bare tree in autumn, the twilight after sunset, and the glowing embers of a fire.
2. The beloved's love is stronger with the realization that the speaker must die soon.

Interpreting Meanings
3. Night is "Death's second self" because night "seals up all in rest," or sleep, just as death seals up all in permanent rest.
4. Answers will vary. Line 12 might be paraphrased: "The fire's flames are choked by ashes from the wood that nourished the fire," meaning, "I am consumed by life itself (or time), which nour-

ished me."
5. The turn occurs with "This thou perceivest" (line 13).
   In three metaphors (lines 1–12), the speaker says, "I am growing old and must die soon." The statements after the turn say, "Therefore, you love me more because you will soon be without me."
6. They reinforce the sonnet's somber, melancholy tone.

USING THE AUDIOCASSETTE
Play the recording as students follow in their books.

A. Metaphor
In "Bare ruined choirs," the speaker is not referring to the actual ruins of a church choir, but is speaking metaphorically of the trees' bare branches.

B. Syntax
Note the parallel syntax. Each metaphor begins with words that say, in effect, "You see in me. . . ."

C. Interpreting
What do all three metaphors (lines 1–12) have in common? (They describe the end of something: the year, the day, a fire.) Why are they appropriate for the speaker's message? (He is talking about the end of his life.)

Again, in Sonnet 73 the speaker dwells on his advanced years. But this sonnet is richer in striking metaphors than Sonnet 71. Here each quatrain develops a single metaphor.

Sonnet 73

That time of year thou mayst in me behold
When yellow leaves, or none, or few, do hang
Upon those boughs which shake against the cold,
A   Bare ruined choirs° where late the sweet birds sang.
5   In me thou see'st the twilight of such day
As after sunset fadeth in the west,
Which by-and-by black night doth take away,
Death's second self, that seals up all in rest.
B   In me thou see'st the glowing of such fire
10   That on the ashes of his youth doth lie,
As the deathbed whereon it must expire,
Consumed with that which it was nourished by.
      This thou perceivest, which makes thy love more
         strong,
C   To love that well which thou must leave ere long.

4. **choirs:** parts of a church or abbey. The landscape of Shakespeare's England was dotted with ecclesiastical ruins resulting from Henry VIII's abolition of religious orders.

Responding to the Poem

Analyzing the Poem

Identifying Details
1. What three **metaphors** describe the speaker?
2. What should make love even stronger?

Interpreting Meanings
3. In what sense can night (line 7) be called "Death's second self" (line 8)?
4. The idea of line 12 is somewhat compressed. **Paraphrase** it in your own words, after you have thought

about what originally fed ("nourished") the speaker's fires—fires that are now choked ("consumed").
5. Where is the **turn** in this sonnet? What is the logical relationship between the statements coming after the turn and those coming before it?
6. How do the seasonal and daily **imagery** contribute to the **tone** of this poem?

ANALYZING THE POEM
Identifying Details
1. Love is a seamark (line 5) and a star (the North Star) that sailors use to navigate (line 7). Love's not Time's fool (line 9).
2. Lines 2–4 and 9–11.
3. Time is a reaper with a sickle who "cuts down" rosy lips and cheeks (lines 9–10).

Interpreting Meanings
4. The turn occurs between lines 12 and 13.
    Suggestions about the speaker's voice will vary. Have students demonstrate the change by reading aloud the last six lines.
5. The final couplet gives emphasis to the rest of the poem, shows how strongly the speaker believes what he is saying,

and reveals that the speaker is both a writer and a lover.
6. Love's steadfastness.
7. The emphasis on the steadfastness of true love makes light of the disparity in ages. Lines 11–12 suggest that true love continues even after the death of one of the lovers.
8. Answers will vary. You might use this question as a journal assignment.

Perhaps the most famous of Shakespeare's sonnets, Sonnet 116 contains an idealized description of true love under the metaphor of a "marriage of true minds" (line 1). To such a love there can be no *impediments* (line 2), a word taken from the priest's remarks to the congregation at a Church of England wedding: "If any of you know cause or just impediment why these persons should not be joined together. . . ."

Sonnet 116

    Let me not to the marriage of true minds
A Admit impediments. Love is not love
    Which alters when it alteration finds
    Or bends with the remover to remove.
5 O, no! It is an ever-fixèd mark,°
    That looks on tempests and is never shaken;
    It is the star to every wand'ring bark,°
    Whose worth's° unknown, although his height° be taken.
B Love's not Time's fool, though rosy lips and cheeks
10 Within his bending sickle's compass° come.
C Love alters not with his brief hours and weeks,
    But bears it out° even to the edge of doom.°
      If this be error, and upon me proved,
      I never writ, nor no man ever loved.

5. **mark:** seamark, a prominent object on shore that serves as a guide to sailors.

7. **bark:** boat.

8. **worth:** value. **height:** altitude measured (taken) by a navigational instrument.

10. **compass:** sweep, reach.

12. **bears it out:** survives. **doom:** the Last Judgment.

Responding to the Poem

Analyzing the Poem

Identifying Details
1. What **metaphors** does the speaker use to describe the steadiness of love?
2. Where does the speaker define love by what it is *not*, and by what it does *not* do?
3. How is time **personified** in the poem?

Interpreting Meanings
4. Between which lines does the **turn**—the change in **moods**—occur? Describe how the speaker's voice might change.
5. What is the function of the final **couplet**?
6. What single quality of true love does the sonnet emphasize?
7. How does the sonnet solve the problem of a disparity in the ages of two lovers, or the death of one of them?
8. Do you agree with this definition of love? Explain.

Phillus and Philander. Woodcut.

A. Definition
In defining "true love," Shakespeare begins by telling what love is *not* (lines 2–4). This negative definition continues in lines 9–11.

B. Synecdoche
The rosy lips and cheeks stand for the beautiful young people who eventually are cut down by Time. (A *synecdoche* is a figure of speech in which a part is used to represent a whole.)

C. Hyperbole
❓ How is this statement an exaggeration? (Love lasts beyond death, till the Last Judgment.) Is Shakespeare being ironic or sincere?

D. About the Woodcut
In an old ballad, Philander was the lover of Phillus. The name we spell Phyllis today means "leaf"; the masculine name Philander (no longer in use) means "lover." Today, *to philander* means "to engage lightly in love affairs."

D

1. The sun (her eyes), coral (her lips), snow (her breasts), roses (her cheeks), perfume (her breath), music (her voice).

Interpreting Meanings
2. Students' descriptions should be unflattering to the mistress.
3. The comical descriptions include the

reference to her hair as "wires," the description of her breath, and the understatement of her treading "on the ground."

The sonnet is humorous as a whole because it reverses conventional romantic conceits.
4. The couplet shows that the speaker is passionately devoted to his mistress despite his negative descriptions.

A. Internal Rhyme

How many times can you hear the sound of *why* in lines 3 and 4? (Four: "white," "why," "wires," "wires")

B. Alliteration

Find the alliteration here. (The repeated *g*'s)

C. Paraphrase

Paraphrase lines 13–14. (And yet, by heaven, I think my love is as rare as any of those who have been misrepresented with false comparisons.)

This sonnet ridicules the fashionable excesses being committed by some of Shakespeare's fellow poets, the exaggerated metaphors they were using to describe the women they loved: Your eyes are suns that set me on fire, your cheeks are roses, your lips are coral, your breasts are snowballs, you are a goddess—that sort of thing. Such metaphors, or *conceits*, as they were called, are ultimately traceable to Petrarch, but by 1600 they had become, through repetition, tiresome or laughable.

Sonnet 130

My mistress' eyes are nothing like the sun;
Coral is far more red than her lips' red;
A [If snow be white, why then her breasts are dun;°
  [If hairs be wires, black wires grow on her head.
5   I have seen roses damasked,° red and white,
But no such roses see I in her cheeks;
And in some perfumes is there more delight
Than in the breath that from my mistress reeks.°
I love to hear her speak; yet well I know
10   That music hath a far more pleasing sound.
B [I grant I never saw a goddess go:
  [My mistress, when she walks, treads on the ground.
C [And yet, by heaven, I think my love as rare
  [As any she belied° with false compare.°

3. **dun:** brown.

5. **damasked:** variegated.

8. **reeks:** is exhaled.

14. **belied:** misrepresented. **compare:** comparison.

Responding to the Poem

Analyzing the Poem

Identifying Details

1. Shakespeare uses the classic objects of comparison in describing his mistress. What are they?

Interpreting Meanings

2. Describe what the speaker's mistress might look like.
3. Some of the ways the speaker chooses to praise his mistress are humorous. Which descriptions did you find comical? How is the sonnet as a whole humorous?
4. Why is the **couplet** absolutely necessary to keep the sonnet from being misunderstood?

Writing About the Poems

A Creative Response

1. **Writing a Parody.** Sonnet 130 is a witty parody of love poems popular in Shakespeare's day. You might write your own parody of love songs popular today. Before you write, make a list of the characteristics of the songs; you might consider **imagery, repetition, story line, tone, melody.**

A Critical Response

2. **Comparing Poems.** Read the following poem carefully and write an essay in which you (a) discuss its speaker and (b) compare the speaker in this poem with the

CLOSURE
Based on this small sampling of sonnets,
students should be able to explain how
Shakespeare was concerned with love,
time, and loss. They should then be able
to quote lines to support their opinions.

Portrait of a Young Woman (detail). Artist unknown (1569). Oil.

The Tate Gallery, London.

A. Humanities Connection: Responding to the Fine Art
This anonymous portrait tells us a good deal about fashions for wealthy young women in 1569. Note that the young woman's "best" outfit displays some of the fine decorative work of embroidery and jewelry of the period and that her elaborate collar, bodice, and hat look restrictive.
? How old do you think she is? Do any details in the portrait make her seem "contemporary"? Could the young women in your class stand being dressed like this? Would the young men find the girl attractive? What do you imagine this young Elizabethan might think of fashions today?

speaker in Shakespeare's Sonnet 71. Which of the two speakers seems to be the more attractive person?

Foolish Tears

Come not, when I am dead,
　To drop thy foolish tears upon my grave,
To trample round my fallen head,
　And vex the unhappy dust thou wouldst not
　　save.
5　There let the wind sweep and the plover cry;
　But thou, go by.

Child, if it were thine error or thy crime
　I care no longer, being all unblest;
Wed whom thou wilt, but I am sick of Time,
10　And I desire to rest.
Pass on, weak heart, and leave me where I lie:
　Go by, go by.

　　　　　　　　　　—Alfred, Lord Tennyson

3. Analyzing Poetic Technique. In an essay, discuss Shakespeare's use of the elements of poetry in these sonnets. Include in your discussion these elements:

a. Rhymes, half rhymes, end rhymes, and internal rhymes
b. Meter and variations in meter to avoid a sing-song effect
c. Use of sound effects like onomatopoeia and alliteration
d. Use of figurative language

You cannot cover every element in every sonnet, but if you choose wisely, you should find at least one good example of each element.

1. **BUILDING ON PRIOR KNOWLEDGE.** Refer students to text page 177 of the Introduction, and have them reread the section on songs. Note also the title page of *Tottel's Miscellany* (text page 176), which gives the songs equal billing with the sonnets.

2. **ESTABLISHING A PURPOSE.** Since *Mac-beth* contains no songs, students have no example of the contexts in which these songs are sung. As they read the songs that follow, ask students to think about the kinds of music that might have accompanied them. Have them also compare the songs to lyrics popular today.

A. Types of Songs
Shakespeare's plays include the following types of songs: aubades (morning songs); pastoral invitations; love songs; ballads; and dirges (funeral songs).

B. About the Illustration
These bright colors are typical of the brilliant illumination (hand-painted lettering and decoration) of manuscripts produced before the invention of the printing press. The *Roman de la Rose* was a medieval French allegorical poem. In Part One, Idleness conducts the Lover to a garden of roses, where he meets such characters as Pleasure, Riches, and Sweet-Looks. The Lover wishes to pick a rosebud, but Cupid explains that he must first undergo the sufferings required by the code of courtly love—her indifference to his noble deeds, secrecy, and the impossibility of ever attaining the lady in marriage. (See also page 360).

Songs from Shakespeare's Plays

When people went to the Globe, the Swan, or any other London theater, they expected not only to see a tragedy or comedy acted, but also to hear music, both vocal and instrumental. Trumpets announced the beginning of the play and important arrivals and departures within the play. High up in the tower above the inner stage, musicians played between the acts and at other appropriate times during the performance. And scattered throughout most of the plays, especially the comedies, there were songs. We have reason to believe that these songs were well sung, since many of them are for women, and all the women's parts were taken by boys who had been trained to sing as well as act.

The songs in Shakespeare's plays are the best of this kind that have come down to us, for Shakespeare excelled in lyric and in dramatic poetry. He included a great variety of songs in his plays, as the selections here illustrate: sad, happy, comic, thoughtful songs, full of the sights and sounds of the English countryside. Each song is particularly adapted to the play and scene in which it occurs and to the character who performs it. Some of the songs advance the dramatic action, some help establish the mood of a scene, some reveal character. All of them are fresh and spontaneous, not contrived and artificial. Unfortunately, most of the original music for Shakespeare's songs has been lost, but just as the plays themselves have inspired many composers of music for opera, orchestra, and ballet, so have the songs in the plays been set to music by many composers right up to the present time.

Dreamer Enters the Garden (detail) from *Roman de la Rose* (c. 1487–95). French manuscript.

The British Library.

ANALYZING THE POEM
Identifying Details
1. Visual images include icicles; Dick blowing on his hands and Tom lugging logs; frozen milk; messy roads; birds brooding; greasy Joan (the cook); Marian's raw red nose. Images of sound include the owl's song, the blowing wind, the coughing, the hissing crab apples. We feel the cold with Dick's fingers, frozen milk, nipped blood, blowing wind.

Interpreting Meanings
2. Answers will vary. Most will say the general effect is to suggest bleakness and cold, though others might feel the hissing apples and Joan's pot redeem the scene a bit.
3. In general, the song depicts winter as a time of discomfort and difficulty.

4. There were shepherds working outdoors; they burned logs to keep warm; roads were bad in winter; people went to cold churches to listen to sermons; they ate roasted apples and some sort of stew. Women seemed to work in the kitchen; men did the outdoor work. Indoors and outdoors, it was cold.

Ordinarily, the songs in Shakespeare's plays do not have titles; they are known only by their first lines. "Winter," an exception to this rule, is the second of two songs with the same metrical form sung at the end of Shakespeare's early comedy *Love's Labor's Lost*, the first being titled "Spring." The two songs are said to be "in praise of the owl and the cuckoo."

Winter

A   When icicles hang by the wall
       And Dick the shepherd blows his nail°
   And Tom bears logs into the hall,
       And milk comes frozen in pail,
5   When blood is nipped and ways° be foul,
   Then nightly sings the staring owl,
           Tu-who;

B   Tu-whit, tu-who: A merry note,
   While greasy Joan doth keel° the pot.

   When all aloud the wind doth blow,
10   And coughing drowns the parson's saw,°
   And birds sit brooding in the snow,
     And Marian's nose looks red and raw,
   When roasted crabs° hiss in the bowl,
   Then nightly sings the staring owl,
           Tu-who;

15   Tu-whit, tu-who: A merry note
   While greasy Joan doth keel the pot.

2. **blows his nail:** breathes on his fingers to warm them.

5. **ways:** roads, paths.

8. **keel:** stir.

10. **saw:** wise but tedious sayings.

13. **crabs:** crab apples.

A. Syntax
Describe the syntax in the two verses. (A long introductory adverb clause is followed by subject and predicate in inverted order.)

B. Onomatopoeia
Note the onomatopoeia (lines 6–8) to imitate the owl's voice.

Responding to the Poem

Analyzing the Poem

Identifying Details

1. What **images** does Shakespeare use to help us see and hear this winter scene? What images help us feel the cold?

Interpreting Meanings

2. The owl's note is said to be merry, although the sound of an owl hooting at night is usually regarded as mournful and melancholy. Perhaps the owl's call seems merry only in contrast to the other wintry **images** in the poem. What is the general effect of these images?

3. What is the poet's **attitude** toward winter?
4. What does this song tell you about sixteenth-century life? What do you suppose Joan is stirring in that pot? Why do you think she is greasy?

Writing About the Poem

A Creative Response

Imitating the Writer's Technique. Write a song or a paragraph in which you describe a winter scene you are familiar with. Include **images** that will help your readers to see and hear the scene, and to feel its temperature.

**A. Humanities
Connection:
Discussing the
Illustration**
(See also the an-
notation on em-
broidery on
page 233.) This
detail is especially
interesting for its
mixture of different
nuts and fruits on
the central tree,
and its inclusion of
animals we consid-
er mythical (the
unicorn) right along
with goats, birds,
etc. Have students
identify as many
fruits and beasts
as they can. Do
they catch from the
work a feeling of
exuberant delight
in all living things?
When students
have read the
song on the facing
page, they might
also consider how
the embroidery
does or does not
illustrate the poem.

Fruiting Trees, Animals, and Birds (17th century). Embroidery.

The Metropolitan Museum of Art. New York.
Gift of Irwin Untermyer. 1964. (64.101.1305).

ANALYZING THE POEM
Identifying Details
1. Winter and rough weather.
2. Lines 9–12 suggest a human life in harmony with nature: A person seeks the food he eats and is pleased with what he gets. The sweet bird's song and the image of "living in the sun" also suggest this idea of harmony in nature.

Interpreting Meanings
3. Answers will vary. Students may suggest "merry note" (line 3), "Come hither, . . ." (line 5), "loves to live i' the sun" (line 10), and "Seeking the food . . . what he gets" (lines 11–12).
4. The song suggests that life in the forest may be idyllic and joyful.
5. Answers will vary. Students should observe that both poems are pastoral and idealize the natural setting. In both poems the speaker tries to convince another person to join him in the pastoral setting.

Songs in plays could be useful as well as entertaining when their words described the scene. Since there were no painted sets, as in the modern picture-frame stage, a song like "Under the Greenwood Tree" could take the place of scenery. In the very first line the singer tells his audience that they are watching a woodland scene. "Imagine," the singer says, "a great leafy tree, and come and lie down under it with me." A character named Amiens sings this song in *As You Like It*, a comedy about a group of sophisticated courtiers exiled from their palaces and living in a very comfortable wilderness, the Forest of Arden.

Under the Greenwood Tree

       Under the greenwood tree
       Who loves to lie with me,
       And turn his merry note
       Unto the sweet bird's throat,°
5   Come hither, come hither, come hither:
       Here shall he see
       No enemy
       But° winter and rough weather.

       Who doth ambition shun
10   And loves to live i' the sun,
       Seeking the food he eats,
       And pleased with what he gets,
       Come hither, come hither, come hither:
       Here shall he see
15   No enemy
       But winter and rough weather.

4. **turn . . . throat:** that is, sing in harmony with a bird's song.

8. **But:** except.

A. **Symbolism**
What do you think the word *ambition* symbolizes here? (A whole way of life associated with court, politics, money; this way of life is seen as undesirable.)

B. **Responding**
Do you think the poem's message is dated, or does it still appeal? How does this song relate to the concept of paradise (a happy life in a garden setting, without pain or trouble)?

Responding to the Poem

Analyzing the Poem

Identifying Details
1. Who is the only "enemy" in this song?
2. Which **images** suggest harmony with nature?

Interpreting Meanings
3. Which words or phrases in this song give it a light and upbeat feeling?

4. What comment does the song make on the life led by the exiles in the forest?
5. Relate this song to Christopher Marlowe's "The Passionate Shepherd to His Love." What do the two works have in common?

ANALYZING THE POEM
Identifying Details
1. The speaker criticizes ingratitude, false friendship, and the folly of love.
2. The wind's bite is kinder than man's and not so keen (lines 1–5); the sky's bite is not as close (to the bone) as the bite of human ingratitude (11–13); its sting is not as sharp as being forgotten by a friend.

3. The wind is personified with mention of its "tooth" (line 3) and "breath" (line 6). The sky is personified with reference to its "bite" (line 12) and "sting" (line 15).

Interpreting Meanings
4. Answers will vary. Some students may see Amiens as bitter, distrustful, and cynical.
5. Most students will agree that the para-

phrase seems more complex than the original. Be sure to have them write their own paraphrases, perhaps as group work.
6. The chorus contrasts with the serious, cynical statements about human nature in the preceding verses. Most students will agree that Shakespeare is deliberately creating some sort of clash, or paradoxical effect.

A. Context
The song is sung in Act Two, Scene 5.

B. Apostrophe
Note the apostrophe (direct address) to the wind.
? What else is addressed in this way? (The sky in the second stanza)

C. Refrain
Have students identify the refrain (lines 7–10). See question 6.

A Like "Under the Greenwood Tree," this song is from *As You Like It*, and it also is sung by Amiens, who is not a professional singer but one of the exiled courtiers who performs only when asked to. Together, the two songs give a good impression of Amiens's temperament. "Blow, Blow" also makes a playful comment on a common human failing: ingratitude. In comparison with people's ungrateful behavior, the cruel winter weather seems kind—unexpectedly kind, because the weather is naturally cruel whereas human beings are supposed to resist their naturally ungrateful instincts.

Blow, Blow, Thou Winter Wind

B
Blow, blow, thou winter wind,°
Thou art not so unkind
        As man's ingratitude;
Thy tooth is not so keen,
5   Because thou art not seen,
        Although thy breath be rude.

C
Heigh-ho! Sing, heigh-ho! Unto the green holly:
Most friendship is feigning, most loving mere folly:
Then, heigh-ho, the holly!
10   This life is most jolly.

Freeze, freeze, thou bitter sky,
That dost not bite so nigh
        As benefits forgot:
Though thou the waters warp°
15   Thy sting is not so sharp
        As friend remembered not.
Heigh-ho! sing, etc.

1. **wind:** pronounced to rhyme with *find*.

14. **warp:** make rough by freezing.

Responding to the Poem

Analyzing the Poem

Identifying Details
1. Which aspects of human nature does the singer criticize?
2. How does the singer compare man's bite with winter's?
3. What details **personify** the wind and sky?

Interpreting Meanings
4. "Under the Greenwood Tree" and "Blow, Blow, Thou Winter Wind" are probably the first dramatic songs used to characterize the singer, a practice that since Shakespeare's day has been common and expected in musical comedy and opera. What can you deduce from the songs about Amiens's character?
5. Samuel Johnson **paraphrased** lines 4–5 of this song as follows: "Thy rudeness gives the less pain as thou art not seen, as thou art an enemy that dost not brave us with thy presence, and whose unkindness is therefore not aggravated by insult." Explain whether this paraphrase helps you understand lines 4–5.
6. How does the merry-sounding chorus with its nonsense words modify the impression made by the preceding verse?

PREREADING JOURNAL. After they have read this song, ask students to write about whether they think things have changed much since Shakespeare's day. Are there lines in the song that a young man might use today? What might a young woman say in response? Five minutes or so of freewriting can prepare students for the writing assignment at the bottom of this page.

ANALYZING THE POEM
Identifying Details
1. The speaker is singing to his mistress, who is twenty years old.
2. The answer describes love as a phenomenon of the present; whatever else it may be, it does not exist in delay or in the uncertain "hereafter."

Interpreting Meanings
3. The reasons are that the future is unsure and that there is no fulfillment in delay.
4. Answers will vary. Students should point out that a "song of good life" would probably preach a moral; this song is an invitation to find pleasure in the present.

A. Connections
This song is in the carpe diem (Latin for "seize the day") tradition. The man's argument can be summarized as, "Love me now, for tomorrow we may all be dead." Alert students to Andrew Marvell's "To His Coy Mistress," text page 436; and Robert Herrick's "To the Virgins, to Make Much of Time," text page 385.

In the comedy *Twelfth Night*, two roistering knights called Sir Andrew Aguecheek and Sir Toby Belch ask the clown Feste to sing them a song. "Would you have a love song or a song of good life?" asks Feste. For once the drunken knights agree:

Toby. A love song, a love song.
Andrew. Ay, ay! I care not for good life.

The following song, which Feste sings for them, is a kind of poem widely practiced in antiquity and in the Renaissance, the invitation to love.

O Mistress Mine

O mistress mine, where are you roaming?
O, stay and hear; your true-love's coming,
   That can sing both high and low.
Trip no further, pretty sweeting;°
5 Journeys end in lovers meeting,
   Every wise man's son doth know . . .

A What is love? 'tis not hereafter;
   Present mirth hath present laughter;
    What's to come is still unsure:
10 In delay there lies no plenty;
   Then come kiss me, sweet and twenty!
    Youth's a stuff will not endure.

4. **sweeting:** sweetheart.

Responding to the Poem

Analyzing the Poem

Identifying Details

1. To whom is the singer speaking? How old is this person?
2. In the beginning of the second stanza the singer asks "What is love?" How is the question answered?

Interpreting Meanings

3. Though the song is not in the form of an argument, as so many invitations to love are, it does include some reasons for loving now rather than later. What are they?

4. Explain how Feste's song is not a "song of good life." Use lines from the song to back up your answer.

Writing About the Poem

A Creative Response

Answering the Speaker. Write a song or a prose paragraph answering the singer. Speak as if you are the woman he is trying to persuade to stay with him.

A. Metaphor
Note the metaphor in lines 3–4; it would appeal directly to the humblest laborers. ("Thy worldly task" or work is life; "home" is the grave; and the "wages" are rest and cease from worry.)

B. Metonymy
This line is often used as an example of metonymy (see definition page 1266).

C. Connections / Puns
Students who have seen the 1964 movie *Mary Poppins* will recall the grime of the dancing chimney sweeps. Compare lines 5–6 with A. E. Housman's "With Rue My Heart Is Laden," text page 843. Note Shakespeare's sly pun on the word *dust* (the dust of the grave and the dust in a chimney).

D. Vocabulary
A *thunderstone* is a meteorite.

This song in Shakespeare's late play *Cymbeline* is not sung, but is recited by two young princes, Guiderius and Arviragus. They claim they cannot sing because their voices have suddenly "got the mannish crack," or as we would say, have started to change. And so they take turns reciting the lines, as indicated, over the body of their sister Imogen, who looks very dead but as it turns out later is only under a spell. *Cymbeline* is that sort of play.

This poem is an *elegy*—a kind of poem lamenting and commemorating the dead and consoling the living. When such a poem is designed to be sung or performed in the presence of the dead person's body, it is usually called a *dirge*. Some of the content of this particular dirge is traditional, such as the "death the leveler" theme, which makes the point that we all die, high and low, rich and poor; and the "consolation" theme, which enumerates unpleasant experiences in life that we all have from which the dead person has now escaped.

Fear No More the Heat o' the Sun

Guiderius	Fear no more the heat o' the sun
	Nor the furious winter's rages;
	Thou thy worldly task hast done,
	Home art gone, and ta'en thy wages.
5	Golden lads and girls all must,
	As° chimney sweepers, come to dust.

6. **As:** like.

Arviragus	Fear no more the frown o' the great;
	Thou art past the tyrant's stroke.
	Care no more to clothe and eat;
10	To thee the reed° is as the oak.
	The scepter, learning, physic, must
	All follow this and come to dust.

10. **reed:** a proverbially frail plant.

Guiderius	Fear no more the lightning flash—
Arviragus	Nor th' all-dreaded thunderstone;°
15 **Guiderius**	Fear not slander, censure rash;
Arviragus	Thou hast finished joy and moan.
Both	All lovers young, all lovers must
	Consign to° thee and come to dust.

14. **thunderstone:** falling stones, that supposedly caused the noise of thunder.

18. **consign to:** agree with.

Guiderius	No exorciser° harm thee!
20 **Arviragus**	Nor no witchcraft charm thee!
Guiderius	Ghost unlaid° forbear thee!
Arviragus	Nothing ill come near thee!
Both	Quiet consummation° have,
	And renowned be thy grave!

19. **exorciser:** conjurer, magician.

21. **unlaid:** not properly laid to rest in the grave, hence forced to walk about.

23. **consummation:** finality.

354

354 The Renaissance

ANALYZING THE POEM
Identifying Details

1. The dead person need no longer fear the summer's heat, the rages of the winter, the displeasure of great tyrants, the need to eat and be clothed, lightning and thunder, slander and disapproval.
2. Advantages: The dead person need not fear all the threats that make human life unpleasant. Dangers: The dead person might be disturbed by exorcisers, witchcraft, and ghosts.

Interpreting Meanings
3. Lines 5–6, 11–12, and 17–18.
4. "Golden lads and girls" connotes wealth, handsomeness, good luck. "Chimney sweepers" connotes humble social status, dirt, poverty.
5. The "scepter" is the king; "learning" is a schoolmaster or scholar; "physic" is the doctor.
6. The dirge reflects the time of the play by its apparent belief in exorcism and witchcraft (lines 19–20).

A. About the Fine Art
Another detail from this manuscript appears on text page 338. The Lover is apparently depositing a heart (this one without wings) in a flower or decorative basket in a garden. Ask students what lines in the song the illustration might relate to. (Lines 16–18)

A

Emblems and Devices of Love (detail) by Pierre Sala. Manuscript.

The British Library.

Responding to the Poem

Analzying the Poem

Identifying Details

1. What are the things the dead person can no longer fear?
2. According to this dirge, what are the advantages of being dead? What are the dangers?

Interpreting Meanings

3. Identify the lines that carry the **theme** of death as a leveler.
4. In the famous **simile** in lines 5–6, what are the connotations of "golden lads and girls" and of "chimney sweepers"? How are they different?
5. Who are the "scepter," "learning," and "physic"?
6. The events in *Cymbeline* supposedly take place long before Christianity was introduced into Britain. How does the dirge reflect the time of the play?

William Shakespeare 355

ANALYZING THE POEM
Identifying Details
1. At the bottom of the sea.
2. Images of sight include coral and pearls. Images of sound include the ringing of the knell and the onomatopoeic "ding-dong."

Interpreting Meanings
3. Answers will vary. Some students

may mention lines 5 or 8–9.
4. The *f* sound is repeated ("full," "fathom," "five," and "father"). Note also the repeated *th* and *l* sounds.
5. The body of Alonso turns from a decaying corpse into a gem-studded, "rich and strange" marvel.

CLOSURE
Ask students to identify each song's tone (serious, ironic, merry, etc.) and its "message." Then ask three students to suggest singers or groups popular today who might sing three of the songs.

A. Assonance
Besides the remarkable alliteration in line 1, have students note the repeated long *i* sound ("five," "thy," "lies") repeated with "eyes" in line 3.

B. Vocabulary
Sea change here means "a change made within the sea and by the sea." A wrecked ship, for example, undergoes a sea change as it rusts and decays. Today the phrase *sea change* is often used to mean a major upheaval and change in someone's life, especially a change for the better.

C. Onomatopoeia
Note the onomatopoeia of *ding-dong.* The nursery-rhyme language of the last two lines provides a marked contrast to the rich language and imagery of lines 1–7.

Ariel, the "airy spirit" of *The Tempest,* sings this brief but memorable dirge to Prince Ferdinand, who has lost his father in the dreadful storm at sea that opens the play. But the father, King Alonso of Naples, is not really dead. Unknown to Ferdinand, he has been washed up onto the island where the play takes place. This circumstance reminds us of the false death of Imogen in *Cymbeline,* but unlike her dirge there are no traditional materials in this one except the mention of the knell. Otherwise, this dirge is a pure product of Shakespeare's remarkable imagination.

Full Fathom Five

A Full fathom five thy father lies;
  Of his bones are coral made:
Those are pearls that were his eyes:
  Nothing of him that doth fade,
B But doth suffer a sea change
Into something rich and strange.
Sea nymphs hourly ring his knell:°
C Ding-dong.
Hark! Now I hear them—Ding-dong, bell.

7. **knell:** the tolling of bells at a funeral.

Responding to the Poem

Analyzing the Poem

Identifying Details
1. Where does Ariel say Ferdinand's father is?
2. What **images** of sight and sound do you find in the poem?

Interpreting Meanings
3. Which lines of this dirge suggest Ariel's playful and cheerful character?

4. What examples of **alliteration** make the first line so interesting?
5. The subject of this dirge, King Alonso, is a thoroughly bad man who, during the course of the play, turns into a good man. What other "sea change" takes place in this dirge?

THE ENGLISH LANGUAGE

by John Algeo

S hakespeare's language is an early form of Modern English, the same basic kind of English that we speak, although it is now archaic in many ways. We can still read Shakespeare's plays and poetry without their being translated because he and we speak the same language. But we need explanations for some words and phrases because English has changed during the past four hundred years.

Speaking the Speech: Shakespeare's Pronunciation

The actors who pronounced Shakespeare's lines on the stage of the Globe Theater would not have sounded like modern actors, American or British. We need not be concerned with the details of their pronunciation, but some differences are obvious even from the written text of the plays. For example, Shakespeare's contemporaries, like English speakers today, used a great many contractions. But we contract in different ways. Nowadays, we especially favor the contraction of *not* into *n't,* as in "She isn't"; and the contraction of verbs, as in "She's here," "They've gone," and "We'll try," where *'s, 've,* and *'ll* represent *is, have,* and *will,* respectively.

Shakespeare contracted verbs too, as in *Macbeth:* "When all's done" and "Thou'lt be afraid to hear it" for *thou wilt* (that is, "you will"). But Shakespeare also liked to contract the pronouns that begin with vowels (*us* and *it*), as the following examples show:

> . . . we / Shall take upon's what else remains to do . . .
> . . . To mend it or be rid on't [of it].
> . . . for't must be done tonight.
> What is't that moves your highness?   **A**

Shakespeare also frequently omitted unstressed syllables from the middle of words (as we still do in words like *fam'ly*):

> . . . o'er the rest . . .
> . . . will these hands ne'er be clean?
> . . . my near'st [nearest] of life . . .
> Thou marvel'st at my words . . .

A whole syllable could be omitted from the beginning of a word if it was unstressed (as also in modern *'cause* for *because,* an omission that Shakespeare also makes):

> . . . 'cause he fail'd . . .
> Point against point, rebellious arm 'gainst arm . . .
> . . . 'Twixt this and supper.

Shakespeare's Language

John Philip Kemble as Hamlet by Sir Thomas Lawrence. Oil.

The Tate Gallery, London.

A. Examples
Throughout the essay, you might ask students (working in pairs or small groups) to look for other examples in the play.

B. Humanities Connection: Discussing the Portrait
Sir Thomas Lawrence (1769–1830), the most fashionable English portraitist of his day, achieved royal patronage and even knighthood. John Philip Kemble (1757–1823) was educated for the priesthood but turned instead to acting. He debuted in London as Hamlet in 1783, and in 1788 became manager of the Drury Lane Theatre. His sister Mrs. Sarah Kemble Siddons (see text page 252) often acted there with him.

A. Humanities Connection: Responding to the Fine Art
Henry Fuseli (fyōo′ zĭ·lē) (1741–1825) was an Anglo-Swiss painter who took holy orders but never practiced the priesthood. His paintings reveal a fascination with the weird, terrifying, and visionary—elements clearly visible in this painting. Note the painting's dramatic lighting and unusual perspective, which draw the viewer's eyes to the witches and the sword.

? Who do you think stands next to Macbeth? (Banquo) Compare these witches to those in an actual production (text page 259).

B. Expansion
Ask students to give examples from Spanish, French, and other modern languages that still distinguish an intimate *you* and a formal *you*.

A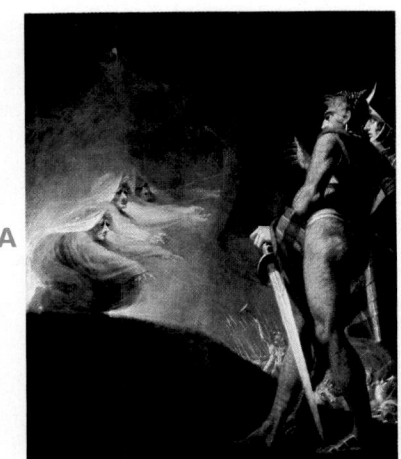

Macbeth and the Witches
by Henry Fuseli. Oil.

National Trust, Pentworth House, England.

Some of Shakespeare's words are stressed on different syllables from those we would now accent. For example, in "Stop up th' *access* and passage to remorse," the iambic rhythm of the line shows us that Shakespeare pronounced the word acCESS, rather than ACcess, as we would.

Other words have changed their form in various minor ways since Shakespeare's day. In *Macbeth* we find *afeard* for "afraid," *aweary* for "weary," and *alarum* for "alarm."

Shakespeare's Grammar

Although Shakespeare's grammar is essentially the same as ours, it differed in numerous minor ways.

Today, we use *who* to refer to persons and *which* (as a relative pronoun) to refer to things: "The doctor *who* treated me; the medicine *which* he gave me." Shakespeare, however, could use *which* for both purposes, and occasionally did so: " . . . the slave / Which nev'r shook hands." He could also use *the which*, especially of broad or unstated antecedents: "He only lived but till he was a man; / The which [his manhood] no sooner had his prowess confirmed, . . . / But like a man he died." Shakespeare could also use the pronoun *who* in an indefinite sense, for which we need *he who*: "Who was the thane lives yet."

In present-day English, we use *mine* as a pronoun and *my* to modify a noun: "It's mine" but "It's my book." Shakespeare used both forms to modify nouns: *mine* before words beginning with a vowel, and *my* before words beginning with a consonant, just as we do *an* and *a* today ("an orange, a lemon"): "Ha! They pluck out *mine* eyes! / Will all great Neptune's ocean wash this blood / Clean from *my* hand?"

Today, English generally uses only a single pronoun for the person or people we talk to: *you* (with its possessives *your* and *yours*). Shakespeare had a choice between *th*-forms (*thou, thee, thy, thine*) and *y*-forms (*ye, you, your, yours*). *Thou* and *ye* were subject forms, like *I; thee* and *you* were object forms, like *me.*

B *Th*-forms were used in talking to one person with whom the speaker was intimate (wife or husband, bosom buddy) or to whom the speaker was socially superior (child, servant, subject). *Y*-forms were used in talking to several persons, or to one person who was a social equal but not an intimate friend, or who was a superior (parent, boss, king). In the singular, the *th*-forms showed intimacy or superiority; the *y*-forms showed equality or servility.

Shakespeare made careful use of the different connotations of *th*- and *y*-forms. When Macbeth and Banquo meet the weird Sisters (Act 1, Scene 3), they address the witches with *y*-forms because the two soldiers are in awe of these supernatural women; the witches, however, use *th*-forms for Macbeth and Banquo, thereby asserting their superiority over the mere mortals.

Macbeth and Banquo normally address one another with *y*-forms because, though equals, they are not intimates. At the beginning of Act 3, however, when Banquo is thinking about the foul deeds that Macbeth has obviously used to come to the throne, he uses *th*-forms for Macbeth, since he regards Macbeth's murderous actions as having made a moral inferior of him. Banquo can think what he wants, but when Macbeth actually appears, Banquo addresses him with *y*-forms again. For Banquo to have called King Macbeth *thou* to his face would have been an insulting breach of etiquette.

The verb in Shakespeare's day had a special ending to go with *thou* as a subject, *-st,* thus: "Thou know'st," "thou didst," and "Thou hast." It also had an alternative ending, *-th,* for the third-person singular *-s* that we still use today. Shakespeare could use "he knows" or "knoweth," "he does" or "doth," and "he has" or "hath." The two forms meant the same thing, although the *-s* ending was more common, and the *-th* probably sounded rather formal or old-fashioned even in Shakespeare's day. Sometimes Shakespeare used the two together: "The earth hath bubbles as the water has," with no apparent difference.

Today we make a sentence negative by contracting *not* with the first auxiliary verb in the sentence: "They are trying" and "They aren't trying." We make a statement into a question by inverting the order of the subject and the first auxiliary verb: "They are trying" and "Are they trying?" If there is no auxiliary verb in the sentence (as in "They try"), we have to add an otherwise meaningless *do* as a filler for negative sentences ("They don't try") and questions ("Do they try?"). Shakespeare, however, did not have to use the filler *do.* He could say "They try not" and "Try they?" which are impossible in our language:

> Live you? [Do you live?]
> How goes the night, boy? [How does the night go?]
> Ride you this afternoon? [Do you ride this afternoon?]

On the other hand, we cannot use *do* as an auxiliary in unemphatic affirmative statements. We can say "They *do* try" with emphasis on *do* if we want to contradict someone who has suggested that they do not try, but we cannot say "They do try" without emphasis on *do.* Shakespeare, however, could use *do* that way, and frequently did. For him, "They try" and "They do try" (with unstressed *do*) were simply alternative ways of saying exactly the same thing, as shown by these examples:

> . . . swimmers that do cling together . . .
> . . . such things here as we do speak about . . .
> His wonders and his praises do contend . . .
> . . . the earth / Was feverous and did shake.

Shakespeare had a wider choice of past participles than we do today in standard English, although some of Shakespeare's forms have survived even today in nonstandard speech:

> . . . I have spoke [for *spoken*]
> And his great love . . . hath holp him . . . [for *has helped*]

Today we make perfect tenses *(have come, has seen, had hoped)* by combining a form of the verb *have* with the past participle of

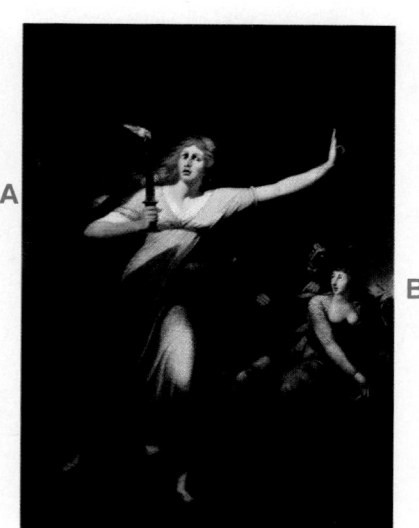

Lady Macbeth by Henry Fuseli. Oil.

Louvre, Paris.

A. Example
See line 2 of Sonnet 73 for an example of this use of *do*: "When yellow leaves, or none, or few, do hang . . . ." This possibility for using or omitting the single-syllable *do* helped poets maintain a meter.

B. Humanities Connection: Discussing the Fine Art
Have students compare and contrast this sleepwalking Lady Macbeth with Schussele's (text page 337) and Polanski's (text page 318). Note the strong light and shadow in the painting.

? What does Lady Macbeth's dramatic arm gesture suggest to you? (She is determined; she won't be held back.) Who are the figures in the background? (The doctor and lady-in-waiting)

A. Humanities Connection: About the Fine Art

Students should realize that the painting, the elaborate marginal decorations, and the lettering of these manuscripts were all done by hand. Have students turn to text pages 67 and 348 for other details from the exquisite *Roman de la Rose*. Students should be able to connect the manuscript with the Renaissance's intense interest in the subject of love.

A

The Lover and His Rose from *Roman de la Rose* (c. 1487–95). French manuscript.

The British Library.

the main verb. English speakers in Shakespeare's day generally made them the same way. However, if the main verb indicated motion, they used forms of the verb *be* instead of *have*: "They *are* not yet *come* back."

Where we would say "Come on, *let's go* to the King," Shakespeare has simply "Come, *go we* to the King." Shakespeare's use is an old first-person plural command that is more direct than the *let's* form we now prefer.

In both Shakespeare's English and ours, noun phrases may consist of a determiner (like *the, a, my*), an adjective, and a noun ("the old house"). However, in short expressions used to address a person, Shakespeare could put the adjective first: "Gentle my lord" [for "My gentle lord"] and "Gracious my lord" [for "My gracious lord"].

Some of the "mistakes" we make today are also in Shakespeare. They are different ways of using English that have fallen out of favor in standard English, or at least among some people who use standard English, but are still much used:

> There's daggers in men's smiles . . . [There *are* daggers . . .]
> Who I myself struck down . . . [*Whom* I myself struck down]
> . . . asked for who . . . [for *whom*]

Shakespeare's Words

In some respects, Shakespeare's vocabulary was more complex than ours. We commonly use three words for location: *here, there,* and *where*. Shakespeare had nine because in addition to those three, six others were available that are now rare, if not archaic: *hence, thence, whence* ("from here, there, where") and *hither, thither, whither* ("to here, there, where"):

> Whence cam'st thou, worthy thane? [Where did you come from?]
> . . . I will thither. [I will go (to) there.]
> Whither should I fly? [Where should I fly (to)?]

These other six words must have lost some of their effect already by Shakespeare's time, because he sometimes used unnecessary prepositions with them:

> . . . a place / From whence himself does fly? [a place whence or from where he himself flies]
> . . . I must be from thence! [I had to be away from there!]

Shakespeare uses other words that are now rare or obsolete:

> . . . I say *sooth* . . . [I tell the truth; we still have *sooth* in the form *soothsayer* ("truth teller").]
> This diamond he greets your wife *withal* [with] . . .
> Send out *moe* [more] horses. . . . [In early English, *moe* referred to number, *more* to size.]

Some of the words in Shakespeare's plays that strike us as "fancy" were fancy even when he used them. They were "inkhorn

A. Shakespeare's Words

Shakespeare's works contain numerous original phrases, familiar today, but once fresh from his pen: "It was Greek to me" (*Julius Caesar*); "salad days" (*Antony and Cleopatra*); "green-ey'd jealousy" (*The Merchant of Venice*); "the crack of doom" (*Macbeth*); etc.

A word like *multitudinous* is a reminder that Shakespeare used one of the largest vocabularies of any English writer—some 30,000 words. (Estimates vary, but an educated person today probably has a vocabulary of 15,000 words.) He was, in his own phrase, "a man of fire-new words." New in the sixteenth century and appearing in his works were *armada, demonstrate, dire, emphasis, prodigious,* and *vast.* Other words that appeared in print for the first time in his First Folio were *accommodation, assassination, dexterously, dislocate, indistinguishable, reliance,* and *submerged.*

terms''—words borrowed from the classical languages and used for their mouth-filling and impressive sounds, as well as their subtleties of meaning. After he has just stabbed King Duncan, Macbeth says that his hand will never be clean again, but will rather

The multitudinous seas incarnadine . . .

He means that the blood on his hands would "make the many seas red," but the word *multitudinous* seems to mean far more than the short word *many,* and the literal meaning of *incarnadine* ("to turn into the blood-red color of raw flesh") is especially appropriate to Macbeth's actions and state of mind. Shakespeare was using fancy words—but for a purpose.

The trickiest words in Shakespeare, however, are those that look familiar but have a different meaning from their present-day versions. There are a great many of them, and they may make a Shakespeare play seem to be slightly askew. They are false friends that make us think we understand what the language means, while in fact meaning something different from what we expect. More than any other single thing, they make Shakespeare difficult to read. Here are a few examples out of many:

Sweno, the Norway's king, craves *composition* . . . [agreement, peace terms].

[Banquo to the weird Sisters:] Are ye *fantastical* [illusory, imaginary], or that indeed / Which outwardly ye *show* [seem, appear]?

Say from whence / You *owe* [own, have] this strange *intelligence* [information]?

Sleep that *knits up* [straightens out] the *raveled sleave* [tangled thread] of care . . . [The image of reknitting the sleeve of a sweater that has unraveled makes sense, but is wrong.]

Because of differences like these between Shakespeare's English and ours, it takes some effort for us to read his plays and poetry. What we can get from the reading, however, is well worth the effort.

A

"But the script says 'Lay on Macduff.'"

B

B. About the Cartoon
Most students will need no help enjoying the actor's confusion of a spoken line with a stage direction. (Have them look up *Macbeth,* Act V, Scene 8, line 33, text page 328.)
? What does "Lay on" mean in *Macbeth*? ("Let's go" or "Let's fight"—roughly the opposite of our phrase "Lay off") What's wrong with this picture? (The cartoonist has the actors wearing Viking costumes. The sign on the wall says Act V, Scene 7; but the line occurs in Scene 8.) Many people today confuse the verbs *lie* and *lay.* What does each mean? (In the present tense, *lie* means "to recline," and *lay* means "to put an object down.")

Analyzing Language

Find an example in Shakespeare's poetry (other than those in the essay on his language) of each of the following:

a. A contraction that we would not use today

b. The omission of a syllable from the middle or beginning of a word

c. A word stressed differently from the way we pronounce it today

d. An unusual use of *who* or *which*

e. *Mine* where we would use *my*

f. *Thou, thee, thy,* or *thine* (notice who is talking to whom)

g. The *-th* and *-st* forms of verbs

h. A negative like "They try not" (instead of "They don't try")

i. A question like "Try they?" (instead of "Do they try?")

j. An unemphatic statement like "They do try" (instead of "They try")

k. An unusual form of a verb (like "I have spoke")

l. A word we no longer have or no longer use in the same meaning

Before beginning the remainder of the unit, review "Decline of the Renaissance," text page 186. Elizabethans, ruled by a queen of great tact and flexibility, had lived in a world of order and stability. James and Charles Stuart, however, attempted to stamp out religious and political dissent during a time of rising religious controversy. The social turmoil that resulted stimulated activity, especially in the area of theological disputation. In literature there was a decline of drama and an increase in prose. In the rest of the unit, therefore, students will see sharp distinctions in literary styles and much concern with religious topics.

A. Expansion
A career in the Church of England, the military, or politics required such an oath; scholarship did not.

B. The Conceit
Recall that *conceited* (from Italian *concetto*, "thought") here refers not to egocentric vanity but to an elaborate intellectual image or metaphor. (See the definition of *conceit* and examples in the headnote, text page 366.)

John Donne (1572–1631)

Donne (a Welsh name pronounced Dun) wrote learned, passionate, argumentative poetry most of which he never published, since he never was ambitious to be known publicly as a poet. His first aim in life was to be "courtier"—that is, a member of the Queen's government. But he had one bad handicap: He was born into a prominent Roman Catholic family, his great uncle being no less a person than Sir (or Saint) Thomas More, the author of *Utopia* and the Lord Chancellor whom Henry VIII had beheaded for not supporting him in his quarrels with the Pope.

A When we first hear of Donne from his earliest biographer, Izaak Walton, he was only twelve years old but already studying at Oxford. Catholic boys went to the University very young, so that they would not have to take the oath of allegiance to the Queen, whom the Pope had excommunicated. After a few terms at Oxford, and perhaps also at Cambridge, Donne returned to his native city of London and at the age of seventeen became a law student at Lincoln's Inn, one of the "Inns of Court" where lawyers were trained. He had no financial worries, since his father, a prosperous iron merchant, had died and left him some money. We can think of him now as "Jack" Donne, a handsome, well dressed youth who devoted his mornings to heavy reading in philosophy and foreign literature and his afternoons to circulating in society. A friend later in life remembered him as being "a great visitor of ladies, a great frequenter of plays, a **B** great writer of conceited verses."

Eventually, in 1598, after various adventures such as taking part in two naval expeditions against Spain, Donne became confidential secretary to the Lord Chancellor, Sir Thomas Egerton. This was an important post, the starting point for what could become a brilliant career in government, for by now Donne had abandoned his Catholicism. But he blasted all his hopes and ambitions when, in 1602, he secretly married Anne More, a seventeen-year-old niece of the Lord Chancellor's wife. Marriage with a minor, without her father's consent, was a serious crime against both Church and state. As soon as

Title page to John Donne's *Sermons* (1640). Engraving.

Anne's father discovered what had happened, he had Jack Donne arrested, jailed, and dismissed from his position. In jail, Donne wrote his shortest poem:

> John Donne,
> Anne Donne,
> Undone.

In his head-on confrontation with society, Donne blundered badly. Of course he was not kept in prison long, but he never did recover his position, and for years he and Anne had to live off the bounty of friends and relatives, Donne's own money being all gone. They certainly needed what help they could get, since they eventually had twelve children, five of whom died in infancy.

In the early 1600's Donne continued to read voraciously, to write poetry for private circulation, and prose for public, though he did publish two long poems in memory of a dead little girl, the daughter of one of his patrons. In prose, he wrote against the Church of Rome so effectively that he became known as an important defender of the Church of England. The new King, James I, was impressed, and he began to put pressure on Donne to become a clergyman. And so, in 1615, Donne was ordained a priest. His brilliant, theatrical sermons immediately won his advancement in the church, and he rose to be Dean of St. Paul's in London, the principal cathedral of England. Thus Jack Donne became Dr. John Donne, with an honorary degree from Cambridge University and important ecclesiastical positions. He preached outdoors in the open space before the cathedral, and he preached before the King, always with great effect, for he brought to his sermons the same surprising inventiveness that he showed in his poems. He died full of years and honors, and his monument, showing how he looked in the winding sheet put about his dead body, may still be seen in St. Paul's.

A

Preaching at Old St. Paul's Cathedral (ca. 1616). Oil.

Society of Antiquaries of London.

A. St. Paul's Cathedral
A Saxon cathedral built in seventh-century London on the site of a Roman temple burned in 1087 and was replaced by this Norman church (see the round arches). In 1561, fire struck again, and in 1628 the architect Inigo Jones (see page 182) began repairs. Note that in the foreground of the painting is Paul's Cross, a gazebo-like pulpit, from which a bishop is preaching to the king and court.

St. Paul's was again so severely damaged (by the Great Fire of London in 1666) that architect Christopher Wren (1632–1723) was ordered to replace it with an entirely new structure. Wren's cathedral was damaged by World War II bombs but has since been restored.

The Elements of Literature

METAPHYSICAL POETRY

In the 1590's, when Donne started writing, most poets tried to make their works as sweet, smooth, and musical-sounding as possible. The opening lines of some of Shakespeare's songs show how one poet achieved the "sugared sweetness" that many poets aspired to:

> "Come unto these yellow sands"
> "It was a lover and his lass"
> "When daffodils begin to peer"
> "Full merrily the humble bee doth sing"

Sidney, Spenser, Campion, Raleigh, and dozens of others assumed that the language and rhythms of poetry should be as pleasing to the ear as music. But Donne would have none of this. In one of his poems he says, "I sing not siren-like, to tempt, for I am harsh." For his poems he invented a new style, a style that some later critics would call metaphysical.

For the most part, Donne based his most characteristic poems not on music but on the rhythms of colloquial—that is, spoken—English. "For God's sake hold your tongue and let me love," he begins one of his poems. "I wonder," he begins another, "what thou and I did till we loved." The speaker in his poems frequently sounds blunt and angry, or he broods to himself, or he seems to be thinking out loud. At times the speaker sounds like a lecturer, explaining difficult matters to the woman who is presumably listening to him. But whatever he sounds like, Donne's speaker is always using his brains and bringing into the poem ideas from books he has read, especially books of philosophy and theology. He also brings in images from everyday activities, trades, occupations, and learned disciplines—law, medicine, science, geography. Metaphysical poems, then, are not only impassioned; they are also intellectual, and reading them is frequently like figuring out the solution to a riddle.

PREPARATION

BUILDING ON PRIOR KNOWLEDGE. Have students read the headnote and review Marlowe's poem (text page 232) before reading "The Bait."

A. Imagery
How does the speaker's love compare to the sun and moon? (She gives a greater light.)

B. Responding
What do you think of Donne's description of the sport of fishing in lines 17–24?

CLOSURE
Have one student explain to the class who or what the bait is and who the fish are.

ANALYZING THE POEM
Identifying Details
1. By the woman's eyes. The fish will stay near her.
2. Her beauty is the bait.
3. In line 8.

Interpreting Meanings
4. Alluring, sensual, magical.

5. She can catch the fish by simply bathing in the river.
6. Line 6. Shakespeare wrote "My mistress' eyes are nothing like the sun."
7. Answers will vary. The lady is being complimented on her appearance, but the speaker says that those who escape her lures are far wiser than he.
8. Responses will vary.

The opening of this poem tells us that it was inspired by Christopher Marlowe's "The Passionate Shepherd to His Love." The first lines of the two poems are identical; after that each poem goes its own way, and as usual with Donne it is an original way for the most part, although the notion that a woman's beauty can influence natural phenomena is very common among Donne's predecessors and contemporaries.

The Bait

Come live with me, and be my love,
And we will some new pleasures prove,
Of golden sands, and crystal brooks,
With silken lines, and silver hooks.

5   There will the river whispering run,
Warmed by thy eyes more than the sun,
And there the enamored fish will stay,
Begging themselves they may betray.

When thou wilt swim in that live bath,
10 Each fish, which every channel hath,
Will amorously to thee swim,
Gladder to catch thee, than thou him.

A   If thou, to be so seen, beest loth,
By sun or moon, thou darkenest both;

15 And if myself have leave to see,
I need not their light, having thee.

Let others freeze with angling reeds,
And cut their legs with shells and weeds,
Or treacherously poor fish beset
20 With strangling snare, or windowy net.

Let coarse bold hands from slimy nest
The bedded fish in banks out-wrest,
Or curious° traitors, sleave-silk° flies,
Bewitch poor fishes' wand'ring eyes.

25 For thee, thou need'st no such deceit,
For thou thyself art thine own bait;
The fish that is not catched thereby,
Alas, is wiser far than I.

23. **curious:** made with great care. **sleave-silk:** raveled silk used to make artificial flies.

B

Responding to the Poem

Analyzing the Poem

Identifying Details
1. According to the second stanza, how will the river be warmed? How will the fish behave?
2. Explain why the lady does not need "deceit."
3. Where in the poem is the **syntax** or word order of a sentence shifted about to accommodate the **rhyme** and **meter**?

Interpreting Meanings
4. What **tone** do the adjectives "golden," "crystal," "silken," and "silver" establish for the poem as a whole?
5. Why would the woman in the poem be a very desirable companion on a fishing trip?
6. Which line of this poem could Shakespeare have been thinking of when he wrote Sonnet 130?
7. Explain why the compliment paid to the lady in the last stanza is a rather dubious one.

8. Some people regard this poem as cold, clammy, unattractive. Do you agree?

Writing About the Poem

A Creative Response
1. **Constructing a Conceit.** Donne's "The Bait" relies almost entirely on an extended conceit: The lady is her own "bait." Write a short poem or prose paragraph that is structured around an extended conceit. Try to make your conceit ingenious and original.

A Critical Response
2. **Comparing Two Poems.** In a brief essay, explain whether this poem is an answer to Marlowe's "The Passionate Shepherd to His Love," an imitation of it, or neither. Remember to support your views with specific references to the texts of both poems.

BUILDING ON PRIOR KNOWLEDGE. Ask students to read the headnote, and make sure they understand what *hyperbole* is before they read the poem.

SUPPLEMENTARY SUPPORT MATERIALS
1. Vocabulary Activity Worksheet (*CCB*)
2. Review and Response Worksheet: Hyperbole (*CCB*)
3. Selection Test (*CCB*)

DEVELOPING VOCABULARY
The following word from the poem is tested in the Selection Test. (See also Vocabulary Activity Worksheet.)
cleft

Donne's love poems are collectively known as his "Songs and Sonnets." This is a rather misleading title because most of the poems in the collection are too intellectually demanding to be called songs, and none of them is a proper sonnet as that term is defined today. Yet we must accept the fol-lowing poem as a song because it was set to music in a contemporary manuscript. Unlike a great many Renaissance songs that idealize women, Donne's "Song," which contains many examples of exaggeration or hyperbole (pronounced hī·pur′bə·lē), satirizes them.

Song

Go and catch a falling star,
　　Get with child a mandrake° root,
Tell me where all past years are,
　　Or who cleft the devil's foot,
5　Teach me to hear mermaids singing,
　　Or to keep off envy's stinging,
A　　　　And find
　　　　What wind
　Serves to advance an honest mind.

10　If thou be'st born to strange sights,
　　Things invisible to see,
　Ride ten thousand days and nights,
　　Till age snow white hairs on thee,
　Thou, when thou return'st, wilt tell me

15　　All strange wonders that befell thee,
　　　And swear
　　　No where
　Lives a woman true and fair.

　If thou find'st one, let me know;
20　　Such a pilgrimage were sweet.
　Yet do not; I would not go,
　　Though at next door we might meet.
　Though she were true when you met her,
　And last till you write your letter,
25　　　Yet she
　　　Will be
　False, ere I come, to two or three.

---

2. **mandrake:** a plant whose forked root is said to resemble a human being's trunk and legs.

Responding to the Poem

Analyzing the Poem

Identifying Details

1. What commands does the speaker make in the first stanza? What do the commands have in common?
2. What does the speaker say about the ideal of a woman both "true" and "fair" in the second stanza?
3. What does the speaker say he will not do in the last stanza? Why?

Interpreting Meanings

4. What examples of **hyperbole,** or exaggeration for rhetorical effect, can you find in the poem?

5. What song-like qualities does the poem possess, in your view?
6. How would you describe the speaker's **tone**? What keeps the song from being offensive in the way it characterizes women?

Writing About the Poem

A Creative Response

Using Hyperbole. Imitate the first stanza of Donne's song by constructing some **hyperbolic** statements of your own to show the impossibility of something. You might want to answer Donne.

ANALYZING THE POEM
Identifying Details
1. There is a total of seven commands (one each in lines 1–6; one in lines 7–9).
　They are all impossible.
2. She lives nowhere.
3. He would not go to see a true and fair woman because she will be false by the time he arrives.

Interpreting Meanings
4. The commands in stanza 1; ten thousand days and nights (line 12); the exaggeration in lines 25–27.
5. It has strong rhythm, rhyme, and repetition.
6. Most will agree the tone is cynical. Some may find the song offensive; others may feel that it is not to be taken seriously.

A. Pronunciation/Interpretation
❓ Based on the poem's rhyme scheme, how should *wind* be pronounced? (Short *i* vowel sound, as in *win*) How is this injunction, like the others in this verse, impossible? (Wind cannot affect honesty.)

PREPARATION

1. BUILDING ON PRIOR KNOWLEDGE.   Have students read the headnote and the side glosses before reading the poem. Then ask students to watch as you draw a circle with a compass and to pay close attention to the relative movements of the two legs of the instrument.

2. ESTABLISHING A PURPOSE.   Ask stu-

dents to look for the images and conceits used to characterize the love of the speaker and his wife.

SUPPLEMENTARY SUPPORT MATERIALS

1. Vocabulary Activity Worksheet (CCB)
2. Review and Response Worksheet: Figurative Language (CCB)
3. Selection Test (CCB)

DEVELOPING VOCABULARY

The following word from the poem is tested in the Selection Test. (See also Vocabulary Activity Worksheet.)
refined

CLOSURE

Ask students to summarize Donne's various attitudes toward love and women.

A. Interpreting
❓ Why does the speaker consider silence the most fitting way for him and his wife to separate? (A show of anxiety would profane or "deconsecrate" their love and trust.)

B. Connotations
❓ What kind of love does the word *refined* suggest? (Superior, spiritual, sensitive, purified, restrained)

This poem is typical of Donne in having a dramatic situation, a particular occasion on which the poem is spoken. Here the speaker, a man, must take leave of the woman he loves, to go away from her on a long trip. In the poem he is saying goodbye (pronouncing a "valediction") and telling her not to cry or feel sad ("forbidding mourning"). In reading the poem, notice particularly that the entire first stanza is a *simile* introduced by *As* and followed in the second stanza by *So*. The dying men in this stanza are not part of the poem's drama; they and their friends provide only a situation analogous to that of the two lovers who are being separated.

According to Izaak Walton this poem is autobiographical. Donne wrote it for his wife when he was leaving England as a member of a diplomatic mission to France. She urged him not to go because she was pregnant and unwell. Yet he went, because of his obligations to the leader of the mission, Sir Robert Drury. Two days after arriving in Paris, Donne had a vision which he described as

follows to Sir Robert: "I have seen my dear wife pass twice by me through this room, with her hair hanging about her shoulders, and a dead child in her arms." A messenger sent back to England returned with the news that "Mrs. Donne after a long and dangerous labor . . . had been delivered of a dead child" on the very day when Donne had the vision.

Whether autobiographical or not, "A Valediction: Forbidding Mourning" contains the most famous of all metaphysical *conceits*. These are odd and surprising figures of speech in which something is said to be something else that seems to be very unusual and unlikely. Here are some examples of such conceits: The tears dropping from a lover's eyes are newly minted coins; a man is a world; the king's court is a bowling-alley; lovers are holy saints. In this poem the lovers are said to be "stiff twin compasses"—not the kind of compass used for finding directions, but the kind of compass with two legs used by geometers and others to draw circles.

A Valediction: Forbidding Mourning

As virtuous men pass mildly away,
　　And whisper to their souls to go,
Whilst some of their sad friends do say
　　"The breath goes now," and some say, "No";

5 A
So let us melt, and make no noise,
　　No tear-floods, nor sigh-tempests move,
'Twere profanation of our joys
　　To tell the laity° our love.

10
Moving of th' earth° brings harms and fears,
　　Men reckon what it did and meant;°
But trepidation of the spheres,°
　　Though greater far, is innocent.°

Dull sublunary° lovers' love
　　(Whose soul° is sense°) cannot admit
15
Absence, because it doth remove
　　Those things which elemented° it.

B
But we by a love so much <u>refined</u>
　　That our selves know not what it is,
Inter-assuréd of the mind,
20
　　Care less, eyes, lips, and hands to miss.

8. **laity:** lay persons, those unable to understand the "religion" of true love.
9. **moving of th' earth:** earthquake.
10. **meant:** "What does it mean" was a question ordinarily asked of any unusual phenomena.
11. **trepidation of the spheres:** irregularities in the movements of remote heavenly bodies.
12. **innocent:** unobserved and harmless compared with earthquakes.
13. **sublunary:** under the moon, therefore subject to change.
14. **soul:** essence. **sense:** the body with its five "senses."
16. **elemented:** comprised, composed.

ANALYZING THE POEM
Identifying Details
1. A man who is about to go on a journey is addressing his wife.
2. Just as virtuous men die in peaceful silence, so now let us part in silence and tranquillity.
3. Other couples fear separation because their love is based on sense experience, but he and his wife are bound by a spiritual love, one that is not affected by separation.
4. Compasses are used to draw perfect circles.

Donne compares himself and his wife to the two legs of a compass: She leans toward him when he moves away, but he always returns to her at her fixed position in the center of his life.

Interpreting Meanings
5. These references to earthly upheavals underscore the trauma that "dull sublunary lovers" feel during separation.

This separation of the speaker and his wife is like "trepidation of the spheres."
6. To emphasize the sense of union, harmony, and trust that he and his beloved feel.
7. "Melt": to separate but not in a violent way; "inter-assured": mutually assured; "airy-thinness": so thin or fragile as to be almost invisible (spoken of thin gold wire).
8. Have them read lines 25–36 aloud to hear the run-on lines and the syncopated rhythm that prevent monotony.
9. The rhythm is iambic tetrameter with occasional irregularities.
10. In "Song," the speaker despairs of finding a lady who is fair and true; in this poem the speaker loves and trusts his wife.
11. Possible answers: ardent, idealistic, intellectual.

Our two souls therefore, which are one,
　　Though I must go, endure not yet
A breach, but an expansion,
　　Like gold to airy thinness beat.

25　If they be two, they are two so
　　As stiff twin compasses are two;
Thy soul, the fixed foot, makes no show
　　To move, but doth, if th' other do.

And though it in the center sit,
30　Yet when the other far doth roam,
It leans and hearkens after it,
　　And grows erect, as that comes home.

Such wilt thou be to me, who must
　　Like th' other foot, obliquely° run;
35　Thy firmness° makes my circle just,°
　　And makes me end where I begun.

34. **obliquely:** off-course.
35. **firmness:** fidelity. **just:** perfect. A circle symbolizes perfection: hence wedding rings.

Responding to the Poem

Analyzing the Poem

Identifying Details

1. Who is the speaker in this poem? Whom is he addressing, and on what occasion?
2. Paraphrase the **simile** in the first two stanzas.
3. How does the speaker distinguish himself and his lover from other couples in the fourth and fifth stanzas?
4. What are compasses used for? Explain the conceit Donne uses in the final stanzas, and show how it applies to the couple's situation.

Interpreting Meanings

5. What is the point of the references to irregular events on earth and irregular events in the spheres (or outer space) in lines 9–12? What kind of event is like the separation of the lovers?
6. Why does the speaker insist that the lovers—obviously two people—are actually one?
7. Comment on the way these words are used in the poem: "melt" (line 5); "inter-assuréd" (line 19, a coinage of Donne's); "airy thinness" (line 24).

8. How does Donne enliven the stanzas on the compasses, so that they do not become mechanical?
9. Comment on the **rhythm** of the poem.
10. How does the attitude toward the lover here contrast with the attitude in "Song"?
11. How would you describe the personality of the speaker of this poem? Does the poem give you any hints?

Writing About the Poem

A Creative Response

1. **Writing a Farewell.** Assume that you, like Donne, are leaving a loved one behind for a long, possibly dangerous journey. Write your own "valediction" in a brief letter.

A Critical Response

2. **Analyzing Conceits.** In a brief essay, identify and analyze the metaphysical "conceits" Donne employs in "A Valediction: Forbidding Mourning." Conclude by evaluating the effectiveness of these conceits in the poem as a whole.

1. BUILDING ON PRIOR KNOWLEDGE.
Remind students that a meditation is a reflection on a serious subject.

2. ESTABLISHING A PURPOSE. "Jack" Donne, the young rake, wrote "Song"; John Donne, the devoted husband, wrote "Valediction." Ask students to consider which "Donne" wrote this.

SUPPLEMENTARY SUPPORT MATERIALS
1. Vocabulary Activity Worksheet (*CCB*)
2. Review and Response Worksheet: Metaphor (*CCB*)
3. Selection Test (*CCB*)
4. Audiocassette recording

DEVELOPING VOCABULARY
The following words from the meditation are tested in the Selection Test. (See also Vocabulary Activity Worksheet.)

contention	to defray
to intermit	tribulation
clod	recourse
covetousness	

A. Responding
This extended metaphor is often quoted.
❓ What is your personal reaction to this comparison? Do you find it an important concept? (It may help to avoid references to religion and to ask students to relate the text to popular songs like "We Are the World.")

B. Allusions
References to this well-known meditation appear in many literary works. Ernest Hemingway chose the title *For Whom the Bell Tolls* for his novel about an American who fights in the bloody Spanish Civil War.

C. Theme
❓ How can one person profit from the suffering of another? (By seeing it as a reminder that suffering and death will come to him or her as well)

CLOSURE
Ask students to discuss the meaning of the two famous metaphors: "No man is an island . . ." and "never send to know for whom the bell tolls. . . ."

MEDITATION 17

In 1623 Donne wrote a series of meditations prompted by a serious illness. It is important to know that in Donne's time, church bells would ring out to announce the death of someone in the parish.

Nunc lento sonitu dicunt, Morieris.

Now, this bell tolling softly for another, says to me, Thou must die.

Perchance he for whom this bell tolls may be so ill as that he knows not it tolls for him; and perchance I may think myself so much better than I am, as that they who are about me and see my state may have caused it to toll for me, and I know not that. The Church is Catholic, universal, so are all her actions; all that she does belongs to all. When she baptizes a child, that action concerns me; for that child is thereby connected to that Head[1] which is my Head too, and engrafted into that body, whereof I am a member. And when she buries a man, that action concerns me: All mankind is of one Author, and is one volume; when one man dies, one chapter is not torn out of the book, but translated into a better language; and every chapter must be so translated. God employs several translators; some pieces are translated by age, some by sickness, some by war, some by justice; but God's hand is in every translation; and his hand shall bind up all our scattered leaves again, for that Library where every book shall lie open to one another. As therefore the bell that rings to a sermon calls not upon the preacher only, but upon the congregation to come; so this bell calls us all: but how much more me, who am brought so near the door by this sickness. There was a contention as far as a suit[2] (in which both piety and dignity, religion and estimation,[3] were mingled) which of the religious orders should ring to prayers first in the morning; and it was determined that they should ring first that rose earliest. If we understand aright the dignity of this bell that tolls for our evening prayer, we would be glad to make it ours, by rising early, in that application, that it might be ours as well as his, whose indeed it is. The bell doth toll for him that thinks it doth; and though it intermit again, yet from that minute that that occasion wrought upon him, he is united to God. Who casts not up his eye to the sun when it rises? but who takes off his eye from a comet when that breaks out?[4] Who bends not his ear to any bell, which upon any occasion rings? but who can remove it from that bell which is passing a piece of himself out of this world? No man is an island, entire of itself; every man is a piece of the continent, a part of the main;[5] if a clod be washed away by the sea, Europe is the less, as well as if a promontory were, as well as if a manor of thy friends or of thine own were; any man's death diminishes me because I am involved in mankind; and therefore never send to know for whom the bell tolls; it tolls for thee. Neither can we call this a begging of misery or a borrowing of misery, as though we were not miserable enough of ourselves, but must fetch in more from the next house, in taking upon us the misery of our neighbors. Truly it were an excusable covetousness if we did; for affliction is a treasure, and scarce any man hath enough of it. No man hath affliction enough that is not matured and ripened by it, and made fit for God by that affliction. If a man carry treasure in bullion, or in a wedge of gold, and have none coined into current monies, his treasure will not defray him as he travels. Tribulation is treasure in the nature of it, but it is not current money in the use of it, except we get nearer and nearer our home, Heaven, by it. Another man may be sick too, and sick to death, and this affliction may lie in his bowels, as gold in a mine, and be of no use to him; but this bell that tells me of his affliction digs out and applies that gold to me, if by this consideration of another's danger I take mine own into contemplation, and so secure myself by making my recourse to my God, who is our only security.

1. **Head:** Christ.
2. **suit:** lawsuit.
3. **estimation:** self esteem.
4. Comets were regarded as signs of disaster to come.
5. **main:** mainland.

ANALYZING THE MEDITATION
Identifying Facts
1. The tolling of a bell to announce death.
2. He is a part of the body of which Christ is the Head; a page in a book that God has translated; a piece of the continent.
3. Affliction is a treasure because it helps us to get nearer to our ultimate home, heaven.

Interpreting Meanings
4. He intends to remind us that we must all die and that another's death should remind us of that fact.
5. We are all interconnected; we all must die; we must not resent affliction, for it helps us to get to heaven. Student opinions will vary.

6. Answers will vary. The message of brotherhood (no man is an island) is certainly relevant to the civil rights struggle of our time.
7. The speaker's tone might be described as dignified and optimistic. He holds profoundly religious values, including a belief in an afterlife and in divine protection and mercy.

Le Chateau de Maintenon (detail) by Hubert Robert (1808). Oil.

Sotheby's, New York.

A. Humanities Connection: Responding to the Fine Art
Hubert Robert (1733–1808) was a French painter and landscape artist who helped plan the Versailles gardens. He was jailed during the French Revolution but escaped death because a man of the same name was guillotined instead.
? How are the subject and mood of this painting suited to Donne's meditation? What can you infer the various people are doing? (The building is a church, and the figures in white appear to be giving alms. The mood, set by the darkness of the scene, is one of almost solemn calmness.)

Responding to the Meditation

Analyzing the Meditation

Identifying Facts

1. What sound prompts the speaker to begin his meditation?
2. List the **metaphors** used to show that the speaker is part of all humanity and not an isolated individual.
3. Why does the speaker feel that affliction is a treasure? In what ways is tribulation like money?

Interpreting Meanings

4. How would you explain what Donne means by saying "the bell . . . tolls for thee"?
5. What are Donne's **main ideas** in this meditation? Do you agree with all of them?
6. Do you think any lines from this meditation should have particular relevance to life in the late twentieth century? Explain.
7. How would you describe this speaker's **tone?** Is it depressed, angry, resigned, or something else? What beliefs and values account for the tone?

Writing About the Meditation

A Critical Response

Analyzing Metaphors. In a brief essay, take two of the metaphors in this meditation and show how Donne uses them to make his points. Be sure to explain the terms of each metaphor and to show how Donne extends them.

Analyzing Language and Style

Context Clues

Context clues can be found in several places: (1) the unfamiliar word might be defined in an appositive; (2) the sentences surrounding the unfamiliar word might give you a clue to its meaning; (3) the structure of the word itself might help you figure out what it means. Locate where Donne uses the following words. What does Donne use each word to mean? Check all your guesses in a dictionary.

perchance	contention	covetousness
Catholic	aright	bullion
leaves	intermit	

1. BUILDING ON PRIOR KNOWLEDGE.
Discuss with students what they know about the Biblical accounts of the Last Judgment. You might refer them to Revelation 7 (the source of imagery for this poem) or to Isaiah 34 and 35.

2. ESTABLISHING A PURPOSE. Ask students to look for the reason why the speaker focuses on the Last Judgment. What is he concerned about?

___

SUPPLEMENTARY SUPPORT MATERIALS
1. Review and Response Worksheet: Sonnet Structure (*CCB*)
2. Selection Test (*CCB*)

Writing Assignment
Ask students to imagine a particular character who is about to have his or her life's worth judged. Have them write a speech in which their character tries to explain the value of his or her life.

___

A. Humanities Connection: Responding to the Fine Art
Jan Van Eyck (c. 1390–1441) was a Flemish painter who exerted tremendous influence on the generation of European painters that followed him. He advanced the technique of oil painting and astonished the art world of his day with his minute detail and subtle differentiations of texture and light.

? Ask students to locate details in Van Eyck's painting that correspond to details of the Last Judgment presented in the first four lines of Donne's poem. (The angels and trumpets are at the top, rising dead at the bottom.)

Donne's Sonnets

The Last Judgment (detail) by Jan Van Eyck (c. 1430). Oil.

The Metropolitan Museum of Art, New York, Fletcher Fund, 1933. (33.92b).

In Donne's collected poems the individual works are arranged by kind, into categories such as epigrams, songs and sonnets, verse letters, satires, and so on. One important category is "Divine Poems," and among these perhaps the finest are twenty-six "Holy Sonnets." Donne never published his "Holy Sonnets," and so we do not know the order in which he wanted us to read them. They are arranged in different ways in the contemporary manuscripts and in the books printed after his death. Consequently, they are most conveniently referred to not by number, as Shakespeare's sonnets are, but by their first words.

A

ANALYZING THE POEM
Identifying Details
1. In the octave he addresses the angels (line 2); the numberless dead souls (lines 2–7); and those who are alive (lines 7–8).
   In the sestet he addresses Christ (Lord).
2. The speaker changes his mind in line 9, where the sestet begins.

3. He refers to Christ's redemption of humanity through the crucifixion.
   He is addressing Christ.

Interpreting Meanings
4. Time to repent his sins.
5. The sound and rhythm in lines 1–8 are bright and syncopated, as the speaker conjures up the sound of the angels' trumpets and the roll call of the dead. In lines 9–14 the sound and rhythm become more somber.

CLOSURE
Have students summarize what the speaker is asking for.

In "At the Round Earth's Imagined Corners" the speaker first calls for the tremendous events that will happen, according to biblical prophecies, at the end of time: the return of Christ to the Earth and the Last Judgment of both the living and the dead. Then, having called rather flamboyantly for the end of the world, the speaker changes his mind.

The "last busy day," as he once called it, fascinated Donne, as it has many other writers and painters. Like practically everybody in his time, he was confident that the great event would soon occur, perhaps even before his own death. The prospect of God's judgment lends urgency to many of his sermons and poems.

A. Identifying Details
? What is listed or cataloged in lines 5–7? (The various ways in which the souls called to judgment met their death)

B. Theme
? What does the speaker request in these last two lines? (That Christ teach him how to repent while he is still alive)

At the Round Earth's Imagined Corners

At the round earth's imagined corners,° blow
Your trumpets, angels, and arise, arise
From death, you numberless infinities
Of souls, and to your scattered bodies° go,
5   All whom the flood did, and fire shall o'erthrow,
A   All whom war, dearth,° age, agues,° tyrannies,
  Despair, law, chance hath slain, and you whose eyes
Shall behold God, and never taste° death's woe.
But let them sleep, Lord, and me mourn a space,
10 For, if above all these, my sins abound,
'Tis late to ask abundance of thy grace,
When we are there;° here on this lowly ground,
B   Teach me how to repent; for that's as good
  As if thou hadst sealed my pardon with thy blood.

1. **imagined corners:** A globe has no corners, though the Bible (Revelation 7.1) mentions the four corners of the earth.

4. **scattered bodies:** scattered because the bodies to be resurrected on the last day will be mainly dust and bones.
6. **dearth:** famine. **agues:** sicknesses.

8. **never taste:** Those who are alive on the last day will not die (I Corinthians 15.51-52).

12. **there:** at the Last Judgment.

Responding to the Poem

Analyzing the Poem

Identifying Details

1. Whom does the speaker address in the **octave** of the sonnet? Whom does he address in the **sestet**?
2. Where does the speaker change his mind in the sonnet? How does Donne use the sonnet form to signal this change of mind?
3. To what event does the speaker refer in the last line? Whom is he addressing here?

Interpreting Meanings

4. Essentially, the poem is a plea for more time. Time for what?
5. Explain how the sound of the poem changes as it moves from its beginning to its end.

1. BUILDING ON PRIOR KNOWLEDGE. Some students who know the Bible might recognize the Biblical echoes in this sonnet, such as the following: "The last enemy that shall be destroyed is death" (1 Corinthians 15:26); ". . . Death is swallowed up in victory. O Death where is thy sting? O grave, where is thy victory?" (1 Corinthians 15:54-55); "And God shall wipe away all tears from their eyes; and there shall be no more death" (Revelation 21:4).

2. ESTABLISHING A PURPOSE. Use the headnote to prepare students to look for the ways in which Donne denigrates or diminishes death.

SUPPLEMENTARY SUPPORT MATERIALS
1. Review and Response Worksheet: Paradox (*CCB*)
2. Selection Test (*CCB*)

CLOSURE
Show how this poem is a Shakespearean sonnet. See text page 338.

ANALYZING THE POEM
Identifying Details
1. Death doesn't kill anyone.
Death serves fate, chance, kings, etc.

Interpreting Meanings
2. Lines 3–4: Death doesn't actually kill anyone. Lines 5–8: Death is like rest and sleep, therefore pleasurable. Lines 9–12: Death is powerless. Lines 13–14: Death will die because there is eternal life.
3. In rest and sleep the body is immobile; in sleep we are not conscious.
4. The paradox is resolved if one assumes that there is eternal life.
5. American journalist John Gunther's moving account (1949) of his son's death.

For those who believe in immortality, death is merely an episode in the progress of the soul, the moment of its delivery from the confines of the body and into eternal life. This belief, which Donne held firmly, permits him to belittle and denigrate death in this sonnet. The sonnet finds a modern echo in a well-known poem by Dylan Thomas, "And Death Shall Have No Dominion."

Death Be Not Proud

Death be not proud, though some have called thee
Mighty and dreadful, for thou art not so,
For those whom thou think'st thou dost overthrow
Die not, poor death, nor yet canst thou kill me;
5 From rest and sleep, which but thy pictures° be,
Much pleasure,° then from thee, much more must flow,
And soonest our best men with thee do go,
Rest of their bones, and soul's delivery.°
Thou art slave to fate, chance, kings, and desperate men,
10 And dost with poison, war, and sickness dwell,
And poppy,° or charms° can make us sleep as well,
And better than thy stroke; why swellest° thou then?
One short sleep past, we wake eternally,
And death shall be no more, Death thou shalt die.

5. **pictures:** A sleeping person can resemble a dead person.
6. **much pleasure:** That is, rest and sleep give much pleasure.
8. **Rest . . . delivery:** Death gives the body rest and delivers the soul from the bondage of the body.

11. **poppy:** opium. **charms:** magic, hypnotism.

12. **swellest:** swell with pride.

Responding to the Poem

Analyzing the Poem

Identifying Details

1. According to the poem, why should death not be proud? Whom must death serve as a slave?

Interpreting Meanings

2. Show how, as the sonnet develops, the speaker shifts the grounds of his attack on death.
3. Explain how rest and sleep are the "pictures" of death (line 5).
4. The sonnet seems to involve a **paradox,** or contradiction: Those who die do not die, but *Death* itself will die. Explain how the paradox can be resolved.
5. What book uses this poem's opening lines as its title? How is the title appropriate to that book?

Writing About the Poem

A Critical Response

Comparing Two Sonnets. In a brief essay, compare the attitude toward death in "At the Round Earth's Imagined Corners" and "Death Be Not Proud." What religious convictions seem to underlie both sonnets?

PREPARATION

1. BUILDING ON PRIOR KNOWLEDGE. See if your students know the Christian concept of the Trinity: the Father, Son, and Holy Spirit (Holy Ghost) all making up one God. See also if they know about Satan seeking to turn people from God.

2. ESTABLISHING A PURPOSE. Ask students to pay close attention to rhythm and sound effects and to think about how the sound reflects the poem's meaning.

SUPPLEMENTARY SUPPORT MATERIALS
1. Vocabulary Activity Worksheet (*CCB*)
2. Review and Response Worksheet: Sound Effects (*CCB*)
3. Selection Test (*CCB*)

DEVELOPING VOCABULARY
The following word from the poem is tested in the Selection Test. (See also Vocabulary Activity Worksheet.)
to usurp

CLOSURE
Ask each student to make a list of common themes in Donne's poems. Then have them discuss their lists and make a class master list. Which themes did everyone mention?

This sonnet, perhaps the most personal-sounding of Donne's sonnets, is an impassioned prayer. The speaker implores God both to destroy him and to remake him. The poem is based on the distinction frequently made in the New Testament between the sinful person and the saved person, and the need of the former, with God's help, to become the latter. Instead of using the Biblical language of being "born again" or "putting off the old man" and "putting on the new man," Donne invents his own metaphors for the complete change which he begs God to make.

Batter My Heart

Batter my heart, three-personed God; for you
As yet but knock, breathe, shine, and seek to mend;
That I may rise and stand, o'erthrow me, and bend
Your force, to break, blow, burn, and make me new.
5 I, like an <u>usurped</u> town, to another due,
Labor to admit you, but oh, to no end,
Reason your viceroy in me, me should defend,
But is captived, and proves weak or untrue;
Yet dearly I love you, and would be loved fain,
10 But am betrothed unto your enemy.
Divorce me, untie, or break that knot again,
Take me to you, imprison me, for I,
Except you enthrall me, never shall be free,
Nor ever chaste, except you ravish me.

Responding to the Poem

Analyzing the Poem

Identifying Details

1. What does the speaker ask God to do to him?
2. Explain the **simile** in line 5. Where else in the poem does the **image** of the siege of a town seem appropriate?

Interpreting Meanings

3. Comment on the poem's use of **alliteration**.
4. How does Donne use **paradox** throughout the sonnet?
5. Why is God "three-personed" in line 1? Who is the "enemy" in line 10?
6. Does this seem like the prayer of a weak person or of a strong person, in your view? Explain your answer.

Writing About the Poem

A Critical Response

Analyzing Rhythm and Sound Effects. In a brief essay, analyze Donne's use of **rhythm** and **sound effects** in this sonnet.

ANALYZING THE POEM
Identifying Details
1. To make him new, to imprison him, to ravish him.
2. The speaker's heart is like a conquered town.
   In lines 7–8, where reason is "captivated."

Interpreting Meanings
3. See examples in lines 4, 7, 9. (In line 4 the repeated "b" sounds suggest hammering.)
4. Line 3: God should overthrow him so he can rise and stand. Line 4: God should break him, etc., to make him new. Lines 9–10: He loves God but is betrothed to God's enemy. Lines 13–14: God must imprison him to make him free and ravish him to make him chaste.
5. God is the Holy Trinity.
   Satan.
6. Most students will agree that the imagery makes these the words of a strong person. Others may feel that only a strong person would have the courage to admit to moral weaknesses.

A. Expansion

Jonson's first play, *Every Man in His Humour* (each character in the comedy had one overriding *humour*, or character trait), was performed in 1598 with Will Shakespeare in the cast. It led to several similar plays and a "war of the theatres" in which Jonson and two other playwrights caricatured one another. Jonson abandoned the war when he began writing masques. He wrote twenty-one of the thirty-three masques performed at court between 1605 and 1640. King James's wife, Anne of Denmark, not only encouraged masques, but often took part as chief dancer. The masque began to disappear in the 1640's as political turmoil grew. Toward the end of his career, Jonson wrote his best comedies, including *Volpone, or The Fox* (1606) and *The Alchemist* (1610).

Ben Jonson (1572–1637)

Although Jonson was christened Benjamin, he was, and is, always known as Ben. He was born in the same year as his friend John Donne, and if his friend William Shakespeare had never existed, he would probably be regarded as the chief dramatist of the age.

Ben was a posthumous son; that is, his father died before he was born. His stepfather, a bricklayer, intended to make him into a bricklayer too, but while still a boy, he became acquainted with William Camden, an eminent scholar and headmaster of the Westminster School, one of the best in the kingdom. Camden enrolled young Ben in his school and educated him at his own expense. When he grew up, Jonson addressed a poem to Camden, beginning:

> Camden, most reverend head, to whom I owe
> All that I am in arts, all that I know.

Jonson, his contemporaries all agreed, knew a great deal, despite never having attended university. He had an immense knowledge of Latin literature and a somewhat smaller acquaintance with Greek. But he was no mere pedant or bookish recluse. After leaving Westminster School, he joined the English army and fought against the Spanish in the Low Countries. There, while the two massed armies watched, he engaged in single combat with the Spanish champion and killed him. Back in England, he became a playwright and an actor, specializing in loud and roaring parts. He had two brushes with the law: once when he killed a fellow actor in a duel and escaped hanging by demonstrating that he could read, and once when he went to prison for making derogatory remarks about Scotland in a play. In short, Jonson was very much a part of the tough, violent life of the time. We think of him as a complete Londoner, like a later writer with the same surname (but differently spelled), Samuel Johnson. Samuel held forth in the Miter Tavern in the eighteenth century, and more than a hundred years before, Ben held forth at the Mermaid, where his witty combats with Shakespeare and others are mentioned in contemporary writings.

Ben Jonson after Abraham van Blyenberch. Oil.

Gradually, Jonson became well known as a dramatist. He was particularly good at devising masques for the court of King James. Masques were elaborate, expensively mounted productions combining the efforts of poets, musicians, professional and amateur actors and dancers, scene designers, choreographers, and even engineers and architects. Jonson provided the words, which he naturally regarded as the most important part of a masque. This opinion involved him in many conflicts with his collaborators, especially with Inigo Jones, an eminent designer. In addition to his masques, Jonson wrote tragedies and comedies for the public theaters.

A

Jonson's attitude toward his writing was different from Donne's and Shakespeare's; Jonson was more like today's writers, who are, for the most part, very eager to publish. In 1616 Jonson assembled a number of his plays and poems and published them, to the astonishment of the reading public, under the title *Works*. Up to that time, this was a label reserved for more intellectual subjects, such as theology and history. Numerous people scoffed at Jonson, among them one who asked,

Pray tell me, Ben, where does the mystery
lurk?
What others call a play, you call a work.

This was probably the reaction Jonson wanted,
because he was making the point that poems and
plays *are* serious works of art, as serious in their
own way as history and theology, and as worthy
of high regard. Jonson wanted to be a professional writer, a man who lived by his pen, not a
gentleperson who wrote on the side for other
gentlepersons. He depended on patrons for his
livelihood, members of the gentry and nobility to
whom he dedicated his writings and from whom
he received gifts. In 1616 no less a person than
King James became patron, for in that year Jonson was named Poet Laureate.

At the height of his career, Jonson was a sort
of literary dictator in London—opinionated and
crusty but admired by a number of younger writers. These younger writers became known as the
"Tribe of Ben" or the "Sons of Ben." They
stood by Jonson in his old age, when he was
sick, poor, and neglected because his blunt and
forthright manner had made him many enemies.
The "Sons of Ben" also put together a second
large folio volume of his *Works* (1640). Meantime, Jonson had been buried near Chaucer in
Westminster Abbey, in what later became known
as the "Poet's Corner." His inscription required
only four words: "O Rare Ben Jonson."

**A. Humanities
Connection:
Responding to
the Engraving**
The scene depic-
ted conveys the
camaraderie of so-
cial gatherings like
those of Ben Jon-
son and his friends
at the Mermaid
and of Samuel
Johnson and com-
pany at the Miter.
The Mermaid, on
Bread Street in
Cheapside, was
the meeting place
for the literary and
the clever men of
the day. These in-
cluded Sir Walter
Raleigh (text page
194), Francis
Beaumont and
John Fletcher (text
page 183), and
possibly Shake-
speare. In his
"Lines to Ben Jon-
son," Beaumont
praised the nimble
wit of the company
at the Mermaid.

At the "Devil" Tavern (1876). Engraving.

A

SUPPLEMENTARY SUPPORT MATERIALS
1. Vocabulary Activity Worksheet (*CCB*)
2. Review and Response Worksheet: Epigrams (*CCB*)
3. Selection Test (*CCB*)

DEVELOPING VOCABULARY
The following word from the epigram is tested in the Selection Test. (See also Vocabulary Activity Worksheet.)
strike

A. Meaning
Jonson dismisses the person as a fool or knave. His praise does not "stroke" Jonson; his criticism doesn't strike.

B. Meaning
The speaker claims that King James is superior to Martial's emperor because James cannot be moved by flattery (or because he is so superior that statements intended to flatter really state the truth). By saying James cannot be flattered, Jonson is flattering him.

C. James I
The son of Mary Queen of Scots, James Stuart (1566–1625) ruled Scotland for twenty years before he succeeded Queen Elizabeth in 1603. His awkwardness, pedantry, and Scottish accent were against him from the start; and his insistence on the divine right of kings and attempts to make peace with Spain created great resentment. He was called "the Wisest Fool in Christendom" because of his literary ambitions.

This is one of Jonson's many epigrams, which he called "the ripest of his studies" and which he included among his published *Works*. Some of the epigrams pay elaborate compliments to Jonson's friends in all walks of life; others are satirical, like his stage comedies, making fun of foolish or knavish (dishonest or deceitful) behavior. Though never stuffy or preachy, Jonson is most of the time a hard-core moralist; he knows exactly what sort of conduct he approves of and what sort of conduct he disapproves of. What does Jonson think of the person he is addressing in this biting epigram? **A**

To Fool or Knave

Thy praise or dispraise is to me alike:
One doth not stroke me, nor the other <u>strike</u>.

Like many other Renaissance writers, Jonson drew inspiration from the works of ancient Latin and Greek writers and used them as models for his own poems. For his epigrams, he was particularly indebted to the Roman poet Martial (40?– 104?), who wrote an enormous number of little poems, some of them nasty. Martial lived during the reign of the Emperor Domitian (81–96). How does this epigram actually flatter King James? **B**

C

To the Ghost of Martial

Martial, thou gavest far nobler epigrams
To thy Domitian than I can my James.
But in my royal subject I pass thee:
Thou flattered'st thine, mine cannot flattered be.

James I (detail) by
John de Critz
(1623). Oil.

Hatfield House.

ESTABLISHING A PURPOSE. Ask students to see how the bereaved father copes with the loss of his only son.

SUPPLEMENTARY SUPPORT MATERIALS
1. Vocabulary Activity Worksheet (CCB)
2. Review and Response Worksheet: Theme (CCB)
3. Selection Test (CCB)

DEVELOPING VOCABULARY
The following word from the poem is tested in the Selection Test. (See also Vocabulary Activity Worksheet.)
lament

We know very little about the woman Jonson married when he was 22; he once described her, with characteristic candor, as "a shrew, yet honest"—that is, bossy, yet faithful to her marriage vows. The Jonsons apparently had only two children, a son, Benjamin, who died of the plague on his seventh birthday and a daughter, Mary, who died in infancy. Among Jonson's epigrams is this little poem on Benjamin, whose name in Hebrew means "a child of the right hand" (line 1) and, ironically, connotes "a lucky, clever child."

On My First Son

Farewell, thou child of my right hand, and joy;
A My sin was too much hope of thee, loved boy:
Seven years thou wert lent to me, and I thee pay,°
Exacted° by thy fate, on the just° day.
5 O could I lose all father° now! for why
B Will man lament the state he should envy,
To have so soon 'scaped world's and flesh's rage,
And, if no other misery, yet age?
Rest in soft peace, and asked, say, "Here doth lie
10 Ben Jonson his best piece of poetry."
For whose sake henceforth all his vows be such
As what he loves may never like too much.

3. **thee pay:** pay thee back.
4. **Exacted:** forced. **just:** exact. Loans were often made for exactly seven years.
5. **father:** sense of fatherhood, need to mourn like a father.

A. Interpreting
⁇ Why do you suppose he calls this a sin? (Because he lost sight of the fragility of life; his dashed hopes are now a source of acute pain)

B. Interpreting
⁇ What state is Jonson referring to here? (Death)

ANALYZING THE POEM
Identifying Details
1. Jonson comforts himself with the thought that his son has escaped the troubles of the world and illness and old age.
   No.

Interpreting Meanings
2. Because the name Benjamin connotes good fortune.
3. Many students will agree that a child is more beautifully crafted and meaningful than a poem, which a child resembles in a figurative sense.

Responding to the Poem

Analyzing the Poem

Identifying Details

1. What comfort does Jonson provide himself in lines 7–8? Is this comfort sufficient to make him "lose all father"?

Interpreting Meanings

2. Why can the early death of a boy named *Benjamin* be regarded as **ironic**?
3. Jonson borrowed some of the poem's features from Latin works: the direct address to the dead boy in line 9 and the first three words of the **epitaph**, or inscription, "Here doth lie. . . . " But the idea that the son is his best poem is original with Jonson. What do you think of this statement?

Writing About the Poem

A Critical Response

Responding to a Theme. In the last line Jonson resolves never again to love what he cannot bear to lose. Is this a sound resolution? What kind of person would he become if he did this? Write a paragraph answering this question. Consider also the opinion of a later English poet, Alfred, Lord Tennyson, who wrote, " 'Tis better to have loved and lost than never to have loved at all."

SUPPLEMENTARY SUPPORT MATERIALS
1. Review and Response Worksheet:
Figurative Language (*CCB*)
2. Selection Test (*CCB*)

A. Metaphor
? What is "The thirst that from the soul doth rise"? (The longing for love)

B. Interpreting
? What is a rosy wreath? (A little circlet, adorned with roses) Note that "I sent thee late" means "I sent thee recently."

ANALYZING THE POEM
Interpreting Meanings
1. Traditionally, the meeting of lovers' eyes can convey a world of meaning: Here they pledge their faithfulness.
2. "Thine" refers to the lady's "nectar," or, by extension, to her love.
3. The speaker sent the wreath in the hope that it would never wither.
   Celia has the magical power to keep the wreath forever fresh.
4. Celia breathed on the wreath, and now it exudes her fragrance.

Jonson once said that he always wrote out his poems in prose before turning them into verse, just as his master Camden had taught him to. At times, it must be admitted, the prose that he versified was not his own but someone else's. This poem, for instance, Jonson made out of five different passages that he found in an obscure old book, the *Epistles* of Philostratus, a Greek philosopher of the third century A.D. Throughout his life, Jonson's enemies taunted him for once being a bricklayer. In a sense, he remained a bricklayer all his creative life, a builder whose tiniest construction, like this poem, is solid and seamless.

Jonson's songs are not as numerous as Shakespeare's, nor have they attracted as many composers. But this one has a very famous tune that many people still know.

Song: To Celia

Drink to me only with thine eyes,
And I will pledge with mine;
Or leave a kiss but in the cup,
And I'll not look for wine.
A
5 The thirst that from the soul doth rise,
Doth ask a drink divine:
But might I of Jove's nectar° sup,
I would not change° for thine.

B I sent thee late a rosy wreath,
10 Not so much honoring thee,
As giving it a hope, that there
It could not withered be.
But thou thereon did'st only breathe,
And sent'st it back to me;
15 Since when it grows and smells, I swear,
Not of itself, but thee.

7. **Jove's nectar:** ambrosia, the drink of the gods that kept them immortal.
8. **change:** exchange.

Responding to the Poem

Analyzing the Poem

Interpreting Meanings

1. Explain how a woman might drink to a man with her eyes and how the man could "pledge" himself to her with his eyes in return.
2. What does "thine" refer to in line 8?
3. Why did the speaker send the wreath? What powers does he attribute to Celia?
4. How did Celia transform the wreath?

Box embroidered with scenes representing the five senses (1650–75).

The Metropolitan Museum of Art, New York. Rogers Fund, 1929. (29.231.1).

PREPARATION
1. BUILDING ON PRIOR KNOWLEDGE. Ask students if men today have preferences in women's clothing.

2. ESTABLISHING A PURPOSE. Ask students to discover what "look" the poet prefers and to compare their own preferences with his.

SUPPLEMENTARY SUPPORT MATERIALS
1. Vocabulary Activity Worksheet (CCB)
2. Review and Response Worksheet: Figurative Language (CCB)
3. Selection Test (CCB)

DEVELOPING VOCABULARY
The following words from the poem are tested in the Selection Test. (See also Vocabulary Activity Worksheet.)
sound   adulteries
grace

One of the characters in Jonson's comedy *The Silent Woman* sings this song, which expresses Jonson's firm opinions about women's appearances. Although he lived in an age that strove for an artificial effect in both men's and women's dress, he admired the opposite—a natural appearance—and he regarded cosmetics as a form of hypocrisy. Robert Herrick, one of Ben's "sons," imitated this poem in "A Sweet Disorder in the Dress."

Song: Still to Be Neat

Still° to be neat, still to be dressed
As you were going to a feast,
Still to be powdered, still perfumed,
Lady, it is to be presumed,
5 Though art's hid causes are not found,
A All is not sweet, all is not <u>sound</u>.

Give me a look, give me a face
That makes simplicity a <u>grace</u>:
Robes loosely flowing, hair as free,
10 Such sweet neglect more taketh me
Than all the <u>adulteries</u> of art.
They strike mine eyes, but not my heart.

1. **still:** always.

CLOSURE
Based on the poems they have read, ask students to identify three of Jonson's themes or subjects that are still "current" today.

A. Inference
Since makeup and costume conceal what is underneath, their users must have something to hide.

ANALYZING THE POEM
Identifying Details
1. She is hiding something not sweet and not sound.
2. A simple face, loose robes, hair free.

Interpreting Meanings
3. Elaborate dresses, powder, and perfume.
4. "Adulteries" (deceptions) of art.
5. See lines 5–6.
6. Adultery suggests infidelity in marriage.

Responding to the Poem

Analyzing the Poem

Identifying Details

1. What does the speaker presume about a woman who is always neat and dressed up?
2. What kind of "look" does the speaker prefer?

Interpreting Meanings

3. What is the "art" in line 11?
4. What does "they" refer to in line 12?
5. How does Jonson show he may have known the old proverb, "He who always smells good doesn't smell good"?

6. What **connotations** of the word *adulteries* do you think Jonson might have expected his readers to recognize?

Writing About the Poem

A Creative Response

Responding to the Main Idea. Write a letter to Jonson telling him how you feel about his advice. Do you think a woman might have a different opinion? Might she have some advice for *men*?

A. **Expansion**
Herrick is a happy
poet. While some
of his poems deal
with the inevitabili-
ty of age and
death (e.g., "To
the Virgins," "Co-
rinna's Going A-
Maying," and "To
Daffodils"), he
treats the theme
gently, inviting one
to enjoy life's fleet-
ing beauty. His
love poems do not
suggest the tragic
possibilities of a
grand passion, and
his religious poems
are honest and
touching but not
cries from the
depths.

Robert Herrick
(1591–1674)

In many ways, Robert Herrick's life parallels the life of George Herbert. Almost the same age, both poets were brought up by widowed mothers, both graduated from Cambridge University, both became clergymen, and both produced a single volume of poems. But they were born into different ranks of society—Herrick into the prosperous merchant class, Herbert into the aristocracy—and the temper of their lives and of their poems is quite different.

We first hear of Herrick as an apprentice to his uncle, a London goldsmith and jeweler; it is pleasant to think that the future poet may have acquired his taste for small, beautiful things in his uncle's workshop. Herrick apparently lacked ambition and drive, since he did not enter the university until he was 22, a very late age in those days, and he did not leave it until he was 29. For the next few years, so far as we know, he had no regular occupation, but enjoyed himself in London as a member of Ben Jonson's circle of young friends. At some point, he was ordained a priest, but the serious part of Herrick's life did not begin until he was 38. He was then called to a parish in Dean Prior, in Devonshire, far from London, in the "West Country," which Londoners habitually regarded as wretched and barbaric. According to some of Herrick's poems, this was an intolerable exile; according to others, it was heaven on earth. At any rate, Herrick's stay in Dean Prior came abruptly to an end in 1647 with the arrival of the Parliamentary Army, which deprived him of his parish and substituted in his place a clergyman of a more puritanical stripe. (It would not be easy to find a less puritanical priest than Herrick.) When the King was restored some thirteen years later, so was Herrick, and he lived on at Dean Prior until he died at the age of 83.

While deprived of his parish and living in London, Herrick published a fat little book containing 1399 poems, with the title *Hesperides, or the Works Both Human and Divine of Robert Herrick, Esq.* (1648). Less than a fourth of the poems fit into the "divine" category, and these are mainly witty verses on biblical characters

and events; all the rest of the poems are definitely "human." The word *Hesperides* in the title is borrowed from classical mythology; it is the collective name for the sisters who live in a garden somewhere in the West, where they watch over a tree that bears golden apples. The title implies that Herrick's book is a garden full of precious things.

Herrick borrowed more than his title from classical antiquity. He was so steeped in Latin poetry that he frequently wrote his poems as if he were an ancient Roman, imposing pagan customs, creeds, and rituals on the English country people and his own household. He imitated the Latin love poets, especially Catullus, when he addressed poems to beautiful women with such classical names as Julia, Corinna, Perilla, Anthea, and Electra. But regardless of how erotic he sounds, Herrick knew only imaginary ladies; never a breath of scandal touched his own bachelor life.

Her Bed
See'st thou that cloud as silver clear,
Plump, soft, and swelling everywhere?
'Tis Julia's bed, and she sleeps there.

A poem like this is immediately recognizable as a pretty fantasy, an imaginative way of saying "Julia is a goddess." But not all Herrick's poems are pretty, for he was also drawn to the crude and grotesque elements in Latin poetry.

Upon Blanch
Blanch swears her husband's lovely; when a scald
Has bleared his eyes; besides, his head is bald.
Next, his wild ears, like leathern wings full spread,
Flutter to fly and bear away his head.

Herrick writes about his small house, his small spaniel named Tracy, his cat, his small maid Prudence Baldwin, the royal family in far-off London, the work and play of country people—whatever came into his mind. Except for

dividing his poems into the categories of "divine" and "human," he never bothered to arrange them in any order at all, so that his book is a jumble full of surprises. If some poems seem to be trifles, they are trifles on which their author has lavished much care.

His Desire
Give me a man that is not dull,
When all the world with rifts[1] is full,

But unamazed dares clearly sing
When as the roof's a tottering;

And, though it falls, continues still
Tickling the cittern[2] with his quill.

Altogether, Herrick's poems give us a picture of "Merrie England," which is not so much the England of any particular time or place but an ideal, pastoral state where sadness is momentary and pleasure innocent.

A

---

1. **rifts:** faults.
2. **cittern:** guitar.

Village Celebration by Jan Brueghel the Elder
(16th century). Oil.

Sabauda Gallery, Turin, Italy.

A. Expansion
It is said that Herrick never wrote an ugly line. His lyrics are perfect miniatures of the world he says he will describe in the opening poem of *Hesperides:* "I sing of brooks, blossoms, birds, and bowers . . . / I sing of May-poles, hock-carts, wassails, wakes . . . ."

B. Humanities Connection: Discussing the Fine Art
Another painting by the Flemish painter Jan Brueghel the Elder (1568–1625) is on text page 217. Ask students to relate the tone of the painting to what the text biography says about Herrick's life and poetry.

❓ What do you see happening in the scene? (Note the fish being cleaned in the foreground and the dancing couples.) Is there a modern counterpart to this kind of gathering? (A county fair, a street fair, a July Fourth celebration, etc.)

B

Remind students of Jonson's "Still to Be Neat." This is another poem in which a man delivers opinions on how a woman should dress.

2. ESTABLISHING A PURPOSE. Ask students to read to discover how Herrick's views compare with Jonson's.

SUPPLEMENTARY SUPPORT MATERIALS
1. Vocabulary Activity Worksheet (*CCB*)
2. Review and Response Worksheet: Oxymoron (*CCB*)
3. Selection Test (*CCB*)

DEVELOPING VOCABULARY
The following words from the poem are tested in the Selection Test. (See also Vocabulary Activity Worksheet.)
to kindle   tempestuous
to enthrall

A. Word Choice
Find words throughout the poem that suggest the opposite of order. (*Disorder, wantonness, distraction, erring, neglectful, confusedly, tempestuous, careless, wild*) Note that *wantonness* can also mean something like "sexiness."

B. Half Rhyme
? Find examples of half rhymes (also called near-rhymes or approximate rhymes). (*Dress, wantonness; thrown, distraction; there, stomacher; thereby, confusedly, tie, civility*)

This poem protests—if that is not too strong a word—against the way most ladies dressed themselves in Herrick's day. Women with sufficient means spent vast sums on elaborately formal clothing, which made them look stiff and unapproachable, like idols. Men, of course, were just as richly and rigidly fitted out as women, but Herrick doesn't care what they look like. He is interested only in describing the kind of female dress that he finds attractive. It is tempting to derive Herrick's general attitude toward life from his ideas about dress. He would have known the negative connotation of *precise* (line 14); this adjective suggested too great a fuss over unimportant questions of conduct. Puritans were sometimes called Precisians.

Delight in Disorder

A   A sweet disorder in the dress
    Kindles in clothes a wantonness.
B   A lawn° about the shoulders thrown
    Into a fine distraction,
5   An erring° lace, which here and there
    Enthralls the crimson stomacher,°
    A cuff neglectful, and thereby
    Ribbons to flow confusedly,
    A winning wave, deserving note,
10 In the tempestuous petticoat,
    A careless shoestring, in whose tie
    I see a wild civility,
    Do more bewitch me than when art
    Is too precise in every part.

3. **lawn:** fine linen scarf.

5. **erring:** wandering.
6. **stomacher:** the lower part of a tightly laced garment worn around the middle of the body, to accentuate the waist.

Responding to the Poem

Analzying the Poem

Identifying Details

1. What is the effect of a slightly disordered dress?

Interpreting Meanings

2. This poem makes use of a figure of speech called **oxymoron.** This is a group—usually a pair—of words that seem contradictory; *cruel kindness* is often given as an example. Find the oxymoron in "Delight in Disorder." How does it sum up the poem's **message**?

Writing About the Poem

A Creative Response

1. **Writing a Parody.** Every work of literature can be parodied—or made fun of. (Some people say no subject is too solemn for laughter.) Write a parody of this poem or of Jonson's, in which you parody the message. You might use a young woman of today as your speaker. In your parody, be sure to use some of Herrick's or Jonson's words.

A Critical Response

2. **Comparing Poems.** As one of Ben Jonson's most successful "sons," Herrick certainly knew his mentor's song "Still to Be Neat." The resemblance between Jonson's poem and Herrick's "Delight in Disorder" has often been noticed. Write an essay in which you compare the two, emphasizing the differences rather than the similarities. Consider **message, imagery,** and **tone.**

ANALYZING THE POEM
Identifying Details
1. It bewitches the speaker.

Interpreting Meanings
2. Line 12: "wild civility."

The figure of speech sums up the total effect of the opposites the speaker mentions: disorder and delight; carelessness and precision; nature and art.

A. Humanities Connection: Discussing the Art

This is a detail from the little box shown on text page 378. Embroidery experts might notice that this is an example of crewel work, in which twisted wool yarn is used on linen.

? Which of the five senses is suggested in this scene? (Hearing) What effect does the music seem to have on the animals? (Lion, leopard, stag all seem peaceful as the lute is played.)

A

Detail (flute player) of box embroidered with scenes representing the five senses (1650–75).

The Metropolitan Museum of Art, New York. Rogers Fund. (29.23.1).

1. BUILDING ON PRIOR KNOWLEDGE. Recall with students all the love poems they've read in which an ardent lover importunes a reluctant lady. Ask students if love songs popular today still express this urgency to "seize the day" and make the most of youth and beauty.

2. ESTABLISHING A PURPOSE. After students have read the first line of the poem, ask them to predict what they think will be the overall advice given in the poem.

SUPPLEMENTARY SUPPORT MATERIALS
1. Vocabulary Activity Worksheet (*CCB*)
2. Review and Response Worksheet: Symbols (*CCB*)
3. Selection Test (*CCB*)

A. Humanities Connection: Discussing the Fine Art

Lucas van Valkenborch (1540–1597) was a Netherlandish painter, the most prominent member of a family of genre and landscape painters. *Spring* is typical of the northern European paintings of the sixteenth century, with its rich colors, its meticulous details (especially its rendering of the subject's hair and dress), and its voluptuousness of texture.

? What is this woman doing and thinking? (She appears to be making potpourri; note the shorn flower stems at her feet and the little bowl on her lap filling up with petals. As for thoughts, she does seem to be thinking of love, as would be appropriate in the season of spring). Notice the unusual touch provided by the formal bouquet of flowers in an ornamental urn in this outdoor scene. Ask students what images this same painter might choose to depict winter, summer, and autumn.

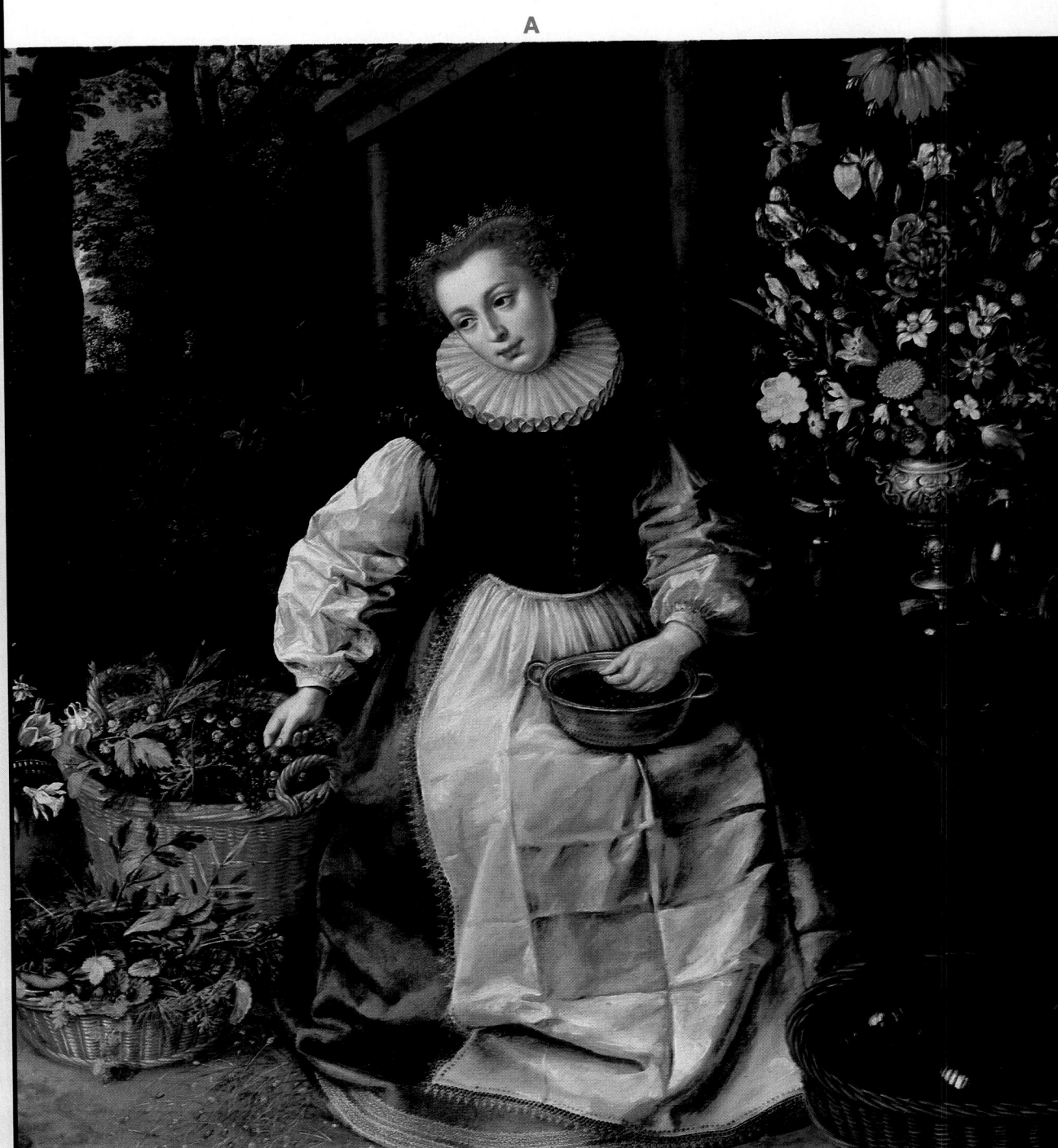

A

Spring (detail) by Lucas van Valkenborch (1595). Oil.

ANALYZING THE POEM
Identifying Details
1. The flower that blooms today will die tomorrow.
2. The higher the sun mounts in the sky, the nearer it is to setting.
3. The best age is the first, when youth and blood are warm.
4. The virgins should marry and not be coy (aloof). When they are old it may be too late for them to marry.

Interpreting Meanings
5. Perhaps line 14, "go marry," reflects the poet's profession as a clergyman.
6. Answers will vary. Encourage them to discuss the *carpe diem* theme.

A. Allusion
In Greek mythology, the sun god Helios (often confused with Apollo) drove a fiery chariot across the heavens each day. It was pulled by his four horses, Fiery, Flaming, Orient, and Blazing.

B. Theme
What does the speaker expect from life after youth is over? (He expects everything to get worse.) Do you agree or disagree? Explain why.

The first line of this little lyric, Herrick's most popular poem, has been a metaphorical part of our language ever since, in the nineteenth century, Herrick was "discovered" by people interested in Renaissance literature. "To the Virgins" is related thematically to a large number of poems by many poets in which a male speaker addresses a particular woman and urges her to love him. Instead of courting one woman, Herrick addresses all "virgins," or young women.

To the Virgins, to Make Much of Time

Gather ye rosebuds while ye may,
    Old time is still a-flying;
And this same flower that smiles today
    Tomorrow will be dying.

5   The glorious lamp of heaven, the sun,
A   The higher he's a-getting,
    The sooner will his race be run,
      And nearer he's to setting.

    That age is best which is the first,
10   When youth and blood are warmer;
B   But being spent, the worse, and worst
     Times still° succeed the former.

    Then be not coy,° but use your time,
     And, while ye may, go marry;
15   For having lost but once your prime,
     You may forever tarry.

12. **still:** always.

13. **coy:** cold, inaccessible, aloof.

Responding to the Poem

Analyzing the Poem

Identifying Details

1. What warning does the speaker give the virgins in the first stanza?
2. What solar **image** does he use to enforce his point in the second stanza?
3. How does the speaker feel about age in the third stanza?
4. What warning does he sign off with?

Interpreting Meanings

5. Which line of the poem seems to reflect Herrick's profession as a priest?
6. How would you respond to Herrick's urgent advice?

Writing About the Poem

A Creative Response

1. **Extending the Poem.** In a paragraph, describe the situation that you imagine gave rise to this poem.
2. **Answering the Poet.** Write an answer to the poet, in prose or poetry, and let your speaker be an older woman.

FOR FURTHER READING
Edward Rutherford's *Sarum: The Novel of England* (1987) is a panoramic account of the Salisbury area in southwest England, from the Ice Age to the twentieth century. Rutherford covers old Sarum (a Roman outpost), the Salisbury plain and Stonehenge, and the cathedral town of Salisbury itself. In later chapters, the Herbert family is discussed several times. For teachers or students, the book is especially good at conveying the religious conflicts of the sixteenth and seventeenth centuries and the history and importance of English class distinctions, such as the aristocratic allegiances that aroused conflict within Herbert.

A. Expansion
Herbert was highly esteemed as a model of what a priest should be, despite one of his frequent themes—the conflict he felt between living up to his priestly calling and pride in his ancestry and achievements.

B. Expansion
Herbert's poems show a trusting, intimate friendliness with God. He draws his symbols and images from church ritual, farming, the trades, science, and (as Herrick did) from everyday household pursuits. He is also known for his metrical inventiveness and "pattern poems," such as the well-known "Easter Wings" (1633) and "The Altar" (text page 388).

George Herbert (1593–1633)

George Herbert was an Anglican priest, and all his poems have religious subjects. He was born into a high-spirited and illustrious Welsh family, the sort of people who expect their sons to become political or military leaders. In his youth, Herbert apparently accepted his family's worldly values. He attended Westminster School and then took two degrees, with distinction, at Cambridge University. After graduation, he stayed on at the university as Public Orator, an official who had to make elaborate speeches in Latin whenever an important personage, like the King, came to visit. This was a promising position from which Herbert might readily have moved into public life and national prominence. But after ten years as Orator, Herbert turned away from his worldly career, married for love rather than for material advantage, and in 1630 was ordained a priest in the national church.

A For the remaining three years of his life, he was in charge of a small church and parish in Bemerton, a village near the cathedral city of Salisbury. There he became an exemplary country pastor, ministering to his flock, writing his poems, and walking regularly to Salisbury, where, according to Izaak Walton, he went to "sing and play his part at an appointed private music meeting." "Holy Mr. Herbert," Walton calls him. In his final illness, Herbert trusted a manuscript of his poems to a friend, who had them published after the poet's death under the title *The Temple* (1633).

Many literary historians have linked George Herbert with John Donne, and indeed there are several connections between the two poets. Herbert's mother, a pious and learned lady named Magdalen, was a great friend of Donne; Donne addressed letters and poems to her and preached an eloquent sermon at her funeral. Another bond between the two poets is Izaak Walton, who wrote the first biographies of both men, presenting them as inspirational models. Finally, there are enough resemblances between the works of the two writers to justify calling them both "metaphysical" poets. This means that both use **conceits**—ingenious and often daring metaphors that join together widely different ideas and images. Both poets also imitate spoken English in their poems. But there are also important differences. Herbert is much quieter, more assured, and less violent than Donne. If a poem by Herbert registers an emotional disturbance, it is a small one, and calm is soon restored. Instead of arguing and showing off his knowledge of many things, Herbert humbly accepts the teaching of his religion. Those who do not share Herbert's beliefs still find much to admire in his poems, especially their neat, tidy workmanship. **B**

PREPARATION

1. BUILDING ON PRIOR KNOWLEDGE. Discuss briefly with students their definition of *virtue*.

2. ESTABLISHING A PURPOSE. Ask students to look for the answer to the question: How can virtue conquer time?

SUPPLEMENTARY SUPPORT MATERIALS
1. Vocabulary Activity Worksheet (*CCB*)
2. Review and Response Worksheet: Theme (*CCB*)
3. Selection Test (*CCB*)

DEVELOPING VOCABULARY
The following words from the poem are tested in the Selection Test. (See also Vocabulary Activity Worksheet.)
rash   gives
compact

This poem is a good example of Herbert's simplicity, the kind of simplicity that only a great artist can attain. Like hundreds of other lyric poems in English, it is about the passing of time and the inevitable end that awaits all lovely and admirable things—except one. Even a rose (stanza 2), whose brave, defiant color suggests that it is defying time, will soon wither.

Virtue

Sweet day, so cool, so calm, so bright,
The bridal of the earth and sky:
The dew shall weep thy fall tonight,
    For thou must die.

5 Sweet rose, whose hue, angry and brave,
Bids the rash gazer wipe his eye:
Thy root is ever in its grave,
    And thou must die.

Sweet spring, full of sweet days and roses,
10 A box where sweets° compacted lie;
My music shows ye have your closes,°
    And all must die.

A Only a sweet and virtuous soul,
Like seasoned timber, never gives;
15 But though the whole world turn to coal,°
    Then chiefly lives.

10. **sweets:** sweet smells.
11. **closes:** closing sounds.

15. **turn to coal:** that is, burn up at the Last Judgment.

A. Simile
? How is a virtuous soul like seasoned timber? (Seasoned wood does not rot or dry out; neither does a virtuous soul "give" or yield to sin.)

ANALYZING THE POEM
Identifying Details
1. The day, the rose, the spring, all die.
2. The sweet and virtuous soul will live forever.

Interpreting Meanings
3. It reinforces the theme: that virtue is of primary importance because it outlives physical beauty.
4. Possible answer: A virtuous soul endures for eternity, even after the Day of Judgment when the world will be burned.
5. The last line stresses life (not death, as in the other stanzas).
6. Herbert's poem recommends the exact opposite: Virtue is superior to the passing pleasures of the senses.

Responding to the Poem

Analyzing the Poem

Identifying Details

1. What examples does the speaker give to prove his statement that "all must die"?
2. According to the last stanza, what kind of soul will live forever?

Interpreting Meanings

3. What does the **title** add to the message of the poem?
4. How would you **paraphrase** the last stanza?
5. What is the effect of the twist in the last line of the last stanza? How is it different from the final lines of the other stanzas?

6. Many poems on the passage of time end with the advice, "Let us eat, drink, and be merry, for tomorrow we die"—or words to that effect. How does Herbert's poem differ from these others?

Analyzing Language and Style

Figures of Speech

How many figures of speech can you list from this brief poem? Consider examples of the following:

1. Metaphors
2. Metaphors that are personifications
3. Similes

PREPARATION

1. BUILDING ON PRIOR KNOWLEDGE. After students have read the headnote, make sure they recognize that the poem has the shape of an altar. Discuss the uses of an *altar* today and in the past.

2. ESTABLISHING A PURPOSE. Ask students to be alert for the ways in which the poem answers question 3.

SUPPLEMENTARY SUPPORT MATERIALS
1. Vocabulary Activity Worksheet (*CCB*)
2. Review and Response Worksheet: Shaped Verse (*CCB*)
3. Selection Test (*CCB*)

DEVELOPING VOCABULARY
The following word from the poem is tested in the Selection Test. (See also Vocabulary Activity Worksheet.)
frame

A. Imagery
? Why is the altar "broken"? (Perhaps because the builder is imperfect)

ANALYZING THE POEM
Identifying Details
1. A heart cemented by tears.
2. The power of the Lord.
3. To praise the Lord's name.

Interpreting Meanings
4. Students may note immediately the shape on the page of the poem. Line 2 further indicates the speaker may not be describing an altar used in religious worship.
   The words of the poem.
5. Natural stones might represent the purity and integrity of God; they are in the shape God put them in, not in the shape man has imposed on them.
6. His hard heart is, paradoxically, the material with which he builds his altar. The word *broken* in line 1 and the mention of tears might signify that this stony heart was broken to make building blocks for the altar praising God.

This is an example of a "picture poem," sometimes called "shaped verse" or, in its French version, a *calligramme*. In a picture poem, typography is so distributed as to shape a pyramid, a wing, an hour-glass, or whatever provides a relevant visual extension of the poem's subject. Poems in the shape of objects have been composed by ancient Greeks as well as by twentieth-century poets like Guillaume Apollinaire and Dylan Thomas.

"The Altar" is also an example of a devotional poem—one in which the speaker praises God and, in the same breath, confesses his unworthiness to do so.

The Altar

A   A broken altar, Lord, Thy servant rears,
     Made of a heart and cémented with tears;
       Whose parts are as Thy hand did <u>frame</u>;
       No workman's tool° hath touched the same.
5   A   heart   alone
           Is   such   a   stone
           As   nothing   but
           Thy power doth cut.
           Wherefore each part
10   Of my hard heart
           Meets in this frame
           To praise Thy name;
     That if I chance to hold my peace,
     These stones to praise Thee may not cease.
15   Oh, let Thy blessed sacrifice be mine,
     And sanctify this altar to be Thine.

4. **workman's tool:** God said to Moses (Exodus 20:25) that He wanted His altars of earth: "And if thou wilt make me an altar of stone, thou shalt not build it of hewn stone: for if thou lift up thy tool upon it, thou hast polluted it."

Responding to the Poem

Analyzing the Poem

Identifying Details
1. What is the speaker's altar made of?
2. According to the speaker, what alone can "cut" a stony heart?
3. What is the purpose of the altar the speaker is building?

Interpreting Meanings
4. When does it become apparent to you that the altar is the *poem*? What does the speaker mean, **metaphorically**, by the stones in line 14?
5. Why might an altar of "hewn stone" be less acceptable than one made of natural stones that are not chipped away at?
6. Of someone lacking in compassion, we say that he or she has "a heart of stone." What are the ways in which Herbert plays with that idea?

Writing About the Poem

A Creative Response
Writing a "Picture Poem." Try to write a poem in the shape of its subject: "Picture poems" have been written in such shapes as moths, rain, hearts, and apples.

PREPARATION
1. BUILDING ON PRIOR KNOWLEDGE. Have students describe a pulley—a wheel with a rope or cable that can lift a weight.

2. ESTABLISHING A PURPOSE. Have students think about how Herbert explains the reason for human unhappiness or dissatisfaction.

SUPPLEMENTARY SUPPORT MATERIALS
1. Vocabulary Activity Worksheet (*CCB*)
2. Review and Response Worksheet: Diction (*CCB*)
3. Selection Test (*CCB*)
4. Audiocassette recording

DEVELOPING VOCABULARY
The following word from the poem is tested in the Selection Test. (See also Vocabulary Activity Worksheet.)
to repine

When writing this poem, Herbert may have been thinking of the well-known Pandora, the first woman in some Greek myths. Zeus gave into Pandora's keeping a mysterious box, and told her never to open it. But she did, and her curiosity let out all the evils and woes that ever since have caused human beings to be unhappy. Herbert gives this old story an entirely new twist.

The Pulley

When God at first made man,
Having a glass of blessings standing by,
Let us, said he, pour on him all we can.
A   Let the world's riches, which dispersèd lie,
5   Contract into a span.°

So strength first made a way,
Then beauty flowed, then wisdom, honor, pleasure.
When almost all was out, God made a stay,
Perceiving that alone of all his treasure
10   Rest in the bottom lay.

For if I should, said he,
Bestow this jewel also on my creature,
He would adore my gifts instead of me,
And rest in nature, not the God of nature:
15   So both should losers be.

Yet let him keep the rest,
B   But keep them with repining restlessness.
Let him be rich and weary, that at least
If goodness lead him not, yet weariness
20   May toss him to my breast.

5. **span:** a small space.

A. Interpreting
❓ What is the *span*? (A human being)

B. Responding
❓ Do you agree that people can be rich but still unhappy?

ANALYZING THE POEM
Identifying Details
1. God poured a glass of blessings on man and gave him the world's riches.
2. Strength, beauty, wisdom, honor, pleasure.
3. He believed that man might adore God's gifts instead of God.
4. To ensure that weariness, if not goodness, would lead man to God.

Interpreting Meanings
5. In line 16, *rest* has the simple meaning; it has the complex meaning in lines 10 and 14.
6. God suspects men would become complacent and idolatrous.
7. God has put man on a "pulley" to pull him back to God's breast.

Responding to the Poem

Analyzing the Poem

Identifying Details

1. According to stanza 1, what did God do for man?
2. According to stanza 2, what specific riches did he pour into man?
3. Why didn't God bestow His "jewel" on man?
4. Why, according to the last stanza, did God make man "rich and weary" with "repining restlessness"?

Interpreting Meanings

5. The word *rest,* as it is used in this poem, has two possible meanings: the simple one, "remainder," and a more complex one containing the ideas of peace, repose, satisfaction, absence of restlessness, and the like. Locate all the places in the poem where *rest* is used. Where in the poem does *rest* have the simple meaning? Where the more complex one?

6. Why, according to the poem, does God not give human beings "rest" in the complex sense?
7. Explain the connection between the poem and the **title**.

Writing About the Poem

A Critical Response

Supporting the Main Idea. It has often been observed that people's wants and desires are insatiable. Show in a paragraph how the poem accounts for this common human failing, and how it suggests that the failing may actually be a blessing in disguise.

PREPARATION
ESTABLISHING A PURPOSE. Have students read the poems aloud so that they can hear their easy rhythms and conversational tone.

SUPPLEMENTARY SUPPORT MATERIALS
1. Review and Response Worksheet: Tone (CCB)
2. Selection Test (CCB)

CLOSURE
Describe the attitude toward love revealed in both of Suckling's poems. Let students discuss whether these opinions are current among both men and women today.

A. Metaphor
? What is time compared with? (A bird that is molting—losing its feathers)

Sir John Suckling (1609–1642) Richard Lovelace (1618–1657)

It is convenient to consider these two poets together because they were Royalists; that is, they supported King Charles in the Civil Wars of the 1630's and 1640's. Because of their politics, they are sometimes called Cavalier Poets, "Cavalier" being the nickname for a supporter of the King, as "Roundhead" is for a supporter of Parliament. But these poets had more than politics in common; they shared a common literary goal, which was to write poems that sound like elegant conversation. In the next century, Alexander Pope, looking back at the work of the poets of the mid-seventeenth century, referred to them as "the mob of gentlemen who wrote with ease." Pope should have said that they *seemed* to write with ease, because he knew better than most people how hard it is make any kind of writing, and especially poetry, sound easy and at the same time be technically accomplished.

John Suckling was born rich, but he gambled away his money and spent a lot of it on extravagant clothes. Suckling's military career included service as a mercenary soldier on the Continent and as commander of a troop of cavalry fighting in Scotland for King Charles. He plotted unsuccessfully to deliver one of the King's chief advisers from the Tower of London; then he fled to France. There, at the age of 33, he died—or was perhaps murdered. Suckling's poems, which were mostly published after his death, are lighthearted, as was his life. Dryden praised him, saying that he had "the conversation of a gentleman." He is said to be the inventor of cribbage, a card game.

Lovelace (pronounced love-less) was altogether a more serious person than the playboy Suckling; one of his contemporaries even compared him with that paragon of chivalry, Sir Philip Sidney. Unlike Sidney, whose pock marks everybody pretended not to see, Lovelace was very handsome. Like his fellow Cavalier Poets, he was very rich, at least at the beginning of his life. He was also a conoisseur of music, painting, and horsemanship. While still a student at Oxford, he made such an impression on King Charles and Queen Henrietta Maria, who were visiting the university, that the royal couple ordered the authorities to confer on him the Master of Arts degree at once. Lovelace became an ardent Royalist, and when the Civil War broke out, he fought bravely for the King. The Roundheads caught him twice and imprisoned him both times. His last days were sad, his health and fortune ruined in the service of a lost cause.

"Out upon it!" is an interjection expressing anger, indignation, and self-disgust. The speaker in Sir John Suckling's poem is reproaching himself because he has been faithful to one particular woman for what, to him, has been a very long time.

Out Upon It!

Out upon it! I have loved
   Three whole days together;
And am like to love three more,
   If it prove fair weather.

A
5 Time shall molt away his wings,
   Ere he shall discover
In the whole wide world again
   Such a constant lover.

But the spite on 't is, no praise
10   Is due at all to me:
Love with me had made no stays
   Had it any been but she.

Had it any been but she,
   And that very face,
15 There had been at least ere this
   A dozen dozen in her place.
          —Sir John Suckling

Comment from a Critic
According to one critic, Cavalier poetry sounds as if it had been written while falling off a horse. This remark isn't completely unfair; the Cavalier poets did try to give the impression of having dashed off flawless poems with little effort.

Inspired by the inherited code of the gentleman (see the biography of Sidney, text page 214), the Cavaliers empha-
sized *sprezzatura,* or fine, careless elegance. Have students read these poems by Suckling and Lovelace—and perhaps try writing a poem of equal smoothness.

In Renaissance literature, and perhaps in the actual life of the time, many young men suffered horribly from the pangs of unrequited love. The women they admired showed no pity toward them, but consistently ignored their pleas for attention. As a result, they became "pale" and "wan"—that is, sickly looking—like the young fellow being addressed in this poem by Sir John Suckling.

Why So Pale and Wan, Fond Lover?

> Why so pale and wan, fond° lover?
>   Prithee, why so pale?
> Will, when looking well can't move her,
>   Looking ill prevail?
> 5   Prithee, why so pale?
>
> Why so dull and mute, young sinner?
>   Prithee, why so mute?
> Will, when speaking well can't win her,
>   Saying nothing do't?
> 10   Prithee, why so mute?
>
> Quit, quit, for shame! this will not move:
>   This cannot take her.
> If of herself she will not love,
>   Nothing can make her:
> 15   The devil take her!
>   —Sir John Suckling

1. **fond:** foolish.

An Unknown Youth by Nicholas Hilliard (16th century). Oil.

Fitzwilliam Museum, Cambridge, England.

A. Humanities Connection: Discussing the Fine Art
Information on Hilliard is on page 194.

? What details suggest that this young man could be the wan lover in Suckling's poem? (He is pale, looks as if he has a stomachache, and appears to have nothing to say.)

ANALYZING THE POEM
Interpreting Meanings
1. In the first stanza, the speaker brags about being faithful for a total of six days; in the last stanza he admits that if his lady hadn't been so beautiful he would have loved dozens of women by now.
2. He tells the lover to quit being so ill and dull and mute, since pain will not change the lady's mind.
The tone is sarcastic and cynical.
3. Answers will vary. Students may cite the surprise ending.

Responding to the Poems

Analyzing the Poems

Interpreting Meanings

1. It has been said of "Out Upon It!" that in the very act of claiming his devotion and constancy, the speaker gives us good reasons to doubt that he is temperamentally capable of either. Where, in the poem, are these "good reasons" to be found?

2. What advice does the speaker give the pale lover? What is his **tone**?
3. This poem lacks interesting **metaphors** and **similes** and it is barren of other poetic devices and decorations. What, then, makes it a likeable poem? (How did you respond to it?)

PREPARATION

ESTABLISHING A PURPOSE. Have students look for how this man, departing for war, reasons with the woman he leaves behind.

SUPPLEMENTARY SUPPORT MATERIALS
1. Vocabulary Activity Worksheet (*CCB*)
2. Review and Response Worksheet: Paradox and Theme (*CCB*)
3. Selection Test (*CCB*)

DEVELOPING VOCABULARY
The following word from the poem is tested in the Selection Test. (See also Vocabulary Activity Worksheet.)
inconstancy

ANALYZING THE POEM
Identifying Details
1. The first foe he meets on the battlefield.
2. A sword, a horse, and a shield.
3. Because it is a sign of his honor.

Interpreting Meanings
4. The paradoxes are resolved in the last stanza, lines 11–12. He is suggesting that a woman cannot expect a man to be loyal to her if he does not honor his other commitments.
5. Most students will point to line 10.

In the background of this poem by Richard Lovelace are the English Civil Wars, and the poem itself resembles John Donne's "A Valediction: Forbidding Mourning" in being a lover's goodbye to his beloved. The speakers in both poems try to console the women being left behind and make them accept and understand the separation about to take place. Lovelace's speaker appeals to a higher commitment than the one he has made to Lucasta. He must leave her because of his honor, a concept that includes not only his loyalty to the woman he loves but also his duties to King, country, and his own manhood. It is tempting to identify Lovelace himself with this speaker, for the poet was just such an idealist, ready to sacrifice his happiness, fortune, and life, to maintain the high standards of behavior he set for himself.

To Lucasta on Going to the Wars

Tell me not, sweet, I am unkind,
    That from the nunnery°
Of thy chaste breast and quiet mind
    To war and arms I fly.

5 True, a new mistress now I chase,
    The first foe in the field;
And with a stronger faith embrace
    A sword, a horse, a shield.

Yes this inconstancy is such,
10   As you too shall adore;
I could not love thee, dear, so much,
    Loved I not honor more.
               —Richard Lovelace

2. **nunnery:** a metaphor for a pure, safe place.

Responding to the Poem

Analyzing the Poem

Identifying Details

1. What new mistress is the speaker about to chase?
2. Instead of Lucasta, what is he about to embrace?
3. Why will Lucasta adore his inconstancy, or unfaithfulness?

Interpreting Meanings

4. The poem implies the **paradox** that inconstancy (line 9) is really constancy, that loyalty to a woman is dependent on loyalty to something else. Explain these paradoxes.

5. Can you find in the poem evidence for believing that Lucasta has the same values as the speaker and will therefore not whine or scold him for leaving her?

Writing About the Poem

A Creative Response

Responding to the Speaker. Write out a modern Lucasta's answer.

PREPARATION

ESTABLISHING A PURPOSE. Have students look at lines 25–26 and read to find out how the poet explains this paradox.

SUPPLEMENTARY SUPPORT MATERIALS
1. Vocabulary Activity Worksheet (CCB)
2. Review and Response Worksheet: Paradox (CCB)
3. Selection Test (CCB)

DEVELOPING VOCABULARY
The following words from the poem are tested in the Selection Test. (See also Vocabulary Activity Worksheet.)
to allay   to tipple
draught

CLOSURE
Assign three students to define paradox and provide examples from each of Lovelace's poems.

This is also a famous poem by Lovelace, who followed the fashion, set by Sidney and Jonson, of calling the women in his poems by classical names. Whether real women are hidden behind the names Lucasta and Althea we do not know, nor does it matter, for there is little or no connection between having a love affair and the ability to write a good poem. We do know that Lovelace was imprisoned during the Civil Wars, and it seems likely that a man as attractive as he would be visited by a female admirer.

To Althea, from Prison

When love with unconfinèd wings
    Hovers within my gates,
And my divine Althea brings
    To whisper at the grates;
5   When I lie tangled in her hair,
    And fettered to her eye,
The birds that wanton in the air
    Know no such liberty.

When flowing cups run swiftly round
10   With no allaying Thames,°
Our careless heads with roses bound,
    Our hearts with loyal flames;
When thirsty grief in wine we steep,
    When healths and draughts go free,
15 Fishes that tipple in the deep
    Know no such liberty.

When, like committed linnets,° I
    With shriller throat shall sing
The sweetness, mercy, majesty,
20   And glories of my king;
When I shall voice aloud how good
    He is, how great should be,
Enlargèd winds, that curl the flood,°
    Know no such liberty.

25 Stone walls do not a prison make,
    Nor iron bars a cage:
Minds innocent and quiet take
    That for a hermitage;°
If I have freedom in my love,
30   And in my soul am free,
Angels alone that soar above
    Enjoy such liberty.

—Richard Lovelace

10. **allaying Thames:** That is, the wine is not diluted with water from the Thames River.

17. **committed linnets:** caged birds.
23. **flood:** sea.
28. **hermitage:** holy refuge.

Responding to the Poem

Analyzing the Poem

Identifying Details

1. In stanzas 1–3, the last two lines make a **comparison**. What two things are being compared in each stanza?

Interpreting Meanings

2. What **message** is the speaker sending Althea from prison?
3. How would you explain line 6?
4. The poem's most famous lines, lines 25–26, state a **paradox**. What is it? Explain why the prisoner does not feel imprisoned.

5. According to the implication made in the poem, what *does* make a prison? How do you feel about this idea?

Writing About the Poem

A Critical Response

Relating the Poem to Current Events. Does this poem about liberty and bondage have any relevance to life in the late twentieth century? In a brief essay, give your opinion on this question, and cite specific passages from the poem to support your views.

ANALYZING THE POEM
Identifying Details
1. Stanza 1: The speaker's freedom is compared to that of birds. Stanza 2: The lovers' abandon is compared to that of fishes in the deep. Stanza 3: The speaker's voice is compared to sea winds.

Interpreting Meanings
2. Despite his imprisonment, he is free in his heart and mind.
3. The speaker has eyes for Althea alone and is, figuratively, "chained" to her glance.
4. Stone walls and iron bars cannot imprison a mind. He feels free because he may still love Althea and praise his king.
5. The poem implies that mental conformity or abandoning one's personal values creates a prison far more confining than a jail.

A. About the Title Page
Copies of the King James Bible printed today are modernized in spelling and typography. Students with good eyesight may notice the spelling of "Conteyning" *(containing)* and the *f*-like *s* in the word *Testament.* Note the twelve tribes of Israel on the left and the twelve disciples of Jesus on the right. The four seated men are Matthew, Mark, Luke, and John.

B. Researching Bible Translations
Students interested in the history of English translations should look up "Bible" in an encyclopedia for an overview. References at the end of the article will suggest more specific materials.

C. Locating Biblical Passages
Many students do not know there are reference books for locating biblical passages. These are biblical concordances, which are usually shelved in the reference section of a library. A biblical concordance indexes phrases in the same manner as the index at the back of *Bartlett's Familiar Quotations.* The only difference is that a Bible is needed to look up the quotation in full. Perhaps the most widely used concordances for the King James Bible are *Strong's Exhaustive Concordance of the Bible* and *Young's Analytical Concordance.*

The King James Bible (1611)

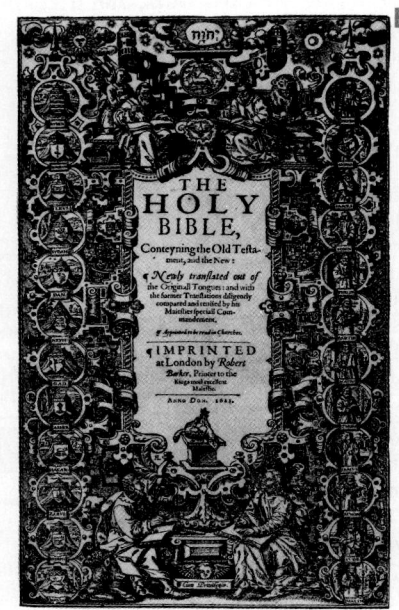

Frontispiece King James Bible (1611). Engraving.

New York Public Library.

One of the first acts of James I after he was crowned king of England was to call a conference of clergymen and scholars, to discuss, among other matters, a new translation of the Bible into English. Of course there already existed several translations of the Bible, but the king and others disliked the interpretive comments printed in them. Moreover, Renaissance scholars and humanists had made everybody more historically minded and sensitive to textual inaccuracies. The new translation would be checked against the most authoritative Hebrew and Greek texts available, and, to keep it from sounding too unfamiliar, it would incorporate much of the language of its predecessors, but without their partisan commentary.

To accomplish this task, the King appointed a team of fifty-four learned clergymen. They broke up into groups, each with a section of the scriptures to translate and each with a pair of scholars to check the work of the others. Then a committee of bishops gave it a final review, and the new translation was published, seven years after it was commissioned. It has become known variously as the "King James Bible" because James sponsored it; as the "Authorized Version" because the Anglican Church authorized its use in their services; and simply as the "English Bible" because it has been so important to English literature and also to the civilization and literature of all countries where English is spoken, especially the United States and Canada. Like the Hebrews, speakers of English could be called "people of the Book," the word *Bible* being derived from a Greek word meaning *book.* If people living before our own time read anything at all, they read the English Bible; and if they read nothing themselves, they regularly heard the Bible read in church.

For over three hundred and fifty years, most writers of poetry, fiction, and drama have been consciously or unconsciously influenced by the English Bible. They have quoted from it, echoed it, paraphrased it, alluded to it, imitated it, and retold its fascinating stories over and over. Milton and Bunyan based their most important works directly upon it. If the Bible had never existed, how different would be the works of many other English writers: Dryden, Pope, Blake, Byron, Browning, Hardy, George Eliot—but the list is endless.

Common speech is full of words and phrases from the English Bible: "loving kindness," "tender mercy," "long suffering." We "cast pearls before swine" and "wait until the eleventh hour" before doing something. We speak of the "wisdom of Solomon" and the "patience of Job." Many biblical words now embedded in our language (such as the word *scapegoat*) are used without any knowledge of their source: People often do not know when they are using biblical language.

But the King James Bible was never "the Bible in modern English," to use an expression often heard today. Even when it was first published, its language was far from being up to date: It preserved much of the style of William Tyndale, a Bible translator who had been dead for over seventy years—years in which the language had changed rapidly. In 1611 English people were be-

A. Humanities Connection: About the Fine Art

Call students' attention to the color and decorativeness of both the Gutenberg Bible and the illuminated letter from the Flemish manuscript. Remind them that illuminated manuscripts were completely written and decorated by hand, usually by monks who devoted their lives to creating gorgeous manuscripts for wealthy patrons and monastery libraries.

The first typefaces, which we often find difficult to read, attempted to imitate medieval hand lettering. Some students may be able to pick out an occasional word from the Gutenberg page (e.g., *prologus* in the first line). The language is Latin.

ginning to address each other as "you," but the new Bible kept the archaic verb forms and the old second-person pronouns *thou, thy, thine,* and *thee:* "Thou shalt not covet," says one of the Ten Commandments. It even used the old word *ye* for the second-person plural: "Ye are the salt of the earth." Many sentences in the new Bible sounded old fashioned to 1611 ears: "The earth is the Lord's and the fullness thereof, the world and they that dwell therein."

Of course, over the years the language of the King James Bible has become more and more distant from ordinary English. For some readers this remoteness makes it seem dignified and impressive; even when it is incompletely understood, it is more moving and evokes more sublime feelings than a Bible in the vernacular. The King James Bible stands with Shakespeare as an exemplar of English when the language was—as many people believe—more flexible and eloquent than at any other time, and more capable of stirring people's hearts and minds. There is "one English book, and one only," said Matthew Arnold, a nineteenth-century poet and essayist, in which "perfect plainness of speech is allied with perfect nobleness; and that book is the Bible."

A

The letter "P" from an illuminated Bible. Flemish manuscript (ca. 1500).

Victoria and Albert Museum, London.

B

A page from the Gutenberg Bible (1453–56).

B. The King James Bible

The King James Bible has been a major force in stabilizing the English language since the seventeenth century. Part of its effectiveness lies in its limited vocabulary. In contrast with the 30,000-word vocabulary of Shakespeare's First Folio, the King James Bible uses only 8,000 words. Some seventeenth-century religious dissenters even attempted to limit their vocabulary to that of the King James Bible—a program destined to fail, since words were needed for a great many things unheard of in biblical times (e.g., *parliament, theater,* and the names of New World plants and animals).

A. The Editors of Genesis

Some biblical scholars believe that four major writers or editors worked on various parts of Genesis; two of them are represented in this selection. Students who wish to do their own analysis should read the first two chapters of Genesis from any translation, noting that a recounting of the creation begins in Chapter 2, verse 4. They may also investigate the blending together of two accounts of the Flood in Genesis 6 through 8 (e.g., different lengths of the rainy period, different numbers of animals).

B. Humanities Connection: Discussing the Fine Art

After students have read the selection, ask them to cite the specific lines the painting illustrates. (The passage describing the fifth day)

[?] Do any creatures seem fanciful or imaginary? How would you account for their presence here? (Many of the aquatic creatures, in particular, seem fanciful. Perhaps the artist wanted to emphasize the imagination with which God created the world. Perhaps, too, the creatures seem probable, given the scientific knowledge of the unknown artist's day.)

FROM **GENESIS**

The first book of the Bible is called Genesis, which means "coming into being." Genesis opens with two accounts of God's creation, one of them emphasizing the cosmos or universe, the other the earth and humanity. Although Moses is the traditional author of Genesis, many biblical scholars now say that two different writers recorded the two creation accounts, which may well be regarded as complementary. Both narratives are very spare, pared to the bone, simple but somehow elevated in style. It would be interesting to have some additional authentic details about Adam, Eve, the Garden, the serpent, and the act of disobedience to God. But it is the very nature of ancient narratives, which originated long before people began to write, not to provide the sorts of details we enjoy today in novels and short stories.

The first chapters of Genesis are concerned with much more important matters than entertainment. They tell us how the physical universe we know came into being, how and why human beings were created, and especially why individual members of the human race must suffer and die, and why the history of the whole race has been so bloody and troubled.

The Creation of the Animals by an unknown Flemish artist. Oil.

Museo Archeologico, Pamplona, Spain.

PREPARATION

1. BUILDING ON PRIOR KNOWLEDGE. Most students know that Genesis, the first book of the Old Testament, contains an account of the creation of the world and the first human beings.

2. ESTABLISHING A PURPOSE. Tell students that their purpose is to study the Genesis account for its literary qualities, not for its religious doctrine. Have them read question 8 on text page 399.

SUPPLEMENTARY SUPPORT MATERIALS

1. Vocabulary Activity Worksheet (*CCB*)
2. Review and Response Worksheet: Style (*CCB*)
3. Selection Test (*CCB*)

DEVELOPING VOCABULARY
The following words from the narrative are tested in the Selection Test. (See also Vocabulary Activity Worksheet.)

void	to encompass
abundantly	to cleave
dominion	subtile
to replenish	to beguile
to sanctify	enmity

A In the beginning God created the heaven and the earth. And the earth was without form, and void; and darkness was upon the face of the deep. And the spirit of God moved upon the face of the waters.[1] And God said, "Let there be **B** light": and there was light. And God saw the light, that it was good: and God divided the light from the darkness. And God called the light Day, and the darkness he called Night. And the evening and the morning were the first day.

And God said, "Let there be a firmament[2] in the midst of the waters, and let it divide the waters from the waters." And God made the firmament, and divided the waters which were under the firmament from the waters which were above the firmament: and it was so. And God called the firmament Heaven. And the evening and the morning were the second day.

And God said, "Let the waters under the heaven be gathered together unto one place, and let the dry land appear": and it was so. And God called the dry land Earth; and the gathering together of the waters called he Seas: and God saw that it was good. And God said, "Let the earth bring forth grass, the herb[3] yielding seed, and the fruit tree yielding fruit after his kind, whose seed is in itself, upon the earth": and it was so. And the earth brought forth grass, and herb yielding seed after his[4] kind, and the tree yielding fruit, whose seed was in itself, after his kind: and God saw that it was good. And the evening and the morning were the third day.

And God said, "Let there be lights in the firmament of the heaven to divide the day from the night; and let them be for signs, and for seasons, and for days, and years: and let them be for lights in the firmament of the heaven to give light upon the earth": and it was so. And God made two great lights; the greater light to rule the day, and the lesser light to rule the night: he made the stars also. And God set them in the firmament of the heaven to give light upon the earth, and to rule over the day and over the night, and to divide the light from the darkness: and God saw that it was good. And the evening and the morning were the fourth day.

And God said, "Let the waters bring forth abundantly the moving creature[5] that hath life, and fowl that may fly above the earth in the open firmament of heaven." And God created great whales, and every living creature that moveth, which the waters brought forth abundantly, after their kind,[6] and every winged fowl after his kind: and God saw that it was good. And God blessed them, saying, "Be fruitful, and multiply, and fill the waters in the seas, and let fowl multiply in the earth." And the evening and the morning were the fifth day.

And God said, "Let the earth bring forth the living creature after his kind, cattle, and creeping thing, and beast of the earth after his kind": and it was so. And God made the beast of the earth after his kind, and cattle after their kind, and every thing that creepeth upon the earth after his kind: and God saw that it was good. And God said, **C** "Let us make man in our image, after our likeness: and let them have dominion over the fish of the sea, and over the fowl of the air, and over the cattle, and over all the earth, and over every creeping thing that creepeth upon the earth." So God created man in his own image, in the image of God created he him; male and female created he them. And God blessed them, and God said unto them, "Be fruitful, and multiply, and replenish the earth, and subdue it: and have dominion over the fish of the sea, and over the fowl of the air, and over every living thing that moveth upon the earth." And God said, "Behold, I have given you every herb bearing seed, which is upon the face of all the earth, and every tree, in the which is the fruit of a tree yielding seed; to you it shall be for meat.[7] And to every beast of the earth, and **D** to every fowl of the air, and to every thing that creepeth upon the earth, wherein there is life, I have given every green herb for meat:" and it was so. And God saw every thing that he had made, and, behold, it was very good. And the evening and the morning were the sixth day.

Thus the heavens and the earth were finished, and all the host[8] of them. And on the seventh day **E** God ended his work which he had made; and he rested on the seventh day from all his work which

---

1. **waters:** There was only water before the Creation began.
2. **firmament:** sky. Since the sky is blue, it is natural to suppose that there are waters above it. Where, otherwise, would the rain come from?
3. **herb:** vegetation.
4. **his:** its (*Its* is a word that came into common use late in the seventeenth century).

5. **creature:** created beings; an old plural without the *s*.
6. **kind:** nature.
7. **meat:** food. What we call meat, the Bible calls *flesh*.
8. **host:** multitude.

A. Vocabulary
In Hebrew the words used here are *tohu* and *bohu*, "trackless waste" and "emptiness." The images imply the concept of "creation from nothing."

B. Repetition
Note throughout the account the refrains that repeat certain themes and phrases, concerning time, rest, and the goodness of creation.

C. Vocabulary
The common name for God in Hebrew is *Elohim*, a plural form. The plural here might be the use of the royal "We."

D. Interpreting
This was a Golden Age, when humans and animals were at peace; all ate only plants.

E. The Sabbath
The Sabbath (*shabbat,* "rest," in Hebrew) is thus of divine institution. The Jews count Saturday as the seventh day. Christians observe the Sabbath on Sunday, the day of Christ's resurrection. Muslims observe Friday as their weekly holy day.

Literature and Language: Using Transitional Expressions for Coherence

Point out that in the King James Bible account of *Genesis*, nearly every sentence begins with *and*. Explain that this use of *and* was a poetic way of keeping the narrative flowing.

Remind students that today writers use transitional expressions for coherence, joining sentences to emphasize the relationships among them:

1. **Adding a similar idea:** *and, also, another, besides, moreover, in addition*
2. **Linking opposite ideas:** *although, but, however, in spite of, yet, instead*
3. **Indicating a reason:** *because, since, hence, for this reason, thus*
4. **Indicating a result:** *so, then, therefore, as a result, consequently*
5. **Indicating time:** *at once, before, eventually, finally, first of all, next*

Have students work in groups to write a contemporary version of the passage on page 398, using transitional expressions to ensure coherence. Have students begin in column 2 with *Now the serpent* and end with *and made themselves aprons*. Encourage the groups to share their work.

A. Expansion
This second creation narrative (Genesis 2:4) describes the primordial tragedy that explains the human condition.

B. Vocabulary
Eden is a geographical name, but the place cannot be identified. Note that Paradise is pictured as an oasis in the desert. (John Steinbeck took the title of his novel *East of Eden* from this account.)

C. Names
In some translations the third river is named Tigris. The Tigris and Euphrates are actual rivers, but the others are unknown.

D. Names
Adam means "of the soil."

E. Play on Words
In Hebrew this is a play on similar sounding words: *ishshah* (woman) and *ish* (man).

F. Expansion
"Now the serpent" begins Chapter 3 of Genesis. "Subtil" *(subtle)* means "cunning."

G. Reading Closely
Note that at no time is the fruit identified as an apple.

he had made. And God blessed the seventh day, and <u>sanctified</u> it: because that in it he had rested from all his work which God created and made.

A These are the generations of the heavens and of the earth when they were created, in the day that the LORD God made the earth and the heavens, and every plant of the field before it was in the earth, and every herb of the field before it grew: for the LORD God had not caused it to rain upon the earth, and there was not a man to till the ground. But there went up a mist from the earth, and watered the whole face of the ground. And the LORD God formed man of the dust of the ground, and breathed into his nostrils the breath of life; and man became a living soul.

B And the LORD God planted a garden eastward in Eden; and there he put the man whom he had formed. And out of the ground made the LORD God to grow every tree that is pleasant to the sight, and good for food; the tree of life also in the midst of the garden, and the tree of knowledge of good and evil. And a river went out of Eden to water the garden; and from thence it was parted, and became into four heads. The name of the first is Pison:[9] that is it which compasseth the whole land of Havilah, where there is gold; and the gold of that land is good: there is bdellium[10] and the onyx[11] stone. And the name of the second river is Gihon: the same is it that <u>compasseth</u> the whole **C** land of Ethiopia. And the name of the third river is Hiddekel: that is it which goeth toward the east of Assyria. And the fourth river is Euphrates. And the LORD God took the man, and put him into the garden of Eden to dress it and to keep it. And the LORD God commanded the man, saying, "Of every tree of the garden thou mayest freely eat: but of the tree of the knowledge of good and evil, thou shalt not eat of it: for in the day that thou eatest thereof thou shalt surely die."

And the LORD God said, "It is not good that the man should be alone; I will make him an help meet[12] for him." And out of the ground the LORD God formed every beast of the field, and every fowl of the air; and brought them unto Adam to **D** see what he would call them: and whatsoever Adam called every living creature, that was the name thereof. And Adam gave names to all cattle, and to the fowl of the air, and to every beast of the field; but for Adam there was not found an help meet for him. And the LORD God caused a deep sleep to fall upon Adam, and he slept: and he took one of his ribs, and closed up the flesh instead thereof; and the rib, which the LORD God had taken from man, made he a woman, and brought her unto the man. And Adam said, "This is now bone of my bones, and flesh of my flesh: she shall be called Woman, because she was taken **E** out of Man." Therefore shall a man leave his father and his mother, and shall <u>cleave</u> unto his wife: and they shall be one flesh. And they were both naked, the man and his wife, and were not ashamed.

Now the serpent[13] was more <u>subtil</u> than any beast **F** of the field which the LORD God had made. And he said unto the woman, "Yea, hath God said, 'Ye shall not eat of every tree of the garden'?" And the woman said unto the serpent, "We may eat of the fruit of the trees of the garden: but of the fruit of the tree which is in the midst of the garden, God hath said, 'Ye shall not eat of it, neither shall ye touch it, lest ye die.' " And the serpent said unto the woman, "Ye shall not surely die: for God doth know that in the day ye eat thereof, then your eyes shall be opened, and ye shall be as gods, knowing good and evil." And when the woman saw that the tree was good for food, and that it was pleasant to the eyes, and a tree to be desired to make one wise, she took of **G** the fruit thereof, and did eat, and gave also unto her husband with her; and he did eat. And the eyes of them both were opened, and they knew that they were naked; and they sewed fig leaves together, and made themselves aprons. And they heard the voice of the LORD God walking in the garden in the cool of the day: and Adam and his wife hid themselves from the presence of the LORD God amongst the trees of the garden. And the LORD God called unto Adam, and said unto

---

9. **Pison:** This and the other geographical names (except for Ethiopia, for which modern translations say *Cush*) locate the Garden of Eden in Mesopotamia (modern Iraq).
10. **bdellium:** a precious substance, either a stone or a resin.
11. **onyx:** a gemstone.
12. **meet:** mate.

13. **serpent:** traditionally understood to be possessed by Satan. Satan used to be the angel Lucifer, who was expelled from Heaven because of his enmity to God.

ANALYZING THE NARRATIVE
Identifying Details

1. God repeatedly utters a command starting with "Let."
2. In the first, God creates man and woman from nothing, in His own image and likeness. In the second, God first creates Adam from dust and breathes a soul into him; later He creates Eve from Adam's rib as company for Adam.

3. The serpent is the subtlest (most cunning) animal.
4. Adam is condemned to a life of toil, to till ground that grows thorns and thistles, and to certain death; Eve will experience great sorrow and pain in childbirth and will be under Adam's dominion; the serpent is compelled to move on its belly and eat dust, and the woman's seed will hate it and crush it.

Interpreting Meanings
5. Omnipotence, majesty, benevolence, justice.
6. Adam's creation from dust foreshadows the return of his body to dust after death.
7. Perhaps the serpent thinks that Eve may be more susceptible to flattery, or that the most effective way to influence Adam is through Eve.

8. It accounts for human suffering, pain in childbirth, barren soil, toil, guilt, death, self-consciousness, separation from God, and the knowledge of both good and evil.

A. Responding
What familiar human tendency is presented here? (The tendency to "pass the buck," that is, to blame others for our own failings)

him, "Where art thou?" And he said, "I heard thy voice in the garden, and I was afraid, because I was naked; and I hid myself." And he said, "Who told thee that thou wast naked? Hast thou eaten of the tree, whereof I commanded thee that thou shouldest not eat?" And the man said, "The woman whom thou gavest to be with me, she gave me of the tree, and I did eat." And the LORD God said unto the woman, "What is this that thou hast done?" And the woman said, "The serpent beguiled me, and I did eat." And the LORD God said unto the serpent, "Because thou hast done this, thou art cursed above all cattle,[14] and above every beast of the field; upon thy belly shalt thou go, and dust shalt thou eat all the days of thy life: and I will put enmity between thee and the woman, and between thy seed and her seed; it shall bruise thy head, and thou shalt bruise his heel." Unto the woman he said, "I will greatly multiply thy sorrow and thy conception;[15] in sorrow thou shalt bring forth children; and thy desire shall be to thy husband, and he shall rule over thee." And unto Adam he said, "Because thou hast hearkened unto[16] the voice of thy wife, and hast eaten of the

tree, of which I commanded thee, saying, Thou shall not eat of it: cursed is the ground for thy sake; in sorrow shalt thou eat of it all the days of thy life; thorns also and thistles shall it bring forth to thee; and thou shalt eat the herb of the field; in the sweat of thy face shalt thou eat bread, till thou return unto the ground; for out of it wast thou taken: for dust thou art, and unto dust shalt thou return." And Adam called his wife's name Eve; because she was the mother of all living. Unto Adam also and to his wife did the LORD God make coats of skins, and clothed them.

And the LORD God said, "Behold, the man[17] is become as one of us, to know good and evil: and now, lest he put forth his hand, and take also of the tree of life,[18] and eat, and live for ever": therefore the LORD God sent him forth from the garden of Eden, to till the ground from whence he was taken. So he drove out the man; and he placed at the east of the garden of Eden Cherubims,[19] and a flaming sword which turned every way, to keep the way of[20] the tree of life.

—Genesis 1–3

---

14. **cattle:** animals.
15. **conception:** pains in childbearing.
16. **hearkened unto:** listened and obeyed.

---

17. **man:** i.e., both man and woman.
18. **tree of life:** the first mention of this forbidden tree.
19. **Cherubims:** Large, fierce angels, quite unlike the modern idea of a cherub.
20. **keep the way of:** prevent access to.

Responding to the Narrative

Analyzing the Narrative

Identifying Details

1. How is the creation an example of divine *fiat*, or decree?
2. Contrast the two accounts of the creation of man.
3. Of all animals, why is the serpent able to tempt Eve?
4. What punishment does God mete out to Adam, Eve, and the serpent?

Interpreting Meanings

5. What characteristics or qualities of God does the narrative reveal? (In your answer consider the phrases "and it was so" and "it was good.")

6. How does Adam's creation from dust **foreshadow** his ultimate fate?
7. Why do you think the serpent tempts Eve instead of Adam?
8. What aspects of the human condition does the story of Adam and Eve account for?

A. The Psalms

Explain to students that the Hebrew title of the book of Psalms is *Tehillim,* meaning "hymns." The English word *Psalms* comes from Latin *psalmi,* coming in turn from Greek *psalmoi,* "sacred songs chanted with accompaniment." Martin Luther called Psalms "the immortal song book of the human heart," and John Calvin praised Psalms as "the mirror of man." Historically, the Gospels and Psalms have been the two books of the Bible most often published as separate volumes. *The Bay Psalm Book* (1640) was the first book published in America.

FOR FURTHER READING
TEACHERS
Buckner B. Trawisk, *The Bible as Literature: The Old Testament and the Apocrypha* (1970)

B. Biblical Poetry

Poems appear even in books of the Bible that are essentially prose (e.g., David's lament for Saul and Jonathan in 2 Samuel 1:19–27, Mary's "Magnificat" in Luke 1:46–55). Much of the "wisdom" literature (Job, Proverbs, Song of Songs, Ecclesiastes) and prophetic literature (Isaiah, Jeremiah) of the Bible is also lyrical.

C. Humanities Connection: Responding to the Fine Art

David was not born into a royal family; as a boy, he shepherded his father's flocks. He came to the attention of King Saul, his predecessor, by volunteering to fight Goliath, a giant warrior of the enemy Philistines. The account of their battle appears in I Samuel 17 and is depicted in this engraving.

? Which character looks more likely to win the battle? (Goliath) Why, then, does David appear so confident? (He is trusting God [see Psalm 91, at right]; he believes that his cause is just.)

A *Psalms*

Folio 523v (13th century). Illuminated manuscript.

Courtesy of British Library, London.

B The Bible is full of poetry. Every book of it contains poems or fragments of poems inserted into the prose text, and much of the prose itself is highly rhythmical. One book, the Psalms, consists entirely of poems, some of which were set to music and sung during worship services in the ancient temple in Jerusalem. Psalms preserves 150 of these songs, a fraction of the total number that the ancient Hebrews knew and sang. Seventy-three of the psalms are said, in the ancient texts, to be "for David" or "concerning David," phrases that led King James's translators and others to assume that they were written by David, who was the most heroic of the Hebrew kings. Modern scholars doubt David's authorship; the psalms are anonymous, they say, and the "I" or speaker in them should be understood as any person praying, praising, lamenting, or rejoicing.

A collection of psalms is called a psalter (the *p* is silent as in the word *psalm* itself). There have been dozens of English psalters besides the one in the King James Bible, but none of them has lasted so well and so long. King James's translators did not try to impose rhyme on their versions because there is no rhyme in the originals. Instead, they imitated such Hebrew poetic devices as repetition (as in Psalm 8 opposite) and **parallel structure** (the use of sentences or phrases that are similar in structure);

> Let the floods clap their hands,
> Let the hills be joyful together.
> —from Psalm 98

The psalmists were fond of saying essentially the same thing twice, in different words ("babes and sucklings" and "man and son of man" in Psalm 8 or "rod and staff" in 23). By the way, the King James Bible uses the numbering of the ancient Hebrew manuscripts; some other Bibles use a different numbering derived from a Greek translation of the Hebrew, and these Bibles have an extra psalm, number 151.

Biblical poetry, then, is much like modern free verse in that it does not have rhyme and meter but it does have other patterns of repetition, balance, antithesis, and parallelism. Metaphors and similes abound, and so do images drawn from nature and everyday experience:

> My God, in him will I trust.
> Surely he shall deliver thee from the snare of the fowler,
> And from the noisome pestilence.
> He shall cover thee with his feathers,
> And under his wings shalt thou trust;
> His truth shall be thy shield and buckler.
> Thou shalt not be afraid for the terror by night,
> Nor for the arrow that flieth by day,
> Nor for the pestilence that walketh in darkness,
> Nor for the destruction that wasteth at noonday.
> —from Psalm 91

PREPARATION
ESTABLISHING A PURPOSE. Like all psalms, this one is a hymn of praise meant to be chanted or sung aloud. Ask students to read to find out how the psalmist describes the place human beings have in God's creation.

SUPPLEMENTARY SUPPORT MATERIALS
1. Vocabulary Activity Worksheet (*CCB*)
2. Review and Response Worksheet: Biblical Imagery (*CCB*)
3. Selection Test (*CCB*)

DEVELOPING VOCABULARY
The following word and phrase from the psalm are tested in the Selection Test. (See also Vocabulary Activity Worksheet.)
avenger   have dominion over

Psalm 8 is a hymn, designed to be sung in the temple in praise of God, whose strength and glory are shown in his creation. Compared to God, a human being is only an infant, though paradoxically a human being holds a very high position in the creation.

Psalm 8

O LORD our Lord,
How excellent is thy name in all the earth!
Who hast set thy glory above the heavens.
Out of the mouth of babes and sucklings° hast thou
    ordained strength
5 Because of thine enemies,
That thou mightest still° the enemy and the avenger.
When I consider thy heavens, the work of thy fingers,
The moon and the stars, which thou hast ordained;°
What is man, that thou art mindful of him?
10 And the son of man, that thou visitest him?
For thou hast made him a little lower than the angels,
And hast crowned him with glory and honor.
A Thou madest him to have dominion over the works of
    thy hands;
Thou hast put all things under his feet:
15 All sheep and oxen,
Yea, and the beasts of the field;
The fowl of the air, and the fish of the sea,
And whatsoever passeth through the paths of the seas.
O LORD our Lord,
20 How excellent is thy name in all the earth!

4. **sucklings:** infants.

6. **still:** put down, silence.

8. **ordained:** decreed (i.e., created by speaking).

B

The Terrestrial Paradise (detail) by Jan Brueghel the Elder. Oil.

Museo Lazar Galdiano, Madrid.

A. Theme
Recall the concept of the Great Chain of Being (see note on text page 184). The idea that there is an order of excellence within every possible category of creation is echoed in this psalm. In the Great Chain of Being, the king is superior to his subjects, gold to other metals, the eagle to other birds, and so on.

B. Humanities Connection: About the Fine Art
This painting suggests the "peaceable kingdom" described in Isaiah 11:6–9: "The wolf also shall dwell with the lamb, and the leopard shall lie down with the kid; and the calf and the young lion and the fatling together, and a little child shall lead them. . . . They shall not hurt nor destroy in all my holy mountain: for the earth shall be full of the knowledge of the Lord."
  Students may also wish to compare this painting with other works by Flemish painter Jan Brueghel (1568–1625) on text pages 217 and 381.

ESTABLISHING A PURPOSE. Most students will have heard some version of this well-known psalm, either read or sung. Ask them to read to find out why this psalm is so often recited at funerals and other difficult times.

SUPPLEMENTARY SUPPORT MATERIALS
1. Vocabulary Activity Worksheet (*CCB*)
2. Review and Response Worksheet: Biblical Imagery (*CCB*)
3. Selection Test (*CCB*)

DEVELOPING VOCABULARY
The following words from the psalm are tested in the Selection Test. (See also Vocabulary Activity Worksheet.)
righteousness   to anoint

A. Expansion
Sheep will not drink from turbulent waters.

B. Expansion
Anointing a guest (dusty from travel) with oil was a gesture of hospitality.

C. Humanities Connection:
About the Mosaic
A mosaic is a picture made of tiny bits of colored glass, stone, or tile. In ancient Egypt, mosaics were used to decorate objects; in Greece and Italy, they were used to decorate floors. The art of mosaic reached its height in Byzantine (Constantinople) culture with the addition of gold. During the fifth and sixth centuries, gorgeous mosaics (many of which still stand) decorated the churches of Ravenna, Italy.

The identification of the king with a shepherd is deeply rooted in Eastern literary tradition. One of the earliest images in Christian symbolism is that of Jesus as the Good Shepherd. (See John 10:11–14: "I am the good shepherd: the good shepherd giveth his life for the sheep. . . .")

This song of trust, affirming the speaker's faith and confidence in God, is the best known religious poem in the world. The opening verses, depicting God as a shepherd, employ the kind of pastoral imagery found throughout the Bible—very appropriate for the Hebrews and for the original readers of the King James Bible. Then the metaphors change, and the Lord becomes a host providing a banquet for the speaker, whose enemies watch him enviously as he eats, not daring to harm him. Among the rich and varied images of the poem, there is also a suggestion of the speaker as a pilgrim traveling through a dangerous world.

Psalm 23

The LORD is my shepherd; I shall not want.
He maketh me to lie down in green pastures:
A He leadeth me beside the still waters.
He restoreth my soul:
He leadeth me in the paths of righteousness for his
5   name's sake.°
Yea, though I walk through the valley of the shadow of
death,
I will fear no evil: for thou art with me;
Thy rod and thy staff they comfort me.

Thou preparest a table before me in the presence of
B   mine enemies:
10 Thou anointest my head with oil; my cup runneth over.
Surely goodness and mercy shall follow me all the days
of my life:
And I will dwell in the house of the LORD for ever.

5. **his name's sake:** i.e., he will live up to his name as shepherd.

The Good Shepherd. Mosaic.

Mausoleum of Galla Placida, Ravenna, Italy.

C

ESTABLISHING A PURPOSE. Remind students that the psalms were originally composed to be sung to the accompaniment of a musical instrument. With that in mind, have them listen to the psalm read aloud to hear its dignified cadence (produced by repetition) and to note its use of military imagery.

SUPPLEMENTARY SUPPORT MATERIALS
1. Review and Response Worksheet: Biblical Imagery (*CCB*)
2. Selection Test (*CCB*)
3. Audiocassette recording

A. Interpreting
? What kind of behavior will exclude a person from entrance into the Temple? (Impurity, vanity, deceit)

B. Rhetorical Devices
? In the last stanza, find examples of an apostrophe (lines 14–15); of repetition (note especially lines 14–15, 16–17, 18–19; the last five lines in part repeat lines 14–19); and of a rhetorical question (line 17).

C. A Musical Setting
The last verse was set to music by George Frederick Handel (1685–1759) in his oratorio *The Messiah*.

Psalm 24 falls into three parts, as indicated by the spaces in the text below. Some scholars believe that the psalm was sung by the procession entering the temple, which was on the hill of Zion (line 5). After a brief choral hymn (lines 1–4), a priest chants a question and another priest answers it, giving a description of the sort of person who is entitled to worship in the temple. This part of the psalm illustrates the close connection between religion and morality which we take for granted but which was first made by the ancient Hebrews. The final part of the song, as the procession goes through the temple gates, continues the dialogue pattern.

Psalm 24

The earth is the LORD'S, and the fulness thereof;°
The world, and they that dwell therein.
For he hath founded it upon the seas,
And established it upon the floods.°

5   Who shall ascend into the hill of the LORD?
    And who shall stand in his holy place?
A   He that hath clean hands, and a pure heart;
    Who hath not lifted up his soul unto vanity,
    Nor sworn deceitfully.
10 He shall receive the blessing from the LORD,
    And righteousness from the God of his salvation.
    This is the generation of them that seek him,
    That seek thy face, O Jacob.° Selah.°

    Lift up your heads, O ye gates;
15 And be ye lift up, ye everlasting doors;
    And the King of glory shall come in.
B   Who is this King of glory?
    The LORD strong and mighty,
    The LORD mighty in battle.
20 Lift up your heads, O ye gates;
    Even lift them up, ye everlasting doors;
    And the King of glory shall come in.
    Who is this King of glory?
    The LORD of hosts, he is the King of glory. Selah.

C

1. **fulness thereof:** the whole of it.

4. **seas . . . floods:** the primal waters mentioned in Genesis.

13. **Jacob:** i.e., the "God of Jacob." Jacob was a Hebrew patriarch, grandson of the first patriarch Abraham. **Selah:** a word used seventy times in the whole Psalter, but whose meaning is unknown (pronounced say-lah). Traditionally, it has been interpreted as a blessing meaning "forever."

PREPARATION

BUILDING ON PRIOR KNOWLEDGE.
Although most contemporary Americans have not personally experienced exile or loss of homeland, many of their ancestors have. This experience of the Hebrews in captivity was particularly meaningful to black American slaves. Some students might recognize the opening words as the title of a futuristic story by

the American writer Stephen Vincent Benét.

SUPPLEMENTARY SUPPORT MATERIALS
1. Vocabulary Activity Worksheet (*CCB*)
2. Review and Response Worksheet: Biblical Imagery (*CCB*)
3. Selection Test (*CCB*)

DEVELOPING VOCABULARY
The following word from the psalm is tested in the Selection Test. (See also Vocabulary Activity Worksheet.)
wasted

CLOSURE
The exercise Reading Aloud on page 405 is an appropriate exercise in closure.

A. Interpreting
Without his right hand and tongue, he would be unable to play his harp and sing.

B. Expansion
According to the Book of Daniel, mysterious handwriting appeared on the wall of the palace of Belshazzar, king of Babylon, warning of the city's fall. In 539 B.C. Babylon was captured by the Persians and part of the city eventually destroyed for its continued rebelliousness. Babylon fell into complete ruin sometime around 200 B.C. Today the government of Iraq has rebuilt part of the famous Hanging Gardens of Babylon, once one of the Seven Wonders of the World.

C. Interpreting
❓ How does this line change in meaning if the word *thy* is emphasized? (It suggests that the singer has seen his or her own babies dashed to death by the captors.)

In the sixth century B.C. Nebuchadnezzar, king of Babylonia, deported the Hebrews to Babylon, a great ancient city now a ruin near Baghdad on the Euphrates River. The speaker of Psalm 137 is a captive Hebrew, bitterly lamenting his people's exile. The captors have asked the Hebrews to sing, but what do they have to sing about? Instead, the psalmist curses himself should he ever forget Jerusalem, and then calls on God to destroy Jerusalem's enemies.

Psalm 137

By the rivers of Babylon, there we sat down, yea, we wept,
When we remembered Zion.°
We hanged our harps
Upon the willows in the midst thereof.
For there they that carried us away captive required of
5   us a song;
And they that wasted us required of us mirth,
Saying, "Sing us one of the songs of Zion."
How shall we sing the LORD'S song
In a strange land?
10 If I forget thee, O Jerusalem,
A ⌈ Let my right hand forget her cunning.
    If I do not remember thee,
   ⌊ Let my tongue cleave to the roof of my mouth;
If I prefer not Jerusalem above my chief joy.
Remember, O Lord, the children of Edom° in the day of
15   Jerusalem;
Who said, "Raze it,° raze it, even to the foundation thereof."
B ⌈ O daughter of Babylon, who art to be destroyed;
    Happy shall he be, that rewardeth thee
   ⌊ As thou hast served us.
20   Happy shall he be, that taketh
C ⌊ And dasheth thy little ones against the stones.

2. **Zion:** a hill in Jerusalem, the center of government, worship, and public life.

15. **children of Edom:** The Edomites, neighbors of the Hebrews, rejoiced when the Hebrews were conquered and deported.
16. **Raze it:** Level it to the ground.

Responding to the Psalms

Analyzing the Psalms

Identifying Details

1. In Psalm 8 which **images** suggest the enormous power of God?
2. In Psalm 23 which **images** show that God will protect the psalmist?
3. In Psalm 24 which **images** describe God in military terms?

4. In Psalm 137 which lines refer to the speaker's loss of talent as a harpist and singer?

Interpreting Meanings

5. In what ways does Psalm 8 resemble the creation narratives in Genesis?
6. How does the **figurative language** used to describe God in Psalms 23 and 24 affect the psalms' **tone**?

ANALYZING THE PSALMS

Identifying Details

1. The moon and stars, which God made; God's glory above the heavens; and the catalog of gifts that God ordained.

2. The Lord as his shepherd, who leads him beside still waters; the rod and the staff that comfort the psalmist in the valley of the shadow of death; the preparation of a feast for the psalmist; the anointing of his head with oil; his overflowing cup.

3. "The Lord mighty in battle" and the "Lord of hosts."

4. Lines 3–4 and 8–9.

Interpreting Meanings

5. Both show God as the omnipotent creator. Lines 7–8 of the psalm refer to the creation of the heavens, and lines 12–18, to aspects of earthy creation.

6. The figurative language in Psalm 23, describing the Lord as a shepherd, creates a consolatory tone. In Psalm 24, God is figuratively described as a triumphant military commander, creating a tone of joy and praise.

7. Homesickness in lines 1–2 and 10–14; revenge in lines 15–21. Reactions to the final line will vary.

Isaiah's Vision of the Destruction of Babylon by Gustave Doré. Engraving.

7. The speaker in Psalm 137 is both homesick and revengeful. Which lines convey these emotions most vividly to you? How did you react to the final line?

Reading Aloud

Prepare the psalms for oral recitation. Pay particular attention to the way **repetition** and **parallel structures** are used to create rhythm. How many speakers will you assign to each psalm?

Writing About the Psalms

A Critical Response

Comparing Another Translation. The following version of Psalm 23 appeared in a Psalter translated by the Massachusetts Puritans and published in *The Bay Psalm Book* (1640). Write an essay comparing it to the King James Version. Tell which version you prefer and why.

The Lord to me a shepherd is; want therefore shall not I.
He in the folds of tender grass doth cause me down to lie.
To waters calm me gently leads, restore my soul doth he;
He doth in paths of righteousness for his name's sake lead me.
5 Yea, though in valley of death's shade I walk, none ill I'll fear
Because thou art with me; thy rod and staff my comfort are.
For me a table thou hast spread in presence of my foes;
Thou dost anoint my head with oil; my cup it overflows.
Goodness and mercy surely shall all my days follow me,
10 And in the Lord's house I shall dwell so long as days shall be.

The King James Bible 405

405

1. **BUILDING ON PRIOR KNOWLEDGE.** Since most students will have some knowledge of the story of Jonah, ask them to begin by writing down what they remember of the plot.

2. **ESTABLISHING A PURPOSE.** Have students read with these questions in mind: How does Jonah get into the sea in the first place? Does he ever get to Nineveh? How is Jonah getting along with God at the end of the story?

SUPPLEMENTARY SUPPORT MATERIALS
1. Vocabulary Activity Worksheet (*CCB*)
2. Review and Response Worksheet: Theme (*CCB*)
3. Selection Test (*CCB*)

DEVELOPING VOCABULARY
The following words from the narrative are tested in the Selection Test. (See also Vocabulary Activity Worksheet.)
to beseech   gourd
affliction   vehement

A. Expansion
Going to Tarshish would be like going to the end of the earth.

B. Expansion
A *lot* could involve holding a drawing, picking the short straw, throwing dice, tossing coins, or something similar. The "winner" (or loser) is the one upon whom "the lot" falls. (The notion that a ship is endangered by having a guilty man on it is an old one.)

C. Characterization
Note the good nature and piety of these pagan sailors. They do not immediately leap at Jonah's suggestion, but work to avert its necessity. See how they worship Jonah's God in the passage that follows.

JONAH

Of all the kinds of writing in the Bible—poems, songs, riddles, philosophical and theological discourses, codes of behavior, history, proverbs, drama—the most memorable are the stories. Even people who do not read the Bible or attend a church regularly have heard of baby Moses in the bulrushes, Noah and his ark, young Joseph and his multi-colored coat, young David and the sling he used in slaying the giant Goliath, and the strong man Samson who lost his strength when Delilah cut off his hair. English authors take it for granted that their readers are familiar with these and dozens of other biblical stories from the Old Testament. Among the most famous biblical figures is Jonah, who, as everybody knows, was swallowed by a whale (the King James Bible says a "great fish") and after spending three days in its belly, was vomited up on the shore. Unfortu-

nately, this is all that many people know about this unusual story, though it is far from being the most important incident in it.

Jonah's story is told in the very short biblical book named after him. There are two main characters in the story: God and Jonah, a prophet. The chief duty of a Hebrew prophet was to go through the land calling on people to abandon their wicked ways, and warning them that God was about to destroy them. As the story opens, God has ordered Jonah to go and prophesy disaster to Nineveh, then the capital of Assyria and a vast city with a bad reputation. But Jonah, for reasons that are not exactly clear, does not want to go to Nineveh. Instead, he disobeys God and sets out for Tarshish, in the opposite direction from Nineveh and far off to the west, perhaps in Spain.

N
ow the word of the LORD came unto Jonah the son of Amittai, saying, "Arise, go to Nineveh, that great city, and cry against it; for their wickedness is come up before me." But Jonah rose up to flee unto Tarshish from the presence of the LORD, and went down to Joppa; and he found a ship going to Tarshish. So he paid the fare thereof, and went down into it, to go with them unto Tarshish from the presence of the LORD. But the LORD sent out a great wind into the sea, and there was a mighty tempest in the sea, so that the ship was like to be broken. Then the mariners were afraid, and cried every man unto his god, and cast forth the wares that were in the ship into the sea, to lighten it of them. But Jonah was gone down into the sides of the ship; and he lay, and was fast asleep.

So the shipmaster came to him, and said unto him, "What meanest thou, O sleeper? Arise, call upon thy God, if so be that God will think upon us, that we perish not." And they said every one to his fellow, "Come, and let us cast lots, that we may know for whose cause this evil is upon us." So they cast lots, and the lot fell upon Jonah. Then

said they unto him, "Tell us, we pray thee, for whose cause this evil is upon us? What is thine occupation? And whence comest thou? What is thy country? And of what people art thou?" And he said unto them, "I am an Hebrew; and I fear the LORD, the God of heaven, which hath made the sea and the dry land." Then were the men exceedingly afraid, and said unto him, "Why hast thou done this?" For the men knew that he fled from the presence of the LORD, because he had told them. Then said they unto him, "What shall we do unto thee, that the sea may be calm unto us?" for the sea wrought,[1] and was tempestuous. And he said unto them, "Take me up, and cast me forth into the sea; so shall the sea be calm unto you: for I know that for my sake this great tempest is upon you."

Nevertheless, the men rowed hard to bring it to the land; but they could not, for the sea wrought, and was tempestuous against them. Wherefore they cried unto the LORD, and said, "We beseech thee, O LORD, we beseech thee, let

---

1. **wrought:** was stirred up, agitated.

READING CHECK TEST
1. God orders Jonah to go to Nineveh, but Jonah disobeys. (T)
2. Jonah tells the men on the ship to throw him into the sea so that the storm will cease. (T)
3. God speaks to the great fish and Jo-
nah is vomited out upon dry land. (T)
4. Because the people of Nineveh refuse to listen to Jonah's warning, God destroys the city. (F)
5. Jonah is pleased with the decision that God made regarding Nineveh. (F)

Jonah Thrown Up by the Whale (detail). Manuscript illumination (15th century).

Musée Condé, Chantilly, France.

A. Humanities Connection: Responding to the Fine Art
❓ How does this medieval artist's understanding of the story differ from your own mental images of Jonah's ordeal? (Many students may recall the scene from Disney's *Pinocchio* or a scene from one of the *Star Wars* movies of the 1970's, which depicts the interior of a whale or large beast as a great cavern.)

B. Connections
❓ Compare Jonah's prayer (the indented lines) with the psalms you have read. What examples of imagery, repetition, and parallel structure show that this prayer is written like a psalm? Could this prayer be extended to many situations, even in life today? Note that Jack Abbott called his account of his experiences in prison *In the Belly of the Beast* (1982).

A

us not perish for this man's life, and lay not upon us innocent blood: for thou, O LORD, hast done as it pleased thee.'' So they took up Jonah, and cast him forth into the sea: and the sea ceased from her raging. Then the men feared the LORD exceedingly, and offered a sacrifice unto the LORD, and made vows. Now the LORD had prepared a great fish to swallow up Jonah. And Jonah was in the belly of the fish three days and three nights.

Then Jonah prayed unto the LORD his God out of the fish's belly, and said,

B

"I cried by reason of mine <u>affliction</u> unto the
    LORD, and he heard me;
Out of the belly of hell cried I, and thou heardest
    my voice.
For thou hadst cast me into the deep, in the
    midst of the seas;
And the floods compassed me about:
All thy billows and thy waves passed over me.
Then I said, I am cast out of thy sight;
Yet I will look again toward thy holy temple.
The waters compassed me about, even to the
    soul:

The depth closed me round about,
The weeds were wrapped about my head.
I went down to the bottoms of the mountains;
The earth with her bars was about me forever:
Yet hast thou brought up my life from corrup-
    tion, O LORD my God.
When my soul fainted within me I remembered
    the LORD:
And my prayer came in unto thee, into thine
    holy temple.
They that observe lying vanities forsake their
    own mercy.
But I will sacrifice unto thee with the voice of
    thanksgiving;
I will pay that that I have vowed.
Salvation is of the LORD.''

And the LORD spake unto the fish, and it vomited out Jonah upon the dry land.

And the word of the LORD came unto Jonah the second time, saying, ''Arise, go unto Nineveh, that great city, and preach unto it the preaching that I bid thee.'' So Jonah arose, and went unto Nineveh, according to the word of the LORD. Now

1. At first, Jonah disobeys God and sets out for Tarshish, but God causes a great storm on the sea, and Jonah is swallowed by a great fish. Jonah cries out to the Lord, who then causes the fish to vomit him up. When God again orders Jonah to Nineveh, he goes.
2. The people repent and God changes his mind and witholds his punishment from them.

Interpreting Meanings

3. Probably because he feels that God has used him unnecessarily.
4. The audience could be those who interpret prophecy too rigidly.

The lesson has to do with repentance and the great mercy of God. (Note that God is merciful even to Jonah, the rebellious prophet.)

A. Expansion
That is, it took three days on foot to cross the city.

B. Word Choice
? How is the word *repent* used here? (It refers to God's change of plan and His forgiveness of the people of Nineveh.)

C. Translations
In the Jerusalem Bible this is a castor-oil plant.

D. Expansion
A score is 20; the population (possibly just the number of children in Nineveh) is thus more than 120,000.

A Nineveh was an exceeding great city of three days' journey. And Jonah began to enter into the city a day's journey, and he cried, and said, "Yet forty days, and Nineveh shall be overthrown." So the people of Nineveh believed God, and proclaimed a fast, and put on sackcloth,[2] from the greatest of them even to the least of them. For word came unto the king of Nineveh, and he arose from his throne, and he laid his robe from him, and covered him with sackcloth, and sat in ashes.[3] And he caused it to be proclaimed and published through Nineveh by the decree of the king and his nobles, saying, "Let neither man nor beast, herd nor flock, taste anything: Let them not feed, nor drink water. But let man and beast be covered with sackcloth, and cry mightily unto God. Yea,
B let them turn everyone from his evil way, and from the violence that is in their hands. Who can tell if God will turn and repent, and turn away from his fierce anger, that we perish not?" And God saw their works, that they turned from their evil way; and God repented of the evil that he had said that he would do unto them; and he did it not.

But it displeased Jonah exceedingly, and he was very angry. And he prayed unto the LORD, and said, "I pray thee, O LORD, was not this my saying when I was yet in my country? Therefore

---

2. **sackcloth:** ugly, uncomfortable clothing worn to symbolize sorrow and repentance.
3. **ashes:** symbols of repentence.

I fled before unto Tarshish, for I knew that thou art a gracious God, and merciful, slow to anger, and of great kindness, and repentest thee of the evil. Therefore now, O Lord, take, I beseech thee, my life from me; for it is better for me to die than to live." Then said the LORD, "Doest thou well to be angry?" So Jonah went out of the city, and sat on the east side of the city, and there made him a booth, and sat under it in the shadow, till he might see what would become of the city. And
C the LORD God prepared a gourd, and made it to come up over Jonah, that it might be a shadow over his head, to deliver him from his grief. So Jonah was exceeding glad of the gourd. But God prepared a worm when the morning rose the next day, and it smote the gourd that it withered. And it came to pass, when the sun did arise, that God prepared a vehement east wind; and the sun beat upon the head of Jonah, that he fainted, and wished in himself to die, and said, "It is better for me to die than to live." And God said to Jonah, "Doest thou well to be angry for the gourd?" And he said, "I do well to be angry, even unto death." Then said the LORD, "Thou hast had pity on the gourd, for the which thou hast not labored, neither madest it grow; which came up in a night, and perished in a night. And should not I spare Nineveh, that great city, wherein are more than six-
D score thousand persons that cannot discern between their right hand and their left hand, and also much cattle?"

Responding to the Narrative

Analyzing the Narrative

Identifying Details

1. How does God persuade Jonah to go to Nineveh?
2. What miraculous events occur as a result of Jonah's warning the people of Nineveh?

Interpreting Meanings

3. Jonah claims to believe that God is "gracious and merciful"; why, then, does he become infuriated when God spares Nineveh?
4. Who do you think is the **audience** for the story of Jonah? What **lesson** do you think the story is teaching?

Writing About the Narrative

A Critical Response

Discussing the Theme. For at least two thousand years the story of Jonah has been interpreted and reinterpreted many times. One problem is that it seems incomplete; it ends abruptly, almost like a modern short story, without any final comment. What do you think is the theme of the story? What is the narrator's attitude toward Jonah? What is the story saying about God and God's relationship to human beings? Write a brief essay in which you discuss the theme of the story of Jonah, using any of these questions that you find helpful.

The Parables

The preceding biblical selections in this book have all been from the Hebrew Bible, which Christians call the Old Testament; this is the longer of the two main divisions of the Christian Bible. In the New Testament—which was originally written in Greek—a characteristic literary form is the **parable**, a short fictitious narrative illustrating spiritual or moral truths. The most memorable parables are those told by Jesus. Instead of speaking abstractly and philosophically, Jesus frequently taught his followers by means of realistic, down-to-earth parables about everyday events: A poor woman loses a coin, a sheep strays from the flock, a crooked steward cheats his employer, a man builds his house on a sandbank, bridesmaids are asleep when the bridal party arrives, a father forgives his wastrel son. On the surface the parables may seem to be simple, even superficial, stories. Looked at closely, they concern the profound truths and moral laws on which human happiness depends.

A Shepherd and Stray Sheep (1469).

Bibliothèque Municipale, Dijon, France.

A

A. Humanities Connection: Discussing the Fine Art
The parable of the lost sheep occurs in Luke 15:4–7. It is part of a trio of stories (the others are the story of the lost drachma and the story of the prodigal son). One moral of all three stories is that Heaven rejoices when a "lost" sinner repents. By implication, another point of the stories has to do with the love and mercy of God, which is not bounded by human conventions. Jesus Christ is often equated with a shepherd, notably in John 10:11–14.
❓ Although this medieval illustration has a Biblical basis, ask students if they perceive any non-Biblical elements in it. (The castle and landscape suggest Europe; the leisurely pipe-player anticipates the pastoral conventions of Renaissance poetry. See, for example, the illustration on text page 233.)

ESTABLISHING A PURPOSE. Have students look for the lesson of the parable.

SUPPLEMENTARY SUPPORT MATERIALS
1. Vocabulary Activity Worksheet (*CCB*)
2. Review and Response Worksheet: Parable (*CCB*)
3. Selection Test (*CCB*)

DEVELOPING VOCABULARY
The following word from the parable is tested in the Selection Test. (See also Vocabulary Activity Worksheet.)
raiment

CLOSURE
Ask students to think about this parable in the context of contemporary society. Why do most people in big cities, for example, not stop to help distressed people they see on the street? Are they behaving in the same way as the priest and the Levite?

A. Expansion
A *lawyer* was an expert in the Mosaic law, not an attorney in the modern sense. The word *tempted* here means *tested*.

B. Interpreting
In other words, the man wanted to justify himself for having asked the question.

ANALYZING THE PARABLE
Identifying Details
1. "Who is my neighbor?"
2. To show mercy to others, no matter who they may be.

Interpreting Meanings
3. The audience would have expected the priest and the Levite to be sensitive to the higher demands of charity, even though it would mean defiling themselves. But the Samaritan, an outsider, regarded as a heretic (he does not obey Mosaic law), is the one who has compassion for the wounded man. He obeys the higher law that requires us to be merciful.
4. Answers will vary. In general, many students will suggest "everyone."

THE PARABLE OF THE GOOD SAMARITAN

To understand this parable, you have to know that a Levite was a member of the priestly tribe. The priest and the Levite would be considered unclean, according to law, if they touched a dead person. Samaritans were people from Samaria; they had a mixed ancestry and mixed religion. They had adopted the Torah of the Hebrew Bible as their scriptures, but the Hebrews to the South frowned upon their "mixed religious practices."
The lawyer is questioning Jesus.

A And, behold, a certain lawyer stood up, and tempted him, saying, Master, what shall I do to inherit eternal life?

He said unto him, What is written in the law? how readest thou?

And he answering said, Thou shalt love the Lord thy God with all thy heart, and with all thy soul, and with all thy strength, and with all thy mind; and thy neighbor as thyself.

And he said unto him, Thou hast answered right: this do, and thou shalt live.

B But he, willing to justify himself, said unto Jesus, And who is my neighbor?

And Jesus answering said, A certain man went down from Jerusalem to Jericho, and fell among thieves, which stripped him of his <u>raiment</u>, and wounded him, and departed, leaving him half dead.

And by chance there came down a certain priest that way; and when he saw him, he passed by on the other side.

And likewise a Levite, when he was at the place, came and looked on him, and passed by on the other side.

But a certain Samaritan, as he journeyed, came where he was; and when he saw him, he had compassion on him.

And went to him, and bound up his wounds, pouring in oil and wine, and set him on his own beast, and brought him to an inn, and took care of him.

And on the morrow when he departed, he took out two pence, and gave them to the host, and said unto him, Take care of him: and whatsoever thou spendest more, when I come again, I will repay thee.

Which now of these three, thinkest thou, was neighbor unto him that fell among the thieves?

And he said, He that showed mercy on him. Then said Jesus unto him, Go, and do thou likewise.

—Luke 10:25–37

Responding to the Parable

Analyzing the Parable

Identifying Details
1. What question is the parable answering?
2. What are the hearers of the parable asked to do?

Interpreting Meanings
3. Why is it **ironic** that the priest and the Levite ignore the wounded man, but the Samaritan helps him?
4. After reading the parable, how do you answer the question: Who is my neighbor?

1. BUILDING ON PRIOR KNOWLEDGE. Talk with students about the ways they view their childhoods. Do they see childhood as a Golden Age, that time of purity, peace, and bliss described by Ovid and other ancient writers? (Remind them also of the description of the sixth day of creation in Genesis, on text page 397.) Also, discuss the meanings the word *retreat* can have.

2. ESTABLISHING A PURPOSE. As students read the poem, ask them to look for the ways in which the poet characterizes childhood.

SUPPLEMENTARY SUPPORT MATERIALS
1. Vocabulary Activity Worksheet (*CCB*)
2. Review and Response Worksheet: Tone (*CCB*)
3. Selection Test (*CCB*)

Henry Vaughan (1622–1695)

A Henry Vaughan was a country physician in Wales. With his twin brother Thomas he dabbled in alchemy and other secret philosophies, exploring the hidden relations between the world of creatures (plants, animals, human beings) and the world of spirits. Except for the time he spent as a student in Oxford and London and as a soldier fighting for the King in the Civil Wars, Vaughan lived out his long life in Wales. His poetical career was short, and the titles of his two principal books of poems are odd. The first is *Silex Scintillans* (1650), whose Latin title might be translated as "sparkling flint"—and these are, indeed, bright sparks of poetry struck out of the Welsh countryside. The second volume is *Olor Iscanus* (1651), which means "swan of Usk," Usk being a small river near Vaughan's native town. There are a great many verbal echoes of George Herbert in these two volumes, but Vaughan differs from Herbert in having a more individual and less institutional feeling for religion. To Herbert, the Church is all; to Vaughan, nature—the so-called "book of creatures"—is also a place where God can be experienced. Vaughan's poems are more uneven than Herbert's; they contain great lines (a poem about his dead friends begins "They are all gone into the world of night") interspersed among less interesting lines.

CLOSURE
Ask three students to debate whether this is essentially a sorrowful or hopeful poem. They must cite lines from the poem to support their views.

A. Expansion
Having strong local loyalties, Vaughan called himself "the Silurist" in honor of the Celtic tribe (*Silures*) that once inhabited his native Wales. He experienced a sort of religious awakening after going to war, falling ill, and losing his younger brother. Vaughan, like Donne, Herbert, and Marvell (text page 435), is considered a metaphysical poet.

B. Multiple Meanings
When students finish the poem, see if they can suggest another meaning for the word *retreat* that might apply to the poem.

C. Imagery
❓ What does the image "a white, celestial thought" suggest to you? (Purity, divinity, spirituality)

The speaker in this poem by Henry Vaughan believes that before he was born, his soul existed in heaven, in a state of blessedness. This state continued while he was an infant, before he learned to understand his "second race" (line 4), by which he means his existence in this world.

Commentators on this poem have often compared it with a later poem, William Wordsworth's "Ode: Intimations of Immortality," but the two poems are really not much alike. Vaughan's is Christian; Wordsworth's is pagan, derived from an idea he found in the Greek philosopher Plato.

B # The Retreat

Happy those early days! when I
Shined in my angel infancy.
Before I understood this place
Appointed for my second race,
5 Or taught my soul to fancy aught°
C But a white, <u>celestial</u> thought:
When yet I had not walked above
A mile or two from my first love,
And looking back, at that short space,
10 Could see a glimpse of His bright face;
When on some <u>gilded</u> cloud or flower
My gazing soul would dwell an hour,
And in those weaker glories spy
Some shadows of eternity:

5. **aught:** anything.

DEVELOPING VOCABULARY
The following words from the poem are
tested in the Selection Test. (See also
Vocabulary Activity Worksheet.)

celestial   to tread
gilded   enlightened
to dispense

**A. Humanities
Connection:
Responding to
the Fine Art**
Ask students to
study the painting
first in relation to
Vaughan's "The
Retreat."

❓ What details in
the painting
suggest inno-
cence? (The guile-
less look of the
children, the cra-
dling of the apple,
the sharing of the
grapes) What other
human qualities
does this image
suggest? (Family
ties, love, pride in
children) What
does the painting
reveal about life in
the sixteenth cen-
tury? (Student re-
sponses may in-
clude the evident
wealth of the fami-
ly, the fine crafts-
manship in clothing
and jewelry, the
uncomfortable col-
lars, the formality,
the "adult" costum-
es and poses of
the children.)

A

Baron Cobham and His Family (detail). Attributed to the
Master of the Countess of Warwick (1567). Oil on panel.

Reproduced by permission of the Marquess of Bath,
Longleat House, Warminster, Wiltshire, Great Britain.

1. "Angel infancy" (line 2), "a white, celestial thought" (line 6), "had not walked above a mile or two" (lines 7–8), the gaze on a "gilded cloud or flower" (lines 11–12), and "bright shoots of everlastingness" (line 20).
2. A wounding tongue (line 15), a guilty conscience (line 16), and sins of the senses (lines 17–18).
3. The speaker longs to "travel back" to his earlier innocence and proximity to God.

He says he cannot do it because his soul is "drunk" with the intoxication of the adult world and staggers as it tries to go back.

Interpreting Meanings
4. "Retreat" refers to the backward movement in time that the speaker desires to make, to regain his former purity.
5. The "first love" refers to God.
6. The tone is one of nostalgia, longing, and regret.
7. Answers will vary. Some will suggest that the speaker is longing for the happy, innocent Edenic state we all live in before our "fall" from grace. This state of innocence is symbolized by infancy in the poem.

A. Imagery
? What does "fleshly dress" refer to? (The body) What is suggested by "bright shoots of everlastingness"? (Memories of an immortal and spiritual state)

B. Responding
? What do you think of this idea? Do most people want to go forward, to see the future, or do they wish to retreat to childhood? (Answers will vary. Students should back up their opinions with reasons or examples.)

FOR FURTHER READING STUDENTS
You might refer students to Dylan Thomas's poem "Fern Hill" on text page 1125.

```
15      Before I taught my tongue to wound
        My conscience with a sinful sound,
        Or had the black art to dispense
        A several° sin to every sense,
A  ┌    But felt through all this fleshly dress
20 └    Bright shoots of everlastingness.
           O, how I long to travel back,
        And tread again that ancient track!
        That I might once more reach that plain
        Where first I left my glorious train,°
25      From whence th' enlightened spirit sees
        That shady city° of palm trees.
        But, ah! my soul with too much stay°
        Is drunk, and staggers in the way.
B  ┌    Some men a forward motion love;
30 └    But I by backward steps would move,
        And when this dust falls to the urn,°
        In that state I came, return.
```

18. **several:** different.

24. **train:** the company of angels.

26. **city:** the Celestial City of Heaven.
27. **stay:** residence in the world.

31. **urn:** container for human ashes. This is a poetic way of speaking since bodies were not cremated at this time.

Responding to the Poem

Analyzing the Poem

Identifying Details

1. In lines 1–20, list the **images** and details that describe infancy.
2. In lines 15–18, list the **images** and details that characterize adult life.
3. What does the speaker long to do? Why does he say he cannot do it?

Interpreting Meanings

4. What does the **title** refer to, in terms of the poem?
5. Who or what is the "first love" in line 8?
6. How would you describe this speaker's **tone**?
7. What connections can you see between this poem and the account of creation given in Genesis?

Writing About the Poem

A Critical Response

Evaluating the Main Idea. In two or three paragraphs, tell whether you agree or disagree with Vaughan's characterization of infancy and of adult life. Is infancy always a time of happiness and innocence? Must adulthood be sinful? Support your statements with reasons based on your own observations and reading.

A. Milton's Themes
Note the connection with Milton's theme in *Paradise Lost*. In the section reprinted here, Eve has the ability to choose, and she chooses evil.

John Milton (1608–1674)

John Milton by Robert Streater (c. 1650). Oil.

The Metropolitan Museum of Art, New York.
Gift of Mrs. Wheeler Smith, 1908. (08.237.1).

The Young Poet

Early in his life John Milton resolved to be a great poet. His teachers and his parents encouraged him in this ambition because they believed, as Milton said later in his life, that he "might perhaps leave something so written to aftertimes as they should not willingly let it die." Time has confirmed his parents' and his teachers' confidence in him: Milton's *Paradise Lost* is one of the most brilliant achievements in English poetry and perhaps the richest and most intricately beautiful poem in the world. Posterity has not willingly let *Paradise Lost* die.

Milton was fortunate in his parents. His father, a musician and a prosperous merchant, had him educated at St. Paul's School (which he loved) and Cambridge University (which he hated). Indulged in every way by his parents, Milton spent the next eight years after college (1632–1640) continuing his education by himself, since he firmly believed that a poet must be a person of learning, familiar with ancient and contemporary philosophy, history, languages, and literatures. He made a leisurely tour of Italy, whose language and culture he had long admired, and there he visited many interesting people, including the astronomer Galileo. And throughout this period he wrote poems, in English, Latin, Greek, and Italian. Some of these he collected and published in 1646. It has become customary to refer to them as Milton's "Minor Poems," but they would not be minor if anyone else had written them.

The two outstanding poems of Milton's early career are known today by their short titles: *Comus* and *Lycidas*. *Comus* is a masque, an elaborate pageant of the sort that Ben Jonson was famous for writing. *Comus* was presented with speeches, songs, and dances at Ludlow Castle in 1634, for and by the Earl of Bridgewater's family. It opens with two brothers and a sister—played by the Earl's children—lost in a forest. The sister, separated from her brothers, is invited by a flashy magician named Comus to join his troop. Comus flatters the girl and praises the carefree life of pleasure that he is offering her, but she is able to resist all his blandishments because she has inner strength of character: Her heart is pure. *Comus* gave Milton an early opportunity to dramatize an idea that he firmly believed: Human beings have been given the ability and freedom to choose between good and evil, and so long as they choose the good they will remain strong and free.

Just as *Comus* surpasses all other Renaissance masques by the beauty of its language and the profundity of its thought, so does *Lycidas* surpass all other pastoral elegies written in English. An **elegy** celebrates the memory of a dead person; this poem remembers Edward King, a fellow student of Milton's who was shipwrecked and drowned in the Irish Sea in 1637. The elegy is called pastoral because it imitates certain ancient elegies in using imagery of shepherds and their flocks. Milton and Edward King (renamed Lycidas) are the young shepherds feeding their flock. This poetic practice, used by Percy Bysshe Shelley and many other English poets, seems natural enough if we recall that the word *pastor* which is often applied to clergymen literally means "shepherd," and that, as students, both Milton and King were preparing themselves for the Church. Milton changed his mind and King—a most promising youth—was killed. To lament this loss, Milton combines and harmonizes both classical and Christian views of

A

Milton as a Family Man

Milton has been described as a noble but difficult man who was least admirable in his personal relationships. In June 1642, at the age of 34, he married Mary Powell, a very young girl from a down-at-the-heels Royalist family. She left him within six weeks (she returned to her parents) and did not return until 1645—an experience that liberalized Milton's views on divorce. After bearing him three daughters (to whom Milton showed little understanding or consideration) and a son who died in infancy, Mary Powell died in 1652. In 1656, Milton married Katherine Woodcock, who died in childbirth in 1658. (He lamented her passing in his last sonnet.) In 1663, blind, impoverished and discredited, Milton married his third wife, Elizabeth Minshull, who survived him by many years. You might enjoy Robert Graves's fictionalized but meticulously researched story of Milton's first marriage, *Wife to Mr. Milton* (1984).

---

death, in a way very characteristic of Christian Humanists. But the poem is more about life than death because it celebrates a human being's capacity to create something significant even in a short lifetime.

Milton's Political Activity

In the 1640's an ongoing struggle between King Charles and his Parliament came to a head. Milton, believing that a poet must be active in the life of his time, entered the paper warfare that accompanied the conflict and started publishing prose works—some of them very elaborate and a few of them very insulting—in support of the Parliamentary Party. For this reason some people have referred to Milton as a Puritan, but this is a label that has only limited application to a person of Milton's stature. If he shared some of the Puritans' ideas and attitudes, such as their extreme dislike of kings and bishops, he also differed greatly from them in other important ways. For instance, he advocated divorce for incompatible married couples and he argued that the press should be free from governmental censorship and interference. Although we take these freedoms for granted nowadays, most people in the seventeenth century, particularly most Puritans, considered them dangerously radical. Altogether, Milton wrote about twenty prose works between 1641 and 1660, some of them considerable volumes. Also during part of this period Milton served in the government of England under Oliver Cromwell, who, with the title of Lord Protector, ruled England after the Parliamentary Party had won the Civil War and executed King Charles. As Latin Secretary to the Council of State, Milton was responsible for all correspondence with foreign countries, Latin then being the language of diplomacy. But his eyesight was gradually failing; by 1652 he could distinguish day from night. Otherwise, by the age of forty-four, he was totally blind.

To Milton, the ideal government was a republic in which the most capable, intelligent, and virtuous men would serve as leaders. To establish and maintain such a government in England, he devoted most of his intelligence and energy for twenty years. Then suddenly, in 1660, the cause for which he had worked so hard became totally discredited; the English recalled their dead King's son from exile and crowned him as King Charles II. Overnight, Milton found himself stripped of his possessions and under arrest as a traitor. Fortunately, influential friends, including the poet Andrew Marvell, intervened, and Milton was allowed to go into retirement rather than to the scaffold. From then on his life was more like what we ordinarily imagine a poet's life to be. He lived privately with his three daughters and his third wife, his first two wives and only son having died. By reading aloud to him, in foreign languages as well as English, his daughters enabled him to carry on the studies he thought necessary for a poet.

Milton's Epics

Being a poet, in Milton's view, was not a matter of writing short lyrics that expressed his private feelings and insights; being a poet meant emulating the great authors of antiquity, the epic poets Homer and Virgil and the Greek dramatists Aeschylus, Sophocles, and Euripides. Because they chose subjects drawn from their own nations' history, Milton first pondered various English subjects for his works, especially King Arthur and the knights of the Round Table. But finally, after years of thinking and reading, Milton decided that King Arthur's exploits were mainly fictitious, and so he settled on subjects drawn from the Bible. Milton thought the Bible alone contained everything people needed to know for the practice of true religion; he rejected not only the Roman Catholic Church and the Church of England, but also the immense number of churches—Puritan or otherwise—that had proliferated in the century since the Reformation began. While the Christian religion was the most important matter in life, to Milton it was a matter involving only God, God's Word (the Bible), and the individual human being. The classics and the Bible provided Milton with the inspiration he needed for his major poems: *Samson Agonistes, Paradise Lost,* and *Paradise Regained.*

Milton published *Paradise Lost* twice: first in a ten-book version in 1667 and then in twelve books in 1674, the year of his death. It's no exaggeration to say that Milton in one way or another worked on this epic all his life; he made many different plans and even once thought of it as a tragedy with Satan, the fallen archangel transformed into the chief devil, as its protagonist. In the finished poem Satan is still very con-

A. Areopagitica

Milton's most famous prose work is *Areopagitica* (1644), an eloquent and idealistic document that supports freedom of the press and attacks censorship of books before publication (Milton allows for censorship to protect the common good). The word comes from *areopagus*, "the supreme tribunal of Athens," and refers to any group of persons whose judgments are authoritative.

B. The End of the Civil War

Winston Churchill describes tersely Cromwell's achievements: "By the end of 1648 all was over. Cromwell was Dictator. The Royalists were crushed; Parliament was a tool; the Constitution was a figment; the Scots were rebuffed, the Welsh back in their mountains; the Fleet was reorganized, London overawed. King Charles, at Carisbrooke Castle, where the donkey treads the water wheel, was left to pay the bill. It was mortal."

A. **Humanities Connection: Responding to the Fine Art**
Michaly von Munkacsy (mē′həl·ya von moon′kə·chē) (1844–1909) was a Hungarian painter of genre and historical subjects.
? Imagine yourselves in this scene: How old is each daughter? What time of day is it? What is happening right now? How do the three daughters share the work? How do they feel about John Milton as a father? Students might record their answers in their response journals. (Note that Milton had trouble with his daughters. He does not seem to have been an easy man to live with.)

spicuous. The first two books are devoted mainly to him, he appears frequently in books three to ten, and Milton lavishes on him some of his most glorious writing. It's not surprising, then, that many readers have regarded Satan as the secret hero of the poem, especially since he receives no such grand treatment in the Bible. "Milton was of the Devil's party without knowing it," asserted the poet and artist William Blake. But this argument is convincing only to those who concentrate on part of the poem and ignore the rest of it. Moreover, in literary works evil frequently seems more interesting than good, and if any part of *Paradise Lost* fails from a literary point of view, it is Milton's portrayal of God, who represents absolute good, just as Satan represents absolute evil.

In *Paradise Lost* Milton took relatively few verses from the Bible, mainly from Genesis, and developed them into a 10,565-line poem. He used the conventions and devices of the classical epic to make the poem a work of art; he used his prodigious learning and wide experience of human affairs to make the poem profound. Although the poem ranges back and forth between Hell and Heaven, the most important action takes place on Earth, where the first human beings, Adam and Eve, are given the choice of obeying or disobeying God. They chose, as everybody knows, to disobey, and having done so, they accept their punishment and make the best of the life that is left to them. They are the heroes of Milton's epic, and they represent us all.

Though it has always had its admirers, *Paradise Regained* (1671) is altogether a less impressive poem and arguably an unnecessary one because before *Paradise Lost* ends, Adam and Eve regain what they lost through disobedience: They attain a wonderful "paradise within," a spiritual paradise within themselves which is far superior to the physical Eden that they had forfeited. But Milton had an orderly mind, and he may have felt that he needed to complete his epic by showing how Christ, at the very beginning of his mission on Earth, defeated Satan. *Paradise Regained,* then, is a brief epic of 2070 lines based on an incident in the New Testament Book of Luke, in which Christ resists the temptations that Satan offers him, including the gift of "all the kingdoms of the earth."

A

The Blind Milton Dictating Paradise Lost *to His Daughters* by Michaly von Munkacsy (19th century). Oil.

PREPARATION

1. BUILDING ON PRIOR KNOWLEDGE. How do students imagine a *writer* who has lost his or her eyesight might feel? Given the fact that there were no typewriters, word processors, or even recorded books or tapes available in the seventeenth century, what impact would blindness have on a writer's life and work?

2. ESTABLISHING A PURPOSE. The final line of this sonnet is often quoted. Have students read to find out what this sentiment has to do with the speaker's blindness.

SUPPLEMENTARY SUPPORT MATERIALS

1. Vocabulary Activity Worksheet (*CCB*)
2. Review and Response Worksheet: Theme (*CCB*)
3. Selection Test (*CCB*)

DEVELOPING VOCABULARY

The following words from the poem are tested in the Selection Test. (See also Vocabulary Activity Worksheet.)

spent	to exact
bent	bidding
to chide	to post

Altogether, Milton wrote eighteen sonnets in English and five in Italian. In form and subject matter, his sonnets differ from those of his predecessors: Sidney, Spenser, and Shakespeare. Their sonnets are written in an English form unlike the models brought from Italy, where the sonnet was invented, and they are about love. Milton's sonnets closely follow the Italian (Petrarchan) model, and they are about events and persons in his public and private life.

This sonnet is about the calamity that hit Milton in middle age: he went blind long before he had accomplished his life's work. Deeply religious, and believing firmly in the accountability of all people to God, Milton asks, "How can I, handicapped as I am, do the work that God expects of me?" But it's a foolish question, he realizes, and may even sound like a "murmur" or complaint against God. To forestall further protest, the part of his conscience personified as Patience takes over and puts his suffering in perspective.

On His Blindness

When I consider how my light is <u>spent</u>
　Ere half my days in this dark world and wide,°
　And that one talent° which is death to hide
　Lodged with me useless, though my soul more bent
5 To serve therewith my Maker, and present
　My true account, lest He returning <u>chide</u>,
　"Doth God <u>exact</u> day-labor, light denied?"
A 　I fondly ask. But Patience, to prevent
　That murmur, soon replies, "God doth not need
10 Either man's work or His own gifts. Who best
　Bear His mild yoke,° they serve Him best. His state
　Is kingly: Thousands° at His <u>bidding</u> speed,
　　And <u>post</u> o'er land and ocean without rest;
　　They also serve who only stand and wait."

2. **wide:** A blind person's world is without limits.
3. **talent:** Milton's writing ability and also a punning allusion to the talent, or coin, for which the lazy servant in the parable (Matthew 25) was scolded for hiding rather than investing to increase its value.

11. **mild yoke:** easy harness. Jesus said (Matthew 11:30), "My yoke is easy, and my burden is light."
12. **Thousands:** of angels. (*Angel* comes from a Greek word meaning "messenger.")

A. Vocabulary
Fondly means "foolishly."

ANALYZING THE POEM
Identifying Details
1. The poet and a personification of patience.
2. His blindness prevents him from using his writing ability to serve God.
　Patience tells him that he will serve God best if he bears God's yoke patiently.

Interpreting Meanings
3. Milton slightly varies the structure by changing the direction of the sonnet in the middle of line 8, rather than at line 9.
4. The word *stand* carries connotations of respect, forbearance, and attentiveness.
5. Answers will vary. Some students might say that Milton's sense of pride in his work and talent wouldn't allow him to be reassured; others might say that, having been reminded of his duty to God, he would be reassured.
6. The statement is often applied to those too old or young or ill to defend their country.

Responding to the Poem

Analyzing the Poem

Identifying Details

1. Who are the speakers in the poem?
2. What worries Milton in the sonnet? How is this worry answered, and by whom?

Interpreting Meanings

3. Analyze the structure of this sonnet. How does Milton slightly vary the usual divisions into **octave** and **sestet**?
4. Suppose the word "sit" were substituted for "stand" in line 14. What difference would that make?
5. If you were in Milton's position, would you have been reassured by the words of Patience?

6. To what other situations in a person's life could this famous last line be applied?

Writing About the Poem

A Critical Response

Paraphrasing the Poem. Write a prose paraphrase of the sonnet. Put the figures of speech in plain, literal English, and rewrite the sentences so that they reflect the kind of syntax you hear in ordinary speech today. You will also have to supply some missing words. Write your paraphrase in the first person.

1. BUILDING ON PRIOR KNOWLEDGE. Ask students to discuss the monuments that have been built to honor great people, wars, or ideals. What should a monument do for the viewer? Have them think of how a person's writings themselves could be a kind of monument.

2. ESTABLISHING A PURPOSE. Ask stu-

dents to read to find out what the famous last line of the sonnet means.

SUPPLEMENTARY SUPPORT MATERIALS
1. Vocabulary Activity Worksheet (*CCB*)
2. Review and Response Worksheet: Theme (*CCB*)
3. Selection Test (*CCB*)

DEVELOPING VOCABULARY
The following words and expressions from the poem are tested in the Selection Test. (See also Vocabulary Activity Worksheet.)

relics	to sepulcher
to endeavor	pomp

CLOSURE
Have one student explain to another the meaning of the sonnet's final line.

A. Interpreting
❓ What does Milton mean by "slow-endeavoring art"? (All poets except Shakespeare, probably including himself)

ANALYZING THE POEM
Identifying Details
1. Why does Shakespeare, whose plays are living reminders of the man, need a stone pyramid as a monument?
2. His works.
3. "Thy unvalued book" (line 11).

Interpreting Meanings
4. Shakespeare's metrical facility ("easy numbers") and imagination.
5. He calls him "my Shakespeare," implying a close, almost familial, connection.

Critics and scholars have located thousands of connections between Shakespeare's works and Milton's, so it's clear that Milton was an admirer of the older poet. Moreover, Milton was born on Bread Street in London, the same street where the Mermaid Tavern, a favorite haunt of Shakespeare's, was located. Is it too fanciful to suppose that the boy Milton may have seen or even spoken to the man Shakespeare? At any rate, in 1632,

when Shakespeare's friends were republishing his collected works (the first collection came out in 1623), Milton contributed this poem to the volume, according to the pleasant custom of the time. It is interesting to find a poet with Milton's religious beliefs praising a dramatist; the Puritans hated the theaters and closed them down for eighteen years (1642–1660).

On Shakespeare

What needs my Shakespeare for his honored bones
The labor of an age in pilèd stones,
Or that his hallowed <u>relics</u> should be hid
Under a star-ypointing° pyramid?°
5   Dear son of Memory,° great heir of Fame,
What need'st thou such weak witness of thy name?
Thou in our wonder and astonishment
Hast built thyself a livelong monument.
A   For whilst to the shame of slow–endeavoring art
10   Thy easy numbers flow, and that each heart
Hath from the leaves of thy unvalued book
Those Delphic° lines with deep impression took,
Then thou, our fancy of itself bereaving,°
Dost make us marble° with too much conceiving;°
15   And so <u>sepulchered</u> in such <u>pomp</u> dost° lie,
That kings for such a tomb would wish to die.

4. **-ypointing:** pointing; Milton copied the *y* form of the participle from Spenser. It gave him the extra syllable he needed. **pyramid:** Many old monuments are pyramidal in shape, surmounted by stars.
5. **son of Memory:** brother of the Muses, who were daughters of Memory.

12. **Delphic:** truly poetical, inspired by Apollo of Delphi.
13. **bereaving:** depriving.
14. **make us marble:** turn us into marble statues about your monument. **conceiving:** imagining.
15. **dost:** that is, thou dost.

Responding to the Poem

Analyzing the Poem

Identifying Details
1. Paraphrase the questions the speaker asks in lines 1–6.
2. According to the poem, what is Shakespeare's true monument?
3. What hints does Milton give that Shakespeare was not adequately appreciated in his lifetime?

Interpreting Meanings
4. What qualities in Shakespeare does Milton admire?
5. What comparison does Milton imply might be made between Shakespeare and himself?

Writing About the Poem

A Critical Response
Comparing Poems. In a brief essay, compare "On Shakespeare" with Shakespeare's own Sonnet 55, beginning "Not marble, nor the gilded monuments." In your essay, tell what each poem says about the power of poetry. Could Shakespeare's sonnet be seen as a reply to those who wish to erect marble monuments to the dead?

Statue of William Shakespeare in Stratford-on-Avon.

A

A. Discussing the Photograph

? What would Milton say about statues of Shakespeare such as this one? (He might call them "weak witness" to Shakespeare's name. For Milton, Shakespeare's works were sufficient monument: "kings for such a tomb would wish to die.")

Samuel Johnson, the eighteenth-century writer and lexicographer (see text page 553), wrote about Milton:

"He seems to have been well acquainted with his own genius, and to know what it was that nature had bestowed upon him more bountifully than upon others: the power of displaying the vast, illuminating the splendid, enforcing the awful, darkening the gloomy, and aggravating the dreadful. He therefore chose a subject on which too much could not be said, on which he might tire his fancy without the censure of extravagance.

"The appearances of nature, and the occurrences of life, did not satiate his appetite of greatness. To paint things as they are requires a minute attention, and employs the memory rather than the fancy. Milton's delight was to sport in the wide regions of possibility; reality was a scene too narrow for his mind. He sent his faculties out upon discovery, into worlds where only imagination can travel, and delighted to form new modes of existence, and furnish sentiment and action to superior beings, to trace the counsels of hell, or accompany the choirs of heav-

A. Syntax

As the text states, the first sentence is very complicated. Have students try to rewrite this part of the sentence in conventional English word order (subject, verb, object). Note that the subject is understood ("you"), that the verb is "sing" (line 6), and that the prepositional phrase beginning "of man's first disobedience" (lines 1–5) follows the verb. The clause beginning "That" (line 6) modifies "Muse."

Paradise Lost

There is a formal, set way to begin an epic. At the outset an epic poet does two things: The speaker invokes the Muse to speak or sing through the poet (the Muse being one of the nine Greek goddesses who inspire poets, musicians, dancers, and any practitioner of the arts and sciences), and the speaker states the subject of the poem. Milton does both these things in the first complicated sentence (lines 1–16) of *Paradise Lost*. Grammatically, this sentence begins in line 6 with the command, "Sing, Heavenly Muse"; the epic is metaphorically a song, though far too long and complex to be literally sung. "Sing," says Milton, and now we move back to line 1, "Of man's first disobedience," which is Adam's and Eve's first act of disobedience against God, who had forbidden them to eat the fruit of a particular tree in Eden (see the selection from Genesis, Chapter 2). The result, or "fruit," a kind of pun in line 1, of their disobedience was expulsion from and loss of Paradise, another name for the Garden of Eden. Yet all was not lost because a "greater Man" (line 4), Jesus Christ, has restored the possibility of Paradise to the human race.

7. **Oreb . . . Sinai:** mountains where Moses received heavenly inspiration.
8. **shepherd:** Moses. **chosen seed:** the Jews.
10. **Sion hill:** where David had his palace in Jerusalem.
11. **Siloa's brook:** It flowed past God's "oracle," the Temple in Jerusalem.

15. **Aonian mount:** Helicon, the Muses' residence.

17. **Spirit:** the Holy Spirit, or Holy Ghost, who, with the Father and the Son, makes up the Trinity, the three-personed God.

> **A**
> Of man's first disobedience, and the fruit
> Of that forbidden tree whose mortal taste
> Brought death into the world, and all our woe,
> With loss of Eden, till one greater Man
> 5 Restore us, and regain the blissful seat,
> Sing, Heavenly Muse, that, on the secret top
> Of Oreb, or of Sinai,° didst inspire
> That shepherd° who first taught the chosen seed°
> In the beginning how the Heavens and Earth
> 10 Rose out of Chaos: or, if Sion hill°
> Delight thee more, and Siloa's brook° that flowed
> Fast by the oracle of God, I thence
> Invoke thy aid to my adventurous song,
> That with no middle flight intends to soar
> 15 Above th' Aonian mount,° while it pursues
> Things unattempted yet in prose or rhyme.
> And chiefly thou, O Spirit,° that dost prefer
> Before all temples th' upright heart and pure,
> Instruct me, for thou know'st; thou from the first
> 20 Wast present, and, with mighty wings outspread,
> Dovelike sat'st brooding on the vast abyss,
> And mad'st it pregnant: what in me is dark
> Illumine; what is low, raise and support;
> That, to the height of this great argument,
> 25 I may assert Eternal Providence,
> And justify the ways of God to men.

It's easy to agree with Milton when he calls this argument "great" (line 24), for he is attempting to resolve an interesting dilemma that has puzzled many people throughout the ages. On the one hand, we are told that through His Providence (line 25) God takes loving care of creation; on the other hand, we know that there are many very bad things in the world, such as war, crime, poverty, disease, oppression, injustice, death—the list is endless.

en.

"But he could not always be in other worlds: he must sometimes revisit earth, and tell of things visible and known. When he cannot raise wonder by the sublimity of his mind, he gives delight by its fertility.

"Whatever be his subject, he never fails to fill the imagination. But his images and descriptions of the scenes or operations of nature do not seem to be always copied from original form, nor to have the freshness, raciness, and energy of immediate observation. He saw nature, as Dryden expresses it, *through the spectacles of books;* and on most occasions calls learning to his assistance. The garden of Eden brings to his mind the vale of *Enna,* where Proserpine was gathering flowers. Satan makes his way through fighting elements, like *Argo* between the *Cyanean* rocks, or *Ulysses* between the two *Sicilian* whirlpools. . . . The mythological allusions have been justly censured, as not being always used with notice of their vanity; but they contribute variety to the narration, and produce an alternate exercise of the memory and the fancy.

(Continued on next page.)

In *Paradise Lost* Milton asserts that God is not responsible for these evils; instead, Adam's and Eve's disobedience to God's command "Brought death into the world, and all our woe" (line 3). God gave Adam and Eve the freedom to choose between good and evil, and the strength to resist evil; yet they chose evil, and their offspring, including all of us, have suffered the effects of their choice ever since. This explanation of course is not original to Milton; most Christians have accepted it for many centuries.

It must be emphasized that an individual reader need not accept this traditional explanation of the evil in the world in order to enjoy and admire the poem; the poem is interesting whether the explanation is "true" or not. Indeed, some readers have found evidence in the poem that Milton himself did not really believe the explanation. The poem is rich enough to provide support for many different interpretations. And the introduction, full of great sounds and lofty references, tells us that something truly big is beginning, "Things unattempted yet in prose or rhyme" (line 16).

A

Reading *Paradise Lost*

Although Milton knew Latin as well as he knew English, he decided after deliberation to write his epic in his native language. The example of Shakespeare may have been influential with him because he also decided to write in Shakespeare's meter, which is **blank verse** or unrhymed iambic pentameter. Though blank verse was the usual meter in dramatic poetry, it was not used at all for non-dramatic poems in Milton's day and for long after. Like any other poetry, it requires a reader to be alert to sentences not written in normal English word order (subject-verb-object). Most of Milton's sentences are long and many of them require patience to sort out the syntax. Then there is Milton's vocabulary, which includes both big and little words not used in ordinary prose today. In some passages Milton sprinkles unfamiliar proper nouns, and though these are explained in the notes, they still have to be understood in the context of the lines where they appear.

Readers will understand the epic better if they know about Milton's heroic, optimistic view of life. God purposely let Satan escape from Hell and establish himself on Earth, not only so that Satan's deeds would damn him further, but also so that human beings would have something to fight against—and with God's help triumph over. Goodness, to Milton, was not goodness unless it resulted from a struggle to overcome evil. In one of his prose tracts, *Aeropagitica* (1644), Milton wrote this sentence, now famous:

> I cannot praise a fugitive and cloistered virtue, unexercised and unbreathed, that never sallies out and sees her adversary, but slinks out of the race where that immortal garland is to be run for, not without dust and heat.

Here Milton describes life as a race in which good must compete

A. Expansion
Another religious concept connected with the sin of Adam and Eve is the idea of *felix culpa* (happy fault) of the Exsultet, a hymn still sung at the Easter Vigil in Roman Catholic services: "O truly needful sin of Adam, which was blotted out by the death of Christ! O happy fault that merited so great a Redeemer!"

(Continued from previous page.)

"His similes are less numerous, and more various, than those of his predecessors. But he does not confine himself within the limits of rigorous comparison: his great excellence is amplitude, and he expands the adventitious image beyond the dimensions which the occasion required. Thus, comparing the shield of Satan to the orb of the moon, he crowds the imagination with the discovery of the telescope, and all the wonders which the telescope discovers."

A. Humanities Connection: About the Engraving

The name Lucifer, found in Isaiah 14:12, means "bright star." The Hebrew word *Satan* means simply "adversary," and occurs in only four places in the Old Testament.

In the New Testament, Satan is taken for granted, but all tradition about Satan has its basis in a single New Testament passage, Revelation 12:7–9: "And there was war in heaven: Michael [an archangel] and his angels fought against the dragon; and the dragon fought and his angels, and prevailed not; neither was their place found any more in heaven. And the great dragon was cast out, that old serpent, called the Devil, and Satan, which deceiveth the whole world: he was cast out into the earth, and his angels were cast out with him."

with bad. Virtue, he says, is not virtue unless it is won in the "heat and dust" of the conflict with evil. And so, when Adam and Eve lose Paradise, they also gain something: the opportunity to prove themselves in the real world. The Archangel Michael, who comes to dispossess them of the perfect garden where they have lived so happily, tells them how to live in the new, imperfect world. Practice good deeds, he says, and patience, temperance, faith, and love, and

> then will thou be not loath
> To leave this Paradise, but shalt possess
> A Paradise within thee, happier far.

Illustration from *Paradise Lost* (17th century). Engraving.

Rare Books and Manuscripts Division, The New York Public Library.

A

422

422   **The Renaissance**

PREPARATION

1. BUILDING ON PRIOR KNOWLEDGE.
Review the Genesis account of the fall of
Adam and Eve on text page 399.

2. ESTABLISHING A PURPOSE. Ask students to pay particular attention to Satan's reasons for tempting Eve and Eve's
reasons for rising to the serpent's bait.

SUPPLEMENTARY SUPPORT MATERIALS
1. Vocabulary Activity Worksheet (*CCB*)
2. Review and Response Worksheet:
Characterization (*CCB*)
3. Selection Test (*CCB*)
4. Audiocassette recording

DEVELOPING VOCABULARY
The following words from the epic are
tested in the Selection Test. (See also
Vocabulary Activity Worksheet.)

dalliance   abject
oblique   capacious
fraudulent   importune
insatiate   delusive
guileful   comely

The following long excerpt from Book IX of *Paradise Lost* narrates Satan's successful temptation of Eve. Milton adds many details to the bare outline of the incident as it is given in Genesis, not only to make the story more interesting but also to make his readers better understand Eve's behavior.

In the preceding books of *Paradise Lost*, Satan, the former archangel Lucifer, has been cast out of Heaven for waging a civil war (epics always have warfare) against God. In Hell he and the other fallen angels, now devils, hold a conference to plan further campaigns against God. Wisely deciding not to attack God directly, they determine to seek revenge by attacking His new creation on Earth, which they have heard about. Satan, all alone, escapes from Hell and searches for Earth (a typical epic "dark voyage"). When he finds it, he spies on Adam and Eve. They, meantime, have been visited by the archangel Raphael, who tells them all about themselves: how God created them, put them in charge of the Earth, gave them free will. (Flashbacks of this kind are usual in epics.) Raphael also warns them against Satan, now loose from Hell and coming toward them. After hearing all this, Adam and Eve express their confidence in their ability to resist Satan and obey God's ban on the fruit of the Tree of the Knowledge of Good and Evil. Satan, of course, does not play fair: He approaches Eve in the disguise of a beautiful serpent, an animal that originally did not crawl on his belly but rolled along erect, glittering and waving fantastic plumes.

The Temptation of Eve

A
Since first break of dawn, the Fiend,
Mere serpent in appearance, forth was come,
And on his quest, where likeliest he might find
The only two of mankind, but in them

5   The whole included race, his purposed prey.
In bower and field he sought, where any tuft
Of grove or garden-plot more pleasant lay,
Their tendance° or plantation for delight;
By fountain or by shady rivulet

B
10   He sought them both, but wished his hap° might find
Eve separate; he wished, but not with hope
Of what so seldom chanced; when to his wish,
Beyond his hope, Eve separate he spies,

C
Veiled in a cloud of fragrance, where she stood,
15   Half spied, so thick the roses bushing round
About her glowed, oft stooping to support
Each flower of slender stalk, whose head though gay
Carnation, purple, azure, or specked with gold,
Hung drooping unsustained, them she upstays

D
20   Gently with myrtle band, mindless the while
Herself, though fairest unsupported flower,
From her best prop so far, and storm so nigh.
Nearer he drew, and many a walk traversed
Of stateliest covert,° cedar, pine, or palm;
25   Then voluble° and bold, now hid, now seen
Among thick-woven arborets° and flowers
Embordered on each bank, the hand° of Eve:

8. **tendance:** tending.

10. **hap:** luck.

24. **covert:** shade.
25. **voluble:** rolling.
26. **arborets:** bushes.
27. **hand:** handiwork.

A. Word Choice
❓ What words in the first five lines suggest Satan's evil nature and purpose? ("Fiend," "mere serpent in appearance," "prey") Note that *mere* means "pure."

B. Plot
❓ What was the purpose of Satan's search in the garden? (He wished to find Eve alone and to prey upon her.)

C. Imagery
Here is a beautiful example of Milton's lush, sensuous imagery. Note the appeals to sight and smell and touch.

D. Characterization/Foreshadowing
Question 6 on text page 434 asks about this famous metaphor. Note the foreshadowing of trouble with the words "and storm so nigh."

A. Simile

❓ To whom is Satan, newly arrived in the lovely garden, compared? (To a pent-up city dweller, delighting in the pleasures of the countryside)

B. Plot

❓ What is Satan's initial reaction to the sight of beautiful Eve? (Even he is disarmed by her innocence and momentarily distracted from his evil purpose.) Note the phrase "stupidly good."

C. Characterization

❓ Is Milton's characterization of Adam and Eve justified in Genesis? (Only by implication)

Spot more delicious than those gardens feigned
Or of revived Adonis, or renowned

30 Alcinous,° host of old Laertes' son,°
Or that, not mystic,° where the sapient king°
Held <u>dalliance</u> with his fair Egyptian spouse.
Much he the place admired, the person more.

As one who long in populous city pent,
35 Where houses thick and sewers annoy° the air,
Forth issuing on a summer's morn to breathe
Among the pleasant villages and farms
Adjoined, from each thing met conceives delight,
The smell of grain, or tedded° grass, or kine,
40 Or dairy, each rural sight, each rural sound;
If chance with nymphlike step fair virgin pass,
What pleasing seemed, for° her now pleases more,
She most, and in her look sums all delight.

A

Such pleasure took the serpent to behold
45 This flowery plot, the sweet recess of Eve
Thus early, thus alone; her heavenly form
Angelic, but more soft and feminine,
Her graceful innocence, her every air
Of gesture or least action overawed
50 His malice, and with rapine° sweet bereaved
His fierceness of the fierce intent it brought.
That space the evil one abstracted stood
From his own evil, and for the time remained
Stupidly good, of enmity disarmed,
55 Of guile, of hate, of envy, of revenge.

B

But the hot Hell that always in him burns,
Though in mid Heaven, soon ended his delight,
And tortures him now more, the more he sees
Of pleasure not for him ordained; then soon
60 Fierce hate he recollects, and all his thoughts
Of mischief, gratulating,° thus excites:
    "Thoughts, whither have ye led me? With what sweet
Compulsion thus transported to forget
What hither brought us? Hate, not love, nor hope
65 Of Paradise for Hell, hope here to taste
Of pleasure, but all pleasure to destroy,
Save what is in destroying; other joy
To me is lost. Then let me not let pass
Occasion which now smiles; behold alone
70 The woman, opportune° to all attempts,
Her husband, for I view far round, not nigh,
Whose higher intellectual more I shun,
And strength, of courage haughty, and of limb
Heroic built, though of terrestrial mold;°
75 Foe not informidable, exempt from wound,°
I not; so much hath Hell debased, and pain
Enfeebled me, to what I was in Heaven.
She fair, divinely fair, fit love for gods,
Not terrible, though terror be in love

C

29–30. **Adonis . . . Alcinous:** mythological inhabitants of gardens, or owners of them.
30. **Laertes' son:** Ulysses visited Alcinous in the *Odyssey.*
31. **mystic:** mythological. **sapient king:** Solomon (1 Kings 3:1), known for his wisdom (sapience).

35. **annoy:** dirty.

39. **tedded:** dried.

42. **for:** because of.

50. **rapine:** force.

61. **gratulating:** rejoicing.

70. **opportune:** open.

74. **mold:** make.
75. **exempt from wound:** invulnerable.

Satan in His Original Glory by William Blake.

The Tate Gallery, London.

A

A. **Humanities Connection: Responding to the Fine Art**
A biography of William Blake, eighteenth-century artist, poet, and mystic, appears on text page 617. Over the course of his life, Blake produced hundreds of paintings and engravings, many of them illustrations for the work of other poets, such as this and the one on text page 431. Some other fine examples are his illustrations for *The Canterbury Tales* (see text pages 86–87), for the Book of Job, and for Dante's epic.

This painting captures Satan as Lucifer, "bright star," shining with glory before his fall from heaven.

? What elements of the painting suggest Lucifer's preeminent status among the angels? (His size; the tiny representations of the other angels, busy about their duties; but above all, the quality of light that shines from his image) Why, given this image of Satan, was his fall so tragic? (Satan's original potential for goodness was a tragic waste.)

"Like most morally coherent writers, Milton is careful to distinguish the human from the demonic, even when what he is showing is the relationship between them. As it may be difficult to feel this distinction without examples we may take an analogy from Shakespeare. Cleopatra in Shakespeare is all the things that the critics of Milton say Eve is. She is vain and frivolous and light-minded and capricious and extravagant and irresponsible and a very bad influence on Antony, who ought to be out chasing Parthians instead of wasting his time with her. She is morally a most deplorable character, yet there is something about her which is obstinately likable. Perhaps that makes her more dangerous, but it's no good: we cannot feel that Cleopatra is evil in the way that Goneril and Regan are evil. For one thing, Cleopatra can always be unpredictable, and as long as she can be that she is human. Goneril and Regan are much closer to what is meant in religion by lost souls, and what that means dramatically is that they can no longer be unpredictable. Everything they do or say is coarse and ugly and cruel, but still it also has about it something of the styl-

A. Description

How does Milton describe the serpent as it approaches Eve? How does it differ from serpents as we know them? (It was crested, dazzling, and bejeweled, moving about the ground in spiraling coils.)

B. Plot

How does Satan use Eve's beauty as bait to tempt her? (He tells her that her beauty is such that she should have more than beasts and one man to admire her; rather, she should be a goddess with angels to attend her.)

80 And beauty, not° approached by stronger hate,
Hate stronger, under show of love well feigned,
The way which to her ruin now I tend."
    So spake the enemy of mankind, enclosed
In serpent, inmate bad, and toward Eve
85 Addressed his way, not with indented wave,
Prone on the ground, as since, but on his rear,
Circular base of rising folds, that towered
Fold above fold a surging maze; his head

A

Crested aloft, and carbuncle° his eyes;
90 With burnished neck of verdant gold, erect
Amidst his circling spires,° that on the grass
Floated redundant. Pleasing was his shape,
And lovely; never since of serpent kind
Lovelier. . . . With tract° oblique
95 At first, as one who sought access, but feared
To interrupt, sidelong he works his way.
As when a ship by skillful steersman wrought
Nigh river's mouth or foreland, where the wind
Veers oft, as oft so steers, and shifts her sail,
100 So varied he, and of his tortuous train
Curled many a wanton wreath in sight of Eve,
To lure her eye; she busied heard the sound
Of rustling leaves, but minded not, as used
To such disport before her through the field,
105 From every beast, more duteous at her call,
Than at Circean° call the herd disguised.
He bolder now, uncalled before her stood,
But as in gaze admiring; oft he bowed
His turret° crest, and sleek enameled neck,
110 Fawning, and licked the ground whereon she trod.
His gentle dumb expression turned at length
The eye of Eve to mark his play; he, glad
Of her attention gained, with serpent tongue
Organic,° or impulse of vocal air,°
115 His fraudulent temptation thus began.
    "Wonder not, sovereign mistress, if perhaps
Thou canst, who art sole wonder, much less arm
Thy looks, the heaven of mildness, with disdain,
Displeased that I approach thee thus, and gaze
120 Insatiate, I thus single, nor have feared
Thy awful° brow, more awful thus retired.

B

Fairest resemblance of thy Maker fair,
Thee all things living gaze on, all things thine
By gift, and thy celestial beauty adore
125 With ravishment beheld, there best beheld
Where universally admired; but here
In this enclosure wild, these beasts among,
Beholders rude, and shallow to discern
Half what in thee is fair, one man except,
130 Who sees thee? (And what is one?) Who shouldst be
    seen

80. **not:** if not.

89. **carbuncle:** bright red.

91. **spires:** coils.

94. **tract:** course.

106. **Circean:** pertaining to Circe, an enchantress in the *Odyssey* who turned men to swine.

109. **turret:** towering.

114. **organic:** natural. **vocal air:** wind sounding like a voice.

121. **awful:** demanding respect.

ized grandeur of the demonic, something of the quality that Milton's devils have and that his human beings do not have. At the same time Cleopatra is a part of something far more sinister than herself: this comes out of the imagery attached to Egypt, if not in the characterization attached to her. Putting the two together, what we see is the human contained by the demonic, a fascinating creature of infinite variety who is still, from another point of view, sprung from the equivocal generation of the Nile.

"It is the same with Adam and Eve. Theologically and conceptually, they have committed every sin in the calendar. In *The Christian Doctrine* Milton sets it all down: there was nothing bad that they omitted to do when they ate that wretched apple:

It comprehended at once distrust in the divine veracity, and a proportionate credulity in the assurances of Satan; unbelief; ingratitude; disobedience; gluttony; in the man excessive uxoriousness, in the woman a want of proper regard for her husband, in both an insensibility to the welfare of their offspring, and that offspring the whole hu-

(Continued on next page.)

> A goddess among gods, adored and served
> By angels numberless, thy daily train.''
>   So glozed° the tempter, and his proem° tuned;
> Into the heart of Eve his words made way,
> 135 Though at the voice much marveling; at length,
> Not unamazed, she thus in answer spake.
> "What may this mean? Language of man pronounced
> By tongue of brute, and human sense expressed?
> The first at least of these I thought denied
> 140 To beasts, whom God on their creation-day
> Created mute to all articulate sound;
> The latter I demur,° for in their looks
> Much reason, and in their actions oft appears.
> Thee, serpent, subtlest beast of all the field
> 145 I knew, but not with human voice endued:°
> Redouble then this miracle, and say,
> How cam'st thou speakable of mute,° and how
> To me so friendly grown above the rest
> Of brutal kind, that daily are in sight?
> 150 Say, for such wonder claims attention due.''
>   To whom the guileful tempter thus replied:
> "Empress of this fair world, resplendent Eve!
> Easy to me it is to tell thee all
> What thou command'st and right thou shouldst be
>   obeyed:
> 155 I was at first as other beasts that graze
> The trodden herb, of abject thoughts and low,
> As was my food, nor aught but food discerned
> Or sex, and apprehended nothing high:
> Till on a day, roving the field, I chanced
> 160 A goodly tree far distant to behold
> Loaden with fruit of fairest colors mixed,
> Ruddy and gold; I nearer drew to gaze;
> When from the boughs a savory odor blown,
> Grateful to appetite, more pleased my sense
> 165 Than smell of sweetest fennel,° or the teats°
> Of ewe or goat dropping with milk at even,
> Unsucked of° lamb or kid, that tend° their play.
> To satisfy the sharp desire I had
> Of tasting those fair apples, I resolved
> 170 Not to defer; hunger and thirst at once,
> Powerful persuaders, quickened at the scent
> Of that alluring fruit, urged me so keen.
> About the mossy trunk I wound me soon,
> For, high from ground, the branches would require
> 175 Thy utmost reach, or Adam's: Round the tree
> All other beasts that saw, with like desire
> Longing and envying stood, but could not reach.
> Amid the tree now got, where plenty hung
> Tempting so nigh, to pluck and eat my fill
> 180 I spared° not; for such pleasure till that hour
> At feed or fountain never had I found.

133. **glozed:** praised excessively. **proem:** introduction.

142. **demur:** doubt.

145. **endued:** endowed.

147. **of mute:** after being dumb.

165. **fennel:** a plant supposedly attractive to snakes. **teats:** udders.

167. **of:** by. **tend:** go about.

180. **spared:** refrained.

A. Plot
What does Eve ask the serpent to explain here? (Why he can speak and why he has come to her in such a friendly manner)

B. Plot
In the lines that follow, how does the serpent explain his ability to speak? (He says he gained it by eating the fruit of a very special tree. See the serpent's speech to page 428, through line 196.)

C. Imagery
What various senses does Milton appeal to here? (Note sight, smell, and taste.) You might ask students to write their own descriptions of this forbidden fruit.

man race; parricide, theft, invasion of the rights of others, sacrilege, deceit, presumption in aspiring to divine attributes, fraud in the means employed to attain the object, pride, and arrogance.

Yet there is something that it is wholly impossible for us to feel or realize dramatically, nor does Milton attempt to make us do so. Eve may have been a

silly girl but she is still our general mother, still quite obviously the same kind of human being we are."

—Northrop Frye,
The Return of Eden

A. Characterization

? How is the serpent flattering Eve? (By calling her Empress, which suggests power as well as splendor)

B. Imagery

? How does the sinuous movement of the serpent reflect his purpose? (While appearing well-intentioned, he is indirectly appealing to Eve's weaknesses to gain his crooked end.)

C. Foreshadowing/Irony

Note again the foreshadowing of the cosmic tragedy about to take place. Note also the dramatic irony: We feel intensely sad about what is about to occur, but Eve is absolutely innocent. Note also how Milton intensifies our feelings by calling Eve our "credulous mother."

D. Word Play

? Explain the pun in line 232. (The word *fruitless* is used to mean both "without fruit" and "useless," since Eve recognizes that this is the fruit that has been forbidden.)

Sated at length, ere long I might perceive
Strange alteration in me, to degree
Of reason in my inward powers, and speech
185   Wanted not long, though to this shape retained.°
Thenceforth to speculations high or deep
I turned my thoughts, and with capacious mind
Considered all things visible in Heaven,
Or Earth, or middle, all things fair and good:
190   But all that fair and good in thy divine
Semblance, and in thy beauty's heavenly ray
United I beheld; no fair° to thine
Equivalent or second, which compelled
Me thus, though importune perhaps, to come
195   And gaze, and worship thee of right declared
Sovereign of creatures, universal dame."
     So talked the spirited° sly snake; and Eve
Yet more amazed, unwary thus replied:
     "Serpent, thy overpraising leaves in doubt
200   The virtue of that fruit, in thee first proved.
But say, where grows the tree, from hence how far?
For many are the trees of God that grow
In Paradise, and various, yet unknown
To us; in such abundance lies our choice,
205   As leaves a greater store of fruit untouched,
Still hanging incorruptible, till men
Grow up to their provision, and more hands
Help to disburden Nature of her bearth."°
A   To whom the wily adder, blithe and glad:
210   "Empress, the way is ready, and not long,
Beyond a row of myrtles, on a flat,
Fast by a fountain, one small thicket past
Of blowing° myrrh and balm: If thou accept
My conduct,° I can bring thee thither soon."
215   "Lead then," said Eve. He leading swiftly rolled
B   In tangles, and made intricate seem straight,
To mischief swift. Hope elevates, and joy
Brightens his crest; as when a wandering fire°
Compact° of unctuous° vapor, which the night
220   Condenses, and the cold environs round,
Kindled through agitation to a flame
(Which oft, they say, some evil spirit attends),
Hovering and blazing with delusive light,
Misleads th' amazed night-wanderer from his way
225   To bogs and mires, and oft through pond or pool,
There swallowed up and lost, from succor° far.
So glistered the dire snake, and into fraud
C   Led Eve our credulous mother, to the tree
Of prohibition, root of all our woe;
230   Which when she saw, thus to her guide she spake:
     "Serpent, we might have spared our coming hither,
D   Fruitless to me, though fruit be here to excess,
The credit of° whose virtue rest with thee;

185. **retained:** confined.

192. **fair:** fairness.

197. **spirited:** possessed by a spirit.

208. **bearth:** what the tree bears, fruit.

213. **blowing:** blooming.
214. **conduct:** escort.

218. **fire:** will-o-the-wisp.
219. **compact:** composed. **unctuous:** oily.

226. **succor:** help.

233. **credit of:** belief in.

Wondrous indeed, if cause of such effects!
235   But of this tree we may not taste nor touch;
God so commanded, and left that command
Sole daughter of his voice; the rest, we live
Law to ourselves; our reason is our law.''
        To whom the Tempter guilefully replied:
240   ''Indeed? Hath God then said that of the fruit
Of all these garden trees ye shall not eat,
Yet lords declared of all in Earth or air?''
        To whom thus Eve, yet sinless: ''Of the fruit
Of each tree in the garden we may eat,
245   But of the fruit of this fair tree amidst
The garden, God hath said, 'Ye shall not eat
Thereof, nor shall ye touch it, lest ye die.' ''
A   She scarce had said, though brief, when now more
              bold,
The tempter, but with show of zeal and love
250   To man, and indignation at his wrong,
New parts puts on,° and as to passion moved,
Fluctuates disturbed, yet comely, and in act
Raised,° as of some great matter to begin.
As when of old some orator renowned
255   In Athens or free Rome, where eloquence
Flourished, since mute, to some great cause addressed,
Stood in himself collected, while each part,
Motion, each act, won audience ere the tongue,
Sometimes in height began, as no delay
260   Of preface brooking,° through his zeal of right.
So standing, moving, or to height upgrown
The tempter all impassioned thus began:
        ''O sacred, wise, and wisdom-giving plant,
Mother of science!° Now I feel thy power
265   Within me clear, not only to discern
Things in their causes, but to trace the ways
Of highest agents, deemed° however wise.
Queen of this universe! Do not believe
Those rigid threats of death. Ye shall not die;
270   How should ye? By the fruit? it gives you life
To° knowledge; by the Threatener?° Look on me,
Me who have touched and tasted, yet both live,
B And life more perfect have attained than Fate
Meant me, by venturing higher than my lot.
275   Shall that be shut to man, which to the beast
Is open? Or will God incense his ire°
For such a petty trespass, and not praise
Rather your dauntless virtue, whom the pain
Of death denounced, whatever thing death be,
280   Deterred not from achieving what might lead
To happier life, knowledge of good and evil?
Of good, how just! Of evil, if what is evil
Be real, why not known, since easier shunned?
God therefore cannot hurt ye, and be just;

251. **New . . . on:** assumes a new role, that of friend to man and woman.

253. **Raised:** standing erect.

260. **brooking:** tolerating.

264. **science:** knowledge.

267. **deemed:** judged.

271. **To:** in addition to. **Threatener:** Satan's sarcastic name for God.

276. **incense his ire:** increase his anger.

A. Characterization

? What is the serpent doing in lines 248–262? What comparison is drawn? (He is generally puffing himself up and preening like a classical orator about to give an important speech.)

B. Theme
Note the serpent's subtle appeal to Eve's pride and ambition.

A. Responding

? What do you think is the significance of this phrase "knowing both good and evil"? (Understanding the nature of good and evil, perhaps) Why is such knowledge characteristic of the gods but not of Adam and Eve in their original states? (Adam and Eve knew no evil originally and were, therefore, innocent.)

B. Motivation

? What factors are already weakening Eve's resolve not to eat the fruit? (The serpent's wily arguments, her hunger, and the beauty and fragrance of the fruit)

285   Not just, not God; not feared then, nor obeyed:
Your fear itself of death removes the fear.°
Why then was this forbid? Why but to awe,
Why but to keep ye low and ignorant,
His worshipers? He knows that in the day
290   Ye eat thereof, your eyes that seem so clear,
Yet are but dim, shall perfectly be then
A   Opened and cleared, and ye shall be as gods,°
Knowing both good and evil, as they know.
That ye should be as gods, since I as man,
295   Internal° man, is but proportion meet,°
I, of brute, human; ye, of human, gods.
So ye shall die perhaps, by putting off
Human, to put on gods: Death to be wished,
Though threatened, which no worse than this can bring.
300   And what are gods that man may not become
As they, participating godlike food?
The gods are first, and that advantage use
On our belief, that all from them proceeds.
I question it; for this fair Earth I see,
305   Warmed by the sun, producing every kind,
Them nothing. If they all things° who enclosed
Knowledge of good and evil in this tree,
That whoso eats thereof forthwith attains
Wisdom without their leave? And wherein lies
310   Th' offense, that man should thus attain to know?
What can your knowledge hurt him, or this tree
Impart against his will if all be his?
Or is it envy, and can envy dwell
In heavenly breasts? These, these, and many more
315   Causes import your need of this fair fruit.
Goddess humane, reach then, and freely taste!''
  He ended, and his words, replete with guile,
Into her heart too easy entrance won:
Fixed on the fruit she gazed, which to behold
320   Might tempt alone, and in her ears the sound
Yet rung of his persuasive words, impregned°
B   With reason, to her seeming, and with truth;
Meanwhile the hour of noon drew on, and waked
An eager appetite, raised by the smell
325   So savory of that fruit, which with desire,
Inclinable now grown to touch or taste,
Solicited her longing eye; yet first
Pausing a while, thus to herself she mused:
  "Great are thy virtues, doubtless, best of fruits,
330   Though kept from man, and worthy to be admired,
Whose taste, too long forborn,° at first essay°
Gave elocution to the mute, and taught
The tongue not made for speech to speak thy praise.
Thy praise he also who forbids thy use,
335   Conceals° not from us, naming thee the Tree
Of Knowledge, knowledge both of good and evil;

286. **removes the fear:** takes away the fear of God.

292. **gods:** Satan avoids saying *God,* but speaks like a pagan about *gods.*

295. **Internal:** He says that internally (mentally) he is a human being. **meet:** appropriate.

306. **If . . . things:** if they produced all things.

321. **impregned:** impregnated.

331. **forborn:** avoided. **essay:** trial.

335. **Conceals:** She is saying that God does not hide the tree's virtues; just by naming the tree he makes it attractive.

1. The Fiend first finds Eve looking at the Tree of Knowledge. (F)

2. The serpent's only remaining joy is to destroy pleasures denied to him. (T)

3. Eve is frightened by the serpent because he is ugly. (F)

4. The serpent says he can speak because he has eaten the fruit of a particular tree. (T)

5. The serpent has already tried to tempt Adam but has failed. (F)

6. The serpent decides to tempt Eve because he hates women. (F)

7. Eve says God has commanded her and Adam not to touch or eat the fruit of this particular tree. (T)

8. The serpent says he ate of the fruit and is still alive. (T)

9. As soon as Eve tastes the fruit, the serpent slinks away. (T)

10. Eve decides to have Adam share in her disobedience because she cannot endure life without him. (T)

Angel of Divine Presence Clothing Adam and Eve with Coats of Skin by William Blake.

A. Humanities Connection: Responding to the Fine Art
This painting illustrates events after Adam, too, has eaten the fruit, and he and Eve must leave Eden. (See the account from Genesis, Chapter 3, which begins on text page 398 with the paragraph, "Now the serpent was. . . .")

When students have completed Milton's description of the temptation of Eve, you might have them reread Genesis 3.

How has Milton's poem affected your visualization and interpretation of the temptation of Eve, and of subsequent events, such as God's words to the serpent? What is the scene Blake depicts here? (God is clothing the pair in skins after they feel shame for the first time.) Does Blake suggest an angry, vengeful God, or a loving one? Where do you think this sad scene is set? (At the entrance—or exit—to the Garden)

CLOSURE

Ask a panel of students to cite all the arguments used by Satan to persuade Eve to eat the forbidden fruit. Which arguments do they think are most persuasive?

ANALYZING THE POEM

Identifying Details

1. In a grove of beautiful rose bushes.

2. Satan has lost all joy except the pleasure of destruction, and he will try to tempt Eve by concealing his hatred under the guise of admiration.

3. Satan tells Eve not to believe any threats of death because he ate and still lives. He then argues that eating the fruit increased his knowledge and made him perfect. He tells Eve that God will probably applaud her initiative if she eats the fruit and that God has deliberately forbidden Eve to eat because He wants to keep her in submission. He tells Eve that she will be godlike if she eats the fruit, just as Satan, a serpent, has acquired human powers. Finally, he asks Eve what harm can exist in a desire for knowledge.

4. She rationalizes by saying that God's prohibition makes the fruit more desir-

---

A. Irony

❓ What is ironic about Eve's speech? (Everything she asserts about the serpent is the complete opposite of what the reader knows to be true: He is envious, full of guile, malice, and deceit; and the fruit, rather than a cure, will be a curse.)

B. Climax

Here is the dramatic climax of the story.

❓ Note what happens to Earth. (It is wounded.) What do you think Nature does to give signs of woe that "all is lost"? (Perhaps a storm, earthquake, shadow over the sun, etc.) In an understatement, Milton describes the villain's exit from the scene. Notice the verb *slunk*.

C. Simile

❓ After she has eaten the fruit, what is Eve's state compared to? (To the state of intoxication caused by too much wine)

Forbids us then to taste; but his forbidding
Commends thee more, while it infers the good
By thee communicated, and our want:
340 For good unknown sure is not had, or had
And yet unknown, is as not had at all.
In plain° then, what forbids he but to know?
Forbids us good, forbids us to be wise!
Such prohibitions bind not. But if Death
345 Bind us with after-bands, what profits then
Our inward freedom? In the day we eat
Of this fair fruit, our doom is, we shall die.
How dies the serpent? He hath eaten and lives,
And knows, and speaks, and reasons, and discerns,
350 Irrational till then. For us alone
Was death invented? Or to us denied
This intellectual food, for beasts reserved?
[A] For beasts it seems; Yet that one beast which first
Hath tasted, envies not, but brings with joy
355 The good befallen him, author unsuspect,°
Friendly to man, far from deceit or guile.
What fear I then, rather what know to fear
Under this ignorance of good and evil,
Of God or death, of law or penalty?
360 Here grows the cure of all, this fruit divine,
Fair to the eye, inviting to the taste,
Of virtue° to make wise; what hinders then
To reach, and feed at once both body and mind?"
    So saying, her rash hand in evil hour,
365 [B] Forth reaching to the fruit, she plucked, she eat.°
Earth felt the wound, and Nature from her seat
Sighing through all her works gave signs of woe,
That all was lost. Back to the thicket slunk
The guilty serpent, and well might, for Eve
370 Intent now wholly on her taste, naught else
Regarded; such delight till then, as seemed,
In fruit never tasted, whether true
Or fancied so, through expectation high
Of knowledge; nor was godhead° from her thought.
375 Greedily she engorged without restraint,
And knew not eating death. Satiate at length,
And heightened as with wine, jocund and boon,°
[C] Thus to herself she pleasingly began:
    "O sovereign, virtuous, precious of all trees
380 In Paradise! Of operation blest
To sapience,° hitherto obscured, infamed,°
And thy fair fruit let hang, as to no end
Created; but henceforth my early care,
Not without song each morning, and due praise
385 Shall tend thee, and the fertile burden ease
Of thy full branches offered free to all;
Till dieted by thee I grow mature
In knowledge, as the gods who all things know;

---

342. **In plain:** in plain language.

355. **author unsuspect:** an authority beyond suspicion.

362. **virtue:** power.

365. **eat:** pronounced *et*, meaning ate—an old past tense of *eat*.

374. **godhead:** godhood, which Eve hoped to attain.

377. **jocund and boon:** jolly and merry.

381. **sapience:** wisdom. **infamed:** without fame.

432

able and that prohibitions against attaining knowledge are not binding. Since the serpent has eaten the fruit and is not dead, why should she fear death if she eats it? Finally, she accepts the serpent's apparent good will and guilelessness.

5. Earth feels her wound, and Nature sighs and gives signs of woe.

Interpreting Meanings

6. Eve is far away from Adam, her supporter.

The storm of Satan's temptation is nigh.

7. Milton may be awed by love's power—at least of human love inspired by physical beauty.

8. Satan flatters Eve by praising her beauty and comparing her to a goddess.

Eve does not detect his lies because she is distracted by the serpent's ability to speak, and she seems subject to his flattery.

9. He insinuates that God is tyrannical and envious.

Satan says that by eating the fruit Eve will not die as a human but live as a god.

The greatest inconsistency is that God, (*Answers continue on next page.*)

Though others envy what they cannot give:
390   For had the gift been theirs, it had not here
Thus grown. Experience, next to thee I owe,
Best guide; not following thee I had remained
In ignorance; thou open'st Widsom's way,
And giv'st access, though secret she retire.
395   And I perhaps am secret; Heaven is high,
A   High and remote to see from thence distinct
Each thing on Earth; and other care perhaps
May have diverted from continual watch
Our great Forbidder,° safe with all his spies
400   About him. But to Adam in what sort°
Shall I appear? Shall I to him make known
As yet my change, and give him to partake
Full happiness with me, or rather not,
But keep the odds° of knowledge in my power
405   Without copartner? So to add what wants°
B   In female sex, the more to draw his love,
And render me more equal, and perhaps,
A thing not undesirable, sometime
Superior; for, inferior, who is free?
410   This may be well. But what if God have seen
And death ensue? Then I shall be no more,
And Adam, wedded to another Eve,
Shall live with her enjoying, I extinct;
C   A death to think. Confirmed then I resolve,
415   Adam shall share with me in bliss or woe.
So dear I love him, that with him all deaths
I could endure, without him live no life."
    So saying, from the tree her step she turned,
But first low reverence done, as to the power
420   That dwelt within, whose presence had infused
Into the plant sciental° sap, derived
From nectar, drink of gods. Adam the while
Waiting desirous her return, had wove
Of choicest flowers a garland to adorn
425   Her tresses . . . .

399. **Forbidder:** like Satan, Eve now coins unkind names for God.
400. **sort:** way.

404. **odds:** advantage.
405. **wants:** is missing.

421. **sciental:** wisdom-giving.

A. Characterization

⁇ What guilty hope does Eve express here? (That God did not see her eat the fruit) She is already practicing deceit.

B. Characterization

⁇ What does Eve hope for now? (Equality with Adam; perhaps superiority to him; freedom. She also wants to "draw his love," something she never thought about before.)

C. Motivation

⁇ What fear finally induces Eve to share her knowledge with Adam? (Her fear that if she dies, he will marry "another Eve") who is all-powerful and all-good, would experience envy and deceive Adam and Eve.

10. She glories in the taste of the fruit and gorges herself. She then savors her new power, becomes competitive and deceitful, and wonders if she should share her power with Adam.

11. Eating the forbidden fruit is symbolic of pride and rebellion against God.

Eve's greed, lust for power, fear, and envy show that the consequence of her act is to make the human race a victim to destructive passions.

12. Eve's susceptibility to Satan's flattery and her wish to become divine.

Definitions of *pride* will vary. It can have positive and negative connotations.

13. He is a master of persuasion, of clever argument, and of subtle flattery, and he can appeal to self-interest.

14. There is an underlying assumption that Eve was an easier target for Satan than Adam would have been. (See lines 70–74.)

Eve has the human frailties of pride, envy, fear of death, and lust for power.

Responding to the Poem

Analyzing the Poem

Identifying Details

1. Where does Satan first catch sight of Eve?
2. What information does Satan give about himself in his first speech? (Lines 62–82)
3. What arguments does Satan use to persuade Eve to eat the fruit? (Lines 263–316)
4. How does Eve rationalize her decision to eat the fruit? (Lines 329–363)
5. What is the reaction of earth and nature when Eve eats the forbidden fruit?

Interpreting Meanings

6. What does Milton mean when he **metaphorically** calls Eve the "fairest unsupported flower, / From her best prop so far"? (Lines 21–22) What "storm" is nigh? (Line 22)
7. How would you describe Milton's attitude toward love, as expressed in lines 79–80?
8. In what ways does Satan flatter Eve? Why doesn't Eve detect his lies?
9. How does Satan prejudice Eve's mind against God? What is his explanation of death? Are there any inconsistencies in the statements he makes to Eve?
10. How does the fruit affect Eve, both physically and morally?
11. Why is eating the forbidden fruit such a serious crime? What do Eve's feelings after eating it tell us about the crime?
12. It has been said that the sin committed in Eden was the sin, not of mere disobedience, but of pride. What details in Milton's epic support that view? How would you define *pride*?
13. In literature, Satan is often depicted as a shrewd lawyer. From the way he is **characterized** here, can you explain why?
14. Is Milton's **characterization** of Eve sexist at all? What universal human frailties does Eve manifest?

Writing About the Poem

A Creative Response

1. **Extending the Narrative.** Suppose Eve saw through the tempter and refused the fruit. Write out her response to his honeyed argument.

A Critical Response

2. **Paraphrasing a Speech.** Choose one of the long speeches in this excerpt from *Paradise Lost*: for example, the speech of Satan (lines 116–132) or the monologue of Eve (lines 329–363). Rewrite the speech you select in a prose paraphrase.
3. **Researching Sources.** Read the biblical account of this episode in Genesis 3:1–7. In a brief essay, comment on the similarities and differences between this account and Milton's version.

Analyzing Language and Style

Milton's Poetic Style

1. **Epic Similes.** The word *as* in Milton's epic tells us that a simile is coming, an elaborate **epic simile,** in which something in the poem is compared to something quite outside the poem—often an animal, sometimes a human being or human action. These epic similes allowed Milton to bring into his epic a variety of non-biblical material. Explain the two terms of the comparisons in the epic similes in lines 34–46; 97–102; 218–229; and 254–262.
2. **Syntax.** To accommodate the demands of his meter, Milton often inverts his sentences, so they do not follow the normal subject-verb-complement order. In addition, Milton's sentences are long, and often words are omitted which have to be supplied by the reader.

   a. In lines 1–2, what are the subject and verb?
   b. What additional words must be supplied to make sense of the rest of this sentence, in lines 2–5?
   c. How would you rephrase lines 13; 33; 59–61; and 179–181, using normal English syntax?
   d. What missing words must you supply to make sense of lines 69–71; 134–135; and 139–143? (It might help if you read the lines in context.)

3. **Blank Verse.** Milton used **blank verse,** or **unrhymed iambic pentameter,** to give his epic an exalted tone. Iambic pentameter means that each line of the poem is ten syllables in length, with five strong stresses alternating with five weaker stresses (the lines begin with an unstressed syllable and end with a stressed one). An **iamb** is an unstressed syllable followed by a stressed one, as in the word refér.

   a. Scan lines 245–247 to show that they are written in perfect iambic pentameter.
   b. Choose a passage to read aloud so you can hear the beat of the iambs. Where does Milton vary the meter to give his verse variety and to prevent a sing-song rhythm?

Andrew Marvell
(1621–1678)

Marvell, whose very English name should be accented on its first syllable, like *marvelous,* was the son of a clergyman, who sent him to Cambridge University. There he must have received an excellent education because the poet John Milton, who was not easily impressed by other men's learning, said that he was "well read in the Greek and Latin classics." After receiving his B.A., he traveled for a time on the continent, just how long and how far are not known. There is, surprisingly, no record of Marvell's having been involved in the great upheaval of the 1640's. He seems to have survived the Civil War without belonging to either the Royal or the Parliamentary side. About 1650 he became a tutor to Mary Fairfax, an heiress and a daughter of Sir Thomas Fairfax, who had served as Lord General of the Parliamentary armies. The Fairfaxes had several large estates, one of them at a place called Nun Appleton, and there Marvell wrote a remarkable long poem, "Upon Appleton House." But he did not publish this or any other of the poems that are so highly regarded today. In the best Renaissance fashion, he wrote only for his friends' and his own entertainment.

After leaving the Fairfax household, where presumably he wrote his best poems, Marvell became tutor to a ward of Oliver Cromwell, the Lord Protector and virtual dictator of England in the 1650's. Then, in 1657 he became assistant to John Milton, who needed help in carrying out his duties as Latin Secretary to the Council of State because he was blind. When King Charles II was restored and the Commonwealth government dissolved in 1660, Marvell somehow had enough influence with the Royalists to save Milton's life. Under Charles II, Marvell became active in politics and served until his death as Member of Parliament for his native city, Hull. At this point in his career he did begin to publish verse satires against his political opponents and prose pamphlets on issues of the day. But his lyric poems remained in manuscript until after his death, when his housekeeper, who called herself Mary Marvell and claimed to be his wife, sold them to a publisher, who brought them out.

Andrew Marvell by an unknown artist (c. 1655–60). Oil.

A

Marvell's posthumous volume, called *Miscellaneous Poems,* made little impression when it appeared in 1681. Styles in poetry had changed after 1660, so that Marvell's witty, ingenious metaphors must have seemed old-fashioned to readers who admired the lucid, rational poems of John Dryden (see Unit Four) and other Restoration writers. Today we are in a better position to appreciate Marvell. To many judicious critics his poems seem to sum up much that is admirable in Renaissance lyric poetry. Like Jonson, he is a master craftsman, always in control of his materials. His poems have the precision, urbanity, and lightness of touch associated with the "sons of Ben." Many of Marvell's poems are also, under their graceful surfaces, deep and thoughtful, like Donne's and Herbert's. No wonder that Marvell is sometimes called the "most major" of all the minor poets in English.

A. Humanities Connection: Discussing the Portrait
The portrait clearly places Marvell in an age later than that of Elizabeth. It was a time of plainer religion, plainer dress, and political instability.
? What details make this portrait more like that of John Milton (text page 414) than like those of Raleigh and Sidney (text pages 194 and 214, respectviely)? (Simple collar and plain hairstyle; portraits of Raleigh and Sidney show them to be more elaborately dressed and more fashionably coiffed.)

1. BUILDING ON PRIOR KNOWLEDGE. Ask students to review what they know of Marlowe's "The Passionate Shepherd to His Love" (text page 232) and Herrick's "To the Virgins, to Make Much of Time" (text page 385).

2. ESTABLISHING A PURPOSE. Ask students to consider how this poem resembles these other *carpe diem* poems and how it differs from them.

SUPPLEMENTARY SUPPORT MATERIALS

1. Vocabulary Activity Worksheet (*CCB*)
2. Review and Response Worksheet: The Renaissance Poem (*CCB*)
3. Selection Test (*CCB*)

DEVELOPING VOCABULARY

The following words from the poem are tested in the Selection Test. (See also Vocabulary Activity Worksheet.)

coy	to sport
quaint	to languish
hue	

A. Poetic Effects

? What is the effect of placing the woman by the side of the Ganges River in India and the man on the banks of the Humber in northern England? (It emphasizes that they have time enough even to be apart; it also humorously underscores her romantic dallying and his humble patience.)

B. Personification

? How is time personified? (As a charioteer, an ancient convention) These lines are among the most famous in English poetry.

C. Imagery

? What are some of the images of emptiness and death in lines 24–32? ("Deserts of vast eternity," "marble vault," "echoing song," "worms," "dust," "ashes," "grave")

CLOSURE

Have students, working in groups, prepare brief statements telling how this poem is like and unlike other *carpe diem* poems, and how lines 21–22 and 31–32 relate to the poem's theme.

This poem is the most famous "invitation to love" in English. Its speaker urges a woman to give herself to him because he and she are now in the prime of life, and they cannot afford to wait because time will soon make them old, unattractive, and finally dead. The theme of the poem is an ancient one; the Romans called it *carpe diem* (pronounced kär′pā dē′em). *Carpe diem* poems are the literary counterpart of the human skull which was sometimes part of the decor when Romans gave wild parties. The skull reminded them of the fate that lies in store for all living things.

"To His Coy Mistress" is such a perfect example of its kind that nobody has ever taken it to be autobiographical. Nobody has poked around in old records trying to find the name of the woman to whom Marvell, a bachelor, might have addressed it. But at the same time it is a much deeper poem than others of its kind. Its speaker dwells on the details of human mortality with morbid exactitude, to make the woman listening to him feel that even immoral behavior while she is still alive is preferable to being good but dead.

The title means "To his cold, stand-offish girl friend." In Renaissance England calling a woman a "mistress" did not mean that she was necessarily having a sexual affair with a man; she could be, and almost always was, just a friend, as in this poem.

To His Coy Mistress

Had we but world° enough, and time,
This coyness,° lady, were no crime.
We would sit down, and think which way
To walk, and pass our long love's day.

5 **A**   Thou by the Indian Ganges' side
Shouldst rubies find; I by the tide
Of Humber° would complain.° I would
Love you ten years before the flood,
And you should, if you please, refuse
10 Till the conversion of the Jews.°
My vegetable° love should grow
Vaster than empires and more slow;
An hundred years should go to praise
Thine eyes, and on thy forehead gaze;
15 Two hundred to adore each breast,
But thirty thousand to the rest;
An age at least to every part,
And the last age should show your heart.
For, lady, you deserve this state,°
20 Nor would I love at lower rate.

B   But at my back I always hear
Time's wingéd chariot hurrying near;
And yonder all before us lie
Deserts of vast eternity.
25 Thy beauty shall no more be found,
C   Nor, in thy marble vault, shall sound

1. **world:** geographical space.
2. **coyness:** disdain toward the speaker.

7. **Humber:** river in the northern part of England. **complain:** utter complaints about not being loved.

10. **conversion of the Jews:** Christians once believed that before the world would end, all Jews would become Christians.
11. **vegetable:** having the power to grow very large, like oak trees.

19. **state:** ceremony.

ANALYZING THE POEM
Identifying Details
1. The lovers would dawdle over decisions; he would complain of her rejection for years; his "vegetable love" would grow slowly. Centuries would be spent praising her eyes, her beauties, and her heart.
2. "Time's winged chariot."

Interpreting Meanings
3. The first words are "Had" (if), "But," and "Now."
They state a hypothetical condition (the existence of unlimited time), a challenge to that hypothesis, and a conclusion urging action now.
4. The first major division displays many examples of exaggeration (lines 7–10, 11–12). An example of understatement

occurs in lines 31–32.
They add wit and a wry note to the poem.
5. Lines 11–12 mock this conceit.
6. By enjoying the present.
7. Answers will vary. The mention of marriage would introduce a solemn note into a poem that is obviously intended to commend freedom and "pleasure."

My echoing song; then worms shall try
That long-preserved virginity,
And your quaint honor turn to dust,
30   And into ashes all my lust:
The grave's a fine and private place,
But none, I think, do there embrace.
    Now therefore, while the youthful hue
Sits on thy skin like morning dew,
35   And while thy willing soul transpires°
At every pore with instant fires,
Now let us sport us while we may,
And now, like amorous birds of prey,
Rather at once our time devour
40   Than languish in his slow-chapped power.°
A   Let us roll all our strength and all
Our sweetness up into one ball,
And tear our pleasures with rough strife
Through the iron gates of life:
45   Thus, though we cannot make our sun
Stand still,° yet we will make him run.

35. **transpires:** breathes out.

40. **his slow-chapped power:** time's slowly chewing jaws.

45–46. **sun stand still:** as it did once, according to Joshua 10:13.

Responding to the Poem

Analyzing the Poem

Identifying Details

1. If time were unlimited, how would the lover and his friend spend it?
2. What does the speaker always hear at his back?

Interpreting Meanings

3. What is the first word of each major division of the poem? How do these three words indirectly serve to underline the structure and theme of the poem?
4. The poem contains both **exaggeration** and **understatement.** Find examples of each rhetorical device, and explain what they contribute to the poem's effect on the reader.
5. Where in the poem does Marvell seem to be making fun of certain kinds of love poems? (Hint: A common conceit referred to love growing like the bark of trees upon which the name of the beloved was carved.)
6. How, according to the poem, can human beings become masters rather than victims of time?
7. Notice that the speaker does not mention—let alone suggest—marriage. Suppose he had proposed marriage to the woman. What difference would that make in the poem?

Writing About the Poem

A Creative Response

1. **Writing a Response.** Beginning with the words "Had we but world enough, and time," write a response to the speaker of the poem. What title will you give your response?

A Critical Response

2. **Comparing and Contrasting Poems.** In an essay, compare and contrast this poem with these poems which are also on the *carpe diem* theme:

   a. Marlowe's "The Passionate Shepherd to His Love"
   b. Herrick's "To the Virgins, to Make Much of Time"

   Before you write, list the ways the poems are alike or unlike in terms of their **subjects, themes, tones, sounds,** and **figures of speech.**

A. Learning English Grammar
Discuss with students their own experiences with the study of English grammar and usage.
? What kinds of grammar books did you have? (Answers will vary.) What kind of grammar teaching do you think is most effective? (Answers may include teaching that relies on example more than theory and that is applicable to the kind of writing students actually do.) What kinds have you found least helpful? (Answers may include complicated diagrams.)

B. Dictionary Entries
See question 1 on page 444 for an activity involving the different kinds of information in a modern dictionary.

THE ENGLISH LANGUAGE
by John Algeo

The Growth of Modern English

> " **D**ifficult as it may be for some of us to understand today, English speakers were fascinated by grammars of their language."

During the seventeenth century, English speakers became increasingly aware of their own language—of what it was and of what it could be. Interest in the English language and its study grew rapidly; English scholars pursued vigorously study of the grammar, vocabulary, and style of written English.

The First Grammars and Dictionaries

The first grammars of English appeared shortly before the end of the sixteenth century. These small books imitated widely used Latin grammars and were intended to help English-speaking students learn Latin and foreigners learn English. The first such grammar was William Bullokar's *Pamphlet for Grammar* (1586). Although it would not compare well with the best grammars of our language written today, four hundred years later, it was no small achievement for its day. To write a grammar of a language for which there were no other grammar books was an accomplishment.

By the end of the seventeenth century, a great many grammar books had been written, and more continued to appear through the eighteenth and nineteenth centuries. Difficult as it may be for some of us to understand today, English speakers were fascinated by grammars of their language. Popular as grammar books were, however, readers and writers of English were far more interested in dictionaries.

The first English dictionary appeared at the beginning of the seventeenth century. In 1604 Robert Cawdrey published *A Table Alphabeticall . . . of Hard Usuall English Wordes*. As its title suggests, the earliest dictionaries made no effort, as a modern dictionary does, to list all the words in the English language. Rather they were simply lists of "hard" words—learned, often borrowed words—that a reader might come across but that would be difficult for the ordinary person to understand.

The first dictionaries gave only a familiar synonym for each hard word. Gradually, dictionaries began to expand the number of words they listed and the kinds of information they gave about each word. Definitions increased from single-word synonyms to fuller descriptions of meaning. In the eighteenth century, efforts were made to include all the words of the language and to define all their uses, rather than treat only "hard" words. New sorts of information added to the entry for a word included its etymology (origin and history), its part of speech, quotations illustrating its use, and its pronunciation.

As English dictionaries increased the number of words they included and the kind, amount, and quality of information they gave about each word, they became better and better. Today English has the best dictionaries of any language on earth. The greatest of English dictionaries is *The Oxford English Dictionary,* seventeen large volumes. It attempts with good success to trace the history of every English word from its first appearance in the language until today. The biggest dictionary a high-school student is likely to need is one like the Merriam-Webster *Third New International Dictionary,* and for most ordinary uses, smaller desk dictionaries serve very well.

A

The Battle of Styles: Ornate Vs. Plain

The seventeenth century was an age of social unrest. In England, the Cavaliers, who supported the King and the established Anglican church, were opposed by the Puritans, who supported Parliament and a congregational form of church. The Cavaliers dressed elegantly, ate with gusto, attended the theater, and generally lived a high life; they were the Beautiful People of the seventeenth century. Puritans, on the other hand, dressed and ate plainly, thought the theater was wicked, and generally lived sober, God-fearing, dull lives. There was bound to be trouble between them. And so there was, the Puritans eventually gaining control of Parliament, executing the King, closing the theaters, and establishing a military and church dictatorship in England, something like that established by the Moslem fundamentalists in Iran in recent times.

B

C

Queen Elizabeth in Progress
(detail) attributed to Robert Peake.

By permission of Simon Wingfield
Digby, Sherborne Castle,
Wiltshire, England.

A. Expansion
Most high school students have never seen the *Oxford English Dictionary (O.E.D.).* Borrow several volumes from your library, if you can, for classroom browsing. Or reproduce several pages from the *O.E.D.* and go over them in class.

B. Vocabulary
? What do the words *cavalier* and *puritan* mean today? (*Cavalier* is usually used as an adjective meaning "casual" or "free and easy." A *puritan* is a person who is unusually strict regarding morals or religion.)

C. Discussing the Fine Art
"In progress" means "in a procession." Clearly, these Elizabethans were, in style, the "ornate" people. In contrast, some "plain style" Puritan types are pictured on text page 449 (note the tall black hats). Milton (page 414) is in sober Puritan black.
? Is there any relationship today between what one wears and one's politics? (Think of Richard Nixon's comment on his wife's plain Republican cloth coat.)

A. Vocabulary
Be sure students distinguish between *euphuism* ("high-flown, artificial-sounding speech or writing") and *euphemism* ("a word or phrase used instead of one that is considered offensive or distasteful"). *Pass away,* for example, is a euphemism for *die.*

John Lyly (1554?–1606) wrote a two-part prose romance about the wanderings and adventures of Euphues. The work has little plot, many discourses and letters, and is a precursor of the English novel.

B. About the Embroidery
This is the embroidered binding of a book. Students will find other examples of embroidery of the period (the Elizabethans were highly skilled at the decorative arts) on pages 233, 378, and 383. Compare this cover with the covers put on books today, all of which, of course, are mass produced.

B

A

Embroidered binding.

Folger Shakespeare Library, Washington, D.C.

The difference in life styles between the Cavaliers and the Puritans was echoed in a difference in language styles used in England: an ornate style versus a plain style, although there was by no means a simple equivalence between Cavaliers and ornate style versus Puritans and plain style. Indeed, in some cases, it was the other way around.

The **ornate style** had various aspects. Large numbers of words were borrowed from foreign languages, and learned words were introduced into ordinary speech and writing, thus creating what were scornfully called "inkhorn terms." An inkhorn was a container made from the horn of an animal and used to hold ink for writing with a quill pen. Inkhorn terms were words that scholars might use in writing, but that seemed out of place in ordinary conversation. It was such inkhorn terms that were listed in the dictionaries of "hard" words.

Another aspect of the ornate style was called **euphuism** (after Euphues, a character in two books by John Lyly, who used alliteration, balanced expressions, antitheses, fantastic similes, mythological allusions, and other verbal tricks to create an artificial elegance of language). An example of euphuistic language is the following sentence, in which Euphues cites some proverbs cautioning against rash and excessive action: "The vine watered with wine is soon withered, the blossom in the fattest ground is quickly blasted, the goat the fatter she is the less fertile she is; yea, man the more witty he is the less happy he is."

Still another aspect was the **metaphysical conceit,** an extended and exaggerated metaphor, such as those in Donne's poem "The Bait" and Herbert's "The Altar."

In the ornate style, language seemed often to be stretched to the limits of its complexity. Those who wrote in ornate style were as much interested in the way they expressed their ideas as they were in the ideas expressed. Indeed, often they seemed to be more concerned with cleverness and complexity of expression than with communicating clearly. Those who favored **plain style,** on the other hand, thought that the important thing was to write what they had to say as simply, clearly, and straightforwardly as they could.

Plain style came to be favored especially by those with scientific interests. That is natural enough. If you are going to describe a scientific experiment or observation, you are less interested in having people admire your cleverness with language than in having them understand what you did or saw. In the scientific ideal, the experimenter or observer is an invisible person. Scientists try not to intrude personally in any way into the object of study. Their work and their language are supposed to be impersonal and public. (That ideal is impossible of actual attainment, but it is still an ideal to be striven for.)

In the metaphysical or euphuistic ideal, on the other hand, the reader sees the world through the highly personal, individualistic eyes of the writer. The aim of the writer is to surprise the reader by revealing the world in a fresh way. Thus the two styles, contrasting sharply in their aims, contrast also in their techniques.

The plain style was promoted especially through the work of the

440

440   The Renaissance

Alchemist from the Harley
Manuscript (16th century).   **A**

British Library, London.

Royal Society. Founded in the second half of the seventeenth century, it is one of the oldest organizations in Europe for "improving natural knowledge," promoting scientific study. Members of the Society did much to combat the excesses of ornate style. As a result of their work and example, today the plain style is the unchallenged ideal for good prose.   **B**

Some members of the Royal Society, however, went to an extreme themselves. They were so much concerned with clear expression that they considered inventing a new language that would make ambiguity and confusion impossible by having just one meaning for each of its words and just one word for each imaginable concept. They also wanted a new writing system in which the symbols would represent things directly rather than the sounds of words.   **C**

A member of the Society, John Wilkins, invented both such a language and such a writing system, which he presented in an *Essay Towards a Real Character and a Philosophical Language*. By "real" character, he meant written letters standing for things; and

A. Alchemy
Alchemists sought to change base metals into gold.

Their desire to keep trade secrets led alchemists to use cryptic, symbolic, and arcane language to describe their work. Eventually, alchemy fell into disrepute, but today it is regarded as an ancestor of the modern science of chemistry.

B. Modern Scientific Writing
❓ Do today's scientific journals and papers exhibit "the plain style"? (Most are so filled with technical jargon that they are inaccessible to lay readers.)

C. Symbol Writing
Have volunteers research early forms of writing to see if there ever was a writing system that used symbols to stand for objects. Students might enjoy trying to create such a system, or creating rebuses (puzzles made up of pictures and letters) that have to do with the literature they've studied so far.

A. Style
Note that this dis-
cussion of style is
relevant to stu-
dents' writing.
Take time to read
and discuss these
two pages in class.
You might ask stu-
dents for additional
examples.

B. Definition
Note the definition
of *style* here. Stu-
dents have difficul-
ty seeing "plain" or
"ornate" styles in
older writings pre-
cisely because it is
not their native
way of speaking
and writing. You
might ask them to
bring to class para-
graphs from con-
temporary writing
that exemplify
"plain" and "or-
nate" writing
styles. Ernest
Hemingway was a
famous advocate
of a spare style in
American litera-
ture. In contrast,
students might
look at F. Scott
Fitzgerald's more
poetic style and at
Henry James's ele-
gant, ornate style.

"*If*
we want to mention
our male parent,
we can call him
*father, dad, papa, sire,
pater, pop, my old man,*
or various other names."

by "philosophical" language he meant one free from ambiguity. Wilkins and the Royal Society were later satirized by Jonathan Swift in the third voyage of *Gulliver's Travels,* in which Gulliver meets a group of learned nincompoops who live on an island that floats in the sky and who are so abstracted in thought that servants have to hit them on the head to remind them to talk. Wilkins, however, was no nincompoop. For example, he foresaw that human beings might one day travel to the moon. Moreover, his work was the basis for Roget's *Thesaurus.*

What Is Style?

Although today a plain style is our ideal, we still find other kinds of style in use. What is a style? What makes one different from another? And what is the use of different styles?

Despite the Royal Society's aspiration to have just one word for each concept, all languages have more than one way to say a thing. When we talk or write, we have a choice of ways to express our meaning. For example, if we want to mention our male parent, we can call him *father, dad, papa, sire, pater, pop, my old man,* or various other names. Obviously, those words, although they all mean the "same" thing in that they can all refer to the same person, are very different from one another in how they are used. If you are filling out an employment questionnaire, it is not going to ask you, "What is your daddy's name?" If you are telling a friend why you can't use the family car tonight, you are probably not going to say, "My sire is using it."

We may have a choice also in pronunciation. We may say *greasy* as either "greazy" or "greassy." *Either* can be "ee-ther" or "eye-ther." *What do you think?* can be "watt doo ewe think?" or "whacha think?" In each case, however, the choice we make tells something about us or about the situation in which we are speaking.

There are also grammatical choices. We can say, "I like to go to the movies" or "What I like to do is go to the movies" or "I like going to the movies" or "It's the movies that I like going to" or various other sentences that all mean the same thing, but that are not necessarily used the same way. English gives us a lot of choices. We have to decide which ones to take in any given set of circumstances.

The options that we take in talking or writing determine the style of our language. **Style** is the choice we make among alternative ways of saying the same thing.

Types and Elements of Style

Some styles are formal, the sort we use with strangers or on important occasions; others are informal, the sort we use everyday with people we know well and with whom we are comfortable. Some styles are appropriate for talking and others for writing. Some styles are used for particular subjects, for example, reporting a

**FURTHER READING
FOR STUDENTS**
For year-round reference, have several
classroom copies of E. B. White and
William Strunk's classic manual *Elements of Style* (1979), which teaches
simplicity and clarity in writing.

football game or writing a recipe. Some styles are used with particular media of communication, for example, talking on the telephone or sending a telegram.

Writers choose their style to create an effect that they want: Some writers may use short sentences. They may use simple words. They may repeat the same pattern in their sentences. Their statements may be literal and clear.

Another writer may interweave many disparate ideas into a single sentence, expressed in complex, technical diction, with a variety of grammatical constructions and metaphors running in and out of each other, like the warp and woof of a loom or the gossamer strands of a spider web.

For different purposes and different tastes, there are different styles. None is inherently better or worse than any other, though some may be better adapted for a particular use. **A**

Among the elements that make up a style are options like these: **B**

1. Short and simple versus long and complex sentences. A sequence of short, simple sentences is likely to seem childish or simple-minded, but many long, complex ones are likely to seem—and, in fact, to be—confused.

2. Active versus passive verbs, as in "The Puritans chopped off King Charles's head," versus "King Charles's head was chopped off." Passive verbs are especially useful for telling that something happened without telling who did it. They are favorites of scientific and bureaucratic writers, but many other people find them mealy-mouthed.

3. Direct versus qualified statements. Direct statements tell the facts just as they are. Qualified statements add words like *perhaps, possibly, it seems, it would appear, it is likely that, generally, make an effort to,* and so on. Writers may think that using qualifications will get them off the hook if they say something wrong. But readers find the result wishy-washy.

4. Noun- versus verb-centeredness. We can *agree* on something, or *reach an agreement* about it. We can *wash* the car, or *give it a wash.* We can *decide* to go, or *come to a decision* to do so. We can *promise* our friends something, or *make a promise to* them *about* it. When we put the main meaning into the verb, we have a more direct and forceful sentence. But putting the main meaning into a noun after the verb lets us get that meaning near the end of the sentence, which is the position of greatest emphasis.

5. Plain versus fancy words. Plain words like *newspaper, home, watery,* and *to run* are more comfortable than fancy words like *periodical, domicile, aqueous,* and *to course.* There are times, to be sure, when we want our language to be fancy. The danger in using fancy words, however, is that we will use them not quite right, and the result will be not fancy, but unintentionally funny.

There are many other elements of style. These five are examples, only. But they show the sort of choices we have to make every time we open our mouths or put marks on paper. Every such choice is one step in the creation of a style, simple or fancy, plain or ornate, formal or informal, appropriate or awkward.

A. Clarification
This is a point many students will have trouble accepting. Try to make explicit the style you expect for written assignments. (You might mention such features as clarity of ideas; absence of unnecessary repetition; smoothly flowing connection of ideas.) Emphasize that style is only one part of the writing task: Content and the organization of ideas are the other major writing tasks.

B. Writing Style
Before they revise writing assignments, have students refer to these five points. You might create a checklist (or have students create one) of other stylistic problems that recur in students' writing.

> " **P**lain words
> like *newspaper, home,
> watery,* and *to run*
> are more comfortable
> than fancy words like
> *periodical, domicile,
> aqueous,* and *to course.*"

Analyzing Language

1. The English dictionary began its development during the seventeenth century with lists of "hard" words and their easy meanings. Look at the entry for a word in a modern desk dictionary. You can choose any word you like, but the following are suggestions:

atom	dwarf	hopefully	learn
map	sphinx	tackle	

   What different kinds of information does the entry give you about the word? To start off, you will find the spelling of the word and its pronunciation. What else? (You will find somewhat different kinds of information in the entries for various words and for the same word in various dictionaries.)

2. The language of the King James Bible and of the Book of Common Prayer has been influential on the way we use English. What do the following expressions mean? Find the passage in which the expressions were originally used (it is indicated in parentheses).

   a. Helpmate/helpmeet (Genesis 2:18; look up the first form in a dictionary)
   b. My brother's keeper (Genesis 4:9)
   c. A stranger in a strange land (Exodus 2:22)
   d. A land flowing with milk and honey (Exodus 3:8)
   e. An eye for an eye and a tooth for a tooth (Exodus 21:24)
   f. The apple of one's eye (Deuteronomy 32:10; Psalm 17:8)
   g. Pride goes before a fall. (Proverbs 16:18)
   h. Put one's house in order (2 Kings 20:1; Isaiah 38:1)
   i. Escape by the skin of one's teeth (Job 19:20)
   j. The valley of the shadow of death (Psalm 23:6)
   k. The meek shall inherit the earth (Psalm 37:11)
   l. Cast your bread upon the waters (Ecclesiastes 11:1)
   m. Beat swords into plowshares (Isaiah 2:4)
   n. Holier than thou (Isaiah 65:5)
   o. Balm in Gilead (Jeremiah 8:22)
   p. Feet of clay (Daniel 2:33)

3. Compare the style either of John Donne's "A Valediction . . ." and Ben Jonson's "Song: To Celia," or of the King James account of the temptation and fall of Adam and Eve and Milton's account of the same story in *Paradise Lost*. Note differences in vocabulary (ordinary words versus unusual); length and complexity of sentences; repeated versus varied patterns of language; simple and direct statements versus involved and indirect ones; and the use of descriptive adjectives and adverbs (few versus many). Which work in each pair seems to be in plain style, and which in ornate style?

ANALYZING A POET'S WORK

Writing Assignment

Write a five- to seven-paragraph report in which you analyze at least three poems by one poet. The purpose of your paper is to show what distinguishes this poet's work from that of other poets.

Background

Every person has certain characteristics that distinguish him or her from other people. The person may walk, talk, dress, and even gesture with a particular manner. In much the same way, artists, in their work, tend to have distinguishing characteristics. Someone who is familiar with modern art can walk through a museum, look at a work, and recognize the melancholy people of Picasso's "blue period," the haystacks and lighting of Monet, the vivid colors of Renoir, and so on.

Like painters, poets also have distinguishing characteristics. The works of a particular poet often can be recognized by the repetition of themes, subjects, forms, imagery—the elements of poetry. By analyzing a number of poems, you can identify the characteristics that set one poet apart from another.

Prewriting

Using Primary Sources. Begin by selecting one of the poets whose poems you have read in this unit. Then choose at least three of his poems. You can use the poems in this book, but you might need an additional source. If so, search your library's computer or card catalog under the poet's name for a collection of his poetry. You might also look under the subject heading *Poetry* for a collection of sixteenth-century British poetry.

As you read the poems, ask yourself the following questions:

1. What common **themes** are expressed in the poems?
2. How are the **speakers, situations, subjects, figures of speech,** and kinds of **imagery** similar in the poems? (Note specific examples.)
3. In what form are the poems written? (Petrarchan sonnet, Shakespearean sonnet, lyric, narrative, and so on)

Jot down specific details from the poems to support your answers. For example, if the eternal nature of love is a common theme for one poet, cite particular lines and figures of speech from the poems that show this theme.

Using Secondary Sources. You might also want to look for two kinds of information about the poet's life:

1. How did the poet's life affect his poetry? (Are the distinctive themes or any other elements the result of known events in the poet's life?)
2. Is the poet remembered for a particular accomplishment in poetry? Spenser, for example, invented a new kind of stanza that is named after him.

To answer these questions, you will need to use books other than the poems themselves. **Secondary sources** are books and articles about a writer and the writer's works. Encyclopedias are considered secondary sources, but they will give you only the most general information, such as dates of the poet's birth and death. The best sources are reference books such as *The Oxford Companion to English Literature*, books about the individual poet, and books about sixteenth-century poets.

Read critically the information that you find. Remember that you are not looking for just any information about the poet's life. You are looking for events in the poet's life that affected his poetry.

Carefully record the source for each piece of information that you use, including the author and title of the book and the number of the page from which you took the information. (Your teacher may ask you to record additional details about the source.) If you use this information in your essay, you will need to give credit to the source.

Writing

In the first paragraph of your essay, name the poet whose works you are analyzing. Write a **thesis statement** summarizing the characteristics that distinguish this particular poet. If the poet is known for a particular accomplishment, mention it in this first paragraph. In each of the next three paragraphs, you might discuss how each of the three poems illustrates these characteristics. Use specific details from the poems to support your points.

Another approach is to discuss the poet's common themes and subjects in one paragraph, citing examples from the three poems. In the next paragraphs, you might discuss each of the following elements as they are used

A. Style
In recognizing the works of an artist, one is recognizing the artist's *style*. Bring to class books of the paintings of Vincent Van Gogh or Edgar Degas to give students some understanding of how we can distinguish one artist's work from another's.

B. Choosing Poems to Analyze
To make their writing easier, students should select three poems that are alike in some respects. They should also select poems they have a strong feeling about (preferably poems they like). It can be tedious to work on materials one does not have much interest in.

C. Biographical Criticism
Note that this question will lead students to find out more about the poet's life, but caution them about jumping to conclusions on the basis of little evidence.

Revising Essays
As students revise their essays, refer them to **Grammar, Usage, and Mechanics: A Reference Guide** at the back of their books.

Exercises in Critical Thinking and Writing/*cont.*

in the poems: forms, figurative language, and imagery. If events in the poet's life influenced his use of certain subjects, themes, forms, etc., mention these events in the appropriate paragraph.

In your last paragraph, summarize what you think are the distinguishing characteristics of the poet's work.

Documenting Sources. Be sure to follow your teacher's directions for documenting sources. The following example shows a method of documenting a secondary source directly in the text of your paper. Work the title and author of the source into a sentence and put the page number(s) on which the information appears in parentheses at the end of the sentence.

According to Herbert Grierson and J. C. Smith in *A Critical History of English Poetry*, Spenser's development of the Spenserian stanza was a "stroke of genius" that influenced other poets for centuries to come (83).

Revising and Proofreading

For help in revising and proofreading your essay, see the section on **Writing About Literature** at the back of this book.

THE RESTORATION
AND THE
EIGHTEENTH CENTURY
1660–1800

Procession of the Members of the Order of the Bath in Front of Westminster Abbey by Antonio Canaletto (18th century). Oil.

Westminster Abbey. London.

UNIT FOUR

HUMANITIES CONNECTION: RESPONDING TO THE FINE ART
Canaletto (1697–1768) was Venetian, but he had important English connections and worked in England from 1746 to c. 1756. Some students may be familiar with his impressive, beautifully ordered views of Venice. The Order of Bath, founded in 1399 and revived in 1725, was an association of knights who had been specially honored by the king.
❓ What might the various elements of this picture suggest about the literature in Unit Four? (The tone might be formal, and structure and form might be important.)

TEACHING EIGHTEENTH-CENTURY LITERATURE

This period of English literature, encompassing a relatively unwieldy mass of historical/socioeconomic data and literary samplings, can probably best be managed for student comprehension by breaking the material into several subperiods. The Restoration, a relatively short subperiod, dates from 1660, the year in which Charles II returned from France to assume the long-vacant throne of England. Bringing with him a highly developed taste for French theater and life style, Charles, in his accession to the throne, influenced greatly both the life style and literature of his subjects, long under the sway of Puritan thought. This period is one of contradictions. The modern reader is most likely to associate it with the plays of Sheridan and Congreve and with the poetry of the Earl of Rochester. Certainly this perception is accurate in part; there *was* a relaxation of the Puritan legalistic strictures. Nevertheless, there is a tendency to forget that both *Paradise Lost* and *The Pilgrim's Progress* were published after the accession of Charles II. Thus, the period must be thought of as one of contrasts, able to encompass both Bunyan and Dryden.

One of the major goals of the unit is to develop in the students an awareness of the classical tradition.

A second item of major relevance to the American high-school student is the connection of eighteenth-century thought and culture to the American experience. Students should realize that their own experience is related to the English heritage, whether they claim English blood or not.

OBJECTIVES OF THE RESTORATION UNIT

1. To improve reading proficiency and expand vocabulary
2. To gain exposure to notable authors and works of the period
3. To define and identify significant literary techniques: allegory, apostrophe, autobiography, classicism, Neoclassicism, canto, couplet, heroic couplet, diary, elegy, epic, mock epic, epigram, epitaph, essay, irony, novel, satire, and wit
4. To interpret and respond to fiction, nonfiction, and poetry, orally and in writing, through analysis of its elements
5. To practice the following critical thinking and writing skills:
   a. Evaluating essays
   b. Responding to criticism
   c. Analyzing diary entries
   d. Comparing storytelling techniques
   e. Evaluating a short story
   f. Analyzing a character
   g. Analyzing an elegy
   h. Writing a response to criticism

447

SUPPLEMENTARY SUPPORT MATERIALS: UNIT FOUR
1. Unit Introduction Test (*CCB*)
2. English Language Test (*CCB*)
3. Word Analogies Test (*CCB*)
4. Unit Review Test (*CCB*)
5. Critical Thinking and Writing Test (*CCB*)
6. Instructional Overhead Transparencies

A. About the Quotation

The quotation is from Pope's *An Essay on Man* (see also text page 530). Pope's lines sum up the period's values of order, reason, and harmony. The quotation derives from the premise widely held during the Enlightenment that all things in the universe are good and purposeful, fitting together like the parts of a well-run clock.

B. Humanities Connection: Discussing Music

Point out to students that the balanced, elegant qualities of the music of the Neoclassic period—for example, those pieces composed by Henry Purcell (1659–1695) and George Frederick Handel (1685–1759)—are thoroughly consistent with the style of the period's literature and philosophy. Both Purcell and Handel often turned to ancient classical motifs for inspiration: Examples are Purcell's opera *Dido and Aeneas* and Handel's *Julius Caesar* and *Xerxes*.

THE RESTORATION AND THE EIGHTEENTH CENTURY 1660–1800

by C. F. Main

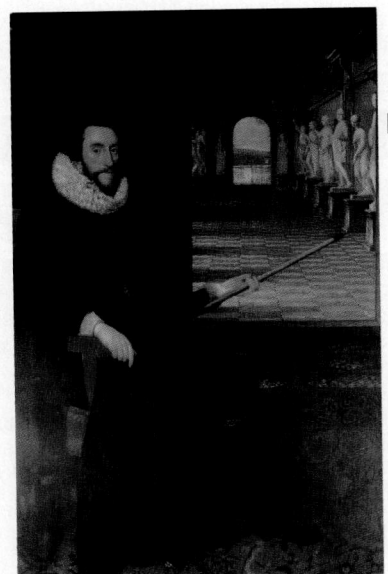

Thomas Howard, Earl of Arundel by Daniel Mytens (1614). Oil.

National Portrait Gallery, London.

A

> *All Nature is but art, unknown to thee;*
> *All chance, direction, which thou canst not see;*
> *All discord, harmony not understood;*
> *All partial evil, universal good:*
> *And, spite of pride, in erring reason's spite,*
> *One truth is clear, Whatever is, is right.*
>
> —Alexander Pope

H ow is the period of the Restoration and the eighteenth century different from the Renaissance that preceded it and the Romantic Age that followed? This question demands a detailed answer, because no single sentence can sum up the long period that runs from 1660 to 1800. Literary historians have applied several labels to this period: The Augustan Age, The Neoclassical Period, The Enlightenment, and The Age of Reason. But such labels are more convenient than accurate—each applies to some characteristics of the period, but none applies to all.

Augustan and Neoclassical

B

These two terms refer to real and imagined similarities between England and its literature in this period and ancient Rome and its literature, especially in the reign of the Emperor Octavius (63 B.C.– A.D. 14). When he became Emperor, Octavius took the high-sounding title *Augustus,* meaning "the magnificent, grand, and exalted one." Augustus restored peace and order to Rome after the tumult and civil wars that followed Julius Caesar's assassination. Similarly, the Stuart monarchs of England restored peace and order to England after the civil wars that led up to and followed the execution of King Charles I in 1649. The people of both Rome and England were weary of their quarrels, suspicious of revolutionaries and extremists, and ready to settle down, make money, and enjoy life. The Roman Senate had hailed Augustus as the second founder of Rome; the English people brought back the son of Charles I from his exile in France, crowned him as Charles II and restored the title of king, and hailed him as their savior. As a warning to revolutionaries, they dug up the dead Lord Protector, Oliver Cromwell, who had ruled England between Charles I and Charles II, and cut off his head. The poet John Dryden, drawing an exact parallel between Charles and Augustus, exclaimed:

> O happy age! O times like those alone
> By fate reserved for great Augustus' throne!

There were literary similarities as well as political ones. In this age many English writers consciously modeled their works on the Latin classics, which they had studied in school and in the universities. The classics, it was generally agreed, were valuable be-

A. Expansion
You may want to remind students that Shakespeare, for all his originality, was heavily influenced by the Latin classics, especially Plautus, Terence, Ovid, and Seneca.

B. Pathetic Fallacy
As a conscious literary device, this view was later termed the "pathetic fallacy."

The execution of King Charles I at Whitehall, London, January 30, 1649. Woodcut.

cause they represented what was permanent and universal in human experience. All educated people knew the classics better than they knew English literature, and one of their pleasures in reading a new work in English was recognizing its similarities to old works in Latin and occasionally Greek. These new works were called **neoclassical**—that is, "new classical." (Of course many Renaissance writers had also produced neoclassical works, but they are not the most famous products of the Renaissance period.)

Reason and Enlightenment

Labels like "The Age of Reason" and "The Enlightenment" reveal how people were gradually changing their view of themselves and the world. For instance, Shakespeare, the greatest writer of the Renaissance, expressed a commonly held view when he described the unusual events that preceded the assassination of Julius Caesar—"a tempest dropping fire" and "blue lightning." These unnatural events, says a character in the play *Julius Caesar,* are "instruments of fear and warning." For centuries people had believed that before a great public disaster like the assassination of a ruler, earth and sky gave warnings. Most people in antiquity, in the Middle Ages, and in the Renaissance believed that unusual events such as earthquakes, comets, and even babies born with

A. Expansion
Among the early, prominent members of the Royal Society were the scientist Robert Boyle, the architect Christopher Wren, and the poet John Dryden.

B. Expansion
An "orrery" was a mechanical apparatus that resembled a miniature planetarium.

malformations had some kind of meaning and were sent as punishment for past misdoings or warning of future troubles. They did not ask, "*How* did this unusual event take place?" but "*Why* did this unusual event take place, and what does it *mean*?"

Gradually, during the Enlightenment, people stopped asking "Why?" questions and started asking "How?" questions. The answers to the "How?" questions are much less frightening and superstitious. For instance, the astronomer Edmund Halley (1656–1742) took the terror out of celestial phenomena by computing when they were going to occur. He predicted that a solar eclipse would take place on May 2, 1721—and it did. He computed, with "immense labor," he said, the orbit of the comet that still bears his name. He predicted it would appear in 1758, 1834, 1910, and 1986—and it did. And how did he know it would reappear at 76-year intervals? Because that was the time it took to complete its orbit. Such a reasonable, mathematical explanation made no connection at all between the comet and human affairs; it paid no attention to "Why?" It paid no attention to the *meaning* of the comet.

Attempts like Halley's to answer questions about the universe were systematized when, in 1662, King Charles II chartered a group of philosophers interested in finding out how things work. This was called the Royal Society of London for the Improving of Natural Knowledge. The members of the Royal Society advocated a kind of writing that was precise and exact, and not decorated with the elaborate metaphors or odd allusions of their predecessors. Above all, these new scientists wanted to shorten the endless sentences of their predecessors. And so in this age was born what we think of as modern English prose.

A

B

A Philosopher Giving a Lecture in the Orrery by Joseph Wright of Derby (1764–66). Oil.

Derby Art Gallery.

Changes in Religion

The new scientific and rational explanations of phenomena gradually began to affect some people's religious views. If God didn't send comets to warn people, perhaps He didn't interfere at all in human affairs. Perhaps the universe was like an immense piece of clockwork, set in motion by a Creator who more or less withdrew from his perfect mechanism and let it run by itself. Such a view, part of a complex of ideas known as *Deism,* could make people feel self-satisfied and complacent, especially if they believed, as Alexander Pope said in his long poem *Essay on Man,* that "Whatever is, is right." Some philosophers even argued that "All is for the best in the best of all possible worlds"—a view that the French writer Voltaire made fun of in his novel *Candide* (1759).

But despite a tiny minority of "enlightened" rationalists and materialists, most people, including great philosophers and scientists like Sir Isaac Newton (1642–1727) and John Locke (1632–1704), remained religious. The Christian religion in its various forms continued to exercise an undiminished power over almost all Europeans in this period, as it had in the Middle Ages and the Renaissance.

Religion and Politics

Religion determined people's politics in this period, and vice versa: the two were indistinguishably connected with each other and with literature. When Charles II was restored to the throne in 1660, he also reestablished the Church of England as the official church of the country. With the approval of Parliament, he attempted to outlaw all the various Puritan and Independent sects—dozens of them, all happily disagreeing among themselves—that had caused so much uproar during the preceding thirty years. Persecution of these people, sometimes severe and sometimes nominal, continued throughout the eighteenth century, the severity depending partly on each monarch's temperament. For instance, throughout the Restoration period (1660–1700), the Quakers were very severely persecuted, even though some aristocratic people such as William Penn belonged to their sect.

The Bloodless Revolution

Charles II had no proper heir, although he did have a number of illegitimate children; unlike England's present rulers, the Stuarts were not models of domesticity. Moreover, he apparently wavered between support of the Church of England and support of the Church of Rome, and was therefore an object of suspicion to some of his subjects. When he died in 1685, he was succeeded by his brother James II, a practicing Roman Catholic. Most English people were utterly opposed to James, just as most Americans today would be violently upset if somehow a proclaimed Communist were

A

B

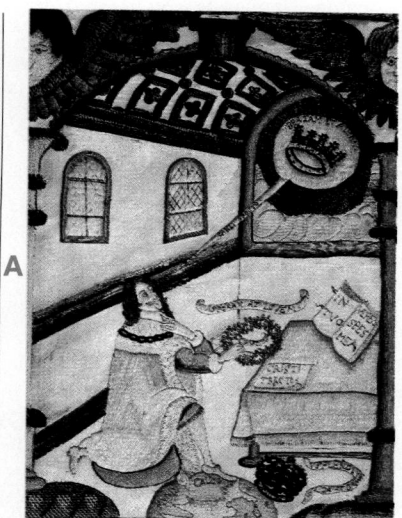

Charles II Kneeling (detail).
17th century stumpwork (embroidery).

Victoria and Albert Museum,
London.

A. Expansion
For additional comments on *An Essay on Man* and for a selection from Pope's poem, see text page 530.

B. Expansion
James II, before his accession, held the title of Duke of York. It was in his honor that New Amsterdam was renamed New York by the English.

A. **Expansion**
You may want to tell students of the Gunpowder Plot of 1605, in which the Catholic Guy Fawkes was convicted of attempting to blow up Parliament.

B. **Expansion**
Remind students that Queen Elizabeth II is still the titular head of the Church of England. It was the Church prohibition against divorce and remarriage that led to the abdication of her uncle, Edward VIII, in 1936.

A

to become President of the United States. After all, it was widely believed that Roman Catholics had not only set fire to London (see Pepys's *Diary*), and caused other disasters, but were actively plotting to hand the country over to the Pope. When James's Queen produced a little boy—a Catholic heir—pressure on the royal family became so great that they suddenly fled to France, and the "Glorious (Bloodless) Revolution" (1688) was accomplished.

Ever since, the rulers of England have been, at least nominally, Anglicans. James II was succeeded by his Protestant daughter Mary and her husband William of Orange. Being childless, they were succeeded by Mary's sister Anne. Anne, after the fashion of those times, had many children, but none of them survived infancy. Upon her death, Parliament went to an extreme to insure the Protestant line: it invited Anne's remote cousin, a German, George,

B

Elector of Hanover, to be King. For the rest of the century, the English kings were all Georges; in fact, the third of that name was the ruler when the American colonies won their independence from England.

Writers and Religion

Most writers of this period, as in most of English history, belonged to the Church of England. Jonathan Swift, a clergyman, and Samuel Johnson, a very devout man, were conspicuously Anglican. However, the two greatest poets of the period were Roman Catholic: John Dryden at the end of his life and Alexander Pope at the beginning and the end of his. (Pope was also interested in the new rational religion.) John Bunyan and Daniel Defoe, two other important writers, were Dissenters, the name now given to members of the various religious groups that did not agree with the Church of England.

The Age of Dryden

It is convenient to divide the long period from 1660 to 1800 into three parts and to label each part according to its most important writer. The first important writer is John Dryden, who died in 1700.

When one thinks of Restoration literature, one thinks first of plays, especially the comedies, which reflected the life of the rich and leisured people of that time—the Frenchified, pleasure-loving upper classes and their servants and hangers-on. During the exile of the court in France, the King, Charles II, had become addicted to theater-going, and so one of the first things he did upon regaining his throne was to repeal the ban on play performances imposed by the Puritan-dominated Parliament in 1642. Charles and his brother James established the patronized companies of actors. Unlike the earlier English theater, in which boys and men had acted all the female roles, the new theater had real actresses, and the new plays emphasized the sexual relations of men and women

A. **Humanities Connection: About the Fine Art**
William Hogarth (1697–1764) was one of England's great portraitists of society and manners. Many of his paintings show the seamy underside of eighteenth-century life; when Hogarth portrayed the upper classes, as here, he often did so with an ironic or satirical eye.

B. **Restoration Comedies**
Other notable writers of Restoration comedy include George Etherege, George Farquhar, and John Vanbrugh, who was also the architect of Blenheim Palace, the birthplace of Winston Churchill.

C. **The "Unities"**
The "unities" were three: time, place, and action. In fact, French critics went considerably beyond their classical sources by positing the unities as "rules" of drama, and their discussions of the matter often degenerated to the ludicrous: for example, a debate on whether the time frame of a tragic play could occupy twelve or twenty-four hours.

A

in very unsentimental and unromantic ways. These plays, such as *The Country Wife* by William Wycherly (1640?–1716) and *The Way of the World* by William Congreve (1670–1729), are very outspoken and rarely included in secondary-school textbooks, although they do exemplify such "Augustan" qualities as cleverness, urbanity, and worldliness.

Dryden wrote many comedies of this kind, as well as the best tragedy of the age, *All for Love* (1677), a neoclassical version of Shakespeare's *Antony and Cleopatra*. In this period, Shakespeare himself, though dead for decades, was gradually attaining the stature of England's preeminent dramatist and poet. Shakespeare's very English example in playwriting kept writers from following the **dramatic unities**—those strict literary "rules" that some countries, such as France, had extracted from the works of ancient writers.

Of course, in this age there were other kinds of writing besides drama; the new Augustan poetry described below was one of them. And there were a vast number of both prose and verse writers, many of them Dissenters, who did not cater to the tastes of sophisticated people but wrote solely for ordinary people. Among these writers was John Bunyan, whose genius has lifted him out of the obscurity into which the rest of this group of writers have fallen. Bunyan's life and works are a whole world apart from the frivolity and debauchery we usually associate with the age he lived in.

B *The Lady's Last Stake* by William Hogarth (1758–59). Oil.

Albright-Knox Art Gallery, Buffalo, New York. Gift of Seymour H. Knox.

C

A. Humanities Connection: About the
Fine Art and Music

How does the Hogarth scene on this
page compare with the one on the
preceding page? (Among the similarities
are that the figures are carefully posed
and the costumes are rich and elegant;
the scenes are different in that in the one
on page 453, the man is petitioning the
woman, and in the one on page 454, the
women are peti-
tioning the men.
The women in this
scene are trying to
get their lover, who
is a criminal, out of
jail and saved from
the hangman's
noose. This scene
is set in prison, as
you can tell if you
examine the back-
ground carefully.)
You may want to
tell students that
*The Beggar's
Opera,* composed
by John Gay and
produced in 1728,
was a brilliantly
successful ballad
opera that took
London by storm.
With its lower-class
characters and set-
ting at Newgate
Prison, it was an
ironic distortion of
the traditional ro-
mantic love story
that served as the
plot for many Ital-
ian operas of the
period. Kurt Weil's
*The Threepenny
Opera* (1928) is a
jazz version of
Gay's opera;
Weil's hard-edged
score is very differ-
ent from John
Gay's lyrical melo-
dies.

The Age of Pope and Swift

A Scene from The Beggar's Opera by
William Hogarth (c. 1728). Oil.

Paul Mellon Collection, National
Gallery, Washington, D.C.

The poet Alexander Pope, who died in 1744, must share preeminence in this age with Jonathan Swift, who died in 1745. Today Pope and Swift are regarded as the most accomplished literary artists of the early eighteenth century, and they have had a profound influence on many succeeding writers. Yet it is somewhat ironic to name the age after them because they were frequently out of harmony with its values and often criticized it severely.

Although Alexander Pope addressed his works exclusively to the educated and leisured classes, he also attacked the members of these classes for their immorality and their bad taste, two failings that were usually associated in Pope's mind. Pope loved order, discipline, and craftsmanship; both he and Swift were appalled by the squalor and shoddiness—in art, manners, and morals—that underlay the polished surfaces of Augustan life. This violent and filthy underside of eighteenth-century life is copiously illustrated in the paintings and engravings of William Hogarth (1697–1764). Jonathan Swift shared many of Pope's attitudes and ideals, and in his exposure of the mean and sordid in human behavior his works resemble Hogarth's art. Neither writer, then, felt smug or satisfied with the world, as did many of the Augustans. They deplored the corrupt politics of the time and the growing commercialism and materialism of the English people.

In contrast with Swift and Pope and their aristocratic values, another prominent writer of the Restoration, Daniel Defoe, stood for values that we think of as being middle class: thrift, prudence, industry, and respectability. Defoe had no interest in such Augustan values as polished manners and social poise. It is not surprising, then, that Swift and Pope looked down their noses at him. "Defoe has written a number of things," Pope once said, "and none of them excellent except *Robinson Crusoe.*"

A

Defoe, like Joseph Addison and Richard Steele, followed a new profession: journalism. Eighteenth-century journalists did not merely describe contemporary political and social matters; they also saw themselves as reformers of public manners and morals.

Augustan Poetry

> "Augustan poets had no desire to expose their souls; they thought of poetry as having a public rather than a private function."

It is useful to think of the poetry written in the Age of Dryden and Pope as **Augustan.** Augustan poetry is not what we think of as lyric poetry. Today when we think of great poetry, we inevitably think of the great lyrics: the sonnets of Shakespeare, Keats, and Wordsworth, the religious poems of Donne and Herbert, the private poems of Emily Dickinson, the works of such twentieth-century poets as T. S. Eliot and Robert Frost, and so on. These poets seem to reveal in their poems their innermost thoughts and feelings, their honest and original responses to life. "Genuine poetry," said Matthew Arnold, a nineteenth-century poet and critic, "is conceived in the soul."

Arnold disparaged the poetry of Swift, Pope, and Dryden because, he said, it was "conceived and composed in their wits"—that is, in their minds, not their souls. But Pope, Swift, and Dryden did not define poetry in Arnold's way and so should not be judged by his standards. They had no desire to expose their souls; they thought of poetry as having a public rather than a private function.

Augustan poets were very conscious of the kinds of poetry available to them. They would write not merely a poem, but a particular kind of poem. They decided in advance what kind of poem they wanted to write, much as a carpenter decides on the kind of chair to make before getting his tools and materials together. The best Augustan poems are like things artfully made for a particular purpose, usually a public purpose.

If, for instance, a grand person such as a general or a titled lady died, all the poets would celebrate that dead person in **elegies,** the appropriate kind of poem for the occasion. Augustan elegies did not tell the "truth" about a dead person, even if the truth could be determined; rather, they said the very best things that the poet could think of saying.

At the opposite extreme, a poet might decide that a certain type of behavior, or even a certain conspicuous person, should be exposed to public ridicule. The poet would then write a **satire,** the kind of writing that does not make a just and balanced judgment of people and their behavior, but rather says the worst things about them that the poet can think of saying. The satire would be meant to reform, and the more ridiculous an offense was made out to be, the more likely it was to be changed.

Many of the popular kinds of poetry were inherited from classical antiquity. The greatest kind of poetry, everyone agreed, was the **epic,** such as Virgil's *Aeneid* and Milton's *Paradise Lost.* Indeed, when critics used the word *poem* in the eighteenth century, they usually were referring to an epic. What we call a "poem" an Augustan would probably call a "song" or a "paper of verses."

A

B

A. The Concept of Genres
It was, in fact, during this period that the concept of *genres,* or the distinct types of literature, was elaborated in English literary criticism.

B. The Epic
The Augustan veneration for the epics was so great that it led Henry Fielding (1707–1754), one of the first English novelists, to "trace" the pedigree of what was really a new form back to a lost comic epic of Homer (see Fielding's Preface to *Joseph Andrews,* 1742).

1. During the Enlightenment, people became more concerned with how things happened than with why they happened. (T)
2. Religion and politics were totally unrelated during the Enlightenment. (F)
3. Many comedic plays of the Restoration reflected the life of the rich and leisured people of the time. (T)
4. Elegies, satire, epics, and odes are typical kinds of Augustan poems. (T)
5. The novels popular during the Age of Johnson rarely gave insights into the nature of life at the time and demonstrated little understanding of the human experience. (F)

A. Humanities Connection: About the Fine Art

Henry Fuseli (1741–1825) was a Swiss painter who settled in England. His works, including the one here, often suggested a grotesque or macabre tone. Fuseli is famous for the series of striking illustrations he did for Shakespeare's *Macbeth*.

B. Pindar's Odes

The classical model for the ode was the Greek poet Pindar (c. 518–443 B.C.), whose poems celebrated the victors in the ancient Olympic games.

Woman in 17th Century Costume by Henry Fuseli (1791). Watercolor.

Victoria and Albert Museum, London.

Another important kind of poem was the **ode**—an ambitious, often pompous poetic utterance expressing a public emotion, like the jubilation felt after a great naval victory. Since odes could be written in a variety of meters and rhyme schemes, they enabled poets to escape from the usual heroic couplets.

Many of the popular kinds of poetry could be inverted, so to speak, and used for trivial, amusing purposes. Alexander Pope's *Rape of the Lock* and Thomas Gray's "Ode on the Death of a Favorite Cat, Drowned in a Tub of Goldfishes" are mock-epic and mock-ode, respectively.

Poets took for granted that each kind of poetry had its own style or form of expression. For instance, the style of **pastoral poetry**—poetry dealing with country life—was supposed to be simpler than the style of the epic or ode, and its language sweeter and more refined than the language of satire. But regardless of its kind, every poem had to be carefully and artificially constructed; every poem had to be dressed in exact **meter** and **rhyme**. Poems were not to sound like spontaneous and impromptu utterances, just as people were not to appear in public except in fancy dress. Those who could afford it adorned themselves with vast wigs, beribboned and bejeweled clothing, and red shoes with high heels. People's movements were dignified and stately in public, the gentlemen encumbered with long swords and the ladies with voluminous skirts and headdresses. Nothing was what we would call "natural."

1660	1660–1666	1673–1678	1687
Charles II restored to throne, 1660 **Pepys begins his diary, 1660**	Actresses appear on stage for the first time in Germany and England, 1660 Plague claims 68,000 in London, 1665 Great Fire in London, 1666	The Test Act excludes Roman Catholics from holding public office in England, 1673 **Bunyan publishes *The Pilgrim's Progress*, 1678**	Newton's *Mathematical Principles of Natural Philosophy* proposes a system for using reason to explain everything, 1687

1688–1709	1711–1719	1726–1735	1740–1749
Protestant rulers William and Mary replace King James II, a Catholic, 1688 **First issue of Addison and Steele's *The Tatler*, 1709**	**First issue of Addison and Steele's *The Spectator*, 1711** Defoe's *Robinson Crusoe*, 1719	Swift's *Gulliver's Travels*, 1726 **Swift's "A Modest Proposal," 1729** Paul Revere born in Boston, 1735	Samuel Richardson's *Pamela, or Virtue Rewarded*, first English novel, 1740 Henry Fielding's novel *The History of Tom Jones*, 1749

1750–1755	1762–1763	1766–1776	1789–1798
Gray's "Elegy Written in a Country Churchyard," 1750 **Johnson's *Dictionary of the English Language*, 1755**	At the age of six, Mozart tours Europe as a performer, 1762 **Boswell meets Johnson for the first time, 1763**	Oliver Goldsmith's novel *The Vicar of Wakefield*, 1766 Jane Austen born, 1775 American Revolution begins, 1776	French Revolution begins, 1789 **Boswell's *Life of Johnson*, 1791** Publication of *Lyrical Ballads*, 1798

FOR FURTHER READING

STUDENTS

The following selections are from *The Norton Anthology of English Literature, Volume 1*, 1986:

John Dryden, "Absalom and Achitophel: A Poem" (1681).

Daniel Defoe, from *Roxana* (1724).

Jonathan Swift, *A Tale of a Tub* (1704).

Alexander Pope, *Epistle to Dr. Arbuthnot* (1735).

Joseph Addison, "Wit: True, False, Mixed," from *The Spectator* (1711).

Richard Steele, "Dueling," from *The Tatler* (1709).

Samuel Johnson, *Rasselas* (1759).

Thomas Gray, "Ode on a Distant Prospect of Eton College."

James Boswell, *Boswell on the Grand Tour* (1764).

The following are available in numerous editions:

Jane Austen, *Pride and Prejudice* (1813).

Oliver Goldsmith, *The Vicar of Wakefield* (1766).

The Age of Johnson

Samuel Johnson is only one of the several great prose writers of the last part of the eighteenth century, which also produced Johnson's biographer James Boswell as well as the philosopher David Hume (1711–1776), the economist Adam Smith (1723–1790), the historian Edward Gibbon (1737–1794), and the political thinker Edmund Burke (1729–1797). And the Age of Johnson is as well known for its fiction as for its nonfiction. Authorities disagree as to whether *Robinson Crusoe* and Defoe's other fictional narratives are true novels, but everybody agrees that the **novel** began either with Defoe or with the writers of the next generation. Three of these novelists are famous: Samuel Richardson (1689–1761), who wrote *Pamela* (1740) and *Clarissa* (1747–1748); Henry Fielding (1707–1754), who wrote *Joseph Andrews* (1742) and *Tom Jones* (1749); and Laurence Sterne (1713–1768), who wrote *Tristram Shandy* (1761–1767) and *Sentimental Journey* (1768). Each of these novels tells us something of what life at this time was like, and each of them helps us understand human experience in all ages. Richardson was perhaps the first novelist to explore in great detail the emotional life of his characters, especially his heroines. Fielding's pages are crammed with rough and rowdy incidents, but he manages to make his good characters seem good but not goody-goody. Sterne's odd, whimsical novels are like no others, except those of his many imitators.

Why, then, if there were so many other important writers in this period, do we name it after Johnson? We do so not only because Johnson, like Dryden before him, excelled in all the literary genres of his day, but also because he was, and is, a commanding figure who speaks with authority about many of the things that matter to men and women: about their relationships to themselves, to God, and to one another. Like Shakespeare and Milton, Johnson used language superbly well to explore these great themes. He was, in Boswell's words, "a majestic teacher of moral and religious wisdom"—wisdom of the kind that is eternal, not useful only in a particular era. Johnson's views of humanity were conservative and traditional. He combated such tendencies of his time as the belief in progress (the belief that things are inevitably getting better) and the assumption that men and women are naturally good (the assumption that if society is reformed, people will automatically do what is right). By the time of Johnson's death in 1784, writers were developing new interests. They were turning, for instance, to external nature and writing about the effect of the natural landscape on the human psyche. They were looking back at the colorful past and searching out the simple poems and songs composed by nameless, uneducated "folk" poets. They were even becoming interested in the literary possibilities of the humble life and trying to enter into the consciousness of the poor and simple. Nothing could be less Augustan than these tendencies. In short, a new literary age was already beginning during the lifetime of the last great representative of the older ages.

A

> "**F**ielding's pages are crammed with rough and rowdy incidents, but he manages to make his good characters seem good but not goody-good."

A. Epistolary Form

You may want to tell students that Richardson's novels illustrate the *epistolary* form; that is, they are cast in the form of letters. The letter itself was highly regarded in this period as a vehicle of literary expression. (For an outstanding example, see Samuel Johnson's "Letter to Lord Chesterfield," text page 559.)

A. Dryden's Translations
Dryden's most celebrated translation was his version of Virgil's epic, *The Aeneid*, which remains widely admired today.

B. Literary Criticism
In addition to his other distinctions, Dryden can be regarded as the father of English literary criticism in prose. His two most notable works in this genre are the essays *Of Dramatic Poetry* (1668) and *A Discourse Concerning the Origin and Progress of Satire* (1693). In the latter, Dryden coined the famous description of satire as "lashing vice into reformation."

C. The Poet Laureate
The first Poet Laureate in the modern sense was Ben Jonson. However, Dryden was the first to be given the title officially.

John Dryden (1631–1700)

A — John Dryden was a poet, a dramatist, a critic, and a translator of foreign works into English. In short he was an all-around "man of letters" and perhaps the first Englishman to deserve that title. Dryden is one of those writers who are not only conspicuous in their own lifetimes but who seem, to later generations, to speak for their entire age. His literary career covered the last forty years of the seventeenth century, and many of his works are concerned with the political and religious crises of that period.

B — Dryden is the least personal and introspective of all England's great poets. He did not look into his heart and write; rather, he used poetry to express his opinions about issues that were before the public at the moment and about events that might be interpreted more than one way. It was as though Dryden were a commentator informing and instructing his fellow citizens and telling them what to think.

By temperament and education, he was well qualified for this role. His prosperous Puritan family sent him to the Westminster School, and after completing the rigorous classical course there he proceeded to Trinity College, Cambridge, from which he graduated in 1654. Then, since his parents had supported the Parliamentary party in the Civil War, he obtained a minor position in Cromwell's government.

Like almost all his poems, Dryden's first important poem was **occasional**—that is, it was written for a specific occasion, the death of Oliver Cromwell—*Heroic Stanzas to the Glorious Memory of Oliver* (1659). This poem praised the dead warrior and statesman, commending particularly the way he restored order to the war-torn country. The next occasion which Dryden celebrated in verse was the restoration of King Charles II to the throne: *Astrea Redux* (1660), or "Justice Restored." This was followed by an ambitious poem on Charles's coronation, *To His Sacred Majesty* (1662). Then, a few years later, Dryden published *Annus Mirabilis* (1667) ("Year of Wonders"), in which he described the two sensational events of 1666, a war between England and Holland and the Great

John Dryden by C. E. Wagstaff (19th century). Stipple engraving.

Fire of London. Dryden also praised King Charles's behavior during both these crises. For C — these poems and other services to the government, Dryden was made Poet Laureate in 1668. His enemies—anyone with as powerful a pen as Dryden's is bound to make enemies—accused him of being an unprincipled turncoat, because he praised first Cromwell and then Charles. But in his defense it can be said, as Samuel Johnson was to say a hundred years later, that if Dryden had changed, so had the whole nation. The English were delighted to have their king back on the throne.

The Poet Laureateship was a considerable honor, but the stipend it carried was not large enough to support Dryden, even if it had been regularly paid (and it wasn't). Since he had meantime married a woman with a title, the Lady Elizabeth Howard, and had established a household, Dryden especially needed money. And so he turned to the theater and started writing plays. Like Shakespeare, he became a professional dramatist, although unlike Shakespeare none of his thirty or so plays has been regularly performed since his death.

In addition to his plays, Dryden wrote a number of longish poems concerned with the literary, political, and religious issues of the time. These include *MacFlecknoe* (written about 1678 but published in 1682), *Absalom and Achitophel* (1681), *The Medal* (1682), *Religio Laici, or a Layman's Faith* (1682), and *The Hind and the Panther* (1687). These poems—each quite different from the other in style—are of great interest to specialists in seventeenth-century history and literature, and Dryden's considerable reputation as a poet is mainly dependent upon them. These works represent Dryden at his very best. But they assume so much background knowledge and they require so much annotation (of contemporary references) to make them intelligible that they do not readily fit into an anthology like this one, which surveys all of English literature.

About 1685 Dryden converted to Roman Catholicism, a religion that was barely tolerated in England. Although Catholics could not vote and were otherwise discriminated against, Dryden's enemies again accused him of insincerity. They said that he had left the Church of England only to retain the favor of King James II, a Catholic who had recently ascended the throne upon the death of his brother Charles. But Dryden actually gained no material advantage from changing his religion. His reappointment as Poet Laureate had already been confirmed before he announced his conversion, and his new faith became even more a handicap when James was forced to abdicate in 1688. Deprived of the Laureateship, as well as the post of Historiographer Royal, Dryden again turned to playwriting and translation to support himself and his three sons. He died famous, but poor, in the first year of the new century.

Dryden's achievement was to perfect the technique of English poetry, to regularize meter and make diction precise. He was also a master of explaining ideas, of reasoning in verse. The voice one hears in his poems is civilized, judicious, and energetic—but calm. Dryden provided models, especially in satire, for his great successor Alexander Pope, and he set standards that most of the poets of the next century aspired to.

Dryden uses poetry to express general ideas about human beings, their government and social organization, and their relationship with God. Many of his greatest poems are arguments in which he reasons with his readers to convince them that he is speaking the truth. Such poems might be called propaganda, but propaganda of a very high order. Dryden does not insult his readers by assuming that they are stupid, as most propagandists do; instead, he treats them as equals. He assumes that, like himself, they are sensible, intelligent, and capable of following a line of thought to its conclusion.

Dryden loved order. Like the majority of his contemporaries, he feared that England might relapse into the chaos of its Civil War days, when dozens of different political parties and religious sects clamored and struggled for control so that they could remake the country according to their own notions. Against these elements, some of which had survived the Restoration, Dryden was a spokesman for peace, quiet, stability, and tradition. This passage from *Absalom and Achitophel* typifies both the substance and style of his message:

> All other errors but disturb a state,
> But innovation is the blow of fate.
> When ancient fabrics nod, and threat to fall,
> To patch the flaws and buttress up the wall
> Thus far, 'tis duty; but here fix the mark:
> For all beyond it is to touch our Ark
> To change foundations, cast the frame anew,
> Is work for rebels who base ends pursue;
> At once divine and human laws control,
> And mend the parts by ruin of the whole.
> The tampering world is subject to this curse,
> To physic their disease into a worse.

Here Dryden reasons by analogy and metaphor. He presents England's government as a venerable "fabric"—a fortress protecting the citizens. Unfortunately, mad people are opposed to maintaining and repairing this building; instead of preserving it, they want to make innovative "improvements" in it. But the building is sacred, like the Ark in which the ancient Hebrews kept the tablets of their law, the ten commandments that God had given them.

Dryden argues that the only people who want to change the government are those who stand to profit from such change. They are fixing something that already works well, and their medicine will only make the disease worse. Notice how forcibly and clearly Dryden expresses his ideas with the aid of such poetic devices as imagery and metaphor. He has made poetry out of political philosophy.

A. Satire
Perhaps the most accessible of these poems is *MacFlecknoe,* written to satirize Dryden's successor as Poet Laureate, the mediocre poet and dramatist Thomas Shadwell.

B. Vocabulary
For "fix the mark," we would probably say, "draw the line," i.e., establish both a standard and a limit.

C. Couplets
Call students' attention to the elements of balance, antithesis, and elegant allusion in the heroic couplets.

PREPARATION

1. **BUILDING ON PRIOR KNOWLEDGE.** Before students begin reading, ask them what they think is Shakespeare's single greatest virtue as a dramatist and his single greatest fault.

2. **ESTABLISHING A PURPOSE.** Have students read question 4. This will help establish a purpose for their reading.

SUPPLEMENTARY SUPPORT MATERIALS
1. Vocabulary Activity Worksheet (*CCB*)
2. Review and Response Worksheet: Argumentation (*CCB*)
3. Selection Test (*CCB*)

DEVELOPING VOCABULARY
The following words from the essay are tested in the Selection Test. (See also Vocabulary Activity Worksheet.)
comprehensive   insipid
laboriously   to degenerate
commendation

A. Humanities Connection: About the Fine Art
Over the centuries, *As You Like It* has been set in many different times. Here it takes place in an eighteenth-century setting. The scene depicted is from Act I, Scene 2 of the play, when Orlando has thrown the Duke's champion Charles to the ground while a delighted Celia and Rosalind look on. Remind students that many productions of Shakespeare's plays in our day use "updated," twentieth-century settings and costumes.

SHAKESPEARE

Dryden made his critical observations on Shakespeare in his *Of Dramatic Poesy: An Essay* (1668). (The word *poesy* in this title means *literature*.) In order to appreciate Dryden's observations, you must remember that Shakespeare had been dead only fifty years when Dryden wrote. Shakespeare's plays were not being studied in every English-speaking school, read in translation in countries all over the world, and constantly performed by professionals and amateurs everywhere. Shakespeare was then only one of many dramatists of the preceding age, and far from being the most popular one at that. Today we may agree that Shakespeare was England's greatest poet, but Dryden had no such consensus to fall back on. When he praised Shakespeare highly, he was not echoing a commonly held opinion; he was advancing a new idea—sticking his neck out, so to speak. In the midst of such high praise, notice how cleverly Dryden acknowledges Shakespeare's weaknesses while simultaneously causing those weaknesses to appear insignificant.

A

The Wrestling Scene (from Shakespeare's *As You Like It*) by Francis Hayman (1758–59). Oil.

The Tate Gallery, London.

READING CHECK TEST

1. Dryden says that Shakespeare's readers can both see and feel whatever he describes. (T)
2. Dryden defends Shakespeare's lack of formal learning. (T)
3. Dryden states that Shakespeare's works were consistently great. (F)

4. Dryden states that Shakespeare was the most popular and best liked of his contemporaries. (F)
5. Dryden states that many courtiers believed Shakespeare was a superior writer to the popular Ben Jonson. (T)

CLOSURE

Have students summarize Dryden's main reasons for feeling that Shakespeare is a great writer.

ANALYZING THE CRITIQUE
Identifying Facts

1. Dryden says that Shakespeare is often flat and insipid and that his comic scenes often degenerate into puns. Dryden also says that Shakespeare's "serious swelling" is sometimes so inflated that it becomes "bombast."

Interpreting Meanings

2. Citing these three different kinds of authorities has the effect of drawing on a representative range of opinion.

Perhaps actors and theatergoers.
3. Arguments are usually much more persuasive when they confront opposing viewpoints.
4. Shakespeare had immense powers of imagination, since "all the images of nature were present to him." This generalization is meant to influence readers favorably.

To begin, then, with Shakespeare: He was the man who of all modern, and perhaps ancient poets, had the largest and most comprehensive soul. All the images of nature were still [always] present to him, and he drew them not laboriously, but luckily; when he describes anything, you more than see it, you feel it too. Those who accuse him to have wanted [lacked] learning give him the greater commendation: He was naturally learned; he needed not the spectacles of books to read nature;[1] he looked inwards, and found her there. I cannot say he is everywhere alike; were he so, I should do him injury to compare him with the greatest of mankind. He is many times flat, insipid; his comic wit degenerating into clenches [puns], his serious swelling into bombast. But he is always great when some great occasion is presented to him; no man can say he ever had a fit subject for his wit,[2] and did not then raise himself as high above the rest of poets,

as cypresses often do among bending osiers.[3]

The consideration of this made Mr. Hales[4] of Eton say that there was no subject of which any poet ever writ, but he would produce it much better treated of in Shakespeare; and however others are now generally preferred before him, yet the age wherein he lived, which had contemporaries with him Fletcher and Jonson,[5] never equaled them to him in their esteem. And in the last King's court, when Ben's reputation was at highest, Sir John Suckling,[6] and with him the greater part of the courtiers, set our Shakespeare far above him.

---

1. **nature:** Dryden is referring to human nature as well as the natural universe.

2. **wit:** creative imagination.
3. **as cypresses . . . osiers:** a quotation translated from Virgil's *Eclogues. Osiers* are willows.
4. **Mr. Hales:** John Hales, provost of Eton College, England's best-known public school.
5. **Fletcher and Jonson:** Shakespeare's fellow dramatists, John Fletcher and Ben Jonson.
6. **Sir John Suckling:** a poet and courtier during the reign of Charles I.

Responding to the Critique

Analyzing the Critique

Identifying Facts

1. What weaknesses of Shakespeare does Dryden acknowledge?

Interpreting Meanings

2. In this short critical excerpt, Dryden uses several techniques of **argumentation.** For example, he cites the opinions of a respected poet, of a literary scholar, and of royal courtiers (then considered arbiters of taste). What is the effect of citing these three kinds of authorities? Can you think of another kind of authority whose opinion could have lent weight to Dryden's argument?
3. Would you have found Dryden's praise more convincing if he had not dealt with **opposing viewpoints**—the opinions of "those who accuse" Shakespeare? Why or why not?

4. What do you think Dryden means by writing that Shakespeare had "the largest and most comprehensive soul"? How does Dryden use this **generalization** to sway his readers?

Writing About the Critique

A Critical Response

Applying a Generalization. Dryden speaks about Shakespeare in a very general way, neither referring to any particular play nor using quotations to illustrate any of the points he makes. Dryden lived in an age that admired generalizations. In contrast, we are skeptical of generalizations unless they are immediately supported with evidence in the form of specific details. Develop, in an essay, one of Dryden's general statements. Take one of Dryden's observations, explain what you think it means, and support your analysis of it with specific references to, and quotations from, Shakespeare's tragedy *Macbeth.*

A. Theme
Point out to students that the motif of divinities wandering the earth in disguise and testing mortals is a common theme in world mythology and folklore.

B. Archaism
Note the archaic meanings of the noun *settle* (line 28) and the adjective *officious* (line 30).

Dryden translated this poem, about a very pleasant old married woman named Baucis (pronounced bō′kəs) and her equally agreeable husband Philemon (fi′lē·mən), from the Latin of the Roman poet Ovid (43 B.C.–A.D. 17). It is one of the many mythological stories Ovid versified for his book *Metamorphoses*—marvelous stories about human and divine transformations. Dryden wasn't interested in word-for-word translations, which are impossible in poetry anyway. Rather, he takes the old poem and transforms it into an entirely new one. The American poet Robert Frost once defined poetry as "what gets lost in translation." In Dryden's translation a lot of Ovid does "get lost"; but the gaps are well filled with a lot of Dryden. Thus, the poem itself is a metamorphosis.

from Baucis and Philemon

In *Phrygian* ground°
Two neighb'ring trees, with walls encompassed round,
Stand on a mod'rate rise, with wonder shown,
One a hard oak, a softer linden one: . . .
5   Not far from thence is seen a lake, the haunt
Of coots, and of the fishing cormorant:°
A ⌈ Here *Jove*° with *Hermes*° came; but in disguise
     Of mortal men concealed their deities;
     One laid aside his thunder, one his rod;
10 And many toilsome steps together trod:
For harbor at a thousand doors they knocked,
Not one of all the thousand but was locked.
At last an hospitable house they found,
A homely shed; the roof, not far from ground,
15 Was thatched with reeds, and straw together bound.
There *Baucis* and *Philemon* lived, and there
Had lived long married, and a happy pair:
Now old in love, though little was their store,°
Inured to want, their poverty they bore,
20 Nor aimed at wealth, professing to be poor.
For master or for servant here to call,
Was all alike, where only two were all.
Command was none, where equal love was paid,
Or rather both commanded, both obeyed.
25   From lofty roofs the gods repulsed before,
Now stooping, entered through the little door:
The man (their hearty welcome first expressed)
B ⌈ A common settle° drew for either guest,
     Inviting each his weary limbs to rest.
30 ⌊ But e'er they sat, officious° *Baucis* lays
Two cushions stuffed with straw, the seat to raise;
Coarse, but the best she had; then rakes the load
Of ashes from the hearth, and spreads abroad
The living coals; and, lest they should expire,
35 With leaves and barks she feeds her infant-fire:

1. *Phrygian* (frij′ē·ən) **ground:** Phrygia was an ancient country in Asia Minor.

6. **coots, cormorants:** water birds.

7. **Jove:** Jupiter, the chief Roman god, who throws thunderbolts. *Hermes:* the messenger of the gods, with his rod (staff) or *caduceus,* which is now the emblem of physicians.

18. **store:** supplies.

28. **settle:** bench.

30. **officious:** busy.

SUPPLEMENTARY SUPPORT MATERIALS
1. Vocabulary Activity Worksheet (*CCB*)
2. Review and Response Worksheet: Theme (*CCB*)
3. Selection Test (*CCB*)

DEVELOPING VOCABULARY
The following words from the poem are tested in the Selection Test. (See also Vocabulary Activity Worksheet.)

inured	impiety
to cull	sepulcher
suppliant	

A

Windsor Forest by Paul Sandby (c. 1763). Watercolor.

Victoria and Albert Museum, London.

A. Humanities Connection: Responding to the Fine Art
Note that Dryden has set the poem squarely in a rural, seventeenth-century locale (rather than in ancient Greece). The man on horseback is actually King George III; Windsor Forest surrounds Windsor Castle on the Thames River. Windsor has been one of the principal residences of British monarchs since the end of the seventeenth century.

? How does the painting relate to the story? (The trees might be the old couple; the traveler might be a divinity in disguise.)

A. A Seventeenth-Century Meal

Based on this account, what might people living in seventeenth-century England have eaten? (The people might have eaten boiled bacon, berries pickled in wine, salads much like our own, cottage cheese, and roasted eggs. According to the next page, in the second course they ate honeycomb, fruits, and nuts. They would, according to line 117, have roasted a goose except that the god saved it.)

It smokes; and then with trembling breath she blows,
Till in a cheerful blaze the flames arose.
With brush-wood and with chips she strengthens these,
And adds at last the boughs of rotten trees.

40 The fire thus formed, she sets the kettle on,
(Like burnished gold the little seether° shone)
Next took the coleworts° which her husband got
From his own ground (a small well-watered spot);
She stripped the stalks of all their leaves; the best

45 She culled, and then with handy-care she dressed.
High o'er the hearth a chine° of bacon hung;
Good old *Philemon* seized it with a prong,
And from the sooty rafter drew it down,
Then cut a slice, but scarce enough for one;

50 Yet a large portion of a little store,
Which for their sakes alone he wished were more.
This in the pot he plunged without delay,
To tame the flesh, and drain the salt away.
The time between, before the fire they sat,

55 And shortened the delay by pleasing chat.
    A beam there was, on which a beechen pail°
Hung by the handle, on a driven nail:
This filled with water, gently warmed, they set
Before their guests; in this they bathed their feet,

60 And after with clean towels dried their sweat:
This done, the host produced the genial bed,°
Sallow° the feet, the borders, and the stead,°
Which with no costly coverlet they spread;
But coarse old garments, yet such robes as these

65 They laid alone,° at feasts, on holydays.
The good old huswife tucking up her gown,
The table sets; th' invited gods lie down.°
The trivet-table of a foot was lame,
A blot° which prudent *Baucis* overcame,

70 Who thrusts beneath the limping leg, a sherd,°
So was the mended board exactly reared:
Then rubbed it o'er with newly-gathered Mint,
A wholesome Herb, that breathed a grateful scent.
Pallas° began the feast, where first was seen

75 The parti-colored° Olive, black, and green:
Autumnal cornels° next in order served,
In lees° of wine well pickled, and preserved.
A garden-salad was the third supply,
A   Of endive, radishes, and succory:°

80 Then curds° and cream, the flow'r of country fare,
And new-laid eggs, which *Baucis* busy care
Turned by a gentle fire, and roasted rear.°
All these in earthenware° were served to board;
And next in place, an earthen Pitcher stored

85 With liquor of the best the cottage could afford.
This was the table's ornament, and pride,

41. **seether:** boiler.
42. **coleworts:** a kind of cabbage.

46. **chine:** a large piece, including the backbone.

56. **beechen pail:** wooden bucket.

61. **genial bed:** the marriage bed, an expression Dryden borrowed from Milton.
62. **sallow:** made of willow-wood. **feet . . . borders . . . stead:** the foot, sides, and head and legs of the bed.
65. **alone:** only; that is, coarse as these coverings are, they are used only on special occasions.
67. **lie down:** in antiquity, people reclined while they ate.
69. **blot:** blemish.
70. **sherd:** shard; a chip or other small piece of something.

74. *Pallas:* Athena, wise in the arts of war and peace. They invoke her blessing.
75. **parti-colored:** variegated.
76. **cornels:** berries.
77. **lees:** dregs.

79. **succory:** chicory, a lettuce-like vegetable.
80. **Curds:** cottage cheese.

82. **rear:** rare.
83. **earthenware:** pottery.

READING CHECK TEST

1. Jove and Hermes visit Baucis and Philemon because they've heard how hospitable the couple is. (F)
2. Baucis and Philemon suspect that their unexpected guests are really gods in disguise. (F)
3. Jove tells his gracious hosts that they alone will be spared from punishment for impiety. (T)
4. Jove tells the couple to flee to the mountains. (T)
5. Jove, angered by the couple's request to die together, turns them into marble statues. (F)

With figures wrought: Like pages at his side
Stood beechen bowls; and these were shining clean,
Varnished with wax without, and lined within.
90   By this the boiling kettle had prepared,
And to the table sent the smoking lard;°
On which with eager appetite they dine,
A sav'ry bit, that served to relish° wine:
95   The wine itself was suiting to the rest,
Still working in the must,° and lately pressed.
The second course succeeds like that before,
Plums, apples, nuts, and of their wintry store,
Dry figs, and grapes, and wrinkled dates were set
In canisters,° t' enlarge the little treat:
100   All these a milk-white honey-comb surround,
Which in the midst the country-banquet crowned:
But the kind hosts their entertainment grace
With hearty welcome, and an open face:
In all they did, you might discern with ease,
105   A willing mind, and a desire to please.
    Meantime the beechen bowls went round, and still
Though often emptied, were observed to fill;
Filled without hands, and of their own accord
Ran without feet, and danced about the board.
110   Devotion seized the pair, to see the feast
With wine, and of no common grape, increased;
And up they held their hands, and fell to pray'r,
Excusing as they could, their country fare.
    One goose they had ('twas all they could allow)
115   A wakeful sentry,° and on duty now,
Whom to the gods for sacrifice they vow:
Her, with malicious zeal, the couple viewed;
She ran for life, and limping they pursued:
Full well the fowl perceived their bad intent,
120   And would not make her masters compliment;
But persecuted, to the pow'rs she flies,
And close between the legs of *Jove* she lies:
He with a gracious ear the <u>suppliant</u> heard,
And saved her life; then what he was declared,
125   And owned the god. The neighborhood, said he,
Shall justly perish for <u>impiety</u>:
You stand alone exempted; but obey
With speed, and follow where we lead the way:
Leave these accursed; and to the mountains height
130   Ascend; nor once look backward in your flight.
    They haste, and what their tardy feet denied,
The trusty staff (their better leg) supplied.
An arrow's flight they wanted to the top,
And there secure, but spent with travel, stop;
135   Then turn their now no more forbidden eyes;
Lost in a Lake the floated level lies:
A wat'ry desert covers all the Plains,

A

B

C

91. **lard:** bacon.

93. **relish:** add flavor to.

95. **must:** new grape juice.

99. **canisters:** small reed baskets.

115. **sentry:** Geese make very good "watchdogs."

A. Setting and Foreshadowing

❓ How does Dryden's use of details in the passage suggest that Baucis and Philemon live close to nature and are in harmony with it? What may this motif foreshadow about how the gods will treat them? (The use of details stresses natural products, such as fruits and vegetables. This motif may foreshadow the gods' kindly treatment of the couple, since they are portrayed as living a natural, simple life.)

B. Parody
You may want to point out that several elements in the goose episode parody the standard scene of supplication in ancient epics. For example, the goose is said to lie "close between the legs of Jove"; the classic gesture of supplication in epics was to clasp the knees of the person whose favor was being sought.

C. Parallels
❓ What parallels can you note between Ovid's mythological flood and the biblical flood in Genesis? (Have students look at Genesis, Chapters 7 and 8.)

John Dryden   465

CLOSURE
Have one student tell the rest of the
class: (1) the moral lesson contained in
"Baucis and Philemon," and (2) the
metamorphosis that is central to the
myth.

ANALYZING THE POEM
Identifying Details
1. Among the details students should
mention are the following: the low,
thatched roof; the small size; the simple
benches; the fire; the sooty rafters; the
marriage bed and its coverlets.
2. Philemon seats the guests and helps
with the cooking.
    Baucis makes the guests comfortable

with cushions and prepares the food.
3. Baucis and Philemon served boiled
cabbage leaves and bacon, olives, berries, salad, eggs, and wine.
4. At line 106, they observe the bowls
magically refilling themselves and dancing around the table. Devotion seizes the
couple, and they fall to prayer.
5. They ask to serve at the gods' shrine
and to die within the same hour. The

A. The Epic Form
The syntax of line
147 reproduces
the formulaic
speech introduc-
tions of classical
epic, as in Homer's
Iliad and *Odyssey*
and Virgil's *Aen-
eid.* Remind stu-
dents that Ovid
was writing very
much in the tradi-
tion of classical
epic: He envisioned
his long poem, the
Metamorphoses,
as a cosmic epic
that would move
from mythological
time to legendary
and historical time.
Thus, the poem
features several
creation stories in
Book I and con-
cludes with the
metamorphosis of
the assassinated
Julius Caesar into
a comet in Book
XV. The story of
Baucis and Phile-
mon can be found
in Book VIII.

**B. Characteriza-
tion**
What does this
speech show
about Philemon's
character? (He is
pious and devoted
to his wife.)

	Their cot° alone, as in an Isle, remains:	138. **cot:** cottage.
	Wond'ring with weeping eyes, while they deplore	
140	Their neighbors' Fate, and country now no more,	
	Their little shed, scarce large enough for two,	
	Seems, from the ground increased, in height and bulk to grow.	
	A stately temple shoots within the skies,	
	The crotches° of their cot in columns rise:	144. **crotches:** props.
145	The pavement polished marble they behold,	
	The gates with sculpture graced, the spires and tiles of gold.	

A ⌐ Then thus the sire of gods, with look serene,
Speak thy desire, thou only just of men;
And thou, O woman, only worthy found
150 To be with such a man in marriage bound.
    A while they whisper; then to *Jove* addressed,   152. **prefers:** puts forward.
Philemon thus prefers° their joint request.
⌐ We crave to serve before your sacred shrine,
And offer at your altars rites divine:
155 And since not any action of our life
   Has been polluted with domestic strife,
B We beg one hour of death; that neither she
With widow's tears may live to bury me,
Nor weeping I, with withered arms may bear
160 ⌐ My breathless *Baucis* to the sepulcher.
    The godheads sign their suit.° They run their race   161. **suit:** consent.
In the same tenor° all th' appointed space: 162. **tenor:** manner, style.
Then, when their hour was come, while they relate
These past adventures at the temple gate,
165 Old *Baucis* is by old *Philemon* seen
Sprouting with sudden leaves of spritely green:
Old *Baucis* looked where old *Philemon* stood,
And saw his lengthened arms a sprouting wood:
New roots their fastened feet begin to bind,
170 Their bodies stiffen in a rising rind:
Then e'er the bark above their shoulders grew,
They give and take at once their last adieu:
At once, Farewell, O faithful spouse, they said;
At once th' incroaching rinds their closing lips invade.
175 Ev'n yet, an ancient *Tyanæan°* shows   175. **Tyanæan:** an inhabitant of that region.
A spreading oak, that near a linden grows;
The neighborhood confirm the prodigy,°   177. **prodigy:** marvel.
Grave men, not vain of tongue, or like° to lie.   178. **like:** likely.
I saw myself the garlands on their boughs,
180 And tablets hung for gifts of granted vows;
And off'ring fresher up, with pious prayer,
The good, said I, are God's peculiar care,
And such as honor Heav'n, shall heav'nly honor share.

gods grant their request and turn them into trees.

Interpreting Meanings

6. The moral, pronounced by the speaker of the poem in the last two lines, is that piety will be rewarded.

7. Answers will vary. In general, the metamorphosis into trees is appropriate because trees symbolize growth and rest

(or shade). The oak tree might stand for strength, while the linden might symbolize beauty.

8. Jove's sparing of the goose perhaps foreshadows the gods' kindly granting of Philemon's request.

9. Other metamorphoses include the gods changing into mortal form, the bowls refilling themselves, the valley turning into a lake, and the old couple's

cottage turning into a shrine. The final metamorphosis, especially, contributes to the theme of piety being rewarded.

10. Most students will agree that Dryden seems to admire the old couple and that the tone of the poem, while occasionally light, is predominantly serious.

11. Answers will vary. Encourage an imaginative response.

Responding to the Poem

Analyzing the Poem

Identifying Details

1. Using details in the poem, describe Baucis and Philemon's house.
2. Using details from the poem, describe Philemon's contribution to the successful marriage. Describe Baucis's.
3. Dryden is very specific about the meal. What did Baucis and Philemon serve for dinner?
4. How do Philemon and Baucis realize they are entertaining gods?
5. What request does the old couple make of the gods? How is it met?

Interpreting Meanings

6. Fables frequently provide a **moral** for the reader. What is the moral of this fable, and who speaks it?
7. Why do you suppose Philemon and Baucis were changed into trees? Consider why the gods chose the oak tree for Philemon and the linden tree for Baucis; what do these trees **symbolize**?
8. Do you think the goose in the story is important? Does it function in any way besides offering **comic relief**?
9. The metamorphosis of the old couple is just one of the metamorphoses in this story. What are some others, and how do they contribute to the **theme**?
10. Does Dryden poke fun at the old couple, or does he admire them? What is the **tone** of the poem?
11. Line 55 mentions the ''pleasing chat'' that Baucis, Philemon, and the gods had. What do you suppose they talked about? What did the gods tell the couple? What did the couple tell the gods?

Writing About the Poem

A Creative Response

1. **Changing the Setting.** In your own words, retell the story of Baucis and Philemon in prose, keeping the plot but giving it a modern (perhaps urban) setting and characters. If you think that a metamorphosis into trees is inappropriate for a city, have your old couple change into something more appropriate.

A Critical Response

2. **Analyzing Characterization.** Dryden uses many complimentary adjectives in describing Baucis and Philemon. In addition, he uses the less direct, but perhaps more effective, technique of letting their actions speak for them. In an essay, analyze some of the details Dryden provides about the old couple's way of life and their ways of dealing with each other. What do these details imply about the personalities of Baucis and Philemon?

A. Expansion
Remind students
that the Royal
Navy continued to
be critical to Eng-
lish world power all
through the seven-
teenth and eigh-
teenth centuries
(as, for example, in
England's wars
against Holland
and in the Napo-
leonic Wars
against France).

B. Expansion
Pepys bequeathed
his diary to Magda-
lene College, Cam-
bridge. It was not
until 1825 that the
shorthand code
was deciphered.
An unbowdlerized
edition of the *Diary*
was published only
in 1970.

C. Expansion
Remind students
that King Charles II
himself led the up-
per classes in their
enthusiasm for
Restoration drama.

Samuel Pepys (1633–1703)

For nine years—1660 to 1669—Samuel Pepys, whose name is pronounced "peeps," kept a secret diary which, when published long after his death, made him very famous. Pepys was not a writer but an official in the government office that maintained the Royal Navy and provided it with ships and supplies. The head of the office was Pepys's cousin Edward Montague, a great friend and supporter of King Charles II, who bestowed on him the title of first Earl of Sandwich. (It was a later earl, not this one, who invented the sandwich.) This Earl (Pepys always calls him "My Lord" in the *Diary*) obtained for Pepys his first appointment in the Navy Office, but Pepys's own diligence and skill accounted for his rapid advancement. He did much to increase the honesty and efficiency of naval supply and maintenance, so much that one of his contemporaries called him "the right hand of the Navy," and a modern historian has hailed him as its "Savior." Along with his public career, Pepys's private affairs also prospered. Starting humbly in life as the son of a tailor who managed to send him to preparatory school and then to Oxford University, Pepys became so rich that when he was forced to retire in 1688, for political reasons, he could live the rest of his life like a gentleman, in leisure, comfort, and elegance.

Many people kept detailed diaries in the seventeenth century, and a surprisingly large number of these diaries have survived, most of them concerned with religion. The pious people whom we now call "Puritans" used their diaries to analyze their moral behavior and record their spiritual progress. In contrast, Pepys in his *Diary* pays little attention to the state of his soul or to his personal relationship with God, though he almost always mentions going to church on Sundays, often with disparaging comments ("a sorry, silly sermon"), and he sometimes mentions family prayers. But Pepys was not an introspective or contemplative person; his *Diary* is interesting because it tells us what he saw, and heard, and said, and did.

Pepys had an insatiable appetite for experience, a vast capacity for pleasure, and an im-

Samuel Pepys by Greenhill. Oil.

Courtesy the Master and Fellows,
Magdalene College, Cambridge University.

mense desire for learning—languages, literature, science, and everything connected with his naval occupation. Small things delighted him. When he heard "a fellow whistle like a bird exceeding well," he resolved to take lessons in bird whistling. Of a new watch he said, "I could not forbear carrying it in my hand and seeing what o'clock it was a hundred times." His house was full of creatures: cats, two dogs, a whistling blackbird, canaries, even for a time an eagle. He owned many books, carpenters' tools, maps and charts, a telescope, and several musical instruments which he could play—a flageolet, a lute, a flute, a small harpsichord (which he never mastered). He composed a few songs which are still regarded as singable, he was proud of his dancing, he liked expensive clothes and oil paintings. In everything he sought pleasure, and he usually found it. Whenever his head ached from business or his wife was angry at him for flirting with other women, he took refuge in the theater. He saw so many plays and recorded his impressions of them so accurately that the *Diary* is now regarded as an important document for theater history.

Historians of all kinds find the *Diary* useful because Pepys was a first-hand observer of public events and contemporary life. He was a member of the delegation of Englishmen who went to The Hague in 1660 to bring King Charles back to England. He witnessed joyous occasions like Charles's coronation (1660) and national disasters like the plague (1665) and the great fire (1666). These important public happenings he recorded in his *Diary* along with trivial personal ones. For instance, the entry for New Year's Day, 1662, begins:

> Waking this morning out of my sleep on a sudden, I did with my elbow hit my wife a great blow over her face and nose, which waked her with pain—at which I was sorry. And so to sleep again.

On another occasion he records something that happened at the theater:

> I went to Mr. Crew's house and thence to the theater, where I saw again *The Lost Lady,* which doth now please me better than before. And here, I sitting behind in a dark place, a lady spat backward upon me by a mistake, not seeing me. But after seeing her to be a very pretty lady, I was not troubled at all.

According to the *Diary* Pepys's life was full of unexpected little events like this one. Looking over Pepys's shoulder we see the lively panorama of Restoration London—and in many of his observations, we also see ourselves.

A

A. Expansion
Although Pepys did not intend his diary for publication, his care and attention to the ordinary—even the trivial—details of everyday life remarkably anticipate literary developments a half century later, when such details would become staples of the personal essay and the novel.

B. About the Illustration
Pepys wrote in Shelton's system of shorthand, with occasional words in longhand. (Some are visible here.) These are the first pages of the *Diary*.

B

Shorthand pages from Pepys's Diary (1659–60).

Courtesy the Master and Fellows, Magdalene College, Cambridge University.

1. BUILDING ON PRIOR KNOWLEDGE. Before students begin reading, ask them to recall other diaries they have read (for example, the journals of Anne Frank, or of Puritan writers such as Mary Rowlandson or William Bradford). What are the purposes of a diary? Do most people write diaries with an audience of some kind in mind?

2. ESTABLISHING A PURPOSE. Before students begin reading, you may want to direct their attention to question 10 on text page 479. Ask students to read to compare and contrast the attitudes and values of Pepys's time with modern attitudes and values. This will help establish a purpose for their reading.

3. PREREADING JOURNAL. Before they read, have students write a list of three or four categories of events, feelings, and observations that they would include if they were keeping a private diary.

A. Expansion
Hanged, drawn, and quartered was a common form of execution. The victim was hanged, eviscerated (drawn), and the body cut into four parts (quartered). (Sometimes it was pulled apart by horses going in different directions.) Discuss with students their reactions to the fact that executions were witnessed by the public.

B. Expansion
Remind students of the background of the English Civil War and of the execution of King Charles I in 1649 (see the woodcut on text page 449).

FROM THE DIARY OF SAMUEL PEPYS

Unlike many other diaries, Pepys's really was a secret one. He wrote it only for his own use, and in a kind of shorthand that had recently been invented. He doubly safeguarded the most intimate details of his life by recording them in a private foreign language that appears to mix together Latin, French, and Spanish words. Yet, since he did not destroy the *Diary* at the end of his life but bequeathed it along with his other books to Cambridge University, he must have recognized its value as literature and history. He must, in other words, have imagined people reading it. But not until the 1970's was it possible to read everything in the *Diary* because earlier editors could not bring themselves to transcribe and print the more personal entries. Though it covers only nine years the *Diary* is immense; in the 1970's and 1980's it was published, along with notes, commentaries, and indexes, in eleven fat volumes.

In 1660, when he began the *Diary*, Pepys was twenty-seven, married to twenty-year-old Elizabeth St. Michel and in the service of Edward Montague. Until recently he and his wife had been living in a turret room in Whitehall Palace, without servants or proper facilities for washing and cooking.

Nine years later, when he stopped keeping the *Diary* because of eye trouble, Pepys and his family had their own handsome townhouse, one of a complex of buildings that comprised the Navy Office. Their household was not much like most modern ones because they had several live-in servants who did most of their work: three housemaids, a waiting woman for Elizabeth, a footboy for Samuel, a coachman to drive and look after their coach and horses. Although Pepys and his wife unfortunately had no children, their house was always full of people.

October 13, 1660
A Public Execution, A Private Explosion

To my Lord's[1] in the morning, where I met with Captain Cuttance. But my Lord not being up, I went out to Charing Cross to see Major General Harrison[2] hanged, drawn, and quartered—which was done there—he looking as cheerfully as any man could do in that condition. He was presently cut down and his head and his heart shown to the people, at which there was great shouts of joy. It is said that he said that he was sure to come shortly at the right hand of Christ to judge them that now have judged him. And that his wife doth expect his coming again.[3]

Thus it was my chance to see the King beheaded at Whitehall and to see the first blood shed in revenge for the blood of the King at Charing Cross. From thence to my Lord's and took Captain Cuttance and Mr. Shebly to the Sun tavern and did give them some oysters. After that I went by water home, where I was angry with my wife for her things lying about, and in my passion kicked the little fine basket which I bought her in Holland and broke it, which troubled me after I had done it.

Within all the afternoon, setting up shelves in my study. At night to bed.

---

1. **my Lord:** Edward Montague, Earl of Sandwich, a cousin of Pepys and his superior at the Naval Office.
2. **Harrison:** one of the people responsible for the execution of King Charles I.

3. **coming again:** with Christ, on Christ's return to earth.

SUPPLEMENTARY SUPPORT MATERIALS
1. Vocabulary Activity Worksheet (*CCB*)
2. Review and Response Worksheet: Primary Sources (*CCB*)
3. Selection Test (*CCB*)

DEVELOPING VOCABULARY
The following words from the diary are tested in the Selection Test. (See also Vocabulary Activity Worksheet.)

scepter	covetous
cavalcade	infinite
gallant	combustible

April 23, 1661
The Coronation of Charles II

About four in the morning I rose, and got to the Abbey,[4] where I followed Sir J. Denham the surveyor with some company that he was leading in. And with much ado, by the favor of Mr. Cooper his man, did get up into a great scaffold across the north end of the Abbey—where with a great deal of patience I sat from past four till eleven before the King came in. And a pleasure it was to see the Abbey raised in the middle, all covered with red and a throne (that is a chair) and footstool on the top of it. And all the officers of all kinds, so much as the very fiddlers, in red vests.

At last comes in the dean and prebends of Westminster with the bishops (many of them in cloth-of-gold copes[5]); and after them the nobility all in their Parliament robes, which was a most magnificent sight. Then the Duke[6] and the King with a scepter (carried by my Lord of Sandwich) and sword and mond[7] before him, and the crown too.

The King in his robes, bareheaded, which was very fine. And after all had placed themselves—there was a sermon and the service. And then in the quire at the high altar he passed all the ceremonies of the coronation—which, to my very great grief, I and most in the Abbey could not see. The crown being put upon his head, a great shout begun. And he came forth to the throne and there passed more ceremonies: as, taking the oath and having things read to him by the Bishop,[8] and his lords (who put on their caps as soon as the king put on his crown) and bishops came and kneeled before him.

And three times the King-at-arms went to the three open places on the scaffold and proclaimed that if anyone could show any reason why Ch. Steward [Charles Stuart] should not be King of England, that now he should come and speak.

And a general pardon also was read by the Lord Chancellor; and medals flung up and down by my Lord Cornwallis—of silver; but I could not come by any.

But so great a noise, that I could make but little of the music; and indeed, it was lost to everybody. But I had so great a list to piss, that I went out a little while before the King had done all his ceremonies and went round the Abbey to Westminster Hall, all the way within rails, and 10,000 people, with the ground covered with blue cloth—and scaffolds all the way. Into the hall I got—where it was very fine with hangings and scaffolds, one upon another, full of brave ladies. And my wife in one little one on the right hand.

Here I stayed walking up and down; and at last, upon one of the side stalls, I stood and saw the King come in with all the persons (but the soldiers) that were yesterday in the cavalcade; and a most pleasant sight it was to see them in their several robes. And the King came in with his crown on and his scepter in his hand—under a canopy borne up by six silver staves, carried by Barons of the Cinqueports—and little bells at every end.

And after a long time he got up to the farther end, and all set themselves down at their several tables—and that was also a rare sight. And the King's first course carried up by the Knights of the Bath. And many fine ceremonies there was of the Heralds leading up people before him and bowing; and my Lord of Albimarles going to the kitchen and eat a bit of the first dish that was to go to the King's table.

But above all was these three Lords, Northumberland and Suffolk and the Duke of Ormond, coming before the courses on horseback and staying so all dinner time; and at last, to bring up Dymock, the King's Champion, all in armor on horseback, with his spear and target carried before him. And a herald proclaim that if any dare deny Ch. Steward to be lawful King of England, here was a champion that would fight with him; and with those words the champion flings down his gantlet;[9] and all this he doth three times in his going up toward the King's table. At last, when he is come, the King drinks to him and then sends him the cup, which is of gold; and he drinks it off and then rides back again with the cup in his hand.

I went from table to table to see the bishops

---

4. **Abbey:** Westminster Abbey, where all monarchs of England are crowned, and where many of them are buried.
5. **copes:** ecclesiastical robes.
6. **Duke:** James, Duke of York—the King's brother.
7. **mond:** golden orb and cross, a symbol of royal power.
8. **Bishop:** the Bishop of London. The Archbishop of Canterbury was too infirm to officiate.

9. **gantlet:** gauntlet, a metal glove.

A. Specific Details
❓ Based on the details in this passage, how would you summarize the relationship between the church and the state in England? (In England, the king is closely linked to the established Church.)

B. Style
You might discuss with students the archaic grammar, syntax, and diction of this passage.

A

A. Humanities Connection: Responding to the Fine Art

Note the elements of balance and order in the illustration. Remind students that this is a representation of Whitehall—still the center of official, governmental London. Note the private park stocked with game, the guards drilling, and the elegantly dressed personage (Charles I) out for a walk, surrounded by his advisers (or admirers).

? In what ways is this scene like something you might see in America today? (This scene suggests what might take place during presidential appearances or summit conferences.)

Whitehall from St. James Park (detail) by Hendrick Danckaerts (ca. 17th century). Oil.

472   The Restoration and the Eighteenth Century

Duke of Roxburghe Collection.

A. Characteriza-
tion

❓ What does this
passage show
about Pepys's
character? (That
he is skeptical of
attributing too
much to God)

and all others at their dinner, and was infinite
pleased with it. And at the Lords' table I met with
Wll. Howe and he spoke to my Lord for me and
he did give him four rabbits and a pullet; and so I
got it, and Mr. Creed[10] and I got Mr. Michell to
give us some bread and so we at a stall eat it, as
everybody else did what they could get.

I took a great deal of pleasure to go up and
down and look upon the ladies—and to hear the
music of all sorts; but above all, the twenty-four
violins.

About six at night they had dined; and I went
up to my wife and there met with a pretty lady
(Mrs. Frankelyn, a doctor's wife, a friend of Mr.
Bowyer's) and kissed them both—and by and by
took them down to Mr. Bowyer's. And strange it
is, to think that these two days have held up fair
till now that all is done and the King gone out of
the hall; and then it fell a-raining and thundering
and lightning as I have not seen it do some years—
which people did take great notice of God's blessing of the work of these two days—which is a
foolery, to take too much notice of such
things. . . .   **A**

At Mr. Bowyer's, a great deal of company;
some I knew, others I did not. Here we stayed
upon the leads[11] and below till it was late, expecting to see the fireworks; but they were not
performed tonight. Only, the City had a light like
a glory round about it, with bonfires.

At last I went to Kingstreet; and there sent
Crockford[12] to my father's and my house to tell
them I could not come home tonight, because of
the dirt and a coach could not be had.

And so after drinking a pot of ale alone at Mrs.
Harper's, I returned to Mr. Bowyer's; and after a
little stay more, I took my wife and Mrs. Frankelyn (who I preferred the civility of lying with
my wife at Mrs. Hunt's tonight) to Axe Yard. In
which, at the further end, there was three great
bonfires and a great many great <u>gallants</u>, men and
women; and they laid hold of us and would have
us drink the King's health upon our knee, kneeling
upon a faggot;[13] which we all did, they drinking
to us one after another—which we thought a
strange frolic. But these gallants continued thus a

---

10. **Wll. Howe . . . Mr. Creed:** fellow workers in the Navy
Office.
11. **leads:** rooftop.
12. **Crockford:** apparently a servant.
13. **faggot:** a bundle of twigs or sticks used to make a bonfire.

Samuel Pepys 473

A. Theme

❓ What lesson does Pepys draw from his experiences on Coronation Day? (He concludes that the coronation was the greatest event he had ever witnessed.) Do you think you would have drawn the same lesson if you had witnessed the events Pepys describes? Why or why not? (Some students may be impressed with the pomp and ceremony of the occasion; other students may feel that the details Pepys notes before reaching this conclusion offset the glory of the occasion.)

B. Vocabulary

❓ What is a *theorbo*? (A lute) How do you know? (Context clues)

C. Specific Details

❓ What everyday errands does Pepys perform on October 28? How does he amuse himself? (Pepys works in the office, has his lute fixed, and buys a belt. For amusement, he attends the theater.)

D. Vocabulary

The *beaver* is a beaver hat.

great while, and I wondered to see how the ladies did tipple.

At last I sent my wife and her bedfellow to bed, and Mr. Hunt and I went in with Mr. Thornbury (who did give the company all their wines, he being yeoman of the wine cellar to the King) to his house; and there, with his wife and two of his sisters and some gallant sparks that were there, we drank the King's health and nothing else, till one of the gentlemen fell down stark drunk and there lay spewing. And I went to my Lord's pretty well. But no sooner abed with Mr. Sheply but my head begun to turn and I to vomit, and if ever I was foxed it was now—which I cannot say yet, because I fell asleep and sleep till morning—only, when I waked I found myself wet with my spewing. Thus did the day end, with joy everywhere; and blessed be God, I have not heard of any mischance to anybody through it all, but only to Serjeant Glynne,[14] whose horse fell upon him yesterday and is like to kill him; which people do please themselves with, to see how just God is to punish that rogue at such a time as this—he being now one of the King's Serjeants and rode in the Cavalcade with Maynard, to whom people wished the same fortune.

There was also this night, in Kingstreet, [a woman] had her eye put out by a boy's flinging of a firebrand into the coach.

A Now after all this, I can say that besides the pleasure of the sight of these glorious things, I may now shut my eyes against any other objects, or for the future trouble myself to see things of state and show, as being sure never to see the like again in this world.

Waked in the morning with my head in a sad taking through the last night's drink, which I am very sorry for. So rise and went out with Mr. Creed to drink our morning draft, which he did give me in chocolate to settle my stomach. And after that to my wife, who lay with Mrs. Frankelyn at the next door to Mrs. Hunt's.

And they were ready, and so I took them up in a coach and carried the lady to Paul's and there set her down; and so my wife and I home—and I to the office.

October 28–29, 1661
Two Ordinary Days

At the office all the morning, and dined[15] at home; **B** and so to Paul's churchyard to Hunt's,[16] and there find my therobo done. Which pleases me very well, and costs me 26s to the altering—but now he tells me it is as good a lute as any is in England, and is worth well 10l. Hither I sent for Captain Ferrers to me, who comes with a friend of his and they and I to the theater and there saw *Argalus and Parthenia*;[17] where a woman acted Parthenia and came afterward on the stage in man's clothes, and had the best legs that ever I saw; and I was very well pleased with it. Thence to the Ringo **C** alehouse, and thither sent for a beltmaker and bought of him a handsome belt for second mourning,[18] which cost me 24s and is very neat. So home and to bed.

This day I put on my half-cloth black stockings and my new coat of the fashion, which pleases me **D** well; and with my beaver I was (after office was done) ready to go to my Lord Mayor's feast,[19] as we are all invited; but the Sir Wms.[20] were both loath to go because of the crowd, and so none of us went; and I stayed and dined with them, and so home; and in the evening, by consent, we met at the Dolphin, where other company came to us and would have been merry; but their wine was so naught and all other things out of order, that we were not so; but stayed long at night and so home and to bed. My mind not pleased with the spending of this day, because I had proposed a great deal of pleasure to myself this day at Guild Hall.

---

14. **Serjeant Glynne:** the title is legal rather than military. Sir John Glynne and Sir John Maynard were unpopular because they had been prominent judges during the Commonwealth period.

15. **dined:** dinner was eaten at midday.
16. **Hunt's:** Hunt, a musical instrument maker, repaired and altered Pepys's lute, or therobo.
17. *Argalus and Parthenia:* an old play by Henry Glapthorne, revived with women instead of boys acting the women's parts.
18. **second mourning:** apparently less solemn than the deep mourning Pepys had been wearing for his Uncle Robert.
19. **Lord Mayor's feast:** an annual event held at the Guild Hall.
20. **Sir Wms.:** Sir William Penn and Sir William Batten, both officials in the Navy Office.

Literature and Language: Writing Complete Sentences

Point out several places on page 475 in which Samuel Pepys did not write complete sentences. Suggest that the fragments occurred because he was writing for his own personal use—and perhaps because he preferred not to be bound by the rules of grammar. Emphasize, however, the general importance of writing in complete sentences except, perhaps, when recording conversation.

Have students rewrite these sentence fragments by adding material to make each one a complete sentence. Encourage them to share their new sentences and to note the variety of responses.

1. Having left the square, to school where I had a class in journalism.
2. Later, back home and ate dinner with the family.
3. In the middle of the night, I in a great sweat and nightmare about falling off a mountain.
4. The following day after not having rested much, two classes in science and one in history, at which I did rather well, considering my condition.
5. No one, after spending such a day at school, to sleep more than I.

This Lord Mayor, it seems, brings up again the custom[21] of Lord Mayors going the day of their installment to Paul's,[22] and walking round about the cross and offering something at the altar.

July 11, 1664
A Bad Night

Home, weary; and not being very well, I betimes[23] to bed.

And there fell into a most mighty sweat in the night, about eleven o'clock; and there, knowing what money[24] I have in the house and hearing a noise, I begin to sweat worse and worse, till I melted almost to water. I rung, and could not in half an hour make either of the wenches hear me; and this made me fear the more, lest they might be gagged; and then I begin to think that there was some design in a stone being flung at the window over our stairs this evening, by which the thieves meant to try what looking there would [be] after them and know our company. These thoughts and fears I had, and do hence apprehend the fears of all rich men that are covetous and have much money by them. At last Jane[25] rose and then I understand it was only the dog wants a lodging and so made a noise. So to bed, but hardly slept; at last did, and so till morning.

September 2, 1666
The First Day of the Great Fire of London

Lord's Day. Some of our maids sitting up late last night to get things ready against our feast today, Jane called us up, about three in the morning, to tell us of a great fire they saw in the City.[26] So I rose, and slipped on my nightgown and went to her window, and thought it to be on the back side of Marklane at the furthest; but being unused to such fires as followed, I thought it far enough off, and so went to bed again and to sleep. About seven rose again to dress myself, and there looked out at the window and saw the fire not so much as it was, and further off. So to my closet[27] to set things to rights after yesterday's cleaning. By and by Jane comes and tells me that she hears that above three hundred houses have been burned down tonight by the fire we saw, and that it was now burning down all Fishstreet by London Bridge. So I made myself ready presently, and walked to the Tower[28] and there got up upon one of the high places, Sir J. Robinson's little son going up with me; and there I did see the houses[29] at that end of the bridge all on fire, and an infinite great fire on this and the other side the end of the bridge—which, among other people, did trouble me for poor little Michell and our Sarah[30] on the bridge. So down, with my heart full of trouble, to the Lieutenant of the Tower, who tells me that it begun this morning in the King's bakers house in Pudding Lane, and that it hath burned down St. Magnes Church and most part of Fishstreet already. So I down to the waterside and there got a boat and through bridge, and there saw a lamentable fire. Poor Michell's house,[31] as far as the Old Swan, already burned that way and the fire running further, that in a very little time it got as far as the Stillyard while I was there. Everybody endeavoring to remove their goods, and flinging into the river or bringing them into lighters that lay off. Poor people staying in their houses as long as till the very fire touched them, and then running into boats or clambering from one pair of stairs by the waterside to another. And among other things, the poor pigeons I perceive were loath to leave their houses, but hovered about the windows and balconies till they were some of them burned, their wings, and fell down.

Having stayed, and in an hour's time seen the

A. Vocabulary
Wenches are young serving girls.

B. Generalization
❓ What generalization does Pepys make in conjunction with this description of a "bad night"? (He reflects that rich men are prone to fears of having their goods stolen.)

---

21. **custom:** these ceremonies had not been observed during the Commonwealth period.
22. **Paul's:** St. Paul's Cathedral. A huge cross stood in the square before the cathedral.
23. **betimes:** early.
24. **money:** about £1,000—a very large sum.
25. **Jane:** Jane Birch, the Pepyses' servant.
26. **City:** London itself. The Great Fire started in a bakery, raged for four days and four nights, and destroyed some thirteen thousand residences. It leveled four fifths of the city and made about one hundred thousand people homeless.

27. **closet:** private room.
28. **Tower:** the Tower of London, a short walk from Pepys's house.
29. **houses:** shops and dwellings were built on London Bridge.
30. **Sarah:** a maid (family name unknown) whom Mrs. Pepys discharged on December 5, 1662. Pepys wrote, "The wench cried, and I was ready to cry too."
31. **Michell's house:** Betty Michell, wife of Michael, whose tavern was destroyed in the fire. Pepys admired Betty's good looks.

A. Humanities
Connection:
Discussing the
Fine Art
Discuss with stu-
dents the major
details of the paint-
ing: the huddling
crowds on the left,
the height of the
flames, the ghastly
reflection of the fire
in the Thames,
and so on.
? What mood do
these details
convey? (Horror,
fear, destruction)

B. Characteriza-
tion
Note Pepys's posi-
tion as an intimate
of the King and the
Lord Mayor.

A

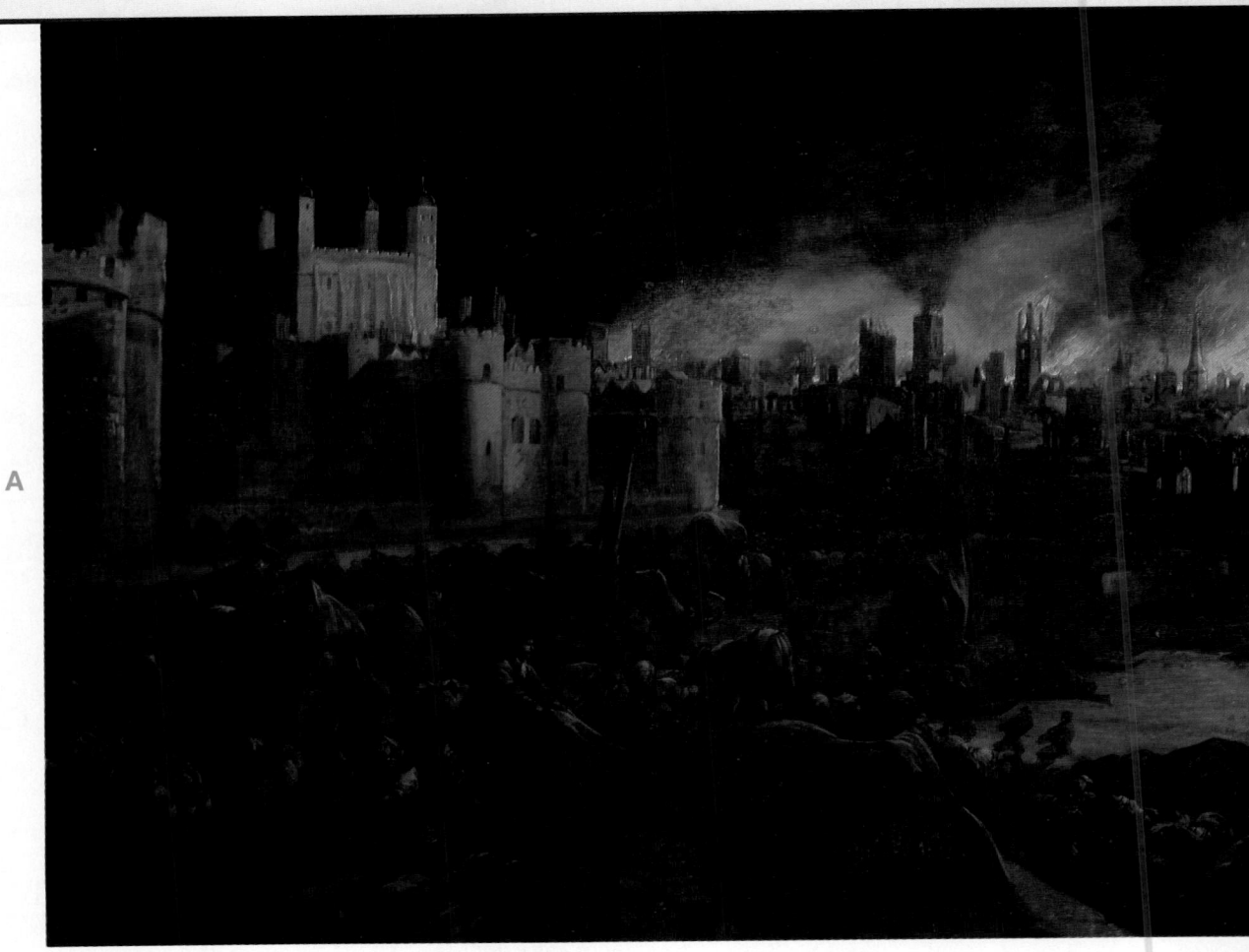

The Fire of London by an unknown artist (ca. 1667–70). Oil.

fire rage every way, and nobody to my sight endeavoring to quench it, but to remove their goods
and leave all to the fire: and having seen it get as
far as the Stillyard, and the wind mighty high and
driving it into the city, and everything, after so
long a drought, proving combustible, even the
very stones of churches, and among other things,
the poor steeple by which pretty Mrs. —— lives,
and whereof my old school-fellow Elborough is
parson, taken fire in the very top and there burned
till it fall down—I to Whitehall with a gentleman
with me who desired to go off from the Tower to
see the fire in my boat—to Whitehall, and there
up to the King's closet in the chapel, where people
came about me and I did give them an account
dismayed them all; and word was carried in to the
King, so I was called for and did tell the King and
Duke of York what I saw, and that unless his
Majesty did command houses to be pulled down,

nothing could stop the fire. They seemed much
troubled, and the King commanded me to go to
my Lord Mayor from him and command him to
spare no houses but to pull down before the fire
every way. The Duke of York bid me tell him that
if he would have any more soldiers, he shall; and
so did my Lord Arlington afterward, as a great
secret. Here meeting with Captain Cocke, I in his
coach, which he lent me, and Creed with me, to
Paul's; and there walked along Watling Street as
well as I could, every creature coming away
loaden with goods to save—and here and there
sick people carried away in beds. Extraordinary
good goods carried in carts and on backs. At last
met my Lord Mayor in Canning Street, like a man
spent, with a hankercher about his neck. To the
King's message, he cried like a fainting woman,
"Lord, what can I do? I am spent. People will not
obey me. I have been pull[ing] down houses. But

B

1. Pepys witnesses the hanging of a man involved in the execution of King Charles I. (T)
2. Pepys says he never becomes angry or loses his temper. (F)
3. Pepys attends the coronation of King Charles II. (T)
4. Pepys says women weren't allowed

to attend the coronation. (F)
5. Pepys seems to appreciate attractive women. (T)
6. Pepys declares that he never feared being robbed. (F)
7. Pepys advises the King to stop the fire in London by pulling down houses. (T)

8. Pepys states that the pigeons of London had more sense than many of the people. (F)
9. Pepys, distressed about all the destruction he had seen, cannot eat. (F)
10. Pepys states that he was lucky he didn't have to move any of his goods or money out of the house. (F)

The Museum of London.

A. Characterization

? Comment on the juxtaposition of fear and anxiety with Pepys's remark that they enjoyed "an extraordinary good dinner." Does this contrast make the writer seem callous and insensitive, or does it serve to humanize him further? (Answers will vary, though students may suggest that this attempt to inject a sense of normalcy—a sense that life goes on—does indeed humanize Pepys.)

the fire overtakes us faster then we can do it." That he needed no more soldiers; and that for himself, he must go and refresh himself, having been up all night. So he left me, and I him, and walked home—seeing people all almost distracted and no manner of means used to quench the fire. The houses too, so very thick thereabouts, and full of matter for burning, as pitch and tar, in Thames Street—and warehouses of oil and wines and brandy and other things. Here I saw Mr. Isaccke Houblon,[32] that handsome man—prettily dressed and dirty at his door at Dowgate, receiving some of his brother's things whose houses were on fire; and as he says, have been removed twice already, and he doubts (as it soon proved)

that they must be in a little time removed from his house also—which was a sad consideration. And to see the churches all filling with goods, by people who themselves should have been quietly there at this time.

By this time it was about twelve o'clock, and so home and there find my guests, which was Mr. Wood and his wife, Barbary Shelden, and also Mr. Moone—she mighty fine, and her husband, for aught I see, a likely man. But Mr. Moone's design and mine, which was to look over my closet and please him with the sight thereof, which he hath long desired, was wholly disappointed, for we were in great trouble and disturbance at this fire, not knowing what to think of it. However, we had an extraordinary good dinner, and as merry as at this time we could be. **A**

While at dinner, Mrs. Batelier came to inquire after Mr. Woolfe and Stanes (who it seems are

---

32. **Houblon:** Houblon and others mentioned in the following paragraphs were substantial Londoners, all friends or acquaintances of Pepys.

ANALYZING THE DIARY
Identifying Facts
1. Harrison was executed because he had participated in the execution of King Charles I in 1649.
2. There was a violent thunderstorm.
3. On July 11, 1664, he was afraid that thieves had broken into the house and were stealing his money.
4. During the Great Fire, his greatest

fear was that his treasure would be destroyed.
Among the buildings that were destroyed were St. Magnes Church, most of Fishstreet, and hundreds of private houses.

Interpreting Meanings
5. Answers may vary. In general, we may suppose that Harrison, having par-

A. Characterization

❓ Tell whether you think that Pepys is more concerned for the general welfare or for the safety of his own "goods." Are the writer's feelings understandable and human? (Answers will vary. It is possible for students to understand his feelings without agreeing with them.)

related to them), whose houses in Fishstreet are all burned, and they in a sad condition. She would not stay in the fright.

As soon as dined, I and Moone away and walked through the City, the streets full of nothing but people and horses and carts laden with goods, ready to run over one another, and removing goods from one burned house to another—they now removing out of Canning Street (which received goods in the morning) into Lumbard Street and further; and among others, I now saw my little goldsmith Stokes receiving some friend's goods, whose house itself was burned the day after. We parted at Paul's, he home and I to Paul's Wharf, where I had appointed a boat to attend me; and took in Mr. Carcasse and his brother, whom I met in the street, and carried them below and above bridge, to and again, to see the fire, which was now got further, both below and above, and no likelihood of stopping it. Met with the King and Duke of York in their Barge, and with them to Queen-Hith and there called Sir Rd. Browne to them. Their order was only to pull down houses apace, and so below bridge at the waterside; but little was or could be done, the fire coming upon them so fast. Good hopes there was of stopping it at the Three Cranes[33] above, and at Buttolphs Wharf below bridge, if care be used; but the wind carries it into the City, so as we know not by the waterside what it doth there. River full of lighter[s] and boats taking in goods, and good goods swimming in the water; and only, I observed that hardly one lighter or boat in three that had the goods of a house in, but there was a pair of virginals[34] in it. Having seen as much as I could now, I away to Whitehall by appointment, and there walked to St. James's Park, and there met my wife and Creed and Wood and his wife and walked to my boat, and there upon the water again, and to the fire up and down, it still increasing and the wind great. So near the fire as we could for smoke; and all over the Thames, with one's face in the wind you were almost burned with a shower of fire-drops—this is very true—so as houses were burned by these drops and flakes of fire, three or four, nay five or six houses, one from another. When we could endure no more upon the water, we to a little alehouse on the bankside over against

the Three Cranes, and there stayed till it was dark almost and saw the fire grow; and as it grew darker, appeared more and more, and in corners and upon steeples and between churches and houses, as far as we could see up the hill of the City, in a most horrid malicious bloody flame, not like the fine flame of an ordinary fire. Barbary and her husband away before us. We stayed till, it being darkish, we saw the fire as only one entire arch of fire from this to the other side the bridge, and in a bow up the hill, for an arch of above a mile long. It made me weep to see it. The churches, houses, and all on fire and flaming at once, and a horrid noise the flames made, and the cracking of houses at their ruin. So home with a sad heart, and there find everybody discoursing and lamenting the fire; and poor Tom Hater came with some few of his goods saved out of his house, which is burned upon Fishstreet hill. I invited him to lie at my house, and did receive his goods: but was deceived in his lying there, the noise coming every moment of the growth of the fire, so as we were forced to begin to pack up our own goods and prepare for their removal. And did by moonshine (it being brave, dry, and moonshine and warm weather) carry much of my goods into the garden, and Mr. Hater and I did remove my money and iron-chests into my cellar—as thinking that the safest place. And got my bags of gold into my office ready to carry away, and my chief papers of accounts also there, and my tallies into a box by themselves. So great was our fear, as Sir W. Batten had carts come out of the country to fetch away his goods this night. We did put Mr. Hater, poor man, to bed a little; but he got but very little rest, so much noise being in my house, taking down of goods.

About four o'clock in the morning, my Lady Batten sent me a cart to carry away all my money and plate and best things to Sir W. Rider's at Bednall Green; which I did, riding myself in my nightgown in the cart; and Lord, to see how the streets and the highways are crowded with people, running and riding and getting of carts at any rate to fetch away thing[s]. I find Sir W. Rider tired with being called up all night and receiving things from several friends. His house full of goods—and much of Sir W. Batten and Sir W. Penn's. I am eased at my heart to have my treasure so well secured. Then home with much ado to find a way. Nor any sleep all this night to me nor my poor wife.

A

---

33. **Three Cranes:** the name of a set of stairs that led down to the river.
34. **virginals:** keyboard instruments.

6. In the first entry, Pepys records his irritation with his wife because of things "lying about the house." In a fit of anger, he kicks and breaks a fine little Dutch basket that he had given her as a present. In the entry for April 23, 1661, Coronation Day, Pepys records getting so drunk that he vomited and awoke with a terrible hangover the following morning.

7. Both occasions are elaborately ceremonial, witnessed by large crowds, and climaxed with parties, fireworks, and so on. Both the president and the king take oaths. However, the inauguration of a president is held in front of the Capitol, rather than in a cathedral, and the president, naturally, does not receive a crown.

8. Answers will vary, but most students will agree that this account by an eyewitness would be extremely valuable for a historian. Note that Pepys himself is directly involved in the official efforts to contain the fire.

9. Most of the entries where Pepys mentions his wife seem to suggest that they did not have an especially close relationship: Note that he scolds her for being untidy, and that he drops her off to sleep at a friend's house one night, while he goes off drinking with male friends.

10. Answers will vary. Encourage students to point to specific parallels and differences, and to support their comments on values.

Responding to the Diary

Analyzing the Diary

Identifying Facts

1. Why was Major General Harrison executed?
2. What happened at the end of the coronation day that caused people to "take great notice of God's blessing"?
3. What fear woke Pepys one night?
4. What was Pepys's greatest fear during the Great Fire? Name some of the buildings, large or small, that were destroyed in the Great Fire.

Interpreting Meanings

5. Pepys gives very few details in the *Diary* about the execution that he witnessed. Why do you suppose he didn't devote much space to it?
6. In the *Diary*, Pepys is surprisingly honest and frank about himself. In which of the entries does he record behavior that is somewhat less than admirable?
7. How is the inauguration of a President in the United States both like and unlike the coronation of the English king?
8. Of what use would Pepys's account be as a **primary source** for a later historian of the Great Fire?
9. Look at the various places where Pepys mentions his wife Elizabeth in these excerpts from the *Diary*. From these references, what can you conclude about their relationship?
10. How is Pepys's life like life in your own time? How is it different? Do you think that the attitudes and values of eighteenth-century life, as Pepys describes it, are similar to those of your own time, or different? Explain your answers.

Writing About the Diary

A Creative Response

1. **Planning a Diary.** If you were to keep a diary, what sort of material would you put into it? What would you omit? Write two or more paragraphs describing the plan for your diary, explaining why you would make a record of some matters (the weather, disasters) but not others (mistakes you make, moments of self-satisfaction). Explain whether you would include public events or only private occurrences, and whether you would keep track of routine work as well as leisure activities. Would you need to safeguard the privacy of your diary? If not, why not? Think what you might want to read twenty-five years from now about your life at the present time.

A Critical Response

2. **Using a Primary Source.** Using the diary excerpts as evidence, evaluate Pepys's character: What kind of man does he seem to be socially, politically, religiously, and personally? Present your conclusions in an essay, using citations from the *Diary* to support your statements. Be sure to open your character study with a thesis statement.

Analyzing Language and Style

Eighteenth-Century Usage

These extracts from Pepys's *Diary* have been modernized for ease of reading: That is, the archaic spellings have been brought up to date. For example, in the first entry, the words *abbey, followed, surveyor, chair, footstool,* and *fiddlers* are spelled *abby, fallowed, surveyour, chaire, footstoole,* and *fidlers* by Pepys.

Capitalization has also been modernized; Pepys tended to capitalize indiscriminately, especially nouns.

1. Here are some other words from these entries (including a surname), spelled as Pepys spelled them. How would each word be spelled today? From these and other original spellings, what inferences can you make about how some words might have been pronounced in Pepys's day?

bonefyres	turne	alter
musique	themselfs	noyse
frolique	shewe	loaden
tiple	Frankelyn	ruine

2. Look over the diary entries and find examples of archaic syntax—sentence structures that would not be used in formal English today.
3. Find examples of verb forms that are different from standard verb forms used today.

A. Expansion
It is interesting to note that the misinterpretation of Defoe's satire in this pamphlet parallels the misunderstanding risked by Swift in "A Modest Proposal" (see text page 518).

B. Expansion
The Scandal Club, a fictitious assemblage devised by Defoe for *The Review,* prefigures the famous club in Addison and Steele's *Spectator.*

Daniel Defoe (1660?–1731)

Daniel Foe—he added the gentlemanly prefix *De* to his name when he was about thirty-five—originally intended to be a Presbyterian minister. His father, a London candle manufacturer and merchant, sent him to an excellent academy where he studied history, law, economics, geography, and natural science, rather than the Latin and Greek classics offered by Cambridge and Oxford. Defoe's family were Dissenters—as Protestants who did not approve of the Church of England were called then—and so he was barred from attending either of the two English universities. When he was around twenty, he evidently changed his mind about becoming a clergyman, and set himself up instead as a merchant, trading in a variety of commodities, including haberdashery, brandy, wool, real estate, and eventually civet cats. He married when he was twenty-four. Meantime, he became a political activist and a journalist. By 1702 he was notorious as the author of a pamphlet called *The Shortest Way with the Dissenters,* which called for the punishment of the Dissenters—Defoe's own party—and confiscation of their property. At first, the Church of England party applauded and admired the pamphlet; then they discovered, to their anger, that it was ironic, meaning exactly the opposite of what it said. The government had Defoe arrested, exposed in the pillory for three days, and then jailed—indefinitely. He was released on the condition that he become a spy and a writer for the very government which had locked him up because of his satire.

All his long life Defoe was a very busy person, sometimes successful in business, sometimes bankrupt and hiding from his creditors. He often traveled about the country as an unofficial agent or spy for one prominent statesman or another. He even performed such services for his favorite monarch, King William III. And he constantly wrote and wrote, and wrote—altogether over four hundred different works, including a news pamphlet, *The Review,* which he put out three times a week for over nine years (1704–1713). Most of his works are what is called today nonfiction, books of advice offered for the

Daniel Defoe (17th century). Engraving.

London Library.

improvement of the people and their lives. He touched on every conceivable subject: the choice of a wife, the history of the Devil, the manufacture of glass. A great many of his works are political; Defoe wrote propaganda for both of the major political parties, sometimes defending both sides of a particular public issue. Some of his works are in poetry: *The True-Born Englishman* (1701) is a long poem that scolds the English people for their antipathy to King William because he was Dutch. Defoe argues that all the English are, in a sense, foreigners.

Defoe's innumerable writings might be roughly classified into four groups. A large number of them, like *The Shortest Way with the Dissenters,* are concerned with the political and religious controversies of the time. The works in a second group advise people on how to become virtuous as well as rich: *The Family Instructor*

(1715, 1728), for example, and *The Complete English Tradesman* (1725, 1727). A third group is made up of journalistic accounts of sensational events, such as *A Journal of the Plague Year* (1722), part of which is included in this book, and *A True Relation of the Apparition of One Mrs. Veal* (1706). (This last was long thought to be only a ghost story that Defoe invented, but scholars now know that the Mrs. Veal mentioned in the title actually lived in Dover, and that a day after her death she allegedly visited a friend named Mrs. Bargrave, who lived some miles distant in the town of Canterbury. The matter-of-fact style Defoe uses in telling this remarkable story makes it seem sensational.) The fourth group contains Defoe's fiction. *Robinson Crusoe* (1719) is generally considered the first novel written in English. Defoe followed it with

A several other novels, including *Moll Flanders* (1722).

In a general way, the story of Robinson Crusoe is well known: a sailor is shipwrecked on a tropical island and for many years manages to lead a more or less civilized life there, without human companionship, until a young "cannibal" whom he names Friday arrives. This classic book, which has been filmed many times and often re-written and simplified for very young readers, has an almost universal appeal because it portrays a single strong individual who, all alone, triumphs over his barren, hostile surroundings. Readers of the book are bound to ask themselves such questions as "Could I survive if I were cast away on an island by myself?" "Do I have the energy and resourcefulness to make a human existence for myself, or would I start walking on all fours and become little better than an animal?"

The appeal of *Robinson Crusoe* is also great because Defoe presents Crusoe's story as a true account of what happened to a real person. Many people believe that Defoe modeled Robinson Crusoe on an actual man, a Scottish sailor named Alexander Selkirk. Selkirk quarreled with his commanding officer and, at his own request, was abandoned on an uninhabited Pacific island. There he stayed for almost five years (1704–1709), and after his rescue and return to England he was interviewed by journalists, including Sir Richard Steele and possibly even Defoe himself. But it was only the *idea* of a marooned man that Defoe used. Though he presents Crusoe's experiences as true autobiography, they are entirely Defoe's own invention; the episodes in the book have nothing to do with Selkirk or with anyone else. It is a tribute to Defoe's skill that many readers have assumed the tale to be true.

Though his fiction sold especially well, Defoe bounced from one financial crisis to another during his later years. He and his wife, Mary, had a large family to support, and Defoe had a talent for getting into disastrous business deals. Late in 1730 he went into hiding to avoid debtor's prison. After several months he secretly returned to London, where he died, aged sixty, early in 1731. An irony of literary history becomes apparent when one realizes that, in spite of his voluminous contributions to literature, Defoe is usually remembered as the author of only one book, the popular *Robinson Crusoe*.

Defoe in the Pillory. From a broadsheet (17th century). British Library, London.

A. Expansion
The full title of *Moll Flanders*, obviously devised to boost sales, is *The Fortunes and Misfortunes of the Famous Moll Flanders, &c., Who was Born in Newgate, and during a Life of continu'd Variety for Threescore Years, beside her Childhood, was Twelve Year a Whore, five times a Wife (whereof once to her own Brother), Twelve Year a Thief, Eight Year a Transplanted Felon in Virginia, at last grew Rich, liv'd Honest, and died a Penitent, Written from her own Memorandums.*

B. About the Illustration
The ancient Romans claimed satire was their own invention, rather than a genre of literature borrowed from the Greeks. Originally, *satura* seems to have meant a mixture, or medley (like a tossed salad). But it was soon assimilated to the word *satyr*, a half goat and half man. Satire thus acquired connotations of roughness and violence.

1. BUILDING ON PRIOR KNOWLEDGE. Before students begin reading, call on volunteers to share their impressions of this well-known story from prior reading or from movie versions.

2. ESTABLISHING A PURPOSE. Before students begin reading, have them read question 4 on text page 495. This will help establish a purpose for their reading.

3. PREREADING JOURNAL. Before they read, have students write two or three sentences describing what they think a person's mental and physical condition would be after fourteen years on a deserted island.

A. About the Photograph
The photograph shows the actual island on which Alexander Selkirk was marooned for almost five years. See the essay by Sir Richard Steele on text page 550.

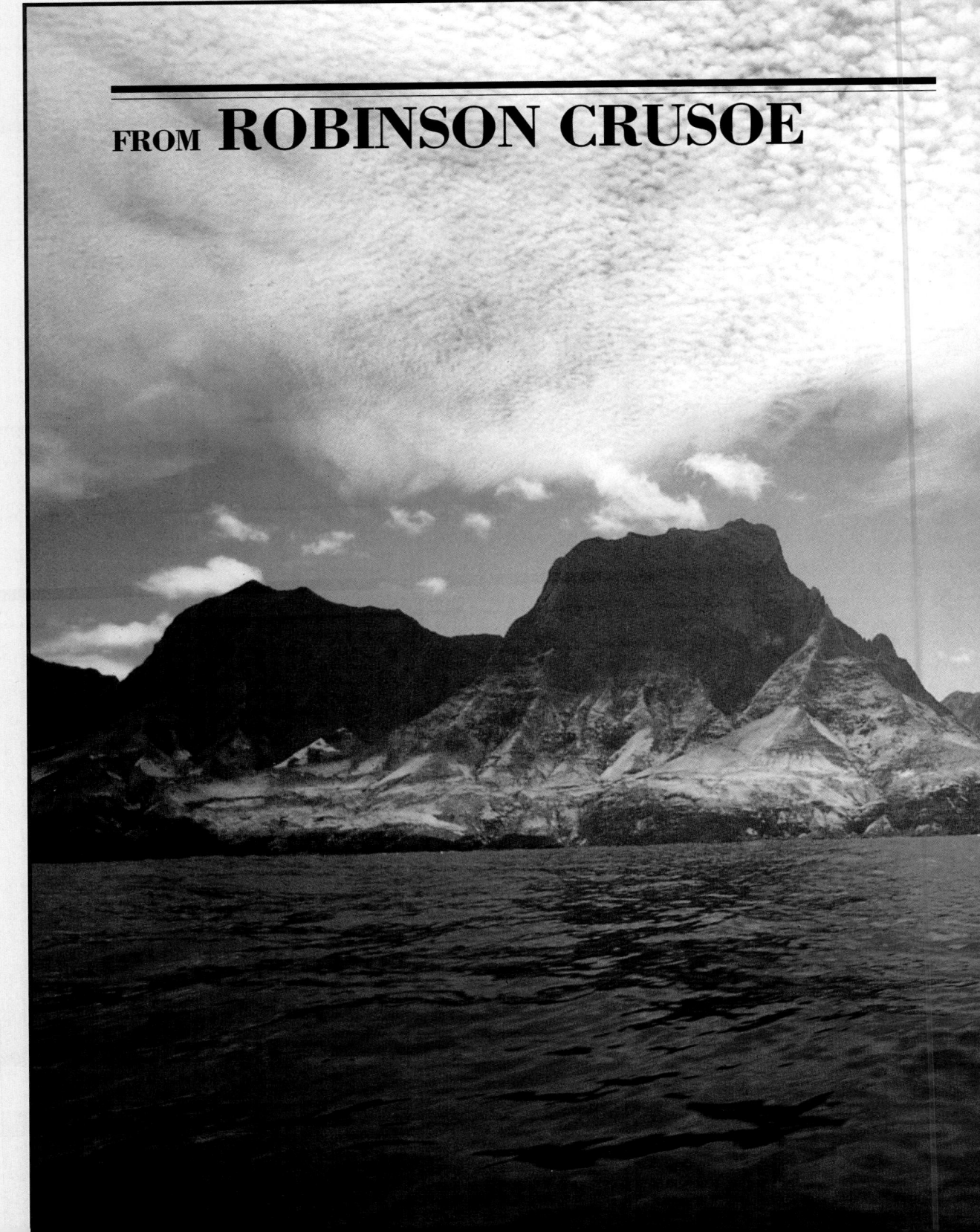

FROM **ROBINSON CRUSOE**

SUPPLEMENTARY SUPPORT MATERIALS
1. Vocabulary Activity Worksheet (CCB)
2. Review and Response Worksheet:
Point of View (CCB)
3. Language Skills Worksheet: Homonyms (CCB)
4. Selection Test (CCB)

DEVELOPING VOCABULARY
The following words from the story are
tested in the Selection Test. (See also
Vocabulary Activity Worksheet.)

to solace	mortification
to abate	unwieldy
sustenance	despondency
ravenous	prodigious
destitute	to inter

A. Conflict

Identify the external conflict established in this passage. (The external conflict is between Crusoe and his seemingly barren, desolate, and potentially dangerous environment.) Does Crusoe's external conflict lead to an internal one? How do you know? (His external conflict does lead to an internal one. The words "and this threw me into terrible agonies of mind, that for a while I run about like a madman" indicate an internal conflict.)

In the first thirty-five or so pages of the book, Crusoe tells the story of his early life, up to the time he is shipwrecked, in September 1659. In the next hundred and twenty pages—the most fascinating part of the book—Crusoe describes his solitary existence, which went on for about twenty-five years. The final eighty pages recount Crusoe's adventures when "savages" (also called "cannibals" and "Indians") arrive on the island, and later on, an English ship whose crew is mutinying. After the mutiny has been put down, this ship takes Crusoe and Friday off the island, in December 1686, more than twenty-seven years after Crusoe was marooned.

In the first of our excerpts from the book, a storm has just driven Crusoe's ship aground on a reef, and only he, of all the crew and passengers, has managed to swim ashore. Imagine yourself as this young man. Would you behave in the same manner?

Crusoe Provides for Himself

I walked about on the shore, lifting up my hands, and my whole being, as I may say, wrapped up in the contemplation of my deliverance, making a thousand gestures and motions which I cannot describe, reflecting upon all my comrades that were drowned, and that there should not be one soul saved but myself; for, as for them, I never saw them afterward, or any sign of them except three of their hats, one cap, and two shoes that were not fellows.

I cast my eyes to the stranded vessel, when the breach and froth of the sea being so big, I could hardly see it, it lay so far off, and considered, Lord! how was it possible I could get on shore?

A   After I had solaced my mind with the comfortable part of my condition, I began to look round me to see what kind of place I was in, and what was next to be done, and I soon found my comforts abate, and that in a word I had a dreadful deliverance; for I was wet, had no clothes to shift me,[1] nor anything either to eat or drink to comfort me, neither did I see any prospect before me but

that of perishing with hunger, or being devoured by wild beasts; and that which was particularly afflicting to me was that I had no weapon either to hunt and kill any creature for my sustenance, or to defend myself against any other creature that might desire to kill me for theirs: In a word, I had nothing about me but a knife, a tobacco pipe, and a little tobacco in a box; this was all my provision, and this threw me into terrible agonies of mind, that for a while I run about like a madman. Night coming upon me, I began with a heavy heart to consider what would be my lot if there were any ravenous beasts in that country, seeing at night they always come abroad for their prey.

All the remedy that offered to my thoughts at that time was to get up into a thick bushy tree like a fir, but thorny, which grew near me, and where I resolved to set[2] all night, and consider the next day what death I should die, for as yet I saw no prospect of life. I walked about a furlong[3] from the shore, to see if I could find any fresh water to drink, which I did, to my great joy; and having drank and put a little tobacco in my mouth to prevent hunger, I went to the tree, and getting up into it, endeavored to place myself so as that if I should sleep I might not fall; and having cut me a short stick, like a truncheon, for my defense, I took up my lodging, and having been excessively fatigued, I fell fast asleep, and slept as comfortably as, I believe, few could have done in my condition, and found myself the most refreshed with it, that I think I ever was on such an occasion.

When I waked it was broad day, the weather clear, and the storm abated, so that the sea did not rage and swell as before. But that which surprised me most was that the ship was lifted off in the night from the sand where she lay, by the swelling of the tide, and was driven up almost as far as the rock which I first mentioned, where I had been so bruised by the dashing of me against it. This being within about a mile from the shore where I was, and the ship seeming to stand upright still, I wished myself on board, that, at least, I might save some necessary things for my use. . . .

A little after noon I found the sea very calm, and the tide ebbed so far out that I could come within a quarter of a mile of the ship; and here I found a fresh renewing of my grief, for I saw evidently that if we had kept on board we had

---

1. **shift me:** change into.

2. **set:** stay seated.
3. **furlong:** one eighth of a mile.

**A. Characteriza-
tion**

❓ How does the
author hint at
Crusoe's practical
nature in this pas-
sage? (Crusoe de-
cides that it is use-
less to lament his
fate, and he sets
about building a
raft.)

**B. Specific
Details/
Responding**

❓ Why do you
think that Defoe
includes such a
detailed list of the
provisions here?
(Some readers find
that this is one of
the most pleasur-
able parts of the
novel—imagining
what one could do
with this store of
bread, rice, three
cheeses, five
pieces of goat
meat, and so on.
Notice how the
narrative continues
to list the provi-
sions that will help
the castaway to
survive. This item-
ization of re-
sources seems to
be a common motif
in survival stories.
Perhaps it is a
means of creating
order out of chaos.
Crusoe's list on
text page 487 is
another means to
the same end.)

been all safe, that is to say, we had all got safe on
shore, and I had not been so miserable as to be
left entirely <u>destitute</u> of all comfort and company,
as I now was. This forced tears from my eyes
again, but as there was little relief in that, I resolved, if possible, to get to the ship; so I pulled
off my clothes, for the weather was hot to extremity, and took the water, but when I came to the
ship, my difficulty was still greater to know how
to get on board, for as she lay aground, and high
out of the water, there was nothing within my
reach to lay hold of. I swam round her twice, and
the second time I spied a small piece of a rope,
which I wondered I did not see at first, hang down
by the forechains[4] so low as that with great difficulty I got hold of it, and by the help of that rope
got up into the forecastle[5] of the ship. Here I found
that the ship was bulged,[6] and had a great deal of
water in her hold, but that she lay so on the side
of a bank of hard sand, or rather earth, that her
stern lay lifted up upon the bank, and her head
low almost to the water. By this means all her
quarter[7] was free, and all that was in that part was
dry; for you may be sure my first work was to
search and to see what was spoiled and what was
free. And first I found that all the ship's provisions
were dry and untouched by the water, and being
very well disposed to eat, I went to the bread
room and filled my pockets with biscuit, and eat
it as I went about other things, for I had no time
to lose; I also found some rum in the great cabin,
of which I took a large dram, and which I had
indeed need enough of to spirit me for what was
before me. Now I wanted nothing but a boat to
furnish myself with many things which I foresaw
would be very necessary to me.

A It was in vain to sit still and wish for what was
not to be had, and this extremity roused my application. We had several spare yards, and two or
three large spars[8] of wood, and a spare topmast
or two in the ship. I resolved to fall to work with
these, and I flung as many of them overboard as
I could manage for their weight, tying every one
with a rope that they might not drive away. When
this was done I went down the ship's side, and
pulling them to me, I tied four of them fast together at both ends as well as I could in the form

of a raft, and laying two or three short pieces of
plank upon them crossways, I found I could walk
upon it very well, but that it was not able to bear
any great weight, the pieces being too light. So I
went to work, and with the carpenter's saw I cut
a spare topmast into three lengths, and added
them to my raft, with a great deal of labor and
pains; but hope of furnishing myself with necessaries encouraged me to go beyond what I should
have been able to have done upon another occasion.

My raft was now strong enough to bear any
reasonable weight. My next care was what to load
it with, and how to preserve what I laid upon it
from the surf of the sea; but I was not long considering this. I first laid all the plank or boards
upon it that I could get, and having considered
well what I most wanted, I first got three of the
seamen's chests, which I had broken open and
emptied, and lowered them down upon my raft.
B The first of these I filled with provision, *viz.*[9]
bread, rice, three Dutch cheeses, five pieces of
dried goat's flesh, which we lived much upon, and
a little remainder of European corn which had
been laid by for some fowls which we brought to
sea with us, but the fowls were killed. There had
been some barley and wheat together, but, to my
great disappointment, I found afterward that the
rats had eaten or spoiled it all. As for liquors, I
found several cases of bottles belonging to our
skipper, in which were some cordial waters, and
in all about five or six gallons of rack;[10] these I
stowed by themselves, there being no need to put
them into the chest, nor no room for them. While
I was doing this, I found the tide began to flow,
though very calm, and I had the <u>mortification</u> to
see my coat, shirt, and waistcoat, which I had left
on shore upon the sand, swim away; as for my
breeches which were only linen and open-kneed,
I swam on board in them and my stockings. However, this put me upon rummaging for clothes, of
which I found enough, but took no more than I
wanted for present use, for I had other things
which my eye was more upon, as, first, tools to
work with on shore; and it was after long searching that I found out the carpenter's chest, which
was indeed a very useful prize to me, and much

---

4. **forechains:** where the leadsman stands in the bow.
5. **forecastle:** the part of a ship in front of the foremast.
6. **bulged:** leaking.
7. **quarter:** back part of a ship.
8. **yards, spars:** parts of the rigging.

9. *viz:* Latin abbreviation meaning "namely."
10. **rack:** arrack, a drink made in the Far East.

more valuable than a ship loading of gold would have been at that time. I got it down to my raft, even whole as it was, without losing time to look into it, for I knew in general what it contained.

My next care was for some ammunition and arms. There were two very good fowling pieces[11] in the great cabin, and two pistols; these I secured first, with some powder horns, and a small bag of shot, and two old rusty swords. I knew there were three barrels of powder in the ship, but knew not where our gunner had stowed them; but with much search I found them, two of them dry and good, the third had taken water. Those two I got to my raft, with the arms, and now I thought myself pretty well freighted, and began to think how I should get to shore with them, having neither sail, oar, or rudder, and the least capful of wind would have overset all my navigation.

I had three encouragements: 1. A smooth calm sea. 2. The tide rising and setting in to the shore. 3. What little wind there was blew me toward the land. And thus, having found two or three broken oars belonging to the boat, and besides the tools which were in the chest, I found two saws, an ax, and a hammer, and with this cargo I put to sea. For a mile, or thereabouts, my raft went very well, only that I found it drive a little distant from the place where I had landed before, by which I perceived that there was some indraft of the water, and consequently I hoped to find some creek or river there which I might make use of as a port to get to land with my cargo. . . .

At length I spied a little cove on the right shore of the creek, to which with great pain and difficulty I guided my raft, and at last got so near, as that, reaching ground with my oar, I could thrust her directly in. But here I had like to have dipped all my cargo in the sea again; for that shore lying pretty steep, that is to say sloping, there was no place to land but where one end of my float, if it run on shore, would lie so high, and the other sink lower as before, that it would endanger my cargo again. All that I could do was to wait 'til the tide was at highest, keeping the raft with my oar like an anchor to hold the side of it fast to the shore, near a flat piece of ground, which I expected the water would flow over; and so it did. As soon as I found water enough, for my raft drew about a foot water, I thrust her on upon that flat piece of

ground, and there fastened or moored her by sticking my two broken oars into the ground; one on one side near one end, and one on the other side near the other end; and thus I lay 'til the water ebbed away, and left my raft and all my cargo safe on shore.

My next work was to view the country, and seek a proper place for my habitation, and where to stow my goods to secure them from whatever might happen. Where I was I yet knew not, whether on the continent or on an island, whether inhabited or not inhabited, whether in danger of wild beasts or not. There was a hill not above a mile from me, which rose up very steep and high, and which seemed to overtop some other hills which lay as in a ridge from it northward. I took out one of the fowling pieces, and one of the pistols, and a horn of powder, and thus armed I traveled for discovery up to the top of that hill, where, after I had with great labor and difficulty got to the top, I saw my fate to my great affliction, (viz.) that I was in an island environed every way with the sea, no land to be seen, except some rocks which lay a great way off, and two small islands less than this, which lay about three leagues[12] to the west.

I found also that the island I was in was barren, and, as I saw good reason to believe, uninhabited except by wild beasts, of whom however I saw none, yet I saw abundance of fowls, but knew not their kinds, neither when I killed them could I tell what was fit for food, and what not. At my coming back, I shot at a great bird which I saw sitting upon a tree on the side of a great wood; I believe it was the first gun that had been fired there since the creation of the world. I had no sooner fired, but from all the parts of the wood there arose an innumerable number of fowls of many sorts, making a confused screaming, and crying every one according to his usual note; but not one of them of any kind that I knew. As for the creature I killed, I took it to be a kind of a hawk, its color and beak resembling it, but had no talons or claws more than common; its flesh was carrion,[13] and fit for nothing.

Contented with this discovery, I came back to my raft, and fell to work to bring my cargo on shore, which took me up the rest of that day; and what to do with myself at night I knew not, nor

A. Suspense

? How does Defoe create suspense here? (Defoe leaves his readers eager to learn if Crusoe will be able to guide the raft safely to shore.)

B. Archaism
Note the archaic diction and syntax of Defoe's style.

---

11. **fowling pieces:** guns for shooting birds (fowls).

12. **leagues:** one league is equal to about three miles.
13. **carrion:** like decayed meat, inedible.

486

A. Repetition
Note the repetition of the motif of the fear of wild beasts (see also text page 483).

B. Humor
? What is amusing about Crusoe's expression, "I called a council"? How does Crusoe himself acknowledge the inappropriateness of this expression? (The phrase is amusing because Crusoe is alone; he immediately glosses the expression by saying, "that is to say, in my thoughts.")

A indeed where to rest; for I was afraid to lie down on the ground, not knowing but some wild beast might devour me, though, as I afterward found, there was really no need for those fears.

However, as well as I could, I barricaded myself round with the chests and boards that I had brought on shore, and made a kind of hut for that night's lodging. As for food, I yet saw not which way to supply myself, except that I had seen two or three creatures like hares run out of the wood where I shot the fowl.

I now began to consider that I might yet get a great many things out of the ship which would be useful to me, and particularly some of the rigging, and sails, and such other things as might come to land, and I resolved to make another voyage on board the vessel, if possible; and as I knew that the first storm that blew must necessarily break her all in pieces, I resolved to set all other things apart, 'til I got everything out of the ship that I **B** could get. Then I called a council, that is to say, in my thoughts, whether I should take back the raft, but this appeared impracticable; so I resolved to go as before, when the tide was down, and I did so, only that I stripped before I went from my hut, having nothing on but a checkered shirt, and a pair of linen drawers, and a pair of pumps[14] on my feet.

I got on board the ship, as before, and prepared a second raft, and having had experience of the first, I neither made this so unwieldy, nor loaded it so hard, but yet I brought away several things very useful to me; as, first, in the carpenter's stores I found two or three bags full of nails and spikes, a great screwjack,[15] a dozen or two of hatchets, and above all, that most useful thing called a grindstone. All these I secured together, with several things belonging to the gunner, particularly two or three iron crows,[16] and two barrels of musket bullets, seven muskets, and another fowling piece, with some small quantity of powder more; a large bag full of small shot, and a great roll of sheet lead; but this last was so heavy, I could not hoist it up to get it over the ship's side.

Besides these things, I took all the men's clothes that I could find, and a spare foretopsail, a hammock, and some bedding; and with this I loaded my second raft, and brought them all safe on shore to my very great comfort.

I was under some apprehensions during my absence from the land that at least my provisions might be devoured on shore; but when I came back, I found no sign of any visitor, only there sat a creature like a wild cat upon one of the chests, which when I came toward it, ran away a little distance, and then stood still; she sat very composed, and unconcerned, and looked full in my face, as if she had a mind to be acquainted with me. I presented my gun at her, but as she did not understand it, she was perfectly unconcerned at it, nor did she offer to stir away; upon which I tossed her a bit of biscuit, though by the way I was not very free of it, for my store was not great. However, I spared her a bit, I say, and she went to it, smelled of it; and ate it, and looked (as pleased) for more, but I thanked her, and could spare no more; so she marched off.

Having got my second cargo on shore, though I was fain[17] to open the barrels of powder, and bring them by parcels, for they were too heavy, being large casks, I went to work to make me a little tent with the sail and some poles which I cut for that purpose, and into this tent I brought everything that I knew would spoil, either with rain or sun, and I piled all the empty chests and casks up in a circle round the tent, to fortify it from any sudden attempt, either from man or beast.

When I had done this, I blocked up the door of the tent with some boards within, and an empty chest set up on end without, and spreading one of the beds upon the ground, laying my two pistols just at my head, and my gun at length by me, I went to bed for the first time, and slept very quietly all night, for I was very weary and heavy; for the night before I had slept little, and had labored very hard all day, as well to fetch all those things from the ship, as to get them on shore.

I had the biggest magazine of all kinds now that ever were laid up, I believe, for one man; but I was not satisfied still, for while the ship sat upright in that posture, I thought I ought to get everything out of her that I could. So every day at low water I went on board, and brought away some

---

14. **pumps:** low shoes.
15. **screwjack:** portable machine used for raising heavy objects.
16. **crows:** crowbars.

17. **fain:** compelled.

thing or other. But particularly the third time I went, I brought away as much of the rigging as I could, as also all the small ropes and rope twine I could get, with a piece of spare canvas, which was to mend the sails upon occasion, the barrel of wet gunpowder; in a word, I brought away all the sails first and last, only that I was fain to cut them in pieces, and bring as much at a time as I could; for they were no more useful to be sails, but as mere canvas only.

But that which comforted me more still was that at last of all, after I had made five or six such voyages as these, and thought I had nothing more to expect from the ship that was worth my meddling with, I say, after all this, I found a great hogshead of bread and three large runlets[18] of rum or spirits, and a box of sugar, and a barrel of fine flour; this was surprising to me, because I had given over expecting any more provisions, except what was spoiled by the water. I soon emptied the hogshead of that bread, and wrapped it up parcel by parcel in pieces of the sails, which I cut out; and, in a word, I got all this safe on shore also.

The next day I made another voyage; and now having plundered the ship of what was portable and fit to hand out, I began with the cables; and cutting the great cable into pieces, such as I could move, I got two cables and a hawser on shore, with all the iron work I could get; and having cut down the spritsailyard, and the mizzenyard, and everything I could to make a large raft, I loaded it with all those heavy goods, and came away. But my good luck began now to leave me; for this raft was so unwieldy, and so overloaded, that after I was entered the little cove where I had landed the rest of my goods, not being able to guide it so handily as I did the other, it overset, and threw me and all my cargo into the water. As for myself, it was no great harm, for I was near the shore; but as to my cargo, it was great part of it lost, especially the iron, which I expected would have been of great use to me. However, when the tide was out, I got most of the pieces of cable ashore, and some of the iron, though with infinite labor; for I was fain to dip[19] for it into the water, a work which fatigued me very much. After this I went everyday on board, and brought away what I could get.

I had been now thirteen days on shore, and had

been eleven times on board the ship; in which time I had brought away all that one pair of hands could well be supposed capable to bring, though I believe verily, had the calm weather held, I should have brought away the whole ship piece by piece. But preparing the twelfth time to go on board, I found the wind begin to rise; however at low water I went on board, and though I thought I had rummaged the cabin so effectually, as that nothing more could be found, yet I discovered a locker with drawers in it, in one of which I found two or three razors, and one pair of large scissors, with some ten or a dozen of good knives and forks; in another I found about thirty-six pounds value in money, some European coin, some Brazil, some pieces of eight, some gold, some silver.

I smiled to myself at the sight of this money, "O drug!" said I aloud, "what art thou good for? Thou art not worth to me, no, not the taking off of the ground; one of those knives is worth all this heap. I have no manner of use for thee; e'en remain where thou art, and go to the bottom as a creature whose life is not worth saving." However, upon second thoughts, I took it away, and wrapping all this in a piece of canvas, I began to think of making another raft. . . .

A

Crusoe Takes Stock and Becomes Comfortable

I now began to consider seriously my condition, and the circumstance I was reduced to, and I drew up the state of my affairs in writing, not so much to leave them to any that were to come after me, for I was like to have but few heirs, as to deliver my thoughts for daily poring upon them, and afflicting my mind; and as my reason began now to master my despondency, I began to comfort myself as well as I could, and to set the good against the evil, that I might have something to distinguish my case from worse, and I stated it very impartially, like debtor and creditor, the comforts I enjoyed against the miseries I suffered, thus:

B

Evil	Good
I am cast upon a horrible desolate island, void of all hope of recovery.	*But I am alive, and not drowned as all my ship's company was.*

---

18. **runlets:** casks.
19. **dip:** dive.

A. Characterization

? What does Crusoe's change of heart regarding the money suggest about how he views his situation? (It suggests that he views his situation as temporary. It indicates he is hopeful that he will again reenter civilization, where he will have use for the money.)

B. Responding
Discuss with students how very "eighteenth-century" this list is—it is an act of reason, not of emotion. It reduces life to an accountant's ledger; it imposes the human intellect on the chaos of nature.

? Have you ever made a list of pros and cons or pluses and minuses like Crusoe's? What was your motivation for doing so? Did the list help you to achieve your goal? Explain.

A. Responding

❓ What infer-
ences can you
make from Cru-
soe's list about his
religious faith? (He
believes in Provi-
dence—that is, he
feels confident that
God has spared
his life and will
provide for his
needs on the
island.)

**B. Characteriza-
tion**

❓ Why might this
remark be con-
sidered psychologi-
cally significant for
a person in Cru-
soe's predica-
ment? (The remark
indicates that Cru-
soe thinks he has
freed himself from
his preoccupation
with rescue.)

C. Interpreting

❓ How does this
passage reflect
some of the
premises of the
"Age of Reason"?
(It places empha-
sis on reason,
mathematics, and
mastery of "every
mechanic art.")

I am singled out and separated, as it were, from all the world to be miserable.

I am divided from mankind, a solitaire, one banished from humane society.

I have not clothes to cover me.

I am without any defense or means to resist any violence of man or beast.

A [*I have no soul to speak to, or relieve me.*

But I am singled out too from all the ship's crew to be spared from death; and He that miraculously saved me from death, can deliver me from this condition.

But I am not starved and perishing on a barren place, affording no sustenance.

But I am in a hot climate, where if I had clothes I could hardly wear them.

But I am cast on an island, where I see no wild beasts to hurt me, as I saw on the coast of Africa; and what if I had been ship-wrecked there?

But God wonderfully sent the ship in near enough to the shore, that I have gotten out so many necessary things as will either supply my wants, or enable me to supply myself even as long as I live.

Upon the whole, here was an undoubted testimony, that there was scarce any condition in the world so miserable, but there was something negative or something positive to be thankful for in it; and let this stand as a direction from the experience of the most miserable of all conditions in this world, that we may always find in it something to comfort our selves from, and to set in the description of good and evil, on the credit side of the account.

B [Having now brought my mind a little to relish my condition, and given over[20] looking out to sea to see if I could spy a ship; I say, giving over these things, I began to apply my self to accommodate my way of living, and to make things as easy to me as I could.

I have already described my habitation, which was a tent under the side of a rock, surrounded with a strong pale[21] of posts and cables, but I might now rather call it a wall, for I raised a kind

of wall up against it of turfs, about two foot thick on the outside, and after some time, I think it was a year and a half, I raised rafters from it leaning to the rock, and thatched or covered it with bows of trees, and such things as I could get to keep out the rain, which I found at some times of the year very violent.

I have already observed how I brought all my goods into this pale, and into the cave which I had made behind me. But I must observe too, that at first this was a confused heap of goods, which as they lay in no order, so they took up all my place, I had no room to turn myself; so I set my self to enlarge my cave and work farther into the earth, for it was a loose sandy rock, which yielded easily to the labor I bestowed on it; and so when I found I was pretty safe as to beasts of prey, I worked sideways to the right hand into the rock, and then turning to the right again, worked quite out and made me a door to come out, on the outside of my pale or fortification.

This gave me not only egress and regress, as it were a back way to my tent and to my storehouse, but gave me room to stow my goods.

And now I began to apply myself to make such necessary things as I found I most wanted, as particularly a chair and a table; for without these I was not able to enjoy the few comforts I had in the world; I could not write, or eat, or do several things with so much pleasure without a table.

So I went to work; and here I must needs observe, that as reason is the substance and original of the mathematics, so by stating and squaring everything by reason, and by making the most rational judgment of things, every man may be in time master of every mechanic art. I had never handled a tool in my life, and yet in time, by labor, application, and contrivance, I found at last that I wanted nothing but I could have made it, especially if I had had tools; however, I made abundance of things, even without tools, and some with no more tools than an adze and a hatchet, which perhaps were never made that way before, and that with infinite labor. For example, if I wanted a board, I had no other way but to cut down a tree, set it on an edge before me, and hew it flat on either side with my ax, till I had brought it to be thin as a plank, and then dub it smooth with my adze. It is true, by this method I could make but one board out of a whole tree, but this I had no remedy for but patience, anymore than I had for the prodigious deal of time and labor which it **C**

---

20. **given over:** stopped.
21. **pale:** enclosure.

A. Vocabulary
Note that in this passage the word *magazine* means "storehouse."

B. Narrative Technique

? Why is the device of Crusoe keeping a journal especially necessary in this novel? (The device serves as a plausible frame for the narrator's recollection of events that happened over a long period of time.)

took me up to make a plank or board. But my time or labor was little worth, and so it was as well employed one way as another.

However, I made me a table and a chair, as I observed above, in the first place, and this I did out of the short pieces of boards that I brought on my raft from the ship. But when I had wrought out some boards, as above, I made large shelves of the breadth of a foot and [a] half one over another, all along one side of my cave, to lay all my tools, nails, and ironwork, and in a word, to separate everything at large in their places, that I must come easily at them; I knocked pieces into the wall of the rock to hang my guns and all things that would hang up.

A So that had my cave been to be seen, it looked like a general magazine of all necessary things, and I had everything so ready at my hand, that it was a great pleasure to me to see all my goods in such order, and especially to find my stock of all necessaries so great.

B And now it was when I began to keep a journal of every day's employment, for indeed at first I was in too much hurry, and not only hurry as to labor, but in too much discomposure of mind, and my journal would ha' been full of many dull things. For example, I must have said thus: "Sept. the 30th. After I got to shore and had escaped drowning, instead of being thankful to God for my deliverance, having first vomited with the great quantity of salt water which was gotten into my stomach, and recovering myself a little, I ran about the shore, wringing my hands and beating my head and face, exclaiming at my misery, and crying out; 'I was undone, undone,' 'til tired and faint I was forced to lie down on the ground to repose, but durst not sleep for fear of being devoured.''

C Some days after this, and after I had been on board the ship, and got all that I could out of her, yet I could not forbear getting up to the top of a little mountain and looking out to sea in hopes of seeing a ship, then fancy at a vast distance I spied a sail, please myself with the hopes of it, and then after looking steadily 'til I was almost blind, lose it quite, and sit down and weep like a child, and thus increase my misery by my folly.

But having gotten over these things in some measure, and having settled my household stuff and habitation, made me a table and a chair, and all as handsome about me as I could, I began to keep my journal. . . .

King Crusoe in the Fourteenth Year of His Reign

D It would have made a stoic[22] smile to have seen me and my little family sit down to dinner; there was my majesty the prince and lord of the whole island; I had the lives of all my subjects at my absolute command; I could hang, draw,[23] give liberty, and take it away, and no rebels among all my subjects.

Then to see how like a king I dined too, all alone, attended by my servants. Poll, as if he had been my favorite, was the only person permitted to talk to me. My dog, who was now grown very old and crazy,[24] and had found no species to multiply his kind upon, sat always at my right hand, and two cats, one on one side the table, and one on the other, expecting now and then a bit from my hand, as a mark of special favor.

But these were not the two cats which I brought on shore at first, for they were both of them dead, and had been <u>interred</u> near my habitation by my own hand; but one of them having multiplied by I know not what kind of creature, these were two which I had preserved tame, whereas the rest run wild in the woods, and became indeed troublesome to me at last; for they would often come into my house, and plunder me too, till at last I was obliged to shoot them, and did kill a great many; at length they left me. With this attendance and in this plentiful manner I lived; neither could I be said to want anything but society, and of that, in some time after this, I was like to have too much.

I was something impatient, as I have observed, to have the use of my boat;[25] though very loath to run anymore hazards; and therefore sometimes I sat contriving ways to get her about the island, and at other times I sat myself down contented enough without her. But I had a strange uneasiness in my mind to go down to the point of the island, where, as I have said, in my last ramble, I went up the hill to see how the shore lay, and how the current set, that I might see what I had to do. This inclination increased upon me every day, and at length I resolved to travel thither by land, fol-

---

22. **stoic:** person who doesn't show feelings, who is indifferent to both pain and pleasure.
23. **draw:** to pull out their inner organs.
24. **crazy:** weak, feeble.
25. **boat:** Crusoe had built a boat, but it was too big and heavy for him to launch.

C. Characterization

? Compare this passage with Crusoe's statement on the previous page that he had "given over looking out to sea." What does this suggest about Crusoe's state of mind? (The two passages seem to contradict each other. This contradiction suggests that Crusoe still clings, perhaps unconsciously, to the hope of seeing a rescue ship.)

D. Humor

? How does this passage indicate Crusoe's sense of humor? (Crusoe displays humor by using the word *subjects* to mean the little family he has gathered in his new "kingdom": parrot, dog, and cats.)

A. **Responding**

❓ What additional details can you imagine about Crusoe's physical appearance? (Answers will vary but should confirm Crusoe's own picture of himself as rough and rather barbarous-looking.)

B. **Responding**

❓ If you were in Crusoe's position, what emotions would the sight of a footprint inspire in you? (Like Crusoe, one might be confused and fearful; one also might feel some hope—perhaps the footprint is that of a rescuer.)

C. **Irony**

❓ What irony is felt when Crusoe uses the word *castle* to describe his home? (His home is anything but a castle, and Crusoe in his reeking goatskins is anything but a king.)

lowing the edge of the shore. I did so: but had anyone in England been to meet such a man as I was, it must either have frighted them, or raised a great deal of laughter; and as I frequently stood still to look at myself, I could not but smile at the notion of my traveling through Yorkshire with such an equipage,[26] and in such a dress. Be pleased to take a sketch of my figure, as follows.

I had a great high shapeless cap, made of a goat's skin, with a flap hanging down behind, as well to keep the sun from me as to shoot the rain off from running into my neck; nothing being so hurtful in these climates as the rain upon the flesh under the clothes.

I had a short jacket of goatskin, the skirts coming down to about the middle of my thighs, and a pair of open-kneed breeches of the same; the breeches were made of the skin of an old he-goat, whose hair hung down such a length on either side that like pantaloons it reached to the middle of my legs; stockings and shoes I had none, but had made me a pair of something, I scarce know what to call them, like buskins, to flap over my legs and lace on either side like spatter-dashes;[27] but of a most barbarous shape, as indeed were all the rest of my clothes.

I had on a broad belt of goatskin dried, which I drew together with two thongs of the same, instead of buckles, and in a kind of a frog[28] on either side of this, instead of a sword and a dagger, hung a little saw and a hatchet, one on one side, one on the other. I had another belt not so broad, and fastened in the same manner, which hung over my shoulder; and at the end of it, under my left arm, hung two pouches, both made of goatskin too; in one of which hung my powder, in the other my shot. At my back I carried my basket, on my shoulder my gun, and over my head a great clumsy ugly goatskin umbrella, but which, after all, was the most necessary thing I had about me, next to my gun. As for my face, the color of it was really not so moletta-like[29] as one might expect from a man not at all careful of it, and living within nine or ten degrees of the equinox.[30] My beard I had once suffered to grow till it was about a quarter of a yard long; but as I had both scissors and

razors sufficient, I had cut it pretty short, except what grew on my upper lip, which I had trimmed into a large pair of Mahometan whiskers, such as I had seen worn by some Turks who I saw at Sallee;[31] for the Moors did not wear such, though the Turks did; of these mustachioes or whiskers I will not say they were long enough to hang my hat upon them; but they were of a length and shape monstrous enough, and such as in England would have passed for frightful. . . .

Crusoe Finds a Footprint

It happened one day about noon going toward my boat, I was exceedingly surprised with the print of a man's naked foot on the shore, which was very plain to be seen in the sand. I stood like one thunderstruck, or as if I had seen an apparition; I listened, I looked round me, I could hear nothing, nor see anything; I went up to a rising ground to look farther; I went up the shore and down the shore, but it was all one, I could see no other impression but that one. I went to it again to see if there were any more, and to observe if it might not be my fancy; but there was no room for that, for there was exactly the very print of a foot, toes, heel, and every part of a foot; how it came thither I knew not, nor could in the least imagine. But after innumerable fluttering thoughts, like a man perfectly confused and out of myself, I came home to my fortification, not feeling, as we say, the ground I went on, but terrified to the last degree, looking behind me at every two or three steps, mistaking every bush and tree, and fancying every stump at a distance to be a man; nor is it possible to describe how many various shapes affrighted imagination represented things to me in, how many wild ideas were found every moment in my fancy, and what strange unaccountable whimsies came into my thoughts by the way.

When I came to my castle, for so I think I called it ever after this, I fled into it like one pursued; whether I went over by the ladder as first contrived, or went in at the hole in the rock which I called a door, I cannot remember; no, nor could I

---

26. **equipage:** outfit.
27. **spatter-dashes:** leather leggings.
28. **frog:** loop for hanging things from a belt.
29. **moletta-like:** dark, like a mulatto.
30. **equinox:** equator.

31. **Sallee:** a seaport in Morocco.

Illustration by N.C. Wyeth for *Robinson Crusoe* (1920).

A

A. Responding to the Illustration

N. C. Wyeth (1882–1945) was an American mural painter and illustrator noted primarily for his illustrations of such classics of Western literature as *Treasure Island* and the *Odyssey*. N. C. Wyeth was father and teacher to the famous American painter Andrew Wyeth.

❓ What do you think is going through Crusoe's mind as he looks at the footprint he has just discovered? Does this illustration match Crusoe's description of himself on the opposite page? Explain. (Students should note that the hand to his mouth and the look on his face do convey a sense of concern and perhaps even fear.)

A. Characterization

[?] What presumption does Crusoe make in this passage? (He presumes that the men who came in the canoes are hostile.)

B. Plot

[?] What are the men doing to the "two miserable wretches"? (They are preparing to eat them.)

remember the next morning, for never frighted hare fled to cover, or fox to earth, with more terror of mind than I to this retreat.

I slept none that night; the farther I was from the occasion of my fright, the greater my apprehensions were, which is something contrary to the nature of such things, and especially to the usual practice of all creatures in fear: but I was so embarrassed with my own frightful ideas of the thing, that I formed nothing but dismal imaginations to myself, even though I was now a great way off of it. Sometimes I fancied it must be the devil; and reason joined in with me upon this supposition; for how should any other thing in human shape come into the place? Where was the vessel that brought them? What mark was there of any other footsteps? And how was it possible a man should come there?

Crusoe Rescues Friday

I was surprised one morning early with seeing no less than five canoes all on shore together on my side the island, and the people who belonged to them all landed, and out of my sight. The number of them broke all my measures, for seeing so many, and knowing that they always came four or six or sometimes more in a boat, I could not tell what to think of it, or how to take my measure to attack twenty or thirty men singlehanded; so I lay still in my castle, perplexed and discomforted. However, I put myself into all the same postures for an attack that I had formerly provided, and was just ready for action, if anything had presented. Having waited a good while, listening to hear if they made any noise, at length being very impatient, I set my guns at the foot of my ladder, and clambered up to the top of the hill, by my two stages as usual, standing so, however, that my head did not appear above the hill, so that they could not perceive me by any means; here I observed by the help of my perspective glass that they were no less than thirty in number, that they had a fire kindled, that they had had meat dressed. How they had cooked it, that I knew not, or what it was; but they were all dancing in I know not how many barbarous gestures and figures, their own way, round the fire.

While I was thus looking on them, I perceived by my perspective two miserable wretches dragged from the boats, where it seems they were laid by, and were now brought out for the slaughter. I perceived one of them immediately fell, being knocked down, I suppose, with a club or wooden sword, for that was their way, and two or three others were at work immediately cutting him open for their cookery, while the other victim was left standing by himself, till they should be ready for him. In that very moment this poor wretch seeing himself a little at liberty, nature inspired him with hopes of life, and he started away from them, and ran with incredible swiftness along the sands directly toward me, I mean toward that part of the coast where my habitation was.

I was dreadfully frighted (that I must acknowledge) when I perceived him to run my way, and especially when as I thought I saw him pursued by the whole body, and now I expected that part of my dream was coming to pass, and that he would certainly take shelter in my grove; but I could not depend by any means upon my dream for the rest of it, (*viz.*) that the other savages would not pursue him thither, and find him there. However, I kept my station, and my spirits began to recover when I found that there was not above three men that followed him, and still more was I encouraged when I found that he outstripped them exceedingly in running, and gained ground of them, so that if he could but hold it for half an hour, I saw easily he would fairly get away from them all.

There was between them and my castle the creek which I mentioned often at the first part of my story, when I landed my cargoes out of the ship; and this I saw plainly he must necessarily swim over, or the poor wretch would be taken there. But when the savage escaping came thither he made nothing of it, though the tide was then up, but plunging in, swam through in about thirty strokes or thereabouts, landed, and ran on with exceeding strength and swiftness. When the three persons came to the creek, I found that two of them could swim, but the third could not, and that, standing on the other side, he looked at the other, but went no further; and soon after went softly[32] back again, which, as it happened, was very well for him in the main.

I observed that the two who swam were yet more than twice as long swimming over the creek as the fellow was that fled from them. It came now very warmly upon my thoughts, and indeed irre-

---

32. **softly:** slowly.

1. Crusoe is certain he will find other survivors. (F)
2. Because he is sure there is nothing to fear, Crusoe spends his first night on the beach. (F)
3. Crusoe builds a raft and loads it with provisions from the ship. (T)
4. Crusoe discovers he is on an apparently uninhabited island. (T)
5. Crusoe leaves the useless gold coins on the ship. (F)
6. Crusoe lists evil versus good things about his situation. (T)
7. After making a table and chair, Crusoe begins a journal. (T)
8. Crusoe saves an intended victim from some cannibals. (T)
9. Crusoe reveals that the "victim's" voice is the first he has heard, besides his own, for over twenty-five years. (T)
10. Although the man he saved seems friendly, Crusoe stays awake all night to guard him. (F)

A sistibly, that now was my time to get me a servant, and perhaps a companion or assistant; and that I was called plainly by Providence to save this poor creature's life. I immediately run down the ladders with all possible expedition, fetches my two guns, for they were both but at the foot of the ladders, as I observed above, and getting up again with the same haste to the top of the hill, I crossed toward the sea; and having a very short cut, and all downhill, clapped myself in the way between the pursuers and the pursued, hallowing[33] aloud to him that fled, who, looking back, was at first perhaps as much frighted at me, as at them. But I beckoned with my hand to him to come back; and in the meantime I slowly advanced toward the two that followed; then rushing at once upon the foremost, I knocked him down with the stock of my piece. I was loath to fire, because I would not have the rest hear; though at that distance it would not have been easily heard, and being out of sight of the smoke too, they would not have easily known what to make of it. Having knocked this fellow down, the other who pursued with him stopped, as if he had been frighted, and I advanced apace toward him; but as I came nearer, I perceived presently he had a bow and arrow, and was fitting it to shoot at me; so I was then necessitated to shoot at him first, which I did, and killed him at the first shoot. The poor savage who fled, but had stopped, though he saw both his enemies fallen and killed, as he thought, yet was so frighted with the fire and noise of my piece, that he stood stock-still, and neither came forward or went backward, though he seemed rather inclined to fly still than to come on. I hollowed again to him, and made signs to come forward, which he easily understood, and came a little way, then stopped again, and then a little farther, and stopped again, and I could then perceive that he stood trembling, as if he had been taken prisoner, and had just been to be killed, as his two enemies were. I beckoned him again to come to me, and gave him all the signs of encouragement that I could think of, and he came nearer and nearer, kneeling down every ten or twelve steps in token of acknowledgment for my saving his life. I smiled at him, and looked pleasantly, and beckoned to him to come still nearer; at length he came close to me, and then he kneeled down again, kissed the ground, and laid his head upon the ground, and taking me by

the foot, set my foot upon his head. This, it seems, was in token of swearing to be my slave forever. I took him up, and made much of him, and encouraged him all I could. But there was more work to do yet, for I perceived the savage who I knocked down was not killed, but stunned with the blow, and began to come to himself; so I pointed to him, and showing him the savage, that he was not dead, upon this he spoke some words to me; and though I could not understand them, yet I thought they were pleasant to hear, for they were the first sound of a man's voice that I had heard, *my own excepted,* for above twenty-five years. But there was no time for such reflections now. The savage who was knocked down recovered himself so far as to sit up upon the ground, and I perceived that my savage began to be afraid; but when I saw that, I presented my other piece at the man, as if I would shoot him, upon this *my* savage, for so I call him now, made a motion to me to lend him my sword, which hung naked in a belt by my side; so I did. He no sooner had it but he runs to his enemy, and at one blow cut off his head as cleverly, no executioner in Germany could have done it sooner or better; which I thought very strange for one who I had reason to believe never saw a sword in his life before, except their own wooden swords. However, it seems, as I learned afterward, they make their wooden swords so sharp, so heavy, and the wood is so hard, that they will cut off heads even with them, aye, and arms, and that at one blow too. When he had done this, he comes laughing to me in sign of triumph, and brought me the sword again, and with abundance of gestures which I did not understand laid it down with the head of the savage that he had killed just before me.

But that which astonished him most was to know how I had killed the other Indian so far off; so pointing to him, he made signs to me to let him go to him. So I bade him go, as well as I could. When he came to him, he stood like one amazed, looking at him, turned him first on one side, then on t'other, looked at the wound the bullet had made, which, it seems, was just in his breast, where it had made a hole, and no great quantity of blood had followed, but he had bled inwardly, for he was quite dead. He took up his bow, and arrows, and came back; so I turned to go away, and beckoned to him to follow me, making signs to him that more might come after them.

---

33. **hallowing:** shouting.

A. Characterization

? What does this conclusion show about Crusoe's religious beliefs? (Crusoe believes in Divine Providence and in the values of mercy and charity.)

B. Responding

? Do you consider this episode realistic? Why or why not? Does the realism, or lack of it, have any effect on your enjoyment of the story? (Students should be able to understand why the overall story is enjoyable, even if they consider the scene unrealistic to modern readers.)

Have students sum up Defoe's characterization of Robinson Crusoe in a few sentences. Then call on volunteers to explain reasons for the enduring appeal of Defoe's novel.

A. Responding to the Illustration

Compare Wyeth's picture with the details of the narrative on text page 493. Given the description in the narrative, how would you characterize Crusoe's feelings toward Friday? Are any words with unfavorable connotations used? Does Defoe show a stereotyped view of the "noble savage" (an eighteenth-century idea)?

ANALYZING THE STORY
Identifying Facts

1. Over the course of thirteen days, Crusoe makes eleven expeditions to the ship. Among the stores he salvages from the ship are biscuits, rum, cheeses, corn, carpenter's tools, guns, saws, a hammer, an ax, nails, a grindstone, clothes, ammunition, gunpowder, sails, rope, canvas, twine, sugar, flour, cables, ironwork, razors, scissors, cutlery, and money.

2. He smiles to himself, recognizing that money is of no use to him and may as well go to the bottom of the sea.

He takes the money with him to the island.

3. His only companions are a dog and two cats.

Illustration by N.C. Wyeth for *Robinson Crusoe* (1920).

494

494 The Restoration and the Eighteenth Century

Interpreting Meanings

4. The advantage is the immediacy of a personal narrative.

The limitations are that we, the readers, are restricted to knowing only what Crusoe can observe.

5. Among the activities students may mention are the construction of the rafts, the building and extension of the cave, the making of a chair and a table, and the fashioning of flat boards or planks from trees.

Student answers will vary. Good qualities might include religious faith, foresight, practicality, and confidence in reason. Bad qualities might include periodic inclinations to despair. Defoe makes these qualities clear through Crusoe's assorted activities and through the first-person narrator's own comments about his situation.

6. Crusoe himself describes Friday as a handsome man, about twenty-six years old, quite tall, with a pleasing smile. If Friday had been old or feeble, he would not have been able to outrun the cannibals who were pursuing him.

7. By *negative*, he seems to mean unfortunate or unfavorable; by *positive*, he means favorable or compensatory.

Student answers will vary. Ask the students to support their opinions with reasons.

8. Again, student answers will vary. Most students will probably agree that Crusoe's behavior is plausible, at least in the main; his initial self-pity, his fears, and then his practical, patient actions to come to terms with his condition seem convincing. Ask students to give reasons for any differences they observe between Crusoe's behavior and what students imagine other people's reactions would be.

Upon this he signed to me that he should bury them with sand, that they might not be seen by the rest if they followed; and so I made signs again to him to do so. He fell to work, and in an instant he had scraped a hole in the sand with his hands big enough to bury the first in, and then dragged him into it, and covered him, and did so also by the other; I believe he had buried them both in a quarter of an hour. Then calling him away, I carried him not to my castle, but quite away to my cave, on the farther part of the island; so I did not let my dream come to pass in that part, *viz.* that he came into my grove for shelter.

Here I gave him bread and a bunch of raisins to eat, and a draft of water, which I found he was indeed in great distress for by his running; and having refreshed him, I made signs for him to go lie down and sleep, pointing to a place where I had laid a great parcel of rice straw, and a blanket upon it, which I used to sleep upon myself sometimes; so the poor creature laid down, and went to sleep.

He was a comely handsome fellow, perfectly well made, with straight strong limbs, not too large, tall and well-shaped, and, as I reckon, about twenty-six years of age. He had a very good countenance, not a fierce and surly aspect, but seemed to have something very manly in his face; and yet he had all the sweetness and softness of a European in his countenance too, especially when he smiled.

Responding to the Story

Analyzing the Story

Identifying Facts

1. Though Robinson Crusoe is often thought of as living a primitive life, he actually retrieves from the ship many of the civilized trappings of seventeenth-century England. What items of civilization help him live on the island?
2. When Crusoe finds money on the ship, what is his first reaction? His second?
3. What companionship does Crusoe have before he rescues Friday?

Interpreting Meanings

4. *Robinson Crusoe* is told from the **first-person point of view.** What is the advantage of this point of view? What are its limitations?
5. What activities show Crusoe to be a man of great patience? What other qualities, both bad and good, does Crusoe have? How does Defoe make those qualities clear?
6. Describe Friday. Why do you suppose Defoe **characterizes** Friday as young, strong, and capable? How would the action have to change if Friday were old, or ugly, or feeble?
7. After listing both the good and the evil things in his life, Crusoe concludes that "there was scarce any condition in the world so miserable, but there was something negative or something positive to be thankful for in it." What does he mean by *negative* and *positive*? Do you agree or disagree with this conclusion? Give reasons for your opinion.
8. Is Crusoe's behavior plausible to you? In what ways is his behavior like what most people's would be on such an occasion? In what ways is it different?

Writing About the Story

A Creative Response

1. **Narrating a Different Outcome.** After thirteen years on the island, Crusoe is in good health and good spirits. What if he had not been so lucky? Imagine that Crusoe had lost either his health or his sanity. How would the excerpt written in the fourteenth year of his "reign" have been different? Rewrite the excerpt, describing how Crusoe lost his health or his sanity. Change details to fit the turn of events you have introduced.

A Critical Response

2. **Explaining Literary Appeal.** James Sutherland, an authority on eighteenth-century literature, has said:

> Much of the appeal of *Robinson Crusoe* to readers living in a world of modern technology and mass production lies in the return to a primitive society, in which a man must turn his own hand to everything that has to be done.
>
> —James Sutherland

Daniel Defoe **495**

A. Irony
Note that both Defoe and Cowper have their castaways speak of themselves in terms of monarchs. Cowper's first four lines are ironic, however, when compared with the next four lines.

B. Specific Details
The speaker misses the sound of human speech. The animals are indifferent to him.

C. Apostrophe
The speaker addresses society, friendship, and love. In line 33, he apostrophizes the wind.

D. Personification
The rocks and valleys are described as if they could hear, sigh, and smile.

E. Theme
The speaker at last seems to remember God's mercy during the restfulness of night.

Write an essay in which you agree or disagree with Sutherland. If you disagree, you must explain why *Robinson Crusoe* appeals to the modern reader. Is it the descriptive **style** of the writing, the adventurous **plot**, or the **theme** of survival?

3. **Analyzing a Character's Responses.** Before Friday arrived, Crusoe was completely cut off from human contact for a long period of time. On one occasion he laments his condition as follows:

> The anguish of my soul at my condition would break out upon me on a sudden, and my very heart would die within me, to think of the woods, the mountains, the deserts I was in, and how I was a prisoner locked up with the eternal bars and bolts of the ocean, in an uninhabited wilderness, without redemption. In the midst of the greatest composures of my mind this would break out upon me like a storm, and make me wring my hands and weep like a child.
>
> —from *Robinson Crusoe*,
> Daniel Defoe

Write an essay in which you explain some of the means by which Crusoe manages to cope with the psychological effects of his solitary state. Include also an explanation of what you would do to keep yourself sane if you suddenly found yourself in a similarly isolated situation for a year.

4. **Comparing and Contrasting Two Treatments of Solitude.** Another of the many literary treatments of the man isolated on an uninhabited island is this poem by William Cowper (1731–1800). Cowper (pronounced "cooper") wrote many other poems, including hymns, in a style simpler and less polished than Pope's and his imitators'. In a brief essay, compare and contrast this cast-off with Crusoe. Consider the effect of meter and rhyme on this rather gloomy poem. How does Cowper's speaker manage to avoid sinking into a complete depression? What, on the other hand, did Crusoe do?

Verses
Supposed to be Written by Alexander Selkirk, During his Solitary Abode in the Island of Juan Fernandez

I am monarch of all I survey,
  My right there is none to dispute;
From the center all round to the sea,
  I am lord of the fowl and the brute.
5 Oh, solitude! where are the charms
  That sages have seen in thy face?
Better dwell in the midst of alarms,
  Than reign in this horrible place.

10 I am out of humanity's reach,
  I must finish my journey alone,
Never hear the sweet music of speech;
  I start at the sound of my own.
The beasts that roam over the plain
  My form with indifference see;
15 They are so unacquainted with man,
  Their tameness is shocking to me.

Society, friendship, and love,
  Divinely bestowed upon man,
Oh, had I the wings of a dove,
20   How soon would I taste you again!
My sorrows I then might assuage
  In the ways of religion and truth,
Might learn from the wisdom of age,
  And be cheered by the sallies° of youth.

25 Religion! what treasure untold
  Resides in that heavenly word!
More precious than silver and gold,
  Or all that this earth can afford.
But the sound of the church-going bell
30   These valleys and rocks never heard,
Ne'er sighed at the sound of a knell,
  Or smiled when a sabbath appeared.

Ye winds, that have made me your sport,
  Convey to this desolate shore
35 Some cordial endearing report
  Of a land I shall visit no more.
My friends, do they now and then send
  A wish or a thought after me?
O tell me I yet have a friend,
40   Though a friend I am never to see.

How fleet is a glance of the mind!
  Compared with the speed of its flight,
The tempest itself lags behind,
  And the swift winged arrows of light.
45 When I think of my own native land,
  In a moment I seem to be there;
But alas! recollection at hand
  Soon hurries me back to despair.

But the sea-fowl is gone to her nest,
50   The beast is laid down in his lair,
Even here is a season of rest,
  And I to my cabin repair.
There is mercy in every place;
  And mercy, encouraging thought!
55 Gives even affliction a grace,
  And reconciles man to his lot.

—William Cowper

---

24. **sallies:** lively talk and activities.

1. BUILDING ON PRIOR KNOWLEDGE. Before students begin reading the text, have them read the headnote carefully. Some of them might remember Edgar Allan Poe's "The Masque of the Red Death," a story about a group of people who tried to escape a plague by retreating to a country estate. Sadly, students will probably be reminded of twentieth-century "plagues"; most will easily notice this account's relevance to our own time.

2. ESTABLISHING A PURPOSE. Before students begin reading, you might have them read question 12 on text page 504. This will help establish a purpose for their reading.

3. PREREADING JOURNAL. Assign students to write two or three sentences about what they think it would be like to live through a plague or epidemic of the proportions described in the headnote.

A. Vocabulary
A *visitation* is a special instance of divine wrath or favor, or a severe trial.

B. Simile
❓ How effective is Defoe's simile here? (It appeals to both the reader's visual and tactile senses, thereby conveying a vivid and precise image.)

FROM A JOURNAL OF THE PLAGUE YEAR

This work, which Defoe published in 1722, pretends to be a firsthand account of an epidemic of bubonic plague that had ravaged London fifty-seven years before, in 1665, when Defoe was five years old. To tell the story, Defoe invented a narrator called "H. F.," who may be Henry Foe, an uncle of Defoe's who may have lived in London during the epidemic and who may have told Defoe about it. "H. F." is said to be a saddler, one who manufactures, repairs, or sells horses' saddles—in other words, an ordinary citizen.

Altogether Defoe had four kinds of materials to aid his powerful imagination: his own childhood memories; the reminiscences of his uncle Henry and other older people; city records; and printed matter such as pamphlets, books, and sermons about the plague. He worked these materials into a convincing narrative that seems to be related by somebody who is actually experiencing, from day to day, the grim events that he describes.

The events were grim indeed. When the plague was raging at its worst, in August and September of 1665, it may have killed as many as ten thousand people every week—an enormous toll in a city whose total population was less than half a million. During the plague, people who could afford to leave London did so, in large numbers. Wherever they went, to outlying villages and towns, they terrified the local inhabitants, who believed that they could become infected from any city dweller, sick or well. Inside London, if any member of a family came down with the plague, the whole family was confined by law to its dwelling.

Quarantines of this kind were totally ineffective. Although everybody in those days assumed that plague could be caught from another person, modern medical research now tells us that it is primarily a disease of rats, transmitted from rat to rat and from rat to person by fleas. Fleas prefer to bite rats, but when rats become scarce (because they die of plague), the fleas bite people. When the last rat has died of plague, then people stop dying. Since Defoe and his contemporaries did not understand how the plague was communicated, the disease seemed not only horrible, but also mysterious and irrational, as though an angry God were punishing them for their wrongdoings. And since the disease was almost always fatal, its victims suffered in their minds as well as in their bodies. Many people became mad when the very painful and discolored buboes (swellings) first appeared on them, for they knew they were doomed to die very soon.

Would the tone of this *Journal* have been different if it had really been written daily during such a crisis?

---

1. The Infection Spreads

One man who may have really received the infection and knows it not, but goes abroad and about as a sound person, may give the plague to a thousand people, and they to greater numbers in proportion, and neither the person giving the infection or the persons receiving it know anything of it, and perhaps not feel the effects of it for several days after.

For example, many persons in the time of this visitation never perceived that they were infected [A] till they found, to their unspeakable surprise, the tokens come out upon them; after which they seldom lived six hours, for those spots they called the tokens were really gangrene spots, or mortified [B] flesh in small knobs as broad as a little silver penny, and hard as a piece of callous or horn; so that, when the disease was come up to that length, there was nothing could follow but certain death, and yet, as I said, they knew nothing of their being

SUPPLEMENTARY SUPPORT MATERIALS
1. Vocabulary Activity Worksheet (*CCB*)
2. Review and Response Worksheet: Tone (*CCB*)
3. Language Skills Worksheet: Run-on Sentences and Fragments (*CCB*)
4. Selection Test (*CCB*)

DEVELOPING VOCABULARY
The following words from the journal are tested in the Selection Test. (See also Vocabulary Activity Worksheet.)

contagious	to importune
inimitable	promiscuously
garret	countenance
distemper	malignity
discourse	calamitous

A. Responding
In your opinion, are these brief "dismal scenes" convincingly described?

B. Responding
What types of sources is Defoe likely to have used for this description of the plague's physical effects?

C. Vocabulary
Drawn means that the pus was forced out of the inflamed area by cutting.

D. Vocabulary
Tokens are the symptoms of the disease.

infected, nor found themselves so much as out of order, till those mortal marks were upon them. But everybody must allow that they were infected in a high degree before, and must have been so some time, and consequently their breath, their sweat, their very clothes, were contagious for many days before. . . .

2. Dismal Scenes

I had some little obligations, indeed, upon me to go to my brother's house, which was in Coleman Street[1] parish, and which he had left to my care, and I went at first every day, but afterward only once or twice a week.

In these walks I had many dismal scenes before my eyes, as particularly of persons falling dead in the streets, terrible shrieks and screechings of women, who, in their agonies, would throw open their chamber windows and cry out in a dismal, surprising manner. It is impossible to describe the variety of postures in which the passions of the poor people would express themselves.

Passing through Tokenhouse Yard, in Lothbury, of a sudden a casement violently opened just over my head, and a woman gave three frightful screeches, and then cried, "Oh! death, death, death!" in a most inimitable tone, and which struck me with horror and a chillness in my very blood. There was nobody to be seen in the whole street, neither did any other window open, for people had no curiosity now in any case, nor could anybody help one another, so I went on to pass into Bell Alley.

Just in Bell Alley, on the right hand of the passage, there was a more terrible cry than that, though it was not so directed out at the window; but the whole family was in a terrible fright, and I could hear women and children run screaming about the rooms like distracted, when a garret window opened, and somebody from a window on the other side the alley called and asked, "What is the matter?" upon which, from the first window it was answered, "O Lord, my old master has hanged himself!" The other asked again, "Is he quite dead?" and the first answered, "Aye, aye, quite dead; quite dead and cold!" This person was a merchant and a deputy alderman, and very

rich. I care not to mention the name, though I knew his name too, but that would be a hardship to the family, which is now flourishing again.

But this is but one; it is scarce credible what dreadful cases happened in particular families every day. People in the rage of the distemper, or in the torment of their swellings, which was indeed intolerable, running out of their own government,[2] raving and distracted, and oftentimes laying violent hands upon themselves, throwing themselves out at their windows, shooting themselves, etc.; mothers murdering their own children in their lunacy, some dying of mere grief as a passion, some of mere fright and surprise without any infection at all, others frighted into idiotism and foolish distractions, some into despair and lunacy, others into melancholy madness.

The pain of the swelling was in particular very violent, and to some intolerable; the physicians and surgeons may be said to have tortured many poor creatures even to death. The swellings in some grew hard, and they applied violent drawing-plasters or poultices to break them, and if these did not do they cut and scarified them in a terrible manner. In some those swellings were made hard partly by the force of the distemper and partly by their being too violently drawn, and were so hard that no instrument could cut them, and then they burnt them with caustics, so that many died raving mad with the torment, and some in the very operation. In these distresses, some, for want of help to hold them down in their beds, or to look to them, laid hands upon themselves, as above. Some broke out into the streets, perhaps naked, and would run directly down to the river, if they were not stopped by the watchmen or other officers, and plunge themselves into the water wherever they found it.

It often pierced my very soul to hear the groans and cries of those who were thus tormented, but of the two this was counted the most promising particular in the whole infection, for, if these swellings could be brought to a head, and to break and run, or, as the surgeons call it, to digest, the patient generally recovered; whereas those who, like the gentlewoman's daughter, were struck with death at the beginning, and had the tokens come out upon them, often went about indifferent easy till a little before they died, and some till the mo-

---

1. **Coleman Street:** This place and other places Defoe names are all within the old City of London, unless otherwise noted.

2. **out of their own government:** unable to control themselves.

Lord, have mercy on London. Woodcut.

A. Humanities
Connection:
Discussing the
Fine Art
? Identify the ele-
ments in the
woodcut that are
paralleled in the
details of Defoe's
narrative. (People
lying dead in the
streets, people
prevented from
fleeing by the
watchmen or other
officers, and so on)
What details indi-
cate that the
plague is a retribu-
tion from God?
(The black cloud
and the lightning)

ment they dropped down, as in apoplexies and epilepsies is often the case. Such would be taken suddenly very sick, and would run to a bench or bulk,[3] or any convenient place that offered itself, or to their own houses if possible, as I mentioned before, and there sit down, grow faint, and die. This kind of dying was much the same as it was with those who die of common mortifications,[4] who die swooning, and, as it were, go away in a dream. Such as died thus had very little notice of their being infected at all till the gangrene[5] was spread through their whole body; nor could physicians themselves know certainly how it was with them, till they opened their breasts or other parts of their body, and saw the tokens.

---

3. **bulk:** low structure projecting from a wall.
4. **mortifications:** fainting, loss of consciousness.
5. **gangrene:** a decay of soft tissues from lack of blood.

3. Escape from Quarantine

I remember one citizen who, having . . . broken out of his house in Aldersgate Street or therea-bout, went along the road to Islington;[6] he at-tempted to have gone in at the Angel Inn, and after that at the White Horse, two inns known still by the same signs, but was refused; after which he came to the Pied Bull, an inn also still contin-uing the same sign. He asked them for lodging for one night only, pretending to be going into Lin-colnshire,[7] and assuring them of his being very sound and free from the infection, which also at that time had not reached much that way.

---

6. **Islington:** a suburb north of London.
7. **Lincolnshire:** a county on the east coast of England.

A. **Responding**

? What moral dilemmas does this story of the man at the inn pose? (Students should discuss the ethical questions raised by the man endangering others and by the refusal of people to give shelter to the sick.)

They told him they had no lodging that they could spare but one bed up in the garret, and that they could spare that bed but for one night, some drovers being expected the next day with cattle; so, if he would accept of that lodging, he might have it, which he did. So a servant was sent up with a candle with him to show him the room. He was very well dressed, and looked like a person not used to lie in a garret; and when he came to the room he fetched a deep sigh, and said to the servant, "I have seldom lain in such a lodging as this." However, the servant assuring him again that they had no better, "Well," says he, "I must make shift; this is a dreadful time; but it is but for one night." So he sat down upon the bedside, and bade the maid, I think it was, fetch him up a pint of warm ale. Accordingly the servant went for the ale, but some hurry in the house, which perhaps employed her other ways, put it out of her head, and she went up no more to him.

The next morning, seeing no appearance of the gentleman, somebody in the house asked the servant that had showed him upstairs what was become of him. She started. "Alas!" says she, "I never thought more of him. He bade me carry him some warm ale, but I forgot." Upon which, not the maid, but some other person was sent up to see after him, who, coming into the room, found him stark dead and almost cold, stretched out across the bed. His clothes were pulled off, his jaw fallen, his eyes open in a most frightful posture, the rug of the bed being grasped hard in one of his hands, so that it was plain he died soon after the maid left him; and 'tis probable, had she gone up with the ale, she had found him dead in a few minutes after he sat down upon the bed. The alarm was great in the house, as anyone may suppose, they having been free from the distemper till that disaster, which, bringing the infection to the house, spread it immediately to other houses round about it. . . .

4. Burial Pits and Dead-Carts

There was a strict order to prevent people coming to those pits, and that was only to prevent infection. But after some time that order was more necessary, for people that were infected and near their end, and delirious also, would run to those pits, wrapped in blankets or rugs, and throw themselves in, and, as they said, bury themselves. . . .

This may serve a little to describe the dreadful condition of that day, though it is impossible to say anything that is able to give a true idea of it to those who did not see it, other than this, that it was indeed very, very, very dreadful, and such as no tongue can express.

I got admittance into the churchyard[8] by being acquainted with the sexton who attended, who, though he did not refuse me at all, yet earnestly persuaded me not to go, telling me very seriously,

8. **churchyard:** location of the cemeteries.

Londoners fleeing into the countryside to escape from the plague. Woodcut.

for he was a good, religious, and sensible man, that it was indeed their business and duty to venture, and to run all hazards,[9] and that in it[10] they might hope to be preserved; but that I had no apparent call to it but my own curiosity, which, he said, he believed I would not pretend was sufficient to justify my running that hazard. I told him I had been pressed in my mind to go, and that perhaps it might be an instructing sight, that might not be without its uses. "Nay," says the good man, "if you will venture upon that score, name of God go in; for, depend upon it, 'twill be a sermon to you, it may be, the best that ever you heard in your life. 'Tis a speaking sight," says he, "and has a voice with it, and a loud one, to call us all to repentance"; and with that he opened the door and said, "Go, if you will."

His discourse had shocked my resolution a little, and I stood wavering for a good while, but just at that interval I saw two links come over from the end of the Minories, and heard the bellman,[11] and then appeared a dead-cart, as they
A⌐called it, coming over the streets; so I could no
 └longer resist my desire of seeing it, and went in. There was nobody, as I could perceive at first, in the churchyard, or going into it, but the buriers and the fellow that drove the cart, or rather led the horse and cart; but when they came up to the pit they saw a man go to and again, muffled up in a brown cloak, and making motions with his hands under his cloak, as if he was in a great agony, and the buriers immediately gathered about him, supposing he was one of those poor delirious or desperate creatures that used to pretend, as I have said, to bury themselves. He said nothing as he walked about, but two or three times groaned very deeply and loud, and sighed as he would break his heart.

When the buriers came up to him they soon found he was neither a person infected and desperate, as I have observed above, or a person distempered in mind, but one oppressed with a dreadful weight of grief indeed, having his wife and several of his children all in the cart that was just come in with him, and he followed in an agony and excess of sorrow. He mourned heartily, as it was easy to see, but with a kind of masculine grief that could not give itself vent by tears; and calmly

defying the buriers to let him alone, said he would only see the bodies thrown in and go away, so they left importuning him. But no sooner was the cart turned round and the bodies shot into the pit promiscuously, which was a surprise to him, for he at least expected they would have been decently laid in, though indeed he was afterward convinced that was impracticable; I say, no sooner did he see the sight but he cried out aloud, unable to contain himself. I could not hear what he said, but he went backward two or three steps and fell down in a swoon.[12] The buriers ran to him and took him up, and in a little while he came to himself, and they led him away to the Pie Tavern over against the end of Houndsditch, where, it seems, the man was known, and where they took care of him. He looked into the pit again as he went away, but the buriers had covered the bodies so immediately with throwing in earth, that though there was light enough, for there were lanterns, and candles in them, placed all night round the sides of the pit, upon heaps of earth, seven or eight, or perhaps more, yet nothing could be seen.

This was a mournful scene indeed, and affected⌐
me almost as much as the rest; but the other was ⌐B
awful and full of terror. The cart had in it sixteen┘
or seventeen bodies; some were wrapped up in linen sheets, some in rags, some little other than naked, or so loose that what covering they had fell from them in the shooting out of the cart, and they fell quite naked among the rest; but the matter was not much to them, or the indecency much to anyone else, seeing they were all dead, and were to be huddled together into the common grave of mankind, as we may call it, for here was no difference made, but poor and rich went together; there was no other way of burials, neither was it possible there should, for coffins were not to be had for the prodigious numbers that fell in such a calamity as this.

5. A Poor Piper

John Hayward . . . was at that time under-sexton of the parish of St. Stephen, Coleman Street. By under-sexton was understood at that time gravedigger and bearer of the dead. This man carried,

---

9. **hazards:** risks.
10. **in it:** in doing it (going up to the rim of the pits).
11. **bellman:** bell ringer who accompanied the dead-cart.

12. **swoon:** faint.

A. **Responding**

How do you feel about the narrator's curiosity here? Could his attitude be called morbid? If so, what about the attitude of the curious reader of the *Journal* itself? (Students probably will agree that many readers would approach this work with a mix of distaste and fascination.)

B. **Interpreting**

Does the episode, in fact, have a "sermonlike" effect on the narrator, the way the sexton predicted? (Despite the sexton's prediction, the narrator does not feel moved to repentance; he does, however, feel sympathy for the dead and sobered by the reminder of human mortality.)

READING CHECK TEST
1. The effects of the plague showed up immediately on an infected person. (F)
2. If tokens (buboes) were opened and drained, people often recovered from the disease. (T)
3. People were allowed to go to the burial pits, since the plague could not be spread by corpses. (F)
4. One man was cured of the plague after an arduous swim in the Thames River. (T)
5. Even after the plague had diminished, people were afraid to touch or even talk to each other. (F)

A. Narrative Technique
Note how Defoe distinguishes between various sources here, increasing the impression of accuracy.

B. Responding
❓ How do you respond to the story of the piper? How would you describe this episode? Is it ironic? Grotesque? Funny? Pathetic? (Students probably will note the strong sense of black humor in this tale.)

A

or assisted to carry, all the dead to their graves which were buried in that large parish, and who were carried in form,[13] and after that form of burying was stopped, went with the dead-cart and the bell to fetch the dead bodies from the houses where they lay. . . .

It was under this John Hayward's care, and within his bounds, that the story of the piper,[14] with which people have made themselves so merry, happened, and he assured me that it was true. It is said that it was a blind piper; but, as John told me, the fellow was not blind, but an ignorant, weak, poor man, and usually walked his rounds about ten o'clock at night and went piping along from door to door, and the people usually took him in at public houses[15] where they knew him, and would give him drink and victuals,[16] and sometimes farthings;[17] and he in return would pipe and sing and talk simply, which diverted the people; and thus he lived. It was but a very bad time for this diversion while things were as I have told, yet the poor fellow went about as usual, but was almost starved; and when anybody asked how he did he would answer, the dead-cart had not taken him yet, but that they had promised to call for him next week.

It happened one night that this poor fellow, whether somebody had given him too much drink or no—John Hayward said he had not drink in his house, but that they had given him a little more victuals than ordinary at a public house in Coleman Street—and the poor fellow, having not usually had a bellyful for perhaps not a good while, was laid all along upon the top of a bulk or stall, and fast asleep, at a door in the street near London Wall, towards Cripplegate, and that upon the same bulk or stall the people of some house, in the alley of which the house was a corner, hearing a bell, which they always rang before the cart came, had laid a body really dead of the plague just by him, thinking, too, that this poor fellow had been a dead body, as the other was, and laid there by some of the neighbors.

Accordingly, when John Hayward with his bell and the cart came along, finding two dead bodies lie upon the stall, they took them up with the instrument they used and threw them into the cart, and all this while the piper slept soundly.

From hence they passed along and took in other dead bodies, till, as honest John Hayward told me, they almost buried him alive in the cart; yet all this while he slept soundly. At length the cart came to the place where the bodies were to be thrown into the ground, which, as I do remember, was at Mount Mill; and as the cart usually stopped some time before they were ready to shoot out the melancholy load they had in it, as soon as the cart stopped the fellow awaked and struggled a little to get his head out from among the dead bodies, when, raising himself up in the cart, he called out, "Hey! where am I?" This frighted the fellow that attended about the work; but after some pause John Hayward, recovering himself, said, "Lord, bless us! There's somebody in the cart not quite dead!" So another called to him and said, "Who are you?" The fellow answered, "I am the poor piper. Where am I?" "Where are you?" says Hayward. "Why, you are in the dead-cart, and we are going to bury you." "But I an't dead though, am I?" says the piper, which made them laugh a little, though, as John said, they were heartily frighted at first; so they helped the poor fellow down, and he went about his business.

I know the story goes he set up his pipes in the cart and frighted the bearers and others so that they ran away; but John Hayward did not tell the story so, nor say anything of his piping at all; but that he was a poor piper, and that he was carried away as above I am fully satisfied of the truth of. . . .

B

6. A Violent Cure

I heard of one infected creature who, running out of his bed in his shirt in the anguish and agony of his swellings, of which he had three upon him, got his shoes on and went to put on his coat; but the nurse resisting, and snatching the coat from him, he threw her down, ran over her, ran downstairs and into the street, directly to the Thames in his shirt, the nurse running after him, and calling to the watch to stop him; but the watchman, frighted at the man, and afraid to touch him, let him go on; upon which he ran down to the Stillyard stairs, threw away his shirt, and plunged into the Thames, and, being a good swimmer, swam quite over the river; and the tide being coming in, as

---
13. **in form:** according to the customary burial rites.
14. **piper:** bagpiper.
15. **public houses:** taverns.
16. **victuals** (vit′′lz): food.
17. **farthings:** small British coins (no longer in use), worth a quarter of a penny.

ANALYZING THE JOURNAL
Identifying Facts

1. Defoe informs the reader that the *Journal* was written at a later date when he speaks in the first section of "the time of this visitation." In the third section, he introduces an episode by saying "I remember." In the fourth section, he refers to his audience as "those who did not see it," implying that he is writing at a lat-

er time.

The explanation lies in the fact of Defoe's attempting to lend an element of truth to his narrative, which is at least partly stylized.

2. The four characters are the citizen who tries to escape from the quarantine, the bereaved husband in the brown cloak, the poor piper, and the man who swam the Thames and back.

The citizen who tries to escape from quarantine lies about his condition and is found dead the following morning. The bereaved husband is shocked at the burial of his wife and children in a common grave. The poor piper wakes up in the dead-cart and asks if he is really dead. The man who swims across the Thames is infected with the plague, but his *(Answers continue on next page.)*

A. Style
Note Defoe's plain but balanced prose style in this passage.

B. Responding
? How would you paraphrase the narrator's "coarse" verse? (Responses should read something like this: "Although 100,000 people died in the London plague of '65, I survived!")

they call it, that is, running westward, he reached the land not till he came about the Falcon stairs, where landing, and finding no people there, it being in the night, he ran about the streets there, naked as he was, for a good while, when, it being by that time high water,[18] he takes the river again, and swam back to the Stillyard, landed, ran up the streets again to his own house, knocking at the door, went up the stairs and into his bed again; and that this terrible experiment cured him of the plague, that is to say, that the violent motion of his arms and legs stretched the parts where the swellings he had upon him were, that is to say, under his arms and his groin, and caused them to ripen and break, and that the cold of the water abated the fever in his blood. . . .

7. The Plague Diminishes

The contagion despised all medicine; death raged in every corner; and had it gone on as it did then, a few weeks more would have cleared the town of all, and everything that had a soul. Men everywhere began to despair; every heart failed them for fear; people were made desperate through the anguish of their souls, and the terrors of death sat in the very faces and countenances of the people.

In that very moment, when we might very well say, "Vain was the help of man"—I say, in that very moment it pleased God, with a most agreeable surprise, to cause the fury of it to abate, even of itself; and the malignity declining, as I have said, though infinite numbers were sick, yet fewer died, and the very first week's bill[19] decreased 1,843; a vast number indeed!

It is impossible to express the change that appeared in the very countenances of the people that Thursday morning when the weekly bill came out. It might have been perceived in their countenances that a secret surprise and smile of joy sat on everybody's face. They shook one another by the hands in the streets, who would hardly go on the same side of the way with one another before. Where the streets were not too broad, they would open their windows and call from one house to another, and ask how they did, and if they had heard the good news that the plague was abated.

Some would return, when they said good news, and ask, "What good news?" and when they answered that the plague was abated and the bills decreased almost two thousand, they would cry out, "God be praised," and would weep aloud for joy, telling them they had heard nothing of it; and such was the joy of the people that it was, as it were, life to them from the grave. I could almost set down as many extravagant things done in the excess of their joy as of their grief; but that would be to lessen the value of it. . . .

8. I'm Alive!

I shall conclude the account of this calamitous year . . . with a coarse but sincere stanza of my own, which I placed at the end of my ordinary memorandums the same year they were written:

> A dreadful plague in London was
>   In the year sixty-five,
> Which swept an hundred thousand souls
>   Away; yet I alive!

H. F.

18. **high water:** high tide.
19. **bill:** count of the dead, published every week so long as the plague raged.

strenuous exercise apparently caused the swellings to burst, and he recovers after the poison drains from his body.

3. The symptoms included gangrenous swellings, or boils.

4. Citizens who had been exposed to the infection were quarantined; doctors tried to get the swelling to come to a head so that it would burst and run.

Interpreting Meanings

5. The tone is predominantly sober.

6. The techniques are suspense, foreshadowing, "eyewitness" accounts, direct quotation, and the citation of statistics.

Students would probably agree that Defoe uses many of the same techniques in *Robinson Crusoe*.

7. A dead person, presumably, would not care about the manner of his body's

burial. The manner of burial, however, can make a difference to the living.

8. This story would be improved because the bit about the playing of the pipes would add an extra touch of ironic humor. The narrator refuses to include it because he insists on the factual accuracy and authenticity of the details he reports.

(Answers continue in left-hand column.)

(Continued from top.)

9. The expression connotes an excessive interest in details involved in violence, illness, death, or an accident.

The narrator seems to be morbidly curious in the fourth section, when he persuades the sexton to allow him to observe the burials at the churchyard.

Students' answers will vary. Possibilities include violence on television, "rubbernecking" on the highways after an accident, interest in details about violent crimes, and so on. Ask students to give reasons for how they account for this type of curiosity.

10. He calls it "coarse" because it is unpolished.

11. Answers will vary.

12. Possible answer: It might make people less afraid of death because they might realize that all the fretting in the world cannot prevent it.

Responding to the Journal

Analyzing the Journal

Identifying Facts

1. Though the title *A Journal of the Plague Year* implies a daily account of events, the book is written as a narrative years after the plague is over. Where does Defoe let the reader know his *Journal* is being written at a later date? How does he explain this change in form?
2. These excerpts from the *Journal* are a series of dramatic scenes introduced by the narrator's general observations of the condition of London's citizens during the epidemic. Who are the four characters which the narrator features? How does each of their situations differ?
3. What were the symptoms of the disease?
4. What attempts were made to cure people?

Interpreting Meanings

5. What is the **tone** of the *Journal*? Do you think the tone would have been different if the *Journal* really had been written during the plague?
6. What literary techniques does Defoe use to make his journal seem authentic? Are these techniques similar to those he uses in *Robinson Crusoe*?
7. Why does Defoe, or his narrator, say that the manner of burial makes no difference to a dead person? To whom do you think the manner of burial *does* make a difference?
8. Why would the story of the piper be improved if it contained the bit about his playing the pipes while he was in the dead-cart? Why, then, does the narrator refuse to include this bit?
9. What do we mean by the expression "morbid curiosity"? In which of the incidents recounted here does the narrator appear to be morbidly curious? Where does this kind of curiosity often appear in contemporary life and how do you account for it? (Are people morbidly curious because they enjoy seeing others suffer? Or is there another explanation?)
10. Why does H. F. call his little poem "coarse"?
11. If you had been living in London in 1665 and had survived the plague, what would you have done to celebrate?
12. How would experiencing a plague of this sort change a person's attitude toward life and death?

Writing About the Journal

A Creative Response

1. **Narrating from Primary Sources.** Examine several accounts (from newspapers, magazines, or television or radio) of a recent natural disaster in which lives were lost. Then, write a narrative of the event as though you were an observer or participant. Be as creative as you wish, but make sure you include the details that will make your story believable: names, dates, places, times, causes, effects, motives, and so on.

A Critical Response

2. **Comparing and Contrasting Literary Works.** In an essay, compare and contrast Defoe's *A Journal of the Plague Year* and Pepys's diary entry about the Great Fire of London. Gather information for your essay by filling out a chart like the one below.

	Pepys's *Diary*	Defoe's *Journal*
Tone		
Informal or formal style		
Use of specific details		
Point of view		
Objectivity vs. subjectivity		

Conclude your essay by deciding how good (or bad) a job Defoe does of imitating a personal journal.

3. **Supporting an Opinion.** Some people are opposed to books like Defoe's *A Journal of the Plague Year*—books that describe, in rich detail, calamities, atrocities, and disasters that befall the human race. After all, these people argue, life itself is often very disagreeable, so why should we have to read about dreadful, depressing events? Wouldn't it be better just to forget them and remember only the pleasant things that have happened? How do you feel about this point of view? Using the events in the *Journal* as support, write an essay in which you either defend or attack this position.

Jonathan Swift
(1667–1745)

Jonathan Swift is the principal prose writer of
the early eighteenth century and England's
A greatest satirist. He was an Anglo-Irishman, a label applied to people who live in Ireland but
who regard themselves as more English than
Irish. Swift was born in Dublin, of English parents, seven months after the death of his father,
a lawyer. As was customary at the time, his
mother entrusted him to the care of a nurse.
This well-intentioned but irresponsible woman
kidnapped him and took him to England, where
he spent almost four years before being brought
back to his family. And so the pattern of Swift's
life was established very early: He was to move
back and forth from Ireland to England, never
feeling completely at home in either country and
never obtaining the rewards to which he felt his
genius entitled him.

Although poor himself, Swift had prosperous
Anglo-Irish uncles who paid for his education,
first at an excellent private grammar school at
Kilkenny, Ireland, and then at Trinity College,
Dublin. After that, in order to advance himself,
he went to England and became secretary to Sir
William Temple, a distant relative. Temple was a
writer, a wealthy country gentleman, and a
statesman and diplomat. At Moor Park, his
handsome estate near London, he maintained a
large household of interesting people. Here Swift
helped him arrange his papers and manage his
correspondence. The job gave Swift the opportunity to mingle with public figures, read, and look
about for a more important and permanent position. Unfortunately, nothing came of Temple's
patronage, in either England or Ireland. After
several years of disappointment, Swift took his
life into his own hands, obtained a Master's degree from Oxford University, and was ordained a
priest in the Church of Ireland, a branch of the
Church of England.

B Swift seemed fated to live in Ireland, although
he desperately wanted a career in England.
Now, as a priest, Swift was assigned to remote
parishes in the Irish countryside. To Swift, Ireland seemed a cultural desert, inhabited mainly
by Roman Catholic natives and Scottish Presby-

Jonathan Swift by C. Jervas (c. 1718). Oil.

National Portrait Gallery, London.

terian immigrants—people whom Swift neither
admired nor respected. And so he escaped to
England whenever possible. His longest period
of absence from Ireland was from 1710 to 1713,
when he was in London writing pamphlets defending the political party then in power, in
which he had friends. Swift hoped to be made an
English bishop as a reward, but his political
friends fell from power, and the only appointment he could obtain was back in Ireland, as the
Dean of St. Patrick's Cathedral in Dublin. Swift
returned to his native city, was installed as
Dean, and held that office for the remaining
thirty years of his life.

In Dublin, Swift made the best of his disappointment, busying himself with his parishioners
in what we would now call the "inner city" and
conducting the cathedral's services.

Swift did not write for fame or money; most
of his books and pamphlets were published
anonymously. Nor did he write simply to divert
or entertain, though most of his works are
marked by his powerful imagination and many of
them are amusing. Swift's aim in writing was to

A. Satire
Direct students' at-
tention to the es-
say on satire as
one of the ele-
ments of literature,
text page 516.

B. Expansion
One of the mani-
fold contradictions
of Swift's life is
that, although disil-
lusioned by his ca-
reer in Ireland, he
was moved to
write a savagely
indignant satire on
the English for
their cruel treat-
ment of the Irish:
see "A Modest
Proposal" (text
page 518).

A. Expansion
You may want to
have students
compare and con-
trast the form, dic-
tion, and theme of
this poem with
those of Andrew
Marvell's "To His
Coy Mistress" (text
page 436).

improve human conduct, to make people more decent and humane, to persuade them to believe as he did and agree with him on controversial issues. He produced a vast amount of excellent journalism defending his religious and political beliefs. His first important book, *The Tale of a Tub* (1704), is a lively, outspoken exposure of "gross corruptions in religion and learning," to quote Swift's own words. It scandalized many respectable readers when they discovered that a clergyman had written it, because it seemed to treat sacred matters irreverently. *Gulliver's Travels* (1726) attacks many different varieties of human misbehavior, vice, and folly. Swift even became an Irish patriot in his pamphlets defending the Irish against the oppressive policies of their English rulers. One series of pamphlets, *The Drapier's Letters* (1724–1725), protested the debased coinage that the English government imposed on Ireland. These *Letters* made Swift famous as a defender of Irish rights—a role that he had never sought but found himself playing because of his deep commitment to the ideals of justice and humanity. The most famous of his pamphlets, *A Modest Proposal* (1729), satirizes the British by proposing a particularly cruel solution to their "Irish problem." In a letter to Pope, Swift justified these pro-Irish writings: "What I do is owing to perfect rage and resentment, and the mortifying sight of slavery, folly, and baseness about me, among which I am forced to live."

Swift has always been a controversial figure to his biographers, who have attacked him, defended him, and speculated wildly about his life, especially about his relationships with women. Some biographers have claimed that he was married to Esther Johnson, a friend whom Swift always called Stella. Fourteen years younger than he, Stella was just a child when Swift first met her at Sir William Temple's house and began to supervise her education. Eventually they became so deeply attached to each other—though there was always a third person present whenever they met—that at Swift's suggestion she moved to Dublin, where she lived with a Mrs. Dingley, who had also been a member of Temple's household. There is no evidence at all that Swift and Stella ever married. However odd their relationship may appear, many letters, journals, and poems exist to prove that it was a very satisfactory one for both Swift and Stella.

Swift wrote many comic and serious poems, including several celebrating Stella's various birthdays. Here are the opening stanzas of the last of the birthday poems; before her next birthday, Stella was dead—at the age of forty-seven.

This day, whate'er the Fates decree,
Shall still be kept with joy by me:
This day, then, let us not be told
That you are sick, and I grown old,
Nor think on our approaching ills,
And talk of spectacles and pills;
Tomorrow will be time enough
To hear such mortifying stuff.
Yet, since from reason may be brought
A better and more pleasing thought,
Which can in spite of all decays,
Support a few remaining days:
From not the gravest of Divines,
Accept for once some serious Lines.

Although we now can form no more
Long schemes of life, as heretofore;
Yet you, while time is running fast,
Can look with joy on what is past.

Were future happiness and pain,
A mere contrivance of the brain,
As atheists argue, to entice
And fit their proselytes for vice
(The only comfort they propose,
To have companions in their woes):
Grant this the case, yet sure 'tis hard,
That virtue, styled its own reward,
And by all sages understood
To be the chief of human good,
Should acting, die, nor leave behind
Some lasting pleasure in the mind,
Which by remembrance will assuage,
Grief, sickness, poverty, and age;
And strongly shoot a radiant dart,
To shine through life's declining part. . . .
          —from "Stella's Birthday"

As the years passed, Swift made fewer and fewer visits to London, though he continued to correspond with Alexander Pope and with many other literary friends. His last days were sad: He suffered from a disease of the inner ear which made him dizzy, deaf, and disoriented. He was buried in his cathedral in Dublin, where troops of tourists now pause every day of the year to read his epitaph.

1. BUILDING ON PRIOR KNOWLEDGE. Before students begin reading, remind them that *Gulliver's Travels* grew directly out of the popular eighteenth-century prose form of the travelogue. Other works inspired by this form include Defoe's *Robinson Crusoe* and Samuel Johnson's *Rasselas* (1759). The form also enjoyed a vogue on the Continent, notably in Voltaire's *Candide* (1759). Travel writing as a respected literary form seems to be coming back into its own in our time: Direct students' attention to the works of Graham Greene (see text page 1010), V. S. Naipaul (see text page 1033), and Paul Theroux. Ask students to comment on the distinctive features of this genre.

2. ESTABLISHING A PURPOSE. Before students begin to read, you may want to direct their attention to the Comment on text pages 512–513. Have students read to try to detect the elements of satire in "A Voyage to Lilliput."

FROM GULLIVER'S TRAVELS

Illustration from a 19th-century edition of *Gulliver's Travels*.

A. Responding to the Illustration

This illustration shows Gulliver during Book I, the Voyage to Lilliput. Notice that the Lilliputians, one-twelfth the size of humans, have erected a platform in order to converse with the bound Gulliver.

? What emotions does the expression on Gulliver's face suggest? (Fascination; amusement) Write a paragraph describing what you see, from the viewpoint of one of two little men on top of Gulliver's chest and leg.

A

SUPPLEMENTARY SUPPORT MATERIALS
1. Vocabulary Activity Worksheet (*CCB*)
2. Review and Response Worksheet:
Parody (*CCB*)
3. Selection Test (*CCB*)

DEVELOPING VOCABULARY
The following words from the story are
tested in the Selection Test. (See also
Vocabulary Activity Worksheet.)

ligature	intrepidity
to conjecture	diminutive
prudent	disapprobation
oration	potent
submissive	to foment

A. Responding

❓ What do you think is Gulliver's probable frame of mind in this passage? (Confusion, surprise, and curiosity)

B. Style

❓ What does the made-up language contribute to the report? (It makes it seem authentic.)

The full title which Swift gave to his work is *Travels to Several Remote Nations of the World. In Four Parts. By Lemuel Gulliver, First a Surgeon, and then a Captain of Several Ships.* **Immediately upon publication it was a sensational success. It seemed so convincing that some readers went about claiming that they had heard of, or even met, its "author," Lemuel Gulliver. But Gulliver is, of course, a figment of Swift's imagination.**

One reason why the book seems to be a true account of actual adventures is Swift's inclusion of many realistic-sounding details and even maps of the places Gulliver visits. The first part of the book, describing the visit to Lilliput, opens with a very circumstantial account of Gulliver's early life: his birth, parentage, and schooling. After studying medicine, Gulliver becomes a ship's doctor and embarks on a long voyage; when the ship breaks up in a storm, he manages to swim ashore and, exhausted, falls into a deep sleep. What could be more convincing?

From
Part 1

A Voyage to Lilliput

I lay down on the grass, which was very short and soft, where I slept sounder than ever I remember to have done in my life, and, as I reckoned, above nine hours; for when I awaked, it was just daylight. I attempted to rise, but was not able to stir: for, as I happened to lie on my back, I found my arms and legs were strongly fastened on each side to the ground; and my hair, which was long and thick, tied down in the same manner. I likewise felt several slender ligatures across my body, from my armpits to my thighs. I could only look upward; the sun began to grow hot, and the light offended my eyes. I heard a confused noise about me, but in the posture I lay, could see nothing except the sky. In a little time I felt something alive moving on my left leg, which advancing gently forward over my breast, came almost up to my chin; when bending my eyes downward as much as I could, I perceived it to be a human creature not six inches high, with a bow and arrow in his hands, and a quiver at his back. In the meantime, I felt at least forty more

of the same kind (as I conjectured) following the first. I was in the utmost astonishment, and roared so loud, that they all ran back in a fright; and some of them, as I was afterward told, were hurt with the falls they got by leaping from my sides upon the ground. However, they soon returned, and one of them, who ventured so far as to get a full sight of my face, lifting up his hands and eyes by way of admiration, cried out in a shrill but distinct voice, *Hekinah degul:*[1] the others repeated the same words several times, but I then knew not what they meant. I lay all this while, as the reader may believe, in great uneasiness: at length, struggling to get loose, I had the fortune to break the strings, and wrench out the pegs that fastened my left arm to the ground; for, by lifting it up to my face, I discovered the methods they had taken to bind me, and at the same time, with a violent pull, which gave me excessive pain, I a little loosened the strings that tied down my hair on the left side, so that I was just able to turn my head about two inches. But the creatures ran off a second time, before I could seize them; whereupon there was a great shout in a very shrill accent, and after it ceased, I heard one of them cry aloud, *Tolgo phonac;* when in an instant I felt above a hundred arrows discharged on my left hand, which pricked me like so many needles; and besides they shot another flight into the air, as we do bombs in Europe, whereof many, I suppose, fell on my body (though I felt them not) and some on my face, which I immediately covered with my left hand. When this shower of arrows was over, I fell a groaning with grief and pain, and then striving again to get loose, they discharged another volley larger than the first, and some of them attempted with spears to stick me in the sides; but, by good luck, I had on me a buff jerkin,[2] which they could not pierce. I thought it the most prudent method to lie still, and my design was to continue so till night, when, my left hand being already loose, I could easily free myself: and as for the inhabitants, I had reason to believe I might be a match for the greatest armies they could bring against me, if they were all of the same size with him that I saw. But fortune disposed otherwise of me. When the people observed I was quiet, they

---

1. *Hekinah degul:* This and other examples of the Lilliputian tongue are mainly nonsense words. Swift was very fond of puns, word-games, pig-Latin, and other kinds of nonsense.
2. **buff jerkin:** a short, close-fitting leather jacket often without sleeves.

discharged no more arrows; but, by the noise I heard, I knew their numbers increased; and about four yards from me, over against my right ear, I heard a knocking for above an hour, like that of people at work; when turning my head that way, as well as the pegs and strings would permit me, I saw a stage erected, about a foot and a half from the ground, capable of holding four of the inhabitants, with two or three ladders to mount it: from whence one of them, who seemed to be a person of quality, made me a long speech, whereof I understood not one syllable. But I should have mentioned, that before the principal person began his oration, he cried out three times, *Langro dehul san* (these words and the former were afterward repeated and explained to me). Whereupon immediately about fifty of the inhabitants came, and cut the strings that fastened the left side of my head, which gave me the liberty of turning it to the right, and of observing the person and gesture of him that was to speak. He appeared to be of a middle age, and taller than any of the other three who attended him, whereof one was a page that held up his train, and seemed to be somewhat longer than my middle finger; the other two stood one on each side to support him. He acted every part of an orator, and I could observe many periods of threatenings, and others of promises, pity, and kindness. I answered in a few words, but in the most submissive manner, lifting up my left hand and both my eyes to the sun, as calling him for a witness; and being almost famished with hunger, having not eaten a morsel for some hours before I left the ship, I found the demands of nature so strong upon me, that I could not forbear showing my impatience (perhaps against the strict rules of decency) by putting my finger frequently on my mouth, to signify that I wanted food. The *Hurgo*[3] (for so they call a great lord, as I afterward learnt) understood me very well. He descended from the stage, and commanded that several ladders should be applied to my sides, on which above a hundred of the inhabitants mounted, and walked toward my mouth, laden with baskets full of meat,[4] which had been provided, and sent thither by the King's orders, upon the first intelligence[5] he received of me. I observed there

was the flesh[6] of several animals, but could not distinguish them by the taste. There were shoulders, legs, and loins, shaped like those of mutton, and very well dressed, but smaller than the wings of a lark. I ate them by two or three at a mouthful, and took three loaves at a time, about the bigness of musket bullets. They supplied me as they could, showing a thousand marks of wonder and astonishment at my bulk and appetite. I then made another sign that I wanted drink. They found by my eating that a small quantity would not suffice me, and being a most ingenious people, they slung up with great dexterity one of their largest hogsheads, then rolled it toward my hand, and beat out the top; I drank it off at a draft, which I might well do, for it did not hold half a pint, and tasted like a small wine of Burgundy, but much more delicious. They brought me a second hogshead, which I drank in the same manner, and made signs for more, but they had none to give me. When I had performed these wonders, they shouted for joy, and danced upon my breast, repeating several times as they did at first, *Hekinah degul*. They made me a sign that I should throw down the two hogsheads, but first warning the people below to stand out of the way, crying aloud, *Borach mivola,* and when they saw the vessels in the air, there was a universal shout of *Hekinah degul*. I confess I was often tempted, while they were passing backward and forward on my body, to seize forty or fifty of the first that came in my reach, and dash them against the ground. But the remembrance of what I had felt, which probably might not be the worst they could do, and the promise of honor I made them, for so I interpreted my submissive behavior, soon drove out these imaginations. Besides, I now considered myself as bound by the laws of hospitality to a people who had treated me with so much expense and magnificence. However, in my thoughts I could not sufficiently wonder at the intrepidity of these diminutive mortals who durst venture to mount and walk upon my body, while one of my hands was at liberty, without trembling at the very sight of so prodigious a creature as I must appear to them. After some time, when they observed that I made no more demands for meat, there appeared

---

3. *Hurgo:* This Lilliputian word is perhaps a partial anagram of the English word *rogue*. It would be characteristic of Swift to call a "great lord" a rogue.
4. **meat:** food.
5. **intelligence:** news.

6. **flesh:** meat.

A. **Responding**

? Do you find Gulliver's ability to communicate through sign language and gestures convincing? Why or why not? (Students may feel that the communication of his hunger was convincing, for it brought about the desired response, whereas his swearing his sincerity might fail to cross cultural distinctions.)

B. **Conflict**

? What is Gulliver's internal conflict? (His internal conflict is one of mixed emotions of violence, fear, and respect for the laws of hospitality.)

A. Humor

🅿 What humorous details enliven this description of the Lilliputians? (The dancing on Gullivers' hand, the game of hide and seek in his hair)

B. Satire

🅿 How does the description of the rope-dancing introduce the element of political satire? (The description serves as Swift's satirical "cue," namely that this game is practiced by those who are ambitious at court.)

before me a person of high rank from his Imperial Majesty. His Excellency, having mounted on the small of my right leg, advanced forward up to my face, with about a dozen of his retinue. And producing his credentials under the Signet Royal, which he applied close to my eyes, spoke ten minutes, without any signs of anger, but with a kind of determinate resolution; often pointing forward, which, as I afterward found, was toward the capital city, about half a mile distant, whither it was agreed by his majesty in council that I must be conveyed. I answered in few words, but to no purpose, and made a sign with my hand that was loose, putting it to the other (but over his Excellency's head, for fear of hurting him or his train) and then to my own head and body, to signify that I desired my liberty. It appeared that he understood me well enough, for he shook his head by way of disapprobation, and held his hand in a posture to show that I must be carried as a prisoner. However, he made other signs to let me understand that I should have meat and drink enough, and very good treatment. Whereupon I once more thought of attempting to break my bonds, but again, when I felt the smart of their arrows upon my face and hands, which were all in blisters, and many of the darts still sticking in them, and observing likewise that the number of my enemies increased, I gave tokens to let them know that they might do with me what they pleased. Upon this the *Hurgo* and his train withdrew with much civility and cheerful countenances. Soon after I heard a general shout, with frequent repetitions of the words, *Peplom selan,* and I felt great numbers of the people on my left side relaxing the cords to such a degree, that I was able to turn upon my right, and to ease myself with making water; which I very plentifully did, to the great astonishment of the people, who conjecturing[7] by my motions what I was going to do, immediately opened to the right and left on that side, to avoid the torrent which fell with such noise and violence from me. But before this, they had daubed my face and both my hands with a sort of ointment very pleasant to the smell, which in a few minutes removed all the smart of their arrows. These circumstances, added to the refreshment I had received by their victuals and drink, which were very nourishing, disposed me

to sleep. I slept about eight hours, as I was afterward assured; and it was no wonder, for the physicians, by the Emperor's order, had mingled a sleepy potion in the hogsheads of wine. . . .

My gentleness and good behavior had gained so far on the emperor and his court, and indeed upon the army and people in general, that I began to conceive hopes of getting my liberty in a short time. I took all possible methods to cultivate this favorable disposition. The natives came by degrees to be less apprehensive of any danger from me. I would sometimes lie down, and let five or six of them dance on my hand. And at last the boys and girls would venture to come and play at hide and seek in my hair. I had now made a good progress in understanding and speaking their language. The emperor had a mind one day to entertain me with several of the country shows; wherein they exceed all nations I have known, both for dexterity and magnificence. I was diverted with none so much as that of the rope-dancers,[8] performed upon a slender white thread, extended about two foot, and twelve inches from the ground. Upon which, I shall desire liberty, with the reader's patience, to enlarge a little.

This diversion is only practiced by those persons, who are candidates for great employments, and high favor, at court. They are trained in this art from their youth, and are not always of noble birth, or liberal education. When a great office is vacant, either by death or disgrace (which often happens), five or six of those candidates petition the emperor to entertain his Majesty and the court with a dance on the rope; and whoever jumps the highest without falling, succeeds in the office. Very often the chief ministers themselves are commanded to show their skill, and to convince the emperor that they have not lost their faculty. Flimnap, the Treasurer, is allowed to cut a caper on the strait rope, at least an inch higher than any other lord in the whole empire. I have seen him do the somersault several times together, upon a trencher[9] fixed on the rope, which is no thicker than a common packthread in England. My friend Reldresal, principal Secretary for Private Affairs, is, in my opinion, if I am not partial, the second after the Treasurer; the rest of the great officers are much upon a par.

---

7. **conjecturing:** reasoning.

8. **rope-dancers:** tight-rope dancers.
9. **trencher:** wooden platter.

READING CHECK TEST

1. Gulliver discovers that his body is fastened to the ground. (T)
2. Gulliver is surprised that his captors don't have any weapons. (F)
3. Gulliver can understand only a few of his captors' words. (F)
4. Gulliver's captors provide him with both food and drink. (T)

5. Gulliver eventually learns that his captors had put a sleeping potion in his drink. (T)
6. Gulliver says government offices are filled by the winners of a tight-rope contest. (T)
7. Gulliver describes a contest in which the prizes were threads. (T)

8. The Principal Secretary says there are no opposing political parties in the kingdom. (F)
9. He also says some citizens did not abide by a new law regarding the breaking of eggs. (T)
10. Gulliver will not support the king against the invading enemy. (F)

These diversions are often attended with fatal accidents, whereof great numbers are on record. I myself have seen two or three candidates break a limb. But the danger is much greater, when the ministers themselves are commanded to show their dexterity: for, by contending to excel themselves and their fellows, they strain so far, that there is hardly one of them who hath not received a fall; and some of them two or three. I was assured, that a year or two before my arrival, Flimnap would have infallibly broke his neck, if one of the king's cushions, that accidentally lay on the ground, had not weakened the force of his fall.

There is likewise another diversion, which is only shown before the emperor and empress, and first minister, upon particular occasions. The emperor lays on a table three fine silken threads, of six inches long. One is blue, the other red, and the third green. These threads are proposed as prizes, for those persons whom the emperor hath a mind to distinguish by a peculiar mark of his favor. The ceremony is performed in his Majesty's great chamber of State; where the candidates are to undergo a trial of dexterity very different from the former, and such as I have not observed the least resemblance of in any other country of the Old or the New World. The emperor holds a stick in his hands, both ends parallel to the horizon, while the candidates advancing one by one, sometimes leap over the stick, sometimes creep under it backward and forward several times, according as the stick is advanced or depressed. Sometimes the emperor holds one end of the stick, and his first minister the other; sometimes the minister hath it entirely to himself. Whoever performs his part with most agility, and holds out the longest in leaping and creeping, is rewarded with the blue-colored silk; the red is given to the next, and the green to the third, which they all wear girt twice round about the middle; and you see few great persons about this court, who are not adorned with one of these girdles. . . .

One morning, about a fortnight after I had obtained my liberty, Reldresal, Principal Secretary (as they style him) of Private Affairs, came to my house, attended only by one servant. He ordered his coach to wait at a distance, and desired I would give him an hour's audience;[10] which I readily consented to, on account of his quality, and per-

sonal merits, as well as of the many good offices he had done me during my solicitations at court. I offered to lie down, that he might the more conveniently reach my ear; but he chose rather to let me hold him in my hand during our conversation. He began with compliments on my liberty; said, he might pretend to some merit in it; but, however, added, that if it had not been for the present situation of things at court, perhaps I might not have obtained it so soon. "For," said he, "as flourishing a condition as we appear to be in to foreigners, we labor under two mighty evils; a violent faction at home, and the danger of an invasion by a most <u>potent</u> enemy from abroad. As to the first, you are to understand, that for above seventy moons past, there have been two struggling parties in this empire, under the names of Tramecksan, and Slamecksan, from the high and low heels on their shoes, by which they distinguish themselves.

"It is alleged indeed, that the high heels are most agreeable to our ancient constitution: but however this be, his Majesty hath determined to make use of only low heels in the administration of the Government, and all offices in the gift of the Crown; as you cannot but observe; and particularly, that his Majesty's imperial heels are lower at least by a *drurr* than any of his court. (*Drurr* is a measure about the fourteenth part of an inch.) The animosities between these two parties run so high, that they will neither eat nor drink, nor talk with each other. We compute the Tramecksan, or high-heels, to exceed us in number; but the power is wholly on our side. We apprehend his Imperial Highness, the heir to the crown, to have some tendency toward the high-heels; at least we can plainly discover one of his heels higher than the other; which gives him a hobble in his gait. Now, in the midst of these intestine[11] disquiets, we are threatened with an invasion from the island of Blefuscu, which is the other great empire of the universe, almost as large and powerful as this of his Majesty. For as to what we have heard you affirm, that there are other kingdoms and states in the world, inhabited by human creatures as large as yourself, our philosophers are in much doubt; and would rather conjecture, that you dropped from the moon, or one of the stars; because it is certain, that a hundred mortals of your bulk, would, in a short time, de-

10. **audience:** conversation; interview.

11. **intestine:** internal.

A. Satire

❓ What seems to be Swift's satirical point in describing the "diversion" with the blue, red, and green threads? (Swift pokes fun at the courtiers' "agility"—namely their ability at flattery and sidestepping responsibility.)

B. Author's Purpose

❓ What might be Swift's purpose in distinguishing, under the guise of a travelogue, the two "mighty evils" of violent faction at home and the danger of invasion from abroad? (Swift's purpose is to make fun of English prejudices against the Roman Catholics at home and the French abroad.)

CLOSURE

Have students define satire as a literary mode. Then ask students to give four or five illustrations of satire from "A Voyage to Lilliput."

ANALYZING THE STORY
Identifying Facts

1. They are less than six inches high—about one-twelfth the size of humans.

Gulliver fears that the Lilliputians may renew their attack with the darts; he also begins to feel bound by the laws of hospitality after the Lilliputians have fed him, and he wonders at their courage.

2. Flimnap is the treasurer, and Reldre-

sal is the principal secretary for Private Affairs.

3. Reldresal identifies the two evils that threaten Lilliput as violent faction at home and the danger of an invasion from abroad by a powerful enemy.

4. The Lilliputians decreed that all eggs must be opened at the small end. But certain rebels disobeyed this edict and continued to open their eggs at the big

A. Satire

? How might this passage about religion be interpreted as a satirical burlesque of certain religious trends in Swift's own time? (Swift is parodying the use of narrow-minded appeals to Scripture to justify religious prejudice.)

stroy all the fruits and cattle of his Majesty's dominions. Besides, our histories of six thousand moons make no mention of any other regions, than the two great empires of Lilliput and Blefuscu. Which two mighty powers have, as I was going to tell you, been engaged in a most obstinate war for six and thirty moons past. It began upon the following occasion. It is allowed on all hands that the primitive way of breaking eggs[12] before we eat them was upon the larger end: but his present Majesty's grandfather, while he was a boy, going to eat an egg, and breaking it according to the ancient practice, happened to cut one of his fingers. Whereupon the emperor his father, published an edict, commanding all his subjects, upon great penalties, to break the smaller end of their eggs. The people so highly resented this law, that our histories tell us, there have been six rebellions raised on that account; wherein one emperor lost his life, and another his crown. These civil commotions were constantly <u>fomented</u> by the monarchs of Blefuscu; and when they were quelled, the exiles always fled for refuge to that empire. It is computed that eleven thousand persons have, at several times, suffered death, rather than submit to break their eggs at the smaller end. Many hundred large volumes have been published upon this controversy: but the books of the Big-Endians have been long forbidden, and the whole party rendered incapable by law of holding employments. During the course of these troubles, the emperors of Blefuscu did frequently expostulate by their ambassadors, accusing us of making a

schism[13] in religion, by offending against a fundamental doctrine of our great prophet Lustrog, in the fifty-fourth chapter of the *Brundrecal*, (which is their *Alcoran*[14]). This, however, is thought to be a mere strain upon the text: for the words are these; 'That all true believers shall break their eggs at the convenient end': and which is the convenient end, seems in my humble opinion, to be left to every man's conscience, or at least in the power of the chief magistrate to determine. Now the Big-Endian exiles have found so much credit in the Emperor of Blefuscu's court; and so much private assistance and encouragement from their party here at home, that a bloody war hath been carried on between the two empires for six and thirty moons with various success; during which time we have lost forty capital ships, and a much greater number of smaller vessels, together with thirty thousand of our best seamen and soldiers; and the damage received by the enemy is reckoned to be somewhat greater than ours. However, they have now equipped a numerous fleet, and are just preparing to make a descent upon us: and his Imperial Majesty, placing great confidence in your valor and strength, hath commanded me to lay this account of his affairs before you.''

I desired the secretary to present my humble duty to the emperor, and to let him know, that I thought it would not become me, who was a foreigner, to interfere with parties; but I was ready, with the hazard of my life, to defend his person and state against all invaders.

A

---

12. **breaking eggs:** The English eat a boiled egg by standing it up in an egg cup, cutting off one end with a knife, and scooping out the contents with a spoon.

---

13. **schism:** division.
14. *Alcoran:* sacred writing, scripture.

A Comment on the Story

Swift's contemporaries immediately understood that Swift was doing two things in this part of *Gulliver's Travels.* Under the pretense of describing politics in Lilliput, he was indirectly referring to politicians and political events in his own country. Swift's first readers were quick to identify the actual statesmen lurking behind such made-up names as Reldresal and Flimnap, and they saw parallels between events in Lilliput and events in England.

While it is interesting to know something about the real political background of *Gulliver's Travels,* it is much more important to understand that Swift is **satirizing** certain characteristics to be found in the political struggles of all countries and at all times in history. For instance, in the imaginary Lilliput there are two major parties, distinguished by a trivial detail: the height of the heels on the shoes they wear. Similarly, in many actual countries there are also two major parties that struggle for end. The kingdom of Blefuscu alienated Lilliput by giving sanctuary and aid to the Big-Endians.

Interpreting Meanings
5. Students can point to almost any part of the introductory episode as illustrating parody of these two kinds of materials.
6. These officials are expected to be able to jump nimbly in rope-dancing.

They also must leap over or creep under a stick, which is held by the king or the first minister.

The comparison implies that English officials are servile, inconsistent, unscrupulous, and hypocritical.
7. In these contexts, *big* might be said to mean "noble," "generous," or "honest." *Small* might be said to mean "dishonest" or "mean-spirited."

Connotations of *big*: outlandish, threatening, disproportionate, ugly. Connotations of *small*: ridiculous, mean, dishonest, silly.
8. Most students will agree that the physical smallness of the Lilliputians also suggests their silliness and pettiness.
9. It is apparent from the passage that Swift thinks that such squabbles are futile and small-minded.

The passage suggests that Swift thinks that these differences are often overstated and ridiculous.

Student answers will vary. Encourage the students to give reasons for their opinions.
10. Student answers will vary. Encourage them to make their parallels as specific as possible.

---

power. Swift wants us to think about what distinguishes such real political parties from each other. Are the issues important or minor?

Later in this section Gulliver discovers another characteristic that distinguishes the two parties: the way they eat their eggs. The Big-Endians always cut open the big end of a boiled egg, and the Little-Endians always cut open the little end. These parties have had a long and bitter history: One emperor has lost his life, another his throne, and many Lilliputians have had to go live in another country, Blefuscu. All these details suggest that Swift was thinking of specific events in English history, and these events determined what he said about Lilliput. It is even possible to identify the parallels between Swift's fictions and historical facts. Lilliput, for example, represents England; and Biefuscu represents France, where some English Catholics lived in exile. The Big-Endians are people loyal to Catholicism, England's old religion, and the Little-Endians are those loyal to Anglicanism, England's new religion. The Emperor who lost his life can be identified with Charles I; the one who lost his throne is James II.

Any narrative incorporating parallels of this kind is called an **allegory**. But again, knowing how to interpret the allegory in a particular way is much less important than understanding the general meaning of the satire, which is directed against follies and excesses wherever they are found.

Responding to the Story

Analyzing the Story

Identifying Facts

1. How large are the Lilliputians? Why doesn't Gulliver seize and harm the Lilliputians who come close to his free hand?
2. What positions do Flimnap and Reldresal hold in this tiny kingdom?
3. Describe the two evils which threaten Lilliput, according to Reldresal.
4. Explain how the war between Lilliput and Blefuscu began.

Interpreting Meanings

5. In the first episode here, Swift is **parodying**—imitating and making fun of—contemporary travel books. Such books were notorious for containing two kinds of materials: fantastic lies about strange places, and trivial details about the traveler's daily life there. Show how this section parodies both kinds of travel materials.
6. In the second episode, Swift begins to use the travel book as a medium for **satire**. He expects his readers to find similarities between what goes on in Lilliput and what goes on at home. The travel-book device enables him to comment indirectly on political matters in England. What qualifications are the officials of Lilliput expected to have in order to hold high office? What does Swift's comparison say about English officials?
7. When people act in a mean, sneaky way, other people say, "That wasn't very big of them," or "That was a small way to behave." What do *big* and *small* mean in these contexts? List some connotations of *big* and *small* as they are used by Swift.

8. Is there any relationship between the physical size of the Lilliputians and the way Swift wants us to evaluate their behavior? In other words, does their size **symbolize** some other kind of "smallness"? Explain.
9. What does Swift think of squabbles over politics and religion? What does he think of the differences that divide people into factions? Do you agree or disagree with his implications?
10. The critical comment following this selection explains how Lilliputian politics paralleled British politics of Swift's time. Can you detect any parallels between Lilliput and what you know of modern politics, either in this country or some other one?

Writing About the Story

A Creative Response

Using First-Person Point of View. The device of having characters awaken from a deep sleep to find themselves in strange circumstances is not uncommon in fiction. In *Metamorphosis* by Franz Kafka, for example, the hero awakens to discover that overnight he has somehow been changed into a beetle-like insect. The rest of the novel concerns his adjustment to his new condition.

Imagine that overnight something surprising has happened to you, and write a first-person narrative of at least three pages about it. You need not try to be fantastic; instead, describe the circumstances in straightforward, sober language of the sort that Swift uses. You need not explain how or why the change has occurred; rather, concentrate on the details of the change itself and on your responses to them.

Jonathan Swift   513

1. **Establishing A Purpose.** Before students read the selection from "A Voyage to Brobdingnag," ask them to think about whether or not Gulliver can be trusted as a reliable narrator. Have them read to note where Gulliver may be regarded as the target of Swift's satire.

SUPPLEMENTARY SUPPORT MATERIALS
1. Vocabulary Activity Worksheet (*CCB*)
2. Review and Response Worksheet: Characterization (*CCB*)
3. Language Skills Worksheet: Repetition and Wordiness (*CCB*)
4. Selection Test (*CCB*)
5. Audiocassette recording

DEVELOPING VOCABULARY
The following words from the story are tested in the Selection Test. (See also Vocabulary Activity Worksheet.)

copious	viscous
schism	perfidiousness
to contrive	to recapitulate
scourge	panegyric
odious	pernicious

A. Characterization

? How does Gulliver's vehement defense of England affect your opinion of him and your assessment of his reliability as a narrator? (Gulliver's uncritical chauvinism casts some doubt on his reliability as a narrator.)

On his second voyage Gulliver finds himself marooned in Brobdingnag, which is pronounced as it is spelled, in three syllables. Here everything—people, animals, buildings—is ten times larger than in England or anywhere else in the known world. The situation in Part 1 is now completely reversed, and Gulliver discovers what it is like to be a petty, insignificant, timid midget among giants. He also learns that nothing is either big or little except by comparison. All sorts of humiliating accidents happen to him: A baby picks him up and tries to suck on his head; a monkey stuffs him with food and carries him up onto a roof; he is almost drowned in a bowl of cream; a farmer exhibits him for money, as though he were a trained flea. Finally he goes to live at court, where he tries to impress the king and queen with his importance, and especially with the importance of England and its civilization, which nobody in Brobdingnag has ever heard of.

Two of the following excerpts are from Chapter 3 of the second part of the Travels. *The third excerpt, in which the Brobdingnagian king comments on England's history, government, and ruling classes, comes from Chapter 4. Although its inhabitants look like immense ugly brutes, Brobdingnag is a kind of utopia, a model civilization with an enlightened and benevolent king. Notice how the king treats Gulliver in spite of his opinion of Gulliver's size and civilization.*

From
Part 2

A Voyage to Brobdingnag

It is the custom, that every Wednesday, (which as I have before observed, was their sabbath) the king and queen, with the royal issue of both sexes, dine together in the apartment of his Majesty; to whom I was now become a favorite; and, at these times my little chair and table were placed at his left hand before one of the salt-cellars.[1] This prince took a pleasure in conversing with me; enquiring into the manners, religion, laws, government, and learning of Europe, wherein I gave him the best account I was able. His apprehension was so clear, and his judgment so exact, that he made very wise reflections and observations upon all I said. But, I confess, that after I had been a little too copious in talking of my own beloved country; of our trade, and wars by sea and land, of our schisms in religion, and parties in the State; the prejudices of his education prevailed so far, that he could not forbear taking me up in his right hand and stroking me gently with the other; after a hearty fit of laughing, asked me whether I were a Whig or a Tory.[2] Then turning to his first minister, who waited behind him with a white staff, near as tall as the mainmast of the *Royal Sovereign*,[3] he observed, how contemptible a thing was human grandeur, which could be mimicked by such diminutive insects as I: "And yet," said he, "I dare engage, those creatures have their titles and distinctions of honor; they contrive little nests and burrows that they call houses and cities; they make a figure in dress and equipage;[4] they love, they fight, they dispute, they cheat, they betray." And thus he continued on, while my color came and went several times with indignation to hear our noble country, the mistress of arts and arms, the scourge of France, the arbitress of Europe, the seat of virtue, piety, honor, and truth, the pride and envy of the world, so contemptuously treated.

A

But, as I was not in a condition to resent injuries, so, upon mature thoughts, I began to doubt whether I were injured or no. For, after having been accustomed several months to the sight and converse of this people, and observed every object upon which I cast mine eyes, to be of proportionable magnitude; the horror I had first conceived from their bulk and aspect was so far worn off, that if I had then beheld a company of English lords and ladies in their finery and birthday clothes[5] acting their several parts in the most courtly manner of strutting, and bowing, and prating;[6] to say the truth, I should have been strongly tempted to laugh as much at them as this king and his grandees did at me. Neither indeed could I forbear smiling at myself, when the queen used to

---

1. **salt-cellars:** dishes of salt.

2. **Whig . . . Tory:** the two chief political parties of England at that time.
3. *Royal Sovereign:* one of the largest British warships.
4. **equipage:** ceremonious display.
5. **birthday clothes:** new outfits worn on a royal birthday.
6. **prating:** talking pompously.

READING CHECK TEST

1. Gulliver was never invited to dine with the king and queen. (F)
2. Gulliver explains that he and the prince had many conversations about manners, religion, government, and other matters. (T)
3. The king asks Gulliver whether all

the people of his country are as brave as he. (F)
4. Gulliver is grateful there are no flies in the kingdom, since they'd have been as big as he. (F)
5. The king decides Gulliver's countrymen are an admirable people. (F)

CLOSURE
Call on students to comment on the irony of Swift's use of first-person point of view in this excerpt from *Gulliver's Travels*.

place me upon her hand toward a looking-glass, by which both our persons appeared before me in full view together; and there could nothing be more ridiculous than the comparison: so, that I really began to imagine myself dwindled many degrees below my usual size. . . .

I was frequently rallied[7] by the queen upon account of my fearfulness; and she used to ask me whether the people of my country were as great cowards as myself. The occasion was this. The kingdom is much pestered with flies in summer; and these odious insects, each of them as big as a Dunstable lark, hardly gave me any rest while I sat at dinner, with their continual humming and buzzing about mine ears. They would sometimes alight upon my victuals, and leave their loathsome excrement or spawn behind, which to me was very visible, although not to the natives of that country, whose large optics were not so acute as mine in viewing smaller objects. Sometimes they would fix upon my nose or forehead, where they stung me to the quick, smelling very offensively; and I could easily trace that viscous matter which our naturalists tell us enables those creatures to walk with their feet upward upon a ceiling. I had much ado to defend myself against these detestable animals, and could not forbear starting when they came on my face. It was the common practice of the dwarf to catch a number of these insects in his hand, as schoolboys do among us, and let them out suddenly under my nose, on purpose to frighten me, and divert the queen. My remedy was to cut them in pieces with my knife as they flew in the air; wherein my dexterity was much admired. . . .

He [the King] was perfectly astonished with the historical account I gave him of our affairs during the last century, protesting it was only a heap of conspiracies, rebellions, murders, massacres, rev-

olutions, banishments, the very worst effects that avarice, faction, hypocrisy, perfidiousness, cruelty, rage, madness, hatred, envy, lust, malice, or ambition could produce.

His Majesty in another audience was at pains to recapitulate the sum of all I had spoken, compared the questions he made with the answers I had given, then taking me into his hands, and stroking me gently, delivered himself in these words, which I shall never forget nor the manner he spoke them in: "My little friend Grildrig,[8] you have made a most admirable panegyric upon your country; you have clearly proved that ignorance, idleness, and vice may be sometimes the only ingredients for qualifying a legislator; that laws are best explained, interpreted, and applied by those whose interest and abilities lie in perverting, confounding, and eluding them. I observe among you some lines of an institution which in its original might have been tolerable, but these half erased and the rest wholly blurred and blotted by corruptions. It doth not appear from all you have said how any one virtue is required toward the procurement of any one station among you; much less that men are ennobled on account of their virtue, that priests are advanced for their piety or learning, soldiers for their conduct or valor, judges for their integrity, senators for the love of their country, or counselors for their wisdom. As for yourself," continued the king, "who have spent the greatest part of your life in traveling, I am well disposed to hope you may hitherto have escaped many vices of your country. But by what I have gathered from your own relation, and the answers I have with much pains wringed and extorted from you, I cannot but conclude the bulk of your natives to be the most pernicious race of little odious vermin that nature ever suffered to crawl upon the surface of the earth."

---

7. **rallied:** kidded.

8. **Grildrig:** the Brobdingnagian name for Gulliver.

A. Responding
Do you find this digression on the enormous flies amusing or disgusting? Why?

B. Characterization/Satire
Discuss how this passage is both consistent with the characterization of the king of Brobdingnag and a vehicle for the author's satire on contemporary English society. (The passage is consistent because it continues to show the king as a kindly, sensible man; it is satirical because the king's criticisms have pointed relevance to the England of Swift's day.)

1. The king first compares Gulliver to an insect.

2. According to Gulliver, English people think of themselves as noble, creative, powerful, virtuous, honorable, and truthful.

3. He can use his knife to cut to pieces the huge flies that annoy him.

4. According to the king, the qualifications for English legislators are ignorance, idleness, and vice.

Interpreting Meanings

5. The implication is that the king finds that the distinction between the two political factions, taken so seriously in British life, is silly and trivial.

6. He observes that the flies in Brobding-nag are as big as Dunstable larks.

7. Swift characterizes the king of Brobdingnag as philosophical and reflective. The king is also extremely intelligent and perceptive, as shown by his speeches to Gulliver. The action of taking Gulliver in his hand and stroking him gently may portray the king as kindly, or it may perhaps imply condescension.

(*Answers continue in left-hand column.*)

(*Continued from top.*)

8. Instances of verbal irony may include the following: Gulliver's indignation that the reputation of England for honor and virtue is being sullied by the king; the account of the immense flies; and Gulliver's reference to the history of the last century, followed by the king's reaction. Another instance of irony occurs toward the end of the section, where the king supposes that Gulliver's travels have made him wiser than his countrymen: In fact, Gulliver has learned little or nothing.

9. These incidents share a common, repulsive motif.

10. The principal evidence is to be found in Gulliver's indignant reaction to the king's comparison of human beings with insects.

11. Answers will vary.

Responding to the Story

Analyzing the Story

Identifying Facts

1. To what form of life does the king first compare Gulliver?
2. In comparison, what do English people think of themselves, according to Gulliver?
3. What feat of dexterity can Gulliver perform that impresses the Brobdingnagians?
4. From Gulliver's defense of England, the king evaluates English officials and institutions. According to the king, what are the qualifications for English legislators?

Interpreting Meanings

5. Explain why the king roars with laughter when he asks Gulliver whether he is a Whig or a Tory.
6. Why does Gulliver begin to think of himself as small?
7. How does Swift **characterize** the king of Brobdingnag? Which actions show the king's personality traits?

8. Point out some instances of **verbal irony** in this section of *Gulliver's Travels*.
9. What connections can you make between Gulliver's experience with the Brobdingnagian flies and the king's dismissal of humanity as "little odious vermin"?
10. What evidence can you find in the text to suggest that Gulliver is learning little or nothing from his experiences in Brobdingnag?
11. What do you think of the Brobdingnagian royal family? What faults and virtues do you see in them?

Writing About the Story

A Creative Response

Varying a Plot. Imagine a situation in which Gulliver, because of his relatively tiny size, would have a great advantage over the giants. Use this situation as the basis of a story in which Gulliver becomes a hero.

The Elements of Literature

SATIRE

A **satire** is any piece of writing designed to make its readers feel critical—of themselves, of their fellow human beings, of their society. Some satires are intended to make us laugh at human follies and weaknesses; others make us angry and indignant at human vices and crimes. In his long poem *The Rape of the Lock,* Alexander Pope provides many examples of the good-natured, laughable kind of satire. Like Pope's, Swift's satire also provokes, laughter, but often laughter of a bitter kind.

While satire is usually directed at humanity in general, or at groups of people such as clumsy surgeons or greedy lawyers, it also can be aimed at a particular individual. Pope, for instance, satirized a contemporary nobleman called Lord Hervey, whose foolish, simpering face and manner he found disgusting. Pope called him "Sporus" and "Lord Fanny" and ridiculed him in a couplet:

Eternal smiles his emptiness betray,
As shallow streams run dimpling all the way.

—Alexander Pope

In the same name-calling manner, Swift made fun of an actual politician whom he believed to be corrupt, the prime minister Sir Robert Walpole. He put Walpole in *Gulliver's Travels* and called him "Flimnap."

Satirists are dissatisfied with things as they are, and they want to make them better. Satirists differ from other people who want to do good, such as moralists, preachers, missionaries, crusaders, and the like, because instead of giving constructive advice, they emphasize what is wrong with the world and its inhabitants. They don't say, "Be good!" "Obey the Golden Rule!" "Put others before yourself!" Rather, they make fun of vicious, selfish, mean-spirited people in the hope that we—the readers—will see ourselves in such people and mend our ways. Satirists perform an important function in society when they expose errors and absurdities that we no longer

My little friend Grildrig, you have made a most admirable panegyric upon yourself and Country, but from what I can gather from your own relation & the answers I have with much pains wringed & extorted from you, I cannot but conclude you to be one of the most pernicious, little-odious reptiles, that nature ever suffer'd to crawl upon the surface of the Earth.

George III as the king of Brobdingnag inspects Napoleon as Gulliver.

A

notice because custom and familiarity have blinded us to them.

Many books have been written about the devices that satirists use to make folly and vice appear ridiculous and therefore unattractive. One of the most common of these devices is **exaggeration.** We must not expect satirists to be objective, to give both sides of a question, to show the good as well as the bad traits of a character. Instead, satirists are likely to exaggerate by picturing all politicians as corrupt, all clergymen as hypocritical, all teachers as pedantic, all young adults as irresponsible. They realize, of course, that such generalizations about professions and age groups cannot be a hundred percent accurate, but for satirical purposes exceptions do not count. Wildly exaggerated satire is conspicuous in such popular magazines as *Mad*—though *Mad's* satire lacks the moral purposes of Swift's and Pope's satire. It also lacks the subtlety of the best satire.

The great satirists expect their readers to be alert and intelligent enough to detect the presence of satire even when there is no exaggeration. For instance, Swift once wrote, without any explanation at all, this sentence: "Last week I saw a woman flayed, and you will hardly believe how much it altered her appearance for the worst." Since to "flay" a person is to peel off all her skin (a common form of capital punishment in those days), Swift's remark is a complete **understatement**—the opposite of an exag-

geration. Such a cruel act would seem to demand a much stronger response than merely saying it "altered her appearance for the worst." Actually, flaying would render a person horrible; it would kill her. By making the statement sound casual and off-handed, Swift implies that extreme cruelty is common, but that people do not become upset by it. Swift expresses his deep concern by pretending to have no concern at all.

Understatement is a form of **irony,** the device of saying one thing and meaning just the opposite. When irony is particularly cruel or cutting, it can come close to sarcasm. "Great!" we say sarcastically, when we actually mean "Terrible!" In literature, irony is extended far beyond mere sarcasm. Swift, for instance, once wrote a satirical pamphlet called *Directions for Servants,* which is ironic throughout. Under the pretense of telling servants how to behave, it actually tells them how to misbehave—and in great detail. Here, for instance, is how he advises servants to respond to their master's or a guest's request for a drink:

> When you carry a glass of liquor to any person who hath called for it, do not bob him on the shoulder, or cry, "Sir, or madam, here's the glass!" That would be unmannerly, as if you had a mind to force it down one's throat. But stand at the person's left shoulder and wait his time; and if he strikes it down with his elbow by forgetfulness, that was his fault and not yours.

—Jonathan Swift

Every house of any size at all had live-in servants in Swift's day; they did a lot of the work that our appliances do for us. Lacking telephones, people who needed to call a coach to their door would send a servant out to look for one. Here is how Swift advises a servant to carry out this errand:

> When you are ordered to call a coach, although it be midnight, go no farther than the door, for fear of being out of the way when you are wanted. And stand there bawling, "Coach! Coach!" for half an hour.

—Jonathan Swift

Since advice of this sort would result in nothing but noise and mess in a household, we know that Swift is using verbal irony. And there's a simple reason why he does so: Ironic advice is more amusing and much more effective than straightforward and sincere advice. Swift's instructions are much more memorable than saying "Be careful when you are serving a drink not to spill it" or "At midnight don't stand on the front doorstep and shout."

Of course, a writer who habitually uses irony runs the risk of being misunderstood, especially by people who cannot think and who are otherwise mentally inert. As an ironist, Swift earned a reputation for being scandalous, irresponsible, and even irreligious. Yet, he claimed he never wrote anything "without a moral view."

A. Discussing the Illustration

Put this cartoon in the political context of the times (seventy years after the publication of Swift's *Gulliver's Travels*). George III (1738–1820), of course, was the king who presided over the loss of the American colonies. Here, as the king of Brobdingnag (an admirable character), he inspects a tiny Napoleon and uses the words Swift gave the king (see text page 515). Napoleon (1769–1821) seized power after the French Revolution and eventually made himself emperor of France, extending his rule over most of Europe. The British finally defeated Napoleon at Waterloo in 1815.

? Is the cartoonist mocking Napoleon or the king? (Napoleon) Cite details from the text that help you interpret the cartoonist's message. If this cartoon were to be drawn today, who might be in Napoleon's place? (Any number of potentates or tyrants)

PREPARATION

1. BUILDING ON PRIOR KNOWLEDGE.
Before students begin reading, review with them the biographical information on Swift and his complex attitudes toward Ireland (see text pages 505–506). Ask students to predict what position Swift might be expected to have taken toward social misery in Ireland.

2. ESTABLISHING A PURPOSE. Before students begin reading, you might have them read the third writing assignment ("Relating the Essay to Current Events") on text page 524. This will help establish a purpose for their reading.

3. PREREADING JOURNAL. Before they read, have students write at least three sentences in which they tell how the engraving on text page 518 makes them feel.

A MODEST PROPOSAL

This is the best and most famous pamphlet that Swift wrote describing the desperate conditions in Ireland and protesting the English treatment of the Irish. For three years before Swift published the pamphlet in 1729, the Irish harvests had been so poor that little or nothing remained for the farmers after they had sold their crops to pay the rents demanded by their English landlords. Beggars were everywhere, many of them accompanied by starving children. Money was in short supply. Swift argued that most of the money was shipped off to England, where the landlords lived, and little remained in Ireland to be spent on Irish goods. English policies kept the Irish poor and hungry.

In *A Modest Proposal*, Swift offers an outrageous solution to these problems of human misery—perhaps the most outrageous solution ever offered. But there is nothing outrageous about Swift's manner. In his pamphlet, he assumes the role of a practical economic planner, pretending to be knowledgeable and objective, reasonable and fair, full of common sense and even benevolence. It is this difference between its straightforward style and its appalling content that gives the pamphlet its force.

Ultimately, Swift is protesting against a purely statistical view of humanity—a view that would reduce people to breeders and babies to meat. Swift risks appearing as a monster himself in order to expose the monstrous behavior of others. As you read, notice where in the story you first realize what Swift's modest proposal is.

A Weaver's Cottage by Charles Grignion (18th century). Engraving.

British Library.

SUPPLEMENTARY SUPPORT MATERIALS
1. Vocabulary Activity Worksheet (*CCB*)
2. Review and Response Worksheet: Elements of Satire (*CCB*)
3. Selection Test (*CCB*)

DEVELOPING VOCABULARY
The following words from the essay are tested in the Selection Test. (See also Vocabulary Activity Worksheet.)

rudiments   expedient
collateral   to disgress
to repine   to enumerate
scrupulous   inclemency
to censure

It is a melancholy object to those who walk through this great town[1] or travel in the country, when they see the streets, the roads, and cabin doors crowded with beggars of the female sex, followed by three, four, or six children, all in rags, and importuning every passenger for an alms.[2] These mothers, instead of being able to work for their honest livelihood, are forced to employ all their time in strolling to beg sustenance for their helpless infants; who, as they grow up, either turn thieves for want of work; or leave their dear native country to fight for the Pretender[3] in Spain, or sell themselves to the Barbadoes.[4]

I think it is agreed by all parties that this prodigious number of children in the arms, or on the backs, or at the heels of their mothers, and frequently of their fathers, is in the present deplorable state of the kingdom a very great additional grievance; and therefore, whoever could find out a fair, cheap, and easy method of making these children sound and useful members of the commonwealth would deserve so well of the public as to have his statue set up for a preserver of the nation.

But my intention is very far from being confined to provide only for the children of professed beggars: It is of a much greater extent, and shall take in the whole number of infants at a certain age who are born of parents in effect as little able to support them as those who demand our charity in the streets.

As to my own part, having turned my thoughts for many years upon this important subject, and maturely weighed the several schemes of other projectors,[5] I have always found them grossly mistaken in their computation. It is true, a child just dropped from its dam[6] may be supported by her milk for a solar year[7] with little other nourishment; at most not above the value of two shillings; which the mother may certainly get, or the value in scraps, by her lawful occupation of begging: and it is exactly at one year old that I propose to provide for them in such a manner, as, instead of being a charge upon their parents or the parish, or wanting[8] food and raiment[9] for the rest of their lives; they shall, on the contrary, contribute to the feeding and partly to the clothing of many thousands.

There is likewise another great advantage in my scheme, that it will prevent those voluntary abortions, and that horrid practice of women murdering their bastard children, alas! too frequent among us; sacrificing the poor innocent babes, I doubt,[10] more to avoid the expense than the shame; which would move tears and pity in the most savage and inhuman breast.

The number of souls[11] in Ireland being usually reckoned one million and a half; of these I calculate there may be about two hundred thousand couples whose wives are breeders; from which number I subtract thirty thousand couples who are able to maintain their own children, although I apprehend there cannot be so many under the present distresses of the kingdom; but this being granted, there will remain a hundred and seventy thousand breeders. I again subtract fifty thousand for those women who miscarry, or whose children die by accident or disease within the year. There only remain a hundred and twenty thousand children of poor parents annually born: The question therefore is, how this number shall be reared, and provided for? Which, as I have already said, under the present situation of affairs, is utterly impossible by all the methods hitherto proposed: For we can neither employ them in handicraft[12] or agriculture; we neither build houses (I mean in the country) nor cultivate land: They can very seldom pick up a livelihood by stealing until they arrive at six years old; except where they are of towardly parts;[13] although, I confess, they learn the rudiments much earlier; during which time they can, however, be properly looked upon only as probationers;[14] as I have been informed by a principal gentleman in the county of Cavan,[15] who protested to me that he never knew above one or two instances under the age of six, even in a part of the

---

1. **town:** Dublin.
2. **importuning . . . alms:** asking for a handout.
3. **the Pretender:** a son of the deposed King James II, who repeatedly tried to gain the English throne.
4. **sell themselves to the Barbadoes:** go to the West Indies and work as slaves to pay their passage.
5. **projectors:** speculators, schemers.
6. **dam:** mother (ordinarily used only of animals).
7. **solar year:** from the first day of spring in one year to the last day of spring in the next.

8. **wanting:** lacking, needing.
9. **raiment:** clothing.
10. **doubt:** suspect.
11. **souls:** people.
12. **handicraft:** manufacturing.
13. **towardly parts:** precocious abilities.
14. **probationers:** apprentices.
15. **Cavan:** an inland county in Ireland, remote from the civilization of Dublin.

A. Relevance
? Review this paragraph and discuss details that are relevant to social problems, and attitudes toward them, in our own day.

B. Purpose
? After finishing this paragraph, comment on Swift's purpose in writing his essay.

C. Irony
? How do these remarks about stealing reveal Swift's irony? (Swift mocks the English stereotype of the Irish as dishonest.) Is this attitude toward the poor common in our own day?

Literature and Language: Using Comparative Forms of Adjectives and Adverbs in Persuasive Writing
When one writes to persuade, using the wrong comparative forms—or using them too often—can detract from one's argument. Point out that in "A Modest Proposal" Jonathan Swift uses comparatives both correctly and sparingly, thus making his words appear moderate and sincere.

Point out as examples *quickest, last, tolerably, eminent, least, more thrifty,* and *highly* on page 520.

Have students form groups to rewrite this paragraph, reducing the number of comparatives and correcting the rest to achieve a tone similar to Swift's.

It should be our most highest priority to reduce the number of children named A and B in our more larger cities. First, the most lazy As and Bs must be zealously trimmed from the population, and the more influentialer immediately dispatched. Then all but the least lazy must be sent to other cities with a larger ratio of As and Bs to normalest citizens.

A. Responding

❓ What does footnote 18 reveal about the commonly held image of an American in Swift's time? What is Swift implying about Americans in this passage? (That they are cannibals—an obvious exaggeration)

B. Irony

❓ How do the mathematical and statistical references enhance the irony of the author's style? (They make the writer seem precise and "scientific," even as he proposes a shocking solution to the problem.)

C. Allusion

Note Swift's allusion to Lent, the period of fasting and penance before Easter. *Prolific* refers to the alleged capacity of fish to increase fertility. During Lent, people would abstain from meat and eat a lot of fish.

D. Emotional Effects

❓ What effect do these two paragraphs have on your feelings and moral sensitivities? (Distaste—but that may be a calculated response.)

kingdom so renowned for the quickest proficiency in that art.[16]

I am assured by our merchants that a boy or a girl before twelve years old is no salable commodity; and even when they come to this age, they will not yield above three pounds, or three pounds and half a crown at most, on the exchange, which cannot turn to account[17] either to the parents or the kingdom; the charge of nutriment and rags, having been at least four times that value.

I shall now therefore humbly propose my own thoughts; which I hope will not be liable to the least objection.

I have been assured by a very knowing American[18] of my acquaintance in London, that a young healthy child, well nursed is, at a year old, a most delicious, nourishing, and wholesome food, whether stewed, roasted, baked, or boiled; and I make no doubt that it will equally serve in a fricasee,[19] or ragout.[20]

I do therefore humbly offer it to public consideration, that of the hundred and twenty thousand children already computed, twenty thousand may be reserved for breed; whereof only one fourth part to be males; which is more than we allow to sheep, black cattle, or swine; and my reason is, that these children are seldom the fruits of marriage, a circumstance not much regarded by our savages; therefore, one male will be sufficient to serve four females. That the remaining hundred thousand, may at a year old be offered in sale to the persons of quality and fortune through the kingdom; always advising the mother to let them suck plentifully in the last month so as to render them plump and fat for a good table. A child will make two dishes at an entertainment for friends; and when the family dines alone, the fore or hind quarter will make a reasonable dish; and seasoned with a little pepper or salt, will be very good boiled on the fourth day, especially in winter.

I have reckoned upon a medium, that a child just born will weigh twelve pounds; and in a solar year, if tolerably nursed, increaseth to twenty-eight pounds.

I grant this food will be somewhat dear,[21] and therefore very proper for landlords; who, as they have already devoured[22] most of the parents, seem to have the best title to the children.

Infant's flesh will be in season throughout the year; but more plentiful in March, and a little before and after: for we are told by a grave author,[23] an eminent French physician, that fish being a prolific diet, there are more children born in Roman Catholic countries about nine months after Lent than at any other season: Therefore reckoning a year after Lent, the markets will be more glutted than usual; because the number of Popish[24] infants is at least three to one in this kingdom; and therefore it will have one other collateral advantage; by lessening the number of Papists among us.

I have already computed the charge of nursing a beggar's child (in which list I reckon all cottagers,[25] laborers, and four fifths of the farmers) to be about two shillings per annum, rags included; and I believe no gentleman would repine to give ten shillings for the carcass of a good fat child; which, as I have said, will make four dishes of excellent nutritive meat when he hath only some particular friend, or his own family, to dine with him. Thus the squire will learn to be a good landlord, and grow popular among his tenants; the mother will have eight shillings net profit, and be fit for work till she produceth another child.

Those who are more thrifty (as I must confess the times require) may flay[26] the carcass; the skin of which, artificially[27] dressed, will make admirable gloves for ladies and summer boots for fine gentlemen.

As to our city of Dublin; shambles[28] may be appointed for this purpose in the most convenient parts of it, and butchers we may be assured will not be wanting; although I rather recommend buying the children alive and dressing them hot from the knife, as we do roasting pigs.

A very worthy person, a true lover of his country, and whose virtues I highly esteem, was lately pleased, in discoursing on this matter, to offer a refinement upon my scheme. He said that many gentlemen of this kingdom, having of late de-

16. **art:** stealing.
17. **turn to account:** be profitable.
18. **American:** To Swift's readers, this label would suggest a barbaric person.
19. **fricasee:** a stew with a light gravy.
20. **ragout:** a highly flavored stew.
21. **dear:** expensive.

22. **devoured:** destroyed by charging high rents.
23. **author:** François Rabelais (1490?–1553), a French satirist.
24. **Popish:** Roman Catholic.
25. **cottagers:** tenant farmers.
26. **flay:** remove the skin.
27. **artificially:** skillfully.
28. **shambles:** slaughterhouses.

stroyed their deer; he conceived that the want of venison might be well supplied by the bodies of young lads and maidens not exceeding fourteen years of age, nor under twelve; so great a number of both sexes in every county being ready to starve for want of work and service:[29] and these to be disposed of by their parents, if alive, or otherwise by their nearest relations. But with due deference to so excellent a friend and so deserving a patriot, I cannot be altogether in his sentiments. For as to the males, my American acquaintance assured me from frequent experience that their flesh was generally tough and lean, like that of our schoolboys, by continual exercise, and their taste disagreeable; and to fatten them would not answer the charge. Then, as to the females, it would, I think with humble submission,[30] be a loss to the public, because they soon would become breeders themselves: And besides it is not improbable that some scrupulous people might be apt to censure such a practice (although indeed very unjustly) as a little bordering upon cruelty; which, I confess, hath always been with me the strongest objection against any project, how well soever intended.

But in order to justify my friend; he confessed that this expedient was put into his head by the famous Salmanaazor,[31] a native of the island Formosa, who came from thence to London above twenty years ago, and in conversation told my friend that in his country when any young person happened to be put to death, the executioner sold the carcass to persons of quality as a prime dainty, and that, in his time, the body of a plump girl of fifteen, who was crucified for an attempt to poison the emperor, was sold to his Imperial Majesty's prime minister of state, and other great mandarins[32] of the court, in joints[33] from the gibbet[34] at four hundred crowns. Neither indeed can I deny, that if the same use were made of several plump young girls in this town, who, without one single groat to their fortunes, cannot stir abroad without a chair,[35] and appear at the playhouse, and assemblies in foreign fineries, which

they never will pay for; the kingdom would not be the worse.

Some persons of a desponding spirit are in great concern about that vast number of poor people who are aged, diseased, or maimed; and I have been desired to employ my thoughts what course may be taken to ease the nation of so grievous an encumbrance. But I am not in the least pain upon that matter; because it is very well known that they are every day dying and rotting by cold and famine and filth and vermin[36] as fast as can be reasonably expected. And as to the younger laborers, they are now in almost as hopeful[37] a condition: They cannot get work, and consequently pine away for want of nourishment to a degree that if at any time they are accidentally hired to common labor they have not strength to perform it; and thus the country, and themselves, are in a fair way[38] of being delivered from the evils to come.

I have too long digressed; and therefore shall return to my subject. I think the advantages by the proposal which I have made are obvious and many, as well as of the highest importance.

For first, as I have already observed, it would greatly lessen the number of Papists, with whom we are yearly overrun; being the principal breeders of the nation, as well as our most dangerous enemies; and who stay at home on purpose, with a design to deliver the kingdom to the Pretender; hoping to take their advantage by the absence of so many good Protestants[39] who have chosen rather to leave their country than stay at home and pay tithes[40] against their conscience to an idolatrous Episcopal curate.

Secondly, the poorer tenants will have something valuable of their own, which, by law, may be made liable to distress[41] and help to pay their landlord's rent; their corn and cattle being already seized and money a thing unknown.

Thirdly, whereas the maintenance of a hundred thousand children from two years old and upward cannot be computed at less than ten shillings

---

29. **service:** employment as servants.
30. **with humble submission:** with all due respect to those who hold such opinions.
31. **Salmanaazor:** George Pslamanazar, a Frenchman who pretended to be a Formosan and whose writings were eventually exposed as fraudulent.
32. **mandarins:** officials.
33. **joints:** pieces of meat.
34. **gibbet:** gallows.
35. **chair:** sedan chair, a covered seat carried by servants.

36. **vermin:** pests such as lice, fleas, and bedbugs.
37. **hopeful:** hopeless.
38. **are in a fair way:** have a good chance.
39. **good Protestants:** that is, in Swift's view, bad Protestants, because they object to the Church of Ireland's bishops and regard them as "idolatrous Episcopal curate."
40. **tithes:** one tenth of one's income donated to the church.
41. **liable to distress:** that is, the money from the sale of their children may be seized by their landlords.

A. Irony

What is the ironic effect of the word *reasonably* in this passage? (The fact that the old are dying and rotting by cold and famine and filth and vermin is hardly a "reasonable" situation at all. It makes a reasonable person sick.) How does Swift combine this irony with emotionally loaded language? (He combines the irony with emotionally loaded words such as *filth* and *vermin*.)

B. Irony/Style

Note the ironic phrasing of Swift's second "advantage." Direct students' attention to the final observation that landlords have already seized the tenants' corn, cattle, and money.

A. Connotations

The exercise on language and style on text page 524 provides opportunity to examine the loaded language Swift uses throughout the essay, particularly in describing the Irish people in terms commonly used for animals.

B. Responding

[?] Are the other "expedients" listed here constructive suggestions? Why does Swift dismiss them? (His purpose is ironical; he suggested these other civilized remedies and they were rejected.) This passage reveals some biases of the eighteenth century: Note the cynical references to Laplanders and Brazilians (regarded as barbarians) and Jews.

apiece per annum, the nation's stock will be thereby increased fifty thousand pounds per annum; besides the profit of a new dish introduced to the tables of all gentlemen of fortune in the kingdom who have any refinement in taste; and the money will circulate among ourselves, the goods being entirely of our own growth and manufacture.[42]

Fourthly, the constant breeders, besides the gain of eight shillings sterling per annum by the sale of their children, will be rid of the charge of maintaining them after the first year.

Fifthly, this food would likewise bring great custom to taverns, where the vintners[43] will certainly be so prudent as to procure the best receipts for dressing it to perfection; and consequently, have their houses frequented by all the fine gentlemen who justly value themselves upon their knowledge in good eating; and a skillful cook, who understands how to oblige his guests, will contrive to make it as expensive as they please.

Sixthly, this would be a great inducement to marriage, which all wise nations have either encouraged by rewards or enforced by laws and penalties. It would increase the care and tenderness of mothers toward their children, when they were sure of a settlement for life to the poor babes provided in some sort by the public, to their annual profit instead of expense. We should soon see an honest emulation[44] among the married women, which of them could bring the fattest child to the market. Men would become as fond of their wives during the time of their pregnancy as they are now of their mares in foal, their cows in calf, or sows when they are ready to farrow;[45] nor offer to beat or kick them (as is too frequent a practice) for fear of a miscarriage.

Many other advantages might be enumerated. For instance, the addition of some thousand carcasses in our exportation of barreled beef: The propagation of swine's flesh, and improvement in the art of making good bacon; so much wanted among us by the great destruction of pigs, too frequent at our tables, and are no way comparable in taste or magnificence to a well-grown, fat, yearling child; which, roasted whole, will make a considerable figure at a Lord Mayor's feast, or any other public entertainment. But this, and many others, I omit, being studious of brevity.

Supposing that one thousand families in this city would be constant customers for infants' flesh, besides others who might have it at merry meetings, particularly weddings and christenings; I compute that Dublin would take off, annually, about twenty thousand carcasses; and the rest of the kingdom (where probably they will be sold somewhat cheaper) the remaining eighty thousand.

I can think of no one objection that will possibly be raised against this proposal; unless it should be urged that the number of people will be thereby much lessened in the kingdom. This I freely own; and it was indeed one principal design in offering it to the world. I desire the reader will observe, that I calculate my remedy for this one individual kingdom of Ireland, and for no other that ever was, is, or, I think, ever can be upon earth. Therefore, let no man talk to me of other expedients.[46] Of taxing our absentees[47] at five shillings a pound; of using neither clothes, nor household furniture, except what is of our own growth and manufacture; of utterly rejecting the materials and instruments that promote foreign luxury; of curing the expensiveness of pride, vanity, idleness, and gaming[48] in our women; of introducing a vein of parsimony,[49] prudence, and temperance; of learning to love our country, wherein we differ even from Laplanders and the inhabitants of Topinamboo;[50] of quitting our animosities and factions,[51] nor act any longer like the Jews, who were murdering one another at the very moment their city[52] was taken; of being a little cautious not to sell our country and consciences for nothing; of teaching landlords to have at least one degree of mercy

---

42. **own growth and manufacture:** home-grown edible children, not imported ones.
43. **vintners:** wine merchants.
44. **emulation:** competition.
45. **farrow:** produce piglets.

46. **other expedients:** At one time or another, Swift advocated all these expedients or measures for the relief of Ireland, but they had all been ignored by the government.
47. **absentees:** English people who refused to live on their Irish property.
48. **gaming:** gambling.
49. **parsimony:** economy.
50. **Topinamboo:** in Brazil.
51. **factions:** political parties.
52. **city:** Jerusalem, which the Roman Emperor Titus destroyed in A.D. 70, while Jewish factions fought one another.

READING CHECK TEST
1. Swift's proposal takes into account only the children of beggars. (F)
2. Swift says that the 120,000 children born to poor parents in Ireland could become useful, productive citizens if they were well-fed. (F)

3. The majority of male children would be saved for breeding purposes. (F)
4. Swift points out that one advantage of the proposal would be an increase in marriages. (T)
5. Swift recommends against exporting the new commodity. (T)

CLOSURE
Have students summarize the modest proposal and briefly discuss whether or not the shock value of the essay contributes to the effectiveness of its satire.

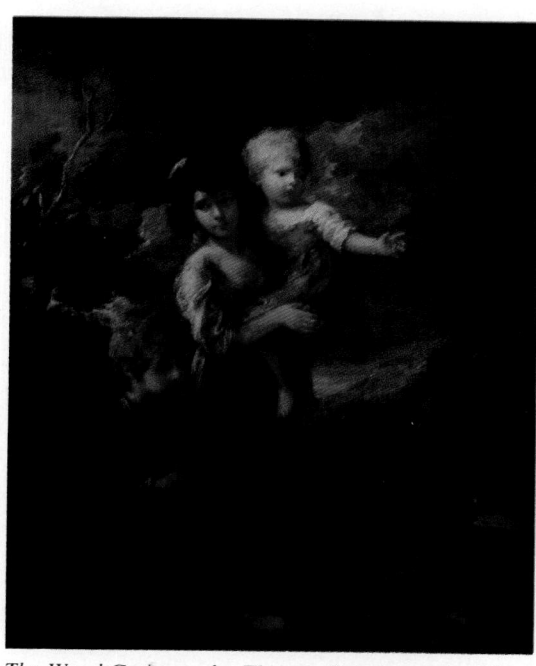

The Wood Gatherers by Thomas Gainsborough. Oil.

The Metropolitan Museum of Art, New York.
Bequest of Mary Stillman Harkness, 1950. (50.145.17).

toward their tenants. Lastly, of putting a spirit of honesty, industry, and skill into our shopkeepers; who, if a resolution could now be taken to buy only our native goods would immediately unite to cheat and exact[53] upon us in the price, the measure; and the goodness; nor could ever yet be brought to make one fair proposal of just dealing, though often and earnestly invited to it.

Therefore I repeat, let no man talk to me of these and the like expedients; till he hath, at least, a glimpse of hope that there will ever be some hearty and sincere attempt to put them in practice.

But as to myself; having been wearied out for many years with offering vain, idle, visionary thoughts; and at length utterly despairing of success, I fortunately fell upon this proposal; which, as it is wholly new, so it hath something solid and real, of no expense and little trouble, full in our own power; and whereby we can incur no danger in disobliging England: for this kind of commodity will not bear exportation; the flesh being of too tender a consistency, to admit a long continuance in salt; although perhaps I could name a country[54] which would be glad to eat up our whole nation without it.

After all, I am not so violently bent upon my own opinion as to reject any offer proposed by wise men which shall be found equally innocent, cheap, easy, and effectual. But before something of that kind shall be advanced in contradiction to my scheme and offering a better, I desire the author, or authors, will be pleased maturely to consider two points. First, as things now stand, how they will be able to find food and raiment for a hundred thousand useless mouths and backs. And secondly, there being a round million of creatures in human figure throughout this kingdom; whose whole subsistence,[55] put into a common stock, would leave them in debt two millions of pounds sterling; adding those, who are beggars by profession to the bulk of farmers, cottagers, and laborers with their wives and children, who are beggars in effect; I desire those politicians who dislike my overture, and may perhaps be so bold to attempt an answer, that they will first ask the parents of these mortals whether they would not at this day think it a great happiness to have been sold for food at a year old in the manner I prescribe; and thereby have avoided such a perpetual scene of misfortunes as they have since gone through; by the oppression of landlords; the impossibility of paying rent without money or trade; the want of common sustenance[56] with neither house nor clothes, to cover them from the <u>inclemencies</u> of the weather; and the most inevitable prospect of entailing[57] the like, or greater miseries, upon their breed forever.

I profess, in the sincerity of my heart, that I have not the least personal interest in endeavoring to promote this necessary work, having no other motive than the public good of my country by advancing our trade, providing for infants, relieving the poor, and giving some pleasure to the rich. I have no children by which I can propose to get a single penny; the youngest being nine years old and my wife past childbearing.

A. Humanities Connection: Responding to the Fine Art
Britain's Thomas Gainsborough (1727–1788) is among the most prominent portraitists and landscape painters of the eighteenth century. Among Gainsborough's early works are portraits of his sisters in a landscape. Generally, Gainsborough's landscapes are of idyllic scenes. During his later years, he painted seascapes and idealized full-size portraits of country children.

❓ What do you think may have been the experiences and feelings of the three young children shown in the painting? How does the landscape in the background reinforce the dominant mood?

B. Author's Purpose
❓ What do you think is the purpose of Swift's concluding paragraph? (It is for Swift to once again adopt the pose of an unbiased, benevolent advocate.)

53. **exact:** impose.

54. **country:** England.
55. **whole subsistence:** all their possessions.
56. **sustenance:** support for life.
57. **entailing:** passing on to the next generation.

1. The narrator says that the landlords should have the first claim on the flesh of the children, since the landlords have already devoured the parents.
2. The males are too tough and lean and their taste is disagreeable. Females would be a loss to the breeding population. Also, some think the practice borders on cruelty.
3. He says that they are dying off quickly enough in the natural course of events, due to cold, famine, filth, and vermin.
4. (1) Reduces number of Papists; (2) gives poor a tangible asset; (3) aids the economy; (4) breeders have to raise children for only one year; (5) increases tavern business; (6) encourages marriage.
5. The narrator anticipates the objection that the proposal, if carried out, would diminish the population.

Interpreting Meanings
6. Both the expression of the wish and the description of the proposal as "modest" are ironic, given the outlandish, monstrous character of the proposal. *(Answers continue in left-hand column.)*

(Continued from top.)
7. Restrained, judicious, constructive.
   See paragraph 1, sentence 1; paragraph 3, sentence 1; last paragraph, sentence 1.
8. The writer's underlying purpose is to criticize the cruelty and insensitivity of the English.
9. The purpose is ironic; Swift forces us to recognize Britain's failure to mount constructive programs to improve the miserable conditions in Ireland.
10. Answers should note Swift's efforts to reveal the bankruptcy of Britain's policy.
11. Answers will vary. Some students may feel that Swift's presentation is so extreme that it undermines the nonsatirical point he is trying to make.

Responding to the Essay

Analyzing the Essay

Identifying Facts

1. Why does the narrator think the food he proposes to be "very proper for landlords"?
2. Why does the narrator object to the suggestion of selling and eating the twelve- to fourteen-year-old children?
3. Why is the narrator not concerned about old people who are suffering from sickness, poverty, and neglect?
4. About midway in the pamphlet, the narrator lists the advantages to his proposal. What are the six principal advantages?
5. Describe the one objection which the narrator anticipates to his proposal.

Interpreting Meanings

6. Just as the narrator is about to make his "modest proposal," he says that he hopes it "will not be liable to the least objection." Why does he express this wish? Why does he call his proposal "modest"?
7. What impression does the speaker want readers to have of him? Find sentences in which the speaker **characterizes** himself favorably and claims to possess certain virtues that—considering the nature of his proposal—he could not possibly have.
8. Describe the narrator's purpose in asserting that England will not mind if Ireland kills and eats its babies. What element of **satire** is evident here?
9. Near the end of the pamphlet the speaker lists "other expedients" that might help lessen the present distress in Ireland. Some of these options are very constructive. Why, then, does the narrator say, "Let no man talk to me of other expedients"?
10. How would you state the **purpose** of this essay?
11. Do you think Swift goes too far in the essay? Why or why not?

Writing About the Essay

A Creative Response

1. **Writing a Newspaper Editorial.** Imagine that you do not get the point of *A Modest Proposal,* that you do not understand the irony but read the pamphlet as a straightforward plan for solving social and economic problems. Write a reply to Swift in the form of a modern newspaper editorial. Focus your attention on details that seem particularly cruel and horrible to you, and attack Swift for his complete lack of human-ity. You might give your reply a long, informative title, modeled on the one Swift gave his own pamphlet. Your editorial essay should be at least three paragraphs long.
2. **Responding to the Essay.** Suppose you are one of the poor Irish men or women discussed in the essay. Write a response to Swift. Will you applaud his efforts, or will you take another point of view?

A Critical Response

3. **Relating the Essay to Current Events.** Does *A Modest Proposal* have any relevance to contemporary problems? In a brief essay, describe how the essay could, or could not, be applied to some serious ethical or moral dilemma of today. Cite passages from the *Proposal* in your discussion. If you think the essay has contemporary relevance, you might try rewriting certain passages to illustrate its application to today's problem.

Analyzing Language and Style

Diction and Connotations

In an essay meant to persuade readers to accept a particular point of view, **diction,** or word choice, is important. Swift is particularly skillful in choosing words with strong **connotations**—that is, words loaded with strong feelings, associations, or even judgments. The essay is sprinkled with insulting remarks about mothers, fathers, husbands, landlords, cooks, shopkeepers, and so on. Here are some of Swift's loaded words:

savages	beggars	filth
male and female	rags	idolatrous
Popish infants	breeders	carcasses

In each instance, another word could have been chosen to create a different, less harsh effect. For the words *male* and *female,* for example, substitute the words *man* and *woman. Male* and *female,* used constantly throughout the essay, make us think of animals, not human beings, which is Swift's intention.

1. Find the passages where the words listed above are used. What is the effect of the word choice in each case?
2. What other words could have been used to create different emotional effects?

Alexander Pope (1688–1744)

Alexander Pope, the most important poet of the early eighteenth century, was a child prodigy. As a very little boy, he later admitted, he "lisped in numbers." That is, he could speak in meter even before he could pronounce English properly. Such a talented youth would ordinarily be educated at Cambridge or Oxford. But Pope's family was Roman Catholic, and the English laws at that time prohibited Roman Catholics from attending the universities as well as from voting and holding public office—and even from practicing their religion.

Pope's father, a retired linen merchant, could afford to educate his son at home, which was perhaps the best place for him since his health was very delicate. When little more than a baby, Pope was playing with some stones when a cow gored and trampled him. Even before that, he had contracted a kind of tuberculosis, probably from milk, which could easily become infected in those days before pasteurization. This disease dwarfed him and disfigured his body, so that eventually his servants had to lace him into a canvas brace before he could sit upright. Since he continually suffered pains in his head, bones, and joints, it is no wonder he spoke of his life as "this long disease." Yet the references to his health that Pope makes in his letters are always good-humored, even joking at times.

For a person as handicapped as he was, Pope led a remarkably busy and productive life. The best modern edition of his poems runs to eleven volumes, and of his letters to five. All his writings are the product of great care and study. He learned to read Italian and French, he taught himself Greek, and he mastered and consciously modeled many of his own poems on famous works in Latin. When he was sixteen, he began his poetic career, as the Roman poet Virgil did, by writing **pastorals**—poems describing the countryside. When he was twenty-three, he published *An Essay on Criticism,* a poem inspired in part by the Latin poet Horace's *Art of Poetry.* At twenty-four, he published a miniature classical epic, *The Rape of the Lock.* And before he was thirty, he had not only written two long poems

Alexander Pope by W. Hoare (17th century). Oil.

inspired by the Latin poet Ovid—*Eloisa to Abelard* and *Elegy to the Memory of an Unfortunate Lady*—but he had also translated into English two enormous Greek epics, Homer's *Iliad* and, with the help of two assistants, Homer's *Odyssey.* In these works, Pope was not at all limited by his classical models, but used them to make works that are new and original. For this reason, he is sometimes referred to as a neoclassical (that is, new classical) poet.

Pope's early, brilliant successes inspired envy in lesser writers, who lampooned and ridiculed him, especially after he had published an edition of Shakespeare that indeed contained some flaws. To defend himself he turned to satire, a kind of writing highly congenial to his temperament. *The Rape of the Lock* is a good-natured, comical kind of satire. The great satires of Pope's maturity include ambitious (and harsher) poems. *The Dunciad* (1728, enlarged and revised in 1742) attacks dull, uninteresting writers of all kinds and shows the forces of stupidity, ignorance, and folly taking over the whole world. The *Moral Essays* (1731–1735) pass moral judgments on certain kinds of men and women as

A. Imitation in Art

Discuss with students the neoclassical theory of "imitation," derived from the ancient Greek emphasis of *mimesis.* Remind students that, even in the Renaissance, "imitation" in art was not considered plagiarism; rather, the study and adaptation of worthy models could aid the artist in achieving a significant, new work. It was not until the Romantic period that modern theories of "originality" in the arts began to predominate.

B. Satire

John Dryden drew the distinction between Horatian (light, elegant) and Juvenalian (rough, savage) satire, referring to the Roman poets Horace (65–8 B.C.) and Juvenal (60–c. 136 A.D.) as the two great classical models for the genre. Although Pope was more attracted temperamentally to the Horatian type of satire, *The Dunciad* includes bitter, dark passages that might be called Juvenalian.

PREPARATION

1. BUILDING ON PRIOR KNOWLEDGE. Before students begin reading, remind them of the elements of balance and antithesis found in heroic couplets.

2. ESTABLISHING A PURPOSE. Before students begin reading, you might have them read question 1 on text page 528. Looking for familiar sayings will help students establish a purpose for their reading.

SUPPLEMENTARY SUPPORT MATERIALS

1. Vocabulary Activity Worksheet (*CCB*)
2. Review and Response Worksheet: Meaning (*CCB*)
3. Selection Test (*CCB*)

A. Humanities Connection: Responding to the Fine Art
Pope's house at Twickenham was famed for its beautiful gardens. Pope's many visitors from London would arrive on barges down the Thames.

❓ How would you describe the mood conveyed by this engraving? (Elegant, serene) Does the style of the house and grounds remind you of plantations in the American South? (Note the houses at the right and left used by servants or tenant farmers.)

well as on very rich people who lack common sense and good taste. Finally, *An Epistle from Mr. Pope to Dr. Arbuthnot* (1735), addressed to a fellow writer who was also a physician to Queen Anne and a man of general good sense, contains both a defense of Pope's career as a writer and attacks on his literary enemies. Among those attacked is Joseph Addison, whose ''character'' in the *Epistle* is quoted in the biography of Addison later in this unit.

As a man, Pope was, and still is, both loved and hated. In his lifetime, and long after, he had a reputation for cruelty, malice, and ill nature. It now seems clear that he had none of these bad qualities but could appear to have them when provoked—as a caged tiger would have them when poked with a stick. We now know that he was often goaded into writing satire, but that

does not necessarily prove that Pope himself was peevish and mean. On the contrary, Pope had a large circle of friends, men and women, including some of the best writers of the day, who found him good-natured, generous, and brilliant in conversation. His agreeable manners, his large expressive eyes, his way of dressing elegantly in bright colors, all made people forget his physical handicaps. Although he never married, he had intense relationships with two women: Martha Bount and Lady Mary Wortley Montague. At his beautiful estate on the bank of the Thames below London, he entertained important writers, artists, and political figures of the day. Pope became rich and famous; as for the people who raged against him, most of them are remembered today only because they disliked Alexander Pope.

A

Alexander Pope's House at Twickenham (18th century). Engraving.

Guildhall Library, London.

DEVELOPING VOCABULARY
The following words from the couplets are tested in the Selection Test. (See also Vocabulary Activity Worksheet.)
to err   to incline   amuck

CLOSURE
Have each student memorize one of these couplets. Then have them explain the basic features of the heroic couplet as a verse form.

A. Verse Form
Note the comparatively rare use of the triplet here.

B. Allusion
The allusion to the Pierian spring, said in antiquity to have inspired the nine Muses, is typical of Pope's style. Remind students that Pope (as opposed to Defoe, Bunyan, or even Addison) wrote for a highly educated, upper-class audience. Such classical allusions were considered elegant, rather than pretentious, by his readers.

C. Rhythm
Note the retardation of the rhythm in the second line of the couplet. How does this rhythmical effect subtly mirror the sense? (The pauses dictated by the commas correspond to the idea of suspended hope.)

D. Expansion/Style
The admiration for Newton is thoroughly typical of writers such as Pope in the early eighteenth century, to whom Newton's laws seemed proof of the orderliness of nature on a universal scale. Notice Pope's elegant, and yet respectful, "turn" on the famous divine command in Genesis: "Let there be light."

Pope is the greatest master of the *heroic couplet*, so called because both he and his predecessor Dryden used this verse form in their translations of the epic poems of antiquity. Each heroic couplet consists of two rhymed lines of iambic pentameter. (For variety, Pope occasionally introduces a *triplet*.) Many express a thought in a complete sentence; such a couplet is called *closed*:

Trust not yourself; but your defects to know,
Make use of every friend—and every foe.

Although this couplet, from *An Essay on Criticism*, is part of a long and carefully organized explanation, it still makes good sense when it is plucked out of its context and allowed to stand by itself. Yet removing couplets from the poems in which they are embedded is dangerous, because it may lead us to think of the poems as strings of beads that can be easily broken apart. In reality, Pope's couplets are so carefully arranged into verse-paragraphs that they are more like the forged links of an iron chain than separable units.

Heroic Couplets

1

A
Music resembles poetry: in each
Are nameless graces[1] which no methods[2] teach,
And which a master-hand alone can reach.
    —*An Essay on Criticism,*
    lines 143–145

2

B
A little learning is a dangerous thing;
Drink deep, or taste not the Pierian[3] spring.
    —*An Essay on Criticism,*
    lines 215–216

3

Be not the first by whom the new are tried,
Nor yet the last to lay the old aside.
    —*An Essay on Criticism,*
    lines 335–336

4

Be thou the first true merit to befriend;
His praise is lost, who stays till all commend.
    —*An Essay on Criticism,*
    lines 474–475

5

Good nature and good sense must ever join:
To err is human; to forgive, divine.
    —*An Essay on Criticism,*
    lines 524–525

6

Hope springs eternal in the human breast:
Man never is, but always to be, blessed. C
    —*An Essay on Man,*
    Epistle I, lines 95–96

7

'Tis education forms the common mind:
Just as the twig is bent the tree's inclined.
    —*Moral Essays,*
    Epistle I, lines 149–150

8

Nature[4] and Nature's laws lay hid in night:
God said, "Let Newton[5] be!" and all was light. D
    —*The Present State of the
    Republic of Letters*

9

But when to mischief mortals bend their will,
How soon they find fit instruments of ill!
    —*The Rape of the Lock,*
    Canto III, lines 125–126

10

Satire's my weapon, but I'm too discreet
To run amuck, and tilt at all I meet.
    —*Imitations of Horace, Satire I,*
    Book II, lines 69–70

---

1. **nameless graces:** pleasing passages that cannot be explained.
2. **methods:** instruction books showing how to write poems.
3. **Pierian:** the spring that inspired the Muses.

4. **Nature:** the physical world.
5. **Newton:** Sir Isaac Newton (1642–1727), the English mathematician and physicist who formulated the laws of gravity.

ANALYZING THE COUPLETS
Identifying Details
1. Student answers will vary.
2. a. Couplet 3; b. Couplet 1; c. Couplet 6; d. Couplet 3 might be construed as doing so; e. Couplet 7; f. Couplet 5; g. Couplet 8, which echoes the first chapter of Genesis, in which God says, "Let there be light."

Interpreting Meanings
3. For one example, someone who knows a little bit about medicine decides on his own treatment and gets sicker.

On the one hand, drinking "deep" implies a detailed knowledge of a subject; on the other hand, drinking superficially implies a fragmentary, imperfect knowledge that may lead its possessor into error or danger.

4. The word *night* suggests obscurity and ignorance; the word *light* suggests intellectual understanding and true reason.
5. The rhyme in couplet 5 shows that the word *join* was pronounced in Pope's day to rhyme with *divine*.
6. Answers will vary. Most students will agree that Pope gains the values of pithi- (*Answers continue in left-hand column.*)

(Continued from top.)
ness and memorability. Many of the couplets are so compressed and artfully constructed that they might qualify as epigrams.
7. Answers will vary. Encourage students to explain and support their opinions.

Responding to the Couplets

Analyzing the Couplets

Identifying Details

1. List some of the old sayings that you recognized in the couplets.
2. Tell in which of the couplets Pope does each of the following:

   a. Advocates a mean between two extremes.
   b. Suggests that geniuses are born, not made.
   c. Explains why people are never satisfied with what they have.
   d. Compares writing to putting on clothes.
   e. Shows how important education is for the young.
   f. Advises critics to be generous.
   g. Assumes that his readers know the Biblical story of creation.

Interpreting Meanings

3. Give some examples showing how a little learning can be dangerous (Couplet 2). What is the difference between drinking "deep" and drinking superficially from the Pierian spring on Mt. Olympus, Greece, from which the Muses drew their inspiration?
4. In the couplet on Newton, explain the difference between what is suggested by the words *night* and *light*.
5. Which couplet shows that the pronunciation of a common word has changed since Pope's day?
6. Pope compresses a large amount of meaning into the twenty or so syllables of his couplets. Try writing out, in your own words, the idea expressed in any couplet that you find hard to understand. What does Pope gain by compressing his meaning?
7. Do you find the advice in these couplets useful, or does it seem out of date? Explain your response.

Analyzing Language and Style

Pope's Poetics

Although heroic couplets follow a rigid metrical pattern, Pope takes pains to keep them from being monotonous. For instance, he varies the location of the main pause within the line, as in this quotation from a poem about a dead woman (note the position of the commas):

> Poets themselves must fall, like those they sung:
> Deaf the praised ear, and mute the tuneful tongue.
> Even he, whose soul now melts in mournful lays,
> Shall shortly want the generous tear he pays.

Some lines move fast; some are slow:

> See the bold youth strain up the threating steep,
> Rush through the thickets, down the valleys sweep,
> Hand o'er their coursers' heads with eager speed,
> And earth rolls back beneath the flying steed.

In the first line of this passage Pope uses language that imitates the effort of riding a horse uphill; in the second, the speed of riding downhill. For variety, Pope occasionally introduces *triplets*—three rhymed lines instead of two.

1. Find examples of pauses located in different places within the lines in the couplets.
2. Find an example of a rhymed triplet.
3. Find an example in the couplets of a line that moves along quickly. What words create the effect? (Consider assonance and alliteration as well as length of words.)

Pope habitually expresses himself in **antitheses** (an·ti' thə·sēs). An antithesis uses parallel structures to present a balanced contrast: "Give me liberty, or give me death." ("Give me liberty or kill me" fails as an antithesis because it isn't parallel or balanced.) List all the antitheses you can find in these couplets.

Pope had a dog named Bounce, one of whose puppies he gave to his friend Frederick, Prince of Wales. Pope had this couplet engraved on the puppy's collar. An epigram is a short poem, often satirical, which ends in a witticism or clever turn of thought. Kew is where the Prince lived. To whom do you think the epigram is addressed? (Don't say, "the Prince," because surely the Prince knows his own dog.)

> **Epigram Engraved on the Collar of a Dog**
> I am his Highness' dog at Kew.
> Pray tell me, sir, whose dog are you?

PREPARATION
ESTABLISHING A PURPOSE. See question 2.

DEVELOPING VOCABULARY
The following words from the poem are tested in the Selection Test. (See also Vocabulary Activity Worksheet.)
surge   torrent   to scour

CLOSURE
Hold a brief class discussion in which students give their opinions of Pope's theory that the sound and form of poetry can mirror the sense, or content.

SUPPLEMENTARY SUPPORT MATERIALS
1. Vocabulary Activity Worksheet (CCB)
2. Review and Response Worksheet: Meaning (CCB)
3. Selection Test (CCB)

In this *verse essay*, a long poem of 744 lines, Pope tells literary critics how to distinguish between good and bad writing. In the following excerpt, Pope is speaking to poets as well as to their critics. He tells them that in a good poem the elements of sound and sense must be perfectly compounded so that one reinforces the other.

Pope has in mind particular passages in Homer's and Virgil's epics which describe physical actions. Like those famous poets of antiquity, Pope wants his verses to be read aloud. As you read aloud, listen for the sounds that help you understand the meaning of the poem.

from An Essay on Criticism

True ease in writing comes from art, not chance,
As those move easiest who have learned to dance.
'Tis not enough no harshness gives offense,
The sound must seem an echo to the sense:
5 Soft is the strain when Zephyr° gently blows,
And the smooth stream in smoother numbers° flows;
But when loud surges lash the sounding shore,
The hoarse, rough verse should like the torrent roar:
When Ajax° strives some rock's vast weight to throw,
10 The line too labors, and the words move slow;
A Not so, when swift Camilla° scours the plain,
Flies o'er the unbending corn,° and skims along the main.°

5. **Zephyr:** a soft, gentle breeze.
6. **numbers:** rhythms.
9. **Ajax:** a strong warrior in Homer's *Iliad*.
11. **Camilla:** a warrior-maiden in Virgil's *Aeneid*.
12. **corn:** wheat. **main:** here, a flat expanse of land.

Responding to the Poem

Analyzing the Poem

Identifying Details
1. What, according to Pope, do writing poetry and dancing have in common?
2. Summarize the advice Pope gives to poets here.

Interpreting Meanings
3. In what ways have both poetry and dancing changed since Pope's day? Think of ways in which the changes in these two activities may be related.

Writing About the Poem

A Creative Response
Creating Sounds. List some subjects for poems that, according to Pope's advice, would require smooth and soft sounds. List other subjects that would require harsh, rough sounds. Then try writing a line or two using both kinds of sound.

A. Sound Effects/Rhythm
How are the sound and rhythm of lines 9–12 elegantly adapted to the sense? (The long vowels in lines 9–10 slow the lines down; the spondees in the one-syllable words also give the lines a slow, heavy beat. The s sounds suggest the sound of wind blowing, and the iambs in lines 11–12 give these lines a lilting, swift beat.)

ANALYZING THE POEM
Identifying Details
1. Poetry and dancing both depend on learning and art.
2. Pope advises that the sound of a poem must harmoniously echo and reinforce its meaning; in other words, a poem's form must be suited to its content.

Interpreting Meanings
3. Student answers will vary. In general, most students will agree that both dancing and poetry have become freer, or at least more flexible, in form.

PREPARATION

ESTABLISHING A PURPOSE. Before students begin reading, have them read question 4.

SUPPLEMENTARY SUPPORT MATERIALS
1. Vocabulary Activity Worksheet (*CCB*)
2. Review and Response Worksheet: Meaning (*CCB*)
3. Selection Test (*CCB*)
4. Instructional Overhead Transparency

DEVELOPING VOCABULARY

The following words from the poem are tested in the Selection Test. (See also Vocabulary Activity Worksheet.)

to presume	to deem
isthmus	chaos

A. Metaphor

[?] How is the word *isthmus* especially appropriate here? (An isthmus is a narrow strip of land bordered on both sides by water. According to Pope, man is bordered by angels and beasts, or heaven and hell.)

ANALYZING THE POEM

Identifying Details

1. Possibilities include wisdom, knowledge, judgment, and the ability to reason.

Possibilities include weakness, doubt, error, ignorance, and passion.

2. There are two sentences in the verse.

Interpreting Meanings

3. Student answers will vary. Ask them to explain the specific possibilities that they suggest.

4. Again, answers will vary. Possibilities might include "ambiguous," "paradoxical," "contradictory," "middle," "wonder-miserable," and so on.

5. Encourage students to give reasons for their opinions as they discuss the couplet.

An Essay on Man is Pope's long (1,304 lines) philosophical poem, published when he was forty-five. A lifetime of reading, in both English and foreign languages, went into its composition. The poem is concerned not only with "man," by which Pope means the whole human race, but with the entire universe as well. It's important to know that the ideas in the poem are not merely the private notions of Pope and his friends, but that they come from many authors including Plato, Aristotle, St. Thomas Aquinas, Dante, Erasmus, Shakespeare, Bacon, and Milton.

In the following lines from the *Essay,* Pope generalizes about the human race. Pope's "man" is all of us. Do you agree that everyone has the characteristics Pope describes?

from An Essay on Man

Know then thyself,° presume not God to scan;°
The proper study of mankind is Man.
A Placed on this isthmus of a middle state.°
A being darkly wise, and rudely great:
5   With too much knowledge for the skeptic° side,
With too much weakness for the Stoic's pride,°
He hangs between; in doubt to act, or rest,
In doubt to deem himself a god, or beast;
In doubt his mind or body to prefer,
10 Born but to die, and reasoning but to err;
Alike in ignorance, his reason such,
Whether he thinks too little, or too much:
Chaos of thought and passion, all confused;
Still° by himself abused, or disabused;°
15 Created half to rise, and half to fall;
Great lord of all things, yet a prey to all;
Sole judge of truth, in endless error hurled:
The glory, jest, and riddle of the world!

1. **Know . . . thyself:** a moral precept of Socrates and other ethical philosophers. **scan:** pry into, speculate about.
3. **middle state:** that is, having the rational intellect of angels and the physical body of beasts.
5. **skeptic:** The ancient Skeptics doubted that humans can gain accurate knowledge of anything. They emphasized the limitations of human knowledge.
6. **Stoic's pride:** The ancient Stoics' ideal was a calm acceptance of life; human beings should be indifferent to both pain and pleasure. Stoics are called proud because they refused to recognize human limitations.

14. **Still:** always, continually. **disabused:** undeceived.

Responding to the Poem

Analyzing the Poem

Identifying Details

1. In almost every sentence of this passage, Pope says something flattering about the human race, only to follow it with something insulting. What characteristics does he think we should be proud of? What should we be ashamed of?

2. How many sentences are in this verse?

Interpreting Meanings

3. In what ways do you think human beings could be seen as the "glory" of this world? As its "jest"? As its "riddle"?

4. What one word would you use to summarize the human condition as Pope describes it? Why do you choose this word?

5. Discuss your opinion of Pope's opening couplet.

Writing About the Poem

A Creative Response

Writing an Illustration. Write an account of an experience which could illustrate Pope's analysis of the conflicting aims and desires within human beings. Perhaps you have been confronted with a choice between doing what you ought to do and doing what you like to do. You may write in the first person about yourself or invent a character.

READING CHECK TEST

1. Pope states that superficial learning is better than none. (F)
2. Pope encourages the reader to be the first to try new things. (F)
3. Pope tells poets that sound is as important as sense (meaning). (T)

4. Pope states that man should study himself before speculating about God. (T)
5. Pope states that man is a riddle who exists in a "middle state" between angels and beasts. (T)

CLOSURE
Have students memorize the first two lines and briefly explain why Pope makes this statement.

Alexander Pope. Self-portrait. Oil.   Bryn Mawr College, Bryn Mawr, Pennsylvania.

A

A. Humanities Connection: Responding to the Fine Art
In this portrait, Pope is seen reflecting among the ruins of Rome and holding in his hand a sepia drawing of the Prodigal Son.
? What elements of the self-portrait show Pope's allegiance to classical antiquity for aesthetic models? (Roman architecture and statuary) What mood is suggested by the pose of the figure and the expression on the face? (Contemplative, relaxed) How does Pope deal with his physical deformity in the painting? (He props himself up against the statuary. His legs look pitifully thin and bent. His hump is hidden.) What may be the purpose of the skull and the plaque above the figure's head and of the broken statue at Pope's feet? (Reminders that life and fame are fleeting. Note also the Latin inscription *Sic transit gloria mundi,* "thus passes the glory of the world.")

Alexander Pope   531

Discuss the elements of classical epic with which students may be familiar from previous reading of such epics as Homer's *Iliad* and *Odyssey*. For example: the invocation to the muse, the use of the supernatural, the hero, a descent to the underworld, battle scenes, speech introductions, extended epic similes, pro-phetic dreams, and formulaic scenes of sacrifice and supplication.

2. ESTABLISHING A PURPOSE. Remind students that by writing about a quarrel in real life, Pope risked the displeasure and misunderstanding of those involved. Therefore, an especially critical element of *The Rape of the Lock* is the author's tone. Ask students to be sensitive to the tone of the mock epic as they read.

3. PREREADING JOURNAL. Before they read, have students write at least three sentences describing an incident that could be described as "making a mountain out of a molehill" or "a tempest in a teapot."

A. Humanities Connection: About the Fine Art

In trying to visualize the invisible sylphs, illustrators previous to Stothard had recalled comparable creatures from ancient and Renaissance art: cupids and cherubim, for example. Stothard, in converting sylphs to winged fairylike creatures, is one of the first illustrators to provide fairies with wings like those of a butterfly, an innovation copied by subsequent artists.

When Pope wrote about people, he wrote mainly about the rich, perhaps because the general public which he addressed in his works found it more interesting to read about the rich than about the poor. (Things have not changed much since Pope's day. Notice the newspapers and magazines at the supermarket checkout counter: They are mainly concerned with rich and famous people, those in politics, sports, show business, and society. Ordinary Americans are even very much interested in royalty.)

The chief characters in *The Rape of the Lock* all belong to the leisured classes; they spend their time amusing themselves rather than working for a living.

The title of Pope's comic masterpiece means "the violent theft of a lock of hair." The poem is based on a real incident. The lock in question belonged to a certain rich and fashionable young lady named Arabella Fermor. The theft in question was committed by a certain rich and fashionable young man named Robert, Lord Petre. When Robert snipped a curl from Arabella's hairdo he set off a quarrel between the Fermor and the Petre families. Had the two families been less sensible, their row might have escalated into the bitter hatred that destroyed Romeo and Juliet in Shakespeare's tragedy. As it turned out, the feud subsided into laughter—thanks to Alexander Pope.

At the suggestion of a friend of the two families and a patron of Pope's, Pope composed *The Rape of the Lock*, changing the name of Arabella to Belinda and calling Robert "the Baron." To make the warring families realize how trivial the so-called "rape" actually was, Pope treated it very, very seriously. He dressed his poem in all the trappings of heroic poetry, as though he were Homer or Virgil writing an epic of the fall of Troy.

Pope's contemporaries had the pleasure of recognizing many similarities between the poem and serious epics like the *Iliad* and the *Aeneid*, works which were then familiar to all educated readers. For instance, such readers would recognize that Pope's poem begins like a proper epic, with a statement of the subject and an invocation to the muse—a female deity who was supposed to inspire poets and other artists and make them "creative." Such readers would also recognize the epic device of a warning dream; such a dream comes to Belinda from a supernatural being. The classical ep-

Cutting the Lock by Thomas Stothard (1798). Watercolor.   **A**

Robert Halsband Collection, New York.

ics all have gods and goddesses who intervene in human affairs. Milton, in *Paradise Lost*, uses several kinds of angels as his superhuman agents. Following these models, Pope invents some tiny, airy spirits called sylphs, who try in vain to prevent the rape from taking place. Since epics always include battles, Pope inserts a card-game into his poem as well as a screaming match after Belinda loses her curl. In the complete poem of 794 lines (254 of which appear here), there are many such parallels to serious epics.

A poem like *The Rape of the Lock* is called a *mock epic*. The comedy of a mock epic arises from the discrepancy between the subject and its treatment: the subject is trivial; the treatment is grandiose. In mock epics, fleas become elephants and cracked tea cups become major catastrophes. Using in a comic way the traditional epic devices, which Pope respected and admired very much, he was able to give them new life in an age when they were rapidly becoming obsolete.

SUPPLEMENTARY SUPPORT MATERIALS
1. Vocabulary Activity Worksheet (*CCB*)
2. Review and Response Worksheet:
Mock Epic (*CCB*)
3. Selection Test (*CCB*)
4. Audiocassette recording

DEVELOPING VOCABULARY
The following words from the poem are
tested in the Selection Test. (See also
Vocabulary Activity Worksheet.)

dire	to interpose
to plait	assignation
labyrinth	pungent
to ogle	ponderous
stratagem	to ravish

from The Rape of the Lock

Canto I

A

What <u>dire</u> offense from amorous causes springs,
What mighty contests rise from trivial things,
I sing—This verse to Caryll,° Muse! is due:
This, even Belinda may vouchsafe° to view:

5 Slight is the subject, but not so the praise,
If she inspire, and he approve my lays.
　　Say what strange motive, Goddess! could compel
A well-bred lord to assault a gentle belle?°
Oh, say what stranger cause, yet unexplored,

10 Could make a gentle belle reject a lord?
In tasks so bold can little men engage,
And in soft bosoms dwells such mighty rage?

B

　　Sol° through white curtains shot a timorous ray,
and oped those eyes that must eclipse the day.

15 Now lapdogs give themselves the rousing shake,
And sleepless lovers just at twelve awake:
Thrice rung the bell, the slipper knocked the ground,°
And the pressed watch° returned a silver sound.
Belinda still her downy pillow pressed,

20 Her guardian Sylph prolonged the balmy rest:
'Twas he had summoned to her silent bed
The morning dream that hovered o'er her head.
A youth more glittering than a birthnight beau°
(That even in slumber caused her cheek to glow)

25 Seemed to her ear his winning lips to lay,
And thus in whispers said, or seemed to say:
　　"Fairest of mortals, thou distinguished care
Of thousand bright inhabitants of air! . . .
Hear and believe! thy own importance know,

30 Nor bound thy narrow views to things below. . . .
Know, then, unnumbered spirits round thee fly,
The light militia of the lower sky:
These, though unseen, are ever on the wing,
Hang o'er the box,° and hover round the ring.°

35 Think what an equipage° thou hast in air,
And view with scorn two pages and a chair.° . . .
　　"Of these am I, who thy protection claim,
A watchful sprite, and Ariel° is my name.
Late, as I ranged the crystal wilds of air,

40 In the clear mirror of thy ruling star°
I saw, alas! some dread event impend,
Ere to the main° this morning sun descend,
But Heaven reveals not what, or how, or where:
Warned by the Sylph, O pious maid, beware!

45 This to disclose is all thy guardian can:
Beware of all, but most beware of Man!"

3. **Caryll:** John Caryll, who suggested that Pope write this poem.
4. **vouchsafe:** condescend.

8. **belle:** beautiful young woman.

13. **Sol:** the sun.

17. **ground:** floor. Belinda beats the floor with her slipper to summon her maid, who has ignored the bell.
18. **watch:** one that chimes when its stem is pressed.

23. **birthnight beau:** a young man splendidly dressed in honor of a royal birthday.

34. **box:** seat in a theater. **ring:** circular drive in London's Hyde Park, where fashionable people rode.
35. **equipage:** a splendid carriage with attending footmen and other uniformed servants.
36. **chair:** compared with her supernatural attendants, Belinda's sedan chair and two pages are a contemptible equipage.
38. **Ariel:** Pope derives this name for an attendant spirit from Shakespeare's comedy *The Tempest.*
40. **star:** the planet governing Belinda that day, according to astrology.
42. **main:** ocean. Ariel is saying that, before sunset, disaster will strike.

A. Style

[?] How does this passage imitate the classical epic's invocation to the muse? (It imitates the invocation in that it mentions the Muse and contains the words *I sing* and the inverted syntax.)

B. Setting

[?] How do these lines immediately set the scene for the level of society about which Pope is writing? (The details of the curtains, the lapdogs, the watch, and the lovers sleeping till noon indicate an upperclass society.)

A. What "epic"
significance
does the word *voy-
age* have in the ti-
tle of this painting,
and how is its use
here comically
overstated? (A
voyage in the *Od-
yssey,* for exam-
ple, is an overseas
voyage that is filled
with monsters and
storms. Belinda is
simply taking a
comfortable barge
to another stately
home down the riv-
er.)

B. Humor

B. Why does Pope
juxtapose Belin-
da's reading of the
billet-doux with the
disappearance of
the warning vision?
What is amusing
about this juxtapo-
sition? (Pope im-
plies that Belinda's
flirtatiousness is in-
compatible with the
"divine" protection
of the sylphs.)

C. Parody

C. Which details in
these lines
about Belinda's
dressing table par-
ody descriptions of
religious ritual in
serious epic? (De-
tails are: "head un-
covered," the
"heavenly image,"
the "inferior priest-
ess at her altar's
side," and the "sa-
cred rites.")

*Belinda on Her Voyage to Hampton
Court* by Thomas Stothard
(1798). Watercolor.

Robert Halsband Collection, New York.

A

He said; when Shock, who thought she slept too long,
Leaped up, and waked his mistress with his tongue.
'Twas then, Belinda, if report say true,
50 Thy eyes first opened on a billet-doux;°
B Wounds, charms, and ardors were no sooner read,
But all the vision vanished from thy head.
    And now, unveiled, the toilet° stands displayed,
Each silver vase in mystic order laid.
55 First, robed in white, the nymph intent adores,
With head uncovered, the cosmetic powers.
A heavenly image in the glass appears;
To that she bends, to that her eyes she rears.
C The inferior priestess,° at her altar's side,
60 Trembling begins the sacred rites of Pride.
Unnumbered treasures ope at once, and here
The various offerings of the world appear;
From each she nicely culls with curious° toil,
And decks the goddess with the glittering spoil.
65 This casket° India's glowing gems unlocks,
And all Arabia° breathes from yonder box.

50. **billet-doux:** love letter.

53. **toilet:** dressing table.

59. **priestess:** Betty, the maid.

63. **curious:** careful.

65. **casket:** jewel box.
66. **Arabia:** a source of scents.

The tortoise here and elephant unite,
Transformed to combs, the speckled and the white.
Here files of pins extend their shining rows,
70 Puffs, powders, patches,° Bibles,° billet-doux.
Now awful Beauty puts on all its arms;°
The fair each moment rises in her charms,
Repairs her smiles, awakens every grace,
And calls forth all the wonders of her face;
75 Sees by degrees a purer blush arise,
And keener lightnings quicken in her eyes.
The busy Sylphs surround their darling care,
These set the head, and those divide the hair,
Some fold the sleeve, whilst others plait the gown;
A
80 And Betty's praised for labors not her own.

Canto II

. . . This nymph, to the destruction of mankind,
Nourished two locks which graceful hung behind
In equal curls, and well conspired to deck
With shining ringlets the smooth ivory neck.
5 Love in these labyrinths his slaves detains,
And mighty hearts are held in slender chains.
With hairy springes° we the birds betray.
Slight lines of hair surprise the finny prey,°
Fair tresses man's imperial race ensnare,
10 And beauty draws us with a single hair.
  The adventurous Baron the bright locks admired,
He saw, he wished, and to the prize aspired.
Resolved to win, he meditates the way,
By force to ravish, or by fraud betray;
15 For when success a lover's toil attends,
B Few ask if fraud or force attained his ends. . . .

Canto III

Close by those meads, forever crowned with flowers,
Where Thames with pride surveys his rising towers,
There stands a structure° of majestic frame,
Which from the neighboring Hampton takes its name.
5 Here Britain's statesmen oft the fall foredoom
Of foreign tyrants and of nymphs at home;
Here thou, great Anna!° whom three realms obey,
C Dost sometimes counsel take—and sometimes tea.
  Hither the heroes and the nymphs° resort,
10 To taste awhile the pleasures of a court:
In various talk th' instructive hours they passed,
Who gave the ball, or paid the visit last;
One speaks the glory of the British Queen,
And one describes a charming Indian screen;
15 A third interprets motions, looks, and eyes;
At every word a reputation dies.

70. **patches:** tiny rounds of black silk, stuck on the face to cover blemishes or enhance beauty (called "beauty marks"). **Bibles:** small editions of the Bible, with decorated bindings and metal clasps. An incongruous item on this list.
71. **arms:** Pope is parodying the traditional scene in epics where the hero dons his armor and weapons.

7. **springes** (sprin'jəs): traps.
8. **finny prey:** fish.

3. **structure:** Hampton Court, on the Thames upstream from London, in Pope's day was a royal residence. It is now a museum.

7. **Anna:** Queen Anne, who ruled Great Britain and Ireland, and claimed to rule France.
9. **nymphs:** young ladies.

A. Tone
❓ What would you say is the tone of line 80? (Ironic, amusing, tongue-in-cheek)

B. Generalization
❓ What generalization does Pope express in lines 15–16 of Canto II? Do you agree or disagree with this generalization? (Pope implies that "all is fair" in love, provided a suit by a male lover is successful.)

C. Zeugma
The rhetorical figure of zeugma (zōōg'mə) is used in lines 7–8. A zeugma (from Greek for "yoking") occurs when a verb has two subjects or objects, or an adjective modifies two nouns, although only one is appropriate, as in "to wage war and peace." Here, *take* governs two sharply different direct objects, *counsel* and *tea.*

A. Foreshadow-
ing/Tone

? How does the
interjection of
the author in lines
29–32 foreshadow
the outcome? (The
comment implies
that Belinda exults
prematurely and
will come to grief.)
In context, what is
the tone of this au-
thorial comment?
(The tone is hu-
morous.)

B. Allusion

? Explain the ap-
propriateness of
the classical allu-
sion to Nisus and
Scylla. (Pope's
readers would
have been familiar
with their story,
which is found in
Book VIII of Ovid's
Metamorphoses.
The tale concerns
Scylla's tragic
shearing of her fa-
ther Nisus's hair.)

Snuff,° or the fan,° supply each pause of chat,
With singing, laughing, ogling, and all that.
    Meanwhile, declining from the noon of day,
20 The sun obliquely shoots his burning ray;
The hungry judges soon the sentence sign,
And wretches hang that jurymen may dine. . . .
Belinda now, whom thirst of fame invites,
Burns to encounter two adventurous knights,
25 At omber° singly to decide their doom;
And swells her breast with conquests yet to come. . . .
The nymph exulting fills with shouts the sky;
The walls, the woods, and long canals reply.
    O thoughtless mortals; ever blind to fate,
30 Too soon dejected, and too soon elate.
A Sudden, these honors shall be snatched away,
And cursed forever this victorious day.
    For lo! the board with cups and spoons is crowned,
The berries° crackle, and the mill° turns round;
35 On shining altars of Japan° they raise
The silver lamp; the fiery spirits blaze;
From silver spouts the grateful liquors glide,
While China's earth° receives the smoking tide.°
At once they gratify their scent and taste,
40 And frequent cups prolong the rich repast.
Straight hover round the fair her airy band;
Some, as she sipped, the fuming liquor fanned,
Some o'er her lap their careful plumes displayed,
Trembling, and conscious of the rich brocade.
45 Coffee (which makes the politician wise,
And see through all things with his half-shut eyes)
Sent up in vapors to the baron's brain
New stratagems the radiant locks to gain.
    Ah, cease, rash youth! desist ere 'tis too late,
50 Fear the just gods, and think of Scylla's fate!°
B Changed to a bird, and sent to flit in air,
She dearly pays for Nisus' injured hair!
    But when to mischief mortals bend their will,
How soon they find fit instruments of ill!
55 Just then Clarissa drew with tempting grace
A two-edged weapon from her shining case:
So ladies in romance assist their knight,
Present the spear, and arm him for the fight.
He takes the gift with reverence, and extends
60 The little engine on his fingers' ends;
This just behind Belinda's neck he spread,
As o'er the fragrant steams she bends her head.
Swift to the lock a thousand sprites repair,
A thousand wings, by turns, blow back the hair;
65 And thrice they twitched the diamond in her ear;
Thrice she looked back, and thrice the foe drew near.
Just in that instant, anxious Ariel sought
The close recesses of the virgin's thought;

17. **snuff:** Both sexes indulged in this tobacco product. **fan:** standard equipment for ladies.

25. **omber:** a three-handed card game.

34. **berries:** coffee beans. **mill:** coffee grinder.
35. **altars of Japan:** small laquered tables.

38. **China's earth:** china cups, made of earthenware. **smoking tide:** coffee.

50. **Scylla's fate:** Scylla was punished by being turned into a seabird after she betrayed her father Nisus by cutting off his purple lock of hair, on which his life depended.

A

The Rape of the Lock by William Hamilton (1790). Oil.

Private collection.

❓ Who are the two major figures represented in the painting? (Belinda and the Baron) What emotions or attitudes do they express? (Anger on the part of Belinda; triumph on the part of the Baron) Find a line from the poem that could serve as a caption. (Lines 83–84 next page)

A. Antithesis

? In lines 75–76, what is particularly clever in the use of antithesis regarding the scissors? (He *spreads* the scissors to *enclose* the lock, and he *joins* the scissors to *divide* the lock from Belinda's head. The verbs name contradictory actions.)

As on the nosegay in her breast reclined,
70 He watched th' ideas rising in her mind.
    Sudden he viewed, in spite of all her art,
    An earthly lover lurking at her heart.
    Amazed, confused, he found his power expired,
    Resigned to fate, and with a sigh retired.
75 The peer now spreads the glittering *forfex*° wide,
A   T' enclose the lock; now joins it, to divide.
    E'en then, before the fatal engine closed,
    A wretched sylph too fondly <u>interposed</u>:
    Fate urged the shears, and cut the sylph in twain,
80 (But airy substance soon unites again).
    The meeting points the sacred hair dissever
    From the fair head, forever, and forever!
        Then flashed the living lightning from her eyes,
    And screams of horror rend th' affrighted skies.
85 Not louder shrieks to pitying Heaven are cast,
    When husbands, or when lapdogs breathe their last;
    Or when rich China vessels, fallen from high,
    In glittering dust and painted fragments lie!
        "Let wreaths of triumph° now my temples twine,"
90 The victor cried; "the glorious prize is mine!
    While fish in streams, or birds delight in air,
    Or in a coach and six the British fair,
    As long as *Atalantis*° shall be read,
    Or the small pillow grace a lady's bed,
95 While visits shall be paid on solemn days,
    When numerous wax lights in bright order blaze,
    While nymphs take treats, or <u>assignations</u> give,
    So long my honor, name, and praise shall live!
    What Time would spare, from steel receives its date,°
100 And monuments, like men, submit to fate!"

75. *forfex:* shears.

89. **wreaths of triumph:** like the ones worn by ancient athletic heroes.

93. *Atalantis:* a fashionable novel which thinly disguised some contemporary scandals.

99. **date:** destruction.

In Canto IV, Pope describes an incident that occurs in all proper epics: a descent into the underworld. Just as Virgil had Aeneas go down to Hades, Pope has a "melancholy sprite" called Umbriel go down to a dismal imaginary place called the "Cave of Spleen." (Spleen was the eighteenth century's name for what we call depression; rich, idle people were particularly subject to spleen in Pope's day.) In the cave, Umbriel obtains an immense bag, which somewhat resembles the bag of winds in Homer's Odyssey, *full of "sighs, sobs, and passions," as well as a vial of "soft sobs, melting griefs, and flowing tears." Umbriel then returns to the surface of the earth and empties the contents of the bag and vial over Belinda and her girlfriend, who is even more angry than Belinda is. The Canto ends with Belinda lamenting to the Baron:*

> O, hadst thou, cruel, been content to seize
> Hairs less in sight, or any hairs but these!

The Baron ignores her pleas: "Fate and Jove have stopped the Baron's ears."

1. Ariel, a sprite, warns Belinda to beware of man. (T)
2. When Belinda arises, she "arms" herself with her cosmetics. (T)
3. The Baron is determined to have one of Belinda's curls. (T)
4. Belinda spends an afternoon at Hampton Court. (T)

5. Although Ariel sees the Baron approach Belinda with a two-edged weapon, he cannot help her. (T)
6. After the Baron cuts off one of Belinda's curls, she faints. (F)
7. A sprite named Umbriel pours a bag of sobs, grief, and tears over Belinda and her girlfriend. (T)

8. Belinda tells the Baron she would have given him the curl if he had asked her for it. (F)
9. Belinda demands the Baron return her lock of hair. (T)
10. Belinda's lock of hair became a star in the sky, and the poet tells her to stop mourning its loss. (T)

A

Sir Plume Demands the Restoration of the Lock by C.R. Leslie (1854). Oil.

Private collection.

A. Humanities Connection: Discussing the Fine Art
Born in London to American parents, Charles Robert Leslie (1794–1859) returned to the United States when he was five years old. In 1811, Leslie went back to London to study art at the Royal Academy, where he received two silver medals for his work. Leslie is best known for his cabinet pictures, which depict scenes from the works of Shakespeare, Cervantes, Molière, and Pope. **?** Comment on the elegance of the costumes, decorations, and furnishings in the picture. How does this painting contrast in tone with Hamilton's illustrations? (Hamilton's are much funnier, more melodramatic, and simpler in detail.)

Canto V

"To arms, to arms!" the fierce virago° cries,
And swift as lightning to the combat flies.
All side in parties, and begin th' attack;
Fans clap, silks rustle, and tough whalebones° crack;
5 Heroes' and heroines' shouts confus'dly rise,
And bass and treble voices strike the skies.
No common weapons in their hands are found,
Like gods they fight, nor dread a mortal wound.°. . .

1. **virago:** a fierce woman. Here, Belinda's girlfriend, who leads the attack on the Baron and his friends.

4. **whalebones:** used to stiffen women's clothing.

8. **mortal wound:** Like gods, who are immortal, these fighters do not fear the wounds inflicted by words.

1. Pope gives the excuse that he will think his work well done if his friend John Caryll approves of it, and if it pleases the real-life Belinda (the young and fashionable Arabella Fermor).
2. Ariel warns Belinda that a mysterious, dread event is to occur; she is to beware of Man.

3. The guardian sylph is powerless to defend the lock when he notices that Belinda is thinking about a lover.
4. Belinda defeats the Baron "in battle" with a pinch of snuff. The weapon is especially appropriate because taking snuff was a somewhat pretentious habit of the aristocracy in Pope's day.
5. The objects include the wits of heroes and beaux (fashionable gentlemen), bro-

ken vows, deathbed alms, and lovers' hearts, which are bound with bits of ribbon.

If it is not there, the Muse says that it has been transformed into a comet in the sky.

The ultimate fate of the lock is supposed to soothe Belinda's grief because at least it will confer immortal fame on her.

A. Anticlimax

❓ Describe Belinda's first act of revenge on the Baron. What is anticlimactic about it? (Belinda uses a pinch of snuff to make the Baron sneeze. The revenge proves to be trivial.)

B. Parody

Pope's conclusion is also a parody, or amusing transposition, of an episode in classical epic: this time, from the conclusion of Ovid's *Metamorphoses*, where the recently assassinated Julius Caesar is transformed into a comet.

CLOSURE

Have students describe the poet's tone in these selections from *The Rape of the Lock*. Have some volunteers identify at least three instances where Pope seems gently or amusingly mocking; have others pick out three places where the satire has a harder, more biting tone.

> See fierce Belinda on the Baron flies,
> 10 With more than usual lightning in her eyes;
> Nor feared the chief th' unequal fight to try,
> Who sought no more than on his foe to die.
> But this bold lord with manly strength endued,
> She with one finger and a thumb subdued:
> 15 Just where the breath of life his nostrils drew,
> A charge of snuff the wily virgin threw;
> The gnomes direct, to every atom just,
> The pungent grains of titillating dust.
> Sudden, with starting tears each eye o'erflows,
> 20 And the high dome re-echoes to his nose.
>   "Now meet thy fate," incensed Belinda cried,
> And drew a deadly bodkin° from her side. . . .
>   "Boast not my fall," he cried, "insulting foe!
> Thou by some other shalt be laid as low;
> 25 Nor think to die dejects my lofty mind;
> All that I dread is leaving you behind!
> Rather than so, ah, let me still survive,
> And burn in Cupid's flames—but burn alive."
>   "Restore the lock!" she cries; and all around
> 30 "Restore the lock!" the vaulted roofs rebound.
> Not fierce Othello° in so loud a strain
> Roared for the handkerchief that caused his pain.
> But see how oft ambitious aims are crossed,
> And chiefs contend till all the prize is lost!
> 35 The lock, obtained with guilt, and kept with pain,
> In every place is sought, but sought in vain.
> With such a prize no mortal must be blessed,
> So Heav'n decrees! with Heav'n who can contest?
>   Some thought it mounted to the lunar sphere,
> 40 Since all things lost on earth are treasured there.
> There heroes' wits are kept in ponderous vases,
> And beaux'° in snuffboxes and tweezer cases;
> There broken vows and deathbed alms are found,
> And lovers' hearts with ends of riband bound. . . .
> 45   But trust the Muse—she saw it upward rise,
> Though marked by none but quick, poetic eyes. . . .
> A sudden star, it shot through liquid air,
> And drew behind a radiant trail of hair. . . .
>   Then cease, bright nymph! to mourn thy ravished hair,
> 50 Which adds new glory to the shining sphere!
> Not all the tresses that fair head can boast,
> Shall draw such envy as the lock you lost.
> For, after all the murders° of your eye,
> When, after millions slain, yourself shall die;
> 55 When those fair suns shall set, as set they must,
> And all those tresses shall be laid in dust:
> This lock, the Muse shall consecrate to fame,
> And 'midst the stars inscribe Belinda's name.

22. **bodkin:** a small, pointed instrument.

31. **Othello:** Shakespeare's tragic hero Othello gave his wife a handkerchief, which his enemy stole and then used as evidence of the wife's unfaithfulness.

42. **beaux':** fashionable gentlemen's.

53. **murders:** Just as Belinda's eyes are said to "eclipse the day" (Canto I, line 14), here they are said to murder the young men who admire her. Both compliments are ancient and trite in love poetry.

Interpreting Meanings

6. Most students will agree that Pope's tone is one of amusement: The underlying comparison of the lady's toilette to a religious rite is humorous, rather than scornful.

7. The purpose is to poke light, satirical fun at the importance that fashionable ladies like Belinda attach to their appearance.

8. Most students will agree that Pope is tolerantly amused. The humor is especially evident in the juxtaposition of important and utterly trivial elements in many of the couplets (for example, in line 6, the mention of the fall of foreign tyrants and the fall of nymphs at home, or the mention of counsel and tea in line 8).

9. Belinda's victory over the Baron might also be said to be ironic because the lock, which Belinda wanted restored, cannot be found.

10. The effect of the juxtaposition in this line is humorous.

Students may mention various passages. Among the possibilities are the mention of counsel and tea at III.8, the mention of the British queen and an Indian screen at III.13–14, the mention of hanging judges and jurymen's dinners at III.21–22, and the description of the sylph's being cut in two (but soon uniting again) at III.79–80.

11. The targets are cruel, insensitive judges and crafty politicians, respectively.

12. The effect is to "deflate" the solemnity of royal councils of state with the mention of a common, everyday activity—drinking tea.

13. The narrator implies that Belinda is victorious, since she will have undying fame.

14. The theme comments on the silly, petty disputes and vanities that sometimes preoccupy us.

Most students will have no difficulty in finding such passages. Ask them to be as specific as they can.

Responding to the Poem

Analyzing the Poem

Identifying Details

1. At the beginning of Canto I, Pope admits that his subject is "slight" or trivial (line 5). What excuses does he give for writing on such a slight subject?
2. Why does the guardian sylph Ariel warn Belinda? What causes her to forget the warning?
3. What renders the guardian sylph powerless to defend the lock?
4. How does Belinda defeat the Baron in battle? What makes the weapon she chooses seem particularly appropriate?
5. In Canto V, lines 39–44, Pope describes a kind of lunar limbo. What sort of lost objects are to be found there? If the stolen lock is not there, where, according to the Muse, is it? How is this ultimate fate of the lock supposed to soothe Belinda's grief?

Interpreting Meanings

6. *The Rape of the Lock* is a famous example of **satire**. The **tone** of satire can either be angry or good-natured, vicious or mild. Consider the description of Belinda at her dressing table (Canto I, lines 53–80). What is Pope's tone in describing this common human activity? Is he amused or contemptuous? How can you tell?
7. Examine the language of this passage and notice all the words associated with religion. What is Pope's purpose in using this language?
8. Another **satirical** passage is the description of the court at the beginning of Canto III. Again, what is Pope's **tone**—his attitude toward the Queen and her courtiers? Is he scornful or tolerantly amused? How can you tell?
9. Belinda's victory at cards (Canto III, lines 23–28) and her cries of triumph are said to be **ironic** because her happiness is so momentary; it's about to be shattered by the rape of her lock. **Irony** always involves a discrepancy of some kind, here between what Belinda expects—a "victorious day"—and what actually happens, the sad loss of her lock. Explain why Belinda's victory over the Baron (Canto V, lines 13–22) might similarly be considered ironic.
10. In Canto III, Pope juxtaposes—that is, places side by side—dying husbands and dying lapdogs (line 86). What is the effect of this juxtaposition? Find other juxtapositions of this kind in the poem.
11. In the complete poem, Pope frequently makes **satirical** remarks about the world outside the privileged ranks to which Belinda and her friends belong. An example of such a remark, in the excerpts printed here, occurs in Canto III, lines 21–22 and lines 45–46. Who or what are Pope's targets in these couplets?
12. The world outside the poem and the world inside it come together in Canto III, lines 7–8. What is the effect of the three words after the dash?
13. Who, if anyone, is victorious by the end of the action?
14. How would you state Pope's **theme** in this epic—based on the extracts you have read? Does the epic apply in any way to any aspects of contemporary life? Can you find passages that could serve as satiric commentaries on people's behavior in the late twentieth century?

Writing About the Poem

A Creative Response

1. **Using the Mock-Heroic Style.** In Canto III, Pope describes making and drinking coffee in rich, elevated, and roundabout language (lines 33–40). This **mock-heroic** writing style breaks the elementary rule saying writers must try to use simple, direct language when describing simple activities. As an exercise in mock-heroic writing, write a prose description of a common activity (such as riding a bicycle or cooking and eating a hamburger) using inflated language and rich images. Do not strain for comic effects; instead, try to be elegant. Study the way Pope uses these two words: *sleepless* (Canto I, line 16) and *instructive* (Canto III, line 11). Try to use one of your words in this way.

A Critical Response

2. **Analyzing a Satire.** In an essay, identify the targets of Pope's satire in this mock-epic and describe the devices Pope uses to ridicule these targets. Consider what Pope says about social role playing and about the foolishness of human behavior in general.
3. **Comparing and Contrasting Epics.** Compare Pope's mock-epic with a serious epic: *Beowulf,* or, if you know them well, Homer's *Iliad* or *Odyssey.* Consider these elements of the epic in your discussion:

   a. Invocation to the muse
   b. Statement of subject
   c. Intervention of gods and goddesses
   d. Epic battles
   e. A hero or heroine who reflects the values of a particular society
   f. Use of elevated language

A. Expansion
You may want to call attention to the etymology of the word *wit,* derived from Greek *oida* (I know) and Latin *video* (I see). The etymology underscores the value accorded by neoclassic writers to the qualities of knowledge and perception.

B. Responding
Be sure students respond to this definition of literature. If this is a true definition, what kinds of writings popular today would not qualify? (Answers might include science fiction and fantasy novels, comic books, or even how-to magazines and technical manuals.)

C. Responding
Ask students how a bad writer can "defraud" the reading public. You might mention, for example, "trashy" novels that offer simple solutions to complex problems, or that present people as stereotyped characters, not genuine human beings with all our complications. Remember that Pope is also talking here about the mediocre or manipulative use of language. Have students use these ideas to begin considering this question: "Why do we study literature in school?"

The Elements of Literature

WIT

Pope and his contemporaries admired a quality they called **wit.** Writers and other people who possessed wit were intellectually brilliant. Their ability to detect resemblances enabled them to write in images, similes, metaphors, and other figures of speech. Their language was polished and exact; their manner, cool and controlled.

The opposite of wit was *dullness,* and Pope wrote a long, brilliant, and insulting poem called the *Dunciad* which ridiculed the dull writers of his day, calling them dunces. The chief dunce of the first version of the *Dunciad* (1728) was Lewis Theobald (pronounced "tibbald"), an editor of Shakespeare whom Pope called "piddling" because he was so concerned with the minute details of Shakespeare's texts. In 1742, when Pope reissued the *Dunciad,* Theobald was replaced as chief dunce by Colley Cibber, an actor and playwright who promoted his own career by publishing an egotistical biography. Theobald and Cibber lacked wit; Pope and such friends of his as Jonathan Swift and John Gay had wit.

Wit, then, meant cleverness. But it also meant something more serious:

True wit is Nature to advantage dressed:
What oft was thought, but ne'er so well expressed.

In this couplet from *An Essay on Criticism* (lines 258–259), Pope describes something he calls "true wit." The nearest modern equivalent of true wit is what we think of as great literature, or the classics. According to Pope, these great works express ideas that people have always accepted as true ("what oft was thought"). In great works, these familiar thoughts are not expressed in dull language, but are "to advantage dressed." The term *Nature* in this couplet refers not only to what we now think

of as nature—the great outdoors with its birds, beasts, trees, plants, oceans, deserts—but also to human nature and the experiences of human beings.

The couplet on true wit might be summarized as follows: "A great work of literature presents familiar human experiences and perceptions in interesting and distinguished language. A great work reminds us, in an exciting and memorable way, of what we already know about the universe and its inhabitants."

But Pope did not regard wit as the most important quality a person can have:

A wit's a feather and a chief's a rod;
An honest man's the noblest work of God.

In this couplet, from Pope's *An Essay on Man* (Epistle IV, lines 247–248), the word *wit* is used as the name of a person, a writer. The writer is compared with a chief (a great leader, such as a general, king, or president) and with an honest man. Of the three, Pope gives first place to the honest man, God's noblest work. In comparison with this virtuous person, a wit is a mere "feather"—a light and flighty decoration—and a great man of action is a mere "rod"—a defender and corrector of society. Pope came to believe that virtue and morality are more important than intellectual brilliance (though he always was inclined to feel that second-rate writing is a kind of immorality because a bad writer defrauds the reading public). Pope spoke his final words on morality while lying on his deathbed, when he said to the attending priest, "There is nothing that is meritorious but virtue and friendship, and indeed friendship itself is only part of virtue."

To summarize, Pope thought of wit as the power enabling a writer to represent the familiar world in language that is correct, interesting, and memorable. Though he thought it important to be a wit, he thought it more important to be a virtuous person.

Sir Richard Steele (1672–1729)
Joseph Addison (1672–1719)

Richard Steele and Joseph Addison are paired in most people's minds because they were the first important English writers of the periodical essay, a very popular kind of journalism in the eighteenth century, and a forerunner of both the modern newspaper and the modern magazine. Each issue of a periodical essay consisted of a single printed sheet that came out at least once a week and usually contained a single piece of writing: an essay for the most part, very rarely a poem or a story. Steele was the founder of, and Addison a contributor to, *The Tatler,* which appeared three times a week from April 1709 until January 1711. Then both men founded *The Spectator,* which appeared daily except Sunday from March 1, 1711, until December 6, 1712. Other periodical essays of the eighteenth century bore such catchy titles as *The Bee* and *The Adventurer.* Defoe wrote *The Review,* Swift *The Examiner,* and Samuel Johnson *The Rambler* and *The Idler.* But the honor of making the periodical essay into an important form of writing belongs to Steele and Addison. They were of the same age, and although of very different temperament, they were always good friends except when they quarreled over politics in the last years of Addison's life.

Steele, born of English parents in Dublin and orphaned early, was sent over to London as a boy to be educated by a privately endowed school, the Charterhouse. There he first met his future collaborator Joseph Addison, who was the son of an English clergyman. Addison was a brilliant student; he entered Oxford University when he was only fifteen. Steele followed him to Oxford two years later, but left the university before graduating and returned to London, where he became an officer in the Horse Guards and a young man about town. After serving in the army at home and abroad, Steele devoted himself to politics, journalism, and the management of a theater. He even became a member of

Sir Richard Steele by Sir Godfrey Kneller (1711).

National Portrait Gallery, London.

Parliament, and for a time edited the *London Gazette,* the government's official newspaper. Though *The Tatler* and *The Spectator* secured his future fame, he was also known as the author of numerous other works: poems and pamphlets, a moral tract entitled *The Christian Hero* (1701), and several stage comedies, the best being *The Conscious Lovers* (1722). Steele was a warmhearted, jovial, impulsive man, devoted to his wife, who was considered a great beauty. He was often short of money; being knighted by George I in 1715 did not make him any richer. In debt and suffering the effects of a stroke, he was miserable during the last years of his life.

Addison was a quite different sort of man, with a reputation for being cold and haughty. After receiving his bachelor's and master's degrees from Oxford, he wrote poems and dedicated them to various statesmen, in the hopes of advancing his career in government. Eventually his literary talents brought him notice, and he was elected to Parliament and held a number of important offices, the most impressive being Secretary of State. Like Steele, Addison wrote plays, but his were not comedies; his best known work

A. Expansion
The Spectator enjoyed a strong circulation of 3,000 copies a day—no mean feat if we take account of historians' estimates that each copy was shared by as many as ten readers.

B. Expansion
When Steele found favor after the accession of George I, one of his interesting posts was as the supervisor of the Drury Lane Theater, which was the renowned playhouse where David Garrick, later in the century, made his reputation as an actor (see the illustration on text page 561).

A. Expansion
Samuel Johnson, however, had a different verdict on Addison in his *Lives of the Poets* (1781), saying that "Whoever wishes to attain an English style . . . must give his days and nights to the volumes of Addison."

B. Comment from the Author
Addison also described his objectives as follows: "I shall be ambitious to have it said of me, that I have brought philosophy out of closets and libraries, schools and colleges, to dwell in clubs and assemblies, at teatables and coffeehouses." Note the essentially middle-class values that Addison and Steele supported.

C. Expansion
One of their vehicles of entertainment was casting the essays in the form of conversations between members of a fictitious club. These gentlemen included Sir Andrew Freeport (representing the rich trading class), Sir Roger de Coverly (representing the conservative, landed gentry), and Captain Sentry (representing the army). The club prefigures, to some degree, Charles Dickens's novelistic device in *The Pickwick Papers* (1837).

for the stage is *Cato,* an immensely successful tragedy first performed in 1713. This play was based on Roman history, but readers and theatergoers interpreted it as referring to contemporary politics. In both politics and literature Addison was successful, and from a worldly point of view so was he in his private life. He retired on a large pension, and after years of bachelorhood he married a rich, widowed countess. We can never know whether he was a happy man, but we do know that he quarreled with, and died without being reconciled to, his partner Steele and his good friends Jonathan Swift and Alexander Pope. Years after Addison died, Pope condemned him under the name of Atticus in *An Epistle to Dr. Arbuthnot* (1735). Atticus, Pope said, was cold and cautious, the sort of critic who would

> Damn with faint praise, assent with civil leer,
> And without sneering, teach the rest to sneer;
> Willing to wound, and yet afraid to strike,
> Just hint at fault, and hesitate dislike;
> Alike reserved to blame or to commend,
> A timorous foe and a suspicious friend.

But this is not the Addison who appears in *The Tatler* and *The Spectator.*

Although both Steele and Addison were deeply involved in politics, they avoided political discussion in *The Tatler* and *The Spectator.* In their periodical essays they did not try to change their readers' political views, but sought to improve their minds, their manners, their morals, and their taste. In the first issue of *The Tatler,* Steele said,

> The general purpose of this paper is to expose the false arts of life, to pull off the disguises of cunning, vanity, and affectation, and to recommend a general simplicity in our dress, our discourse, and our behavior.

And in Number 10 of *The Spectator,* Addison said,

> I shall endeavor to enliven morality with wit and temper wit with morality.

Their aim was "to make morality fashionable," as a famous French literary critic once observed, and they were successful. Historians agree that they were at least partly responsible for the general improvement in public behavior and morality that occurred in their lifetime. They en-

Joseph Addison by Sir Godfrey Kneller (before 1717).

National Portrait Gallery, London.

couraged frugality and discouraged wasteful expense, they ridiculed hypocrisy and false pride and promoted honesty and simplicity, and they praised marriage and the family, unlike some writers of the immediate past who had made bad jokes about both those institutions. But neither was preachy; they knew they had to entertain their readers if they wanted to sell their essays.

The topics of the essays are extremely varied. Steele wrote on problems of love, marriage, and domestic life. He gave advice on education and dress, and he made fun of fads and fashions that he considered vulgar or excessive. Addison's contributions were somewhat more thoughtful; for instance, he wrote a series of essays on the necessity of being a good-natured person. Both authors described scenes and events of everyday life in London and the rest of the country, thus making the essays a rich source of information about how people lived at the time. Many essays are devoted to literary subjects. Addison wrote a distinguished series on *Paradise Lost,* and Steele told people what plays to see, what actors to admire, and why the Italian opera was ridiculous.

PREPARATION

1. BUILDING ON PRIOR KNOWLEDGE.
Discuss with students the use of violence and sentiment in plays today, including TV plays and movies. (Be sure they know that *artifice* means "trick" or "device.") What artifices do directors use today to keep the audience glued to its seat, or to keep them from changing channels?

2. ESTABLISHING A PURPOSE. Before students begin reading, you might have them read question 8 on text page 549. Ask students to read the essay with the question of unnecessary violence in mind.

3. PREREADING JOURNAL. Before they read, have students write at least three sentences summarizing how they feel about violence in popular entertainment.

ARTIFICES IN TRAGEDY

The following essay, one of Addison's pieces of literary criticism, is Number 44 of *The Spectator.* It develops an idea that the Greek philosopher Aristotle (384–322 B.C.) sets forth in his *Poetics:* An audience watching a tragedy in the theater feels the emotions of pity and terror. Aristotle argues that tragedy "purges" the audience of these potentially dangerous emotions. In his essay Addison describes some of the *artifices* and *devices* dramatists use to make their audiences experience pity and terror. Notice how Addison's remarks can be related to contemporary plays and movies.

The Spectator

Number 44

Among the several artifices which are put in practice by the poets to fill the minds of an audience with terror, the first place is due to thunder and lightning, which are often made use of at the descending of a god or the rising of a ghost, at the vanishing of a devil or at the death of a tyrant. I have known a bell introduced into several tragedies with good effect; and have seen the whole assembly in a very great alarm all the while it has been ringing. But there is nothing which delights and terrifies our English theater so much as a ghost, especially when he appears in a bloody shirt. A specter has very often saved a play, though he has done nothing but stalked across the stage, or rose through a cleft of it and sunk again without speaking one word. There may be a proper season[1] for these several terrors; and when they only come in as aids and assistances to the poet, they are not only to be excused, but to be applauded. Thus the sounding of the clock in *Venice Preserved,*[2] makes the hearts of the whole audience quake, and conveys a stronger terror to the mind than it is possible for words to do. The appearance of the ghost in *Hamlet* is a masterpiece in its kind, and wrought up with all the circumstances that can create either attention or horror. The mind of the reader is wonderfully prepared for his reception by the discourses that precede it: his dumb[3] behavior at his first entrance strikes the imagination very strongly; but every time he enters, he is still more terrifying. Who can read the speech with which young Hamlet accosts him without trembling?

> Hor. Look, my lord, it comes!
> Ham. Angels and ministers of grace defend us!
>   Be thou a spirit of health, or goblin damned;
>   Bring with thee airs from Heav'n or blasts from Hell;
>   Be thy events wicked or charitable:[4]
>   Thou com'st in such a questionable shape
>   That I will speak to thee. I'll call thee Hamlet,
>   King, Father, Royal Dane: Oh! Oh! Answer me,
>   Let me not burst in ignorance; but tell
>   Why thy canonized[5] bones, hearsed[6] in death,
>   Have burst their cerements?[7] Why the sepulcher,
>   Wherein we saw thee quietly interred,
>   Hath oped his ponderous and marble jaws
>   To cast thee up again! What may this mean?
>   That thou dead corse again in complete steel[8]
>   Revisit'st thus the glimpses of the moon,
>   Making night hideous!

I do not therefore find fault with the artifices above-mentioned when they are introduced with skill and accompanied by proportionable sentiments and expressions in the writing.

For the moving of pity, our principal machine is the handkerchief; and indeed in our common

---

1. **season:** time and place.
2. *Venice Preserved:* a tragedy by Thomas Otway first produced in 1682. The bell tolls while the hero is being executed.
3. **dumb:** silent.

4. **charitable:** good.
5. **canonized:** revered.
6. **hearsed:** buried.
7. **cerements:** waxed cloths used to wrap dead bodies.
8. **steel:** the dead king is wearing armor.

A

SUPPLEMENTARY SUPPORT MATERIALS
1. Vocabulary Activity Worksheet (*CCB*)
2. Review and Response Worksheet: Tone (*CCB*)
3. Selection Test (*CCB*)

DEVELOPING VOCABULARY
The following words from the essay are tested in the Selection Test. (See also Vocabulary Activity Worksheet.)

specter	censure
disconsolate	to extenuate
obdurate	

A. Humanities Connection: About the Fine Art

Sir Joshua Reynolds (1723–1792) studied art in Italy. When he returned to London in the 1750's, he became the most successful portrait painter of the day and was elected the first president of the Royal Academy in 1768. The Tragic Muse (one of the classical nine) was named Melpomene. Mrs. Sarah Kemble Siddons (1755–1831) was the eldest daughter of a traveling actor. Hired by David Garrick at the Drury Lane Theater, Mrs. Siddons was rapidly acclaimed as the best tragic actress of her day. One of her leading roles was Lady Macbeth, and she has left us a fascinating account of her preparations and rehearsals for acting this part. Thomas Gainsborough, as well as Sir Joshua Reynolds, painted a major portrait of her.

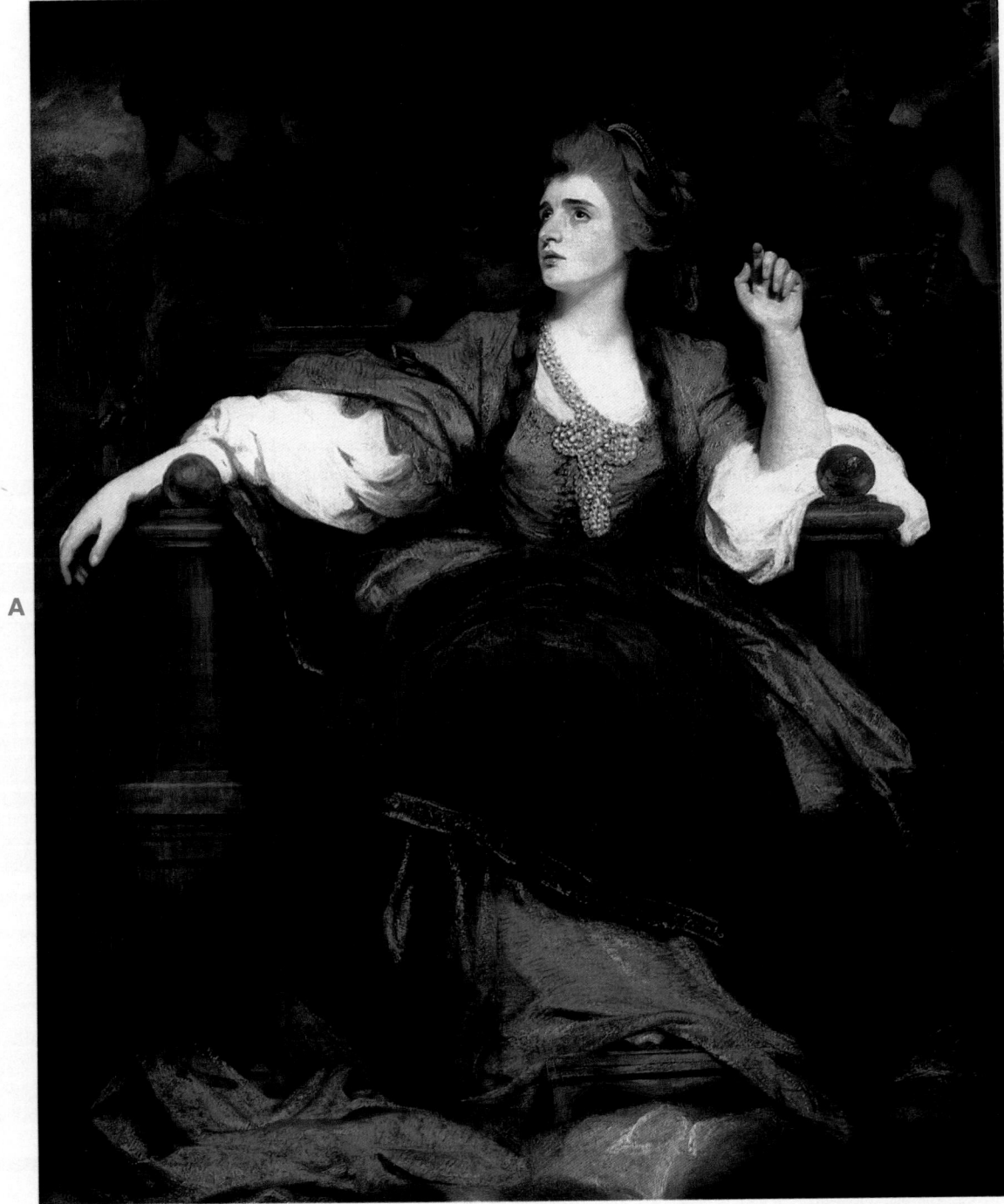

A

Mrs. Siddons as the Tragic Muse by Sir Joshua Reynolds (1784). Oil.

The Huntington Library and Art Collection, San Marino, California.

READING CHECK TEST
1. Addison believes a ghost is the most delightful and terrifying device in a tragedy. (T)
2. Addison says that dramatists can resort to ridiculous means of extracting pity by including sorrowful mothers and their children. (F)
3. Addison objects to the number of murders and executions that occur on the English stage. (T)
4. Addison complains that the French are as bad as the English with regard to stage violence. (F)
5. Addison says tragedy is easier to write than comedy. (F)

tragedies, we should not know very often that the persons are in distress by anything they say, if they did not from time to time apply their handkerchiefs to their eyes. Far be it from me to think of banishing this instrument of sorrow from the stage; I know a tragedy could not subsist without it: All that I would contend for is to keep it from being misapplied. In a word, I would have the actor's tongue sympathize with his eyes.

A disconsolate mother with a child in her hand has frequently drawn compassion from the audience, and has therefore gained a place in several tragedies. A modern writer, that observed how this had took in other plays, being resolved to double the distress and melt his audience twice as much as those before him had done, brought a princess upon the stage with a little boy in one hand and a girl in the other. This too had a very good effect. A third poet, being resolved to outwrite all his predecessors, a few years ago introduced three children with great success. And, as I am informed, a young gentleman, who is fully determined to break the most obdurate hearts, has a tragedy by him where the first person that appears upon the stage is an afflicted widow in her mourning-weeds[9] with half a dozen fatherless children attending her, like those that usually hang about the figure of Charity. Thus several incidents that are beautiful in a good writer become ridiculous by falling into the hands of a bad one.

But among all our methods of moving pity or terror, there is none so absurd and barbarous, and what more exposes us to the contempt and ridicule of our neighbors, than that dreadful butchering of one another which is so very frequent upon the English stage. To delight in seeing men stabbed, poisoned, racked, or impaled is certainly the sign of a cruel temper. And as this is often practiced before the British audience, several French critics, who think these are grateful[10] spectacles to us, take occasion from them to represent us as a people that delight in blood. It is indeed very odd to see our stage strewn with carcasses in the last scene of a tragedy; and to observe in the wardrobe of the playhouse several daggers, poniards, wheels,[11] bowls for poison, and many other instruments of death. Murders and executions are always transacted behind the scenes in the French theater; which in general is very agreeable to the manners of a polite and civilized people: But as there are no exceptions to this rule on the French stage, it leads them into absurdities almost as ridiculous as that which falls under our present censure. I remember in the famous play of *Corneille*,[12] written upon the subject of the *Horatii* and *Curiatii*,[13] the fierce young hero who had overcome the Curiatii one after another, (instead of being congratulated by his sister for his victory, being upbraided by her for having slain her lover) in the height of his passion and resentment kills her. If anything could extenuate so brutal an action, it would be the doing of it on a sudden, before the sentiments of nature, reason, or manhood could take place in him. However, to avoid public bloodshed, as soon as his passion is wrought to its height, he follows his sister the whole length of the stage and forbears killing her till they are both withdrawn behind the scenes. I must confess, had he murdered her before the audience, the indecency might have been greater; but as it is it appears very unnatural and looks like killing in cold blood. To give my opinion upon this case; the fact ought not to have been represented but to have been told, if there was any occasion for it.

It may not be unacceptable to the reader to see how Sophocles[14] has conducted a tragedy under the like delicate circumstances. Orestes was in the same condition with Hamlet in Shakespeare, his mother having murdered his father and taken possession of his kingdom in conspiracy with her adulterer. That young prince therefore, being determined to revenge his father's death upon those who filled his throne, conveys himself by a beautiful stratagem into his mother's apartment, with a resolution to kill her. But because such a spectacle would have been too shocking for the audience, this dreadful resolution is executed behind the scenes. The mother is heard calling out to her son for mercy; and the son answering her, that she showed no mercy to his father. After which she shrieks out that she is wounded, and by what follows we find that she is slain. I do not remember

A. Interpreting
Students who have read *Hamlet* might note an inconsistency between Addison's comment about the "dreadful butchering" on the English stage and his earlier praise of *Hamlet* in this essay. By the end of *Hamlet,* the stage is strewn with corpses: Hamlet has skewered the king and Laertes; Laertes has killed Hamlet; and the queen has taken poison.

B. Expansion
Pierre Corneille (kor·nā′yə) (1606–1684) was widely regarded as the master of French classical tragedy. Perhaps his most famous play was *Le Cid* (1637).

---

9. **weeds:** clothes.
10. **grateful:** pleasing.
11. **wheels:** devices used for torture.

12. **Corneille:** French dramatist (1606–1684).
13. ***Horatii* and *Curiatii*:** warring Roman factions.
14. **Sophocles:** Greek dramatist (496?–406 B.C.). Addison is describing Sophocles's *Electra*.

ANALYZING THE ESSAY
Identifying Facts
1. These artifices should be introduced with skill (as in Shakespeare's *Hamlet*) and accompanied with appropriate sentiments and expressions in the text of the play.
2. Addison criticizes the device of bringing onstage a disconsolate mother who is accompanied by one or more children.

3. Addison singles out the habit of murdering and butchering characters on stage as "absurd and barbarous."
Addison says that on the French stage murders and executions are always carried out behind the scenes.
4. Addison says that Horace's rule—banning onstage deaths—should generally be adhered to, but not pressed to an extreme, as in some of French drama-

A. Expansion
Remind students that Horace's *Art of Poetry*, even more than Aristotle's *Poetics*, was admired in the eighteenth century as the classic formulation of the "rules" of drama.

B. Expansion
Notice that, even though Addison is writing for a broader audience than Dryden or Pope, he still expects that many of his readers will be able to cope with the lengthy Latin quotation from Horace.

that in any of our plays there are speeches made behind the scenes, though there are other instances of this nature to be met with in those of the ancients. And I believe my reader will agree with me that there is something infinitely more affecting in this dreadful dialogue between the mother and her son behind the scenes than could have been in anything transacted before the audience. Orestes immediately after meets the usurper at the entrance of his palace; and by a very happy thought of the poet avoids killing him before the audience by telling him that he should live some time in his present bitterness of soul before he would dispatch him, and by ordering him to retire into that part of the palace where he had slain his father, whose murder he would revenge in the very same place where it was committed. By this means the poet observes that decency, which Horace[15] afterward established by a rule, of forbearing to commit parricides or unnatural murders before the audience.

> *Nec coram populo natos Medea trucidet.*
> Let not Medea draw her murdering knife,
> And spill her children's blood upon the stage.

The French have therefore refined too much upon Horace's rule, who never designed to banish all kinds of death from the stage; but only such as had too much horror in them, and which would have a better effect upon the audience when transacted behind the scenes. I would therefore recommend to my countrymen the practice of the ancient poets, who were very sparing of their public executions, and rather chose to perform them behind the scenes if it could be done with as great an effect upon the audience. At the same time I

must observe, that though the devoted persons of the tragedy were seldom slain before the audience, which has generally something ridiculous in it, their bodies were often produced after their death, which has always in it something melancholy or terrifying; so that the killing on the stage does not seem to have been avoided only as an indecency, but also as an improbability.

> *Nec pueros coram populo Medea trucidet,*
> *Aut humana palam coquat exta nefarius Atreus,*
> *Aut in avem Procne vertatur, Cadmus in anguem,*
> *Quodcunque ostendis mihi sic, incredulus odi.*—Horace.
> Medea[16] must not draw her murdering knife,
> Nor Atreus[17] there his horrid feast prepare.
> Cadmus[18] and Procne's[19] metamorphosis,
> (She to a swallow turned, he to a snake)
> And whatsoever contradicts my sense,
> I hate to see, and never can believe.—Lord Roscommon.[20]

I have now gone through the several dramatic inventions which are made use of by the ignorant poets to supply the place of tragedy, and by the skillful to improve it; some of which I could wish entirely rejected, and the rest to be used with caution. It would be an endless task to consider comedy in the same light, and to mention the innumerable shifts that small wits put in practice to raise a laugh. Bullock in a short coat, and Norris[21] in a long one, seldom fail of this effect. In ordinary comedies, a broad and a narrow brimmed hat are different characters. Sometimes the wit of the scene lies in a shoulder-belt, and

---

15. **Horace:** Roman poet (65–8 B.C.) whose *Art of Poetry* contained rules for poets.

16. **Medea:** In a tragedy by Euripides (479?–406? B.C.), the sorceress Medea kills her two children in revenge for her husband's desertion.
17. **Atreus:** In Greek legend, Atreus's wife was seduced by her husband's brother, Thyestes. In revenge, Atreus killed and cooked Thyestes' sons and served their flesh to Thyeste in a banquet.
18. **Cadmus:** In Greek legend, he begged the gods to relieve his miseries, and they turned him into a snake.
19. **Procne:** In Greek legend, Procne was the wife of Tereus, who raped Procne's sister Philomela and cut out her tongue. Eventually Tereus was turned into a hoopoe, Philomela into a nightingale, and Procne into a swallow.
20. **Roscommon:** Wentworth Dillon, Earl of Roscommon (died 1685), is the translator of these lines from Horace.
21. **Bullock . . . Norris:** William Bullock and Henry Norris, well-known actors.

turgy (Addison cites a play of Corneille as an example).

To demonstrate the correct application of Horace's rule, Addison gives the example of Sophocles's tragedy *Electra*.
5. Addison says that this would be an endless task, since "the objects that make us laugh are infinitely more numerous than those that make us weep." In addition, greater indulgence and latitude

ought to be allowed to comic poets than to tragedians.

Interpreting Meanings
6. Addison is referring to a common experience of spectators at the theater, particularly of the audience at a tragic play. At the same time as we are terrified by the events of the play, we are "delighted" by the skills of the actors, the artistry of

the composition—and, perhaps, by the Aristotelian "catharsis," or purgation, of our emotions that the tragedy provides.
7. Students may propose several reasons: The action may be ludicrous, improbable, or overdone; we may laugh out of nervousness or anxiety; and so on.
8. Most students will agree with Addison's view, but some may propose that such a practice would compromise realism in contemporary drama. Have students defend their opinions with arguments.
9. Most students will agree that violence tends to be handled overtly and explicitly on stage and on screen today. Ask students for their opinions on the effects of this violence. Do the students think that such violence tends to jade people, or to harden their emotions? Do the students think that violence on stage or on screen may be a factor in delinquency and violent crime? Encourage students to defend their opinions.

---

sometimes in a pair of whiskers. A lover[22] running about the stage with his head peeping out of a barrel was thought a very good jest in King Charles the Second's time; and invented by one

of the first wits of that age. But because ridicule is not so delicate as compassion, and because the objects that make us laugh are infinitely more numerous than those that make us weep, there is a much greater latitude for comic than tragic artifices, and by consequence a much greater indulgence to be allowed them.

---

22. **lover:** in Sir George Etherege's *The Comical Revenge, or Love in a Tub*, first produced in 1664.

Responding to the Essay

Analyzing the Essay

Identifying Facts

1. According to Addison, what should introduce and accompany the common artifices of ghosts and bells if they are to be used in a tragedy to provoke terror?
2. What device for provoking pity does Addison say is being overused and made to appear ridiculous?
3. What is the most "absurd and barbarous" of all practices on the English stage? How is this practice different from practices on the French stage?
4. What does Addison recommend as the correct interpretation of Horace's rule? What example does he give?
5. Why doesn't Addison provide a detailed treatment of comic artifices?

Interpreting Meanings

6. Addison speaks of being delighted and terrified at the same time. How can this be, since delight is pleasant and terror unpleasant?
7. Why do people sometimes laugh when they see something that is supposed to inspire feelings of terror or pity? Can you think of examples from the contemporary stage or from movies or TV?
8. Do you agree with Addison that "unnatural murders" should be committed out of the view of the audience? Explain.
9. How is such violence handled on stage or on screen today? What do you think is its effect on the audience?

Writing About the Essay

A Critical Response

Describing Comic Devices. Imagine you are a critic of contemporary television situation comedies, and you have decided to comment on the devices used to make the audience laugh. Write an essay describing the devices and evaluating their effectiveness. Be specific, as Addison has been, pointing to particular television shows to support your thesis.

Before you write, watch a few comedies and take notes on the devices you observe. Which devices make you laugh? Which ones make you groan? Which ones do you see on every show? Which ones are new and refreshing? Observe plots, characters, settings, costumes, and actions.

Analyzing Language and Style

Satirical Techniques and Tone

Find examples of Addison's use of the following satirical techniques: **hyperbole, understatement, sarcasm.**

1. What tone do these techniques create for the essay?
2. At what point in the essay does the **tone** first become clear?
3. Where (if anywhere) in the essay does the tone shift?

PREPARATION

1. Building On Prior Knowledge.
Before students begin reading, direct
their attention to the comments on the
role of Selkirk in inspiring Daniel Defoe's
Robinson Crusoe (see text page 481).

2. Establishing A Purpose. Steele's
essay is an early example of a journalist's interview and impressions of a celebrity. Given Selkirk's background, have
students discuss what they think an interviewer might or should have asked him.
Students can then read the essay to see
if Steele's report of the interview matches
their expectations.

Supplementary Support Materials
1. Vocabulary Activity Worksheet (*CCB*)
2. Review and Response Worksheets:
Tone; Characterization and Theme
(*CCB*)
3. Selection Test (*CCB*)

A. Style

? How does
Steele get his
readers' attention
in the opening
paragraph of the
essay? (He says
that Selkirk's expe-
rience is unique.)

B. Style

? How does this
factual listing of
Selkirk's posses-
sions increase the
believability of
Steele's account?
(The list implies
that Steele took
notes from an ac-
curate, reliable
source—Selkirk
himself.)

ALEXANDER SELKIRK

Alexander Selkirk was sailing master on the privateer *Cinque Ports* ("Five Ports") under Captain
Thomas Stradling. The two men were apparently
incompatible; indeed, their relations became so
strained that Selkirk, after several months at sea,
demanded to be put ashore. In September 1704,
he was marooned on Juan Fernandez, a group of
three small uninhabited islands four hundred
miles off the coast of Peru. There he stayed, all
alone, until 1709, when he was picked up by another British privateer and taken back to England. He arrived home in 1711, on a ship
commanded by a friend of Sir Richard Steele.

Two years later, in 1713, Steele published the
following essay on Selkirk in *The Englishman*, a
periodical that he established after *The Spectator*
ceased publication. Two other contemporary writers besides Steele published accounts of Selkirk's
ordeal, and a third, Daniel Defoe, also knew his
history.

It is not very difficult to explain Alexander Selkirk's appeal: At one time or another most people
have wondered how it would feel to be totally isolated, cut off not only from human companionship
but from all the comforts and conveniences of civilization. This is a particularly interesting speculation for us in the twentieth century, living, as we
do, in an almost completely artificial environment
and depending so much on technology, even for
our entertainment.

The Englishman

Number 26

Under the title of this paper,[1] I do not think
it foreign to my design to speak of a man
born in Her Majesty's dominions, and relate an adventure in his life so uncommon that it's
doubtful whether the like has happened to any
other of human race. The person I speak of is
Alexander Selkirk, whose name is familiar to men
of curiosity from the fame of his having lived four
years and four months alone in the island of Juan
Fernandez. I had the pleasure frequently to converse with the man soon after his arrival in
England in the year 1711. It was matter of great
curiosity to hear him, as he is a man of good sense,
give an account of the different revolutions in his
own mind in that long solitude. When we consider
how painful absence from company for the space
of but one evening is to the generality of mankind,
we may have a sense how painful this necessary
and constant solitude was to a man bred a sailor
and ever accustomed to enjoy and suffer, eat,

drink, and sleep, and perform all offices of life in
fellowship and company. He was put ashore from
a leaky vessel, with the captain of which he had
had an irreconcilable difference; and he chose
rather to take his fate in this place than in a crazy
vessel under a disagreeable commander. His portion were a sea chest, his wearing clothes[2] and
bedding, a firelock,[3] a pound of gunpowder, a large
quantity of bullets, a flint and steel,[4] a few pounds
of tobacco, a hatchet, a knife, a kettle, a Bible,
and other books of devotion, together with pieces
that concerned navigation and his mathematical
instruments. Resentment against his officer, who
had ill used him, made him look forward on this
change of life as the more eligible one, till the
instant in which he saw the vessel put off; at which
moment, his heart yearned within him and melted
at the parting with his comrades and all human
society at once. He had in provisions for the sustenance of life but the quantity of two meals, the
island abounding only with wild goats, cats, and
rats. He judged it most probable that he should
find more immediate and easy relief by finding
shellfish on the shore than seeking game with his

---

1. **this paper:** *The Englishman*.

2. **wearing clothes:** the clothes he had on.
3. **firelock:** a gun with a lock.
4. **flint and steel:** for making fires.

DEVELOPING VOCABULARY
The following words from the essay are tested in the Selection Test. (See also Vocabulary Activity Worksheet.)

irreconcilable   precipitance
languid   to discern·
promontory

READING CHECK TEST
1. Selkirk, abandoned on an island, was being punished for a minor infraction he committed on the ship on which he worked. (F)
2. Selkirk was given provisions including his clothes, a gun, and a Bible. (T)
3. Selkirk did not become depressed about being alone until he had been on the island for three years. (F)
4. After Selkirk's clothes wore out, he went naked because of the island's temperate climate. (F)
5. Selkirk once stated that he was happier when he had less money. (T)

gun. He accordingly found great quantities of turtles, whose flesh is extremely delicious, and of which he frequently ate very plentifully on his first arrival, till it grew disagreeable to his stomach, except in jellies.[5] The necessities of hunger and thirst were his greatest diversions from the reflection on his lonely condition. When those appetites were satisfied, the desire of society was as strong a call upon him, and he appeared to himself least necessitous when he wanted[6] everything; for the supports of his body were easily attained, but the eager longings for seeing again the face of man during the interval of craving bodily appetites were hardly supportable. He grew dejected, languid, and melancholy, scarce able to refrain from doing himself violence, till by degrees, by the force of reason, and frequent reading of the scriptures, and turning his thoughts upon the study of navigation, after the space of eighteen months he grew thoroughly reconciled to his condition. When he had made this conquest, the vigor of his health, disengagement from the world, a constant, cheerful, serene sky, and a temperate air made his life one continual feast, and his being much more joyful than it had before been irksome. He now taking delight in everything, made the hut in which he lay, by ornaments which he cut down from a spacious wood, on the side of which it was situated, the most delicious bower, fanned with continual breezes and gentle aspirations of wind, that made his repose after the chase equal to the most sensual pleasures.

I forgot to observe that during the time of his dissatisfaction, monsters of the deep, which frequently lay on the shore, added to the terrors of his solitude; the dreadful howlings and voices seemed too terrible to be made for human ears; but upon the recovery of his temper he could with pleasure not only hear their voices, but approach the monsters themselves with great intrepidity. He speaks of sea lions, whose jaws and tails were capable of seizing or breaking the limbs of a man if he approached them: But at that time his spirits and life were so high, and he could act so regularly and unconcerned, that merely from being unruffled in himself he killed them with the greatest ease imaginable: For observing that though their jaws and tails were so terrible, yet the animals being mighty slow in working themselves round,

he had nothing to do but place himself exactly opposite to their middle, and as close to them as possible, and he dispatched them with his hatchet at will.

The precaution which he took against want, in case of sickness, was to lame kids when very young so as that they might recover their health but never be capable of speed. These he had in great numbers about his hut; and when he was himself in full vigor, he could take at full speed the swiftest goat running up a promontory, and never failed of catching them but on a descent.

His habitation was extremely pestered with rats, which gnawed his clothes and feet when sleeping. To defend him against them, he fed and tamed numbers of young kitlings,[7] who lay about his bed and preserved him from the enemy. When his clothes were quite worn out, he dried and tacked together the skins of goats, with which he clothed himself, and was inured to pass through woods, bushes, and brambles with as much carelessness and precipitance as any other animal. It happened once to him that, running on the summit of a hill, he made a stretch to seize a goat, with which under him he fell down a precipice and lay senseless for the space of three days, the length of which time he measured by the moon's growth since his last observation. This manner of life grew so exquisitely pleasant that he never had a moment heavy upon his hands; his nights were untroubled and his days joyous from the practice of temperance and exercise. It was his manner to use stated hours and places for exercises of devotion, which he performed aloud, in order to keep up the faculties of speech, and to utter himself with greater energy.

When I first saw him, I thought, if I had not been let into his character and story, I could have discerned that he had been much separated from company from his aspect and gesture; there was a strong but cheerful seriousness in his look, and a certain disregard to the ordinary things about him, as if he had been sunk in thought. When the ship which brought him off the island came in, he received them with the greatest indifference, with relation to the prospect of going off with them, but with great satisfaction in an opportunity to refresh and help them. The man frequently bewailed his return to the world, which could not,

A (margin bracket)
B (margin bracket)

A. Responding
Comment on Steele's summary of Selkirk's progression of feelings, from need to dejection to vigor and joy. (Responses will vary. Students probably will find the progression natural, though some may feel that his final state of joy seems a bit extreme to modern readers.)

B. Responding
What does the essay gain from Steele's injection of his personal reactions in this paragraph? (It gains credibility and an easy informality of tone.)

---

5. **in jellies:** cooked and eaten cold.
6. **wanted:** lacked.

7. **kitlings:** cats.

CLOSURE
Have students sum up the theme of Steele's essay in two or three sentences, and cite one passage that supports the theme.

ANALYZING THE ESSAY
Identifying Facts
1. He needed food and companionship.
2. He found turtles on the shore to satis-fy his hunger, and he read the Scriptures to fight off the melancholy caused by his solitude.
   After an initial period of dejection, Selkirk began to take pleasure in all his daily activities (such as making his hut and the ornaments for it) and in his natural surroundings.
3. He did not want to surrender the happiness and tranquility he had there.

Interpreting Meanings
4. He describes him as intelligent, devout, determined, and practical.
   Note his physical endurance, his determination, and his religious faith.
5. Students may point out a number of details: the making of the hut, for example, as well as the searches for food and the characters' mastery of their natural (Answers continue in left-hand column.)

(Continued from top.)
surroundings.
6. Most students will agree that this quotation adequately sums up the theme. One statement of the theme might be: To be happy, we should confine our desires to natural necessities.
7. Student answers will vary.
   Most students will probably disagree that everyone would respond like Selkirk. Students may suggest that less determined, impractical people would give in to despair or suffer a nervous breakdown.
8. Student answers will vary. Encourage them to be specific when they point out similarities and differences.

he said, with all its enjoyments, restore him to the tranquillity of his solitude. Though I had frequently conversed with him, after a few months absence he met me in the street, and though he spoke to me, I could not recollect that I had seen him; familiar converse in this town had taken off the loneliness of his aspect, and quite altered the air of his face.

This plain man's story is a memorable example, that he is happiest who confines his wants to natural necessities; and he that goes further in his desires increases his wants in proportion to his acquisitions; or to use his own expression, *I am now worth eight hundred pounds, but shall never be so happy as when I was not worth a farthing.*

Responding to the Essay

Analyzing the Essay

Identifying Facts
1. What were Selkirk's two kinds of needs? How did he satisfy those needs?
2. What did he do to avoid becoming bored?
3. When the rescue ship arrived, why was Selkirk unwilling to leave his island?

Interpreting Meanings
4. How does Steele describe the **character** of Selkirk? What personal qualities enabled Selkirk to survive on the island?
5. What details from this account of Selkirk's experience can you see used in Defoe's *Robinson Crusoe*?
6. How well do you think the quotation from Selkirk at the end sums up the **theme** of the article? State the theme in your own words.
7. Do you ever feel that you would enjoy being alone for an extended period of time? Do you think everyone would respond to solitude as Selkirk did?
8. How are Selkirk's means of adjustment to solitude like or unlike the means used by contemporary survivors, prisoners, or hostages?

Writing About the Essay

A Critical Response
Examining a Conclusion. Steele concludes from his account of Selkirk that the happiest people confine their wants to "natural necessities." Write a paragraph or two explaining what Steele means by "natural necessities." Then, in another paragraph, explain why you agree or disagree with Steele's conclusion.

Selkirk Teaching His Cats and Goats to Dance

Analyzing Language and Style

Precise Meanings
This essay was written in 1713 and some of Steele's language would strike us as old-fashioned today. In a good dictionary, find the definitions of these words and tell what precise meaning each has in this essay. What word would more likely be used in each case today?

1. ". . . the different *revolutions* in his own mind . . ."
2. ". . . the *generality* of mankind . . ."
3. ". . . perform all *offices* of life . . ."
4. ". . . the most delicious *bower* . . ."
5. ". . . gentle *aspirations* of wind . . ."
6. ". . . familiar *converse* . . ."

Samuel Johnson (1709–1784)

Samuel Johnson was the dominant literary figure in England during the latter part of the eighteenth century. Johnson is famous not for one or two masterpieces, but for a great variety of writings of many kinds and for three large projects: *A Dictionary of the English Language* (1755); an edition of Shakespeare's plays (1765) with an important critical preface and interesting notes; and *The Lives of the Poets* (1779–1781) in ten volumes, a series of biographical-critical introductions. A wise man, a moralist, a talker, an eminent writer and critic, a beloved friend of people rich, poor, young, and old, Johnson became in his own day an English institution. Even today, his personality is vivid because so many of his contemporaries recorded their impressions of him. We think of him as a large, imposing person of untidy appearance and odd mannerisms, very fond of drinking tea—he avoided wine because he could not drink moderately—and discoursing with his friends on just about every subject that concerns human beings.

Of course he was not always like that. Johnson's beginnings were humble and unpromising. The son of an unsuccessful bookshop proprietor in the small city of Litchfield, he was a puny, weak infant who suffered from the effects of smallpox and scrofula, an infection of the lymph glands of the neck, which made him blind in one eye and deaf in one ear. Scrofula, it was believed, could be cured by the "royal touch"; and so Mrs. Johnson took her young son to London, where Queen Anne touched him along with two hundred other suffering children, and hung around his neck a thick gold medal on a ribbon, showing the archangel Michael. Johnson wore this medal through most of his life.

Despite his early weaknesses, Johnson grew into a sturdy youth, gradually exhibiting the qualities that characterized him as an adult: vigor, courage, pride, bossiness, and dedication to learning. He had to leave Oxford after only one year because he lacked money to continue; after that, he was spectacularly unsuccessful as a teacher in a private school. In 1737 he went to London with one of his pupils, David Garrick,

Samuel Johnson by Sir Joshua Reynolds (1756). Oil.

The Tate Gallery, London.

who was to become the greatest actor and theatrical entrepreneur of the age. Meantime, Johnson had married Elizabeth Porter, a widow twenty years his senior, whom he called Tetty and loved passionately.

To support himself and his wife, Johnson wrote a tragedy, *Irene*, which was moderately successful. For many years he did hack work for periodicals, especially the *Gentleman's Magazine*, often called the first magazine. Here he published "Debates in the Senate of Lilliputia," which pretended to be fictions but were really disguised accounts of debates in Parliament. (It was illegal to print the actual speeches.) In these years, while Johnson was struggling for recognition, he became addicted to the city life in London, and began to disparage life in the countryside and provincial cities. "There is in London," he once said, "all that life can afford"; and "when a man is tired of London, he is tired of life."

People came to enjoy listening to Johnson because he talked so well; he apparently always knew what he was going to say before he started to speak, and his words came out in beautifully

A. Expansion
Johnson is often referred to as "Dr. Johnson," because late in his lifetime Oxford University conferred on him an honorary LL.D (Doctorate of Laws). He also earned the nickname "The Great Cham" (for "Champion") of literature. On the other hand, Johnson himself suffered from no illusions about the difficulty of writing. He struggled for years to make a decent living, and Boswell reports that he once said that "no man but a blockhead" ever wrote except for money.

B. Humanities Connection: About the Fine Art
It was Sir Joshua Reynolds who suggested the idea of forming the Literary Club to Johnson. His *Discourses,* delivered to students of the Academy between 1769 and 1790, are considered valuable documents of neoclassic aesthetic criticism, especially for their discussion of the role of the "sublime" in the arts. Reynolds paid tribute to Johnson by saying that "he cleared my mind of a great deal of rubbish."

? In the artist's most famous portrait of his friend (one of five), what does the expression on Johnson's face and the position of his hands suggest about his character? (Possibly that he is sensitive or dramatic)

A. Boswell

A. Boswell
For numerous entertaining anecdotes about Johnson's life and conversation, we are most indebted to James Boswell's *Life* (see text page 576). Boswell did not meet Johnson until 1763, when Johnson was in middle age and already famous. But the *Life*, published seven years after Johnson's death, affords us perhaps the most detailed and intimate view of any major literary figure in history.

A. Boswell
For numerous entertaining anecdotes about Johnson's life and conversation, we are most indebted to James Boswell's *Life* (see text page 576). Boswell did not meet Johnson until 1763, when Johnson was in middle age and already famous. But the *Life*, published seven years after Johnson's death, affords us perhaps the most detailed and intimate view of any major literary figure in history.

B. Expansion
Boswell records that Johnson wrote *Rasselas* in a week to pay the expenses of his mother's funeral. The short novel derives from the form of the travelogue, and it may be compared with Voltaire's *Candide,* published in the same year. But *Rasselas* is also notable for numerous important statements on morals and literary criticism.

C. Expansion
Johnson's private religious reflections and his personal struggles to live a more disciplined, Christian life are movingly evident in his *Diaries and Prayers.*

rounded sentences, just as though he were writing. He knew his own mind, and he expressed his opinions as though they were facts. When asked a question, he would reply with great firmness and vigor:

> *Questioner:* "How did you acquire your great facility in Latin?"
> *Johnson:* "My master whipt me very well. Without that, Sir, I should have done nothing."

A All sorts of people started coming to Johnson for advice. Johnson's friend Mrs. Hester Piozzi records this anecdote:

> A young gentleman called on him one morning, and told him that his father having, just before his death, dropped suddenly into the enjoyment of an ample fortune, he, the son, was willing to qualify himself for genteel society by adding some literature to his other endowments, and wished to be put in an easy way of obtaining it. Johnson recommended the university: "for you read Latin, sir, with *facility.*" "I read it a little to be sure, sir." "But do you read it *with facility,* I say?" "Upon my word, sir, I do not very well know, but I rather believe not." Mr. Johnson now began to recommend other branches of science, when he found languages at such an immeasurable distance, and advising him to study natural history, there arose some talk about animals, and their divisions into oviparous and viviparous. "And the cat here, sir," said the youth who wished for instruction, "pray in which class is she?" Our doctor's patience and desire of doing good began now to give way to the natural roughness of his temper. "You would do well (said he) to look for some person to be always about you, sir, who is capable of explaining such matters, and not come to us [there were some literary friends present as I recollect] to know whether the cat lays eggs or not: Get a discreet man to keep you company, there are so

many who would be glad of your table and fifty pounds a year." The young gentleman retired, and in less than a week informed his friends that he had fixed on a preceptor to whom no objections could be made.

Gradually Johnson's days of poverty and obscurity came to an end. In 1750 he began publishing, twice a week, a series of essays called *The Rambler.* These made him famous as "a teacher of moral and religious wisdom," to quote his biographer, James Boswell. Other essay series followed: *The Adventurer* (1753–1754), *The Idler* (1759), and an oriental tale entitled *History of Rasselas, Prince of Abyssinia* (1759). **B** Meanwhile, his prodigious *Dictionary* (1755) had been published, and in 1762, in recognition of his services to literature, King George III—an English monarch that most Americans have heard of—awarded him a life pension of three hundred pounds a year. Sad to say, Tetty did not live to see her husband famous, prosperous, and the recipient of honorary degrees from Oxford University and Trinity College, Dublin.

C Johnson shared his prosperity with others, for he was always a devout man and his religion required him to be charitable. He also could not stand to be alone, with no one to talk to. He took into his household and maintained a number of unfortunate people, including a Mrs. Williams, who was old and blind, and an obscure, shy man named Robert Levet, who practiced medicine among the London poor. At the other social extreme, he numbered among his intimates the great painter Sir Joshua Reynolds, the statesman Edmund Burke, the historian Edward Gibbon, the actor David Garrick, and his fellow writer Oliver Goldsmith. These eminent men formed a club that met regularly for elegant dinners and agreeable conversation. Johnson also frequently enjoyed the hospitality of Henry and Hester Thrale, a rich brewer and his wife. After Johnson's death Mrs. Thrale published her *Anecdotes* about him, in which she said, "no man loved laughing better."

PREPARATION
ESTABLISHING A PURPOSE. Before students begin reading, you might have them read questions 8 and 9 on text page 558.

SUPPLEMENTARY SUPPORT MATERIALS
1. Vocabulary Activity Worksheet (*CCB*)
2. Selection Test (*CCB*)

FROM A DICTIONARY OF THE ENGLISH LANGUAGE

A. About the Illustration
Draw students' attention to the resemblances between portable bookstalls of Johnson's time and modern ones. If the figure in the center is the bookseller, he will also have been a publisher, since the printing and retailing of books were undertaken by the same entrepreneur in the eighteenth century. This sign in the tree suggests that these books might be from the library of someone who has died.

Johnson's *Dictionary*—the first comprehensive and authoritative one in English—contains about 40,000 words and many, many definitions. The verb *to take*, for instance, has one hundred and thirteen different meanings, and *to set*, sixty-six. Most of these definitions Johnson wrote himself; those he took from the word books of his predecessors he is careful to identify. Before Johnson's time, academies of scholars in France and in Italy had produced large dictionaries of French and Italian, but there was no such academy in England. Therefore, Johnson took on the job himself: England must have its own dictionary, and Johnson was the man to write it!

How did he do it? He first read an enormous number of literary, religious, philosophical, scientific, and technical books, most of them borrowed from friends. As he read, he marked passages and underlined a key word in each passage; this was the word he intended to define. Next, his copyists—he had six of them, all Scotsmen except one—copied out the marked passages on slips of paper and filed each slip alphabetically according to the key word. Then the slips were pasted into eighty large notebooks. Finally, using the passages, Johnson wrote definitions of the key words. There were originally about 240,000 passages—too many to be printed. When the *Dictionary* was finally put out in 1755 by a combination of five publishing firms, it contained about 114,000 illustrative passages.

Johnson's *Dictionary* was, and is, a prodigious accomplishment. Forty members of the French Academy worked for forty-five years on the French dictionary; Johnson and his six copyists worked for about nine years on the English one. The *Dictionary* made Johnson's name familiar to every literate person in England and the American colonies. It was the basis of all subsequent English dictionaries, including those of the American Noah Webster (1758–1843), who did little else in his lifetime except compile dictionaries that contained thousands of definitions and illustrative quotations taken without acknowledgement from

A Portable Bookstall (ca. 1700). Engraving.

Johnson. Johnson's *Dictionary* was not completely superseded until 1928, when the last of the ten volumes of *A New English Dictionary* was published. This work, revised in thirteen volumes, is now called *The Oxford English Dictionary* (OED).

Though superseded, Johnson's *Dictionary* lives on because a few of the definitions reflect his interesting character and sense of humor. None of the selections given here is a complete entry; there are no etymologies or origins of the words, no definitions reflecting the various shades of meaning, and no illustrative quotations. For an example of a complete definition, here is the entry for the words *giggle* and *giggler*:

The two boxes on pages 556 and 557 show two entries from the original dictionary. The definition of *oats,* on text page 557, is a famous one, showing Johnson's opinion of Scotland, a country for which he regularly expressed his contempt. (The *s* that looks like an *f* reflects the old Gothic script.)

1. Johnson's *Dictionary* was the first comprehensive dictionary in English. (T)
2. Johnson derived most of his dictionary definitions from the work of his predecessors. (F)
3. Johnson chose the words for his *Dictionary* by asking friends what words they had the most difficulty with. (F)

4. Because of the *Dictionary,* Johnson's name became familiar to every literate person in England and the American colonies. (T)
5. Johnson's dictionary was the basis of all subsequent English dictionaries, except those of Noah Webster. (F)

A. Distinctions
❓ What *is* the difference between an alligator and a crocodile? (A crocodile's snout comes to a point in front; an alligator's snout is rounded. The American crocodile is only about two-thirds as heavy as an alligator, and can move much more quickly.)

B. Word Histories
❓ What word used today does this word look like? (Apricot) Are the two words related? (Yes. Both are from the Latin *apricum,* "a sunny place.") How might the apricot have gotten its name? (From its sunny color)

C. Slang
Here is a "low" word, or slang.
❓ Is *budge* considered slang today? What does this indicate about language? (Usage once considered inappropriate is frequently later accepted in "polite society.")

D. Word Changes
The word *pickle* in the British Isles often refers to any pungent sauce used to heighten the flavor of meat.

To GI'GGLE. *v. n.* [*gichgelen,* Dutch.] To laugh idly ; to titter ; to grin with merry levity. It is retained in Scotland.
GI'GGLER. *n. ʃ.* [from *giggle.*] A laugher ; a titterer ; one idly and foolishly merry.

> A sad wise valour is the brave complexion,
> That leads the van, and swallows up the cities:
> The *giggler* is a milk-maid, whom infection,
> Or the fir'd beacon, frighteth from his ditties.   *Herbert.*
> We shew our present, joking, *giggling* race ;
> True joy consists in gravity and grace.   *Garrick's Epilogue.*

A **alligator.** The crocodile. This name is chiefly used for the crocodile of America, between which, and that of Africa, naturalists have laid down this difference, that one moves the upper, and the other the lower jaw; but this is now known to be chimerical,[1] the lower jaw being equally moved by both.

amulet. A thing hung about the neck, or any other part of the body, for preventing or curing of some particular diseases.

and. The particle by which sentences or terms are joined, which it is not easy to explain by any synonymous word.

B **to apricate.** To bask in the sun.

athletic. Strong of body; vigorous; lusty; robust.

autopsy. Ocular demonstration; seeing a thing oneself.

balderdash. Anything jumbled together without judgment; rude mixture; a confused discourse.

bedpresser. A heavy lazy fellow.

bee. The animal that makes honey, remarkable for its industry and art.

to blab. To tell what ought to be kept secret.

board. A piece of wood of more length and breadth than thickness.

C **to budge.** To stir; to move off the place: a low word.

D **catsup.** A kind of pickle, made from mushrooms.

companion. A familiar term of contempt, a fellow.

cough. A convulsion of the lungs, vellicated by some sharp serosity. It is pronounced *coff.*

dedication. A servile address to a patron.

den. A cavern or hollow running horizontally, or with small obliquity, underground; distinct from a hole, which runs down perpendicularly.

dull. Not exhilarating; not delightful; as *To make dictionaries is* dull *work.*

eel. A serpentine slimy fish, that lurks in mud.

essay. A loose sally of the mind; an irregular indigested piece; not a regular and orderly composition.

excise. A hateful tax levied upon commodities, and adjudged not by the common judges of property, but wretches hired by those to whom excise is paid.

favorite. One chosen as a companion by his superior; a mean wretch whose whole business is by any means to please.

fillip. A jerk of the finger let go from the thumb.

frightfully. Disagreeably; not beautifully. A woman's word.

fun. (A low cant[2] word.) Sport; high merriment; frolicsome delight.

gambler. (A cant word, I suppose, for *game,* or *gamester.*) A knave whose practice it is to invite the unwary to game and cheat them.

1. **chimerical** (ki·mir′i·k′l): fanciful.

2. **cant:** a word used to describe language that the writer or speaker disapproves of.

ANALYZING THE DEFINITIONS
Identifying Facts
1. Possibilities include *autopsy, balderdash, companion, dedication, essay, favorite, fillip, jogger, pension, period, vivacious,* and *worm.*
2. Possibilities include *budge, fun, gamble, immaterial, lesser, lingo, slim,* and *traipse.*
3. Possibilities include *bedpresser, mer-*

rythought, mushroom, and *suds.*
4. Possibilities include *cant, cough, den, network, smoke, sneeze,* and *soup.*
5. He includes moral advice when he defines *palmistry* and *slim.*
6. Possibilities include *bee, blab, pompous,* and *romp.*
(Answers continue on next page.)

to giggle. To laugh idly; to titter; to grin with merry levity. It is retained in Scotland.

A **goose.** A large waterfowl, proverbially noted, I know not why, for foolishness.

gravy. The serous juice that runs from flesh not much dried by the fire.

B **hiss.** To utter a noise like that of a serpent and some other animals. It is remarkable that this word cannot be pronounced without making the noise it signifies.

immaterial. Unimportant; without weight; impertinent; without relation. This sense has crept into the conversation and writings of barbarians, but ought to be utterly rejected.

C **jogger.** One who moves heavily and dully.

lesser. A barbarous corruption of *less,* formed by the vulgar from the habit of terminating comparatives in *er;* afterward adopted by poets and then by writers of prose.

lexicographer. A writer of dictionaries; a harmless drudge that busies himself in tracing the original, and detailing the signification of words.

to lift. To rob; to plunder.

lingo. Language; tongue; speech. A low cant word.

lunch, luncheon. As much food as one's hand can hold.

merrythought. A forked bone on the body of fowls; so called because boys and girls pull in play at the two sides, the longest part broken off betokening priority of marriage.

mouth. The aperture in the head of any animal at which the food is received.

mushroom. An upstart; a wretch risen from the dunghill; a director of a company.

network. Anything reticulated or decussated, at equal distances, with interstices between the intersections.

oats. A grain, which in England is generally given to horses, but in Scotland supports the people.

osprey. The sea-eagle, of which it is reported, that when he hovers in the air, all the fish in the

water turn up their bellies and lie still for him to seize which he pleases.

palmistry. The cheat of foretelling fortune by the palm of the hand.

parody. A kind of writing in which the words of an author or his thoughts are taken, and by a slight change adapted to some new purpose.

pastern. The knee of a horse.

pat. Fit, convenient; exactly suitable either as to time or place. This is a low word, and should not be used but in burlesque writings.

patron. One who countenances, supports, or protects. Commonly a wretch who supports with insolence, and is paid with flattery.

pension. An allowance made to anyone without an equivalent. In England it is generally understood to mean pay given to a state hireling for treason to his country.

to period. To put an end to. A bad word.

pompous. Splendid; magnificent; grand.

rhinoceros. A vast beast in the East Indies armed with a horn in its front.

river. A land current of water bigger than a brook.

romance. A tale of wild adventures in love and war.

to romp. To play rudely, noisily, and boisterously.

slim. (A cant word as it seems, and therefore not to be used.) Slender; thin of shape.

smoke. The visible effluvium or sooty exhalation from anything burning.

to sneeze. To emit wind audibly by the nose.

sonnet. A short poem consisting of fourteen lines, of which the rhymes are adjusted by a particular rule. It is not very suitable to the English language, and has not been used by any man of eminence since Milton.

soup. Strong decoction of flesh for the table.

stammel. Of this word I know not the meaning.

suds. A lixivium of soap and water.

tiny. Little; small; puny. A burlesque word.

tittletwattle. Tattle; gabble. A vile word.

torpedo. A fish which while alive, if touched even

OATS. *n. f.* [aʒen, Saxon.] A grain, which in England is generally given to horſes, but in Scotland ſupports the people.

A. Proverbs
? What do you think is the proverbial connection of geese with foolishness? ("Silly as a goose")

B. Echoic Words
Hiss is an example of what lexicographers today call an echoic word. Poets use such words for onomatopoeia.

C. Changes in Meaning
? How is this word used today? (A jogger is one who runs for sport or to enjoy health benefits.)

D. Definitions
? What are some other, modern meanings of the word *pat*? (Tap; small, molded mass; apt; firm)

E. Tone
Compare this definition with the sentiments expressed in the letter on text page 559.

F. Writing Definitions
Words like *sneeze* and *cough* are very hard to define. You might have students suggest other such words and then attempt to define them.

Interpreting Meanings

7. Johnson displays an unfavorable attitude toward slang.

8. Possibilities include the definitions of *hiss, lexicographer, lunch,* and *osprey.*

9. Possibilities include the definitions of *excise, oats, pension, tory,* and *whig.*

10. Possibilities include the definitions of *catsup* and *rhinoceros.*

11. Student answers will vary. Students should include in their discussion some comments about the "living," changing aspects of language. You might want to supplement the discussion with some reference to Johnson's own comments on the *Dictionary,* in which he protested against the concept (then much in vogue with the French Academy) that language was a fossilized, unchanging element that ought to be preserved pure and inviolate.

---

with a long stick, benumbs the hand that so touches it, but when dead is eaten safely.

tory. (A cant term, derived, I suppose, from an Irish word signifying a savage.) One who adheres to the ancient constitution of the state, and the apostolical hierarchy of the Church of England, opposed to a whig.

to traipse. A low word, I believe, without any etymology. To walk in a careless or sluttish manner.

tree. A large vegetable rising, with one woody stem, to a considerable height.

unkindly. Unnatural; contrary to nature.

vivacious. Long-lived.

whale. The largest of fish.

whig. The name of a faction.

whist. A game at cards, requiring close attention and silence.

to worm. To deprive a dog of something, nobody knows what, under his tongue, which is said to prevent him, nobody knows why, from running mad.

zed. The name of the letter *z.*

Responding to the Definitions

Analyzing the Definitions

Identifying Facts

1. Which words in these excerpts from the *Dictionary* have undergone extensive changes in meaning since Johnson's day?
2. Which words did Johnson label as improper but are no longer so regarded?
3. Which words do we regard as slangy but which Johnson apparently accepted as standard English?
4. Which words are defined by terms that are themselves too strange and complex to be understood?
5. In which definitions does Johnson include moral advice?
6. What common words does Johnson define in a sensible, economical way?

Interpreting Meanings

7. What is Johnson's attitude toward slang, which he calls "low words" or "cant"?
8. Which definitions show Johnson's sense of humor?
9. Which definitions show Johnson's political and religious preferences?
10. Which definitions contain what we would regard as errors of fact?

11. From the answers you gave to these questions, what inferences can you make about language, especially about the way it changes?

Writing About the Dictionary

A Creative Response

1. **Writing Dictionary Definitions.** Make your own dictionary of twenty words. In each entry, first give the part of speech; second, give at least one common definition; last, write a complete sentence that illustrates how the word is used. The only rule for this exercise is that you cannot look in a dictionary until after your definitions are finished. Include in your twenty words these: *apple, door, growl, nose, song, turtle.*

A Critical Response

2. **Drawing Inferences.** Study Johnson's definitions and write a long paragraph in which you describe the character of the man who wrote them. Consider these questions: What is he interested in? What are his likes and dislikes and biases? Is he proud? Is he capable of laughing at himself? Is he ever modest? Cite parts of the dictionary excerpts to illustrate your points.

PREPARATION

ESTABLISHING A PURPOSE.   Have students read question 5 on text page 560.

SUPPLEMENTARY SUPPORT MATERIALS
1. Vocabulary Activity Worksheet (*CCB*)
2. Review and Response Worksheet: Purpose (*CCB*)
3. Selection Test (*CCB*)

DEVELOPING VOCABULARY
The following words from the letter are tested in the Selection Test. (See also Vocabulary Activity Worksheet.)
proprietor   to encumber
to repulse

CLOSURE
Have students explain what Johnson's letter to Lord Chesterfield is about.

LETTER TO LORD CHESTERFIELD

Long before Johnson completed work on his dictionary, he put out a pamphlet entitled *Plan of a Dictionary of the English Language* (1747). The pamphlet was dedicated, at his publisher's suggestion, to Philip Dormer Stanhope, fourth Earl of Chesterfield—an accomplished, rich, elegant, and learned nobleman. The publisher, Robert Dodsley, wanted Chesterfield's patronage, or financial support, of this very expensive venture. But nothing came of the attempt to capture the great man's interest, although Johnson called on him a few times and at least once was denied entrance. He received only a token contribution from Chesterfield: ten pounds.

Eight years later, just before the finished dictionary actually appeared, Dodsley again approached Chesterfield, who by this time had probably forgotten all about the *Plan* and its dedication to him. After all, Chesterfield was a very important and busy man. This time he did respond, though not by giving money. Without ever having seen the dictionary, he published two letters praising it in a weekly newspaper.

Johnson, not knowing that Dodsley had again approached Chesterfield, read the two generous letters with surprise and indignation. They could easily be misconstrued; the public might conclude from them that Chesterfield had given what nowadays would be called a "grant" to Johnson. The letters put Johnson in an embarrassing position because he had asserted in the preface to the *Dictionary* that he had received no "patronage of the great." And so he wrote Chesterfield a letter that has since become famous. The language of the letter is very formal; how would you describe its tone?

To the Right Honorable the Earl of Chesterfield, February 7, 1755.

My Lord, I have been lately informed, by the proprietor of the World,[1] that two papers, in which my Dictionary is recommended to the public, were written by your Lordship. To be so distinguished is an honor, which, being very little accustomed to favors from the great, I know not well how to receive, or in what terms to acknowledge.

When, upon some slight encouragement, I first visited your Lordship, I was overpowered, like the rest of mankind, by the enchantment of your address, and could not forbear to wish that I might boast myself *Le vainqueur du vainqueur de la terre*,[2] that I might obtain that regard for which I saw the world contending; but I found my attendance so little encouraged that neither pride nor modesty would suffer me to continue it. When I had once addressed your Lordship in public, I had exhausted all the art of pleasing which a retired and uncourtly scholar can possess. I had done all that I could; and no man is well pleased to have his all neglected, be it ever so little.

Seven years, my Lord, have now passed since I waited in your outward rooms, or was repulsed from your door; during which time I have been pushing on my work through difficulties of which it is useless to complain, and have brought it at last to the verge of publication without one act of assistance, one word of encouragement, or one smile of favor. Such treatment I did not expect, for I never had a patron before.

The shepherd in Virgil[3] grew at last acquainted with Love, and found him a native of the rocks.

---

1. **World:** the name of the newspaper in which Chesterfield published his letters praising the *Dictionary*.
2. *Le vainqueur . . . terre:* The conqueror of the conqueror of the world. Chesterfield would recognize that Johnson is quoting the first line of a French poem.

3. **The shepherd in Virgil:** A shepherd in one of Virgil's pastoral poems discovered that love is unkind; Johnson similarly discovered that patrons are unkind.

A. Expansion
Chesterfield (1694–1773) achieved considerable literary distinction for his *Letters* to his son, which commented on gentlemanly manners and deportment.

B. Irony
Note Johnson's heavily ironic use of the word *patron*.

ANALYZING THE LETTER
Identifying Facts
1. He stopped because he received no encouragement or tangible aid from Chesterfield.
2. He ironically defines a patron as someone who looks with indifference on a drowning man, and then, once the man has reached ground, "encumbers" him with help.

3. Johnson says that Providence has enabled him to complete his task himself.
4. Johnson says that, at least in this situation, hope was a dream.

Interpreting Meanings
5. Most students will probably agree that Johnson's purpose was to set the record straight.
6. Johnson uses irony in the first para-

graph, where he speaks of not knowing how to receive the "honor" that Chesterfield has paid him. He is also ironic when he defines a patron in the fifth paragraph.
    The tone of the letter might be described as one of dignified reproach.
7. Modesty, simplicity; he has no important connections.
8. Some students may suggest that
(Answers continue in left-hand column.)

Is not a patron, my Lord, one who looks with unconcern on a man struggling for life in the water, and, when he has reached ground, encumbers him with help? The notice which you have been pleased to take of my labors, had it been early, had been kind; but it has been delayed till I am indifferent, and cannot enjoy it; till I am solitary,[4] and cannot impart it; till I am known and do not want[5] it. I hope it is no very cynical asperity[6] not to confess obligations where no benefit has been received, or to be unwilling that the public should consider me as owing that to a patron, which Providence has enabled me to do for myself.

Having carried on my work thus far with so little obligation to any favorer of learning, I shall not be disappointed though I should conclude it, if less be possible, with less; for I have been long wakened from that dream of hope, in which I once boasted myself with so much exultation.

> My Lord,
> Your Lordship's most humble
> Most obedient servant,
> SAM. JOHNSON

---

4. **solitary:** Johnson's wife had been dead for three years.
5. **want:** need.
6. **asperity:** bitterness, sharpness.

Responding to the Letter

Analyzing the Letter

Identifying Facts

1. Johnson says that he had asked the Earl for help, but stopped. Why did he stop?
2. How does Johnson define a patron?
3. To whom does Johnson give credit for his accomplishment?
4. What does Johnson say about hope at the letter's end?

Interpreting Meanings

5. What, apparently, was Johnson's **purpose** in writing the letter? To set the record straight? To annoy Chesterfield? To rebuke him? To gloat over him?
6. Where in the letter does Johnson use **irony**? How would you describe the letter's **tone**?
7. Johnson refers to himself as an "uncourtly scholar." What traits does such a person typically possess?
8. Chesterfield did not take offense at the letter, but kept it lying on a table in his office, where any visitor might read it. Why do you suppose he didn't become angry?

Writing About the Letter

A Creative Response

1. **Replying to a Letter.** Imagine that you are Lord Chesterfield. Write a reply to Johnson explaining why you did not support his efforts and why you later wrote the letters to the newspapers. Write in formal language, as befits an earl.
2. **Paraphrasing a Letter.** Johnson was a master of both written and oral language, and this letter illustrates his formal style of writing. Rewrite Johnson's letter into a less formal, more contemporary style, retaining all of his meaning. You may restructure his sentences, but try to make your letter flow smoothly and sound pleasant to the ear.

A Critical Response

3. **Identifying Satirical Elements.** What elements of **satire** do you find in this letter? In a short essay explain how Johnson uses satire. Use quotations from the letter to illustrate your points.

PREPARATION

1. BUILDING ON PRIOR KNOWLEDGE. Ask students to comment on what they have read of Shakespeare in anthologies, in paperback books, in annotated editions, or in editions of collected works. Have students read Dryden's earlier comments on Shakespeare on text page 460.

2. ESTABLISHING A PURPOSE. Ask students to read the discussion of style in the essay on Elements of Literature (text page 565). Review the following elements: Latinate words, parallel structure, exact expressions, and strong metaphors. Have students be aware of these elements of style as they read Johnson's essay.

3. PREREADING JOURNAL. Before they read, have students write at least three sentences summarizing what they think of Shakespeare's characters and themes. If they can remember only *Macbeth,* limit the assignment to *Macbeth.*

FROM THE PREFACE TO SHAKESPEARE

A. Responding to the Medallion

❓ What mixture of moods do the poses of the figures on the medallion suggest? (Tragic and comic) Where is Shakespeare? (On the pedestal) What sorts of awards are given to actors today, and how do they compare with this? (Oscar, Tony, Emmy. They are mass-produced, and this is unique. They are statues for public display; this is to be worn as a piece of jewelry.)

An enamel medallion presented to David Garrick by his fellow artists at Drury Lane in 1777.

Folger Shakespeare Library, Washington, D.C.

SUPPLEMENTARY SUPPORT MATERIALS
1. Vocabulary Activity Worksheet (*CCB*)
2. Review and Response Worksheet: Style (*CCB*)
3. Selection Test (*CCB*)

DEVELOPING VOCABULARY
The following words from the essay are tested in the Selection Test. (See also Vocabulary Activity Worksheet.)

invective   progeny
infallible   depravity
approbation   exigency
satiety

A. Expansion
The pettiness of some of these critics was epitomized by Thomas Rymer (1641–1713) in *A Short View of Tragedy* (1692). Rymer criticized the hero's jealousy in *Othello* as improperly motivated and remarked that the lesson provided by Desdemona's handkerchief was that "ladies should look to their linen." Johnson referred to such censures as "the petty cavils of petty minds."

B. Generalization
[?] Analyze carefully the generalizations presented in this central paragraph. Do you agree with Johnson's opinion?

C. Main Idea
Be sure students can paraphrase this famous line, which might be said to contain the main idea of the essay.

Almost none of the books that people wrote and published in the past can be bought in bookstores today. Though a few old books may be found in secondhand shops, most of them can be obtained only in large libraries. They are "out of print," as bookish people say. Shakespeare's works are among the handful of exceptions to this rule. His poems and plays have always stayed "in print," ever since they were first published. Each succeeding age has produced Shakespeare—on the stage or screen or in books—in ways that satisfied people's needs at that time. And so like Pope before him, Johnson "edited" a set of Shakespeare's works.

Editing consists of a number of intellectual tasks that Johnson was well qualified to perform. For example, in a few places the texts of the plays were originally misprinted; to make them intelligible, the editor must restore the words that Shakespeare probably wanted there. Since for some plays more than one version exists, the editor must also determine which version or combination of versions is to be printed. Finally, the editor must clarify many difficult matters: obsolete words and expressions, references to people and events that have been forgotten, customs and practices long out of use.

Above all, Johnson the editor, being convinced of Shakespeare's preeminence as a dramatic poet, wanted to explain to others just why Shakespeare is so great, why he has lasted such a long time and has held the interest of readers and audiences. This is the subject of the excerpt from Johnson's preface which follows.

[A] Today, of course, practically everybody acknowledges that Shakespeare is England's greatest writer. But in Johnson's time, and just before that time, a group of critics attacked Shakespeare for his alleged irregularities and errors: They accused Shakespeare of violating the so-called "unity of time" in plays that cover many years. They accused him of violating the "unity of place" by moving the action in his plays from one locale to another (*Antony and Cleopatra* covers most of the Mediterranean basin). Worst of all, they accused Shakespeare of violating the "unity of action" by combining comic and tragic elements in the same play. Out of his vast fund of common sense Johnson argued that all of these artificial "unities" are irrelevant to the genuine pleasure and profit that Shakespeare's plays provide.

The poet[1] of whose works I have undertaken the revision may now begin to assume the dignity of an ancient,[2] and claim the privilege of established fame and prescriptive veneration. He has long outlived his century, the term commonly fixed as the test of literary merit.[3] Whatever advantages he might once derive from personal allusions, local customs, or temporary opinions have for many years been lost; and every topic of merriment or motive of sorrow, which the modes of artificial life afforded him, now only obscure the scenes which they once illuminated. The effects of favor and competition are at an end; the tradition of his friendships and his enmities has perished; his works support no opinion with arguments, nor supply any faction with invectives; they can neither indulge vanity nor gratify malignity, but are read without any other reason than the desire of pleasure, and are therefore praised only as pleasure is obtained; yet, thus unassisted by interest or passion, they have passed through variations of taste and changes of manners and, as they devolved from one generation to another, have received new honors at every transmission.

But because human judgment, though it be gradually gaining upon certainty, never becomes infallible, and approbation, though long continued, may yet be only the approbation of prejudice or fashion, it is proper to inquire by what peculiarities of excellence Shakespeare has gained and kept the favor of his countrymen.

[B] Nothing can please many, and please long, but just representations of general nature.[4] Particular manners can be known to few, and therefore few only can judge how nearly they are copied. The irregular combinations of fanciful invention may delight a while by that novelty of which the common satiety of life sends us all in quest; but the pleasures of sudden wonder are soon exhausted, and the mind can only repose on the stability of truth.

[C] Shakespeare is, above all writers, at least above all modern writers, the poet of nature; the poet that holds up to his readers a faithful mirror of manners and of life. His characters are not mod-

---

1. **poet:** Shakespeare.
2. **an ancient:** a great writer who lived in antiquity, such as Homer.
3. **merit:** the Roman poet Horace said that an author has merit who is still read a century after his or her time.
4. **general nature:** Johnson's term for the way people in general behave; *nature* here means human nature.

READING CHECK TEST

1. According to Johnson, Shakespeare depicts life and human nature as they really are. (T)
2. Shakespeare's plays provide a great deal of instruction through their practical axioms and domestic wisdom. (T)

3. Shakespeare focuses most of his attention upon the emotion of love. (F)
4. Shakespeare's characters are unusually distinctive from each other. (T)
5. Even when Shakespeare writes of things that are not possible, he does so in a believable manner. (T)

A. Interpreting

❓ Explain the point Johnson is making in this anecdote. (Shakespeare's greatness is seen better in the large issues—for example, in themes and in the development of character over the course of a play—than in small matters, such as phrasing and word choice in a given line.)

B. Responding

❓ Would people today agree that Shakespeare's characters, despite their archaic usage, exhibit ease, naturalness, and simplicity in their dialogue? Explain. (Students should note that Shakespeare's characters continue to make new friends in each generation of readers.)

C. Responding

❓ The apparent dismissal of love as "only one of many passions" that has "no great influence upon the sum of life" is one of the most controversial aspects of Johnson's critique. How do you respond to Johnson's statements here? (Many students will disagree with Johnson's seeming trivialization of love.) What kind of love is he talking about specifically? (The way love was portrayed on the stage of his time)

D. Responding

❓ Does this statement still apply to dramatists today? (Consider TV and movie dramatists, as well as those of the legitimate theater.)

ified by the customs of particular places, unpracticed by the rest of the world; by the peculiarities of studies or professions, which can operate but upon small numbers; or by the accidents of transient fashions or temporary opinions; they are the genuine <u>progeny</u> of common humanity, such as the world will always supply and observation will always find. His persons act and speak by the influence of those general passions and principles by which all minds are agitated and the whole system of life is continued in motion. In the writings of other poets a character is too often an individual; in those of Shakespeare it is commonly a species.

It is from this wide extension of design that so much instruction is derived. It is this which fills the plays of Shakespeare with practical axioms and domestic wisdom. It was said of Euripides[5] that every verse was a precept; and it may be said of Shakespeare that from his works may be collected a system of civil and economical prudence. Yet his real power is not shown in the splendor of particular passages, but by the progress of his fable and the tenor of his dialogue; and he that tries to recommend him by select quotations will succeed like the pedant in Hierocles,[6] who, when he offered his house to sale, carried a brick in his pocket as a specimen.

It will not easily be imagined how much Shakespeare excels in accommodating his sentiments to real life, but by comparing him with other authors. It was observed of the ancient schools of declamation that the more diligently they were frequented, the more was the student disqualified for the world, because he found nothing there which he should ever meet in any other place. The same remark may be applied to every stage[7] but that of Shakespeare. The theater, when it is under any other direction, is peopled by such characters as were never seen, conversing in a language which was never heard, upon topics which will never arise in the commerce of mankind. But the dialogue of this author is often so evidently determined by the incident which produces it, and is pursued with so much ease and simplicity, that it seems scarcely to claim the merit of fiction, but

to have been gleaned by diligent selection out of common conversation and common occurrences.

Upon every other stage the universal agent is love, by whose power all good and evil is distributed and every action quickened or retarded. To bring a lover, a lady, and a rival into the fable; to entangle them in contradictory obligations, perplex them with oppositions of interest, and harass them with violence of desires inconsistent with each other; to make them meet in rapture and part in agony; to fill their mouths with hyperbolical joy and outrageous sorrow; to distress them as nothing human ever was distressed; to deliver them as nothing human ever was delivered: is the business of a modern dramatist. For this probability is violated, life is misrepresented, and language is depraved. But love is only one of many passions, and, as it has no great influence upon the sum of life, it has little operation in the dramas of a poet, who caught his ideas from the living world and exhibited only what he saw before him. He knew that any other passion, as it was regular or exorbitant, was a cause of happiness or calamity.

Characters thus ample and general were not easily discriminated and preserved, yet perhaps no poet ever kept his personages more distinct from each other. I will not say with Pope[8] that every speech may be assigned to the proper speaker, because many speeches there are which have nothing characteristical; but, perhaps, though some may be equally adapted to every person, it will be difficult to find any that can be properly transferred from the present possessor to another claimant. The choice is right, when there is reason for choice.

Other dramatists can only gain attention by hyperbolical or aggravated characters, by fabulous and unexampled excellence or <u>depravity</u>, as the writers of barbarous romances invigorated the reader by a giant and a dwarf; and he that should form his expectations of human affairs from the play, or from the tale, would be equally deceived. Shakespeare has no heroes; his scenes are occupied only by men who act and speak as the reader thinks that he should himself have spoken or acted on the same occasion. Even where the agency is

5. **Euripides:** a Greek tragic dramatist, whose precepts (moral observations) were praised by Cicero, a Roman philosopher and statesman.
6. **Hierocles:** a Greek philosopher.
7. **stage:** in the sense of a body of plays; a playwright's works considered as a whole.

8. **Pope:** In the preface to his edition of Shakespeare, Alexander Pope implied that every one of Shakespeare's characters has an individual way of speaking.

Have students explain what Johnson means by his claim that Shakespeare is "above all the poet of nature."

ANALYZING THE ESSAY
Identifying Facts
1. Among the reasons are the following: personal allusions, local customs, friendship, the championing of popular causes or issues, the taste and manners of the time, prejudice, and fashion.
2. The reason is the universality of their characters who resemble species rather than individuals.
3. In the fifth paragraph, Johnson praises the memorable quality of Shakespeare's dialogue.
4. In the sixth paragraph, Johnson commends the realism of Shakespeare's plays.
5. Johnson is highly critical of the manner in which the dramatists of his own time portray love.

Johnson says that love is only one of several passions, and that "it has no great influence on the sum of life." (It should be remembered here that Johnson—a deeply religious and sympa-
(Answers continue in left-hand column.)

(Continued from top.)
thetic man who was devoted to his wife and who often maintained homeless people in his own household—is speaking of ludicrously exaggerated portrayals of romantic love on the eighteenth-century stage.)
6. In the eighth paragraph, Johnson commends Shakespeare for individualizing his characters and keeping them distinct from one another.

Interpreting Meanings
7. What Johnson seems to be saying in this passage is that the *sentiments* expressed by Shakespeare's characters are universal and natural, and that these sentiments are appropriate to the characters' particular situations.
8. Student answers will vary. Some students may suggest "romance novels," science fiction novels, television soap operas, and so on.
Possible reasons include escape, vicarious pleasure, and ignorance.

supernatural the dialogue is level with life. Other writers disguise the most natural passions and most frequent incidents, so that he who contemplates them in the book will not know them in the world. Shakespeare approximates the remote, and familiarizes the wonderful; the event which he represents will not happen, but if it were possible, its effects would be probably such as he has assigned; and it may be said that he has not only shown human nature as it acts in real <u>exigencies</u>, but as it would be found in trials to which it cannot be exposed.

This therefore is the praise of Shakespeare, that his drama is the mirror of life; that he who has mazed his imagination in following the phantoms which other writers raise up before him may here be cured of his delirious ecstasies by reading human sentiments in human language, by scenes from which a hermit may estimate the transactions of the world, and a confessor[9] predict the progress of the passions.

---

9. **confessor:** priest, who presumably, being celibate, has little direct experience of passion.

Responding to the Essay

Analyzing the Essay

Identifying Facts

1. In the first and second paragraphs, Johnson deals with the reasons why writers may be popular in their own time. Explain in your own words some of his reasons.
2. In the third and fourth paragraphs, Johnson explains why writers who have long been dead still remain popular. What is this reason?
3. Having asserted that Shakespeare represents "general nature" in his plays, Johnson (in his fifth paragraph) commends the plays for another important quality. What is this quality?
4. For what accomplishments does Johnson commend Shakespeare's plays in the sixth paragraph?
5. In the seventh paragraph, Johnson comments on love as it is represented on the stage and, by implication, in literature generally. What does he think of love as writers portray it? Why does he think that love should *not* be the most frequently treated emotion in literature?
6. For what does Johnson commend Shakespeare in the eighth paragraph?

Interpreting Meanings

7. Is it difficult to agree with Johnson's remark, in paragraph nine, that Shakespeare's characters "act and speak as the reader thinks that he should himself have spoken or acted on the same occasion"? Look back at *Macbeth* and see whether you can find a speech that you yourself might have made.
8. What are the present-day equivalents to the "barbarous romances" that Johnson mentions? Why do you think people read "barbarous romances"?

Writing About the Essay

A Critical Response

Analyzing a Character. Johnson's "Preface to Shakespeare" could have been written only by Johnson. Both the subject matter and the style contain many clues to Johnson's character and interests. Write an essay in which you either agree or disagree with these statements. In your essay explain what the preface tells (or does not tell) us about Johnson himself.

Hall's Library at Margate by T. Maiton (1789). Aquatint.

The British Library.

A. About the Illustration
Remind students that the eighteenth century witnessed the birth of circulating libraries, which were established to accommodate a rapidly expanding reading public.
? Are there any details in Hall's Library that would not be present in a photograph of a library today? (The dogs, the people talking. There seems to be a shop in the front.)

The Elements of Literature

STYLE

Like most important writers, Johnson developed an individual style, a way of writing and speaking like nobody else's. Johnson's style is more complicated than the plain, simple style of Swift. Johnson ordinarily wrote long but carefully constructed sentences, like this one from the preface to his *Dictionary*:

Such is the exuberance of signification which many words have obtained, that it was scarcely possible to collect all their senses; sometimes the meaning of derivatives must be sought in the mother term, and sometimes deficient explanations of the primitive may be supplied in the train of derivation.

This sentence illustrates Johnson's fondness for:

1. Longish words of Latinate derivation: *excellence, signification, derivatives, deficient, explanations.*
2. Parallel structure: the two clauses beginning *sometimes.*
3. Exact expression: the words *exuberance of signification* may sound strange, but they say exactly what Johnson means.

Like Sir Francis Bacon in the century before him, Johnson could also sum up an idea in a very few words, so that it has the sound of an adage or proverb:

If you are idle, be not solitary; if you are solitary, be not idle.

Notice how one part of this sentence is both balanced against the other and contrasted with the other. Here are two more sentences by Johnson, in which the contrasts are held in balance:

Let me smile with the wise, and feed with the rich.
Marriage has many pains, but celibacy has no pleasures.

But at times Johnson could be pompous and wordy. Instead of saying "Charity begins at home," he would say, "A man should first relieve those who are nearly connected with him, by whatever tie; and then, if he has anything to spare, may extend his bounty to a wider circle."

And finally, like all great writers, Johnson is a master inventor of metaphors. During a conversation about Shakespeare and a forgotten minor writer, for instance, Johnson remarked, "We must not compare the noise of your teakettle here with the roaring of the ocean."

If you reread the "Preface to Shakespeare," you should be able to find good examples of Johnson's use of

1. Long, Latin-based words
2. Parallel structure and balance in sentences
3. Unusual, but exact, expressions
4. Concise statements of ideas
5. Strong metaphors

A. Expansion
The impact of West's death on Gray suggests three notable parallels from English literary history. The death by drowning of his Cambridge friend Edward King inspired the young Milton to write his first great poem, the pastoral elegy "Lycidas" (1637). Alfred, Lord Tennyson spent seventeen years trying to deal with the inner anguish caused by the death of his college friend Arthur Hallam; the result was his great poetic cycle *In Memoriam* (1850) (see text page 794). Finally, the death of John Keats in 1821 inspired perhaps the finest elegy of the Romantic period, Shelley's *Adonais*.

B. Ode
Perhaps Gray's most notable ode is "Ode on a Distant Prospect of Eton College" (1747). The popularity of the ode form in the second half of the eighteenth century prefigures in several ways the early stages of Romanticism. Gray also wrote a comic parody of the ode, "Ode on the Death of a Favorite Cat Drowned in a Tub of Gold Fishes."

Thomas Gray (1716–1771)

Thomas Gray is perhaps the best lyric poet of the mid-eighteenth century, an age that is not known for its great lyric poets. The son of a London merchant, he spent nine years at one of the great English "public schools," Eton College, which is neither public nor a college. (It is the equivalent, in American terms, of a prep school for boys who expect to go to Cambridge or Oxford.) At eighteen Gray entered Cambridge University, where he lived for the remaining thirty-seven years of his life, reading literature in a variety of languages; studying archeology, law, history, botany, and zoology; painting landscapes; playing the harpsichord; and growing geraniums in his window boxes. In a quiet, inconspicuous way, he became very learned. These years were interrupted only briefly by a Grand Tour of France, Switzerland, and Italy with two other young men: Richard West, his best friend from Eton days, and Horace Walpole, a son of England's Prime Minister, who paid the expenses.

A   The great crisis of Gray's life came when West, at the age of twenty-four, died of tuberculosis. Gray sought consolation in writing poetry. He was always reluctant to publish his verses; although he carefully and fastidiously revised and rewrote them, they never seemed to him to be quite finished. Moreover, he was painfully shy and, unlike most writers, he really did not want the world's applause. Imagine his distress when his "Elegy Written in a Country Churchyard" made him famous. Gray's other poems—only thirteen of which he published during his
B   lifetime—were also widely admired. Most of them are elegant, gloomy, and artificial: exactly what mid-century taste demanded. Few of these other poems are of much interest today except to historians of English poetry, who find that in several ways Gray anticipated the Romantic age to come.

Thomas Gray by John Giles Eccardt (1748).

National Portrait Gallery, London.

Gray led a quiet, frugal, low-key existence. Unlike everybody else in his century, he was never on the back of a horse. Although he was made professor of history at Cambridge, he never delivered any lectures, which is all that a professor did in those days. He spent his vacations in London, reading in the British Museum (now the British Library), or in the Lake District (a picturesque part of northern England made famous by the poets of the next age), or in Stoke Poges, a village where his mother and aunt lived. There he is buried, beside his mother, in the cemetery that he immortalized in his "Elegy."

PREPARATION

1. BUILDING ON PRIOR KNOWLEDGE. Before students begin reading, have them discuss what they already understand by the term *elegy.* See the Elements of Literature essay on text page 573. Be sure they know what a churchyard is (refer them to text page 570).

2. ESTABLISHING A PURPOSE. Before students begin to read the poem, direct their attention to the second creative writing assignment on text page 572. Ask them to read the poem and look for how Gray imagined the people in this old churchyard once lived. Have them keep in mind the image of the speaker and his setting as they read his meditation.

3. PREREADING JOURNAL. Before they read, have students write two or three sentences describing what they think of when they stand in a cemetery. (This may sound ghoulish, but it need not be. All of us at some point in our lives have some experience with death. We all have thoughts about those who have passed before us. And we all have thoughts of "what might have been.")

Gray had this poem published anonymously in 1751, and only because a copy of it had fallen into the hands of an unscrupulous magazine editor who threatened to print it with Gray's name on it. The poem immediately became a great favorite of readers, a position it still maintains because it sounds so beautiful and because what it says about death is so true. Everybody dies: the famous people of the earth are no different from the rest of us in that respect. We all eventually come to the same dusty end. Painfully obvious truths of this kind are called *truisms,* and a poet can be forgiven his truisms only if he utters them memorably. Gray's "Elegy" exemplifies Pope's definition of true wit: "What oft was thought but ne'er so well expressed."

Gray wanted this poem printed without any spaces between stanzas "because the sense is in some places continued beyond them." The fact that it is almost never printed in this way perhaps justifies Gray's misgivings about publishers and makes the reading of lines 61–73 a bit more difficult than it should be.

Elegy Written in a Country Churchyard

A
The curfew tolls the knell of parting day,
    The lowing herd wind slowly o'er the lea,°
The plowman homeward plods his weary way,
    And leaves the world to darkness and to me.

5 Now fades the glimmering landscape on the sight,
    And all the air a solemn stillness holds,
Save where the beetle wheels his droning flight,
    And drowsy tinklings lull the distant folds;

Save that from yonder ivy-mantled tower
10   The moping° owl does to the moon complain
Of such, as wandering near her secret bower,
    Molest her ancient solitary reign.

Beneath those rugged elms, that yew tree's shade,
    Where heaves the turf in many a moldering heap,
15 **B** Each in his narrow cell forever laid,
    The rude° forefathers of the hamlet sleep.

The breezy call of incense-breathing morn,
    The swallow twittering from the straw-built shed,°
The cock's shrill clarion, or the echoing horn,°
20   No more shall rouse them from their lowly bed.

C
For them no more the blazing hearth shall burn,
    Or busy housewife ply her evening care;
No children run to lisp their sire's return,
    Or climb his knees the envied kiss to share.

25 Oft did the harvest to their sickle yield,
    Their furrow oft the stubborn glebe° has broke;
How jocund did they drive their team afield!
    How bowed the woods beneath their sturdy stroke!

2. **lea:** meadow.

10. **moping:** melancholy.

16. **rude:** uneducated, unpolished.

18. **shed:** nest.
19. **horn:** hunting horn.

26. **glebe:** soil.

A. Tone
? What tone is immediately established in the first stanza? What details create that tone? (The tone might be described as sober, perhaps even melancholy. It would be hard to describe a tolling bell, the end of day, a weary plowman, and darkness without sounding a note of loss and therefore of sadness.) What is the meter of the poem? (Iambic pentameter) What is the rhyme scheme? (*abab* for each verse)

B. Interpreting
? What is the "narrow cell"? (Their graves; "cell" connotes a religious community.)

C. Atmosphere/ Mood
? List all the specific details the speaker thinks of in lines 21–28. What kind of people is the speaker thinking of? (The ordinary, everyday poor)

SUPPLEMENTARY SUPPORT MATERIALS
1. Vocabulary Activity Worksheet (*CCB*)
2. Review and Response Worksheet: Imagery and Theme (*CCB*)
3. Selection Test (*CCB*)
4. Audiocassette recording

DEVELOPING VOCABULARY
The following words from the poem are tested in the Selection Test. (See also Vocabulary Activity Worksheet.)

knell	annals
bower	to impute
clarion	to circumscribe
jocund	to sequester
homely	dirge

A. Responding

❓ This is one of the often-quoted lines from the elegy. (See also those noted in question 14 on text page 572.) Do you agree that the stories of the poor are "short" and "simple"?

B. Metaphor

❓ What is the "mansion"? (The body)

C. Meaning

Note that here the speaker begins to imagine what these people might have been if they had *not* been born poor. The reasons they did not rule empires, and so on, are cited in the next stanza.

D. Theme

These lines are important because they sum up one of the poet's messages.

E. Allusion

Note the historical allusions in lines 57–60. Line 59 is a famous one: What is a "mute" Milton? (One that is unable to use language or speak)

Let not Ambition mock their useful toil,
30   Their homely joys, and destiny obscure;
Nor Grandeur hear with a disdainful smile
A   The short and simple annals of the poor.

The boast of heraldry,° the pomp of power,
    And all that beauty, all that wealth e'er gave,
35 Awaits alike the inevitable hour.
    The paths of glory lead but to the grave.

Nor you, ye proud, impute to these the fault,
    If Memory o'er their tomb no trophies° raise,
Where through the long-drawn aisle and fretted vault°
40   The pealing anthem swells the note of praise.

B Can storied urn° or animated° bust
    Back to its mansion call the fleeting breath?
Can Honor's voice provoke° the silent dust,
    Or Flattery soothe the dull cold ear of Death?

45 Perhaps in this neglected spot is laid
    Some heart once pregnant with celestial fire;
C Hands that the rod of empire might have swayed,
    Or waked to ecstasy the living lyre.

But Knowledge to their eyes her ample page
50   Rich with the spoils of time did ne'er unroll;
Chill Penury° repressed their noble rage,°
    And froze the genial current° of the soul.

D Full many a gem of purest ray serene,
    The dark unfathomed caves of ocean bear:
55 Full many a flower is born to blush unseen,
    And waste its sweetness on the desert air.

Some village Hampden,° that with dauntless breast
    The little tyrant of his fields withstood;
E Some mute inglorious Milton here may rest,
60   Some Cromwell° guiltless of his country's blood.

The applause of listening senates to command,
    The threats of pain and ruin to despise,
To scatter plenty o'er a smiling land,
    And read their history in a nation's eyes,

65 Their lot forbade: nor circumscribed alone
    Their growing virtues, but their crimes confined;
Forbade to wade through slaughter to a throne,
    And shut the gates of mercy on mankind,

---

33. **heraldry:** coats of arms and other symbols of nobility.

38. **trophies:** monuments.
39. **aisle and fretted vault:** aristocrats were buried inside the church, with its high, ornamented vaults.

41. **storied urn:** an urn with an inscription on it. **animated:** lifelike.

43. **provoke:** evoke, call forth.

51. **Penury:** poverty. **rage:** emotion, feeling.
52. **genial current:** warm impulses.

57. **village Hampden:** an obscure person who, with opportunity, might have been famous like John Hampden, who fought in the English Civil War.
60. **Cromwell:** Lord Protector Oliver Cromwell, who ruled England from 1653 to 1658.

The struggling pangs of conscious° truth to hide,
70   To quench the blushes of ingenuous° shame,
Or heap the shrine of Luxury and Pride
        With incense° kindled at the Muse's flame.

A ⎡ Far from the madding° crowd's ignoble strife,
   ⎢   Their sober wishes never learned to stray;
75   Along the cool sequestered vale of life
        They kept the noiseless tenor° of their way.

Yet even these bones from insult to protect
        Some frail memorial° still° erected nigh,
With uncouth rhymes and shapeless sculpture decked,
80   Implores the passing tribute of a sigh.

Their name, their years, spelt by the unlettered Muse,°
        The place of fame and elegy supply:
And many a holy text around she strews,
        That teach the rustic moralist to die.

85 ⎡ For who to dumb Forgetfulness a prey,
   ⎢   This pleasing anxious being e'er resigned,
B ⎢ Left the warm precincts° of the cheerful day,
   ⎣   Nor cast one longing lingering look behind?

On some fond breast the parting soul relies,
90   Some pious drops° the closing eye requires;
Even from the tomb the voice of Nature cries,
        Even in our ashes live their wonted fires.

C ⎡ For thee, who mindful of the unhonored dead
   ⎢   Dost in these lines their artless tale relate;
95 ⎢ If chance, by lonely contemplation led,
   ⎣   Some kindred spirit shall inquire thy fate,

Haply some hoary-headed swain° may say,
        "Oft have we seen him at the peep of dawn
Brushing with hasty steps the dews away
100   To meet the sun upon the upland lawn.°

"There at the foot of yonder nodding beech
        That wreathes its old fantastic roots so high,
His listless length at noontide would he stretch,
D ⎡ And pore upon the brook that babbles by.

105   "Hard° by yon wood, now smiling as in scorn,
        Muttering his wayward fancies he would rove,
Now drooping, woeful wan, like one forlorn,
        Or crazed with care, or crossed in hopeless love.

---

69. **conscious:** conscientious.
70. **ingenuous:** innocent.

72. **incense:** tributes paid to them by poets.

73. **madding:** frenzied.

76. **tenor:** course.

78. **frail memorial:** modest tombstone.
still: always.

81. **unlettered Muse:** the humble engraver of the tombstone.

87. **precincts:** regions.

90. **drops:** mourners' tears.

97. **hoary-headed swain:** white-haired countryman.

100. **lawn:** field.

105. **Hard:** close.

A. Allusions
Gray's "Elegy" has been repeatedly quoted, memorized by generations of schoolchildren, and alluded to by countless other writers. Thomas Hardy, for example, took the title of his first popularly successful novel— *Far from the Madding Crowd* (1874)—from line 73.

B. Rhetorical Question
? What is the significance of the rhetorical question in lines 85–88? (It emphasizes that love of life and fear of death are common to rich and poor alike.)

C. Interpreting
Here the speaker begins to address himself. See question 10, text page 572.

D. Alliteration
? What words alliterate here, and what sound do they imitate? (The *b*'s suggest the sound of the brook. Note the possible pun on the words *pore/pour*.) Read aloud lines 97 and 107–108 to hear the alliteration there.

Have each student select at least four lines to memorize (they should choose complete thoughts). Have them deliver their lines in class and explain the part of the elegy to which they belong.

ANALYZING THE POEM
Identifying Details

1. The speaker is in a country church-yard at dusk.

He sees the glimmering landscape at dusk and the beetle's flight; he hears the tinklings of bells from the sheepfolds and the hooting complaint of the owl.

2. Among the things that the poor people will never again experience are the twittering of the swallow, the crowing of the cock, the sound of the hunting horn, the sight of the blazing hearth, the sight of the housewife, the greetings of their children, the experience of driving their team to the fields, and the labor of planting and harvesting.

3. The poet warns Ambition not to mock the people's toil or their homely joys and obscure destiny; he warns Grandeur not to smile disdainfully at these people's short and simple history.

He warns the proud not to blame the

A. Humanities Connection: Responding to the Fine Art
American landscapist J. F. Cropsey (1823–1900) was one of many artists belonging to the Hudson River school of painting. This school, which included Thomas Doughty, Asher Durand, and Thomas Cole, celebrated the natural beauty of the American landscape, specifically the Hudson River Valley, and had as one of its goals to become independent of European schools of painting.

? How did you picture Gray's setting? Does your mental image differ from Cropsey's? What would you add to or subtract from this painting?

A

Ode to a Country Churchyard (Gray's Elegy) by J. F. Cropsey (1883).

Newington-Cropsey Foundation.

humble people if they did not have elaborate funerals or monuments erected on their graves.

4. Among the examples of personification are the following: Honor (line 43), Flattery (line 44), Knowledge (line 49), Penury (line 51), Luxury and Pride (line 71), Forgetfulness (line 85), Nature (line 91), Earth (line 117), Science (line 119), Melancholy (line 120), Misery (line 123).

5. He asks rhetorically whether monuments, honor, or flattery can bring the dead back to life.

6. The speaker imagines that one might have become an emperor, another a poet, and another a soldier.

The details of the neglected gems and flowers show that excellence and virtue often go unrecognized or are unfulfilled. Just as the gems lie neglected on the ocean floor and the flowers bloom, unappreciated, in the desert, the potential distinction of the humble people buried in the churchyard was never achieved.

7. Their place in life forbade them to experience high political office and commemoration in their nation's history. Their lot also "circumscribed," or limited, both their virtues and their crimes; none of them, at least, became tyrants, slaughterers, or worshipers of luxury and pride.

8. According to these lines, the simple, rudely unlettered epitaphs on the graves show that the humble people also wish to be remembered. The poet reflects that such a wish is universal among humankind.

9. He imagines that the swain may remember him after his death as a humble and good man, just as he is now remembering the other dead who are buried in the churchyard.

Interpreting Meanings

10. Most students will agree that it is not necessary to make this assumption in order to understand the poem. On the other hand, the assumption is attractive, since it provides an elegant structural parallel between the speaker's own situation and the situation he is describing in the poem.

11. He offers the defense that he was generous, sincere, and pious.

12. Student answers will vary. Most students will agree that the stereotype of the poet as a dreamy, mel-

(*Answers continue on next page.*)

---

110   "One morn I missed him on the customed hill,
        Along the heath and near his favorite tree;
      Another came; nor yet beside the rill,°
        Nor up the lawn, nor at the wood was he;

      "The next with dirges due in sad array
        Slow through the churchway path we saw him borne.
115   Approach and read (for thou canst read°) the lay,
        Graved on the stone beneath yon aged thorn,"°

                    The Epitaph

      Here rests his head upon the lap of Earth
        A youth to Fortune and to Fame unknown.
      Fair Science° frowned not on his humble birth,
120   *And Melancholy marked him for her own.*

      Large was his bounty, and his soul sincere,
        Heaven did a recompense as largely send:
      He gave to Misery all he had, a tear,
        He gained from Heaven ('twas all he wished) a friend.

125   *No farther seek his merits to disclose,*
        Or draw his frailties from their dread abode
      (There they alike in trembling hope repose),
        The bosom of his Father and his God.

111. **rill:** brook.

115. **thou canst read:** the "swain" who is speaking is apparently illiterate.
116. **thorn:** hawthorn bush.

119. **Science:** learning.

Responding to the Poem

Analyzing the Poem

Identifying Details

1. Where is the speaker and what time of day is it? What, according to the **images** in stanzas 2 and 3, does he hear?
2. In the fourth through eighth stanzas, the speaker describes the poor people in the churchyard. Name the various things they will never again experience.
3. The poet **personifies** Ambition and Grandeur in lines 29 and 31. What does he warn them not to do? What does he warn the proud about in lines 37–40?
4. What other examples of **personification** can you find in the poem?
5. What questions does the speaker ask in lines 41–44?
6. What does the speaker imagine these humble people might have become, if they'd had the opportunity (lines 45–60)? What do the details in lines 53–56 have to do with this idea?
7. What did their "lot" or place in life forbid the poor people to experience, according to lines 61–72?
8. According to lines 77–92, what evidence on their gravestones shows that the humble also wish to be remembered?

571

ancholy, and intensely reflective person hardly fits the facts of these poets' lives as we know them. Encourage the students to offer their own opinions and to support them with examples.

13. Gray's purpose in the "Elegy" seems to involve a bit of both. However, most students will agree that, on balance, the poem is seeking to establish a certain

mood and to prompt an emotional response in the reader; in this respect, the "Elegy" is more Romantic than Neoclassical.

14. The quotations relate to the poem's message by underscoring the sentiments that life is transient and that excellence may easily be ignored or remain unfulfilled.

---

9. What does the speaker imagine an old man (the "hoary-headed swain") might say of him one day (lines 98–116)?

Interpreting Meanings

10. Many readers of the "Elegy" have assumed that Gray himself is the poet whose epitaph is given in the final lines. Is it necessary to make this assumption to understand the poem? Why does the assumption seem attractive?
11. Suppose that Gray is being autobiographical. What defense does he give of his life?
12. From Gray's time almost to the present, many people have thought of poets as possessing the characteristics described in lines 98–112. Gray established here a **stereotype** that the public long accepted as genuine. Does this stereotype fit any of the poets you have so far studied in this book? (Think particularly of Chaucer, Shakespeare, Donne, Milton, Pope, and Swift.)
13. In one sense, most neoclassical writers thought the purpose of literature was to convey ideas; most Romantic writers, by contrast, thought the purpose of literature was to convey emotions. Judging by his "Elegy," in which group does Gray seem to fit?
14. The poem contains at least two statements that are still frequently quoted:

   a. The paths of glory lead but to the grave. (line 36)
   b. Full many a flower is born to blush unseen,
   And waste its sweetness on the desert air. (lines 55–56)

   How do these lines relate to the **message** of the poem?

Writing About the Poem

A Creative Response

1. **Writing an Epitaph.** Suppose one of the villagers was allowed to speak his or her epitaph. Write out what he or she might say to the poet. You might consider these characters: the busy housewife; the children's sire; the person once full of "celestial fire"; the person that might have ruled an empire; the person that might have "waked" the lyre; the village Hampden; the mute inglorious Milton; the Cromwell; the hoary-headed swain.
2. **Imitating the Writer's Technique.** Suppose you were standing in a graveyard today. Write a brief meditation about the experience, including a description of the place, of the imagined lives of the people buried there, and of your feelings about death. Be sure to describe the time of day, the weather, and the sounds you hear. (If you don't want to use yourself as the speaker, make up a speaker.)

A Critical Response

3. **Comparing and Contrasting Poems.** In a brief essay, discuss the similarities and differences between Gray's "Elegy" and another famous elegy, "The Seafarer," on page 49. Consider the elements of **speaker, theme,** and **tone.**

Analyzing Language and Style

A Poetic Style

Many words in this poem were regarded—until the twentieth century—as particularly "poetic." Examples of such words are *oft* (line 25), *e'er* (line 34), and *ye* (line 37).

1. List the other "poetic" words you find in the elegy. What words would be used in their place today?
2. What effect do such words have on you as you read this poem?

In many of Gray's sentences, the normal word order of English (subject-predicate-complement) is violated. Gray writes "The air a solemn stillness holds" instead of "The air holds a solemn stillness."

3. Find other examples of this practice.
4. Can you propose reasons why Gray took such liberties with idiomatic English?

Perhaps the most difficult lines to sort out syntactically are lines 61–72. The following outline might help to clarify the syntax of these lines:

"Their lot forbade" them
   "to command" "the applause of listening senates"
   "to despise" "the threats of pain and ruin"
   "to scatter plenty o'er a smiling land,
   And read their history in a nation's eyes."

"Nor" has their lot ever

   "circumscribed alone
   Their growing virtues, but their crimes confined."

Their lot also forbade them

   "To hide" "the struggling pangs of conscious truth"
   "To quench the blushes of ingenuous shame,
   Or heap the shrine of Luxury and Pride
   With incense kindled at the Muse's flame."

5. Try now to **paraphrase** these lines, using conventional syntax and as many sentences as you need.

THE ELEGY

The term **elegy** originally referred to a poem written in a particular meter; in Roman literature elegies are frivolous and sexy. By Gray's time the term *elegy* was applied to longish, serious poems reflecting on death—either death in general or the death of a particular person. Gray ends his "Elegy" with an epitaph—a poem short enough to be inscribed on a particular person's tombstone.

Gray's "Elegy" combined elements from several literary traditions. First of all, it is a **pastoral** elegy. Like Milton's famous elegy *Lycidas,* its setting is outdoors in a beautiful summery landscape. The poet keeps a certain distance from the dirt and bad smells of actual country life. His rural people are not individuals but types: the weary plowman, the busy housewife, the hoary-headed swain. These figures are idealized; oafs and boors do not appear. Rural life in a pastoral is always placid and civilized.

Another element in the "Elegy" is the **Gothic,** which supplies the moping owl, the graveyard, and the general gloominess. But unlike most Gothic writers, Gray isn't interested in giving his readers shivers and thrills; he is trying instead to create an atmosphere.

Finally, like many other writers of his time, Gray decorates his poem with polished **generalizations** about life and death: "The paths of glory lead but to the grave." These generalizations give the elegy the solidity of classical architecture.

A. Humanities Connection: Responding to the Fine Art
The distinguishing characteristics of British portraitist and landscapist John Linnell's (1792–1882) work are the originality and pathos he imparted to it. In addition to his work in oil, Linnell executed many miniatures on ivory.
❓ What connections do you see between elements in the painting and the pastoral elegy, as it is described in the essay on the Elements of Literature on this page? (It is set outdoors and in the summer, and the scene is placidly idealized.) How does this pastoral scene contrast with the one on text page 233? (It focuses on the activities of an individual rather than a community—indeed, this is a much less "busy" scene. This painting also does not contain the mythological elements of the earlier embroidery.) What images, nevertheless, are similar? (Both scenes idealize common labor—or, at least, show it as highly civilized.)

A

Landscape by J. Linnell. Oil.

The Tate Gallery, London.

Boswell's and Johnson's Trip to Scotland

In August of 1773 Boswell and Johnson toured the highlands of Scotland, and during the following September and October they visited some of the Hebrides, islands lying off the northwest coast. For several years they had been discussing this trip, whose purpose, according to Johnson, was "to contemplate a system of life almost totally different from what we had been accustomed to see." Boswell, perhaps, doubted that they would ever go: After all, Johnson cared little for Scotland. Although he had never been there, he habitually made disparaging remarks about Scotland and the Scots. When, for instance, he heard a Scotsman praise the noble "prospects" (scenes, vistas, panoramas) of his native land, Johnson reprimanded him: "Sir, I believe you have a great many noble wild prospects. Norway too has some noble wild prospects; and Lapland is remarkable for prodigious noble wild prospects. But, Sir, I believe the noblest prospect that a Scotsman ever sees is the road which leads him to England!" It was, then, with some surprise and delight that Boswell found himself and his men-

A. Expansion
Although other writers, including Johnson himself, had written brief lives of literary figures, Boswell's *Life* has a fair claim to being the first full-length English biography, in the modern sense of the genre.

B. Expansion
Johnson wrote his own account of the tour in his highly entertaining *A Journey to the Western Islands of Scotland* (1775). It is available today in Penguin paperback.

James Boswell (1740–1795)

James Boswell was a Scotsman, the heir to a large fortune, and eldest son of Lord Auchinleck, a strait-laced judge who expected his son to settle down in Scotland and carry on the family profession of law. Young Boswell had other plans. While studying law and classics at Glasgow and Edinburgh, he yearned to travel, to write, to visit great cities, to know famous people and become famous himself, to frequent taverns, and to pursue beautiful women. Lord Auchinleck was totally unsympathetic to these desires, but finally, in 1762, he capitulated and allowed the twenty-two-year-old Boswell to escape to London. There, a year later, Boswell met Samuel Johnson, then aged fifty-four and famous for his *Dictionary*. Gradually Boswell discovered a serious purpose for his life: He would become familiar with Johnson, study his character and personality, record his ideas and opinions, and eventually write his biography.

Boswell had the talent and energy to realize his ambitions. Although as a young man he disappointed his father by his neglect of the law and by his notorious debaucheries and excesses, he did become friends with many illustrious people and he did write one of the greatest biographies in English—*The Life of Samuel Johnson* (1791).

In addition to the biography of Johnson, Boswell published *An Account of Corsica* (1768) and *A Journal of a Tour to the Hebrides* (1785). *Corsica* describes his visit to that Mediterranean island, whose people were then revolting against their rulers in the Republic of Genoa. Boswell interviewed their leader, General Paoli, and represented him as an exemplary freedom fighter. The book was translated into many languages and provided its author, for a year or so, with the nickname "Corsica Boswell." The *Hebrides* book describes an autumnal tour of the islands off the western coast of Scotland, which Boswell undertook with Johnson in 1773.

Johnson advised Boswell not only to read in the literal sense of that word, but also to "read diligently the great book of mankind." This Boswell did, in Scotland and England; in Hol-

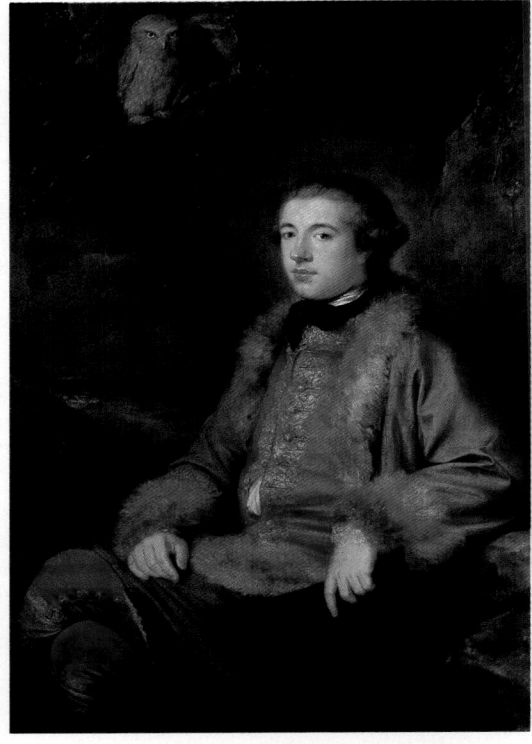

James Boswell by George Willison (1765). Oil.

Scottish National Portrait Gallery, Edinburgh.

land, where he pleased his father by studying law for a year; and in Germany, Switzerland, and Italy, which he visited while he was on what the age called the "Grand Tour." Eventually Lord Auchinleck had his way: Boswell undertook a law practice in Edinburgh, married, and produced a family. But as often as he could, he visited London, for conviviality and intellectual refreshment with Johnson and his friends, and for the freedom to indulge his frailties that a large city provides. Eventually, after Johnson's death, he moved to London with his family to complete work on his great biography.

At an early age, Boswell began to keep a written record of his own and other people's behavior and conversation. To avoid taking notes in public, he trained his memory to recall the exact details of an event and the exact words of a conversation. These he wrote down in private, so that by the time he reached middle age he had accumulated an immense number of jourtor actually traveling about in the wilder parts of Scotland, on foot or horseback or in open boats. Though sedentary, overweight, sixty-four years old, and completely "urbanized," Johnson thoroughly enjoyed himself on the trip. After it was over he wrote to Boswell, "Shall we ever have another frolic like our journey to the Hebrides?"

nals, memoranda to himself, and letters—thousands of pages of personal writing. Although he used some of this material in three published books, he died with most of it unpublished. His heirs and executor did not, apparently, recognize the value of these old papers, though they did not destroy them as literary scholars for over a hundred years had assumed. Boswell's papers were stored in such places as an old croquet box and the loft over a stable until—between 1920 and 1949—they were purchased from Boswell's heirs and deposited in the Yale University Library. Now that many of them have been published, we have available more firsthand information on Boswell than perhaps any other person, living or dead.

"Good Heaven! What is Boswell?" he once asked in a letter to a friend. Any answer to this question must emphasize the contradictions and contrasts in his character. In public he often seemed egotistical and pushy, yet his journals show that he actually lacked self-confidence and suffered from extreme insecurity. Although he loved carousing and could be immensely jovial in company, he was frequently subject to depression and irrational fears. After an evening of highly moral conversation with Johnson, he would prowl for the rest of the night in the more disreputable parts of London. He told his journal that he wanted to appear cool, easy, and serene, but he often behaved in a loud and brash manner. Once, before the beginning of a play, he entertained a theater audience by mooing like a cow. The journal records times when he felt composed, manly, firm, genteel, valiant, and dignified, as well as times when he felt just the opposite: giddy and vain, or mean, timid, bashful, awkward, uneasy, and dissipated. Often he would not restrain himself from "effusions of ludicrous nonsense and intemperate mirth." In short, to some of his contemporaries he seemed to be an uncouth buffoon. We know better.

A. Expansion
Like Samuel Pepys, Boswell recorded many of his own excesses in intimate detail, and it may be some time before a complete, unbowdlerized edition of his papers appears.

B. About the Illustration
The first recorded coffeehouse in England was located in Oxford in 1650. By 1730, there were 500 coffeehouses in London. Some of the most popular ones were named Garraway's, Slaughter's, and White's. Men who shared certain professions would meet at certain houses: Writers, for example, usually met at Will's. Note the details that reveal so much about late seventeenth-century life: the server holding the fistful of clay pipes (they were disposable), the pitchers of coffee warming at the fire, the wigs, the pages being read by candlelight, the absence of women (except for the woman in the booth).

The social center of the middle class was the coffeehouse, like this London establishment (1668). Watercolor.

British Museum, London.

PREPARATION

1. BUILDING ON PRIOR KNOWLEDGE. Before students begin reading, review with them what they have already learned about Johnson's personality, especially his habits of conversation and his eccentricities.

2. ESTABLISHING A PURPOSE. Before students begin reading, you might have them read question 9 on text page 581. Ask students to evaluate Johnson's social behavior and what it reveals about his personality as they read.

3. PREREADING JOURNAL. Before they read, have students write three or four questions they would address to a person who lived in the eighteenth century. (If that seems unreasonable, ask them to address the questions to a famous "taste-setter" of today.)

A. Characterization

❓ What might Boswell's opening sentence show about his personality? (He is self-effacing.)

FROM THE LIFE OF SAMUEL JOHNSON

To call Boswell a successful biographer is to say that he possessed several literary talents. He was, first of all, an accurate historian. The *Life of Samuel Johnson* was based on a great mass of journals, records, letters, notes, and memoranda, all of which Boswell verified, digested, and condensed to produce a reliable account not only of Johnson but of the whole age. Johnson had circles of friends from all walks of life, but Boswell emphasized his relations with people whose names are still well known: among many others, the painter Sir Joshua Reynolds, the actor David Garrick, the statesman Edmund Burke, the musicologist Charles Burney, and the novelist and dramatist Oliver Goldsmith. All study of the artistic and intellectual life of the times begins with Boswell's biography.

Boswell was not only a recorder of facts; he was also a masterful storyteller with an eye for the rich details that make an incident interesting. Boswell brings to life the whole Johnson household: the wretched Dr. Levet, whom Johnson supported; the blind Miss Williams, who made her home with Johnson and, who, when she poured tea, put her finger in the cup to tell when it was full; the black servant Francis Barber, who was Johnson's friend and heir—even the cat Hodge, who loved oysters. Thanks to Boswell we know of Johnson's deep attachments to women; first, to his wife, and after her death to others, especially Hes-ter Thrale, who disappointed him so bitterly by marrying a singing teacher.

One kind of detail sets Boswell's *Life* apart from other biographies: the large number of actual conversations he reports. We have more of Johnson's ordinary talk than that of any other person who lived before the invention of tape recorders. Of course, Johnson's talk was never "ordinary"; it was original, forthright, vigorous, astonishing, and well worth preserving.

In the biography we often see Boswell provoking Johnson to speak out on a topic, or manipulating the conversation for dramatic effect, in much the same way as a playwright manages the dialogue of his characters. Perhaps the most brilliant parts of the *Life* are the civilized conversations it records.

Finally, Boswell aimed to show Johnson "more completely than any man who has ever lived." To do so, he had to be a "psychologist" in the popular sense of that word, a person who listens to, understands, and feels deep sympathy for other people. Boswell appreciated Johnson's sudden outbursts of anger, his fits of depression, his morbid fear of madness and death, just as he appreciated Johnson's cheerfulness, cleverness, and fatherly feelings toward himself. What is more important, Boswell's literary talent enabled him to capture in words all the inconsistency and astonishing humanity of Samuel Johnson.

Boswell's First Meeting with Johnson, 1763

This is to me a memorable year; for in it I had the happiness to obtain the acquaintance of that extraordinary man whose memoirs I am now writing; an acquaintance which I shall ever esteem as one of the most fortunate circumstances in my life. Though then but two and twenty, I had for several years read his works with delight and instruction, and had the highest reverence for their author, which had grown up in my fancy into a kind of mysterious veneration, by figuring to myself a state of solemn elevated abstraction, in which I supposed him to live in the immense metropolis of London. . . .

Mr. Thomas Davies the actor, who then kept a bookseller's shop in Russel Street, Covent Garden, told me that Johnson was very much his friend, and came frequently to his house, where he more than once invited me to meet him; but by some unlucky accident or other he was prevented from coming to us.

A

SUPPLEMENTARY SUPPORT MATERIALS

1. Vocabulary Activity Worksheet (*CCB*)
2. Review and Response Worksheet: Dialogue (*CCB*)
3. Selection Test (*CCB*)

DEVELOPING VOCABULARY

The following words from the biography are tested in the Selection Test. (See also Vocabulary Activity Worksheet.)

to conciliate   noxious
abasement   to coddle
to mortify   tremulous
slovenly   vociferation
mode   candor

A. Responding to the Illustration

Johnson's home on the north of Fleet Street, in what is now a busy commercial district of London, can still be visited today. In his famous article in the *Encyclopaedia Britannica,* Thomas Babington Macaulay said: "In the garret was his library, a large and miscellaneous collection of books, falling to pieces and begrimed with dust. On a lower floor he sometimes, but very rarely, regaled a friend with a plain dinner—a veal pie, or a leg of lamb and spinach, and a rice pudding. Nor was the dwelling uninhabited during his long absences. It was the home of the most extraordinary assemblage of inmates that ever was brought together." (See the biography on text page 554 for more details on Johnson's household.) Notice the details of the engraving, including the architecture and the way the people are dressed. Compare this town house with the dwellings in modern cities. (Some eighteenth-century-style buildings survive in Boston, Philadelphia, and New York.) Note the beggars at the right of the stair.

A

Samuel Johnson's home in London. Engraving.

A. Expansion
Johnson's prejudices, including his aversions to Scotland and America, were well-known among his contemporaries. It is often hard to decide whether he was really prejudiced or whether he fostered these dislikes simply for the sake of witty remarks or *bon mots*. For example, when Johnson was asked which of the French philosophers he favored, Voltaire or Rousseau, he replied, "It is difficult to decide the proportion of iniquity between them."

B. Expansion
Garrick, later to become one of the most famous actors of his day (see text page 561), had been one of Johnson's school pupils.

At last, on Monday the 16th of May, when I was sitting in Mr. Davies's back parlor, after having drunk tea with him and Mrs. Davies, Johnson unexpectedly came into the shop; and Mr. Davies having perceived him through the glass door in the room in which we were sitting, advancing toward us—he announced his awful[1] approach to me, somewhat in the manner of an actor in the part of Horatio, when he addresses Hamlet on the appearance of his father's ghost, "Look, my Lord, it comes." I found that I had a very perfect idea of Johnson's figure from the portrait of him painted by Sir Joshua Reynolds soon after he had published his *Dictionary,* in the attitude of sitting in his easy chair in deep meditation, which was the first picture his friend did for him, which Sir Joshua very kindly presented to me, and from which an engraving has been made for this work. Mr. Davies mentioned my name, and respectfully introduced me to him. I was much agitated: and recollecting his prejudice against the Scotch, of which I had heard much, I said to Davies, "Don't tell where I come from." "From Scotland," cried Davies roguishly. "Mr. Johnson," said I, "I do indeed come from Scotland, but I cannot help it." I am willing to flatter myself that I meant this as light pleasantry to soothe and conciliate him, and not as a humiliating abasement at the expense of my country. But however that might be, this speech was somewhat unlucky; for with that quickness of wit for which he was so remarkable, he seized the expression "come from Scotland," which I used in the sense of being of that country; and, as if I had said that I had come away from it, or left it, retorted, "That, sir, I find, is what a very great many of your countrymen cannot help." This stroke stunned me a good deal; and when we had sat down, I felt myself not a little embarrassed, and apprehensive of what might come next. He then addressed himself to Davies: "What do you think of Garrick? He has refused me an order for the play for Miss Williams, because he knows the house will be full, and that an order would be worth three shillings." Eager to take any opening to get into conversation with him, I ventured to say, "O sir, I cannot think Mr. Garrick would grudge such a trifle to you." "Sir," said he, with a stern look, "I have known David Garrick longer than you have done: and I know no right you have to talk to me on the subject." Perhaps I deserved this check; for it was rather presumptuous in me, an entire stranger, to express any doubt of the justice of his animadversion[2] upon his old acquaintance and pupil. I now felt myself much mortified, and began to think that the hope which I had long indulged of obtaining his acquaintance was blasted. And, in truth, had not my ardor been uncommonly strong, and my resolution uncommonly persevering, so rough a reception might have deterred me forever from making any further attempts. Fortunately, however, I remained upon the field not wholly discomfited.

I was highly pleased with the extraordinary vigor of his conversation, and regretted that I was drawn away from it by an engagement at another place. I had, for a part of the evening, been left alone with him, and had ventured to make an observation now and then, which he received very civilly; so that I was satisfied that though there was a roughness in his manner, there was no ill nature in his disposition. Davies followed me to the door, and when I complained to him a little of the hard blows which the great man had given me, he kindly took upon him to console me by saying, "Don't be uneasy. I can see he likes you very well." . . .

Boswell's First Visit to Johnson

A few days afterward I called on Davies, and asked him if he thought I might take the liberty of waiting on Mr. Johnson at his chambers in the Temple.[3] He said I certainly might, and that Mr. Johnson would take it as a compliment. So upon Tuesday the 24th of May, I boldly repaired to Johnson. His chambers were on the first floor of No. 1, Inner-Temple-lane, and I entered them with an impression given me by the Reverend Dr. Blair,[4] of Edinburgh, who had been introduced to him not long before, and described his having "found the Giant in his den"; an expression

---

1. **awful:** producing awe.

2. **animadversion:** critical comment.
3. **Temple:** An area in London where lawyers and other professional people live and work.
4. **Blair:** Hugh Blair, a Presbyterian clergyman and writer.

which, when I came to be pretty well acquainted with Johnson, I repeated to him, and he was diverted by this picturesque account of himself.

He received me very courteously; but, it must be confessed that his apartment and furniture and morning dress were sufficiently uncouth. His brown suit of clothes looked very rusty; he had on a little old shriveled unpowdered wig, which was too small for his head; his shirt neck and knees of his breeches were loose; his black worsted stockings ill drawn up; and he had a pair of unbuckled shoes by way of slippers. But all these slovenly particularities were forgotten the moment that he began to talk. Some gentlemen, whom I do not recollect, were sitting with him; and when they went away, I also rose; but he said to me, "Nay, don't go." "Sir," said I, "I am afraid that I intrude upon you. It is benevolent to allow me to sit and hear you." He seemed pleased with this compliment, which I sincerely paid him, and answered, "Sir, I am obliged to any man who visits me." I have preserved the following short minute of what passed this day:

"Madness frequently discovers itself merely by unnecessary deviation from the usual modes of the world. My poor friend Smart[5] showed the disturbance of his mind by falling upon his knees and saying his prayers in the street, or in any other unusual place. Now although, rationally speaking, it is greater madness not to pray at all than to pray as Smart did, I am afraid there are so many who do not pray that their understanding is not called in question."

Concerning this unfortunate poet, Christopher Smart, who was confined in a madhouse, he had, at another time, the following conversation with Dr. Burney:[6] *Burney:* "How does poor Smart do, sir; is he likely to recover?" *Johnson:* "It seems as if his mind had ceased to struggle with the disease; for he grows fat upon it." *Burney:* "Perhaps, sir, that may be from want of exercise." *Johnson:* "No, sir; he has partly as much exercise as he used to have, for he digs in the garden. Indeed, before his confinement, he used for exercise to walk to the alehouse; but he was *carried* back again. I did not think he ought to be shut up. His infirmities were not noxious to society. He insisted on people praying with him; and I'd as

lief pray with Kit Smart as anyone else. Another charge was that he did not love clean linen; and I have no passion for it." Johnson continued. "Mankind have a great aversion to intellectual labor; but even supposing knowledge to be easily attainable, more people would be content to be ignorant than would take even a little trouble to acquire it." . . .

Boswell Quizzes Johnson

I know not how so whimsical a thought came into my mind, but I asked, "If, sir, you were shut up in a castle, and a newborn child with you, what would you do?" *Johnson:* "Why, sir, I should not much like my company." *Boswell:* "But would you take the trouble of rearing it?" He seemed, as may well be supposed, unwilling to pursue the subject: but upon my persevering in my question, replied, "Why yes, sir, I would; but I must have all conveniences. If I had no garden, I would make a shed on the roof, and take it there for fresh air. I should feed it, and wash it much, and with warm water to please it, not with cold water to give it pain." *Boswell:* "But, sir, does not heat relax?" *Johnson:* "Sir, you are not to imagine the water is to be very hot. I would not *coddle* the child. No, sir, the hardy method of treating children does no good. I'll take you five children from London, who shall cuff five Highland children. Sir, a man bred in London will carry a burden or run or wrestle as well as a man brought up in the hardiest manner in the country." *Boswell:* "Good living, I suppose, makes the Londoners strong." *Johnson:* "Why, sir, I don't know that it does. Our chairmen[7] from Ireland, who are as strong men as any, have been brought up upon potatoes. Quantity makes up for quality." *Boswell:* "Would you teach this child that I have furnished you with, anything?" *Johnson:* "No, I should not be apt to teach it." *Boswell:* "Would not you have a pleasure in teaching it?" *Johnson:* "No, sir, I should *not* have a pleasure in teaching it." *Boswell:* "Have you not a pleasure in teaching men? *There* I have you. You have the same pleasure in teaching men, that I should have in teaching children." *Johnson:* "Why, something about that." . . .

---

5. **Smart:** Christopher Smart, a poet.
6. **Dr. Burney:** Charles Burney, a musicologist and father of the novelist Fanny Burney.

7. **chairmen:** porters who conveyed people through the London streets in sedan chairs.

A. Expansion
Although apparently prejudiced in some matters, Johnson exhibited remarkable tolerance (for the age) in others. He himself suffered from a lifelong fear of madness, and this perhaps explains his empathy with Christopher Smart.

B. Characterization
This episode illustrates the remarkable talent Boswell had for "drawing Johnson out," even on extremely hypothetical or trivial issues. Although Boswell occasionally looks foolish, it is clear that both men enjoyed each other's conversation, and that Boswell himself was an accomplished conversationalist.

A

B

READING CHECK TEST
1. Johnson is completely gracious and polite when Boswell first meets him. (F)
2. Boswell finds Johnson's clothes, his furniture, and his apartment shabby and unkept. (T)
3. When quizzed by Boswell, Johnson states he would never have anything to do with raising a child. (F)

4. One of Johnson's strange habits was counting his steps when preparing to go through a door. (T)
5. Johnson always made serious efforts to avoid argument or contradiction. (F)

ANALYZING THE BIOGRAPHY
Identifying Facts
1. Boswell felt awed and apprehensive.
2. Johnson was dressed in a rather disorderly brown suit and had on an unpowdered wig that was too small for his head; his clothes did not fit well; and he wore a pair of unbuckled shoes for slippers.

CLOSURE
Have students briefly describe three of Dr. Johnson's character traits, and three of Boswell's.

A. Responding
❓ Are the "eccentricities" as Boswell describes them really that eccentric? Do you think that habits such as these are relatively harmless?

B. Expansion
Thrale here is Henry Thrale—the rich brewer in whose house Johnson often found hospitality. Mrs. Thrale, an admirer and friend, was an accomplished writer, who published a memoir entitled *Anecdotes of the Late Samuel Johnson* two years after Johnson's death.

Johnson's Eccentricities

Talking to himself was, indeed, one of his singularities ever since I knew him. I was certain that he was frequently uttering pious ejaculations; for fragments of the Lord's Prayer have been distinctly overheard. His friend Mr. Thomas Davies, of whom Churchill[8] says, "That Davies hath a very pretty wife," when Dr. Johnson muttered "lead us not into temptation," used with waggish and gallant humor to whisper to Mrs. Davies, "You, my dear, are the cause of this."

He had another particularity, of which none of his friends ever ventured to ask an explanation. It appeared to me some superstitious habit, which he had contracted early, and from which he had never called upon his reason to disentangle him. This was his anxious care to go out or in at a door or passage by a certain number of steps from a certain point, or at least so as that either his right or his left foot (I am not certain which) should constantly make the first actual movement when he came close to the door or passage. Thus I conjecture: for I have, upon innumerable occasions, observed him suddenly stop, and then seem to count his steps with a deep earnestness; and when he had neglected or gone wrong in this sort of magical movement, I have seen him go back again, put himself in a proper posture to begin the ceremony, and, having gone through it, break from his abstraction, walk briskly on, and join his companion. A strange instance of something of this nature, even when on horseback, happened when he was in the isle of Sky.[9] Sir Joshua Reynolds[10] has observed him to go a good way about, rather than cross a particular alley in Leicester-fields;[11] but this Sir Joshua imputed to his having had some disagreeable recollection associated with it.

That the most minute singularities which belonged to him, and made very observable parts of his appearance and manner, may not be omitted, it is requisite to mention that while talking or even musing as he sat in his chair, he commonly held his head to one side toward his right shoulder and shook it in a tremulous manner, moving his body backward and forward, and rubbing his left knee in the same direction with the palm of his hand. In the intervals of articulating he made various sounds with his mouth, sometimes as if ruminating, or what is called chewing the cud, sometimes giving a half whistle, sometimes making his tongue play backward from the roof of his mouth as if clucking like a hen, and sometimes protruding it against his upper gums in front as if pronouncing quickly under his breath, *too, too, too*: all this accompanied sometimes with a thoughtful look, but more frequently with a smile. Generally when he had concluded a period, in the course of a dispute, by which time he was a good deal exhausted by violence and vociferation, he used to blow out his breath like a whale. This I supposed was a relief to his lungs; and seemed in him to be a contemptuous mode of expression, as if he had made the arguments of his opponent fly like chaff before the wind.

I am fully aware how very obvious an occasion I here give for the sneering jocularity of such as have no relish of an exact likeness; which to render complete, he who draws it must not disdain the slightest strokes. But if witlings should be inclined to attack this account, let them have the candor to quote what I have offered in my defense. . . .

Johnson's Love of Argument

I mentioned a new gaming club,[12] of which Mr. Beauclerk[13] had given me an account, where the members played to a desperate extent. *Johnson:* "Depend upon it, sir, this is mere talk. *Who* is ruined by gaming? You will not find six instances in an age. There is a strange rout made about deep play: whereas you have many more people ruined by adventurous trade,[14] and yet we do not hear such an outcry against it." *Thrale:* "There may be few people absolutely ruined by deep play; but very many are much hurt in their circumstances by it." *Johnson:* "Yes, sir, and so are very many by other kinds of expense." I had heard him talk

---

8. **Churchill:** Charles Churchill, author of satirical and comical poems.
9. **Sky:** one of the Hebrides Islands, off the coast of Scotland.
10. **Sir Joshua Reynolds:** the painter (1723–1792).
11. **Leicester-fields:** a square in London. *Leicester* is pronounced "lester."

12. **gaming club:** gambling club.
13. **Beauclerk:** Topham Beauclerk, a fashionable gentleman and descendant of King Charles II.
14. **trade:** business.

3. Johnson had the peculiar habit of passing through a doorway or passage with a particular number of steps.
4. He held his head toward his right shoulder and spoke in a tremulous manner; he moved his body backward and forward and rubbed his left knee; and he made various unusual sounds and movements with his tongue. When he had ended what he had to say, he blew out his breath like a whale.
5. According to Boswell, Johnson did this to exercise and display his ingenuity.

Interpreting Meanings
6. When Boswell actually met Johnson, he found the celebrated man to be down-to-earth, rather slovenly, and far less awe-inspiring than he had expected.
7. Student answers will vary. Johnson's friends may have found his eccentricities refreshing, and they were very probably afraid to risk his ire by trying to persuade him to become more conventional.
8. He says that he has the goal of being accurate.
Student answers will vary.
9. Student answers will vary. Most students will agree that Johnson was not really impolite.

10. We mean that someone departs—in an unexpected or amusing or somewhat trivial way—from the usual or conventional norms of social behavior. The word *insanity* denotes true madness, a complete separation from reality.
11. Most students will agree that Johnson would have been less interesting if his behavior had been conventional.
Student answers will vary. Traditionally, the British have been thought to be especially tolerant of eccentrics. Americans are thought to demand more conformity.

once before in the same manner; and at Oxford he said, "he wished he had learnt to play at cards." The truth, however, is, that he loved to display his ingenuity in argument; and therefore would sometimes in conversation maintain opinions which he was sensible were wrong, but in supporting which, his reasoning and wit would be most conspicuous. He would begin thus: "Why, sir, as to the good or evil of card-playing—"

"Now (said Garrick), he is thinking which side he shall take." He appeared to have a pleasure in contradiction, especially when any opinion whatever was delivered with an air of confidence; so that there was hardly any topic, if not one of the great truths of religion and morality, that he might not have been incited to argue, either for or against. . . .

Responding to the Biography

Analyzing the Biography

Identifying Facts

1. How did Boswell feel as he was about to meet Johnson?
2. How was Johnson dressed when Boswell first visited him in his study?
3. What superstitious habit did Johnson have?
4. Describe the peculiar mannerisms Johnson exhibited when he was talking.
5. Why, according to Boswell, did Johnson sometimes express opinions which he did not really believe?

Interpreting Meanings

6. Before meeting Johnson, Boswell thought that he lived in "a state of solemn elevated abstraction."

Explain how the actual experience of meeting and talking with Johnson differed from Boswell's expectations.
7. Why didn't Boswell or any of Johnson's other friends ask him about his eccentricities, or attempt to make him more conventional?
8. What defense does Boswell offer for describing Johnson's eccentricities in the *Life*? Do you think the defense is valid?
9. Was Johnson an impolite person, or did he only seem rude? Discuss.
10. What do we mean when we call someone an "eccentric"? How is *eccentricity* different from *insanity*?
11. Would Johnson have been more or less interesting had his behavior been conventional? Why is eccentricity of behavior important to society? (How do you think eccentricity is regarded in society today?)

Writing About the Biography

A Creative Response

1. **Writing a Biographical Sketch.** Write a two- or three-page biographical sketch of someone you know well. Include an account of your first meeting and any other interesting anecdotes that will help a reader to know the person you are writing about. As Boswell does, record some of your subject's words and incorporate them into your sketch as **dialogue.**

A Critical Response

2. **Writing an Explanation.** Write an explanation of whether you would, or would not, have liked to be a friend of Samuel Johnson's, had you lived in the eighteenth century. Consider Johnson's own writings as well as Boswell's biographical accounts.

Samuel Johnson and James Boswell in Edinburgh in 1773 by Thomas Rowlandson. Engraving.

James Boswell **581**

A. **Expansion**
The Pilgrim's Progress was one of the first books brought by the Puritans to America.

B. **Responding**
? Name some other famous books that were written by imprisoned authors. (Cervantes's *Don Quixote,* Malory's *Morte Darthur*)

John Bunyan (1628–1688)

Unlike most of the other writers represented in this anthology, Bunyan came from England's lowest social class. He worked with his hands as a brazier or tinker, a maker and mender of cooking pots and pans. Yet he was not just an ordinary tinker, but the author of a book that, next to the Bible, has been the most widely read of all English books: *The Pilgrim's Progress from This World to That Which Is to Come* (1678), commonly called *The Pilgrim's Progress.*

A

What we know about Bunyan comes mainly from his autobiographical work *Grace Abounding to the Chief of Sinners* (1666), the "Chief of Sinners" being himself. In this book he describes his childhood poverty, his service in the army fighting against King Charles I, and his marriage when he was still a teen-ager. He and his wife, he tells us, were "as poor as poor might be, with not so much household stuff as a dish or spoon betwixt us both." Aside from a very few details like these, *Grace Abounding* is concerned entirely with the state of Bunyan's soul and his relationship with God. To Bunyan, these were the only really important matters in life.

Although he had never been formally educated or ordained as a minister, Bunyan felt called to preach to his fellow Baptists. He began holding services in private houses and then, as his eloquence and piety attracted many people, in the woods outside his home town of Bedford. Such Puritan sects as the Baptists flourished during the years when England was without a king (1649–1660), but with the Restoration of Charles II, the government soon reestablished the Church of England and outlawed all other forms of religion. Inevitably, Bunyan found it impossible to obey the law requiring attendance at the Church of England and forbidding all other religious gatherings; in 1660 he was arrested and jailed for preaching without a license.

It looks to us today as though Bunyan brought these troubles upon himself. The sheriff did not want to arrest him, nor did the magistrate want to sentence him. Most of all, they did not want to keep him in jail. They would gladly

John Bunyan by Thomas Sadler. Oil.

have released him had he promised to give up public preaching, to attend church, and occasionally to receive the sacraments. Moreover, there were strong personal reasons why Bunyan should have been eager to leave the jail and resume support of his family. Conditions at home were not ideal: about a year earlier, his first wife had died, leaving a number of small children, one of them blind, to be taken care of. His second wife was pregnant, and the news of her husband's arrest caused her to miscarry. He was, in short, desperately needed at home. Yet his principles did not permit him to obey the law; thus, for twelve years he remained imprisoned, preaching to the other inmates and writing religious books. A short period of freedom followed this imprisonment—a time when the authorities were lax in enforcing the laws. Then, in 1675, Bunyan was locked up again.

During his second confinement, he wrote *The Pilgrim's Progress,* which was such a great success that, like the producers of popular movies

B

today, he published a second part. Both parts have been translated into many languages and republished countless times.

All together, Bunyan wrote sixty books and pamphlets. And, as the laws against nonconformists were relaxed, he also became famous as a preacher, even in London, where an audience of several thousand would go to hear him on a Sunday. When told about Bunyan, King Charles expressed astonishment that a tinker could draw such crowds.

How can we account for Bunyan's enormous appeal? He spoke to, and wrote for, people who believed that every individual human being is engaged in a continuous battle against the forces of evil. Bunyan and his listeners believed that the whole aim of life is to win this battle. Although, in this belief, the evil forces are powerful, they are not so powerful as God; with God's help, the battle can be won and eternal life attained. And so Bunyan told his readers what they most wanted to hear: how they could defeat evil and how God could save them. He expressed his message in language familiar to his readers, drawn from their daily experience and from the Bible, folk tales, and popular literature. In Bunyan's books his readers recognized their own lives, made surprising and interesting.

A. Responding to the Illustration

❓ What does the frontispiece of *The Pilgrim's Progress* suggest about the nature of the work? (That it will deal with spiritual matters and will recount adventures containing obstacles to be overcome) What is the entire title of the work? What do you think the quotation from the prophet Hosea means? (Bunyan is writing *allegory*, a kind of similitude, or comparison.)

A

Rare Books and Manuscripts Division, The New York Public Library.

1. BUILDING ON PRIOR KNOWLEDGE.
Before students begin reading, ask them to discuss what they know about allegory (see also the essay on allegory in The Elements of Literature on text page 590). What do students know about a *pilgrim*—consider not only the American pilgrims and Chaucer's pilgrims, but also contemporary pilgrims.

2. ESTABLISHING A PURPOSE. Since the story is an allegory, students should read with an awareness of the narrative's "double meaning." On one level we have an adventure story; on a deeper allegorical level we have a story about a person who fights despair.

3. PREREADING JOURNAL. Before they read, have students write two or three sentences describing what they think places like the Delectable Mountains, the Slough of Despond, the Hill of Difficulty, and Vanity Fair stand for. What contemporary experiences could relate to each of these "places"? Then have them write a brief reflection on how we are all "pilgrims." See Chaucer's quotation on text page 68.

A. Humanities Connection: Responding to the Fine Art
In addition to being a great poet, William Blake was a talented artist and engraver (see text page 617).
❓ What words would you use to describe this painting? (Heavy, gloomy, depressing, burdensome, torturous) What elements of the painting make you feel this way? (The hunched over posture of the figure and the expression on his face, the resemblance of the burden on his back to claws digging into his flesh, the sparse use of vivid colors, such as red, orange, and yellow, in comparison to the predominant use of drab, pale blues, greens, and browns)

FROM THE PILGRIM'S PROGRESS

A

Christian Reading in His Book by William Blake. Watercolor.

Copyright The Frick Collection.

SUPPLEMENTARY SUPPORT MATERIALS
1. Vocabulary Activity Worksheet (CCB)
2. Review and Response Worksheet: Allegory (CCB)
3. Selection Test (CCB)

DEVELOPING VOCABULARY
The following words from the story are tested in the Selection Test. (See also Vocabulary Activity Worksheet.)

to deride	cudgel
to chide	to abide
evangelist	to moderate
surly	discourse
diffidence	jurisdiction

A. Expansion
Here is evidence that people in Bunyan's day handled their problems in much the same way as many families today handle theirs. That is to say, they hesitate to share their emotional burdens with spouse and children until they reach a bursting point and can no longer bear the stress.

The narrator of *The Pilgrim's Progress* is a dreamer. Asleep, he dreams about a man called Christian who lives with his family in a city called Destruction. Besides living in a city with this appalling name, Christian has another problem: on his back he bears an immense burden that he cannot get rid of. It is like a part of himself. And so he decides to leave home and go on a "progress," or journey, to a wonderful place that he has heard of called the Celestial City. On this trip, which takes up most of the book, he has a few pleasant experiences such as his visit to House Beautiful and the Delectable Mountains, but most of his adventures are unpleasant and even dangerous. He falls into the Slough (rhymes with "cow") (or mudhole) of Despond, he has to climb the Hill Difficulty, he has to fight a dragon-like monster called Apollyon, and he is arrested and unjustly punished in a prosperous, busy place called Vanity Fair. But his most insidious encounters are with characters who try to distract him from his progress: Mr. Worldly Wiseman, Talkative, Little-Faith, and Ignorance. Finally, all these obstacles overcome, Christian enters the Celestial City, where he will dwell eternally in bliss, and where he is eventually joined by his wife Christiana and their children. Bunyan describes their journey in the second part of *The Pilgrim's Progress*.

This excerpt describes how Christian and his companion Hopeful become lost, wander into a giant's domain, fall asleep there, and encounter the giant Despair.

Christian Begins His Pilgrimage

As I walked through the wilderness of this world, I lighted on a certain place where was a Den,[1] and I laid me down in that place to sleep: and as I slept I dreamed a dream. I dreamed, and behold I saw a man clothed with rags, standing in a certain place, with his face from his own house, a book in his hand, and a great burden upon his back. I looked, and saw him open the book and read therein; and as he read, he wept and trembled; and not being able longer to contain, he brake out with a lamentable cry, saying, "What shall I do?"

In this plight, therefore, he went home and refrained himself as long as he could, that his wife and children should not perceive his distress; but he could not be silent long, because that his trouble increased. Wherefore at length he brake his mind to his wife and children; and thus he began to talk to them. "O my dear wife," said he, "and you the children of my bowels,[2] I, your dear friend, am in myself undone by reason of a burden that lieth hard upon me; moreover, I am for certain informed that this our city will be burned with fire from heaven, in which fearful overthrow both myself, with thee my wife, and you my sweet babes, shall miserably come to ruin, except (the which yet I see not) some way of escape can be found, whereby we may be delivered." At this his relations were sore amazed; not for that they believed that what he had said to them was true, but because they thought that some frenzy distemper[3] had got into his head; therefore, it drawing toward night, and they hoping that sleep might settle his brains, with all haste they got him to bed. But the night was as troublesome to him as the day; wherefore, instead of sleeping, he spent it in sighs and tears. So, when the morning was come, they would know how he did. He told them, "Worse and worse": he also set to talking to them again: but they began to be hardened. They also thought to drive away his distemper by harsh and surly carriages[4] to him; sometimes they would deride, sometimes they would chide, and sometimes they would quite neglect him. Wherefore he began to retire himself to his chamber, to pray for and pity them, and also to condole his own misery; he would also walk solitarily in the fields, sometimes reading, and sometimes praying: and thus for some days he spent his time.

Now I saw, upon a time when he was walking in the fields, that he was (as he was wont[5]) reading in his book, and greatly distressed in his mind; and as he read, he burst out, as he had done before, crying, "What shall I do to be saved?"

A

---

1. **Den:** the jail.

2. **bowels:** thought to be the seat of tender feelings and family affection.
3. **frenzy distemper:** insanity.
4. **harsh . . . carriages:** angry behavior.
5. **wont:** accustomed.

A. Vocabulary

? What is an evangelist? (A preacher of the Gospel; or, specifically Matthew, Mark, Luke, or John. It could also be any preacher.) (The word comes from the Greek *evangelion*, meaning "goodness.")

B. Vocabulary

? What would a character named Diffidence be like? (An archaic meaning of *diffidence* is "distrustful," and a character would exhibit such tendencies.)

C. Paraphrase

? Paraphrase the sentence beginning "So when he arose," to show you understand the archaic diction and syntax. (So when he arose, he got a strong stick made from a crab apple tree and went down into the dungeon to them, and there first scolded them as if they were dogs, although they had never given him reason to dislike them.)

I saw also that he looked this way and that way, as if he would run; yet he stood still, because (as I perceived) he could not tell which way to go. I looked then, and saw a man named Evangelist coming to him, who asked, "Wherefore dost thou cry?"

He answered, "Sir, I perceive by the book in my hand that I am condemned to die, and after that to come to judgment, and I find that I am not willing to do the first, nor able to do the second."

Then said Evangelist, "Why not willing to die, since this life is attended with so many evils?" The man answered, "Because I fear that this burden that is upon my back will sink me lower than the grave, and I shall fall into Tophet.[6] And, sir, if I be not fit to go to prison, I am not fit to go to judgment, and from thence to execution; and the thoughts of these things make me cry."

Then said Evangelist, "If this be thy condition, why standest thou still?" He answered, "Because I know not whither to go." Then he gave him a parchment roll, and there was written within, "Fly from the wrath to come."

The man therefore read it, and looking upon Evangelist very carefully, said, "Whither must I fly?" Then said Evangelist, pointing with his finger over a very wide field, "Do you see yonder wicket-gate?" The man said, "No." Then said the other, "Do you see yonder shining light?" He said, "I think I do." Then said Evangelist, "Keep that light in your eye, and go up directly thereto: so shalt thou see the gate; at which when thou knockest it shall be told thee what thou shalt do." So I saw in my dream that the man began to run. Now, he had not run far from his own door, but his wife and children perceiving it, began to cry after him to return; but the man put his fingers in his ears, and ran on, crying, "Life! life! eternal life!" So he looked not behind him, but fled toward the middle of the plain. . . .

Doubting Castle and Giant Despair

At last, lighting under a little shelter, they [Christian and Hopeful] sat down there till the day brake; but being weary, they fell asleep. Now there was, not far from the place where they lay, a castle called Doubting Castle, the owner whereof was Giant Despair; and it was in his grounds they now were sleeping: wherefore he, getting up in the morning early, and walking up and down in his fields, caught Christian and Hopeful asleep in his grounds. Then with a grim and surly voice he bid them awake, and asked them whence they were and what they did in his grounds. They told him they were pilgrims and that they had lost their way. Then said the Giant, "You have this night trespassed on me by trampling in and lying on my grounds, and therefore you must go along with me." So they were forced to go, because he was stronger than they. They also had but little to say, for they knew themselves in a fault. The Giant therefore drove them before him and put them into his castle, into a very dark dungeon, nasty and stinking to the spirits of these two men. Here then they lay from Wednesday morning till Saturday night, without one bit of bread, or drop of drink, or light, or any to ask how they did; they were therefore here in evil case,[7] and were far from friends and acquaintance. Now in this place Christian had double sorrow, because 'twas through his unadvised haste that they were brought into this distress.

Now Giant Despair had a wife, and her name was Diffidence. So when he was gone to bed, he told his wife what he had done; to wit, that he had taken a couple of prisoners and cast them into his dungeon for trespassing on his grounds. Then he asked her also what he had best to do further to them. So she asked him what they were, whence they came, and whither they were bound; and he told her. Then she counseled him that when he arose in the morning he should beat them without any mercy. So when he arose, he getteth him a grievous crabtree cudgel, and goes down into the dungeon to them, and there first falls to rating[8] of them as if they were dogs, although they never gave him a word of distaste. Then he falls upon them and beats them fearfully, in such sort that they were not able to help themselves, or to turn them upon the floor. This done, he withdraws and leaves them there to condole their misery and to mourn under their distress. So all that day they spent the time in nothing but sighs and bitter lamentations. The next night she talking with her husband about them further, and understanding they were yet alive, did advise him to counsel them to

---

6. **Tophet:** Hell.

7. **case:** condition.
8. **rating:** scolding.

make away[9] themselves. So when morning was come, he goes to them in a surly manner as before, and perceiving them to be very sore with the stripes[10] that he had given them the day before, he told them that since they were never like to come out of that place, their only way would be forthwith to make an end of themselves, either with knife, halter,[11] or poison. "For why," said he, "should you choose life, seeing it is attended with so much bitterness?" But they desired him to let them go. With that he looked ugly upon them, and rushing to them, had doubtless made an end of them himself, but that he fell into one of his fits (for he sometimes in sunshine weather fell into fits), and lost for a time the use of his hand; wherefore he withdrew, and left them as before to consider what to do. Then did the prisoners consult between themselves, whether 'twas best to take his counsel or no; and thus they began to discourse:

Christian: "Brother," said Christian, "what shall we do? The life that we now live is miserable. For my part I know not whether it is best to live thus, or to die out of hand. 'My soul chooseth strangling rather than life,'[12] and the grave is more easy for me than this dungeon. Shall we be ruled by the Giant?"

Hope: "Indeed our present condition is dreadful, and death would be far more welcome to me than thus forever to abide; but yet let us consider, the Lord of the country to which we are going hath said, 'Thou shalt do no murder': no, not to another man's person; much more then are we forbidden to take his counsel to kill ourselves. Besides, he that kills another can but commit murder upon his body; but for one to kill himself is to kill body and soul at once. And moreover, my brother, thou talkest of ease in the grave; but hast thou forgotten the hell whither for certain the murderers go? For 'no murderer hath eternal life,'[13]etc. And let us consider again that all the law is not in the hand of Giant Despair. Others, so far as I can understand, have been taken by him, as well as we; and yet have escaped out of his hand. Who knows but that God that made the world may cause that Giant Despair may die? Or

that at some time or other he may forget to lock us in? Or but he may in short time have another of his fits before us, and may lose the use of his limbs? And if ever that should come to pass again, for my part, I am resolved to pluck up the heart of a man,[14] and to try my utmost to get from under his hand. I was a fool that I did not try to do it before; but however, my brother, let's be patient, and endure a while. The time may come that may give us a happy release; but let us not be our own murderers." With these words Hopeful at present did moderate the mind of his brother; so they continued together (in the dark) that day, in their sad and doleful condition.

Well, toward evening the Giant goes down into the dungeon again, to see if his prisoners had taken his counsel; but when he came there he found them alive; and truly, alive was all; for now, what for want of bread and water, and by reason of the wounds they received when he beat them, they could do little but breathe. But, I say, he found them alive; at which he fell into a grievous rage, and told them that, seeing they had disobeyed his counsel, it should be worse with them than if they had never been born.

At this they trembled greatly, and I think that Christian fell into a swoon; but coming a little to himself again, they renewed their discourse about the Giant's counsel; and whether yet they had best to take it or no. Now Christian again seemed to be for doing it, but Hopeful made his second reply as followeth:

Hope: "My brother," said he, "rememberest thou not how valiant thou hast been heretofore? Apollyon could not crush thee, nor could all that thou didst hear, or see, or feel, in the Valley of the Shadow of Death. What hardship, terror, and amazement hast thou already gone through, and art thou now nothing but fear? Thou seest that I am in the dungeon with thee, a far weaker man by nature than thou art; also this Giant has wounded me as well as thee, and hath also cut off the bread and water from my mouth; and with thee I mourn without the light. But let us exercise a little more patience; remember how thou playedst the man[15] at Vanity Fair, and wast neither

---

9. **make away:** kill.
10. **stripes:** blows.
11. **halter:** noose
12. **'My soul . . . life':** quotation from Job 7:15.
13. **no murderer . . . life:** quotation from John 3:15.

14. **pluck . . . man:** be brave.
15. **playedst the man:** was brave.

A. **Reading Aloud/Logical Argument**
You might assign two students to read the following dialogue aloud. Note Hopeful's optimism. Note also Hopeful's logical progression of arguments against despair. Have students trace his reasoning. (Remember that suicide at the time was considered a mortal sin, self-murder.)

B. **Expansion**
Apollyon was a dragonlike monster, called the "Destroyer." See Revelation 9:11.

READING CHECK TEST
1. Christian's family believes him when he tells them of the impending destruction of their city. (F)
2. Christian leaves his family even though they beg him not to. (T)
3. After beating Christian and Hopeful, Giant Despair offers to let them work for their freedom. (F)

4. Giant Despair's wife pleads with him to let the prisoners go because they are so brave. (F)
5. Christian, using a key called Promise, unlocks the dungeon door and an iron gate, enabling him and Hopeful to escape. (T)

A. Symbolism
? What is symbolically significant about the time scheme and the day of the week? (The setting early on Sunday morning may be intended to suggest a symbolic "resurrection," by analogy with Christ's resurrection Easter Sunday morning.)

B. Interpreting
? What is the significance of Promise as the key to escape from Despair? (Promise suggests a future, hope, certainty of better things to come; recall God's promises in the Bible to redeem humankind from evil and sin.)

John Bunyan Dreams a Dream by William Blake. Watercolor.

Copyright The Frick Collection.

afraid of the chain, nor cage, nor yet of bloody death. Wherefore let us (at least to avoid the shame that becomes not a Christian to be found in) bear up with patience as well as we can."

Now night being come again, and the Giant and his wife being in bed, she asked him concerning the prisoners, and if they had taken his counsel. To which he replied, "They are sturdy rogues, they choose rather to bear all hardship than to make away themselves." Then said she, "Take them into the castle yard tomorrow, and show them the bones and skulls of those that thou hast already dispatched, and make them believe, ere a week come to an end, thou also wilt tear them in pieces, as thou hast done their fellows before them."

So when the morning was come, the Giant goes to them again, and takes them into the castle yard, and shows them, as his wife had bidden him. "These," said he, "were pilgrims as you are once, and they trespassed in my grounds, as you have done; and when I thought fit, I tore them in pieces, and so within ten days I will do you. Go, get you down to your den again"; and with that he beat them all the way thither. They lay therefore all day on Saturday in a lamentable case, as before.

Now when night was come, and when Mrs. Diffidence and her husband the Giant were got to bed, they began to renew their discourse of their prisoners; and withal the old Giant wondered that he could neither by his blows nor his counsel bring them to an end. And with that his wife replied, "I fear," said she, "that they live in hope that some will come to relieve them, or that they have picklocks about them, by the means of which they hope to escape." "And sayest thou so, my dear?" said the Giant; "I will therefore search them in the morning."

Well, on Saturday about midnight they began to pray, and continued in prayer till almost break of day.

Now a little before it was day, good Christian, as one half amazed, brake out in this passionate speech: "What a fool (quoth he) am I, thus to lie in a stinking dungeon, when I may as well walk at liberty! I have a key in my bosom called Promise, that will (I am persuaded) open any lock in Doubting Castle." Then said Hopeful, "That is good news, good brother; pluck it out of thy bosom and try." Then Christian pulled it out of his bosom, and began to try at the dungeon door, whose bolt (as he turned the key) gave back, and

1. Christian's problem is that he feels an intolerable burden on his back.

He obeys the Evangelist's command and sets out on a pilgrimage.
2. The giant is stronger than they are.
3. They are held captive for four days, from Wednesday to Sunday.

The giant beats them because his wife, Diffidence, advises him to do so.
4. They escape on Sunday morning, using a key called "Promise."

Interpreting Meanings
5. The book is probably the Bible.
6. A spiritual interpretation might equate the burden with sin or guilt for sin.
7. Possibly the wife's constant grilling of her husband.

8. Because Bunyan describes the family unsympathetically and identifies with Christian's quest for salvation.
9. It may symbolize a crisis of faith and a temptation to give in to despair.

The key called "Promise."
10. Student answers will vary. The discovery of a key may seem silly, but this *is* an allegory.

We often do not realize that we have the means to solve a problem if we focus on a single aspect of it.

the door flew open with ease, and Christian and Hopeful both came out. Then he went to the outward door that leads into the castle yard, and with his key opened that door also. After, he went to the iron gate, for that must be opened too; but that lock went *damnable* hard, yet the key did open it. Then they thrust open the gate to make their escape with speed, but that gate, as it opened, made such a creaking that it waked Giant Despair, who, hastily rising to pursue his prisoners, felt his limbs to fail, for his fits took him again, so that he could by no means go after them. Then they went on and came to the King's highway, and so were safe because they were out of his jurisdiction. . . .

Responding to the Story

Analyzing the Story

Identifying Facts

1. What is Christian's problem? How does he set about resolving it?
2. Why do Christian and Hopeful go with the giant? Why don't they resist?
3. How long are Christian and Hopeful held captive? Why does the giant beat them?
4. How, and on what day, do they escape?

Interpreting Meanings

5. What do you think the book is that so upsets Christian?
6. Most commentators on this story agree that such realistic details as the rags Christian wears are to be interpreted spiritually: the rags signify the desperate condition of Christian's soul, not the desperate condition of his pocketbook. What would be a spiritual interpretation of the heavy burden on Christian's back?
7. In the account of the giant and his wife, which details do *not* seem to have spiritual meaning?
8. Christian abandons his wife and children to go on his pilgrimage. How do you know that Bunyan approved of his values?
9. In thinking about Doubting Castle, remember that doubt is the opposite of faith. How, then, should the place be interpreted **allegorically**? Why are Christian and Hopeful shut up in Doubting Castle? What helps them escape?
10. What do you think of the way Christian and Hopeful escape the giant? Is it psychologically realistic that Christian would have forgotten his "key" for so long? Why or why not?

Writing About the Story

A Creative Response

1. **Changing a Character.** What if Christian's companion had been named Happy or Practical or Ferocious rather than Hopeful? How would the character be different, and how would his personality change the events in the story? Write a new version of one of the nights Christian and his companion spend in Doubting Castle, changing the name, and therefore the personality and actions, of Christian's companion. Write at least two pages, and try to use dialogue, as Bunyan does, to show your new character's personality. How will this new character affect the outcome of the story?

2. **Outlining an Allegory.** Suppose you wanted to write an allegory which presented in story form the account of a person who learned to love. Outline your allegory, including these details:

   a. The hero or heroine's name
   b. The allegorical form the hero or heroine's "burden" (or problem) takes
   c. The pitfalls the traveler meets on the quest to win the ability to love (give names, like the Hill of Difficulty or the Slough of Despond)
   d. The people the traveler meets (give names)

3. **Recasting the Story.** Suppose Bunyan had wanted to deliver his message in a sermon, instead of in a story. Write out the sermon he might have preached on Despair and how to conquer it.

A. Allegory

An allegory is distinguished from a metaphor by its being sustained longer and by its being more fully developed. In addition to Bunyan's *The Pilgrim's Progress,* other elaborate and successful examples of allegory are Spenser's *Faerie Queen,* Swift's *Tale of a Tub,* and Addison's *Vision of Mizra.*

ALLEGORY

A *The Pilgrim's Progress* is an **allegory,** a story developed out of a metaphor. Bunyan's allegory (often regarded as the best example of this kind of writing in English) grows out of the metaphor "Life is a journey." Bunyan did not, of course, invent this metaphor, but like other such metaphors ("Life is a game" or "Life is a play"), it is so ancient that its origin is unknown. When we hear such expressions as "the road of life" or "the crossroads of life," we hardly recognize them as metaphors, but they are variants of the same figure of speech Bunyan based his book on. *The Pilgrim's Progress,* then, joins the two ideas "life" and "journey."

In Bunyan's view, as has already been said, the most important part of human life is the religious part; he was more interested in the spiritual experiences that take place inside people—their thoughts and feelings—than in actual events. But how could he portray such spiritual experiences, which are mental and emotional states, in a way that would interest ordinary readers? In the poetic "Apology for His Book" that he prefixed to *The Pilgrim's Progress* he says this:

> I writing of the way
> And race of saints in this our Gospel day,
> Fell suddenly into an allegory
> About their journey and the way to glory.

The allegory of a journey allowed Bunyan to portray spiritual experiences as though they were physical.

Christian and Christiana, Bunyan's heroes, are ordinary human beings who suddenly feel the need for a closer relationship with God. Bunyan expresses this feeling allegorically; that is, he has his heroes set out on a journey that will bring them physically nearer to God. Their pilgrimage is not at all like the one undertaken by Chaucer's group of pilgrims, whose goal is the city of Canterbury in the southeast part of England. Chaucer's pilgrims start from London, a place on the map; Bunyan's pilgrims start from Destruction, an abstract noun. Instead of real places, Christian travels through such allegorical places as the Valley of Humiliation, where he learns the value of being humble. Christiana climbs the Hill Lucre, where she learns that money cannot save her soul.

Far from being realistic, the proper names in an allegory are direct clues to meaning. Mr. Talkative is a man who speaks much but says little, Madam Bubble is always frivolous, Valiant is always brave and strong, Atheist is always irreligious, and Hypocrisy is always two-faced. The characters are aspects of Christian's own consciousness; they never change, and they disappear from the story after they have helped or hindered him on his journey.

Allegory thus enables Bunyan to tell two stories at the same time. One, the *surface story,* involves a journey through a landscape that is fantastic, yet convincing because it is described in detail. This story is an adventure story. The other story, the *submerged* one, involves the spiritual development of typical human beings who don't go anywhere, but try to lead religious lives, avoiding the obstacles, distractions, and temptations that get in their way. This second story might be called a psychological story, since it is concerned with mental and emotional processes. Yet, in the experience of reading, the two stories become one.

1. What is the plot for the submerged story of Christian and Hopeful's encounter with the giant?
2. What is the allegorical significance of the giant's fits? How is it appropriate that they happen "in sunshine weather"?
3. What does *diffidence* mean? Why is it allegorically appropriate that Diffidence is wedded to Despair?
4. What is the significance of the key that is called "Promise"?

THE ENGLISH LANGUAGE
by **John Algeo**

I n the eighteenth century, some English speakers believed that the English language had become as good as it could become. Therefore, they should try to prevent any more changes, which could only lead to the degeneration of the language. It was a foolish opinion, but some people today still hold it. Only, they think that English has reached perfection in *our* time, so that any change from the way *we* talk and write will lead to the death of our language.

Change, Degeneration, and Growth

A language does not die or degenerate because it changes. Language degenerates when the number of people who speak it decrease and it is used for talking about fewer and fewer things. A language dies only when nobody talks it at all. The oft-predicted death of English is like that of Mark Twain, who read his own obituary in an American newspaper while he was in England. He cabled the newspaper: "The reports of my death are greatly exaggerated." So are reports of the "death" of English.

Throughout its history, the English language has been spoken by more and more people, and has been used for more and more purposes around the world. Today, English as a native language is distributed more widely than any other; as a second language, it is used by more people than any other language. English is used for more purposes—scientific, technical, commercial, and personal—than any other language. Far from being in danger of degenerating or dying, English is the most vital of all human languages.

Change in language is natural; no living language is free from it. It is, moreover, a good thing, for without change, a language would indeed die. Change in language has many causes. When English speakers first settled America, they found new animals, plants, land formations, and other things for which they had no names. To talk about the new world, they had to adapt old words, coin new words, or borrow words from other languages.

Americans have done all three things. English sailors had used the word *bluff* as an adjective to mean "broad and flat"; Americans adapted it as a noun to mean "cliff," of which they encountered a good many. To name the action of reorganizing an election district for the unfair advantage of one party, Americans coined the word *gerrymander* (from Elbridge *Gerry,* a nineteenth-century governor of Massachusetts, who helped carve out an election district that looked like a *salamander*). In the Southwest, English-speaking cowboys learned from their Spanish-speaking co-workers how to

Decorum and Order

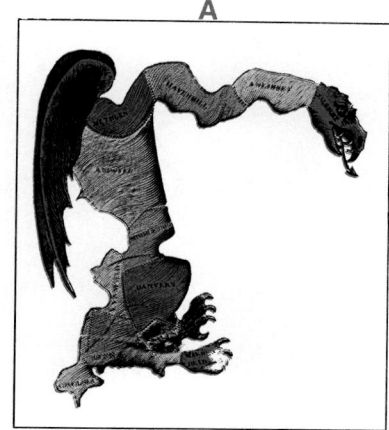

The Gerry-Mander! by Elkanah Tisdale (1812). Cartoon comment on the action of carving the state of Massachusetts into new voting districts.

" **W** ithout change, a language would indeed die."

A. About the Illustration
Born in Connecticut, Elkanah Tisdale (1771–?) was a painter, designer, and engraver of miniatures. Note the fine lines of *The Gerry-Mander!* that demonstrate the artist's skill.

B. Expansion
English is the language used for international aviation. In addition, English, along with Arabic, Chinese, French, Russian, and Spanish, is one of the official languages of the United Nations.

C. Borrowed Words
Among the words borrowed from Native American languages are: *succotash* (a dish consisting of lima beans and corn), *toboggan* (a long, narrow sled without runners), and *skunk.*

American Frederic Remington's (1861–1909) specialty was depicting the American Indian, the cowboy, and the United States soldier as seen on the western plains. Remington's works have been widely reproduced, including reproduction in media other than the original (note that this illustration is a wood engraving based on a drawing). Remington is also noted for several volumes of stories, including *Pony Tracks* (1895), *Crooked Trails* (1898), and *John Ermine of the Yellowstone* (1902).

Roping in a Horse-Corral after a drawing by Frederic Remington (1888). Wood engraving.

catch horses and cattle with a long rope that had a running noose at one end. They borrowed the Spanish name for the rope: *lasso*.

Another cause of change is a natural drift in the way we use language. As each new generation learns English, it introduces changes. We could say that we all learn our language a little bit wrong, but it would be more accurate to say that we "restructure" our language as we learn it. We do not at first learn English out of grammar books and dictionaries. Rather, as infants we hear it spoken about us, and we strive to make sense out of the noises that bombard our ears.

Each of us is like a computer programmer who has to write a program for the language spoken around us. We write our own subconscious grammar and compile our own subconscious dictionary. We are likely to do the job in a somewhat different fashion from the way our parents did it in their time. And so over the generations, a language gradually changes, until one day we realize that some very big and important changes have happened over a thousand years, although none of the thirty generations who lived during that time was aware of using language very differently from those who came before or after them.

Change in language, far from being a sign of degeneracy, can be thought of as the way language adapts to new conditions and new speakers. It is the way language stays alive. Change is not degeneration; it is growth. All living things must grow through change. Languages are no exception.

Refining, Ascertaining, and Fixing English

Some English speakers today are obsessed with the fear that the changes they notice in English mean that the language is about to slip into incoherence and disintegrate, unless we do something about it—and fast. That obsession first became a large-scale concern of English speakers during the eighteenth century. People then thought that they should refine, ascertain, and fix the English language.

By *refine,* the eighteenth-century grammarians meant that they should rub off any rough edges, to correct anything they thought might be amiss. In practice this generally meant telling other people that they should talk and write in the same way that the refiner did.

By *ascertain,* the grammarians meant to write rules that would describe how the English language puts words together into sentences, and to be sure that there was only one acceptable way to do the job. We have already seen that English offers us a great many different ways of saying the same thing. But some people don't like options and the freedom to choose. Valuing unity over diversity, they would prefer that there be just one right way to use language, instead of many. So some eighteenth-century writers set themselves up as authorities who would determine which one way was right and which other ways were wrong. They would promote the unity of English.

By *fix,* the grammarians meant that they wanted to stop any further changes in the language once it had been sufficiently refined and ascertained. They hoped to prevent English from ever becoming different. We have already considered the impossibility, and undesirability, of this goal.

Jonathan Swift was one of the writers of this period who was concerned about the well-being of English and the dangers he saw for it. He especially disliked the idea that a language should be "perpetually changing." So Swift wrote *A Proposal for Correcting, Improving, and Ascertaining the English Tongue* (1712), in which he suggested that a group of persons should take on themselves the responsibility of overseeing the language, improving it, unifying it, and above all stabilizing it so that it would stop changing. A number of other countries in Europe had or were to develop such groups, usually called "Academies": Italy, France, and Spain were prime examples.

The idea of an English Academy never caught on, however. Part of the reason for its failure was the individualism of many English speakers, who were loath to let anybody else tell them how they ought to talk. And part of the reason was the rapid development

> " **C**hange
> is the way
> language stays alive.
> Change
> is not degeneration;
> it is growth."

A

> " **S**ome English
> speakers
> today are obsessed with
> the fear that the language
> is about to slip
> into incoherence
> and disintegrate,
> unless we do something
> about it—and fast."

A. Expansion
In spite of a similar fear French speakers have for their own language, American words such as *hamburger* and *weekend* continue to make their way into spoken French.

A. Expansion

In 1604, Robert Cawdrey, a school-teacher, prepared the first English dictionary, which he called *The Table Alphabeticall of Hard Words*. This book defined approximately 3,000 difficult English words that had been taken from other languages. Later in the 1600's, larger dictionaries that offered more information were published. In 1721, in an attempt to include *all* English words rather than only hard ones, Nathan Bailey produced a dictionary containing approximately 60,000 words.

First edition title page of Johnson's Dictionary of the English Language *(1755).*

The British Library.

of English dictionaries. English dictionaries, especially from Samuel Johnson's great dictionary of 1755 on, became "authorities" to which English speakers who were insecure about their own language looked for advice about what they should say and write.

The Dictionary

The tradition of making English dictionaries reached a high point of development with Samuel Johnson, who in 1755 published his two-volume *Dictionary of the English Language*. This dictionary included more words than any previous dictionary had; it gave more information about each entry; and, instead of merely defining a word, it included quotations from English writers to show how the word was actually used.

In America, Noah Webster produced a dictionary which came to fill the place in American life that Johnson's dictionary filled in Great Britain. Webster was especially good at writing definitions, and he wanted to produce a dictionary that would record the English of the New World, not that of the mother country. Webster's dictionary was so successful that his name has become almost synonymous with the word *dictionary* itself. People sometimes say, "It's in Webster's" or "Webster says . . ." when all they mean is that the information is in some dictionary or other.

(Nowadays many dictionaries use *Webster* in their titles, but none of them preserve anything from old Noah's book. *Webster* in a dictionary's title is no guarantee of anything—it is only an advertising technique to take advantage of the fact that people associate Webster with dictionaries. Of no other work is it truer that you can't tell a book by its cover.)

In the nineteenth century, a group of English scholars began to work on a dictionary to replace Johnson's, which had become very outdated. Their work eventually developed into the greatest dictionary in the world: *The Oxford English Dictionary*. It was completed in 1933 in thirteen volumes. Recently four new supplementary volumes have been published, making seventeen in all, and now the whole dictionary is being put into computer form to be kept up-to-date and accessible to computer users.

Samuel Johnson wrote his dictionary almost single-handedly and by candlelight. Today, teams of lexicographers cooperate in producing dictionaries with the latest computer techniques. As the language changes, so do the ways we keep up with it.

Change All Around Us

Jonathan Swift was not able to stop English from changing, however much he wanted to. Nor can anyone else. The nature of languages is to change, and we can see change going on around us today.

Pronunciation is constantly changing. Not long ago, many Americans pronounced the words *horse* and *hoarse* or *morning* and *mourning* differently from one another; today most pronounce them alike. Today most Americans still pronounce the words *cot* and *caught* or *pond* and *pawned* differently, but increasingly many of us are pronouncing them alike. In a hundred years or so, it is likely that such pairs will be **homophones** (words that sound the same, but are spelled differently) for the majority of our fellow citizens. *Forehead* used to be generally pronounced to rhyme with *horrid;* today it usually rhymes with *more bread.*

A

The very words we use are also changing. We make up new words out of elements already in English, like *to eyeball, feedback,* and *minibike.* We borrow others from foreign languages, like *karate*

B

from Japanese, *klutz* from Yiddish, and *macho* from Spanish. Words also change their meaning, or disappear altogether if we stop using them, often because the things they name have changed or disappeared. For example, people used to preserve food by keeping it cold in a chest packed with blocks of ice; such a chest was called an *icebox.* When gas and electric refrigerators were invented, some people continued to use the old word for them, thus changing the meaning of *icebox.* But gradually the word has been disappearing, so that it is rare today and soon will probably drop out of the language altogether.

We also change our grammar, or the way we combine words into sentences. For example, the older past tense of the verb *dive* is *dived.* But today we use a new past form, *dove,* invented by analogy with irregular verbs like *drive,* whose past tense is *drove.* Another case is with English adverbs. Some adverbs describe how a subject does something: "She skied down the slope *quickly.*" Others tell how the speaker feels about something: "*Fortunately,* she knew how to ski," meaning, "I think it is fortunate that she knew how to ski." *Hopefully* was once used only the first way: "She entered the contest *hopefully,*" meaning, "She was hopeful when she entered it." But recently it has come to be used in the second sense also: "*Hopefully,* she will win the race," meaning, "I am hopeful that she will win it."

The words we use, the way we use them, and the way we say them are all changing constantly. Often, when a change begins, many people do not like it. It sounds odd, sloppy, mistaken. And new uses do often begin as mistakes. But whether the new use has been deliberately introduced or slipped into the language as an error, if many people adopt it, it becomes part of the language— just one more option we have for saying things. When a change is new or has not yet been widely accepted, we need to be careful about using it, because some people will be so distracted by the way we are talking that they will fail to hear what we are saying.

What Is Good English?

Good English is English that communicates the ideas and effects we want to get across. Bad English is language that does not communicate successfully. Bad English may be ambiguous: "Mike lost his textbook, but somebody found it and put it in his locker."

A. Homophones/ Homographs

Homophones are not to be confused with homographs, which are words that are spelled the same but that have different meanings and different origins. An example of a homographic pair is *bluff,* meaning "a steep bank or cliff," and *bluff,* meaning "to fool or mislead." The former meaning of *bluff* is derived from the Dutch *blaf,* meaning "flat, broad"; the latter meaning is derived from the Dutch *bluffen* or *verbluffen,* meaning "to baffle, mislead."

B. Word Changes

❓ Suggest other words that are made up out of elements already in English. (To backtrack, hardware, software)

> "**W**e borrow some words from foreign languages, like *karate* from Japanese, *klutz* from Yiddish, and *macho* from Spanish."

Often, distinctions such as these are made depending upon the mode of communication used. For example, what might be considered "bad English" is more likely to be heard in speech; what might be considered "good English" is more likely to be written.

A

Whose locker did the book go in, Mike's or somebody's? Bad English may actually be clear, but distracting: "Everybody should have his own textbook." Is everybody male? Aren't there any females around? If we say, "Everybody should have their own textbook," someone will object that *everybody* is singular, whereas *their* is plural, so the two don't go together. If we say, "Everybody should have his or her own textbook," someone else will object that the statement sounds too formal, too legalistic.

Each of the choices above is likely to distract someone who hears or reads it. All of them may interfere with communication, and therefore all of them are, to that extent, bad English. The best English in such cases avoids the problem by rewording the statement: "Everybody should have a textbook" or "All students should have their own textbooks." Good English does not get in the way; it does not call attention to itself and away from the message. Good English communicates just what we want to communicate, and nothing else.

Analyzing Language

1. Compare the sample entry for the word *giggle* in Johnson's *Dictionary* with the entry for that word in a modern dictionary. What kinds of information does the modern dictionary give that Johnson did not? How do the meanings Johnson gives compare with those in the modern dictionary?

2. Choose any one of the sample definitions from Johnson's *Dictionary* and compare it with the most similar definition of the same word in a modern dictionary. Tell how the two definitions differ.

3. The following words and expressions are all relatively new to the English language. How many of them are familiar to you? Which of them are listed in the dictionary you use?

   catch-22   dinner theater   ego-trip   granola
   laptop   play hardball   schlepp   ten-speed

4. The following are words about whose correct use people disagree. Do you know what the disagreement is? Look up these words in at least two dictionaries to see what is said about them.

   contact (verb)   data   hopefully   irregardless

5. Why is it impossible to stop the language we use from changing?

USING LOGICAL REASONING TO WRITE A PERSUASIVE ESSAY

Writing Assignment

Each of the following generalizations has at one time or another been made about works of literature in this unit. Choose one of these generalizations (or one that your teacher assigns) and write a persuasive essay. In your essay, use logical reasoning to persuade readers that the generalization is *not* a valid one. Use specific evidence to support your argument.

1. *Samuel Pepys' diary tells us nothing of significance; it mostly satisfies Pepys' desire for gossip.*
2. *Robinson Crusoe is a simple adventure story for very young readers.*
3. *The Rape of the Lock is nothing more than a silly poem that does not deserve its place in literary history.*
4. *Thomas Gray's "Elegy Written in a Country Churchyard" is too depressing.*
5. *The Pilgrim's Progress has meaning only to very religious people.*

Background

The purpose of a persuasive essay is to convince your reader that your point of view is valid. You are to support your case by using logical arguments. (Emotional appeals are something else.) Much of the strength of your argument will come from the kind and amount of evidence you use to support it.

As you gather evidence to develop your argument, be wary of committing these two common logical fallacies. They can weaken your argument.

1. **Hasty generalization.** A hasty generalization is one made without considering all the evidence. (All Republicans favor the rich. Democrats are all for socialized medicine.) The generalizations in the list above are hasty generalizations.

2. **Circular reasoning.** Circular thinking is the basis of much faulty reasoning. If you argue that something is true simply because it is true, you are using circular reasoning: "'Elegy Written in a Country Churchyard' is depressing because it is filled with depressing images."

Prewriting

To gather ideas for your essay, you might have to do library research. In this research, look for two kinds of information:

1. **Look for the critics' general opinions about a work.** Use the critics' opinions about a work to *support* your own evaluations, not to replace them. For example, if you are convinced that a particular movie is silly and contrived, don't argue against your generalization merely on the basis that most critics say that it is a brilliant, clever comedy. Instead, keeping the critics' ideas in mind, think about the movie again. Do you find support for the critics' viewpoint? Or do you still find reasons to stick to your own views? Be convinced yourself before you set out to convince others.

2. **Look up specific references to politics, religion, or literature.** To refute some of these generalizations, you will need to understand allusions to eighteenth-century politics, to religion, and to the classics and the Bible. Some of these references are explained in this textbook, either glossed in the margin or discussed in the introductions to the selections. You can find other references explained in editions of the work itself or in critical comments on the work. Before you begin writing, read carefully through the work. List all the details that support your argument. Your notes should be either direct quotations and appear in quotation marks, or they should be a paraphrase of the material in your own words.

Writing

In developing your essay, you may use either inductive or deductive reasoning. **Inductive reasoning** begins with the reasons and facts that support a final conclusion. **Deductive reasoning** begins with your general statement that is then supported by specific details.

In this assignment, your thesis statement should state the generalization you are refuting and the counterargument you are going to develop. If your essay is inductive, your thesis statement should appear at the end

A. Circular Reasoning

? What are some other examples of circular reasoning? (Example: "This is a short story because it isn't very long.")

B. Thesis Statement

In general, a thesis statement should be worded as a positive statement.

A. Conclusion
Remind students that the purpose of a conclusion is to leave the reader with a sense of completeness.

Revising Essays
As students revise their essays, refer them to **Grammar, Usage, and Mechanics: A Reference Guide** at the back of their books.

Exercises in Critical Thinking and Writing/*cont.*

A of the essay. In this case, think of the essay as a kind of pyramid that begins with supporting details and leads eventually to a generalization, or conclusion. (Think of the generalization as the widest part of the pyramid, in this case the base.)

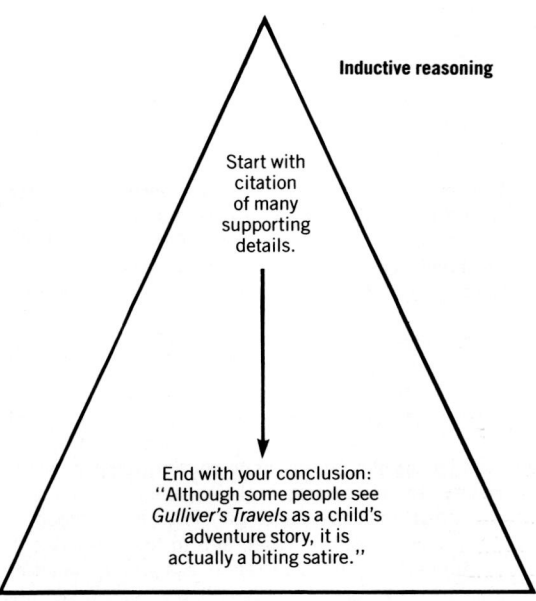

If your essay is deductive, your thesis statement should appear at the beginning of the essay. This type of essay can be visualized as an upside-down pyramid. It begins with the generalization (the widest part of the pyramid), which is then supported by many specific details.

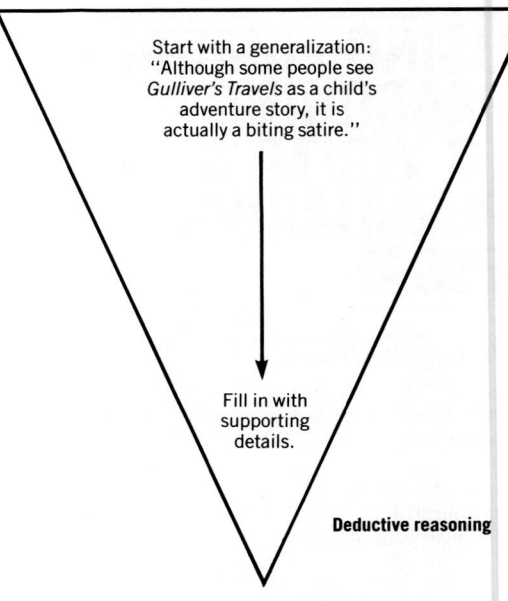

Revision and Proofreading

For help revising and proofreading your essay, see the section on Writing About Literature in the back of the textbook.

THE ROMANTIC PERIOD
1798–1832

The Wanderer by Caspar David Friedrich. Oil.   Hamburger Kunsthalle, Hamburg.

UNIT FIVE

HUMANITIES CONNECTION: RESPONDING TO THE FINE ART
German painter Caspar David Friedrich (1744–1840) is best known for his Romantic landscapes, which art historian Fredrick Hartt says show "an immense and impersonal world, responsive to no human emotion save sadness."

❓ What is the relationship of the man in the painting to his setting? (He is dwarfed by it; he is solid and it seems ephemeral.) What does the title of the painting indicate about the man? What might he be thinking? Why do you suppose the artist painted the man in near silhouette and from behind? (The painting is more mysterious this way; the emphasis is on what the figure sees, rather than on the figure itself.)

TEACHING ROMANTIC LITERATURE

The Romantic Period was actually a movement from one way of thinking to another. The main tenets of Romanticism included a shift from faith in reason to faith in the senses, feelings, and imagination; from interest in urban society and its sophistication to an interest in the rural and natural; from public, impersonal poetry to subjective poetry; and from concern with the scientific and mundane to interest in the mysterious and infinite. The most important tenets of Romanticism, however, were belief in the importance of the individual, imagination, and intuition.

The Romantic Period is usually thought to have begun with the publication of Wordsworth's *Lyrical Ballads* in 1798. However, the era is characterized by more than just a new slant on poetry. It was also a time of optimism and historic turbulence in England. The Romantic movement was at odds with the Industrial Revolution, with the corruption and pollution of the growing large cities, and with the capitalistic motives of many businessmen. Out of its opposition to such changes, the literature of the movement reflected society's conflicts. The Romantic Period also saw the resurgence of revolt and radical political thought that sought to change the status quo.

Before beginning a study of Romantic poets and their works, students may need to review such elements of poetry as speaker, purpose, structure, diction, figurative language, and imagery.

OBJECTIVES OF THE ROMANTIC UNIT

1. To improve reading proficiency and expand vocabulary
2. To gain exposure to notable authors and works of the period
3. To define and identify significant literary techniques and elements (imagery, rhyme, meter, theme, mood, and tone)
4. To interpret and respond to poetry, orally and in writing, through analysis of its elements
5. To practice the following critical thinking and writing skills:
   a. Analyzing a poet's purpose
   b. Analyzing a poem's theme
   c. Analyzing the structure of a poem
   d. Evaluating the point of view chosen by a poet
   e. Analyzing the use of imagery
   f. Analyzing the use of symbolism
   g. Imitating a poet's technique
   h. Analyzing metrics
   i. Responding to criticism

SUPPLEMENTARY SUPPORT MATERIALS: UNIT FIVE

1. Unit Introduction Test (*CCB*)
2. English Language Test (*CCB*)
3. Word Analogies Test (*CCB*)
4. Unit Review Test (*CCB*)
5. Critical Thinking and Writing Test (*CCB*)
6. Study Guide to *Jane Eyre*
7. Instructional Overhead Transparencies

A. Responding to the Quotation

The quotation is from Blake's letters.

❓ Paraphrase Blake's idea in your own words. Do you agree or disagree that the imagination is the "real world"? What do you think Blake means by "vegetable universe"? ("Vegetable" is a generic term for matter in the world that will die and decay—unlike the work of the imagination, which lives forever.)

B. Expansion

Coleridge said his name "stinks" because he was a radical in a time when Britain feared radical sentiments because of the French Revolution. The penniless, already married Coleridge was about to become a Unitarian minister, a post he did not relish, when he received a grant from the wealthy Wedgwood family, giving him a life income of 150 pounds a year to explore his talents. This surprising windfall enabled Coleridge to make the journey to Germany and to devote his life to literature.

THE ROMANTIC PERIOD
1798–1832

by **Donald Gray** *and*
John Malcolm Brinnin

> "**A**s Samuel Coleridge told the printer: 'Wordsworth's name is nothing . . . mine *stinks*.' "

A *The divine arts of imagination, imagination, the real & eternal world of which this vegetable universe is but a faint shadow.*

—William Blake

During the spring of 1798, in southwestern England, two young poets, aged 27 and 25, sold some of their poems to raise money for a trip to Germany. Each had published books of poetry, but this new joint work was to be anonymous. As **B** Samuel Taylor Coleridge, the younger of the pair, told the printer: "Wordsworth's name is nothing . . . mine *stinks*."

Soon after they left England, their book, *Lyrical Ballads, With a Few Other Poems,* appeared. Among the "few other poems" was Coleridge's *The Rime of the Ancient Mariner* and a last-minute addition, Wordsworth's "Lines Composed a Few Miles Above Tintern Abbey." Both these works are now among the most important poems in English literature.

So began what is now called the "Romantic period." Literary historians have found other momentous events to mark its beginning and end, but we should remember the casual, modest appearance of *Lyrical Ballads* as we consider the Romantic period and the writers associated with it.

Political and Economic Changes

Another way to date the Romantic period is to say that it started with the French Revolution in 1789 and ended with the Parliamentary reforms of 1832 that laid the political foundations for modern Britain. However it is dated, it remains the shortest major era of English literary history. The era was dominated by six poets: three (William Blake, William Wordsworth, and Samuel Taylor Coleridge) were born before the period began and lived through most or all of it, while three others (the "second generation" of Percy Bysshe Shelley, John Keats, and George Gordon, Lord Byron) began their short careers in the second decade of the new century but died before 1825. It was a turbulent age, one in which England changed from an agricultural society to an industrial nation; with a large and restless working class concentrated in the teeming mill towns in central and north England.

We think about this era in terms of some important historical occurrences. Beginning in America in 1776, an age of revolution swept across Western Europe, releasing political, economic, and social forces that produced, during the next century, some of the most radical changes ever experienced in human life.

The revolution in America lost for England her thirteen colonies in North America. This was a loss of great economic proportions, but it was also a loss of prestige and of confidence. The more radical revolution in France, which started on July 14, 1789, with

A. Responding to the Illustration

This engraving depicts one of the many grisly executions that so alarmed English conservatives and disillusioned idealists who had originally sympathized with the French Revolution. The civil wars of the Vendée took place between 1793 and 1796 in the Loire region of western France. Rioting began in response to conscription acts drafting men into the Revolutionary Army. Soon the largely Catholic populace in Vendée was in open revolt against the government. During the spring and summer of 1793, the Vendéans captured several towns in the Loire Valley. In December, government forces killed more than 15,000 Vendéans and cruelly executed prisoners.

? What are the people in the lower right-hand corner of the engraving doing? (Looking up at the people being thrown off the ramparts) If the artist had omitted these figures, how would the impact of the engraving be different? (You would not be able to tell how high the tower was, and you would not feel the horror of publicly witnessed executions.)

Destruction of the Vendeans, French Revolution. Engraving.

A

B. Connotations

? What associations does the word *democratic* have for you? Why did the English ruling class fear democracy? (They feared that the masses of uneducated poor would overthrow the stable government, take away their riches, and threaten their lives.)

C. Expansion

Wordsworth added, "France standing on the top of golden hours / and human nature seeming born again." (From *The Prelude,* Book XI)

the storming of the prison called the Bastille, had far more serious repercussions. For the ruling classes in England, the French Revolution came to represent their worst fears: the overthrow of an anointed king by a democratic "rabble." To English conservatives, the French Revolution meant the triumph of radical principles, and they feared that the revolutionary fever would spread across the Channel. One English king, Charles I, had lost his head in 1649; the thought of another bloody rebellion against vested authority was more than most power-holders in England could bear.

B

Not all the English people were horrified at the news coming from France. Democratic idealists and liberals like Wordsworth were exhilarated. During the revolution's early years, they even made trips to France to view the "new regime" at first hand, as if it were a tourist attraction like the Acropolis in Greece. "Bliss was it in that dawn to be alive," Wordsworth later wrote, "but to be young was very heaven."

C

Even Wordsworth became disillusioned, however, when in 1792 the "September Massacre" took place in France. Hundreds of French aristocrats—some with the most tenuous ties to the regime of Louis XVI—had their heads severed from their bodies by a new French invention, the guillotine.

And that wasn't the end of it. In the midst of the blood and turmoil and calls for worldwide revolution from France, control of

" **F**or the ruling classes in England, the French Revolution came to represent their worst fears: the overthrow of an anointed king by a democratic 'rabble.' "

A. Allusion

? What does the expression "to meet your Waterloo" mean? (To be completely defeated or stymied by someone or something. *Waterloo* is one of those specific words that have taken on a general meaning: "any decisive defeat.")

B. Discussing the Engraving

Make sure students understand that the engraving shows an artist's vision of what factories in England *should* look like. Actual factories were dark, cramped, crowded, and filthy. Note that men and women have distinctly different jobs.

? Who is the figure wearing the top hat? (The foreman or owner of the factory) How does this idealized nineteenth-century factory compare with modern-day factories? (Students may cite the lack of automation, the absence of assembly lines, and the difference between men's and women's work in the nineteenth-century factory.)

the country changed hands again. Napoleon Bonaparte, an officer in the French army, emerged first as dictator and then, in 1804, as emperor of France. In the end, Napoleon—whose very name today suggests a tyrant—became as ruthless as the executed king himself.

All of these bewildering changes made conservatives more rigid than ever. Severe repressive measures were instituted in England, and a twenty-two year war was waged against Napoleon. Napoleon's navy was defeated by England at the Battle of Trafalgar in 1805; and in 1815, at Waterloo in Belgium, Napoleon's armies were outmaneuvered by British forces.

The conservatives in England felt they had saved their country from a despot and from chaos; the supporters of the Revolution, like Wordsworth and others, felt betrayed. For them, Waterloo was simply the defeat of one despot by another.

Other changes in English life were being caused by the Industrial Revolution. This meant that there was a shift in manufacturing, that is, in the production of goods. Goods up till this time had been made by hand, at home. Now, production switched to factories, where machines worked at many times the rate human beings could work by hand. Since factories were in cities, the city populations increased, with housing conditions that would appall even the most hardened social worker today.

In addition, the once communal land used by small farmers was

Model Textile Mills at Tewkesbury, England (19th century). Color engraving.

Comment from Wordsworth

"Emphatically may it be said of the poet, as Shakespeare hath said of man, 'that he looks before and after.' He is the rock of defense of human nature; an upholder and preserver, carrying everywhere with him relationship and love. In spite of difference of soil and climate, of language and manners, of laws and customs, in spite of things silently gone out of mind and things violently destroyed, the poet binds together by passion and knowledge the vast empire of human society, as it is spread over the whole earth and over all time. The objects of the poet's thoughts are everywhere; though the eyes and senses of man are, it is true, his favorite guides, yet he will follow wheresoever he can find an atmosphere of sensation in which to move his wings. Poetry is the first and last of all knowledge—it is as immortal as the heart of man."

—from *Lyrical Ballads*

taken over by private owners. Some of these rich private owners transformed the fields into vast private parks, generously stocked with deer for private Christmas hunts. Others divided the land into neatly demarcated fields. Whatever happened to the land, it was no longer communally held. This resulted in large numbers of landless people. Just as the unemployed and homeless do today, these landless people migrated to cities in search of factory work. Or they went on the dole.

The economic philosophy that kept all this misery going was a policy called laissez-faire, "let it alone." According to this policy, economic laws should be allowed to operate freely without government interference. The result of laissez-faire was that the rich grew richer, and the poor suffered even more. The system, of course, had the most tragic effects on the helpless, especially children. Small children of the poor were often used like beasts of burden. In the coal pits, for example, very small children were even harnessed to carts for dragging coal, just as if they had been small donkeys.

Frustrated by England's resistance to political and social change, the Romantic poets turned from the formal, public verse of the eighteenth-century Augustans to a more private, spontaneous, lyric poetry. These lyrics expressed the Romantics' belief that imagination, rather than mere reason, was the best response to the forces of change. Wordsworth spoke of imagination this way:

> . . . spiritual love acts not nor can exist
> Without imagination, which, in truth,
> Is but another name for absolute power
> And clearest insight, amplitude of mind,
> And reason in her most exalted mood.
>
> —from *The Prelude*

We can add details and colors to this broad sketch of the era by considering the following concepts:

1. The term *romantic*
2. The interrelationship of nature, the human mind, and the imagination
3. The idea of the poet
4. Romanticism

The Term "Romantic"

The term *Romantic* is like Janus, the Roman god of doorways, who had two faces, one looking backward and one looking forward. The term suggests a look backward and forward in time. *Romantic* is a word signifying both beginnings and endings.

The first generation of English poets who came to be called Romantics lived well into the new century: Wordsworth was the last of them to die, in 1850 at the age of eighty. Like many nineteenth-century thinkers, these poets were conscious of living in two centuries and two worlds: one gone, the other (to quote the Victorian Matthew Arnold) "powerless to be born."

A

Child Labor in England (detail) (19th century).

B

C

D

A. Humanities Connection: Responding to the Art

❓ How do you know this shows "child labor"? (The child is holding out her hand to receive a few coins, probably for housework. Note her ragged dress.) Dickens often wrote about child household servants who brought their pittances home to an impoverished family. Victor Hugo's little Cosette is a child laborer in *Les Misérables* (1862).

B. Vocabulary

Laissez-faire (les'ā·fer'): French, literally, "Let (people) do (as they please)."

C. Interpreting

❓ Paraphrase these lines, and compare Wordsworth's ideas here to Blake's in the introductory quotation on text page 600. (Real power lies in the power of the imagination not, by implication, in material power. This is Blake's point of view.)

D. Expansion

See the comment from the introduction to *Lyrical Ballads* above.

From "Intimations of Immortality . . ."
An example of the Romantic interest in childhood and innocence is found in Wordsworth's long poem "Intimations of Immortality from Recollections of Early Childhood," which opens:

There was a time when meadow, grove,
    and stream,
The earth, and every common sight,
       To me did seem
    Appareled in celestial light,
The glory and the freshness of a dream.
It is not now as it hath been of yore;
    Turn wheresoe'er I may,
      By night or day,
The things which I have seen I now can
      see no more.

A. Vocabulary
Romance comes from the Old French word *romanz (escrire),* referring to writing in Roman, which was the vernacular, the language of the people (as contrasted with Latin).

? What are some of the modern meanings of the word *romance?* (A love affair; a love story)

B. Expansion
See the note above about "Intimations of Immortality from Recollections of Early Childhood."

> " **T**oday, the word *romantic* is often a derogatory label used to describe sentimental writing, particularly those best-selling paperback 'romances' about love— a subject that many people mistakenly think the Romantic poets popularized."

The first-generation Romantics found few models in eighteenth-century poetry to guide them, so they looked back to Milton and Shakespeare for their inspiration. Yet their great achievement was to create new forms of lyric poetry. Here they could search for "recompense" (Wordsworth's term) for the destruction of their youthful optimism, caused by England's resistance to change. The second generation of poets, whose lives were cut short by illness or accident, felt that their elders, particularly Wordsworth, had betrayed the revolutionary spirit of the age. This second generation never made peace with the repressive atmosphere in England following the end of the Napoleonic Wars in 1815. However, they too looked forward and backward. Their poetry looked forward in being more extravagant and visionary than Wordsworth's and Coleridge's; it was matched in these respects by the poetry of Blake in the first generation. Yet Keats and Shelley, like their immediate predecessors, also looked back to Shakespeare and Milton as the greatest of poets. (Byron differed from all the other Romantics in believing that the Augustans were the best poetic models.)

A   The word *Romantic* comes from the term *romance,* one of the most popular genres of medieval literature. (See page 147.) Later Romantic writers self-consciously used the elements of romance in an attempt to go back beyond the refinements of Neoclassical literature to older types of writing that they saw as more "genuine." The romance genre also allowed writers to explore new, more psychological and mysterious aspects of human experience. The American Romantic Nathaniel Hawthorne (1804–1864), for example, called his rather audacious prose fictions "romances." (He says, in the Preface to *The House of the Seven Gables,* subtitled *A Romance,* that the book has "a great deal more to do with the clouds overhead than with any portion of the actual soil of the County of Essex.")

Today, the word *romantic* is often a derogatory label used to describe sentimental writing, particularly those best-selling paperback "romances" about love—a subject that many people mistakenly think the Romantic poets popularized. As an historical term, however, *romantic* has at least three useful meanings, all of them relevant to the Romantic poets.

B   **1.** The term *romantic* signifies a fascination with youth and innocence, with "growing up" by exploring and learning to trust our emotions and our sense of will and identity.

2. The term *romantic* is applied to a stage in the cyclical development of societies: This is the stage when people need to question tradition and authority in order to imagine better—that is, healthier, fairer, and happier—ways to live. *Romantic* in this sense is associated with idealism. (The 1966—1975 period in America might be called a "romantic" era.)

3. In the so-called Romantic period of the first half of the nineteenth century (up to the Civil War in America), Western societies reached the conditions necessary for industrialization. This demanded that people acquire a stronger and stronger awareness of *change* and that they try to find ways to adapt to it. In this sense, we still live with the legacy of the Romantic period.

The Interrelationship of Nature, the Mind, and the Imagination

Lyrical Ballads did not remain unnoticed or anonymous for long. In 1800, with Coleridge looking over his shoulder, Wordsworth composed a "Preface" for the expanded collection. Distressed by the effect of current events on literature, Wordsworth found hope in "certain inherent and indestructible qualities of the human mind, and likewise . . . certain powers in the great and permanent objects that act upon it, which are equally inherent and indestructible." In other words, there is nature and there are human beings to experience nature.

The Romantics are often called nature poets. This description is misleading if it suggests that their poetry is full of charming scenes of forests, mountains, and streams—like the scenic overlooks on auto trips or the pictures on the calendars that hardware stores give away. We can get a sharper sense of the idea of nature behind Wordsworth's statement by comparing three different views of nature, or the world that is different from the human world.

First, the nature most familiar to us is ecological—a complex, interdependent system of mysterious forces at work. Do something to one part of it, and there may be large, unforeseen results like the greenhouse effect or acid rain, which threaten us. Naturalists talk about killing nature through pollution and radioactivity. But nature doesn't die. It is the agent of death.

Second, the nature common to the Enlightenment (see Unit Four) is a beautiful, intricate system like an immense piece of

A *A Scene in Leigh Woods* by Francis Danby (1822). Oil.

City of Bristol Museum and Art Gallery.

B

A. **Interpreting**
? Give some examples to clarify these statements. (Droughts, soil erosion, fish kills, mudslides, avalanches, hurricanes, and so on) Compare this view of nature later with Thomas Hardy's idea of nature as a timeless and implacable force, neither cruel nor kind, completely indifferent to human life.

B. **Humanities Connection: Responding to the Fine Art**
Francis Danby (1793–1861) was born in Wexford in Ireland, but as a young man he moved to England to study art. Note the minutely detailed foliage and the different shades of green that indicate the play of light.
? What do the human figures add to the painting? (You'll notice that most landscape painters add a human figure somewhere in the scene to add focus and perspective and to allow the viewer to "enter" the painting.)

605

"I have said that poetry is the spontaneous overflow of powerful feelings: it takes its origin from emotion recollected in tranquillity: the emotion is contemplated till by a species of reaction the tranquillity gradually disappears, and an emotion, kindred to that which was before the subject of contemplation, is gradually produced, and does itself actually exist in the mind. In this mood successful composition generally begins, and in a mood similar to this it is carried on. . . ."

—from *Lyrical Ballads*

A. Humanities Connection: About the Fine Art

Blake was both an artist and poet, and he often illustrated his own work, as is evidenced here (see text pages 617–619 for Blake's biography).

B. Expansion

Wordsworth also said that "All good poetry is the spontaneous overflow of powerful feelings." This now-famous statement deliberately stressed his rejection of the impersonal "public" poems of the eighteenth century. See the whole comment above.

C. Imagery

The Romantic poets attempted to render images of nature in specific, concrete detail. Blake once wrote, referring to his painting, "To generalize is to be an idiot; to particularize is the alone distinction of merit."

"The Lamb" from *Songs of Innocence* by William Blake.

clockwork. People believed that since neither the clock nor nature could have come into being by chance, there must be a designer or planner, called a clockmaker or God. Even if we don't know where the creator is, the beauty and order of what was created assures us that the maker exists, and that the plan is still there to be understood.

The third view of nature is that of the Romantics. Romantics were skeptical about the cleverness that inferred the clockmaker from the clock, but they prized experiences of the beauty and majesty of nature. They did not think of nature as hostile, but they had a strong sense of its mysterious forces, partly because these forces hinted at the causes of change. The Romantics sought reassurance in the face of change by thinking about the relationship between the human mind and what is out there, rather than concentrating on nature itself.

But the Romantics also had their own conception of nature, which might be called psychological. They were intrigued by the fact that nature and the human mind always act upon each other. In the *Preface,* Wordsworth says that the poet "considers man and nature as essentially adapted to each other, and the mind of man as naturally a mirror of the fairest and most interesting properties of nature." Though, as we'll see, this is not quite the whole picture, it does tell us that the Romantics were nature poets because they were "mind poets"; they were fascinated by the "how" problems of thought and feeling.

We can conclude this account of the Romantics' psychological view of nature by considering two ways of thinking about the relation between the mind and objects outside the mind. From a religious point of view, the cause of what happens in both mind and nature is some higher power. It is this viewpoint that Wordsworth is thinking about in his poem "Tintern Abbey" when he refers rather vaguely to "something far more deeply interfused" in both nature and the mind. This something, whether it is the traditional divine being or simply some great power, is not a clockmaker, but an active power that makes things happen, perhaps a mind that continually creates a world of human minds and nature by thinking them. A second answer, which doesn't rule out the first, is that human beings have a limited power to create thoughts too. While most of what we know comes from "out there," some of it comes from "in here." That creative power is **imagination.**

Each of the Romantic poets had his own special view of the imagination and of the ways in which the human mind was adapted to nature. You will notice that the poems usually present imaginative experiences as very powerful or moving. This suggests that, in addition to being a special faculty of the mind, the imagination is also a kind of desire, a motive that drives the mind to learn and to know things it cannot learn by rational and logical thinking. So, although, as Wordsworth thought, the mind is naturally a "mirror" of nature, the imagination actually moves the mind in mysterious ways to imitate (without being sacrilegious) the powers of its Maker. The purpose of this imitation is to create new realities in the mind and (as a result) in poetry.

". . . I ask what is meant by the word poet. What is a poet? To whom does he address himself? And what language is to be expected from him? He is a man speaking to men: a man, it is true, endued with more lively sensibility, more enthusiasm and tenderness, who has a greater knowledge of human nature, and a more comprehensive soul, than are supposed to be common among mankind; a man pleased with his own passions and volitions, and who rejoices more than other men in the spirit of life that is in him; delighting to contemplate similar volitions and passions as manifested in the goings-on of the universe, and habitually impelled to create them where he does not find them. To these qualities he has added a disposition to be affected more than other men by absent things as if they were present, an ability of conjuring up in himself passions, which . . . do more nearly resemble the passions produced by real events than anything which, from the motions of their own minds merely, other men are accustomed to feel in themselves. . . . "

—from *Lyrical Ballads*

The Idea of the Poet

In 1802, in order to clarify his remarks about poetry, Wordsworth added a long section to his *Preface* on the question, *What is a poet?* His answer: "He is a man speaking to men." Wordsworth's statement may seem paradoxically both simple and exalted. It becomes more revealing if, for a moment, we concentrate on what it assumes about the relationship between poet and reader. With a little imagination, we can get a better idea of what the phrase "speaking to" implies.

Imagine someone outside your classroom washing the windows. The window washer performs the job very conscientiously, taking days to do all the windows. Later you find out that the window washer took this course in English literature last year but dropped out of school. He became a window washer in order to spy on the class lectures and discussions while pretending to wash the windows.

Our idea that the spy was pretending to do one thing—washing the windows—while really doing something else—learning about English literature—suggests a curious and tricky aspect of the craft of writing. For in order to succeed in the pretense, the window washer would have to do a convincing job of washing the windows—right? Likewise, Wordsworth's short definition of the poet may be paraphrased to suggest something about the "pretense" involved in lyric poetry: "A poet is someone who writes a poem in which there is a 'man speaking to men' *in order to accomplish something else.*"

If this seems strange, consider what happens in a good many of the poems in this section. There is a person—we will call him the "speaker" to distinguish him from the poet—in the poem who is "speaking to" someone or something else: a young highland girl, a baby asleep in a cottage, a skylark, even a Greek vase or a season of the year.

Each poem of this type not only asks us to imagine (pretend) that the "speaking" is taking place; the poem also makes us consider what *kind* of speaking is taking place. Is the speaker praising, or confessing, or complaining, or worshipping, or envying? That is, what is the speaker doing by "speaking"?

The Romantic poets wrote in a number of lyric forms using this special sense of speaker and speaking. We can contrast this form of poetry with the more traditional "narrative" forms found in poems such as Samuel Taylor Coleridge's *The Rime of the Ancient Mariner*, John Keats's "The Eve of St. Agnes," and George Gordon, Lord Byron's *Don Juan*. In these narrative poems, the speaker is a storyteller, such as we find in novels and short stories. In fact, one of the reasons for the development of lyric poetry in the Romantic period is that during the eighteenth century the novel, or prose fiction, had become an important literary art form and had begun taking over the storytelling role traditionally associated with poetry.

The speaking in lyric poetry is not the Augustan reasoning in verse. It is a more passionate speaking from the heart. It has been said that we do not *hear* lyric poetry so much as *overhear*

A

B

P O E M S,

CHIEFLY IN THE

SCOTTISH DIALECT,

BY

R O B E R T   B U R N S.

THE Simple Bard, unbroke by rules of Art,
He pours the wild effusions of the heart:
And if inspir'd, 'tis Nature's pow'rs inspire;
Her's all the melting thrill, and her's the kindling fire.

ANONYMOUS.

KILMARNOCK:
PRINTED BY JOHN WILSON.

M,DCC,LXXXVI.

Title page of Robert Burns's *Poems*, First Edition (1786).

A. Responding
Wordsworth, of course, used the language conventions of his time, which accounts for the exclusion of women from his answer. See the quote in context above.

How would people today reply to Wordsworth's question? (They might say someone who makes a statement or poses a question about human experience.)

B. Inferring
From the quotation on the title page, how would you guess Burns would reply to Wordsworth's question, "What is a poet?" (A person who speaks from the heart, whose art of poetry is inspired by nature)

1. This wasn't a good period for kings. Which one was beheaded? (King Louis XVI of France, in 1793) Which one was declared insane? (King George III of England, in 1812)

2. What popular English novelist was born the year the Brothers Grimm published their *Fairy Tales?* (Charles Dickens, in 1812)
3. Emily Dickinson and William Blake are sometimes referred to as eccentrics. Did they ever meet? (No. Blake died in 1827; Dickinson was born in 1830.)
4. Did Keats attend Shelley's funeral? (No. Keats died in 1821; Shelley died in 1822.)

5. When Jane Austen was writing *Pride and Prejudice,* could she have looked up words in Noah Webster's *American Dictionary of the English Language?* (No. Austen's novel was published in 1813; Webster's dictionary appeared in 1828.)

A. The Voice of Feeling

? Name some poets you have read who use the "language of the heart." (Emily Dickinson, Walt Whitman, Robert Frost, W. B. Yeats)

B. Expansion

The context of the quotation is this: "[Men] talk of poetry as of a matter of amusement and idle pleasure; who will converse with us as gravely about a *taste* for poetry, as they express it, as if it were a thing as indifferent as a taste for rope-dancing, or Frontiniac or sherry. Aristotle, I have been told, hath said, that poetry is the most philosophic of all writing: it is so: its object is truth, not individual and local, but general, and operative; not standing upon external testimony, but carried alive into the heart by passion; truth which is its own testimony, which gives strength and divinity to the tribunal to which it appeals, and receives them from the same tribunal. Poetry is the image of man and nature."

> "The Romantic lyric speaks in what has been called the true voice of feeling or the language of the heart."

A

it—as if (using our imagination again) we were eavesdropping on a private conversation or on someone talking to himself or herself out loud. The Romantic lyric, then, speaks in what has been called the true voice of feeling or the language of the heart. In writing this way, the Romantics created a kind of poetry that poets today continue to use.

B

For lyric poetry to be successful, the speaker and the speaking must be convincing—just as in our example, the window washer must convince us that he is really washing the windows. Thus the poet must create an artful illusion of the voice of the speaker which conveys certain truths or ideas. Though they did not reason in verse like the Neoclassic poets, the Romantics were deeply concerned with the truths of the heart and the imagination—with truth, as Wordsworth said, "carried alive into the heart by passion." Or, as Keats once wrote to a friend: "What the imagination seizes as beauty must be truth whether it existed before or not."

Wordsworth's deceptively simple definition of the poet as "a man speaking to men" was thus a revolutionary conception in a number of ways. If we think of the speaker (not the poet) as an ordinary person, then it is a very democratic definition. Poetry is to be about human experience, about the fundamental relationship between the mind (including the heart and the imagination) and other people and other things. The speaking should be convincing

1786–1789	1789–1790	1793–1794	1798
Burns's *Poems, Chiefly in the Scottish Dialect,* 1786 Blake's *Songs of Innocence,* 1789	French Revolution begins with storming of Bastille, 1789 Wordsworth visits France, 1790	King Louis XVI beheaded in France, 1793 Blake's *Songs of Experience,* 1793	Wordsworth and Coleridge publish *Lyrical Ballads* anonymously, with *The Rime of the Ancient Mariner* as its opening selection, 1798

1811–1812	1812	1812–1813	1814
Jane Austen's novel *Sense and Sensibility,* 1811 Byron's *Childe Harold's Pilgrimage,* 1812 The Brothers Grimm publish *Fairy Tales,* 1812	Charles Dickens born, 1812 America at war with England, 1812	King George III declared insane; Regency begins, 1812 Austen's novel *Pride and Prejudice,* 1813	Edmund Kean, the most famous actor of the nineteenth century, makes his debut as Shylock in Shakespeare's *The Merchant of Venice,* at the Drury Lane Theater in London, 1814

1821	1822–1824	1825–1828	1829–1830
John Keats dies in Rome, 1821 Shelley's "Adonais," an elegy on the death of Keats, 1821	Shelley drowns in Gulf of Spezia, 1822 Byron dies of fever at Missolonghi, attempting to aid the Greeks in their war of independence, 1824	*The Diaries of Samuel Pepys* published, 1825 William Blake dies, 1827 Noah Webster's *American Dictionary of the English Language,* 1828	Catholic Emancipation Act allows Catholics in England to hold public office, 1829 Emily Dickinson born in Amherst, Massachusetts, 1830

1. Wordsworth and other young English liberals became disillusioned with the __French Revolution__ .

2. __Lyrical Ballads__ , an important book of poems by Wordsworth and Coleridge, appeared in 1798.

3. During the Romantic period, England moved from an agricultural economy to a(n) __industrial__ one.

4. The Romantics most often wrote __lyric or personal__ poems, as distinguished from the impersonal, philosophical poems of the eighteenth century.

5. During this period, the Brontë sisters and Jane Austen wrote several __novels__ that are still popular today.

FOR FURTHER READING STUDENTS

Rupert Christiansen, *Romantic Affinities: Portraits from an Age 1780–1830* (1988).

Jonathan Wordsworth, Michael C. Jaye, and Robert Woolf, *William Wordsworth and the Age of English Romanticism* (1987). A beautiful book produced by the Wordsworth Project.

The following selections can be found in *The Norton Anthology of English Literature, Volume 2,* 1986:

Robert Burns, "To a Louse" (1786), "Afton Water" (1792), "A Red, Red Rose" (1796), "Auld Lang Syne" (1796).

William Blake, "The Little Black Boy" (1789), "Holy Thursday" (1789, 1794), "The Sick Rose" (1794), "A Poison Tree" (1794).

William Wordsworth, "Michael" (1800), "Ode: Intimations of Immortality from Recollections of Early Childhood" (1807), "It Is a Beauteous Evening" (1807), "The World Is Too Much with Us" (1807).

Samuel Taylor Coleridge, "Frost at Midnight" (1798), "Dejection: An Ode" (1802), "Christabel" (1816).

George Gordon, Lord Byron, "When We Two Parted" (1816), additional excerpts from *Childe Harold's* *(Continues on next page.)*

so that it can seem a genuine and sincere account of that experience, no matter how special or extravagant the experience may appear to be.

Romanticism

In saying that the poet is "a man speaking to men," Wordsworth did not mean that the poet is just a man. In the *Preface,* it is clear that the poet is a special person, "endowed with more lively sensibility, more enthusiasm and tenderness . . . a greater knowledge of human nature, and a more comprehensive soul, than are supposed to be common among mankind." Though the word *supposed* may suggest that Wordsworth thought his countrymen had too low an estimate of much of humankind, all of the Romantic poets described the poet in such lofty terms.

For William Blake, for example, the poet was the bard, an inspired revealer and teacher. The poet, wrote Coleridge, "brings the whole soul of man into activity" by employing "that synthetic and magical power . . . the imagination." Shelley called poets "the unacknowledged legislators of the world." Keats wrote that a poet is a "physician to all men" and "pours out a balm upon the world." Nothing, wrote Wordsworth,

1800	1802	1804–1805	1808–1810
Napoleon conquers Italy, 1800	Cotton textile industry is first to mechanize; by 1802 Britain imports 60 million pounds of cotton a year, most from the Southern United States	**Nathaniel Hawthorne born in Massachusetts, 1804**	U.S. bans importing of slaves from Africa, 1808
Thomas Jefferson elected U.S. President, 1800		Admiral Nelson defeats Napoleon's navy at Battle of Trafalgar, 1805	**Sir Walter Scott's novel *The Lady of the Lake*, 1810**

1814–1815	1818–1819	1819	1819–1821
British forces burn Washington, D.C., 1814	**Mary Shelley's novel *Frankenstein*, 1818**	**Keats writes his greatest poems, January–September 1819**	**Sir Walter Scott's novel *Ivanhoe*, 1819**
Napoleon defeated by British forces at Waterloo, 1815	Karl Marx born in Prussia, 1818	Factory act of 1819 prohibits employment of children under 9 years of age in cotton mills	**Washington Irving's story "Rip Van Winkle," 1819**
	Walt Whitman born in New York, 1819		Terrorist activities between Greeks and Turks, 1821

1830–1831	1831	1832
The society of Mormons founded by Joseph Smith, 1830	Charles Darwin sails to South America, Australia, and New Zealand to study plant and animal life, 1831	First Reform Bill passed in Parliament, extending vote to more Englishmen and curtailing political privileges of aristocracy, 1832
Edgar Allan Poe's *Poems*, 1831		

(Continued from previous page.)
Pilgrimage (1812–1818) and *Don Juan* (1819–1824).

Percy Bysshe Shelley, "Hymn to Intellectual Beauty" (1817), "The Cloud" (1820), "To Night" (1824), "A Song: 'Men of England'" (1839).

John Keats, "Ode on Melancholy" (1820), "Ode on Indolence" (1848).

TEACHERS
Kenneth R. Johnston and Gene W. Ruoff, eds. *The Age of William Wordsworth: Critical Essays on the Romantic Tradition* (1987). A useful book produced by the Wordsworth Project.

Leslie A. Marchand, ed., *Lord Byron, Selected Letters and Journals* (1984). Byron wrote wonderful letters; here are

about three hundred of his best, along with some journal entries.

Elizabeth Hardwick, *Seduction and Betrayal* (1974). An analysis of Dorothy Wordsworth's mind and achievements.

A. The Novel
You might assign one of the following novels to be read in conjunction with this unit: *Frankenstein* by Mary Shelley; *Pride and Prejudice, Emma,* or *Northanger Abbey* by Jane Austen; *Jane Eyre* by Charlotte Brontë (see the *Study Guide*); *Wuthering Heights* by Emily Brontë; *Ivanhoe* by Sir Walter Scott.

> . . . can breed such fear and awe
> As fall upon us often when we look
> Into our Minds, into the Mind of Man—
> My haunt, and the main region of my song.
> —from *The Recluse,*

The poet, in sum, is someone human beings cannot do without. The Romantic poets sought for a new vision of the relationship of the mind and nature. They did this by turning toward more lyric forms of poetry, where the imagination was freer to seek these visions. Through the artful illusion of their poems, they explored new aspects of human experience.

As you study the poetry of the Romantic period, consider the possibility that these writers created something enduring which we might call "Romanticism." Scholars of the period have debated the nature of Romanticism for some time, and they still find themselves disagreeing about it. Did the poets have a common view of things, or were they united only in being born into this short but hectic time and forced to deal with its problems?

One teasing possibility is that each poet found a way through the imagination to fulfill the poet's traditional role as "prophet, priest, and king" in a time of change. Some envisioned a new world about to be born; others saw only disaster ahead.

The Forms of Literature in the Romantic Period

The literature of the Romantic period is rich in its variety of literary forms, and many of these forms are not represented in our selections. The **novel** advanced through the works of Jane Austen, Sir Walter Scott, and Charlotte and Emily Brontë. Charles Lamb and William Hazlitt, as well as Coleridge, were among the important literary critics and essayists of the age. Coleridge, Wordsworth, and Keats wrote plays for the stage, and Byron and Shelley wrote poetic dramas to be read rather than performed. The unit does provide a sample of the private forms—journals and letters—and calls attention to two of the many writers who were women: Dorothy Wordsworth and Mary Wollstonecraft Shelley.

As the biographical sketches suggest, the major Romantic poets were no less concerned with public matters than their predecessors were. Their works include not only lectures, pamphlets, essays, and journalism on current events, but many poems that were clearly topical, provoked by events and problems of the moment. For the most part, these poems have lost their power for us because of their topicality and because the presence of such concerns drew the poets away from considerations of lyric art to matters of contemporary debate. Although in these topical poems the author might more obviously assume the voice of "a man speaking to men," the genius of the Romantics, and their best responses to their times, are to be found in their more lyrical works.

Jane Austen.

Robert Burns
(1759–1796)

Robert Burns, a Scottish farmer, thrust himself into the Scottish and English literary worlds in 1786 with *Poems, Chiefly in the Scottish Dialect*. In the preface to his volume, now called the "Kilmarnock" edition after its place of publication (a Scottish town near the farm Burns and his brother managed), Burns said he had written the dialect poems "to amuse himself with the little creations of his own fancy, amid the toil and fatigues of a laborious life."

Within a year, the farmboy had left his native Ayrshire (in southwestern Scotland) for the first time and become the toast of the city of Edinburgh. He seized the moment to issue a new edition of his poems (1787) with the same title but with an Edinburgh publisher. In a new preface to this edition he proclaimed, "The poetic genius of my country found me . . . at the plow; and threw her inspiring mantle over me. She bade me sing the loves, the joys, the rural scenes and rural pleasures of my natal soil, in my native tongue: I tuned my wild, artless notes, as she inspired."

Burns was certainly eager to cultivate an audience among the "literati" of Edinburgh. He carefully excluded from these first two editions poems which he thought might offend a cultured reader. He also consciously reinforced his "image" as an untutored rustic inspired by Scotland herself. But he was far from naive. He was fully aware that his immediate fame in the world of letters would probably be temporary, as it was. After this auspicious beginning to his poetic career, Burns's stature declined. He actually wrote relatively little poetry afterward. Instead, he devoted himself to the huge task of collecting, editing, rewriting and (in many instances) creating over 300 Scottish folk songs, most set to music or "airs." It is this later work which established Burns's most enduring reputation. Scottish immigrants to North America and elsewhere took his song collections with them, and they sang and celebrated Burns's words to remember their homeland in a New World.

Less than ten years after his first success, Burns died at the age of 37 of rheumatic heart

Robert Burns (19th century). Engraving.

disease. Though Burns's reputation includes credible legends of heavy drinking, it is clear that poor nutrition and the physical hardships of tenant farming on poor soil led to his early death. From boyhood, he endured long hours as the principal laborer—he was the oldest son—on his father's leased farm. In all, as man and boy, Burns worked behind the plow on four different farms. (At times, his despair at being unsuccessful as a farmer and a poet made him think of emigrating to Jamaica.) From 1789 to 1791, he made one last try at farming. When this failed, he made his living in the final years of his life as a tax inspector: One of his tasks was to apprehend smugglers.

By the early nineteenth century, Burns was well on the way to becoming the single most important symbol of Scottish literature. Eventually, he became known to millions who perhaps had never read more than a few lines of his poetry. In Britain and the United States, he is still remembered annually at "Burns suppers" in honor of his birthday. Indeed, anyone who marks the New Year by singing the song "Auld Lang Syne" is commemorating Robert Burns, in a fashion Burns would probably have approved.

Burns's significance as a symbol, *and* as a late eighteenth century Scottish poet, will perhaps be clearer if we consider the difference between the "literary culture" of late eighteenth-

A. Expansion
Burns originally published his book to raise money to emigrate to Jamaica, where he planned to farm. He sold 612 copies of the Kilmarnock edition by subscription (see the title page on text page 607). Burns's book caused enough of a stir to make him think twice about leaving Scotland.

B. Expansion
Burns was the oldest of seven children. His father, an overworked tenant farmer, guided his children's reading. As a boy, Burns read Pope, Locke, and Shakespeare as well as the Scottish poets.

C. Vocabulary
The Scottish words *auld lang syne* literally mean "old long since." The expression has come to mean "the good old days, the times of one's youth."

George Saintsbury, Professor of Literature at the University of Edinburgh, wrote:

"Burns felt and saw too much to have much time for thinking, even if he had been educated that way. And very fortunate this is. The time did not want thought; it wanted nature and song, and he gave it both."

A. About the Photograph
Burns was born in Alloway, a small town that is now a suburb of Ayr on the west coast of Scotland. The Burns Museum and Monument in Alloway and various memorials in Ayr are popular tourist attractions. Burns is still highly esteemed as Scotland's national poet.

Robert Burns's Monument and Tea Gardens in Alloway, Scotland.

century Scotland and England, and the literary culture of our own time. In our literary culture, the novel is the dominant form and it is preeminently the product of what we can call a "print culture." Highly specialized means of production and distribution enable novelists to reach large masses of the "reading public." One of the persistent appeals of poetry, on the the other hand, even in our own day, is that it seems to come from a different sort of literary culture, one we might call "oral."

In an oral literary culture—even one where the technology of printing is reasonably well developed—the poet is often regarded as speaking for the "people." The poet is the channel through which the "poetic genius" of the country or region speaks. He or she may be the prophet or "bard," as William Blake thought himself to be, or the poet may be the humble person, "bred to the plow" (as Burns said of himself), who sings "wild artless notes" out of an ordinary life.

Robert Burns was an extraordinary poet in part because Scottish culture, both popular and refined, seems to have spoken through him. He grew up with the folk culture of the small isolated Scottish villages and farms, where "the toil and fatigues of a laborious life" made the few pleasures all the more precious. Much of what Wordsworth noted as the "presence of human life" in Burns's work comes from his immersion in the lives of ordinary human beings. The pleasure we take from Burns's work results in part from our recognition of things common and enduring in human experience.

At the same time, Burns himself was quite aware of the tradition of Scottish literature. This tradition had declined from its high point in the fifteenth and sixteenth centuries, but it was undergoing a studied revival in eighteenth-century Scotland. Burns had the benefit of some excellent (though short-lived) formal education before he was needed full time for farm labor, and he was substantially read in English authors. The apparent artlessness of what he wrote and the simple pose he adopted as the humble plowman singing his simple songs masks a mastery of literary forms, some particularly indigenous to Scottish literature. Burns, in fact could write adeptly in the "literary English" of his time, as well as in a range of "Scots," from heavy dialect to a beautiful blending of folk idioms and literary language.

PREPARATION

1. ESTABLISHING A PURPOSE. As you read the poem aloud, have students listen for its lilting, musical sounds. Note that the poem tells of an event from which the poet draws a meaning. Have students look for the main idea of the poem.

2. PREREADING JOURNAL. Have students write two or three sentences describing how they feel when they kill a cockroach or a mosquito or trap a mouse or a rat.

SUPPLEMENTARY SUPPORT MATERIALS
1. Vocabulary Activity Worksheet (*CCB*)
2. Review and Response Worksheet: Sound Effects and Tone (*CCB*)
3. Selection Test (*CCB*)
4. Audiocassette recording

DEVELOPING VOCABULARY
The following word from the poem is tested in the Selection Test. (See also Vocabulary Activity Worksheet.)
timorous

A When used as thickly and consistently as Robert Burns uses it here, dialect sounds like a foreign language. Yet, while the poems seem to call for translation, they also contain some passages, easy to read, that will help you understand those passages that are not easy to grasp. The meanings of some words can be figured out by their sounds, or their place in the context of a phrase or a line. Others are so deeply rooted in their Gaelic origins that a dictionary will be essential.

Dialect is speech native to particular geographical areas. Many people born and brought up in these places know no other kind of speech, and need no other—even though the transactions of government, law, and educated society are conducted in an official language. In the case of Scotland, that official language is English.

As an educated and well-read man, Burns had the option of using either Scots dialect or "the King's English." Depending on the subject or occasion of a poem, he proceeded to use both. But there is little question that, if it were not for his poems in dialect, he would figure in literary history as no more than a pleasant poet who accepted the genteel conventions of his time and its sentimental distortions of "the simple life."

The difficulties of poems in dialect have caused some well-meaning instructors to translate them into contemporary language. They make the verses palatable by adding touches of modern slang. But attempts to render dialect poetry into plain English often fail. This is simply because the logic of a poem is only one part of what it means to convey. When sound is divorced from sense, qualities of rhythm, music, and color are diminished and meaning becomes prosaic.

To enjoy and relish "To a Mouse" and "John Anderson," listen to them read aloud in their own lilting Scottish dialect.

A. Dialect
Braid Scots, the dialect that Burns uses in this and the next poem, is a dialect of English spoken in southern Scotland.

B. Vocabulary
Sleekit means "smooth." Line 3 can be translated, "Thou need not start away so hasty. . . ."

C. Interpreting
❓ Paraphrase the third stanza. (The speaker acknowledges the mouse's right to live and says that he'll be blessed for leaving it bits of grain.)

To a Mouse

On Turning Her up in Her Nest With the Plow, November 1785

B
Wee, sleekit, cow'rin', tim'rous beastie.
O, what a panic's in thy breastie!
Thou need na start awa sae hasty
    Wi' bickering brattle!°
5 I wad be laith° to rin an' chase thee
    Wi' murd'ring pattle!°

I'm truly sorry man's dominion
Has broken Nature's social union,
An' justifies that ill opinion
10   Which makes thee startle
At me, thy poor, earth-born companion,
    An' fellow mortal!

C
I doubt na, whiles,° but thou may thieve;
What then? poor beastie, thou maun° live!
15 A daimen-icker in a thrave°
    'S a sma' request:
I'll get a blessin' wi' the lave,°
    And never miss 't!

4. **bickering brattle:** headlong scamper.
5. **laith:** loath.
6. **pattle:** plowstaff.

13. **whiles:** sometimes.
14. **maun:** must.
15. **daimen-icker in a thrave:** occasional bit of grain in a bundle.
17. **lave:** remainder.

CLOSURE
Have students state the theme of the
poem and cite the lines that contain it.

**A. Humanities
Connection:
About the Fine
Art**
Paul Gustave Doré
(1833–1883) was
a successful
French engraver
and illustrator.
Doré illustrated
*The Rime of the
Ancient Mariner*
(see text pages
655–675), as well
as the Bible, *The
Divine Comedy,
Paradise Lost,* and
Don Quixote.

B. Interpreting
❓ Why can't the
mouse simply
build a new home?
(It's November,
and there's nothing
green to use for
building.)

Scottish Landscape by Gustave Doré (1873). Oil.   Louvre, Paris.

Thy wee-bit housie, too, in ruin!
20   Its silly° wa's the win's are strewin'!
B An' naething, now, to big° a new ane,
        O' foggage° green!
    An' bleak December's winds ensuin',
        Baith snell° an' keen!

25   Thou saw the fields laid bare and waste,
    An' weary winter comin' fast,
    An' cozie here, beneath the blast,
        Thou thought to dwell,
    Till crash! the cruel coulter° passed
30   Out through thy cell.

20. **silly:** feeble.
21. **big:** build.
22. **foggage:** moss.

24. **snell:** bitter.

29. **coulter:** cutter-blade.

ANALYZING THE POEM
Identifying Details
1. His plow has destroyed her nest.
2. For both mice and men, plans are not always fruitful. The mouse, however, is fortunate because it only deals with the present. Man looks backward to failure and forward to the fear of failure.

Interpreting Meanings
3. The tone changes in the last stanza, from lightheartedness to self-pity.
 The past is dreary; he guesses at the future and fears it.
4. (He might also be saying that people can never be in total control of their lives.)
 These lines are the source of Steinbeck's *Of Mice and Men*.

5. The speaker is sorry that he has destroyed the mouse's home. He understands why the mouse is afraid of him and is sorry.
 Dominion refers to human rule over the earth's creatures; *union* to the fact that we are fellow creatures.
 Humans are part of nature but their need for dominance breaks that union.
6. He combines alliteration and dialect in lines 4, 29, and 33.
 For comedy, try lines 4, 19–20, 31–36.

> That wee-bit heap o' leaves an' stibble
> Has cost thee mony a weary nibble!
> Now thou's turned out, for a' thy trouble,
> But° house or hald,
> 35 To thole° the winter's sleety dribble,
> An' cranreuch° cauld!
>
> But Mousie, thou art no thy lane,°
> In proving foresight may be vain:
> The best-laid schemes o' mice an' men
> 40 Gang aft a-gley,°
> An' lea'e us nought but grief an' pain,
> For promised joy.
>
> Still thou art blest compared wi' me!
> The present only toucheth thee:
> 45 But och! I backward cast my e'e
> On prospects drear!
> An' forward though I canna see,
> I guess an' fear!

34. **But:** without.
35. **thole:** endure.
36. **cranreuch:** hoarfrost.

37. **lane:** lone.

40. **Gang aft a-gley:** go oft awry.

Responding to the Poem

Analyzing the Poem

Identifying Details

1. What has happened to the mouse that engages the speaker's sympathy?
2. What comparisons between the mouse and himself does the speaker make in the last two stanzas?

Interpreting Meanings

3. Where does the speaker's **tone** change? What does the speaker imply about his own past and his prospects for the future in the last stanza?
4. The best-known lines of this poem are lines 39–40. Do you agree with the philosophy expressed in these lines? Does the speaker seem to be saying that it makes no sense to make any plans for the future at all, or is he simply commenting on what another British writer, Thomas Hardy, was to call "the persistence of the unforeseen"? (Do you recognize in these lines the title of a novel by John Steinbeck?)
5. Paraphrase the meaning of the second stanza. What are the meanings of the words *dominion* and *union* here, in your view? What attitude about man and nature does the use of these words imply?
6. Identify some uses of **alliteration** in the poem. How does Burns combine alliteration with dialect? Are any of the poem's sound effects comical?

Writing About the Poem

A Creative Response

1. **Imitating the Writer's Technique.** Have another speaker address another creature—fly, cockroach, spider, moth. Imitate Burns, and imagine what the creature is thinking of the encounter. Can the speaker see a connection between the creature and himself?

A Critical Response

2. **Responding to the Poem.** In an essay, explain your response to this poem, including its use of dialect. Be as frank as you want to be, but you must support your response with specific reasons and quotations from the poem when pertinent.

CLOSURE
Have students tell who is speaking in the poem and what her message is. What does *jo* mean in the title?

ANALYZING THE POEM
Identifying Details
1. John Anderson's wife is addressing John Anderson.
2. They climbed "the hill" together and had many a merry day. Now they must go down "the hill" and sleep at its foot.

Interpreting Meanings
3. The foot of the hill is death.
4. In general, the speaker accepts old age and death after many joyous years with her husband.

Instead of Shakespeare's seven ages of man, this lyric deals with only two ages: youth and age. In prose, the "message" of the poem could be reduced to a sentence or two. But with repetitions and the play of a limited number of rhymes, Burns weaves a little garland of words as sweetly sentimental as a Valentine.

John Anderson, My Jo

John Anderson my jo,° John,
   When we were first acquent,
Your locks were like the raven,
   Your bonie brow was brent;°
5 But now your brow is beld,° John,
   Your locks are like the snow;
But blessings on your frosty pow,°
   John Anderson, my jo.

John Anderson my jo, John,
10   We clamb the hill thegither;
And mony a canty° day, John,
   We've had wi' ane anither:
Now we maun <u>totter</u> down, John,
   And hand in hand we'll go,
15 And sleep thegither at the foot,
   John Anderson, my jo.

1. **jo:** joy.

4. **brent:** smooth.
5. **beld:** bald.

7. **pow** (pō): head.

11. **canty:** merry.

Responding to the Poem

Analyzing the Poem

Identifying Details
1. Who is addressing whom in the poem?
2. According to the speaker, what did the lovers used to do? What must they do now?

Interpreting Meanings
3. What **symbolic** meaning might be suggested by line 15?
4. What attitude toward old age seems to be held by the speaker, in your view? Do you think this attitude is prevalent today?

Writing About the Poem

A Creative Response
1. **Changing the Point of View.** Write a paragraph answering the speaker. Use the point of view of John Anderson.

A Critical Response
2. **Rewriting Dialect.** Rewrite the poem in standard English, and comment on the change in effect.

A. Expansion
Here is the entire poem. Ask students to
identify the speaker (a poet) and to tell
why he has written his poems.

Piping down the valleys wild,
  Piping songs of pleasant glee,
On a cloud I saw a child,
  And he laughing said to me:

"Pipe a song about a Lamb!"
  So I piped with merry cheer.
"Piper, pipe that song again;"
  So I piped: he wept to hear.

"Drop thy pipe, thy happy pipe;
  Sing thy songs of happy cheer:"
So I sang the same again,
  While he wept with joy to hear.

"Piper, sit thee down and write
  In a book, that all may read,"
So he vanished from my sight,
  And I plucked a hollow reed,

And I made a rural pen,
  And I stained the water clear,
And I wrote my happy songs
  Every child may joy to hear.

William Blake (1757–1827)

A
> And I made a rural pen,
> And I stained the water clear,
> And I wrote my happy songs
> Every child may joy to hear.
> —from "Introduction,"
> *Songs of Experience*

B
William Blake's life was not as "romantic" or "poetic" as the lives of Coleridge, Shelley, and Keats were. Aside from one terrifying brush with the law as a result of a quarrel with a soldier in 1803, the surface of Blake's personal history seems comparatively uneventful. By all accounts, he was happily married to the same woman all of his life. He never traveled and he lived outside of London, where he was born and raised, for only three unhappy years (1800–1803). He began his artistic training at ten and worked steadily at his craft as an engraver throughout a long life, in good times and bad. During his lifetime, his work received very little attention, and a great deal of his poetry was never published in the sense of being "public." When his work was noticed, readers and viewers too often decided that it, and therefore Blake himself, was weird, confused, or mad. It was only in the last decade of his life that a group of young artists appreciated his work sufficiently to become admirers and disciples. What we really know of Blake—from the enormous energy and variety of the poetry, paintings, drawings, and engravings he produced, work much more available to us than it was to his contemporaries—is that he was quite simply a great artist in the fullest sense.

Is the imaginative creation of a work of art the only real life an artist has? This question led Keats to describe the poet as "the most unpoetical of God's creatures," because imagination is always projecting the poet into his visions. A woman at a gathering is said to have asked Blake *where* he had come upon the scene he had just vividly described to her. "*Here*, madam," he said, pointing his finger at his forehead. To paraphrase Blake: *If we see with imagination, we see all things in the infinite. But if we see only with reason, we see only ourselves.* Blake's

William Blake by Thomas Phillips (1807). Oil.

ordinary life seems "unpoetic" because *we* have come to see that his real life was lived in and through his imagination and the creation of works of art. In these works, he did not see only himself; he saw everything.

Perhaps their works are the surest accounts artists can provide of their own lives. Keats also said, "A man's life of any worth is a continual allegory—and very few eyes can see the mystery . . . [which like the Bible is] figurative . . ." If we take the time simply to *look* at Blake's work, from the simple illustrated poems represented here, to his illustrations for others' works, to his large, magnificent, and sometimes unfinished "prophetic" poems, we can "see" (with the eyes of our imagination) more of the "mystery" of who he was. "I know that this world is a world of imagination & vision," he wrote.

> I see everything I paint in this world, but everybody does not see alike. To the eyes of a miser, a guinea [a coin] is more beautiful than the sun, & a bag worn with the use of money has more beautiful proportions than a vine filled with grapes. . . . But to the eyes of the

In a letter to the Rev. H. F. Cary in 1818, Samuel Taylor Coleridge wrote:

"I have this morning been reading a strange publication—*viz.* Poems with very wild and interesting pictures as swathing, etched (I suppose) but it is said printed and painted by the author, W. Blake. He is a man of Genius—and I apprehend a Swedenborgian [Emanuel Swedenborg, a Swedish mystic and religious philosopher]—certainly a mystic *emphatically.* You may perhaps smile at *my* calling another poet a Mystic; but verily I am in the very mire of commonplace commonplace compared with Mr. Blake, apo- or rather—ana-calyptic Poet, and Painter!"

A. Expansion

Blake, the second son of a wealthy man who ran a hosiery shop, saw visions all his life. When he was four, he was frightened by the face of God at his window; at eight, he told his father that he'd seen a tree filled with bright-winged angels.

As an adult, Blake continued to have visions. He claimed that the spirit of his dead brother spoke to him daily. Mrs. Blake once wrote, "I have very little of Mr. Blake's company. He is always in Paradise."

B. Dramatic Irony

In the *Songs of Innocence,* the speaker is often a child. In many poems, the poet's view is different from the speaker's. This discrepancy is called *dramatic irony.* Ask students to watch for dramatic irony as they read the poems that follow.

A — man of imagination nature is imagination itself. As a man is, so he sees. . . . To me this world is all one continued vision of fancy or imagination.

If we search for William Blake in his art, we are soon aware of the truth of his statement "Everybody does not see alike." One of the purposes of Blake's art was to change the way people "see" and thus to open up new worlds to them—"one continued vision" of what had once been ordinary and commonplace, but would become "imagination itself." One of Blake's most famous statements about his art (in the prophetic poem *Jerusalem*) is "I must create a system or be enslaved by another man's." But in creating the "system" for his works, Blake was also aware that he himself could be trapped by it. The line which follows the one above is, "I will not reason & compare: my business is to create."

B — In the *Songs of Innocence and Experience,* we may find something of Blake in the poet who is the "speaker" in some poems and a narrator in others. In "The Chimney Sweeper" poems, he is a recorder in the first poem and a narrator and brief questioner ("Where are thy father & mother? Say?") in the second. Here, Blake's art is to force us to hear and thus "see" the two young boys from the perspectives of innocence and experience. In "The Lamb," the speaker is a gentle questioner and teacher fulfilling the poet's task of singing the "happy songs" of innocence. In "The Tyger" he is the poet, filled with fear and wonder when he thinks of that other strenuous artist who created the "fearful symmetry" of the animal. Here he is showing us another of the poet's perspectives, the one boldly announced in the introductory poem to *Songs of Experience:*

Hear the voice of the bard!
Who present, past, & future sees,
Whose ears have heard
The holy word
That walked among the ancient trees.

Perhaps the most revealing personal account can be found in "London," where we imagine the speaker wandering despondently and angrily about Blake's native city, feeling compassion for the poor, wretched people he encounters and perhaps feeling a futility about what can be done to improve their lives. Here we can accompany Blake's speaker and "see" with his eyes a world we might prefer to ignore. In doing so, we experience the speaker's anger and despair.

We would not be wrong if we "saw" in these poems Blake's own gentleness and humility, his anger and righteousness, his sympathy and perceptiveness, and his sense of the varying tasks of a poet. All of these were characteristics of William Blake. But what is most common to all of these poems is that Blake the artist uses contrasts to force us to "see" in new and disturbing ways. Our sense of "seeing" is intensified when we read these poems with Blake's own illustrations for them at hand.

Blake's life may also seem less "romantic" or "poetic" to us because, unlike the other Romantics, he was a fulltime professional artist. His father, a London shopkeeper, sent him to one of the best drawing schools and at fourteen William was apprenticed to an engraver. Although he tried his hand at running a print shop for a while, for most of his life he lived on what he could earn from commissions for illustrations and drawing lessons. He seems to have made a reasonable living until the late 1790's when his declining income led him to move to a Sussex village at the invitation of an exploitive patron who had no real appreciation for Blake's work. When he moved back to London, his fortunes did not improve. Though it is clear that he continued to work steadily at both his art and writing, the period of his life when he was in his fifties and early sixties is obscured by poverty and isolation.

The history of Blake the poet cannot really be separated from that of Blake the visual artist. Not only did he provide illustrations for most of his poems, he printed much of his poetry himself (and sometimes only for himself), using engraving methods he had created himself. Only his earlier collection of poems, *Poetical Sketches,* published in 1783, was not under his control. Blake's illuminated poems really began with an unpublished satirical work, *An Island in the Moon,* which he worked on between 1785 and 1788. For this unpublished work, he created some short lyric poems which were quite out of character with the rest of the work. It was these pieces which led to the creation of the first of Blake's many illuminated books, *Songs of Innocence* (1789). According to Blake's nineteenth-

Comment from W. B. Yeats

In 1903 the Irish poet and playwright
W. B. Yeats wrote:

"... when one reads Blake, it is as
though the spray of an inexhaustible
fountain of beauty was blown into our
faces, ...

"He cried again and again that everything that lives is holy, and that nothing is
unholy except things that do not live—le-
thargies, and cruelties, and timidities, and
that denial of the imagination which is the
root they grew from in old times. Passions, because most living, are most
holy—and this was a scandalous paradox in his time—and man shall enter
eternity born upon their wings."

---

century biographer Alexander Gilchrist, "the
poet and his wife did everything in making the
book—writing, designing, printing, engraving—
everything except manufacturing the paper; the
very ink, or color rather, they did make. Never
before surely was a man so literally the author
of his own book."

In *The Book of Thel,* another illuminated work
produced in 1789, Blake used for the first time a
specially conceived character. He would create
such characters extensively in his later prophetic
and symbolic works. *The Marriage of Heaven
and Hell,* written in the early 1790's, is perhaps
the best introduction to both his later poetic
"system," and to the idea, as the poem states it,
that "Without contraries is no progression."
This idea helps us understand the way the "contraries" of "innocence" and "experience"
work. Blake's first great prophetic book, *America,* was completed in 1794, the same year he
issued the combined *Songs of Innocence and
Experience.*

A As Blake's remarks about imagination and
vision suggest, a good deal of what he wrote
outside of his poems is cryptic and needs illustration from his art. But one characteristic of the
man himself shines through clearly—the optimism sustained by his continuous joy in the
"one continued vision" of his art. In 1799, when
things were not going well, he could report his
lack of work to a friend, yet assure him, "I feel
myself happy & contented let what will come;
having passed now near twenty years in ups &
downs, I am used to them, & perhaps a little
practice in them may turn out to benefit. . . .
Though I laugh at fortune I am persuaded that
she alone is governor of worldly riches, & when
it is fit she will call on me; till then I wait with
patience, in hopes that she is busied among my
friends." In 1804, when he felt his artistic powers returning after his unhappy absence from
London and his traumatic brush with the law, he
wrote, "excuse my enthusiasm or rather madness, for I am really drunk with intellectual vision whenever I take a pencil or graver into my
hand, even as I used to be in my youth, and as I
have not been for twenty dark, but very profitable years. I thank God that I courageously pursued my course through darkness." In 1824,
Samuel Palmer visited Blake and found the
sixty-seven-year-old artist confined by a leg injury, lying "like one of the antique patriarchs or

a dying Michaelangelo" in a bed covered with
books "making in a great book the sublimest designs. . . . He designed them (100 I think) during
a fortnight's illness."

The American Romantic writer Henry Thoreau
tells a fable of an artist who vowed to create a
perfect work of art even if he should do nothing
else in his life. When he was finished, "he had
made a new system in making [the work], a
world with full and fair proportions. . . . For him
and his work . . . time had been an illusion. . . .
The material was pure, and his art was pure;
how could the result be other than wonderful?"
It is said that Blake on his deathbed was still at
work coloring a print from his poem of the
1790's, *Europe.* Finally he put it down saying,
"There, that will do! I cannot mend it."

In a letter to Alexander Gilchrist, Palmer said
of Blake, "He was a man without a mask; his
aim single, his path straightforward, and his
wants few; so he was free, noble, and happy."

Self-portrait by William Blake for a page of
his notebook.

In a catalog for
an exhibit of his
paintings, Blake
wrote:

" 'What,' it will
be questioned,
'When the sun
rises, do you not
see a round disc of
fire somewhat like
a guinea?' O no,
no, I see an innu-
merable company
of the heavenly
host crying, 'Holy,
Holy, Holy is the
Lord God Al-
mighty.' "

PREPARATION

1. ESTABLISHING A PURPOSE. See the headnote and the first writing assignment on text page 621.

2. PREREADING JOURNAL. Have students list the connotations, feelings, and images (including animals and plants) they associate with the words *innocence* and *experience*.

DEVELOPING VOCABULARY
The following words from the poem are tested in the Selection Test. (See also Vocabulary Activity Worksheet.)
symmetry   sinews
to aspire   dread

CLOSURE
Assign the poem for memorization and have six students recite it for the class, verse by verse.

A. Humanities Connection: Discussing the Etching
Songs of Innocence was the first book Blake produced using his new engraving technique. Blake printed and hand-colored the engravings himself, and his books were sold only at his home. The few people who were aware of Blake's work during his lifetime thought of him primarily as an artist—not a poet.
? What other animals might Blake have chosen to represent demonic or divine energy, or an elemental force of nature?

B. Imagery
? Find examples of images of fire associated with the tiger. (Lines 2, 6, 8, 14)

Blake's Poems

"The Tyger" from *Songs of Experience* by William Blake (1793). Hand-colored etching.

Blake published the *Songs of Innocence* in 1789 and the *Songs of Experience* in 1793. After 1793 they were always issued together in one volume, the title page promising a demonstration of "the two contrary states of the human soul."

Blake conceived the first of these states, "Innocence," as a state of genuine love and naive trust toward all humankind, accompanied by unquestioned belief in Christian doctrine. Though a firm believer in Christianity, Blake recognized that its doctrines were being used by the English Church and other institutions as a form of social control: to encourage among the people passive obedience and acceptance of oppression, poverty, and inequality. Recognition of this marks what Blake called the state of "Experience," a profound disillusionment with human nature and society. One entering the state of "Experience" sees cruelty and hypocrisy only too clearly, but is unable to imagine a way out. Blake also conceived of a third, higher stage of consciousness he called "Organized Innocence," which is expressed in his later works. In this state, one's sense of the divinity of humanity coexists with oppression and injustice, though involving continued recognition of and active opposition to them.

When reading the *Songs of Innocence* and, to a lesser extent, the *Songs of Experience,* it is important to remember that Blake intended them not as simple expressions of religious faith. The poems are demonstrations of viewpoints that are necessarily limited or distorted by each narrator's or speaker's state of consciousness.

While almost everyone agrees that "The Tyger" is one of the most powerful of Blake's *Songs of Experience*, there has been much disagreement about the meaning of the poem's central symbol, the tiger itself. One possibility is that the tiger represents a strong revolutionary energy that can enlighten and transform society—a positive but dangerous force Blake believed was operating in the French Revolution. The narrator of this poem, at any rate, cannot comprehend such a startling energy, and can only wonder whether it is demonic or godlike.

The Tyger

B Tyger! Tyger! burning bright
In the forests of the night,
What immortal hand or eye
Could frame thy fearful <u>symmetry</u>?

5   In what distant deeps or skies
Burnt the fire of thine eyes?
On what wings dare he <u>aspire</u>?
What the hand dare seize the fire?

1. In essence, the speaker asks who created such a fearful creature and did its creator also make the lamb.
2. God as creator is suggested in lines 3 and 19–20.
    A demonic creator (from Hell) is suggested in lines 5–12.
    Stanza 4 suggests a blacksmith or goldsmith (hammer, chain, furnace, anvil, grasp).

Interpreting Meanings
3. Possibly its stripes.
4. *Could* becomes *dare.*
    Dare suggests something risky or forbidden.
5. Enlightenment: burning bright / In the forests of the night; fire; wings. Violence: deadly terrors.
6. Simple meter and rhyme; vivid description of the tiger.
7. The speaker is attracted to the power and repulsed by the tiger's destructive capability.

And what shoulder, and what art,
10   Could twist the sinews of thy heart?
And when thy heart began to beat,
What dread hand? and what dread feet?

What the hammer? what the chain?
In what furnace was thy brain?
15   What the anvil? what <u>dread</u> grasp
Dare its deadly terrors clasp?

When the stars threw down their spears,
And watered heaven with their tears,°
Did he smile his work to see?
20   Did he who made the Lamb make thee?

Tyger! Tyger! burning bright
In the forests of the night,
What immortal hand or eye
Dare frame thy fearful symmetry?

18. A reference to the fallen angels who, after losing the war in Heaven, threw down their spears.

Responding to the Poem

Analyzing the Poem

Identifying Details

1. What questions does the speaker ask the tiger?
2. Where in the poem does the speaker wonder if the tiger may have been created by God? What **imagery** tells us that the speaker also suspects that the tiger could be a demonic creation? What images suggest a human creator—like a blacksmith or goldsmith?

Interpreting Meanings

3. What do you think is meant by the tiger's "fearful symmetry"?
4. The last stanza of the poem virtually repeats the first. In your view, what is the significance of the one word that is changed in the last stanza?
5. What **imagery** suggests that the tiger could be a force of enlightenment? Of violence?
6. This poem has always appealed to children, as well as to adults. What reasons can you think of for the poem's appeal to younger as well as older readers?
7. How does the poem testify to the simultaneous attraction to and repulsion from evil?

Writing About the Poem

A Critical Response

1. **Analyzing the Poem.** In a brief essay, state what you think is the meaning of the poem's central **symbol,** the tiger. Support your statement with arguments drawn from the text of the poem.
2. **Comparing and Contrasting Two Versions of a Poem.** In an early draft of this poem, Blake inserted the following lines after the third stanza:

> Could fetch it from the furnace deep
> And in thy horrid ribs dare steep
> In the well of sanguine wee
> In what clay and in what mold
> Were thy eyes of fury rolled?
>
> —William Blake

This early version also lacked the fifth stanza of the final version. Compare and contrast the early draft and the final version of "The Tyger," commenting on why you think Blake made the changes he did.

A. The Passover Lamb

Just before the Exodus from Egypt, the Israelites smeared the blood of a lamb on their doorposts so the angel of God "passed over" their homes and did not slay their firstborn sons (Exodus 12). (This event is commemorated at Passover.) Jesus is identified with the paschal lamb.

ANALYZING THE POEM

Identifying Details

1. The creator gave the lamb life, food, clothing (fleece), and a "tender voice."
2. It tells the lamb Christ made it.
3. He's a child.

Interpreting Meanings

4. It is a lamb in a literal sense and also a symbol of innocence, purity, and meekness.
5. The young speaker may die soon.
6. This speaker is neither meek nor submissive.

PREPARATION

ESTABLISHING A PURPOSE. Students should note how this poem is similar to and different from "The Tyger."

SUPPLEMENTARY SUPPORT MATERIALS

1. Review and Response Worksheet: The Speaker (*CCB*)
2. Selection Test (*CCB*)

CLOSURE

Have students explain who is speaking in "The Lamb," what question is asked, and how it is answered.

One of the *Songs of Innocence*, this poem has often been read as a statement of Christian faith. However, we know that Blake's other writings show Christ as an active fighter against injustice, not the "meek and mild" lamb—a common symbol for Christ—with which this innocent narrator identifies. The speaker's viewpoint is thus an incomplete one.

The Lamb

Little Lamb who made thee
    Dost thou know who made thee?
Gave thee life and bid thee feed,
By the stream and o'er the mead;°
5 Gave thee clothing of delight,
Softest clothing wooly bright;
Gave thee such a tender voice,
Making all the vales° rejoice!
    Little Lamb who made thee
10   Dost thou know who made thee?

    Little Lamb I'll tell thee,
    Little Lamb I'll tell thee!
A   He° is called by thy name,
    For he calls himself a Lamb:
15 He is meek and he is mild,
He became a little child:
I a child and thou a lamb,
We are called by his name.
    Little Lamb God bless thee.
20   Little Lamb God bless thee.

4. **mead:** meadow.

8. **vales:** valleys.

13. **He:** Christ.

Responding to the Poem

Analyzing the Poem

Identifying Details

1. What did its creator do for the lamb in the first stanza?
2. How does the second stanza respond to the question posed in the first?
3. What do you know about the **speaker** of the poem?

Interpreting Meanings

4. How is the lamb both a literal object and a **symbol** in this poem?
5. Christ called himself a lamb because, like the Passover lamb slain to save the people of Israel, he sacrificed himself for the people. What might this imply about the fate of the young speaker in this poem?

6. Blake wrote a two-line poem called "An Answer to the Parson" in which the parson (preacher) asks, "Why, of the sheep, you do not learn peace?" The narrator replies, "Because I don't want you to shear my fleece!" How would the narrator of this poem disagree with the narrator of "The Lamb"?

Writing About the Poem

A Critical Response

Comparing and Contrasting Two Poems. In a brief essay, explain how both "The Tyger" and "The Lamb," although they seem to be simple lyrics, are concerned with very profound questions of religion. Be sure to comment on the structure and imagery in the two poems.

PREPARATION
1. BUILDING ON PRIOR KNOWLEDGE. Refer students to the illustration on text page 603 and to the time line on text page 609, which notes that the Factory Act of 1819 prohibited employment in cotton mills of children under nine years of age.

2. ESTABLISHING A PURPOSE. Students should note the speaker's tone and identity.

SUPPLEMENTARY SUPPORT MATERIALS
1. Review and Response Worksheet: Tone (CCB)
2. Selection Test (CCB)

CLOSURE
Ask each student to give one example of Blake's use of irony in the poem.

In Blake's London, buildings were heated by coal or wood-burning fireplaces, so every house had at least one chimney that had to be cleaned regularly. Children were often employed as chimney sweepers because they could more easily fit into the narrow chimneys. Some poor parents—as the second line of this poem implies—did sell their children to "masters" who managed crews of young chimney sweepers. The work was dirty and dangerous, and the children, poorly fed and badly clothed by masters concerned only with profits, were social outcasts. Blake's chimney sweeper, like the other narrators of the *Songs of Innocence*, is able to take comfort for the time being in his belief in the heaven that he has been taught awaits him after death.

The Chimney Sweeper

When my mother died I was very young,
And my father sold me while yet my tongue
Could scarcely cry weep weep weep weep.°
So your chimneys I sweep and in soot I sleep.

5　There's little Tom Dacre, who cried when his head
A　That curled like a lamb's back, was shaved, so I said
Hush Tom never mind it, for when your head's bare,
You know that the soot cannot spoil your white hair.

And so he was quiet, and that very night,
10　As Tom was a sleeping he had such a sight,
That thousands of sweepers Dick, Joe, Ned, and Jack
Were all of them locked up in coffins of black,

And by came an Angel who had a bright key,
And he opened the coffins and set them all free.
15　Then down a green plain leaping laughing they run
And wash in a river and shine in the sun.

Then naked and white, all their bags left behind,
They rise upon clouds, and sport in the wind.
B　And the Angel told Tom if he'd be a good boy,
20　He'd have God for his father and never want° joy.

And so Tom awoke and we rose in the dark
And got with our bags and our brushes to work.
C　Though the morning was cold, Tom was happy and warm,
D　So if all do their duty, they need not fear harm.

3. **weep . . . weep:** the child's attempt at the chimney sweeper's cry: "Sweep! Sweep!"

20. **want:** lack

A. Imagery
? Given what you've learned from "The Lamb," what significance can you find in this comparison of Tom to a lamb? (Tom is an innocent child, a child of God.)

B. Vocabulary
Here, the verb *want* means "be without."

C. Tone
? How happy do you think Tom is? (He does not seem happy; all he has to look forward to is dying.)

D. Responding
? What is your opinion of this moral? It is ironic? How does it relate to your own experiences and observations? (It is ironic; the boy should enjoy life, not the prospect of death.)

1. His mother died when he was young, and his father sold him off as a chimney sweeper. The speaker sweeps and sleeps in the soot.
2. He tells Tom that he will be spared the discomfort and ugliness of sooty blond hair.
3. Tom dreams that sweepers locked in coffins are set free by angels, wash in a river, and play on clouds. The angel tells him that if he's a good boy, God will be his father, and he'll always be happy.
4. If a person performs earthly duties, he "need not fear harm"—i.e., God will care for him.

Interpreting Meanings
5. In the dream Tom is clean and plays in heaven, trouble free. In actuality, he exists in the narrow, filthy, and harmful confines of chimneys.
6. He is without a parent. Most significantly, the idea of God as the "good father" directly contrasts with the speaker's earthly father.
7. The speaker means to say "sweep," but unknowingly reveals his spiritual and *(Answers continue in left-hand column.)*

(Continued from top.)
physical condition with the word "weep." Although the speaker comforts Tom, his cry "weep" pervades the entire scene.
8. In the final line, he derives his moral from the dream.
9. Students may feel that in this case doing his duty, i.e., working as a chimney sweep, *is* doing him harm.

A. Humanities Connection: About the Fine Art
The brush in the child's right hand was used to clean the sooty chimney.

This illustration looks blurred because it is an enlargement of a detail from a tiny etching approximately 4½ by 2¾ inches. After printing each etching, Blake or his wife would hand-color it with watercolors and touch it up with pen.

A

"The Chimney Sweeper" (detail) from *Songs of Innocence* by William Blake (1794). Color relief etching.

Responding to the Poem

Analyzing the Poem

Identifying Details

1. What do we learn about the speaker in the first stanza?
2. In the second stanza, how does the speaker try to reassure Tom Dacre?
3. Describe Tom's dream. How does the angel reassure him?
4. What moral lesson does this speaker draw from his dream?

Interpreting Meanings

5. How does Tom's dream of heaven contrast with the actual condition of his daily life?
6. Why would the angel's promise that Tom (and presumably any "good" boy) can "have God for his father" be especially significant for this speaker?
7. Reread line 3 carefully. How is the child's mispronunciation of the chimney sweep's cry at once poignant and **ironic**? Is it possible, in your view, that the irony here establishes a certain **tone** for the entire poem? What is that tone?
8. Where in this poem does the speaker try to make the best of a degrading situation? Does his reasoning convince you?
9. How does the final line affect you?

PREPARATION
ESTABLISHING A PURPOSE. As students
read this poem, have them compare it
with the previous one.

CLOSURE
Students should be able to describe the
difference between the two chimney
sweeper poems.

ANALYZING THE POEM
Identifying Details
1. As a "little black thing" weeping in the
snow.
2. They put him in the "clothes of death"

and taught him to sing sad notes because he was happy in the country.

Interpreting Meanings
3. The child weeps "notes of woe"
though he claims to be happy.
4. Soot-blackened clothes.
5. It can mean "to invent or pretend." It
can also mean that the parents make a
heaven out of his misery.

They create an
ironic, bitter con-
clusion.
6–7. Answers will
vary. Blake might
be attacking child
labor.

A. Imagery
The child is like a
bird (weep weep/
peep peep).

Unlike the chimney sweeper in *Songs of Innocence*, this chimney sweeper in the *Songs of Experience* no longer accepts oppression and poverty
because it will gain him a reward in heaven. This
little speaker has recognized that the people who
pray for him are the same ones (his parents) who
sold him into a life of hard labor. The first three
lines of this poem are spoken by an adult who
finds the child. The rest of the poem represents
the bitter and ironic response of the young chimney sweeper.

The Chimney Sweeper

A A little black thing among the snow:
Crying weep, weep, in notes of woe!
Where are thy father and mother? say?
They are both gone up to the church to pray.

5 Because I was happy upon the heath,°
And smiled among the winter's snow:
They clothed me in the clothes of death,
And taught me to sing the notes of woe.

And because I am happy, and dance and sing,
10 They think they have done me no injury;
And are gone to praise God and his Priest and King,
Who make up a heaven of our misery.

5. **heath:** open land in the country.

Responding to the Poem

Analyzing the Poem

Identifying Details

1. How does the speaker of the first three lines describe
the young chimney sweeper?
2. What does the child say his parents did to him, and
why?

Interpreting Meanings

3. How do the first two lines of the poem help you to
realize that the chimney sweeper's statement in line
9 must be **ironic**?
4. What are the "clothes of death" (line 7)?
5. What are the different meanings of the phrase "who
make up" (line 12)? How do these different meanings
of the phrase affect your interpretation of the final
line of the poem?
6. How do you imagine the sweeper's story affected the
narrator of the poem?
7. What do you think was Blake's **purpose** in writing this
poem?

Writing About the Poems

A Creative Response

1. **Writing a Narrative.** Based on the details in Blake's
two poems about the chimney sweeper, write a short
prose narrative about the childhood of such a boy in
Blake's London. Your narrative might be structured as
the opening chapter of a novel.

A Critical Response

2. **Writing an Analysis.** Although Blake's lyrics use simple
diction and striking imagery, their philosophical content is often complex. For example, it is obvious from
the chimney sweeper poems that Blake profoundly
respected religious faith even as he was skeptical of
what he regarded as hypocrisy in organized religion.
It is equally clear that Blake found the existence of
earthly misery hard to reconcile with the grace and
love of a merciful God. In a brief essay, comment on
how Blake expresses these philosophical tensions in
the two poems on the chimney sweeper.

William Blake   625

PREPARATION

1. ESTABLISHING A PURPOSE. Question 2 will set a purpose for students' reading.

2. PREREADING JOURNAL. Ask students to list some images they associate either with their own community or with a large American city. When they finish, ask students to evaluate the tones of their lists.

SUPPLEMENTARY SUPPORT MATERIALS
1. Vocabulary Activity Worksheet (*CCB*)
2. Review and Response Worksheet: Imagery and Tone (*CCB*)
3. Selection Test (*CCB*)

DEVELOPING VOCABULARY
The following words from the poem are tested in the Selection Test. (See also Vocabulary Activity Worksheet.)
manacles   hapless   to blight

A. Connotation
The adjective *chartered* is used twice here. Note that the law restricts the streets and the very river itself. Blake uses the word *chartered* with irony: This kind of law is a tyranny that results only in woe.

B. Vocabulary
Hapless means "luckless" or "unfortunate."

C. Irony
Note the ironic juxtaposition of *marriage* and *hearse* (see question 5).

D. Form
❓ Describe the poem's structure. Which part deals with general ideas? (Lines 1–8) Which part gives specific examples? (Lines 9–16)

CLOSURE
Have three students discuss, in front of the class, whether Blake's poem applies to society today.

The effects of oppression on the human spirit are visible and audible to the speaker of "London." He sees and hears the signs of this oppression coming back to haunt the society responsible for perpetuating it. Blake thought that certain institutions in his society reinforced the assumptions that poverty, war, and the "inferiority" of women were natural and inevitable in the "order of things." In accepting these teachings ("the mind-forged manacles"), many oppressed people lost the hope that they could change their condition. This sense of hopelessness seems to affect the speaker of this poem. Like most of the other speakers of the *Songs of Experience*, he cannot offer a way out.

London

A I wander through each chartered° street,
Near where the chartered Thames does flow,
And mark° in every face I meet
Marks of weakness, marks of woe.

5 In every cry of every man,
In every infant's cry of fear,
In every voice, in every ban,°
The mind-forged manacles I hear.

How the chimney sweeper's cry
10 Every blackning church appalls,°
B And the hapless soldier's sigh
Runs in blood down palace walls.

But most through midnight streets I hear
How the youthful harlot's curse°
15 Blasts the newborn infant's tear
C And blights with plagues the marriage hearse.

D

1. **chartered:** controlled by law.
3. **mark:** notice.
7. **ban:** legal prohibition, public condemnation, or curse; also, a marriage announcement (spelled *banns*).
10. **appalls:** causes to lose color; also, dismays, terrifies, weakens.
14. **harlot's curse:** the curse upon the harlot by a hypocritical society which pushed women into prostitution and then condemned them for it, and the curse the harlot utters in return. A very real form of the "curse" is disease.

Responding to the Poem

Analyzing the Poem

Identifying Details

1. What specific **images** describe what the speaker sees in London?

Interpreting Meanings

2. Blake uses specific, concrete images to stand for larger concepts and institutions. Identify figures or images of war; of oppression and restriction; of prostitution; and of anger.

3. What do you think the "mind-forged manacles" are (line 8)?
4. Where does Blake use **images** of darkness in this poem? What do you think darkness **symbolizes**?
5. In Blake's time, sexually transmitted diseases were often incurable. If the husband had previously been infected by a prostitute, he infected his wife and the disease then "blasted" (infected) their children's "tear" (the disease caused infants to be blind from birth). In Blake's time, the word *hearse* could mean both a carriage and a funeral bier. Given all this information, how would you explain the poem's final line?

ANALYZING THE POEM

Identifying Details

1. "Chartered street"; "chartered Thames"; faces of woe, weakness, fear; "blackning church"; "blood down palace walls"; "midnight streets."

Interpreting Meanings

2. War: lines 11–12; oppression and restriction: lines 1–8; prostitution: lines 13–16; anger: lines 9–10, 13–16.

3. Answers will vary. The metaphor refers to the attitudes and institutions that condone oppression.

4. These images occur in lines 10, 13, 16 (black hearse). Darkness could symbolize ignorance, oppression, sin, evil.

5. It refers to venereal disease transmitted to the husband, infecting his wife and children (plague), and thus blighting the marriage. Marriage is seen as a carriage (hearse) carrying its inhabitants to death.

Children Leaving School by Benjamin Vautier.

Victoria and Albert Museum, London.

A. Humanities Connection: Responding to the Fine Art
German painter and illustrator Benjamin Vautier (1829–1898) was a genre painter—a painter of scenes from everyday life. ❓ Describe the mood of this painting. (Sentimental, carefree; some might detect an ominous note in the painting's coldness and dark tones) How do these children relate to those Blake describes? (These children are in school, not working.)

Writing About the Poem

A Creative Response

1. **Writing a Description.** Assume that you were planning, like Blake himself, to illustrate this poem with a painting or woodcut. Basing your details on the images in the poem, write a brief description of the various elements you would put into your illustration.

A Critical Response

2. **Comparing Two Poems.** Read the following passage describing London from James Thomson's *The City of Dreadful Night* (1874):

> The street lamps burn amidst the baleful glooms,
>   Amidst the soundless solitudes immense
> Of rangéd mansions dark and still as tombs.
>   The silence which benumbs or strains the sense
> Fulfills with awe the soul's despair unweeping;
> Myriads of habitants are ever sleeping,
>   Or dead, or fled from nameless pestilence!
>
> —from *The City of Dreadful Night*
> James Thomson

In a brief essay, compare this passage with Blake's "London." Explain how the contrasting **images** (silence for Thomson, cries and curses for Blake) are used for two entirely different approaches and statements.

Analyzing Language and Style

Puns

Puns are plays on the multiple meanings of words. In line 7, for example, the word *ban* means "a legal restriction," as in "a ban on parking." But the word also refers to the marriage *banns* which in Blake's day were announced three times in church before a wedding. When we catch the pun here, we understand lines 7–8 on another level.

1. The word *pall* can mean a burial robe. What pun might be intended, then, for line 10?
2. According to the side note to line 14, how many meanings of the word "curse" might Blake intend us to think about?

PREPARATION

1. BUILDING ON PRIOR KNOWLEDGE. Have students tell what they know about Jerusalem, the holy city for three great world religions: Judaism, Christianity, and Islam. Jerusalem was the site of the Temple for the ancient Jews; the place where Jesus died; and the city from which the prophet Mohammed is believed to have ascended into heaven.

2. ESTABLISHING A PURPOSE. Go over the headnote in class. Then have students read the poem to see what kind of battle Blake is describing.

SUPPLEMENTARY SUPPORT MATERIALS

1. Vocabulary Activity Worksheet (CCB)
2. Review and Response Worksheet: Symbolism (CCB)
3. Selection Test (CCB)

DEVELOPING VOCABULARY

The following word from the poem is tested in the Selection Test. (See also Vocabulary Activity Worksheet.)
countenance

CLOSURE

Have students explain what the speaker means by "mental fight."

A. Expansion
This is the hymn sung in the movie Chariots of Fire, which takes its title from line 12. It is also sung by the Borstal boys in the movie of Alan Sillitoe's Loneliness of the Long Distance Runner.

B. Imagery
Identify the pastoral images that contrast with the "dark Satanic mills." (Lines 2, 4, 16)

A Although Blake originally published this poem as part of the preface to his epic poem *Milton,* it has since been set to music and become a popular English hymn. The poem is Blake at his most prophetic—the voice of that highest state of consciousness he called "Organized Innocence." The first two stanzas refer to an ancient legend that Jesus Christ visited England during his lifetime. But here Blake uses the figure of Christ symbolically (as he does in many of his other writings).

The figure of Christ stands for poetic inspiration, an external force that Blake believed could transform human society into a kind of heaven on earth he called "Jerusalem." The "dark Satanic mills" (line 8) represent not only the actual mills of the Industrial Revolution, but also more broadly the mechanistic, scientific, and rational world view that Blake and the other Romantics opposed.

Jerusalem

And did those feet in ancient time
    Walk upon England's mountains green?
And was the holy Lamb of God
    On England's pleasant pastures seen?

5 And did the countenance divine
    Shine forth upon our clouded hills?
And was Jerusalem builded here
B   Among these dark Satanic mills?

10 Bring me my bow of burning gold!
    Bring me my arrows of desire!
Bring me my spear! O clouds, unfold!
    Bring me my chariot of fire!

I will not cease from mental fight,
    Nor shall my sword sleep in my hand,
15 Till we have built Jerusalem
    In England's green and pleasant land.

Responding to the Poem

Analyzing the Poem

Identifying Details

1. What ancient legend does the speaker recall in the first two stanzas?
2. What does the speaker call for in the third stanza?
3. According to the last stanza, what is the speaker resolved to do?

Interpreting Meanings

4. What is the **tone** of the third stanza? In line 13, how does Blake clarify the kind of battle he is talking about here?
5. What do you think Jerusalem **symbolizes** in the poem?
6. How would you describe the speaker's attitude toward the present state of society? How would you compare this attitude to the attitudes of the narrators of the

Songs of Innocence and to those of the *Songs of Experience?*
7. What is there about the poem, in your view, that makes it especially suitable to an adaptation as a hymn?

Writing About the Poem

A Critical Response

Comparing Visions. In the following passage from the Book of Revelation in the Bible, John describes his vision of a "new heaven and a new earth." In a paragraph, compare the **diction** and **imagery** used by Blake in "Jerusalem" with the diction and imagery in John's passage from the Bible. Can you propose a reason why the city of Jerusalem, of all the cities in the world, was chosen by each writer as a symbol?

ANALYZING THE POEM
Identifying Details
1. That Jesus visited England.
2. For a bow, arrows, spear, and chariot.
3. To build a new Jerusalem or holy land in England.

Interpreting Meanings
4. The tone is passionate, emphatic, and imperative.

He makes specific reference to a mental or imaginative battle.
5. Jerusalem could symbolize redemption or heaven reestablished on earth.
6. The speaker sees society as fallen from innocence but proclaims a will to alter the state of affairs.

In *Innocence* and *Experience,* the speakers either accept their condition and/or ironically comment on it.

7. It is a rhymed, metrically regular lyric and adaptable to music and song. It also contains elements of a hymn: religious fervor and a call to righteousness.

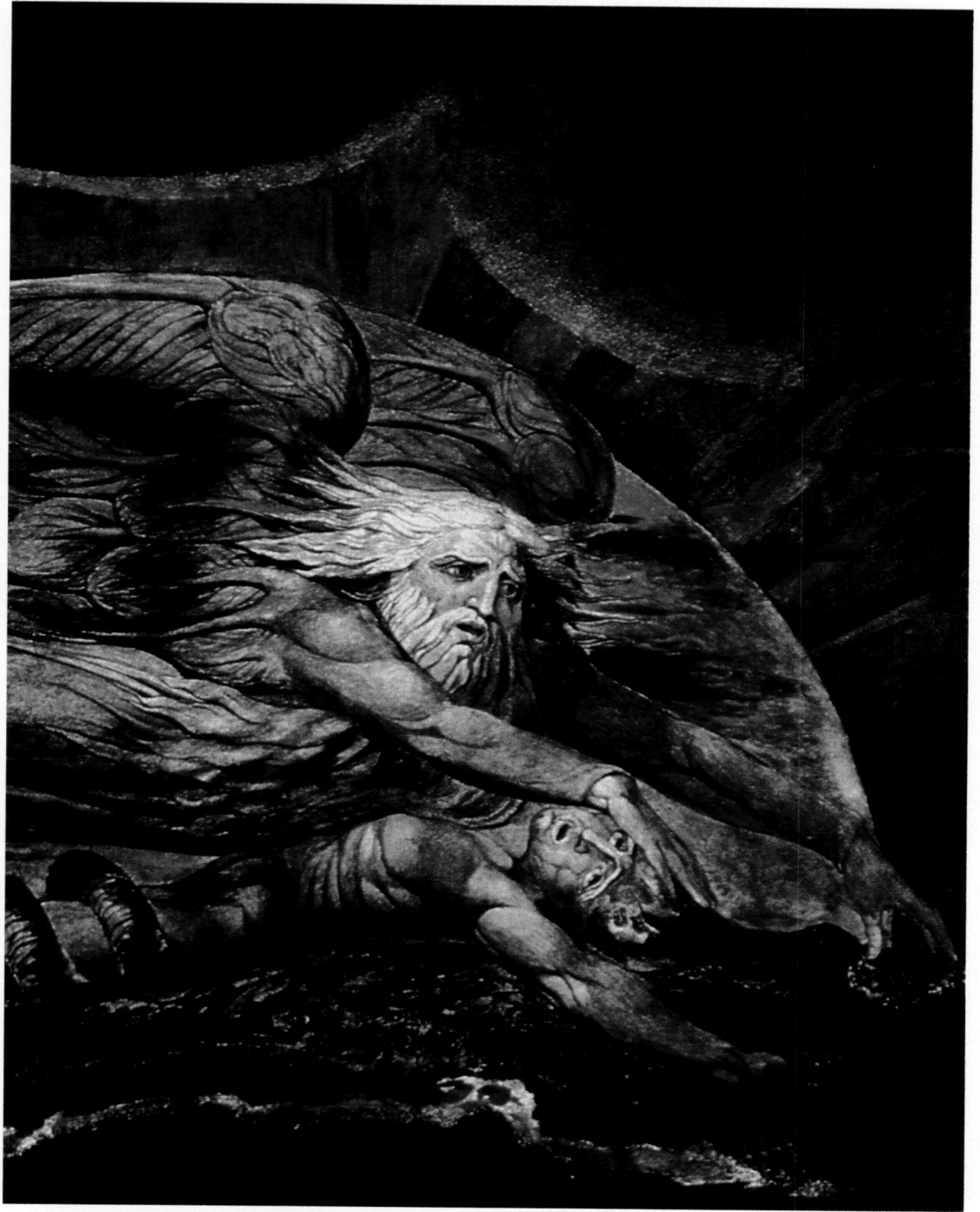

Elohim Creating Adam by William Blake (1795). Color-printed monotype.

A

A. Humanities Connection: Discussing the Fine Art
Elohim (e·lō′him) is the Hebrew word for God. This illustration is a detail from a large monoprint, one of a series of twelve that Blake did in about 1795. In the full-size print, a snake is wound around Adam's left leg. God has a magnificent pair of wings, behind which are green clouds with a red and blue finlike design. Note the mud that appears to engulf Adam. You might compare this dynamic Elohim with Michelangelo's God the creator on text page 167.

❓ What do you think the serpent is here for? (It might represent the tempter; it might show the demon's pull on Adam; it might foreshadow Adam's fall.)

Comment from the Poet

In August 1799 Blake wrote to a clergyman who had criticized his visionary art:

"... I know that this world is a world of imagination and vision. I see everything I paint in this world, but everybody does not see alike. To the eyes of a miser, a guinea is more beautiful than the sun, and a bag worn with the use of money has more beautiful proportions than a vine filled with grapes. The tree which moves some to tears of joy is in the eyes of others only a green thing that stands in the way."

A. Expansion
Snowden is a mountain in Wales. The contemporary Argentine writer Jorge Luis Borges imagined the last Anglo-Saxon to have survived in Britain (see text page 58).

B. Connections
Blake's Canterbury Pilgrims referred to here are reproduced on text pages 86–87.

> And I saw a new heaven and a new earth: for the first heaven and the first earth were passed away; and there was no more sea.
> And I John saw the holy city, new Jerusalem, coming down from God out of heaven, prepared as a bride adorned for her husband.
> And I heard a great voice out of heaven saying, Behold, the tabernacle of God is with men, and he will dwell with them, and they shall be his people, and God himself shall be with them, and be their God.
> And God shall wipe away all tears from their eyes; and there shall be no more death, neither sorrow, nor crying, neither shall there be any more pain: for the former things are passed away.
> —Revelation 21: 1–4

For example, much of "The Tyger" consists of questions that start with the word *what*. Sometimes the questions occupy one or two full verses; occasionally, Blake varies them so that one verse is split into two questions.

1. What examples of parallelism can you find in "The Lamb"?
2. How does Blake use parallelism in a narrative poem like "The Chimney Sweeper (*Innocence*)"?
3. Identify at least two examples of parallelism in "London."
4. How does Blake use a series of questions and commands to create parallelism in "Jerusalem"? What is the emotional effect of this series of questions and then of commands?

Analyzing Language and Style

Parallelism

When words are arranged in balanced, similar structures, they are said to be parallel. Blake was especially fond of parallelism, and the use of this device contributes to the childlike simplicity on the surface of his poems.

Primary Sources
"Blake is a real name . . ."

To Bernard Barton

"Blake is a real name, I assure you, and a most extraordinary man, if he be still living. He is the Robert [William] Blake, whose wild designs accompany a splendid folio edition of the 'Night Thoughts,' which you may have seen, in one of which he pictures the parting of soul and body by a solid mass of human form floating off, God knows how, from a lumpish mass (facsimile to itself) left behind on the dying bed. He paints in water colors marvelous strange pictures, visions of his brain, which he asserts that he has seen. They have great merit. He has seen the old Welsh bards on Snowden—he has seen the beautifulest, the strongest, and the ugliest man, left alone from the massacre of the Britons by the Romans, and has painted them from memory (I have seen his paintings), and asserts them to be as good as the figures of Raphael and Angelo, but not better, as they had precisely the same retro-visions and prophetic visions with himself. The painters in oil (which he will have it that neither of them practiced) he affirms to have been the ruin of art, and affirms that all the while he was engaged in his water paintings, Titian was disturbing him, Titian the III Genius of Oil Painting. His pictures—one in particular, the Canterbury Pilgrims (far above Stothard's)—have great merit, but hard, dry, yet with grace. He has written a catalogue of them with a most spirited criticism on Chaucer, but mystical and full of vision. His poems have been sold hitherto only in manuscript. I never read them; but a friend at my desire procured the 'Sweep Song.' There is one to a tiger, which I have heard recited, beginning:

Tiger, Tiger, burning bright,
Thro' the desarts of the night,

which is glorious, but, alas! I have not the book; for the man is flown, whither I know not—to Hades or a madhouse. But I must look on him as one of the most extraordinary persons of the age. . . ."

—Charles Lamb

William Wordsworth
(1770–1850)

> . . . so wide appears
> The vacancy between me and those days
> Which yet have such self-presence in my
> mind,
> That, musing on them, often do I seem
> Two consciousnesses, conscious of myself
> And of some other Being.
>
> —from *The Prelude*

Surveying Wordsworth's life can be like walking around a large statue, awed by its presence and puzzled by its apparent importance. Sometimes Wordsworth must have felt the same way.

Through his long poem on the "growth of a poet's mind," *The Prelude,* Wordsworth turned the first third of his life into a literary monument. He hit upon the exploration of his own experiences as a lasting poetic occupation in his mid-twenties, most likely during the period (1797–1798) when he was in almost daily contact with his friend Samuel Taylor Coleridge. During the following decade, he composed his great poem and wrote most of his best poetry, including all of the selections here. Sometime after 1805, his poetic powers began to decline. His greatness as a poet was in his fascination with the complexity and wonder of experience itself and it gave his best work freshness and energy. There is a note of resignation in his work after his beloved brother John died at sea in 1805. But the gradual decline in the quality of his poetry was probably the result of losing, by simply outgrowing it, the sheer delight in

> . . . the mighty world
> Of eye, and ear—both what they half create,
> And what perceive . . .

As Wordsworth thought about his early life and recreated it in *The Prelude,* he understandably felt a strange duality, as if he were "two consciousnesses"—one remembering, the other one remembered. To us, his life and work have a similar doubleness.

When Wordsworth's mother died in 1778, he and his three brothers were sent to Hawkshead to school. His sister Dorothy, aged seven, had to live with relatives. When their father died in

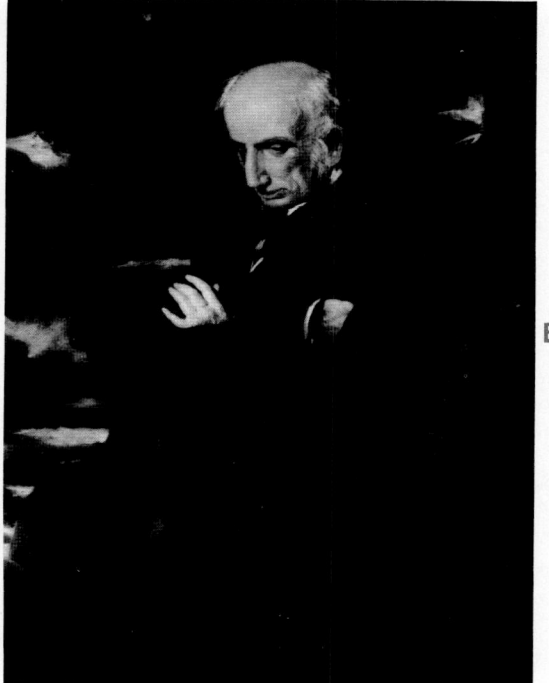

William Wordsworth by Benjamin Robert Haydon (1842). Oil.

1783, the children and their financial resources were placed under the guardianship of two uncles. William and Dorothy were not reunited until 1787, shortly before William left the Lake District for the first time to study at Cambridge. He managed to get a degree in 1791, but had little interest in the few careers open to him—the main one being the church—as an educated young man with no title, wealth, or head for business. He'd taken a walking tour on the Continent before his last year at university, so in late 1791 he returned to France to learn the language and, as it turned out, the "bliss" of being young in that time of birth and rebirth known as the French Revolution. This was the beginning of ten years of painful growth, as he searched for and eventually found his vocation as a poet.

By the time Wordsworth was in his forties, his life was centered on his family; his duties as a minor government official in the Lake District, where he settled for good in 1800; and his unflagging diligence as a poet. As his writing lost its energy and his political opinions grew more

A. **Connections**
See the biography of Dorothy Wordsworth on text page 748.

B. **Humanities Connection: Discussing the Fine Art**
Benjamin Robert Haydon (1786–1846) was the first artist to sketch the Elgin Marbles (classical Greek friezes taken from the Acropolis by Lord Elgin and transported to London in the early 1800's). Haydon urged that the government buy them from Greece. (There is still controversy over these marbles; they remain in the British Museum.) Imprisoned on four occasions for excessive debt, Haydon was forced to do genre paintings instead of the historical and religious paintings he preferred. **?** From this painting, what impression do you get of Wordsworth's personality? (Serious, brooding, withdrawn)

Critical Comment
The reception of *Lyrical Ballads* was
lukewarm at best. In 1799, the Reverend
Charles Burney said "Tintern Abbey" was
". . . poetical, beautiful, and philosophical: but somewhat tinctured with gloomy,
narrow, and unsociable ideas of seclusion from the commerce of the world: as
if men were born to live in woods and
wilds, unconnected with each other."

Comment from the Poet
Regarding the reception of *Lyrical Ballads,* Wordsworth consoled himself by
accusing the reading public:
   "It is an awful truth, that there neither
is, nor can be, any genuine enjoyment of
poetry among nineteen out of twenty of
those persons who live, or wish to live, in
the broad light of the world—among
those who either are, or are striving to

make themselves, people of consideration in society. This is a truth, and an
awful one, because to be incapable of a
feeling of poetry, in my sense of the
word, is to be without love of human nature and reverence for God."

A. Connections
This is the trip that
Wordsworth refers
to in the first few
lines of "Tintern
Abbey" (see text
page 633).

B. Connections
See Coleridge's
touching account
of his addiction on
text page 677.

C. Expansion
Wordsworth comes
back to this idea
frequently in
poems (see "Tin-
tern Abbey," lines
143–159; and "I
Wandered Lonely
as a Cloud," text
page 643, lines
19–24).

conservative, he became a sort of literary monument. His last and largest poetical work published in his lifetime was *The Excursion* (1814).

By the Victorian era, Wordsworth was the
Poet Laureate (1843), a cartoon image of an old
gentleman delighting in daffodils and butterflies
while wandering about the Lake District. This
ideal image of "the poet" was preserved from
contradiction by the family's suppression of the
fact that he had fathered a child in France in
1792 to a young woman he never married.

The truth seems to be that Wordsworth's life
was double. His early years (until his thirties)
were erratic and difficult; his later life, uneventful. When he returned from France in 1793, he
was sickened by the war between France and
England and gradually became deeply disillusioned about his hopes for change. Late that
year he went on a long walking tour which included his first visit to the Wye River valley in
southern Wales. The experience—and the collapse of his radical hope of perfecting society—
drove him back to poetry. Luckily, he was reunited with his sister Dorothy, who became a constant companion and inspiration.

In 1795, his fortunes began to change. He inherited some money from a friend, he and Dorothy took up residence in a rent-free house, and
Coleridge suddenly burst upon their lives. By
June 1797, when he and Dorothy moved to a
comfortable country house four miles from the
village where Coleridge lived, Wordsworth had
produced a good deal of new poetry, none yet
published, including a play and some stark narratives. Coleridge and Wordsworth quickly became powerful influences on each other's work.
Coleridge had the gift of a wide-ranging, philosophic mind, and Wordsworth the talent and
steady diligence of a writer. *Lyrical Ballads* was
the fruit of their friendship and mutual influence.
Coleridge's *The Rime of the Ancient Mariner*
was his greatest effort to match, in his own way,
Wordsworth's creativity. "Tintern Abbey"
shows how crucial Coleridge's effect on Wordsworth would be. Although it was one of the
most wonderful literary collaborations we know
of, it could not survive the real differences
between the two men. Wordsworth's ability
eventually provoked Coleridge's envy, and
Wordsworth could not endure watching Coleridge squander his talents in indecision and drug
addiction.

The distinguishing quality of Wordsworth's
best lyric poetry comes from another sort of
duality. He found delight in the simple miracles
of perception and experience, and in the way the
mind and nature are "adapted" to each other.
He conveyed this delight in vivid, direct, and
seemingly immediate images and descriptions.
Yet most of his poems are in the past tense,
showing his reverence for the mind's power to
preserve and enrich what would otherwise be
passing sense experiences. In *The Prelude* and
elsewhere, Wordsworth revealed the power of
what he called "spots of time."

> In spots like these it is we prize
> Our memory, feel that she hath eyes.
> —from "To a Highland Girl"

The poet's ability to recreate these important
moments, no matter how uneventful they may
seem, assures us that nothing will be lost, and
that in every moment there is "life and fold /
For future years."

The poems on the following pages reflect the
"two consciousnesses" of Wordsworth's work.
The mature products of several years of searching and of his crucial collaboration with Coleridge, they are at the same time examples of
what is fundamental to the Romantic—the simple delight in the nature of experience itself and
the mind's instinctive capacity to shape everyday experience into something lasting and poetic. As such, they exemplify Wordsworth's
conception of poetry in the "Preface" to *Lyrical
Ballads*. Poetry, he wrote, is the "spontaneous
overflow of powerful feelings"; but, he added,
poems of lasting value are only produced by
someone who has "thought long and deeply."

[Poetry] takes its origin from emotion recollected in tranquillity: the emotion is contemplated till . . . the tranquillity gradually
disappears, and an emotion, kindred to that
which was before the subject of contemplation, is gradually produced, and does itself actually exist in the mind. In this mood
successful composition generally begins. . . .

Immediacy and contemplation, emotion and
tranquillity, spontaneity and composition. The
reconciliation of this doubleness, as Coleridge
recognized, made Wordsworth "the poet of the
age."

A. Aural Imagery
? What words suggest the sounds the speaker hears? (*Rolling, soft, murmur*—all describing a water sound)

B. Visual Imagery
? What images does Wordsworth use to "paint" the rural scene? (Dark sycamore, plots of cottage-ground, green orchard-tufts, hedgerows, green farms, wreaths of smoke)

"Tintern Abbey" (the ruined abbey mentioned only in the title) is one of the most important short lyric works in English literature. A major step forward in Wordsworth's writing and a definitive statement of some of the Romantics' ideas, it has inspired and guided many poets since. The ease with which Wordsworth wrote it is therefore even more astonishing.

In July 1798 Wordsworth and his sister Dorothy went on a vigorous walking tour in southern Wales. Shortly after leaving the Wye River valley, Wordsworth, by his account, began to compose this poem about revisiting the valley, concluding it "just as I was entering Bristol in the evening, after a ramble of four or five days. . . . Not a line of it was altered, and not any part of it written down till I reached Bristol. It was published almost immediately after."

Wordsworth had previously written two long descriptive poems and a few other descriptive lyrics, but nothing quite like this. He had been hard at work on a play and the narrative ballads that make up *Lyrical Ballads* when he went off on his tour. But he had learned something from two poems by Coleridge: the use of a flowing blank verse (later employed so grandly in *The Prelude*), and the easy maneuvering of the meditative poem.

The apparent ease of its composition hides the art of this poem, evident even in the title, which asks us to imagine that these lines were poured out at the time the speaker returned to the Wye valley after five years' absence. The many days of composition on the way back to Bristol were spent creating a poem in which we seem to hear the easy, immediate utterance of what is going on in the heart and mind of the speaker.

Lines Composed a Few Miles Above Tintern Abbey

On Revisiting the Banks of the Wye During a Tour, July 13, 1798

Five years have past; five summers, with the length
Of five long winters! and again I hear
These waters, rolling from their mountain springs
With a soft inland murmur. Once again
5 Do I behold these steep and lofty cliffs,
That on a wild secluded scene impress
Thoughts of more deep seclusion; and connect
The landscape with the quiet of the sky.
The day is come when I again repose
10 Here, under this dark sycamore, and view
These plots of cottage-ground, these orchard-tufts,
Which at this season, with their unripe fruits,
Are clad in one green hue, and lose themselves
'Mid groves and copses.° Once again I see
15 These hedgerows,° hardly hedgerows, little lines
Of sportive wood run wild: these pastoral farms,
Green to the very door; and wreaths of smoke
Sent up, in silence, from among the trees!
With some uncertain notice, as might seem
20 Of vagrant dwellers in the houseless woods,
Or of some Hermit's cave, where by his fire
The Hermit sits alone.

14. **copses:** areas densely covered with shrubs and small trees.
15. **hedgerows:** rows of bushes, shrubs and small trees that in England serve as fences.

A. About the Photograph

Tintern Abbey was founded in 1131 for Cistercian monks from France. The photograph shows the ruins of its church, which was once noted for its graceful lines and proportions. King Henry VIII dissolved Tintern Abbey and other Roman Catholic monasteries in 1537. The abbey disappeared completely; the ruined church was bought by the British government in 1900.

B. Meditative Lyric

Wordsworth's thought shifts to the role the landscape has played in his life during the past five years.

C. Simile

Note that the powerful simile is used as a negative comparison.

? Why is the scene *not* like a landscape to a blind man? (Unlike a blind man, the speaker has seen the landscape in vivid detail and can re-create it in his memory.)

D. Meaning

Lines 35–49 describe the sublime transcendental feeling Wordsworth finds in nature.

The ruins of Tintern Abbey in Monmouthshire, Wales.

B   These beauteous forms,
     Through a long absence, have not been to me
C   As is a landscape to a blind man's eye:
25   But oft, in lonely rooms, and 'mid the din
     Of towns and cities, I have owed to them
     In hours of weariness, sensations sweet,
     Felt in the blood, and felt along the heart;
     And passing even into my purer mind,
30   With tranquil restoration: feelings too
     Of unremembered pleasure: such, perhaps,
     As have no slight or trivial influence
     On that best portion of a good man's life,
     His little, nameless, unremembered acts
35   Of kindness and of love. Nor less, I trust,
     To them I may have owed another gift,
     Of aspect more sublime; that blessed mood
     In which the burden of the mystery,
     In which the heavy and the weary weight
40   Of all this unintelligible world,
D   Is lightened: that serene and blessed mood,
     In which the affections° gently lead us on,
     Until, the breath of this corporeal° frame
     And even the motion of our human blood
45   Almost suspended, we are laid asleep
     In body, and become a living soul:
     While with an eye made quiet by the power
     Of harmony, and the deep power of joy,
     We see into the life of things.

42. **affections:** feelings.
43. **corporeal:** bodily.

"I have not wanted to call this poem an ode," Wordsworth wrote, but he did hope that its "transitions" along with "the impassioned music of the versification" would make "Tintern Abbey" sound enough like an ode to take its place in the literature of praise and lofty sentiment.

The "transitions" to which Wordsworth refers are the divisions into which the poem falls. Lines 1–22 recapitulate the remembered scene. Lines 22–65 confirm the role of the landscape in Wordsworth's life during the preceding five years. Lines 65–83 invoke the days when, as a boy, he participated in nature without thinking about it. Lines 83–114 indicate Wordsworth's awareness of the play of mind and "Of eye, and ear" that can "half create" what they respond to. Lines 115–159 are addressed to his sister Dorothy, who, he hopes, will eventually share the exalted sense of nature to which his meditation is a testament.

                                        If this
50   Be but a vain belief, yet, oh! how oft—
      In darkness and amid the many shapes
      Of joyless daylight; when the fretful stir
      Unprofitable, and the fever of the world,
      Have hung upon the beatings of my heart—
55   How oft, in spirit, have I turned to thee,
      O sylvan° Wye! thou wanderer thro' the woods,
      How often has my spirit turned to thee!

         And now, with gleams of half-extinguished thought,
      With many recognitions dim and faint,
60   And somewhat of a sad perplexity,
      The picture of the mind° revives again:
      While here I stand, not only with the sense
      Of present pleasure, but with pleasing thoughts
      That in this moment there is life and food
65   For future years. And so I dare to hope,
      Though changed, no doubt, from what I was when first
      I came among these hills; when like a roe°
      I bounded o'er the mountains, by the sides
      Of the deep rivers, and the lonely streams,
70   Wherever nature led: more like a man
      Flying from something that he dreads than one
      Who sought the thing he loved. For nature then
      (The coarser pleasures of my boyish days,
      And their glad animal movements all gone by)
75   To me was all in all. I cannot paint
      What then I was. The sounding cataract°
      Haunted me like a passion: the tall rock,
      The mountain, and the deep and gloomy wood,
      Their colors and their forms, were then to me
80   An appetite; a feeling and a love,
      That had no need of a remoter charm,
      By thought supplied, nor any interest
      Unborrowed from the eye. That time is past,
      And all its aching joys are now no more,
85   And all its dizzy raptures. Not for this
      Faint° I, nor mourn nor murmur; other gifts
      Have followed; for such loss, I would believe,
      Abundant recompense. For I have learned
      To look on nature, not as in the hour
90   Of thoughtless youth; but hearing oftentimes
      The still, sad music of humanity,
      Nor harsh nor grating, though of ample power
      To chasten and subdue. And I have felt
      A presence that disturbs me with the joy
95   Of elevated thoughts; a sense sublime
      Of something far more deeply interfused,
      Whose dwelling is the light of setting suns,
      And the round ocean and the living air,
      And the blue sky, and in the mind of man:

56. sylvan: associated with the forest or woodlands.

61. picture of the mind: primarily the picture in the mind, but also the picture the individual mind has of itself.

67. roe: deer.

76. cataract: waterfall.

86. Faint: become faint, lose heart.

<!-- side notes -->

A. Interpreting
Note how Wordsworth evokes the past, present, and future.

B. Simile
Identify the two similes in lines 67–72. (Wordsworth compares himself to a roe; he compares himself to a man flying from something he dreads.)

C. A Famous Line
Note how Wordsworth says his attitude toward nature has changed. This famous phrase is often quoted.

D. Interpreting
What is the "sense sublime" Wordsworth refers to in this passage? (Students should recall lines 37–49.)

Have three students summarize (1) the
role nature plays in this poem, (2) the
changes that have taken place in the
poet since his first visit, and (3) the main
idea of the poem.

ANALYZING THE POEM
Identifying Details

1. He hears the murmur of springs and
sees the steep cliffs, quiet sky, sycamore
tree, orchard thickets, and hedgerows
that mark the boundaries of small farms.

2. Unlike a blind man, the speaker has
seen the landscape firsthand and has
been able to experience it emotionally
and reorganize it through memory.

3. He has lost the purity and innocence
of his youth. He is older and responds to
nature meditatively rather than spontaneously.

4. He sees the passion of the "shooting
lights / Of thy wild eyes" (lines 118–
119)—her spontaneous joy of nature.

5. The meter is unrhymed iambic pentameter, or blank verse. Instances of run-on lines are numerous: e.g., lines 3, 9,

A. Vocabulary
Sense refers to
"the senses."
Identify the
metaphors in
lines 109–111.
(Nature is identi-
fied with an an-
chor, nurse, guide,
guardian, and
soul.)

B. Interpreting
Why does Dor-
othy remind
Wordsworth of his
former self? (She
is seeing the
scene for the first
time with great joy
and "wild eyes."
Wordsworth has
already let "these
wild ecstasies . . .
be matured into a
sober pleasure,"
lines 138–139.)

100 A motion and a spirit, that impels
   All thinking things, all objects of all thought,
   And rolls through all things. Therefore am I still
   A lover of the meadows and the woods,
   And mountains; and of all that we behold
105 From this green earth; of all the mighty world
   Of eye, and ear—both what they half create,
   And what perceive; well pleased to recognize
   In nature and the language of the sense
   The anchor of my purest thought, the nurse,
110 The guide, the guardian of my heart, and soul
   Of all my moral being.
           Nor perchance,
   If I were not thus taught, should I the more
   Suffer my genial° spirits to decay:
   For thou art with me here upon the banks
115 Of this fair river; thou my dearest Friend,°
   My dear, dear Friend; and in thy voice I catch
   The language of my former heart, and read
   My former pleasures in the shooting lights
   Of thy wild eyes. Oh! yet a little while
120 May I behold in thee what I was once,
   My dear, dear Sister! and this prayer I make,
   Knowing that Nature never did betray
   The heart that loved her; 'tis her privilege,
   Through all the years of this our life, to lead
125 From joy to joy: for she can so inform
   The mind that is within us, so impress
   With quietness and beauty, and so feed
   With lofty thoughts, that neither evil tongues,
   Rash judgments, nor the sneers of selfish men,
130 Nor greetings where no kindness is, nor all
   The dreary intercourse° of daily life,
   Shall e'er prevail against us, or disturb
   Our cheerful faith, that all which we behold
   Is full of blessings. Therefore let the moon
135 Shine on thee in thy solitary walk;
   And let the misty mountain winds be free
   To blow against thee: and, in after years,
   When these wild ecstasies shall be matured
   Into a sober pleasure; when thy mind
140 Shall be a mansion for all lovely forms,
   Thy memory be as a dwelling place
   For all sweet sounds and harmonies; oh! then,
   If solitude, or fear, or pain, or grief,
   Should be thy portion, with what healing thoughts
145 Of tender joy wilt thou remember me,
   And these my exhortations!° Nor, perchance—
   If I should be where I no more can hear
   Thy voice, nor catch from thy wild eyes these gleams
   Of past existence—wilt thou then forget
150 That on the banks of this delightful stream

113. **genial:** creative.

115. **my dearest Friend:** Wordsworth's
sister Dorothy.

131. **intercourse:** dealings, social contacts.

146. **exhortations:** strong recommendations.

Interpreting Meanings

6. The reference is to the mystery of an "unintelligible world."

It seems evident that Keats shared this idea.

7. The gifts are the gifts of understanding and maturity. He continues to perceive nature with joy, but not with the rapture of the past. Nature is seen as a moral guide.

The themes of loss and gain are of prime importance.

8. The speaker's sister is used as a window into his own past.

Her role as an intermediary between the speaker and nature is a contrivance. The figures in Coleridge's poem seem less contrived, since their presence, or absence, inspired the poem.

9. The speaker expresses his love of nature and says that what is taken in through the senses is half-created by imagination (lines 106–107). He comments on his sister's innocent reaction to nature and on nature's guarding and healing effect. He asks his sister to remember him and his love of nature when she is alone, in fear, in pain.

We stood together; and that I, so long
A worshiper of Nature, hither came
Unwearied in that service: rather say
With warmer love—oh, with far deeper zeal
155   Of holier love. Nor wilt thou then forget,
That after many wanderings, many years
Of absence, these steep woods and lofty cliffs,
And this green pastoral landscape, were to me
More dear, both for themselves and for thy sake!

Responding to the Poem

Analyzing the Poem

Identifying Details

1. Briefly sketch what the speaker hears and sees as he beholds "once again" the scene in the first verse paragraph (lines 1–22).
2. Why are these "beauteous forms" not, for the speaker, "As is a landscape to a blind man's eye" (line 24)?
3. What has the speaker lost since he first "came among these hills" (line 67)?
4. What does the speaker see in his "dear Sister" that makes him more aware of what he "was once" (line 120)?
5. Describe the **meter** of the poem. Pick out at least four instances of **run-on lines** that keep the poem from sounding mechanical and sing-song.

Interpreting Meanings

6. What do you think is meant by "the burden of the mystery" (line 38)? Do you think Keats understood this phrase in the same way? (See Keats's poems beginning on page 709.)
7. What "gifts" (line 86) and "abundant recompense" (line 88) does the speaker believe he has received for his "loss" (line 87)? How important is the **theme** of loss and gain in this poem?
8. What role does the speaker's sister play in the poem? Compare this role with that of the silent figures in Coleridge's "This Lime-Tree Bower My Prison" (page 652). Does Dorothy's presence here seem more or less contrived than the presence of the silent figures in Coleridge's poem?
9. Summarize and comment on the significance of the speaker's conclusion, beginning with line 102. Have you ever been in a situation where you felt you wanted to have some reassurance and recompense for the sense of losing part of your past?

Writing About the Poem

A Creative Response

1. **Describing a Scene.** Write a description of a scene from nature that prompts a strong emotional response in you. Be sure to include vivid sensory details.

A Critical Response

2. **Analyzing the Structure of a Poem.** In a brief essay, trace and comment on the progression of thought in "Tintern Abbey." Be sure to analyze the significance of the poem's division into verse paragraphs.

Analyzing Language and Style

Verse Paragraphs

Wordsworth's **blank verse** is best read in the long, rolling movements of his verse paragraphs, which mark the major transitions of thought.

In the first paragraph of "Tintern Abbey," the poet unifies the long clauses of the section by repeating the word *again* in lines 4, 9, and 14. The function of the paragraph is to establish the time interval between the speaker's visits to the Wye (five years) and to describe the scene. In the second paragraph, notice that Wordsworth makes his thought easier to follow by repeating a phrase ("blessed mood," lines 37 and 41).

1. Slowly and carefully reread aloud one of the verse paragraphs of "Tintern Abbey," observing the punctuation and the **run-on lines.** Then see if you can map out on a sheet of paper the major "movements" of the paragraph.
2. Write a few sentences stating whether or not you think that the verse paragraph you have chosen is unified by one main idea. If so, state the main idea.

PREPARATION

1. ESTABLISHING A PURPOSE. Have students read question 7 on text page 640 to set a purpose for reading.

2. PREREADING JOURNAL. Have students write two or three sentences in their journals describing their general responses to movies, television shows, plays, and novels that deal with death or loss.

SUPPLEMENTARY SUPPORT MATERIALS
1. Vocabulary Activity Worksheet (*CCB*)
2. Review and Response Worksheet: Imagery and Theme (*CCB*)
3. Selection Test (*CCB*)

DEVELOPING VOCABULARY
The following word from the poem is tested in the Selection Test. (See also Vocabulary Activity Worksheet.)
diurnal

A. Symbolism
? Trace the images of the horse's movement and the moon's movement. (As the horse nears the cottage, the moon drops lower.)

B. Mood
? What images create a peaceful, dreamy mood? (The sweet dream and the regular motion of the horse's hoofs) How is this mood suddenly shattered? (The moon drops, and the speaker thinks of Lucy's death.)

C. Responding
? How does this last line make you feel? Were you prepared for it, or did it surprise you? (Students might think of a time they were happy and afraid something might happen to spoil their happiness.)

These graceful and suggestive lyrics were written during Wordsworth's stay in Germany in 1799, and published together in the expanded 1800 *Lyrical Ballads*. The second of the three was called simply "Song," while the other two were not given titles. Together with two other poems, they are now called the "Lucy poems." From 1815 on, Wordsworth classified the first two as "Poems Founded on the Affections," while the last was grouped with "Poems of the Imagination."

As in other "literary mysteries" where we suspect that a hidden connection between the writer's life and his work will supply a clue, there has been much speculation about who "Lucy" was beyond the characteristics the poems give her.

When Coleridge read the third poem, he called it an "epitaph," which underscores the idea of death on which the speaker meditates in each poem. He also thought Wordsworth might have written the poem "in some gloomier moment," when he "fancied the moment when his sister might die." In reading these poems, it is much more important to focus on the workings of the speaker's imagination than it is to think about the identity of Lucy.

Strange Fits of Passion Have I Known

Strange fits of passion have I known:
And I will dare to tell,
But in the lover's ear alone,
What once to me befell.

5　When she I loved looked every day
Fresh as a rose in June,
I to her cottage bent my way,
Beneath an evening moon.

A　Upon the moon I fixed my eye,
10　All over the wide lea;°
With quickening pace my horse drew nigh
Those paths so dear to me.

And now we reached the orchard plot;
And, as we climbed the hill,
15　The sinking moon to Lucy's cot°
Came near, and nearer still.

B　In one of those sweet dreams I slept,
Kind Nature's gentlest boon!
And all the while my eyes I kept
20　On the descending moon.

My horse moved on; hoof after hoof
He raised, and never stopped:
When down behind the cottage roof,
At once, the bright moon dropped.

25　What fond° and wayward thoughts will slide
Into a lover's head!
"O mercy!" to myself I cried,
C　"If Lucy should be dead!"

10. **lea:** meadowland.

15. **cot:** cottage.

25. **fond:** foolish.

She Dwelt Among the Untrodden Ways

She dwelt among the untrodden ways
   Beside the springs of Dove,°
A maid whom there were none to praise
   And very few to love:

5   A violet by a mossy stone
   Half hidden from the eye!
  —Fair as a star, when only one
   Is shining in the sky.

She lived unknown, and few could know
10   When Lucy ceased to be;
But she is in her grave, and, oh,
   The difference to me!

2. **Dove:** an English river.

A. Metaphor/Simile
The violet metaphor suggests a shy, hidden beauty in a tiny almost unnotable aspect of nature. The star simile suggests a cosmic beauty and solitude. The difference between a violet and a sun is huge.

B. Speaker
We are unaware of the speaker until the last line, when Lucy's death suddenly becomes a deep personal loss.

C. Humanities Connection: Responding to the Fine Art
John Constable (1776–1837) was one of the two great English landscape painters of the period. (J. M. W. Turner was the other.) Constable, the son of a well-to-do miller, spent his life painting and sketching the landscape of the Stour Valley in Suffolk. Unlike English landscape painters before him, Constable introduced vivid color into his landscapes and tried to depict the interplay of light and shadow.

Salisbury, England by John Constable. Oil.

Victoria and Albert Museum, London.

CLOSURE
Have students describe the personal feelings Wordsworth expresses in the Lucy poems.

ANALYZING THE POEM
Identifying Details
1. Lovers (line 3), and hence perhaps everyone.
2. Lucy's death makes a difference in

the speaker's life.
3. She has died.

Interpreting Meanings
4. The moon's movement corresponds to or directs the speaker's mood. As the mood drops in the sky, the speaker gets closer and closer to Lucy's cottage. Its sinking triggers his fear of her disappearance/death.

5. He uses a metaphor (lines 5–6) and simile (line 7–8). Lucy's beauty is both hidden like the violet in a forest and unsurpassed like the single star.
6. The "human fears" are fears of mortality. His lack of such fear makes Lucy's death ironic.
7. Recurring themes are love, loss, and death. Recurring images are of night *(Answers continue in left-hand column.)*

(Continued from top.)
(moon and star); of flowers (rose and violet).
    The subject and themes link the poems into a unit.
8. In one poem, Lucy is specifically his lover.
    She lives alone, is not known, is little loved.
    The speaker loves Lucy. That fact alone is enough to justify his concern.
9. The poems offer no consolation, unless Lucy's escape from the "touch of earthly years" and her absorption as part of the natural cycle is a comfort.
    The speaker shares his feelings, perhaps to ease his pain.

A Slumber Did My Spirit Seal

A slumber did my spirit seal;
    I had no human fears:
She seemed a thing that could not feel
    The touch of earthly years.

5   No motion has she now, no force;
    She neither hears nor sees;
Rolled round in earth's <u>diurnal°</u> course,
    With rocks, and stones, and trees.

7. **diurnal:** daily.

Responding to the Poems

Analyzing the Poems

Identifying Details
1. Who is the intended **audience** of "Strange Fits of Passion Have I Known"?
2. What does "difference" in the last line of "She Dwelt Among the Untrodden Ways" refer to?
3. What has happened to the woman in "A Slumber Did My Spirit Seal"?

Interpreting Meanings
4. Explain the role of the moon in "Strange Fits of Passion Have I Known."
5. What two contrasting **figures of speech** does the speaker use to characterize Lucy in the second poem? How could one person be both of these very different things?
6. Why does the speaker of "A Slumber Did My Spirit Seal" specify that the "fears" he refers to are "human"?
7. What connections among **themes** and recurring **images** do you note in these three poems? Do you think the poems should be read together as a unit? Why?

8. Why is "Lucy" special to the speaker? How much do we learn about her in the poems? Is this information enough on its own to justify the speaker's concern for her?
9. Do the poems offer any consolation for the sadness they explore? Why do you think the speaker has said what he has?

Writing About the Poems

A Creative Response
1. **Using Another Point of View.** Write a response to the speaker from Lucy's first-person point of view.

A Critical Response
2. **Analyzing Romantic Themes.** In a brief essay, identify the themes and images of Wordsworth's "Lucy poems" that you would classify as typically Romantic. Be sure to explain your reasons.

ESTABLISHING A PURPOSE. Ask students to read the poem to discover why Wordsworth addresses Milton in the opening lines.

SUPPLEMENTARY SUPPORT MATERIALS
1. Vocabulary Activity Worksheet (CCB)
2. Review and Response Worksheet: Metaphor and Simile (CCB)
3. Selection Test (CCB)

DEVELOPING VOCABULARY
The following words from the poem are tested in the Selection Test. (See also Vocabulary Activity Worksheet.)
stagnant   to forfeit

CLOSURE
Have students explain why Wordsworth chose to address Milton in this poem.

During a brief peace in the Napoleonic Wars (1801–1803), English travelers were able to go to France. Wordsworth made a trip across the channel to Calais where he was reunited with Annette Vallon and their child, Caroline, whom he had not seen for nearly ten years. The meeting helped Wordsworth make peace with the past. This was necessary before he could go forward with his marriage to Mary Hutchison, a childhood friend from the Lake District, in October 1802.

On his return to England, Wordsworth was struck with the "vanity and parade of our own country . . . as contrasted with . . . the desolation that the Revolution had produced in France." This sonnet does not directly attack the English smugness and materialism of the time. Rather, as an address to the poet John Milton—a great spokesman in his time—it shows the need for a new and powerful poetic "voice" in Wordsworth's own time to correct these weaknesses.

London, 1802

Milton! thou shouldst be living at this hour:
England hath need of thee: she is a fen°
Of stagnant waters: altar, sword, and pen,
Fireside, the heroic wealth of hall and bower,°
5   Have forfeited their ancient English dower°
Of inward happiness. We are selfish men;
Oh! raise us up, return to us again;
And give us manners, virtue, freedom, power.
Thy soul was like a star, and dwelt apart;
10   Thou hadst a voice whose sound was like the sea:
Pure as the naked heavens, majestic, free,
So didst thou travel on life's common way,
In cheerful godliness; and yet thy heart
The lowliest duties on herself did lay.

2. fen: marsh.

4. bower: cottage, rural dwelling.

5. dower: endowment.

[Handwritten annotations: Wishing Milton alive / England is unhappy / apostrophe / stagnant, not as powerful as before / simile / You, Milton, were pure + majestic. Travelled life's journey cheerfully. Milton was heroic for having pure qualities. England needs a poetic voice like Milton's again / Milton description]

ANALYZING THE POEM
Identifying Details
1. John Milton.
2. England needs someone to restore its manners, virtue, freedom, and power.
   England is a stagnant swamp (lines 2–3).
3. To return from death and help restore England's manners, virtue, freedom, strength.
4. His soul was like a star; his voice like the sea; he was pure, cheerful, godly, humble.

Interpreting Meanings
5. Deep, resounding, inspiring, powerful.
6. Altar is religion; sword is the military; pen is writers; fireside is commoners; hall and bower are the aristocracy. These are excellent examples of *metonymy*.
7. The line could refer to Milton's humility, especially in regard to his blindness.

Responding to the Poem

Analyzing the Poem

Identifying Details

1. To whom is the poem addressed?
2. According to lines 2–6, why does England need Milton now? What striking **metaphor** characterizes the country?
3. What does the speaker ask Milton to do?
4. According to the speaker, what kind of man was Milton?

Interpreting Meanings

5. What would a "voice . . . like the sea" (line 10) sound like?
6. What does each of the following objects in lines 3–4

symbolize: "altar, sword, and pen, / Fireside, [and] the heroic wealth of hall and bower"?
7. What do you think the "lowliest duties" are in the last line?

Writing About the Poem

A Creative Response

Writing an Apostrophe. The first two lines of this sonnet have frequently been imitated. Write a poem or prose paragraph of your own that is an apostrophe, or address to someone not present. Open with Wordsworth's first lines, but substitute another person's name for Milton, and another place for England. Whom would you want to call back to correct the problems you see today?

SUPPLEMENTARY SUPPORT MATERIALS
1. Review and Response Worksheet: Visual Imagery (*CCB*)
2. Selection Test (*CCB*)

A. Humanities Connection: Discussing the Fine Art

In 1802 Constable became the first painter to do quick oil sketches outdoors; before then, artists painted landscapes in their studios. In 1821–1822, Constable painted a series of cloud studies after reading scientific papers on cloud formations.

? Compare the sky shown here with that in the painting on page 639. How are the skies different? (The brush strokes are different; here they are more prominent and interesting. The colors are different; here they are more vibrant.)

Written in 1804, first published in 1807 without a title, and later grouped with other "Poems of the Imagination," this poem is one of Wordsworth's best known. Its main appeal undoubtedly rests on its vivid imagery. Its final stanza celebrates the powers of memory to turn fleeting experiences into "spots of time," as in "Tintern Abbey" and "The Solitary Reaper." See also Dorothy Wordsworth's fine description of this scene—a different sort of interiorization—in her journal for April 1802, later in this unit.

I Wandered Lonely as a Cloud

A

Study of Sky and Trees by John Constable. Victoria and Albert Museum, London.

CLOSURE

Have a student explain to the class what Wordsworth means by "that inward eye."

A. Figure of Speech

? What makes this figure of speech so effective? (The speaker compares his motion and mood to two aspects of a solitary cloud: its slow, wandering motion and its isolation in the huge blue sky.)

A ☐ I wandered lonely as a cloud
That floats on high o'er vales° and hills,
When all at once I saw a crowd,
A host,° of golden daffodils;
5   Beside the lake, beneath the trees,
Fluttering and dancing in the breeze.

Continuous as the stars that shine
And twinkle on the milky way,
They stretched in never-ending line
10   Along the margin of a bay:
Ten thousand saw I at a glance,
Tossing their heads in sprightly dance.

The waves beside them danced; but they
Outdid the sparkling waves in glee:
15   A poet could not but be gay,
In such a jocund° company:
I gazed—and gazed—but little thought
What wealth the show to me had brought:

For oft, when on my couch I lie
20   In vacant or in pensive mood,
They flash upon that inward eye
Which is the bliss of solitude;
And then my heart with pleasure fills,
And dances with the daffodils.

2. **vales:** wide valleys.
4. **host:** multitude.

16. **jocund:** cheerful, merry.

ANALYZING THE POEM
Identifying Details
1. Lonely, sad.
2. To the stars of the Milky Way; *dance*
3. How valuable the experience will be as a memory.
4. Memory can transform the present.

Interpreting Meanings
5. "Vacant," "pensive mood," "solitude." It suggests a solitariness or isolation.
6. *Dance.* Dance suggests a triumph over the pull of earth.
7. Memory and imagination. It transforms solitude into joy.
8. Try ear; voice; door; computer.

Responding to the Poem

Analyzing the Poem

Identifying Details

1. Describe the speaker's **mood** in the first stanza.
2. What does the speaker compare the daffodils to in the second stanza? What word in this stanza **personifies** the flowers?
3. What does the speaker *not* realize at the end of the third stanza?
4. How does the speaker describe the effect of memory in the last stanza?

Interpreting Meanings

5. What details in the last stanza echo the word "lonely" in line 1? What might this echo suggest about the speaker's personality?
6. What word is repeated in each stanza? What could be the significance of this repetition?
7. What do you think the speaker means by the "inward eye"? (line 21) Why can the inward eye be called "the bliss of solitude"?
8. Would you describe that faculty known as "the inward eye" as an *eye,* or as something else?

Writing About the Poem

A Creative Response

1. **Creating a Simile.** See if you can create five similes based on the famous simile that opens this poem. Wordsworth quite naturally drew his figures of speech from nature. Other poets draw theirs from the scenes they know well. American poet Phyllis McGinley, for example, once said *she* wandered lonely as a fareless cabby.

A Critical Response

2. **Comparing Poems.** In a brief essay, compare the experience described in this poem with the case made for the importance of memory in "Tintern Abbey."
3. **Evaluating a Metaphor.** In a paragraph, explain in what sense a cloud might be lonely.

SUPPLEMENTARY SUPPORT MATERIALS
1. Review and Response Worksheet:
Sound Effects and Mood (CCB)
2. Selection Test (CCB)
3. Instructional Overhead Transparency

Critical Comment
American poet Mark Van Doren said:
"He [Wordsworth] had lived in London
once, and had rejected it as ugly and untrue. Yet here it was, a great, calm, almost holy thing, a breathing creature with
its eyes closed, as patient and wise as
any landscape he had been worshipping
in his northern retreat."

A. Form
Identify the type of sonnet and its
rhyme scheme. (Italian; *abba abba
cdc dcd*)

CLOSURE
Have students summarize Wordsworth's
feelings about the city of London.

ANALYZING THE POEM
Identifying Details
1. Ships, towers,
domes, theaters,
temples, smoke-
less air, river,
silence.
2. The city wears
beauty "like a gar-
ment"; the houses
sleep; its heart is
still.

Interpreting Meanings
3. Deeply moved.
4. A heart cannot
be still and alive.
5. The city's maj-
esty, beauty, and
calm.

Additional Writing Assignment
Compare the son-
net to Dorothy
Wordsworth's jour-
nal entry for July
30, 1802:
    "It was a beauti-
ful morning. The
city, St. Paul's,
with the river, and
a multitude of little
boats, made a
most beautiful
sight as we
crossed Westmin-
ster Bridge; the
houses, not over-
hung by their
clouds of smoke,
were spread out
endlessly; yet the
sun shone so
brightly, with such
a pure light, that
there was some-
thing of the purity
of one of nature's
own grand
spectacles."

First published in 1807, this sonnet shows that
Wordsworth, the nature lover, could also be
moved by the majesty of a sleeping city, in this
case London. But this is clearly a different London from the one in Blake's poem and from the

city known as the "great wen [boil]" that shocked
many of Wordsworth's contemporaries because of
its filth and poverty.
    Again, it is the speaker's imaginative impres-
sion which counts here.

Composed upon Westminster Bridge
September 3, 1802

Earth has not anything to show more fair: a
Dull would he be of soul who could pass by   b
A sight so touching in its majesty: b
This city now doth, like a garment, wear   a
5   The beauty of the morning; silent, bare,   a
Ships, towers, domes, theaters, and temples lie   b
Open unto the fields, and to the sky;   b
All bright and glittering in the smokeless air.   a
Never did sun more beautifully steep   c
10   In his first splendor, valley, rock, or hill;   d
Ne'er saw I, never felt, a calm so deep!   c
The river glideth at his own sweet will: d
Dear God! the very houses seem asleep;   c
And all that mighty heart is lying still!   d

[Handwritten annotations: "Octave" "Description of the city" "Sestet Reaction to city"]

[Handwritten annotation: "A person would have to have no soul to pass by the majesty of the city. City - personified"]

A

Responding to the Poem

Analyzing the Poem

Identifying Details
1. What details and features of the city are noticed by
the speaker?
2. What details **personify** the city?

Interpreting Meanings
3. What seems to be the **mood** of the speaker in this
poem?
4. What **paradox** do you find in the poem's last line?

5. What quality or characteristic of the scene seems to
move the speaker most?

Writing About the Poem

A Creative Response
Imitating the Writer's Technique. Write a prose description
or a poem of a city or town that a speaker is looking at
from afar. Use **personification** to characterize your city or
town. You might open with Wordsworth's first line: "Earth
has not anything to show more fair."

PREPARATION
1. BUILDING ON PRIOR KNOWLEDGE. Be sure students know what a reaper is and what the Scottish Highlands are. You might refer to an encounter with another Highland girl in Dorothy Wordsworth's journal entry (text page 750).

2. ESTABLISHING A PURPOSE. In contrast to "Composed upon Westminster

Bridge," this poem is about sound. Listen to the poem read aloud to hear its beautiful verbal music.

SUPPLEMENTARY SUPPORT MATERIALS
1. Vocabulary Activity Worksheet (*CCB*)
2. Review and Response Worksheet: Structure (*CCB*)
3. Selection Test (*CCB*)
4. Audiocassette recording

DEVELOPING VOCABULARY
The following word from the poem is tested in the Selection Test. (See also Vocabulary Activity Worksheet.)
plaintive

A. Diction
Find four details revealing the girl's aloneness. (Single, solitary, by herself, alone)

B. Interpreting
The speaker cannot understand Erse, the Scottish Gaelic.

C. Connections
Where else has Wordsworth written of such a remembrance? ("Tintern Abbey," "I Wandered Lonely as a Cloud")

CLOSURE
Have students explain how this poem is like "I Wandered Lonely as a Cloud" in terms of what it says about the power of memory.

Unlike many of Wordsworth's poems that reflect upon something he saw or experienced, this poem was not the result of a personal experience. It was provoked by a passage in a manuscript account of someone else's experiences in Scotland.

As in other poems by Wordsworth, this speaker finds consolation in the assurance (provided by the poem itself) that an experience will endure in the speaker's heart (and imagination).

The young woman in the poem speaks Gaelic, which explains why her words are unintelligible to the traveler from England.

The Solitary Reaper

A
Behold her, single in the field,
Yon solitary Highland Lass!
Reaping and singing by herself;
Stop here, or gently pass!
5 Alone she cuts and binds the grain,
And sings a melancholy strain;
O listen! for the Vale profound°
Is overflowing with the sound.

No Nightingale did ever chaunt°
10 More welcome notes to weary bands
Of travelers in some shady haunt,°
Among Arabian sands:
A voice so thrilling ne'er was heard
In springtime from the Cuckoo-bird,
15 Breaking the silence of the seas
Among the farthest Hebrides.°

B
Will no one tell me what she sings?
Perhaps the plaintive numbers° flow
For old, unhappy, far-off things,
20 And battles long ago:
Or is it some more humble lay,°
Familiar matter of today?
Some natural sorrow, loss, or pain,
That has been, and may be again?

25 Whate'er the theme, the Maiden sang
As if her song could have no ending;
I saw her singing at her work,
And o'er the sickle bending:
I listened, motionless and still;
30 And, as I mounted up the hill,
C The music in my heart I bore,
Long after it was heard no more.

7. **Vale profound:** deep valley.

9. **chaunt:** chant.

11. **haunt:** often-visited place.

16. **Hebrides:** islands off the northwest coast of Scotland; here, a far-off place with hard weather where spring is especially welcome.
18. **numbers:** phrases of music.

21. **lay:** short song.

Identifying Details
1. She is reaping and singing.
2. The song is melancholy (line 6).
   Lines 18–24 state that she either sings an old song of long-ago woes or a song of personal sorrows.
3. It shifts from present to past.
   The second and fourth lines begin with spondees (two accented syllables) in-

stead of iambs; also, each line ends with an unaccented syllable.

Interpreting Meanings
4. A possible answer is that the song was more beautiful than any bird song and that therefore it became part of his memory. (The poet seems to suggest that her natural, unaffected song is as powerful as poetry.)

A. The Speakers in the Poems
The bard or prophet is heard in "London," "Jerusalem," "London, 1802," "England in 1819." The wanderer is heard in "Tintern Abbey," "I Wandered Lonely as a Cloud," "Westminster Bridge," "The Solitary Reaper." The traveler is heard in "Kubla Khan," *The Rime of the Ancient Mariner, Childe Harold's Pilgrimage,* "Ozymandias," "La Belle Dame Sans Merci." The esthete is heard in "Ode to the West Wind," "To a Skylark," "On First Looking into Chapman's Homer," "Ode to a Nightingale," "Ode on a Grecian Urn," and "To Autumn."

Responding to the Poem

Analyzing the Poem

Identifying Details

1. What is the Highland Lass doing?
2. Is the girl's song happy or melancholy? How do you know?
3. What shift in verb tense occurs in the fourth stanza? How does the speaker alter the **rhythm** in the second and fourth lines of this stanza?

Interpreting Meanings

4. Why do you think the speaker wanted to recapture this brief experience in a poem? (Is there any significance in the fact that the girl and the speaker are both *singers?*)

5. How does this poem, and others in this selection from Wordsworth, comment on the problem of experiences which too quickly fade away?

Writing About the Poem

A Critical Response

Comparing Poems. In an essay, tell whether "The Solitary Reaper" and "I Wandered Lonely as a Cloud" show these characteristics of the meditative lyric:

1. An experience is described.
2. An insight is gained in the discovery of a "recompense" for the inevitable end of the experience.
3. The resolution of the conflict is celebrated and its "spirit" is hailed.

The Elements of Literature

ROMANTIC LYRICS

The poems in this section represent a number of lyric forms—from variations of traditional sonnet schemes and experiments with the ode to the distinctive Romantic lyric form, the "meditative poem."

The **sonnet** was popular in Romantic poetry as a traditional type of occasional poem written for an important subject, public or private. Milton, for example, had used the sonnet in this way. But for the Romantics the sonnet was also used for experimentation. Coleridge's early sonnets, called "effusions" to excuse their looseness, helped him to create the meditative poem. Keats's sonnets shaped the stanza forms for his odes. The main sonnet form was the **Italian,** or **Petrarchan,** composed of an octave (eight lines) and a sestet (six lines). But the Romantics also used the **Shakespearean** sonnet of three quatrains and a couplet.

The Romantic **ode** was a self-conscious use of a classical form that had been brought into English literature in the seventeenth and eighteenth centuries by such writers as Abraham Cowley, John Dryden, and Thomas Gray. The structure of the Romantic ode was certainly influenced by the Romantic meditative poem. Sometimes a poem in the manner of an ode was called a "hymn."

There are two distinctive features of the ode. (1) It uses heightened, impassioned language, and (2) it addresses some object. The ode may speak to, or **apostrophize,** objects (an urn), creatures (a skylark, a nightingale), and presences or powers (intellectual beauty, autumn, the west wind). The speaker first invokes the object and then creates a relationship with it, either through praise or prayer.

The **meditative poem** is a form the Romantics developed and passed on to later generations of poets. It is the best example of the "artful illusion" of the lyric in which we are to imagine a person speaking. The prototypes of the form—Coleridge's "This Lime-Tree Bower My Prison" and Wordsworth's "Tintern Abbey"—are in a flowing **blank verse** in which the stanzas are the equivalent of paragraphs, beginning and ending where sense, rather than strict form, dictates. The tone of these lyrics is much easier and more colloquial than the tone of the odes. Coleridge called one of his meditative lyrics a "conversation poem."

As you read the poems here, think about the various speakers in Romantic lyric poems: the bard or prophet who speaks about matters of great concern; the wanderer who happens upon something that turns out to be revealing; the traveler who returns from far-off lands with his tale to tell; and the esthete or lover of poetic experiences who finds beauty in common or special subjects.

A

Samuel Taylor Coleridge (1772–1834)

He was "the most wonderful man that I have ever known," said Wordsworth. Charles Lamb, another friend who had known him closely since their school days, thought the world would never see another person like him. The Victorian philosopher John Stuart Mill called him one of the two great "seminal minds" of the age. "The class of thinkers," he declared, "has scarcely yet arisen by whom he is to be judged."

The three poems that follow are only a snapshot in comparison to the full portrait of a man who was unquestionably a genius. When scholars finish collecting Coleridge's works, including letters, journals, and even comments made in the margins of books, there will be over thirty volumes, more than most encyclopedias.

The youngest child of a village parson in southwestern England, Coleridge was destined to follow in his father's footsteps, though with giant and erratic strides. When his father died in 1781, Coleridge was sent to school in London. Having begun his classical education at home, when he arrived at Cambridge University in 1791 he already had a reputation for insatiable curiosity and wide reading, especially in "out-of-the-way" books.

At Cambridge he became a radical and won a prize for an ode in Greek on the abolition of slavery. He left the university in 1794 without a degree, but with a commitment to a utopian colony in America. The experiment never materialized, but Coleridge gave radical lectures and married one of the prospective utopians. In 1797 he moved to a village in Somerset, with two books of poetry published but no prospects of a career. The next twenty months, which ended when he went to Germany to study, were a time of miracles.

By June 1797 he had persuaded Wordsworth to live nearby. They became catalysts for each other, and the friendship helped Coleridge write most of his best poems, including two that had a profound effect on Wordsworth. But convinced that Wordsworth was "the best poet of the

Samuel Taylor Coleridge by Peter Vandyke (1797). Oil.

A

age," the poet in Coleridge hid in the "giant's" shadow ever after. After the year in Germany, Wordsworth returned to his native Lake District in northwestern England. Coleridge abandoned his own roots and followed (as he told a friend) "a great, a true poet—I am only a kind of metaphysician."

Despite this characteristic self-disparagement, Coleridge was, if only in brief periods, a "true poet," and, moreover, a profound philosopher. The middle period of his life, from 1800 to 1818, is a record of great achievement, most notably his lectures on Shakespeare and the *Biographia Literaria*, a work on philosophy and criticism disguised as his literary life and opinions. These works laid the foundations of twentieth-century literary theory.

This period was also a time of pain and despair, memorialized in "Dejection: An Ode" (1802) and played out in the collapse of his marriage, his increasing addiction to opium, and his inability to discipline his wonderful mind to concentrate.

Coleridge was a formidable figure, the "Sage of Highgate" as he came to be known after 1816

A. Humanities Connection: Discussing the Fine Art
Peter Vandyke (1729–?) was a Flemish portrait painter who came to England to work as Sir Joshua Reynolds's assistant.

Have students compare Vandyke's portrait with Coleridge's own description of himself:

"As to me, my face, unless animated by immediate eloquence, expresses great sloth, and great, indeed almost idiotic, good nature. 'Tis a mere carcase of a face: fat, flabby, and expressive chiefly of inexpression. Yet I am told that my eyes, eyebrows, and forehead are physiognomically good; but of this the Deponent knoweth not. As to my shape, 'tis a good shape enough, if measured—but my gait is awkward, and the walk of the whole man indicates *indolence capable of energies* . . . I cannot breathe through my nose, so my mouth with sensual thick lips is almost always open."

According to Martin Gardner:

"Coleridge and Wordsworth were a study in contrast. Coleridge: outgoing, impulsive, emotional, unstable, weak-willed, impractical, helpless, careless; at times a liar and a hypocrite, but always fun-loving and lovable.

"Wordsworth: cool, rational, industrious physically as well as intellectually, cautious, reserved, grim. Coleridge was as compulsive a talker as he was a reader. (Lamb once imagined himself button-holed by Coleridge and forced to escape by snipping off the button. Five hours later he returns, finds Coleridge, eyes closed, still holding the button and talking eloquently.) Surely Wordsworth must have been a compulsive listener.

"Yet the two men had much in common: a Protestant outlook, a love of nature, a love of poetry, enormous talent, and, it must also be said, a common conviction that Wordsworth was potentially the greatest poet in England."

---

when he began to live in a rural suburb north of London with a kindly physician, Dr. James Gillman. Keats met Coleridge accidentally on nearby Hampstead Heath on an April Sunday in 1819, and was astonished by Coleridge's powers of conversation: "I walked with him a[t] his alderman-after-dinner pace. . . . In those two miles he broached a thousand things." The meeting is a wonderful emblem of the Romantic period itself. The legendary creator of the "sadder but wiser" Ancient Mariner with his "strange powers of speech" had written his greatest poetry twenty years earlier. The doomed young poet walking with him was just then writing his "great odes" in a remarkably similar burst of intense artistic energy.

When he met Keats, Coleridge had already accomplished more than enough to fill two careers—as poet, critic, journalist, essayist, and philosopher. He would spend the next fifteen years pushing his philosophic powers to higher insights. He hoped to realize his lifelong ambition to produce "one great work" that would clarify the major problems of his age. Along the way, he became an influential theologian and political theorist. Through his extraordinary conversation at his "Thursday evenings," he made a lasting impression on a stream of visitors, including the young American Ralph Waldo Emerson, who came to hear him.

It is natural to compare Coleridge to Samuel Johnson. If the Romantic period had been longer and less turbulent, it might have been called the "Age of Coleridge" as the late eighteenth-century was called the "Age of Johnson." Both men were great talkers of unmeasured influence. Both had wide-ranging interests and an ability to see the heart and connections of every problem. Both were deeply and naturally religious, and acutely, even morbidly, self-critical. Perhaps both were so interested in literature itself that their greatest contributions had to be as critics and scholars rather than as artists.

But the comparison with Johnson also reveals the distressing side of Coleridge, the side that troubled his friends, affected his reputation, and undoubtedly tortured him in his frequent bouts of self-recrimination. Coleridge's life was dogged by both his awareness of his great intellectual talents and by his clear inability to live up to them.

Genius means a "guiding spirit." Like the spirit of the South Pole in his *Rime of the Ancient Mariner,* Coleridge's guiding spirit was powerful in its effect on himself and others, and lonely as well. The loneliness came from a life-long need for the affection and support of others—a need that made the isolation of the writer's life often unbearable for him. His addiction to laudanum (a mixture of alcohol and opium) that began before he was thirty was not controlled until his residence with the Gillmans.

Living at a time when common pains are easily and safely dispatched by aspirin, it is difficult for us to imagine the need for a painkiller like laudanum, which was commonly used in Coleridge's time, even given to infants. Little was known at the time about what we call "withdrawal symptoms." Coleridge's addiction, and his hypochondria, were made worse by the laudanum he took to relieve the discomforts he suffered when he tried to stop using the drug. Although scholars disagree about the destructive effect of opium on his achievements, there is no question that he was badly addicted.

As a thinker and as a writer, Coleridge was truly magnanimous, generous of his intellect and spirit and devoted to the good of his fellow human beings as only a youthful utopian and son of a parson can be. The pity is that we must be content with snapshots. The size of the full portrait—and the breadth of the man's learning and interests—are too great for anyone to master. Anyone, that is, except someone like Coleridge himself.

PREPARATION

1. BUILDING ON PRIOR KNOWLEDGE. Kublai Khan (1216?–1294) was the Mongol emperor of China for more than thirty years (see the portrait on text page 651). He was the grandson of Genghis Khan, the Mongol conqueror of central Asia (a name students might know). *Khan* comes from a Turkic word meaning "prince" or "sovereign."

2. ESTABLISHING A PURPOSE. Have students evaluate critic William Empson's belief that "Kubla Khan" is really about the role of the artist in society.

SUPPLEMENTARY SUPPORT MATERIALS
1. Vocabulary Activity Worksheet (*CCB*)
2. Review and Response Worksheet: Imagery (*CCB*)
3. Selection Test (*CCB*)

DEVELOPING VOCABULARY
The following word from the poem is tested in the Selection Test. (See also Vocabulary Activity Worksheet.)
tumult

Certainly one of the most enchanting poems ever written, "Kubla Khan" is lyric in tone and manner, resembling a meditative poem and an ode. Full of mystery and dread, "Kubla Khan" was composed at about the same time (late 1797 or early 1798) as *The Rime of the Ancient Mariner*.

"Kubla Khan" has always intrigued readers, including Byron who, after reading it in manuscript, apparently prevailed on Coleridge to publish it in 1816. At that time, Coleridge added a prose introduction that offered a rational account of the origins of the poem. He claimed it was written in a reverie brought on by opium after reading a provocative passage in a seventeenth-century travel book. Coleridge contended that the composition of the poem, after he awoke from his dream, was interrupted by a visitor and that only a fragment of his original vision could be reproduced.

Kubla Khan

In Xanadu did Kubla Khan
A stately pleasure-dome decree:
Where Alph,° the sacred river, ran
Through caverns measureless to man
5   Down to a sunless sea.
So twice five miles of fertile ground
With walls and towers were girdled round:
And there were gardens bright with sinuous rills,°
Where blossomed many an incense-bearing tree;
10 And here were forests ancient as the hills,
Enfolding sunny spots of greenery.

But oh! that deep romantic chasm which slanted
Down the green hill athwart a cedarn cover!°
A A savage place! as holy and enchanted
15 As e'er beneath a waning moon was haunted
By woman wailing for her demon lover!
    And from this chasm, with ceaseless turmoil seething,
As if this earth in fast thick pants were breathing,
A mighty fountain momently° was forced:
20 Amid whose swift half-intermitted burst
Huge fragments vaulted like rebounding hail,
Or chaffy grain beneath the thresher's flail:°
And 'mid these dancing rocks at once and ever
It flung up momently the sacred river.
25 Five miles meandering with a mazy motion
Through wood and dale the sacred river ran,
Then reached the caverns measureless to man,
And sank in tumult to a lifeless ocean:
B And 'mid this <u>tumult</u> Kubla heard from far
30 Ancestral voices prophesying war!
    The shadow of the dome of pleasure
    Floated midway on the waves;
    Where was heard the mingled measure°
    From the fountain and the caves.
35 It was a miracle of rare device,
A sunny pleasure-dome with caves of ice!

3. **Alph:** probably a reference to the Greek river Alpheus, which flows into the Ionian Sea, and whose waters are fabled to rise up again in Sicily.

8. **sinuous rills:** winding streams.

13. **athwart a cedarn cover:** cutting diagonally across the cedar-covered hill.

19. **momently:** at each moment.

22. **thresher's flail:** a heavy, whiplike tool used to beat (thresh) grain in order to separate the kernels from their husks (chaff).

33. **measure:** rhythmic sound.

A. Imagery
Note the opposites and demonic imagery in these lines, which, combined with the exotic setting, create an air of mystery and magic. (The demon lover motif is found in Elizabeth Bowen's story on text page 994.)

B. Tone
The prophecies of approaching war strike an ominous note of contrast with the pleasure dome.

The Composition of "Kubla Khan"

"In consequence of a slight indisposition, an anodyne had been prescribed, from the effects of which he fell asleep in his chair at the moment that he was reading the following sentence . . . 'Here the Khan Kubla commanded a palace to be built, and a stately garden thereunto. And thus ten miles of fertile ground were inclosed with a wall.' The author continued for about three hours in profound sleep . . . during which time he has the most vivid confidence that he could not have composed less than from two to three hundred lines. . . . On awaking he appeared to himself to have a distinct recollection of the whole, and taking his pen, ink, and paper, instantly and eagerly wrote down the lines that are here preserved. At this moment he was unfortunately called out by a person on business . . . and on his return to his room found . . . that . . . with the exception of some eight or ten scattered lines and images, all the rest had passed away like the images on the surface of a stream into which a stone has been cast. . . ."

—Samuel Taylor Coleridge

A. Humanities Connection: About the Fine Art

The *Livre de Merveilles* is a French illuminated manuscript containing descriptions of voyages to exotic lands made in the thirteenth and fourteenth centuries, including Marco Polo's journeys.

B. Meaning

Here the thought shifts abruptly.

❓ How is this section of the poem connected to the preceding section? (Coleridge connects the two sections in lines 45–47: The speaker wants to re-create the vision of the pleasure dome.)

A

The Palace of Kublai Khan at Peking (14th century). Miniature from the *Livre de Merveilles*.

A damsel with a dulcimer°
In a vision once I saw:
It was an Abyssinian° maid.
40 And on her dulcimer she played,
Singing of Mount Abora.°
Could I revive within me
Her symphony and song,
B   To such a deep delight 'twould win me,
45 That with music loud and long.
I would build that dome in air,
That sunny dome! those caves of ice!
And all who heard should see them there,
And all should cry, Beware! Beware!
50 His flashing eyes, his floating hair!
Weave a circle round him thrice,
And close your eyes with holy dread,
For he on honeydew hath fed,
And drunk the milk of Paradise.

37. **dulcimer:** stringed instrument.

39. **Abyssinian:** Ethiopian.

41. **Mount Abora:** probably a modified reference to Milton's *Paradise Lost*, Book IV, where the Ethiopian "Mount Amara" is a type of mythical earthly paradise.

Have students debate whether this poem (especially the last part) is really about the role of the artist in our lives. If so, what does it say about the artist?

ANALYZING THE POEM
Identifying Details
1. The images include the pleasure dome, sacred river, gardens, streams, blossoming fragrant trees, sunny spots of greenery.
2. Within it ceaseless turmoil seethes. In line 30, distant voices prophesy war.
3. He sees a damsel with a dulcimer. He imagines himself re-creating her song and building the dome in air.
4. The rhyme scheme in the first stanza is *abaabccdbdb;* it varies later in the poem. The meter is iambic with varying numbers of feet per line.
   Lines 19, 22, 27, and 50 provide a few examples of the poem's rich alliteration.

Interpreting Meanings
5. The speaker is an artist who wants to create beauty, just as Kubla Khan created the pleasure dome.
6. She represents imagination.
   The speaker can re-create the dome with music (words).
   The dome may symbolize creation of some sort.
7. The people protect themselves with magic ritual (line 51) and regard the poet with fear and awe. He has drunk the milk of Paradise.
8. Examples occur in lines 14, 26, 47.
   The tone in the last stanza suggests a lack of tension: The song synthesizes all opposites.
9. Most critics say the poem is an accomplished whole and believe Coleridge was making up the story of the fragment.

Responding to the Poem

Analyzing the Poem

Identifying Details

1. What **images** recreate the earthly paradise that Kubla Khan decrees in the first stanza?
2. Why is the "deep romantic chasm" of line 12 called a "savage place"? What ominous note is introduced toward the end of the second stanza?
3. What does the speaker see in a vision in the third stanza? How does the speaker imagine himself in this stanza?
4. Describe the **rhyme scheme** and **meter** of the poem. Can you find examples of **alliteration** that add to the poem's music?

Interpreting Meanings

5. Who is the speaker of the poem? Compare him with Kubla Khan.
6. Why is the "damsel with a dulcimer" important to the speaker? How could the speaker "build that dome in air"? What could the "pleasure dome" **symbolize**?
7. Many ancient cultures regarded poets as seers who had a special relationship with the gods and were thus to be treated with special reverence. How may Coleridge be alluding to such beliefs in the closing lines of the last stanza?
8. Where does the poet use contrasting **images** (of greenery and ice, of tranquility and of turmoil, etc.)? In your view, does he offer any synthesis of these images in the concluding stanza?
9. Does the poem seem to you to bear out Coleridge's own description of it as a "fragment"? Or do you think that these lines were all the poet really intended to write? Explain.

Writing About the Poem

A Creative Response

1. **Completing the Poem.** Suppose that we take Coleridge at his word and assume that "Kubla Khan" is really an unfinished fragment. Basing your idea on the existing lines, write a summary in prose of how the poem

Kublai Khan (Yüan Dynasty, China). Painting on silk.

might be completed. Specify what you imagine the story line might be.

A Critical Response

2. **Analyzing the Poem.** There is general agreement that one of the major themes of "Kubla Khan" concerns the imagination. In a brief essay, analyze how Coleridge develops this theme in the poem. What symbolic hints does he provide about the powers, dangers, and limits of the human imagination?

1. BUILDING ON PRIOR KNOWLEDGE. Remind students of the characteristics of a meditative lyric: blank verse, verse paragraphs, a conversational tone. See text page 646.

2. ESTABLISHING A PURPOSE. Have students read to find out what prison the title refers to. See question 6 on text page 654.

3. PREREADING JOURNAL. Ask students to write two or three sentences about the images they associate with the words *lime-tree bower* and *prison*.

SUPPLEMENTARY SUPPORT MATERIALS
1. Vocabulary Activity Worksheet (*CCB*)
2. Review and Response Worksheet: Tone (*CCB*)
3. Selection Test (*CCB*)

DEVELOPING VOCABULARY
The following word from the poem is tested in the Selection Test. (See also Vocabulary Activity Worksheet.)
usurp

A. Tone
Note the colloquial, conversational beginning: "Well, . . ."

B. Structure
The speaker says he has lost "Beauties and feelings." Note that the rest of the poem recounts these beauties and feelings— he is remembering and imagining them.

C. Interpreting
? Why might he "never more meet again" his friends in this place? (Coleridge hints at his own mortality.)

It is curious that this poem, first written in the summer of 1797, was not included in *Lyrical Ballads*. Quite likely, Coleridge's philosophic, religious side worried over the precision and orthodoxy of the revelation imagined in lines 38–43. This is the first great romantic "meditative poem," a development from some similar but less successful poems that Coleridge had written in the preceding two years.

The "bower" was located between Coleridge's cottage in Nether Stowey, Somerset, a village at the foot of the Quantock Hills in southwestern England, and the home of Thomas Poole, a local tanner and Coleridge's loyal supporter. The "wide landscape" depicted in the poem can be experienced today from the north side of the Quantocks looking out over the Bristol Channel, which separates England from southern Wales. The two tiny islands are still there, but the "fair bark" would probably be a motorboat today.

The "friends" referred to in the poem are William and Dorothy Wordsworth, who had recently taken up residence in the neighborhood, and Coleridge's friend from their London schooldays, Charles Lamb. Lamb's "strange calamity" refers obliquely to a horrible event that took place in September 1796 when Lamb's sister, Mary, in a temporary fit of insanity, killed her mother. Lamb made a long-wished-for visit to Coleridge's rural retreat in June 1797.

This Lime-Tree Bower My Prison

A Well, they are gone, and here must I remain,
This lime-tree bower my prison! I have lost
B Beauties and feelings, such as would have been
Most sweet to my remembrance even when age
5 Had dimmed mine eyes to blindness! They, meanwhile,
C Friends, whom I never more may meet again,
On springy heath,° along the hilltop edge,
Wander in gladness, and wind down, perchance,
To that still roaring dell,° of which I told;
10 The roaring dell, o'erwooded, narrow, deep,
And only speckled by the midday sun;
Where its slim trunk the ash from rock to rock
Flings arching like a bridge; that branchless ash,
Unsunned and damp, whose few poor yellow leaves
15 Ne'er tremble in the gale, yet tremble still,
Fanned by the waterfall! and there my friends
Behold the dark green file° of long lank weeds,
That all at once (a most fantastic sight!)
Still nod and dip beneath the dripping edge
Of the blue claystone.

20   Now, my friends emerge
Beneath the wide wide heaven—and view again
The many-steepled tract° magnificent
Of hilly fields and meadows, and the sea,
With some fair bark,° perhaps, whose sails light up
25 The slip° of smooth clear blue betwixt two isles
Of purple shadow!° Yes! they wander on
In gladness all; but thou, methinks, most glad,

7. **heath:** open, uncultivated land covered with low vegetation.

9. **dell:** small, deep valley. (In the locale in which this poem was written, these dells are called "combs," are usually overgrown, and are therefore only speckled with sunlight.)

17. **file:** series of rows.

22. **tract:** expanse. It is "many-steepled" because of the churches in the small villages that dot the landscape.
24. **bark:** small boat.
25. **slip:** strip.
26. **purple shadow:** two islands seen dimly in the distance.

CLOSURE
Have students compare this poem with
Alexander Pope's poems (or any earlier
poem) to get a strong sense of how the
meditative lyric was a radical departure in
English poetry.

A My gentle-hearted Charles! for thou hast pined
And hungered after Nature, many a year,
30 In the great city pent,° winning thy way
With sad yet patient soul, through evil and pain

B And strange calamity! Ah! slowly sink
Behind the western ridge, thou glorious sun!
Shine in the slant beams of the sinking orb,
35 Ye purple heathflowers! richlier burn, ye clouds!
Live in the yellow light, ye distant groves!
And kindle, thou blue ocean! So my friend
Struck with deep joy may stand, as I have stood,
Silent with swimming sense;° yea, gazing round
40 On the wide landscape, gaze till all doth seem
Less gross than bodily;° and of such hues
As veil the Almighty Spirit, when yet he makes
Spirits perceive his presence.

A delight
C Comes sudden on my heart, and I am glad
45 As I myself were there! Nor in this bower,
This little lime-tree bower, have I not marked
Much that has soothed me. Pale beneath the blaze
Hung the transparent foliage; and I watched
Some broad and sunny leaf, and loved to see
50 The shadow of the leaf and stem above
Dappling its sunshine! And that walnut tree
Was richly tinged, and a deep radiance lay
Full on the ancient ivy, which usurps
Those fronting elms, and now, with blackest mass
55 Makes their dark branches gleam a lighter hue
Through the late twilight: and though now the bat
Wheels silent by, and not a swallow twitters,
Yet still the solitary humblebee
Sings in the beanflower! Henceforth I shall know

D 60 That Nature ne'er deserts the wise and pure;
No plot so narrow, be but Nature there,
No waste° so vacant, but may well employ
Each faculty of sense, and keep the heart
Awake to love and beauty! and sometimes
65 'Tis well to be bereft° of promised good,
That we may lift the soul, and contemplate
With lively joy the joys we cannot share.
My gentle-hearted Charles! when the last rook°
Beat its straight path along the dusky air
70 Homewards, I blest it! deeming its black wing
(Now a dim speck, now vanishing in light)
Had crossed the mighty orb's° dilated glory,
While thou stood'st gazing; or, when all was still,
Flow creeking° o'er thy head, and had a charm
75 For thee, my gentle-hearted Charles, to whom
No sound is dissonant which tolls of life.

30. **pent:** imprisoned. In Milton's Paradise Lost, Book IX, Satan leaves Hell and enters Eden, enjoying it "As one who long in populous city pent" enjoys the country.

39. **swimming sense:** blurred sight, presumably because of the different types of light playing on the landscape.
41. **less gross than bodily:** less solid than a physical object (Coleridge's effort to be philosophically precise).

62. **waste:** wasteland.

65. **bereft:** deprived.

68. **rook:** crow.

72. **orb's:** sun's.

74. **creeking:** squawking.

A. Expansion
Charles Lamb (see text page 736) was known for his wit and practical jokes. To his close friend Coleridge, whom he had known since boyhood, Lamb complained: "Don't make me ridiculous any more by terming me gentle-hearted in print, or do it in better verses. Substitute drunken dog, ragged-head, self-shaven, odd-eyed, stuttering, or any other epithet which truly and properly belongs to the gentleman in question."
Coleridge addresses "my gentle-hearted Charles" three times in this poem.

B. Tone
[?] Note the exclamation marks. What does the speaker command? (He commands the sun and other natural objects to put on a gorgeous display for Charles.)

C. Setting
The scene switches back to the bower, upon which Coleridge focuses closely.

D. Theme
These lines state the poem's theme.

1. The speaker is sitting in a lime-tree bower, his friends have gone for a walk without him. They will see the fields and villages, the sea and two islands.
2. It is sunset.
  The passage of time is from daylight to nightfall.
3. He sees light playing on leaves, branches, and trees.
4. He addresses Charles—specifically Charles Lamb.
5. He blesses the rook because Charles has seen its beauty.

Interpreting Meanings
6. The speaker feels he is trapped there while his friends go away.
  Age (lines 4–5), the dark valley (lines 9–20), city (line 30), evil and pain (line 31), and grief (lines 64–65) are "prisons" of sorts.
  One escapes them by being awake to love and beauty (lines 60–64).
7. Even dissonance (sorrow, loss, and so on) is part of life.
8. He has learned that nature frees and cares for those who open themselves *(Answers continue in left-hand column.)*

(Continued from top.)
up to her beauty.
9. Lines 1–9 have a mournful tone; lines 32–43 are joyful and celebratory; lines 59–67 are contemplative; lines 68–76 are gentle and comforting.
10. Answers may vary in all three cases.
  (a) The statement reflects the Romantics' feeling that cities are corrupt and evil while the country is filled with goodness and beauty. Those who live in the country will be protected by Nature.
  (b) Rural students may disagree; students from urban areas, where vacant lots are sometimes turned into gardens, may agree.
  (c) All is beautiful in life. Students who have experienced tragedies may disagree.

Responding to the Poem

Analyzing the Poem

Identifying Details

1. What is the situation at the beginning of the poem? Describe the scene the speaker imagines his friends will see when they "emerge / Beneath the wide wide heaven" (lines 20–26).
2. What time of day is it in lines 32–37? Can you tell approximately how much time passes in lines 43–59?
3. Describe in your own words the scene the speaker sees from his bower in lines 43–59.
4. Whom does the speaker address by name in the poem?
5. Why does the speaker bless the "last rook" in lines 68–70? What consolation does he suggest the rook brings?

Interpreting Meanings

6. In what sense is the bower a prison? What other prisons, literal or figurative, are alluded to in the poem? How does the poem suggest that one can escape from them?
7. How does the wording of the final line, especially the verb *tolls,* suggest a **paradox,** or apparent contradiction?
8. Paraphrase what the speaker seems to have learned from his own experience. Look carefully at the statement beginning, "Henceforth I shall know . . ." (line 59).
9. How does the speaker's **tone** change in different sections of the poem? Look again at these four sections: lines 1–9, 32–43, 59–67, and 68–76.

10. How do you respond to these statements from the poem?
  a. "Nature ne'er deserts the wise and pure"
  b. "No plot so narrow, be but Nature there, No waste so vacant, but may well employ Each faculty of sense, and keep the heart Awake to love and beauty!"
  c. "No sound is dissonant which tolls of life."

Writing About the Poem

A Creative Response

1. **Writing a Description.** Write a description in which the contemplation of nature produces a strong, emotional response in a speaker. Be sure to include vivid sensory details in your description. At the end of the description, try to sum up what the speaker may have learned after examining his or her emotions.

A Critical Response

2. **Comparing Two Meditative Lyrics.** In a brief essay, compare and contrast Coleridge's "This Lime-Tree Bower My Prison" with Wordsworth's meditative lyric "Lines Composed a Few Miles Above Tintern Abbey."
3. **Supporting a Topic Statement.** In a brief essay, cite details from the poem that support this statement about its purpose:

   From pleasant and painful ingredients, Coleridge has created an imaginative meditation on the justification of evil.

PREPARATION

1. BUILDING ON PRIOR KNOWLEDGE. Ask students if they know the account of Cain (Genesis 4:1–15), who was marked by God in punishment for the crime of fratricide and doomed ever after to be a wanderer over the earth (see text page 30). The Ancient Mariner, or sailor, has been compared to Cain.

2. ESTABLISHING A PURPOSE. Note that the poem is a narrative and so has the elements of plot, character, and setting. Have students read Part I to answer these questions: What is the "frame story"? What is the setting? Who is the Mariner? What is his "crime"?

SUPPLEMENTARY SUPPORT MATERIALS
1. Vocabulary Activity Worksheet (*CCB*)
2. Review and Response Worksheet: Narrative Poetry (*CCB*)
3. Selection Test (*CCB*)
4. Audiocassette recording

A. Expansion
Four of the twenty-three poems in *Lyrical Ballads* (all anonymous) were by Coleridge. Not until 1817 was this poem published naming Coleridge as author.

B. Connotation
What do you associate with a "glittering eye"? (The "evil eye," hypnosis, the glittering eyes of snakes or of cats)

A The most famous of Coleridge's poems, *The Rime of the Ancient Mariner* was written as part of the collaboration with Wordsworth in 1797–1798 that culminated in *Lyrical Ballads*. Twenty years later, in the *Biographia Literaria*, Coleridge recalled that he and Wordsworth had made a poetic division of labor based on their interest in the two powers of poetry: (1) to represent ordinary events and objects in an unfamiliar way so as to make them fresh and interesting; and (2) to make believable the unfamiliar and strange.

Coleridge's task was to write about "persons and characters supernatural, or at least romantic; yet so far as to transfer from our inward nature a human interest and semblance of truth sufficient to procure for these shadows of imagination that willing suspension of disbelief for the moment, which constitutes poetic faith." "With this view," he said, "I wrote the Ancient Mariner." The poem was the first item in the 1798 *Lyrical Ballads*. But partly due to Wordsworth's discomfort with the incongruity between it and the rest of the poems in the volume, Coleridge modernized many of the deliberately old-fashioned words he had used to give the poem the flavor of an ancient and previously undiscovered ballad. The marginal notes were added in 1817, and need to be imagined as "modern" and rational comments on the mariner's tale.

Coleridge's poem no doubt reflects his avid reading of "out-of-the-way" books, including travelers' accounts of strange lands. It was apparently Wordsworth who suggested the use of the albatross. It is helpful in reading this hypnotic narrative to keep in mind three things. First, there is no explanation for the killing of the albatross. The results of the act, rather than the act itself, are important. Second, the "moral" of the story, pronounced by the mariner at the end, is, as Coleridge later observed, too much and too little; that is, it is too obtrusive and yet not adequate. Finally, the poem must be seen in the light of Coleridge's own more settled religious convictions (as reflected in "This Lime-Tree Bower My Prison"), which contrast with the spiritual despair of the mariner who found himself

Alone on a wide wide sea:
So lonely 'twas, that God himself
Scarce seemed there to be.

The Rime of the Ancient Mariner

Summary

How a ship having passed the line [equator] was driven by storms to the cold country toward the South Pole; and how from thence she made her course to the tropical latitude of the great Pacific Ocean; and of the strange things that befell; and in what manner the Ancient Mariner came back to his own country.

Part I

It is an ancient Mariner,
And he stoppeth one of three.
"By thy long gray beard and glittering eye,
Now wherefore stopp'st thou me?

B

An ancient Mariner meeteth three gallants bidden to a wedding feast, and detaineth one.

5   The Bridegroom's doors are opened wide,
And I am next of kin;
The guests are met, the feast is set:
May'st hear the merry din."

A. Vocabulary
Here, *loon* means an "ill-bred, awkward person."

B. Expansion
These two lines were written by Wordsworth.

C. Setting
Kirk, a Scottish word, suggests that the voyage originates in Scotland.

D. Plot
What is the effect of this interruption and switch to the wedding scene? (The interruption creates suspense; the joyful scene contrasts with the somber tone of the Mariner's tale.)

E. Form
Note the variation in the basic stanza form.

He holds him with his skinny hand,
10   "There was a ship," quoth he.
A   "Hold off! unhand me, gray-beard loon!"
  Eftsoons° his hand dropt he.

He holds him with his glittering eye—
The Wedding Guest stood still,
15 And listens like a three years' child:
B   The Mariner hath his will.

The Wedding Guest sat on a stone:
He cannot choose but hear;
And thus spake on that ancient man,
20   The bright-eyed Mariner.

"The ship was cheered, the harbor cleared,
Merrily did we drop
C Below the kirk,° below the hill,
  Below the lighthouse top.

25 The Sun came up upon the left,
Out of the sea came he!
And he shone bright, and on the right
Went down into the sea.

Higher and higher every day,
30 Till over the mast at noon—"
The Wedding Guest here beat his breast,
For he heard the loud bassoon.

D The bride hath paced into the hall,
Red as a rose is she;
35 Nodding their heads before her goes
The merry minstrelsy.°

The Wedding Guest he beat his breast,
Yet he cannot choose but hear;
And thus spake on that ancient man,
40   The bright-eyed Mariner.

"And now the Storm blast came, and he
Was tyrannous and strong;
He struck with his o'ertaking wings,
And chased us south along.

45 With sloping masts and dipping prow,
As who° pursued with yell and blow
Still° treads the shadow of his foe.
E And forward bends his head,
The ship drove fast, loud roared the blast.
50 And southward aye° we fled.

12. **eftsoons:** at once.

The Wedding Guest is spellbound by the eye of the old seafaring man, and constrained to hear his tale.

23. **kirk:** church.
The Mariner tells how the ship sailed southward with a good wind and fair weather, till it reached the line.

The Wedding Guest heareth the bridal music; but the Mariner continueth his tale.

36. **minstrelsy:** group of musicians.

The ship driven by a storm toward the South Pole.

46. **who:** one.
47. **Still:** always.

50. **aye:** continually.

Wordsworth, his sister Dorothy, and Coleridge planned *The Ancient Mariner* on a late afternoon walk in the autumn of 1797. Coleridge had told his friends about a neighbor's strange dream of a skeleton ship with ghastly figures.

Wordsworth recalls: "Much the greatest part of the [poem's] story was Mr. Coleridge's invention, but certain parts I suggested; for example, some crime was to be committed which should bring upon the Old Navigator, as Coleridge afterwards delighted to call him, the spectral persecution, as a consequence of that crime and his own wanderings."

Wordsworth had been reading a travel book that mentioned "a disconsolate black albatross." " 'Suppose,' said I, 'you represent him as having killed one of these birds on entering the South Sea, and that the tutelary spirits of these regions take upon them to avenge the crime.' "

The Rime of the Ancient Mariner, illustration by Gustave Doré. Engraving.

A

B
> And now there came both mist and snow,
> And it grew wondrous cold:
> And ice, mast-high, came floating by,
> As green as emerald.

The land of ice, and of fearful sounds where no living thing was to be seen.

55   And through the drifts° the snowy clifts°
    Did send a dismal sheen:
    Nor shapes of men nor beasts we ken°—
    The ice was all between.

55. **drifts:** icebergs (or possibly patches of fog driven by the wind).   **clifts:** crevasses; large cracks in the ice.
57. **ken:** saw.

    The ice was here, the ice was there,
60   The ice was all around:
C
> It cracked and growled, and roared and howled,
> Like noises in a swound!°

62. **swound:** swoon.

    At length did cross an Albatross,
D
> Thorough the fog it came;
65   As if it had been a Christian soul,
    We hailed it in God's name.

Till a great seabird, called the Albatross, came through the snow-fog, and was received with great joy and hospitality.

A. Humanities Connection: Responding to the Illustration
The illustrations for the poem are by Paul Gustave Doré (1833–1883), a French illustrator, painter, and sculptor. Doré also did a series of illustrations for the Bible, *The Divine Comedy, Paradise Lost,* and *Don Quixote.* The engraving on this page illustrates lines 1–2 of the poem.
❓ What mood is suggested by the engraving? (Some students may suggest an ominous, mysterious mood.) Note the alarmed glance of the guest who's escaped.

B. Imagery
Coleridge had never been to sea when he wrote this poem. These descriptions and images have been traced back to travel books about the Antarctic regions that Coleridge had read.

C. Sound Effects
Note the onomatopoeia and sound imagery in this line.

D. Archaism
Thorough is an archaic form of *through.*

Melville's Albatross

In a footnote to *Moby-Dick*, Herman Melville describes his first encounter with an albatross. Melville had not yet read *The Ancient Mariner*: ". . . I saw a regal, feathery thing of unspotted whiteness. . . . Though bodily unharmed, it uttered cries, as some king's ghost in supernatural distress. Through its inexpressible, strange eyes, methought I peeped to secrets which took hold of God."

A. Variations

In the original version, this line was, "The Mariners gave it biscuit-worms." (Biscuits are crackers.)

B. The Speakers

Note that the speaker changes in line 79. Here the Wedding Guest addresses the old sailor.

C. Motivation

The shooting of the albatross is the event that causes the problem in the narrative. The Mariner's motivation, however, is never made clear.

? Why do you think the Mariner shoots the albatross? (Students may say that the Mariner despises living creatures or that he is annoyed by the bird's daily presence.)

D. Humanities Connection: Responding to the Illustration

Doré's engraving illustrates lines 272–273 (see text page 664). You might have students supply captions for these Doré engravings, using lines from the poem. Note in this one how huge the albatross is.

READING CHECK TEST: PART I

1. An Ancient Mariner tells his tale to a Wedding Guest. (T)
2. The Mariner tells of a terrible storm that forced his ship to sail to a land of ice and cold. (T)
3. All of the sailors were cruel to an albatross that came out of the fog. (F)
4. The albatross proved to be a good omen and followed the ship. (T)
5. The Mariner admits he shot the albatross because he was jealous of the attention it was getting. (F)

A It ate the food it ne'er had eat,
And round and round it flew.
The ice did split with a thunder-fit;
70   The helmsman steered us through!

And a good south wind sprung up behind;
The Albatross did follow,
And every day, for food or play,
Came to the mariner's hollo!

75   In mist or cloud, or mast or shroud,°
It perched for vespers° nine;
Whiles all the night, through fog-smoke white,
Glimmered the white Moonshine.''

B "God save thee, ancient Mariner!
80   From the fiends, that plague thee thus!
C Why look'st thou so?''—With my crossbow
I shot the Albatross.

And lo! the Albatross proveth a bird of good omen, and followeth the ship as it returned northward through fog and floating ice.

75. shroud: support rope that stretches from the top of the mast to the side of the ship.
76. vespers: evenings; also, evening prayers.

The ancient Mariner inhospitably killeth the pious bird of good omen.

D

The Rime of the Ancient Mariner, illustration by Gustave Doré. Engraving.

A. Setting/Speaker
The ship has rounded Cape Horn, the most southerly part of South America, and is now sailing north. Note that the Mariner is speaking.

B. Plot
❓ How do you account for the change in the shipmates' attitudes in lines 93–102? (The shipmates see the albatross's death as the cause of the calm and fog. [Remember that this is a sailing ship and needs the wind to move and the stars to navigate.] When all is well, they support the bird; when things go wrong, they blame it.)

C. Alliteration/Internal Rhyme
Note the alliteration and internal rhyme, which help create the powerful music of the poem.

D. Setting
The sun's location suggests that the ship is becalmed at the equator.

E. A Famous Verse
Here is one of the most frequently quoted stanzas from the poem. You might suggest some of these verses for memorization.

Part II

A
The Sun now rose upon the right:
Out of the sea came he,
85   Still hid in mist, and on the left
Went down into the sea.

And the good south wind still blew behind,
But no sweet bird did follow.
Nor any day for food or play
90   Came to the mariners' hollo!

And I had done a hellish thing,
And it would work 'em woe:
For all averred,° I had killed the bird
That made the breeze to blow.
95   Ah wretch! said they, the bird to slay,
That made the breeze to blow!

B
Nor dim nor red, like God's own head,
The glorious Sun uprist:°
Then all averred, I had killed the bird
100   That brought the fog and mist.
'Twas right, said they, such birds to slay,
That bring the fog and mist.

C
The fair breeze blew, the white foam flew,
The furrow° followed free;
105   We were the first that ever burst
Into that silent sea.

Down dropt the breeze, the sails dropt down,
'Twas sad as sad could be;
And we did speak only to break
110   The silence of the sea!

D
All in a hot and copper sky,
The bloody Sun, at noon,
Right up above the mast did stand,
No bigger than the Moon.

115   Day after day, day after day,
We stuck, nor breath nor motion;
As idle as a painted ship
Upon a painted ocean.

E
Water, water, everywhere,
120   And all the boards did shrink;
Water, water, everywhere,
Nor any drop to drink.

93. **averred:** asserted, claimed.
His shipmates cry out against the ancient Mariner for killing the bird of good luck.

98. **uprist:** rose up.
But when the fog cleared off, they justify the same, and thus make themselves accomplices in the crime.

The fair breeze continues; the ship enters the Pacific Ocean, and sails northward, even till it reaches the line.
104. **furrow:** the ship's wake.

The ship hath been suddenly becalmed.

And the Albatross begins to be avenged.

READING CHECK TEST: PART II

1. The Mariner's shipmates believed the albatross had brought them good luck. (T)
2. When the fog cleared, the shipmates praised the Mariner for killing the bird. (T)
3. Suddenly, the breeze stopped, and the ship's sails dropped. (T)
4. The crew had plenty of water to drink but suffered from a lack of fresh vegetables. (F)
5. The shipmates hung the dead albatross around the Mariner's neck as a good-luck charm. (F)

A. Expansion
In reality, the albatross is too large a bird to be hung around a person's neck. Coleridge may not have realized the bird's size.

B. Diction
This stanza first appeared in Coleridge's collected poems *Sybilline Leaves* (1818).
❓ What is the effect of the repetition of *weary*? (It emphasizes the exhaustion and slow passage of time.)

C. Plot
❓ Why does the Mariner bite his arm and drink the blood? (So that he can moisten his dry throat to speak)

The very deep did rot: O Christ!
That ever this should be!
125 Yea, slimy things did crawl with legs
Upon the slimy sea.

About, about, in reel and rout°
The death-fires° danced at night;
The water, like a witch's oils,
130 Burnt green, and blue and white.

And some in dreams assuréd were
Of the Spirit that plagued us so;
Nine fathom deep he had followed us
From the land of mist and snow.

135 And every tongue, through utter drought,
Was withered at the root;
We could not speak, no more than if
We had been choked with soot.

Ah! well a-day!° what evil looks
140 Had I from old and young!
A ⎡Instead of the cross, the Albatross
  ⎣About my neck was hung.

127. **rout:** chaotic movement, uproar.
128. **death-fires:** probably the ghostly glow that actually is emitted by some rotting substances, said to be seen in graveyards.

A Spirit had followed them; one of the invisible inhabitants of this planet, neither departed souls nor angels; concerning whom the learned Jew, Josephus, and the Platonic Constantinopolitan, Michael Psellus, may be consulted. They are very numerous, and there is no climate or element without one or more.

139. **well a-day:** an exclamation of sorrow; alas.
The shipmates, in their sore distress, would fain throw the whole guilt on the ancient Mariner: in sign whereof they hang the dead seabird round his neck.

Part III

There passed a weary time. Each throat
Was parched, and glazed each eye.
145 A weary time! a weary time!
B How glazed each weary eye,
When looking westward, I beheld
A something in the sky.

At first it seemed a little speck,
150 And then it seemed a mist;
It moved and moved, and took at last
A certain shape, I wist.°

A speck, a mist, a shape, I wist!
And still it neared and neared:
155 As if it dodged a water-sprite,
It plunged and tacked and veered.°

With throats unslaked, with black lips baked,
We could nor laugh nor wail;
Through utter drought all dumb we stood!
160 ⎡I bit my arm, I sucked the blood,
C ⎣And cried, A sail! a sail!

The ancient Mariner beholdeth a sign in the element afar off.

152. **wist:** knew.

156. **tacked and veered:** turned toward and then away from the wind.
At its nearer approach, it seemeth him to be a ship; and at a dear ransom, he freeth his speech from the bonds of thirst.

With throats unslaked,° with black lips baked,
Agape they heard me call:
Gramercy!° they for joy did grin,
165   And all at once their breath drew in,
As they were drinking all.

See! see! (I cried) she tacks no more!
Hither to work us weal;°
Without a breeze, without a tide,
170   She steadies with upright keel!

The western wave was all aflame.
The day was well nigh done!
Almost upon the western wave
Rested the broad bright Sun;
175   When that strange shape drove suddenly
Betwixt us and the Sun.

And straight the Sun was flecked with bars.
(Heaven's Mother send us grace!)
As if through a dungeon-grate he peered
180   With broad and burning face.

Alas! (thought I, and my heart beat loud)
How fast she nears and nears!
Are those *her* sails that glance in the Sun,
Like restless gossameres?°

185   Are those *her* ribs through which the Sun
Did peer, as through a grate?
And is that Woman all her crew?
A   Is that a Death? and are there two?
Is Death that woman's mate?

190   *Her* lips were red, *her* looks were free,
Her locks were yellow as gold:
B   Her skin was as white as leprosy,
The Nightmare Life-in-Death was she,
Who thicks man's blood with cold.

195   The naked hulk alongside came,
And the twain were casting dice;
C   "The game is done! I've won! I've won!"
Quoth she, and whistles thrice.

The Sun's rim dips; the stars rush out:
200   At one stride comes the dark;
With far-heard whisper, o'er the sea,
Off shot the specter-bark.

We listened and looked sideways up!
Fear at my heart, as at a cup,

162. **unslaked:** unrelieved of thirst.

164. **Gramercy:** an exclamation of great thanks.
A flash of joy.

And horror follows. For can it be a ship that comes onward without wind or tide?
168. **work us weal:** do us good.

It seemeth him but the skeleton of a ship.

184. **gossameres:** filmy cobwebs.

And its ribs are seen as bars on the face of the setting Sun. The Specter-Woman and her Deathmate, and no other on board the skeleton ship.

Like vessel, like crew!

Death and Life-in-Death have diced for the ship's crew, and she (the latter) winneth the ancient Mariner.

No twilight within the courts of the Sun.

At the rising of the Moon,

A. Symbolism
In line 188, *Death* means "skeleton." The Mariner soon realizes that what he sees is not an ordinary skeleton, but Death itself.

B. Vocabulary
Free means "lewd, licentious."

C. Plot
❓ What do you think is going to happen to the ship's crew and to the Ancient Mariner? Why?

A. Humanities
Connection:
About the
Illustration
Doré's engraving
illustrates line 153.
The ship of death
can be dimly seen
on the horizon.

The Rime of the Ancient Mariner, illustration by Gustave Doré. Engraving.

READING CHECK TEST: PART III
1. The mariners are dying of thirst. (T)
2. Death and Life-in-Death approached in a mysterious ship. (T)
3. Life-in-Death exclaimed that she had won their game of dice. (T)
4. All the crew except the Mariner dropped dead on the deck. (T)
5. The Mariner was taken on to the mysterious ship as a prisoner. (F)

205   My lifeblood seemed to sip!
The stars were dim, and thick the night,
The steersman's face by his lamp gleamed white;
From the sails the dew did drip—

A   Till clomb° above the eastern bar
210   The hornéd° Moon, with one bright star
Within the nether tip.

209. **clomb:** climbed.
210. **hornéd:** crescent.

One after one, by the star-dogged Moon,
Too quick for groan or sigh,
Each turned his face with a ghastly pang,
215   And cursed me with his eye.

One after another,

Four times fifty living men,
(And I heard nor sigh nor groan)
With heavy thump, a lifeless lump,
They dropped down one by one.

His shipmates drop down dead.

220   The souls did from their bodies fly,
They fled to bliss or woe!
And every soul, it passed me by,
Like the whizz of my crossbow!

But Life-in-Death begins her work on the ancient Mariner.

Part IV

"I fear thee, ancient Mariner!
225   I fear thy skinny hand!
B   And thou art long, and lank, and brown,
As is the ribbed sea-sand.

The Wedding Guest feareth that a Spirit is talking to him;

I fear thee and thy glittering eye,
And thy skinny hand, so brown."—
230   Fear not, fear not, thou Wedding Guest!
This body dropt not down.

But the ancient Mariner assureth him of his bodily life, and proceedeth to relate his horrible penance.

C   Alone, alone, all, all alone,
Alone on a wide wide sea!
And never a saint took pity on
235   My soul in agony.

The many men, so beautiful!
And they all dead did lie:
And a thousand thousand slimy things
Lived on; and so did I.

He despiseth the creatures of the calm,

240   I looked upon the rotting sea,
And drew my eyes away;
I looked upon the rotting deck,
And there the dead men lay.

And envieth that they should live, and so many lie dead.

A. Expansion
The *eastern bar* is the eastern horizon. Coleridge explained: "It is a common superstition among sailors, 'that something evil is about to happen, whenever a star dogs the moon.'"

B. Expansion
Wordsworth wrote these two lines during the walk in which the poem was planned.

C. Repetition/ Imagery
Coleridge uses just a few words to create this powerful image of human isolation. Note the alliteration and assonance, caused mostly by repetition.

Samuel Taylor Coleridge   663

A. Mood

? How does the mood of the poem change with the rising of the moon? (The moon-rise brings with it a feeling of calm and softness and heal-ing in contrast to the "bloody sun.")

B. Plot

Here is the turning point of the narra-tive.

? What action does the Mari-ner take that be-gins his "rebirth"? (He loves the wa-ter snakes and blesses them.)

245 I looked to heaven, and tried to pray;
But or° ever a prayer had gushed,
A wicked whisper came, and made
My heart as dry as dust.

250 I closed my lids, and kept them close,
And the balls like pulses beat;
For the sky and the sea, and the sea and the sky
Lay like a load on my weary eye,
And the dead were at my feet.

255 The cold sweat melted from their limbs,
Nor rot nor reek did they:
The look with which they looked on me
Had never passed away.

260 An orphan's curse would drag to hell
A spirit from on high;
But oh! more horrible than that
Is the curse in a dead man's eye!
Seven days, seven nights, I saw that curse,
And yet I could not die.

265 **A** The moving Moon went up the sky,
And nowhere did abide:
Softly she was going up,
And a star or two beside—

270 Her beams bemocked the sultry main,°
Like April hoarfrost° spread;
But where the ship's huge shadow lay,
The charméd water burnt alway°
A still and awful red.

275 Beyond the shadow of the ship,
I watched the water snakes:
They moved in tracks of shining white,
And when they reared, the elfish light
Fell off in hoary flakes.

280 Within the shadow of the ship
I watched their rich attire:
Blue, glossy green, and velvet black,
They coiled and swam; and every track
Was a flash of golden fire.

285 **B** O happy living things! no tongue
Their beauty might declare:
A spring of love gushed from my heart,
And I blessed them unaware:
Sure my kind saint took pity on me,
And I blessed them unaware.

245. **or:** before.

But the curse liveth for him in the eye of the dead men.

In his loneliness and fixedness he yearneth toward the journeying Moon, and the stars that still sojourn, yet still move onward; and everywhere the blue sky belongs to them, and is their appointed rest, and their native country and their own natural homes, which they enter unannounced, as lords that are certainly expected and yet there is a silent joy at their arrival.
267. **main:** open sea.
268. **hoarfrost:** white ("hoar") deposits from freezing dew; frost.
270. **alway:** always.

By the light of the Moon he beholdeth God's creatures of the great calm.

Their beauty and their happiness.

He blesseth them in his heart.

1. The Wedding Guest fears the Mariner is a ghost. (T)
2. The Mariner rejoiced that his own life was spared. (F)
3. The bodies of the crew rotted quickly, so the Mariner was surrounded by skeletal remains. (F)
4. The Mariner cursed the water snakes and killed them. (F)
5. When the Mariner discovered he could pray, the albatross fell from his neck into the sea. (T)

290
The selfsame moment I could pray;
And from my neck so free
The Albatross fell off, and sank
Like lead into the sea.

Part V

A
Oh sleep! it is a gentle thing,
Beloved from pole to pole!
To Mary Queen the praise be given!
295
She sent the gentle sleep from Heaven
That slid into my soul.

The silly° buckets on the deck,
That had so long remained,
I dreamt that they were filled with dew;
300
And when I awoke, it rained.

My lips were wet, my throat was cold,
My garments all were dank;
Sure I had drunken in my dreams,
And still my body drank.

305
I moved, and could not feel my limbs:
I was so light—almost
I thought that I had died in sleep,
And was a blessèd ghost.

And soon I heard a roaring wind:
310
It did not come anear;
But with its sound it shook the sails,
That were so thin and sere.°

The upper air burst into life!
And a hundred fire flags sheen,
315
To and fro they were hurried about!
And to and fro, and in and out,
The wan stars danced between.°

And the coming wind did roar more loud,
And the sails did sigh like sedge;°
320
And the rain poured down from one black cloud;
The Moon was at its edge.

The thick black cloud was cleft, and still
The Moon was at its side:
Like waters shot from some high crag,
325
The lightning fell with never a jag,
A river steep and wide.

The spell begins to break.

By grace of the holy Mother, the ancient Mariner is refreshed with rain.
297. **silly:** pathetic (because they had remained useless for so long).

He heareth sounds and seeth strange sights and commotions in the sky and the element.

312. **sere:** threadbare.

313–317. This stanza apparently describes the shifting lights of an aurora, which sometimes resemble waving, luminous folds of fabric.
319. **sedge:** reedy plants.

A. A Famous Stanza
This stanza is frequently quoted.
? How is sleep represented? (As something gentle, sent by the Virgin Mary, and beloved the world over)

A. Vocabulary
Inspired here means "inspirited," which is the word Coleridge used in the first printing of the glosses.

B. Plot
Wordsworth claimed that it was his idea to have the ship run by dead sailors. Tales of ships manned by the dead were common among sailors.

C. Speaker
Note that the Wedding Guest interrupts again.
❓ What does the Mariner tell him? (That it was not the dead men's souls that animated their corpses, but the holy spirits)

D. Vocabulary
Note the interesting origin of the word *jargon*.

The loud wind never reached the ship,
Yet now the ship moved on!
Beneath the lightning and the Moon
330 The dead men gave a groan.

They groaned, they stirred, they all uprose,
Nor spake, nor moved their eyes;
It had been strange, even in a dream,
To have seen those dead men rise.

335 The helmsman steered, the ship moved on;
Yet never a breeze upblew;
The mariners all 'gan work the ropes,
Where they were wont° to do;
They raised their limbs like lifeless tools—
340 We were a ghastly crew.

The body of my brother's son
Stood by me, knee to knee:
The body and I pulled at one rope,
But he said nought to me.

345 "I fear thee, ancient Mariner!"
Be calm, thou Wedding Guest!
'Twas not those souls that fled in pain,
Which to their corses° came again,
But a troop of spirits blest:

350 For when it dawned—they dropped their arms,
And clustered round the mast;
Sweet sounds rose slowly through their mouths,
And from their bodies passed.

Around, around, flew each sweet sound,
355 Then darted to the Sun;
Slowly the sounds came back again,
Now mixed, now one by one.

Sometimes a-dropping from the sky
I heard the skylark sing;
360 Sometimes all little birds that are,
How they seemed to fill the sea and air
With their sweet jargoning!°

And now 'twas like all instruments,
Now like a lonely flute:
365 And now it is an angel's song,
That makes the heavens be mute.

It ceased; yet still the sails made on
A pleasant noise till noon,
A noise like of a hidden brook

The bodies of the ship's crew are inspired and the ship moves on.

338. **wont:** accustomed.

But not by the souls of the men, nor by demons of earth or middle air, but by a blessed troop of angelic spirits, sent down by the invocation of the guardian saint.
348. **corses:** corpses.

362. **jargoning:** twittering.

The Rime of the Ancient Mariner, illustration by Gustave Doré. Engraving.

A

READING CHECK TEST: PART V

1. After the Mariner awakened, rain refreshed him. (T)
2. When the ship moved, the dead crew rose and began working. (T)
3. The Mariner's nephew, working beside him, repeatedly cursed his uncle. (F)

4. A strong wind caused the ship to sail smoothly. (F)
5. The Mariner heard a voice say that he still had more penance to do for his crime. (T)

A. Plot
? Who or what is moving the ship? (A water spirit from the South Pole)

B. Meaning
In line 394, *have not* means "am not able." In line 395, *living life* contrasts with death-in-life.

C. Interpreting
? Whose are the voices here and at the beginning of Part VI? (The voices belong to the Polar spirit's "fellow demons.")

D. Allusion
The reference is to Christ.

E. Predicting Outcomes
? What further penance do you predict the Mariner will have to do?

370   In the leafy month of June,
      That to the sleeping woods all night
      Singeth a quiet tune.

      Till noon we quietly sailed on,
      Yet never a breeze did breathe:
375   Slowly and smoothly went the ship,
      Moved onward from beneath.

A

      Under the keel nine fathom deep,
      From the land of mist and snow,
      The spirit slid: and it was he
380   That made the ship to go.
      The sails at noon left off their tune,
      And the ship stood still also.

      The Sun, right up above the mast,
      Had fixed her° to the ocean:
385   But in a minute she 'gan stir,
      With a short uneasy motion—
      Backwards and forwards half her length
      With a short uneasy motion.

      Then like a pawing horse let go,
390   She made a sudden bound:
      It flung the blood into my head,
      And I fell down in a swound.

      How long in that same fit I lay,
B   I have not to declare;
395   But ere my living life returned,
      I heard and in my soul discerned
C   Two voices in the air.

      "Is it he?" quoth one, "Is this the man?
D   By him who died on cross.
400   With his cruel bow he laid full low
      The harmless Albatross.

      The spirit who bideth by himself
      In the land of mist and snow,
      He loved the bird that loved the man
405   Who shot him with his bow."

      The other was a softer voice,
      As soft as honeydew:
E   Quoth he, "The man hath penance done,
      And penance more will do."

The lonesome Spirit from the South Pole carries on the ship as far as the line, in obedience to the angelic troop, but still requireth vengeance.

384. **fixed her:** that is, seemed to hold the ship motionless, as if by hypnotic power.

The Polar Spirit's fellow demons, the invisible inhabitants of the element, take part in his wrong; and two of them relate, one to the other, that penance long and heavy for the ancient Mariner hath been accorded to the Polar Spirit, who returneth southward.

PREPARATION

ESTABLISHING A PURPOSE. As they read
Parts VI and VII, ask students to think
about the poem's message.

Part VI

A

First Voice

410   "But tell me, tell me! speak again,
       Thy soft response renewing—
       What makes that ship drive on so fast?
       What is the ocean doing?"

Second Voice

       "Still as a slave before his lord,
415   The ocean hath no blast;°
       His great bright eye most silently
       Up to the Moon is cast—

B

       If he may know which way to go;
       For she guides him smooth or grim.
420   See, brother, see! how graciously
       She looketh down on him."

First Voice

       "But why drives on that ship so fast,
       Without or wave or wind?"°

Second Voice

       "The air is cut away before,
425   And closes from behind.

       Fly, brother, fly! more high, more high!
       Or we shall be belated:
       For slow and slow that ship will go.

C   When the Mariner's trance is abated."

430   I woke, and we were sailing on
       As in a gentle weather:
       'Twas night, calm night, the moon was high;
       The dead men stood together.

       All stood together on the deck,
435   For a charnel dungeon° fitter:
       All fixed on me their stony eyes,
       That in the Moon did glitter.

       The pang, the curse, with which they died,
       Had never passed away:
440   I could not draw my eyes from theirs,
       Nor turn them up to pray.

       And now this spell was snapped: once more
       I viewed the ocean green,
       And looked far forth, yet little saw
445   Of what had else° been seen—

---

415. **blast:** wind.

The Mariner hath been cast into a trance; for the angelic power causeth the vessel to drive northward faster than human life could endure.
423. **Without . . . wind:** with neither wave nor wind.

The supernatural motion is retarded: the Mariner awakes, and his penance begins anew.

435. **charnel dungeon:** burial vault.

The curse is finally expiated [removed, after penance is done].

445. **had else:** would have otherwise, or at another time.

A. Voices
? Whose voices are we hearing now? (Notice that these are not the Mariner or the Wedding Guest, but disembodied voices that are watching the mysterious ship move through the sea. They are the two spirits who spoke in lines 398–409.)

B. Personification
? How are the ocean and the moon personified in these stanzas? (The ocean is looking up to the moon for guidance. The sea is personified in line 414 as a slave to the moon.)

C. Connections
Note that the magical, swift motion of the ship while the Mariner is in a trance resembles Odysseus's homeward voyage in Homer's *Odyssey* (Book 13). The gods cause Odysseus to fall into a trance while they speed his ship home to Ithaca.

1. Death and Rebirth. Maud Bodkin sees the poem as an archetypal story—that is, a narrative that is found in all cultures. She believes its theme has to do with death and rebirth. Trace with the students the poem's powerful images of death and rebirth in the natural world: sleep and waking, the death of winter and rebirth of spring, the cycle of night and day, the death and rebirth of the moon.

2. Crime and Punishment. Martin Gardner calls this the "rebirth pattern of sin-suffering-death-repentance-rebirth-penance-salvation." In his book *The Romantic Imagination,* Cecil M. Bowra suggests that readers might ask why there is "all this 'pother about a bird.'" Bowra goes on to say, "The poem is a myth of a guil-ty soul and marks in clear stages the passage from crime through punishment to such redemption as is possible in this world." Some critics suggest that the Mariner's crime represents original sin.

3. The Supernatural Elements. As students state the theme of the poem, be sure they take into account its supernatural elements. What could Coleridge be saying about the importance of the

A. Alliteration/ Assonance
Have students read this stanza aloud to hear its alliteration and as-sonance.

The Rime of the Ancient Mariner, illustration by Gustave Doré. Engraving.

Like one, that on a lonesome road
Doth walk in fear and dread,
And having once turned round walks on,
And turns no more his head;
450   Because he knows, a frightful fiend
Doth close behind him tread.

But soon there breathed a wind on me,
Nor sound nor motion made:
Its path was not upon the sea,
455   In ripple or in shade.

It raised my hair, it fanned my cheek
Like a meadow gale of spring—
It mingled strangely with my fears,
Yet it felt like a welcoming.

460   Swiftly, swiftly flew the ship,
A   Yet she sailed softly too:
Sweetly, sweetly blew the breeze—
On me alone it blew.

"shadow world" and about its influence on our "daylit" lives?

4. The Wanderer Archetype. American critic Harold Bloom says that the story Coleridge tells in this poem is clearly related "to a major Romantic archetype, the Wanderer, the man with the mark of Cain [see text page 30], or the mocker of Christ, who must expiate in a perpetual cycle of guilt and suffering, and whose

torment is in excess of its usually obscure object and source."

Have students relate the Mariner to this Wanderer archetype. See also text pages 42–46.

5. The Creative Imagination. American poet and novelist Robert Penn Warren sees a secondary theme of the creative imagination. He believes that the death of the albatross represents the poet's

"crime against his imagination," which leaves the poet unable to write. In this case, what might the wind, the serpents, and the sea symbolize?

465
A
Oh! dream of joy! is this indeed
The lighthouse top I see?
Is this the hill? is this the kirk?
Is this mine own countree?

We drifted o'er the harbor bar,
And I with sobs did pray—
470 O let me be awake, my God!
Or let me sleep alway.

The harbor bay was clear as glass,
So smoothly it was strewn!°
And on the bay the moonlight lay,
475 And the shadow of the Moon.

The rock shone bright, the kirk no less,
That stands above the rock:
The moonlight steeped in silentness
B The steady weathercock.°

480 And the bay was white with silent light,
Till rising from the same,
Full many shapes, that shadows were,
In crimson colors came.

A little distance from the prow
485 Those crimson shadows were:
I turned my eyes upon the deck—
Oh, Christ! what saw I there!

Each corse lay flat, lifeless and flat,
And, by the holy rood!°
490 A man all light, a seraph-man,°
C On every corse there stood.

This seraph band, each waved his hand:
It was a heavenly sight!
They stood as signals to the land,
495 Each one a lovely light;

D This seraph band, each waved his hand,
No voice did they impart—
No voice; but oh! the silence sank
Like music on my heart.

500 But soon I heard the dash of oars,
I heard the Pilot's cheer;
My head was turned perforce away
And I saw a boat appear.

And the ancient Mariner beholdeth his native country.

473. **strewn:** spread out in a sheet, calmed.

479. **weathercock:** rooster-shaped weather-vane.

The angelic spirits leave the dead bodies,

And appear in their own forms of light.

489. **rood:** crucifix.
490. **seraph-man:** angel of the highest rank.

A. Imagery
In lines 23–24, when the ship departed, the lighthouse, hill, and kirk are mentioned in reverse order.

B. Vocabulary
A *steady weathercock* means that there is no wind.

C. Imagery
The powerful image of a crowd of corpses and angels might seem gruesome.
❓ What phrases create instead a surprising, positive atmosphere? ("A lively light"; "like music on my heart")

D. Interpreting
The Mariner's boat waits in the harbor for the Pilot's boat to guide it to shore. The seraphim are signaling for the Pilot's boat to come.

A. Character

? Why do you think this Hermit is introduced? (Confessing to him will be part of the Mariner's "penance yet to come.") A hermit was a holy man who had retreated to the woods to pray. The early Fathers of the Christian Church were called hermits.

B. Plot

? At the end of Part VI, what is the Mariner's urgent hope? (That the Hermit will release him from his guilt)

C. Speaker

The Hermit and the Pilot are talking as they approach the Mariner's ship. Remember that the ship is littered with corpses.

D. Simile

? What makes this simile so eerie? (The ship's thin, dry sails are compared to the "skeletons" of leaves that float on brooks in winter. A further threatening image is provided by the owl that eats the wolf's young.)

E. Irony

Coleridge is using dramatic irony: *We* know what these characters will find on board the ship.

READING CHECK TEST: PART VI

1. When the Mariner woke, the crew was standing together on the deck. (T)
2. The ship sailed on and the Mariner reached his homeland again. (T)
3. The Mariner saw an angel standing on top of each corpse. (T)
4. The angels brought the corpses back to life. (F)
5. The Mariner now must go to the Hermit to confess his sin. (T)

505   The Pilot and the Pilot's boy,
I heard them coming fast:
Dear Lord in Heaven! it was a joy
The dead men could not blast.

I saw a third—I heard his voice:
A It is the Hermit good!
510   He singeth loud his godly hymns
That he makes in the wood.
B He'll shrieve° my soul, he'll wash away
The Albatross's blood.

512. **shrieve:** release from guilt, following confession.

Part VII

515   This Hermit good lives in that wood
Which slopes down to the sea.
How loudly his sweet voice he rears!
He loves to talk with marineres
That come from a far countree.

520   He kneels at morn, and noon, and eve—
He hath a cushion plump:
It is the moss that wholly hides
The rotted old oak stump.

The Hermit of the Wood,

The skiff-boat° neared: I heard them talk,
C "Why, this is strange, I trow!°
525   Where are those lights so many and fair,
That signal made but now?"

523. **skiff-boat:** rowboat.
524. **trow:** believe.

"Strange, by my faith!" the Hermit said—
"And they answered not our cheer!
The planks looked warped! and see those sails,
530   How thin they are and sere!
I never saw aught° like to them,
Unless perchance it were

Approacheth the ship with wonder.

531. **aught:** anything.

D Brown skeletons of leaves that lag°
My forest brook along;
535   When the ivy tod° is heavy with snow,
And the owlet whoops to the wolf below,
That eats the she-wolf's young."

533. **lag:** drift (more slowly than the current).
535. **ivy tod:** clump of ivy.

E "Dear Lord! it hath a fiendish look—
(The Pilot made reply)
540   I am afeared"—"Push on, push on!"
Said the Hermit cheerily.

1. The Hermit tells the frightened Pilot not to approach the ship. (F)
2. With a loud sound the ship sinks, but the Mariner is saved. (T)
3. The Mariner's penance is to continue to live and to tell his tale. (T)
4. The Mariner advises the Wedding Guest to love all things that God has created. (T)
5. The Wedding Guest invites the Mariner to go with him to the wedding feast. (F)

The boat came closer to the ship,
But I nor spake nor stirred;
The boat came close beneath the ship,
545 And straight° a sound was heard.

Under the water it rumbled on,
Still louder and more dread:
It reached the ship, it split the bay;
The ship went down like lead.

550 Stunned by that loud and dreadful sound,
Which sky and ocean smote,
Like one that hath been seven days drowned
My body lay afloat;
But swift as dreams, myself I found
555 Within the Pilot's boat.

Upon the whirl, where sank the ship,
The boat spun round and round;
And all was still, save that the hill
Was telling of the sound.

560 I moved my lips—the Pilot shrieked
And fell down in a fit;
The holy Hermit raised his eyes,
And prayed where he did sit.

A I took the oars: the Pilot's boy,
565 Who now doth crazy go,
Laughed loud and long, and all the while
His eyes went to and fro.
"Ha! ha!" quoth he, "full plain I see,
The Devil knows how to row."

570 And now, all in my own countree,
I stood on the firm land!
The Hermit stepped forth from the boat,
And scarcely he could stand.

"O shrieve me, shrieve me, holy man!"
575 The Hermit crossed° his brow.
"Say quick," quoth he, "I bid thee say—
What manner of man art thou?"

B

Forthwith° this frame of mine was wrenched
With a woeful agony,
580 Which forced me to begin my tale;
And then it left me free.

Since then, at an uncertain hour,
That agony returns:
C And till my ghastly tale is told,
585 This heart within me burns.

545. **straight:** straightaway, at once.

The ship suddenly sinketh.

The ancient Mariner is saved in the Pilot's boat.

The ancient Mariner earnestly entreateth the Hermit to shrieve him; and the penance of life falls on him.
575. **crossed:** made the sign of the cross.

578. **Forthwith:** at once.

And ever and anon throughout his future life an agony constraineth him to travel from land to land;

A. Character
? Describe the reactions of the three people in the Pilot's boat. (The Pilot faints, the Pilot's boy goes crazy, the Hermit remains calm but makes the sign of the cross to protect himself.)

B. Climax
Here is the Mariner's catharsis: He tells his tale to the Hermit.

C. Inferring
? According to these lines, why has the Mariner forced the Wedding Guest to listen to his story? (The periodic agony that overcomes him goes away only when he tells his story.)

1. The poem begins with an omniscient narrator, but from line 41 on, the narrator is the Ancient Mariner, who tells his story to the Wedding Guest.

The Mariner killed an albatross—the embodiment of love and good fortune. Because of his act of irrational destruction, he is punished with a life of permanent alienation. The crew die but continue to sail the ship. The mariner's journey continues as he does penance for his sin. Eventually he returns home, but he is fated always to travel. In his travels he must retell (as he does to the Wedding Guest) his story (thereby reliving his horrors and shame), and through his story he must teach love and reverence for all living things.

2. The ship is becalmed; the Mariner and the crew suffer from heat and thirst.

3. He fears the Mariner was one of those who died and is now a ghost.

The Mariner assures him that he is alive, that his body was not one of those that fell.

4. A woman (Life-in-Death) and Death are the occupants.

A. Setting

? What is the effect of cutting once again to the wedding scene? (There is a sharp contrast in mood and setting as the narrative returns to the frame story to close the poem.)

B. Humanities Connection: Responding to the Illustration

Doré's engraving illustrates lines 618–620.

? What does it make you feel for the Ancient Mariner? (Pity probably)

I pass, like night, from land to land;
I have strange power of speech;
That moment that his face I see,
I know the man that must hear me:
590   To him my tale I teach.

A

What loud uproar bursts from that door!
The wedding guests are there:
But in the garden bower the bride
And bridemaids singing are:
595   And hark the little vesper bell,
Which biddeth me to prayer!

O Wedding Guest! this soul hath been
Alone on a wide wide sea:
So lonely 'twas, that God himself
600   Scarce seemèd there to be.

B

The Rime of the Ancient Mariner,
illustration by Gustave Doré.
Engraving.

The crewmen die one by one.
5. A "wicked whisper" makes his heart "as dry as dust."

When he shifts his focus away from himself and his circumstances, he blesses the water snakes; then he is able to pray.
6. They are afraid of the Mariner.

The Mariner asks the Hermit to shrieve him—to hear his confession and give him God's forgiveness.
7. He says he is destined to travel from land to land telling his tale as penance.

To love all God's creatures.

Interpreting Meanings
8. In the beginning of the poem and at the end.

The joy of the wedding is contrasted with the Mariner's grim tale. Also, the Mariner's crime is a lack of love; the wedding is a celebration of love.
9. He begins by seeing himself as cursed and his surroundings as ugly. When he recognizes the beauty of the water snakes and blesses them, he begins to love, and the albatross falls from him.

Yes. In his isolation he recognizes his need for other living beings; focusing only on himself— his regret and shame and guilt— is deadly. Focusing on others offers him life, which is symbolized by his ability to pray.
10. Shame is the feeling you have done something wrong or have lost the respect of oth- er people. Guilt is a feeling of self- reproach for hav- ing done some- thing unethical or immoral.

He experiences shame after he kills the albatross. He feels guilt when he acknowledges the great harm he has caused to the albatross.
11. His immediate penance is to suf- fer alone on the ship.

His lifetime pen- ance is to be an outcast, wandering and telling his sto- ry to relieve his ag- ony (his "burning heart").
12. Answers will vary. Generally, one who loves generously and completely will live happily and there- fore well. Nothing needs to be added to the conclusion. Prayer, here, implies life in general.
(Answers continue on next page.)

O sweeter than the marriage feast,
'Tis sweeter far to me,
To walk together to the kirk
With a goodly company!—

605   To walk together to the kirk,
And all together pray,
While each to his great Father bends,
Old men, and babes, and loving friends
And youths and maidens gay!

610   Farewell, farewell! but this I tell
To thee, thou Wedding Guest!
He prayeth well, who loveth well
Both man and bird and beast.

He prayeth best, who loveth best
615   All things both great and small;
For the dear God who loveth us,
He made and loveth all.

The Mariner, whose eye is bright,
Whose beard with age is hoar,
620   Is gone: and now the Wedding Guest
Turned from the bridegroom's door.

He went like one that hath been stunned,
And is of sense forlorn:
A sadder and a wiser man,
625   He rose the morrow morn.

And to teach, by his own example, love and reverence to all things that God made and loveth.

Responding to the Poem

Analyzing the Poem

Identifying Details

1. Who is presented as the **narrator** of the ballad? To whom is he telling his story? Summarize the Mariner's story.
2. According to Part II, what consequences follow the Mariner's killing of the albatross?
3. Explain the Wedding Guest's fear at the opening of Part IV. How does the Ancient Mariner reassure him?
4. Who are the occupants of the strange ship that appears in Part III? What results from their appearance?
5. In Part IV, why is the Mariner unable to pray? What happens that enables him to pray?
6. What is the reaction of the Pilot and the Hermit to the Mariner's homecoming? What does the Mariner plead with the Hermit to do?
7. At the end of the ballad, how does the Mariner describe his current life? What lesson does he draw for the Wedding Guest from this tale?

Interpreting Meanings

8. Where in the poem is the wedding mentioned? How does this context for the ballad affect your response to it?

13. He is sad because he has heard a tragic story, wiser because he has learned the importance of loving others.

Kubla Khan hears ancestral voices prophesying war. In "This Lime-Tree Bower," the speaker is addressing his friend Charles.

14. Students may feel the sidenotes are helpful in summarizing the plot. Reading them should not, however, alter the meaning of the poem.

15. The following effects might be noted.

Simile: lines 33–34 compare the bride to a rose to describe her radiant beauty.

Metaphor: in lines 195–199 Death and Life-in-Death cast dice for the Mariner's life.

Personification: lines 41–44 describe the storm as a living being.

Alliteration: in lines 171–173 the *w*'s speed up the rhythm and suggest the absent breeze.

Assonance: lines 521–522 emphasize the stump and add to the lyrical quality of the stanza.

Internal rhyme: in line 381 *noon* and *tune* break up the line, reflecting the sudden stopping of the ship.

---

9. Describe in detail the changing states of the Mariner in Part IV. Given the circumstances, are these changes believable?

10. After he shoots the albatross, the Mariner experiences both shame and guilt. What is the difference between these two emotions? Where in the poem does he experience each emotion?

11. What is the Mariner's "penance" (line 408)? What penance does he have left to do? Does it seem fair that he should have to do any sort of penance? Explain.

12. Explain in your own terms the Mariner's **moral** (lines 612–617). Does the story indicate that he ought to have added something to his moral conclusion? Explain.

13. Why is the Wedding Guest sadder but wiser after hearing the Mariner's tale? What other figures in Coleridge's poems in this selection are also listening to a speaker?

14. What do you think of Coleridge's side notes to the poem? Do you think reading them alters the meaning of the poem? Should they be consulted in a careful reading of the poem? Why or why not?

15. This ballad is famous for its use of vivid **imagery** and memorable **sound effects.** Pick out and comment on several especially effective examples of **simile, metaphor, personification, alliteration, assonance,** and **internal rhyme.**

16. For the most part, the form of the poem is the regular **ballad stanza.** Occasionally, however, Coleridge varies the **meter** of the lines and the length of the stanzas. Pick out several examples of such variations and comment on the effect of each.

17. There was a time in American history when almost every schoolchild could recite *The Rime of the Ancient Mariner*, or parts of it. Find some stanzas that strike you as particularly quotable. What situations in life could you apply the lines to?

18. Do you think that this poem has something universal to say about human conduct? Explain.

Writing About the Poem

A Creative Response

1. **Extending the Poem.** The Ancient Mariner has much in common with other legendary figures, such as the Flying Dutchman, who are condemned to wander the world in a quest for atonement or expiation. Imagine that the Mariner ultimately finds peace. Describe in a brief narrative how this might occur.

A Critical Response

2. **Analyzing Plot.** Although Coleridge keeps the plot moving along briskly in this ballad, he ignores characters' motives that other writers might have explained. For example, how could the Mariner tell that the Wedding Guest was a fit audience for his tale? Why did the Mariner shoot the albatross? How can the Mariner's punishment be regarded as fitting his crime? In a brief essay, analyze these or other questions that you think are unsatisfactorily resolved by the ballad. Does Coleridge succeed in distracting our attention from these issues so that they do not interfere with our enjoyment of his poem?

3. **Identifying Allegory.** An **allegory** is a prose or verse tale in which the characters, actions, and settings are symbolic; that is, they have both a literal and a figurative meaning. Could Coleridge's ballad be regarded as an allegory? If so, what do the various elements in the ballad symbolize? How may the tale as a whole be interpreted on an allegorical level? In a brief essay, explain your answers.

Analyzing Language and Style

Archaic Words

To give his ballad an antique flavor, Coleridge used many words that were archaic even at the time of his writing, and which, of course, are very archaic today.

1. Here is a list of archaic words from the poem. Note what each one means, and then substitute a modern synonym in the poem in place of each one. How does the flavor of the ballad change?

   a. *eftsoons* (line 12)   **g.** *wont* (line 338)
   b. *swound* (line 62)   **h.** *corses* (line 348)
   c. *uprist* (line 98)   **i.** *rood* (line 489)
   d. *wist* (line 152)   **j.** *shrieve* (line 512)
   e. *Gramercy* (line 164)   **k.** *trow* (line 524)
   f. *clomb* (line 209)

2. Are any forms of these words still in use today?

3. Sometimes the archaic meaning of a word gives us a clue to the history of a word in current use. Look at the use of the word *jargoning* in line 362. What does the word *jargon* mean today? How is contemporary "jargon" like bird twittering? (Check the derivation of the word in a dictionary.)

16. Lines 45–50, 91–102, 111–122, and 589–590 exemplify the breaks in the pattern. These shifts call attention to the events described. The varied stanzas also help to avoid a singsong quality that could lull the readers into a daze.

17. Answers will vary. These sections might be cited:

Lines 115–118: The feeling of being completely isolated from everything and everyone around you.

Lines 285–291: The feeling of overcoming a terrible burden and beginning to find happiness in life again.

18. The poem suggests that human beings must avoid destructive behavior. To live fully and happily, we must love all living creatures.

Primary Sources
Coleridge Describes His Affliction

Joseph Cottle was a close friend of the poet.

A To Joseph Cottle   *April 26, 1814*

B "You have poured oil in the raw and festering wound of an old friend's conscience, Cottle! but it is oil of vitriol! I but barely glanced at the middle of the first page of your Letter, & have seen no more of it—not from resentment (God forbid!) but from the state of my bodily & mental sufferings, that scarcely permitted human fortitude to let in a new visitor of affliction. The object of my present reply is to state the case just as it is—first, that for years the anguish of my spirit has been indescribable, the sense of my danger *staring*, but the conscience of my GUILT worse, far worse than all!—I have prayed with drops of agony on my brow, trembling not only before the justice of my Maker, but even before the mercy of my Redeemer. 'I gave thee so many talents. What hast thou done with them'?—Secondly—that it is false & cruel to say (overwhelmed as I am with the sense of my direful infirmity), that I attempt or ever have attempted to *disguise* or conceal the cause. On the contrary, not only to friends have I stated the whole case with tears & the very bitterness of shame; but in two instances I have warned young men, mere acquaintances who had spoken of having taken laudanum, of the direful consequences, by an ample exposition of its tremendous effects on myself—Thirdly, tho before God I dare not lift up my eyelids, & only do not despair of his mercy because to despair would be adding crime to crime; yet to my fellow-men I may say, that I was seduced into the ACCURSED habit ignorantly.—I had been almost bed-ridden for many months with swellings in my knees—in a medical journal I unhappily met with an account of a cure performed in a **C** similar case (or what to me appeared so) by rubbing in of laudanum, at the same time taking a given dose internally—It acted like a charm, like a miracle! I recovered the use of my limbs, of my appetite, of my spirits—& this continued for near a fortnight—At length, the un-usual stimulus subsided—the complaint returned—the supposed remedy was recurred to——but I can not go thro the dreary history—suffice it to say, that effects were produced, which acted on me by *terror & cowardice* of PAIN & sudden death, not (so help me God!) by any temptation of pleasure, or expectation or desire of exciting pleasurable sensations. On the very contrary, Mrs. Morgan & her sister will bear witness so far, as to say that the longer I abstained, the higher my spirits were, the keener my enjoyments—till the moment, the direful moment, arrived, when my pulse began to fluctuate, my heart to palpitate, & such a dreadful *falling abroad*, as it were, of my whole frame, such intolerable restlessness & incipient bewilderment, that in the last of my several attempts to abandon the dire poison, I exclaimed in agony, what I now repeat in seriousness & solemnity—'I am too poor to hazard this! Had I but a few hundred pounds, but 200 £, half to send to Mrs. Coleridge, & half to place myself in a private madhouse, where I could procure nothing but what a physician thought proper, & where a medical attendant could be constantly with me for two or three months (in less than that time life or death would be determined) then there might be hope. Now there is none!'—O God! how willingly would I place myself under Dr. Fox in his establishment—for my case is a species of madness, only that it is a derangement, an utter impotence of the *volition,* & not of the intellectual faculties—You bid me rouse myself—go, bid a man paralytic in both arms rub them briskly together, & that will cure him. Alas! (he would reply) that I cannot move my arms is my complaint & my misery.—

"My friend, Wade, is not at home—& I sent off all the little money, I had—or I would with this have inclosed the 10 £ received from you.—

"May God bless you | & | Your affectionate & | most afflicted

—S. T. Coleridge"

A. Expansion
Coleridge was forty-two when he wrote this letter. Two years later he was confined to a physician's home, hopelessly addicted to opium, his personal life and his writing career in ruins.

B. Metaphor
Oil of vitriol is concentrated sulphuric acid.

C. Vocabulary
Laudanum, a form of opium, was once used by doctors to cure a variety of ills before they knew it was addictive.

A. Humanities Connection:
About the Fine Art
Thomas Phillips (1770–1845) was a prosperous English portrait painter who counted among his clients Napoleon, William Blake, Sir Walter Scott, and Robert Southey. This is one of two portraits he did of Byron. (The second portrait, painted in 1814, shows Byron without a moustache and in conventional clothes.)

Byron is shown here in Albanian dress. In Canto II of *Childe Harold*, the poet records his journey on horseback through Albania, which was practically *terra incognita* to the English in those days.

One of Byron's friends said he was the only man to whom he would apply the word *beautiful*. Coleridge said "if you had seen him you could scarce disbelieve him . . . his eyes the open portals of the sun—things of light."

B. Expansion
Byron's 1815 marriage to Annabella Milbanke, a well-educated young heiress, was stormy from the start. After their daughter Augusta was born, Lady Byron believed her husband's violent and eccentric behavior indicated madness. When Byron ejected his wife from their home, Lady Byron demanded a separation, a scandalous decision at this time. Later documents (published by Harriet Beecher Stowe) seem to show that his wife accused Byron of incest with his half-sister Augusta Byron.

C. Expansion
Byron traveled through Spain, Greece, Turkey, and Italy. In a much vaunted feat, he swam across the Dardanelles (the one-to-four-mile-wide strait that separates the Aegean Sea and the Sea of Marmara in Turkey) in imitation of the legendary Greek hero Leander.

George Gordon, Lord Byron (1788–1824)

George Gordon Byron undoubtedly inherited the flamboyance and unconventional behavior of his grandfather and father, but until one fateful day in 1794 he seemed destined to grow up confined by humble surroundings and by the harsh Calvinism of Scotland. (His mother had fled back to her Scottish family to escape her brutish husband.) On that day in 1794, Byron's cousin was killed in a battle in Corsica and young George became first in line to be the sixth Baron Byron of Rochdale. He assumed the title on the death of his grand-uncle when he was ten years old.

His literary elevation came no less suddenly than his aristocracy. In 1812, the mid-point of the Romantic period, Byron became a celebrity with the publication of the first two cantos of a poem called *Childe Harold's Pilgrimage*, based on his recent travels in Europe and Asia Minor. Byron awoke one morning, as he later said, to find himself famous.

Like his admiral grandfather (known as "Foulweather Jack") and his father (a sea captain, a psychopath, and a spender of women's fortunes), George seems to have had an obsessive determination to prove himself in every way. Extraordinarily handsome, he was born with a deformity (which is said to have been a club foot) and in compensation he learned swimming, boxing, and horseriding. His lifestyle aggravated a glandular problem and a tendency toward grotesque obesity, so he would go on brutal periodic binge diets.

Once his inherited title was clear, young George's life changed. He was groomed for his aristocratic role with an education at Harrow and Cambridge and the required Grand Tour of Europe. These preparations, when combined with his native genius, outfitted him for his later extraordinary achievements and behavior. But pride in birth and class resulted in a stuffiness which seems curious in light of his notorious unconventional behavior. Byron was, in his way, a genuine aristocrat—he was conscious of his stature, particularly on the Continent, as the English

George Gordon, Lord Byron
by Thomas Phillips. Oil.

"M'Lord," and of his obligation to uphold a code of conduct. In Switzerland, in 1816, for example, he was shocked when Percy Shelley signed himself (in Greek) on hotel registers as "Democrat" and "Atheist." Byron later said of the younger poet, "Surely he has talent and honor, but [he] is crazy against religion and morality." Yet as an aristocrat, Byron was aware that his own behavior was virtually unchallengeable. Whatever George Gordon Byron did, he would always be Lord Byron.

The shocking aspects of Byron's private life have become legendary as a result of his literary fame, not the reverse. But they are shocking nevertheless—and sometimes rather sad. Scandal concerning Byron's unhappy marriage, and some of his radical, pro-French political views made life in England uncomfortable and he left for the Continent in 1816. He was never to return to England.

But Byron eventually subsided, by 1819, into a kind of premature middle age as the congenial "escort" of a beautiful but shrewish young Italian noblewoman.

Lord Byron was both a celebrity ("famous for being famous") and by far the most widely recognized literary figure of the age. As is often the case with such figures, there was a good deal more to Byron than can be seen in his flamboyant life. One acquaintance, expecting to find aristocratic haughtiness and romantic melancholy, encountered "the most unaffected and gentlemanly ease . . . He is all sunshine, and good humor with which the elegance of his language and the brilliancy of his wit cannot fail to inspire those who are near him." Byron himself observed, "What I think of myself is that I am so changeable, being everything in turns and nothing long—I am such a strange [mixture] of good and evil, that it would be difficult to describe me. There are but two sentiments to which I am constant—a strong love of liberty and a detestation of cant [insincere idealism], and neither is calculated to gain me friends."

We must resist the temptation to find the "real" Byron in the characters and voices in his poetry. As a lyricist, he was as adept as his contemporaries in creating the fictive "speaker" in his poems. Byron also wrote well in two other literary forms, satire and drama, where the personal and private are not on display. Since much of his poetry, including his masterpiece, *Don Juan* (jo͞o′ən), is narrative, readers have also looked for Byron in the teller, if not in the main characters, of the stories. The real Byron is more likely revealed in the wit, humor, and inventiveness of these works.

Byron's career began modestly in 1807 with a small collection of short lyric pieces which was harshly reviewed by the *Edinburgh Review*, the leading literary magazine of the day. In response, Byron wrote his first satire, *English Bards and Scotch Reviewers* (1800), which revealed the vein of wit which helped cast Byron as the clever and rebellious mocker of established conventions. His target in this satire was not only the *Edinburgh Review*; he also took on such Romantic icons as Sir Walter Scott, William Wordsworth, and Samuel Taylor Coleridge. Following the overnight success of his two cantos of *Childe Harold* in 1812, he produced a series of exotic Near-East tales and some lyrics, *Hebrew Melodies*, to be set to music. But for the most part, his life between 1812 and 1816 was as the notorious social figure rather than the poet.

When Byron left England in 1816, he was drawn into contact with Percy Shelley and his wife Mary in Switzerland. This fortuitous meeting was arranged by Claire Clairmont, Mary's stepsister, who had thrown herself at Byron. Because of the association with Shelley, Byron's writing life began in earnest. It intensified when he moved to Italy after the Shelleys returned to England. The Byron we can just glimpse in these years, despite the debauchery and the circus-like menagerie he kept about him in Venice, is a man who worked very hard, sometimes quite obsessively, at his writing. His wildness and aristocratic ease obscure what was, in fact, a period of great literary productivity, including the completion of the fourth canto of *Childe Harold;* a tragedy, *Manfred;* and the revival of an old verse form—the *ottava rima*—in a short satiric work, *Beppo*. He later used this verse form brilliantly in *Don Juan*, his greatest work and the poem he continued to write for the rest of his life. "To how many cantos [it] may extend," Byron said, "I know not, nor whether (even if I live) I shall complete it."

As a poet, Byron was not a "Romantic" in style. His masters, in fact, were the Neo-classical writers whose wit and precision he admired (and even burlesqued) more than the lyric qualities of his contemporaries. His greatest talent was for longer works—dramas, satires, and rambling narratives. Yet throughout the nineteenth century Byron was regarded as the incarnation of "Romantic."

All of the major Romantics were involved in public life, but none led a more public life (in both the personal and literary senses) than Lord Byron. Because of his consciousness of his social class, he had the strongest and surest sense of being a public person. One reason for Shelley's admiration for Byron, in fact, was that Byron could successfully attract an audience (Shelley felt *he* was not attractive to people). On a personal level, Byron (like Coleridge) drew people to him naturally and excelled in conversation.

Byron's death came in conspicuous public service. With much preparation, including the creation of special military uniforms for himself and his party, Byron set off in July 1823 to support the Greek nationalists in their struggle for independence from Turkey. In a marshy town in Greece called Missolonghi, he came down with a series of fevers which took his life only a few days after his thirty-sixth birthday.

A. Speaker
In *Don Juan* the fictive storyteller-speaker is the source of biting satire. Toward the end of *Childe Harold*, Byron remarked that he had given up trying to separate his own character from that of the hero; Canto III contains many comments on Byron's personal life.

B. Expansion
Byron wrote Cantos I and II of *Don Juan* with a long, scathing "dedication" to Robert Southey, England's Poet Laureate, whom Byron despised. The dedication was so vitriolic that the publisher omitted it in the first edition.

C. Expansion
Byron's heart was buried at Missolonghi and his body laid beneath the village church of Hucknall-Torkard.

Authorities would not allow him burial in Westminster Abbey, and there is no statue of Byron in the Poet's Corner. In 1969, however, a white marble memorial was laid in the floor in the Poet's Corner in his memory.

ESTABLISHING A PURPOSE. Have students read the poem to identify the figures of speech and the imagery that help create a verbal portrait of this dark lady.

SUPPLEMENTARY SUPPORT MATERIALS
1. Vocabulary Activity Worksheet (*CCB*)
2. Review and Response Worksheet: Simile (*CCB*)
3. Selection Test (*CCB*)

DEVELOPING VOCABULARY
The following word from the poem is tested in the Selection Test. (See also Vocabulary Activity Worksheet.)
raven

CLOSURE
Have students summarize the qualities that Byron found attractive in this woman.

A. Expansion
Mrs. Horton was a young widow and Byron's cousin by marriage, whom he met for the first time at the ball. He sent her this poem the next morning. The manuscript (in the Pierpont Morgan Library in New York City) is torn where she broke the seal.

B. Imagery
Note the dark-light imagery in stanzas 1 and 2.

ANALYZING THE POEM
Identifying Details
1. She is like the night.
2. Her eyes, hair, cheek, brow, and smile.
3. That she is sweet, innocent, and at peace.

Interpreting Meanings
4. It is garish, compared to the night.
5. See lines 7, 13–14, and 15–16.
6. He means "on earth."
7. Answers will vary. Some students will feel any love poem is mushy. Phrases that seem like clichés may not have been clichés when this was written.

A "She Walks in Beauty"—by now one of Byron's most famous poems—is supposed to have been inspired by Lady Wilmot Horton, a beautiful woman whom Byron saw at a ball, perhaps in the spring of 1814. Lady Horton was in mourning, and, in the fashion of the times, was dressed in black. This particular dress was decorated with glittering spangles.

She Walks in Beauty

1

She walks in beauty, like the night
  Of cloudless climes° and starry skies;
And all that's best of dark and bright
  Meet in her aspect° and her eyes:
5 Thus mellowed to that tender light
B   Which heaven to gaudy day denies.

2

One shade the more, one ray the less,
  Had half impaired the nameless grace
Which waves in every raven tress,
10   Or softly lightens o'er her face;
Where thoughts serenely sweet express
  How pure, how dear their dwelling place.

3

And on that cheek, and o'er that brow,
  So soft, so calm, yet eloquent,
15 The smiles that win, the tints that glow,
  But tell of days in goodness spent,
A mind at peace with all below,
  A heart whose love is innocent!

2. **climes:** atmospheres.

4. **aspect:** face, look.

Responding to the Poem

Analyzing the Poem

Identifying Details

1. What **simile** does the speaker use to describe the woman in the first stanza?
2. What aspects of the woman's physical appearance does the speaker mention?
3. What does the woman's appearance suggest to the speaker about her character and personality?

Interpreting Meanings

4. What does the speaker imply about day when he calls it "gaudy"?
5. "Dark and bright" (line 3) suggests a balance of opposites. How is this idea developed in other details?
6. What does the speaker mean by "below" in line 17?
7. This poem has sometimes been criticized as overly sentimental and dependent on clichés. Tell whether or not you agree and why.

PREPARATION
1. ESTABLISHING A PURPOSE. The speaker in this poem makes himself a promise. Have students read to discover what that promise is and why the speaker makes it.
2. PREREADING JOURNAL. Have students write two or three sentences describing what they think they will be like when they are thirty.

SUPPLEMENTARY SUPPORT MATERIALS
1. Review and Response Worksheet: Rhythm and Tone (*CCB*)
2. Selection Test (*CCB*)

CLOSURE
Have students discuss the ironic contrast in the poem's message and the mood of the sound effects.

ANALYZING THE POEM
Identifying Details
1. He has decided to cease roving. He feels worn out.

If these lines are addressed to anyone, it is to the poet himself. They were written when Byron, just turned twenty-nine, was deeply aware of the passing of his youth and perhaps slightly penitential about the sensual indulgences of his free-wheeling life.

The specific occasion of the poem was the coming of Lent after a carnival season in Venice where the poet, having "lived it up," was suddenly weary and in a mood to chastise himself—in a mixture of anapests and iambs and a song-like refrain. **A**

So We'll Go No More A-Roving

1
So we'll go no more a-roving
　So late into the night,
Though the heart be still as loving,
　And the moon be still as bright.

B
2
5　For the sword outwears its sheath,
　And the soul wears out the breast,
And the heart must pause to breathe,
　And love itself have rest.

3
Though the night was made for loving,
10　And the day returns too soon,
Yet we'll go no more a-roving
　By the light of the moon.

Interpreting Meanings
2. He means carousing.
3. He is saying that each needs its rest. They stand for lust and passion.
4. Night is a time for love and sensual indulgence; day is for somber behavior. The speaker also implies that time is fleeting and that life ends too soon.

A. Refrain
Byron used the refrain of an old Scottish song "The Jolly Beggar": "And we'll gang nae mair a roving / Sae late into the nicht . . ."

B. Metaphor
In a letter to an old friend, Byron wrote, "I find the 'sword wearing out the scabbard,' though I have but just turned the corner of twenty-nine."

Responding to the Poem

Analyzing the Poem

Identifying Details

1. What decision has the speaker made in the first stanza? What are the reasons for that decision, as given in the second stanza?

Interpreting Meanings

2. What do you think the speaker means by "roving"?
3. What single point is the speaker driving at with his examples of the sword, the soul, and the heart in the second stanza? What do you think the sword and the sheath stand for?
4. What attitude toward time does the speaker imply in this poem? Do you agree or disagree with this attitude?

Writing About the Poem

A Critical Response

Analyzing Techniques. In an essay, analyze the poet's use of **meter, rhyme,** and other forms of **repetition** in this poem. Tell what you think the emotional effect of the lyric is.

PREPARATION

ESTABLISHING A PURPOSE. Read aloud the biblical description of the battle in II Kings 18–19. Then have students read the poem to see what Byron did with this story. Be sure to note the poem's five powerful similes.

SUPPLEMENTARY SUPPORT MATERIALS
1. Vocabulary Activity Worksheet (CCB)
2. Review and Response Worksheet: Simile and Theme (CCB)
3. Selection Test (CCB)

DEVELOPING VOCABULARY
The following word from the poem is tested in the Selection Test. (See also Vocabulary Activity Worksheet.)
cohorts

A. Humanities Connection: Discussing the Fine Art

This relief shows how the Assyrians used art for factual reporting. Note that there is no effort to create the illusion of depth.

? What can you infer about the ancient Assyrians from looking at this fragment? (They maintained an army; the soldier is elaborately groomed; he wears armor and carries metal weapons, such as a dagger and lance; his horse is carefully groomed and decorated. The artist seems to have a feeling for nature: See the fish.) What do you guess accounts for the unusual (and conventional) details of the soldier's beard? (It may not have been possible to carve the stone in a way that resembled hair. Also, the artist may have been trying to represent curly hair or a kind of ornamentation that was popular then.)

In both Kings and Chronicles, the Bible tells the story of the Assyrian king Sennacherib's [sə·nak′ər·ibz] attempt to capture and enslave Jerusalem. When his mighty army, encamped nearby, was about to descend upon the city, "the Angel of Death"—in the form of a sudden pestilence or plague—killed man and beast alike, yet spared Sennacherib himself. But the disgrace his failure had brought upon "Ashur," i.e., Assyria, was so great that, upon his return, the king was murdered by his own sons.

The poem is a prime example of the use of bouncy anapestic rhythms which, popular in the nineteenth century, have been almost totally absent from the work of serious poets ever since.

The Destruction of Sennacherib

A

Cavalryman Fording a Stream. Fragment of a wall relief from the Palace of Sennacherib at Nineveh, Assyria (8th-7th centuries B.C.). Limestone.

The Metropolitan Museum of Art, New York. Gift of John D. Rockefeller, Jr., 1932. (32.143.8).

CLOSURE
Have students read three stanzas aloud to demonstrate the strong anapestic measure.

ANALYZING THE POEM
Identifying Details
1. They are attacking the Israelites. They have died.
   "Like the wolf on the fold," "Like the leaves of the forest when summer is green," "Like the leaves of the forest when autumn hath blown."
2. The Angel of Death.

3. It is terrible and silent, strewn with the bodies of soldiers and horses.
4. Sennacherib and the Assyrian troops. See line 24.

Interpreting Meanings
5. Anapestic tetrameter (four feet).
   It imitates the galloping of horses and has a military beat.

The Assyrian came down like the wolf on the fold,
And his cohorts were gleaming in purple and gold;
And the sheen of their spears was like stars on the sea,
When the blue wave rolls nightly on deep Galilee.

5 Like the leaves of the forest when summer is green,
That host with their banners at sunset were seen:
Like the leaves of the forest when autumn hath blown,
That host on the morrow lay withered and strown.

For the Angel of Death spread his wings on the blast,
10 And breathed in the face of the foe as he passed;
And the eyes of the sleepers waxed deadly and chill,
And their hearts but once heaved, and forever grew still.

And there lay the steed with his nostril all wide,
But through it there rolled not the breath of his pride;
15 And the foam of his gasping lay white on the turf,
And cold as the spray of the rock-beating surf.

And there lay the rider distorted and pale,
With the dew on his brow, and the rust on his mail:°
And the tents were all silent, the banners alone,
20 The lances unlifted, the trumpet unblown.

And the widows of Ashur are loud in their wail,
And the idols are broke in the temple of Baal;°
And the might of the Gentile,° unsmote by the sword,
Hath melted like snow in the glance of the Lord!

A

B

18. **mail:** a kind of armor made of linked metal.

22. **Baal:** the Assyrian god.
23. **Gentile:** Sennacherib and the Assyrians (non-Hebrews).

A. Contrasts
? What contrasting similes are used here? (One is based on summer imagery; the other on autumn.)

B. Diction
? What words emphasize stillness? (*Sleepers, lay, cold, rust, silent, unlifted, unblown*)

Responding to the Poem

Analyzing the Poem

Identifying Details

1. What are the Assyrians doing in the first stanza? What has happened to them in the second stanza? What **similes** describe the army in these two stanzas?
2. According to stanza 3, who or what is created with the victory?
3. What does the field look like after the battle is over?
4. What is "the Gentile" in the last stanza? What **simile** describes how the Gentile was conquered?

Interpreting Meanings

5. Describe the **meter** of the poem. How does the movement of the meter help reinforce the action of the poem?

Writing About the Poem

A Critical Response

Analyzing Similes. In a brief essay, list and analyze all the explicit similes in "The Destruction of Sennacherib." How would you defend or qualify the view that the powerful visual impact of this poem derives primarily from its use of vivid similes?

women." Don Juan is the hero of Mozart's opera *Don Giovanni*.

2. ESTABLISHING A PURPOSE. Students should read to enjoy the poem, and to discover what Byron satirizes in this "unheroic epic."

SUPPLEMENTARY SUPPORT MATERIALS
1. Vocabulary Activity Worksheet (*CCB*)
2. Review and Response Worksheet: Satire (*CCB*)
3. Selection Test (*CCB*)

A. Setting
Byron spends several stanzas describing the island's peaceful setting in contrast to the storm and shipwreck.

B. Tone
❓ What do you think is the purpose of this comment on the narrator's wandering attention? (The effect is a comic contrast with the serious narration.)

C. Connections
Byron describes with *un-* words, as in "Sennacherib," line 20.

D. Character
They (line 17) are Haidée, the pirate's daughter, and Don Juan.

The following stanzas represent a sampling of the longest satirical poem in English literature. Its stanza form—eight rhymed iambic pentameter lines ending in a rhymed couplet—is based on the Italian *ottava rima*. While Byron adheres strictly to the demands of the form, his tone is loosely conversational, colloquial, and continually punctuated by digressions. One of the charms of the poem is that it moves at a pace appropriate to the narrator's quick shifts of attention. He is confident that the reader will stay with him, when, every now and then, he slows down and dawdles over something he sees in the corner of his eye.

Ostensibly, this is another version of the legend of Don Juan (in Spanish, "hwän"), the man whose passion and persistence made him the greatest lover in history. But Byron's *Don Juan* ("jōō'ən") is actually a livelier portrait of the man who tells the story than of his chosen hero. And Byron's Don Juan is different from other Don Juans in history. His hero is an innocent who

becomes involved in many amorous adventures simply because he is so handsome and irresistible.

The form that the poem would take came to Byron late in his comparatively brief life. But once he had got the hang of it, he found that it accommodated everything he wanted to say about the world he knew, and just how to put it. The result was a poem of enormous popularity and scandalous interest. In contrast with the solemnity and pure lyricism of his contemporaries, Byron hearkened back to the age of Alexander Pope and its penchant for wit as both a social grace and as a weapon against folly.

Don Juan, left unfinished at Byron's death, comprises sixteen long divisions, called cantos, and a part of a seventeenth. This extract comes from the early part of the poem, where the hero finds himself shipwrecked on a Greek island. These stanzas describe how Haidée, the daughter of a pirate, falls in love with Don Juan.

To enjoy the fun, read the poem aloud.

from **Don Juan, Canto II**

A

It was a wild and breaker-beaten coast,
    With cliffs above, and a broad sandy shore,
Guarded by shoals and rocks as by an host,
    With here and there a creek, whose aspect wore
5   A better welcome to the tempest tost;
    And rarely ceased the haughty billow's roar,
Save on the dead long summer days, which make
The outstretched ocean glitter like a lake.

. . .

B

The coast—I think it was the coast that I
10   Was just describing—Yes, it *was* the coast—
Lay at this period quiet as the sky,

C

    The sands untumbled, the blue waves untossed,
And all was stillness, save the sea bird's cry,
    And dolphin's leap, and little billow crossed
15   By some low rock or shelve, that made it fret
Against the boundary it scarcely wet.

D

And forth they wandered, her sire being gone,
    As I have said, upon an expedition;
And mother, brother, guardian, she had none,
20   Save Zoe, who, although with due precision

DEVELOPING VOCABULARY

The following word from the poem is
tested in the Selection Test. (See also
Vocabulary Activity Worksheet.)
dissipation

The Plot

Byron's picaresque tale begins in Don
Juan's native Spain. After a romance
with his mother's married friend, the sixteen-year-old Juan must leave his native
Seville. A storm at sea sinks the ship and
forces everyone into a boat. After an episode of cannibalism (Juan's tutor is
eaten by the survivors), Juan reaches a
desert island, where he is secretly
cared for by Haidée. This leads to his
sale into slavery and to Haidée's death.
As a slave in Turkey, Juan faces the advances of the sultan's favorite wife. He
joins the Russian army, and his exploits
bring him to the court of the Empress
Catherine the Great. She sends him as
her representative to London, where he
has many adventures in English society.

She waited on her lady with the sun,
   Thought daily service was her only mission,
Bringing warm water, wreathing her long tresses,
A   And asking now and then for cast-off dresses.

25 It was the cooling hour, just when the rounded
    Red sun sinks down behind the azure hill,
Which then seems as if the whole earth it bounded,
B   Circling all nature, hushed, and dim, and still,
With the far mountain crescent half surrounded
30   On one side, and the deep sea calm and chill
Upon the other, and the rosy sky
With one star sparkling through it like an eye.

And thus they wandered forth, and hand in hand,
   Over the shining pebbles and the shells,
35 Glided along the smooth and hardened sand,
   And in the worn and wild receptacles
Worked by the storms, yet worked as it were planned
   In hollow halls, with sparry° roofs and cells,
They turned to rest; and, each clasped by an arm,
40 Yielded to the deep twilight's purple charm.

They looked up to the sky, whose floating glow
   Spread like a rosy ocean, vast and bright;
They gazed upon the glittering sea below,
   Whence the broad moon rose circling into sight;
45 They heard the waves splash, and the wind so low,
   And saw each other's dark eyes darting light
Into each other—and, beholding this,
Their lips drew near, and clung into a kiss;

A long, long kiss, a kiss of youth, and love,
50   And beauty, all concentrating like rays
Into one focus, kindled from above;
   Such kisses as belong to early days,
Where heart, and soul, and sense, in concert move,
   And the blood's lava, and the pulse a blaze,
55 Each kiss a heart quake—for a kiss's strength,
I think, it must be reckoned by its length

C By length I mean duration; theirs endured
   Heaven knows how long—no doubt they never reck-
    oned;
And if they had, they could not have secured
60   The sum of their sensations to a second:
They had not spoken, but they felt allured,
   As if their souls and lips each other beckoned,
Which, being joined, like swarming bees they clung—
Their hearts the flowers from whence the honey sprung.

38. **sparry:** made of shiny rock.

A. Tone

❓ What is comic
about line 24?
(It comes as a sur-
prise; the lines be-
fore and after
seem serious.)

B. Setting/Tone

❓ Does Byron's
description of
the setting sound
as sincere as
Wordsworth's de-
scriptions of na-
ture? Or, do you
think Byron is ex-
aggerating to sati-
rize the Romantics
on Nature?
Explain.

C. Speaker

At this moment of
high passion, the
narrator disgresses
for comic effect.

Character

Byron's hero is based on the legendary Don Juan, famous for his prowess as a ladies' man and his lack of conscience. Don Juan was surely a figure Byron must have identified with, for his own scandalous love affairs had made him the talk of England. Unlike the Don Juan who is a heartless seducer of women, Byron's innocent hero never takes the initiative; it is the women who pursue him.

The second major "character" is the narrator. This worldly-wise character comments sardonically on Don Juan's adventures, on life, on human values—on *everything.* The narrator's satiric voice exposes the foibles of society and humankind.

Theme

In a critical essay on "Irony and Image in *Don Juan,*" Ernest J. Lovell, Jr., identifies the unifying principle of the poem as "the basically ironic theme of appearance versus reality, the difference between what things seem to be (or are said or thought to be) and what they actually are."

A. Satire

? What is Byron satirizing here? (The women of his own society, demanding promises and vows from their lovers)

B. Tone

The sardonic tone of lines 102–103 is Byron, the womanizer's.

C. Allusion

? To whom is Byron referring with the words "our first parents"? (Adam and Eve)

65 They were alone, but not alone as they
       Who shut in chambers think it loneliness;
    The silent ocean, and the starlight bay,
       The twilight glow, which momently° grew less,
    The voiceless sands, and dropping° caves, that lay
70   Around them, made them to each other press,
    As if there were no life beneath the sky
    Save theirs, and that their life could never die.

    They feared no eyes nor ears on that lone beach;
       They felt no terrors from the night; they were
75 All in all to each other: though their speech
       Was broken words, they *thought* a language there—
    And all the burning tongues the passions teach
       Found in one sigh the best interpreter
    Of nature's oracle—first love—that all
80 Which Eve has left her daughters since her fall.

A
85
    Haidée spoke not of scruples, asked no vows,
       Nor offered any; she had never heard
    Of plight° and promises to be a spouse,
       Or perils by a loving maid incurred;
    She was all which pure ignorance allows,
       And flew to her young mate like a young bird;
    And, never having dreamt of falsehood, she
    Had not one word to say of constancy.

    She loved, and was belovéd—she adored,
90   And she was worshiped after nature's fashion—
    Their intense souls, into each other poured,
       If souls could die, had perished in that passion,
    But by degrees their senses were restored,
       Again to be o'ercome, again to dash on;
95 And, beating 'gainst *his* bosom, Haidée's heart
    Felt as if never more to beat apart.

    Alas! they were so young, so beautiful,
       So lonely, loving, helpless, and the hour
    Was that in which the heart is always full,
100   And, having o'er itself no further power,
    Prompts deeds eternity cannot annul,

B
       But pays off moments in an endless shower
    Of hell fire—all prepared for people giving
    Pleasure or pain to one another living.

105 Alas! for Juan and Haidée! they were
       So loving and so lovely—till then never,

C
    Excepting our first parents, such a pair
       Had run the risk of being damned for ever:

68. **momently:** at each moment.
69. **dropping:** dripping.

83. **plight:** engagement.

686

Comment from the Poet

In an 1819 letter to John Murray, the publisher of Cantos I and II, Byron makes his purpose clear: "You ask me for the plan of Donny Johnny: I *have* no plan—I *had* no plan; but I had or have materials. . . . You are too earnest and eager about a work never intended to be serious. Do you suppose that I could have any intention but to giggle and make giggle?—a playful satire with as little poetry as could be helped, was what I meant."

Comment from Shelley

In August 1821, Shelley was visiting Byron in Ravenna—perhaps in response to Byron's invitation in the letter on text page 693. In a letter to his wife Mary, Shelley wrote about Byron and *Don Juan:* "It sets him not above but far above all the poets of the day: every word is stamped with immortality. I despair of rivaling Lord Byron, as well I may, and there is no other with whom it is worth contending."

Portrait of Haidée. Engraving.

READING CHECK TEST
1. Don Juan's beloved's name is Haidée.
2. This part of the story is set on a <u>wild</u> coast.
3. Haidée's father is a <u>pirate</u>.

4. Is Haidée an innocent young girl or an older woman who wants to marry Juan? (The former)
5. The tone of this story is <u>humorous</u>, <u>satiric</u>, etc.

CLOSURE
Have students explain what is being satirized in *Don Juan.* Ask them to name some ways in which this story is like the romance novels popular today.

A. Satire

❓ What is the narrator's attitude toward women in this and the following passages? (He sees them as completely dependent on men, living solely for love, quick to revenge. In lines 153–160, he seems sympathetic but really belittles women.)

110

And Haidée, being devout as well as fair,
    Had, doubtless, heard about the Stygian river,°
And Hell and Purgatory—but forgot
Just in the very crisis she should not.

. . .

And when those deep and burning moments passed,
    And Juan sunk to sleep within her arms,
115
    She slept not, but all tenderly, though fast,°
Sustained his head upon her bosom's charms
And now and then her eye to Heaven is cast,
    And then on the pale cheek her breast now warms,
Pillowed on her o'erflowing heart, which pants
120
With all it granted, and with all it grants.

An infant when it gazes on a light,
    A child the moment when it drains the breast,
A devotee when soars the Host° in sight,
    An Arab with a stranger for a guest,
125
A sailor when the prize has struck in fight,°
    A miser filling his most hoarded chest,
Feel rapture; but not such true joy are reaping
As they who watch o'er what they love while sleeping.

For there it lies so tranquil, so beloved,
130
    All that it hath of Life with us is living;
So gentle, stirless, helpless, and unmoved,
    And all unconscious of the joy 't is giving;
All it hath felt, inflicted, passed, and proved,
    Hushed into depths beyond the watcher's diving:
135
There lies the thing we love with all its errors
And all its charms, like death without its terrors.

The Lady watched her lover—and that hour
    Of Love's, and Night's, and Ocean's solitude
O'erflowed her soul with their united power;
140
    Amidst the barren sand and rocks so rude°
She and her wave-worn love had made their bower,°
    Where nought upon their passion could intrude,
And all the stars that crowded the blue space
Saw nothing happier than her glowing face.

145

A

Alas! the love of women! it is known
    To be a lovely and a fearful thing;
For all of theirs upon that die° is thrown,
    And if 't is lost, life hath no more to bring
To them but mockeries of the past alone,
150
    And their revenge is as the tiger's spring,
Deadly, and quick, and crushing; yet, as real
Torture is theirs—what they inflict they feel.

110. **Stygian river:** the river Styx (in Greek mythology) which flows through Hell.

115. **fast:** fixed in place.

123. **Host:** the Eucharistic wafer in the Anglican or Roman Catholic ritual, which is lifted up by the priest at one moment in the Mass.
125. **prize . . . fight:** captured enemy ship has lowered its flag in surrender.

140. **rude:** rough.
141. **bower:** rustic dwelling.

147. **die:** one of a pair of dice.

ANALYZING THE POEM
Identifying Details
1. He describes a rocky coast with cliffs and a sandy shore.
2. Zoe. Haidée's father is on an expedition.
3. Adjectives, metaphors, similes, hyperbole.
4. First love is in the oracle. One sigh is the best interpreter.

5. She did not give or ask for promises. She had never dreamed of false-hood—she didn't know it could exist.
6. She should have remembered the Stygian River, Hell, and Purgatory.
7. The infant, child, devotee, Arab, sailor, and miser are among those students might mention.
8. A sleeping beloved.
9. They take revenge. Some take lovers,

drink, or pray; some look after their households; others turn to dissipation; some run away, play the devil, and write novels.
Women are correct in behaving this way because men treat them unjustly.
10. The priest was solitude; the nuptial torches were stars; the witness was the ocean; their bed was the cave.
(Answers continue on next page.)

155
A

They are right; for man, to man so oft unjust,
  Is always so to women: one sole bond
Awaits them—treachery is all their trust;°
  Taught to conceal, their bursting hearts despond
Over their idol, till some wealthier lust
  Buys them in marriage—and what rests beyond?
A thankless husband—next, a faithless lover—
Then dressing, nursing, praying—and all 's over.

160

155. **all their trust:** that is, all man will be in return for woman's trust.

165
B

Some take a lover, some take drams° or prayers,
  Some mind their household, others dissipation,
Some run away, and but exchange their cares,
  Losing the advantage of a virtuous station;
Few changes e'er can better their affairs,
  Theirs being an unnatural situation,
From the dull palace to the dirty hovel:
Some play the devil, and then write a novel.

161. **drams:** shots of liquor.

170

Haidée was nature's bride, and knew not this;
  Haidée was passion's child, born where the sun
Showers triple light, and scorches even the kiss
  Of his gazelle-eyed daughters; she was one
Made but to love, to feel that she was his
  Who was her chosen: what was said or done
Elsewhere was nothing. She had nought to fear,
Hope, care, nor love, beyond—her heart beat *here*.

175

180
C

And oh! that quickening of the heart, that beat!
  How much it costs us! yet each rising throb
Is in its cause as its effect so sweet,
  That wisdom, ever on the watch to rob
Joy of its alchemy, and to repeat
  Fine truths; even conscience, too, has a tough job
To make us understand each good old maxim,
So good—I wonder Castlereagh° don't tax 'em.

185

190

And now 't was done—on the lone shore were plighted
  Their hearts; the stars, their nuptial torches, shed
Beauty upon the beautiful they lighted:
  Ocean their witness, and the cave their bed,
By their own feelings hallowed and united,
  Their priest was solitude, and they were wed:
And they were happy—for to their young eyes
Each was an angel, and earth Paradise.

184. **Castlereagh:** British foreign secretary from 1812–1822, who was much disliked by radicals, including Byron and Shelley.

A. Tone
❓ What do you think of Byron's view of marriage and the relationship between the sexes? Note how he sums up a woman's life in two lines. (Point out that his description of marriage is quite accurate for the time he lived in. In many places women did not even have the right to own property.)

B. Allusion
In 1816, Lady Caroline Lamb published a very amateurish novel (*Glenarvon*) based on her scandalous affair with Byron. She included Byron's letter breaking off the relationship.

C. Satire
Note how the tone shifts again.
❓ What is the narrator satirizing in these passages? (Marriage)

Interpreting Meanings

11. Innocence implies freedom from sin and actions that are morally wrong; ignorance implies lack of knowledge.

12. The two are alone in "Paradise." It is as if they are the only beings on earth. Innocence and downfall are alluded to.

13. The rhyme scheme is *abababcc*. For examples of alliteration, see lines 38,

49, 106, 141. Humor is created in the end rhymes of the final couplets in lines 159–160, 183–184.

14. Answers will vary. Some students may feel there are no real exaggerations. Others may cite lines like "blood [is] lava" (line 54).

15. She only works during the day, and she asks Haidée for old dresses.

16. The tone is exaggerated, oversentimental, perhaps satirical.

17. Some of Byron's targets are the characters of men and women and the love between them, indulgence, lust, morality, and religion.

The Romantic tradition is satirized with exaggerated sincerity, the relationship between man and nature, and the discussion of love.

Responding to the Poem

Analyzing the Poem

Identifying Details

1. How does the speaker describe the **setting** in lines 1–8?
2. Who is Haidée's only companion? Where has her father gone?
3. What exaggerated **figures of speech** are used to describe that kiss beginning on line 49?
4. According to line 79, what is nature's oracle and what best interprets it?
5. In what ways is Haidée, lines 81–88, described as totally innocent? Why doesn't she ask her lover for a vow of constancy, or faithfulness?
6. What does the narrator say Haidée should have remembered, but did not (lines 110–112)?
7. Identify all the exaggerated **similes** in lines 121–126.
8. In lines 129–136, what does "it" refer to?
9. According to lines 145–168, what do women do when their love is lost? Why, according to the poem, are women correct in behaving this way?
10. Describe the nuptials that Haidée and Juan celebrate in lines 185–191.

Interpreting Meanings

11. Why does the speaker link Haidée with "pure ignorance"? (What is the difference between "ignorance" and "innocence"?)
12. In what way could this story be analogous to the account of Adam and Eve? Is there evidence in the poem that Byron intended it to be?
13. Describe the stanzas' **rhyme scheme** and find examples of **alliteration**. Where does Byron use sound devices to create humor?
14. Which of Byron's **figures of speech** do you think are comically exaggerated?

15. Where does Byron say things that surprise you, in that they catch you off guard and make you laugh? For example, what about his description of Zoe, the servant, in lines 20–24?
16. What seems to be the speaker's **tone** as he describes Don Juan and Haidée falling in love?
17. If *Don Juan* is in part witty **satire**, who or what are Byron's targets? Can you find some barbs directed at the whole Romantic tradition, as exemplified by Wordsworth and Coleridge? Explain.

Writing About the Poem

A Creative Response

1. **Continuing the Story.** In a brief sequel, summarize what you think may be the future of Don Juan and Haidée. How will he treat her, and she him? Base your sequel on hints offered in this selection. You might want to tell the story to make some satirical jabs of your own at the popular romance novels that always top the best-seller lists today.

A Critical Response

2. **Comparing Epics.** In an essay, compare and contrast Byron's story with the story told by Alexander Pope in the selection from *The Rape of the Lock* (in Unit Four). Consider at least two of these elements of the stories in your essay:

   a. Verse forms
   b. Tones
   c. Targets of satire
   d. Use of irony

PREPARATION

1. BUILDING ON PRIOR KNOWLEDGE.
Recall that Byron left England for Europe as part of the separation agreement with his wife. Childe Harold's wanderings mimic Byron's own travels.

2. ESTABLISHING A PURPOSE. As they read, have students pay special attention to the sound of the poem.

3. PREREADING JOURNAL. Ask students to imagine they are at the ocean. Have them write a few sentences describing what they see and how they feel.

SUPPLEMENTARY SUPPORT MATERIALS
1. Vocabulary Activity Worksheet (CCB)
2. Review and Response Worksheet: Byronic Hero (CCB)
3. Selection Test (CCB)

DEVELOPING VOCABULARY
The following word from the poem is tested in the Selection Test. (See also Vocabulary Activity Worksheet.)
to protract

The long poem that made Byron suddenly "famous" in 1812 was published in divisions, called cantos, and was a thinly disguised autobiographical account of Byron's own journeys. The pilgrim, called Childe Harold, became the prototype for the moody, dashingly handsome character type in European Romantic literature who would eventually be dubbed "the Byronic hero."

In the thirteenth and fourteenth centuries, "child" appears to have been a term applied to a young noble awaiting knighthood. Byron uses it to mean a youth of "gentle" birth, a kind of title (like Lord, or Sir).

In Canto IV, published in 1818, the speaker digresses to apostrophize one of the grandest aspects of nature, the ocean. The last two verses here are Byron's personal conclusion to the whole narrative. By this time, Byron said, he had ceased trying to separate himself from the figure of Childe Harold.

from Childe Harold's Pilgrimage

Canto IV

A. Apostrophe
See page 700 for a discussion of apostrophe.

B. Sound
Note that Byron's vowels imitate the open, rolling sound of the sea.

C. Diction
Byron is using a series of *un-* words again.

D. Alliteration
Note the *b* sounds in lines 21–23.

E. Metaphor
Here is the answer to question 3: The sea is a horse.

1

There is a pleasure in the pathless woods,
There is a rapture on the lonely shore,
There is society, where none intrudes,
By the deep sea, and music in its roar:
5 I love not man the less, but nature more,
From these our interviews, in which I steal
From all I may be, or have been before,
To mingle with the universe, and feel
What I can ne'er express—yet can not all conceal.

2

A
10 Roll on, thou deep and dark blue ocean—roll!
B Ten thousand fleets sweep over thee in vain;
Man marks the earth with ruin—his control
Stops with the shore;—upon the watery plain
The wrecks are all thy deed, nor doth remain
15 A shadow of man's ravage, save his own,
When, for a moment, like a drop of rain,
He sinks into thy depths with bubbling groan—
C Without a grave—unknelled,° uncoffined, and unknown.

18. **unknelled:** without the traditional ringing of a church bell to announce his death.

3

And I have loved thee, ocean! and my joy
20 Of youthful sports was on thy breast to be
D Borne, like thy bubbles, onward: from a boy
I wantoned with thy breakers—they to me
Were a delight; and if the freshening° sea
Made them a terror—'twas a pleasing fear,
25 For I was as it were a child of thee,
And trusted to thy billows far and near,
E And laid my hand upon thy mane—as I do here.

24. **freshening:** becoming rough as the wind comes up.

ANALYZING THE POEM
Identifying Details
1. The speaker loves nature.
2. Man destroys the earth.
   Man cannot destroy the sea, but the sea can destroy man—causing shipwrecks and death.
3. He recalls playing in the ocean.
   He uses a metaphor: A wave is the horse's mane.

4. He describes himself as tired and old. The poem is finished, but he wishes it were worthier.
5. He hopes he will be remembered.
6. The rhyme scheme for all the stanzas are *ababbcbcc*. The last line in each stanza is iambic hexameter; the first eight lines are iambic pentameter.

A. Speaker

? Who is the speaker in these two stanzas? (Byron, the poet; he separates himself from Childe Harold by referring to him as "the pilgrim" in line 40.)

B. Interpreting

? What do you think the speaker means by "I am not now / That which I have been"? (He has aged and changed.) What might the "glow" in line 36 be? (Perhaps his inspiration; perhaps his life force)

4

A ⌈ My task is done—my song hath ceased—my theme
    ⌊ Has died into an echo; it is fit
30   The spell should break of this <u>protracted</u> dream.
      The torch shall be extinguished which hath lit
      My midnight lamp—and what is writ, is writ,—
    ⌈ Would it were worthier! but I am not now
    | That which I have been—and my visions flit
B |
35 | Less <u>palpably</u> before me—and the glow
    ⌊ Which in my spirit dwelt is fluttering, faint, and low.

5

      Farewell! a word that must be, and hath been—
      A sound which makes us linger;—yet—farewell!
      Ye! who have traced the pilgrim to the scene
40   Which is his last—if in your memories dwell
      A thought which once was his—if on ye swell
      A single recollection—not in vain
      He wore his sandal shoon, and scallop shell;°
      Farewell! with *him* alone may rest the pain,
45   If such there were—with *you*, the moral of his strain.°

43. **Sandals** (*shoon* is shoes) and a **scallop shell** worn on a hat were traditional emblems of pilgrims. (The scallop shell is a symbol of St. James, whose shrine in Spain was a great attraction to pilgrims.)
45. **strain:** passage of poetry or song.

Responding to the Poem

Analyzing the Poem

Identifying Details

1. According to the first stanza, how does the speaker feel about nature?
2. In stanza 2, what does the speaker say man does to earth? What can man do to the sea—or the sea do to him?
3. What experience from his childhood does the speaker recall in the third stanza? What **figure of speech** describes the sea as a horse here?
4. What does the speaker say about himself and his poem in the fourth stanza?
5. What does the speaker hope for in the last stanza?
6. Describe the **rhyme scheme** of each stanza. How does the last line of each stanza differ in **rhythm** from the preceding eight lines?

Interpreting Meanings

7. What single aspect of the ocean does the speaker repeatedly emphasize in these stanzas?
8. In spite of the ocean's destructive aspects, the speaker professes that he loves it passionately. What might this tell you about the speaker's personality?
9. What link does the speaker imply between himself and the pilgrim in the final two stanzas?
10. From the little you have read, what would you guess the speaker's pilgrimage was in search of?
11. Can the fierce identification and rapture experienced by this speaker in the presence of nature be felt today? Do any of these lines strike you with particular **irony**, considering what has happened to the environment in some places in the twentieth century?

7. He emphasizes its depth and bound-lessness.

8. It seems to reveal his love of nature, a characteristic of the Romantic spirit.

9. The two are about to embark on the final journey—that is, die.

10. Student answers will vary. Most would recognize that, as a Byronic hero, the speaker was on a quest to under-stand himself and to find meaning in life.

11. Students who have visited places like the Grand Canyon or the Rocky Mountains may feel it is possible.

Lines 12–13, about Man's ability to ruin not extending to the ocean, seem ironic in this age of massive oil spills and dumping.

Writing About the Poem

A Creative Response

1. Writing an Apostrophe. Choose some other element of nature—wind, snow, fire, rain. Using stanzas 2 and 3 as a model, write a prose apostrophe, or address, to the element you have selected. Try to convey some of your speaker's personal feelings about the element.

A Critical Response

2. Analyzing a Stanza Form. The verse form Byron uses in *Childe Harold's Pilgrimage* is called the **Spenserian stanza,** because it was first used extensively in English by Edmund Spenser in *The Faerie Queene.* In a few paragraphs, describe the technical requirements of this verse form, and then show how Byron used it.

Primary Sources
Byron Writes to Shelley

Keats had died in Rome on February 23, 1821. Here is Byron's response to the news. (The child mentioned in the first sentence is Allegra, the daughter Byron had with Claire Clairmont, Mary Shelley's half-sister. Allegra would not live long.)

Ravenna, April 26, 1821.

"The child continues doing well, and the accounts are regular and favorable. It is gratifying to me that you and Mrs. Shelley do not disapprove of the step which I have taken, which is merely temporary.

A   "I am very sorry to hear what you say of Keats—is it *actually* true? I did not think criticism had been so killing. Though I differ from you essentially in your estimate of his performances, I so much abhor all unnecessary pain, that I would rather he had been seated on the highest peak of Parnassus than have perished in such a manner. Poor fellow! though with such inordinate self-love he would probably have not been very happy. I read the review of *Endymion* in the *Quarterly.* It was severe—but surely not so severe as many reviews in that and other journals upon others.

". . . I have published a pamphlet on the Pope controversy, which you will not like. Had I known Keats was dead—or that he was alive and so sensitive—I should have omitted some remarks upon his poetry, to which I was provoked by his *attack* upon *Pope,* and my disapprobation of *his own* style of writing.

"You want me to undertake a great poem—I have not

Byron Among the Ruins (19th century).
French steel engraving.

the inclination nor the power. As I grow older, the indif-ference—*not* to life, for we love it by instinct—but to the **B** stimuli of life, increases. Besides, this late failure of the Italians has latterly disappointed me for many reasons—some public, some personal. My respects to Mrs. S.

Yours ever,
B.

"P.S.—Could not you and I contrive to meet this summer? Could not you take a run here *alone?*"

A. Expansion
When he wrote his long elegy for Keats, *Adonais* (1821), Shelley mistakenly attribut-ed Keats's illness and death to a scathing review of *Endymion* that ap-peared in *The Quarterly* in April 1818. In fact, Keats died from tu-berculosis, which he contracted while nursing his brother Tom.

B. Expansion
Byron had given up his wild ways ("So We'll Go No More A-Roving" was written in 1817) and was liv-ing fairly quietly in Ravenna.

Shelley was the firstborn son of a Sussex country squire, who had been a conservative member of Parliament. Bysshe, as his family called him, stood to inherit his grandfather's wealth and title of baronet. Young Shelley lived quite happily with his four sisters on their parents' estate. At ten, he went to boarding school and then to Eton, where older boys taunted him because he was slim and short and not good at sports.

Mary Shelley's Description of Her Husband

"His life was spent in the contemplation of nature, in arduous study, or in acts of kindness and affection. . . . He knew every plant by its name, and was familiar with the history and habits of every production of the earth; he could interpret without a fault each appearance in the sky; and the varied phenomena of heaven and earth filled him with deep emotion. He made his study and reading room of the shadowed copse, the stream, the lake, the waterfall. . . ."

A. Expansion

After only six months at Oxford, Shelley and a friend were expelled because they refused to answer questions about the pamphlet *The Necessity of Atheism.*

B. Expansion

For a time, Harriet and Shelley lived in Dublin, where they worked for the vote for Catholics and for better living conditions for the poor.

C. Connections

This is Mary Wollstonecraft Shelley, the author of *Frankenstein* (see text page 741).

Percy Bysshe Shelley (1792–1822)

When young Percy Shelley arrived at Oxford in 1810, his father introduced him to that bookish town's most important bookseller: "My son here," he said, "has a literary turn; he's already an author . . . do pray indulge him in his printing freaks."

A   By spring, one of those "freaks"—an unsigned pamphlet on atheism—got Percy expelled and started a lifelong quarrel with his father. It was the first of many upheavals in the short, ill-fated life of an "author" who followed his "literary turn" wherever it led. In his own time, this "author" was better known for his shocking domestic life and opinions than for the impressive body of writing he created in the next twelve years.

It is tempting to see Shelley's life as a microcosm of the era into which he was born—an epoch of revolutionary energies and events. Suprahuman powers seemed to be disrupting and changing the world, and Shelley's life, no less than his poetry, seems to exemplify the statement in his great meditative poem, "Mont Blanc" (1816):

> All things that move and breathe with toil and
>   sound
> Are born and die; revolve, subside and swell.
> Power dwells apart in its tranquillity
> Remote, serene, and inaccessible . . .
>   —from "Mont Blanc"

Yet we should also remember that from his early political activism to his pronouncement in *A Defense of Poetry* (1821) that "Poets are the unacknowledged legislators of the world," Shelley was convinced that human thought and expression had the power to change human life for the better. And neither the upheavals of his personal life nor the strenuous reaching of his imagination toward a cosmic vision ever subverted his energies or optimism.

B   At nineteen, already estranged from his family, Shelley embarked on a career of courting the unconventional. To "rescue" her from a tyrannical father, he eloped with sixteen-year-old Harriet Westbrook, a classmate of his sisters. Three years later, he ran away with sixteen-year-old Mary Godwin, daughter of two of the most important radicals of the 1790's, Mary Wollstonecraft and William Godwin. The aging Godwin was a rationalist who had been Percy's intellectual idol before he became his money-grubbing father-in-law. Percy's alliance with Mary also involved responsibility for Mary's sixteen-year-old half-sister Jane (soon changed to Claire) Clairmont, who accompanied the pair on their elopement to Switzerland. Claire's brief affair with Byron brought Shelley and Byron together in Switzerland in 1816 in one of the age's most important literary relationships.   C

Shortly after their return to England from Switzerland, Mary's older half-sister Fanny committed suicide. Then Harriet, only twenty-one years old, drowned herself in a pond in Hyde Park. Percy was now free to marry Mary, but was denied custody of his children with Harriet.

In 1818, after eighteen months of semi-seclusion and self-examination in England, Shelley had completed his first major poetic work, *The Revolt of Islam.* Shelley now fled his debts and notoriety in England and returned to the Continent for the third and last time. The next four years were his most productive. One inspired work followed another, including four major long poems, *Julian and Maddalo* (1818), *Prometheus Unbound* (1819), and *Epipsychidion* and *Hellas* (1821). In the brief periods when he could not create, he nourished his energies with enormous reading, much of it in modern languages, with impressive accomplishments in translation.

Through their years of self-imposed exile in Italy (1818–1822), the Shelleys were shaken by the deaths of four children, including Clara and William, Mary's first two children with Percy. (A third child, Percy Florence, born in 1819, lived to inherit his grandfather's title and to care for his mother in later years.)

In 1822, when he was not yet even thirty years old, Shelley and a companion, Edward Williams, drowned when their sailing boat, the *Ariel,* went down in a storm off the northwestern coast of Italy. Twelve days later, Shelley's body washed ashore, a copy of Sophocles in one pocket and of Keats in the other. The body was burned in a pyre on the beach while friends stood by, and Shelley's ashes were buried in the Protestant cemetery in Rome.

Shelley's literary career, though obscured at

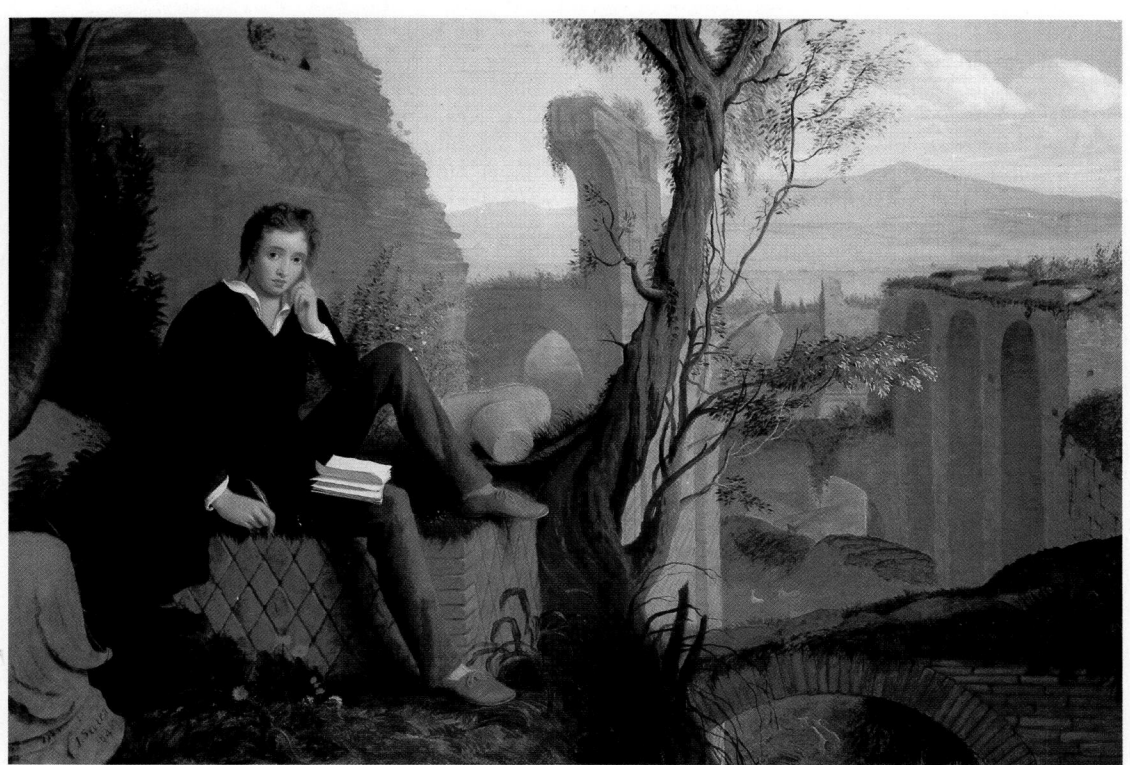

Shelley Composing Prometheus Unbound by Joseph Severn (1845). Keats-Shelley Memorial House, Rome.

A. Humanities Connection: Responding to the Fine Art
British artist Joseph Severn (1793–1879) was a successful portrait painter whose subjects also included John Keats (see text page 707).

Prometheus Unbound is Shelley's long verse drama about the Titan of Greek mythology, chained to a rock and tortured by Zeus for having given fire to human beings. Shelley began writing his play in Italy in 1818.

? Note that Severn painted this portrait twenty-three years after Shelley died. What mood does the painting evoke? (A very young-looking Shelley seems pensive, peaceful, and somewhat sad. The ruins and twisted tree are standard Romantic motifs to suggest the relentless passage of time, perhaps death.)

the time by the soap-opera character of his life, is all the more remarkable because of it. At eighteen he had published poetry and Gothic fiction, and his "literary turn" endured through all the upheavals of his restless life. In this he differed markedly from his fellow romantics: Coleridge and Keats enjoyed only brief, intense periods of poetic power; Wordsworth saw his powers decline; and Byron treated his writing as a gentlemanly avocation. Shelley's literary productivity was, with a few slow periods, unceasing. He was rarely without one or more important writing projects at hand, and his experience, enriched by wide reading, travel, and curiosity, constantly supplied new materials and ideas.

As his father recognized, Shelley was certainly an "author." His works include political pamphlets, topical satire, and powerful lyric poetry on contemporary events. He was equally capable of deeply personal and philosophic forms of poetry, and the great stylistic range of his work includes plays and lyric dramas, odes and meditative poems, including his highly wrought elegy for Keats, "Adonais" (1821). He also wrote epics and tragedies, verse epistles, and philosophic and literary essays.

Shelley's literary life is also remarkable for his inability to find an audience for his enormous output. Consequently, he relied on the small circle close to him for a sense of his "public." In 1812 he flung copies of his pamphlet supporting Irish independence from his balcony into passing carriages and sent off his pamphlet on human rights in bottles, toy boats, and even a miniature hot air balloon. *Julian and Maddalo* and *Epipsychidion,* among other works, were not published until after his death. "Adonais" sold so poorly in England that the publisher merely used copies of the privately printed first edition Shelley had had done in Italy.

There are a number of reasons why Shelley's works, most of which are far from "literary freaks," did not find their rightful audience at the time, making his pursuit of the vocation of

In a letter he wrote in 1823, Byron expressed his admiration for Shelley:

"He was the most gentle, most amiable, and least worldly-minded person I ever met; full of delicacy, disinterested beyond all other men, and possessing a degree of genius, joined to a simplicity, as rare as it is admirable. He had formed to himself a *beau ideal* of all that is fine, high-minded, and noble, and he acted up to this ideal even to the very letter. . . . I have seen nothing like him, and never shall again, I am certain."

A. Imagery
The English critic John Stuart Mill compared Shelley's imagery with Wordsworth's:
"Never did a fancy so teem with sensuous imagery as Shelley's. Wordsworth economizes an image, and detains it until he has distilled all the poetry out of it, and it will not yield a drop more. Shelley lavishes his with a profusion which is unconscious because it is inexhaustible. The one like a thrifty housewife, uses all his materials and wastes none; the other scatters them with a reckless prodigality of wealth of which there is perhaps no similar instance."

"author" a rather lonely one. First, the government feared radical opinions of any sort, particularly those concerning the monarchy or the established religion. Virtually any unconventional position was labeled seditious, with the first to suffer prosecution (and frequently imprisonment) being the printer-publisher. Living in Italy, Shelley found it even harder to get his publisher to take full responsibility for issuing work in the face of government repression.

A second reason was Shelley's self-exile during what turned out to be his mature poetic period. In 1819, when news of the "Peterloo Massacre" reached Italy, Shelley sensed how detached he had become from events at home, and in the opening lines of a powerful political poem, he rebukes himself:

As I lay asleep in Italy
There came a voice from over the sea,
And with great power it forth led me
To walk in the visions of poesy.
—from "The Mask of Anarchy"

Finally, as Shelley grew older he became, as one of his biographers observes, less active and more speculative. Like Coleridge, Shelley was a philosopher. His response to the forces of the time was to think and write about what seemed to him ultimate questions. He strained at times the resources of poetic language to their limits. The astonishing richness of his imagery bears witness to this, and to his lifelong conviction that poetry must strive to enlarge human understanding so that men and women might improve their lives by knowing their true bearings in the universe.

A

It is said that the Italian sailors who encountered Shelley's boat in the storm on July 8, 1822, offered in vain to take Shelley and Williams on board. When this offer was refused, the sailors pleaded with the Englishmen to furl their sails lest they be lost. As Williams tried to do so, Shelley seized his arm and stopped him. We must certainly regret Shelley's untimely death, but at the same time, we can't help but wonder at his power to capture, and be captured by, the great dark forces that so fascinated him.

Peterloo Massacre (1819). St. Peter's Fields, Manchester, England.

1. BUILDING ON PRIOR KNOWLEDGE. See if students know what kind of wind a "wild west wind" is (usually warm and moist). Shelley said the poem was chiefly written "in a wood that skirts the Arno, near Florence, and on a day when that tempestuous wind, whose temperature is at once mild and animating, was collecting the vapors which pour down the autumnal rains." Some students might have heard the beautiful sixteenth-century song that begins "O Western Wind, when wilt thou blow, / The small rain down can rain?"

2. ESTABLISHING A PURPOSE. Suggest that students concentrate on enjoying the lush beauty of Shelley's sound and imagery as they read the poem.

SUPPLEMENTARY SUPPORT MATERIALS
1. Vocabulary Activity Worksheet (*CCB*)
2. Review and Response Worksheet: Extended Apostrophe (*CCB*)
3. Selection Test (*CCB*)

One of Shelley's major lyric achievements, this poem was written in late October 1819. It was provoked by the sight of an oncoming storm near Florence, Italy, where Shelley was living. It marks, in his creative life, a temporary note of exaltation after a period of grief over the death of his three-year-old son, William. The ode demands to be read aloud.

Ode to the West Wind

I

A
B O wild West Wind, thou breath of Autumn's being,
Thou, from whose unseen presence the leaves dead
Are driven, like ghosts from an enchanter fleeing,

Yellow, and black, and pale, and hectic° red,
5 Pestilence-stricken multitudes: O Thou,
C Who chariotest to their dark wintry bed

The winged seeds, where they lie cold and low,
Each like a corpse within its grave, until,
D Thine azure° sister of the Spring shall blow

10 Her clarion° o'er the dreaming earth, and fill
(Driving sweet buds like flocks to feed in air)
With living hues and odors plain and hill:

Wild Spirit, which art moving everywhere;
Destroyer and Preserver; hear, O hear!

II

15 Thou on whose stream, 'mid the steep sky's commotion,
Loose clouds like Earth's decaying leaves are shed,
E Shook from the tangled boughs of Heaven and Ocean,

Angels of rain and lightning: there are spread
On the blue surface of thine aery surge,
20 Like the bright hair uplifted from the head
F
Of some fierce Maenad,° even from the dim verge
Of the horizon to the zenith's height,
The locks of the approaching storm. Thou Dirge

Of the dying year, to which this closing night
25 Will be the dome of a vast sepulcher,
Vaulted with all thy congregated might

Of vapors, from whose solid atmosphere
G Black rain and fire and hail will burst: O hear!

4. **hectic:** wasting or consuming; from the "hectic flush" of the face of tuberculosis sufferers.

9. **azure:** the color of the cloudless sky.

10. **clarion:** a call, loud and clear, as well as the trumpet capable of making such a shrill sound.

21. **Maenad:** in Greek mythology, a woman who performs frenzied dances in the workship of Dionysus, god of wine.

A. Apostrophe
Note that throughout the poem, the wind is personified and addressed directly.

B. Structure
Each of the first three sections describes the wind in relation to a natural element: I: leaves; II: clouds; III: sea.

C. Personification
[?] What words personify the wind and leaves? (The wind drives a chariot, the leaves are being driven to a bed.)

D. Imagery
Note that line 9 marks the turning point of spring: rebirth.

E. Vocabulary
Tangled boughs are waterspouts.

F. Interpreting
[?] Why is the autumn wind a "Dirge"? (The growing cycle is ended; the trees are getting barren. Life is going underground.)

G. Refrain
Notice that the first three sections end with the words "O hear!" What does the speaker want the wind to hear? (His ode—and his request)

CLOSURE
In 1834 Henry Taylor compared reading Shelley's poems to gazing on "so many gorgeously colored clouds in an evening sky. Surpassingly beautiful they were whilst before [the reader's] eyes; but forasmuch as they had no relevancy to his life, past or future, the impression upon the memory barely survived that upon the senses. . . ." Read this comment to the class, and ask if they think it applies to "Ode to the West Wind."

A. Expansion
Baiae is a district west of Naples.

B. Repetition
Note how Shelley neatly reviews the subjects of section I–III (see also line 53).

C. Metaphor
This line is often quoted, either to confirm Shelley as the most romantic of the Romantic poets, or to caricature him as a man whose celebration of his own feelings is less moving than comical.

D. Speaker
The speaker moves from thinking himself a passive object of the wind (section 4) to the powerful view of himself as a lyre for the universe.

III

Thou who didst waken from his summer dreams
30   The blue Mediterranean, where he lay,
Lulled by the coil of his crystalline streams,

A Beside a pumice° isle in Baiae's bay,
And saw in sleep old palaces and towers
Quivering within the wave's intenser day,

35   All overgrown with azure moss and flowers
So sweet, the sense faints picturing them! Thou
For whose path the Atlantic's level powers

Cleave themselves into chasms, while far below
The sea-blooms and the oozy woods which wear
40   The sapless foliage of the ocean, know

Thy voice, and suddenly grow gray with fear,
And tremble and despoil themselves: O hear!

IV

If I were a dead leaf thou mightest bear;
B If I were a swift cloud to fly with thee;
45   A wave to pant beneath thy power, and share

The impulse of thy strength, only less free
Than thou, O Uncontrollable! If even
I were as in my boyhood, and could be

The comrade of thy wanderings over Heaven,
50   As then, when to outstrip thy skiey speed
Scarce seemed a vision; I would ne'er have striven

As thus with thee in prayer in my sore need.
Oh! lift me as a wave, a leaf, a cloud!
C I fall upon the thorns of life! I bleed!

55   A heavy weight of hours has chained and bowed
One too like thee: tameless, and swift, and proud.

V

Make me thy lyre,° even as the forest is:
What if my leaves are falling like its own!
The tumult of thy mighty harmonies

60   Will take from both a deep, autumnal tone,
D Sweet though in sadness. Be thou, Spirit fierce,
My spirit! Be thou me, impetuous one!

Drive my dead thoughts over the universe
Like withered leaves to quicken a new birth!
65   And, by the incantation of this verse,

32. **pumice:** the volcanic substance of islands in the Bay of Naples. These islands were once summer resorts for Roman nobility and, in Shelley's time, were notable for their ruins of ancient villas and monumental baths.

57. **lyre:** the Aeolian harp, a stringed instrument that emits sound when the wind blows across its strings: a favorite Romantic symbol.

ANALYZING THE POEM
Identifying Details
1. He implores the wind to listen.
2. The wind blows the leaves, stirs the clouds to a storm, wakens the ocean from its summer sleep and causes great waves.
3. He is "tameless, and swift, and proud."
4. He prays the wind to make him its instrument, to drive his "dead thoughts over the universe," and to scatter his wind-inspired words "among mankind."

Interpreting Meanings
5. It serves the final death to autumn leaves and it preserves seeds by carrying them to earth.
6. The clouds form a blanket over the sky, thus closing in the earth. Line 24 mentions the dying or waning year. Line 25's reference to a tomb also hints at coming winter.
7. They are the surface of the ocean.
8. Life's pain, suffering, and sorrows.
9. It is a ritual chant, designed to produce some effect.
   As in prayer, an incantation requests something from a force outside of and *(Answers continue on next page.)*

Scatter, as from an unextinguished hearth°
Ashes and sparks, my words among mankind!
Be through my lips to unawakened Earth

The trumpet of a prophecy! O Wind,
70   If Winter comes, can Spring be far behind?

66. **unextinguished hearth:** from *A Defense of Poetry:* "the mind in creation is as a fading coal which some invisible influence, like an inconstant wind, awakens to transitory brightness."

A. Interpreting
❓ What do you think the "prophecy" is in line 69? (A just society free from oppression)

A Comment on the Poem

This ode is both an expression of Shelley's sense of purpose as a public poet, and a personal meditation on the role. In what a biographer calls a moment of both "triumph and defiance," he copied a Greek phrase from the dramatist Euripides in his notebook after finishing the poem: "By virtuous power, I, a mortal, vanquish thee a mighty god."

A genuine ode in its overall style and arrangement, the form of this poem is special. It consists of five sonnets in *terza rima*, with each section ending, as a Shakespearean sonnet does, with a couplet. Each group of three lines picks up the rhyme of the second line of the preceding three lines.

Even Shelley's admirers have been a little embarrassed by the exaggerated self-dramatization of "I fall upon the thorns of life! I bleed!" (line 54). But the poem is full of such heightened effects. They are consistent with the manner of the ode, with its large scale—the earth, the air, and the sea—with its imagery, and with the situation of the speaker, who is striving in "sore need" in prayer with a higher power.

"Ode to the West Wind" expresses Shelley's fascination with power and with those forces—both destroyers and preservers—that inspire the same powers within the poet.

B. Humanities Connection: Responding to the Fine Art
Joseph Mallord William Turner (1775–1851) was born in London, the son of a barber. Turner's landscapes and paintings of ships at sea are often made up of masses of swirling, vibrant color, which the art historian Frederick Hartt calls "a kind of color music."
❓ How has the artist created a sense of vast openness and space? (You can see for a great distance with nothing obstructing the view; the sky is cloudless; the sky and river have the same soft, glowing white color.)

Panorama of Florence by J. M. W. Turner (19th century).

greater than the person.

10. In section 5, the speaker does state that he needs the power of the wind to make poetry of transformative power. However, nowhere in the poem is it suggested that poetry needs an outer inspiration. And in specific reference to this poem, the west wind is commonly interpreted as inner inspiration.

11. The first three sections describe the wind's effects. In the fourth and fifth sections, the speaker asks the wind to empower him.

12. An unextinguished hearth contains both ashes (comparable to dead leaves) and sparks (comparable to seeds). The speaker contains within him elements of both death (dead thoughts) and life (the trumpet of a prophecy).

13. The speaker continues to ask the wind to speak through him, to give him the voice of prophecy. He wants more than anything the power of expression. He is in a dormant state—winter—and concludes by asking rhetorically if spring (poetry, expression, life) will come after winter (grief, silence).

Responding to the Poem

Analyzing the Poem

Identifying Details

1. What does the speaker ask the wind to do at the end of sections 1, 2, and 3?
2. What does the wind do to the leaves, the clouds, and the sea?
3. How is the speaker like the wind, according to section 4?
4. In the final section, what does the poet pray the wind to do?

Interpreting Meanings

5. How is the wind both a "Destroyer and Preserver" (line 14)?
6. Why does the sky become a "vast sepulcher" (line 25)? How do lines 24 and 25 hint at the time the poem may have been written?
7. What are the "level powers" of line 37?
8. What are the "thorns of life" (line 54)?
9. What is an *incantation* (line 65)? How is it related to a prayer?
10. Does the ode argue that poetry cannot come into being unless the poet is inspired by a force greater than himself or herself? Explain.
11. How do the fourth and fifth sections of the poem differ in their approach and emphasis from the first three sections?
12. In line 67, the speaker describes his words as "ashes and sparks." How can you explain this **paradox**?
13. What do you think lines 68–70 mean?

Writing About the Poem

A Critical Response

Analyzing Sound Effects. Shelley's poetry has often been acclaimed for its musical qualities. In a brief essay, cite what you think are the outstanding examples of the poet's use of sound effects (**alliteration, onomatopoeia, assonance,** and **rhyme**) in "Ode to the West Wind," and analyze the effectiveness of each example in context.

Analyzing Language and Style

Terza Rima and the Sonnet

"Ode to the West Wind" should be read aloud to hear the remarkable chiming effects of Shelley's adaptation of *terza rima* to the sonnet form. Shelley the technician adjusts sound to sense in passages of onomatopoeic beauty, while Shelley the thinker dramatizes the cycles of death and rebirth.

1. **Terza rima** consists of sequences of three lines of interlocking rhyme. Identify Shelley's rhyme scheme in each 14-line section. Are the schemes all the same?
2. Each section is also a **sonnet.** Review the forms of the Italian and Shakespearean sonnets and tell how Shelley has adapted the forms to suit his own purposes.
3. Sonnets **turn** their thoughts or arguments at some place in the 14 lines. Does Shelley do this in his ode?

The Elements of Literature

APOSTROPHE

Apostrophe is a figure of speech in which a writer directly addresses an absent person, a personified inanimate object, or an abstract idea. For example, Shelley's "Ode to the West Wind" begins with an apostrophe, the speaker's invocation of the wind in line 1. This device recurs in lines 2, 5, 13, 15, 23, 29, 36, 47, 52, 57, 61, 62, and 69. In fact this poem, like quite a few others of Shelley's, might be called an **extended apostrophe.**

Perhaps the origins of apostrophe lie in prayer. Formulas of prayer in both ancient and modern religions are built around repeated invocations in which the faithful call upon God to hear them. It is probably no accident that many Romantic poems are titled or otherwise described as "hymns," since apostrophe was a favorite device of the Romantics.

Romantic "empathy"—or the notion of deep sympathy or identification with another person or object—raises an interesting question about apostrophe. When Shelley, for example, addresses the West Wind, he closes with an ecstatic prayer to *be* or *become* the object addressed. His empathy is so intense that the idea of apostrophe begins to break down—for a moment, the speaker *is* the object, or at least we can imagine that the object is actually in the speaker's presence.

PREPARATION

1. ESTABLISHING A PURPOSE. Ask students to read the poem to find out how the skylark's song is different from the poet's song. (The skylark's song is unpremeditated, always joyous, without pain or fear. It sings for itself, not for an audience.)

2. PREREADING JOURNAL. Have students write in their journals two or three sentences explaining the symbolic significance one might bestow upon a songbird (line 2).

SUPPLEMENTARY SUPPORT MATERIALS
1. Review and Response Worksheet: Simile (*CCB*)
2. Selection Test (*CCB*)
3. Audiocassette recording

This poem was composed during Shelley's summer residence on the northwestern coast of Italy in June 1820.

The singing bird is a favorite romantic comparison or *analogue* for the poet: The human singer seeks to capture or approximate the ethereal beauty of the bird's song, but often finds, as here, that human life can never be the source of such pure song. (See also John Keats's "Ode to a Nightingale.")

Here, as elsewhere, we are aware that the Romantic poets, though lovers of nature, were not interested in making exact and detailed observations of natural phenomena. They were more inclined to see in nature manifestations of some higher order of being, harmony, and divinity.

To a Skylark

A
     Hail to thee, blithe° Spirit!
          Bird thou never wert—
     That from Heaven, or near it,
          Pourest thy full heart
5   In profuse strains of unpremeditated art.

B
     Higher still and higher
          From the earth thou springest
     Like a cloud of fire;
          The blue deep thou wingest,
10   And singing still dost soar, and soaring ever singest.

C
     In the golden lightning
          Of the sunken sun—
     O'er which clouds are brightening,
          Thou dost float and run;
15   Like an unbodied joy whose race is just begun.

D
     The pale purple even°
          Melts around thy flight,
     Like a star of Heaven°
          In the broad daylight
20   Thou art unseen—but yet I hear thy shrill delight,

     Keen as are the arrows
          Of that silver sphere,°
     Whose intense lamp narrows
          In the white dawn clear
25   Until we hardly see—we feel that it is there.

     All the earth and air
          With thy voice is loud,
     As when night is bare
          From one lonely cloud
     The moon rains out her beams—and Heaven is over-
30   flowed.

1. **blithe:** joyful.

16. **even:** evening.

18. **star of Heaven:** evening star.

22. **silver sphere:** morning star.

A. Meaning
? How does the poet explain his opening statement? (He sees the lark as being from Heaven and its song as art.)

B. Rhyme/ Rhythm
? Identify the pattern of rhyme and rhythm in each stanza. (Rhyme: *ababb*: Rhythm: four short [three-foot] trochaic lines followed by a long [six-foot] flowing line, perhaps in imitation of the skylark's song)

C. Setting
? What is the time of day? (Sundown)

D. Diction
Note the many different ways Shelley refers to the bird's joyful song. (Lines 3–5, 10, 15, 20, 26–27, 35, 65)

Share with students that the Romantic poets often took liberties with word order to achieve rhyme and rhythm. To help the reader follow their train of thought, they made certain that each pronoun had a recognizable antecedent. Point out *it* and *world* in lines 39 and 40, *maiden* and *her* in lines 41 and 43, as well as examples from the facing page such as *glow-worm* and *Its, rose* and *its*, and *Bird* and *thine*.

Have volunteers orally correct the following sentences by adding words that include an antecedent for each pronoun. (Note: A noun in one sentence cannot be the antecedent for a pronoun in a later one.)

1. When singing, her voice is sweet and sad.
2. The symphony ends, and their final flourish echoes through the concert hall.
3. The audience applauds at its final haunting notes.
4. All the way home they hear the last bugle call of the evening.
5. Throughout her next rehearsal the sharp, sweet bugle notes linger.

A. Humanities Connection: Discussing the Fine Art

Robert Collinson (b. 1832) was an English painter known for his detailed genre paintings—that is, realistically rendered scenes from everyday life. Collinson had a long and successful career as a painter, exhibiting his work at the Royal Academy of Art from 1858 to 1890.

❓ Much like a photograph, this painting seems to capture a silent moment in a golden, lush forest. What do the two rabbits add to the painting? (A mood of stillness and peace; a center of interest in the foreground; a sense of size and distance; a startling solid black and white among the many gradations of green, gold, and brown)

B. Structure/Simile

Note that this question introduces a series of four similes (lines 36–60).

A

B

What thou art we know not;
  What is most like thee?
From rainbow clouds there flow not
  Drops so bright to see
35 As from thy presence showers a rain of melody.

Like a poet hidden
  In the light of thought,
Singing hymns unbidden,
  Till the world is wrought
40 To sympathy with hopes and fears it heeded not:

Like a high-born maiden
  In a palace tower,
Soothing her love-laden

Rabbits in the Woods
by Robert Collinson.

Victoria and Albert Museum, London.

The Skylark as a Symbol

Shelley's choice of the skylark as a symbol of "unembodied joy" is remarkably apt. The skylark is a small bird resembling a sparrow. It seldom lights in trees or shrubs but soars high above the ground, singing a very long, melodious song as it flies. Often, the skylark soars so high that it cannot be seen; only its song can be heard. Skylarks have been introduced to North America, but they've survived only on Vancouver Island.

Soul in secret hour,

45   With music sweet as love—which overflows her bower:

Like a glow-worm golden
  In a dell° of dew,
Scattering unbeholden
  Its aerial hue

50   Among the flowers and grass which screen it from the
       view:

Like a rose embowered
  In its own green leaves—
By warm winds deflowered—
  Till the scent it gives
Makes faint with too much sweet heavy-winged

55   thieves:

A

Sound of vernal° showers
  On the twinkling grass,
Rain-awakened flowers,
  All that ever was

60   Joyous, and clear and fresh, thy music doth surpass.

Teach us, Sprite or Bird,
  What sweet thoughts are thine;
I have never heard
  Praise of love or wine

65   That panted forth a flood of rapture so divine:

Chorus Hymeneal°
  Or triumphal chaunt°
Matched with thine would be all
  But an empty vaunt,°

70   A thing wherein we feel there is some hidden want.

B

What objects are the fountains
  Of thy happy strain?°
What fields or waves or mountains?
  What shapes of sky or plain?

75   What love of thine own kind? what ignorance of pain?

With thy clear keen joyance°
  Languor cannot be—
Shadow of annoyance
  Never came near thee;

80   Thou lovest—but ne'er knew love's sad satiety.°

Waking or asleep,
  Thou of death must deem
Things more true and deep
  Than we mortals dream,

85   Or how could thy notes flow in such a crystal stream?

---

47. **dell:** small but deep valley.

56. **vernal:** occurring in the spring.

66. **Chorus Hymeneal:** wedding song (from Hymen, Greek god of marriage).
67. **chaunt:** chant.

69. **vaunt:** boast.

72. **strain:** melody.

76. **joyance:** rejoicing.

80. **satiety:** the feeling of weariness due to overfulfillment of appetite or desire.

A. Meaning
In line 53, the warm winds literally take away the flower and are therefore called "thieves" (line 55).

B. Meaning
What does the speaker want the skylark to teach us? (The source of its transcendent joy)

ANALYZING THE POEM
Identifying Details
1. The similes occur in lines 6–8, 15, 18–19, 21–22, 28–30, 33–35, 36–38, 41–45, 46–50, and 51–55.
2. He asks it what the objects of its song are (lines 71–75). He asks how it could sing so purely without knowledge of life and death (lines 81–85).
He asks the bird to teach its thoughts

(line 61–62), its gladness (lines 101–105).
3. Wedding songs and triumphal chants.
4. The skylark's song is happy; the sweetest human songs are sad.
5. He would have to be free from hate, pride, fear, and sorrow.
(Answers continue in left-hand column.)

(Continued from top.)
Interpreting Meanings
6. We learn that its song is spontaneous (5); far away (15). It sings for itself (38); is rarely seen (48); is untouched by pain (75). Its song is free of love's melancholy (80); and of earthly concerns (100).
7. Student answers will vary. Possible details include those found in lines 21–24, 27–30, 35, 46–50, 55, 61–65.
8. Such passages occur in lines 1–5, 36–40, 46–50, 61–65.
9. Answers will vary. Students should have no difficulties thinking of examples of the first two lines. For the next two, analysis of a few current jokes will probably reveal the anger that is often hidden in or used by humor.
Popular music, especially ballads and, above all, country-and-western songs, is filled with examples of how much we enjoy pain. Most of these are "sweet" in the sense of "popular."

We look before and after,
    And pine for what is not—
Our sincerest laughter
    With some pain is fraught—
90   Our sweetest songs are those that tell of saddest
      thought.

Yet if we could scorn
    Hate and pride and fear;
If we were things born
    Not to shed a tear,
95   I know not how thy joy we ever should come near.

Better than all measures
    Of delightful sound—
Better than all treasures
    That in books are found—
100 Thy skill to poet were, thou Scorner of the ground!

Teach me half the gladness
    That thy brain must know,
Such harmonious madness
    From my lips would flow
105 The world should listen then—as I am listening now.

Responding to the Poem

Analyzing the Poem

Identifying Details

1. Identify the different **similes** that the poet uses to describe the skylark.
2. What questions does the speaker ask the bird? What does he ask the bird to teach him?
3. What kinds of songs would be an "empty vaunt" (line 69) compared to the song of the skylark?
4. Why are humans' "sweetest songs" (line 90) not the same as the song of the skylark?
5. What, according to lines 91–95, would be necessary for "harmonious madness" to flow from the speaker of the poem?

Interpreting Meanings

6. What do we learn about the skylark and its song from the following words used to describe it: "unpremeditated" (line 5), "unbodied" (line 15), "unbidden" (line 38), "unbeholden" (line 48), "ignorance" (line

75), "ne'er knew love's sad satiety" (line 80), and "Scorner of the ground" (line 100)?
7. What details of this poem do you think suggest the special quality of the skylark's music?
8. What passages in the poem seem to reflect the Romantics' esteem for spontaneity in poetry?
9. Lines 86–90 of this poem are among the most-quoted lines in English poetry. Do you agree with what this stanza says about humans? What examples can you provide that support line 90?

Writing About the Poem

A Critical Response

Comparing Poems. In a brief essay, tell why you think the speaker of this poem asserts that the skylark must know things "more true and deep" (line 83) than human beings do. Compare this contention with Keats's "Thou wast not born for death, immortal Bird!" (line 61 of "Ode to a Nightingale").

PREPARATION
ESTABLISHING A PURPOSE. Question 6 will help set a purpose for reading.

SUPPLEMENTARY SUPPORT MATERIALS
1. Vocabulary Activity Worksheet (CCB)
2. Review and Response Worksheet: Figures of Speech (CCB)
3. Selection Test (CCB)

DEVELOPING VOCABULARY
The following word from the poem is tested in the Selection Test. (See also Vocabulary Activity Worksheet.)
dregs

CLOSURE
Ask students to identify the tone of the poem and to cite details to support their answers.

A. Syntax
This sonnet is a single sentence. There are eight compound subjects in lines 1–12. The predicate appears in the final couplet.

B. Responding
❓ Until the last line, did you expect a note of hope for the future?

ANALYZING THE POEM
Identifying Details
1. The king is old, mad, and despised. The royalty are a dull race, scorned by the people.
   Shelley uses metaphors (dregs, mud) and simile (leechlike).
2. The people are starved and killed; the army inflicts pain and oppression; laws are corrupt; religion is Christless and Godless.

Interpreting Meanings
3. Princes are the last of an incompetent and dying institution: royalty. Rulers feed off the people.
4. Answers will vary. Note the similarity to King Lear.
5. The paradox is in the fact that life can burst forth from a grave. The oppressive statute may cause the people to react with a revolution.
6. Haiti, South Africa, China, and Germany have been tyrannies at various times.

This sonnet was unpublished until after 1832, the year of the first great reform measures passed by the English parliament.

The shock of the Peterloo Massacre (see line 7) had awakened Shelley's anger. On August 16, 1819, mounted soldiers charged into a crowd gathered in St. Peter's Field, near Manchester, to rally for the reform of parliament. At least six people were killed and more than eighty injured.

"Peterloo" is a bitterly ironic reference to the Battle of Waterloo (1815), in which the English commander, Lord Wellington, vanquished Napoleon's armies for the last time.

The king in line 1 is George III, the same king who presided over the loss of the American colonies. His insanity had been acknowledged in 1811. The king died in 1820.

England in 1819

A   An old, mad, blind, despised, and dying King;
     Princes, the dregs of their dull race, who flow
     Through public scorn—mud from a muddy spring;
     Rulers who neither see nor feel nor know,
5   But leechlike to their fainting country cling
     Till they drop, blind in blood, without a blow.
     A people starved and stabbed in th'untilled field;
     An army, whom liberticide° and prey
     Makes as a two-edged sword to all who wield;
10   Golden and sanguine laws° which tempt and slay;
     Religion Christless, Godless—a book sealed;
     A senate, time's worst statute,° unrepealed—
B   Are graves from which a glorious Phantom° may
     Burst, to illumine our tempestuous day.

8. **liberticide:** murder of liberty.
10. **Golden and sanguine laws:** apparently, laws written to protect financial interests and those which lead to bloodshed.
12. **time's worst statute:** probably the law or laws that imposed restrictions on people who did not belong to the Church of England, specifically Roman Catholics.
13. **Phantom:** spirit (of revolution).

Responding to the Poem

Analyzing the Poem

Identifying Details

1. What does the speaker say about kings and rulers of England? What **figures of speech** are used to describe them?
2. What does the speaker say about the people, the army, the laws, and religion?

Interpreting Meanings

3. Why are the "princes" described as "dregs of their dull race" (line 2), and the "rulers" as "leechlike" (line 5)?
4. Analyze the effectiveness of Shelley's choice of adjectives that describe King George III in line 1.

5. Explain the **paradox** in line 13: that "graves" might give birth to the glorious Phantom.
6. Can you think of any other periods in history to which Shelley's invective might apply?

Analyzing Language and Style

Connotations

Make a list of all the words in this sonnet that are loaded with negative associations and that are used to describe the rulers of England. Try substituting a less powerful word in each case and comment on the resultant change in tone.

ESTABLISHING A PURPOSE. Have students read the poem to identify its tone and theme.

CLOSURE
Have students state the main idea of "Ozymandias."

A. Syntax
This clause beginning with "that" is difficult and can be used to test your students' reading skills. What is the objective of "survive"? (The "hand" and the "heart") Whose hand and heart? (The sculptor's) *Mocked* can mean "imitated" as well as "derided."

B. Expansion
According to an ancient Greek historian, the statue was inscribed: "I am Ozymandias, king of kings; if anyone wishes to know what I am and where I lie, let him surpass me in some of my exploits."

ANALYZING THE POEM
Identifying Details
1. He sees the ruins of a huge statue in a vast desert.
2. See lines 10–11. Nothing remains except the ruined statue.
3. There are three speakers: the narrator, the traveler, and Ozymandias.

Interpreting Meanings
4. The passions are the king's bitterness and contempt for others.
5. Disdain and haughtiness.
6. The king boasted of his mighty works; only a ruined statue remains.
7. Answers will vary. There are many possibilities.

Theme: Transience of earthly fame + power
: Time + eternity erase the mightiest works of human beings

Romantic: faraway place

Shelley wrote relatively few sonnets, and this is certainly one of his best. It is all the more interesting since it was written as part of a friendly and informal poetry competition with Keats in the winter of 1817. The general topic of the competition was Egypt: Some extraordinary fragments of the Empire of the several kings of Egypt named Rameses (fourteenth to eleventh centuries B.C.)

had recently been put on display at the British Museum in London.

Ozymandias is the Greek name for Rameses II (ruled 1292–1225 B.C.), who left monuments all over Egypt, including the temples of Karnak and Luxor. Rameses is probably the pharaoh mentioned in the Bible who contended with Moses at the time of the Hebrews' Exodus from Egypt.

Traveler
Speaker
Ozymandias

Ozymandias *(Ramses II)*

a I met a traveler from an antique land,
b Who said—"Two vast and trunkless legs° of stone
a Stand in the desert. . . . Near them, on the sand,
b Half sunk a shattered visage lies, whose frown,   *face*
a 5 And wrinkled lip, and sneer of cold command,
c ⌜Tell that its sculptor well those passions read
d A │Which yet survive, stamped on these lifeless things,
c ⌞The hand that mocked them, and the heart° that fed;   *imitated*
e And on the pedestal, these words appear:
d 10 ⌜My name is Ozymandias, King of Kings,   *Ozy speaks his words*
e B ⌞Look on my works, ye mighty, and despair!
f ⌠Nothing beside remains. Round the decay
e ⌡Of that colossal wreck, boundless and bare
f The lone and level sands stretch far away."

2. **trunkless legs:** that is, the legs without the rest of the body.

The sculptor read the expression well of the model

8. **hand . . . heart:** the hand of the sculptor and the heart of Ozymandias.

Hand is the sculptor
the heart is of Ozy
He fed the passions.
It was these passions the sculptor created in the stone, yet they were destroyed

Passions— bitterness
confidence contempt
pride
haughtiness

11 lines - set up his picture of human arrogance.
3 lines - ironic commentary
*   Time + eternity erase the mightiest works of human beings.*

Responding to the Poem

Analyzing the Poem

Identifying Details
1. Explain in your own words what the traveler has seen.
2. What words are on the pedestal? What works remain?
3. Even in the brief space of a sonnet, Shelley suggests a number of **narrative frames:** How many speakers do you hear in this poem?

Interpreting Meanings
4. What do you think are the passions that the sculptor read and embodied in the "visage"?

5. What kind of pride is condemned by the poem?
6. Explain the fundamental **irony** of the sonnet.
7. Could this poem apply to any contemporary figures that wield political power?

Writing About the Poem

A Critical Response
Comparing and Contrasting Sonnets. In a brief essay, compare and contrast the **structure, subject, theme,** and **tone** of Shelley's two sonnets with those of any Renaissance writer.

SUPPLEMENTARY SUPPORT MATERIALS
1. Review and Response Worksheet: Theme (*CCB*)
2. Selection Test (*CCB*)

A. Humanities Connection: About the Fine Art

Joseph Severn (1793–1879) was the friend who accompanied Keats to Rome in the fall of 1820 after Keats's doctor warned that he would not survive another English winter. They reached Rome after a difficult six-week journey, but Keats died in the spring. Severn was with him when he died.

Severn worked on this portrait for two years after Keats's death. The artist's concern with the effects of light and shadow is reminiscent of the work of the seventeenth-century Dutch painter Jan Vermeer.

B. Expansion

Wentworth Place, a semi-detached house in Hampstead in northwest London, is now the Keats Museum. In December 1818, Keats moved to Wentworth Place. In the spring a widow and her three children moved into the adjoining house. The oldest was eighteen-year-old Fanny Brawne; by the fall of 1819 she and Keats were engaged.

John Keats (1795–1821)

It is surprising Keats became a poet at all, and surely a wonder that, when he died at the age of twenty-five, he had accomplished enough to become one of our major poets.

John Keats did not have most of the advantages a poet often needs to get started. His parents ran a London livery stable and both died before he was fifteen. After two years in a school where his literary interests were encouraged, he was apprenticed at the age of fifteen to learn medicine. Keats saw something of his own country as a young man, but his only foreign travel was a desperate trip to Italy when he was dying, enduring what he called a "posthumous existence." He had friends and supporters who recognized his poetic genius, but he never enjoyed a close collaborative relationship with another poet. He seems to have been always conscious of his small physical stature (he was five feet and three-quarters of an inch tall), and there can be no doubt that he lived in close acquaintance with death and the fragile nature of human life.

We have to measure Keats's life in weeks and months, not in years. He was forced to grow up and make his mind up about important things so quickly that it seems he grew from a child to a man without the chance to be young, to make mistakes, and to grow.

His short life was clogged with troubles. Tuberculosis killed his mother in 1810, his brother Tom in 1818, and John himself in 1821. His mother's death left the family finances tied up in legal complications and inaccessible to the Keats children. George (born in 1797) emigrated to Kentucky in 1818. This left only John to care for the dying Tom. Fanny, fifteen, lived with a guardian, and John saw his sister infrequently.

In 1816, not yet twenty-one, Keats completed his medical studies at Guy's Hospital in London. Before he could be legally licensed as a surgeon and apothecary, he made the momentous decision to become a poet. The harsh reviews of his first book of poetry (1818) stung him and added to the periodic doubts that made his dedication to poetry sometimes seem an awful burden.

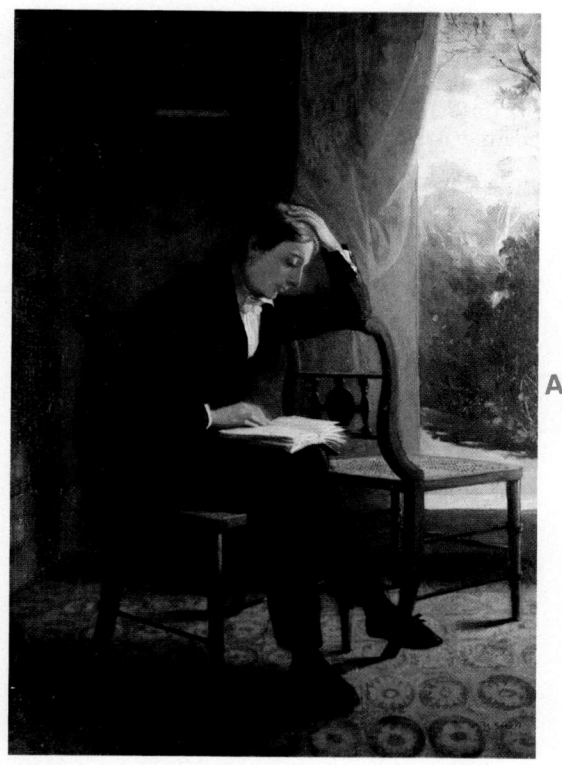

John Keats at Wentworth Place
by Joseph Severn (1821-23). Oil.

After Tom's death in December 1818, Keats had little more than a year to make what he could of his determination to lead a "literary life." Great passages and nearly perfect poems poured from him in that miraculous time. Already in failing health, he never knew the greatness of his achievements, which might have given him at least the consolation of literary success. He had fallen in love—her name was Fanny Brawne—but his poor health and money problems kept him from marrying. "I am three and twenty," he wrote despairingly in March 1819, "with little knowledge and middling intellect. It is true that in the height of enthusiasm I have been cheated into some fine passages, but that is nothing."

In the next eight months he wrote six of the eight glorious poems in our selection. Yet he lamented in a November letter to George, "Nothing could have in all its circumstances fallen out worse for me than the last year has done, or

In an 1818 letter to a friend (reprinted as written), Keats wrote about poetry: "1st. I think Poetry should surprise by a fine excess and not by Singularity—it should strike the Reader as a wording of his own highest thoughts, and appear almost a Remembrance—2nd. Its touches of Beauty should never be half way thereby making the reader breathless instead of content: the rise, the progress, the setting of imagery should like the Sun come natural to him—shine over him and set soberly although in magnificence leaving him in the Luxury of twilight—but it is easier to think what Poetry should be than to write it—and this leads me to another axiom. That if Poetry comes not as naturally as the Leaves to a tree it had better not come at all."

Recall that Homer, the semilegendary author of the *Iliad* and the *Odyssey*, lived during the eighth century B.C. Keats could not read Homer in the original Greek, but he was familiar with Alexander Pope's translation.

A. Expansion
His companion was Joseph Severn, the artist who painted the portrait on text page 707.

B. Keats's Epitaph
As he lay dying, Keats asked Severn to inscribe this epitaph on his grave: "Here lies one whose name was writ in water."

C. Keats's Letters
In May 1818 Keats wrote to Leigh Hunt, "I have asked myself so often why I should be a poet more than other men, seeing how great a thing it is—how great things are to be gained by it, what a thing to be in the mouth of Fame. . . ."

D. Keats's Genius
The poet Gerard Manley Hopkins (see text page 827) wrote to a friend in 1878: "Keats's genius was so astonishing, unequalled at his age and scarcely surpassed at any, that one may surmise whether if he had lived he would have rivaled Shakespeare."

---

could be more damping to my poetical talent." Three months later he coughed up blood. His medical training and the nursing of Tom made the truth obvious: "That drop of blood is my death warrant." His only chance, a slim one, was to live in a warmer climate.

He was unable to accept an invitation from the Shelleys to join them in Pisa, Italy. After a long and exhausting sea journey, Keats and a companion settled in Rome in late 1820. There he died in February 1821. Before the summer was over, Shelley had written his powerful elegy for Keats, "Adonais," in which he described the Protestant cemetery in Rome where Keats was buried. That "camp of death," as Shelley called it, seems like the tomb of the young Romantics. Shelley's young son William was buried there in 1819; Shelley himself in 1822.

The stark sadness of Keats's life heightens, by contrast, our awareness of the distinguishing qualities of his poems. They are not bleak, but rich in sensuous detail. They are not subdued, but exciting representations of intense emotional experiences. They are not heavy with resignation, but full of courageous hope for what the imagination, with what Keats called "the ardor of pursuit," can seize and enjoy in life. Above all, they show us what Keats was able to wrest from his troubled life by singlemindedly working at the art of poetry.

When Keats set out at eighteen to be a poet, he had published but one sonnet, and what he had written did not show exceptional promise. He was learning from his contemporaries, but his real masters were Spenser, Milton, and Shakespeare, a burden of ambition that was heavy. His letters show his obsession with his calling as a poet and his determination to become one. The letters have become works of literature in themselves because he poured himself into what he wrote to those close to him, and because he left behind fewer published works than most great poets.

What is most striking in Keats's letters is his unerring sense of the tension between the imaginative escape from life provided by his writing, and his unflinching courage in accepting the harsh realities of day-to-day experience. His earlier letters celebrate the gusto of the creative life of "sensations" rather than thought, and the happy loss of self-consciousness in intense experiences of beauty. But he rapidly saw the importance of what he called "speculations," or thinking deeply into what Wordsworth called, in "Tintern Abbey," the "burden of the mystery." Confronted with Wordsworth's achievements, Keats longed for some assurance that he too might grow and develop into a maturer poet. His speculations took the form of two allegories of human life found in his letters: life as a "mansion of many apartments" and as a "vale of soul making."

Keats's actual development alternated between pushing himself to write and allowing what he called "the genius of poetry" to work out its "salvation" in him. That salvation began with a sonnet—one of more than sixty Keats wrote—on reading Chapman's translation of Homer. The hard work began soon after, in 1817, with his writing of *Endymion*, a romance he was determined would reach four thousand lines. When it was published with some of his other works in 1818, and generally scorned by reviewers, Keats had already found a new direction. He began a long epic in the manner of Milton. It was never completed and eventually abandoned for another long poem, *The Fall of Hyperion*. *Hyperion* was also unfinished and teases us with what it suggests about the kind of poetry Keats might have written if he had lived longer.

Keats's most mature finished works come from the extraordinary flowering of his genius in 1819, which produced the great odes and a romance, "The Eve of St. Agnes." Lyric in nature, these poems show a hard-won discipline, strengthened by his work in sonnets, which curbed the extravagance of his earlier poetry.

In 1820, Keats published his new poems in what has been called "one of the richest volumes in the history of English poetry." He had already set his sights higher, hoping to nurture his "little dramatic skill" in the writing of a few more narrative poems to "nerve me up to the writing of a few fine plays—my greatest ambition." He had done so much in the little time he had; now he longed to follow Shakespeare into "the fierce dispute / Betwixt damnation and impassioned clay."

Our tragedy is that he could not. Our wonder must be that none of the great poets who came before him—Chaucer, Spenser, Shakespeare, Milton, Pope, or Wordsworth—would be found in this book if they had died at twenty-five.

2. PREREADING JOURNAL. Suggest that students write two or three sentences describing how a book, play, movie, or TV show moved them deeply.

CLOSURE
Have students state in their own words how Keats felt when he first read Homer.

SUPPLEMENTARY SUPPORT MATERIALS
1. Vocabulary Activity Worksheet (*CCB*)
2. Review and Response Worksheet: Extended Figures of Speech (*CCB*)
3. Selection Test (*CCB*)

DEVELOPING VOCABULARY
The following word from the poem is tested in the Selection Test. (See also Vocabulary Activity Worksheet.)
fealty

Keats had been writing poetry for nearly three years when, in October 1816, just before his twenty-first birthday, he produced this sonnet. It was his first work of high quality and he wrote it in a few hours. Though he knew, as he said fifteen months later, "it is easier to think what poetry should be than to write it," his conviction—borne out by this poem and the "great odes" of 1819— was that "if poetry comes not as naturally as the leaves to a tree, it had better not come at all."

It is revealing that Keats's ease in writing this poem was connected with an exciting literary experience. Charles Cowden Clarke, Keats's favorite teacher, invited his pupil-turned-poet to spend an evening reading a translation of Homer's *Iliad* by George Chapman, a contemporary of Shakespeare. Clarke and Keats stayed up all night enjoying the "famousest" passages. Keats went home at dawn and by ten that morning sent his sonnet to his teacher.

On First Looking into Chapman's Homer

A

Much have I traveled in the realms of gold,
   And many goodly states and kingdoms seen;
   Round many western islands have I been
Which bards in <u>fealty</u> to Apollo° hold.
5 Oft of one wide expanse had I been told
   That deep-browed Homer ruled as his demesne;°
   Yet did I never breathe its pure serene°
Till I heard Chapman speak out loud and bold:

B

Then felt I like some watcher of the skies
10   When a new planet swims into his ken;°
   Or like stout Cortez° when with eagle eyes
   He stared at the Pacific—and all his men
Looked at each other with a wild surmise—
   Silent, upon a peak in Darien.

4. **bards in fealty to Apollo:** poets in loyal service (as feudal tenants to their lord) to Apollo, the Greek god of poetry.
6. **demesne:** domain, estate.
7. **serene:** clear air.

10. **ken:** range of vision.
11. **Cortez:** sixteenth-century Spanish explorer. Keats is confusing him with Balboa, another Spanish explorer, who was the first European to see the Pacific Ocean, from the heights of Darien in Panama.

A. Figurative Language
Note the figures of speech that have to do with travel.

B. Expansion
William Herschel discovered the planet Uranus in 1781.

ANALYZING THE POEM
Identifying Details
1. He has read many great poets, but has only secondhand knowledge of Homer.
2. He feels like the discoverer of a new planet or like Cortez when he discovered the Pacific Ocean.
3. The rhyme scheme is abbaabba cdcdcd.

Interpreting Meanings
4. "Realms of gold" are imaginative lands.
5. The speaker feels like an astronomer or an explorer, both of whom search for the undiscovered. (Poetry is compared to a voyage of discovery.)

Responding to the Poem

Analyzing the Poem

Identifying Details

1. What does the speaker say he had already experienced before he read Homer?
2. How does the speaker say he felt on reading Homer?
3. Describe the **rhyme scheme** of the sonnet.

Interpreting Meanings

4. What do you think "realms of gold" are? (line 1)
5. What significance can you find in those two famous **similes** that tell how the speaker felt on reading Homer? (By implication, what is he comparing the experience of reading poetry to?)

Writing About the Poem

A Creative Response

1. **Writing Similes.** Keats compares his emotions in this first experience to those of an astronomer and an explorer. Think of two other extended similes that would be apt for this context.

A Critical Response

2. **Analyzing the Poem's Structure.** In a paragraph, explain the relationship between the first eight lines (the octet) of this sonnet, and the last six lines (the sestet).

PREPARATION

BUILDING ON PRIOR KNOWLEDGE. This poem was written by a young man who had fallen deeply in love. Ask students whether people in love long for change and adventure, or do they merely wish things "never to change"? Is the latter desire possible?

SUPPLEMENTARY SUPPORT MATERIALS
1. Review and Response Worksheet: Personification (*CCB*)
2. Selection Test (*CCB*)

CLOSURE
Have students summarize what the speaker tells the star.

A. Expansion
The last line of an earlier version was "Half-passionless, and so swoon to death."

B. Imagery
Contrast the images in the octave with those in the sestet. (Octave: distant, inanimate; sestet: intimate, human)

ANALYZING THE POEM
Identifying Details
1. He wants the steadfastness or permanence of the star.

He does not want the star's aloneness or splendor.
2. He wants to live forever (or to die of love) with his love.
3. The star is personified as a hermit; the waters are priests who pour cleansing waters on the earth (as priests do in baptism).

Interpreting Meanings
4. *Steadfast* is "watchfulness."

In the sestet, the speaker clarifies his meaning by saying he wants the star's "unchangeableness," or permanence.
5. For the speaker, death is the only alternative to the impossible permanence he wishes for.

In the late summer of 1818, Keats met eighteen-year-old Fanny Brawne and soon fell in love with her. One of the most poignant, but perhaps overemphasized, aspects of Keats's last years was his failure to establish a full and steady relationship with Fanny because of problems with his health and his finances. This sonnet was written in 1819, most likely during a period of separation from Fanny.

Bright Star, Would I Were Steadfast as Thou Art

Bright star, would I were steadfast as thou art—
    Not in lone splendor hung aloft the night,
And watching, with eternal lids apart,
    Like nature's patient, sleepless eremite,°
5 The moving waters at their priestlike task
    Of pure ablution° round earth's human shores,
Or gazing on the new soft-fallen mask
    Of snow upon the mountains and the moors;
No—yet still steadfast, still unchangeable,
10 Pillowed upon my fair love's ripening breast,
To feel forever its soft swell and fall,
    Awake forever in a sweet unrest,
Still, still to hear her tender-taken breath,
A And so live ever—or else swoon to death.

B

4. **eremite:** religious hermit.

6. **ablution:** ritual cleansing.

Responding to the Poem

Analyzing the Poem

Identifying Details

1. What characteristics of the star does the speaker want to resemble? Which ones does he *not* want to emulate?
2. What does the speaker really want?
3. How is the star **personified**? How are the waters personified?

Interpreting Meanings

4. How does the octet (lines 1–8) define the meaning of *steadfast*? How does the sestet clarify further what the speaker means by the wish in line 1?
5. What is ominous about the mention of death as an alternative in the last line?

Writing About the Poem

A Critical Response

Analyzing Figures of Speech. In a brief essay, identify and comment on all the major figures of speech in this sonnet: **simile, metaphor, apostrophe, personification.**

SUPPLEMENTARY SUPPORT MATERIALS
1. Review and Response Worksheet: Tone and Theme (*CCB*)
2. Selection Test (*CCB*)

CLOSURE
Have students summarize Keats's feelings when he wrote this sonnet.

A. Expansion
This is Keats's first Shakespearean sonnet; his others are Italian.

B. Imagery
Note this famous and powerful image of loneliness. Compare it to the figure of the Wanderer (see text page 599).

The facts of Keats's life lend poignancy to the "fears" expressed here, since his death at the age of twenty-five confirmed them. His aspirations to "love," as well as to "fame" (which here should be regarded not as a hunger for celebrity but as a hope of fulfillment) would both be frustrated. John Keats would "cease to be" within three years of writing this sonnet.

A # When I Have Fears

> When I have fears that I may cease to be
>   Before my pen has gleaned my teeming brain,
> Before high-pilèd books, in charact'ry,°
>   Hold like rich garners the full-ripened grain;
> 5 When I behold, upon the night's starred face,
>   Huge cloudy symbols of a high romance,
> And think that I may never live to trace
>   Their shadows, with the magic hand of chance;
> And when I feel, fair creature of an hour,
> 10   That I shall never look upon thee more,
> Never have relish in the faery° power
>   Of unreflecting love!—then on the shore
> B Of the wide world I stand alone, and think
> Till love and fame to nothingness do sink.

3. **charact'ry:** the characters of the alphabet.

11. **faery:** here, supernatural or unearthly.

ANALYZING THE POEM
Identifying Details
1. He may never have written all he wants to write, never have "relished" love, and may never see his lover again.
2. The simile compares the books to harvests of grain.
3. He is addressing his lover (lines 9–10).

Interpreting Meanings
4. The last line suggests that, in the face of death, love and fame no longer matter.
5. The tone might be described as anxious and melancholy.
The end of the poem is sad but calm.

Responding to the Poem

Analyzing the Poem

Identifying Details

1. What experiences that he may never have make the speaker stand "on the shore / Of the wide world" alone?
2. What **simile** describes the books the speaker hopes to write?
3. Whom is the speaker addressing in this poem, and what line tells you?

Interpreting Meanings

4. What do you think the last line signifies?
5. Describe the speaker's **tone.** Does it remain constant or become more intense? Explain.

Writing About the Poem

A Creative Response

1. **Answering the Speaker.** From your perspective—nearly two hundred years after this sonnet was written—write a letter to the speaker and answer his fears.

A Critical Response

2. **Analyzing the Poem's Structure.** In a brief essay, show how this poem follows the structure of the Shakespearean sonnet. Be sure to identify where the shift in focus or attention occurs.

1. BUILDING ON PRIOR KNOWLEDGE. Have students describe other female tempters, from other works of literature or from movies or TV shows. (Students might remember the loathsome Duessa in *The Faerie Queene*, text page 201. They might also recall the witch Circe who changed men into swine in the *Odyssey*.)

2. ESTABLISHING A PURPOSE. Have students read to answer question 1 on text page 714, which will alert them to the fact that there are two speakers.

SUPPLEMENTARY SUPPORT MATERIALS
1. Review and Response Worksheet: Imagery and Theme (*CCB*)
2. Selection Test (*CCB*)

A. Speaker
The poem is in dialogue form with two speakers: The first speaker addresses a knight in stanzas 1–3; the knight responds in the rest of the poem.

B. Repetition
Note the repeated lines and syntax, both of which are characteristic of ballads.

C. Metaphor
❓ What do the metaphors "a lily on thy brow" and "a fading rose" describe? (The knight's paleness) Note how the nature imagery associated with the knight is decaying, just as the landscape is.

D. Character
Call students' attention to the details describing the lady. Notice how she is associated not with autumn and decay, but with flowers and fruitfulness. (See lines 25–28 also.)

E. Meaning
❓ Does *as* mean "as if" or "while"? How would the answer affect the sense of the poem?

Like Coleridge's story about the Ancient Mariner, this ballad attempts to recreate the air of mystery and enchantment associated with the medieval ballad. Like many of Wordsworth's ballads, it presents its story with a seemingly direct simplicity. The poem looks back to older literature, but the story told in songlike verse is just as common in today's folk music repertoire.

The figure of the woman as temptress has appeared and reappeared in many stories. In most tellings, the woman is irresistibly beautiful, but emotionally cold. Indifferent to the fate of those who come under her spell, she vanishes as swiftly and mysteriously as she arrives, leaving her victim spiritless and deprived of his manhood. In this poem, the man is also threatened by a fear of mortality, as suggested by the "death-pale" kings, princes, and warriors in the dream.

The poem's title, translated as "The Beautiful Woman Without Pity," repeats the title of a poem by the French poet Alain Chartier. Keats's poem, written in the spring of 1819, probably was influenced by Keats's own fascination with the "self-destroying" experiences of intense passion.

La Belle Dame Sans Merci

1

A O what can ail thee, knight-at-arms,
    Alone and palely loitering?
The sedge° has withered from the lake,
    And no birds sing.

3. **sedge:** reedy plants.

2

B
5 O what can ail thee, knight-at-arms,
    So haggard and so woebegone?
The squirrel's granary is full,
    And the harvest's done.

3

I see a lily on thy brow
10   With anguish moist and fever dew,
C And on thy cheeks a fading rose
    Fast withereth too.

4

I met a lady in the meads,°
    Full beautiful, a fairy's child;
15 Her hair was long, her foot was light,
D   And her eyes were wild.

13. **meads:** meadowlands.

5

I made a garland for her head,
    And bracelets too, and fragrant zone;°
E She looked at me as she did love,
20   And made sweet moan.

18. **zone:** belt or girdle.

A

A. Humanities
Connection:
Discussing the
Fine Art

A. **Humanities
Connection:
Discussing the
Fine Art**
Walter Crane
(1845–1915) was
an English painter
and illustrator best
known for his
children's book
illustrations. He
also created ornate
designs for wallpa-
per and fabrics
(see the rich detail
on the armor, sad-
dle, and horse's
trappings).

? What stanza in
the poem has
Crane illustrated?
(Stanza 4) Do the
characters look the
way you imagined
them? Should the
lady be less
"substantial" look-
ing? Do you think
Crane has shown
her as evil, as
innocent, or as
something else
entirely? (Answers
will vary. She ap-
pears to be moving
away from him,
which suggests
that she is afraid
and, therefore, in-
nocent. Her smile
and the position of
her right arm, how-
ever, seem open
to interpretation.)

6

I set her on my pacing steed,
  And nothing else saw all day long,
For sidelong would she bend, and sing
  A fairy's song.

7

25 She found me roots of relish sweet,
  And honey wild, and manna dew,°
And sure in language strange she said—
  I love thee true.

8

  She took me to her elfin grot,°
30 And there she wept, and sighed full sore,
And there I shut her wild wild eyes
  With kisses four.

La Belle Dame Sans Merci by
Walter Crane (19th century).

26. **manna dew:** probably a sweet syrup
made from tree sap.

29. **grot:** cave.

READING CHECK TEST

1. The speaker asks a knight why he is so pale and sad. (T)
2. The knight has met a beautiful lady in the meadowlands. (T)
3. The lady took the knight to her cave. (T)

4. There the knight saw all the happy kings and princes who had also loved the lady. (F)
5. The knight kills the lady when he awakens. (F)

CLOSURE

Have students explain who La Belle Dame Sans Merci was and what she had done to the knight.

A. Imagery

What makes the images in lines 37–42 so gruesome? (The figures resemble skeletons or images of death.)

ANALYZING THE POEM

Identifying Details

1. The first speaker (stanzas 1–3) is the narrator. The second (stanzas 4–12) is a knight.

The first speaker asks the knight what is troubling him.
2. Late autumn.
3. Loneliness, pallor, aimlessness, fatigue, depression, feverishness.
4. They loved each other and went to the lady's "elfin grot."

He had been enchanted and enslaved. (By a demon?)

Interpreting Meanings

5. Answers will vary. Have they been consigned to "death-in-life"?
6. The meter varies in the last line of each stanza.

It pulls the reader up short, breaking the lulling rhythm of the first three lines.

Additional Writing Assignments

Compare this poem and its depiction of women with "Lord Randall" on text page 78, or with *Sir Gawain and the Green Knight* on text page 133.

9

And there she lulled me asleep,
    And there I dreamed—Ah! woe betide!
35 The latest° dream I ever dreamed
    On the cold hill's side.

10

I saw pale kings, and princes too,
    Pale warriors, death pale were they all;
They cried—"La belle dame sans merci
40   Hath thee in thrall!"°

11

I saw their starved lips in the gloam°
    With horrid warning gaped wide,
And I awoke and found me here
    On the cold hill's side.

12

45 And this is why I sojourn here,
    Alone and palely loitering,
Though the sedge is withered from the lake,
    And no birds sing.

35. **latest:** last.

40. **in thrall:** enslaved.

41. **gloam:** twilight.

Responding to the Poem

Analyzing the Poem

Identifying Details

1. Who are the two speakers in the poem? Where does the first speaker stop and the other start? What is the first speaker's question?
2. At the opening of the poem, what time of year is it?
3. What **images** help you visualize the knight?
4. According to the knight's story, what happened when he went off with the enchantress? What did he learn from his dream?

Interpreting Meanings

5. What do you infer happened to the pale kings and princes?
6. Where does Keats vary the **meter** of each ballad stanza? What is the effect of this change in rhythm?

Writing About the Poem

A Creative Response

1. **Setting a Ballad to Music.** Try to improvise a musical setting for "La Belle Dame Sans Merci." You do not need to know musical notation: Simply try to imagine what you think would be an effective melody for each stanza.
2. **Writing a Short Story.** Are you satisfied with the knight's explanation of his problem? Write your own version of what "ails" the knight-at-arms.

1. BUILDING ON PRIOR KNOWLEDGE. Recall with students the Romantic attitude toward nature as discussed on text pages 605–606. Note that there are no nightingales in North America. This unearthly, sad, sweet song can only be heard in central and western Europe.

2. ESTABLISHING A PURPOSE. Ask students to use their imaginations as they think of the rich imagery in the poem.

3. PREREADING JOURNAL. Have students list some of the sensory images they might hear, see, smell, and touch if they were sitting in a garden on a warm summer night. Have them write two or three sentences telling how the experience might make them feel.

SUPPLEMENTARY SUPPORT MATERIALS
1. Review and Response Worksheet: Imagery (*CCB*)
2. Selection Test (*CCB*)
3. Audiocassette recording

Like other poems that have become part of the spiritual and imaginative life of many educated men and women, this one is not the utterance of a godlike being, but of a human being who seized upon the experience of a moment and, with all the art at his command, tried to turn his thoughts and feelings into words and patterns that might outlast the moment.

When Keats was twenty-three years old, he spent a few months in Hampstead—now a suburb of London—at Wentworth House, the home of his friend Charles Brown, who left us a recollection of a particular morning: "In the spring of 1819 a nightingale had built her nest near my house. Keats felt a tranquil and continual joy in her song, and one morning he took his chair from the breakfast table to the grass plot under a plum tree, where he sat for two or three hours. When he came into the house, I perceived he had some scraps of paper in his hand, and these he was quietly thrusting behind the books. On inquiry, I found those scraps, four or five in number, contained his poetic feeling on the song of our nightingale."

Ode to a Nightingale

1

My heart aches, and a drowsy numbness pains
  My sense, as though of hemlock° I had drunk,
Or emptied some dull opiate to the drains°
  One minute past, and Lethewards° had sunk:
'Tis not through envy of thy happy lot,   5
  But being too happy in thine happiness,
    That thou, light-winged Dryad° of the trees,
      In some melodious plot
Of beechen green, and shadows numberless,
    Singest of summer in full-throated ease.   10

2

O, for a draught of vintage! that hath been
  Cooled a long age in the deep-delved earth,
Tasting of Flora° and the country green,
  Dance, and Provençal° song, and sunburnt mirth!
O for a beaker full of the warm South,   15
  Full of the true, the blushful Hippocrene,°
    With beaded bubbles winking at the brim,
      And purple-stained mouth;
That I might drink, and leave the world unseen,
    And with thee fade away into the forest dim: 20

3

Fade far away, dissolve, and quite forget
  What thou among the leaves hast never known,
The weariness, the fever, and the fret
Here, where men sit and hear each other groan;
Where palsy° shakes a few, sad, last gray hairs,   25

---

2. **hemlock:** a powerful sedative made from the poisonous hemlock plant.
3. **drains:** dregs.
4.. **Lethewards:** toward Lethe; in Greek mythology, the river in Hell whose waters cause forgetfulness.

7. **Dryad:** in Greek mythology, a female spirit of the forest.

13. **Flora:** the richness of flowers (Flora is the Latin goddess of flowers).
14. **Provençal:** from Provence, a region in southern France known in the Middle Ages for its troubadors singing songs of love.
16. **Hippocrene:** in Greek mythology, the fountain of the muses; waters of inspiration, referring here to rosy-colored ("blushful") wine.

25. **palsy:** a disease of the nervous system, causing partial paralysis and involuntary shaking.

A. Mood
❓ How does the speaker feel as the poem opens? (Melancholic, heart-sore, numb, as if drunk or drugged)

B. Meaning
❓ What is a "draught of vintage"? (A glass of wine) What is "deep-delved earth"? (Soil that has been spaded)

C. Meaning
❓ What does this mean? (He wants a glassful of wine that reminds him of the warm southern place the grapes came from.)

D. Meaning
❓ Why does the speaker long for wine? (To take him away with the nightingale, away from worldly cares)

E. Alliteration
Lines 21–23 contain repeated *f* sounds and *w* sounds.

F. Imagery
This famous image sums up old age in a single line. Note that the speaker imagines that the nightingale has never known mortality and mortal cares (the "fever and the fret").

Here is part of an analysis of the poem by Cleanth Brooks and Robert Penn Warren:

"This poem is essentially a reverie induced by the poet's listening to the song of the nightingale. In the first stanza the poet is just sinking into the reverie; in the last stanza, he comes out of the reverie and back to a consciousness of the actual world in which he and all other human beings live. The first lines of the poem and the last, therefore, constitute a sort of frame for the reverie proper.

"The poet has chosen to present his reverie largely in terms of imagery—imagery drawn from nature—the flowers and leaves, etc., associated with the bird actually, or imaginatively in myth and story. The images are elaborate and decorative and the poet dwells upon them lovingly and leisurely, developing them in some detail as pictures. . . . The loving elaboration and slowed movement resemble the slowed movement of a meditative trance, or dream, and therefore is appropriate to the general mood of this poem."

A. Reference
Keats's younger brother Tom had died of tuberculosis several months before Keats wrote this poem.

B. Tone
Note how the tone changes from lethargy and melancholy to animation and hope. The poet will escape, not with wine, but with poetry.

C. Setting
Where does the speaker find himself? (It's night in a woodland or garden.)

D. Sensory Details
Note the many smells evoked in this amazing catalog and the image of sound in line 50. The speaker can't see but must use his other senses.

The Nightingale (19th century). Wood engraving.

A
    Where youth grows pale, and specter-thin, and dies;
      Where but to think is to be full of sorrow
        And leaden-eyed despairs,
    Where Beauty cannot keep her lustrous eyes,
30   Or new Love pine at them beyond tomorrow.

4

B
Away! away! for I will fly to thee,
    Not charioted by Bacchus and his pards,°
But on the viewless° wings of Poesy,
    Though the dull brain perplexes and retards:
35 Already with thee! tender is the night,
    And haply the Queen-Moon is on her throne,
      Clustered around by all her starry Fays;°
        But here there is no light,
C
Save what from heaven is with the breezes blown
40   Through verdurous° glooms and winding mossy ways.

5

I cannot see what flowers are at my feet,
    Nor what soft incense hangs upon the boughs,
But, in embalmed° darkness, guess each sweet
    Wherewith the seasonable month endows
45 The grass, the thicket, and the fruit-tree wild;
D
    White hawthorn, and the pastoral eglantine;°
      Fast fading violets covered up in leaves;
        And mid-May's eldest child,
    The coming° musk-rose, full of dewy wine,
50   The murmurous haunt of flies on summer eves.

32. **Not . . . pards:** not by getting drunk. Bacchus, the Greek god of wine, was sometimes pictured in a chariot pulled by leopards ("pards").
33. **viewless:** invisible.

37. **Fays:** fairies.

40. **verdurous:** full of green foliage.

43. **embalmed:** perfumed.

46. **eglantine:** a kind of rose.

49. **coming:** soon to bloom.

CLOSURE
Have the students discuss writing assignment 1 on text page 718. Jot down students' suggestions on the chalkboard, and ask them to cite evidence from the poem to support their ideas of what the nightingale symbolizes.

ANALYZING THE POEM
Identifying Details
1. The setting is a garden in summer. The speaker is melancholy and lethargic.
2. The speaker wants to leave his world and join the nightingale.
3. In the third stanza, the speaker wants to escape from worry, aging, and death.

In stanza four, the speaker thinks of poetry as a means of escape.

4. The speaker is tempted by the prospect of death.

He resolves the temptation by realizing that even death would not be equivalent to the bird's song; his symbolic ideal of sustained unconsciousness of pain—the nightingale—would remain nonetheless alive, and he would be unable to relish it. *(Answers continue on next page.)*

6

A
Darkling° I listen; and, for many a time
   I have been half in love with easeful Death,
Called him soft names in many a mused rhyme,
   To take into the air my quiet breath;
55 Now more than ever seems it rich to die,
   To cease upon the midnight with no pain,
     While thou art pouring forth thy soul abroad
      In such an ecstasy!
   Still wouldst thou sing, and I have ears in vain—
60   To thy high requiem° become a sod.°

7

B
Thou wast not born for death, immortal Bird!
   No hungry generations tread thee down;
The voice I hear this passing night was heard
   In ancient days by emperor and clown:
65 Perhaps the selfsame song that found a path
C
   Through the sad heart of Ruth,° when, sick for home,
     She stood in tears amid the alien corn;°
     The same that ofttimes hath
   Charmed magic casements,° opening on the foam
70   Of perilous seas, in fairy lands forlorn.

8

D
Forlorn! the very word is like a bell
   To toll me back from thee to my sole self!
Adieu! the fancy cannot cheat so well
   As she is famed to do, deceiving elf.
75 Adieu! adieu! thy plaintive anthem fades
   Past the near meadows, over the still stream,
     Up the hillside; and now 'tis buried deep
     In the next valley-glades:
   Was it a vision, or a waking dream?
80   Fled is that music: Do I wake or sleep?

51. **Darkling:** in the dark; here a form of address.

60. **requiem:** a Mass or song for the dead. **sod:** a piece of sod or earth.

66. **Ruth:** a young widow in the biblical Book of Ruth, who left her own people to accompany her mother-in-law to a strange land.
67. **corn:** the English generic term for grain.
69. **casements:** hinged windows, a favorite Keats image.

A. Interpreting
According to the next lines, why does it seem rich to die now? (Death would come as the bird sings in ecstasy.) What would happen to the bird if the speaker died? (It would sing on.)

B. Interpreting
In what ways is the bird immortal? (Its song has been heard through the ages. Compare with "Dover Beach," lines 15–20, text page 813.)

C. Allusion
You might have students memorize this beautiful and famous allusion to Ruth.

D. Diction
What word ties together stanzas 7 and 8? (The word *forlorn*)

A Comment on the Poem

Keats's completed poem is not "about" or "on" the nightingale, but, as the title tells us, "to" the nightingale. The speaker seems, as the poem opens, to have already passed beyond the limit of ordinary experience and become "too" happy in the experience conveyed in the nightingale's song. The poem consists of a series of propositions, each containing its own rejection as to how the speaker might imitate the "ease" of the song he hears—wine, poetry, even death are considered. Each time, the speaker in his humanness is drawn back to his "sole self," to a preference for poetry as a celebration, not of "summer," but of human life as a process of "soul making."

(Answers begin on previous page.)

5. In ancient empires, in Biblical times, and in fairy tales.
6. The nightingale flies away, beyond the speaker's sight and hearing.

Interpreting Meanings
7. The night is "tender" because it is springtime; it is "mid-May."
8. The speaker imagines himself as

dead—part of the earth.
9. The speaker wants to capture the nightingale's "ease" because it represents a unity with nature and an escape from worldly trouble.

He is, however, "too happy" because he realizes that his identification with the bird is illusory, not real.
10. The speaker's is a realm of time, awareness, and decay; the nightingale's

is a realm of eternity and happy unconsciousness.
11. He realizes that there is absolute difference between the world of the nightingale—whether real or imagined—and his own human world. When the nightingale flies away, he is left with a question and a lonely sense of self. The question is: Is he waking to reality, or is (Answers continue in left-hand column.)

(Continued from top.)
he returning to his lack of awareness or sleep?
12. The speaker's moods shift back and forth from despair to hope. He sees himself bereft; then imagines a series of escapes from his pain, each one of which turns out to be impossible. At the end of the poem, he seems a bit more exalted than at the beginning.
13. Answers will vary, but the best guess is that he is both awake and asleep. The speaker's symbolic experience has been a combination of dream and reality.

Responding to the Poem

Analyzing the Poem

Identifying Details

1. Describe the outward **setting** and the emotions of the speaker as they are portrayed in the first stanza.
2. According to the second stanza, what state of feeling does the speaker want to have?
3. What misfortunes does the speaker want to escape in the third stanza? What means of escape are considered in the fourth stanza?
4. What thoughts about death does the speaker have in stanza 6? How does he resolve these temptations?
5. Where does the speaker imagine the song of the nightingale has been heard in the seventh stanza?
6. What is happening in the final stanza?

Interpreting Meanings

7. Why is the night already "tender" (line 35) for the nightingale? What time of year is it?
8. Why would the speaker become a "sod" to the bird's "high requiem" (line 60)?
9. Why does the speaker want to capture or imitate the nightingale's "ease"? Why is he "too happy in thine happiness"?
10. What differences does the poem emphasize between the realm (or experience) of the nightingale and those of the speaker?
11. What does the speaker realize by the end of the poem?
12. What are the different **moods** of this speaker? Does he seem to be more, or less, exalted at the end than at the beginning?
13. How would you answer the speaker's question at the end of the poem?

Writing About the Poem

A Critical Response

1. **Analyzing Symbolism.** In a brief essay, explain how the nightingale is both a concrete object and a symbol in Keats's ode. What, in your view, does the nightingale represent for the speaker?

2. **Comparing and Contrasting Odes.** Both Keats's "Ode to a Nightingale" and Shelley's "Ode to the West Wind" are concerned, at least partially, with poetic inspiration. In a brief essay, write a comparison of these two odes. Focus on how each poem treats the subject.
3. **Comparing and Contrasting Poems.** Shelley also addressed a poem to a bird—a skylark. In an essay, compare and contrast Keats's ode with Shelley's poem. In your essay, consider these elements of the poems:

a. Subject
b. Theme
c. Tone

Analyzing Language and Style

Imagery

This poem is one of the most famous in the English language for its lush imagery. Several of its images, in fact, have been used by other writers as titles. (The American novelist F. Scott Fitzgerald used Tender Is the Night as the title of one of his tragic love stories.)

1. How does the poet use concrete imagery to conjure up two quite different historical periods in the seventh stanza?
2. In the figure of speech with the long name of **synaesthesia,** one phrase contains an image that appeals simultaneously to two different senses (for example, sight and touch). How many examples of synaesthesia can you find in this ode?

1. BUILDING ON PRIOR KNOWLEDGE. Talk with students briefly about ancient Greek vases (see text page 720) and the scenes painted on them (chiefly mythological). At the time this ode was written, Keats was fascinated by the Elgin Marbles, marble friezes from the Parthenon in Athens that Lord Elgin had carted back to London. No one knows what vase

Keats had in mind when he wrote the ode. The critic W. Jackson Bate says that the urn may be a combination of the Sosibios Vase and the Townley Vase in the British Museum, and of the Borghese Vase in the Louvre (Keats had seen engravings of it).

2. ESTABLISHING A PURPOSE. Ask students to read to discover two things:

what the speaker sees on the vase, and what he says to the vase.

SUPPLEMENTARY SUPPORT MATERIALS
1. Review and Response Worksheet: Figures of Speech (*CCB*)
2. Selection Test (*CCB*)

As we read this poem, we absorb its words in order to "read" its pictures. We glimpse the ancient people the speaker finds depicted on the urn and become aware that, in the record of the speaker's contemplation of a work of art, Keats manages to create another, equally permanent, work of art.

Urns have traditionally been used for planting and for burial. In this one, life and death are joined, but not confined. Through the medium of art (poetry or pottery), life and death find their

reflection in the mind and eye of the beholder.

If you have ever been to a museum and looked at the antique Greek vases, you will be able to imagine the scene that Keats describes in this poem. The Greek vases are usually black in color and are painted in a reddish color. Usually, the paintings on the vases have to do with mythological subjects—we often see on them gods, goddesses, heroes, and the men and women who were involved in their adventures.

Ode on a Grecian Urn

1

A
Thou still unravished bride of quietness,
   Thou foster child of silence and slow time,
Sylvan° historian, who canst thus express
   A flowery tale more sweetly than our rhyme:

5
What leaf-fringed legend haunts about thy shape
   Of deities or mortals, or of both,
      In Tempe or the dales of Arcady?°
   What men or gods are these? What maidens loath?
What mad pursuit? What struggle to escape?

B

10
      What pipes and timbrels?° What wild ecstasy?

2

C
Heard melodies are sweet, but those unheard
   Are sweeter; therefore, ye soft pipes, play on;
Not to the sensual ear, but, more endeared,
   Pipe to the spirit ditties° of no tone:

15
Fair youth, beneath the trees, thou canst not leave
   Thy song, nor ever can those trees be bare;
      Bold lover, never, never canst thou kiss,
   Though winning near the goal—yet, do not grieve;
      She cannot fade, though thou hast not thy bliss,

D

20
Forever wilt thou love, and she be fair!

3

Ah, happy, happy boughs! that cannot shed
   Your leaves, nor ever bid the spring adieu;
And, happy melodist, unwearied,
   Forever piping songs forever new;

25
More happy love! more happy, happy love!
   Forever warm and still to be enjoyed,
      Forever panting, and forever young;
All breathing human passion far above,
   That leaves a heart high-sorrowful and cloyed,°

30
      A burning forehead, and a parching tongue.

E

3. Sylvan: associated with the forest (the urn is decorated with leafy branches).

7. Tempe . . . dales of Arcady: valleys in ancient Greece; ideal types of rural beauty.

10. timbrels: tambourines.

14. ditties: poems intended to be set to music.

29. cloyed: satiated, wearied with excess.

Handwritten annotations:
Apostrophe — directly addresses the urn —
The urn is not ruined by time; it has lasted for centuries; it has preserved the history of nature
Historian — Urn can express itself better than the poet
Gods or mortals?
Where?
What is on the Urn?
Men + gods, unwilling maidens, a chase, a struggle, musicians
Paradox — power of imagination
Pipes play an eternal song.
Fair youth cannot leave
lover never reach the girl
Youth + girl will always be exactly the same.
Trees — Eternal Spring
Melodist — Piper — Eternal music joy happiness
On the urn nothing changes
Emotional tone

A. Address
❓ The speaker addresses the urn as "a still unravished bride of quietness," a "foster child," and a "sylvan historian." What does each mean? (The urn is not ruined by time; it has lasted for centuries; and it has preserved the history of nature.) Note that *still* might be an adverb or adjective.

B. The Scene
❓ Describe what is on the urn. (Men and gods, unwilling maidens, a chase, a struggle, musicians)

C. Responding
❓ Can an imagined experience be "sweeter" than a real one? Why? (Answers will vary, but most will cite the power of the imagination.)

D. Interpreting
❓ How does this line sum up the main point of this stanza? (The youth and girl will always remain exactly as they are now.)

E. Tone
❓ Describe the tone of this stanza. (Emotional) How is actual life different from what is on the urn? (On the urn, nothing ever changes.)

John Keats **719**

Ask three students to cite the most important passages from the poem and to justify their choices.

ANALYZING THE POEM
Identifying Details

1. The urn can tell a tale "more sweetly than our rhyme."
2. In the first stanza, the poem describes an idyllic Grecian scene with "men and gods" in "mad pursuit" of "maidens loath." The second stanza describes a lover under a tree about to kiss his lover.
   These actions are "frozen" in time.
3. The speaker has reached a state of high excitement not unlike those states he sees on the urn.
4. The fourth stanza describes a priest and others about to sacrifice a calf. The speaker imagines their empty village.
5. The urn will remain, just as it is, even when the speaker is no more.
   The urn's message: Beauty and truth are one. That is all we know and all we need to know.

Interpreting Meanings

6. The "unheard" melodies appeal to "the spirit" or imagination rather than to the ear, and as such triumph over time.

A. Expansion
The speaker is now looking at another side of the urn.

❓ What does he see? (People going to present a sacrifice. The poet imagines that their town is still and empty.)

B. Interpreting
The thought of the little town and its desolation and silence seems to bring the speaker to a melancholy realization that loneliness is found even on his urn. "Cold pastoral" means/ "cold scene."

C. Expansion
"I am certain of nothing," Keats wrote to a friend two years before he wrote this poem, "but of the holiness of the Heart's affections, and the truth of Imagination. What the Imagination seizes as Beauty must be truth—whether it existed before or not—for I have the same idea of all our passions as of love: They are all in their sublimity, creative of essential beauty."

[handwritten: Looking at side of another the urn]

4

A

Who are these coming to the sacrifice?
　　To what green altar, O mysterious priest,
Lead'st thou that heifer lowing° at the skies,
　　And all her silken flanks with garlands dressed?
35　What little town by river or seashore,
　　Or mountain-built with peaceful citadel,
　　　Is emptied of this folk, this pious morn?
And, little town, thy streets forevermore
　　Will silent be; and not a soul to tell
40　　　Why thou art desolate, can e'er return.

33. **lowing:** mooing.

[handwritten: Sacrifice scene / Priest - heifer]

[handwritten: Town - empty + still]

5

B
45

C
50

O Attic° shape! Fair attitude!° with brede°
　　Of marble men and maidens overwrought,°
With forest branches and the trodden weed;
　　Thou, silent form, dost tease us out of thought
As doth eternity: Cold Pastoral!°　*immortal*
　　When old age shall this generation waste,
　　Thou shalt remain, in midst of other woe
Than ours, a friend to man, to whom thou say'st,
"Beauty is truth, truth beauty"—that is all
　　Ye know on earth, and all ye need to know.

41. **Attic:** Athenian; classically elegant. **attitude:** posture. **brede:** interwoven design (with a pun on *breed*, species or type).
42. **overwrought:** elaborated or decorated to excess (with a double meaning in reference to the maidens: worked up, over-excited).
45. **Pastoral:** an artwork depicting idealized rural life; also an instructional letter or book concerning spiritual health.

[handwritten: Athenian style urn / decorated / w/ men, women / trees, foliage]

[handwritten: loneliness / found even / on the urn]

[handwritten: ⤷ Urn, Art will remain / even after humans / die]

Ancient Greek water jar showing women at a fountain house (Athens, ca. 520 B.C.).

The whole poem suggests tension between timelessness in an ideal world and change or loss in the actual world.

Refer to Blake's quote on text page 600. The Romantics saw in the imagination the possibility of triumph over change and time. See text page 606.

7. Answers will vary. The words *happy* and *forever* produce a strong, repetitive rhythm that suggests the urgency of the speaker's feelings and conflicts.

8. "Out of thought" would be lifelessness—ironically, the opposite of the vivacity and life the speaker had seen in the urn.

This state is presumably not better than thinking because it is the equivalent of death (eternity also teases us out of thought).

9. When old age has wasted this generation, the vase will remain, in the midst of troubles different from those we know today. The vase will be our friend, telling us that all we need to know is that only beauty is true and real. (The vase in this sense is like a poem.)

10. If the former, the urn speaks for itself; if the latter, the speaker draws this conclusion.

A Comment on the Poem

This poem depicts a beautiful curve of emotion and engagement, that begins and ends with detachment. At its center, it abandons all restraints, including those of art itself, to live in that world which is "happy" and "forever." By itself, the third stanza seems "overwrought" (a word used in the more detached fifth stanza)—so much so that we feel that all controls have been lost. But this is precisely the nature of the speaker's experience. Bit by bit, a miniature world of human passions comes alive, only to remind us that it is as dead as the clay on which it is represented. Keats has shown us that in the midst of change, art seems to provide the only truth. Yet this is a truth that depends not on sensory experience, but on the human imagination.

Responding to the Poem

Analyzing the Poem

Identifying Details

1. The urn is called a "sylvan historian" in line 3. What does the speaker say about its ability to tell a tale?
2. Describe the details represented on the urn according to the first and second stanzas. What actions are "frozen" in time on the vase?
3. What is suggested about the speaker's state by the last three lines of the third stanza?
4. Describe the picture on the urn according to the fourth stanza.
5. According to stanza 5, what will happen to the urn when the speaker is dead? What message does the urn give to people?

Interpreting Meanings

6. Why are "unheard" melodies (line 11) sweeter than heard ones? How does this relate to the poem? How could this idea be said to be typically Romantic?
7. How would you respond to the criticism that the third stanza is badly written because Keats used *happy* and *forever* too many times?
8. If the urn could "tease us out of thought," what state would we be in? Would this state be better than thinking? Explain.
9. How would you paraphrase the last five lines of the final stanza? In what sense are truth and beauty the same?
10. There is a famous textual difficulty surrounding the last two lines of this poem. Based on the manuscripts, some critics suggest that the quotation marks should enclose the entire couplet, rather than simply "Beauty is truth, truth beauty." Explain what differences in meaning the different punctuation would cause.

Writing About the Poem

A Creative Response

1. **Imitating the Writer's Technique.** Select a painting, perhaps one in this book. In a brief paragraph, describe what is taking place in the painting, and pose questions about what will *never* happen in the painting. Describe your feelings on looking at the painting. Structure your paragraph in the form of a direct address to the painting, just as Keats addresses the vase.

A Critical Response

2. **Analyzing a Main Idea.** Many of Keats's odes resemble interior monologues: They portray the speaker in a state of tension or ambiguity—a state that is explored and then tentatively resolved at the end of the poem. In a brief essay, analyze how this idea of tension is central to "Ode on a Grecian Urn." What positive and negative aspects of human art does Keats explore in the ode?

BUILDING ON PRIOR KNOWLEDGE. What feelings do students associate with autumn? Ask them to imagine that they are creating a video on autumn. What images would they include? What music might they have in the background? How does autumn make them feel? If they had to decide on a season for Paradise, which would it be, and why?

A. Assonance
Read these lines aloud to hear the assonance (see text page 1260).

B. Onomatopoeia
? Find examples of onomatopoeia in these lines. (The bee-like *z* and *s* sounds) Note that *clammy* means "moist" (they are full of honey).

C. Interpreting
Note the calmness of the scene, instead of the labor usually associated with the harvest.

D. Interpreting
Lines 23–24 hint that the seasons may also symbolize the span of human life; the speaker seems to be consoling autumn here, who is no longer young.

E. Onomatopoeia
? What words here echo their sense? (*Wailful, mourn, bleat, sing, whistles, twitter*) Note that though the effect is melancholic, it is not anguished (as it is in Keats's other odes). In fact, ask students if these images of life can exist in other seasons too. (Only the grown lambs are specific to autumn.)

SUPPLEMENTARY SUPPORT MATERIALS
1. Review and Response Worksheet: Personification (*CCB*)
2. Selection Test (*CCB*)

CLOSURE
Have students compare the tone of this poem with that of "Ode on a Grecian Urn."

Keats on Autumn
"How beautiful the season is now—How fine the air. A temperate sharpness about it. . . . I never lik'd stubble fields so much as now—Aye better than the chilly green of the spring. Somehow a stubble plain looks warm—in the same way that some pictures look warm—this struck me so much in my Sunday's walk that I composed upon it."

This poem was written some months after all of the other odes. It is strikingly different from them and suggests a new, serene manner in Keats's poetry which seems to predict the kind of poetry he might have explored more fully had he lived longer. "To Autumn" is remarkable among all the lyric poems written by the Romantics in its air of detachment. It looks backward to the techniques of personification common in eighteenth-century poetry. But it looks forward, beyond the Romantic absorption in the self and its emotional turbulence, to a very modern attitude toward nature as something independent of human beings' longings and fantasies.

To Autumn

1

A
Season of mists and mellow fruitfulness,
    Close bosom-friend of the maturing sun;
Conspiring with him how to load and bless
    With fruit the vines that round the thatch-eves° run;
5 To bend with apples the mossed cottage-trees,°
    And fill all fruit with ripeness to the core;
      To swell the gourd, and plump the hazel shells
    With a sweet kernel; to set budding more,
B
And still more, later flowers for the bees,
10 Until they think warm days will never cease,
      For summer has o'er-brimmed their clammy cells.

4. **thatch-eves:** the overhang of a thatched roof.
5. **mossed cottage-trees:** moss-covered trees next to a cottage.

2

Who hath not seen thee oft amid thy store?°
    Sometimes whoever seeks abroad may find
C
Thee sitting careless on a granary° floor,
15   Thy hair soft-lifted by the winnowing° wind;
Or on a half-reaped furrow sound asleep,
    Drowsed with the fume of poppies, while thy hook°
      Spares the next swath° and all its twined flowers:
And sometimes like a gleaner° thou dost keep
20   Steady thy laden head across a brook;
    Or by a ciderpress, with patient look,
      Thou watchest the last oozings hours by hours.

12. **store:** accumulations (from the harvest).
14. **granary:** storehouse for grain.
15. **winnowing:** separating the grain kernels from their husks. The grain is tossed in the air to allow the dry husks to drift off in the wind.
17. **hook:** scythe, a long-handled curved blade for cutting.
18. **swath:** strip of vegetation covered by a sweep of the scythe.
19. **gleaner:** one who gathers up the grain left in the field by the reapers.

3

D
Where are the songs of spring? Aye, where are they?
    Think not of them, thou hast thy music too,
25 While barred° clouds bloom° the soft-dying day,
    And touch the stubble-plains° with rosy hue;
Then in a wailful choir the small gnats mourn
    Among the river sallows,° borne aloft
E
      Or sinking as the light wind lives or dies;
30 And full-grown lambs loud bleat from hilly bourn;°
    Hedge-crickets sing; and now with treble soft
    The red-breast whistles from a garden-croft;°
      And gathering swallows twitter in the skies.

25. **barred:** streaked. **bloom:** cause to glow.
26. **stubble-plains:** reaped fields with only the lower part of the wheat stalks left standing.
28. **sallows:** willows.
30. **bourn:** region or boundary (of a farm).
32. **garden-croft:** small piece of enclosed land, usually next to a cottage.

ANALYZING THE POEM
Identifying Details
1. The speaker is in the country in autumn.

He mentions cottages, an apple orchard, vines, fruits and nuts, flowers, bees, lambs, a river, crickets, birds. Also a granary, poppies, stubble plain, and gnats.
2. There are five sentences, which are all addressed to autumn itself.
3. In stanza 1, autumn is personified as a conspiratorial friend of the sun; in stanza 2, autumn is sitting or sleeping amid the harvest; in stanza 3, autumn is personified as a maker of music.
4. The songs of autumn are the "wailful" choir of gnats, bleats of lambs, cricket songs, bird whistles and twitters.

Interpreting Meanings
5. The "songs of spring" might be of young animals, bird songs, rivers rushing, soft breezes, etc. They could also include many of the songs here.

Autumn's songs are generally mournful, but Keats's are not.
6. The speaker feels an attraction to the luxuriant bounty and fullness of autumn. (Bate says that here at last Keats has found something of a genuine Paradise.)

Perhaps the poem also refers to the last stages of human life; the harvests are like the end of human productiveness, yet we have the notion that growth continues.
7. The poem gives both a pleasant picture of autumn (a time of ripeness) and a vaguely ominous sense of it as a time of decay. Autumn is, of course, both. Most people regard autumn as a time of both fruition and of the onset of cold and darkness; responses, however, will vary, and may note that autumn is the beginning of the traditional academic calendar.

A. Humanities Connection: Responding to the Fine Art
George Stubbs (1724–1806) is best known for his realistic paintings of animals. You might compare Stubbs's scene with details in Keats's ode.
? Does Keats suggest activity or repose? Are the colors in Stubbs like the colors suggested by Keats?

The Harvest Wagon by George Stubbs (18th century). Oil.

Roy Milnes Fine Paintings, London.

A

Responding to the Poem

Analyzing the Poem

Identifying Details

1. Where is the speaker of this ode? Describe the landscape.
2. How many sentences are there in the poem? To whom are these sentences addressed?
3. What details **personify** autumn in each stanza?
4. According to stanza 3, what are the songs of autumn?

Interpreting Meanings

5. What might the "songs of spring" be? How would they differ from the songs of autumn?
6. How does this speaker feel about autumn? Do you think by extension the speaker is also talking about a human season? Explain.
7. Does this poem give too mellow and pleasant a picture of this season of harvest and the beginning of decay and loss? How would you characterize autumn? How do most people regard autumn, and why?

Writing About the Poem

A Creative Response

1. **Writing a Description.** Select one of the other seasons and write a short address to it. Include a personified figure of the season itself, and tell how you feel about the season.

A Critical Response

2. **Analyzing Poetic Techniques.** Read Keats's ode "To Autumn" slowly out loud. In a brief essay, identify the **meter**, the **rhyme scheme**, and the poet's use of other sound effects, such as **assonance** and **onomatopoeia**. How do the ode's sound effects subtly contribute to its mood?

1. BUILDING ON PRIOR KNOWLEDGE. Have students discuss what they know about romances (see text page 147) and what they recall of Shakespeare's *Romeo and Juliet.* In "The Eve of St. Agnes," Keats tells a romance set in medieval times. (Appropriately, Keats uses the Spenserian stanza form; see text page 200.) Keats wrote this poem in January right around the eve of St. Agnes.

2. ESTABLISHING A PURPOSE. Have students read the headnote, the comment that follows the poem, and the second writing assignment on text page 735. As they read (and enjoy) the poem, they should keep these plot elements in mind. Note that Keats wished his romance to be different from the "sugary" romances popular at the time.

SUPPLEMENTARY SUPPORT MATERIALS
1. Vocabulary Activity Worksheet (*CCB*)
2. Review and Response Worksheet: Evaluating a Poem (*CCB*)
3. Selection Test (*CCB*)

A. Setting
Note that the poem begins outside the castle with the animals and then moves indoors, to the chapel, like a movie camera approaching a house.

B. Theme
Immediately, we have mentions of death (lines 8, 14, 22).

C. Contrasts
❓ Why do you think Keats opens his poem with the beadsman? (The humble beadsman contrasts with the drunken revelers.) Note the foreshadowing of the old man's death.

There's a story here, a romantic one, with suspense and a degree of menace.

The story is based on an ancient legend associated with a thirteen-year-old Christian martyr. Saint Agnes, daughter of a noble Roman family of the fourth century, was put to death for refusing the attentions of a man she did not love. According to the legend, this sacrifice of innocence led to two different kinds of rituals. One, performed by unmarried girls on January 20, the night before the feast of Saint Agnes, would enable them to see in their dreams the faces of their future husbands. The second was the presentation of lambs at the church altar, whose wool would be shorn and woven into neckbands worn by archbishops.

In Keats's story, written early in 1819, dream and reality become one. The hopeful Madeline is rewarded for her observation of ritual by the appearance of Porphyro, but not before Porphyro conquers the fading of his emotions brought on by their very intensity. The happy and magical result of their union is their escape from the castle as they slide, dreamlike, through mysteriously opened doors into a new realm of existence.

The Eve of St. Agnes

1

A
St. Agnes' Eve—Ah, bitter chill it was!
The owl, for all his feathers, was a-cold;
The hare limped trembling through the frozen grass,
And silent was the flock in woolly fold:°
5 Numb were the beadsman's° fingers, while he told
His rosary,° and while his frosted breath,
Like pious incense from a censer° old,
B
Seemed taking flight for heaven, without a death,
Past the sweet Virgin's picture, while his prayer he saith.

4. **fold:** group of sheep in a fenced enclosure.
5. **beadsman:** one who is paid to say prayers for his employer.
6. **told his rosary:** counted the beads of his rosary necklace to keep track of his prayers.
7. **censer:** a vessel in which incense used in religious ceremonies is kept.

2

10 His prayer he saith, this patient, holy man;
Then takes his lamp, and riseth from his knees,
And back returneth, meager, barefoot, wan,
Along the chapel aisle by slow degrees:
The sculptured dead,° on each side, seem to freeze,
15 Emprisoned in black, purgatorial rails:
Knights, ladies, praying in dumb orat'ries,
He passeth by; and his weak spirit fails
To think how they may ache in icy hoods and mails.

14. **sculptured dead:** Lines 14–18 describe the tombs set in small, silent chapels ("dumb orat'ries") that jut out on each side of a church. Each tomb is surrounded by an iron railing, and the sculptures on top of the tombs depict husbands and wives lying side by side in attitudes of prayer, the women in hooded gowns and the men in suits of armor made of interlocking metal rings ("mails").

3

Northward he turneth through a little door,
20 And scarce three steps, ere Music's golden tongue
C
Flattered to tears this aged man and poor;
But no—already had his deathbell rung;
The joys of all his life were said and sung:
His was harsh penance on St. Agnes' Eve:
25 Another way he went, and soon among
Rough ashes sat he for his soul's reprieve,
And all night kept awake, for sinners' sake to grieve.

DEVELOPING VOCABULARY
The following words from the poem are
tested in the Selection Test. (See also
Vocabulary Activity Worksheet.)
sumptuous   ethereal   sagacious

4

That ancient beadsman heard the prelude soft;
And so it chanced, for many a door was wide,
30   From hurry to and fro. Soon, up aloft,
A   The silver, snarling trumpets 'gan to chide:
The level° chambers, ready with their pride,
Were glowing to receive a thousand guests:
The carved angels, ever eager-eyed,
35   Stared, where upon their heads the cornice° rests,
With hair blown back, and wings put crosswise on their
        breasts.

32. **level:** ground floor.

35. **cornice:** horizontal molding or ornamental band just below the ceiling.

5

At length burst in the argent revelry,°
With plume, tiara, and all rich array,
B   Numerous as shadows haunting fairily
40   The brain, new stuffed, in youth, with triumphs gay
Of old romance. These let us wish away,
And turn, sole-thoughted, to one lady there,
C   Whose heart had brooded, all that wintry day,
On love, and winged St. Agnes' saintly care,
45 As she had heard old dames full many times declare.

37. **argent revelry:** silver–clad party participants.

6

They told her how, upon St. Agnes' Eve,
Young virgins might have visions of delight,
And soft adornings from their loves receive
D   Upon the honeyed middle of the night,
50   If ceremonies due° they did aright;
As, supperless to bed they must retire,
And couch supine° their beauties, lily white;
Nor look behind, nor sideways, but require
Of heaven with upward eyes for all that they desire.

50. **due:** owed as a duty; proper.

52. **couch supine:** lay to rest horizontally.

7

55   Full of this whim was thoughtful Madeline:
The music, yearning like a god in pain,
She scarcely heard: her maiden eyes divine,
Fixed on the floor, saw many a sweeping train°
Pass by—she heeded not at all: in vain
60   Came many a tiptoe, amorous cavalier,
And back retired, not cooled by high disdain;
But she saw not: her heart was otherwhere:
She sighed for Agnes' dreams, the sweetest of the year.

58. **train:** long, trailing skirt.

8

She danced along with vague, regardless eyes,
65   Anxious her lips, her breathing quick and short:
The hallowed hour was near at hand: She sighs
Amid the timbrels,° and the thronged resort°

67. **timbrels:** tambourines. **thronged resort:**
crowded gathering.

A. Imagery
The setting opens
in chilly black and
white, but soon
turns to lush color.
Here is the first
mention of silver.
Tell students to be
alert to the con-
trasting silver-crim-
son imagery
throughout the
poem.

B. Contrast
Notice the contrast
with the opening
scene in the chill,
silent night.

C. Character
❓ How does
Keats introduce
the first of the two
main characters?
(Without naming
her and by de-
scribing her as
brooding on love
and the legend)

D. Exposition
Keats here tells
the St. Agnes Eve
legend, which is
central to the plot.

726

A. Reference
The headnote explains the reference to the lambs.

B. Character
Here is the second main character. Note that he, like Madeline, is "outside" the action of the ball.
❓ What do we learn immediately about this character? (He is in love with Madeline.)

C. Conflict
Students should begin to see similarities to the story of *Romeo and Juliet*. Notice that both young couples meet at a party and that neither young man is welcome.

D. Character
❓ In what ways does the "old beldame" resemble the nurse in *Romeo and Juliet*? (She is old and friendly to Porphyro; she helps the lovers.)

E. Suspense
❓ How does the old lady's speech create suspense? (She points out the great danger Porphyro is in; we worry about him. We now have some villains: dwarfish Hildebrand and gray-haired Lord Maurice.)

Of whisperers in anger, or in sport;
'Mid looks of love, defiance, hate, and scorn,
70 Hoodwinked° with fairy fancy; all amort,°
A Save to St. Agnes and her lambs unshorn,
And all the bliss to be before tomorrow morn.

9

So, purposing each moment to retire,
She lingered still. Meantime, across the moors,
75 Had come young Porphyro, with heart on fire
For Madeline. Beside the portal doors,
B Buttressed from moonlight, stands he, and implores
All saints to give him sight of Madeline,
But for one moment in the tedious hours,
80 That he might gaze and worship all unseen;
Perchance speak, kneel, touch, kiss—in sooth° such
    things have been.

10

He ventures in: Let no buzzed whisper tell:
All eyes be muffled, or a hundred swords
Will storm his heart, Love's feverous citadel:
85 For him, those chambers held barbarian hordes,
Hyena foemen,° and hot-blooded lords,
C Whose very dogs would execrations° howl
Against his lineage: not one breast affords
Him any mercy, in that mansion foul,
90 Save one old beldame,° weak in body and in soul.

11

D Ah, happy chance! the aged creature came,
Shuffling along with ivory-headed wand,
To where he stood, hid from the torch's flame,
Behind a broad hall pillar, far beyond
95 The sound of merriment and chorus bland:
He startled her; but soon she knew his face,
And grasped his fingers in her palsied hand,
Saying, "Mercy, Porphyro! hie thee from this place;
They are all here tonight, the whole bloodthirsty race!

12

100 "Get hence! get hence! there's dwarfish Hildebrand;
He had a fever late, and in the fit
E He cursed thee and thine, both house and land:
Then there's that old Lord Maurice, not a whit
More tame for his gray hairs—Alas me! flit!
105 Flit like a ghost away."—"Ah, Gossip° dear,
We're safe enough; here in this armchair sit,
And tell me how"—"Good Saints! not here, not here;
Follow me, child, or else these stones will be thy
    bier."°

70. **Hoodwinked:** blindfolded. **all amort:** as though she were dead.

81. **sooth:** truth.

86. **foemen:** enemies.
87. **execrations:** curses.

90. **beldame:** old woman.

105. **Gossip:** godmother or old friend.

108. **bier:** stretcher on which a corpse is laid.

13

He followed through a lowly arched way,
110   Brushing the cobwebs with his lofty plume,
And as she muttered "Well-a—well-a-day!"°
A He found him in a little moonlight room,
Pale, latticed,° chill, and silent as a tomb.
"Now tell me where is Madeline," said he,
115   "O tell me, Angela, by the holy loom
Which none but secret sisterhood may see,
When they St. Agnes' wool are weaving piously."

14

"St. Agnes! Ah! it is St. Agnes' Eve—
B Yet men will murder upon holy days:
120   Thou must hold water in a witch's sieve,°
And be liege-lord° of all the Elves and Fays,°
To venture so: it fills me with amaze
To see thee, Porphyro!—St. Agnes' Eve!
C God's help! my lady fair the conjuror plays
125   This very night: good angels her deceive!
But let me laugh awhile, I've mickle° time to grieve."

15

Feebly she laugheth in the languid moon,
While Porphyro upon her face doth look,
Like puzzled urchin on an aged crone
130   Who keepeth closed a wond'rous riddle book,
As spectacled she sits in chimney nook.
But soon his eyes grew brilliant, when she told
His lady's purpose; and he scarce could brook°
Tears, at the thought of those enchantments cold,
135   And Madeline asleep in lap of legends old.

16

Sudden a thought came like a full-blown° rose,
Flushing his brow, and in his pained heart
D Made purple riot: then doth he propose
A stratagem, that makes the beldame start:
140   "A cruel man and impious thou art:
Sweet lady, let her pray, and sleep, and dream
Alone with her good angels, far apart
From wicked men like thee. Go, go!—I deem
Thou canst not surely be the same that thou didst
    seem."

17

145   "I will not harm her, by all saints I swear,"
Quoth Porphyro: "O may I ne'er find grace
When my weak voice shall whisper its last prayer,
E If one of her soft ringlets I displace,

---

111. **well-a-day:** exclamation of sorrow; "alas."

113. **latticed:** with windows made up of small, diamond-shaped panes.

120. **sieve:** strainer.
121. **liege-lord:** a lord to whom allegiance is owed. **Fays:** fairies.

126. **mickle:** much.

133. **brook:** usually "endure," though Keats probably means "restrain."

136. **full-blown:** in full bloom.

A. Imagery
These images echo the death-chill-tomb imagery of the opening stanzas.

B. Expansion
Witches were believed to be able to carry water in a sieve.

C. Interpreting
Madeline is playing the magician in hopes of conjuring up the face of her future husband.

D. Suspense/Predicting
❓ Why doesn't Keats reveal the "stratagem"? (To create suspense) What might the "stratagem" be? (Most students will guess that it has to do with visiting Madeline.)

E. Character
Note Porphyro's vow not to harm Madeline or even to displace one of her curls, or even (see next page) to look with passion in her face.

❓ How likely is this hot-blooded youth to be true to these vows? (Answers may vary. Hot-blooded or not, he waited "tedious hours" for a chance to see her, so he surely has patience.)

A. Plot/Predicting
Angela seems to
have some special
connection with
Porphyro, but its
nature is not made
clear.
? What might the
connection be?
(Answers will vary.
She may be a rela-
tive or a former
nurse.)

B. Plot
The "stratagem"
mentioned in line
139 is revealed.

C. Interpreting
? What is she
saying? (After
he sees Madeline
in her bedroom,
Porphyro must
marry her, or An-
gela won't go to
heaven.)

D. Character
Keats makes An-
gela a figure of
some fun. Even
the couplet here is
funny.

150

Or look with ruffian passion in her face:
Good Angela, believe me by these tears;
Or I will, even in a moment's space,
Awake, with horrid shout, my foemen's ears,
And beard° them, though they be more fanged than
    wolves and bears.''

153. **beard:** defiantly oppose.

18

155

"Ah! why wilt thou affright a feeble soul?
A poor, weak, palsy-stricken, churchyard thing,
Whose passing-bell° may ere the midnight toll;
Whose prayers for thee, each morn and evening,
Were never missed.''—Thus plaining,° doth she bring
A gentler speech from burning Porphyro;

160

So woeful, and of such deep sorrowing,
That Angela gives promise she will do
Whatever he shall wish, betide her weal or woe.°

156. **passing-bell:** a bell rung when someone dies.

162. **betide her weal or woe:** whether happiness or sorrow comes to her as a result.

19

165

Which was, to lead him, in close secrecy,
Even to Madeline's chamber, and there hide
Him in a closet, of such privacy
That he might see her beauty unespied,
And win perhaps that night a peerless bride,
While legioned fairies paced the coverlet,
And pale enchantment held her sleepy-eyed.

170

Never on such a night have lovers met,
Since Merlin paid his Demon all the monstrous debt.°

171. **Since Merlin . . . debt:** probably referring to the episode in the King Arthur legends in which Merlin, a magician and the son of the demon, pays the "monstrous debt" of his own life ("owed" to his father) when his beloved Vivien turns one of his own spells against him.
173. **cates:** delicacies.
174. **tambour frame:** circular frame for embroidery.

20

"It shall be as thou wishest," said the Dame:
"All cates° and dainties shall be stored there
Quickly on this feast night; by the tambour frame°

175

Her own lute thou wilt see: no time to spare,
For I am slow and feeble, and scarce dare
On such a catering trust my dizzy head.
Wait here, my child, with patience; kneel in prayer

180

The while: Ah! thou must needs the lady wed,
Or may I never leave my grave among the dead.''

21

So saying, she hobbled off with busy fear.
The lover's endless minutes slowly passed;
The dame returned, and whispered in his ear
To follow her; with aged eyes aghast

185

From fright of dim espial.° Safe at last,
Through many a dusky gallery, they gain
The maiden's chamber, silken, hushed, and chaste;
Where Porphyro took covert, pleased amain.°

189

His poor guide hurried back with agues° in her brain.

185. **espial:** spying.

188. **amain:** greatly.
189. **agues:** fevers, hot and cold spells.

Literature and Language: Using Different Parts of Speech
Explain that one way Keats achieves his lush and eloquent style is by using words creatively, often by taking a word into a less familiar part of speech. Point out *garlanded, diamonded,* and *damasked* in stanza 24; note that *garland, diamond,* and *damask,* the usual forms of these words, are all nouns. Discuss with stu-

dents how using the adjective form adds a new dimension or connotation to each word.

Have students work in groups to change the part of speech of one or more words in each of the following sentences. Allow the class to discuss how each group's "new" words add life and freshness to the images.

Tapestries of lemon and turquoise, pearl and jet swirled through the ballroom with the dancers. The air was heady with the rainbow scents of jasmine, musk, and orange that perfumed the night, oppressive yet cool. Inside the colonnade all was bright and full of music; outside, darkness and silence waited.

22

190   Her falt'ring hand upon the balustrade,°
    Old Angela was feeling for the stair,
    When Madeline, St. Agnes' charmed maid,
    Rose, like a missioned spirit, unaware:
    With silver taper's light, and pious care,
195   She turned, and down the aged gossip led

A   To a safe level matting.° Now prepare,
    Young Porphyro, for gazing on that bed;
    She comes, she comes again, like ring-dove frayed° and
      fled.

190. **balustrade:** bannister, railing.

196. **level matting:** carpeted floor, but "level" may also refer to a lower floor in the castle.
198. **frayed:** frightened.

23

B   Out went the taper as she hurried in;
200   Its little smoke, in pallid moonshine, died:
    She closed the door, she panted, all akin
    To spirits of the air, and visions wide:
    No uttered syllable, or, woe betide!
    But to her heart, her heart was voluble,
205   Paining with eloquence her balmy side;

C   As though a tongueless nightingale should swell
    Her throat in vain, and die, heart-stifled, in her dell.

24

D   A casement° high and triple-arched there was,
    All garlanded with carven imageries
210   Of fruits, and flowers, and bunches of knotgrass,
    And diamonded with panes of quaint device,
    Innumerable of stains and splendid dyes,
    As are the tiger-moth's deep-damasked° wings;
    And in the midst, 'mong thousand heraldries,
215   And twilight saints, and dim emblazonings,
    A shielded scutcheon° blushed with blood of queens
      and kings.

208. **casement:** window frame.

213. **deep-damasked:** richly decorated.

216. **shielded scutcheon:** shield-shaped coat of arms.

25

    Full on this casement shone the wintry moon,
    And threw warm gules° on Madeline's fair breast,
    As down she knelt for heaven's grace and boon;
220   Rose-bloom fell on her hands, together prest,
    And on her silver cross soft amethyst,°
    And on her hair a glory,° like a saint:
    She seemed a splendid angel, newly dressed,
    Save wings, for heaven: Porphyro grew faint;
225   She knelt, so pure a thing, so free from mortal taint.

218. **gules:** red (a term from heraldry).

221. **amethyst:** purple.
222. **glory:** halo of light.

26

    Anon his heart revives: her vespers° done;
    Of all its wreathed pearls her hair she frees;
    Unclasps her warmed jewels one by one;

226. **vespers:** evening prayers.

A. Connections
Keats echoes the scene in Shakespeare's *Cymbeline* where the evil Iachimo prepares to spy on Imogen.
❓ How different is Porphyro from the conventional lovers of romance? (Think of the virtuous Gawain. Romance heroes would not resort to this deception.)

B. Imagery
❓ Find two death images in this stanza. ("Out went the taper", "pallid moonshine")

C. Simile
❓ What is compared to the tongueless nightingale? (Madeline's feelings, which are "making her burst" because she cannot express them) See text page 216 for the myth of the tongueless nightingale.

D. Imagery
Point out the richness of the visual imagery in this magnificent description of a stained glass window. This window might be in the parish church in Enfield, which Keats had seen often when he was a boy.

A. Revision

Keats had trouble finding the right words here. He tried these lines before settling on the one quoted: "Loosens her boddice from her. . . ," "Loosens her Boddice lace string," "Loosens her Boddice and her bosom bare," and "Loosens her bursting boddice."

B. Revision

This once read "Half hidden like a Syren of the Sea." (Madeline, however, was no siren, so Keats changed it to "mermaid.")

C. Imagery

❓ What do lines 241–243 mean? (They are images of the closeness with which sleep envelops the sleeper; the loss of consciousness; the restorative powers of sleep.)

D. Imagery

Keats is masterful at creating images of color and sound. The noises without emphasize the quiet within Madeline's room, where even her breathing is audible.

E. Sound

❓ What gives this description its rich lushness? (Repeated *s* sounds and assonance; names of exotic fruits)

A
230
   Loosens her fragrant bodice;° by degrees
   Her rich attire creeps rustling to her knees:

B
   Half-hidden, like a mermaid in seaweed,
   Pensive awhile she dreams awake, and sees,
   In fancy, fair St. Agnes in her bed,
But dares not look behind, or all the charm is fled.

27

235
Soon, trembling in her soft and chilly nest,
In sort of wakeful swoon, perplexed she lay,
Until the poppied warmth of sleep oppressed
Her soothed limbs, and soul fatigued away;
Flown, like a thought, until the morrow-day;

240
Blissfully havened both from joy and pain;

C
Clasped like a missal where swart Paynims° pray;
Blinded alike from sunshine and from rain,
As though a rose should shut, and be a bud again.

28

Stolen to this paradise, and so entranced,

245
Porphyro gazed upon her empty dress,
And listened to her breathing, if it chanced
To wake into a slumberous tenderness;
Which when he heard, that minute did he bless,
And breathed himself: then from the closet crept,

250
Noiseless as fear in a wide wilderness,
And over the hushed carpet, silent, stept,
And 'tween the curtains peeped, where, lo!—how fast
   she slept.

29

D
255

Then by the bedside, where the faded moon
Made a dim, silver twilight, soft he set
A table, and, half anguished, threw thereon
A cloth of woven crimson, gold, and jet:°
O for some drowsy Morphean amulet!°
The boisterous, midnight, festive clarion,°
The kettledrum, and far-heard clarionet,

260
Affray° his ears, though but in dying tone:
The hall door shuts again, and all the noise is gone.

30

E
265

And still she slept an azure–lidded° sleep,
In blanched linen, smooth, and lavendered,
While he from forth the closet brought a heap°
Of candied apple, quince,° and plum, and gourd;°
With jellies soother° than the creamy curd,
And lucent° syrops, tinct° with cinnamon;

229. **bodice:** corset, tight-fitting vest.

241. **Clasped . . . Paynims:** held tightly (or kept shut and hidden) like a Christian prayerbook ("missal") in a land of dark–skinned "pagans" ("swart Paynims").

256. **jet:** black.
257. **Morphean amulet:** a sleep-inducing charm (in Latin mythology, Morpheus is god of sleep).
258. **clarion:** shrill trumpet.

260. **Affray:** startle.

262. **azure-lidded:** apparently because her skin is so fair (a common Romantic ideal of feminine beauty) that the tiny veins beneath the surface give her eyelids a bluish tint.
264–273. According to the legend of St. Agnes' Eve, the dream lover would bring the virgin an exotic feast.
265. **quince:** applelike fruit. **gourd:** melon.
266. **soother:** smoother.
267. **lucent:** clear. **tinct:** tinged.

Manna° and dates, in argosy° transferred
From Fez;° and spiced dainties, every one,
270 From silken Samarkand° to cedared Lebanon.

31

These delicates he heaped with glowing hand
On golden dishes and in baskets bright
Of wreathed silver: <u>sumptuous</u> they stand
A In the retired quiet of the night,
275 Filling the chilly room with perfume light.
"And now, my love, my seraph° fair, awake!
Thou art my heaven, and I thine eremite:°
Open thine eyes, for meek St. Agnes' sake,
Or I shall drowse beside thee, so my soul doth ache."

32

280 Thus whispering, his warm, unnerved arm
Sank in her pillow. Shaded was her dream
By the dusk curtains:—'twas a midnight charm
Impossible to melt as iced stream:
The lustrous salvers° in the moonlight gleam;
285 Broad golden fringe upon the carpet lies:
It seemed he never, never could redeem
From such a steadfast spell his lady's eyes;
So mused awhile, entoiled° in woofed° fantasies.

33

Awakening up, he took her hollow lute,
290 Tumultuous, and, in chords that tenderest be,
He played an ancient ditty, long since mute,
B In Provence° called, "La belle dame sans merci":
Close to her ear touching the melody;
Wherewith disturbed, she uttered a soft moan:
295 He ceased—she panted quick—and suddenly
Her blue affrayed eyes wide open shone:
Upon his knees he sank, pale as smooth-sculptured
     stone.

34

C Her eyes were open, but she still beheld,
Now wide awake, the vision of her sleep:
300 There was a painful change, that nigh expelled
The blisses of her dream so pure and deep:
At which fair Madeline began to weep,
And moan forth witless words with many a sigh;
While still her gaze on Porphyro would keep;
305 Who knelt, with joined hands and piteous eye,
Fearing to move or speak, she look'd so dreamingly.

268. **Manna:** in this case, probably a sweet syrup made from tree sap.   **argosy:** a large merchant ship.
269. **Fez:** a city in Morocco.
270. **Samarkand:** a city (now in the south central Soviet Union) on the silk-traders' route from China.

276. **seraph:** an angel of the highest rank.
277. **eremite:** religious hermit.

284. **salvers:** trays.

288. **entoiled:** tangled.   **woofed:** woven.

292. **Provence:** a region of southern France, known in the Middle Ages for its troubadours.

A. Imagery
Note again the image of chill. An image of warmth occurs in line 280.

B. Connections
Keats wrote this poem about three months before he wrote "La Belle Dame Sans Merci" (on April 21, 1819). See text page 712.

C. Plot
Madeline had been dreaming of Porphyro.

"Keats's own partial identification with the lover is obvious enough. Madeline, it is true, is no Fanny Brawne. In fact she is significantly different: Madeline timid and subdued, Fanny 'flying in all directions'; Madeline serious and devout, Fanny with her delight in clothes, her concern for fashion, and her quick tongue—'calling people such names.' In entering into the character of Porphyro, Keats is able to take some vicarious pleasure in the lover's 'stratagem'; and when Woodhouse later objected to the seduction scene, Keats waywardly replied (as the distressed Woodhouse went on to tell John Taylor) that he would 'despise a man who would be such an eunuch in sentiment as to leave a maid, with that Character about her, in such a situation: & sho^d despise himself to write about it &c &c &c—and all this sort of Keats-like rhodomontade [boasting].' "

—W. Jackson Bate

A. Theme
Porphyro has changed now that reality has replaced the dream. (But *he* "melts" into *her* dream, not the opposite.) Though innocence is lost, the two lovers are not miserable. Actual happiness is impossible without an awakening from dream to reality.

B. Setting
The scene switches at the key moment: The frozen outdoor storm contrasts with the sweet warmth of Madeline's room. St. Agnes's moon has set.

C. Conflict
? Why is Madeline upset? (She thought she was dreaming of Porphyro; awake, she realizes she has been deceived and her reputation ruined, and she hears that he will leave her.)

D. Character
Porphyro reassures Madeline and asks her to marry him. Like Romeo, he compares himself to a pilgrim (a journeyer to a religious shrine).

E. Speaker
? Who speaks? (Porphyro)

35

> "Ah, Porphyro!" said she, "but even now
> Thy voice was at sweet tremble in mine ear,
> Made tunable with every sweetest vow;
> 310 And those sad eyes were spiritual and clear:
> How changed thou art! how pallid, chill, and drear!
> Give me that voice again, my Porphyro,
> Those looks immortal, those complainings dear!
> Oh leave me not in this eternal woe,
> 315 For if thou diest, my love, I know not where to go."

36

> Beyond a mortal man impassioned far
> At these voluptuous accents, he arose,
> Ethereal, flushed, and like a throbbing star
> Seen mid the sapphire heaven's deep repose;
> 320 Into her dream he melted, as the rose
> Blendeth its odor with the violet,
> Solution sweet: meantime the frost wind blows
> Like Love's alarum pattering the sharp sleet
> Against the windowpanes; St. Agnes' moon hath set.

37

> 325 'Tis dark: quick pattereth the flaw-blown° sleet;
> "This is no dream, my bride, my Madeline!"
> 'Tis dark: the iced gusts still rave and beat:
> "No dream, alas! alas! and woe is mine!
> Porphyro will leave me here to fade and pine.
> 330 Cruel! what traitor could thee hither bring?
> I curse not, for my heart is lost in thine,
> Though thou forsakest a deceived thing;
> A dove forlorn and lost with sick unpruned° wing."

38

> "My Madeline! sweet dreamer! lovely bride!
> 335 Say, may I be for aye thy vassal blest?
> Thy beauty's shield, heart-shaped and vermeil° dyed?
> Ah, silver shrine, here will I take my rest
> After so many hours of toil and quest,
> A famished pilgrim, saved by miracle.
> 340 Though I have found, I will not rob thy nest
> Saving of thy sweet self; if thou think'st well
> To trust, fair Madeline, to no rude infidel.

39

> "Hark! 'tis an elfin-storm from fairyland,
> Of haggard seeming, but a boon indeed:
> 345 Arise—arise! the morning is at hand;
> The bloated wassailers° will never heed:

325. **flaw-blown:** blown by a gust of wind.

333. **unpruned:** unpreened; with disorderly feathers.

336. **vermeil:** vermilion; red.

346. **wassailers:** rowdy party participants (*wassail* is spiced ale).

READING CHECK TEST
1. On St. Agnes's Eve, women hoped to see visions of their future husbands. (T)
2. Porphyro has been forbidden to see Madeline because of his age. (F)
3. The old woman helps Porphyro hide in Madeline's bedroom. (T)

4. Porphyro doesn't want Madeline to wake and see him. (F)
5. Madeline's father finally agrees to let her marry Porphyro. (F)

CLOSURE
Have students imagine they are telling one of their friends about this poem and the friend asks, "What is it about?" Let one student give the class his or her answer.

A

350

Let us away, my love, with happy speed;
There are no ears to hear, or eyes to see,
Drowned all in Rhenish° and the sleepy mead:°
Awake! arise! my love, and fearless be,
For o'er the southern moors I have a home for thee.''

40

She hurried at his words, beset with fears,
For there were sleeping dragons all around,
At glaring watch, perhaps, with ready spears—
355   Down the wide stairs a darkling° way they found.
In all the house was heard no human sound.
A chain-drooped lamp was flickering by each door;
The arras,° rich with horseman, hawk, and hound,
Fluttered in the besieging wind's uproar;
360   And the long carpets rose along the gusty floor.

41

They glide, like phantoms, into the wide hall;
Like phantoms, to the iron porch, they glide;
Where lay the Porter, in uneasy sprawl,

349. **Rhenish:** Rhine wine.   **mead:** a heavy liquor made from honey.

355. **darkling:** in the dark.

358. **arras:** hanging tapestry.

The Eve of St. Agnes
by William Holman Hunt. Oil.

Guildhall Art Gallery, London.

A. Plot
❓ What is Porphyro's plan? (To run away with Madeline while all are drunk; to live somewhere "o'er the southern moors")

B. Humanities Connection: Responding to the Fine Art
In 1848 William Holman Hunt (1827–1910) helped found the Pre-Raphaelite Brotherhood, a group of young painters who believed in the direct study of nature, attention to minute detail, and expression of serious ideas. Hunt painted historical scenes and made several journeys to Egypt and Palestine to paint biblical scenes.
❓ What scene from the poem is illustrated here? (The lovers are fleeing, stanza 41.) Do Madeline and Porphyro look the way you imagined them? Why or why not?

B

John Keats   733

1. The chapel of an old castle on a bitterly cold January night.
2. Madeline is brooding upon love. She must skip supper, lie in bed, and look upward to heaven.
3. An old feud between their families.
4. He wants to see Madeline.
5. Angela conducts Porphyro to Madeline's room and hides him there.
6. The sight of Madeline at prayer.
7. Madeline undresses, falls asleep, and dreams of Porphyro. He emerges from the closet, sets out food, wakes her with a song, and proclaims his love.
8. Porphyro and Madeline sneak out of the castle.
   Madeline's father and his guests.
9. The Baron and his guests have nightmares about death; the beadsman and Angela die.

Interpreting Meanings
10. The castle might symbolize Madeline's virginity, or tradition, including its confinements and prejudices.
11. No. The storm might symbolize the actual world. Or it might symbolize death *(Answers continue in left-hand column.)*

(Continued from top.)
or chaos, the world beyond Eden.
12. The castle, the crone, the maiden, the true lovers, the evil enemies, the dreams, the dangerous father.

A. Responding
? Are you satisfied with the poem's ending? Do you know whether the lovers escaped? (No.) Why do you suppose Keats ends with the death of the two old people? (Answers will vary. They might include the parallel between the end of a life and the end of this poem or an attempt to reflect the anti-life atmosphere of the castle.)

365
With a huge empty flagon° by his side:
The wakeful bloodhound rose, and shook his hide,
But his sagacious eye an inmate owns:°
By one, and one, the bolts full easy slide:
The chains lie silent on the footworn stones;
The key turns, and the door upon its hinges groans.

364. **flagon:** large wine bottle.

366. **an inmate owns:** recognizes a member of the household.

42

370

A

375
And they are gone: Aye, ages long ago
These lovers fled away into the storm.
That night the Baron dreamt of many a woe,
And all his warrior-guests, with shade and form
Of witch, and demon, and large coffin worm,
Were long be-nightmared. Angela the old
Died palsy-twitched, with meager face deform;
The Beadsman, after thousand aves° told,
For aye° unsought for slept among his ashes cold.

377. **aves:** prayers that begin, "Ave Maria" ("Hail Mary").
378. **For aye:** forever.

A Comment on the Poem

Keats's preoccupation with love is natural. He was young and his passion for Fanny Brawne was great. But throughout his poetic career, Keats was, as a writer and thinker, also fascinated with the possibility that the most intense moments in life might—in some other realm, of art or life after death—last forever. We cannot be sure just what sort of existence "these lovers fled away" to. They left the mortality-haunted castle of Madeline's father, the Baron, who, with his like, dreamt only of death. But where did they go?

The Baron and his friends, foemen to the love-seeking and dream-seeking Porphyro, seem to represent those who cling to ordinary life as the sole source of reassurance and pleasure. There is also the old beadsman, praying himself to death in anticipation of a post-mortal existence, and old Angela—the protective old woman like the nurse in Shakespeare's *Romeo and Juliet*—who takes the lovers under her wing but cannot follow them into the world outside the castle. Beyond these deftly limned portraits, atmosphere, created by rich details and glowing descriptions, becomes the most lasting effect of the poem, as though the story had been told in a hundred windows of stained glass rather than in words.

Responding to the Poem

Analyzing the Poem

Identifying Details

1. Describe the opening **setting** of the story.
2. What do we learn at once about "one lady," Madeline, in lines 42–44? What have the old wives told her must be done in order to have visions that night?
3. Explain what keeps Porphyro and Madeline apart, according to lines 82–89.
4. Describe Porphyro's strategem.
5. What role does Angela the nurse play in bringing Porphyro and Madeline together?
6. What sight of Madeline in her room makes Porphyro grow faint?
7. Describe what happens in Madeline's room.
8. Describe the elopement. Who are the "sleeping dragons" all around?
9. What does the last stanza suggest happens to those who are still in the castle?

Interpreting Meanings

10. What do you think the castle in this love story might **symbolize**?
11. Do you think it is a weakness of the poem that Keats does not show us what happens to Madeline and Porphyro after they leave the castle? Do you think the storm they flee into has any **symbolic** significance?
12. What particular elements of this story remind you of old fairy tales and legends?

Writing About the Poem

A Creative Response

1. **Creating and Staging a Dramatic Version.** Outline a dramatized version of the narrative in "The Eve of St. Agnes." Then write some notes on how you would stage the poem as a play.

A Critical Response

2. **Comparing Stories.** Review Shakespeare's *Romeo and Juliet*, and write a brief essay in which you show the similarities and differences between Keats's poem and Shakespeare's play. Consider these elements:

a. The main characters and their problem
b. Solution to the problem
c. Other characters in the story
d. Resolution to the plot
e. Theme

3. **Supporting a Statement.** *Keats was profoundly influenced by an idealized vision of the Middle Ages.* In an essay, show how this interest in the Middle Ages is shown in "The Eve of St. Agnes" and "La Belle Dame Sans Merci." Consider the **settings,** the **characters,** and the use of the **supernatural.**

Analyzing Language and Style

Imagery

List images from the poem that appeal to the senses of sight, hearing, smell, taste, and touch.

After you have your list of images, examine them to see if you can answer these questions:

1. Does any one color dominate?
2. Do any of the images present contrasts?
3. What images in the story present a sense of menace?
4. What atmospheres do the images create for different settings of the poem?

Primary Sources
Keats's Last Letter

Rome, 30 November 1820

A "My dear Brown,

" 'Tis the most difficult thing in the world to me to write a letter. My stomach continues so bad, that I feel it worse on opening any book, yet I am much better than I was in quarantine. Then I am afraid to encounter the pro-ing and con-ing of anything interesting to me in England. I have an habitual feeling of my real life having passed, and that I am leading a posthumous existence. God knows how it would have been—but it appears to me—however, I will not speak of that subject. I must have been at Bedhampton nearly at the time you were writing to me from Chichester—how unfortunate—and to pass on the river too! There was my star predominant! I cannot answer anything in your letter, which followed me from Naples to Rome, because I am afraid to look it over again. I am so weak (in mind) that I cannot bear the sight of any handwriting of a friend I love so much as I do you. Yet I ride the little horse, and, at my worst, even in quarantine, summoned up more puns, in a sort of desperation, in one week than in any year of my life. There

B is one thought enough to kill me; I have been well, healthy, alert, etc., walking with her, and now—the knowledge of contrast, feeling for light and shade, all

that information (primitive sense) necessary for a poem, are great enemies to the recovery of the stomach. There, you rogue, I put you to the torture; but you must bring your philosophy to bear, as I do mine, really, or how should I be able to live? Dr. Clark is very attentive to me; he says, there is very little the matter with my lungs, but my stomach, he says, is very bad. I am well disappointed in hearing good news from George, for it runs in my head we shall all die young. I have not written to Reynolds yet, which he must think very neglectful; being anxious to send him a good account of my health, I have delayed it from week to week. If I recover, I will do all in my power to correct the mistakes made during sickness; and if I should not, all my faults will be forgiven. Severn is very well, though he leads so dull a life with me. Remember me to all friends, and tell Haslam I should not have left London without taking leave of him, but from being so low in body and mind. Write to George as soon you receive this, and tell him how I am, as far as you can guess; and also a note to my sister—who walks about my imagination like a ghost—she is so like Tom. I can scarcely bid you goodbye, even in a letter. I always made an awkward bow.
God bless you!
John Keats"

A. Expansion
The letter is to Charles Brown Keats's good friend. Keats lived with Brown in Wentworth House from December 1818 until he left for Rome in the fall of 1820. Keats died at No. 26 in the Piazza di Spagna, which is now the Keats-Shelley Memorial House.

B. Clarification
The reference is to Fanny Brawne, whom Keats loved. Keats had asked Brown on September 30 to be a friend to Fanny after he died.

C. Expansion
Dr. Clark must have been pacifying Keats. According to another of Keats's friends, Joseph Severn, an autopsy revealed that Keats's "lungs were entirely destroyed—the cells were quite gone."

D. Tone
Keats is being ironic here. George is Keats's younger brother, who left England in June 1818 to live in Kentucky with his bride.

In a letter to Wordsworth in 1801, Lamb tells why he prefers city life:

"I have passed all my days in London, until I have formed as many and intense local attachments as any of you mountaineers can have done with dead Nature. The lighted shops of the Strand and Fleet Street; the innumerable trades, tradesmen and customers, coaches, wagons, playhouse; all the bustle and wickedness round about Covent Garden; . . . the crowds, the very dirt and mud, the sun shining upon houses and pavements, the print shops, the old bookstalls, parsons cheapening books, coffeehouses, steams of soups from kitchens . . . —all these things work themselves into my mind and feed me, without a power of satiating me. The wonder of these sights impels me into night walks about her crowded streets, and I often shed tears in the motley Strand from fullness of joy at so much life. All these emotions must be strange to you. So are your rural emotions to me."

A. Expansion

Christ's Hospital was a free boarding school in London for the sons of middle-class parents who were unable to pay for their sons' educations.

B. Connections

See Coleridge's "This Lime-Tree Bower My Prison" (text page 652), in which Coleridge addresses Lamb and refers to this tragedy. When the stabbing occurred, Lamb was only twenty-two; his sister Mary was thirty-two.

Charles Lamb (1775–1834)

The great achievements of the Romantic poets have tended to overshadow the development of prose in the early nineteenth century. But that cluster of imaginative responses that we call Romanticism had a major effect on many prose forms: the letter, the novel, and, in particular, the essay. In the "Neoclassic" period, the prose essay had been largely devoted to travel, moral subjects, and literary criticism. During the Romantic period, this focus widened to include a host of imaginative topics. Perhaps the most accomplished Romantic essayist was Charles Lamb.

A Born in London, Lamb formed an enduring friendship with Samuel Taylor Coleridge when the two were schoolboys at Christ's Hospital. At seventeen, Lamb went to work at East India House, a huge commercial firm where he remained as an official for thirty-three years.

B Charles's older sister Mary suffered from emotional instability. The tragic turning point of Lamb's life occurred in 1796, when his sister stabbed their invalid mother to death in a violent episode of insanity. The sequel to this shocking horror would be remarkable for any time and place. Assuming custody and responsibility for Mary, Charles lived with her for nearly forty years. Gently nurturing his sister in her illness, he never married for fear of passing on her mental disease to another generation. During her periods of lucidity, Lamb collaborated with his sister on literary projects.

Perhaps the most celebrated result of these collaborations was *Tales from Shakespeare,* published in 1807 and intended as an introduction to the plays for children.

Charles himself wrote sonnets, plays, and newspaper reviews. His imaginative insights, his friendships with Coleridge and Wordsworth, and the hospitality of his salon—which often welcomed other leading Romantic writers—soon established Lamb as an influential figure in English letters.

But it was not until 1820 that Lamb's most celebrated writing—his essays—began to appear. At East India House, he had known an Italian clerk named Elia, and, taking this name as a pseudonym, he began to contribute personal essays to the *London Magazine* on a wide variety of topics. The first series of these essays, entitled *Essays of Elia,* were collected for book publication in 1823. Their imaginative wit and keen perception inspired both popular and critical admiration. A second series of essays followed ten years later.

What, in particular, makes Lamb's essays "Romantic"? The prominence of the writer's personality, the essays' flexibility of form, and their emphasis on memory and imagination are three possible answers. But it is also important to bear in mind that Lamb's reflections, apparently so personal and spontaneous, are—like much Romantic poetry—carefully crafted. As you read "Dream Children," for example, you will see that the writer deliberately structures the essay to lead up to a surprise ending. Perhaps Lamb's greatest gift was to strike such a harmonious balance between the particular and the general, between his own personality and the objective world around him.

PREPARATION

1. BUILDING ON PRIOR KNOWLEDGE. Ask students if they have ever had dreams that seemed very real to them. Discuss with students how dreams usually combine elements of fantasy with bits of ordinary reality from everyday life. Have them comment on how "real" the illusory world of dreams can seem. How dangerous can it also be?

2. ESTABLISHING A PURPOSE. Have students read question 9 on text page 740 to set a purpose for their reading.

SUPPLEMENTARY SUPPORT MATERIALS
1. Vocabulary Activity Worksheet (*CCB*)
2. Review and Response Worksheet: Tone (*CCB*)
3. Selection Test (*CCB*)

DEVELOPING VOCABULARY
The following words from the essay are tested in the Selection Test. (See also Vocabulary Activity Worksheet.)
to upbraid   concourse   mettlesome

DREAM CHILDREN: A REVERIE

The literal meaning of "reverie" is dream, and the use of the word in this title might prepare you for a surprise ending. The faithful "Bridget" at the end is really Lamb's sister, Mary.

A. Expansion
Lamb's great-grandmother was named Mary Field. Norfolk is a county in eastern England near the North Sea.

B. Title
? Do you think these are the dream children of the title? (They seem to be; but perhaps Lamb is deliberately misleading us here.)

Children love to listen to stories about their elders, when *they* were children; to stretch their imagination to the conception of a traditionary great-uncle or grandame, whom they never saw. It was in this spirit that my little ones crept about me the other evening to hear about their great-grandmother Field, who lived in a great house in Norfolk (a hundred times bigger than that in which they and papa lived) which had been the scene—so at least it was generally believed in that part of the country—of the tragic incidents which they had lately become familiar with from the ballad of the Children in the Wood.[1] Certain it is that the whole story of the children and their cruel uncle was to be seen fairly carved out in wood upon the chimneypiece of the great hall, the whole story down to the Robin Redbreasts, till a foolish rich person pulled it down to set up a marble one of modern invention in its stead, with no story upon it. Here Alice put out one of her dear mother's looks, too tender to be called upbraiding. Then I went on to say, how religious and how good their great-grandmother Field was, how beloved and respected by everybody, though she was not indeed the mistress of this great house, but had only the charge of it (and yet in some respects she might be said to be the mistress of it too) committed to her by the owner, who preferred living in a newer and more fashionable mansion which he had purchased somewhere in the adjoining county; but still she lived in it in a manner as if it had been her own, and kept up the dignity of the great house in a sort while she lived, which afterward came to decay, and was nearly pulled down, and all its old ornaments stripped and carried away to the owner's other house, where they were set up, and looked as awkward as if someone were to carry away the old tombs they had seen lately at the Abbey, and stick them up in Lady C.'s tawdry gilt drawing room. Here John smiled, as much as to say, "that would be foolish indeed." And then I told how, when she came to die, her funeral was attended by a concourse of all the poor, and some of the gentry too, of the neighborhood for many miles round, to show their respect for her memory, because she had been such a good and religious woman; so good indeed that she knew all the Psaltery by heart, aye, and a great part of the Testament besides. Here little Alice spread her hands. Then I told what a tall, upright, graceful person their great-grandmother Field once was; and how in her youth she was esteemed the best dancer—here Alice's little right foot played an involuntary movement, till upon my looking grave, it desisted—the best dancer, I was saying, in the county, till a cruel disease, called a cancer, came, and bowed her down with pain; but it could never bend her good spirits, or make them stoop, but they were still upright, because she was so good and religious.

Then I told how she was used to sleep by herself in a lone chamber of the great lone house; and how she believed that an apparition of two infants was to be seen at midnight gliding up and down the great staircase near where she slept, but she said "those innocents would do her no harm"; and how frightened I used to be, though in those days I had my maid to sleep with me, because I was never half so good or religious as she—and yet I never saw the infants. Here John expanded

---

1. In this popular sixteenth-century ballad, a gentleman of Norfolk on his deathbed leaves his fortune to his two young children. The children's uncle then arranges to have the children killed, so he can inherit the money. But one murderer repents, and instead of killing the children, he kills the other would-be murderer and leaves the children in the forest. They die, and a Robin Redbreast covers their little bodies with leaves.

READING CHECK TEST

1. The dream children are really Lamb's children who died young. (F)
2. Lamb tells the children about their great-grandmother. (T)
3. The children cry over the story of Uncle John. (T)

4. Lamb tells the children that he courted a woman named Alice, who became the children's mother. (T)
5. After the children tell Lamb they are only what might have been, he awakens from his dream. (T)

A. Humanities Connection: Discussing the Fine Art
Joshua Reynolds (1723–1792) began painting portraits at the age of seventeen and, after studying in Italy for three years, established himself as a London portrait painter. He was extremely ambitious and soon had more commissions than he could handle. In 1768, Reynolds became the first president of the Royal Academy and was knighted. ▓ Does the painting idealize the child or is it satiric? Is the child poor or well-to-do? (The painter idealizes childhood; note the child's open, relaxed pose and the soft, rounded beauty of his features. Master Hare is not poor.) Students may be astonished to find that the portrait is of a boy. In those days, boys' hair was kept uncut and they were clothed in dresses until they were about five.

A

Master Hare by Sir Joshua Reynolds. Oil.   The Louvre, Paris.

all his eyebrows and tried to look courageous. Then I told how good she was to all her grandchildren, having us to the great house in the holidays, where I in particular used to spend many hours by myself, in gazing upon the old busts of the Twelve Caesars, that had been Emperors of Rome, till the old marble heads would seem to live again, or I to be turned into marble with them; how I never could be tired with roaming about that huge mansion, with its vast empty rooms,

CLOSURE
Have students state Lamb's purpose in writing the essay, as they see it.

ANALYZING THE ESSAY
Identifying Details
1. The speaker remembers a recent evening when he told his children about their great-grandmother.
2. She was religious, good, respected

and beloved by everyone, tall and graceful, and a fine dancer.
Uncle John was handsome, spirited, considerate, and caring.
3. They are interested and involved with the stories.
4. They say that Alice's children call someone else father, that they are only dreams, "what might have been."

Interpreting Meanings
5. They are on the shores of Lethe.
6. The subtitle refers to the fact that the narrator is relating a daydream. The children of the title are the children he might have had.
7. They were apparently in love, but never married.
8. Answers will vary. He is thinking of (Answers continue on next page.)

with their worn-out hangings, fluttering tapestry, and carved oaken panels, with the gilding almost rubbed out—sometimes in the spacious old-fashioned gardens, which I had almost to myself, unless when now and then a solitary gardening man would cross me—and how the nectarines and peaches hung upon the walls, without my ever offering to pluck them, because they were forbidden fruit, unless now and then—and because I had more pleasure in strolling about among the old melancholy-looking yew trees, or the firs, and **A** picking up the red berries, and the fir apples, which were good for nothing but to look at—or in lying about upon the fresh grass, with all the fine garden smells around me—or basking in the orangery, till I could almost fancy myself ripening too along with the oranges and the limes in that grateful warmth—or in watching the dace that darted to and fro in the fishpond, at the bottom of the garden, with here and there a great sulky pike hanging midway down the water in silent state, as if it mocked at their impertinent friskings—I had **B** more pleasure in these busy-idle diversions than in all the sweet flavors of peaches, nectarines, oranges, and suchlike common baits of children. Here John slyly deposited back upon the plate a bunch of grapes, which, not unobserved by Alice, he had meditated dividing with her, and both seemed willing to relinquish them for the present as irrelevant. Then in somewhat a more heightened tone, I told how, though their great-grandmother Field loved all her grandchildren, yet in an especial manner she might be said to love **C** their uncle, John L——, because he was so handsome and spirited a youth, and a king to the rest of us; and, instead of moping about in solitary corners, like some of us, he would mount the most mettlesome horse he could get, when but an imp no bigger than themselves, and make it carry him half over the county in a morning, and join the hunters when there were any out—and yet he loved the old great house and gardens too, but had too much spirit to be always pent up within their boundaries—and how their uncle grew up to man's estate as brave as he was handsome, to the admiration of everybody, but of their great-grandmother Field most especially; and how he used to carry me upon his back when I was a lame-footed boy—for he was a good bit older than me—many a mile when I could not walk for pain; and how in after life he became lame-footed too, and I did not always (I fear) make allowances enough for

him when he was impatient, and in pain, nor remember sufficiently how considerate he had been to me when I was lame-footed; and how when he died, though he had not been dead an hour, it seemed as if he had died a great while ago, such a distance there is betwixt life and death; and how I bore his death as I thought pretty well at first, but afterward it haunted and haunted me; and though I did not cry or take it to heart as some do, and as I think he would have done if I had died, yet I missed him all day long, and knew not till then how much I had loved him.

I missed his kindness, and I missed his crossness, and wished him to be alive again, to be quarreling with him (for we quarreled sometimes), rather than not have him again, and was as uneasy without him, as he their poor uncle must have been when the doctor took off his limb. Here the children fell a crying, and asked if their little mourning which they had on was not for Uncle John, and they looked up, and prayed me not to go on about their uncle, but to tell them some stories about their pretty dead mother. Then I told how for seven long years, in hope sometimes, sometimes in despair, yet persisting ever, I **D** courted the fair Alice W——n; and, as much as children could understand, I explained to them what coyness, and difficulty, and denial meant in maidens—when suddenly, turning to Alice, the soul of the first Alice looked out at her eyes with such a reality of represosentment, that I became in doubt which of them stood there before me, or whose that bright hair was; and while I stood gazing, both the children gradually grew fainter to my view, receding, and still receding till nothing at last but two mournful features were seen in the uttermost distance, which, without speech, strangely impressed upon me the effects of speech: "We are not of Alice, nor of thee, nor are we children at all. The children of Alice call Bartrum father. We are nothing; less than nothing, and dreams. We are only what might have been, and must wait upon the tedious shores of Lethe[2] millions of ages before we have existence, and a **E** name"—and immediately awaking, I found myself quietly seated in my bachelor armchair, where I had fallen asleep, with the faithful Bridget unchanged by my side—but John L. (or James Elia) was gone forever.

---

2. **Lethe:** river of forgetfulness in Greek mythology, where the dead wait in hopes of returning to mortal life.

A. Vocabulary
Fir apples are pine cones.

B. Diction
Note Lamb's oxymoron (a figure of speech made up of contradictory words that still make sense): busy-idle diversions.

C. Theme
John L— is Charles Lamb's eldest brother John Lamb, who died shortly before Lamb wrote this essay. The essay's theme has to do with loss (from death and from what has never happened).

D. Expansion
Lamb is probably referring to Ann Simmons, whom he loved as a young man.

E. Responding
How do you feel about this ending? Were you surprised? Satisfied? Explain.

progeny and generations and ties to the past and future through children. The grandmother who never was a grand-mother to Lamb's children adds special poignancy.

9. Mention of children, elders, and imagi-nation sets a tone of nostalgia and yearning.

10. Answers will vary. Given the trage-dies of Lamb's life, the ending would move most readers.

A. Expansion
The Bluecoat School is Christ's Hospital, the Lon-don boarding school Lamb and Coleridge attended as boys. The stu-dents were called Bluecoat Boys be-cause of their uni-forms of long blue gowns.

B. Expansion
Lamb did give up writing poetry and turned his attention to writing essays.

Responding to the Essay

Analyzing the Essay
Identifying Facts

1. Describe the situation at the beginning of the essay.
2. What qualities of their great-grandmother Field does the narrator single out to tell the children? What does he say to the children about their Uncle John?
3. How do the children respond to the father's story of the "old days"?
4. What do the children say as they disappear?

Interpreting Meanings

5. According to the reader, where are all the people who might have existed but weren't born?
6. Tell what the essay's title and subtitle mean.
7. What do you infer happened between the speaker and Alice W.?
8. What significance can you find in the fact that the stories Lamb is telling the children are stories about his grandmother? (What would have been lost if he had been telling them about King Arthur, or the history of England?)
9. How does the first sentence of the essay establish its **tone**? How would you describe this tone?
10. What impression do you have of the ending? Is it overly sentimental? Clever? Touching? Given Lamb's life story, how did the essay make you feel?

Writing About the Essay
A Creative Response

Writing a Reverie. Use Lamb's essay as a model and write a first-person short reverie, or daydream, of your own. You might imagine another speaker who dreams about people who, for one reason or another, never existed.

Analyzing Language and Style
The Familiar Essay

Essays are generally divided into two classes: the formal essay and the familiar (or informal) essay. The formal essay has an objective style and uses dignified, formal language. The formal essay is also apt to be logically and clearly structured. The familiar essay, by contrast, uses a conversational tone and a looser structure, and gives an impression of the writer's personality.

1. See if you can trace the structure of the essay in the progression of ideas till it comes to the main point.
2. Locate instances where the writer digresses.
3. Where do the sentences become longer and longer, piling up details as the speaker remembers them?
4. Find details that give the essay a personal and con-versational tone.
5. How do the details about the children's gestures and facial expressions contribute to its tone?

Primary Sources
Lamb's Letter to Coleridge

On September 17, 1796, Charles Lamb wrote this letter to his friend Samuel Coleridge:

"My dearest friend—White or some of my friends or the public papers by this time may have informed you of the terrible calamities that have fallen on our family. I will only give you the outlines. My poor dear dearest sister in a fit of insanity has been the death of her own mother. I was at hand only time enough to snatch the knife out of her grasp. She is at present in a madhouse, from whence I fear she must be moved to a hospital. God has preserved to me my senses—I eat and drink and sleep, and have my judgment I believe very sound.

"My poor father was slightly wounded, and I am left to take care of him and my aunt. Mr. Norris of the Blue-coat School has been very kind to us, and we have no other friend, but thank God I am very calm and composed and able to do the best that remains to do. Write—as religious a letter as possible—but no mention of what is gone and done with—with me the former things are passed away, and I have something more to do that [than] to feel——mention nothing of poetry. I have destroyed every vestige of past vanities of that kind. Do as you please, but if you publish, publish mine (I give free leave) without name or initial, and never send me a book, I charge you, you [your] own judgment will convince you not to take any notice of this yet to your dear wife. You look after your family. I have my reason and strength left to take care of mine. I charge you don't think of coming to see me. Write. I will not see you if you come. God almighty love you and all of us——

"God almighty

have us all in
his keeping——

C. Lamb"

"Night waned upon this talk, and even the witching hour had gone by, before we retired to rest. When I placed my head on my pillow, I did not sleep, nor could I be said to think. My imagination, unbidden, possessed and guided me, gifting the successive images that arose in my mind with a vividness far beyond the usual bounds of reverie. I saw—with shut eyes but acute mental vision—I saw the pale student of unhallowed arts kneeling beside the thing he had put together. I saw the hideous phantasm of a man stretched out, and then, on the working of some powerful engine, show signs of life and stir with an uneasy, half vital motion. Frightful must it be, for supremely frightful would be the effect of any human endeavor to mock the stupendous mechanism of the Creator of the world. His success would terrify the artist; he would rush away from his odious handiwork, horror-stricken. He would hope that, left to itself, the slight spark of life which he had communicated would fade; that this thing, which had received such imperfect animation, would subside into dead mat-

(Continued on next page.)

Mary Wollstonecraft Shelley (1797–1851)

The Romantic period was one of intense, over-powering expectations. It is hard to imagine a single figure of this period who inherited greater expectations and demands for her own life than Mary Wollstonecraft Shelley.

Her mother, who died shortly after Mary was born, was a talented writer and a courageous advocate for women's rights and revered by Mary's own generation. Her father, William Godwin, was one of the leading political philosophers of the first Romantic generation and the author of one of its most important works, *Political Justice,* which influenced Coleridge and Wordsworth and the young Percy Shelley.

Astonished in 1812 to discover that Godwin was still alive, Percy Shelley began a correspondence with him and soon sought out his idol in London. In 1814, Percy met Mary, who had spent the previous two years living with a family in Scotland. Already married and heir to a baronetcy, Percy was estranged from his wife Harriet and becoming independent from the philosophic influence of Godwin. Sixteen-year-old Mary was attractive, with large, hazel eyes, an open brow, and a fairness which gave her a serene appearance. Beneath this serene appearance lay an independent, highly sensitive spirit, and a strength of conviction that enabled her, at an early age, to embark on nearly a decade of adventure and tragedy that seems a working out of an extraordinary Romantic heritage.

Mary had grown up in a household astream with visitors coming to exchange views with her father on the great social and scientific issues of the day. "I was nursed and fed with a love of glory," she said. "To be something great and good was the precept given me by my father; Shelley reiterated it . . ."

Despite her father and stepmother's opposition—and amidst Percy's theatrical and love-lorn threats of suicide—Mary dramatically (at her mother's gravesite) declared her love for the twenty-two-year-old poet and eloped with him on July 14, 1814. Accompanying them was Mary's half-sister Jane (soon to call herself Claire) Clairmont, who was to be a member of the young

Mary Wollstonecraft by Richard Rothwell (1841). Oil.

Shelleys' household until 1820. Mrs. Godwin, Mary's stepmother, followed the elopers and tried to persuade them to give up their rebellion, but they refused and set off on a tour through France, Switzerland, and Germany. The trio read to each other—often from Mary's mother's travel writings—and kept journals. Mary eventually used hers for her first publication, *History of a Six Weeks Tour* (1817).

The elopement, of course, was scandalous. When they returned to England, the young couple was shunned by their families and friends. Mary's father lost no time in making up for the loss of Percy's discipleship by calling upon *him* for financial assistance. The death of Percy's grandfather, Sir Bysshe Shelley, stabilized the couple's economic situation somewhat, but Percy's father, now Sir Timothy, still violently opposed his son's alliance with Mary.

The couple's first child, a daughter, died shortly after her birth. But a second child, William, who was to be nicknamed "Willmouse" by his parents, seemed to thrive. The impetuous Claire had by this time struck up an affair with Lord Byron. Byron soon left for the Continent,

(Continued from previous page.)
ter; and he might sleep in the belief that the silence of the grave would quench forever the transient existence of the hideous corpse which he had looked upon as the cradle of life. . . .

"I opened mine [eyes] in terror. The idea so possessed my mind, that a thrill of fear ran through me. . . . I could not so easily get rid of my hideous phantom: still it haunted me. I must try to think of something else. I recurred to my ghost story—my tiresome unlucky ghost story! O! if I could only contrive one which would frighten my reader as I myself had been frighted that night!

"Swift as light and as cheering was the idea that broke in upon me. 'I have found it! What terrified me will terrify others, and I need only describe the specter which had haunted my midnight pillow.'"

A. Connections
Prometheus, who also is the central character in her husband's long verse drama, *Prometheus Unbound*, is the Titan who created humans from clay and water and who stole fire from the gods for human use.

B. Expansion
The novel appeared in three volumes with a preface by Percy Bysshe Shelley. Mary Shelley dedicated the novel to her father.

and the Shelleys and Claire followed in May and joined Byron in Switzerland on the shore of Lake Geneva. That summer marked the beginning of Shelley and Byron's literary relationship.

One stormy night at Byron's Villa Diodati, their host read aloud from a book of ghost stories and suggested that each of them write one. Listening to Shelley and Byron speak of Erasmus Darwin's experiments in creating life, Mary conceived a vision of a monster made by man and dedicated to evil. Although horrified by the idea, the next day she began to write down her vision. At the end of the summer, the Shelleys returned to England and Mary completed what was to become her best-known work, *Frankenstein,* which she subtitled *The Modern Prometheus.*

A [

Back in England, she gave birth to a third child, a daughter Clara, and began creating a household in their first attempt at an extended residence. But distress and sadness followed. In October, Mary's half-sister on her mother's side, Fanny Imlay, committed suicide. Two months later, Shelley's wife Harriet killed herself by drowning. Percy and Mary were now free to marry, which they did in December 1816.

Condemned for his scandalous behavior by the Lord Chancellor (who also disliked Shelley's political views), and denied custody of his children with Harriet, Shelley fled England. He and Mary, with their servants, children, and Claire and Claire's infant, set off for Italy. *Frankenstein* was published anonymously in early 1818.

B [

Over the next four years, the Shelleys and the ever-present Claire lived and traveled in Italy, enjoying a small circle of friends, the beautiful, historic towns and villages where they lived, and the sensuous Italian landscape—a productive environment in which to write. Mary finished a second novel, *Valperga* (1823), and sent it off to her importunate father to arrange its publication and keep the profits for himself.

But her relationship with Percy was shaken by the deaths of both their children. Mary withdrew into herself, and Percy turned to others for companionship. Another son, Percy Florence, was born in November 1819, and lived to be a comfort to his mother in her later years. But for the most part, Mary struggled during these years to keep her domestic life together.

On July 1, 1822, Percy drowned when his boat capsized in a storm in the Gulf of Spezia. Sixteen years later, in her journal, Mary summarized the effect of this loss on her life: "I was left alone. . . . My total friendlessness, my horror of pushing, and inability to put myself forward unless led, cherished, and supported—all this . . . sunk me in a state of loneliness no other human being ever before, I believe, endured—except Robinson Crusoe." One might add that Mary herself had painted an even more overwhelming portrait of loneliness and isolation in her most famous work, *Frankenstein.*

The eight years between her elopement with Percy and his death, when she was only twenty-four, in some ways must have seemed a lifetime for Mary. In her intellectual and emotional openness to life, she had lived in tune with the extraordinary expectations she felt as the daughter and wife of such forceful persons. She returned to England with her child and devoted her life to his care and education, to the dissemination of her husband's work, and to her own writing. It was not until old Sir Timothy Shelley died in 1844 that her financial situation, and that of her son as well, was secure.

While Percy was alive, Mary had faithfully, and with no small cost to her own work, performed the task of fair copying his works. After his death, she edited and saw to publication much of what we now regard as his most important creations, works which were not published during his lifetime. She herself published five novels, over twenty short fictional works, and several travel books. In comparison with her early adult years, the remainder of Mary Shelley's life was uneventful and calm.

PREPARATION

1. BUILDING ON PRIOR KNOWLEDGE. More than twenty-eight movies and television plays related to *Frankenstein* have been produced since 1910. Have students tell about any they have seen. Note that ever since *The Bride of Frankenstein*, a 1935 sequel to the 1931 movie with Boris Karloff as the monster, the name Frankenstein has been mistakenly used for the Monster rather than for his creator.

Have students discuss some ways in which modern scientists have created or altered life forms. (Such techniques include genetic engineering, resulting in altered animal and plant forms, and hybridization of food plants and decorative plants, resulting in better crops and more beautiful foliage and flowers.)

2. ESTABLISHING A PURPOSE. Have students read to discover what Mary Shelley seems to be saying about the role of the scientist and the origin of evil.

FROM **FRANKENSTEIN**

Though you might have seen the Hollywood movie *Frankenstein*, you will find that the movie differs from Shelley's novel. In Shelley's story, the narrator is Dr. Frankenstein, a scientist. In this extract, the doctor narrates the history of his "filthy creation."

From
Chapter IV

One of the phenomena which had peculiarly attracted my attention was the structure of the human frame, and, indeed, any animal endued with life. Whence, I often asked myself, did the principle of life proceed? It was a bold question, and one which has ever been considered as a mystery. Yet with how many things are we upon the brink of becoming acquainted, if cowardice or carelessness did not restrain our inquiries. I revolved these circumstances in my mind, and determined thenceforth to apply myself more particularly to those branches of natural philosophy which relate to physiology. Unless I had been animated by an almost supernatural enthusiasm, my application to this study would have been irksome, and almost intolerable. To examine the causes of life, we must first have recourse to death. I became acquainted with the science of anatomy, but this was not sufficient. I must also observe the natural decay and corruption of the human body. In my education my father had taken the greatest precautions that my mind should be impressed with no supernatural horrors. I do not ever remember to have trembled at a tale of superstition, or to have feared the apparition of a spirit. Darkness had no effect upon my fancy and a churchyard was to me merely the receptacle of bodies deprived of life, which, from being the seat of beauty and strength, had become food for the worm. Now I was led to examine the cause and progress of this decay, and forced to spend days and nights in vaults and charnel houses. My attention was fixed upon every object the most insupportable to the delicacy of the human feelings. I saw how the fine form of man was degraded and wasted. I beheld the corruption of death succeed to the blooming cheek of life. I saw how the worm inherited the wonders of the eye and brain. I paused, examining and analyzing all the minutiae of causation, as exemplified in the change from life to death, and death to life, until from the midst of this darkness a sudden light broke in upon me— a light so brilliant and wondrous, yet so simple, that while I became dizzy with the immensity of the prospect which it illustrated, I was surprised, that among so many men of genius who had directed their inquiries toward the same science, that I alone should be reserved to discover so astonishing a secret.

Remember, I am not recording the vision of a madman. The sun does not more certainly shine in the heavens, than that which I now affirm is true. Some miracle might have produced it, yet the stages of the discovery were distinct and probable. After days and nights of incredible labor and fatigue, I succeeded in discovering the cause of generation and life. Nay, more. I became myself capable of bestowing animation upon lifeless matter.

The astonishment which I had at first experienced on this discovery soon gave place to delight and rapture. After so much time spent in painful labor, to arrive at once at the summit of my desires was the most gratifying consummation of my toils. But this discovery was so great and overwhelming that all the steps by which I had been progressively led to it were obliterated, and I beheld only the result. What had been the study and desire of the wisest men since the creation of the world was now within my grasp. Not that, like a magic scene, it all opened upon me at once. The information I had obtained was of a nature rather to direct my endeavors so soon as I should point them toward the object of my search, than to exhibit that object already accomplished. I was like the Arabian who had been buried with the dead[1] and found a pas-

---

1. **Arabian . . . dead:** from "The Fourth Voyage of Sindbad the Sailor," in *The Thousand and One Nights*.

A. Theme
❓ What does Frankenstein set out to discover? (The principle of life) Why is this "a bold question"? (Many would say it is a question humans should not ask: that life comes from God.)

B. Connotation
Note that *supernatural* appears twice in this paragraph.
❓ What other details create an otherworldly mood? (Death, superstition, spirit, darkness, bodies, nights in graveyards, and so on)

C. Plot
❓ What exactly does Frankenstein discover? (The ability to create life)

SUPPLEMENTARY SUPPORT MATERIALS
1. Vocabulary Activity Worksheet (*CCB*)
2. Review and Response Worksheet: Theme (*CCB*)
3. Language Skills Worksheet: Varying Sentence Length; Revision Worksheet 3 (*CCB*)
4. Selection Test (*CCB*)

DEVELOPING VOCABULARY
The following words from the novel are tested in the Selection Test. (See also Vocabulary Activity Worksheet.)

minutiae	alloy
to obliterate	lassitude
insensible	to palpitate
to disquiet	

The Gothic Novel
The word *Gothic* (literally, of the Goths, a medieval Germanic people) was originally applied to architecture, specifically to those huge, atmospheric medieval cathedrals with their glowing stained glass, pointed arches, and gargoyles. Gothic novels have an atmosphere of mystery and use elements of the supernatural. *Frankenstein* is a classic example.

A. Allusion
According to the custom of the land in which he finds himself, Sindbad is buried alive in a large underground cave when his wife dies. He sustains himself by taking food from the newly arrived bereaved spouses, but eventually escapes by following a dim light at the end of a long passage.

B. Details
The author, a teenager untrained in science, does not even try to give details of Frankenstein's "secret."

C. Theme
Here is a direct statement of Shelley's theme.

Boris Karloff in the 1931 movie of *Frankenstein*.

A sage to life, aided only by one glimmering, and seemingly ineffectual, light.

I see by your eagerness, and the wonder and hope which your eyes express, my friend, that you expect to be informed of the secret with which B I am acquainted. That cannot be. Listen patiently until the end of my story, and you will easily perceive why I am reserved upon that subject. I will not lead you on, unguarded and ardent as I then was, to your destruction and infallible misery. Learn from me, if not by my precepts, at least by my example, how dangerous is the acquirement of knowledge, and how much happier that man is C who believes his native town to be the world, than he who aspires to become greater than his nature will allow.

When I found so astonishing a power placed within my hands, I hesitated a long time concerning the manner in which I should employ it. Although I possessed the capacity of bestowing animation, yet to prepare a frame for the reception of it, with all its intricacies of fibers, muscles, and veins, still remained a work of inconceivable difficulty and labor. I doubted at first whether I should attempt the creation of a being like myself, or one of simpler organization, but my imagination was too much exalted by my first success to permit me to doubt of my ability to give life to an animal as complex and wonderful as man. The materials at present within my command hardly appeared adequate to so arduous an undertaking, but I doubted not that I should ultimately succeed. I prepared myself for a multitude of reverses. My operations might be incessantly baffled, and at last my work be imperfect. Yet, when I considered the improvement which every day takes place in science and mechanics, I was encouraged to hope my present attempts would at least lay the foundations of future success. Nor could I consider the magnitude and complexity of my plan as any argument of its impracticability. It was with these feelings that I began the creation of a human

Theme

In their introduction to the Everyman edition of *Frankenstein*, R. E. Dowse and D. J. Palmer identify "the central theme of the fable [*Frankenstein*]: that man's desire to understand and control the world around him is conditioned by his inability to understand and control himself. The precondition of rational and scientific exploration is the creative imagination, and, as in all romantic writing, this is a moral issue." The novel as a whole, they go on to say, deals with the Romantic hero in quest of his own soul.

being. As the minuteness of the parts formed a great hindrance to my speed, I resolved, contrary to my first intention, to make the being of a gigantic stature. That is to say, about eight feet in height, and proportionally large. After having formed this determination, and having spent some months in successfully collecting and arranging my materials, I began.

No one can conceive the variety of feelings which bore me onward, like a hurricane, in the first enthusiasm of success. Life and death appeared to me ideal bounds, which I should first break through, and pour a torrent of light into our dark world. A new species would bless me as its creator and source. Many happy and excellent natures would owe their being to me. No father could claim the gratitude of his child so completely as I should deserve theirs. Pursuing these reflections, I thought, that if I could bestow animation upon lifeless matter, I might in process of time (although I now found it impossible) renew life where death had apparently devoted the body to corruption.

These thoughts supported my spirits, while I pursued my undertaking with unremitting ardor. My cheek had grown pale with study, and my person had become emaciated with confinement. Sometimes, on the very brink of certainty, I failed. Yet still I clung to the hope which the next day or the next hour might realize. One secret which I alone possessed was the hope to which I had dedicated myself, and the moon gazed on my midnight labors, while, with unrelaxed and breathless eagerness, I pursued nature at her hiding places. Who shall conceive the horrors of my secret toil, as I dabbled among the unhallowed damps of the grave or tortured the living animal to animate the lifeless clay? My limbs now tremble and my eyes swim with the remembrance, but then a resistless, and almost frantic, impulse urged me forward. I seemed to have lost all soul or sensation but for this one pursuit. It was indeed but a passing trance that only made me feel with renewed acuteness so soon as, the unnatural stimulus ceasing to operate, I had returned to my old habits. I collected bones from charnel houses and disturbed, with profane fingers, the tremendous secrets of the human frame. In a solitary chamber, or rather cell, at the top of the house, and separated from all the other apartments by a gallery and staircase, I kept my workshop of filthy creation. My eyeballs were starting from their sockets in attending to the details of my employment. The dissecting room and the slaughterhouse furnished many of my materials and often did my human nature turn with loathing from my occupation, while still urged on by an eagerness which perpetually increased, I brought my work near to a conclusion.

The summer months passed while I was thus engaged, heart and soul, in one pursuit. It was a most beautiful season. Never did the fields bestow a more plentiful harvest, or the vines yield a more luxuriant vintage. But my eyes were insensible to the charms of nature. And the same feelings which made me neglect the scenes around me caused me also to forget those friends who were so many miles absent, and whom I had not seen for so long a time. I knew my silence disquieted them and I well remembered the words of my father. "I know that while you are pleased with yourself, you will think of us with affection and we shall hear regularly from you. You must pardon me if I regard any interruption in your correspondence as a proof that your other duties are equally neglected."

I knew well, therefore, what would be my father's feelings, but I could not tear my thoughts from my employment, loathsome in itself, but which had taken an irresistible hold of my imagination. I wished, as it were, to procrastinate all that related to my feelings of affection until the great object, which swallowed up every habit of my nature, should be completed.

I then thought that my father would be unjust if he ascribed my neglect to vice, or faultiness on my part, but I am now convinced that he was justified in conceiving that I should not be altogether free from blame. A human being in perfection ought always to preserve a calm and peaceful mind, and never to allow passion or a transitory desire to disturb his tranquillity. I do not think that the pursuit of knowledge is an exception to this rule. If the study to which you apply yourself has a tendency to weaken your affections, and to destroy your taste for those simple pleasures in which no alloy can possibly mix, then that study is certainly unlawful, that is to say, not befitting the human mind. If this rule were always observed, if no man allowed any pursuit whatsoever to interfere with the tranquillity of his domestic affections, Greece had not been enslaved, Caesar would have spared his country, America would have been discovered more gradually, and the empires of Mexico and Peru had not been destroyed.

A. Character
Frankenstein is guilty of *hubris* (overweening pride), the character flaw of many heroes in ancient Greek tragedies.

B. Details
Note the writer's powerful suggestion. She does not describe the horrors in detail, but rather leaves them to the reader's imagination.

C. Diction
Filthy is the perfect word here; try to substitute others.

D. Imagery
Note the strong contrast between nature and the speaker's work.

E. Theme
Again, Shelley is being didactic and stating her theme directly.

READING CHECK TEST

1. Frankenstein is a scientist. (T)
2. Frankenstein wanted to discover the cause of life and perhaps in time bring the dead to life. (T)
3. Frankenstein was in league with Satan. (F)

4. Even though his creature was ugly, Frankenstein loved it. (F)
5. Frankenstein immediately kills his creation. (F)

ANALYZING THE NOVEL
Identifying Facts

1. First he studied anatomy, and then he studied the natural decay of the human body after death.
2. He wants to give life to the inanimate.
   He hesitates because of the difficulties in preparing a suitable "frame" to animate.
   He decides, at last, to create a man

A. Character

Victor is only twenty years old. Does this surprise you? Explain. (Many will say they are surprised that one so young can be so dedicated.)

B. Character

Note how the narrator has changed.

C. Expansion

This is the first sentence Shelley wrote when she began her novel.

D. Symbolism

Elizabeth is the narrator's fiancée; Ingolstadt is the German town in which Frankenstein is experimenting.

What do you think this dream means? (Students will provide their own interpretations that suggest the narrator's experiments have hurt him.)

E. Interpreting

What do you think the monster wants? (Perhaps he only wants to chat.)

CLOSURE

Ask three students to (1) identify who Frankenstein is, (2) describe what he created and why, and (3) explain the main idea in this part of the story.

But I forget that I am moralizing in the most interesting part of my tale and your looks remind me to proceed.

My father made no reproach in his letters and only took notice of my silence by inquiring into my occupations more particularly than before. Winter, spring, and summer passed away during my labors, but I did not watch the blossom or the expanding leaves—sights which before always yielded me supreme delight—so deeply was I engrossed in my occupation. The leaves of that year had withered before my work drew near to a close and now every day showed me more plainly how well I had succeeded. But my enthusiasm was checked by my anxiety, and I appeared rather like one doomed by slavery to toil in the mines, or any other unwholesome trade, than an artist occupied by his favorite employment. Every night I was oppressed by a slow fever, and I became nervous to a most painful degree. The fall of a leaf startled me, and I shunned my fellow creatures as if I had been guilty of a crime. Sometimes I grew alarmed at the wreck I perceived that I had become. The energy of my purpose alone sustained me. My labors would soon end, and I believed that exercise and amusement would then drive away incipient disease. I promised myself both of these when my creation should be complete.

From
Chapter V

It was on a dreary night of November that I beheld the accomplishment of my toils. With an anxiety that almost amounted to agony, I collected the instruments of life around me, that I might infuse a spark of being into the lifeless thing that lay at my feet. It was already one in the morning. The rain pattered dismally against the panes and my candle was nearly burned out, when, by the glimmer of the half-extinguished light, I saw the dull yellow eye of the creature open. It breathed hard and a convulsive motion agitated its limbs.

How can I describe my emotions at this catastrophe, or how delineate the wretch whom with such infinite pains and care I had endeavored to form? His limbs were in proportion, and I had selected his features as beautiful. Beautiful! Great God! His yellow skin scarcely covered the work of muscles and arteries beneath. His hair was of a lustrous black, and flowing. His teeth of a pearly whiteness. But these luxuriances only formed a more horrid contrast with his watery eyes, that seemed almost of the same color as the dun white sockets in which they were set, his shriveled complexion and straight black lips.

The different accidents of life are not so changeable as the feelings of human nature. I had worked hard for nearly two years, for the sole purpose of infusing life into an inanimate body. For this I had deprived myself of rest and health. I had desired it with an ardor that far exceeded moderation, but now that I had finished, the beauty of the dream vanished, and breathless horror and disgust filled my heart. Unable to endure the aspect of the being I had created, I rushed out of the room, and continued a long time traversing my bedchamber, unable to compose my mind to sleep. At length lassitude succeeded to the tumult I had before endured and I threw myself on the bed in my clothes, endeavoring to seek a few moments of forgetfulness. But it was in vain. I slept, indeed, but I was disturbed by the wildest dreams. I thought I saw Elizabeth, in the bloom of health, walking in the streets of Ingolstadt. Delighted and surprised, I embraced her, but as I imprinted the first kiss on her lips, they became livid with the hue of death, her features appeared to change, and I thought that I held the corpse of my dead mother in my arms. A shroud enveloped her form, and I saw the grave worms crawling in the folds of the flannel. I started from my sleep with horror. A cold dew covered my forehead, my teeth chattered and every limb became convulsed. When, by the dim and yellow light of the moon, as it forced its way through the window shutters, I beheld the wretch—the miserable monster whom I had created. He held up the curtain of the bed and his eyes, if eyes they may be called, were fixed on me. His jaws opened, and he muttered some inarticulate sounds, while a grin wrinkled his cheeks. He might have spoken, but I did not hear. One hand was stretched out, seemingly to detain me, but I escaped and rushed downstairs. I took refuge in the courtyard belonging to the house which I inhabited, where I remained during the rest of the night walking up and down in the greatest agitation, listening attentively, catching and fearing each sound as if it were to announce the approach of the demoniacal corpse to which I had so miserably given life.

Oh! no mortal could support the horror of that countenance. A mummy again endued with ani-because he is convinced of his ultimate success.

3. He becomes pale, thin, sickly, and extremely nervous.

4. He is horrified. He runs out of the room and paces in his bedroom.

5. His skin is yellow; his hair is black; his teeth are "pearly" white. His eyes are watery; his skin is shriveled; his lips are black. He makes inarticulate noises, grins, and stretches out his hand to Frankenstein.

6. Frankenstein is frantically walking through the streets, afraid that his creation might appear.

Interpreting Meanings

7. Students' answers will vary. One striking element of Frankenstein's behavior is his growing sense of autonomy, which parallels his delight in viewing himself as the omnipotent creator. Mad and morbid do not necessarily describe him at all. Studying the human body—even the decaying body—is not morbid; it is essential in advancing scientific knowledge of living creatures. It is through this knowledge that Frankenstein actually does create life.

He is not necessarily mad at all; he is living out the fantasy of many men—to assume women's natural power of giving birth. And, godlike, he hopes to create his own species.

8. Answers will vary. Frankenstein expects to feel thrilled, joyous, and powerful.

Shelley was perhaps exploring our desire for power over life itself and our ultimate fear of that power. She may also have been expressing the disappointment that occurs when something fantasized becomes real.

---

mation could not be so hideous as that wretch. I had gazed on him while unfinished. He was ugly then, but when those muscles and joints were rendered capable of motion, it became a thing such as even Dante[2] could not have conceived.

I passed the night wretchedly. Sometimes my pulse beat so quickly and hardly that I felt the palpitation of every artery. At others, I nearly sank to the ground through languor and extreme weakness. Mingled with this horror, I felt the bitterness of disappointment. Dreams that had been my food and pleasant rest for so long a space were now becoming a hell to me. And the change was so rapid, the overthrow so complete!

Morning, dismal and wet, at length dawned, and discovered to my sleepless and aching eyes the church of Ingolstadt, its white steeple and clock, which indicated the sixth hour. The porter opened the gates of my court, which had that night been my asylum, and I ran into the streets, pacing them with quick steps, as if I sought to avoid the wretch whom I feared every turn of the street would present to my view. I did not dare return to the apartment which I inhabited, but felt impelled to hurry on, although drenched by the rain which poured from a black and comfortless sky.

I continued walking in this manner for some time, endeavoring, by bodily exercise, to ease the load that weighed upon my mind. I traversed the streets, without any clear conception of where I was, or what I was doing. My heart palpitated in the sickness of fear and I hurried on with irregular steps, not daring to look about me.

"Like one who, on a lonely road,
  Doth walk in fear and dread,
And, having once turned round, walks on,
  And turns no more his head;
Because he knows a frightful fiend
  Doth close behind him tread."[3]

---

2. **Dante:** Italian poet Dante Alighieri (1265–1321), author of *The Divine Comedy.* Shelley is here alluding to the part of the epic set in Hell.

3. From *The Rime of the Ancient Mariner,* by English poet Samuel Taylor Coleridge (1772–1834).

Responding to the Novel

Analyzing the Novel

Identifying Facts

1. Summarize the overall steps that Frankenstein took in order to discover the secret of human life.
2. Once Frankenstein has gained his knowledge, what does he want to do with it? Why does he hesitate? What finally moves him to carry out his plan?
3. Describe how Frankenstein changes physically during the two years he works on his creation.
4. What is Frankenstein's first response as the monster begins to breathe? Describe his next response.
5. What does Frankenstein's monster look like? Describe how it moves, talks, etc.
6. Briefly describe the scene that is taking place as the selection ends.

Interpreting Meanings

7. Frankenstein begins his study with the rational curiosity of a scientist. However, as his project develops, Frankenstein's motives and behavior change. Explain whether you believe his behavior warrants the adjectives "mad" or "morbid."
8. What feeling does Frankenstein expect to be left with when his creation comes alive? What do you think Shelley was trying to express about human nature?

Writing About the Novel

A Creative Response

1. **Extending the Story.** In two or three paragraphs, describe at least two possible ways Dr. Frankenstein's story might end.

A Critical Response

2. **Identifying a Theme.** In a brief essay, and based only on the fragment of the story you've just read, explain what theme you think Shelley is revealing in this story about the creation of life in a laboratory. Take into consideration her subtitle: *The Modern Prometheus.* (Who was Prometheus? What did he have to do with the creation of life? How did he suffer?)

A. Expansion
Nevertheless, she read Chaucer, Shakespeare, and Spenser. A typical journal entry (November 24, 1801) reads as follows: "I read a little of Chaucer, prepared the goose for dinner, and then we all walked out."

B. Expansion
In a letter to a friend, Dorothy wrote, "I have not those powers which Coleridge thinks I have—I know it. My only merits are my devotedness to those I love and I hope a charity toward all mankind."

C. Expansion
Relatives felt that a young girl could not properly be raised in an all-male household.

D. About the Drawing
This portrait was done by Samuel Crosthwaite in 1833, when Dorothy was sixty-two years old.

E. Expansion
Dorothy may have had something like Alzheimer's disease. She made strange noises and was given to violence, rages, and obscenities.

Dorothy Wordsworth (1771–1855)

William Wordsworth's depiction of his sister in "Tintern Abbey" as someone "I was once" refers to the shadow of his fame, which obscured Dorothy Wordsworth's own literary achievements. Dorothy Wordsworth had her own special eye for things and her own voice to express them. Readers of Wordsworth and Coleridge have long known that the lives and works of the two poets were strongly influenced by Dorothy Wordsworth's presence, but her writings occupy only a minor place in the history of the Romantic Period.

As a woman, she was not provided with the education most of the male writers of the age received. Her literary art is expressed in forms—journals and letters—not considered "publishable" in the ways that the work of her female contemporaries—Mary Wollstonecraft Shelley, Jane Austen, or Charlotte Brontë—found an audience. Like Mary Shelley, Dorothy Wordsworth often spent more time transcribing the manuscripts of the male writer in the household than she spent on her own. The writing that she did leave for us has, unfortunately, often been treated only as source material for the study of Wordsworth and Coleridge.

The spare details of Dorothy Wordsworth's life may be enriched by a fuller reading of her letters, journals, and other works, but they are mainly defined by the bold outlines of the life of her brother. She was born on Christmas Day, 1771, less than two years after her brother, and she was the only girl of the five Wordsworth children. When she was seven, her mother died and she was separated from her brothers and moved from relative to relative until, at the age of 24, she was reunited with William. Their long life together began in a little cottage in Dorsetshire. Two years later they were living near Coleridge in Somerset, and it was during this period that the bond between the three friends was formed, and their mutual influence was strongest. After the brief excursion to Germany financed by the sale of *Lyrical Ballads*, Dorothy and William returned to their native Lake District in May 1799, and took up residence in a cottage in Grasmere. Dorothy's relationship with William was, of course, changed, though not radically, by his marriage in 1802 to Mary Hutchinson, Dorothy's long-time friend. She continued to be part of their growing family through several relocations within the Lake District.

In 1836, she was stricken with an illness which made her an invalid and sadly altered her loving and placid temperament. Once so vigorous and adventurous, Dorothy Wordsworth spent the last twenty years of her life being cared for by others, including William, whom she outlived by five years. Ironically, her brother was reluctant to proceed finally with the publication of her journal of the Scottish tour (1803) because he did not wish to call public attention to her illness. It has therefore been the special pleasure of twentieth-century readers to discover in her now-published work, Dorothy Wordsworth's eye and voice. They remain for us, not simply as reminders of the "former" pleasures of her brother, but more truly as revealing "gleams / Of past existence" which are Dorothy Wordsworth's own.

1. BUILDING ON PRIOR KNOWLEDGE. The journal excerpts in the text give Dorothy Wordsworth's perspective on one experience that inspired her brother's poem "I Wandered Lonely as a Cloud" (text page 642). You may wish to have students re-read the poem quickly before beginning Dorothy's journal entries.

2. ESTABLISHING A PURPOSE. Ask students to read the entries to find the ways Wordsworth describes her daily life and her feelings.

SUPPLEMENTARY SUPPORT MATERIALS
1. Review and Response Worksheet: Analyzing the Journals (*CCB*)
2. Language Skills Worksheet: Transitional Expressions (*CCB*)
3. Selection Test (*CCB*)

A

FROM THE JOURNALS

Dorothy Wordsworth's special gift was for the delicate and patient rendering of the things that "matter" in everyday life. The daffodils in the first excerpt are the same ones William describes in "I Wandered Lonely as a Cloud." The text reproduces the writer's unorthodox punctuation.

Thursday, April 15th, 1802. It was a threatening misty morning—but mild. We set off after dinner from Eusemere. Mrs. Clarkson went a short way with us but turned back. The wind was furious and we thought we must have returned. We first rested in the large boathouse, then under a furze bush opposite Mr. Clarkson's. Saw the plow going in the field. The wind seized our breath the lake was rough. There was a boat by itself floating in the middle of the bay below Water Millock. We rested again in the Water Millock Lane. The hawthorns are black and green, the birches here and there greenish but there is yet more of purple to be seen on the twigs. We got over into a field to avoid some cows—people working, a few primroses by the roadside, woodsorrel flower, the anemone, scentless violets, strawberries, and that starry yellow flower which Mrs. C. calls pile wort. When we were in the woods beyond Gowbarrow Park we saw a few daffodils close to the water side. We fancied that the lake had floated the seeds ashore and that the little colony had so sprung up. But as we went along there were more and yet more and at last under the boughs of the trees, we saw that there was a long belt of them along the shore, about the breadth of a country turnpike road. I never saw daffodils so beautiful they grew among the mossy stones about and about them, some rested their heads upon these stones as on a pillow for weariness and the rest tossed and reeled and danced and seemed as if they verily laughed with the wind that blew upon them over the lake, they looked so gay ever glancing ever changing. This wind blew directly over the lake to them. There was here and there a little knot and a few stragglers a few yards higher up but they were so few as not to disturb the simplicity and unity and life of that one busy highway. . . . Rain came on—we were wet when we reached Luffs but we called in.

B

Luckily all was cheerless and gloomy so we faced the storm—we *must* have been wet if we had waited—put on dry clothes at Dobson's. I was very kindly treated by a young woman, the landlady looked sour but it is her way. She gave us a goodish supper. Excellent ham and potatoes. We paid 7/ when we came away. William was sitting by a bright fire when I came downstairs. . . . We had a glass of warm rum and water. We enjoyed ourselves and wished for Mary. . . .

C

September 24th, 1802. Mary first met us in the avenue. She looked so fat and well that we were made very happy by the sight of her. Then came Sara, and last of all Joanna. Tom was forking corn standing upon the corn cart. We dressed ourselves immediately and got tea—the garden looked gay with asters and sweet peas. I looked at everything with tranquillity and happiness—was ill on Saturday and on Sunday and continued to be during most of the time of our stay. Jack and George came on Friday Evening 1st October. On Saturday 2nd we rode to Hackness, William Jack George and Sara single, I behind Tom. On Sunday 3rd Mary and Sara were busy packing. On Monday 4th October 1802, my Brother William was married to Mary Hutchinson. I slept a good deal of the night and rose fresh and well in the morning. At a little after 8 o'clock I saw them go down the avenue towards the church. William had parted from me upstairs. I gave him the wedding ring—with how deep a blessing! I took it from my forefinger where I had worn it the whole of the night before—he slipped it again onto my finger and blessed me fervently. When they were absent my dear little Sara prepared the breakfast. I kept myself as quiet as I could, but when I saw the two men running up the walk, coming to tell us it was over, I could stand it no longer and threw myself on the bed where I lay in stillness, neither hearing or seeing anything, till Sara came upstairs to me

D

A. Expansion
The first two excerpts are from Dorothy Wordsworth's *Grasmere Journal* (1800–1803), which she began when she was twenty-eight. The excerpt on text page 750 is from her *Recollections of a Tour Made in Scotland* (1803).

B. Connections
See "I Wandered Lonely as a Cloud," text page 642.

C. Expansion
This is Mary Hutchinson, Dorothy Wordsworth's dear childhood friend and her brother William's future wife.

D. Responding
❓ Dorothy, who was thirty-two years old at the time, did not attend William's wedding. What do you suppose she is feeling here? Are several interpretations possible? (Yes, she may be feeling happy, sad, or merely anxious, among other emotions.)

READING CHECK TEST
1. Dorothy Wordsworth describes the daffodils as dancing. (T)
2. She joyfully attended her brother's wedding to Mary Hutchinson. (F)
3. She describes her envy of Mary Hutchinson. (F)
4. The Wordsworths disliked their trip to Loch Lomond. (F)
5. The author's experiences in Scotland left her with favorable impressions. (T)

CLOSURE
Have students provide three examples showing how Dorothy Wordsworth's keen powers of observation are manifested in her writing.

A. Connections
Compare this experience to "The Solitary Reaper" (text page 645). (Students may mention that in "The Solitary Reaper" there was only *one* girl, the reaper, and that she did not talk to, in fact was not even aware of, the speaker of the poem.) Wordsworth's poem written about this experience on August 28, 1803, is called "The Highland Girl."

B. Expansion
Erse, a Scottish form of Gaelic, could not be understood by these speakers of English. William Wordsworth asks in "The Solitary Reaper," "Will no one tell me what she sings?"

C. Vocabulary
Sprigged means "flowered" (embroidering was called "sprigging"). Lindsey is a fabric made of cotton and wool.

and said "They are coming." This forced me from the bed where I lay and I moved I knew not how straight forward, faster than my strength could carry me till I met my beloved William and fell upon his bosom. He and John Hutchinson led me to the house and there I stayed to welcome my dear Mary. . . .

A **August 28th, 1803.** When beginning to descend the hill towards Loch Lomond, we overtook two girls, who told us we could not cross the ferry till evening, for the boat was gone with a number of people to church. One of the girls was exceedingly beautiful; and the figures of both of them, in gray plaids falling to their feet, their faces only being uncovered, excited our attention before we spoke to them; but they answered us so sweetly that we were quite delighted, at the same time that they stared at us with an innocent look of wonder. I think I never heard the English language sound more sweetly than from the mouth of the elder of these girls, while she stood at the gate answering our inquiries, her face flushed with the rain; her pronunciation was clear and distinct: without difficulty, yet slow, like that of a foreign speech. They told us we might sit in the ferry-house till the return of the boat, went in with us, and made a good fire as fast as possible to dry our wet clothes. We learnt that the taller was the sister of the ferryman, and had been left in charge with the house for the day, that the other was his wife's sister, and was come with her mother on a visit—an old woman, who sate in a corner beside the cradle, nursing her little grandchild. We were glad to be housed, with our feet upon a warm hearthstone; and our attendants were so active and good-humored that it was pleasant to have to desire them to do anything. The younger was a delicate and unhealthy-looking girl; but there was an uncommon meekness in her countenance, with an air of premature intelligence, which is often seen in sickly young persons. The other made me think of Peter Bell's Highland Girl:

> As light and beauteous as a squirrel,
> As beauteous and as wild!

She moved with unusual activity, which was chastened very delicately by a certain hesitation in her looks when she spoke, being able to understand us but imperfectly. They were both exceedingly desirous to get me what I wanted to make me comfortable. I was to have a gown and petticoat of the mistress's; so they turned out her whole wardrobe upon the parlor floor, talking Erse to **B** one another, and laughing all the time. It was long before they could decide which of the gowns I was to have; they chose at last, no doubt thinking that it was the best, a light-colored sprigged cotton, **C** with long sleeves, and they both laughed while I was putting it on, with the blue lindsey petticoat, and one or the other, or both together, helped me to dress, repeating at least half a dozen times, "You never had on the like of that before." They held a consultation of several minutes over a pair of coarse woollen stockings, gabbling Erse as fast as their tongues could move, and looked as if uncertain what to do: at last, with great diffidence, they offered them to me, adding, as before, that I had never worn "the like of them." When we entered the house we had been not a little glad to see a fowl stewing in barley-broth; and now when the wettest of our clothes were stripped off, began again to recollect that we were hungry, and asked if we could have dinner. "Oh yes, ye may get that," the elder replied, pointing to the pan on the fire.

. . . The hut was after the Highland fashion, but without anything beautiful except its situation; the floor was rough, and wet with the rain that came in at the door, so that the lasses' bare feet were as wet as if they had been walking through street puddles, in passing from one room to another; the windows were open, as at the other hut; but the kitchen had a bed in it, and was much smaller, and the shape of the house was like that of a common English cottage, without its comfort; yet there was no appearance of poverty—indeed, quite the contrary. The peep out of the open door-place across the lake made some amends for the want of the long roof and elegant rafters of our boatman's cottage, and all the while the waterfall, which we could not see, was roaring at the end of the hut, which seemed to serve as a sounding-board for its noise, so that it was not unlike sitting in a house where a mill is going. The dashing of the waves against the shore could not be distinguished; yet in spite of my knowledge of this I could not help fancying that the tumult and storm came from the lake, and went out several times to see if it was possible to row over in safety.

After long waiting we grew impatient for our dinner; at last the pan was taken off, and carried into the other room; but we had to wait at least another half hour before the ceremony of dishing up was completed; yet with all this bustle and

ANALYZING THE JOURNAL
Identifying Facts
1. The two saw an amazing quantity of daffodils.
   She uses personification.
2. She stayed quietly at home—apparently in a state of mixed emotions.

Interpreting Meanings
3. The speaker seems Romantic in spirit. She becomes involved with what she observes in nature, and there is an emotional content to her descriptions. On the morning of April 15th, for example, the wind is "furious." She uses a great deal of personification, which reflects her imaginative desire to "humanize" nature.
4. The entries suggest that she was extremely close to her brother.
   It seems that she had mixed emotions over her brother's marriage, though we can only conjecture what her real feelings were. She certainly loved his wife.
5. They have open hearths, wear sprigged cotton dresses and lindsey petticoats and coarse woolen stockings. They eat chicken stewing in barley broth. Their houses are not beautiful: rough floor that was wet from rain, bed in kitchen. They entertain in a "parlor."

difficulty, the manner in which they (and particularly the elder of the girls) performed everything, was perfectly graceful. . . .

The hospitality we had met with at the two cottages and Mr. Macfarlane's gave us very favorable impressions on this our first entrance into the Highlands, and at this day the innocent merriment of the girls, with their kindness to us, and the beautiful figure and face of the elder, come to my mind whenever I think of the ferryhouse and waterfall of Loch Lomond, and I never think of the two girls but the whole image of that romantic spot is before me, a living image, as it will be to my dying day. The following poem was written by Wm. not long after our return from Scotland:

Sweet Highland Girl, a very shower
Of beauty is thy earthly dower!

Responding to the Journal

Analyzing the Journal

Identifying Facts

1. What did William and Dorothy see on April 15, 1802, in the woods beyond Gowbarrow Park? What **figures of speech** does Dorothy Wordsworth use to describe the sight?
2. Tell what Dorothy did as her brother was married to Mary Hutchinson.

Interpreting Meanings

3. Describe the writer's attitude toward what she observes in nature. Does she seem "Romantic" in spirit, or more like an objective observer? Explain your answer with specific references to the journal entries.

4. What do Dorothy Wordsworth's entries on the day of William's wedding suggest about her relationship with her brother? What do you think her emotions were as her brother was married?
5. What do these journal entries reveal to you about life in eighteenth-century England? In the Highlands?

Writing About the Journal

A Critical Response

Comparing the Journal to the Poem. In a brief essay, explain how you think Dorothy Wordsworth's journal can illuminate "I Wandered Lonely as a Cloud." Are there any passages in the journals that make you wonder how much of William's poetry was also Dorothy's?

Primary Sources
Dorothy Wordsworth Describes Coleridge

A This letter was written to the woman who would later become William's wife. She was Dorothy's closest and life-long friend. Coleridge, by the way, returned Dorothy's admiration.

Racedown, June, 1797
". . . You had a great loss in not seeing Coleridge. He is a wonderful man. His conversation teems with soul, mind, and spirit. Then he is so benevolent, so good tempered and cheerful, and, like William, interests himself so much about every little trifle. At first I thought him very plain, that is, for about three minutes: he is pale and thin, has a wide mouth, thick lips, and not very good teeth, longish loose-growing half-curling rough black hair. But if you hear him speak for five minutes you think no more of them. His eye is large and full, not dark but gray; such an eye as would receive from a heavy soul the dullest expression; but it speaks every emotion of his animated mind; it has more of the 'poet's eye in a fine frenzy rolling' than I ever witnessed. He has fine dark eyebrows, and an overhangng forehead. . . ."

A. Comment from Coleridge
In July 1797 Coleridge had known Dorothy less than a month when he wrote:
   "Wordsworth and his exquisite sister are with me. She is a woman indeed!—in mind, I mean, and heart. . . . if you expected to see a pretty woman, you would think her ordinary; if you expected to find an ordinary woman, you would find her pretty!"

A. Connections
See, for example, Coleridge's "Kubla Khan" (text page 649) and Keats's "The Eve of St. Agnes" (text page 724).

B. Connections
Burns's best poetry is written in dialect. William and Dorothy Wordsworth both mention the Scottish language of the Highland people (see, for example, "The Solitary Reaper," text page 645).

C. Language
Students may be more familiar with the terms *levels of usage* and *formal* and *informal language*.

THE ENGLISH LANGUAGE
by John Algeo

Variety in Language

A William Wordsworth wrote a preface to *Lyrical Ballads* in which he talked about the kind of poetry he and Samuel Taylor Coleridge tried to produce, especially about its subjects and its language. He said that their subject matter was to be "incidents and situations from common life" and that their language was to be that "really used" by ordinary people. A twofold aspect of the Romantic movement was its fascination, on the one hand, with the exotic or mysterious—the East and the Middle Ages—and, on the other hand, with common, especially rural, life and customs, with earthiness, with simple people and their language.

B In Germany the brothers Jakob and Wilhelm Grimm collected the folk stories that we know as *Grimm's Fairy Tales* and also studied the dialects in which those stories had been told. The study of dialect was encouraged by a Romantic conviction that simple country life is better than complex city life. As a result, we often think of dialect as a form of language spoken by uneducated rural people. But in fact it is something much broader than that.

What Are Dialects?

We have already seen that language has many variations, many ways of saying the same thing. They all fall, however, into two broad types. On the one hand, we vary the way we use language according to the people we talk to (strangers or friends), where we talk (in a classroom, on a playing field, at home, in a disco), the subjects we talk about (the weather, dates, a car accident we had), whether we talk face-to-face or over the telephone, or if we are putting words on paper, whether we are writing a postcard, a diary, **C** a note, or a report. Such kinds of variation, by which we adapt our language to the circumstances around us, are called **registers.**

On the other hand, how we talk also depends on where we come from (Maine, California, Texas), what ethnic or social group we belong to, whether we are male or female, what education we have had, and how old we are. Such kinds of variation are not dependent on the special circumstance in which we find ourselves. They depend rather on *who* we are. They are called **dialects.**

Dialects, then, are the special way we have of using language, depending on the region and group we belong to. Everybody speaks in a dialect, or sometimes several dialects. There are regional dialects, ethnic dialects, class dialects, sex dialects, educational dialects, and age-group dialects. Dialects are the various forms in which a language exists, not some peculiar or quaint versions of it.

> "Everybody speaks in a dialect, or sometimes several dialects. There are regional dialects, ethnic dialects, class dialects, sex dialects, educational dialects, and age-group dialects."

A language is like ice cream; it comes in many flavors. If you want ice cream, you ask for chocolate, vanilla, butter pecan, peppermint, or a lot of other flavors. But it would make no sense to say, "I just want plain ice cream—none of those flavors, just the real stuff." Ice cream comes only in flavors; apart from its flavors, no ice cream exists. In the same way, a language comes only in the form of one dialect or another; apart from its dialects, no language exists.

Many of us think that the way we talk is real English, whereas the way others talk is some odd dialect. However, we all talk dialects, none intrinsically odder (or better) than any of the others. The more different someone else's speechways are from ours, however, the odder they are likely to seem to us. And conversely, the odder we will seem to them. But dialect is not just the way Snuffy Smith talks. We all speak some dialect.

How Odd You Should Say That

Dialects differ among themselves in the words they use, the way they pronounce words, and the way they put words together.

Depending on where you come from, a *porch* may be a *gallery*, *piazza*, *stoop*, or *veranda*. A *dragonfly* may be a *darning needle*, *mosquito hawk*, *snake doctor*, or *snake feeder*. *Pancakes* may be *batter cakes*, *flannel cakes*, *fritters*, *griddlecakes*, or *hotcakes*.

In most parts of the United States, *rubber band* is the term for an elastic loop that holds things together; but if you are from the Minneapolis–St. Paul area, you may call it a *rubber binder*. *Soft drink* is what most of us call a flavored carbonated beverage, though it may also be *soda*, *pop*, or *soda pop*; an old-fashioned term is *phosphate*. If you are from New England, you may call it *tonic*, which means something more specific ("quinine water") in the rest of the country.

Most Americans pronounce *fog*, *hog*, and *log* as *fawg*, *hawg*, and *lawg*, with the same vowel they use in *law*, *paw*, and *raw*. But they use a different vowel sound in *lock*, *pot*, and *top*. In parts of New York and the north central states, however, *fog*, *hog*, *log* have the same vowel as *lock*, *pot*, *top*, whereas *law*, *paw*, *raw* have a different sound. In eastern New England, and in western Pennsylvania and some places westward from there, including most of the Far West, all of those words may be pronounced with the same vowel (either an *aw*-like or an *ah*-like sound).

Those who come from the southern United States tend to pronounce *greasy* as *greazy*, whereas those from the northern part tend to make it sound like *greassy*. TV ads for dishwasher detergents generally use the northern pronunciation, which seems to be gaining ground. Some people, having heard both pronunciations, use them both, but may develop special meanings for the two ways of saying the word. They may think that *greassy* means literally "coated with grease," while using *greazy* as a metaphor meaning "untrustworthy, disagreeable." In this way two pronunciations of the same word may eventually turn into different words, as hap-

"A host? You call that a host! Why, back in the States . . ."

Cartoon by Mike Williams. © Punch. Courtesy Rothco.

> " **D**epending on where you come from, a *porch* may be a *gallery, piazza, stoop, or veranda.*"

A. **Dialect**
This point needs to be emphasized: No one dialect is "superior" to another. Though we teach students the rules of standard English for written language, we and they must remain open-minded to spoken language that is different from ours.

B. **Dialect**
❓ Which of the following terms do you use? (See also Analyzing Language activities on text page 756.) Students who have moved from region to region will probably find that they use the term from the region in which they grew up.

C. **Allusion**
❓ To which poem is the cartoonist alluding? (Wordsworth's "I Wandered Lonely as a Cloud")

You may wish to have students who are familiar with other languages give examples of words used for *you* singular and *you* plural. In some languages, there are even different words for the familiar form of *you*, which is addressed to family and close friends. (See the discussion of *thou/you* in Shakespeare on text page 358.)

B. Discussing the Cartoon

What is jargon? (It can be the specialized language of a group, such as computer users, short-order cooks, and sailors. Or it can refer to language that is incomprehensible gibberish, such as bureaucratic language or language used by people trying to seem more learned than they are.) What kind of jargon do you think is meant here? What attitude toward American English does the cartoon suggest? What is it making fun of? (Note: UK means "United Kingdom.")

> " **W**hether you are sick *to, at, in,* or *on* your stomach depends mainly on where you learned to talk. So also does how you tell time— whether you say a quarter *of, till,* or *to* the hour."

A

B

WHAT DO YOU WANT TO SAY?— I'LL TRANSLATE IT INTO JARGON FOR HIM

Cartoon by Colin Wheeler, Daily Telegraph, London. © Rothco.

pened long ago with *shade* and *shadow, of* and *off,* and *flour* and *flower.*

Prepositions are especially subject to dialect variation. Whether you are sick *to, at, in,* or *on* your stomach depends mainly on where you learned to talk. So also does how you tell time—whether you say a quarter *of, till,* or *to* the hour. In most of the United States, people stand *in line,* but in New York City, they stand *on line.* Most Americans, when they are not away, are *at home,* but some are *to home.*

For a long time English has had a problem with the second-person pronoun *you.* We make one word do double duty—for both the singular and the plural, for talking to one person and for talking to many. Some dialects, however, have tried to distinguish between the singular and plural forms. In certain parts of the North, especially in cities, some people say *youse* or *yuzz* for the plural; in the Appalachian Mountain region some people say *you'uns.* But neither of these forms has ever made much headway in educated use. Throughout the South, however, the plural form *y'all* is widely used by the best-educated speakers, only, however, when referring to more than one person. Another new plural form that is gaining ground, especially among younger people and for informal use, is *you guys.*

American Regional Dialects

The first English settlers in America brought with them the dialects that they spoke in the British Isles. As soon as they settled into their new country, however, they began to develop new dialects. They encountered new things and had new experiences that needed to be named. They met people speaking other languages—the native American Indian languages, as well as other nonnative tongues like Dutch, French, Spanish, and African languages. They talked with one another and thus influenced one another's language. Eventually a new set of specifically American dialects came into existence.

Today, regional dialect boundaries are clearest along the eastern coast of the United States, which was settled first by English speakers. The boundaries are increasingly less clear to the West, which was settled later. It takes time for dialects to become established, so it is not surprising that the boundaries are fuzzy in the West. In the East, however, there are clearly three important dialect areas: Northern, Midland, and Southern.

The Northern dialect area includes all the territory from northern New Jersey and Pennsylvania northward. It includes as subdialect areas eastern New England and especially the Boston area, western New England and upstate New York, the Hudson Valley area, and New York City.

The Midland dialect area includes southern New Jersey and Pennsylvania and northern Delaware and Maryland. West of these states, however, it dips sharply southward and divides into two subareas: north Midland and south Midland. North Midland includes parts of Ohio, Indiana, and Illinois. South Midland includes the Appalachian Mountain regions of West Virginia and the western parts of Virginia, North and South Carolina, and northern Georgia.

The Southern dialect area includes the coastal regions from southern Maryland through eastern Virginia, the Carolinas, east and south Georgia, and westward through southern Alabama and Mississippi.

Nowadays, some of the traditional differences among these regions are disappearing as our lifestyle changes and becomes more uniform. What used to be called a *skillet* in the South and a *spider* in parts of the North is now almost everywhere a *frying pan* or a *fry pan*. When horses pulled wagons, the horizontal crossbar by which the wagon was attached to the animals' harness was called a *singletree* or *swingletree* in the South and a *whippletree* or *whiffletree* in the North. But now the object is foreign to the experience of most of us, so we have no name whatever for it.

New dialect terms, however, will doubtless come into existence. For example, we might expect dialect variation in the terms we use for limited-access highways, for the rest areas along them, and for the center barrier that divides the two directions of traffic. In addition, there will be varied terms for a small neighborhood store that is open early and late hours, or for an informal kind of open shoe that has a strap between the big toe and the other toes. Such objects have many names.

Some dialect differences will always exist. Yet in the future, mass communications, mass transportation, and shared education may inhibit many new regional differences from coming into existence, thus strengthening the older regional dialects. Regional dialects have never been very pronounced in the United States and are likely to become even less so in the future. But they will probably never fade away altogether.

American Ethnic Dialects

Another important kind of dialect is ethnic speech. People who share a common cultural heritage tend to talk alike, and unlike those with a different heritage. When the Irish moved to America, they brought their Irish English with them, and features of it have survived on this side of the Atlantic not as a regional dialect, which it is in the British Isles, but as an ethnic dialect.

Almost every immigrant group has its own ethnic dialect, preserved more or less strongly, depending on the cohesion of the group. Among the larger and more enduring ethnic dialects are Yiddish English, spoken by many Jews; Hispanic English, spoken in several variations by Chicanos from Mexico and by Cuban-Americans, especially in Florida; and Black English, a mixture of African influences, Southern dialect, and features that developed in the black American community.

Among the features of Black English (which are, however, by no means found in the speech of all blacks) are the following. In pronunciation, final clusters of consonants are simplified, usually

A

" **W**hat used to be called a *skillet* in the South and a *spider* in parts of the North is now almost everywhere a *frying pan* or a *fry pan*."

B

A. Dialect Terms

What words do you use to name each of the places and objects mentioned here? (Answers may include, respectively: service roads; rest stops; islands; bodega; sandal.)

B. Ethnic Dialects

The essay goes on to give specific examples of the pronunciation, syntax, and vocabulary of Black English. You may wish to ask those students who can to give some examples from other dialects mentioned in this paragraph.

> "**S**ome words from Black English have become a part of the standard English vocabulary: *chigger* ('sand flea'), *goober* (Southern and Midland for 'peanut'), *gumbo, jazz, juke(box), nitty-gritty*, and *zombie*."

by dropping all except the first consonant: *most* becomes *mose*, and *find* becomes *fine*. *Nice* and *mine* become something like *nahs* and *mahn*. The article *a* is used instead of *an* before words beginning with a vowel: *a orange, a apple*. All of these features are typical of the Southern dialect, too.

Other features, although found elsewhere in Southern speech, are much more common in Black English. The ending *-s* is frequently omitted from verbs, possessive nouns, and plural nouns that have a number before them: "He work hard," "my brother car," "four ticket." The verb *be* is either omitted altogether or is used in the unchanged form of *be*, rather than *am, is, are*. These two uses, however, mean different things: "She here" means "She is here right now," whereas "She be here" means "She is usually or regularly here."

Black English also has a distinctive vocabulary. Some words from Black English have become a part of the standard English vocabulary: *chigger* ("sand flea"), *goober* (Southern and Midland for "peanut"), *gumbo, jazz, juke(box), nitty-gritty*, and *zombie*. Other uses are known outside the black community and are sometimes used as slang; for example, *bad* pronounced with a drawn-out vowel (*baaaad*) meaning "very good." The black ethnic vocabulary and idiom change freely and continue to grow.

As new influences come to bear on the life and language of the nation, new dialects are likely to arise. It is the nature of language to change continually. But it changes in different ways among different groups—and that is why dialects exist.

Analyzing Language

1. Which of the following columns contains words that seem most familiar to you?

pail	bucket	bucket
quarter of	quarter till	quarter to
angleworm	fishing worm	wiggler
mud wasp	mud dauber	dirt dauber
fussbudget	fuss-button	fussbox
haycock	hayrick	shock
brook, crick	run	branch

The first column is of predominantly Northern words, the second of Midland words, and the third of Southern words.

2. Here are some words with special meanings in dialect use. Look up these words in the *Dictionary of American Regional English* to find out where they are used and what they mean.

acknowledge the corn	bayou	cabbage salad
Adam's off-ox	bismarck	chill bumps
all in	blinky	commie

3. The Romantics were concerned with change in life and society. Some of them were also concerned with varieties of dialects. Can you think of any way those two concerns might be connected?

INTERPRETING POETRY

Writing Assignment

Write an essay in which you explain the meaning of one of the poems in this unit. In your essay, discuss how the elements of poetry you have studied so far in this unit contribute to the meaning of the poem. Discuss also your response to the poem.

Background

To **interpret** a poem means to explain its meaning. The first step in interpretation is to understand the poem's literal meaning, or what it says. To do this, you must be able to identify both the speaker and the situation of the poem. You should also be able to give a line-by-line paraphrase of the poem, "translating" difficult or unusual vocabulary words and sentence structures into your own words.

Being able to paraphrase a poem is not sufficient to understand it fully, however. To grasp the total experience of the poem, you must analyze the poetic elements. Which elements—meter and rhythm, sound effects, imagery, and so on—are used by the poet? What effects do these elements have on the ideas expressed in the poem? How do they affect your response to the poem?

Responding to Poetry. As you analyze the poem to determine its meaning, you respond to the poem on an intellectual level. Appreciation of poetry also calls for a more personal response. What emotional impact does the poem have on you? Can you identify with the ideas and emotions expressed in the poem? How do you respond to the poet's use of language? Are the images clear and specific enough so that you share the poet's experience? How do the other elements of the poem help you to share in the experience of the poem?

Prewriting

One way to gather details for your essay is to ask yourself questions about the poem and its elements. The following questions and notes are for an essay on the meaning of William Blake's poem "The Chimney Sweeper," from *Songs of Innocence*.

1. **Who is the speaker?** A chimney sweeper—mother died when he was young; sold by father.
2. **What is the situation?** Speaker telling about another sweep, young Tom Dacre, and a dream of Tom's—thousands of young sweeps freed from coffins, taken to heavenlike place.
3. **What is the literal meaning of the poem?**

   a. **Stanza 1.** Speaker telling about his own experience—mother died when he was young; father sold him.

   b. **Stanza 2.** Tom Dacre, another sweep—Tom's curly hair cut; speaker comforts him.

   c. **Stanzas 3–5.** Speaker telling about Tom's dream—young chimney sweeps freed from coffins, taken to heavenlike place. Tom told by angel that he will one day have God for his father and that he will be happy if he is a "good boy."

   d. **Stanza 6.** Comfort Tom feels from his dream; speaker makes comment about sweeps' doing their duty and not fearing harm.

4. **What is the tone of the poem?** Irony? Contrast between speaker's attitude of happiness in next life and poet's depiction of miserable unhappiness of children in this one.

5. **What poetic elements are used by the poet? What effect do these elements have on the ideas expressed in the poem? How do these elements help to shape your response to the poem?**

   a. **Regular meter and rhyme scheme.** Make poem seem like speech; seem to fit speaker's simple advice about duty.

   b. **Sound.** "S" sounds in first stanza reinforce simple rhythmic quality of lines, contrast with reality of what's happening to children. Repetition of word *weep* in first stanza brings out unhappiness of children.

   c. **Imagery.** Poet paints dark picture of children's condition (sleeping in soot, black coffin, rising in dark, coldness of morning); suggests innocence of children (Tom's hair like lamb's back, Angel, children running and playing); contrast between everyday life for children and freedom and happiness in next life (running and playing, clouds and wind, green plain, sun and water).

   d. **Response.** Strong reaction to condition of children's lives—can't forget picture of child sleeping in soot, thousands of children locked in black coffins. Re-

A. Paraphrase
In class, have students practice this line-by-line paraphrasing for one of the short poems in the unit. Suggest that for longer poems, such as "Tintern Abbey," line-by-line paraphrasing is not necessary. Students may briefly summarize ideas, feelings, and actions in the order in which they are presented.

B. Elements of Poetry
Elicit from students the elements of poetry, and have a volunteer record them on the chalkboard. They are as follows: speaker, situation, imagery, symbol, figurative language (metaphor, simile, personification, and so on), sound effects (rhyme, rhythm, alliteration, assonance, onomatopoeia, and so on), tone, theme, and form.

C. Prewriting
Have students reread the poem (text page 623) before they read and discuss prewriting notes.

A. Organization
Make sure stu-
dents understand
that they can
choose either of
the two suggested
organizations—dis-
cussing each stan-
za separately (or-
ganization 1), or
dealing with the
poem as a whole
(organization 2).

B. Model
The model gives
only the opening
and closing para-
graphs of an essay
based on the pre-
writing notes on
text page 757. You
might ask students
to complete the
body of this essay
of analysis.

Revising Essays
As students revise
their essays, refer
them to Grammar,
Usage, and Me-
chanics: A Refer-
ence Guide at the
back of their
books.

Exercises in Critical Thinking and Writing/*cont.*

minds me of pictures of hungry, sick children I have seen. Disagree with speaker—children deserve a life in this world and a chance to be happy and free from misery.

Writing

In the first paragraph of your essay, cite the poem and the poet. Summarize briefly the literal meaning of the poem and tell how the elements of the poem affect what the poem says. In the remaining paragraphs of your essay, choose one of the following types of organization:

A

Organization 1. Explain the literal meaning of each stanza. For each stanza, discuss how poetic elements affect the meaning. Discuss also your response to each stanza.

Organization 2. Explain in detail the literal meaning of the entire poem. Then discuss the poet's use of significant elements and the effect of these elements on the meaning. Conclude the essay with a discussion of your response to the elements and to the poem as a whole.

Below are the opening and closing paragraphs for an essay on "The Chimney Sweeper" (*Innocence*).

B

William Blake's "The Chimney Sweeper," from *Songs of Innocence,* is about the plight of young chimney sweeps in eighteenth-century England. On a literal level, the speaker of the poem seems to suggest that the children should accept their lives, do their duty, and look forward to the next life. This next life is depicted, in a young chimney sweep's dream, as one of freedom and joy. Through sound and imagery, however, the poet contrasts this vision with the real-world horror of the children's lives. This contrast leads readers to question the speaker's attitude. Does the poet really agree with this attitude? . . .

Introduction

Summary of literal meaning

Effect of elements on meaning

In my opinion, William Blake succeeds in conveying the tragedy of these children's lives. Through Blake's imagery, I could see the speaker sleeping in the soot of the chimney, and I could hear young Tom Dacre crying as his curly white hair was shaved. Most tragic, though, are the thousands of children locked in "coffins of black." Because of these images, I couldn't accept the speaker's advice about children doing their duty. Blake's imagery also left me with the strong feeling that he, too, could not accept this advice. Blake and I would agree, I think, that these innocent children deserve much more from life.

Discussion of reader's response

Specific details about elements

Effect of elements on reader's response

Identification with statement of poet

Revision and Proofreading

For help revising and proofreading your essay, see the section on **Writing About Literature** in the back of this book.

THE VICTORIAN PERIOD
1832–1901

The Triumph of Steam and Electricity (1897). Lithograph.

UNIT SIX

HUMANITIES CONNECTION: RESPONDING TO THE FINE ART

Ask students to examine closely the lithograph on text page 759.

? How does the lithograph justify its title? (Each pair of panels shows a technological advancement that improved the quality of life. The steamship replaced the sailing ship; the locomotive replaced the horse; electric lights replaced gas.) What more modern technological changes could the panels on the right illustrate? (Cars, planes, subways, computers)

TEACHING VICTORIAN LITERATURE

Most teachers would agree that the Victorian period provides the richest array of selections of interest to secondary school students and that it is the most easily and happily "mineable" of all the periods of English literature.

An anthology has only a limited number of pages, so we can only offer here a sampling of Victorian literature. Poetry and drama dominate the unit; the presumption is that you will assign at least one of the great Victorian novels for outside reading. (See the recommended list on page 772.) Selections in this unit of Victorian prose include an extract from Thomas Macaulay's *History of England;* an early chapter from Charles Dickens's *David Copperfield,* in which the repulsive Murdstone sends Davy away; and what is perhaps one of Rudyard Kipling's finest stories, "The Miracle of Purun Bhagat." The great woman novelist of the period, George Eliot, so difficult to extract for an anthology, should be one of your outside assignments.

No Victorian survey would be complete without a study of what was happening to drama at the end of the century. (See Robert Anderson's introduction to Victorian Drama on text page 867.) This anthology includes Oscar Wilde's hilarious satiric farce, *The Importance of Being Earnest,* a perfect play, by the way, for student performance.

OBJECTIVES OF THE VICTORIAN UNIT

1. To recognize the changes that occured in British poetry following the Romantic period, including
   a. changes in diction
   b. changes in themes, including views of nature and religion
   c. changes in form, including the introduction of the dramatic monologue
2. To recognize the new diversity in the forms and uses of prose
3. To compare the themes that dominate Victorian writings
4. To recognize the elements of satirical drawing-room comedy

SUPPLEMENTARY SUPPORT MATERIALS: UNIT SIX

1. Unit Introduction Test (*CCB*)
2. English Language Test (*CCB*)
3. Word Analogies Test (*CCB*)
4. Unit Review Test (*CCB*)
5. Critical Thinking and Writing Test (*CCB*)

6. Study Guide to *The Return of the Native*
7. Instructional Overhead Transparencies

A. Discussing the Quotation

You might tell students some of the background of Tennyson's elegiac cycle, *In Memoriam,* which was completed in 1850 (see text page 794). Point out that this type of mid-century optimism changes with the poets of later years.

? What does this quotation from the period's leading poet suggest about the mood of the day?

B. Responding to the Illustration

? Do you think this scene is idealized for proper Victorian eyes? (We certainly don't see the children laborers, nor feel the effects of the noise and dust and long hours. See text page 767.)

THE VICTORIAN PERIOD 1832–1901

by **Harley Henry, John Malcolm Brinnin,** *and* **Robert Anderson**

Model Textile Mill at Tewkesbury, England (19th century). Color engraving.

A
> *So many worlds, so much to do,*
> *So little done, such things to be . . . .*
>
> —from *In Memoriam*
> Alfred, Lord Tennyson

Many Victorians thought of themselves as living in a time of great change. They were right. But the changes during Queen Victoria's long reign (1837–1901) occurred in a period of political and social stability, and many were the results of conditions that began before Victoria and most of her subjects were born.

Peace and Economic Growth

The Victorian era was a time of peace and economic growth. After Napoleon's defeat at Waterloo in 1815, Britain was not involved in a major European war until World War I began in 1914. The Empire that began in the eighteenth century with British interests in India and North America grew steadily, until by 1900 Victoria was Queen-Empress of more than two hundred million people living outside Great Britain. The Industrial Revolution of the eighteenth century greatly expanded during the Victorian period. It moved through booms and depressions, but over the course of the century it steadily created new towns, new goods, new wealth, and new jobs for tens of thousands of people climbing through the complicated levels of the middle class.

B

The movement toward political democracy, an outgrowth of the American and French Revolutions, was deflected into political reforms that left the monarchy and aristocracy in place. Piece by piece, middle-class and ultimately working-class politicians and voters achieved political power.

The Idea of Progress

This selection of Victorian literary texts opens with Thomas Babington Macaulay's description (which was published in 1844) of the London streets of 1685. Macaulay's judgments about the past reflect some of the powerful ideas and feelings of his time. Many Victorians regretted or disputed Macaulay's confident tone and materialistic standards. But they would have acknowledged that in his satisfaction with the improvements time had brought to London and to England as a whole, his views were typical of his contemporaries.

History for Macaulay meant progress, and progress largely meant material improvement that could be seen and touched, counted and measured. (Better an acre in Sussex, he once wrote, than a principality in Utopia.) Macaulay admired cleanliness and order. He wanted the London streets free of garbage, drained and paved, lighted at night, and patrolled by a sober police force. He wanted the city planned so that residents of respectable neighborhoods did not live next to hovels and were not annoyed by beggars and peddlers. He would have the houses numbered and a population literate enough to read signs. He did not claim that his own time had entirely met these standards of material comfort and security, but his cool, almost amazed regard of seventeenth-century disorder and squalor conveyed his sense of progress: How could those people have lived like that? How different we are; how far we have come.

Problems of Victoria's Reign

Whatever its advances, the first decade of Victoria's reign was full of troubles. Victoria came to the throne in the first year of a depression that by 1842 had put a million and a half unemployed workers and their families (in a population of sixteen million in England and Wales) on some form of poor relief. Government commissions investigating working conditions learned of children mangled when they fell asleep at machines at the end of a twelve-hour working day. They discovered young girls and boys hauling sledges of coal through narrow mine tunnels, working shifts so long that in winter they saw the sun only on Sunday.

In 1845, the potato blight caused a famine in Ireland that killed perhaps half a million people and forced two million others—nearly twenty percent of Ireland's population—to emigrate. Some went to English cities, where they lived ten or twelve people to a room in slums that had two toilets for every 250 people.

Queen Victoria.

> "**S**ome of the Irish went to English cities, where they lived ten or twelve people to a room in slums that had two toilets for every 250 people."

A. Expansion
As a reminder of America's role in democratic government, note the dates of the American (1775–1781) and French (1789–1794) revolutions.

B. Responding
Do you agree or disagree with this sentiment? How would you rephrase it so it would be pertinent today? (Better a two-bedroom cottage in suburbia than a kingdom in Utopia.)

C. About the Photograph
In this famous photograph, Queen Victoria is at the peak of her rule as empress of India and sovereign of numerous other overseas colonies. Note her crown, her ornate dress, her medals, and her quintessentially Victorian fan.

A. About the Photograph

Notice that the boys are dressed in suits—not the work clothes that miners wear today. At this time (and in remote parts of the British Isles still), men wore old formal suits and jackets for work. The idea of special "work clothes" is a recent one.

B. Victorian Society

Cities were important in Victorian society—a result of the rise of industry and increasing wealth. Remind students that Liverpool and Manchester are still industrial centers today. Some novelists, notably Dickens, dealt memorably with life in urban settings. Others, such as George Eliot and Thomas Hardy, continued to turn to village and country life for the sources of their fiction.

A

Pit boys waiting to go to work in the coal mines in Derbyshire.

B

" **In the 1850's Parliament had sometimes to adjourn from its new riverside building because of the stench from the Thames.** "

The rapid growth of other cities often made them as filthy and disorderly as the London Macaulay wrote about. Nearly two million people lived in London during the 1840's, and commercial and industrial cities such as Manchester and Liverpool expanded rapidly. In Manchester in the 1840's forty percent of the streets were still unpaved. The Thames River in London was polluted by sewage, industrial waste, and the drainage from graveyards where bodies were buried in layers six or eight deep. In the 1850's Parliament had sometimes to adjourn from its new riverside building because of the stench from the Thames.

The Movement for Reform

Violence broke out at massive political rallies called in the 1840's to protest government policies that kept the price of bread and other food high and deprived most working men (and all women) of the vote and representation in Parliament. In 1848, a year of revolution in Europe, nervous British politicians got the army ready and armed the staffs of museums and government offices when working-class political reformers organized what they called a monster rally in London to petition Parliament and the Queen.

Still, most Victorians of Macaulay's temperament believed that things were better than in the past, and that they were going to be better yet in the future. Their opinion was in part founded on a steady improvement throughout the Victorian era in the material condition of people in all social classes. The price of food dropped after mid-century, largely because of trade with other countries and the growing Empire. Diet improved as meat, fruit, and margarine (a Victorian invention) began to appear regularly in working-class households. Factories and railroads made postage, newspapers, clothing, furniture, travel, and other goods and services cheap.

A series of political reforms gave the vote to almost all adult males by the last decades of the century. In 1832 the First Reform Bill extended the vote to all men who owned property worth ten pounds or more in yearly rent. Continued pressure led to the Second Reform Act in 1867, which gave the right to vote to all working-class men except for agricultural workers. Women had to wait until 1928 for universal adult suffrage; organized political action by women was another Victorian invention.

A series of Factory Acts limited child labor and reduced the usual working day to ten hours, with a half-holiday on Saturday. State-supported schools were established in 1870, made compulsory in 1880, and free in 1891. In 1859 forty percent of the couples getting married could not write their names on their marriage certificates. By 1900, using that simple definition of literacy, more than ninety percent of the population was literate.

Decorum and Authority

Many Victorians thought of themselves as progressing morally and intellectually as well as materially. Macaulay's admiration of cleanliness and order was part of a powerful, mostly middle-class obsession with gentility or decorum that has made *prudery* almost a synonym for *Victorianism*. Book publishers and magazine editors deleted or obscured words and episodes that might, in the phrase of the day, bring a blush to the cheek of a young person. In popular fiction sex, birth, and death were softened by sentimental conventions into tender courtships, joyous motherhoods, and deathbed scenes in which old people became saints and babies became angels. In the real world, people were arrested for distributing information about sexually transmitted diseases. Victorian society regarded seduced or adulterous women (but not their male partners) as "fallen" and pushed them to the margins of respectability.

Victorian decorum also supported powerful ideas about authority. Many Victorians were uneasy about giving strong authority to a central government (although it is revealing of the fundamental decorum of British society that its version of the 1848 revolutions

A. Blake's Poems
You might refer back to Blake's poems on text pages 623, 625, and 626 in discussing child labor.

B. Responding
❓ Do you think contemporary attitudes about censorship are significantly different from Victorian attitudes?

A

B

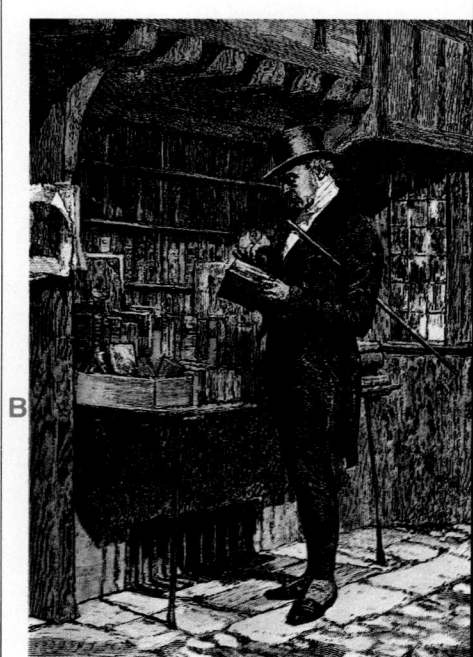

A Treasure at the Bookstall (19th century). Color engraving.

A. Humanities Connection: Responding to the Fine Art

James Jacques Joseph Tissot (1836–1902) was born in France and worked in England. Much of his work depicts the opulent life of Victorian high society.

? Contrast this painting depicting one part of Victorian society with the Doré wood engraving on the next page, which depicts another class altogether. Could the same contrasts be noted in society today? (Students probably will agree but should be encouraged to give specific examples that illustrate today's class contrasts.)

B. Expansion

For a biography of Elizabeth Barrett Browning, see text page 808. For Mr. Murdstone, see the selection from *David Copperfield* on text page 846.

C. Women in English Literature

As an indication of the growing role of women in English literature, review the women writers cited in the table of contents of this anthology. Notice that it was only in the nineteenth century, during the Romantic period, that women writers were published and so came to prominence.

The Artist's Wives by James Jacques Tissot (1885). Oil.

Gift of Walter P. Chrysler, Jr., and the Grandy Fund, Landmark Communications Fund and "An Affair to Remember" 1982. © 1983 The Chrysler Museum, Norfolk, Virginia.

was a meeting to petition Parliament). In Victorian private lives, however, the autocratic father of middle-class households is a vivid figure in both fact (Elizabeth Barrett Browning's father, for example) and fiction (Mr. Murdstone of Dickens's *David Copperfield*).

Women were also subject to male authority. Middle-class women especially were expected to marry and make their homes a comfortable refuge for their husbands from the male domains of business, politics, and the professions. Women who did not marry had few occupations open to them. Working-class women could find jobs as servants in affluent households, while unmarried middle-class ladies could become governesses or teachers. Many middle-class women remained unmarried because of the surplus of women in the British population after mid-century. The problem of these "redundant women," as they were called, was painful, although in literature, especially literature written by men, the figure of the middle-aged maiden was often played for comedy (as is Miss Prism of Oscar Wilde's *The Importance of Being Earnest*).

The excesses, cruelties, and hypocrisies of all these repressions were obvious to many Victorians in their own time. But the codes and barriers of decorum changed slowly because they were part of the ideology of progress. Prudery and social order were intended to control the licentiousness that Victorians associated with the political revolutions of the eighteenth century and the social corruption of the Regency period in the 1820's. The Victorian idea of decorum grew from the conviction that life would be improved if, like Macaulay's London streets, it steadily became more refined, more rationally organized, better policed, and therefore safer.

Intellectual Progress: The March of Mind

The intellectual advances of the Victorian period were dramatically evident to those living in it. Humans began to understand the earth, its creatures, and its natural laws. Geologists worked out the history written in rocks and fossils. From countless observations, Charles Darwin and other biologists theorized about the evolution of species. The industrialization of England depended on and supported science and technology, especially chemistry (in the iron and textile industries) and engineering. Those who made and used scientific and technological knowledge had a confidence of their own. Thomas Huxley, a variously accomplished scientist who wrote and lectured frequently on the necessity of scientific education, imagined science as an exhilarating, high-stakes chess game with the physical universe.

The chessboard is the world, the pieces are the phenomena of the universe, the rules of the game are what we call the laws of Nature. The player on the other side is hidden from us. We know that his play is always fair, just, and patient. But we also know, to our cost, that he never overlooks a mistake, or makes the smallest allowance for ignorance. To the man who plays well, the highest stakes are paid, with that sort of generosity with which the strong shows delight in strength. And one who plays ill is checkmated without haste, but without remorse.

—from "A Game of Chess,"
Thomas Huxley

A

Huxley resembles those confident Victorians who built railways and sewers, organized markets and schools, and pushed through electoral reforms and laws regulating the condition of work. These reformers believed that the world offered a challenging set of problems that could be understood by human intelligence and solved by science, government, and other human institutions. Huxley made the game exciting by warning that humans could lose. But so long as the problems were material and immediately at hand—an unanalyzed chemical substance, a dirty street, an illiterate child—there was no reason why human beings should fail to figure out how to make the world yield what was needed to live in it with increasing knowledge and comfort.

Over London by Rail after Gustave Doré (1872). Colored wood engraving.

A. Responding

How does this view of life as a chess game strike you? (Since so many aspects of life are competitive, the image of life as a competitive game is fair.) Is such an outlook fundamentally optimistic or pessimistic? (It can be either, depending on how strong the individual is or feels he or she is and the perceived nature of the adversary.) Who or what are the players in Huxley's chess game? (The individual vs. the impersonal laws of the physical universe)

This view of the poet is, in fact, a very old one, with roots in widely disparate ancient cultures (Greek, Hindu, and Jewish).

? What is the role of the poet or writer in society today? (Answers will vary but may include that of teacher, entertainer, or inspirational orator.)

B. Responding

? Based on this paragraph, cite five questions posed in Victorian literature. (1. Does material comfort fully satisfy human needs? 2. Is the achievement of these material comforts worth the exploitation of the earth? 3. Are our codes of decorum and authority acceptable, or are they hypocritical? 4. Do our materialistic ideas overlook the spirit or soul that makes life beautiful and just? 5. Is there really a coherence in history and nature?) Are these questions still relevant today? Do various writers (and movies and TV shows) still make you think about these questions? (Encourage specific titles.)

Victorian and Romantic Literature

> " The Victorian period, and especially its literature, was filled with voices asking questions and raising doubts."

A

B

In two important ways the literature of the Victorian period reflected the continuity of nineteenth-century British experience. First, unlike the Romantic writers before 1830, the principal poets, novelists, and essayists of the Victorian period did not think it necessary to break sharply from the practices and traditions of their immediate predecessors. They continued to write within the broad range of literary forms and styles they inherited from the Romantic period. The poetry of Alfred Tennyson, Matthew Arnold, and Gerard Manley Hopkins grew from the complicated meditations and carefully worked harmonies of William Wordsworth, Percy Bysshe Shelley, and John Keats. The apparent simplicity of the poems of Christina Rossetti and A. E. Housman is like that of William Blake; the colloquial wit and dissonances of Robert Browning's work look back to the poetry of Lord Byron. Novelists in both periods—from Jane Austen to Charles Dickens and George Eliot—told stories of the ordinary but intense difficulties of childhood, growing up, courtship, marriage, and growing old.

The second feature of Victorian writing is an idea about literature that was also inherited from Romantic writers. In *A Defense of Poetry* (1821) Shelley wrote, "Poets are the unacknowledged legislators of the world." The nineteenth-century writers imagined themselves as seers or sages who saw deeply into the fundamental nature of existence. They believed that their writing could change how people acted in their moral, social, and even political lives by changing their awareness of what was happening to themselves and in the world around them. Sometimes the lessons of literature were open and direct, as in the essays of Mary Wollstonecraft, Thomas Carlyle, and John Ruskin. More often, Romantic and Victorian writers offered images and stories that either reassured or troubled their readers by suggesting what they should worry or be happy about, what they should fear, and what they should hope for and strive to become.

Questions and Doubts

The Victorian period, and especially its literature, was filled with voices asking questions and raising doubts. Speaking for many of their contemporaries, and speaking to others they thought shallow and complacent, Victorian writers asked whether material comfort fully satisfied human needs and wishes. They questioned the cost of exploiting the earth and human beings to achieve such comfort. They protested or mocked codes of decorum and authority. In the first half of the period, some writers complained that materialist ideas of reality completely overlooked the spirit or soul that made life beautiful and just. Later in the century writers like Hardy and Housman thought that Macaulay's and Huxley's ideas of history and nature presupposed a coherence and generosity that did not really exist. Literature in Victorian culture often reassured its readers that, rightly perceived, the universe made sense. But some writers unsettled their readers by telling them that they were not rightly perceiving the universe, or by asking them to consider whether human life and the natural world made as much sense as they had once hoped.

Charles Dickens, the most popular and most important figure in Victorian literature, is a case in point. The son of an improvident clerk, Dickens lived out one of the favorite plots of Victorian progress by rising through his own enormous talents and energy to become a wealthy and famous man. His was a peculiarly Victorian success, made possible by the increasing affluence and literacy that gave him a large reading public, and by improved printing and distribution that made book publishing a big business.

The conventional happy endings of Dickens's novels satisfied his readers', and probably his own, conviction that things usually work out well for decent people. But from the beginning of his career in the 1830's to the publication of his last complete novel in 1865, many of Dickens's most memorable scenes showed decent people neglected, abused, and exploited. The hungry Oliver Twist asks for more gruel in the workhouse; the crippled Tiny Tim in *A Christmas Carol* cheerfully hobbles toward death; and David Copperfield is beaten and exiled by the cold, dark Mr. Murdstone.

In his later novels Dickens also created characters and scenes to show that even the winners in the competition for material gain had reason to be as desperate and unhappy as the losers. In *Our Mutual Friend,* his last novel, he describes a dinner party at the home of a family called the Veneerings. They are "bran-new people in a bran-new house in a bran-new quarter of London."

> The great looking-glass above the sideboard reflects the table and the company. Reflects the new Veneering crest, in gold and eke in silver, frosted and also thawed, a camel of all work. The Heralds' College found out a Crusading ancestor for Veneering who had a camel on his shield (or might have done it if he had thought of it), and a caravan of camels take charge of the fruits and flowers and candles, and kneel down to be loaded with the salt. Reflects Veneering, forty, wavy-haired, dark, tending to corpulence, sly, mysterious, filmy. . . . Reflects Mrs. Veneering, fair, aquiline-nosed and fingered, not so much light hair as she might have, gorgeous in raiment and jewels. . . . Reflects Podsnap, prosperously feeding, two little light-colored wiry wings, one on either side of his else bald head, looking as like hairbrushes as his hair. . . . Reflects Mrs. Podsnap, quantity of bone, neck, and nostrils like a rocking horse, hard features, majestic head-dress in which Podsnap has hung golden offerings. . . . Reflects . . . mature young gentleman, with too much nose in his face, too much ginger in his whiskers, too much sparkle in his studs, his eyes, his buttons, his talk, and his teeth.

—from *Our Mutual Friend,*
Charles Dickens

Attacks like Dickens's on the hollowness, glitter, superficiality, and excesses of Victorian affluence were common in Victorian literature. Such attacks are evident in Robert Browning's portrayal

Illustration by Everett Shinn for
A Christmas Carol by Charles Dickens.

Print Collection, Miriam and Ira D. Wallach Division of Art, Prints, and Photographs, The New York Public Library.

A

> " **M**any of Dickens's most memorable scenes showed decent people neglected, abused, and exploited."

A. Responding

? What is the significance of the name *Veneering*? (A *veneer* is a surface overlay of wood; it does not go very deep. The Veneerings are "surface" people, interested only in appearances.) Do you think that Dickens in this passage seems to agree or disagree with Huxley's ideas on text page 764? (Dickens is more cynical than Huxley. His vulgarians, not the people Huxley admires, are winning the game.) Do people today still behave and dress like those at this dinner party? (People still show off their material possessions and themselves.) Do people today, for example, still commission coats-of-arms to lend distinction to their lineage? (Some might.)

A. Humanities Connection: About the Fine Art

Versailles, built by King Louis XIV of France (1638–1715), was a glittering symbol of royalty, not only in France but in England and Europe generally. This painting reveals the prosperity and extravagance of the age.

B. John Ruskin

John Ruskin (1819–1900) wrote on social, political, and artistic topics. His proposals for social improvement were less grand and aggressive than those of that other critic of society, Thomas Carlyle (1795–1881). Carlyle admired strong national leaders like Cromwell and Frederick the Great, but Ruskin urged individual actions, like boycotting the products of industrial and economic systems that demeaned human labor.

Ruskin's ideas influenced many late-nineteenth-century writers and political thinkers and reached into the twentieth century to affect the ideas and tactics of Gandhi, the Indian nationalist.

A

Dinner at Versailles Given Queen Victoria by Napoleon III by E. Lami (1855). Oil.

B

of the murderously acquisitive Duke in "My Last Duchess" and in Oscar Wilde's sport with Lady Bracknell's gentility in *The Importance of Being Earnest*.

Dickens also raised questions about the costs of progress in his descriptions of the huddle and waste of cities and the smoke and fire of industrial landscapes. Here, too, he was joined by other writers. In 1871 the art historian and social critic John Ruskin noted a new phenomenon that we call smog; he called it the plague wind, or "the storm-cloud of the nineteenth century":

> . . . the sky is covered with greasy cloud; not raincloud, but a dry black veil, which no ring of sunshine can pierce; partly diffused in feeble mist, enough to make distant objects unintelligible, yet without any substance, or wreathing, or color of its own. And everywhere the leaves of the trees are shaking fitfully, . . . not violently, but enough to show the passing to and fro of a strange, bitter, blighting wind. . . . It looks partly as if it were made of poisonous smoke; very possibly it may be; there are at least two hundred furnace chimneys in a square of two miles on either side of me. But mere smoke would not blow to and fro in that wild way. It looks more to me as if it were made of dead men's souls.

—from "The Storm-Cloud of the Nineteenth Century," John Ruskin

The materialism, secularism, vulgarity, and sheer waste that accompanied Victorian progress led some writers to wonder if their culture was really advancing by any measure. In "Locksley Hall," an early poem of the 1840's, Alfred Tennyson rescued his young hero from despondency over a frustrated love affair by figuratively putting him on the railroad train of the great forward movements of Empire, science, and technology:

Not in vain the distance beckons. Forward, forward let us range,
Let the great world spin forever down the ringing grooves of change.
Thro' the shadow of the globe we sweep into the younger day;
Better fifty years of Europe than a cycle of Cathay.
　　　　　—from "Locksley Hall,"
　　　　　　Alfred, Lord Tennyson

In 1886, Tennyson returned to his hero, now an old man, to speak his own disillusion in a civilization threatened by political and moral anarchy. The wonders of technology have become commonplace. From science the hero has learned not that he is riding forward on a train, but that he is drifting in a vast history commanded by forces beyond human control.

Forward, backward, backward, forward, in the unmeasurable sea.
Swayed by vaster ebbs and flows than can be known to you or me. . . .
Evolution ever climbing after some ideal good;
And Reversion ever dragging Evolution in the mud.
　　　　　—from "Locksley Hall Sixty Years After,"
　　　　　　Alfred, Lord Tennyson

B

A

View of Birmingham (detail) (19th century) from *Our Own Country,* Cassell and Co. Ltd., London.

Victorian Literature and Victorian Life

Tennyson settled the problems he considered in "Locksley Hall Sixty Years After" in the way he usually resolved his poems of doubt about the beneficent purpose of human life. He ended by trusting that "That which made us meant us to be mightier by and by," if not on earth, then in heaven.

Tennyson's trust in a transcendental power was characteristic of the early Victorian writers. They were the immediate heirs of the Romantic idea of a finite, natural world surrounded by and interfused with an infinite, ideal, transcendental reality. The highest purpose of a poet, of any writer, was to make readers aware of the connection between earth and heaven, body and soul, material and ideal. Fundamentally, as Thomas Carlyle wrote in his essay "The Poet as Hero," reality is spiritual, a divine idea. "All Appearances, from the starry sky to the grass of the field, but especially the Appearance of Man and his work, is but the *vesture,* the embodiment that renders it [the divine idea] possible." The poet pene-

A. Expansion/ Responding
The two sets of lines from Tennyson set the philosophical stage for the unit in a uniquely revealing manner. Here is the spokesman for the Victorian Age acting, as Shelley said a poet should, as a "legislator," and going back to rewrite his "legislation" after forty-six years. He still believes in evolution and in Europe, but his "railroad" has become more like a meandering stream. *Reversion* means "a stance of turning the opposite way or of returning to an original position."
❓ Paraphrase the line that concludes the first verse. (More can be accomplished in Europe in fifty years than in many more years in China.) Do the last two lines still apply today? (No.)

B. About the Illustration
Birmingham was the center of industry in England. Note the churches rising out of the crowded streets and the factory smoke.

770   The Victorian Period

A. Expansion
The Kipling story is on text page 859.

B. Discussing the Time Line
One way to use the time line, which reveals the great creativity of these years, is to develop a discussion or a debate on the question of the most important contributions listed on the chart as judged from our present-day vantage point.

❓ Which events, discreetly cited on the chart, had earth-shattering effects on our own day? (Students might mention the telegraph, the Irish famine, *The Communist Manifesto,* Darwin's theory, the emancipation of American slaves, the birth of Gandhi, the telephone, the electric light, the first Ford.)

trates to the divine idea and makes it palpable in language and story to those of lesser power and vision. "That is always his message; he is to reveal that to us—that sacred mystery which he more than others lives ever present with."

With some exceptions—Hopkins is one and Christina Rossetti another—writers younger than Tennyson and Ruskin found it increasingly difficult to believe in an infinite power and order that made sense of material and human existence. Some simply thought it unnecessary. Algernon Charles Swinburne and Rudyard Kipling, in their different ways, celebrated a relation between humans and the natural world that could be joyous and even redemptive. In Kipling's short story "The Miracle of Purun Bhagat," a saintly Buddhist's oneness with nature enables him to save the lives of a whole village.

Other writers at mid-century were saddened by what seemed to them to be the withdrawal of the divine from the world. The dominant note of much mid-Victorian writing was struck by Arnold in his poem "Dover Beach": "The Sea of Faith," Arnold wrote, had ebbed. There was no certainty, or if there was, what was certain was that existence was not governed by a benevolent intelligence that cared for its creatures.

By the end of the century, this skepticism and denial had become pervasive in the works of such writers as Thomas Hardy, A. E. Housman, and others. Early- and mid-Victorian novelists such

> " **O**ther writers at mid-century were saddened by what seemed to them to be the withdrawal of the divine from the world."

1832–1833	1834	1837	1838–1839
First Reform Bill passes Parliament, 1832 Telegraph invented, 1833	Victor Hugo's *The Hunchback of Notre Dame* is the best-selling novel in Europe, 1834	Dickens's novel *Pickwick Papers* and Carlyle's history *The French Revolution*, 1837 Victoria becomes Queen of England and reigns for over 60 years, 1837–1901	Dickens's *Oliver Twist* (1838) and *Nicholas Nickleby* (1839) Edgar Allan Poe's story "The Fall of the House of Usher," 1839
1847	1847	1848–1849	1850
Ten Hours Act establishes 10-hour working day for women and for children under age of 18 in textile factories, 1847	Charlotte Brontë's novel *Jane Eyre*, Emily Brontë's novel *Wuthering Heights*, and William Makepeace Thackery's novel *Vanity Fair*, 1847	Publication of *The Communist Manifesto*, by Karl Marx and Friedrich Engels, 1848 Dickens's *David Copperfield*, 1849	Elizabeth B. Browning's *Sonnets from the Portuguese* and Hawthorne's novel *The Scarlet Letter*, 1850 Tennyson succeeds Wordsworth as Poet Laureate, 1850
1867	1868–1869	1876–1881	1883–1884
Second Reform Bill passed, giving the vote to most city industrial workers (servants, farmworkers, and women still excluded), 1867 Arnold's "Dover Beach," 1867	Leo Tolstoy publishes his great realistic novel *War and Peace*, in Russia, 1868–1869 Gandi born in India, 1869	Alexander Graham Bell invents the telephone, 1876 Hardy's novel *The Return of the Native*, 1878 Pablo Picasso born in Spain, 1881	Robert Louis Stevenson's novel *Treasure Island*, 1883 Mark Twain's novel *The Adventures of Huckleberry Finn*, 1884

READING CHECK TEST

1. The Victorian era was a time of __c__.
   a. increased hardships for all classes
   b. civil wars at home
   c. peace and economic growth
   d. warfare with France
2. Victorian decorum supported strong ideas about __d__.

a. sex
b. the place of women
c. authority
d. all of the above

3. Most Victorians believed that history meant __b__.
   a. regression   c. tragedy
   b. progress   d. hardship

4. In his *Defense of Poetry* (1824), Percy Bysshe Shelley compared poets to __b__.
   a. journalists   c. actors
   b. legislators   d. novelists

as Dickens and Eliot had dramatized a human ideal achieved through sympathy and unselfishness. They made sad or frightening examples of people like the Murdstones in *David Copperfield* and Godfrey Cass in *Silas Marner*—all hard surface and no soul. Their heroes and heroines learned to find happiness in nurturing marriages and in small communities of family and friends. But there were few such marriages and communities in the fiction and poetry of Hardy and Housman. These late Victorian writers told stories of lovers and friends bereft and betrayed by unfaithfulness, war, and the other troubles that humans add to the natural troubles of mortal life.

Victorian writers had purposes as various as the ideas of reality they believed in. Some writers wanted to scare or shame readers into effective moral and political actions that they optimistically believed were possible. Some wanted to show readers what it is like to live in a pleasurable moment of intense feeling like that caught in a lyric or in the interesting perspectives of a character in a dramatic monologue or novel. Victorian literature entertained, informed, warned, and reassured.

Even the playfulness of Lewis Carroll and Oscar Wilde shows the two most important and consistent purposes or effects of Victorian literature. The first was to make readers hope or wonder if reality was really like that—really as whole and satisfying as in Tennyson's *In Memoriam,* as briskly coherent as in a poem by Browning or an

A

" **T**hese late Victorian writers told stories of lovers and friends bereft and betrayed by unfaithfulness, war, and the other troubles that humans add to the natural troubles of mortal life."

A. George Eliot
The real name of George Eliot (1819–1880) was Mary Ann Evans. Her use of a pseudonym was one of a series of self-defining acts. After her father's death, she left her family's strongly religious household and went to London to edit an important magazine of liberal intellectual opinion. Eliot became one of the most accomplished Victorian novelists. Her most attractive fiction is based on her close knowledge of the small worlds of families and provincial towns. Her novels include *Adam Bede* (1859), *The Mill on the Floss* (1860), *Silas Marner* (1861), and *Middlemarch* (1872). The last is about the emotional and ethical growth of a young woman who comes to maturity in a tightly confined society.

Cass in *Silas Marner* is a squire who seduces and abandons a young woman. Their child is found and reared by a miser, Silas Marner. The novel tells of Silas's redemption through love.

1841	1842	1843–1845	1845–1847
Browning's *Pippa Passes*, Dickens's *The Old Curiosity Shop*, and Poe's "The Murders in the Rue Morgue," 1841	Treaty of Nanking ends the Opium War between England and China and makes Hong Kong a British colony, 1842 Tennyson's *Morte d'Arthur* and *Locksley Hall*, 1842	Wordsworth appointed England's Poet Laureate, 1843 John Henry Newman, well-known Anglican clergyman, becomes a Roman Catholic, 1845	Failure of Irish potato crops (beginning in 1845) causes the death of over 500,000 people in Ireland

1852–1854	1859	1861	1863–1865
Dickens's novel *Bleak House*, 1852 Tennyson's "The Charge of the Light Brigade," 1854	Dickens's *A Tale of Two Cities*, Tennyson's *Idylls of the King*, 1859 Darwin publishes his theory of evolution in *On the Origin of Species by Natural Selection*, 1859	Dickens's *Great Expectations* and Eliot's *Silas Marner*, 1861	Abraham Lincoln's Emancipation Proclamation frees all slaves in the United States, 1863 Lewis Carroll's *Alice's Adventures in Wonderland*, 1865

1886–1887	1887–1893	1894–1895	1895–1901
Karl Marx's study of capitalism, *Das Kapital*, 1886 Sir Arthur Conan Doyle's *A Study in Scarlet*, the first of his stories about Sherlock Holmes, 1887	Thomas Edison produces an electric lamp, 1887 Henry Ford builds his first car in Detroit, Michigan, 1893	Kipling's *The Jungle Book* and Shaw's *Arms and the Man*, 1894 H. G. Wells's novel *The Time Machine*, 1895	Wilde's *The Importance of Being Earnest*, 1895 Queen Victoria dies and is succeeded by her son Edward VII, 1901

FOR FURTHER READING

STUDENTS

The following are available in numerous hardbound and paperback editions:

Charlotte Brontë, *Jane Eyre* (1847).
Charles Dickens, *David Copperfield* (1850).
_____, *Great Expectations* (1861).

George Eliot, *Adam Bede* (1859).
_____, *Silas Marner* (1861).
_____, *Middlemarch* (1872).
Thomas Hardy, *The Return of the Native* (1878).
Rudyard Kipling, *Kim* (1901).
_____, *The Jungle Books* (1894–1895).

_____, *Captains Courageous* (1897).
Robert Louis Stevenson, *The Strange Case of Dr. Jekyll and Mr. Hyde* (1886).
_____, *Kidnapped* (1886).
_____, *Treasure Island* (1881).
William Makepeace Thackeray, *Vanity Fair* (1848).

A. Responding to the Cartoon

Two years after this cartoon appeared, in 1845, the young novelist Benjamin Disraeli (later to become prime minister of England and a close friend of Queen Victoria) published his novel *Sybil* with the subtitle "The Two Nations"—in pointed reference to the gulf between rich and poor.

? List five details that are important in the cartoon. (Be sure students note the maimed men, the babies in the pit, the bags of gold, the small figures in the mine shafts, which might be children, and the fat overseer.) What emotional impact does the pampered dog in the "capital" section create? Who might the woman with the anchor be? (Britannia) What might the hook in the picture's center be for? (To lift the babies to the level of the mine shafts for work)

Capital and Labor (1843). Cartoon, inspired by government report on the state of the workers in the coal mines.

A

> " In every successful act of writing and reading literature, one more satisfyingly coherent thing in the world is created or discovered."

essay by Macaulay, as baffling and precarious as a conversation with Humpty Dumpty. The second principal purpose or effect was to demonstrate that, however bleak and disorderly reality seemed to be, the writer and reader could make a pleasing order in it. Even when a story or poem said that the world was ugly or made no sense, the story or the poem could seem beautiful and make sense to its writer and reader. In every successful act of writing and reading literature, one more satisfyingly coherent thing in the world is created or discovered.

Finally, it is important to remember that these purposes and effects happened first to readers who were living Victorian lives. The poems, stories, novel excerpts, plays, and essays that make up this selection of Victorian literature did not exist above or outside the comfortable and often confident lives of their readers. Many of the people who read Dickens settled down with his books after dining in rooms as garishly decorated as the Veneerings'. Most of the young men and women who thrilled to Dante Gabriel Rossetti's sensualism and to A. E. Housman's tender gloom probably moved on to make proper and modestly happy marriages and to find worthy occupations. People who were making a lot of money listened to Carlyle and Ruskin telling them that they were foolish and damned. People who were disturbed by how much money was being made listened to Macaulay reminding them that a century or so before they might not have been able to afford, or even read, his book. Victorian literature needs to be read not just as a comment on the complexity of its culture, but also as an important part of that culture. Its writers sent their words to work in the world to alter, to reinforce, to challenge, to enlarge, or to relieve the ideas and feelings with which their contemporaries managed their lives.

Thomas Babington Macaulay (1800–1859)

Almost all of Thomas Babington Macaulay's writing carries the tone of satisfaction with Victorian civil and material progress that is evident in his description of seventeenth-century London streets. In a way, he was born to the belief that A the conditions of human life steadily improve because people work to improve them. His family was distinguished for its work in religious and political causes, especially the abolition of slavery in British possessions in the early nineteenth century.

After his graduation from Cambridge University, Macaulay began writing for relatively liberal intellectual and literary journals. He was admitted to the practice of law and elected to Parliament in 1830. In 1834 he went out to India as a member of the Supreme Council, its governing body. Before he returned to England in 1838, he had helped to organize the Indian educational system and had written the criminal code of British Imperial India.

On his return Macaulay entered Parliament again and served in several high government offices. In 1849, his first two volumes of a *History of England from the Succession of James II* were enormously successful. Readers were attracted by his liberal faith in progress, his use of narrative and biography, and his smooth, forceful style. Booksellers in the United States wrote to tell him that the sales of the *History* were second only to those of the Bible, and a group of British workers whose employer had had the book read to them wrote to thank Macaulay for writing a history they could understand. He published two other equally successful volumes in 1855, but the work remained unfinished at his death.

Macaulay eloquently voices the middle-class Victorian attitude toward government, history,

and civilization. He strongly believed that England's hopes for progress lay in free enterprise and not in government. "Our rulers will best promote the improvement of the nation," he wrote in 1830, "by strictly confining themselves to their own legitimate duties, by leaving capital to find its most lucrative course, commodities their fair price, industry and intelligence their natural reward, idleness and folly their natural punishment, by maintaining peace, by defending property, by diminishing the price of law, and by observing strict economy in every department of the State. Let the Government do this; the People will assuredly do the rest." Notice that Macaulay's prose style is that of a debater determined to persuade his audience. His writing is energetic and forceful, characterized by rhetorical devices such as simplification, exaggeration, and balance.

In 1857 Thomas Babington Macaulay was made a peer and was Lord Macaulay until his death in 1859.

B

A. Responding

? Do you see the world this way? (Answers will vary.) Do you think this view is held by the majority of people in America today? (Many people believe in less government rather than more. Others believe government regulations keep people and their businesses honest.) Why might it be important for some people to persuade themselves that they hold this view even if they really don't? (People often pretend to subscribe to the views of their bosses as a way of currying favor.)

B. Responding

? How do you think that Macaulay, who was considered liberal in his own day, would be classified today? (As a conservative)

PREPARATION

1. BUILDING ON PRIOR KNOWLEDGE. Before students begin reading the essay, refer them back to the introductory comments on Macaulay's views and their importance (text page 761). Students can also be reminded of what they know about London from earlier literature: See if they recall the *Diary* of Samuel Pepys, a contemporary of King Charles II (see text page 470), or Wordsworth's sonnet "Composed upon Westminster Bridge" (see text page 644).

2. ESTABLISHING A PURPOSE. Ask students to try to form visual images of these London streets and to compare these images with what they know of city life today.

3. PREREADING JOURNAL. Before they read, have students write two or three sentences describing how they feel their own community has changed in the past twenty-five years. Be sure they note whether they think the quality of human life has been improved by the changes, or worsened by them. (See writing assignments on text page 776.)

A. London Districts

Covent Garden was the site of the open-air fruit and vegetable market in London. In 1974 it was moved to a new site. The old warehouses were demolished, and the whole area is now "gentrified" with boutiques and shops. *Pygmalion* (text page 1148) opens in Covent Garden; the Royal Opera House is situated at the edge of the old market area; Lincoln's Inn Fields (see below) is a garden square in the lawyers' district.

B. About the Illustration

Employing more than forty woodcutters and producing over ninety illustrated books, Gustave Doré (1832–1883) is best known for his wood-engraved illustrations for the Bible and for Dante's *Inferno*.

? In what ways is this scene similar to one that might take place in a twentieth-century city? In what ways is it different?

C. Vocabulary

A *mountebank* was a peddler of quack medicines.

LONDON STREETS

Macaulay begins this passage by drawing attention to how much more important London was, compared to other towns in England, in the reign of King Charles II: that is, nearly two hundred years before Macaulay wrote. His vivid re-creation of seventeenth-century London emphasizes the progress of Victorian London.

The position of London, relative to the other towns of the empire, was, in the time of Charles II, far higher than at present. For at present the population of London is little more than six times the population of Manchester or of Liverpool. In the days of Charles II, the population of London was more than seventeen times the population of Bristol or of Norwich. It may be doubted whether any other instance can be mentioned of a great kingdom in which the first city was more than seventeen times as large as the second. There is reason to believe that in 1685 London had been, during about half a century, the most populous capital in Europe. The inhabitants, who are now at least nineteen hundred thousand, were then probably little more than half a million. . . .

We should greatly err if we were to suppose that any of the streets and squares then bore the same aspect as at present. The great majority of the houses, indeed, have, since that time, been wholly, or in great part, rebuilt. If the most fashionable parts of the capital could be placed before us, such as they then were, we should be disgusted by their squalid appearance, and poisoned by their noisome atmosphere. In Covent Garden a filthy and noisy market was held close to the dwellings of the great. Fruit women screamed, carters fought, cabbage stalks and rotten apples accumulated in heaps at the thresholds of the Countess of Berkshire and of the Bishop of Durham.

The center of Lincoln's Inn Fields was an open space where the rabble congregated every eve-

Congestion at Ludgate by Gustave Doré from *London, a Pilgrimage* by Doré and Jerrold (1860's).

ning, within a few yards of Cardigan House and Winchester House, to hear mountebanks harangue, to see bears dance, and to set dogs at oxen. Rubbish was shot[1] in every part of the area. Horses were exercised there. The beggars were as noisy and importunate as in the worst-governed cities of the Continent. A Lincoln's Inn mumper[2] was a proverb. The whole fraternity knew the arms and liveries of every charitably disposed grandee in the neighborhood, and, as soon as his lordship's coach and six appeared, came hopping and crawling in crowds to persecute him. These disorders lasted, in spite of many accidents, and of some legal proceedings, till, in the reign of George II, Sir Joseph Jekyll, Master of the Rolls,

---

1. **shot:** dumped.
2. **mumper:** a beggar who pretended to be disabled.

SUPPLEMENTARY SUPPORT MATERIALS
1. Vocabulary Activity Worksheet (CCB)
2. Review and Response Worksheet: Rhetorical Devices (CCB)
3. Language Skills Worksheet: Varying Sentence Structure (CCB)
4. Selection Test (CCB)

DEVELOPING VOCABULARY
The following words from the essay are tested in the Selection Test. (See also Vocabulary Activity Worksheet.)

squalid   facetious
to harangue   pugnacious
importunate   impunity
grandee   dissolute
offal   to execute

READING CHECK TEST
1. Life in seventeenth-century London was orderly and comfortable. (F)
2. Gangs and beggars roamed the streets. (T)
3. Houses were not numbered because few people could read. (T)
4. Watchmen were supposed to patrol the streets at night. (T)

Print Collection, Miriam and Ira D. Wallach Division of Art, Prints, and Photographs, New York Public Library.

was knocked down and nearly killed in the middle of the square. Then at length palisades[3] were set up and a pleasant garden laid out.

Saint James' Square was a receptacle for all the offal and cinders, for all the dead cats and dead dogs of Westminster. At one time a cudgel player[4] kept the ring there. At another time an impudent squatter settled himself there, and built a shed for rubbish under the windows of the gilded saloons in which the first magnates of the realm, Norfolk, Ormond, Kent, and Pembroke, gave banquets and balls. It was not till these nuisances had lasted through a whole generation, and till much had been written about them, that the inhabitants ap-

plied to Parliament for permission to put up rails, and to plant trees.

When such was the state of the region inhabited by the most luxurious portion of society, we may easily believe that the great body of the population suffered what would now be considered as insupportable grievances. The pavement was detestable; all foreigners cried shame upon it. The drainage was so bad that in rainy weather the gutters soon became torrents. Several facetious poets have commemorated the fury with which these black rivulets roared down Snow Hill and Ludgate Hill, bearing to Fleet Ditch a vast tribute of animal and vegetable filth from the stalls of butchers and greengrocers. This flood was profusely thrown to right and left by coaches and carts. To keep as far from the carriage road as possible was therefore the wish of every pedes-

---

3. **palisades:** a fence made of large, pointed stakes.
4. **cudgel player:** a performer who challenged passers-by to try to beat him in a match using short staffs or clubs.

Thomas Babington Macaulay 775

Have students summarize Macaulay's reasons for asserting that conditions in London have improved.

ANALYZING THE ESSAY
Identifying Facts
1. He offers population statistics: In Charles II's time, London's population was six times that of Manchester or Liv-

erpool. In 1865, London was the most populous European capital, with a little more than half a million people; in Macaulay's day it had at least nineteen hundred thousand.
2. Residences were close to the filthy, noisy market of Covent Garden and the rabble gathered in Lincoln's Inn Fields every evening. The streets were full of rubbish and dead animals, and residents

dumped their chamber pots into the streets. Beggars, theives, and gangs of young ruffians bothered people walking in the streets.
3. Many of the residents, especially workers who had to locate houses, could not read.
(Answers continue in left-hand column.)

(Continued from top.)
Interpreting Meanings
4. Answers will vary. Some may conclude from the words he uses to describe the seventeenth-century poor (*rabble, the ignorant, noisy and importunate, impudent squatter*) that Macaulay was hardly a liberal reformer in sympathy with the poor, but was instead allied with maintaining the status quo for the wealthy, privileged, and educated upper classes.
5. Students may mention the many specific details about everyday life not usually given in a history text and Macaulay's clean and easy-to-read prose style.

trian. The mild and timid gave the wall. The bold and athletic took it. If two roisterers met, they cocked their hats in each other's faces and pushed each other about till the weaker was shoved toward the kennel.[5] If he was a mere bully he sneaked off, muttering that he should find a time. If he was pugnacious, the encounter probably ended in a duel behind Montague House.

The houses were not numbered. There would indeed have been little advantage in numbering them; for of the coachmen, chairmen,[6] porters, and errand boys of London, a very small proportion could read. It was necessary to use marks which the most ignorant could understand. The shops were therefore distinguished by painted or sculptured signs, which gave a gay and grotesque aspect to the streets. The walk from Charing Cross to Whitechapel lay through an endless succession of Saracens' Heads, Royal Oaks, Blue Bears, and Golden Lambs, which disappeared when they were no longer required for the direction of the common people.

When the evening closed in, the difficulty and danger of walking about London became serious indeed. The garret windows were opened and pails

were emptied, with little regard to those who were passing below. Falls, bruises, and broken bones were of constant occurrence. For, till the last year of the reign of Charles II [1685], most of the streets were left in profound darkness. Thieves and robbers plied their trade with impunity; yet they were hardly so terrible to peaceable citizens as another class of ruffians. It was a favorite amusement of dissolute young gentlemen to swagger by night about the town, breaking windows, upsetting sedans, beating quiet men, and offering rude caresses to pretty women. Several dynasties of these tyrants had, since the Restoration, domineered over the streets. The Muns and Tityre Tus had given place to the Hectors, and the Hectors had been recently succeeded by the Scourers. At a later period rose the Nicker, the Hawcubite, and the yet more dreaded name of Mohawk. The machinery for keeping the peace was utterly contemptible. There was an act of Common Council which provided that more than a thousand watchmen should be constantly on the alert in the city, from sunset to sunrise, and that every inhabitant should take his turn of duty. But this act was negligently executed. Few of those who were summoned left their homes; and those few generally found it more agreeable to tipple in alehouses than to pace the streets.

---

5. **kennel:** gutter.
6. **chairmen:** bearers of sedan chairs in which affluent Londoners were carried through the streets.

Responding to the Essay

Analyzing the Essay

Identifying Facts

1. What statistics does Macaulay offer to measure the importance of London as a city under Charles II and under Queen Victoria?
2. What are some of the "insupportable grievances" that the population of London suffered in the seventeenth century, according to Macaulay?
3. In the seventeenth century, why would it have been useless to place numbers on the houses?

Interpreting Meanings

4. What would you guess Macaulay's politics to have been?
5. Given this sample of it, why do you think that Macaulay's *History* was so popular?

Writing About the Essay

A Creative Response

1. **Conducting an Interview.** Select an older person in your family or community, and interview him or her about the physical appearance of the area where you live, compared to its appearance some years ago. Before the interview, prepare a list of specific questions.

A Critical Response

2. **Presenting an Oral Report.** Use the results of your interview and other appropriate reference sources in the library to prepare and deliver an oral report comparing and contrasting the physical appearance of your community now with its appearance some years ago. In your report, be sure to touch on the concept of "progress."

Alfred, Lord Tennyson (1809–1892)

A When Alfred Tennyson learned that Lord Byron had died while on his adventure to help Greek nationalist rebels, he went out to the woods and carved on a piece of sandstone, "Byron is dead." Tennyson was fourteen years old. He felt sure that he would be a poet, and he was already practicing the dramatic gestures of the Romantic poets he admired.

Tennyson grew up in a Lincolnshire village, where his father was a clergyman of good family but little money. His father, given to serious bouts of emotional instability and depression, educated his large family (seven sons and four daughters) at home. He encouraged young Alfred's interest in poetry, and in 1827 Alfred and his brother Charles published anonymously *Poems by Two Brothers*. That same year Tennyson entered Cambridge University.

"That man must be a poet," someone remarked on seeing Tennyson at Cambridge. Tennyson was six feet tall (an unusual height at that time) and dark, his strong head crowned by a wavy mane of hair, his shyness masked by an air of preoccupation and self-possession. Tennyson
B soon joined a group of young intellectuals who called themselves The Apostles and met to discuss literature, religion, philosophy, and politics. Tennyson's new friends urged him to write poems based on "the broad and common interests of the time" and believed that he was destined to become the greatest poet of their generation.

In 1831, when Tennyson's father died, lack of funds forced him to leave Cambridge without graduating. His father's death began a troubled period for Tennyson. He lived at home with his mother, sisters, and some of his brothers. In 1832 he published his first significant book of poems. Some of its reviewers derided his melancholy themes and his weak imitations of Keats's language. The next year Tennyson was devastated by the sudden death of his closest friend,
C Arthur Henry Hallam. Tennyson became engaged to marry in 1838, but the marriage was postponed for twelve years because of his uncertain prospects. In 1843 he lost most of his fami-

Caricature of Alfred, Lord Tennyson by Frederick Waddy (1872).

ly's little money in a wood-carving business that failed. Finally, his physical and mental health broken, he entered a private hospital to undergo a curious treatment of being immersed in hot and cold baths and then wrapped in wet sheets.

During all these difficult years, Tennyson apparently never thought about working at anything but poetry. He disciplined and polished the style of his early poems until he developed the melodious line and rich imagery of poems like "The Lady of Shalott" and "Now Sleeps the Crimson Petal." He wrote some new poems in the vigorous dramatic style of "Ulysses," and he began the long series of lyric and reflective poems that finally became his elegy for Hallam, *In Memoriam*. Tennyson published almost nothing during his "ten years of silence" from 1832 to 1842, but the friends to whom he read his poems remained convinced of his promise.

Gradually, Tennyson began to make his way. His *Poems in Two Volumes* (1842) was favorably

D **A. Lord Byron**
Byron's biography is on text page 678.

B. "The Apostles"
The Apostles continued into the twentieth century, when famous members included the economist John Maynard Keynes, the reforming journalist Leonard Woolf, the biographer Lytton Strachey, the philosopher Bertrand Russell, and the novelist E. M. Forster.

C. Expansion
Some scholars have suggested that an additional reason for the postponement was Tennyson's own fear of inheriting his family's melancholia and instability.

D. Responding to the illustration
? "Read" this caricature and tell what you think it is saying about Tennyson. (Perhaps that his name and popularity keep him swinging high in the heavens of poetry) What caption would you write for this caricature? (Example: "High, Higher, Highest")

A. Expansion
The Latin title *In Memoriam* means "in memory."

B. Further Reading
If students are interested in exploring Tennyson's fascinating epic *Idylls of the King,* recommend that they first review the material on Thomas Malory on text page 148. Then urge them to sample Tennyson's long poem by beginning with "The Passing of Arthur."

A reviewed, and three years later the government granted him an annual pension of two hundred pounds. In 1850 he published *In Memoriam,* which was immediately successful, going through three editions in the first year. That same year he was named Poet Laureate (after Wordsworth's death), and he finally married. Tennyson settled into the long, successful career that had been expected of him, and for the rest of his life he was considered the greatest living English poet.

Occasionally Tennyson wrote directly about public matters, as he did in "The Charge of the Light Brigade," a poem about a battle during the Crimean War. Usually he told stories. *In Memoriam* is the story of his own recovery of faith in the immortality of the soul and the harmony of creation—despite the evidence of science and his deep sense of the unfairness of Hallam's death.

B *The Idylls of the King,* twelve episodes that Tennyson began publishing in 1859 and brought together in one book in 1885, makes the rise, fall, and possible return of King Arthur into a kind of parable of the moral qualities of good political leaders and of their betrayal by the rest of us. "Ulysses" is about a brave, or foolish, or brave and foolish response to the securities and comforts of an orderly life very like that of middle-class mid-Victorian England.

In the forty years before his death in 1892, Tennyson published nearly a dozen volumes of poems along with the *Idylls* and some plays. His books sold like best-selling novels and made him rich. He lived in the country like an affluent gentleman. Occasionally, he went to London to walk around in his black cloak and broad-brimmed hat and to meet with distinguished writers, scientists, churchmen, politicians, and sometimes the Queen. Tourists hung around his country house on the Isle of Wight and climbed trees to get a glimpse of him. People sent him mountains of poetry; he once estimated that he had received a verse for every three minutes of his life. In 1883, he was made a peer of the realm and took his seat in the House of Lords as Alfred, Lord Tennyson.

Tennyson never lost the melancholy and sense of chaos that friends and reviewers found in him and his poems in the 1830's and 1840's. Characteristically, his poems are about how to respond to the losses and disorders of love, death, old age, the passing of leaders, and challenges to old standards of political and moral authority. He was immensely popular with his contemporaries because he spoke in a beautiful, measured language of their sense of the precariousness and sadness of life. And he also assured his readers that his own experience of sadness and disorder had taught him that everything was part of a benevolent plan in which eventually all losses will be made good.

PREPARATION

ESTABLISHING A PURPOSE Before students read "Tears, Idle Tears," ask them to read question 6. As they read have them decide if the speaker feels a loss of faith or of human love. (You might assign the poem for memorization; it once could be recited by heart by thousands of Tennyson's avid readers.)

SUPPLEMENTARY SUPPORT MATERIALS
1. Vocabulary Activity Worksheet (*CCB*)
2. Review and Response Worksheet: Imagery and Connotations (*CCB*)
3. Selection Test (*CCB*)

DEVELOPING VOCABULARY
The following word from the poem is tested in the Selection Test. (See also Vocabulary Activity Worksheet.)
casement

CLOSURE
Have three students discuss in class the source of the speaker's "divine despair."

This lyric is from *The Princess,* a long narrative poem about the education and emancipation of women. The narrative is interspersed with eleven lyric songs, of which this is the most famous. Tennyson wrote this poem while visiting Tintern Abbey in the autumn, the same site contemplated by Wordsworth in his famous meditation "Lines Composed a Few Miles Above Tintern Abbey." While Tennyson's poem is similarly elegiac, its theme and tone are more somber than Wordsworth's pastoral lines.

Tears, Idle Tears

Tears, idle tears, I know not what they mean,
Tears from the depth of some divine despair
Rise in the heart, and gather to the eyes,
In looking on the happy autumn-fields,
5 And thinking of the days that are no more.

Fresh as the first beam glittering on a sail,
That brings our friends up from the underworld,
Sad as the last which reddens over one
That sinks with all we love below the verge;
10 So sad, so fresh, the days that are no more.

Ah, sad and strange as in dark summer dawns
The earliest pipe of half-awakened birds
To dying ears, when unto dying eyes
The casement slowly grows a glimmering square;
15 So sad, so strange, the days that are no more.

Dear as remembered kisses after death,
And sweet as those by hopeless fancy feigned
On lips that are for others; deep as love,
Deep as first love, and wild with all regret;
20 O Death in Life, the days that are no more!

Responding to the Poem

Analyzing the Poem

Identifying Details

1. What does the speaker gaze on in the first stanza? What memory prompts his tears?
2. Stanzas 2–4 present a series of comparisons that attempt to make concrete the abstract memory of "days that are no more." What are these comparisons?

Interpreting Meanings

3. How does the sequence of **images** in this poem result in an increasingly darker tone?

4. Explain and comment on the meaning of the poem's last line.
5. Analyze the structure of "Tears, Idle Tears." What is the scene of each stanza? Why do you think Tennyson arranges the scenes and events in the order he does?
6. What do you think the "divine despair" is in line 2? Do you think Tennyson is alluding to the account of the Fall of Adam and Eve in Genesis here? Would that account explain the poet's existential sadness?

ANALYZING THE POEM
Identifying Details
1. The autumn fields.
  The days that are no more.
2. Stanza 2: The days that are no more are as fresh as the first beam of the rising sun and as sad as the last sunbeam. In stanza 3, they are as sad as the morning sound of birds to dying ears, as sad as the morning light to dying eyes. In stanza 4, they are as dear as kisses remembered after death, as sweet as imagined kisses, as deep as first love, as wild as regret.
3. The poem moves from simple images of autumn fields, to images of boats carrying the dead, to images of birds singing to dying ears, to intimate images of a dead loved one.
4. Time past is like death in the midst of life.
5. The poem begins with a statement of an emotion (lines 1–3) and then analyzes the cause of that emotion.
6. See also Hopkins's "Spring and Fall" on text page 828.

A. **Allusion**

? What erotic motif is suggested by the allusion to Zeus and Danaë? (Physical love)

PREPARATION

ESTABLISHING A PURPOSE. Questions 1 and 2 should set a purpose for reading this love poem.

SUPPLEMENTARY SUPPORT MATERIALS
1. Vocabulary Activity Worksheet (*CCB*)
2. Review and Response Worksheet: Imagery (*CCB*)
3. Selection Test (*CCB*)

CLOSURE

Have three students paraphrase the poem for the rest of the class. Allow the class a chance to evaluate the paraphrases.

ANALYZING THE POEM

Identifying Details
1. Night.
2. To his beloved. He asks her to become part of him.

Interpreting Meanings
3. The "palace walk," decorated fountain, and peacock suggest wealth.
4. The light of the stars "showers down" upon the Earth.
5. The first and final stanzas end with a command to the lover. Each stanza begins with the word *Now* followed by a present-tense verb; each stanza ends with a prepositional phrase ending in *me*.
6. Answers will vary. Students may note that, except for the commonplace firefly, the images in stanzas 1 and 2 are exotic and ornate; those in stanzas 3 and 4 are of heavenly objects. Some students may say that the mood of the poem is mysterious and sensuous.

This poem, which is also from *The Princess,* was set to music several times in the Victorian period.

It is a good example of Tennyson's use of finely wrought images and melodious sounds.

Now Sleeps the Crimson Petal

Now sleeps the crimson petal, now the white;
Nor waves the cypress in the palace walk;
Nor winks the gold fin in the porphyry° font.°
The firefly wakens; waken thou with me.

5   Now droops the milk-white peacock like a ghost,
And like a ghost she glimmers on to me.

Now lies the Earth all Danaë° to the stars,
And all thy heart lies open unto me.

A ☐ Now slides the silent meteor on, and leaves
10   A shining furrow, as thy thoughts in me.

Now folds the lily all her sweetness up,
And slips into the bosom of the lake.
So fold thyself, my dearest, thou, and slip
Into my bosom and be lost in me.

3. **porphyry** (por′fər·ē): a deep red or purple stone. **font:** fountain.

7. **Danaë** (dan′ə·ē′): in Greek mythology, a princess on whom the god Zeus descended in the form of a shower of gold.

Responding to the Poem

Analyzing the Poem

Identifying Details
1. What time of day is described in the poem?
2. Whom is the speaker talking to? What does the speaker ask in the last two lines of the poem?

Interpreting Meanings
3. Various details in the poem hint at the setting, or at least at the social position or rank of the speaker. What are these hints?
4. Explain the meaning of line 7. How can the Earth lie "all Danaë to the stars"?
5. Identify the instances of **repetition** and **parallel syntax** in the poem.
6. Pick out two or three lines whose **images** and sounds you think are especially remarkable. How do these lines help create the mood of the poem?

Writing About the Poem

A Creative Response
1. **Setting the Lyric to Music.** Experiment with making up a melody for this lyric. You do not need to know musical notation; simply try to find a pleasing melody that fits the words of the song's stanzas.

A Critical Response
2. **Analyzing Words and Images.** Write a brief composition analyzing the emotional effect of Tennyson's choice of words and images in this poem. (Remember that both words and images can have powerful positive or negative *connotations*, or emotional associations.) Use a statement of the poem's mood as your thesis statement. Then support this statement with specific examples of the poet's choice of words and images.

ESTABLISHING A PURPOSE. The headnote sets up a purpose for reading. Be sure students picture the speaker in his setting as they read. (On a cliff overlooking the wild sea)

SUPPLEMENTARY SUPPORT MATERIALS
1. Vocabulary Activity Worksheet (*CCB*)
2. Review and Response Worksheet: Atmosphere (*CCB*)
3. Selection Test (*CCB*)

DEVELOPING VOCABULARY
The following word from the poem is tested in the Selection Test. (See also Vocabulary Activity Worksheet.)
crag

CLOSURE
Have three students suggest one adjective each that describes the tone of the lyric. Have three other students cite details that contribute to the tone.

This poem is a kind of elegy—a mournful hymn in which instances of vigorous life remind the speaker of a personal loss that has left him still able to observe, but not to participate. Read the poem aloud, and listen to how the sound is related to the sense. How do the sounds of lines 1–2 and 13–14 contrast with the rest of the poem?

Break, Break, Break

A
Break, break, break,
   On thy cold gray stones, O Sea!
And I would that my tongue could utter
   The thoughts that arise in me.

5   O, well for the fisherman's boy,
   That he shouts with his sister at play!
O, well for the sailor lad,
   That he sings in his boat on the bay!

And the stately ships go on
10   To their haven under the hill;
But O for the touch of a vanished hand,
   And the sound of a voice that is still!

B
Break, break, break,
   At the foot of thy crags, O Sea!
15   But the tender grace of a day that is dead
   Will never come back to me.

A. Meter/ Alliteration
Notice how the spondees in lines 1–2 and 13 suggest the crashing of waves.

B. Sound and Mood
The harsh force in lines 1–2 and 13–14 contrast with the basically anapestic lilt of the other lines.

ANALYZING THE POEM
Identifying Details
1. At the seashore, watching the waves break.
2. For the touch of a vanished hand and the sound of a stilled voice.

Interpreting Meanings
3. The speaker's heart is breaking. A relationship has broken up.
4. The two boys suggest the joy of life and youth; the ships suggest serenity.
   The speaker is grieving.
5. Some students may say that the sorrow remains the same. Others may feel that the speaker seems to be somewhat more resigned to his loss.

Responding to the Poem

Analyzing the Poem

Identifying Details
1. Where is the speaker as the poem begins?
2. In the third stanza, what does the speaker grieve for?

Interpreting Meanings
3. The words of the title are repeated twice: at the beginning of the first and fourth stanzas, when the speaker calls on the waves of the sea to "break, break, break." Considering the **atmosphere** and **tone** of the poem, what else might we imagine to be "breaking" in this lyric?
4. What moods are suggested by the **images** of the fisherman's boy (line 5), the sailor lad (line 7), and the stately ships (line 9)? How do these moods contrast with the speaker's emotions?
5. Has the speaker's sorrow changed in any way from the beginning of the poem to its end? If so, how?

Writing About the Poem

A Critical Response
Analyzing the Poem's Structure. Write an essay analyzing the structure of this four-stanza lyric. In your essay, focus on the poem's syntax, including Tennyson's use of parallelism, apostrophe, interjection, and repetition.

PREPARATION

ESTABLISHING A PURPOSE. Have students read the first writing assignment. As they read the poem aloud, they should think of how it affects them.

SUPPLEMENTARY SUPPORT MATERIALS
1. Review and Response Worksheet: Imagery and Theme (CCB)
2. Selection Test (CCB)

CLOSURE
Have students identify the basic metaphor of the poem. (What is death compared with?) What does the title mean?

ANALYZING THE POEM
Identifying Details
1. He wishes that there will be no moaning of the bar when he puts out to sea.
2. He hopes to see his Pilot when he has crossed the bar.

Interpreting Meanings
3. The "Pilot," or someone who acts as a guide, refers to God.
4. The voyage is a metaphor for the journey from life to death.
5. Student responses will vary. They should note that the rhythm is

A. Meaning
❓ What could the famous "moaning" be? (People moaning? The sounds that the water makes because the bar is shallow?)

B. Meaning
❓ What is "that"? (The soul) What is suggested by the word *home*? (Possibly Heaven, God)

C. Archaism
Bourne might have reminded Tennyson's readers of Hamlet's famous image for death as "The undiscovered country, from whose bourn / No traveler returns" (Act III, Scene 1, line 79).

Tennyson wrote this poem in 1889, at the age of eighty, while crossing the channel that separates England from the Isle of Wight. Just before his death in 1892, Tennyson directed that this poem be printed at the end of all editions of his collected verse.

A bar is a sandbar at the mouth of a harbor. Beyond the bar is deep sea.

Crossing the Bar

Sunset and evening star,
    And one clear call for me!
A And may there be no moaning of the bar,
    When I put out to sea,

5   But such a tide as moving seems asleep,
    Too full for sound and foam,
B When that which drew from out the boundless deep
    Turns again home.

Twilight and evening bell,
10   And after that the dark!
And may there be no sadness of farewell,
    When I embark;

C For though from out our bourne° of Time and Place
    The flood may bear me far,
15 I hope to see my Pilot° face to face
    When I have crossed the bar.

13. **bourne** (bôrn): (archaic) boundary.

15. **Pilot:** a person who knows the local waters and guides a ship as it enters or leaves a harbor.

Responding to the Poem

Analyzing the Poem

Identifying Details
1. What does the speaker wish in the first stanza?
2. What hope does the speaker express in the final stanza?

Interpreting Meanings
3. Who might the "Pilot" (line 15) be?
4. What is the speaker's sea voyage a **metaphor** for?
5. Analyze the rhythm of the poem and comment on how it affected you.

basically iambic with a pattern of shorter lines (3 feet) followed by longer lines (4 and 5 feet). The soothing rhythm seems to imitate the ebb and flow of the tide, or wave action.

Sunset on Wet Sand (detail) by J. M. W. Turner (1845). Watercolor over pencil.

The Whitworth Art Gallery, University of Manchester, England.

A. Humanities Connection: About the Fine Art
Joseph Mallord William Turner (1775–1851) was the most admired English painter of the nineteenth century, and arguably the greatest landscape painter that England has ever produced. Although he is usually described as a "Romantic" artist, he actually foreshadowed the French Impressionists of the last third of the nineteenth century (especially Claude Monet) in his radical experiments with light and color.

Writing About the Poem

A Creative Response

1. **Writing a Letter.** Imagine that this poem was sent to you in a letter by the poet himself. Write a reply to Tennyson, expressing your reactions to the poem's theme.

A Critical Response

2. **Comparing and Contrasting Imagery.** In a brief essay, compare and contrast Tennyson's use of the sea in this poem and in "Break, Break, Break." How are the seas in each poem different? How does the image of the sea help to create the tone and meaning of each poem?

PREPARATION

1. BUILDING ON PRIOR KNOWLEDGE. The Victorians, like their Romantic predecessors, were fascinated with medieval legends and settings. Students should discuss what they recall of the Arthurian cycle of legends (What was Camelot?) and especially of the medieval code of chivalry (see text pages 71, 147, and 148–155).

2. ESTABLISHING A PURPOSE. Before students read "The Lady of Shalott," you may want to direct them to the Comment on the Poem (text page 788). They should be alert to symbolic or allegorical meanings as they read.

3. PREREADING JOURNAL. Have students record in their journals all the connotations that the word *shadow* has for them. Share the responses in class.

A. Humanities Connection: Discussing the Fine Art
The figures of British artist John William Waterhouse (1847–1917) reflect an imaginative power and a very personal style. For the most part, Waterhouse's paintings are illustrations of classic myths treated with fantasy. Three Waterhouse works, *St. Eulalia, The Magic Circle,* and *Consulting the Oracle,* hang in the National Gallery of British Art.

After they finish the poem, have students go back to the painting and see if Tennyson explains the chain, the tapestry, the crucifix, and the candles.

Tennyson wrote this ballad in 1832 and revised it extensively in 1842. He said of the imaginary Lady in the poem: "Her newborn love for something, for someone in the wide world from which she had been so long secluded, takes her out of the region of shadows into that of realities." The contrast of shadow and reality is one of several oppositions in the poem. As you read this ballad, look also for contrasts between the Lady's isolation and the activity of the broader community, between her work as an artist and the labor of the reapers.

The Lady of Shalott by John William Waterhouse (1888). Oil.   The Tate Gallery, London.

The Lady of Shalott

Part I

On either side the river lie
Long fields of barley and of rye,
That clothe the wold° and meet the sky;
And through the field the road runs by
5   To many-towered Camelot;°
And up and down the people go,
Gazing where the lilies blow°
Round an island there below,
    The island of Shalott.

3. **wold:** a plain or open hilly region.

5. **Camelot:** a legendary city, site of King Arthur's court and the capital of Arthur's kingdom.
7. **blow:** blossom.

SUPPLEMENTARY SUPPORT MATERIALS
1. Vocabulary Activity Worksheet (*CCB*)
2. Review and Response Worksheet: Sensory Details (*CCB*)
3. Language Skills Worksheet: Nouns (*CCB*)
4. Selection Test (*CCB*)
5. Audiocassette recording

DEVELOPING VOCABULARY
The following words from the poem are tested in the Selection Test. (See also Vocabulary Activity Worksheet
sheaves   to burnish   seer

10
Willows whiten,° aspens quiver,
Little breezes dusk and shiver
Through the wave that runs forever
By the island in the river

A
    Flowing down to Camelot.
15
Four gray walls, and four gray towers,
Overlook a space of flowers,
And the silent isle imbowers°
    The Lady of Shalott.

By the margin, willow-veiled,
20
Slide the heavy barges trailed
By slow horses; and unhailed
The shallop° flitteth silken-sailed
    Skimming down to Camelot:
But who hath seen her wave her hand?
25
Or at the casement seen her stand?
Or is she known in all the land,
    The Lady of Shalott?

Only reapers, reaping early
In among the bearded barley,
30
Hear a song that echoes cheerly
From the river winding clearly,
B
    Down to towered Camelot:
And by the moon the reaper weary,
Piling <u>sheaves</u> in uplands airy,
35
Listening, whispers "'Tis the fairy
    Lady of Shalott."

Part II

C
There she weaves by night and day
A magic web with colors gay.
She has heard a whisper say,
40
A curse is on her if she stay
    To look down to Camelot.
She knows not what the curse may be,
And so she weaveth steadily,
And little other care hath she,
45
    The Lady of Shalott.

D
And moving through a mirror clear°
That hangs before her all the year,
Shadows of the world appear.
There she sees the highway near
50
    Winding down to Camelot;
There the river eddy whirls,
And there the surly village churls,°
And the red cloaks of market girls,
    Pass onward from Shalott.

10. whiten: show the white undersides of their leaves, blown by the wind.

17. imbowers: shelters with trees, gardens, and flowers.

22. shallop: a small, open boat.

46. mirror clear: Weavers worked on the back of the tapestry so that they could easily knot their yarns. In order to see their designs, weavers looked in a mirror that reflected the front of the tapestry.

52. churls: peasants; country folk.

A. Setting
? What details make the locale especially vivid? (White willows, quivering aspens, breezes, waves, gray walls and towers, flowers, silence) What contrast is established in lines 10–18? (The details in lines 10–14 suggest color and movement; the details in lines 15–18 suggest drabness and silence.) Note the alliteration in line 10.

B. Rhyme
The slant rhymes in this stanza are famous (*early/barley, weary/airy*).

C. Interpreting
The Lady's "magic web" is interpreted as her art.

D. Interpreting
The artist experiences life only as through a mirror—second hand.

A. **Responding**
[?] How do the last two lines in this stanza reinforce our sense of the Lady's melancholy isolation? (They sharply contrast with the "social" scenes of ordinary life above.)

B. **Turning Point**
Here is the turning point of the story. Tennyson himself said that these lines are key to the poem's meaning.

C. **Connections**
Recall the knight called Redcrosse in Spenser's *The Faerie Queene.* (The yellow field is the field of barley on the shore near the Lady's island.)

D. **Alliteration**
Note the sound effects created by alliteration in these lines. (G's and b's)

55 Sometimes a troop of damsels glad,
An abbot on an ambling pad,°
Sometimes a curly shepherd-lad,
Or long-haired page in crimson clad,
    Goes by to towered Camelot;
60 And sometimes through the mirror blue
The knights come riding two and two:

A   She hath no loyal knight and true,
      The Lady of Shalott.

But in her web she still delights
65 To weave the mirror's magic sights,
For often through the silent nights
A funeral, with plumes and lights
    And music, went to Camelot;
Or when the moon was overhead,
70 Came two young lovers lately wed:

B   "I am half sick of shadows," said
      The Lady of Shalott.

Part III

A bow-shot from her bower-eaves,
He rode between the barley sheaves,
75 The sun came dazzling through the leaves,
And flamed upon the brazen greaves°
    Of bold Sir Lancelot.

C   A red-cross knight° for ever kneeled
To a lady in his shield,
80 That sparkled on the yellow field,
    Beside remote Shalott.

The gemmy bridle glittered free,
Like to some branch of stars we see
Hung in the golden Galaxy.°

D   85 The bridle bells rang merrily
    As he rode down to Camelot:
And from his blazoned baldric° slung
A mighty silver bugle hung,
And as he rode his armor rung.
90   Beside remote Shalott.

All in the blue unclouded weather
Thick-jeweled shone the saddle-leather,
The helmet and the helmet-feather
Burned like one burning flame together,
95   As he rode down to Camelot.
As often through the purple night,
Below the starry clusters bright,
Some bearded meteor, trailing light,
    Moves over still Shalott.

56. **pad:** an easy-gaited horse.

76. **greaves:** armor for the legs from ankle to knee.

78. **red-cross knight:** The red cross is the emblem of St. George, England's patron saint.

84. **Galaxy:** the Milky Way.

87. **blazoned baldric:** a richly decorated belt worn diagonally over one shoulder for carrying a bugle or sword.

READING CHECK TEST
1. The Lady of Shalott has been seduced and abandoned by Sir Lancelot.
(F)
2. The Lady of Shalott will be cursed if
she stops her weaving. (F)
3. The Lady sees shadows of the world
through her mirror. (T)

4. After the Lady of Shalott looks toward Camelot to watch Sir Lancelot, the
mirror cracks. (T)
5. The Lady of Shalott dies in her tower
and is put in a boat by her servants. (F)

100   His broad clear brow in sunlight glowed;
       On burnished hooves his warhorse trode;
       From underneath his helmet flowed
       His coal-black curls as on he rode,
            As he rode down to Camelot.
105   From the bank and from the river
       He flashed into the crystal mirror,
       "Tirra lirra," by the river
            Sang Sir Lancelot.

       She left the web, she left the loom,
110   She made three paces through the room,
       She saw the water lily bloom,
       She saw the helmet and the plume,
A   She looked down to Camelot.
       Out flew the web and floated wide;
115   The mirror cracked from side to side;
       "The curse is come upon me," cried
            The Lady of Shalott.

Part IV

       In the stormy east-wind straining,
B   The pale yellow woods were waning,
120   The broad stream in his banks complaining,
       Heavily the low sky raining
            Over towered Camelot;
       Down she came and found a boat
       Beneath a willow left afloat,
125   And round about the prow she wrote
            The Lady of Shalott.

       And down the river's dim expanse
       Like some bold seer in a trance,
       Seeing all his own mischance—
130   With a glassy countenance
            Did she look to Camelot.
       And at the closing of the day
       She loosed the chain, and down she lay;
       The broad stream bore her far away,
135   The Lady of Shalott.

       Lying, robed in snowy white
       That loosely flew to left and right—
       The leaves upon her falling light—
       Through the noises of the night
140   She floated down to Camelot:
       And as the boathead wound along
       The willowy hills and fields among,
       They heard her singing her last song,
            The Lady of Shalott.

A. Climax
The sight of the
handsome knight
has made the Lady
do what was for-
bidden: She looks
directly at Camelot.
Notice the conse-
quences in the
next lines.

**B. Pathetic
Fallacy**
Here is a good ex-
ample of the "pa-
thetic fallacy" as a
literary device.
(The pathetic falla-
cy occurs when a
writer uses nature
to mirror human
feelings or emo-
tions.)

Have students illustrate Tennyson's musical sound effects by preparing the poem for an oral reading. They could arrange it for three voices: a chorus, the Lady, and Lancelot.

ANALYZING THE POEM
Identifying Details
1. The setting is a castle ("Four gray walls, and four gray towers") on an island in a river that leads to Camelot. On either side of the river are fields of barley and rye; lilies, willows, and aspens surround the island castle.
2. She "weaveth steadily" by night and day.

Reflected in the mirror are the shadows of the world. The poet mentions specifically the highway to Camelot, the river, the village people, knights, a funeral, and two newlyweds.
3. She stops weaving and sets off to Camelot by boat.

She dies mysteriously (her blood froze) on her journey to Camelot. When she arrives, everyone comes down to see her. The royal celebration ends, the knights cross themselves in fear, and Lancelot utters a blessing for her.

A. Symbol
What do you think is the significance of the repeated emphasis on the mirror, the tapestry, and this song? (They all can symbolize the artist who creates a world that mirrors the real one. The art is the tapestry and the song. When the artist turns from his or her art to the ordinary world, his or her song dies.)

B. Irony
How do you respond to Lancelot's valedictory prayer? What mood does it establish for the conclusion of the story? (Ironic, for it is only at her death that the Lady of Shalott comes face to face with Lancelot, the object of her desire and indirect cause of her death)

> 145 Heard a carol, mournful, holy,
> Chanted loudly, chanted lowly,
> Till her blood was frozen slowly,
> And her eyes were darkened wholly,
>   Turned to towered Camelot.
> 150 For ere she reached upon the tide
> The first house by the waterside,
> **A** Singing in her song she died,
>   The Lady of Shalott.
>
> Under tower and balcony,
> 155 By garden wall and gallery,
> A gleaming shape she floated by,
> Dead-pale between the houses high,
>   Silent into Camelot.
> Out upon the wharfs they came,
> 160 Knight and burgher,° lord and dame,
> And round the prow they read her name,
>   *The Lady of Shalott.*
>
> Who is this? and what is here?
> And in the lighted palace near
> 165 Died the sound of royal cheer;
> And they crossed themselves for fear,
>   All the knights at Camelot:
> But Lancelot mused a little space;
> **B** He said, "She has a lovely face;
> 170 God in his mercy lend her grace,
>   The Lady of Shalott."

160. **burgher:** citizen.

A Comment on the Poem

Readers may differ in regard to the meaning or moral of the simple story this richly ornamented and carefully wrought poem tells. But no one should disregard the clue offered by Tennyson himself: "Her newborn love for something," he said of the Lady of Shalott, "for someone in the wide world from which she had been so long secluded, takes her out of the region of shadows into that of realities." He is referring particularly to the last lines of Part II when, having watched a young bride and groom in the moonlight, the Lady declares that she is "half sick of shadows."

Like the weaving that perpetually occupies the heroine—"A magic web with colors gay"—the narrative moves from scene to scene with a tapestried grace that quietly captures the romantic heart of the Age of Chivalry. The Lady is appropriately beautiful, wan, sequestered, and mysterious. Sir Lancelot, panoplied to the hilt with every object in the book of heraldry, is less a man than a vision of a man. And Camelot itself, "many-towered," exists like a little city afloat in time.

The "mirror clear" in line 46 is crucial to both the poem's narrative line and to its meaning. In the custom of weavers, the Lady has placed this mirror in a spot facing the loom from which she is able to see at a glance how her work is going. But, for the purposes of the story, the more important function of the mirror is to allow the Lady glimpses or "Shadows of the world" in which she takes no part.

4. The poem is written chiefly in iambic tetrameter. (The last line of each stanza is iambic trimeter.) For emphasis, many lines are trochaic and open with a stressed syllable. (See lines 7–8, 10–17, etc.) The rhyme scheme is *aaaabcccb*.

The short, rhythmic lines and the three lines of consecutive rhyming words, plus the repetition of *Camelot, Shalott,* and *Lancelot,* create the poem's music.

5. Here the Lady notices two young lovers and is envious of them.

When she says she is "half sick of shadows," she means she is tired of living her life apart (with illusions) and wants to experience life firsthand in the real world. She acts on these feelings when she falls in love with Lancelot and leaves her tower.

6. The Lady must die if she leaves her weaving and her isolated existence for the real world.

The artist does not lead a "normal" human life, but instead observes and records life as if through a mirror.

7. The sun flames on his "brazen greaves"; his shield sparkles; his bridle glitters like a branch of stars.

Lancelot contrasts with the Lady's world of shadows. Even her castle is gray.

8. The Lady lives alone in a world of shadows, seeing the world only as a reflection in a mirror. The churls, the market girls, the abbot, and the court go down the road to Camelot.

The Lady's remark "I am half sick of shadows" might indicate the poet believes any participation in life is preferable to nonparticipation.

Responding to the Poem

Analyzing the Poem

Identifying Details

1. How does the poet describe the **setting** for the ballad in Part I?

2. In Part II, what is the Lady of Shalott said to do? What does she see in the mirror?

3. What is the Lady's reaction to the appearance of Sir Lancelot in Part III? According to Part IV, what are the consequences of her reaction?

Interpreting Meanings

4. Describe the **rhythm** and the **rhyme scheme** of the poem. How do both rhythm and rhyme produce an especially musical quality in this lyric?

5. Explain why lines 69–72 might be said to **foreshadow** the whole second half of the poem. What yearning do you think the Lady expresses when she exclaims, "I am half sick of shadows" (line 71)?

6. What do you think the Lady's "curse" is? Explain how the poem as a whole can be interpreted as Tennyson's comment on the role and the life of the artist in relation to society.

7. Find examples of **images** used to describe Lancelot in Part III that are associated with bright, shining light. What is this dazzling imagery contrasted with in other parts of the poem?

8. In what ways does Tennyson contrast the Lady's life with that of the village churls and of the court in Camelot? Do you think that Tennyson indicates any preference for any of these ways of life? Explain.

Writing About the Poem

A Creative Response

1. Filming the Poem. "The Lady of Shalott" is full of vivid, highly descriptive, sensory details. The poem contains only a few lines of directly quoted speech. Try to write a screenplay for a filmed version of the poem, expressing its theme entirely through a sequence of camera "shots." Decide in advance on a coherent sequence, and then write a short screenplay, basing your directions on the action and imagery in the text.

A Critical Response

2. Analyzing the Ending. When Tennyson published the first version of this poem in 1832, the last stanza read:

> They crossed themselves, their stars they blest,
> Knight, minstrel, abbot, squire, and guest.
> There lay a parchment on her breast,
> That puzzled more than all the rest,
>   The well-fed wits at Camelot.
> *"The web has broken curiously,*
> *The charm is broken utterly,*
> *Draw near and fear not—this is I,*
>   *The Lady of Shalott."*

In an essay, compare this ending with the final stanza in the text. Which ending do you think is more moving? More effective? Do you think that Tennyson significantly changed the poem's meaning when he revised its ending? Explain.

Watercolor illustration by Walter Crane for *The Lady of Shalott* (1858).

PREPARATION

ESTABLISHING A PURPOSE. Tell students to try to put themselves into the eagle's place, to see what he sees.

CLOSURE
Explain how a sea can be wrinkled and how an eagle is like a thunderbolt.

SUPPLEMENTARY SUPPORT MATERIALS
1. Review and Response Worksheet: Style and Meaning (*CCB*)
2. Selection Test (*CCB*)

A. Simile
A *thunderbolt* is a flash of lightning and the thunder that follows.
❓ What does this comparison suggest about the eagle? (It is swift and deadly.) Compare the effect if the word had been *stone* or *meteor* or *guided missile*.

ANALYZING THE POEM

Identifying Details
1. The eagle is perched on a high mountaintop.
2. The sea crawls along, and the eagle leaves his perch and falls.

Interpreting Meanings
3. Lonely, isolated, majestic, powerful, and so on. The eagle is alone, looking down on the rest of the world.

Although Tennyson called this poem a fragment, its organization gives it a feeling of completeness: three lines with one rhyme, and then three lines with another. The eagle and the world are at rest in the first stanza, and moving in the second.

The Eagle: A Fragment

He clasps the crag with crooked hands;
Close to the sun in lonely lands,
Ringed with the azure world, he stands.

The wrinkled sea beneath him crawls;
He watches from his mountain walls,
A And like a thunderbolt he falls.

Responding to the Poem

Analyzing the Poem

Identifying Details

1. Describe the physical **setting** in the poem.
2. What movement or action takes place in stanza 2?

Interpreting Meanings

3. Tennyson uses no adjectives to describe the eagle. What two or three adjectives would you use, and why? What happens in the poem, and what ideas about eagles do you bring to it, that make your adjectives appropriate?

Writing About the Poem

A Creative Response

1. Extending the Poem. Suppose this poem were really a fragment, and you found more of the manuscript of which it is a part. How might the poem continue? What actions or descriptions would extend the ideas of the eagle and the natural world that Tennyson dramatizes in "The Eagle"? Write a paragraph or stanza.

2. Imitating the Writer's Technique. Each stanza in this poem is a **tercet:** a group of three lines all having the same end rhyme. Tercets are somewhat uncommon, although they are not all that difficult to write. Experiment with writing a poem in two stanzas with each stanza comprising a tercet. Try to write two stanzas that have contrasting moods or actions, as in "The Eagle."

A Critical Response

3. Interpreting the Poem. This "fragment" has the quality of a cinematic close-up, a sharply focused look at an extraordinary creature obeying nothing but its own instincts. Yet the words *hands, lonely, azure,* etc. refer to things comprehensible only to humans. Consequently, the eagle takes on characteristics explicable mainly in terms of human nature and becomes a metaphor open to interpretation. Is Tennyson talking about a bird? A force? Or a phenomenon in which, from an observer's standpoint, both are united? Write a paragraph.

PREPARATION
1. BUILDING ON PRIOR KNOWLEDGE. Review what students know of the *Odyssey*. Remind them of Teiresias's prophecy in Book 11, that Odysseus will go on another journey until he comes to men who know nothing of the sea: "Death will come to you from the sea in some altogether unwarlike way."

2. ESTABLISHING A PURPOSE. As they read, have students focus on the characterization of the speaker.

SUPPLEMENTARY SUPPORT MATERIALS
1. Vocabulary Activity Worksheet (*CCB*)
2. Review and Response Worksheet: Characterization (*CCB*)
3. Selection Test (*CCB*)

DEVELOPING VOCABULARY
The following word from the poem is tested in the Selection Test. (See also Vocabulary Activity Worksheet.)
to smite

Ulysses (*Odysseus* in Greek) is one of the Greek leaders who fought in the ten-year Trojan War. He is also the hero of Homer's epic poem the *Odyssey,* which tells of his equally long journey home from Troy to Ithaca. In this poem, Ulysses is old, a king who had not tended to his people for two decades. Now he wants to leave home again for a final journey in a ship with loyal followers to see the far-flung world and sail beyond the sun. Tennyson said of this poem, "'Ulysses' was written soon after Arthur Hallam's death, and gave my feeling about the need of going forward, and braving the struggle of life perhaps more simply than anything in *In Memoriam*."

Ulysses

It little profits that an idle king,
By this still hearth, among these barren crags,
Match'd with an aged wife, I mete and dole°
A Unequal laws unto a savage race,
5 That hoard, and sleep, and feed, and know not me.
I cannot rest from travel; I will drink
B Life to the lees. All times I have enjoy'd
Greatly, have suffer'd greatly, both with those
That loved me, and alone; on shore, and when
10 Thro' scudding drifts the rainy Hyades°
Vext the dim sea. I am become a name;
For always roaming with a hungry heart
Much have I seen and known, cities of men
And manner, climates, councils, governments,
15 Myself not least, but honor'd of them all,
And drunk delight of battle with my peers,
Far on the ringing plains of windy Troy.
C I am a part of all that I have met;
D Yet all experience is an arch wherethro'
20 Gleams that untravel'd world whose margin fades
Forever and forever when I move.
How dull it is to pause, to make an end,
To rust unburnish'd, not to shine in use!
As tho' to breathe were life! Life piled on life
25 Were all too little, and of one to me
Little remains; but every hour is saved
From that eternal silence, something more,
A bringer of new things; and vile it were
For some three suns to store and hoard myself,
30 And this gray spirit yearning in desire
E To follow knowledge like a sinking star,
Beyond the utmost bound of human thought.
    This is my son, mine own Telemachus,°
To whom I leave the scepter and the isle,°
35 Well-loved of me, discerning to fulfill
This labor, by slow prudence to make mild
A rugged people, and thro' soft degrees
Subdue them to the useful and the good.
Most blameless is he, centered in the sphere

3. **mete and dole:** measure and give out.

10. **Hyades** (hī'ə·dēz'): stars that were thought to indicate the approach of the rainy season when they appeared at sunrise.

33. **Telemachus** (tə·lem'ə·kəs): Ulysses's son.
34. **isle:** Ithaca, Ulysses's island kingdom off the west coast of Greece.

A. Expansion
The laws are unequal or unfair because his subjects are savages.

B. Vocabulary
Lees means "dregs," or the sediment left in a glass of wine. Students might guess the meaning from context.

C. Paraphrasing
? Paraphrase line 18. (All of what I have experienced has made me what I am.)

D. A Famous Metaphor
These lines are frequently quoted. See question 2.

E. Interpreting
? What does Ulysses want? (To follow knowledge beyond the limits of the human mind)

READING CHECK TEST
1. The speaker is the youthful Ulysses. (F)
2. Ulysses wants to spend the rest of his life in retirement. (F)
3. Ulysses regrets leaving his kingdom to his son. (F)

4. Ulysses says it is not too late to seek a newer world. (T)
5. The old king is going to return to Troy. (F)

ANALYZING THE POEM
Identifying Details
1. He is old and considers himself an "idle king" ruling over savages.

His present life is boring and unfulfilling compared with his past.
2. All experience is an arch through which he sees a boundless, untraveled world.
3. He says Telemachus is his well-loved

A. Interpreting
Tennyson suggests two archetypal ways of looking at the world here—one "domestic" and one "questing."

B. Interpreting
How does Ulysses's attitude toward his companions contrast with his earlier comments on his son? (Ulysses feels different from his son but at one with his fellow seafarers.)

C. Allusion
Tennyson's allusion to Achilles intentionally departs from Homer's story, since in Book 11 of the *Odyssey* the hero encounters the shade (ghost) of Achilles in the Underworld.

CLOSURE
(1) Have students describe the character of Ulysses as portrayed in the poem. (2) Have them recite three passages that they think best reveal his character.

40   Of common duties, decent not to fail
      In offices of tenderness, and pay
 A   Meet adoration to my household gods,
      When I am gone. He works his work, I mine.
         There lies the port; the vessel puffs her sail;
45   There gloom the dark, broad seas. My mariners,
      Souls that have toil'd, and wrought, and thought with
            me,
 B   That ever with a frolic welcome took
      The thunder and the sunshine, and opposed
      Free hearts, free foreheads, you and I are old;
50   Old age hath yet his honor and his toil.
      Death closes all; but something ere the end,
      Some work of noble note, may yet be done,
      Not unbecoming men that strove with Gods.
      The lights begin to twinkle from the rocks;
55   The long day wanes; the slow moon climbs; the deep
      Moans round with many voices. Come, my friends,
      'Tis not too late to seek a newer world.
      Push off, and sitting well in order smite
      The sounding furrows;° for my purpose holds
60   To sail beyond the sunset, and the baths°
      Of all the western stars, until I die.
      It may be that the gulfs will wash us down;
      It may be we shall touch the Happy Isles,°
 C   And see the great Achilles,° whom we knew.
65   Tho' much is taken, much abides; and tho'
      We are not now that strength which in old days
      Moved earth and heaven, that which we are, we are,
      One equal temper of heroic hearts,
      Made weak by time and fate, but strong in will
70   To strive, to seek, to find, and not to yield.

59. **smite . . . furrows:** row against the waves.
60. **baths:** seas.

63. **Happy Isles:** in Greek mythology, Elysium, where dead heroes lived for eternity.
64. **Achilles** (ə·kil'ēz): Greek warrior and leader in the Trojan War.

Responding to the Poem

Analyzing the Poem

Identifying Details

1. In lines 1–5, how does Ulysses describe his life in the present? How does his present life contrast with his past adventures?
2. What does Ulysses claim about "all experience" in lines 19–21?
3. How does Ulysses describe his son Telemachus in lines 33–43?
4. Whom does Ulysses address in the second half of the poem? In the concluding lines of the poem, what qualities does he emphasize that he shares with his mariners?

Interpreting Meanings

5. In the *Odyssey*, Homer lays great stress on the hero's powers of endurance and his insatiable curiosity. Where does Tennyson emphasize these characteristics of Ulysses?
6. What seem to be Ulysses's underlying feelings toward his son? Find and comment on the speaker's sole reference to his wife. How does he feel toward her?
7. How would you **characterize** Ulysses?
8. Ulysses knows that his journey is like pursuing the horizon. Do you think he is foolish for setting out on a journey in which he cannot arrive at the destination he pursues? Explain.

heir, who is discerning, prudent, and decent. Telemachus seems to have a quiet, plodding personality in contrast to Ulysses's tempestuous nature.
4. He addresses "my mariners" (line 45), the loyal old sailors who sailed with him in the past.

Ulysses and the mariners have heroic hearts and are strong-willed.

Interpreting Meanings
5. Lines 6–7, 12, 30–32, 45–48, 51–52, 56–57, 59–64, 65–70.
6. He says he loves Telemachus but seems to have somewhat negative feelings for him.

In line 3, he calls her "aged." He seems to have ambivalent feelings.
7. Student answers will vary. Many will see him as self-centered and selfish;

others may view him more positively.
8. Student answers will vary. Have them support their views. Discussion may touch on old age, death, and the purpose of human life.

Ulysses Deriding Polyphemus by J. M. W. Turner. Oil. The National Gallery, London. **A**

A. Humanities Connection: Discussing the Fine Art
Have students read Book 9 of the *Odyssey* to see who Polyphemus was (the Cyclops who imprisoned Odysseus and his men).
? Where is the giant in this famous painting? (Behind the crag on the left) What happened as a result of this incident? (Polyphemus cursed Odysseus so that not one of his men made it home alive.)

Writing About the Poem

A Creative Response

1. Extending the Poem. Write Telemachus's reply (in either prose or poetry) to his father's speech. Give him words to speak, and an order of argument, that fit the kind of man you think he is.

A Critical Response

2. Comparing Heroes. To create his dramatic monologue, Tennyson borrowed events, scenic details, and some of the character traits of Ulysses (Odysseus in Greek), the hero of Homer's *Odyssey.* Inevitably, however, he cast his imaginative version of Ulysses in a distinctly nineteenth-century mold. Research the plot of Homer's *Odyssey,* and read selected portions of the epic in translation, especially from Books 8, 13, and 19. Then write an essay comparing the hero-figures of Homer and Tennyson. In your essay, comment on some of the ways in which Tennyson has markedly *altered* the character traits of the Homeric hero. What seems to you especially significant about these changes?

Alfred, Lord Tennyson 793

1. **BUILDING ON PRIOR KNOWLEDGE.** Before students begin reading, review with them the biography of Tennyson on text pages 777–778, paying special attention to the circumstances that led him to compose *In Memoriam.*

2. **ESTABLISHING A PURPOSE.** Remind students that *In Memoriam* was com-

posed over a seventeen-year period. Tell them to note how these stanzas show the speaker's coming to terms with human mortality.

3. **PREREADING JOURNAL.** Before they read, have students write in their journals two or three sentences expressing their responses to poetry that explores feelings about mortality. (See the Writing As-

signment on text page 797.)

A. Paraphrasing
Paraphrased, this stanza might read: "Doesn't our wish that there be life beyond the grave come from the divinity within our souls?"

B. Metaphor
? What metaphor is central to this stanza? (Life is compared to an altar stair that leads through darkness to God.)

C. Vocabulary
Chaff is the worthless husk of grain that is thrown away in the winnowing process.

In Memoriam (Latin for "in memory of") is Tennyson's elegy for Arthur Hugh Hallam, his closest friend at Cambridge and his sister's fiancé. Hallam, who died of a sudden fever, was supposed to be an extraordinarily promising young man. In the separate lyrics (131 in all) of his elegy, Tennyson asks and gradually answers profound questions about the meaning of life and death and the immortality of the soul.

from **In Memoriam**

55

A
The wish, that of the living whole
  No life may fail beyond the grave,
  Derives it not from what we have
The likest God within the soul?

5 Are God and Nature then at strife,
  That Nature lends such evil dreams?
  So careful of the type° she seems,
So careless of the single life,

That I, considering everywhere
10 Her secret meaning in her deeds,
  And finding that of fifty seeds
She often brings but one to bear,

B
I falter where I firmly trod,
  And falling with my weight of cares
15 Upon the great world's altar-stairs
That slope through darkness up to God,

C
I stretch lame hands of faith, and grope,
  And gather dust and chaff, and call
  To what I feel is Lord of all,
20 And faintly trust the larger hope.°

56

"So careful of the type?" but no.
  From scarpéd° cliff and quarried stone
  She° cries, "A thousand types are gone;
I care for nothing, all shall go.

5 "Thou makest thine appeal to me:
  I bring to life, I bring to death;
  The spirit does but mean the breath:
I know no more." And he, shall he,

7. **type:** species.

20. **larger hope:** Tennyson explains this phrase in his *Memoirs:* "that the whole human race would through, perhaps, ages of suffering, be at length purified and saved."

2. **scarpéd:** eroded to a steep slope.
3. **She:** Nature.

SUPPLEMENTARY SUPPORT MATERIALS
1. Vocabulary Activity Worksheet (*CCB*)
2 Review and Response Worksheet: Theme (*CCB*)
3. Selection Test (*CCB*)

DEVELOPING VOCABULARY
The following word from the poem is tested in the Selection Test. (See also Vocabulary Activity Worksheet.)
diffusive

10   Man, her last work, who seemed so fair,
           Such splendid purpose in his eyes,
           Who rolled the psalm to wintry skies,
       Who built him fanes° of fruitless prayer,

A   Who trusted God was love indeed
           And love Creation's final law—
15   Though Nature, red in tooth and claw°
       With ravine, shrieked against his creed—

       Who loved, who suffered countless ills,
           Who battled for the True, the Just,
           Be blown about the desert dust,
20   Or sealed within the iron hills?°

       No more? A monster then, a dream,
           A discord. Dragons of the prime,
           That tare° each other in their slime,
       Were mellow music matched with him.

25   O life as futile, then, as frail!
           O for thy voice to soothe and bless!
B   What hope of answer, or redress?
       Behind the veil,° behind the veil.

                      95

C   By night we lingered on the lawn,
           For underfoot the herb was dry;
           And genial warmth; and o'er the sky
       The silvery haze of summer drawn:

5   And calm that let the tapers burn
           Unwavering: not a cricket chirred;
           The brook alone far off was heard,
       And on the board the fluttering urn.°

       And bats went round in fragrant skies,
10   And wheeled or lit the filmy shapes°
           That haunt the dusk, with ermine capes
       And woolly breasts and beaded eyes;

       While now we sang old songs that pealed
           From knoll to knoll, where, couched at ease,
15   The white kine° glimmered, and the trees
       Laid their dark arms about the field.

       But when those others, one by one,
           Withdrew themselves from me and night,
           And in the house light after light
20   Went out, and I was all alone,

12. **fanes:** temples.

15. **red . . . claw:** The phrase refers to the view of all life as a ruthless struggle for survival.

20. **sealed . . . hills:** preserved like fossils in rock.

23. **tare:** (archaic) tore.

28. **veil:** the veil of death.

8. **fluttering urn:** a teapot or coffee urn heated by a candle.

10. **filmy shapes:** moths.

15. **kine:** cattle.

A. A Famous Personification
"Nature red in tooth and claw" is frequently quoted. Notice how nature is personified as a person (or beast) bloody with ravine, or ravaging, shrieking against man's belief.

B. Rhetorical Question
Be sure students realize that line 28 is the answer to the rhetorical question posed in line 27.

C. Interpreting
The "we" are Tennyson and his friends.

CLOSURE

Have three students explain to the class (1) what the title *In Memoriam* means, (2) whom the poem was written for, and (3) what its message is (insofar as they can tell from these stanzas).

ANALYZING THE POEM
Identifying Details

1. The speaker wishes to believe in life after death but finds no evidence of it in Nature. Nature has no regard for the individual life but is only "careful of the type."
2. Nature claims not even to be interested in the type; a thousand types come and go and she doesn't care. All that she does is bring life and death. She doesn't believe the spirit survives after death.
3. The setting is the lawn of a country house on a summer night, where people talk and sing.

At the poem's end, the speaker is alone in the same setting. The final stanza describes the light of dawn.
4. He feels confident that he is in some way forever united with Hallam.

A. Interpreting
What are the "fallen leaves which kept their green"? (Hallam's letters)

B. Paradox
Note the paradoxes in "silent-speaking words" and "love's dumb cry."

C. Interpreting
What has been happening to the speaker? (Hallam's letters reminded him that love and faith are bold enough to drive away doubts. He experiences a kind of spiritual awakening, though his "trance" ends and doubt returns.)

D. Personification
How is the breeze personified in lines 54–61? (It moves the sycamore, elms, rose, and lilies and says "The dawn, the dawn.")

A
A hunger seized my heart; I read
  Of that glad year which once had been
  In those fallen leaves which kept their green,
The noble letters of the dead.

B
25 And strangely on the silence broke
      The silent-speaking words, and strange
      Was love's dumb cry defying change
    To test his worth; and strangely spoke

The faith, the vigor, bold to dwell
30   On doubts that drive the coward back,
      And keen through wordy snares to track
    Suggestion to her inmost cell.

So word by word, and line by line,
      The dead man touched me from the past,
35   And all at once it seemed at last
    The living soul° was flashed on mine.

And mine in this was wound, and whirled
      About empyreal° heights of thought,
      And came on that which is, and caught
40   The deep pulsations of the world,

C
Aeonian° music measuring out
      The steps of Time—the shocks of Chance—
      The blows of Death. At length my trance
    Was canceled, stricken through with doubt.

45 Vague words! but ah, how hard to frame
      In matter-molded forms of speech,
      Or even for intellect to reach
    Through memory that which I became.

Till now the doubtful dusk revealed
50   The knolls once more where, couched at ease,
      The white kine glimmered, and the trees
    Laid their dark arms about the field;

D
And sucked from out the distant gloom
      A breeze began to tremble o'er
55   The large leaves of the sycamore,
    And fluctuate all the still perfume,

And gathering freshlier overhead,
      Rocked the full-foliaged elms, and swung
      The heavy-folded rose, and flung
60   The lilies to and fro, and said,

36. **The living soul:** Originally, the phrase read "His living soul." Tennyson said he changed it because he wanted the soul to be not Hallam's but the soul of "the Deity, maybe."
38. **empyreal** (em·pir′ē·əl): heavenly.

41. **Aeonian** (ē·ō′nē·ən): eternal.

5. The rhyme scheme is *abba*.
Answers about the effect will vary. Many will think that the short lines and stanzas and frequent rhymes add to the poem's music and sense of reason applied to a difficult subject.
6. In the earlier lyrics, Nature is portrayed as a cold, unfeeling force that denies the possibility of a soul or of life after death. In Lyric 130, Nature is seen as a positive force no longer in conflict with God. The speaker feels and hears his friend Hallam's soul diffused throughout Nature; and the images of air, water, sunrise, sunset, star, and flower are positive images.
7. Student answers will vary; this is a difficult question. Help them to see that Lyrics 55 and 56 express the speaker's anguish, doubt, and despair. Lyric 130 expresses his joyful celebration of faith in life after death.

"The dawn, the dawn," and died away;
    And East and West, without a breath,
    Mixed their dim lights, like life and death,
To broaden into boundless day.

130

A

Thy° voice is on the rolling air,
    I hear thee where the waters run;
    Thou standest in the rising sun,
And in the setting thou art fair.

5   What art thou then? I cannot guess;
    But though I seem in star and flower
    To feel thee some <u>diffusive</u> power,
I do not therefore love thee less.

    My love involves the love before;
10   My love is vaster passion now;
    Though mixed with God and Nature thou,
I seem to love thee more and more.

B

    Far off thou art, but ever nigh;
    I have thee still, and I rejoice;
15   I prosper, circled with thy voice;
    I shall not lose thee though I die.

1. **Thy:** Hallam's.

A. Interpreting
? Where does the speaker now find his friend? (In the air, waters, sun; he is at one with nature.)

B. Paradoxes
Note the paradoxes again: His friend is far yet near, and even if he dies he will not lose him.

Responding to the Poem

Analyzing the Poem

Identifying Details

1. In Lyric 55, why does the poet envision the possibility that God and Nature may be "at strife"? What complaint does the speaker voice against Nature in this poem?
2. How does Nature answer this complaint in Lyric 56?
3. Describe the **setting** at the beginning of Lyric 95. How does this setting contrast with that at the end of the poem?
4. Of what is the speaker confident in Lyric 130?

Interpreting Meanings

5. Describe the **rhyme scheme** of these lyrics. What do you think is the effect of the short lines and stanzas and the frequent rhymes?

6. What is the difference between the aspects of nature described in Lyrics 55 and 56 and in Lyric 130?
7. Consider the structure of Lyric 95, its move from a particular, local scene to "empyreal heights of thought" and then its return to the original scene. How is this movement related to the speaker's mood in Lyrics 55 and 56? In Lyric 130?

Writing About the Poem

A Critical Response

Writing an Essay. This poem was popular because it satisfied readers who believed poetry should deal with serious subjects. In an essay, tell whether you agree or disagree with such expectations for poetry. If you disagree, what do you think are the proper functions of poetry?

A. **Percy Bysshe Shelley**
Ask students to review the biography of Shelley and the selections from his work (see text pages 694–706).

B. **Elizabeth Barrett Browning**
For a biography of Elizabeth Barrett Browning, see text page 808.

C. **Responding**
❓ Contrast this description of Browning with what you have learned about Tennyson's psychological makeup. (Tennyson in general is more melancholy and introspective and tries to accept, not change, things.)

Robert Browning (1812–1889)

Robert Browning wrote of his first published book, a long poem about the spiritual development of a poet, that it was part of a "foolish plan." He intended, he said, to write in many forms and under different names: "Meanwhile the world was never to guess that 'Brown, Smith, Jones & Robinson' . . . the respective authors of this poem, the other novel, such an opera, such a speech, etc., etc., were no other than one and the same individual." Browning gave up the idea of writing under different names and in different forms, but he held on to his ambition of dazzling the world with his range and variety.

Browning's education allowed him to indulge his wide-ranging interests in music, art, the history of medicine, drama, literature, insects, and other oddly assorted topics. His father, a clerk in the Bank of England, collected books and drawings and had a library of six thousand volumes. Browning attended boarding school briefly but was mainly educated at home in a London suburb by tutors and by his omnivorous reading in his father's library. As a teen-ager, Browning was brilliant, undisciplined, and determined to be a poet like his idol Shelley. After a term at the University of London, he published (at his family's expense) three long poems, some plays, and a series of pamphlets containing plays and short poems. The long poems won him mostly the reputation of being a difficult poet, and the few plays that were produced closed almost immediately. It was not until he began to write the short dramatic monologues of the 1840's—poems like "My Last Duchess" and "Porphyria's Lover"—that Browning found his proper form. While Browning struggled to gain recognition for his writing, he lived comfortably at home, supported by his parents. He did not leave home until he married at thirty-four.

In 1845 Browning wrote to Elizabeth Barrett, already an established poet: "I love your verse with all my heart, dear Miss Barrett, and I love you too." At thirty-eight, Barrett lived as a semi-invalid in her father's London house and submitted, with a mixture of affection and fear,

Robert Browning by Michele Gordigiani (1858). Oil.

to his sternly protective care. Four months after they began their correspondence, Browning was taken to meet her. He fell in love with the woman as well as the poet, and she with him. They conducted their courtship in letters and twice-weekly visits and in secrecy from the jealously overprotective Mr. Barrett. Browning began to press for a happy ending: "Oh, dearest, let us marry soon, very soon, and end all this!" He arranged a secret wedding in 1846, after which Elizabeth returned to her father's house. A week later the Brownings eloped to Italy. Mr. Barrett never acknowledged the marriage, never saw his daughter again, and never opened the letters she sent to him explaining her act and asking his forgiveness.

Browning's happy marriage confirmed his belief that only by acting boldly can one wrest what is good from the pettiness and selfishness that obscures the good in an imperfect world. "I was ever a fighter," he wrote in "Prospice." He liked to see himself in strenuous but joyous contests with difficulties. In his dramatic poems he also liked to emphasize the error, weakness, and even the viciousness of his characters and the difficulties they encounter or create. His standing as a poet grew slowly in the 1840's and 1850's. Readers did not know how to react to speakers like the Duke in "My Last Duchess" and "Porphyria's Lover," who act boldly but for selfish and perverse motives. It was also hard for readers used to Tennyson's melodic lyrics to hear the music in Browning's quick, rough sound.

Browning lived in Italy until Elizabeth's death in 1861, when he returned to England with their thirteen-year-old son. During the 1860's his fame began to grow; the dramatic monologues of *Men and Women* (1855) and *Dramatis Personae* (1864) began to find readers. His first immediate success came with *The Ring and the Book* (1868–1869), a long poem in twelve books spoken by characters involved in a seventeenth-century murder in Rome. Gradually, it became clear to many readers that by asking them to figure out and judge wicked men like the Duke of Ferrara in "My Last Duchess," Browning was really challenging them to discover what is virtuous and healthy, when love nourishes, and when and why it kills. Browning believed that human beings must act by a moral standard, just as he believed (in "Prospice") that those who love constantly and act bravely will be rewarded.

During the 1880's admirers all over England and America founded Browning Societies and met to read and discuss his work and philosophy. By the time of his death in 1889, Browning had won a place next to Tennyson as the other great Victorian poet. Like Tennyson, he was read as a kind of sage who assured his contemporaries that "This world's no blot for us, / Nor blank; it means intensely, and means good" ("Fra Lippo Lippi"). Tennyson usually wrote of the sadness of experiencing the difficulties and losses of life. Browning (like the hero in Tenny-son's "Ulysses") usually wrote of the invigorating pleasures of contesting and surviving those troubles.

Although the affirmative and optimistic themes of Browning's poems were eventually apparent to his readers, his style remained difficult and often obscure. Browning once told a reader who asked about the meaning of a passage that when he wrote the lines, only God and he had known what they meant, and now only God knew. Browning liked odd rhymes, unusual words, broken rhythms, and the imperfect syntax and quick shifts of subject and diction characteristic of actual speech. He often tried for the effect of immediacy: the look of things not obviously arranged to make a pretty picture, the sound of someone speaking directly, or a moment of intense and unexamined feeling.

Browning was the principal and most accomplished writer of the dramatic monologue in Victorian literature. The speaker of a dramatic monologue is obviously someone other than the poet. Instead of commenting directly on the speaker, Browning provides us with clues and expects us to make inferences. We are required to think about the character of the speaker, to reconstruct the situation in which he or she speaks, and to guess at the speaker's motives. Browning's dramatic monologues also require us to assess the truth and worth of the speaker's words by taking into account who is talking, and in what context, and why.

The dramatic monologue is a useful form for poets who want their readers to think about the moral meaning of experience. It was an especially appropriate form for Browning, who delighted in both the rough surfaces of material and mortal existence and the promise of order and harmony that he believed judgment and right conduct could win.

A. Verse Forms and Diction
Browning's experimentation with verse forms and diction was regarded reverentially by many of the modernist poets at the beginning of the twentieth century.

B. Dramatic Monologue
Since three of the selections from Browning in this text are dramatic monologues, make sure that students are familiar with the essential elements of this verse form.

PREPARATION
1. BUILDING ON PRIOR KNOWLEDGE. Review with the class what they know about the Italian Renaissance (see text page 166). The intrigues that marked the rules of some of these Renaissance princes are legendary.

2. ESTABLISHING A PURPOSE. Have students study the headnote to set a purpose for their reading.

SUPPLEMENTARY SUPPORT MATERIALS
1. Vocabulary Activity Worksheet (CCB)
2. Review and Response Worksheet: Dramatic Monologue (CCB)
3. Selection Test (CCB)

DEVELOPING VOCABULARY
The following words from the poem are tested in the Selection Test. (See also Vocabulary Activity Worksheet.)
officious   warrant
munificence   to avow

A. Syntax
Inversion makes these lines difficult. Translated into normal order, the subject, verb, and object are: "Strangers never read that pictured countenance."

B. Actions
Note the speaker's actions here and in lines 5, 47, and 53–54.

C. Characterization
? What do these lines suggest about the Duchess? (Perhaps she was unfaithful.)

D. Characterization
? What do these lines reveal about the Duke? (He is proud and vain and jealous.)

"My Last Duchess" is one of Robert Browning's earliest and most popular dramatic monologues. In most of his dramatic monologues, Browning has the speaker reveal something about himself that he does not intend, or something about his situation that he does not fully comprehend. The speaker in this poem is Alfonso II, Duke of Ferrara, a powerful Italian nobleman of the Renaissance. As you read the poem, look beyond the speaker's words and ask: To whom is he talking? Why is he saying all this? What does he want? What is really going on?

My Last Duchess

Ferrara

That's my last Duchess painted on the wall,
Looking as if she were alive. I call
That piece a wonder, now: Frà Pandolf's° hands
Worked busily a day, and there she stands.
5   Will't please you sit and look at her? I said
    "Frà Pandolf" by design, for never read
    Strangers like you that pictured countenance,
    The depth and passion of its earnest glance,
    But to myself they turned (since none puts by
10   The curtain I have drawn for you, but I)
    And seemed as they would ask me, if they durst,
    How such a glance came there; so, not the first
    Are you to turn and ask thus. Sir, 'twas not
    Her husband's presence only, called that spot
15   Of joy into the Duchess' cheek: perhaps
    Frà Pandolf chanced to say, "Her mantle° laps
    Over my lady's wrist too much," or "Paint
    Must never hope to reproduce the faint
    Half-flush that dies along her throat": such stuff
20   Was courtesy, she thought, and cause enough
    For calling up that spot of joy. She had
    A heart—how shall I say?—too soon made glad,
    Too easily impressed; she liked whate'er
    She looked on, and her looks went everywhere.
25   Sir, 'twas all one! My favor° at her breast,
    The dropping of the daylight in the West,
    The bough of cherries some officious fool
    Broke in the orchard for her, the white mule
    She rode with round the terrace—all and each
30   Would draw from her alike the approving speech,
    Or blush, at least. She thanked men—good! but thanked
    Somehow—I know not how—as if she ranked
    My gift of a nine-hundred-years-old name
    With anybody's gift. Who'd stoop to blame
35   This sort of trifling? Even had you skill

3. **Frà Pandolf:** Brother Pandolf, an imaginary painter and monk.

16. **mantle:** cloak.

25. **favor:** a ribbon or some other gift given as a token of love.

1. The Duke of Ferrara, the speaker, is talking to the Count's representative to work out the terms of a marriage between the Duke and the Count's daughter.
2. He says she was cheerful and courteous, delighted with everyone.
3. He gave commands (line 45) and her smiling stopped.

Interpreting Meanings
4. Iambic pentameter couplets.
   Student choices will vary. Note the lines in which he interrupts himself (e.g., lines 22, 31–32).
5. He presents himself as cultured, confident, wealthy—probably to ensure his marriage to the Count's daughter.

6. Students may say he is evil, amoral, jealous, insecure.
   Lines 13–15 and 19–45 reveal his true character.
7. The references to art are ironic. We find it horrible that in the same breath the Duke can confess to his wife's murder and brag about his possessions.

In speech—(which I have not)—to make your will
Quite clear to such an one, and say, "Just this
Or that in you disgusts me; here you miss,
Or there exceed the mark"—and if she let
40 Herself be lessoned so, not plainly set
Her wits to yours, forsooth,° and made excuse
A ⌐—E'en then would be some stooping; and I choose
  ⌐Never to stoop. Oh sir, she smiled, no doubt,
Whene'er I passed her; but who passed without
45 Much the same smile? This grew; I gave commands;
Then all smiles stopped together. There she stands
B ⌐As if alive. Will't please you rise? We'll meet
The company below, then. I repeat,
The Count your master's known <u>munificence</u>
50 Is ample <u>warrant</u> that no just pretense
Of mine for dowry will be disallowed;
Though his fair daughter's self, as I <u>avowed</u>
At starting, is my object. Nay, we'll go
Together down, sir. Notice Neptune,° though,
55 Taming a sea horse, thought a rarity,
Which Claus of Innsbruck° cast in bronze for me!

41. **forsooth:** (archaic) in truth.

54. **Neptune:** Roman god of the sea.
56. **Claus of Innsbruck:** an imaginary sculptor.

A. Characterization
[?] How does this reveal the element of pride in the Duke's character? (He refused to "stoop" for anyone.)

B. Implied Actions
[?] What is happening here and in lines 53–54? (The emissary from the Count is rising. In the last lines he and the Duke are descending the stairs.)

CLOSURE
Have students define a dramatic monologue. Then have them summarize the story contained in "My Last Duchess."

Responding to the Poem

Analyzing the Poem

Identifying Details

1. Describe the occasion for this monologue. Who is speaking to whom, in what circumstances, and for what purpose?
2. How does the Duke describe the personality of his "last Duchess"?
3. What happened to the last Duchess, according to the Duke?

Interpreting Meanings

4. Describe the **rhyme** and **rhythm** of the poem. Pick out a few passages which seem to you to be especially striking examples of colloquial, natural speech.
5. What impression of himself do you think the Duke intends to create in his remarks to the Count's emissary? Why would he choose so to present himself?
6. What kind of man do you think the Duke really is? Which lines reveal his true **character**?
7. What is the effect of having the Duke's **monologue** begin and end by referring to works of art?

Writing About the Poem

A Creative Response

1. **Writing a Dramatic Monologue.** Write a dramatic monologue in prose using the "last Duchess" as the speaker. Base your monologue on an imaginary incident, and take into account the personality portraits of both the Duchess and the Duke in Browning's poem.

A Critical Response

2. **Analyzing the Theme.** In a brief essay, analyze what you take to be the theme of Browning's "My Last Duchess."

PREPARATION
1. **BUILDING ON PRIOR KKNOWLEDGE.**
Review with the class the techniques
Browning uses to characterize the Duke
in "My Last Duchess." Tell students that
this poem is similar to "My Last Duchess" in subject matter and form.

2. **ESTABLISHING A PURPOSE.** Tell students to focus on the motivations of the

speaker in this monologue.

3. **PREREADING JOURNAL.** Before they
read, have students write two or three
sentences about what it feels like to be
jealous.

SUPPLEMENTARY SUPPORT MATERIALS
1. Vocabulary Activity Worksheet (*CCB*)
2. Review and Response Worksheet:
Atmosphere (*CCB*)
3. Selection Test (*CCB*)

A. Conflict
Here is Porphyria's
conflict—and the
reason for the
speaker's deep
unhappiness.

B. Interpreting
? Contrast the
speaker here
with the speaker in
"My Last Duch-
ess." (The speaker
here is sure Por-
phyria worships
him. The speaker
in "My Last Duch-
ess" is sure his
Duchess doesn't
worship him; he
believes she had a
roving eye and
was flirtatious.)

Like his American contemporary Edgar Allan
Poe, Browning had a taste for morbid psychology,
as is evident in this dramatic monologue. The
speaker is a man whose character and identity we
can deduce only by what he says. Impressed by
the directness of the man's speech and a manner
of address that remains even and unruffled
throughout, we are apt to gape at what we learn
late in the poem, yet we continue to hear the man
out—fascinated, however uneasy.

Porphyria's Lover

    The rain set early in tonight,
        The <u>sullen</u> wind was soon awake,
    It tore the elm-tops down for spite,
        And did its worst to <u>vex</u> the lake:
5   I listened with heart fit to break.
    When glided in Porphyria; straight
        She shut the cold out and the storm,
    And kneeled and made the cheerless grate
        Blaze up, and all the cottage warm;
10   Which done, she rose, and from her form
    Withdrew the dripping cloak and shawl,
        And laid her soiled gloves by, untied
    Her hat and let the damp hair fall,
        And, last, she sat down by my side
15   And called me. When no voice replied,
    She put my arm about her waist,
        And made her smooth white shoulder bare,
    And all her yellow hair displaced,
        And, stooping, made my cheek lie there,
20   And spread, o'er all, her yellow hair,

A   Murmuring how she loved me—she
        Too weak, for all her heart's endeavor,
    To set its struggling passion free
        From pride, and vainer ties dissever,
25   And give herself to me forever.

    But passion sometimes would prevail,
        Nor could tonight's gay feast restrain
    A sudden thought of one so pale
        For love of her, and all in vain:
30   So, she was come through wind and rain.

B   Be sure I looked up at her eyes
        Happy and proud; at last I knew
    Porphyria worshiped me: surprise
        Made my heart swell, and still it grew
35   While I debated what to do.
    That moment she was mine, mine, fair,
        Perfectly pure and good: I found
    A thing to do, and all her hair
        In one long yellow string I wound
40   Three times her little throat around,

DEVELOPING VOCABULARY
The following words from the poem are tested in the Selection Test. (See also Vocabulary Activity Worksheet.)
sullen   to vex

READING CHECK TEST

1. The speaker anxiously awaits Porphyria's arrival. (T)
2. When Porhphyria speaks to her lover, he doesn't answer her. (T)
3. The speaker is never convinced that Porphyria worships him. (F)
4. The speaker strangles Porphyria with her own hair. (T)

5. The speaker says he killed Porphyria because she was deceiving him. (F)

April Love by Arthur Hughes. Oil.

The Tate Gallery, London.

A

A. Humanities Connection: Responding to the Fine Art

A "genre painting" is one that depicts a scene from everyday life in meticulous, realistic details. Like most genre paintings, this one suggests a story.

❓ What do you think has happened before this scene, and what is likely to happen after? What mood is suggested by the background and foreground? Do you think this painting makes a good illustration for Browning's poem? Explain. (In this painting, the mood of mystery or foreboding complements the dark deed described in the poem.)

ANALYZING THE POEM
Identifying Details

1. Sad and irritable.
  Students may say that he seems to cheer up, but this is never stated directly.
2. Apparently, he wishes to preserve forever the moment when she is totally his and perfectly pure. He complains (lines 21–24) that she is too weak to commit herself to him forever.

A. Responding

? How did you feel as you read this line? Were you at all expecting this murder? (Most students will feel startled at this point; they would not have expected this murder.)

CLOSURE

Have students give a brief summary of the motivations and actions of the speaker.

3. After she is dead, her blue eyes laughed (lines 44–45) and her cheek blushed bright (lines 47–48).

Interpreting Meanings

4. The speaker seems to realize the awfulness of his deed, though he does not repent. The line implies that he is not totally insane.
5. It makes the speaker's action a bit

less unexpected and shocking. It also tells what happened to him after Porphyria's death was discovered.
  Students will probably say in a country house.
6. Browning is definitely relating the crime and insanity.
  Student answers will vary.

A ⌐ And strangled her. No pain felt she;
          I am quite sure she felt no pain.
    As a shut bud that holds a bee,
          I warily oped her lids: again
45   Laughed the blue eyes without a stain.
    And I untightened next the tress
          About her neck; her cheek once more
    Blushed bright beneath my burning kiss:
          I propped her head up as before,
50   Only, this time my shoulder bore
    Her head, which droops upon it still:
          The smiling rosy little head,
    So glad it has its utmost will,
          That all it scorned at once is fled,
55   And I, its love, am gained instead!
    Porphyria's love: she guessed not how
          Her darling one wish would be heard.
    And thus we sit together now,
          And all night long we have not stirred,
60   And yet God has not said a word!

Responding to the Poem

Analyzing the Poem

Identifying Details

1. What is the speaker's mood at the opening of the poem? How does his mood change when Porphyria comes to him?
2. What reasons does the speaker give for strangling Porphyria?
3. What leads the speaker to assert that Porphyria "felt no pain"?

Interpreting Meanings

4. "And yet God has not said a word!" Why do you think the speaker expects God to say something? What does this line tell you about the speaker's character and his awareness of what he has done?
5. Browning first published this poem, along with another dramatic monologue, under the general title *Madhouse Cells.* How does a knowledge of that **setting** affect your response to and interpretation of the poem? Where did you think the poem was set before you knew about Browning's original title?
6. What do you think Browning is saying about the relationship of crime to madness or mental instability? Do you agree or disagree? Explain why.

Writing About the Poem

A Creative Response

1. **Extending the Poem.** Based on the evidence in the poem, write a short composition in which you imaginatively reconstruct the relationship between Porphyria and her lover before Porphyria's last visit.

A Critical Response

2. **Comparing and Contrasting Two Dramatic Monologues.** In a brief essay, compare the themes and techniques of "My Last Duchess" and "Porphyria's Lover." Tell which poem you consider the more effective dramatic monologue, and why.

PREPARATION

ESTABLISHING A PURPOSE. Have students read question 4 to set a purpose for reading the poems.

SUPPLEMENTARY SUPPORT MATERIALS
1. Review and Response Worksheet: Imagery and Tone (*CCB*)
2. Selection Test (*CCB*)

CLOSURE

Ask students to discuss whether or not these two lyrics could have been spoken by the Duke or Porphyria's lover. What attitude toward women do all three speakers reveal?

A. Imagery

List the images in this poem and the senses they appeal to. (Sight, sound, touch, smell) Note how onomatopoeia in lines 6 and 9 contributes to the imagery.

ANALYZING THE POEMS
Identifying Details
1. The speaker rows a boat to a cove, crosses a mile of beach, three fields. He meets his lover at her farm.
2. The speaker says that he "has need of a world of men."

Interpreting Meanings
3. "As I gain the cove with pushing prow, . . . "; "two hearts beating each to each."
    "The quick sharp scratch" suggests that she is waiting anxiously for him.
4. "Meeting at Night" seems hurried and tense. "Parting at Morning" seems lighter, easier, and more relaxed.
5. The speaker is no longer so obsessed with being with her; he is eager to leave.
6. Responses will vary, possibly according to students' own experiences.

Paired, as they were meant to be, these short poems tell a love story in quickly presented, care-fully selected details. Both poems, according to Browning, are spoken by the man.

Meeting at Night

A
The gray sea and the long black land;
And the yellow half-moon large and low;
And the startled little waves that leap
In fiery ringlets from their sleep,
5   As I gain the cove with pushing prow,
And quench its speed i' the slushy sand.

Then a mile of warm sea-scented beach;
Three fields to cross till a farm appears;
A tap at the pane, the quick sharp scratch
10 And blue spurt of a lighted match,
And a voice less loud, through its joys and
    fears,
Than the two hearts beating each to each!

Parting at Morning

Round the cape of a sudden came the sea,
And the sun looked over the mountain's rim;
And straight was a path of gold for him,°
And the need of a world of men for me.

---

3. **him:** the sun.

Responding to the Poems

Analyzing the Poems

Identifying Details

1. Describe the speaker's journey in "Meeting at Night." Where does he finally meet his beloved?
2. Why does the speaker leave his love at the end of "Parting at Morning"?

Interpreting Meanings

3. In "Meeting at Night," what words underscore the speaker's restless anxiety to gain his destination? What words emphasize the anxiety of his beloved?
4. Compare the **rhythms** of the second stanza of "Meeting at Night," especially lines 9–12, with those of "Parting at Morning." How do the rhythms of each poem create and fit the mood of each episode of the love story?
5. Why do you think the beloved is not explicitly mentioned in "Parting at Morning"?
6. Do the episodes of the love story described here ring true to you? Explain.

Writing About the Poems

A Creative Response

1. **Extending the Poems.** In a short composition, fill in some of the details of the love story that Browning omits: for example, the age of the lovers, their personalities, etc. Be sure that the details you invent fit with the facts and feelings that Browning uses to tell the story.
2. **Using Another Point of View.** How would the mood and meaning of the poems change if they were spoken by the other person? Write a poem (or prose paragraph) from the other person's point of view that dramatizes your idea of how the change in perspective might alter the meaning and tone.

PREPARATION

1. ESTABLISHING A PURPOSE. Have students read to discover why the poem is called "Prospice."

2. PREREADING JOURNAL. You might have students write three sentences describing the way they think most people would respond to Browning's opening question.

A. Humanities Connection: Discussing the Fine Art

❓ Describe the emotions of the men on the boat. Are they fearful? Determined? Anxious? Exhilarated? What detail in the painting suggests possible disaster? (The broken mast in the water)

SUPPLEMENTARY SUPPORT MATERIALS
1. Vocabulary Activity Worksheet (*CCB*)
2. Review and Response Worksheet: Imagery and Theme (*CCB*)
3. Selection Test (*CCB*)
4. Audiocassette recording

DEVELOPING VOCABULARY
The following words from the poem are tested in the Selection Test. (See also Vocabulary Activity Worksheet.)
to denote   brunt   arrears

CLOSURE
Have students explain the meaning of the poem's title.

Prospice (prō·spik′ē) is Latin for "Look forward." Despite his pleasure in "glad life," Browning here looks forward to death as an opportunity to show himself a brave man and to be reunited with his wife, "thou soul of my soul" (line 27). Browning wrote this poem soon after Elizabeth Barrett Browning died in Italy in 1861.

Prospice

Dogger Bank by Clarkson Stanfield (1846). Oil.

Victoria and Albert Museum, London.

1. Fog in his throat and mist in his face; a storm with snowy blasts.

Barriers that fall and a battle to fight before the reward can be gained; the heroes of old.
2. He wants to experience it fully.
3. Being reunited with his dead wife.

4. There is a listener whom the speaker is addressing; the speaker is about to reveal his innermost thoughts.
5. Lines 1–10 contain images of a storm; these lines contain many heavily stressed syllables. The imagery in lines 21–28 is of the storm's cease; there are fewer heavily stressed syllables.

The differences reflect the movement from battle, anguish, and night to peace, love, and light.
6. The speaker will give up his burdens to God and enjoy a peaceful existence.
7. Student answers will vary. Responses may include fear, confrontation, and challenge, among others.

ADDITIONAL WRITING ASSIGNMENT
Other comparisons could be made with John Donne's "Death Be Not Proud" (text page 372) and with Dylan Thomas's "Do Not Go Gentle into That Good Night" (text page 1130).

Fear death?—to feel the fog in my throat,
    The mist in my face,
When the snows begin, and the blasts denote
    I am nearing the place,
5   The power of the night, the press of the storm,
    The post of the foe;
Where he stands, the Arch Fear° in a visible form,
    Yet the strong man must go:
For the journey is done and the summit attained,
10   And the barriers fall,
Though a battle's to fight ere the guerdon° be gained,
    The reward of it all.
I was ever a fighter, so—one fight more,
    The best and the last!
15 I would hate that death bandaged my eyes, and forbore,
    And bade me creep past.
No! let me taste the whole of it, fare like my peers
    The heroes of old,
Bear the brunt, in a minute pay glad life's arrears
20   Of pain, darkness, and cold.
For sudden the worst turns the best to the brave,
    The black minute's at end,
And the elements' rage, the fiend-voices° that rave,
    Shall dwindle, shall blend,
25 Shall change, shall become first a peace out of pain,
    Then a light, then thy breast,
O thou soul of my soul! I shall clasp thee again,
    And with God be the rest!

7. **Arch Fear:** death.

11. **guerdon** (gur'd'n): (archaic) reward.

23. **fiend-voices:** According to legend, fiends or evil spirits try to seize the soul as it leaves the body.

Responding to the Poem

Analyzing the Poem

Identifying Details

1. What concrete **images** does the poet use in lines 1–6 to suggest the approach of death? What images later in the poem suggest that death is a battle?
2. Why does the speaker want to be conscious at the moment of his death?
3. What does Browning look forward to after death?

Interpreting Meanings

4. What is the effect of the abrupt, colloquial beginning of this monologue, in your opinion?
5. Consider the images and rhythms of lines 1–10, the fight with death, and of lines 21–28, the results of the battle. How are these passages different? How do the differences affect the poem's point and feeling?

6. What is your interpretation of the last line, "And with God be the rest"?
7. What do you think of the speaker's **attitude** toward death?

Writing About the Poem

A Critical Response

Comparing and Contrasting Two Poets' Views. In a short essay, compare and contrast the attitudes toward death and toward life after death expressed in Browning's "Prospice" and in Alfred, Lord Tennyson's "Crossing the Bar" and the selections from *In Memoriam*. In your essay be sure to include specific references to the poems' themes and images.

A. Expansion
She is said to have known by heart 18,000 verses of ancient Greek poetry.

B. Expansion
They made their home in Florence at a villa named the Casa Guidi.

FOR FURTHER READING STUDENTS
Students would enjoy Rudolph Fleish's *The Barretts of Wimpole Street,* a popular play about the Brownings' elopement. Virginia Woolf's little book called *Flush,* a biography of the Brownings' dog, can be recommended to advanced students.

Elizabeth Barrett Browning (1806–1861)

Elizabeth Barrett Browning by Michele Gordigiani (1858). Oil.

Elizabeth Barrett Browning was one of the most famous poets of her day, more successful during her lifetime than her husband Robert Browning. She is remembered today for her *Sonnets from the Portuguese,* of which "How Do I Love Thee" is the best known. She wrote the forty-four sonnets during the months before her marriage and elopement to Italy in 1846, but she thought them so personal that she did not show them to her husband until three years later. When Browning urged her to publish the poems, she was reluctant because they were so intimate and autobiographical. She deliberately gave them a title that suggested the poems were not really hers, but a translation into English from an original Portuguese source.

During her lifetime she was well known as an audacious, versatile poet who frequently wrote on intellectual, religious, and political matters. As a girl she had studied Greek, Latin, French, Italian, history, and philosophy—an uncommon education for a woman in nineteenth-century England. She published translations of Greek plays, long narratives, a novel in verse, and poems full of striking and excited language. Her poems dealt with such diverse topics as the abolition of slavery, the exploitation of children in factories, the power of religious belief, and the promise of Italian nationalism.

Through the first half of her busy literary career, she was a semi-invalid. Her illnesses have been variously diagnosed, and it is certain that their effect was enlarged by the sometimes bullying protectiveness of her father. She wrote to

Robert Browning during their courtship, "Papa says sometimes when he comes into this room unexpectedly and convicts me of having dry toast for dinner, . . . that obstinacy and dry toast have brought me to my present condition, and if I *pleased* to have porter and beefsteaks instead, I should be as well as ever I was, in a month!"

In 1845 she met Robert Browning, and the next year they married secretly and went to live in Italy. Her father never forgave her for her marriage, nor did he ever see her again. She flourished in Italy and bore a son. Through the publication of new poems and several successful collected editions of her poetry, she continued to hold her place as one of the principal poets of mid-Victorian England.

PREPARATION
1. ESTABLISHING A PURPOSE. Have students read the poem as an answer to the question posed in line 1.

2. PREREADING JOURNAL. Have students write three sentences that might answer the question in line 1.

SUPPLEMENTARY SUPPORT MATERIALS
1. Review and Response Worksheet: Theme (*CCB*)
2. Selection Test (*CCB*)

CLOSURE
Have students list at least four of the ways in which Browning says she loves.

ANALYZING THE POEM
Identifying Details
1. Seven plus love after death (lines 13–14).
2. Lines 9–12, 13–14.

Interpreting Meanings
3. The pauses through line 11 indicate the end of a thought or a natural pause. The pauses in lines 12–13 indicate an emotional interruption.
The effect is one of contrast.
4. She does not suggest (as her husband does) that dying is a struggle.
In fact, both poets look forward to a reunion after death. Robert Browning is defiant. He will triumph over death. Elizabeth Browning's passion will simply continue.

Elizabeth Barrett Browning wrote this sonnet and all the *Sonnets from the Portuguese* in traditional Petrarchan, or Italian, sonnet form. The sonnets have a rhyme scheme of *abba abba* in the octave (first eight lines) and *cdcdcd* in the sestet (last six lines). She does not observe the usual break or "turn," which introduces some new aspect of the topic in the last six lines. Rather, she breaks the poem into short units of thought (usually a line or two) until the very end.

from Sonnets from the Portuguese

43

How do I love thee? Let me count the ways.
I love thee to the depth and breadth and height
My soul can reach, when feeling out of sight
For the ends of Being and ideal Grace.
5   I love thee to the level of everyday's
Most quiet need, by sun and candle light.
I love thee freely, as men strive for Right;
I love thee purely, as they turn from Praise.
I love thee with the passion put to use
10   In my old griefs, and with my childhood's faith.
I love thee with a love I seemed to lose
With my lost saints°—I love thee with the breath,
Smiles, tears, of all my life!—and, if God choose,
I shall but love thee better after death.

12. **lost saints:** a reference to the innocent faith and love of childhood.

Responding to the Poem

Analyzing the Poem

Identifying Details

1. How many distinct ways does the speaker say that she loves her beloved?
2. Which lines indicate the speaker's religious faith?

Interpreting Meanings

3. How are the pauses in the last three lines different from those in the rest of the poem? What do you think is the effect of these differences?
4. Compare the ending of this poem to that of Robert Browning's "Prospice." How does each speaker treat the movement from life to death? Do you find one ending more attractive than the other? Explain.

Writing About the Poem

A Creative Response

1. **Extending the Poem.** The rhetorical question of line 1 and the answers to it hint that Browning is attempting to be all-inclusive in her description of love. Has she described all of the important aspects and emotions of love, in your opinion? Write a short composition extending Browning's description.

A Critical Response

2. **Analyzing Concrete and Abstract Words.** In a brief essay, analyze the poet's use of concrete and abstract words in this sonnet.

A. **Expansion**
Rugby School as-
sumed virtually
legendary dimen-
sions in the nine-
teenth century.
Founded in 1567,
it was the birth-
place of rugby
football. The ethos
of the school under
Dr. Thomas Arnold
(headmaster from
1828 to 1841) in-
spired Thomas
Hughes's popular
memoir, *Tom
Brown's School-
days* (1857).

B. **Expansion**
Arnold also paid
attention to the ed-
ucational systems
on the Continent
(where he visited
in 1859 and 1867).
In his reports, he
argued that En-
gland badly
needed more edu-
cational organiza-
tion and could
learn much from
European models.

Matthew Arnold (1822–1888)

Unlike the other major Victorian poets, Matthew Arnold achieved fame as both a poet and a critic. He is as famous today for his essays on literary and social criticism as he is for his poetry. In a letter written to his mother in 1869, Arnold assessed his accomplishments as a poet: "It might be fairly urged that I have less poetic sentiment than Tennyson, and less intellectual vigor and abundance than Browning; yet, because I have perhaps more of a fusion of the two than either of them, and have more regularly applied that fusion to the main line of modern development, I am likely enough to have my turn, as they have had theirs." He was right. His poems stand with those of Tennyson and Browning as one of the principal achievements of Victorian literature. Their quiet tones and carefully shaped lines and figures of speech express his reflections on what Victorian society was like, what it would come to, and what it had cost.

Arnold was the son of a famous father and had a hard time in his youth living up to his father's expectations. Dr. Thomas Arnold—a clergyman, historian, and educational reformer—was one of the leading thinkers of the Victorian A era and headmaster of Rugby School. At Rugby, Arnold was an uneven student, but in 1841 won a scholarship to Oxford University. Although he was less than enthusiastic as a student, he seemed to enjoy thoroughly playing the role of a dandy. His performance at Oxford was a failure by Rugby standards, and he graduated without knowing clearly what he wanted to do. In 1847 he became private secretary to Lord Landsowne, head of the Council of Education.

Arnold had won prizes for his poetry at Rugby when he was a teen-ager and later at Oxford. In 1849 he published his first book of poems, *The Strayed Reveller,* to mixed reviews. Two more volumes of poetry followed in 1852 and 1853, and as a result Arnold was elected a Professor of Poetry at Oxford in 1857.

When he married in 1851, Arnold looked for a B job that would support a family. He became a government inspector of schools for poor children, a job he held for thirty-five years. He

wrote to his wife after his first months on the job: "I think I shall get interested in the schools after a little time; their effects on the children are so immense, and their future effects in civilizing the next generation of the lower classes, who, as things are going, will have most of the political power of the country in their hands, may be so important." Arnold's job was exhausting, requiring him to travel all over England and write daily reports. Though he continued to write poetry in his free time, he found it increasingly difficult. In 1853 he told a friend, "I am past thirty, and three parts iced over—and my pen, it seems to me is even stiffer and more cramped than my feeling."

After 1860 Arnold almost completely stopped writing poetry; he began his second career as a critic. Arnold's travels and his work had given him firsthand knowledge of pressing social problems. He became a prolific and energetic essayist and lecturer on literary, political, social, and religious topics. His first essays were literary criticism: *Essays in Criticism* was published in 1865; a second series appeared after his death in 1888. During the 1870's Arnold published essays on religion and on education. In *Culture and Anarchy* (1869) and in his essays on literature and religion, Arnold urged his readers to acquire a knowledge of the past and to read the Greeks, Dante, and Shakespeare. A study of "the best that has been thought and said in the world" would help them judge ideas and personal conduct, he believed. Without the steadying influence of what he called culture, Arnold warned that the technological and political changes of the nineteenth century would accelerate into a grossly materialistic democracy. He feared also an intellectual anarchy in which every opinion was seen to be as good as any other.

In his poetry Arnold wrote with equal point

and force but without much joy or hope. The speaker of "Dover Beach" stands in a world in which the battle against anarchy has already been lost, a world without faith or certitude. The speaker of "To Marguerite—Continued" is left without even the solace of a lover.

All through his life Arnold was capable of knowing and feeling both the excitement of trying to change the temper and direction of his time and the loneliness of someone who was not wholly at home in his time. Lionel Trilling, the twentieth-century literary critic, wrote of Arnold: "Of the literary men of the great English nineteenth century, there are few who have stayed quite so fresh, so immediate, and so relevant as Matthew Arnold. . . . As a poet he reaches us not more powerfully but, we sometimes feel, more intimately than any other. As a critic he provided us with the essential terms for our debate in matters of taste and judgment."

A. Expansion
Arnold thus takes his place among the distinguished English poet-critics: Sir Philip Sidney, John Dryden, Alexander Pope, Samuel Johnson, Samuel Taylor Coleridge, T. S. Eliot, and Philip Larkin. Note that, like Eliot, Arnold's focus on literary criticism gradually expanded to include broad social and cultural issues.

B. Humanities Connection: Responding to the Fine Art
What values and interests of the period are reflected in this painting? (The costumes and attentive postures of the figures, the neatly arranged art on the walls, and the opulent nature of the hall itself reflect the high value Victorians placed on material and intellectual advancement and on gentility and decorum.)

A Private View by William Powell Frith.   Wrackelford House, Dorchester.

1. BUILDING ON PRIOR KNOWLEDGE. Refer students back to the introduction (text pages 766–772) to review the questions and doubts that beset the Victorians, especially in regard to the conflict between faith and the new discoveries of science. Remind them also of Tennyson's grappling with doubt in *In Memoriam* (text pages 794–797).

2. ESTABLISHING A PURPOSE. Have students read question 8 on text page 814 before they read the poem. You might also direct them to the Comment on the Poem (text page 814).

1. Vocabulary Activity Worksheet (*CCB*)
2. Review and Response Worksheet: Analyzing a Poem (*CCB*)
3. Selection Test (*CCB*)
4. Audiocassette recording

A. Humanities Connection: About the Fine Art

After studying in Aberdeen, Edinburgh, and London, Scottish painter William Dyce (1806–1864) visited Italy. Dyce's Italian studies led him to a style of primitive simplicity and repose, evident in the work shown here.

The cliffs in this painting are strongly reminiscent of the white cliffs of Dover on England's southeast coast. Strolling on the beach was a popular Victorian pastime, and during this period many of the popular seaside resorts, such as Brighton, were developed.

A *Pegwell Beach* by William Dyce (1858). Oil.

The Tate Gallery, London.

DEVELOPING VOCABULARY
The following words from the poem are
tested in the Selection Test. (See also
Vocabulary Activity Worksheet.)
to blanch   turbid
cadence   to furl

CLOSURE
Ask five students to select the lines from
this poem that they think are most significant or, to them, most memorable.

ADDITIONAL WRITING ASSIGNMENTS
1. Have students compare Arnold's
"eternal note of sadness" with Gerard
Manley Hopkins's poem "Spring and
Fall" (text page 828) and with Robert
Frost's "Nothing Gold Can Stay" (text
page 51).
2. Compare "Dover Beach" with W. B.
Yeats's "The Second Coming" on text
page 1092.

Compared with the characteristic poems of Romantic and Victorian writers, "Dover Beach" is
low-keyed, spoken largely in tones of quiet conversation. For all its conversational tone, however,
the poem is remarkably ambitious in its claim to
render a universal condition.

Dover Beach

The sea is calm tonight.
The tide is full, the moon lies fair
Upon the straits°—on the French coast the light
Gleams and is gone; the cliffs of England stand,
5 Glimmering and vast, out in the tranquil bay.
Come to the window, sweet is the night air!
Only, from the long line of spray
Where the sea meets the moon-blanched land,
Listen! you hear the grating roar
10 Of pebbles which the waves draw back, and fling,
At their return, up the high strand,°
Begin, and cease, and then again begin,
With tremulous cadence slow, and bring
The eternal note of sadness in.

15 Sophocles° long ago
Heard it on the Aegean,° and it brought
Into his mind the turbid ebb and flow
Of human misery; we
Find also in the sound a thought,
20 Hearing it by this distant northern sea.

The Sea of Faith
Was once, too, at the full, and round earth's shore
Lay like the folds of a bright girdle° furled.
But now I only hear
25 Its melancholy, long, withdrawing roar,
Retreating, to the breath
Of the night wind, down the vast edges drear
And naked shingles° of the world.

Ah, love, let us be true
30 To one another! for the world, which seems
To lie before us like a land of dreams,
So various, so beautiful, so new,
Hath really neither joy, nor love, nor light,
Nor certitude, nor peace, nor help for pain;
35 And we are here as on a darkling plain
Swept with confused alarms of struggle and flight,
Where ignorant armies clash by night.°

3. **straits:** the Strait of Dover, a body of
water separating southeastern England and
France.

11. **strand:** shore.

15. **Sophocles** (säf'ə·klēz'): (496?–406 B.C.)
one of the principal writers of ancient Greek
tragedies.
16. **Aegean** (ē·jē'ən): sea between Greece
and Turkey.

23. **girdle:** belt.

28. **shingles:** beaches covered with pebbles.

37. **ignorant armies . . . night:** an episode in
a history by the classical Greek historian
Thucydides. During a battle fought at night,
soldiers killed friend as well as foe, for they
could not know one from the other in the
dark.

A. Sound and
Sense
Notice how the use
of onomatopoeia
("grating roar")
and of repetition
re-creates the very
movement and
sound of the
waves as they
wash over the peb-
bles on the strand.
(When the water
washes away from
the pebbly beach,
a sort of slurping
sound is heard.
See line 25.)

B. Memorization
Encourage stu-
dents to memorize
this stanza. The
poem was pub-
lished in 1867, well
before the tragic
wars of the twenti-
eth century.
[?] In what ways
does this fa-
mous stanza seem
prophetic? (In the
complicated strug-
gles of the 20th
century, friends be-
come enemies and
enemies become
friends. World War
II enemies
Germany and Ja-
pan are now
friends. World War
II ally Russia be-
came an enemy
and is now a
friend.)

1. It is night in a room in Dover, England, overlooking the sea.

The speaker is an educated man addressing his beloved.

2. He contrasts the Sea of Faith in the past and in the present.

3. He urges that he and his love be true to one another because life is difficult, painful, and chaotic.

Interpreting Meanings

4. Calm, peaceful, perhaps joyful.

Line 7 begins with the word *Only,* suggesting that a contrast will follow. The imperative *Listen!* (line 9) also suggests a change.

5. He says that the same sound could be heard centuries ago and in a different place.

Allusion: the tragedies of the ancient Greek playwright Sophocles (*Oedipus the King, Antigone*).

6. The Sea of Faith (religious belief; the metaphor) once surrounded the earth, encompassing it like the folds of a bright belt (the simile) that enclosed and decorated the earth.

(Answers continue in left-hand column.)

(Continued from top.)

Stanza 1: The sound of the waves and the pebbles in a "grating roar" and a sad sound. Stanza 3: The sound is a "withdrawing roar" and a melancholy sound.

7. The lines in each stanza rhyme but not in a repeated pattern; the rhythm is also irregular. There is a cadence, but the irregularities create the effect of natural speech.

8. He sees the world as a chaotic, painful place without joy or peace.

Yes, because the political struggles of established nations and emerging countries have erupted into local wars, which constantly threaten to spread.

A Comment on the Poem

More than any other poem written in the nineteenth century, "Dover Beach" continues to echo through the consciousness of every generation of the twentieth century. To say why involves matters of both technique and meaning.

Compared with the characteristic product of the Romantic or Victorian poets, "Dover Beach" is low-keyed. The speaker's tone is largely that of quiet conversation in which iambs and anapests are congenially mixed.

Unlike his predecessors and contemporaries, Arnold neither reaches for the sublime nor dwells upon the sentimental in this poem. Instead, he writes a love poem which, incidentally, expresses the crisis of conscience brought about by the dwindling of religion—"the Sea of Faith"—and the rise of science. Science has transformed human life by industrialism and by the mass warfare that scientific inventions made possible. Against these bewildering developments, Arnold poses the notion that love is itself a faith to cling to and, by implication, that individual integrity and a humanistic vision broad enough to include the tragic conclusions of Sophocles are the only defense against a world moving toward anarchy.

Responding to the Poem

Analyzing the Poem

Identifying Details

1. What is the **setting** of the first stanza? Who is the speaker, and whom is he addressing?

2. What contrast does the speaker draw in the third stanza?

3. What does the speaker urge in the last stanza, and why?

Interpreting Meanings

4. What is the **mood** evoked by the first six lines? How does Arnold begin to change this mood in the second half of the first stanza?

5. How does Arnold make the speaker's **mood** at the end of the first stanza seem timeless and universal? Explain the literary **allusion** in the second stanza.

6. Explain the **metaphor** and **simile** in lines 21–23. How do lines 24–28 relate to the sound the speaker hears at the end of the first stanza?

7. Describe the **rhyme scheme** and the **rhythm** of the poem. What is the effect of their irregularity?

8. What is the speaker's view of his world as it is presented in the last stanza? Do you think this view is relevant to today's world? Explain why or why not.

Writing About the Poem

A Critical Response

Analyzing a Problem. Arnold starts with a specific setting and situation and moves quietly to make a series of generalizations about human life and faith and love. He concludes the poem by returning to the lovers' specific relationship. Write a short essay about your views of a contemporary problem or issue of broad significance. In your essay, try to imitate the structure of this poem by starting with a specific, concrete image, then moving to a generalization, and returning at the end to the specific.

PREPARATION
ESTABLISHING A PURPOSE.   Direct students' attention to question 7.

SUPPLEMENTARY SUPPORT MATERIALS
1. Vocabulary Activity Worksheet (*CCB*)
2. Review and Response Worksheet: Tone and Theme (*CCB*)
3. Selection Test (*CCB*)

DEVELOPING VOCABULARY
The following words from the poem are tested in the Selection Test. (See also Vocabulary Activity Worksheet.)
mirth   ample

CLOSURE
Have students list the characteristics of the woman the speaker laments.

ANALYZING THE POEM
Identifying Details
1. The woman described in the poem has just died.
2. She appeared merry but was not. She was always busy and yearned for peace.

As in "Dover Beach," the outer world is contrasted with the inner world in this brief lyric. As you read "Requiescat," try to identify the qualities in the dead person that the speaker hints may have made her unhappy when she was alive. *Requiescat* is Latin for "may she rest."

Requiescat

Strew on her roses, roses,
  And never a spray of yew!°
In quiet she reposes;
  Ah, would that I did too!

5 Her mirth the world required;
  She bathed it in smiles of glee.
But her heart was tired, tired,
  And now they let her be.

Her life was turning, turning,
10   In mazes of heat and sound.
But for peace her soul was yearning,
  And now peace laps her round.

Her cabined,° ample spirit,
  It fluttered and failed for breath.
15 Tonight it doth inherit
  The vasty° hall of death.

2. **yew:** a dark evergreen tree traditionally associated with death.

13. **cabined:** confined within narrow limits or space.

16. **vasty:** vast, immense, huge.

Interpreting Meanings
3. She "bathed" the world in smiles of glee (line 6) and is "bathed" in peace (line 12).
4. *Inherit* here means "to come into possession of" and "to receive something of value from a person who has died."
5. Lines 1, 7, 9.
   The poet may have wanted to emphasize the seriousness and finality of death, so he abandoned the singsong repetition. Perhaps he wanted to emphasize that the woman's soul was finally at rest.
6. The images of death create a serious tone.
7. Death brings rest and peace.
   Opinions will vary.

Responding to the Poem

Analyzing the Poem

Identifying Details

1. What appears to be the occasion for this poem?
2. What contrast between the woman's inner world and the outer world does the poet emphasize in the second and third stanzas?

Interpreting Meanings

3. Explain the **metaphor** in line 6. How does the poet echo this metaphor in line 12?
4. What makes the use of the word *inherit* appropriate in line 15?
5. The poet uses **repetition** in each of the first three stanzas. Identify the instances of repetition. Why do you think the poet does not continue this pattern in the last stanza?
6. The bouncy pace of the first three stanzas makes them sound much like the verses on greeting cards found in drugstores and supermarkets. How does the poem's **tone** change in the fourth stanza?
7. What attitude toward death emerges from this brief elegy? What do you think of this attitude?

Writing About the Poem

A Creative Response

1. **Writing a Character Sketch.** From the evidence of Arnold's poem, write a brief character sketch in prose of the woman he laments.

A Critical Response

2. **Contrasting Poems.** In a brief essay, contrast "Requiescat" with "She Dwelt Among the Untrodden Ways" by William Wordsworth (page 639).

PREPARATION

1. BUILDING ON PRIOR KNOWLEDGE. Review with students the figurative uses of the sea in the poems by Arnold and Tennyson.

2. ESTABLISHING A PURPOSE. Direct students' attention to question 4 on text page 818. Have them pause after stanza 1 and identify the metaphors used to describe life (the sea) and individuals (islands).

3. PREREADING JOURNAL. Before they read, have students write two or three sentences about our dependence on others and our solitariness. Do they agree with the lines quoted in the headnote?

SUPPLEMENTARY SUPPORT MATERIALS
1. Vocabulary Activity Worksheet (CCB)
2. Review and Response Worksheet: Extended Metaphor and Theme (CCB)
3. Selection Test (CCB)

A. Connections
These images and those in lines 15–16 bear a strong resemblance to those used by John Donne in "Meditation 17" (sometimes called his "No man is an island" essay) on text page 368.

B. Tone
❓ What is the tone of the last stanza? (Possible answers: bitter, angry, puzzled) Compare this stanza with Tennyson's questions and answers in *In Memoriam* (see text page 794).

Arnold wrote a series of poems in 1847 to 1849 to Marguerite, the name he gave to a woman he met in Switzerland before his marriage. Nothing is known about the relationship except that he and Marguerite finally separated. The experience seems to have confirmed Arnold's idea that in our most authentic and private identity each of us is alone. In "Isolation: To Marguerite," another poem in this series, Arnold writes:

This truth—to prove, and make thine own:
"Thou hast been, shalt be, art, alone."

To Marguerite– Continued

A
Yes! in the sea of life enisled,°
With echoing straits between us thrown,
Dotting the shoreless watery wild,
We mortal millions live *alone*.
5   The islands feel the enclasping flow,
And then their endless bounds° they know.

But when the moon their hollows lights,
And they are swept by balms of spring,
And in their glens, on starry nights,
10   The nightingales divinely sing;
And lovely notes, from shore to shore,
Across the sounds and channels pour—

Oh! then a longing like despair
Is to their farthest caverns sent;
15   For surely once, they feel, we were
Parts of a single continent!
Now round us spreads the watery plain—
Oh might our marges° meet again!

B
20   Who ordered, that their longing's fire
Should be, as soon as kindled, cooled?
Who renders vain their deep desire?
A God, a God their severance ruled!
And bade betwixt their shores to be
The unplumbed,° salt, <u>estranging</u> sea.

---

1. **enisled:** each made into a separate island.
6. **endless bounds:** Someone walking the boundaries of an island will walk in a circle.
18. **marges:** borders.
24. **unplumbed:** unexplored; unmeasured.

Fingall's Cave, Island of Staffa, Scotland by Thomas Moran (1884-85). Oil.

DEVELOPING VOCABULARY
The following word from the poem is tested in the Selection Test. (See also Vocabulary Activity Worksheet.)
to estrange

CLOSURE
Have students summarize Arnold's message to Marguerite in this poem.

A

The High Museum of Art, Atlanta, Georgia.
Purchased with Friends of Art Fund.

Matthew Arnold   817

ANALYZING THE POEM
Identifying Details
1. They are compared to islands.
2. The islands long to touch each other, to be joined.
3. The speaker says that "a God" ruled that humans should be isolated.

Interpreting Meanings
4. Human beings are islands separated

by a sea.
5. The beautiful, calm, romantic images of the second stanza create a mood of peace and beauty. In the third stanza, the interjection *Oh*, the two exclamatory sentences, and the word *despair* sharply break the tranquil mood of the preceding stanza.
6. Some may think *unplumbed* has negative connotations (something unexplored

may be dangerous), while others believe it is positive (the unexplored is exciting). *Salt* is a neutral word, but it is necessary to animal life (positive) yet stings when it touches an open wound (negative). *Estranging* has negative connotations.

If students view *unplumbed* as positive, then there is a progression from positive through neutral to negative. *(Answers continue in left-hand column.)*

(Continued from top.)
7. Yes. The institutions that held society together— religion, school, and family—are no longer as strong as they were. People's dependence on drugs, their lack of responsibility for each other, and their economic problems contribute to their sense of isolation.

Responding to the Poem

Analyzing the Poem

Identifying Details

1. To what are human beings compared in the first stanza?
2. What is the "longing like despair" of line 13?
3. In the last stanza, whom or what does the speaker identify as the cause of human isolation?

Interpreting Meanings

4. What **extended metaphor** runs throughout the entire poem?
5. How does the poet establish two contrasting **moods** in the second and third stanzas?
6. Comment on the three adjectives for the sea in the last line of the poem. What are the **connotations** of each adjective? Why do you think the poet chose this particular order for these three words?
7. Is Arnold's view of human isolation and estrangement relevant to today's world, in your view? Support your answer with reasons.

Writing About the Poem

A Creative Response

1. **Writing an Extended Metaphor.** Arnold uses the sea to construct an extended metaphor that dominates the poem. Write a short prose passage in which you use the sea, or another natural phenomenon of your choice, as the basis for an extended metaphor. Make sure that your passage is unified by a single theme and a consistent tone.

A Critical Response

2. **Comparing and Contrasting Two Poems.** One difference between this poem and "Dover Beach" is that the lovers in "To Marguerite—Continued" are separated. In what other ways are the poems different? How are they similar? In an essay, compare and contrast the theme and tone of these two works.

Dante Gabriel Rossetti (1828–1882)

When Dante Gabriel Rossetti's beautiful young wife died (a probable suicide) in 1862, he remorsefully placed in her coffin the manuscripts of his poems, many of them still unpublished. He thought that writing the poems had made his wife unhappy and had distracted him from caring for her. Seven years later, in order to publish his first collected edition of his poetry, he had his manuscripts exhumed from his wife's grave. This episode is typical of the unconventional and sometimes erratic character of Rossetti's life.

A He was born in London into a literary household. His father, an exiled Italian patriot, wrote commentaries on Dante; and his sister Christina and his brother William also became well-known writers.

B Dante Gabriel Rossetti first came to public attention as a self-consciously rebellious painter. As an art student in 1848, he helped found a movement called the Pre-Raphaelite Brotherhood. The aim of this small group of young painters was to break from the contemporary conventions of painting and return to the natural light and accurate detail of the fourteenth- and fifteenth-century Italian religious painters who preceded the Italian painter Raphael (hence, pre-Raphaelites). In the 1850's Rossetti's paintings of mythological and medieval subjects were criticized for being awkwardly composed, harshly lighted, and cluttered with antique objects. By the 1860's, however, the pre-Raphaelite style had begun to be accepted, and Rossetti started to make a moderately comfortable living as a painter.

C Rossetti was doubly talented as an artist and as a poet. He published a few of his early stories and nearly a dozen poems, including an early version of "The Blessed Damozel," in *The*

Dante Gabriel Rossetti by William Holman Hunt.

Germ, the Pre-Raphaelite Brotherhood's magazine. Critics attacked his poems, especially in the 1870's, as unhealthy and immoral in their emphasis on sensual detail. One critic referred to Rossetti as the leader of the "Fleshly School of Poetry."

"The Blessed Damozel" accurately represents the style of Rossetti's painting and many of his poems in its strong color and glittering surface, its use of unusual details and words (Rossetti called them "stunners"), its insistence on flesh, and its theme of separation and yearning. All these features make Rossetti's paintings and poems more characteristic of mainstream mid-Victorian taste than his critics, or perhaps Rossetti himself, would have acknowledged.

A. Expansion
See text pages 825–826 for a biography of Christina and a sample of her poetry.

B. Expansion
Other notable members of this group included the painters J. E. Millais (see text page 829), William Holman Hunt, and Sir Edward Burne-Jones. The Pre-Raphaelites had a significant effect on the aesthetic theories of the "art for art's sake" movement, led by English artist William Morris and essayist Walter Pater.

C. Connections
This kind of double talent is rare. Recall poet-artist William Blake (text page 617).

1. BUILDING ON PRIOR KNOWLEDGE. Recall with students the information on the Pre-Raphaelite movement and the discussion of "The Blessed Damozel" in the last three paragraphs of Rossetti's biography (text page 819).

2. ESTABLISHING A PURPOSE. Before they read the poem, have students turn to Rossetti's painting on text page 822 and note that it is the poet's own illustration for his poem. Ask them to speculate, from looking at the painting, what the poem is about. Have them read to answer these two questions: (1) Who is the blessed damozel? (A young woman who has died and gone to Heaven) (2) Why does the poet call her blessed? (Because she is in Heaven)

A. Symbol
Note the lilies and stars (only six stars show) in Rossetti's painting.
❓ What might they symbolize? (Student guesses will vary. The lilies and white rose might symbolize purity; the stars might be a celestial halo, as Rossetti pictures them in the painting. Three and seven are "magic numbers" in folklore and fairy tales.)

B. Archaic Diction
Note that *Herseemed* and *meetly* (line 10) are examples of archaic diction. Have students look for other examples (*haply* in line 115 and *Herself* in line 121) as preparation for the second writing assignment.

C. Speaker
Make sure that students realize that the parentheses here indicate a change in speaker: the damozel's beloved, who is alive on earth. Alert them to watch for parentheses throughout the poem.

"The Blessed Damozel" offers a kind of anthology of the features of pre-Raphaelite literary style in its deliberate, semi-mystical quaintness of language; its use of precise but mysterious symbols; its clear, strong colors; and the romantic archaism of the ballad form.

Many years after he wrote this poem, Rossetti explained that its theme was suggested by Edgar Allan Poe's poem "The Raven." "I saw at once," he wrote, "that Poe had done the utmost it was possible to do with the grief of the lover on earth, and I determined to reverse the conditions and give utterance to the yearnings of the loved one in heaven." As you read "The Blessed Damozel," note that the earthly lover's words are enclosed in parentheses.

The Blessed Damozel

The blessed damozel° leaned out
   From the gold bar of heaven;
Her eyes were deeper than the depth
   Of waters stilled at even;
5 She had three lilies in her hand,
   And the stars in her hair were seven.

Her robe, ungirt from clasp to hem,
   No wrought flowers did adorn,
But a white rose of Mary's gift,
10   For service meetly° worn;
Her hair that lay along her back
   Was yellow like ripe corn.°

Herseemed° she scarce had been a day
   One of God's choristers;
15 The wonder was not yet quite gone
   From that still look of hers;
Albeit, to them she left, her day
   Had counted as ten years.

(To one, it is ten years of years.
20   . . . Yet now, and in this place,
Surely she leaned o'er me—her hair
   Fell all about my face. . . .
Nothing: the autumn-fall of leaves.
   The whole year sets apace.)

25 It was the rampart of God's house
   That she was standing on;
By God built over the sheer depth
   The which is Space begun;
So high, that looking downward thence
30   She scarce could see the sun.

It lies in heaven, across the flood
   Of ether, as a bridge.
Beneath the tides of day and night

1. **damozel:** an early word form of the French *demoiselle*, which means "maiden."

10. **meetly:** appropriately.

12. **corn:** grain.

13. **Herseemed:** It seemed to her.

SUPPLEMENTARY SUPPORT MATERIALS
1. Vocabulary Activity Worksheet (*CCB*)
2. Review and Response Worksheet: Atmosphere (*CCB*)
3. Selection Test (*CCB*)

DEVELOPING VOCABULARY
The following word from the poem is tested in the Selection Test. (See also Vocabulary Activity Worksheet.)
abash

35
A
> With flame and darkness ridge
> The void, as low as where this earth
> Spins like a fretful midge.°

B
40
> Around her, lovers, newly met
> 'Mid deathless love's acclaims,
> Spoke evermore among themselves
> Their heart-remembered names;
> And the souls mounting up to God
> Went by her like thin flames.

45
C
> And still she bowed herself and stooped
> Out of the circling charm;
> Until her bosom must have made
> The bar she leaned on warm,
> And the lilies lay as if asleep
> Along her bended arm.

50
> From the fixed place of heaven she saw
> Time like a pulse shake fierce
> Through all the worlds. Her gaze still strove
> Within the gulf to pierce
> Its path; and now she spoke as when
> The stars sang in their spheres.°

55
60
> The sun was gone now; the curled moon
> Was like a little feather
> Fluttering far down the gulf; and now
> She spoke through the still weather.
> Her voice was like the voice the stars
> Had when they sang together.

D
> (Ah, sweet! Even now, in that bird's song,
> Strove not her accents there,
> Fain to be harkened? When those bells
> Possessed the midday air,

65
> Strove not her steps to reach my side
> Down all the echoing stair?)

E
70
> "I wish that he were come to me,
> For he will come," she said.
> "Have I not prayed in heaven?—on earth,
> Lord, Lord has he not prayed?
> Are not two prayers a perfect strength?
> And shall I feel afraid?

75
> "When round his head the aureole° clings,
> And he is clothed in white,
> I'll take his hand and go with him
> To the deep wells of light;
> As unto a stream we will step down,
> And bathe there in God's sight.

36. **midge:** gnat or small fly.

54. **stars . . . spheres:** According to an ancient belief, the stars make music as they move across the sky.

73. **aureole:** halo.

A. Simile
Have students explain the simile. (The earth, seen from heaven, looks like a gnat.)
? Why is it *fretful*? (The earth is troubled, beset with problems.)

B. Interpreting
She is surrounded by lovers who are happily and forever united in death. (Have students note the background images of lovers in the painting on text page 822.)

C. Imagery
Here's an example of the "fleshly" imagery that so outraged some Victorians.

D. Connections
The earthly lover feels his lost love in nature (the bird's song), as does Tennyson in *In Memoriam*: "Thy voice is on the rolling air,/I hear thee where the waters run. . . ."

E. Structure
Here begins the damozel's reverie (continuing through line 132) about what she and her lover will do once he has died and joined her in heaven.

A. Humanities Connection: Responding to the Fine Art

See the suggestion (top page 820) on using this painting to establish a purpose for reading.

? Who do you think are the figures embracing in the background? (They might be the reunited lovers mentioned in lines 37–40, but they are all the same couple and they must be the damozel's memories of her lover and herself.) Who are the three figures at the bottom? (Angels—notice the wings.)

Blessed Damozel by Dante Gabriel Rossetti (1871-77). Oil.

The Fogg Art Museum, Harvard University, Bequest of Grenville L. Winthrop.

"We two will stand beside that shrine,
80   Occult,° withheld, untrod,
Whose lamps are stirred continually
    With prayer sent up to God;
And see our old prayers, granted, melt
    Each like a little cloud.

85   "We two will lie i' the shadow of
    That living mystic tree°
Within whose secret growth the Dove°
    Is sometimes felt to be,
While every leaf that His plumes touch
90   Saith His Name audibly.

80. **Occult:** mysterious; beyond human understanding.

86. **mystic tree:** the tree of life, whose leaves are "for the healing of nations" (Revelation 22:2).
87. **Dove:** symbol of the Holy Spirit.

Humanities Connection: Music
In 1903 the French composer Claude
Debussy (1862–1918) wrote very beautiful music (called *La Damoiselle Élue*) for
an adaptation of this poem by Frank
Damrosch. In Damrosch's adaptation, the
earthly lover's lines are omitted, and the
words are slightly changed and abridged,
but most of the poem remains intact. A
narrator and the blessed damozel sing

the solo parts; a chorus sings the rest of
the words.
    If you can get hold of the music, play it
in class. Ask students how well they think
Debussy has interpreted the mystical,
longing mood of the poem.

CLOSURE
Ask students to identify at least five images of sound in the poem. (There are

many: stars singing in their spheres,
bird's song, bells ringing, songs, sweet
symphonies, angels singing, citherns and
citoles, weeping)

"And I myself will teach to him,
　　I myself, lying so,
The songs I sing here, which his voice
　　Shall pause in, hushed and slow,
95　And find some knowledge at each pause,
　　Of some new thing to know."

A [(Alas! We two, we two, thou say'st!
　　Yea, one wast thou with me
That once of old. But shall God lift
100　To endless unity
The soul whose likeness with thy soul
　　Was but its love for thee?)]

"We two," she said, "will seek the groves
　　Where the lady Mary is,
105　With her five handmaidens, whose names
　　Are five sweet symphonies,
Cecily, Gertrude, Magdalen,
　　Margaret, and Rosalys.°

"Circlewise sit they, with bound locks
110　And foreheads garlanded;
Into the fine cloth white like flame
　　Weaving the golden thread,
B [To fashion the birthrobes for them
　　Who are just born, being dead.]

115　"He shall fear, haply, and be dumb;
　　Then will I lay my cheek
To his, and tell about our love,
　　Not once abashed or weak;
And the dear Mother will approve
120　My pride, and let me speak.

"Herself shall bring us, hand in hand,
　　To Him round whom all souls
Kneel, the clear-ranged unnumbered heads
　　Bowed with their aureoles;
125　And angels meeting us shall sing
　　To their citherns and citoles.°

"There will I ask of Christ the Lord
　　Thus much for him and me—
Only to live as once on earth
130　With Love—only to be,
As then awhile, forever now,
　　Together, I and he."

She gazed and listened and then said,
　　Less sad of speech than mild—
135　"All this is when he comes." She ceased.

108. **Cecily . . . Rosalys:** names of saints,
chosen for their musical sound.

126. **citherns and citoles:** medieval stringed
instruments of the guitar family.

A. Interpreting
Ask students to try
to interpret the
earthly lover's
comment in these
lines. (He seems
not nearly so en-
thusiastic about in-
finite togetherness
as the damozel.
He says that the
only thing they had
in common was
their love for each
other.)

B. Paradox
Explain the par-
adox in these
lines. (The death
of earthly life is the
beginning, or birth,
of eternal life.)

ANALYZING THE POEM
Identifying Details
1. She is in heaven.
  Ten years.
2. A pulse that shakes the world.
3. She prays that her lover will join her in Heaven.

Interpreting Meanings
4. Student answers will vary. They may describe the mood as melancholy, ethereal, mystical, sensuous.
  Possible answers: The three lilies and seven stars are mystical. The description of the damozel is sensuous.
5. He says the only way in which they were alike was that they loved each other while she was alive.
6. The first and last sentences are those of the earthly lover, who is so mystically "in tune" with the damozel that he is aware of her emotions ten years after her death.
7. Students may say yes. Lovers are meeting in heaven; her bosom is warm even though she is dead; she longs for her lover; when he comes they will live with love as on earth.

The light thrilled toward her, filled
With angels in strong, level flight.
  Her eyes prayed, and she smiled.

(I saw her smile.) But soon their path
140   Was vague in distant spheres;
And then she cast her arms along
  The golden barriers,
And laid her face between her hands,
  And wept. (I heard her tears.)

A Comment on the Poem

The maiden lady of the title is, prosaically speaking, a damsel, as in the familiar term of mock humor, "a damsel in distress." But the predicament in which this damsel finds herself is not "fraught with peril," as was the case with many other Victorian heroines awaiting rescue by a manly hero, but quite the reverse. This damsel, newly ensconced in Heaven, is concerned about "saving" the man who loves her and about securing "forever now" the relationship which on earth lasted but "awhile."

Her unusual circumstance is spelled out by the man in the form of a fantasy into which, at crucial moments, he parenthetically introduces himself and expresses reactions of which his deceased love is unaware.

The poem is based in genuine Christian faith, but comes close to heresy in suggesting that the loss of earthly love might be a cause for dissatisfaction in Heaven. Nevertheless, Rossetti's intention is consonant with his belief: a conviction that romantic love can "move heaven and earth."

Responding to the Poem

Analyzing the Poem

Identifying Details

1. Where is the blessed damozel? How long has she been separated from her lover?
2. To what is time compared in line 50?
3. For what does the damozel pray?

Interpreting Meanings

4. How would you describe the **mood,** or **atmosphere,** of this poem? What details in the first three stanzas help to establish this mood?
5. What is the reason for the lover's doubts expressed in lines 97–102?
6. Describe the structure of the final stanza. What is especially effective about this structure?
7. Victorian critics sometimes complained of the sensualism of "The Blessed Damozel." Do the relationship of the lovers, and the damozel's condition in heaven, support a description of the poem as sensual, in your view?

Writing About the Poem

A Creative Response

1. **Illustrating the Poem.** If you were illustrating this poem, which episodes and details would you choose for your picture? Why? What do your choices reveal about what you think are the important themes and feelings of the poem?

A Critical Response

2. **Analyzing the Poem.** Write a brief essay in which you analyze Rossetti's use of metaphor, archaic diction, and symbolism in "The Blessed Damozel." Cite specific images that you consider especially striking.

Christina Rossetti (1830–1894)

Christina Rossetti was the youngest of the Rossetti children. Her father, an exiled Italian patriot, devoted himself to politics and poetry, especially the works of Dante. In the years when Christina was growing up, the Rossetti home in London was the center of a lively group of Italian exiles, who met to argue about culture and politics. Christina and both of her brothers—Dante Gabriel and William Michael—developed an early interest in poetry and art. Her pleasurable, energetic life changed radically when their father became an invalid, and suddenly the family was short of money. As a teen-ager, Christina's own health worsened, and she became exceedingly religious, giving up such frivolous pursuits as theater and the opera.

A Christina Rossetti's religious convictions were deep. Despite the fact that she deeply loved one of her suitors, she refused two offers of marriage at least in part because she was unsure of her suitors' religious beliefs. She lived at home with her mother, occasionally visiting the houses and studios of London writers and painters, and sometimes modeling for her brother's drawings.

B The color, strong imagery, and clarity of Christina Rossetti's poems may be partly due to the influence of the pre-Raphaelite artists led by her brother, Dante Gabriel Rossetti. In the 1860's and 1870's, she published a volume of poems for children; several volumes of simple lyrics; and "Goblin Market," a strangely disturbing poem about sensual temptation. For the rest of her life, she wrote mostly religious verse and commentary, some of it published by a missionary agency of the Church of England.

Christina Rossetti by Lewis Carroll. Photograph.

Much of her poetry deals with her inner emotional experiences and reflects the narrowness and asceticism of her life. Two dominant themes in her poetry are a longing for death and a frustration at being shut out from joy and fulfillment. But almost all of her poetry can also be read as expressing the feelings of a deeply religious person. She writes often of a yearning for communion with an absolutely satisfying presence, and (as in "A Birthday") of her joy and sense of being reborn when that presence comes near.

A. Expansion
The unfortunate suitor whom she deeply loved was James Collinson, an original member of the Pre-Raphaelite Brotherhood. Christina Rossetti, a devout Anglican, broke off her engagement to him in 1850 when he rejoined the Roman Catholic Church.

B. Further Reading
"Goblin Market" (1862) is a lengthy verse fairy tale that recounts the story of two sisters tempted by goblins. The poem has often been interpreted allegorically and was made into an off-Broadway musical.

C. About the Photograph
Lewis Carroll was a scholarly professor, a writer of fantasy, and a talented amateur photographer.

PREPARATION

1. ESTABLISHING A PURPOSE. Have students look for the figures of speech and lush imagery that make this poem memorable.

2. PREREADING JOURNAL. Before they read, ask students to brainstorm (in writing for perhaps two minutes) with the word *birthday.* Suggest that they think of images and feelings, perhaps wishes they associate with birthdays, especially their own.

SUPPLEMENTARY SUPPORT MATERIALS
1. Vocabulary Activity Worksheet (*CCB*)
2. Review and Response Worksheet: Imagery (*CCB*)
3. Selection Test (*CCB*)

DEVELOPING VOCABULARY
The following word from the poem is tested in the Selection Test. (See also Vocabulary Activity Worksheet.)
dais

ANALYZING THE POEM
Identifying Details
1. Her heart is like a singing bird, an apple tree, and a rainbow seashell.
2. Both lines end with "my love is come to me" and explain why she is happy.

Interpreting Meanings
3. Possible answers: her actual birthday, a new beginning, a religious turning point.
4. Stanza 1: common, everyday images of nature. Stanza 2: exotic images of rare, expensive things.
5. Neither interpretation (love poem or religious lyric) is contradicted by anything in the poem.
 The love is Jesus Christ.
 The birthday might be the beginning of faith or participation in a religious ritual.
6. Both poems are about preparing for a major change; both have a tone of willingness and fervor. The imagery differs.

CLOSURE
Have each student write three adjectives describing the poem's tone.

Read this poem twice: once as a love poem, and the second time as an expression of religious faith.

In either case, what is the significance of the "birth" day?

A Birthday

My heart is like a singing bird
  Whose nest is in a watered shoot:
My heart is like an apple tree
  Whose boughs are bent with thickset fruit;
5 My heart is like a rainbow shell
  That paddles in a halcyon° sea;
My heart is gladder than all these
  Because my love is come to me.

Raise me a <u>dais</u> of silk and down;
10 Hang it with vair° and purple dyes;
Carve it in doves and pomegranates,
  And peacocks with a hundred eyes;
Work it in gold and silver grapes,
  In leaves and silver fleurs-de-lys;°
15 Because the birthday of my life
  Is come, my love is come to me.

6. **halcyon** (hal′sē·ən): tranquil.

10. **vair:** squirrel fur used in medieval times to trim the robes of nobility.

14. **fleurs-de-lys** (flur′də·lē′): an emblem resembling a lily, used on coats of arms.

Responding to the Poem

Analyzing the Poem

Identifying Details
1. What three **similes** describe the speaker's heart in the first stanza?
2. How does the last line of the second stanza echo the last line of the first?

Interpreting Meanings
3. How would you interpret the phrase "birthday of my life"?

4. What is the difference between the kinds of **images** used in the first and second stanzas?
5. How can the lyric be read as both a conventional love poem, and as a religious lyric? When read as a religious lyric, who is the "love" referred to so often? What "birth" is anticipated?
6. How does this poem compare with Donne's "Batter My Heart" (page 373), in **subject, imagery,** and **tone?**

826

Gerard Manley Hopkins (1844–1889)

Hopkins was the eldest son of highly educated parents, who were devoted to the Church of England. His father, Consul-General of the Hawaiian Islands to Great Britain, sent the young Hopkins to Highgate, a London boarding school, where he won a poetry prize and later a scholarship to study classics at Oxford University. Hopkins intended to prepare himself for the Anglican ministry, but after much soul searching, converted to Roman Catholicism in 1866. He graduated from Oxford with high honors and taught for a while in a school of the religious order administered by John Henry Newman.

In 1868, when he entered the Jesuit order, Hopkins burned almost all of his poetry (a few poems remain) and "resolved to write no more, as not belonging to my profession, unless it were by the wish of my superiors." He wrote no poetry for seven years, but in 1875 was asked to write an ode in memory of five Franciscan nuns who had drowned at sea. He sent "The Wreck of the *Deutschland*" to a Jesuit periodical, whose editors "dared not print it."

Hopkins, an unusually conscientious man, was ordained as a Jesuit priest in 1877 and devoted himself to the immediate demands of his priesthood. He served in parishes in poor sections of English and Scottish cities, writing sermons and ministering to the sick. As a teacher of classics at a Jesuit seminary and later as Professor of Greek at the Roman Catholic university in Dublin, Hopkins worked hard at lecturing, grading papers, and planning a series of scholarly papers. In 1889, at the age of forty-four, he died of typhoid fever in Dublin.

Hopkins published one of his poems in 1863, the year he entered college, but only a few insignificant poems appeared during his lifetime. He composed a small but very powerful body of poetry that he sent to friends with careful instructions about how to understand them. In his letters he elaborated on his ideas about using the stock of native English words for the diction of his verse. Hopkins's poems are also characterized by what he called sprung rhythm, and by assonance, alliteration, and internal rhyme. Rob-

ert Bridges, a friend and fellow poet, published the first edition of Hopkins's poems in 1918—almost thirty years after Hopkins's death.

Hopkins attempted in his **sprung rhythm** to imitate the sound of natural speech. He explained: "It consists in scanning by accents alone or stresses alone, so that a foot may be one strong syllable or it may be many light and one strong." In conventional metrics, a foot consists of a prescribed number of stressed and unstressed syllables (an *iamb*, for example, is an unstressed syllable followed by a stressed syllable). Sprung rhythm is not concerned with using only one kind of foot in a poem; in Hopkins's poems, a line may consist of many kinds of feet: iambs, trochees, dactyls, spondees.

For a while literary critics regarded Hopkins as a twentieth-century poet because of his strongly individual language, compression of meaning, unconventional forms, and singular sound. But Hopkins is unmistakably rooted in the nineteenth century. In his almost ecstatic love of nature, his passionate conviction in a transcendental power, and his striving for individuality, Hopkins resembled the Romantic poets. In the "terrible sonnets" of his last four years, Hopkins also expressed the doubts and spiritual anguish of many late nineteenth-century writers.

A. Expansion
The charismatic John Henry Cardinal Newman (1801–1890) played a major role in the social and religious thought of the times. A High Anglican with a distinguished career at Oxford, he shocked many of his contemporaries by converting to the Roman Catholic Church in 1845.

B. Literary Elements
Given the importance of these elements in Hopkins's verse, this may be a good time to review with the class the following terms: assonance, alliteration, and internal rhyme.

C. Sprung Rhythm/Free Verse
You may want to compare Hopkins's concept of sprung rhythm to the technique of free verse (see text pages 1101, 1265). The two techniques are similar in that they both allow for far more rhythmical flexibility than conventional meter permits.

PREPARATION

1. BUILDING ON PRIOR KNOWLEDGE.
Review with students Hopkins's explanation of sprung rhythm (text page 827) and explain that the accent marks in the text indicate where the stress should fall if the words are spoken aloud. Encourage volunteers to prepare oral readings of the poem.

2. ESTABLISHING A PURPOSE. Hopkins's thoughts are so compressed that many students will find this poem difficult to follow. Read the poem aloud and ask students to listen to its sound effects as they try to follow its meaning. Then go over the couplets and ask students to paraphrase each one. (See the writing assignment below.)

SUPPLEMENTARY SUPPORT MATERIALS
1. Vocabulary Activity Worksheet (CCB)
2. Review and Response Worksheet: Sound Effects and Theme (CCB)
3. Selection Test (CCB)

A. Feminine Rhyme
Have students note the predominantly feminine rhyme (an unstressed syllable at the end of the line). Hopkins may have used this falling rhythm to suggest sadness.

B. Paraphrasing
Ask students to paraphrase these difficult lines. (Nobody told you, and you did not even think it; but your heart and soul have intuited it.)

CLOSURE
Ask each student to write one sentence summarizing the poem's theme.

In this short, deceptively simple lyric, an adult speaker comments on a young girl's sadness over the falling autumn leaves. The speaker then relates the girl's sorrow over death in the natural world to her coming awareness of death and pain in the human life cycle. Read the poem slowly and carefully, since it is full of words with multiple meanings.

Spring and Fall

To a Young Child

A
Márgarét, are you grieving
Over Goldengrove unleaving?°
Leáves, líke the things of man, you
With your fresh thoughts care for, can you?
5 Áh! ás the heart grows older
It will come to such sights colder
By and by, nor spare a sigh
Though worlds of wanwood° leafmeal° lie;
And yet you wíll weep and know why.
10 Now no matter, child, the name:
Sórrow's spríngs áre the same.
B
Nor° mouth had, no nor mind, expressed
What heart heard of, ghost° guessed:
It ís the blight man was born for,
15 It is Margaret you mourn for.

2. **Goldengrove unleaving:** a grove of trees whose autumn leaves are falling.

8. **wanwood:** gloomy, pale wood. **leafmeal:** reduced to decaying leaves.

12. **Nor:** neither.
13. **ghost:** soul (of a living person).

Responding to the Poem

Analyzing the Poem

Identifying Details

1. What is Margaret grieving for at the opening?
2. What does the speaker predict about Margaret's feelings when her "heart grows older"?
3. Whom does the speaker say she is really grieving for?
4. Identify at least four examples of **alliteration** and **assonance** in the poem.

Interpreting Meanings

5. Discuss the multiple meanings of *spring, fall,* and *leaves* in the poem.
6. What does the speaker mean by saying "sorrow's springs are the same" (line 11)?

7. What is the "blight man was born for" in line 14?
8. Explain how the speaker's attitude toward Margaret and her grief shifts in the course of the poem. How would you interpret the poem's last line?

Writing About the Poem

A Critical Response

Writing a Paraphrase. Try to rewrite Hopkins's poem in a prose paraphrase, using normal syntax. Be sure to include every major idea of the poem in your paraphrase, and restate the figures of speech in literal language.

ANALYZING THE POEM
Identifying Details
1. She is grieving for the autumn leaves fallen from the trees.
2. That she will grow "colder" and not care about fallen leaves.
3. Herself.
4. Examples can be found in almost every line.

Interpreting Meanings
5. *Spring* and *fall* refer to the seasons. *Springs* (line 11) is the source of water, or sorrow. The *fall* of man is suggested in line 14. *Leaves* are the leaves of trees and the verb *leaves* ("goes away").
6. All sorrows have the same source (probably original sin).
7. The line refers to the biblical fall: All human beings are destined to struggle, to experience sorrow, and to die.
8. Lines 1–8 suggest Margaret will outgrow her sensitivity because her heart will grow colder. In lines 10–12 the speaker realizes that Margaret's sadness is an intuited grief for her future losses.
Margaret is grieving for the loss of her innocence and youth, for her own death and the death of loved ones.

A. Humanities Connection: Discussing the Fine Art
Most Victorian Realists confined themselves to painting the world they saw around them, but John Everett Millais (1829–1896) also used the Realist technique to paint religious, historical, and literary subjects. Millais's most famous painting, *Ophelia* (1852), depicts the drowning of Ophelia in *Hamlet*.
? What connections can you draw between Millais's scene of autumn leaves and Hopkins's lyric on "Goldengrove unleaving"? (Both create a mood of sadness, contemplation of lost time, knowledge that all must die.)

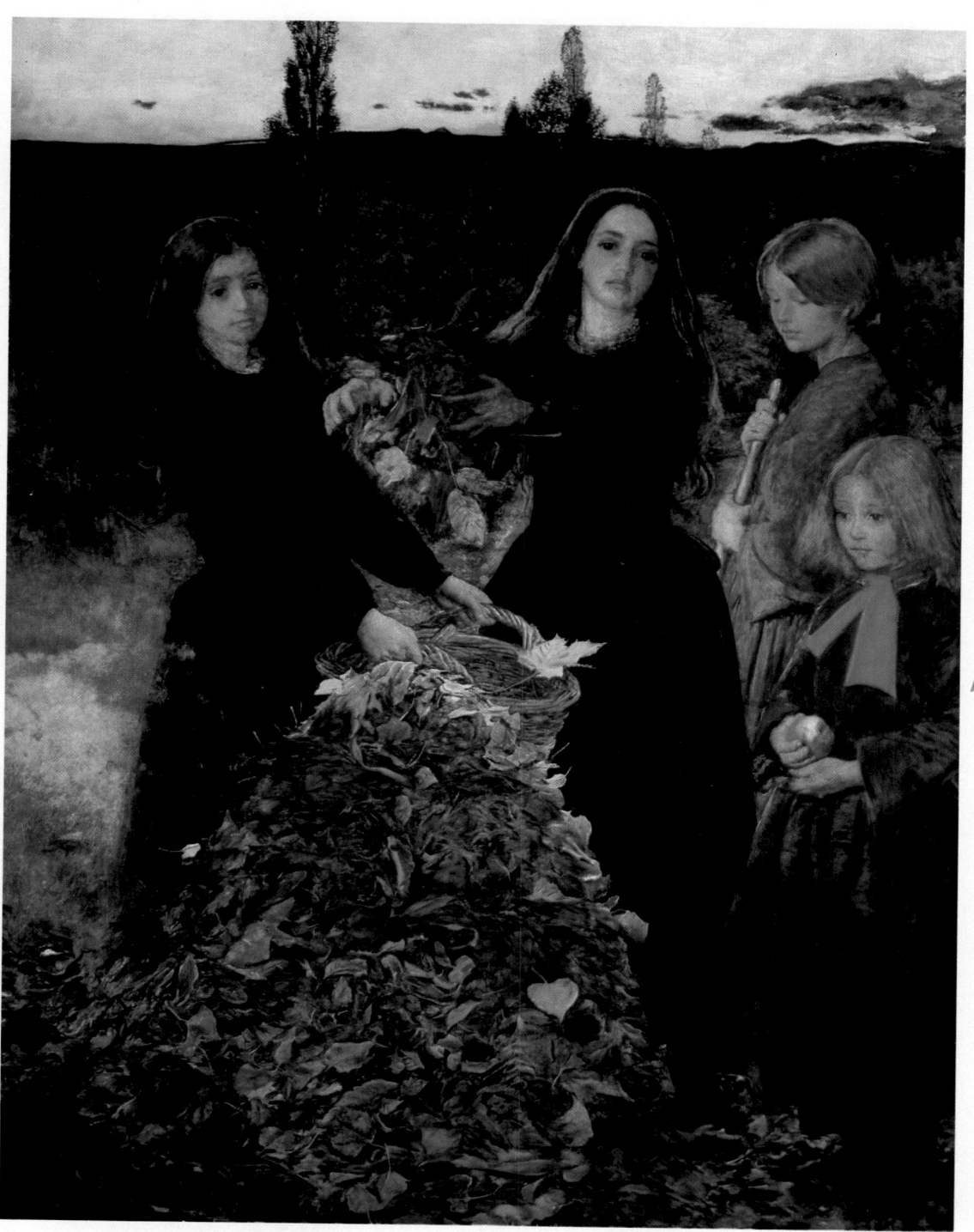

Autumn Leaves by J. E. Millais (1856). Oil.

City Art Gallery, Manchester, England.

PREPARATION

1. Building On Prior Knowledge.
Recall that Hopkins was a Roman Catholic priest who served in a number of humble, industrial parishes (including the slums of Liverpool).

2. Establishing A Purpose. Ask students to read the poem to see what it says about the meaning of suffering.

SUPPLEMENTARY SUPPORT MATERIALS
1. Vocabulary Activity Worksheet (*CCB*)
2. Review and Response Worksheet: Elements of Style and Tone (*CCB*)
3. Selection Test (*CCB*)
4. Audiocassette recording

DEVELOPING VOCABULARY
The following words from the poem are tested in the Selection Test. (See also Vocabulary Activity Worksheet.)
to pine   reprieve

A. Sound Effects
Ask students to point out examples of alliteration, rhyme, assonance, and repetition in this first quatrain.

B. Expansion
Hopkins is referring to Extreme Unction, or the last rites. This Roman Catholic sacrament consists of the anointing of various parts of the body and prayers for the salvation of the ill person's soul.

C. Dialect
"All road ever" is Lancashire dialect from northwestern England, where Liverpool is.

D. Theme
[?] What does the speaker learn from Felix Randal's suffering? (The interconnectedness of all human beings; the needs we have and comfort we can give)

Closure
Explain in a sentence or two your response to this poem: is it a sad, depressing poem, or an affirmation of life?

The subject of this poem is a blacksmith who has died. Hopkins, a priest, remembers Felix Randal's illness and the sacraments he administered to the gravely sick man. A farrier is a blacksmith.

Felix Randal

A
Felix Randal the farrier, O he is dead then? my duty all ended,
Who have watched his mould of man, big-boned and hardy-handsome
<u>Pining</u>, pining, till time when reason rambled in it and some
Fatal four disorders, fleshed there, all contended?

5 B
Sickness broke him. Impatient he cursed at first, but mended
Being anointed° and all; though a heavenlier heart began some
Months earlier, since I had our sweet <u>reprieve</u> and ransom°
C
Tendered to him. Ah well, God rest him all road ever° he offended!

10 D
This seeing the sick endears them to us, us too it endears.
My tongue had taught thee comfort, touch had quenched thy tears,
Thy tears that touched my heart, child, Felix, poor Felix Randal;

How far from then forethought of, all thy more boisterous years,
When thou at the random° grim forge, powerful amidst peers,
Didst fettle° for the great gray drayhorse his bright and battering sandal!

---

6. **anointed:** given the sacrament in which a priest prays for and anoints with oil a dying or gravely ill person.
7. **sweet reprieve and ransom:** Holy Communion preceded by confession and absolution.
8. **all road ever:** (dialect) in whatever way.
13. **random:** built with stones of irregular size and shape.
14. **fettle:** make ready; prepare.

A Comment on the Poem

In the form of a loose-jointed **sonnet**, Hopkins produces an elegy in which the relationship between priest and parishioner at a critical time is reviewed. Helpless to arrest the physical decline of the man, the priest can only watch the progress of the "fatal four disorders" which caused his death and offer the spiritual comfort of Communion, "our sweet reprieve and ransom." When Felix Randal dies, the image he leaves behind is not that of an invalid, but of a "big-boned and hardy-handsome" man of heroic proportions who might be working in the blazing light of Vulcan's forge. This outsized portrait is achieved by a sudden shift from the tripping, almost dainty, consonants of the third stanza to the broad, open, organ-roll vowels of the final stanza. The music of **onomatopoeia** not only supports the sentiments expressed, but also lends power to the action that closes the poem.

ANALYZING THE POEM
Identifying Details
1. He comforted him, gave him Holy Communion and absolution.

   He was impatient and cursed (line 5). Later he had a "heavenlier heart" (lines 6–7). He wept (line 11), but he was "mended" by being anointed (line 6).
2. ". . . God rest him all road ever he offended!" (line 8).

3. Healthy at work in his forge.

Interpreting Meanings
4. Section 1: news of Randal's death and the speaker's thoughts about him during his last days. Section 2: course of Randal's illness. Section 3: thoughts about comforting the sick, comforting Felix. Section 4: Felix healthy at the forge.

   The turn of the poem is from the dying man back to when he was healthy with no thought of death.
5. Some may say that Felix is a child of God; others that, like a child, he weeps in fear and needs comforting.

   It helps us to identify with Felix Randal since we are all God's children.
6. They are grateful for our visits.
7. Student responses will vary. It is a powerful, triumphant image that emphasizes life, not death.

A. Humanities Connection: Discussing the Fine Art
British painter Joseph Mallord William Turner (1775–1851), perhaps the greatest of the nineteenth-century landscape artists, was original in his use of light and color. (See text page 699 for another Turner painting and biographical information.) Have students note the golden glow that bathes this painting. Color is limited to a range of gold, brown, and black; greens and blues are eliminated completely.

❓ This painting of the blacksmith is like a snapshot of him in context. What details de-emphasize the blacksmith? (The women turn away from him; his face is not seen; the figure of the white horse seems to dominate the painting.)

A Country Blacksmith (detail) by J. M. W. Turner. Oil.

The Tate Gallery, London.

Responding to the Poem

Analyzing the Poem

Identifying Details

1. How does the speaker say that he took care of Felix Randal? What were the stages of Randal's reaction to his illness?
2. What prayer does the speaker offer for Felix Randal?
3. How is Felix Randal described in lines 12–14?

Interpreting Meanings

4. Hopkins here uses a conventional, fourteen-line **sonnet** form. What is the topic of each of the four sections of the poem? What is the "turn" of the poem, the difference between the subject of the first eight lines and the subject of the last six lines?
5. Why does Hopkins refer to the farrier as "child" in line 11? What is the effect of this reference?
6. It is clear enough how "seeing the sick endears them to us" (line 9). What does Hopkins mean by saying that "us too it endears"?
7. Why do you think Hopkins decided to end the sonnet with images of Felix Randal whole and healthy at his forge? What is the effect of this ending?

PREPARATION

1. BUILDING ON PRIOR KNOWLEDGE.
Discuss Hopkins's use of sound effects and unusual words in the preceding two poems.

2. ESTABLISHING A PURPOSE. Have students read question 9 before they read the poem.

SUPPLEMENTARY SUPPORT MATERIALS

1. Vocabulary Activity Worksheet (*CCB*)
2. Review and Response Worksheet: Imagery and Theme (*CCB*)
3. Selection Test (*CCB*)
4. Instructional Overhead Transparency

DEVELOPING VOCABULARY

The following word from the poem is tested in the Selection Test. (See also Vocabulary Activity Worksheet.)
dappled

ANALYZING THE POEM
Identifying Details
1. A brinded cow, rose-colored spots on trout, roasted chestnuts, etc.
2. As the creator whose beauty is unchanging.
3. Because God is the creator of all beauty, and because God's beauty is unchanging.

Interpreting Meanings
4. The adjectives *dappled, couple-color, brinded, stipple, plotted,* and *pieced* reinforce the title and theme of God's creativity.
5. All things strange, unlike the norm.
6. The beauty of the physical world is transitory; God's beauty is eternal.
7. The line has three pairs of words with opposite meanings. Two pairs repeat *s* and *sw* sounds; one pair repeats the *d* sound.
8. Its abruptness creates emphasis.
9. All praise God's creations.

CLOSURE
Have students explain how they feel Hopkins would define *beauty*.

This is Hopkins's song of praise to God for the beauty of all things that are *pied*, or covered with spots of two or more colors. The first line states the poem's theme, which is then followed by many specific examples. Images follow one another with the kind of instantaneousness and clarity achieved by the movie camera.

Pied Beauty

Glory be to God for dappled things—
  For skies of couple-color as a brinded° cow;
    For rose-moles all in stipple° upon trout that swim;
Fresh-firecoal chestnut-falls;° finches' wings;
5   Landscape plotted and pieced°—fold, fallow, and plow;
    And áll trádes, their gear and tackle and trim.

All things counter, original, spare, strange,
  Whatever is fickle, freckled (who knows how?)
    With swift, slow; sweet, sour; adazzle, dim;
10 He fathers-forth° whose beauty is past change:
    Praise him.

2. **brinded:** streaked with a darker color.
3. **stipple:** random dots or spots.
4. **Fresh-firecoal chestnut-falls:** freshly fallen chestnuts roasted in a fire.
5. **pieced:** parceled into fields.

10. **fathers-forth:** creates.

Responding to the Poem

Analyzing the Poem

Identifying Details
1. What specific examples of pied beauty does the poet mention in lines 2–6?
2. How does the poet describe God in line 10?
3. Why does the poet offer glory and praise to God?

Interpreting Meanings
4. What phrases and **images** do you think serve to reinforce the poem's title and its **theme**? Give at least four specific examples to support your answer.
5. What do you think the poet means by "all things counter" (line 7)?
6. In line 10, what contrast does the poet suggest between the "pied beauty" of the physical world and the beauty of God the creator?
7. Explain how the poet combines **alliteration** with **antithesis** (opposites) in line 9.
8. How does the **rhythm** of the last line make it especially effective?
9. How is this poem like the psalms from the King James Bible (Unit Three)—which are "praise songs"?

Writing About the Poem

A Creative Response
1. **Extending the Poem.** In the first stanza, Hopkins names a number of "dappled things" whose beauty he celebrates. Make your own list of beautiful things that are "dappled," in the sense of the word that Hopkins intends.

A Critical Response
2. **Analyzing Diction.** Hopkins's poem contains a number of unusual words, such as *pied, dappled, brinded, stipple, fallow, trim, adazzle.* The poet also coins some compound words: *couple-color, fresh-firecoal, chestnut-falls, fathers-forth.* Research the usage and denotations of these terms and make a list of definitions for each word or phrase.

Thomas Hardy (1840–1928)

Thomas Hardy was one of the principal novelists of late-Victorian Britain, but he began and ended his literary career as a poet. The oldest of four children, Hardy was born in a small village in Dorsetshire in the southwest of England, the setting (under its ancient name of Wessex) of many of his novels and poems. His father was a stonemason and building contractor who loved music and taught Hardy to play the violin. Hardy went to the village school until he was sixteen, when he became an apprentice to an architect. He read widely on his own for the next six years, "reading the *Iliad,* the *Aeneid,* or the Greek Testament from six to eight in the morning, would work at Gothic architecture all day, and then in the evening rush off with his fiddle under his arm . . . to play at country dances. . . ." In 1861 Hardy began working as an architect in London, writing poems and stories in his free time. He tried unsuccessfully to publish his poems, but by the time he returned to Dorset in 1867 as an architect specializing in church restoration, he had started to publish fiction.

A Hardy's second novel, *Far from the Madding Crowd* (1874), was enough of a popular success to enable him to stop working as an architect. In the next twenty years he published ten novels and three collections of stories. The plots and themes of Hardy's fiction, like those of his poetry, express his belief in a world governed by chance and natural laws that are not hostile, but simply indifferent, to what humans want and deserve. Chance gives us pain when we try for gladness or glory; sometimes in his novels the entire course of lives is determined by coincidence. Hardy liked to play the big scenes of his novels against the backdrop of powerful natural forces that take no account of human life, such as the vast heath of *The Return of the Native* (1878). To chance and the indifference of nature, humans add the folly of war, the cruelty of ingratitude and neglect, and the irrationality of laws and customs that frustrate talent and desire. Finally, the central characters' own weaknesses—Henchard in *The Mayor of Casterbridge* (1886), Jude in *Jude the Obscure* (1896), even

Tess in *Tess of the D'Urbervilles* (1891)—make them vulnerable to the destructive powers of nature and society.

The bleakness, pessimism, and irony of Hardy's novels disturbed many of his readers. In 1892, after reading an unfavorable review of *Tess of the D'Urbervilles,* he wrote, "Well, if this sort of thing continues no more novel-writing for me. A man must be a fool to deliberately stand up to be shot at." In 1895 when *Jude the Obscure* was severely denounced by readers and critics (some called it "Jude the Obscene"), Hardy decided to have his say thereafter in poetry: "Perhaps I can express more fully in verse ideas and emotions which run counter to the inert crystallized opinion—hard as a rock—which the vast body of men have vested interests in supporting."

He began collecting old, new, and revised poems in a series of volumes. He published the first in 1898 and was putting together an eighth collection thirty years later, the year of his death. "My poetry was revolutionary," he wrote, "in the sense that I meant to avoid the jeweled line. . . ." Twentieth-century critics have praised Hardy's poems for their simple, compressed forms and their sad, ironic tone.

A. Allusion
The title comes from line 73 of Thomas Gray's "Elegy Written in a Country Churchyard" (see text page 567).

B. Hardy's Novels
Another important theme of Hardy's mature novels was a bittersweet nostalgia for the passing of an older, more rural way of life.

C. Expansion
One Bishop of the Church of England is said to have thrown his copy into the fire in disgust. Probably the most shocking aspect of *Jude the Obscure* for Hardy's readers was his pessimistic treatment of marriage as a social institution. In this regard, the novelist was almost certainly drawing on personal experience, since his thirty-year marriage to Emma Gifford had soured. In 1912, when Emma died, Hardy married Florence Dugdale, who became his biographer.

1. BUILDING ON PRIOR KNOWLEDGE. Have students discuss the word *darkling* in the title (see question 4). You might want to refer them to the uses of this word in Keats's "Ode to a Nightingale" (line 51, text page 717) and Arnold's "Dover Beach" (line 35, text page 813).

2. ESTABLISHING A PURPOSE. Ask stu-dents to focus on mood and tone as they read the poem.

SUPPLEMENTARY SUPPORT MATERIALS
1. Vocabulary Activity Worksheet (*CCB*)
2. Review and Response Worksheet: Setting and Tone (*CCB*)
3. Selection Test (*CCB*)
4. Audiocassette recording

DEVELOPING VOCABULARY
The following words from the poem are tested in the Selection Test. (See also Vocabulary Activity Worksheet.)
gaunt   terrestrial

ANALYZING THE POEM
Identifying Details
1. "Coppice gate," "Frost," "Winter's dregs," "weakening eye of day."
2. In the third stanza.
   He hears his joyful song.
3. It suggests the thrush knows of "some blessed Hope."

Interpreting Meanings
4. *Darkling* means "in the dark" and suggests gloom as well as darkness.
   Answers will vary.
5. Answers will vary. Most will feel the thrush's song gives him hope; others may feel his hopeless mood remains.

CLOSURE
Have students describe in one sentence the theme of "The Darkling Thrush."

Hardy wrote this poem on the last day of the nineteenth century ("the Century's corpse" in line 10). His thrush, like the century, is worn out and diminished—but still singing.

The Darkling Thrush

I leant upon a coppice° gate
　　When Frost was specter-gray,
And Winter's dregs made desolate
　　The weakening eye of day.
5　The tangled bine-stems° scored the sky
　　Like strings of broken lyres,
And all mankind that haunted nigh
　　Had sought their household fires.

The land's sharp features seemed to be
10　The Century's corpse outleant,
His crypt the cloudy canopy,
　　The wind his death-lament.
The ancient pulse of germ° and birth
　　Was shrunken hard and dry,
15　And every spirit upon earth
　　Seemed fervorless as I.

At once a voice arose among
　　The bleak twigs overhead
In a fullhearted evensong
20　　Of joy illimited;
An aged thrush, frail, gaunt, and small,
　　In blast-beruffled plume,
Had chosen thus to fling his soul
　　Upon the growing gloom.

25　So little cause for carolings
　　Of such ecstatic sound
Was written on terrestrial things
　　Afar or nigh around,
That I could think there trembled through
30　　His happy good-night air
Some blessed Hope, whereof he knew
　　And I was unaware.

---

1. **coppice:** thicket of small trees or shrubs.
5. **bine-stems:** stems of plants that have twined around the trees.
13. **germ:** seed or bud.

Responding to the Poem

Analyzing the Poem

Identifying Details
1. What details in the first stanza establish the **setting** for the poem?
2. Where in the poem is the thrush introduced? How does the bird first come to the attention of the speaker?
3. What does the speaker say about the "air" of the thrush in the last stanza?

Interpreting Meanings
4. What is the significance of the word *darkling* in the poem's title? Do you think the thrush's song seems hopeful or hopeless? Explain.
5. Does the speaker's mood change significantly in the course of the poem? If so, how?

Writing About the Poem

A Creative Response
1. **Writing a Prediction.** Imagine that you are in a creative mood on the final evening of the twentieth century. Write a short essay or poem summing up your view of the past and your hopes or fears for the future.

A Critical Response
2. **Comparing and Contrasting Two Poems.** In a brief essay, compare "The Darkling Thrush" to any of the poems in this anthology in which poets use the conventional Romantic images of bird and song (for example, Keats's "Ode to a Nightingale" or Shelley's "To a Skylark"). Which elements of Hardy's poem are most important when you consider how it is like or different from the poem you are comparing it to?

PREPARATION

1. Building On Prior Knowledge. Before students begin reading, remind them that Hardy's poetry often derives its power from the use of an unusual or unexpected point of view.

2. Establishing A Purpose. Ask the students to read the poem to determine what point Hardy is making about war.

Supplementary Support Materials

1. Review and Response Worksheet: Irony (*CCB*)
2. Selection Test (*CCB*)

Closure

Have students summarize the poem's theme—Hardy's attitude toward war.

The subject of this poem is the testing of guns at sea and on the shores of the English Channel.

Hardy wrote the poem in April of 1914, four months before World War I began.

Channel Firing

That night your great guns, unawares,
Shook all our coffins as we lay,
And broke the chancel° window-squares,
We thought it was the Judgment Day

5   And sat upright. While drearisome
Arose the howl of wakened hounds:
The mouse let fall the altar-crumb,
The worms drew back into the mounds,

The glebe° cow drooled. Till God called,
    "No;
10 It's gunnery practice out at sea
Just as before you went below;
The world is as it used to be:

"All nations striving strong to make
Red war yet redder. Mad as hatters
15 They do no more for Christés sake
Than you who are helpless in such matters.

"That this is not the judgment hour
For some of them's a blessed thing,
For if it were they'd have to scour
20 Hell's floor for so much threatening. . . .

"Ha, ha. It will be warmer when
I blow the trumpet (if indeed
I ever do; for you are men,
And rest eternal sorely need)."

25 So down we lay again. "I wonder.
Will the world ever saner be,"
Said one, "than when He sent us under
In our indifferent century!"

And many a skeleton shook his head.
30 "Instead of preaching forty year,"
My neighbor Parson Thirdly said,
"I wish I had stuck to pipes and beer."

Again the guns disturbed the hour.
Roaring their readiness to avenge,
35 As far inland as Stourton Tower,
And Camelot, and starlit Stonehenge.

---

3. **chancel:** part of a church around the altar.
9. **glebe:** land attached to a church or its rectory. Apparently, the clergyman keeps a cow on the glebe of this church.

Responding to the Poem

Analyzing the Poem

Identifying Details

1. Who is the speaker? Who are the *we* in line 4?
2. In the first stanza, why are the people afraid?
3. What does God say about the Judgment Day in the fifth stanza?

Interpreting Meanings

4. What do you make of God's irritation at those who fire the guns?
5. Point out at least three examples of **irony** in the poem.
6. What do you think this poem says about war?

Writing About the Poem

A Creative Response

1. **Writing an Editorial.** Hardy's poem indirectly makes a point about war through the use of fantasy, dialogue, and irony. Write a persuasive editorial about war.

A Critical Response

2. **Analyzing Point of View.** In a short essay, analyze the poet's use of point of view in "Channel Firing." Given what you think the poem says about war, what does Hardy gain for his argument by telling the poem from the point of view of the dead?

Analyzing The Poem
Identifying Details
1. The speaker is one of the dead (*we* in line 4) buried in a church near the English Channel.
2. They hear the noises of the guns and think it's Judgment Day.
3. It is a good thing it's not Judgment Day for some of the living, who would be doomed to scour the floors of Hell.

Interpreting Meanings
4. It is a pointless activity that accomplishes no more than the actions of a dead man.
5. The guns disturb the dead but not the living; the Parson wishes he had stuck to pipes and beer; the guns avenge a time that is long gone.
6. War is foolish, mad, unjustifiable, and an eternal human activity.

1. BUILDING ON PRIOR KNOWLEDGE. Elicit what students know about the sinking of the *Titanic* in 1912. Some students may be familiar with the ship's recent rediscovery on the ocean floor.

2. ESTABLISHING A PURPOSE. Before they read Hardy's poem, ask students to read John Malcolm Brinnin's prose account of the sinking of the *Titanic* (text page 838). Have them read the poem to compare the two accounts of the sinking.

SUPPLEMENTARY SUPPORT MATERIALS
1. Vocabulary Activity Worksheet (*CCB*)
2. Review and Response Worksheet: Imagery and Theme (*CCB*)
3. Selection Test (*CCB*)

DEVELOPING VOCABULARY
The following words from the poem are tested in the Selection Test. (See also Vocabulary Activity Worksheet.)
opulent   august

A. Diction
Note the unusual uses of *deep, stilly,* and *couches.*

B. Metaphor
🔋 Explain the difficult metaphors and imagery in these lines. (Ocean water threads its way through the ship's boilers, which are compared to lyres.)

C. Stanza Form
Hardy uses an irregular tercet stanza throughout. (Compare Tennyson's "The Eagle," text page 790.)

D. Alliteration
Ask students to find examples of alliteration throughout the poem.

Hardy wrote this poem shortly after the *Titanic* struck an iceberg and sank on April 15, 1912, during its maiden voyage from Southampton, England, to New York City. The *Titanic*, the largest and most luxurious ocean liner ever built, had been designed to be unsinkable. More than 1500 people died in the disaster. Of all the poems, songs, and eulogies inspired by the *Titanic* disaster, Hardy's is the one that most profoundly reflects the awe and disbelief that event engendered across the breadth of "two hemispheres."

The Convergence of the Twain

Lines on the Loss of the Titanic

1

A

    In a solitude of the sea
    Deep from human vanity,
And the Pride of Life that planned her, stilly couches she.

2

B

5
    Steel chambers, late the pyres
    Of her salamandrine fires,°
Cold currents thrid,° and turn to rhythmic tidal lyres.

3

C

    Over the mirrors meant
    To glass the opulent
The seaworm crawls—grotesque, slimed, dumb, indifferent.

4

10
    Jewels in joy designed
    To ravish the sensuous mind

D

Lie lightless, all their sparkles bleared and black and blind.

5

    Dim moon-eyed fishes near
    Gaze at the gilded gear
15 And query: "What does this vaingloriousness down here?" . . .

6

    Well: while was fashioning
    This creature of cleaving wing,
The Immanent Will° that stirs and urges everything

---

5. **salamandrine fires:** fires so hot that only a salamander, a lizard said to be able to live in fire, could survive.
6. **thrid:** thread through.
18. **Immanent Will:** Hardy's name for the power that created and determines life and history.

1. Hardy mentions that the ship "stilly couches" deep in the sea. He mentions steel chambers, mirrors, and sunken jewels.
2. "What does this vaingloriousness down here?"

He answers the question in all of the rest of the poem. He says that The Im-manent Will fashioned an iceberg at the same time that the ship was being built and determined the two should collide.

Interpreting Meanings
3. The first half describes the sunken ship and ends with the question in line 15. The second half answers that question.
4. It was no accident but fate.

5. The Spinner of the Years (also called The Immanent Will) is an illusion to the Fates in Greek mythology, who controlled human destiny and life.
6. The twain are the *Titanic* and the ice-berg. The convergence is their collision.
7. Student responses will vary, de-pending on their notions of free will, chance, and fate. (Hardy says they were created for "consummation.")

A. Imagery
You may wish to note that Hardy uses sexual im-ages (*mate, intimate, twin halves, consummation*) to describe the collision.

B. Diction
Why is Hardy's choice of the word *august* sur-prising here? (The word usually sug-gests religious reverence.)

C. Multiple Meanings
Hemispheres reso-nates with two meanings here: geographical halves of the world; "twin halves" of one event (line 30).

CLOSURE
Ask students to discuss their ideas about fate. Have them consider whether events are fated, whether they occur by chance, or whether we con-trol events.

7

A

20   Prepared a sinister mate
For her—so gaily great—
A Shape of Ice, for the time far and dissociate.

8

And as the smart ship grew
In stature, grace, and hue,
In shadowy silent distance grew the Iceberg too.

9

25   Alien they seemed to be:
No mortal eye could see
The intimate welding of their later history,

10

Or sign that they were bent
By paths coincident

B

30   On being anon twin halves of one august event,

11

Till the Spinner of the Years
Said "Now!" And each one hears,

C   And consummation comes, and jars two hemispheres.

Responding to the Poem

Analyzing the Poem

Identifying Details

1. What physical details does Hardy use in his descrip-tion of the *Titanic* in the first four stanzas?
2. What question does the poet ask in line 15? Where and how does he answer this question?

Interpreting Meanings

3. How does Hardy divide the poem into two halves? How does this structure reinforce the poem's mean-ing?
4. According to Hardy's poem, was the sinking of the *Titanic* an accident? Explain.
5. Who is the "Spinner of the Years" (line 31)?
6. How would you explain the poem's **title**?
7. What is your response to Hardy's **main idea**?

Writing About the Poem

A Creative Response

1. **Writing a Commentary.** Consider some recent disas-trous event like the sinking of the *Titanic*. What les-sons do you think can be drawn from this recent event? Are these the same (or similar) lessons that Hardy draws in his poem?

A Critical Response

2. **Writing an Essay.** According to the commentary on the next page, the disaster of the *Titanic* had a great public effect because it challenged assumptions about the power of technology and the invulnerability of wealth and privilege. Are these the lessons that Hardy draws from the disaster? In a brief essay, dis-cuss the point of view in each of the two texts.

A

"For ten lethal seconds on the night of April 14, 1912, the starboard hull of the greatest ship of the high seas came into contact with the submerged shelf of a drifting island of ice. Smudged with a bit of paint from the shipyards of Belfast, the iceberg then slid back into the dark and floated away on the Labrador Current. Her engines stopped, her signals silent as she continued to travel on the momentum of 46,000 tons, the ship began to fill, to lurch into a list that would never be righted. Through a gash three hundred feet long, torrents of sea water were already pouring in. 'All of a sudden the starboard side came in upon us,' said one of the stokers. 'It burst like a big gun going off; the water came pouring in and swilled our legs.'

"The encounter was as brief as a glancing blow; the meeting of ice and steel a matter of dreadful efficiency. Three hours later the 882-foot-long *Titanic* stood almost vertical, a weird black and white column in the middle of the ocean. Then she dived down, head first. Trapped in the dark companionways and wooden dormitories of the third-class quarters, hundreds of emigrants were first overwhelmed, then entombed. On the upright afterdecks, passengers clinging to stanchions and ventilators were washed from the ship like insects from the trunk of a tree. The water temperature was 28 degrees Fahrenheit.

B

"Adrift in lifeboats, some seven hundred other people heard the tumbling crash of boilers and engines dragging the ship under, then a vast silence like a sudden intake of breath, then 'one long continuous wailing chant' as their shipmates succumbed to the cold or drowned among pieces of wreckage. To one man in a lifeboat, the sound they made was like that of 'locusts on a mid-summer's night.' To another, theirs was 'a cry that called to heaven for the very injustice of its own existence; a cry that clamored for its own destruction.' An accident at sea was already on its way to becoming a metaphor: the arm of a wrathful God lifted against the vanity of earthly riches and the presumptions of science.

C

"In simple fact, the loss of the *Titanic* was a maritime disaster without equal. But in the broad resonance of its notoriety, the sinking of the *Titanic* became an event in the psychological make-up of a generation. 'The pleasure and comfort which all of us enjoyed upon this floating palace,' said one passenger, 'seemed an ominous feature to many of us, including myself, who felt it almost too good to last without some terrible retribution inflicted by the hand of an angry omnipotence.' In the space of three appalling hours, vague guilts and elusive anxieties that had dogged one hundred years of material progress came into focus.

D

"The unsinkable ship, the most superb technological achievement of her time, the dreamed-of sign and symbol that man's mechanical skill would carry him into a luminous new world of power, freedom, and affluence, had become, in the words of one contemporary dirge, 'the most imposing mausoleum that ever housed the bones of men since the Pyramids rose from the sand.' Nothing had gone wrong. Everything had gone wrong. The odds on a ship such as the *Titanic* hitting an iceberg and foundering under the blow were calculated at a million to one. With devastating and absolute precision the *Titanic* and her officers had in the space of four days surmounted these odds. Designed to survive anything that man or nature could bring to bear against her, the great ship could not survive even the first voyage of the twenty-five or thirty long years of seagoing for which she was built.

"Courts of inquiry on both sides of the Atlantic would sift every detail, rehearse every movement, accuse, exonerate, and recommend. Yet all of their columns of facts would be swamped by an overwhelming sense of incredulity, all their tediously rational explanations would be surrendered with a primitive bow toward the irrational. To the man in the street, not one of the answers to the more than twenty-five thousand questions asked in court about the loss of the *Titanic* would do. The only explanation was Fate, a bolt from the sky that conclusively demolished two of his most important articles of faith: an awed belief in the sovereignty of science, a generous conviction that the rights and privileges of wealth were both real and deserved. When scores of the richest and most influential men on earth, men 'to whom life itself seemed subservient and obedient,' could freeze to death clinging to pieces of wreckage in the middle of the ocean, something in the order of things was amiss. The unfolding marvels of science and the Olympian preserves of privilege were suddenly made human, vulnerable, and hardly worth his affection or his fealty."

—from *The Sway of the Grand Saloon: A Social History of the North Atlantic,* John Malcolm Brinnin

---

A. Expansion
The *Titanic* was traveling at approximately twenty-five miles per hour when it struck the iceberg.

B. Expansion
The *Titanic* had only 1,178 lifeboat spaces for the 2,224 persons aboard.

C. Expansion
As a result of the disaster, the first International Convention for Safety of Life at Sea was convened in 1913. It established regulations on lifeboat drills, adequate lifeboat spaces, and 24-hour radio watch.

D. Expansion
It had a double-bottomed hull divided into sixteen watertight compartments. Four of these could be flooded without jeopardizing the ship's buoyancy.

PREPARATION

1. BUILDING ON PRIOR KNOWLEDGE.
Review with students the definitions and examples of the three different types of irony (see text page 1265).

2. ESTABLISHING A PURPOSE. Tell students that this poem is a dialogue, and ask them to identify the two speakers and the type of irony (situational irony).

SUPPLEMENTARY SUPPORT MATERIALS
1. Review and Response Worksheet: Tone (*CCB*)
2. Language Skills Worksheet: Pronouns (*CCB*)
3. Selection Test (*CCB*)

CLOSURE
Have students explain the poem's irony in a single sentence. (What is the speaker's expectation? What is the reality?)

The power of Hardy's poetry often depends on irony and on an abrupt shift of point of view. In the following lyric, the poet challenges our conventional beliefs, not only about the dead, but also about our own expectations of what people may say about us after we die.

Ah, Are You Digging on My Grave?

"Ah, are you digging on my grave,
  My loved one?—planting rue?"°
—"No: yesterday he went to wed
One of the brightest wealth has bred.
5 'It cannot hurt her now,' he said,
  'That I should not be true.' "

"Then who is digging on my grave?
  My nearest dearest kin?"
—"Ah, no: they sit and think, 'What use!
10 What good will planting flowers produce?
No tendance of her mound can loose
  Her spirit from Death's gin.' "°

"But someone digs upon my grave?
  My enemy?—prodding sly?"
15 —"Nay: when she heard you had passed
    the Gate
That shuts on all flesh soon or late,
She thought you no more worth her hate,
  And cares not where you lie."

"Then, who is digging on my grave?
20 Say—since I have not guessed!"
—"O it is, my mistress dear,
Your little dog, who still lives near,
And much I hope my movements here
  Have not disturbed your rest?"

25 "Ah yes! *You* dig upon my grave . . .
  Why flashed it not on me
That one true heart was left behind!
What feeling do we ever find
To equal among human kind
30 A dog's fidelity!"

"Mistress, I dug upon your grave
  To bury a bone, in case
I should be hungry near this spot
When passing on my daily trot.
35 I am sorry, but I quite forgot
  It was your resting place."

2. **rue:** a yellow-flowered herb associated with grief.
12. **gin:** trap.

ANALYZING THE POEM
Identifying Details
1. Her husband (or lover), a beloved relative, her sly enemy.
2. To bury a bone.

Interpreting Meanings
3. For each guess the dead woman hopefully makes, the persons are far from devoting themselves to grief.
4. Students should agree that the tone is wry, ironic, perhaps even bitter.
  Lines 2–6 (Rue is a bitter-tasting herb); lines 7–10; lines 25–30.

Responding to the Poem

Analyzing the Poem

Identifying Details

1. The dead woman who speaks one part of the dialogue in this poem tries three guesses about the identity of the person digging on her grave. Whom does she guess?
2. In the last stanza, what reason does the dog give for digging on the grave?

Interpreting Meanings

3. **Anticlimax,** or *bathos,* is the deflating effect we feel when our lofty expectations are let down. Comment on how Hardy employs the device of *bathos* in each of the first three stanzas.
4. How would you characterize the **tone** of this poem?

Which two or three passages do you think are most important in establishing this tone?

Writing About the Poem

A Creative Response

1. **Writing a Character Sketch.** Write a short character sketch of the woman who is the speaker in "Ah, Are You Digging on My Grave?"

A Critical Response

2. **Analyzing Irony.** In **irony of situation,** there is a sharp discrepancy between the expected result of a statement or action and its actual result. In a brief essay, analyze Hardy's use of situational irony in this poem.

A. Expansion
In fact, even within that small world, Housman deliberately chose abstruse subjects for his contributions to classical scholarship. He compiled editions of the works of three first-century minor Latin poets: Manilius, Lucan, and Juvenal.

B. Expansion
Housman's outlook is similar to Walter Pater's exaltation of style and the movement known as *l'art pour l'art* ("art for art's sake"). Another champion of this movement was the poet Algernon Charles Swinburne (1837–1909).

A. E. Housman (1859–1936)

Housman said that he was careful not to think of poetry while he was shaving, for "if a line of poetry strays into my memory, my skin bristles so that the razor ceases to act." For Housman, poetry was all feeling. The feelings produced physical effects (he also described shivers along the spine, tears, the sensation of being pierced by a spear) that came from what Housman said was the source of his own poems, "the pit of the stomach."

Housman's poetry is more restrained than his comments suggest. His poems evoke a narrow range of subdued feelings that are controlled by simple, tight verse forms and clear language and syntax. Although he uses simple words, his diction is precise and carefully polished: Each word is the right word in the right place.

Alfred Edward Housman was born in Worcestershire in western England, the oldest of seven children. He was close to his mother, who died on his twelfth birthday. His father, a lawyer, allowed his practice, money, and talent to dwindle away in despondency and drink. At sixteen, Housman won a scholarship to Oxford, where he prepared for a career as a scholar and teacher of classical literature. But he attended classes irregularly, preferring to study on his own, and failed his final examinations.

In 1882 Housman entered the civil service as a clerk in the patent office, determined to prove himself as a classical scholar despite his failure at Oxford. For the next ten years he set himself a rigorous program: writing and publishing papers on Greek and Latin literature while working as a patent clerk. In 1892 his series of scholarly papers won him an appointment as Professor of Latin at the University of London. He stayed until 1911, when he moved to Cambridge University as Professor of Latin and Fellow at Trinity College. Housman spent the rest of his life as a formal and rather aloof teacher, a reserved participant in the small world of his college, and

Alfred Edward Housman by Francis Dodd (1936). Pencil drawing.

an authority in the yet smaller world of classical scholarship.

During his lifetime, Housman published only two books of poems containing a little over one hundred poems. His first collection, *A Shropshire Lad* (1896), became popular because its graceful recollection of youthful pleasures and their transience fit a late-century mood of disillusionment in a world which has "much good, but much less good than ill." In "Terence, This Is Stupid Stuff," Housman acknowledged that his poems could be dismissed as self-indulgent belly aching. The test of poetry, he believed, is not what is said but how it is said. In the refined elegance of his poems, he expressed his pessimism about the cold emptiness of the world. Unlike the major Romantic and Victorian poets who preceded him, Housman saw no hope of improvement or change, but only the possibility of enduring and making bearable the conditions of human experience.

1. BUILDING ON PRIOR KNOWLEDGE. Before students begin reading Housman's lyrics, review with them the summary of Victorian life and literature in the Introduction on text pages 769–772. Remind students that Housman, together with other late Victorians like Thomas Hardy, had a far less optimistic view of human behavior than those writers who lived earlier in the century, such as Macaulay.

2. ESTABLISHING A PURPOSE. A major theme that runs throughout Housman's poetry is the failure of early promise: Youth is doomed to old age and death, love is doomed to disappointment, etc. Ask students to look for this theme as they read the next three poems.

SUPPLEMENTARY SUPPORT MATERIALS
1. Review and Response Worksheet: Tone and Theme (CCB)
2. Selection Test (CCB)

CLOSURE
Have students explain the effect of Housman's use of repetition in the poem.

The tone of Housman's poetry is often nostalgic and bittersweet. This brief lyric is a good example.

When I Was One-and-Twenty

When I was one-and-twenty
  I heard a wise man say,
"Give crowns and pounds and guineas°
  But not your heart away;
5 Give pearls away and rubies
  But keep your fancy free."
But I was one-and-twenty,
  No use to talk to me.

When I was one-and-twenty
10 I heard him say again,
"The heart out of the bosom
  Was never given in vain;
'Tis paid with sighs a plenty
  And sold for endless rue."°
15 And I am two-and-twenty,
  And oh, 'tis true, 'tis true.

A

3. **crowns . . . pounds . . . guineas:** units of money in Great Britain.

14. **rue:** sorrow; regret.

Responding to the Poem

Analyzing the Poem

Identifying Details

1. In the first stanza, what advice did the wise man give the speaker?
2. How much time has passed between the first and the second stanza?

Interpreting Meanings

3. What has the speaker learned, in your opinion?
4. What do you think of the wise man's advice that it is better to give away money than to fall in love? Explain.

5. What is the effect of Housman's use of **repetition** in the last line of the poem? What other kinds of repetition do you find in the poem?
6. What do you think is the poem's **theme,** or message? Do you think Housman is being serious or ironic or humorous in his attitude toward falling in love?

A. Tone
Which of the following adjectives best characterizes the speaker's tone: *ironic, regretful, bitter, nostalgic, melancholy*? Explain.

ANALYZING THE POEM
Identifying Details
1. Not to give his heart away and to keep his "fancy free."
2. A year (or part of a year).

Interpreting Meanings
3. That love can be painful.
4. Some students might agree that the experience of being in love is worth the pain they feel when the relationship ends.
5. The repetition of " 'tis true" emphasizes the speaker's agreement, suggests the pain of the experience he has had without giving any information about that experience, and brings the poem to an emphatic close.
Students should note the repetition of whole lines (1 and 9), similar lines (2 and 10), and syntax in the two stanzas.
6. Humorous and ironic.

SUPPLEMENTARY SUPPORT MATERIALS
1. Review and Response Worksheet:
Extended Metaphor (*CCB*)
2. Selection Test (*CCB*)

A. Interpreting
Who is "he" in this line and "His" in line 11? (Dick, who has died. Students' understanding of the poem depends on their awareness that Dick is the subject of this second stanza.)

ANALYZING THE POEM
Identifying Details
1. It is November 30th.
2. Dick has died.
3. The rhyme scheme is *abcabc*.

Interpreting Meanings
4. The connotations of icy cold and darkness are unpleasant.
5. The earth, which covers the body of Dick, is Dick's clothing: his winter robe, his overcoat.
6. Winterfalls suggests the beginnings of many winters as nightfall suggests the beginning of night.
It suggests the quick passing of years.
7. Possible answer: The troubles that plague us soon disappear, for our life on earth is short, and nothing troubles us in the grave.

In the following lyric, Housman's typical nostalgia is colored by pessimism.

The Night Is Freezing Fast

The night is freezing fast,
    Tomorrow comes December;
        And winterfalls of old
Are with me from the past;
5   And chiefly I remember
        How Dick would hate the cold.

A Fall, winter, fall; for he,
    Prompt hand and headpiece clever,
        Has woven a winter robe,
10 And made of earth and sea
    His overcoat forever,
        And wears the turning globe.

Responding to the Poem

Analyzing the Poem

Identifying Details
1. According to the evidence of the first stanza, what day is it?
2. What has happened to Dick?
3. Describe the **rhyme scheme** of the poem.

Interpreting Meanings
4. What are the connotations of the poem's title?

5. Explain the **extended metaphor** that dominates the second stanza.
6. What do you think *winterfalls* (line 3) means? How do you interpret the phrase "Fall, winter, fall" (line 7)?
7. What would you say is the poem's **theme**, or message? Is it about winter, or Dick, or something else entirely?

ANALYZING THE POEM
Identifying Details
1. He mourns the friends of his youth who have died.
2. Beside "brooks too broad for leaping"; in "fields where roses fade."

Interpreting Meanings
3. The boys are "lightfoot" and are appropriately buried beside brooks too broad for leaping. The girls are "rose-lipt" and appropriately buried in fields where roses (like themselves) are fading.
4. Students may suggest that the regular variation of strong and weak rhymes adds to the poem's musical quality.

In eight lines, Housman gives fresh expression to a universal emotion: sorrow for friends who are lost to the passage of time.

With Rue My Heart Is Laden

With rue my heart is laden
   For golden friends I had,
For many a rose-lipt maiden
   And many a lightfoot lad.

By brooks too broad for leaping
   The lightfoot boys are laid;
The rose-lipt girls are sleeping
   In fields where roses fade.

A

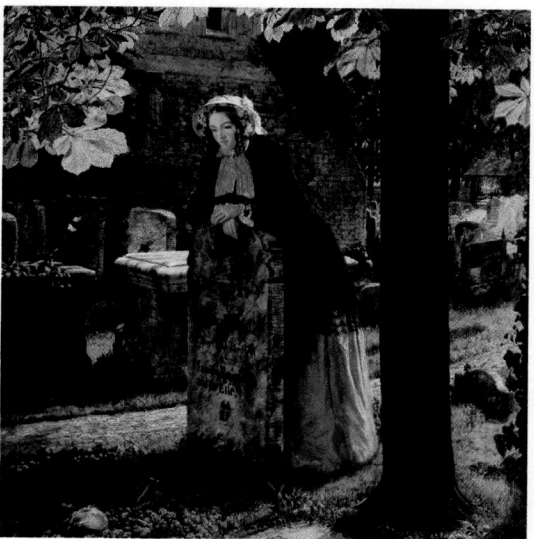

The Doubt by Henry Alexander Bowler.

The Tate Gallery, London.

A. Connections
Have students compare this poem with Tennyson's "Tears, Idle Tears" (text page 779). (The feelings of the speakers are similar, though Housman is more focused. Housman's ideas are expressed almost tersely; Tennyson is discursive.)

B. Humanities Connection: Responding to the Fine Art
[?] The painting is titled "The Doubt." What do you imagine this woman is doubting? What feelings do you get from looking at the painting? (Responses will vary. The woman is sad, but the cemetery seems almost cheerful with its greenery and dappled sunlight.)

B

Responding to the Poem

Analyzing the Poem

Identifying Details

1. Why is the speaker mournful?
2. According to the second stanza, where are the boys laid to rest? Where do the girls lie?

Interpreting Meanings

3. Given the burial places where the boys and girls are said to lie in the second stanza, what is appropriate about the adjectives used to describe them?
4. The **rhythm** of the poem is perfectly regular, even in the variations of lines 1, 3, 5, and 7, where Housman adds an extra final syllable to create a feminine **rhyme** (on an unstressed syllable). What is the effect of this regular variation of strong and weak rhymes?

Writing About the Poems

A Creative Response

1. **Imitating the Writer's Technique.** Imagine that twenty or thirty years have passed and that you are looking back on your teen-age years. Pick one aspect of youth to write about: perhaps friendship, discovery, dreams, self-doubt, or first love. Write a brief poem about the aspect of youth you select.

A Critical Response

2. **Comparing and Contrasting Poems.** In a brief essay, compare and contrast the themes, tones, and imagery of these three poems by Housman: "When I Was One-and-Twenty," "The Night Is Freezing Fast," and "With Rue My Heart Is Laden."

A. E. Housman   843

PREPARATION
ESTABLISHING A PURPOSE. Have students notice the details Housman uses to establish the setting of the poem.

SUPPLEMENTARY SUPPORT MATERIALS
1. Review and Response Worksheet: Tone and Theme (*CCB*)
2. Selection Test (*CCB*)

CLOSURE
Have students state the contrast between the setting in the poem and the events the poem portrays.

ANALYZING THE POEM
Identifying Details
1. Criminals were once hanged at the crossroads; now they are hanged in Shrewsbury jail.
2. He will be hanged in the morning.
3. He will stay awake on the heath and think of his friend.

Interpreting Meanings
4. The past is described in pastoral terms; the present in terms of prisons.
5. He is a friend.
6. Students should notice the harshly accented syllables in lines 19 and 21. These two stanzas are set off from the story that the speaker tells.
7. Because people's actions are often determined by their circumstances, potentially good people still can end up as criminals.

In this lyric, Housman combines a Romantic evocation of the past and a pastoral setting with realistic, almost macabre, motifs. Housman recalls a time when convicted criminals were hanged in public and left on display as a warning against crime.

On Moonlit Heath and Lonesome Bank

On moonlit heath and lonesome bank
  The sheep beside me graze;
And yon the gallows used to clank
  Fast by the four crossways.

5 A careless shepherd once would keep
  The flocks by moonlight there,
And high amongst the glimmering sheep
  The dead man stood on air.

They hang us now in Shrewsbury jail:
10 The whistles blow forlorn,
And trains all night groan on the rail
  To men that die at morn.

There sleeps in Shrewsbury jail tonight,
  Or wakes, as may betide,
15 A better lad, if things went right,
  Than most that sleep outside.

And naked to the hangman's noose
  The morning clocks will ring
A neck God made for other use
20 Than strangling in a string.

And sharp the link of life will snap,
  And dead on air will stand
Heels that held up as straight a chap
  As treads upon the land.

25 So here I'll watch the night and wait
  To see the morning shine,
When he will hear the stroke of eight
  And not the stroke of nine;

And wish my friend as sound a sleep
30 As lads' I did not know,
That shepherded the moonlit sheep
  A hundred years ago.

Responding to the Poem

Analyzing the Poem

Identifying Details
1. What differences between the past and present does the speaker remark on?
2. What does the speaker say will happen to the young man in Shrewsbury jail?
3. In the final two stanzas, what does the speaker say he will do?

Interpreting Meanings
4. What seems to be the speaker's attitude toward the past, as compared to the present?
5. What is the speaker's relationship to the condemned man?
6. How are the sounds of the fifth and sixth stanzas different from those of the stanzas that precede and follow them? Explain the purpose and effect of this difference.
7. Do you think this poem has any contemporary applications, given what you know about crime and punishment in our society?

Writing About the Poem

A Critical Response
1. **Writing a Paraphrase.** Write a brief paraphrase in prose of this poem. Be sure to include all the major points of the poem in your paraphrase.
2. **Analyzing the Effects of Setting.** In a brief essay, discuss the effect of the details of setting. How does the setting affect the poem's mood and theme?

Charles Dickens
(1812–1870)

When Charles Dickens was twelve years old, his father, a clerk in the Navy Pay Office, was imprisoned for debt. His wife and younger children lived with him in debtors' prison, while Charles (the second of eight children) was put to work in a warehouse pasting labels on bottles of shoe polish six days a week. "It is wonderful to me how I could have been so easily cast away at such an age," he wrote in a fragment of autobiography that led to his writing *David Copperfield*. "It is wonderful to me that . . . no one had compassion enough on me—a child of singular abilities, quick, eager, delicate, and soon hurt, bodily or mentally—to suggest that something might have been spared . . . to place me at any common school."

Three months later Dickens left the warehouse and returned to school when sympathetic relatives rescued his imprisoned family. At fifteen, he began working as a law clerk and learned shorthand, which he used as a court reporter. At nineteen, he became a parliamentary reporter for a London newspaper. For a while he thought of becoming an actor, but settled into a writing career when magazines began to buy his prose sketches (signed "Boz") of London life. In 1836 his collected *Sketches by Boz* appeared, and Dickens began to write monthly installments of his very successful first novel, *Posthumous Papers of the Pickwick Club* (1836–1837). He began publishing *Oliver Twist* (1838) in magazine installments before he finished *Pickwick*. It became his pattern to start publishing a new novel in serial installments before he had finished writing it, and for most of his life he wrote steadily for weekly and monthly deadlines.

In 1850 Dickens founded a weekly magazine in which he serialized *A Tale of Two Cities* (1859) and *Great Expectations* (1860–1861). Other novels, like *David Copperfield* (1850), *Bleak House* (1852–1853), and *Our Mutual Friend* (1864–1865) were published in monthly installments that took nearly two years to complete their run.

Dickens's first success was as a comic writer, and he continued to entertain his readers with

Charles Dickens's Legacy to England
(19th century). Color engraving.

eccentric characters and elaborately fanciful descriptions, like that of the metallic Miss Jane Murdstone in *David Copperfield*. From the beginning of his career, Dickens also used humor to attack moral and social injustices. In all of his novels he included scenes in which people—often children—suffered because of neglect, incompetence, or cruelty. In his novels in the 1850's and 1860's, Dickens increasingly attacked what he saw as injustice without being funny.

Dickens's popularity as a writer was extraordinary in the 1840's. The monthly installments of his novels sold as many as one hundred thousand copies each in England, and crowds gathered on the New York City docks to buy them as soon as they arrived. Although his later novels were not as immediately popular, Dickens maintained his eminence as the best known and most widely read British writer of the period.

His early ambition to be an actor was founded on genuine theatrical talent. In the 1860's he began a series of readings from his works that were as intense, flamboyant, and vivid as the high-powered passages he chose to read. The readings were also physically exhausting. After a successful tour of the United States in 1867–1868, his health broke during a reading tour of England in 1869. He began publishing *The Mystery of Edwin Drood* in 1870, but died before he had written more than half the installments.

A. Imagery
This childhood experience made a deep and lasting impression on Dickens. Numerous memorable scenes in his novels deal literally with poverty and imprisonment, and images of prison and jailers loom large in his fiction. Tell students to look for such images in the selection from *David Copperfield*.

B. Expansion
Some critics have suggested that this was a contributing cause of the great length of some of the novels.

1. Building On Prior Knowledge. Before students begin reading, ask them to discuss works by Dickens with which they are familiar. Many students, for example, will have seen movie or television adaptations of *Great Expectations, A Christmas Carol,* and *A Tale of Two Cities.*

2. Establishing A Purpose. As they read the chapter, ask students to focus on the characterization of David, his mother, Mr. Murdstone, and Miss Jane Murdstone.

3. Prereading Journal. Before they read, have students write two or three sentences in their journals recalling a time in childhood when they felt especially sad or lonely.

A. Literary Genre
Point out to students that *David Copperfield,* together with *Oliver Twist* and *Great Expectations,* is in the literary form of a *Bildungsroman* (German for "novel of education"). This type of novel chronicles the progress of a young child to adulthood. Joyce's *A Portrait of the Artist as a Young Man* is another novel of this type. (See text page 966.)

B. Character
Little Em'ly is Peggotty's niece, whom David meets when he visits Peggotty's family in Yarmouth.

C. Humor
One of Dickens's favorite comic devices is making a character scramble a well-known phrase in a *malapropism.* (The term comes from Mrs. Malaprop, a character in Richard Brinsley Sheridan's play *The Rivals,* 1775.) Peggotty, of course, means to say, "*ever be truly sorry.*"

FROM DAVID COPPERFIELD

Only three years before Dickens wrote *David Copperfield,* the English novelist Charlotte Brontë had pioneered using a child as protagonist in her novel *Jane Eyre* (1847). Dickens titled his novel *The Personal History of David Copperfield* and referred to it as his "favorite child." "I seem to be sending some part of myself into the Shadowy World," he said. The novel clearly incorporates some autobiographical elements, such as Dickens's painful experiences as a twelve-year-old apprentice in a blacking warehouse. In the fragment of autobiography that preceded his writing *David Copperfield,*

Dickens remarked, "I do not write resentfully or angrily: for I know how all these things have worked together to make me what I am."

Davy is eight years old when he and the maid Peggotty are sent away for two weeks to visit Peggotty's relatives, who live in Yarmouth. When they return home, Davy discovers that his pretty widowed mother has married Mr. Murdstone, whom Davy dislikes and distrusts. Mr. Murdstone has moved Davy's bed far away from his mother's room.

I Fall into Disgrace

Chapter 4

If the room to which my bed was removed were a sentient thing that could give evidence, I might appeal to it at this day—who sleeps there now, I wonder!—to bear witness for me what a heavy heart I carried to it. I went up there, hearing the dog in the yard bark after me all the way while I climbed the stairs, and, looking as blank and strange upon the room as the room looked upon me, sat down with my small hands crossed, and thought.

I thought of the oddest things. Of the shape of the room, of the cracks in the ceiling, of the paper on the wall, of the flaws in the window-glass making ripples and dimples on the prospect, of the washing stand being rickety on its three legs, and having a discontented something about it, which reminded me of Mrs. Gummidge[1] under the influence of the old one. I was crying all the time, but, except that I was conscious of being cold and dejected, I am sure I never thought why I cried. At last in my desolation I began to consider that I was dreadfully in love with little Em'ly, and had been torn away from her to come here where no one seemed to want me, or to care about me, half

as much as she did. This made such a very miserable piece of business of it, that I rolled myself up in a corner of the counterpane, and cried myself to sleep.

I was awakened by somebody saying "Here he is!" and uncovering my hot head. My mother and Peggotty had come to look for me, and it was one of them who had done it.

"Davy," said my mother. "What's the matter?"

I thought it was very strange that she should ask me, and answered, "Nothing." I turned over on my face, I recollect, to hide my trembling lip, which answered her with greater truth.

"Davy," said my mother. "Davy, my child!"

I daresay no words she could have uttered would have affected me so much, then, as her calling me her child. I hid my tears in the bedclothes, and pressed her from me with my hand, when she would have raised me up.

"This is your doing, Peggotty, you cruel thing!" said my mother. "I have no doubt at all about it. How can you reconcile it to your conscience, I wonder, to prejudice my own boy against me, or against anybody who is dear to me? What do you mean by it, Peggotty?"

Poor Peggotty lifted up her hands and eyes, and only answered, in a sort of paraphrase of the grace I usually repeated after dinner, "Lord forgive you, Mrs. Copperfield, and for what you have said this minute, may you never be truly sorry!"

---

1. **Mrs. Gummidge:** a widow who lives in Peggotty's brother's household. She becomes exceedingly depressed whenever she thinks of "the old 'un," her late husband.

SUPPLEMENTARY SUPPORT MATERIALS
1. Vocabulary Activity Worksheet (CCB)
2. Review and Response Worksheet: Characterization (CCB)
3. Language Skills Worksheet: Participles and Participial Phrases (CCB)
4. Selection Test (CCB)

DEVELOPING VOCABULARY
The following words from the chapter are tested in the Selection Test. (See also Vocabulary Activity Worksheet.)

sentient	bane
inveterate	to wallow
pettish	stoical
compunction	vise
nominally	atrocious

"It's enough to distract me," cried my mother. "In my honeymoon, too, when my most inveterate enemy might relent, one would think, and not envy me a little peace of mind and happiness. Davy, you naughty boy! Peggotty, you savage creature! Oh, dear me!" cried my mother, turning from one of us to the other, in her pettish, willful manner. "What a troublesome world this is, when one has the most right to expect it to be as agreeable as possible!"

I felt the touch of a hand that I knew was neither hers nor Peggotty's, and slipped to my feet at the bedside. It was Mr. Murdstone's hand, and he kept it on my arm as he said:

"What's this! Clara, my love, have you forgotten? Firmness, my dear!"

"I am very sorry, Edward," said my mother. "I meant to be very good, but I am so uncomfortable."

"Indeed!" he answered. "That's a bad hearing, so soon, Clara."

"I say it's very hard I should be made so now," returned my mother, pouting; "and it is—very hard—isn't it?"

He drew her to him, whispered in her ear, and kissed her. I knew as well, when I saw my mother's head lean down upon his shoulder, and her arm touch his neck—I knew as well that he could mold her pliant nature into any form he chose, as I know, now, that he did it.

"Go you below, my love," said Mr. Murdstone. "David and I will come down, together. My friend," turning a darkening face on Peggotty, when he had watched my mother out, and dismissed her with a nod and a smile: "do you know your mistress's name?"

"She has been my mistress a long time, sir," answered Peggotty. "I ought to know it."

"That's true," he answered. "But I thought I heard you, as I came upstairs, address her by a name that is not hers. She has taken mine, you know. Will you remember that?"

Peggotty, with some uneasy glances at me, curtseyed herself out of the room without replying, seeing, I suppose, that she was expected to go, and had no excuse for remaining. When we two were left alone, he shut the door, and, sitting on a chair, and holding me standing before him, looked steadily into my eyes. I felt my own attracted, no less steadily, to his. As I recall our being opposed thus, face to face, I seem again to hear my heart beat fast and high.

"David," he said, making his lips thin by pressing them together, "if I have an obstinate horse or dog to deal with, what do you think I do?"

"I don't know."

"I beat him."

I had answered in a kind of breathless whisper, but I felt, in my silence, that my breath was shorter now.

"I make him wince and smart. I say to myself, 'I'll conquer that fellow,' and if it were to cost him all the blood he had, I should do it. What is that upon your face?"

"Dirt," I said.

He knew it was the mark of tears as well as I. But if he had asked the question twenty times, each time with twenty blows, I believe my baby heart would have burst before I would have told him so.

"You have a good deal of intelligence for a little fellow," he said, with a grave smile that belonged to him, "and you understood me very well, I see. Wash that face, sir, and come down with me."

He pointed to the washing stand, which I had made out to be like Mrs. Gummidge, and motioned me with his head to obey him directly. I had little doubt then, and I have less doubt now, that he would have knocked me down without the least compunction, if I had hesitated.

"Clara, my dear," he said, when I had done his bidding, and he walked me into the parlor, with his hand still on my arm, "you will not be made uncomfortable anymore, I hope. We shall soon improve our youthful humors."[2]

God help me, I might have been improved for my whole life, I might have been made another creature perhaps for life, by a kind word at that season. A word of encouragement and explanation, of pity for my childish ignorance, of welcome home, of reassurance to me that it *was* home, might have made me dutiful to him in my heart henceforth, instead of in my hypocritical outside, and might have made me respect instead of hate him. I thought my mother was sorry to see me standing in the room so scared and strange, and that, presently, when I stole to a chair, she followed me with her eyes more sorrowfully still—missing, perhaps, some freedom in my childish tread—but the word was not spoken, and the time for it was gone.

We dined alone, we three together. He seemed

---

2. **humors:** temperament; disposition.

A. Characterization

? What does this passage indicate about the character of David's mother? (She is naive, childish, and self-pitying.)

B. Vocabulary

A "bad hearing" is a Victorian expression meaning "Sorry to hear that."

C. Characterization

? What does this passage reveal about Mr. Murdstone's character? (He has a streak of brutality.)

D. Style

Have students stop to focus on Dickens's style in this paragraph. Note the elements of balance, concrete details, and pathos, especially in the concluding sentence.

**A. Plot:
Exposition**
Notice how well
Dickens incorpo-
rates exposition
with narrative in
this passage.

**B. Characteriza-
tion/Style**
This paragraph is
an example of
Dickens's remark-
able powers of
characterization.
Point out that the
key word is *metal-
lic*, which is fore-
shadowed by the
"hard brass nails,"
the "hard steel
purse," and "the
heavy chain."

You may want to
read the passage
aloud and have
students make
quick sketches of
Miss Murdstone.

C. Metaphor
Ask students to
identify the figure
of speech Dickens
uses here. (Meta-
phor: He compares
her early rising to
that of a lark.)

to be very fond of my mother—I am afraid I liked him none the better for that—and she was very fond of him. I gathered from what they said that an elder sister of his was coming to stay with them, and that she was expected that evening. I am not certain whether I found out then or afterward that, without being actively concerned in any business, he had some share in, or some annual charge upon the profits of, a wine-merchant's house in London, with which his family had been connected from his great-grandfather's time, and in which his sister had a similar interest, but I may mention it in this place, whether or no.

After dinner, when we were sitting by the fire, and I was meditating an escape to Peggotty without having the hardihood to slip away, lest it should offend the master of the house, a coach drove up to the garden gate, and he went out to receive the visitor. My mother followed him. I was timidly following her, when she turned round at the parlor door, in the dusk, and taking me in her embrace as she had been used to do, whispered me to love my new father and be obedient to him. She did this hurriedly and secretly, as if it were wrong, but tenderly, and, putting out her hand behind her, held mine in it, until we came near to where he was standing in the garden, where she let mine go, and drew hers through his arm.

It was Miss Murdstone who was arrived, and a gloomy looking lady she was: dark, like her brother, whom she greatly resembled in face and voice, and with very heavy eyebrows, nearly meeting over her large nose, as if, being disabled by the wrongs of her sex from wearing whiskers, she had carried them to that account. She brought with her two uncompromising hard black boxes, with her initials on the lids in hard brass nails. When she paid the coachman she took her money out of a hard steel purse, and she kept the purse in a very jail of a bag which hung upon her arm by a heavy chain, and shut up like a bite. I had never, at that time, seen such a metallic lady altogether as Miss Murdstone was.

She was brought into the parlor with many tokens of welcome, and there formally recognized my mother as a new and near relation. Then she looked at me, and said:

"Is that your boy, sister-in-law?"

My mother acknowledged me.

"Generally speaking," said Miss Murdstone, "I don't like boys. How d'ye do, boy?"

Under these encouraging circumstances, I re-

plied that I was very well, and that I hoped she was the same, with such an indifferent grace, that Miss Murdstone disposed of me in two words:

"Wants manner!"

Having uttered which with great distinctness, she begged the favor of being shown to her room, which became to me from that time forth a place of awe and dread, wherein the two black boxes were never seen open or known to be left unlocked, and where (for I peeped in once or twice when she was out) numerous little steel fetters and rivets, with which Miss Murdstone embellished herself when she was dressed, generally hung upon the looking-glass in formidable array.

As well as I could make out, she had come for good, and had no intention of ever going again. She began to "help" my mother next morning, and was in and out of the store closet all day, putting things to rights, and making havoc in the old arrangements. Almost the first remarkable thing I observed in Miss Murdstone was her being constantly haunted by a suspicion that the servants had a man secreted somewhere on the premises. Under the influence of this delusion, she dived into the coal cellar at the most untimely hours, and scarcely ever opened the door of a dark cupboard without clapping it to again, in the belief that she had got him.

Though there was nothing very airy about Miss Murdstone, she was a perfect lark in point of getting up. She was up (and, as I believe to this hour, looking for that man) before anybody in the house was stirring. Peggotty gave it as her opinion that she even slept with one eye open, but I could not concur in this idea, for I tried it myself after hearing the suggestion thrown out, and found it couldn't be done.

On the very first morning after her arrival she was up and ringing her bell at cock crow. When my mother came down to breakfast and was going to make the tea, Miss Murdstone gave her a kind of peck on the cheek, which was her nearest approach to a kiss, and said:

"Now, Clara, my dear, I am come here, you know, to relieve you of all the trouble I can. You're much too pretty and thoughtless"—my mother blushed but laughed, and seemed not to dislike this character—"to have any duties imposed upon you that can be undertaken by me. If you'll be so good as give me your keys, my dear, I'll attend to all this sort of thing in the future."

From that time, Miss Murdstone kept the keys

Omnibus Life in London by William Maw Egley (1859).

Tate Gallery, London/Art Resource, New York.

A

A. Humanities Connection: Responding to the Fine Art

William Maw Egley (1826–1916) was one of the famous historical genre painters of nineteenth-century London. He produced more than a thousand paintings, many of them scenes of contemporary London life.

❓ What are some similarities and differences between this painting and the scenes Dickens "draws" in *David Copperfield*? (The people in the painting look pleasant, fashionable, and kind; most of the characters in the story are mean, ugly, and brutal.)

❓ Since Egley was a contemporary of Dickens, the two were dealing with similar subject matter. How do you account for the differences between the two? (Perhaps Egley painted the pleasant, colorful surface of things, but Dickens saw beneath the civilized surface into people's dark hearts and gloomy lives.)

A. Style
Notice the way in
which Dickens
plays with the word
firmness in this
ironic paragraph,
applying it to differ-
ent characters.

B. Responding
❓ How do you
feel about Clara
as this scene pro-
gresses? What ad-
vice would you
give her? (She is
weak and child-
like. She needs to
be assertive and
demand her rights
as mistress of the
house. She is also
a poor judge of
character.)

C. Vocabulary
❓ What does
base mean
here? ("Ignoble,"
"mean")

in her own little jail all day, and under her pillow
all night, and my mother had no more to do with
them than I had.

My mother did not suffer her authority to pass
from her without a shadow of protest. One night
when Miss Murdstone had been developing certain household plans to her brother, of which he
signified his approbation, my mother suddenly began to cry, and said she thought she might have
been consulted

"Clara!" said Mr. Murdstone sternly. "Clara!
I wonder at you."

"Oh, it's very well to say you wonder, Edward!" cried my mother, "and it's very well for
you to talk about firmness, but you wouldn't like
it yourself."

Firmness, I may observe, was the grand quality
on which both Mr. and Miss Murdstone took their
stand. However I might have expressed my comprehension of it at that time, if I had been called
upon, I nevertheless did clearly comprehend, in
my own way, that it was another name for tyranny,
and for a certain gloomy, arrogant, devil's humor,
that was in them both. The creed, as I should state
it now, was this. Mr. Murdstone was firm; nobody
in his world was to be so firm as Mr. Murdstone;
nobody else in his world was to be firm at all, for
everybody was to be bent to his firmness. Miss
Murdstone was an exception. She might be firm,
but only by relationship, and in an inferior and
tributary degree. My mother was another exception. She might be firm, and must be, but only in
bearing their firmness, and firmly believing there
was no other firmness upon earth.

"It's very hard," said my mother, "that in my
own house——"

"*My* own house?" repeated Mr. Murdstone.
"Clara!"

"*Our* own house, I mean," faltered my mother,
evidently frightened—"I hope you must know
what I mean, Edward—it's very hard that in *your*
own house I may not have a word to say about
domestic matters. I am sure I managed very well
before we were married. There's evidence," said
my mother sobbing, "ask Peggotty if I didn't do
very well when I wasn't interfered with!"

"Edward," said Miss Murdstone, "let there be
an end of this. I go tomorrow."

"Jane Murdstone," said her brother, "be silent!
How dare you to insinuate that you don't know
my character better than your words imply?"

"I am sure," my poor mother went on at a

grievous disadvantage, and with many tears, "I
don't want anybody to go. I should be very miserable and unhappy if anybody was to go. I don't
ask much. I am not unreasonable. I only want to
be consulted sometimes. I am very much obliged
to anybody who assists me, and I only want to be
consulted as a mere form, sometimes. I thought
you were pleased, once, with my being a little
inexperienced and girlish, Edward—I am sure you
said so—but you seem to hate me for it now, you
are so severe."

"Edward," said Miss Murdstone again, "let
there be an end of this. I go tomorrow."

"Jane Murdstone," thundered Mr. Murdstone.
"Will you be silent? How dare you?"

Miss Murdstone made a jail delivery[3] of her
pocket handkerchief, and held it before her eyes.

"Clara," he continued, looking at my mother,
"you surprise me! You astound me! Yes, I had a
satisfaction in the thought of marrying an inexperienced and artless person, and forming her
character, and infusing into it some amount of that
firmness and decision of which it stood in need.
But when Jane Murdstone is kind enough to come
to my assistance in this endeavor, and to assume,
for my sake, a condition something like a housekeeper's, and when she meets with a base
return——"

"Oh, pray, pray, Edward," cried my mother,
"don't accuse me of being ungrateful. I am sure I
am not ungrateful. No one ever said I was before.
I have many faults, but not that. Oh, don't, my
dear!"

"When Jane Murdstone meets, I say," he went
on, after waiting until my mother was silent, "with
a base return, that feeling of mine is chilled and
altered."

"Don't, my love, say that!" implored my
mother very piteously. "Oh, don't Edward! I can't
bear to hear it. Whatever I am, I am affectionate.
I know I am affectionate. I wouldn't say it if I
wasn't certain that I am. Ask Peggotty. I am sure
she'll tell you I'm affectionate."

"There is no extent of mere weakness, Clara,"
said Mr. Murdstone in reply, "that can have the
least weight with me. You lose breath."

"Pray let us be friends," said my mother. "I
couldn't live under coldness or unkindness. I am
so sorry. I have a great many defects, I know, and

---

3. **jail delivery:** Dickens imagines Miss Murdstone's purse as
a jail from which objects must be liberated.

it's very good of you, Edward, with your strength of mind, to endeavor to correct them for me. Jane, I don't object to anything. I should be quite brokenhearted if you thought of leaving——'' My mother was too much overcome to go on.

"Jane Murdstone,'' said Mr. Murdstone to his sister, "any harsh words between us are, I hope, uncommon. It is not my fault that so unusual an occurrence has taken place tonight. I was betrayed into it by another. Nor is it your fault. You were betrayed into it by another. Let us both try to forget it. And as this,'' he added, after these magnanimous words, "is not a fit scene for the boy—David, go to bed!''

I could hardly find the door, through the tears that stood in my eyes—I was so sorry for my mother's distress—but I groped my way out, and groped my way up to my room in the dark, without even having the heart to say good night to Peggotty, or to get a candle from her. When her coming up to look for me, an hour or so afterward, awoke me, she said that my mother had gone to bed poorly, and that Mr. and Miss Murdstone were sitting alone.

Going down next morning rather earlier than usual, I paused outside the parlor door on hearing my mother's voice. She was very earnestly and humbly entreating Miss Murdstone's pardon, which that lady granted, and a perfect reconciliation took place. I never knew my mother afterward to give an opinion on any matter, without first appealing to Miss Murdstone, or without having first ascertained, by some sure means, what Miss Murdstone's opinion was, and I never saw Miss Murdstone, when out of temper (she was infirm that way), move her hand toward her bag as if she were going to take out the keys and offer to resign them to my mother, without seeing that my mother was in a terrible fright.

The gloomy taint that was in the Murdstone blood darkened the Murdstone religion, which was austere and wrathful. I have thought, since, that its assuming that character was a necessary consequence of Mr. Murdstone's firmness, which wouldn't allow him to let anybody off from the utmost weight of the severest penalties he could find any excuse for. Be this as it may, I well remember the tremendous visages with which we used to go to church, and the changed air of the place. Again, the dreaded Sunday comes round, and I file into the old pew first, like a guarded captive brought to a condemned service.[4] Again,

Miss Murdstone, in a black velvet gown that looks as if it had been made out of a pall,[5] follows close upon me; then my mother; then her husband. There is no Peggotty now, as in the old time. Again, I listen to Miss Murdstone mumbling the responses, and emphasizing all the dread words with a cruel relish. Again, I see her dark eyes roll round the church when she says "miserable sinners,'' as if she were calling all the congregation names. Again, I catch rare glimpses of my mother, moving her lips timidly between the two, with one of them muttering at each ear like low thunder. Again, I wonder with a sudden fear whether it is likely that our good old clergyman can be wrong, and Mr. and Miss Murdstone right, and that all the angels in Heaven can be destroying angels. Again, if I move a finger or relax a muscle of my face, Miss Murdstone pokes me with her prayer book, and makes my side ache.

Yes, and again, as we walk home, I note some neighbors looking at my mother and at me, and whispering. Again, as the three go on arm-in-arm, and I linger behind alone, I follow some of those looks, and wonder if my mother's step be really not so light as I have seen it, and if the gaiety of her beauty be really almost worried away. Again, I wonder whether any of the neighbors call to mind, as I do, how we used to walk home together, she and I, and I wonder stupidly about that, all the dreary, dismal day.

There had been some talk on occasions of my going to boarding school. Mr. and Miss Murdstone had originated it, and my mother had of course agreed with them. Nothing, however, was concluded on the subject yet. In the meantime I learnt lessons at home.

Shall I ever forget those lessons? They were presided over nominally by my mother, but really by Mr. Murdstone and his sister, who were always present, and found them a favorable occasion for giving my mother lessons in that miscalled firmness, which was the bane of both our lives. I believe I was kept at home for that purpose. I had been apt enough to learn, and willing enough, when my mother and I had lived alone together. I can faintly remember learning the alphabet at her knee. To this day, when I look upon the fat black letters in the primer, the puzzling novelty of their shapes, and the easy good-nature of O and Q and

---

4. **condemned service:** service for prisoners sentenced to die.
5. **pall:** a covering for a casket.

A. Setting
Here Dickens is dramatizing the role in Victorian life of two kinds of middle-class women: the typical demure wife who did not want to offend, and the spinster aunt who was ready to take charge.
? Do you think either of these character types exists today? (Yes, although women are learning to be more assertive. Also, the spinster aunt today would probably have a job.)

B. Style
Have students note the artfully contrived shift into the present tense.
? What is the effect of the present-tense verbs? (Vividness, immediacy)

C. Expansion
Children of the middle and upper classes were often educated at home. State-supported schools were not established until 1870 (see text page 763), twenty years after Dickens wrote this scene.

A. Satire/Style
Dickens reserves his most scathing satire for the teaching methods used both at home and in private schools. Note again the shift to the present tense, serving to make the scene even more vivid.

B. Characterization
❓ Do you find this passage believable? Explain why or why not. What prevents David from reciting his lessons correctly? (He finds them unintelligible; he is frightened and tense; he dreads the scene to come.)

S, seem to present themselves again before me as they used to do. But they recall no feeling of disgust or reluctance. On the contrary, I seem to have walked along a path of flowers as far as the crocodile book,[6] and to have been cheered by the gentleness of my mother's voice and manner all the way. But these solemn lessons which succeeded those, I remember as the deathblow at my peace, and a grievous daily drudgery and misery. They were very long, very numerous, very hard—perfectly unintelligible, some of them, to me—and I was generally as much bewildered by them as I believe my poor mother was herself.

Let me remember how it used to be, and bring one morning back again.

I come into the second-best parlor after breakfast, with my books, and an exercise book, and a slate. My mother is ready for me at her writing desk, but not half so ready as Mr. Murdstone in his easy chair by the window (though he pretends to be reading a book), or as Miss Murdstone, sitting near my mother stringing steel beads. The very sight of these two has such an influence over me, that I begin to feel the words I have been at infinite pains to get into my head, all sliding away, and going I don't know where. I wonder where they *do* go, by-the-by?

I hand the first book to my mother. Perhaps it is a grammar, perhaps a history or geography. I take a last drowning look at the page as I give it into her hand, and start off aloud at a racing pace while I have got it fresh. I trip over a word. Mr. Murdstone looks up. I trip over another word. Miss Murdstone looks up. I redden, tumble over half-a-dozen words, and stop. I think my mother would show me the book if she dared, but she does not dare, and she says softly:

"Oh, Davy, Davy!"

"Now, Clara," says Mr. Murdstone, "be firm with the boy. Don't say, 'Oh, Davy, Davy!' That's childish. He knows his lesson, or he does not know it."

"He does *not* know it," Miss Murdstone interposes awfully.

"I am really afraid he does not," says my mother.

"Then, you see, Clara," returns Miss Murdstone, "you should just give him the book back, and make him know it."

---

6. **crocodile book:** a book about crocodiles that Davy used to read in the happy days before his mother married Mr. Murdstone.

"Yes, certainly," says my mother, "that is what I intend to do, my dear Jane. Now, Davy, try once more, and don't be stupid."

I obey the first clause of the injunction by trying once more, but am not so successful with the second, for I am very stupid. I tumble down before I get to the old place, at a point where I was all right before, and stop to think. But I can't think about the lesson. I think of the number of yards of net in Miss Murdstone's cap, or of the price of Mr. Murdstone's dressing gown, or any such ridiculous problem that I have no business with, and don't want to have anything at all to do with. Mr. Murdstone makes a movement of impatience which I have been expecting for a long time. Miss Murdstone does the same. My mother glances submissively at them, shuts the book, and lays it by as an arrear to be worked out when my other tasks are done.

There is a pile of these arrears very soon, and it swells like a rolling snowball. The bigger it gets, the more stupid *I* get. The case is so hopeless, and I feel that I am wallowing in such a bog of nonsense, that I give up all idea of getting out, and abandon myself to my fate. The despairing way in which my mother and I look at each other, as I blunder on, is truly melancholy. But the greatest effect in these miserable lessons is when my mother (thinking nobody is observing her) tries to give me the cue by the motion of her lips. At that instant, Miss Murdstone, who has been lying in wait for nothing else all along, says in a deep warning voice:

"Clara!"

My mother starts, colors, and smiles faintly. Mr. Murdstone comes out of his chair, takes the book, throws it at me or boxes my ears with it, and turns me out of the room by the shoulders.

Even when the lessons are done, the worst is yet to happen, in the shape of an appalling sum. This is invented for me, and delivered to me orally, by Mr. Murdstone, and begins, "If I go into a cheesemonger's shop, and buy five thousand double-Gloucester cheeses at fourpence-half-penny each, present payment"—at which I see Miss Murdstone secretly overjoyed. I pore over these cheeses without any result or enlightenment until dinnertime, when, having made a mulatto of myself by getting the dirt of the slate into the pores of my skin, I have a slice of bread to help me out with the cheeses, and am considered in disgrace for the rest of the evening.

It seems to me, at this distance of time, as if my unfortunate studies generally took this course. I could have done very well if I had been without the Murdstones, but the influence of the Murdstones upon me was like the fascination of two snakes on a wretched young bird. Even when I did get through the morning with tolerable credit, there was not much gained but dinner, for Miss Murdstone never could endure to see me untasked, and if I rashly made any show of being unemployed, called her brother's attention to me by saying, "Clara, my dear, there's nothing like work—give your boy an exercise," which caused me to be clapped down to some new labor there and then. As to any recreation with other children of my age, I had very little of that, for the gloomy theology of the Murdstones made all children out to be a swarm of little vipers (though there *was* a child once set in the midst of the Disciples), and held that they contaminated one another.

The natural result of this treatment, continued, I suppose, for some six months or more, was to make me sullen, dull, and dogged. I was not made the less so, by my sense of being daily more and more shut out and alienated from my mother. I believe I should have been almost stupefied but for one circumstance.

It was this. My father had left a small collection of books in a little room upstairs, to which I had access (for it adjoined my own), and which nobody else in our house ever troubled. From that blessed little room, Roderick Random, Peregrine Pickle, Humphrey Clinker, Tom Jones, the Vicar of Wakefield, Don Quixote, Gil Blas, and Robinson Crusoe[7] came out, a glorious host, to keep me company. They kept alive my fancy, and my hope of something beyond that place and time—they, and the *Arabian Nights,* and the *Tales of the Genii*—and did me no harm, for whatever harm was in some of them was not there for me; *I* knew nothing of it. It is astonishing to me now, how I found time, in the midst of my porings and blunderings over heavier themes, to read those books as I did. It is curious to me how I could ever have consoled myself under my small troubles (which

were great troubles to me) by impersonating my favorite characters in them—as I did—and by putting Mr. and Miss Murdstone into all the bad ones—which I did too. I have been Tom Jones (a child's Tom Jones, a harmless creature) for a week together. I have sustained my own idea of Roderick Random for a month at a stretch, I verily believe. I had a greedy relish for a few volumes of *Voyages and Travels*—I forget what, now—that were on those shelves, and for days and days I can remember to have gone about my region of our house, armed with the centerpiece out of an old set of boot-trees—the perfect realization of Captain Somebody, of the Royal British Navy, in danger of being beset by savages, and resolved to sell his life at a great price. The Captain never lost dignity from having his ears boxed with the Latin Grammar. I did, but the Captain was a Captain and a hero, in despite of all the grammars of all the languages in the world, dead or alive.

This was my only and my constant comfort. When I think of it, the picture always rises in my mind, of a summer evening, the boys at play in the churchyard, and I sitting on my bed, reading as if for life. Every barn in the neighborhood, every stone in the church, and every foot of the churchyard, had some association of its own, in my mind, connected with these books, and stood for some locality made famous in them. I have seen Tom Pipes go climbing up the church steeple; I have watched Strap, with the knapsack on his back, stopping to rest himself upon the wicket gate; and I *know* that Commodore Trunnion held that club with Mr. Pickle,[8] in the parlor of our little village alehouse.

The reader now understands, as well as I do, what I was when I came to that point of my youthful history to which I am now coming again.

One morning when I went into the parlor with my books, I found my mother looking anxious, Miss Murdstone looking firm, and Mr. Murdstone binding something round the bottom of a cane—a lithe and limber cane, which he left off binding when I came in, and poised and switched in the air.

---

7. The first three names are the heroes (and the titles of novels) created by Tobias Smollett. Henry Fielding wrote *Tom Jones,* Oliver Goldsmith wrote *The Vicar of Wakefield,* and Daniel Defoe wrote *Robinson Crusoe.* All are eighteenth-century British novels that Dickens read excitedly as a boy. *Don Quixote* is by Miguel de Cervantes; *Gil Blas* is by the eighteenth-century French novelist Alain René LeSage.

8. **Tom Pipes, Commodore Trunnion, Mr. Pickle:** characters in *Peregrine Pickle* by Tobias Smollett. **Strap:** a character in Smollett's *Roderick Random.*

A. Simile/ Metaphor

? Identify the simile in these lines. (The Murdstones lay in wait, watching with malicious intent, like two snakes watching a young bird.) What metaphor toward the end of this paragraph presents a related image? (Children are a swarm of little vipers.)

B. Expansion
Dickens's rhapsody on the joys of reading is definitely autobiographical. A similar passage occurs in *A Christmas Carol,* when Scrooge remembers how reading books such as these comforted him when he was a heartsick boy left alone at school during the Christmas holidays.

READING CHECK TEST

1. David is happy when his widowed mother marries Mr. Murdstone. (F)
2. Miss Murdstone, the sister of David's stepfather, moves in and runs the household. (T)
3. According to David, Mr. Murdstone's creed is kindness. (F)
4. After biting Mr. Murdstone's hand, David is confined to his room for five days. (T)
5. Before David is sent away to school, his mother promises him that she will get even with Mr. Murdstone. (F)

A. Plot: Foreshadowing

❓ What clues does Dickens give for what is about to happen to David? (His mother's anxiety, the cane, and the conversation all suggest that David is about to be caned.)

B. Simile

Students should identify the simile (David's thoughts flee as if they were on roller skates) and note that it's a fresh and extremely apt comparison.

C. Responding

❓ Do you think Dickens's recurring theme of cruelty (often involving beating) to innocent children is relevant today? (Students should cite the frequent news of cases of child abuse.)

D. Descriptive Details

Notice the way in which Dickens reinforces the notion of Miss Murdstone as a prison guard. She has been associated with images of jail since we first met her (see text page 848).

A "I tell you, Clara," said Mr. Murdstone, "I have been often flogged myself."

"To be sure, of course," said Miss Murdstone.

"Certainly, my dear Jane," faltered my mother, meekly. "But—but do you think it did Edward good?"

"Do you think it did Edward harm, Clara?" asked Mr. Murdstone gravely.

"That's the point," said his sister.

To this my mother returned, "Certainly, my dear Jane," and said no more.

I felt apprehensive that I was personally interested in this dialogue, and sought Mr. Murdstone's eye as it lighted on mine.

"Now, David," he said—and I saw that cast again as he said it—"you must be far more careful today than usual." He gave the cane another poise, and another switch, and having finished his preparation of it, laid it down beside him, with an impressive look, and took up his book.

This was a good freshener to my presence of mind, as a beginning. I felt the words of my lessons slipping off, not one by one, or line by line, but by the entire page; I tried to lay hold of them, but they seemed, if I may so express it, to have put skates on, and to skim away from me with a smoothness there was no checking.

B We began badly, and went on worse. I had come in with an idea of distinguishing myself rather, conceiving that I was very well prepared, but it turned out to be quite a mistake. Book after book was added to the heap of failures, Miss Murdstone being firmly watchful of us all the time. And when we came at last to the five thousand cheeses (canes he made it that day, I remember), my mother burst out crying.

"Clara!" said Miss Murdstone, in her warning voice.

"I am not quite well, my dear Jane, I think," said my mother.

I saw him wink, solemnly, at his sister, as he rose and said, taking up the cane:

"Why, Jane, we can hardly expect Clara to bear, with perfect firmness, the worry and torment that David has occasioned her today. That would be stoical. Clara is greatly strengthened and improved, but we can hardly expect so much from her. David, you and I will go upstairs, boy."

As he took me out at the door, my mother ran toward us. Miss Murdstone said, "Clara! are you a perfect fool?" and interfered. I saw my mother stop her ears then, and I heard her crying.

He walked me up to my room slowly and gravely—I am certain he had a delight in that formal parade of executing justice—and when we got there, suddenly twisted my head under his arm.

"Mr. Murdstone! Sir!" I cried to him. "Don't! Pray don't beat me! I have tried to learn, sir, but I can't learn while you and Miss Murdstone are by. I can't indeed!"

"Can't you, indeed, David?" he said. "We'll try that."

He had my head as in a vise, but I twined round him somehow, and stopped him for a moment, entreating him not to beat me. It was only for a moment that I stopped him, for he cut me heavily an instant afterward, and in the same instant I caught the hand with which he held me in my mouth, between my teeth, and bit it through. It sets my teeth on edge to think of it.

C He beat me then, as if he would have beaten me to death. Above all the noise we made, I heard them running up the stairs, and crying out—I heard my mother crying out—and Peggotty. Then he was gone, and the door was locked outside, and I was lying, fevered and hot, and torn, and sore, and raging in my puny way, upon the floor.

How well I recollect, when I became quiet, what an unnatural stillness seemed to reign through the whole house! How well I remember, when my smart and passion began to cool, how wicked I began to feel!

I sat listening for a long while, but there was not a sound. I crawled up from the floor, and saw my face in the glass, so swollen, red, and ugly that it almost frightened me. My stripes were sore and stiff, and made me cry afresh when I moved, but they were nothing to the guilt I felt. It lay heavier on my breast than if I had been a most atrocious criminal, I daresay.

D It had begun to grow dark, and I had shut the window (I had been lying, for the most part, with my head upon the sill, by turns crying, dozing, and looking listlessly out), when the key was turned, and Miss Murdstone came in with some bread and meat and milk. These she put down upon the table without a word, glaring at me the while with exemplary firmness, and then retired, locking the door after her.

Long after it was dark I sat there, wondering whether anybody else would come. When this appeared improbable for that night, I undressed, and went to bed, and there I began to wonder fearfully

854

Share with students that using gerunds (verb forms that function as nouns) and participles (verb forms that function as adjectives) can provide variety in narrative writing. Point out Charles Dickens's use of *ringing, opening, shutting, murmuring, laughing, whistling,* and *singing* to offset his much more common use of the past tense below.

Have pairs or groups of students work together on the passage below to add gerunds and participles or to use them in place of some past-tense verbs. Later, have students share their improvements.

She was a happy child, who jumped and skipped most of the time when she might have walked, or ran when she more properly ought to have paced. In spite of our efforts to control her, however, she continued to hop, jump, prance, and leap down the sidewalk, much to the annoyance of her elders and the amusement of other children. Oddly enough, it was this very cheerfulness that caught John's eye as she cavorted one day down the churchyard walk. With a smile on his face, he called to his butler, "Bring that joyful child here!"

A

what would be done to me. Whether it was a criminal act that I had committed? Whether I should be taken into custody, and sent to prison? Whether I was at all in danger of being hanged?

I never shall forget the waking next morning, the being cheerful and fresh for the first moment, and then the being weighed down by the stale and dismal oppression of remembrance. Miss Murdstone reappeared before I was out of bed, told me, in so many words, that I was free to walk in the garden for half an hour and no longer, and retired, leaving the door open, that I might avail myself of that permission.

I did so, and did so every morning of my imprisonment, which lasted five days. If I could have seen my mother alone, I should have gone down on my knees to her and besought her forgiveness, but I saw no one, Miss Murdstone excepted, during the whole time, except at evening prayers in the parlor, to which I was escorted by Miss Murdstone after everybody else was placed, where I was stationed, a young outlaw, all alone by myself near the door, and whence I was solemnly conducted by my jailer, before anyone arose from the devotional posture. I only observed that my mother was as far off from me as she could be, and kept her face another way, so that I never saw it, and that Mr. Murdstone's hand was bound up in a large linen wrapper.

B

The length of those five days I can convey no idea of to anyone. They occupy the place of years in my remembrance. The way in which I listened to all the incidents of the house that made themselves audible to me: the ringing of bells, the opening and shutting of doors, the murmuring of voices, the footsteps on the stairs; to any laughing, whistling, or singing outside, which seemed more dismal than anything else to me in my solitude and disgrace; the uncertain pace of the hours, especially at night, when I would wake thinking it was morning, and find that the family were not yet gone to bed, and that all the length of night had yet to come; the depressed dreams and nightmares I had; the return of day, noon, afternoon, evening, when the boys played in the churchyard, and I watched them from a distance within the room, being ashamed to show myself at the window lest they should know I was a prisoner; the strange sensation of never hearing myself speak; the fleeting intervals of something like cheerfulness, which came with eating and drinking, and went away with it; the setting in of rain one evening, with a fresh smell, and its coming down faster and faster between me and the church, until it and gathering night seemed to quench me in gloom, and fear, and remorse—all this appears to have gone round and round for years instead of days, it is so vividly and strongly stamped on my remembrance.

On the last night of my restraint, I was awakened by hearing my own name spoken in a whisper. I started up in bed, and, putting out my arms in the dark, said:

"Is that you, Peggotty?"

There was no immediate answer, but presently I heard my name again, in a tone so very mysterious and awful, that I think I should have gone into a fit, if it had not occurred to me that it must have come through the keyhole.

I groped my way to the door, and, putting my own lips to the keyhole, whispered:

"Is that you, Peggotty, dear?"

"Yes, my own precious Davy," she replied. "Be as soft as a mouse, or the Cat'll hear us."

I understood this to mean Miss Murdstone, and was sensible of the urgency of the case, her room being close by.

"How's Mama, dear Peggotty? Is she very angry with me?"

I could hear Peggotty crying softly on her side of the keyhole, as I was doing on mine, before she answered. "No. Not very."

"What is going to be done with me, Peggotty dear? Do you know?"

"School. Near London," was Peggotty's answer. I was obliged to get her to repeat it, for she spoke it the first time quite down my throat, in consequence of my having forgotten to take my mouth away from the keyhole and put my ear there, and though her words tickled me a good deal, I didn't hear them.

"When, Peggotty?"

"Tomorrow."

"Is that the reason why Miss Murdstone took the clothes out of my drawers?" which she had done, though I have forgotten to mention it.

"Yes," said Peggotty. "Box."

"Shan't I see Mama?"

"Yes," said Peggotty. "Morning."

Then Peggotty fitted her mouth close to the keyhole, and delivered these words through it with as much feeling and earnestness as a keyhole has ever been the medium of communicating, I will venture to assert, shooting in each broken little sentence in a convulsive little burst of its own.

A. Characterization
Note the overdramatic thoughts typical of a child David's age.

B. Concrete Details
Examine this passage for vivid, concrete details that describe the feeling of imprisonment. (Possible answers: "the ringing of bells," "never hearing myself speak," "fleeting intervals of cheerfulness," and so on.)

Charles Dickens 855

Have students briefly summarize what happens in this chapter. Then ask each student to answer this question: Are the events that Dickens described dated, or could they still happen today? Explain.

ANALYZING THE CHAPTER
Identifying Facts
1. Students may mention any of the fol-lowing: David's bed is moved; Jane Murdstone arrives and takes control of the household; Peggotty no longer goes to church with David and his mother; the Murdstones preside over David's lessons.
2. Students should mention that the Murdstones make David so nervous he invariably forgets his lessons. David's mother does the teaching. At the end of each lesson, Mr. Murdstone poses a diffi-cult arithmetic problem David can't do.
3. She bursts into tears and runs toward David and Mr. Murdstone as they are leaving the room.

He entreats Mr. Murdstone not to beat him, and after the first blow bites Mr. Murdstone's hand.

A. Humanities Connection: Responding to the Illustration
Nineteenth-century British genre paint-er Gertrude De-main Hammond is best known for her watercolor draw-ings and paintings. Ask students to note the use of light and the color white in this painting.
? What mood is suggested by the scenes in the room and outside the window? (The mood is sentimen-tal, nostalgic.) Note that David is a very young child here. The illustra-tion is of an earlier chapter in the hap-py days before David's mother married Mr. Murdstone.

B. Character
Throughout the novel, Peggotty is portrayed as com-pletely good—a warm and loving force in David's life. Peggotty's dia-lect is that of Yar-mouth, a fishing village about 110 miles north of London.

A

Illustration for *David Copperfield* by Gertrude Demain Hammond.   © Harrap, Ltd., London.

B

''Davy, dear. If I ain't been azackly as intimate with you. Lately, as I used to be. It ain't because I don't love you. Just as well and more, my pretty poppet. It's because I thought it better for you. And for someone else besides. Davy, my darling, are you listening? Can you hear?''

''Ye—ye—ye—yes, Peggotty!'' I sobbed.

''My own!'' said Peggotty, with infinite com-passion. ''What I want to say, is. That you must never forget me. For I'll never forget you. And I'll take as much care of your mama, Davy. As ever I took of you. And I won't leave her. The day may come when she'll be glad to lay her poor head. On her stupid, cross, old Peggotty's arm again. And I'll write to you, my dear. Though I ain't no scholar. And I'll—I'll——'' Peggotty fell to kissing the keyhole, as she couldn't kiss me.

''Thank you, dear Peggotty!'' said I. ''Oh, thank you! Thank you! Will you promise me one thing, Peggotty? Will you write and tell Mr. Peg-gotty and little Em'ly, and Mrs. Gummidge and Ham, that I am not so bad as they might suppose, and that I sent 'em my love—especially to little Em'ly? Will you, if you please, Peggotty?''

The kind soul promised, and we both of us kissed the keyhole with the greatest affection—I patted it with my hand, I recollect, as if it had been her honest face—and parted. From that night there grew up in my breast a feeling for Peggotty which I cannot very well define. She did not re-place my mother—no one could do that—but she came into a vacancy in my heart, which closed upon her, and I felt towards her something I have never felt for any other human being. It was a sort of comical affection, too, and yet if she had died, I cannot think what I should have done, or how I should have acted out the tragedy it would have been to me.

Only one new character (Jane Murdstone) is introduced in this chapter, and Dickens describes her appearance in detail. Dickens doesn't use direct characterization in this chapter: He develops his characters by telling what they say and do (or don't do) and letting us draw our own conclusions.

5. The first-person narrator is the adult David Copperfield, looking back at his life. This point of view makes us feel much sympathy for young David. We are limited, however, by not being able to know the thoughts, feelings, and motivations of other characters.

6. Student opinions will vary. The Murdstones seem to be total villains with no redeeming qualities at all. Like many of Dickens's characters, they seem simply to have been born horrible.

In the morning Miss Murdstone appeared as usual, and told me I was going to school, which was not altogether such news to me as she supposed. She also informed me that when I was dressed, I was to come downstairs into the parlor, and have my breakfast. There I found my mother, very pale and with red eyes, into whose arms I ran, and begged her pardon from my suffering soul.

"Oh, Davy!" she said. "That you could hurt anyone I love! Try to be better, pray to be better! I forgive you, but I am so grieved, Davy, that you should have such bad passions in your heart."

They had persuaded her that I was a wicked fellow, and she was more sorry for that than for my going away. I felt it sorely. I tried to eat my parting breakfast, but my tears dropped upon my bread and butter, and trickled into my tea. I saw my mother look at me sometimes, and then glance at the watchful Miss Murdstone, and then look down, or look away.

"Master Copperfield's box there!" said Miss Murdstone, when wheels were heard at the gate.

I looked for Peggotty, but it was not she; neither she nor Mr. Murdstone appeared. My former acquaintance, the carrier, was at the door; the box was taken out to his cart, and lifted in.

"Clara!" said Miss Murdstone, in her warning note.

"Ready, my dear Jane," returned my mother. "Goodbye, Davy. You are going for your own good. Goodbye, my child. You will come home in the holidays, and be a better boy"

"Clara!" Miss Murdstone repeated.

"Certainly, my dear Jane," replied my mother, who was holding me. "I forgive you, my dear boy. God bless you!"

"Clara!" Miss Murdstone repeated.

Miss Murdstone was good enough to take me out to the cart, and to say on the way that she hoped I would repent, before I came to a bad end, and then I got into the cart, and the lazy horse walked off with it.

A. Oral Reading
Suggest that students act out this final scene or read it aloud, taking parts. Have students discuss the irony and pathos in this scene.

Responding to the Chapter

Analyzing the Chapter

Identifying Facts

1. Name several changes that occur in the household as a result of Clara Copperfield's marriage to Mr. Murdstone.
2. Describe a typical lesson for David.
3. How does David's mother respond when Mr. Murdstone is about to flog David? What does David do?

Interpreting Meanings

4. By the end of Chapter 4, how do you feel about each of the following characters: David's mother, Peggotty, Mr. Murdstone, Jane Murdstone? How has Dickens managed to make you feel this way? (Discuss the **images** associated with each character as well as Dickens's methods of **characterization**.)
5. Discuss the advantages and disadvantages of the **point of view** Dickens uses for this novel. How does Dickens overcome the limitations of a child-narrator?
6. Why do you think the Murdstones are so insensitive to David? Are they simply hard and cruel people, or is there some additional reason for their behavior toward him? Do you find their types in the world today?

Writing About the Chapter

A Creative Response

1. **Predicting Outcomes.** What kind of school do you think the Murdstones have selected for David, and what will happen to him there? Write a synopsis of a short episode during David's first week at school.

A Critical Response

2. **Analyzing Character.** Write a brief character sketch of either David's mother or Mr. Murdstone. Identify two character traits, and support each trait by referring to specific incidents in the novel.

A. Expansion
Remind students
that England con-
solidated its rule
over India in the
eighteenth century.
The vast subconti-
nent remained a
British possession
until it achieved in-
dependence in
1947.

B. Ambiguity
In his fascination
for the ambiguities
of empire, Kipling
foreshadowed
such writers as Jo-
seph Conrad (see
text page 921) and
E. M. Forster,
whose novel *A
Passage to India*
(1924) remains
one of the most
moving treatments
of the subject.

C. Expansion
While this view
might seem pater-
nalistic today, it
was liberal for its
time.

**FOR FURTHER
READING
STUDENTS**
Students who like
this story might
enjoy *Plain Tales
from the Hills*
(1888) or other
anthologies of
Kipling's stories.
He was a poet as
well. Students
might sample
"Recessional,"
"Gunga Din," and
"Mandalay."

Rudyard Kipling (1865–1936)

A Rudyard Kipling was born in Bombay, India,
where his father was a professor at the University of Bombay. Since it was customary for
Anglo-Indians (English citizens living in India) to
send their children home for their education, the
six-year-old Kipling and his sister were left in
the care of foster parents in England. Kipling recalled some of the unhappiness and rebelliousness of his school years in a novel called *Stalky
& Co.* (1899).

At seventeen, Kipling returned to India to
work as a journalist on a newspaper in Lahore.
He quickly became popular for his stories,
sketches, and poems that were published in
newspapers and then collected in cheap editions
sold at Indian railroad stations. His books were
distributed in England as well, preparing the way
for his return to England as a writer in 1889.
Barrack-Room Ballads (1892), his first collection
of poems published in England, went into three
editions in its first year, and fifty more editions
were published during the next thirty years. By
the end of Queen Victoria's reign, Kipling had
become the most popular British poet since Tennyson, and the most popular prose writer since
Dickens. Kipling's popularity and public influence can be attributed in part to his strong en-
dorsement of the British Empire.

B But Kipling's ideas about Empire were not
simple. He was fascinated by the contrast and
conflict of European civilization with the ancient
cultures of the strange places into which it intruded. This conflict is the theme of many of his

Rudyard Kipling by Philip Burne-Jones (1899). Oil.

Indian stories, beginning with *Plain Tales from
the Hills* (1888) and continuing in *Kim* (1901), his
novel about a British boy submerged in the mystery of India. Kipling did not always see European culture as superior, and he also knew that
empires fall. He urged readers not to trust in
guns to justify their dominion over large parts of
the earth. The purpose of the British Empire, he
cautioned, was not to make the imperial nation
rich, but rather to extend British efficiency, decency, and comfort throughout the world. C

In 1907, Kipling became the first British
writer to win the Nobel Prize in literature.

1. BUILDING ON PRIOR KNOWLEDGE. Before students begin reading, ask for volunteers to share with the class what they know about the geography, religion, customs, and culture of India.

2. ESTABLISHING A PURPOSE. Remind students that Kipling's story is a fable in the sense that it teaches a moral, or lesson about life. Ask students to read to identify the moral that might also be called the story's theme.

3. PREREADING JOURNAL. Before they read, have students write two or three sentences in their journals about how they regard the notions of self-sacrifice and self-denial.

THE MIRACLE OF PURUN BHAGAT

This story first appeared in Kipling's second series of *The Jungle Books* (1894, 1895), stories for young readers. The story is full of instruction about Indian ways and words. It is also a very sophisticated fable about Kipling's recurrent theme: the difference between East and West, and the value of each culture.

A

B

A. Fable
Discuss with students the definition of a fable as a brief story that teaches a moral or lesson about life.

B. Responding to the Photograph
[?] What are some of the exotic elements in the photograph? (The ornate chair, the turban on the man's head, his jewelry) What seem to be the emotions of the ruler who is pictured? (He looks tense and perhaps anxious.)

Rudyard Kipling 859

859

SUPPLEMENTARY SUPPORT MATERIALS
1. Vocabulary Activity Worksheet (CCB)
2. Review and Response Worksheet: Theme (CCB)
3. Language Skills Worksheet: Prepositions and Prepositional Phrases (CCB)
4. Selection Test (CCB)

DEVELOPING VOCABULARY
The following words from the fable are tested in the Selection Test. (See also Vocabulary Activity Worksheet.)

caste	flue
subordinate	caress
bastion	haunch
lionized	plashy
shrine	brethren

A. Fable
The opening line is a variation on the typical beginning of a fable or fairy tale: "Once upon a time . . ."

B. Caste
Point out to students that the notion of inherited caste, so foreign to American democracy, has for centuries played a powerful role in Indian culture. Although caste distinctions were officially abolished by the Indian Constitution after independence, caste continues to affect village life.

C. Connections
Compare this narrative about "progress" with Macaulay's comments on progress in England (see "London Streets," text page 774).

D. Expansion
The viceroy was the highest British official in the colony. The last viceroy of India was Count Earl Mountbatten, who presided over the difficult transition to independence and the partitioning of India and Pakistan.

A
B

There was once a man in India who was Prime Minister of one of the semi-independent native States[1] in the northwestern part of the country. He was a Brahmin,[2] so high-caste that caste ceased to have any particular meaning for him; and his father had been an important official in the gay-colored tag-rag and bobtail of an old-fashioned Hindu Court. But as Purun Dass grew up he felt that the old order of things was changing, and that if anyone wished to get on in the world he must stand well with the English, and imitate all that the English believed to be good. At the same time a native official must keep his own master's favor. This was a difficult game, but the quiet, close-mouthed young Brahmin, helped by a good English education at a Bombay University, played it coolly, and rose, step by step, to be Prime Minister of the kingdom. That is to say, he held more power than his master, the Maharajah.

When the old king—who was suspicious of the English, their railways and telegraphs—died, Purun Dass stood high with his young successor, who had been tutored by an Englishman; and between them, though he always took care that his master should have the credit, they established schools for little girls, made roads, and started State dispensaries and shows of agricultural implements, and published a yearly blue book[3] on the "Moral and Material Progress of the State," and the Foreign Office and the Government of India were delighted. Very few native States take up English progress altogether, for they will not believe, as Purun Dass showed he did, that what was good for the Englishman must be twice as good for the Asiatic. The Prime Minister became the honored friend of Viceroys and Governors, and Lieutenant-Governors, and medical missionaries, and common missionaries, and hard-riding English officers who came to shoot in the State preserves, as well as of whole hosts of tourists who traveled up and down India in the cold weather, showing how things ought to be managed. In his spare time he would endow scholarships for the study of

C

medicine and manufactures on strictly English lines, and write letters to the *Pioneer,* the greatest Indian daily paper, explaining his master's aims and objects.

At last he went to England on a visit, and had to pay enormous sums to the priests when he came back; for even so high-caste a Brahmin as Purun Dass lost caste[4] by crossing the black sea. In London he met and talked with everyone worth knowing—men whose names go all over the world—and saw a great deal more than he said. He was given honorary degrees by learned universities, and he made speeches and talked of Hindu social reform to English ladies in evening dress, till all London cried, "This is the most fascinating man we have ever met at dinner since cloths were first laid."

When he returned to India there was a blaze of glory, for the Viceroy himself made a special visit to confer upon the Maharajah the Grand Cross of the Star of India—all diamonds and ribbons and enamel; and at the same ceremony, while the cannon boomed, Purun Dass was made a Knight Commander of the Order of the Indian Empire; so that his name stood Sir Purun Dass, K.C.I.E.

D

That evening, at dinner in the big Viceregal tent, he stood up with the badge and the collar of the Order on his breast, and replying to the toast of his master's health, made a speech few Englishmen could have bettered.

Next month, when the city had returned to its sun-baked quiet, he did a thing no Englishman would have dreamed of doing; for, so far as the world's affairs went, he died. The jeweled order of his knighthood went back to the Indian Government, and a new Prime Minister was appointed to the charge of affairs, and a great game of General Post began in all the subordinate appointments. The priests knew what had happened and the people guessed; but India is the one place in the world where a man can do as he pleases and nobody asks why; and the fact that Dewan Sir Purun Dass, K.C.I.E., had resigned position, palace, and power, and taken up the begging-bowl

1. **native States:** Some former states remained under the rule of their hereditary kings, but the British imperial government appointed a political officer to advise each state, and the states were subject to certain restrictions.
2. **Brahmin:** a member of the priestly Hindu caste (inherited social class), which is the highest.
3. **blue book:** The British Parliament's reports on social and economic matters were bound in blue covers.

4. **lost caste:** lost status by defiling oneself with people and interests outside those of one's own caste.

Share with students that although a subordinate clause is not the most important clause in a sentence, the details it can add to an independent clause often make the difference between boring and interesting prose. Point out the details that the subordinate clauses at the top of the first column on this page add to their main clauses. Discuss what the resulting sentences would have lost without them.

Have students use **Grammar, Usage, and Mechanics: A Reference Guide** to review the kinds of subordinate clauses. Then ask volunteers to add details in subordinate clauses to the following sentences.

1. Purun Bhagat believed (noun clause).
2. (Adverbial clause telling *when*), he felt no sense of loss.
3. Purun Bhagat felt a oneness with the universe (adverbial clause beginning with *since* + noun clause beginning with *that*).
4. The holy man (adjectival clause beginning with *who*) was well loved by all.
5. Purun Bhagat's miracle was (noun clause beginning with *that*).

---

and ocher-colored dress of a Sunnyasi or holy man, was considered nothing extraordinary. He had been as the Old Law[5] recommends, twenty years a youth, twenty years a fighter—though he had never carried a weapon in his life—and twenty years head of a household. He had used his wealth and his power for what he knew both to be worth; he had taken honor when it came his way; he had seen men and cities far and near, and men and cities had stood up and honored him. Now he would let these things go, as a man drops the cloak he no longer needs.

Behind him, as he walked through the city gates, an antelope skin and brass-handled crutch under his arm, and a begging-bowl of polished brown *coco-de-mer*[6] in his hand, barefoot, alone, with eyes cast on the ground—behind him they were firing salutes from the bastions in honor of his happy successor. Purun Dass nodded. All that life was ended; and he bore it no more ill will or good will than a man bears to a colorless dream of the night. He was a Sunnyasi—a houseless wandering mendicant, depending on his neighbors for his daily bread; and so long as there is a morsel to divide in India neither priest nor beggar starves. He had never in his life tasted meat, and very seldom eaten even fish. A five-pound note would have covered his personal expenses for food through any one of the many years in which he had been absolute master of millions of money. Even when he was being lionized in London he had held before him his dream of peace and quiet—the long, white, dusty Indian road, printed all over with bare feet, the incessant, slow-moving traffic, and the sharp-smelling wood smoke curling up under the fig trees in the twilight, where the wayfarers sit at their evening meal.

When the time came to make that dream true the Prime Minister took the proper steps, and in three days you might more easily have found a bubble in the trough of the long Atlantic seas than Purun Dass among the roving, gathering, separating millions of India.

At night his antelope skin was spread where the darkness overtook him—sometimes in a Sunnyasi monastery by the roadside; sometimes by a mud pillar shrine of Kala[7] Pir, where the Jogis, who are another misty division of holy men, would receive him as they do those who know what castes and divisions are worth; sometimes on the outskirts of a little Hindu village, where the children would steal up with the food their parents had prepared; and sometimes on the pitch of the bare grazing-grounds, where the flame of his stick fire waked the drowsy camels. It was all one to Purun Dass—or Purun Bhagat,[8] as he called himself now. Earth, people, and food were all one. But unconsciously his feet drew him away northward and eastward; from the south to Rohtak; from Rohtak to Kurnool; from Kurnool to ruined Samanah, and then upstream along the dried bed of the Gugger River that fills only when the rain falls in the hills, till one day he saw the far line of the great Himalayas.

Then Purun Bhagat smiled, for he remembered that his mother was of Rajput Brahmin birth, from Kulu way—a Hill woman, always homesick for the snows—and that the least touch of Hill blood draws a man at the end back to where he belongs.

"Yonder," said Purun Bhagat, breasting the lower slopes of the Sewaliks, where the cacti stand up like seven-branched candlesticks—"yonder I shall sit down and get knowledge"; and the cool wind of the Himalayas whistled about his ears as he trod the road that led to Simla.

The last time he had come that way it had been in state, with a clattering cavalry escort, to visit the gentlest and most affable of Viceroys; and the two had talked for an hour together about mutual friends in London, and what the Indian common folk really thought of things. This time Purun Bhagat paid no calls, but leaned on the rail of the Mall, watching that glorious view of the Plains spread out forty miles below, till a native Mohammedan[9] policeman told him he was obstructing traffic; and Purun Bhagat salaamed[10] reverently to the Law, because he knew the value of it, and was seeking for a Law of his own. Then he moved on, and slept that night in an empty hut at Chota Simla, which looks like the very last end of the earth, but it was only the beginning of his journey.

He followed the Himalaya-Tibet road, the little ten-foot track that is blasted out of solid rock, or strutted out on timbers over gulfs a thousand feet

---

A

B

A. Sensory Details

? Cite the sensory details Kipling uses to create a vivid image of the setting. ("Long, white, dusty Indian road, printed all over with bare feet," "the incessant, slow-moving traffic," "sharp-smelling wood smoke curling up under the fig trees in the twilight," and so on)

B. Characterization

Note the portrayal of Purun Bhagat as a quester.

? What "law" do you think Purun Bhagat is seeking? (A "law" that will show him how to live the remainder of his life)

---

5. **Old Law:** a code of behavior for Brahmins.
6. *coco-de-mer:* sea coconut.
7. **Kala** (Hindi): time. Kipling is preparing for Purun Bhagat's service to the goddess Kali, who symbolizes eternal time in which life is given and destroyed.

8. **Bhagat:** a Hindu holy person or saint.
9. **Mohammedan:** member of the Moslem religion.
10. **salaamed:** bowed low with the right palm to the forehead, a gesture of respect.

A. Simile

Notice that Kipling earlier mentioned railways as one of the "foreign" improvements made by the English in India (see text page 860).

B. Interpreting

❓ Why do you think that Purun Bhagat chose this particular place to settle? (Unlike the lodgings he had been accustomed to, this place is uncluttered and simple, and will not be a distraction as he seeks his new "law.")

deep; that dips into warm, wet, shut-in valleys, and climbs out across bare, grassy hill-shoulders where the sun strikes like a burning-glass; or turns through dripping, dark forests where the tree ferns dress the trunks from head to heel, and the pheasant calls to his mate. And he met Tibetan herdsmen with their dogs and flocks of sheep, each sheep with a little bag of borax on his back, and wandering wood-cutters, and cloaked and blanketed Lamas[11] from Tibet, coming into India on pilgrimage, and envoys of little solitary Hill states, posting furiously on ring-streaked and piebald ponies, or the cavalcade of a Rajah paying a visit; or else for a long, clear day he would see nothing more than a black bear grunting and rooting below

A in the valley. When he first started, the roar of the world he had left still rang in his ears, as the roar of a tunnel rings long after the train has passed through; but when he had put the Mutteeanee Pass behind him that was all done, and Purun Bhagat was alone with himself, walking, wondering, and thinking, his eyes on the ground, and his thoughts with the clouds.

One evening he crossed the highest pass he had met till then—it had been a two days' climb—and came out on a line of snowpeaks that banded all the horizon—mountains from fifteen to twenty thousand feet high, looking almost near enough to hit with a stone, though they were fifty or sixty miles away. The pass was crowned with dense, dark forest—deodar, walnut, wild cherry, wild olive, and wild pear, but mostly deodar, which is the Himalayan cedar; and under the shadow of the deodars stood a deserted shrine to Kali[12]— who is Durga, who is Sitala, who is sometimes worshiped against the smallpox.

B Purun Dass swept the stone floor clean, smiled at the grinning statue, made himself a little mud fireplace at the back of the shrine, spread his antelope skin on a bed of fresh pine-needles, tucked his *bairagi*—his brass-handled crutch—under his armpit, and sat down to rest.

Immediately below him the hillside fell away, clean and cleared for fifteen hundred feet, where a little village of stone-walled houses, with roofs of beaten earth, clung to the steep tilt. All round it the tiny terraced fields lay out like aprons of patchwork on the knees of the mountain, and

cows no bigger than beetles grazed between the smooth stone circles of the threshing floors. Looking across the valley, the eye was deceived by the size of things, and could not at first realize that what seemed to be low scrub, on the opposite mountain flank, was in truth a forest of hundred-foot pines. Purun Bhagat saw an eagle swoop across the gigantic hollow, but the great bird dwindled to a dot ere it was halfway over. A few bands of scattered clouds strung up and down the valley, catching on a shoulder of the hills, or rising up and dying out when they were level with the head of the pass. And "Here shall I find peace," said Purun Bhagat.

Now, a Hill man makes nothing of a few hundred feet up or down, and as soon as the villagers saw the smoke in the deserted shrine, the village priest climbed up the terraced hillside to welcome the stranger.

When he met Purun Bhagat's eyes—the eyes of a man used to control thousands—he bowed to the earth, took the begging bowl without a word, and returned to the village, saying, "We have at last a holy man. Never have I seen such a man. He is of the Plains—but pale-colored—a Brahmin of the Brahmins." Then all the housewives of the village said, "Think you he will stay with us?" and each did her best to cook the most savory meal for the Bhagat. Hill food is very simple, but with buckwheat and Indian corn, and rice and red pepper, the little fish out of the stream in the valley, and honey from the flue-like hives built in the stone walls, and dried apricots, and turmeric, and wild ginger, and bannocks[13] of flour, a devout woman can make good things, and it was a full bowl that the priest carried to the Bhagat. Was he going to stay? asked the priest. Would he need a *chela*—a disciple—to beg for him? Had he a blanket against the cold weather? Was the food good?

Purun Bhagat ate, and thanked the giver. It was in his mind to stay. That was sufficient, said the priest. Let the begging bowl be placed outside the shrine, in the hollow made by those two twisted roots, and daily should the Bhagat be fed; for the village felt honored that such a man—he looked timidly into the Bhagat's face—should tarry among them.

That day saw the end of Purun Bhagat's wan-

---

11. **Lamas:** Tibetan priests or monks.
12. **Kali:** a Hindu goddess, viewed both as destroying life and as giving it.

13. **bannocks:** loaves.

derings. He had come to the place appointed for him—the silence and the space. After this, time stopped, and he, sitting at the mouth of the shrine, could not tell whether he were alive or dead; a man with control of his limbs, or a part of the hills, and the clouds, and the shifting rain and sunlight. He would repeat a Name softly to himself a hundred hundred times, till, at each repetition, he seemed to move more and more out of his body, sweeping up to the doors of some tremendous discovery; but, just as the door was opening, his body would drag him back, and, with grief, he felt he was locked up again in the flesh and bones of Purun Bhagat.

Every morning the filled begging bowl was laid silently in the crutch of the roots outside the shrine. Sometimes the priest brought it; sometimes a Ladakhi trader, lodging in the village, and anxious to get merit, trudged up the path; but, more often, it was the woman who had cooked the meal overnight; and she would murmur, hardly above her breath: "Speak for me before the gods, Bhagat. Speak for such a one, the wife of so-and-so!" Now and then some bold child would be allowed the honor, and Purun Bhagat would hear him drop the bowl and run as fast as his little legs could carry him, but the Bhagat never came down to the village. It was laid out like a map at his feet. He could see the evening gatherings, held on the circle of the threshing floors because that was the only level ground; could see the wonderful unnamed green of the young rice, the indigo blues of the Indian corn, the docklike patches of buckwheat, and, in its season, the red bloom of the amaranth, whose tiny seeds, being neither grain nor pulse,[14] make a food that can be lawfully eaten by Hindus in time of fasts.

When the year turned, the roofs of the huts were all little squares of purest gold, for it was on the roofs that they laid out their cobs of the corn to dry. Hiving and harvest, rice-sowing and husking, passed before his eyes, all embroidered down there on the many-sided plots of fields, and he thought of them all, and wondered what they all led to at the long last.

Even in populated India a man cannot a day sit still before the wild things run over him as though he were a rock; and in that wilderness very soon the wild things, who knew Kali's Shrine well,

came back to look at the intruder. The *langurs,* the big gray-whiskered monkeys of the Himalayas, were, naturally, the first, for they are alive with curiosity; and when they had upset the begging bowl, and rolled it round the floor, and tried their teeth on the brass-handled crutch, and made faces at the antelope skin, they decided that the human being who sat so still was harmless. At evening, they would leap down from the pines, and beg with their hands for things to eat, and then swing off in graceful curves. They liked the warmth of the fire, too, and huddled round it till Purun Bhagat had to push them aside to throw on more fuel; and in the morning, as often as not, he would find a furry ape sharing his blanket. All day long, one or other of the tribe would sit by his side, staring out at the snows, crooning and looking unspeakably wise and sorrowful.

After the monkeys came the *barasingh,* that big deer which is like our red deer, but stronger. He wished to rub off the velvet of his horns against the cold stones of Kali's statue, and stamped his feet when he saw the man at the shrine. But Purun Bhagat never moved, and, little by little, the royal stag edged up and nuzzled his shoulder. Purun Bhagat slid one cool hand along the hot antlers, and the touch soothed the fretted beast, who bowed his head, and Purun Bhagat very softly rubbed and raveled off the velvet. Afterward, the *barasingh* brought his doe and fawn—gentle things that mumbled on the holy man's blanket—or would come alone at night, his eyes green in the fire-flicker, to take his share of fresh walnuts. At last, the musk deer, the shyest and almost the smallest of the deerlets, came, too, her big rabbity ears erect; even brindled, silent *mushick-nabha* must needs find out what the light in the shrine meant, and drop her mooselike nose into Purun Bhagat's lap, coming and going with the shadows of the fire. Purun Bhagat called them all "my brothers," and his low call of *"Bhai! Bhai!"* would draw them from the forest at noon if they were within earshot. The Himalayan black bear, moody and suspicious—Sona, who has the V-shaped white mark under his chin—passed that way more than once; and since the Bhagat showed no fear, Sona showed no anger, but watched him, and came closer, and begged a share of the caresses, and a dole of bread or wild berries. Often, in the still dawns, when the Bhagat would climb to the very crest of the pass to watch the red day walking along the peaks of the snows, he would find Sona

---

14. **pulse:** edible seeds, such as peas and beans, of plants with pods.

A. Interpreting
You may want to tell students that the repetition of a name or phrase (called a *mantra*) is an important element of Hindu mysticism.

What do you think may be the "tremendous discovery" that Purun Bhagat is seeking? (Perhaps spiritual enlightenment, or a oneness with the universe)

B. Theme
Purun Bhagat's harmony with the universe is exemplified in his relationship with these animals. He calls them "brother," and even the shyest become his friends.

READING CHECK TEST
1. Purun Dass retains his wealth and position when he becomes a Sunnyasi holy man. (F)
2. Purun Bhagat ends his wandering in a big city in southern India. (F)
3. Purun Bhagat becomes "brothers" with various wild beasts, including a huge bear. (T)

4. One night Purun Bhagat saves all the villagers from being killed in a land-slide. (T)
5. After his death, the villagers finally learn the true identity of their "saint." (F)

CLOSURE
Note that Purun Bhagat is an Eastern hero and that our concept of hero comes from Western literature. Ask students to list two ways in which Purun Bhagat resembles a typical Western hero (he is brave; he is on a quest) and two ways in which he is different (his goal is spiritual enlightenment; he completely withdraws from the world).

A. Responding

? What do you think of this statement? How would you define a "miracle"? Do you think miracles are possible in today's world? (Students may suggest that all of life is a miracle. Miracles sometimes can be defined in ways that are not necessarily supernatural. The peace that lifelong enemies ultimately forge can be considered a miracle.)

B. Style/Theme
Notice how the style and details in this passage serve almost to obliterate the concept of time.

? What connection might there be between "time-lessness" and the theme of this fable? (To achieve true enlightenment, human beings must free them-selves—at least mentally—from the possessions, ambition, and the pres-sures of human society. All of these are involved in "human time," as distinguished from the "natural time" of the pass-ing days, seasons, and years.)

shuffling and grunting at his heels, thrusting a cu-rious forepaw under fallen trunks, and bringing it away with a *whoof* of impatience; or his early steps would wake Sona where he lay curled up, and the great brute, rising erect, would think to fight, till he heard the Bhagat's voice and knew his best friend.

Nearly all hermits and holy men who live apart from the big cities have the reputation of being able to work miracles with the wild things, but all the miracle lies in keeping still, in never making a hasty movement, and, for a long time, at least, in never looking directly at a visitor. The villagers saw the outline of the *barasingh* stalking like a shadow through the dark forest behind the shrine; saw the *minaul,* the Himalayan pheasant, blazing in her best colors before Kali's statue; and the *langurs* on their haunches, inside, playing with the walnut shells. Some of the children, too, had heard Sona singing to himself, bear-fashion, be-hind the fallen rocks, and the Bhagat's reputation as a miracle-worker stood firm.

A Yet nothing was further from his mind than miracles. He believed that all things were one big Miracle, and when a man knows that much he knows something to go upon. He knew for a cer-tainty that there was nothing great and nothing little in this world; and day and night he strove to think out his way into the heart of things, back to the place whence his soul had come.

B So thinking, his untrimmed hair fell down about his shoulders, the stone slab at the side of the antelope skin was dented into a little hole by the foot of his brass-handled crutch, and the place between the tree trunks, where the begging bowl rested day after day, sunk and wore into a hollow almost as smooth as the brown shell itself; and each beast knew his exact place at the fire. The fields changed their colors with the seasons; the threshing floors filled and emptied, and filled again and again; and again and again, when winter came, the *langurs* frisked among the branches feathered with light snow, till the mother-monkeys brought their sad-eyed little babies up from the warmer valleys with the spring. There were few changes in the village. The priest was older, and many of the little children who used to come with the beg-ging dish sent their own children now; and when you asked of the villagers how long their holy man had lived in Kali's Shrine at the head of the pass, they answered, "Always."

Then came such summer rains as had not been known in the Hills for many seasons. Through three good months the valley was wrapped in cloud and soaking mist—steady, unrelenting downfall, breaking off into thundershower after thundershower. Kali's Shrine stood above the clouds, for the most part, and there was a whole month in which the Bhagat never saw his village. It was packed away under a white floor of cloud that swayed and shifted and rolled on itself and bulged upward, but never broke from its piers—the streaming flanks of the valley.

All that time he heard nothing but the sound of a million little waters, overhead from the trees, and underfoot along the ground, soaking through the pine needles, dripping from the tongues of draggled fern, and spouting in newly torn muddy channels down the slopes. Then the sun came out, and drew forth the good incense of the deodars and the rhododendrons, and that far-off, clean smell which the Hill people call "the smell of the snows." The hot sunshine lasted for a week, and then the rains gathered together for their last downpour, and the water fell in sheets that flayed off the skin of the ground and leaped back in mud. Purun Bhagat heaped his fire high that night, for he was sure his brothers would need warmth; but never a beast came to the shrine, though he called and called till he dropped asleep, wondering what had happened in the woods.

It was in the black heart of the night, the rain drumming like a thousand drums, that he was roused by a plucking at his blanket, and, stretch-ing out, felt the little hand of a *langur.* "It is better here than in the trees," he said sleepily, loosening a fold of blanket; "take it and be warm." The monkey caught his hand and pulled hard. "Is it food, then?" said Purun Bhagat. "Wait a while, and I will prepare some." As he kneeled to throw fuel on the fire the *langur* ran to the door of the shrine, crooned, and ran back again, plucking at the man's knee.

"What is it? What is thy trouble, Brother?" said Purun Bhagat, for the *langur's* eyes were full of things that he could not tell. "Unless one of thy caste be in a trap—and none set traps here—I will not go into that weather. Look, Brother, even the *barasingh* comes for shelter!"

The deer's antlers clashed as he strode into the shrine, clashed against the grinning statue of Kali. He lowered them in Purun Bhagat's direction and

ANALYZING THE STORY
Identifying Facts
1. He establishes schools for little girls, builds roads, opens health clinics, exhibits agricultural tools, endows scholarships.
2. *Langurs*, gray-whiskered monkeys; *barasingh*, red deer; *mushick-nabha*, musk deer; *Sona*, a black bear; *minaul*, pheasants.

3. A monkey wakes him and pulls his hand. A deer pushes him toward the door just before the floor gives way.
4. Brahmin, Sunnyasi, *coco-de-mer*, Bhagat, *bairagi*, *chela*, *langurs*, *bara-singh*, *mushick-nabha*, *minaul*, Bhai! Bhai!

Interpreting Meanings
5. The miracle is the holy man's saving

all of the villagers' lives. Students may name other miracles: that Purun Bhagat dies in the very attitude in which Sunnyasis must be buried; that he can communicate with the animals; that he transforms himself so completely.
6. Student answers will vary, and some may even disagree with the statement.
7. His mother was from the hill country, *(Answers continue on next page.)*

stamped uneasily, hissing through his half-shut nostrils.

"Hai! Hai! Hai!" said the Bhagat, snapping his fingers. "Is *this* payment for a night's lodging?" But the deer pushed him toward the door, and as he did so Purun Bhagat heard the sound of something opening with a sigh, and saw two slabs of the floor draw away from each other, while the sticky earth below smacked its lips.

"Now I see," said Purun Bhagat. "No blame to my brothers that they did not sit by the fire tonight. The mountain is falling. And yet—why should I go?" His eye fell on the empty begging bowl, and his face changed. "They have given me good food daily since—since I came, and, if I am not swift, tomorrow there will not be one mouth in the valley. Indeed, I must go and warn them below. Back there, Brother! Let me get to the fire."

The *barasingh* backed unwillingly as Purun Bhagat drove a pine torch deep into the flame, twirling it till it was well lit. "Ah! ye came to warn me," he said, rising. "Better than that we shall do; better than that. Out, now, and lend me thy neck, Brother, for I have but two feet."

He clutched the bristling withers of the *bara-singh* with his right hand, held the torch away with his left, and stepped out of the shrine into the desperate night. There was no breath of wind, but the rain nearly drowned the flare as the great deer hurried down the slope, sliding on his haunches. As soon as they were clear of the forest more of the Bhagat's brothers joined them. He heard, though he could not see, the *langurs* pressing about him, and behind him the *uhh! uhh!* of Sona. The rain matted his long white hair into ropes; the water splashed beneath his bare feet, and his yellow robe clung to his frail old body, but he stepped down steadily, leaning against the *bara-singh*. He was no longer a holy man, but Sir Purun Das, K.C.I.E., Prime Minister of no small State, a man accustomed to command, going out to save life. Down the steep, plashy path they poured all together, the Bhagat and his brothers, down and down, till the deer's feet clicked and stumbled on the wall of a threshing floor, and he snorted because he smelt Man. Now they were at the head of the one crooked village street, and the Bhagat beat with his crutch on the barred windows of the blacksmith's house as his torch blazed up in the shelter of the eaves. "Up and out!" cried Purun

Bhagat; and he did not know his own voice, for it was years since he had spoken aloud to a man. "The hill falls! The hill is falling! Up and out, oh, you within!"

"It is our Bhagat," said the blacksmith's wife. "He stands among his beasts. Gather the little ones and give the call."

It ran from house to house, while the beasts, cramped in the narrow way, surged and huddled round the Bhagat, and Sona puffed impatiently.

The people hurried into the street—they were no more than seventy souls all told—and in the glare of the torches they saw their Bhagat holding back the terrified *barasingh,* while the monkeys plucked piteously at his skirts, and Sona sat on his haunches and roared.

"Across the valley and up the next hill!" shouted Purun Bhagat. "Leave none behind! We follow!"

Then the people ran as only Hill folk can run, for they knew that in a landslip you must climb for the highest ground across the valley. They fled, splashing through the little river at the bottom, and panted up the terraced fields on the far side, while the Bhagat and his brethren followed. Up and up the opposite mountain they climbed, calling to each other by name—the roll-call of the village—and at their heels toiled the big *bara-singh,* weighted by the failing strength of Purun Bhagat. At last the deer stopped in the shadow of a deep pine wood, five hundred feet up the hillside. His instinct, that had warned him of the coming slide, told him he would be safe here.

Purun Bhagat dropped fainting by his side, for the chill of the rain and that fierce climb were killing him; but first he called to the scattered torches ahead, "Stay and count your numbers"; then, whispering to the deer as he saw the lights gather in a cluster: "Stay with me, Brother. Stay—till—I—go!"

There was a sigh in the air that grew to a mutter, and a mutter that grew to a roar, and a roar that passed all sense of hearing, and the hillside on which the villagers stood was hit in the darkness, and rocked to the blow. Then a note as steady, deep, and true as the deep C of the organ drowned everything for perhaps five minutes, while the very roots of the pines quivered to it. It died away, and the sound of the rain falling on miles of hard ground and grass changed to the muffled drum of water on soft earth. That told its own tale.

A. Characterization
Kipling fuses the two "personas" of Purun Bhagat at the moment of crisis: that is, his Western practicality and experience, and his Eastern mysticism.

B. Climax/Theme
The climax of the story is the death of Purun Bhagat. Yet in this paragraph, Kipling chooses to hint at this event by describing the natural world.
❓ How might this description of Purun Bhagat's death hint at an important theme of the story? (It suggests the important theme of the unity of all nature.)

and he remembers how she was always homesick for it.

The villagers and animals make him feel welcome.

8. Students' statements of theme will vary. Here is one possible answer: What is most important in this life is to achieve a sense of oneness with the universe, which is not possible if one is caught up in the daily struggle for wealth, power, and success. A person who has achieved this inner peace deserves high respect.

9. Purun Bhagat leaves the hurry and rush of civilization to find peace in a timeless landscape. In her role as creator, Kali enables the villagers, plants, and animals to thrive and grow as the days pass and the seasons change. As destroyer, she is responsible for the passing of time, which leads inexorably to death.

A. Satire
Note Kipling's jibe at learned and scientific societies.

Never a villager—not even the priest—was bold enough to speak to the Bhagat who had saved their lives. They crouched under the pines and waited till the day. When it came they looked across the valley and saw that what had been forest, and terraced field, and track-threaded grazing ground was one raw, red, fan-shaped smear, with a few trees flung head-down on the scarp.[15] That red ran high up the hill of their refuge, damming back the little river, which had begun to spread into a brick-colored lake. Of the village, of the road to the shrine, of the shrine itself, and the forest behind, there was no trace. For one mile in width and two thousand feet in sheer depth the mountainside had come away bodily, planed clean from head to heel.

And the villagers, one by one, crept through the wood to pray before their Bhagat. They saw the *barasingh* standing over him, who fled when they came near, and they heard the *langurs* wailing in the branches, and Sona moaning up the hill; but their Bhagat was dead, sitting cross-legged, his back against a tree, his crutch under his armpit, and his face turned to the northeast.

The priest said: "Behold a miracle after a miracle, for in this very attitude must all Sunnyasis be buried! Therefore where he now is we will build the temple to our holy man."

They built the temple before a year was ended—a little stone-and-earth shrine—and they called the hill the Bhagat's Hill, and they worship there with lights and flowers and offerings to this day. But they do not know that the saint of their worship is the late Sir Purun Dass, K.C.I.E., D.C.L.,[16] Ph.D., etc., once Prime Minister of the progressive and enlightened State of Mohiniwala, and honorary or corresponding member of more learned and scientific societies than will ever do any good in this world or the next.

A

---

15. **scarp:** eroded slope.

16. **D.C.L.:** Doctor of Civil Laws, one of Purun Bhagat's honorary degrees from a Western university.

Responding to the Story

Analyzing the Story

Identifying Facts

1. What improvements does Purun Dass make when he is Prime Minister?
2. Name the animals that share the mountain shelter of Purun Bhagat. Use both the English and the Indian names.
3. How does Purun Bhagat find out about the catastrophe that is about to befall the village?
4. Make a list of the Indian words and customs that you have learned by reading this story.

Interpreting Meanings

5. Explain and comment on the meaning of the story's **title.**
6. Why would no English person "have dreamed of doing" what Dewan Sir Purun Dass, K.C.I.E. does?
7. Why does Purun Bhagat feel at home when he reaches the hill country? How is this feeling of being at home related to his reception by the villagers and the animals?
8. What do you think is the story's **theme?**

9. The Hindu goddess Kali, who represents time, is both a creator and destroyer. Why is she an appropriate figure in this story?

Writing About the Story

A Creative Response

1. **Writing a Story or a Personal Narrative.** The wish to get away from it all and retreat to some secluded and quiet place is very common. Write a story about yourself (either a real story or an imagined one) in which you retreat for a while from the responsibilities of school, family, friends, and work. Why do you go? Where do you go? What do you find out about yourself and your life?

A Critical Response

2. **Supporting an Opinion.** Do you think that Kipling is simple-minded and sentimental in his description of nature and rural life in this story? Write a brief essay in which you use evidence from the story to support your opinion.

Victorian Drama

Though Queen Victoria, who came to the throne in 1837, loved the theater, it was she who once remarked, "We are not amused." And certainly the theater of the early part of her reign provided little to amuse anyone. Comedy must have license to explore, to expose, to look under the bed, and to ridicule, but Victoria's England was marked by prudery, "good taste," repression of natural feelings, "high-mindedness," and official censorship. It was a period of the Industrial Revolution, the British Empire, the worship of commerce and trade.

The operettas William S. Gilbert wrote to Arthur Sullivan's music, beginning with *Trial by Jury* (1875), provided some delightful comic relief. Though today we think of these operettas (such as *The Pirates of Penzance, Patience,* and *H.M.S. Pinafore*) merely as charming, tuneful, witty entertainments, in their period they irreverently ridiculed the law, the Navy, the world of esthetes, and the aristocracy. Intrinsic to the Gilbert and Sullivan operettas was a world-turned-on-its-head view of life that would influence both Oscar Wilde and Bernard Shaw. In Gilbert and Sullivan, as often as Wilde and Shaw,

> Things are seldom what they seem.
> Skim milk masquerades as cream.

Coming into the era of Oscar Wilde and Bernard Shaw, drama was moving toward realism, which has been the predominant dramatic mode for the last hundred years. In England and in Europe, fiction writers were dealing with the social realities of the time—Charles Dickens among others in England, Emile Zola in France. From Scandinavia came the revolutionary voices of Henrik Ibsen in such plays as *Ghosts* (1881) and *The Enemy of the People* (1882), and August Strindberg in *Marriage* (1886) and *The Father* (1887).

While some playwrights were assimilating new points of view and style, the theaters were also undergoing changes to accommodate the new plays. For years, London had been dominated by two huge theaters, Covent Garden and Drury Lane, each seating well over three thousand people. The size of the theaters had to some extent dictated the types of plays produced; they were not congenial to intimate realistic drama. (Today, the usual Broadway theater for plays seats between eight hundred and a thousand people.) Also, candlelight was too theatrical a method of illumination for naturalistic or realistic plays.

In the early part of the nineteenth century, new, smaller theaters were built. The forestage or apron was removed, and gaslight (and soon electricity) took the place of candles. These changes cleared the way for the staging of smaller-scale realistic dramas, which an audience might view as though through an invisible "fourth wall." (The setting constituted three walls of a room. When the curtain went up, it was as though the fourth wall had been removed, and the audience was eavesdropping on the action.) In smaller theaters, on such a stage with the new lighting, playwrights could now achieve an illusion of reality.

A

B

C

A. Connections
The operetta *H.M.S. Pinafore* opened in May of 1878 and after a slow start played to packed houses. In its comic plot and satire on Victorian class consciousness, *Pinafore* resembles Oscar Wilde's *The Importance of Being Earnest* (text page 870). You might play some Gilbert and Sullivan songs to the class to give a sample of their unique form of satire.

B. Expansion
Have students recall the much smaller size and different design of the Globe Theater (see text pages 241–243).

C. Theater Design
This development in theater design had a revolutionary impact on literary drama. The actor was able to withdraw further into the created illusion of the play, and his character became a part of it. In the mid-nineteenth century, when it was possible to dim the house lights, the illusion became complete.

A. Expansion
This is a macabre fantasy about a man's evil deeds that leave their mark only on his portrait, while he remains looking like Adonis. The novel was extremely controversial—a fact that (as in modern times) contributed to its popular success. Wilde deliberately challenged conventional Victorian morality when he declared in the preface: "There is no such thing as a moral or an immoral book. Books are well written or badly written. That is all."

FOR FURTHER READING STUDENTS
If students enjoy *The Importance of Being Earnest*, suggest they try Wilde's first stage success, *Lady Windermere's Fan* (1892). For an altogether different glimpse of Wilde's many talents, they might read *The Ballad of Reading Gaol* (1898), the long poem Wilde wrote as a result of his two years' imprisonment.

Oscar Wilde (1854–1900)

Oscar Fingal O'Flahertie Wills Wilde was born in Dublin. His father was a celebrated surgeon and his mother a poet and member of Dublin's literary set. Wilde was an outstanding student of classical literature at Trinity College in Dublin and later at Oxford University. His travels through Greece and Italy after his father's death influenced his book of poems published in 1881. On his return to London, he became part of the social world of artists and intellectuals, wrote essays on art and literature, and championed the cause of Aestheticism, a movement critical of the crass commercialism of the time. Wilde's motto was "Art for art's sake."

Gilbert and Sullivan satirized him and the whole overprecious Aesthetic movement in *Patience* (1881). To publicize the American tour of this operetta, Wilde was persuaded to travel across America giving lectures. He was an enormous success both as a showman and a lecturer, shocking his audiences with his unconventional views and dress. He usually wore knee breeches and sported a flowing tie and a sunflower in his buttonhole, or carried a lily.

He lived for a while in Paris and led the Bohemian life while studying art, the poetry of Charles Baudelaire, and the novels of Balzac. Returning to London, he married Constance Lloyd in 1884 and set up a fashionable home. Wilde wrote fairy tales for his two children, book reviews, and essays. In 1887 he became the editor of *The Woman's World* and in the next few years wrote essays in criticism, short stories, and the famous novel *The Picture of Dorian Gray* (1891).

A In 1891, needing money to support his extravagances, Wilde turned to the theater where he could cash in on the wit he had been giving away for nothing as a dandy around town. His first play produced in London was *Lady Windermere's Fan* (1892), a problem play about a "woman with a past" and a sentimental comedy. The play is filled with (one might almost say smothered by) paradoxical epigrams in which the conventional view of things is turned upside-down.

Oscar Wilde. Photo by Napolean Sarony.

Wilde wrote two more plays using the same ingredients: *A Woman of No Importance* (1893) and *The Ideal Husband* (1894). Though both plays are filled with the standard claptrap of Victorian melodrama (stolen letters, blackmail, "shocking" revelations, and intrigue), Wilde peppered his dialogue with barbs ridiculing Victorian ideas of respectability. The lines are fresh, impertinent, and witty: "One should never take sides in anything, Mr. Kelvil. Taking sides is the beginning of sincerity, and earnestness follows shortly afterwards, and the human being becomes a bore." "Duty is what one expects of others; it is not what one does oneself."

In 1895, the Marquess of Queensberry, enraged by Wilde's friendship with his son, began to persecute Wilde and blacken his name around London. Wilde was finally persuaded to sue him for libel, but he lost his case and was instead sentenced to two years in prison for immoral conduct.

The Importance of Being Earnest (1895) was closed at the height of its success, and Wilde was ruined. After his release from prison, he lived in France under the name of Sebastian Melmoth and wrote a long poem about prison life, "The Ballad of Reading Gaol." Oscar Wilde died, deserted by all but a few friends, in a Paris hotel in November 1900.

The Importance of Being Earnest

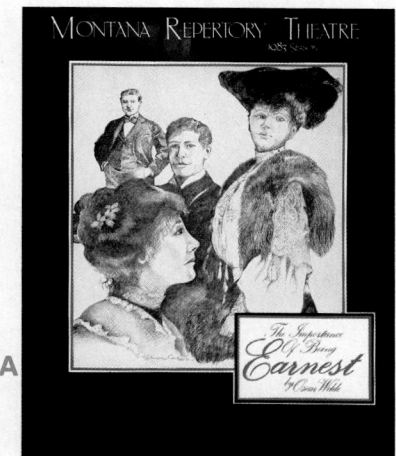

Wilde subtitled this play *A Trivial Comedy for Serious People* and set aside all seriousness. The whole play is an exercise in manner and absurdity, a high-wire act with no net. Usually a play concerns characters with whom we become emotionally involved. The characters find themselves in some kind of crisis and struggle to achieve a meaningful goal. The playwright introduces conflict and creates suspense as events change the characters' relationships. The story progresses because of the characters, grows out of their personalities and their psychological complexities.

In *The Importance of Being Earnest,* we really don't care much about Algernon and Jack or whether they succeed in winning and marrying Cecily and Gwendolen. Our main interest and suspense come from wondering what Wilde will say next (almost all the characters speak in Wilde's voice). In most plays, it is impossible to quote "good lines" out of context because the lines are only intelligible in terms of the characters and the ongoing story. But in this play almost everyone speaks in epigrams, and it makes no difference in whose mouth they are put.

Our interest and suspense also come from wondering what ridiculous situation Wilde will dream up next as these characters sail through "urbane nonsense," exercising the greatest seriousness over such trifles as cucumber sandwiches and muffins. The essence of all good comedy is seriousness. The audience laughs; the actors must not.

Wilde once wrote, "The aim of social comedy is to mirror the manners, not reform the morals, of the day." In this play he is painting a picture of an idle class that has outgrown its time, much as Chekhov portrayed a similar class in Russia in *The Cherry Orchard* (1904). Wilde treats these aristocratic drifters with such obvious enjoyment that it is difficult to sense any ridicule—real or implied. In *The Cherry Orchard* Chekhov presents one character who represents the norm against which the others can be judged. In *The Importance of Being Earnest,* there is no such norm: Everyone and everything is ridiculous—and yet very human.

Wilde is also having great fun with the very conventions that he followed so seriously in his earlier plays: the woman with a past, "lost" mothers, and mistaken identities. He sums up all the supercilious grand ladies of the earlier plays in Lady Bracknell, one of the great comic characters in the English theater.

The Importance of Being Earnest is a **farce,** a highly exaggerated comedy. In a farce, the plot is everything and must move rapidly. There are no characters to probe, no meaningful relationships to develop or change. The question in the audience's mind is the simple one of a child listening to a story: "What happens next?" Wilde keeps things happening delightfully and absurdly as Algernon and Jack pursue their goals, meeting obstacles and overcoming them only to find new obstacles. The surprise ending is as happily contrived as the rest of the play, and the audience of the day must have guffawed at Wilde's "sending up" one of the conventions of Victorian drama, which Gilbert and Sullivan also satirized in *The Pirates of Penzance* (1880).

A. Epigram
Discuss epigrams with the class. You might want to refer back to some of the verse epigrams of Alexander Pope (see text page 527).

B. Connections
The plot of the play depends on a comic device with ancient roots: the idea of the look-alike, or double. This motif is prevalent in comedy (see, for example, Shakespeare's *Comedy of Errors* and Nikolai Gogol's *The Inspector General*) as well as in serious fiction (see Joseph Conrad's *The Secret Sharer*, text page 925).

1. BUILDING ON PRIOR KNOWLEDGE. Before students begin reading, ask them if they have ever seen a live play. Discuss the kinds of drama with which the students are familiar (television, movies, opera, radio shows, puppet drama). Explain the difference between farce and comedy (see text page 869) and the differences between pun, paradox, and epigram (see the Handbook of Literary Terms, beginning on text page 1259). Have students give their own examples of each of these literary terms.

2. ESTABLISHING A PURPOSE. Tell students that Wilde wrote about this play: "It is exquisitely trivial, a delicate bubble of fancy, and it has its philosophy . . . that we should treat all the trivial things of life seriously, and all the serious things of life with sincere and studied triviality." Ask students to read the play to enjoy Wilde's humor and clever language.

A. About the Photograph
You may want to identify the figures in the photograph after students read the cast of characters: From left to right they are: Gwendolen, John Worthing (Ernest), Algernon, and Lady Bracknell.
? What characteristically Victorian details can you find in the stage set and costumes in the photograph? (Elegantly and tastefully appointed drawing room; fashionably dressed ladies and gentlemen)

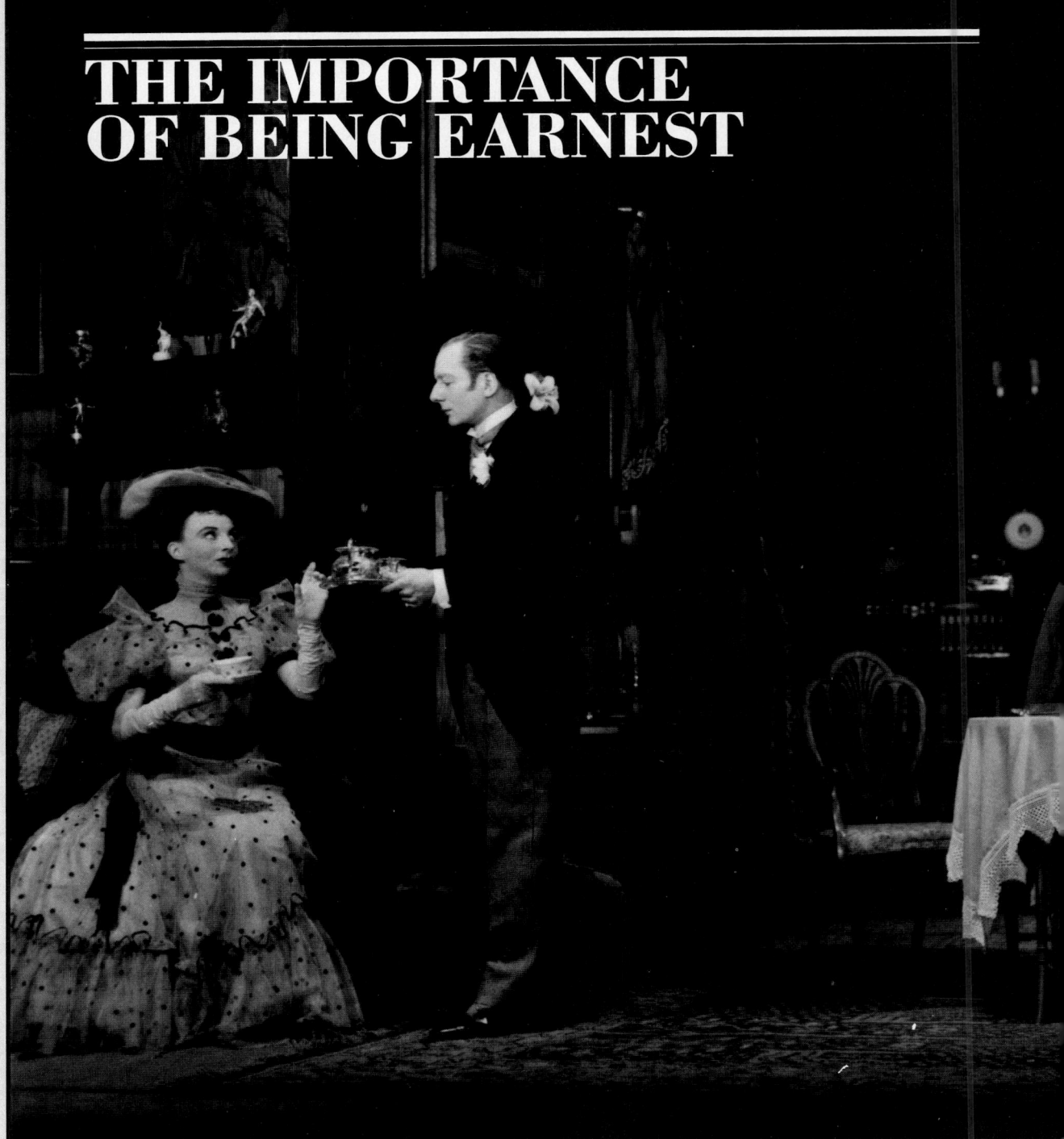

THE IMPORTANCE OF BEING EARNEST

The photographs illustrating the play are from the 1947 revival at the Royale Theater in New York, starring Margaret Rutherford as Lady Bracknell and Sir John Gielgud as Ernest.

A

SUPPLEMENTARY SUPPORT MATERIALS
1. Vocabulary Activity Worksheet (*CCB*)
2. Review and Response Worksheets: Characterization; Complications; Farce; Wit (*CCB*)
3. Language Skills Worksheet: Diction (*CCB*)
4. Selection Test (*CCB*)

DEVELOPING VOCABULARY
The following words from the play are tested in the Selection Test. (See also Vocabulary Activity Worksheet.)

forte	melodramatic
provincial	confirmation
pulpit	canonical
demeanor	ostentatious
to vacillate	to dote

Characters

John Worthing, alias Ernest Worthing
Algernon Moncrieff, friend of John
Lady Bracknell, Algernon's aunt
Honorable[1] Gwendolen Fairfax, daughter of Lady Bracknell
Cecily Cardew, ward of John Worthing
Miss Prism, governess to Cecily
The Reverend Canon Chasuble, rector
Lane, Algernon's butler
Merriman, butler at Manor House

Act One

Morning room[2] in ALGERNON'*s flat on Half-Moon Street. The room is luxuriously and artistically furnished. The sound of a piano is heard in the adjoining room.* LANE *is arranging afternoon tea on the table, and after the music has ceased,* ALGERNON *enters.*

A

Algernon. Did you hear what I was playing, Lane?
Lane. I didn't think it polite to listen, sir.
Algernon. I'm sorry for that, for your sake. I don't play accurately—anyone can play accurately—but I play with wonderful expression. As far as the piano is concerned, sentiment is my <u>forte</u>. I keep science for life.

B

Lane. Yes, sir.
Algernon. And, speaking of the science of life, have you got the cucumber sandwiches cut for Lady Bracknell?
Lane. Yes, sir. (*Hands them on a salver[3]*)
Algernon (*inspects them, takes two, and sits down on the sofa*). Oh! . . . By the way, Lane, I see from your book that on Thursday night, when Lord Shoreman and Mr. Worthing were dining with me, eight bottles of champagne are entered as having been consumed.
Lane. Yes, sir; eight bottles and a pint.
Algernon. Why is it that at a bachelor's establish-

1. **Honorable:** title of the daughter of a Viscount or Baron.
2. **Morning room:** an informal sitting room for daytime use.
3. **salver:** serving tray.

A. Plot: Exposition
In the opening scene of a play, the playwright must let the audience know something about the characters, their situation, their relationships, the setting. Have students watch for the kind of information Wilde reveals in this scene between Algernon and his butler. (Algernon, a bachelor, lives in luxury, and spends his time amusing himself. He is expecting a visit from Lady Bracknell.)

B. Pun
Since the piano was still occasionally called the *pianoforte*, Algernon is punning here on the word *forte*.

The act takes place in Algernon Moncrieff's bachelor apartment in London. The opening dialogue between Algernon and his manservant Lance introduces the witty, satirical tone of the play. Algernon's friend Jack (also known as Ernest) Worthing arrives and says that he is about to propose to Gwendolen Fairfax, Algernon's cousin. Because of a lost cigarette case, Jack is forced to reveal to Algernon that his name is really Jack and that he has invented a brother (Ernest) as an excuse to leave his country home. He also reveals that he is the guardian of young Cecily Cardew. Algernon, in return, tells about his imaginary friend Bunbury, whom he uses as an excuse to get out of engagements.

Gwendolen arrives with her mother, Lady Bracknell. Alone with her for a few minutes, Jack proposes and Gwendolen accepts. But when Lady Bracknell interviews Jack, she finds him totally unacceptable because his parentage is unknown. (As an infant, Jack was found in a handbag in a railroad station.) Gwendolen and Lady Bracknell leave, but Gwendolen returns briefly to assure Jack that she loves him because his name is

A. Satire
Wilde's first target is the institution of marriage as a come-down from the bachelor life.

❓ Whom, or what, is Wilde satirizing in this passage about social class and moral responsibility? (The snobbery and self-centeredness of the upper classes; the existence of social classes)

B. Exposition
Here is the first hint of the plot to come.

C. Humor
Algernon's statement reverses the well-known saying that marriages are made in heaven.

ment the servants invariably drink the champagne? I ask merely for information.

Lane. I attribute it to the superior quality of the wine, sir. I have often observed that in married households the champagne is rarely of a first-rate brand.

Algernon. Good heavens! Is marriage so demoralizing as that?

Lane. I believe it *is* a very pleasant state, sir. I have had very little experience of it myself up to the present. I have only been married once. That was in consequence of a misunderstanding between myself and a young person.

Algernon (*languidly*). I don't know that I am much interested in your family life, Lane.

Lane. No, sir; it is not a very interesting subject. I never think of it myself.

Algernon. Very natural, I am sure. That will do, Lane, thank you.

Lane. Thank you, sir. (*LANE goes out.*)

A **Algernon.** Lane's views on marriage seem somewhat lax. Really, if the lower orders don't set us a good example, what on earth is the use of them? They seem, as a class, to have absolutely no sense of moral responsibility.

[*Enter* LANE.]

Lane. Mr. Ernest Worthing.

[*Enter* JACK. LANE *goes out*.]

Algernon. How are you, my dear Ernest? What brings you up to town?

Jack. Oh, pleasure, pleasure! What else should bring one anywhere? Eating as usual, I see, Algy!

Algernon (*stiffly*). I believe it is customary in good society to take some slight refreshment at five o'clock. Where have you been since last Thursday?

Jack (*sitting down on the sofa*). In the country.

Algernon. What on earth do you do there?

Jack (*pulling off his gloves*). When one is in town, one amuses oneself. When one is in the country, one amuses other people. It is excessively boring.

Algernon. And who are the people you amuse?

Jack (*airily*). Oh, neighbors, neighbors.

Algernon. Got nice neighbors in your part of Shropshire?

Jack. Perfectly horrid! Never speak to one of them.

Algernon. How immensely you must amuse them! (*Goes over and takes sandwich*) By the way, Shropshire is your county, is it not?

Jack. Eh? Shropshire? Yes, of course. Hallo! Why all these cups? Why cucumber sandwiches? Why such reckless extravagance in one so young? Who is coming to tea?

Algernon. Oh! Merely Aunt Augusta and Gwendolen.

Jack. How perfectly delightful!

B **Algernon.** Yes, that is all very well; but I am afraid Aunt Augusta won't quite approve of your being here.

Jack. May I ask why?

Algernon. My dear fellow, the way you flirt with Gwendolen is perfectly disgraceful. It is almost as bad as the way Gwendolen flirts with you.

Jack. I am in love with Gwendolen. I have come up to town expressly to propose to her.

Algernon. I thought you had come up for pleasure? . . . I call that business.

Jack. How utterly unromantic you are!

Algernon. I really don't see anything romantic in proposing. It is very romantic to be in love. But there is nothing romantic about a definite proposal. Why, one may be accepted. One usually is, I believe. Then the excitement is all over. The very essence of romance is uncertainty. If ever I get married, I'll certainly try to forget the fact.

Jack. I have no doubt about that, dear Algy. The Divorce Court[4] was specially invented for people whose memories are so curiously constituted.

C **Algernon.** Oh! There is no use speculating on that subject. Divorces are made in heaven——(JACK *puts out his hand to take a sandwich.* ALGERNON *at once interferes.*) Please don't touch the cucumber sandwiches. They are ordered specially for Aunt Augusta. (*Takes one and eats it*)

Jack. Well, you have been eating them all the time.

Algernon. That is quite a different matter. She is my aunt. (*Takes plate from below*) Have some bread and butter. The bread and butter is for Gwendolen. Gwendolen is devoted to bread and butter.

Jack (*advancing to table and helping himself*). And very good bread and butter it is too.

Algernon. Well, my dear fellow, you need not eat as if you were going to eat it all. You behave as if you were married to her already. You are not married to her already, and I don't think you ever will be.

---

4. **Divorce Court:** established in 1857. Divorce was frowned upon by the Church of England; before 1857 divorce could only be granted by an act of Parliament.

Ernest (which, of course, it isn't). Jack gives her his country address so they can write; Algernon writes down the address.

Jack. Why on earth do you say that?

A **Algernon.** Well, in the first place, girls never marry the men they flirt with. Girls don't think it right.

Jack. Oh, that is nonsense!

Algernon. It isn't. It is a great truth. It accounts for the extraordinary number of bachelors that one sees all over the place. In the second place, I don't give my consent.

Jack. Your consent!

Algernon. My dear fellow, Gwendolen is my first cousin. And before I allow you to marry her, you will have to clear up the whole question of Cecily. *(Rings bell)*

Jack. Cecily! What on earth do you mean? What do you mean, Algy, by Cecily! I don't know anyone of the name of Cecily.

[*Enter* LANE.]

Algernon. Bring me that cigarette case Mr. Worthing left in the smoking room the last time he dined here.

Lane. Yes, sir. *(LANE goes out.)*

Jack. Do you mean to say you have had my cigarette case all this time? I wish to goodness you had let me know. I have been writing frantic letters to Scotland Yard[5] about it. I was very nearly offering a large reward.

Algernon. Well, I wish you would offer one. I happen to be more than usually hard up.

Jack. There is no good offering a large reward now that the thing is found.

[*Enter* LANE *with the cigarette case on a salver.* ALGERNON *takes it at once.* LANE *goes out.*]

Algernon. I think that is rather mean of you, Ernest, I must say. *(Opens case and examines it)* However, it makes no matter, for, now that I look at the inscription inside, I find that the thing isn't yours after all.

B **Jack.** Of course it's mine. *(Moving to him)* You have seen me with it a hundred times, and you have no right whatsoever to read what is written inside. It is a very ungentlemanly thing to read a private cigarette case.

Algernon. Oh! It is absurd to have a hard and fast rule about what one should read and what one shouldn't. More than half of modern culture depends on what one shouldn't read.

Jack. I am quite aware of the fact, and I don't propose to discuss modern culture. It isn't the sort

of thing one should talk of in private. I simply want my cigarette case back.

Algernon. Yes; but this isn't your cigarette case. This cigarette case is a present from someone of the name of Cecily, and you said you didn't know anyone of that name.

Jack. Well, if you want to know, Cecily happens to be my aunt.

C **Algernon.** Your aunt!

Jack. Yes. Charming old lady she is, too. Lives at Tunbridge Wells. Just give it back to me, Algy.

Algernon *(retreating to back of sofa).* But why does she call herself little Cecily if she is your aunt and lives at Tunbridge Wells? *(Reading)* "From little Cecily with her fondest love."

Jack *(moving to sofa and kneeling upon it).* My dear fellow, what on earth is there in that? Some aunts are tall, some aunts are not tall. That is a matter that surely an aunt may be allowed to decide for herself. You seem to think that every aunt should be exactly like your aunt! That is absurd. For heaven's sake, give me back my cigarette case. *(Follows* ALGERNON *round the room)*

Algernon. Yes. But why does your aunt call you her uncle? "From little Cecily, with her fondest love to her dear Uncle Jack." There is no objection, I admit, to an aunt being a small aunt, but why an aunt, no matter what her size may be, should call her own nephew her uncle, I can't quite make out. Besides, your name isn't Jack at all; it is Ernest.

Jack. It isn't Ernest; it's Jack.

D **Algernon.** You have always told me it was Ernest. I have introduced you to everyone as Ernest. You answer to the name of Ernest. You look as if your name was Ernest. You are the most earnest-looking person I ever saw in my life. It is perfectly absurd your saying that your name isn't Ernest. It's on your cards. Here is one of them: *(taking it from case)* "Mr. Ernest Worthing, B.4, The Albany, W." I'll keep this as a proof that your name is Ernest if ever you attempt to deny it to me, or to Gwendolen, or to anyone else. *(Puts the card in his pocket)*

Jack. Well, my name is Ernest in town and Jack in the country, and the cigarette case was given to me in the country.

Algernon. Yes, but that does not account for the fact that your small Aunt Cecily, who lives at Tunbridge Wells, calls you her dear uncle. Come, old boy, you had much better have the thing out at once.

---

5. **Scotland Yard:** headquarters of the London police.

A. Epigrams
The conversation between these two is full of Wilde's barbed one-liners. Ask students to look for other examples. (For example, "I don't propose to discuss modern culture. It isn't the sort of thing one should talk of in private.")

B. Expansion
This line plays on the Victorian (and to some extent modern) conviction that reading other people's mail is an unforgivable breach of social decorum.

C. Responding
Do you think Jack is telling the truth in this scene? How can you tell? (Jack is not telling the truth because he does not want Algernon to read the inscription in his cigarette case.)

D. Interpreting
Why do you think that Wilde chose the name Ernest for his character? (It provides a pun and also the opportunity to poke some fun at the Victorian values of earnestness and sincerity.)

A. Coinage

Wilde teases us by not explaining "Bunburyist" right away; he makes us wonder what on earth it could be. (His explanation follows in the middle of the next column.)

B. Plot: Exposition

Note how crisply Wilde provides background information. Jack's birth and parentage are important to the plot.

C. Epigram

Wilde mocks the rather pompous morality and self-righteousness of his time.

D. Satire

❓ How does Wilde revenge himself on literary critics? (He says, snobbishly, that they haven't been at a university.)

E. Vocabulary

Be sure students understand the Victorian meaning of the phrase "sent down." Victorians regarded the seating arrangements at dinner as a matter of great importance.

Jack. My dear Algy, you talk exactly as if you were a dentist.[6] It is very vulgar to talk like a dentist when one isn't a dentist. It produces a false impression.

Algernon. Well, that is exactly what dentists always do. Now, go on! Tell me the whole thing. I may mention that I have always suspected you of being a confirmed and secret Bunburyist; and I am quite sure of it now.

Jack. Bunburyist? What on earth do you mean by a Bunburyist?

Algernon. I'll reveal to you the meaning of that incomparable expression as soon as you are kind enough to inform me why you are Ernest in town and Jack in the country.

Jack. Well, produce my cigarette case first.

Algernon. Here it is. *(Hands cigarette case)* Now produce your explanation, and pray make it improbable. *(Sits on sofa)*

Jack. My dear fellow, there is nothing improbable about my explanation at all. In fact it's perfectly ordinary. Old Mr. Thomas Cardew, who adopted me when I was a little boy, made me in his will guardian to his granddaughter, Miss Cecily Cardew. Cecily, who addresses me as her uncle from motives of respect that you could not possibly appreciate, lives at my place in the country under the charge of her admirable governess, Miss Prism.

Algernon. Where is that place in the country, by the way?

Jack. That is nothing to you, dear boy. You are not going to be invited. . . . I may tell you candidly that the place is not in Shropshire.

Algernon. I suspected that, my dear fellow! I have Bunburyed all over Shropshire on two separate occasions. Now, go on. Why are you Ernest in town and Jack in the country?

Jack. My dear Algy, I don't know whether you will be able to understand my real motives. You are hardly serious enough. When one is placed in the position of guardian, one has to adopt a very high moral tone on all subjects. It's one's duty to do so. And as a high moral tone can hardly be said to conduce very much to either one's health or one's happiness, in order to get up to town I have always pretended to have a younger brother of the name of Ernest, who lives in the Albany, and gets into the most dreadful scrapes. That, my dear Algy, is the whole truth pure and simple.

Algernon. The truth is rarely pure and never simple. Modern life would be very tedious if it were either, and modern literature a complete impossibility!

Jack. That wouldn't be at all a bad thing.

Algernon. Literary criticism is not your forte, my dear fellow. Don't try it. You should leave that to people who haven't been at a University. They do it so well in the daily papers. What you really are is a Bunburyist. I was quite right in saying you were a Bunburyist. You are one of the most advanced Bunburyists I know.

Jack. What on earth do you mean?

Algernon. You have invented a very useful younger brother called Ernest, in order that you may be able to come up to town as often as you like. I have invented an invaluable permanent invalid called Bunbury, in order that I may be able to go down into the country whenever I choose. Bunbury is perfectly invaluable. If it wasn't for Bunbury's extraordinary bad health, for instance, I wouldn't be able to dine with you at Willis' tonight, for I have been really engaged[7] to Aunt Augusta for more than a week.

Jack. I haven't asked you to dine with me anywhere tonight.

Algernon. I know. You are absurdly careless about sending out invitations. It is very foolish of you. Nothing annoys people so much as not receiving invitations.

Jack. You had much better dine with your Aunt Augusta.

Algernon. I haven't the smallest intention of doing anything of the kind. To begin with, I dined there on Monday, and once a week is quite enough to dine with one's own relations. In the second place, whenever I do dine there I am always treated as a member of the family, and sent down[8] with either no woman at all, or two. In the third place, I know perfectly well whom she will place me next to, tonight. She will place me next Mary Farquhar, who always flirts with her own husband across the dinner table. That is not very pleasant. Indeed, it is not even decent . . . and that sort of thing is

---

6. **dentist:** Dentists, doctors, and merchants were looked down on by the snobbish elite of society.

7. **engaged:** having an engagement or appointment.
8. **sent down:** asked to escort a lady to the dining room. If there were few men at a dinner party, family members were asked to escort two ladies.

enormously on the increase. The amount of women in London who flirt with their own husbands is perfectly scandalous. It looks so bad. It is simply washing one's clean linen in public. Besides, now that I know you to be a confirmed Bunburyist I naturally want to talk to you about Bunburying. I want to tell you the rules.

Jack. I'm not a Bunburyist at all. If Gwendolen accepts me, I am going to kill my brother, indeed I think I'll kill him in any case. Cecily is a little too much interested in him. It is rather a bore. So I am going to get rid of Ernest. And I strongly advise you to do the same with Mr. . . . with your invalid friend who has the absurd name.

Algernon. Nothing will induce me to part with Bunbury, and if you ever get married, which seems to me extremely problematic, you will be very glad to know Bunbury. A man who marries without knowing Bunbury has a very tedious time of it.

Jack. That is nonsense. If I marry a charming girl like Gwendolen, and she is the only girl I ever saw in my life that I would marry, I certainly won't want to know Bunbury.

Algernon. Then your wife will. You don't seem to realize that in married life three is company and two is none.

Jack (*sententiously*[9]). That, my dear young friend, is the theory that the corrupt French drama has been propounding for the last fifty years.[10]

Algernon. Yes; and that the happy English home has proved in half the time.

Jack. For heaven's sake, don't try to be cynical. It's perfectly easy to be cynical.

Algernon. My dear fellow, it isn't easy to be anything nowadays. There's such a lot of beastly competition about. (*The sound of an electric bell is heard.*) Ah! That must be Aunt Augusta. Only relatives, or creditors, ever ring in that Wagnerian[11] manner. Now, if I get her out of the way for ten minutes, so that you can have an opportunity for proposing to Gwendolen, may I dine with you tonight at Willis'?

Jack. I suppose so, if you want to.

Algernon. Yes, but you must be serious about it. I hate people who are not serious about meals. It is so shallow of them.

[*Enter* LANE.]

Lane. Lady Bracknell and Miss Fairfax.

[ALGERNON *goes forward to meet them. Enter* LADY BRACKNELL *and* GWENDOLEN.]

Lady Bracknell. Good afternoon, dear Algernon, I hope you are behaving very well.

Algernon. I'm feeling very well, Aunt Augusta.

Lady Bracknell. That's not quite the same thing. In fact the two things rarely go together. (*Sees* JACK *and bows to him with icy coldness*)

Algernon (*to* GWENDOLEN). Dear me, you are smart!

Gwendolen. I am always smart! Am I not, Mr. Worthing?

Jack. You're quite perfect, Miss Fairfax.

Gwendolen. Oh! I hope I am not that. It would leave no room for developments, and I intend to develop in many directions. (GWENDOLEN *and* JACK *sit down together in the corner.*)

Lady Bracknell. I'm sorry if we are a little late, Algernon, but I was obliged to call on dear Lady Harbury. I hadn't been there since her poor husband's death. I never saw a woman so altered; she looks quite twenty years younger. And now I'll have a cup of tea and one of those nice cucumber sandwiches you promised me.

Algernon. Certainly, Aunt Augusta. (*Goes over to tea table*)

Lady Bracknell. Won't you come and sit here, Gwendolen?

Gwendolen. Thanks, Mama, I'm quite comfortable where I am.

Algernon (*picking up empty plate in horror*). Good heavens! Lane! Why are there no cucumber sandwiches? I ordered them specially.

Lane (*gravely*). There were no cucumbers in the market this morning, sir. I went down twice.

Algernon. No cucumbers!

Lane. No, sir. Not even for ready money.

Algernon. That will do, Lane, thank you.

Lane. Thank you, sir. (*Goes out*)

Algernon. I am greatly distressed, Aunt Augusta, about there being no cucumbers, not even for ready money.

Lady Bracknell. It really makes no matter, Algernon. I had some crumpets[12] with Lady Harbury,

---

9. **sententiously:** tersely; expressing a great deal in few words.
10. **corrupt . . . years:** The "love triangle" was the basis for many late-nineteenth-century plays.
11. **Wagnerian** (väg·nir′ē·ən): loud and discordant; resembling the music of Richard Wagner (1813–1883), a German composer.

12. **crumpets:** soft, flat rolls similar to English muffins.

A. Responding
Stop at this point and ask students what they think of Wilde's humor so far.

? Do you think Wilde's humor is dated or still funny? (It is still funny because the objects of Wilde's wit—pretension and pretentious people—still exist.) Students will need to know the idiom "washing one's dirty linen in public" to appreciate this line.

B. Epigram
Point out that in these lines Wilde gives a new twist to the expression "Two's company and three's a crowd."

C. Characterization
Have students watch for the acid-tongued Lady Bracknell's matching wits with Algernon and Jack.

? Who seems to be the "winner" whenever she tangles with one of the young men? (She does.)

D. Pun
The word *smart* here has the additional meaning of "fashionable," "elegant."

A. Epigram
This line is another example of Wilde twisting a familiar saying to create a satirical epigram.

B. Characterization/Satire
In the characterization of Lady Bracknell, Wilde works with double-edged satire. Although she is caricatured as an imperious snob, she also is made to deliver quite perceptive, deflating comments on the pretentiousness of others.

who seems to me to be living entirely for pleasure now.

A

Algernon. I hear her hair has turned quite gold from grief.

Lady Bracknell. It certainly has changed its color. From what cause I, of course, cannot say. (AL-GERNON *crosses and hands tea.*) Thank you, I've quite a treat for you tonight, Algernon. I am going to send you down with Mary Farquhar. She is such a nice woman, and so attentive to her husband. It's delightful to watch them.

Algernon. I am afraid, Aunt Augusta, I shall have to give up the pleasure of dining with you tonight after all.

Lady Bracknell (*frowning*). I hope not, Algernon. It would put my table completely out. Your uncle would have to dine upstairs. Fortunately he is accustomed to that.

Algernon. It is a great bore, and, I need hardly say, a terrible disappointment to me, but the fact is I have just had a telegram to say that my poor friend Bunbury is very ill again. (*Exchanges glances with* JACK*) They seem to think I should be with him.

Lady Bracknell. It is very strange. This Mr. Bunbury seems to suffer from curiously bad health.

Algernon. Yes; poor Bunbury is a dreadful invalid.

B

Lady Bracknell. Well, I must say, Algernon, that I think it is high time that Mr. Bunbury made up his mind whether he was going to live or to die. This shilly-shallying with the question is absurd. Nor do I in any way approve of the modern sympathy with invalids. I consider it morbid. Illness of any kind is hardly a thing to be encouraged in others. Health is the primary duty of life. I am always telling that to your poor uncle, but he never seems to take much notice . . . as far as any improvement in his ailments goes. I should be much obliged if you would ask Mr. Bunbury, from me, to be kind enough not to have a relapse on Saturday, for I rely on you to arrange my music for me. It is my last reception, and one wants something that will encourage conversation, particularly at the end of the season when everyone has practically said whatever they had to say, which, in most cases, was probably not much.

Algernon. I'll speak to Bunbury, Aunt Augusta, if he is still conscious, and I think I can promise you he'll be all right by Saturday. Of course the music is a great difficulty. You see, if one plays good music, people don't listen, and if one plays bad music, people don't talk. But I'll run over the program I've drawn out, if you will kindly come into the next room for a moment.

Lady Bracknell. Thank you, Algernon. It is very thoughtful of you. (*Rising, and following* ALGER-NON*) I'm sure the program will be delightful, after a few expurgations. French songs I cannot possibly allow. People always seem to think that they are improper, and either look shocked, which is vulgar, or laugh, which is worse. But German sounds a thoroughly respectable language, and indeed I believe is so. Gwendolen, you will accompany me.

Gwendolen. Certainly, Mama.

[LADY BRACKNELL *and* ALGERNON *go into the music room;* GWENDOLEN *remains behind.*]

Jack. Charming day it has been, Miss Fairfax.

Gwendolen. Pray don't talk to me about the weather, Mr. Worthing. Whenever people talk to me about the weather, I always feel quite certain that they mean something else. And that makes me so nervous.

Jack. I do mean something else.

Gwendolen. I thought so. In fact, I am never wrong.

Jack. And I would like to be allowed to take advantage of Lady Bracknell's temporary absence . . .

Gwendolen. I would certainly advise you to do so. Mama has a way of coming back suddenly into a room that I have often had to speak to her about.

Jack (*nervously*). Miss Fairfax, ever since I met you I have admired you more than any girl . . . I have ever met since . . . I met you.

Gwendolen. Yes, I am quite aware of the fact. And I often wish that in public, at any rate, you had been more demonstrative. For me you have always had an irresistible fascination. Even before I met you I was far from indifferent to you. (JACK *looks at her in amazement.*) We live, as I hope you know, Mr. Worthing, in an age of ideals. The fact is constantly mentioned in the more expensive monthly magazines, and has reached the provin-cial pulpits, I am told; and my ideal has always been to love someone of the name of Ernest. There is something in that name that inspires absolute confidence. The moment Algernon first mentioned to me that he had a friend called Ernest, I knew I was destined to love you.

Jack. You really love me, Gwendolen?

Gwendolen. Passionately!

Jack. Darling! You don't know how happy you've made me.

Gwendolen. My own Ernest!

Jack. But you don't really mean to say that you couldn't love me if my name wasn't Ernest?

Gwendolen. But your name is Ernest.

Jack. Yes, I know it is. But supposing it was something else? Do you mean to say you couldn't love me then?

Gwendolen (glibly). Ah! That is clearly a metaphysical speculation,[13] and like most metaphysical speculations has very little reference at all to the actual facts of real life, as we know them.

Jack. Personally, darling, to speak quite candidly, I don't much care about the name of Ernest. . . . I don't think the name suits me at all.

Gwendolen. It suits you perfectly. It is a divine name. It has a music of its own. It produces vibrations.

Jack. Well, really, Gwendolen, I must say that I think there are lots of other much nicer names. I think Jack, for instance, a charming name.

Gwendolen. Jack? . . . No, there is very little music in the name Jack, if any at all, indeed. It does not thrill. It produces absolutely no vibrations. . . . I have known several Jacks, and they all, without exception, were more than usually plain. Besides, Jack is a notorious domesticity[14] for John! And I pity any woman who is married to a man called John. She would probably never be allowed to know the entrancing pleasure of a single moment's solitude. The only really safe name is Ernest.

Jack. Gwendolen, I must get christened at once— I mean we must get married at once. There is no time to be lost.

Gwendolen. Married, Mr. Worthing?

Jack (astounded). Well . . . surely. You know that I love you, and you led me to believe, Miss Fairfax, that you were not absolutely indifferent to me.

Gwendolen. I adore you. But you haven't proposed to me yet. Nothing has been said at all about marriage. The subject has not even been touched on.

Jack. Well . . . may I propose to you now?

---

13. **metaphysical speculation:** highly abstract philosophical question.
14. **notorious domesticity:** well-known nickname.

Gwendolen. I think it would be an admirable opportunity. And to spare you any possible disappointment, Mr. Worthing, I think it only fair to tell you quite frankly beforehand that I am fully determined to accept you.

Jack. Gwendolen!

Gwendolen. Yes, Mr. Worthing, what have you got to say to me?

Jack. You know what I have got to say to you.

Gwendolen. Yes, but you don't say it.

Jack (goes on his knees). Gwendolen, will you marry me?

Gwendolen. Of course I will, darling. How long you have been about it! I am afraid you have had very little experience in how to propose.

Jack. My own one, I have never loved anyone in the world but you.

Gwendolen. Yes, but men often propose for practice. I know my brother Gerald does. All my girlfriends tell me so. What wonderfully blue eyes you have, Ernest! They are quite, quite blue. I hope you will always look at me just like that, especially when there are other people present.

[Enter LADY BRACKNELL.]

Lady Bracknell. Mr. Worthing! Rise, sir, from this semirecumbent posture. It is most indecorous.

Gwendolen. Mama! (He tries to rise; she restrains him.) I must beg you to retire. This is no place for you. Besides, Mr. Worthing has not quite finished yet.

Lady Bracknell. Finished what, may I ask?

Gwendolen. I am engaged to Mr. Worthing, Mama. (They rise together.)

Lady Bracknell. Pardon me, you are not engaged to anyone. When you do become engaged to someone, I, or your father, should his health permit him, will inform you of the fact. An engagement should come on a young girl as a surprise, pleasant or unpleasant, as the case may be. It is hardly a matter that she could be allowed to arrange for herself. . . . And now I have a few questions to put to you, Mr. Worthing. While I am making these inquiries, you, Gwendolen, will wait for me below in the carriage.

Gwendolen (reproachfully). Mama!

Lady Bracknell. In the carriage, Gwendolen! (GWENDOLEN goes to the door. She and JACK blow kisses to each other behind LADY BRACKNELL's back. LADY BRACKNELL looks vaguely about as if she could not understand what the noise was.

A. Plot: Conflict
Note that this passage provides the first obstacle to Jack's pursuit of Gwendolen.

B. Names
Though they've been calling each other by their first names, note that Gwendolen switches back to addressing Jack formally as Mr. Worthing, and he responds by calling her Miss Fairfax. Gwendolen is keeping things formal until he actually proposes.

C. Expansion
Point out to students that Lady Bracknell's comments on "arranged marriages" reflect the significant number of such marriages during the Victorian period (at least among the upper classes).

A. Satire
In this famous scene, Wilde satirizes the custom of having a member of the bride's family (usually her father) interview the prospective bridegroom to determine his "suitability" for the match.

B. Satire
This line reflects a different society's attitude toward smoking—long before it was revealed as a deadly habit.

? Why does Lady Bracknell call smoking "an occupation"? (Wilde is making fun of the idle rich, who literally have nothing to do.)

"Gwendolen, the carriage!"

Finally turns round) Gwendolen, the carriage!
Gwendolen. Yes, Mama. *(Goes out, looking back at* JACK*)*
Lady Bracknell *(sitting down).* You can take a seat, Mr. Worthing. *(Looks in her pocket for notebook and pencil)*
Jack. Thank you, Lady Bracknell, I prefer standing.
Lady Bracknell *(pencil and notebook in hand).* I feel bound to tell you that you are not down on my list of eligible young men, although I have the same list as the dear Duchess of Bolton has. We work together, in fact. However, I am quite ready to enter your name, should your answers be what a really affectionate mother requires. Do you smoke?
Jack. Well, yes, I must admit I smoke.
Lady Bracknell. I am glad to hear it. A man should always have an occupation of some kind. There are far too many idle men in London as it is. How old are you?
Jack. Twenty-nine.
Lady Bracknell. A very good age to be married at. I have always been of opinion that a man who desires to get married should know either everything or nothing. Which do you know?

Jack (*after some hesitation*). I know nothing, Lady Bracknell.

Lady Bracknell. I am pleased to hear it. I do not approve of anything that tampers with natural ignorance. Ignorance is like a delicate exotic fruit; touch it and the bloom is gone. The whole theory of modern education is radically unsound. Fortunately in England, at any rate, education produces no effect whatsoever. If it did, it would prove a serious danger to the upper classes, and probably lead to acts of violence in Grosvenor Square.[15] What is your income?

Jack. Between seven and eight thousand a year.

Lady Bracknell (*makes a note in her book*). In land or in investments?

Jack. In investments, chiefly.

Lady Bracknell. That is satisfactory. What between the duties[16] expected of one during one's lifetime, and the duties exacted from one after one's death, land has ceased to be either a profit or a pleasure. It gives one position and prevents one from keeping it up. That's all that can be said about land.

Jack. I have a country house with some land, of course, attached to it, about fifteen hundred acres, I believe; but I don't depend on that for my real income. In fact, as far as I can make out, the poachers are the only people who make anything out of it.

Lady Bracknell. A country house! How many bedrooms? Well, that point can be cleared up afterward. You have a town house, I hope? A girl with a simple, unspoiled nature, like Gwendolen, could hardly be expected to reside in the country.

Jack. Well, I own a house in Belgrave Square, but it is let by the year to Lady Bloxham. Of course, I can get it back whenever I like, at six months' notice.

Lady Bracknell. Lady Bloxham? I don't know her.

Jack. Oh, she goes about very little. She is a lady considerably advanced in years.

Lady Bracknell. Ah, nowadays that is no guarantee of respectability of character. What number in Belgrave Square?

Jack. One hundred and forty-nine.

Lady Bracknell (*shaking her head*). The unfashionable side. I thought there was something. However, that could easily be altered.

Jack. Do you mean the fashion, or the side?

Lady Bracknell (*sternly*). Both, if necessary, I presume. What are your politics?

Jack. Well, I am afraid I really have none. I am a Liberal Unionist.[17]

Lady Bracknell. Oh, they count as Tories.[18] They dine with us. Or come in the evening, at any rate. Now to minor matters. Are your parents living?

Jack. I have lost both my parents.

Lady Bracknell. To lose one parent, Mr. Worthing, may be regarded as a misfortune; to lose both looks like carelessness. Who was your father? He was evidently a man of some wealth. Was he born in what the Radical papers call the purple of commerce,[19] or did he rise from the ranks of the aristocracy?

Jack. I am afraid I really don't know. The fact is, Lady Bracknell, I said I had lost my parents. It would be nearer the truth to say that my parents seem to have lost me. . . . I don't actually know who I am by birth. I was . . . well, I was found.

Lady Bracknell. Found!

Jack. The late Mr. Thomas Cardew, an old gentleman of a very charitable and kindly disposition, found me and gave me the name of Worthing, because he happened to have a first-class ticket for Worthing in his pocket at the time. Worthing is a place in Sussex. It is a seaside resort.

Lady Bracknell. Where did the charitable gentleman who had a first-class ticket for this seaside resort find you?

Jack (*gravely*). In a handbag.

Lady Bracknell. A handbag?

Jack (*very seriously*). Yes, Lady Bracknell. I was in a handbag—a somewhat large, black leather handbag, with handles to it—an ordinary handbag in fact.

Lady Bracknell. In what locality did this Mr. James, or Thomas, Cardew come across this ordinary handbag?

Jack. In the cloakroom[20] at Victoria Station. It was given to him in mistake for his own.

---

15. **Grosvenor** (grōv′nər) **Square:** a wealthy, upper-class residential area.
16. **duties:** the duties of a landowner to his tenants, followed by death duties, or taxes.

17. **Liberal Unionist:** member of a group in the Liberal party who opposed home rule for Ireland in 1886.
18. **Tories:** members of a conservative political party associated with upholding established institutions and limited social and economic reform.
19. **purple of commerce:** wealthy businessmen who were given titles in the late Victorian period.
20. **cloakroom:** room where luggage can be checked.

A. Simile/ Epigram
Note the way in which Wilde combines simile and epigram here.

B. Pun
Be sure that students understand the pun on *duties* here (as "responsibilities" and "inheritance taxes").

C. Irony
Explain the irony in this line. (We have seen that Gwendolen is neither simple nor unspoiled. Also, someone with a simple, unspoiled nature *would* be perfectly suited for country life.)

D. Plot: Details
Be sure that students read this passage carefully, since this apparently ludicrous detail is critical for the resolution of the plot in Act Three.

The Importance of Being Earnest, Act One 879

READING CHECK TEST: ACT ONE

1. Jack confesses to Algernon that he is known as Ernest in town and Jack in the country. (T)

2. Ernest Worthing and Bunbury have something in common: They are both Algernon's relatives. (F)

3. Jack proposes to Gwendolen, and she accepts. (T)

4. Lady Bracknell approves of Jack as a possible suitor for her daughter. (F)

5. Jack is adopted and doesn't know who his natural parents are. (T)

A. Style
You might read this speech aloud to call students' attention to the diction, rhythm, and irony.

B. Dialogue
Wilde gave Lady Bracknell one of the best exit lines ever written.

C. Epigram
Here's another of Wilde's tart epigrams. Notice how natural it sounds; we've come to expect such acid wit from Algernon.

D. Interpreting
❓ What do you think Wilde means here? (Women often end up repeating their mothers' mistakes. Men would be better off if they were softer and more sensitive like their mothers.)

E. Style
Suggest to students that through Algernon, Wilde is commenting ironically on his own style. (Remind students that Wilde agreed with those who championed "style" as the chief element of a literary work.)

Lady Bracknell. The cloakroom at Victoria Station?

Jack. Yes. The Brighton line.

Lady Bracknell. The line is immaterial. Mr. Worthing, I confess I feel somewhat bewildered by what you have just told me. To be born, or at any rate bred, in a handbag, whether it had handles or not, seems to me to display a contempt for the ordinary decencies of family life that reminds one of the worst excesses of the French Revolution. And I presume you know what that unfortunate movement led to? As for the particular locality in which the handbag was found, a cloakroom at a railway station might serve to conceal a social indiscretion—has probably, indeed, been used for that purpose before now—but it could hardly be regarded as an assured basis for a recognized position in good society.

Jack. May I ask you then what you would advise me to do? I need hardly say I would do anything in the world to ensure Gwendolen's happiness.

Lady Bracknell. I would strongly advise you, Mr. Worthing, to try and acquire some relations as soon as possible, and to make a definite effort to produce at any rate one parent, of either sex, before the season is quite over.

Jack. Well, I don't see how I could possibly manage to do that. I can produce the handbag at any moment. It is in my dressing room at home. I really think that should satisfy you, Lady Bracknell.

Lady Bracknell. Me, sir! What has it to do with me? You can hardly imagine that I and Lord Bracknell would dream of allowing our only daughter—a girl brought up with the utmost care—to marry into a cloakroom, and form an alliance with a parcel. Good morning, Mr. Worthing!

[LADY BRACKNELL *sweeps out in majestic indignation.*]

Jack. Good morning! (ALGERNON, *from the other room, strikes up the Wedding March.* JACK *looks perfectly furious, and goes to the door.*) For goodness' sake, don't play that ghastly tune, Algy! How idiotic you are!

[*The music stops, and* ALGERNON *enters cheerily.*]

Algernon. Didn't it go off all right, old boy? You don't mean to say Gwendolen refused you? I know it is a way she has. She is always refusing people. I think it is most ill-natured of her.

Jack. Oh, Gwendolen is as right as a trivet.[21] As far as she is concerned, we are engaged. Her mother is perfectly unbearable. Never met such a Gorgon.[22] . . . I don't really know what a Gorgon is like, but I am quite sure that Lady Bracknell is one. In any case, she is a monster, without being a myth, which is rather unfair. . . . I beg your pardon, Algy, I suppose I shouldn't talk about your own aunt in that way before you.

Algernon. My dear boy, I love hearing my relations abused. It is the only thing that makes me put up with them at all. Relations are simply a tedious pack of people, who haven't got the remotest knowledge of how to live, nor the smallest instinct about when to die.

Jack. Oh, that is nonsense!

Algernon. It isn't!

Jack. Well, I won't argue about the matter. You always want to argue about things.

Algernon. That is exactly what things were originally made for.

Jack. Upon my word, if I thought that, I'd shoot myself. . . . (*A pause*) You don't think there is any chance of Gwendolen becoming like her mother in about a hundred and fifty years, do you, Algy?

Algernon. All women become like their mothers. That is their tragedy. No man does. That's his.

Jack. Is that clever?

Algernon. It is perfectly phrased! And quite as true as any observation in civilized life should be.

Jack. I am sick to death of cleverness. Everybody is clever nowadays. You can't go anywhere without meeting clever people. The thing has become an absolute public nuisance. I wish to goodness we had a few fools left.

Algernon. We have.

Jack. I should extremely like to meet them. What do they talk about?

Algernon. The fools? Oh! About the clever people, of course.

Jack. What fools.

Algernon. By the way, did you tell Gwendolen the truth about your being Ernest in town and Jack in the country?

Jack (*in a very patronizing manner*). My dear fellow, the truth isn't quite the sort of thing one tells

---

21. **right as a trivet:** steady or firm as a trivet, a short three-legged stand for holding hot pots and kettles.
22. **Gorgon:** in Greek mythology, one of three sisters who had snakes for hair. Anyone looking at a Gorgon would be turned to stone.

1. Jack tells Algernon that his real name is Jack and that he is known as Ernest in town and Jack in the country. Jack explains further that in order to come to town, he has invented a younger brother named Ernest, who lives in town and gets into terrible scrapes. Jack uses Ernest as an excuse to leave the country frequently.

2. Algernon has invented a sick friend named Bunbury, who lives in the country. "Bunburying" is Algernon's telling people that he is going to the country to take care of Bunbury when he is really doing something else.

3. She asks him numerous questions, including whether he smokes, how old he is, whether he knows everything or noth-ing, what his income is, etc. (See text pages 878–880.)

She advises him to produce one parent before the season is over.

4. He must convince Gwendolen's parents that he is an acceptable husband for Gwendolen. He must produce at least one parent and also get rid of his imaginary brother Ernest. He must tell Gwen-

(Answers continue on next page.)

---

to a nice, sweet, refined girl. What extraordinary ideas you have about the way to behave to a woman!

Algernon. The only way to behave to a woman is to make love[23] to her, if she is pretty, and to someone else, if she is plain.

Jack. Oh, that is nonsense.

Algernon. What about your brother? What about the profligate[24] Ernest?

Jack. Oh, before the end of the week I shall have got rid of him. I'll say he died in Paris of apoplexy.[25] Lots of people die of apoplexy, quite suddenly, don't they?

Algernon. Yes, but it's hereditary, my dear fellow. It's a sort of thing that runs in families. You had much better say a severe chill.

Jack. You are sure a severe chill isn't hereditary, or anything of that kind?

Algernon. Of course it isn't!

Jack. Very well, then. My poor brother Ernest is carried off suddenly, in Paris, by a severe chill. That gets rid of him.

Algernon. But I thought you said that . . . Miss Cardew was a little too much interested in your poor brother Ernest? Won't she feel his loss a good deal?

Jack. Oh, that is all right. Cecily is not a silly romantic girl, I am glad to say. She has got a capital appetite, goes for long walks, and pays no attention at all to her lessons.

Algernon. I would rather like to see Cecily.

Jack. I will take very good care you never do. She is excessively pretty, and she is only just eighteen.

Algernon. Have you told Gwendolen yet that you have an excessively pretty ward who is only just eighteen?

Jack. Oh! One doesn't blurt these things out to people. Cecily and Gwendolen are perfectly certain to be extremely great friends. I'll bet you anything you like that half an hour after they have met, they will be calling each other sister.

Algernon. Women only do that when they have called each other a lot of other things first. Now, my dear boy, if we want to get a good table at Willis', we really must go and dress. Do you know it is nearly seven?

Jack *(irritably).* Oh! It always is nearly seven.

Algernon. Well, I'm hungry.

Jack. I never knew you when you weren't. . . .

Algernon. What shall we do after dinner? Go to a theater?

Jack. Oh, no! I loathe listening.

Algernon. Well, let us go to the club?

Jack. Oh, no! I hate talking.

Algernon. Well, we might trot round to the Empire[26] at ten?

Jack. Oh, no! I can't bear looking at things. It is so silly.

Algernon. Well, what shall we do?

Jack. Nothing!

Algernon. It is awfully hard work doing nothing. However, I don't mind hard work where there is no definite object of any kind.

[*Enter* LANE.]

Lane. Miss Fairfax.

[*Enter* GWENDOLEN. LANE *goes out.*]

Algernon. Gwendolen, upon my word!

Gwendolen. Algy, kindly turn your back. I have something very particular to say to Mr. Worthing.

Algernon. Really, Gwendolen, I don't think I can allow this at all.

Gwendolen. Algy, you always adopt a strictly immoral attitude toward life. You are not quite old enough to do that. (ALGERNON *retires to the fireplace.*)

Jack. My own darling!

Gwendolen. Ernest, we may never be married. From the expression on Mama's face I fear we never shall. Few parents nowadays pay any regard to what their children say to them. The old-fashioned respect for the young is fast dying out. Whatever influence I ever had over Mama, I lost at the age of three. But although she may prevent us from becoming man and wife, and I may marry someone else, and marry often, nothing that she can possibly do can alter my eternal devotion to you.

Jack. Dear Gwendolen!

Gwendolen. The story of your romantic origin, as related to me by Mama, with unpleasing comments, has naturally stirred the deeper fibers of my nature. Your Christian name has an irresistible fascination. The simplicity of your character makes you exquisitely incomprehensible to me.

---

23. **to make love:** to court or woo.
24. **profligate** (präf′lə·git): shamelessly immoral.
25. **apoplexy** (ap′ə·plek′sē): a stroke.

26. **the Empire:** a popular theater or amusement hall.

A. Plot
The death of the imaginary Ernest is material for much of the comedy of Act Two.

B. Character
Notice how Wilde arouses our curiosity about Cecily before we meet her.
? Do you think she will be like Gwendolen or very different from her? Explain why. (She will be very like Gwendolen since all the characters are witty and sophisticated.)

C. Responding
? Do you agree or disagree? Do you find Jack and Algernon sympathetic or not? Explain. (Wilde pokes fun at everyone— those who work as well as those who do not. Jack and Algernon are sympathetic because they are charming and witty but unsympathetic because they lead idle, useless lives. They should, however, be judged not as real people but as types.)

D. Wilde's Wit
Ask students to explain how this sentence gives a new twist to a familiar saying. (It is often said that the young have no respect for the old.)

The Importance of Being Earnest, Act One   881

dolen about his ward Cecily. He intends to kill off his brother Ernest.

Interpreting Meanings
5. The dialogue is witty and fast-paced. Serious topics are satirized.
6. Lady Bracknell, who is trying to make sure her daughter "marries well," is the blocking figure.

7. Examples and answers will vary.
8. Students may mention finding out whether Jack and Gwendolen manage to get together and whether Jack's true identity is revealed.

A. Predicting Outcomes
? What do you think Algernon is planning to do? (Visit the forbidden Cecily at Jack's country home)

B. Stereotype
Lane is, of course, a stereotype of the discreet Victorian butler—but with one distinct difference: He spouts witty epigrams as easily as his master. Notice how Lane's appearances frame the act.

C. Responding
? Do you agree or disagree with Algernon's statement about nonsense? Thus far in the play, what have the characters talked about that isn't nonsense? (Serious subjects—love, marriage, social classes—have been satirized.) Act Two ends with the same remark— Jack accuses Algernon of talking nonsense.

Your town address at the Albany I have. What is your address in the country?
Jack. The Manor House, Woolton, Hertfordshire.

A [ALGERNON, *who has been carefully listening, smiles to himself, and writes the address on his shirt cuff. Then picks up the Railway Guide.*]

Gwendolen. There is a good postal service, I suppose? It may be necessary to do something desperate. That, of course, will require serious consideration. I will communicate with you daily.
Jack. My own one!
Gwendolen. How long do you remain in town?
Jack. Till Monday.
Gwendolen. Good! Algy, you may turn round now.
Algernon. Thanks, I've turned round already.
Gwendolen. You may also ring the bell.
Jack. You will let me see you to your carriage, my own darling?
Gwendolen. Certainly.
Jack (*to* LANE, *who now enters*). I will see Miss Fairfax out.
Lane. Yes, sir. (JACK *and* GWENDOLEN *go off.*)

[LANE *presents several letters on a salver to* ALGERNON. *It is to be surmised that they are bills, as* ALGERNON, *after looking at the envelopes, tears them up.*]

Algernon. A glass of sherry, Lane.
Lane. Yes, sir.
Algernon. Tomorrow, Lane, I'm going Bunburying.

Lane. Yes, sir.
Algernon. I shall probably not be back till Monday. You can put up my dress clothes, my smoking jacket,[27] and all the Bunbury suits. . . .
Lane. Yes, sir. (*Handing sherry*)
Algernon. I hope tomorrow will be a fine day, Lane.
Lane. It never is, sir.
Algernon. Lane, you're a perfect pessimist.
Lane. I do my best to give satisfaction, sir.

B

[*Enter* JACK. LANE *goes off.*]

Jack. There's a sensible, intellectual girl! The only girl I ever cared for in my life. (ALGERNON *is laughing immoderately.*) What on earth are you so amused at?
Algernon. Oh, I'm a little anxious about poor Bunbury, that is all.
Jack. If you don't take care, your friend Bunbury will get you into a serious scrape some day.
Algernon. I love scrapes. They are the only things that are never serious.
Jack. Oh, that's nonsense, Algy. You never talk anything but nonsense.
Algernon. Nobody ever does.

C

[JACK *looks indignantly at him, and leaves the room.* ALGERNON *lights a cigarette, reads his shirt cuff, and smiles.*]

---

27. **smoking jacket:** a velvet or silk jacket worn on informal occasions.

Responding to the Play

Analyzing Act One

Identifying Facts
1. What does Jack reveal to Algernon about his name?
2. Who is Bunbury, and what is "Bunburying"?
3. What questions does Lady Bracknell ask Jack in her inquisition of him? What does she advise him to do if he wants to marry Gwendolen?
4. At the end of Act One, what are the **obstacles** that Jack must overcome in his pursuit of Gwendolen? What is the first step he intends to take?

Interpreting Meanings
5. In what ways does the brief opening scene with the butler **foreshadow** the **tone** of the play?
6. Comedies often include a **blocking figure** who opposes the wishes of the young lovers. Who is the blocking figure here, and what is her **motive**?
7. Give some examples of Wilde's use of **epigrams** in Act One. Which epigrams strike you as the cleverest? Are they only throwaway lines, or do some of them contain a grain of truth?
8. What do you look forward to happening next? How has Wilde piqued your curiosity about future events?

The setting is the garden of Jack's country home. Jack's eighteen-year-old ward Cecily and her governess, Miss Prism, are discussing a variety of topics, including Jack's wayward brother Ernest. Dr. Chasuble, the rector, arrives and goes for a walk with Miss Prism. Algernon arrives, posing as the fictional Ernest Worthing, Jack's brother. He and Cecily converse wittily and are attracted to each other. When the two go into the house, Miss Prism and Dr. Chasuble return. Jack arrives, claiming that his brother Ernest has died in Paris from a severe chill. He also arranges with Chasuble to be christened as Ernest later in the day.

Cecily appears and informs Jack that Ernest is in the dining room. Jack is furious with Algernon and tells him to leave, but Algernon delays. Alone together, Cecily informs Algernon (alias Ernest) that they have been engaged for the past three months. She tells him she loves him because of his name, and he goes off (like Jack) to find Chasuble to arrange a christening.

Gwendolen arrives and is welcomed by Cecily. They get along very well until *(Continued on next page.)*

Act Two

Garden at the Manor House. A flight of gray stone steps leads up to the house. The garden, an old-fashioned one, full of roses. Time of year, July. Basket chairs, and a table covered with books, are set under a large yew tree.

MISS PRISM discovered seated at the table. CECILY is at the back, watering flowers.

A **Miss Prism** *(calling).* Cecily, Cecily! Surely such a utilitarian occupation as the watering of flowers is rather Moulton's[1] duty than yours? Especially at a moment when intellectual pleasures await you. Your German grammar is on the table. Pray open it at page fifteen. We will repeat yesterday's lesson.

Cecily *(coming over very slowly).* But I don't like German. It isn't at all a becoming language. I know perfectly well that I look quite plain after my German lesson.

Miss Prism. Child, you know how anxious your guardian is that you should improve yourself in every way. He laid particular stress on your German, as he was leaving for town yesterday. Indeed, he always lays stress on your German when he is leaving for town.

Cecily. Dear Uncle Jack is so very serious! Sometimes he is so serious that I think he cannot be quite well.

Miss Prism *(drawing herself up).* Your guardian enjoys the best of health, and his gravity of demeanor is especially to be commended in one so comparatively young as he is. I know no one who has a higher sense of duty and responsibility.

Cecily. I suppose that is why he often looks a little bored when we three are together.

Miss Prism. Cecily! I am surprised at you. Mr. Worthing has many troubles in his life. Idle merriment and triviality would be out of place in his conversation. You must remember his constant anxiety about that unfortunate young man, his brother.

Cecily. I wish Uncle Jack would allow that unfortunate young man, his brother, to come down here sometimes. We might have a good influence over him, Miss Prism. I am sure you certainly would.

You know German and geology, and things of that kind influence a man very much. (CECILY *begins to write in her diary.*)

Miss Prism *(shaking her head).* I do not think that even I could produce any effect on a character that according to his own brother's admission is irretrievably weak and vacillating. Indeed I am not sure that I would desire to reclaim him. I am not in favor of this modern mania for turning bad people into good people at a moment's notice. As a man sows, so let him reap. You must put away your diary, Cecily. I really don't see why you should keep a diary at all.

Cecily. I keep a diary in order to enter the wonderful secrets of my life. If I didn't write them down, I should probably forget all about them.

Miss Prism. Memory, my dear Cecily, is the diary that we all carry about with us.

Cecily. Yes, but it usually chronicles the things that have never happened, and couldn't possibly have happened. I believe that memory is responsible for nearly all the three-volume novels that Mudie[2] sends us.

B **Miss Prism.** Do not speak slightingly of the three-volume novel,[3] Cecily. I wrote one myself in earlier days.

Cecily. Did you really, Miss Prism? How wonderfully clever you are! I hope it did not end happily?

C I don't like novels that end happily. They depress me so much.

Miss Prism. The good ended happily, and the bad unhappily. That is what fiction means.

Cecily. I suppose so. But it seems very unfair. And was your novel ever published?

Miss Prism. Alas! No. The manuscript unfortunately was abandoned. (CECILY *starts.*) I used the word in the sense of lost or mislaid. To your work, child, these speculations are profitless.

Cecily *(smiling).* But I see dear Dr. Chasuble coming up through the garden.

Miss Prism *(rising and advancing).* Dr. Chasuble! This is indeed a pleasure.

D [*Enter* CANON CHASUBLE.]

Chasuble. And how are we this morning? Miss Prism, you are, I trust, well?

Cecily. Miss Prism has just been complaining of a slight headache. I think it would do her so much

---

1. **Moulton:** the gardener, a minor character in the original four-act version of the play.

2. **Mudie:** a lending library in London.
3. In an essay, "The Critic as Artist," Oscar Wilde wrote: "Anybody can write a three-volume novel. It merely requires a complete ignorance of both life and literature."

A. Interpreting
? What does the name "Prism" suggest? (That she is prim or prissy, or both. See the answers to question 1, The Play as a Whole, text page 906.)

B. Plot: Details
Until the 1920's long novels were published in a number of volumes, rather than as one hefty book. Miss Prism's novel is a significant detail for the climax and resolution of the play.

C. Paradox
? Explain the paradox in these lines. (Wilde again reverses the accepted norm. This remark is meant to be witty rather than truthful.)

D. Expansion
Canon Chasuble has a "speaking name"—that is, a name with meanings appropriate to his character. A *chasuble* is a vestment worn by priests of the Roman Catholic Church and the Church of England for the celebration of Mass. *Canon* is an honorific title given to some priests in the Church of England.

(Continued from previous page.)

both say they are engaged to Ernest Worthing. After they quarrel during tea, Jack and Algernon enter and the mix-up is unraveled. When both young men reveal that their names are not Ernest, the girls go off in a huff. The act ends with the young men bickering over christenings and muffins.

A. Responding to the Photograph

? Who are the characters shown here? (Cecily, Canon Chasuble, Miss Prism) Describe how you imagined these characters' appearance. Based on the caption, how would you say Canon Chasuble feels about Miss Prism? (There may be another love interest brewing here.) Note that in the stage direction on page 885, Wilde says that Miss Prism *glares* at Canon Chasuble in response to his compliment.

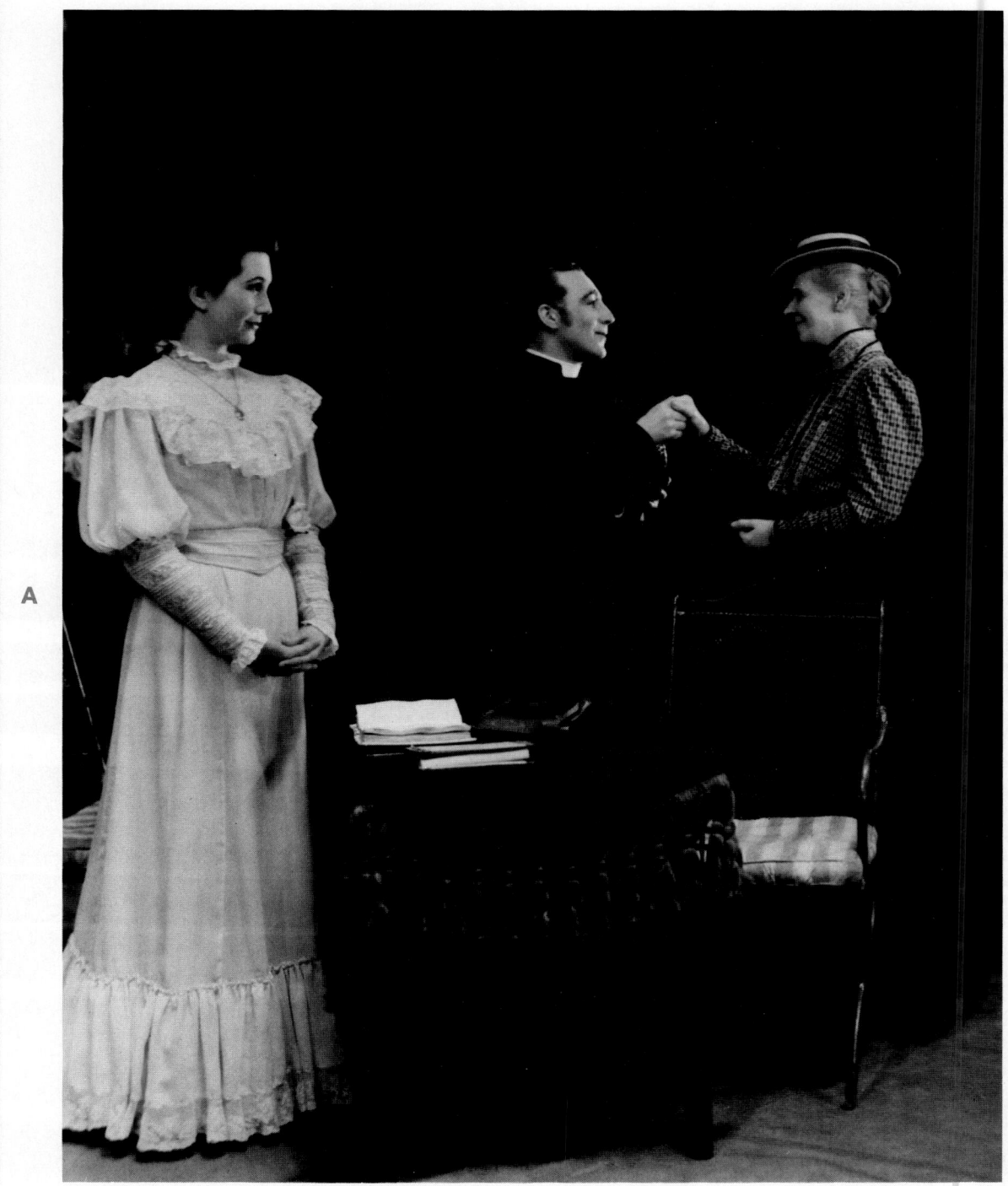

A

"Were I fortunate enough to be Miss Prism's pupil, I would hang upon her lips."

good to have a short stroll with you in the park, Dr. Chasuble.

Miss Prism. Cecily, I have not mentioned anything about a headache.

Cecily. No, dear Miss Prism, I know that, but I felt instinctively that you had a headache. Indeed I was thinking about that, and not about my German lesson, when the Rector came in.

Chasuble. I hope, Cecily, you are not inattentive.

Cecily. Oh, I am afraid I am.

Chasuble. That is strange. Were I fortunate enough to be Miss Prism's pupil, I would hang upon her lips. (MISS PRISM *glares.*) I spoke metaphorically. My metaphor was drawn from bees. Ahem! Mr. Worthing, I suppose, has not returned from town yet?

Miss Prism. We do not expect him till Monday afternoon.

Chasuble. Ah, yes, he usually likes to spend his Sunday in London. He is not one of those whose sole aim is enjoyment, as, by all accounts, that unfortunate young man his brother seems to be. But I must not disturb Egeria[4] and her pupil any longer.

Miss Prism. Egeria? My name is Laetitia, Doctor.

Chasuble (*bowing*). A classical allusion merely, drawn from the pagan authors. I shall see you both no doubt at Evensong?[5]

Miss Prism. I think, dear Doctor, I will have a stroll with you. I find I have a headache after all, and a walk might do it good.

Chasuble. With pleasure, Miss Prism, with pleasure. We might go as far as the schools and back.

Miss Prism. That would be delightful. Cecily, you will read your political economy in my absence. The chapter on the fall of the rupee[6] you may omit. It is somewhat too sensational. Even these metallic problems have their <u>melodramatic</u> side. (*Goes down the garden with* DR. CHASUBLE)

Cecily (*picks up books and throws them back on table*). Horrid political economy! Horrid geography! Horrid, horrid German!

[*Enter* MERRIMAN *with a card on a salver.*]

Merriman. Mr. Ernest Worthing has just driven over from the station. He has brought his luggage with him.

---

4. **Egeria** (i·jir′ē·ə): a woman adviser; in Roman mythology, Egeria was the nymph who advised the second legendary king of Rome.
5. **Evensong:** evening prayer service.
6. **rupee** (roo·pē′): monetary unit of India.

Cecily (*takes the card and reads it*). "Mr. Ernest Worthing, B.4, The Albany, W." Uncle Jack's brother! Did you tell him Mr. Worthing was in town?

Merriman. Yes, miss. He seemed very much disappointed. I mentioned that you and Miss Prism were in the garden. He said he was anxious to speak to you privately for a moment.

Cecily. Ask Mr. Ernest Worthing to come here. I suppose you had better talk to the housekeeper about a room for him.

Merriman. Yes, miss. (MERRIMAN *goes off.*)

Cecily. I have never met any really wicked person before. I feel rather frightened. I am so afraid he will look just like everyone else. (*Enter* ALGERNON, *very gay and debonair.*) He does!

Algernon (*raising his hat*). You are my little cousin Cecily, I'm sure.

Cecily. You are under some strange mistake. I am not little. In fact, I believe I am more than usually tall for my age. (ALGERNON *is rather taken aback.*) But I am your cousin Cecily. You, I see from your card, are Uncle Jack's brother, my cousin Ernest, my wicked cousin Ernest.

Algernon. Oh! I am not really wicked at all, Cousin Cecily. You mustn't think that I am wicked.

Cecily. If you are not, then you have certainly been deceiving us all in a very inexcusable manner. I hope you have not been leading a double life, pretending to be wicked and being really good all the time. That would be hypocrisy.

Algernon (*looks at her in amazement*). Oh! Of course I have been rather reckless.

Cecily. I am glad to hear it.

Algernon. In fact, now you mention the subject, I have been very bad in my own small way.

Cecily. I don't think you should be so proud of that, though I am sure it must have been very pleasant.

Algernon. It is much pleasanter being here with you.

Cecily. I can't understand how you are here at all. Uncle Jack won't be back till Monday afternoon.

Algernon. That is a great disappointment. I am obliged to go up by the first train on Monday morning. I have a business appointment that I am anxious . . . to miss!

Cecily. Couldn't you miss it anywhere but in London?

Algernon. No, the appointment is in London.

Cecily. Well, I know, of course, how important it is not to keep a business engagement, if one wants

A

B

C

D

A. Satire

❓ What is Wilde poking fun at here? (Chasuble's silly metaphor about bees and his obscure classical allusions are examples of the ostentatious display of knowledge that Wilde detested.)

B. Responding

❓ What do you think of Cecily so far?

C. Motivation/ Theme

❓ What do you suppose Algernon is up to, masquerading as the imaginary Ernest? (He may be just having fun at Jack's expense, but it soon becomes clear that he's interested in Cecily.) So far in the play, how is the subject of identity (or false identity) important to the plot? (Both Algernon and Jack have invented false characters/ identities. Jack's ignorance of his true identity handicaps him as a suitor for Gwendolen.)

D. Irony

Note Wilde's topsy-turvy definition of *hypocrisy*. It's usually the other way around.

A. Plot
Here is Jack's solution for getting rid of the imaginary Ernest.

B. Epigram
Another of Wilde's delicious barbs. Note how smoothly he works these into the dialogue.

C. Humor
Ask students to comment on the humor in this courtship scene. (Characters spar and exchange witticisms as in the rest of the play.)

D. Vocabulary/ Motive
Students need to know that a *misanthrope* is a person who hates and distrusts men (that is, all human beings). Miss Prism has just made up a *neologism* (new word) for a woman hater.

? What is Miss Prism up to in this scene? (She's trying to convince Chasuble to marry; she may have staked him out for herself.)

E. Repetition/ Humor
Note that Miss Prism's line echoes almost exactly Canon Chasuble's earlier remark about his metaphor from bees.

to retain any sense of the beauty of life, but still I think you had better wait till Uncle Jack arrives. I know he wants to speak to you about your emigrating.

Algernon. About my what?

Cecily. Your emigrating. He has gone up to buy your outfit.

Algernon. I certainly wouldn't let Jack buy my outfit. He has no taste in neckties at all.

Cecily. I don't think you will require neckties. Uncle Jack is sending you to Australia.[7]

Algernon. Australia! I'd sooner die.

Cecily. Well, he said at dinner on Wednesday night that you would have to choose between this world, the next world, and Australia.

Algernon. Oh, well! The accounts I have received of Australia and the next world are not particularly encouraging. This world is good enough for me, Cousin Cecily.

Cecily. Yes, but are you good enough for it?

Algernon. I'm afraid I'm not that. That is why I want you to reform me. You might make that your mission, if you don't mind, Cousin Cecily.

Cecily. I'm afraid I've no time, this afternoon.

Algernon. Well, would you mind my reforming myself this afternoon?

Cecily. It is rather Quixotic[8] of you. But I think you should try.

Algernon. I will. I feel better already.

Cecily. You are looking a little worse.

Algernon. That is because I am hungry.

Cecily. How thoughtless of me. I should have remembered that when one is going to lead an entirely new life, one requires regular and wholesome meals. Won't you come in?

Algernon. Thank you. Might I have a buttonhole[9] first? I never have any appetite unless I have a buttonhole first.

Cecily. A Maréchal Niel?[10] *(Picks up scissors)*

Algernon. No, I'd sooner have a pink rose.

Cecily. Why? *(Cuts a flower)*

Algernon. Because you are like a pink rose, Cousin Cecily.

Cecily. I don't think it can be right for you to talk to me like that. Miss Prism never says such things to me.

Algernon. Then Miss Prism is a shortsighted old lady. *(CECILY puts the rose in his buttonhole.)* You are the prettiest girl I ever saw.

Cecily. Miss Prism says that all good looks are a snare.

Algernon. They are a snare that every sensible man would like to be caught in.

Cecily. Oh, I don't think I would care to catch a sensible man. I shouldn't know what to talk to him about.

[*They pass into the house.* MISS PRISM *and* DR. CHASUBLE *return.*]

Miss Prism. You are too much alone, dear Dr. Chasuble. You should get married. A misanthrope I can understand—a womanthrope, never!

Chasuble *(with a scholar's shudder).* Believe me, I do not deserve so neologistic[11] a phrase. The precept as well as the practice of the Primitive Church[12] was distinctly against matrimony.

Miss Prism *(sententiously).* That is obviously the reason why the Primitive Church has not lasted up to the present day. And you do not seem to realize, dear Doctor, that by persistently remaining single, a man converts himself into a permanent public temptation. Men should be more careful; this very celibacy leads weaker vessels astray.

Chasuble. But is a man not equally attractive when married?

Miss Prism. No married man is ever attractive except to his wife.

Chasuble. And often, I've been told, not even to her.

Miss Prism. That depends on the intellectual sympathies of the woman. Maturity can always be depended on. Ripeness can be trusted. Young women are green. *(DR. CHASUBLE starts.)* I spoke horticulturally. My metaphor was drawn from fruits. But where is Cecily?

Chasuble. Perhaps she followed us to the schools.

[*Enter* JACK *slowly from the back of the garden.*

---

7. **Australia:** From 1787 to the mid-nineteenth century, British convicts and other offenders were sent to live in Australia.
8. **Quixotic** (kwik·sät'ik): rash, idealistic, and impractical; from the hero of *Don Quixote*, a seventeenth-century satire on the romance.
9. **buttonhole:** flower worn in a lapel buttonhole.
10. **Maréchal Niel:** a climbing yellow rose.

---

11. **neologistic:** newly invented (word or phrase), from *neo-*, "new," and *logos*, "word."
12. **Primitive Church:** the early Christian church during the first three centuries.

A

He is dressed in the deepest mourning, with crepe hatband and black gloves.]

Miss Prism. Mr. Worthing!

Chasuble. Mr. Worthing?

Miss Prism. This is indeed a surprise. We did not look for you till Monday afternoon.

Jack *(shakes* MISS PRISM's *hand in a tragic manner)*. I have returned sooner than I expected. Dr. Chasuble, I hope you are well?

Chasuble. Dear Mr. Worthing, I trust this garb of woe does not betoken some terrible calamity?

Jack. My brother.

Miss Prism. More shameful debts and extravagance?

Chasuble. Still leading his life of pleasure?

B

Jack *(shaking his head)*. Dead!

Chasuble. Your brother Ernest dead?

Jack. Quite dead.

Miss Prism. What a lesson for him! I trust he will profit by it.

Chasuble. Mr. Worthing, I offer you my sincere condolence. You have at least the consolation of knowing that you were always the most generous and forgiving of brothers.

Jack. Poor Ernest! He had many faults, but it is a sad, sad blow.

Chasuble. Very sad indeed. Were you with him at the end?

Jack. No. He died abroad; in Paris, in fact. I had a telegram last night from the manager of the Grand Hotel.

Chasuble. Was the cause of death mentioned?

Jack. A severe chill, it seems.

Miss Prism. As a man sows, so shall he reap.

Chasuble *(raising his hand)*. Charity, dear Miss Prism, charity! None of us are perfect. I myself am peculiarly susceptible to drafts. Will the interment take place here?

Jack. No. He seems to have expressed a desire to be buried in Paris.

Chasuble. In Paris. *(Shakes his head)* I fear that hardly points to any very serious state of mind at the last. You would no doubt wish me to make some slight allusion to this tragic domestic affliction next Sunday. (JACK *presses his hand convulsively.)* My sermon on the meaning of the manna in the wilderness can be adapted to almost any occasion, joyful, or, as in the present case, distressing. *(All sigh.)* I have preached it at harvest

C

celebrations, christenings, confirmations, on days of humiliation and festal days. The last time I delivered it was in the Cathedral, as a charity sermon on behalf of the Society for the Prevention of Discontent among the Upper Orders. The Bishop, who was present, was much struck by some of the analogies I drew.

Jack. Ah! That reminds me, you mentioned christenings, I think, Dr. Chasuble? I suppose you know how to christen all right? (DR. CHASUBLE *looks astounded.)* I mean, of course, you are continually christening, aren't you?

D

Miss Prism. It is, I regret to say, one of the Rector's most constant duties in this parish. I have often spoken to the poorer classes on the subject. But they don't seem to know what thrift is.

Chasuble. But is there any particular infant in whom you are interested, Mr. Worthing? Your brother was, I believe, unmarried, was he not?

Jack. Oh, yes.

Miss Prism *(bitterly)*. People who live entirely for pleasure usually are.

Jack. But it is not for any child, dear Doctor. I am very fond of children. No! The fact is, I would like to be christened myself, this afternoon, if you have nothing better to do.

Chasuble. But surely, Mr. Worthing, you have been christened already?

Jack. I don't remember anything about it.

Chasuble. But have you any grave doubts on the subject?

Jack. I certainly intend to have. Of course, I don't know if the thing would bother you in any way, or if you think I am a little too old now.

Chasuble. Not at all. The sprinkling and, indeed, the immersion of adults is a perfectly canonical practice.

Jack. Immersion!

Chasuble. You need have no apprehensions. Sprinkling is all that is necessary, or indeed I think advisable. Our weather is so changeable. At what hour would you wish the ceremony performed?

Jack. Oh, I might trot round about five if that would suit you.

Chasuble. Perfectly, perfectly! In fact I have two similar ceremonies to perform at that time. A case of twins that occurred recently in one of the outlying cottages on your own estate. Poor Jenkins the carter, a most hard-working man.

Jack. Oh! I don't see much fun in being christened along with other babies. It would be childish. Would half-past five do?

A. Visual Humor
In live performances, the audience start to laugh as soon as they see Jack because they can guess from his clothes what's coming next.

B. Dramatic Irony
Our enjoyment of this scene and situation is heightened because we know what none of the characters onstage know: Ernest (Algernon) is inside the house with Cecily.

C. Satire
Wilde is lampooning the all-purpose sermon completely unrelated to real-life problems. No matter what the occasion, Chasuble has the same sermon ready to go.

D. Predicting Outcomes
? What do you guess Jack is up to here? (Officially changing his name to Ernest to keep Gwendolen's love)

A. Dramatic Irony
We know what some of the characters onstage don't: that Algernon is an impostor. Our knowledge of what's true heightens the humor of Algernon's deception.

B. Irony
❓ Explain the irony of Chasuble's lines. (The reconciliation is hardly "perfect," and the men are not brothers.)

Chasuble. Admirably! Admirably! *(Takes out watch)* And now, dear Mr. Worthing, I will not intrude any longer into a house of sorrow. I would merely beg you not to be too much bowed down by grief. What seems to us bitter trials are often blessings in disguise.

Miss Prism. This seems to me a blessing of an extremely obvious kind.

[Enter CECILY *from the house.]*

Cecily. Uncle Jack! Oh, I am pleased to see you back. But what horrid clothes you have got on. Do go and change them.

Miss Prism. Cecily!

Chasuble. My child! My child! (CECILY *goes toward* JACK; *he kisses her brow in a melancholy manner.)*

Cecily. What is the matter, Uncle Jack? Do look happy! You look as if you had a toothache, and I have got such a surprise for you. Who do you think is in the dining room? Your brother!

Jack. Who?

Cecily. Your brother Ernest. He arrived about half an hour ago.

Jack. What nonsense! I haven't got a brother.

Cecily. Oh, don't say that. However badly he may have behaved to you in the past he is still your brother. You couldn't be so heartless as to disown him. I'll tell him to come out. And you will shake hands with him, won't you, Uncle Jack? *(Runs back into the house)*

Chasuble. These are very joyful tidings.

Miss Prism. After we had all been resigned to his loss, his sudden return seems to me peculiarly distressing.

Jack. My brother is in the dining room? I don't know what it all means. I think it is perfectly absurd.

[Enter ALGERNON *and* CECILY *hand in hand. They come slowly up to* JACK.]

Jack. Good heavens! *(Motions* ALGERNON *away)*

Algernon. Brother John, I have come down from town to tell you that I am very sorry for all the trouble I have given you, and that I intend to lead a better life in the future. (JACK *glares at him and does not take his hand.)*

Cecily. Uncle Jack, you are not going to refuse your own brother's hand?

Jack. Nothing will induce me to take his hand. I think his coming down here disgraceful. He knows perfectly well why.

Cecily. Uncle Jack, do be nice. There is some good in everyone. Ernest has just been telling me about his poor invalid friend, Mr. Bunbury, whom he goes to visit so often. And surely there must be much good in one who is kind to an invalid, and leaves the pleasures of London to sit by a bed of pain.

Jack. Oh! He has been talking about Bunbury, has he?

Cecily. Yes, he has told me all about poor Mr. Bunbury, and his terrible state of health.

Jack. Bunbury! Well, I won't have him talk to you about Bunbury or about anything else. It is enough to drive one perfectly frantic.

Algernon. Of course I admit that the faults were all on my side. But I must say that I think that Brother John's coldness to me is peculiarly painful. I expected a more enthusiastic welcome, especially considering it is the first time I have come here.

Cecily. Uncle Jack, if you don't shake hands with Ernest, I will never forgive you.

Jack. Never forgive me?

Cecily. Never, never, never!

Jack. Well, this is the last time I shall ever do it. *(Shakes hands with* ALGERNON *and glares)*

Chasuble. It's pleasant, is it not, to see so perfect a reconciliation? I think we might leave the two brothers together.

Miss Prism. Cecily, you will come with us.

Cecily. Certainly, Miss Prism. My little task of reconciliation is over.

Chasuble. You have done a beautiful action today, dear child.

Miss Prism. We must not be premature in our judgments.

Cecily. I feel very happy. *(They all go off except* JACK *and* ALGERNON.*)*

Jack. You young scoundrel, Algy, you must get out of this place as soon as possible. I don't allow any Bunburying here.

[Enter MERRIMAN.]

Merriman. I have put Mr. Ernest's things in the room next to yours, sir. I suppose that is all right?

Jack. What?

Merriman. Mr. Ernest's luggage, sir. I have unpacked it and put it in the room next to your own.

Jack. His luggage?

Merriman. Yes, sir. Three portmanteaus,[13] a

---

13. **portmanteaus** (pôrt·man′tōz): suitcases.

dressing case, two hatboxes, and a large luncheon basket.

Algernon. I am afraid I can't stay more than a week this time.

Jack. Merriman, order the dogcart[14] at once. Mr. Ernest has been suddenly called back to town.

Merriman. Yes, sir. *(Goes back into the house)*

Algernon. What a fearful liar you are, Jack. I have not been called back to town at all.

Jack. Yes, you have.

Algernon. I haven't heard anyone call me.

Jack. Your duty as a gentleman calls you back.

Algernon. My duty as a gentleman has never interfered with my pleasures in the smallest degree.

Jack. I can quite understand that.

Algernon. Well, Cecily is a darling.

Jack. You are not to talk of Miss Cardew like that. I don't like it.

Algernon. Well, I don't like your clothes. You look perfectly ridiculous in them. Why on earth don't you go up and change? It is perfectly childish to be in deep mourning for a man who is actually staying for a whole week with you in your house as a guest. I call it grotesque.

Jack. You are certainly not staying with me for a whole week as a guest or anything else. You have got to leave . . . by the four-five train.

Algernon. I certainly won't leave you so long as you are in mourning. It would be most unfriendly. If I were in mourning, you would stay with me, I suppose. I should think it very unkind if you didn't.

Jack. Well, will you go if I change my clothes?

Algernon. Yes, if you are not too long. I never saw anybody take so long to dress, and with such little result.

Jack. Well, at any rate, that is better than being always overdressed as you are.

Algernon. If I am occasionally a little overdressed, I make up for it by being always immensely over-educated.

Jack. Your vanity is ridiculous, your conduct an outrage, and your presence in my garden utterly absurd. However, you have got to catch the four-five, and I hope you will have a pleasant journey back to town. This Bunburying, as you call it, has not been a great success for you. *(Goes into the house)*

Algernon. I think it has been a great success. I'm in love with Cecily, and that is everything. *(Enter* CECILY *at the back of the garden. She picks up the can and begins to water the flowers.)* But I must see her before I go, and make arrangements for another Bunbury. Ah, there she is.

Cecily. Oh, I merely came back to water the roses. I thought you were with Uncle Jack.

Algernon. He's gone to order the dogcart for me.

Cecily. Oh, is he going to take you for a nice drive?

Algernon. He's going to send me away.

Cecily. Then have we got to part?

Algernon. I am afraid so. It's a very painful parting.

Cecily. It is always painful to part from people whom one has known for a very brief space of time. The absence of old friends one can endure with equanimity. But even a momentary separation from anyone to whom one has just been introduced is almost unbearable.

Algernon. Thank you.

[*Enter* MERRIMAN.]

Merriman. The dogcart is at the door, sir.

[ALGERNON *looks at* CECILY *appealingly.*]

Cecily. It can wait, Merriman . . . for . . . five minutes.

Merriman. Yes, miss. *(Exit.)*

Algernon. I hope, Cecily, I shall not offend you if I state quite frankly and openly that you seem to me to be in every way the visible personification of absolute perfection.

Cecily. I think your frankness does you great credit, Ernest. If you will allow me, I will copy your remarks into my diary. *(Goes over to table and begins writing in diary)*

Algernon. Do you really keep a diary? I'd give anything to look at it. May I?

Cecily. Oh, no. *(Puts her hand over it)* You see, it is simply a very young girl's record of her own thoughts and impressions, and consequently meant for publication. When it appears in volume form, I hope you will order a copy. But pray, Ernest, don't stop. I delight in taking down from dictation. I have reached "absolute perfection." You can go on, I am quite ready for more.

Algernon *(somewhat taken aback)*. Ahem! Ahem!

Cecily. Oh, don't cough, Ernest. When one is dictating one should speak fluently and not cough. Besides, I don't know how to spell a cough. *(Writes as* ALGERNON *speaks)*

---

14. **dogcart:** a light, open horse-drawn carriage; originally with a special seat for a hunting dog.

A. Character
Note that Algernon is engaging in what's called "the pot calling the kettle black": He has been lying all through this act.

B. Farce
In a farce, actions are exaggerated and hardly credible. Algernon's love at first sight brings the total couples up to three.

❓ How do you think Cecily will respond to Algernon's declaration of love? (Positively)

C. Paradox
Ask students to explain the paradox in this speech and to tell whether they think there's any truth to what Cecily says. (Wilde is mocking the idea of love at first sight.)

D. Satire
Wilde is satirizing the Victorian practice (especially common among women) of keeping a journal, some of which were apparently published. Wilde has another funny bit about diaries in Gwendolen's speech on text page 893 at the top of the right column.

A. Responding

❓ Do you think that Cecily's speech is completely silly, or does it contain a grain of truth? What do you think of Cecily's passion for the imaginary Ernest (Algernon)? (The characters in this play are not meant to be real, but rather comic versions of real types and attitudes.)

B. Expansion

Notice that the date is, appropriately, Valentine's Day.

C. Satire

❓ What do you think is the point of Cecily's description of her imaginary engagement? (Wilde is satirizing the romantic imagination of women. Cecily, who seemed so down-to-earth and likable earlier in the act, is shown to be just as silly and absurd as Gwendolen.)

D. Title

Gwendolen made nearly the same speech to Jack near the end of Act One. (What a reason for loving a man!) Now we begin to understand the title.

Algernon (*speaking very rapidly*). Cecily, ever since I first looked upon your wonderful and incomparable beauty, I have dared to love you wildly, passionately, devotedly, hopelessly.

Cecily. I don't think that you should tell me that you love me wildly, passionately, devotedly, hopelessly. Hopelessly doesn't seem to make much sense, does it?

Algernon. Cecily.

[*Enter* MERRIMAN.]

Merriman. The dogcart is waiting, sir.

Algernon. Tell it to come round next week, at the same hour.

Merriman (*looks at* CECILY, *who makes no sign*). Yes, sir. (MERRIMAN *retires.*)

Cecily. Uncle Jack would be very much annoyed if he knew you were staying on till next week, at the same hour.

Algernon. Oh, I don't care about Jack. I don't care for anybody in the whole world but you. I love you, Cecily. You will marry me, won't you?

Cecily. You silly boy! Of course. Why, we have been engaged for the last three months.

Algernon. For the last three months?

Cecily. Yes, it will be exactly three months on Thursday.

Algernon. But how did we become engaged?

Cecily. Well, ever since dear Uncle Jack first confessed to us that he had a younger brother who was very wicked and bad, you, of course, have formed the chief topic of conversation between myself and Miss Prism. And of course a man who is much talked about is always very attractive. One feels there must be something in him, after all. I daresay it was foolish of me; but I fell in love with you, Ernest.

Algernon. Darling. And when was the engagement actually settled?

Cecily. On the fourteenth of February last. Worn out by your entire ignorance of my existence, I determined to end the matter one way or the other, and after a long struggle with myself, I accepted you under this dear old tree here. The next day I bought this little ring in your name, and this is the little bangle with the true lovers' knot I promised you always to wear.

Algernon. Did I give you this? It's very pretty, isn't it?

Cecily. Yes, you've wonderfully good taste, Ernest. It's the excuse I've always given for your leading such a bad life. And this is the box in which I keep all your dear letters. (*Kneels at table, opens box, and produces letters tied up with blue ribbon*)

Algernon. My letters! But, my own sweet Cecily, I have never written you any letters.

Cecily. You need hardly remind me of that, Ernest. I remember only too well that I was forced to write your letters for you. I wrote always three times a week, and sometimes oftener.

Algernon. Oh, do let me read them, Cecily?

Cecily. Oh, I couldn't possibly. They would make you far too conceited. (*Replaces box*) The three you wrote me after I had broken off the engagement are so beautiful, and so badly spelled, that even now I can hardly read them without crying a little.

Algernon. But was our engagement ever broken off?

Cecily. Of course it was. On the twenty-second of last March. You can see the entry if you like. (*Shows diary*) "Today I broke off my engagement with Ernest. I feel it is better to do so. The weather still continues charming."

Algernon. But why on earth did you break it off? What had I done? I had done nothing at all. Cecily, I am very much hurt indeed to hear you broke it off. Particularly when the weather was so charming.

Cecily. It would hardly have been a really serious engagement if it hadn't been broken off at least once. But I forgave you before the week was out.

Algernon (*crossing to her, and kneeling*). What a perfect angel you are, Cecily.

Cecily. You dear romantic boy. (*He kisses her, she puts her fingers through his hair.*) I hope your hair curls naturally, does it?

Algernon. Yes, darling, with a little help from others.

Cecily. I am so glad.

Algernon. You'll never break off our engagement again, Cecily?

Cecily. I don't think I could break it off now that I have actually met you. Besides, of course, there is the question of your name.

Algernon (*nervously*). Yes, of course.

Cecily. You must not laugh at me, darling, but it had always been a girlish dream of mine to love someone whose name was Ernest. (ALGERNON *rises*, CECILY *also.*) There is something in that name that seems to inspire absolute confidence. I pity any poor married woman whose husband is not called Ernest.

Algernon. But, my dear child, do you mean to say you could not love me if I had some other name?
Cecily. But what name?
Algernon. Oh, any name you like—Algernon—for instance . . .
Cecily. But I don't like the name of Algernon.
Algernon. Well, my own dear, sweet, loving little darling, I really can't see why you should object to the name of Algernon. It is not at all a bad name. In fact, it is rather an aristocratic name. Half of the chaps who get into the Bankruptcy Court are called Algernon. But seriously, Cecily *(moving to her),* if my name was Algy, couldn't you love me?

Cecily *(rising).* I might respect you, Ernest, I might admire your character, but I fear that I should not be able to give you my undivided attention.
Algernon. Ahem! Cecily! *(Picking up hat)* Your Rector here is, I suppose, thoroughly experienced in the practice of all the rites and ceremonials of the church?
Cecily. Oh, yes. Dr. Chasuble is a most learned man. He has never written a single book, so you can imagine how much he knows.
Algernon. I must see him at once on a most important christening—I mean on most important business.

A. Repetition/ Humor
One of Wilde's most effective comic devices is repetition. Note that Gwendolen has told Jack the same thing in Act One.

B. Plot
Here's another parallel.
? What is Algernon up to? (He's going to be rechristened as Ernest.)

C. Responding to the Photograph
? What's ironic about Cecily's talk of her "true love"? (She doesn't love Algernon at all—only a fiction of an imaginary man. She refuses to love the flesh-and-blood Algernon unless his name is Ernest.)

"*. . . and this is the little bangle with the true lovers' knot I promised you always to wear.*"

A. Irony
This famous scene between Gwendolen and Cecily involves two ironic reversals; have students watch for them.

B. Oral Reading
You might call on volunteers to read this scene aloud.

Cecily. Oh!

Algernon. I shan't be away more than half an hour.

Cecily. Considering that we have been engaged since February the fourteenth, and that I only met you today for the first time, I think it is rather hard that you should leave me for so long a period as half an hour. Couldn't you make it twenty minutes?

Algernon. I'll be back in no time. *(Kisses her and rushes down the garden)*

Cecily. What an impetuous boy he is! I like his hair so much. I must enter his proposal in my diary.

[*Enter* MERRIMAN.]

Merriman. A Miss Fairfax just called to see Mr. Worthing. On very important business, Miss Fairfax states.

Cecily. Isn't Mr. Worthing in his library?

Merriman. Mr. Worthing went over in the direction of the Rectory some time ago.

Cecily. Pray ask the lady to come out here; Mr. Worthing is sure to be back soon. And you can bring tea.

Merriman. Yes, miss. *(Goes out)*

Cecily. Miss Fairfax! I suppose one of the many good elderly women who are associated with Uncle Jack in some of his philanthropic work in London. I don't quite like women who are interested in philanthropic work. I think it is so forward of them.

[*Enter* MERRIMAN.]

Merriman. Miss Fairfax.

A [*Enter* GWENDOLEN. *Exit* MERRIMAN.]

Cecily *(advancing to meet her).* Pray let me introduce myself to you. My name is Cecily Cardew.

Gwendolen. Cecily Cardew? *(Moving to her and shaking hands)* What a very sweet name! Something tells me that we are going to be great friends. I like you already more than I can say. My first impressions of people are never wrong.

B **Cecily.** How nice of you to like me so much after we have known each other such a comparatively short time. Pray sit down.

Gwendolen *(still standing up).* I may call you Cecily, may I not?

Cecily. With pleasure!

Gwendolen. And you will always call me Gwendolen, won't you?

Cecily. If you wish.

Gwendolen. Then that is all quite settled, is it not?

Cecily. I hope so. *(A pause. They both sit down together.)*

Gwendolen. Perhaps this might be a favorable opportunity for my mentioning who I am. My father is Lord Bracknell. You have never heard of Papa, I suppose?

Cecily. I don't think so.

Gwendolen. Outside the family circle, Papa, I am glad to say, is entirely unknown. I think that is quite as it should be. The home seems to me to be the proper sphere for the man. And certainly once a man begins to neglect his domestic duties he becomes painfully effeminate, does he not? And I don't like that. It makes men so very attractive. Cecily, Mama, whose views on education are remarkably strict, has brought me up to be extremely shortsighted; it is part of her system; so do you mind my looking at you through my glasses?

Cecily. Oh! Not at all, Gwendolen. I am very fond of being looked at.

Gwendolen *(after examining* CECILY *carefully through a lorgnette[15]).* You are here on a short visit, I suppose.

Cecily. Oh, no! I live here.

Gwendolen *(severely).* Really? Your mother, no doubt, or some female relative of advanced years resides here also?

Cecily. Oh, no! I have no mother, nor, in fact, any relations.

Gwendolen. Indeed?

Cecily. My dear guardian, with the assistance of Miss Prism, has the arduous task of looking after me.

Gwendolen. Your guardian?

Cecily. Yes, I am Mr. Worthing's ward.

Gwendolen. Oh! It is strange he never mentioned to me that he had a ward. How secretive of him! He grows more interesting hourly. I am not sure, however, that the news inspires me with feelings of unmixed delight. *(Rising and going to her)* I am very fond of you, Cecily; I have liked you ever since I met you! But I am bound to state that now that I know that you are Mr. Worthing's ward, I cannot help expressing a wish you were—well, just a little older than you seem to be—and not quite so very alluring in appearance. In fact, if I may speak candidly——

---

15. **lorgnette** (lôr·nyet′): a pair of hand-held eyeglasses attached to a handle.

Cecily. Pray do! I think that whenever one has anything unpleasant to say, one should always be quite candid.

Gwendolen. Well, to speak with perfect candor, Cecily, I wish that you were fully forty-two, and more than usually plain for your age. Ernest has a strong upright nature. He is the very soul of truth and honor. Disloyalty would be as impossible to him as deception. But even men of the noblest possible moral character are extremely susceptible to the influence of the physical charms of others. Modern, no less than ancient history, supplies us with many most painful examples of what I refer to. If it were not so, indeed, history would be quite unreadable.

Cecily. I beg your pardon, Gwendolen, did you say Ernest?

Gwendolen. Yes.

Cecily. Oh, but it is not Mr. Ernest Worthing who is my guardian. It is his brother—his elder brother.

Gwendolen (*sitting down again*). Ernest never mentioned to me that he had a brother.

Cecily. I am sorry to say they have not been on good terms for a long time.

Gwendolen. Ah! That accounts for it. And now that I think of it, I have never heard any man mention his brother. The subject seems distasteful to most men. Cecily, you have lifted a load from my mind. I was growing almost anxious. It would have been terrible if any cloud had come across a friendship like ours, would it not? Of course you are quite, quite sure that it is not Mr. Ernest Worthing who is your guardian?

Cecily. Quite sure. (*A pause*) In fact, I am going to be his.

Gwendolen (*inquiringly*). I beg your pardon?

Cecily (*rather shy and confidingly*). Dearest Gwendolen, there is no reason why I should make a secret of it to you. Our little country newspaper is sure to chronicle the fact next week. Mr. Ernest Worthing and I are engaged to be married.

Gwendolen (*quite politely, rising*). My darling Cecily, I think there must be some slight error. Mr. Ernest Worthing is engaged to me. The announcement will appear in the *Morning Post* on Saturday at the latest.

Cecily (*very politely, rising*). I am afraid you must be under some misconception. Ernest proposed to me exactly ten minutes ago. (*Shows diary*)

Gwendolen (*examines diary through her lorgnette carefully*). It is very curious, for he asked me to be his wife yesterday afternoon at five-thirty. If you would care to verify the incident, pray do so. (*Produces diary of her own*) I never travel without my diary. One should always have something sensational to read in the train. I am so sorry, dear Cecily, if it is any disappointment to you, but I am afraid I have the prior claim.

Cecily. It would distress me more than I can tell you, dear Gwendolen, if it caused you any mental or physical anguish, but I feel bound to point out that since Ernest proposed to you he clearly has changed his mind.

Gwendolen (*meditatively*). If the poor fellow has been entrapped into any foolish promise, I shall consider it my duty to rescue him at once, and with a firm hand.

Cecily (*thoughtfully and sadly*). Whatever unfortunate entanglement my dear boy may have got into, I will never reproach him with it after we are married.

Gwendolen. Do you allude to me, Miss Cardew, as an entanglement? You are presumptuous. On an occasion of this kind it becomes more than a moral duty to speak one's mind. It becomes a pleasure.

Cecily. Do you suggest, Miss Fairfax, that I entrapped Ernest into an engagement? How dare you? This is no time for wearing the shallow mask of manners. When I see a spade, I call it a spade.

Gwendolen (*satirically*). I am glad to say that I have never seen a spade. It is obvious that our social spheres have been widely different.

[*Enter* MERRIMAN, *followed by the footman. He carries a salver, tablecloth, and plate stand.* CECILY *is about to retort. The presence of the servants exercises a restraining influence, under which both girls chafe.*]

Merriman. Shall I lay tea here as usual, miss?

Cecily (*sternly, in a calm voice*). Yes, as usual. (MERRIMAN *begins to clear table and lay cloth. A long pause.* CECILY *and* GWENDOLEN *glare at each other.*)

Gwendolen. Are there many interesting walks in the vicinity, Miss Cardew?

Cecily. Oh, yes! A great many. From the top of one of the hills quite close one can see five counties.

Gwendolen. Five counties! I don't think I should like that; I hate crowds.

Cecily (*sweetly*). I suppose that is why you live in town? (GWENDOLEN *bites her lip, and beats her foot nervously with her parasol.*)

A. Humor

❓ Comment on the humor of Gwendolen's remark about history. (Gwendolen reads history only for its soap-opera details of romance.)

B. Plot: Reversals

Here begins the first reversal. The young women who have been so friendly are soon hating each other.

C. Tone

❓ At what point in this scene should Gwendolen's tone of voice become less friendly? (Early in the scene, when she learns that the young and pretty Cecily is Mr. Worthing's ward) When does she become angry? (With this line) When does Cecily first show anger? (In her next speech)

A. Visual Humor
Note that once again the audience can "see" the humor as Cecily does the opposite of what she's been told.

B. Repetition/Irony
❓ How is the echo of Gwendolen's first speech in the scene amusingly ironic here? (Gwendolen uses very similar language to reverse sharply her previous declaration of friendship for Cecily on text page 892.)

C. Dramatic Structure
Midway through Act Two some of the confusion is cleared up, but point out to students that the more significant revelations are reserved for Act Three.

D. Plot: Reversal
The second reversal begins here. The two young women who began as friends, then became furious with each other, will soon be friends again.

E. Motivation
❓ Why do the two young women recoil from their lovers? (They are horrified by their "non-Ernest" names.)

Gwendolen (*looking round*). Quite a well-kept garden this is, Miss Cardew.

Cecily. So glad you like it, Miss Fairfax.

Gwendolen. I had no idea there were any flowers in the country.

Cecily. Oh, flowers are as common here, Miss Fairfax, as people are in London.

Gwendolen. Personally I cannot understand how anybody manages to exist in the country, if anybody who is anybody does. The country always bores me to death.

Cecily. Ah! This is what the newspapers call agricultural depression,[16] is it not? I believe the aristocracy are suffering very much from it just at present. It is almost an epidemic amongst them, I have been told. May I offer you some tea, Miss Fairfax?

Gwendolen (*with elaborate politeness*). Thank you. (*Aside*) Detestable girl! But I require tea!

Cecily (*sweetly*). Sugar?

Gwendolen (*superciliously*). No, thank you. Sugar is not fashionable anymore. (CECILY *looks angrily at her, takes up the tongs and puts four lumps of sugar into the cup.*)

Cecily (*severely*). Cake or bread and butter?

Gwendolen (*in a bored manner*). Bread and butter, please. Cake is rarely seen at the best houses nowadays.

Cecily (*cuts a very large slice of cake and puts it on the tray*). Hand that to Miss Fairfax.

[MERRIMAN *does so, and goes out with footman.* GWENDOLEN *drinks the tea and makes a grimace. Puts down cup at once, reaches out her hand to the bread and butter, looks at it, and finds it is cake. Rises in indignation.*]

Gwendolen. You have filled my tea with lumps of sugar, and though I asked most distinctly for bread and butter, you have given me cake. I am known for the gentleness of my disposition, and the extraordinary sweetness of my nature, but I warn you, Miss Cardew, you may go too far.

Cecily (*rising*). To save my poor, innocent, trusting boy from the machinations of any other girl, there are no lengths to which I would not go.

Gwendolen. From the moment I saw you I distrusted you. I felt that you were false and deceitful. I am never deceived in such matters. My first impressions of people are invariably right.

---

16. **agricultural depression:** (a play on words) British farming was in a severe recession at the time.

Cecily. It seems to me, Miss Fairfax, that I am trespassing on your valuable time. No doubt you have many other calls of a similar character to make in the neighborhood.

[*Enter* JACK]

Gwendolen (*catches sight of him*). Ernest! My own Ernest!

Jack. Gwendolen! Darling! (*Offers to kiss her*)

Gwendolen (*drawing back*). A moment! May I ask if you are engaged to be married to this young lady? (*Points to* CECILY)

Jack (*laughing*). To dear little Cecily! Of course not! What could have put such an idea into your pretty little head?

Gwendolen. Thank you. You may! (*Offers her cheek*)

Cecily (*very sweetly*). I knew there must be some misunderstanding, Miss Fairfax. The gentleman whose arm is at present round your waist is my dear guardian, Mr. John Worthing.

Gwendolen. I beg your pardon?

Cecily. This is Uncle Jack.

Gwendolen (*receding*). Jack! Oh!

[*Enter* ALGERNON]

Cecily. Here is Ernest.

Algernon (*goes straight over to* CECILY *without noticing anyone else*). My own love! (*Offers to kiss her*)

Cecily (*drawing back*). A moment, Ernest! May I ask you—are you engaged to be married to this young lady?

Algernon (*looking round*). To what young lady? Good heavens! Gwendolen!

Cecily. Yes, to good heavens, Gwendolen. I mean to Gwendolen.

Algernon (*laughing*). Of course not. What could have put such an idea into your pretty little head?

Cecily. Thank you. (*Presenting her cheek to be kissed*) You may. (ALGERNON *kisses her.*)

Gwendolen. I felt there was some slight error, Miss Cardew. The gentleman who is now embracing you is my cousin, Mr. Algernon Moncrieff.

Cecily (*breaking away from* ALGERNON). Algernon Moncrieff! Oh!

[*The two girls move toward each other and put their arms round each other's waists as if for protection.*]

Cecily. Are you called Algernon?

Algernon. I cannot deny it.

READING CHECK TEST: ACT TWO
1. For a time, Gwendolen and Cecily believe they are both engaged to the same man. (T)
2. Algernon tells Cecily that he is Jack's brother Ernest. (T)
3. Cecily informs Algernon ("Ernest") that they have been engaged for three months. (T)
4. At the end of the act, Gwendolen and Cecily realize the young men have deceived them about their real names. (T)
5. Jack and Algernon both intend to have Dr. Chasuble christen them as Ernest. (T)

"We are both engaged to be married to your brother Ernest...."

A

Cecily. Oh!

Gwendolen. Is your name really John?

Jack *(standing rather proudly).* I could deny it if I liked. I could deny anything if I liked. But my name certainly is John. It has been John for years.

Cecily *(to* GWENDOLEN*).* A gross deception has been practiced on both of us.

B **Gwendolen.** My poor, wounded Cecily!

Cecily. My sweet, wronged Gwendolen!

Gwendolen *(slowly and seriously).* You will call me sister, will you not?

[*They embrace,* JACK *and* ALGERNON *groan and walk up and down.*]

Cecily *(rather brightly).* There is just one question I would like to be allowed to ask my guardian.

Gwendolen. An admirable idea! Mr. Worthing, there is just one question I would like to be permitted to put to you. Where is your brother Ernest? We are both engaged to be married to your brother Ernest, so it is a matter of some importance to us to know where your brother Ernest is at present.

Jack *(slowly and hesitatingly).* Gwendolen—Cecily—it is very painful for me to be forced to speak the truth. It is the first time in my life that I have ever been reduced to such a painful position, and I am really quite inexperienced in doing anything

C

A. About the Photograph
Call students' attention to the details of the costumes. Point out that the elaborate, decorative, frilly, and flounced clothing is typical of upper-class Victorian tastes.
[?] Women's clothing has changed a great deal. How much has men's clothing changed? Why do you suppose this is true? (Men wore elaborate clothing until the 20th century. Perhaps the role of man as serious provider demanded simple, serious clothing.)

B. Humor/Irony
Ask students to explain the humor of this second, ironic reversal in the relations between Gwendolen and Cecily. (The relationship between the women is as fleeting and insincere as the relationships between the men and women.)

C. Character
Here is Jack's "moment of truth."
[?] How believable is he here? (Even in this moment of truth, Jack resorts to exaggeration.)

1. In Jack's country house, Manor House.
2. Answers will vary. Miss Prism is Cecily's governess, a serious and very wordy woman. Dr. Chasuble is a somewhat addle-brained country rector, her obvious admirer.
3. He announces to Miss Prism and Dr. Chasuble that Ernest is dead.

Algernon has already arrived, introducing himself to Cecily as Jack's brother Ernest. Jack is forced to accept Algernon as Ernest, and Algernon soon announces that he is in love with Cecily.
4. They argue about Ernest, for both claim to be engaged to him.
Their respective lovers come in and are identified. When it is revealed that neither of them is named Ernest, the

young women are repulsed and sympathize with each other at their having been deceived. When Jack is forced to admit that he has never had a brother named Ernest, the two women are further united against the men.

Interpreting Meanings
5. Possible answers: popular literature of his day (three-volume novels), the rec-

A. Irony
The outcome of the play will, of course, make these lines ironic in retrospect.

B. Oxymoron
Jack suggests that a "serious Bunburyist" is an oxymoron—a figure of speech that combines contradictory or opposite ideas.

C. Parallels
In this conversation Jack's and Algernon's situations are seen to be remarkably parallel.

D. Repetition
The muffin-eating scene echoes the cucumber-sandwich scene in Act One. Both of these scenes embody one of Wilde's stated goals: "treating all the trivial things of life seriously."

E. Responding
❓ What do you think of Algernon's remarks about eating and unhappiness? (They mock people who say they lose their appetite when they have problems with loved ones.)

A of the kind. However, I will tell you quite frankly that I have no brother Ernest. I have no brother at all. I never had a brother in my life, and I certainly have not the smallest intention of ever having one in the future.
Cecily (*surprised*). No brother at all?
Jack (*cheerily*). None!
Gwendolen (*severely*). Had you never a brother of any kind?
Jack (*pleasantly*). Never. Not even of any kind.
Gwendolen. I am afraid it is quite clear, Cecily, that neither of us is engaged to be married to anyone.
Cecily. It is not a very pleasant position for a young girl suddenly to find herself in. Is it?
Gwendolen. Let us go into the house. They will hardly venture to come after us there.
Cecily. No, men are so cowardly, aren't they?

[*They retire into the house with scornful looks.*]

Jack. This ghastly state of things is what you call Bunburying, I suppose?
Algernon. Yes, and a perfectly wonderful Bunbury it is. The most wonderful Bunbury I have ever had in my life.
B **Jack.** Well, you've no right whatsoever to Bunbury here.
Algernon. That is absurd. One has a right to Bunbury anywhere one chooses. Every serious Bunburyist knows that.
Jack. Serious Bunburyist? Good heavens!
Algernon. Well, one must be serious about something, if one wants to have any amusement in life. I happen to be serious about Bunburying. What on earth you are serious about I haven't got the remotest idea. About everything, I should fancy. You have such an absolutely trivial nature.
Jack. Well, the only small satisfaction I have in the whole of this wretched business is that your
C friend Bunbury is quite exploded. You won't be able to run down to the country quite so often as you used to do, dear Algy. And a very good thing too.
Algernon. Your brother is a little off color, isn't he, dear Jack? You won't be able to disappear to London quite so frequently as your wicked custom was. And not a bad thing either.
Jack. As for your conduct toward Miss Cardew, I must say that your taking in a sweet, simple, innocent girl like that is quite inexcusable. To say nothing of the fact that she is my ward.

Algernon. I can see no possible defense at all for your deceiving a brilliant, clever, thoroughly experienced young lady like Miss Fairfax. To say nothing of the fact that she is my cousin.
Jack. I wanted to be engaged to Gwendolen, that is all. I love her.
Algernon. Well, I simply wanted to be engaged to Cecily. I adore her.
Jack. There is certainly no chance of your marrying Miss Cardew.
Algernon. I don't think there is much likelihood, Jack, of you and Miss Fairfax being united.
Jack. Well, that is no business of yours.
Algernon. If it was my business, I wouldn't talk about it. (*Begins to eat muffins*) It is very vulgar to talk about one's business. Only people like stockbrokers do that, and then merely at dinner parties.
D **Jack.** How you can sit there, calmly eating muffins when we are in this horrible trouble, I can't make out. You seem to me to be perfectly heartless.
Algernon. Well, I can't eat muffins in an agitated manner. The butter would probably get on my cuffs. One should always eat muffins quite calmly. It is the only way to eat them.
Jack. I say it's perfectly heartless your eating muffins at all, under the circumstances.
E **Algernon.** When I am in trouble, eating is the only thing that consoles me. Indeed, when I am in really great trouble, as anyone who knows me intimately will tell you, I refuse everything except food and drink. At the present moment I am eating muffins because I am unhappy. Besides, I am particularly fond of muffins. (*Rising*)
Jack (*rising*). Well, there is no reason why you should eat them all in that greedy way. (*Takes muffins from* ALGERNON)
Algernon (*offering teacake*). I wish you would have teacake instead. I don't like teacake.
Jack. Good heavens! I suppose a man may eat his own muffins in his own garden.
Algernon. But you have just said it was perfectly heartless to eat muffins.
Jack. I said it was perfectly heartless of you, under the circumstances. That is a very different thing.
Algernon. That may be. But the muffins are the same. (*He seizes the muffin dish from Jack.*)
Jack. Algy, I wish to goodness you would go.
Algernon. You can't possibly ask me to go without having some dinner. It's absurd. I never go without my dinner. No one ever does, except vegetar-

tor's adaptable sermons, the relationship between men and women, and the notion of falling in love at first sight.

6. Student answers will vary. Students may note that Miss Prism seems to be trying to entrap Dr. Chasuble, while Algernon and Cecily and Jack and Gwendolen move in and out of love very quickly.

7. Students may note Jack's and Al-

gernon's muffin-eating orgy, which echoes the cucumber-sandwich scene in Act One. Also, at the end of Act One new obstacles arise to prevent the lovers from being united.

A. Responding
Have students try to follow the rapid-fire wit here.
[?] Is either character being logical and convincing? Or is the conversation totally absurd? (It is once again an opportunity for Wilde to be clever and amusing. None of the characters is ever meant to be convincing as a character.)

B. Repetition
Notice how Jack's line about Algy's talking nonsense echoes the concluding lines of Act One.

C. About the Illustration
Challenge students to identify the figures caricatured here. (From left to right: Gwendolen or Cecily; Canon Chasuble; Lady Bracknell; and Algy or Jack, or possibly one of the butlers)

A **Jack.** My dear fellow, the sooner you give up that nonsense the better. I made arrangements this morning with Dr. Chasuble to be christened at five-thirty, and I naturally will take the name of Ernest. Gwendolen would wish it. We can't both be christened Ernest. It's absurd. Besides, I have a perfect right to be christened if I like. There is no evidence at all that I have ever been christened by anybody. I should think it extremely probable I never was, and so does Dr. Chasuble. It is entirely different in your case. You have been christened already.

Algernon. Yes, but I have not been christened for years.

Jack. Yes, but you have been christened. That is the important thing.

Algernon. Quite so. So I know my constitution can stand it. If you are not quite sure about your ever having been christened, I must say I think it rather dangerous your venturing on it now. It might make you very unwell. You can hardly have

ians and people like that. Besides I have just made arrangements with Dr. Chasuble to be christened at a quarter to six under the name of Ernest.

forgotten that someone very closely connected with you was very nearly carried off this week in Paris by a severe chill.

Jack. Yes, but you said yourself that a severe chill was not hereditary.

Algernon. It usen't to be, I know—but I daresay it is now. Science is always making wonderful improvements in things.

Jack *(picking up the muffin dish).* Oh, that is nonsense; you are always talking nonsense. **B**

Algernon. Jack, you are at the muffins again! I wish you wouldn't. There are only two left. *(Takes them)* I told you I was particularly fond of muffins.

Jack. But I hate teacake.

Algernon. Why on earth then do you allow teacake to be served up for your guests? What ideas you have of hospitality!

Jack. Algernon! I have already told you to go. I don't want you here. Why don't you go!

Algernon. I haven't quite finished my tea yet! And there is still one muffin left.

[JACK *groans, and sinks into a chair.* ALGERNON *still continues eating.*]

Responding to the Play

Analyzing Act Two

Identifying Facts

1. Where does the second act take place?
2. Describe Miss Prism and Dr. Chasuble.
3. When Jack arrives, what does he say about his brother Ernest? How does this soon lead to **complications**?
4. What do Gwendolen and Cecily argue about? How is their argument swiftly and comically **reversed**?

Interpreting Meanings

5. Name some of the targets of Wilde's **satire** in this act.
6. How does Wilde incorporate the age-old **comic motif** of the "battle of the sexes" in this act?
7. What echoes, or **repetitions,** of the first act occur near the end of the second? What could be the reason for these echoes?

C

Illustration by Alfred Frueh for the 1947 New York production.

This act follows Act Two immediately. The setting is the morning room of Jack's country home. Gwendolen and Cecily console each other until Algernon and Jack enter and begin to explain themselves. The girls forgive them, and the couples are reunited.

Lady Bracknell arrives to retrieve Gwendolen. She objects to Algernon's engagement to Cecily until Jack reveals that his ward Cecily is extremely rich. Jack refuses to give his consent as Cecily's guardian unless the Bracknells let him marry Gwendolen.

Chasuble enters prepared for the "Ernest christenings." He mentions Miss Prism, whom Lady Bracknell summons and quickly recognizes. Lady Bracknell and Miss Prism reveal that years ago Miss Prism mixed up an infant and a three-volume novel, checking the infant in a handbag in Victoria Station and leaving the novel in the baby carriage.

Jack produces the handbag in which he was found, and his true identity is revealed: He is Lady Bracknell's nephew and Algernon's older brother. Jack further discovers that his real name (he was christened before he was lost) is Ernest.

A. Setting
Point out that the dialogue indicates that Act Three follows Act Two almost immediately.

B. Style
Note that this line echoes Wilde's own aesthetic creed of "art for art's sake."

Act Three

Morning room at the Manor House. GWENDOLEN *and* CECILY *are at the window, looking into the garden.*

A

Gwendolen. The fact that they did not follow us at once into the house, as anyone else would have done, seems to me to show that they have some sense of shame left.

Cecily. They have been eating muffins. That looks like repentance.

Gwendolen (*after a pause*). They don't seem to notice us at all. Couldn't you cough?

Cecily. But I haven't got a cough.

Gwendolen. They're looking at us. What effrontery!

Cecily. They're approaching. That's very forward of them.

Gwendolen. Let us preserve a dignified silence.

Cecily. Certainly. It's the only thing to do now.

[*Enter* JACK *followed by* ALGERNON. *They whistle some dreadful popular air from a British opera.*]

Gwendolen. This dignified silence seems to produce an unpleasant effect.

Cecily. A most distasteful one.

Gwendolen. But we will not be the first to speak.

Cecily. Certainly not.

Gwendolen. Mr. Worthing, I have something very particular to ask you. Much depends on your reply.

Cecily. Gwendolen, your common sense is invaluable. Mr. Moncrieff, kindly answer me the following question. Why did you pretend to be my guardian's brother?

Algernon. In order that I might have an opportunity of meeting you.

Cecily (*to* GWENDOLEN). That certainly seems a satisfactory explanation, does it not?

Gwendolen. Yes, dear, if you can believe him.

Cecily. I don't. But that does not affect the wonderful beauty of his answer.

B

Gwendolen. True. In matters of grave importance, style, not sincerity, is the vital thing Mr. Worthing, what explanation can you offer to me for pretending to have a brother? Was it in order that you might have an opportunity of coming up to town to see me as often as possible?

Jack. Can you doubt it, Miss Fairfax?

Gwendolen. I have the gravest doubts upon the subject. But I intend to crush them. This is not the moment for German skepticism.[1] (*Moving to* CECILY) Their explanations appear to be quite satisfactory, especially Mr. Worthing's. That seems to me to have the stamp of truth upon it.

Cecily. I am more than content with what Mr. Moncrieff said. His voice alone inspires one with absolute credulity.

Gwendolen. Then you think we should forgive them?

Cecily. Yes. I mean no.

Gwendolen. True! I had forgotten. There are principles at stake that one cannot surrender. Which of us should tell them? The task is not a pleasant one.

Cecily. Could we not both speak at the same time?

Gwendolen. An excellent idea! I nearly always speak at the same time as other people. Will you take the time from me?

Cecily. Certainly. (GWENDOLEN *beats time with uplifted finger.*)

Gwendolen and Cecily (*speaking together*). Your Christian names are still an insuperable[2] barrier. That is all!

Jack and Algernon (*speaking together*). Our Christian names! Is that all? But we are going to be christened this afternoon.

Gwendolen (*to* JACK). For my sake you are prepared to do this terrible thing?

Jack. I am.

Cecily (*to* ALGERNON). To please me you are ready to face this fearful ordeal?

Algernon. I am!

Gwendolen. How absurd to talk of the equality of the sexes! Where questions of self-sacrifice are concerned, men are infinitely beyond us.

Jack. We are. (*Clasps hands with* ALGERNON)

Cecily. They have moments of physical courage of which we women know absolutely nothing.

Gwendolen (*to* JACK). Darling!

Algernon (*to* CECILY). Darling! (*They fall into each other's arms.*)

[*Enter* MERRIMAN. *When he enters, he coughs loudly, seeing the situation.*]

---

1. **German skepticism:** a school of philosophy led by Immanuel Kant, which taught that all knowledge is uncertain: that we never know reality, only what seems to be.
2. **insuperable** (in·sōō′pər·ə·b'l): impossible to overcome; insurmountable.

The act ends with the promise of three marriages (Gwendolen-Jack, Cicely-Algernon, and Miss Prism-Dr. Chasuble).

Merriman. Ahem! Ahem! Lady Bracknell.
Jack. Good heavens!

[*Enter* LADY BRACKNELL. *The couples separate in alarm. Exit* MERRIMAN.]

A

Lady Bracknell. Gwendolen! What does this mean?
Gwendolen. Merely that I am engaged to be married to Mr. Worthing, Mama.
Lady Bracknell. Come here. Sit down. Sit down immediately. Hesitation of any kind is a sign of mental decay in the young, of physical weakness in the old. (*Turns to* JACK) Apprised, sir, of my daughter's sudden flight by her trusty maid, whose confidence I purchased by means of a small coin, I followed her at once by a luggage train. Her unhappy father is, I am glad to say, under the impression that she is attending a more than usually lengthy lecture by the University Extension Scheme on the Influence of a Permanent Income on Thought. I do not propose to undeceive him. Indeed I have never undeceived him on any question. I would consider it wrong. But of course, you will clearly understand that all communication between yourself and my daughter must cease immediately from this moment. On this point, as indeed on all points, I am firm.
Jack. I am engaged to be married to Gwendolen, Lady Bracknell!
Lady Bracknell. You are nothing of the kind, sir. And now as regards Algernon! . . . Algernon!
Algernon. Yes, Aunt Augusta.

B

Lady Bracknell. May I ask if it is in this house that your invalid friend Mr. Bunbury resides?
Algernon (*stammering*). Oh! No! Bunbury doesn't live here. Bunbury is somewhere else at present. In fact, Bunbury is dead.
Lady Bracknell. Dead! When did Mr. Bunbury die? His death must have been extremely sudden.
Algernon (*airily*). Oh! I killed Bunbury this afternoon. I mean poor Bunbury died this afternoon.
Lady Bracknell. What did he die of?
Algernon. Bunbury? Oh, he was quite exploded.
Lady Bracknell. Exploded! Was he the victim of a revolutionary outrage? I was not aware that Mr. Bunbury was interested in social legislation. If so, he is well punished for his morbidity.
Algernon. My dear Aunt Augusta, I mean he was found out! The doctors found out that Bunbury could not live, that is what I mean—so Bunbury died.
Lady Bracknell. He seems to have had great con-

fidence in the opinion of his physicians. I am glad, however, that he made up his mind at the last to some definite course of action, and acted under proper medical advice. And now that we have finally got rid of this Mr. Bunbury, may I ask, Mr. Worthing, who is that young person whose hand my nephew Algernon is now holding in what seems to me a peculiarly unnecessary manner?
Jack. That lady is Miss Cecily Cardew, my ward. (LADY BRACKNELL *bows coldly to* CECILY.)
Algernon. I am engaged to be married to Cecily, Aunt Augusta.
Lady Bracknell. I beg your pardon?
Cecily. Mr. Moncrieff and I are engaged to be married, Lady Bracknell.

C

Lady Bracknell (*with a shiver, crossing to the sofa and sitting down*). I do not know whether there is anything peculiarly exciting in the air of this particular part of Hertfordshire, but the number of engagements that go on seems to me considerably above the proper average that statistics have laid down for our guidance. I think some preliminary inquiry on my part would not be out of place. Mr. Worthing, is Miss Cardew at all connected with any of the larger railway stations in London? I merely desire information. Until yesterday I had no idea that there were any families or persons whose origin was a Terminus.[3] (JACK *looks perfectly furious, but restrains himself.*)
Jack (*in a cold, clear voice*). Miss Cardew is the granddaughter of the late Mr. Thomas Cardew of 149 Belgrave Square, S.W.; Gervase Park, Dorking, Surrey; and the Sporran, Fifeshire, N.B.[4]
Lady Bracknell. That sounds not unsatisfactory. Three addresses always inspire confidence, even in tradesmen. But what proof have I of their authenticity?
Jack. I have carefully preserved the Court Guides[5] of the period. They are open to your inspection, Lady Bracknell.
Lady Bracknell (*grimly*). I have known strange errors in that publication.
Jack. Miss Cardew's family solicitors are Messrs. Markby, Markby, and Markby.
Lady Bracknell. Markby, Markby, and Markby? A firm of the very highest position in the profession. Indeed I am told that one of the Mr. Markbys is

---

3. **Terminus:** a railway terminal. It is used here as a paradox, for *terminus* in Latin means "end."
4. **N.B.:** North Britain.
5. **Court Guides:** books containing the names and addresses of people in high society.

A. Plot: Reversal
Just when everything seems happily resolved, Lady Bracknell bears down upon the couples, who spring apart in alarm. Recall that she is the "blocking figure" in the play.

? How do you think she can be won over? (By learning Cecily has an aristocratic background and an ample fortune)

B. Parallels
Note that since Jack has had to do away with Ernest, it's only fair that Bunbury be eliminated. Students should enjoy Algernon's evident discomfort in this scene.

C. Oral Interpretation
This is one of the funniest speeches in the play. Ask for a volunteer (or several students) to read it in Lady Bracknell's acid tones.

A. Characteriza-
tion

❓ Comment on
Lady Brack-
nell's amusing re-
versal here. What
quality in her char-
acter is Wilde satir-
izing? (Greed)

"There are distinct social possibilities in your profile."

occasionally to be seen at dinner parties. So far I am satisfied.

Jack *(very irritably).* How extremely kind of you, Lady Bracknell! I have also in my possession, you will be pleased to hear, certificates of Miss Cardew's birth, baptism, whooping cough, registration, vaccination, confirmation, and the measles; both the German and the English variety.

Lady Bracknell. Ah! A life crowded with incident, I see; though perhaps somewhat too exciting for a young girl. I am not myself in favor of premature experiences. *(Rises, looks at her watch)* Gwendolen! The time approaches for our departure. We have not a moment to lose. As a matter of form, Mr. Worthing, I had better ask you if Miss Cardew has any little fortune?

Jack. Oh! About a hundred and thirty thousand pounds in the Funds.[6] That is all. Goodbye, Lady Bracknell. So pleased to have seen you.

Lady Bracknell *(sitting down again).* A moment,

---

6. **Funds:** government bonds.

Mr. Worthing. A hundred and thirty thousand pounds! And in the Funds! Miss Cardew seems to me a most attractive young lady, now that I look at her. Few girls of the present day have any really solid qualities, any of the qualities that last, and improve with time. We live, I regret to say, in an age of surfaces. *(To* CECILY*)* Come over here, dear. *(*CECILY *goes across.)* Pretty child! Your dress is sadly simple, and your hair seems almost as nature might have left it. But we can soon alter all that. A thoroughly experienced French maid produces a really marvelous result in a very brief space of time. I remember recommending one to young Lady Lancing, and after three months her own husband did not know her.

Jack. And after six months nobody knew her.

Lady Bracknell *(glares at* JACK *for a few moments. Then bends, with a practiced smile, to* CECILY*).* Kindly turn round, sweet child. *(*CECILY *turns completely round.)* No, the side view is what I want. *(*CECILY *presents her profile.)* Yes, quite as I expected. There are distinct social possibilities in your profile. The two weak points in our age are its want of principle and its want of profile. The chin a little higher, dear. Style largely depends on the way the chin is worn. They are worn very high, just at present. Algernon!

Algernon. Yes, Aunt Augusta!

Lady Bracknell. There are distinct social possibilities in Miss Cardew's profile.

Algernon. Cecily is the sweetest, dearest, prettiest girl in the whole world. And I don't care twopence about social possibilities.

Lady Bracknell. Never speak disrespectfully of Society, Algernon. Only people who can't get into it do that. (*To* CECILY) Dear child, of course you know that Algernon has nothing but his debts to depend upon. But I do not approve of mercenary marriages. When I married Lord Bracknell, I had no fortune of any kind. But I never dreamed for a moment of allowing that to stand in my way. Well, I suppose I must give my consent.

Algernon. Thank you, Aunt Augusta.

Lady Bracknell. Cecily, you may kiss me!

Cecily (*kisses her*). Thank you, Lady Bracknell.

Lady Bracknell. You may also address me as Aunt Augusta for the future.

Cecily. Thank you, Aunt Augusta.

Lady Bracknell. The marriage, I think, had better take place quite soon.

Algernon. Thank you, Aunt Augusta.

Cecily. Thank you, Aunt Augusta.

Lady Bracknell. To speak frankly, I am not in favor of long engagements. They give people the opportunity of finding out each other's character before marriage, which I think is never advisable.

Jack. I beg your pardon for interrupting you, Lady Bracknell, but this engagement is quite out of the question. I am Miss Cardew's guardian, and she cannot marry without my consent until she comes of age. That consent I absolutely decline to give.

Lady Bracknell. Upon what grounds, may I ask? Algernon is an extremely, I may almost say an ostentatiously, eligible young man. He has nothing, but he looks everything. What more can one desire?

Jack. It pains me very much to have to speak frankly to you, Lady Bracknell, about your nephew, but the fact is that I do not approve at all of his moral character. I suspect him of being untruthful.

[ALGERNON *and* CECILY *look at him in indignant amazement.*]

Lady Bracknell. Untruthful! My nephew Algernon? Impossible! He is an Oxonian.[7]

Jack. I fear there can be no possible doubt about the matter. This afternoon during my temporary absence in London on an important question of romance, he obtained admission to my house by means of the false pretense of being my brother. Under an assumed name he drank, I've just been informed by my butler, an entire pint bottle of my Perrier-Jouet, Brut, '89; wine I was specially reserving for myself. Continuing his disgraceful deception, he succeeded in the course of the afternoon in alienating the affections of my only ward. He subsequently stayed to tea, and devoured every single muffin. And what makes his conduct all the more heartless is that he was perfectly well aware from the first that I have no brother, that I never had a brother, and that I don't intend to have a brother, not even of any kind. I distinctly told him so myself yesterday afternoon.

Lady Bracknell. Ahem! Mr. Worthing, after careful consideration I have decided entirely to overlook my nephew's conduct to you.

Jack. That is very generous of you, Lady Bracknell. My own decision, however, is unalterable. I decline to give my consent.

Lady Bracknell (*to* CECILY). Come here, sweet child. (CECILY *goes over.*) How old are you, dear?

Cecily. Well, I am really only eighteen, but I always admit to twenty when I go to evening parties.

Lady Bracknell. You are perfectly right in making some slight alteration. Indeed, no woman should ever be quite accurate about her age. It looks so calculating. . . . (*In a meditative manner*) Eighteen, but admitting to twenty at evening parties. Well, it will not be very long before you are of age and free from the restraints of tutelage. So I don't think your guardian's consent is, after all, a matter of any importance.

Jack. Pray excuse me, Lady Bracknell, for interrupting you again, but it is only fair to tell you that according to the terms of her grandfather's will Miss Cardew does not come legally of age till she is thirty-five.

Lady Bracknell. That does not seem to me to be a grave objection. Thirty-five is a very attractive age. London society is full of women of the very highest birth who have, of their own free choice,

---

7. **Oxonian:** student or graduate of Oxford University, one of England's most prestigious universities.

A. Epigram
Here's another of Wilde's pithy statements.

❓ Has this kind of high society altogether disappeared, or does it still exist today? (It exists, as students may know from society news, debutante balls, etc.)

B. Connotations
❓ Why might "Augusta" be a thoroughly appropriate name for Lady Bracknell? (The name suggests *august,* connoting an imperial—or imperious—image.)

C. Plot: Predicting Outcomes
Here's the final obstacle for Algernon and Cecily.

❓ What do you think it will take for Jack to give his consent? (Lady Bracknell's permission for him to marry Gwendolen)

D. Expansion
The wine in question is champagne; Perrier-Jouët is still in business. Students should note that '89 here means 1889; the play is about one hundred years old.

A. Plot: Conflict
The conflict seems insoluble! Ask students to predict how Wilde might manage to make the play end happily.

B. Plot
Note the role of chance in determining everyone's happiness. Lady Bracknell's being where she can hear Miss Prism's name mentioned (at the home of a stranger, far from London) is extremely unlikely, yet that is the device on which the plot's resolution depends.

C. Diction
Chasuble is consistently pedantic: The phrase "she is nigh" was archaic even in Victorian times.

D. Plot: Resolution
Here begins the final unraveling of the plot in this recognition scene.
? What problem remains to be solved? (Lady Bracknell must give her consent to Jack's marriage to Gwendolen before Jack will consent to Cecily's marriage to Algernon.)

remained thirty-five for years. Lady Dumbleton is an instance in point. To my own knowledge she has been thirty-five ever since she arrived at the age of forty, which was many years ago now. I see no reason why our dear Cecily should not be even still more attractive at the age you mention than she is at present. There will be a large accumulation of property.

Cecily. Algy, could you wait for me till I was thirty-five?

Algernon. Of course I could, Cecily. You know I could.

Cecily. Yes, I felt it instinctively, but I couldn't wait all that time. I hate waiting even five minutes for anybody. It always makes me rather cross. I am not punctual myself, I know, but I do like punctuality in others, and waiting, even to be married, is quite out of the question.

Algernon. Then what is to be done, Cecily?

Cecily. I don't know, Mr. Moncrieff.

Lady Bracknell. My dear Mr. Worthing, as Miss Cardew states positively that she cannot wait till she is thirty-five—a remark which I am bound to say seems to me to show a somewhat impatient nature—I would beg of you to reconsider your decision.

Jack. But my dear Lady Bracknell, the matter is entirely in your own hands. The moment you consent to my marriage with Gwendolen, I will most gladly allow your nephew to form an alliance with my ward.

Lady Bracknell (*rising and drawing herself up*). You must be quite aware that what you propose is out of the question.

Jack. Then a passionate celibacy is all that any of us can look forward to.

Lady Bracknell. That is not the destiny I propose for Gwendolen. Algernon, of course, can choose for himself. (*Pulls our her watch*) Come, dear (GWENDOLEN *rises*), we have already missed five, if not six, trains. To miss any more might expose us to comment on the platform.

[*Enter* DR. CHASUBLE.]

Chasuble. Everything is quite ready for the christenings.

Lady Bracknell. The christenings, sir! Is not that somewhat premature?

Chasuble (*looking rather puzzled, and pointing to* JACK *and* ALGERNON). Both these gentlemen have expressed a desire for immediate baptism.

Lady Bracknell. At their age? The idea is gro-

tesque and irreligious! Algernon, I forbid you to be baptized. I will not hear of such excesses. Lord Bracknell would be highly displeased if he learned that that was the way in which you wasted your time and money.

Chasuble. Am I to understand then that there are to be no christenings at all this afternoon?

Jack. I don't think that, as things are now, it would be of much practical value to either of us, Dr. Chasuble.

Chasuble. I am grieved to hear such sentiments from you, Mr. Worthing. They savor of the heretical views of the Anabaptists,[8] views that I have completely refuted in four of my unpublished sermons. However, as your present mood seems to be one peculiarly secular, I will return to the church at once. Indeed, I have just been informed by the pew-opener that for the last hour and a half Miss Prism has been waiting for me in the vestry.

Lady Bracknell (*starting*). Miss Prism! Did I hear you mention a Miss Prism?

Chasuble. Yes, Lady Bracknell. I am on my way to join her.

Lady Bracknell. Pray allow me to detain you for a moment. This matter may prove to be one of vital importance to Lord Bracknell and myself. Is this Miss Prism a female of repellent aspect, remotely connected with education?

Chasuble (*somewhat indignantly*). She is the most cultivated of ladies, and the very picture of respectability.

Lady Bracknell. It is obviously the same person. May I ask what position she holds in your household?

Chasuble (*severely*). I am a celibate, madam.

Jack (*interposing*). Miss Prism, Lady Bracknell, has been for the last three years Miss Cardew's esteemed governess and valued companion.

Lady Bracknell. In spite of what I hear of her, I must see her at once. Let her be sent for.

Chasuble (*looking off*). She approaches; she is nigh.

[*Enter* MISS PRISM *hurriedly.*]

Miss Prism. I was told you expected me in the vestry, dear Canon. I have been waiting for you there for an hour and three-quarters. (*Catches sight of* LADY BRACKNELL, *who has fixed her with a stony glare.* MISS PRISM *grows pale and quails.*

---

8. **Anabaptists:** a sixteenth-century religious sect founded in Switzerland, whose members believed in adult baptism rather than infant baptism.

She looks anxiously round as if desirous to escape.)

Lady Bracknell *(in a severe, judicial voice)*. Prism! *(MISS PRISM bows her head in shame.)* Come here, Prism! *(MISS PRISM approaches in a humble manner.)* Prism! Where is that baby? *(General consternation. The CANON starts back in horror. ALGERNON and JACK pretend to be anxious to shield CECILY and GWENDOLEN from hearing the details of a terrible public scandal.)* Twenty-eight years ago, Prism, you left Lord Bracknell's house, Number 104, Upper Grosvenor Square, in charge of a perambulator that contained a baby of the male sex. You never returned. A few weeks later, through the elaborate investigations of the Metropolitan police, the perambulator was discovered at midnight standing by itself in a remote corner of Bayswater. It contained the manuscript of a three-volume novel of more than usually revolting sentimentality. *(MISS PRISM starts in involuntary indignation.)* But the baby was not there. *(Everyone looks at MISS PRISM.)* Prism! Where is that baby? *(A pause)*

Miss Prism. Lady Bracknell, I admit with shame that I do not know. I only wish I did. The plain facts of the case are these. On the morning of the day you mention, a day that is forever branded on my memory, I prepared as usual to take the baby out in its perambulator. I had also with me a somewhat old, but capacious, handbag in which I had intended to place the manuscript of a work of fiction that I had written during my few unoccupied hours. In a moment of mental abstraction, for which I can never forgive myself, I deposited the manuscript in the bassinette and placed the baby in the handbag.

Jack *(who has been listening attentively)*. But where did you deposit the handbag?

Miss Prism. Do not ask me, Mr. Worthing.

Jack. Miss Prism, this is a matter of no small importance to me. I insist on knowing where you deposited the handbag that contained that infant.

Miss Prism. I left it in the cloakroom of one of the larger railway stations in London.

Jack. What railway station?

Miss Prism *(quite crushed)*. Victoria. The Brighton line. *(Sinks into a chair)*

Jack. I must retire to my room for a moment. Gwendolen, wait here for me.

Gwendolen. If you are not too long, I will wait here for you all my life. *(Exit JACK in great excitement.)*

Chasuble. What do you think this means, Lady Bracknell?

Lady Bracknell. I dare not even suspect, Dr. Chasuble. I need hardly tell you that in families of high position strange coincidences are not supposed to occur. They are hardly considered the thing.

[Noises heard overhead as if someone was throwing trunks about. Everyone looks up.]

Cecily. Uncle Jack seems strangely agitated.

Chasuble. Your guardian has a very emotional nature.

Lady Bracknell. This noise is extremely unpleasant. It sounds as if he was having an argument. I dislike arguments of any kind. They are always vulgar, and often convincing.

Chasuble *(looking up)*. It has stopped now.

[The noise is redoubled.]

Lady Bracknell. I wish he would arrive at some conclusion.

Gwendolen. This suspense is terrible. I hope it will last.

[Enter JACK with a handbag of black leather in his hand.]

Jack *(rushing over to MISS PRISM)*. Is this the handbag, Miss Prism? Examine it carefully before you speak. The happiness of more than one life depends on your answer.

Miss Prism *(calmly)*. It seems to be mine. Yes, here is the injury it received through the upsetting of a Gower Street omnibus in younger and happier days. Here is the stain on the lining caused by the explosion of a temperance beverage, an incident that occurred at Leamington. And here, on the lock, are my initials. I had forgotten that in an extravagant mood I had had them placed there. The bag is undoubtedly mine. I am delighted to have it so unexpectedly restored to me. It has been a great inconvenience being without it all these years.

Jack *(in a pathetic voice)*. Miss Prism, more is restored to you than this handbag. I was the baby you placed in it.

Miss Prism *(amazed)*. You?

Jack *(embracing her)*. Yes . . . Mother!

Miss Prism *(recoiling in indignant astonishment)*. Mr. Worthing. I am unmarried!

Jack. Unmarried! I do not deny that is a serious blow. But after all, who has the right to cast a

A. Identifying

Where was Miss Prism's novel first mentioned? (At the beginning of Act Two).

B. Epigram/Pun

Comment on Lady Bracknell's epigram here. On what two senses of the word *argument* is Wilde punning? ("Dispute" and "persuasive theory")

C. Suspense

Here Gwendolen voices the feeling of readers and movie- and theater-going audiences today as well as a hundred years ago.

Do you agree or disagree with Gwendolen? Why do you think suspense is such a delicious feeling? (While we want the story to be resolved, we also want it to continue.)

D. Plot

What mistake in reasoning does Jack make here? (He jumps to the conclusion that Miss Prism, who lost him as a baby, is his mother.)

1. At the beginning of this act, Gwendolen and Cecily readily forgive Jack and Algernon. (T)
2. Jack tells Lady Bracknell that he will consent to the marriage of Cecily and Algernon only if she agrees to let Jack marry Gwendolen. (T)

3. Jack jumps to the conclusion that Lady Bracknell is his mother. (F)
4. Algernon turns out to be Jack's first cousin. (F)
5. Jack discovers that he was christened Ernest as an infant. (T)

CLOSURE

Reread Wilde's comment in Establishing a Purpose (top, page 870), and ask students to identify at least two trivial topics Wilde has treated seriously (names, cucumbers, muffins) and two serious topics he's treated trivially (marriage, love, identity, etc.).

A. Plot: Resolution

Wilde's resolution of the play gently pokes fun at another common motif in comic as well as serious literature: the search for one's identity. (Note Jack's request to Lady Bracknell to "kindly inform me who I am.")

B. Responding

❓ Does Wilde make Gwendolen a sympathetic character, or is he critical of her? Describe your response to her. (He is being critical of her as he is being critical of everyone.)

C. Plot: Climax

Ask students to identify the play's climax (see the discussion on text page 1261).

❓ Do you think the climax occurs when Jack finds out he's Algy's brother, or when he finds out his name is Ernest? (Opinions will vary.)

D. Paradox

Here's another. Ask students to explain. (Wilde is merely being witty. In fact, people both tell the truth and lie.)

stone against one who has suffered? Cannot repentance wipe out an act of folly? Why should there be one law for men and another for women? Mother, I forgive you. (*Tries to embrace her again*)

Miss Prism (*still more indignant*). Mr. Worthing, there is some error. (*Pointing to* LADY BRACKNELL.) There is the lady who can tell you who you really are.

A

Jack (*after a pause*). Lady Bracknell, I hate to seem inquisitive, but would you kindly inform me who I am?

Lady Bracknell. I am afraid that the news I have to give you will not altogether please you. You are the son of my poor sister, Mrs. Moncrieff, and consequently Algernon's elder brother.

Jack. Algy's elder brother! Then I have a brother after all. I knew I had a brother! I always said I had a brother! Cecily—how could you have ever doubted that I had a brother? (*Seizes hold of* ALGERNON) Dr. Chasuble, my unfortunate brother. Miss Prism, my unfortunate brother. Gwendolen, my unfortunate brother. Algy, you young scoundrel, you will have to treat me with more respect in the future. You have never behaved to me like a brother in all my life.

Algernon. Well, not till today, old boy, I admit. I did my best, however, though I was out of practice. (*Shakes hands*)

Gwendolen (*to* JACK). My own! But what own are you? What is your Christian name, now that you have become someone else?

Jack. Good heavens! . . . I had quite forgotten that point. Your decision on the subject of my name is irrevocable, I suppose?

B

Gwendolen. I never change, except in my affections.

Cecily. What a noble nature you have, Gwendolen!

Jack. Then the question had better be cleared up at once. Aunt Augusta, a moment. At the time when Miss Prism left me in the handbag, had I been christened already?

Lady Bracknell. Every luxury that money could buy, including christening, had been lavished on you by your fond and doting parents.

Jack. Then I was christened! That is settled. Now, what name was I given? Let me know the worst.

Lady Bracknell. Being the eldest son you were naturally christened after your father.

Jack (*irritably*). Yes, but what was my father's Christian name?

Lady Bracknell (*meditatively*). I cannot at the present moment recall what the General's Christian name was. But I have no doubt he had one. He was eccentric, I admit. But only in later years. And that was the result of the Indian climate, and marriage, and indigestion, and other things of that kind.

Jack. Algy! Can't you recollect what our father's Christian name was?

Algernon. My dear boy, we were never even on speaking terms. He died before I was a year old.

Jack. His name would appear in the Army Lists of the period, I suppose, Aunt Augusta?

Lady Bracknell. The General was essentially a man of peace, except in his domestic life. But I have no doubt his name would appear in any military directory.

Jack. The Army Lists of the last forty years are here. These delightful records should have been my constant study. (*Rushes to bookcase and tears the books out*) M. Generals . . . Mallam, Maxbohm, Magley—what ghastly names they have—Markby, Migsby, Mobbs, Moncrieff! Lieutenant 1840, Captain, Lieutenant-Colonel, Colonel, General 1869, Christian names, Ernest John. (*Puts book very quietly down and speaks quite calmly*) I always told you, Gwendolen, my name was Ernest, didn't I? Well, it is Ernest after all. I mean it naturally is Ernest.

C

Lady Bracknell. Yes, I remember now that the General was called Ernest. I knew I had some particular reason for disliking the name.

Gwendolen. Ernest! My own Ernest! I felt from the first that you could have no other name!

Jack. Gwendolen, it is a terrible thing for a man to find out suddenly that all his life he has been speaking nothing but the truth. Can you forgive me?

D

Gwendolen. I can. For I feel that you are sure to change.

Jack. My own one!

Chasuble (*to* MISS PRISM). Laetitia! (*Embraces her*)

Miss Prism (*enthusiastically*). Frederick! At last!

Algernon. Cecily! (*Embraces her*) At last!

Jack. Gwendolen! (*Embraces her*) At last!

Lady Bracknell. My nephew, you seem to be displaying signs of triviality.

Jack. On the contrary, Aunt Augusta. I've now realized for the first time in my life the vital Importance of Being Earnest.

1. He reveals that Cecily has about a hundred and thirty thousand pounds in the Funds.

2. Dr. Chasuble remarks that Miss Prism has been waiting for him in the vestry. Lady Bracknell, overhearing the remark, asks to see Miss Prism.

3. Algernon and Cecily, Jack and Gwen-dolen, and Miss Prism and Dr. Chasuble will marry.

Interpreting Meanings

4. There is, of course, a play on the name Ernest and the word *earnest.* Students should note that instead of demonstrating the importance of being earnest (hardworking, sincere, serious, and intense), the play celebrates wit, idleness, and deception.

5. Students should note similarities between the two characters' point of view and lifestyle.

6. Answers will vary. Ask students to give reasons for their choice.

7. Miss Prism is the character whose revelations bring the play to a sudden surprise resolution. Student responses to *(Answers continue on next page.)*

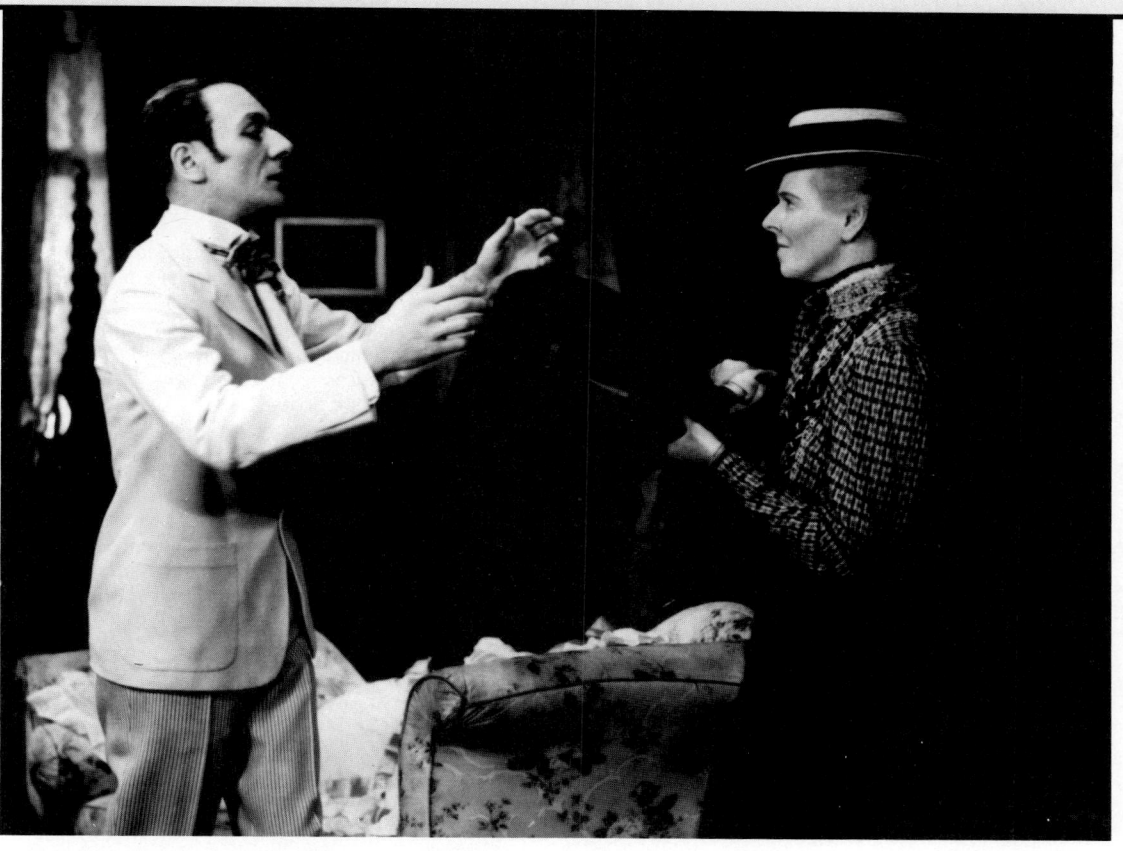

"Miss Prism, more is restored to you than this handbag."

A. Responding

Do you agree with Wilde's "truth" regarding the function of literature? Why or why not? In your opinion, what is the function of literature? (Wilde's "lies" can be seen as the artist's desire to impose order out of the chaos of "reality" and thus create a new reality. An artist creates literature to provide reasons and answers for people who do not have them, to express a point of view, to join ideas and concepts in a new way.)

A Comment on the Play

What, after all, is the importance of *The Importance of Being Earnest*? Jack's reply to Lady Bracknell's accusation that he is "displaying signs of triviality" does not help much. Jack replies that for the first time he has realized "the vital Importance of Being Earnest." Beyond the obvious play on words, the closing line seems to mean nothing at all. We need to remember, however, that throughout the play the dialogue has been turning conventional and "earnest" attitudes upside down. The traditional values connected with love, marriage, birth, death, sin, truth, sincerity, and so forth have been "trivialized" by means of burlesque, parody, verbal nonsense, and wit. But the term "trivialized" requires redefinition.

The subtitle of Wilde's play is "A Trivial Play for Serious People." If by this term Wilde means "negligible" or "inconsequential," Wilde would be applying the same standards of judgment as his Philistine critics. If by "trivial," however, we mean a susceptibility to artistic form, the delicate patterns of language, the artificial elegances of living, we come much closer to Wilde's meaning. The sort of "earnestness" that Wilde is rejecting in this play is the sort of stuffiness, priggishness, and hypocrisy that he detected in Victorian society.

Wilde's drama demonstrates the dictum that "Lying, the telling of beautiful untrue things, is the proper aim of Art" (from his essay "The Decay of Lying"). For example, at the end of the play Jack asks Gwendolen's forgiveness when he realizes that all of his life he has been telling the truth. Gwendolen replies that she can forgive him for she feels that he is certain to change. Jack has in reality discovered the importance of *not* being earnest. He has discovered the truth that Wilde set forth in "The Decay of Lying" and "The Critic as Artist": that just as it is "the function of literature to create, from the rough material of actual existence, a new world that will be more marvelous, more enduring, and more true than the world that common eyes look upon," so it is the function of man to create by "imaginative lying" and the cultivation of the beautiful forms of life, a personality that will realize the highest aims of art.

—Donald H. Ericksen

A

(Answers begin on previous page.)
the ending may vary.

Students should agree that the ending is in keeping with the ironic, humorous tone of the play. Their explanations may vary.

The Play as a Whole
1. Responses will vary. Jack is certainly not very worthy (Worthing). Algernon

Moncrieff sounds very upper-class. A *chasuble* is a sleeveless outer garment worn by priests during Mass, an appropriate last name for Dr. Chasuble. Miss Prism's last name suggests that she is very prim or prissy, which she is.
2. Responses will vary. Students should note that these devices are typical of much of comedy. The obstacles that separate the lovers are finally overcome, and

the play ends in the lovers' impending marriage—in this case, three marriages.
3. The play's subtitle is *A Trivial Comedy for Serious People.* Students may point out passages, such as the dialogue between Jack and Algernon near the end of Act One, that begins with Jack's saying, "I am sick to death of cleverness. Everybody is clever nowadays. . . ."
Responses will vary.

Responding to the Play

Analyzing Act Three

Identifying Facts

1. What does Jack reveal that causes Lady Bracknell to change her mind about the proposed marriage of Algernon and Cecily?
2. What chance remark leads to the revelation that Jack and Algernon are, indeed, brothers?
3. What weddings do we look forward to at the end of the play?

Interpreting Meanings

4. Explain the **irony** of the play's title.
5. What clues might have led you to expect, especially from their behavior, that Jack and Algernon were brothers all along?
6. As an actor or actress, which role would you like to play in *The Importance of Being Earnest*? Which role seems to offer the best comic possibilities?
7. In a **farce,** the situations become so entangled and complicated that the ending is often purely arbitrary or a trick. In ancient Greek and Roman drama, the ending was sometimes brought about by a god descending from the heavens in some kind of device or machine. Hence, these arbitrary endings are called **deus ex machina** endings. Who is the deus ex machina in this play, and were you disappointed in the ending? Was it in keeping with the **tone** of the rest of the play?

The Play as a Whole

1. Look back over the characters' proper names. What is significant about some of them?
2. Certain strands in Wilde's **plot** are so often found in comedy that they might be called elements of comedy. How does Wilde use these comic motifs: **disguise; mistaken identity; mysterious parentage; triangle of boy-girl-and-obstinate-parent?** In what ways are these motifs used today?
3. Wilde hints several times that the play is not to be taken seriously. What are these hints? In spite of them, do you think the play may have a serious message, or theme? What might it be?

Writing About the Play

A Creative Response

1. **Writing Epigrams.** Select a number of epigrams from Wilde's play and study them carefully, focusing on the

diction (choice of words) and rhythmical structure as well as the content. Then try to write a few epigrams of your own on a subject of your choice.
2. **Writing a Sequel.** Describe the weddings that we anticipate at the end of the play. How are the characters dressed? What comic hitches might develop? How does Aunt Augusta behave?

A Critical Response

3. **Writing an Analysis.** In a brief essay, analyze the play's relationship to its historical period. Could anything of comparable effect be written today in America, in your opinion? If so, give a brief sketch of possible settings, characters, and subjects. If not, explain why not.

Analyzing Language and Style

Puns and Paradoxes

Wilde's **epigrams** (short, witty statements) are often **puns,** or plays on words. A pun depends upon a word's multiple meanings or on two words that sound alike but have different meanings. The title, for example, is a play on the words *earnest* and the name Ernest; it really refers to both. Some of Wilde's puns, obvious to his contemporaries, are no longer clear today. See the footnote for *agricultural depression* in Act Two.

Wilde also has his characters speak in **paradoxes,** statements that are apparently contradictory but are nonetheless true. When Cecily says in Act Two, "I don't like novels that end happily. They depress me so much," the lines surprise us because *depress* is not the word we associate with happy endings. Yet Wilde presents us with a new thought: that a series of silly novels with happy endings can indeed be depressing.

Tell whether each of the following lines from Act I involves either a pun or a paradox.

1. **Algernon.** . . . The very essence of romance is uncertainty. If ever I get married, I'll certainly try to forget the fact.
2. **Jack.** . . . It is very vulgar to talk like a dentist when one isn't a dentist. It produces a false impression.
3. **Lady Bracknell.** . . . I do not approve of anything that tampers with natural ignorance. Ignorance is like a delicate exotic fruit; touch it and the bloom is gone.
4. **Algernon.** . . . It is awfully hard work doing nothing. However, I don't mind hard work where there is no definite object of any kind.

Find three more examples of puns and paradoxes in Acts II and III of the play.

906

THE ENGLISH LANGUAGE

by **John Algeo**

Although the spread of English outside the British Isles began in the early seventeenth century, it was during the Victorian Age and the establishment of the British Empire that English became a world language. Primarily because of the Empire, English became the first or an important second language in the British Isles, the United States, and Canada, and also in Jamaica, Trinidad and Tobago, Australia, New Zealand, Malaysia, Singapore, Burma, India, Sri Lanka, Pakistan, Israel, Ghana, Sierra Leone, Nigeria, Sudan, Kenya, Tanzania, Malawi, Zambia, Zimbabwe, Swaziland, and South Africa. American expansion, although modest by comparison, extended English to the Philippines, Liberia, and a few other places.

English as an International Language

English first spread around the world as a result of political and commercial activities, empire-building, and colonization. In addition, scientific and technological advances, movies and television programs, popular music, and fashions of clothing have all served to reinforce the prestige of English as an international language. Today English is used more widely and for more purposes as a second language than any other human tongue.

To take only one example: English is the language of international aviation. If a Swedish pilot is landing an airplane in Greece, he carries on his conversation with the controller on the ground in English. Having a single language for international aviation is obviously sensible. It would not do for a pilot who spoke only Swedish to ask for landing instructions from a ground control run by people who spoke only Greek. A common language is needed as a safety measure for international flights, and English was chosen because of the prominence of English-speaking people in making and flying airplanes. It is for such reasons that English has become the most widely used international language.

Dialects of English

Today there are dialects of English all over the world. Each place where it is spoken has its own variety of the language, and old countries like England or large ones like the United States have many regional dialects. However, standard English—the English found in books, magazines, and large newspapers—is relatively uniform. That uniformity also helps to make English useful as an international language. Differences exist, to be sure, but they are minor fluctuations in what is obviously a single language.

One Language— Many Nations

A. "The Queen's English"
It was during the Victorian Age that the notion of "the Queen's English" arose—the spoken standard to which all, even the lower classes, could aspire.

B. Indian English
The Constitution of India, established in 1947, recognized English as an "associate" official language. With approximately two hundred native languages, India needs English to unify its peoples. A prominent Indian professor, a proponent of Indian English, has said, "More Indians speak English and write English than in England itself. . . ."

C. British English
❓ What does this sign stand for in England today? (*Underground* is the British name for what we call a *subway*.) Refer students to the section on British English on the next page.

A. British and American English

In many parts of the world (Japan and Saudi Arabia, for example), a student must choose which type of English to learn: British or American.

B. Expansion

While British and American English are closely related, there are, in fact, so many differences between the two that the American news agency the Associated Press and the British news agency Reuters have to translate English into English.

Each country in which English is the main language of communication has its own national standard that differs in small, but recognizable, ways from the standard of other English-speaking lands. Among these national standards are those of Australia, Canada, Great Britain (England, Scotland, Wales, and North Ireland), Jamaica, New Zealand, Republic of Ireland, and the United States.

Two Close Cousins: British and American English

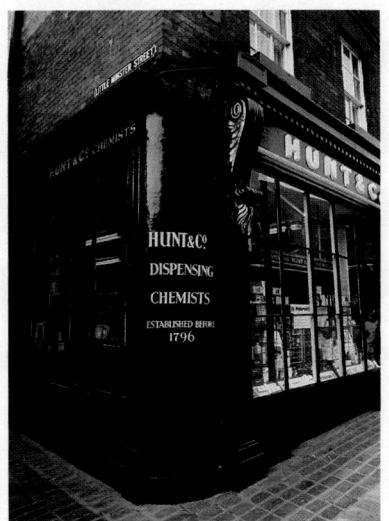

A The two most important national standards are those of Great Britain and the United States: British and American English. The differences between them can be illustrated by a few expressions:

American	British
baby stroller	push chair
baked potato	jacket potato
barrette	hair slide
coffee with cream	coffee white
daylight saving time	summer time
divided highway	dual carriage way
elevator	lift
hood (of a car)	bonnet
Main Street	High Street
pharmacist	dispensing chemist
public rest room	convenience
quiche	flan
savings and loan association	building society
subway	underground *or* tube
traffic circle	roundabout
trunk (of a car)	boot
wastepaper basket	bin
Watch your step.	Mind the step.
whole wheat bread	brown bread
yield (highway sign)	give way

The differences tend to occur especially in technical areas like automotive terms, in domestic matters like food names, and in specialized commercial terms like names for kinds of businesses. The specialized terminologies of American and British English differ considerably, but the words of the ordinary language—the everyday nouns and most verbs, adverbs, adjectives, and grammatical words like prepositions and conjunctions—are very much alike in the two national standards.

B Each national standard also has words for which there is no exact equivalent in the other. For example, in England a *bap* is a soft roll that may be used to make a sandwich; a *crumpet* is a kind of muffin; a *gateau* is a kind of cake; a *scone* is a type of biscuit; a *free house* is a *pub* or bar where more than one brand of beer is sold; and a *purveyor* is a company that sells or deals in some product.

Each country has influenced the language of the other. In America, people who drive foreign cars may begin to use British automotive terms because they are in the operating manuals for cars from England. The expression "Not to worry" is a Briticism that has become popular here. On the other hand, American expressions like "nitty-gritty" turn up in England, as do many technical terms.

Strange combinations of the two national standards sometimes emerge. American clothing, food, and television programs, like *Dallas,* are very popular in England. A store in the Chelsea area of London announces itself as the "Texas Lone Star Saloon, Purveyors of the Best Chili, Tacos, Nachos." Everything about the store's sign is pure American—except the word *purveyors,* which is as British as crumpets and scones.

Pronunciation, Spelling, and Grammar

British and American English obviously differ in pronunciation. The British pronounce words like *bath, class,* and *can't* with the vowel sound of *father,* rather than with the vowel sound of *cat.* Like people from eastern New England, New York City, and the coastal South, but unlike most other Americans, the British drop *r* sounds unless they have a vowel after them, so that *poppa* and *popper* sound alike. American English tends to have more stresses on its words than does British English; so we pronounce *secretary* as sek′rə·ter′ē whereas the British say it as sek′rə·trē′. Perhaps the most striking difference between the two national standards, however, is in intonation, the "tune" of the sentence. To British ears, American speech sounds flat and dull—we have a more uniform, lower pitch and minimize the difference between our high and low notes. To American ears, British sounds fluting, high-pitched, quavering, and slightly hysterical—they have a more varied, higher pitch and exaggerate the difference between high and low notes.

Spelling also differs slightly in the two countries. British English uses -*our* in words like *colour* and *honour,* where American English uses -*or.* British uses -*re* in words like *centre* and *metre,* where American uses -*er.* British doubles the *l* at the end of unstressed syllables before adding a suffix beginning with a vowel in words like *travelling,* for which American usage typically keeps a single *l, traveling.* There are also a few miscellaneous differences: British *pyjamas* versus American *pajamas.* The differences are all trivial, although the British often insist that American books published in England be reset in British spelling. Americans seldom notice the difference.

Grammatical differences between the two countries are also few and unimportant. The British sometimes omit the definite article where we would use it: "in hospital" (British) versus "in the hospital" (American). They use a plural verb with some collective nouns (the word *government* and names of sports teams) for which we use a singular verb: "The government *have* decided. . . ." "Ne-

A

B

C

"A store in the Chelsea area of London announces itself as the 'Texas Lone Star Saloon, Purveyors of the Best Chili, Tacos, Nachos.' "

A. Pronunciation
In the transition from British to American English, the word *missile* lost the emphasis British speakers place on the last syllable. It is now pronounced like *missal.*

B. Rate of Speaking
In addition, British and American English differ in the speed with which they are spoken. Britons speak rather quickly; Americans speak more deliberately.

C. Spelling
It is to Noah Webster that we credit these changes.

A. "Common Source"/Grimm's Law

Linguists believe that the languages of approximately one third of the human race come from an Indo-European "common source." Some of the languages that derive from this source are the European descendants of Latin—French, Spanish, Italian, and Portuguese; Russian; the Celtic languages Irish and Scots Gaelic; and various offshoots of German, among them, Dutch and English.

It was folklorist Jakob Grimm who established that the German word *vater* (the English word *father*) has the same root as the Sanskrit/Latin *pitar/pater*. This breakthrough, known as Grimm's law, supports the thesis of Indo-European as a common source.

"**O**scar Wilde said that the English 'have really everything in common with America nowadays, except, of course, language.'"

A

braska *are* winning the bowl game." They treat *have* as a special verb that does not require an auxiliary in questions: "Have you the answer?" versus "Do you have the answer?" The British use only the past participle *got,* whereas we use both *got* and *gotten,* in different ways: "I've got it" versus American "I've got it" (meaning "I have it") and "I've gotten it" (meaning "I've obtained it"). None of the other grammatical differences are more important than these.

The differences between British and American English have often been exaggerated, as they were by Oscar Wilde, who said that the English "have really everything in common with America nowadays, except, of course, language." In fact, not only these two countries, but all the nations of the English-speaking world share a common linguistic heritage that goes back to the Anglo-Saxons and before them to Proto-Indo-European tribes wandering from Asia across Europe. Today, despite the linguistic differences that divide us—the small distinctions of grammar, spelling, and pronunciation, and the greater but still not insuperable ones of terminology—English is a unified language. The core of English—our basic words and how we use them—is one.

Analyzing Language

1. On the left are some words from British English with their American counterparts on the right (though not in the same order). Look up the British words in a dictionary, and match them with their American equivalents.

accumulator	car battery
banger	gobble up
flog	high rubber boots
nous	line
queue	property taxes
rates	sausage
scoff	savvy, intelligence
toffee-nosed	sell
wellies	stuck-up

2. The following sentences in British English have grammatical constructions that differ from American use. What part of each sentence seems unusual to you? Rewrite each sentence as you would say it.

   a. He has been in hospital for a week.
   b. "It's good to be home again." "Yes, isn't it just?"
   c. At the weekend, they stayed with friends in the mountains.

   d. What had you in mind to do this afternoon?
   e. She says she tried to call us, but she can't have done.
   f. It looks like being a close vote.
   g. Everybody was issued with an identity card.
   h. After long discussions, they agreed the plan.
   i. I carry two pencils in case one goes missing.

3. The following words are spelled in British fashion. Write the corresponding American spelling.

ageing	centre	labour
analyse	gaol	marvelled

4. The following words come from several different national varieties of English. Look up the words in a dictionary to see what they mean and where they originated.

boomerang	kiwi	trek
boondocks	thug	walkabout

Exercises in Critical Thinking and Writing

DEVELOPING AND SUPPORTING GENERALIZATIONS

Writing Assignment

Write an essay in which you develop and support a valid generalization about one of the works you have read in this unit. In your essay, discuss your response to the work.

Background

A **generalization** is a general conclusion based on a body of specific details. In analyzing literature, you often make generalizations about its elements—plot, characters, theme, imagery, and so on. You may, for example, make the following generalizations about literature in the Victorian Age:

1. *In the poem "Dover Beach," Matthew Arnold describes the world much as it is today.*
2. *The imagery of Tennyson's "Ulysses" makes the reader sympathize with Ulysses's desire to experience the world once again.*
3. *Dickens's novels are filled with autobiographical details.*

Generalizations such as these are **valid** (true) if they meet both of the following criteria:

A
1. Sufficient evidence supports the generalization.
2. The generalization covers all the evidence.

When you read any work of literature, you have a personal **response** to it: The work may evoke a feeling or personal memory; you may decide that you like or dislike the work. Often, a specific image or quality of character may begin to shape your response. In Tennyson's "Ulysses," for example, when you read the image "How dull it is to pause, to make an end, / To rust unburnish'd, not to shine in use," you may begin to feel sympathy with the plight of Ulysses. Additional images like "And this gray spirit yearning in desire / To follow knowledge like a sinking star" might develop and reinforce your feeling of sympathy.

Prewriting

As a first step, be certain that your generalization is adequately focused. You should be able to find sufficient evidence (details, quotations, images, characters) to support your generalization.

1. **Begin by stating a first draft of your generalization:**

   The Importance of Being Earnest is an indictment of the shallowness and hypocrisy of the attitudes of Victorian society.

2. **Consider whether your generalization is too broad.** For example, does *The Importance of Being Earnest* indict *all* attitudes of the Victorians?

3. **Focus your generalization so that it is limited enough to support easily.**

   The Importance of Being Earnest is an indictment of the shallowness and hypocrisy of the attitudes of Victorian society about relationships between the sexes and marriage and family life.   **B**

   Before you begin planning your essay, study the following model essay about *The Importance of Being Earnest*. This essay was planned for an audience that is already familiar with the play. The student's thoughts in developing the essay appear in the margin.

In *The Importance of Being Earnest*, two young men named Algernon and Jack learn the importance of being named Ernest. As they do, the audience learns Oscar Wilde's views about some Victorian ideas. In Jack's and Algernon's words and actions, as well as those of other characters in the play, Wilde indicts the shallowness and hypocrisy of many Victorian attitudes. Attitudes about relationships between the sexes and marriage and family life all come in for their share of ridicule.

I'm summarizing the plot here and attracting reader interest.

This sentence and the next sentence express my focused generalization. They are also my thesis statement. I depend on my readers' knowledge to some extent.   **C**

A. Hasty Generalization
Caution students to avoid making a hasty generalization based on insufficient evidence. A hasty generalization is based on only a small number of samples.

B. Thesis Statement
Students should recognize that the thesis statement of an essay is usually a generalization; so is the topic sentence of a paragraph.

C. Using the Model Essay
Go over the essay in class, and discuss the marginal comments. Note especially how the writer has cited specific incidents and characters in the play to support general statements.

A. Cue Words
Other examples of cue words are *on the other hand, nevertheless,* and *as a result.*

Revising Essays
As students revise their essays, refer them to **Grammar, Usage, and Mechanics: A Reference Guide** at the back of their books.

Exercises in Critical Thinking and Writing/*cont.*

The shallowness and hypocrisy of Victorian attitudes about relationships between the sexes are shown in the relationships between the pairs of lovers in the play—Algernon and Cecily, and Jack and Gwendolen. In fact, the shallowness of their relationships is the very premise of the play. The ideal of both Gwendolen and Cecily, for example, is nothing more than to love someone named Ernest. Both Algernon and Jack go along with this nonsense in their willingness to be baptized to gain the name Ernest. The words and actions of individual characters also reveal shallowness and hypocrisy in attitudes about the sexes. From the beginning, for example, Algernon makes disparaging remarks about women and how they should be treated. At one point he says to Jack, "The only way to behave to a woman is to make love to her, if she is pretty, and to someone else, if she is plain."

Much of Wilde's indictment of Victorian attitudes toward home and family life is seen through Lady Bracknell. She reveals her shallow attitudes when she questions Jack, who has just asked to marry her niece Gwendolen. Lady Bracknell's questions reveal what she considers important in a marriage. She asks, for example, whether Jack smokes and who his parents are. When she learns that Jack has lost his parents, she refuses to let the marriage take place. Also significant is Lady Bracknell's comment about a recently widowed friend on whom she has just called: "I never saw a woman so altered; she looks quite twenty years younger."

In spite of its indictment of Victorian society, the play seems to be a comedy in the truest sense and I enjoyed its wit and humor. In this, as in Shakespeare's comedies, the lovers encounter problems that are solved by the play's end. Jack discovers his true relations—he is Algernon's older brother and his real name is Ernest. This discovery removes Lady Bracknell's objection to his marrying Gwendolen and leaves Algernon free to marry Cecily. Even Miss Prism and Dr. Chasuble are to be married. With this happy ending, it is difficult to believe that Oscar Wilde found Victorian society completely beyond redemption.

This is my topic sentence. It announces to my readers that I'm dealing with the first part of my thesis statement.

I'm giving a specific example to clarify the general point in the preceding sentence.

This quotation supports the point made in the preceding sentence.

This topic sentence makes the content of the paragraph clear, but, for variety, I am wording it differently from the last topic sentence.

The quotation here is not particularly significant, so I'm paraphrasing.

This quotation supports the point just made.

In this paragraph, I give my response to the play.

This is support for my feeling that the play is a comedy.

This is how I think the playwright must have felt.

Writing

Although you should support your generalization with specific details, your essay should be more than a string of quotations. Notice how, in the model essay, the writer has paraphrased many of the characters' words. Quotations are used when they make a point especially well.

Also, be aware of cues that you can use to help readers follow your ideas. A thesis statement and topic sentences announce the content of the essay and of each paragraph.

Words like *for example* indicate that a specific example is being used to support a point. Words like *and, also, because,* and *however* point out relationships between ideas.

Revising and Proofreading

For help in revising and proofreading your essay, see the section on **Writing About Literature** at the back of the book.

THE TWENTIETH CENTURY

Untitled by Joseph Cornell (1965–68).
Collage and oil on masonite.

The University of Iowa.
Museum of Art.

UNIT SEVEN

HUMANITIES CONNECTION: DISCUSSING THE FINE ART

Joseph Cornell (1903–1973) was an American sculptor born in Nyack, New York. Although without formal art training, he made a significant contribution to the development of modern sculpture. Like the surrealists, he often juxtaposed objects in surprising ways, but unlike them, his works often evoked a nostalgia for a lost past. His miniature box sculptures, containing fragments of beautiful and precious objects, were the forerunners of the art of assemblage, in which sculptors incorporated ready-made objects from the everyday world in their original works.

? Ask students to consider the connections between the kettle and the constellation of stars in this collage. (Note the juxtaposition of the domestic and cosmic elements.) Why might this work have been chosen to open a unit on twentieth-century literature?

TEACHING TWENTIETH-CENTURY LITERATURE

Modern British literature actually had its genesis in the last decade of the nineteenth century. From that time on, writers became increasingly concerned with the place of the individual in mass society. Much literature focused on the lonely, isolated, and thoughtful individual, fighting to find peace and security in a threatening world. Literature seemed to turn away from the idealism nurtured by the Romantic movement and to focus instead on social and psychological issues. In the early 1900's came the first so-called "world" war, and with it came the desire and need to look inward in the hopes of securing some understanding of human nature, which was already being reduced and dissected by psychiatrists, evolutionists, and Marxists.

The early twentieth century was also a period of experimentation in literary technique. Such devices as stream of consciousness were developed by writers like James Joyce and Virginia Woolf. In fiction, the characters' psychological makeup was elevated to a level of preeminence previously enjoyed only by plot and story line. Alienation from an uncaring world became a frequent theme in prose, poetry, and drama.

Some poets, such as Dylan Thomas and T. S. Eliot, looked back to past forms of expression. Thomas tried to return poetry to the incandescent language of the Romantics; Eliot called for a return to the elaborate wordplay and religious imagery of the metaphysical poets.

Despite their differences, the goal of all these twentieth-century writers has not been mere helpless remonstrance against societal evil. All of these writers write—as writers always have—to discover order in the midst of chaos, to give voice to the vexing questions of who we are, where we should be going, and what values should guide us as we try to get there.

OBJECTIVES OF THE TWENTIETH-CENTURY UNIT

1. To improve reading proficiency and expand vocabulary
2. To gain exposure to notable authors and works of the period
3. To define and identify significant literary techniques and movements: the modern short story, the marginal hero, stream of consciousness, the theater of the absurd
4. To interpret and respond to fiction, poetry, and drama, orally and in writing
5. To practice the following critical thinking and writing skills:
   a. Extending a short story beyond its ending
   b. Analyzing a story's theme
   c. Analyzing a character in a story
   d. Comparing and contrasting characters
   e. Evaluating the points of view chosen by a writer
   f. Writing a comparison of poems
   g. Imitating a writer's techniques
   h. Analyzing dialogue
   i. Analyzing an adaptation
   j. Responding to criticism

SUPPLEMENTARY SUPPORT MATERIALS: UNIT SEVEN
1. Unit Introduction Test *(CCB)*
2. Word Analogies Test *(CCB)*
3. Unit Review Test *(CCB)*
4. Critical Thinking and Writing Test *(CCB)*

5. Study Guide to *A Portrait of the Artist as a Young Man*
6. Instructional Overhead Transparencies

A. Discussing the Quotation
This quotation from Virginia Woolf sums up her intent to capture in her writing the stream of thoughts and feelings flowing through the minds of her characters—what has come to be called the stream-of-consciousness technique.
? How realistically do you think the workings of the human mind can be conveyed by a writer?

B. Humanities Connection: Discussing the Fine Art
Call students' attention to the works of art on pages 914 and 915. Each depicts a well-known site in London.
? Note the date of each work. How do the styles differ? (Note use of perspective, architectural subject, and Romantic treatment of people in one and the minimalistic detail, with a geometric/elliptical pattern imposed on human forms, in the other.)

THE TWENTIETH CENTURY

A

by **Robert Anderson,**
John Malcolm Brinnin,
and **John Leggett**

B

Hyde Park by Sybil Andrews (1931). Linoleum cut.

Mary Ryan Gallery, New York.

> *Let us record the atoms as they fall upon the mind in the order in which they fall, let us trace the pattern, however disconnected and incoherent in appearance, which each sight or incident scores upon the consciousness.*
>
> —Virginia Woolf

What a story of change, of the erosion of a proud, complacent, well-ordered society, is told by the early years of the twentieth century in England!

If we had lived in the era of Victoria, which ended with the great queen's death in 1901, or during the ten-year reign of her son, Edward VII, we would have believed that England, with her moral and economic dominance of the world, would sail on majestically forever. But of course that is the misconception of every stable age and society—that life will go on much as it has in the past.

Even during this long, fairly comfortable period in England, though, profound changes were taking place, both externally and internally. Although the British imperial policy remained much the same throughout the Victorian era, several major colonies—Australia, South Africa, and New Zealand—gained their independence. Internally, England was experiencing social reforms that were to have far-reaching consequences. The rise in literacy, the growing power and influence of the Labor Party, the widespread interest in socialist ideology—all were to alter dramatically England and the world.

Darwin, Marx, and Freud

Many of the social and intellectual changes that were taking place had their roots in the nineteenth-century work of three men: Charles Darwin, Karl Marx, and Sigmund Freud.

Darwin's *Origin of Species* (1859) propounded a theory of the evolution of animal species based upon natural selection—those species which successfully adapted to their environments survived, those which did not became extinct. This theory, which seemed to contradict the Biblical account of the special creation of each species, fueled a debate between science and religion that has continued from Victorian times to the present. "Social Darwinism," the notion that in society, as in nature, only the fittest should survive and flourish, became a controversial aspect of political, social, and economic thought.

In *Das Kapital* (1867), Karl Marx, a German philosopher and political economist who spent the last twenty years of his life in London, advocated the abolition of private property. He traced economic injustices to the capitalist system of ownership and argued that workers should own the means of production. His

Trafalgar Square is named for its monument to British naval hero Lord Horatio Nelson. The square was built during Victoria's reign, when many of London's old, unsanitary, rabbit-warren streets were transformed into spacious new squares and thoroughfares. (Earlier, this area was known as Porridge Island.) In this painting, the church of St. Martin-in-the-Fields is seen, with its famous open portico and clock tower. The church was designed by James Gibb and built in 1721–1726. It survived the London blitz and still looks very much like this today. Next to the church is the South Africa building, now an embassy. The church faces the great National Gallery and the National Portrait Gallery.

? Do American cities have similar squares? (Journal Square in Cleveland, Times Square in New York City, etc.) What advantages do they provide? (Light, air, a pleasant place to walk)

A

Trafalgar Square by H. E. Tidmarsh (1898). Oil.

Guildhall Art Gallery, London.

theories of social and economic justice revolutionized political thought and eventually led to sweeping changes in many governments and economic systems, including those of England.

Sigmund Freud's psychological theories were equally revolutionary and far-reaching in their effects. In *The Interpretation of Dreams* (1900) and later works, Freud found the motives for human behavior not in our rational, conscious minds, but in the irrational and sexually driven realm of the unconscious, which is visible to us only in our dreams. Conservative Victorian sensibilities were outraged by his claims of the importance of sex in behavior, but artists and writers found the notion of the unconscious and its mysterious, illogical workings fascinating.

The work of these thinkers helped to undermine the political, religious, and psychological ideas which had served as the foundation of British society and the British Empire for generations. With the calamity of the Great War and the events that followed, that foundation was largely swept away.

A. Humanities Connection: Discussing the Fine Art

Stanley Spencer (1891–1959) served with the British Army in Macedonia in World War I and was commissioned to paint pictures based on his experiences there. This picture is one of those. "Travoys" are primitive stretchers. As a war memorial, he also painted a series of murals for a specially built chapel in Burghclere in Berkshire.

? What does this picture express about war? How are the men in the painting portrayed? What element in the painting is its focus? The pale operating room? The dark, ominous horses? The stretchers with their suffering blanketed forms? (The focus of the painting is the stretchers; the artist is lamenting the pain and death of soldiers, who are the victims of war.)

Travoys Arriving with Wounded at a Dressing Station at Smol, Macedonia by Stanley Spencer (1919). Oil.

Imperial War Museum, London.

The Great War

The truly great disaster of the first half of the century was the breakdown of the European balance of power. In 1914, England, France, and Russia, bound by treaties, were locked in opposition to Germany, Austria-Hungary, and Italy. The confrontation plunged the whole of Europe into what has come to be known as The Great War.

The Victorian writer Rudyard Kipling celebrated the British character as essentially patriotic, and he was right. When war broke out, a young Englishman felt that to be called upon to defend his nation was likely to be the most exalted experience of his life. For centuries, in all sorts of wars and skirmishes, the most ordinary youths of England had donned smart uniforms and marched off to faraway battlefields, just as they might to major sports events. There they would perform heroic acts. For the most part, these soldiers returned to be honored and to add their tales to the romantic lore of their regiments.

When Britain declared war on Germany in 1914, young Britons crowded to the recruiting stations to enlist. Six months later, hordes of them lay slaughtered in the miserable, rain-soaked, vermin-infested trenches of France. Sixty thousand young British men were killed or wounded on the first day of the Battle of the Somme

A

A. Expansion
Ypres (ē'pr') is a city in northwestern Belgium, near the French border.

B. Responding

? Can you think of a period later in the century in which American youth rejected the values of their elders and questioned involvement in a war? (The "hippie" and Vietnam protest movements of the 1960's)

alone. Three hundred thousand were killed, wounded, or frozen to death at the Battle of Ypres. The generals would not stop the terrible, and in the end futile, carnage, and over the course of four years an entire generation of young Englishmen was fed to the insatiable furnace of the war.

With the armistice in 1918 a new cynicism arose. The old values of national honor and glory had endorsed a war whose results were gradually recognized as a weakened economy, a tottering colonial empire, and a loss of life worse than that caused by any plague. Out of disillusionment came a pessimism about the state and the individual's relation to society. A new realism arose, an antidote to the "romantic nonsense" of the past and in particular to the propaganda machine that had led a whole people into war.

Experimentation in the Arts

The decade before the War had seen the beginnings of a transformation in all the arts, especially on the Continent. In Paris in 1905, Henri Matisse and other new painters exhibiting at the Salon d'Automne were called *les fauves* ("the wild beasts") by critics for their bold new use of line and color. Picasso's first cubist painting, *Les Demoiselles d'Avignon,* was finished in 1907, the year John Millington Synge's play *The Playboy of the Western World* caused a riot at its premiere at Dublin's Abbey Theater. In 1913, Stravinsky's revolutionary ballet, *The Rite of Spring,* which was marked by strong, primitive rhythms and dissonant harmonies, caused a riot at *its* premiere in Paris. The year after that, Joyce's *Dubliners,* containing stories written up to a decade before, finally found an Irish publisher brave enough to publish it. All of these works challenged traditional notions of beauty and order, and opened new avenues of expression.

Following the War, those artists who survived ("there died a myriad," American poet Ezra Pound wrote of the War) continued to develop in new directions, and the next fifteen years or so saw a flowering of genius that has seldom been equaled. In England, while traditional writers such as H. G. Wells and Arnold Bennett continued to produce, a new generation, impatient with both traditional subject matter and traditional narrative method, was emerging.

The new novelists, such as Joseph Conrad, were moving from a concern with society to a focus on introspection, the probing of the depths of the individual spirit. Virginia Woolf was even rejecting traditional chronological order in storytelling. Experimenting with structure and with a shifting point of view, Woolf portrayed, with striking success, the inner lives of her characters.

In his novels D. H. Lawrence was writing out his own strong resentment against traditional British society, with its class system, industrialism, militarism, and prudery. Lawrence shocked the English with his beliefs about the opposing aspects of human nature, and with his glorification of the senses and of relations between the sexes.

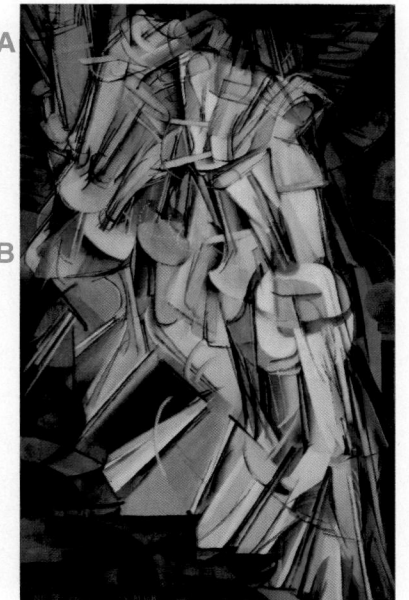

Nude Descending a Staircase, No. 2 by Marcel Duchamp (1912). Oil.

Philadelphia Museum of Art. Louise and Walter Arensberg Collection.

C. Humanities Connection: Discussing the Fine Art
French painter Marcel Duchamp (1887–1968) was associated in the early twentieth century with futurism, a movement in literature and art that wished to break with the past by embracing the discoveries of modern science and expressing in art the dynamic movement of machines and of the human body. Here Duchamp, in futurist fashion, repeats various portions of the human form and fragments these with shafts of dynamic movement. Ask students if they can think of other ways in which a painter can suggest movement on canvas. (Showing objects and people stretched, flattened, or otherwise distorted by momentum, or in positions gravity would not permit them to hold for long)

" **D. H. Lawrence shocked the English with his beliefs about the opposing aspects of human nature, and with the glorification of the senses and of relations between the sexes.** "

A. Discussing the Caricature

Joyce allowed the Spanish artist Cesar Abin to draw him for his fiftieth birthday, even though it was an occasion that made Joyce very dejected. The portrait turned out to be the classical figure of the artist in a dressing gown. So Joyce suggested changes. He said that Paul Léon had said he looked like a question mark when he stood on street corners. Someone else had called him a blue-nosed comedian, so he had the artist put a star at the end of his nose to illuminate it. He requested the black derby with the number 13 and cobwebs to suggest his mourning for his father, who had just died in Ireland. The roll of paper sticking out of his pocket is the song "Let me like a soldier fall..." The patches suggest his poverty. The point of the question mark is shaped like the world with only one country visible—Ireland. Dublin is marked in black.

You might suggest that students describe the way they'd have their own caricatures drawn.

A

Caricature of Joyce by Cesar Abin.

Most influential of all was the Irish poet and novelist James Joyce whose novel *Ulysses* appeared to a storm of controversy in 1922. *Ulysses,* based on Homer's *Odyssey,* narrates the events in a single day in the lives of a Jewish Dubliner named Leopold Bloom and a young man named Stephen Dedalus, as they unwittingly recapitulate the actions of Homer's Odysseus and his son Telemachus. Joyce drew, in a wholly revolutionary way, upon myth and symbol, upon Freudian explorations of sexuality, and upon new conceptions of time and the workings of human consciousness.

The book, now regarded as one of the masterpieces of modern literature, had a stormy reception. "How can one plow through such stuff?" said novelist George Moore after trying to read it. Critic Edmund Gosse called Joyce "a literary charlatan of the extremest order." *Ulysses,* he wrote, "is an anarchical production, infamous in taste, in style, in everything." Other critics, such as John Middleton Murry and Arnold Bennett, lauded the work, and most younger writers recognized its genius. Ernest Hemingway called it "a wonderful book," and T. S. Eliot, whose poem *The Waste Land* was influenced by *Ulysses,* praised the book extravagantly to his friends. "How could anyone write again," he asked Virginia Woolf, "after achieving the immense prodigy of the last chapter?" Eliot claimed that *Ulysses* finally destroyed nineteenth-century novelistic style and subject matter, and so, to a large extent, it did.

1901	1902–1905	1907–1908	1910–1913
Queen Victoria dies, is succeeded by her son, Edward VII, 1901 Ragtime music becomes popular in U.S., then in England, 1901	**Conrad's novel *Heart of Darkness*, 1902** **Shaw's *Mrs. Warren's Profession* opens in New York City and is closed by police after one performance, 1905**	**Rudyard Kipling receives Nobel Prize, 1907** Sigmund Freud visits U.S. to lecture on psychoanalysis, 1908	South Africa gains independence from Britain, 1910 **Shaw's *Pygmalion*, 1912** **D. H. Lawrence's novel *Sons and Lovers*, 1913**

1922	1923–1925	1926–1927	1929
Britain refuses to grant Ireland republic status; Civil War begins in Ireland, 1922 **Joyce's *Ulysses*, Eliot's *The Waste Land*, 1922**	**Yeats receives Nobel Prize, 1923** **E. M. Forster's novel *A Passage to India*, 1924** **Shaw receives Nobel Prize, 1925**	Fascist youth organizations formed in Italy and Germany, 1926 **Woolf's novel *To the Lighthouse*, 1927**	**Woolf's *A Room of One's Own* and Ernest Hemingway's *A Farewell to Arms*, 1929**

1939–1940	1940–1945	1945	1947–1948
Joyce's *Finnegans Wake*, 1939 Germany invades Poland; World War II begins, 1939 "The Battle of Britain," 1940	**Greene's novel *The Power and the Glory*, 1940** U.S. declares war on Italy, Germany, and Japan, 1941 Germany surrenders, 1945	Atom bombs dropped over Hiroshima and Nagasaki, ending World War II, 1945 **George Orwell's novel *Animal Farm*, 1945**	India granted independence from Great Britain, 1947 Republic of Israel created, 1948 Mohandas Gandhi assassinated in India, 1948

The Rise of Dictatorships

The Great War, which had been called "the war to end war," ironically led to another war. The League of Nations, the idealistic dream of America's President Wilson, had no sooner been created than it was abandoned by a newly isolationist United States government. A worldwide economic depression which began in 1929 encouraged the rise of dictators in Germany, Italy, and Russia.

In Italy and Germany, the form of totalitarianism that developed was Fascism, a type of government that relies on the rule of a single dictator whose power is absolute and backed by force. Benito Mussolini, who came to power in Italy in 1922, held control through brutality and manipulation. Adolf Hitler and the Nazi party capitalized on Germany's economic woes to convince many Germans that their problems were caused by Jews, Communists, and immigrants.

Russia's totalitarian government, based on the political theories of economist Karl Marx, was Communist rather than Fascist. Its founder, Nikolai Lenin, had sought, in the 1920's, to create a society without a class system, one in which the state would distribute the country's wealth equally among the people. But in reality, the new government became as repressive as the rule of the Czars had been. In 1941 Joseph Stalin became Premier and continued to rule with an iron fist.

A

" **The Great War, which had been called 'the war to end war,' ironically led to another war.**"

A. Expansion
Stalin was the virtual dictator of the U.S.S.R. from the death of Lenin in 1923 to his own death in 1953. In 1941 Stalin named himself premier of the Soviet Union.

1913–1914	1914–1916	1916–1917	1917–1918
In New York City, the Armory Show introduces Post-Impressionism and Cubism in art, 1913	World War I begins, 1914	Easter Rebellion in Dublin, 1916	T. S. Eliot's *The Love Song of J. Alfred Prufrock*, 1917
	Einstein's General Theory of Relativity, 1915	U.S. enters the war in Europe, 1917	World War I ends with 8 million dead, 1918
James Joyce's *Dubliners*, 1914	**Joyce's *A Portrait of the Artist as a Young Man*, 1916**	Russian Revolution, 1917	Vote in England extended to women over 30, 1918

1930	1931–1933	1933–1938	1936–1937
Auden's *Poems*, Noel Coward's play *Private Lives*, and Eliot's *Ash Wednesday*, 1930	Banks close and financial crisis begins in Europe, triggering a worldwide Depression, 1931	Adolf Hitler appointed chancellor in Germany, 1933	Civil War in Spain, 1936–1939
American Sinclair Lewis receives Nobel Prize, 1930	**After being banned for 11 years, Joyce's *Ulysses* is allowed into U.S., 1933**	Stalinist purges in Russia result in 8 million people sent to labor camps, 1934–1938	**Dylan Thomas's *Twenty-Five Poems*, 1936**
			Orwell's *The Road to Wigan Pier*, 1937

1948–1949	1953–1954	1960	1969–1980
Auden's *The Age of Anxiety*, 1948	**Winston Churchill receives Nobel Prize for Literature, 1953**	Nigeria gains independence from Britain, 1960	**Samuel Beckett receives Nobel Prize, 1969**
Eliot receives Nobel Prize, 1948	**Beckett's *Waiting for Godot*, 1954**	British singing group the Beatles revolutionize popular music, 1960's	British colony of Southern Rhodesia in Africa gains independence and is called Zimbabwe, 1980
Most of Ireland wins independence, 1949			

READING CHECK TEST

1. Which of the following was *not* characteristic of Victorian times?
a. social equality   b. prosperity
c. imperialism   (a)
2. Whose theories on the origin of species rocked the Victorian world?
a. Sigmund Freud   b. Arnold Bennett
c. Charles Darwin   (c)
3. In what spirit did the young go off to fight the First World War?
a. patriotically   b. cynically
c. pessimistically   (a)
4. Which word best describes the post-war mood of the survivors?
a. idealistic   b. defeated
c. disillusioned   (c)
5. Which of the following revolutionized the structure of the English novel?
a. Charles Dickens   b. H. G. Wells
c. James Joyce   (c)

By 1939, the Nazis were sweeping through Europe with their motorized army and crack air force. Hitler's plan for the systematic destruction of the Jews and other minorities, scapegoats on whom he blamed Germany's economic woes, resulted in the Holocaust, which led to the deaths of millions of innocent men, women, and children—six million of them Jews. Only twenty years after "the war to end war," the world had again plunged into a bloody, brutal conflict. It ended in the ultimate horror. On August 6, 1945, the entire Japanese city of Hiroshima was wiped out by a single atomic bomb dropped from an American plane. Small wonder, then, that the literature following this second world war has often been dark and pessimistic.

Contemporary British Writing

The most conspicuous literary figures in England before World War II were poets W. H. Auden, Stephen Spender, and Christopher Isherwood. They shared a common intellectual background and a left-wing anti-fascist political point of view. Following the war, although these writers continued to produce, a group of younger figures emerged who shared an antipathy to the Auden group's values. These writers, who became known as "The Angry Young Men," criticized both the pretensions of intellectuals and the bland lives of the newly prosperous middle class. Kingsley Amis's novel *Lucky Jim* (1953) was a scathing satire of British university life. John Wain's novel *Hurry On Down* (1953) and John Braine's *Room at the Top* (1958) presented dark portraits of middle-class Britain.

The period since the 1960's has been marked by great diversity, from the sharp and witty novels of Muriel Spark (*The Prime of Miss Jean Brodie,* 1961) to the moral and linguistic experiments of Anthony Burgess (*A Clockwork Orange,* 1962) or the harsh satirical novels of Kingsley Amis (*The Old Devils,* 1987) and his son Martin (*Money: A Suicide Note,* 1984).

An important development in the years since the war is the appearance of writers from Britain's former dependencies. One result of Britain's empire was the spread of English around the world. We are now reaping the benefits of that spread, as writers from the Caribbean (V. S. Naipaul, Derek Walcott), Africa (Doris Lessing, Wole Soyinka, Nadine Gordimer, Chinua Achebe, William Boyd, Ben Okri), India (R. K. Narayan, Ruth Prawer Jhabvala, Salman Rushdie, Santha Rama Rau), and other outposts of the British Empire challenge and enrich us all.

" **W**riters from the Caribbean (V. S. Naipaul, Derek Walcott), Africa (Doris Lessing, Wole Soyinka, Nadine Gordimer, Chinua Achebe, William Boyd, Ben Okri), India (R. K. Narayan, Ruth Prawer Jhabvala, Salman Rushdie, Santha Rama Rau), and other outposts of the British Empire challenge and enrich us all."

FICTION

Joseph Conrad (1857–1924)

"Faith is a myth," Joseph Conrad once wrote ominously, and much of his fiction deals with the modernist themes of alienation, loneliness, and isolation. As a master fiction writer, crafting his novels and stories to achieve dramatic and sometimes disturbing effects, Conrad and his psychological realism profoundly influenced some of the greatest writers of our time, including T. S. Eliot, William Faulkner, F. Scott Fitzgerald, and Graham Greene.

Conrad was born Józef Konrad Korzeniowski in the Polish Ukraine. In that year, 1857, Poland was a divided and conquered nation, much of it under Russian rule. The boy's father, Apollo Korzeniowski, was an intellectual, a translator of Victor Hugo, Charles Dickens, and William Shakespeare, and an ardent Polish patriot. In 1861 he was arrested by the Russian police for conspiring to free Poland and was exiled to Russia. Surprisingly, his wife Evelina and their three-year-old son were allowed to join him in the prison camp at Valogda. Evelina contracted tuberculosis, and she died when Jozef was eight, leaving him to his father's care. The father, who was also critically ill with tuberculosis, prescribed a rigorous course of study for the boy and read to him from his own favorite authors. For all this closeness to his father, Conrad was robbed of a childhood. He was miserably lonely, full of sickness, confinement, and despair for Poland's future. "I don't know what would have become of me if I had not been a reading boy," he wrote later. ". . . I read! What did I not read!"

When his father died, leaving him an eleven-year-old orphan, Conrad yearned for freedom and faraway places. As ward of a kindly uncle, Thaddeus Bobrowski, he completed his school-

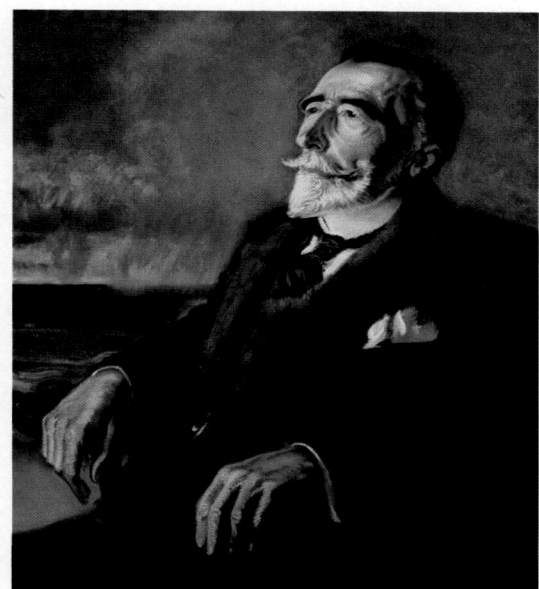

Joseph Conrad by Walter Tittle (1923–24). Oil.

ing listlessly, complaining that his teachers "were not only middle-aged, but looked to me as if they had never been young." Only geography interested him. Putting his finger onto a map at random he touched the heart of Africa and announced, "When I grow up, I shall go *there*."

At the age of fifteen he alarmed his uncle and other relatives by announcing that he wished to go to sea. At seventeen, despite all entreaties, he left Poland for the French port of Marseille, where his uncle had apprenticed him to a banking and shipping company. In 1875 he made his first voyage as apprentice seaman aboard the bark *Mont Blanc*. It was a grueling, six-month cruise to the West Indies, but it confirmed his love for the sea and began two decades of life under sail.

Conrad was an unusual sailor. An aristocratic manner, elegant dress, Slavic good looks, and a free hand with his money earned him the nickname "The Count." According to Conrad's own account, he was soon fulfilling his most vivid dreams of adventure. He claims that, with friends, he bought a fast boat, the *Tremolino,* and ran contraband guns to the Carlist army fighting to regain control of Spain. These daring exploits, furthermore, were said to have culminated in a love affair with a rich, beautiful woman whom he called Doña Rita. His exploits. ended in disaster—the shipwreck of the *Tremolino,* the loss of Rita, possibly in a duel over her affections, and the disappearance of his remaining funds into the roulette wheels at Monte Carlo.

But are these adventures true? Conrad, who so brilliantly writes of evasion and concealment in his fiction, has left an ambiguous record of his own life.

At the age of twenty, Conrad joined the crew of the British ship *Mavis* and learned English from his shipmates as he worked his way to England. Ashore there, he spent his wages foolishly and wrote to Poland for help. His uncle Thaddeus refused: "I have no money for drones and have no intention of working so that someone else may enjoy himself at my expense. . . . Arrange your budget within the limits of what I give you, for I will give no more. . . . You have forfeited my confidence. Work now to regain it."

Conrad turned again to the sea. Determined to become fluent in English, he acquired a complete set of Shakespeare and sought berths on British ships. He made many voyages and thrived on the adventure. When his ship the *Palestine* caught fire and blew up in the Indian Ocean, he had his first command, that of a lifeboat which he guided on its fifteen-day journey into Singapore. In 1886, he received his master's papers and became a naturalized British citizen.

During the long waits between voyages, Conrad made his first attempts at writing in English. Then, aboard a ship sailing between Singapore and Malaysia, he found the subject for his first novel. One of his acquaintances was a Dutchman who became the character Almayer in *Almayer's Folly.* "If I had not got to know Almayer pretty well" said Conrad later, "it is almost certain there would never have been a line of mine in print."

In 1889, while waiting in London for a ship, he began writing Almayer's story. Like all of

Conrad's subsequent fiction, it told of a failed dream, of the hopelessness of human aspiration. His writing was interrupted by another voyage, an arduous tour of duty on a small steamboat plying the waters of the Upper Congo. This was the chance to visit Africa he had dreamed about ever since touching his finger to the map as a teen-ager. Later, these experiences in the Congo would figure in one of his most famous novels. But the trip ruined his health—he came down with fever and wracking dysentery—and in effect, it ended his nautical career.

Returning to London, he resumed work on *Almayer's Folly,* finishing it in 1894, when he was thirty-seven. Conrad sent the manuscript to the London publisher Fisher Unwin, and then he went looking for a ship. No one could have been more surprised than Conrad when, three months later, Unwin accepted the book. The source of enthusiasm at the publishing house was a young reader, Edward Garnett. "You have written one book," he told Conrad. "It is very good. Why not write another?" Thinking it over, Conrad agreed he could write *one* more. His second novel, *An Outcast of the Islands,* was finished in 1895.

That same year, *Almayer's Folly* was published, receiving critical praise but small sales. Conrad's life was about to change in another way. He found himself drawn to Jessie George, a twenty-one-year-old secretary working in London. One afternoon, while they had sought refuge in the National Gallery from a downpour, Conrad said to her, "Look here, my dear, we had better get married and out of this. Look at the weather. We will get married at once and go over to France. How soon can you be ready?" In 1896 they were married.

While Conrad yearned for another sea assignment, he had renounced the life of adventure to begin a new life as a writer. He was writing for his and Jessie's sustenance now, and he found it was hard, nerve-wracking work.

"I don't know what to make of the pages I am sending you," he wrote Garnett. "Mostly they fill me with dismay. . . . is the plan utterly wrong? I doubt the sincerity of my own impressions. I dream for hours, hours! over a sentence, and even then can't put it together so as to satisfy the cravings of my soul."

The Conrads settled in an Essex farmhouse and, full of self-doubt, he wrote away at a novel

A. **Humanities Connection: Discussing the Fine Art**
British painter Paul Nash (1889–1946) had a poetic and imaginative inclination, which was not immediately at home with the abstractionist tendencies of continental art. His experiences of trench warfare in World War I, however, shocked him out of his poetic languors. He was invalided out of the war in 1917 and returned with a graphic record of his experiences. These war paintings are deeply felt descriptions of the terrible destruction and fragmentation of the "no man's land" of war. Later, in the 1930's, Nash found an outlet for his poetic tendencies in a personal surrealistic style that stresses illustrative, moody landscapes with dreamlike qualities. Ask students to suggest the predominant mood of this painting. What about it suggests a dream? (The indistinct shapes; the mix of natural and fantastic elements) What do they think the two birds represent? (Note that one—or both—seems to be a falcon or other bird of prey.)

called *The Nigger of the Narcissus.* "I am getting more sophisticated from day to day," he wrote Garnett, "and more uncertain! I am more conscious of my own unworthiness and also of my desire of perfection which—from the conditions of the case—is so unattainable."

"And the end!" he rejoiced to Garnett in 1897. "I can't eat—I dream—nightmares—and scare my wife. . . . But I think it will do! It will do!"

The Nigger of the Narcissus appeared at the end of that year, again to favorable reviews and small sales. But Conrad's literary reputation was on the rise. His stories were appearing in magazines, and he counted writers John Galsworthy, Henry James, and Stephen Crane among his friends.

In 1898, a son, Borys, was born, and Conrad began work on his novel *Lord Jim,* in which he explores the theme that is constant in his greatest fiction: In various ways, our dreams must connect us with other people, or we are wrecked as human beings. Conrad now entered the era of his career that brought forth his masterworks:

Youth (1902), for which he drew on the sinking of the *Palestine; Heart of Darkness* (1902), about the brutal exploitation of Africans in the Belgian Congo (a novel used by Frances Ford Coppola as the basis of his film about the Vietnam War, *Apocalypse Now*); and the ambitious political novel *Nostromo* (1904). In all of these novels, the recurring theme has to do with the remorse that springs from a knowledge of dreams lost, of duty failed. It is a theme perhaps related to Conrad's own sense of failure in, first, having abandoned his country in the time of its misfortune, and, second, of having achieved his fame in a new language.

Ironically, popular success did not come to Conrad until 1914. In that year his novel *Chance* was published, and it marked a double turning point in Conrad's career, one common among productive writers. The books that followed—*Victory* (1915) and *The Arrow of Gold* (1923)—were all popular successes, yet they were inferior to his earlier novels, which for eighteen years, had lain, largely unwanted, in the bookstalls.

A

Landscape from a Dream by Paul Nash (1936–38). Oil.

The Tate Gallery, London.

PREPARATION

1. BUILDING ON PRIOR KNOWLEDGE. Ask students to recall other stories or movies that take place on sailing ships, such as *Moby-Dick* or *Two Years Before the Mast.* Ask them to think about why a ship setting lends itself to dramatic situations. Remind students that a ship at sea forms an enclosed world that is cut off from the restraining laws and customs of land society. While at sea, the captain has absolute authority.

2. ESTABLISHING A PURPOSE. Introduce the theme of the double by having students read question 6 on page 948. Alert them to look for passages that describe the relationship between the captain and Leggatt.

3. PREREADING JOURNAL. (Challenging) Ask students to write a paragraph on how they might feel if they met their "double." Would it be an occasion for happiness or dread?

(Less Challenging) Ask students to write three questions they would ask a long-lost twin if they were unexpectedly reunited.

A. Humanities Connection: Discussing the Fine Art

German painter, graphic artist, and sculptor Emil Nolde (1869–1956) was a member of the German Expressionist group called *Die Brücke* (the Bridge), who were interested primarily in expressing emotional reactions to the visual world. Later, after visiting Siberia, China, Japan, and the South Seas, he developed a mystical and visionary style, particularly in his watercolors.

? What mood is expressed by this painting? What does it have in common with the setting of the novel? (Water is an important element in both.)

Reflections by Emil Nolde (c. 1930). Watercolor.

SUPPLEMENTARY SUPPORT MATERIALS
1. Vocabulary Activity Worksheet (*CCB*)
2. Review and Response Worksheet:
Point of View (*CCB*)
3. Language Skills Worksheets: Verb
Tenses; Commas; Revision Worksheet
4 (*CCB*)
4. Selection Test (*CCB*)

DEVELOPING VOCABULARY
The following words from the novel are
tested in the Selection Test. (See also
Vocabulary Activity Worksheet.)

domain	eccentric
impeccable	compunction
monotonous	opaque
arduous	pestiferous
caprice	confabulation

© 1987 The Detroit Institute of Arts.
Bequest of Robert H. Tannahill.

THE SECRET SHARER

This novel is based on a famous crime at sea that happened in 1880 aboard a ship called *Cutty Sark*. The mate of the *Cutty Sark* killed a seaman for insubordination. The captain of the *Sark* allowed the killer, a man named Sidney Smith, to escape to an American ship, the *Colorado*. But the captain of the *Sark* was so filled with remorse at this dereliction of his duty that he jumped overboard and drowned. The murderer was later tried for his crime and was sentenced to seven years on a manslaughter charge.

Conrad uses this incident as a framework for a story about a search for identity. His captain forms a relationship with the criminal, who becomes his "double," perhaps as a projection of the captain's own outlaw tendencies and desires for freedom.

As you read you'll discover that Conrad's story probes for the answers to some tricky moral and psychological questions.

1. Does an act of violence reflect the secret, dark places in the hearts of everyone?
2. When we feel sympathy for a criminal, are we really feeling sympathy for ourselves?
3. Who should judge the guilt or innocence of a person accused of a crime?

I

On my right hand there were lines of fishing stakes resembling a mysterious system of half-submerged bamboo fences, incomprehensible in its division of the domain of tropical fishes, and crazy of aspect as if abandoned forever by some nomad tribe of fishermen now gone to the other end of the ocean; for there was no sign of human habitation as far as the eye could reach. To the left a group of barren islets, suggesting ruins of stone walls, towers, and blockhouses, had its foundations set in a blue sea that itself looked solid, so still and stable did it lie below my feet;

A. Expansion
Projection, as a psychological process, means the attributing of one's own ideas or feelings to another, often for the purpose of escaping feelings of guilt.

B. Setting and Mood
The first three paragraphs describe the physical setting and create the mood of isolation, mystery, and danger. See also question 12 on page 948.

Joseph Conrad   925

925

A. Theme
Point out that this
passage indicates
that the captain
and his ship will
undergo some kind
of dangerous test.
It also introduces
the recurring
theme of judgment.

B. Character
❓ How are the
chief and the
second mate de-
scribed? (The chief
as a fool, the mate
as silent and
sneering) How well
does the captain
know these men?
(Very little) Do you
think the captain
will grow closer to
them as the story
develops? (He will
probably know
them better. He
may not get closer
to them.)

C. Interpreting
❓ What does the
captain mean
when he says that
he is a stranger to
himself? (He does
not know himself
or know of what he
is capable.) How
does he relate this
to the test he be-
lieves he will face?
(He will learn to
know himself
through the test of
experience.)

even the track of light from the westering sun shone smoothly, without that animated glitter which tells of an imperceptible ripple. And when I turned my head to take a parting glance at the tug which had just left us anchored outside the bar,[1] I saw the straight line of the flat shore joined to the stable sea, edge to edge, with a perfect and unmarked closeness, in one leveled floor half brown, half blue under the enormous dome of the sky. Corresponding in their insignificance to the islets of the sea, two small clumps of trees, one on each side of the only fault in the impeccable joint, marked the mouth of the river Meinam we had just left on the first preparatory stage of our homeward journey; and, far back on the inland level, a larger and loftier mass, the grove surrounding the great Paknam pagoda,[2] was the only thing on which the eye could rest from the vain task of exploring the monotonous sweep of the horizon. Here and there gleams as of a few scattered pieces of silver marked the windings of the great river; and on the nearest of them, just within the bar, the tug steaming right into the land became lost to my sight, hull and funnel and masts, as though the impassive earth had swallowed her up without an effort, without a tremor. My eye followed the light cloud of her smoke, now here, now there, above the plain, according to the devious curves of the stream, but always fainter and farther away, till I lost it at last behind the miter-shaped[3] hill of the great pagoda. And then I was left alone with my ship, anchored at the head of the Gulf of Siam.

She floated at the starting point of a long journey, very still in an immense stillness, the shadows of her spars flung far to the eastward by the setting sun. At that moment I was alone on her decks. There was not a sound in her—and around us nothing moved, nothing lived, not a canoe on the water, not a bird in the air, not a cloud in the sky. In this breathless pause at the threshold of a long passage we seemed to be measuring our fitness for a long and arduous enterprise, the appointed task of both our existences to be carried out, far from all human eyes, with only sky and sea for spectators and for judges.

There must have been some glare in the air to interfere with one's sight, because it was only just before the sun left us that my roaming eyes made out beyond the highest ridge of the principal islet of the group something which did away with the solemnity of perfect solitude. The tide of darkness flowed on swiftly; and with tropical suddenness a swarm of stars came out above the shadowy earth, while I lingered yet, my hand resting lightly on my ship's rail as if on the shoulder of a trusted friend. But, with all that multitude of celestial bodies staring down at one, the comfort of quiet communion with her was gone for good. And there were also disturbing sounds by this time—voices, footsteps forward; the steward flitted along the main deck, a busily ministering spirit; a hand bell tinkled urgently under the poop deck.[4] . . .

I found my two officers waiting for me near the supper table, in the lighted cuddy.[5] We sat down at once, and as I helped the chief mate, I said:

"Are you aware that there is a ship anchored inside the islands? I saw her mastheads above the ridge as the sun went down."

He raised sharply his simple face, overcharged by a terrible growth of whisker, and emitted his usual ejaculations: "Bless my soul, sir! You don't say so!"

My second mate was a round-cheeked, silent young man, grave beyond his years, I thought; but as our eyes happened to meet I detected a slight quiver on his lips. I looked down at once. It was not my part to encourage sneering on board my ship. It must be said, too, that I knew very little of my officers. In consequence of certain events of no particular significance, except to myself, I had been appointed to the command only a fortnight before. Neither did I know much of the hands forward. All these people had been together for eighteen months or so, and my position was that of the only stranger on board. I mention this because it has some bearing on what is to follow. But what I felt most was my being a stranger to the ship; and if all the truth must be told, I was somewhat of a stranger to myself. The youngest man on board (barring the second mate), and untried as yet by a position of the fullest responsibility, I was willing to take the adequacy of the others for granted. They had simply to be equal

---

1. **bar:** sandbar.
2. **pagoda:** temple with a pyramid-shaped tower.
3. **miter-shaped:** shaped like a bishop's cap; like a tall, pointed arch.

4. **poop deck:** a raised deck at the stern of a ship.
5. **cuddy:** cabin.

to their tasks; but I wondered how far I should turn out faithful to that ideal conception of one's own personality every man sets up for himself secretly.

Meantime the chief mate, with an almost visible effect of collaboration on the part of his round eyes and frightful whiskers, was trying to evolve a theory of the anchored ship. His dominant trait was to take all things into earnest consideration. He was of a painstaking turn of mind. As he used to say, he "liked to account to himself" for practically everything that came in his way, down to a miserable scorpion he had found in his cabin a week before. The why and the wherefore of that scorpion—how it got on board and came to select his room rather than the pantry (which was a dark place and more what a scorpion would be partial to), and how on earth it managed to drown itself in the inkwell of his writing desk—had exercised him infinitely. The ship within the islands was much more easily accounted for; and just as we were about to rise from the table he made his pronouncement. She was, he doubted not, a ship from home lately arrived. Probably she drew too much water to cross the bar except at the top of spring tides. Therefore she went into that natural harbor to wait for a few days in preference to remaining in an open roadstead.

"That's so," confirmed the second mate, suddenly, in his slightly hoarse voice. "She draws over twenty feet. She's the Liverpool ship *Sephora* with a cargo of coal. Hundred and twenty-three days from Cardiff."

We looked at him in surprise.

"The tugboat skipper told me when he came on board for your letters, sir," explained the young man. "He expects to take her up the river the day after tomorrow."

After thus overwhelming us with the extent of his information he slipped out of the cabin. The mate observed regretfully that he "could not account for that young fellow's whims." What prevented him telling us all about it at once, he wanted to know.

I detained him as he was making a move. For the last two days the crew had had plenty of hard work, and the night before they had very little sleep. I felt painfully that I—a stranger—was doing something unusual when I directed him to let all hands turn in without setting an anchor watch. I proposed to keep on deck myself till one o'clock or thereabouts. I would get the second mate to relieve me at that hour.

"He will turn out the cook and the steward at four," I concluded, "and then give you a call. Of course at the slightest sign of any sort of wind we'll have the hands up and make a start at once."

He concealed his astonishment. "Very well, sir." Outside the cuddy he put his head in the second mate's door to inform him of my unheard-of caprice to take a five hours' anchor watch on myself. I heard the other raise his voice incredulously: "What? The captain himself?" Then a few more murmurs, a door closed, then another. A few moments later I went on deck.

My strangeness, which had made me sleepless, had prompted that unconventional arrangement, as if I had expected in those solitary hours of the night to get on terms with the ship of which I knew nothing, manned by men of whom I knew very little more. Fast alongside a wharf, littered like any ship in port with a tangle of unrelated things, invaded by unrelated shore people, I had hardly seen her yet properly. Now, as she lay cleared for sea, the stretch of her main deck seemed to me very fine under the stars. Very fine, very roomy for her size, and very inviting. I descended the poop and paced the waist,[6] my mind picturing to myself the coming passage through the Malay Archipelago, down the Indian Ocean, and up the Atlantic. All its phases were familiar enough to me, every characteristic, all the alternatives which were likely to face me on the high seas—everything! . . . except the novel responsibility of command. But I took heart from the reasonable thought that the ship was like other ships, the men like other men, and that the sea was not likely to keep any special surprises expressly for my discomfiture.

Arrived at that comforting conclusion, I bethought myself of a cigar and went below to get it. All was still down there. Everybody at the after end of the ship was sleeping profoundly. I came out again on the quarterdeck,[7] agreeably at ease in my sleeping suit on that warm breathless night, barefooted, a glowing cigar in my teeth, and, going forward, I was met by the profound silence of the fore end of the ship. Only as I passed the door of

---

6. **waist:** the ship's midsection.
7. **quarterdeck:** a raised deck near the stern of a ship, usually including the poop deck. The quarterdeck is usually reserved for the ship's officers.

A. Character
"Unconventional" is an understatement! As we can tell by the chief mate's and second mate's astonishment, the captain's decision to keep watch himself is bizarre. It would be inconceivable that a captain, who has supreme authority and is always treated with complete deference by the crew, would do such a lowly chore as keep watch at night when the seas are calm. His decision does, however, establish the captain's generous nature.

❓ Do you question the captain's wisdom in this decision, in light of his uneasiness as a newcomer among the crew? (It is important to note that this is the first aspect of the captain's behavior that makes the crew suspicious of him.)

B. Irony
Prepare students for what is coming by telling them that this statement is ironic. The sea will shortly yield something very unexpected.

A

B

Joseph Conrad 927

A. Suspense
Have students note the details of tranquility in this passage. ("Trustful sigh," "great security of the sea," "untempted life," "moral beauty," "clear, untroubled . . . . confident and bright") Conrad has placed hints of trouble in his exposition—the captain's insecurity, phrases such as "tide of darkness" and "mysterious shades of night." The reader senses that something will happen to disrupt the captain's peace.

B. Language and imagery
❓ What words and images are used to describe what the captain sees on the side of the boat? What effect do these produce? (*Fishlike, phosphorescent, cadaverous, corpse*—producing an eerie and menacing effect)

the forecastle[8] I heard a deep, quiet, trustful sigh of some sleeper inside. And suddenly I rejoiced in the great security of the sea as compared with the unrest of the land, in my choice of that untempted life presenting no disquieting problems, invested with an elementary moral beauty by the absolute straightforwardness of its appeal and by the singleness of its purpose.

The riding light in the fore-rigging burned with a clear, untroubled, as if symbolic, flame, confident and bright in the mysterious shades of the night. Passing on my way aft along the other side of the ship, I observed that the rope side ladder, put over, no doubt, for the master of the tug when he came to fetch away our letters, had not been hauled in as it should have been. I became annoyed at this, for exactitude in small matters is the very soul of discipline. Then I reflected that I had myself peremptorily dismissed my officers from duty, and by my own act had prevented the anchor watch being formally set and things properly attended to. I asked myself whether it was wise ever to interfere with the established routine of duties even from the kindest of motives. My action might have made me appear <u>eccentric</u>. Goodness only knew how that absurdly whiskered mate would "account" for my conduct, and what the whole ship thought of that informality of their new captain. I was vexed with myself.

Not from <u>compunction</u> certainly, but, as it were mechanically, I proceeded to get the ladder in myself. Now a side ladder of that sort is a light affair and comes in easily, yet my vigorous tug, which should have brought it flying on board, merely recoiled upon my body in a totally unexpected jerk. What the devil! . . . I was so astounded by the immovableness of that ladder that I remained stock-still, trying to account for it to myself like that imbecile mate of mine. In the end, of course, I put my head over the rail.

The side of the ship made an <u>opaque</u> belt of shadow on the darkling glassy shimmer of the sea. But I saw at once something elongated and pale floating very close to the ladder. Before I could form a guess a faint flash of phosphorescent light, which seemed to issue suddenly from the naked body of a man, flickered in the sleeping water with the elusive, silent play of summer lightning in a night sky. With a gasp I saw revealed to my stare a pair of feet, the long legs, a broad livid back immersed right up to the neck in a greenish cadaverous glow. One hand, awash, clutched the bottom rung of the ladder. He was complete but for the head. A headless corpse! The cigar dropped out of my gaping mouth with a tiny plop and a short hiss quite audible in the absolute stillness of all things under heaven. At that I suppose he raised up his face, a dimly pale oval in the shadow of the ship's side. But even then I could only barely make out down there the shape of his black-haired head. However, it was enough for the horrid, frost-bound sensation which had gripped me about the chest to pass off. The moment of vain exclamations was past, too. I only climbed on the spare spar and leaned over the rail as far as I could, to bring my eyes nearer to that mystery floating alongside.

As he hung by the ladder, like a resting swimmer, the sea lightning played about his limbs at every stir; and he appeared in it ghastly, silvery, fishlike. He remained as mute as a fish, too. He made no motion to get out of the water, either. It was inconceivable that he should not attempt to come on board, and strangely troubling to suspect that perhaps he did not want to. And my first words were prompted by just that troubled incertitude.

"What's the matter?" I asked in my ordinary tone, speaking down to the face upturned exactly under mine.

"Cramp," it answered, no louder. Then slightly anxious, "I say, no need to call anyone."

"I was not going to," I said.

"Are you alone on deck?"

"Yes."

I had somehow the impression that he was on the point of letting go the ladder to swim away beyond my ken—mysterious as he came. But, for the moment, this being appearing as if he had risen from the bottom of the sea (it was certainly the nearest land to the ship) wanted only to know the time. I told him. And he, down there, tentatively:

"I suppose your captain's turned in?"

"I am sure he isn't," I said.

He seemed to struggle with himself, for I heard something like the low, bitter murmur of doubt. "What's the good?" His next words came out with a hesitating effort.

"Look here, my man. Could you call him out quietly?"

I thought the time had come to declare myself.

---

8. **forecastle** (fōk'səl): the forward section of the ship, where the crew's quarters are located.

Literature and Language: Varying Sentence Structure
Conrad's elegant prose could serve as a model for student writers. Some passages will also be useful for a close analysis of sentence structure. Before students examine the novel's style, they might review the material on the sentence in **Grammar, Usage, and Mechanics: A Reference Guide.**

On this page, you might concentrate on the paragraph beginning "Before entering the cabin." As a group exercise, analyze with students the varieties of sentences used in this one paragraph. Notice the correct placement of a participial phrase in the first sentence: What word does the phrase modify? ("I") Which sentence in the paragraph curiously inverts the subject and verb? (The

fifth one)
As a writing exercise, have students rewrite the paragraph, restructuring all the sentences. Have them read their versions of Conrad's paragraph aloud.

"*I* am the captain."

I heard a "By Jove!" whispered at the level of the water. The phosphorescence flashed in the swirl of the water all about his limbs, his other hand seized the ladder.

"My name's Leggatt."

A The voice was calm and resolute. A good voice. The self-possession of that man had somehow induced a corresponding state in myself. It was very quietly that I remarked:

"You must be a good swimmer."

"Yes. I've been in the water practically since nine o'clock. The question for me now is whether I am to let go this ladder and go on swimming till I sink from exhaustion, or—to come on board here."

I felt this was no mere formula of desperate speech, but a real alternative in the view of a strong soul. I should have gathered from this that he was young; indeed, it is only the young who are ever confronted by such clear issues. But at the time it was pure intuition on my part. A mysterious communication was established already between us two—in the face of that silent, darkened tropical sea. I was young, too; young enough to make no comment. The man in the water began suddenly to climb up the ladder, and I hastened away from the rail to fetch some clothes.

Before entering the cabin I stood still, listening in the lobby at the foot of the stairs. A faint snore came through the closed door of the chief mate's room. The second mate's door was on the hook, but the darkness in there was absolutely soundless. He, too, was young and could sleep like a stone. Remained the steward, but he was not likely to wake up before he was called. I got a sleeping suit out of my room and, coming back on deck, saw the naked man from the sea sitting on the main hatch, glimmering white in the darkness, his elbows on his knees and his head in his hands. In a moment he had concealed his damp body in a sleeping suit of the same gray-stripe pattern as the one I was wearing and followed me like my double on the poop. Together we moved right aft, barefooted, silent.

"What is it?" I asked in a deadened voice, taking the lighted lamp out of the binnacle,[9] and raising it to his face.

"An ugly business."

He had rather regular features; a good mouth; light eyes under somewhat heavy, dark eyebrows; a smooth, square forehead; no growth on his cheeks; a small, brown mustache, and a well-shaped, round chin. His expression was concentrated, meditative, under the inspecting light of the lamp I held up to his face; such as a man thinking hard in solitude might wear. My sleeping suit was just right for his size. A well-knit young fellow of twenty-five at most. He caught his lower lip with the edge of white, even teeth.

"Yes," I said, replacing the lamp in the binnacle. The warm, heavy tropical night closed upon his head again.

"There's a ship over there," he murmured.

"Yes, I know. The *Sephora*. Did you know of us?"

"Hadn't the slightest idea. I am the mate of her—" He paused and corrected himself. "I should say I *was*."

"Aha! Something wrong?"

"Yes. Very wrong indeed. I've killed a man."

"What do you mean? Just now?"

"No, on the passage. Weeks ago. Thirty-nine south. When I say a man—"

"Fit of temper," I suggested, confidently. B

The shadowy, dark head, like mine, seemed to nod imperceptibly above the ghostly gray of my sleeping suit. It was, in the night, as though I had been faced by my own reflection in the depths of a somber and immense mirror.

"A pretty thing to have to own up to for a Conway boy,"[10] murmured my double, distinctly. C

"You're a Conway boy?"

"I am," he said, as if startled. Then, slowly . . . "Perhaps you too—"

It was so; but being a couple of years older I had left before he joined. After a quick interchange of dates a silence fell; and I thought suddenly of my absurd mate with his terrific whiskers and the "Bless my soul—you don't say so" type of intellect. My double gave me an inkling of his thoughts by saying:

"My father's a parson in Norfolk. Do you see me before a judge and jury on that charge? For myself I can't see the necessity. There are fellows that an angel from heaven—— And I am not that. He was one of those creatures that are just simmering all the time with a silly sort of wickedness.

A. Theme
Tell students that this is the first example of identification between the captain and the intruder. Ask them to look for other examples as they occur.

B. Character
[?] The captain is already supplying a reason for the stranger's crime, without even hearing the story. Why might he be doing this? (He has already identified with this stranger and is perhaps looking for ways to excuse his criminal behavior. Note the word *confidently*—the captain does not want to suspect someone whom he has already grown to respect.)

C. The Double
At this point, the captain is calling Leggatt his "double" because they are wearing identical sleeping suits.

---

9. **binnacle:** stand that holds the ship's compass.

10. **Conway boy:** The *Conway* was a British merchant marine training ship.

A. Conflict

? What reasons does Leggatt give for killing the seaman? (He refused to do his duty.) How do Leggatt's feelings for this man parallel the captain's feelings for his officers? (Both are contemptuous of the other men.)

B. Motivation

? How does Leggatt think a judge and jury would react to the story of the killing? (They would be shocked and disapproving.)

C. Character

? What effect does the fact that Leggatt is a clergyman's son have on him? On others? (He feels it as a burden. Others expect superior behavior from him.)

Miserable devils that have no business to live at all. He wouldn't do his duty and wouldn't let anybody else do theirs. But what's the good of talking! You know well enough the sort of ill-conditioned snarling cur—''

He appealed to me as if our experiences had been as identical as our clothes. And I knew well enough the pestiferous danger of such a character where there are no means of legal repression. And I knew well enough also that my double there was no homicidal ruffian. I did not think of asking him for details, and he told me the story roughly in brusque, disconnected sentences. I needed no more. I saw it all going on as though I were myself inside that other sleeping suit.

"It happened while we were setting a reefed[11] foresail, at dusk. Reefed foresail! You understand the sort of weather. The only sail we had left to keep the ship running; so you may guess what it had been like for days. Anxious sort of job, that. He gave me some of his cursed insolence at the sheet.[12] I tell you I was overdone with this terrific weather that seemed to have no end to it. Terrific, I tell you—and a deep ship. I believe the fellow himself was half crazed with funk. It was no time for gentlemanly reproof, so I turned round and felled him like an ox. He up and at me. We closed just as an awful sea made for the ship. All hands saw it coming and took to the rigging, but I had him by the throat, and went on shaking him like a rat, the men above us yelling, 'Look out! look out!' Then a crash as if the sky had fallen on my head. They say that for over ten minutes hardly anything was to be seen of the ship—just the three masts and a bit of the forecastle head and of the poop all awash driving along in a smother of foam. It was a miracle that they found us, jammed together behind the forebits. It's clear that I meant business, because I was holding him by the throat still when they picked us up. He was black in the face. It was too much for them. It seems they rushed us aft together, gripped as we were, screaming 'Murder!' like a lot of lunatics, and broke into the cuddy. And the ship running for her life, touch and go all the time, any minute her last in a sea fit to turn your hair gray only a-looking at it. I understand that the skipper, too, started raving like the rest of them. The man had been deprived of sleep for more than a week, and to

have this sprung on him at the height of a furious gale nearly drove him out of his mind. I wonder they didn't fling me overboard after getting the carcass of their precious shipmate out of my fingers. They had rather a job to separate us, I've been told. A sufficiently fierce story to make an old judge and a respectable jury sit up a bit. The first thing I heard when I came to myself was the maddening howling of that endless gale, and on that the voice of the old man. He was hanging on to my bunk, staring into my face out of his sou'wester.[13]

'' 'Mr. Leggatt, you have killed a man. You can act no longer as chief mate of this ship.' ''

His care to subdue his voice made it sound monotonous. He rested a hand on the end of the skylight to steady himself with, and all that time did not stir a limb, so far as I could see. "Nice little tale for a quiet tea party," he concluded in the same tone.

One of my hands, too, rested on the end of the skylight; neither did I stir a limb, so far as I knew. We stood less than a foot from each other. It occurred to me that if old "Bless my soul—you don't say so" were to put his head up the companion[14] and catch sight of us, he would think he was seeing double, or imagine himself come upon a scene of weird witchcraft; the strange captain having a quiet confabulation by the wheel with his own gray ghost. I became very much concerned to prevent anything of the sort. I heard the other's soothing undertone.

"My father's a parson in Norfolk," it said. Evidently he had forgotten he had told me this important fact before. Truly a nice little tale.

"You had better slip down into my stateroom now," I said, moving off stealthily. My double followed my movements; our bare feet made no sound; I let him in, closed the door with care, and, after giving a call to the second mate, returned on deck for my relief.

"Not much sign of any wind yet," I remarked when he approached.

"No, sir. Not much," he assented, sleepily, in his hoarse voice, with just enough deference, no more, and barely suppressing a yawn.

"Well, that's all you have to look out for. You have got your orders."

"Yes, sir."

---

11. **reefed:** partly rolled up.
12. **sheet:** rope attached to a sail.

13. **sou'wester:** waterproof coat.
14. **companion:** a stairway between the cabins and the deck.

I paced a turn or two on the poop and saw him take up his position face forward with his elbow in the ratlines[15] of the mizzen-rigging before I went below. The mate's faint snoring was still going on peacefully. The cuddy lamp was burning over the table on which stood a vase with flowers, a polite attention from the ship's provision merchant—the last flowers we should see for the next three months at the very least. Two bunches of bananas hung from the beam symmetrically, one on each side of the rudder casing. Everything was as before in the ship—except that two of her captain's sleeping suits were simultaneously in use, one motionless in the cuddy, the other keeping very still in the captain's stateroom.

It must be explained here that my cabin had the form of the capital letter L, the door being within the angle and opening into the short part of the letter. A couch was to the left, the bedplace to the right; my writing desk and the chronometers' table faced the door. But anyone opening it, unless he stepped right inside, had no view of what I call the long (or vertical) part of the letter. It contained some lockers surmounted by a bookcase; and a few clothes, a thick jacket or two, caps, oilskin coat, and such like, hung on hooks. There was at the bottom of that part a door opening into my bathroom, which could be entered also directly from the saloon.[16] But that way was never used.

The mysterious arrival had discovered the advantage of this particular shape. Entering my room, lighted strongly by a big bulkhead lamp swung on gimbals above my writing desk, I did not see him anywhere till he stepped out quietly from behind the coats hung in the recessed part.

"I heard somebody moving about, and went in there at once," he whispered.

I, too, spoke under my breath.

"Nobody is likely to come in here without knocking and getting permission."

He nodded. His face was thin and the sunburn faded, as though he had been ill. And no wonder. He had been, I heard presently, kept under arrest in his cabin for nearly seven weeks. But there was nothing sickly in his eyes or in his expression. He was not a bit like me, really; yet, as we stood leaning over my bedplace, whispering side by side, with our dark heads together and our backs

to the door, anybody bold enough to open it stealthily would have been treated to the uncanny sight of a double captain busy talking in whispers with his other self.

"But all this doesn't tell me how you came to hang on to our side ladder," I inquired, in the hardly audible murmurs we used, after he had told me something more of the proceedings on board the *Sephora* once the bad weather was over.

"When we sighted Java Head I had had time to think all those matters out several times over. I had six weeks of doing nothing else, and with only an hour or so every evening for a tramp on the quarterdeck."

He whispered, his arms folded on the side of my bedplace, staring through the open port. And I could imagine perfectly the manner of this thinking out—a stubborn if not a steadfast operation; something of which I should have been perfectly incapable.

"I reckoned it would be dark before we closed with the land," he continued, so low that I had to strain my hearing, near as we were to each other, shoulder touching shoulder almost. "So I asked to speak to the old man. He always seemed very sick when he came to see me—as if he could not look me in the face. You know, that foresail saved the ship. She was too deep to have run long under bare poles. And it was I that managed to set it for him. Anyway, he came. When I had him in my cabin—he stood by the door looking at me as if I had the halter around my neck already—I asked him right away to leave my cabin door unlocked at night while the ship was going through Sunda Straits. There would be the Java coast within two or three miles, off Angier Point. I wanted nothing more. I've had a prize for swimming my second year in the Conway."

"I can believe it," I breathed out.

"God only knows why they locked me in every night. To see some of their faces you'd have thought they were afraid I'd go about at night strangling people. Am I a murdering brute? Do I look it? By Jove! If I had been he wouldn't have trusted himself like that into my room. You'll say I might have chucked him aside and bolted out, there and then—it was dark already. Well, no. And for the same reason I wouldn't think of trying to smash the door. There would have been a rush to stop me at the noise, and I did not mean to get into a confounded scrimmage. Somebody else might have got killed—for I would not have bro-

---

15. **ratlines:** rope ladders used for climbing the rigging. (Rats would use the ropes to gain entrance to the ship.)
16. **saloon:** officers' dining room.

A. Mood

? What atmosphere does the whispering of Leggatt and the captain create? (Guilt, danger, intimacy)

B. Character
Note that the captain of the *Sephora* also behaves guiltily.

? Why does Leggatt think the captain could not look him in the face? (Because the captain knew that he himself had panicked in a crisis)

A. **Discussing the Photograph**
This dramatic photograph should give students an idea of how dangerous sailors' jobs were in the days of the sailing ships. A clipper ship, for example, would have as many as six rows of these sails to a mast. Many sailors plummeted to death from the high masts. Note the rope ladders and the complexity of ropes and pulleys.

B. **Motivation**
Here Leggatt explains why he thinks the old captain would not agree to let him escape.
? Contrast these reasons with the young captain's willingness to help him. (The old captain is afraid of his men, the law, and his wife. The young captain risks all.)

A

The *Kilmalie* (1893).   National Maritime Museum, Greenwich, England.

ken out only to get chucked back, and I did not want any more of that work. He refused, looking more sick than ever. He was afraid of the men, and also of that old second mate of his who had been sailing with him for years—a gray-headed old humbug; and his steward, too, had been with him devil knows how long—seventeen years or more—a dogmatic sort of loafer who hated me like poison, just because I was the chief mate. No chief mate ever made more than one voyage in the *Sephora*, you know. Those two old chaps ran the ship. Devil only knows what the skipper wasn't afraid of (all his nerve went to pieces altogether in that hellish spell of bad weather we

B

had)—of what the law would do to him—of his wife, perhaps. Oh, yes! She's on board. Though I don't think she would have meddled. She would have been only too glad to have me out of the ship in any way. The 'brand of Cain' business, don't you see. That's all right. I was ready enough to go off wandering on the face of the earth—and that was price enough to pay for an Abel of that sort.[17] Anyhow, he wouldn't listen to me. 'This

_____

17. **brand of Cain . . . an Abel of that sort:** In the Bible, Cain slew his brother Abel. As punishment, God made Cain a fugitive, driving him out ''from the face of the earth.'' So that Cain would not be slain, the Lord set a mark, or brand, upon him (Genesis, Chapter 4).

thing must take its course. I represent the law here.' He was shaking like a leaf. 'So you won't?' 'No!' 'Then I hope you will be able to sleep on that,' I said, and turned my back on him. 'I wonder that *you* can,' cries he, and locks the door.

"Well, after that, I couldn't. Not very well. That was three weeks ago. We have had a slow passage through the Java Sea; drifted about Carimata for ten days. When we anchored here they thought, I suppose, it was all right. The nearest land (and that's five miles) is the ship's destination; the consul would soon set about catching me; and there would have been no object in bolting to these islets there. I don't suppose there's a drop of water on them. I don't know how it was, but tonight that steward, after bringing me my supper, went out to let me eat it, and left the door unlocked. And I ate it—all there was, too. After I had finished I strolled out on the quarterdeck. I don't know that I meant to do anything. A breath of fresh air was all I wanted, I believe. Then a sudden temptation came over me. I kicked off my slippers and was in the water before I had made up my mind fairly. Somebody heard the splash and they raised an awful hullabaloo. 'He's gone! Lower the boats! He's committed suicide! No, he's swimming.' Certainly I was swimming. It's not so easy for a swimmer like me to commit suicide by drowning. I landed on the nearest islet before the boat left the ship's side. I heard them pulling about in the dark, hailing, and so on, but after a bit they gave up. Everything quieted down and the anchorage became as still as death. I sat down on a stone and began to think. I felt certain they would start searching for me at daylight. There was no place to hide on those stony things— and if there had been, what would have been the good? But now I was clear of that ship, I was not going back. So after a while I took off all my clothes, tied them up in a bundle with a stone inside, and dropped them in the deep water on the outer side of that islet. That was suicide enough for me. Let them think what they liked, but I didn't mean to drown myself. I meant to swim till I sank—but that's not the same thing. I struck out for another of these little islands, and it was from that one that I first saw your riding light. Something to swim for. I went on easily, and on the way I came upon a flat rock a foot or two above water. In the daytime, I dare say, you might make it out with a glass from your poop. I scrambled up on it and rested myself for a bit. Then I made

another start. That last spell must have been over a mile."

His whisper was getting fainter and fainter, and all the time he stared straight out through the porthole, in which there was not even a star to be seen. I had not interrupted him. There was something that made comment impossible in his narrative, or perhaps in himself; a sort of feeling, a quality, which I can't find a name for. And when he ceased, all I found was a futile whisper: "So you swam for our light?"

"Yes—straight for it. It was something to swim for. I couldn't see any stars low down because the coast was in the way, and I couldn't see the land, either. The water was like glass. One might have been swimming in a confounded thousand-feet deep cistern with no place for scrambling out anywhere; but what I didn't like was the notion of swimming round and round like a crazed bullock before I gave out; and as I didn't mean to go back . . . No. Do you see me being hauled back, stark naked, off one of these little islands by the scruff of the neck and fighting like a wild beast? Somebody would have got killed for certain, and I did not want any of that. So I went on. Then your ladder—"

"Why didn't you hail the ship?" I asked, a little louder.

He touched my shoulder lightly. Lazy footsteps came right over our heads and stopped. The second mate had crossed from the other side of the poop and might have been hanging over the rail, for all we knew.

"He couldn't hear us talking—could he?" My double breathed into my very ear, anxiously.

His anxiety was an answer, a sufficient answer, to the question I had put to him. An answer containing all the difficulty of that situation. I closed the porthole quietly, to make sure. A louder word might have been overheard.

"Who's that?" he whispered then.

"My second mate. But I don't know much more of the fellow than you do."

And I told him a little about myself. I had been appointed to take charge while I least expected anything of the sort, not quite a fortnight ago. I didn't know either the ship or the people. Hadn't had the time in port to look about me or size anybody up. And as to the crew, all they knew was that I was appointed to take the ship home. For the rest, I was almost as much of a stranger on board as himself, I said. And at the moment I

A. Symbolism
By saying that it was something to swim toward, Conrad presents the light as a goal, an inspiration, and a source of hope.

B. Interpreting
? Instead of acting responsibly at the conclusion of this tale of murder and flight from justice, the captain makes an inane remark. How would you explain this response? (Again, the captain sees himself reflected in Leggatt. Blaming Leggatt would be blaming himself. The "feeling, or quality, that [he] can't find a name for" may be his sense of the ship's light as a symbol of Leggatt's deliverance, and of his own role as Leggatt's savior.) Would you justify Leggatt's crime as the captain is doing? (Before they answer, students should look back to page 930, where Leggatt describes the man he killed as having "no business of living at all." He does not seem to repent of his crime.)

A. Plot Structure and Mood
Part of the air of mystery in this story comes from the pattern of unexpected coincidences or incidents of good fortune. Look for such examples in this paragraph. They contribute to a fatalistic mood—a feeling that events are moving, as they must, to a predetermined end.

felt it most acutely. I felt that it would take very little to make me a suspect person in the eyes of the ship's company.

A   He had turned about meantime; and we, the two strangers in the ship, faced each other in identical attitudes.

"Your ladder—" he murmured, after a silence. "Who'd have thought of finding a ladder hanging over at night in a ship anchored out here! I felt just then a very unpleasant faintness. After the life I've been leading for nine weeks, anybody would have got out of condition. I wasn't capable of swimming round as far as your rudder chains. And, lo and behold! there was a ladder to get hold of. After I gripped it I said to myself, 'What's the good?' When I saw a man's head looking over I thought I would swim away presently and leave him shouting—in whatever language it was. I didn't mind being looked at. I—I liked it. And then you speaking to me so quietly—as if you had expected me—made me hold on a little longer. It had been a confounded lonely time—I don't mean while swimming. I was glad to talk a little to somebody that didn't belong to the *Sephora*. As to asking for the captain, that was a mere impulse. It could have been no use, with all the ship knowing about me and the other people pretty certain to be round here in the morning. I don't know—I wanted to be seen, to talk with somebody, before I went on. I don't know what I would have said. . . . 'Fine night, isn't it?' or something of the sort."

"Do you think they will be round here presently?" I asked with some incredulity.

"Quite likely," he said, faintly.

He looked extremely haggard all of a sudden. His head rolled on his shoulders.

"H'm. We shall see then. Meantime get into that bed," I whispered. "Want help? There."

It was a rather high bedplace with a set of drawers underneath. This amazing swimmer really needed the lift I gave him by seizing his leg. He tumbled in, rolled over on his back, and flung one arm across his eyes. And then, with his face nearly hidden, he must have looked exactly as I used to look in that bed. I gazed upon my other self for a while before drawing across carefully the two green serge curtains which ran on a brass rod. I thought for a moment of pinning them together for greater safety, but I sat down on the couch, and once there I felt unwilling to rise and hunt for a pin. I would do it in a moment. I was extremely

tired, in a peculiarly intimate way, by the strain of stealthiness, by the effort of whispering and the general secrecy of this excitement. It was three o'clock by now and I had been on my feet since nine, but I was not sleepy; I could not have gone to sleep. I sat there, fagged out, looking at the curtains, trying to clear my mind of the confused sensation of being in two places at once, and greatly bothered by an exasperating knocking in my head. It was a relief to discover suddenly that it was not in my head at all, but on the outside of the door. Before I could collect myself the words "Come in" were out of my mouth, and the steward entered with a tray, bringing in my morning coffee. I had slept, after all, and I was so frightened that I shouted, "This way! I am here, steward," as though he had been miles away. He put down the tray on the table next the couch and only then said, very quietly, "I can see you are here, sir." I felt him give me a keen look, but I dared not meet his eyes just then. He must have wondered why I had drawn the curtains of my bed before going to sleep on the couch. He went out, hooking the door open as usual.

I heard the crew washing decks above me. I knew I would have been told at once if there had been any wind. Calm, I thought, and I was doubly vexed. Indeed, I felt dual more than ever. The steward reappeared suddenly in the doorway. I jumped up from the couch so quickly that he gave a start.

"What do you want here?"

"Close your port, sir—they are washing decks."

"It is closed," I said, reddening.

"Very well, sir." But he did not move from the doorway and returned my stare in an extraordinary, equivocal manner for a time. Then his eyes wavered, all his expression changed, and in a voice unusually gentle, almost coaxingly:

"May I come in to take the empty cup away, sir?"

"Of course!" I turned my back on him while he popped in and out. Then I unhooked and closed the door and even pushed the bolt. This sort of thing could not go on very long. The cabin was as hot as an oven, too. I took a peep at my double, and discovered that he had not moved, his arm was still over his eyes; but his chest heaved; his hair was wet; his chin glistened with perspiration. I reached over him and opened the port.

"I must show myself on deck," I reflected.

Of course, theoretically, I could do what I liked, with no one to say nay to me within the whole circle of the horizon; but to lock my cabin door and take the key away I did not dare. Directly I put my head out of the companion I saw the group of my two officers, the second mate barefooted, the chief mate in long india-rubber boots, near the break of the poop, and the steward halfway down the poop ladder talking to them eagerly. He happened to catch sight of me and dived, the second ran down on the main deck shouting some order or other, and the chief mate came to meet me, touching his cap.

There was a sort of curiosity in his eye that I did not like. I don't know whether the steward had told them that I was "queer" only, or downright drunk, but I know the man meant to have a good look at me. I watched him coming with a smile which, as he got into point-blank range, took effect and froze his very whiskers. I did not give him time to open his lips.

"Square the yards by lifts and braces before the hands go to breakfast."

It was the first particular order I had given on board that ship; and I stayed on deck to see it executed, too. I had felt the need of asserting myself without loss of time. That sneering young cub got taken down a peg or two on that occasion, and I also seized the opportunity of having a good look at the face of every foremast man as they filed past me to go to the after braces. At breakfast time, eating nothing myself, I presided with such frigid dignity that the two mates were only too glad to escape from the cabin as soon as decency permitted; and all the time the dual working of my mind distracted me almost to the point of insanity. I was constantly watching myself, my secret self, as dependent on my actions as my own personality, sleeping in that bed, behind that door which faced me as I sat at the head of the table. It was very much like being mad, only it was worse because one was aware of it.

I had to shake him for a solid minute, but when at last he opened his eyes it was in the full possession of his senses, with an inquiring look.

"All's well so far," I whispered. "Now you must vanish into the bathroom."

He did so, as noiseless as a ghost, and I then rang for the steward, and facing him boldly, directed him to tidy up my stateroom while I was having my bath—"and be quick about it." As my tone admitted of no excuses, he said, "Yes, sir,"

and ran off to fetch his dustpan and brushes. I took a bath and did most of my dressing, splashing, and whistling softly for the steward's edification, while the secret sharer of my life stood drawn up bolt upright in that little space, his face looking very sunken in daylight, his eyelids lowered under the stern, dark line of his eyebrows drawn together by a slight frown.

When I left him there to go back to my room the steward was finishing dusting. I sent for the mate and engaged him in some insignificant conversation. It was, as it were, trifling with the terrific character of his whiskers; but my object was to give him an opportunity for a good look at my cabin. And then I could at last shut, with a clear conscience, the door of my stateroom and get my double back into the recessed part. There was nothing else for it. He had to sit still on a small folding stool, half smothered by the heavy coats hanging there. We listened to the steward going into the bathroom out of the saloon, filling the water bottles there, scrubbing the bath, setting things to rights, whisk, bang, clatter—out again into the saloon—turn the key—click. Such was my scheme for keeping my second self invisible. Nothing better could be contrived under the circumstances. And there we sat; I at my writing desk ready to appear busy with some papers, he behind me, out of sight of the door. It would not have been prudent to talk in daytime; and I could not have stood the excitement of that queer sense of whispering to myself. Now and then, glancing over my shoulder, I saw him far back there, sitting rigidly on the low stool, his bare feet close together, his arms folded, his head hanging on his breast—and perfectly still. Anybody would have taken him for me.

I was fascinated by it myself. Every moment I had to glance over my shoulder. I was looking at him when a voice outside the door said:

"Beg pardon, sir."

"Well!" . . . I kept my eyes on him, and so, when the voice outside the door announced, "There's a ship's boat coming our way, sir," I saw him give a start—the first movement he had made for hours. But he did not raise his bowed head.

"All right. Get the ladder over."

I hesitated. Should I whisper something to him? But what? His immobility seemed to have been never disturbed. What could I tell him he did not know already? . . . Finally I went on deck.

A. Theme
Insanity is another recurring theme or motif.
❓ Why might the crew think the captain unbalanced? (He is behaving strangely and secretively.) In this passage what reason does the captain give for feeling "insane"? (His mind is split between himself and his double.)

B. Interpreting
Many of the statements in the story have more than one level of meaning.
❓ What is the literal meaning of "keeping my second self invisible"? (Hiding Leggatt) How else might these words be interpreted? (Keeping a part of oneself concealed from others)

Critic Adam Gillon states "The story is a strange mixture of suspense and comedy, especially in scenes with the old captain of the *Sephora*, who is ridiculed. Yet it is Leggatt's captain who upholds the law while the young captain breaks it. The old captain performs a painful duty though he also resents the chief mate who is a Conway boy, not like himself, who has risen through the ranks. The young captain does not seem to be bothered by the fact that Leggatt is a killer. Though he, like old Captain Archbold, represents the law aboard *his* ship, he chooses not to enforce it; he chooses, moreover, the path of duplicity, deceiving his whole crew and Captain Archbold, thereby becoming Leggatt's accomplice."

Ask students what elements of comedy they can find in the scene between the captain of the *Sephora* and the young captain. Who do they think acted with the most authority in this scene—who "won" the encounter?

A. Character
Note that the narrator describes the captain of the *Sephora* in the same disdainful manner as Leggatt described him. The "doubles" often display a superior attitude toward those who are different from them.

B. Plot
The captain's gesture graphically illustrates that the dead man was undoubtedly strangled because the tongue of the corpse was sticking out of its mouth.

II

The skipper of the *Sephora* had a thin red whisker all round his face, and the sort of complexion that goes with hair of that color; also the particular, rather smeary shade of blue in the eyes. He was not exactly a showy figure; his shoulders were high, his stature but middling—one leg slightly more bandy than the other. He shook hands, looking vaguely around. A spiritless tenacity was his main characteristic, I judged. I behaved with a politeness which seemed to disconcert him. Perhaps he was shy. He mumbled to me as if he were ashamed of what he was saying; gave his name (it was something like Archbold—but at this distance of years I hardly am sure), his ship's name, and a few other particulars of that sort, in the manner of a criminal making a reluctant and doleful confession. He had had terrible weather on the passage out—terrible—terrible—wife aboard, too.

By this time we were seated in the cabin and the steward brought in a tray with a bottle and glasses. "Thanks! No." Never took liquor. Would have some water, though. He drank two tumblerfuls. Terrible thirsty work. Ever since daylight had been exploring the islands round his ship.

"What was that for—fun?" I asked, with an appearance of polite interest.

"No!" He sighed. "Painful duty."

As he persisted in his mumbling and I wanted my double to hear every word, I hit upon the notion of informing him that I regretted to say I was hard of hearing.

"Such a young man, too!" he nodded, keeping his smeary blue, unintelligent eyes fastened upon me. What was the cause of it—some disease? he inquired, without the least sympathy and as if he thought that, if so, I'd got no more than I deserved.

"Yes; disease," I admitted in a cheerful tone which seemed to shock him. But my point was gained, because he had to raise his voice to give me his tale. It is not worthwhile to record that version. It was just over two months since all this had happened, and he had thought so much about it that he seemed completely muddled as to its bearings, but still immensely impressed.

"What would you think of such a thing happening on board your own ship? I've had the *Sephora* for these fifteen years. I am a well-known shipmaster."

He was densely distressed—and perhaps I should have sympathized with him if I had been able to detach my mental vision from the unsuspected sharer of my cabin as though he were my second self. There he was on the other side of the bulkhead, four or five feet from us, no more, as we sat in the saloon. I looked politely at Captain Archbold (if that was his name), but it was the other I saw, in a gray sleeping suit, seated on a low stool, his bare feet close together, his arms folded, and every word said between us falling into the ears of his dark head bowed on his chest.

"I have been at sea now, man and boy, for seven-and-thirty years, and I've never heard of such a thing happening in an English ship. And that it should be my ship. Wife on board, too."

I was hardly listening to him.

"Don't you think," I said, "that the heavy sea which, you told me, came aboard just then might have killed the man? I have seen the sheer weight of a sea kill a man very neatly, by simply breaking his neck."

"Good God!" he uttered, impressively, fixing his smeary blue eyes on me. "The sea! No man killed by the sea ever looked like that." He seemed positively scandalized at my suggestion. And as I gazed at him, certainly not prepared for anything original on his part, he advanced his head close to mine and thrust his tongue out at me so suddenly that I couldn't help starting back.

After scoring over my calmness in this graphic way he nodded wisely. If I had seen the sight, he assured me, I would never forget it as long as I lived. The weather was too bad to give the corpse a proper sea burial. So next day at dawn they took it up on the poop, covering its face with a bit of bunting; he read a short prayer, and then, just as it was, in its oilskins and long boots, they launched it amongst those mountainous seas that seemed ready every moment to swallow up the ship herself and the terrified lives on board of her.

"That reefed foresail saved you," I threw in.

"Under God—it did," he exclaimed fervently. "It was by a special mercy, I firmly believe, that it stood some of those hurricane squalls."

"It was the setting of that sail which—" I began.

"God's own hand in it," he interrupted me. "Nothing less could have done it. I don't mind telling you that I hardly dared give the order. It seemed impossible that we could touch anything without losing it, and then our last hope would have been gone."

The terror of that gale was on him yet. I let him go on for a bit, then said, casually—as if returning to a minor subject:

"You were very anxious to give up your mate to the shore people, I believe?"

He was. To the law. His obscure tenacity on that point had in it something incomprehensible and a little awful; something, as it were, mystical, quite apart from his anxiety that he should not be suspected of "countenancing any doings of that sort." Seven-and-thirty virtuous years at sea, of which over twenty of immaculate command, and the last fifteen in the *Sephora,* seemed to have laid him under some pitiless obligation.

"And you know," he went on, groping shame-facedly amongst his feelings, "I did not engage that young fellow. His people had some interest with my owners. I was in a way forced to take him on. He looked very smart, very gentlemanly, and all that. But do you know—I never liked him, somehow. I am a plain man. You see, he wasn't exactly the sort for the chief mate of a ship like the *Sephora.*"

I had become so connected in thoughts and impressions with the secret sharer of my cabin that I felt as if I, personally, were being given to understand that I, too, was not the sort that would have done for the chief mate of a ship like the *Sephora.* I had no doubt of it in my mind.

"Not at all the style of man. You understand," he insisted, superfluously, looking hard at me.

I smiled urbanely. He seemed at a loss for a while.

"I suppose I must report a suicide."

"Beg pardon?"

"Sui-cide! That's what I'll have to write to my owners directly I get in."

"Unless you manage to recover him before to-morrow," I assented, dispassionately. . . . "I mean, alive."

He mumbled something which I really did not catch, and I turned my ear to him in a puzzled manner. He fairly bawled:

"The land—I say, the mainland is at least seven miles off my anchorage."

"About that."

My lack of excitement, of curiosity, of surprise, of any sort of pronounced interest, began to arouse his distrust. But except for the felicitous

pretense of deafness I had not tried to pretend anything. I had felt utterly incapable of playing the part of ignorance properly, and therefore was afraid to try. It is also certain that he had brought some ready-made suspicions with him, and that he viewed my politeness as a strange and unnatural phenomenon. And yet how else could I have received him? Not heartily! That was impossible for psychological reasons, which I need not state here. My only object was to keep off his inquiries. Surlily? Yes, but surliness might have provoked a point-blank question. From its novelty to him and from its nature, punctilious[18] courtesy was the manner best calculated to restrain the man. But there was the danger of his breaking through my defense bluntly. I could not, I think, have met him by a direct lie, also for psychological (not moral) reasons. If he had only known how afraid I was of his putting my feeling of identity with the other to the test! But, strangely enough—(I thought of it only afterward)—I believe that he was not a little disconcerted by the reverse side of that weird situation, by something in me that reminded him of the man he was seeking—suggested a mysterious similitude to the young fellow he had distrusted and disliked from the first.

However that might have been, the silence was not very prolonged. He took another oblique step.

"I reckon I had no more than a two-mile pull to your ship. Not a bit more."

"And quite enough, too, in this awful heat," I said.

Another pause full of mistrust followed. Necessity, they say, is mother of invention, but fear, too, is not barren of ingenious suggestions. And I was afraid he would ask me point-blank for news of my other self.

"Nice little saloon, isn't it?" I remarked, as if noticing for the first time the way his eyes roamed from one closed door to the other. "And very well fitted out, too. Here, for instance," I continued, reaching over the back of my seat negligently and flinging the door open, "is my bathroom."

He made an eager movement, but hardly gave it a glance. I got up, shut the door of the bathroom, and invited him to have a look round, as if I were very proud of my accommodation. He had to rise and be shown round, but he went through the business without any raptures whatever.

---

18. **punctilious:** exact; careful.

A. Maritime Law
The captain commits an inexcusable breach of maritime law by hiding the refugee. By all the laws of the sea and the British Merchant Marine Service, the captain should have given up Leggatt to the proper authorities.

B. Conflict
❓ What psychological reason(s) would have made it difficult for the captain to deny the presence of the fugitive? (He would, in a sense, be denying his own existence.)

C. Making Inferences
❓ What is the captain of the *Sephora* hinting at here? (He is really asking the young captain if he has seen any sign of the murderer, since the two ships are only two miles apart. The young captain, however, avoids the question so he does not have to lie.)

Literature and Language: Punctuating Dialogue
You might use the dialogue on this page to review (with students who need help) the rules of punctuating dialogue. For reference see **Grammar, Usage, and Mechanics: A Reference Guide.** In addition, as a reading exercise, you might see if students can identify the speakers in the dialogue reprinted here. Notice that

Conrad does not always state the speaker's name.

A. Responding
These passages reveal the reactions of the crew to the story of the murder. The captain is mainly bent on protecting Leggatt from discovery.
? Whom do you sympathize with at this point? Do you hope Leggatt will escape? (Students may sympathize with Leggatt, who acted to save his ship, but they also may believe that murder is never justified. They may sympathize with the captain, who is caught up in a situation he cannot control.)

B. Plot
Note that the captain's sense of duality has grown to the point where he cannot bear to be separated from his other self. They are able to communicate only with their eyes—an ability that is possible only between two people who are mysteriously close.

"And now we'll have a look at my stateroom," I declared, in a voice as loud as I dared to make it, crossing the cabin to the starboard side with purposely heavy steps.

He followed me in and gazed around. My intelligent double had vanished. I played my part.

"Very convenient—isn't it?"

"Very nice. Very comf . . ." He didn't finish, and went out brusquely as if to escape from some unrighteous wiles of mine. But it was not to be. I had been too frightened not to feel vengeful; I felt I had him on the run, and I meant to keep him on the run. My polite insistence must have had something menacing in it, because he gave in suddenly. And I did not let him off a single item; mate's room, pantry, storerooms, the very sail locker which was also under the poop—he had to look into them all. When at last I showed him out on the quarterdeck he drew a long, spiritless sigh, and mumbled dismally that he must really be going back to his ship now. I desired my mate, who had joined us, to see to the captain's boat.

The man of whiskers gave a blast on the whistle which he used to wear hanging round his neck, and yelled, "*Sephora* away!" My double down there in my cabin must have heard, and certainly could not feel more relieved than I. Four fellows came running out from somewhere forward and went over the side, while my own men, appearing on deck too, lined the rail. I escorted my visitor to the gangway ceremoniously, and nearly overdid it. He was a tenacious beast. On the very ladder he lingered, and in that unique, guiltily conscientious manner of sticking to the point:

"I say . . . you . . . you don't think that—"

I covered his voice loudly:

"Certainly not. . . . I am delighted. Goodbye."

I had an idea of what he meant to say, and just saved myself by the privilege of defective hearing. He was too shaken generally to insist, but my mate, close witness of that parting, looked mystified and his face took on a thoughtful cast. As I did not want to appear as if I wished to avoid all communications with my officers, he had the opportunity to address me.

"Seems a very nice man. His boat's crew told our chaps a very extraordinary story, if what I am told by the steward is true. I suppose you had it from the captain, sir?"

"Yes. I had a story from the captain."

"A very horrible affair—isn't it, sir?"

"It is."

"Beats all these tales we hear about murders in Yankee ships."

"I don't think it beats them. I don't think it resembles them in the least."

"Bless my soul—you don't say so! But of course I've no acquaintance whatever with American ships, not I, so I couldn't go against your knowledge. It's horrible enough for me. . . . But the queerest part is that those fellows seemed to have some idea the man was hidden aboard here. They had really. Did you ever hear of such a thing?"

"Preposterous—isn't it?"

We were walking to and fro athwart the quarterdeck. No one of the crew forward could be seen (the day was Sunday), and the mate pursued:

"There was some little dispute about it. Our chaps took offense. 'As if we would harbor a thing like that,' they said. 'Wouldn't you like to look for him in our coal hole?' Quite a tiff. But they made it up in the end. I suppose he did drown himself. Don't you, sir?"

"I don't suppose anything."

"You have no doubt in the matter, sir?"

"None whatever."

I left him suddenly. I felt I was producing a bad impression, but with my double down there it was most trying to be on deck. And it was almost as trying to be below. Altogether a nerve-trying situation. But on the whole I felt less torn in two when I was with him. There was no one in the whole ship whom I dared take into my confidence. Since the hands had got to know his story, it would have been impossible to pass him off for anyone else, and an accidental discovery was to be dreaded now more than ever. . . .

The steward being engaged in laying the table for dinner, we could talk only with our eyes when I first went down. Later in the afternoon we had a cautious try at whispering. The Sunday quietness of the ship was against us; the stillness of air and water around her was against us; the elements, the men were against us—everything was against us in our secret partnership; time itself— for this could not go on forever. The very trust in Providence was, I suppose, denied to his guilt. Shall I confess that this thought cast me down very much? As to the chapter of accidents which counts for so much in the book of success, I could only hope that it was closed. For what favorable accident could be expected?

"Did you hear everything?" were my first

words as soon as we took up our position side by side, leaning over my bedplace.

He had. And the proof of it was his earnest whisper, "The man told you he hardly dared to give the order."

I understood the reference to be to that saving foresail.

"Yes. He was afraid of it being lost in the setting."

"I assure you he never gave the order. He may think he did, but he never gave it. He stood there with me on the break of the poop after the main-topsail blew away, and whimpered about our last hope—positively whimpered about it and nothing else—and the night coming on! To hear one's skipper go on like that in such weather was enough to drive any fellow out of his mind. It worked me up into a sort of desperation. I just took it into my own hands and went away from him, boiling, and—But what's the use telling you? *You* know! . . . Do you think that if I had not been pretty fierce with them I should have got the men to do anything? Not it! The bosun[19] perhaps? Perhaps! It wasn't a heavy sea—it was a sea gone mad! I suppose the end of the world will be something like that; and a man may have the heart to see it coming once and be done with it—but to have to face it day after day— I don't blame anybody. I was precious little better than the rest. Only—I was an officer of that old coal-wagon, anyhow—"

"I quite understand," I conveyed that sincere assurance into his ear. He was out of breath with whispering; I could hear him pant slightly. It was all very simple. The same strung-up force which had given twenty-four men a chance, at least, for their lives, had, in a sort of recoil, crushed an unworthy mutinous existence.

But I had no leisure to weigh the merits of the matter—footsteps in the saloon, a heavy knock. "There's enough wind to get under way with, sir." Here was the call of a new claim upon my thoughts and even upon my feelings.

"Turn the hands up," I cried through the door. "I'll be on deck directly."

I was going out to make the acquaintance of my ship. Before I left the cabin our eyes met— the eyes of the only two strangers on board. I pointed to the recessed part where the little

---

19. **bosun:** the boatswain, an officer in charge of the ship's deckhands.

campstool awaited him and laid my finger on my lips. He made a gesture—somewhat vague—a little mysterious, accompanied by a faint smile, as if of regret.

This is not the place to enlarge upon the sensations of a man who feels for the first time a ship move under his feet to his own independent word. In my case they were not unalloyed. I was not wholly alone with my command; for there was that stranger in my cabin. Or rather, I was not completely and wholly with her. Part of me was absent. That mental feeling of being in two places at once affected me physically as if the mood of secrecy had penetrated my very soul. Before an hour had elapsed since the ship had begun to move, having occasion to ask the mate (he stood by my side) to take a compass bearing of the Pagoda, I caught myself reaching up to his ear in whispers. I say I caught myself, but enough had escaped to startle the man. I can't describe it otherwise than by saying that he shied. A grave, preoccupied manner, as though he were in possession of some perplexing intelligence, did not leave him henceforth. A little later I moved away from the rail to look at the compass with such a stealthy gait that the helmsman noticed it—and I could not help noticing the unusual roundness of his eyes. These are trifling instances, though it's to no commander's advantage to be suspected of ludicrous eccentricities. But I was also more seriously affected. There are to a seaman certain words, gestures, that should in given conditions come as naturally, as instinctively as the winking of a menaced eye. A certain order should spring on to his lips without thinking; a certain sign should get itself made, so to speak, without reflection. But all unconscious alertness had abandoned me. I had to make an effort of will to recall myself back (from the cabin) to the conditions of the moment. I felt that I was appearing an irresolute commander to those people who were watching me more or less critically.

And, besides, there were the scares. On the second day out, for instance, coming off the deck in the afternoon (I had straw slippers on my bare feet) I stopped at the open pantry door and spoke to the steward. He was doing something there with his back to me. At the sound of my voice he nearly jumped out of his skin, as the saying is, and incidentally broke a cup.

"What on earth's the matter with you?" I asked, astonished.

A. Motivation

❓ What additional justification for his actions does Leggatt give in this passage? (The captain lost his nerve in the terrible weather, and it was up to Leggatt to save them all. Keyed up under this heavy responsibility, he killed someone who was thwarting his life-saving efforts.)

B. Plot

These passages and the following give examples of ways in which the captain was behaving strangely or in a manner that the crew would find hard to understand.

A. Character

This description of Leggatt as "self-controlled, calm—almost invulnerable" shows that the captain respects him, and it is this continued admiration of Leggatt's stoicism—which the captain believes he himself shares—that feeds the captain's determination to help Leggatt. Ask students whether they think the captain might have changed his mind if Leggatt had been anxious and quivering instead of controlled.

B. Suspense

❓ What details of suspense are created in this episode? (There are many—Conrad makes the reader as terrified as the captain is that the steward will discover Leggatt. Note that we feel relief after the captain warns Leggatt with his loud orders—even though they sound inane to the others—but our suspense is immediately renewed when the steward seems to dawdle in the captain's stateroom.)

He was extremely confused. "Beg your pardon, sir. I made sure you were in your cabin."

"You see I wasn't."

"No, sir. I could have sworn I had heard you moving in there not a moment ago. It's most extraordinary . . . very sorry, sir."

I passed on with an inward shudder. I was so identified with my secret double that I did not even mention the fact in those scanty, fearful whispers we exchanged. I suppose he had made some slight noise of some kind or other. It would have been miraculous if he hadn't at one time or another. And yet, haggard as he appeared, he looked always perfectly self-controlled, more than calm—almost invulnerable. On my suggestion he remained almost entirely in the bathroom, which, upon the whole, was the safest place. There could be really no shadow of an excuse for anyone ever wanting to go in there, once the steward had done with it. It was a very tiny place. Sometimes he reclined on the floor, his legs bent, his head sustained on one elbow. At others I would find him on the campstool, sitting in his gray sleeping suit and with his cropped dark hair like a patient, unmoved convict. At night I would smuggle him into my bedplace, and we would whisper together, with the regular footfalls of the officer of the watch passing and repassing over our heads. It was an infinitely miserable time. It was lucky that some tins of fine preserves were stowed in a locker in my stateroom; hard bread I could always get hold of; and so he lived on stewed chicken, paté de foie gras,[20] asparagus, cooked oysters, sardines—on all sorts of abominable sham delicacies out of tins. My early morning coffee he always drank; and it was all I dared do for him in that respect.

Every day there was the horrible maneuvering to go through so that my room and then the bathroom should be done in the usual way. I came to hate the sight of the steward, to abhor the voice of that harmless man. I felt that it was he who would bring on the disaster of discovery. It hung like a sword over our heads.

The fourth day out, I think (we were then working down the east side of the Gulf of Siam, tack for tack,[21] in light winds and smooth water)—the fourth day, I say, of this miserable juggling with

the unavoidable, as we sat at our evening meal, that man, whose slightest movement I dreaded, after putting down the dishes ran up on deck busily. This could not be dangerous. Presently he came down again; and then it appeared that he had remembered a coat of mine which I had thrown over a rail to dry after having been wetted in a shower which had passed over the ship in the afternoon. Sitting stolidly at the head of the table I became terrified at the sight of the garment on his arm. Of course he made for my door. There was no time to lose.

"Steward," I thundered. My nerves were so shaken that I could not govern my voice and conceal my agitation. This was the sort of thing that made my terrifically whiskered mate tap his forehead with his forefinger. I had detected him using that gesture while talking on deck with a confidential air to the carpenter. It was too far to hear a word, but I had no doubt that this pantomime could only refer to the strange new captain.

"Yes, sir," the pale-faced steward turned resignedly to me. It was this maddening course of being shouted at, checked without rhyme or reason, arbitrarily chased out of my cabin, suddenly called into it, sent flying out of his pantry on incomprehensible errands, that accounted for the growing wretchedness of his expression.

"Where are you going with that coat?"

"To your room, sir."

"Is there another shower coming?"

"I'm sure I don't know, sir. Shall I go up again and see, sir?"

"No! never mind."

My object was attained, as of course my other self in there would have heard everything that passed. During this interlude my two officers never raised their eyes off their respective plates; but the lip of that confounded cub, the second mate, quivered visibly.

I expected the steward to hook my coat on and come out at once. He was very slow about it; but I dominated my nervousness sufficiently not to shout after him. Suddenly I became aware (it could be heard plainly enough) that the fellow for some reason or other was opening the door of the bathroom. It was the end. The place was literally not big enough to swing a cat in. My voice died in my throat and I went stony all over. I expected to hear a yell of surprise and terror, and made a movement, but had not the strength to get on my legs. Everything remained still. Had my second

---

20. **paté de foie gras** (pä·tä′ də fwä grä): a rich goose-liver paste.
21. **tack for tack:** a technique of sailing against the wind in a zigzag course.

A

B

Heaving Up the Anchor by T. W. Ward. Drawing.

From *Merchant Sailing Ships 1815–1850* by David R. MacGregor. Copyright © Argus Books, Ltd., and David MacGregor.

A. Character

❓ What mixed emotions does the captain experience when the steward fails to discover Leggatt? (Relief, fear that Leggatt has gone)

B. Imagery and Theme

❓ Here the hidden double is described in ghostly imagery. How is that imagery appropriate to the situation? (Ghosts suggest fear, mystery, and death.) How does it reinforce the themes of insanity and guilt? (Seeing ghosts might suggest madness, and ghosts are associated with unquiet consciences.)

self taken the poor wretch by the throat? I don't know what I would have done next moment if I had not seen the steward come out of my room, close the door, and then stand quietly by the sideboard.

A Saved, I thought. But, no! Lost! Gone! He was gone!

I laid my knife and fork down and leaned back in my chair. My head swam. After a while, when sufficiently recovered to speak in a steady voice, I instructed my mate to put the ship round at eight o'clock himself.

"I won't come on deck," I went on. "I think I'll turn in, and unless the wind shifts I don't want to be disturbed before midnight. I feel a bit seedy."

"You did look middling bad a little while ago," the chief mate remarked without showing any great concern.

They both went out, and I stared at the steward clearing the table. There was nothing to be read on that wretched man's face. But why did he avoid my eyes I asked myself. Then I thought I should like to hear the sound of his voice.

"Steward!"

"Sir!" Startled as usual.

"Where did you hang up that coat?"

"In the bathroom, sir." The usual anxious tone. "It's not quite dry yet, sir."

For some time longer I sat in the cuddy. Had my double vanished as he had come? But of his coming there was an explanation, whereas his disappearance would be inexplicable. . . . I went slowly into my dark room, shut the door, lighted the lamp, and for a time dared not turn round. When at last I did I saw him standing bolt upright in the narrow recessed part. It would not be true to say I had a shock, but an irresistible doubt of his bodily existence flitted through my mind. Can it be, I asked myself, that he is not visible to other eyes than mine? It was like being haunted. Mo- **B**

A. Character
Here is an example in which the captain judges his double to be different, even better, than himself.

❓ What quality does the captain admire in the other? (His composure, his sanity)

B. Theme
Here Leggatt asserts his belief that no ordinary judge and jury have a right to judge him. He, in effect, has acted as his own judge, sentencing himself to lifelong exile.

C. Plot
The captain has deliberately changed the direction of the ship to get closer to land. Since this is a dangerous and unnecessary move, the mate is puzzled and concerned about the captain's competence.

tionless, with a grave face, he raised his hands slightly at me in a gesture which meant clearly, "Heavens! what a narrow escape!" Narrow indeed. I think I had come creeping quietly as near insanity as any man who has not actually gone over the border. That gesture restrained me, so to speak.

The mate with the terrific whiskers was now putting the ship on the other tack. In the moment of profound silence which follows upon the hands going to their stations I heard on the poop his raised voice: "Hard alee!" and the distant shout of the order repeated on the main deck. The sails, in that light breeze, made but a faint fluttering noise. It ceased. The ship was coming round slowly; I held my breath in the renewed stillness of expectation; one wouldn't have thought that there was a single living soul on her decks. A sudden brisk shout, "Mainsail haul!" broke the spell, and in the noisy cries and rush overhead of the men running away with the main brace we two, down in my cabin, came together in our usual position by the bedplace.

He did not wait for my question. "I heard him fumbling here and just managed to squat myself down in the bath," he whispered to me. "The fellow only opened the door and put his arm in to hang the coat up. All the same—"

"I never thought of that," I whispered back, even more appalled than before at the closeness of the shave, and marveling at that something unyielding in his character which was carrying him through so finely. There was no agitation in his whisper. Whoever was being driven distracted, it was not he. He was sane. And the proof of his sanity was continued when he took up the whispering again.

"It would never do for me to come to life again."

It was something that a ghost might have said. But what he was alluding to was his old captain's reluctant admission of the theory of suicide. It would obviously serve his turn—if I had understood at all the view which seemed to govern the unalterable purpose of his action.

"You must maroon me as soon as ever you can get amongst these islands off the Cambodje[22] shore," he went on.

22. **Cambodje** (kam·böj′): French name for Cambodia, then part of the French colony of Indochina.

"Maroon you! We are not living in a boy's adventure tale," I protested. His scornful whispering took me up.

"We aren't indeed! There's nothing of a boy's tale in this. But there's nothing else for it. I want no more. You don't suppose I am afraid of what can be done to me? Prison or gallows or whatever they may please. But you don't see me coming back to explain such things to an old fellow in a wig and twelve respectable tradesmen, do you? What can they know whether I am guilty or not— or of *what* I am guilty, either? That's my affair. What does the Bible say? 'Driven off the face of the earth.' Very well. I am off the face of the earth now. As I came at night so I shall go."

"Impossible!" I murmured. "You can't."

"Can't? . . . Not naked like a soul on the Day of Judgment. I shall freeze on to this sleeping suit. The Last Day is not yet—and . . . you have understood thoroughly. Didn't you?"

I felt suddenly ashamed of myself. I may say truly that I understood—and my hesitation in letting that man swim away from my ship's side had been a mere sham sentiment, a sort of cowardice.

"It can't be done now till next night," I breathed out. "The ship is on the offshore tack and the wind may fail us."

"As long as I know that you understand," he whispered. "But of course you do. It's a great satisfaction to have got somebody to understand. You seem to have been there on purpose." And in the same whisper, as if we two whenever we talked had to say things to each other which were not fit for the world to hear, he added, "It's very wonderful."

We remained side by side talking in our secret way—but sometimes silent or just exchanging a whispered word or two at long intervals. And as usual he stared through the port. A breath of wind came now and again into our faces. The ship might have been moored in dock, so gently and on an even keel she slipped through the water, that did not murmur even at our passage, shadowy and silent like a phantom sea.

At midnight I went on deck, and to my mate's great surprise put the ship round on the other tack. His terrible whiskers flitted round me in silent criticism. I certainly should not have done it if it had been only a question of getting out of that sleepy gulf as quickly as possible. I believe he told the second mate, who relieved him, that it was a

Symbolism
It is important to note that the captain does not dress on this day and continues to wear his sleeping suit, as does Leggatt. The similarity of the outfits (and the fact that they both belong to the captain) links them as one, and poses irony, since they are soon to separate forever. The sleeping suit—the clothing one wears to sleep—could represent the subconscious where all communication between the "light soul" and the "dark soul" takes place (represented by the captain and Leggatt—the captain's "dark self"). Also note that the suits are gray, which emphasizes the "gray area" between the subconscious and the conscious.

great want of judgment. The other only yawned. That intolerable cub shuffled about so sleepily and lolled against the rails in such a slack, improper fashion that I came down on him sharply.

"Aren't you properly awake yet?"

"Yes, sir! I am awake."

"Well, then, be good enough to hold yourself as if you were. And keep a lookout. If there's any current we'll be closing with some islands before daylight."

The east side of the gulf is fringed with islands, some solitary, others in groups. On the blue background of the high coast they seem to float on silvery patches of calm water, arid and gray, or dark green and rounded like clumps of evergreen bushes, with the larger ones, a mile or two long, showing the outlines of ridges, ribs of gray rock under the dark mantle of matted leafage. Unknown to trade, to travel, almost to geography, the manner of life they harbor is an unsolved secret. There must be villages—settlements of fishermen at least—on the largest of them, and some communication with the world is probably kept up by native craft. But all that forenoon, as we headed for them, fanned along by the faintest of breezes, I saw no sign of man or canoe in the field of the telescope I kept on pointing at the scattered group.

At noon I gave no orders for a change of course, and the mate's whiskers became much concerned and seemed to be offering themselves unduly to my notice. At last I said:

"I am going to stand right in. Quite in—as far as I can take her."

The stare of extreme surprise imparted an air of ferocity also to his eyes, and he looked truly terrific for a moment.

"We're not doing well in the middle of the gulf," I continued, casually. "I am going to look for the land breezes tonight."

"Bless my soul! Do you mean, sir, in the dark amongst the lot of all them islands and reefs and shoals?"

"Well—if there are any regular land breezes at all on this coast one must get close inshore to find them, mustn't one?"

"Bless my soul!" he exclaimed again under his breath. All that afternoon he wore a dreamy, contemplative appearance which in him was a mark of perplexity. After dinner I went into my stateroom as if I meant to take some rest. There we two bent our dark heads over a half-unrolled chart lying on my bed.

"There," I said. "It's got to be Koh-ring. I've been looking at it ever since sunrise. It has got two hills and a low point. It must be inhabited. And on the coast opposite there is what looks like the mouth of a biggish river—with some town, no doubt, not far up. It's the best chance for you that I can see."

"Anything. Koh-ring let it be."

He looked thoughtfully at the chart as if surveying chances and distances from a lofty height—and following with his eyes his own figure wandering on the blank land of Cochin-China,[23] and then passing off that piece of paper clean out of sight into uncharted regions. And it was as if the ship had two captains to plan her course for her. I had been so worried and restless running up and down that I had not had the patience to dress that day. I had remained in my sleeping suit, with straw slippers and a soft floppy hat. The closeness of the heat in the gulf had been most oppressive, and the crew were used to see me wandering in that airy attire.

"She will clear the south point as she heads now," I whispered into his ear. "Goodness only knows when, though, but certainly after dark. I'll edge her in to half a mile, as far as I may be able to judge in the dark—"

"Be careful," he murmured, warningly—and I realized suddenly that all my future, the only future for which I was fit, would perhaps go irretrievably to pieces in any mishap to my first command.

A

I could not stop a moment longer in the room. I motioned him to get out of sight and made my way on the poop. That unplayful cub had the watch. I walked up and down for a while thinking things out, then beckoned him over.

"Send a couple of hands to open the two quarterdeck ports," I said, mildly.

He actually had the impudence, or else so forgot himself in his wonder at such an incomprehensible order, as to repeat:

"Open the quarterdeck ports! What for, sir?"

"The only reason you need concern yourself about is because I tell you to do so. Have them open wide and fastened properly."

---

23. **Cochin-China:** another part of Indochina, now in Vietnam.

A. Motivation
For the first time, the captain seems to realize the danger involved in his helping Leggatt. The reader has to question seriously at this point the captain's motivation—can the desire to help someone with whom you identify and sympathize be enough to risk your career and even your life? Why hasn't the captain realized, or considered, the danger before? As readers, we must draw the conclusion that Leggatt is not only uncannily similar to the captain, but actually represents a part of the captain—his "dark self." For the captain, saving Leggatt is necessary to save his own character, although he does not realize this consciously. Accepting responsibility for his dark self is crucial to his maturation as a person. (See the note on symbolism above.)

A. Setting

? What are the details of the night setting, and what mood or atmosphere do they evoke? ("Breeze was loaded with dew," "night . . . sparkled darkly," "opaque, lightless patches shifting slowly," "one more distant and shadowily imposing by the great space of sky it eclipsed"— an atmosphere of foreboding)

B. Theme

? How would you describe the leave-taking of the captain and Leggatt? (Tender, poignant, as close friends or brothers)

He reddened and went off, but I believe made some jeering remark to the carpenter as to the sensible practice of ventilating a ship's quarterdeck. I know he popped into the mate's cabin to impart the fact to him because the whiskers came on deck, as it were by chance, and stole glances at me from below—for signs of lunacy or drunkenness, I suppose.

A little before supper, feeling more restless than ever, I rejoined, for a moment, my second self. And to find him sitting so quietly was surprising, like something against nature, inhuman.

I developed my plan in a hurried whisper.

"I shall stand in as close as I dare and then put her round. I shall presently find means to smuggle you out of here into the sail locker, which communicates with the lobby. But there is an opening, a sort of square for hauling the sails out, which gives straight on the quarterdeck and which is never closed in fine weather, so as to give air to the sails. When the ship's way is deadened in stays and all the hands are aft at the main braces you shall have a clear road to slip out and get overboard through the open quarterdeck port. I've had them both fastened up. Use a rope's end to lower yourself into the water so as to avoid a splash— you know. It could be heard and cause some beastly complication."

He kept silent for a while, then whispered, "I understand."

"I won't be there to see you go," I began with an effort. "The rest . . . I only hope I have understood, too."

"You have. From first to last," and for the first time there seemed to be a faltering, something strained in his whisper. He caught hold of my arm, but the ringing of the supper bell made me start. He didn't, though; he only released his grip.

After supper I didn't come below again till well past eight o'clock. The faint, steady breeze was loaded with dew; and the wet, darkened sails held all there was of propelling power in it. The night, clear and starry, sparkled darkly, and the opaque, lightless patches shifting slowly against the low stars were the drifting islets. On the port bow there was a big one more distant and shadowily imposing by the great space of sky it eclipsed.

On opening the door I had a back view of my very own self looking at a chart. He had come out of the recess and was standing near the table.

"Quite dark enough," I whispered.

He stepped back and leaned against my bed with a level, quiet glance. I sat on the couch. We had nothing to say to each other. Over our heads the officer of the watch moved here and there. Then I heard him move quickly. I knew what that meant. He was making for the companion; and presently his voice was outside my door.

"We are drawing in pretty fast, sir. Land looks rather close."

"Very well," I answered. "I am coming on deck directly."

I waited till he was gone out of the cuddy, then rose. My double moved too. The time had come to exchange our last whispers, for neither of us was ever to hear each other's natural voice.

"Look here!" I opened a drawer and took out three sovereigns. "Take this, anyhow. I've got six and I'd give you the lot, only I must keep a little money to buy some fruit and vegetables for the crew from native boats as we go through Sunda Straits."

He shook his head.

"Take it," I urged him, whispering desperately. "No one can tell what—"

He smiled and slapped meaningly the only pocket of the sleeping jacket. It was not safe, certainly. But I produced a large old silk handkerchief of mine, and tying the three pieces of gold in a corner, pressed it on him. He was touched, I suppose, because he took it at last and tied it quickly round his waist under the jacket, on his bare skin.

Our eyes met; several seconds elapsed, till, our glances still mingled, I extended my hand and turned the lamp out. Then I passed through the cuddy, leaving the door of my room wide open. . . . "Steward!"

He was still lingering in the pantry in the greatness of his zeal, giving a rub-up to a plated cruet stand the last thing before going to bed. Being careful not to wake up the mate, whose room was opposite, I spoke in an undertone.

He looked round anxiously. "Sir!"

"Can you get me a little hot water from the galley?"

"I am afraid, sir, the galley fire's been out for some time now."

"Go and see."

He fled up the stairs.

"Now," I whispered, loudly, into the saloon— too loudly, perhaps, but I was afraid I couldn't make a sound. He was by my side in an instant— the double captain slipped past the stairs—through

Comment from a Critic
You might have students discuss a point that critic C. B. Cox describes as "the crux of the narrative": "Why does the captain sail his ship so near to the black hill of Koh-ring? The obvious reply is that he wishes to give Leggatt every chance to swim safely ashore; but Leggatt has proved himself an excellent swimmer, and so there is no necessity for the ship to shave the land so dangerously close. The captain admits that his heart was in his mouth, and under any other circumstances he would not have held on a moment longer. The crew are convinced they are doomed. The plain fact is that for moral or psychological reasons the captain endangers his ship and the lives of his men unnecessarily, and they are only saved by the lucky accident that the floppy hat, dropped in his escape by Leggatt, serves as a marker in the water. Is this irresponsible piece of daring a sign of maturity, of his competence to assume the role of the captain of the ship? It could be said he behaves like a madman. Why?"

A. Climax
By taking the ship so close to shore, the captain is risking grounding and destroying her. He is pushing himself, the crew, and the ship to the limit. This is the test that was alluded to earlier. The captain is risking death in an ultimate test of his fitness to command a ship.

the tiny dark passage . . . a sliding door. We were in the sail locker, scrambling on our knees over the sails. A sudden thought struck me. I saw myself wandering barefooted, bareheaded, the sun beating on my dark poll. I snatched off my floppy hat and tried hurriedly in the dark to ram it on my other self. He dodged and fended off silently. I wonder what he thought had come to me before he understood and suddenly desisted. Our hands met gropingly, lingered united in a steady, motionless clasp for a second. . . . No word was breathed by either of us when they separated.

I was standing quietly by the pantry door when the steward returned.

"Sorry, sir. Kettle barely warm. Shall I light the spirit lamp?"

"Never mind."

I came out on deck slowly. It was now a matter of conscience to shave the land as close as possible—for now he must go overboard whenever the ship was put in stays. Must! There could be no going back for him. After a moment I walked over to leeward[24] and my heart flew into my mouth at the nearness of the land on the bow. Under any other circumstances I would not have held on a minute longer. The second mate had followed me anxiously.

I looked on till I felt I could command my voice.

"She will weather," I said then in a quiet tone.

"Are you going to try that, sir?" he stammered out incredulously.

I took no notice of him and raised my tone just enough to be heard by the helmsman.

"Keep her good full."

"Good full, sir."

The wind fanned my cheek, the sails slept, the world was silent. The strain of watching the dark loom of the land grow bigger and denser was too much for me. I had shut my eyes—because the ship must go closer. She must! The stillness was intolerable. Were we standing still?

When I opened my eyes the second view started my heart with a thump. The black southern hill of Koh-ring seemed to hang right over the ship like a towering fragment of the everlasting night. On that enormous mass of blackness there was not a gleam to be seen, not a sound to be heard.

It was gliding irresistibly toward us and yet seemed already within reach of the hand. I saw the vague figures of the watch grouped in the waist, gazing in awed silence.

"Are you going on, sir?" inquired an unsteady voice at my elbow.

I ignored it. I had to go on.

"Keep her full. Don't check her way. That won't do now," I said warningly.

"I can't see the sails very well," the helmsman answered me, in strange, quavering tones.

Was she close enough? Already she was, I won't say in the shadow of the land, but in the very blackness of it, already swallowed up as it were, gone too close to be recalled, gone from me altogether.

"Give the mate a call," I said to the young man who stood at my elbow as still as death. "And turn all hands up."

My tone had a borrowed loudness reverberated from the height of the land. Several voices cried out together: "We are all on deck, sir."

Then stillness again, with the great shadow gliding closer, towering higher, without a light, without a sound. Such a hush had fallen on the ship that she might have been a bark[25] of the dead floating in slowly under the very gate of Erebus.[26]

"My God! Where are we?"

It was the mate moaning at my elbow. He was thunderstruck, and as it were deprived of the moral support of his whiskers. He clapped his hands and absolutely cried out, "Lost!"

"Be quiet," I said sternly.

He lowered his tone, but I saw the shadowy gesture of his despair. "What are we doing here?"

"Looking for the land wind."

He made as if to tear his hair, and addressed me recklessly.

"She will never get out. You have done it, sir. I knew it'd end in something like this. She will never weather, and you are too close now to stay. She'll drift ashore before she's round. O my God!"

I caught his arm as he was raising it to batter his poor devoted head, and shook it violently.

"She's ashore already," he wailed, trying to tear himself away.

24. **leeward** (lōo′ərd): the side of the ship facing away from the wind.
25. **bark:** boat.
26. **Erebus** (er′ə·bəs): according to Greek mythology, the dark place under the earth, through which the dead passed before entering Hades.

READING CHECK TEST

1. The young captain is commanding his ship on a journey off the coast of South America. (F)
2. He and his crew have worked together for eighteen months. (F)
3. The young captain is unsure of his ability to command a ship. (T)
4. When he reached the side of the ship, Leggatt was unnerved and unable to speak to the captain. (F)
5. The captain felt a mysterious bond with the swimmer. (T)
6. The crew finds the captain's behavior unusual and doubts his ability. (T)
7. The second mate is the only member of the crew who trusts the captain. (F)
8. Leggatt wishes to stay on board until the ship returns to its home port. (F)
9. The crew catches Leggatt as he slips off the ship into the water. (F)
10. A hat saves the ship from doom. (T)

A. Resolution

? How did the hat that the captain had given to Leggatt turn out to be of benefit to himself? (It helped him to save his ship.) What does this suggest about the nature of their relationship? (It was a good one for both men).

B. Responding

? Do you think the encounter of the Captain and Leggatt was mutually beneficial or mutually destructive?

Critical Comment

Critic Edward W. Said wrote that Conrad "focused on brooding and graphic enigmas" and that "the significantly repeated patterns in [his] fiction are obsessive." Ask students to find examples in *The Secret Sharer* of a pattern or motif that is repeated so often as to be obsessive.

Closure

Ask students to discuss what the narrator learns about himself as a result of his encounter with his "double."

"Is she? . . . Keep good full there!"

"Good full, sir," cried the helmsman in a frightened, thin, childlike voice.

I hadn't let go the mate's arm and went on shaking it. "Ready about, do you hear? You go forward"—shake—"and stop there"—shake—"and hold your noise"—shake—"and see these head sheets properly overhauled"—shake, shake—shake.

And all the time I dared not look toward the land lest my heart should fail me. I released my grip at last and he ran forward as if fleeing for dear life.

I wondered what my double there in the sail locker thought of this commotion. He was able to hear everything—and perhaps he was able to understand why, on my conscience, it had to be thus close—no less. My first order "Hard alee!" re-echoed ominously under the towering shadow of Koh-ring as if I had shouted in a mountain gorge. And then I watched the land intently. In that smooth water and light wind it was impossible to feel the ship coming-to. No! I could not feel her. And my second self was making now ready to slip out and lower himself overboard. Perhaps he was gone already . . . ?

The great black mass brooding over our very mastheads began to pivot away from the ship's side silently. And now I forgot the secret stranger ready to depart, and remembered only that I was a total stranger to the ship. I did not know her. Would she do it? How was she to be handled?

I swung the mainyard and waited helplessly. She was perhaps stopped, and her very fate hung in the balance, with the black mass of Koh-ring like the gate of the everlasting night towering over her taffrail.[27] What would she do now? Had she way on her yet? I stepped to the side swiftly, and on the shadowy water I could see nothing except a faint phosphorescent flash revealing the glassy smoothness of the sleeping surface. It was impossible to tell—and I had not learned yet the feel of my ship. Was she moving? What I needed was something easily seen, a piece of paper, which I could throw overboard and watch. I had nothing on me. To run down for it I didn't dare. There was no time. All at once my strained, yearning stare distinguished a white object floating within

---

27. **taffrail:** the rail around the ship's stern.

---

a yard of the ship's side. White on the black water. A phosphorescent flash passed under it. What was that thing? . . . I recognized my own floppy hat. It must have fallen off his head . . . and he didn't bother. Now I had what I wanted—the saving mark for my eyes. But I hardly thought of my other self, now gone from the ship, to be hidden forever from all friendly faces, to be a fugitive and a vagabond on the earth, with no brand of the curse on his sane forehead to stay a slaying hand . . . too proud to explain.

And I watched the hat—the expression of my sudden pity for his mere flesh. It had been meant to save his homeless head from the dangers of the sun. And now—behold—it was saving the ship, by serving me for a mark to help out the ignorance of my strangeness. Ha! It was drifting forward, warning me just in time that the ship had gathered sternway.

"Shift the helm," I said in a low voice to the seaman standing still like a statue.

The man's eyes glistened wildly in the binnacle light as he jumped round to the other side and spun round the wheel.

I walked to the break of the poop. On the overshadowed deck all hands stood by the forebraces waiting for my order. The stars ahead seemed to be gliding from right to left. And all was so still in the world that I heard the quiet remark "She's round," passed in a tone of intense relief between two seamen.

"Let go and haul."

The foreyards ran round with a great noise, amidst cheery cries. And now the frightful whiskers made themselves heard giving various orders. Already the ship was drawing ahead. And I was alone with her. Nothing! no one in the world should stand now between us, throwing a shadow on the way of silent knowledge and mute affection, the perfect communion of a seaman with his first command.

Walking to the taffrail, I was in time to make out, on the very edge of a darkness thrown by a towering black mass like the very gateway of Erebus—yes, I was in time to catch an evanescent glimpse of my white hat left behind to mark the spot where the secret sharer of my cabin and of my thoughts, as though he were my second self, had lowered himself into the water to take his punishment: a free man, a proud swimmer striking out for a new destiny.

1. The captain feels like a stranger to them. He suspects that the chief mate and the second mate are privately chuckling over his inexperience.

The captain feels diffident and tentative. At the same time, he feels excited and looks forward to this new stage of his career.

2. Leggatt served as a chief mate on the *Sephora*. In the middle of a terrific storm, the crewman, who had been habitually impudent, started an altercation with him. Leggatt hit the insubordinate sailor, who then rushed to attack him. In the struggle, Leggatt throttled the man to death. The captain then dismissed him and confined him to quarters, saying that Leggatt would have to be surrendered to the authorities. Leggatt, however, slipped overboard.

3. Archbold is a stickler for the law, and he is also afraid of a blot on his own career.

4. He becomes stealthy, secretive, and apprehensive.

The inexplicable oddities and eccentricities of the captain's behavior cause the crew to be suspicious of him. Some of them probably think he has been drinking.

5. Student answers will vary. In general, the captain is motivated by compassion and a feeling of kinship with Leggatt. He thinks that both he and Leggatt are outsiders and is struck by their remarkable physical resemblance. Also he admires Leggatt's courage.

Again, student answers will vary. The captain gains the satisfaction of helping Leggatt. Since Leggatt is repeatedly described as the narrator's "double," the captain has also, in some sense, helped himself. The end of the story, featuring Leggatt's hat, also implies that the captain has achieved a newfound confidence in his handling of his ship. Students may suggest, however, that with the disappearance of Leggatt into the unknown, the captain has symbolically lost a part of himself as well: his innocence, perhaps.

(Answers continue on next page.)

A Comment on the Novel
The Marginal Hero

One way to approach *The Secret Sharer* is to note the recurrence of a key word: *stranger.* This word, in several forms (*strange, strangeness*), occurs about fourteen times in this story. It is repeated several times at the beginning of the story in the narrator's description of himself: "my position was that of the only stranger on board . . . what I felt most was my being a stranger to the ship; and if all the truth must be told, I was somewhat of a stranger to myself." Being a stranger to the ship and a stranger to himself are related. He is young, untried in both his crew's eyes and his own. This voyage will be a test not only of his skills but of his self-image: "I wondered," he tells us, "how far I should turn out faithful to that ideal conception of one's own personality every man sets up for himself secretly." The narrator needs to demonstrate his abilities to his crew, and he needs to come to a degree of self-knowledge as well.

Leggatt, when he arrives, seems to complicate both of these tasks. The narrator, in choosing to hide him, must engage in increasingly suspicious and unprofessional behavior, and he realizes that the crew is becoming distrustful. Leggatt challenges his self-image, too. "He was not a bit like me, really," the narrator says, yet he is struck, over and over, by the resemblances. They are the "two strangers in the ship." Leggatt, though, is a stranger in a profound sense, for Leggatt has killed a man.

Leggatt has killed a man in morally ambiguous circumstances. Is he guilty or not? Who is to judge? The sea sometimes puts people in situations where simple moral actions are impossible, and the storm the *Sephora* endured was one of them. The captain failed to act at all, if Leggatt is to be believed. "He never gave it" [the order to set sail], he says. "He stood there with me on the break of the poop . . . and whimpered about our last hope. . . . To hear one's skipper go on like that in such weather was enough to drive any fellow out of his mind. It worked me up into a sort of desperation." Faced with the possibility of saving twenty-four people by killing one, Leggatt acted. Who can understand or judge his actions? Not the captain, who, faced with the same situation, flinched. Not those ashore, either, who have never faced such a situation. "But you don't see me coming back to explain such things to an old fellow in a wig and twelve respectable tradesmen, do you?" Leggatt asks the narrator. "What can they know whether I am guilty or not—or of *what* I am guilty, either? That's my affair."

The truth to be found in extreme situations, at the margins of life, so to speak, cannot easily be apprehended or understood by most people. The psychological dangers are too great. Who wants to face the murderer within? This is why Captain Archbold is so eager to dispose of Leggatt to the land authorities. To identify with Leggatt, to understand him, would be to admit that there is a dark, violent side of his own makeup. That would threaten the captain's cozy and orderly life, and this he is not willing to do. As a result, though, the captain remains a limited man. The narrator does identify with Leggatt, however, despite the very real psychological dangers. During the interview with Archbold, he identifies with Leggatt more closely than before, but the process frightens him. "If he [Archbold] had only known how afraid I was of his putting my feeling of identity with the other to the test!" he exclaims. At one point, he begins to doubt whether Leggatt really exists at all, and comes close to madness: "I think I had come creeping quietly as near insanity as any man who has not actually gone over the border."

To face the truth, then, you have to sail close to the edge, which the narrator does, both psychologically and in his actions. If *stranger* is the word most used in the beginning of the story, *understand* in its variations is the one most used at the end. "You have understood thoroughly. Didn't you?" Leggatt asks. "I may say truly that I understood," the narrator tells us in reply, and Leggatt responds, "As long as I know that you understand. . . . It's a great satisfaction to have got somebody to understand." And finally, when the narrator brings the ship in so close to the shore that he risks wrecking it, he tells us that Leggatt "was able to hear everything—and perhaps he was able to understand why, on my conscience, it had to be thus close—no less." The narrator, too, has a truth to find, for both himself and his ship, and this is something the secret sharer of his thoughts should understand. Such sympathy, such communication, is the reward for facing the dangers involved in seeing ourselves whole, moral ambiguities and all. For the narrator, one aspect of this is his complete understanding of his ship at the story's end: "no one in the world should stand now between us, throwing a shadow on the way of silent knowledge and mute affection, the perfect communion of a seaman with his first command."

For Joseph Conrad, as for other twentieth-century novelists, truth and significant action are often to be found at the margins of life. Heroes in modern fiction are apt not to be people who engage in traditionally heroic activities—fighting glorious wars, or going on dangerous adventures, for example—but people who face more complex but less obvious psychological dangers. The great voyages of twentieth-century fiction are to the interior, to, as Conrad put it, "The Heart of Darkness."

(Answers begin on previous page.)

6. There are numerous passages in the story that indicate that Leggatt is the captain's double. First, the two men are remarkably similar in physical appearance. The captain dresses Leggatt in a sleeping suit that is identical to his own. They occupy the same quarters, eat the same food, and sleep in the same bed. The captain says at one point that he felt "more dual than ever." The narrator refers to Leggatt several times as the "secret sharer" of his life, echoing the title of the story. Finally, the captain senses a kinship in their position vis-à-vis the crew as the "only two strangers on board." However, Leggatt is unlike the captain in that the captain is a figure of authority, whereas Leggatt is a fugitive. The captain's admiration for Leggatt's long swim implies that Leggatt may be athletically superior to the captain.

Students may suggest that, as a result of his experience with Leggatt, the captain has grown in maturity and achieved more profound understanding.

7. The story implies that the captain had to take the risk so that he could prove to himself that he was capable of sacrifice and of confronting danger.

Responding to the Novel

Analyzing the Novel

Identifying Facts

1. The captain (the "I" of this story) tells us that he "had been appointed to the command only a fortnight before." What is the captain's relationship with the rest of the crew, especially with the chief mate and the second mate? How does the captain feel about himself and his new career?
2. Outline the details of Leggatt's story. What, if any, are the extenuating circumstances of his crime?
3. Why is Archbold seeking Leggatt, when Leggatt really saved the ship?
4. How do the captain's thoughts and feelings toward his crew change after he has hidden Leggatt on board? How does the crew perceive the captain?

Interpreting Meanings

5. The captain risks his ship and his career to help Leggatt. What are his **motivations** for taking these risks? What does he gain in the end? Has he lost anything? Explain.
6. A meeting with one's **double** is a recurring motif in literature. What passages indicate that Leggatt is the captain's double? How is Leggatt like the captain, and how is he different? When a character meets his double, he usually gains a new perspective; the meeting often changes his life, for better or worse. How do these aspects of the "double" motif apply to *The Secret Sharer*?
7. Leggatt is an excellent swimmer, so there was no need for the ship to go so dangerously close to land. Why, then, do you think the captain sailed his ship so near to the black hill of Koh-ring?
8. One famous critic of Conrad, R. W. Stallman, writes that "everything in *The Secret Sharer* is charged with symbolic purpose." What **symbolic** significance can you find in the captain's floppy white hat? In Leggatt's sleeping suit? In the sea itself?
9. Locate in *The Secret Sharer* the several **allusions** to the Biblical story of Cain and Abel. Is the "brand of Cain" a punishment worse than death, or is it also a blessing? What do these allusions contribute to your understanding of Conrad's story?
10. In his letter to Richard Curle (see "Primary Sources," next page), Conrad complains that the classification of his stories as "sea yarns" causes readers to overlook the stories' true subject matter. He worries that Americans, especially, will fail to see past the nautical settings. *The Secret Sharer* is, of course, set on board a ship, yet it is not primarily about ships or the sea. How would you state the **theme** of *The Secret Sharer*? Did you find the theme easy to overlook, or do you think Conrad made it obvious?
11. From what **point of view** is *The Secret Sharer* told? How does this point of view affect the impact of the story? Does it have any limitations? Explain.
12. The first three paragraphs of this story have often been analyzed. How would you describe the **atmosphere** or **mood** created by these paragraphs? What details contribute to that mood?

Writing About the Novel

A Creative Response

1. **Extending the Story.** Imagine that you are Leggatt at the conclusion of *The Secret Sharer*. You have reached the Cambodian shore and have pushed inland where no European or English speaker has ever been before. Describe the kind of life you are leading. How does it compare with your former life as chief mate of a British merchant ship? What understanding would you now have of what it means to be Cain—that is, "to be a fugitive and a vagabond on the earth"? The narrator says that Leggatt "had lowered himself into the water to take his punishment." What are the implications of this punishment in his new life?
2. **Writing About a Secret Sharer.** American poet Delmore Schwartz wrote a poem called "The Heavy Bear Who Goes with Me," which is about a double who represents a dark aspect of the speaker's character. In a paragraph or more, describe some person's "secret sharer." Will this double represent something negative or positive in the character? Will you represent the double as a person, as Conrad did, or as an animal, as Schwartz did? (You might want to represent the double as a mirror image.)

A Critical Response

3. **Analyzing a Theme.** On one level, *The Secret Sharer* is about a physical adventure. On another level, it is about a psychological adventure—what one critic has termed a "journey within." In a brief essay, explain how *The Secret Sharer* is a psychological adventure, referring to details of the story to back up your interpretation. What discovery does this "traveler" make? What theme does the inner journey reveal?
4. **Analyzing a Character.** One expert on Conrad believes that Conrad's main characters go through a series of stages as they identify and deal with a crisis. First, they find themselves isolated from society or from people around them. Second, within this hostile

8. The hat is a symbol of pity and acceptance of our "dark self" and salvation.

The sleeping suit symbolizes the "double" motif, since it is identical to the captain's own.

The sea may symbolize danger and the unknown.

9. The first allusion to Cain and Abel occurs toward the end of section I of the story, when Leggatt explains to the captain why Archbold's wife would have been only too glad to have Leggatt off the ship. The second allusion occurs when Leggatt refers to the Biblical words about Cain, "driven off the face of the earth" (Genesis 4:12), and says that he wishes to be marooned at night. Students will differ in their reactions to the significance of the "brand of Cain" in the story. Conrad perhaps intends these references to be ambiguous.

10. Most students will agree that Conrad has deliberately conveyed the theme in an oblique fashion, perhaps in an effort to parallel the captain's gradual maturation. One statement of the theme might run as follows: It is only by confronting the danger of our dark side and of the unknown that we can achieve mature moral sense.

11. The novel is told from the first-person point of view of the captain.

The point of view adds vividness and immediacy to the story.

The limitations are that we cannot know for sure what Leggatt and the other characters are thinking and how they are reacting. The result is to reinforce the impression of Leggatt in the story as something of a "mystery" figure.

12. The mood might be described as exotic, mysterious, and disturbing.

Among the details students may cite are the following: the "incomprehensible" lines of fishing stakes, the barren islets, the setting sun, the description of the Paknam pagoda, the image of the "impassive earth" swallowing the tug, the immense stillness, the breathless silence, the sudden tide of darkness, and the "disturbing sounds" heard by the captain.

world, they recognize their situation. Finally, after learning something about themselves, they resolve their problem or yield to it. Using details of the story, write an essay showing the stages of isolation, recognition, and resolution that the narrator of *The Secret Sharer* goes through. Explain how he is transformed at the novel's end.

5. Analyzing Imagery. Conrad uses a wealth of rich descriptive detail. These details not only create a vivid and realistic picture, but also operate as **imagery** to reinforce the **themes** of the story. Using either the opening three paragraphs of the story or the closing eight paragraphs, write an essay explaining how the imagery reinforces the story's theme.

6. Interpreting the Ending. In a brief essay, explain your interpretation of the story's ending. In your essay, comment on this interpretation offered by a critic of Conrad. (Who is the "reflection in the mirror"?)

The meaning of the end is not so easy to figure out as some writers on Conrad have suggested. I feel that as Leggatt swims away into the darkness it is as if Conrad is saying farewell to some essential element in his artistic identity. The reflection in the mirror bears the soul away.

—C. B. Cox

Primary Sources

"I wish that all those ships of mine were given a rest"

Conrad wrote this letter to his friend Richard Curle, who had written an extended study of Conrad's works.

Oswalds
July 14th, 1923.

"My Dearest Dick,

"I am returning you the article with two corrections as to matters of fact and one of style.

"As it stands I can have nothing against it. As to my feelings that is a different matter; and I think that, looking at the intimate character of our friendship and trusting to the indulgence of your affection, I may disclose them to you without reserve.

"My point of view is that this is an opportunity, if not unique then not likely to occur again in my lifetime. I was in hopes that on a general survey it could also be made an opportunity for me to get freed from that infernal tale of ships and that obsession of my sea life, which has about as much bearing on my literary existence, on my quality as a writer, as the enumeration of drawing rooms which Thackeray frequented could have had on his gift as a great novelist. After all, I may have been a seaman, but I am a writer of prose. Indeed, the nature of my writing runs the risk of being obscured by the nature of my material. I admit it is natural; but only the appreciation of a special personal intelligence can counteract the superficial appreciation of the inferior intelligence of the mass of readers and critics. Even Doubleday was considerably disturbed by that characteristic as evidenced in press notices in America, where such headings as 'Spinner of sea yarns—master mariner—seaman writer,' and so forth, predominated. I must admit that the letterpress had less emphasis than the headings; but that was simply because they didn't know the facts. That the connection of my ships with my writing stands, with my concurrence I admit, recorded in your book is of course a fact. But that was biographical matter, not literary. And where it stands it can do no harm. Undue prominence has been given to it since, and yet you know yourself very well that in the body of my work barely one tenth is what may be called sea stuff, and even of that, the bulk, that is *Nigger* and *Mirror,* has a very special purpose which I emphasize myself in my Prefaces.

"Of course there are seamen in a good many of my books. That doesn't make them sea stories any more than the existence of de Barral in *Chance* (and he occupies there as much space as Captain Anthony) makes that novel a story about the financial world. I do wish that all those ships of mine were given a rest, but I am afraid that when the Americans get hold of them they will never, never, never get a rest. . . ."

1. Building on Prior Knowledge. Ask students to think back to their childhood. How did they feel about the rules and restraints put upon them by adults? Could they always see how these strictures were for their own good? Tell them that this is a story about a ten-year-old boy who is governed by a particularly restrictive and unloving relative.

2. Establishing a Purpose. Ask students to look for the ways in which the child tries to free himself from his guardian's domination. Does he succeed in the end? How?

3. Prereading Journal. **(Challenging)** Ask students if they can remember a game, person, or scene they made up when they were children. Have them write a description of what they imagined and explain why they might have imagined it.

(Less Challenging) Ask students to recall a children's story in which an animal comes to the aid of a child. Have them write a summary of the story.

Hector Hugh Munro (Saki) (1870–1916)

Hector Hugh Munro was born in Burma, the third child of a British army officer. When he was two, his mother died, and the three children were taken back to England to live with their paternal grandmother and their two aunts. There Munro was raised in a large country house, Broadgate Villa in Devonshire. There were servants, a governess, gardens, and access to the sea, but Munro's recollections of the time were of frequent illnesses and the nattering constraints of his aunts, who show up later in various unflattering guises in his stories.

Munro was happy at boarding school in spite of its discipline. He enjoyed writing in particular and was singled out for his fastidiousness and facility with language. Nevertheless, he was to look back on his boarding school days with growing skepticism about traditional preparatory schools and about the values of the British upper class they perpetuated.

When Munro was twenty-three, his father arranged for him to return to Burma and take a post with the military police. After three years of policing and a bout with malaria, Munro returned to England with a contempt for colonial bureaucracy and a determination to become a writer.

His first project, a history of Russia, was scorned by the academic establishment for a certain flippancy toward religion. He then abandoned scholarship for political satire, which he wrote under the penname Saki. (Saki was the bearer of wine, and hence of pleasure, in the Persian poem *The Rubáiyát of Omar Khayyám.*)

From 1902 until 1907, Munro covered the Balkans, Poland, and Russia as a foreign correspondent for the *Morning Post*. Then he turned to fiction and for the next seven years wrote and published a profusion of stories that were popular for their clever satire, wit, and occasional moments of horror.

With the outbreak of World War I in 1914, Munro enlisted as a private in the British Army, even though he was forty-four years old. For two years, he fought in the dismal and terrifying trenches of France. On November 14, 1916, on a dark winter morning, he was killed by a sniper after shouting to a friend, ''Put that bloody cigarette out!''

SUPPLEMENTARY SUPPORT MATERIALS
1. Vocabulary Activity Worksheet *(CCB)*
2. Review and Response Worksheet: Style *(CCB)*
3. Language Skills Worksheet: Clauses *(CCB)*
4. Selection Test *(CCB)*

DEVELOPING VOCABULARY
The following words from the story are tested in the Selection Test. (See also Vocabulary Activity Worksheet.)

effete	abode
foregoing	precept
to succumb	furtive
rampant	paean
irksome	waning

SREDNI VASHTAR

Munro chose a pseudonym with overtones of the ornate and elegant: One can imagine him offering his stories as delicacies to a refined readership, just as Saki the cupbearer offered refreshment to the sultan's guests in old Persia. The same ornate overtones mark Saki's writing style. As you read, notice the long, complex sentences, the elevated diction, and the formal tone. Which character in this little story of horror seems to share Saki's taste for the ornate?

A

Conradin was ten years old, and the doctor had pronounced his professional opinion that the boy would not live another five years. The doctor was silky and <u>effete</u>, and counted for little, but his opinion was endorsed by Mrs. De Ropp, who counted for nearly everything. Mrs. De Ropp was Conradin's cousin and guardian, and in his eyes she represented those three-fifths of the world that are necessary and disagreeable and real; the other two-fifths, in perpetual antagonism to the <u>foregoing</u>, were summed up in himself and his imagination. One of these days Conradin supposed he would <u>succumb</u> to the mastering pressure of wearisome necessary things—such as illnesses and coddling restrictions and drawn-out dullness. Without his imagination, which was <u>rampant</u> under the spur of loneliness, he would have succumbed long ago.

Mrs. De Ropp would never, in her honestest moments, have confessed to herself that she disliked Conradin, though she might have been dimly aware that thwarting him "for his good" was a duty which she did not find particularly <u>irksome</u>. Conradin hated her with a desperate sincerity which he was perfectly able to mask. Such few pleasures as he could contrive for himself gained an added relish from the likelihood that they would be displeasing to his guardian, and from the realm of his imagination she was locked out—an unclean thing, which should find no entrance.

In the dull, cheerless garden, overlooked by so many windows that were ready to open with a message not to do this or that, or a reminder that medicines were due, he found little attraction. The few fruit trees that it contained were set jealously apart from his plucking, as though they were rare specimens of their kind blooming in an arid waste; it would probably have been difficult to find a market-gardener who would have offered ten shillings for their entire yearly produce. In a forgotten corner, however, almost hidden behind a dismal shrubbery, was a disused toolshed of respectable proportions, and within its walls Conradin found a haven, something that took on the varying aspects of a playroom and a cathedral. He had peopled it with a legion of familiar phantoms, evoked partly from fragments of history and partly from his own brain, but it also boasted two inmates of flesh and blood. In one corner lived a ragged-plumaged Houdan hen,[1] on which the boy lavished an affection that had scarcely another outlet. Further back in the gloom stood a large hutch, divided into two compartments, one of which was fronted with close iron bars. This was the <u>abode</u> of a large polecat-ferret, which a friendly butcher boy had once smuggled, cage and all, into its present quarters, in exchange for a long-secreted hoard of small silver. Conradin was dreadfully afraid of the lithe, sharp-fanged beast, but it was his most treasured possession. Its very presence in the toolshed was a secret and fearful joy, to be kept scrupulously from the knowledge of the Woman, as he privately dubbed his cousin. And one day, out of Heaven knows what material, he spun the beast a wonderful name, and from that moment it grew into a god and a religion. The Woman indulged in religion once a week at a church nearby, and took Conradin with her, but to him the church service was an alien rite in the House of Rimmon.[2] Every Thursday, in the dim and musty silence of the toolshed, he worshiped with mystic and elab-

B

---

1. **Houdan hen:** a fairly common breed of black-and-white domestic fowl.
2. **House of Rimmon:** the temple of a Syrian (pagan) god mentioned in several books of the Old Testament.

A. Conflict
This passage summarizes the conflict at the center of the story. It is a battle between the forces of repression and respectability represented by Mrs. De Ropp and those of freedom, fun, and imagination represented by Conradin.
❓ In terms of the percentages given, who seems to have the advantage? (Mrs. De Ropp and the forces of respectability)

B. Noting Specific Details
In his imagination Conradin gave the ferret the attributes of a god.
❓ What kind of god did he imagine it to be? (Fearsome and awe-inspiring) What does his choice of the name Sredni Vashtar suggest? (A powerful, mysterious, and vengeful force)

A. Discussing
the Photograph
? Ask students if
this photo of an
outbuilding on a
farm resembles
what they imagine
the home of a
powerful oriental
god to look like.
When students say
no, point out that
the actual tool-
shed home of
Sredni Vashtar in
the story is proba-
bly as humble as
this one but that
Conradin's imagi-
nation transforms it
into the exotic
dwelling place of a
powerful god.

A

orate ceremonial before the wooden hutch where dwelt Sredni Vashtar,[3] the great ferret. Red flowers in their season and scarlet berries in the wintertime were offered at his shrine, for he was a god who laid some special stress on the fierce impatient side of things, as opposed to the Woman's religion, which, as far as Conradin could observe, went to great lengths in the contrary direction. And on great festivals powdered nutmeg was strewn in front of his hutch, an important feature of the offering being that the nutmeg had to be stolen. These festivals were of irregular occurrence, and were chiefly appointed to celebrate some passing event. On one occasion, when Mrs. De Ropp suffered from acute toothache for three days, Conradin kept up the festival during the entire three days, and almost succeeded in persuading himself that Sredni Vashtar was personally responsible for the toothache. If the malady had lasted for another day the supply of nutmeg would have given out.

The Houdan hen was never drawn into the cult of Sredni Vashtar. Conradin had long ago settled that she was an Anabaptist.[4] He did not pretend to have the remotest knowledge as to what an Anabaptist was, but he privately hoped that it was dashing and not very respectable. Mrs. De Ropp was the ground plan on which he based and detested all respectability.

After a while Conradin's absorption in the toolshed began to attract the notice of his guardian. "It is not good for him to be pottering down there in all weathers," she promptly decided, and at breakfast one morning she announced that the Houdan hen had been sold and taken away overnight. With her short-sighted eyes she peered at Conradin, waiting for an outbreak of rage and sorrow, which she was ready to rebuke with a flow of excellent precepts and reasoning. But Conradin said nothing: there was nothing to be said. Something perhaps in his white set face gave her a momentary qualm, for at tea that afternoon there was toast on the table, a delicacy which she usually banned on the ground that it was bad for him; also because the making of it "gave trouble," a deadly offense in the middle-class feminine eye.

"I thought you liked toast," she exclaimed,

with an injured air, observing that he did not touch it.

"Sometimes," said Conradin.

In the shed that evening there was an innovation in the worship of the hutch-god. Conradin had been wont to chant his praises, tonight he asked a boon.

"Do one thing for me, Sredni Vashtar."

The thing was not specified. As Sredni Vashtar was a god he must be supposed to know. And choking back a sob as he looked at that other empty corner, Conradin went back to the world he so hated.

And every night, in the welcome darkness of his bedroom, and every evening in the dusk of the toolshed, Conradin's bitter litany went up: "Do one thing for me, Sredni Vashtar."

Mrs. De Ropp noticed that the visits to the shed did not cease, and one day she made a further journey of inspection.

"What are you keeping in that locked hutch?" she asked. "I believe it's guinea pigs. I'll have them all cleared away."

Conradin shut his lips tight, but the Woman ransacked his bedroom till she found the carefully hidden key, and forthwith marched down to the shed to complete her discovery. It was a cold afternoon, and Conradin had been bidden to keep to the house. From the furthest window of the dining room the door of the shed could just be seen beyond the corner of the shrubbery, and there Conradin stationed himself. He saw the Woman enter, and then he imagined her opening the door of the sacred hutch and peering down with her short-sighted eyes into the thick straw bed where his god lay hidden. Perhaps she would prod at the straw in her clumsy impatience. And Conradin fervently breathed his prayer for the last time. But he knew as he prayed that he did not believe. He knew that the Woman would come out presently with that pursed smile he loathed so well on her face, and that in an hour or two the gardener would carry away his wonderful god, a god no longer, but a simple brown ferret in a hutch. And he knew that the Woman would triumph always as she triumphed now, and that he would grow ever more sickly under her pestering and domineering and superior wisdom, till one day nothing would matter much more with him, and the doctor would be proved right. And in the sting and misery of his defeat, he began to chant

---

3. **Sredni Vashtar:** a made-up name suggesting a Hindu god.
4. **Anabaptist:** a member of a radical religious reform movement of the sixteenth and seventeenth centuries.

A. Irony
Conradin's religion is an ironic version of conventional religion.
❓ What does he pray for? (The continuation of his cousin's toothache.) How is this opposed to the conventional view of the purpose of prayer? (Usually people pray for good to come to others and to themselves.)

B. Character
❓ What was Mrs. De Ropp's true motive for taking things away from Conradin? (She wanted to be in control of him.) Was she really interested in what was good for him? (No)

C. Plot
❓ What do you think Conradin is praying for right here? (The death of his cousin) Do you think he will get what he wants? (No, because the animal is in a cage. Yes, because the boy has endowed it with great power.)

D. Theme
Here Conradin associates the victory of his aunt and all she stands for with death or with a life not worth living.

READING CHECK TEST

1. From whom did Conradin get the ferret?
a. the doctor b. his cousin
c. the butcher d. the gardener (c)
2. What kind of person was Conradin's cousin?
a. sentimental b. domineering
c. disreputable d. lazy (b)

3. What kind of person was Conradin?
a. imaginative b. obedient
c. cruel d. robust (a)
4. Where did the name Sredni Vashtar come from?
a. It was the name of an ancient Egyptian king.
b. It was a name made up by the boy

to sound like a Hindu god.
c. It was the name of an animal totem.
d. It was the name of a rare breed of Asian ferret. (b)
5. What did Conradin want from Sredni Vashtar?
a. revenge b. companionship
c. gifts d. sympathy (a)

CLOSURE
Conradin tried to cope with a painful situation by exercising his imagination. He fantasized the death of his insensitive guardian. Ask students to discuss whether or not he had any other means to improve his situation.

A. Conflict and Resolution
To Conradin's surprise the ferret emerges from the hut, not his cousin.
❓ How does he describe the ferret in this passage? (As fierce, calm, and triumphant) What has apparently happened to Mrs. De Ropp? (She has been killed by the ferret-god.)

B. Responding
❓ Were you surprised by the ending? Why? (Yes, because fantasies rarely become reality. No, because the story has been building to this end.) Whom did you wish to emerge victorious? (The boy)

loudly and defiantly the hymn of his threatened idol:

> Sredni Vashtar went forth,
> His thoughts were red thoughts and his teeth were white.
> His enemies called for peace, but he brought them death.
> Sredni Vashtar the Beautiful.

And then of a sudden he stopped his chanting and drew closer to the windowpane. The door of the shed still stood ajar as it had been left, and the minutes were slipping by. They were long minutes, but they slipped by nevertheless. He watched the starlings running and flying in little parties across the lawn; he counted them over and over again, with one eye always on that swinging door. A sour-faced maid came in to lay the table for tea, and still Conradin stood and waited and watched. Hope had crept by inches into his heart, and now a look of triumph began to blaze in his eyes that had only known the wistful patience of defeat. Under his breath, with a furtive exultation, he began once again the paean of victory and devastation. And presently his eyes were rewarded: out through that doorway came a long, low, yellow-and-brown beast, with eyes a-blink at the waning daylight, and dark wet stains around

the fur of jaws and throat. Conradin dropped on his knees. The great polecat-ferret made its way down to a small brook at the foot of the garden, drank for a moment, then crossed a little plank bridge and was lost to sight in the bushes. Such was the passing of Sredni Vashtar.

"Tea is ready," said the sour-faced maid; "where is the mistress?"

"She went down to the shed some time ago," said Conradin.

And while the maid went to summon her mistress to tea, Conradin fished a toasting-fork out of the sideboard drawer and proceeded to toast himself a piece of bread. And during the toasting of it and the buttering of it with much butter and the slow enjoyment of eating it, Conradin listened to the noises and silences which fell in quick spasms beyond the dining room door. The loud foolish screaming of the maid, the answering chorus of wondering ejaculations from the kitchen region, the scuttering footsteps and hurried embassies for outside help, and then, after a lull, the scared sobbings and the shuffling tread of those who bore a heavy burden into the house.

"Whoever will break it to the poor child? I couldn't for the life of me!" exclaimed a shrill voice. And while they debated the matter among themselves, Conradin made himself another piece of toast.

Responding to the Story

Analyzing the Story

Identifying Facts

1. Praying to a wild animal seems an act born of desperation. What desperate circumstances in Conradin's life have led up to this behavior?
2. What prompts Mrs. De Ropp to offer Conradin toast at teatime? What is her excuse for not making toast more often?
3. What does Conradin do after he sees Sredni Vashtar emerge from the doorway and vanish into the undergrowth?

Interpreting Meanings

4. Saki develops his characters by using both **direct characterization,** in which he states directly what the characters are like, and **indirect characterization,** in which he lets the characters' actions speak for themselves. Find examples in the story of both kinds of character description. How would you summarize the aunt's character?
5. What would you say is Saki's message, or **theme,** in telling this strange story?
6. Munro's sister (see "Primary Sources," next page) says that people detect an element of cruelty in his

1. Conradin is lonely and alienated from his aunt, who regiments his life. He has also been told by the doctor that it would be surprising if he lived for five years. The imaginative, sensitive child has no friends or playmates.
2. She feels guilty about having told Conradin that the hen has been taken away and sold. She thinks that toast is bad for Conradin; she also thinks that making toast "makes trouble."
3. He makes himself a piece of toast and enjoys eating it.

Interpreting Meanings
4. Students should be able to find copious examples of both methods of characterization.

The aunt is cruel and insensitive.
5. One statement of the theme might be this: You corner a person or animal at your peril. See also the critic's note about the conflict between imagination and reality.
6. Many students may agree with this comment, suggesting that the aunt's behavior is cruel and that the boy's "prayer" for her death is also cruel.

Saki's cruelty is really directed, however, at the insensitivity of the aunt.
7. The aunt is "religious," yet her cruelty is counter to all religious tenets. Conradin's sincere "religion" is rewarded.
8. The conclusion of the story, in which we learn of the aunt's death and Conradin's ignorance of it, is an example of dramatic irony.
9. Student answers will vary. Ask the students to explain the reasons for the questions on their lists.

A. Discussing Primary Sources
This is an account by the author's sister in which she describes the actual aunts who took care of her and her brother when they were children. Ask students to discuss how closely the description of the aunt in "Sredni Vashtar" resembles the aunt described in Ethel Munro's last paragraph.

---

stories. Do you see any cruelty in this story? If so, at whom is the cruelty directed, and what is its nature?

7. **Situational irony** refers to a twist of events—a contradiction between what is expected and what happens. Why is there such irony in Conradin's worship of an animal in a locked cage? What other situational ironies exist in "Sredni Vashtar"?

8. Find in the story an example of **dramatic irony,** in which an event reveals something to the readers that a character does not realize. Explain how your example shows dramatic irony.

9. An expert on modern British literature once said that the mark of an excellent critic is knowing how to ask the right questions. List the questions that you would ask readers of this story.

Writing About the Story

A Creative Response

1. **Recasting the Story.** Rewrite a portion of "Sredni Vashtar" so that it reveals the theme of "the triumph of reality over imagination" (see the critical comment that follows). Rewrite either the beginning of the story (the first three paragraphs) or the end of the story (starting with Mrs. De Ropp's ransacking of Conradin's bedroom for the key to the hutch). Change elements of **characterization** and **plot** as necessary in order to express the new theme.

A Critical Response

2. **Responding to a Critical Comment.** Write a brief essay in which you respond to the main idea in this comment by a Saki critic. Support your responses with details from the story.

> . . . in this story what finally wins is not simply the boy, but the force of his imagination. In fact, almost all that we see of him is his imagination in conflict with the real world, just as all that we see of Mrs. De Ropp is her reality, reason, and respectability—the virtues of the real world—in conflict with Conradin's imagination. The forces, therefore, which are opposed in the central conflict are *imagination* and *reality,* "reality" being the literal and the commonplace.
>
> —Robert Stanton

Primary Sources
Aunt Tom and Aunt Augusta

Munro's sister wrote this about their aunts:

"So much has been said, in reviews of Hector's books, about the cruelty element in them, an element which, personally, I cannot see, that an account of the aunts' characters may perhaps throw some light on the environment of his early years.

"Our grandmother, a gentle, dignified old lady, was entirely overruled by her turbulent daughters, who hated each other with a ferocity and intensity worthy of a bigger cause. How it was they were not consumed by the strength of their feelings I don't know. . . .

"Aunt Tom was the most extraordinary woman I have ever known—perhaps a reincarnation of Catherine of Russia. What she meant to know or do, that she did. She had no scruples, never saw when she was hurting people's feelings, was possessed of boundless energy, and had not a day's real illness until she was seventy-six.

"Her religious convictions would fit into any religion ever invented. She took us regularly to Pilton Church on Sunday mornings. For a long time I was struck by her familiarity with the Psalms, which she apparently repeated without looking at her book, but one day I discovered she was merely murmuring, without saying a word at all, and had put on her long-distance glasses in order to take good stock of the congregation and its clothes. A walk back after church with various neighbors provided material for a dramatic account to Granny (not that she was interested) of the doings of the neighborhood. Whatever Aunt Tom did was dramatic, and whatever story she repeated, she embroidered. No use to try to get to the end before she intended you should. Without any sense of humor whatever, she was the funniest storyteller I've ever met. She was a colossal humbug, and never knew it.

"The other aunt, Augusta, is the one who, more or less, is depicted in 'Sredni Vashtar.' She was the autocrat of Broadgate—a woman of ungovernable temper, of fierce likes and dislikes, imperious, a moral coward, possessing no brains worth speaking of, and a primitive disposition. Naturally the last person who should have been in charge of children."

—Ethel M. Munro

A

James Joyce
(1882–1941)

James Joyce's masterpiece, *Ulysses* (1922), has had greater effect upon the fiction of the twentieth century than any other work of our times. Yet while he lived, Joyce was known largely as the author of an unintelligible and scandalous book.

It is in retrospect that readers have seen Joyce's genius so clearly—his mastery of language, his originality and wit, and his innovations in narrative method. *Ulysses,* based on Homer's great epic of the ancient world, describes the events of a single day, June 16, 1904, in Dublin, the city where Joyce grew up. "Ulysses" in Joyce's book is a Jewish Dubliner named Leopold Bloom. The rounds Bloom makes in Dublin on June 16 correspond to the stages of Ulysses's journey in the ancient Mediterranean world, as various monsters and temptations keep him from getting home to Ithaca. Just as Homer's epic story interpreted the world of the ancient Greeks, so does Joyce's epic mirror and interpret for us our own lives in the twentieth century.

Joyce was born in Rathgar, a Dublin suburb, at a time of great strife in Ireland over independence from Britain. At the time, many people in Ireland had rallied behind a gifted nationalist leader named Charles Stewart Parnell. Joyce's father, John, was a loyal Parnell follower and was rewarded with a post of tax collector, which brought him a comfortable income. However, the elder Joyce was also careless with money, a lover of pubs and good times, a shirker of duty, and often a brute of a husband, so that James grew up in a family of ten children amidst quarrels and forever-sinking fortunes. Despite his father's chaotic effect on his family, James loved him and used him in almost all of his writings. John Joyce, heavily disguised, is supposed to have been the model for the uncle in "Araby."

As a child of six-and-a-half, James was sent to Clongowes, a boarding school run by the Jesuits, and Ireland's best. James flourished there but, for lack of tuition, he had to drop out when he was nine years old. For two years, James went to a school run by the Christian Brothers on

James Joyce by J. E. Blanche (1935). Oil.

North Richmond Street (see the setting of "Araby"), but he hated his time there and used to overlook those years in talking about his childhood. When he was eleven, the Jesuits arranged for him to enter a Jesuit day-school, Belvedere College. James did well there, although by the time he graduated he had lost his Catholic faith.

At University College, Dublin, Joyce read adventurously and began to write verse and some short prose pieces he called "epiphanies," or sudden spiritual revelations. He polished his style and published an occasional article, but he tended to follow his father's pleasure-loving ways. When these combined with his preoccupation with writing, his studies suffered and he barely passed his examinations.

Realizing the need to support himself, Joyce decided to become a doctor, but he was discouraged by the medical lectures he attended in Dublin. He went off to Paris hoping to enroll in medical school there, but he lacked both the registration fees and the qualifications.

Nevertheless, Joyce found he could exist frugally in France by giving English lessons and by writing book reviews. He found his pleasure in the St. Genevieve library, reading Gustave Flaubert, Thomas Aquinas, and Aristotle.

In the spring of 1903, Joyce returned home to Dublin to see his mother, who died of cancer that summer. Joyce stayed on in Dublin, trying his hand at teaching while living with Oliver St. John Gogarty in the Martello Tower, on the coast near Dublin, a site that has now become Ireland's famous Joyce museum.

Here, in the tower, he began to write a novel he called *Stephen Hero* in which he described his own chaotic youth. He wrote some short stories as well, also about Dublin, some of which were published a decade later in the volume he called *Dubliners* (1914).

Joyce's brother Stanislaus described him as:

[having] extraordinary moral courage—courage so great that I have hoped that he will one day become the Rousseau of Ireland. . . . His great passion is a fiérce scorn of what he calls the "rabblement"—a tiger-like, insatiable hatred. He has a distinguished appearance and bearing and many graces, a musical singing and especially speaking voice (a tenor), a good undeveloped talent in music, and witty conversation. He has a distressing habit of saying quietly to those with whom he is familiar the most shocking things about himself and others and, moreover, of selecting the most shocking times for saying them, not because they are shocking merely, but because they are true. . . . But few people will love him, I think, in spite of his graces and his genius and whosoever exchanges kindnesses with him is likely to get the worst of the bargain.

In June of 1904, he met a Galway girl named Nora Barnacle and fell in love with her. Nora worked at Finn's hotel in Dublin and was neither a great beauty nor an intellectual. She admired his sweet voice and once said, "Jim should have stuck to music instead of bothering with writing." The date of their second meeting and the beginning of Joyce's courtship was June 16, 1904, which was later to become Bloomsday, the date on which *Ulysses* takes place. This day is now celebrated annually by Joyce lovers throughout the literary world.

When the debts and complexities of Joyce's life mounted, he decided to travel. He persuaded Nora to leave Ireland and her family, and, although Joyce was penniless, the couple set out for Europe. Joyce was never to live in Ireland again.

After much difficulty, Joyce found a job at a Berlitz language school near Trieste, a largely Italian city, then part of the Austro-Hungarian empire. During these years in Trieste, Joyce wrote stories and continued to work on the *Stephen Hero* novel. Explaining his love of neologisms, or new words, he felt that although English was the best of languages, it restrained him:

For example, take the word *battlefield*. A battlefield is a field where the battle is raging. When the battle is over and the field is covered with blood, it is no longer a battlefield but a *bloodfield*.

While Nora had little understanding of his work and was miserably homesick for Ireland, Joyce admired her and loved her for her trust in him. It was here in Trieste that their two children, Giorgio and Anna Lucia, were born.

Joyce's book of poems *Chamber Music* was published in 1907, but it brought him no royalties. The completed short-story collection *Dubliners* failed to find a publisher, and disillusioned with *Stephen Hero,* Joyce decided to rewrite the novel as *A Portrait of the Artist as a Young Man* (1916).

When Italy entered World War I in 1915, the Joyce family was able to escape into Switzerland. Here, in Zurich, Joyce gave English lessons, and while he worked on the early chapters of *Ulysses* his luck began to turn.

The luck had much to do with Joyce's discovery by the influential American poet Ezra Pound, who soon determined to find an audience for him. It was Pound who persuaded the editor of the British magazine *The Egoist* to serialize *A Portrait of the Artist as a Young Man,* whereupon the Irish publisher who had procrastinated over *Dubliners* for three years decided to publish the book.

Joyce also began to receive substantial sums of money—a grant from the Royal Literary Fund and sizable gifts from anonymous well-wishers. But as his financial troubles eased, his physical problems increased. His eyes were a particular

PREPARATION

1. BUILDING ON PRIOR KNOWLEDGE. Ask students if they can recall from their younger days a "crush" they had on someone they hardly knew. Was their romantic idealization of the person ever challenged?

2. ESTABLISHING A PURPOSE. As students read the story, ask them to distinguish the actual details of the narrator's surroundings from those things that feed his imagination and seem to lift him out of his environment.

3. PREREADING JOURNAL. (Challenging) Ask students to recall a time when they were really looking forward to an event or an outing, which, when it actually happened, was not at all what they had expected. Ask them to write a journal entry describing how they felt when their expectations were disappointed.

(Less Challenging) Ask students to recall an event or a person who did not live up to their expectations. Ask them to write what they expected in one column and what they actually experienced in the opposite column.

agony to him. Between 1917 and 1930 he endured twenty-five operations for glaucoma and cataracts. Sometimes he was totally blind. Yet he kept up his spirits and some of the most comical passages of *Ulysses* were written when he was in greatest pain.

The completed *Ulysses* did not find its way easily into print. Indeed the printers in England found the book so scandalous they were unwilling to set it in type. When the American *Little Review* began to serialize it in 1918, The New York Society for the Prevention of Vice went to court to suppress its further publication.

Joyce despaired of ever seeing the book published in either England or the U.S. But in Paris, Sylvia Beach, the American owner of a bookstore called Shakespeare & Co., agreed to put out an edition of one thousand copies and so became the book's original publisher. Beach published *Ulysses* on February 2, 1922, Joyce's fortieth birthday.

The reviews, many of them favorable, added to the scandal. They were admiring of Joyce's genius, learning, and originality, but sensitive to the book's obscenity and, for most readers, its difficulty. One critic called it "the foulest book that has ever appeared in print." Another hailed it as "the biggest event in the history of the English novel since *Jude*" (Thomas Hardy's novel *Jude the Obscure*).

But *Ulysses* was banned from sale in both Britain and the United States. Copies of the French edition were seized and destroyed by customs officers of both nations. Copies smuggled into the United States were passed from hand to hand until they fell apart.

Meanwhile, in spite of frightful eye pain and intermittent blindness, Joyce began to work on a new novel about a Dublin barkeep, Earwicker, his wife, and three children. This was to become *Finnegans Wake* (1939) and would take sixteen years to write.

Then, in 1933, the American publisher Bennett Cerf, encouraged by the venturesome lawyer Morris Ernst, sought a test case for *Ulysses*. In the most famous of all literary court judgments, Judge John Woolsey decided that *Ulysses* was "a sincere and honest book":

. . . whilst in many places the effect of *Ulysses* on the reader undoubtedly is somewhat emetic, nowhere does it tend to be an aphrodisiac. *Ulysses* may therefore be admitted to the United States.

—Judge John Woolsey

Cerf's Random House published *Ulysses* in February of 1934 and in two months sold thirty-three thousand copies. A British edition soon followed and the book's fame spread rapidly throughout the world.

Joyce procrastinated for years over *Finnegans Wake*. Even his admirers found the early chapters, with their merging of dreams and reality and their extraordinary language, impenetrable. Although he finished it in 1932, it was not published until 1939 and then to inconclusive reviews. Some critics took it as a bad joke, others as madness, and Joyce, who considered it his masterpiece, grew morose over the dismal response.

The Joyces had been living in Paris but with the fall of France in World War II they returned to Zurich. The move was made partly out of concern for their daughter, Lucia, who had become hopelessly ill with schizophrenia. The anguished parents hoped she might benefit from psychiatric treatment in Switzerland.

Joyce himself was also ill. His eye troubles and disappointment over the fate of *Finnegans Wake* were complicated by a duodenal ulcer. He died on January 13, 1941, a month short of his fifty-ninth birthday.

The final passage from *A Portrait of the Artist as a Young Man* is often cited as embodying Joyce's hope for his art:

April 26. Mother is putting my new second-hand clothes in order. She prays now, she says, that I may learn in my own life and away from home and friends what the heart is and what it feels. Amen. So be it. Welcome, O life! I go to encounter for the millionth time the reality of experience and to forge in the smithy of my soul the uncreated conscience of my race.

April 27. Old father, old artificer, stand me now and ever in good stead.

SUPPLEMENTARY SUPPORT MATERIALS
1. Vocabulary Activity Worksheet (*CCB*)
2. Review and Response Worksheet: Connotations (*CCB*)
3. Language Skills Worksheets: Pronoun-Antecedent Agreement; Appositives and Appositive Phrases (*CCB*)
4. Selection Test (*CCB*)
5. Audiocassette recording

DEVELOPING VOCABULARY
The following words from the story are tested in the Selection Test. (See also Vocabulary Activity Worksheet.)

imperturbable	to chafe
to diverge	garrulous
litanies	salver
chalice	to deride
to impinge	

ARABY

On May 14–19, 1894, a bazaar called "Araby" came to Dublin. The name refers to Arabia, regarded as a mysterious, exotic place, very different from the dark, all-too-real streets of Dublin. The bazaar was held to raise funds for charity. The house in this story is one which Joyce and his family actually lived in. The Christian Brothers' school was at the end of the blind (or dead-end) street. When the Joyce children were moved to this musty, dark house, they missed the open fields and woods of their old home. Notice how much of this famous story is about loss.

A. Humanities Connection: Writing About the Fine Art
Dame Laura Knight (1877–1970) was a well-known English painter in the 1920's, 1930's, and 1940's. She was particularly attracted to circus, ballet, and gypsy subjects. She and her painter husband, Harold Knight, lived in Cornwall from 1908 to 1918, the location of *Penzance Fair*. After World War II, she was sent to Nuremberg as the official British painter. She is noted for her straightforward presentation of the details of daily life.
? Tell students that this painting depicts a country fair in Cornwall. Have them list the types of people they see and what they appear to be experiencing at the fair. Fairs, carnivals, circuses, bazaars of the type Joyce describes in "Araby"—all have been used by writers and artists to symbolize an ironic world of distorted romance.

Penzance Fair by Dame Laura Knight (1917). Oil.

Richard Green Galleries, London.

A. **Setting**
The fact that North Richmond Street is a blind or dead-end street mirrors the restricted lives of its inhabitants who have little hope of escaping its confines.

B. **Imagery**
❓ What images link the boy's feeling for Mangan's sister with religious devotion? ("Chalice," "strange prayers and praises," and "confused adoration")

A

N orth Richmond Street, being blind,[1] was a quiet street except at the hour when the Christian Brothers' School set the boys free. An uninhabited house of two stories stood at the blind end, detached from its neighbors in a square ground. The other houses of the street, conscious of decent lives within them, gazed at one another with brown imperturbable faces.

The former tenant of our house, a priest, had died in the back drawing room. Air, musty from having been long enclosed, hung in all the rooms, and the waste room behind the kitchen was littered with old useless papers. Among these I found a few paper-covered books, the pages of which were curled and damp: *The Abbot,* by Walter Scott, *The Devout Communicant,* and *The Memoirs of Vidocq.*[2] I liked the last best because its leaves were yellow. The wild garden behind the house contained a central apple tree and a few straggling bushes under one of which I found the late tenant's rusty bicycle pump. He had been a very charitable priest; in his will he had left all his money to institutions and the furniture of his house to his sister.

When the short days of winter came dusk fell before we had well eaten our dinners. When we met in the street the houses had grown somber. The space of sky above us was the color of ever-changing violet and toward it the lamps of the street lifted their feeble lanterns. The cold air stung us and we played till our bodies glowed. Our shouts echoed in the silent street. The career of our play brought us through the dark muddy lanes behind the houses where we ran the gauntlet of the rough tribes from the cottages, to the back doors of the dark dripping gardens where odors arose from the ashpits, to the dark odorous stables where a coachman smoothed and combed the horse or shook music from the buckled harness. When we returned to the street light from the kitchen windows had filled the areas. If my uncle was seen turning the corner we hid in the shadow until we had seen him safely housed. Or if Mangan's sister came out on the doorstep to call her

brother in to his tea we watched her from our shadow peer up and down the street. We waited to see whether she would remain or go in and, if she remained, we left our shadow and walked up to Mangan's steps resignedly. She was waiting for us, her figure defined by the light from the half-opened door. Her brother always teased her before he obeyed and I stood by the railings looking at her. Her dress swung as she moved her body and the soft rope of her hair tossed from side to side.

Every morning I lay on the floor in the front parlor watching her door. The blind was pulled down to within an inch of the sash so that I could not be seen. When she came out on the doorstep my heart leaped. I ran to the hall, seized my books and followed her. I kept her brown figure always in my eye and, when we came near the point at which our ways diverged, I quickened my pace and passed her. This happened morning after morning. I had never spoken to her, except for a few casual words, and yet her name was like a summons to all my foolish blood.

Her image accompanied me even in places the most hostile to romance. On Saturday evenings when my aunt went marketing I had to go to carry some of the parcels. We walked through the flaring streets, jostled by drunken men and bargaining women, amid the curses of laborers, the shrill litanies of shopboys who stood on guard by the barrels of pigs' cheeks, the nasal chanting of street singers, who sang a *come-all-you* about O'Donovan Rossa,[3] or a ballad about the troubles in our native land. These noises converged in a single sensation of life for me: I imagined that I bore my chalice safely through a throng of foes. Her name sprang to my lips at moments in strange prayers and praises which I myself did not understand. My eyes were often full of tears (I could not tell why) and at times a flood from my heart seemed to pour itself out into my bosom. I thought little of the future. I did not know whether I would ever speak to her or not or, if I spoke to her, how I could tell her of my confused adoration. But my

B

---

1. **blind:** dead-end.
2. ***The Abbott . . . Vidocq:*** a historical romance, a religious manual, and the memoirs (mostly fictional) of a criminal who became a detective.

3. ***come-all-you . . . Rossa:*** A *come-all-you* (kum·al′yə) is an Irish ballad that usually opens with the words "Come all you [young lovers, rebels, etc.]." O'Donovan Rossa was Jeremiah O'Donovan from Ross Carberry in County Cork. He was active in Ireland's struggle against British rule in the mid-nineteenth century.

Literature and Language: Varying Sentences

Joyce, of course, is the great stylist of the twentieth century. As a class or group exercise, you might analyze some passages from "Araby" to see how Joyce has constructed his famous sentences. This page offers possibilities in the passages beginning "One evening I went" and "What innumerable follies." Before

you start your analysis, have students review the discussion of the sentence in **Grammar, Usage, and Mechanics: A Reference Guide.** Here are some possible activities:

1. Describe the structure of each sentence in the passage (simple, compound, complex, compound-complex).
2. Which sentences open with a word or phrase other than the subject?

3. Is there a mixture of long and short sentences? What is the effect of the short sentences?
4. Does Joyce use any parallel structures to lend a cadence to his story? Assign groups to rewrite the passages, using different sentence structures. Read the rewritten passages aloud for class evaluation.

body was like a harp and her words and gestures were like fingers running upon the wires.

One evening I went into the back drawing room in which the priest had died. It was a dark rainy evening and there was no sound in the house. Through one of the broken panes I heard the rain impinge upon the earth, the fine incessant needles of water playing in the sodden beds. Some distant lamp or lighted window gleamed below me. I was thankful that I could see so little. All my senses seemed to desire to veil themselves and, feeling that I was about to slip from them, I pressed the palms of my hands together until they trembled, murmuring: "*O love! O love!*" many times.

At last she spoke to me. When she addressed the first words to me I was so confused that I did not know what to answer. She asked me was I going to *Araby*. I forgot whether I answered yes or no. It would be a splendid bazaar, she said she would love to go.

"And why can't you?" I asked.

While she spoke she turned a silver bracelet round and round her wrist. She could not go, she said, because there would be a retreat that week in her convent.[4] Her brother and two other boys were fighting for their caps and I was alone at the railings. She held one of the spikes, bowing her head toward me. The light from the lamp opposite our door caught the white curve of her neck, lit up her hair that rested there and, falling, lit up the hand upon the railing. It fell over one side of her dress and caught the white border of a petticoat, just visible as she stood at ease.

"It's well for you,"[5] she said.

"If I go," I said, "I will bring you something."

What innumerable follies laid waste my waking and sleeping thoughts after that evening! I wished to annihilate the tedious intervening days. I chafed against the work of school. At night in my bedroom and by day in the classroom her image came between me and the page I strove to read. The syllables of the word *Araby* were called to me through the silence in which my soul luxuriated and cast an Eastern enchantment over me. I asked

for leave to go to the bazaar on Saturday night. My aunt was surprised and hoped it was not some Freemason[6] affair. I answered few questions in class. I watched my master's face pass from amiability to sternness; he hoped I was not beginning to idle. I could not call my wandering thoughts together. I had hardly any patience with the serious work of life which, now that it stood between me and my desire, seemed to me child's play, ugly monotonous child's play.

On Saturday morning I reminded my uncle that I wished to go to the bazaar in the evening. He was fussing at the hallstand, looking for the hatbrush, and answered me curtly:

"Yes, boy, I know."

As he was in the hall I could not go into the front parlor and lie at the window. I left the house in bad humor and walked slowly toward the school. The air was pitilessly raw and already my heart misgave me.

When I came home to dinner my uncle had not yet been home. Still it was early. I sat staring at the clock for some time and, when its ticking began to irritate me, I left the room. I mounted the staircase and gained the upper part of the house. The high cold empty gloomy rooms liberated me and I went from room to room singing. From the front window I saw my companions playing below in the street. Their cries reached me weakened and indistinct and, leaning my forehead against the cool glass, I looked over at the dark house where she lived. I may have stood there for an hour, seeing nothing but the brown-clad figure cast by my imagination, touched discreetly by the lamplight at the curved neck, at the hand upon the railings and at the border below the dress.

When I came downstairs again I found Mrs. Mercer sitting at the fire. She was an old garrulous woman, a pawnbroker's widow, who collected used stamps for some pious purpose. I had to endure the gossip of the tea table. The meal was prolonged beyond an hour and still my uncle did not come. Mrs. Mercer stood up to go: she was sorry she couldn't wait any longer, but it was after

---

4. **retreat . . . convent:** This means that the students and teachers at the convent school she attends will go on a retreat—that is, withdraw from worldly life for a week to devote time to prayer, meditation, and religious studies.
5. **"It's well for you":** "You're lucky" (usually said out of envy or bitterness).

6. **Freemason:** The Masons, a secret, exclusively Protestant society that often did charitable work, were often hostile to Catholics. Ironically, the aunt does not know that the bazaar is being held to help a Roman Catholic hospital.

A. Comparing Characters

❓ What similarities do you see in the way the narrator of this story and Conradin in "Sredni Vashtar" cope with the restrictions of their surroundings? (They fantasize in search of relief from intolerable situations.)

B. Theme

❓ What does the description of the lamplight falling on the woman remind you of? (It is a romantic, idealized depiction of a loved one.) What effect did it have on the boy? (The boy seems to be in a worshipful trance.)

READING CHECK TEST

1. The former tenant of the narrator's house was a ___priest___.
2. The narrator wanted to go to the bazaar to buy a gift for ___Mangan's sister___.
3. The word *Araby* suggested ___romance or enchantment___ to the young narrator.
4. Waiting for his ___uncle___ caused the boy to leave late for the bazaar.
5. At the end of the story, the boy rebukes himself for his ___vanity___.

CLOSURE

Assign three students to discuss the ways in which "Araby" is a story about an epiphany. (See the note on page 963.)

A. Plot

? What interpretation did the boy put on his uncle's behavior? (The uncle had too much to drink.)

B. Character

? How would you characterize the aunt and uncle's treatment of the boy? (Kind enough but inattentive and unimaginative)

C. Crisis

The boy arrives late to the bazaar; the stalls are closing; the wares seem ordinary.

? Why does the conversation between the young girl and boy seem to shatter any remnants of romance? (It is so trivial that not even the boy's imagination could fit it into a romantic setting.)

D. Ironic Resolution

? What emotions overwhelm the boy at the end? (Disillusionment, humiliation, futility) How do they differ from what he expected? (He expected to buy a gift that would make the girl value and esteem him.)

eight o'clock and she did not like to be out late, as the night air was bad for her. When she had gone I began to walk up and down the room, clenching my fists. My aunt said:

"I'm afraid you may put off your bazaar for this night of Our Lord."

A   At nine o'clock I heard my uncle's latchkey in the halldoor. I heard him talking to himself and heard the hallstand rocking when it had received the weight of his overcoat. I could interpret these signs. When he was midway through his dinner I asked him to give me the money to go to the bazaar. He had forgotten.

"The people are in bed and after their first sleep now," he said.

I did not smile. My aunt said to him energetically:

"Can't you give him the money and let him go? You've kept him late enough as it is."

B   My uncle said he was very sorry he had forgotten. He said he believed in the old saying: "All work and no play makes Jack a dull boy." He asked me where I was going and, when I had told him a second time he asked me did I know *The Arab's Farewell to His Steed*.[7] When I left the kitchen he was about to recite the opening lines of the piece to my aunt.

I held a florin[8] tightly in my hand as I strode down Buckingham Street toward the station. The sight of the streets thronged with buyers and glaring with gas recalled to me the purpose of my journey. I took my seat in a third-class carriage of a deserted train. After an intolerable delay the train moved out of the station slowly. It crept onward among ruinous houses and over the twinkling river. At Westland Row Station a crowd of people pressed to the carriage doors; but the porters moved them back, saying that it was a special train for the bazaar. I remained alone in the bare carriage. In a few minutes the train drew up beside an improvised wooden platform. I passed out on to the road and saw by the lighted dial of a clock that it was ten minutes to ten. In front of me was a large building which displayed the magical name.

I could not find any sixpenny entrance and, fearing that the bazaar would be closed, I passed in quickly through a turnstile, handing a shilling to a weary-looking man. I found myself in a big

hall girdled at half its height by a gallery. Nearly all the stalls were closed and the greater part of the hall was in darkness. I recognized a silence like that which pervades a church after a service. I walked into the center of the bazaar timidly. A few people were gathered about the stalls which were still open. Before a curtain, over which the words *Café Chantant*[9] were written in colored lamps, two men were counting money on a salver. I listened to the fall of the coins.

Remembering with difficulty why I had come I went over to one of the stalls and examined porcelain vases and flowered tea sets. At the door of the stall a young lady was talking and laughing with two young gentlemen. I remarked their English accents and listened vaguely to their conversation.

"O, I never said such a thing."

"O, but you did!"

"O, but I didn't!"

"Didn't she say that?"

"Yes. I heard her."

"O, there's a . . . fib!"

C

Observing me the young lady came over and asked me did I wish to buy anything. The tone of her voice was not encouraging; she seemed to have spoken to me out of a sense of duty. I looked humbly at the great jars that stood like eastern guards at either side of the dark entrance to the stall and murmured:

"No, thank you."

The young lady changed the position of one of the vases and went back to the two young men. They began to talk of the same subject. Once or twice the young lady glanced at me over her shoulder.

I lingered before her stall, though I knew my stay was useless, to make my interest in her wares seem the more real. Then I turned away slowly and walked down the middle of the bazaar. I allowed the two pennies to fall against the sixpence in my pocket. I heard a voice call from one end of the gallery that the light was out. The upper part of the hall was now completely dark.

D   Gazing up into the darkness I saw myself as a creature driven and derided by vanity; and my eyes burned with anguish and anger.

---

7. ***The Arab's . . . Steed:*** a popular sentimental poem by Caroline Norton (1808–1877).
8. **florin:** a coin worth two shillings, which at the time was the equivalent of fifty cents.

9. ***Café Chantant:*** a coffeehouse with musical entertainment.

1. The narrator is an adult who remembers an episode from his childhood. The narrator is older than the hero, indicated by the use of past tense.

2. Sensory adjectives include *quiet, square, brown, imperturbable, musty, old, curled, damp, yellow, wild, straggling, rusty, short, somber, feeble, cold,* *silent, dark, muddy, rough, dripping, odorous, buckled.* Colors include yellow, brown, and violet. Among the adjectives painting a gloomy scene are *brown, somber, rusty, musty, old, damp, wild, rough, muddy, silent, dark,* and *feeble.* Among the repeated adjectives are *silent* and *dark.*

3. The object of the "quest" is to buy a gift at the bazaar for Mangan's sister.

The obstacles include the uncle's lateness, Mrs. Mercer's visit, the train's delay, and the narrator's failure to find a sixpenny entrance to the bazaar.

4. The sentence is "The syllables of the word *Araby* were called to me through the silence in which my soul luxuriated and cast an Eastern enchantment over me" (page 961). He found the bazaar to be a great dark hall, with most of the stalls closed. Few people were there, and the hall was eerily silent.

Responding to the Story

Analyzing the Story

Identifying Facts

1. Who is the narrator of the story? Is the narrator the same age as the hero? Find evidence to support your answer.

2. The first two-and-a-half paragraphs describe the **setting** and establish the story's **atmosphere.** List the specific sensory adjectives in these paragraphs. (You should be able to find at least thirty, excluding such adjectives as *two, former, few, its, all.*) What colors are named? Which adjectives paint a gloomy scene? Which adjectives are repeated?

3. Describe the object of the hero's "quest." What are the obstacles that keep him from getting to the bazaar on time?

4. Cite the sentence that tells you what **connotations** the word *Araby* had for the hero. In your own words, describe in detail what he actually discovered the bazaar to be like.

Interpreting Meanings

5. Has the main character changed by the story's end? Use details from the story to support your answer.

6. How often have the hero and Mangan's sister spoken to each other? How would you describe the hero's relationship with her?

7. In what ways are the lives of these characters narrow or restricted?

8. How does the hero deal with intrusions of reality into his fantasy—at the market, for example, or at school?

9. What do you think is the purpose of including the dead priest in the story? List all the other religious references you can find in the story. What do you think they contribute to the significance of the boy's quest?

10. In what ways could the story be seen as presenting a conflict between romance and reality? How would you state the **theme** of the story? (In your statement of theme, use the word *Araby.*)

11. What do you see as the central **irony** in this story? How would you describe the writer's **tone**—his attitude toward the characters and what happens to them?

12. The story is set many years ago in Dublin. Does it relate to American life today? If it were to be set in America in the 1990's, would any details of **plot** have to change? Would the **characters** have to be different, or could they remain the same? Explain.

Writing About the Story

A Creative Response

1. **Changing the Setting.** Read the comment by Ezra Pound under "Primary Sources" (page 965). Then recall your answer to question 12, and choose a part of "Araby" to rewrite, changing the setting to your own town today. You might share your work with others in class and discuss whether, after trying to apply it, you agree with Pound's statement.

A Critical Response

2. **Analyzing the Story.** Joyce called the moments of revelation that occur in his stories "epiphanies," from a Greek word meaning "a showing forth, or revelation." Here is an excerpt from an early draft of Joyce's semi-autobiographical novel, in which his hero explains what he means by "epiphany":

> A young lady was standing on the steps of one of those brown brick houses which seem the very incarnation of Irish paralysis. A young gentleman was leaning on the rusty railings of the area. Stephen as he passed on his quest heard the following fragment of colloquy out of which he received an impression keen enough to afflict his sensitiveness very severely.
>
> The Young Lady—(drawling discreetly) . . . O, yes . . . I was . . . at the . . . cha . . . pel . . .
>
> The Young Gentleman—(inaudibly) . . . I . . . (again inaudibly) . . . I . . .
>
> The Young Lady—(softly) . . . O . . . but you're . . . ve . . . ry . . . wick . . . ed . . .
>
> This triviality made him think of collecting many such moments together in a book of epiphanies. By an epiphany he meant a sudden spiritual manifestation, whether in the vulgarity of speech or of gesture or in a memorable phase of the mind itself. He believed that it was for the man of letters to record these epiphanies with extreme care, seeing that they themselves are the most delicate and evanescent of moments.
>
> —from *Stephen Hero,*
> James Joyce

In an essay, use Joyce's definition of the epiphany, and show how "Araby" fits or does not fit the definition. At the end of your essay, tell whether you think such epiphanies occur in the fiction of other writers.

5. Most students will agree that the main character has changed, because he has recognized his romantic dreams as illusions. He feels a sense of burning shame for having indulged this "vanity."

6. The narrator has spoken only a few casual words to Mangan's sister. The relationship might be described as unrequited "puppy love."

7. Young people are restricted physically by their elders. Both young and old are restricted by the elders' insensitivity and lack of imagination.

8. At the market, the hero imagines that he bears his "chalice" safely through a throng of foes. At school, his thoughts wander, and he considers the classwork "child's play."

9. The dead priest accentuates the gloominess of the hero's house and emphasizes the burdens of religion. (*Answers continue on next page.*)

The boy imagines himself bearing a "chalice"; the narrator may not be able to go to the bazaar on "this night of our Lord"; Mangan's sister cannot go because of a retreat at her convent. Students will differ about what these references signify to the boy's quest. See also "Irony" below.

10. The boy's vision of Mangan's sister and his concept of *Araby* represent romance; his disappointment at the bazaar and his failure to buy the gift represent reality.

11. The central irony is that the boy's vision of a beautiful, exotic place *(Araby)* turns out to be reversed: The bazaar is quiet, dreary, and disappointing.

Student answers will vary. On the whole, the tone might be described as sympathetic and melancholy.

12. Young people are still experiencing restrictions, first love, and disillusion. Adults are still unimaginative and insensitive.

---

3. Analyzing a Character. At the end of the story, the narrator sees himself "driven and derided by vanity." One meaning of *vanity* is "the state of being empty, idle, valueless." Another meaning is "exaggerated self-love." Still another is "hunger for praise or admiration." In an essay, explain how all these definitions could apply to the hero.

4. Analyzing a Theme. In medieval legends a knight often rode off on a quest to prove himself worthy to his beloved, whom he idealized and worshiped from afar. How does the hero of "Araby" act like a knight on a quest? How is the story actually the distortion of a quest story? Give specific details to support your answers in one or two well-developed paragraphs.

5. Comparing Characters. The main characters in the stories presented in this section so far have all been isolated in one way or another, and all for different reasons. Choose one of these main characters (the narrator of *The Secret Sharer,* Conradin in "Sredni Vashtar," and the hero of "Araby") and in a three-paragraph essay explain the reasons for his isolation. Is the problem of the character **resolved** or made worse by the end of the story?

The Elements of Literature

IRONY

Here is the plot of a story: A boy develops a crush on a girl who lives across the street. The first time he has a chance to talk to her, he promises to bring her something back from a local bazaar. He goes to the bazaar, but gets there late. They are shutting down for the night, and the young man is unable to buy anything. The story ends with him standing in the darkened hall of the bazaar.

This is, of course, the plot of "Araby" boiled down to its skeleton, and in outline it is clear that it is not much of a story, at least not in any traditional sense. Traditionally, a story deals with some significant action, but "Araby" deals not with a significant action but with a thwarted action. The goal the protagonist works toward is not reached, and in the end he is revealed to himself as the very opposite of the person he had dreamed he was. "Araby" is in its form and in many of its details ironic, and as such it is representative of a good deal of modern fiction.

Irony is a difficult term that can refer to several related things. In Greek comedy, an *eiron* was a character who was not what he appeared to be, and irony in all its meanings refers to things that are not what they appear to be. The commonest form of irony, for example, is **verbal irony** in which you say the opposite of what you really mean. Asked how you feel after a really terrible day, you might say, "I feel just great." We'd know by the tone of your voice that you feel anything but great. **Sarcasm** is a very broad and more cutting form of this kind of irony.

Another form is **irony of situation,** in which things turn out differently from what is expected. In its simplest form this can involve a cartoon character laughing so hard at someone who has slipped on a banana peel that he walks into an open manhole. In its most sophisticated form, as in Sophocles's *Oedipus Rex,* it can involve a man who, in trying to escape a curse, brings it down upon himself.

Behind irony of situation is the disjunction, or disparity, between expectation and reality.

A third form of irony, **dramatic irony,** occurs when we as readers know something that a character does not know. In "Little Red Riding Hood," readers know that the wolf has dressed in the grandmother's clothes and climbed into her bed, but Little Red Riding Hood does not. This disjunction between what the readers know and what the character knows creates a sense of irony and a great deal of dramatic tension.

The principal disjunction in "Araby" is between the young man's romantic view of things and the way things really are. His love for Mangan's sister is obviously overblown. It is an adolescent reaction that he thinks is something more noble, and because of this his journey to the bazaar becomes an ironic quest. In pursuit of his love he seeks some exotic gift from Araby, just as a medieval knight might have gone on a quest for an exotic gift from the east for his lady. In fact, though, he has just taken a suburban train trip to a hospital bazaar and returned empty-handed. We might consider the source of the irony, then, to be the difference between an adolescent view of things and an adult view, and in part this is true. Moreover, the adult view of love is presented throughout the story by the narrator's aunt and uncle. Love—at least married love in Dublin—is not the ideal the boy imagines. It is, rather, a marriage to a man who comes home late and drunk.

But the ironies in "Araby" go further than this. Mangan's sister is directly associated with religion, and the narrator's worship of her is as much a religious act as an emotional one. Walking through the streets, he says, "I imagined that I bore my chalice safely through a throng of foes. Her name sprang to my lips at moments in strange prayers and praises which I myself did not understand." At one point, he goes into the back drawing room to think of her. "I pressed the palms of my hands together until they trembled," he says, "murmuring: '*O love! O love!*' many times." The last sentence of the story can be fully understood only in this light. "I saw myself as a creature driven and derided by vanity. . . ." "Vanity" here is not egotism, but the dark emptiness of Ecclesiastes in the Bible: "Vanity of vanities, saith the Preacher, vanity of vanities, all is vanity. What profit hath a man of all his labor which he taketh under the sun? . . . All is vanity and vexation of spirit." The narrator's disillusion is not just with love, but with the church and the spiritual values the church represents.

This insight enables us to understand a part of the story that appears extraneous, the mention of the former tenant of the house, a priest. The priest had died in the back drawing room (where the narrator goes to "pray" to love), leaving behind only musty air, some useless papers, and a bicycle pump. Just as the narrator's aunt and uncle present the reality of married love, the reality of the religious part of the narrator's quest is presented by the dead priest and his rusty bicycle pump.

For Joyce, modern Ireland—social, religious, and cultural Ireland—was in a state of decay. The disjunction between the ideals of Ireland's past and the reality of its current state was the source of his irony. While the ideals, and the language in which those ideals were expressed, remained, the reality was far different.

This ironic view of current reality is not Joyce's alone. It is a characteristic of many modern writers. One cause of this (less important to Joyce than to many other writers) was World War I, a horrible demonstration of the disjunction between a romantic ideal and a sordid reality. A whole generation of British youth went off to this war filled with ideals of honor, glory, and patriotism. "If I should die," wrote Rupert Brooke in a poem called "The Soldier," "think only this of me, / That there's some corner of a foreign field / That is forever England." But such ideals could not survive the reality of the drawn-out trench warfare that killed virtually an entire generation of young men (there were five million Allied deaths). Ernest Hemingway's narrator in *A Farewell to Arms* (a novel based on his own experience in the war) says that he was always embarrassed by the words *sacred, glorious,* and *sacrifice.* "I had seen nothing sacred, and the things that were glorious had no glory and the sacrifices were like the stockyards at Chicago if nothing was done with the meat except to bury it."

Irony had been a dominant mode of modern fiction and of modern world views even before World War I. Some poets and novelists, in fact, were looking at the world with new and critical eyes well before the turn of the century. Conrad's *Lord Jim* was published in 1900, A. E. Housman's dark *A Shropshire Lad* in 1896. And "Araby" was written nine years before the outbreak of the war. The war, tragically, provided graphic proof that the ideals of the past seldom lived up to the reality of the present.

A. **Responding to Primary Sources** In this critical excerpt, Ezra Pound praises Joyce for his realism, his lack of sentimentality, and his lean style. Ask students to read other stories from *The Dubliners* and to evaluate one of them in the light of Pound's comments. If students have seen the movie version of the last story in the collection, *The Dead,* they may want to concentrate on that story.

Primary Sources
Ezra Pound Reviews Dubliners

A
The following excerpt is from Ezra Pound's article "*Dubliners* and Mr. James Joyce," published in *The Egoist* on July 15, 1914.

"Mr. Joyce's merit, I will not say his chief merit but his most engaging merit, is that he carefully avoids telling you a lot that you don't want to know. He presents his people swiftly and vividly, he does not sentimentalize over them, he does not weave convolutions. He is a realist. He does not believe 'life' would be all right if we stopped vivisection or if we instituted a new sort of 'economics.' He gives the thing as it is. He is not bound by the tiresome convention that any part of life, to be interesting, must be shaped into the conventional form of a 'story.' Since de Maupassant we have had so many people trying to write 'stories' and so few people presenting life. Life for the most part does not happen in neat little diagrams and nothing is more tiresome than the continual pretense that it does.

"Mr. Joyce's 'Araby,' for instance, is much better than a 'story,' it is a vivid waiting.

"It is surprising that Mr. Joyce is Irish. One is so tired of the Irish or 'Celtic' imagination (or 'fantasy' as I think they now call it) flopping about. Mr. Joyce does not flop about. He defines. He is not an institution for the promotion of Irish peasant industries. He accepts an international standard of prose writing and lives up to it.

"He gives us Dublin as it presumably is. He does not descend to farce. He does not rely upon Dickensian caricature. He gives us things as they are, not only for Dublin, but for every city. Erase the local names and a few specifically local allusions, and a few historic events of the past, and substitute a few different local names, allusions, and events, and these stories could be retold of any town.

"That is to say, the author is quite capable of dealing with things about him, and dealing directly, yet these details do not engross him, he is capable of getting at the universal element beneath them."

—Ezra Pound

1. BUILDING ON PRIOR KNOWLEDGE. Ask students to try to recall how they felt or what they noticed around them on an important day in their childhood, such as the first day of school.

2. ESTABLISHING A PURPOSE. The voice in this excerpt is that of six-year-old Stephen. As you read, try to discover how the child thinks, what he is feeling, and what is important to him.

3. PREREADING JOURNAL. (Challenging) Ask students to write an account of a childhood memory from the point of view of the child.

(Less Challenging) Ask students to write down all they can remember of their first day of school. What did they see, hear, touch, and feel on that day?

FROM A PORTRAIT OF THE ARTIST AS A YOUNG MAN

In this brief excerpt from the beginning of Joyce's autobiographical novel *A Portrait of the Artist as a Young Man*, six-year-old Stephen Dedalus is in his first semester of boarding school at Ireland's prestigious Clongowes Wood College. Part of the appeal of this selection is Joyce's extraordinary use of the *stream-of-consciousness* technique. Notice how he recreates the flow of thoughts, feelings, and memories within a child's mind. As you read, be alert for evidence of young Stephen's fascination with language.

SUPPLEMENTARY SUPPORT MATERIALS
1. Vocabulary Activity Worksheet (CCB)
2. Review and Response Worksheet:
Stream of Consciousness (CCB)
3. Selection Test (CCB)

DEVELOPING VOCABULARY
The following word from the story is
tested in the Selection Test. (See also
Vocabulary Activity Worksheet.)
refectory

A

All the boys seemed to him very strange. They had all fathers and mothers and different clothes and voices. He longed to be at home and lay his head on his mother's lap. But he could not: and so he longed for the play and study and prayers to be over and to be in bed.

He drank another cup of hot tea and Fleming said:

—What's up? Have you a pain or what's up with you?

—I don't know, Stephen said.

—Sick in your breadbasket, Fleming said, because your face looks white. It will go away.

—O yes, Stephen said.

B

But he was not sick there. He thought that he was sick in his heart if you could be sick in that place. Fleming was very decent to ask him. He wanted to cry. He leaned his elbows on the table and shut and opened the flaps of his ears. Then he heard the noise of the refectory[1] every time he opened the flaps of his ears. It made a roar like a train at night. And when he closed the flaps the roar was shut off like a train going into a tunnel. That night at Dalkey the train had roared like that and then, when it went into the tunnel, the roar stopped. He closed his eyes and the train went on, roaring and then stopping; roaring again, stopping. It was nice to hear it roar and stop and then roar out of the tunnel again and then stop.

Then the higher line fellows began to come down along the matting in the middle of the refectory. Paddy Rath and Jimmy Magee and the Spaniard who was allowed to smoke cigars and the little Portuguese who wore the woolly cap. And then the lower line tables and the tables of the third line. And every single fellow had a different way of walking.

He sat in a corner of the playroom pretending to watch a game of dominos and once or twice he was able to hear for an instant the little song of the gas. The prefect was at the door with some boys and Simon Moonan was knotting his false sleeves. He was telling them something about Tullabeg.

Then he went away from the door and Wells came over to Stephen and said:

—Tell us, Dedalus, do you kiss your mother before you go to bed?

Stephen answered:

—I do.

Wells turned to the other fellows and said:

—O, I say, here's a fellow says he kisses his mother every night before he goes to bed.

The other fellows stopped their game and turned round, laughing. Stephen blushed under their eyes and said:

—I do not.

Wells said:

—O, I say, here's a fellow says he doesn't kiss his mother before he goes to bed.

C

They all laughed again. Stephen tried to laugh with them. He felt his whole body hot and confused in a moment. What was the right answer to the question? He had given two and still Wells laughed. But Wells must know the right answer for he was in third of grammar.[2] He tried to think of Wells's mother but he did not dare to raise his eyes to Wells's face. He did not like Wells's face. It was Wells who had shouldered him into the square ditch the day before because he would not swap his little snuffbox for Wells's seasoned hacking chestnut, the conqueror of forty.[3] It was a mean thing to do; all the fellows said it was. And how cold and slimy the water had been! And a fellow had once seen a big rat jump plop into the scum.

The cold slime of the ditch covered his whole body; and, when the bell rang for study and the lines filed out of the playrooms, he felt the cold air of the corridor and staircase inside his clothes. He still tried to think what was the right answer. Was it right to kiss his mother or wrong to kiss his mother? What did that mean, to kiss? You put your face up like that to say good night and then his mother put her face down. That was to kiss. His mother put her lips on his cheek; her lips were soft and they wetted his cheek; and they made a tiny little noise: kiss. Why did people do that with their two faces?

Sitting in the study hall he opened the lid of his desk and changed the number pasted up inside from seventy-seven to seventy-six. But the Christmas vacation was very far away: but one time it would come because the earth moved round always.

There was a picture of the earth on the first

---

1. **refectory:** dining room.

2. **third of grammar:** third form (grade) of grammar school.
3. The boys play with chestnuts strung on strings, knocking them together until one chestnut breaks.

A. Character

⟦?⟧ At first what is it about the other boys that is most striking to Stephen? (How different they all are from him and one another)

B. Stream of Consciousness

⟦?⟧ Stephen's senses are very attuned to what is going on around him. Which of his senses is engaged in this paragraph? (His hearing) Look for examples of other sensations that Stephen experiences in the rest of the selection.

C. Mood

⟦?⟧ Besides homesickness, what other unpleasant emotions is Stephen feeling? (Confusion, the pain of ridicule)

READING CHECK TEST
1. The excerpt is written from the point of view of a ten-year-old boy. (F)
2. The homesick boy is awed by his new school and schoolmates. (T)
3. The boy narrator is very observant and aware of what is going on around him. (T)
4. Fleming, a fellow student, writes serious poetry. (F)
5. The narrator shows signs of being a gifted student. (T)

CLOSURE
Ask students to read aloud passages of this story that show the use of a stream-of-consciousness technique.

A. Stream of Consciousness
Stephen is looking at a picture of the earth in a geography book. His own small nursery world is widening. He is becoming aware of the vastness of the outer world and of the existence of others. He is wondering how he fits into this larger world.

B. Responding
❓ What kind of person does the last paragraph suggest that Stephen will become? (A poet, a philosopher, a seeker of truth)

page of his geography: a big ball in the middle of clouds. Fleming had a box of crayons and one night during free study he had colored the earth green and the clouds maroon. That was like the two brushes in Dante's press,[4] the brush with the green velvet back for Parnell and the brush with the maroon velvet back for Michael Davitt.[5] But he had not told Fleming to color them those colors. Fleming had done it himself.

A ⌐ He opened the geography to study the lesson; but he could not learn the names of places in America. Still they were all different places that had those different names. They were all in different countries and the countries were in continents and the continents were in the world and the world was in the universe.

He turned to the flyleaf of the geography and read what he had written there: himself, his name, and where he was.

> *Stephen Dedalus*
> *Class of Elements*
> *Clongowes Wood College*
> *Sallins*
> *County Kildare*
> *Ireland*
> *Europe*
> *The World*
> *The Universe*

---

4. **Dante's press:** Dante's closet. Dante was the children's governess at home.
5. **Parnell . . . Davitt:** Irish political leaders; both fierce nationalists.

That was in his writing: and Fleming one night for a cod[6] had written on the opposite page:

> *Stephen Dedalus is my name,*
> *Ireland is my nation.*
> *Clongowes is my dwelling place*
> *And heaven my expectation.*

B ⌐ He read the verses backward but then they were not poetry. Then he read the flyleaf from the bottom to the top till he came to his own name. That was he: and he read down the page again. What was after the universe? Nothing. But was there anything round the universe to show where it stopped before the nothing place began? It could not be a wall but there could be a thin thin line there all round everything. It was very big to think about everything and everywhere. Only God could do that. He tried to think what a big thought that must be but he could think only of God. God was God's name just as his name was Stephen. *Dieu* was the French for God and that was God's name too; and when anyone prayed to God and said *Dieu* then God knew at once that it was a French person that was praying. But though there were different names for God in all the different languages in the world and God understood what all the people who prayed said in their different languages still God remained always the same God and God's real name was God.

---

6. **cod:** joke.

Responding to the Story

Analyzing the Story

Identifying Facts

1. What details show how Stephen is different from his classmates?
2. Why is Stephen "sick in his heart"?
3. What topics do Stephen's thoughts touch on?

Interpreting Meanings

4. How would you describe the **point of view** from which these experiences are narrated? How would the effect have been different if a different point of view had been used?
5. In what ways is identity one of the key topics in this selection?
6. Do you think that Joyce tries to show how the artist is present in young Stephen? Explain.
7. What examples of **free association** do you find in this recreation of the child's thoughts? Did you find the narration convincing?
8. How did you feel about Stephen as he's presented in this extract? How would you describe Joyce's **tone** toward his young hero?

1. Stephen is sensitive and easily picked on; one of the classmates shoves him into a ditch, and some of the boys tease him about kissing his mother every night.
2. He is lonely, homesick, and confused about the boys' remarks and behavior toward him.
3. Being bullied, kissing, the sounds in the refectory (dining room), the appearance and habits of the other boys, learning geography, poetry, the universe, and God.

Interpreting Meanings
4. A limited third-person point of view, focusing on Stephen.

A first-person point of view might make Stephen sound extremely self-conscious and self-analytical.
5. Again, student answers will vary. Most obviously, Stephen's identification of his name and location on the flyleaf of his geography book indicates a concern with his identity and his place in the world. He tries to understand the behavior of the other boys and their remarks toward him. He is painfully shy and anxious about fitting in at school.

6. Student answers will vary. His self-consciousness, sensory perceptions, and reflective personality might be indicators of the budding "artist" within Stephen.
7. His thoughts about a train, Wells shoving him into a ditch, his mother's kiss, God and the universe.
8. He is sympathetic and likely to suffer because he is more sensitive and thoughtful than his peers.

In general, the tone is gentle and affectionate.

A. About the Cartoon
F. Scott Fitzgerald met Joyce in 1928 and tried to exhibit his respect by offering to jump out the window in tribute. Joyce said, "That young man must be mad—I'm afraid he'll do himself some injury."

Writing About the Story

A Creative Response

1. **Using the Stream-of-Consciousness Technique.** You may have found something strangely familiar in Stephen's abstracted little mental voice, endlessly recording, recalling, associating, attempting to fit things together. Perhaps, as you read, you began to remember your own first days in school. Try writing a narrative recording the stream of consciousness of another six-year-old child—perhaps yourself. Include ideas and statements that interest and puzzle your character, and remember that the mind's connections are not always logical. As Joyce does, limit yourself as much as possible to a six-year-old's vocabulary and speech patterns. (For more information on stream of consciousness, see the material under "The Elements of Literature" below.)

A Critical Response

2. **Comparing and Contrasting Characters.** How is Stephen Dedalus like the hero of "Araby"? How is he different? Could the hero of "Araby" be an older version of Stephen Dedalus? In a brief essay, compare and contrast the two characters. Cite passages from both selections to support your main ideas.

The Elements of Literature

THE STREAM OF CONSCIOUSNESS

Language for Joyce had an important psychological and social element. For Joyce (following St. Thomas Aquinas, who was following Aristotle), there is nothing in the mind which does not enter through the senses. We come to know the world through our senses, and our thought processes follow a pattern of association based on what we experience through our senses. Here is young Stephen thinking about the castle on the school grounds, for example:

> It was nice and warm to see the lights in the castle. [*Sight*] It was like something in a book. Perhaps Leicester Abbey was like that. [*Association*]

This is followed by a series of associations of warmth and cold:

> It would be nice to lie on the hearthrug before the fire, leaning his head upon his hands. . . . He shivered as if he had cold slimy water next his skin. That was mean of Wells to shoulder him into the square ditch because he would not swop his little snuffbox for Wells's seasoned hacking chestnut, the conqueror of forty. How cold and slimy the water had been! A fellow had once seen a big rat jump into the scum. Mother was sitting at the fire with Dante waiting for Brigid to bring in the tea. She had her feet on the fender and her jewelly slippers were so hot and they had such a lovely warm smell!

> —from *A Portrait of the Artist as a Young Man*, James Joyce

Joyce and His Friends by F. Scott Fitzgerald (1928).

Here physical sensations and mental associations call each other up.

Joyce's use of point of view and his presentation of thoughts directed by association led to the best-known characteristic of his mature style, called **stream of consciousness.** This is an attempt to portray the thinking mind directly, without "organizing" the thoughts and without the intervention of the author. *A Portrait of the Artist as a Young Man* contains the beginnings of this—germs of stream of consciousness are present even in the paragraph above, as young Stephen's thoughts move from the cold water to the warmth of his mother's sitting room. The technique is most apparent, though, in Joyce's sec-

Oral Reading
Be sure to have
students read
some of these pas-
sages aloud. They
will be surprised at
how much more
sense the pas-
sages make when
they are spoken.

A. About the Photograph
You might tell stu-
dents that Joyce
had to have type-
setters in Paris set
type for *Ulysses,*
because typeset-
ters in Dublin and
London regarded
the book as
obscene and
would not touch it.
Consequently, this
most complicated
book was set by
people who did not
know the English
language. And
Joyce's handwrit-
ing, to make mat-
ters even worse,
was not always
legible (as you can
see by this page of
manuscript). Only
recently have
scholars returned
to Joyce's original
manuscript and
had the text of
Ulysses reset to
correct errors.

ond novel, *Ulysses.* Much of the action in this novel is presented through the thoughts of its protagonists. Here, for example, is one of the main characters, Leopold Bloom, standing in front of a tea shop reading the labels on cans of tea and thinking:

> So warm. His right hand once more slowly went over his brow and hair. Then he put on his hat again, relieved: and read again: choice blend, made of the finest Ceylon brands. The far east. Lovely spot it must be: the garden of the world, big lazy leaves to float about on, cactuses, flowery meads, snaky lianas they call them. Wonder is it like that . . . Where was the chap I saw in that picture somewhere? Ah yes, in the dead sea floating on his back, reading a book with a parasol open. Couldn't sink if you tried: so thick with salt. Because the weight of the water, no, the weight of the body in the water is equal to the weight of the what? Or is it the volume is equal to the weight? It's a law something like that. Vance in High School crack-ing his finger joints, teaching. The college curriculum. Cracking curriculum. What is weight really when you say the weight? Thirty-two feet per second per second. Law of falling bodies: per second per second. They all fall to the ground. The earth. It's the force of gravity of the earth is the weight.

—from *Ulysses,*
James Joyce

Bloom's mind moves by association from the tea label to the Far East to the picture he saw of a man who, he realizes, wasn't in the Far East but in the Near East, on the Dead Sea. This makes him think of the principles behind floating and falling, which reminds him of his school days and of a teacher who cracked his knuckles. Bloom's mind, as this passage demonstrates, contains a mix of personal memories, sensations, and half-remem-bered bits of information.

Joyce's last novel was *Finnegans Wake.* When it ap-peared, some critics claimed that it announced the death of the novel as a literary form. In the book, the author has completely disappeared, and the consciousness is that of a dreamer. The associations are much more rapid, and the stream of consciousness is often diverted by **puns,** or wordplays, often in a number of languages. Finnegan is a hod carrier (a bricklayer's helper) who falls from a ladder and dies on the first page of the novel. Here is the description of his death:

> The great fall of the offwall entailed at such short notice the pftjschute of Finnegan, erse solid man, that the humptyhillhead of humself promptly sends an un-quiring one well to the west in quest of his tumpty-tumtoes: and their upturnpikepointandplace is at the knock out in the park where oranges have been laid to rust upon the green since devlinsfirst loved livvy.

—from *Finnegans Wake,*
James Joyce

A

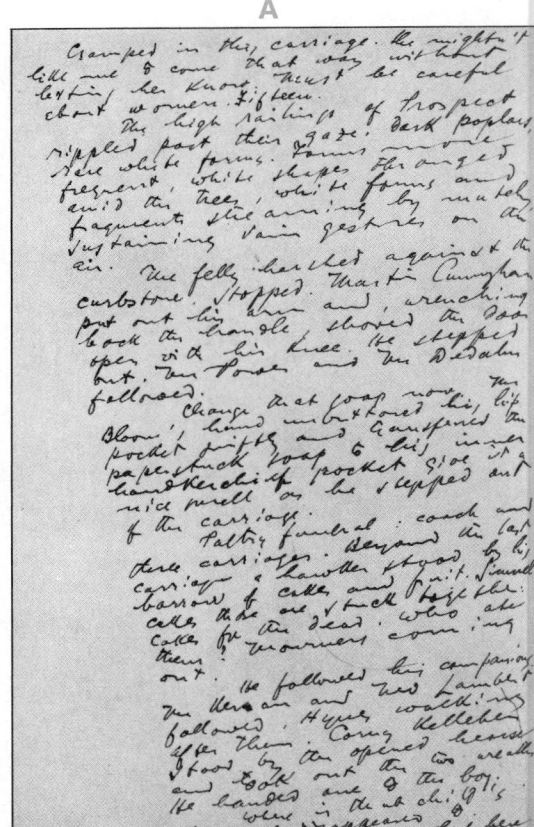

Manuscript of *Ulysses* in Joyce's handwriting.

Translated, this means that Finnegan has fallen ("pftjschute") in Phoenix Park, in Dublin. His head lies at the Hill of Howth, his feet far to the west, by the Castle of Knock, at a cemetery where the Orangemen (Northern invaders) have been buried. The similarities between Fin-negan's fall and Humpty Dumpty's (from "humptyhill-head" to "tumptytumtoes") are so strong that they affect even unrelated words, so that *himself* becomes *humself* (with the overtone of humming), *promptly* becomes *prumptly,* and *enquiring* becomes *unquiring.* Here lan-guage is at times virtually reinvented, in a manner that is intense and playful. Joyce claimed that most difficul-ties in understanding the language of *Finnegans Wake* disappear when the book is read aloud, and it is true that reading aloud makes much of the language play under-standable. But one needs a vast knowledge of history, myth, and several languages to appreciate all of the book's complexities.

D. H. Lawrence
(1885–1930)

David Herbert Lawrence was born in the English Midlands, the frailest of the five children of an earthy miner and his disappointed wife, Lydia, whose ambition was to keep her sons out of the mines and her daughters from household service. Bertie, as the family called David, grew up fulfilling his mother's wish. He was an able scholar, he became a schoolmaster, and he resented the ugliness the mine owners had made, not just of town and countryside but also of the hopes and relationships of the people.

In 1912, Lawrence decided to leave his teaching job and go to Germany. Hoping to secure a lectureship there, he called on his former French teacher, Ernest Weekley, before leaving England. In the course of the visit, he became enchanted with Weekley's young wife Frieda. Frieda was a German baroness from the von Richthofen family, a blond beauty with tartar eyes, a continental manner, and an exotic voice. She was also the mother of three children.

It took only a few weeks for Frieda Weekley to decide to say goodbye to her children and flee with Lawrence to Germany. For the next several years, Lawrence and Frieda traveled around Austria and Italy. There he finished his novel *Sons and Lovers* (1913) and began work on two others, *The Rainbow* (1915) and *Women in Love* (1920).

Reviews of *Sons and Lovers* were cautiously favorable, but already the moral controversy over Lawrence's work was heating up. Henry James did not like it. Rebecca West was enthusiastic. John Galsworthy found "the love parts too graphic."

While he was basking in the Italian sunshine, Lawrence began to see industrialized England as corrosive and oppressive. He embraced a belief in "blood knowledge," in putting one's animal self in balance with one's intellect. He saw the Victorian world he had known in England as an over-civilized and prudish world, and now he took aim at it.

Returning to England, Lawrence announced that "the source of all life and knowledge is in man and woman, and the source of all living is in the interchange and the meeting and mingling of these two."

In the year 1914, England entered World War I. Lawrence despised the war and resented the bullying and conformity it thrust upon his countrymen and women. Meanwhile, there was plenty of warring in Lawrence's personal life. The quarrels between Lawrence and Frieda were becoming legendary, and they seemed to live in a tide of curses and hurtling crockery.

A limited edition of *Women in Love* was published in 1920 to what was becoming the usual controversy. One critic in London judged it "a loathsome study of sex depravity leading youth to unspeakable disaster." Lawrence's friend John Middleton Murry described it as "five hundred pages of passionate vehemence, wave after wave of turgid, exasperated writing impelled toward some distant, invisible end."

Around this time, a wealthy American, Mabel Dodge Luhan, invited Lawrence to come to Taos, New Mexico. Luhan was passionately interested in art and Indian culture and her generosity was overwhelming. She had read

1. **BUILDING ON PRIOR KNOWLEDGE.** Ask students to think about the characteristics of the fairy tale or of stories that are frequently told to children. Remind them that in fairy tales problems are often solved by magic or by the intervention of supernatural forces, such as fairy godmothers or wizards. Have students contrast these solutions with how people in real life usually solve their problems.

2. **ESTABLISHING A PURPOSE.** As students read, ask them to watch for ways in which this story resembles a fairy tale and also for ways in which it departs from the traditional form of the fairy tale.

3. **PREREADING JOURNAL.** (Challenging) Ask students to think about the many different ways that children try to please their parents. Ask them to make a list of three of these and to give an example of each.

(Less Challenging) Ask students to recall a story or to make one up in which a child tries to please or help a parent and fails.

Lawrence's work and particularly liked *Sea and Sardinia,* in which he had written that to be a whole, humans must move forward to the "unknown, unworked lands where the salt has not lost its savor."

Lawrence accepted the invitation and he found New Mexico gorgeous: "The moment I saw the brilliant proud morning sun shine high up over the deserts of Santa Fe, something stood still in my soul." But he had his doubts about Americans, calling them "a host of people who must all have a sense of inferiority complex somewhere, striving to make good over everybody else."

In New York, what Lawrence called "the vice people" had been trying to suppress publication of *Women in Love,* and Lawrence rejoiced to learn that a magistrate had declared in court, "I do not find anything in these books which may be considered obscene." On the contrary, he found they made a "distinct contribution to the literature of the present day."

But Lawrence was growing inured to the fusillade of invective that was produced on each publication day. J. B. Priestley declared that most of Lawrence's admirers were adolescents, but Lawrence felt he had an audience now that was not made up of fools and cultists. Moreover, his income from his uncompromising books and articles permitted him to travel as he pleased. But then he lost his health; there was no longer any doubt that he had incurable tuberculosis.

Knowing he had only a few years remaining, Lawrence left America for the last time and found a house near Genoa, Italy. He now wrote continuously, producing *Lady Chatterley's Lover* (1928), the work by which he is best remembered. The novel draws upon his favorite theme—that of the sleeping beauty, the sexual awakening of a woman. It is the story of the mistress of an English manor house who falls in love with her husband's gamekeeper. Lawrence made the husband, Sir Clifford Chatterley, an industrialist and an intellectual (he despised both types), while the gamekeeper was his admired "natural" man. The novel was to become one of the most notable books of the twentieth century.

Lawrence expected *Lady Chatterley's Lover* to bring forth new waves of anger from the censors. Even the typist had refused to proceed with her work beyond Chapter Five. And reaction to an edited version of the book was as hostile as he had anticipated. One reviewer called it "a landmark of evil," finding it "the most evil outpouring that has ever besmirched the literature of our country. The sewers of French pornography would be dragged in vain to find a parallel in beastliness."

American customs officers seized the books as they arrived on the docks. In Parliament, the Home Secretary justified suppressing the book under the Obscene Publications Act, and it was banned in Britain. As a result of this tremendous publicity, a new, unabridged edition was prepared in Paris (1929) and all of Lawrence's work, including his poetry, was in demand in the bookstores.

Although Lawrence rejoiced in the new interest in his work, tuberculosis was sapping the last of his strength. "I intend to find God; I wish to realize my relation with him. The hatred which my books have aroused comes back to me and gets me here," he said, tapping his chest. He gave in at last to the doctors' advice and in early 1930 retreated to a sanitarium in southern France where he wrote every day until his life's end. On March 2, 1930, with Frieda at his bedside, Lawrence died. He is buried at Taos.

His friend Richard Aldington tried to explain Lawrence's sharp mockery of so many people and things: "It was created in him by the spirit of persecution and hostility which met nearly everything he wrote . . . but I am indeed glad that he never wasted time in replying to literary 'attacks,' that he made the only reply an artist need make—writing another fine book."

SUPPLEMENTARY SUPPORT MATERIALS
1. Vocabulary Activity Worksheet (*CCB*)
2. Review and Response Worksheet: Characterization (*CCB*)
3. Language Skills Worksheet: Infinitives and Infinitive Phrases (*CCB*)
4. Selection Test (*CCB*)

DEVELOPING VOCABULARY
The following words from the story are tested in the Selection Test. (See also Vocabulary Activity Worksheet.)

bonny	to parry
discreet	to reiterate
smirking	uncanny
pram	to writhe
brazening	to remonstrate

THE ROCKING-HORSE WINNER

Lawrence saw men and women as torn between the voice of their instinct (which he saw as natural and therefore good) and the voice of their "education" (which he saw as destructive). As you read this story—which is told like a modern fable—notice which voices permeate the house, and what their effects are.

There was a woman who was beautiful, who started with all the advantages, yet she had no luck. She married for love, and the love turned to dust. She had bonny children, yet she felt they had been thrust upon her, and she could not love them. They looked at her coldly, as if they were finding fault with her. And hurriedly she felt she must cover up some fault in herself. Yet what it was that she must cover up she never knew. Nevertheless, when her children were present, she always felt the center of her heart go hard. This troubled her, and in her manner she was all the more gentle and anxious for her children, as if she loved them very much. Only she herself knew that at the center of her heart was a hard little place that could not feel love, no, not for anybody. Everybody else said of her: "She is such a good mother. She adores her children." Only she herself, and her children themselves, knew it was not so. They read it in each other's eyes.

There were a boy and two little girls. They lived in a pleasant house, with a garden, and they had discreet servants, and felt themselves superior to anyone in the neighborhood.

Although they lived in style, they felt always an anxiety in the house. There was never enough money. The mother had a small income, and the father had a small income, but not nearly enough for the social position which they had to keep up. The father went into town to some office. But though he had good prospects, these prospects never materialized. There was always the grinding sense of the shortage of money, though the style was always kept up.

At last the mother said, "I will see if *I* can't make something." But she did not know where to begin. She racked her brains, and tried this thing and the other, but could not find anything successful. The failure made deep lines come into her face. Her children were growing up, they would have to go to school. There must be more money, there must be more money. The father, who was always very handsome and expensive in his tastes, seemed as if he never *would* be able to do anything worth doing. And the mother, who had a great belief in herself, did not succeed any better, and her tastes were just as expensive.

And so the house came to be haunted by the unspoken phrase: *There must be more money! There must be more money!* The children could hear it all the time, though nobody said it aloud. They heard it at Christmas, when the expensive and splendid toys filled the nursery. Behind the shining modern rocking horse, behind the smart doll's house, a voice would start whispering: "There *must* be more money! There *must* be more money!" And the children would stop playing, to listen for a moment. They would look into each other's eyes to see if they had all heard. And each one saw in the eyes of the other two that they too had heard. "There *must* be more money! There *must* be more money!"

It came whispering from the springs of the still-swaying rocking horse, and even the horse, bending his wooden, champing head, heard it. The big doll, sitting so pink and smirking in her new pram, could hear it quite plainly, and seemed to be smirking all the more self-consciously because of it. The foolish puppy, too, that took the place of the teddy bear, he was looking so extraordinarily foolish for no other reason but that he heard the secret whisper all over the house: "There *must* be more money!"

Yet nobody ever said it aloud. The whisper was

A. Character
Ask students to try to discover as they read what the mother is lacking.

B. Theme
Have students note the recurrent use of the word *anxiety* in connection with the house and the mother. Also ask students to note all the ways in which the attractive, pleasant surface of things is contradicted by an underlying worry and unhappiness.

C. Conflict
? Why is a pervasive whispering in the house a good image for the family's problem? (The problem was persistent, troubling, and never spoken of openly.)

A. Plot
Notice that Paul's series of questions about the source and solution to the mother's problems ends with the mention of God. Ask students to be alert to how Paul will call on God or something beyond earthly powers for help.

B. Theme
? What is it that the boy wants from his mother and does not get? (Warmth, love, and attention)

C. Character
? Who does the boy resemble in his heedless, self-absorbed rocking and intense desire for luck? (His mother)

D. Language and Theme
Note the frequent use of words like *mad, furious, frenzy* to describe not only Paul's riding but also his state of mind.

everywhere, and therefore no one spoke it. Just as no one ever says: "We are breathing!" in spite of the fact that breath is coming and going all the time.

"Mother," said the boy Paul one day, "why don't we keep a car of our own? Why do we always use uncle's, or else a taxi?"

"Because we're the poor members of the family," said the mother.

"But why *are* we, mother?"

"Well—I suppose," she said slowly and bitterly, "it's because your father has no luck!"

The boy was silent for some time.

"Is luck money, mother?" he asked, rather timidly.

"No, Paul. Not quite. It's what causes you to have money."

"Oh!" said Paul vaguely. "I thought when Uncle Oscar said *filthy lucker,* it meant money."

"*Filthy lucre*[1] does mean money," said the mother. "But it's lucre, not luck."

"Oh!" said the boy, "Then what *is* luck, mother?"

"It's what causes you to have money. If you're lucky you have money. That's why it's better to be born lucky than rich. If you're rich, you may lose your money. But if you're lucky, you will always get more money."

"Oh! Will you? And is father not lucky?"

"Very unlucky, I should say," she said bitterly.

The boy watched her with unsure eyes.

"Why?" he asked.

"I don't know. Nobody ever knows why one person is lucky and another unlucky."

"Don't they? Nobody at all? Does *nobody* know?"

"Perhaps God. But He never tells."

"He ought to, then. And aren't you lucky either, mother?"

"I can't be, if I married an unlucky husband."

"But by yourself, aren't you?"

"I used to think I was, before I married. Now I think I am very unlucky indeed."

"Why?"

"Well—never mind! Perhaps I'm not really," she said.

The child looked at her, to see if she meant it. But he saw, by the lines of her mouth, that she was only trying to hide something from him.

---

1. **Filthy lucre** (lōō'kər): riches, used in a derogatory sense.

"Well, anyhow," he said stoutly, "I'm a lucky person."

"Why?" said his mother, with a sudden laugh.

He stared at her. He didn't even know why he had said it.

"God told me," he asserted, brazening it out.

"I hope He did, dear!" she said, again with a laugh, but rather bitter.

"He did, mother!"

"Excellent!" said the mother, using one of her husband's exclamations.

The boy saw she did not believe him; or rather, that she paid no attention to his assertion. This angered him somewhere, and made him want to compel her attention.

He went off by himself, vaguely, in a childish way, seeking for the clue to "luck." Absorbed, taking no heed of other people, he went about with a sort of stealth, seeking inwardly for luck. He wanted luck, he wanted it, he wanted it. When the two girls were playing dolls in the nursery, he would sit on his big rocking horse, charging madly into space, with a frenzy that made the little girls peer at him uneasily. Wildly the horse careered, the waving dark hair of the boy tossed, his eyes had a strange glare in them. The little girls dared not speak to him.

When he had ridden to the end of his mad little journey, he climbed down and stood in front of his rocking horse, staring fixedly into its lowered face. Its red mouth was slightly open, its big eye was wide and glassy-bright.

"Now!" he would silently command the snorting steed. "Now, take me to where there is luck! Now take me!"

And he would slash the horse on the neck with the little whip he had asked Uncle Oscar for. He *knew* the horse could take him to where there was luck, if only he forced it. So he would mount again, and start on his furious ride, hoping at last to get there. He knew he could get there.

"You'll break your horse, Paul!" said the nurse.

"He's always riding like that! I wish he'd leave off!" said his elder sister Joan.

But he only glared down on them in silence. Nurse gave him up. She could make nothing of him. Anyhow he was growing beyond her.

One day his mother and his Uncle Oscar came in when he was on one of his furious rides. He did not speak to them.

Merry-Go-Round by Mark Gertler (1916). Oil.

The Ben-Guri Gallery, London.

A

A. Humanities Connection: Discussing the Fine Art
English painter Mark Gertler (1891–1939) tried to reconcile his own predilection for realism with his European contemporaries' emphasis on defined form and heightened color. *Merry-Go-Round,* for example, has elements of English genre painting, but its emphasis on design and movement connects it to continental trends.
❓ Ask students if they think the people in the painting are enjoying themselves. What aspect of riding a merry-go-round is being emphasized? How does the painting relate to "The Rocking-Horse Winner"? With what other visual images might students have illustrated this story?

A. Theme
Notice again the
association of reli-
gion with Paul's
behavior.

B. Character
❓ How does Un-
cle Oscar's atti-
tude toward Paul
differ from Bas-
sett's? (The former
is amused and
skeptical; the latter
is a serious believ-
er in Paul's knowl-
edge.)

"Hallo, you young jockey! Riding a winner?"
said his uncle.

"Aren't you growing too big for a rocking
horse? You're not a very little boy any longer, you
know," said his mother.

But Paul only gave a blue glare from his big,
rather close-set eyes. He would speak to nobody
when he was in full tilt. His mother watched him
with an anxious expression on her face.

At last he suddenly stopped forcing his horse
into the mechanical gallop, and slid down.

"Well, I got there!" he announced fiercely, his
blue eyes still flaring, and his sturdy long legs
straddling apart.

"Where did you get to?" asked his mother.

"Where I wanted to go," he flared back at her.

"That's right, son!" said Uncle Oscar. "Don't
you stop till you get there. What's the horse's
name?"

"He doesn't have a name," said the boy.

"Gets on without all right?" asked the uncle.

"Well, he has different names. He was called
Sansovino last week."

"Sansovino, eh? Won the Ascot.[2] How did you
know his name?"

"He always talks about horse races with Bassett," said Joan.

The uncle was delighted to find that his small
nephew was posted with all the racing news. Bassett, the young gardener, who had been wounded
in the left foot in the war and had got his present
job through Oscar Cresswell, whose batman[3] he
had been, was a perfect blade of the "turf."[4] He
lived in the racing events, and the small boy lived
with him.

Oscar Cresswell got it all from Bassett.

A   "Master Paul comes and asks me, so I can't do
more than tell him, sir," said Bassett, his face
terribly serious, as if he were speaking of religious
matters.

"And does he ever put anything on a horse he
fancies?"

"Well—I don't want to give him away—he's a
young sport, a fine sport, sir. Would you mind
asking him himself? He sort of takes a pleasure in
it, and perhaps he'd feel I was giving him away,
sir, if you don't mind."

---

2. **Ascot:** a famous horse race held annually at Ascot Heath in
England.
3. **batman:** an officer's orderly.
4. **blade of the "turf":** good-looking young racing fan.

Bassett was serious as a church.

The uncle went back to his nephew, and took
him off for a ride in the car.

"Say, Paul, old man, do you ever put anything
on a horse?" the uncle asked.

The boy watched the handsome man closely.

"Why, do you think I oughtn't to?" he parried.

"Not a bit of it! I thought perhaps you might
give me a tip for the Lincoln."

The car sped on into the country, going down
to Uncle Oscar's place in Hampshire.

"Honor bright?" said the nephew.

"Honor bright, son!" said the uncle.

"Well, then, Daffodil."

"Daffodil! I doubt it, sonny. What about
Mirza?"

"I only know the winner," said the boy.
"That's Daffodil."

"Daffodil, eh?"

There was a pause. Daffodil was an obscure
horse comparatively.

"Uncle!"

"Yes, son?"

"You won't let it go any further, will you? I
promised Bassett."

"Bassett be damned, old man! What's he got
to do with it?"

"We're partners. We've been partners from the
first. Uncle, he lent me my first five shillings,
which I lost. I promised him, honor bright, it was
only between me and him; only you gave me that
ten-shilling note I started winning with, so I
thought you were lucky. You won't let it go any
further, will you?"

The boy gazed at his uncle from those big, hot,
blue eyes, set rather close together. The uncle
stirred and laughed uneasily.

B

"Right you are, son! I'll keep your tip private.
Daffodil, eh? How much are you putting on him?"

"All except twenty pounds," said the boy. "I
keep that in reserve."

The uncle thought it a good joke.

"You keep twenty pounds in reserve, do you,
you young romancer? What are you betting,
then?"

"I'm betting three hundred," said the boy
gravely. "But it's between you and me, Uncle
Oscar! Honor bright?"

The uncle burst into a roar of laughter.

"It's between you and me all right, you young
Nat Gould," he said, laughing. "But where's your
three hundred?"

"Bassett keeps it for me. We're partners."

"You are, are you! And what is Bassett putting on Daffodil?"

"He won't go quite as high as I do, I expect. Perhaps he'll go a hundred and fifty."

"What, pennies?" laughed the uncle.

"Pounds," said the child, with a surprised look at his uncle. "Bassett keeps a bigger reserve than I do."

Between wonder and amusement Uncle Oscar was silent. He pursued the matter no further, but he determined to take his nephew with him to the Lincoln races.

"Now, son," he said, "I'm putting twenty on Mirza, and I'll put five for you on any horse you fancy. What's your pick?"

"Daffodil, uncle."

"No, not the fiver on Daffodil!"

"I should if it was my own fiver," said the child.

"Good! Good! Right you are! A fiver for me and a fiver for you on Daffodil."

The child had never been to a race meeting before, and his eyes were blue fire. He pursed his mouth tight, and watched. A Frenchman just in front had put his money on Lancelot. Wild with excitement, he flayed his arms up and down, yelling "*Lancelot! Lancelot!*" in his French accent.

Daffodil came in first, Lancelot second, Mirza third. The child, flushed and with eyes blazing, was curiously serene. His uncle brought him four five-pound notes, four to one.

"What am I to do with these?" he cried, waving them before the boy's eyes.

"I suppose we'll talk to Bassett," said the boy. "I expect I have fifteen hundred now; and twenty in reserve; and this twenty."

His uncle studied him for some moments.

"Look here, son!" he said. "You're not serious about Bassett and that fifteen hundred, are you?"

"Yes, I am. But it's between you and me, uncle. Honor bright!"

"Honor bright all right, son! But I must talk to Bassett."

"If you'd like to be a partner, uncle, with Bassett and me, we could all be partners. Only, you'd have to promise, honor bright, uncle, not to let it go beyond us three. Bassett and I are lucky, and you must be lucky, because it was your ten shillings I started winning with. . . ."

Uncle Oscar took both Bassett and Paul into Richmond Park for an afternoon, and there they talked.

"It's like this, you see, sir," Bassett said. "Master Paul would get me talking about racing events, spinning yarns, you know, sir. And he was always keen on knowing if I'd made or if I'd lost. It's about a year since, now, that I put five shillings on Blush of Dawn for him: and we lost. Then the luck turned, with that ten shillings he had from you: that we put on Singhalese. And since that time, it's been pretty steady, all things considering. What do you say, Master Paul?"

"We're all right when we're sure," said Paul. "It's when we're not quite sure that we go down."

"Oh, but we're careful then," said Bassett.

"But when are you *sure*?" smiled Uncle Oscar.

"It's Master Paul, sir," said Bassett, in a secret, religious voice. "It's as if he had it from heaven. Like Daffodil, now, for the Lincoln. That was as sure as eggs."

"Did you put anything on Daffodil?" asked Oscar Cresswell.

"Yes, sir. I made my bit."

"And my nephew?"

Bassett was obstinately silent, looking at Paul.

"I made twelve hundred, didn't I, Bassett? I told uncle I was putting three hundred on Daffodil."

"That's right," said Bassett, nodding.

"But where's the money?" asked the uncle.

"I keep it safe locked up, sir. Master Paul he can have it any minute he likes to ask for it."

"What, fifteen hundred pounds?"

"And twenty! And *forty,* that is, with the twenty he made on the course."

"It's amazing!" said the uncle.

"If Master Paul offers you to be partners, sir, I would, if I were you: if you'll excuse me," said Bassett.

Oscar Cresswell thought about it.

"I'll see the money," he said.

They drove home again, and, sure enough, Bassett came round to the garden house with fifteen hundred pounds in notes. The twenty pounds reserve was left with Joe Glee, in the Turf Commission deposit.

"You see, it's all right, uncle, when I'm *sure!* Then we go strong, for all we're worth. Don't we, Bassett?"

"We do that, Master Paul."

"And when are you sure?" said the uncle, laughing.

"Oh, well, sometimes I'm *absolutely* sure, like about Daffodil," said the boy; "and sometimes I

A. Character
Note again that Bassett connects Paul's knowledge with heaven.

❓ Of the three, whose attitude is most down-to-earth? (Uncle Oscar's)

A. Character
? What does this detail about the mother's sketching job reveal about her character? (She impatiently wants rewards without waiting or working for them.)

B. Language and Theme
Note the repeated use of words like *hard, cold, stone, expressionless* in connection with the mother.
? In what terms are the boy's eyes repeatedly described? ("Uncanny cold fire") How are the two descriptions related? (Both are cold, driven, and unhappy.)

have an idea; and sometimes I haven't even an idea, have I, Bassett? Then we're careful, because we mostly go down."

"You do, do you! And when you're sure, like about Daffodil, what makes you sure, sonny?"

"Oh, well, I don't know," said the boy uneasily. "I'm sure, you know, uncle; that's all."

"It's as if he had it from heaven, sir," Bassett <u>reiterated</u>.

"I should say so!" said the uncle.

But he became a partner. And when the Leger was coming on Paul was "sure" about Lively Spark, which was a quite inconsiderable horse. The boy insisted on putting a thousand on the horse, Bassett went for five hundred, and Oscar Cresswell two hundred. Lively Spark came in first, and the betting had been ten to one against him. Paul had made ten thousand.

"You see," he said, "I was absolutely sure of him."

Even Oscar Cresswell had cleared two thousand.

"Look here, son," he said, "this sort of thing makes me nervous."

"It needn't uncle! Perhaps I shan't be sure again for a long time."

"But what are you going to do with your money?" asked the uncle.

"Of course," said the boy, "I started it for mother. She said she had no luck because father is unlucky, so I thought if *I* was lucky, it might stop whispering."

"What might stop whispering?"

"Our house. I *hate* our house for whispering."

"What does it whisper?"

"Why—why"—the boy fidgeted—"why, I don't know. But it's always short of money, you know, uncle."

"I know it, son, I know it."

"You know people send mother writs,[5] don't you, uncle?"

"I'm afraid I do," said the uncle.

"And then the house whispers, like people laughing at you behind your back. It's awful, that is! I thought if I was lucky——"

"You might stop it," added the uncle.

The boy watched him with big blue eyes, that had an <u>uncanny</u> cold fire in them, and he said never a word.

---

5. **writs:** legal documents demanding payment of debts.

"Well, then!" said the uncle. "What are we doing?"

"I shouldn't like mother to know I was lucky," said the boy.

"Why not, son?"

"She'd stop me"

"I don't think she would."

"Oh!"—and the boy <u>writhed</u> in an odd way— "I *don't* want her to know, uncle."

"All right, son! We'll manage it without her knowing."

They managed it very easily. Paul, at the other's suggestion, handed over five thousand pounds to his uncle, who deposited it with the family lawyer, who was then to inform Paul's mother that a relative had put five thousand pounds into his hands, which sum was to be paid out a thousand pounds at a time, on the mother's birthday, for the next five years.

"So she'll have a birthday present of a thousand pounds for five successive years," said Uncle Oscar. "I hope it won't make it all the harder for her later."

Paul's mother had her birthday in November. The house had been "whispering" worse than ever lately, and, even in spite of his luck, Paul could not bear up against it. He was very anxious to see the effect of the birthday letter, telling his mother about the thousand pounds.

When there were no visitors, Paul now took his meals with his parents, as he was beyond the nursery control. His mother went into town nearly every day. She had discovered that she had an odd knack of sketching furs and dress materials, so she worked secretly in the studio of a friend who was the chief "artist" for the leading drapers. She drew the figures of ladies in furs and ladies in silk and sequins for the newspaper advertisements. This young woman artist earned several thousand pounds a year, but Paul's mother only made several hundreds, and she was again dissatisfied. She so wanted to be first in something, and she did not succeed, even in making sketches for drapery advertisements.

She was down to breakfast on the morning of her birthday. Paul watched her face as she read her letters. He knew the lawyer's letter. As his mother read it, her face hardened and became more expressionless. Then a cold, determined look came on her mouth. She hid the letter under the pile of others, and said not a word about it.

Literature and Language: Using Exclamatory Sentences for Variety and Tone

Have students skim the beginning of "The Rocking-Horse Winner" to find where D. H. Lawrence occasionally intersperses his more ordinary sentences with exclamations. As the story continues, students should note that the exclamations become more frequent and more agitated as the child persists in his riding. The result is an increasingly desperate and despairing tone as the child eventually rides the horse to his death.

Have students rewrite the following paragraph, adding exclamations to approach the variety and tone that D. H. Lawrence achieved.

She reached the top of the hill and looked down. The sidewalk stretched away, a concrete ribbon unfurling to the street below. Seeing it filled the child with both delight and dread. She started down, skates making their familiar metallic grating. Down and down. Trees and houses became a blur. Cars zipped by, indistinguishable in the speed of her racing. Vainly she wondered where the bottom was.

"Didn't you have anything nice in the post for your birthday, mother?" said Paul.

"Quite moderately nice," she said, her voice cold and absent.

She went away to town without saying more.

But in the afternoon Uncle Oscar appeared. He said Paul's mother had had a long interview with the lawyer, asking if the whole five thousand could not be advanced at once, as she was in debt.

"What do you think, uncle?" said the boy.

"I leave it to you son,"

"Oh, let her have it, then! We can get some more with the other," said the boy.

"A bird in the hand is worth two in the bush, laddie!" said Uncle Oscar.

"But I'm sure to *know* for the Grand National; or the Lincolnshire; or else the Derby. I'm sure to know for *one* of them," said Paul.

So Uncle Oscar signed the agreement, and Paul's mother touched the whole five thousand. Then something very curious happened. The voices in the house suddenly went mad, like a chorus of frogs on a spring evening. There were certain new furnishings, and Paul had a tutor. He was *really* going to Eton, his father's school, in the following autumn. There were flowers in the winter, and a blossoming of the luxury Paul's mother had been used to. And yet the voices in the house, behind the sprays of mimosa and almond-blossom, and from under the piles of iridescent cushions, simply trilled and screamed in a sort of ecstasy: "There *must* be more money! Oh-h-h; there *must* be more money. Oh, now, now-w! Now-w-w—there *must* be more money!—more than ever! More than ever!"

It frightened Paul terribly. He studied away at his Latin and Greek with his tutors. But his intense hours were spent with Bassett. The Grand National had gone by: he had not "known," and had lost a hundred pounds. Summer was at hand. He was in agony for the Lincoln. But even for the Lincoln he didn't "know," and he lost fifty pounds. He became wild-eyed and strange, as if something were going to explode in him.

"Let it alone, son! Don't you bother about it!" urged Uncle Oscar. But it was as if the boy couldn't really hear what his uncle was saying.

"I've got to know for the Derby! I've got to know for the Derby!" the child reiterated, his big blue eyes blazing with a sort of madness.

His mother noticed how overwrought he was.

"You'd better go to the seaside. Wouldn't you like to go now to the seaside, instead of waiting? I think you'd better," she said, looking down at him anxiously, her heart curiously heavy because of him.

But the child lifted his uncanny blue eyes.

"I couldn't possibly go before the Derby, mother!" he said. "I couldn't possibly!"

"Why not?" she said, her voice becoming heavy when she was opposed. "Why not? You can still go from the seaside to see the Derby with your Uncle Oscar, if that's what you wish. No need for you to wait here. Besides, I think you care too much about these races. It's a bad sign. My family has been a gambling family, and you won't know till you grow up how much damage it has done. But it has done damage. I shall have to send Bassett away, and ask Uncle Oscar not to talk racing to you, unless you promise to be reasonable about it: go away to the seaside and forget it. You're all nerves!"

"I'll do what you like mother, so long as you don't send me away till after the Derby," the boy said.

"Send you away from where? Just from this house?"

"Yes," he said, gazing at her.

"Why, you curious child, what makes you care about this house so much, suddenly? I never knew you loved it."

He gazed at her without speaking. He had a secret within a secret, something he had not divulged, even to Bassett or to his Uncle Oscar.

But his mother, after standing undecided and a little bit sullen for some moments, said:

"Very well, then! Don't go to the seaside till after the Derby, if you don't wish it. But promise me you won't let your nerves go to pieces. Promise you won't think so much about horse racing and *events,* as you call them!"

"Oh, no," said the boy casually. "I won't think much about them, mother. You needn't worry. I wouldn't worry, mother, if I were you."

"If you were me and I were you," said his mother, "I wonder what we *should* do!"

"But you know you needn't worry, mother, don't you?" the boy repeated.

"I should be awfully glad to know it," she said wearily.

"Oh, well, you *can,* you know. I mean, you *ought* to know you needn't worry," he insisted.

A. Plot

What happened as a result of Paul's giving his mother money for her birthday? (The mother went on a spending spree.) Did the whispering stop? (No, it increased wildly.) What can you conclude about the nature of the mother's problem? (She is a compulsive spender.)

B. Irony

What is ironic about Paul's mother telling him he cares too much about winning races? (She cares too much about material things herself.)

C. Irony

Tell students that these passages ironically underscore the identification between mother and son. He is trying to help her, but since he does not understand the true nature of her problem, he is destroying himself (as she is) in a reckless pursuit of money. She senses that he is in danger but is incapable of giving the one thing that would save them both.

CLOSURE

Ask students to discuss as a group what kind of child Paul was and if his tragic ending might have been averted. How might another child have acted in the same circumstances?

1. Paul's mother lacks _____.
a. peace of mind   b. ambition
c. opportunity   d. beauty (a)
2. The relationship between Paul's father and mother seems _____.
a. loving   b. stormy
c. distant   d. practical (c)
3. After speaking with his mother, Paul believes that _____ is what the family needs.
a. help   b. luck
c. work   d. prayers (b)
4. What is Uncle Oscar's attitude toward Paul's death?
a. great sadness   b. outrage
c. indifference   d. resignation (d)

A. Character

? Paul's mother has begun to be anxious not only about money but about him. What do you think is the basis of her anxiety about Paul? (Perhaps guilt)

B. Climax

Tell students that all the recurrent themes of the story come together in this climactic scene—Paul's madness, a kind of inherited disease, and her inability to attend to her children in a life-giving way.

"Ought I? Then I'll see about it," she said.

Paul's secret of secrets was his wooden horse, that which had no name. Since he was emancipated from a nurse and nursery governess, he had had his rocking horse removed to his own bedroom at the top of the house.

"Surely, you're too big for a rocking horse!" his mother had remonstrated.

"Well, you see, mother, till I can have a *real* horse, I like to have *some* sort of animal about," had been his quaint answer.

"Do you feel he keeps you company?" she laughed.

"Oh, yes! He's very good, he always keeps me company, when I'm there," said Paul.

So the horse, rather shabby, stood in an arrested prance in the boy's bedroom.

The Derby was drawing near, and the boy grew more and more tense. He hardly heard what was spoken to him, he was very frail, and his eyes were really uncanny. His mother had sudden strange seizures of uneasiness about him. Sometimes, for half an hour, she would feel a sudden anxiety about him that was almost anguish. She wanted to rush to him at once, and know he was safe.

A Two nights before the Derby, she was at a big party in town, when one of her rushes of anxiety about her boy, her firstborn, gripped her heart till she could hardly speak. She fought with the feeling, might and main, for she believed in common sense. But it was too strong. She had to leave the dance and go downstairs to telephone to the country. The children's nursery governess was terribly surprised and startled at being rung up in the night.

"Are the children all right, Miss Wilmot?"

"Oh, yes, they are quite all right."

"Master Paul? Is he all right?"

"He went to bed as right as a trivet. Shall I run up and look at him?"

"No," said Paul's mother reluctantly. "No! Don't trouble. It's all right. Don't sit up. We shall be home fairly soon." She did not want her son's privacy intruded upon.

"Very good," said the governess.

It was about one o'clock when Paul's mother and father drove up to their house. All was still. Paul's mother went to her room and slipped off her white fur cloak. She had told her maid not to wait up for her. She heard her husband downstairs, mixing a whiskey and soda.

And then, because of the strange anxiety at her heart, she stole upstairs to her son's room. Noiselessly she went along the upper corridor. Was there a faint noise? What was it?

She stood, with arrested muscles, outside his door, listening. There was a strange, heavy, and yet not loud noise. Her heart stood still. It was a soundless noise, yet rushing and powerful. Something huge, in violent, hushed motion. What was it? What in God's name was it? She ought to know. She felt that she knew the noise. She knew what it was.

Yet she could not place it. She couldn't say what it was. And on and on it went, like a madness.

Softly, frozen with anxiety and fear, she turned the door handle. The room was dark. Yet in the space near the window, she heard and saw something plunging to and fro. She gazed in fear and amazement.

Then suddenly she switched on the light, and saw her son, in his green pajamas, madly surging on the rocking horse. The blaze of light suddenly lit him up, as he urged the wooden horse, and lit her up, as she stood, blond, in her dress of pale green and crystal, in the doorway.

"Paul!" she cried, "Whatever are you doing?"

"It's Malabar!" he screamed, in a powerful, strange, voice. "It's Malabar!"

B His eyes blazed at her for one strange and senseless second, as he ceased urging his wooden horse. Then he fell with a crash to the ground, and she, all her tormented motherhood flooding upon her, rushed to gather him up.

But he was unconscious, and unconscious he remained, with some brain fever. He talked and tossed, and his mother sat stonily by his side.

"Malabar! It's Malabar! Bassett, Bassett, I *know*! It's Malabar!"

So the child cried, trying to get up and urge the rocking horse that gave him his inspiration.

"What does he mean by Malabar?" asked the heart-frozen mother.

"I don't know," said the father stonily.

"What does he mean by Malabar?" she asked her brother Oscar.

"It's one of the horses running for the Derby," was the answer.

And, in spite of himself, Oscar Cresswell spoke to Bassett, and himself put a thousand on Malabar: at fourteen to one.

The third day of the illness was critical: they were waiting for a change. The boy, with his rather

ANALYZING THE STORY
Identifying Facts

1. The woman's love had turned to dust; she found herself unable to love her children; she felt flawed.

Lawrence tells us that the woman was ambitious and eager for social position; she was not as rich as she hoped and was continually dissatisfied; also she had expensive tastes.

2. She says that luck is what causes people to have money.

Paul cannot understand why God doesn't reveal the reason why one person is lucky and another is not. He confuses "luck" and "lucre."

3. He bets on horses. He asks his uncle to make an anonymous birthday present to his mother of a thousand pounds a year for five years.

Disappointed that she has not received the whole amount, the mother appears cold and indifferent.

4. Bassett is the gardener and Paul's partner at the races.

Bassett respects the boy as a "young sport."

5. Paul fails to resolve his mother's problem because her receipt of the money leads only to the desire for more money.

long, curly hair, was tossing ceaselessly on the pillow. He neither slept nor regained consciousness, and his eyes were like blue stones. His mother sat, feeling her heart had gone, turned actually into a stone.

In the evening, Oscar Cresswell did not come, but Bassett sent a message, saying could he come up for one moment, just one moment? Paul's mother was very angry at the intrusion, but on second thought she agreed. The boy was the same. Perhaps Bassett might bring him to consciousness.

The gardener, a shortish fellow with a little brown mustache, and sharp little brown eyes, tiptoed into the room, touched his imaginary cap to Paul's mother, and stole to the bedside, staring with glittering, smallish eyes at the tossing, dying child.

"Master Paul!" he whispered. "Master Paul. Malabar came in first all right, a clean win. I did as you told me. You've made over seventy thousand pounds, you have; you've got over eighty thousand. Malabar came in all right, Master Paul."

"Malabar! Malabar! Did I say Malabar, mother? Did I say Malabar? Do you think I'm lucky, mother? I knew Malabar, didn't I? Over eighty thousand pounds! I call that lucky, don't you, mother? Over eighty thousand pounds! I knew, didn't I know I knew? Malabar came in all right. If I ride my horse till I'm sure, then I tell you, Bassett, you can go as high as you like. Did you go for all you were worth, Bassett?"

"I went a thousand on it, Master Paul."

"I never told you, mother, that if I can ride my horse, and *get there*, then I'm absolutely sure—oh, absolutely! Mother, did I ever tell you? I *am* lucky!"

"No, you never did," said the mother.

But the boy died in the night.

And even as he lay dead, his mother heard her brother's voice saying to her: "My God, Hester, you're eighty-odd thousand to the good, and a poor devil of a son to the bad. But, poor devil, poor devil, he's best gone out of a life where he rides his rocking horse to find a winner."

Responding to the Story

Analyzing the Story

Identifying Facts

1. In the style of a fairy tale, the opening of the story tells about a woman who "had no luck." How had she been unlucky? What else does the writer tell us directly about the mother's **character**?
2. How does Paul's mother define luck when Paul asks her what it means? What is Paul's confusion about the word *luck*?
3. What step does Paul take to ease his mother's anxiety over the family's debts? How does she react when she learns of her birthday surprise?
4. Who is Bassett? Why does he keep Paul's secret?
5. Does Paul solve his mother's problem? Why or why not?

Interpreting Meanings

6. Why do you suppose only Paul and his sisters hear and react to the whispering of the walls? How would you describe what has happened to Paul?

7. What might the rocking horse **symbolize**?
8. What do you think the story means? Do you agree that the **theme** has something to do with an inability to love? How would you state the story's theme?
9. How would you describe the **tone** of Lawrence's story? If you detect a **satiric** tone, who or what is Lawrence's target?
10. In what ways is the story's ending a distortion of the usual fairy-tale ending? What do you think of Lawrence's decision to end it as he did?

Writing About the Story

A Creative Response

1. **Writing a New Resolution.** Is it possible to write a happy ending for the story? Try it, imitating Lawrence's style as closely as possible. Be prepared to explain which conclusion—the happy one you have written or the sad one that Lawrence wrote—is more satisfying to the reader, and why.

Interpreting Meanings

6. The fact that only the children hear and react to the whispering underscores the parents' obliviousness to their own materialism.

He has willed himself into a psychic trance.

7. Possibilities include material pursuit or even the demonic imagination.

8. The theme has to do with materialism in conflict with our instinctual need for love and with the dark powers of the soul. Compare with "Snake" on page 1099.

9. The tone might be described as ominous.

Materialism and greed may be the targets of Lawrence's satire.

10. The typical fairy tale ends "They lived happily ever after." But here Paul dies, and the uncle comments that "he's best gone out of a life where he rides his rocking horse to find a winner."

Answers will vary. Ask if the story would be as interesting if Paul had lived and gone on winning for years.

A. Humanities Connection: Discussing the Fine Art

William Roberts (1885–1980) was influenced by the theories of Vorticism developed by writer and artist Wyndham Lewis. Lewis said that Vorticism aimed at creating "a visual language as abstract as music" and that "the world of machinery" could be a source of inspiration.Roberts began painting abstract geometrical forms but later created paintings that seemed to shape the incidents and people of everyday life into a frenzied and mechanized ballet.

? What activities are the people performing in this painting? What is the overall effect produced by the composition? How does the painting comment on modern life? How does it reinforce a theme of "The Rocking-Horse Winner"?

B. Responding to Primary Sources

In this letter by D. H. Lawrence, he explains how the avid pursuit of money kills life and happiness. Ask students to respond to this letter as if it had been written to them, offering their views on Lawrence's ideas.

A

People at Play by William Roberts (1936). Oil.

Private collection.

A Critical Response

2. **Analyzing a Character.** *The mother's extravagance results partly from social pressure—the need to keep up appearances. Her hunger for material wealth might also be a way to compensate for her inability to love.* Find evidence in the story to support this topic statement, and write a brief essay presenting what you find.

3. **Applying a Quotation to a Story.** In his sonnet "The World Is Too Much with Us" (Unit Five), William Wordsworth writes, "Getting and spending, we lay waste our powers." In a brief essay, discuss the ways Lawrence's story illustrates this statement. Before you write, be sure you understand what Wordsworth means by "getting," "spending," and "powers."

4. **Comparing and Contrasting Characters.** In a brief essay, compare Mrs. De Ropp's feeling for Conradin in Saki's story "Sredni Vashtar" with the mother's feeling for Paul. In your essay, consider how the two boys react to maternal indifference, and what accounts for the differences in their reactions.

Primary Sources
D. H. Lawrence on Money

A theme that runs through nearly all of Lawrence's works is the celebration of life—the human energy and force that express the joy of existence. Opposing this natural energy is materialism, which Lawrence believed misdirects one's energies and warps the soul.

B   Rolf Gardiner, one of Lawrence's first admirers, managed a large farm in Dorset. In 1926, Lawrence wrote to Gardiner: "And don't be too ernest—earnest—how does one spell it?—nor overburdened by a mission: neither too self-willed. One must be simple and direct, and a bit free from oneself above all."

In a letter to Rolf Gardiner, Lawrence makes a rare, brief mention of the evils of materialism.

Villa Mirenda, Scandicci
Florence
18 Dec., 1927

"Dear Rolf Gardiner,

". . . If I were talking to the young, I should say only one thing to them: Don't you live just to make money, either for yourself or for anybody else. Don't look on yourself as a wage slave. Try to find out what life itself is, and live. Repudiate the money idea.

"And then I'd teach 'em, if I could, to dance and sing together. The togetherness is important.

"But they must first overthrow in themselves the money-fear and money-lust. . . ."

Katherine Mansfield (1888–1923)

Katherine Mansfield was born Kathleen Mansfield Beauchamp in New Zealand, the third child of a hearty, ambitious Wellington merchant. Even as a girl, she was aware of the extraordinary rugged beauty of her island home, but she shared her mother's distaste for being "out here," oceans away from England, the source of their culture.

At home she was "difficult," a lonely, resentful child, subject to nightmares and unreasonable fears, and seeing her father as an adversary. At school she was moody and had few friends. She had her father's head for figures and could memorize verse at sight, yet she was a slovenly scholar. One teacher described her as "dumpy and unattractive, not even cleverly naughty." The neighbor boys called her "Fatty."

When Mansfield was fifteen, the Beauchamp family sailed for England to put the three oldest girls into finishing school at the progressive Queen's College in London. Mansfield was delighted with every aspect of her new life.

She made many new friends, including Ida Baker, who was to be her loyal shadow for the rest of an ardent life. She also developed a crush on her German instructor; read the "decadents," Walter Pater and Oscar Wilde; played the cello; and regarded a day as wasted if she had not written something.

When, in 1906, it came time to return to New Zealand, Mansfield pleaded to be left behind, but her father would not hear of it. She accepted the return to Wellington in bad grace. Once home, she made outrageous scenes before the family and was deliberately rude to guests. She closeted herself in her room, grieved for lost London, burned incense, and thought of writing a novel. It was to be "unreal but wholly possible," a book that "raises in the hearts of the readers emotions, sensations too vivid not to have effect, which causes a thousand delicate tears, a thousand sweet chimes of laughter."

In 1908, when she was nineteen, her father gave in and permitted her to return to London alone. The homely child had become a beauty, with porcelain skin and eyes brimming with in-

telligence. With an allowance of one hundred pounds a year, she was painfully poor, always inadequately dressed, and frequently ailing. She complained that her father was "the richest man in New Zealand, and the meanest."

Her first literary encouragement came in 1911, when A. R. Orage, editor of the progressive journal *New Age,* accepted several of her stories. These stories, which showed the strong influence of the Russian writer Anton Chekhov, were collected in a volume called *In a German Pension* (1911).

About the same time, an Oxford undergraduate named John Middleton Murry accepted a story and some of her poems for his new literary magazine *Rhythm.* Mansfield was soon sharing Murry's interest in *Rhythm,* and she convinced him to drop out of Oxford to give full attention to the magazine. Murry, who was even poorer than Mansfield, began a long and stormy relationship with the young writer. Eventually, Mansfield and Murry married and became publishing partners.

PREPARATION

1. BUILDING ON PRIOR KNOWLEDGE Ask students to recall a time when they were alone in a public place and passed the time by observing other people. Did the scene make them feel happy or sad? What do they think affected their feelings about what they saw and heard?

2. ESTABLISHING A PURPOSE. As students read, ask them to try to form a mental picture of Miss Brill. How old is she? What does she look like? What kind of life does she lead?

You might read Robert Burns's lines from "To a Louse": "O would some power the giftie gie us/To see oursels as others see us!" Does this idea apply to Miss Brill?

3. PREREADING JOURNAL. Ask students to think about what being alone means to them. Are there ways in which being alone offers an opportunity? Have students write their thoughts in their journals, perhaps in the form of a short poem.

The couple became close friends with D. H. Lawrence, and they were witnesses at his marriage to Frieda Weekley in 1914. Frieda found Mansfield "so exquisite and complete with her firm, brown hair, delicate skin, and brown eyes." She gave Mansfield her wedding ring from her former marriage, and Mansfield wore it the rest of her life. Lawrence convinced them to become their neighbors in Cornwall, but it did not prove to be a pleasant experience. Lawrence was prone to frequent rages, and he made onerous demands on Murry, so Mansfield and Murry left. Lawrence, in turn, ridiculed them; he used them as models for Gudrun Brangwen and Gerald Crich—a couple with a destructive relationship in his novel *Women in Love*.

World War I brought a tragic event that would have a major effect on Mansfield's writing. Her younger brother Leslie joined a British regiment and came to England for training. Katherine and Leslie had a joyous time together recalling their childhood before Leslie's regiment was sent to fight in France. Only a week later, her brother was killed. His last words were, "Lift my head, Katie, I can't breathe."

Mansfield was overwhelmed by grief. When she at last emerged from it, she was changed. She vowed from then on to write about New Zealand as "a sacred debt, because my brother and I were born there." She called it "a debt of love. . . . I shall tell everything, even of how the laundry basket squeaked."

As her stories were published in periodicals, and later in her many collections, Mansfield came to be recognized as a supremely gifted writer and an innovator of the short story. Just as her contemporaries Virginia Woolf and James Joyce were changing the concept of the novel, so Mansfield was remaking the short-story form. Drawn from autobiographical material—often the world of childhood—her stories depend on the revelation of interior moods and on the evocative power of language. Up to this time, the short story had been seen as merely a finger exercise for the novel. People expected stories to have strong, chronological plots, and the clever, tricky ending was popular. Mansfield's stories eliminated attention to plot and action; instead, she tried to illuminate moments of significance. Some people would complain that in stories like Mansfield's "nothing happened." But Murry spoke of the "peculiar quality of her work"

which he described as "a kind of *purity*. It is as though the glass through which she looked upon life were crystal-clear."

Mansfield's own life, however, continued to be troubled. In September 1917 she learned that she had tuberculosis and must never endure another English winter. In spring of 1918, she and Murry were married, but three weeks later they separated. She wrote him, complaining that their marriage

was to have shone, apart from all else in my life. And it really was only part of the nightmare after all. You never held me in your arms and called me your wife. In fact the whole affair was like my silly birthday. I had to keep on making you remember it.

As Mansfield's health worsened, she sought the sunnier climate of the French Riviera. Her characteristic verve gave way to loneliness, anger, and fear of death. She nursed a grievance against D. H. Lawrence, and described this time as "the worst days of my life."

As Mansfield, at thirty-four, entered the final year of her life, her pain was in remission, and she was reconciled to her illness. Again affectionate with Murry, she became newly compassionate in her writing and reached new levels of skill in such stories as "The Young Girl," "Miss Brill," and "The Stranger."

Despairing of the care she was receiving in France, she went to the Swiss Alps, where her health improved. There, in the brief period of time left to her, she wrote some of her finest stories, many with New Zealand backgrounds, which are collected in *The Garden Party and Other Stories* (1922). The reviews were glowing; some reviewers recognized that she was dealing with death in these stories, and that she had brought not just skill but also tenderness to her task.

A belief that some miracle might save her led Mansfield to a healer named George Gurdjieff. In January 1923, she was a patient at his institute in France when Murry came for a visit. As she was retiring for the night, Mansfield was overcome by a fit of coughing, which ended in a gush of blood from her mouth. She was able to whisper to Murry that she believed she was going to die, and those were her last words. She was buried in the nearby cemetery at Fontainebleau.

SUPPLEMENTARY SUPPORT MATERIALS
1. Vocabulary Activity Worksheet (*CCB*)
2. Review and Response Worksheet: Theme (*CCB*)
3. Language Skills Worksheet: Subject-Verb Agreement/Adverb Clauses (*CCB*)
4. Selection Test (*CCB*)

DEVELOPING VOCABULARY
The following words from the story are tested in the Selection Test. (See also Vocabulary Activity Worksheet.)

elderdown	ermine
dab	brute
to tingle	to hobble
to swoop	invalid
gravely	resolute

MISS BRILL

Many of us go about life silently imagining the lives of others. Sometimes these fantasies are what psychologists call projection—that is, putting one's own ideas or feelings into other people's minds. In "Miss Brill" the main character imagines that she knows the circumstances of her fellow strollers in a public park, unaware that she too plays a part in the drama of life.

Although it was so brilliantly fine—the blue sky powdered with gold and great spots of light like white wine splashed over the Jardins Publiques[1]—Miss Brill was glad that she had decided on her fur. The air was motionless, but when you opened your mouth there was just a faint chill, like a chill from a glass of iced water before you sip, and now and again a leaf came drifting—from nowhere, from the sky. Miss Brill put up her hand and touched her fur. Dear little thing! It was nice to feel it again. She had taken it out of its box that afternoon, shaken out the moth powder, given it a good brush, and rubbed the life back into the dim little eyes. "What has been happening to me?" said the sad little eyes. Oh, how sweet it was to see them snap at her again from the red eiderdown[2] . . . But the nose, which was of some black composition, wasn't at all firm. It must have had a knock, somehow. Never mind—a little dab of black sealing wax when the time came—when it was absolutely necessary. . . . Little rogue! Yes, she really felt like that about it. Little rogue biting its tail just by her left ear. She could have taken it off and laid it on her lap and stroked it. She felt a tingling in her hands and arms, but that came from walking, she supposed. And when she breathed, something light and sad—no, not sad, exactly—something gentle seemed to move in her bosom.

There were a number of people out this afternoon, far more than last Sunday. And the band sounded louder and gayer. That was because the Season had begun. For although the band played all the year round on Sundays, out of season it was never the same. It was like someone playing with only the family to listen; it didn't care how it played if there weren't any strangers present. Wasn't the conductor wearing a new coat, too? She was sure it was new. He scraped with his foot and flapped his arms like a rooster about to crow, and the bandsmen sitting in the green rotunda[3] blew out their cheeks and glared at the music. Now there came a little "flutey" bit—very pretty!—a little chain of bright drops. She was sure it would be repeated. It was; she lifted her head and smiled.

Only two people shared her "special" seat: a fine old man in a velvet coat, his hands clasped over a huge carved walking stick, and a big old woman, sitting upright, with a roll of knitting on her embroidered apron. They did not speak. This was disappointing, for Miss Brill always looked forward to the conversation. She had become really quite expert, she thought, at listening as though she didn't listen, at sitting in other people's lives just for a minute while they talked round her.

She glanced, sideways, at the old couple. Perhaps they would go soon. Last Sunday, too, hadn't been as interesting as usual. An Englishman and his wife, he wearing a dreadful Panama hat and she button boots. And she'd gone on the whole time about how she ought to wear spectacles; she knew she needed them; but that it was no good getting any; they'd be sure to break and they'd never keep on. And he'd been so patient. He'd suggested everything—gold rims, the kind that curved round your ears, little pads inside the bridge. No, nothing would please her. "They'll always be sliding down my nose!" Miss Brill had wanted to shake her.

---

1. **Jardins Publiques** (zhär·dän′ püb·lēk′): French for "public gardens."
2. **eiderdown:** a quilt stuffed with soft feathers (down) from eider ducks.

3. **rotunda:** round structure with a dome.

A. Setting
Call students' attention to the opening description of the day: It was fine but there was a faint chill.

B. Character
Miss Brill is wearing a fur piece around her neck, which includes the head and tail of the animal.
❓ What does the fact that Miss Brill talks to and seems to sympathize with the dead animal suggest about her? (She is lonely and she identifies with the creature.)

C. Language and Theme
Notice the frequent use of the word *sad*, often followed by a denial that *sad* is the right word.

D. Character
❓ What conclusion do you draw about Miss Brill from her habit of listening to other people's conversations? (Perhaps she is lonely or bored or prefers to live through others.)

A. Humanities Connection: Discussing the Fine Art

Gustave Caillebotte (1848–1894) was a French painter and collector who exhibited with the Impressionists. He was a prolific producer of town and country views, still lifes, and boating scenes. He bequeathed his large collection of Impressionist paintings to the French nation after his death.

? Study the male figure sitting alone in this outdoor scene and the female bystander. Discuss whether the two know each other and what the overall mood of the painting is. (They appear to be strangers focused on their own worlds. The contrast of light and shade adds a feeling of isolation.) How does the theme of the painting relate to that of "Miss Brill"? (This scene is much like the one Miss Brill sees—until she realizes she herself is being watched and thought about.)

B. Character

? How does Miss Brill judge the older people she sees in the park? (They seem to her to be odd, silent, and detached from life.) Does she include herself in this judgment? (No, seemingly not)

The Orange Trees (detail) by Gustave Caillebotte (1878). Oil on canvas, 61″ × 46″.

The Museum of Fine Arts, Houston. The John A. and Audrey Jones Beck Collection.

The old people sat on the bench, still as statues. Never mind, there was always the crowd to watch. To and fro, in front of the flowerbeds and the band rotunda, the couples and groups paraded, stopped to talk, to greet, to buy a handful of flowers from the old beggar who had his tray fixed to the railings. Little children ran among them, <u>swooping</u> and laughing; little boys with big white silk bows under their chins, little girls, little French dolls, dressed up in velvet and lace. And sometimes a tiny staggerer came suddenly rocking into the open from under the trees, stopped, stared, as suddenly sat down "flop," until its small high-stepping mother, like a young hen, rushed scolding to its rescue. Other people sat on the benches and green chairs, but they were nearly always the same, Sunday after Sunday, and—Miss Brill had often noticed—there was something funny about nearly all of them. They were odd, silent, nearly all old, and from the way they stared they looked as though they'd just come from dark little rooms or even—even cupboards!

Behind the rotunda the slender trees with yellow leaves down drooping, and through them just a line of sea, and beyond the blue sky with gold-veined clouds.

Tum-tum-tum tiddle-um! tiddle-um! tum tiddley-um tum ta! blew the band.

Two young girls in red came by and two young soldiers in blue met them, and they laughed and paired and went off arm-in-arm. Two peasant women with funny straw hats passed, gravely, leading beautiful smoke-colored donkeys. A cold, pale nun hurried by. A beautiful woman came along and dropped her bunch of violets, and a little boy ran after to hand them to her, and she took them and threw them away as if they'd been poisoned. Dear me! Miss Brill didn't know whether to admire that or not! And now an ermine toque[4] and a gentleman in gray met just in front of her. He was tall, stiff, dignified, and she was wearing the ermine toque she'd bought when her hair was yellow. Now everything, her hair, her face, even her eyes, was the same color as the shabby ermine, and her hand, in its cleaned glove, lifted to dab her lips, was a tiny yellowish paw. Oh, she was so pleased to see him—delighted! She rather thought they were going to meet that afternoon. She described where she'd been—everywhere, here, there, along by the sea. The day was so charming—didn't he agree? And wouldn't he, perhaps? . . . But he shook his head, lighted a cigarette, slowly breathed a great deep puff into her face, and, even while she was still talking and laughing, flicked the match away and walked on. The ermine toque was alone; she smiled more brightly than ever. But even the band seemed to know what she was feeling and played more softly, played tenderly, and the drum beat, "The Brute! The Brute!" over and over. What would she do? What was going to happen now? But as Miss Brill wondered, the ermine toque turned, raised her hand as though she'd seen someone else, much nicer, just over there, and pattered away. And the band changed again and played more quickly, more gaily than ever, and the old couple on Miss Brill's seat got up and marched away, and such a funny old man with long whiskers hobbled along in time to the music and was nearly knocked over by four girls walking abreast.

Oh, how fascinating it was! How she enjoyed it! How she loved sitting here, watching it all! It was like a play. It was exactly like a play. Who could believe the sky at the back wasn't painted? But it wasn't till a little brown dog trotted on solemn and then slowly trotted off, like a little "theater" dog, a little dog that had been drugged,

that Miss Brill discovered what it was that made it so exciting. They were all on the stage. They weren't only the audience, not only looking on; they were acting. Even she had a part and came every Sunday. No doubt somebody would have noticed if she hadn't been there; she was part of the performance after all. How strange she'd never thought of it like that before! And yet it explained why she made such a point of starting from home at just the same time each week—so as not to be late for the performance—and it also explained why she had quite a queer, shy feeling at telling her English pupils how she spent her Sunday afternoons. No wonder! Miss Brill nearly laughed out loud. She was on the stage. She thought of the old invalid gentleman to whom she read the newspaper four afternoons a week while he slept in the garden. She had got quite used to the frail head on the cotton pillow, the hollowed eyes, the open mouth and the high pinched nose. If he'd been dead she mightn't have noticed for weeks; she wouldn't have minded. But suddenly he knew he was having the paper read to him by an actress! "An actress!" The old head lifted; two points of light quivered in the old eyes. "An actress—are ye?" And Miss Brill smoothed the newspaper as though it were the manuscript of her part and said gently: "Yes, I have been an actress for a long time."

The band had been having a rest. Now they started again. And what they played was warm, sunny, yet there was just a faint chill—a something, what was it?—not sadness—no, not sadness—a something that made you want to sing. The tune lifted, lifted, the light shone; and it seemed to Miss Brill that in another moment all of them, all the whole company, would begin singing. The young ones, the laughing ones who were moving together, they would begin, and the men's voices, very resolute and brave, would join them. And then she too, she too, and the others on the benches—they would come in with a kind of accompaniment—something, low, that scarcely rose or fell, something so beautiful—moving. . . . And Miss Brill's eyes filled with tears and she looked smiling at all the other members of the company. Yes, we understand, we understand, she thought—though what they understood she didn't know.

Just at that moment a boy and a girl came and sat down where the old couple had been. They were beautifully dressed; they were in love. The

---

4. **toque** (tōk): a woman's small, round, close-fitting hat. Here, it refers to the woman as well.

A. Plot

❓ How would you describe the lady in the ermine toque? (Worn, shabbily genteel, falsely cheerful) How does the man treat her? (He coldly and cruelly walks away.) How does she resemble Miss Brill? (They are very similar except that the former might try harder to get involved with others.)

B. Theme

Miss Brill describes her Sunday afternoon in the park as a delightful play in which even she has an important part.

❓ What role has she been playing up till now? (The spectator)

C. Conflict and Irony

Miss Brill thinks she is an actress in the play of life that is going on in the park, and indeed she is part of a pretense.

❓ What is Miss Brill pretending? (That she is a real participant in what is going on and that she is enjoying herself)

Katherine Mansfield   987

987

1. Miss Brill goes to the park on __Sunday__ afternoons.
2. Although it was warm, Miss Brill decided to wear her __furpiece__.
3. While in the park, Miss Brill liked to listen to people's __conversations__.

4. As Miss Brill watched the people in the park, she felt as if she was part of a __play__.
5. Miss Brill overhead a __boy and girl or young couple__ making fun of her and her appearance.

CLOSURE

Ask students to write their thoughts about the last line in the story in which Miss Brill hears something crying. Since she is alone, what can this line mean? Have students share their interpretations.

A. Crisis
Here Miss Brill actually becomes a participant in the drama going on around her in a very painful way.

How is she viewed by the young couple? (As silly, stupid, and in the way)

B. Resolution
Ask students to imagine how Miss Brill felt when she returned to her room after hearing the young man's words. They might try pantomiming the scene described in the last paragraph. (Answers will vary, but students should understand that she is suffering from shock. She now knows that others do not see her as she sees herself.)

hero and heroine, of course, just arrived from his father's yacht. And still soundlessly singing, still with that trembling smile, Miss Brill prepared to listen.

A

"No, not now," said the girl. "Not here, I can't."

"But why? Because of that stupid old thing at the end there?" asked the boy. "Why does she come here at all—who wants her? Why doesn't she keep her silly old mug at home?"

"It's her fu-fur which is so funny," giggled the girl. "It's exactly like a fried whiting."[5]

"Ah, be off with you!" said the boy in an angry whisper. Then: "Tell me, ma petite cherie——"[6]

"No, not here," said the girl. "Not *yet*."

5. **whiting:** a kind of fish.
6. **ma petite chérie** (French): "my little darling."

On her way home she usually bought a slice of honeycake at the baker's. It was her Sunday treat. Sometimes there was an almond in her slice, sometimes not. It made a great difference. If there was an almond it was like carrying home a tiny present—a surprise—something that might very well not have been there. She hurried on the almond Sundays and struck the match for the kettle in quite a dashing way.

B

But today she passed the baker's by, climbed the stairs, went into the little dark room—her room like a cupboard—and sat down on the red eiderdown. She sat there for a long time. The box that the fur came out of was on the bed. She unclasped the necklet quickly; quickly, without looking, laid it inside. But when she put the lid on she thought she heard something crying.

A Critical Comment

"In Katherine Mansfield's 'Miss Brill,' there is only one character and only one situation. The narrative is simple, Miss Brill's action consists nearly altogether in sitting down; she does nothing but go and sit in the park, return home and sit on her bed in her little room. Yet considerably more of a story is attempted by this lesser-to-do than Crane attempted in 'Yellow Sky';[1] its plot is all implication.

" 'Miss Brill' is set on a stage of delight. 'Although it was so brilliantly fine—the blue sky powdered with gold and great spots of light like white wine splashed over the Jardins Publiques—Miss Brill was glad that she had decided on her fur. . . . [She] put up her hand and touched her fur. Dear little thing!' We see right off that for Miss Brill delight is a kind of coziness. She sits listening to the band, her Sunday habit, and 'Now there came a little "flutey" bit—very pretty!—a little chain of bright drops. She was sure it would be repeated. It was; she lifted her head and smiled.'

"Miss Brill has confidence in her world—anticipation: What will happen next? Ah, but she knows. She's delighted but safe. She sees the others from her little perch, her distance—the gay ones and then those on benches: 'Miss Brill had often noticed—there was something funny

1. Stephen Crane's "The Bride Comes to Yellow Sky," which Welty was also discussing in this essay.

about nearly all of *them*. They were odd, silent, nearly all old, and from the way they stared they looked as though they'd just come from dark little rooms or even—even cupboards!' For she hasn't identified herself at all.

"The drama is slight in this story. There is no collision. Rather the forces meeting in the Jardins Publiques have, at the story's end, passed through each other and come out the other side; there has not been a collision, but a change—something much more significant. This is because, though there is one small situation going on, a very large and complex one is implied—the outside world, in fact.

"One of the forces in the story is life itself, . . . life in the setting of a park on Sunday afternoon in Paris. All it usually does for Miss Brill is promenade stylishly while the band plays, form little tableaux, separate momently into minor, rather darker encounters, and keep in general motion with bright colors and light touches—there are no waving pistols at all, to storm and threaten.

"Yet, being life, it does threaten. In what way, at last? Well, how much more deadly to Miss Brill than a flourished pistol is an overheard remark—about *her*. Miss Brill's vision—a vision of love—is brought abruptly face to face with another, ruder vision of love. The boy and girl in love sit down on her bench, but they cannot go on with what they have been saying because of her, though

1. The park is located in Paris, France.
Her name suggests that she is not French; the fact that she has "English pupils" suggests that she is English.
2. The basic situation is that Miss Brill takes regular Sunday outings to the park, where she sits on a bench and observes her surroundings.

Students may mention the English couple discussing spectacles, the two girls in red meeting the soldiers, the beautiful woman dropping her violets and then throwing them away after the small boy picks them up and returns them to her, the woman in the ermine toque and her meeting with the elderly man, and the rich young boy and girl making fun of Miss Brill's fox collar.

Interpreting Meanings
3. Evidence includes her regular expeditions to the park, always at the same hour on Sundays, and her customary purchase of cake on the way home.
Her delight in the park, her pleasure in the band music, and her reading to the invalid gentleman are evidence of Miss Brill's kind heart.
4. She does not realize that she, too, is part of the "show."
5. Miss Brill's fox collar is a precious, beloved possession that she has cherished. The mockery of it by the young girl causes Miss Brill deep sorrow.
6. Basically, the protagonist, who had always thought of herself as an amused, detached spectator of the people around her, is rudely confronted by an unpleasant aspect of the outside world; she herself is "observed," and her prize possession is mocked.
Students' statements of theme may vary. In general, the theme has to do with human vulnerability and the harm that a casual, thoughtless remark may inflict.
7. Most students will agree that Miss Brill is crying.
The ambiguity reinforces the motif of "observing" in the story; by having Miss Brill think that "she heard someone crying," Mansfield refers once again to the ambiguous situation of Miss Brill as a spectator and, in turn, as the subject of observation herself.
8. Student answers will vary.

'still soundlessly singing, still with that trembling smile, Miss Brill prepared to listen.'

" 'No, not now,' said the girl. 'Not here, I can't.'

" 'But why? Because of that stupid old thing at the end there? . . . Why does she come here at all—who wants her? Why doesn't she keep her silly old mug at home?'

" 'It's her fu-fur which is so funny,' giggled the girl. 'It's exactly like a fried whiting.'

" 'Ah, be off with you!' said the boy in an angry whisper.

"So Miss Brill, she who could spare even pity for this world, in her innocence—pity, the spectator's emotion—is defeated. She had allowed herself occasional glimpses of lives not too happy, here in the park, which had moved her to little flutters of sadness. But that too had been coziness—coziness, a remedy visitors seek to take the chill off a strange place with. She hadn't known it wasn't good enough. All through the story she has sat in her 'special seat'—another little prop to endurance—and all unknown to her she sat in mortal danger. This is the story. The danger nears, a word is spoken, the blow falls—and Miss Brill retires, ridiculously easy to mow down, as the man with the pistols was easy to stare down in 'Yellow Sky,' for comedy's sake. But Miss Brill was from the first defenseless and on the losing side, and her defeat is the deeper for it, and one feels sure it is forever."

—Eudora Welty

Responding to the Story

Analyzing the Story

Identifying Facts

1. The story takes place in a public park, where Miss Brill is in many ways an outsider. In what country is this park located? What clues reveal Miss Brill's nationality?

2. "Miss Brill" is a story without much plot or action; rather, it focuses, as do many of Mansfield's stories, on the small human dramas within an ordinary situation. What is the **basic situation** in this story? Describe some of the human dramas the reader is permitted to see.

Interpreting Meanings

3. Miss Brill is unmarried and getting on in years. What evidence indicates that she is set in her ways—a creature of habit? What evidence indicates her kind heart?

4. What is **ironic** about Miss Brill's observations of the "other people" who sit on the benches and chairs every Sunday?

5. In *The Secret Sharer* by Conrad, the narrator's hat takes on **symbolic** meaning. What symbolic meaning is given to Miss Brill's fox collar? Pay close attention to its description at the beginning and end of the story.

6. In her critical comment, Eudora Welty maintains that a great deal happens in "Miss Brill," even though "its plot is all implication" and the action "consists nearly altogether in sitting down." What happens in "Miss Brill"? How would you state the story's **theme**?

7. Note that the last line of the story does not, as it easily might have, tell you exactly who or what is crying. Who do you think is crying? What is the effect of the **ambiguity** here?

8. How did this story make you feel about Miss Brill? Do you think there are characters like Miss Brill in the world as you know it?

Writing About the Story

A Creative Response

1. **Narrating What Happens Next.** Miss Brill's visits to the park have been a Sunday ritual. But will she return? Describe the scene that takes place in Miss Brill's room on the Sunday following the one in the story, several moments before her usual time of departure.

A Critical Response

2. **Analyzing Point of View.** In a brief essay, describe the point of view from which "Miss Brill" is told, and tell how it helps you understand Miss Brill's **character.** Include in your essay an explanation of how the impact of the story might have changed if Mansfield had chosen to tell the story from the point of view of the couple or from Miss Brill's own first-person point of view.

A. Responding to Primary Sources
In these excerpts from her journal and letters, Mansfield discusses what she tries to achieve in her writing. She is very concerned with the effect of every detail and of the overall sound of her prose. Have students read "Miss Brill" aloud as Mansfield did and judge if each word and image fits smoothly into the whole.

Primary Sources
Letters and Journals

The following extracts are from *The Letters and Journals of Katherine Mansfield: A Selection.* The first is a journal entry dated May 30, 1917; the second and third are letters to her painter friend Richard Murry.

"*May 30*   To be alive and to be a 'writer' is enough. Sitting at my table just now I saw one person turning to another, smiling, putting out his hand—speaking. And suddenly I clenched my fist and brought it down on the table and called out—There is *nothing* like it!"

17 January 1921

". . . It's a very queer thing how *craft* comes into writing. I mean down to details. Par exemple. In 'Miss Brill' I choose not only the length of every sentence, but even the sound of every sentence. I choose the rise and fall of every paragraph to fit her, and to fit her on that day at that very moment. After I'd written it I read it aloud—numbers of times—just as one would *play over* a musical composition—trying to get it nearer and nearer to the expression of Miss Brill—until it fitted her.

"Don't think I'm vain about the little sketch. It's only the method I wanted to explain. I often wonder whether other writers do the same—If a thing has really come off it seems to me there mustn't be one single word out of place, or one word that could be taken out. That's how I AIM at writing. It will take some time to get anywhere near there."

20 June 1921

". . . About the old masters. What I feel about them (all of them—writers too, of course) is the more one *lives* with them the better it is for one's work. It's almost a case of living *into* one's ideal world—the world that one desires to express. Do you know what I mean? For this reason I find that if I stick to men like Chaucer and Shakespeare and Marlowe and even Tolstoi, I keep much nearer what I want to do than if I confuse things with reading a lot of lesser men. I'd like to make the old masters my *daily* bread—in the sense in which it's used in the Lord's Prayer, really—to make them a kind of essential nourishment. All the rest is—well—it *comes after*. . . ."

—Katherine Mansfield

The Elements of Literature

THE MODERN SHORT STORY

People have been telling stories since the first campfire and writing them down since the invention of the alphabet. Stories, sketches, incidents, and episodes are the building blocks of narrative, as a reading of any long work, such as an epic, will demonstrate. During most of literary history, though, the short story did not exist as a separate form. Individual unconnected stories were sometimes linked together to form a larger whole, as in Boccaccio's *Decameron* or Chaucer's *Canterbury Tales,* but short works were seldom intended to stand on their own. The short story as a form is really an invention of the nineteenth century. A number of factors probably contributed to the rise of the short story, including growing literacy and the consequent popularity of magazines, but the form's flexibility and its appeal to a wide variety of artistic temperaments and visions has doubtless been responsible for its continued success.

We cannot really place the invention of the short story in a particular country or with a particular author. It developed and flourished at roughly the same time in Germany, France, and the United States, in the hands of writers such as E. T. A. Hoffman, Gustave Flaubert, Honoré de Balzac, Nathaniel Hawthorne, and Edgar Allan Poe. It was Poe, though, who created the most influential theoretical foundations for the short story in his 1842 review of Hawthorne's *Twice-Told Tales.* In this essay, Poe claimed not only that the story should be considered the equivalent of longer narratives such as the novel, but that it should be considered their superior. "The ordinary novel," he wrote, "is objectionable, from its length. . . . As it cannot be read at one sitting, it deprives itself . . . of the immense force derivable from *totality*." He argued that the story, which could be read at a single sitting, could have a more unified esthetic effect on the reader, and a **unified effect** was, to Poe, the most important literary goal. "The artist," he wrote, "having conceived, with deliberate care, a certain unique or single *effect* to be wrought out . . . then invents such incidents—he then combines such events as may best aid him in establishing this preconceived effect. If his very initial sentence tend not to the outbringing of this effect, then he has failed in his first step. In the whole composition there should be no word written, of which the tendency, direct or indirect, is not to the one pre-established design." The effect that Poe aimed for in most of his stories was usually shock or horror.

Other nineteenth-century story writers did not necessarily share Poe's thematic interests, but they would probably have agreed with his formulations. The nineteenth-century short story was painted with broad strokes. It frequently involved people in extreme states—either physically or emotionally, or both. It was not unusual for characters to go mad or die at the end. Such grand events satisfied both writers' and readers' need for a sense of **closure**, or the feeling that one has reached a fitting and satisfactory conclusion. This sense was provided by some writers, such as Guy de Maupassant in France and O. Henry in the United States, through the use of a **trick ending.** Whether it was character-oriented or plot-oriented, though, you *knew* when you had reached the conclusion of a nineteenth-century story.

Realism, a literary movement that developed in the latter part of the nineteenth century, served to constrain some of the psychological and narrative excesses of earlier writers. The realists strove to portray life as it really was, not as we might wish or fear it to be. Some realists, such as the Russian Anton Chekhov, whose work had a great influence on short-story writers in this century, frequently wrote stories that had no strong beginning or end, but merely portrayed the events of daily life. For these writers, the short story was not so much a form as it was a container. A form would falsify experience by forcing it into a shape it did not have. These **slice-of-life** stories provided readers with snapshots of life as it was lived in a great variety of regions and social classes. The American Henry James wrote thoroughly realistic stories, not only in their depiction of settings and ways of life, but in their faithful representation of his characters' perceptions and motivations. This **psychological realism,** like the realism of slice-of-life writers, had a great effect on the modern short story.

In the twentieth century, the short story has proven to be as popular and significant a form to serious writers as the novel. Few writers today, though, would agree with Poe that effect is the most important aspect of a story. Poe's theory was concerned with manipulating the reader's emotions. The modern story more often aims not at effect on the reader but at *revelation* to the reader—the revelation of some essential truth implicit in the story. The main character of the story may remain ignorant of this truth even at the end, and **irony,** the result of the reader knowing more than the character, is a characteristic element in modern fiction. Externally the story may not appear to have the unity of form that Poe espoused, but closer examination would probably reveal a coherence of **language, theme,** and **imagery** that is not obvious at first. Indeed, the less obviously unified a story is by form,

the more important unity of language, theme, and imagery becomes.

Mansfield's "Miss Brill" is a good example of these elements at work. One way to understand this is to look at two subtle participants in Miss Brill's afternoon—a faint chill and a gentle sadness. The chill appears in the weather in the first paragraph as "a faint chill, like a chill from a glass of iced water before you sip." Shortly later, we learn of a certain instability in Miss Brill's emotional state, something she is only faintly aware of: "when she breathed, something light and sad—no, not sad, exactly—something gentle seemed to move in her bosom." These two details—the faint chill beneath the surface warmth and the gentle not-quite-sadness beneath Miss Brill's composed exterior—come together in the music the band plays at the climax of the story, when Miss Brill is happiest. "And what they played was warm, sunny, yet there was just a faint chill—a something, what was it?—not sadness—no, not sadness—a something that made you want to sing." Miss Brill, who is still unaware of the chill and sadness under the surface of her own life, misinterprets these portents, but the reader does not.

The appearance of the fur in "Miss Brill" is an example of the importance of **symbol** in the modern short story. The fur is closely associated with Miss Brill's public self, carefully kept in its box at home, and somewhat the worse for wear. Miss Brill thinks of it as alive, as a "little rogue." She sees the ermine toque of a woman in the audience as representing the woman: "she was wearing the ermine toque she'd bought when her hair was yellow. Now everything, her hair, her face, even her eyes, was the same color as the shabby ermine, and her hand, in its cleaned glove, lifted to dab her lips, was a tiny yellowish paw." But while the reader is aware of how this applies to Miss Brill, she herself is not. Only when the girl makes fun of the fur at the end is the connection between herself and her fur revealed to Miss Brill.

Generalizations about a form as varied as the short story in the twentieth century are apt to be misleading. Nevertheless, in a general sense, we can say three things about the modern short story:

1. It is more likely to be concerned with the nuances of character than with the construction of a tricky or fast-paced plot.

2. It is more apt to imply than to state.

3. It is more apt to move toward a revelation than toward an effect.

While Poe would find some elements of the modern story puzzling, he would certainly recognize the continuation of his own interest in coherence and care for detail: "If a thing has really come off," Katherine Mansfield wrote of "Miss Brill," "it seems to me there mustn't be one single word out of place, or one word that could be taken out." With that sentiment, Poe would heartily agree.

Elizabeth Bowen
(1899–1973)

Elizabeth Bowen always thought of herself as the same age as the century. She was born in Dublin, Ireland, and spent her early years in County Cork, on her family's country estate, called Bowen's Court, a splendid house surrounded by beautiful gardens. Elizabeth was an only child, looked after by a governess, taken to the Anglican church on Sundays, taught to dance, wear gloves, and pay attention to manners. On her mother's orders, she was not taught to read until she was seven.

Elizabeth's father, Henry Bowen, practiced law. Overworked at his law practice, he behaved with increasing irrationality and once hurled all his papers from his office window. When Elizabeth was seven, he was confined to a mental hospital, but Elizabeth was not allowed to dwell on this or subsequent misfortunes. By Elizabeth's twelfth year, her father had recovered but her mother had contracted fatal cancer. ("Good news," her mother is reported to have remarked in her characteristic vigorous optimism. "Now I'm going to see what Heaven's like.") Elizabeth was not allowed to attend her mother's funeral in 1912 or to mourn her.

In fact, Elizabeth maintained an unsinkable cheerfulness for the rest of her days, but she also developed a pronounced stutter that never left her. On a few words she would stall out altogether; one of these words was *mother*. Describing the Bowen family later, Elizabeth wrote that they strove "to live as though living gave them no trouble." Stylishness, vanity, discipline, energy, a dislike of cant, independence, and courage were all Bowen qualities, and they were also very much Elizabeth's own.

Bowen's fiction also bears the stamp of her early years. Much of her writing is concerned with the processes of growing up, of losing innocence, of coming to terms with reality. Her main characters are often wealthy, sensitive, and well-mannered women, yet her novels also reveal a sense of insecurity, a feeling that life cannot be trusted, that existence is a struggle. Dislocation is a major theme, as is the brittleness of romance.

Perhaps because as a child she was always kept unknowing and in the power of others, Bowen feared that she would never become a grown-up. In the preface to her first collection of stories, *Encounters* (1923), she wrote that this fear actually "egged her on" to write, because she was writing as a way to become an adult. At seventeen, after finishing at boarding school in England, she began her adult life. With no further formal education, she moved to London to write stories.

In London, she attended readings at the Poetry Bookshop and there made the first of the literary friendships that were to become the fabric of her life. Among these literary friends were Rose Macauley, Edith Sitwell, Ezra Pound, and Aldous Huxley. In the year *Encounters* was published to little notice, she married Alan Cameron, a teacher. Cameron was not an intellectual, but he was an intelligent man and he adored his wife.

For the next ten years the Camerons lived in the university town of Oxford, where Bowen wrote industriously. Her short stories appeared regularly and her first novel, *The Hotel,* was published in 1927. Thereafter, she produced nearly a novel a year.

In these Oxford days, Bowen fell seriously in love with a younger man; she later explained it on one level as the writer's need for experience. (She drew on this experience for her novel *The House in Paris,* published in 1935.) As a writer, she often fused the role of watched and watcher, and she noted, "It is hard for me (being a writer before I am a woman) to realize that anything—friendship or love especially—in which I participate imaginatively isn't a book too. Isn't, I mean, something I make what it is by my will, that it shall be like that."

In 1935, the Camerons moved back to London, where Elizabeth became a notable hostess of the literary world. Returning from his job at the BBC, Alan would find the hallway festooned with the hats of Elizabeth's admirers. While he did resent those hats, the clouds of World War II were threatening, and in the face of this new danger, the Camerons' dependency on each other deepened.

The war, with its nightly air raids on London, had a profound effect on Bowen's feelings about writing. "These days," she said, "one feels rather a revulsion against psychological intricacies for their own sakes." She was also wary of people who called forth a remark customarily addressed to adolescents: "For heaven's sake stop fussing over yourself and try to get on with something more important."

Amidst the destruction, Bowen was a dedicated air-raid warden, policing the neighborhood each night for dangerous leaks of light. But she also went right on giving parties. Once while entertaining guests on her balcony, she took no notice of the sky ablaze with magnesium flares, but when she had gathered everyone inside she said, in a typical understatement, "I feel I should apologize for the noise."

Perhaps her best novel, *The Heat of the Day* (1949), is a classic story of wartime London that drew upon her relationship with Charles Ritchie, a Canadian diplomat. Moved to tears by the novel, Bowen's friend Rosamond Lehmann wrote her, "I suppose you must know, inside you, what you've done. . . . You really do, write about love. Who else does today?"

At the same time, she was writing the stories later published in 1945 in the collection called *The Demon Lover.* She wrote that this collection was a "diary" she kept of her reactions to the war period, and she described the stories as "flying particles of something enormous and inchoate."

Following the war, Elizabeth and Alan decided to return to a quieter life in Ireland at Bowen's Court. They had barely begun this new, serene era, when Alan died of a heart attack. As might have been predicted, Elizabeth became more active than ever. She traveled to Europe and the United States, visited her many friends and her American publishers Alfred and Blanche Knopf, and taught and lectured at Princeton, Wisconsin, Vassar, and Bryn Mawr. All the while she wrote steadily, continuing to produce novels, stories, and magazine articles. Though her literary output was tremendous, Bowen found that she could no longer afford to maintain her beloved Bowen's Court, and she was obliged to sell the beautiful estate in 1959.

Although she had been strong and irrepressibly healthy all her life, a persistent cough proved to be a symptom of lung cancer. She died in 1973, and was buried in the Irish churchyard beside her father and her husband.

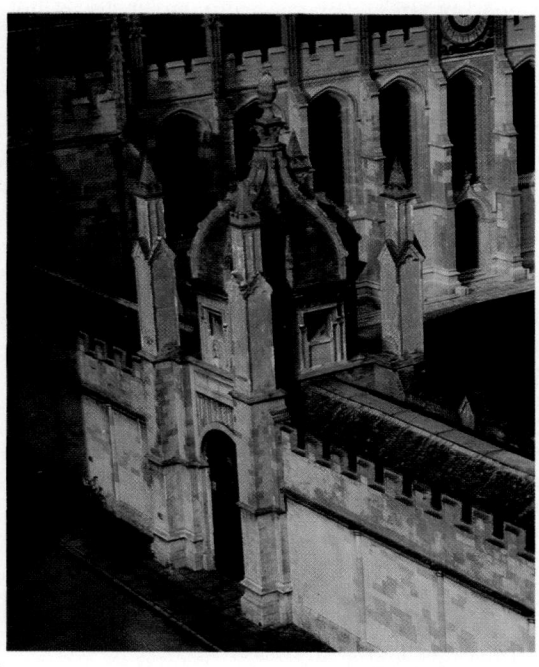

Remind students that a demon is an evil spirit who appears in fairy tales or folk tales to do harm to humans. Demons are associated with hell and the devil's revenge. The word *demon* is sometimes used to refer to an internal drive or obsession that leads a person into excess or danger.

2. ESTABLISHING A PURPOSE. Ask students to be alert for details that suggest departure from the normal or expected routines of domestic life. Is Mrs. Drover as ordinary and her life as predictable as she would like? Who or what is lurking in the shadows?

A. Mood and Atmosphere

? What is the effect of statements like, "No human eye watched Mrs. Drover's return"? (A sense of menace, fear, and suspense)

B. Language and Theme

Note the choice of the expression "she stopped dead" to describe Mrs. Drover's reaction when she sees the letter.

THE DEMON LOVER

"The Demon Lover" has been compared to an Alfred Hitchcock movie. Hitchcock was a master of style, mood, and suspense in film. From the first paragraph of Bowen's story, it is evident that she is a master of these same qualities in fiction. An amusing idiosyncrasy of Hitchcock's films is that he places himself somewhere in each as a walk-on character. Generations of moviegoers have delighted in trying to discover Hitchcock's fleeting but very recognizable presence. In a simi-larly brief and unobtrusive way, Elizabeth Bowen is present in her work for those readers who recognize her. As you read "The Demon Lover," watch for a few words of description or a bit of emotional content that suddenly reminds you of something you read in her biography. You are forgiven, of course, if, as often happens to viewers of a Hitchcock movie, you are too caught up in suspense to notice.

Toward the end of her day in London Mrs. Drover went round to her shut-up house to look for several things she wanted to take away. Some belonged to herself, some to her family, who were by now used to their country life. It was late August; it had been a steamy, showery day: at the moment the trees down the pavement glittered in an escape of humid yellow afternoon sun. Against the next batch of clouds, already piling up ink-dark, broken chimneys and parapets stood out. In her once familiar street, as in any unused channel, an unfamiliar queerness had silted up; a cat wove itself in and out of railings, but no human eye watched Mrs. Drover's return. Shifting some parcels under her arm, she slowly forced round her latchkey in an unwilling lock, then gave the door, which had warped, a push with her knee. Dead air came out to meet her as she went in.

The staircase window having been boarded up, no light came down into the hall. But one door, she could just see, stood ajar, so she went quickly through into the room and unshuttered the big window in there. Now the prosaic[1] woman, looking about her, was more perplexed than she knew by everything that she saw, by traces of her long former habit of life—the yellow smoke-stain up the white marble mantelpiece, the ring left by a vase on the top of the *escritoire*;[2] the bruise in the wallpaper where, on the door being thrown open widely, the china handle had always hit the wall.

The piano, having gone away to be stored, had left what looked like claw marks on its part of the parquet. Though not much dust had seeped in, each object wore a film of another kind; and, the only ventilation being the chimney, the whole drawing room smelled of the cold hearth. Mrs. Drover put down her parcels on the escritoire and left the room to proceed upstairs; the things she wanted were in a bedroom chest.

She had been anxious to see how the house was—the part-time caretaker she shared with some neighbors was away this week on his holiday, known to be not yet back. At the best of times he did not look in often, and she was never sure that she trusted him. There were some cracks in the structure, left by the last bombing, on which she was anxious to keep an eye. Not that one could do anything——

A shaft of refracted daylight now lay across the hall. She stopped dead and stared at the hall table—on this lay a letter addressed to her.

She thought first—then the caretaker *must* be back. All the same, who, seeing the house shuttered, would have dropped a letter in at the box? It was not a circular, it was not a bill. And the post office redirected, to the address in the country, everything for her that came through the post. The caretaker (even if he *were* back) did not know she was due in London today—her call here had been planned to be a surprise—so his negligence in the manner of this letter, leaving it to wait in the dusk and the dust, annoyed her. Annoyed, she picked up the letter, which bore no stamp. But it cannot be important, or they would know . . . She

---

1. **prosaic** (prō·zā′ik): dull and ordinary.
2. *escritoire* (es·krē′twär): writing desk.

SUPPLEMENTARY SUPPORT MATERIALS
1. Vocabulary Activity Worksheet (*CCB*)
2. Review and Response Worksheet:
Flashback and Foreshadowing (*CCB*)
3. Language Skills Worksheet: Parallel
Sentence Structure (*CCB*)
4. Selection Test (*CCB*)

DEVELOPING VOCABULARY
The following words from the story are
tested in the Selection Test. (See also
Vocabulary Activity Worksheet.)

parapet	to plight
to refract	troth
rank	stint
intermittent	arboreal
precipitately	hinterland

A

A Lady in an Interior by Carl Holsoe. Oil.

Private collection.

A. Humanities Connection: Discussing the Fine Art

? Does this painting of a woman reading alone in a room convey the mood of "The Demon Lover"? (It does resemble the scene in the empty bedroom in the late afternoon. The space and lighting suggest isolation.) What does the woman's posture in the painting suggest about her situation? (The curves of her body contrast with the horizontal and vertical lines of the room, suggesting vulnerability.) What is the effect of the mirror facing the door? (The mirror confirms the emptiness of the room.) What does the angle of perspective from which the picture is painted suggest? (It suggests she is being observed by someone in the hall.) What do you think will happen next? (Answers will vary. The observer may interrupt her or may decide to leave her to her thoughts.)

A. Plot

❓ What signifi-
cance could
there be in Mrs.
Drover's going to
her former bed-
room and sitting on
the bed to read the
letter? (Uncon-
sciously she knows
it is from her
former lover.)

B. Tone

❓ How would you
describe the
tone of this letter?
(Implacable, deter-
mined, knowing)
What do you ex-
pect will happen
"at the hour ar-
ranged"?

C. Flashback

Here the narrative
moves abruptly to
the past.

❓ How does the
description of
the parting of the
girl and the soldier
differ from conven-
tional romantic ver-
sions of the same
scene? (She does
not look at his
face; he is not
kind; she wished
him gone; they do
not kiss.)

D. Conflict

❓ What does the
soldier promise
will inevitably hap-
pen? (They will
definitely be re-
united.) What
seems to be the
girl's strongest de-
sire throughout this
meeting? (To get
away)

took the letter rapidly upstairs with her, without
a stop to look at the writing till she reached what
had been her bedroom, where she let in light. The
room looked over the garden and other gardens:
the sun had gone in; as the clouds sharpened and
lowered, the trees and rank lawns seemed already
to smoke with dark. Her reluctance to look again
at the letter came from the fact that she felt intruded upon—and by someone contemptuous of
her ways. However, in the tenseness preceding
the fall of rain she read it: it was a few lines.

> Dear Kathleen: You will not have forgotten that
> today is our anniversary, and the day we said.
> The years have gone by at once slowly and fast.
> In view of the fact that nothing has changed, I
> shall rely upon you to keep your promise. I was
> sorry to see you leave London, but was satisfied
> that you would be back in time. You may expect
> me, therefore, at the hour arranged. Until
> then . . .   K.

Mrs. Drover looked for the date: it was today's.
She dropped the letter on to the bedsprings, then
picked it up to see the writing again—her lips,
beneath the remains of lipstick, beginning to go
white. She felt so much the change in her own
face that she went to the mirror, polished a clear
patch in it and looked at once urgently and stealthily in. She was confronted by a woman of forty-
four, with eyes starting out under a hatbrim that
had been rather carelessly pulled down. She had
not put on anymore powder since she left the shop
where she ate her solitary tea. The pearls her
husband had given her on their marriage hung
loose round her now rather thinner throat, slipping
in the V of the pink wool jumper her sister knitted
last autumn as they sat round the fire. Mrs. Drover's most normal expression was one of controlled worry, but of assent. Since the birth of the
third of her little boys, attended by a quite serious
illness, she had had an intermittent muscular
flicker to the left of her mouth, but in spite of this
she could always sustain a manner that was at
once energetic and calm.

Turning from her own face as precipitately as
she had gone to meet it, she went to the chest
where the things were, unlocked it, threw up the
lid and knelt to search. But as rain began to come
crashing down she could not keep from looking
over her shoulder at the stripped bed on which
the letter lay. Behind the blanket of rain the clock
of the church that still stood struck six—with rapidly heightening apprehension she counted each
of the slow strokes. "The hour arranged . . . My
God," she said, "*what* hour? How should I . . .?
After twenty-five years. . . ."

The young girl talking to the soldier in the garden
had not ever completely seen his face. It was dark;
they were saying goodbye under a tree. Now and
then—for it felt, from not seeing him at this intense moment, as though she had never seen him
at all—she verified his presence for these few moments longer by putting out a hand, which he each
time pressed, without very much kindness, and
painfully, on to one of the breast buttons of his
uniform. That cut of the button on the palm of her
hand was, principally, what she was to carry away.
This was so near the end of a leave from France
that she could only wish him already gone. It was
August 1916. Being not kissed, being drawn away
from and looked at intimidated Kathleen till she
imagined spectral glitters in the place of his eyes.
Turning away and looking back up the lawn she
saw, through branches of trees, the drawing room
window alight: she caught a breath for the moment
when she could go running back there into the
safe arms of her mother and sister, and cry: "What
shall I do, what shall I do? He has gone."

Hearing her catch her breath, her fiancé said,
without feeling: "Cold?"

"You're going away such a long way."

"Not so far as you think."

"I don't understand?"

"You don't have to," he said. "You will. You
know what we said."

"But that was—suppose you—I mean, suppose."

"I shall be with you," he said, "sooner or later.
You won't forget that. You need do nothing but
wait."

Only a little more than a minute later she was
free to run up the silent lawn. Looking in through
the window at her mother and sister, who did not
for the moment perceive her, she already felt that
unnatural promise drive down between her and
the rest of all humankind. No other way of having
given herself could have made her feel so apart,
lost and foresworn.[3] She could not have plighted
a more sinister troth.

Kathleen behaved well when, some months
later, her fiancé was reported missing, presumed

---

3. **foresworn:** having lied under oath.

killed. Her family not only supported her but were able to praise her courage without stint because they could not regret, as a husband for her, the man they knew almost nothing about. They hoped she would, in a year or two, console herself—and had it been only a question of consolation things might have gone much straighter ahead. But her trouble, behind just a little grief, was a complete dislocation from everything. She did not reject other lovers, for these failed to appear: for years she failed to attract men—and with the approach of her thirties she became natural enough to share her family's anxiousness on this score. She began to put herself out, to wonder; and at thirty-two she was very greatly relieved to find herself being courted by William Drover. She married him, and the two of them settled down in this quiet, <u>arboreal</u> part of Kensington: in this house the years piled up, her children were born and they all lived <u>till they were driven out by the bombs of the next war. Her movements as Mrs. Drover were circumscribed, and she dismissed any idea that they were still watched.</u>

As things were—dead or living the letter-writer sent her only a threat. Unable, for some minutes, to go on kneeling with her back exposed to the empty room, Mrs. Drover rose from the chest to sit on an upright chair whose back was firmly against the wall. The desuetude[4] of her former bedroom, her married London home's whole air of being a cracked cup from which memory, with its reassuring power, had either evaporated or leaked away, made a crisis—and at just this crisis the letter-writer had, knowledgeably, struck. The hollowness of the house this evening canceled years on years of voices, habits, and steps. Through the shut windows she only heard rain fall on the roofs around. To rally herself, she said she was in a mood—and for two or three seconds shutting her eyes, told herself that she had imagined the letter. But she opened them—there it lay on the bed.

On the supernatural side of the letter's entrance she was not permitting her mind to dwell. Who, in London, knew she meant to call at the house today? Evidently, however, this had been known. The caretaker, *had* he come back, had had no cause to expect her: he would have taken the letter in his pocket, to forward it, at his own time, through the post. There was no other sign that the caretaker had been in—but, if not? Letters dropped in at doors of deserted houses do not fly or walk to tables in halls. They do not sit on the dust of empty tables with the air of certainty that they will be found. There is needed some human hand—but nobody but the caretaker had a key. Under circumstances she did not care to consider, a house can be entered without a key. It was possible that she was not alone now. She might be being waited for, downstairs. Waited for—until when? Until "the hour arranged." At least that was not six o'clock: six has struck.

She rose from the chair and went over and locked the door.

The thing was, to get out. To fly? No, not that: she had to catch her train. As a woman whose utter dependability was the keystone of her family life she was not willing to return to the country, to her husband, her little boys and her sister, without the objects she had come up to fetch. Resuming work at the chest she set about making up a number of parcels in a rapid, fumbling-decisive way. These, with her shopping parcels, would be too much to carry; these meant a taxi—at the thought of the taxi her heart went up and her normal breathing resumed. I will ring up the taxi now; the taxi cannot come too soon: I shall hear the taxi out there running its engine, till I walk calmly down to it through the hall. I'll ring up—But no: the telephone is cut off . . . She tugged at a knot she had tied wrong.

The idea of flight . . . He was never kind to me, not really. I don't remember him kind at all. Mother said he never considered me. He was set on me, that was what it was—not love. Not love, not meaning a person well. What did he do, to make me promise like that? I can't remember—But she found that she could.

She remembered with such dreadful acuteness that the twenty-five years since then dissolved like smoke and she instinctively looked for the weal[5] left by the button on the palm of her hand. She remembered not only all that he said and did but the complete suspension of *her* existence during that August week. I was not myself—they all told me so at the time. She remembered—but with one white burning blank as where acid has dropped on a photograph: *under no conditions* could she remember his face.

So, wherever he may be waiting, I shall not

---

4. **desuetude** (des′wi·tōōd′): disuse.

5. **weal**: a ridge or lump caused by a blow.

A. Theme
This sentence reveals that Mrs. Drover has had the sense from time to time of being watched. Look for other signs that she is not always able to maintain her desired calm state of mind.

B. Conflict
❓ What kind of relationship does Mrs. Drover recall? (A loveless determination to be together) How was the promise extracted? (By force, both mental and physical)

Critical Comment
Eudora Welty has said that "Elizabeth Bowen's awareness of place, *of where she was*, seemed to approach the siesmetic [capable of registering minute changes or vibrations]; it was equaled only by her close touch with the passage, the pulse, of time. . . . Her characters she invented, in consequence [of their time and place]." Ask students to write an explanation of how the time and place of this story help to shape the characters.

READING CHECK TEST
1. Mrs. Dover was returning to the home of her childhood on a humid August day. (F)
2. The empty, closed-up house made Mrs. Drover uneasy. (T)
3. After reading the letter, Mrs. Drover became increasingly fearful. (T)

4. The letter writer was someone she had loved passionately when they were both young. (F)
5. Mrs. Drover was a strong person who did not bend to the will of others. (F)

CLOSURE
Ask students to write two or three sentences explaining what they think the demon lover represented.

A. Mood and Atmosphere

❓ Look for details that give the last part of the story the feel of a dream or a nightmare. ("Unnatural pace"; the taxi "appeared already to be waiting for her"; "the clock struck seven")

B. Climax

❓ What is particularly horrible about the final, face-to-face encounter in the taxi? (We are not told who or what she sees—only that she screams.) What is the effect of the use of the word *eternity*? (It suggests her death.)

know him. You have no time to run from a face you do not expect.

The thing was to get to the taxi before any clock struck what could be the hour. She would slip down the street and round the side of the square to where the square gave on the main road. She would return in the taxi, safe, to her own door, and bring the solid driver into the house with her to pick up the parcels from room to room. The idea of the taxi driver made her decisive, bold: she unlocked her door, went to the top of the staircase and listened down.

She heard nothing—but while she was hearing nothing the passé⁶ air of the staircase was disturbed by a draft that traveled up to her face. It emanated from the basement: down there a door or window was being opened by someone who chose this moment to leave the house.

The rain had stopped; the pavements steamily shone as Mrs. Drover let herself out by inches from her own front door into the empty street. The unoccupied houses opposite continued to meet her look with their damaged stare. Making toward the thoroughfare and the taxi, she tried not to keep looking behind. Indeed, the silence was so intense—one of those creeks of London silence exaggerated this summer by the damage of war—that no tread could have gained on hers unheard. **A** Where her street debouched⁷ on the square where

---

6. **passé:** (French) "belonging to the past."
7. **debouched** (di·bōōshd): emptied out.

---

people went on living, she grew conscious of, and checked, her unnatural pace. Across the open end of the square two buses impassively passed each other: women, a perambulator, cyclists, a man wheeling a barrow signalized, once again, the ordinary flow of life. At the square's most populous corner should be—and was—the short taxi rank. This evening, only one taxi—but this, although it presented its blank rump, appeared already to be alertly waiting for her. Indeed, without looking round the driver started his engine as she panted up from behind and put her hand on the door. As she did so, the clock struck seven. The taxi faced the main road: to make the trip back to her house it would have to turn—she had settled back on the seat and the taxi *had* turned before she, surprised by its knowing movement, recollected that she had not "said where." She leaned forward to scratch at the glass panel that divided the driver's head from her own.

The driver braked to what was almost a stop, turned round and slid the glass panel back: the jolt of this flung Mrs. Drover forward till her face was almost into the glass. Through the aperture driver and passenger, not six inches between them, remained for an eternity eye to eye. Mrs. Drover's mouth hung open for some seconds before she could issue her first scream. After that she continued to scream freely and to beat with her gloved hands on the glass all round as the taxi, accelerating without mercy, made off with her into the hinterland of deserted streets. **B**

Responding to the Story

Analyzing the Story

Identifying Facts

1. In some stories, the **setting** is much more than a description of physical background—it also creates a particular **mood**. In "The Demon Lover" an atmosphere of foreboding is established immediately. List the **images** in the first paragraph that help create this strong sense of foreboding.
2. Why has the Drover family been dislocated from their home? Cite two places in the text that make the reason clear. For what purpose has Mrs. Drover returned?

3. Explain the circumstances surrounding the arrival of the letter. Before Mrs. Drover reads the letter, how does she feel about its being in the house? How do her feelings change after she reads the letter?
4. A tale that begins with the promise of a meeting between two former lovers could easily lead the reader to expect a sentimental love story. But the reader of "The Demon Lover" never for a moment expects this. What details in the description of the lovers' last meeting **foreshadow** a sinister, threatening reunion? What does Mrs. Drover tell us about her fiancé that explains why she is terrified of him?

1. Students may list the shut-up house, the "steamy, showery day," the batch of clouds that pile up "ink-dark," the broken chimney and parapets, the references to the unwilling lock, the warped door, and the dead air inside the house.

2. The family has been dislocated because of the wartime bombings of London. Note the part-time caretaker and the family's growing used to their country life. Also the detail of the cracks in the wall, caused by the recent bombing.

She has returned to pick up some things from the house.

3. Mrs. Drover sees the letter on the hall table. She cannot understand how it got there, since the caretaker has not been in the house, and, even if he return-ed, he would not have known of Mrs. Drover's unplanned visit. As she picks up the letter, Mrs. Drover feels mystified. She becomes terrified as she reads.

4. Students may mention the lack of kindness with which the lover presses Mrs. Drover's hand, the spectral glitters that she imagines in place of his eyes, and the ambivalence with which the lover *(Answers continue on next page.)*

---

5. The use of an **omniscient narrator** allows Bowen to give her readers information about Mrs. Drover's psychological makeup that Mrs. Drover herself is not consciously aware of. Find several such passages in the text.

Interpreting Meanings

6. World War I and World War II bracket this story like bookends. During each war, Mrs. Drover experiences confusion, dislocation, and disorientation. During each war, the demon lover is part of her life. Yet the demon lover doesn't appear during the intervening twenty-five years. Use these strands of the story (the war, Mrs. Drover's inner turmoil, and the appearances of the demon lover) in a statement of the **theme** of the story.

7. Dramatic irony occurs when the audience is aware of a situation that a character in the story is not aware of. What is the dramatic irony of the story?

8. One aspect of "The Demon Lover" that contributes to its richness and depth is the interplay between present and past. Locate the place in the story where Bowen uses a **flashback** to tell what happened earlier in Mrs. Drover's life. Note that Bowen does not provide a smooth transition into the flashback. Do you think the abrupt shift into the past is effective in this story, or merely confusing? Why?

9. One possible, decidedly psychological, interpretation of "The Demon Lover" is that Mrs. Drover's experience is an hallucination. Another way of looking at the story is to consider it a frank ghost story. Which interpretation do you favor, or do you have another? Support your interpretation with evidence from the text.

Writing About the Story

A Creative Response

1. Describing a Character. At no time in the story are we given a description of the demon lover's face. When he is Mrs. Drover's fiancé, his face is in a shadow and she feels as though "she had never seen him at all." Twenty-five years later, we are told that *"under no conditions* could she remember his face." At the end of the story, however, when Mrs. Drover is finally within six inches of his face, she begins to scream. Describe what you imagine Mrs. Drover saw.

2. Mixing Media. Suppose yourself the producer-director of a movie version of "The Demon Lover." You have to consider these tasks:

a. Casting both the younger and older Mrs. Drover, her lover, and the minor characters of the family

b. Creating scenery, lighting, and background music to establish atmosphere

A

Letter Ghost by Paul Klee (1937). Colored paste (mixture of pigment, chalk, and starch) on newspaper, 13″ × 19¼″.

Collection, The Museum of Modern Art, New York. Purchase.

c. Creating suspense by such means as the chiming of the clock

d. Telling your screenwriters how you would expand certain parts of the story for a feature-length film

Write a proposal outlining your ideas on how you'd convert the story into a film. Will you film the story as a horror story, or as a psychological study of love?

A Critical Response

3. Comparing Literature. "The Demon Lover" is also the title of the following famous old ballad. In an essay, compare the ballad to Bowen's story. Before you write, gather the material for your comparison by filling out a chart like the one below.

	Bowen Story	Ballad
Characters		
Plot		
Mood		
Theme		

Conclude your essay by telling whether or not you believe the story is based in any way on the old song.

**James Harris
(The Demon Lover)**

"O where have you been, my long, long love,
  This long seven years and mair?"°
"O I'm come to seek my former vows
  Ye granted me before."

---

2. **mair:** more.

A. Humanities Connection: Discussing the Fine Art
Paul Klee (1879–1940) is one of the master draughtsmen of this century. A lover of fantasy, Klee's playful, seemingly improvised drawings combine a childlike imagination and a sophisticated wit. Born in Switzerland of a Swiss mother and a Bavarian father, Klee was also a talented violinist and, in his mature years, taught at the famous Bauhaus, a German school that had a powerful impact on modern graphic design.

? In what way is the letter in "The Demon Lover" a "letter ghost"? (The letter arrived on the day she would visit the house and was placed on a table inside the house.) Do you think the mood of the drawing fits the mood of the story? Why or why not? (Answers will vary. Some will find the drawing too cartoon-like, others may find parallels between the simplicity of its forms and the quiet, empty feeling in the story.)

says, "I shall be with you sooner or later."

She feels that she promised herself to him unnaturally; also he has threatened to come back sooner or later to reclaim her.

5. References to Mrs. Drover as a "prosaic woman," the explanation of her "intermittent muscular flicker," and the descriptions of her reactions to her fiance.

Interpreting Meanings

6. A possible answer might be that the story reveals the psychological dislocations experienced by people during the disruptions of wartime.

7. The dramatic irony is that the reader suspects that the taxi driver must be the demon lover; Mrs. Drover does not. Even though she is unnerved by the letter and by her fear of her lover's return, she feels

safe until the driver turns around. Then she screams in horror.

8. The flashback begins with the sentence, "The young girl talking to the soldier in the garden had not ever completely seen his face." The abrupt shift is perhaps appropriate, given Mrs. Drover's disorientation and excited frame of mind.

9. Students' answers will vary. The (*Answers continue in left-hand column.*)

(Continued from top.)

hallucination theory, which must cover the letter as well as the taxi, is supported by the atmosphere of the house, with its "dead air" and memories, and by the fact that she is completely alone. The ghost story, while it too draws on the atmosphere of the house, is supported by the existence of the letter and the final scene. Ask students to support their interpretations with citations from the story.

5
"O hold your tongue of your former vows,
   For they will breed sad strife;
O hold your tongue of your former vows,
   For I am become a wife."

He turned him right and round about,
10
   And the tear blinded his ee:°
"I wad never hae trodden on Irish ground,
   If it had not been for thee.

"I might hae had a king's daughter,
   Far, far beyond the sea;
15
I might have had a king's daughter,
   Had it not been for love o thee."

"If ye might have had a king's daughter,
   Yer sel° ye had to blame;
Ye might have taken the king's daughter,
20
   For ye kend° that I was nane.°

"If I was to leave my husband dear,
   And my two babes also,
O what have you to take me to,
   If with you I should go?"

25
"I hae seven ships upon the sea—
   The eighth brought me to land—
With four-and-twenty bold mariners,
   And music on every hand."

She has taken up her two little babes,
30
   Kissed them baith cheek and chin:
"O fair ye weel, my ain two babes,
   For I'll never see you again."

She set her foot upon the ship,
   No mariners could she behold;
35
But the sails were o the taffetie,
   And the masts o the beaten gold.

They had not sailed a league, a league,
   A league but barely three,
When dismal grew his countenance,
40
   And drumlie° grew his ee.

They had not sailed a league, a league,
   A league but barely three,
Until she espied his cloven foot,
   And she wept right bitterlie.

45
"O hold your tongue of your weeping," says he,
   "Of your weeping now let me be;
I will show you how lilies grow
   On the banks of Italy."

"O what hills are yon, yon pleasant hills,
50
   That the sun shines sweetly on?"
"O yon are the hills of heaven," he said,
   "Where you will never win."

"O whaten mountain is yon," she said,
   "All so dreary wi frost and snow?"
55
"O yon is the mountain of hell," he cried,
   "Where you and I will go."

He strack the tap-mast wi his hand,
   The fore-mast wi his knee,
And he brake that gallant ship in twain,
60
   And sank her in the sea.

---

10. **ee:** eye.
18. **yer sel:** yourself.
20. **kend:** knew. **nane:** none.

40. **drumlie:** dark and gloomy.

Frank O'Connor
(1903–1966)

Frank O'Connor was born Michael John O'Donovan in Cork City, Ireland. He was the only child of a tall, bitterly poor man, Michael O'Donovan, and his long-suffering wife, Minnie. The memory of his parents' battling shadowed his life. "In those days," he wrote in his autobiography *An Only Child* (1961),

> the house would be a horror. Only when he had money for drink would we have peace for an hour. . . . When I was old enough to go to school, I would come back at three o'clock and scout around to make sure that he was not at home. . . . When I talked of him to Mother, I always called him "he" or "him," carefully eschewing the name of "Father," which would have seemed like profanation to me.
>
> "You must not speak like that of your father, child," Mother would say severely. "Whatever he does he's still your father." I resented her loyalty to him. I wanted her to talk to me about him the way I knew the neighbors talked. They could not understand why she did not leave him. I realize now that to do so she would have had to take a job as housekeeper and put me into an orphanage. . . .

O'Connor read endlessly, first boys' magazines and then, finding his way to the library, books of all kinds. Ironically, he particularly enjoyed stories of English schoolboys, and while he knew there would never be money for any such education in his own life, he imagined its privileges and yearned to be an educated man.

The reality of his own schooling was not half so appealing. One schoolmaster "combined the sanctimoniousness of a reformed pirate with the brutality of a half-witted drill sergeant. With him the cane was never a mere weapon; it was a real extension of his personality."

However, another teacher, a writer named Daniel Corkery, was kind to young O'Donovan. It was Corkery who later drew him into the literary and political life that was to change the face of Ireland.

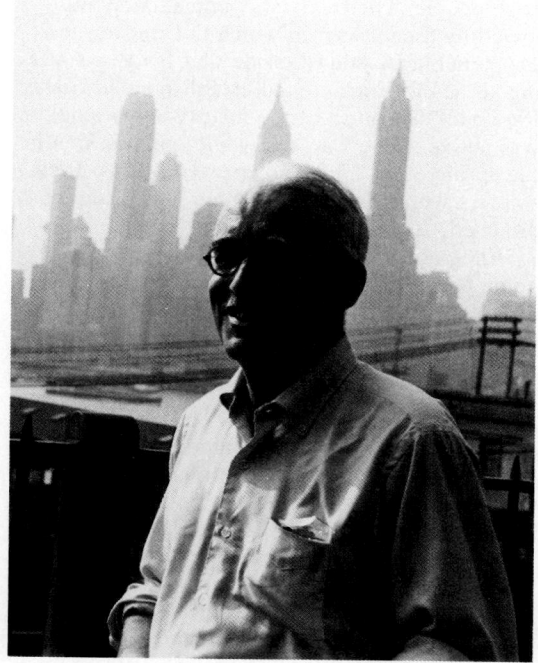

In the end, O'Donovan gave up on school, feeling it was a place where he would be always "useless, frightened, or hurt." But at fourteen, he also had no intention of abandoning his dream of an education. He took a series of clerk's jobs that gave him money to buy the books he needed to educate himself.

In 1916, the hostility between England and Ireland flared into open rebellion, and O'Donovan was caught up in the new patriotism. As his countrymen were executed by the British for their part in the uprising, he read Irish history with new fervor and, along with other young Irish men, he thought of heroism.

"I was improvising an education I could not afford," he said later, "and the country was improvising a revolution it could not afford." When England brought up its artillery and "blew the center of Dublin flat . . . the country had to content itself with a make-believe revolution and I had to content myself with a make-believe education and the curious thing is that it was the make-believe that succeeded."

The truce with England came in 1921 when O'Donovan was just short of eighteen, but its

1. BUILDING ON PRIOR KNOWLEDGE. Direct students' attention to the headnote below, which explains the Oedipus complex. You might ask students if they have ever noticed a young child behaving jealously toward a parent.

2. ESTABLISHING A PURPOSE. Everything in this story is seen from the point of view of the little boy. As you read, note his feelings for his mother and for his father and how his feelings change.

3. PREREADING JOURNAL. **(Challenging)** Ask students to write a short description of a five-year-old child they know. What does he or she like to do? What does a child want from his or her parents?

(Less Challenging) Ask students to think about the world of a five-year-old child. Perhaps they can remember their own childhood or that of a brother or sister. Have them summarize in a few sentences what they think is most important to a child at this age.

---

terms were unacceptable to a large number of Irish people. The treaty was immediately followed by a civil war, in which O'Donovan took the Republican side (the side that favored severing all ties to England and establishing an Irish Republic). Throughout the next two years he was active in the war, and while on a mission in the spring of 1923 he was arrested by two Irish soldiers who were "on the other side" and imprisoned.

When at last he was released and returned home to see his mother, he had become a man. He went on to educate himself further and to take part in the Irish literary revival, a movement that tried to restore the Irish language (it had been wiped out by the English), and to create a purely Irish literature. As a penname, he chose his mother's maiden name.

O'Connor began writing stories, and in 1935, with his friend the poet W. B. Yeats, he became director of the Abbey Theatre in Dublin. The theater was the heart of the Irish revival, which also involved Lady Gregory, Sean O'Casey, Sean O'Faolain, and Liam O'Flaherty.

In his writing, O'Connor sought to capture the essence of Irish lyrical speech. His stories are all set in Ireland because, "I know to a syllable how everything in Ireland can be said." O'Connor became a richly productive literary figure, bringing forth volumes of poetry, stories, a novel, an autobiography, plays, criticism, and translations. He was a regular contributor to such American magazines as *The New Yorker, The Atlantic Monthly,* and *Esquire.* Speaking of his mastery of the short-story form, Yeats said, "O'Connor is doing for Ireland what Chekhov did for Russia."

O'Connor came to the United States in 1952. He taught in his later years at Harvard, Northwestern, and Stanford universities. For a poor boy with very little formal education, he had done very well.

SUPPLEMENTARY SUPPORT MATERIALS
1. Vocabulary Activity Worksheet (*CCB*)
2. Review and Response Worksheet: Conflict (*CCB*)
3. Language Skills Worksheets: Ornate and Plain Style; Punctuating Dialogue (*CCB*)
4. Selection Test (*CCB*)

DEVELOPING VOCABULARY
The following words from the story are tested in the Selection Test. (See also Vocabulary Activity Worksheet.)

pertrified	intercession
to muster	guffaw
remote	placidly
to pummel	hullabaloo
to cajole	magnanimous

MY OEDIPUS COMPLEX

In Greek mythology, Oedipus was the king of Thebes who, unaware of his true parentage, killed his father and married his mother. The term *Oedipus complex* was first used in 1899 by the Austrian physician and "father of psychoanalysis," Sigmund Freud, to describe the unconscious desire of a child for the exclusive love of the parent of the opposite sex. This desire results in rivalry with the parent of the same sex. In psychoanalytic theory, the Oedipus complex is an important part of normal human development, lasting from about age three to age five or six, and ending when the child identifies with the parent of the same sex.

Father was in the army all through the war—the first war, I mean—so, up to the age of five, I never saw much of him, and what I saw did not worry me. Sometimes I woke and there was a big figure in khaki peering down at me in the candlelight. Sometimes in the early morning I heard the slamming of the front door and the clatter of nailed boots down the cobbles of the lane. These were Father's entrances and exits. Like Santa Claus he came and went mysteriously.

In fact, I rather liked his visits, though it was an uncomfortable squeeze between Mother and him when I got into the big bed in the early morning. He smoked, which gave him a pleasant musty smell, and shaved, an operation of astounding interest. Each time he left a trail of souvenirs—model tanks and Gurkha knives with handles made of bullet cases, and German helmets and cap badges and button-sticks, and all sorts of military equipment—carefully stowed away in a long box on top of the wardrobe, in case they ever came in handy. There was a bit of the magpie[1] about Father; he expected everything to come in handy. When his back was turned, Mother let me get a chair and rummage through his treasures. She didn't seem to think so highly of them as he did.

The war was the most peaceful period of my life. The window of my attic faced southeast. My mother had curtained it, but that had small effect. I always woke with the first light and, with all the responsibilities of the previous day melted, feeling myself rather like the sun, ready to illumine and rejoice. Life never seemed so simple and clear and full of possibilities as then. I put my feet out from under the clothes—I called them Mrs. Left and Mrs. Right—and invented dramatic situations for them in which they discussed the problems of the day. At least Mrs. Right did; she was very demonstrative, but I hadn't the same control of Mrs. Left, so she mostly contented herself with nodding agreement.

They discussed what Mother and I should do during the day, what Santa Claus should give a fellow for Christmas, and what steps should be taken to brighten the home. There was that little matter of the baby, for instance. Mother and I could never agree about that. Ours was the only house in the terrace without a new baby, and Mother said we couldn't afford one till Father came back from the war because they cost seventeen and six. That showed how simple she was. The Geneys up the road had a baby, and everyone knew they couldn't afford seventeen and six. It was probably a cheap baby, and Mother wanted something really good, but I felt she was too exclusive. The Geneys' baby would have done us fine.

Having settled my plans for the day, I got up, put a chair under the attic window, and lifted the frame high enough to stick out my head. The window overlooked the front gardens of the terrace behind ours, and beyond these it looked over a deep valley to the tall, red-brick houses terraced up the opposite hillside, which were all still in shadow, while those at our side of the valley were all lit up, though with long strange shadows that made them seem unfamiliar; rigid and painted.

After that I went into Mother's room and

---

1. **magpie:** a bird that picks up all kinds of unlikely materials to build its nest.

A. Character
This passage shows that at this point the son believes that he and his mother are of one mind on all matters, even where his father is concerned.

B. Plot
Describe the boy's morning ritual before his father's return from the war. (Up at dawn, "talked" with his toes, opened window, went to mother's room) What was it that he enjoyed so much about these mornings? (His freedom to do as he pleased)

C. Expansion
Terrace here means "a row of houses." See the photograph on page 1002.

A

B

C

A. Conflict

?　How did the boy's life change when his father came home from the war? (He was no longer able to have long talks with his mother in her bed in the early morning.) What had the boy lost that he could not regain? (The exclusive attention of his mother)

B. Irony

?　Why is the boy's exasperation with his father's self-absorption so amusing and ironic? (Because the boy himself is so totally self-absorbed)

C. Comparing Stories

?　How is this conversation between Larry and his mother similar to the conversation between Paul and his mother regarding luck in "The Rocking-Horse Winner"? (Both children ask a series of questions and look to God for solutions to their need to get their mothers' attention.)

climbed into the big bed. She woke and I began to tell her of my schemes. By this time, though I never seem to have noticed it, I was petrified in my nightshirt, and I thawed as I talked until, the last frost melted, I fell asleep beside her and woke again only when I heard her below in the kitchen, making the breakfast.

After breakfast we went into town; heard Mass at St. Augustine's and said a prayer for Father, and did the shopping. If the afternoon was fine we either went for a walk in the country or a visit to Mother's great friend in the convent, Mother St. Dominic. Mother had them all praying for Father, and every night, going to bed, I asked God to send him back safe from the war to us. Little, indeed, did I know what I was praying for!

A One morning, I got into the big bed, and there, sure enough, was Father in his usual Santa Claus manner, but later, instead of uniform, he put on his best blue suit, and Mother was as pleased as anything. I saw nothing to be pleased about, because, out of uniform, Father was altogether less interesting, but she only beamed, and explained that our prayers had been answered, and off we went to Mass to thank God for having brought Father safely home.

B The irony of it! That very day when he came in to dinner he took off his boots and put on his slippers, donned the dirty old cap he wore about the house to save him from colds, crossed his legs, and began to talk gravely to Mother, who looked anxious. Naturally, I disliked her looking anxious, because it destroyed her good looks, so I interrupted him.

"Just a moment, Larry!" she said gently.

This was only what she said when we had boring visitors, so I attached no importance to it and went on talking.

"Do be quiet, Larry!" she said impatiently. "Don't you hear me talking to Daddy?"

This was the first time I had heard those ominous words, "talking to Daddy," and I couldn't help feeling that if this was how God answered prayers, he couldn't listen to them very attentively.

"Why are you talking to Daddy?" I asked with as great a show of indifference as I could muster.

"Because Daddy and I have business to discuss. Now, don't interrupt again!"

In the afternoon, at Mother's request, Father took me for a walk. This time we went into town instead of out the country, and I thought at first,

in my usual optimistic way, that it might be an improvement. It was nothing of the sort. Father and I had quite different notions of a walk in town. He had no proper interest in trams,[2] ships, and horses, and the only thing that seemed to divert him was talking to fellows as old as himself. When I wanted to stop he simply went on, dragging me behind him by the hand; when he wanted to stop I had no alternative but to do the same. I noticed that it seemed to be a sign that he wanted to stop for a long time whenever he leaned against a wall. The second time I saw him do it I got wild. He seemed to be settling himself forever. I pulled him by the coat and trousers, but, unlike Mother who, if you were too persistent, got into a wax and said: "Larry, if you don't behave yourself, I'll give you a good slap," Father had an extraordinary capacity for amiable inattention. I sized him up and wondered would I cry, but he seemed to be too remote to be annoyed even by that. Really, it was like going for a walk with a mountain! He either ignored the wrenching and pummeling entirely, or else glanced down with a grin of amusement from his peak. I had never met anyone so absorbed in himself as he seemed.

At teatime, "talking to Daddy" began again, complicated this time by the fact that he had an evening paper, and every few minutes he put it down and told Mother something new out of it. I felt this was foul play. Man for man, I was prepared to compete with him anytime for Mother's attention, but when he had it all made up for him by other people it left me no chance. Several times I tried to change the subject without success.

"You must be quiet while Daddy is reading, Larry," Mother said impatiently.

It was clear that she either genuinely liked talking to Father better than talking to me, or else that he had some terrible hold on her which made her afraid to admit the truth.

C "Mummy," I said that night when she was tucking me up, "do you think if I prayed hard God would send Daddy back to the war?"

She seemed to think about that for a moment.

"No, dear," she said with a smile. "I don't think he would."

"Why wouldn't he, Mummy?"

"Because there isn't a war any longer, dear."

"But, Mummy, couldn't God make another war, if He liked?"

---

2. **trams:** streetcars.

A

B

"He wouldn't like to, dear. It's not God who makes wars, but bad people."

"Oh!" I said.

I was disappointed about that. I began to think that God wasn't quite what he was cracked up to be.

Next morning I woke up at my usual hour, feeling like a bottle of champagne. I put out my feet and invented a long conversation in which Mrs. Right talked of the trouble she had with her own father till she put him in the Home. I didn't quite know what the Home was but it sounded the right place for Father. Then I got my chair and stuck my head out of the attic window. Dawn was just breaking, with a guilty air that made me feel I had caught it in the act. My head bursting with stories and schemes, I stumbled in next door, and in the half-darkness scrambled into the big bed. There was no room at Mother's side so I had to get between her and Father. For the time being I had forgotten about him, and for several minutes

I sat bolt upright, racking my brains to know what I could do with him. He was taking up more than his fair share of the bed, and I couldn't get comfortable, so I gave him several kicks that made him grunt and stretch. He made room all right, though. Mother waked and felt for me. I settled back comfortably in the warmth of the bed with my thumb in my mouth.

"Mummy!" I hummed, loudly and contentedly.

"Sssh! dear," she whispered. "Don't wake Daddy!"

This was a new development, which threatened to be even more serious than "talking to Daddy." Life without my early-morning conferences was unthinkable.

"Why?" I asked severely.

"Because poor Daddy is tired."

This seemed to me a quite inadequate reason, and I was sickened by the sentimentality of her "poor Daddy." I never liked that sort of gush; it always struck me as insincere.

A. Discussing the Photograph

❓ In what ways does the boy in the photo express the spirit of the narrator of this story? (He stands apart from the others, even turning his back on them. He seems to want things to be another way.) Why do you think he is standing apart from the other children? (He may not want to give up his independence to be part of a group.) Is there any significance in the way he is dressed? (By covering his ears and limiting his vision, the hat accentuates his isolation.) How would you describe the expression on his face? (Answers will vary. Is he happily imagining a dream world or at the point of tears?)

B. Plot

❓ What are some of the ways in which the boy tries to oust his father and win his mother? (Kicking his father, snuggling up to his mother like a baby) Watch how the father's reaction to the boy's behavior changes from a distant tolerance to active annoyance.

A. Irony and
Conflict

❓ This statement
is an example
of comic irony.
How does it sum
up the source of
the story's conflict
and its humor?
(The boy thinks of
himself as a true
rival and equal of
his father in the
battle for his moth-
er's attention.)

B. Interpreting

❓ What feelings
and sensations
is the child experi-
encing this morn-
ing? (Impatience,
boredom, discom-
fort, deprivation)
How might an
adult handle the
same situation dif-
ferently? (By talk-
ing about the prob-
lem and/or taking
care of his own
needs)

"Oh!" I said lightly. Then in my most winning tone: "Do you know where I want to go with you today, Mummy?"

"No, dear," she sighed.

"I want to go down the Glen and fish for thornybacks with my new net, and then I want to go out to the Fox and Hounds, and—"

"Don't-wake-Daddy!" she hissed angrily, clapping her hand across my mouth.

But it was too late. He was awake, or nearly so. He grunted and reached for the matches. Then he stared incredulously at his watch.

"Like a cup of tea, dear?" asked Mother in a meek, hushed voice I had never heard her use before. It sounded almost as though she were afraid.

"Tea?" he exclaimed indignantly. "Do you know what the time is?"

"And after that I want to go up the Rathcooney Road," I said loudly, afraid I'd forget something in all those interruptions.

"Go to sleep at once, Larry!" she said sharply.

I began to snivel. I couldn't concentrate, the way that pair went on, and smothering my early-morning schemes was like burying a family from the cradle.

Father said nothing, but lit his pipe and sucked it, looking out into the shadows without minding Mother or me. I knew he was mad. Every time I made a remark Mother hushed me irritably. I was mortified. I felt it wasn't fair; there was even something sinister in it. Every time I had pointed out to her the waste of making two beds when we could both sleep in one, she had told me it was healthier like that, and now here was this man, this stranger, sleeping with her without the least regard for her health!

He got up early and made tea, but though he brought Mother a cup he brought none for me.

"Mummy," I shouted, "I want a cup of tea, too."

"Yes, dear," she said patiently. "You can drink from Mummy's saucer."

That settled it. Either Father or I would have to leave the house. I didn't want to drink from Mother's saucer; I wanted to be treated as an equal in my own home, so, just to spite her, I drank it all and left none for her. She took that quietly, too.

But that night when she was putting me to bed she said gently:

"Larry, I want you to promise me something."

"What is it?" I asked.

"Not to come in and disturb poor Daddy in the morning. Promise?"

"Poor Daddy" again! I was becoming suspicious of everything involving that quite impossible man.

"Why?" I asked.

"Because poor Daddy is worried and tired and he doesn't sleep well."

"Why doesn't he, Mummy?"

"Well, you know, don't you, that while he was at the war Mummy got the pennies from the Post Office?"

"From Miss MacCarthy?"

"That's right. But now, you see, Miss Mac-Carthy hasn't any more pennies, so Daddy must go out and find us some. You know what would happen if he couldn't?"

"No," I said, "tell us."

"Well, I think we might have to go out and beg for them like the poor old woman on Fridays. We wouldn't like that, would we?"

"No," I agreed. "We wouldn't."

"So you'll promise not to come in and wake him?"

"Promise."

Mind you, I meant that. I knew pennies were a serious matter, and I was all against having to go out and beg like the old woman on Fridays. Mother laid out all my toys in a complete ring round the bed so that, whatever way I got out, I was bound to fall over one of them.

When I woke I remembered my promise all right. I got up and sat on the floor and played—for hours, it seemed to me. Then I got my chair and looked out the attic window for more hours. I wished it was time for Father to wake; I wished someone would make me a cup of tea. I didn't feel in the least like the sun; instead, I was bored and so very, very cold! I simply longed for the warmth and depth of the big featherbed.

At last I could stand it no longer. I went into the next room. As there was still no room at Mother's side I climbed over her and she woke with a start.

"Larry," she whispered, gripping my arm very tightly, "what did you promise?"

"But I did, Mummy," I wailed, caught in the very act. "I was quiet for ever so long."

"Oh, dear, and you're perished!" she said

READING CHECK TEST

1. When the story begins, there is only one child in the family. (T)
2. The narrator refuses to pray for the safe return of his father from the war. (F)
3. After the father returns, the mother immediately forbids the boy to come

into her bed in the mornings. (F)
4. The father as well as the son behaves jealously. (T)
5. The mother feels torn between the demands of father and son. (T)

sadly, feeling me all over. "Now, if I let you stay will you promise not to talk?"

"But I want to talk, Mummy," I wailed.

"That has nothing to do with it," she said with a firmness that was new to me. "Daddy wants to sleep. Now, do you understand that?"

I understood it only too well. I wanted to talk, he wanted to sleep—whose house was it, anyway?

"Mummy," I said with equal firmness, "I think it would be healthier for Daddy to sleep in his own bed."

That seemed to stagger her, because she said nothing for a while.

"Now, once for all," she went on, "you're to be perfectly quiet or go back to your own bed. Which is it to be?"

The injustice of it got me down. I had convicted her out of her own mouth of inconsistency and unreasonableness, and she hadn't even attempted to reply. Full of spite, I gave Father a kick, which she didn't notice but which made him grunt and open his eyes in alarm.

"What time is it?" he asked in a panic-stricken voice, not looking at Mother but at the door, as if he saw someone there.

"It's early yet," she replied soothingly. "It's only the child. Go to sleep again. . . . Now, Larry," she added, getting out of bed, "you've wakened Daddy and you must go back."

This time, for all her quiet air, I knew she meant it, and knew that my principal rights and privileges were as good as lost unless I asserted them at once. As she lifted me, I gave a screech, enough to wake the dead, not to mind Father. He groaned.

"That damn child! Doesn't he ever sleep?"

"It's only a habit, dear," she said quietly, though I could see she was vexed.

"Well, it's time he got out of it," shouted Father, beginning to heave in the bed. He suddenly gathered all the bedclothes about him, turned to the wall, and then looked back over his shoulder with nothing showing only two small, spiteful, dark eyes. The man looked very wicked.

To open the bedroom door, Mother had to let me down, and I broke free and dashed for the farthest corner, screeching. Father sat bolt upright in bed.

"Shut up, you little puppy!" he said in a choking voice.

I was so astonished that I stopped screeching. Never, never had anyone spoken to me in that

tone before. I looked at him incredulously and saw his face convulsed with rage. It was only then that I fully realized how God had codded[3] me, listening to my prayers for the safe return of this monster.

"Shut up, you!" I bawled, beside myself.

"What's that you said?" shouted Father, making a wild leap out of the bed.

"Mick, Mick!" cried Mother. "Don't you see the child isn't used to you?"

"I see he's better fed than taught," snarled Father, waving his arms wildly. "He wants his bottom smacked."

All his previous shouting was as nothing to these obscene words referring to my person. They really made my blood boil.

"Smack your own!" I screamed hysterically. "Smack your own! Shut up! Shut up!"

At this he lost his patience and let fly at me. He did it with the lack of conviction you'd expect of a man under Mother's horrified eyes, and it ended up as a mere tap, but the sheer indignity of being struck at all by a stranger, a total stranger who had cajoled his way back from the war into our big bed as a result of my innocent intercession, made me completely dotty. I shrieked and shrieked, and danced in my bare feet, and Father, looking awkward and hairy in nothing but a short gray army shirt, glared down at me like a mountain out for murder. I think it must have been then that I realized he was jealous too. And there stood Mother in her nightdress, looking as if her heart was broken between us. I hoped she felt as she looked. It seemed to me that she deserved it all.

From that morning out my life was a hell. Father and I were enemies, open and avowed. We conducted a series of skirmishes against one another, he trying to steal my time with Mother and I his. When she was sitting on my bed, telling me a story, he took to looking for some pair of old boots which he alleged he had left behind him at the beginning of the war. While he talked to Mother I played loudly with my toys to show my total lack of concern. He created a terrible scene one evening when he came in from work and found me at his box, playing with his regimental badges, Gurkha knives, and button-sticks. Mother got up and took the box from me.

"You mustn't play with Daddy's toys unless he

---

3. **codded:** tricked.

A. Point of View
From the child's point of view, the father appears wicked, a monster. Is he really? Why or why not? (No; the father ends up giving the child "a mere tap.")

B. Character
? Do you think the child is correct when he surmises that Daddy is jealous too? Use details from the story to support your point of view. (He competes with the child for attention by losing his boots and making a fuss about his box of war treasures.)

ANALYZING THE STORY
Identifying Facts
1. By the end of the second paragraph, it is clear that the narrator is a five-year-old boy.
2. Larry awakens with the first light, feeling liberated from the previous day's responsibilities. He sticks his feet out from under the bedclothes and invents dramatic dialogues for them. Then he settles

his plans for the day, looks out of the window, and goes to his mother's room, where he climbs into her bed.

His mother pays him less attention and scolds him for interrupting his father.
3. Students might point to Mick's ill-tempered resentment of Larry's talking and his visits to their bedroom in the morning.
4. The mother's attention to the new

baby makes Larry's father feel neglected. Feeling kinship with Larry, he crawls into bed with the boy, and Larry decides to forgive his father.

Interpreting Meanings
5. Larry does not understand how babies are born and assumes that they are purchased for "seventeen and six." He also doesn't understand why his parents

A. Theme
What is amusing and touching about Larry's predicament is that he mistakenly thinks he is the center and cause of everything in his world, even the arrival of the new baby.

B. Resolution
? What finally makes Larry and his father allies? (The mother's doting attention to the new baby)

lets you, Larry," she said severely. "Daddy doesn't play with yours."

For some reason Father looked at her as if she had struck him and then turned away with a scowl.

"Those are not toys," he growled, taking down the box again to see had I lifted[4] anything. "Some of those curios are very rare and valuable."

But as time went on I saw more and more how he managed to alienate Mother and me. What made it worse was that I couldn't grasp his method or see what attraction he had for Mother. In every possible way he was less winning than I. He had a common accent and made noises at his tea. I thought for a while that it might be the newspapers she was interested in, so I made up bits of news of my own to read to her. Then I thought it might be the smoking, which I personally thought attractive, and took his pipes and went round the house dribbling into them till he caught me. I even made noises at my tea, but Mother only told me I was disgusting. It all seemed to hinge round that unhealthy habit of sleeping together, so I made a point of dropping into their bedroom and nosing round, talking to myself, so that they wouldn't know I was watching them, but they were never up to anything that I could see. In the end it beat me. It seemed to depend on being grown up and giving people rings, and I realized I'd have to wait.

But at the same time I wanted him to see that I was only waiting, not giving up the fight. One evening when he was being particularly obnoxious, chattering away well above my head, I let him have it.

"Mummy," I said, "do you know what I'm going to do when I grow up?"

"No, dear," she replied. "What?"

"I'm going to marry you," I said quietly.

Father gave a great guffaw out of him, but he didn't take me in. I knew it must only be pretense. And Mother, in spite of everything, was pleased. I felt she was probably relieved to know that one day Father's hold on her would be broken.

"Won't that be nice?" she said with a smile.

"It'll be very nice," I said confidently. "Because we're going to have lots and lots of babies."

"That's right, dear," she said placidly. "I think we'll have one soon, and then you'll have plenty of company."

I was no end pleased about that because it

showed that in spite of the way she gave in to Father she still considered my wishes. Besides, it would put the Geneys in their place.

It didn't turn out like that, though. To begin with, she was very preoccupied—I suppose about where she would get the seventeen and six—and though Father took to staying out late in the evenings it did me no particular good. She stopped taking me for walks, became as touchy as blazes, and smacked me for nothing at all. Sometimes I wished I'd never mentioned the confounded baby—I seemed to have a genius for bringing calamity on myself.

And calamity it was! Sonny arrived in the most appalling hullabaloo—even that much he couldn't do without a fuss—and from the first moment I disliked him. He was a difficult child—so far as I was concerned he was always difficult—and demanded far too much attention. Mother was simply silly about him, and couldn't see when he was only showing off. As company he was worse than useless. He slept all day, and I had to go round the house on tiptoe to avoid waking him. It wasn't any longer a question of not waking Father. The slogan now was "Don't-wake-Sonny!" I couldn't understand why the child wouldn't sleep at the proper time, so whenever Mother's back was turned I woke him. Sometimes to keep him awake I pinched him as well. Mother caught me at it one day and gave me a most unmerciful flaking.[5]

One evening, when Father was coming in from work, I was playing trains in the front garden. I let on not to notice him; instead, I pretended to be talking to myself, and said in a loud voice: "If another bloody baby comes into this house, I'm going out."

Father stopped dead and looked at me over his shoulder.

"What's that you said?" he asked sternly.

"I was only talking to myself," I replied, trying to conceal my panic. "It's private."

He turned and went in without a word. Mind you, I intended it as a solemn warning, but its effect was quite different. Father started being quite nice to me. I could understand that, of course. Mother was quite sickening about Sonny. Even at mealtimes she'd get up and gawk at him in the cradle with an idiotic smile, and tell Father to do the same. He was always polite about it, but

---

4. **lifted:** stolen.

5. **flaking:** spanking.

share the same bed. When Larry decides to make his father jealous by saying that he is going to marry mother one day and have many children, the results are hilariously ironic.

6. As the young narrator sees Father, he is somewhat gross and unrefined, as well as selfish and tyrannical with his mother and himself.

7. Larry becomes friends with his father and "forgives" him; Sonny occupies the mother's attentions; and Father buys Larry a model railway for Christmas. The birth of Sonny has made Father jealous.

8. Student answers will vary. Many students may suggest that the story, which is really a humorous series of "take-offs," or burlesques, on the Oedipal theme, has no serious theme, but is intended rather as an entertaining sketch of family life.

he looked so puzzled you could see he didn't know what she was talking about. He complained of the way Sonny cried at night, but she only got cross and said that Sonny never cried except when there was something up with him—which was a flaming lie, because Sonny never had anything up with him, and only cried for attention. It was really painful to see how simple-minded she was. Father wasn't attractive, but he had a fine intelligence. He saw through Sonny, and now he knew that I saw through him as well.

One night I woke with a start. There was someone beside me in the bed. For one wild moment I felt sure it must be Mother, having come to her senses and left Father for good, but then I heard Sonny in convulsions in the next room, and Mother saying: "There! There! There!" and I knew it wasn't she. It was Father. He was lying beside me, wide awake, breathing hard and apparently as mad as hell.

After a while it came to me what he was mad about. It was his turn now. After turning me out of the big bed, he had been turned out himself. Mother had no consideration now for anyone but that poisonous pup, Sonny. I couldn't help feeling sorry for Father. I had been through it all myself, and even at that age I was <u>magnanimous</u>. I began to stroke him down and say: "There! There!" He wasn't exactly responsive.

"Aren't you asleep either?" he snarled.

"Ah, come on and put your arm around us, can't you?" I said, and he did, in a sort of way. Gingerly, I suppose, is how you'd describe it. He was very bony but better than nothing.

At Christmas he went out of his way to buy me a really nice model railway.

A. Irony
This passage is amusingly ironic because in a role reversal the son is comforting the distraught father.

B. Resolution
The story ends warmly with a new bond of affection developing between father and son.

Responding to the Story

Analyzing the Story

Identifying Facts

1. How far into the story must you read before you can identify the **narrator** and determine his age?
2. Larry describes the war, ironically, as the most peaceful period of his life. Outline the details of Larry's peaceful morning ritual during the war. How does his life change when his father comes home?
3. At one point in the story, Larry realizes that he and his father are conducting "a series of skirmishes against one another, he trying to steal my time with Mother and I his." What details justify Larry's conclusion that his father is really jealous of him?
4. What event finally resolves the **conflict** between Larry and his father?

Interpreting Meanings

5. The story is full of comic **irony**, including Larry's rueful remarks about sharing his mother with his father. Find some of Larry's comments about his mother and his father and explain what it is that Larry doesn't understand in each case. (Include his remarks about the cost of a baby.)
6. How would you describe Father's **character** as the young narrator sees it?

7. How does the end of the story indicate that the Oedipal stage of the narrator's development is over? But what new problem has arisen in the household?
8. How would you state the **theme** of this story?

Writing About the Story

A Creative Response

1. **Using a Different Point of View.** Reread the scene that culminates in Larry's father finally hitting him. Then write one paragraph in which you let his mother reveal what *she* is feeling after that episode, and another paragraph revealing his father's feelings.

A Critical Response

2. **Comparing and Contrasting Characters.** The young heroes of "Araby" and "My Oedipus Complex," although not the same age, are similar in some ways. In a brief essay that uses references from the stories to support your interpretations, discuss the heroes' similarities and differences.
3. **Responding to the Story.** Do you think O'Connor is writing a serious story about an Oedipal conflict, or is he having a bit of fun with psychiatry? In a brief essay give your opinion on O'Connor's intent in this story.

1. BUILDING ON PRIOR KNOWLEDGE. The story takes place in a London neighborhood that was bombed by the Germans in World War II. The remnants of the bombed-out buildings have not been cleared away, and the destructive impact of the war remains. Perhaps students have seen newsreels of the London blitz or of the effects of similar bombings of cities, such as Beirut, Teheran, etc. Also, students who are familiar with the film *Hope and Glory* might want to compare its child's view of the London blitz with the one in this story.

2. ESTABLISHING A PURPOSE. This story is about a relentless and pitiless act of destruction. As you read, try to discover the motive for the act and how the author feels about it.

3. PREREADING JOURNAL. (Challenging) Ask students to consider whether there can be pleasure in destroying as well as in creating. Ask them to think of an example of a person being destructive and enjoying it. Then have them write an explanation of the source of the enjoyment.

(Less Challenging) Ask students what

Graham Greene (1904–1991)

For his serious idealistic novels dealing with contemporary moral dilemmas and for his light "entertainments" and thrillers, Graham Greene has won a rare combination of popular and critical admiration. There may not be a storyteller writing today who can rival his ability to plot a narrative and to keep his readers suspended in anxiety over its conclusion. As you will see in the story that follows, Greene often wrote about life's losers—at least those whom we conventionally think of as losers.

Henry Graham Greene was born to a comfortable family in Berkhamsted, Hertfordshire. His mother was an elegant, aloof woman whom he recalls as smelling of cologne and making occasional "state visits" to the nursery. His father was the headmaster of Berkhamsted School, which Greene attended. For reasons that are not clear, as Greene grew into adolescence, he also grew increasingly depressed and unhappy at school, which he described as his first impression of hell. After he tried to run away, he was sent to London to undergo psychoanalysis. He would later recall those six months in London as among the happiest of his life.

While he was still at Berkhamsted, he had a story published by a local newspaper, and he recalled feeling a sense of pure literary triumph "for the first and last time." This "publication experience" convinced him to become a professional writer. Greene attended Oxford University, wrote a novel that failed to find a publisher, and published a book of poems in 1925, the year he graduated. As an apprenticeship for a writing career, he went to work as a reporter for the Nottingham *Journal*.

In 1926 he became engaged to a Roman Catholic woman, Vivien Dayrell-Browning, and agreed to take instruction in her faith. Although Greene had been a confirmed atheist, he took a great liking to the priest who was instructing him. In January 1926 he became convinced of "the probable existence of something we call God." His Catholic faith would turn out to be an important factor in his writing.

Greene took a job with the London *Times* and worked there until his first novel, *The Man Within,* was published in 1929. His next books were adventure stories, competent derivations of John Buchan and Robert Louis Stevenson, but they received little attention. Greene began to come into his own with the thriller *Orient Express* (1932). This story of a train journey to Istanbul was organized in a cinematic manner, and it was the first of many of Greene's works that would be made into movies.

Greene brought his religious concerns into his fiction with the novel *Brighton Rock* (1938), in which he explored the nature of good and evil and the inexplicable workings of divine grace. Pursuing the theme further in the story of a "spoiled priest" who dies as a saint in *The Power and the Glory* (1940), Greene revealed an unorthodox kind of Catholicism in which naturally sinful men and women, living in a fallen world, are often given a last-minute chance at redemption. As one critic noted, Greene's characters live "on the border between love and hate, good and evil, heaven and hell." Though

DEVELOPING VOCABULARY
The following words from the story are tested in the Selection Test. (See also Vocabulary Activity Worksheet.)

ignoble	restive
impromptu	joist
implacable	facade
altruistic	rheumatics
estuary	dithery

A. Character
Note that it is T.'s silence and lack of emotion that impresses the other boys and sets him apart from them.
❓ How does the younger boy Mike differ from T.? (He is unable to control his emotions as well as T. does.)

Greene is sometimes labeled a "Roman Catholic writer," he preferred to be seen as a novelist who happened to be Roman Catholic. "I'm not a religious man, though it interests me," he once said. "Religion is important, as atomic science is."

During World War II, Greene worked for the British Foreign Office, and afterward he became a director for a publishing house. During the 1950's he was a celebrated foreign correspondent, assigned to Malaysia, Indochina, Africa, and Cuba for such publications as *Life* magazine, *Paris Match,* the London *Times,* and *Le Figaro.* His experiences as a journalist were reflected in novels such as *The Quiet American* (1955), which prophetically dealt with the impli-cations of the American involvement in Vietnam.

Greene's novels came out steadily: *The Heart of the Matter* (1948), *The End of the Affair* (1951), *A Burnt-Out Case* (1961). Many of his books have been made into films, including *The Third Man* (1950) and *Our Man in Havana* (1958).

In his autobiography, *A Sort of Life* (1971), Greene revealed his motives for writing fiction as "a desire to reduce the chaos of experience to some sort of order, and a hungry curiosity. We cannot love others, so the theologians teach, unless in some degree we can love ourselves, and curiosity too begins at home."

THE DESTRUCTORS

At one point in this story, the word *beautiful* appears several times. As readers, we are struck by the word's incongruity. We recognize, as do certain characters in the story, that the word somehow doesn't belong here. Until this scene and in all the scenes that follow, we are immersed in what has come to be known as Greene's "seediness," his characteristic use of coarse imagery and language to describe his vision of the world—a world full of drabness and shabby violence. Greene's intention in his writing was to tell the truth, which he saw as a primary duty of the artist. As you read, decide if *beautiful* belongs to the shabby world Greene has created. Then notice the painstaking accuracy with which Greene describes beauty's fate.

The story takes place around 1954, about nine years after the end of World War II, during which the Germans had firebombed London. Even at this time, evidence of the firebombing was still to be seen in the half-wrecked houses on some of London's blitzed streets.

1

It was on the eve of August Bank Holiday that the latest recruit became the leader of the Wormsley Common Gang. No one was surprised except Mike, but Mike at the age of nine was surprised by everything. "If you don't shut your mouth," somebody once said to him, "you'll get a frog down it." After that Mike kept his teeth tightly clamped except when the surprise was too great.

The new recruit had been with the gang since the beginning of the summer holidays, and there were possibilities about his brooding silence that all recognized. He never wasted a word even to tell his name until that was required of him by the rules. When he said "Trevor" it was a statement of fact, not as it would have been with the others a statement of shame or defiance. Nor did anyone laugh except Mike, who finding himself without support and meeting the dark gaze of the newcomer opened his mouth and was quiet again. There was every reason why T., as he was afterward referred to, should have been an object of mockery—there was his name (and they substituted the initial because otherwise they had no

A

A. Motivation
Keep in mind when trying to figure out T.'s motives that Trevor's father is a former architect and his mother thinks she is better than her neighbors.

❓ What do you think was the dominant emotion in T.'s home? (Resentment)

B. Setting
Note that Mr. Thomas's house was one of the few houses left standing in the immediate area, although it too suffered some damage.

C. Character
Mr. Thomas, like his house, is a shaken survivor. As you continue to read, decide whether you think he deserves his nickname of *Old Misery*.

D. Interpreting
❓ What reasons do the boys propose for Mr. Thomas's having given them candy? (The candy is dirty, stolen, or meant as a bribe.) What does this tell us about the kind of treatment they expect from other people? (They expect unkindness and dishonesty.)

A excuse not to laugh at it), the fact that his father, a former architect and present clerk, had "come down in the world," and that his mother considered herself better than the neighbors. What but an odd quality of danger, of the unpredictable, established him in the gang without any ignoble ceremony of initiation?

The gang met every morning in an impromptu car-park, the site of the last bomb of the first blitz.[1] The leader, who was known as Blackie, claimed to have heard it fall, and no one was precise enough in his dates to point out that he would have been one year old and fast asleep on the down platform of Wormsley Common Underground Station. On one side of the car-park leaned

B the first occupied house, No. 3, of the shattered Northwood Terrace—literally leaned, for it had suffered from the blast of the bomb and the side walls were supported on wooden struts. A smaller bomb and some incendiaries[2] had fallen beyond, so that the house stuck up like a jagged tooth and carried on the further wall relics of its neighbor, a dado,[3] the remains of a fireplace. T., whose words were almost confined to voting "Yes" or "No" to the plan of operations proposed each day by Blackie, once startled the whole gang by saying broodingly, "Wren built that house, father says."

"Who's Wren?"

"The man who built St. Paul's."

"Who cares?" Blackie said. "It's only Old Misery's."

C Old Misery—whose real name was Thomas—had once been a builder and decorator. He lived alone in the crippled house, doing for himself: Once a week you could see him coming back across the common with bread and vegetables, and once as the boys played in the car-park he put his head over the smashed wall of his garden and looked at them.

"Been to the lav," one of the boys said, for it was common knowledge that since the bombs fell something had gone wrong with the pipes of the house and Old Misery was too mean to spend money on the property. He could do the redecorating himself at cost price, but he had never learned plumbing. The lav was a wooden shed at

---

1. **blitz:** the bombing of London by the German air force in World War II.
2. **incendiaries:** fire bombs.
3. **dado** (dā′dō): an architectural term referring to the wood along the lower part of the walls of a room.

the bottom of the narrow garden with a star-shaped hole in the door: it had escaped the blast which had smashed the house next door and sucked out the window frames of No. 3.

The next time the gang became aware of Mr. Thomas was more surprising. Blackie, Mike, and a thin yellow boy, who for some reason was called by his surname Summers, met him on the common coming back from the market. Mr. Thomas stopped them. He said glumly, "You belong to the lot that play in the car-park?"

Mike was about to answer when Blackie stopped him. As the leader he had responsibilities. "Suppose we are?" he said ambiguously.

D "I got some chocolates," Mr. Thomas said. "Don't like 'em myself. Here you are. Not enough to go round, I don't suppose. There never is," he added with somber conviction. He handed over three packets of Smarties.

The gang was puzzled and perturbed by this action and tried to explain it away. "Bet someone dropped them and he picked 'em up," somebody suggested.

"Pinched 'em and then got in a bleeding funk," another thought aloud.

"It's a bribe," Summers said. "He wants us to stop bouncing balls on his wall."

"We'll show him we don't take bribes," Blackie said, and they sacrificed the whole morning to the game of bouncing that only Mike was young enough to enjoy. There was no sign from Mr. Thomas.

Next day T. astonished them all. He was late at the rendezvous, and the voting for that day's exploit took place without him. At Blackie's suggestion the gang was to disperse in pairs, take buses at random and see how many free rides could be snatched from unwary conductors (the operation was to be carried out in pairs to avoid cheating). They were drawing lots for their companions when T. arrived.

"Where you been, T.?" Blackie asked. "You can't vote now. You know the rules."

"I've been *there*," T. said. He looked at the ground, as though he had thoughts to hide.

"Where?"

"At Old Misery's." Mike's mouth opened and then hurriedly closed again with a click. He had remembered the frog.

"At Old Misery's?" Blackie said. There was nothing in the rules against it, but he had a sensation that T. was treading on dangerous ground. He asked hopefully, "Did you break in?"

"No. I rang the bell."

"And what did you say?"

"I said I wanted to see his house."

"What did he do?"

"He showed it me."

"Pinch anything?"

"No."

"What did you do it for then?"

The gang had gathered round: it was as though an impromptu court were about to form and try some case of deviation. T. said, "It's a beautiful house," and still watching the ground, meeting no one's eyes, he licked his lips first one way, then the other.

"What do you mean, a beautiful house?" Blackie asked with scorn.

"It's got a staircase two hundred years old like a corkscrew. Nothing holds it up."

"What do you mean, nothing holds it up. Does it float?"

"It's to do with opposite forces, Old Misery said."

"What else?"

"There's paneling."

"Like in the Blue Boar?"

"Two hundred years old."

"Is Old Misery two hundred years old?"

Mike laughed suddenly and then was quiet again. The meeting was in a serious mood. For the first time since T. had strolled into the car-park on the first day of the holidays his position was in danger. It only needed a single use of his real name and the gang would be at his heels.

"What did you do it for?" Blackie asked. He was just, he had no jealousy, he was anxious to retain T. in the gang if he could. It was the word *beautiful* that worried him—that belonged to a class world that you could still see parodied at the Wormsley Common Empire by a man wearing a top hat and a monocle, with a haw-haw accent. He was tempted to say, "My dear Trevor, old chap," and unleash his hell hounds. "If you'd broken in," he said sadly—that indeed would have been an exploit worthy of the gang.

"This was better," T. said. "I found out things." He continued to stare at his feet, not meeting anybody's eye, as though he were absorbed in some dream he was unwilling—or ashamed—to share.

"What things?"

"Old Misery's going to be away all tomorrow and Bank Holiday."

Blackie said with relief, "You mean we could break in?"

"And pinch things?" somebody asked.

Blackie said, "Nobody's going to pinch things. Breaking in—that's good enough, isn't it? We don't want any court stuff."

"I don't want to pinch anything," T. said. "I've got a better idea."

"What is it?"

T. raised eyes, as gray and disturbed as the drab August day. "We'll pull it down," he said. "We'll destroy it."

Blackie gave a single hoot of laughter and then, like Mike, fell quiet, daunted by the serious <u>implacable</u> gaze. "What'd the police be doing all the time?" he said.

"They'd never know. We'd do it from inside. I've found a way in." He said with a sort of intensity, "We'd be like worms, don't you see, in an apple. When we came out again there'd be nothing there, no staircase, no panels, nothing but just walls, and then we'd make the walls fall down—somehow."

"We'd go to jug," Blackie said.

"Who's to prove? and anyway we wouldn't have pinched anything." He added without the smallest flicker of glee, "There wouldn't be anything to pinch after we'd finished."

"I've never heard of going to prison for breaking things," Summers said.

"There wouldn't be time," Blackie said. "I've seen housebreakers at work."

"There are twelve of us," T. said. "We'd organize."

"None of us know how . . ."

"I know," T. said. He looked across at Blackie. "Have you got a better plan?"

"Today," Mike said tactlessly, "we're pinching free rides . . ."

"Free rides," T. said. "Kid stuff. You can stand down, Blackie, if you'd rather . . ."

"The gang's got to vote."

"Put it up then."

Blackie said uneasily, "It's proposed that tomorrow and Monday we destroy Old Misery's house."

"Here, here," said a fat boy called Joe.

"Who's in favor?"

A. Character

❓ What does T. do and say during and after his visit to the Thomas house that none of the others would have done or said? (Asks to see the house but doesn't steal anything; calls the house beautiful) Do you think T. knows what is beautiful?

B. Imagery and Theme

Here T. describes the kind of destruction he wants to accomplish.

❓ What image does he use? How does his statement make you feel?

C. Character

❓ After hearing T.'s plan, what is Blackie concerned about? (Going to jail) What is it about T. that gains him the leadership of the gang? (His daring, planning ability, and confidence)

A. Plot

❓ Why does Blackie finally decide to join in T.'s plan of destruction? (His desire for fame) Do you think T. would share his motive?

B. Theme

❓ What does this passage say about the difference between Blackie and T.? (Blackie is emotional, and T. is joyless and efficient.) Is there a way in which they represent different aspects of evil? (Once again, answers will vary. Blackie might be said to represent those for whom evil seems to be an end in itself. T. seems motivated by the desire to destroy things he cannot have.)

T. said, "It's carried."

"How do we start?" Summers asked.

"He'll tell you," Blackie said. It was the end of his leadership. He went away to the back of the car-park and began to kick a stone, dribbling it this way and that. There was only one old Morris in the park, for few cars were left there except lorries:[4] without an attendant there was no safety. He took a flying kick at the car and scraped a little paint off the rear mudguard. Beyond, paying no more attention to him than to a stranger, the gang had gathered round T.; Blackie was dimly aware of the fickleness of favor. He thought of going home, of never returning, of letting them all discover the hollowness of T.'s leadership, but suppose after all what T. proposed was possible—nothing like it had ever been done before. The fame of the Wormsley Common car-park gang would surely reach around London. There would be headlines in the papers. Even the grown-up gangs who ran the betting at the all-in wrestling and the barrow-boys would hear with respect of how Old Misery's house had been destroyed. Driven by the pure, simple, and altruistic ambition of fame for the gang, Blackie came back to where T. stood in the shadow of Old Misery's wall.

A

T. was giving his orders with decision: It was as though this plan had been with him all his life, pondered through the seasons, now in his fifteenth year crystalized with the pain of puberty. "You," he said to Mike, "bring some big nails, the biggest you can find, and a hammer. Anybody who can better bring a hammer and a screwdriver. We'll need plenty of them. Chisels too. We can't have too many chisels. Can anybody bring a saw?"

"I can," Mike said.

"Not a child's saw," T. said. "A real saw."

Blackie realized he had raised his hand like any ordinary member of the gang.

"Right, you bring one, Blackie. But now there's a difficulty. We want a hacksaw."

"What's a hacksaw?" someone asked.

"You can get 'em at Woolworth's," Summers said.

The fat boy called Joe said gloomily, "I knew it would end in a collection."

"I'll get one myself," T. said. "I don't want your money. But I can't buy a sledgehammer."

Blackie said, "They are working on No. 15. I know where they'll leave their stuff for Bank Holiday."

"Then that's all," T. said. "We meet here at nine sharp."

"I've got to go to church," Mike said.

"Come over the wall and whistle. We'll let you in."

2

On Sunday morning all were punctual except Blackie, even Mike. Mike had a stroke of luck. His mother felt ill, his father was tired after Saturday night, and he was told to go to church alone with many warnings of what would happen if he strayed. Blackie had difficulty in smuggling out the saw, and then in finding the sledgehammer at the back of No. 15. He approached the house from a lane at the rear of the garden, for fear of the policeman's beat along the main road. The tired evergreens kept off a stormy sun: another wet Bank Holiday was being prepared over the Atlantic, beginning in swirls of dust under the trees. Blackie climbed the wall into Misery's garden.

There was no sign of anybody anywhere. The lav stood like a tomb in a neglected graveyard. The curtains were drawn. The house slept. Blackie lumbered nearer with the saw and the sledgehammer. Perhaps after all nobody had turned up: the plan had been a wild invention: they had woken wiser. But when he came close to the back door he could hear a confusion of sound hardly louder than a hive in swarm: a clickety-clack, a bang bang, a scraping, a creaking, a sudden painful crack. He thought: it's true, and whistled.

They opened the back door to him and he came in. He had at once the impression of organization, very different from the old happy-go-lucky ways under his leadership. For a while he wandered up and down stairs looking for T. Nobody addressed him: he had a sense of great urgency, and already he could begin to see the plan. The interior of the house was being carefully demolished without touching the outer walls. Summers with hammer and chisel was ripping out the skirting-boards[5] in the ground floor dining room: he had already smashed the panels of the door. In the same room

B

---

4. **lorries:** trucks.

5. **skirting-boards:** the narrow edgings of cement placed along the base of the wall of a room.

Joe was heaving up the parquet blocks, exposing the soft wood floorboards over the cellars. Coils of wire came out of the damaged skirting and Mike sat happily on the floor clipping the wires.

On the curved stairs two of the gang were working hard with an inadequate child's saw on the banisters—when they saw Blackie's big saw they signaled for it wordlessly. When he next saw them a quarter of the banisters had dropped into the hall. He found T. at last in the bathroom—he sat moodily in the least cared-for room in the house, listening to the sounds coming up from below.

"You've really done it," Blackie said with awe. "What's going to happen?"

"We've only just begun," T. said. He looked at the sledgehammer and gave his instructions. "You stay here and break the bath and the washbasin. Don't bother about the pipes. They come later."

Mike appeared at the door. "I've finished the wires, T.," he said.

"Good. You've just got to go wandering round now. The kitchen's in the basement. Smash all the china and glass and bottles you can lay hold of. Don't turn on the taps—we don't want a flood—yet. Then go into all the rooms and turn out drawers. If they are locked get one of the others to break them open. Tear up any papers you find and smash all the ornaments. Better take a carving knife with you from the kitchen. The bedroom's opposite here. Open the pillows and tear up the sheets. That's enough for the moment. And you, Blackie, when you've finished in here crack the plaster in the passage up with your sledgehammer."

"What are you going to do?" Blackie asked.

"I'm looking for something special," T. said.

It was nearly lunchtime before Blackie had finished and went in search of T. Chaos had advanced. The kitchen was a shambles of broken glass and china. The dining room was stripped of parquet, the skirting was up, the door had been taken off its hinges, and the destroyers had moved up a floor. Streaks of light came in through the closed shutters where they worked with the seriousness of creators—and destruction after all is a form of creation. A kind of imagination had seen this house as it had now become.

Mike said, "I've got to go home for dinner."

"Who else?" T. asked, but all the others on one excuse or another had brought provisions with them.

They squatted in the ruins of the room and swapped unwanted sandwiches. Half an hour for lunch and they were at work again. By the time Mike returned they were on the top floor, and by six the superficial damage was completed. The doors were all off, all the skirtings raised, the furniture pillaged and ripped and smashed—no one could have slept in the house except on a bed of broken plaster. T. gave his orders—eight o'clock next morning, and to escape notice they climbed singly over the garden wall, into the carpark. Only Blackie and T. were left: the light had nearly gone, and when they touched a switch, nothing worked—Mike had done his job thoroughly.

"Did you find anything special?" Blackie asked.

T. nodded. "Come over here," he said, "and look." Out of both pockets he drew bundles of pound notes. "Old Misery's savings," he said. "Mike ripped out the mattress, but he missed them."

"What are you going to do? Share them?"

"We aren't thieves," T. said. "Nobody's going to steal anything from this house. I kept these for you and me—a celebration." He knelt down on the floor and counted them out—there were seventy in all. "We'll burn them," he said, "one by one," and taking it in turns they held a note upward and lit the top corner, so that the flame burnt slowly toward their fingers. The gray ash floated above them and fell on their heads like age. "I'd like to see Old Misery's face when we are through," T. said.

"You hate him a lot?" Blackie asked.

"Of course I don't hate him," T. said. "There'd be no fun if I hated him." The last burning note illuminated his brooding face. "All this hate and love," he said, "it's soft, it's hooey. There's only things, Blackie," and he looked round the room crowded with the unfamiliar shadows of half things, broken things, former things. "I'll race you home, Blackie," he said.

3

Next morning the serious destruction started. Two were missing—Mike and another boy whose parents were off to Southend and Brighton in spite of the slow warm drops that had begun to fall and the rumble of thunder in the estuary like the first

A. Theme
This key passage gives us some idea of the author's view of T.'s behavior. He sees T. as an artist of destruction.
❓ What qualities does T. share with a creative artist? (Determination, vision, imagination, skill, awareness of beauty)

B. Character
In this passage T. reveals his sense of values.
❓ What is important to him and what is not? (He desires to be effective without feeling anything. He enjoys destroying what others value. He does not feel for other people.) What particular act in the general destruction did he find "special"? (Burning the money)

A

B

A. **Theme**

▣ What does this passage reveal about the kind of destruction T. desires? (Total destruction) Would you say his desire is a whim or an obsession? (Obsession)

B. **Climax**

▣ For the first time, T. has lost control of his emotions. Why? (He fears not being able to complete his vision of total destruction because of Mr. Thomas's return.)

C. **Plot**

Blackie resumes leadership and makes it possible for T. to complete his plan.

▣ Why do you think Blackie wishes to continue? (Answers may vary. Being leader once again, he has a greater stake in the outcome.)

guns of the old blitz. "We've got to hurry," T. said.

Summers was <u>restive</u>. "Haven't we done enough?" he asked. "I've been given a bob for slot machines. This is like work."

"We've hardly started," T. said. "Why, there's all the floors left, and the stairs. We haven't taken out a single window. You voted like the others. We are going to *destroy* this house. There won't be anything left when we've finished."

They began again on the first floor picking up the top floorboards next the outer wall, leaving the <u>joists</u> exposed. Then they sawed through the joists and retreated into the hall, as what was left of the floor heeled and sank. They had learned with practice, and the second floor collapsed more easily. By the evening an odd exhilaration seized them as they looked down the great hollow of the house. They ran risks and made mistakes: when they thought of the windows it was too late to reach them. "Cor,"[6] Joe said, and dropped a penny down into the dry rubble-filled well. It cracked and span amongst the broken glass.

"Why did we start this?" Summers asked with astonishment; T. was already on the ground, digging at the rubble, clearing a space along the outer wall. "Turn on the taps," he said. "It's too dark for anyone to see now, and in the morning it won't matter." The water overtook them on the stairs and fell through the floorless rooms.

It was then they heard Mike's whistle at the back. "Something's wrong," Blackie said. They could hear his urgent breathing as they unlocked the door.

"The bogies?"[7] Summers asked.

"Old Misery," Mike said. "He's on his way." He put his head between his knees and retched. "Ran all the way," he said with pride.

"But why?" T. said. "He told me . . ." He protested with the fury of the child he had never been, "It isn't fair."

"He was down at Southend," Mike said, "and he was on the train coming back. Said it was too cold and wet." He paused and gazed at the water. "My, you've had a storm here. Is the roof leaking?"

"How long will he be?"

"Five minutes. I gave Ma the slip and ran."

---

6. **Cor:** (British dialect) an exclamation of strong surprise or irritation.
7. **bogies:** much-dreaded evil beings.

"We better clear," Summers said. "We've done enough, anyway."

"Oh no, we haven't. Anybody could do this—" "this" was the shattered hollowed house with nothing left but the walls. Yet walls could be preserved. <u>Facades</u> were valuable. They could build inside again more beautifully than before. This could again be a home. He said angrily, "We've got to finish. Don't move. Let me think."

"There's no time," a boy said.

"There's got to be a way," T. said. "We couldn't have got this far . . ."

"We've done a lot," Blackie said.

"No. No, we haven't. Somebody watch the front."

"We can't do anymore."

"He may come in at the back."

"Watch the back too." T. began to plead. "Just give me a minute and I'll fix it. I swear I'll fix it." But his authority had gone with his ambiguity. He was only one of the gang. "Please," he said.

"Please," Summers mimicked him, and then suddenly struck home with the fatal name. "Run along home, Trevor."

T. stood with his back to the rubble like a boxer knocked groggy against the ropes. He had no words as his dreams shook and slid. Then Blackie acted before the gang had time to laugh, pushing Summers backward. "I'll watch the front, T.," he said, and cautiously he opened the shutters of the hall. The gray wet common stretched ahead, and the lamps gleamed in the puddles. "Someone's coming, T. No, it's not him. What's your plan, T.?"

"Tell Mike to go out to the lav and hide close beside it. When he hears me whistle he's got to count ten and start to shout."

"Shout what?"

"Oh, 'Help,' anything."

"You hear, Mike," Blackie said. He was the leader again. He took a quick look between the shutters. "He's coming, T."

"Quick, Mike. The lav. Stay here, Blackie, all of you, till I yell."

"Where are you going, T.?"

"Don't worry. I'll see to this. I said I would, didn't I?"

Old Misery came limping off the common. He had mud on his shoes and he stopped to scrape them on the pavement's edge. He didn't want to soil his house, which stood jagged and dark between the bomb sites, saved so narrowly, as he believed, from destruction. Even the fanlight had been left unbroken by the bomb's blast. Somewhere somebody whistled. Old Misery looked sharply round. He didn't trust whistles. A child was shouting: it seemed to come from his own garden. Then a boy ran into the road from the car-park. "Mr. Thomas," he called, "Mr. Thomas."

"What is it?"

"I'm terribly sorry, Mr. Thomas. One of us got taken short, and we thought you wouldn't mind, and now he can't get out."

"What do you mean, boy?"

"He's got stuck in your lav."

"He'd no business . . . . Haven't I seen you before?"

"You showed me your house."

"So I did. So I did. That doesn't give you the right to . . ."

"Do hurry, Mr. Thomas. He'll suffocate."

"Nonsense. He can't suffocate. Wait till I put my bag in."

"I'll carry your bag."

"Oh no, you don't. I carry my own."

"This way, Mr. Thomas."

"I can't get in the garden that way. I've got to go through the house."

"But you *can* get in the garden this way, Mr. Thomas. We often do."

"You often do?" He followed the boy with a scandalized fascination. "When? What right . . .?"

"Do you see . . .? The wall's low."

"I'm not going to climb walls into my own garden. It's absurd."

"This is how we do it. One foot here, one foot there, and over." The boy's face peered down, an arm shot out, and Mr. Thomas found his bag taken and deposited on the other side of the wall.

"Give me back my bag," Mr. Thomas said. From the loo a boy yelled and yelled. "I'll call the police."

"Your bag's all right, Mr. Thomas. Look. One foot there. On your right. Now just above. To your left." Mr. Thomas climbed over his own garden wall. "Here's your bag, Mr. Thomas."

"I'll have the wall built up," Mr. Thomas said, "I'll not have you boys coming over here, using my loo." He stumbled on the path, but the boy caught his elbow and supported him. "Thank you, thank you, my boy," he murmured automatically. Somebody shouted again through the dark. "I'm coming, I'm coming," Mr. Thomas called. He said

to the boy beside him, "I'm not unreasonable. Been a boy myself. As long as things are done regular. I don't mind you playing round the place Saturday mornings. Sometimes I like company. Only it's got to be regular. One of you asks leave and I say Yes. Sometimes I'll say No. Won't feel like it. And you come in at the front door and out at the back. No garden walls."

"Do get him out, Mr. Thomas."

"He won't come to any harm in my loo," Mr. Thomas said, stumbling slowly down the garden. "Oh, my <u>rheumatics</u>," he said. "Always get 'em on Bank Holiday. I've got to go careful. There's loose stones here. Give me your hand. Do you know what my horoscope said yesterday? 'Abstain from any dealings in first half of week. Danger of serious crash.' That might be on this path," Mr. Thomas said. "They speak in parables and double meanings." He paused at the door of the loo. "What's the matter in there?" he called. There was no reply.

"Perhaps he's fainted," the boy said.

"Not in my loo. Here, you, come out," Mr. Thomas said, and giving a great jerk at the door he nearly fell on his back when it swung easily open. A hand first supported him and then pushed him hard. His head hit the opposite wall and he sat heavily down. His bag hit his feet. A hand whipped the key out of the lock and the door slammed. "Let me out," he called, and heard the key turn in the lock. "A serious crash," he thought, and felt <u>dithery</u> and confused and old.

A voice spoke to him softly through the star-shaped hole in the door. "Don't worry, Mr. Thomas," it said, "we won't hurt you, not if you stay quiet."

Mr. Thomas put his head between his hands and pondered. He had noticed that there was only one lorry in the car-park, and he felt certain that the driver would not come for it before the morning. Nobody could hear him from the road in front, and the lane at the back was seldom used. Anyone who passed there would be hurrying home and would not pause for what they would certainly take to be drunken cries. And if he did call "Help," who, on a lonely Bank Holiday evening, would have the courage to investigate? Mr. Thomas sat on the loo and pondered with the wisdom of age.

After a while it seemed to him that there were sounds in the silence—they were faint and came from the direction of his house. He stood up and

A. Irony
How is the reference to "danger of serious crash" in Mr. Thomas's horoscope an example of black humor? (He is unaware that his house is being dismantled.) Look for other instances of black humor, or bitter irony, in the story.

A

READING CHECK TEST

1. Before Trevor's arrival, _____ was the leader of the gang.
a. Mike   b. Blackie   c. Summers
(b)

2. Mike was not taken seriously by the other gang members because he was

too _____.
a. fat   b. unreliable   c. emotional   (c)

3. Blackie wanted to wreck the house for _____.
a. profit   b. fun   c. fame   (c)

4. Mr. Thomas was a _____ man.
a. rich   b. gullible   c. cheerful   (b)

5. The tone of "The Destructors" can best be described as _____.
a. ironic   b. tragic   c. comic   (a)

A. Motivation

The passage describes the final job of destroying the house as "long, tiring, and unamusing."

❓ Why do you think all but Mike stick to it? (They all have become infected with T.'s obsession.)

B. Responding

❓ Does the fact that the boys give Mr. Thomas food and a blanket make them seem more humane? Why or why not? (Although destroying the man's home seems inhumane to us, they have done it for very different reasons. In dealing with the man himself, they are almost kind.)

peered through the ventilation hole—between the cracks in one of the shutters he saw a light, not the light of a lamp, but the wavering light that a candle might give. Then he thought he heard the sound of hammering and scraping and chipping. He thought of burglars—perhaps they had employed the boy as a scout, but why should burglars engage in what sounded more and more like a stealthy form of carpentry? Mr. Thomas let out an experimental yell, but nobody answered. The noise could not even have reached his enemies.

4

Mike had gone home to bed, but the rest stayed. The question of leadership no longer concerned the gang. With nails, chisels, screwdrivers, anything that was sharp and penetrating, they moved around the inner walls worrying at the mortar between the bricks. They started too high, and it was Blackie who hit on the damp course and realized the work could be halved if they weakened the joints immediately above. It was a long, tiring, unamusing job, but at last it was finished. The gutted house stood there balanced on a few inches of mortar between the damp course and the bricks.

There remained the most dangerous task of all, out in the open at the edge of the bomb site. Summers was sent to watch the road for passers-by, and Mr. Thomas, sitting on the loo, heard clearly now the sound of sawing. It no longer came from his house, and that a little reassured him. He felt less concerned. Perhaps the other noises too had no significance.

A voice spoke to him through the hole. "Mr. Thomas."

"Let me out," Mr. Thomas said sternly.

"Here's a blanket," the voice said, and a long gray sausage was worked through the hole and fell in swathes over Mr. Thomas's head.

"There's nothing personal," the voice said. "We want you to be comfortable tonight."

"Tonight," Mr. Thomas repeated incredulously.

"Catch," the voice said. "Penny buns—we've buttered them, and sausage rolls. We don't want you to starve, Mr. Thomas."

Mr. Thomas pleaded desperately. "A joke's a joke, boy. Let me out and I won't say a thing. I've got rheumatics. I got to sleep comfortable."

Devastation by Graham Sutherland (1940). Ink and chalk.

"You wouldn't be comfortable, not in your house, you wouldn't. Not now."

"What do you mean, boy?" But the footsteps receded. There was only the silence of night: no sound of sawing. Mr. Thomas tried one more yell, but he was daunted and rebuked by the silence— a long way off an owl hooted and made away again on its muffled flight through the soundless world.

At seven next morning the driver came to fetch his lorry. He climbed into the seat and tried to start the engine. He was vaguely aware of a voice shouting, but it didn't concern him. At last the engine responded and he backed the lorry until it touched the great wooden shore that supported Mr. Thomas's house. That way he could drive right out and down the street without reversing. The lorry moved forward, was momentarily

A. Humanities Connection: Discussing the Fine Art

Born in London, Graham Sutherland (1903–1980) began as an engineer but turned to etching and later to drawing, painting, and designing posters, textiles, and decorative objects. A great admirer of Blake and Picasso, it was not until the 1930's that he found in Surrealism a medium for his original vision. This 1940 creation captures the destructive forces unleashed on civilian life by the Nazi bombing in World War II. Do you think it also suggests the kind of destructive force at work in this story? Why or why not? (Answers may vary. Discuss the differences, if any, between wartime destruction of lives and property and the more orderly destruction described in the story.)

B. Responding

This lorry driver cannot help laughing at the utter destruction around him. He compares the former dignity of the house with a man in a top hat who is at one moment standing and in the next flat on the floor—perhaps from sliding on a banana peel.

❓ Can you see humor in this final scene? (It is the kind of physical humor found in some Buster Keaton films. The almost instant disappearance of a whole building has a shock value that can provoke laughter.) Was Mr. Thomas the kind of pompous character who is often pulled down in comedies? (Mr. Thomas is a recluse and a miser, but he is not like those characters—often seen on TV—who are foolish and irritating and who invite disaster.)

CLOSURE

All the characters in the story, with the exception of the rather helpless Mr. Thomas, are destructors. Ask students to imagine introducing another character into the story who is constructive or creative. Have a class discussion on this new character and how he or she would alter the plot of the story.

A

Cheltenham Art Gallery and Museums, Cheltenham, England.

checked as though something were pulling it from behind, and then went on to the sound of a long rumbling crash. The driver was astonished to see bricks bouncing ahead of him, while stones hit the roof of his cab. He put on his brakes. When he climbed out the whole landscape had suddenly altered. There was no house beside the car-park, only a hill of rubble. He went round and examined the back of his lorry for damage, and found a rope tied there that was still twisted at the other end round part of a wooden strut.

The driver again became aware of somebody shouting. It came from the wooden erection which was the nearest thing to a house in that desolation of broken brick. The driver climbed the smashed wall and unlocked the door. Mr. Thomas came out of the loo. He was wearing a gray blanket to which flakes of pastry adhered. He gave a sobbing cry. "My house," he said. "Where's my house?"

"Search me," the driver said. His eye lit on the remains of a bath and what had once been a dresser and he began to laugh. There wasn't anything left anywhere.

"How dare you laugh," Mr. Thomas said. "It was my house. My house."

"I'm sorry," the driver said, making heroic efforts, but when he remembered the sudden check to his lorry, the crash of bricks falling, he became convulsed again. One moment the house had stood there with such dignity between the bomb sites like a man in a top hat, and then, bang, crash, there wasn't anything left—not anything. He said, "I'm sorry. I can't help it, Mr. Thomas. There's nothing personal, but you got to admit it's funny."

B

1. The narrator says that Blackie would have been a year old at the time of the bombing (in 1940) and that Trevor is fifteen. From this, we can deduce that the story takes place around 1954.

2. The flavor of the gang's interactions is suggested by the brusque treatment of Mike; the difference between Trevor and the rest of the gang is suggested by the comments about his name; the reasons for the difference are hinted at in the comments about Trevor's background.

3. It was built by the renowned seventeenth-century architect Christopher Wren.

Since Old Misery used to be a builder and decorator, he was able to buy materials for the restoration at cost.

4. At the opening of the story, Blackie is the leader of the gang.

The leadership of the gang passes to Trevor when he proposes the destruction of Old Misery's house.

The new leadership is almost lost when Summers mocks Trevor and Trevor is undecided about a plan for the final phase of destruction.

The criterion that seems to determine leadership is the boldness of the leader's proposals.

5. On the first day, they destroy the banisters, slash the beds and pillows, smash the dishes and glasses, break the bath and washbasin, and tear up the papers. On the second day, they

proceed to more structural demolition.

Tricking him, they manage to lock the old man up for the night in the shed.

Interpreting Meanings

6. The boys are not trying to harm him physically, nor do they want revenge.

Since they burn the money, the boys are not interested in material gain.

7. Student answers will vary. Greene

never explicitly reveals Trevor's motives. Some may suggest that Trevor takes perverse pleasure in the complete destruction of beauty, as represented by the house.

8. Trevor is talented at organization and leadership and displays considerable technical knowledge.

9. The fact that the father was an architect, or builder, sharply contrasts with the

---

Responding to the Story

Analyzing the Story

Identifying Facts

1. Assuming Blackie is about the same age as Trevor, what clues in the story would help you approximate the year the story takes place?
2. The first two paragraphs of this story are remarkable for the amount of information they communicate. The writer manages (a) to convey the flavor of the gang's interactions, (b) to explain how Trevor is different from the rest of the gang, and (c) to hint at the reasons for the difference. List the details that supply these three kinds of information.
3. Why is Old Misery's house valuable? Why was Old Misery able to restore certain parts of the house inexpensively?
4. Who is the leader of the gang at the opening of the story? At what point does the leadership change hands? When is the new leadership almost lost? What criterion determines who leads the gang?
5. How does the gang go about its destructive project? What does it do to Old Misery himself?

Interpreting Meanings

6. Trevor's **motives** for destroying Old Misery's house are important. Several details shed light on what these motives *are not*. What motive do you rule out based on the way the boys treat Old Misery? What motives do you rule out based on what the boys do with the money?
7. What do you think Trevor's motives *are* for destroying Old Misery's house?
8. It is **ironic** that the abilities Trevor exhibits in destroying the house are highly prized by society. What are Trevor's talents?
9. Why is it **ironic** that Trevor's father was once an architect? In light of the history of Old Misery's house, what is ironic about its destruction? What is ironic about Old Misery's horoscope reading?
10. What significance does the name *Wormsley Common* have in the story? What are the **connotations** of these two words? What details in the story back up your answer?
11. When Blackie asks Trevor whether Trevor hates Mr. Thomas, he answers, "Of course I don't. . . . There'd be no fun if I hated him." How would you explain Trevor's answer?
12. The gang is an entity, and as such has its own set of values. What are its values? Is the gang's antisocial stance merely one of poor versus rich, or does it spring from something deeper? Explain.

13. Consider the following excerpt from the story:

> Streaks of light came in through the closed shutters where they worked with the seriousness of creators—and destruction after all is a form of creation. A kind of imagination had seen this house as it had now become.

How close do you think this statement comes to expressing the **theme** of "The Destructors"? Explain.
14. Some people feel that the story should have ended differently, so that the destructors are punished. Do you think this would have been a better ending, or is the story more powerful as is? Explain.
15. Do such acts of destruction, for similar motives, take place today in the world as you know it? Who or what might be today's "destructors"?

Writing About the Story

A Creative Response

1. **Using Another Point of View.** Imagine you are Mr. Thomas. In two or three paragraphs, tell a friend about the central incident in the story as you saw and experienced it. Include your perceptions of the gang members and their motives.

A Critical Response

2. **Explaining Imagery.** The image of hollowness—of rotting from within—pervades the story. In an essay, cite the images of rotting or nothingness, and explain how they pertain not only to the house but to the characters in the story as well.

Analyzing Language and Style

Slang

Greene writes convincing dialogue for his young characters by having them use the slang popular in England in the 1950's (and, in most cases, still popular today). Using a good dictionary, explain what each of the following slang words means. What is the derivation of each?

1. "'Been to the *lav* . . .'"
2. "'*Pinched* 'em and then got in a *bleeding funk*. . . .'"
3. "'. . . a man . . . with a *haw-haw* accent.'"
4. "'We'd go to *jug*.'"
5. "'I've been given a *bob* for slot machines.'"

Do Americans have slang expressions for these same things?

son's talent for destruction.

It is ironic that this house, which survived the German bombings in World War II, is destroyed by a gang of local boys.

The "serious crash" comes about unexpectedly (and literally) when the house crashes to the ground in a heap of rubble.

10. The gang is known as the "Wormsley Common" gang, which suggests worms, and, by extension, destruction and corruption. Trevor uses the following simile: "We'd be like worms, don't you see, in an apple." The word "common" suggests vulgarity, perhaps hinting at the lower-class origins of the boys.

11. Student answers will vary. They should point out that the answer makes Trevor's actions even more ominous. Devoid of even the passion of hatred, his destructiveness is frighteningly malicious.

12. They value sensation and money in their pockets. They seem to find pleasure in cruelty.

The gang's antisocial stance reflects the wider breakdown of social order and the conflict between old and new values. The orderly society of England's past is being eroded, just as surely as Old Misery's house is pulled down by the gang of ruffians. Greene is also showing us how the imagination can be put to demonic use.

13. Many students will agree that this quotation is closely related to the paradoxical theme of the story: Destruction, just like creation, requires planning, organization, and effective implementation.

14. Some may suggest that the boys ought to have been punished, but others may argue that then the story's ironic tone and effect would be lost.

15. You might discuss ways in which we are all destructors: in warfare, in ruining our environment, in our neglect of the innocent, in our indifference to the aged, in our rejection of the past, etc.

Doris Lessing (1919 –)

Doris Lessing was born in Persia (now Iran), where her British father had moved with his wife to escape the narrowness and provincialism of England. When she was five, her father, who lived on impulses, grew tired of the corruption in Persia and longed for a freer life. He gave up his job running a bank and moved his family to a three-thousand-acre farm in Southern Rhodesia (now Zimbabwe), on which he planned to grow maize. The farm employed some thirty to fifty African laborers, each of whom earned the equivalent in American money of approximately $1.50 a month. The laborers lived in mud huts that had no sanitation.

In Africa, Lessing's mother was terribly lonely for England and was often ill, and her father's behavior became increasingly eccentric. Lessing describes her childhood as "hellishly lonely." The district in which the farm was located was very sparsely populated, with the nearest neighbor miles away. Only as an adult did she come to realize that her childhood had been extraordinarily lucky. Because she lacked company, she gave herself a very good education by slowly reading the classics of European and American fiction.

At the age of fifteen, Lessing quit school and went to work in Salisbury, the capital city of Rhodesia, first as a nursemaid, then as a stenographer and telephone operator. Salisbury had a white population of about ten thousand, and a larger black population that Lessing discovered "didn't count." When her first marriage collapsed, she entered radical politics. At twenty-six, she married a second time, but that marriage also ended in divorce. "I do not think," she has said, "that marriage is one of my talents."

England was always in her thoughts. "I can't remember a time when I didn't want to come to England," she recalled. "England was for me a grail. I would lie in bed and dream about England. . . . That England was almost entirely filled with rather dangerous night clubs which had a strong literary flavor."

In 1949 she left Africa for England with her two-year-old son and the manuscript of her first

novel, *The Grass Is Singing.* The story of a complex relationship between a white farmer's wife and her black servant, the novel, published in 1950, commanded attention as one of the earliest novels about Africa's racial problems.

From that time on, Lessing supported herself and her son by writing. In all of her work there is evidence of the responsibility she feels, as a writer, to be "an instrument of change." "It is not merely a question of preventing evil," she says, "but of strengthening a vision of a good which may defeat the evil."

Many of her short stories, collected in a book called *African Stories* (1964), take place in the district in Southern Rhodesia (now Zimbabwe) where she was brought up. *Children of Violence* (1952–1969), a quintet of novels, tells the story of the aptly named Martha Quest, who, like her creator, spent her childhood in Africa and her mature life in postwar Britain. The entire narrative proceeds through the present to an apocalyptic ending in an unnamed city in 2000 A.D.

Lessing's most widely read and discussed book by far is *The Golden Notebook* (1962). This big, ambitious, and complexly structured work combines fiction, parody, and factual reporting

1. BUILDING ON PRIOR KNOWLEDGE. Ask students to read the headnote to learn the setting and the social relationships among the main characters in this story. The status of blacks in colonial Rhodesia was similar to the long-time status of blacks in South Africa, although black exclusion in Rhodesia was not as systematic nor as totally supported by the legal system as it was in South Africa.

2. ESTABLISHING A PURPOSE. Since this is a story about the relationships of black and white people in British Rhodesia, ask students to pay close attention to the shifting tides of closeness and distance between the Farquars and their African cook Gideon, especially in the relationship between Gideon and Teddy Farquar.

3. PREREADING JOURNAL. Ask students to think about the differences in the relationship between an employer and an employee and between two people who are friends. Can employers and employees ever become true friends? Have them write two or three sentences on these questions.

A. Character

Gideon's pleasure in Teddy's birth is the first reason given for the warmth that the Farquars feel for Gideon. Look for other ways in which the employers and the servant share common bonds. (Shared religious and family values)

B. Plot

? Why do you think that Mrs. Farquar was pleased when Gideon said "we"? (Because he seemed to share her joy in her son) What information is given in the following sentence that partly explains why Gideon might have felt at home on the Farquars' farm? (He had his wife and children with him.)

to explore the writer's concerns with politics, mental illness, and the problems of women in modern life.

In her later novels, like *Briefing for a Descent into Hell* (1971), Lessing departs from psychological realism and introduces her readers to "inner-space fiction," in which an individual mental breakdown is related to a wider social breakdown.

Her most recent series, *Canopus in Argos* (1983), is a sequence of fantasies set in outer space. A reviewer has remarked, however, that these books show a relationship, not to the Buck Rogers type of space fiction, but to the Book of Revelation in the Bible.

Asked what advice she would give to young writers, Lessing answered, ". . . writing can't be a way of life; the important part of writing is living. You have to live in such a way that your writing emerges from it."

NO WITCHCRAFT FOR SALE

This story is from *African Stories* and it takes place in Southern Rhodesia at a time when that part of Africa was still under British rule. The servants in the story are black Africans, the Farquars are part of the British ruling class. In her Preface to *African Stories*, Lessing writes: "If people had been prepared to listen, two decades earlier, to the small, but shrill-enough, voices crying out for the world's attention, perhaps the present suffering in South Africa and Southern Rhodesia could have been prevented. Britain, who is responsible, became conscious of her responsibility too late; and now the tragedy must play itself out."

This story, which is not about witchcraft at all, reads like a contemporary parable.

The Farquars had been childless for years when little Teddy was born; and they were touched by the pleasure of their servants, who brought presents of fowls and eggs and flowers to the homestead when they came to rejoice over the baby, exclaiming with delight over his downy golden head and his blue eyes. They congratulated Mrs. Farquar as if she had achieved a very great thing, and she felt that she had—her smile for the lingering, admiring natives was warm and grateful.

Later, when Teddy had his first haircut, Gideon the cook picked up the soft gold tufts from the ground, and held them reverently in his hand. Then he smiled at the little boy and said: "Little Yellow Head." That became the native name for the child. Gideon and Teddy were great friends from the first. When Gideon had finished his work, he would lift Teddy on his shoulders to the shade of a big tree, and play with him there, forming curious little toys from twigs and leaves and grass, or shaping animals from wetted soil. When Teddy learned to walk it was often Gideon who crouched before him, clucking encouragement, finally catching him when he fell, tossing him up in the air till they both became breathless with laughter. Mrs. Farquar was fond of the old cook because of his love for her child.

There was no second baby; and one day Gideon said: "Ah, missus, missus, the Lord above sent this one; Little Yellow Head is the most good thing we have in our house." Because of that "we" Mrs. Farquar felt a warm impulse toward her cook; and at the end of the month she raised his wages. He had been with her now for several years; he was one of the few natives who had his wife and children in the compound and never wanted to go home to his kraal,[1] which was some

1. **kraal** (kräl): a native village.

SUPPLEMENTARY SUPPORT MATERIALS
1. Vocabulary Activity Worksheet (*CCB*)
2. Review and Response Worksheet: Irony (*CCB*)
3. Language Skills Worksheet: Verbs (*CCB*)
4. Selection Test (*CCB*)

DEVELOPING VOCABULARY
The following words from the story are tested in the Selection Test. (See also Vocabulary Activity Worksheet.)

impulse	efficacy
compound	perfunctory
intoxication	uncouth
inevitable	perversely
protuberance	eminent

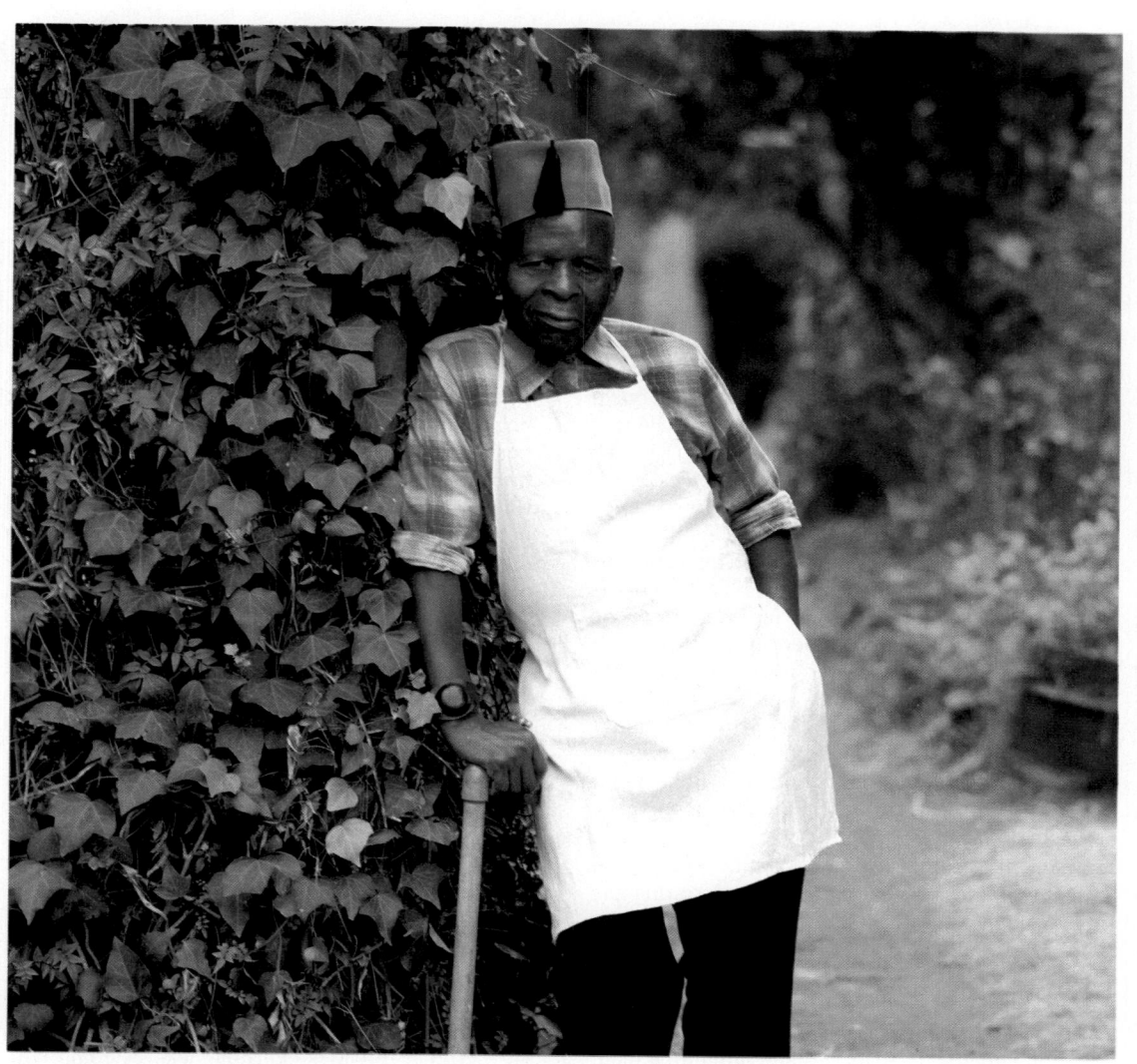

A. Imagery
❓ In what ways might Teddy's fair hair seem "miraculous" to a black child? (The color, texture, and straightness of the hair would be very different from the hair of the child's friends and family. The writer is saying this with some irony. The white child's hair, of course, is no more miraculous than the hair of the black child.)

B. Expansion
Calling Gideon a mission boy means that he attended a school run by Christian missionaries where he was taught the religion of his employers.

A   hundreds of miles away. Sometimes a small piccanin[2] who had been born the same time as Teddy, could be seen peering from the edge of the bush, staring in awe at the little white boy with his miraculous fair hair and Northern blue eyes. The two little children would gaze at each other with a wide, interested gaze, and once Teddy put out his hand curiously to touch the black child's cheeks and hair.

Gideon, who was watching, shook his head

wonderingly, and said: "Ah, missus, these are both children, and one will grow up to be a baas,[3] and one will be a servant"; and Mrs. Farquar smiled and said sadly, "Yes, Gideon, I was thinking the same." She sighed. "It is God's will," said Gideon, who was a mission boy. The Farquars   B were very religious people; and this shared feeling about God bound servant and masters even closer together.

Teddy was about six years old when he was

2. **piccanin** (from the Portuguese *pequeño,* meaning "small"): a native child.

3. **baas:** South African dialect for "boss."

? How does Ted-
dy's inability to
apologize to Gide-
on reflect the rela-
tionship between
black and white
adults in this soci-
ety? (It empha-
sizes the inequality
of status and the
lack of a single
standard of behav-
ior toward all.)
How does the rela-
tionship between
these two change
as Teddy grows
older? (It becomes
more formal and
distant.)

B. Plot

? What state was
Mrs. Farquar in
when her remedy
failed to help the
stricken Teddy?
(Panic-stricken)
How was this a re-
versal of the usual
relationship be-
tween mistress
and servant? (She
was helpless, and
he was knowl-
edgeable and in
charge.)

given a scooter, and discovered the <u>intoxications</u> of speed. All day he would fly around the home-stead, in and out of flowerbeds, scattering squawking chickens and irritated dogs, finishing with a wide dizzying arc into the kitchen door. There he would cry: "Gideon, look at me!" And Gideon would laugh and say: "Very clever, Little Yellow Head." Gideon's youngest son, who was now a herdsboy, came especially up from the compound to see the scooter. He was afraid to come near it, but Teddy showed off in front of him. "Piccanin," shouted Teddy," get out of my way!" And he raced in circles around the black child until he was frightened, and fled back to the bush.

"Why did you frighten him?" asked Gideon, gravely reproachful.

Teddy said defiantly: "He's only a black boy," and laughed. Then, when Gideon turned away from him without speaking, his face fell. Very soon he slipped into the house and found an orange and brought it to Gideon, saying: "This is for you." He could not bring himself to say he was sorry; but he could not bear to lose Gideon's affection either. Gideon took the orange unwillingly and sighed. "Soon you will be going away to school, Little Yellow Head," he said wonderingly, "and then you will be grown up." He shook his head gently and said, "And that is how our lives go." He seemed to be putting a distance between himself and Teddy, not because of resentment, but in the way a person accepts something <u>inevitable</u>. The baby had lain in his arms and smiled up into his face: the tiny boy had swung from his shoulders and played with him by the hour. Now Gideon would not let his flesh touch the flesh of the white child. He was kind, but there was a grave formality in his voice that made Teddy pout and sulk away. Also, it made him into a man: With Gideon he was polite, and carried himself formally, and if he came into the kitchen to ask for something, it was in the way a white man uses toward a servant, expecting to be obeyed.

But on the day that Teddy came staggering into the kitchen with his fists to his eyes, shrieking with pain, Gideon dropped the pot full of hot soup that he was holding, rushed to the child, and forced aside his fingers. "A snake!" he exclaimed. Teddy had been on his scooter, and had come to a rest with his foot on the side of a big tub of plants. A tree snake, hanging by its tail from the roof, had spat full into his eyes. Mrs. Farquar came running when she heard the commotion. "He'll go blind," she sobbed, holding Teddy close against her. "Gideon, he'll go blind!" Already the eyes, with perhaps half an hour's sight left in them, were swollen up to the size of fists: Teddy's small white face was distorted by great purple oozing <u>protuberances</u>. Gideon said: "Wait a minute, missus, I'll get some medicine." He ran off into the bush.

Mrs. Farquar lifted the child into the house and bathed his eyes with permanganate.[4] She had scarcely heard Gideon's words; but when she saw that her remedies had no effect at all, and remembered how she had seen natives with no sight in their eyes because of the spitting of a snake, she began to look for the return of her cook, remembering what she heard of the <u>efficacy</u> of native herbs. She stood by the window, holding the terrified, sobbing little boy in her arms, and peered helplessly into the bush. It was not more than a few minutes before she saw Gideon come bounding back, and in his hand he held a plant.

"Do not be afraid, missus," said Gideon, "this will cure Little Yellow Head's eyes." He stripped the leaves from the plant, leaving a small white fleshy root. Without even washing it, he put the root in his mouth, chewed it vigorously, and then held the spittle there while he took the child forcibly from Mrs. Farquar. He gripped Teddy down between his knees, and pressed the balls of his thumbs into the swollen eyes, so that the child screamed and Mrs. Farquar cried out in protest: "Gideon, Gideon!" But Gideon took no notice. He knelt over the writhing child, pushing back the puffy lids till chinks of eyeball showed, and then he spat hard, again and again, into first one eye, and then the other. He finally lifted Teddy gently into his mother's arms, and said: "His eyes will get better." But Mrs. Farquar was weeping with terror, and she could hardly thank him: It was impossible to believe that Teddy could keep his sight. In a couple of hours the swellings were gone: The eyes were inflamed and tender but Teddy could see. Mr. and Mrs. Farquar went to Gideon in the kitchen and thanked him over and over again. They felt helpless because of their gratitude: It seemed they could do nothing to express it. They gave Gideon presents for his wife and children, and a big increase in wages, but these things could not pay for Teddy's now com-

---

4. **permanganate** (pər·mang′gə·nāt′): a dark purple chemical compound used as a disinfectant.

READING CHECK TEST

1. The story takes place in a city in Southern Rhodesia. (F)
2. The Farquars were religious people with strong family bonds. (T)
3. Teddy Farquar was afraid of Gideon when he was a child. (F)
4. It was just good luck that made it possible for Gideon to save Teddy's eyes. (F)
5. The scientist did not expect to find out which herb Gideon had used. (T)

pletely cured eyes. Mrs. Farquar said: "Gideon, God chose you as an instrument for His goodness," and Gideon said: "Yes, missus, God is very good."

Now, when such a thing happens on a farm, it cannot be long before everyone hears of it. Mr. and Mrs. Farquar told their neighbors and the story was discussed from one end of the district to the other. The bush is full of secrets. No one can live in Africa, or at least on the veld,[5] without learning very soon that there is an ancient wisdom of leaf and soil and season—and, too, perhaps most important of all, of the darker tracts of the human mind—which is the black man's heritage. Up and down the district people were telling anecdotes, reminding each other of things that had happened to them.

"But I saw it myself, I tell you. It was a puff adder[6] bite. The kaffir's[7] arm was swollen to the elbow, like a great shiny black bladder. He was groggy after a half a minute. He was dying. Then suddenly a kaffir walked out of the bush with his hands full of green stuff. He smeared something on the place, and next day my boy was back at work, and all you could see was two small punctures in the skin."

This was the kind of tale they told. And, as always, with a certain amount of exasperation, because while all of them knew that in the bush of Africa are waiting valuable drugs locked in bark, in simple-looking leaves, in roots, it was impossible to ever get the truth about them from the natives themselves.

The story eventually reached town; and perhaps it was at a sundowner party, or some such function, that a doctor, who happened to be there, challenged it. "Nonsense," he said, "These things get exaggerated in the telling. We are always checking up on this kind of story, and we draw a blank every time."

Anyway, one morning there arrived a strange car at the homestead, and out stepped one of the workers from the laboratory in town, with cases full of test-tubes and chemicals.

Mr. and Mrs. Farquar were flustered and pleased and flattered. They asked the scientist to lunch, and they told the story all over again, for the hundredth time. Little Teddy was there too,

his blue eyes sparkling with health, to prove the truth of it. The scientist explained how humanity might benefit if this new drug could be offered for sale; and the Farquars were even more pleased: They were kind, simple people, who liked to think of something good coming about because of them. But when the scientist began talking of the money that might result, their manner showed discomfort. Their feelings over the miracle (that was how they thought of it) were so strong and deep and religious, that it was distasteful to them to think of money. The scientist, seeing their faces, went back to his first point, which was the advancement of humanity. He was perhaps a trifle perfunctory: It was not the first time he had come salting the tail[8] of a fabulous bush secret.

Eventually, when the meal was over, the Farquars called Gideon into their living room and explained to him that this baas, here, was a Big Doctor from the Big City, and he had come all that way to see Gideon. At this Gideon seemed afraid; he did not understand; and Mrs. Farquar explained quickly that it was because of the wonderful thing he had done with Teddy's eyes that the Big Baas had come.

Gideon looked from Mrs. Farquar to Mr. Farquar, and then at the little boy, who was showing great importance because of the occasion. At last he said grudgingly: "The Big Baas want to know what medicine I used?" He spoke incredulously, as if he could not believe his old friends could so betray him. Mr. Farquar began explaining how a useful medicine could be made out of the root, and how it could be put on sale, and how thousands of people, black and white, up and down the continent of Africa, could be saved by the medicine when that spitting snake filled their eyes with poison. Gideon listened, his eyes bent on the ground, the skin of his forehead puckering in discomfort. When Mr. Farquar had finished he did not reply. The scientist, who all this time had been leaning back in a big chair, sipping his coffee and smiling with skeptical good humor, chipped in and explained all over again, in different words, about the making of drugs and the progress of science. Also, he offered Gideon a present.

There was silence after this further explanation, and then Gideon remarked indifferently that he

---

5. **veld:** a South African grassland.
6. **puff adder:** a type of poisonous snake.
7. **kaffir:** a black African native.

8. **salting the tail:** trying to catch (the truth).

A. Interpreting
This paragraph describes what has been called "the bush telegraph." What exactly is being described? (How information spreads by word of mouth through the African community)

B. Character
What was the Farquars' initial reaction to the visit of the scientist? (Pleasure) Why did they want to help him? (To benefit humanity) Read the following passages carefully to find out what the scientist really wanted and what he expected to happen. (Money; he would fail to obtain the name of the herb.)

C. Conflict and Crisis
Why did Gideon feel that the Farquars were betraying him when they asked him to tell the scientist what plant he had used to cure Teddy? (In Gideon's culture, the knowledge of healing was confined to particular individuals [called witch doctors by Westerners], who only passed on their knowledge to selected heirs.)

1. At the start of the story, Gideon and Teddy are great friends. The cook plays with the child and teaches him to walk. A change occurs when Teddy, riding his scooter, frightens Gideon's son. When Gideon reproaches the boy, Teddy answers that "he's only a black boy." After this, Gideon's attitude toward Teddy

grows more distant.
2. The reality is the compulsory separation of the races at that time practiced in Rhodesia.
3. A venomous tree snake sprays him in the eyes.
4. Gideon chews a root, and then rubs the spittle in the boy's eyes. Within a short time, his eyes are cured.
5. The Farquars cannot understand why

Gideon would not want to share his knowledge as a benefit for humanity. They feel he is unreasonable (see pages 1025–1026).
6. The quest fails, after Gideon leads the scientist and the Farquars six miles from the house, only to hand the scientist some common blue flowers.
7. As he grows up, the relationship becomes more formal, polite, and guarded.

A. Theme

? Why did the Farquars get annoyed with Gideon's refusal to divulge the medicinal plant? (They thought he was just being stubborn.) How is this an example of a cultural misunderstanding? (They did not understand the importance of the knowledge to Gideon and to the black community.)

B. Motivation

? Why is the scientist eager to believe that there is no curative plant? (He does not want to admit that an African could have knowledge that he lacks.)

C. Character

Here another African reports that Gideon, the son of a medicine man, is considered an accomplished healer by his people.

? How does this explain why for a while Gideon behaves "like an unwilling servant"?

CLOSURE

Ask students to discuss the limits that existed in the relationship between Gideon and the Farquars. What were these limits, and what was their source?

A

could not remember the root. His face was sullen and hostile, even when he looked at the Farquars, whom he usually treated like old friends. They were beginning to feel annoyed; and this feeling annulled the guilt that had been sprung into life by Gideon's accusing manner. They were beginning to feel that he was unreasonable. But it was at that moment that they all realized that he would never give in. The magical drug would remain where it was, unknown and useless except for the tiny scattering of Africans who had the knowledge, natives who might be digging a ditch for the municipality in a ragged shirt and a pair of patched shorts, but who were still born to healing, hereditary healers, being the nephews or sons of the old witch doctors whose ugly masks and bits of bone and all the <u>uncouth</u> properties of magic were the outward signs of real power and wisdom.

The Farquars might tread on that plant fifty times a day as they passed from house to garden, from cow kraal to mealie⁹ field, but they would never know it.

But they went on persuading and arguing, with all the force of their exasperation; and Gideon continued to say that he could not remember, or that there was no such root, or that it was the wrong season of the year, or that it wasn't the root itself, but the spit from his mouth that had cured Teddy's eyes. He said all these things one after another, and seemed not to care they were contradictory. He was rude and stubborn. The Farquars could hardly recognize their gentle, lovable old servant in this ignorant, <u>perversely</u> obstinate African, standing there in front of them with lowered eyes, his hands twitching his cook's apron, repeating over and over whichever one of the stupid refusals that first entered his head.

And suddenly he appeared to give in. He lifted his head, gave a long, blank angry look at the circle of whites, who seemed to him like a circle of yelping dogs pressing around him, and said: "I will show you the root."

They walked single file away from the homestead down a kaffir path. It was a blazing December afternoon, with the sky full of hot rain clouds. Everything was hot: The sun was like a bronze tray whirling overhead, there was a heat shimmer over the fields, the soil was scorching underfoot, the dusty wind blew gritty and thick and warm in

---

9. **mealie:** South African name for Indian corn.

their faces. It was a terrible day, fit only for reclining on a veranda with iced drinks, which is where they would normally have been at that hour.

From time to time, remembering that on the day of the snake it had taken ten minutes to find the root, someone asked: "Is it much further, Gideon?" And Gideon would answer over his shoulder, with angry politeness: "I'm looking for the root, baas." And indeed, he would frequently bend sideways and trail his hand among the grasses with a gesture that was insulting in its perfunctoriness. He walked them through the bush along unknown paths for two hours, in that melting destroying heat, so that the sweat trickled coldly down them and their heads ached. They were all quite silent; the Farquars because they were angry, the scientist because he was being proved right again; there was no such plant. His was a tactful silence.

B

At last, six miles from the house, Gideon suddenly decided they had had enough; or perhaps his anger evaporated at that moment. He picked up, without an attempt at looking anything but casual, a handful of blue flowers from the grass, flowers that had been growing plentifully all down the paths they had come.

He handed them to the scientist without looking at him, and marched off by himself on the way home, leaving them to follow him if they chose.

When they got back to the house, the scientist went to the kitchen to thank Gideon: he was being very polite, even though there was an amused look in his eyes. Gideon was not there. Throwing the flowers casually into the back of his car, the <u>eminent</u> visitor departed on his way back to his laboratory.

Gideon was back in his kitchen in time to prepare dinner, but he was sulking. He spoke to Mr. Farquar like an unwilling servant. It was days before they liked each other again.

The Farquars made enquiries about the root from their laborers. Sometimes they were answered with distrustful stares. Sometimes the natives said: "We do not know. We have never heard of the root." One, the cattle boy, who had been with them a long time, and had grown to trust them a little, said: "Ask your boy in the kitchen. Now, there's a doctor for you. He's the son of a famous medicine man who used to be in these parts, and there's nothing he cannot cure." Then he added politely: "Of course, he's not as good

C

Interpreting Meanings

8. Most students will agree that, even though Lessing does not condemn the Farquars, there is some irony in her attitude toward them.

Students will have differing opinions.
9. This passage vividly points up the economic disparity between the races in South Africa.
10. See page 1026, col. 1. The plant

is for those "born to healing." It is not for commercial use.
11. Student answers will vary.
12. The culture of white Europe clashes with that of black Africa. They clash in values, religion, responses to nature, ways of dealing with one another, etc.

The comment tells us that Gideon, better than anyone else in the story, understands the sad realities of condi-

tions in Rhodesia and the human divisions and suffering that they cause.
13. One statement of the theme might be this: All too often, social prejudice and social institutions erect insuperable barriers between people.

as the white man's doctor, we know that, but he's good for us."

After some time, when the soreness had gone from between the Farquars and Gideon, they began to joke: "When are you going to show us the snake root, Gideon?" And he would laugh and shake his head, saying, a little uncomfortably: "But I did show you, missus, have you forgotten?"

Much later, Teddy, as a schoolboy, would come into the kitchen and say: "You old rascal, Gideon!

Do you remember that time you tricked us all by making us walk miles all over the veld for nothing? It was so far my father had to carry me!"

And Gideon would double up with polite laughter. After much laughing, he would suddenly straighten himself up, wipe his old eyes, and look sadly at Teddy, who was grinning mischievously at him across the kitchen: "Ah, Little Yellow Head, how you have grown! Soon you will be grown up with a farm of your own . . ."

A

A. Irony
There is irony in this statement by Gideon.
? In what important sense did Gideon totally reveal the power of the curing plant and of his own knowledge? (There was no reluctance to show his knowledge at the moment when it was truly needed.)

Responding to the Story

Analyzing the Story

Identifying Facts

1. Describe the relationship between Gideon and Teddy at the start of the story. What incident signals a change in their relationship?
2. Mrs. Farquar and Gideon share a sense of sadness about the reality of their children's future lives. What is the reality that gives these two characters, and this whole story, a feeling of sadness?
3. What happens to Teddy that sets the action of the **plot** in motion?
4. What does Gideon do for Teddy?
5. Although Lessing makes it clear that the Farquars feel close to Gideon, when the "Big Doctor" arrives from the city, it also becomes apparent that they do not really understand Gideon at all. Cite the sentences that express their puzzlement over Gideon's behavior.
6. What happens to the scientist's quest for the plant?
7. How does Teddy's relationship with Gideon change as he grows up?

Interpreting Meanings

8. How do you think Lessing feels about the Farquars: Does she really feel that they are people of good will, or is there some **irony** in her attitude? How did you respond to them?
9. What implicit criticism can you detect in the fact that while Teddy is riding on a scooter, Gideon's son of the same age is a herdsboy?
10. Why do you think Gideon refuses to share his wisdom with the Farquars?
11. Describe how you feel about the "Big Doctor." Did you find yourself identifying with him, with the Far-

quars, or with Gideon? Explain your responses.
12. In what ways is this story about a clash of cultures? Reread Gideon's comment at the end of the story. What does it tell us about Gideon's understanding of the relationship between the two cultures?
13. How would you state the **theme** of this story?

Writing About the Story

A Creative Response

1. **Extending a Character.** When Gideon hears the arguments for sharing his knowledge, he remains sullen. Imagine what he would have said if he were on an equal footing with his employers. In two paragraphs, write Gideon's refusal speech.

A Critical Response

2. **Analyzing Conflict.** The conflict in the story between the scientist and the Farquars on one hand and Gideon on the other comes about because Gideon does not wish to share his knowledge. It is not even a conflict between right and wrong, or between good and evil. Nor is it a conflict between enlightened and unenlightened viewpoints. Rather, it is over cultural differences. In an essay, discuss the similarities and differences between the Farquars' and scientist's point of view and Gideon's. Be sure to use quotations from the story to back up your opinions.
3. **Analyzing Point of View.** In a brief essay, tell whether the story is told from the **omniscient** or the **limited third-person** point of view. Cite passages to support your analysis. How would the story's impact have differed if it had been narrated by Gideon or by the adult Teddy Farquar?

FURTHER READING FOR STUDENTS
For a work with a similar theme, direct students to the play *Master Harold . . . and the Boys,* written by the white South African playwright Athol Fugard. This play also deals powerfully with the relationship between a white child and a black man who works for the boy's family. Other plays by Fugard and much of the fiction of Nadine Gordimer also deal with the corrosive effects of institutional racism in South Africa.

1. BUILDING ON PRIOR KNOWLEDGE. Tell students that this story is about a young man who has to face life after the loss of a leg. Ask them to recall movies or plays they have seen and stories they have read about people coping with disabilities or crippling illnesses, such as *The Miracle Worker.* What are the various ways in which the characters try to cope with their loss? How important is it that people facing tragedy be honest about what they are feeling?

2. ESTABLISHING A PURPOSE. Since this is a story in which more is implied than is stated directly, ask students to pay very close attention to what is suggested by the title and by the symbolism of the garden setting.

3. PREREADING JOURNAL. Ask students to think about what it might feel like to become suddenly ill and to try to express these feelings in the form of a diary entry. Ask them to try to write about how, when we're hurt or upset, we try to project our feelings of anger about our situation upon someone else.

Nadine Gordimer (1923–   )

Nadine Gordimer was born in Springs, a small town thirty miles from Johannesburg, on the gold mining ridge that has brought South Africa much of its wealth. Her father was Jewish, a jeweler who had emigrated from Lithuania as a teen-ager; her mother was a native of England. Gordimer grew up in a middle-class colonial society that imitated European conventions and values. She has said that she spent much of her childhood reading because she found that atmosphere extremely dull.

She began writing at the age of nine when, as a sickly child, she was taken out of school for a time. Her first published story appeared in a Johannesburg weekly when she was fifteen. Her first internationally published collection of short stories, *The Soft Voice of the Serpent and Other Stories,* appeared in 1952. Critics hailed Gordimer as a strong new voice who could draw fresh, authentic perceptions of African life. Her first novel, *The Lying Day,* was published the following year to favorable reviews.

Since then, Gordimer has continued to win praise, culminating in her winning the Nobel Prize in literature in 1991. She is known for her ability to show, as one critic said, "the infinite variety of human character, the rich and surprising drama inherent in human personality and in the clash of personality." She has been compared to Virginia Woolf for her talent in capturing moments in people's lives that reveal significant emotions. Critic Robert F. Haugh called it "the illuminating moment, the quick perceptive glance of the author which sparkles like a gem."

Although she deals with universal themes and uses a wide variety of settings, much of Gordimer's writing concerns her own troubled nation. "Our father's culture," she has observed, "white culture imported from Europe—never had a chance in the South African context. . . . All it did was to harm black culture. . . . In the process we suffered more than they." Gordimer has inevitably been drawn to writing about the effects of apartheid on South Africa. One critic commented that she is "one of the very few links between white and black in South Africa. She is a bearer of culture in a barbaric society. And she is a luminous symbol of at least one white person's understanding of the black man's burden." Yet her great achievement is the ability to deal with South Africa's problems from a literary rather than a political perspective.

"Here I live in a society which is fundamentally out of joint. One can't but be politically concerned," she has said, but she disclaims a political allegiance. "I don't understand politics except in terms of what politics does to influence lives. What interests me is the infinite variety of effects apartheid has on men and women."

Among her best-known works are *A Guest of Honor* (1970) and *July's People* (1981), the latter set in an unnamed future when whites in South Africa become the servants of the blacks.

Although Gordimer is respected around the world, she has been a thorn in the side of her own country's government. One critic noted that her novels "have stirred the foes of apartheid with words that slash at the system." Indeed, three of her novels were banned in South Africa. Gordimer says that she considers herself "an intensely loyal South African. I care deeply for my country. If I didn't, I wouldn't still be there."

SUPPLEMENTARY SUPPORT MATERIALS
1. Vocabulary Activity Worksheet (*CCB*)
2. Review and Response Worksheet: Protagonist and Theme (*CCB*)
3. Language Skills Worksheet: Noun Clauses (*CCB*)
4. Selection Test (*CCB*)

DEVELOPING VOCABULARY
The following words from the story are tested in the Selection Test. (See also Vocabulary Activity Worksheet.)

fervently	hypnotic
pungent	lugubrious
tiered	pulsation
vehement	aperture
unobtrusive	to parry

THE SOFT VOICE OF THE SERPENT

The conflict in this story is so subtle that it can be overlooked easily in a quick first reading. The title refers to the serpent's tempting of Eve in the Garden of Eden. Why do you think Gordimer calls the serpent's voice "soft"? As you read, decide who or what brings the soft voice of temptation to this modern couple.

The Equatorial Jungle by Henri Rousseau (1909). Oil.

National Gallery of Art. Chester Dale Collection, Washington, D.C.

A. Humanities Connection: Responding to the Fine Art
French painter Henri Rousseau (1844–1910) worked as a customs inspector. In his spare time, he painted. In 1891, he began a series of unique, highly evocative jungle paintings. A tour of army duty in Mexico may have inspired his tropical settings, but the plants were in the Paris botanical gardens and the wild animals in zoo photographs. The paintings, with their lush outsized vegetation and mysterious lurking animals, have the entrancing power of a dream.

? Ask students if they find the painting both inviting and menacing. Do the animals seem shy or waiting to pounce? What associations do they make with the word *garden*? (See if anyone mentions Eden.)

A

1. The young man and his loved ones believed it would be good for him to spend time in the ___garden___.
2. He felt his ___leg___ missing under the rug or chair covering.
3. A locust frightened the young wife while she was ___sewing___.
4. The young man felt that he ___understood___ what the locust was feeling.
5. At the end, the young man's mood turns ___irritable___.

CLOSURE

Ask students to discuss what they think the young man should do in the future and whether or not it would be healthy for him to spend the rest of his life as he passed these first days in the garden with his wife.

A. Plot

A young man, recovering from an injury, is completing his convalescence in the garden. He wonders if there is any parallel between his situation and Adam's in the Garden of Eden. Have students consider this question as they read.

B. Interpreting

The young man says he feels as he did when he was a little boy.

❓ What is there about his current situation that is similar to childhood? (He is being wheeled about by a woman in a protected environment.)

C. Conflict

❓ What realization does the young man want to avoid? (That he once had two legs)

D. Plot

❓ How would you describe the time the husband and wife spend together in the garden? (Peaceful, companionable, and restorative)

E. Conflict

❓ What disturbs the serenity of the couple in the garden? (The appearance of the locust)

A

He was only twenty-six and very healthy and he was soon strong enough to be wheeled out into the garden. Like everyone else, he had great and curious faith in the garden: "Well, soon you'll be up and able to sit out in the garden," they said, looking at him _fervently_, with little understanding tilts of the head. Yes, he would be out . . . in the garden. It was a big garden enclosed in old dark, sleek, _pungent_ firs, and he could sit deep beneath their _tiered_ fringes, down in the shade, far away. There was the feeling that there, in the garden, he would come to an understanding; that it would come easier, there. Perhaps there was something in this of the old Eden idea; the tender human adjusting himself to himself in the soothing impersonal presence of trees and grass and earth, before going out into the stare of the world.

B

The very first time it was so strange; his wife was wheeling him along the gravel path in the sun and the shade, and he felt exactly as he did when he was a little boy and he used to bend and hang, looking at the world upside down, through his ankles. Everything was vast and open, the sky, the wind blowing along through the swaying, trembling greens, the flowers shaking in _vehement_ denial. Movement . . .

A first slight wind lifted again in the slack, furled sail of himself; he felt it belly gently, so gently he could just feel it, lifting inside him.

So she wheeled him along, pushing hard and not particularly well with her thin pretty arms—but he would not for anything complain of the way she did it or suggest that the nurse might do better, for he knew that would hurt her—and when they came to a spot that he liked, she put the brake on the chair and settled him there for the morning. That was the first time and now he sat there every

C

day. He read a lot, but his attention was arrested sometimes, quite suddenly and compellingly, by the sunken place under the rug where his leg used to be. There was his one leg, and next to it, the rug flapped loose. Then looking, he felt his leg not there; he felt it go, slowly, from the toe to the thigh. He felt that he had no leg. After a few minutes he went back to his book. He never let the realization quite reach him; he let himself realize it physically, but he never quite let it get at _him_. He felt it pressing up, coming, coming, dark, crushing, ready to burst—but he always turned away, just in time, back to his book. That was his system; that was the way he was going to do it.

He would let it come near, irresistibly near, again and again, ready to catch him alone in the garden. And again and again he would turn it back, just in time. Slowly it would become a habit, with the reassuring strength of a habit. It would become such a habit never to get to the point of realizing it, _that he never would realize it_. And one day he would find that he had achieved what he wanted: _He would feel as if he had always been like that_.

Then the danger would be over, forever.

In a week or two he did not have to read all the time; he could let himself put down the book and look about him, watching the first part silkily as a child's fine straight hair in the wind, watching the small birds tightroping the telephone wire, watching the fat old dove trotting after his refined patrician[1] gray women, purring with lust. His wife came and sat beside him, doing her sewing, and sometimes they spoke, but often they sat for hours, a whole morning, her movements at work small and _unobtrusive_ as the birds', he resting his head back and looking at a blur of sky through half closed eyes. Now and then her eye, habitually looking inward, would catch the signal of some little happening, some point of color in the garden, and her laugh or exclamation drawing his attention to it would suddenly clear away the silence. At eleven o'clock she would get up and put down her sewing and go into the house to fetch their tea; crunching slowly away into the sun up the path, going easily, empowered by the sun rather than her own muscles. He watched her go, easily . . . He was healing. In the static quality of his gaze, in the relaxed feeling of his mouth, in the upward-lying palm of his hand, there was annealment[2] . . .

D

E

One day a big locust[3] whirred drily past her head, and she jumped up with a cry, scattering her sewing things. He laughed at her as she bent about picking them up, shuddering. She went into the house to fetch the tea, and he began to read. But presently he put down the book and, yawning, noticed a reel of pink cotton that she had missed, lying in a rose bed.

He smiled, remembering her. And then he became conscious of a curious old mannish little face, fixed upon him in a kind of _hypnotic_ dread. There, absolutely stilled with fear beneath his glance, crouched a very big locust. What an amus-

---

1. **patrician:** from a high social class, with fine breeding.
2. **annealment:** strengthening, toughening.
3. **locust:** a type of grasshopper that often travels in swarms.

ANALYZING THE STORY
Identifying Facts
1. His wife wheels him into the garden, where he takes the air and reads. Whenever he becomes consciously aware that he has lost his leg, he quickly turns back to his book. He thinks that by ignoring his amputation, he will soon feel as if he had always been one-legged.
2. "Dark" and "crushing."

3. Since the locust is also missing one leg, the man feels that the locust is like himself.

Interpreting Meanings
4. Like Adam, he is situated in a comparatively safe, cocoon-like atmosphere in the garden.
5. The "understanding" that he has suffered no real loss. By the story's end, the man realizes that the comparison between himself and the locust was false, since the locust can fly and he is one-legged and earthbound.
6. The wife's sympathetic interest in the locust, despite her initial repulsion, and the husband's not suggesting that the nurse would wheel him more skillfully.
7. The locust looked like a little person (*Answers continue on next page.*)

ing face the thing had! A lugubrious long face, that somehow suggested a bald head, and such a glum mouth. It looked like some little person out of a Disney cartoon. It moved slightly, still looking up fearfully at him. Strange body, encased in a sort of old-fashioned creaky armor. He had never realized before what ridiculous-looking insects locusts were! Well, naturally not; they occur to one collectively, as a pest—one doesn't go around looking at their faces.

The face was certainly curiously human and even expressive, but looking at the body, he decided that the body couldn't really be called a body at all. With the face, the creature's kinship with humans ended. The body was flimsy paper stretched over a frame of matchstick, like a small boy's homemade airplane. And those could not be thought of as legs—the great saw-toothed back ones were like the parts of an old crane, and the front ones like—like one of her hairpins, bent in two. At that moment the creature slowly lifted up one of the front legs, and passed it tremblingly over its head, stroking the left antenna down. Just as a man might take out a handkerchief and pass it over his brow.

He began to feel enormously interested in the creature, and leaned over in his chair to see it more closely. It sensed him and beneath its stiff, plated sides, he was surprised to see the pulsations of a heart. How fast it was breathing . . . He leaned away a little, to frighten it less.

Watching it carefully, and trying to keep himself effaced from its consciousness by not moving, he became aware of some struggle going on in the thing. It seemed to gather itself together in muscular concentration: this coordinated force then passed along its body in a kind of petering[4] tremor, and ended in a stirring along the upward shaft of the great back legs. But the locust remained where it was. Several times this wave of effort currented through it and was spent, but the next time it ended surprisingly in a few hobbling, uneven steps, undercarriage—airplanelike again—trailing along the earth.

Then the creature lay, fallen on its side, antennae turned stretched out toward him. It groped with its feet, feeling for a hold on the soft ground, bending its joints and straining. With a heave, it righted itself, and as it did so, he saw—leaning forward again—what was the trouble. It was the

---

4. **petering:** gradually diminishing.

same trouble. His own trouble. The creature had lost one leg. Only the long upward shaft of its left leg remained, with a neat round aperture where, no doubt, the other half of the leg had been attached.

Now as he watched the locust gather itself again and again in that concentration of muscle, spend itself again and again in a message that was so puzzlingly never obeyed, he knew exactly what the creature felt. Of course he knew that feeling! That absolute certainty that the leg was there: one had only to lift it . . . The upward shaft of the locust's leg quivered, lifted; why then couldn't he walk? He tried again. The message came; it was going through, the leg was lifting, now it was ready—now! . . . The shaft sagged in the air, with nothing, nothing to hold it up.

He laughed and shook his head: He *knew* . . . Good Lord, *exactly* like— He called out to the house—"Come quickly! Come and see! You've got another patient!"

"What?" she shouted. "I'm getting tea."

"Come and look!" he called. "Now!"

". . . What is it?" she said, approaching the locust distastefully.

"Your locust!" he said. She jumped away with a little shriek.

"Don't worry—it can't move. It's as harmless as I am. You must have knocked its leg off when you hit out at it!" He was laughing at her.

"Oh, I didn't!" she said reproachfully. She loathed it but she loathed to hurt, even more. "I never even touched it! All I hit was air . . . I couldn't possibly have hit it. Not its leg off."

"All right then. It's another locust. But it's lost its leg, anyway. You should just see it . . . It doesn't know the leg isn't there. God, I know exactly how that feels . . . I've been watching it, and honestly, it's uncanny. I can see it feels just like I do!"

She smiled at him, sideways; she seemed suddenly pleased at something. Then, recalling herself, she came forward, bent double, hands up on her hips.

"Well, if it can't move . . ." she said, hanging over it.

"Don't be frightened," he laughed. "Touch it."

"Ah, the poor thing," she said, catching her breath in compassion. "It can't walk."

"Don't encourage it to self-pity," he teased her.

She looked up and laughed. "Oh you—" she parried, assuming a frown. The locust kept its

A. Symbolism
In what terms is the locust described? (In human terms as a sad old man who has a flimsy body like a model airplane)

B. Character
What feeling does the young man have toward the locust after he discovers that it has lost a leg? (He identifies with it; he thinks he knows how it feels.)

C. Character
What feelings toward the locust does the wife reveal? (Distaste, fear, guilt, pity, superiority) Suggest that these reactions may throw light on her unstated and perhaps unconscious feelings toward her husband.

Comment from the Writer
Nadine Gordimer has said, "I'm fascinated by observed moments of tension between people; my mind immediately invents causes for the tension. I like to compose alternate lives."

out of a Disney cartoon; its body was like a small boy's homemade airplane; its back legs were like the parts of an old crane; its front legs were like one of the wife's hairpins; it passed a leg over its head, just as a man might wipe his brow with his handkerchief. Student opinions on the significance of the similes in context will differ.

8. Student answers will vary. Most obviously, the locust plays the tempter, and the temptation is the seductive idea that the man has suffered no real loss.

9. Student answers will vary. In general, the story asks how capable we really are at coping with personal tragedy and implies that most people, like the husband in the story, really need the assistance of illusions in doing so.

A. Mood and Tone

? What is the mood of the conversation between husband and wife concerning the locust? (Lighthearted amusement)

B. Mood

? How does the mood change after the wife flicks the locust away? (Both become uneasy and alarmed.)

C. Theme

The couple forgot that locusts can fly.

? How may the couple's tendency to forget cause them more problems? (They cannot cope with the loss of the leg unless they both acknowledge that fact with all its ramifications.)

---

solemn silly face turned to her. "Shame, isn't he a funny old man," she said. "But what will happen to him?"

A "I don't know," he said, for being in the same boat absolved him from responsibility or pity. "Maybe he'll grow another one. Lizards grow new tails, if they lose them."

"Oh, *lizards,*" she said. "—But not these. I'm afraid the cat'll get him."

"Get another little chair made for him and you can wheel him out here with me."

"Yes," she laughed. "Only for him it would have to be a kind of little cart, with wheels."

"Or maybe he could be taught to use crutches. I'm sure the farmers would like to know that he was being kept active."

"The poor old thing," she said, bending over the locust again. And reaching back somewhere into an inquisitive childhood she picked up a thin wand of twig and prodded the locust, very gently. "Funny thing is, it's even the same leg, the left one." She looked round at him and smiled.

"I know," he nodded, laughing. "The two of us . . ." And then he shook his head and, smiling, said it again: "The two of us."

B She was laughing and just then she flicked the twig more sharply than she meant to and at the touch of it there was a sudden flurried papery whirr, and the locust flew away.

She stood there with the stick in her hand, half afraid of the creature again, and appealed, unnerved as a child, "What happened. What happened."

C There was a moment of silence.
"Don't be a fool," he said irritably.
They had forgotten that locusts can fly.

Responding to the Story

Analyzing the Story

Identifying Facts

1. Describe the **protagonist's,** or main character's, daily routine. What is his plan for coping with the loss of his leg?
2. In the fourth paragraph of the story, what adjectives let the reader know the kinds of feelings the protagonist is trying to avoid?
3. What discoveries does the man make about the locust?

Interpreting Meanings

4. At the end of the first paragraph, the narrator compares the garden in which the story takes place to the Biblical Garden of Eden. How do you think the **protagonist** is like Adam?
5. What "understanding" does the man hope he'll come to? What knowledge does he actually achieve by the story's end?
6. Find the details which imply that the husband and wife do not want to hurt each other.
7. The description of the locust contains a number of **similes.** List the similes and then discuss their significance in the story.
8. The **title** of the story refers to the serpent's temptation of Eve in the Garden of Eden. Who or what plays the tempter in this story? What is the temptation?
9. "The Soft Voice of the Serpent" raises a question about human nature in its attempt to cope with personal tragedy. What question is raised, and what answer is implied? Try to combine this question and answer in a statement of the **theme** of the story.

Writing About the Story

A Creative Response

1. **Using Similes in a Description.** In two paragraphs, describe a living creature that is familiar to you. Try to choose one that your readers might not know very well. You might want to begin by doing some careful observation at a pet store, an aquarium, or a zoo. Then, as Gordimer does, use **similes** to put the unfamiliar traits of the creature—its appearance and actions—into familiar terms.

A Critical Response

2. **Analyzing a Character.** In a three-paragraph essay, discuss the abrupt ending of the story. What has the main character learned about himself and his condition? Has his relationship with his wife changed subtly? Is he now ready to go "out into the stare of the world"? Why?

1. BUILDING ON PRIOR KNOWLEDGE. Ask students what they know about calypso and reggae, two popular types of West Indian music. Note that calypso traditionally has impromptu lyrics, composed on the spot by the performer, so that the calypso singer is something like an improvisational actor. In the following story, the title character earns a living by playing calypso music at island festivals.

2. ESTABLISHING A PURPOSE. As students read Naipaul's story, ask them to look for the attitudes that B. Wordsworth displays. Encourage them to consider how those attitudes compare with attitudes found in the poetry of William Wordsworth (pages 633–645) and how they affect the young narrator.

3. PREREADING JOURNAL. Ask students to think about the qualities they would expect to find in the personality of a poor, unknown poet in today's world. Have students use their journals to create a rough verbal character sketch of such a person.

V. S. Naipaul (1932–   )

V. S. (Vidiadhar Surajprasad) Naipaul was born on the Caribbean island of Trinidad, at a time when that island was still under the colonial rule of England. Naipaul's family had gone to Trinidad from East India in the nineteenth century, to work as indentured servants on the English sugar estates. In nationality East Indian and Hindu in religion, they felt themselves to be members of a transplanted society. As a result, from his earliest days, Naipaul felt a rootlessness. He also felt in Trinidad a sense of the world as a kind of prison.

Fortunately, he was an outstanding student. Scholastic honors won him a place at Trinidad's Queen's Royal College and, in 1949, provided him the chance to quit the island for England. He was given a scholarship to the prestigious Oxford University. Naipaul was one of a few dark-skinned Indians at a university famed for educating England's privileged white Protestant males.

Naipaul's father had had a faltering career as an island journalist, and this provided Naipaul with the idea of becoming a writer. Leaving Oxford in 1954, with no desire to return to Trinidad's narrow possibilities, he sought his identity in writing. He worked part time for the BBC and tried his hand at writing fiction about the island life he had fled. His first short stories, which later became *Miguel Street,* went begging until he was able, in 1957 and 1958, to publish his two early Trinidad novels.

Naipaul's first masterpiece, *A House for Mr. Biswas,* came along in 1961. The novel, which some critics compared to Dickens's comic satires, created a character much like his father. It tells about a poor, ineffectual Trinidadian who finds stability by marrying into an influential family. Mr. Biswas is deprived of independence, however, and his rebellion takes shape in the desperate quest for a house of his own.

A House for Mr. Biswas revealed Naipaul's special gifts as a storyteller: his unique, ironic voice; his clear vision of so-called third-world people; and his understanding of life's essentials. The book established him as a major novelist throughout the world of letters.

Naipaul's search for his ideological roots sent him traveling, first back to the West Indies, then to Africa, the Middle East, and India itself, as he pursued the meaning of his own mixed heritage. These voyages and inquiries have led Naipaul to produce a score of books, both fiction and nonfiction, including *A Bend in the River* (a novel set in Africa) and *India: A Million Mutinies Now* (a travel book about his return to India in 1989). All of Naipaul's works have been acclaimed for their clear, bitter, yet compassionate insights into modern humankind's struggle for survival.

Naipaul has won almost all the major British literary prizes available to a prose writer.

A. Expansion Explain that after slavery was abolished in the British Empire (1833), many poor people from India—which then also was under British rule—came to Trinidad as indentured servants. These immigrants agreed to a period of service in exchange for passage to a new land. Today, about two-fifths of Trinidad's people are of Indian background; most others are of African descent.

B. For Further Reading Students In addition to the collection of stories in Naipaul's *Miguel Street,* students might enjoy the stories of Samuel Selvon, another Trinidadian. Selvon now lives in Britain, but he has set many of his tales in Trinidad.

SUPPLEMENTARY SUPPORT MATERIALS
1. Vocabulary Activity Worksheet (*CCB*)
2. Review and Response Worksheet: Characterization and Theme (*CCB*)
3. Language Skills Worksheet: Narrative Paragraph (*CCB*)
4. Selection Test (*CCB*)

DEVELOPING VOCABULARY
The following words from the story are tested in the Selection Test. (See also Vocabulary Activity Worksheet.)
hospitable   rite   distill
rogue   patronize

A. Character

? What do the tidy clothing and odd request suggest about the visitor? (He differs from the beggars to whom the narrator is accustomed; he seems to have less pragmatic interests.)

B. Vernacular

Point out that the narrator speaks in the vernacular of Trinidad, a creole English that includes words and structures from other languages. In the early part of the story, at least, you might have students restate the narrator's speeches in more traditional English.

C. Character/ Interpreting

? What does the stranger's proper English reveal about him? (He is well educated, whether through schooling or self-education, and he seems fond of using language with precision and care.)

? Why is the mother suspicious of him? (An educated beggar is an oddity; also, his request probably makes her question his motives.)

B. WORDSWORTH

"B. Wordsworth" is a story about the magical world of childhood innocence. It brims with all the possibility, surprise, and joy that children feel when they first glimpse a road to the future opening before their eyes.

The humor in this story, of which there is plenty, springs from the contrast between the boy-narrator's view of things and the more cynical point of view of his mother. Ma has *been* there, and she knows this funny old geezer at the back gate is at best a nut, at worst, a thief, and in either case he is trouble she doesn't need.

But what excitement for the boy! He sees a poet, a man who lives for beauty, for mango trees, for the stars of heaven, and for ice cream. He sees a man with a wildly romantic and tragic history, a man who can feel for all creatures of the world. What a role model! What an opening of a boy's narrow horizons!

The outcome of this odd friendship is somehow satisfying, too. Note the way in which B. Wordsworth says goodbye to the boy, and how it is when the old man is gone. The boy has nothing left then but the memory—so like a dream.

Before you read, review what you know of another Wordsworth, the one with the first initial "W." You might reread pages 631–646 of this book.

Three beggars called punctually every day at the hospitable houses in Miguel Street. At about ten an Indian came in his dhoti[1] and white jacket, and we poured a tin of rice into the sack he carried on his back. At twelve an old woman smoking a clay pipe came and she got a cent. At two a blind man led by a boy called for his penny.

Sometimes we had a rogue. One day a man called and said he was hungry. We gave him a meal. He asked for a cigarette and wouldn't go until we had lit it for him. That man never came again.

The strangest caller came one afternoon at about four o'clock. I had come back from school and was in my home clothes. The man said to me, "Sonny, may I come inside your yard?"

He was a small man and he was tidily dressed. He wore a hat, a white shirt, and black trousers.

I asked, "What you want?"

He said, "I want to watch your bees."

We had four small gru-gru palm trees[2] and they were full of uninvited bees.

I ran up the steps and shouted, "Ma, it have a man outside here. He say he want to watch the bees."

My mother came out, looked at the man and asked in an unfriendly way, "What you want?"

The man said, "I want to watch your bees."

His English was so good, it didn't sound natural, and I could see my mother was worried.

She said to me, "Stay here and watch him while he watch the bees."

The man said, "Thank you, Madam. You have done a good deed today."

He spoke very slowly and very correctly as though every word was costing him money.

We watched the bees, this man and I, for about an hour, squatting near the palm trees.

The man said, "I like watching bees. Sonny, do you like watching bees?"

I said, "I ain't have the time."

He shook his head sadly. He said, "That's what I do, I just watch. I can watch ants for days. Have you ever watched ants? And scorpions, and centipedes, and *congorees*[3]—have you watched those?"

I shook my head.

---

1. **dhoti** (dō'tē): a loincloth worn by Hindu men.
2. **gru-gru palm trees:** tropical spiny palm trees.

3. *congorees:* long, thin, burrowing insects.

The Trial by Julio Larraz (1986). Oil on canvas.

© Julio Larraz. courtesy Nohra Haime Gallery. New York City.

I said, "What you does do, mister?"
He got up and said, "I am a poet."
I said, "A good poet?"
He said, "The greatest in the world."
"What your name, mister?"
"B. Wordsworth."
"B for Bill?"
"Black. Black Wordsworth. White Wordsworth was my brother. We share one heart. I can watch a small flower like the morning glory and cry."
I said, "Why you does cry?"
"Why, boy? Why? You will know when you grow up. You're a poet, too, you know. And when you're a poet you can cry for everything."
I couldn't laugh.

He said, "You like your mother?"
"When she not beating me."
He pulled out a printed sheet from his hip pocket and said, "On this paper is the greatest poem about mothers and I'm going to sell it to you at a bargain price. For four cents."
I went inside and I said, "Ma, you want to buy a poetry for four cents?"
My mother said, "Tell that blasted man to haul his tail away from my yard, you hear."
I said to B. Wordsworth, "My mother say she ain't have four cents."
B. Wordsworth said, "It is the poet's tragedy."
And he put the paper back in his pocket. He didn't seem to mind.

Like many Larraz paintings, *The Trial* uses oblique lighting and a stark setting.

? What can you infer about the man in this painting from his clothing, posture, and expression? (He is clean, precise, old and somewhat infirm, and is—or was—married.) In what ways might this man be like B. Wordsworth? (Both are thoughtful, kind, calm, and caring. It may also be that both men carry the weight of a past romance that had a tragic ending.)

B. Allusion
? Who is "White Wordsworth," and what do the two "Wordsworths" share? ("White Wordsworth" is William Wordsworth, the British Romantic poet. The "Wordsworths" share "one heart"—a love of poetry and nature.)

C. Humor
The narrator's rewording of his mother's angry and colorful refusal helps the story to achieve its sense of humor.

A. Motivation

? B. Wordsworth is quite different from the narrator's mother. How might this factor into the narrator's desire to see B. Wordsworth again? (The poet opens new horizons by offering an idealized way of looking at the world, one that is far less harsh and cynical than the mother's practical approach.)

B. Setting/Theme

? What Romantic attitudes are stressed in Naipaul's description of Wordsworth's lawn? (Answers include a love for nature and a dislike for modern urban life)

C. Irony

By turning the officer's demand into a philosophical question, Wordsworth amuses his young companion, thus easing the tension of the moment.

D. Expansion

Explain that since the stories of *Miguel Street* are interconnected, there are occasional references to details in earlier stories. George is a neighborhood character who sleeps in an unfurnished room.

I said, "Is a funny way to go round selling poetry like that. Only calypsonians[4] do that sort of thing. A lot of people does buy?"

He said, "No one has yet bought a single copy."

"But why you does keep on going round, then?"

He said, "In this way I watch many things, and I always hope to meet poets."

I said, "You really think I is a poet?"

"You're as good as me," he said.

A And when B. Wordsworth left, I prayed I would see him again.

About a week later, coming back from school one afternoon, I met him at the corner of Miguel Street.

He said, "I have been waiting for you for a long time."

I said, "You sell any poetry yet?"

He shook his head.

He said, "In my yard I have the best mango tree in Port of Spain.[5] And now the mangoes are ripe and red and very sweet and juicy. I have waited here for you to tell you this and to invite you to come and eat some of my mangoes."

B He lived in Alberto Street in a one-roomed hut placed right in the center of the lot. The yard seemed all green. There was the big mango tree. There was a coconut tree and there was a plum tree. The place looked wild, as though it wasn't in the city at all. You couldn't see all the big concrete houses in the street.

He was right. The mangoes were sweet and juicy. I ate about six, and the yellow mango juice ran down my arms to my elbows and down my mouth to my chin and my shirt was stained.

My mother said when I got home, "Where you was? You think you is a man now and could go all over the place? Go cut a whip for me."

She beat me rather badly, and I ran out of the house swearing that I would never come back. I went to B. Wordsworth's house. I was so angry, my nose was bleeding.

B. Wordsworth said, "Stop crying, and we will go for a walk."

I stopped crying, but I was breathing short. We went for a walk. We walked down St. Clair Avenue to the Savannah[6] and we walked to the racecourse.

B. Wordsworth said, "Now, let us lie on the grass and look up at the sky, and I want you to think how far those stars are from us."

I did as he told me, and I saw what he meant. I felt like nothing, and at the same time I had never felt so big and great in all my life. I forgot all my anger and all my tears and all the blows.

When I said I was better, he began telling me the names of the stars, and I particularly remembered the constellation of Orion the Hunter, though I don't really know why. I can spot Orion even today, but I have forgotten the rest.

Then a light was flashed into our faces, and we saw a policeman. We got up from the grass.

The policeman said, "What you doing here?"

C B. Wordsworth said, "I have been asking myself the same question for forty years."

We became friends, B. Wordsworth and I. He told me, "You must never tell anybody about me and about the mango tree and the coconut tree and the plum tree. You must keep that a secret. If you tell anybody, I will know, because I am a poet."

I gave him my word and I kept it.

D I liked his little room. It had no more furniture than George's front room, but it looked cleaner and healthier. But it also looked lonely.

One day I asked him, "Mister Wordsworth, why you does keep all this bush in your yard? Ain't it does make the place damp?"

He said, "Listen, and I will tell you a story. Once upon a time a boy and girl met each other and they fell in love. They loved each other so much they got married. They were both poets. He loved words. She loved grass and flowers and trees. They lived happily in a single room, and then one day, the girl poet said to the boy poet, 'We are going to have another poet in the family.' But this poet was never born, because the girl died, and the young poet died with her, inside her. And the girl's husband was very sad, and he said

---

4. **calypsonians:** West Indian folk musicians who compose impromptu songs.
5. **Port of Spain:** the capital of Trinidad.

6. **Savannah:** Queen's Park Savannah—two hundred acres of grassy playing fields, including the racecourse.

READING CHECK TEST

1. Wordsworth is a famous Trinidadian poet. (F)
2. The old man asks to watch bees in the boy's yard. (T)
3. The boy's mother welcomes the old man's friendship with her son. (F)
4. Wordsworth makes his living by singing calypsos. (F)
5. After Wordsworth's death, all signs of his house disappear. (T)

CLOSURE
Discuss with students how knowing B. Wordsworth has changed the narrator. Encourage volunteers to suggest careers that the narrator might choose when he grows up. (Answers might include poet, writer, artist, and natural scientist.)

A. Theme
❓ What do Wordsworth's attitudes—so obvious to the child—suggest about how a poet should face everyday experiences? (A poet should bring to the day-to-day world a fresh eye and a sense of wonder or reverence.)

he would never touch a thing in the girl's garden. And so the garden remained, and grew high and wild.''

I looked at B. Wordsworth, and as he told me this lovely story, he seemed to grow older. I understood his story.

We went for long walks together. We went to the Botanical Gardens and the Rock Gardens. We climbed Chancellor Hill in the late afternoon and watched the darkness fall on Port of Spain, and watched the lights go on in the city and on the ships in the harbor.

A He did everything as though he were doing it for the first time in his life. He did everything as though he were doing some church <u>rite</u>.

He would say to me, ''Now, how about having some ice cream?''

And when I said yes, he would grow very serious and say, ''Now, which café shall we <u>patronize</u>?'' As though it were a very important thing. He would think for some time about it, and finally say, ''I think I will go and negotiate the purchase with that shop.''

The world became a most exciting place.

One day, when I was in his yard, he said to me, ''I have a great secret which I am now going to tell you.''

I said, ''It really secret?''

''At the moment, yes.''

I looked at him, and he looked at me. He said, ''This is just between you and me, remember. I am writing a poem.''

''Oh.'' I was disappointed.

He said, ''But this is a different sort of poem. This is the greatest poem in the world.''

I whistled.

He said, ''I have been working on it for more than five years now. I will finish it in about twenty-two years from now, that is, if I keep on writing at the present rate.''

Papiamento by Julio Larraz (1987). Oil on canvas.   © Julio Larraz, courtesy Nohra Haime Gallery, New York City.

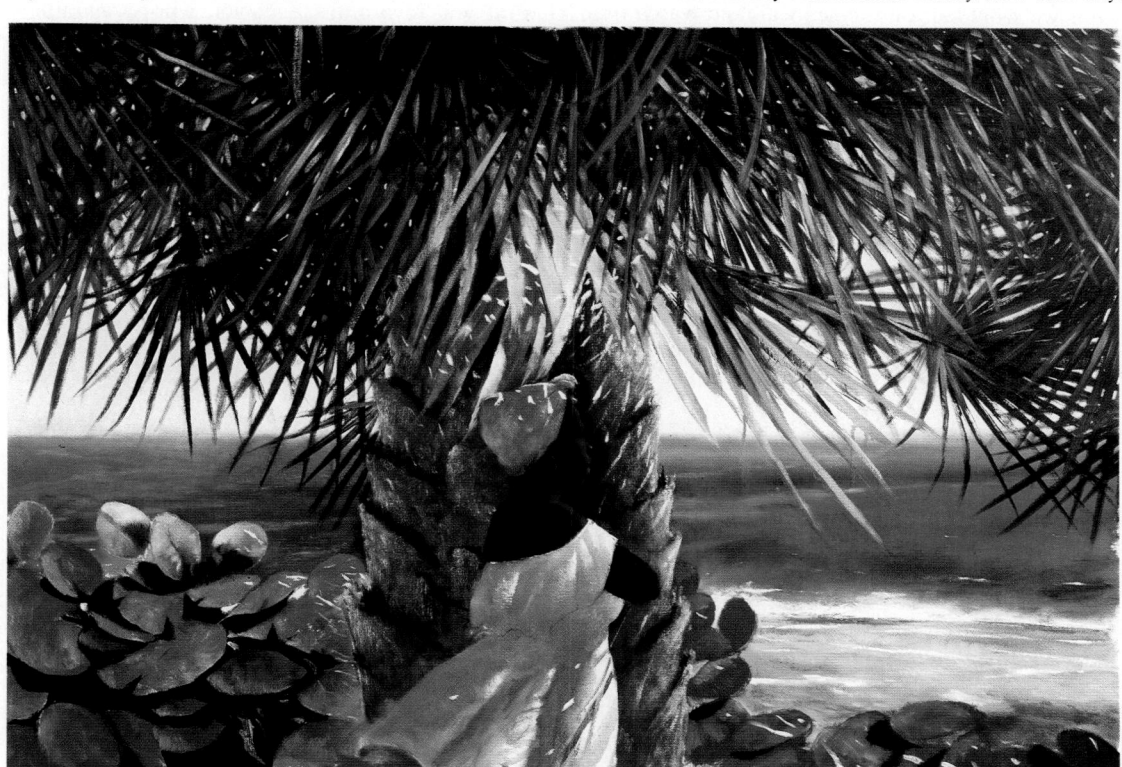

1. A poet who refers to himself as "Black Wordsworth," he connects with his namesake in that they share "one heart." In their lives, both demonstrated the quality of extreme sensitivity.

Interpreting Meanings
2. From Wordsworth he learns sensitivity to the world and begins to grasp his place in it. He also comes to see his own worth as a person—and as a poet.
3. The story has the ring of truth, and the narrator reacts to it as if it were true.
Wordsworth may later deny it due to bitterness over having achieved so little before his death.
4. He responds that he has spent forty years pondering the same question.

He is questioning the purpose of his life and of human existence in general—questions to which many poets seek an answer.
5. Wordsworth states that poetry involves observation (watching the natural world), enjoying experience (eating from the mango tree), sharing experience, questioning, and remembering. In short, poetry touches all aspects of life.

A. Symbol
? What might the sinking of the pin represent? (The rules by which the real world operates, as opposed to the poet's idealized view)

B. Expansion
Explain that the calypso "season" in Trinidad is Carnival, the period of merrymaking (including Mardi Gras) just before Lent. In Trinidad calypso performances are a standard feature of Carnival festivities.

C. Theme
Emphasize that the boy's intensely emotional response to life embraces great grief (at this moment) as well as great joy (earlier in the story). The narrator's response is poetic because of its all-encompassing sensitivity.

D. Setting/ Symbol
? What do these changes signify? (The encroachments of modern city life upon nature and the tendency of modern life to stifle ideals)

"You does write a lot, then?"

He said, "Not any more. I just write one line a month. But I make sure it is a good line."

I asked, "What was last month's good line?"

He looked up at the sky, and said, *"The past is deep."*

I said, "It is a beautiful line."

B. Wordsworth said, "I hope to distill the experiences of a whole month into that single line of poetry. So, in twenty-two years, I shall have written a poem that will sing to all humanity."

I was filled with wonder.

Our walks continued. We walked along the sea wall at Docksite one day, and I said, "Mr. Wordsworth, if I drop this pin in the water, you think it will float?"

A He said, "This is a strange world. Drop your pin, and let us see what will happen."

The pin sank.

I said, "How is the poem this month?"

But he never told me any other line. He merely said, "Oh, it comes, you know. It comes."

Or we would sit on the sea wall and watch the liners come into the harbor.

But of the greatest poem in the world I heard no more.

I felt he was growing older.

"How you does live, Mr. Wordsworth?" I asked him one day.

He said, "You mean how I get money?"

When I nodded, he laughed in a crooked way.

B He said, "I sing calypsos in the calypso season."

"And that last you the rest of the year?"

"It is enough."

"But you will be the richest man in the world when you write the greatest poem?"

He didn't reply.

One day when I went to see him in his little house, I found him lying on his little bed. He looked so old and so weak, that I found myself wanting to cry.

He said, "The poem is not going well."

He wasn't looking at me. He was looking through the window at the coconut tree, and he was speaking as though I wasn't there. He said, "When I was twenty I felt the power within myself." Then, almost in front of my eyes, I could see his face growing older and more tired. He said, 'But that—that was a long time ago."

And then—I felt it so keenly, it was as though I had been slapped by my mother. I could see it clearly on his face. It was there for everyone to see. Death on the shrinking face.

He looked at me, and saw my tears and sat up.

He said, "Come." I went and sat on his knees.

He looked into my eyes, and he said, "Oh, you can see it, too. I always knew you had the poet's eye."

He didn't even look sad, and that made me burst out crying loudly.

He pulled me to his thin chest, and said, "Do you want me to tell you a funny story?" and he smiled encouragingly at me.

But I couldn't reply.

He said, "When I have finished this story, I want you to promise that you will go away and never come back to see me. Do you promise?"

I nodded.

He said, "Good. Well, listen. That story I told you about the boy poet and the girl poet, do you remember that? That wasn't true. It was something I just made up. All this talk about poetry and the greatest poem in the world, that wasn't true, either. Isn't that the funniest thing you have heard?"

But his voice broke.

C I left the house, and ran home crying, like a poet, for everything I saw.

D I walked along Alberto Street a year later, but I could find no sign of the poet's house. It hadn't vanished, just like that. It had been pulled down, and a big, two-storied building had taken its place. The mango tree and the plum tree and the coconut tree had all been cut down, and there was brick and concrete everywhere.

It was just as though B. Wordsworth had never existed.

6. Answers will vary. The name implies that words have a value deeper than their surface meaning. It's a good name for a writer, since writers take language seriously; and it's especially good for the poet in the story, for whom words are so important that he writes only one line a month.

7. Answers will vary. Discuss the various aspects of B. Wordsworth's charac- ter, including the depth of his love and sorrow.

8. The mother is pragmatic; Wordsworth is a visionary. When Wordsworth offers to sell a poem about mothers, for example, she reacts with scorn. She beats her son; the poet takes him out and shows him the stars.

9. Answers might include the image of palm trees humming with bees; the poet's yard; and the clear, starry skies.

10. The influence of people like Words- worth—people who looked for beauty in the world—may have influenced him a great deal. Like the boy in this story, perhaps Naipaul, too, was encouraged to see, feel, and remember his experiences.

The last scene in the story suggests that the role of a poet includes being a witness (through writing), so that the things he or she has seen will not be forgotten.

Responding to the Story

Analyzing the Story

Identifying Facts

1. Who is B. Wordsworth and how does he explain his connection with W. Wordsworth, the great Romantic poet of the nineteenth century?

Interpreting Meanings

2. What does the boy learn from B. Wordsworth?
3. Do you think B. Wordsworth's tragic love story is true? If it is true, why would he deny it?
4. What does B. Wordsworth say to the policeman who asks "What you doing here"? What deeper significance do you see in his reply? (Is this what poets also seek to know?)
5. Find some of the statements B. Wordsworth makes about poetry. Then think about the **theme** of this short story—that is, what could Naipaul want to re- veal about the nature of poetry?
6. Examine the name *Wordsworth* and discuss whether you think it's an especially good name for any writer, and in particular for the poet in this story.
7. How did this story make you feel about B. Words- worth?
8. Find passages in the story that **contrast** the mother's no-nonsense ways with the poetic vision of B. Words- worth. Do you find these two types of people in your own world? Explain.
9. The story's **setting** is the back streets of Port of Spain, the capital of the Caribbean island of Trini- dad. What specific pictures of the place are most vivid in your mind? If you had to illustrate the story, what **images** would you concentrate on?
10. Naipaul grew up in Trinidad and certainly knew a street like Miguel Street in Port of Spain. If we think of the boy in the story as the author's recollection of himself at that age, what does that suggest about the influences that made him a writer? What does it suggest about his view of the poet's position and role in society?

Writing About the Story

A Creative Response

1. **Writing a Character Sketch.** Naipaul has immortalized an old poet by describing him in words. Think of a character you have known who is different in some way, and whom you would like to rescue from oblivion. Write a brief character sketch of that person, describ- ing his or her home, appearance, job, personality, and actions. Be sure to tell your reader how you feel about your subject.

A Critical Response

2. **Analyzing a Character.** Write a brief essay in which you analyze the character of B. Wordsworth. Before you write, gather your details by skimming over the story and filling in a chart like the following:

	Details	What character traits they reveal
Actions		
Speech		
Responses of others		
Appearance		
Direct evaluations made by the writer		

Analyzing Language and Style

Vernacular

The manner of speech recorded in this story would cer- tainly sound unusual to anyone who lives outside Trini- dad. What we hear is the **vernacular,** or everyday speech, as it sounds on the streets of Trinidad. The Trinidad vernacular is a creolized language, which means it is a blend of the words, idioms, pronunciations, and gram- matical constructions of the island's English, Spanish, Portuguese, African, and Indian settlers. Find three con- versations in the Trinidad vernacular in this story, and read them aloud to hear their special rhythm. Try to make a generalization describing how this Trinidad vernacular uses verb forms.

1. BUILDING ON PRIOR KNOWLEDGE. Have students discuss how a civil war differs from most other wars. (Civil wars often pit neighbor against neighbor and force civilians to become far more involved than they would be in a war fought abroad.)

2. ESTABLISHING A PURPOSE. Point out that the following story is told from the third-person limited point of view; its telling is confined to the experiences and perceptions of Omovo, a young Nigerian. Because Omovo is a child, he does not always understand what he witnesses. As students read, encourage them to determine the meaning behind events that Omovo himself does not comprehend.

3. PREREADING JOURNAL. Ask students to narrate a simple episode (for example, the absence of a teacher, or a parent's response to a story on an evening newscast) from the point of view of a child. Remind students that children often do not have enough experience to make sense of the things they see and hear.

Ben Okri
(1959–   )

Ben Okri grew up in Lagos, the capital of Nigeria. Although he later moved to London, his stories are set in Nigeria. Okri seems especially haunted by remembrances of the Nigerian Civil War (1967–1970), often called the Biafran War. This war began when the Ibo tribes tried to secede from Nigeria and form their own state, to be called Biafra. Thousands of people were killed in the civil war that ensued, and many more died of starvation. In fact, the very word *Biafra* today suggests images of swollen-bellied children holding up bowls and begging for food. The image of the starving child in Okri's story is a stark reminder of the horror of this war.

Okri first gained recognition in England with the publication of two novels (*Flowers and Shadows* and *The Landscapes Within*) and a collection of short stories (*Incidents at the Shrine*). The short story that follows, "In the Shadow of War," is from *Stars of the New Curfew*, Okri's first book to be published in the United States.

Okri's awards include the Commonwealth Writers' Prize for Africa and the *Paris Review* Aga Khan Prize for fiction.

IN THE SHADOW OF WAR

"In the Shadow of War" takes place in Lagos, the capital of Nigeria, during the Nigerian Civil War. Ben Okri was only eight years old when this war broke out in his homeland, so it is not surprising that the narrator, Omovo, is also a child. War is a frightening, confusing time to children, but a civil war, when neighbor fights neighbor, is especially so. Whom should one trust? Are the soldiers in this story good-hearted or evil? Is the veiled woman a supernatural being or a mere mortal? And if she is a mortal, is she an innocent citizen or a spy?

Lagos is a large metropolis, but right outside the city is the jungle, where magical transformations seem to take place. There are mysteries in this story. Can they be solved, or is their mere existence the author's main point? Read this deceptively simple story slowly and carefully, letting its powers cast their spell.

SUPPLEMENTARY SUPPORT MATERIALS
1. Vocabulary Activity Worksheet (*CCB*)
2. Review and Response Worksheet: Third-Person Limited Point of View (*CCB*)
3. Language Skills Worksheet: Coherence: Spatial Order (*CCB*)
4. Selection Test (*CCB*)

DEVELOPING VOCABULARY
The following words from the essay are tested in the Selection Test. (See also Vocabulary Activity Worksheet.)
stupefying   ostentatious
dispiritedly   livid
to succumb   dementedly

That afternoon three soldiers came to the village. They scattered the goats and chickens. They went to the palm-frond bar and ordered a calabash[1] of palm wine. They drank amidst the flies.

Omovo watched them from the window as he waited for his father to go out. They both listened to the radio. His father had bought the old Grundig[2] cheaply from a family that had to escape the city when the war broke out. He had covered the radio with a white cloth and made it look like a household fetish.[3] They listened to the news of bombings and air raids in the interior of the country. His father combed his hair, parted it carefully, and slapped some after-shave on his unshaven face. Then he struggled into the shabby coat that he had long outgrown.

Omovo stared out of the window, irritated with his father. At that hour, for the past seven days, a strange woman with a black veil over her head had been going past the house. She went up the village paths, crossed the Express road, and disappeared into the forest. Omovo waited for her to appear.

The main news was over. The radio announcer said an eclipse of the moon was expected that night. Omovo's father wiped the sweat off his face with his palm and said, with some bitterness:

"As if an eclipse will stop this war."

"What is an eclipse?" Omovo asked.

"That's when the world goes dark and strange things happen."

"Like what?"

His father lit a cigarette.

"The dead start to walk about and sing. So don't stay out late, eh."

Omovo nodded.

"Heclipses hate children. They eat them."

Omovo didn't believe him. His father smiled, gave Omovo his ten kobo allowance, and said:

"Turn off the radio. It's bad for a child to listen to news of war."

Omovo turned it off. His father poured a libation[4] at the doorway and then prayed to his ancestors. When he had finished he picked up his briefcase and strutted out briskly. Omovo watched him as he threaded his way up the path to the bus stop at the main road. When a danfo bus[5] came, and his father went with it, Omovo turned the radio back on. He sat on the windowsill and waited for the woman. The last time he saw her she had glided past with agitated flutters of her yellow smock. The children stopped what they were doing and stared at her. They had said that she had no shadow. They had said that her feet never touched the ground. As she went past, the children began to throw things at her. She didn't flinch, didn't quicken her pace, and didn't look back.

The heat was stupefying. Noises dimmed and lost their edges. The villagers stumbled about their various tasks as if they were sleepwalking. The three soldiers drank palm wine and played draughts[6] beneath the sun's oppressive glare. Omovo noticed that whenever children went past the bar the soldiers called them, talked to them, and gave them some money. Omovo ran down the stairs and slowly walked past the bar. The soldiers stared at him. On his way back one of them called him.

"What's your name?" he asked.

Omovo hesitated, smiled mischievously, and said:

"Heclipse."

The soldier laughed, spraying Omovo's face with spit. He had a face crowded with veins. His companions seemed uninterested. They swiped flies and concentrated on their game. Their guns were on the table. Omovo noticed that they had numbers on them. The man said:

"Did your father give you that name because you have big lips?"

His companions looked at Omovo and laughed. Omovo nodded.

"You are a good boy," the man said. He paused. Then he asked, in a different voice:

"Have you seen that woman who covers her face with a black cloth?"

"No."

The man gave Omovo ten kobo and said:

"She is a spy. She helps our enemies. If you see her come and tell us at once, you hear?"

---

1. **calabash:** a cup made from a calabash (a type of gourd).
2. **Grundig:** a German brand of radio.
3. **fetish:** an object with magical powers.
4. **libation** (lī·bā′shən): wine poured out on the ground as a sacrifice to the gods.

5. **danfo bus:** a small bus. (*Danfo* means "in disrepair.")
6. **draughts** (drafts): checkers.

A. Characterization
❓ What do these opening details suggest about the soldiers? (At best, they are insensitive to their surroundings.)

B. Motivation
Explain that fetishes are common decor in many Nigerian households. Then ask why Omovo's father might want to make the radio look like a household fetish. (Wartime measures might restrict the use of radios. The owner of a radio might be suspected of espionage.)

C. Interpreting
❓ Notice how the children describe the woman. If they were to call her names at this point, what might those names be? ("Witch" or "devil" would be likely names.)

D. Atmosphere
Okri has carefully chosen details—and words to express those details—to establish a harsh, oppressive, and even unreal atmosphere. Encourage students to discuss this as an appropriate setting in a time of warfare.

READING CHECK TEST
1. Omovo's father hopes that the war will end with the next lunar eclipse. (F)
2. The soldiers tell Omovo that the woman he sees is a spy. (T)
3. When she comes to their cave, the veiled woman is treated with respect by hungry women and children. (T)
4. The soldiers, taking pity on the woman, allow her to escape. (F)
5. The soldiers threaten to harm Omovo if he tells what he has seen. (F)

A. Humanities Connection: Responding to the Photograph
Point out that more than a million Biafran civilians are believed to have died of starvation during their civil war and that the child in the photograph has the distended stomach of someone who is starving. Encourage students to discuss efforts that are being made to alleviate food shortages in the world today.

B. Characterization/Motivation
? What does Omovo's refusal of the soldiers' money suggest about where his sympathies lie? (He takes the side that opposes the soldiers—not because he understands their political differences but probably because he feels some sympathy for the woman and resents being asked to spy on her.)

C. Expansion
If necessary, explain that women in many parts of the world traditionally carry food and other goods in baskets balanced on their heads.

Omovo refused the money and went back upstairs. He repositioned himself on the windowsill. The soldiers occasionally looked at him. The heat got to him and soon he fell asleep in a sitting position. The cocks, crowing dispiritedly, woke him up. He could feel the afternoon softening into evening. The soldiers dozed in the bar. The hourly news came on. Omovo listened without comprehension to the day's casualties. The announcer succumbed to the stupor, yawned, apologized, and gave further details of the fighting.

Omovo looked up and saw that the woman had already gone past. The men had left the bar. He saw them weaving between the eaves of the thatch houses, stumbling through the heat-mists. The woman was further up the path. Omovo ran downstairs and followed the men. One of them had taken off his uniform top. The soldier behind had buttocks so big they had begun to split his pants.

Omovo followed them across the Express road. When they got into the forest the men stopped following the woman, and took a different route. They seemed to know what they were doing. Omovo hurried to keep the woman in view.

He followed her through the dense vegetation. She wore faded wrappers and a gray shawl, with the black veil covering her face. She had a red basket on her head. He completely forgot to determine if she had a shadow, or whether her feet touched the ground.

He passed unfinished estates, with their flaking ostentatious signboards and their collapsing fences. He passed an empty cement factory: blocks lay crumbled in heaps and the workers' sheds were deserted. He passed a baobab[7] tree,

7. **baobab** (bā′ō·bab): a thick-trunked tree, often called the "upside-down tree," since its branches look like roots.

CLOSURE
Have students try to express in one sentence what this story, about a particular war, suggests about warfare in general. (Most students will conclude that Okri depicts war as brutal, unjust, and irrational. Some students may comment upon Okri's implication that those who suffer most have least to do with the politics of war.)

ANALYZING THE STORY
Identifying Facts
1. The world might go dark, and the dead might walk around and sing. He also adds that "heclipses" eat children.
2. They say that she does not have a shadow and that she walks without touching the ground. They seem to believe that she is not human.
  She is captured, tortured, and shot.

Interpreting Meanings
3. The description is subtly unfavorable. Without regard for the chickens and goats that they frighten, they head directly for the bar.
4. Answers will vary. The father's words seem frightening on the surface; but if they keep Omovo inside when going outside would be dangerous, they have (Answers continue on next page.)

under which was the intact skeleton of a large animal. A snake dropped from a branch and slithered through the undergrowth. In the distance, over the cliff edge, he heard loud music and people singing war slogans above the noise.

He followed the woman till they came to a rough camp on the plain below. Shadowy figures moved about in the half-light of the cave. The woman went to them. The figures surrounded her and touched her and led her into the cave. He heard their weary voices thanking her. When the woman reappeared she was without the basket. Children with kwashiorkor[8] stomachs and women wearing rags led her half-way up the hill. Then, reluctantly, touching her as if they might not see her again, they went back.

He followed her till they came to a muddied river. She moved as if an invisible force were trying to blow her away. Omovo saw capsized canoes and trailing waterlogged clothes on the dark water. He saw floating items of sacrifice: loaves of bread in polythene wrappings, gourds of food, Coca-Cola cans. When he looked at the canoes again they had changed into the shapes of swollen dead animals. He saw outdated currencies on the riverbank. He noticed the terrible smell in the air. Then he heard the sound of heavy breathing from behind him, then someone coughing and spitting. He recognized the voice of one of the soldiers urging the others to move faster. Omovo crouched in the shadow of a tree. The soldiers strode past. Not long afterwards he heard a scream. The men had caught up with the woman. They crowded round her.

"Where are the others?" shouted one of them.

The woman was silent.

"You dis witch! You want to die, eh? Where are they?"

She stayed silent. Her head was bowed. One of the soldiers coughed and spat towards the river.

"Talk! Talk!" he said, slapping her.

The fat soldier tore off her veil and threw it to the ground. She bent down to pick it up and stopped in the attitude of kneeling, her head still bowed. Her head was bald, and disfigured with a deep corrugation.[9] There was a livid gash along the side of her face. The bare-chested soldier

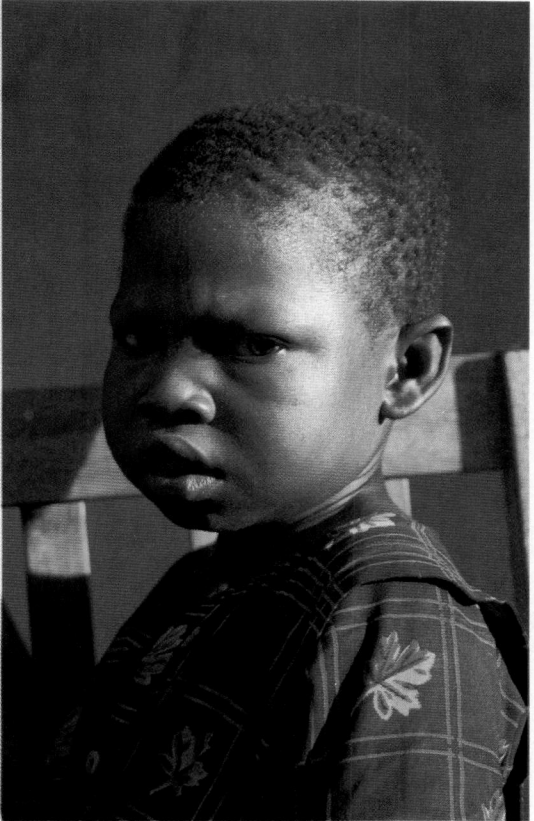

pushed her. She fell on her face and lay still. The lights changed over the forest and for the first time Omovo saw that the dead animals on the river were in fact the corpses of grown men. Their bodies were tangled with river-weed and their eyes were bloated. Before he could react, he heard another scream. The woman was getting up, with the veil in her hand. She turned to the fat soldier, drew herself to her fullest height, and spat in his face. Waving the veil in the air, she began to howl dementedly. The two other soldiers backed away. The fat soldier wiped his face and lifted the gun to the level of her stomach. A moment before Omovo heard the shot a violent beating of wings just above him scared him from his hiding place. He ran through the forest screaming. The soldiers tramped after him. He ran through a mist which seemed to have risen from the rocks. As he ran he saw an owl staring at him from a canopy of leaves. He tripped over the roots of a tree and blacked out when his head hit the ground.

---

8. **kwashiorkor** (kwä'shē·ôr'kôr'): protruding (as a result of malnutrition and slow starvation).
9. **corrugation:** groove or furrow.

A. Interpreting
? What do you think the red basket contained? (Probably food for the refugees) What one word is the key to your interpretation? (The word kwashiorkor)

B. Character/ Motivation
? What might these harsh details indicate about the woman's past and the reasons she carries the basket to the refugee hideout? (She has suffered greatly, perhaps as an earlier victim of the warfare, and she sympathizes with those who are suffering now.)

C. Plot: Climax
Have a volunteer identify this passage as the story's climax, or point of highest tension, where our concern both for the woman and for Omovo reaches its peak.

served as a warning.

Omovo doesn't believe him.

5. The soldiers hope to bribe Omovo into revealing the whereabouts of the veiled woman.

He seems to distrust the soldiers, and he is fascinated by the veiled woman.

6. Omovo, perhaps feeling protective of the woman, is curious about what the soldiers will do to her. She is mysterious in herself, and that adds to his curiosity.

7. These details are evidence of the war's devastating effect upon the landscape and testify that many citizens have fled the country.

8. She is probably bringing them food.

She leaves the cave without the basket, and the cave's inhabitants can be heard thanking her. We also know that she is in a poverty-ridden area, for she is led up the hill by starving children.

9. It is likely that Omovo's childlike view of the world cannot take in the extent of death and brutality that he witnesses. Until he can properly interpret the scene, he masks the horror with gentler images.

10. Answers may include embarrassment, anger, and betrayal.

Omovo's father believes that Omovo is imagining things.

A. Plot: Resolution

? Why is the resolution to this story ironic? (Neither we nor Omovo expects the father to behave in such a friendly manner to the men who are guilty of such brutality.)

When he woke up it was very dark. He waved his fingers in front of his face and saw nothing. Mistaking the darkness for blindness he screamed, thrashed around, and ran into a door. When he recovered from his shock he heard voices outside and the radio crackling on about the war. He found his way to the balcony, full of wonder that his sight had returned. But when he got there he was surprised to find his father sitting on the sunken cane chair, drinking palm wine with the three soldiers. Omovo rushed to his father and pointed frantically at the three men.

"You must thank them," his father said. "They brought you back from the forest."

Omovo, overcome with delirium, began to tell his father what he had seen. But his father, smiling apologetically at the soldiers, picked up his son and carried him off to bed.

A

Responding to the Story

Analyzing the Story

Identifying Facts

1. What does Omovo's father say might happen during an eclipse of the moon?
2. What do the children believe about the veiled woman? What happens to her?

Interpreting Meanings

3. The opening paragraph describes the arrival of the soldiers. Is the description favorable, unfavorable, or neutral? Explain your answer.
4. Do you think Omovo's father is trying to scare Omovo about the eclipse or warn him? What is Omovo's reaction to the warning?
5. Omovo gets ten kobo from his father as an allowance, yet he refuses the same amount of money when the soldier offers it. What is the soldier's **motive** for offering the money? Why does Omovo refuse the offer?
6. Why do you think Omovo follows the soldiers who are following the veiled woman?
7. The story is told from the **third-person limited point of view.** Omovo, through whose eyes we observe the action, is not sophisticated enough to interpret what he sees. How do *you* interpret the significance of the landscape Omovo presents, including "unfinished estates," "an empty cement factory," and the "intact skeleton of a large animal"?
8. What do you think the woman brings to the people in the cave? What clues are provided?
9. How do you account for the transformations that Omovo reports (from canoes to dead animals to dead men)? Is he frightened? Delirious? Or is there some other explanation?
10. At the end of the story Omovo wakes up to find his father drinking with the soldiers. When Omovo tries to tell his father what happened, his father smiles "apologetically at the soldiers." What do you think Omovo's feelings are toward his father at this point? Explain.

Writing About the Story

A Creative Reponse

1. **Using a Third-Person Limited Point of View.** Describe a science class, a sporting event, or any gathering of adults through the eyes of a young child. Use a third-person limited point of view. Be sure to reveal the young child's feelings and confused perceptions of the events.

A Critical Response

2. **Analyzing a Symbol.** The radio plays a symbolic role in Okri's story. Find all the references to the radio and then write a short essay explaining its significance.

Here are some questions to get you started: Why is the brand name of the radio (a trivial detail) given? What is significant about the radio's resembling a fetish? What does Omovo listen to on the radio? What is the difference between hearing a disembodied voice on a radio and actually seeing an event?

PREPARATION

1. BUILDING ON PRIOR KNOWLEDGE. Ask students if they have ever studied a natural object very closely for a long period of time. Perhaps they have observed cloud formations, the veins of a leaf, the shape of a snowflake, or the intricacies of a spiderweb. Did what they see make them think about human life? Students who read "The Soft Voice of the Serpent" may recall the thoughts of the young man who had lost his leg as he watched the locust.

2. ESTABLISHING A PURPOSE. As students read, ask them to be aware of what the moth is doing at each point in the essay and of what thoughts or associations its actions provoke in the writer.

3. PREREADING JOURNAL. (Challenging) Have students concentrate on a part of nature and jot down their observations and associations in their journals. Using this material, have them write an essay or a poem expressing a single idea stimulated by their observations.

(Less Challenging) Ask students to concentrate on something in nature, such as an animal, a tree, a plant, or a flower, and to write down what they see in their journals. Have them take particular note of any similarities or differences they see between the natural and human worlds.

NONFICTION

Virginia Woolf (1882–1941)

Virginia Woolf was born in London in 1882. Her father, Sir Leslie Stephen, was a philosopher and literary critic, and in her youth Virginia enjoyed all the advantages of a financially comfortable and intellectually challenging environment. Too frail to attend school, she was privately tutored and given the luxury of her father's extensive library.

After her father's death in 1904, Virginia, her sister Vanessa, and their two brothers moved to the area of London known as Bloomsbury. A few years later, a group of their friends, later to be known as the Bloomsbury Group, began to meet. This group included writers like E. M. Forster and Roger Fry, artists such as Duncan Grant, and intellectuals like the economist John Maynard Keynes. One member of the group was journalist Leonard Woolf, to whom Virginia was married in 1912.

The Bloomsbury Group was an informal gathering of intellectuals with the highest cultural standards. It helped provide the right environment for Virginia Woolf's sensitive, experimental fiction. Only after her death, when her diaries were published, was it clear how powerful the emotional effect of her friends' praise or criticism had been on her.

She had been writing since she was fourteen, and reviewing books since she was in her early twenties; but it was not until she was thirty-three, in 1915, that her first novel, *The Voyage Out,* was published. Her second, *Night and Day,* appeared in 1919. In 1922, with the publication of *Mrs. Dalloway* and *Jacob's Room,* her position among the foremost writers of her time was made clear. With these novels, and continuing with books such as *To the Lighthouse* (1927) and *The Waves* (1931), she pursued an experimental vision that emphasized personal impressions and the experience of life as it was being led, rather than external events.

Like Joyce, Virginia Woolf used the technique of stream of consciousness, although her version of it was different from his. She was a great admirer of Joyce's *A Portrait of the Artist,* but she considered his *Ulysses* to be an "illiterate, underbred book." Still, she worried that "what I am doing is probably being better done by Mr. Joyce."

There were some similarities of form and style between the two writers. *Mrs. Dalloway,* for example, like *Ulysses,* takes place on a single day; however, it covers, through the thoughts of its characters, an entire lifetime.

Woolf also wrote a great many essays and reviews, and in 1917 she established The Hogarth Press with her husband. This press published many of the most important writers of the time.

Throughout her life, Virginia Woolf suffered from well-concealed bouts with depression and anxiety. In March of 1941, fearful that she was losing her mind, she took her own life.

SUPPLEMENTARY SUPPORT MATERIALS
1. Vocabulary Activity Worksheet (*CCB*)
2. Review and Response Worksheet: Descriptive Details (*CCB*)
3. Language Skills Worksheet: Adjective Clauses (*CCB*)
4. Selection Test (*CCB*)

DEVELOPING VOCABULARY
The following words from the essay are tested in the Selection Test. (See also Vocabulary Activity Worksheet.)

hybrid	diminutive
somber	intricate
fringed	to garnish
vigor	animation
clamor	to right

Comment from the Writer
In an autobiographical piece called "A Sketch of the Past," Virginia Woolf wrote: "I . . . suppose that the shock-receiving capacity is what makes me a writer. . . . I feel that I have had a blow; but it is not . . . simply a blow from an enemy hidden behind the cotton wool of daily life; it is or will become a revelation of some order; it is a token of some real thing behind appearances." Ask students to discuss the shock that the writer receives in this essay. What revelation does the shock bring to the writer?

THE DEATH OF THE MOTH

Many people have had the experience of focusing on a tiny detail in nature and coming to an important realization about human existence. In this es- **say, Woolf's study of the movements of a moth lead her to thoughts about life and death.**

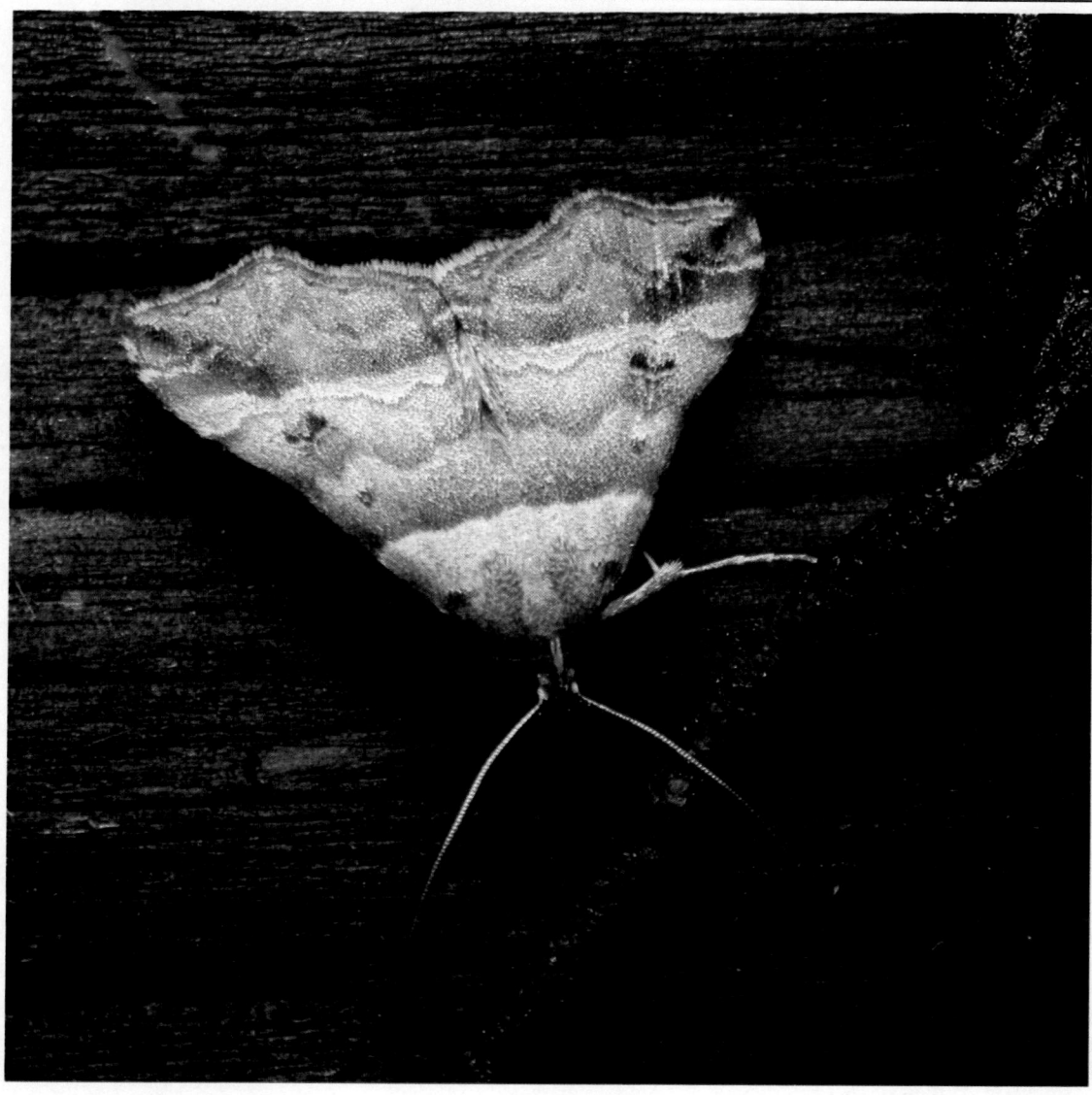

READING CHECK TEST

1. The writer makes her observations at the height of summertime. (F)
2. The writer is a person who sees life as a succession of gloomy days. (F)
3. The moth represents the struggle and the glory of life. (T)
4. At the end of the essay, the moth flies away to freedom. (F)
5. The tone of this essay is reflective. (T)

Moths that fly by day are not properly to be called moths; they do not excite that pleasant sense of dark autumn nights and ivy-blossom which the commonest yellow-underwing asleep in the shadow of the curtain never fails to rouse in us. They are hybrid creatures, neither gay like butterflies nor somber like their own species. Nevertheless the present specimen, with his narrow hay-colored wings, fringed with a tassel of the same color, seemed to be content with life. It was a pleasant morning, mid-September, mild, benignant,[1] yet with a keener breath than that of the summer months. The plow was already scoring[2] the field opposite the window, and where the share[3] had been, the earth was pressed flat and gleamed with moisture. Such vigor came rolling in from the fields and the down[4] beyond that it was difficult to keep the eyes strictly turned upon the book. The rooks[5] too were keeping one of their annual festivities; soaring round the treetops until it looked as if a vast net with thousands of black knots in it had been cast up into the air; which, after a few moments sank slowly down upon the trees until every twig seemed to have a knot at the end of it. Then, suddenly, the net would be thrown into the air again in a wider circle this time, with the utmost clamor and vociferation,[6] as though to be thrown into the air and settle slowly down upon the treetops were a tremendously exciting experience.

The same energy which inspired the rooks, the plowmen, the horses, and even, it seemed, the lean bare backed downs, sent the moth fluttering from side to side of his square of the windowpane. One could not help watching him. One was, indeed, conscious of a queer feeling of pity for him. The possibilities of pleasure seemed that morning so enormous and so various that to have only a moth's part in life, and a day moth's at that, appeared a hard fate, and his zest in enjoying his meager opportunities to the full, pathetic. He flew vigorously to one corner of his compartment, and, after waiting there a second, flew across to the other. What remained for him but to fly to a third corner and then to a fourth? That was all he could do, in spite of the size of the downs, the width of the sky, the far-off smoke of houses, and the romantic voice, now and then, of a steamer out at sea. What he could do he did. Watching him, it seemed as if a fiber, very thin but pure, of the enormous energy of the world had been thrust into his frail and diminutive body. As often as he crossed the pane, I could fancy that a thread of vital light became visible. He was little or nothing but life.

Yet, because he was so small, and so simple a form of the energy that was rolling in at the open window and driving its way through so many narrow and intricate corridors in my own brain and in those of other human beings, there was something marvelous as well as pathetic about him. It was as if someone had taken a tiny bead of pure life and decking it as lightly as possible with down and feathers, had set it dancing and zigzagging to show us the true nature of life. Thus displayed one could not get over the strangeness of it. One is apt to forget all about life, seeing it humped and bossed[7] and garnished and cumbered[8] so that it has to move with the greatest circumspection[9] and dignity. Again, the thought of all that life might have been had he been born in any other shape caused one to view his simple activities with a kind of pity.

After a time, tired by his dancing apparently, he settled on the window ledge in the sun, and, the queer spectacle being at an end, I forgot about him. Then, looking up, my eye was caught by him. He was trying to resume his dancing, but seemed either so stiff or so awkward that he could only flutter to the bottom of the windowpane; and when he tried to fly across it he failed. Being intent on other matters I watched these futile attempts for a time without thinking, unconsciously waiting for him to resume his flight, as one waits for a machine, that has stopped momentarily, to start again without considering the reason of its failure. After perhaps a seventh attempt he slipped from the wooden ledge and fell, fluttering his wings, on to his back on the windowsill. The helplessness of his attitude roused me. It flashed upon me that he was in difficulties; he could no longer raise himself; his legs struggled vainly. But, as I stretched

---

1. **benignant** (bi·nig′nənt): favorable; kindly.
2. **scoring:** marking with notches or lines.
3. **share:** part of a plow that cuts the soil.
4. **down:** expanse of open, grassy land.
5. **rooks:** European birds, similar to American crows.
6. **vociferation** (vō·sif′ər·ā′shən): loud noise.
7. **bossed:** covered with knobs or protrusions.
8. **cumbered:** burdened.
9. **circumspection:** caution.

A. Setting

[?] What kind of day is described in the first paragraph? (A mild September morning with a brisk hint of cooler air)

B. Exposition

[?] What is the energy that Woolf is describing in this passage? (The energy of life, joy, and activity) Why does the writer express pity for the moth? (Its share in the joy of life seems so small.)

C. Theme

[?] How does Woolf see the moth as marvelous here? (He is small and simple, yet fully alive.) In what way might she identify herself with it? (At times she may feel as small and as helpless in the face of death as the moth does.)

D. Theme

Here the writer temporarily forgets about the moth.

[?] What might this forgetting signify? (The way in which we frequently forget about the wonder and the shortness of life while immersed in our daily routines)

ANALYZING THE ESSAY
Identifying Facts
1. The middle of September; ploughmen are notching the fields, rooks are flying.
2. He is a day moth.
3. The moth's environment seems pathetic and confined, compared to the spacious environment at large, which is full of "possibilities."

4. Stillness and quiet replace the previous animation of the landscape.

Interpreting Meanings
5. The phrase "keener breath" foreshadows the moth's death.
6. She hesitates to interfere with its dignity and peace at the moment of its death.

7. The moth is marvelous because it suggests a graceful, simple form of energy, a "tiny bead of pure life." It is pathetic because of its feebleness and vulnerability.

A. Theme
? How does the writer characterize death in this passage? (All-powerful and unavoidable) How does she view the moth's behavior in the face of death? (Brave but futile)

B. Conclusion
? How would you describe Woolf's overall attitude toward life and death? (She is stoical; she sees the beauty in life but knows that it is cut off by death.)

CLOSURE
Ask students to write three adjectives that they feel describe the writer of this essay. Then have them exchange their lists, discuss the entries, and make a master list of words that characterize the writer.

out a pencil, meaning to help him to right himself, it came over me that the failure and awkwardness were the approach of death. I laid the pencil down again.

The legs agitated themselves once more. I looked as if for the enemy against which he struggled. I looked out of doors. What had happened there? Presumably it was midday, and work in the fields had stopped. Stillness and quiet had replaced the previous animation. The birds had taken themselves off to feed in the brooks. The horses stood still. Yet the power was there all the same, massed outside, indifferent, impersonal, not attending to anything in particular. Somehow it was opposed to the little hay-colored moth. It was useless to try to do anything. One could only watch the extraordinary efforts made by those tiny legs against an oncoming doom which could, had it chosen, have submerged an entire city, not merely a city, but masses of human beings; nothing, I knew, had any chance against death. Nevertheless after a pause of exhaustion the legs fluttered again. It was superb this last protest, and

A

so frantic that he succeeded at last in righting himself. One's sympathies, of course, were all on the side of life. Also, when there was nobody to care or to know, this gigantic effort on the part of an insignificant little moth, against a power of such magnitude, to retain what no one else valued or desired to keep, moved one strangely. Again, somehow, one saw life, a pure bead. I lifted the pencil again, useless though I knew it to be. But even as I did so, the unmistakable tokens of death showed themselves. The body relaxed, and instantly grew stiff. The struggle was over. The insignificant little creature now knew death. As I looked at the dead moth, this minute wayside triumph of so great a force over so mean[10] an antagonist filled me with wonder. Just as life had been strange a few minutes before, so death was now as strange. The moth having righted himself now lay most decently and uncomplainingly composed. O yes, he seemed to say, death is stronger than I am.

B

10. **mean:** unimportant.

Responding to the Essay

Analyzing the Essay

Identifying Facts

1. At what time of year does Woolf make her observations? What activities are going on around her?
2. How is the moth different from other species of moths?
3. How does she compare the moth's environment to the environment at large?
4. What changes come over the landscape when the moth begins to die?

Interpreting Meanings

5. How does Woolf's description of the September morning as "mild, benignant, yet with a keener breath than that of the summer months" help to prepare the reader for the experience she is going to relate?
6. When she sees that the moth is turned on its back, Woolf reaches out a pencil to turn it over again. But then she lays the pencil down. Why does she do this?
7. The moth is described as both marvelous and pathetic. What characteristics generate this ambivalent attitude on Woolf's part?

Writing About the Essay

A Creative Response

1. **Imagining a Different Environment.** Without disturbing it, observe an insect in its natural environment. Then write an essay comparing and contrasting its life in its small environment with the environment from which you observe it. If you like, you may imagine instead how a creature much larger than human beings would observe us, contrasting its environment with ours.

A Critical Response

2. **Analyzing the Writer's Discovery.** Midway through the essay, Woolf describes the moth in this way: "It was as if someone had taken a tiny bead of pure life and decking it as lightly as possible with down and feathers, had set it dancing and zigzagging to show us the true nature of life." Write a brief essay discussing "the true nature of life" as revealed to Woolf by her examination of the moth. Does the insect's death at the end make her conclusion in the middle of the essay invalid? Why or why not?

PREPARATION

1. **BUILDING ON PRIOR KNOWLEDGE.** Ask students to remember a very special day from their childhood, such as Christmas or Passover or their birthday. They might imagine that they are telling their own child about that special day from their past. What aspects of the day would stand out in their memory? Would they remember events exactly as they hap-pened? How might their choice of details differ depending on who their listeners were?

2. **ESTABLISHING A PURPOSE.** As students read aloud or listen to a recorded perfor-mance, they should be aware of how the sprightly rhythm and the playful use of language add to the sense of childlike delight, which is the essence of this imaginative recollection.

3. **PREREADING JOURNAL.** (Challenging) Ask students to write a personal essay in which they recall a special day from their childhood or in which they describe a day they would like to share with a child they love.

(Less Challenging) Ask students to talk to a young child about a day that he or she really enjoyed. Have students ask the child questions about the details of the day and have them record these in their journals for a class discussion on what children remember.

A. Point of View
? Is the speaker in the first para-graph a child or an adult? (An adult) How do you know? (He is remember-ing a series of Christmases in the past.)

B. Tone
? Give examples of Thomas's use of exaggera-tion in this para-graph. ("It was al-ways snowing on Christmas"; cats like jaguars; "lynx-eyed hunters") What is the effect of his exaggerating the details? (Heightened vivid-ness and emotion) What overall feel-ing do you think Thomas wishes to convey? (The imaginative free-dom of childhood)

A CHILD'S CHRISTMAS IN WALES

Dylan Thomas

Like all poets, Dylan Thomas seems to have been preoccupied with the sounds of words. Even his prose is filled with words and phrases that turn his sentences into a kind of music. This essay is Thomas's fond remembrance of Christmas in the small town in Wales where he grew up. It is so poetic that it would be best to read it aloud. If that isn't possible, try to hear the sounds and the rhythms of the writer's words. Look for invented words and for odd uses of ordinary words.

A biography of Thomas appears on page 1124, in the section on poetry.

One Christmas was so much like another, in those years around the sea-town corner now and out of all sound except the dis-tant speaking of the voices I sometimes hear a moment before sleep, that I can never remember whether it snowed for six days and six nights when I was twelve or whether it snowed for twelve days and twelve nights when I was six. All the Christ-mases roll down toward the two-tongued sea, like a cold and headlong moon bundling[1] down the sky that was our street; and they stop at the rim of the ice-edged, fish-freezing waves, and I plunge my hands in the snow and bring out whatever I can find. In goes my hand into that wool-white bell-tongued ball of holidays resting at the rim of the carol-singing sea, and out come Mrs. Prothero and the firemen.

It was on the afternoon of the day of Christmas Eve, and I was in Mrs. Prothero's garden, waiting for cats, with her son Jim. It was snowing. It was always snowing at Christmas. December, in my memory, is white as Lapland, though there were no reindeers. But there were cats. Patient, cold, and callous,[2] our hands wrapped in socks, we waited to snowball the cats. Sleek and long as jaguars and horrible-whiskered, spitting and snarl-ing, they would slink and sidle over the white back-garden walls, and the lynx-eyed hunters, Jim and I, fur-capped and moccasined trappers from Hudson Bay, off Mumbles Road, would hurl our deadly snowballs at the green of their eyes. The wise cats never appeared. We were so still, Eskimo-footed arctic marksmen in the muffling silence of the eternal snows—eternal, ever since Wednesday—that we never heard Mrs. Prothero's first cry from her igloo at the bottom of the garden. Or, if we heard it at all, it was, to us, like the far-off challenge of our enemy and prey, the neigh-bor's polar cat. But soon the voice grew louder.

"Fire!" cried Mrs. Prothero, and she beat the dinner gong.

And we ran down the garden, with the snow-balls in our arms, toward the house; and smoke, indeed, was pouring out of the dining room, and the gong was bombilating, and Mrs. Prothero was announcing ruin like a town crier in Pompeii.[3] This was better than all the cats in Wales standing on the wall in a row. We bounded into the house, laden with snowballs, and stopped at the open door of the smoke-filled room. Something was burning all right; perhaps it was Mr. Prothero, who always slept there after midday dinner with a newspaper over his face. But he was standing in the middle of the room, saying, "A fine Christ-mas!" and smacking at the smoke with a slipper.

"Call the fire brigade," cried Mrs. Prothero as she beat the gong.

"They won't be there," said Mr. Prothero, "it's Christmas."

There was no fire to be seen, only clouds of

---

1. **bundling:** rushing.
2. **callous** (kal'əs): without mercy; heartless.

3. **Pompeii** (pom·pā'): an ancient Italian city that was de-stroyed by a volcanic eruption.

SUPPLEMENTARY SUPPORT MATERIALS
1. Vocabulary Activity Worksheet (*CCB*)
2. Review and Response Worksheet: Simile and Metaphor (*CCB*)
3. Language Skills Worksheets: Adjectives; Semicolons and Colons (*CCB*)
4. Selection Test (*CCB*)

DEVELOPING VOCABULARY
The following words from the essay are tested in the Selection Test. (See also Vocabulary Activity Worksheet.)

to sidle	strident
rasping	thrush
poised	festoon
constitutional	to scud
forlorn	to trudge

A. Diction
Here the voice of a child interrupts the reminiscing of the narrator. The child tells of a snowstorm he experienced last year.

❓ How does the speech of the child differ from that of the narrator? (It is simple, unadorned, and unself-conscious.) What does the contrast emphasize about the voice of the narrator? (It is an adult, sophisticated, consciously literary voice.)

B. Figurative Language
This description of the snow-covered town is teeming with similes and metaphors.

❓ List as many of these as you can. ("Shaken from whitewash buckets"; "shawling out"; "snow grew . . . like . . . moss"; "thunderstorm of . . . Chistmas cards")

C. Comparing Diction
Note again how the naive literal expression of the child contrasts with the imaginative, figurative language of the narrator.

---

smoke and Mr. Prothero standing in the middle of them, waving his slipper as though he were conducting.

"Do something," he said.

And we threw all our snowballs into the smoke—I think we missed Mr. Prothero—and ran out of the house to the telephone box.

"Let's call the police as well," Jim said.

"And the ambulance."

"And Ernie Jenkins, he likes fires."

But we only called the fire brigade, and soon the fire engine came and three tall men in helmets brought a hose into the house and Mr. Prothero got out just in time before they turned it on. Nobody could have had a noisier Christmas Eve. And when the firemen turned off the hose and were standing in the wet, smoky room, Jim's aunt, Miss Prothero, came downstairs and peered in at them. Jim and I waited, very quietly, to hear what she would say to them. She said the right thing, always. She looked at the three tall firemen in their shining helmets, standing among the smoke and cinders and dissolving snowballs, and she said: "Would you like anything to read?"

Years and years and years ago, when I was a boy, when there were wolves in Wales, and birds the color of red-flannel petticoats whisked past the harp-shaped hills, when we sang and wallowed all night and day in caves that smelt like Sunday afternoons in damp front farmhouse parlors, and we chased, with the jawbones of deacons,[4] the English and the bears, before the motor car, before the wheel, before the duchess-faced horse, when we rode the daft[5] and happy hills bareback, it snowed and it snowed. But here a small boy says: "It snowed last year, too. I made a snowman and my brother knocked it down and I knocked my brother down and then we had tea."

"But that was not the same snow," I say. "Our snow was not only shaken from whitewash buckets down the sky, it came shawling out of the ground and swam and drifted out of the arms and hands and bodies of the trees; snow grew overnight on the roofs of the houses like a pure and grandfather moss, minutely white-ivied the walls and settled on the postman, opening the gate, like a dumb, numb thunderstorm of white, torn Christmas cards."

"Were there postmen then, too?"

"With sprinkling eyes and wind-cherried noses, on spread, frozen feet they crunched up to the doors and mittened on them manfully. But all that the children could hear was a ringing of bells."

"You mean that the postman went rat-a-tat-tat and the doors rang?"

"I mean that the bells that the children could hear were inside them."

"I only hear thunder sometimes, never bells."

"There were church bells, too."

"Inside them?"

"No, no, no, in the bat-black, snow-white belfries, tugged by bishops and storks. And they rang their tidings over the bandaged town, over the frozen foam of the powder and ice-cream hills, over the crackling sea. It seemed that all the churches boomed for joy under my window; and the weathercocks crew for Christmas, on our fence."

"Get back to the postmen."

"They were just ordinary postmen, fond of walking and dogs and Christmas and the snow. They knocked on the doors with blue knuckles. . . ."

"Ours has got a black knocker. . . ."

"And then they stood on the white Welcome mat in the little, drifted porches and huffed and puffed, making ghosts with their breath, and jogged from foot to foot like small boys wanting to go out."

"And then the Presents?"

"And then the Presents, after the Christmas box. And the cold postman, with a rose on his button-nose, tingled down the tea-tray-slithered run of the chilly glinting hill. He went in his ice-bound boots like a man on fishmonger's slabs.[6] He wagged his bag like a frozen camel's hump, dizzily turned the corner on one foot, and, by God, he was gone."

"Get back to the Presents."

"There were the Useful Presents: engulfing mufflers of the old coach[7] days, and mittens made for giant sloths; zebra scarfs of a substance like silky gum that could be tug-o'-warred down to the galoshes; blinding tam-o'-shanters[8] like patchwork tea cozies and bunny-suited busbies and balaclavas[9] for victims of head-shrinking tribes;

---

4. **deacons:** minor church officials.
5. **daft:** crazy.

6. **fishmonger's slabs:** planks for displaying fish for sale.
7. **coach:** a carriage, like a stagecoach.
8. **tam-o'-shanters:** flat-topped caps.
9. **tea . . . balaclavas:** knitted items.

Discussing the Photograph

🅿 What do you think the children in this photograph are planning to do with the snowballs? What adjectives would you use to describe these children? (Happy, excited, mischievous) Do your adjectives also apply to the boys described in Thomas's essay?

1. What do the narrator and his friends imagine on the afternoon of Christmas?
a. They are hunters in the wilderness.
b. They are the winning athletes.
c. They are in command of spaceships.
d. They are at home safely in beds. (a)

2. What was the emergency at the Prothero house?
a. a family quarrel   b. a lost book
c. a sick child   d. a fire (d)

3. Who always came to the narrator's house on Christmas Day?
a. grandfather   b. uncles
c. the parson   d. the postman (b)

4. How would you describe the narrator and his friends?
a. sad and serious youngsters
b. malicious pranksters
c. deprived children
d. mischievous, fun-loving boys (d)

5. What is the overall tone?
a. happy   b. regretful
c. bitter   d. solemn (a)

A. Exposition

❓ Whom does the narrator meet on the street on Christmas Day? (An old man on his daily walk and two healthy young men with pipes) Why are these encounters so easy to visualize? (The description is so concrete and detailed.)

from aunts who always wore wool next to the skin there were mustached and rasping vests that made you wonder why the aunts had any skin left at all; and once I had a little crocheted[10] nose bag from an aunt now, alas, no longer whinnying with us. And pictureless books in which small boys, though warned with quotations not to, *would* skate on Farmer Giles' pond and did and drowned; and books that told me everything about the wasp, except why."

"Go on to the Useless Presents."

"Bags of moist and many-colored jelly babies and a folded flag and a false nose and a tram-conductor's[11] cap and a machine that punched tickets and rang a bell; never a catapult; once, by mistake that no one could explain, a little hatchet; and a celluloid duck that made, when you pressed it, a most unducklike sound, a mewing moo that an ambitious cat might make who wished to be a cow; and a painting book in which I could make the grass, the trees, the sea and the animals any color I pleased, and still the dazzling sky-blue sheep are grazing in the red field under the rainbow-billed and pea-green birds. Hard-boileds, toffee, fudge and allsorts, crunches, cracknels, humbugs, glaciers, marzipan, and butterwelsh[12] for the Welsh. And troops of bright tin soldiers who, if they could not fight, could always run. And Snakes-and-Families and Happy Ladders. And Easy Hobbi-Games for Little Engineers, complete with instructions. Oh, easy for Leonardo![13] And a whistle to make the dogs bark to wake up the old man next door to make him beat on the wall with his stick to shake our picture off the wall. And a packet of cigarettes: you put one in your mouth and you stood at the corner of the street and you waited for hours, in vain, for an old lady to scold you for smoking a cigarette, and then with a smirk you ate it. And then it was breakfast under the balloons."

"Were there Uncles, like in our house?"

"There are always Uncles at Christmas. The same Uncles. And on Christmas mornings, with dog-disturbing whistle and sugar fags,[14] I would

scour the swatched town for the news of the little world, and find always a dead bird by the white Post Office or by the deserted swings; perhaps a robin, all but one of his fires out. Men and women wading or scooping back from chapel, with taproom[15] noses and wind-bussed cheeks, all albinos, huddled their stiff black jarring feathers against the irreligious snow. Mistletoe hung from the gas brackets[16] in all the front parlors; there was sherry and walnuts and bottled beer and crackers by the dessertspoons; and cats in their fur-abouts watched the fires; and the high-heaped fire spat, all ready for the chestnuts and the mulling pokers. Some few large men sat in the front parlors, without their collars, Uncles almost certainly, trying their new cigars, holding them out judiciously at arms' length, returning them to their mouths, coughing, then holding them out again as though waiting for the explosion; and some few small aunts, not wanted in the kitchen, nor anywhere else for that matter, sat on the very edges of their chairs, poised and brittle, afraid to break, like faded cups and saucers."

Not many those mornings trod[17] the piling streets: an old man always, fawn-bowlered,[18] yellow-gloved and, at this time of year, with spats of snow, would take his constitutional to the white bowling green and back, as he would take it wet or fire on Christmas Day or Doomsday; sometimes two hale[19] young men, with big pipes blazing, no overcoats and wind-blown scarfs, would trudge, unspeaking, down to the forlorn sea, to work up an appetite, to blow away the fumes, who knows, to walk into the waves until nothing of them was left but the two curling smoke clouds of their inextinguishable briars.[20] Then I would be slapdashing home, the gravy smell of the dinners of others, the bird smell, the brandy, the pudding and mince, coiling up to my nostrils, when out of a snow-clogged side lane would come a boy the spit[21] of myself, with a pink-tipped cigarette and the violet past of a black eye, cocky as a bullfinch, leering all to himself. I hated him on sight and sound, and would be about to put my dog whistle to my lips

A

---

10. **crocheted** (krō·shād′): made of interwoven thread in a process similar to knitting.
11. **tram-conductor:** fare collector on a streetcar.
12. **hardboileds . . . butterwelsh:** various treats to eat.
13. **Leonardo:** Leonardo da Vinci (1452–1519), Italian painter, sculptor, engineer, and architect. Thomas is suggesting that the instructions might have been easy for a genius such as da Vinci.
14. **sugar fags:** imitation cigarettes made of sugar.

15. **taproom:** barroom; that is, the red noses typical of people who have been drinking alcohol.
16. **gas brackets:** gas jets used for lighting the house.
17. **trod:** walked heavily on.
18. **fawn-bowlered:** wearing a yellowish-brown bowler, a type of hat in style when Thomas was a child.
19. **hale:** healthy.
20. **briars:** pipes.
21. **spit:** mirror-image.

ANALYZING THE ESSAY
Identifying Facts

1. A fire in the dining room.

The boys threw snowballs into the smoke, then went to a public telephone and alerted the fire brigade.

2. Useful presents: mufflers, mittens, a tam-o'-shanter, a nose bag, and books.

Useless presents: bags of jelly babies, a celluloid duck, a painting book, candy,

tin soldiers, a whistle, candy cigarettes.

Thomas remembers the Useless Presents more fondly; one can tell his preference from the gusto with which he describes them and because they are exactly what little boys would like.

3. The Uncles seem imposing and lazy; they smoked, sat by the fire, and slept.

4. They sing "Good King Wenceslas." A small dry voice joins their singing,

which they think may be the voice of a ghost or of trolls.

5. Invented words: "white-ivied," "tea-tray-slithered," "tug-o'-warred." Ordinary words used in a startling way: "whooed," "rasping vests," "wind-cherried-noses."

Interpreting Meanings

6. Answers will vary. In general, most *(Answers continue on next page.)*

and blow him off the face of Christmas when suddenly he, with a violet wink, put *his* whistle to *his* lips and blew so <u>stridently</u>, so high, so exquisitely loud, that gobbling faces, their cheeks bulged with goose, would press against their tinseled windows, the whole length of the white echoing street. For dinner we had turkey and blazing pudding, and after dinner the Uncles sat in front of the fire, loosened all buttons, put their large moist hands over their watch chains, groaned a little and slept. Mothers, aunts, and sisters scuttled to and fro, bearing tureens.[22] Auntie Bessie, who had already been frightened, twice, by a clock-work mouse,[23] whimpered at the sideboard and had some elderberry wine. The dog was sick. Auntie Dosie had to have three aspirins, but Auntie Hannah, who liked port, stood in the middle of the snowbound back yard, singing like a big-bosomed <u>thrush</u>. I would blow up balloons to see how big they would blow up to; and, when they burst, which they all did, the Uncles jumped and rumbled. In the rich and heavy afternoon, the Uncles breathing like dolphins and the snow descending, I would sit among <u>festoons</u> and Chinese lanterns and nibble dates and try to make a model man-o'-war, following the Instructions for Little Engineers, and produce what might be mistaken for a sea-going tramcar. Or I would go out, my bright new boots squeaking, into the white world, on to the seaward hill, to call on Jim and Dan and Jack and to pad through the still streets, leaving huge deep footprints on the hidden pavements.

"I bet people will think there's been hippos."

"What would you do if you saw a hippo coming down our street?"

"I'd go like this, bang! I'd throw him over the railings and roll him down the hill and then I'd tickle him under the ear and he'd wag his tail."

"What would you do if you saw *two* hippos?"

Iron-flanked and bellowing he-hippos clanked and battered through the <u>scudding</u> snow toward us as we passed Mr. Daniel's house.

"Let's post[24] Mr. Daniel a snowball through his letter box."

"Let's write things in the snow."

"Let's write 'Mr. Daniel looks like a spaniel' all over his lawn."

Or we walked on the white shore. "Can the fishes see it's snowing?"

The silent one-clouded heavens drifted on to the sea. Now we were snow-blind travelers lost on the north hills, and vast dewlapped dogs, with flasks round their necks, ambled and shambled up to us, baying "Excelsior."[25] We returned home through the poor streets where only a few children fumbled with bare red fingers in the wheel-rutted snow and cat-called after us, their voices fading away, as we <u>trudged</u> uphill, into the cries of the dock birds and the hooting of ships out in the whirling bay. And then, at tea the recovered Uncles would be jolly; and the ice cake loomed in the center of the table like a marble grave. Auntie Hannah laced her tea with rum, because it was only once a year.

Bring out the tall tales now that we told by the fire as the gaslight bubbled like a diver. Ghosts whooed like owls in the long nights when I dared not look over my shoulder; animals lurked in the cubbyhole under the stairs where the gas meter ticked. And I remember that we went singing carols once, when there wasn't the shaving of a moon to light the flying streets. At the end of a long road was a drive that led to a large house, and we stumbled up the darkness of the drive that night, each one of us afraid, each one holding a stone in his hand in case, and all of us too brave to say a word. The wind through the trees made noises as of old and unpleasant and maybe webfooted men wheezing in caves. We reached the black bulk of the house.

"What shall we give them? Hark the Herald?"

"No," Jack said. "Good King Wenceslas. I'll count three."

One, two, three, and we began to sing, our voices high and seemingly distant in the snow-felted darkness round the house that was occupied by nobody we knew. We stood close together, near the dark door.

Good King Wenceslas looked out
On the Feast of Stephen . . .

And then a small, dry voice, like the voice of someone who has not spoken for a long time, joined our singing: a small, dry, eggshell voice

A. **Exposition**

❓ How does this long catalog of events and sensations re-create a child's view of the world? (It emphasizes sense experience, and it is told in the episodic fashion in which children often speak.)

B. **Metaphor**

"The iron-flanked and bellowing he-hippos" are the vehicles passing in the street.

C. **Theme**

Here again the imaginative power of children, and by implication of literary artists, is evoked.

---

22. **tureens:** large, deep serving bowls with lids, used for serving soups and stews.
23. **clock-work mouse:** mechanical mouse that rolls on the floor when it is wound up.
24. **post:** mail.

25. **Excelsior:** Latin for "higher."

will agree that the essay is probably part imagination, part fact.

7. Mr. Prothero and the aunts are lethargic and somewhat given to the bottle—rather comic, eccentric figures.

8. The small boy asks if there were postmen; to identify the presents; and if there were uncles. The writer responds to each comment by giving his reminiscences.

A. Mood

? What tendency of children does this incident of the unknown caroler dramatize? (Their pleasure in using their imaginations to scare themselves a little when there is no real danger) Does the telling of this incident seriously darken the mood of the piece? (No)

B. Conclusion

? How does the boy end his wonderful Christmas day? (He looks out the window, turns down the gaslight, and whispers to the darkness.) What does this tell us about the narrator's feeling toward the events he has recorded? (The day ends reverently and peacefully in a kind of prayer before sleep. The narrator respects and cherishes his memories and the sacred state of childhood that they represent.)

Thomas's purpose may have been to suggest that, however disordered and "unfactual" his memories of Christmas may be, there is in fact a common core of Christmas memories that is pretty much the same for everyone. These have more to do with feeling and atmosphere than with specific details of time and place.

CLOSURE

Ask students to list three pleasant sense experiences that the narrator recalls from his childhood Christmases. Have students exchange their lists.

A from the other side of the door: a small dry voice through the keyhole. And when we stopped running we were outside *our* house; the front room was lovely; balloons floated under the hot-water-bottle-gulping gas; everything was good again and shone over the town.

"Perhaps it was a ghost," Jim said.

"Perhaps it was trolls," Dan said, who was always reading.

"Let's go in and see if there's any jelly left," Jack said. And we did that.

Always on Christmas night there was music. An uncle played the fiddle, a cousin sang "Cherry Ripe," and another uncle sang "Drake's Drum."

B It was very warm in the little house. Auntie Hannah, who had got on to the parsnip wine, sang a song about Bleeding Hearts and Death, and then another in which she said her heart was like a Bird's Nest; and then everybody laughed again; and then I went to bed. Looking through my bedroom window, out into the moonlight and the unending smoke-colored snow, I could see the lights in the windows of all the other houses on our hill and hear the music rising from them up the long, steadily falling night. I turned the gas down, I got into bed. I said some words to the close and holy darkness, and then I slept.

(1945, 1950)

Responding to the Essay

Analyzing the Essay

Identifying Facts

1. What happened in the home of Mr. and Mrs. Prothero on Christmas Eve? How did the boys react to this event?
2. What are some of the Useful Presents Thomas lists? What are some of the Useless Presents? Which does he remember more fondly? How can you tell?
3. What kind of people are the Uncles, who were always around on Christmas?
4. What do the boys do in front of Mr. Daniel's house? What response do they get? How do they react?
5. Thomas writes of a fire gong that was "bombilating" and snow that came "shawling" up from the ground. The first is an invented word, and the second is an unusual use of the word *shawl*. Find at least two more examples in the essay of invented words and of ordinary words used in a startling way.

Interpreting Meanings

6. Thomas writes, "...I can never remember whether it snowed for six days and six nights when I was twelve or whether it snowed for twelve days and twelve nights when I was six." How does this statement affect your reaction to the entire essay? Why?
7. Compare Thomas's depiction of his aunts with that of Mr. Prothero. What impression does he want to give in each case? What details in the descriptions support your answer?

8. In the middle of the essay, a small boy says, "It snowed last year, too." What other comments does the boy make? How does the writer respond to each comment? Why did Thomas include this imaginary conversation in his essay? What is he suggesting about the past?

Writing About the Essay

A Creative Response

1. **Writing a Sensory Description.** Choose a past or present scene that you find especially pleasant. Or make up such a scene. Focus on one part of the scene and think about the sensory pleasure it involves. Then write one or two paragraphs that will convey that sensory pleasure to a reader.

A Critical Response

2. **Analyzing the Writer's Style.** Write the names of each of the five senses—sight, hearing, touch, smell, and taste—on five different sheets of paper. Then go through the essay looking for sensory details. Write as many examples as you can find under each of the five headings. (Some examples might easily belong on more than one page.) Then use these notes to write an essay explaining how Thomas uses sensory details to make his memories come alive for a reader. If you like, you may choose the two or three senses with which he works most effectively.

1. BUILDING ON PRIOR KNOWLEDGE. Tell students that this essay is an eyewitness account of the working conditions of coal miners in Britain in the 1930's. To help students understand how important coal was to the British economy at that time, you might compare it with the importance of petroleum to the U.S. economy and the upheaval that occurred as a result of the oil shortage in the 1970's.

2. ESTABLISHING A PURPOSE. Ask students to try to imagine that they are traveling with Orwell through the coal mine and are experiencing the conditions in the mine along with him. Does Orwell make it easy to imagine what it is like in the mine?

3. PREADING JOURNAL. (Challenging) Have students investigate a typical workday of someone they know or do research on a type of work that particularly interests them. Ask them to write a report that focuses on the daily experience of the person doing the job.

(Less Challenging) Ask students to find an interview in a book or magazine with a worker who is doing a job that interests them. Have students summarize the important points made in the interview and report whether it increased or decreased their interest in the job or profession.

George Orwell (1903–1950)

George Orwell was born Eric Blair in Bengal in 1903. His father was a member of the Indian Civil Service at the time. A few years afterward, his family returned to England, and he was educated at Eton. He was a lonely child, who spent a good deal of time making up stories and poems. From the age of five or six, he later wrote, he knew he was going to be a writer.

In 1922, he joined the Indian Imperial Police, serving in Burma until 1927, when he resigned to devote his full time to writing. Returning to Europe, he taught and took part-time jobs in France and England. His first book, *Down and Out in Paris and London,* which was based on these experiences, was published in 1933. This was followed by a novel based on his life in Burma, *Burmese Days.*

Although he had published journalistic pieces under his real name, with *Burmese Days* he began to write under the name George Orwell, and continued to do so until his death. After *Burmese Days,* he wrote two more novels. Then in 1936, he was asked to write a study of conditions in Welsh coal mines for the Left Book Club, a socialist organization run by publisher Victor Gollancz. This became *The Road to Wigan Pier,* a moving portrait of the difficult lives of miners.

The rise of Fascism in the 1930's made Orwell a committed anti-Fascist. He fought against the Fascists in the Spanish Civil War in 1937. The following year, he published a book based on these experiences, *Homage to Catalonia.* "The Spanish war," he wrote, "turned the scale and thereafter I knew where I stood. Every line of serious work that I have written since 1936 has been written, directly or indirectly, *against* totalitarianism and *for* democratic socialism."

His two most famous books, *Animal Farm* (1945) and *1984* (1949) illustrate this point. *Animal Farm* is a political allegory which points up the dangers of totalitarianism of the left or the right. And *1984* has given us an entire vocabulary of the excesses of totalitarian regimes, including such words as *newspeak* and *doublethink.* In this book especially he stressed the connections between language, thought, and power, dramatizing what he had demonstrated in his essay "Politics and the English Language"—how corrupt language can be used to promote political oppression.

SUPPLEMENTARY SUPPORT MATERIALS
1. Vocabulary Activity Worksheet (*CCB*)
2. Review and Response Worksheet: Fact *vs.* Opinion (*CCB*)
3. Language Skills Worksheets: Adverbs; Weak Words and Clichés (*CCB*)
4. Selection Test (*CCB*)

DEVELOPING VOCABULARY
The following words from the essay are tested in the Selection Test. (See also Vocabulary Activity Worksheet.)

metabolism	crick
to taper	to hack
supple	tractable
qualm	stout
to buckle	drudge

A. Fact and Opinion

❓ What attitude toward manual laborers does this paragraph reveal? (Respect) What is the position of the rest of society in relation to the coal miners? (Totally dependent)

B. Expansion
Fillers are the workers who shovel the loosened coal onto a conveyor belt. They work in the deepest portion of the mine and are the first link in the chain of workers that are necessary to bring coal to the surface.

C. Descriptive Details

❓ What are some of the sense impressions that the mine made on Orwell? What did he see, hear, smell, feel, and taste? (Machines roar; "air is black with coal dust"; heat; cramped space)

D. Expansion
The main roads mentioned here are the wider passages in the mine where the coal is transported in tubs that run along a track. The main roads of the mine do not extend to the places where the coal is actually being extracted.

FROM THE ROAD TO WIGAN PIER

This essay is an example of investigative journalism, similar to reports written for newspapers or television to expose social problems that many people often prefer to ignore. Think of such pieces you've read or seen on television. More often than not, the tone of the reporter is one of anger, maybe even outrage. As you read Orwell's essay, pay close attention to his tone. It may be different from what you expect.

Our civilization, *pace* Chesterton,[1] *is* founded on coal, more completely than one realizes until one stops to think about it. The machines that keep us alive, and the machines that make the machines, are all directly or indirectly dependent upon coal. In the metabolism of the Western world the coal miner is second in importance only to the man who plows the soil. He is a sort of grimy caryatid[2] upon whose shoulders nearly everything that is *not* grimy is supported. For this reason the actual process by which coal is extracted is well worth watching, if you get the chance and are willing to take the trouble.

When you go down a coal mine it is important to try and get to the coal face[3] when the "fillers" are at work. This is not easy, because when the mine is working visitors are a nuisance and are not encouraged, but if you go at any other time, it is possible to come away with a totally wrong impression. On a Sunday, for instance, a mine seems almost peaceful. The time to go there is when the machines are roaring and the air is black with coal dust, and when you can actually see what the miners have to do. At those times the place is like hell, or at any rate like my own mental picture of hell. Most of the things one imagines in hell are there—heat, noise, confusion, darkness, foul air, and, above all, unbearably cramped space. Everything except the fire, for there is no fire down there except the feeble beams of Davy lamps and electric torches[4] which scarcely penetrate the clouds of coal dust.

When you have finally got there—and getting there is a job in itself: I will explain that in a moment—you crawl through the last line of pit props[5] and see opposite you a shiny black wall three or four feet high. This is the coal face. Overhead is the smooth ceiling made by the rock from which the coal has been cut; underneath is the rock again, so that the gallery you are in is only as high as the ledge of coal itself, probably not much more than a yard. The first impression of all, overmastering everything else for a while, is the frightful, deafening din from the conveyor belt which carries the coal away. You cannot see very far, because the fog of coal dust throws back the beam of your lamp, but you can see on either side of you the line of half-naked kneeling men, one to every four or five yards, driving their shovels under the fallen coal and flinging it swiftly over their left shoulders. They are feeding it on to the conveyor belt, a moving rubber belt a couple of feet wide which runs a yard or two behind them. Down this belt a glittering river of coal races constantly. In a big mine it is carrying away several tons of coal every minute. It bears it off to some place in the main roads where it is shot into tubs holding half a ton, and thence dragged to the cages and hoisted to the outer air.

---

1. *pace* **Chesterton** (pä′chē, a form of the Latin word for *peace*): Orwell is politely disagreeing with a comment made by the English writer G. K. Chesterton (1874–1936).
2. **caryatid** (kar′ē-at′id): a supporting column carved into the shape of a woman in a gown or drape.
3. **coal face:** the end of a tunnel, where the mining goes on.
4. **Davy lamps and electric torches:** lanterns with enclosed flames and flashlights.
5. **pit props:** wooden supports for the ceiling of a mine.

A. Reasons

Why does the writer envy the fillers? (For their physical skill and stamina)

B. Responding

What simile does the writer use to describe the coal miners? ("Hammered iron statues") What other reactions to the same sight might other viewers have? Do you think Orwell's view is romanticized? Do you think the person who took the photograph on page 1058 saw the miners in the same way as Orwell?

It is impossible to watch the "fillers" at work without feeling a pang of envy for their toughness. It is a dreadful job that they do, an almost super-human job by the standards of an ordinary person. For they are not only shifting monstrous quantities of coal, they are also doing it in a position that doubles or trebles[6] the work. They have got to remain kneeling all the while—they could hardly rise from their knees without hitting the ceiling—and you can easily see by trying it what a tremen-dous effort this means. Shoveling is comparatively easy when you are standing up, because you can use your knee and thigh to drive the shovel along; kneeling down, the whole of the strain is thrown upon your arm and belly muscles. And the other conditions do not exactly make things easier. There is the heat—it varies, but in some mines it is suffocating—and the coal dust that stuffs up your throat and nostrils and collects along your eyelids, and the unending rattle of the conveyor belt, which in that confined space is rather like the rattle of a machine gun. But the fillers look and work as though they were made of iron. They really do look like iron—hammered iron statues—under the smooth coat of coal dust which clings to them from head to foot. It is only when you see miners down the mine and naked that you realize what splendid men they are. Most of them are small (big men are at a disadvantage in that job) but nearly all of them have the most noble bodies: wide shoulders tapering to slender supple waists, and small pronounced buttocks and si-newy thighs, with not an ounce of waste flesh anywhere. In the hotter mines they wear only a pair of thin drawers, clogs,[7] and kneepads; in the hottest mines of all, only the clogs and kneepads. You can hardly tell by the look of them whether they are young or old. They may be any age up to sixty or even sixty-five, but when they are black and naked they all look alike. No one could do their work who had not a young man's body, and a figure fit for a guardsman at that; just a few pounds of extra flesh on the waistline, and the constant bending would be impossible. You can never forget that spectacle once you have seen it—the line of bowed, kneeling figures, sooty black all over, driving their huge shovels under the coal with stupendous force and speed. They are on the job for seven and a half hours, theoretically with-out a break, for there is no time "off." Actually they snatch a quarter of an hour or so at some time during the shift to eat the food they have brought with them, usually a hunk of bread and dripping[8] and a bottle of cold tea. The first time I was watching the "fillers" at work I put my hand upon some dreadful slimy thing among the coal dust. It was a chewed quid of tobacco. Nearly all the miners chew tobacco, which is said to be good against thirst.

Probably you have to go down several coal mines before you can get much grasp of the pro-cesses that are going on round you. This is chiefly because the mere effort of getting from place to place makes it difficult to notice anything else. In some ways it is even disappointing, or at least is unlike what you have expected. You get into the cage, which is a steel box about as wide as a telephone box and two or three times as long. It holds ten men, but they pack it like pilchards[9] in a tin, and a tall man cannot stand upright in it. The steel door shuts upon you, and somebody working the winding gear above drops you into the void. You have the usual momentary qualm in your belly and a bursting sensation in the ears, but not much sensation of movement till you get near the bottom, when the cage slows down so abruptly that you could swear it is going upward again. In the middle of the run the cage probably touches sixty miles an hour; in some of the deeper mines it touches even more. When you crawl out at the bottom you are perhaps four hundred yards under ground. That is to say you have a tolerable-sized mountain on top of you; hundreds of yards of solid rock, bones of extinct beasts, subsoil, flints, roots of growing things, green grass and cows grazing on it—all this suspended over your head and held back only by wooden props as thick as the calf of your leg. But because of the speed at which the cage has brought you down, and the complete blackness through which you have trav-eled, you hardly feel yourself deeper down than you would at the bottom of the Piccadilly tube.[10]

What *is* surprising, on the other hand, is the immense horizontal distances that have to be trav-

---

6. **trebles:** triples.
7. **clogs:** wooden shoes.

8. **bread and dripping:** bread soaked in fat from roasted meat.
9. **pilchards** (pil' chərdz): tiny food fish, similar to sardines.
10. **Piccadilly tube:** the London subway is called the tube; Piccadilly is a busy section of London.

Literature and Language: Pronouns and Point of View
Orwell's essay is written in the unusual second-person point of view. Have students examine in particular the passage on this page beginning "You do not notice." Does the use of the second-person pronoun force you as the reader to imagine you are actually accompanying the speaker on a trip into the mine?

Have students rewrite this passage in the more traditional third-person or first-person point of view. How is the effect changed? You might also have students try to rewrite a passage of "The Death of the Moth" or "A Child's Christmas in Wales" from the second-person point of view. Is it possible?

A. Noting Specific Details
Note how Orwell uses specific details to convey a vivid picture of what a miner does in a day's work.
? List some of these specific details. ("Passages as long as London Bridge to Oxford Circus"; "a mile from pit bottom to coal face")

A

eled underground. Before I had been down a mine I had vaguely imagined the miner stepping out of the cage and getting to work on a ledge of coal a few yards away. I had not realized that before he even gets to his work he may have to creep through passages as long as from London Bridge to Oxford Circus.[11] In the beginning, of course, a mine shaft is sunk somewhere near a seam[12] of coal. But as that seam is worked out and fresh seams are followed up, the workings get farther and farther from the pit bottom. If it is a mile from the pit bottom to the coal face, that is probably an average distance; three miles is a fairly normal one; there are even said to be a few mines where it is as much as five miles. But these distances bear no relation to distances above ground. For in all that mile or three miles as it may be, there is hardly anywhere outside the main road, and not many places even there, where a man can stand upright.

You do not notice the effect of this till you have gone a few hundred yards. You start off, stooping slightly, down the dim-lit gallery, eight or ten feet wide and about five high, with the walls built up

---

11. **London Bridge to Oxford Circus:** a distance of about 2 1/2 miles.
12. **seam:** layer.

dust; there is a dusty fiery smell which seems to be the same in all mines. You see mysterious machines of which you never learn the purpose, and bundles of tools slung together on wires, and sometimes mice darting away from the beam of the lamps. They are surprisingly common, especially in mines where there are or have been horses. It would be interesting to know how they got there in the first place; possibly by falling down the shift—for they say a mouse can fall any distance uninjured, owing to its surface area being so large relative to its weight. You press yourself against the wall to make way for lines of tubs jolting slowly toward the shaft, drawn by an endless steel cable operated from the surface. You creep through sacking[15] curtains and thick wooden doors which, when they are opened, let out fierce blasts of air. These doors are an important part of the ventilation system. The exhausted air is sucked out of one shaft by means of fans, and the fresh air enters the other of its own accord. But if left to itself the air will take the shortest way round, leaving the deeper workings unventilated; so all short-cuts have to be partitioned off.

At the start to walk stooping is rather a joke, but it is a joke that soon wears off. I am handicapped by being exceptionally tall, but when the roof falls to four feet or less it is a tough job for anybody except a dwarf or a child. You have not only got to bend double, you have also got to keep your head up all the while so as to see the beams and girders and dodge them when they come. You have, therefore, a constant crick in the neck, but this is nothing to the pain in your knees and thighs. After half a mile it becomes (I am not exaggerating) an unbearable agony. You begin to wonder whether you will ever get to the end—still more, how on earth you are going to get back. Your pace grows slower and slower. You come to a stretch of a couple of hundred yards where it is all exceptionally low and you have to work yourself along in a squatting position. Then suddenly the roof opens out to a mysterious height—scene of an old fall of rock, probably—and for twenty whole yards you can stand upright. The relief is overwhelming. But after this there is another low stretch of a hundred yards and then a succession of beams which you have to crawl under. You go down on all fours; even this is a relief after the squatting

A

with slabs of shale, like the stone walls in Derbyshire.[13] Every yard or two there are wooden props holding up the beams and girders; some of the girders have buckled into fantastic curves under which you have to duck. Usually it is bad going underfoot—thick dust or jagged chunks of shale, and in some mines where there is water it is as mucky as a farmyard. Also there is the track for the coal tubs, like a miniature railway track with sleepers[14] a foot or two apart, which is tiresome to walk on. Everything is gray with shale

---

13. **Derbyshire:** a county in central England.
14. **sleepers:** railroad ties.

15. **sacking:** a heavy fabric.

Review with students the fact that the active voice imparts a sense of vitality and dynamism to writing whereas the passive voice slows it down and produces a sluggish, weighty effect. Nevertheless, the occasional use of the passive voice can be a welcome change of pace. Refer students to the middle of column 2, page 1061.

Have students work in pairs to rewrite the following paragraph, changing most of the passive-voice verbs to active voice. Allow students to exchange their papers and compare their work.

The drudgery of farming is almost impossible for city-dwellers to grasp. First, the soil must be turned, and seeds must be sown. As crops spring up, the rows have to be hoed and weeded and watered, often in hours of backbreaking labor in the hot sun. Farm animals need daily care: They must be fed and watered, groomed, and given exercise. Broken tools must be mended; farm machinery must be repaired. Such a workday entails fourteen hours of sweat.

A. Audience

? What audience is Orwell addressing in this essay? (Nonminers who know nothing of the miners' lives) Why is he emphasizing the miners' journey to and from the coal face? (It is a good example of the difficulties of their work and one his readers would know nothing about.)

business. But when you come to the end of the beams and try to get up again, you find that your knees have temporarily struck work and refuse to lift you. You call a halt, ignominiously,[16] and say that you would like to rest for a minute or two. Your guide (a miner) is sympathetic. He knows that your muscles are not the same as his. "Only another four hundred yards," he says encouragingly; you feel that he might as well say another four hundred miles. But finally you do somehow creep as far as the coal face. You have gone a mile and taken the best part of an hour; a miner would do it in not much more than twenty minutes. Having got there, you have to sprawl in the coal dust and get your strength back for several minutes before you can even watch the work in progress with any kind of intelligence.

Coming back is worse than going, not only because you are already tired out but because the journey back to the shaft is probably slightly uphill. You get through the low places at the speed of a tortoise, and you have no shame now about calling a halt when your knees give way. Even the lamp you are carrying becomes a nuisance and probably when you stumble you drop it; whereupon, if it is a Davy lamp, it goes out. Ducking the beams becomes more and more of an effort, and sometimes you forget to duck. You try walking head down as the miners do, and then you bang your backbone. Even the miners bang their backbones fairly often. This is the reason why in very hot mines, where it is necessary to go about half naked, most of the miners have what they call "buttons down the back"—that is, a permanent scab on each vertebra. When the track is downhill the miners sometimes fit their clogs, which are hollow underneath, on to the trolley rails and slide down. In mines where the "traveling" is very bad all the miners carry sticks about two and a half feet long, hollowed out below the handle. In normal places you keep your hand on top of the stick and in the low places you slide your hand down into the hollow. These sticks are a great help, and the wooden crash-helmets—a comparatively recent invention—are a godsend. They look like a French or Italian steel helmet, but they are made of some kind of pith[17] and very light, and so strong that you can take a violent blow on the head without feeling it. When finally you get back to the surface you have been perhaps three hours underground and traveled two miles, and you are more exhausted than you would be by a twenty-five-mile walk above ground. For a week afterward your thighs are so stiff that coming downstairs is quite a difficult feat; you have to work your way down in a peculiar sidelong manner, without bending the knees. Your miner friends notice the stiffness of your walk and chaff[18] you about it. ("How'd ta like to work down pit, eh?" etc.) Yet even a miner who has been long away from work—from illness, for instance—when he comes back to the pit, suffers badly for the first few days.

It may seem that I am exaggerating, though no one who has been down an old-fashioned pit (most of the pits in England are old-fashioned) and actually gone as far as the coal face, is likely to say so. But what I want to emphasize is this. Here is this frightful business of crawling to and fro, which to any normal person is a hard day's work in itself; and it is not part of the miner's work at all, it is merely an extra, like the city man's daily ride in the tube. The miner does that journey to and fro, and sandwiched in between there are seven and a half hours of savage work. I have never traveled much more than a mile to the coal face; but often it is three miles, in which cases I and most people other than coal miners would never get there at all. This is the kind of point that one is always liable to miss. When you think of a coal mine you think of depth, heat, darkness, blackened figures hacking at walls of coal; you don't think, necessarily, of those miles of creeping to and fro. There is the question of time, also. A miner's working shift of seven and a half hours does not sound very long, but one has got to add on to it at least an hour a day for "traveling," more often two hours and sometimes three. Of course, the "traveling" is not technically work and the miner is not paid for it; but it is as like work as makes no difference. It is easy to say that miners don't mind all this. Certainly, it is not the same for them as it would be for you or me. They have done it since childhood, they have the right muscles hardened,

A

---

16. **ignominiously** (ig'nə·min'ē·əs·lē): feeling shame or disgrace.
17. **pith:** soft, spongy tissue in the center of certain plant stems.

18. **chaff:** tease.

READING CHECK TEST
1. The writer of this piece desires to become a miner. (F)
2. According to the excerpt, all British comfort and security rely on the continued supply of coal. (T)
3. The difficult conditions in the coal mines do not affect the miners because they are so strong. (F)
4. Those who are dependent on the coal miners' work do not want to be reminded of their dependency. (T)
5. Orwell is most sympathetic to the interests of the nonlaboring classes. (F)

and they can move to and fro underground with a startling and rather horrible agility. A miner puts his head down and *runs,* with a long swinging stride, through places where I can only stagger. At the workings you see them on all fours, skipping round the pit props almost like dogs. But it is quite a mistake to think that they enjoy it. I have talked about this to scores of miners and they all admit that the "traveling" is hard work; in any case when you hear them discussing a pit among themselves the "traveling" is always one of the things they discuss. It is said that a shift always returns from work faster than it goes; nevertheless the miners all say that it is the coming away, after a hard day's work, that is especially irksome. It is part of their work and they are equal to it, but certainly it is an effort. It is comparable, perhaps, to climbing a smallish mountain before and after your day's work.

When you have been down two or three pits you begin to get some grasp of the processes that are going on underground. (I ought to say, by the way, that I know nothing whatever about the technical side of mining: I am merely describing what I have seen.) Coal lies in thin seams between enormous layers of rock, so that essentially the process of getting it out is like scooping the central layer from a Neapolitan ice.[19] In the old days the miners used to cut straight into the coal with pick and crowbar—a very slow job because coal, when lying in its virgin state, is almost as hard as rock. Nowadays the preliminary work is done by an electrically driven coal-cutter, which in principle is an immensely tough and powerful band-saw, running horizontally instead of vertically, with teeth a couple of inches long and half an inch or an inch thick. It can move backward or forward on its own power, and the men operating it can rotate it this way and that. Incidentally it makes one of the most awful noises I have ever heard, and sends forth clouds of coal dust which make it impossible to see more than two or three feet and almost impossible to breathe. The machine travels along the coal face cutting into the base of the coal and undermining it to the depth of five feet or five feet and a half; after this it is comparatively easy to extract the coal to the depth to which it has been undermined. Where it is "difficult getting," however, it has also to be loosened with explosives. A man with an electric drill, like a rather smaller version of the drills used in streetmending, bores holes at intervals in the coal, inserts blasting powder, plugs it with clay, goes round the corner if there is one handy (he is supposed to retire to twenty-five yards distance) and touches off the charge with an electric current. This is not intended to bring the coal out, only to loosen it. Occasionally, of course, the charge is too powerful, and then it not only brings the coal out but brings the roof down as well.

After the blasting has been done the "fillers" can tumble the coal out, break it up, and shovel it on to the conveyor belt. It comes out at first in monstrous boulders which may weigh anything up to twenty tons. The conveyor belt shoots it on to tubs, and the tubs are shoved into the main road and hitched on to an endlessly revolving steel cable which drags them to the cage. Then they are hoisted, and at the surface the coal is sorted by being run over screens, and if necessary is washed as well. As far as possible the "dirt"—the shale, that is—is used for making the roads below. All that cannot be used is sent to the surface and dumped; hence the monstrous "dirt-heaps," like hideous gray mountains, which are the characteristic scenery of the coal areas. When the coal has been extracted to the depth to which the machine has cut, the coal face has advanced by five feet. Fresh props are put in to hold up the newly exposed roof, and during the next shift the conveyor belt is taken to pieces, moved five feet forward and reassembled. As far as possible the three operations of cutting, blasting, and extraction are done in three separate shifts, the cutting in the afternoon, the blasting at night (there is a law, not always kept, that forbids its being done when there are other men working nearby), and the "filling" in the morning shift, which lasts from six in the morning until half-past one.

Even when you watch the process of coal extraction you probably only watch it for a short time, and it is not until you begin making a few calculations that you realize what a stupendous task the "fillers" are performing. Normally each man has to clear a space four or five yards wide. The cutter has undermined the coal to the depth of five feet, so that if the seam of coal is three or four feet high, each man has to cut out, break up and load on to the belt something between seven

---

19. **Neapolitan ice:** ice cream made of varicolored layers of fruit, flavorings, and cream; developed in Naples, Italy.

A. Facts
❓ What does Orwell say is the miners' attitude toward traveling to and from the coal face? (They are capable of doing it, but it is not easy, even for them.)

B. Purpose
Orwell mentions in passing that safety regulations are not always observed.
❓ Why do you think he does not make a bigger issue in this essay of these threats to the miners' safety? (His purpose here is to give a realistic and convincing account of the miners' everyday reality, not of the extraordinary events or risks in the miners' life.)

1. Because visitors are discouraged and because the ubiquitous coal dust makes seeing difficult.
2. The vertical descent in the cage; the immense distances to be traversed while hunched over and oppressed by heat, foul air, and noise.
3. All miners must have a young man's

body in order to do their work, and all are covered with dust.
4. The distance between London Bridge and Oxford Circus.
5. First, the men are extremely tired after their day's work. Second, the return journey is uphill.
6. He compares the shifting of two tons of coal an hour to a gardener shifting two tons of earth in his garden.

7. He mentions the practice of employing pregnant women as miners.

Interpreting Meanings
8. The first paragraph displays a relatively upbeat tone. In contrast, the tone of the rest is serious, even depressing.
9. He evidently admires the miners in his description of their "traveling," of the amount of coal moved by the fillers, and

---

A. Persuasive Techniques

❓ Why does Orwell compare the miners' work to digging in his garden? (To help his readers imagine the enormity of the labor of the miners by relating it to something with which the readers might be familiar)

B. Opinion

❓ Why does Orwell think that the majority of people in society do not wish to hear about the working conditions of the laboring classes? (Knowledge might make them feel guilty, insecure, and uncomfortable.)

C. Opinion

❓ Why does Orwell think it important that the majority learn what mining coal really involves? (Because the survival of Britain's way of life depends on the labors of the miners)

D. Opinion

❓ Why does Orwell say it is "humiliating" for people who are not manual laborers to watch miners working? (Because the watchers are dependent on the miners)

---

and twelve cubic yards of coal. This is to say, taking a cubic yard as weighing twenty-seven hundredweight,[20] that each man is shifting coal at a speed approaching two tons an hour. I have just enough experience of pick-and-shovel work to be able to grasp what this means. When I am digging trenches in my garden, if I shift two tons of earth during the afternoon, I feel that I have earned my tea. But earth is <u>tractable</u> stuff compared with coal, and I don't have to work kneeling down, a thousand feet underground, in suffocating heat and swallowing coal dust with every breath I take; nor do I have to walk a mile bent double before I begin. The miner's job would be as much beyond my power as it would be to perform on the flying trapeze or to win the Grand National. I am not a manual laborer and please God I never shall be one, but there are some kinds of manual work that I could do if I had to. At a pitch I could be a tolerable road-sweeper or an inefficient gardener or even a tenth-rate farm hand. But by no conceivable amount of effort or training could I become a coal miner; the work would kill me in a few weeks.

Watching coal miners at work, you realize momentarily what different universes different people inhabit. Down there where coal is dug it is a sort of world apart which one can quite easily go through life without ever hearing about. Probably a majority of people would even prefer not to hear about it. Yet it is the absolutely necessary counterpart of our world above. Practically everything we do, from eating an ice to crossing the Atlantic, and from baking a loaf to writing a novel, involves the use of coal, directly or indirectly. For all the arts of peace coal is needed; if war breaks out it is needed all the more. In time of revolution the miner must go on working or the revolution must stop, for revolution as much as reaction needs coal. Whatever may be happening on the surface, the hacking and shoveling have got to continue without a pause, or at any rate without pausing for more than a few weeks at the most. In order that Hitler may march the goosestep, that the Pope may denounce Bolshevism, that the cricket crowds may assemble at Lord's, that the Nancy poets may scratch one another's backs, coal has

got to be forthcoming. But on the whole we are not aware of it; we all know that we "must have coal," but we seldom or never remember what coal-getting involves. Here am I, sitting writing in front of my comfortable coal fire. It is April but I still need a fire. Once a fortnight[21] the coal cart drives up to the door and men in leather jerkins[22] carry the coal indoors in <u>stout</u> sacks smelling of tar and shoot it clanking into the coalhole under the stairs. It is only very rarely, when I make a definite mental effort, that I connect this coal with that far-off labor in the mines. It is just "coal"— something that I have got to have; black stuff that arrives mysteriously from nowhere in particular, like manna[23] except that you have to pay for it. You could quite easily drive a car right across the north of England and never once remember that hundreds of feet below the road you are on the miners are hacking at the coal. Yet in a sense it is the miners who are driving your car forward. Their lamp-lit world down there is as necessary to the daylight world above as the root is to the flower.

It is not long since conditions in the mine were worse than they are now. There are still living a few very old women who in their youth have worked underground, with a harness round their waists and a chain that passed between their legs, crawling on all fours and dragging tubs of coal. They used to go on doing this even when they were pregnant. And even now, if coal could not be produced without pregnant women dragging it to and fro, I fancy we should let them do it rather than deprive ourselves of coal. But most of the time, of course, we should prefer to forget that they were doing it. It is so with all types of manual work; it keeps us alive, and we are oblivious[24] of its existence. More than anyone else, perhaps, the miner can stand as the type of the manual worker, not only because his work is so exaggeratedly awful, but also because it is so vitally necessary and yet so remote from our experience, so invisible, as it were, that we are capable of forgetting it as we forget the blood in our veins. In a way it is even humiliating to watch coal miners working. It raises in you momentary doubt about your own status as an "intellectual" and a superior person

---

20. **hundredweight:** 112 pounds in England (100 pounds in U.S.).

21. **fortnight:** two weeks.
22. **jerkins:** sleeveless jackets.
23. **manna:** in the Book of Exodus in the Bible, the food that appeared miraculously as the Israelites crossed the desert.
24. **oblivious:** completely unaware.

of the men enduring the heat. These opinions prepare us for the stark juxtaposition in the last paragraph of the necessary work performed by the miners and the superficialities of cultural and political activity mentioned by Orwell.

10. Students will have different opinions. On the whole, Orwell seems to be employing understatement rather than sarcasm.

11. Student answers will vary. In general, the effect is ironic because of the contrast between the essential work of the miners and the self-indulgent activities mentioned. Many students will agree that the effect is the same in the last sentence. Ask the students to defend their opinions in class.

generally. For it is brought home to you, at least while you are watching, that it is only because miners sweat their guts out that superior persons can remain superior. You and I and the editor of the *Times Lit. Supp.*,[25] and the Nancy poets and the Archbishop of Canterbury and Comrade X, author of *Marxism for Infants*—all of us *really* owe the comparative decency of our lives to poor drudges underground, blackened to the eyes, with their throats full of coal dust, driving their shovels forward with arms and belly muscles of steel.

A

---

25. *Times Lit. Supp.:* the literary supplement of the *London Times,* a publication read by many educated people in England.

Responding to the Essay

Analyzing the Essay

Identifying Facts

1. According to Orwell, why is it difficult to get a good view of coal miners at work?
2. In what way is getting into the mine "a job in itself"?
3. Why did Orwell have trouble telling whether a particular miner was young or old?
4. What comparisons does he use to describe the distance the miners must travel before they begin to work?
5. What two reasons does he give for considering the return trip even worse than going into the mine?
6. What comparison does Orwell use to emphasize the amount of coal each miner produces every day?
7. What recently discontinued practice does he mention in his final paragraph?

Interpreting Meanings

8. Reread the first paragraph. How does the tone of this paragraph contrast with the conditions described in the rest of the essay? Why do you suppose Orwell used this tone as an introduction to the essay?
9. What opinion of the miners does Orwell express when he is describing their physiques? Find at least three other places in the essay where he expresses a similar opinion. In what way are these opinions a preparation for the last paragraph of the essay?
10. Reread the paragraph beginning "It may seem that I am exaggerating, though no one. . . ." The word *traveling* is enclosed in quotation marks several times in that paragraph. One common use of quotation marks is to suggest a sarcastic tone of voice. Explain why you think Orwell is or is not using the word *traveling* sarcastically.

11. Reread the sentence beginning, "In order that Hitler . . . ," in the second to last paragraph. What is the effect of Orwell's joining together the particular activities he mentions? Is he after the same effect, or a different one, when he gives a similar list in his last sentence? Explain your answer.

Writing About the Essay

A Creative Response

1. **Writing About a Social Problem.** Think of some social problem you have read about or seen firsthand. (Or do some research on a problem that interests you.) Write a brief essay in which you describe some aspect of the problem in a way that will make a reader see, hear, or feel some of the things that afflict people who face this problem every day.

A Critical Response

2. **Analyzing a Writer's Technique.** As Orwell suggests, he was writing for people who would rather not think about the horrors of coal mining. As a result, he worked carefully to keep his readers interested, even though he was forcing them to face ugly facts. Write an essay explaining why you think he was or was not successful. Before you write, think about the following questions:

   a. What is Orwell's **tone?**
   b. What does he do to keep readers from feeling they are being lectured?
   c. What is the effect of his reference to women— some of them pregnant—in the mines?
   d. Why doesn't he make suggestions about how working conditions in the mines could be improved?

A. Tone

? How does the tone of this description of the miners vary from the tone of the one on page 1057? (This tone is more realistic and sociological, whereas the other was romantic and aesthetic—more of an artistic reaction than a journalistic one.)

CLOSURE
Ask students to think about how they would react to the experience of visiting these mines. What would their attitude be toward the miners, the mine owners, and the society that needs the coal? Would their response differ from Orwell's? How? Have students exchange their views in class.

PREPARATION

1. BUILDING ON PRIOR KNOWLEDGE. Have a volunteer (using a dictionary, if necessary) define the term *ethnocentric* (considering one's own culture or ethnic group to be superior to others). Encourage students to recall examples of ethnocentric attitudes in history.

2. ESTABLISHING A PURPOSE. Remind students of the headnote comment regarding the origin of the essay's title. Ask students to determine, as they read, how well that title survives its transplantation from Elizabethan England to colonial India. Encourage them to consider both the content and the theme of the essay before they respond.

3. PREREADING JOURNAL. Ask students to imagine teaching school in a culture that is different from their own. Have them list qualities that would make a teacher effective and attitudes that such a teacher should be careful to avoid. Interested students could write a fictional journal entry in which such a teacher looks back at the first day of school in the new position.

A. Expansion
You might explain that India's entire subcontinent—including present-day Pakistan and Bangladesh—was ruled by the British crown from 1857 to 1947. The author's father, a diplomat within the British Empire, was appointed India's ambassador to Japan after India became an independent nation.

B. For Further Reading Students
In addition to E. M. Forster's famous novel, students interested in modern India might read more of Rama Rau's *Gifts of Passage* (the autobiography-cum-travel book that contains the following essay), stories by Rabindranath Tagore and R. K. Narayan, and fiction and nonfiction by Rumer Godden, a British writer who has spent much of her life in India and often writes about it.

Santha Rama Rau (1923–   )

Santha Rama Rau was born in Madras, India, into a wealthy and distinguished family. Her father was a diplomat and her mother an influential social reformer. She was educated in England and the United States, earning her A.B. from Wellesley College in 1944, the same year that her first book, *Home to India,* was published.

Home to India is a record of Rama Rau's return to India in 1939 after many years of living abroad. It is marked by several characteristics that reappear in her later travel writing: a light, graceful style; a particularly personal point of view; and a sensitive insight into the clash of Eastern and Western cultures.

After graduating from college, Rama Rau worked for a time in India and then moved to Japan to accompany her father, who had been named India's ambassador to that country. *East of Home* (1950) describes her Japanese experiences. In 1952, she married an American whom she had met in Japan, and the two began a life of travel and writing. She was a frequent contributor to *Holiday* magazine, and her travel pieces are collected in a number of books, including *View to the Southeast* (1957), *My Russian Journey* (1958), and *Gifts of Passage* (1961).

Her first novel, *Remember the House,* depicts life among the privileged classes in Bombay. The novel reminds some readers of E. M. Forster's *A Passage to India,* which Rama Rau dramatized for London and Broadway productions years later.

SUPPLEMENTARY SUPPORT MATERIALS
1. Vocabulary Activity Worksheet (*CCB*)
2. Review and Response Worksheet: Autobiography (*CCB*)
3. Language Skills Worksheet: The Descriptive Paragraph (*CCB*)
4. Selection Test (*CCB*)

DEVELOPING VOCABULARY
The following words from the essay are tested in the Selection Test. (See also Vocabulary Activity Worksheet.)

to intimidate   palpitating
provincial   incomprehensible
insular   peevishness

BY ANY OTHER NAME

The setting of "By Any Other Name" is India under British rule (before 1950), when educated natives of India were expected to learn English in addition to their own native languages. (Hindi, Urdu, and Gujarati are just a few of the languages spoken in India.) This essay portrays a clash of two cultures in an Anglo-Indian school. The headmistress of this school would be white and British. Many of the students would also be white and British, from families of British civil servants sent to India as colonial rulers.

The title of the essay is from William Shakespeare's *Romeo and Juliet*. Juliet is wishing that Romeo's surname, Montague, were some other name, because the Montagues are sworn enemies of her family. "What's in a name?" she asks. "That which we call a rose/By any other name would smell as sweet."

How important do you think our names are in identifying who we are? What problems would you have if your first name were to be taken from you?

At the Anglo-Indian day school in Zorinabad to which my sister and I were sent when she was eight and I was five and a half, they changed our names. On the first day of school, a hot, windless morning of a north Indian September, we stood in the headmistress's study and she said, "Now you're the *new* girls. What are your names?"

My sister answered for us. "I am Premila, and she"—nodding in my direction—"is Santha."

The headmistress had been in India, I suppose, fifteen years or so, but she still smiled her helpless inability to cope with Indian names. Her rimless half-glasses glittered, and the precarious bun on the top of her head trembled as she shook her head. "Oh, my dears, those are much too hard for me. Suppose we give you pretty English names. Wouldn't that be more jolly? Let's see, now—Pamela for you, I think." She shrugged in a baffled way at my sister. "That's as close as I can get. And for *you*," she said to me, "how about Cynthia? Isn't that nice?"

My sister was always less easily intimidated than I was, and while she kept a stubborn silence, I said, "Thank you," in a very tiny voice.

We had been sent to that school because my father, among his responsibilities as an officer of the civil service, had a tour of duty to perform in the villages around that steamy little provincial town, where he had his headquarters at that time. He used to make his shorter inspection tours on horseback, and a week before, in the stale heat of a typically postmonsoon[1] day, we had waved goodbye to him and a little procession—an assistant, a secretary, two bearers, and the man to look after the bedding rolls and luggage. They rode away through our large garden, still bright green from the rains, and we turned back into the twilight of the house and the sound of fans whispering in every room.

Up to then, my mother had refused to send Premila to school in the British-run establishments of that time, because, she used to say, "you can bury a dog's tail for seven years and it still comes out curly, and you can take a Britisher away from his home for a lifetime and he still remains insular." The examinations and degrees from entirely Indian schools were not, in those days, considered valid. In my case, the question had never come up, and probably never would have come up if Mother's extraordinary good health had not broken down. For the first time in my life, she was not able to continue the lessons she had been giving us every morning. So our Hindi books were put away, the stories of the Lord Krishna as a little boy were left in midair, and we were sent to the Anglo-Indian school.

That first day at school is still, when I think of it, a remarkable one. At that age, if one's name is changed, one develops a curious form of dual personality. I remember having a certain detached

---

1. **postmonsoon:** after the rainy season.

A. Expansion
Explain that *Anglo-Indian* means that the school was open to Indian nationals and to the children of British colonists. As the essay continues, note that the English spoken in India shows British influences. (For example, in the United States we tend to use the term *principal* rather than *headmistress*.)

B. Theme
❓ Why is the behavior of the headmistress insensitive? (She has lived in India for some fifteen years yet knows little of Indian culture. She also shows little respect for the feelings of children, to whom names are very important.)

C. Interpreting/Contrast
❓ What is the mother's attitude toward her own culture? (Proud) What is one of the facts of colonial life that works against that attitude? (The British authorities do not consider tests and degrees from Indian schools valid.)

A. Theme

❓ What do these details suggest about British ethnocentricity? (The attitude is excessive, to the point of creating discomfort. The style of the verandas suggests a loss of national culture. Furthermore, the additional heat could be interpreted symbolically as the day-to-day pressure of colonial rule.)

B. Interpreting

❓ What attitude feared by her mother does young Santha give in to with this decision? (That British styles and customs are superior)

C. Characterization

Santha's inability to give her name encourages the reader's sympathy in two ways: The reader not only understands how Santha might have trouble remembering her odd new name but also feels her shame at being embarrassed in front of her classmates.

D. Expansion

Apple trees do not grow in hot climates, so apples would be unfamiliar to many Indian children.

and disbelieving concern in the actions of "Cynthia," but certainly no responsibility. Accordingly, I followed the thin, erect back of the headmistress down the veranda to my classroom, feeling, at most, a passing interest in what was going to happen to me in this strange, new atmosphere of School.

The building was Indian in design, with wide verandas opening onto a central courtyard, but Indian verandas are usually whitewashed, with stone floors. These, in the tradition of British schools, were painted dark brown and had matting on the floors. It gave a feeling of extra intensity to the heat.

I suppose there were about a dozen Indian children in the school—which contained perhaps forty children in all—and four of them were in my class. They were all sitting at the back of the room, and I went to join them. I sat next to a small, solemn girl who didn't smile at me. She had long, glossy-black braids and wore a cotton dress,[2] but she still kept on her Indian jewelry—a gold chain around her neck, thin gold bracelets, and tiny ruby studs in her ears. Like most Indian children, she had a rim of black kohl around her eyes. The cotton dress should have looked strange, but all I could think of was that I should ask my mother if I couldn't wear a dress to school, too, instead of my Indian clothes.

I can't remember too much about the proceedings in class that day, except for the beginning. The teacher pointed to me and asked me to stand up. "Now, dear, tell the class your name."

I said nothing.

"Come along," she said, frowning slightly. "What's your name, dear?"

"I don't know," I said, finally.

The English children in the front of the class—there were about eight or ten of them—giggled and twisted around in their chairs to look at me. I sat down quickly and opened my eyes very wide, hoping in that way to dry them off. The little girl with the braids put out her hand and very lightly touched my arm. She still didn't smile.

Most of that morning I was rather bored. I looked briefly at the children's drawings pinned to the wall and then concentrated on a lizard clinging to the ledge of the high, barred window behind the teacher's head. Occasionally it would shoot out its long yellow tongue for a fly, and then it would rest, with its eyes closed and its belly palpitating, as though it were swallowing several times quickly. The lessons were mostly concerned with reading and writing and simple numbers—things that my mother had already taught me—and I paid very little attention. The teacher wrote on the easel blackboard words like *bat* and *cat,* which seemed babyish to me; only *apple* was new and incomprehensible.

When it was time for the lunch recess, I followed the girl with braids out onto the veranda. There the children from the other classes were assembled. I saw Premila at once and ran over to her, as she had charge of our lunchbox. The children were all opening packages and sitting down to eat sandwiches. Premila and I were the only ones who had Indian food—thin wheat chapatis,[3] some vegetable curry, and a bottle of buttermilk. Premila thrust half of it into my hand and whispered fiercely that I should go and sit with my class, because that was what the others seemed to be doing.

The enormous black eyes of the little Indian girl from my class looked at my food longingly, so I offered her some. But she only shook her head and plowed her way solemnly through her sandwiches.

I was very sleepy after lunch, because at home we always took a siesta. It was usually a pleasant time of day, with the bedroom darkened against the harsh afternoon sun, the drifting off into sleep with the sound of Mother's voice reading a story in one's mind, and, finally, the shrill, fussy voice of the ayah[4] waking one for tea.

At school, we rested for a short time on low, folding cots on the veranda, and then we were expected to play games. During the hot part of the afternoon we played indoors, and after the shadows had begun to lengthen and the slight breeze of the evening had come up, we moved outside to the wide courtyard.

I had never really grasped the system of competitive games. At home, whenever we played tag or guessing games, I was always allowed to "win"—"because," Mother used to tell Premila, "she is the youngest, and we have to allow for

---

2. The cotton dress would be an English dress. Indian girls would normally not wear English clothes.

3. **chapatis** (chə·pät′ēz): pieces of unleavened bread.
4. **ayah:** a governess or maid.

that." I had often heard her say it, and it seemed quite reasonable to me, but the result was that I had no clear idea of what "winning" meant.

When we played twos-and-threes that afternoon at school, in accordance with my training, I let one of the small English boys catch me but was naturally rather puzzled when the other children did not return the courtesy. I ran about for what seemed like hours without ever catching anyone, until it was time for school to close. Much later I learned that my attitude was called "not being a good sport," and I stopped allowing myself to be caught, but it was not for years that I really learned the spirit of the thing.

When I saw our car come up to the school gate, I broke away from my classmates and rushed toward it yelling, "Ayah! Ayah!" It seemed like an eternity since I had seen her that morning—a wizened, affectionate figure in her white cotton sari, giving me dozens of urgent and useless instructions on how to be a good girl at school. Premila followed more sedately, and she told me on the way home never to do that again in front of the other children.

When we got home we went straight to Mother's high, white room to have tea with her, and I immediately climbed onto the bed and bounced gently up and down on the springs. Mother asked how we had liked our first day in school. I was so pleased to be home and to have left that peculiar Cynthia behind that I had nothing whatever to say about school, except to ask what *apple* meant. But Premila told Mother about the classes and added that in her class they had weekly tests to see if they had learned their lessons well.

I asked, "What's a test?"

Premila said, "You're too small to have them. You won't have them in your class for donkey's years.[5]" She had learned the expression that day and was using it for the first time. We all laughed enormously at her wit. She also told Mother, in an aside, that we should take sandwiches to school the next day. Not, she said, that *she* minded. But they would be simpler for me to handle.

That whole lovely evening I didn't think about school at all. I sprinted barefoot across the lawns with my favorite playmate, the cook's son, to the stream at the end of the garden. We quarreled in

---

5. **for donkey's years:** for a long time (similar to the American expression "for a dog's age").

our usual way, waded in the tepid water under the lime trees, and waited for the night to bring out the smell of the jasmine. I listened with fascination to his stories of ghosts and demons, until I was too frightened to cross the garden alone in the semidarkness. The ayah found me, shouted at the cook's son, scolded me, hurried me in to supper— it was an entirely usual, wonderful evening.

It was a week later, the day of Premila's first test, that our lives changed rather abruptly. I was sitting at the back of my class, in my usual inattentive way, only half listening to the teacher. I had started a rather guarded friendship with the girl with the braids, whose name turned out to be Nalini (Nancy, in school). The three other Indian children were already fast friends. Even at that age it was apparent to all of us that friendship with the English or Anglo-Indian children was out of

A. Responding

Which of these conflicting attitudes toward competition do you find more valid? Why? (Students probably will be more familiar with the British attitude but should note that the Indian attitude has its own virtues.)

B. Idiom

Note that the phrase *for donkey's years* is an idiom—an expression whose meaning differs from the literal meaning of the words that comprise it. Idioms cannot be translated word for word, and they often are the most difficult aspect of learning another language. Encourage students to suggest other examples of idiom (for example, *an arm and a leg* for "expensive" or *raining cats and dogs* for "raining heavily").

C. Setting/ Contrast

Encourage students to comment upon the difference between Santha's classroom (where she has just spent a most unpleasant day) and her home (where familiar activities are pleasant and even fun and where she does not feel alienated.)

READING CHECK TEST
1. The headmistress claimed that Indian names were too hard for her. (T)
2. The girls' parents were eager to send them to British schools. (F)
3. Santha was bored because she already had learned most of the lesson material from her mother. (T)

4. Premila was sent home because she cheated on a test. (F)
5. Santha Rama Rau regretted losing her new identity as "Cynthia" so soon. (F)

CLOSURE
Have students discuss the significance of the essay's title. (It relates specifically to the name-changing practice of the headmistress and symbolically to failed efforts of the British to "Anglicize" the Indians. It also stresses that bigotry remains bigotry, no matter how it is cloaked.)

A. Theme
❓ Why does friendship among the students seem impossible? (Adult prejudices have taught the English children to look down on their Indian classmates.)

B. Character
❓ What chief qualities does each sister display here? (Premila shows courage, pride, and independence; Santha shows loyalty and sensitivity.)

C. Humanities Connection: Responding to the Fine Art
This detail is from a large wall hanging from the Madras region of India. Weaving and embroidery, ancient arts that are mentioned in the Hindu Vedas, were introduced to Europe when Crusaders returned with samples of Eastern fabrics.
❓ How does the seventeenth-century hanging relate to the twentieth-century story? (The headmistress seems to feel that English culture is far superior to Indian culture. This hanging shows that India has a highly advanced culture of its own.)

A the question. Occasionally, during the class, my new friend and I would draw pictures and show them to each other secretly.

The door opened sharply and Premila marched in. At first, the teacher smiled at her in a kindly and encouraging way and said, "Now, you're little Cynthia's sister?"

B Premila didn't even look at her. She stood with her feet planted firmly apart and her shoulders rigid and addressed herself directly to me. "Get up," she said. "We're going home."

I didn't know what had happened, but I was aware that it was a crisis of some sort. I rose obediently and started to walk toward my sister.

"Bring your pencils and your notebook," she said.

I went back for them, and together we left the room. The teacher started to say something just as Premila closed the door, but we didn't wait to hear what it was.

In complete silence we left the school grounds and started to walk home. Then I asked Premila what the matter was. All she would say was "We're going home for good."

It was a very tiring walk for a child of five and a half, and I dragged along behind Premila with my pencils growing sticky in my hand. I can still remember looking at the dusty hedges and the tangles of thorns in the ditches by the side of the road, smelling the faint fragrance from the eucalyptus trees and wondering whether we would ever reach home. Occasionally a horse-drawn

Three women, a detail from *Wall Hanging (Kalamkari): Indian Notable, Wife, and Child* (c. 1640–50). Cotton.

The Metropolitan Museum of Art, New York. Gift of Mrs. Albert Blum, 1920. (20.79).

C

ANALYZING THE POEM
Identifying Facts
1. Indian names were "much too hard."
2. Premila took offense at her teacher's charge that Indians cheated on tests.

Interpreting Meanings
3. Indian parents who wanted British authorities to accept their children's degrees had no other choice.

4. British colonists remained in India but were unaffected by Indian culture.
5. Santha had never seen an apple.
6. At first, she understood only that her kindness in a game was not returned; later she realized the importance of a competitive spirit in British culture.
7. In school the girls received English variations on their names and were encouraged to adopt British tastes in clothing and food. Their Indian heritage was maligned by insults concerning "cheating." They were viewed as parts of a group rather than as individuals.
8. The essay implies racial prejudice—exemplified by the headmistress—stems from misconception and indifference. Culture clash shows in forcing Indian students to sit in the back of the room and subjecting them to suspicion.

tonga[6] passed us, and the women, in their pink or green silks, stared at Premila and me trudging along on the side of the road. A few coolies and a line of women carrying baskets of vegetables on their heads smiled at us. But it was nearing the hottest time of day, and the road was almost deserted. I walked more and more slowly and shouted to Premila from time to time, "Wait for me!" with increasing peevishness. She spoke to me only once, and that was to tell me to carry my notebook on my head, because of the sun.

When we got to our house the ayah was just taking a tray of lunch into Mother's room. She immediately started a long, worried questioning about what are you children doing back here at this hour of the day.

Mother looked very startled and very concerned and asked Premila what had happened.

Premila said, "We had our test today, and She made me and the other Indians sit at the back of the room, with a desk between each one."

---

6. **tonga:** two-wheeled carriage.

Mother said, "Why was that, darling?"

"She said it was because Indians cheat," Premila added. "So I don't think we should go back to that school."

Mother looked very distant and was silent a long time. At last she said, "Of course not, darling." She sounded displeased.

We all shared the curry she was having for lunch, and afterward I was sent off to the beautifully familiar bedroom for my siesta. I could hear Mother and Premila talking through the open door.

Mother said, "Do you suppose she understood all that?"

Premila said, "I shouldn't think so. She's a baby."

Mother said, "Well, I hope it won't bother her."

Of course, they were both wrong. I understood it perfectly, and I remember it all very clearly. But I put it happily away, because it had all happened to a girl called Cynthia, and I never was really particularly interested in her.

A

Responding to the Essay

Analyzing the Essay

Identifying Facts

1. What reason did the headmistress give for changing Premila's and Santha's names?
2. Why did Premila take her sister and leave school permanently?

Interpreting Meanings

3. Explain why parents sent their children to Anglo-Indian schools rather than to entirely Indian schools.
4. What does the mother mean when she says, "you can bury a dog's tail for seven years and it still comes out curly"?
5. Why do you think the word *apple* was "new and incomprehensible" to Santha?
6. What cultural differences about "winning" did Santha discover?
7. List all the ways that Santha and Premila were made to feel like strangers in their own country.
8. In what ways is this a story about a clash of cultures and also about the causes of racial prejudice?

Writing About the Essay

A Creative Response

1. **Persuading a Person.** Imagine that a time machine could take you to the Anglo-Indian school at the moment that Santha and Premila left it for good. Write a brief essay summarizing what you would say to the headmistress to help her understand the damage she was doing to her Indian students. Include what the headmistress might say in her own defense.

A Critical Response

2. **Describing Contrasts.** Santha Rama Rau gives glimpses of her home life as a child and also describes her experiences at school. In a brief essay, explain how Santha's home life contrasts with life at school. Consider these aspects of home and school: kinds of lessons taught, atmosphere, attitude toward children, attitude toward games.

"... there are national differences among poetries as well as linguistic differences, and American poetry has added something new to the store of poetry in the world. The mixed poverty and riches of the United States have brought into being a poetry that differs from that of England. In England—a tiny country, agriculturally cultivated for centuries, architecturally and historically rich; uninvaded in battle since 1066, with a small, homogeneous educated class—a coherent poetry was possible for a number of centuries. In America—an enormous wilderness only recently settled, educationally and ethnically diverse, made and remade by waves of immigrants—poetry was bound to be diffuse, heterogeneous, and, vis-à-vis England, defensive. Although the victories won by American modernists were indisputable, they were won chiefly by Americans who had Europeanized themselves with a vengeance. Pound and Eliot became expatriates; Frost went deliberately to England for three years and published his first book there; Stevens said that French and English constitute a single language. And Williams made himself so pointedly American only because he was by birth and education so

A. Expansion
Europe here means continental Europe, as opposed to the British Isles.

Twentieth-Century Poetry A

British poetry in the early twentieth century was distinguished by the fact that, unlike American poetry, it was barely influenced by the poetry being written in Europe, particularly by the French Symbolists. This difference is not easy to account for. It cannot be explained as an example of British self-satisfaction. And it is not an indication that British poets lacked curiosity and receptiveness to change.

Ironically enough, most British poets were, in fact, better acquainted with French and other foreign languages than Americans were. They were also better informed about the striking new developments in what we know today as modern art and modern poetry.

The strange thing is that the poets' knowledge and awareness of these new kinds of expression did not lead them to the daring adaptations that American poets were quick to make. As a result, poetry in the United States, for the first time since Walt Whitman, was more experimental, more attuned to contemporary consciousness, and altogether more interesting than almost anything produced in Great Britain until the 1930's.

Instead of entering into the international spirit of Modernism, British poets continued to draw upon the vast riches of their own native traditions. After all, poetry in the British Isles (like music in Germany) had for hundreds of years been the form of expression that had made the nation famous. What other culture could match the succession of poets that included Chaucer, Shakespeare, Donne, Milton, Wordsworth, Blake, Keats, and Hopkins?

A few British poets were intrigued by the kinds of psychological shorthand characteristic of the French Symbolists. Notable among these poets was Dame Edith Sitwell, whose collection of poems called *Façade* brought high color and linguistic playfulness into a drab period. Yet, as influences from France began to reshape the poetry of Americans such as Ezra Pound, T. S. Eliot, William Carlos Williams, and Wallace Stevens, most of the British poets kept their distance. As a result, the history of British poetry in the twentieth century is less concerned with new techniques and modes of perception than with subject matter couched in conventional meters and familiar rhyme schemes.

World War I and the Trench Poets

This tendency to accommodate even the most violent responses to experience within entirely conventional forms is found in a number of men who became known as the Trench Poets. The term is precise: Each of the Trench Poets either died in the muddy trenches of World War I or survived as a bitter but articulate ghost trapped by memories from which there was no escape. What these poets wrote was categorized as "war poetry." Yet the poets themselves hoped their works would stand as testaments beyond the usual reach of poetic art—and as warnings.

As Wilfred Owen wrote, "The poetry is in the pity," meaning that the shame of war overwhelms every attempt to make sense of

> "**E**ach of the Trench Poets either died in the muddy trenches of World War I or survived as a bitter but articulate ghost trapped by memories from which there was no escape."

European (his father was English, his mother Puerto Rican, and he had been educated in part in Switzerland). In spite of their American origins, each of these authors had to come to terms in some way with Europe."
—from *Contemporary American Poetry*
    Helen Vendler

A. **Humanities Connection: Discussing the Fine Art** For background information on Paul Nash, see the annotation on page 923. Call students' attention to the ironic title of this painting. Tell them that it is another reflection of the bitter disillusionment that afflicted young World War I veterans like Nash and the Trench Poets. Ask students to think of other appropriate titles for this painting.

A

We Are Making a New World by Paul Nash (1918). Oil.

Imperial War Museum, London.

it, in verse or by any other means. Intimately acquainted with miseries and horrors inconceivable to civilians, the Trench Poets stripped war of its glory. They positioned themselves against the Romantic rhetoric of their immediate predecessor, Rupert Brooke (himself a casualty of The Great War), who put into rhyme the expected patriotic response.

In contrast, the Trench Poets dwelt on the degradation of body and soul caused by trench warfare, and the humiliation that the trenches represented. In their view, the military conflict that began as an assertion of national righteousness and a test of national will became an exercise in slaughter. To them, the war demeaned the very idea of civilization and turned history itself into a "no-man's land"—the few hundred yards of dead terrain that divided German trenches from British trenches, a terrain that bore all the features of Hell. Killed in action, or crippled, blinded, gassed, and shell-shocked, the Trench Poets, dead and alive, spoke to and for the young men of generations to come.

The two poets among them who most clearly showed signs of genius were the young soldiers Wilfred Owen and Isaac Rosenberg. Owen's experiments with half rhyme were unique in British poetry;

A. Expansion
The libretto is the text or the words for a musical work.

B. Eliot and Pound

Eliot became a British citizen in 1927, when he was thirty-nine years old and when his greatest work was behind him. "The Love Song of J. Alfred Prufrock" had appeared in 1915; "The Waste Land" in 1922; and "Ash Wednesday" in 1927, the year of his conversion to the Church of England. Eliot's major work concluded in 1943 with "Four Quartets." Pound and Eliot are both represented in *Elements of Literature: Fifth Course* (The Literature of the United States). For a reassessment of Eliot's contribution to modern poetry and his place as an American in the British establishment, see Cynthia Ozick's essay "A Critic at Large: T. S. Eliot" in *The New Yorker* (Nov. 20, 1989).

A

B

> "**B**ritish readers of poetry in the 1920's were aware of an extraordinary American contribution to an art they had considered their own time-honored preserve."

Stephen Spender reading poetry aloud at an informal dinner party.

Rosenberg's deftness in handling free verse showed that he was a potential master of language. On April 1, 1918, Rosenberg was killed in action. Owen, whose poems later formed the libretto for Benjamin Britten's *War Requiem,* met the same fate six months later.

The American Influence: Eliot and Pound

The unflinching realism of the Trench Poets was distasteful and dismaying to the older generation, even to those who were appalled by the lengthening casualty lists and the realization that the flower of British manhood was being systematically wiped out. But, for the young, the realism of the war poetry sharpened the edge of bitterness echoed by two American poets, Ezra Pound and T. S. Eliot, who would soon be as well known in Great Britain as in their own country. In fact, Pound's "Hugh Selwyn Mauberley" (1920) and Eliot's "The Waste Land" (1922) became more familiar to readers in postwar England than to those in postwar America.

British readers of poetry in the 1920's were aware of an extraordinary American contribution to an art they had considered their own time-honored preserve. They were also cosmopolitan enough to recognize its ingenuity and power, and generous enough to concede that a man from Idaho (Pound) and another from Missouri (Eliot) spoke with an authority that their own poets lacked.

But what might be called the American takeover was brief. It came to an end when British poetry proved that it could absorb American influences and still produce works of a tone and a technique that would turn the tables and lead a whole generation of American poets to emulate it.

The English Group of the 1930's

One of the most exciting developments of the early 1930's was the emergence of four poets popularly known in America as "the English Group." They were given this title even though two of them were Irish and even though they had little in common but a certain political commitment. The group consisted of the British writers W. H. Auden and Stephen Spender, both thoroughly British by ancestry, education, and temperament; and the Irish-born writers Cecil Day Lewis, and Louis MacNeice, both of whom were brought up in the cultural traditions of England and not those of embattled Ireland.

Coming to public attention at more or less the same time, these poets at first seemed to represent poetry as public speech, addressed especially to their immediate contemporaries. This broad audience was a generation that tended to regard the devastation of World War I as a result of the failure of capitalism. This failure, they felt, was made even more apparent in the social unrest of the 1920's and in the economic collapse of 1929 that led to the Great Depression. The audience of the English Group was also the generation that began to look toward socialism as an alternative to Great Britain's capitalist class system, and to the unequal distribution of wealth which perpetuated that system.

As spokesmen for their own generation, Auden, Spender and Day Lewis took a closer look at Marxism as a political philosophy; they also watched developments in the still new (and pre-Stalinist) Soviet Union for signs that its social revolution might serve as a model for other countries. The most important concern in their political thinking, however, was the rise of fascism. Fascism was a dictatorial, militaristic system that would eventually unite the democracies of the world in opposition to it and lead to World War II.

Without quite being aware of the fact, poetry, like everything else, became politicized:

> The qualities which distinguished us from the writers of the previous decade lay not in ourselves, but in the events to which we reacted. These were unemployment, economic crisis, . . . fascism, approaching war. . . . The older writers were reacting . . . to the exhaustion and hopelessness of a Europe in which the old regimes were falling to pieces. We were a "new generation," but it took me some time to appreciate the meaning of this phrase . . . that we had begun . . . in circumstances strikingly different from those of our immediate predecessors and that a consciousness of this was shown in our writing. . . . We were the 1930's.

—Stephen Spender

Already entrenched in Italy and Germany, fascism threatened to spread to Spain when General Francisco Franco overthrew the elected Spanish Republican government in 1936. Franco's move was supported by Benito Mussolini, dictator of Italy, and Adolf Hitler. More than any other event of the decade, the events in Spain unified the artists and intellectuals of a generation in support of Spanish democracy. The Spanish Civil War became *their* war. Some, unwilling to remain bystanders, enlisted as volunteers in the Republican Army and were counted among its casualties. As in World War I, some of the most brilliant poets of an era were silenced before they could fulfill their promise.

The Spanish Civil War was a prelude; it ended in 1939, the same year that World War II began with Hitler's invasion of Poland that September. By that time—in spite of the politically radical outlook that united the poets of Great Britain—it was clear that their interest in Marxism was not a commitment but a mere flirtation.

The members of the English Group were poets of great skill, adept in forms ranging from sonnets to free verse to poetic drama. Yet, with the exception of Auden, they were not innovators. And even Auden's innovation had little in common with the new kinds of poetic expression coming from France, Spain, South America, and elsewhere. Auden's innovation was the miracle that takes place when, out of the resources of his own language and its history, one individual invents an idiom identified with no one but himself. A

Guernica (detail) by Pablo Picasso (1937). Oil.

Museo Picasso, Barcelona, Spain.

A. Humanities Connection:
Discussing the Fine Art
Widely considered the greatest artist of the twentieth century, Pablo Picasso (1881–1973) was born in Malaga, Spain; had his first exhibition in Barcelona at the age of sixteen; and moved to Paris in 1904. During his long career, he excelled as a painter, sculptor, graphic artist, and ceramist. He experimented with many styles and made innovative contributions in each, but it was probably his development of Cubism with Georges Braque that had the greatest impact on the course of modern art. Cubist technique strove to reduce forms to their geomtrical essences and to rearrange them on canvas in an order suggested not by nature but by the mind of the artist. *Guernica,* completed in 1937, was a huge Cubist-Surrealist projection of the horrific results of the aerial bombing of the small Spanish town of Guernica by Franco's forces in the Spanish Civil War. After a long stay in the Museum of Modern Art in New York, the painting was finally returned, at Picasso's request, to Spain after the death of Franco and the restoration of democracy.

What archetypal images of war are seen in this detail? (Note the destruction of the innocent.) Why do you suppose a bull is in the picture?

A. About the Photograph

Christopher Isherwood, who became an American citizen in 1946, wrote the Berlin stories that became the basis of the musical *Cabaret*. Two of Isherwood's Berlin stories were adapted by John Van Druten for his prize-winning play *I Am a Camera* (1951).

B. Expansion

Auden left the States to live in England the last year of his life. Ironically, he had lived in New York City for years without experiencing any of the violence typically attributed to that city; when he returned to what he hoped would be a peaceful life at Oxford, his rooms were vandalized.

A

W. H. Auden, Christopher Isherwood, and Stephen Spender.

" **When Auden became an American citizen, it was the opinion of at least one critic that British poetry was 'up the creek,' but not 'without a paddle.' The paddle that he thought might rescue British poetry was Dylan Thomas.''**

jack-of-all-trades, poetically speaking, Auden was master of each. At first his gift seemed to be a young man's show-off virtuosity; it eventually led to the creation of an unmistakable personal signature that could be recognized at a glance, whether it was attached to a throwaway piece of topical doggerel or to a religious ode.

Dylan Thomas and the New Apocalypse

B When Auden became an American citizen and established residence in New York City, it was the opinion of at least one critic that British poetry was "up the creek," but not "without a paddle." The paddle that he thought might rescue British poetry was Dylan Thomas. This young man from Wales, whose poetic debut was heralded with as much enthusiasm in the United States as in Great Britain, effectively ended one phase of poetic history and set the stage for another.

Never a part of any group, Thomas established his own poetic goals as a very young man. On the evidence of the remarkable notebooks he left behind, he pursued these goals throughout the brief course of his adult life. Yet, in the minds of critics who are more comfortable with poetry when it comes as the product of a "school" or a movement than from an individual of genius, Thomas was associated with certain poets more or less his own age. As time would tell, these other writers were more gifted as theorists than as practitioners.

Ambitious and bold, they called themselves "the New Apocalypse" and quickly found ways to advance their ideas in periodicals and anthologies. In their opinion, it was time to halt the tendency of British poets to be concerned with politics and psychology—a concern that had turned poetry into a form of intellectual debate. They wanted a return to poetry as incandescent language—the language of the great English Romantics. They wanted to render individual experience in sacramental imagery—such as that found in the Psalms and in the high rhetoric of the King James Bible, in the visionary world of William Blake, and in the compacted word-play and religious wit of Gerard Manley Hopkins. The young poets also admired the dream imagery of the subconscious which had been dredged up and used by the spectacular new painters who called themselves Surrealists.

These poets of the New Apocalypse believed that a new wave of Romanticism was about to break, bringing with it a heightening of verbal music and a delight in language for its own sake. They believed that this kind of poetry had been curbed by other kinds of poetry that emulated public speech and demanded clarity, logic, and a message. True to the name they chose, they saw themselves as apocalyptic: They regarded poems not as arguments or conclusions but as revelations, not as commentaries upon experience but, literally, as re-creations of experience still in the process of becoming intelligible.

The poets of the New Apocalypse got their message across, but they did not have the talent to give it the substance which a

READING CHECK TEST

1. The __Trench__ Poets expressed the horrors of war in traditional metrical forms.
2. Auden, Spender, Day Lewis, and MacNeice were called the __English__ Poets.
3. The poets of the 1930's were at- tracted by the economic theories of __Marx or Communism__.
4. __Auden__ was the most innovative of the poets of the 1930's.
5. __American__ poetry of the 1920's was more experimental than British poetry.

significant body of poetry would provide. As they faded from the scene, Dylan Thomas alone was left to carry their ideas to fruition. His famous career brought a new dimension to British poetry, reminding readers that poetry could be both as sensually exciting as music and as philosophically profound as Greek tragedy.

The Contemporary Scene

Soon after the tragic death of Dylan Thomas at the age of thirty-nine, it again became clear that poetry renews itself in brief cycles. The British poets who began publishing under Thomas's wide shadow were so different from him that they constituted an entirely new order of temperament and taste. Rejecting Thomas's linguistic inventions and intricate, formal structures, they retreated into the simple measures, mild wit, and sentiment characteristic of the Georgian poets early in the century. Nevertheless, out of this conservative and technically unadventurous phase of British poetry, two exceptional poetic personalities arose. Each in his own way showed that individual talent can make a mark and still have nothing to do with groups or movements. Each poet also rejected the nineteenth-century belief that—like sermons or editorials—poetry should be morally uplifting, or, at least, addressed to public issues of the moment.

These two poets were Philip Larkin and Ted Hughes, who is now Poet Laureate of England.

Today, British poetry is closer to its twentieth-century beginnings than it has been for many years. British poetry, as we said, was never modern in the energetically experimental ways that produced the extraordinary succession of American poets that includes Ezra Pound, T. S. Eliot, Hart Crane, Wallace Stevens, William Carlos Williams, Robert Lowell, and James Merrill. Instead, British poetry moved from the pretty parochialism of the end-of-century Georgians into a momentary brush with Imagists, then into the several groups of the 1930's through the 1950's. These groups seem, at this point in history, to have been more a matter of convenience than of conviction.

Now that the age of poetic schools, movements, and other kinds of labeled association seems to have run its course, certain poets who followed no program but their own have begun to shine more brightly than ever. Chief among these are Thomas Hardy and D. H. Lawrence, who share renewed luster with Robert Graves and John Betjeman. As it comes full circle, British poetry may have surrendered some of its vitality, but none of its character. The individual voice is still the one to listen for, and the measure of poets is still the degree to which they make our common language sound like their own.

A

With Riding on a Cloud by David Hockney (1960).

Christie's, London.

A. Humanities Connection: Discussing the Fine Art
David Hockney was born in Bradford, Yorkshire, in 1937. He studied at the Bradford School of Art and at the Royal College. He became famous as a painter and etcher in the early sixties even before he left the Royal College. He is known for his use of popular imagery, such as swimming pools, for satirical purposes and is noted for his elegant draughtmanship. He has also produced fine book illustrations, including those for an edition of Grimms' *Fairy Tales.*

? Ask students to find as many images or objects as they can in this work and to suggest why they might have been included. Have them consider also how the painting comments on or reflects the contemporary world.

PREPARATION

1. BUILDING ON PRIOR KNOWLEDGE. Ask students to recall any other anti-war literature or films they may know. Tell them that this poem is a lament for the soldiers who died in the battlefields of World War I. It is also an implicit protest against the war that caused their untimely deaths.

2. ESTABLISHING A PURPOSE. Ask students to sense the mood of the poem by listening to its rhythm and noting the poet's choice of words.

Wilfred Owen
(1893–1918)

Wilfred Owen is one of the most poignant figures in modern literature. "The poetry is in the pity," he said, and this famous remark could serve as his epitaph. Within the few adult years granted to him, Owen pursued a course of development that went from strength to strength. His interest in experimental techniques led him to master the use of half rhyme; this would become his most easily recognizable poetic signature. He also had a gift for lyricism that was bitterly tempered by "the truth untold, / The pity of war, the pity war distilled." The result was a series of elegies and metrical statements as terse and stark as those carved on tombstones.

Like an apprentice determined to master his art, Owen had immersed himself in the long history of English poetry. He had chosen for his model and mentor the poet John Keats, whose astonishing life's work had ended with his death at twenty-six (the same age Shakespeare had reached when he published his first play). As a tutor in France for two years, Owen had studied the French poets who, along with French painters, were producing the tradition-shattering art that would become known as Modernist. But all these literary influences were to become secondary to the devastating impact of a war Owen witnessed firsthand.

World War I broke out when Owen turned twenty-one; he joined the British army and the course of his life was determined. His progress in poetry was not made in the arcades of an ancient university or in the pastoral retreats where his poetic predecessors were privileged to pursue their careers. His progress took place in the muddy purgatory of trench warfare and in the twilight existence of military hospitals.

In one of those hospitals, Craig-lockart, not far from Edinburgh, Owen met the young Siegfried Sassoon, a fellow officer and poet who had already distinguished himself for bravery in battle. Ironically, Sassoon was also the author of some of the most biting antiwar verses ever written. Temperamentally, the two men were far apart. Owen was an idealistic youth thwarted by circumstance; Sassoon was an aristocrat appalled by the wartime complacency of his own class. Even so, they became friends at once, and the relationship continued beyond Owen's death. Sassoon became the first important British writer to herald the younger man's genius and to call attention to what he had accomplished under the most appalling conditions. By that time, events had told the sad story.

In 1918, Owen was listed among those killed in action—a mere seven days before the war ended with a joyous ringing of bells and dancing in the streets.

1. **BUILDING ON PRIOR KNOWLEDGE.** Ask students to think of patriotic songs, poems, or speeches they have heard, particularly those connected with fighting for one's country. Perhaps they have heard veterans make speeches on Memorial Day or remember the sentiments expressed at military funerals. These conventional expressions of the honor and glory of dying for one's country are what this poem rejects.

2. **ESTABLISHING A PURPOSE.** Since the poem is full of strong visual images, ask the students to try to form a mental picture of what the poet is describing in each stanza.

SUPPLEMENTARY SUPPORT MATERIALS
1. Vocabulary Activity Worksheet (*CCB*)
2. Review and Response Worksheet: Figures of Speech and Tone (*CCB*)
3. Selection Test (*CCB*)

The title is from the first words of a poem by the Latin poet Horace ("It is sweet and honorable to die for one's country"). The statement has been used as a morale builder, and as an epitaph, for centuries. Here the motto is given a bitter twist by a soldier-poet who cannot reconcile the thought it expresses with the reality he has experienced. Under the weight of firsthand evidence, the saying loses its consoling and comforting sentiment. After poison gas as a battlefield weapon was used for the first time in World War I, every man in the trenches was equipped with a gas mask. This poem includes a comment on the horrible consequences of not getting the mask on in time.

Dulce et Decorum Est

A
Bent double, like old beggars under sacks,
Knock-kneed, coughing like hags, we cursed through sludge,
Till on the haunting flares we turned our backs
And toward our distant rest began to trudge.
5   Men marched asleep. Many had lost their boots,
B
But limped on, blood-shod. All went lame, all blind;
Drunk with fatigue; deaf even to the hoots
Of tired, outstripped Five-Nines° that dropped behind.

Gas! GAS! Quick, boys!—An ecstasy of fumbling,
10   Fitting the clumsy helmets just in time;
C
But someone still was yelling out and stumbling
And flound'ring like a man in fire or lime . . .
Dim, through the misty panes and thick green light,
As under a green sea, I saw him drowning.

15   In all my dreams, before my helpless sight,
He plunges at me, guttering, choking, drowning.

If in some smothering dreams, you too could pace
Behind the wagon that we flung him in,
And watch the white eyes writhing in his face,
20   His hanging face, like a devil's sick of sin;
If you could hear, at every jolt, the blood
Come gargling from the froth-corrupted lungs
Obscene as cancer, bitter as the cud
Of vile, incurable sores on innocent tongues,—
25   My friend, you would not tell with such high zest
D
To children <u>ardent</u> for some desperate glory,
The old Lie: *Dulce et decorum est*
Pro patria mori.

8. **Five-Nines:** gas shells.

A. Figurative Language
In the first two lines, find two similes that Owen uses to describe the weary men. ("Bent double, like old beggars under sacks"; "coughing like hags")

B. Rhyme Scheme
Note the regular rhyme scheme of *ababcdcd* throughout the poem.

C. Imagery
In the second stanza, one man does not get his gas mask on in time. What image does Owen use to describe the dying man? (Drowning in a green sea)

D. Connotations
Who are the "children" the poet is talking about in line 26? (The very young and naive who are urged by their elders to go off to war) What are the connotations of the words "ardent" and "desperate"? (They express the impatient, romantic enthusiasm of young people who have little real experience of the world.)

DEVELOPING VOCABULARY
The following word from the poem is tested in the Selection Test. (See also Vocabulary Activity Worksheet.)
ardent

ANALYZING THE POEM
Identifying Details
1. The exhausted men, bent double and coughing, march on, even though many have lost their boots and are lame.
2. The panes of the gas mask that the speaker wears.
3. A nightmare, in which he sees one of his fellow soldiers choking on gas.
4. A "friend," probably the reader.

5. The rhyme scheme is *ababcdcde-fefghghijijklklmnmn*. Half rhymes include "in" (line 18) and "sin" (line 20), and "glory" (line 26) and "mori" (line 28).

Interpreting Meanings
6. It compares the tainted blood that pours from the gassed soldier to a cud chewed by a cow; this cud, in turn, is *(Continued in left-hand column.)*

(Continued from top.)
chewed with a cancerous, sore-ridden tongue. The figure of speech reinforces the theme: War and its destruction are a vile disease of humanity.
7. Student answers will vary. Urge the students to support their reactions.
8. Most will agree that the poem could apply to the conditions of modern war, although some may suggest that current technology creates a more impersonal and mechanized war. Many will describe the tone as tormented and angry, or as brutally realistic. Opinions will vary on analogues.

A. Rupert Brooke
Rupert Brooke (1887–1915) wrote "pretty" romantic verses celebrating youth, idealism, and England; if he had lived longer, he might have become a different kind of poet. Some might prefer Brooke's romanticism to Owen's irony, and they are entitled to their opinions, though further reading of poetry might reveal Brooke's limitations.

Responding to the Poem

Analyzing the Poem

Identifying Details
1. Describe the condition and actions of the men in the first stanza.
2. What are "the misty panes" in line 13 through which the speaker glimpses the dying man?
3. What experience does the speaker refer to in lines 15–16?
4. Who is addressed in the final stanza?
5. Analyze the **rhyme scheme** of the poem. Can you find any **half rhymes?**

Interpreting Meanings
6. Explain the **figure of speech** in lines 23–24. How is this **metaphor** relevant to the **theme** of the poem?
7. This poem uncompromisingly contrasts the high-minded ideals of patriotism with the reality of war. What is your personal reaction to this contrast?

8. Could this poem describe the conditions of any modern war? How would you describe the speaker's **tone?** Is it a tone that you sense in war stories today or even in war movies?

Writing About the Poem

A Critical Response
1. **Writing an Essay.** In the next-to-last line, Owen refers to the famous Latin saying as "the old Lie." The phrase from Horace's *Odes* says that "it is sweet and honorable to die for one's country." Do you think this is a lie? Is Owen perhaps stacking the deck by including so many gruesome battle details? Or do you think the poem presents a valid—though perhaps insoluble—conflict? In a brief essay, explain how you would relate this poem to your own concept of patriotism.
2. **Comparing and Contrasting Poems.** In an essay, point out the similarities and the differences between Owen's poem and the following poem by Rupert Brooke, who also served in World War I. (Brooke did not experience trench warfare; he died of blood poisoning en route to Europe.) In your essay, consider these elements of the poems:

   a. Imagery
   b. Theme and sentiments about war
   c. Tone
   d. Sounds
   e. Figurative language

A

The Soldier

If I should die, think only this of me;
  That there's some corner of a foreign field
That is forever England. There shall be
  In that rich earth a richer dust concealed;
A dust whom England bore, shaped, made aware,
  Gave, once, her flowers to love, her ways to roam,
A body of England's breathing English air,
  Washed by the rivers, blest by suns of home.

And think, this heart, all evil shed away,
  A pulse in the eternal mind, no less
    Gives somewhere back the thoughts by England given;
Her sights and sounds; dreams happy as her day;
  And laughter, learnt of friends; and gentleness,
    In hearts at peace, under an English heaven.
                              —Rupert Brooke

SUPPLEMENTARY SUPPORT MATERIALS
1. Vocabulary Activity Worksheet (*CCB*)
2. Review and Response Worksheet: Elements of Style (*CCB*)
3. Selection Test (*CCB*)

DEVELOPING VOCABULARY
The following word from the poem is tested in the Selection Test. (See also Vocabulary Activity Worksheet.)
livid

PREPARATION
1. BUILDING ON PRIOR KNOWLEDGE. Ask students to recall any war movies they may have seen, particularly any that depicted trench warfare. Possibilities include the movie *All Quiet on the Western Front,* based on the 1929 German anti-war novel by Erich Maria Remarque, and Stanley Kubrick's film *Paths of Glory* (1957). (Tell them that this poem is another graphic description of the hellish conditions in the trenches of France in World War I.)

2. ESTABLISHING A PURPOSE. Tell students that the poem recounts a single, very brief incident inside a trench. What occurs is so vividly described that two students might prepare to mime the action while another reads the poem aloud to the class.

Siegfried Sassoon (1886–1967)

Siegfried Sassoon was born into that high level of English society in which lifelong privilege is sustained by the income from landed estates and assured inheritances. Educated at Cambridge University, and under no pressure to adopt a profession, he lived the life of a country gentleman until the outbreak of the war. Along with the pursuit of leisure—which he would later write about in a famous book called *Memoirs of a Fox-Hunting Man* (1928), Sassoon also wrote poetry. He had sufficient skill to win a place in the anthologies of the Georgian movement, in which the value of all things English was celebrated—from scones and honey at tea-time to the bells of Winchester Cathedral.

The war would change all that. For Sassoon, it would also lead to a career entirely at odds with his earlier expectations. Enlisting in the army as a patriot and an idealist determined to put an end to "Teutonic barbarism," he distinguished himself as an officer and was awarded a prestigious medal for bravery under fire. But, within two years of his enlistment, Sassoon's attitude toward the war underwent a change amounting to a total reversal of his earlier commitment. His new attitude was expressed in stark, almost savage poems detailing the brutality and debasement of trench warfare. The publication of these bitter testaments sent a shock wave of doubt across the minds of the English (among them, Winston Churchill, then Minister of Munitions, whose secretary, Edward Marsh, was the leader of the comforting Georgian poets and their most outspoken publicist).

Dissatisfied even with the depth of response his poems evoked, Sassoon was determined to go even further to advertise his conviction that the war was "being deliberately prolonged by those who have the power to end it." In a statement handed to his commanding officer, which Sassoon himself regarded as "an act of willful defiance," he spelled out his disillusion: "I believe that this war, upon which I entered as a war of defense and liberation, has now become a war of aggression and conquest."

Expecting court-martial, and entirely prepared to sacrifice himself for his own cause, Sassoon was thwarted by the unsolicited and unwanted kindness of some of his friends, notably the poet Robert Graves, who shunted him toward a medical board of examiners. Diagnosed as shell-shocked, Sassoon was committed to a military hospital in Scotland. There he met a fellow-patient, Wilfred Owen, and the two began one of the most famous and mutually beneficial relationships in modern literature.

Disgust controlled by irony gives Sassoon's war poems their indelible imprint; the poems stand by themselves in an otherwise pedestrian career marked by one great parenthesis—the Great War itself.

1. In line 11, he says that he is looking for headquarters. The tunnel is fifty feet below ground.
2. The man tugs at his arm because he wants the sleeper to guide him through the tunnel.
3. He discovers that the sleeper is dead.
4. Horror-stricken, the man climbs up through the darkness to the twilight on the battlefield.
5. Examples include "winked" (line 2), "smashed" (line 5), "tripping" (line 8), "humped" (line 9), "tug" (line 10), "staggered" (line 19), "muttering" (line 21), "boom" (line 22), "muffled" (line 22).

Interpreting Meanings

6. The air is unwholesome because the tunnel contains the bodies of dead soldiers.
7. His behavior is brutal because he curses and kicks the sleeper. His behavior is pathetic because of his evident horror at finding that the sleeper is dead and at being lost in the tunnel.
8. These words establish a vivid sense of immediacy and hint at the officer's desperation and powerlessness.

A. Humanities Connection: Discussing the Fine Art
British sculptor and draftsman Henry Moore (1898–1986) found early inspiration in African, Etruscan, and Sumerian sculpture. In 1940 he was commissioned to do a series of drawings of the people who gathered in subway tunnels during the nightly German bombings. In this picture he emphasizes the smooth shapes of the figures under blankets and speckles the surface with a rock-like texture.

? What does the style suggest about these figures? (Some will feel it reflects very deep sleep.) How do the sleepers relate to the narrator's experience in the poem? (They resemble the dead man in the tunnel.) What similarities and differences do you find in the poem and drawing? (The dark, enclosed space and the apparently lifeless bodies; the child and woman and the fact that these people are alive.)

The "he" in this poem is the officer-poet, Siegfried Sassoon himself, recalling in grim detail an episode in the trenches of World War I. On its battlefields, enlisted men lived for weeks, sometimes years, in interconnected underground caverns infested by rats, with no drainage, poor ventilation, and no more than occasional dim shafts of natural light.

The Rear-Guard

A

Sleeping Shelterers by Henry Moore (1941). Water color and chalk.   Fitzwilliam Museum, Cambridge, England.

9. The officer is asking a dead man to be his guide.
10. Perhaps the speaker means that, by ascending to the surface of the earth out of the dark tunnel, he is escaping from an inferno.

CLOSURE

In military terms the rear guard is the detachment that protects the main army from attack from the rear. The term is also used to suggest resistance or reaction to sweeping change or innovation. Ask students why they think Sassoon chose this title. Was he being ironic?

Groping along the tunnel, step by step,
He winked his prying torch° with patching glare
From side to side, and sniffed the unwholesome air.

Tins,° boxes, bottles, shapes too vague to know,
5   A mirror smashed, the mattress from a bed;
And he, exploring fifty feet below
The rosy gloom of battle overhead.
Tripping, he grabbed the wall; saw someone lie
Humped at his feet, half-hidden by a rug,
10 And stooped to give the sleeper's arm a tug.
"I'm looking for headquarters." No reply.
"God blast your neck!" (For days he'd had no sleep.)
"Get up and guide me through this stinking place."
Savage, he kicked a soft, unanswering heap,
15 And flashed his beam across the livid face
Terribly glaring up, whose eyes yet wore
Agony dying hard ten days before;
And fists of fingers clutched a blackening wound.
Alone he staggered on until he found
20 Dawn's ghost that filtered down a shafted stair
To the dazed, muttering creatures underground
Who hear the boom of shells in muffled sound.
At last, with sweat of horror in his hair,
He climbed through darkness to the twilight air,
25 Unloading hell behind him step by step.

A
B
C
D

2. **torch:** flashlight.

4. **Tins:** cans.

A. Setting
? Describe conditions in the trench as they are presented in the first eight lines. (Dark, malodorous, cluttered)

B. Interpreting Meanings
? Why do you think the officer speaks as he does to the reclining figure? (He is exhausted, uncomfortable, scared, and accustomed to giving orders.)

C. Imagery
Livid means "ashen, pale, or pallid."
? What other words or images are used to describe the dead man's body? ("Unanswering heap," "eyes yet wore agony," "fists of fingers clutched a blackening wound")

D. Irony
? What emotion does the officer experience when he climbs out of the trench? (Relief) How is this ironic? (One would expect him to be unhappy to be exposed to enemy gunfire.)

Responding to the Poem

Analyzing the Poem

Identifying Details

1. What is the man looking for in the tunnel? How deep is it?
2. Why does the man tug at the sleeper's arm in line 10?
3. What does the man discover about the sleeper?
4. What does the man do in the final three lines?
5. What words in the poem use **onomatopoeia** to help you hear the sounds in the tunnel?

Interpreting Meanings

6. Why is the air "unwholesome"?
7. How is the officer's behavior simultaneously brutal and pathetic?

8. Look at the present and past participles in the poem—words such as *groping, prying, smashed,* and *tripping.* What effect do these words have on the poem?
9. Explain the **irony** of the quotation in line 13.
10. What does the speaker mean by saying he is "unloading hell"?

Writing About the Poem

A Critical Response

Comparing Two Poems. In an essay, compare the imagery, structure, and sound devices of Wilfred Owen's "Dulce et Decorum Est" with those of "The Rear-Guard."

1. BUILDING ON PRIOR KNOWLEDGE. Ask students if they have seen or heard of the Broadway (originally British) musical *Cats*. Explain that *Cats* was inspired by Eliot's poetry collection *Old Possum's Book of Practical Cats*. Its best-known song, "Memory," contains lines from "Preludes," which follows.

2. ESTABLISHING A PURPOSE. Before students read, ask them what qualities they think make a writer's work enduring rather than merely popular. Have them discuss their responses in class. Then, as they read the two Eliot poems presented here, have them look for poetic ideas that suggest Eliot's influence in the development of modern literature.

FOR FURTHER READING
Students and Teachers
Students should enjoy the humorous poems in *Old Possum's Book of Practical Cats*. Advanced students could read "The Journey of the Magi." After reading and discussing "Preludes" and "The Hollow Men," you may wish to read and discuss "The Waste Land," as well.

A. Connections
Other influential American expatriate writers included Ezra Pound, Ernest Hemingway, F. Scott Fitzgerald, Archibald MacLeish, Sinclair Lewis, and Gertrude Stein. Stein coined the phrase "lost generation" to describe these exiles.

B. Style
The American "Confessional Poets," including Robert Lowell, Sylvia Plath, and Anne Sexton, rejected Eliot's view that poetry should be impersonal.
? Do you think poetry should be primarily a personal or an impersonal expression? (Answers will vary; many students may feel that personal poetry is more meaningful.)

THE INFLUENCE OF T. S. ELIOT
by John Malcolm Brinnin

Unlike poets whose long, outstanding careers eventually turn them into cultural monuments, T. S. Eliot was a monument who later turned into a man. Internationally famous at an early age, he was the product of an aristocratic New England family. The Eliots valued privacy and regarded self-exploitation and public exposure—even fame itself—as a form of vulgarity. Consequently, millions of readers knew T. S. Eliot less as a real personality than as a presence. Eliot was remote, <u>aus</u><u>tere</u>, and self-possessed, a man whose sparse output was nevertheless the most celebrated and influential poetry written in English over a span of three decades.

A

T. S. Eliot was born in St. Louis, Missouri, in 1888, where his father was Chancellor of George Washington University. In spite of this geographical displacement, the Eliots remained New Englanders. They could trace their ancestry back to the first Puritan settlements in the New World. Young Tom Eliot was educated at Harvard College, after which he did graduate studies at the Sorbonne in Paris. Like many other young American writers of his generation, he found life abroad so stimulating that he decided not to return home. Settling in London before World War I, he worked in a bank, married an Englishwoman, and became an editor and a publisher. He made his <u>expatriation</u> complete by becoming a British citizen in 1927. In 1949 he was awarded the Nobel Prize. Not long before his death in 1965, on one of his several visits to the United States, so many people wanted to see and hear Eliot read his poetry that a football stadium had to be taken over to hold the audience.

Eliot had a vast influence as a poet. His techniques, along with those of his friend and fellow American, Ezra Pound, became the hallmarks of "modern poetry." For over thirty years, in classrooms and in critical studies, his was *the* voice that expressed the dislocation and despair of the twentieth century. Eliot's world-weariness, his grave, restrained, and impersonal <u>cadences</u>, so much like the voices he heard in New England pulpits, were widely imitated and instantly recognized. Eliot dominated English literature in a way not seen since the days of Dr. Johnson.

Eliot's critical studies were also far-reaching. He argued against the commonly held view that poets were romantics who had superior powers of observation and expression. Eliot, on the other hand, regarded poets as craftsmen who used traditional literary materials not for personal revelations but for the creation of better-made poems. The poet, according to these theories, was like those anonymous master artisans who made individual contributions to the great medieval cathedrals but who remained personally unknown. Like these humble artisans, the poet is just part of the background. What is important is the poem (or the cathedral), not the worker who made it. This point of view deplored the notion that a search through the poet's life would give clues to the meaning of the work. The work, all important, stood apart from its creator. Submitting to Eliot's instruction, poets, students, and critics for generations studied a poem not for its messages or meaning, but for its method and structure—for its architecture.

B

In 1950, when I was director of New York's Poetry Center, Eliot made a visit to the United States. I recalled the event in a book called *Sextet*:

This late in his life (he was sixty-one) Eliot had given less than a handful of readings in the United States and had read only once before in New York. The response to our announcement of the event suggested that many people thought his reading at the Poetry Center might well be his last. On the morning after we had named his date in The New York *Times*, fifteen or twenty requests were made for every seat available. Pursued and badgered to use my influence to produce tickets, I found that people who'd never read a sonnet since the seventh grade were suddenly lovers of poetry whose devotion I was implored not to dismiss.

SUPPLEMENTARY SUPPORT MATERIALS
1. Vocabulary Activity Worksheet (*CCB*)
2. Review and Response Worksheets: Imagery and Mood; Symbol and Theme (*CCB*)
3. Language Skills Worksheet: Subordinate Clauses (*CCB*)
4. Selection Test (*CCB*)

DEVELOPING VOCABULARY
The following words from the essay are tested in the Selection Test. (See also Vocabulary Activity Worksheet.)
aristocratic   displacement
self-exploitation expatriation
vulgarity   dislocation
austere   cadences

In music, *preludes* are brief works, usually free in form, that introduce larger and more formal compositions. When Eliot chose a musical title, he no doubt meant to suggest that these short poems introduced the mood and method of longer works written in the same period.

The images in *Preludes* are all drawn from city life. Horse-drawn carriages had not yet been replaced by automobiles, nor gas lamps by electricity, but nevertheless the dehumanizing aspects of a growing metropolis like Eliot's Boston were already sadly in evidence. Eliot saw multitudes of workers every day moving to and fro like debris washed in and out by the tides. He saw massive slums that blocked out forever the gentle rural landscapes of a pre-industrial age.

Preludes are the observations of a wanderer through city streets. The speaker attempts to come to some conclusion about the meaning of the life he sees around him, but he finally gives up. But in the process, he gives us "a vision of the street," for which he feels compassion but which, finally, he considers beyond redemption. Eliot wrote these poems when he was in his twenties.

How many images suggest life as a wasteland? How do these descriptions of city life relate to urban landscapes today? (Note, steaks in line 2 were cheap cuts of meat.)

Preludes

I

The winter evening settles down
With smell of steaks in passageways.
Six o'clock.
A The burnt-out ends of smoky days.
5 And now a gusty shower wraps
The grimy scraps
Of withered leaves about your feet
And newspapers from vacant lots;
The showers beat
10 On broken blinds and chimney-pots,
And at the corner of the street
A lonely cab-horse steams and stamps.
And then the lighting of the lamps.

II

The morning comes to consciousness
15 Of faint stale smells of beer
From the sawdust-trampled street
With all its muddy feet that press
To early coffee-stands.
With the other masquerades
20 That time resumes,
One thinks of all the hands
That are raising dingy shades
In a thousand furnished rooms.

III

You tossed a blanket from the bed,
25 You lay upon your back, and waited;
You dozed, and watched the night revealing
B The thousand sordid images
Of which your soul was constituted;

They flickered against the ceiling.
30 And when all the world came back
And the light crept up between the shutters
And you heard the sparrows in the gutters,
You had such a vision of the street
As the street hardly understands;
C 35 Sitting along the bed's edge, where
You curled the papers from your hair,
Or clasped the yellow soles of feet
In the palms of both soiled hands.

IV

His soul stretched tight across the skies
40 That fade behind a city block,
Or trampled by insistent feet
At four and five and six o'clock;
And short square fingers stuffing pipes,
And evening newspapers, and eyes
45 Assured of certain certainties,
The conscience of a blackened street
Impatient to assume the world.

I am moved by fancies that are curled
Around these images, and cling:
50 The notion of some infinitely gentle
Infinitely suffering thing.

D Wipe your hand across your mouth, and laugh;
The worlds revolve like ancient women
Gathering fuel in vacant lots.

A. Implied Metaphor/Tone
❓ To what are the days being compared, and how does this first comparison set the tone for the poem? (An initial comparison to cigarette butts sets a tone of bleakness; it suggests that things—and perhaps people—have been used up.)

B. Connotation
Sordid is just one of the poem's many adjectives with negative connotations. Have students identify other such adjectives from earlier in the poem. (*Burnt-out, grimy, withered, vacant, broken, lonely, faint, stale, sawdust-trampled, muddy,* and *dingy*—almost all the adjectives have negative connotations.)

C. Interpreting
❓ Who do these details suggest the *you* might be? (A woman who has disappointed the speaker, perhaps in love)

D. Contrast
❓ How is the final stanza related to the two lines that precede it? (They express a hope for humanity—a hope that the final stanza refutes.)

A. Epigraph

The sources for the epigram are cited in the headnote, but notice how different they are. What does juxtaposing the quotation from *Heart of Darkness* and a children's chant suggest about the importance of "Mistah Kurtz"? (He is a trivial and perhaps pathetic figure rather than a tragic one.)

B. Speaker

Who is the speaker in this poem, the "we"? (Modern people aware of the emptiness of their lives)

C. Allusion

Explain that these lines allude to *The Divine Comedy*, the epic religious allegory by the great Italian poet Dante. Those who have crossed to "death's other Kingdom" have gone to Paradise; the hollow men have not.

D. Repetition

Notice the repetition of "hollow men" and "stuffed men." How would you describe its effect? (It emphasizes despair—a lack of meaning and purpose.)

There are many references to religion in this poem. You may, for instance, recognize a line from The Lord's Prayer on sight (see lines 77 and 91–94). But Eliot's main concern here is not to affirm his Christianity, but to give us a picture of a world of godless despair, a world without religion or the promise of salvation.

Taken from Joseph Conrad's famous story *The Heart of Darkness*, the first line placed under the title is significant in two ways. First, it calls attention to the story of a man named Kurtz, who journeys to the heart of Africa and falls into degradation. Kurtz is redeemed by self-awareness, only to find that this painful knowledge is not liberating but useless. Second, the line strikes the note of futility heard throughout the poem.

The next line—"A penny for the Old Guy"—refers to one of the most notorious incidents in British history, the Gunpowder Plot. On November 5, 1605, a band of conspirators made plans to kill King James I by planting barrels of gunpowder in the underground vaults of Parliament. The man chosen to light the fuse that would result in a fatal explosion was a soldier named Guy Fawkes. But before the plot could be carried out, the conspirators were discovered. Guy Fawkes was arrested and, in the cruel custom of the day, first hanged, then drawn and quartered.

To commemorate this grisly event, every year, on November 5, huge bonfires are set all over England. When these fires are lit, straw-filled effigies of Fawkes—"the stuffed men" of the poem—that look like scarecrows go up in flames, lighting up the skies. Children join in the fun by becoming beggars who ask passersby to give them "a penny for the guy."

The last two lines of this poem are among the most famous in modern poetry. What is the difference between ending with a "bang," and ending with only a "whimper"?

The Hollow Men

A

Mistah Kurtz—he dead.
—A penny for the Old Guy

I

We are the hollow men
We are the stuffed men
Leaning together
Headpiece filled with straw. Alas!
5 Our dried voices, when
B We whisper together
Are quiet and meaningless
As wind in dry grass
Or rats' feet over broken glass
10 In our dry cellar

   Shape without form, shade without color,
Paralyzed force, gesture without motion;

C Those who have crossed
With direct eyes, to death's other Kingdom

15 Remember us—if at all—not as lost
D Violent souls, but only
As the hollow men
The stuffed men.

II

Eyes I dare not meet in dreams
20 In death's dream kingdom
These do not appear:
There, the eyes are
Sunlight on a broken column
There, is a tree swinging
25 And voices are
In the wind's singing
More distant and more solemn
Than a fading star.

30 Let me be no nearer
In death's dream kingdom
Let me also wear
Such deliberate disguises
Rat's coat, crowskin, crossed staves
In a field
35 Behaving as the wind behaves
No nearer—

Not that final meeting
In the twilight kingdom

III

40 This is the dead land
This is cactus land
A Here the stone images
Are raised, here they receive
The supplication of a dead man's hand
Under the twinkle of a fading star.

45 Is it like this
In death's other kingdom
Waking alone
At the hour when we are
Trembling with tenderness
50 Lips that would kiss
B Form prayers to broken stone.

IV

The eyes are not here
There are no eyes here
In this valley of dying stars
55 In this hollow valley
This broken jaw of our lost kingdoms

In this last of meeting places
We grope together
And avoid speech
60 Gathered on this beach of the tumid river

Sightless, unless
The eyes reappear
As the perpetual star
Multifoliate rose
65 Of death's twilight kingdom

The hope only
Of empty men.

V

C
Here we go round the prickly pear
Prickly pear prickly pear
70 *Here we go round the prickly pear*
At five o'clock in the morning.

Between the idea
And the reality
Between the motion
75 And the act
Falls the Shadow

For Thine is the Kingdom

Between the conception
And the creation
80 Between the emotion
And the response
Falls the Shadow

Life is very long

Between the desire
85 And the spasm
Between the potency
And the existence
Between the essence
And the descent
90 Falls the Shadow

For Thine is the Kingdom

D
For Thine is
Life is
For Thine is the

95 *This is the way the world ends*
This is the way the world ends
This is the way the world ends
Not with a bang but a whimper.

A. Rhythm
Although the poem employs free verse, it lacks a strong rhythm. Show how using stressed first syllables (here and elsewhere) creates a plodding, dirge-like rhythm.

B. Interpreting
What does this image suggest that the hollow men are incapable of feeling? (Love)

C. Allusion
If you ever sang this verse, you may be surprised to find "mulberry bush" replaced by "prickly pear." Why would Eliot change it? (A prickly pear is more in keeping with the poem's barren view.)

D. Interpreting
Look at the use of the word *kingdom.* Why do you think the hollow men cannot say "Kingdom" to complete line 94? (Perhaps they feel so isolated from the Kingdom—the "other kingdom," the "dream kingdom," the "twilight kingdom," the "lost kingdom," "[God's] Kingdom"—that they feel they cannot even pray for it or have forgotten how to pray.)

William Butler Yeats (1865–1939)

William Butler Yeats is generally regarded as the century's greatest poet writing in English. Yeats was an Irishman who—along with his compatriots playwright George Bernard Shaw and novelist James Joyce—gave his small, poor, and oppressed native land a proud place in world literature. Yeats was an artist who never doubted his vocation or underrated the discipline needed to fulfill his ambitions.

Yeats was born in Dublin, the son of a painter, John Butler Yeats—familiarly known as "Jack"—who viewed himself and his own professional career less solemnly than his son was to view his. In what amounted to a reversal of conventional father-son roles, Jack Yeats was a gregarious, easygoing, and slightly disreputable character who became as well known in the barrooms of New York as in the pubs of Dublin; his son, who worshiped at the high altar of art, showed little tolerance for human frailties and indulgences, least of all for self-indulgence.

The younger Yeats came onto the scene when the Pre-Raphaelite movement of the mid-nineteenth century was enjoying a revival under new influences from Europe. In painting and design, this was the phenomenon of Art Nouveau, with its romantic portrayals of women as languid, lily-like beings who looked as though they would be more at home in a glass case than in an ordinary drawing room.

In literature, the revival emphasized the mysterious and unfathomed—especially those recesses of the mind just then being scrutinized by the great pioneers in psychology, Sigmund Freud and Carl Jung. Particularly in poetry, the revival recommended evocation above statement, symbols above facts, musical measures above common speech. It was in this atmosphere that Yeats established a reputation as a lyricist of great delicacy, as well as a versifier of old tales drawn from Irish folklore and mythology.

In *The Celtic Twilight* (1893), his second book of poetry, Yeats was a romantic dreamer, evoking the mythic and heroic past of Ireland. He was determined, at this stage of his career, to make the Irish peasants conscious of their own

heroic past. He came abruptly into a new phase when, in 1914, he listened to the good advice of his American friend, Ezra Pound. Determined to curb his tendency toward dreaminess and prettiness, Yeats set out to create a stark, chiseled, and eloquently resonant kind of poetry. In 1914, Yeats published a volume aptly entitled *Responsibilities*. The man who had once seen himself as the prophet-priest of Ireland's national destiny was now grappling with his own immediate realities. The first of these realities was his loss—to another, more pedestrian suitor—of Maud Gonne, the famous and beautiful Irish political activist whom he had for years idolized and yearned for. The second reality was his marriage, at the age of fifty-two, to Georgina Hyde-Lees ("my wife, George," he called her) who would remain his "delight and comfort" for the next twenty-two years.

With his private life settled, Yeats "went public." He helped his friend Lady Gregory to maintain the nationalistic orientation and high standards of Dublin's landmark Abbey Theatre. From 1922 to 1928, he served as a senator of the Irish Free State; and he toured America giving ritualized readings of the poems for which, in 1923, he was awarded the ultimate accolade of the Nobel Prize for Literature.

As a poet, Yeats may be said to have carved out of the English language a language distinctly his own. Monumentally spare and unadorned, "cold and passionate as the dawn" (in Yeats's own words), it confirms the basic definition of poetry as "heightened speech." At the same time, as some of his younger contemporaries were to learn, Yeats's poetry stubbornly resists emulation or imitation.

Yeats was also a playwright, who dealt in poetic drama, allegories, and other nonrealistic approaches to drama, often making adaptations of the ceremonial choreography of the Japanese Noh theater. While Yeats's dramas are more properly regarded as theater-pieces than as plays, they continue to be produced by small theater groups. Some audiences may agree with Yeats himself that some of his most memorable poems are embedded, like gems, in the working scripts of these dramas.

A philosopher of sorts, in 1925 Yeats produced *A Vision,* a book which details a cyclical theory of history based on the writings of the fourteenth-century Italian, Giambattista Vico. According to many scholars, this book laid the groundwork for the epic poem Yeats did not live to write.

Yeats dramatized himself in the grand manner, which, in his case, was entirely in keeping with his aristocratic pretensions and his unquestioned accomplishments. Nearly ten years after he died in the south of France, his body was disinterred and returned to Ireland, like that of a primitive king, with full ceremony and military pomp, on the deck of a battleship.

1. BUILDING ON PRIOR KNOWLEDGE. Ask students to think of other stories or works of art that feature enchanted islands or remote lands offering escape from the burdens of civilization. They might consider *Robinson Crusoe, Walden, The Tempest,* or the paintings of Gauguin. Tell them that his poem is in the same romantic tradition that finds restoration in nature.

2. ESTABLISHING A PURPOSE. Ask the students to read the poem aloud to hear the music of the verse. If possible, you might also play for them the recording of Yeats himself reading this poem.

A. Interpreting Meaning

? What kind of life does the poet wish to lead on the island? (Simple, solitary, and peaceful)

B. Figurative Language

? What is the implied comparison in lines 5–6? (Peace drops like morning dew.)

C. Theme

In the last lines, the poet says that he hears the sounds of the lake water within him even when he is in the city.

? What does this suggest about his relationship with nature? (It suggests a mystical connection or basic identification that has been artificially severed by civilization.)

SUPPLEMENTARY SUPPORT MATERIALS
1. Vocabulary Activity Worksheet (*CCB*)
2. Review and Response Worksheet: Tone (*CCB*)
3. Selection Test (*CCB*)

DEVELOPING VOCABULARY
The following word from the poem is tested in the Selection Test. (See also Vocabulary Activity Worksheet.)
glade

As a young man, Yeats inherited much of the vocabulary and many of the poetic postures of his nineteenth-century predecessors. Phrases like "veils of the morning" and "midnight's all a glimmer" come from this old-fashioned vocabulary; and Innisfree itself represents all the impossibly idyllic great good places that weary Victorians "on the roadway, or on the pavements gray" yearned for. Nevertheless, Yeats's lyrical skills give the poem a charm and authority that have made his "Lake Isle" a famous symbol of escape from worldly cares.

Innisfree is a real island in Sligo, the beautiful county in the West of Ireland where Yeats spent many summers as a child, visiting his grandparents. Yeats says the poem came to him when he was in London on a dreary day. He passed a store display that used dripping water in a fountain, and he thought at once of the lake island of his childhood.

The Lake Isle of Innisfree

A
I will arise and go now, and go to Innisfree,
And a small cabin build there, of clay and wattles° made:
Nine bean-rows will I have there, a hive for the honey-bee,
And live alone in the bee-loud glade.

B
5 And I shall have some peace there, for peace comes dropping slow,
Dropping from the veils of the morning to where the cricket sings;
There midnight's all a glimmer, and noon a purple glow,
And evening full of the linnet's wings.

C
I will arise and go now, for always night and day
10 I hear lake water lapping with low sounds by the shore;
While I stand on the roadway, or on the pavements gray,
I hear it in the deep heart's core.

2. **wattles:** twigs.

Responding to the Poem

Analyzing the Poem

Identifying Details

1. In the first stanza, what does the speaker say he will do?
2. What sounds does the speaker describe in the poem?
3. How do the surroundings of the lake island contrast with the speaker's actual location?

Interpreting Meanings

4. Why do you think the speaker cannot find peace in the city setting?

5. How would you describe the **tone** of this poem? Do you think it could be called a Romantic poem? Explain why or why not.

Writing About the Poem

A Creative Response

1. Imitating the Writer's Technique. The first line of this poem is often quoted. Write a poem or a paragraph of your own, opening with the words "I will arise and go now." In your poem or paragraph, describe your own ideal place of peace.

Identifying Details
1. The speaker will go to Innisfree, build a small cabin there, and live alone.
2. In line 4, the speaker refers to the sound of the bees in the glade. Line 6 refers to the singing of the cricket. Line 10 mentions the sound of the lake water lapping the shore.
3. The lake island is beautiful, natural,
and tranquil. The speaker's actual location, by contrast, is urban and dreary (line 11).

Interpreting Meanings
4. The speaker is evidently a lover of nature. He finds the city setting grim and dreary.
5. Lyrical, escapist, nostalgic, yearning, quiet. Because the speaker evidently val-
ues the tranquility and beauty of natural surroundings, many students will agree that the poem could be called a Romantic work.

A Critical Response
2. **Comparing Poems.** Write a brief essay comparing "The Lake Isle of Innisfree" with one of these two Romantic poems. Comment on the images used by each poet to describe a place.

  a. "Kubla Khan" by Samuel Taylor Coleridge
  b. "La Belle Dame Sans Merci" by John Keats

Analyzing Language and Style

Assonance and Alliteration
The music of this poem comes in part from Yeats's use of **assonance**—the repetition of similar vowel sounds to
create an effect. The poem is also notable for a famous line of **alliteration**.

1. What vowel sound do you think dominates the first stanza?
2. What vowel sounds are repeated in the rhyming words?
3. In line 10, what repeated consonant sounds echo the sound of lake water?
4. How would you describe the total effect of the vowel sounds in the poem? (How would the poem have been different if the poet had used more hard consonants, like *k, d,* or *p*?)

PREPARATION

1. BUILDING ON PRIOR KNOWLEDGE. Ask students to read the headnote to get the setting of the poem. Ask students if they can recall looking at the same natural scene year after year, such as the blooming of cherry blossoms or the turning of the maple leaves. What thoughts and feelings do repeated experiences of this kind arouse in them?

2. ESTABLISHING A PURPOSE. Ask students to note a shift from present to past and the emotions evoked by each.

DEVELOPING VOCABULARY
The following word from the poem is tested in the Selection Test. (See also Vocabulary Activity Worksheet.)
clamorous

SUPPLEMENTARY SUPPORT MATERIALS
1. Vocabulary Activity Worksheet (*CCB*)
2. Review and Response Worksheet: Symbol and Theme (*CCB*)
3. Selection Test (*CCB*)

A. Interpreting Meaning
❓ What stage of life do you think the speaker of the poem has reached? (Middle age)

B. Mood
❓ What is the dominant emotion expressed in the third stanza? (Regret, disappointment, loss)

C. Figurative Language
In stanza 4, the speaker compares himself with the swans.
❓ What do they seem to have that he lacks? (They are paired in a lasting union that remains exciting and satisfying.)

D. Expansion
Note that the view of the swans in lines 25–29 seems more impersonal and distant. They seem to be approaching the status of works of art to "delight men's eyes."

Yeats's good friend Lady Gregory was a woman of culture and modest literary accomplishment who lived on an estate in County Galway known as Coole Park. When he first visited her there in 1897, he was in love with Maud Gonne, the beautiful activist for Irish independence, who was more interested in her political career than in marriage. This poem, written in 1916, recalls Yeats's first view of the swans; now, nineteen years later, he realizes that "All's changed."

The swans are "wild," or migratory. Like the poet, they return annually to familiar places. Yeats knew that swans are monogamous, that "lover by lover" they continue to live in a state of mated bliss denied to him. But the larger meanings of the poem lie in the relation between human concerns of memory, time, loss, and the inflexible patterns of natural life as represented by the swans.

The Wild Swans at Coole

A
The trees are in their autumn beauty,
The woodland paths are dry,
Under the October twilight the water
Mirrors a still sky;
5 Upon the brimming water among the stones
Are nine-and-fifty swans.

The nineteenth autumn has come upon me
Since I first made my count;
I saw, before I had well finished,
10 All suddenly mount
And scatter wheeling in great broken rings
Upon their clamorous wings.

B
I have looked upon those brilliant creatures,
And now my heart is sore.
15 All's changed since I, hearing at twilight,
The first time on this shore,
The bell-beat of their wings above my head,
Trod with a lighter tread.

C
Unwearied still, lover by lover,
20 They paddle in the cold
Companionable streams or climb the air;
Their hearts have not grown old;
Passion or conquest, wander where they will,
Attend upon them still.

D
25 But now they drift on the still water,
Mysterious, beautiful;
Among what rushes will they build,
By what lake's edge or pool
Delight men's eyes when I awake some day
30 To find they have flown away?

ANALYZING THE POEM
Identifying Details
1. The speaker describes trees by a lake or pond in the autumn. Fifty-nine swans swim in the water. After a while, they rise into the sky. Autumn (end of summer) corresponds with twilight (end of day).
2. He feels melancholy. Line 18 indicates that he then "trod with a lighter tread."

3. The swans are unwearied and their hearts have not grown old. They seem unaffected by time.
4. He wonders where the swans will have gone and where they will have built their nests, when the speaker realizes one day that they will have flown away.

Interpreting Meanings
5. Hints include the image of nineteen autumns, which means he's much older. Line 14 suggests emotional pain. Line 15 suggests that everything in his life is now changed. Line 18 suggests he once walked more lightly. Lines 22–24 suggest his heart has grown old; perhaps he's lost a lover or his ability to love. Unlike him, the swans have lovers, are companionable, and can feel and conquer.

Students may suggest that the speaker rues his advancing age, or possibly has had disappointment in love. In general, the stanzas suggest that the speaker has undergone a sobering, sad experience.
6. He envies their brilliance, their timelessness, their mystery, and their ability to delight men's eyes. Perhaps the swans symbolize beauty and changelessness to the speaker.
7. The word implies that the speaker's life is as fleeting as a dream—thus, the word *awake*, paradoxically, could connote the speaker's death.
8. The theme, which relates to the speaker's contemplation of his own mortality, is indirectly reinforced by the setting of twilight in the autumn, a symbol for old age or decline.

Responding to the Poem

Analyzing the Poem

Identifying Details

1. Describe the scene depicted in the first stanza. How does the time of year correspond to the time of day?
2. How is the speaker feeling as he gazes at the swans? How did he feel nineteen years earlier when he heard the beating of their wings?
3. In what ways have the swans remained unchanged?
4. What question does the speaker ask in the last stanza?

Interpreting Meanings

5. The second, third, and fourth stanzas offer some hints about the speaker's personal experience that underlies the poem. What are these hints? Why do you think the speaker's heart is "sore" (line 14)?
6. What qualities of the swans do you think the speaker envies? Why? What might the swans **symbolize** to the speaker?

7. The word *awake* in the next-to-last line is mysterious at first reading. Do you think it signifies that the poem has all been a dream? Or could it mean something else? How might this word offer a clue to the **theme** of the poem?
8. How are the time of year and the time of day appropriate to the theme of the poem?

Writing About the Poem

A Critical Response

1. **Comparing Poems.** In a brief essay, compare the themes, imagery, and progression of thought in "The Wild Swans at Coole" with those of Keats's "Ode to a Nightingale."
2. **Analyzing a Poem.** In a brief essay, discuss how this poem could be said to be in the elegiac mode. How does it relate in theme and tone and imagery to any of the other famous elegies in this book?

PREPARATION

1. BUILDING ON PRIOR KNOWLEDGE. The headnote below explains the Christian concept of the Second Coming. Some students may be able to relate this concept to messianic elements in their own tradition.

2. ESTABLISHING A PURPOSE. Ask students to think of the speaker of this poem as a modern-day prophet decrying the state of the world.

SUPPLEMENTARY SUPPORT MATERIALS
1. Vocabulary Activity Worksheet (*CCB*)
2. Review and Response Worksheet: Imagery and Theme (*CCB*)
3. Selection Test (*CCB*)

DEVELOPING VOCABULARY
The following word from the poem is tested in the Selection Test. (See also Vocabulary Activity Worksheet.)
anarchy

A. Interpreting Meaning
? Besides the flying falcon, what else is spinning out of control? (Human society) What might lines 2–8 suggest is missing from modern society? (Possibly restraint, reflection, reason, tolerance, belief in absolute values, or faith)

B. Expansion
You might wish to tell students that lines 13–14 suggest St. John the Baptist, who lived in the desert and is traditionally depicted wearing an animal skin. Also, his function in the New Testament was to announce the coming of Christ. The lines also suggest the Egyptian sphinx, which had a man's head and a lion's body and represented the enigmatic and mysterious.

C. Responding
The poem is most often read as not holding out much hope for the salvation of the world. However, less pessimistic interpretations are possible.
? How do you read the last four lines?

"The Second Coming" refers to the Christian hope that Jesus Christ will return to earth one day and will usher in an era of peace and justice and faith. This Second Coming is prophesied in the Book of Revelation in the New Testament of the Bible. The "first coming," of course, was the Nativity of Jesus in Bethlehem of Judea, nearly two thousand years ago.

The poem alludes to the elaborate cosmology (theory of the cosmos, or universe) devised by Yeats and eventually set down in the graphic systems and schematic tables of his book *A Vision*. Nevertheless, the power of "The Second Coming" lies not in its allusions to history or mythology, but in the simple grandeur of its rough iambics, in the tonal variations within its twenty-two lines, and in the passion and eloquence of the speaker's pessimism.

The first two lines present an image and introduce a theme. The central image is of a falconer who is unable to limit the flight of his released hawk as it spirals "out of control." Like the falconer, civilization has lost the means to halt the descent into chaos signified by World War I and by the vast social disruptions caused by communism and fascism.

Having made a grim statement in stanza 1 and come to a melancholy conclusion, Yeats steps back for a moment, draws a well-timed dramatic breath, then enters upon a speculation that ends in neither hope nor promise, but with a threat in the form of an unanswerable question.

The Second Coming

A
Turning and turning in the widening gyre°
The falcon cannot hear the falconer;
Things fall apart; the center cannot hold;
Mere <u>anarchy</u> is loosed upon the world,
5 The blood-dimmed tide is loosed, and everywhere
The ceremony of innocence is drowned;
The best lack all conviction, while the worst
Are full of passionate intensity.

Surely some revelation is at hand;
10 Surely the Second Coming is at hand.
The Second Coming! Hardly are those words out
When a vast image out of *Spiritus Mundi*°
B
Troubles my sight: somewhere in sands of the desert
A shape with lion body and the head of a man,
15 A gaze blank and pitiless as the sun,
Is moving its slow thighs, while all about it
Reel shadows of the indignant desert birds.
The darkness drops again; but now I know
C
That twenty centuries of stony sleep
20 Were vexed to nightmare by a rocking cradle,°
And what rough beast, its hour come round at last,
Slouches toward Bethlehem to be born?

1. **gyre:** circle or spiral.

12. ***Spiritus Mundi:*** Latin for "the world's soul or spirit"; for Yeats, the collective reservoir of human memory from which artists draw their images.

20. **cradle:** a reference to the birth of Christ.

ANALYZING THE POEM
Identifying Details
1. The speaker offers a bleak picture of a world of anarchy, warfare, loss of traditional values, and strife.
2. The speaker offers a frightening image of a violent beast emerging from the desert, half lion and half man. Specific words: "blank," "pitiless," "reel," "indignant," "stony," "rough," and "slouches."

Interpreting Meanings
3. He probably means "moral center," or that scheme of civilized values that helps to stave off anarchy and chaos.
The falcon flies in widening circles around the falconer. That the bird can no longer hear its master corresponds to the fact that humanity has lost its moral "center" and has raged out of control with warfare, sin, and violence.
4. The word *mere*, used to describe anarchy, has the ironic force of understatement. The verb *slouches* carries ominous connotations.
5. The "blood-dimmed tide" probably refers to warfare. Student answers will vary. Some may suggest that the phrase obliquely refers to Christian baptism.
6. The idea becomes frighteningly ironic because Yeats is suggesting that the Second Coming—traditionally thought of as the day of the Last Judgment—may actually turn out to be the advent of a cruel, sinister "god" who will preside over the loss of civilization.
7. The creature's gaze, "blank and pitiless as the sun," implies that the creature is merciless and powerful. The darkness dropping carries menacing undertones.
8. Student answers will vary.

A. Humanities Connection: Discussing the Fine Art
Francis Bacon was born in Dublin in 1910 and grew up there. He had his first exhibition in London in 1949. Bacon's eccentric painting focuses on the unwelcome, nightmarish aspects that he sees just beyond the conventional surface of reality. He wishes to startle his viewers into seeing what they would rather not see.
? What aspects of this picture are unlikely and seemingly inexplicable? Note that the title of the painting suggests a study of a human figure.

Responding to the Poem

Analyzing the Poem

Identifying Details

1. In your own words, describe the picture of the world that the speaker offers in the first stanza.
2. What **image** of the Second Coming troubles the speaker in the second half of the poem? Name some of the specific words that make this image especially vivid.

Interpreting Meanings

3. What do you think the poet means by the word *center* in line 3? Why, in this poem's context, is the image of the falcon especially appropriate?
4. Comment on the force of the words *mere* in line 4 and *slouches* in line 22.

A

Figure Study II by Francis Bacon (1945–46).

Huddersfield Art Gallery, West Yorkshire, England.

5. What might the "blood-dimmed tide" in line 5 refer to? What could the "ceremony of innocence" in line 6 mean?
6. How does the idea of the Second Coming become frighteningly **ironic** in the second half of the poem?
7. Like some monster in a horror movie, Yeats's "shape with lion body and the head of a man" begins to move "its slow thighs" and start upon a path of destruction that human beings are helpless to halt or stall. What hints in the poem indicate that this creature has the power to paralyze its enemies and overcome their defenses?
8. If you know enough about the history of the twentieth century, tell who might be counted among "the best" and among "the worst."

Writing About the Poem

A Creative Response

1. **Evaluating the Effect of a Poem.** In its deliberate evocation of the origins of Christianity, set against the apocalyptic image of a barbarous, perhaps satanic age, "The Second Coming" is a bold, even shocking work. In a brief essay, explain how a reading of this poem affects your ideas about human progress and the future.

A Critical Response

2. **Comparing and Contrasting Two Works.** You might want to read several chapters of the Biblical account of the end of the world in the Book of Revelation. Then compare and contrast the themes and imagery of these chapters with "The Second Coming."
3. **Commenting on Famous Lines.** Lines from this poem are frequently quoted. (Some of them have been used as titles. American writer Joan Didion, for example, entitled one of her essay collections *Slouching Toward Bethlehem*.) Comment on how each of the following lines from the poem could relate to life today:

   a. "Things fall apart."
   b. "The center cannot hold."

PREPARATION

1. BUILDING ON PRIOR KNOWLEDGE. Tell students that the ancient Eastern city of Byzantium has connotations similar to those suggested by "Araby" in James Joyce's story. Both names conjure up images of exotic, mysterious places of great sensual beauty. In addition, Byzantium, since it became the center of Eastern Christianity under Constantine, has religious and artistic associations for Yeats.

2. ESTABLISHING A PURPOSE. Tell students that the speaker of this poem is entering old age and is struggling with the feelings that this fact arouses in him. As they read, ask them to look for what the speaker is saying about youth and age and the concerns of each.

SUPPLEMENTARY SUPPORT MATERIALS
1. Vocabulary Activity Worksheet (*CCB*)
2. Review and Response Worksheet: Theme (*CCB*)
3. Selection Test (*CCB*)
4. Audiocassette recording

A. Theme
Although the speaker in the first stanza expresses envy for and admiration of the young in their natural, summer world, he also sees a flaw in their existence.
? What is the flaw in their idyll? (The young are subject to death and aging, and they are absorbed with things that will fade and die.)

B. Interpreting Meaning
Paltry here means "insignificant" or "trivial."
? How can an old man avoid being useless according to the poet? (By studying the great works of human genius)

C. Expansion
Note that in the third stanza the speaker asks the sages to come from the holy fire and "consume" his heart, presumably by fire. He wishes to shed the flesh and its desires and to be purified by fire, as metals are.

D. Theme
In the final stanza, the poet makes it clear that he is speaking of a transformation into a golden object of art.

Byzantium—later Constantinople and now Istanbul—was famous for the exquisite skills of its craftspeople: sculptors, gem-cutters, silversmiths, and goldsmiths. To those aware of history, the very name *Byzantium* has connotations of mystery, splendor, elegance, and sensuality. This poem was written when Yeats was sixty-two years old.

Sailing to Byzantium

1

That is no country for old men. The young
In one another's arms, birds in the trees
—Those dying generations—at their song,
The salmon-falls, the mackerel-crowded seas,
Fish, flesh, or fowl, commend all summer long
Whatever is begotten, born, and dies.
Caught in that sensual music all neglect
Monuments of unaging intellect.

2

An aged man is but a paltry thing,
A tattered coat upon a stick, unless
Soul clap its hands and sing, and louder sing
For every tatter in its mortal dress,
Nor is there singing school but studying
Monuments of its own magnificence;
And therefore I have sailed the seas and come
To the holy city of Byzantium.

3

O sages standing in God's holy fire
As in the gold mosaic of a wall,
Come from the holy fire, perne in a gyre,°
And be the singing-masters of my soul.
Consume my heart away; sick with desire
And fastened to a dying animal
It knows not what it is; and gather me
Into the artifice of eternity.

4

Once out of nature I shall never take
My bodily form from any natural thing,
But such a form as Grecian goldsmiths make
Of hammered gold and gold enameling
To keep a drowsy Emperor awake;
Or set upon a golden bough to sing
To lords and ladies of Byzantium
Of what is past, or passing, or to come.

Scythian gold pectoral (chest ornament) (4th century B.C.).

19. **perne in a gyre:** come spinning to my side.

1094

DEVELOPING VOCABULARY

The following words from the poem are tested in the Selection Test. (See also Vocabulary Activity Worksheet.)

paltry   sage

ANALYZING THE POEM
Identifying Details

1. The young have no regard for anything except sensual pleasure.

They neglect "monuments of unaging intellect," or the products of the intelligence and the imagination.

2. The old can give in to physical decrepitude, or they can celebrate the inner life of the mind and the imagination.

He is sailing on an imaginary voyage to Byzantium to celebrate the power of art and the imagination.

3. He prays that the sages and saints will take him out of his aging, physical body and trasmute him into the eternal realm of art.

4. He imagines himself transformed into a bird, fashioned from gold and enamel, who will sit upon a golden bough and sing of the past, present, and future to the court of Byzantium.

Interpreting Meanings

5. The speaker's physical body.

6. References to song and singing occur in lines 3, 11, 13, 20, and 30. This image is drawn from the realm of art, creativity, and the imagination.

The spiritual song of the speaker/bird (as opposed to the "sensual music" of the first stanza) perhaps symbolizes wisdom, art, or timelessness.

7. He seems to uphold spiritual and artistic values, as opposed to sensual, physical, or worldly values.

8. See the Comment on the Poem on this page. Lines 30–32 suggest that the poem is about poetry.

CLOSURE

Ask students to summarize Yeats's views on nature and art. What evolution in his views is reflected in the four poems reprinted here?

A Comment on the Poem

The first lines of this poem show the poet at a point of decision. Aware of his age, and of the beautiful country (Ireland) where he no longer feels at home, he decides to take an imaginary trip to the ancient city of Byzantium. There, rid of his passions and his envy of the young, he sees that the only beauty to survive over time is not natural beauty, but that represented in objects of art. To secure his own immortality, he begs the saints and wise men he sees in the brilliant church mosaics to come to his side and teach his soul to sing, to relieve him of his declining years and make him one with "the artifice of eternity." Once free of nature, including human nature, he vows to exist forever as a kind of toy bird of "gold and gold enameling" placed on a golden branch with no other purpose than to entertain those who will listen to his mechanical song.

The theme—art in relation to life, the natural in relation to the artificial—is set when the young, "caught in that sensual music," pay no attention to enduring masterpieces by long dead artists. Since he can himself no longer enjoy the life of the senses, the poet turns to art and its "monuments," not only to study and praise them but, as a final wish, to become one of them.

Responding to the Poem

Analyzing the Poem

Identifying Details

1. In the first stanza, what is the speaker's complaint about the young? What happens to people caught in "that sensual music"?
2. In the second stanza, what does the speaker say are the alternatives that confront the old? Why is he sailing to Byzantium?
3. Paraphrase the speaker's prayer to the sages or wise men and saints in the third stanza.
4. How does the speaker imagine himself in the fourth stanza?

Interpreting Meanings

5. What is the "dying animal" in line 22?
6. Explain how the **image** of singing helps to unify the poem. What do you think this song symbolizes?
7. What values does the speaker seem to uphold in the poem?
8. Is this poem primarily a protest against the ravages of time, is it a celebration of art, or does its major **theme** lie elsewhere? Explain your answer.

Writing About the Poem

A Creative Response

1. **Describing a Symbolic Setting.** Yeats describes his Byzantium in a highly symbolic fashion, possibly to emphasize that his imaginative journey there is motivated by an abstract ideal. Choose a past or present setting that represents an ideal for you. Describe the setting, using at least one symbol to underline the ideal nature of the place.

A Critical Response

2. **Comparing and Contrasting Two Poems.** In an essay, compare and contrast the **imagery, theme,** and **tone** of "Sailing to Byzantium" with those of John Keats's "Ode on a Grecian Urn."
3. **Exploring a Symbol.** In Book 6 of Virgil's *Aeneid,* the golden bough is a charm that the epic hero Aeneas must carry to ensure his safe passage through the underworld. The bough, an artificial metallic object, thrives on a living tree, and thus may symbolize a fusion of art and nature. A generation before Yeats wrote "Sailing to Byzantium," Sir James Frazer entitled his pioneering comparative study of myth and folklore *The Golden Bough.* Frazer's monumental work had a remarkable influence on early twentieth-century literature, not least on the poetry of Yeats. Using the research resources in your library, see what you can find out about the golden bough. Write a report summarizing your findings.

1. BUILDING ON PRIOR KNOWLEDGE. Tell students that the sensibility behind this poem is thoroughly Christian. The sacrificial death of Christ is the poem's central reality, and it is in the light of this reality that all else is seen.

2. ESTABLISHING A PURPOSE. Although this poem was inspired by German bombing raids in World War II, ask students to consider as they read if its descriptions of senseless violence and cruelty have meaning for them today.

SUPPLEMENTARY SUPPORT MATERIALS
1. Vocabulary Activity Worksheet (CCB)
2. Review and Response Worksheet: Figurative Language and Theme (CCB)
3. Selection Test (CCB)

DEVELOPING VOCABULARY
The following words from the poem are tested in the Selection Test. (See also Vocabulary Activity Worksheet.)
to nurture   to smirch

Edith Sitwell (1887–1964)

Edith Sitwell never ceased to regard herself as an embattled rebel. First, she opposed the austere codes of behavior maintained by her aristocratic (and eccentric) family. Later, she stood against the smugness and banality of the verse popular in pre-World War I England. Finally, she showed her contempt of her critics, nearly all of whom she considered to be intellectual pygmies or impertinent nobodies.

In poetry, her earliest love was Swinburne (1837–1909), but her career was soon more deeply influenced by the French Symbolists. She was particularly responsive to two esthetic sources outside of poetry—the post-Impressionist painting being done in France and the Russian ballet which was introduced to England under the auspices of the great impresario, Sergei Diaghilev. Sitwell's most famous poems, a group called *Façade,* reflect her dual interest in their use of extravagantly colored imagery, quickly shifting rhythms, and cacophonous sounds. Recited by its author, with a musical accompaniment by William Walton, the first "performance" of *Façade* was both a sensation and a scandal; it stood as an exotic challenge to the complacency, paleness, and monotony of Georgian poetry, which tended to render experience in the palest of pastel colors and in the most monotonous of metrics.

Once her reputation was established, however, Sitwell put aside the witty playfulness and audacious syncopation that made her work unique in British poetry. In reaction to the German saturation bombing of English cities in World War II—including Sheffield, the one closest to her country estate—and then to the destruction of Hiroshima by the atomic bomb, her poetry became grave, sober, and less experimental. Following her surprising conversion to Roman Catholicism, she tended to interpret current events in terms of Christian history.

In spite of its profound personal motivations, her later poetry, in the eyes of most critics, was shallower and less ingenious than her earlier work. And when the young British poets sensed that this imposing and strange-looking woman

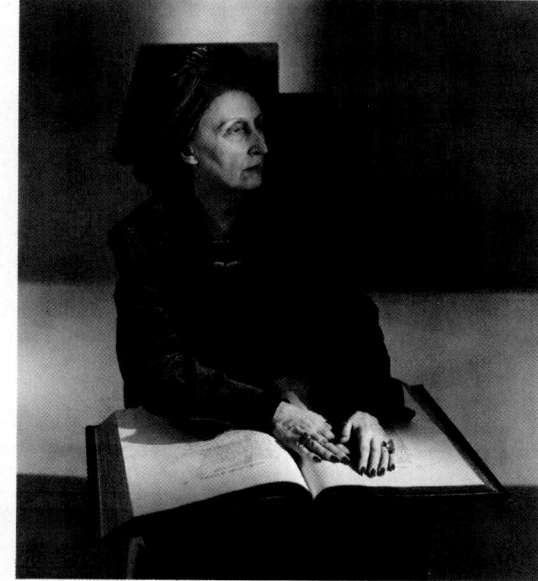

Dame Edith Sitwell (1955).
Photo by Horst.

had dared to set herself up as the voice of the public conscience, they tweaked her pretensions by referring to her as "the Old Jane," a reference to a nonsensical poem in *Façade* beginning "Jane, Jane, tall as a crane. . . ."

Nevertheless, Sitwell's later, high-sounding poetry gained for her a wider audience than she had ever before enjoyed. She became a much-sought-after public figure, particularly as a performer in American lecture halls. She was perhaps as famous for her theatrical demeanor, for her medieval costumes, and for her outspoken opinions as for her poetic skills. Along with her brother, Sir Osbert (who was also a poet), she made a number of trips to the United States where she professed an affection for Americans and American customs.

The final phase of Edith Sitwell's career was marked by irony. The woman who saw herself as the flaming rebel targeted for destruction by the whole conservative British literary establishment became the recipient of one prize and award after another, including an honorary degree from Oxford University. When, on the recommendation of Queen Elizabeth II, she became Dame Edith Sitwell, her journey from rebellion to acquiescence to surrender was completed.

ANALYZING THE POEM
Identifying Details
1. She mentions 1,940 nails, a number that corresponds to the year during World War II in which she wrote the poem.
2. The rain falls on the Potter's Field, the Field of Blood, and at the feet of the Cross.
3. First stanza: *abcb.* Second stanza:

addeaaa. Third stanza: *abffg.* Fourth stanza: *ahhiijdj.* Fifth stanza: *aklmnak.* Sixth stanza: *oap.*
4. The rain might be held to symbolize human sin, violence, war, cruelty, or departure from God's will.

Interpreting Meanings
5. Cain, in the Bible, was the first murderer, who killed his brother Abel.

His mention is appropriate because the subject of the poem is killing among the human family.
6. These references expand the chronological field of reference, emphasizing that cruelty and inhumanity have always been part of human history.
7. The speaker of the last line is the crucified Christ.
(Answers continue on next page.)

In the early days of World War II, the cities of England were subjected to bombing raids by German planes. One of these cities was Sheffield, the manufacturing center famous for articles of silver, including tableware used around the world. Sheffield was not far from Renishaw, the estate that was Edith Sitwell's ancestral home. Night after night, she could observe the lethal "rain" of bombs that all but wiped out the city.

One of the notable things about this poem is the absence of any sense of righteousness or malice toward the enemy. In Sitwell's view—that of a newly converted Roman Catholic—the war was simply another episode in the murderous and self-destructive history of mankind which, for nearly two thousand years, had ignored the peace-loving words of Christ.

Still Falls the Rain

The Raids, 1940. *Night and Dawn*

A

Still falls the Rain—
Dark as the world of man, black as our loss—
Blind as the nineteen hundred and forty nails
Upon the Cross.

B

5   Still falls the Rain
With a sound like the pulse of the heart that is changed
   to the hammer-beat
In the Potter's Field,° and the sound of the impious feet
On the Tomb:
         Still falls the Rain
10 In the Field of Blood where the small hopes breed and
   the human brain
Nurtures its greed, that worm with the brow of Cain.

C

Still falls the Rain
At the feet of the Starved Man hung upon the Cross.
Christ that each day, each night, nails there, have mercy
   on us—
15 On Dives and on Lazarus.°
Under the Rain the sore and the gold are as one.

D

Still falls the Rain—
Still falls the Blood from the Starved Man's wounded
   Side:
He bears in His Heart all wounds—those of the light
   that died,
20 The last faint spark
In the self-murdered heart, the wounds of the sad un-
   comprehending dark,
The wounds of the baited bear°—
The blind and weeping bear whom the keepers beat
On his helpless flesh . . . the tears of the hunted hare.

7. **Potter's Field:** a burial place near Jerusalem where poor people and foreigners were buried. According to the Gospels, it was bought with the money Judas Iscariot received for betraying Christ. Potter's Field is thus called the Field of Blood since it was purchased with blood money.

15. **Dives . . . Lazarus:** two figures in a parable told by Christ. The rich man, Dives, is condemned to hell; the poor man, Lazarus, is allowed to enter heaven.

22. **baited bear:** A medieval form of entertainment was watching a chained bear fight a pack of dogs.

A. Setting and Theme
In the first stanza, the poet sets the scene in a night-shrouded city that is being continually bombarded.
? In what way, other than the literal one, is the world "dark"? (It is confused and troubled.) What is "our loss"? (Peace, clarity, faith)

B. Theme
? In the second stanza, what motive does the poet suggest for the death of Christ and, by implication, for the present sufferings caused by the war? (Petty human greed)

C. Interpreting Meaning
? Why do you think Christ on the cross is called "the Starved Man"? (He has not received the love and understanding of those He came to save.)

D. Expansion
In the fourth stanza, the poet reiterates the same theme, underscoring through repetition that as the bombing continues so does the willful misunderstanding and rejection of the message of love.

(Answers begin on previous page.)

Despite human unworthiness and violence, Christ still loves humanity and is willing to shed His own blood for human redemption.

8. The meter of the poem alternates between rising and falling structures (trochees and anapests), producing an irregular, strained effect. The meter of the refrain (two stressed syllables, followed by an iamb) suggests the steady falling of rain.

9. Student answers will vary. The last three lines, however, suggest the traditional Christian hope that through the sufferings of Christ the fallen world has been redeemed.

A. Resolution
In the fifth stanza, suffering humanity, speaking in the words of the sinner Faustus, finally turns to God and begs for mercy. Note that the context of Faust's agonized speech is on page 229.

? What answer does he receive in the last three lines? (Christ continues to love and redeem the sins of men and women by His death.)

CLOSURE
Lines 15 and 16 suggest that suffering, such as war, falls equally on rich and poor. Ask students to discuss this view. Do they agree or disagree?

---

25   Still falls the Rain—
       Then—O Ile leape up to my God: who pulles me
         doune—
       See, see where Christ's blood streames in the firmament:°
       It flows from the Brow we nailed upon the tree
       Deep to the dying, to the thirsting heart
       That holds the fires of the world—dark-<u>smirched</u> with
30   pain
       As Caesar's laurel crown.

A   Then sounds the voice of One who like the heart of man
       Was once a child who among beasts has lain—
       "Still do I love, still shed my innocent light, my Blood,
       for thee."

27. **O . . . firmament:** a quotation from the play *Faustus* by Christopher Marlowe. Faustus, after selling his soul to Satan, tries to save himself with one last plea to Christ.

Responding to the Poem

Analyzing the Poem

Identifying Details

1. How many nails does the speaker mention in the first stanza? What is the significance of that number?
2. Upon what various items or places does the rain fall?
3. What is the **rhyme scheme** of each stanza of the poem?
4. Each stanza but the last one begins with the same **refrain.** What would you say the *rain* symbolizes? Does it refer to more than one thing?

Interpreting Meanings

5. Who is Cain (line 11)? What does he have to do with the subject of the poem?
6. Why does the poet mention the "baited bear" and the "hunted hare"?
7. The last line is enclosed in quotation marks. Who is the speaker? What is the meaning of the speaker's words?
8. Examine the **meter** of the poem, especially the meter of the refrain. What effect does this meter help to create?
9. Do you think this is an optimistic poem or a pessimistic one?

Writing About the Poem

A Creative Reponse

1. **Preparing a Choral Reading.** Suppose you and two other speakers were going to perform a choral reading of the poem before an audience. What would be the most effective way of assigning the lines of the poem? Write the numbers 1–34 in a list. Then assign each line to one of the three speakers. In some stanzas, it might be more effective to have one reader. In others, each line might be given to a different reader. After you have assigned the lines, write a paragraph explaining why you alloted them the way you did.

A Critical Response

2. **Relating Technique to Theme.** Write an essay explaining how Sitwell uses **sounds** and **imagery** to underscore the **theme** of her poem. Begin by making an explicit statement of what you think her theme is.

PREPARATION

1. BUILDING ON PRIOR KNOWLEDGE. Tell students to think about the powerful effect of the snake image. Remind them that, in the Garden of Eden, a snake was the undoing of Adam and Eve.

2. ESTABLISHING A PURPOSE. As students read, ask them to note the various reactions of the poet to the snake.

SUPPLEMENTARY SUPPORT MATERIALS
1. Vocabulary Activity Worksheet (*CCB*)
2. Review and Response Worksheet: Imagery in Free Verse (*CCB*)
3. Selection Test (*CCB*)

DEVELOPING VOCABULARY
The following words from the poem are tested in the Selection Test. (See also Vocabulary Activity Worksheet.)
trough   perversity
to muse   to convulse
bowels   to expiate
venomous

In this dialogue, a supposedly civilized and educated man, confronted with an emissary of nature that is also a creature from the "underworld" of Satanic legend, painfully examines his feelings and actions, and finds them both mean and cowardly.

The water trough in the first line was part of the fountain in the garden of a house Lawrence occupied for a time in the early 1920's and which gave the property its name—*Fontana Vecchia*, meaning "Old Fountain." This small estate was situated on the outskirts of Taormina, the Sicilian town from which the snow-capped and ever-smoking cone of the volcano Mt. Etna is visible.

The setting is important to the poem in that "the burning bowels of the earth" is not figurative, but a literal description. As one of the world's few active volcanoes, Etna is a reminder of how close to the earth's surface molten lava still churns. And it is from this "infernal region" that the snake emerges, bringing with him the diabolical associations of the Garden of Eden.

Technically, the poem is remarkable for its onomatopoeic renderings of experience, particularly in stanzas 3, 5, and 10.

A biography of Lawrence appears on page 971, in the fiction section.

Snake

D. H. Lawrence

A
> A snake came to my water trough
> On a hot, hot day, and I in pajamas for the heat,
> To drink there.

> In the deep, strange-scented shade of the great dark carob tree
> 5   I came down the steps with my pitcher
B
> And must wait, must stand and wait, for there he was at
>   the trough before me.

> He reached down from a fissure in the earth wall in the gloom
> And trailed his yellow-brown slackness soft-bellied down, over the edge
>   of the stone trough
> And rested his throat upon the stone bottom,
> 10   And where the water had dripped from the tap, in a small clearness,
> He sipped with his straight mouth,
> Softly drank through his straight gums, into his slack long body,
> Silently.

> Someone was before me at my water trough,
> 15   And I, like a second comer, waiting.

C
> He lifted his head from his drinking, as cattle do,
> And looked at me vaguely, as drinking cattle do,
> And flickered his two-forked tongue from his lips, and mused a moment,
> And stooped and drank a little more,
> 20   Being earth-brown, earth-golden from the burning bowels of the earth
> On the day of Sicilian July, with Etna smoking.

> The voice of my education said to me
> He must be killed,
> For in Sicily the black black snakes are innocent, the gold are venomous.

A. Expansion
Alert students to the fact that the speaker meets the snake in a tropical garden. This and the fact that he is not fully clothed recall the Garden of Eden.

B. Symbolism
⚡ What is the possible symbolic significance of the snake's being at the fountain before the man? (This suggests the precedence in time, and possibly in importance, of the nonhuman, natural world over the human.)

C. Mood
⚡ What feelings toward the snake is the poet experiencing in the fifth stanza? (Awe, fascination, some fear)

1. By his water trough.
The speaker was pleasurably fascinated by the snake.
2. Even though he liked the snake, the speaker was warned by the "voice of his education" that the reptile might be poisonous. He throws a log at the snake.
3. The speaker is horrified at the idea that the snake may disappear down the hole into the earth.
He regrets the act because it suddenly strikes him as mean and vulgar.
4. He compares the snake to a king of the underworld.

Interpreting Meanings
5. Images include the snake's "yellow-brown slackness" (line 8), the flickering of the snake's tongue (line 18), the snake licking his lips (line 44), and the snake writhing like lightning (line 60).
The concluding simile, comparing the snake to an exiled king of the underworld, seems especially symbolic.
6. Student answers will vary. In general, the speaker seems to come down on the side of nature, since he calls his human *(Answers continue on next page.)*

A. Theme
? How does the poet's society define manhood? (A man dominates, or kills, what he fears or does not understand.) Consider what alternative definition the whole poem may be offering. (A man protects and reveres what is different from him.)

B. Interpreting
? Why did the poet like the fact that the snake would leave satisfied but "thankless"? (Unlike humans, the snake is serene, untroubled by conflicting emotions or confusions of identify.)

C. Responding
? Why do you think the poet is horrified by the snake's return to the dark earth from which it came? (He may be afraid of death, of being separated from the snake, of the unknown dark powers in nature and in man, or of something else.)

---

25 ⎡ And voices in me said, If you were a man
A ⎣ You would take a stick and break him now, and finish him off.

⎡ But must I confess how I liked him,
  How glad I was he had come like a guest in quiet, to drink at my water
B ⎢   trough
  And depart peaceful, pacified, and thankless
30 ⎣ Into the burning bowels of this earth?

Was it cowardice, that I dared not kill him?
Was it perversity, that I longed to talk to him?
Was it humility, to feel so honored?
I felt so honored.

35 And yet those voices:
If you were not afraid, you would kill him!

And truly I was afraid, I was most afraid,
But even so, honored still more
That he should seek my hospitality
40 From out the dark door of the secret earth.

He drank enough
And lifted his head, dreamily, as one who has drunken,
And flickered his tongue like a forked night on the air, so black,
Seeming to lick his lips,
45 And looked around like a god, unseeing, into the air,
And slowly turned his head,
And slowly, very slowly, as if thrice adream
Proceeded to draw his slow length curving round
And climb the broken bank of my wall face.

50 ⎡ And as he put his head into that dreadful hole,
  And as he slowly drew up, snake-easing his shoulders, and entered further,
  A sort of horror, a sort of protest against his withdrawing into that horrid
C ⎢   black hole,
  Deliberately going into the blackness, and slowly drawing himself after,
⎣ Overcame me now his back was turned.

55 I looked round, I put down my pitcher,
I picked up a clumsy log
And threw it at the water trough with a clatter.

I think it did not hit him;
But suddenly that part of him that was left behind convulsed in undignified
    haste.
60 Writhed like lightning, and was gone
Into the black hole, the earth-lipped fissure in the wall front
At which, in the intense still noon, I stared with fascination.

And immediately I regretted it.
I thought how paltry, how vulgar, what a mean act!

education (the symbol of culture in the poem) "accursed" in line 65. The poem implies that human civilization has involved man in a dangerous split between his "natural" instincts and pleasures and his "civilized" or "educated" inclinations.

Again, student answers will vary. Ask the students to support their suggestions with references to the poem.

7. The simile in lines 68–70 might refer to Hades.

Some students may suggest that the speaker's fascination with the serpent's beauty is an oblique allusion to the tale of the temptation in Genesis.

8. Student answers will vary.

CLOSURE
Have students write down what they think the snake stands for in this poem. Allow them to read one another's interpretations and to discuss them in class.

65 I despised myself and the voices of my accursed
A   human education.

And I thought of the albatross,°
And I wished he would come back, my snake.

For he seemed to me again like a king,
Like a king in exile, uncrowned in the underworld,
70 Now due to be crowned again.

And so, I missed my chance with one of the lords
Of life.
B And I have something to expiate:
A pettiness.

66. **albatross:** an allusion to Samuel Taylor Coleridge's *Rime of the Ancient Mariner.* It shows that the speaker is (accursedly) educated, and that his "civilized" consciousness is separated from the thoughtless indifference of nature (the snake).

Responding to the Poem

Analyzing the Poem

Identifying Details

1. Where did the speaker find the snake? What is the speaker's reaction?
2. What **internal conflict** does the speaker experience? How does he resolve it?
3. Why does the speaker throw the log at the snake? Why does he regret having done so?
4. At the close of the poem, what does the speaker compare the snake to?

Interpreting Meanings

5. What **images** describing the snake seem to you especially realistic? What aspects of the description seem mostly **symbolic**?
6. What does the poem imply about the dichotomy, or split, between culture and nature? Does the poem suggest any resolution of this split?
7. Do you find any **allusions** in this poem to Pluto or Hades, the king of the Underworld in Greek and Roman mythology? Do you detect any allusions to the account of the serpent in Genesis? Explain.
8. Can you think of occasions when the voices of one's "human education" might make one do something that later would be cause for shame or regret?

Writing About the Poem

A Critical Response

1. **Explaining an Allusion.** Why does the speaker think of the albatross? In a brief essay explain this allusion to

Coleridge's *The Rime of the Ancient Mariner* and tell how Coleridge's poem connects to Lawrence's experience.
2. **Comparing and Contrasting Two Poems.** Snakes are the subject of many poems. If you have access to American poet Emily Dickinson's poem "A Narrow Fellow in the Grass," write an essay in which you explain the similarities and differences between it and Lawrence's snake poem.

Analyzing Language and Style

Free Verse

"Free verse" is free only in the sense that it is free from the constraints imposed by meter and by the demands of a regular rhyme scheme. A poet writing in free verse must look for other methods of creating rhythms and of creating sound effects. You will not find meter and strict rhyme schemes used in free verse, but you will find rhyming sounds, onomatopoeia, alliteration, and repetition.

1. Examine "Snake" and find as many examples as you can of **onomatopoeia,** the use of words with sounds that echo their sense.
2. Look also for examples of **alliteration** used to create onomatopoeia.
3. How does the poet use long and short lines for emphasis?
4. Where does the poet use **repetition** to create rhythm?

A. Theme
❓ What particular aspect of his human education do you think the poet is condemning here? (Possibly those values that urge man to dominate nature and to eradicate the forces of nature within himself)

B. Resolution
❓ What pettiness does the speaker have to atone for? (The impulse to assert his will or his ego over the disinterested natural world, represented by the snake)

Additional Research Assignment
Students may be interested in researching the status of snakes as gods in various ancient cultures. Perhaps they can find reproductions of art from a culture that revered the snake. If so, have them share these images and explain to their classmates the status of the snake in the culture they have researched.

1. BUILDING ON PRIOR KNOWLEDGE. Ask
students to recall round songs like "Row,
Row, Row Your Boat" that they may
have sung as children. Tell them that this
poem, like a round song, keeps coming
back to where it started. Note also that
the poem is addressed to children.

2. ESTABLISHING A PURPOSE. As they

read, ask students to be aware of what is
repeated and what is subtly changed
within the poem's circular structure.

SUPPLMENTARY SUPPORT MATERIALS
1. Vocabulary Activity Worksheet (*CCB*)
2. Review and Response Worksheet:
Theme and Repetition (*CCB*)
3. Selection Test (*CCB*)

DEVELOPING VOCABULARY
The following word from the poem is
tested in the Selection Test. (See also
Vocabulary Activity Worksheet.)
tawny

ANALYZING THE POEM
Identifying Details
1. The poem
is addressed to
children.
 The speaker
tells the children
not to undo the
parcel.
2. Inside is a small
island with a fruit
tree.
3. They should not
undo the parcel
because, if they
do, they will find
themselves inside
it.

Interpreting Meanings
4. Lines 2–5 are
repeated in lines
34–37, and lines
6–9 are repeated
in lines 17–20 and
26–30.
 The repetitions
reinforce the
theme of reality *vs.*
imagination.
5. Predominantly
trochaic tetrameter.
 Many will sug-
gest that this
rhythm creates a
sense of playful-
ness.
6. That imagina-
tion cannot be an-
alyzed the way a
parcel can be.
 The human
imagination should
be enjoyed, not
dissected.

Robert Graves (1895–1985)

Robert Graves enjoyed a career spanning much
of the twentieth century. Beginning with an early
association with the Trench Poets, his career
lasted until a time when, entirely independent of
the other movements and groupings of his time,
he stood alone as the grand old man of British
poetry.

 His poems are robust and straightforward and
are distinguished by a fresh approach to the handling of old forms. They often seem like the heritage of another era. Some are written in the
aphoristic style of the ancient Roman poets to
whom, both as poet and novelist, Graves was
powerfully drawn.

 Celebrated primarily for his poetry, Graves
was a man of letters in the broadest sense of the
term. His novels of ancient Rome (*I, Claudius;
Claudius the God*) became the basis for an often-
revived television series. His famous and still
widely read autobiography, *Good-Bye to All That*
(1929), became the standard account of the
Trench Poets' generation. In collaboration with
the American poet Laura Riding, he wrote an influential volume of literary criticism entitled *A
Survey of Modernist Poetry* (1927). This book
brought into focus new examples of experimentation in early twentieth-century poetry. *The*

White Goddess (1948), his highly individual
interpretation of primitive religion, generated
controversy. But even Graves's critics had to admire the scope of his knowledge and the cranky
brilliance of his convictions. If you haven't encountered Robert Graves in one of his novels,
you might have read some of the ancient myths
he has retold in his wry, witty style for young
readers.

Comment from the Writer
In his book *The White Goddess,* Graves wrote, "There seems to be no escape from our difficulties until the industrial system breaks down for some reason or other. . . and nature reasserts herself with grass and trees among the ruins." This is a classic statement of the Romantic temperament. Which other poets included in this unit do you think would

subscribe to these sentiments? Support your answer with examples from their poetry.

CLOSURE
Ask students why they think this poem was addressed to children. What qualities do children have in common with poets? To whom do you think the poet is really speaking?

A. Word Order
Call students' attention to inversions in the word order of lines 2–4 and lines 34–36. Ask them to consider what the poet might be suggesting by this difference in sameness and sameness in difference. (The unity of all reality or the imagination's ability to see and create unity.)

B. Expansion
The poem suggests worlds within worlds and that investigation brings one back to where one started. Line 24 is a key line in discovering the poem's meaning. It seems to be suggesting that when one looks for the world one finds oneself.

C. Theme
Note how often the words *enclosed* or *enclosing* appear in the poem. What is the circle in which the child is enclosed? (Possibly the limits of his own imagination, curiosity, or consciousness)

This is a kind of puzzle poem. Reading it is a bit like unwrapping a package and finding another package, and then another and another, so that, when you come to the last one, you're back where you started. For all of its playfulness, the poem is based on some very serious considerations. One of these is the relationship between what is real and what is *thought* to be real. "Children, leave the string alone!" says the poet, and the reader is teased to figure out what lies behind his warning.

Warning to Children

Children, if you dare to think
Of the greatness, rareness, muchness,
A   Fewness of this precious only
Endless world in which you say
5   You live, you think of things like this:
Blocks of slate enclosing dappled
Red and green, enclosing tawny
Yellow nets, enclosing white
And black acres of dominoes,
10   Where a neat brown paper parcel
Tempts you to untie the string.
In the parcel a small island,
On the island a large tree,
On the tree a husky fruit.
15   Strip the husk and pare the rind off:
In the kernel you will see
Blocks of slate enclosed by dappled
Red and green, enclosed by tawny
Yellow nets, enclosed by white

20   And black acres of dominoes,
Where the same brown paper parcel—
Children, leave the string alone!
For who dares undo the parcel
B   Finds himself at once inside it,
25   On the island, in the fruit,
Blocks of slate about his head,
C   Finds himself enclosed by dappled
Green and red, enclosed by yellow
Tawny nets, enclosed by black
30   And white acres of dominoes,
With the same brown paper parcel
Still unopened on his knee.
And, if he then should dare to think
Of the fewness, muchness, rareness,
35   Greatness of this endless only
Precious world in which he says
He lives—he then unties the string.

Responding to the Poem

Analyzing the Poem

Identifying Details

1. To whom is the poem addressed? What "warning" does the speaker deliver?
2. What is inside the parcel?
3. Why shouldn't the children undo the parcel?

Interpreting Meanings

4. Identify the **repetitions** in the poem. Given the poem's **theme,** what makes the use of repetition especially effective?
5. Comment on the poet's use of **rhythm.** Do you think it gives the poem a somber, serious tone, or does it create a sense of fun and playfulness?

6. What do you think this poem is really all about? What could it be saying about the imagination?

Writing About the Poem

A Creative Response

1. **Writing a Reply.** Imagine that the poet's warning has been delivered to you. In a brief paragraph or poem, write a reply, stating your reaction.
2. **Imitating the Writer's Technique.** What do *you* imagine might be in one of these parcels? Write your own description of the world the child might find if he or she pulled the string.

Robert Graves   1103

1. BUILDING ON PRIOR KNOWLEDGE.
Discuss what Larkin might have meant by comparing Smith's poetry to that of Blake and Nash. Remind students of the mystical nature of Blake's poetry, especially its juxtaposition of childlike innocence and harshly mature realism. Explain that American poet Ogden Nash is best known for wry verse that takes a comical look at nature and satirizes aspects of modern life. Encourage students to make note of their response so that they can review it after they have read "Not Waving but Drowning."

2. ESTABLISHING A PURPOSE. Encourage students to keep the word *communication* in mind as they read. Have them consider what the poem suggests about communication in general and about the kinds of people that have the most difficulty communicating.

3. PREREADING JOURNAL. Have students use their journals to describe an incident (real or imaginary) in which problems arose because one person or group of people failed to understand what someone else was trying to say.

Stevie Smith
(1902–1971)

She was christened Florence Margaret Smith but got the nickname "Stevie" because she was short, like the British jockey Steve Donaghue. She grew up in a suburb of London, abandoned by her father and raised by her mother and an aunt. She lived with "Auntie" for sixty-six years, until the old woman died in 1968. The film *Stevie,* starring Glenda Jackson, portrays the relationship between Stevie and Auntie. It also gives a glimpse of Smith's wit and insight as well as her oblique slant on life.

Smith's early publications—mostly novels— reflect her offbeat outlook and writing style. But it is in her poems that she fully displays her cleverness. The light side of her poetry often reflects a darker side as well, making her verse **serio-comic** (partly serious, partly humorous). Her poems often deal with death, loneliness, or despair, but Smith is never self-pitying. Her humor adds sparkle, allowing her to distance herself from her subject. Smith herself best summed up her paradoxical views when she claimed that she was "straightforward, but not simple." Poet Philip Larkin (see page 1132) described her poems as "William Blake rewritten by Ogden Nash."

CLOSURE

Ask students if, having read the poem, they feel that Larkin's comment applies. (Most students will agree that the poem contains both humor and sharply contrasting images.)

Tell students that Stevie Smith, like Dylan Thomas, participated in a revival of oral poetry, reading her poems aloud all over Britain. Ask students what tone they would try to adopt in an oral presentation of "Not Waving but Drowning" and to explain their choice.

Stevie Smith published ten volumes of verses, but except for this one single poem, most of her poetry is unknown to American readers.

Why—out of a lifetime of work—one particular poem should have become more famous than all of her other poems combined is a question best answered by readers like yourself. Whatever conclusion you may come to about "Not Waving but Drowning," here's what the poet reveals about her state of mind when she wrote the poem:

"I often try to pull myself together, having been well brought up in the stiff-upper-lip school of thought and not knowing either whether other people find Death as merry as I do. But it's a tightrope business, this pulling oneself together, and can give rise to misunderstandings which may prove fatal, as in this poem I wrote about a poor fellow who got drowned. His friends thought he was waving to them but really he was asking for help."

As you read, listen for the different voices speaking in the poem.

Not Waving but Drowning

A ⌐ Nobody heard him, the dead man,
But still he lay moaning:
I was much further out than you thought
And not waving but drowning.

5 Poor chap, he always loved larking
And now he's dead
B ⌐ It must have been too cold for him his heart gave way,
They said.

10 Oh, no no no, it was too cold always ⌐ C
(Still the dead one lay moaning)
I was much too far out all my life
And not waving but drowning.

Blue and Silver-Chopping Channel by James McNeil Whistler (1890's). Watercolor on paper (5½″ × 9½″).

Courtesy of the Freer Gallery of Art, Smithsonian Institution, Washington, D.C. (99.24).

A. Characterization/Interpreting

? What might this line suggest about the personality or identity of the dead man? (*Further out* suggests that he lives on the edge of society.)

B. Symbol/Interpreting

? Beyond a purely literal reading, what might the "cold" represent? (Students may say it refers to a lack of warm human relationships or love.)

C. Tone

Elicit from students that the repeated *no* helps achieve a childlike quality—one that contrasts ironically with the poem's serious subject matter.

D. Humanities Connection: Responding to the Fine Art

American artist James McNeil Whistler (1834–1903), often created harmonies of color more pleasing than the actual colors of a scene.

? How is the painting different from a photograph of the same scene? (A photograph would be sharper, more true-to-life.)

1. Lines 1–2: the author herself, or the speaker she employs in telling this poetic incident.

Lines 3–4: the drowned man.

Lines 5–7: friends of the dead man (possibly bystanders).

Lines 9, 11, 12: the dead man.

Line 10: the poet (or her speaker).

Interpreting Meanings

2. The title refers to the horrible mistake that onlookers made in thinking that the man was merely waving, when in actuality he was signaling for help.

3. Answers will vary; students may suggest that his failure to communicate well even in his lifetime indicates an emotional deadness.

4. The man's signal for help is misunder-stood as "larking." It is suggested that the onlookers are inaccurate in conclud-ing that the cold caused him to have a heart attack. They also seem to have misunderstood his need for closeness to others, as they failed to realize that he had been emotionally "too cold."

5. The man's comment about the cold may mean that his life experiences were *(Answers continue in left-hand column.)*

(Continued from top.)
harsh, largely be-cause of his inabili-ty to connect with other people. He was "too far out" perhaps because he was in some way uncommon or perhaps, paradoxi-cally, because he was locked too far within himself.

6. Students may suggest that there is, in every mo-ment, a possibility for understanding or misunderstand-ing. As much as people try to com-municate in a meaningful way, they may not al-ways communicate perfectly. For this reason, each indi-vidual stands alone.

7. Students proba-bly will agree that there is a dark hu-mor in the poem and that it is sad—both in the fact of the man's death and in the lonely life he seems to have led. Students may point out the truth that people need to be loved and under-stood in order to stay alive emotion-ally. Students also may call the poem economical in that it conveys so many contrasts in such a brief space.

Responding to the Poem

Analyzing the Poem

Identifying Details

1. Who is speaking in lines 1–2? In lines 3–4? In lines 5–7? In lines 9, 11, 12? In line 10?

Interpreting Meanings

2. What does the title of the poem mean?
3. It seems bizarre that a dead man is talking. What might "dead" signify in the poem, besides its literal meaning?
4. Describe all the ways that the dead man is misunder-stood or ignored.
5. What does the speaker mean by "it was too cold always" and "I was much too far out all my life"?
6. How could this poem be a summing up of one's whole life, or of the human condition in general?
7. Stevie Smith once said that good writing had to be "sad, true, economical, and funny." Does the poem meet these criteria? Discuss your responses.

Writing About the Poem

A Creative Response

1. **Writing Verse.** Write a lighthearted or comic poem in which a person is not drowning but waving. (Your poem can be in free verse—that is, without a regular meter or rhyme scheme.) You might call your poem "Not Drowning but Waving." Decide ahead of time who your speaker will be.

A Critical Response

2. **Explaining a Metaphor.** In an essay explain how the sea is often used as a metaphor for life. What comparisons do we often make between living and swimming, float-ing, sinking, diving, or drowning?

Primary Sources
The Truths About Poetry

"Here are some of the truths about poetry. She is an Angel, very strong. It is not poetry but the poet who has a feminine ending, not the Muse who is weak, but the poet. She makes a strong communication. Poetry is like a strong explosion in the sky. She makes a mushroom shape of terror and drops to the ground with a strong infection. Also she is a strong way out. The human creature is alone in his carapace. Poetry is a strong way out. . . .

"Poetry does not like to be up to date, she refuses to be neat. ('Anglo-Saxon,' wrote Gavin Bone, 'is a good language to write poetry in because it is impossible to be neat.') All the poems Poetry writes may be called 'Heaven, a Detail,' or 'Hell, a Detail.' (She only writes about heaven and hell.) . . .

"All Poetry has to do is to make a strong communi-cation. All the poet has to do is to listen. The poet is not an important fellow. There will always be another poet."

—from *Me Again,*
Stevie Smith

W. H. Auden
(1907–1973)

A Wystan Hugh Auden gave a name to his times—
"the Age of Anxiety"—and he lived to see the
day when his influence was so broad and deep
that, as far as poetry was concerned, that same
era became known as "the Age of Auden."

Auden was born in York, a city in northern
England near the city of Leeds. He was the son
of a physician and a nurse who encouraged his
early interest in science and engineering. But in
his adolescence, Auden discovered poetry, and
he studied, with an analytical eye, all the forms
of it from Chaucer onward. By the time he entered Oxford, he was as much a teacher as he
was a student, and he quickly gathered about
himself other young poets, who accepted him as
their leader.

Auden as a poet was difficult to classify, and
he remains so to this day. By the time they have
been recognized and acclaimed, most of the outstanding poets of any generation have produced
individual works by which, rightly or wrongly,
they will be identified. Sometimes these poems
are masterpieces; sometimes they are more or
less run of the mill poems which, for one reason
or another, have caught the popular imagination.
To this, Auden is an exception. In spite of their
virtuosity, uniform excellence, and formal variety, Auden's poems—lyrics, oratorios, ballads—
tend to cohere as a body of work rather than to
distinguish themselves as easily separable enti-
ties. For this reason, Auden is often regarded
less as the author of certain individual poems
than as the creator of a climate in which all
things Audenesque thrive in an atmosphere
uniquely his own.

Auden put his indelible stamp on the poetry
of the 1930's, establishing his preeminence
among the brilliant group of poets that included
Stephen Spender, Louis MacNeice, and Cecil
Day Lewis. Auden caused his countrymen shock
and dismay when, in the critical year of 1939,
when Hitler's divisions were to march through
Poland and initiate World War II, he decided to
make his home in America. In a practical sense,
this decision was prompted by an invitation from
the University of Michigan to join its English

W. H. Auden (1967). Photograph © 1988
by Jill Krementz.

faculty on any teaching terms he chose. In a
broader sense, Auden had come to feel that, as
the rise of fascism made war in Europe inevitable, his chances of enjoying creative freedom
and of making a livelihood were available only in
America. At first merely a temporary measure,
Auden's residence at the University of Michigan
was extended to include teaching positions at
other universities. He became an American citizen in 1946.

For the ten years following, Auden lived
mostly in New York City. He spent his summers
in Kirchstetten, Austria, in a house he bought in
1957 with profits from his extensive reading
tours—the first, and last, home of his own. This
retreat, not far from Vienna, provided him with
much-needed privacy and the opportunity to experience firsthand the culture of Middle Europe.

In England, Auden's immigration to the United
States was, at the time, widely regarded as a de-
fection, if not an outright betrayal. But his countrymen eventually welcomed him back—first by
electing him Professor of Poetry at Oxford, and
later by making it possible for him to live on the
campus of Christ Church College as a guest of
the university whenever he returned to England.

A. *The Age of Anxiety*

This is the title of a long dramatic poem for which Auden won a Pulitzer Prize in 1948. The poem is set in a seedy Third Avenue bar in New York City. Though Auden was a Marxist early in his life, he grad-ually shifted to the faith of Anglo-Catholicism. A famous expression of that faith is found in a poem called "For the Time Being," which is the closing speech in Auden's impressive Christ-mas oratorio of the same title. "The time being" refers to the time be-tween the two great Christian feasts of Christ-mas and Easter, when Auden im-agines people tem-porarily returning to a state of ordi-nariness. "The time being," he says in the poem, is the most trying time of all.

1. BUILDING ON PRIOR KNOWLEDGE. Ask students to study closely the reproduction of Brueghel's painting *The Fall of Icarus* on the bottom of this page. Tell them that Brueghel was a sixteenth-century Flemish painter, meaning he was from the German-speaking area of northern Belgium called Flanders. Auden's poem is concerned with the proper perspective on suffering in human life. It finds its answer in a particular interpretation of Brueghel's painting. Be sure they review what they know of the myth of Icarus.

2. ESTABLISHING A PURPOSE. Ask students to identify the tone of the speaker toward his subject. Is he indignant, despairing, or detached?

SUPPLEMENTARY SUPPORT MATERIALS
1. Vocabulary Activity Worksheet (*CCB*)
2. Review and Response Worksheet: Theme (*CCB*)
3. Selection Test (*CCB*)

DEVELOPING VOCABULARY
The following word from the poem is tested in the Selection Test. (See also Vocabulary Activity Worksheet.)
martyrdom

A. Humanities Connection: Discussing the Fine Art
Flemish painter Pieter Brueghel, or Brueghel the Elder (c. 1525–1569) was a lover of nature and was insatiably curious about his fellow humans. His paintings, well-received in their day, are full of rich details of ordinary life and often have a moral or philosophical message. Brueghel's interest in the lives of the peasants was not of a romantic, escapist nature. His paintings realistically depict both the vigor and the coarseness of country life.

? How is Icarus's death regarded by the rest of the world? (They fail to notice the drowning boy.)

The source and inspiration for this poem is the famous painting by Pieter Brueghel showing Icarus drowning, permanently on display in the fine arts museum (Musée des Beaux Arts) in Brussels, Belgium. The painting depicts a dramatic moment in the Greek legend of Daedalus and his son Icarus. According to the legend, the two were imprisoned on the island of Crete. In order to escape, Daedalus constructed wings of feathers and wax. Together they managed to take off from the island, but Icarus flew so high that the sun's heat melted the wax in his wings, causing him to fall into the sea and drown.

According to one critic, the painting represents "the greatest conception of indifference" in the history of art. The indifference, whether it is the artist's attitude or merely a strategy of technique, lies in its unexpected focus. The painting's center of interest is a peasant plowing a field above the sea. He is handsomely dressed—in medieval rather than in Greek costume—and the furrows he tills are richly realistic. In the lower right-hand corner of the painting, almost as an afterthought, Icarus is seen splashing into the water not far from a passing ship.

Extending Brueghel's painting, Auden picks up its indifference, notes its rightness in regard to suffering, and goes on to confirm in words what the painter expressed with pigment.

Musée des Beaux Arts

The Fall of Icarus by Pieter Brueghel the Elder.

Musée des Beaux Arts, Brussels, Belgium.

ANALYZING THE POEM
Identifying Details

1. The acknowledged geniuses of European painting.

The examples from Brueghel's paintings show individuals' indifference to
events outside their immediate world.

2. The poet refers to Brueghel's painting
The Fall of Icarus.

Interpreting Meanings

3. The title means "museum of fine
arts," perhaps used ironically.

4. In the first painting, the subject is
probably the birth of Christ; the indifferent
children skate on a pond at the edge of a
wood. The subject of the second may be
Christ's crucifixion or the martyrdom of a
saint; unperturbed dogs and horses are
pictured as an ironic counterpoint.

5. One statement of the theme might be
this: Human beings are indifferent to one
another's suffering, as nature and Brueghel's art are. Students' comments will
vary.

6. Consider people's responses to the
homeless in their midst, to disasters in
far-off places, to unemployment in the
next town, to those sick in hospitals, and
so on.

About suffering they were never wrong,
The Old Masters: how well they understood
Its human position; how it takes place
A ⎡ While someone else is eating or opening a window or just walking dully along;
5 How, when the aged are reverently, passionately waiting
B ⎡ For the miraculous birth, there always must be
Children who did not specially want it to happen, skating
On a pond at the edge of the wood:
C ⎡ They never forgot
10 That even the dreadful martyrdom must run its course
Anyhow in a corner, some untidy spot
D ⎡ Where the dogs go on with their doggy life and the torturer's horse
Scratches its innocent behind on a tree.

E ⎡ In Brueghel's *Icarus,* for instance: how everything turns away
15 Quite leisurely from the disaster; the plowman may
Have heard the splash, the forsaken cry,
But for him it was not an important failure; the sun shone
As it had to on the white legs disappearing into the green
Water; and the expensive delicate ship that must have seen
20 Something amazing, a boy falling out of the sky,
Had somewhere to get to and sailed calmly on.

Responding to the Poem

Analyzing the Poem

Identifying Details

1. Who are the "Old Masters" (line 2)? What examples
does the speaker provide to show how they understood
suffering?

2. What example of his theory does the poet offer in lines
14–21?

Interpreting Meanings

3. What is the meaning of the title?

4. Lines 5–13 describe two other paintings by Brueghel.
What do you think are the events that Brueghel portrays? What is the attitude of the bystanders to those
events?

5. Identify and comment on what you think is the overall
theme of the poem.

6. Do you agree with Auden's view of the "human position" of suffering? Explain.

Writing About the Poem

A Creative Response

1. Describing a Painting. Study the reproduction of
Brueghel's *Icarus.* In a paragraph, describe the painting's most significant features. Do you think Auden
has correctly interpreted Brueghel's intent?

A Critical Response

2. Researching a Myth. Read a translation or summary of
Ovid's version of the myth of Daedalus and Icarus in
Book 8 of the *Metamorphoses.* Then, in a brief essay,
relate the original story to Auden's treatment of it.

**A. Interpreting
Events**
❓ What kinds of
actions are
listed in line 4 as
going on while oth-
ers suffer? (Eating,
opening a window,
walking dully
along)

B. Allusion
❓ How do you in-
terpret the ref-
erence to "the mi-
raculous birth" in
line 6? (Probably
Christ's birth) Why
might children be
unenthusiastic
about a birth? (A
new sibling is often
a rival for parents'
attention.)

C. Allusion
❓ To what might
"the dreadful
martyrdom" refer?
(Christ's Crucifix-
ion)

D. Theme
The first stanza
suggests ordinary
life continues in
the midst of suffer-
ing.
❓ According to
lines 12–13,
how is the natural
world affected by
human suffering?
(It is unaffected or
indifferent.)

E. Expansion
There may be sig-
nificance in the
fact that the man
who turns away
from Icarus's fall is
a farmer, an earthy
and a necessary
occupation.

PREPARATION

1. BUILDING ON PRIOR KNOWLEDGE. Tell students that stanzas 3–5 echo traditional ballads, love songs, and love poetry in which the young lover vows everlasting love. Students may be familiar with the song "Twelfth of Never," which contains similar extravagant promises of all-conquering love.

2. ESTABLISHING A PURPOSE. Ask students to look for the speaker's attitude toward human love.

SUPPLEMENTARY SUPPORT MATERIALS
1. Vocabulary Activity Worksheet (*CCB*)
2. Review and Response Worksheet: Figures of Speech (*CCB*)
3. Selection Test (*CCB*)

DEVELOPING VOCABULARY
The following word from the poem is tested in the Selection Test. (See also Vocabulary Activity Worksheet.)
burrow

A. Expansion
The "I" in line 1 is an observer of the life around him. He hears the lover singing in stanza 2.

B. Word Choice
? What is the effect of the choice of the verb "coughs" here? (Time seems an old, skeptical, unromantic force that is mocking the young lovers.)

C. Theme
? How does stanza 8 suggest Time will defeat the lovers? (The wearying, everyday cares of the passing years)

D. Expansion
This stanza could be interpreted as an ironic allusion to Narcissus, who fell in love with his image in a pool of water.

E. Interpreting Meaning
? How do you interpret the word *crooked*? (It suggests aging and certainly imperfection.)

F. Mood
? What is the dominant mood of the last stanza? (Resignation, necessity, detachment)

Love, time, and human destiny are weighty themes for any poem. This one carries them all with a musical beat, a steady step, and rhythms made familiar by generations of ballad writers.

Its metaphors and similes are fanciful; but its sobering conclusion (in the next-to-last stanza) echoes a line Auden wrote much earlier: "We must love one another or die."

Song: As I Walked Out One Evening

A
As I walked out one evening,
  Walking down Bristol Street,
The crowds upon the pavement
  Were fields of harvest wheat.

5 And down by the brimming river
  I heard a lover sing
Under an arch of the railway:
  "Love has no ending.

I'll love you, dear, I'll love you
10   Till China and Africa meet,
And the river jumps over the mountain
  And the salmon sing in the street.

I'll love you till the ocean
  Is folded and hung up to dry,
15 And the seven stars go squawking
  Like geese about the sky.

The years shall run like rabbits,
  For in my arms I hold
The Flower of the Ages,
20   And the first love of the world."

But all the clocks in the city
  Begin to whirr and chime:
"O let not Time deceive you,
  You cannot conquer Time.

25 In the burrows of the Nightmare
  Where Justice naked is,
Time watches from the shadow
B   And coughs when you would kiss.

C
In headaches and in worry
30   Vaguely life leaks away,
And Time will have his fancy
  Tomorrow or today.

Into many a green valley
  Drifts the appalling snow;
35 Time breaks the threaded dances
  And the diver's brilliant bow.

D
O plunge your hands in water,
  Plunge them in up to the wrist;
Stare, stare in the basin
40   And wonder what you've missed.

The glacier knocks in the cupboard,
  The desert sighs in the bed,
And the crack in the tea cup opens
  A lane to the land of the dead.

45 Where the beggars raffle the banknotes
  And the Giant is enchanting to Jack,
And the Lily-white Boy is a Roarer
  And Jill goes down on her back.

O look, look in the mirror,
50   O look in your distress;
Life remains a blessing
  Although you cannot bless.

O stand, stand at the window
  As the tears scald and start;
55 **E** You shall love your crooked neighbor
  With your crooked heart."

F
It was late, late in the evening,
  The lovers they were gone;
The clocks had ceased their chiming
60   And the deep river ran on.

ANALYZING THE POEM
Identifying Details
1. That he will love her forever.
2. The clocks warn the speaker that he cannot conquer the effects of time.

Interpreting Meanings
3. Comparing the crowds to fields of wheat suggests that the lover is in an upbeat, romantic mood; perhaps also that he is inclined to hyperbole.
4. The images of naked justice buried in a nightmare (lines 25–26), the figure of speech of life "leaking away" (line 30), of "appalling snow" (line 34), glacier and desert (lines 41–42), beggars (line 45), and scalding tears (line 54).
5. The first may suggest poverty, while the second probably refers to lovelessness or the waning of passion.

The crack may be a metaphor for the wrinkles, or "cracks," of old age; since the crack leads "to the land of the dead" (line 44), the poet is probably referring to old age and death.
6. The clocks suggest that justice is often thwarted (lines 25–26), human life is beset by anxiety (lines 29–30), and children are often immoral (lines 47–48).
7. The central irony is that time inevitably reverses some of our youthful, optimistic expectations about life and romance.
   Student answers may vary. Many may suggest that, although playful on the surface, the poem is actually quite somber.
8. In lines 55–56, the clocks suggest that, despite human beings' "crookedness" and all their imperfections, they are still capable of love.
9. Student answers will vary. The relatively light form of the poem—quatrains that resemble the ballad stanza, with rhyme scheme *abcb*—ironically contrasts with its somber message.
10. Student answers will vary. Ask them if this seems to be the expression of a young person, or of an older, experienced one.

Big Ear, Big Mouth by Irvin Tepper (1981). White charcoal drawing.

Newport Harbor Art Museum, Newport Beach, California.

Responding to the Poem

Analyzing the Poem

Identifying Details

1. What does the lover declare to the beloved in lines 8–20?
2. How do the clocks of the city respond to the lover's declaration?

Interpreting Meanings

3. What does the **metaphor** in lines 3–4 reveal about the lover's mood as the poem opens?
4. List the **images** and **figures of speech** in the clocks' response that contrast with this metaphor.
5. What do you think the poet means by the glacier that knocks in the cupboard and the desert that sighs in the bed? How would you explain the significance of the crack in the tea cup and where it leads? (See lines 41–44.)

6. What other **reversals** of romantic expectations does the clocks' response give us?
7. How would you explain the central **irony** of the poem? What is the **tone** of the poem?
8. Does a new dimension of love emerge from the clocks' statement? Explain.
9. What effect does the form of the poem—its **sounds** and **metrics**—have on its message?
10. What do you think of the poet's feelings about love, as expressed by the clocks? What experiences might make a person feel this way?

Writing About the Poem

A Creative Response

Responding to the Poem. Write a response to the clocks' comments to the lover, using either prose or metrical verse. What will your tone be?

PREPARATION
1. BUILDING ON PRIOR KNOWLEDGE. Tell students that this poem reads like the official report of a death written by a government worker for some departmental file or like an obituary written by a detached journalist for a government newspaper.

2. ESTABLISHING A PURPOSE. Have students pay attention to the ways in which the dead man is identified. Do they distinguish him from others?

SUPPLEMENTARY SUPPORT MATERIALS
1. Vocabulary Activity Worksheet (*CCB*)
2. Review and Response Worksheet: Satire and Theme (*CCB*)
3. Selection Test (*CCB*)

DEVELOPING VOCABULARY
The following words from the poem are tested in the Selection Test. (See also Vocabulary Activity Worksheet.)
scab   eugenist

A. Word Choice
Note that the dead man's "virtues" are often presented in the negative, as in line 2, where it is reported that "there was *no* official complaint."
❓ What are some other examples? ("Never got fired"; "wasn't a scab")

B. Humanities Connection: Discussing the Fine Art
Eduardo Paolozzi was born in Scotland in 1924. He is known principally as a sculptor and printmaker. Interested in popular culture and modern technology, he is associated with the Pop Art School and with the incorporation of industrial components into his sculpture. He deliberately sought the assistance of technicians when assembling his work to play down the subjective aspect of his creations.
❓ Ask students to list all the images in this work and to suggest what they have in common. (Austrian-born Ludwig Wittgenstein is one of the major philosophers of the twentieth century.)

One of the persistent themes of twentieth-century literature is the anonymity of the individual in an ever more bureaucratic world. Here, Auden mimics the language of officialdom in a report that covers everything except the fact that "the unknown citizen" had a heart and a soul.

The Unknown Citizen

(To JS/07/M/378
This Marble Monument
Is Erected by the State)

He was found by the Bureau of Statistics to be
One against whom there was no official complaint,
And all the reports on his conduct agree
That, in the modern sense of an old-fashioned word, he was a saint,
5   For in everything he did he served the Greater Community.
Except for the War till the day he retired
He worked in a factory and never got fired,
But satisfied his employers, Fudge Motors Inc.

Wittgenstein in New York
by Eduardo Paolozzi.

Editions Alecto, London.

ANALYZING THE POEM
Identifying Details
1. He worked in a factory. He satisfied his employers, held "normal" views, paid his Union dues, liked a drink with his "mates," bought a paper every day, took out insurance, had one hospital stay, bought on the installment plan, served in the war, married and had five children, and never interfered with his children's education.
2. The Bureau of Statistics, the Union, the Social Psychology workers, the press, Producers Research and High-Grade Living, the researchers in Public Opinion, the Eugenist.
3. A government official.

Interpreting Meanings
4. The "old-fashioned" sense of "saint"—piety and an exemplary life—is contrasted with the "modern" sense—normalcy and conformity.
5. An unconventional person; perhaps a friend of the deceased.
6. He was an exemplary citizen, honored by the state.
 Consider its similarity to the Tomb of the Unknown Soldier.
7. Some will sympathize with the citizen, claiming that rigid conformity, rather than the citizen, is Auden's real target.
8. The tone is satirical.
9. The poem sounds like an FBI report.
10. The modern world emphasizes conformity at the expense of individuality, freedom, and happiness.
11. Student answers will vary.
12. Most will agree that mention of social institutions, appliances, and automobiles makes this a twentieth-century poem.

A. Expansion
A *scab* is a person who crosses a picket line and takes the job of a striking worker.

B. Theme
The impersonal voice seems to approve of the dead man's behavior.
❓ What does the voice appear to value in a citizen? (Conformity, obedience, consumption, and complacency)

CLOSURE
On the basis of the poems they have read, ask students if they consider Auden a Romantic or an ironic poet. Have them cite examples of his themes and use of language.

A Yet he wasn't a <u>scab</u> or odd in his views,
10 For his Union reports that he paid his dues,
    (Our report on his Union shows it was sound)
    And our Social Psychology workers found
    That he was popular with his mates and liked a drink.
    The Press are convinced that he bought a paper every day
15 And that his reactions to advertisements were normal in every way.
    Policies taken out in his name prove that he was fully insured,
    And his Health-card shows he was once in hospital but left it cured.
    Both Producers Research and High-Grade Living declare
B   He was fully sensible to the advantages of the Installment Plan
20 And had everything necessary to the Modern Man,
    A phonograph, a radio, a car and a frigidaire.
    Our researchers into Public Opinion are content
    That he held the proper opinions for the time of year;
    When there was peace, he was for peace; when there was war, he went.
25 He was married and added five children to the population,
    Which our <u>Eugenist</u> says was the right number for a parent of his generation,
    And our teachers report that he never interfered with their education.
    Was he free? Was he happy? The question is absurd:
    Had anything been wrong, we should certainly have heard.

Responding to the Poem

Analyzing the Poem

Identifying Details

1. What did the unknown citizen do for a living? What facts are reported on his conduct?
2. What agencies or groups contribute to this report?
3. Who is the speaker of the poem?

Interpreting Meanings

4. What do you think a saint is in the "modern sense" of an old-fashioned word (line 4)?
5. Who do you think might have asked the questions in line 28?
6. What do you make of the inscription under the title? What other "monuments" are you reminded of?
7. The poem seems to depict the "unknown citizen" as a colorless stereotype. Did you, however, sympathize with the citizen? Explain your response to him.
8. Although the poet does not directly state his opinions in this poem, they clearly emerge from the poem's **tone.** How would you describe this tone?
9. What is the effect of the poet's **free verse**? What does it make the poem *sound* like?
10. What is the message or **theme** of this poem?

11. Do you think this poem gives a true depiction of contemporary society, or where society is heading? Explain what details of the poem are or are not paralleled in reality.
12. Could this poem have been written in any other time of history but the twentieth century? Why or why not?

Writing About the Poem

A Creative Response

1. **Shifting the Point of View.** Change the point of view to that of a good friend of the deceased citizen. Write his obituary from this new point of view.
2. **Imitating the Writer's Technique.** Write your own epitaph for an unknown citizen (or soldier, movie star, politician, etc.). Use the questions "Was he or she free? Was he or she happy?" as the focus of your account.

A Critical Response

3. **Analyzing Satire.** In a brief essay, analyze the targets and the methods of Auden's **satire** in this poem. Does Auden manage to combine satire and sympathy? Explain.

Louis MacNeice
(1907–1963)

Louis MacNeice was born in Belfast, Northern Ireland, but he lived most of his life in England. During his years at Oxford University, he became associated with the talented poets of his own age—W. H. Auden, Stephen Spender, and C. Day Lewis—who achieved international prominence as the English Group during the early 1930's. Although he began an academic career as Lecturer in Classics at Birmingham University, MacNeice was drawn to another, more congenial, kind of work. He soon went to London and a lifelong position on the programming staff of the British Broadcasting Corporation.

With the publication of *Poems* in 1935, MacNeice established himself as a poet of urbane grace and wit who had a varied sense of musical measure. He also showed a notably relaxed view of the political causes in which his colleagues were personally enlisted. Never directly involved in the political issues that dominated the 1930's, MacNeice nevertheless made a memorable contribution to the poetry of his generation with his book *Autumn Journal* (1939). These poems were based on the most public of political concerns—the rise of fascism in Europe and its threat to England. According to critic Cyril Connolly, the poems in *Autumn Journal* "preserve forever the uneasy atmosphere of 'Munich.' " Connolly was referring to those months when it became increasingly clear that the pact Prime Minister Neville Chamberlain had made with Adolf Hitler would not be honored. It was a time when preparations for the defense of England were visible everywhere, including freshly dug trenches in the manicured lawn of Hyde Park.

© Rollie McKenna.

Just before the war broke out, MacNeice made several visits to the United States, one of them to teach at Cornell University. On later trips, he read his poems in solo performances, or shared the stage with his wife, Hedli Anderson, a former cabaret singer who became an interpreter of art songs.

Not an orthodox believer, MacNeice saw writing as a kind of participation in the divine act of creation. "This very act of shaping," he once said, "may bring him [the poet] back full circle into something like belief."

PREPARATION

1. BUILDING ON PRIOR KNOWLEDGE. Tell students that the poem has many elements of a conventional prayer. In it, a higher power is addressed and asked to provide protection, nourishment, consolation, guidance, forgiveness, and strength.

2. ESTABLISHING A PURPOSE. As students read, ask them to look for those elements of the poem that are surprising and not typical of a conventional prayer.

SUPPLEMENTARY SUPPORT MATERIALS
1. Vocabulary Activity Worksheet (*CCB*)
2. Review and Response Worksheet: Simile and Metaphor (*CCB*)
3. Selection Test (*CCB*)

DEVELOPING VOCABULARY
The following words from the poem are tested in the Selection Test. (See also Vocabulary Activity Worksheet.)
stoat   to dissipate

The dramatic force of this poem comes from its perspective—a view of the joys and hazards of existence as seen by a child yet to be born. The poem is an *apostrophe*—words spoken to an absent person or a thing. Since it is also a prayer, we assume that it is addressed to a higher power that, although never named, is capable of responding.

The poem's rhetorical flourishes and lofty tone would not have been out of place in the nineteenth century; yet much of what the speaker fears is associated only with life in the twentieth century.

Prayer Before Birth

Even poisons praise thee.
—George Herbert

A
I am not yet born; O hear me.
Let not the bloodsucking bat or the rat or the <u>stoat</u> or
    the club-footed ghoul come near me.

B
I am not yet born, console me.
I fear that the human race may with tall walls wall me,
    with strong drugs dope me, with wise lies lure me, on
        black racks rack me, in bloodbaths roll me.

C
5 I am not yet born; provide me
With water to dandle me, grass to grow for me, trees to
    talk to me, sky to sing to me, birds and a white light
        in the back of my mind to guide me.

D
I am not yet born; forgive me
For the sins that in me the world shall commit, my
    words when they speak me, my thoughts when they
        think me, my treason engendered by traitors
            beyond me, my life when they murder by means
                of my hands, my death when they live me.

I am not yet born; rehearse me
In the parts I must play and the cues I must take when
    old men lecture me, bureaucrats hector me, mountains
        frown at me, lovers laugh at me, the white waves
            call me to folly and the desert calls me to doom
                and the beggar refuses my gift and my
10   children curse me.
I am not yet born; O hear me,
Let not the man who is beast or who thinks he is God
    come near me.

A. Expansion
A *stoat* is a type of weasel. Note that in this first stanza the child fears animals and monsters, fears that a child of any century might express.

B. Imagery
In the second stanza, the child begins to enumerate fears that seem more specific to the twentieth century.
? What do you think the "wise lies" are? (Possibly propaganda, advertising, sweeping ideologies)

C. Imagery
In this stanza, the child seeks the solace of various nurturing forces.
? What do you think is the "white light in the back of my mind"? (Conscience, intuition, or faith)

D. Figurative Language
The fourth stanza contains a series of paradoxes, or seeming contradictions.
? Why do you think the child is asking for forgiveness for the crimes of others? (All humans share in the responsibility for the crimes of humanity.)

Identifying Details

1. An unborn child.

2. In the first, the speaker prays for protection from the physical threats. In the second, he prays for consolation. In the third, he asks to enjoy the beauties of nature. In the fourth, he asks for forgiveness of the sins he may commit. In the fifth, he asks for patience and forbearance. In the last, he asks for the courage to preserve his individuality.

Interpreting Meanings

3. The phrases "I am not yet born" at the beginning of each stanza, the use of "O," and the use of the word "let."

4. Because the speaker's requests grow more complex as he progresses from prayers for physical protection to requests concerning his emotional, intellectual, and moral nature.

The three-word last line shocks because the speaker asks for death if the other requests cannot be fulfilled.

5. "Tall walls wall me," "water to dandle me," "sky to sing to me," "my death when they live me," "mountains frown at me," "dragoon me into a lethal automa- *(Answers continue on next page.)*

A. Humanities Connection: Responding to the Fine Art

David Siqueiros (1898–1974) is one of the great Mexican muralists. His work stresses Mexican history and humanity's struggle for freedom. Beginning in the 1920's, Siqueiros, along with other Mexican artists such as José Orozco and Diego Rivera, painted many murals telling the story of the Mexican Revolution. Their work can be seen on public buildings throughout Latin America.

❓ What similarities are there between Siqueiros's painting and MacNeice's poem? (Both are emotional reactions to a world full of pain, poverty, suffering, injustice, and wars, in which the innocent are frequently the victims.) Does this violent image remind students of similar scenes in the news today?

I am not yet born; O fill me
With strength against those who would freeze my hu-
    manity, would dragoon me into a lethal automaton,
      would make me a cog in a machine, a thing with
        one face, a thing, and against all those who
          would dissipate my entirety, would blow
            me like thistledown hither and thither or
              hither and thither like water held in the
                hands would spill me.

15   Let them not make me a stone and let them not spill me.
    Otherwise kill me.

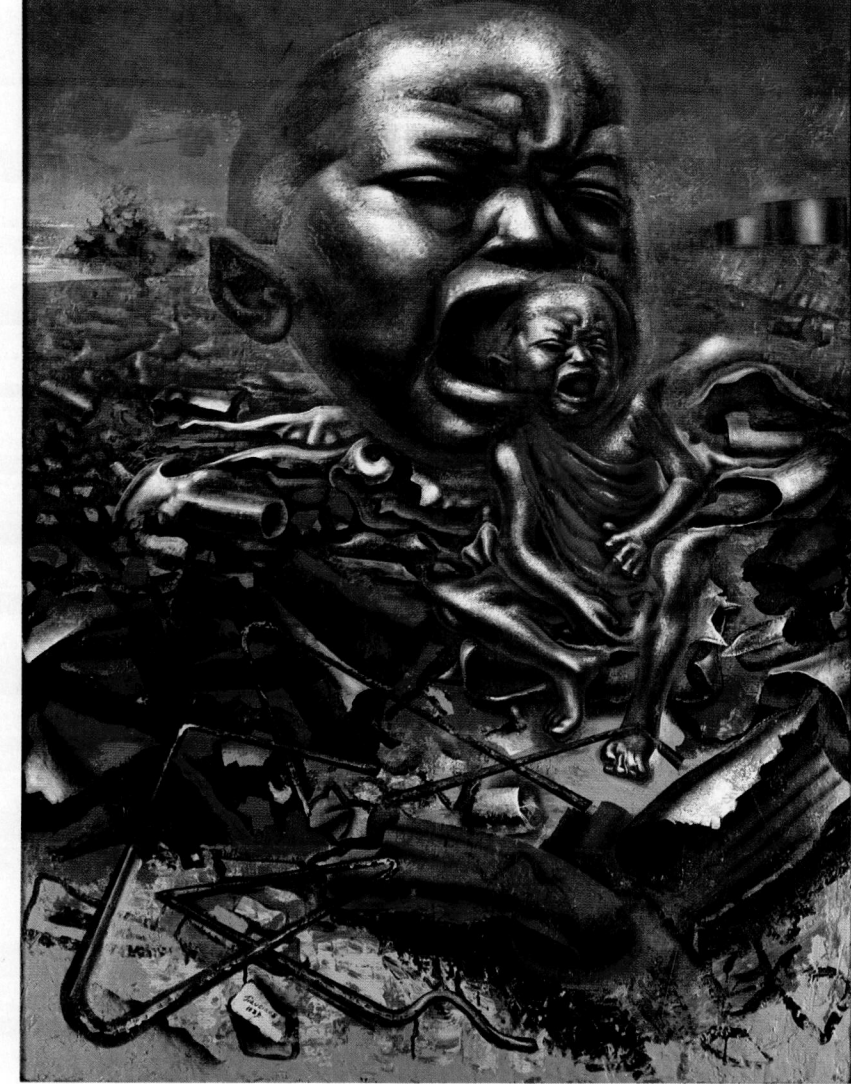

A

Echo of a Scream by David Alfaro Siqueiros (1937). Enamel on wood (48″ × 36″).

Collection. The Museum of Modern Art, New York. Gift of Edward M. M. Warburg.

1116

ton," "blow me like thistledown," "like water held in the hands would spill me."

6. It suggests that even the most obnoxious elements of God's creation—typified by "poisons"—give praise to God. The poet may be implying that human beings, evil as they may sometimes be, still praise God and pray for the strength and courage to be good.

7. Student answers will vary. Most students will agree that the tone is serious.

8. Student answers will vary. Encourage the students to give reasons for their "requests."

Responding to the Poem

Analyzing the Poem

Identifying Details

1. From whose **point of view** is the prayer uttered?

2. Summarize the speaker's prayer in each stanza.

Interpreting Meanings

3. What repetitive structures in the poem can you identify as typical of other prayers you are familiar with?

4. Why do you think the stanzas of the poem grow gradually longer? How and why does the last line clash with this pattern?

5. MacNeice's poem is rich in unusual figurative language. Pick out some especially striking examples of **simile** and **metaphor** in the poem.

6. What is the significance of the **epigraph**?

7. How would you describe the overall **tone** of the poem?

8. If you could have uttered a "prayer before birth," what might you have asked for?

Writing About the Poem

A Creative Response

1. **Using a Different Point of View.** In the epigraph from Herbert, MacNeice invokes a specific paradox and, by extension, the whole tradition of English Metaphysical poetry. After reviewing George Herbert (Unit Three), how do you think this seventeenth-century poet would have reacted to MacNeice's poem? Write a comment that Herbert might have jotted down in his notebook. Base your comment on what you know about Herbert's life, his beliefs, and his poetic technique.

A Critical Response

2. **Connecting Two Poems.** W. H. Auden's "The Unknown Citizen" is written as if it is an epitaph for someone who has died. This poem is written as if it's spoken by someone not yet born. Both poems relate very specifically to the twentieth century. In an essay, tell how you can imagine the two poems are connected. Consider **tone, imagery,** and **theme.**

Analyzing Language and Style

Free Verse

On close reading, you should be able to see how this poet has abandoned strict meter but has, at the same time, continued to use **rhyme, alliteration,** and **onomatopoeia.**

1. Identify as many rhymes in the poem as you can find. How many of them are internal rhymes?

2. What examples of alliteration and onomatopoeia can you find?

3. Where does the poet use a short line for dramatic effect?

CLOSURE
This poem was written over fifty years ago as a kind of prophecy of what the mid-twentieth century would offer its children. Ask students to discuss whether the prophecies came true. Is contemporary life any better or worse than this description? If they could answer the speaker, what would they say?

PREPARATION

1. BUILDING ON PRIOR KNOWLEDGE. Ask students to picture a high-speed express train pulling out of a city train station, gaining speed in the suburbs, and eventually hurtling through the countryside.

2. ESTABLISHING A PURPOSE. Tell students that the poem contains much metaphorical language, which enlarges the significance of the express train. Ask them to be aware of these metaphors as they read the poem initially and to go back afterward and consider the meaning of each.

SUPPLEMENTARY SUPPORT MATERIALS

1. Vocabulary Activity Worksheet *(CCB)*
2. Review and Response Worksheet: Sound Effects and Theme *(CCB)*
3. Selection Test *(CCB)*

Stephen Spender (1909–)

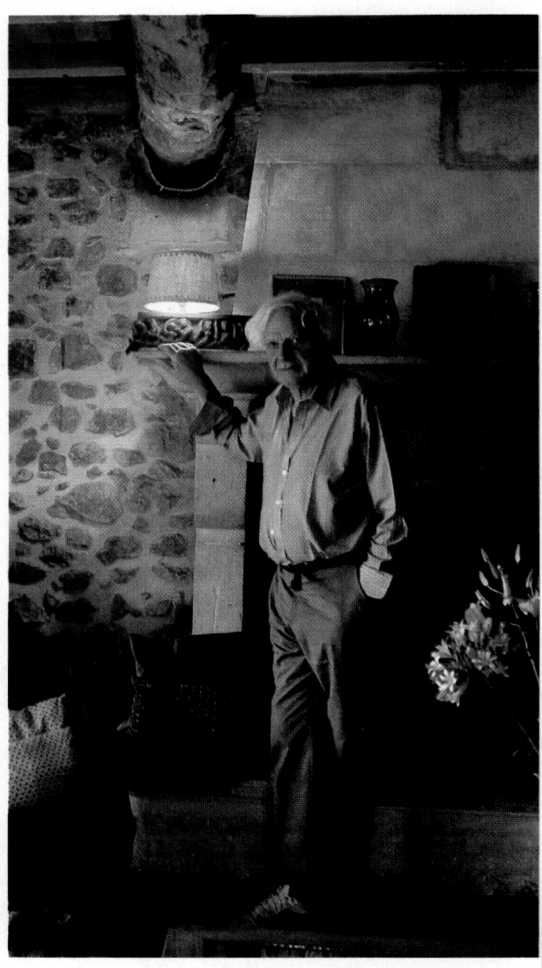

Stephen Spender was recently knighted in official recognition of his long career as poet, critic, and roving ambassador of British letters in conferences and seminars around the world. A pivotal member of that loose association known in America as the English Group, Spender as a young man produced a number of poems of spare power and broad resonance never to be repeated in the many volumes he has published since. He has been one of the most politically minded and, at the same time, the most lyrically romantic poet of his generation.

Spender has been a constant visitor to the United States, where he has held teaching positions from Connecticut to Texas. Consequently, he is familiar with the diversity of American poetry, is personally acquainted with many American poets, and has often assumed the task of explaining Anglo-American differences on both sides of the Atlantic.

Spender was an early champion of radical causes and a sympathetic observer of the great social changes wrought by the Russian Revolution. He was also one of the first European intellectuals to become disillusioned with Communism as the crimes of the Stalin era were brought to light. Joining with other similarly disillusioned writers, he became one of the most outspoken and effective anti-Communists of his time.

Spender was also one of the first writers to expose the kinds of censorship and repression by which, under the pretext of anti-Communism, many reactionary political factions and governments have attained power and curbed artistic freedom. While a full assessment of Spender's contribution to contemporary poetry is still to be made, it seems likely that he may go down in history as the political conscience of a generation. But Spender is aware that bad art, including bad poetry, may come from the most idealistic of intentions. He has been a spokesman for those artists who try to find the point at which humanitarian concerns and esthetic impulses may be joined without compromising either.

DEVELOPING VOCABULARY
The following word from the poem is tested in the Selection Test. (See also Vocabulary Activity Worksheet.)
trajectories

Critical Comment

? John Gross, an editor of *The New York Times Book Review*, wrote that "Spender's most characteristic poetry is marked by a strong vein of idealism and romantic yearning." Do you think this statement applies to "The Express"? Explain your answer.

CLOSURE
Ask students to summarize in a sentence or two what they think the express train stands for in Spencer's mind. What is his overall attitude toward the train—approving, disapproving, indifferent? Have them cite lines from the poem to support their answers.

The machine as an object of beauty equal to the natural beauty of birds, beasts, and flowers has been a recurrent theme for artists since the first decade of this century. Here, an express train, which goes nonstop at high speed from city to city, gradually takes on the character of a mysterious force. As it transforms everything with which it comes in contact, we hardly notice that the train itself is being transformed from an ordinary public conveyance to an object of romance.

The Express

After the first powerful, plain manifesto
The black statement of pistons, without more fuss
A But gliding like a queen, she leaves the station.
Without bowing and with restrained unconcern
5 She passes the houses which humbly crowd outside,
B The gasworks, and at last the heavy page
Of death, printed by gravestones in the cemetery.
Beyond the town, there lies the open country
C Where, gathering speed, she acquires mystery,
10 The luminous self-possession of ships on ocean.
It is now she begins to sing—at first quite low
Then loud, and at last with a jazzy madness—
The song of her whistle screaming at curves,
Of deafening tunnels, brakes, innumerable bolts.
15 And always light, aerial, underneath,
Retreats the elate° meter of her wheels.
D Steaming through metal landscape on her lines,
She plunges new eras of white happiness,
Where speed throws up strange shapes, broad curves
20 And parallels clean like trajectories from guns.
At last, further than Edinburgh or Rome,
Beyond the crest of the world, she reaches night
Where only a low streamline brightness
Of phosphorus on the tossing hills is light.
25 Ah, like a comet through flame, she moves entranced,
Wrapped in her music no bird song, no, nor bough
Breaking with honey buds, shall ever equal.

16. **elate:** elated; joyful.

A. Figurative Language
? What is the simile in lines 3–4? (A queen making a stately exit) What are the houses compared to in line 5? (Onlookers in a crowd that must make way for the passage of an important personage)

B. Figurative Language
? To what is the cemetery compared? (A somber page in a book of death)

C. Imagery
In lines 9–10, the poet suggests that the train moving in the dark acquires the mysterious look of a lighted ship at sea.
? What image does the poet use to describe the sounds the train makes? (A jazz singer)

D. Expansion
To understand lines 17–19, students need to know that the train has a steam engine and that it is white smoke escaping from the engine that is making strange shapes in the air.

Responding to the Poem

Analyzing the Poem

Identifying Details
1. Name the sights the train passes in lines 1–7.
2. Explain the **simile** in line 20. What two things are being compared?
3. What **metaphors** are combined in lines 21–27?

Interpreting Meanings
4. Why do you think the poet chose the word *manifesto* in line 1? What are the **connotations** of this word?
5. The poem makes constant use of **alliteration** to achieve **onomatopoeic** effects. Which lines do you think most clearly show the poet's attempt to fit the sound to the sense?

Identifying Details

1. Houses, gasworks, and the cemetery.
2. The moving train is compared with the trajectory of a bullet from a gun, suggesting speed.
3. "The crest of the world," "the tossing hills," the "streaming brightness of phosphorous," "a comet through flame."

Interpreting Meanings

4. The connotations of the word are philosophical and political. Spender may have chosen the word to set a philosophical tone at the outset.
5. Line 3 ("gliding like a queen"), line 5 ("She passes the houses which humbly crowd"), line 14 ("deafening tunnels, brakes, innumerable bolts"), line 16 ("retreats the elate meter of her wheels"),

and line 24 ("phosphorus on the tossing hills").

6. The poet may be suggesting that the train is as majestic and marvelous as the ship was in an earlier era.
7. Beyond the crest of the world where the train reaches night, speed distorts perception and creates mystery.
8. Answers will vary.

A. Humanities Connection: Discussing the Fine Art

Edward Hopper (1882–1967) was born in Nyack, New York. He was influenced by the Ashcan School, a group of artists active in the early twentieth century. Like them, Hopper wanted to convey the harsh reality of small-town and urban life in America. His paintings and etchings are spare and lit with a harsh light that suggests coldness, impersonality, and emptiness.

❓ What did Hopper choose to include in this painting of a train? What might he have included that he left out? How do you think he feels about this train? Are his feelings similar to those of the speaker in "The Express"? Why or why not? (Some might say that, unlike the speaker, Hopper's view of a train is cold and bleak, as evidenced by his use of dark colors, omission of people, and back—not front—view of the train.)

Railroad Train by Edward Hopper (1908). Oil.

Addison Gallery of American Art, Phillips Academy, Andover, Massachusetts.

6. Even when they have masculine names, ships are always referred to by sailors as though they were female. Why do you suppose the poet uses the feminine pronoun to refer to a railroad train? Line 10 might be a clue.
7. On the evidence supplied by this poem, what does speed do to perception? At what point does mechanical propulsion cease being a convenience and become a mystery?
8. This poem was written long before the countryside became so altered by the presence of railroad tracks and superhighways. Do you agree with Spender's romantic view of the train and her music? Explain.

Writing About the Poem

A Creative Response

1. **Imitating the Writer's Technique.** Write a paragraph or a short poem in which you describe another machine and express your response to its movements, sounds, and power. Include details that personify the machine as a type of person.

A Critical Response

2. **Comparing and Contrasting Poems.** In a short essay, compare and contrast the following poem by the nineteenth-century American poet Emily Dickinson with Spender's express-train poem. Consider imagery, figures of speech, tone, and sound effects.

I like to see it lap the Miles—
And lick the Valleys up—
And stop to feed itself at Tanks—
And then—prodigious step

5   Around a Pile of Mountains—
And supercilious peer
In Shanties—by the sides of Roads—
And then a Quarry pare

To fit its sides
10   And crawl between
Complaining all the while
In horrid—hooting stanza—
Then chase itself down Hill—

And neigh like Boanerges°—
15   Then—prompter than a Star
Stop—docile and omnipotent
At its own stable door—

            —Emily Dickinson

14. **Boanerges** (bō′ə·nur′jēz): "sons of thunder," a name given to James and John, two thundering speakers who were apostles of Jesus.

Henry Reed
(1914–   )

Henry Reed was born and educated in the industrial city of Birmingham. As an adult, he served in the British army and the diplomatic corps. He then began a career as a journalist in London, where he was well known for his wit and satirical imagination. More limited in output than any other significant poet of his generation, Reed's fame rests entirely on a single work. Constantly anthologized everywhere in the English-speaking world, "Naming of Parts" has long been one of the staples of modern poetry. (The story goes that a faculty member, introduced to the poet for the first time, said, "Oh yes, Mr. Reed, I've read your poem.") Excerpted from a longer poem published in Reed's first volume, *A Map of Verona* (1946), "Naming of Parts" contrasts gentleness with rude actuality, the voice of a man of action with the musings of a dreamer. In the process, it transcends the fact that, in spite of its Cockney lilt, the language of most of the poem is as flat as the prose of a training manual.

© Rollie McKenna.

1. BUILDING ON PRIOR KNOWLEDGE. Ask students if they have heard the phrase "flower power" and what they think it means. Remind them that the phrase became popular during the countercultural "hippie" and anti-Vietnam War period of the late 1960's. Tell them that this poem expresses in a more sophisticated way the sentiments summed up in the slogan "flower power."

2. ESTABLISHING A PURPOSE. As students read the words of the two speakers in this dialogue, ask them to imagine the personalities and values of the two speakers.

SUPPLEMENTARY SUPPORT MATERIALS
1. Review and Response Worksheet: Tone *(CCB)*
2. Selection Test *(CCB)*

A. Word Choice

? Use the word's context to make an educated guess at what "Japonica" is. (Students should realize that it is something colorful that grows in a garden. Then you can tell them that it is a blossoming fruit tree, also called Japanese quince.)

B. Interpreting Meaning

? To what do the parts named by the first speaker belong? (A rifle) To what do the parts named by the second speaker belong? (A garden or Nature)

C. Theme

? How do lines 16–18 and 28–29 sum up an important theme of the poem? (The language of the military man is loud and meaningless, like the language of war. The language of the branches and the blossoms is quiet, subtle, and full of meaning.)

CLOSURE

Discuss the "point of balance" that the drill instructor lacks in the view of the trainee. Have students identify the constrasting values of the two men.

Here we have a poem in the form of a most unusual dialogue—words spoken by a military drill instructor and answered silently by the thoughts of a recruit in the first stages of training. In each stanza except the last, the voice of the instructor is heard in the first three or four lines; the unspoken words of the trainee are in the last three or four lines. The final stanza is a kind of summing up. The recruit faithfully reports what he has heard, but gives it all a meaning never intended by the hard-boiled drill sergeant.

As you read, watch carefully for the places where the instructor's words are replaced by the recruit's thoughts. What differences can you identify in the language used by the two men?

Naming of Parts

Today we have naming of parts. Yesterday,
We had daily cleaning. And tomorrow morning,
We shall have what to do after firing. But today,

A Today we have naming of parts. Japonica
5 Glistens like coral in all of the neighboring gardens,
    And today we have naming of parts.

This is the lower sling swivel. And this
Is the upper sling swivel, whose use you will see,
When you are given your slings. And this is the piling swivel,
B 10 Which in your case you have not got. The branches
Hold in the gardens their silent, eloquent gestures,
    Which in our case we have not got.

This is the safety catch, which is always released
With an easy flick of the thumb. And please do not let me
15 See anyone using his finger. You can do it quite easy
C If you have any strength in your thumb. The blossoms
Are fragile and motionless, never letting anyone see
    Any of them using their finger.

And this you can see is the bolt. The purpose of this
20 Is to open the breech, as you see. We can slide it
Rapidly backwards and forwards: we call this
Easing the spring. And rapidly backwards and forwards
The early bees are assaulting and fumbling the flowers:
    They call it easing the Spring.

25 They call it easing the Spring: it is perfectly easy
If you have any strength in your thumb: like the bolt,
And the breech, and the cocking-piece, and the point of balance,
Which in our case we have not got; and the almond-blossom
Silent in all of the gardens and the bees going backwards and forwards,
30   For today we have naming of parts.

ANALYZING THE POEM
Identifying Details
1. The drill instructor speaks the first three and a half lines of each of the first four stanzas; the recruit silently answers in the last two and a half lines. The whole last stanza represents the thoughts of the recruit.
2. The parts include the lower sling swivel, the piling swivel, the safety catch, the bolt, the breech, and the spring.
3. The first half of each of these stanzas is a dry, mechanical recital by the instructor; the second half is the recruit's lyrical, imaginative daydream about a beautiful sight in a spring garden.
4. "Easing the Spring" (line 25) repeats part of line 24; "it is perfectly easy/If you have any strength in your thumb" (lines 25–26) repeats phrases from lines 15–16; the list of parts in lines 26–27 echoes the fourth stanza; the phrase "Which in our case we have not got" (line 28) echoes line 10 and line 12; and line 30 repeats lines 1 and 6.

Interpreting Meanings
5. The phrase could refer to slowly releasing the spring on a weapon and to the signs of the coming of the season of spring.
6. Student answers will vary. Ask them to support their opinions.
7. Most students will say that the poet is protesting war or weapons.
  Students' opinions on the validity of the protest will differ.

A. Humanities Connection: Discussing the Fine Art
Belgian painter René Magritte (1898–1967) participated in the French Surrealist movement of the twenties and went on to develop a very personal style and visual language. In a simple and direct manner, he depicts improbable situations and mysterious encounters, the significances of which are felt but hard to put into words.
? Call students' attention to the title of this painting. How is the title ironic? Is it significant that there is only one rifle? What is the spreading dark stain at the rifle's base? (Blood) What relationships do you see between the painting and the poem?

Responding to the Poem

Analyzing the Poem

Identifying Details

1. Identify the lines spoken by the principal speakers in the poem. What details describe the **setting**?
2. List the "parts" that are named as the poem goes on.
3. How do the first and second halves of stanzas 1–4 contrast with each other?
4. In the last stanza, what phrases are repeated echoed from the preceding four stanzas?

Interpreting Meanings

5. What different meanings does "easing the Spring" have in the poem?
6. Among the poem's elements are irony, bitterness, mockery, humor, and sorrow. Which **tone,** in your opinion, is the dominant one? Explain your answer.
7. What do you think the poet is protesting against? Is the protest valid, in your view?

Writing About the Poem

A Creative Response

Writing a Dialogue. Recast "Naming of Parts" as a dialogue, with the recruit actually voicing his thoughts and the instructor responding to his comments.

Analyzing Language and Style

Diction

A contrast in **diction,** or word choice, marks the language of the two speakers in this poem.

1. What "kinds" of words does the instructor use? (Technical? Poetic? Literary? Hard? Soft?)
2. In contrast, what "kinds" of words does the recruit use?
3. How does the rhythm of the instructor's speech differ from the rhythm of the recruit's?
4. How does the emotional effect produced by the recruit's words differ from the emotional effect produced by the instructor's words?

A

The Survivor by René Magritte (1950).

Dylan Thomas (1914–1953)

Dylan Thomas was born in Swansea, Wales, and died in the course of a fourth consecutive visit to the United States, where he was to collaborate on an opera with Igor Stravinsky.

Thomas was a prodigy—a poet who wrote some of his most famous works before he was twenty. By that time, he had also sketched out in source books themes, ideas, and angles of perspective for poems that he drew upon for the rest of his life. Largely self-educated, he chose the rough-and-tumble life of a newspaper reporter over the comparative serenity of the university education, to which an adolescent of his intellect and talent would have been entitled. His recognition by the leading poets and literary critics of England and America came early, and with it came international fame. Neither was enough to prevent him from having to exist on the edge of poverty—both in the years after he had left Wales for London and when he entered upon a marriage which, in spite of the arrival of three children, was emotionally turbulent. Thomas was to remain seriously troubled by money problems until his death.

The only son of parents who lived by a code of "good appearances" among their neighbors, Thomas as a child was continually torn between a deep-seated wish to live up to the expectations of his schoolmaster father and an equally strong impulse to please his doting mother. At the same time, he rejected both parents' pretensions to gentility, and he disappointed their hopes that he would "make something of himself." This conflict was later intensified by a strangely childish self-indulgence that continually defeated his attempts to be a devoted husband and loving father. This self-indulgence plagued an existence that found temporary solace in alcohol. This led to that "insult to the brain" which, according to the attending physicians, was the cause of his early and sudden death, in St. Vincent's Hospital in New York City.

A man of magical presence, with an endless flow of wit and a transparent hunger for affection, Thomas charmed his English contemporaries. When he first came to America in 1950, he

Dylan Thomas by Augustus John.

National Museum of Wales, Cardiff.

was regarded as the most charismatic literary visitor to come from England since the day in 1885 when Oscar Wilde, asked by a customs officer what he had to declare, answered, "Nothing but my genius."

Thomas's first reading tour of American colleges and universities was followed in succeeding years by ever more extensive trips on which he criss-crossed the continent from Florida to British Columbia. Beyond their response to his personal magnetism, those who attended Thomas's readings heard something new in modern poetry—a kind of expression combining the oratorical *hywl* of the Welsh chapel service with the theatrical delivery of the Victorian actors who once thrilled American audiences with thunderous recitations from Shakespeare and Marlowe.

Thomas enjoyed his role as a performer, but his deeper dedication was to the composition of poems in a mode he had made his own. His works are a mixture of intricate complication and preacher-like eloquence, of sonorous solemnity combined with a playful use of language

PREPARATION

1. BUILDING ON PRIOR KNOWLEDGE. Discuss how a child might feel living on a prosperous farm in a picturesque landscape. Then talk about how the same person might remember the time as an adult living a turbulent existence.

2. ESTABLISHING A PURPOSE. Consider with students the associations and feelings connected with the word *green*. Then ask them to be alert for the use of *green* in the poem.

___

SUPPLEMENTARY SUPPORT MATERIALS
1. Vocabulary Activity Worksheet *(CCB)*
2. Review and Response Worksheet: Personification and Word Play *(CCB)*
3. Selection Test *(CCB)*

DEVELOPING VOCABULARY
The following words from the poem are tested in the Selection Test. (See also Vocabulary Activity Worksheet.)
lilting   heedless

that is apparent in even the most serious of his works.

In his last years, he found that the concentration needed to write poetry was more and more difficult to achieve. Consequently, he turned to less demanding forms of expression and produced two works that became familiar around the world. The first was *Under Milk Wood* (1954), which he called a "play for voices." The second was his lyrical memoir called *A Child's*

Christmas in Wales (1955) (see page 1051), now a holiday classic performed as frequently as *The Nutcracker* ballet.

Idolized, celebrated, sought after by American lecture agencies, and pursued like a rock star, Thomas died at the height of a kind of fame he could neither accept nor enjoy. "Once I was lost and proud," he told a reporter from *The New York Times,* "now I'm found and humble. I prefer that other."

As a child, Thomas spent his summer months among relatives who worked a farm that, in his poem, he named "Fern Hill." Set in an apple orchard, the farmhouse is of the whitewashed stucco typical in Wales, and has a number of outlying barns for livestock and the storage of hay. Not far from the sea, "Fern Hill" looks down upon enormous tidal flats in an ever-changing seascape that provides a bountiful habitat for thousands of water birds of every species.

"Fern Hill" is a memory of childhood joy, a vision of an earthly paradise as well as the playground of a boy for whom every day is an enchanted adventure. Yet, typical of Dylan Thomas, joy is never unadulterated or unshadowed. As he comes to the conclusion of this extended song of praise, "Time" holds him not, as we might expect, "green and growing," but "green and dying." Once more, we have a variation on one of Thomas's persistent themes—the lurking presence of death in life, of the worm in the seed.

Fern Hill

> Now as I was young and easy under the apple boughs
> About the <u>lilting</u> house and happy as the grass was green,
>> The night above the dingle° starry,
>>> Time let me hail and climb
>>> Golden in the heydays of his eyes,
> And honored among wagons I was prince of the apple towns
> And once below a time I lordly had the trees and leaves
>>> Trail with daisies and barley
>>> Down the rivers of the windfall light.

10   And as I was green and carefree, famous among the barns
> About the happy yard and singing as the farm was home,
>> In the sun that is young once only,
>>> Time let me play and be
>>> Golden in the mercy of his means,
15 And green and golden I was huntsman and herdsman, the calves
> Sang to my horn, the foxes on the hills barked clear and cold,
>>> And the sabbath rang slowly
>>> In the pebbles of the holy streams.

A
5

B
C

3. **dingle:** a little valley.

A. Word Choice
Thomas's careful choice and placement of words subtly express a child's spirited world of imagination and play.
? What are some of the games the child plays, and whom does he pretend to be? (Climbing, singing, imagining he was prince, huntsman, herdsman, and lord of all his outdoor world)

B. Language and Theme
Note the use of the word *sabbath* in line 17.
? Look for other words with religious connotations throughout the poem. *(Holy, mercy of his means, blessed, out of grace)* What theme do such words suggest? (The sacred innocence of childhood)

C. Interpreting
Some readers would say the poem has no overarching theme. This is not a flaw of the poem, however. "Fern Hill" can be enjoyed for its imagery, its insights, its songlike quality, etc.

1. An adult who is nostalgically remembering his childhood and youth.
2. "Prince of the apple towns" (line 6), "singing" (line 11), "sang to my horn" (line 16), "ran my heedless ways" (line 40).

His activities included singing, hunting and herding, sleeping under the stars and listening to owls, and running.
3. He failed to realize that time would pass and that his happy childhood would soon be over.
4. In the second, time is said to let the child play; time is "golden" in line 14. But in the sixth stanza, fleeting time deceives the speaker, who refers to himself as "green and dying" (line 53).
5. Lines 29–36 in the fourth stanza.

Interpreting Meanings
6. In lines 4 and 13, Time is obliquely personified as an indulgent parent who allows the boy the freedom to be happy. But in line 53, Time is a parent who holds a dying child in his arms. Thus, Time seems to have intended both for the speaker to be happy and also to grow up, lose the paradise of childhood, and eventually die.

A. Expansion
Note that in this stanza Thomas uses images of the four elements: earth, air, fire, and water. These seem appropriate to his purpose of evoking the simple life of a child on a farm, or of man in a lost paradise.

B. Imagery
❓ What has "come back" in line 29? Look for more than one meaning. (The farm, the boy's consciousness, daylight, playtime)

C. Allusion
❓ What do you associate with the phrases "after the birth of the simple light" and "In the first, spinning place"? (Perhaps the birth of Christ, the creation of the world)

D. Responding
❓ How do you interpret the paradoxical last line? How can the sea be seen as chained, as singing? (It has fixed boundaries; it has a sound.) Why does the speaker say that he "sang" in his "chains"? Is he happy or sad?

A

> All the sun long it was running, it was lovely, the hay
20 Fields high as the house, the tunes from the chimneys, it was air
>   And playing, lovely and watery
>   And fire green as grass.
>   And nightly under the simple stars
> As I rode to sleep the owls were bearing the farm away,
25 All the moon long I heard, blessed among stables, the night-jars
>   Flying with the ricks,° and the horses
>   Flashing into the dark.

26. **ricks:** stacks of hay or straw.

B
> And then to awake, and the farm, like a wanderer white
> With the dew, come back, the cock on his shoulder: it was all
30   Shining, it was Adam and maiden,
>   The sky gathered again
>   And the sun grew round that very day.

C
> So it must have been after the birth of the simple light
> In the first, spinning place, the spellbound horses walking warm
35   Out of the whinnying green stable
>   On to the fields of praise.

> And honored among foxes and pheasants by the gay house
> Under the new made clouds and happy as the heart was long,
>   In the sun born over and over,
40   I ran my <u>heedless</u> ways,
>   My wishes raced through the house high hay
> And nothing I cared, at my sky blue trades, that time allows
> In all his tuneful turning so few and such morning songs
>   Before the children green and golden
45   Follow him out of grace.

> Nothing I cared, in the lamb white days, that time would take me
> Up to the swallow thronged loft by the shadow of my hand,
>   In the moon that is always rising,
>   Nor that riding to sleep
50   I should hear him fly with the high fields
> And wake to the farm forever fled from the childless land.
> Oh as I was young and easy in the mercy of his means,
>   Time held me green and dying
D   Though I sang in my chains like the sea.

Responding to the Poem

Analyzing the Poem

Identifying Details

1. From whose point of view is the poem told?
2. What details tell how the speaker felt when he was "young and easy"? What did he do on the farm?
3. What did the boy fail to realize about time, according to the fifth stanza?
4. How do the statements about time in the second stanza differ from those in the sixth stanza?
5. What lines in the poem seem to refer to the Biblical account of paradise, of the Garden of Eden?

7. Students may mention the speaker's carefree happiness and his joy in nature (represented by the references to river, stars, calves, foxes, owls, pheasants, the hay, etc.).

The boy's "awakening" into the reality of adulthood, with all its disappointments and responsibilities, may be compared to Adam and Eve's loss of Eden.

8. The phrase "green and dying" is paradoxical because it suggests innocent freshness and mortality at the same time.

9. Thomas evidently wants the word *green* to connote nature, freshness, youth, and innocence.

10. This word is used in lines 5, 14, and 44.

Students may suggest associations like "perfection," "preciousness," "value," "warmth."

11. Students may suggest that the poem's lifting rhythm and the variation of long and short lines reinforce the happy, carefree mood of youth.

Examples of alliteration and onomatopoeia occur in lines 2, 3, 7, 14, 15, 19, 20, 26–27, 34, 41, and 51.

12. Most students will agree that the impulse to look back on one's youth nostalgically and to recognize time as fleeting is universal. Some students may point out, however, that not everyone has experienced as idyllic a childhood as Thomas describes here.

13. Student answers will vary. Some students may suggest that this line did not satisfy Thomas because it does not contain an original image or figure of speech or that it seems to be a cliché.

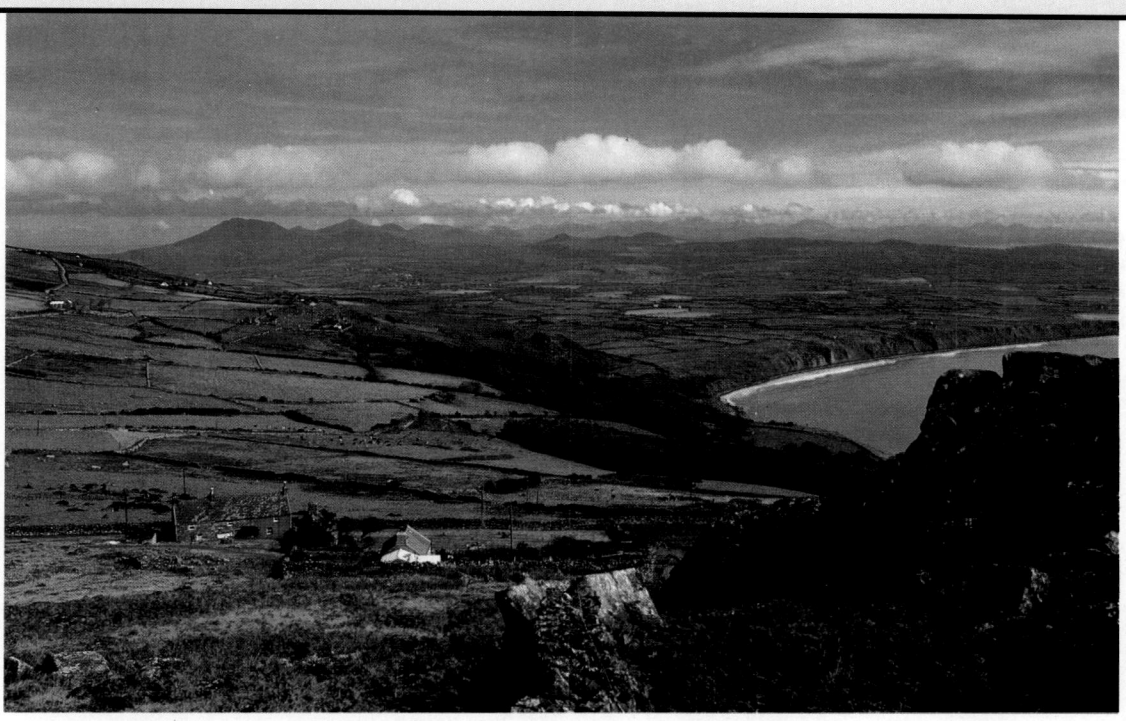

Interpreting Meanings

6. Find where time is **personified** in the poem. Describe the different kinds of intentions Time seems to have in regard to the boy.

7. In what specific ways was the speaker's childhood "Edenic," that is, like the life Adam and Eve led in Eden? In what ways is the boy's "waking" in the last stanza like the "waking" of Adam and Eve as they left the Garden?

8. How would you explain the **paradox** in the next-to-last line?

9. Find where the word *green* occurs in each of the seven stanzas. For a craftsman as meticulous as Thomas, these recurrences are certainly not accidental. Why do you suppose Thomas repeats the word so often? What associations and feelings are connected with the word *green*?

10. Where is *gold* used in the poem? What associations do you have with gold?

11. Read the poem aloud, or listen to a recording of it. How does its **rhythm** match its subject and mood? Where does Thomas use **alliteration** and **onomatopoeia** to provide the sound effects?

12. Is the experience described in this poem universal? Explain.

13. Years after this poem was first published, Thomas told a friend that one line continued to bother him because it was "bloody bad." "What line is it?" asked the friend. "I ran my heedless ways," said Thomas, and he winced as though he had made a mistake from which he would never recover. Why do you think Thomas felt so strongly about a line that most people accept and even quote as part of his most celebrated poem? How do you feel about the line?

Writing About the Poem

A Creative Response

1. Imitating the Writer's Technique. Write a brief memoir of an episode from your own childhood. Try to imitate Thomas's lyrical tone in some of your sentences. Open with the words "Now as I was young and easy . . ."

A Critical Response

2. Analyzing a Theme. In a brief essay, state the theme of this poem and cite the details from the poem that support that theme. In your essay, tell how you respond to Thomas's handling of this theme.

Analyzing Language and Style

Word Play

Even at his most somber, Thomas continually indulges in word play—sometimes turning a **cliché** upside-down, sometimes making chilling or amusing **puns,** sometimes using modifiers in surprising ways, often giving a twist of emphasis and new luster to an old saying. How many instances of this kind of word play can you identify in "Fern Hill"?

2. ESTABLISHING A PURPOSE. Alert students to the need for careful study of the original syntax, unusual rhythm, and verbal invention of this poem to fully grasp Thomas's meaning.

SUPPLEMENTARY SUPPORT MATERIALS
1. Vocabulary Activity Worksheet (CCB)
2. Review and Response Worksheet: Tone and Diction (CCB)
3. Selection Test (CCB)

DEVELOPING VOCABULARY

The following word from the poem is tested in the Selection Test. (See also Vocabulary Activity Worksheet.)
to blaspheme

A. Humanities Connection: About the Fine Art

A firestorm is an intense fire over a large area. The fire is sustained and spread by inrushing winds created by the strong draft of rising hot air. Though this depicts a firestorm in Boston in 1872, firestorms can also be started by aerial bombing, such as in Hamburg and Tokyo during World War II.

❓ You might discuss with students the terror a person would feel, trapped in a firestorm or in a house fire.

Ferrandini's painting is somewhat dreamlike in that the burning urban area is strangely isolated.

Determined to avoid the conventions of grief and mourning in confronting something as monstrous as a little girl being burned to death, Thomas wrote one of the most famous elegies of the century. The tension of his poem comes from a refusal to "blaspheme" the child's memory by a "grave truth"—by offering still another cliché about death, or by making another sermon about how young and innocent she was. Yet, before he is finished, the poet drops his resistance and does exactly what he has said he would not do. He mourns the child's fate and, in effect, buries her among "the first dead."

Some people quite naturally take the final line to mean that after death comes salvation, the eternal life of the soul. Others read the line in another way: once "the first death" is recognized, it has no sequel because all deaths are finally one. Like the child, everyone will eventually join "the first dead."

A Refusal to Mourn the Death, by Fire, of a Child in London

A

Firestorm (Boston 1872) by Robert Ferrandini (1986). Oil.

Courtesy Victoria Munroe Gallery, New York City.

1. Four sentences.
The first: line 1 to line 13, the second: line 14 to 18, the third: line 19 to 23, and the last: line 24.
2. He will not "blaspheme" the child's death by offering a cliché about death or by composing an elegy, mourning her youth and innocence.

He violates it in the last stanza.
3. The "salt seed" is a tear.
The "mother" is the earth.
4. She lies with the "first dead"—with all who have died before her.

Interpreting Meanings
5. The line may mean that "we only die once" or that after our individual death, we live forever.

6. Most students will agree that Thomas is genuinely affected by the girl's death and appears to refuse to mourn only in order to place her death in a larger context.
7. The tone of "Fern Hill" is lyrical and hopeful for the most part; the tone of this poem is somber with a far subtler suggestion of hope.

A ⎡Never until the mankind making
⎢Bird beast and flower
⎣Fathering and all humbling darkness
Tells with silence the last light breaking
5 ⎡And the still hour
B ⎣Is come of the sea tumbling in harness

⎡And I must enter again the round
⎢Zion° of the water bead
C ⎢And the synagogue of the ear of corn
10 ⎢Shall I let pray the shadow of a sound
⎢Or sow my salt seed
⎣In the least valley of sackcloth to mourn

The majesty and burning of the child's death.
I shall not murder
15 The mankind of her going with a grave truth
D ⎡Nor blaspheme down the stations of the breath
⎣With any further
Elegy of innocence and youth.

Deep with the first dead lies London's daughter,
E
20 ⎡Robed in the long friends,
The grains beyond age, the dark veins of her mother,
Secret by the unmourning water
Of the riding Thames.
F ⎡After the first death, there is no other.

8. **Zion:** temple.

A. Alliteration
Note the striking use of alliteration in the first three lines.

B. Theme
? Until when is the speaker refusing to mourn? ("Never until . . . the still hour is come . . .")

C. Imagery
? What associations does the imagery in the second stanza call to mind? (The cycle of birth, growth, death; harvest rituals)

D. Imagery
"The stations of the breath" echo the Christian ritual called "the stations of the cross."

E. Expansion
"The long friends" are usually interpreted as the worms feeding on the dead, an allusion to the natural vegetative cycle.

F. Expansion
One interpretation of the last line sees "the first death" as birth, with actual death merely a return to some former ideal existence, as in Wordsworth's "Ode: Intimations of Immortality."

Responding to the Poem

Analyzing the Poem

Identifying Details

1. How many sentences are in the poem? Where does each one begin and end?
2. In stanza 3, what does the speaker say he will not do? Where does he violate his promise?
3. What is the "salt seed" in line 11? What is the "mother" in line 21?
4. Where, according to the speaker, does "London's daughter" now lie?

Interpreting Meanings

5. What do you think the last line means?
6. Does Thomas's poem minimize the tragedy, or does it endow it with a larger dimension? Explain.
7. How does the **tone** of this poem differ from the tone of "Fern Hill"?

Writing About the Poem

A Creative Response

1. **Relating the Poem to Contemporary Experience.** Thomas's poem is an attempt to come to grips with an inexplicable tragedy. Every day, the mass media bombard us with stories of gruesome disasters to the extent that, unless we have personal connection with the events, we tend to become numb to them. In an essay, discuss your opinions on this modern tendency to become insensible to others' tragedies.

A Critical Response

2. **Paraphrasing the Poem.** In your own words, paraphrase the poem, line by line. Be sure to explain each figure of speech. You can write your paraphrase using the first-person pronoun *I,* as the speaker does, or you can write in the third person, as the outside reader.

1. BUILDING ON PRIOR KNOWLEDGE.
Modern psychology urges acceptance of death but observes that a person must go through several stages, including denial and bargaining, before he or she can reach acceptance. This poem, however, urges protest and struggle in the face of death. Such an "existential" stance echoes views similar to those of the French writers Albert Camus and Jean-Paul Sartre. They urged protest against the terms of human existence.

2. ESTABLISHING A PURPOSE. Ask students to look for the reasons Thomas gives for not facing death with calm, quiet acceptance.

SUPPLEMENTARY SUPPORT MATERIALS
1. Review and Response Worksheet: Theme (*CCB*)
2. Selection Test (*CCB*)

CLOSURE
Have students identify two possible meanings of the title and how each relates to the rest of the poem. ("Do not die gently"; "Do not die, gentle man.")

A. Imagery
Note that death is expressed in images of light and dark in this stanza.

B. Theme
? Why might "wise men" at the end of their lives know that "dark [death] is right"? (Resignation to the inevitability of death seems wise.) Knowing what they do, why do the wise men still not die calmly according to lines 5–6? (Even though they have not yet succeded, they need to continue their efforts.)

C. Imagery
? Who are the "wild men" in line 10? What do they learn too late? (Men who experienced life intensely but who were not fully aware of the fleetingness of their experiences)

D. Responding
? Why does the speaker urge his dying father to stuggle against death? (He may feel that his father, like most men, failed at something in life.)

The typical elegy is a poem mourning a death that has already occurred. This elegy speaks to a dying man, urging him not to surrender to death, but to meet death in a spirit of challenge.

Once more, Thomas gives his own twist to a familiar subject. The poem may invite charges of heresy or irreverence, but its lyrical solemnity, not its argument, is what counts.

Only two end rhymes occur in this poem. Both are simple, blended into iambic pentameter with such skill that the many repetitions of similar sounds become a somber and delicate music of chimes.

Thomas's use of *gentle* instead of the adverb *gently* may seem grammatically suspect. But when, as he insisted, we read the line as "Do not go, gentle, into that good night," we gain the additional meaning of all that is gentle, including the gentle man who was his father.

Do Not Go Gentle into That Good Night

A
Do not go gentle into that good night,
Old age should burn and rave at close of day;
Rage, rage against the dying of the light.

B
Though wise men at their end know dark is right,
5 Because their words had forked no lightning they
Do not go gentle into that good night.

Good men, the last wave by, crying how bright
Their frail deeds might have danced in a green bay,
Rage, rage against the dying of the light.

C
10 Wild men who caught and sang the sun in flight,
And learn, too late, they grieved it on its way,
Do not go gentle into that good night.

Grave men, near death, who see with blinding sight
Blind eyes could blaze like meteors and be gay,
15 Rage, rage against the dying of the light.

D
And you, my father, there on the sad height,
Curse, bless, me now with your fierce tears, I pray.
Do not go gentle into that good night.
Rage, rage against the dying of the light.

1. The speaker's father:
Old age should "burn and rave" at the close of day—old people should protest against the coming of death.
2. These stanzas describe wise men, good men, wild men, and grave men.
The wise men are angry because their counsels failed to influence others; the good men deplore the ineffectuality of their deeds; the wild men learn too late that time is fleeting; the grave men regret their failure to enjoy life.
3. He asks his father to both curse and bless him.

Interpreting Meanings
4. Death:
To catch the meaning of a casual farewell.

It is paradoxical, since Thomas obviously wants his father to protest against death.
5. The phrase hints at a complex relationship, involving both love and anger.
6. Old age burning and raving (line 2), wise men's words forking lightning (line 5), "frail deeds" dancing in a "green bay" (line 8), the singing of the sun in flight (line 10), and the blazing of blind eyes (line 14).
7. Student answers will vary. Urge the students to support their opinions.

A. Humanities Connection: Discussing the Fine Art
For background information on Emil Nolde, see the annotation on page 924.
? Ask students what they think the artist wished to communicate about himself in his self-portrait. What does his choice of colors suggest? What is the effect of his wearing a hat? Do you think he wished to reveal or conceal his character? What do you think Thomas's father's self-portrait would look like? (The picture's lack of definition and the bleeding of the colors might make the man seem old. So might the hat, which puts his eyes in shadow and makes him more mysterious.)

Responding to the Poem

Analyzing the Poem

Identifying Details

1. To whom is the poem addressed? What does the speaker say old age should do?
2. What four types of people are described in stanzas 2–5? How do all these people respond to the dying of the light?
3. What does the speaker pray for in the final stanza?

Interpreting Meanings

4. What is the "good night"? What **pun** on the phrase does Thomas intend you to catch? Given Thomas's feelings about the "good night," do you see anything contradictory in his use of the word *good*?
5. Why would any son beg his father to "Curse, bless, me now with your fierce tears"? What might this strange request indicate about the relationship between this father and son?
6. Identify at least three **metaphors** in the poem.
7. Soon after this poem was finished, Thomas sent it to the Princess Caetani in Rome, hoping that she might publish it in a literary magazine of which she was editor. In an accompanying letter, he wrote: "The only person I can't show the enclosed little poem to is, of course, my father, who doesn't know he's dying." Given the fact that the poem has become one of the most famous elegies of this century, do you think Thomas's reluctance was justified? What would you have done in the same situation?

Writing About the Poem

A Creative Response

1. Responding to the Speaker. Write a response to the advice given in this poem, using the voice of a very old person who is facing death. Your response might be a poem, an essay, or a letter.
2. Writing a Villanelle. You might write your response to Thomas in another villanelle. First think of the lines that you will want to repeat. Then think of the sounds you will want to repeat in your rhyme scheme.

Analyzing Language and Style

The Villanelle

Thomas has written his poem in an old form invented by French poets. At first this form, called a **villanelle** (meaning "rural" or "country-like"), was limited to light, lyric

A

Self Portrait of Emil Nolde. Watercolor.

© 1987 The Detroit Institute of Arts. Bequest of Robert H. Tannahill.

poems about the countryside. Today villanelles are written on many topics, and, as you can see from Thomas's villanelle, they do not have to have a light tone.

The villanelle is a complex form. The trick is to make the poem sound spontaneous and fresh, yet still adhere to the strict limits of the form.

Here are the villanelle's "rules":

1. It has nineteen lines, divided into five three-line stanzas (*tercets*) and a concluding four-line stanza (a *quatrain*).
2. It can use only two end rhymes and it must use this rhyme scheme: *aba aba aba aba aba abaa.*
3. It repeats certain lines: line 1 is repeated in lines 6, 12, and 18. Line 3 is repeated in lines 9, 15, and 19.

How faithfully has Thomas followed the rules of a villanelle? The repeated lines in a villanelle must be significant. Has Thomas repeated an idea important to his poem?

Philip Larkin (1922–1985)

Philip Larkin was the most widely admired poet in the generation succeeding that of Dylan Thomas. Unlike Thomas, Larkin was conservative in his politics, private to the point of anonymity in his personal life, and more inclined to woo his readers than to dazzle them. A man who scrupulously avoided public attention, Larkin refused hundreds of invitations to read or lecture in the United States and Great Britain. He seemed content to cultivate his own talents without reference to the choruses of praise and delight that attended the publication of each of his few but flawless collections of poetry.

Educated at Oxford, Larkin spent most of his life as librarian at the University of Hull. He maintained an uneasy and sometimes yearning bachelorhood, and he wrote of romantic love in terms of bittersweet comedy or outright farce. He came to prominence at the time when the famous "angry young men," notably the novelist Kingsley Amis and the playwright John Osborne, were attacking or ridiculing the spiritual emptiness and diminishing horizons of postwar England. Although Larkin shared much of their disillusionment, he retained a large degree of diffidence in regard to the issues they addressed with passion or to the injustices they scorched with satire.

This diffidence about engaging with wider social issues seemed more a trait of Larkin's character than an absence of conviction. In their quiet, low-keyed way, his poems reflect all the great themes of contemporary experience. In his handling of these themes, Larkin keeps to an intimately human scale, in which the balance lies somewhere between disgust and disdain on the one hand, and heartbreak and despairing humor on the other.

PREPARATION

1. BUILDING ON PRIOR KNOWLEDGE. In this poem, a man visits an empty church and muses about its meaning. Students might remember or imagine themselves in an empty church or synagogue or mosque.

2. ESTABLISHING A PURPOSE. Ask students to pay attention to the speaker's various feelings about the church.

SUPPLEMENTARY SUPPORT MATERIALS

1. Vocabulary and Activity Worksheet (*CCB*)
2. Review and Response Worksheet: Theme (*CCB*)
3. Selection Test (*CCB*)
4. Audiocassette recording

DEVELOPING VOCABULARY

The following words from the poem are tested in the Selection Test. (See also Vocabulary Activity Worksheet.)

chronically   compulsion
buttress   obsolete
to accouter

The speaker's relaxed tone of voice and his casual meandering from point to point almost disguise the fact that this is a deeply religious poem. Curious, skeptical, hungering for spiritual assurance that he is unable to accept, Larkin reveals a temperament common to an age in which science and rationality have made serious inroads on religion and the claims of faith.

Church Going

Once I am sure there's nothing going on
I step inside, letting the door thud shut.
Another church: matting, seats, and stone,
And little books; sprawlings of flowers, cut
5 For Sunday, brownish now; some brass and stuff
Up at the holy end; the small neat organ;
And a tense, musty, unignorable silence,
Brewed God knows how long. Hatless, I take off
My cycle clips in awkward reverence,

10 Move forward, run my hand around the font.°
From where I stand, the roof looks almost new—
Cleaned, or restored? Someone would know: I don't.
Mounting the lectern, I peruse a few
Hectoring° large-scale verses, and pronounce
15 "Here endeth" much more loudly than I'd meant.
The echoes snigger briefly. Back at the door
I sign the book, donate an Irish sixpence,
Reflect the place was not worth stopping for.

Yet stop I did: in fact I often do,
20 And always end much at a loss like this,
Wondering what to look for; wondering, too,
When churches fall completely out of use
What we shall turn them into, if we shall keep
A few cathedrals chronically on show,
25 Their parchment, plate,° and pyx° in locked cases,
And let the rest rent-free to rain and sheep.
Shall we avoid them as unlucky places?

Or, after dark, will dubious women come
To make their children touch a particular stone;
30 Pick simples° for a cancer; or on some
Advised night see walking a dead one?
Power of some sort or other will go on
In games, in riddles, seemingly at random;
But superstition, like belief, must die,
35 And what remains when disbelief has gone?
Grass, weedy pavement, brambles, buttress, sky,

10. font: a bowl or basin used in baptismal services.

14. Hectoring: bullying.

25. plate: silver religious objects. **pyx:** an ornamental container for communion bread.

30. simples: herbs thought to have medicinal power.

A. Expansion
Call students' attention to the rather ordinary, secular language in which the speaker describes the church, which suggests he is a nonbeliever. However, lines 59–63 reveal that he has a degree of respect for the church.

B. Mood
❓ How does stanza 2 suggest that the speaker has conflicting attitudes toward the church? (He is curious, disapproves of "hectoring" verses but signs the book and donates money.)

C. Theme
In the third stanza, the speaker admits that he often visits churches, but he is unsure of what he is looking for. Next he assumes that churches will "fall completely out of use" and wonders what the buildings will be used for then.
❓ Do you think he welcomes their loss? Give examples from the poem to support your answer. (In the last two stanzas, the speaker states that there is nothing in modern life to replace the church.)

ANALYZING THE POEM
Identifying Details

1. The matting, seats, stone, little books, flowers, brass, the font, the organ, and the lectern with the Bible.

He pauses to make sure that there is no service in progress. Then he steps inside, takes off his cycle clips, runs his hand around the font, and mounts the lectern, where he says a few biblical verses. He signs the book and donates an Irish sixpence before he leaves.

2. He wonders what will become of churches when no one uses them anymore for religious services. Perhaps, he reflects, we will keep some cathedrals on show as symbols of the past. Perhaps churches may become superstitious gathering places for women and children.

3. The church might become a sort of antique curio, examined eagerly by "ruin-bibbers," as an archaeological site.

4. Even though he has no idea of the value of the church, he is still pleased to stand there because it is "a serious house on serious earth." The church is a meeting place for human beings, where their "compulsions" blend. It is a proper place to "grow wise in."

5. *ababcadcd.*

A. Discussing the Photograph

? What impression of this church and churchyard is conveyed by the photograph? Does its atmosphere resemble that of the church described in the poem? (The photo shows a church in the British Isles, where picturesque, untended graveyards like this one are common. Notice the beautiful yew trees, which in British poetry are always associated with death.)

B. Tone

? What kind of people does the poet mock in lines 40–44? (Those who value things long after they are gone)

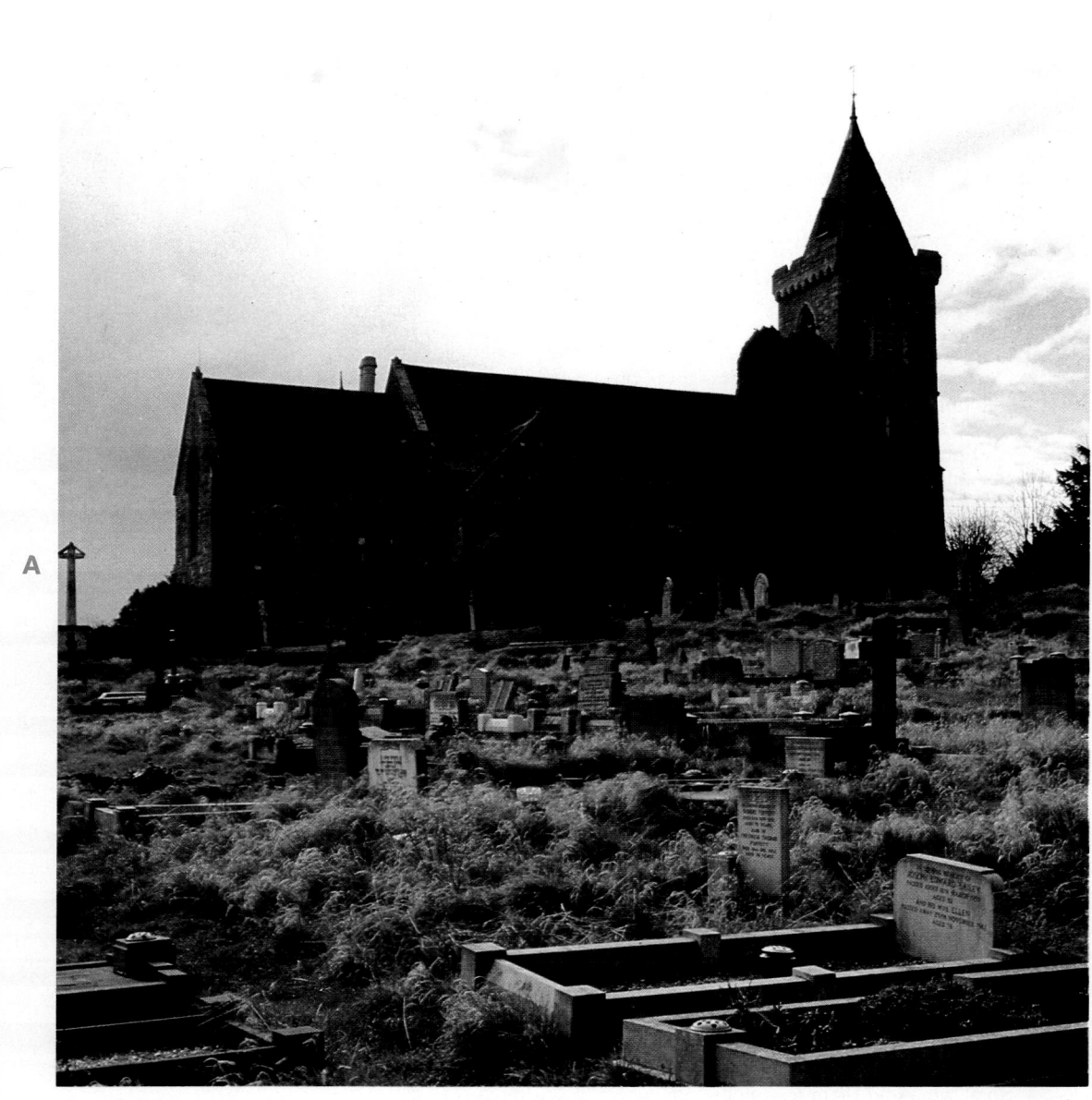

```
     A shape less recognizable each week,
     A purpose more obscure. I wonder who
     Will be the last, the very last, to seek
40   This place for what it was; one of the crew
     That tap and jot and know what rood-lofts were?
B    Some ruin-bibber,° randy for antique,
     Or Christmas-addict, counting on a whiff
     Of gown-and-bands and organ pipes and myrrh?
45   Or will he be my representative,
```

42. **ruin-bibber:** someone who loves old things not because of their beauty or value, but simply because they are old.

Interpreting Meanings

6. It could mean "attending church" or "the disappearing, or fading, church."

7. Because so many are dead in the church; we can at least learn in church that we're mortal too.

The poet is not being disrespectful to the church or to the dead; he is just making an ironic remark on the popular wisdom that death comes to everyone.

8. People in the contemporary secular world are steadily abandoning the church as hollow and "antique." All the same, the speaker suggests that he derived pleasure, consolation, and perhaps a sense of wisdom from visiting the church.

Student answers will vary. Many students will suggest that the speaker, for all of his skepticism and wry humor, is still deeply religious.

9. Students may suggest that he derives a feeling of consolation and tranquility.

10. Students should point out that, in both poems, the speaker notes a general decline of religious faith.

> Bored, uninformed, knowing the ghostly silt
> Dispersed, yet tending to this cross of ground°
> Through suburb scrub because it held unspilt
> So long and equally what since is found
> 50 Only in separation—marriage, and birth,
> And death, and thoughts of these—for whom was built
> This special shell? For, though I've no idea
> What this accoutered frowsty° barn is worth,
> It pleases me to stand in silence here;
>
> 55 A serious house on serious earth it is,
> In whose blent° air all our compulsions meet,
> Are recognized, and robed as destinies.
> And that much never can be obsolete,
> Since someone will forever be surprising
> 60 A hunger in himself to be more serious,
> And gravitating with it to this ground,
> Which, he once heard, was proper to grow wise in,
> If only that so many dead lie round.

47. this cross of ground: The floor plans of most Christian churches are in the form of a cross.

53. frowsty: stale, musty.

56. blent: blended.

A. Theme

In the last two stanzas, what positive functions does the speaker see the church performing? (A place to take seriously the milestones of human life and to ponder the meaning of death)

CLOSURE

Ask students to characterize the tone of this poem. Is the speaker hostile or indifferent to the church? Is he sympathetic or merely curious?

Additional Writing Assignment

Imagine another person visiting an empty church, synagogue, or mosque who has a reaction to the scene completely different from Larkin's. Write a poem or a scene for a short story in which you present an alternative reaction.

Responding to the Poem

Analyzing the Poem

Identifying Details

1. What concrete details does the speaker notice in the church? What does he do there?
2. What questions does the speaker ask in the third and fourth stanzas?
3. According to stanza 5, what might become of the church in the future?
4. According to the final two stanzas, why does it please the speaker to visit the church?
5. What is the **rhyme scheme** of the poem?

Interpreting Meanings

6. What are the two possible meanings of the **title**?
7. In the last two lines of the last stanza, there is an example of humor that some people might find offensive. Why is the church a good place to grow wise in? How would you justify the poet's wry comment to someone who finds it distasteful?
8. What does the speaker seem to be saying about the place of the church, or of faith, in the contemporary secular world? How do you think this outlook might be related to the speaker's own religious faith, or lack of it?
9. Can you think of reasons why the speaker might like to stand in the old church?
10. Can you see any connection between the **tone** of this poem and that of Matthew Arnold's "Dover Beach" (Unit Six)?

Writing About the Poem

A Critical Response

1. **Writing a Character Sketch.** Based on the evidence in the poem, write a brief character sketch of the speaker.
2. **Comparing Two Poems.** In a brief essay, compare the theme and poetic techniques of "Church Going" with those of W. B. Yeats's poem "The Second Coming." In what way might Larkin's poem seem like a response to Yeats's?

1. BUILDING ON PRIOR KNOWLEDGE. Tell students that the poem describes Frederiksted, a port in the U.S. Virgin Islands in the Caribbean. The port was first taken over by tourism and then abandoned by the tourist trade, leaving it worse off than before. Frederiksted today has a population of about 1,500.

2. ESTABLISHING A PURPOSE. Ask students to look for the images of waste, decay, and abandonment that set the mood of the poem.

SUPPLEMENTARY SUPPORT MATERIALS
1. Review and Response Worksheet: Imagery and Theme (*CCB*)
2. Selection Test (*CCB*)

Comment from the Writer
When asked in an interview why he continued to live in and write about the Caribbean area, Derek Walcott answered, "The greatest writers have been at heart parochial, provincial in their rootedness. I think Shakespeare remains a Warwickshire country boy, Joyce a minor bourgeois from Dublin."

Do you agree with Walcott's assertion? How might a strong sense of where you come from help a writer? (Perhaps because it gives the writer a keener awareness of the nuances of the native language, the people, and the local settings.)

Additional Writing Assignment
The person speaking in this poem is a visitor to the port. Who do you think he or she is? Is the person a native of the Caribbean or of a developed European country or of the United States? Using whatever information the poem provides, write an imaginative portrait of the visitor.

Derek Walcott (1930–   )

Derek Walcott was born and raised in St. Lucia, an English-speaking island in the Caribbean, noted for its green valleys, its vast banana plantations, and its sleeping volcano.

One of twin boys, he was the son of a schoolteacher father and a mother who was headmistress of the island's Methodist Infant School. Introduced to the classics of English literature at an early age, Walcott showed early signs of proficiency in the use of language. As he realized as an adult, he also enjoyed the peculiar brand of "Englishness" that belonged to even the most far-flung colonies of the British Empire. In spite of all that, no one guessed that a boy from a remote tropical island would one day be regarded as the premier poet and playwright of the Caribbean, as well as one of the leading poets of his time, anywhere.

Walcott was a scholarship student at the University of the West Indies in Jamaica, and he stayed on after his graduation to teach comparative literature. Then he embarked on an independent career that took him to the island of Trinidad, where he chose to make his permanent home. Later he traveled to the United States, where the scope of his activities has included not only writing poetry, but also writing plays and teaching classes in creative writing at Harvard and at Boston University.

© Rollie McKenna.

Walcott's characteristic language is elegant, gracefully formal, and full of the resourcefulness that comes only from a well-trained talent. But he has also tried, particularly in his plays, to capture the native rhythms, the diction, and the Creole variations of the speech of the islands he knows.

1. Of "life not lost to the American dream," that is, the simplicities of a life blighted by greed and commercialism.
2. A rise in crime.

Interpreting Meanings
3. The dead streets (line 1), "funeral pace" (line 3), "streets blighted with sun" (line 10), "plazas blown dry" (line 11), the condominium drowning in vacancy (lines 12–13), the reference to dust (line 13), and the rusty spinning of the roulette wheels (lines 15–16).
4. Paradoxically, the "free port" has died of tourism, meaning that commercial exploitation has led to the decline of the town's basic values.
5. Because no one lives in them anymore, presumably due to overdevelopment and rising crime.
6. References to the vigorous trade around the pierhead in lines 16–19; line 5, where the speaker evokes the "simplicities" of a vanished way of life.

Commercial greed and a "selling out" to tourism are the culprits. Most will agree that the change is a destructive one.

In this lyric, Walcott describes one of the old port cities on the U. S. Virgin Island of St. Croix [sānt kroi]. Frederiksted is a free port where goods can be purchased by tourists without paying custom duties. The economy of St. Croix, once based on sugar cane, is now dependent on tourism. As you read, remember that *virgins* refers to the Virgin Islands, of which St. Croix is one.

The Virgins

A Down the dead streets of sun-stoned Frederiksted,
    the first free port to die for tourism,
    strolling at funeral pace, I am reminded
    of life not lost to the American dream;
5   but my small-islander's simplicities
B can't better our new empire's civilized
    exchange of cameras, watches, perfumes, brandies
    for the good life, so cheaply underpriced
    that only the crime rate is on the rise
10 in streets blighted with sun, stone arches
C and plazas blown dry by the hysteria
    of rumor. A condominium drowns
    in vacancy; its bargains are dusted,
    but only a jeweled housefly drones
15 over the bargains. The roulettes spin
    rustily to the wind—the vigorous trade
    that every morning would begin afresh
    by revving up green water round the pierhead
D heading for where the banks of silver thresh.

A. Imagery
? "Dead streets" in line 1 has more than one meaning. In what ways are the streets "dead"? (Quiet; devoid of community life) What is the meaning of the phrase "sun-stoned Frederiksted"? (The city has been drugged into torpor by the sun. Note the irony—the sun is usually associated with growth and with prosperity.)

B. Word Choice
? How do you think the poet is using the word *civilized* here? (Ironically)

C. Theme
? What do you think the poet means by "the hysteria of rumor"? (The fear of crime)

D. Imagery
In addition to its agricultural meaning of separating seed from chaff, *thresh* can also mean "to strike repeatedly" or "to toss about."
? What do you think the image "where the banks of silver thresh" means? (Waves, the sea)

Responding to the Poem

Analyzing the Poem

Identifying Facts

1. What is the tourist reminded of, as he strolls the streets of Frederiksted?
2. According to line 9, what, **ironically,** is the result of the "good life"?

Interpreting Meanings

3. List the **images** in the poem that suggest emptiness and decay.
4. How would you explain line 2?
5. Why are the condominiums drowning in vacancy?

6. What **images** remind you of what life was once like in Frederiksted? Who or what is responsible for the change? Is it a change for the better or the worse?

Writing About the Poem

A Critical Response

Supporting a Critical Statement. Laurence Perrine has said that Walcott's poems "are sharpened by his skillful use of irony and of words and phrases of double meanings." Write an essay supporting that statement, citing as examples words and passages from the poem.

1. Building on Prior Knowledge. A hawk is a raptor, or a bird of prey, with hooked beak and strong, curved talons.

2. Establishing a Purpose. As students read, ask them to look for the ways in which the poet sees the hawk as being different from, perhaps even superior to, human beings.

Critical Comment

Critic Denis Donoghue said "It is Hughes's way in poetry to set the vocabulary of human convention in a context which outrages it." "Hawk Roosting" has many examples of this tendency. One example is the line "Now I hold Creation in my foot." Conventionally, God is considered to have Creation in His hands, and humans see themselves as masters of the animal world. Hughes's line turns those relationships upside down, thus outraging conventions of speech and belief. What other lines in the poem outrage convention? ("I kill where I please because it is all mine"—line 14; "my manners are tearing off heads"—line 16)

Ted Hughes (1930–   )

Ted Hughes, who often uses violent nature imagery to symbolize the human condition, has been called "a twentieth-century Aesop whose fables lack an explicit moral." Hughes was born in Yorkshire, where his father was a carpenter. After serving two years in the Royal Air Force, he studied archeology and anthropology at Cambridge. In 1956 he married the now-legendary American poet Sylvia Plath. The couple was separated in 1963, when Plath, ill and depressed, took her own life in an unheated flat during one of the worst winters in London history.

The titles of Hughes's books of poetry reveal his recurring subjects: *The Hawk in the Rain* (1957), *Animal Poems* (1967), *A Few Crows* (1970), and *Cave Birds* (1976). Although Hughes writes of nature, he has nothing in common with the Romantics, who saw in nature a reflection of divine providence and primeval innocence. In Hughes's poems, nature represents the darkest impulses of the human heart; violence is not only an accepted fact of life, but the impulse that links all creatures on earth. Hughes is known as an intensely private writer. In 1984 he was named Poet Laureate of England, succeeding Sir John Betjeman.

ANALYZING THE POEM
Identifying Details
1. A perch at the "top of the wood."
2. Because of the air's buoyancy, the sun's ray, and his wide prospect.
3. He kills where he pleases; he flies in a straight line; the sun is behind him; he is changeless.
   Line 16 says that his "manners" are "tearing off heads."

Interpreting Meanings
4. He has the entire world at his mercy.
   Each has an entirely different effect; the hawk's boast suggests an amoral sense of power, while the notion that God has the world in His hands suggests the benevolent care and protection of an all-powerful God.
5. I am so powerful that I am above the level of rational argument.

6. One meaning is that "the sun supports me." Another is that "I am more powerful than the sun; it must take second place to me."
7. It surveys the world like a powerful master or lord.
   The hawk thinks itself omnipotent.
8. Students' answers will vary. Note lines 14, 20, 23–24.

"If a hawk could speak, this is what it might say." Behind this conceit of a tough old bird with a perfect command of English is a message: There are forces in creation impervious to humankind and oblivious to our moral discriminations. "No arguments assert my right," says the hawk. His grim joke—"The sun is behind me"—suggests that the source of all life encourages even those that destroy life.

Before you read the poem, think about what it means to call a bird like the hawk a "predator."

Hawk Roosting

A
I sit in the top of the wood, my eyes
   closed.
Inaction, no falsifying dream
Between my hooked head and hooked feet:
Or in sleep rehearse perfect kills and eat.

B
5 The convenience of the high trees!
The air's buoyancy and the sun's ray
Are of advantage to me;
And the earth's face upward for my
   inspection.

My feet are locked upon the rough bark.
10 It took the whole of Creation
To produce my foot, my each feather:
Now I hold Creation in my foot

Or fly up, and revolve it all slowly—
I kill where I please because it is all mine.
15 There is no sophistry° in my body:
My manners are tearing off heads—

The allotment of death.
For the one path of my flight is direct
Through the bones of the living.
20 No arguments assert my right:

C
The sun is behind me.
Nothing has changed since I began.
My eye has permitted no change.
I am going to keep things like this.

15. **sophistry:** plausible but unsound reasoning.

Responding to the Poem

Analyzing the Poem

Identifying Details

1. Where is the hawk speaking from?
2. Why does he like his roost?
3. What are his actions? How does he describe his "manners"?

Interpreting Meanings

4. What does the hawk mean by saying he holds Creation in his foot? How is this different from the notion that God has "the whole world in His hands"?
5. How would you **paraphrase** lines 18–19?
6. What two meanings can you propose for the line "the sun is behind me"?
7. What is the hawk's attitude toward the world it surveys? What does it think of itself?

8. In what ways is the hawk's philosophy inhuman, or even nonhuman? In what ways does it resemble the philosophy of some people?

Writing About the Poem

A Creative Response

1. **Writing a Poem.** Select some other animal and, in a short paragraph or poem, let it explain its "philosophy."

A Critical Response

2. **Analyzing Theme.** In a paragraph, state and discuss what you take to be the main theme of the poem. In a second paragraph, discuss your response to the theme.

A. Making Comparisons
? What difference between the hawk and humans is the poet emphasizing in the first stanza? (Unlike man, the hawk lives totally in the present, neither dreaming of nor rehearsing future actions.)

B. Mood
? What is the mood of the second stanza? (Elation, self-assurance, imperiousness)

C. Irony
In the last stanza the hawk speaks as if he is the lord of all Creation.
? How is this a kind of ironic echo of human claims? (This is the same claim to dominion that humans usually make.) What is the essential difference in the poet's mind between human claims to dominion and those of the hawk? (The hawk's claims are buttressed by the laws of Nature, which ultimately cannot be superseded by human desires.)

BUILDING ON PRIOR KNOWLEDGE. Tell students that the speaker in this poem is thinking about how his father and grandfather dug the soil for food and fuel and how their activity compares with his occupation as a writer. In a literal and a figurative sense, the poet is thinking about "roots."

SUPPLEMENTARY SUPPORT MATERIALS
1. Vocabulary Activity Worksheet (*CCB*)
2. Review and Response Worksheet: Imagery (*CCB*)
3. Selection Test (*CCB*)

DEVELOPING VOCABULARY
The following word from the poem is tested in the Selection Test. (See also Vocabulary Activity Worksheet.)
squat

A. Figurative Language

? Why do you think the poet compares his pen with a gun? (Perhaps because his pen is his most powerful weapon in the struggle of life; also his pen gives him a sense of security)

B. Expansion
Tell students that in the first line of stanza 3 the poet's father is digging in the flowerbeds outside the window where the poet sits writing. Starting with the second line, the poet moves in his imagination twenty years earlier to the time when his father was digging potatoes on the family farm. "Drills" here are furrows in which seed is planted.

Seamus Heaney (1939–   )

Seamus Heaney was born in largely Protestant Northern Ireland to Roman Catholic parents. His boyhood on a farm in County Derry contributed profoundly to his identity as a poet. But Heaney has never promoted himself as a rustic or regarded his work as an expression of regionalism. He earned his education as a scholarship student, first at a Catholic preparatory school and then at Queen's University in Belfast where, still in his mid-twenties, he was appointed Lecturer in English.

Instead of leading him away from his roots in Irish soil, Heaney's studies—particularly those having to do with the history and psychology of myth—opened for him a way of seeing anew not only the misty grandeur of his native landscape, but also the figures in it who, unknowingly, unite the past with the present. Heaney is an acute observer of rural life and of life lived on the industrial margins of cities, and he deals with both without romanticizing them.

Regarded by Robert Lowell as "the best Irish poet since William Butler Yeats," Heaney now occupies the chair at Harvard left vacant by Lowell's death in 1977. He divides his time between Cambridge, Massachusetts, and a home in the Irish Republic.

The Irish farmer digs two things in particular: potatoes and turf, or peat. The peat is dug from bogs. These huge soggy areas of decaying vegetable matter have produced for Ireland, especially in centuries gone by, the material that is dried and then burned in fires for cooking and heat. This poet is also "digging," just as his father and grandfather had done before him. But what is he "digging" for? And what is his tool?

Digging

A   Between my finger and my thumb
     The squat pen rests; snug as a gun.

     Under my window, a clean rasping sound
     When the spade sinks into gravelly ground:
5   My father, digging. I look down

B   Till his straining rump among the flowerbeds
     Bends low, comes up twenty years away
     Stooping in rhythm through potato drills
     Where he was digging.

1. His father digging with a spade in a vegetable garden.
2. Taking his grandfather some milk in a bottle, watching him drink it, and then seeing the old man digging turf.
3. "Clean rasping sound" (line 3), the sight of the father's "straining rump" (line 6), the "cool hardness" of the potatoes (line 14), "the cold smell of potato mould" (line 25), and "the squelch and slap of soggy peat" (lines 25–26).
4. He will "dig" with his pen, that is, use his writing ability to create literature.

Interpreting Meanings
5. In line 2, the pen is "snug as a gun," implying its power. In the last line, the pen is compared to a spade, emphasizing creativity and continuity.
6. For memorable incidents that can be turned into poetry.
7. One expects to find a word like *feet* or *yards.* The effect is to emphasize how far back the speaker is remembering.
8. Most students will agree that the speaker feels respectful and admiring, even though their work and his are quite different.

10 The coarse boot nestled on the lug, the shaft
     Against the inside knee was levered firmly.
     He rooted out tall tops, buried the bright edge deep
     To scatter new potatoes that we picked
     Loving their cool hardness in our hands

15 By God, the old man could handle a spade.
     Just like his old man.

     My grandfather cut more turf in a day
     Than any other man on Toner's bog.
     Once I carried him milk in a bottle
20 Corked sloppily with paper. He straightened up
     To drink it, then fell to right away

     Nicking and slicing neatly, heaving sods
     Over his shoulder, going down and down
     For the good turf. Digging.

25 The cold smell of potato mould, the squelch and slap
A   Of soggy peat, the curt cuts of an edge
     Through living roots awaken in my head.
     But I've no spade to follow men like them.

     Between my finger and my thumb
30 The squat pen rests.
B   I'll dig with it.

Responding to the Poem

Analyzing the Poem

Identifying Details

1. Describe what the speaker sees from his window.
2. What scene does the speaker remember involving his grandfather?
3. What **images** in the poem help you to share what the speaker hears, feels, and smells?
4. At the end of the poem, what does the speaker intend to do?

Interpreting Meanings

5. What **figures of speech** compare the speaker's pen to other things? What significance can you find in these comparisons, particularly the last one?
6. What do you think the speaker wants to "dig" for?

7. Why do you think the father comes up "twenty *years*" away in line 7? (What word did you expect to find here?)
8. How would you say this speaker feels about his father and grandfather and the work they did?

Writing About the Poem

A Creative Response

Extending the Poem. Starting with the last two lines of Heaney's poem, write a poem (or prose paragraph, if you prefer) telling what you would like to "dig" with your "pen" (or typewriter, or computer). You might want to start by recalling something about your parents and grandparents.

A. Interpreting Events
❓ What kind of experiences from his childhood does the poet recall, especially in lines 25–27? (Vivid sense experiences) How were these experiences in a way preparing him for his adult occupation? (By providing raw material for his poetry)

B. Theme
The poet clearly respects the work done by his father and grandfather.
❓ Does he feel alienated from his forebears? (No) What does the last stanza suggest about his sense of self-worth and purpose? (He is proud of his work as a writer and sees it as a continuation of the skilled and dedicated labor of his forebears.)

CLOSURE
Ask students to explain the central metaphor of this poem in a few sentences.

PREPARATION

1. BUILDING ON PRIOR KNOWLEDGE. Ask students if they have ever discovered mushrooms on damp lawns, in shady spots, and in other moist areas. Point out that some mushrooms are poisonous, but experts can distinguish edible from poisonous ones. Explain that mushrooms are not the only subject of the poem that follows.

2. ESTABLISHING A PURPOSE. Have students read the headnote, especially the comments about Atwood's basic comparison in "Mushrooms." As they read (and perhaps reread) the poem, have them ask themselves, "Where does poetry come from?" and see how the poem itself responds to that question.

3. PREREADING JOURNAL. Provide students with a few simple metaphors—for example, "Life is a dance" or "Poems are birds." Then have students use their journals to extend the metaphor of their choice by adding more specific details of comparison.

Margaret Atwood (1939–   )

Atwood is a Canadian who grew up in Ottawa and now lives in Toronto. She is a versatile writer who has published volumes of poetry and short stories. Her stories (they are often bizarre) appear frequently in *The New Yorker;* one collection has been published under the title of *Bluebeard's Egg and Other Stories* (1986). Atwood is probably best known as a novelist. Her novel *The Handmaid's Tale* (1985), a nightmarish vision of the future in which women are used chiefly for breeding purposes in a neo-puritanic dictatorship, has been made into a movie.

As a child Atwood spent a good part of each year with her parents in the wilderness. (Her father was an expert on insects.) As a result, she developed a keen eye for nature, as her poem "Mushrooms" demonstrates.

Atwood, in speaking about her poems, said, "I don't think of poetry as a 'rational' activity but as an aural one. My poems usually begin with words or phrases which appeal more because of their sound than their meaning, and the movement and phrasing of a poem are very important to me."

SUPPLEMENTARY SUPPORT MATERIALS
1. Review and Response Worksheet: Diction (CCB)
2. Selection Test (CCB)

CLOSURE
Ask students to consider, based on the poem, how Atwood would define the terms *poet* and *poetry*. Encourage them to suggest comparisons that help them to define these terms for themselves.

This poem is not "about" mushrooms. Its purpose is not to inform or instruct. Rather, it evokes the feelings—the sights, sounds, smells, tastes—that the poet has experienced as she watched mushrooms suddenly appear, propagate, and die.

If there is a main point to this poem, it comes in the final stanza. Then we realize that all of these minutely detailed and elaborate descriptions of mushrooms add up to "this mouth-/ful of dirt, this poetry." The poem, we can see, is an extended metaphor, an implied comparison between one thing and another. It celebrates not only nature and life but, in some mysterious way, poetic creation itself.

The conclusion is not pretty, and the process by which we come to it is as unsentimental as a clinical examination. Any emotional response that we might be expected to have is deliberately held off, then openly invited.

Read the poem aloud, and listen for Atwood's use of sounds.

Mushrooms

i

A
> In this moist season,
> mist on the lake and thunder
> afternoons in the distance

> they ooze up through the earth
> 5 during the night,
B
> like bubbles, like tiny
> bright red balloons
> filling with water;
> a sound below sound, the thumbs of rubber
> 10 gloves turned softly inside out.

> In the mornings, there is the leaf mold
> starred with nipples,
> with cool white fishgills,
> leathery purple brains,
> 15 fist-sized suns dulled to the color of embers,
> poisonous moons, pale yellow.

ii

Where do they come from?

C
> For each thunderstorm that travels
> overhead there's another storm
> 20 that moves parallel in the ground.
> Struck lightning is where they meet.

> Underfoot there's a cloud of rootlets,
> shed hairs or a bundle of loose threads
> blown slowly through the midsoil.

A. Alliteration and Assonance
Although Atwood uses free verse without end rhyme, she supplies other sound effects to link poetic ideas. Note, for example, the repeated *s* sounds in line 1 and *oo* sounds in lines 3–4.

B. Simile and Metaphor
Have students identify the similes ("like bubbles," "like tiny . . . water") and the metaphor ("the thumbs . . . out") that help us picture the mushrooms.

C. Figurative Language
Note that Atwood answers the question in line 17 with language that is both figurative ("another storm," "cloud") and literal ("rootlets," "loose threads").

A. Pronouns
Elicit that *these* refers to the mushrooms; *their*, to the rootlets or loose threads in the preceding lines.

B. Expansion
Since mushrooms do not contain chlorophyll, they do not make their own food as green plants do. Instead, they feed on moist, rotting debris such as the items mentioned here.

C. Contrast
In taking pleasure in describing the mushrooms, what is the speaker embracing? (All aspects of the cycle of life—including the inevitability of death and decay)

A
25   These are their flowers, these fingers
     reaching through darkness to the sky,
     these eyeblinks
     that burst and powder the air with spores.

iii

     They feed in shade, on halfleaves
30   as they return to water,
B   on slowly melting logs,
     deadwood. They glow
     in the dark sometimes. They taste
     of rotten meat or cloves
35   or cooking steak or bruised
     lips or new snow.

iv

     It isn't only
     for food I hunt them
     but for the hunt and because
40   they smell of death and the waxy
C   skins of the newborn,
     flesh into earth into flesh.

     Here is the handful
     of shadow I have brought back to you:
45   this decay, this hope, this mouth-
     ful of dirt, this poetry.

ANALYZING THE POEM
Identifying Details
1. Lines 1–16.
Lines 17–28.
Lines 29–32.
2. The *b* sound.
3. "Soil enriched by decayed leaves."
4. Line 42 refers to the cycle of birth, death, and regeneration.

Interpreting Meanings
5. It appeals to sight, as in the reference to suns, embers, and pale yellow moons (lines 15–16); it appeals to hearing and touch, as in the reference to balloons that are being filled (lines 7–9) and through the choice of such words as *softly* (line 10) and *leathery* (line 14). There is a vivid appeal to taste in lines 33–36 and to smell in lines 40–42.

6. Answers will vary, but most students will identify the photos as looking like (in order of appearance) nipples, fishgills (or brains, but not purple ones), and poisonous moons.
7. Explanations will vary, but students should remember that it is in these lines that Atwood's metaphor is most obvious.

The mushrooms suggest decay because they feed on decaying matter and eventually decay themselves; however, there is hope in their sudden renewal through the spores they have spread. They suggest mouthfuls of dirt because they are nourished in soil (and perhaps because some varieties have an earthy taste). They may suggest poetry in that both embody bright and dark aspects of existence and that their products, while true to their own nature, may not always be palatable.

FURTHER READING FOR STUDENTS
You might recommend Sylvia Plath's poem "Mushrooms," in which the mushrooms are the speakers.

Responding to the Poem

Analyzing the Poem

Identifying Details

1. Which lines of the poem describe the mushrooms' first appearance above ground? Which lines describe the reproduction of mushrooms from spores? Which lines describe the end of their life cycle?
2. In lines 6–10, what repeated consonant suggests the sound of the fingers of rubber gloves turning inside out?
3. "Leaf mold" (line 11) can be defined as "soil enriched by decayed leaves" or "mold that grows on leaves." Which definition applies here?
4. In your own words, tell what biological process line 42 refers to.

Interpreting Meanings

5. What **senses** does the poem appeal to? (Quote examples.)
6. In lines 11–16 the poet tells us what various kinds of mushrooms look like, against the background of leaf mold. Which photographs in this textbook would you match up with Atwood's descriptions? Think up a **metaphor** of your own for each of the photographs. For example, "the mushrooms on page 1143 are shaggy mops."
7. Explain the poem's last four lines. How do the mushrooms suggest decay, hope, mouthfuls of dirt, and poetry?

Writing About the Poem

A Creative Response

Fitting Sounds to Meanings. Choose a simple subject from nature such as "butterflies," "lions," "pigeons," "rocks," "sand," "worms," or one of your own choosing. What sounds do you associate with your subject? Before you write, list words that not only have these sounds but also have some meaning associated with your subject. Then write a short poem about your subject (four lines or so) using these words. Try to use images that will appeal to the senses.

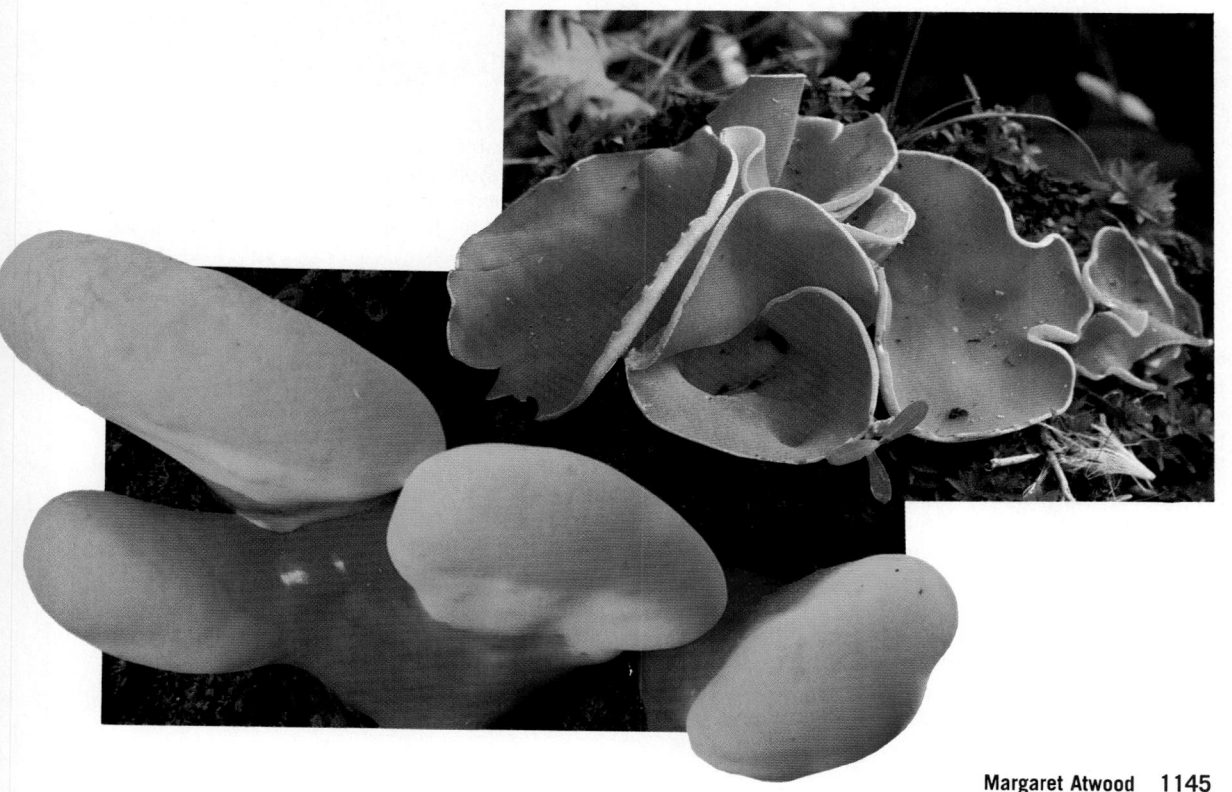

DRAMA

Bernard Shaw (1856–1950)

Bernard Shaw (he disliked his first name, George) described himself as "an upstart son of an alcoholic downstart." Though he came from a Dublin family with claims to a certain position in society, his father's failings led to the family's loss of status, and Shaw was made to feel like an outsider. He decided that the way to "show them" was to succeed in the arts.

When he was sixteen, the family broke up, and Mrs. Shaw, whose one concern in life seemed to be her singing, went to London with her daughter to teach music. After working for four years in Ireland at various uncongenial jobs (such as rent collecting), Shaw also went to London, and lived with his mother. He remained with her as a rather unwelcome boarder until he was married at forty-two. "I did not throw myself into the struggle for life," he was to say later, "I threw my mother into it."

The first nine years in London were bitter and discouraging. Feeling that he was meant for better things, Shaw haunted the museums and the concert halls, and read omnivorously in an attempt to educate himself. He also wrote five novels in six years, and even succeeded in getting one, *Cashel Byron's Profession,* published.

Soon, Shaw was writing reviews of music, art, books, and theater—brilliant reviews that are still interesting to read today. For most of what he saw in the theater, he had nothing but contempt. Looking back in 1933, he wrote,

> In 1889 the London stage had come into shattering collision with the Norwegian giant, Ibsen. I say "shattering" advisedly because nobody could follow up Ibsen. He knocked

the fashionable drama of the day out of countenance without effectively replacing it, because his plays could never be forced on the London theater for more than a fortnight at a time.

In many countries at this time, dissatisfaction was developing with "fashionable drama," which seemed to have little or no relationship to the issues of the day. On the European continent, small theaters were being established to house a new kind of drama. In France there was the Théâtre Libre (1887); in Germany, the Freie Bühne (1889); in Russia, The Moscow Art Theater (1887).

In England in 1891, J. T. Grein, a young journalist, started the private Independent Theater "for the presentment of real human life." Grein's first production was Henrik Ibsen's shocking exposé of the cost of respectability, *Ghosts. Ghosts* raised a furor in the press, but there were defenders, among them Bernard

Shaw. Grein looked to the English playwrights for the kinds of plays he wanted to produce, but he found none until Shaw offered *Widowers' Houses,* an attack on slum landlords. The play's excoriating criticism of social evils was true to Shaw's belief that art did not exist for art's sake. Art, he believed, should be didactic, and it should hope to reform.

This belief tends to make Shaw sound like a dull and chilly preacher, and in fact he has been accused of lacking human passion. What he did *not* lack was a passionate humanitarianism, which for him transcended romance and idealism. For Shaw, love did not conquer all or solve all of life's problems, as it had in most Victorian plays.

And Shaw had wit and a comic eye. His plays are anything but dull. He accomplished his "teaching" in delightful, mischievous comedies that turn things topsy-turvy and debunk one conventional idea after another. Shaw makes us question absolutes and do some hard thinking for ourselves. For example, in *Major Barbara* (1905), Barbara, a Salvation Army officer, scorns the wealth her father has earned from manufacturing munitions, only to find that this same wealth supports her Salvation Army work. In *Arms and the Man* (1894), Shaw deflates the heroic concept of the soldier. His soldier does not carry a gun in his holster. He carries chocolates, because it is more realistic to worry about being hungry than about being killed.

Shaw's art is the art of anticlimax. He leads us to expect a conventional conclusion, and then pulls the rug out from under us, in the process giving us new insights. *Candida* (1895), one of his most delightful and popular plays, is basically a domestic comedy with some debt to Ibsen's *A Doll's House* (1879). Candida is a warm and charming woman in her mid-thirties, married to a rigid, unimaginative minister. She is also being wooed by a flamboyant, romantic young poet, who is forever throwing himself at her feet, begging her to run away with him. In the end, Candida (the "honest" one) says she will choose the weaker man, the one who needs her more. (Presenting a Victorian wife as able to choose to go or to stay was in itself remarkable.) Candida surprisingly chooses her apparently self-sufficient husband, thus making us reconsider the husband's supposed strength. At the same time, Shaw makes one of his favorite points

about the artist standing alone, strong in his own powers and talents.

In his long life, Shaw wrote fifty plays of a variety and quality matched only by Shakespeare. Sometimes the work of reformists dates badly, as the targets of their criticism disappear. This has not been so with Shaw. With the exception of his earliest plays, *Widowers' Houses* and *Mrs. Warren's Profession,* Shaw's plays have borne up well and are constantly revived. At the Theater Guild, an American production company which presented most of Shaw's American premieres, the saying always was, "When in doubt, do Shaw." In 1925, Shaw's achievements earned him the Nobel Prize for literature.

Shaw is still popular for a variety of reasons. In most cases, the evils and follies he attacked are still with us; the manner in which he launched his attacks is brilliant and witty; and he created some extraordinary parts for actors, especially for women. Shaw wrote most of the great parts for the leading actresses of his day— Janet Achurch, Ellen Terry, and Mrs. Patrick Campbell. (With both Ellen Terry and Mrs. Patrick Campbell, he carried on lengthy epistolary love affairs; according to Shaw, this was the best kind.) To this day, actresses relish playing Shaw's St. Joan, Eliza Doolittle, Candida, Cleopatra, and Barbara.

In his later years, after *Heartbreak House* (1919), and his greatest play, *Saint Joan* (1923), Shaw wrote such plays as *The Apple Cart* (1929) and *The Millionairess* (1935), which are little more than discussions, opportunities for him to present and argue ideas that interested him. In these later years, Shaw continued to write about his favorite subjects, marriage and religion. In 1950, the year he died, he was part way through yet another play, *Why She Would Not.*

Toward the end of his life, as the world seemed determined to blow itself up, Shaw looked on in horror. But he was still the reformer who saw human life as a comedy and not as a tragedy. As the apostle of reason, Shaw lived and wrote for the day when society and the world could be brought to their senses through reason. In the Epilogue to *Saint Joan,* the soldier asks what might have been Shaw's prayer:

Oh, God, that madest this beautiful earth,
when will it be ready to receive Thy saints?
How long, oh Lord, how long?

PREPARATION

1. BUILDING ON PRIOR KNOWLEDGE. If students are familiar with the Alan Jay Lerner and Frederick Loewe musical *My Fair Lady,* they will already know the basic plot and theme of *Pygmalion,* on which the musical comedy was based. Remind them also that Shaw gave his play the name of the sculptor in Greek mythology who fell in love with the statue of a beautiful woman that he had created.

2. ESTABLISHING A PURPOSE. Ask students to read a version of the Greek myth of Pygmalion and Galatea. Point out that although the time and place are different there are many similarities between the myth and *Pygmalion.* As they read the play, have students look for these similarities.

3. PREREADING JOURNAL. Ask students to write one or two paragraphs discussing what—if anything—a person's manner of speaking tells us about his or her intelligence and personality. Students should give at least two real-life examples to support each of their generalizations.

PYGMALION
A ROMANCE IN FIVE ACTS

Preface
A Professor of Phonetics

Shaw stipulated that the text of Pygmalion *be reprinted exactly as he wrote it; this means that the British spelling style is retained, and apostrophes are often omitted, as are periods after abbreviations like* Mrs. *and* Mr. *Shaw's will also requires that each time* Pygmalion *is reprinted, the Preface and the Epilogue must be reprinted also.*

A s will be seen later on, Pygmalion needs, not a preface, but a sequel, which I have supplied in its due place.

The English have no respect for their language, and will not teach their children to speak it. They cannot spell it because they have nothing to spell it with but an old foreign alphabet of which only the consonants—and not all of them—have any agreed speech value. Consequently no man can teach himself what it should sound like from reading it; and it is impossible for an Englishman to open his mouth without making some other Englishman despise him. Most European languages are now accessible in black and white to foreigners: English and French are not thus accessible even to Englishmen and Frenchmen. The reformer we need most today is an energetic phonetic enthusiast: that is why I have made such a one the hero of a popular play.

There have been heroes of that kind crying in the wilderness for many years past. When I became interested in the subject towards the end of the eighteen-seventies, the illustrious Alexander Melville Bell, the inventor of Visible Speech,[1] had emigrated to Canada, where his son invented the telephone; but Alexander J. Ellis was still a London patriarch, with an impressive head always covered by a velvet skull cap, for which he would

1. **Visible Speech:** a system of symbols that show the position of the throat, tongue, and lips in making sounds. Bell invented the system to help deaf people learn to speak.

SUPPLEMENTARY SUPPORT MATERIALS

1. Vocabulary Activity Worksheet (*CCB*)
2. Review and Response Worksheets: Exposition; Conflict; Characterization; Plot; Theme (*CCB*)
3. Language Skills Worksheets: Varying Sentence Beginnings; Mechanics: End

Punctuation; Revision Worksheet 5 (*CCB*)
4. Selection Test (*CCB*)

DEVELOPING VOCABULARY

The following words from the play are tested in the Selection Test. (See also Vocabulary Activity Worksheet.)

gumption   mendacity
peremptorily   imprecation
elocutionary   somnambulist

Photographs on this page and pages 1154, 1163, 1170, 1176, and 1194 are from the April 1984 production of *Pygmalion* at the Shaftesbury Theater, London.

Summary of Preface
In the Preface, Shaw gives his views on the spelling and pronunciation of English. He deplores the inadequacy of the alphabet to convey the varied sounds of English and points out how the people of his day snobbishly used speech patterns to classify people socially. He names several phoneticians whom he admires for trying to reform British spelling but notes that they are disregarded both by their fellow academics and by the general public. He describes one phonetician at some length, Henry Sweet, and compares him to his protagonist, Henry Higgins. Finally, he gives his explicit support to the central thesis of his play that speech patterns are learned and that they are not true indicators of a person's identity or worth.

apologize to public meetings in a very courtly manner. He and Tito Pagliardini, another phonetic veteran, were men whom it was impossible to dislike. Henry Sweet, then a young man, lacked their sweetness of character: he was about as conciliatory to conventional mortals as Ibsen or Samuel Butler.[2] His great ability as a phonetician (he was, I think, the best of them all at his job) would have entitled him to high official recognition, and perhaps enabled him to popularize his subject, but for his Satanic contempt for all academic dignitaries and persons in general who thought more of Greek than of phonetics. Once, in the days when the Imperial Institute rose in South Kensington, and Joseph Chamberlain[3] was booming the Empire, I induced the editor of a leading monthly review to commission an article from Sweet on the imperial importance of his subject. When it arrived, it contained nothing but a savagely derisive attack on a professor of language and literature whose chair Sweet regarded as proper to a phonetic expert only. The article, being libellous, had to be returned as impossible; and I had to renounce my dream of dragging its author into the limelight. When I met him afterwards, for the first time for many years, I found to my astonishment that he, who had been a quite tolerably presentable young man, had actually managed by sheer scorn to alter his personal appearance until he had become a sort of walking repudiation of Oxford and all its traditions. It must have been largely in his own despite that he was squeezed into something called a Readership of phonetics there. The future of phonetics rests probably with his pupils, who all swore by him; but nothing could bring the man himself into any sort of compliance with the university to which he nevertheless clung by divine right in an intensely Oxonian way. I daresay his papers, if he has left any, include some satires that may be published without too destructive results fifty years hence. He was, I believe, not in the least an ill-natured man: very much the opposite, I should say; but he would not suffer fools gladly; and to him all scholars who were not rabid phoneticians were fools.

Those who knew him will recognize in my third act the allusion to the Current Shorthand in which he used to write postcards. It may be acquired from a four and sixpenny manual published by the Clarendon Press. The postcards which Mrs. Higgins describes are such as I have received from Sweet. I would decipher a sound which a cockney would represent by *zerr,* and a Frenchman by *seu,* and then write demanding with some heat what on earth it meant. Sweet, with boundless contempt for my stupidity, would reply that it not only meant but obviously was the word Result, as no other word containing that sound, and capable of making sense with the context, existed in any language spoken on earth. That less expert mortals should require fuller indications was beyond Sweet's patience. Therefore, though the whole point of his Current Shorthand is that it can express every sound in the language perfectly, vowels as well as consonants, and that your hand has to make no stroke except the easy and current ones with which you write m, n, and u, l, p, and q, scribbling them at whatever angle comes easiest to you, his unfortunate determination to make this remarkable and quite legible script serve also as a shorthand reduced it in his own practice to the most inscrutable of cryptograms. His true objective was the provision of a full, accurate, legible script for our language; but he was led past that by his contempt for the popular Pitman system of shorthand, which he called the Pitfall system. The triumph of Pitman was a triumph of business organization: there was a weekly paper to persuade you to learn Pitman: there were cheap textbooks and exercise books and transcripts of speeches for you to copy, and schools where experienced teachers coached you up to the necessary proficiency. Sweet could not organize his market in that fashion. He might as well have been the Sybil[4] who tore up the leaves of prophecy that nobody would attend to. The four and sixpenny manual, mostly in his lithographed handwriting, that was never vulgarly[5] advertized, may perhaps some day be taken up by a syndicate and pushed upon the public as The Times pushed the Encyclopædia Britannica; but until then it will certainly not prevail against Pitman. I have bought three copies of it during my lifetime; and I am informed by the publishers that its cloistered existence is still a steady and healthy one. I actually learned the system two several[6] times; and yet the shorthand in

---

2. **Samuel Butler** (1612–1680): English writer noted for his sharp satires on society and human shortcomings.
3. **Joseph Chamberlain** (1836–1914): a member of the British Parliament, and colonial secretary from 1895 to 1903.

4. **Sybil:** in Greek legend, a prophet whose warnings were often ignored.
5. **vulgarly:** popularly.
6. **several:** different.

Lines written by Bernard Shaw in Pitman shorthand.

which I am writing these lines is Pitman's. And the reason is, that my secretary cannot transcribe Sweet, having been perforce taught in the schools of Pitman. In America I could use the commercially organized Gregg shorthand, which has taken a hint from Sweet by making its letters writable (current, Sweet would have called them) instead of having to be geometrically drawn like Pitman's; but all these systems, including Sweet's, are spoilt by making them available for verbatim reporting, in which complete and exact spelling and word division are impossible. A complete and exact phonetic script is neither practicable nor necessary for ordinary use; but if we enlarge our alphabet to the Russian size, and make our spelling as phonetic as Spanish, the advance will be prodigious.

Pygmalion Higgins is not a portrait of Sweet, to whom the adventure of Eliza Doolittle would have been impossible; still, as will be seen, there are touches of Sweet in the play. With Higgins's physique and temperament Sweet might have set the Thames on fire. As it was, he impressed himself professionally on Europe to an extent that made his comparative personal obscurity, and the failure of Oxford to do justice to his eminence, a puzzle to foreign specialists in his subject. I do not blame Oxford, because I think Oxford is quite right in demanding a certain social amenity from its nurslings (heaven knows it is not exorbitant in its requirements!); for although I well know how hard it is for a man of genius with a seriously underrated subject to maintain serene and kindly relations with the men who underrate it, and who keep all the best places for less important subjects which they profess without originality and sometimes without much capacity for them, still, if he overwhelms them with wrath and disdain, he cannot expect them to heap honors on him.

Of the later generations of phoneticians I know little. Among them towered Robert Bridges, to whom perhaps Higgins may owe his Miltonic sym-

pathies, though here again I must disclaim all portraiture. But if the play makes the public aware that there are such people as phoneticians, and that they are among the most important people in England at present, it will serve its turn.

I wish to boast that Pygmalion has been an extremely successful play, both on stage and screen, all over Europe and North America as well as at home. It is so intensely and deliberately didactic, and its subject is esteemed so dry, that I delight in throwing it at the heads of the wiseacres who repeat the parrot cry that art should never be didactic. It goes to prove my contention that great art can never be anything else. **A**

Finally, and for the encouragement of people troubled with accents that cut them off from all high employment, I may add that the change wrought by Professor Higgins in the flowergirl is neither impossible nor uncommon. The modern concierge's daughter who fulfils her ambition by playing the Queen of Spain in Ruy Blas at the Théâtre Français is only one of many thousands of men and women who have sloughed off their native dialects and acquired a new tongue. Our **B** West End shop assistants and domestic servants are bi-lingual. But the thing has to be done scientifically, or the last state of the aspirant may be worse than the first. An honest slum dialect is more tolerable than the attempts of phonetically untaught persons to imitate the plutocracy. Ambitious flower-girls who read this play must not imagine that they can pass themselves off as fine **C** ladies by untutored imitation. They must learn their alphabet over again, and different, from a phonetic expert. Imitation will only make them ridiculous.

Note for Technicians. A complete representation of the play as printed for the first time in this edition is technically possible only on the cinema screen or on stages furnished with exceptionally elaborate machinery. For ordinary theatrical use the scenes separated by rows of asterisks are to be omitted.

In the dialogue an *e* upside down indicates the indefinite vowel, sometimes called obscure or neutral, for which, though it is one of the commonest sounds in English speech, our wretched alphabet has no letter.[7]

---

7. **no letter:** Shaw is referring to the schwa (ə), used in most dictionaries to represent such sounds as *a* in *again, e* in *parent, i* in *purity, o* in *compare,* and *u* in *focus.*

A. Responding

This is worth talking about. Is *Pygmalion* great because it's didactic? Or in spite of it? What is the distinction between something that is "didactic" and something that is a "revelation"? (The difference is a matter of degree. Something that is "didactic" is instructive or informational while something that is a "revelation" is an enlightenment; something that communicates a truth by *experience*.)

B. Expansion

A *concierge* (kän' sē·ʉrzh') is a building custodian or janitor. *Ruy Blas* (Shaw did not use italics) is a play by the French writer Victor Hugo (author of *Lés Misérables*).

C. Responding

Students might relate this controversial comment to the arguments that rage today over the kind of language instruction that should be used in schools.

Summary of Act One
After leaving the theater, a mother and daughter are sheltering from a rainstorm under a church portico while the son tries to find them a cab. Then a military gentleman joins them for the same purpose and is approached to buy flowers by a poor young girl with a pronounced "lower-class" accent. The crowd in attendance notices that another bystander is taking notes. The flower girl becomes alarmed, thinking the bystander a policeman. The note taker turns out to be an expert on dialects whom the Colonel, who shares his interest, has wanted to meet. They decide to go off together, and, when the flower girl complains of her treatment, the professor impulsively gives her a handful of money. Gleefully, she takes a cab home to her dreary room.

A. Expansion
Call students' attention to the way in which Shaw uses comic irony to reveal character. Here the self-satisfied Mother accuses her son of helplessness, the very trait she is exhibiting by relying on him to secure her a taxi.

B. Character
❓ What does this speech reveal about the Daughter's character? (She too is self-satisfied and spoiled.)

C. Responding
Eliza's clothes and appearance are described in detail.
❓ How do you imagine Freddy's sister looks? What kind of clothes do you think she is wearing? (Most students will agree that Freddy's sister is wearing an evening dress and probably has only a shawl or top jacket to keep her warm.)

Act One

London at 11:15 P.M. Torrents of heavy summer rain. Cab whistles blowing frantically in all directions. Pedestrians running for shelter into the portico of St Paul's church (not Wren's cathedral but Inigo Jones's[1] church in Covent Garden vegetable market), among them a lady and her daughter in evening dress. All are peering out gloomily at the rain, except one man with his back turned to the rest, wholly preoccupied with a notebook in which he is writing.

The church clock strikes the first quarter.

The Daughter *(in the space between the central pillars, close to the one on her left).* I'm getting chilled to the bone. What can Freddy be doing all this time? He's been gone twenty minutes.
The Mother *(on her daughter's right).* Not so long. But he ought to have got us a cab by this.
A Bystander *(on the lady's right).* He wont get no cab not until half-past eleven, missus, when they come back after dropping their theatre fares.
The Mother. But we must have a cab. We cant stand here until half-past eleven. It's too bad.
The Bystander. Well it aint my fault, missus.
The Daughter. If Freddy had a bit of gumption, he would have got one at the theatre door.
The Mother. What could he have done, poor boy?
The Daughter. Other people get cabs. Why couldnt he?

[FREDDY *rushes in out of the rain from the Southampton Street side, and comes between them closing a dripping umbrella. He is a young man of twenty, in evening dress, very wet round the ankles.*]

The Daughter. Well, havn't you got a cab?
Freddy. Theres not one to be had for love or money.
The Mother. Oh, Freddy, there must be one. You cant have tried.
The Daughter. It's too tiresome. Do you expect us to go and get one ourselves?
Freddy. I tell you theyre all engaged. The rain was so sudden: nobody was prepared; and everybody had to take a cab. Ive been to Charing Cross one way and nearly to Ludgate Circus the other; and they were all engaged.
The Mother. Did you try Trafalgar Square?
Freddy. There wasnt one at Trafalgar Square.
The Daughter. Did you try?
Freddy. I tried as far as Charing Cross Station. Did you expect me to walk to Hammersmith?
The Daughter. You havnt tried at all.
The Mother. You really are very helpless, Freddy. Go again; and dont come back until you have found a cab.
Freddy. I shall simply get soaked for nothing.
The Daughter. And what about us? Are we to stay here all night in this draught,[2] with next to nothing on? You selfish pig——
Freddy. Oh, very well: I'll go, I'll go. *(He opens his umbrella and dashes off Strandwards, but comes into collision with a flower girl who is hurrying in for shelter, knocking her basket out of her hands. A blinding flash of lightning, followed instantly by a rattling peal of thunder, orchestrates the incident).*
The Flower Girl. Nah then, Freddy: Look wh' y' gowin, deah.
Freddy. Sorry *(he rushes off)*.
The Flower Girl *(picking up her scattered flowers and replacing them in the basket).* Theres menners f' yer! Tǝ-oo banches o voylets trod into the mad.[3] *(She sits down on the plinth[4] of the column, sorting her flowers, on the lady's right. She is not at all a romantic figure. She is perhaps eighteen, perhaps twenty, hardly older. She wears a little sailor hat of black straw that has long been exposed to the dust and soot of London and has seldom if ever been brushed. Her hair needs washing rather badly: its mousy color can hardly be natural. She wears a shoddy black coat that reaches nearly to her knees and is shaped to her waist. She has a brown skirt with a coarse apron. Her boots are much the worse for wear. She is no doubt as clean as she can afford to be; but compared to the ladies she is very dirty. Her features are no worse than theirs; but their condition leaves something to be desired; and she needs the services of a dentist).*
The Mother. How do you know that my son's name is Freddy, pray?

1. **Wren's . . . Jones's:** English architects Christopher Wren (1632–1723) and Inigo Jones (1573–1652).
2. **draught:** draft.
3. **theres . . . mad:** "There's manners for you. Two bunches of violets trod into the mud."
4. **plinth:** the square block at the base of a column.

The Flower Girl. Ow, eez, yə-ooa san, is e? Wal, fewd dan y' d-ooty bawmz a mather should, eed now bettern to spawl a pore gel's flahrzn than ran awy athaht pyin. Will ye-oo py me f'them?[5] *(Here, with apologies, this desperate attempt to represent her dialect without a phonetic alphabet must be abandoned as unintelligible outside London).*

The Daughter. Do nothing of the sort, mother. The idea!

The Mother. Please allow me, Clara. Have you any pennies?

The Daughter. No. Ive nothing smaller than sixpence.

The Flower Girl *(hopefully).* I can give you change for a tanner,[6] kind lady.

The Mother *(to* CLARA*).* Give it to me *(*CLARA *parts reluctantly).* Now *(to the girl).* This is for your flowers.

The Flower Girl. Thank you kindly, lady.

The Daughter. Make her give you the change. These things are only a penny a bunch.

The Mother. Do hold your tongue, Clara. *(To the girl).* You can keep the change.

The Flower Girl. Oh, thank you, lady.

The Mother. Now tell me how you know that young gentleman's name.

The Flower Girl. I didnt.

The Mother. I heard you call him by it. Dont try to deceive me.

The Flower Girl *(protesting).* Who's trying to deceive you? I called him Freddy or Charlie same as you might yourself if you was talking to a stranger and wished to be pleasant.

The Daughter. Sixpence thrown away! Really, mamma, you might have spared Freddy that. *(She retreats in disgust behind the pillar).*

[An elderly gentleman of the amiable military type rushes into the shelter, and closes a dripping umbrella. He is in the same plight as FREDDY, *very wet about the ankles. He is in evening dress, with a light overcoat. He takes the place left vacant by the daughter.]*

The Gentleman. Phew!

The Mother *(to the gentleman).* Oh, sir, is there any sign of its stopping?

The Gentleman. I'm afraid not. It started worse than ever about two minutes ago *(he goes to the plinth beside the flower girl; puts up his foot on it; and stoops to turn down his trouser ends).*

The Mother. Oh dear! *(She retires sadly and joins her daughter).*

The Flower Girl *(taking advantage of the military gentleman's proximity to establish friendly relations with him).* If it's worse, it's a sign it's nearly over. So cheer up, Captain; and buy a flower off a poor girl.

The Gentleman. I'm sorry. I havnt any change.

The Flower Girl. I can give you change, Captain.

The Gentleman. For a sovereign? Ive nothing less.

The Flower Girl. Garn! Oh do buy a flower off me, Captain. I can change half-a-crown. Take this for tuppence.

The Gentleman. Now dont be troublesome: theres a good girl. *(Trying his pockets)* I really havnt any change—Stop: heres three halfpence, if thats any use to you *(he retreats to the other pillar).*

The Flower Girl *(disappointed, but thinking three halfpence better than nothing).* Thank you, sir.

The Bystander *(to the girl).* You be careful: give him a flower for it. Theres a bloke here behind taking down every blessed word youre saying. *(All turn to the man who is taking notes).*

The Flower Girl *(springing up terrified).* I aint done nothing wrong by speaking to the gentleman. Ive a right to sell flowers if I keep off the kerb.[7] *(Hysterically)* I'm a respectable girl: so help me, I never spoke to him except to ask him to buy a flower off me.

[General hubbub, mostly sympathetic to the flower girl, but deprecating her excessive sensibility. Cries of Dont start hollerin. Who's hurting you? Nobody's going to touch you. Whats the good of fussing? Steady on. Easy easy, etc., *come from the elderly staid spectators, who pat her comfortingly. Less patient ones bid her shut her head, or ask her roughly what is wrong with her. A remoter group, not knowing what the matter is, crowd in and increase the noise with question and answer:* Whats the row? What-she-do? Where is he? A tec[8] taking her down. What! him? Yes: him over there: Took money off the gentleman, etc.]*

---

5. **Ow . . . f' them?:** "Oh, he's your son, is he? Well, if you'd done your duty by him as a mother should, he'd know better than to spoil a poor girl's flowers and then run away without paying. Will you pay me for them?" (Try reading the Cockney dialect speeches aloud.)
6. **tanner:** English slang for a sixpence coin.

7. **kerb:** curb
8. **tec:** detective.

A. Conflict

❓ Why does the Daughter disapprove of her mother's behavior? (She is embarrassed that her mother would suspect a link between her brother and a lower-class person.) What does the Mother's action reveal about her character? (She is prying and suspicious.)

B. Character

❓ How does the Gentleman respond to the Flower Girl's requests? (Politely, kindly, and paternalistically) What kind of person do you think he is? (An amiable bachelor, not overly knowledgeable about women)

A. **Conflict**

❓ Why is the Flower Girl frightened? (She is afraid of being charged with soliciting gentlemen on the street.) What conclusion does she and the Bystander draw about the man taking notes? (That he is a policeman)

B. **Expansion**
Point out to students that in this speech the Bystander concludes that the Note Taker is a gentleman by the look of his boots. This is another example of the judgments many of the characters are making about one another on the basis of surface characteristics. The fact that few of the characters are given names underscores Shaw's intent to show how people generally pigeonhole one another on the basis of appearances.

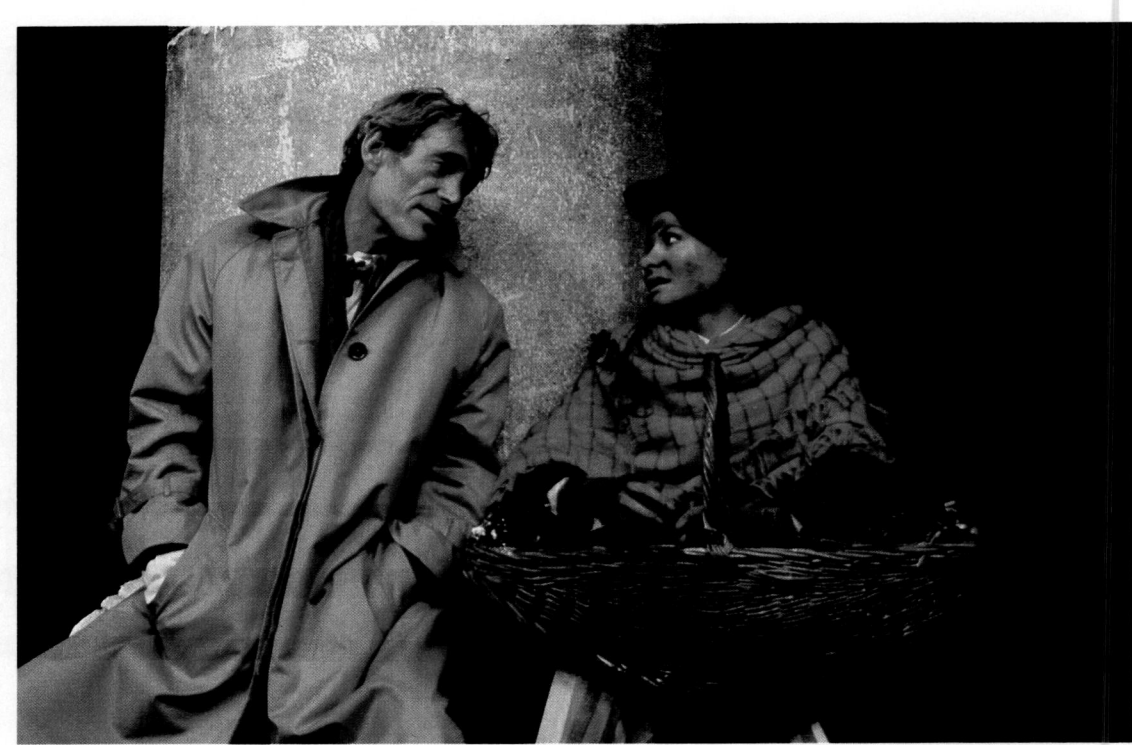

"Oh, shut up, shut up. Do I look like a policeman?"

A

The Flower Girl (*breaking through them to the gentleman, crying wildly*). Oh, sir, dont let him charge me. You dunno what it means to me. Theyll take away my character and drive me on the streets for speaking to gentlemen. They—

The Note Taker (*coming forward on her right, the rest crowding after him*). There! there! there! who's hurting you, you silly girl? What do you take me for?

B

The Bystander. It's aw rawt: e's a genleman: look at his bə-oots. (*Explaining to the note taker*) She thought you was a copper's nark, sir.

The Note Taker (*with quick interest*). Whats a copper's nark?

The Bystander (*inapt at definition*). It's a—well, it's a copper's nark, as you might say. What else would you call it? A sort of informer.

The Flower Girl (*still hysterical*). I take my Bible oath I never said a word——

The Note Taker (*overbearing but good-humored*). Oh, shut up, shut up. Do I look like a policeman?

The Flower Girl (*far from reassured*). Then what did you take down my words for? How do I know

whether you took me down right? You just shew[9] me what youve wrote about me. (*The note taker opens his book and holds it steadily under her nose, though the pressure of the mob trying to read it over his shoulders would upset a weaker man*). Whats that? That aint proper writing. I cant read that.

The Note Taker. I can. (*Reads, reproducing her pronunciation exactly*) "Cheer ap, Keptin; n' baw ya flahr orf a pore gel."

The Flower Girl (*much distressed*). It's because I called him Captain. I meant no harm. (*To the gentleman*) Oh, sir, dont let him lay a charge agen me for a word like that. You——

The Gentleman. Charge! I make no charge. (*To the note taker*) Really, sir, if you are a detective, you need not begin protecting me against molestation by young women until I ask you. Anybody could see that the girl meant no harm.

The Bystanders Generally (*demonstrating against police espionage*). Course they could. What busi-

---

9. **shew:** show.

ness is it of yours? You mind your own affairs. He wants promotion, he does. Taking down people's words! Girl never said a word to him. What harm if she did? Nice thing a girl cant shelter from the rain without being insulted, etc., etc., etc. (*She is conducted by the more sympathetic demonstrators back to her plinth, where she resumes her seat and struggles with her emotion*).

The Bystander. He aint a tec. He's a blooming busy-body: thats what he is. I tell you, look at his bə-oots.

The Note Taker (*turning on him genially*). And how are all your people down at Selsey?

The Bystander (*suspiciously*). Who told you my people come from Selsey?

The Note Taker. Never you mind. They did. (*To the girl*) How do you come to be up so far east? You were born in Lisson Grove.

The Flower Girl (*appalled*). Oh, what harm is there in my leaving Lisson Grove? It wasn't fit for a pig to live in; and I had to pay four-and-six a week. (*In tears*) Oh, boo—hoo—oo——

The Note Taker. Live where you like; but stop that noise.

The Gentleman (*to the girl*). Come, come! he cant touch you: you have a right to live where you please.

A Sarcastic Bystander (*thrusting himself between the note taker and the gentleman*). Park Lane, for instance. I'd like to go into the Housing Question with you, I would.

The Flower Girl (*subsiding into a brooding melancholy over her basket, and talking very low-spiritedly to herself*). I'm a good girl, I am.

The Sarcastic Bystander (*not attending to her*). Do you know where *I* come from?

The Note Taker (*promptly*). Hoxton.

[*Titterings. Popular interest in the note taker's performance increases.*]

The Sarcastic One (*amazed*). Well, who said I didnt? Bly me! you know everything, you do.

The Flower Girl (*still nursing her sense of injury*). Aint no call to meddle with me, he aint.

The Bystander (*to her*). Of course he aint. Dont you stand it from him. (*To the note taker*) See here: what call have you to know about people what never offered to meddle with you?

The Flower Girl. Let him say what he likes. I dont want to have no truck with him.

The Bystander. You take us for dirt under your feet, dont you? Catch you taking liberties with a gentleman!

The Sarcastic Bystander. Yes: tell him where he come from if you want to go fortune-telling.

The Note Taker. Cheltenham, Harrow, Cambridge, and India.

The Gentleman. Quite right.

[*Great laughter. Reaction in the note taker's favor. Exclamations of He knows all about it. Told him proper. Hear him tell the toff*[10] *where he come from? etc.*]

The Gentleman. May I ask, sir, do you do this for your living at a music hall?

The Note Taker. I've thought of that. Perhaps I shall some day.

[*The rain has stopped; and the persons on the outside of the crowd begin to drop off.*]

The Flower Girl (*resenting the reaction*). He's no gentleman, he aint, to interfere with a poor girl.

The Daughter (*out of patience, pushing her way rudely to the front and displacing the gentleman, who politely retires to the other side of the pillar*). What on earth is Freddy doing? I shall get pneumownia if I stay in this draught any longer.

The Note Taker (*to himself, hastily making a note of her pronunciation of "monia"*). Earlscourt.

The Daughter (*violently*). Will you please keep your impertinent remarks to yourself.

The Note Taker. Did I say that out loud? I didnt mean to. I beg your pardon. Your mother's Epsom, unmistakeably.

The Mother (*advancing between the daughter and the note taker*). How very curious! I was brought up in Largelady Park, near Epsom.

The Note Taker (*uproariously amused*). Ha! ha! what a devil of a name! Excuse me. (*To the daughter*) You want a cab, do you?

The Daughter. Dont dare speak to me.

The Mother. Oh, please, please, Clara. (*Her daughter repudiates her with an angry shrug and retires haughtily*). We should be so grateful to you, sir, if you found us a cab. (*The note taker produces a whistle*). Oh, thank you. (*She joins her daughter. The note taker blows a piercing blast*).

The Sarcastic Bystander. There! I knowed he was a plainclothes copper.

The Bystander. That aint a police whistle: thats a sporting whistle.

---

10. **toff:** English slang for a dandy.

A. Conflict

❓ How does the Note Taker classify people? (By their accents, or dialects) How do the Bystander and the Flower Girl react to his questions? (Suspiciously at first)

B. Expansion
Call students' attention to the crowd's changing reaction to the Note Taker's skill. Crowd members now find his ability to pinpoint people through language admirable and entertaining.

A. Character

? What is the
Note Taker's at-
titude toward his
special skill? (He
enjoys and is
proud of his abili-
ty.) What is the
Flower Girl's atti-
tude toward him?
(She disapproves
of him strongly.)

B. Diction

? How would you
characterize the
professor's
speech? (Exagger-
ated, pompous, er-
udite) How does it
contrast with the
Flower Girl's utter-
ances? (Her
speech is emotion-
al and basic, at
times not words at
all.) What is the ef-
fect of the con-
trast? (Humor)

C. Expansion
Tell students that
this speech fore-
shadows the major
action of the play.
It also displays the
arrogant overconfi-
dence and disdain
for others that are
part of the profes-
sor's character.

The Flower Girl (*still preoccupied with her wounded feelings*). He's no right to take away my character. My character is the same to me as any lady's.

The Note Taker. I dont know whether youve noticed it; but the rain stopped about two minutes ago.

The Bystander. So it has. Why didnt you say so before? and us losing our time listening to your silliness! (*He walks off towards the Strand*).

The Sarcastic Bystander. I can tell where you come from. You come from Anwell. Go back there.

The Note Taker (*helpfully*). Hanwell.

The Sarcastic Bystander (*affecting great distinction of speech*). Thenk you, teacher. Haw haw! So long (*he touches his hat with mock respect and strolls off*).

The Flower Girl. Frightening people like that! How would he like it himself?

The Mother. It's quite fine now, Clara. We can walk to a motor bus. Come. (*She gathers her skirts above her ankles and hurries off towards the Strand*).

The Daughter. But the cab——(*her mother is out of hearing*). Oh, how tiresome! (*She follows angrily*).

[*All the rest have gone except the note taker, the gentleman, and the flower girl, who sits arranging her basket, and still pitying herself in murmurs.*]

The Flower Girl. Poor girl! Hard enough for her to live without being worrited and chivied.[11]

The Gentleman (*returning to his former place on the note taker's left*). How do you do it, if I may ask?

The Note Taker. Simply phonetics. The science of speech. Thats my profession: also my hobby. Happy is the man who can make a living by his hobby! You can spot an Irishman or a Yorkshireman by his brogue. *I* can place any man within six miles. I can place him within two miles in London. Sometimes within two streets.

The Flower Girl. Ought to be ashamed of himself, unmanly coward!

The Gentleman. But is there a living in that?

The Note Taker. Oh, yes. Quite a fat one. This is an age of upstarts. Men begin in Kentish Town with £80 a year, and end in Park Lane with a hundred thousand. They want to drop Kentish Town; but they give themselves away every time

---

11. **worrited and chivied:** worried and tormented.

they open their mouths. Now I can teach them——

The Flower Girl. Let him mind his own business and leave a poor girl——

The Note Taker (*explosively*). Woman: cease this detestable boohooing instantly; or else seek the shelter of some other place of worship.

The Flower Girl (*with feeble defiance*). Ive a right to be here if I like, same as you.

The Note Taker. A woman who utters such depressing and disgusting sounds has no right to be anywhere—no right to live. Remember that you are a human being with a soul and the divine gift of articulate speech: that your native language is the language of Shakespear and Milton and The Bible; and dont sit there crooning like a bilious pigeon.

The Flower Girl (*quite overwhelmed, looking up at him in mingled wonder and deprecation without daring to raise her head*). Ah-ah-ah-ow-ow-ow-oo!

The Note Taker (*whipping out his book*). Heavens! what a sound! (*He writes; then holds out the book and reads, reproducing her vowels exactly*) Ah-ah-ah-ow-ow-ow-oo!

The Flower Girl (*tickled by the performance, and laughing in spite of herself*). Garn!

The Note Taker. You see this creature with her kerbstone English: the English that will keep her in the gutter to the end of her days. Well, sir, in three months I could pass that girl off as a duchess at an ambassador's garden party. I could even get her a place as lady's maid or shop assistant, which requires better English.

The Flower Girl. What's that you say?

The Note Taker. Yes, you squashed cabbage leaf, you disgrace to the noble architecture of these columns, you incarnate insult to the English language: I could pass you off as the Queen of Sheba. (*To the* GENTLEMAN) Can you believe that?

The Gentleman. Of course I can. I am myself a student of Indian dialects; and——

The Note Taker (*eagerly*). Are you? Do you know Colonel Pickering, the author of Spoken Sanscrit?

The Gentleman. I am Colonel Pickering. Who are you?

The Note Taker. Henry Higgins, author of Higgins's Universal Alphabet.

Pickering (*with enthusiasm*). I came from India to meet you.

Higgins. I was going to India to meet you.

Pickering. Where do you live?

READING CHECK TEST: Act One

1. The mother and daughter are prepared to go out in the rain to look for a cab for themselves. (F)
2. The flower girl does not know the son Freddy. (T)
3. Colonel Pickering has come under the portico to meet Professor Higgins. (F)
4. The professor is able to identify the area of London in which each person was born. (T)
5. Liza has probably never been in a taxi before. (T)

Higgins. 27A Wimpole Street. Come and see me tomorrow.

Pickering. I'm at the Carlton. Come with me now and lets have a jaw over some supper.

Higgins. Right you are.

The Flower Girl (to PICKERING, as he passes her). Buy a flower, kind gentleman. I'm short for my lodging.

Pickering. I really havnt any change. I'm sorry (he goes away).

Higgins (shocked at the girl's mendacity[12]). Liar. You said you could change half-a-crown.

The Flower Girl (rising in desperation). You ought to be stuffed with nails, you ought. (Flinging the basket at his feet) Take the whole blooming basket for sixpence.

[The church clock strikes the second quarter.]

A

Higgins (hearing in it the voice of God, rebuking him for his Pharisaic[13] want of charity to the poor girl). A reminder. (He raises his hat solemnly; then throws a handful of money into the basket and follows PICKERING).

The Flower Girl (picking up a half-crown). Ah-ow-ooh! (Picking up a couple of florins) Aaah-ow-ooh! (Picking up several coins) Aaaaaah-ow-ooh! (Picking up a half-sovereign) Aaaaaaaaaaaah-ow-ooh!!!

Freddy (springing out of a taxicab). Got one at last. Hallo! (To the girl) Where are the two ladies that were here?

The Flower Girl. They walked to the bus when the rain stopped.

Freddy. And left me with a cab on my hands! Damnation!

The Flower Girl (with grandeur). Never mind, young man. I'm going home in a taxi. (She sails off to the cab. The driver puts his hand behind him and holds the door firmly shut against her. Quite understanding his mistrust, she shews him her handful of money). A taxi fare aint no object to me, Charlie. (He grins and opens the door). Here. What about the basket?

The Taximan. Give it here. Tuppence extra.

Liza. No: I dont want nobody to see it. (She crushes it into the cab and gets in, continuing the conversation through the window) Goodbye, Freddy.

---

12. **mendacity:** deceit.
13. **Pharisaic** (far′ə·sā′ik): The Pharisees were a group among the ancient Jews known for their strict observance of the Mosaic Law. They were sometimes condemned for being more concerned with the letter of the Law than with its spirit.

Freddy (dazedly raising his hat). Goodbye.

Taximan. Where to?

Liza. Bucknam Pellis [Buckingham Palace].

Taximan. What d'ye mean—Bucknam Pellis?

Liza. Dont you know where it is? In the Green Park, where the King lives. Goodbye, Freddy. Dont let me keep you standing there. Goodbye.

Freddy. Goodbye (He goes).

Taximan. Here? Whats this about Bucknam Pellis? What business have you at Bucknam Pellis?

B

Liza. Of course I havnt none. But I wasnt going to let him know that. You drive me home.

Taximan. And wheres home?

Liza. Angel Court, Drury Lane, next Meiklejohn's oil shop.

Taximan. That sounds more like it, Judy. (He drives off).

*   *   *

Let us follow the taxi to the entrance to Angel Court, a narrow little archway between two shops, one of them Meiklejohn's oil shop. When it stops there, Eliza gets out, dragging her basket with her.

Liza. How much?

Taximan (indicating the taximeter). Cant you read? A shilling.

Liza. A shilling for two minutes!!

Taximan. Two minutes or ten: it's all the same.

Liza. Well, I dont call it right.

Taximan. Ever been in a taxi before?

Liza (with dignity). Hundreds of thousands of times, young man.

Taximan (laughing at her). Good for you, Judy. Keep the shilling, darling, with best love from all at home. Good luck! (He drives off).

Liza (humiliated). Impidence!

C

[She picks up the basket and trudges up the alley with it to her lodging: a small room with very old wall paper hanging loose in the damp places. A broken pane in the window is mended with paper. A portrait of a popular actor and a fashion plate of ladies' dresses, all wildly beyond poor ELIZA's means, both torn from newspapers, are pinned up on the wall. A birdcage hangs in the window; but its tenant died long ago: it remains as a memorial only.

These are the only visible luxuries: the rest is the irreducible minimum of poverty's needs: a wretched bed heaped with all sorts of coverings that have any warmth in them, a draped packing case with a basin and jug on it and a little looking

---

A. Character

🅰 Is the professor's giving the flower girl a handful of money surprising? (Somewhat) Does it fit with any aspect of his character already revealed? (He does seem informal, impulsive, and good-natured.)

B. Interpreting

🅱 What does Eliza's request that the taxi take her to Buckingham Palace tell you about her? (She is proud and cares about what upper-class people think about her.)

C. Expansion

Ask students to note the very specific details that Shaw gives in describing Eliza's room. Tell them that not all playwrights specify their settings in this much detail.

1. On a street near St. Paul's in London.
2. Eliza, a flower seller, is trying to make a sale to the Eynsford Hills and Pickering, who are taking shelter from the rain. Higgins, a professor of phonetics, is taking notes on the girl's dialect. She and the bystanders suspect him of being a policeman, and the girl loudly protests her innocence of any crime. Colonel Pickering, the author of a book on Sanskrit, turns out to be an admirer of Higgins's work.

Interpreting Meanings
3. Students' answers will vary. Students may suggest that Higgins's comments about the way he makes a living and the focus on Eliza at the end of the act combine to suggest that Higgins will try to teach the girl standard English.
4. Evidence includes the suspicion and hostility of the bystanders, and also Higgins's comments on the prevalence of social climbing.

Students will probably agree that such judgments are also made in America, despite the fact that most people consider *(Answers continue in left-hand column.)*

(Continued from top.)
such judgments "snobbish."
5. The society girl is spoiled and selfish and contrasts pointedly with the deprived flower girl. Shaw may be preparing us for a surprise: a romantic plot involving the superficially unattractive flower girl.
6. The set reveals that Eliza comes from a very humble background. The detail of the bird cage hints at tenderness in her character; the portrait of the popular actor and the fashion plate of ladies' dresses suggests romantic yearnings.

glass over it, a chair and table, the refuse of some suburban kitchen, and an American alarum clock on the shelf above the unused fireplace: the whole lighted with a gas lamp with a penny in the slot meter. Rent: four shillings a week.]

Here Eliza, chronically weary, but too excited to go to bed, sits, counting her new riches and dreaming and planning what to do with them, until the gas goes out, when she enjoys for the first time the sensation of being able to put in another penny without grudging it. This prodigal mood does not extinguish her gnawing sense of the need for economy sufficiently to prevent her from calculating that she can dream and plan in bed more cheaply and warmly than sitting up without a fire. So she takes off her shawl and skirt and adds them to the miscellaneous bedclothes. Then she kicks off her shoes and gets into bed without any further change.

Responding to the Play

Analyzing Act One

Identifying Facts

1. Where does the first act take place?
2. The **exposition** in a play consists of background information about the locale and the principal characters who will be involved in the action. Shaw handles the exposition brilliantly by inventing an amusing incident that tells us all we need to know. What is the incident, and what do we learn from it about the flower girl, the note taker, and the gentleman? What are these characters' names?

Interpreting Meanings

3. Usually, an opening scene will in some way **foreshadow** the coming conflict. Is there any clue as to what action might arise from what has happened so far?
4. Shaw says in the Preface, ". . . it is impossible for an Englishman to open his mouth without making some other Englishman despise him." What evidence of this statement occurs in Act One? Do we also judge people by their speech and accent in America?
5. What does Shaw seem to think of the "society daughter" in this scene? How does her manner contrast with that of the flower girl? What might Shaw be trying to tell us by this counterpoint? What further developments might he be preparing us for?
6. What do you think the set of Eliza's room reveals about her background and her **character**?

Analyzing Language and Style

Cockney Dialect

People in England say that a Cockney is a person who was born in London within hearing of the sound of the Bow bells—the bells of the old church in the East End called St. Mary-le-Bow.

Centuries ago, the word *cockney* was probably applied contemptuously by country people to city people. The origin of the word is uncertain. Probably it came from *cock's eggs,* a name applied to the small and malformed eggs laid by a young hen. The word also was once applied to a young child nursed by its mother (it was believed such a child would become a simpleton).

The Cockney dialect is distinguished from standard English in these ways:

1. In the nineteenth century, Cockney speakers substituted a *v* for a *w* and a *w* for a *v,* though this is no longer done.
2. Cockneys today substitute an *f* or a *v* for a *th* (*fing* for *thing* and *farver* for *farther*).
3. The vowel sound *ou* is sounded *ah* (*abaht* for *about*).
4. The vowel sound *ai* is sounded *ei* (*dyly* for *daily*).

Cockney speakers also drop the *h* in the front of words (*iggins* for *Higgins*), but this is not peculiar only to Cockney speakers. They do *not* put an *h* in front of words that do not have one (*height* for *eight*), though stage comedians often have Cockneys speak this way.

Cockney speakers also have their own slang and idioms. Part of Eliza's charm in this play comes from her buoyant use of slang that offends (in a later act) the sensitive and well-bred ears of people like Mrs. Eynsford Hill.

1. Examine Eliza's Cockney dialect in the first act, and find examples of the characteristics listed above. Can you make any other observations about her dialect, based on what you observe?
2. Try reading Eliza's Cockney speeches aloud, using Shaw's meticulous phonetic spellings. If you don't hear her speech, you'll miss some of the play's humor.

Summary of Act Two
Eliza goes to Higgins's laboratory to hire him to give her speech lessons so that she can get a job in a flower shop. She intends to pay him with the money he gave her the night before. Higgins wants to prove that he can transform Eliza into the likeness of a duchess. Disregarding his housekeeper's concerns about Eliza's future, Higgins invites her to stay and take speech lessons. Later Eliza's father comes to see Higgins looking to get some monetary benefit from what he sees as his daughter's sudden good fortune. Higgins sees through him but is so delighted by his outrageous locutions and good-natured scheming that he gives him money anyway. After a transforming bath, Eliza's father does not recognize her, and Higgins and Pickering are also pleasantly surprised. Eliza's lessons begin, and she proves an apt pupil.

Act Two

Next day at 11 A.M. HIGGINS's laboratory in Wimpole Street. It is a room on the first floor, looking on the street, and was meant for the drawing room. The double doors are in the middle of the back wall; and persons entering find in the corner to their right two tall file cabinets at right angles to one another against the wall. In this corner stands a flat writing-table, on which are a phonograph, a laryngoscope,[1] a row of tiny organ pipes with a bellows, a set of lamp chimneys for singing flames with burners attached to a gas plug in the wall by an indiarubber tube, several tuning-forks of different sizes, a life-size image of half a human head, shewing in section the vocal organs, and a box containing a supply of wax cylinders for the phonograph.

Further down the room, on the same side, is a fireplace, with a comfortable leather-covered easy-chair at the side of the hearth nearest the door, and a coal-scuttle. There is a clock on the mantelpiece. Between the fireplace and the phonograph table is a stand for newspapers.

On the other side of the central door, to the left of the visitor, is a cabinet of shallow drawers. On it is a telephone and the telephone directory. The corner beyond, and most of the side wall, is occupied by a grand piano, with the keyboard at the end furthest from the door, and a bench for the player extending the full length of the keyboard. On the piano is a dessert dish heaped with fruit and sweets, mostly chocolates.

The middle of the room is clear. Besides the easy-chair, the piano bench, and two chairs at the phonograph table, there is one stray chair. It stands near the fireplace. On the walls, engravings: mostly Piranesi[2] and mezzotint[3] portraits. No paintings.

PICKERING *is seated at the table, putting down some cards and a tuning-fork which he has been using.* HIGGINS *is standing up near him, closing two or three file drawers which are hanging out. He appears in the morning light as a robust, vital, appetizing sort of man of forty or thereabouts, dressed in a professional-looking black frock-coat with a white linen collar and black silk tie. He is of the energetic scientific type, heartily, even violently interested in everything that can be studied as a scientific subject, and careless about himself and other people, including their feelings. He is, in fact, but for his years and size, rather like a very impetuous baby "taking notice" eagerly and loudly, and requiring almost as much watching to keep him out of unintended mischief. His manner varies from genial bullying when he is in a good humor to stormy petulance when anything goes wrong; but he is so entirely frank and void of malice that he remains likeable even in his least reasonable moments.*

Higgins (*as he shuts the last drawer*). Well, I think thats the whole show.
Pickering. It's really amazing. I havnt taken half of it in, you know.
Higgins. Would you like to go over any of it again?
Pickering (*rising and coming to the fireplace, where he plants himself with his back to the fire*). No, thank you: not now. I'm quite done up for this morning.
Higgins (*following him, and standing beside him on his left*). Tired of listening to sounds?
Pickering. Yes. It's a fearful strain. I rather fancied myself because I can pronounce twenty-four distinct vowel sounds; but your hundred and thirty beat me. I cant hear a bit of difference between most of them.
Higgins (*chuckling, and going over to the piano to eat sweets*). Oh, that comes with practice. You hear no difference at first; but you keep on listening, and presently you find theyre all as different as A from B. (MRS PEARCE *looks in; she is* HIGGINS's *housekeeper*). Whats the matter?
Mrs Pearce (*hesitating, evidently perplexed*). A young woman asks to see you, sir.
Higgins. A young woman! What does she want?
Mrs Pearce. Well, sir, she says youll be glad to see her when you know what she's come about. She's quite a common girl, sir. Very common indeed. I should have sent her away, only I thought perhaps you wanted her to talk into your machines. I hope Ive not done wrong; but really you see such queer people sometimes—youll excuse me, I'm sure, sir——
Higgins. Oh, thats all right, Mrs Pearce. Has she an interesting accent?
Mrs Pearce. Oh, something dreadful, sir, really. I dont know how you can take an interest in it.

---

1. **laryngoscope:** an instrument for examining the movements of the larynx during speaking or singing.
2. **Piranesi:** the engravings of Giambattista Piranesi (1720–1778), an Italian artist.
3. **mezzotint:** a copper or steel engraving.

A. Setting
[?] What do the details of the professor's laboratory suggest about his character? (He has a serious and enthusiastic interest in his subject.)

B. Character
After students have read this description of Higgins's character, ask them to be alert for examples in what follows of his bullying, his petulance, and his good-naturedness.

A. Character

? What is Higgins's initial reaction to Eliza's return? (Petulant disappointment) How does she respond to his reception? (Saucily or assertively)

B. Expansion
Point out that Colonel Pickering is unwaveringly polite and sensible and that he avoids the periodic outbursts of emotion that are characteristic of both Higgins and Eliza.

Higgins (*to* PICKERING). Lets have her up. Shew her up, Mrs Pearce (*he rushes across to his working table and picks out a cylinder to use on the phonograph*).

Mrs Pearce (*only half resigned to it*). Very well, sir. It's for you to say. (*She goes upstairs*).

Higgins. This is rather a bit of luck. I'll shew you how I make records. We'll set her talking; and I'll take it down first in Bell's Visible Speech; then in broad Romic; and then we'll get her on the phonograph so that you can turn her on as often as you like with the written transcript before you.

Mrs Pearce (*returning*). This is the young woman, sir.

[*The flower girl enters in state. She has a hat with three ostrich feathers, orange, sky-blue, and red. She has a nearly clean apron and the shoddy coat has been tidied a little. The pathos of this deplorable figure, with its innocent vanity and consequential air, touches* PICKERING, *who has already straightened himself in the presence of* MRS PEARCE. *But as to* HIGGINS, *the only distinction he makes between men and women is that when he is neither bullying nor exclaiming to the heavens against some featherweight cross,[4] he coaxes women as a child coaxes its nurse when it wants to get anything out of her.*]

A **Higgins** (*brusquely, recognizing her with unconcealed disappointment, and at once, babylike, making an intolerable grievance of it*). Why, this is the girl I jotted down last night. She's no use: Ive got all the records I want of the Lisson Grove lingo; and I'm not going to waste another cylinder on it. (*To the girl*) Be off with you: I dont want you.

The Flower Girl. Dont you be so saucy. You aint heard what I come for yet. (*To* MRS PEARCE, *who is waiting at the door for further instructions*) Did you tell him I come in a taxi?

Mrs Pearce. Nonsense, girl! what do you think a gentleman like Mr Higgins cares what you came in?

The Flower Girl. Oh, we are proud! He aint above giving lessons, not him: I heard him say so. Well, I aint come here to ask for any compliment; and if my money's not good enough I can go elsewhere.

Higgins. Good enough for what?

The Flower Girl. Good enough for yə-oo. Now you know, dont you? I'm coming to have lessons, I am. And to pay for em tə-oo: make no mistake.

Higgins (*stupent[5]*). Well!!! (*Recovering his breath with a gasp*) What do you expect me to say to you?

The Flower Girl. Well, if you was a gentleman, you might ask me to sit down, I think. Dont I tell you I'm bringing you business?

Higgins. Pickering: shall we ask this baggage to sit down, or shall we throw her out of the window?

The Flower Girl (*running away in terror to the piano, where she turns at bay*). Ah-ah-oh-ow-ow-ow-oo! (*Wounded and whimpering*) I wont be called a baggage when Ive offered to pay like any lady.

[*Motionless, the two men stare at her from the other side of the room, amazed.*]

Pickering (*gently*). But what is it you want?

The Flower Girl. I want to be a lady in a flower shop stead of sellin at the corner of Tottenham Court Road. But they wont take me unless I can talk more genteel. He said he could teach me. Well, here I am ready to pay him—not asking any favor—and he treats me zif I was dirt.

Mrs Pearce. How can you be such a foolish ignorant girl as to think you could afford to pay Mr Higgins?

The Flower Girl. Why shouldn't I? I know what lessons cost as well as you do; and I'm ready to pay.

Higgins. How much?

The Flower Girl (*coming back to him, triumphant*). Now youre talking! I thought youd come off it when you saw a chance of getting back a bit of what you chucked at me last night. (*Confidentially*) Youd had a drop in,[6] hadnt you?

Higgins (*peremptorily*). Sit down.

The Flower Girl. Oh, if youre going to make a compliment of it——

Higgins (*thundering at her*). Sit down.

Mrs Pearce (*severely*). Sit down, girl. Do as youre told.

The Flower Girl. Ah-ah-ah-ow-ow-oo! (*She stands, half rebellious, half-bewildered*).

Pickering (*very courteous*). Wont you sit down? (*He places the stray chair near the hearthrug between himself and* HIGGINS). B

---

4. **featherweight cross:** a very small burden or inconvenience.

5. **stupent:** dumbfounded.
6. **had a drop in:** been drinking.

Liza (*coyly*). Dont mind if I do. (*She sits down.* PICKERING *returns to the hearthrug*).

Higgins. Whats your name?

The Flower Girl. Liza Doolittle.

Higgins (*declaiming gravely*).

Eliza, Elizabeth, Betsy and Bess,
They went to the woods to get a bird's nes':

Pickering. They found a nest with four eggs in it:

Higgins. They took one apiece, and left three in it.

[*They laugh heartily at their own fun.*]

Liza. Oh, dont be silly.

Mrs Pearce (*placing herself behind* ELIZA'*s chair*). You mustnt speak to the gentleman like that.

Liza. Well, why wont he speak sensible to me?

Higgins. Come back to business. How much do you propose to pay me for the lessons?

Liza. Oh, I know whats right. A lady friend of mine gets French lessons for eighteenpence an hour from a real French gentleman. Well, you wouldn't have the face to ask me the same for teaching me my own language as you would for French; so I wont give more than a shilling. Take it or leave it.

Higgins (*walking up and down the room, rattling his keys and his cash in his pockets*). You know, Pickering, if you consider a shilling, not as a simple shilling, but as a percentage of this girl's income, it works out as fully equivalent to sixty or seventy guineas from a millionaire.

Pickering. How so?

Higgins. Figure it out. A millionaire has about £150 a day. She earns about half-a-crown.

Liza (*haughtily*). Who told you I only——

Higgins (*continuing*). She offers me two-fifths of her day's income for a lesson. Two-fifths of a millionaire's income for a day would be somewhere about £60. It's handsome. By George, it's enormous! it's the biggest offer I ever had.

Liza (*rising, terrified*). Sixty pounds! What are you talking about? I never offered you sixty pounds. Where would I get——

Higgins. Hold your tongue.

Liza (*weeping*). But I aint got sixty pounds. Oh——

Mrs Pearce. Dont cry, you silly girl. Sit down. Nobody is going to touch your money.

Higgins. Somebody is going to touch you, with a broomstick, if you dont stop snivelling. Sit down.

Liza (*obeying slowly*). Ah-ah-ah-ow-oo-o! One would think you was my father.

Higgins. If I decide to teach you, I'll be worse than two fathers to you. Here (*he offers her his silk handkerchief*)!

Liza. Whats this for?

Higgins. To wipe your eyes. To wipe any part of your face that feels moist. Remember: thats your handkerchief; and thats your sleeve. Dont mistake the one for the other if you wish to become a lady in a shop.

[LIZA, *utterly bewildered, stares helplessly at him.*]

Mrs Pearce. It's no use talking to her like that, Mr Higgins: she doesnt understand you. Besides, youre quite wrong: she doesnt do it that way at all (*she takes the handkerchief*).

Liza (*snatching it*). Here! You give me that handkerchief. He gev it to me, not to you.

Pickering (*laughing*). He did. I think it must be regarded as her property, Mrs Pearce.

Mrs Pearce (*resigning herself*). Serve you right, Mr Higgins.

Pickering. Higgins: I'm interested. What about the ambassador's garden party? I'll say youre the greatest teacher alive if you make that good. I'll bet you all the expenses of the experiment you cant do it. And I'll pay for the lessons.

Liza. Oh, you are real good. Thank you, Captain.

Higgins (*tempted, looking at her*). It's almost irresistible. She's so deliciously low—so horribly dirty——

Liza (*protesting extremely*). Ah-ah-ah-ah-ow-ow-oo-oo!!! I aint dirty: I washed my face and hands afore I come, I did.

Pickering. Youre certainly not going to turn her head with flattery, Higgins.

Mrs Pearce (*uneasy*). Oh, dont say that, sir: theres more ways than one of turning a girl's head; and nobody can do it better than Mr Higgins, though he may not always mean it. I do hope, sir, you wont encourage him to do anything foolish.

Higgins (*becoming excited as the idea grows on him*). What is life but a series of inspired follies? The difficulty is to find them to do. Never lose a chance: it doesnt come every day. I shall make a duchess of this draggletailed guttersnipe.

Liza (*strongly deprecating this view of her*). Ah-ah-ah-ow-ow-oo!

Higgins (*carried away*). Yes: in six months—in three if she has a good ear and a quick tongue—I'll take her anywhere and pass her off as anything. We'll start today: now! this moment! Take

A. Responding

Do you find this explanation of the uses of the handkerchief funny? (Answers will vary. Most students will agree that Higgins pokes fun at Eliza's lack of manners. Do you think Higgins is being cruel to Eliza? (Answers will vary. Some students may say he is not being deliberately cruel because he sees her as an object, not as a human being.) If you were directing, how would you play this scene? (Answers will vary. Students might direct the character Higgins to play this scene seriously, sarcastically, or even indignantly.)

B. Plot

Here Pickering takes Higgins up on his boast in the first act and challenges him to turn Eliza into a lady.

A. Tone
Much of the humor in the play is based on ironic implications and unexpected turns of phrase. Here for example, Higgins urges Eliza to abandon modesty if she wishes to pass as a duchess.

? Why is this ironic? (It amounts to a humorous sideswipe at the morals of duchesses.)

B. Expansion
A *zephyr* here is a gentle breeze.

C. Character
? What is Mrs. Pearce's concern here regarding Eliza? (Who she is and how her relatives will react if she stays) How would you describe Mrs. Pearce's character? (Conventional, respectable, cautious)

her away and clean her, Mrs Pearce. Monkey Brand, if it wont come off any other way. Is there a good fire in the kitchen?

Mrs Pearce (*protesting*). Yes; but——

Higgins (*storming on*). Take all her clothes off and burn them. Ring up Whiteley or somebody for new ones. Wrap her up in brown paper til they come.

Liza. Youre no gentleman, youre not, to talk of such things. I'm a good girl, I am; and I know what the like of you are, I do.

A ⌈**Higgins.** We want none of your Lisson Grove prudery here, young woman. Youve got to learn to behave like a duchess. Take her away, Mrs Pearce. If she gives you any trouble, wallop her.⌋

Liza (*springing up and running between* PICKERING *and* MRS PEARCE *for protection*). No! I'll call the police, I will.

Mrs Pearce. But Ive no place to put her.

Higgins. Put her in the dustbin.

Liza. Ah-ah-ah-ow-ow-oo!

Pickering. Oh come, Higgins! be reasonable.

Mrs Pearce (*resolutely*). You must be reasonable, Mr Higgins: really you must. You cant walk over everybody like this.

B ⌈[HIGGINS, *thus scolded, subsides. The hurricane is succeeded by a zephyr of amiable surprise.*]⌋

Higgins (*with professional exquisiteness of modulation*). *I* walk over everybody! My dear Mrs Pearce, my dear Pickering, I never had the slightest intention of walking over anyone. All I propose is that we should be kind to this poor girl. We must help her to prepare and fit herself for her new station in life. If I did not express myself clearly it was because I did not wish to hurt her delicacy, or yours.

[LIZA, *reassured, steals back to her chair.*]

Mrs Pearce (*to* PICKERING). Well, did you ever hear anything like that, sir?

Pickering (*laughing heartily*). Never, Mrs Pearce: never.

Higgins (*patiently*). Whats the matter?

C ⌈**Mrs Pearce.** Well, the matter is, sir, that you cant take a girl up like that as if you were picking up a pebble on the beach.⌋

Higgins. Why not?

Mrs Pearce. Why not! But you dont know anything about her. What about her parents? She may be married.

Liza. Garn!

Higgins. There! As the girl very properly says, Garn! Married indeed! Dont you know that a woman of that class looks a worn out drudge of fifty a year after she's married?

Liza. Whood marry me?

Higgins (*suddenly resorting to the most thrillingly beautiful low tones in his best elocutionary style*). By George, Eliza, the streets will be strewn with the bodies of men shooting themselves for your sake before Ive done with you.

Mrs Pearce. Nonsense, sir. You mustnt talk like that to her.

Liza (*rising and squaring herself determinedly*). I'm going away. He's off his chump, he is. I dont want no balmies teaching me.

Higgins (*wounded in his tenderest point by her insensibility to his elocution*). Oh, indeed! I'm mad, am I? Very well, Mrs Pearce: you neednt order the new clothes for her. Throw her out.

Liza (*whimpering*). Nah-ow. You got no right to touch me.

Mrs Pearce. You see now what comes of being saucy. (*Indicating the door*) This way, please.

Liza (*almost in tears*). I didnt want no clothes. I wouldnt have taken them (*she throws away the handkerchief*). I can buy my own clothes.

Higgins (*deftly retrieving the handkerchief and intercepting her on her reluctant way to the door*). Youre an ungrateful wicked girl. This is my return for offering to take you out of the gutter and dress you beautifully and make a lady of you.

Mrs Pearce. Stop, Mr Higgins. I wont allow it. It's you that are wicked. Go home to your parents, girl; and tell them to take better care of you.

Liza. I aint got no parents. They told me I was big enough to earn my own living and turned me out.

Mrs Pearce. Wheres your mother?

Liza. I aint got no mother. Her that turned me out was my sixth stepmother. But I done without them. And I'm a good girl, I am.

Higgins. Very well, then, what on earth is all this fuss about? The girl doesnt belong to anybody—is no use to anybody but me. (*He goes to* MRS PEARCE *and begins coaxing*). You can adopt her, Mrs Pearce: I'm sure a daughter would be a great amusement to you. Now dont make any more fuss. Take her downstairs; and——

Mrs Pearce. But whats to become of her? Is she to be paid anything? Do be sensible, sir.

Higgins. Oh, pay her whatever is necessary: put it down in the housekeeping book. (*Impatiently*)

A

What on earth will she want with money? She'll have her food and her clothes. She'll only drink if you give her money.

Liza *(turning on him)*. Oh you are a brute. It's a lie: nobody ever saw the sign of liquor on me. *(To* PICKERING) Oh, sir: youre a gentleman: dont let him speak to me like that.

Pickering *(in good-humored remonstrance)*. Does it occur to you, Higgins, that the girl has some feelings?

Higgins *(looking critically at her)*. Oh no, I dont think so. Not any feelings that we need bother about. *(Cheerily)* Have you, Eliza?

Liza. I got my feelings same as anyone else.

Higgins *(to* PICKERING, *reflectively)*. You see the difficulty?

Pickering. Eh? What difficulty?

Higgins. To get her to talk grammar. The mere pronunciation is easy enough.

Liza. I dont want to talk grammar. I want to talk like a lady in a flower-shop.

Mrs Pearce. Will you please keep to the point, Mr Higgins. I want to know on what terms the girl is to be here. Is she to have any wages? And what is to become of her when youve finished your teaching? You must look ahead a little.

Higgins *(impatiently)*. Whats to become of her if I leave her in the gutter? Tell me that, Mrs Pearce.

Mrs Pearce. Thats her own business, not yours, Mr Higgins.

Higgins. Well, when Ive done with her, we can throw her back into the gutter; and then it will be her own business again; so thats all right.

Liza. Oh, youve no feeling heart in you: you dont care for nothing but yourself. *(She rises and takes the floor resolutely)*. Here! Ive had enough of this. I'm going *(making for the door)*. You ought to be ashamed of yourself, you ought.

Higgins *(snatching a chocolate cream from the piano, his eyes suddenly beginning to twinkle with mischief)*. Have some chocolates, Eliza.

Liza *(halting, tempted)*. How do I know what might be in them? Ive heard of girls being drugged by the like of you.

[HIGGINS *whips out his penknife; cuts a chocolate in two; puts one half into his mouth and bolts it;[7] and offers her the other half.*]

Higgins. Pledge of good faith, Eliza. I eat one half: you eat the other. *(LIZA opens her mouth to retort: he pops the half chocolate into it)*. You shall have boxes of them, barrels of them, every day. You shall live on them. Eh?

B

---

7. **bolts it:** chews and swallows it quickly.

A. Conflict and Complications

❓ What is Mrs. Pearce concerned about that neither Higgins nor Eliza seems to be considering? (What Eliza's place in the household will be and what will become of her in the future)

B. Character

Shaw describes Higgins as a baby. ❓ In what ways is Eliza also childish? (She is impulsive, has tantrums, feels sorry for herself, and tries to get her own way.) What do you think this scene of their eating chocolates together suggests about them and their future? (They enjoy each other.) What does the photo above suggest? (Answers will vary. She possibly is a willing but somewhat skeptical student whereas he is enjoying his role as a masterful but beguiling teacher.)

A. Plot
Here Higgins casually predicts a fairy-tale future for Eliza. Mrs. Pearce and Pickering sensibly object.

? Are there other aspects of the fairy tale in this play? How is Eliza a Cinderella figure? (She is transformed from rags to fine clothing and goes to a grand party. Also, her happiness is short-lived.) Will Higgins be her Prince Charming? (Yes, in that he will make her into a lady, but they will not marry and live happily ever after.)

B. Responding
Here Mrs. Pearce predicts unexpected consequences for Eliza and Higgins.

? What do you think these surprises will be?

Liza *(who has disposed of the chocolate after being nearly choked by it)*. I wouldnt have ate it, only I'm too ladylike to take it out of my mouth.

Higgins. Listen, Eliza. I think you said you came in a taxi.

Liza. Well, what if I did? Ive as good a right to take a taxi as anyone else.

Higgins. You have, Eliza; and in future you shall have as many taxis as you want. You shall go up and down and round the town in a taxi every day. Think of that, Eliza.

Mrs Pearce. Mr Higgins: youre tempting the girl. It's not right. She should think of the future.

Higgins. At her age! Nonsense! Time enough to think of the future when you havnt any future to think of. No, Eliza: do as this lady does: think of other people's futures; but never think of your own. Think of chocolates, and taxis, and gold, and diamonds.

Liza. No: I dont want no gold and no diamonds. I'm a good girl, I am. *(She sits down again, with an attempt at dignity)*.

A

Higgins. You shall remain so, Eliza, under the care of Mrs Pearce. And you shall marry an officer in the Guards, with a beautiful moustache: the son of a marquis, who will disinherit him for marrying you, but will relent when he sees your beauty and goodness——

Pickering. Excuse me, Higgins; but I really must interfere. Mrs Pearce is quite right. If this girl is to put herself in your hands for six months for an experiment in teaching, she must understand thoroughly what she's doing.

Higgins. How can she? She's incapable of understanding anything. Besides, do any of us understand what we are doing? If we did, would we ever do it?

Pickering. Very clever, Higgins; but not to the present point. *(To* ELIZA*)* Miss Doolittle——

Liza *(overwhelmed)*. Ah-ah-ow-oo!

Higgins. There! Thats all youll get out of Eliza. Ah-ah-ow-oo! No use explaining. As a military man you ought to know that. Give her her orders: thats enough for her. Eliza: you are to live here for the next six months, learning how to speak beautifully, like a lady in a florist's shop. If youre good and do whatever youre told, you shall sleep in a proper bedroom, and have lots to eat, and money to buy chocolates and take rides in taxis. If youre naughty and idle you will sleep in the back kitchen among the black beetles, and be walloped by Mrs Pearce with a broomstick. At the end of six months you shall go to Buckingham Palace in a carriage, beautifully dressed. If the King finds out youre not a lady, you will be taken by the police to the Tower of London, where your head will be cut off as a warning to other presumptuous flower girls. If you are not found out, you shall have a present of seven-and-sixpence to start life with as a lady in a shop. If you refuse this offer you will be a most ungrateful wicked girl; and the angels will weep for you. *(To* PICKERING*)* Now are you satisfied, Pickering? *(To* MRS PEARCE*)* Can I put it more plainly and fairly, Mrs Pearce?

B

Mrs Pearce *(patiently)*. I think youd better let me speak to the girl properly in private. I dont know that I can take charge of her or consent to the arrangement at all. Of course I know you dont mean her any harm; but when you get what you call interested in people's accents, you never think or care what may happen to them or you. Come with me, Eliza.

Higgins. Thats all right. Thank you, Mrs Pearce. Bundle her off to the bathroom.

Liza *(rising reluctantly and suspiciously)*. Youre a great bully, you are. I wont stay here if I dont like. I wont let nobody wallop me. I never asked to go to Bucknam Palace, I didnt. I was never in trouble with the police, not me. I'm a good girl——

Mrs Pearce. Dont answer back, girl. You dont understand the gentleman. Come with me. *(She leads the way to the door, and holds it open for* ELIZA*)*.

Liza *(as she goes out)*. Well, what I say is right. I wont go near the King, not if I'm going to have my head cut off. If I'd known what I was letting myself in for, I wouldnt have come here. I always been a good girl; and I never offered to say a word to him; and I dont owe him nothing; and I dont care; and I wont be put upon; and I have my feelings the same as anyone else——

[MRS PEARCE *shuts the door; and* ELIZA's *plaints are no longer audible.*]

*   *   *

Eliza is taken upstairs to the third floor greatly to her surprise; for she expected to be taken down to the scullery. There Mrs Pearce opens a door and takes her into a spare bedroom.

Mrs Pearce. I will have to put you here. This will be your bedroom.

Liza. O-h, I couldnt sleep here, missus. It's too good for the likes of me. I should be afraid to touch anything. I aint a duchess yet, you know.

Mrs Pearce. You have got to make yourself as clean as the room: then you wont be afraid of it. And you must call me Mrs Pearce, not missus. *(She throws open the door of the dressingroom, now modernized as a bathroom).*

Liza. Gawd! whats this? Is this where you wash clothes? Funny sort of copper[8] I call it.

Mrs Pearce. It is not a copper. This is where we wash ourselves, Eliza, and where I am going to wash you.

Liza. You expect me to get into that and wet myself all over! Not me. I should catch my death. I knew a woman did it every Saturday night; and she died of it.

Mrs Pearce. Mr Higgins has the gentlemen's bathroom downstairs; and he has a bath every morning, in cold water.

Liza. Ugh! He's made of iron, that man.

Mrs Pearce. If you are to sit with him and the Colonel and be taught you will have to do the same. They wont like the smell of you if you dont. But you can have the water as hot as you like. There are two taps: hot and cold.

Liza *(weeping).* I couldnt. I dursnt. Its not natural: it would kill me. Ive never had a bath in my life: not what youd call a proper one.

Mrs Pearce. Well, dont you want to be clean and sweet and decent, like a lady? You know you cant be a nice girl inside if youre a dirty slut outside.

Liza. Boohoo!!!!

Mrs Pearce. Now stop crying and go back into your room and take off all your clothes. Then wrap yourself in this *(taking down a gown from its peg and handing it to her)* and come back to me. I will get the bath ready.

Liza *(all tears).* I cant. I wont. I'm not used to it. Ive never took off all my clothes before. It's not right: it's not decent.

Mrs Pearce. Nonsense, child. Dont you take off all your clothes every night when you go to bed?

Liza *(amazed).* No. Why should I? I should catch my death. Of course I take off my skirt.

Mrs Pearce. Do you mean that you sleep in the underclothes you wear in the daytime?

Liza. What else have I to sleep in?

Mrs Pearce. You will never do that again as long as you live here. I will get you a proper nightdress.

---

8. **copper:** a large boiler used for washing clothes.

Liza. Do you mean change into cold things and lie awake shivering half the night? You want to kill me, you do.

Mrs Pearce. I want to change you from a frowzy slut to a clean respectable girl fit to sit with the gentlemen in the study. Are you going to trust me and do what I tell you or be thrown out and sent back to your flower basket?

Liza. But you dont know what the cold is to me. You dont know how I dread it.

Mrs Pearce. Your bed wont be cold here: I will put a hot water bottle in it. *(Pushing her into the bedroom)* Off with you and undress.

Liza. Oh, if only I'd a known what a dreadful thing it is to be clean I'd never have come. I didnt know when I was well off. I— *(MRS PEARCE pushes her through the door, but leaves it partly open lest her prisoner should take to flight).*

[MRS PEARCE *puts on a pair of white rubber sleeves, and fills the bath, mixing hot and cold, and testing the result with the bath thermometer. She perfumes it with a handful of bath salts and adds a palmful of mustard. She then takes a formidable looking long-handled scrubbing brush and soaps it profusely with a ball of scented soap.*

ELIZA *comes back with nothing on but the bath gown huddled tightly round her, a piteous spectacle of abject terror.*]

Mrs Pearce. Now come along. Take that thing off.

Liza. Oh I couldn't, Mrs Pearce: I reely couldnt. I never done such a thing.

Mrs Pearce. Nonsense. Here: step in and tell me whether it's hot enough for you.

Liza. Ah-oo! Ah-oo! It's too hot.

Mrs Pearce *(deftly snatching the gown away and throwing* ELIZA *down on her back).* It wont hurt you. *(She sets to work with the scrubbing brush).*

[ELIZA's *screams are heartrending.*]

*   *   *

[*Meanwhile the* COLONEL *has been having it out with* HIGGINS *about* ELIZA. PICKERING *has come from the hearth to the chair and seated himself astride of it with his arms on the back to cross-examine him.*]

Pickering. Excuse the straight question, Higgins. Are you a man of good character where women are concerned?

Higgins *(moodily).* Have you ever met a man of good character where women are concerned?

A. Comic Effects
This bath scene is one of the most amusing in the play.
? Why do you think it is so humorous? (Because Eliza is so frightened and reluctant to do something that most people consider so ordinary. Also tell students that scenes in which rascals or orphans are transformed by soap and kindliness are tried-and-true dramatic conventions that seldom fail to satisfy audiences.)

B. Dialogue
This exchange between Higgins and Pickering is an example of the clever riposte or witty epigrammatic use of language that is associated with Shaw and Oscar Wilde.
? Ask students to find other examples of clever dialogue and unexpected turns of phrase.

A. Character

How does Higgins describe his attitude toward women? (He is immune to their charms.) Ask students to observe as they read whether or not he knows himself very well.

B. Comic Effects

What is the source of humor in this speech? (In the midst of his protestation of never swearing, he swears.) What does it indicate about Higgins's self-knowledge? (He does not know himself well, or pretends not to know.)

Pickering. Yes: very frequently.

Higgins (dogmatically, lifting himself on his hands to the level of the piano, and sitting on it with a bounce). Well, I havnt. I find that the moment I let a woman make friends with me, she becomes jealous, exacting, suspicious, and a damned nuisance. I find that the moment I let myself make friends with a woman, I become selfish and tyrannical. Women upset everything. When you let them into your life, you find that the woman is driving at one thing and youre driving at another.

Pickering. At what, for example?

Higgins (coming off the piano restlessly). Oh, Lord knows! I suppose the woman wants to live her own life; and the man wants to live his; and each tries to drag the other on to the wrong track. One wants to go north and the other south; and the result is that both have to go east, though they both hate the east wind. (He sits down on the bench at the keyboard). So here I am, a confirmed old bachelor, and likely to remain so.

Pickering (rising and standing over him gravely). Come, Higgins! You know what I mean. If I'm to be in this business I shall feel responsible for that girl. I hope it's understood that no advantage is to be taken of her position.

A Higgins. What! That thing! Sacred, I assure you. (Rising to explain) You see, she'll be a pupil; and teaching would be impossible unless pupils were sacred. Ive taught scores of American millionairesses how to speak English: the best looking women in the world. I'm seasoned. They might as well be blocks of wood. I might as well be a block of wood. It's——

[MRS PEARCE opens the door. She has ELIZA's hat in her hand. PICKERING retires to the easy-chair at the hearth and sits down.]

Higgins (eagerly). Well. Mrs Pearce: is it all right?

Mrs Pearce (at the door). I just wish to trouble you with a word, if I may, Mr Higgins.

Higgins. Yes, certainly. Come in. (She comes forward) Dont burn that, Mrs Pearce. I'll keep it as a curiosity. (He takes the hat).

Mrs Pearce. Handle it carefully, sir, please. I had to promise her not to burn it; but I had better put it in the oven for a while.

Higgins (putting it down hastily on the piano). Oh! thank you. Well, what have you to say to me?

Pickering. Am I in the way?

Mrs Pearce. Not at all, sir. Mr Higgins: will you please be very particular what you say before the girl?

Higgins (sternly). Of course. I'm always particular about what I say. Why do you say this to me?

Mrs Pearce (unmoved). No sir: youre not at all particular when youve mislaid anything or when you get a little impatient. Now it doesn't matter before me: I'm used to it. But you really must not swear before the girl.

B Higgins (indignantly). I swear! (Most emphatically) I never swear. I detest the habit. What the devil do you mean?

Mrs Pearce (stolidly). Thats what I mean, sir. You swear a great deal too much. I dont mind your damning and blasting, and what the devil and where the devil and who the devil——

Higgins. Mrs Pearce: this language from your lips! Really!

Mrs Pearce (not to be put off). —but there is a certain word I must ask you not to use. The girl used it herself when she began to enjoy the bath. It begins with the same letter as bath.[9] She knows no better: she learnt it at her mother's knee. But she must not hear it from your lips.

Higgins (loftily). I cannot charge myself with having ever uttered it, Mrs Pearce. (She looks at him steadfastly. He adds, hiding an uneasy conscience with a judicial air) Except perhaps in a moment of extreme and justifiable excitement.

Mrs Pearce. Only this morning, sir, you applied it to your boots, to the butter, and to the brown bread.

Higgins. Oh, that! Mere alliteration, Mrs Pearce, natural to a poet.

Mrs Pearce. Well, sir, whatever you choose to call it, I beg you not to let the girl hear you repeat it.

Higgins. Oh, very well, very well. Is that all?

Mrs Pearce. No, sir. We shall have to be very particular with this girl as to personal cleanliness.

Higgins. Certainly. Quite right. Most important.

Mrs Pearce. I mean not to be slovenly about her dress or untidy in leaving things about.

Higgins (going to her solemnly). Just so. I intended to call your attention to that. (He passes on to PICKERING, who is enjoying the conversation immensely). It is these little things that matter, Pickering. Take care of the pence and the pounds will take care of themselves is as true of personal habits as of money. (He comes to anchor on the

---

9. **same letter as bath:** Mrs. Pearce is referring to the word *bloody*, which, until recently, was considered an obscenity.

hearthrug, with the air of a man in an unassailable position).

Mrs Pearce. Yes, sir. Then might I ask you not to come down to breakfast in your dressing-gown, or at any rate not to use it as a napkin to the extent you do, sir. And if you would be so good as not to eat everything off the same plate, and to remember not to put the porridge saucepan out of your hand on the clean tablecloth, it would be a better example to the girl. You know you nearly choked yourself with a fishbone in the jam only last week.

Higgins *(routed from the hearthrug and drifting back to the piano).* I may do these things sometimes in absence of mind; but surely I dont do them habitually. *(Angrily)* By the way: my dressing-gown smells most damnably of benzine.

Mrs Pearce. No doubt it does, Mr Higgins. But if you will wipe your fingers—

Higgins *(yelling).* Oh very well, very well: I'll wipe them in my hair in future.

Mrs Pearce. I hope youre not offended, Mr Higgins.

Higgins *(shocked at finding himself thought capable of an unamiable sentiment).* Not at all, not at all. Youre quite right, Mrs Pearce: I shall be particularly careful before the girl. Is that all?

Mrs Pearce. No, sir. Might she use some of those Japanese dresses you brought from abroad? I really cant put her back into her old things.

Higgins. Certainly. Anything you like. Is that all?

Mrs Pearce. Thank you, sir. Thats all. *(She goes out).*

A **Higgins.** You know, Pickering, that woman has the most extraordinary ideas about me. Here I am, a shy, diffident sort of man. Ive never been able to feel really grown-up and tremendous, like other chaps. And yet she's firmly persuaded that I'm an arbitrary overbearing bossing kind of person. I cant account for it.

[MRS PEARCE *returns.*]

Mrs Pearce. If you please, sir, the trouble's beginning already. Theres a dustman[10] downstairs, Alfred Doolittle, wants to see you. He says you have his daughter here.

Pickering *(rising).* Phew! I say!

Higgins *(promptly).* Send the blackguard up.

Mrs Pearce. Oh, very well, sir. *(She goes out).*

Pickering. He may not be a blackguard, Higgins.

---

10. **dustman:** a garbage collector.

Higgins. Nonsense. Of course he's a blackguard.

Pickering. Whether he is or not, I'm afraid we shall have some trouble with him.

Higgins *(confidently).* Oh no: I think not. If theres any trouble he shall have it with me, not I with him. And we are sure to get something interesting out of him.

Pickering. About the girl?

Higgins. No. I mean his dialect.

Pickering. Oh!

Mrs Pearce *(at the door).* Doolittle, sir. *(She admits* DOOLITTLE *and retires).*

[ALFRED DOOLITTLE *is an elderly but vigorous dustman, clad in the costume of his profession, including a hat with a back brim covering his neck and shoulders. He has well marked and rather interesting features, and seems equally free from fear and conscience. He has a remarkably expressive voice, the result of a habit of giving vent to his feelings without reserve. His present pose is that of wounded honor and stern resolution.*]

Doolittle *(at the door, uncertain which of the two gentlemen is his man).* Professor Iggins?

Higgins. Here. Good morning. Sit down.

Doolittle. Morning, Governor. *(He sits down magisterially).* I come about a very serious matter, Governor.

Higgins *(to* PICKERING*).* Brought up in Hounslow. Mother Welsh, I should think. *(*DOOLITTLE *opens his mouth, amazed.* HIGGINS *continues).* What do you want, Doolittle?

Doolittle *(menacingly).* I want my daughter: thats what I want. See?

B **Higgins.** Of course you do. Youre her father, arnt you? You dont suppose anyone else wants her, do you? I'm glad to see you have some spark of family feeling left. She's upstairs. Take her away at once.

Doolittle *(rising, fearfully taken aback).* What!

Higgins. Take her away. Do you suppose I'm going to keep your daughter for you?

Doolittle *(remonstrating).* Now, now, look here, Governor. Is this reasonable? Is it fairity to take advantage of a man like this? The girl belongs to me. You got her. Where do I come in? *(He sits down again).*

Higgins. Your daughter had the audacity to come to my house and ask me to teach her how to speak properly so that she could get a place in a flower-shop. This gentleman and my housekeeper have been here all the time. *(Bullying him)* How dare

A. Responding
Here are two views of Higgins's character.

? What do you think Higgins is really like based on what you have seen of him so far in the play?

B. Conflict
? How does Higgins outsmart Eliza's father? (By pretending that he wants to get rid of Eliza) In what way has he beat Mr. Doolittle at his own game? (He has hidden his true motives and desires, as Doolittle also attempts to do.)

A. Motivation

? Why do you think Mr. Doolittle really came to Higgins's house? (To hit up Higgins for a little money)

B. Character

Call students' attention to Mr. Doolittle's ability to bend the truth to his own advantage.

? In what ways is he like Higgins? (Like Higgins, he is a clever man with words who has no real malice in him.)

you come here and attempt to blackmail me? You sent her here on purpose.

Doolittle (*protesting*). No, Governor.

Higgins. You must have. How else could you possibly know that she is here?

Doolittle. Dont take a man up like that, Governor.

Higgins. The police shall take you up. This is a plant—a plot to extort money by threats. I shall telephone for the police. (*He goes resolutely to the telephone and opens the directory*).

Doolittle. Have I asked you for a brass farthing? I leave it to the gentleman here: have I said a word about money?

Higgins (*throwing the book aside and marching down on* DOOLITTLE *with a poser*). What else did you come for?

Doolittle (*sweetly*). Well, what would a man come for? Be human, Governor.

Higgins (*disarmed*). Alfred: did you put her up to it?

Doolittle. So help me, Governor, I never did. I take my Bible oath I aint seen the girl these two months past.

Higgins. Then how did you know she was here?

Doolittle (*"most musical, most melancholy"*). I'll tell you, Governor, if youll only let me get a word in. I'm willing to tell you. I'm wanting to tell you. I'm waiting to tell you.

Higgins. Pickering: this chap has a certain natural gift of rhetoric. Observe the rhythm of his native woodnotes wild. "I'm willing to tell you: I'm wanting to tell you: I'm waiting to tell you." Sentimental rhetoric! thats the Welsh strain in him. It also accounts for his mendacity and dishonesty.

Pickering. Oh, please, Higgins: I'm west country myself. (*To* DOOLITTLE) How did you know the girl was here if you didn't send her?

Doolittle. It was like this, Governor. The girl took a boy in the taxi to give him a jaunt. Son of her landlady, he is. He hung about on the chance of her giving him another ride home. Well, she sent him back for her luggage when she heard you was willing for her to stop here. I met the boy at the corner of Long Acre and Endell Street.

Higgins. Public house.[11] Yes?

Doolittle. The poor man's club, Governor: why shouldnt I?

Pickering. Do let him tell his story, Higgins.

Doolittle. He told me what was up. And I ask you, what was my feelings and my duty as a father? I

---

11. **Public house:** a pub, or saloon.

says to the boy, "You bring me the luggage," I says——

Pickering. Why didnt you go for it yourself?

Doolittle. Landlady wouldnt have trusted me with it, Governor. She's that kind of woman: you know. I had to give the boy a penny afore he trusted me with it, the little swine. I brought it to her just to oblige you like, and make myself agreeable. Thats all.

Higgins. How much luggage?

Doolittle. Musical instrument, Governor. A few pictures, a trifle of jewelry, and a birdcage. She said she didn't want no clothes. What was I to think from that, Governor? I ask you as a parent what was I to think?

Higgins. So you came to rescue her from worse than death eh?

Doolittle (*appreciatively: relieved at being so well understood*). Just so, Governor. Thats right.

Pickering. But why did you bring her luggage if you intended to take her away?

Doolittle. Have I said a word about taking her away? Have I now?

Higgins (*determinedly*). Youre going to take her away, double quick. (*He crosses to the hearth and rings the bell*).

Doolittle (*rising*). No, Governor. Dont say that. I'm not the man to stand in my girl's light. Heres a career opening for her as you might say; and——

[MRS PEARCE *opens the door and awaits orders*.]

Higgins. Mrs Pearce: this is Eliza's father. He has come to take her away. Give her to him. (*He goes back to the piano, with an air of washing his hands of the whole affair*).

Doolittle. No. This is a misunderstanding. Listen here——

Mrs Pearce. He cant take her away, Mr Higgins: how can he? You told me to burn her clothes.

Doolittle. Thats right. I cant carry the girl through the streets like a blooming monkey, can I? I put it to you.

Higgins. You have put it to me that you want your daughter. Take your daughter. If she has no clothes go out and buy her some.

Doolittle (*desperate*). Wheres the clothes she come in? Did I burn them or did your missus here?

Mrs Pearce. I am the housekeeper, if you please. I have sent for some clothes for the girl. When they come you can take her away. You can wait in the kitchen. This way, please.

[DOOLITTLE, *much troubled, accompanies her to the door; then hesitates: finally turns confidentially to* HIGGINS.]

Doolittle. Listen here, Governor. You and me is men of the world, aint we?

Higgins. Oh! Men of the world, are we? Youd better go, Mrs Pearce.

Mrs Pearce. I think so, indeed, sir. (*She goes, with dignity*).

Pickering. The floor is yours, Mr Doolittle.

Doolittle (*to* PICKERING). I thank you, Governor. (*To* HIGGINS, *who takes refuge on the piano bench, a little overwhelmed by the proximity of his visitor; for* DOOLITTLE *has a professional flavor of dust about him*). Well, the truth is, Ive taken a sort of fancy to you, Governor; and if you want the girl, I'm not so set on having her back home again but what I might be open to an arrangement. Regarded in the light of a young woman, she's a fine handsome girl. As a daughter she's not worth her keep; and so I tell you straight. All I ask is my rights as a father; and youre the last man alive to expect me to let her go for nothing; for I can see youre one of the straight sort, Governor. Well, whats a five-pound note to you? and whats Eliza to me? (*He turns to his chair and sits down judicially*).

Pickering. I think you ought to know, Doolittle, that Mr Higgins's intentions are entirely honorable.

Doolittle. Course they are, Governor. If I thought they wasn't, I'd ask fifty.

Higgins (*revolted*). Do you mean to say that you would sell your daughter for £50?

Doolittle. Not in a general way I wouldnt; but to oblige a gentleman like you I'd do a good deal, I do assure you.

Pickering. Have you no morals, man?

Doolittle (*unabashed*). Cant afford them, Governor. Neither could you if you was as poor as me. Not that I mean any harm, you know. But if Liza is going to have a bit out of this, why not me too?

Higgins (*troubled*). I dont know what to do, Pickering. There can be no question that as a matter of morals it's a positive crime to give this chap a farthing. And yet I feel a sort of rough justice in his claim.

Doolittle. Thats it, Governor. Thats all I say. A father's heart, as it were.

Pickering. Well, I know the feeling; but really it seems hardly right——

Doolittle. Dont say that, Governor. Dont look at it that way. What am I, Governors both? I ask you, what am I? I'm one of the undeserving poor: thats what I am. Think of what that means to a man. It means that he's up agen middle class morality all the time. If theres anything going, and I put in for a bit of it, it's always the same story: "Youre undeserving; so you cant have it." But my needs is as great as the most deserving widow's that ever got money out of six different charities in one week for the death of the same husband. I dont need less than a deserving man: I need more. I dont eat less hearty than him; and I drink a lot more. I want a bit of amusement cause I'm a thinking man. I want cheerfulness and a song and a band when I feel low. Well, they charge me just the same for everything as they charge the deserving. What is middle class morality? Just an excuse for never giving me anything. Therefore, I ask you, as two gentlemen, not to play that game on me. I'm playing straight with you. I aint pretending to be deserving. I'm undeserving; and I mean to go on being undeserving. I like it; and thats the truth. Will you take advantage of a man's nature to do him out of the price of his own daughter what he's brought up and fed and clothed by the sweat of his brow until she's growed big enough to be interesting to you two gentlemen? Is five pounds unreasonable? I put it to you; and I leave it to you.

Higgins (*rising, and going over to* PICKERING). Pickering: if we were to take this man in hand for three months, he could choose between a seat in the Cabinet and a popular pulpit in Wales.

Pickering. What do you say to that, Doolittle?

Doolittle. Not me, Governor, thank you kindly. Ive heard all the preachers and all the prime ministers—for I'm a thinking man and game for politics or religion or social reform same as all the other amusements—and I tell you it's a dog's life any way you look at it. Undeserving poverty is my line. Taking one station in society with another, it's—it's—well, it's the only one that has any ginger in it, to my taste.

Higgins. I suppose we must give him a fiver.

Pickering. He'll make a bad use of it, I'm afraid.

Doolittle. Not me, Governor, so help me I wont. Dont you be afraid that I'll save it and spare it and live idle on it. There wont be a penny of it left by Monday: I'll have to go to work same as if I'd never had it. It wont pauperize me, you bet. Just one good spree for myself and the missus,

A. Expansion
Much of the humor in the dialogue arises out of Mr. Doolittle's way of overturning conventional reasoning and morality. He sees things from a poor man's point of view and speaks against the middle-class morality represented by Pickering and Higgins, and presumably shared by the audience.

B. Responding
Do you think Mr. Doolittle makes a convincing case for the needs of the "undeserving poor"? Would you have given him his fiver?

A. Plot

What is Mr. Doolittle's response to Higgins's offer of ten pounds? (He refuses it.) Were you surprised by his response? How does Doolittle explain his action? (Too much money would make him responsible, middle-class, and unhappy.) Do you think his action is consistent with his overall personality?

Dont you give me none of your lip. . . .''

giving pleasure to ourselves and employment to others, and satisfaction to you to think it's not been throwed away. You couldn't spend it better.
Higgins *(taking out his pocket book and coming between* DOOLITTLE *and the piano).* This is irresistible. Lets give him ten. *(He offers two notes to the dustman).*

Doolittle. No, Governor. She wouldn't have the heart to spend ten; and perhaps I shouldnt neither.

Ten pounds is a lot of money: it makes a man feel prudent like; and then goodbye to happiness. You give me what I ask you, Governor: not a penny more, and not a penny less.

Pickering. Why dont you marry that missus of yours? I rather draw the line at encouraging that sort of immorality.

Doolittle. Tell her so, Governor: tell her so. *I*'m willing. It's me that suffers by it. Ive no hold on

READING CHECK TEST: Act Two
1. Professor Higgins summons Eliza to come to his laboratory. (F)
2. Eliza wants to take speech lessons from the professor. (T)
3. Mrs. Pearce does not approve of Eliza's joining the household. (T)
4. Colonel Pickering has no interest in passing off Eliza as a duchess. (F)
5. Eliza is a very slow and lazy student with no aptitude. (F)

her. I got to be agreeable to her. I got to give her presents. I got to buy her clothes something sinful. I'm a slave to that woman, Governor, just because I'm not her lawful husband. And she knows it too. Catch her marrying me! Take my advice, Governor—marry Eliza while she's young and dont know no better. If you dont youll be sorry for it after. If you do, she'll be sorry for it after; but better her than you, because youre a man, and she's only a woman and dont know how to be happy anyhow.

A **Higgins.** Pickering: If we listen to this man another minute, we shall have no convictions left. (*To* DOOLITTLE) Five pounds I think you said.

Doolittle. Thank you kindly, Governor.

Higgins. Youre sure you wont take ten?

Doolittle. Not now. Another time, Governor.

Higgins (*handing him a five-pound note*). Here you are.

Doolittle. Thank you, Governor. Good morning. (*He hurries to the door, anxious to get away with his booty. When he opens it he is confronted with a dainty and exquisitely clean young Japanese lady in a simple blue cotton kimono printed cunningly with small white jasmine blossoms.* MRS PEARCE *is with her. He gets out of her way deferentially and apologizes*). Beg pardon, miss.

The Japanese Lady. Garn! Dont you know your own daughter?

Doolittle ⎱ Bly me! it's Eliza! ⎰ [*exclaiming*
Higgins ⎰ What's that? This! ⎱ *simultaneously*]
Pickering ⎰ By Jove! ⎱

Liza. Dont I look silly?

Higgins. Silly?

Mrs Pearce (*at the door*). Now, Mr Higgins, please dont say anything to make the girl conceited about herself.

Higgins (*conscientiously*). Oh! Quite right, Mrs Pearce. (*To* ELIZA) Yes: damned silly.

Mrs Pearce. Please, sir.

Higgins (*correcting himself*). I mean extremely silly.

Liza. I should look all right with my hat on. (*She takes up her hat; puts it on; and walks across the room to the fireplace with a fashionable air*).

B **Higgins.** A new fashion, by George! And it ought to look horrible!

Doolittle (*with fatherly pride*). Well, I never thought she'd clean up as good looking as that, Governor. She's a credit to me, aint she?

Liza. I tell you, it's easy to clean up here. Hot and cold water on tap, just as much as you like,

there is. Woolly towels, there is; and a towel horse[12] so hot, it burns your fingers. Soft brushes to scrub yourself, and a wooden bowl of soap smelling like primroses. Now I know why ladies is so clean. Washing's a treat for them. Wish they could see what it is for the like of me!

Higgins. I'm glad the bathroom met with your approval.

Liza. It didnt: not all of it; and I dont care who hears me say it. Mrs Pearce knows.

Higgins. What was wrong, Mrs Pearce?

Mrs Pearce (*blandly*). Oh, nothing, sir. It doesnt matter.

Liza. I had a good mind to break it. I didn't know which way to look. But I hung a towel over it, I did.

Higgins. Over what?

Mrs Pearce. Over the looking-glass sir.

Higgins. Doolittle: you have brought your daughter up too strictly.

Doolittle. Me! I never brought her up at all, except to give her a lick of a strap now and again. Dont put it on me, Governor. She aint accustomed to it, you see: thats all. But she'll soon pick up your free-and-easy ways.

Liza. I'm a good girl, I am; and I wont pick up no free-and-easy ways.

Higgins. Eliza: if you say again that youre a good girl, your father shall take you home.

Liza. Not him. You dont know my father. All he come here for was to touch you for some money to get drunk on.

Doolittle. Well, what else would I want money for? To put into the plate in church, I suppose. (*She puts out her tongue at him. He is so incensed by this that* PICKERING *presently finds it necessary to step between them*). Dont you give me none of your lip; and dont let me hear you giving this gentleman any of it neither, or youll hear from me about it. See?

Higgins. Have you any further advice to give her before you go, Doolittle? Your blessing, for instance.

C **Doolittle.** No, Governor: I aint such a mug as to put up my children to all I know myself. Hard enough to hold them in without that. If you want Eliza's mind improved, Governor, you do it yourself with a strap. So long, gentlemen. (*He turns to go*).

---

12. **towel horse:** towel rack; here, with a built-in heater for drying the towels.

A. Conflict
❓ Although Higgins seemed to have the upper hand in the comic confrontation with the scheming Doolittle, who won in the end? (Higgins was won over, and Doolittle went off with exactly what he came for.)

B. Character
❓ What is Higgins's true reaction to Eliza's transformation? (He is impressed, and attracted to her.)

C. Character
Both Higgins and Doolittle talk about beating Eliza if she misbehaves.
❓ Do you think the audience is meant to take these threats seriously? (No) What personality traits do the two men have in common? (Tendencies toward exaggeration, bravado, and willfulness)

1. She hopes he will give her speech lessons so she can work in a genteel flower shop. Higgins treats her preremptorily. Pickering treats her considerately.
2. Pickering and Higgins bet on whether Higgins will be able to pass Eliza off as a duchess at the ambassador's garden party. Pickering will assume all the costs

of the lessons. Then Higgins orders Mrs. Pearce to clean Eliza up and dress her in decent clothes.
3. He says that the moment he makes friends with a woman, she becomes jealous and he becomes selfish.
4. He visits Higgins to retrieve Eliza. He claims he can't afford to have morals because they are too expensive.

Interpreting Meanings
5. A contradiction exists between Doolittle's demand for his daughter and his apparent willingness to allow Eliza to stay if he is paid five pounds. Although he is looking for money, he stubbornly refuses Higgins's offer of ten pounds, saying that too much money would make him feel "prudent" and ruin his happiness.
6. Much of the apparent "morality" of

A. Expansion
Shaw is making fun of social climbers here.

B. Plot
? How does Act Two end? (With Eliza painfully but successfully learning to talk like a lady)

A

Higgins (*impressively*). Stop. Youll come regularly to see your daughter. It's your duty, you know. My brother is a clergyman; and he could help you in your talks with her.
Doolittle (*evasively*). Certainly, I'll come, Governor. Not just this week, because I have a job at a distance. But later on you may depend on me. Afternoon, gentlemen. Afternoon, maam. (*He touches his hat to* MRS PEARCE, *who disdains the salutation and goes out. He winks at* HIGGINS, *thinking him probably a fellow-sufferer from* MRS PEARCE's *difficult disposition, and follows her*).
Liza. Dont you believe the old liar. He'd as soon you set a bulldog on him as a clergyman. You wont see him again in a hurry.
Higgins. I dont want to, Eliza. Do you?
Liza. Not me. I dont want never to see him again, I dont. He's a disgrace to me, he is, collecting dust, instead of working at his trade.
Pickering. What is his trade, Eliza?
Liza. Talking money out of other people's pockets into his own. His proper trade's a navvy;[13] and he works at it sometimes too—for exercise—and earns good money at it. Aint you going to call me Miss Doolittle any more?
Pickering. I beg your pardon, Miss Doolittle. It was a slip of the tongue.
Liza. Oh, I dont mind; only it sounded so genteel. I should just like to take a taxi to the corner of Tottenham Court Road and get out there and tell it to wait for me, just to put the girls in their place a bit. I wouldnt speak to them, you know.
Pickering. Better wait til we get you something really fashionable.
Higgins. Besides, you shouldnt cut your old friends now that you have risen in the world. Thats what we call snobbery.
Liza. You dont call the like of them my friends now, I should hope. Theyve took it out of me often enough with their ridicule when they had the chance; and now I mean to get a bit of my own back. But if I'm to have fashionable clothes, I'll wait. I should like to have some. Mrs Pearce says youre going to give me some to wear to bed at night different to what I wear in the daytime; but it do seem a waste of money when you could get something to shew. Besides, I never could fancy changing into cold things on a winter night.
Mrs Pearce (*coming back*). Now, Eliza. The new things have come for you to try on.

---

13. **navvy** (nav′ē): an unskilled laborer.

Liza. Ah-ow-oo-oooh! (*She rushes out*).
Mrs Pearce (*following her*). Oh, dont rush about like that, girl. (*She shuts the door behind her*).
Higgins. Pickering: we have taken on a stiff job.
Pickering (*with conviction*). Higgins: we have.

* * *

There seems to be more curiosity as to what Higgins's lessons to Eliza were like. Well, here is a sample: the first one.

Picture Eliza, in her new clothes, and feeling her inside put out of step by a lunch, dinner, and breakfast of a kind to which it is unaccustomed, seated with Higgins and the Colonel in the study, feeling like a hospital out-patient at a first encounter with the doctors.

Higgins, constitutionally unable to sit still, discomposes her still more by striding restlessly about. But for the reassuring presence and quietude of her friend the Colonel she would run for her life, even back to Drury Lane.

Higgins. Say your alphabet.
Liza. I know my alphabet. Do you think I know nothing? I dont need to be taught like a child.
Higgins (*thundering*). Say your alphabet.
Pickering. Say it, Miss Doolittle. You will understand presently. Do what he tells you; and let him teach you in his own way.
Liza. Oh well, if you put it like that—Ahyee, bə-yee, cəyee, dəyee——
Higgins (*with the roar of a wounded lion*). Stop. Listen to this, Pickering. This is what we pay for as elementary education. This unfortunate animal has been locked up for nine years in school at our expense to teach her to speak and read the language of Shakespear and Milton. And the result is Ahyee, Bə-yee, Cə-yee, Də-yee. (*To* ELIZA) Say A, B, C, D.
Liza (*almost in tears*). But I'm sayin it. Ahyee, Bəyee, Cə-yee——
Higgins. Stop. Say a cup of tea.
Liza. A cappətə-ee.
Higgins. Put your tongue forward until it squeezes against the top of your lower teeth. Now say cup.
Liza. C-c-c—I cant. C-cup.
Pickering. Good. Splendid, Miss Doolittle.
Higgins. By Jupiter, she's done it at the first shot. Pickering: we shall make a duchess of her. (*To* ELIZA) Now do you think you could possibly say tea? Not tə-yee, mind: if you ever say bə-yee cə-yee də-yee again you shall be dragged round the

B

---

middle-class people is mere respectability and caution. They can use money to conceal their true nature.
7. The major question of the play is: What is to become of Eliza? Higgins has a blithely optimistic, almost indifferent attitude. Student interpretations of his attitude will vary.
8. Shaw portrays Higgins as very amusing and intelligent. Underneath his apparently callous exterior, we suspect that he is generous and completely honest. He views himself as an expert in his profession and uninterested in romance.
9. Colonel Pickering functions as a sensible, kindly "uncle" figure who moderates Higgins's insensitivity toward Eliza as a woman. He also serves as something of a "straight man" for Higgins.
10. Examples are her childlike joy at her first carriage ride, fear of the bath, outrage at being suspected of immorality.
11. The conflict is whether or not Eliza will stay at Higgins's house and start her training. He bribes Eliza with chocolates and tempts her with visions of her future life. The resolution of the conflict leads us to expect that Higgins and Pickering will indeed take Eliza in hand and "present" her as a duchess.

room three times by the hair of your head. (*Fortissimo*[14]) T, T, T, T.
Liza (*weeping*). I cant hear no difference cep that it sounds more genteel-like when you say it.
Higgins. Well, if you can hear that difference, what the devil are you crying for? Pickering: give her a chocolate.
Pickering. No, no. Never mind crying a little, Miss Doolittle: you are doing very well; and the lessons wont hurt. I promise you I wont let him drag you round the room by your hair.

---

14. *Fortissimo:* a musical term in Italian meaning "very loud."

Higgins. Be off with you to Mrs Pearce and tell her about it. Think about it. Try to do it by yourself: and keep your tongue well forward in your mouth instead of trying to roll it up and swallow it. Another lesson at half-past four this afternoon. Away with you.

[ELIZA, *still sobbing, rushes from the room.*]

And that is the sort of ordeal poor Eliza has to go through for months before we meet her again on her first appearance in London society of the professional class.

A

A. Expansion
Shaw obviously wrote his play to be read as well as performed, since a note like this is obviously meant for readers, not directors or actors.

Responding to the Play

Analyzing Act Two

Identifying Facts

1. Why does Eliza come to Higgins's laboratory? How does Higgins treat her? How does Pickering treat her?
2. What is the bet made between Pickering and Higgins? Describe the plan set in action as a result of the bet.
3. What reasons does Higgins give for remaining a "confirmed old bachelor"?
4. Why does Doolittle visit Higgins? What are his problems as a member of the "undeserving poor"?

Interpreting Meanings

5. Point out some of the **paradoxes,** or apparent contradictions, between Doolittle's speeches and his behavior. Where does he vacillate between moral indignation and rascally wheedling?
6. What **satiric** point might Shaw be making in his characterization of Doolittle?
7. Mrs. Pearce several times expresses the major question of the play. What is it? What is Higgins's attitude toward the question? Does he have a point?
8. The **character** of Higgins could be a monster, but obviously Shaw does not see him as such. How does Shaw describe Higgins, and what keeps him from being unbearable? What is Higgins's view of himself?
9. What is the function of Colonel Pickering in the action?

A corner of Higgins's study, set designed by Oliver Smith for *My Fair Lady.*

10. Eliza is a tough street girl, but Shaw goes to great lengths to establish her innocent nature. How does he do this?
11. What is the basic **conflict** of Act Two? What means does Higgins use to gain his end? What does the **resolution** of the conflict lead us to expect about what will happen next?

Henry, anxious to show off the great progress he has made with Eliza, brings her to his mother's home on the day when she receives visitors. The Eynsford Hills, the mother, son, and daughter from Act One, arrive. Eliza, looking beautiful, begins to speak with perfect pronunciation. However, as she warms to her subject, she lapses into her native slang and into unfit subjects like gin and marital relations. The socially insecure Miss Hill takes her patter for the latest fashionable talk. The mother is too shocked to protest, and the son is overwhelmed by Eliza's beauty. After Eliza leaves with Freddy, Mrs. Higgins tries to make her son and Pickering see the dangers to Eliza in their enterprise, but they are enjoying themselves too much to listen. Finally, after further instruction, the two men take Eliza to an embassy party where a fraudulent linguist, named Nepommuck, convinces everyone that Eliza is a princess.

A. Character
Henry admits to lacking the ability to make small talk but imagines that people do not mind. His mother, on the other hand, worries about his "large talk."
❓ What do you think she means by that? (The way he says whatever he feels like without considering the effect on others) How do you imagine Henry behaves in the company of conventional people? (Tactlessly, rudely, and with a relish for unsettling others)

B. Character
❓ Has Henry's attitude toward women consciously changed since the beginning of the play? (No) What about his attitude toward Eliza at this point? (She is the amusing subject of an experiment.)

Act Three

It is MRS HIGGINS's *at-home day.[1] Nobody has yet arrived. Her drawing room, in a flat on Chelsea Embankment, has three windows looking on the river; and the ceiling is not so lofty as it would be in an older house of the same pretension. The windows are open, giving access to a balcony with flowers in pots. If you stand with your face to the windows, you have the fireplace on your left and the door in the right-hand wall close to the corner nearest the windows.*

MRS HIGGINS *was brought up on Morris and Burne Jones,[2] and her room, which is very unlike her son's room in Wimpole Street, is not crowded with furniture and little tables and nicknacks. In the middle of the room there is a big ottoman; and this, with the carpet, the Morris wallpapers, and the Morris chintz window curtains and brocade covers of the ottoman and its cushions, supply all the ornament, and are much too handsome to be hidden by odds and ends of useless things. A few good oil-paintings from the exhibitions in the Grosvenor Gallery thirty years ago (the Burne Jones, not the Whistler[3] side of them) are on the walls. The only landscape is a Cecil Lawson[4] on the scale of a Rubens.[5] There is a portrait of* MRS HIGGINS *as she was when she defied the fashion in her youth in one of the beautiful Rossettian[6] costumes which, when caricatured by people who did not understand, led to the absurdities of popular estheticism in the eighteen-seventies.*

In the corner diagonally opposite the door MRS HIGGINS, *now over sixty and long past taking the trouble to dress out of the fashion, sits writing at an elegantly simple writing-table with a bell button within reach of her hand. There is a Chippendale chair further back in the room between her and the window nearest her side. At the other side of the room, further forward, is an Elizabethan chair roughly carved in the taste of Inigo Jones. On the same side a piano in a decorated case. The corner between the fireplace and the window is occupied by a divan cushioned in Morris chintz.*

It is between four and five in the afternoon.

The door is opened violently; and HIGGINS *enters with his hat on.*

Mrs Higgins (*dismayed*). Henry! (*Scolding him*) What are you doing here today? It is my at-home day: you promised not to come. (*As he bends to kiss her, she takes his hat off, and presents it to him*).

Higgins. Oh bother! (*He throws the hat down on the table*).

Mrs Higgins. Go home at once.

Higgins (*kissing her*). I know, mother. I came on purpose.

Mrs Higgins. But you mustnt. I'm serious, Henry. You offend all my friends: they stop coming whenever they meet you.

Higgins. Nonsense! I know I have no small talk; but people dont mind. (*He sits on the settee*).

Mrs Higgins. Oh! dont they? Small talk indeed! What about your large talk? Really, dear, you mustnt stay.

Higgins. I must. Ive a job for you. A phonetic job.

Mrs Higgins. No use, dear. I'm sorry; but I cant get round your vowels; and though I like to get pretty postcards in your patent shorthand, I always have to read the copies in ordinary writing you so thoughtfully send me.

Higgins. Well, this isnt a phonetic job.

Mrs Higgins. You said it was.

Higgins. Not your part of it. Ive picked up a girl.

Mrs Higgins. Does that mean that some girl has picked you up?

Higgins. Not at all. I dont mean a love affair.

Mrs Higgins. What a pity!

Higgins. Why?

Mrs Higgins. Well, you never fall in love with anyone under forty-five. When will you discover that there are some rather nice-looking young women about?

Higgins. Oh, I cant be bothered with young women. My idea of a lovable woman is somebody as like you as possible. I shall never get into the way of seriously liking young women: some habits lie too deep to be changed. (*Rising abruptly and walking about, jingling his money and his keys in his trouser pockets*) Besides, theyre all idiots.

A

B

---

1. **at-home day:** a day on which a lady receives visitors that do not have specific invitations.
2. **Morris and Burne Jones:** William Morris (1834–1896) and Sir Edward Coley Burne-Jones (1833–1898) were English artists who influenced interior design. Note that Shaw approves of Mrs. Higgins's tastes.
3. **Whistler:** James Abbott McNeill Whistler (1834–1903), a fashionable American portrait painter who spent many years in England.
4. **Cecil Lawson:** Cecil Gordon Lawson (1851–1882), English landscape painter.
5. **Rubens:** Peter Paul Rubens (1577–1640), Flemish painter known for his large paintings.
6. **Rossettian:** a style associated with the paintings of Dante Gabriel Rossetti (1828–1882).

Mrs Higgins. Do you know what you would do if you really loved me, Henry?

Higgins. Oh bother! What? Marry, I suppose.

Mrs Higgins. No. Stop fidgeting and take your hands out of your pockets. *(With a gesture of despair, he obeys and sits down again)*. Thats a good boy. Now tell me about the girl.

Higgins. She's coming to see you.

Mrs Higgins. I dont remember asking her.

Higgins. You didnt. *I* asked her. If youd known her you wouldnt have asked her.

Mrs Higgins. Indeed! Why?

Higgins. Well, it's like this. She's a common flower girl. I picked her off the kerbstone.

Mrs Higgins. And invited her to my at-home!

Higgins *(rising and coming to her to coax her)*. Oh, thatll be all right. Ive taught her to speak properly; and she has strict orders as to her behavior. She's to keep to two subjects: the weather and everybody's health—Fine day and How do you do, you know—and not to let herself go on things in general. That will be safe.

Mrs Higgins. Safe! To talk about our health! about our insides! perhaps about our outsides! How could you be so silly, Henry?

Higgins *(impatiently)*. Well, she must talk about something. *(He controls himself and sits down again)*. Oh, she'll be all right: dont you fuss. Pickering is in it with me. Ive a sort of bet on that I'll pass her off as a duchess in six months. I started on her some months ago; and she's getting on like a house on fire. I shall win my bet. She has a quick ear; and she's been easier to teach than my middle-class pupils because she's had to learn a complete new language. She talks English almost as you talk French.

Mrs Higgins. Thats satisfactory, at all events.

Higgins. Well, it is and it isnt.

Mrs Higgins. What does that mean?

Higgins. You see, Ive got her pronunciation all right; but you have to consider not only how a girl pronounces, but what she pronounces; and thats where—

[*They are interrupted by the parlormaid, announcing guests.*]

The Parlormaid. Mrs and Miss Eynsford Hill. *(She withdraws)*.

Higgins. Oh Lord! *(He rises: snatches his hat from the table; and makes for the door; but before he reaches it his mother introduces him)*.

[MRS *and* MISS EYNSFORD HILL *are the mother and daughter who sheltered from the rain in Covent Garden. The mother is well bred, quiet, and has the habitual anxiety of straitened means. The daughter has acquired a gay air of being very much at home in society: the bravado of genteel poverty.*]

Mrs Eynsford Hill *(to* MRS HIGGINS*)*. How do you do? *(They shake hands)*.

Miss Eynsford Hill. How d'you do? *(She shakes)*.

Mrs Higgins *(introducing)*. My son Henry.

Mrs Eynsford Hill. Your celebrated son! I have so longed to meet you, Professor Higgins.

Higgins *(glumly, making no movement in her direction)*. Delighted. *(He backs against the piano and bows brusquely)*.

Miss Eynsford Hill *(going to him with confident familiarity)*. How do you do?

Higgins *(staring at her)*. Ive seen you before somewhere. I havnt the ghost of a notion where; but Ive heard your voice. *(Drearily)* It doesnt matter. Youd better sit down.

Mrs Higgins. I'm sorry to say that my celebrated son has no manners. You mustnt mind him.

Miss Eynsford Hill *(gaily)*. I dont. *(She sits in the Elizabethan chair)*.

Mrs Eynsford Hill *(a little bewildered)*. Not at all. *(She sits on the ottoman between her daughter and* MRS HIGGINS, *who has turned her chair away from the writing-table)*.

Higgins. Oh, have I been rude? I didnt mean to be.

[*He goes to the central window, through which, with his back to the company, he contemplates the river and the flowers in Battersea Park on the opposite bank as if they were a frozen desert.*

The parlormaid returns, ushering in PICKERING.]

The Parlormaid. Colonel Pickering. *(She withdraws)*.

Pickering. How do you do, Mrs Higgins?

Mrs Higgins. So glad youve come. Do you know Mrs Eynsford Hill—Miss Eynsford Hill? *(Exchange of bows. The* COLONEL *brings the Chippendale chair a little forward between* MRS HILL *and* MRS HIGGINS, *and sits down)*.

Pickering. Has Henry told you what weve come for?

Higgins *(over his shoulder)*. We were interrupted: damn it!

A. Responding
Ask students to predict what they think will happen during Eliza's visit based on Higgins's description of her progress at this point.

B. Character
What is the effect of their limited means on the Eynsford Hills' social confidence? (They are insecure and the daughter is particularly desirous of being accepted.)

C. Noting Specific Details
What kind of bad manners does Higgins display here? (He tactlessly reveals his total disinterest in Miss Hill's presence.) Look for other examples of unacceptable drawing-room behavior on his part in the rest of the scene.

A. Expansion
Point out the complicated and amusing ironies in the fact that Miss Hill, who claims to desire frankness in conversation, is saying not what she believes but what she thinks is fashionable, and Higgins, who rejects the idea of uttering what one really thinks in company, is speaking more honestly.

Mrs Higgins. Oh Henry, Henry, really!

Mrs Eynsford Hill (*half rising*). Are we in the way?

Mrs Higgins (*rising and making her sit down again*). No, no. You couldnt have come more fortunately: we want you to meet a friend of ours.

Higgins (*turning hopefully*). Yes, by George! We want two or three people. Youll do as well as anybody else.

[*The parlormaid returns, ushering* FREDDY.]

The Parlormaid. Mr Eynsford Hill.

Higgins (*almost audibly, past endurance*). God of Heaven! another of them.

Freddy (*shaking hands with* MRS HIGGINS). Ahdedo?

Mrs Higgins. Very good of you to come. (*Introducing*) Colonel Pickering.

Freddy (*bowing*). Ahdedo?

Mrs Higgins. I dont think you know my son, Professor Higgins.

Freddy (*going to* HIGGINS). Ahdedo?

Higgins (*looking at him much as if he were a pickpocket*). I'll take my oath Ive met you before somewhere. Where was it?

Freddy. I dont think so.

Higgins (*resignedly*). It dont matter, anyhow. Sit down.

[*He shakes* FREDDY'*s hand and almost slings him on to the ottoman with his face to the window; then comes round to the other side of it.*]

Higgins. Well, here we are, anyhow! (*He sits down on the ottoman next* MRS EYNSFORD HILL, *on her left*). And now, what the devil are we going to talk about until Eliza comes?

Mrs Higgins. Henry: you are the life and soul of the Royal Society's soirées; but really youre rather trying on more commonplace occasions.

Higgins. Am I? Very sorry. (*Beaming suddenly*) I suppose I am, you know. (*Uproariously*) Ha, ha!

Miss Eynsford Hill (*who considers* HIGGINS *quite eligible matrimonially*). I sympathize. *I* havnt any small talk. If people would only be frank and say what they really think!

Higgins (*relapsing into gloom*). Lord forbid!

Mrs Eynsford Hill (*taking up her daughter's cue*). But why?

Higgins. What they think they ought to think is bad enough, Lord knows; but what they really think would break up the whole show. Do you suppose it would be really agreeable if I were to come out now with what *I* really think?

Miss Eynsford Hill (*gaily*). Is it so very cynical?

Higgins. Cynical! Who the dickens said it was cynical? I mean it wouldnt be decent.

Mrs Eynsford Hill (*seriously*). Oh! I'm sure you dont mean that, Mr Higgins.

Higgins. You see, we're all savages, more or less. We're supposed to be civilized and cultured—to know all about poetry and philosophy and art and science, and so on; but how many of us know even the meanings of these names? (*To* MISS HILL) What do you know of poetry? (*To* MRS HILL) What

"And now what the devil are we going to talk about until Eliza comes?"

do you know of science? (*Indicating* FREDDY) What does he know of art or science or anything else? What the devil do you imagine I know of philosophy?

Mrs Higgins (*warningly*). Or of manners, Henry?

The Parlormaid (*opening the door*). Miss Doolittle. (*She withdraws*).

Higgins (*rising hastily and running to* MRS HIGGINS). Here she is, mother. (*He stands on tiptoe and makes signs over his mother's head to* ELIZA *to indicate to her which lady is her hostess*).

[ELIZA, *who is exquisitely dressed, produces an impression of such remarkable distinction and beauty as she enters that they all rise, quite fluttered. Guided by* HIGGINS's *signals, she comes to* MRS HIGGINS *with studied grace*.]

Liza (*speaking with pedantic correctness of pronunciation and great beauty of tone*). How do you do, Mrs Higgins? (*She gasps slightly in making sure of the H in Higgins, but is quite successful*). Mr Higgins told me I might come.

A

A. Diction

How would you describe Eliza's language in this speech? (It is totally artificial; she is repeating words without understanding their meaning or their suitability to the situation.)

B. Diction

What turn has Eliza's speech taken here? (She has lapsed into her native slang.)

C. Expansion

Point out to students that it is the hilarious contrast between Mrs. Hill's conventional, restrained responses and Eliza's outrageous, colorful assertions that creates the humor in this scene.

Mrs Higgins (*cordially*). Quite right: I'm very glad indeed to see you.

Pickering. How do you do, Miss Doolittle?

Liza (*shaking hands with him*). Colonel Pickering, is it not?

Mrs Eynsford Hill. I feel sure we have met before, Miss Doolittle. I remember your eyes.

Liza. How do you do? (*She sits down on the ottoman gracefully in the place just left vacant by* HIGGINS).

Mrs Eynsford Hill (*introducing*). My daughter Clara.

Liza. How do you do?

Clara (*impulsively*). How do you do? (*She sits down on the ottoman beside* ELIZA, *devouring her with her eyes*).

Freddy (*coming to their side of the ottoman*). Ive certainly had the pleasure.

Mrs Eynsford Hill (*introducing*). My son Freddy.

Liza. How do you do?

[FREDDY *bows and sits down in the Elizabethan chair, infatuated.*]

Higgins (*suddenly*). By George, yes: it all comes back to me! (*They stare at him*). Covent Garden! (*Lamentably*) What a damned thing!

Mrs Higgins. Henry, please! (*He is about to sit on the edge of the table*) Dont sit on my writing-table: youll break it.

Higgins (*sulkily*). Sorry.

[*He goes to the divan, stumbling into the fender and over the fire-irons on his way; extricating himself with muttered imprecations; and finishing his disastrous journey by throwing himself so impatiently on the divan that he almost breaks it.* MRS HIGGINS *looks at him, but controls herself and says nothing.*

A long and painful pause ensues.]

Mrs Higgins (*at last, conversationally*). Will it rain, do you think?

Liza. The shallow depression in the west of these islands is likely to move slowly in an easterly direction. There are no indications of any great change in the barometrical situation.

Freddy. Ha! ha! how awfully funny!

Liza. What is wrong with that, young man? I bet I got it right.

Freddy. Killing!

Mrs Eynsford Hill. I'm sure I hope it wont turn cold. Theres so much influenza about. It runs right through our whole family regularly every spring.

Liza (*darkly*). My aunt died of influenza: so they said.

Mrs Eynsford Hill (*clicks her tongue sympathetically*) !!!

Liza (*in the same tragic tone*). But it's my belief they done the old woman in.

Mrs Higgins (*puzzled*). Done her in?

Liza. Y-e-e-e-es, Lord love you! Why should she die of influenza? She come through diphtheria right enough the year before. I saw her with my own eyes. Fairly blue with it, she was. They all thought she was dead; but my father he kept ladling gin down her throat til she came to so sudden that she bit the bowl off the spoon.

Mrs Eynsford Hill (*startled*). Dear me!

Liza (*piling up the indictment*). What call would a woman with that strength in her have to die of influenza? What become of her new straw hat that should have come to me? Somebody pinched it; and what I say is, them as pinched it done her in.

Mrs Eynsford Hill. What does doing her in mean?

Higgins (*hastily*). Oh, thats the new small talk. To do a person in means to kill them.

Mrs Eynsford Hill (*to* ELIZA, *horrified*). You surely dont believe that your aunt was killed?

Liza. Do I not! Them she lived with would have killed her for a hat-pin, let alone a hat.

Mrs Eynsford Hill. But it cant have been right for your father to pour spirits down her throat like that. It might have killed her.

Liza. Not her. Gin was mother's milk to her. Besides, he'd poured so much down his own throat that he knew the good of it.

Mrs Eynsford Hill. Do you mean that he drank?

Liza. Drank! My word! Something chronic.

Mrs Eynsford Hill. How dreadful for you!

Liza. Not a bit. It never did him no harm what I could see. But then he did not keep it up regular. (*Cheerfully*) On the burst, as you might say, from time to time. And always more agreeable when he had a drop in. When he was out of work, my mother used to give him fourpence and tell him to go out and not come back until he'd drunk himself cheerful and loving-like. Theres lots of women has to make their husbands drunk to make them fit to live with. (*Now quite at her ease*) You see, it's like this. If a man has a bit of a conscience, it always takes him when he's sober; and then it makes him low-spirited. A drop of booze just takes that off and makes him happy. (*To* FREDDY, *who is in convulsions of suppressed laughter*) Here! what are you sniggering at?

Freddy. The new small talk. You do it so awfully well.

Liza. If I was doing it proper, what was you laughing at? *(To* HIGGINS*)* Have I said anything I oughtnt?

Mrs Higgins *(interposing)*. Not at all, Miss Doolittle.

Liza. Well, thats a mercy, anyhow. *(Expansively)* What I always say is——

Higgins *(rising and looking at his watch)*. Ahem!

Liza *(looking round at him; taking the hint; and rising)*. Well: I must go. *(They all rise.* FREDDY *goes to the door).* So pleased to have met you. Goodbye. *(She shakes hands with* MRS HIGGINS*).*

Mrs Higgins. Goodbye.

Liza. Goodbye, Colonel Pickering.

Pickering. Goodbye, Miss Doolittle. *(They shake hands).*

Liza *(nodding to the others)*. Goodbye, all.

Freddy *(opening the door for her)*. Are you walking across the Park, Miss Doolittle? If so——

A | **Liza** *(perfectly elegant diction)*. Walk! Not bloody likely. *(Sensation).* I am going in a taxi. *(She goes out).*

[PICKERING *gasps and sits down.* FREDDY *goes out on the balcony to catch another glimpse of* ELIZA.]

B | **Mrs Eynsford Hill** *(suffering from shock)*. Well, I really cant get used to the new ways.

Clara *(throwing herself discontentedly into the Elizabethan chair)*. Oh, it's all right, mamma, quite right. People will think we never go anywhere or see anybody if you are so old-fashioned.

Mrs Eynsford Hill. I daresay I am very old-fashioned; but I do hope you wont begin using that expression, Clara. I have got accustomed to hear you talking about men as rotters, and calling everything filthy and beastly; though I do think it horrible and unladylike. But this last is really too much. Dont you think so, Colonel Pickering?

Pickering. Dont ask me. Ive been away in India for several years; and manners have changed so much that I sometimes dont know whether I'm at a respectable dinner-table or in a ship's forecastle.

Clara. It's all a matter of habit. Theres no right or wrong in it. Nobody means anything by it. And it's so quaint, and gives such a smart emphasis to things that are not in themselves very witty. I find the new small talk delightful and quite innocent.

Mrs Eynsford Hill *(rising)*. Well, after that, I think it's time for us to go.

[PICKERING *and* HIGGINS *rise*.]

Clara *(rising)*. Oh yes: we have three at-homes to go to still. Goodbye, Mrs Higgins. Goodbye, Colonel Pickering. Goodbye, Professor Higgins.

Higgins *(coming grimly at her from the divan, and accompanying her to the door)*. Goodbye. Be sure you try on that small talk at the three at-homes. Dont be nervous about it. Pitch it in strong.

Clara *(all smiles)*. I will. Goodbye. Such nonsense, all this early Victorian prudery!

Higgins *(tempting her)*. Such damned nonsense!

Clara. Such bloody nonsense!

Mrs Eynsford Hill *(convulsively)*. Clara!

Clara. Ha! ha! *(She goes out radiant, conscious of being thoroughly up to date, and is heard descending the stairs in a stream of silvery laughter).*

Freddy *(to the heavens at large)*. Well, I ask you—— *(He gives it up, and comes to* MRS HIGGINS*).* Goodbye.

Mrs Higgins *(shaking hands)*. Goodbye. Would you like to meet Miss Doolittle again?

Freddy *(eagerly)*. Yes, I should, most awfully.

Mrs Higgins. Well, you know my days.

Freddy. Yes. Thanks awfully. Goodbye. *(He goes out).*

Mrs Eynsford Hill. Goodbye, Mr Higgins.

Higgins. Goodbye. Goodbye.

Mrs Eynsford Hill *(to* PICKERING*)*. It's no use. I shall never be able to bring myself to use that word.

Pickering. Dont. It's not compulsory, you know. Youll get on quite well without it.

Mrs Eynsford Hill. Only, Clara is so down on me if I am not positively reeking with the latest slang. Goodbye.

Pickering. Goodbye. *(They shake hands).*

Mrs Eynsford Hill *(to* MRS HIGGINS*)*. You mustnt mind Clara. *(*PICKERING, *catching from her lowered tone that this is not meant for him to hear, discreetly joins* HIGGINS *at the window)* We're so poor! and she gets so few parties, poor child! She doesnt quite know. *(*MRS HIGGINS, *seeing that her eyes are moist, takes her hand sympathetically and goes with her to the door).* But the boy is nice. Dont you think so?

Mrs Higgins. Oh, quite nice. I shall always be delighted to see him.

Mrs Eynsford Hill. Thank you, dear. Goodbye. *(She goes out).*

Higgins *(eagerly)*. Well? Is Eliza presentable? *(He swoops on his mother and drags her to the otto-*

A. Climax

⁇ What is the climax of this highly comic scene? (Eliza's surprising use of a word that was considered totally vulgar in polite society)

B. Satire

⁇ How do Mrs. Hill and Miss Hill respond to Eliza's unconventional behavior? (They think she is behaving in the latest fashion, which the mother mildly disapproves of and the daughter quickly plans to adopt.) What is Shaw satirizing? (The willingness of conventional people to follow others blindly)

A. Irony

❓ At this point, what is ironic about Pickering telling Higgins that Higgins should know himself? (Pickering himself seems to have lost his good sense in his enthusiasm for transforming Eliza.)

B. Character

Mrs. Pearce and Mrs. Higgins see Eliza's situation more clearly than Higgins and Pickering.

❓ Why do you think this is so? (The men have become emotionally involved without their even realizing it.)

C. Character

❓ What is missing from Higgins and Pickering's absorption with Eliza? (They fail to realize that she is a separate person with feelings of her own.)

man, where she sits down in ELIZA's *place with her son on her left).*

[PICKERING *returns to his chair on her right.*]

Mrs Higgins. You silly boy, of course she's not presentable. She's a triumph of your art and of her dressmaker's; but if you suppose for a moment that she doesn't give herself away in every sentence she utters, you must be perfectly cracked about her.

Pickering. But dont you think something might be done? I mean something to eliminate the sanguinary[7] element from her conversation.

Mrs Higgins. Not as long as she is in Henry's hands.

Higgins *(aggrieved).* Do you mean that my language is improper?

Mrs Higgins. No, dearest: it would be quite proper—say on a canal barge; but it would not be proper for her at a garden party.

Higgins *(deeply injured).* Well I must say——

A **Pickering** *(interrupting him).* Come, Higgins: you must learn to know yourself. I havnt heard such language as yours since we used to review the volunteers in Hyde Park twenty years ago.

Higgins *(sulkily).* Oh, well, if you say so, I suppose I dont always talk like a bishop.

Mrs Higgins *(quieting* HENRY *with a touch).* Colonel Pickering: will you tell me what is the exact state of things in Wimpole Street?

Pickering *(cheerfully: as if this completely changed the subject).* Well, I have come to live there with Henry. We work together at my Indian Dialects; and we think it more convenient——

Mrs Higgins. Quite so. I know all about that: it's an excellent arrangement. But where does this girl live?

Higgins. With us, of course. Where should she live?

Mrs Higgins. But on what terms? Is she a servant? If not, what is she?

Pickering *(slowly).* I think I know what you mean, Mrs Higgins.

Higgins. Well, dash me if *I* do! Ive had to work at the girl every day for months to get her to her present pitch. Besides, she's useful. She knows where my things are, and remembers my appointments and so forth.

---

7. **sanguinary** (sang'gwə·ner'ē): bloody; a reference to Eliza's use of the slang term *bloody.*

Mrs Higgins. How does your housekeeper get on with her?

Higgins. Mrs Pearce? Oh, she's jolly glad to get so much taken off her hands; for before Eliza came, she used to have to find things and remind me of my appointments. But she's got some silly bee in her bonnet about Eliza. She keeps saying "You dont think, sir": doesnt she, Pick? **B**

Pickering. Yes: thats the formula. "You dont think, sir." Thats the end of every conversation about Eliza.

Higgins. As if I ever stop thinking about the girl and her confounded vowels and consonants. I'm worn out, thinking about her, and watching her lips and her teeth and her tongue, not to mention her soul, which is the quaintest of the lot.

Mrs Higgins. You certainly are a pretty pair of babies, playing with your live doll.

Higgins. Playing! The hardest job I ever tackled: make no mistake about that, mother. But you have no idea how frightfully interesting it is to take a human being and change her into a quite different human being by creating a new speech for her. It's filling up the deepest gulf that separates class from class and soul from soul. **C**

Pickering *(drawing his chair closer to* MRS HIGGINS *and bending over to her eagerly).* Yes: it's enormously interesting. I assure you, Mrs Higgins, we take Eliza very seriously. Every week—every day almost—there is some new change. *(Closer again)* We keep records of every stage—dozens of gramophone disks and photographs——

Higgins *(assailing her at the other ear).* Yes, by George: it's the most absorbing experiment I ever tackled. She regularly fills our lives up: doesnt she, Pick?

Pickering. We're always talking Eliza.

Higgins. Teaching Eliza.

Pickering. Dressing Eliza.

Mrs Higgins. What!

Higgins. Inventing new Elizas.

Higgins. You know, she has the most extraordinary quickness of ear: ⎫ [*speaking*
Pickering. I assure you, my dear Mrs Higgins, that girl ⎬ *together*]
Higgins. just like a parrot. Ive tried her with every ⎭
Pickering. is a genius. She can play the piano quite beautifully.

Higgins. possible sort of sound that a human being can make—

Pickering. We have taken her to classical concerts and to music

Higgins. Continental dialects, African dialects, Hottentot

Pickering. halls; and it's all the same to her: she plays everything

Higgins. clicks, things it took me years to get hold of; and

Pickering. she hears right off when she comes home, whether it's

Higgins. she picks them up like a shot, right away, as if she had

Pickering. Beethoven and Brahms or Lehar and Lionel Monckton;

Higgins. been at it all her life.

Pickering. though six months ago, she'd never as much as touched a piano——

[speaking together]

Mrs Higgins (*putting her fingers in her ears, as they are by this time shouting one another down with an intolerable noise*). Sh-sh-sh—sh!

[*They stop.*]

Pickering. I beg your pardon. (*He draws his chair back apologetically*).

Higgins. Sorry. When Pickering starts shouting nobody can get a word in edgeways.

Mrs Higgins. Be quiet, Henry. Colonel Pickering: dont you realize that when Eliza walked into Wimpole Street, something walked in with her?

Pickering. Her father did. But Henry soon got rid of him.

Mrs Higgins. It would have been more to the point if her mother had. But as her mother didnt something else did.

Pickering. But what?

Mrs Higgins (*unconsciously dating herself by the word*). A problem.

Pickering. Oh I see. The problem of how to pass her off as a lady.

Higgins. I'll solve that problem. Ive half solved it already.

Mrs Higgins. No, you two infinitely stupid male

creatures: the problem of what is to be done with her afterwards.

Higgins. I dont see anything in that. She can go her own way, with all the advantages I have given her.

Mrs Higgins. The advantages of that poor woman who was here just now! The manners and habits that disqualify a fine lady from earning her own living without giving her a fine lady's income! Is that what you mean?

Pickering (*indulgently, being rather bored*). Oh, that will be all right, Mrs Higgins. (*He rises to go*).

Higgins (*rising also*). We'll find her some light employment.

Pickering. She's happy enough. Dont you worry about her. Goodbye. (*He shakes hands as if he were consoling a frightened child, and makes for the door*).

Higgins. Anyhow, theres no good bothering now. The thing's done. Goodbye, mother. (*He kisses her, and follows* PICKERING).

Pickering (*turning for a final consolation*). There are plenty of openings. We'll do whats right. Goodbye.

Higgins (*to* PICKERING *as they go out together*). Lets take her to the Shakespear exhibition at Earls Court.

Pickering. Yes: lets. Her remarks will be delicious.

Higgins. She'll mimic all the people for us when we get home.

Pickering. Ripping. (*Both are heard laughing as they go downstairs*).

Mrs Higgins (*rises with an impatient bounce, and returns to her work at the writing-table. She sweeps a litter of disarranged papers out of the way; snatches a sheet of paper from her stationery case; and tries resolutely to write. At the third time she gives it up; flings down her pen; grips the table angrily and exclaims*). Oh, men! men!! men!!!

*   *   *

Clearly Eliza will not pass as a duchess yet; and Higgins's bet remains unwon. But the six months are not yet exhausted; and just in time Eliza does actually pass as a princess. For a glimpse of how she did it imagine an Embassy in London one summer evening after dark. The hall door has an awning and a carpet across the sidewalk to the kerb, because a grand reception is in progress. A small crowd is lined up to see the guests arrive.

A. Conflict

[?] What is Mrs. Higgins's concern about Eliza's future? (That she will have the manners of a lady but not the means to live a lady's life) How do the two men respond to her concern? (They are unworried.)

B. Character

[?] What do these remarks by the two men indicate about their feelings for Eliza? (They are amused by her and desire her company.)

A. Discussing the Photograph

❓ What does the expression on Eliza's face in the photograph suggest about her feelings for Higgins at this point in the play? (She both admires and is intimidated by him.)

A

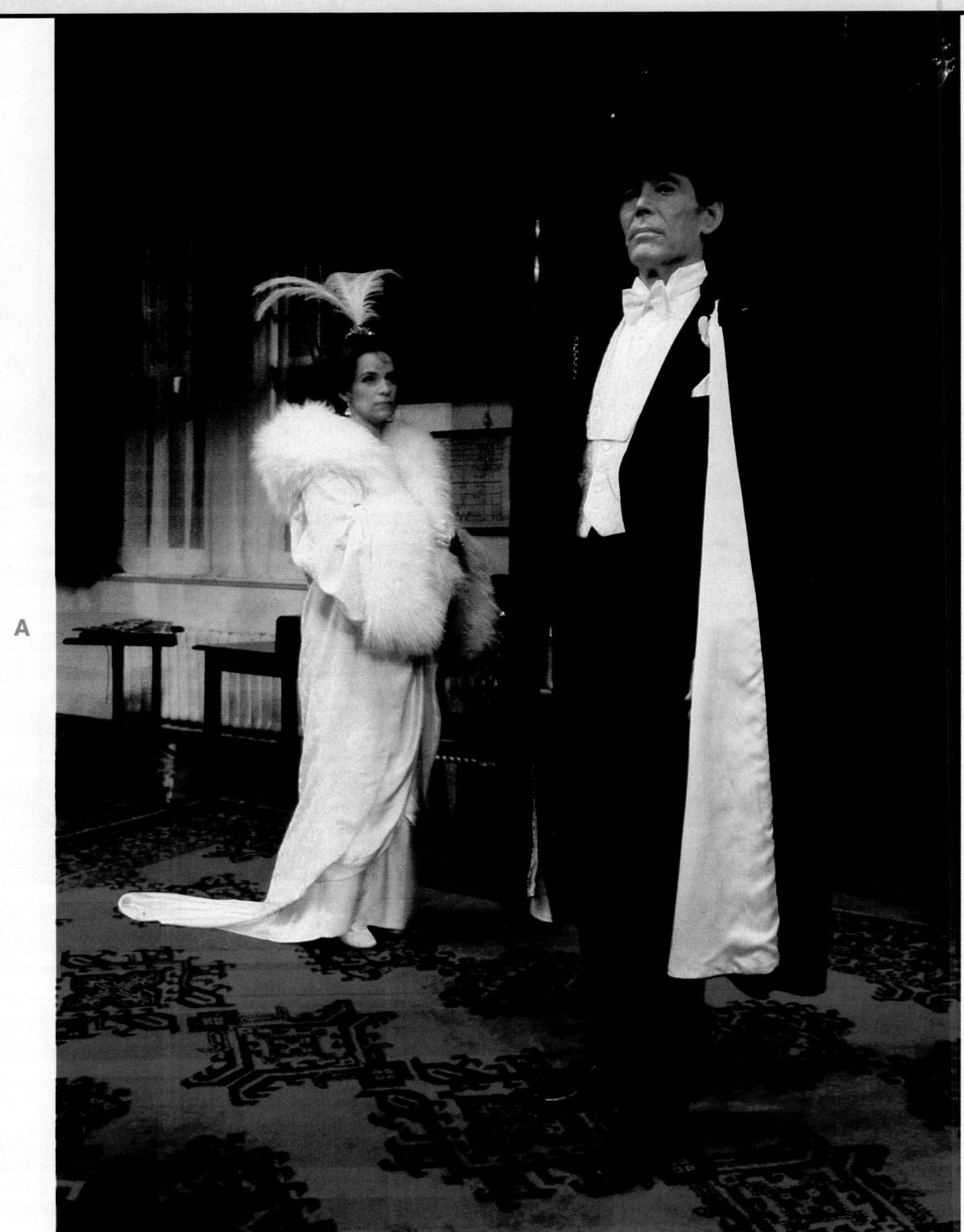

"We shall see. If he finds her out I lose my bet."

READING CHECK TEST: Act Three

1. Mrs. Higgins has an unrealistic, self-centered character like her son. (F)
2. Mrs. Higgins has many of the same concerns about Eliza as Mrs. Pearce had. (T)
3. Eliza is still having great difficulty with her pronunciation. (F)

4. The Eynsford Hill ladies reject Eliza's unusual manners totally. (F)
5. Freddy is thoroughly beguiled by Eliza's charms. (T)

A Rolls-Royce car drives up. Pickering in evening dress, with medals and orders, alights, and hands out Eliza, in opera cloak, evening dress, diamonds, fan, flowers, and all accessories. Higgins follows. The car drives off; and the three go up the steps and into the house, the door opening for them as they approach.

Inside the house they find themselves in a spacious hall from which the grand staircase rises. On the left are the arrangements for the gentlemen's cloaks. The male guests are depositing their hats and wraps there.

On the right is a door leading to the ladies' cloakroom. Ladies are going in cloaked and coming out in splendor. Pickering whispers to Eliza and points out the ladies' room. She goes into it. Higgins and Pickering take off their overcoats and take tickets for them from the attendant.

One of the guests, occupied in the same way, has his back turned. Having taken his ticket, he turns round and reveals himself as an important looking young man with an astonishingly hairy face. He has an enormous moustache, flowing out into luxuriant whiskers. Waves of hair cluster on his brow. His hair is cropped closely at the back, and glows with oil. Otherwise he is very smart. He wears several worthless orders. He is evidently a foreigner, guessable as a whiskered Pandour[8] from Hungary; but in spite of the ferocity of his moustache he is amiable and genially voluble.

Recognizing Higgins, he flings his arms wide apart and approaches him enthusiastically.

Whiskers. Maestro, maestro (*he embraces* Higgins *and kisses him on both cheeks*). You remember me?
Higgins. No I dont. Who the devil are you?
Whiskers. I am your pupil: your first pupil, your best and greatest pupil. I am little Nepommuck, the marvelous boy. I have made your name famous throughout Europe. You teach me phonetic. You cannot forget ME.
Higgins. Why dont you shave?
Nepommuck. I have not your imposing appearance, your chin, your brow. Nobody notices me when I shave. Now I am famous: they call me Hairy Faced Dick.
Higgins. And what are you doing here among all these swells?

8. **Pandour:** an armed servant of a Hungarian nobleman.

Nepommuck. I am interpreter. I speak 32 languages. I am indispensable at these international parties. You are great cockney specialist: you place a man anywhere in London the moment he open his mouth. I place any man in Europe.

[*A footman hurries down the grand staircase and comes to* NEPOMMUCK.]

Footman. You are wanted upstairs. Her Excellency cannot understand the Greek gentleman.
Nepommuck. Thank you, yes, immediately.

[*The footman goes and is lost in the crowd.*]

Nepommuck (*to* HIGGINS). This Greek diplomatist pretends he cannot speak nor understand English. He cannot deceive me. He is the son of a Clerkenwell watchmaker. He speaks English so villainously that he dare not utter a word of it without betraying his origin. I help him to pretend; but I make him pay through the nose. I make them all pay. Ha ha! (*He hurries upstairs*).
Pickering. Is this fellow really an expert? Can he find out Eliza and blackmail her?
Higgins. We shall see. If he finds her out I lose my bet. ⌉ A

[ELIZA *comes from the cloakroom and joins them*.]

Pickering. Well, Eliza, now for it. Are you ready?
Liza. Are you nervous, Colonel?
Pickering. Frightfully. I feel exactly as I felt before my first battle. It's the first time that frightens.
Liza. It is not the first time for me, Colonel. I have done this fifty times—hundreds of times—in my little piggery in Angel Court in my day-dreams. I am in a dream now. Promise me not to let Professor Higgins wake me; for if he does I shall forget everything and talk as I used to in Drury Lane. ⌉ B
Pickering. Not a word, Higgins. (*To* ELIZA) Now ready?
Liza. Ready.
Pickering. Go.

[*They mount the stairs,* HIGGINS *last.* PICKERING *whispers to the footman on the first landing.*]

First Landing Footman. Miss Doolittle, Colonel Pickering, Professor Higgins.
Second Landing Footman. Miss Doolittle, Colonel Pickering, Professor Higgins.

[*At the top of the staircase the Ambassador and his wife, with* NEPOMMUCK *at her elbow, are receiving.*]

A. Plot

? How have Higgins and Pickering decided to settle their wager? (By whether or not Nepommuck can detect Eliza's true origins)

B. Character

? Do you hear a new Eliza in this speech? (Yes) What is different about her expression, beyond her improved pronunciation? (She speaks with sensitive awareness of her past and present situations.)

1. Mrs. Eynsford Hill and her daughter Clara, whom we have seen on the rainy London street in Act One. Later, Colonel Pickering and Freddy Eynsford Hill enter.

2. She says that her aunt was "done in" and that her father was addicted to gin.

Higgins says that it is the new small talk. Freddy is romantically smitten by Eliza.

3. The problem is "what is to be done with her [Eliza] afterwards."

4. Nepommuck, who was Higgins's first pupil, speaks thirty-two languages. He serves as an interpreter at the embassy entertainment. Higgins is afraid he may be able to unmask Eliza because of his knowledge of languages and phonetics.

5. Eliza enters, beautifully dressed with diamonds, flowers, and a fan, and escorted by Higgins and Pickering. Everyone stares at her in admiration, and the Hostess sends Nepommuck to find out all about her. Because of her perfect English, Nepommuck comically makes the assumption that Eliza must be a foreigner, and he pronounces her to be a Hungarian princess.

Higgins wins the bet.

A. Character

? How does Higgins really rate Nepommuck's expertise? (He has a gift for learning languages but has no ability to recognize dialects.)

B. Irony

There are multiple ironies in Nepommuck's calling Eliza a fraud, starting with the fact that he himself is a fraud.

? Look for further ironies in the dialogue that follows. (He says she is not even English but a Hungarian princess trying to conceal her true origins.)

C. Expansion

Point out to students that the Hostess's willingness to take Eliza for a princess parallels the Eynsford Hills' willingness in Act Two to take her speech for the latest fashionable slang. Shaw is revealing in a very humorous way how easily people are misled by appearances and swayed by the opinion of others.

Hostess (taking ELIZA's hand). How d'ye do?

Host (same play). How d'ye do? How d'ye do, Pickering?

Liza (with a beautiful gravity that awes her hostess). How do you do? (She passes on to the drawing room).

Hostess. Is that your adopted daughter, Colonel Pickering? She will make a sensation.

Pickering. Most kind of you to invite her for me. (He passes on).

Hostess (to NEPOMMUCK). Find out all about her.

Nepommuck (bowing). Excellency—— (he goes into the crowd).

Host. How d'ye do, Higgins? You have a rival here tonight. He introduced himself as your pupil. Is he any good?

A **Higgins.** He can learn a language in a fortnight—knows dozens of them. A sure mark of a fool. As a phonetician, no good whatever.

Hostess. How d'ye do, Professor?

Higgins. How do you do? Fearful bore for you this sort of thing. Forgive my part in it. (He passes on).

In the drawing room and its suite of salons the reception is in full swing. Eliza passes through. She is so intent on her ordeal that she walks like a somnambulist in a desert instead of a debutante in a fashionable crowd. They stop talking to look at her, admiring her dress, her jewels, and her strangely attractive self. Some of the younger ones at the back stand on their chairs to see.

The Host and Hostess come in from the staircase and mingle with their guests. Higgins, gloomy and contemptuous of the whole business, comes into the group where they are chatting.

Hostess. Ah, here is Professor Higgins: he will tell us. Tell us all about the wonderful young lady, Professor.

Higgins (almost morosely). What wonderful young lady?

Hostess. You know very well. They tell me there has been nothing like her in London since people stood on their chairs to look at Mrs Langtry.[9]

[NEPOMMUCK joins the group, full of news.]

Hostess. Ah, here you are at last, Nepommuck. Have you found out all about the Doolittle lady?

---

9. **Mrs. Langtry:** Lily Langtry (1852–1929), a famous and beautiful actress of the day.

Nepommuck. I have found out all about her. She is a fraud. **B**

Hostess. A fraud! Oh no.

Nepommuck. YES, yes. She cannot deceive me. Her name cannot be Doolittle.

Higgins. Why?

Nepommuck. Because Doolittle is an English name. And she is not English.

Hostess. Oh, nonsense! She speaks English perfectly.

Nepommuck. Too perfectly. Can you shew me any English woman who speaks English as it should be spoken? Only foreigners who have been taught to speak it speak it well.

Hostess. Certainly she terrified me by the way she said How d'ye do. I had a schoolmistress who talked like that; and I was mortally afraid of her. But if she is not English what is she?

Nepommuck. Hungarian.

All the rest. Hungarian!

Nepommuck. Hungarian. And of royal blood. I am Hungarian. My blood is royal.

Higgins. Did you speak to her in Hungarian?

Nepommuck. I did. She was very clever. She said "Please speak to me in English: I do not understand French." French! She pretends not to know the difference between Hungarian and French. Impossible: she knows both.

Higgins. And the blood royal? How did you find that out?

Nepommuck. Instinct, maestro, instinct. Ony the Magyar races can produce that air of the divine right, those resolute eyes. She is a princess.

Host. What do you say, Professor?

Higgins. I say an ordinary London girl out of the gutter and taught to speak by an expert. I place her in Drury Lane.

Nepommuck. Ha ha ha! Oh, maestro, maestro, you are mad on the subject of cockney dialects. The London gutter is the whole world for you.

Higgins (to the HOSTESS). What does your Excellency say?

Hostess. Oh, of course I agree with Nepommuck. She must be a princess at least. **C**

Host. Not necessarily legitimate, of course. Morganatic[10] perhaps. But that is undoubtedly her class.

Higgins. I stick to my opinion.

---

10. **Morganatic:** a marriage between a member of a royal family and a commoner. Though the marriage is valid, the children do not inherit titles.

Interpreting Meanings

6. Higgins reveals his absent-mindedness and impatience in social situations by flinging himself around the room, stumbling over furniture.

His mother reveals Higgins's absent-mindedness and lack of manners by taking his hat off and presenting it to him.

7. Eliza is becoming more attractive and her speech has become so perfect that she scores a triumph at the embassy. In character, she is portrayed as more romantic and sensitive, especially when she refers to herself as "in a dream."

8. That he is absent-minded and insensitive.

9. They mean that they are working hard to meet the challenges of training her to appear to be a duchess.

Mrs. Higgins is referring to taking Eliza seriously as a human being with feelings and a life of her own.

10. Student answers will vary.

11. Among the possibilities are a romance between Freddy and Eliza (hinted at in Act Two), or an unhappy resolution, in which Higgins might turn Eliza out, after he has won his bet.

12. Higgins flinging himself about the room; his bad manners to the guests; Mrs. Higgins's ironic remarks about her son; Eliza's hilarious remarks about her father and her aunt.

Hostess. Oh, you are incorrigible.

[The group breaks up, leaving HIGGINS *isolated.* PICKERING *joins him.]*

Pickering. Where is Eliza? We must keep an eye on her.

*[*ELIZA *joins them.]*

Liza. I dont think I can bear much more. The people all stare so at me. An old lady has just told me that I speak exactly like Queen Victoria. I am sorry if I have lost your bet. I have done my best; but nothing can make me the same as these people. **A**

Pickering. You have not lost it, my dear. You have won it ten times over.

Higgins. Let us get out of this. I have had enough of chattering to these fools.

Pickering. Eliza is tired; and I am hungry. Let us clear out and have supper somewhere. **B**

Responding to the Play

Analyzing Act Three

Identifying Facts

1. Who are the other guests at Mrs. Higgins's at-home, and where have we seen them before?
2. Eliza's accent and manners are perfect. But what does she say that shocks the other guests—at least some of them? How does Higgins explain Eliza's slang? How does Freddy feel about Eliza?
3. According to Mrs. Higgins, what "problem" walks in the door with Eliza?
4. What role does Nepommuck have in the play at this point?
5. Describe Eliza's triumph at the reception. How is Pickering's bet with Higgins resolved?

Interpreting Meanings

6. **Characters** can be revealed to us by physical activity: by what they say and by what they do, and by the way other characters respond to them. In this act, how does Shaw use physical activity to reveal Higgins's personality? What do his mother's actions in particular reveal about Higgins's nature?
7. How is Eliza changing—in **appearance, speech,** and **character**?
8. What does Mrs. Pearce mean by her comment to Higgins: "You dont think"?
9. What do Higgins and Pickering mean when they assure Mrs. Higgins that they take Eliza seriously? What, on the other hand, is Mrs. Higgins really talking about?
10. How do you feel about Higgins and Pickering at this point in the play?
11. What do you predict is going to happen next? (What are the possibilities?)
12. In *My Fair Lady,* the musical comedy made from *Pygmalion,* the scene at Mrs. Higgins's at-home is a comic triumph. What incongruous elements in that scene would contribute to its comedy? (**Incongruity** refers to the joining of two opposites to create a situation that we don't expect.)

Eliza's costume designed by Ladislas Czettel for the 1956 film version of *Pygmalion.*

A. Irony

❓ What does the audience realize here that Eliza does not? (That she has been accepted and admired) In what ways, which she does not realize, is Eliza different from these society people? (She is capable of feeling honest emotion.)

B. Character

Call students' attention to this expression of concern by Pickering for Eliza's feelings.

Summary of Act Four

Higgins and Pickering are in Higgins's study late at night expressing their relief that the task of transforming Eliza is over. She is feeling very down because Higgins takes her for granted and shows no sensitivity to her feelings. Also, she is uncertain of her position with him now. In his typical self-centered way, Higgins gives orders to Eliza as if she were his servant. She is so enraged that she throws his slippers at him. Later, she manages to provoke him into a temper by threatening to leave. He regains his composure, however, and Eliza leaves the house in a fury. On the street, she meets Freddy, who is in love with her, and they go off together.

A. Character

How is Higgins's behavior about the slippers representative of his general attitude toward Eliza? (He takes her for granted and makes use of her as if she were a servant.)

B. Expansion

This speech and the following underscore Higgins's self-centered disregard for Eliza's feelings.

Act Four

The Wimpole Street laboratory. Midnight. Nobody in the room. The clock on the mantelpiece strikes twelve. The fire is not alight: it is a summer night.

Presently HIGGINS *and* PICKERING *are heard on the stairs.*

Higgins *(calling down to* PICKERING*)*. I say, Pick: lock up, will you? I shant be going out again.
Pickering. Right. Can Mrs Pearce go to bed? We don't want anything more, do we?
Higgins. Lord, no!

[ELIZA *opens the door and is seen on the lighted landing in all the finery in which she has just won* HIGGINS*'s bet for him. She comes to the hearth, and switches on the electric lights there. She is tired: her pallor contrasts strongly with her dark eyes and hair; and her expression is almost tragic. She takes off her cloak; puts her fan and gloves on the piano; and sits down on the bench, brooding and silent.* HIGGINS, *in evening dress, with overcoat and hat, comes in, carrying a smoking jacket which he has picked up downstairs. He takes off the hat and overcoat; throws them carelessly on the newspaper stand; disposes of his coat in the same way; puts on the smoking jacket; and throws himself wearily into the easy-chair at the hearth.* PICKERING, *similarly attired, comes in. He also takes off his hat and overcoat, and is about to throw them on* HIGGINS*'s when he hesitates.*]

Pickering. I say: Mrs Pearce will row if we leave these things lying about in the drawing room.
Higgins. Oh, chuck them over the bannisters into the hall. She'll find them there in the morning and put them away all right. She'll think we were drunk.
Pickering. We are, slightly. Are there any letters?
Higgins. I didnt look. (PICKERING *takes the overcoats and hats and goes downstairs.* HIGGINS *begins half singing half yawning an air from* La Fanciulla del Golden West.[1] *Suddenly he stops and exclaims)* I wonder where the devil my slippers are!

[ELIZA *looks at him darkly; then rises suddenly and leaves the room.*

HIGGINS *yawns again, and resumes his song.*
PICKERING *returns, with the contents of the letterbox in his hand.*]

Pickering. Only circulars, and this coroneted billet-doux[2] for you. (*He throws the circulars into the fender, and posts himself on the hearthrug, with his back to the grate*).
Higgins *(glancing at the billet-doux)*. Money-lender. (*He throws the letter after the circulars*).

[ELIZA *returns with a pair of large down-at-heel slippers. She places them on the carpet before* HIGGINS, *and sits as before without a word.*]

Higgins *(yawning again)*. Oh Lord! What an evening! What a crew! What a silly tomfoolery! (*He raises his shoe to unlace it, and catches sight of the slippers. He stops unlacing and looks at them as if they had appeared there of their own accord*). Oh, theyre there, are they?

A

Pickering *(stretching himself)*. Well, I feel a bit tired. It's been a long day. The garden party, a dinner party, and the reception! Rather too much of a good thing. But youve won your bet, Higgins. Eliza did the trick, and something to spare, eh?
Higgins *(fervently)*. Thank God it's over!

[ELIZA *flinches violently; but they take no notice of her; and she recovers herself and sits stonily as before.*]

Pickering. Were you nervous at the garden party? *I* was. Eliza didnt seem a bit nervous.
Higgins. Oh, she wasnt nervous. I knew she'd be all right. No: it's the strain of putting the job through all these months that has told on me. It was interesting enough at first, while we were at the phonetics; but after that I got deadly sick of it. If I hadnt backed myself to do it I should have chucked the whole thing up two months ago. It was a silly notion: the whole thing has been a bore.

B

Pickering. Oh come! the garden party was frightfully exciting. My heart began beating like anything.
Higgins. Yes, for the first three minutes. But when I saw we were going to win hands down, I felt like a bear in a cage, hanging about doing nothing. The dinner was worse: sitting gorging there for over an hour, with nobody but a damned fool of a fashionable woman to talk to! I tell you, Pick-

---

1. **La Fanciulla del Golden West:** *The Girl of the Golden West,* an opera by Giacomo Puccini.

2. **billet-doux** (bil′ā·dōō′): a love letter.

ering, never again for me. No more artificial duchesses. The whole thing has been simple purgatory.

Pickering. Youve never been broken in properly to the social routine. *(Strolling over to the piano)* I rather enjoy dipping into it occasionally myself: it makes me feel young again. Anyhow, it was a great success: an immense success. I was quite frightened once or twice because Eliza was doing it so well. You see, lots of the real people cant do it at all: theyre such fools that they think style comes by nature to people in their position; and so they never learn. Theres always something professional about doing a thing superlatively well.

Higgins. Yes: thats what drives me mad: the silly people dont know their own silly business. *(Rising)* However, it's over and done with; and now I can go to bed at last without dreading tomorrow.

[ELIZA's *beauty becomes murderous.*]

Pickering. I think I shall turn in too. Still, it's been a great occasion: a triumph for you. Goodnight. *(He goes)*.

Higgins *(following him)*. Goodnight. *(Over his shoulder, at the door)* Put out the lights, Eliza; and tell Mrs Pearce not to make coffee for me in the morning: I'll take tea. *(He goes out)*.

[ELIZA *tries to control herself and feel indifferent as she rises and walks across to the hearth to switch off the lights. By the time she gets there she is on the point of screaming. She sits down in* HIGGINS'S *chair and holds on hard to the arms. Finally she gives way and flings herself furiously on the floor, raging.*]

Higgins *(in despairing wrath outside)*. What the devil have I done with my slippers? *(He appears at the door)*.

Liza *(snatching up the slippers, and hurling them at him one after the other with all her force)*. There are your slippers. And there. Take your slippers; and may you never have a day's luck with them!

Higgins *(astounded)*. What on earth—! *(He comes to her)*. Whats the matter? Get up. *(He pulls her up)*. Anything wrong?

Liza *(breathless)*. Nothing wrong—with you. Ive won your bet for you, havent I? Thats enough for you. *I* dont matter, I suppose.

Higgins. You won my bet! You! Presumptuous insect! *I* won it. What did you throw those slippers at me for?

Liza. Because I wanted to smash your face. I'd like to kill you, you selfish brute. Why didnt you leave me where you picked me out of—in the gutter? You thank God it's all over, and that now you can throw me back again there, do you? *(She crisps her fingers[3] frantically)*.

Higgins *(looking at her in cool wonder)*. The creature is nervous, after all.

Liza *(gives a suffocated scream of fury, and instinctively darts her nails at his face)*!!

Higgins *(catching her wrists)*. Ah! would you? Claws in, you cat. How dare you shew your temper to me? Sit down and be quiet. *(He throws her roughly into the easy-chair)*.

Liza *(crushed by superior strength and weight)*. Whats to become of me? Whats to become of me?

Higgins. How the devil do I know whats to become of you? What does it matter what becomes of you?

Liza. You dont care. I know you dont care. You wouldnt care if I was dead. I'm nothing to you—not so much as them slippers.

Higgins *(thundering)*. Those slippers.

Liza *(with bitter submission)*. Those slippers. I didnt think it made any difference now.

[*A pause.* ELIZA *hopeless and crushed.* HIGGINS *a little uneasy.*]

Higgins *(in his loftiest manner)*. Why have you begun going on like this? May I ask whether you complain of your treatment here?

Liza. No.

Higgins. Has anybody behaved badly to you? Colonel Pickering? Mrs Pearce? Any of the servants?

Liza. No.

Higgins. I presume you don't pretend that *I* have treated you badly?

Liza. No.

Higgins. I am glad to hear it. *(He moderates his tone)*. Perhaps youre tired after the strain of the day. Will you have a glass of champagne? *(He moves toward the door)*.

Liza. No. *(Recollecting her manners)* Thank you.

Higgins *(good-humored again)*. This has been coming on you for some days. I suppose it was natural for you to be anxious about the garden party. But thats all over now. *(He pats her kindly on the shoulder. She writhes)*. There's nothing more to worry about.

---

3. **crisps her fingers:** clenches and unclenches her fists.

A. Irony

❓ What is ironic about Pickering's statement? (He sees the triumph as Higgins's and not Eliza's.) How has he become more like Higgins? (He too seems insensitive to Eliza's feelings.)

B. Conflict and Crisis

Eliza gives way to rage and throws Higgins's slippers at him.

❓ What in his behavior most hurts and enrages her? (His apparent lack of feeling for her as a person)

C. Tone

Note Higgins's change of tone.

❓ What do you think has caused the change? (Eliza has reverted to her former submissiveness.)

Pygmalion, Act Four   1187

1187

A. Conflict
There are feelings between Eliza and Higgins that neither one is acknowledging.
❓ Why does Higgins's expression of relief that the experiment is over make Eliza unhappy? (Because she is no longer sure if he is interested in her and because he is not considering the effort she put in to make the undertaking a success)

Liza. No. Nothing more for you to worry about. *(She suddenly rises and gets away from him by going to the piano bench, where she sits and hides her face).* Oh God! I wish I were dead.

Higgins *(staring after her in sincere surprise).* Why? In heaven's name, why? *(Reasonably, going to her)* Listen to me, Eliza. All this irritation is purely subjective.

Liza. I dont understand. I'm too ignorant.

Higgins. It's only imagination. Low spirits and nothing else. Nobody's hurting you. Nothing's wrong. You go to bed like a good girl and sleep it off. Have a little cry and say your prayers: that will make you comfortable.

Liza. I heard your prayers. "Thank God it's over!" **A**

Higgins *(impatiently).* Well, dont you thank God it's all over? Now you are free and can do what you like.

Liza *(pulling herself together in desperation).* What am I fit for? What have you left me fit for? Where am I to go? What am I to do? Whats to become of me?

Higgins *(enlightened, but not at all impressed).* Oh, thats whats worrying you, is it? *(He thrusts his hands into his pockets, and walks about in his usual manner, rattling the contents of his pockets, as if condescending to a trivial subject out of pure*

"If these belonged to me instead of to the jeweler, I'd ram them down your ungrateful throat."

kindness). I shouldnt bother about it if I were you. I should imagine you won't have much difficulty in settling yourself somewhere or other, though I hadnt quite realized that you were going away. *(She looks quickly at him: he does not look at her, but examines the dessert stand on the piano and decides that he will eat an apple).* You might marry, you know. *(He bites a large piece out of the apple and munches it noisily).* You see, Eliza, all men are not confirmed old bachelors like me and the Colonel. Most men are the marrying sort (poor devils!); and youre not bad-looking: it's quite a pleasure to look at you sometimes—not now, of course, because youre crying and looking as ugly as the very devil; but when youre all right and quite yourself, youre what I should call attractive. That is, to the people in the marrying line, you understand. You go to bed and have a good nice rest; and then get up and look at yourself in the glass; and you wont feel so cheap.

[ELIZA *again looks at him, speechless, and does not stir.*

The look is quite lost on him: he eats his apple with a dreamy expression of happiness, as it is quite a good one.]

Higgins *(a genial afterthought occurring to him).* I daresay my mother could find some chap or other who would do very well.
Liza. We were above that at the corner of Tottenham Court Road.
Higgins *(waking up).* What do you mean?
Liza. I sold flowers. I didnt sell myself. Now youve made a lady of me I'm not fit to sell anything else. I wish youd left me where you found me.
Higgins *(slinging the core of the apple decisively into the grate).* Tosh, Eliza. Dont you insult human relations by dragging all this cant[4] about buying and selling into it. You neednt marry the fellow if you don't like him.
Liza. What else am I to do?
Higgins. Oh, lots of things. What about your old idea of a florist's shop? Pickering could set you up in one: he has lots of money. *(Chuckling)* He'll have to pay for all those togs you have been wearing today; and that, with the hire of the jewelry, will make a big hole in two hundred pounds. Why,

six months ago you would have thought it the millennium[5] to have a flower shop of your own. Come! youll be all right. I must clear off to bed: I'm devilish sleepy. By the way, I came down for something: I forget what it was.
Liza. Your slippers.
Higgins. Oh yes, of course. You shied them at me. *(He picks them up, and is going out when she rises and speaks to him).*
Liza. Before you go, sir——
Higgins *(dropping the slippers in his surprise at her calling him Sir).* Eh?
Liza. Do my clothes belong to me or to Colonel Pickering?
Higgins *(coming back into the room as if her question were the very climax of unreason).* What the devil use would they be to Pickering?
Liza. He might want them for the next girl you pick up to experiment on.
Higgins *(shocked and hurt).* Is that the way you feel towards us?
Liza. I dont want to hear anything more about that. All I want to know is whether anything belongs to me. My own clothes were burnt.
Higgins. But what does it matter? Why need you start bothering about that in the middle of the night?
Liza. I want to know what I may take away with me. I don't want to be accused of stealing.
Higgins *(now deeply wounded).* Stealing! You shouldnt have said that, Eliza. That shews a want of feeling.
Liza. I'm sorry. I'm only a common ignorant girl; and in my station I have to be careful. There cant be any feelings between the like of you and the like of me. Please will you tell me what belongs to me and what doesnt?
Higgins *(very sulky).* You may take the whole damned houseful if you like. Except the jewels. Theyre hired. Will that satisfy you? *(He turns on his heel and is about to go in extreme dudgeon[6]).*
Liza *(drinking in his emotion like nectar, and nagging him to provoke a further supply).* Stop, please. *(She takes off her jewels).* Will you take these to your room and keep them safe? I dont want to run the risk of their being missing.
Higgins *(furious).* Hand them over. *(She puts them into his hands).* If these belonged to me instead

4. **cant:** insincere or meaningless talk.
5. **millenium:** a golden age.
6. **dudgeon:** anger; resentment.

A. Character
❓ What hint is there in this speech that Higgins feels more for Eliza than he is aware of? (He had not considered her going away.)

B. Evaluating Motivation
❓ Why is Eliza pleased when she manages to provoke Higgins? (She knows that she has penetrated his seeming indifference to her.)

READING CHECK TEST: Act Four
1. Both Higgins and Pickering are guilty of insensitivity to Eliza's feelings. (T)
2. Eliza has become helpful to Higgins in practical domestic matters. (T)
3. Eliza is angry at Higgins because he pays too much attention to her. (F)
4. Higgins is indifferent to the idea of Eliza leaving his house. (F)
5. Freddy is ashamed of Eliza's low origins. (F)

A. Conflict

❓ Why does Eliza feel she has triumphed over Higgins this time? (Because she has provoked Higgins into losing his temper and revealing his strong feelings for her.)

B. Setting

Point out that this detailed description of Eliza's room in Higgins's house, which is in such sharp contrast to her old room, underscores how much her situation has changed.

C. Character

❓ Why does Eliza fall back into her former manner of speaking here? (Because she was frightened by the policeman) How much do you think Eliza has really changed? (She has changed on the surface but is still the same person underneath.)

of to the jeweler, I'd ram them down your ungrateful throat. (*He perfunctorily thrusts them into his pockets, unconsciously decorating himself with the protruding ends of the chains*).

Liza (*taking a ring off*). This ring isnt the jeweler's: it's the one you bought me in Brighton. I dont want it now. (*Higgins dashes the ring violently into the fireplace, and turns on her so threateningly that she crouches over the piano with her hands over her face, and exclaims*) Dont you hit me.

Higgins. Hit you! You infamous creature, how dare you accuse me of such a thing? It is you who have hit me. You have wounded me to the heart.

Liza (*thrilling with hidden joy*). I'm glad. Ive got a little of my own back, anyhow.

Higgins (*with dignity, in his finest professional style*). You have caused me to lose my temper: a thing that has hardly ever happened to me before. I prefer to say nothing more tonight. I am going to bed.

Liza (*pertly*). Youd better leave a note for Mrs Pearce about the coffee; for she wont be told by me.

Higgins (*formally*). Damn Mrs Pearce; and damn the coffee; and damn you; and (*wildly*) damn my own folly in having lavished my hard-earned knowledge and the treasure of my regard and intimacy on a heartless guttersnipe. (*He goes out with impressive decorum, and spoils it by slamming the door savagely*).

[ELIZA *goes down on her knees on the hearthrug to look for the ring. When she finds it she considers for a moment what to do with it. Finally she flings it down on the dessert stand and goes upstairs in a tearing rage.*]

* * *

[*The furniture of* ELIZA's *room has been increased by a big wardrobe and a sumptuous dressing-table. She comes in and switches on the electric light. She goes to the wardrobe; opens it; and pulls out a walking dress, a hat, and a pair of shoes, which she throws on the bed. She takes off her evening dress and shoes; then takes a padded hanger from the wardrobe; adjusts it carefully in the evening dress; and hangs it in the wardrobe, which she shuts with a slam. She puts on her walking shoes, her walking dress, and hat. She takes her wrist watch from the dressing-table and fastens it on. She pulls on her gloves; takes her*]

vanity bag; and looks into it to see that her purse is there before hanging it on her wrist. She makes for the door. Every movement expresses her furious resolution.

She takes a last look at herself in the glass.

She suddenly puts out her tongue at herself; then leaves the room, switching off the electric light at the door.

Meanwhile, in the street outside, FREDDY EYNSFORD HILL, *lovelorn, is gazing up at the second floor, in which one of the windows is still lighted.*

The light goes out.]

Freddy. Goodnight, darling, darling, darling.

[ELIZA *comes out, giving the door a considerable bang behind her.*]

Liza. Whatever are you doing here?

Freddy. Nothing. I spend most of my nights here. It's the only place where I'm happy. Dont laugh at me, Miss Doolittle.

Liza. Dont you call me Miss Doolittle, do you hear? Liza's good enough for me. (*She breaks down and grabs him by the shoulders*) Freddy: you dont think I'm a heartless guttersnipe, do you?

Freddy. Oh no, no, darling: how can you imagine such a thing? You are the loveliest, dearest——

[*He loses all self-control and smothers her with kisses. She, hungry for comfort, responds. They stand there in one another's arms.*

An elderly police constable arrives.]

Constable (*scandalized*). Now then! Now then!! Now then!!!

[*They release one another hastily.*]

Freddy. Sorry, constable. Weve only just become engaged.

[*They run away.*]

The constable shakes his head, reflecting on his own courtship and on the vanity of human hopes. He moves off in the opposite direction with slow professional steps.

The flight of the lovers takes them to Cavendish Square. There they halt to consider their next move.

Liza (*out of breath*). He didnt half give me a fright, that copper. But you answered him proper.
Freddy. I hope I havnt taken you out of your way. Where were you going?

ANALYZING ACT FOUR
Identifying Facts
1. Eliza is angry and hurt because Higgins and Pickering do not give her any of the credit for her "triumph."
2. Higgins has been selfish and cruel to raise her hopes in life without thinking of the consequences to her.
3. Freddy rescues her.

Interpreting Meanings
4. She keeps his appointments; he can't find any of his possessions without her help; she has "wounded him to the heart" by causing him to lose his temper.
5. Eliza infuriates Higgins by handing back the things he had given her, including a ring.
    He has lost the air of calm indifference to Eliza's fate.

6. The crisis is Eliza's angry departure from the house without telling anyone of her plans.
7. We continue to think about Eliza's future and of the outcome of Freddy's love for her. We also wonder if Higgins will fall for Eliza, in spite of himself.
8. Student answers will vary. Ask the students to discuss and support their opinions.

Liza. To the river.

Freddy. What for?

Liza. To make a hole in it.

Freddy (*horrified*). Eliza, darling. What do you mean? What's the matter?

Liza. Never mind. It doesn't matter now. Theres nobody in the world now but you and me, is there?

Freddy. Not a soul.

[*They indulge in another embrace, and are again surprised by a much younger constable.*]

Second Constable. Now then, you two! What's this? Where do you think you are? Move along here, double quick.

Freddy. As you say, sir, double quick.

[*They run away again, and are in Hanover Square before they stop for another conference.*]

Freddy. I had no idea the police were so devilishly prudish.

Liza. It's their business to hunt girls off the streets.

Freddy. We must go somewhere. We cant wander about the streets all night.

Liza. Cant we? I think it'd be lovely to wander about forever.

Freddy. Oh, darling.

[*They embrace again, oblivious of the arrival of a crawling taxi. It stops.*]

Taximan. Can I drive you and the lady anywhere, sir?

[*They start asunder.*]

Liza. Oh, Freddy, a taxi. The very thing.

Freddy. But, damn it, Ive no money.

Liza. I have plenty. The Colonel thinks you should never go out without ten pounds in your pocket. Listen. We'll drive about all night; and in the morning I'll call on old Mrs Higgins and ask her what I ought to do. I'll tell you all about it in the cab. And the police wont touch us there.

Freddy. Righto! Ripping. (*To the* TAXIMAN). Wimbledon Common. (*They drive off*).

A. Responding
? Do you think Eliza is really in love with Freddy and has forgotten Higgins? Who do you think would be the better man for her?

B. Predicting Outcomes
? What do you think Mrs. Higgins will advise Eliza to do? How do you think the play will end?

Responding to the Play

Analyzing Act Four

Identifying Facts

1. During this act, Eliza stands onstage saying nothing for a very long time, yet we soon begin to pay more attention to how she is reacting than to what is being said. In his stage directions, how does Shaw show us Eliza's mood and prepare us for what she will eventually say?
2. From Eliza's point of view, what has Higgins done that is wrong?
3. Who "rescues" Eliza as she is about to "make a hole in the river"?

Interpreting Meanings

4. What small indications does Higgins give in Acts Three and Four that he has become attached to Eliza?
5. Plays often move through a series of **reversals**. At the end of this act, a reversal makes us feel that Higgins has in some way been toppled and that Eliza has gained the upper hand. How does she do this? Why is she so happy that Higgins loses his temper?

Set designed by Oliver Smith for the Embassy reception scene in *My Fair Lady*.

6. A **crisis** in a play is a turning point—a moment when the action begins to move toward either a happy ending or a tragic one. What is the crisis in this brief act?
7. The long game is over, and Higgins has won his bet. Why do we continue to be interested in the play? What questions has Shaw put in our minds?
8. How did you feel about Higgins's behavior in this act?

Summary of Act Five
Higgins and Pickering rush to Mrs. Higgins's house alarmed because Eliza has left. Then Eliza's father arrives, dressed for his wedding, with the sad tale of how he has inherited wealth and is now doomed to a sober life of respectability. Mrs. Higgins announces that Eliza is upstairs and chides Higgins and Pickering for the complacent way they have treated Eliza. Eliza confronts the two, praising Pickering for his gentlemanly behavior toward her and sparring with Higgins over his high-handedness. She tries to get Higgins to admit that he needs her but fails. She then tells him that she is going to marry Freddy and give speech lessons. This enrages Higgins, but he gets the last word by refusing to believe that she is really going for good.

A. Character

? What reason does Higgins give for wanting Eliza back? (He needs her to organize his life.) What other reasons might there be for his disturbance over her departure? (He is emotionally attached to her.)

B. Comparing Characters

? What reason does Pickering give for regretting Eliza's departure? (He is concerned about her feelings.) How does it contrast with Higgins's stated concern? (Higgins is apparently only concerned with his own convenience.)

Act Five

MRS HIGGINS's *drawing room. She is at her writing-table as before. The parlormaid comes in.*

The Parlormaid *(at the door).* Mr Henry, maam, is downstairs with Colonel Pickering.
Mrs Higgins. Well, shew them up.
The Parlormaid. Theyre using the telephone, maam. Telephoning to the police, I think.
Mrs Higgins What!
The Parlormaid *(coming further in and lowering her voice).* Mr Henry is in a state, maam. I thought I'd better tell you.
Mrs Higgins. If you had told me that Mr Henry was not in a state it would have been more surprising. Tell them to come up when theyve finished with the police. I suppose he's lost something.
The Parlormaid. Yes, maam *(going).*
Mrs Higgins. Go upstairs and tell Miss Doolittle that Mr Henry and the Colonel are here. Ask her not to come down til I send for her.
The Parlormaid. Yes, maam.

[HIGGINS *bursts in. He is, as the parlormaid has said, in a state.*]

Higgins. Look here, mother: heres a confounded thing!
Mrs Higgins. Yes, dear. Good morning. *(He checks his impatience and kisses her, whilst the parlormaid goes out).* What is it?
Higgins. Eliza's bolted.[1]
Mrs Higgins *(calmly continuing her writing).* You must have frightened her.
Higgins. Frightened her! nonsense! She was left last night, as usual, to turn out the lights and all that; and instead of going to bed she changed her clothes and went right off: her bed wasnt slept in. She came in a cab for her things before seven this morning; and that fool Mrs Pearce let her have them without telling me a word about it. What am I to do?
Mrs Higgins. Do without, I'm afraid, Henry. The girl has a perfect right to leave if she chooses.

A **Higgins** *(wandering distractedly across the room).* But I cant find anything. I dont know what appointments Ive got. I'm—— (PICKERING *comes in.*

---

1. **bolted:** run away suddenly.

MRS HIGGINS *puts down her pen and turns away from the writing-table).*
Pickering *(shaking hands).* Good morning, Mrs Higgins. Has Henry told you? *(He sits down on the ottoman).*
Higgins. What does that ass of an inspector say? Have you offered a reward?
Mrs Higgins *(rising in indignant amazement).* You dont mean to say you have set the police after Eliza?
Higgins. Of course. What are the police for? What else could we do? *(He sits in the Elizabethan chair).*
Pickering. The inspector made a lot of difficulties. I really think he suspected us of some improper purpose.
Mrs Higgins. Well, of course he did. What right have you to go to the police and give the girl's name as if she were a thief, or a lost umbrella, or something? Really! *(She sits down again, deeply vexed).*
Higgins. But we want to find her.
Pickering. We cant let her go like this, you know, Mrs. Higgins. What were we to do? **B**
Mrs Higgins. You have no more sense, either of you, than two children. Why——

[*The parlormaid comes in and breaks off the conversation.*]

The Parlormaid. Mr Henry: a gentleman wants to see you very particular. He's been sent on from Wimpole Street.
Higgins. Oh, bother! I cant see anyone now. Who is it?
The Parlormaid. A Mr Doolittle, sir.
Pickering. Doolittle! Do you mean the dustman?
The Parlormaid. Dustman! Oh no, sir: a gentleman.
Higgins *(springing up excitedly).* By George, Pick, it's some relative of hers that she's gone to. Somebody we know nothing about. *(To the parlormaid)* Send him up, quick.
The Parlormaid. Yes, sir. *(She goes).*
Higgins *(eagerly, going to his mother).* Genteel relatives! now we shall hear something. *(He sits down in the Chippendale chair).*
Mrs Higgins. Do you know any of her people?
Pickering. Only her father: the fellow we told you about.
The Parlormaid *(announcing).* Mr Doolittle. *(She withdraws).*

[DOOLITTLE *enters. He is resplendently dressed as for a fashionable wedding, and might, in fact, be the bridegroom. A flower in his buttonhole, a dazzling silk hat, and patent leather shoes complete the effect. He is too concerned with the business he has come on to notice* MRS HIGGINS. *He walks straight to* HIGGINS, *and accosts him with vehement reproach.*]

Doolittle (*indicating his own person*). See here! Do you see this? You done this.

Higgins. Done what, man?

Doolittle. This, I tell you. Look at it. Look at this hat. Look at this coat.

Pickering. Has Eliza been buying you clothes?

Doolittle. Eliza! not she. Why would she buy me clothes?

Mrs Higgins. Good morning, Mr Doolittle. Wont you sit down?

Doolittle (*taken aback as he becomes conscious that he has forgotten his hostess*). Asking your pardon, maam. (*He approaches her and shakes her proffered hand*). Thank you. (*He sits down on the ottoman, on* PICKERING's *right*). I am that full of what has happened to me that I cant think of anything else.

Higgins. What the dickens has happened to you?

Doolittle. I shouldnt mind if it had only happened to me: anything might happen to anybody and nobody to blame but Providence, as you might say. But this is something that you done to me: yes, you, Enry Iggins.

Higgins. Have you found Eliza?

Doolittle. Have you lost her?

Higgins. Yes.

Doolittle. You have all the luck, you have. I aint found her; but she'll find me quick enough now after what you done to me.

Mrs Higgins. But what has my son done to you, Mr Doolittle?

Doolittle. Done to me! Ruined me. Destroyed my happiness. Tied me up and delivered me into the hands of middle class morality.

Higgins (*rising intolerantly and standing over* DOOLITTLE). Youre raving. Youre drunk. Youre mad. I gave you five pounds. After that I had two conversations with you, at half-a-crown an hour. Ive never seen you since.

Doolittle. Oh! Drunk am I? Mad am I? Tell me this. Did you or did you not write a letter to an old blighter in America that was giving five mil-

lions to found Moral Reform Societies all over the world, and that wanted you to invent a universal language for him?

Higgins. What! Ezra D. Wannafeller! He's dead. (*He sits down again carelessly*).

Doolittle. Yes: he's dead; and I'm done for. Now did you or did you not write a letter to him to say that the most original moralist at present in England, to the best of your knowledge, was Alfred Doolittle, a common dustman?

Higgins. Oh, after your first visit I remember making some silly joke of the kind.

Doolittle. Ah! You may well call it a silly joke. It put the lid on me right enough. Just give him the chance he wanted to shew that Americans is not like us: that they reckonize and respect merit in every class of life, however humble. Them words is in his blooming will, in which, Henry Higgins, thanks to your silly joking, he leaves me a share in his Pre-digested Cheese Trust worth three thousand a year on condition that I lecture for his Wannafeller Moral Reform World League as often as they ask me up to six times a year.

Higgins. The devil he does! Whew! (*Brightening suddenly*) What a lark!

Pickering. A safe thing for you, Doolittle. They wont ask you twice.

Doolittle. It aint the lecturing I mind. I'll lecture them blue in the face, I will, and not turn a hair. It's making a gentleman of me that I object to. Who asked him to make a gentleman of me? I was happy. I was free. I touched pretty nigh everybody for money when I wanted it, same as I touched you, Enry Iggins. Now I am worrited; tied neck and heels; and everybody touches me for money. It's a fine thing for you, says my solicitor.[2] Is it? says I. You mean it's a good thing for you, I says. When I was a poor man and had a solicitor once when they found a pram in the dust cart, he got me off, and got shut of me and got me shut of him as quick as he could. Same with the doctors: used to shove me out of the hospital before I could hardly stand on my legs, and nothing to pay. Now they finds out that I'm not a healthy man and cant live unless they looks after me twice a day. In the house I'm not let do a hand's turn for myself: somebody else must do it and touch me for it. A year ago I hadnt a relative in the world except two or three that wouldnt speak to me. Now Ive

---

2. **solicitor:** lawyer.

A. Plot

Like Eliza, her father has undergone a personal transformation— and his metamorphosis also has had some unexpected results.

? What are some of these changes? (He is well-dressed, sought out by the hard-up, getting married, and concerned with security in his old age.)

B. Plot

? How did Mr. Doolittle come into money? (He inherited it from a wealthy American.) How was Higgins involved? (He had praised Doolittle as an "original moralist" in a letter to the wealthy man.)

C. Character

As in his previous appearance, Doolittle overturns all conventional expectations.

? Why does he complain about his new-found wealth? (He now has responsibilities and worries.)

A. Responding

? Do you think Doolittle's inability to give up his inheritance reveals him to be a fraudulent windbag who really welcomes his new wealth, or do you think he really feels trapped?

"Now, now, Enry Iggins! Have some consideration for my feelings as a middle class man."

fifty, and not a decent week's wages among the lot of them. I have to live for others and not for myself: thats middle class morality. You talk of losing Eliza. Dont you be anxious: I bet she's on my doorstep by this: she that could support herself easy by selling flowers if I wasnt respectable. And the next one to touch me will be you, Enry Iggins. I'll have to learn to speak middle class language from you, instead of speaking proper English. Thats where youll come in; and I daresay thats what you done it for.

Mrs Higgins. But, my dear Mr Doolittle, you need not suffer all this if you are really in earnest. Nobody can force you to accept this bequest. You can repudiate it. Isnt that so, Colonel Pickering?

Pickering. I believe so.

Doolittle *(softening his manner in deference to her sex)*. Thats the tragedy of it, maam. It's easy to say chuck it; but I havnt the nerve. Which of us has? We're all intimidated. Intimidated, maam: thats what we are. What is there for me if I chuck it but the workhouse in my old age? I have to dye my hair already to keep my job as a dustman. If I was one of the deserving poor, and had put by a bit, I could chuck it; but then why should I, acause the deserving poor might as well be millionaires for all the happiness they ever has. They dont know what happiness is. But I, as one of the undeserving poor, have nothing between me and the pauper's uniform but this here blasted three thousand a year that shoves me into the middle class. (Excuse the expression, maam; youd use it yourself if you had my provocation.) Theyve got you every way you turn: it's a choice between the Skilly of the workhouse and the Char Bydis[3] of the middle class; and I havnt the nerve for the workhouse. Intimidated: thats what I am. Broke. Bought up. Happier men than me will call for my dust, and touch me for their tip; and I'll look on helpless, and envy them. And thats what your son has brought me to. *(He is overcome by emotion).*

Mrs Higgins. Well, I'm very glad youre not going

---

3. **Skilly . . . Char Bydis:** Doolittle means Scylla (a dangerous rock) and Charybdis (a whirlpool) in the straits between Sicily and the Italian mainland. To have to "sail between Scylla and Charybdis" means to be in a very tight or dangerous spot.

to do anything foolish, Mr Doolittle. For this solves the problem of Eliza's future. You can provide for her now.

Doolittle (*with melancholy resignation*). Yes, maam: I'm expected to provide for everyone now, out of three thousand a year.

Higgins (*jumping up*). Nonsense! he cant provide for her. He shant provide for her. She doesnt belong to him. I paid him five pounds for her. Doolittle: either youre an honest man or a rogue.

Doolittle (*tolerantly*). A little of both, Henry, like the rest of us: a little of both.

Higgins. Well, you took that money for the girl; and you have no right to take her as well.

Mrs Higgins. Henry: dont be absurd. If you want to know where Eliza is, she is upstairs.

Higgins (*amazed*). Upstairs!!! Then I shall jolly soon fetch her downstairs. (*He makes resolutely for the door*).

Mrs. Higgins (*rising and following him*). Be quiet, Henry. Sit down.

Higgins. I——

Mrs Higgins. Sit down, dear; and listen to me.

Higgins. Oh, very well, very well, very well. (*He throws himself ungraciously on the ottoman, with his face towards the windows*). But I think you might have told us this half an hour ago.

Mrs. Higgins. Eliza came to me this morning. She told me of the brutal way you two treated her.

Higgins (*bouncing up again*). What!

Pickering (*rising also*). My dear Mrs Higgins, she's been telling you stories. We didnt treat her brutally. We hardly said a word to her; and we parted on particularly good terms. (*Turning on* HIGGINS) Higgins: did you bully her after I went to bed?

Higgins. Just the other way about. She threw my slippers in my face. She behaved in the most outrageous way. I never gave her the slightest provocation. The slippers came bang into my face the moment I entered the room—before I had uttered a word. And used perfectly awful language.

Pickering (*astonished*). But why? What did we do to her?

Mrs Higgins. I think I know pretty well what you did. The girl is naturally rather affectionate, I think. Isnt she, Mr Doolittle?

Doolittle. Very tender-hearted, maam. Takes after me.

Mrs Higgins. Just so. She had become attached to you both. She worked very hard for you, Henry. I dont think you quite realize what anything in the nature of brain work means to a girl of her class. Well, it seems that when the great day of trial came, and she did this wonderful thing for you without making a single mistake, you two sat there and never said a word to her, but talked together of how glad you were that it was all over and how you had been bored with the whole thing. And then you were surprised because she threw your slippers at you! *I* should have thrown the fire-irons at you.

Higgins. We said nothing except that we were tired and wanted to go to bed. Did we, Pick?

Pickering (*shrugging his shoulders*). That was all.

Mrs Higgins (*ironically*). Quite sure?

Pickering. Absolutely. Really, that was all.

Mrs Higgins. You didnt thank her, or pet her, or admire her, or tell her how splendid she'd been.

Higgins (*impatiently*). But she knew all about that. We didnt make speeches to her, if thats what you mean.

Pickering (*conscience stricken*). Perhaps we were a little inconsiderate. Is she very angry?

Mrs Higgins (*returning to her place at the writing-table*). Well, I'm afraid she wont go back to Wimpole Street, especially now that Mr Doolittle is able to keep up the position you have thrust on her; but she says she is quite willing to meet you on friendly terms and to let bygones be bygones.

Higgins (*furious*). Is she, by George? Ho!

Mrs Higgins. If you promise to behave yourself, Henry, I'll ask her to come down. If not, go home; for you have taken up quite enough of my time.

Higgins. Oh, all right. Very well. Pick: you behave yourself. Let us put on our best Sunday manners for this creature that we picked out of the mud. (*He flings himself sulkily into the Elizabethan chair*).

Doolittle (*remonstrating*). Now, now, Enry Iggins! Have some consideration for my feelings as a middle class man.

Mrs Higgins. Remember your promise, Henry. (*She presses the bell-button on the writing-table*). Mr Doolittle: will you be so good as to step out on the balcony for a moment. I dont want Eliza to have the shock of your news until she has made it up with these two gentlemen. Would you mind?

Doolittle. As you wish, lady. Anything to help Henry to keep her off my hands. (*He disappears through the window*).

[*The parlormaid answers the bell.* PICKERING *sits down in* DOOLITTLE's *place.*]

A. Irony
? What ironic truth is contained in Pickering's protestation? (It is true that they rarely spoke to her about what she was feeling or what was important to her.)

B. Character
Call students' attention to Mrs. Higgins's clear-sightedness. She is the only character who is level-headed enough to see the whole picture and to explain it to the blinder characters, like her son and Pickering.

C. Predicting Outcomes
? On the basis of his reactions to his mother's explanation of Eliza's behavior, do you think Higgins will change his manner toward Eliza?

A. Character

? How does Higgins behave toward Eliza in this scene? (Bullying) Is his behavior different from before? (No) How is Eliza behaving? (Coolly)

B. Theme

Here Eliza states what she believes good manners to be.

? What is her view? (Self-control and consistent courtesy)

Mrs Higgins. Ask Miss Doolittle to come down, please.

The Parlormaid. Yes, maam. *(She goes out).*

Mrs Higgins. Now, Henry: be good.

Higgins. I am behaving myself perfectly.

Pickering. He is doing his best, Mrs Higgins.

[*A pause.* HIGGINS *throws back his head; stretches out his legs; and begins to whistle.*]

Mrs Higgins. Henry, dearest, you dont look at all nice in that attitude.

Higgins *(pulling himself together).* I was not trying to look nice, mother.

Mrs Higgins. It doesn't matter, dear. I only wanted to make you speak.

Higgins. Why?

Mrs Higgins. Because you cant speak and whistle at the same time.

[HIGGINS *groans. Another very trying pause.*]

Higgins *(springing up, out of patience).* Where the devil is that girl? Are we to wait here all day?

[ELIZA *enters, sunny, self-possessed, and giving a staggeringly convincing exhibition of ease of manner. She carries a little work-basket, and is very much at home.* PICKERING *is too much taken aback to rise.*]

Liza. How do you do, Professor Higgins? Are you quite well?

Higgins *(choking).* Am I—— *(He can say no more).*

Liza. But of course you are: you are never ill. So glad to see you again, Colonel Pickering. *(He rises hastily; and they shake hands).* Quite chilly this morning, isnt it? *(She sits down on his left. He sits besides her).*

Higgins. Dont you dare try this game on me. I taught it to you; and it doesnt take me in. Get up and come home; and dont be a fool.

[ELIZA *takes a piece of needlework from her basket, and begins to stitch at it, without taking the least notice of this outburst.*]

Mrs Higgins. Very nicely put, indeed, Henry. No woman could resist such an invitation.

Higgins. You let her alone, mother. Let her speak for herself. You will jolly soon see whether she has an idea that I havnt put into her head or a word that I havnt put into her mouth. I tell you I have created this thing out of the squashed cabbage leaves of Covent Garden; and now she pre-

tends to play the fine lady with me.

Mrs Higgins *(placidly).* Yes, dear; but youll sit down, wont you?

[HIGGINS *sits down again, savagely.*]

Liza *(to* PICKERING, *taking no apparent notice of* HIGGINS, *and working away deftly).* Will you drop me altogether now that the experiment is over, Colonel Pickering?

Pickering. Oh dont. You mustnt think of it as an experiment. It shocks me, somehow.

Liza. Oh, I'm only a squashed cabbage leaf—

Pickering *(impulsively).* No.

Liza *(continuing quietly).* —but I owe so much to you that I should be very unhappy if you forgot me.

Pickering. It's very kind of you to say so, Miss Doolittle.

Liza. It's not because you paid for my dresses. I know you are generous to everybody with money. But it was from you that I learnt really nice manners; and that is what makes one a lady, isnt it? You see it was so very difficult for me with the example of Professor Higgins always before me. I was brought up to be just like him, unable to control myself, and using bad language on the slightest provocation. And I should never have known that ladies and gentlemen didnt behave like that if you hadn't been there.

Higgins. Well!!

Pickering. Oh, thats only his way, you know. He doesnt mean it.

Liza. Oh, *I* didnt mean it either, when I was a flower girl. It was only my way. But you see I did it; and thats what makes the difference after all.

Pickering. No doubt. Still, he taught you to speak; and I couldnt have done that, you know.

Liza *(trivially).* Of course: that is his profession.

Higgins. Damnation!

Liza *(continuing).* It was just like learning to dance in the fashionable way: there was nothing more than that in it. But do you know what began my real education?

Pickering. What?

Liza *(stopping her work for a moment).* Your calling me Miss Doolittle that day when I first came to Wimpole Street. That was the beginning of self-respect for me. *(She resumes her stitching).* And there were a hundred little things you never noticed, because they came naturally to you. Things about standing up and taking off your hat and opening doors—

Pickering. Oh, that was nothing.

Liza. Yes: things that shewed you thought and felt about me as if I were something better than a scullery-maid; though of course I know you would have been just the same to a scullery-maid if she had been let into the drawing room. You never took off your boots in the dining room when I was there.

Pickering. You mustnt mind that. Higgins takes off his boots all over the place.

A **Liza.** I know. I am not blaming him. It is his way, isnt it? But it made such a difference to me that you didnt do it. You see, really and truly, apart from the things anyone can pick up (the dressing and the proper way of speaking, and so on), the difference between a lady and a flower girl is not how she behaves, but how she's treated. I shall always be a flower girl to Professor Higgins, because he always treats me as a flower girl, and always will; but I know I can be a lady to you, because you treat me as a lady, and always will.

Mrs Higgins. Please dont grind your teeth, Henry.

Pickering. Well, this is really very nice of you, Miss Doolittle.

Liza. I should like you to call me Eliza, now, if you would.

Pickering. Thank you. Eliza, of course.

Liza. And I should like Professor Higgins to call me Miss Doolittle.

Higgins. I'll see you damned first.

Mrs. Higgins. Henry! Henry!

Pickering (*laughing*). Why dont you slang back at him? Dont stand it. It would do him a lot of good.

Liza. I cant. I could have done it once but now I cant go back to it. You told me, you know, that when a child is brought to a foreign country, it picks up the language in a few weeks, and forgets its own. Well, I am a child in your country. I have forgotten my own language, and can speak nothing but yours. Thats the real break-off with the corner of Tottenham Court Road. Leaving Wimpole Street finishes it.

Pickering (*much alarmed*). Oh! but youre coming back to Wimpole Street, arnt you? Youll forgive Higgins?

Higgins (*rising*). Forgive! Will she, by George! Let her go. Let her find out how she can get on without us. She will relapse into the gutter in three weeks without me at her elbow.

[DOOLITTLE *appears at the centre window. With a look of dignified reproach at* HIGGINS, *he comes slowly and silently to his daughter, who, with her back to the window, is unconscious of his approach.*]

Pickering. He's incorrigible, Eliza. You wont relapse, will you?

Liza. No: not now. Never again. I have learnt my lesson. I dont believe I could utter one of the old sounds if I tried. (DOOLITTLE *touches her on her left shoulder. She drops her work, losing her self-possession utterly at the spectacle of her father's splendor*). A-a-a-a-a-ah-ow-ooh!

B

Higgins (*with a crow of triumph*). Aha! Just so. A-a-a-a-ahowooh! A-a-a-a-ahowooh! A-a-a-a-ahowooh! Victory! Victory! (*He throws himself on the divan, folding his arms, and spraddling arrogantly*).

Doolittle. Can you blame the girl? Dont look at me like that, Eliza. It aint my fault. Ive come into some money.

Liza. You must have touched a millionaire this time, dad.

Doolittle. I have. But I'm dressed something special today. I'm going to St George's, Hanover Square. Your stepmother is going to marry me.

Liza (*angrily*). Youre going to let yourself down to marry that low common woman!

Pickering (*quietly*). He ought to, Eliza. (*To* DOOLITTLE) Why has she changed her mind?

Doolittle (*sadly*). Intimidated, Governor. Intimidated. Middle class morality claims its victim. Wont you put on your hat, Liza, and come and see me turned off?

C **Liza.** If the Colonel says I must, I—I'll (*almost sobbing*) I'll demean myself. And get insulted for my pains, like enough.

Doolittle. Dont be afraid: she never comes to words with anyone now, poor woman! respectability has broke all the spirit out of her.

Pickering (*squeezing* ELIZA's *elbow gently*). Be kind to them, Eliza. Make the best of it.

Liza (*forcing a little smile for him through her vexation*). Oh well, just to shew theres no ill feeling. I'll be back in a moment. (*She goes out*).

Doolittle (*sitting down beside* PICKERING). I feel uncommon nervous about the ceremony, Colonel. I wish youd come and see me through it.

Pickering. But youve been through it before, man. You were married to Eliza's mother.

Doolittle. Who told you that, Colonel?

Pickering. Well, nobody told me. But I concluded—naturally——

A. Theme
In this speech, Eliza continues her explanation of what she thinks is really of value in social behavior.
? What sets apart a lady in her view? (The respectful way in which a lady is treated)

B. Character
As Pickering states, Higgins seems incapable of changing his ways, and Eliza, who confidently predicted that she was totally reformed, here slips back into one of her former unrestrained squeals.
? What point do you think Shaw is making about these two characters? (That their true natures are not revealed by their manners—either good or bad)

C. Motivation
? Why doesn't Eliza want to go to her father's wedding? (She dislikes the woman he is marrying.) What reasons does Pickering give her for going? (To be kind and show good will) Her father? (The woman he is marrying is no longer quarrelsome.)

A. Responding

❓ Do you think Higgins is expressing Shaw's view when he says that the most important thing is to treat everyone alike? Do you agree with this viewpoint, or do you think that Higgins ought to behave differently to Eliza?

B. Character

❓ What does Eliza mean when she says she "won't be passed over"? (She refuses to be ignored and treated like household help.)

Doolittle. No: that aint the natural way, Colonel: it's only the middle class way. My way was always the undeserving way. But dont say nothing to Eliza. She dont know: I always had a delicacy about telling her.

Pickering. Quite right. We'll leave it so, if you dont mind.

Doolittle. And youll come to the church, Colonel, and put me through straight?

Pickering. With pleasure. As far as a bachelor can.

Mrs Higgins. May I come, Mr Doolittle? I should be very sorry to miss your wedding.

Doolittle. I should indeed be honored by your condescension, maam; and my poor old woman would take it as a tremenjous compliment. She's been very low, thinking of the happy days that are no more.

Mrs Higgins (*rising*). I'll order the carriage and get ready. (*The men rise, except* HIGGINS). I shant be more than fifteen minutes. (*As she goes to the door* ELIZA *comes in, hatted and buttoning her gloves*). I'm going to the church to see your father married, Eliza. You had better come in the brougham[4] with me. Colonel Pickering can go on with the bridegroom.

[MRS HIGGINS *goes out.* ELIZA *comes to the middle of the room between the centre window and the ottoman.* PICKERING *joins her.*]

Doolittle. Bridegroom! What a word! It makes a man realize his position, somehow. (*He takes up his hat and goes towards the door*).

Pickering. Before I go, Eliza, do forgive Higgins and come back to us.

Liza. I dont think dad would allow me. Would you, dad?

Doolittle (*sad but magnanimous*). They played you off very cunning, Eliza, them two sportsmen. If it had been only one of them, you could have nailed him. But you see, there was two; and one of them chaperoned the other, as you might say. (*To* PICKERING) It was artful of you, Colonel; but I bear no malice: I should have done the same myself. I been the victim of one woman after another all my life, and I dont grudge you two getting the better of Liza. I shant interfere. It's time for us to go, Colonel. So long, Henry. See you in St George's, Eliza. (*He goes out*).

---

4. **brougham** (broom): a four-wheeled carriage.

Pickering (*coaxing*). Do stay with us, Eliza. (*He follows* DOOLITTLE).

[ELIZA *goes out on the balcony to avoid being alone with* HIGGINS. *He rises and joins her there. She immediately comes back into the room and makes for the door; but he goes along the balcony quickly and gets his back to the door before she reaches it.*]

Higgins. Well, Eliza, youve had a bit of your own back, as you call it. Have you had enough? and are you going to be reasonable? Or do you want any more?

Liza. You want me back only to pick up your slippers and put up with your tempers and fetch and carry for you.

Higgins. I havnt said I wanted you back at all.

Liza. Oh, indeed. Then what are we talking about?

Higgins. About you, not about me. If you come back I shall treat you just as I have always treated you. I can't change my nature; and I dont intend to change my manners. My manners are exactly the same as Colonel Pickering's.

Liza. That's not true. He treats a flower girl as if she was a duchess.

Higgins. And I treat a duchess as if she was a flower girl.

Liza. I see. (*She turns away composedly, and sits on the ottoman, facing the window*). The same to everybody.

Higgins. Just so.

Liza. Like father.

Higgins (*grinning, a little taken down*). Without accepting the comparison at all points, Eliza, it's quite true that your father is not a snob, and that he will be quite at home in any station of life to which his eccentric destiny may call him. (*Seriously*) The great secret, Eliza, is not having bad manners or good manners or any other particular sort of manners, but having the same manner for all human souls: in short, behaving as if you were in Heaven, where there are no third-class carriages, and one soul is as good as another.

Liza. Amen. You are a born preacher.

Higgins (*irritated*). The question is not whether I treat you rudely, but whether you ever heard me treat anyone else better.

Liza (*with sudden sincerity*). I dont care how you treat me. I dont mind your swearing at me. I shouldnt mind a black eye: Ive had one before this. But (*standing up and facing him*) I wont be passed over.

Higgins. Then get out of my way; for I wont stop for you. You talk about me as if I were a motor bus.

Liza. So you are a motor bus: all bounce and go, and no consideration for anyone. But I can do without you: dont think I cant.

Higgins. I know you can. I told you you could.

Liza (*wounded, getting away from him to the other side of the ottoman with her face to the hearth*). I know you did, you brute. You wanted to get rid of me.

Higgins. Liar.

Liza. Thank you. (*She sits down with dignity*).

Higgins. You never asked yourself, I suppose, whether *I* could do without you.

Liza (*earnestly*). Dont you try to get round me. You'll to have to do without me.

Higgins (*arrogant*). I can do without anybody. I have my own soul: my own spark of divine fire. But (*with sudden humility*) I shall miss you, Eliza. (*He sits down near her on the ottoman*). I have learnt something from your idiotic notions: I confess that humbly and gratefully. And I have grown accustomed to your voice and appearance. I like them, rather.

Liza. Well, you have both of them on your gramophone and in your book of photographs. When you feel lonely without me, you can turn the machine on. It's got no feelings to hurt.

Higgins. I cant turn your soul on. Leave me those feelings; and you can take away the voice and the face. They are not you.

Liza. Oh, you are a devil. You can twist the heart in a girl as easy as some could twist her arms to hurt her. Mrs Pearce warned me. Time and again she has wanted to leave you; and you always got round her at the last minute. And you dont care a bit for her. And you dont care a bit for me.

Higgins. I care for life, for humanity; and you are a part of it that has come my way and been built into my house. What more can you or anyone ask?

Liza. I wont care for anybody that doesnt care for me.

Higgins. Commercial principles, Eliza. Like (*reproducing her Covent Garden pronunciation with professional exactness*) s'yollin voylets, isn't it?

Liza. Dont sneer at me. It's mean to sneer at me.

Higgins. I have never sneered in my life. Sneering doesnt become either the human face or the human soul. I am expressing my righteous contempt for Commercialism. I dont and wont trade in af-

fection. You call me a brute because you couldnt buy a claim on me by fetching my slippers and finding my spectacles. You were a fool: I think a woman fetching a man's slippers is a disgusting sight: did I ever fetch your slippers? I think a good deal more of you for throwing them in my face. No use slaving for me and then saying you want to be cared for: who cares for a slave? If you come back, come back for the sake of good fellowship; for youll get nothing else. Youve had a thousand times as much out of me as I have out of you; and if you dare to set up your little dog's tricks of fetching and carrying slippers against my creation of a Duchess Eliza, I'll slam the door in your silly face.

Liza. What did you do it for if you didnt care for me?

Higgins (*heartily*). Why, because it was my job.

Liza. You never thought of the trouble it would make for me.

Higgins. Would the world ever have been made if its maker had been afraid of making trouble? Making life means making trouble. Theres only one way of escaping trouble; and thats killing things. Cowards, you notice, are always shrieking to have troublesome people killed.

Liza. I'm no preacher: I dont notice things like that. I notice that you dont notice me.

Higgins (*jumping up and walking about intolerantly*). Eliza: youre an idiot. I waste the treasures of my Miltonic mind by spreading them before you. Once for all, understand that I go my way and do my work without caring twopence what happens to either of us. I am not intimidated, like your father and your stepmother. So you can come back or go to the devil: which you please.

Liza. What am I to come back for?

Higgins (*bouncing up on his knees on the ottoman and leaning over it to her*). For the fun of it. Thats why I took you on.

Liza (*with averted face*). And you may throw me out tomorrow if I dont do everything you want me to?

Higgins. Yes; and you may walk out tomorrow if I dont do everything you want me to.

Liza. And live with my stepmother?

Higgins. Yes, or sell flowers.

Liza. Oh! If I only could go back to my flower basket! I should be independent of both you and father and all the world! Why did you take my independence from me? Why did I give it up? I'm a slave now, for all my fine clothes.

A. Conflict
The question that remains to be resolved is whether Eliza will stay in Higgins's household and, if so, under what terms.

B. Responding
Do you believe Higgins when he says he can do without Eliza, or do you think he is just being stubborn and proud?

C. Responding
Here Eliza and Higgins are arguing about freedom. Which of them is expressing Shaw's views? With which character do you sympathize? Which one do you find more believable?

A. Character

❓ Why is Higgins disturbed by Freddy's feelings for Eliza? (He is probably jealous and does not consider Freddy good enough for his creation.)

B. Conflict

This exchange between Higgins and Eliza turns into a kind of debate over the best form of relations between the sexes.

❓ Summarize the position of each. Which one do you think makes the stronger argument? (Higgins says that to be a lady, Eliza will have to give up ideas of marriage and dedicate herself to independent study—as he does. Eliza says that Higgins knows that she can't go back to the way she used to live, and she can't go on living with a man as cruel as he is. Student answers will vary about which character's argument is stronger.)

Higgins. Not a bit. I'll adopt you as my daughter and settle money on you if you like. Or would you rather marry Pickering?

Liza (*looking fiercely round at him*). I wouldnt marry you if you asked me; and youre nearer my age than what he is.

Higgins (*gently*). Than he is: not "than what he is."

Liza (*losing her temper and rising*). I'll talk as I like. Youre not my teacher now.

Higgins (*reflectively*). I dont suppose Pickering would, though. He's as confirmed an old bachelor as I am.

Liza. Thats not what I want; and dont you think it. Ive always had chaps enough wanting me that way. Freddy Hill writes to me twice and three times a day, sheets and sheets.

A **Higgins** (*disagreeably surprised*). Damn his impudence! (*He recoils and finds himself sitting on his heels*).

Liza. He has a right to if he likes, poor lad. And he does love me.

Higgins (*getting off the ottoman*). You have no right to encourage him.

Liza. Every girl has a right to be loved.

Higgins. What! By fools like that?

Liza. Freddy's not a fool. And if he's weak and poor and wants me, may be he'd make me happier than my betters that bully me and dont want me.

Higgins. Can he make anything of you? Thats the point.

Liza. Perhaps I could make something of him. But I never thought of us making anything of one another; and you never think of anything else. I only want to be natural.

Higgins. In short, you want me to be as infatuated about you as Freddy? Is that it?

Liza. No I dont. Thats not the sort of feeling I want from you. And dont you be too sure of yourself or of me. I could have been a bad girl if I'd liked. Ive seen more of some things than you, for all your learning. Girls like me can drag gentlemen down to make love to them easy enough. And they wish each other dead the next minute.

Higgins. Of course they do. Then what in thunder are we quarrelling about?

Liza (*much troubled*). I want a little kindness. I know I'm a common ignorant girl, and you a book-learned gentleman; but I'm not dirt under your feet. What I done (*correcting herself*) what I did was not for the dresses and the taxis: I did it because we were pleasant together and I come—

came—to care for you; not to want you to make love to me, and not forgetting the difference between us, but more friendly like.

Higgins. Well, of course. Thats just how I feel. And how Pickering feels. Eliza: youre a fool.

Liza. Thats not a proper answer to give me (*she sinks on the chair at the writing-table in tears*).

Higgins. It's all youll get until you stop being a common idiot. If youre going to be a lady, youll have to give up feeling neglected if the men you know dont spend half their time snivelling over you and the other half giving you black eyes. If you cant stand the coldness of my sort of life, and the strain of it, go back to the gutter. Work til youre more a brute than a human being; and then cuddle and squabble and drink til you fall asleep. Oh, it's a fine life, the life of the gutter. It's real: it's warm: it's violent: you can feel it through the thickest skin: you can taste it and smell it without any training or any work. Not like Science and Literature and Classical Music and Philosophy and Art. You find me cold, unfeeling, selfish, dont you? Very well: be off with you to the sort of people you like. Marry some sentimental hog or other with lots of money, and a thick pair of lips to kiss you with and a thick pair of boots to kick you with. If you cant appreciate what youve got, youd better get what you can appreciate.

B

Liza (*desperate*). Oh, you are a cruel tyrant. I cant talk to you: you turn everything against me: I'm always in the wrong. But you know very well all the time that youre nothing but a bully. You know I cant go back to the gutter, as you call it, and that I have no real friends in the world but you and the Colonel. You know well I couldnt bear to live with a low common man after you two; and it's wicked and cruel of you to insult me by pretending I could. You think I must go back to Wimpole Street because I have nowhere else to go but father's. But dont you be too sure that you have me under your feet to be trampled on and talked down. I'll marry Freddy, I will, as soon as I'm able to support him.

Higgins (*thunderstruck*). Freddy!!! that young fool! That poor devil who couldnt get a job as an errand boy even if he had the guts to try for it! Woman: do you not understand that I have made you a consort for a king?

Liza. Freddy loves me: that makes him king enough for me. I dont want him to work: he wasnt brought up to it as I was. I'll go and be a teacher.

Higgins. Whatll you teach, in heaven's name?

READING CHECK TEST: Act Five

1. Eliza does not follow Mrs. Higgins's advice. (F)
2. Higgins is alarmed when he discovers that Eliza has left. (T)
3. Doolittle is willing to give away the money he has inherited. (F)

4. Eliza praises Pickering for the courteous way he has treated her. (T)
5. Higgins is a sentimental man and a true romantic at heart. (F)

Liza. What you taught me. I'll teach phonetics.

Higgins. Ha! ha! ha!

Liza. I'll offer myself as an assistant to that hairy-faced Hungarian.

Higgins (*rising in a fury*). What! That impostor! that humbug! that toadying ignoramus! Teach him my methods! my discoveries! You take one step in his direction and I'll wring your neck. (*He lays hands on her*). Do you hear?

Liza (*defiantly non-resistant*). Wring away. What do I care? I knew youd strike me some day. (*He lets her go, stamping with rage at having forgotten himself, and recoils so hastily that he stumbles back into his seat on the ottoman*). Aha! Now I know how to deal with you. What a fool I was not to think of it before! You can't take away the knowledge you gave me. You said I had a finer ear than you. And I can be civil and kind to people, which is more than you can. Aha! (*Purposely dropping her aitches to annoy him*) Thats done you, Enry Iggins, it az. Now I dont care that (*snapping her fingers*) for your bullying and your big talk. I'll advertize it in the papers that your duchess is only a flower girl that you taught, and that she'll teach anybody to be a duchess just the same in six months for a thousand guineas. Oh, when I think of myself crawling under your feet and being trampled on and called names, when all the time I had only to lift up my finger to be as good as you, I could just kick myself.

Higgins (*wondering at her*). You damned impudent slut, you! But it's better than snivelling; better than fetching slippers and finding spectacles, isnt it? (*Rising*) By George, Eliza, I said I'd make a woman of you; and I have. I like you like this.

Liza. Yes: you can turn round and make up to me now that I'm not afraid of you, and can do without you.

Higgins. Of course I do, you little fool. Five minutes ago you were like a millstone round my neck. Now youre a tower of strength: a consort battleship. You and I and Pickering will be three old bachelors instead of only two men and a silly girl.

[MRS HIGGINS *returns, dressed for the wedding.* ELIZA *instantly becomes cool and elegant.*]

Mrs Higgins. The carriage is waiting, Eliza. Are you ready?

Liza. Quite. Is the Professor coming?

Mrs Higgins. Certainly not. He cant behave himself in church. He makes remarks out loud all the time on the clergyman's pronunciation.

Liza. Then I shall not see you again, Professor. Goodbye. (*She goes to the door*).

Mrs Higgins (*coming to* HIGGINS). Goodbye, dear.

Higgins. Goodbye, mother. (*He is about to kiss her, when he recollects something*). Oh, by the way, Eliza, order a ham and a Stilton cheese, will you? And buy me a pair of reindeer gloves, number eights, and a tie to match that new suit of mine. You can choose the color. (*His cheerful, careless, vigorous voice shews that he is incorrigible*).

Liza (*disdainfully*). Number eights are too small for you if you want them lined with lamb's wool. You have three new ties that you have forgotten in the drawer of your washstand. Colonel Pickering prefers double Gloucester to Stilton; and you dont notice the difference. I telephoned Mrs Pearce this morning not to forget the ham. What you are to do without me I cannot imagine. (*She sweeps out*).

Mrs Higgins. I'm afraid youve spoilt that girl, Henry. I should be uneasy about you and her if she were less fond of Colonel Pickering.

Higgins. Pickering! Nonsense: she's going to marry Freddy. Ha ha! Freddy!! Ha ha ha ha ha!!!!!

[*He roars with laughter as the play ends.*]

Epilogue

The rest of the story need not be shewn in action, and indeed, would hardly need telling if our imaginations were not so enfeebled by their lazy dependence on the ready-mades and reach-me-downs of the ragshop in which Romance keeps its stock of "happy endings" to misfit all stories. Now, the history of Eliza Doolittle, though called a romance because the transfiguration it records seems exceedingly improbable, is common enough. Such transfigurations have been achieved by hundreds of resolutely ambitious young women since Nell Gwynne set them the example by playing queens and fascinating kings in the theatre in which she began by selling oranges. Nevertheless, people in all directions have assumed, for no other reason than that she became the heroine of a romance, that she must have married the hero of it. This is unbearable, not only because her little drama, if acted on such a thoughtless assumption, must be spoiled, but because the true sequel is patent to anyone with a sense of human nature in general, and of feminine instinct in particular.

A. Responding

In a sense, the play ends with Higgins and Eliza still battling but perhaps on more even terms than before.

? Do you find the ending satisfactory or not? Give reasons.

B. Romances

For an exposition of romance as a mode of literature, see page 147. Notice Shaw's cynical tone here.

? How could imaginations be "enfeebled" by romances? (Think of a person who reads only the cheap "romances" available today, in which all problems, no matter how profound, are resolved and the characters live happily ever after. Such fiction demands little mental struggle and little imaginative participation, which is why it is called "escape" fiction. The most interesting and challenging plots are those that do not provide the "easy answer." Some of the best provide no answers at all!)

Summary of Epilogue
In the prose epilogue that follows the play, Shaw explains his intentions and his view of his characters. He strongly rejects the idea of a conventional romantic ending with Higgins and Eliza falling into each other's arms. Shaw explains at great length why Eliza would not choose to marry Higgins. Ask students if they find his reasoning convincing. Next Shaw

explains approvingly why Higgins is reluctant to marry. Since Shaw was a confirmed bachelor until the age of forty-two, there is a ring of self-justification in his argument. Here Shaw develops the reasons why Eliza would choose to marry Freddy. Ask students to list some of Shaw's reasons and to discuss their validity. (Some students may find them cynical; others, realistic.) Then Shaw tells

what lies in store for Eliza's father—a brilliant career of living off the highest of society.

A. Responding

? What do you think of this comment? Is it true of women in this era of "consciousness-raising"? Remember that Shaw himself did not marry until he was forty-two years old.

B. Paraphrasing

? How would you express Shaw's unusual sentiments here in simpler, everyday language? Be sure to refer to the biography of Shaw and review his relationship with his own mother.

C. Interpreting

? What does this mean? (Even if Mrs. Higgins died, her son would have been more interested in Milton and the Universal Alphabet than in Eliza.) According to the next sentence, Higgins has a greater power of loving than Eliza does, and thus "love" [read "sex"] to him is secondary.

D. Vocabulary
Predestinate means "predestined" or "fated."

Eliza, in telling Higgins she would not marry him if he asked, was not coquetting: she was announcing a well-considered decision. When a bachelor interests, and dominates, and teaches, and becomes important to a spinster, as Higgins with Eliza, she always, if she has character enough to be capable of it, considers very seriously indeed whether she will play for becoming that bachelor's wife, especially if he is so little interested in marriage that a determined and devoted woman might capture him if she set herself resolutely to do it. Her decision will depend a good deal on whether she is really free to choose; and that, again, will depend on her age and income. If she is at the end of her youth, and has no security for her livelihood, she will marry him because she must marry anybody who will provide for her. But at Eliza's age a good-looking girl does not feel that pressure: she feels free to pick and choose. She is therefore guided by her instinct in the matter. Eliza's instinct tells her not to marry Higgins. It does not tell her to give him up. It is not in the slightest doubt as to his remaining one of the strongest personal interests in her life. It would be very sorely strained if there was another woman likely to supplant her with him. But as she feels sure of him on that last point, she has no doubt at all as to her course, and would not have any, even if the difference of twenty years in age, which seems so great to youth, did not exist between them.

As our own instincts are not appealed to by her conclusion, let us see whether we cannot discover some reason for it. When Higgins excused his indifference to young women on the ground that they had an irresistible rival in his mother, he gave the clue to his inveterate old-bachelordom. The case is uncommon only to the extent that remarkable mothers are uncommon. If an imaginative boy has a sufficiently rich mother who has intelligence, personal grace, dignity of character without harshness, and a cultivated sense of the best art of her time to enable her to make her house beautiful, she sets a standard for him against which very few women can struggle, besides effecting for him a disengagement of his affections, his sense of beauty, and his idealism from his specifically sexual impulses. This makes him a standing puzzle to the huge number of uncultivated people who have been brought up in tasteless homes by commonplace or disagreeable parents, and to whom, consequently, literature,

painting, sculpture, music, and affectionate personal relations come as modes of sex if they come at all. The word passion means nothing else to them; and that Higgins could have a passion for phonetics and idealize his mother instead of Eliza, would seem to them absurd and unnatural. Nevertheless, when we look round and see that hardly anyone is too ugly or disagreeable to find a wife or a husband if he or she wants one, whilst many old maids and bachelors are above the average in quality and culture, we cannot help suspecting that the disentanglement of sex from the associations with which it is commonly confused, a disentanglement which persons of genius achieve by sheer intellectual analysis, is sometimes produced or aided by parental fascination.

Now, though Eliza was incapable of thus explaining to herself Higgins's formidable powers of resistance to the charm that prostrated Freddy at the first glance, she was instinctively aware that she could never obtain a complete grip of him, or come between him and his mother (the first necessity of the married woman). To put it shortly, she knew that for some mysterious reason he had not the makings of a married man in him, according to her conception of a husband as one to whom she would be his nearest and fondest and warmest interest. Even had there been no mother-rival, she would still have refused to accept an interest in herself that was secondary to philosophic interests. Had Mrs Higgins died, there would still have been Milton and the Universal Alphabet. Landor's remark that to those who have the greatest power of loving, love is a secondary affair, would not have recommended Landor to Eliza. Put that along with her resentment of Higgins's domineering superiority, and her mistrust of his coaxing cleverness in getting round her and evading her wrath when he had gone too far with his impetuous bullying, and you will see that Eliza's instinct had good grounds for warning her not to marry her Pygmalion.

And now, whom did Eliza marry? For if Higgins was a predestinate old bachelor, she was most certainly not a predestinate old maid. Well, that can be told very shortly to those who have not guessed it from the indications she has herself given them.

Almost immediately after Eliza is stung into proclaiming her considered determination not to marry Higgins, she mentions the fact that young Mr Frederick Eynsford Hill is pouring out his love for her daily through the post. Now Freddy is young, practically twenty years younger than Higgins: he is a gentleman (or, as Eliza would qualify him, a toff), and speaks like one. He is nicely dressed, is treated by the Colonel as an equal, loves her unaffectedly, and is not her master, nor ever likely to dominate her in spite of his advantage of social standing. Eliza has no use for the foolish romantic tradition that all women love to be mastered, if not actually bullied and beaten. "When you go to women" says Nietzsche "take your whip with you." Sensible despots have never confined that precaution to women: they have taken their whips with them when they have dealt with men, and been slavishly idealized by the men over whom they have flourished the whip much more than by women. No doubt there are slavish women as well as slavish men; and women, like men, admire those that are stronger than themselves. But to admire a strong person and to live under that strong person's thumb are two different things. The weak may not be admired and hero-worshipped; but they are by no means disliked or shunned; and they never seem to have the least difficulty in marrying people who are too good for them. They may fail in emergencies; but life is not one long emergency: it is mostly a string of situations for which no exceptional strength is needed, and with which even rather weak people can cope if they have a stronger partner to help them out. Accordingly, it is a truth everywhere in evidence that strong people, masculine or feminine, not only do not marry stronger people, but do not shew any preference for them in selecting their friends. When a lion meets another with a louder roar "the first lion thinks the last a bore." The man or woman who feels strong enough for two, seeks for every other quality in a partner than strength.

A

The converse is also true. Weak people want to marry strong people who do not frighten them too much; and this often leads them to make the mistake we describe metaphorically as "biting off more than they can chew." They want too much for too little; and when the bargain is unreasonable beyond all bearing, the union becomes impossible: it ends in the weaker party being either discarded or borne as a cross, which is worse. People who are not only weak, but silly or obtuse as well, are often in these difficulties.

This being the state of human affairs, what is Eliza fairly sure to do when she is placed between Freddy and Higgins? Will she look forward to a lifetime of fetching Higgins's slippers or to a lifetime of Freddy fetching hers? There can be no doubt about the answer. Unless Freddy is biologically repulsive to her, and Higgins biologically attractive to a degree that overwhelms all her other instincts, she will, if she marries either of them, marry Freddy.

And that is just what Eliza did.

Complications ensued; but they were economic, not romantic. Freddy had no money and no occupation. His mother's jointure, a last relic of the opulence of Largelady Park, had enabled her to struggle along in Earlscourt with an air of gentility, but not to procure any serious secondary education for her children, much less give the boy a profession. A clerkship at thirty shillings a week was beneath Freddy's dignity, and extremely distasteful to him besides. His prospects consisted of a hope that if he kept up appearances somebody would do something for him. The somebody appeared vaguely to his imagination as a private secretaryship or a sinecure[1] of some sort. To his mother it perhaps appeared as a marriage to some lady of means who could not resist her boy's niceness. Fancy her feelings when he married a flower girl who had become disclassed under extraordinary circumstances which were now notorious!

B

It is true that Eliza's situation did not seem wholly ineligible. Her father, though formerly a dustman, and now fantastically disclassed, had become extremely popular in the smartest society by a social talent which triumphed over every prejudice and every disadvantage. Rejected by the middle class, which he loathed, he had shot up at once into the highest circles by his wit, his dustmanship (which he carried like a banner), and his Nietzschean transcendence of good and evil. At intimate ducal dinners he sat on the right-hand of the Duchess; and in country houses he smoked in the pantry and was made much of by the butler when he was not feeding in the dining room and being consulted by cabinet ministers. But he found it almost as hard to do all this on three thousand a year as Mrs Eynsford Hill to live in Earlscourt on an income so pitiably smaller that I have not the heart to disclose its exact figure. He absolutely refused to add the last straw to his burden by contributing to Eliza's support.

C

Thus Freddy and Eliza, now Mr and Mrs Eyns-

---

1. **sinecure** (si′nə·kyo͞or): a position that involves little work.

A. Main Idea

? How would you summarize Shaw's main idea in this remarkable paragraph? (A key statement is found in the sentence beginning "Accordingly, it is a truth…") This long digression on the paradoxical power of "weakness" should fuel a discussion. Remember also that Shaw is known for his strong women characters, who, at the climactic moment, always surprise us by refusing to make what was considered the "traditional" feminine choice. (See the biography, pages 1146–1147.)

B. Vocabulary

? What does "disclassed" mean? (Eliza moved from the lowest class in English society to a higher class; some were fooled into thinking that she was of the aristocracy.)

C. Interpretation

Be sure students understand what "social talent" Shaw is ironically referring to. See the next sentence.

A. Interpreting
? Why is Freddy's mother opposed to "retail trade"? (It's considered middle-class. Someone "in trade" would be scorned by the aristocracy, even by an impoverished lady like Mrs. Eynsford Hill. See page 767 for Dickens's satiric description of the newly rich Veneerings, who had made their money in trade. Note also here the amusing image created by the metaphor.)

B. Allusion
Shaw compares modern "conversions" of new theories to the conversion of a large part of the Mediterranean world to Christianity, as described in the Acts of the Apostles in the New Testament.

ford Hill, would have spent a penniless honeymoon but for a wedding present of £500 from the Colonel to Eliza. It lasted a long time because Freddy did not know how to spend money, never having had any to spend, and Eliza, socially trained by a pair of old bachelors, wore her clothes as long as they held together and looked pretty, without the least regard to their being many months out of fashion. Still, £500 will not last two young people forever; and they both knew, and Eliza felt as well, that they must shift themselves in the end. She could quarter herself on Wimpole Street because it had come to be her home; but she was quite aware that she ought not to quarter Freddy there, and that it would not be good for his character if she did.

Not that the Wimpole Street bachelors objected. When she consulted them, Higgins declined to be bothered about her housing problem when that solution was so simple. Eliza's desire to have Freddy in the house with her seemed of no more importance than if she had wanted an extra piece of bedroom furniture. Pleas as to Freddy's character, and the moral obligation on him to earn his own living, were lost on Higgins. He denied that Freddy had any character, and declared that if he tried to do any useful work some competent person would have the trouble of undoing it: a procedure involving a net loss to the community, and great unhappiness to Freddy himself, who was obviously intended by Nature for such light work as amusing Eliza, which, Higgins declared, was a much more useful and honorable occupation than working in the city. When Eliza referred again to her project of teaching phonetics, Higgins abated not a jot of his violent opposition to it. He said she was not within ten years of being qualified to meddle with his pet subject; and as it was evident that the Colonel agreed with him, she felt she could not go against them in this grave matter, and that she had no right, without Higgins's consent, to exploit the knowledge he had given her; for his knowledge seemed to her as much his private property as his watch: Eliza was no communist. Besides, she was superstitiously devoted to them both, more entirely and frankly after her marriage than before it.

It was the Colonel who finally solved the problem, which had cost him much perplexed cogitation. He one day asked Eliza, rather shyly, whether she had quite given up her notion of keeping a flower shop. She replied that she had thought of it, but had put it out of her head, because the Colonel had said, that day at Mrs Higgins's, that it would never do. The Colonel confessed that when he said that, he had not quite recovered from the dazzling impression of the day before. They broke the matter to Higgins that evening. The sole comment vouchsafed by him very nearly led to a serious quarrel with Eliza. It was to the effect that she would have in Freddy an ideal errand boy.

Freddy himself was next sounded on the subject. He said he had been thinking of a shop himself; though it had presented itself to his pennilessness as a small place in which Eliza should sell tobacco at one counter whilst he sold newspapers at the opposite one. But he agreed that it would be extraordinarily jolly to go early every morning with Eliza to Covent Garden and buy flowers on the scene of their first meeting: a sentiment which earned him many kisses from his wife. He added that he had always been afraid to propose anything of the sort, because Clara would make an awful row about a step that must damage her matrimonial chances, and his mother could not be expected to like it after clinging for so many years to that step of the social ladder on which retail trade is impossible.

This difficulty was removed by an event highly unexpected by Freddy's mother. Clara, in the course of her incursions into those artistic circles which were the highest within her reach, discovered that her conversational qualifications were expected to include a grounding in the novels of Mr H. G. Wells.[2] She borrowed them in various directions so energetically that she swallowed them all within two months. The result was a conversion of a kind quite common today. A modern Acts of the Apostles would fill fifty whole Bibles if anyone were capable of writing it.

Poor Clara, who appeared to Higgins and his mother as a disagreeable and ridiculous person, and to her own mother as in some inexplicable way a social failure, had never seen herself in either light; for, though to some extent ridiculed and mimicked in West Kensington like everybody else there, she was accepted as a rational and normal—or shall we say inevitable?—sort of human being. At worst they called her The Pusher; but to them no more than to herself had it ever occurred that she was pushing the air, and pushing

_____

2. **H. G. Wells** (1866–1946): British writer who wrote novels supporting social reform.

Summary of Epilogue (cont.)
On pages 1205–1206, Shaw recounts in great detail how Clara met H. G. Wells and how she launched herself and Eliza and Freddy into business. Then he describes how Freddy and Eliza, with Pickering's financial assistance, finally manage to prosper in their flower shop.

it in a wrong direction. Still, she was not happy. She was growing desperate. Her one asset, the fact that her mother was what the Epsom greengrocer called a carriage lady, had no exchange value, apparently. It had prevented her from getting educated, because the only education she could have afforded was education with the Earlscourt greengrocer's daughter. It had led her to seek the society of her mother's class; and that class simply would not have her, because she was much poorer than the greengrocer, and, far from being able to afford a maid, could not afford even a housemaid, and had to scrape along at home with an illiberally treated general servant. Under such circumstances nothing could give her an air of being a genuine product of Largelady Park. And yet its tradition made her regard a marriage with anyone within her reach as an unbearable humiliation. Commercial people and professional people in a small way were odious to her. She ran after painters and novelists; but she did not charm them; and her bold attempts to pick up and practise artistic and literary talk irritated them. She was, in short, an utter failure, an ignorant, incompetent, pretentious, unwelcome, penniless, useless little snob; and though she did not admit these disqualifications (for nobody ever faces unpleasant truths of this kind until the possibility of a way out dawns on them) she felt their effects too keenly to be satisfied with her position.

Clara had a startling eyeopener when, on being suddenly wakened to enthusiasm by a girl of her own age who dazzled her and produced in her a gushing desire to take her for a model, and gain her friendship, she discovered that this exquisite apparition had graduated from the gutter in a few months time. It shook her so violently, that when Mr H. G. Wells lifted her on the point of his puissant[3] pen, and placed her at the angle of view from which the life she was leading and the society to which she clung appeared in its true relation to real human needs and worthy social structure, he effected a conversion and a conviction of sin comparable to the most sensational feats of General Booth[4] or Gypsy Smith. Clara's snobbery went bang. Life suddenly began to move with her. Without knowing how or why, she began to make friends and enemies. Some of the acquaintances to whom she had been a tedious or indifferent or ridiculous affliction, dropped her: others became cordial. To her amazement she found that some "quite nice" people were saturated with Wells, and that this accessibility to ideas was the secret of their niceness. People she had thought deeply religious and had tried to conciliate on that tack with disastrous results, suddenly took an interest in her, and revealed a hostility to conventional religion which she had never conceived possible except among the most desperate characters. They made her read Galsworthy;[5] and Galsworthy exposed the vanity of Largelady Park and finished her. It exasperated her to think that the dungeon in which she had languished for so many unhappy years had been unlocked all the time, and that the impulses she had so carefully struggled with and stifled for the sake of keeping well with society, were precisely those by which alone she could have come into any sort of sincere human contact. In the radiance of these discoveries, and the tumult of their reaction, she made a fool of herself as freely and conspicuously as when she so rashly adopted Eliza's expletive in Mrs Higgins's drawing room; for the new-born Wellsian had to find her bearings almost as ridiculously as a baby; but nobody hates a baby for its ineptitudes, or thinks the worse of it for trying to eat the matches; and Clara lost no friends by her follies. They laughed at her to her face this time; and she had to defend herself and fight it out as best she could.

When Freddy paid a visit to Earlscourt (which he never did when he could possibly help it) to make the desolating announcement that he and his Eliza were thinking of blackening the Largelady scutcheon[6] by opening a shop, he found the little household already convulsed by a prior announcement from Clara that she also was going to work in an old furniture shop in Dover Street, which had been started by a fellow Wellsian. This appointment Clara owed, after all, to her old social accomplishment of Push. She had made up her mind that, cost what it might, she would see Mr Wells in the flesh; and she had achieved her end at a garden party. She had better luck than so rash an enterprise deserved. Mr Wells came up to her expectations. Age had not withered him, nor could custom stale his infinite variety in half an hour.

---

3. **puissant:** (pyoo'i·sənt): powerful.
4. **General Booth:** the evangelist William Booth (1829–1912), who founded the Salvation Army.

5. **John Galsworthy** (1867–1933): British novelist, playwright, and social critic.
6. **scutcheon:** family coat of arms.

A. Tone
Note Shaw's barely disguised contempt here for young women like Clara.

B. Metaphor
Have students explain the metaphor of Wells's pen as a kind of crane that lifted Clara up so she could see life from a new perspective.
❓ What does it mean that Clara's snobbery "went bang"? (It was punctured, like a balloon.)

A. Tone
Note that Shaw refuses to be labeled a romantic: He almost fell into the trap of providing a happy-ever-after ending, despite his earlier protests about the "ragshop in which romance keeps its stock of 'happy endings.'"

B. Expansion
Richard Porson and Richard Bentley were famous classical scholars.

C. Expansion
Dickensian here means "in the style of Dickens." Note Shaw's scorn of the highly esteemed London School of Economics. When the director (below) suggests that the couple combine the London School with Kew Gardens (where vegetables are grown), he is being sarcastic.

His pleasant neatness and compactness, his small hands and feet, his teeming ready brain, his unaffected accessibility, and a certain fine apprehensiveness which stamped him as susceptible from his topmost hair to his tipmost toe, proved irresistible. Clara talked of nothing else for weeks and weeks afterwards. And as she happened to talk to the lady of the furniture shop, and that lady also desired above all things to know Mr Wells and sell pretty things to him, she offered Clara a job on the chance of achieving that end through her.

And so it came about that Eliza's luck held, and the expected opposition to the flower shop melted away. The shop is in the arcade of a railway station not very far from the Victoria and Albert Museum; and if you live in that neighborhood you may go there any day and buy a buttonhole from Eliza.

Now here is a last opportunity for romance. Would you not like to be assured that the shop was an immense success, thanks to Eliza's charms and her early business experience in Covent Garden? Alas! the truth is the truth: the shop did not pay for a long time, simply because Eliza and her Freddy did not know how to keep it. True, Eliza had not to begin at the very beginning: she knew the names and prices of the cheaper flowers; and her elation was unbounded when she found that Freddy, like all youths educated at cheap, pretentious, and thoroughly inefficient schools, knew a little Latin. It was very little, but enough to make him appear to her a Porson or Bentley, and to put him at his ease with botanical nomenclature. Unfortunately he knew nothing else; and Eliza, though she could count money up to eighteen shillings or so, and had acquired a certain familiarity with the language of Milton from her struggles to qualify herself for winning Higgins's bet, could not write out a bill without utterly disgracing the establishment. Freddy's power of stating in Latin that Balbus built a wall and that Gaul was divided into three parts[7] did not carry with it the slightest knowledge of accounts or business: Colonel Pickering had to explain to him what a cheque book and a bank account meant. And the pair were by no means easily teachable. Freddy backed up Eliza in her obstinate refusal to believe that they could save money by engaging a bookkeeper with some knowledge of the business. How, they ar-

gued, could you possibly save money by going to extra expense when you already could not make ends meet? But the Colonel, after making the ends meet over and over again, at last gently insisted; and Eliza, humbled to the dust by having to beg from him so often, and stung by the uproarious derision of Higgins, to whom the notion of Freddy succeeding at anything was a joke that never palled, grasped the fact that business, like phonetics, has to be learned.

On the piteous spectacle of the pair spending their evenings in shorthand schools and polytechnic classes, learning bookkeeping and typewriting with incipient junior clerks, male and female, from the elementary schools, let me not dwell. There were even classes at the London School of Economics, and a humble personal appeal to the director of that institution to recommend a course bearing on the flower business. He, being a humorist, explained to them the method of the celebrated Dickensian essay on Chinese Metaphysics by the gentleman who read an article on China and an article on Metaphysics and combined the information. He suggested that they should combine the London School with Kew Gardens. Eliza, to whom the procedure of the Dickensian gentleman seemed perfectly correct (as in fact it was) and not in the least funny (which was only her ignorance), took the advice with entire gravity. But the effort that cost her the deepest humiliation was a request to Higgins, whose pet artistic fancy, next to Milton's verse, was calligraphy, and who himself wrote a most beautiful Italian hand, that he would teach her to write. He declared that she was congenitally incapable of forming a single letter worthy of the least of Milton's words; but she persisted; and again he suddenly threw himself into the task of teaching her with a combination of stormy intensity, concentrated patience, and occasional bursts of interesting disquisition on the beauty and nobility, the august mission and destiny, of human handwriting. Eliza ended by acquiring an extremely uncommercial script which was a positive extension of her personal beauty, and spending three times as much on stationery as anyone else because certain qualities and shapes of paper became indispensable to her. She could not even address an envelope in the usual way because it made the margins all wrong.

Their commercial schooldays were a period of disgrace and despair for the young couple. They seemed to be learning nothing about flower shops.

---

7. **Gaul . . . parts:** a reference to the opening sentence of an account of the Gallic Wars written by Julius Caesar and commonly read in advanced Latin classes.

At last they gave it up as hopeless, and shook the dust of the shorthand schools, and the polytechnics, and the London School of Economics from their feet for ever. Besides, the business was in some mysterious way beginning to take care of itself. They had somehow forgotten their objections to employing other people. They came to the conclusion that their own way was the best, and that they had really a remarkable talent for business. The Colonel, who had been compelled for some years to keep a sufficient sum on current account at his bankers to make up their deficits, found that the provision was unnecessary: the young people were prospering. It is true that there was not quite fair play between them and their competitors in trade. Their week-ends in the country cost them nothing, and saved them the price of their Sunday dinners; for the motor car was the Colonel's; and he and Higgins paid the hotel bills. Mr F. Hill, florist and greengrocer (they soon discovered that there was money in asparagus; and asparagus led to other vegetables), had an air which stamped the business as classy; and in private life he was still Frederick Eynsford Hill, Esquire. Not that there was any swank about him: nobody but Eliza knew that he had been christened Frederick Challoner. Eliza herself swanked like anything.

That is all. That is how it has turned out. It is astonishing how much Eliza still manages to meddle in the housekeeping at Wimpole Street in spite of the shop and her own family. And it is notable that though she never nags her husband, and frankly loves the Colonel as if she were his favorite daughter, she has never got out of the habit of nagging Higgins that was established on the fatal night when she won his bet for him. She snaps his head off on the faintest provocation, or on none. He no longer dares to tease her by assuming an abysmal inferiority of Freddy's mind to his own. He storms and bullies and derides; but she stands up to him so ruthlessly that the Colonel has to ask her from time to time to be kinder to Higgins; and it is the only request of his that brings a mulish expression into her face. Nothing but some emergency or calamity great enough to break down all likes and dislikes, and throw them both back on their common humanity—and may they be spared any such trial!—will ever alter this. She knows that Higgins does not need her, just as her father did not need her. The very scrupulousness with which he told her that day that he had become used to having her there, and dependent on her for all sorts of little services, and that he should miss her if she went away (it would never have occurred to Freddy or the Colonel to say anything of the sort) deepens her inner certainty that she is "no more to him than them slippers"; yet she has a sense, too, that his indifference is deeper than the infatuation of commoner souls. She is immensely interested in him. She has even secret mischievous moments in which she wishes she could get him alone, on a desert island, away from all ties and with nobody else in the world to consider, and just drag him off his pedestal and see him making love like any common man. We all have private imaginations of that sort. But when it comes to business, to the life that she really leads as distinguished from the life of dreams and fancies, she likes Freddy and she likes the Colonel, and she does not like Higgins and Mr Doolittle. Galatea never does quite like Pygmalion: his relation to her is too godlike to be altogether agreeable.

A. Expansion
The sculptor was Pygmalion; his creation was Galatea. Students probably could comment on this generalization.

B. Responding
Be sure to urge students to write their own epilogues to the story. They must include Eliza, Higgins, Freddy, the Colonel, Clara, and Doolittle. See writing assignment 1 on page 1209.

A Comment on the Play

Pygmalion (1912) was Shaw's first popular success. Its original run in London was cut short by the beginning of World War I, but it subsequently was played all over the world and finally emerged, in 1956, as the superb musical *My Fair Lady* by Alan Jay Lerner and Frederick Lowe.

People interested in the creative process are always asking writers: Which came first, the story, the characters, or the theme? Apparently, in *Pygmalion,* the juxtaposition of the two main characters came first. In a letter to the actress Ellen Terry in 1897, Shaw wrote:

Caesar and Cleopatra has been driven clean out of my head by a play I want to write for them [the actors Forbes-Robertson and Mrs. Patrick Campbell] in which he shall be a West End gentleman and she an East End dona [a Spanish lady] in an apron and three orange and red ostrich feathers.

The facing off of two characters with opposite natures always makes for a good theatrical situation. But a situation does not make a play. The characters must be

1. From the dialogue at the end of Act Four, we suspect that Eliza and Freddy have ridden around all night in the taxicab and that Eliza is now at Mrs. Higgins's house.
2. Doolittle is now a respectable, nicely dressed gentleman, who has inherited a trust fund from a wealthy American.

He chafes under the restrictions of his new "respectability."
3. She says she learned more about being a lady as a result of Pickering's gentlemanly treatment than from Higgins's speech lessons.
4. Among the examples are Higgins's sitting down on the ottoman near Eliza, his bouncing up on his knees, and his thunderstruck reaction when Eliza re-

veals that she will marry Freddy.
5. He says that people should treat everyone in exactly the same way.
6. They are really arguing about their relationship.

Eliza's main point is that she wants a little kindness.
7. He tells Eliza that he depends on her.

He will adopt her as his daughter and settle money on her.

---

fleshed out, and for Shaw, there had to be a message. In the Preface he wrote to the text of the play, he boasts about the success of this didactic play, but Shaw must have known that the success of *Pygmalion* was due to its appealing Cinderella theme and not to his preaching. (This same kind of perversity and irony appeared years later when Shaw was negotiating a contract with the famous Hollywood producer Samuel Goldwyn. "The trouble, Mr. Goldwyn," said Shaw, "is that you are always thinking about art and I am thinking about money.")

The American playwright Howard Lindsay, who with Russel Crouse wrote *Life with Father,* used to tell young playwrights that it's all right for a play to have a message, but they shouldn't let the characters know it. In other words, no ringing speeches should be made. Sam Goldwyn, another theatrical personage who did not believe in message plays, put it another way: "If you want to send a message, use Western Union."

Shaw had various messages, and he sent many of them via *Pygmalion.* The first message is about his arch-enemy, the upper classes: By having an illiterate flower seller pass as a duchess just by learning how to speak and act properly, Shaw exposed the foolish pretensions of high society. In other words, class is only speech-deep.

Later, Eliza voices a more profound truth when she says to Pickering, "the difference between a lady and a flower girl is not how she behaves, but how she's treated."

The most serious message is expressed in Eliza's constant question, "What's to become of me?" At the time of this play, education in England was becoming increasingly available to all classes; but the educated flower girl would still be a flower girl. The class system would make it difficult for her to find work commensurate with her new talents and education.

A final point seems to be a very personal one with Shaw. In the face of Eliza's emotional appeal to Higgins that he "care" for her, Shaw claims again that the superior person should be allowed to pursue his or her high vocation without getting enmeshed in emotional turmoil. This seems a very cold way of living, but many an artist has struggled to achieve the solitude which creativity demands but to avoid the problem of loneliness. Shaw solved the problem for himself by making a friendly marriage in which, he said, emotion played no part.

For many people, Shaw's insistence on this theme, on keeping Eliza and Higgins apart, almost ruins the play. They expect a play called *Pygmalion* to follow the general outlines of the Greek legend, in which the sculptor, Pygmalion, falls in love with the statue of a beautiful woman he has carved from marble. After asking the gods to bring her to life, he marries her.

The entire movement of *Pygmalion,* the tidal pull of the story, is that Cinderella will break down the reserve of her crusty prince and move off with him into the sunset. But Shaw's message would not allow this. And this was not just perversity on his part. Using his favorite device of anticlimax, Shaw meant to make a point, to

shock us, to disappoint our expectations, and make us see his message. He wanted Eliza to be the New Woman, rising above the conventional comforts of home and the usual wifely duties of fetching slippers. Shaw meant us to rejoice in Eliza's freedom. (Most audiences, however, would rather have seen "girl get boy.") Shaw might have built his story so that we would have been eager for Eliza to go off on her own, but he didn't. He was stuck with the charming story that demanded a fairy-tale ending which he wouldn't allow.

The actors playing Higgins, however, sometimes take matters into their own hands. The actor who originally played the part of Higgins in London threw a rose after the departing Eliza at the play's end. The famous film made from the play fades out on actor Leslie Howard's loving smile as he watches Eliza go. And in *My Fair Lady,* the musical comedy made from the play, the adapters ignored Shaw altogether and brought Eliza and Higgins together in the end.

When Shaw was asked why he allowed a "happy ending" in the movie, he retorted,

I did not. I cannot conceive a less happy ending to the story of *Pygmalion* than a love affair between the middle-class professor, a confirmed bachelor with a mother fixation, and a flower girl of 18.

Change is at the heart of drama. In *Pygmalion* we watch the changes in Eliza and note the possibility of change in Higgins. (Whenever a character declares himself a "confirmed bachelor" in Act One, the audience is bound to say to itself, "We'll see about that.") The normal change of a character in a play is always rewarding, but when the main character changes, in Cinderella fashion, from guttersnipe to duchess, the audience is enraptured. This transformation of the "plain girl" into a beauty has by now been the basis of so many plays and movies that it has become an almost overworked cliché.

Once Shaw put the flower seller together with the West End phonetics teacher, the story practically wrote itself: Girl wants to improve herself. Teacher thinks it a joke to pass her off as a duchess. Obstacles—the basic difficulty of the task and Eliza's unwillingness to be bossed around by an uncaring tyrant.

The plot moves along, as we'd expect in a Cinderella story, toward its **climax** at the ball. (Shaw omitted the ball scene itself as too expensive to produce on stage. In the musical *My Fair Lady,* it is the climactic scene.) Meanwhile, we watch the development of the relationship between Eliza and Higgins. Actually, Shaw shows us little or nothing of the training of Eliza, while *My Fair Lady* uses it for a series of delightful numbers.

The plot of the play is actually completed about halfway through, when Eliza charms everyone at the ball. But the more important story questions, "What is to become of me?" and "What is to become of us?" are not answered until the last scene, when Shaw delivers his message—to our satisfaction or dissatisfaction.

8. Infuriated at the suggestion that Eliza may marry Nepommuck and reveal his professional secrets, Higgins lays hands on her as if to shake her.

Interpreting Meanings

9. Eliza certainly is no longer afraid of Higgins and she knows she can do without him.

10. Some will say that Higgins has remained exactly true to character.

11. Many will agree with the theory that Shaw's intent is ambiguous, since the futures of Eliza and Higgins are left up in the air.

The Play as a Whole

1. Most students will say that Shaw led them to expect a romantic ending. In the epilogue, Shaw defends the outcome by saying that a romantic conclusion would have been a capitulation to stale convention. He says that a marriage between Higgins and Eliza would have been inconsistent with both of their characters. Student responses to Shaw's arguments will differ.

2. Since the play is entitled *Pygmalion*, many will argue that Higgins is the most important character. Some may suggest that Eliza is a more dynamic character than Higgins and is therefore the real protagonist. Since the basic conflict hinges on their relationship, the two characters may be seen as equally important.

3. Among the alterations are making the "metamorphosis" of Eliza include her speech, rather than just her physical appearance; the fact that Higgins does not fall passionately in love with Eliza; the outcome of the play.

Student speculations on why Shaw made these changes will differ.

4. Doolittle functions as a vehicle of comic relief and social commentary; Mrs. Eynsford Hill, as a conventional middle-class matron; Mrs. Pearce, as a kindly "housekeeper" stereotype; and Freddy as the romantic, handsome, young hero.

Shaw probably approves most of Mrs. Pearce's kindness and good sense.

5. She has gained self-respect.

Some may suggest that she has lost a certain quality of innocence and naiveté, which were traits that made her attractive originally.

Responding to the Play

Analyzing Act Five

Identifying Facts

1. At the end of Act Four, Eliza leaves Higgins's house. At the beginning of Act Five, how does Shaw let us know where Eliza is?
2. How has Doolittle been transformed? Why is he miserable with his new station in life?
3. How does Eliza turn the tables on Higgins when she tells Pickering what *really* turned her into a lady?
4. Though Higgins is not about to humble himself when he and Eliza are finally alone together, Shaw reveals how vulnerable Higgins is through certain stage directions. Cite examples of these.
5. Explain in your own words Higgins's theory of how people should behave toward each other.
6. As Eliza and Higgins argue, they seem to slip from subject to subject. What are they really arguing about? What is Eliza's main point?
7. In Act Two, Mrs. Pearce tells us how Higgins can turn on his charm. How does he do it in Act Five? What does he offer Eliza if she comes back?
8. Higgins and Eliza finally do have passionate physical contact. How is it shown?

Interpreting Meanings

9. Are you convinced by Eliza's transition from someone who wants to be cared about to someone who is independent? Explain.
10. Do you see any evidence that Higgins has also changed? Explain.
11. What do you think about the ending of the play? Is Shaw's intent ambiguous, or do you think it is perfectly clear?

The Play as a Whole

1. What kind of ending did Shaw lead you to expect? How does Shaw defend the outcome of his play in the epilogue? How do you feel about his arguments in the epilogue?
2. In your view, who emerges as the play's most important character, or **protagonist**: Eliza or Higgins? Defend your opinion.
3. Look up the myth of Pygmalion in Ovid's *Metamorphoses* or in a reference book. How has Shaw altered the myth? Why might Shaw have made these changes?
4. Look back over the roles of the minor characters in the play. Explain the dramatic function of each of the following characters: Doolittle, Mrs. Eynsford Hill, Mrs. Pearce, Freddy. How are some of these people representative of **character types**? Which types does Shaw approve of?
5. What has Eliza gained as a result of her experience with Higgins? What, if anything, has she lost?
6. Try to state Shaw's **theme**, or underlying message, in two or three sentences. What do you think of his theme?
7. If we think of *Pygmalion* as a **satire**, who or what would you say are Shaw's targets? What is your response to his satire? Do you think it has application to society as you know it today?

Writing About the Play

A Creative Response

1. **Extending the Play.** Shaw has proposed one explanation of what happens between Eliza and Higgins after the final curtain has fallen. Write a sequel to the play, in dialogue or in narrative form, showing what *you* think happens to Eliza, Higgins, and Freddy in the six months after the conclusion of the play.
2. **Updating the Story.** One of the marks of a classic is that it is relevant even after its setting has become outdated. Suppose, however, you wanted to do a modern version of this play, perhaps for a TV special. In a brief essay, discuss the changes that would have to be made in the script in order to make the situation current. In your discussion, consider not only Higgins's profession and Eliza's background and aspirations, but also the relationship.
3. **Adapting Another Myth to the Stage.** Select another myth (perhaps one of the ones listed below), and in an essay describe how you would update it and adapt it to the stage. Consider who your **characters** would be, what their problem or **conflict** would be, and what your **contemporary setting** would be. Would you change any part of the story?

   a. King Midas and the Golden Touch
   b. Demeter and Persephone
   c. Icarus and Daedalus
   d. Orpheus and Eurydice
   e. Phaëthon

A Critical Response

4. **Analyzing Dialogue.** One consistent criticism of Shaw's plays is that they contain too much preaching, philosophizing, or speechifying. Do you think such a criticism is applicable to *Pygmalion*? Explain your opinion in a brief essay.

6. The theme has to do with society's false values. Shaw mocks the English language and English class structure. He also believes that our conventional ideas of romantic love and marriage are ridiculous.

7. Among the targets are hollow social conventions, snobbishness, posturing, and the attitudes of the rich (or the middle class) toward the poor.

Students' reactions to the satire will vary, but most will agree that the satire still has application to today's society.

Poster from a Theatre Guild production of *Pygmalion*, New York City, 1926.

5. Analyzing Themes. Shaw's play is full of themes on a variety of topics, such as (a) social classes, (b) education, (c) language, (d) friendship, (e) poverty, (f) courtesy, and (g) appearance and reality. Select two topics that interest you, and in a brief essay, discuss Shaw's comments on each one. How are his themes relevant to the contemporary world?

6. Analyzing an Adaptation. Listen to a recording of the songs from *My Fair Lady,* the musical based on *Pygmalion.* Select one song that you think expresses Shaw's intentions well, and one that he might have disapproved of. Defend your opinion of the two songs in a brief essay.

7. Responding to Shaw's Women Characters. Actresses have always considered Shaw's women characters "plum" roles. In a three-paragraph essay, write your response to Shaw's depiction of women in *Pygmalion.*

Open with a statement that summarizes your general response to his characterization of women. Support your response with quotations from the play and from the epilogue.

8. Responding to a Critic. Read the following critical review of *Pygmalion,* and then write an essay of at least three paragraphs in which you respond to the critic's **main ideas**. Before you write, make a list of just what this critic's main ideas are, and the details he uses to support them, if any.

Pygmalion's enduring popularity has somewhat embarrassed Shaw's critics. Its fairy-tale atmosphere, traditional form, and romantic undertones, as well as its apparent absence of philosophic weight and social significance, have made it seem rather an anomaly in the dramatist's output, and its very fame in several stage and screen versions has further encouraged the critics to dismiss it as merely a superior piece of commercial theater. Shaw himself abetted this snobbery by calling the play a "shameless potboiler" and by allowing it only a scanty preface, which reduced its meaning to little more than a plea for alphabetical reform. Yet despite the opinion of Shaw the critic and his more deferential followers, the public has been right to esteem this work, which is in fact one of his richest creations not only in its obvious charms but precisely in the depth of its psychological insights, the range of its philosophical implications, and the wit of its many literary allusions. And its apparent lack of the Big Issues in the other major plays only indicates Shaw's achievement here in weaving those issues so finely into the fabric of characterization and structure that one can scarcely talk about the ideas without talking about the people, who happily transcend anything that can be said about them. Moreover, like other true works of art, the play affects us in hidden ways and came from hidden recesses in the writer's own being. It was drawn from depths Shaw has never before reached and was incubated longer than any other play he wrote. His later belittling of the play arose in part from a desire to deflect attention from the ways it incorporated essential aspects of himself. In short, *Pygmalion* is neither the "lucky" hit that one critic has called it, nor yet again the oddly atypical work that others have considered it to be, but rather the one play of them all that Shaw was born to write.

—Arnold Silver

9. Responding to Shaw's Epilogue. Write a response to Shaw's epilogue to the play. You might want to put your response in the form of a letter to Shaw. Before you write, be sure that you have isolated Shaw's **main ideas** in the Epilogue, and that you've decided which of these ideas you want to address your remarks to.

Using the Commentary
This commentary on contemporary British drama was written by American playwright Robert Anderson. You'll find many scenes and speeches reproduced here from landmark contemporary dramas:

Juno and the Paycock by Sean O'Casey (pages 1213–1214)
Private Lives by Noel Coward (pages 1214–1215)
Look Back in Anger by John Osborne (page 1216)
Waiting for Godot by Samuel Beckett (pages 1217–1219)

Harold Pinter
On pages 1221–1222 is the complete text of *That's All,* a sketch by contemporary British dramatist Harold Pinter.

MODERN BRITISH DRAMA
by Robert Anderson

The nineteenth-century American essayist Ralph Waldo Emerson wrote, "All history resolves itself easily into the biography of a few stout and earnest persons." Hindsight makes it relatively easy to say that the only stout and earnest persons in British drama of the eighteenth century were Richard Sheridan and Oliver Goldsmith, and in the nineteenth century, Oscar Wilde and Bernard Shaw.

It is more difficult to know which of the playwrights of the twentieth century will stand the test of time—because we are still in it. Plays are volatile creations, written out of present concerns and emotions to reach an audience in the present. In a changing world with changing fashions, there is no way of knowing how people will respond to plays in the future. The highly regarded play of one generation is often viewed with contempt by the next generation: "How could they have thought that was a great play?"

Departures from Conventions: New Subjects and Forms

Perhaps more significant than the work of any one "great" playwright have been the sweeping changes in the content and form of plays in this century. The subjects that now can be written about have expanded enormously. Censorship of the stage in England ended in 1968, and now there is virtually nothing that playwrights have not written about or cannot write about.

While the broadening of subject matter is probably the most significant breakthrough, some playwrights have been less interested in new subject matter than in new ways to get our attention—to shock us into recognizing old and new truths. These playwrights have followed various paths. Some have broken up the usual linear structure of a story—a beginning, a middle, and an end arranged in that order. In their plays they jump backward and forward in time, hither and yon in space. Some, like the German playwright Bertolt Brecht, do not want to engage our sympathy for any character, but want us to keep our distance. Brecht called this "the alienation effect." Some, like the Irish playwright Samuel Beckett, ignore the usual ingredients of drama—character, conflict, development, and progression to a climax—and present us instead with a static situation. As the British critic Kenneth Tynan pointed out, if they have done nothing else, these new forms have made us reconsider the long-held principles of playwriting.

For centuries in all countries, the theater thrived on presenting a story with a beginning, a middle, and an end, told in that order, and involving conflict among characters who interest us. Playwrights who depart from these conventions take a great risk; they

The Peacock Skirt from *Salome* by Oscar Wilde. Drawing by Aubrey Beardsley (1894).

A

> " **C**ensorship of the stage in England ended in 1968, and now there is virtually nothing that playwrights have not written about or cannot write about."

B

A. Discussing the Drawing
Aubrey Beardsley (1872–1898) is noted for his decorative work, which is closely linked with Art Nouveau. This famous pen-and-ink shows Beardsley's concern with formal design. The influence of Japanese prints on the artist is clear. Note the rhythms and tight interrelationships of the curving lines and sweeping shapes. Beardsley is concerned more with a pleasing design than with a true depiction of reality.

B. Expansion
Call students' attention to this note about censorship, which will probably surprise them. You might assign them to do research on forms of censorship that exist in the United States today. Consider the stage, movies, and TV.

A. The Stained-Glass Window

The Fabian Society, founded in 1884, brought together persons who believed in a gradualist, reformist Socialism (in contrast to revolutionary Communism). Noted Fabians, besides Shaw and Wells, included Sidney Webb (1859–1947) and his wife Beatrice Potter Webb (1858–1943). The society was named for the Roman general Quintus Fabius Maximus Verucosus Cunctator (d. 203 B.C.), known as The Delayer because of his tactic in war of wearing down and harrassing the enemy without actually fighting a decisive battle.

B. The Abbey

The Abbey Theater still exists in Dublin and has recently been completely renovated. A photograph of the original Abbey is on page 1087.

Fabian window at the Beatrice Webb House, Leith Hill, Surrey, England (1910). Stained glass.

Bernard Shaw is pictured on right. H. G. Wells is thumbing his nose on left.

A

are like performers on a very high wire without the safety net of a story. They had better be star performers every time out, or there will be disaster. If they deny their audiences the pleasure of narrative ("Tell me a story!"), they have to keep them fascinated by other means.

Irish Dramatists: Yeats, Synge, and O'Casey

In the period of national awakening starting in the 1880's, Irish drama flourished as an extension of Irish poetry. (Ireland had always been famous for recited poetry, the poetry of the Celtic bards.)

Ireland's first significant playwright was the poet and Nobel laureate William Butler Yeats. Together with Lady Gregory, the influential wife of a member of Parliament and herself a minor writer of folk plays, Yeats founded the Irish Literary Theater in 1899. The first production, Yeats's play *The Countess Cathleen*, was greeted with catcalls, foot-stamping, and a near-riot. The same kind of welcome was later accorded to John Millington Synge's *The Playboy of the Western World* (1907) and Sean O'Casey's *The Plough and the Stars* (1926). (To lessen the noise of the stamping feet, the theater owners finally carpeted the floor.)

B In 1904 the famous Abbey Theater opened its doors in Dublin and joined the other new small theaters throughout Europe—the Moscow Art Theater, the Theatre Libre in France, and Grein's Independent Theater in London. These theaters catered largely to playwrights writing the "new" plays. In much the same way, experimental American drama is now done not in large theaters, but

1212

in small off-Broadway houses or in regional theaters scattered across the country.

John Millington Synge (1871–1909) re-created the stories and legends of Ireland and infused them with a poetry unequaled since Shakespeare. Synge wrote that in Ireland "those of us who wish to write start with a chance that is not given to writers in places where the springtime of local life has been forgotten and the harvest is a mere memory only, and the straw has been turned into bricks." He said he had learned how to catch the colorful speech of the peasants by listening at chinks in the floor above the kitchen, where the servants were gossiping.

Synge's major work, *The Playboy of the Western World*, derives from a folk story he heard in the Aran Islands. A young man, Christy Mahon, arrives at a country pub claiming to have killed his father in a distant village. He is at once regarded as a hero, and two women, Pegeen and the Widow Quinn, set their caps for him. His father then appears, and Christy bashes in his head and "kills" him again. This time the village folk are horrified. A patricide in a distant village is different from one in your own town. But the indestructible father returns yet again and drags off his thoroughly deflated son.

The play is a satire on hero worship and the Irish temperament. It is rich in poetic language and boasts a cast of colorful characters worthy of Dickens or Shakespeare. The members of the first audience stamped their feet to show their outrage: Synge, they felt, was offending Irish womanhood by showing two Irish women vying for the affections of a murderer.

Synge died of cancer in 1909 at the age of thirty-nine, and the Abbey Theater had to wait almost fifteen years for its next giant, Sean O'Casey (1880–1964). The Abbey Theater produced his play *The Shadow of a Gunman* in 1923. Born in the slums of Dublin, O'Casey wrote about the city slums as Synge had written about the country peasants. He depicted their poverty and misery realistically, but his plays are also infused with beauty, energy, and humor.

O'Casey's most famous play is *Juno and the Paycock* (1924), which tells of a near-destitute family of romantic and patriotic Irishmen held together by the wife-mother Juno. Though O'Casey had enlisted in the fighting for a free Ireland, he could be objectively critical of the men who fought and died "gloriously" while leaving their wives and mothers to cope with the more urgent problems of living in misery and poverty.

> **Johnny.** I'd do it agen, Ma. I'd do it agen; for a principle's a principle.
> **Juno.** Ah, you lost your best principle, me boy, when you lost your arm; them's the only sort of principles that's any good to a workin' man.
>
> —from *Juno and the Paycock*,
> Sean O'Casey

Meanwhile, Juno's husband, the Paycock, works very hard at avoiding work and spends his time at the pub with his crony, Joxer. In

" **T**he members of the first audience stamped their feet to show their outrage: Synge, they felt, was offending Irish womanhood by showing two Irish women vying for the affections of a murderer."

A

Awaiting Admission to the Casual Ward by Sir Luke Fildes.

A. **Responding to the Painting**
Sir Luke Fildes (1884–1927) was an English genre and portrait painter.
? What is the principal feeling you take from this painting? Cite at least three qualities of the painting that help evoke your feeling. (The painting will evoke a feeling of sadness in many students. Contributing to the feeling are the somber colors of the painting; the bowed heads of many persons depicted; the child tugging at the mother; etc.)

Private Lives by Noel Coward.

> " The 'shocking' play of one generation often seems mild and slightly musty to the next."

A. Discussing the Photograph
Coward and the great Gertrude Lawrence are shown here on the balcony. Encourage an oral reading of Amanda and Elyot's dialogue on this page and the next, to give students a taste of the Coward wit. You might encourage readers to mimic an upper class British accent. *Private Lives* ends, in the tradition of many great comedies, with the battling lovers, Amanda and Elyot, reunited. *Private Lives* is frequently revived in New York and in regional theaters throughout the United States. You might have *Private Lives* or Coward's comedy *Blithe Spirit* read aloud in the classroom with a capable cast.

the end, their hopes are gone, their son has been dragged out and executed, and Juno is left to cry out:

Juno. Mother o' God, Mother o' God, have pity on us all! Blessed Virgin, where were you when me darlin' son was riddled with bullets? Sacred heart o' Jesus, take away our hearts o' stone, and give us hearts o' flesh! Take away our murtherin' hate and give us Thine own eternal love.

—from *Juno and the Paycock*, Sean O'Casey

English Comedy and Noel Coward

"For a people notoriously well bred," the drama critic John Gassner said, "the English can be delightfully poisonous in comedy, which is perhaps a way of avenging themselves on their breeding." Until recently the great figures in English drama (aside from Shakespeare) have been writers of comedy, not tragedy. The most successful English writer of comedies in this century is Noel Coward (1899–1973).

Coward was a complete theater man—actor, director, playwright, lyricist, and composer. He emerged in the 1920's, the post-World War I period of "flaming youth" and endless parties. His flip, cynical manner, which is the eternal manner of high comedy, suited the times. In 1925, a year after O'Casey's *Juno and the Paycock* had been produced in Dublin, Coward's *The Vortex* was shocking audiences in London. (The "shocking" play of one generation often seems mild and slightly musty to the next.) Coward could also be outrageously sentimental. For more than forty years he alternately shocked and charmed audiences with such plays as *Bitter Sweet* (1929), *Private Lives* (1930), *Cavalcade* (1931), *Design for Living* (1933), and *Blithe Spirit* (1941).

Coward's most successful play was *Private Lives*, in which he appeared with Gertrude Lawrence and Laurence Olivier. It is the story of a divorced couple, each remarried, now finding themselves honeymooning with the new spouses in adjacent suites in a hotel on the French Riviera. Each has married a nice but rather colorless person. On discovering the situation, Elyot and Amanda separately try to persuade their respective spouses, Sybil and Victor, to leave the hotel and flee to Paris. They succeed only in driving Sybil and Victor into a rage. Amanda and Elyot then meet on the balcony between their suites.

Amanda. What's happened to yours?
Elyot. Didn't you hear her screaming? She's downstairs in the dining room, I think.
Amanda. Mine's being grand at the bar.
Elyot. It really is awfully difficult.
Amanda. Have you known her long?
Elyot. About four months. We met at a house party in Norfolk.
Amanda. Very flat, Norfolk.

Elyot. How old is dear Victor?

Amanda. Thirty-four, or five. And Sybil?

Elyot. I blush to tell you only twenty-three.

Amanda. You've gone a mucker all right.

Elyot. I shall reserve my opinion of your choice until I've met dear Victor.

Amanda. I wish you wouldn't go on calling him "dear Victor." It's extremely irritating.

Elyot. That's how I see him. Dumpy and fair, and very considerate, with glasses. Dear Victor.

Amanda. As I said before, I would rather not discuss him. At least I have good taste enough to refrain from making cheap gibes at Sybil.

Elyot. You said Norfolk was flat.

Amanda. That was no reflection on her unless she made it flatter.

—from *Private Lives,*
Noel Coward

The Angry Young Men

But English drama soon turned its back on the charm of Coward and plunged into "the real world" of England in the 1950's.

In 1956 John Osborne's *Look Back in Anger* was produced by George Devine at the Royal Court Theater. English drama has not been the same since. It is convenient to put up a sign and say, "It all started here." But, of course, nothing in the arts is quite that self-starting, and no one can ever really know what gives rise to a certain kind of creativity. One can only look back and discover trends, movements, and sources which may or may not have been influential.

First, certain social conditions may have given rise to the generation of playwrights that came to be known as "the angry young men." England had lost a generation of young men in World War I, had endured World War II and suffered incalculable losses in standing long alone against Hitler, had gone through a devastating depression, and had gradually watched the Empire slip away. It was not a time for rejoicing. But great drama does not often come from rejoicing. It can come from anger, frustration, bewilderment, and despair.

Second, London had seen innovative productions of plays by such European writers as Jean-Paul Sartre, Jean Anouilh, Eugene Ionesco, Bertolt Brecht, Luigi Pirandello, and Samuel Beckett. Earlier, there had been productions of American proletarian playwrights, such as Clifford Odets. Smaller fringe or alternative theaters were also producing offbeat, experimental plays. Chief among these were Joan Littlewood's Stratford East and George Devine's English Stage Company at the Royal Court, which concentrated on new English playwrights, such as John Osborne, Arnold Wesker, Harold Pinter, Edward Bond, and David Storey.

John Osborne's (1929—   ) *Look Back in Anger* represents a

> "**G**reat drama does not often come from rejoicing. It can come from anger, frustration, bewilderment, and despair."

A

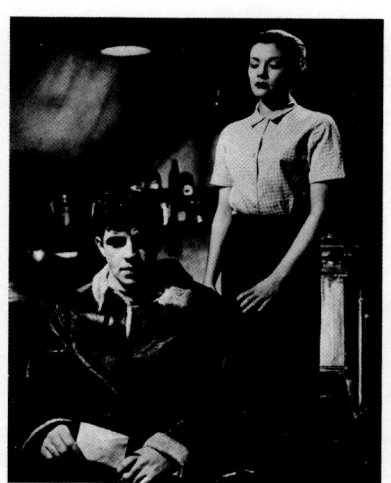

Look Back in Anger by John Osborne.

couple is stylish, formal, elegant; they are perched on the balcony of an expensive hotel in an exotic setting; they are assuming a typical romantic pose, perhaps poised for a kiss. We can imagine moonlight and romantic dance music. Osborne's young couple, Alison and Jimmy, are in everyday working-class dress (the leather jacket on Jimmy suggests an attempt to be macho); they are shown in a dingy, dark flat, and they seem strained and tense with each other. The modern obsession with the ideas of alienation and the difficulty of communication are easily noted in this single photograph.

A. Allusion
See if students recognize the ironic allusion to Wordsworth's famous Romantic lyric (page 642). Note that Jimmy has a different theory of where poetry comes from.

B. Discussing the Photograph
Brecht's *Mother Courage and Her Children* (1939) tells of a mother's attempt to survive with her three children during the horrors of the Thirty Years War (1618–1648). The mother supports the family by selling trifles to soldiers fighting in the war. The children are all killed. The play is divided into twelve episodes.

Brecht (1898–1956) grew up in Germany and gained fame there in the 1920's, especially with *The Threepenny Opera* (1928; an adaptation of John Gay's *The Beggar's Opera* [1728]). During World War II, Brecht lived in the United States. In 1949 he returned to Germany, founding and guiding the highly respected Berliner Ensemble theater company in East Berlin. Brecht's wife, Hélène Weigel (1900–1971), a noted actress, created the role of Mother Courage. Other plays by Brecht include *In the Jungle of Cities* (1924), *The Rise and Fall of the City of Mahagonny* (1929), *The Life of Galileo* (1938–1939), *The Good Woman of Setzuan* (1939–1941), and *The Caucasian Chalk Circle* (1944–1945).

Mother Courage and Her Children
by Bertolt Brecht.

breakthrough in content and style, but not in form. Structurally, it is a conventional well-made play, but the style and mood are different. It is about a different class of people, not the drawing-room class of Coward sophisticates. It deals with the disenchanted, disenfranchised, and angry youth who have great vitality but no sense of purpose: "No good causes left." They are anti-establishment, disgusted with "them," whoever "them" might be.

In the course of the play nothing much happens that hadn't happened in other plays—marital conflict, flirtations, unwanted children. But it is not genteel; it is rough and tumble and caustic and filled with the vitality of its central character, Jimmy Porter.

> **Jimmy.** One day, when I'm no longer spending my days running a sweet stall, I may write a book about us all. It's all here. (*Slapping his forehead*) Written in flames a mile high. And it won't be recollected in tranquility either, picking daffodils with Auntie Wordsworth. It'll be recollected in fire and blood, my blood.
>
> —from *Look Back in Anger,*
> John Osborne

The essence of the angry young men's drama is a kind of left-wing lashing out. Something is wrong with the world, they are saying; something has to be changed. But nobody has a specific program. These plays, which declared war on a whole section of society, had great appeal for the young postwar intellectuals.

Obsorne wrote his next play, *The Entertainer* (1957), for Laurence Olivier. It tells the story of a seedy music hall comic and also serves as the symbolic representation of the plight of modern England. In *The Entertainer*, Osborne shows the influence of the German playwright Bertolt Brecht, whose plays and theories of drama had considerable impact on the English playwrights of the 1960's, 1970's, and 1980's.

Brecht, the author of such plays as *The Threepenny Opera* (1928), *Mother Courage and Her Children* (1941), and *The Caucasian Chalk Circle* (1945), stated that he did not want his audience to identify with his characters, did not want them sitting there almost drugged by emotional involvement with the play. He wanted them not to *feel*, but to *think*. He wanted them always to be aware that they were in a theater watching a play, not behind some imaginary fourth wall eavesdropping on real life. To achieve this end, he often had actors address the audience directly. He interrupted his scenes with songs and broke up the action into short scenes that did not necessarily lead into one another. He called this approach "epic theater." Brecht's emphasis on theater as theater, letting us see the stage lights and the struts holding up the scenery, avoiding all efforts at the illusion of reality, has had great influence on contemporary drama.

It is not, however, the innovative use of forms and theatrical techniques that marks Osborne's continuing work. It is the raw energy and vitality in such plays as *Inadmissible Evidence* (1964), a virtual monologue in which a middle-aged lawyer spews forth his self-loathing and his disgust with the world.

Theater of the Absurd: Samuel Beckett

Though Samuel Beckett (1906–1989) was born in Ireland, he lived most of his life in France and wrote many of his plays in French, which he then translated into English. Whether or not he can be considered a British playwright, his *Waiting for Godot* (1953) is a modern classic, and his work is a prime example of what is known as the Theater of the Absurd.

Deriving to some degree from James Joyce and Surrealism, the Theater of the Absurd is an almost complete departure from the traditional theater of the preceding four hundred years. It should be noted at once that just as there was no "school" of the "angry young men," so there is no "school" of the Absurdist—just a number of writers, perhaps influenced by one another, employing the methods of Absurdism for their own ends.

The Theater of the Absurd, first of all, represents an attitude toward life expressed in part by French writer Albert Camus:

> A world that can be explained by reasoning, however faulty, is a familiar world. But in a universe that is suddenly deprived of illusion and of light, man feels a stranger. . . . This divorce between man and his life . . . truly contributes to the feeling of absurdity.
>
> —from *The Myth of Sisyphus,* Albert Camus

The Absurdists do not want to tell us a story with characters arguing about the emptiness of life. They want instead to *present* us with this emptiness, this absurdity, moment by moment, so that we can experience it. There is usually no progression, no development in an Absurdist play. As we shall see in Beckett's *Waiting for Godot,* the "action" is waiting. The French title for Beckett's play is *En Attendant Godot,* literally, "While Waiting for Godot." The play is about the "while." Since the Absurdists' view is that the world is irrational, unmotivated, without cause and effect, they convey this idea not only as "the message" of the play but in the fragmented, irrational method of the playwriting. *Waiting for Godot* was first produced in Paris in 1953 and in London in 1955. Two tramps, Vladimir and Estragon, are on a stage, bare except for a tree.

Estragon. Charming spot. (*He turns, advances to the front, halts facing auditorium.*) Inspiring prospects. (*He turns to* VLADIMIR.) Let's go.
Vladimir. We can't.
Estragon. Why not?
Vladimir. We're waiting for Godot.
Estragon (*despairingly*). Ah! (*Pause*) You're sure it was here?
Vladimir. What?
Estragon. That we were to wait.
Vladimir. He said by the tree. (*They look at the tree.*) Do you see any others?

A

Samuel Beckett's *Trilogy.*

B

" **In** Beckett's *Waiting for Godot,* the 'action' is waiting."

A. Discussing the Photograph

Stage settings of realistic and nonrealistic plays usually are very different. The setting of a realistic play typically will evoke an actual setting in a specific place and time (for instance, a drawing room in Victorian England). In a nonrealistic play, such as *Waiting for Godot,* the stage setting often will not evoke an actual setting and will be rather bare. The set designer may seek mainly to create a mood among onlookers, partly by actively engaging their imaginations. An abstract design might be significant for its own sake. On the other hand, the symbolism of props and other aspects of the setting might be important. In the set design for this production of *Godot,* for example, the tree may serve in its traditional symbolic role as the "axis of the universe," that is, the link between the underworld, the world about us, and the universe beyond the earth.

A

Waiting for Godot by Samuel Beckett.

Estragon. What is it?
Vladimir. I don't know. A willow.
Estragon. Where are the leaves?
Vladimir. It must be dead.
Estragon. No more weeping.
Vladimir. Or perhaps it's not the season.
Estragon. Looks to me more like a bush.
Vladimir. A shrub.
Estragon. A bush.
Vladimir. A——. What are you insinuating? That we've come to the wrong place?
Estragon. He should be here.
Vladimir. He didn't say for sure he'd come.
Estragon. And if he doesn't come?
Vladimir. We'll come back tomorrow.
Estragon. And then the day after tomorrow.
Vladimir. Possibly.
Estragon. And so on.
Vladimir. The point is——
Estragon. Until he comes.
Vladimir. You're merciless.
Estragon. We came here yesterday.
Vladimir. Ah, no, there you're mistaken.
Estragon. What did we do yesterday?
Vladimir. What did we do yesterday?
Estragon. Yes.
Vladimir. Why . . . (*Angrily*) Nothing is certain when you're about.
Estragon. In my opinion we were here.

Vladimir (*looking around*). You recognize the place?
Estragon. I didn't say that.
Vladimir. Well?
Estragon. That makes no difference.
Vladimir. All the same . . . that tree . . . (*turning toward auditorium*) that bog.
Estragon. You're sure it was this evening?
Vladimir. What?
Estragon. That we were to wait.
Vladimir. He said Saturday. (*Pause*) I think.
Estragon. You think.
Vladimir. I must have made a note of it. (*He fumbles in his pockets, bursting with miscellaneous rubbish.*)
Estragon (*very insidious*). But what Saturday? And is it Saturday? Is it not rather Sunday? (*Pause*) Or Monday? (*Pause*) Or Friday?
Vladimir (*looking wildly about him as though the date was inscribed in the landscape*). It's not possible!
Estragon. Or Thursday?
Vladimir. What'll we do?
Estragon. If he came yesterday and we weren't here you may be sure he won't come again today.
Vladimir. But you say we were here yesterday.
Estragon. I may be mistaken. (*Pause*) Let's stop talking for a minute. Do you mind?
Vladimir (*feebly*). All right.

—from *Waiting for Godot,*
Samuel Beckett

Thus ends one of the series of "riffs" which make up the play. After a few moments' pause, they will start up again, terrified by the silence and the momentary view of nothingness.

Many people find the Absurdists (Beckett, Eugene Ionesco, Jean Gênet, and some of Edward Albee) maddening. They say, "That's not a play!" just as some years ago, steeped in representational painting, we said of Abstract Expressionism, "That's not art!" Our expectations of what a play or a picture should be are deeply rooted in us, planted and nurtured by years of exposure to only one kind of dramatic experience or one kind of painting experience. The best we can do when faced with the strange is to try to remain open to the new, to let it try to educate us and broaden our appreciation, rather than to reject it because it is strange and new.

Who is Godot? When someone asked Beckett this question, he answered that if he had known, he would have revealed it in the play. Possibly Godot is best explained by Tennessee Williams when he has Tom say in *The Glass Menagerie* that the Gentleman Caller is "the long delayed but always expected something that we live for."

Beckett's tramps, like Laurel and Hardy, bicker in scene after scene, sometimes sounding like husband and wife in a standard domestic comedy. They seem to be derived in part from the end-

" Who is Godot? When someone asked Beckett this question, he answered that if he had known, he would have revealed it in the play."

A

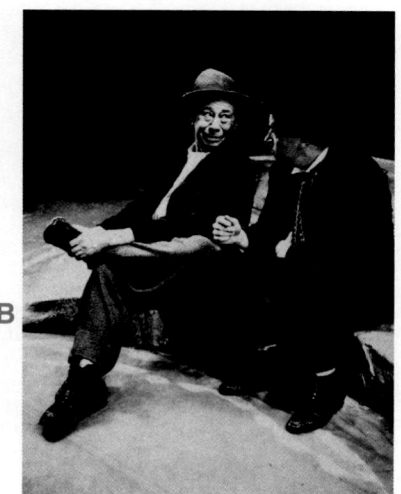

Waiting for Godot by Samuel Beckett.

A. About the Photograph
One of Beckett's famous "clowns" is played in this production by Bert Lahr, whom students might know as the Cowardly Lion in MGM's *The Wizard of Oz.*

B. Expansion
Spend a few moments on this important opinion.
[?] How can this idea be expanded to include art, literature, music, movies, design, even clothing and hair styles? What do you think of this admonition regarding "the new" or "the strange" in art? (Answers will vary, but students probably will find some grounds for agreement with it, as the opinion influences much of contemporary thought.)

A. Discussing the Photograph

The nonrealistic set design for *Endgame* reinforces the psychological relationship of the two characters. (The character in the foreground is the blind autocrat Hamm; the character in the background is Hamm's servant Clov.) The setting has an ominous, nightmarish quality—fitting for a play dealing with a disintegrating world.

The set design of a play can be very important. The set can help establish the play's mood and can reinforce its themes. The set can take on added importance if the script is elliptical or contains many ambiguities: We may look to the set to help explain the words and action of the play. This scene of *Endgame* probably would strike the audience very differently if played on a set of *Pygmalian* (photograph, pages 1176–1177).

"A critic reviewing a Pinter play might start by saying, 'This is a play about a man who did or did not meet a woman a year ago in a restaurant.'"

A

Endgame by Samuel Beckett.

men who used to appear in vaudeville and music halls, bantering jokes and wisecracks back and forth. They also resemble the comedian and the straight man in the comedy teams of movies, radio, and television. Though Beckett discarded all the ideas of progression and dramatic development, he does employ a number of the appealing theatrical tricks of farce and vaudeville. There are pratfalls, difficulty getting shoes on and off, trousers falling down, futile efforts at suicide. The tramps are joined by a bizarre pair, Pozzo and Lucky, one a master, the other a slave on the end of a rope—a vivid theatrical picture.

Toward the end of Act I, a boy arrives from Godot to say he will not arrive today, but "surely tomorrow." Act II is almost a repetition of Act I, except that when Pozzo and Lucky enter, Pozzo is blind and Lucky is dumb. The boy again arrives at the end of the act to say that Godot will not arrive today, but "surely tomorrow."

Beckett regarded habit as "the lightning conductor" of our existence—in other words, the small habitual activities that keep us busy every day, all day, prevent us from being hit with the truth, which (as Beckett sees it) is loneliness, nothingness.

Regarding language, the Absurdist movement is anti-literary. The Absurdists believe that language has broken down and can no longer convey meaning. When asked why, then, he used words, Beckett replied that words are all we have to work with. Actually, although Beckett turned his back on Naturalism (the exact, detailed duplication of real life), he was a Naturalist in his dialogue and sometimes even achieved a kind of poetry by his fidelity to real speech.

The nature of Beckett's work almost demands that it be performed in small, intimate theaters, where every flutter of an eye can register. Beckett's plays are done in such theaters all over the world, and he is the "master," the point of reference for many of the experimenters now working in the theater. He was awarded the Nobel Prize for literature in 1969.

The Plays of Harold Pinter

Harold Pinter (1930—   ), an avowed disciple of Beckett and probably the most influential of the new English playwrights, is on the fringe of the Absurdist Theater. While Beckett deals with often grotesque characters in bizarre settings (the two tramps in *Waiting for Godot*, two old people in ashcans in *Endgame*, a woman buried in sand up to her neck in *Happy Days*), Pinter most often presents us with more or less real settings and identifiable characters speaking everyday language. The whole, however, is stylized in a manner that is now called "Pinteresque."

With Pinter, we are not in a story-telling theater. To summarize what happens in these plays is as meaningless as trying to describe an Abstract Expressionist painting. Pinter's is a drama of ambiguities, implications, and contradictions. A critic reviewing a Pinter play might start by saying, "This is a play about a man who did or did not meet a woman a year ago in a restaurant." It is a world

Performing the Play

Pinter believed that people communicate as much through silence as through words. Have students note all the instructions in *That's All* to "pause." These pauses are a Pinter hallmark. In addition, his dialogues often seem pointless, repetitious, and circular. You might ask these questions:

1. What do conversations like the one in *That's All* say about our ability to communicate on an intimate, personal level?

2. At each pause, what might the characters be thinking? What might they have said, if they had had the words or ability to say it?

3. Who might "she" be?

4. What significance can you find in the play's title?

where the real is menacing, the pregnant pauses (all carefully indicated by Pinter) are full of terror, and the banal speech is full of mystery.

In a traditional play, we watch the gradual unfolding of a character, as though we were watching an onion being peeled, until the psychological center of the person is exposed. In Pinter's plays we are not dealing with the complex psychology of character. Pinter's people are often without pasts—or they have self-contradicting pasts. Though Pinter avoids the conventional dramatic principles of progression and development, he starts from arresting situations, and he sustains mystery and suspense.

But it is Pinter's dialogue that is the hallmark of his art. He has taken the chitchat of everyday speech and stylized it to the point where it becomes a kind of poetry. The following revue sketch entitled *That's All* was first presented on BBC Radio in 1964.

That's All

Mrs. A. I always put the kettle on about that time.

Mrs. B. Yes. (*Pause*)

Mrs. A. Then she comes round.

Mrs. B. Yes. (*Pause*)

Mrs. A. Only on Thursdays.

Mrs. B. Yes. (*Pause*)

Mrs. A. On Wednesdays I used to put it on. When she used to come round. Then she changed it to Thursdays.

Mrs. B. Oh yes.

Mrs. A. After she moved. When she used to live round the corner, then she always came in on Wednesdays, but then when she moved she used to come down to the butcher's on Thursdays. She couldn't find a butcher up there.

Mrs. B. No.

Mrs. A. Anyway, she decided she'd stick to her own butcher. Well, I thought, if she can't find a butcher, that's the best thing.

Mrs. B. Yes. (*Pause*)

Mrs. A. So she started to come down on Thursdays. I didn't know she was coming down on Thursdays until one day I met her in the butcher.

Mrs. B. Oh yes.

Mrs. A. It wasn't my day for the butcher, I don't go to the butcher on Thursday.

Mrs. B. No, I know. (*Pause*)

Mrs. A. I go on Friday.

Mrs. B. Yes. (*Pause*)

Mrs. A. That's where I see you.

Mrs. B. Yes. (*Pause*)

Mrs. A. You're always in there on Fridays.

Mrs. B. Oh yes. (*Pause*)

Mrs. A. But I happened to go in for a bit of meat, it turned out to be a Thursday. I wasn't going in for my usual weekly on Friday. I just slipped in, the day before.

Mrs. B. Yes.

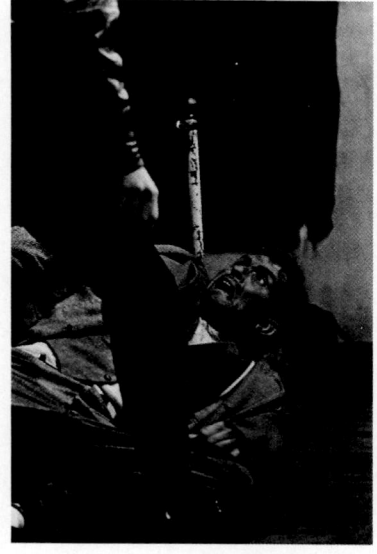

The Caretaker by Harold Pinter.

A

" **P**inter has taken the chitchat of everyday speech and stylized it to the point where it becomes a kind of poetry."

A. About the Photograph

The Caretaker (1959) is set in Aston's cluttered, decaying room in a shabby London neighborhood. The photo shows an elderly tramp, Davies, whom Aston has generously taken in. But Davies is a manipulator: He has no shoes and he uses this as an eternal excuse for not leaving. Eventually, Davies becomes Aston's caretaker. When a scene of violence (pictured here) takes place, Davies is tossed out, but not until he has alienated Aston from his brother. Again, have students note the contrast between this violent photograph and the one of Coward's elegant lovers on page 1214.

1. A well-made play has a beginning, a middle, and an end. (T)
2. John Millington Synge founded the Abbey Theater with W. B. Yeats. (F)
3. John Osborne's play *Look Back in Anger* portrayed the disillusionment of an upper-class hero. (F)

4. The plays of Samuel Beckett employ comic techniques associated with vaudeville or movie slapstick. (T)
5. Pinteresque dialogue suggests that what people do not say is often as important as what they do say. (T)

A. Expansion
British actor Ben Kingsley (he starred in *Gandhi*) is one of the best interpreters of Pinter today. You can hear Pinter's peculiar, halting, and flat dialogue in the movie version of *The Betrayal,* starring Kingsley and Jeremy Irons.

B. Writing Assignment
Some students might be capable of imitating Pinter's dialogue, using a snatch of dialogue from another play in this book. For example, you might suggest that they write the dialogue between Macbeth and Lady Macbeth in Act II, Scene 2, as Pinter might have written it; or the opening dialogue in *The Importance of Being Earnest,* up to Lady Bracknell's entrance on page 875; or the conversation among Mrs. Higgins, Higgins, and the Eynsford Hills in *Pygmalion,* pages 1174–1179.

Mrs. A. That was the first time I found out she couldn't find a butcher up there, so she decided to come back here, once a week, to her own butcher.
Mrs. B. Yes.
Mrs. A. She came on Thursday so she'd be able to get meat for the weekend. Lasted her till Monday, then from Monday to Thursday they'd have fish. She can always buy cold meat, if they want a change.
Mrs. B. Oh yes. (*Pause*)
Mrs. A. So I told her to come in when she came down after she'd been to the butcher's and I'd put a kettle on. So she did. (*Pause*)
Mrs. B. Yes. (*Pause*)
Mrs. A. It was funny because she always used to come in Wednesdays. (*Pause*) Still, it made a break. (*Long pause*)
Mrs. B. She doesn't come in no more, does she? (*Pause*)
Mrs. A. She comes in. She doesn't come in so much, but she comes in. (*Pause*)
Mrs. B. I thought she didn't come in. (*Pause*)
Mrs. A. She comes in. (*Pause*) She just doesn't come in so much. That's all.

—Harold Pinter

It is, of course, questionable how many situations, characters, or subjects can be dealt with in the Pinter manner. It would seem to be limiting. But over the last thirty years, he has written such notable full-length plays as *The Caretaker* (1960), *The Homecoming* (1965), *Old Times* (1971), and *Betrayal* (1978); and a series of highly effective short plays including *The Dumb Waiter* (1960), *The Collection* (1961), *Landscape* (1968), and *Silence* (1969). He has also adapted for motion pictures novels such as *The French Lieutenant's Woman* and *The Last Tycoon.*

British Theater Today

Beckett, Osborne, and Pinter are only three among the many flourishing contemporary playwrights in Great Britain. There are others who are writing in a wide range of styles and forms, more or less influenced by Beckett and Brecht. Yesterday's avant-garde is today's mainstream, and perhaps the avant-garde of tomorrow will be a return to some form of the conventional well-made play.

Americans have always considered London a great theater town, and it still is. Though seasons may vary in quality, in almost any year one may see productions from the rich dramatic literature of the country, past and present. The major British playwrights from Shakespeare to Shaw to Pinter form a galaxy to make Americans envious. Though the contemporary English theater may lack such tragic American masterworks as Eugene O'Neill's *Long Day's Journey into Night,* Arthur Miller's *Death of a Salesman,* and Tennessee Williams's *A Streetcar Named Desire,* we have nothing to match, as yet, the brilliance of Beckett or Pinter. But, as they say in baseball, ''Wait until next year.''

George Bernard Shaw by Feliks Topolski (1939). Drawing.

Art Gallery and Museum, Glasgow, Scotland.

THE ENGLISH LANGUAGE
by John Algeo

In the twentieth century, English has spread all over the world. It has developed from a language spoken by a few wandering tribes to a world language used for more purposes than any other human tongue. Because its uses have continued to grow, it has continued to change. We can see change going on in English right now—especially in its vocabulary.

Tracking New Words: Where They Come From

We are constantly in need of new words—to talk about new things or to talk about old things in new ways. We borrow new words from other languages, or we make them up out of old words already existing in English. Few, if any, new words are ever created out of nothing. Almost all new words are based upon existing words in English or other languages.

The word *nylon* is sometimes mentioned as a word that was just made up as a name for a kind of synthetic material. However, the word has a history. Chemists at the duPont Company invented the material, and the company wanted to call it *no-run,* because it was used for stockings. But since stockings made of it do run, the vowels were switched, making *nuron.* That seemed too much like *neuron,* a nerve cell, so it was changed to *nilon* and then to *nylon.* Thus *nylon* came from *no-run* by various changes that effectively disguise its origin.

Some words echo, not other words, but the sounds of things in the world around us. For example, the word *vroom* began as an imitation of how a car or motorcycle engine sounds when it is being raced. Then it was used as a verb referring to how a vehicle operates at very high speed: "The car vroomed around the corner and disappeared."

Except for those that echo natural sounds, most new words are based on some earlier word material. We borrow many words from other languages. Words that we make up from other English words or word parts are formed in four main ways: by combining earlier words, by shortening words, by blending them, or by shifting the way we use them. We can find some examples of each type of word-making among recent words in English.

Loanwords: Sacking Other Languages

English speakers began to borrow words while they still lived on the Continent—even before they migrated to England. And we have gone on borrowing ever since. Today we have loanwords from most of the languages of the world.

English Today and Tomorrow

" **E**nglish has developed from a language spoken by a few wandering tribes to a world language used for more purposes than any other human tongue."

A

A. Expansion
Another example is the word *plop*. Although *plop* imitates the sound of spooning pudding or a similar substance into a bowl, it also can be the verb used to indicate any heavy falling, such as "I plopped down for a nap."

A. Words Borrowed from French

One result of the Norman victory over the English at the Battle of Hastings in 1066 was that many French words entered the English language, as all important positions in the country became occupied by French-speaking Normans. For example, French words were used in the areas of government *(royal, regal)* and law *(attorney, perjury)*. These words, as well as the more obviously French words *lieutenant* and *colonel*, among others, are an important part of English today. See text pages 159–162.

B. Compounds

❓ Can you suggest other new words formed in this way? (Input, blast off, launch pad, etc.)

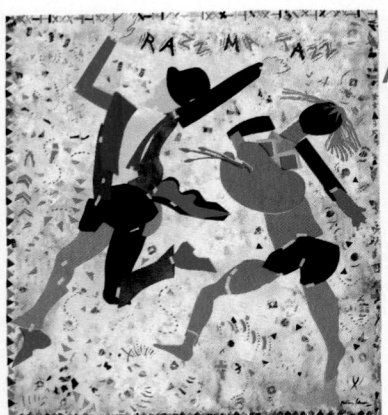

Razz Ma Tazz by Miriam Schapiro (1985). Acrylic on paper.

Courtesy of Bernice Steinbaum Gallery, New York.

A French is the modern language from which we have borrowed most words. They include *chief, choice, honor, machine, menu, picnic, police, prairie, restaurant, soup,* and a great many other familiar words, as well as more obvious loans like *chauffeur, crepe, etiquette, rapport,* and *souvenir.* From Spanish we have taken *canyon, lasso, patio, ranch, rodeo,* and more recently *macho;* from Portuguese, *flamingo, molasses, pagoda,* and others. From Italian we get musical terms like *duet, soprano,* and *trombone,* and a variety of other words, such as *balloon, bandit, carnival, studio, umbrella,* and *volcano.*

Dutch has given us sailing terms like *deck, dock,* and *yacht,* as well as *boss, dollar, knapsack, pickle, Santa Claus,* and *skate.* From German we have borrowed *frankfurter, hamburger, kindergarten, nickel,* and *pretzel.*

From more distant languages we have borrowed *banjo* (African), *boomerang* (native Australian), *coffee* (Turkish from Arabic), *ketchup* (catchup, Malay), *mammoth* (Russian), *pal* (Gypsy), *pecan* (Algonquian), *shawl* (Persian), *shampoo* (Hindustani), *soy* (sauce or bean, Japanese), *tattoo* (Tahitian), *tea* (Chinese), *tom-tom* (Hindi), and *ukulele* (Hawaiian).

English is much richer for all the words we have borrowed from other languages. English is an international language not only because it is used all over the world, but because it has taken words from other languages spoken all over the world. We also, however, make words from our own resources.

Compounds: Stacking Words Together

B We often make new words by joining older ones in a compound. Women's and girls' shoes made of brightly colored flexible plastic are called *jelly bean shoes* because they are shoes with the colors of jelly beans. A camera that uses film, not in a roll but on a disc, is a *disc camera.* A person intensely interested in computers and in nothing else is a *computer nerd.*

A compound may mean something different from the literal sense of its parts. Thus a *blackboard* is not necessarily a black board; it is often green instead.

Compounds have always been a favorite method of word formation in English. In Modern English we have some words that were originally compounds, but whose parts have merged so completely that we no longer recognize their origins. For example, *nostril* comes from an Old English compound, *nosu-thyrel* (literally "nose hole"), and *sheriff* comes from *scir-gerefa* (literally "shire-reeve" or "county official").

Affixes: Tacking Parts On

Instead of combining two whole words to make a new one, we can add a word element (an affix) to the front of a word (as a prefix) or to the end of a word (as a suffix). The suffix *-ster* is used to

1224

1224 The Twentieth Century

make nouns that name a person who does something. Thus a *songster* makes songs, a *trickster* plays tricks, and a *funkster* plays funky music, a popular kind of blues. The suffix *-ist* forms nouns meaning a person who believes in something or who has a particular profession. A *royalist* follows royalty, a *lobbyist* lobbies, and a *flat-earthist* believes that the earth is really flat as a pancake, whatever astronomers and astronauts may think.

Some suffixes were originally independent words that dwindled into mere affixes. The suffix *-ful* is such a dwindling of the word *full,* to which it is still close, though not the same, in meaning. A "handful of pennies" is not the same as a "hand full of pennies." The first is an indefinite number of coins, and the second is a hand with coins in it.

There are fewer prefixes than suffixes in English, but two common ones are *pre-,* meaning "before," and *post-,* meaning "after." We use them in combinations like *pregame* and *postgame, preteen* and *postteen, prepunk* and *postpunk.*

A

Shortenings and Back-Formations: Hacking Parts Off

Instead of adding something to a word (another word or an affix), we can also make new words by removing part of a word and thereby shortening it. This process is quite common, probably because we don't like to use energy in saying long words if short ones will do. *Gymnasium* is shortened to *gym; zoological gardens* becomes *zoo.* From *jelly bean shoes* we omit the *bean* and the *shoe* and come up with *jellies.*

Some shortenings are more complicated. The label *hazardous material* indicates that a container has dangerous chemicals or radioactive matter inside it. But the label is too long—a warning ought to be short and snappy. So both words in the expression are clipped, to produce *Haz-Mat,* a short, easy-to-say, and (provided you know what it means) clear expression. When a phrase is shortened to a word made up of the first parts of each word, the result is called an *acronym* (from two Greek forms meaning "tip-name," that is, a name formed from the tips of other words).

The most extreme kind of acronym includes only the first letter of each original word. The pronunciation may be the individual letter names, like *CB* ("citizens' band") or *RV* ("recreational vehicle"), or said together as a normal word, like *NOW* ("National Organization for Women") or *ZIP* code ("zone improvement plan").

A special kind of shortening occurs when an affix is taken off. Typewriters are a little over a hundred years old now. When they first came into use, the word *typewriter* was used for either the machine or the person who operated it. Then someone decided that a typewriter is for typewriting, and so the verb *to typewrite* was formed by taking off the suffix *-er.* Such words are called *back-formations* because they are formed backward to the usual way of adding affixes.

"*Hmm*" by Inez Storer (1987). Mixed media.

Courtesy of Rena Bransten, San Francisco.

A. Prefixes
Other common prefixes are *anti-,* meaning "against"; *pro-,* meaning "for"; *micro-,* meaning "small"; *macro-,* meaning "large"; *inter-,* meaning "between"; and *intra-,* meaning "within." You may wish to have students supply context sentences for the above-mentioned prefixes.

? How do prefixes affect the meanings of the words *inflammatory* and *intangible*? (The word *inflammatory,* meaning "tending to excite anger or to excite the senses," begins with the prefix *in-,* meaning "within or into." For *intangible,* meaning "not palpable or material," the prefix *in-* means "not.") Of *antiwar* and *antebellum*? (The prefix *anti-* means "against" while the prefix *ante-* means "before." *Antebellum* means "existing before the war" and is often applied to the period preceding the Civil War in the United States.)

A. Portmanteau Words

❓ See if students can figure out the blends that account for *twirl* (*twist* plus *whirl*), *bash* (*bat* plus *mash*), *flare* (*flame* plus *glare*), *smash* (*smack* plus *mash*), *glimmer* (*gleam* plus *shimmer*), and *clash* (*clap* plus *crash*).

B. Blends

Students might enjoy devising their own blends in the areas of science and technology, or in any other area in which they have a special interest.

> " The word *burgle* took a lot of time, more than three hundred years, to work its way out of *burglar*."

A

B

A similar example is *to burgle,* which is what a burglar does. A difference between *burgle* and *typewrite,* however, is that while *typewrite* was shortened from *typewriter* very quickly (within twelve years after the longer word was introduced to English), *burgle* took a lot of time, more than three hundred years, to work its way out of *burglar.* And some people still don't like it.

Blends: Packing Words Together

A *blend* is a word that is made by combining two or more words while omitting part of at least one of them. Familiar examples are *brunch* (*breakfast* plus *lunch*) and *smog* (*smoke* plus *fog*). In *Through the Looking-Glass,* Humpty Dumpty calls such terms *portmanteau words.* A portmanteau is a suitcase with two sides that are folded together to make a single case. Humpty Dumpty said that in a portmanteau word, "There are two meanings packed up into one word," like the suitcase.

A recent example of a scientific blend is *planiverse.* Some scientists have theorized what a world with only two dimensions, a truly flat world, would be like. They have dubbed such a world a *planiverse,* from *plane* (surface) plus *universe.* A technical example is *shuttle craft,* from *space shuttle* plus *spacecraft.* A feminist example is *herstory* (meaning "history told from a woman's point of view"), from *her* plus *history.*

A special kind of blending is *folk etymology.* We sometimes take an unfamiliar word, especially a word borrowed from another language, and change its form by associating it with familiar English words. For example, we borrowed the Dutch word *koolsla* (which means "cabbage salad") as *coleslaw;* but then we associated the first part of the word with the English word *cold* and came up with *cold slaw,* which makes sense because slaw is generally served cold.

Folk etymology does not always involve foreign words, however. In Chaucer's day, English had a word, *bridegome,* meaning "bride's man"; that is, the husband-to-be. *Gome* was an ancient English word meaning "man" that had dropped out of use, except for some fossil remains like *bridegome.* Because the second part of the word had become unrecognizable, English speakers changed it to the more familiar word *groom* (meaning "boy" or "lad") to produce the form we now use: *bridegroom.*

Shifted Words: Racking Up New Meanings

Perhaps the most frequent way of making a new word is to use an old word in a new way. If we greatly change the meaning of a word, we have made a new word because words are not just their sounds and spellings, but also their meanings.

Corn originally meant grain of any kind. The use of the word was specialized in the United States to mean "Indian corn," or "maize." It was specialized in a different way in England, where it means "wheat," and in Scotland, where it means "oats." What in England were called "Corn Laws" we would call "Grain Laws." With respect to its form, *corn* is still one word, but with respect to its meaning, it is now several distinct words.

Shakespeare's language often used words in different meanings from those to which we are accustomed. English used to apply the term *worm* to various creatures without legs, including snakes; now we use it only for insect-like creatures. In Shakespeare, to *want* something was not mainly to desire it, but to need it, a use we keep when we talk about "being in want." Of course if we lack something good, we are very likely to desire it, so it was easy for *want* to make the shift of meaning. Today *censure* means "to judge unfavorably," or "condemn"; in Shakespeare's day it meant simply "to judge or form an opinion."

Shifts of meaning are going on all the time. *Bulletin board* can now be used for an electronic computer service that provides information, instead of just for a wall on which notices are posted. *Skunkworks* may be "a place away from the main plant where a small group of employees work on a difficult problem." There used to be a comic strip called *Li'l Abner* whose hero had a job at the Skunk Works on the outskirts of town; it was not clear what he did, but he came home smelling strong.

A different kind of shift occurs when a word originally belonging to one part of speech is used as another part of speech. For example we use the noun *hand* as a verb in "Hand me that book, please"; the verb *sing* as a noun in "We are having a community sing"; the adjective *brave* as a noun in "the Indian braves"; the noun *fun* as an adjective in "a really fun evening"; the adverb *up* as a verb in "They upped the price," and so on. Such functional shift is an easy and often-used way of making new words in Modern English.

A

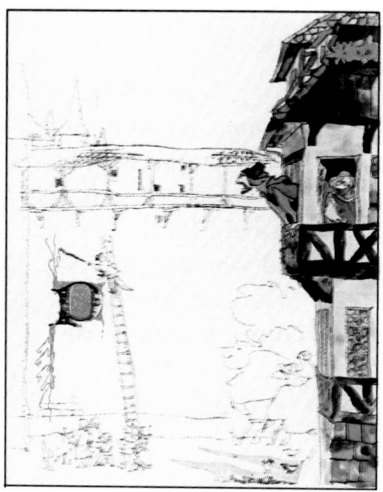

"A bulletin is coming in now, Sir."

Cartoon by Rowland B. Wilson.
Reprinted with permission from
Esquire. © 1960 by Esquire, Inc.

Tomorrow's English

English is changing today even as we use it. Indeed, it is changing *because* we use it. Pronunciation, grammar, and vocabulary are all changing, but the changes in vocabulary are the easiest to see and the quickest to happen.

Each change, however small, makes the language somewhat different from the English of yesterday. As the changes accumulate, little by little, day by day, they eventually make the language very different from what it was. But that is nothing to fear. Languages grow, as they must to live. By the way we talk English today and by the changes we introduce into it, we are creating the English of tomorrow.

B

The thirteen hundred years of recorded history of the English language have seen it spread from a small group of speakers on one island in a remote corner of Europe to hundreds of millions distributed all over the globe. In the future, English will doubtless be spoken by even more millions. Once used mainly to talk about farming and fighting, the weather and children, English is now

A. Shifts and Parts of Speech
This type of shift is also exemplified by the word *outfit*. We use the noun *outfit* in "The child wore an adorable outfit." We use the verb *outfit* in "It is very expensive to outfit an entire family."
? Can *input, impact,* and *interface* be used as nouns and verbs? (Some purists object to these usages as perversions of the language.)

B. The Changing Language
Nevertheless, many *are* afraid, including both Americans and Britons. Fears over the future of English are expressed frequently in newspaper columns and on television talk shows. In addition, in 1978, the British House of Lords held a special debate on the subject.

> " **E**nglish belongs to all those all over the world who speak and write it, who read its literature, and who treasure it. They are the ones who are its tomorrow."

used for every aspect of life, from everyday things to the most technical and scientific matters. In the future, English will doubtless be used for whatever now unimagined subjects human beings will need to communicate about. In the past, English speakers have written some of the greatest literature known to humanity, literature that is read all over the world by people from diverse cultures. In the future, English will doubtless continue to be a medium for the expression of our common anxieties, fears, hopes, aspirations, and exaltations.

The English language, like English literature, is something we can take pride in. This language and this literature do not belong to one nation or to one people only, but are shared by many. English belongs to all those all over the world who speak and write it, who read its literature, and who treasure it. They are the ones who are its tomorrow.

Analyzing Language

1. The following words illustrate various ways in which words are made. Look them up in a dictionary that gives etymologies, and describe their origins.

easel	jeep	pep
escalate	kitty-cornered	scarecrow
gas	motel	lengthwise
hiccup		

2. Words change their meanings over time, but some words keep evidence of their earlier meanings. Try to guess the earlier meanings of the following words from their forms. Then look up their etymologies to see whether your guesses were correct.

business	cupboard	disease
doff	bonfire	

3. Look in a recent newspaper or magazine for words you do not recognize—words that are completely new to you. Find at least three such words, and on a sheet of paper copy the sentences in which the words are used. Underline the unfamiliar words. Then look up the words in a college or unabridged dictionary. If you find them, read their etymologies to find out where they come from. If you do not find them, do you think they may be new words or old but rare words?

4. Several dictionaries and periodicals list new words. Try to locate one of the following lists of new words in a library:

   The Second Barnhart Dictionary of New English, ed. Clarence L. Barnhart, Sol Steinmetz, and Robert K. Barnhart

   12,000 Words: A Supplement to Webster's Third New International Dictionary

   "Among the New Words" (a regular article in the magazine *American Speech*)

   The Barnhart Dictionary Companion (a periodical that lists new words)

   Make a list of five new words from any of these sources, and tell what each new word means.

ANALYZING A WRITER'S STYLE

Writing Assignment

Choose a significant passage from one of the stories that you have read in this unit. Then write an essay of at least five paragraphs in which you analyze the writer's style. Include an evaluation of how effectively the writer's style reflects the substance of the passage.

Background

Style has to do with the kinds of words a writer chooses and the way the writer forms those words into sentences. Words, for example, may be common, everyday words, or they may be multisyllabic words. They may be formal, informal, or somewhere in between. They may be concrete and specific or abstract and general. They may be flowery and ornate or simple and direct.

Sentences vary also. Sentences may be long or short and simple or complex. They may be written in either the active or the passive voice; and the syntax of the sentence may follow the normal subject-verb order of the English language, or it may be inverted in some way.

A Most writers tend to have an identifiable style that clearly distinguishes their writing. At the same time, a writer's style usually varies somewhat within a particular work, depending upon the writer's purpose. Thus, a passage of description is likely to have more concrete, specific words than a passage of dialogue.

For all good writers, the style reflects the substance, or content, of the work. For example, in *The Secret Sharer*, Joseph Conrad writes about some of the complex, psychological problems of human existence. Appropriately, the tangled matters that the main character ponders are reflected by Conrad's long, complex sentences.

Prewriting

Choose a passage that is significant to the story and that is from two to three paragraphs long. (A passage of dialogue should be of equivalent length.) Then read back over the passage carefully, examining the kinds of words

and sentences used by the writer. In note form, write answers to the following questions. (*Note:* For most of these questions you will probably not be able to answer simply *yes* or *no*. Instead, look for a pattern in the writer's use of kinds of words, sentences, and stylistic devices.) **B**

Questions About Words

1. Are the words simple or multisyllabic?
2. Are the words formal or informal? Does the passage contain colloquialisms, slang, or jargon?
3. Are the words concrete (referring to things that can be perceived by the senses), or are they abstract?
4. Are the words specific (referring to particular people, places, things), or are they general?
5. Do the words have any particular connotations? (Do they arouse in the reader positive or negative emotions about the subject?)

Questions About Sentences

1. Are the sentences long or short?
2. Do the sentences have a simple, compound, complex, or compound-complex structure?
3. Are the sentences in the active or passive voice?
4. Do the sentences follow the normal order of English, or is the syntax inverted in some way?

Questions About Stylistic Devices

1. Does the writer use such stylistic devices as repetition or parallelism?
2. Where in the passage are these devices used and what effect do they have?

Writing

In the first paragraph of your essay, identify the passage, its type (narration, description, dialogue, etc.), and the speaker. Include a **thesis statement** in which you briefly describe the writer's style in the passage.

In the body of your essay, discuss the kinds of words, sentences, and stylistic devices used in the passage. Be specific, citing examples and counting numbers of kinds of words and sentences. Discuss how the style reflects the substance of the passage.

In your final paragraph, discuss the purpose of the passage in relationship to the remainder of the story. Evaluate how well the style reflects the substance and purpose of the passage.

In the following essay, the writer analyzes a passage from James Joyce's "Araby."

A. Style
Style can also vary depending on the writer's audience.

B. Style
In fact, a good writer would consciously avoid doing things that would elicit a simple *yes* or *no* answer to these questions. It is the occasional deviation from the pattern, or style, that makes a writer's work interesting.

Revising Essays
As students revise their essays, refer them to **Grammar, Usage, and Mechanics: A Reference Guide** at the back of their books.

Exercises in Critical Thinking and Writing/*cont*.

A Master of Style: James Joyce in "Araby"

In the third paragraph of "Araby," an adult narrator reflects back on his life as a boy playing in the streets of Dublin. In this descriptive passage, Joyce uses a reflective but simple and concise style that is entirely appropriate to the somber and simple life recalled by the narrator.

The simple words used by the narrator are appropriate for a young boy. Most of the nouns in this passage, for example, reflect an ordinary and even somewhat mundane existence—nouns such as *houses, sky, street, lanes, cottages, gardens, ashpits,* and *stables.* In the entire passage, only the word *gauntlet* might be beyond a boy's everyday vocabulary.

The adjectives and descriptive nouns used in the passage (*somber, feeble, silent, dark, muddy,* and *shadow*) suggest the somber aspect of the young hero's life. To heighten the suggestion, both the words *dark* and *shadow* are used three times, and the effect of repeating *dark* is intensified through the word's placement in the parallel phrases "the *dark* muddy lanes," "the *dark* dripping gardens," and "the *dark* odorous stables." In addition, concrete words are carefully chosen to provide a sampling of boyhood sights, sounds, smells, and even textures. Joyce writes, for example, "the houses had grown somber"; the coachman "shook music from the buckled harness"; the stables were "odorous"; and "the cold air stung" the boys.

The sentences of the passage are appropriate to a narrator looking back on a boyhood experience with the greater knowledge and insight of an adult. Of the thirteen sentences in the passage, only two are simple. Of thirty-eight verbs in the passage, only one verb is in the passive voice. The use of active voice makes the boyhood experience seem real and immediate.

It is important to the story to establish that the narrator is a "sadder but wiser" adult telling about his life in Dublin. It is also important that the somber, simple life of the young hero be concisely and clearly depicted, for it is against this background that the boy's attraction to Mangan's sister and, thus, to Araby, seems so natural. Through his masterfully simple and direct but reflective style, Joyce accomplishes both purposes in this passage.

Revising and Proofreading

For help in revising and proofreading your essay, refer to the section on **Writing About Literature** at the back of this book.

Jane Eyre by Charlotte Brontë

For a biography of Charlotte Brontë, further background on the novel, further activities, and tests, see the separate study guide to this novel.

The Novel
STUDY GUIDE

Jane Eyre by Charlotte Brontë

Elements of the Novel

The Themes

Love, independence, and forgiveness—these are the three principal and interrelated themes that Brontë explores in *Jane Eyre*. She also deals with several minor themes, such as the relationship between money and happiness and the effect religious belief has on social conduct.

Of course, in a romance the theme of love is foremost. From the outset Jane is in search of affection. Each of the novel's settings provides the opportunity to explore the nature of love: The Gateshead episodes focus on family relationships and show how jealousy and self-centeredness thwart love. At Lowood Jane enjoys the love of a saintly friend and an ideal teacher. At Thornfield Brontë explores romantic love between a man and a woman and shows that passion must be tempered by reason. At Moor House Brontë presents another example of family relationships. The Rivers are the precise opposites of the Reeds; as a family they are a river of life for Jane whereas her other cousins were brittle reeds. And finally, at Ferndean, Jane and Mr. Rochester achieve a harmonious union in marriage.

Jane emerges independent, not only in her ability to make the best of her disadvantaged childhood and to support herself, but also in her relationships with Mr. Rochester and St. John Rivers. (Rivers' first name is pronounced "sinjin.") In a society that forced women to be economically and emotionally dependent on men for their survival and sense of self-worth, Brontë's heroine

was a bold innovation. Both reason and passion enable Jane to resist St. John's moral blackmail of her, and when she finally does marry, Jane does so freely as her husband's equal.

The theme of forgiveness is most clearly revealed in Jane's dealings with Mrs. Reed. As a child, Jane wanted revenge against her cruel guardian, but under the influence of Helen Burns's spiritual beliefs Jane learns to

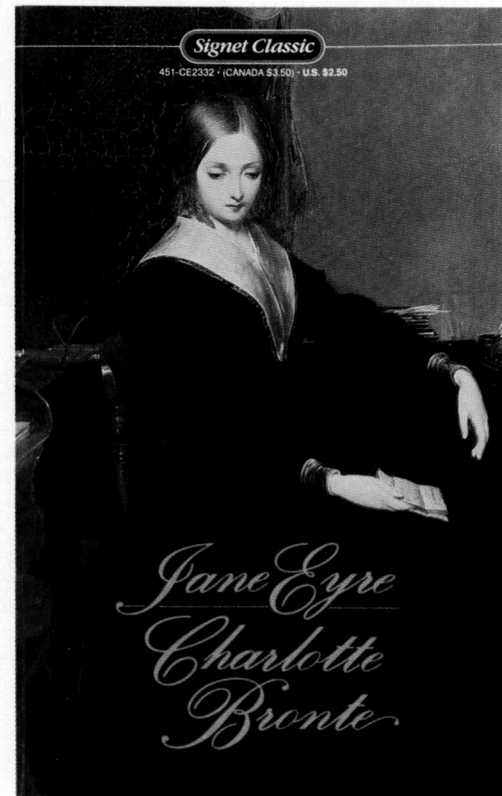

> *"Unless I have something of my own to say, and a way of my own to say it in, I have no business to publish. . . . Unless I can have the courage to use the language of Truth in preference to the jargon of Conventionality, I ought to be silent."*
>
> —Charlotte Brontë

control her natural emotions. When Jane returns as an adult to Gateshead, she is compassionate toward her hateful aunt and expresses her desire for a reconciliation. Just as there can be no true love between unequals, there can be no love without forgiveness. Brontë makes this point elsewhere in the novel as well, especially in her condemnation of the rigid, incompassionate, fire-and-brimstone brand of religion espoused by Mr. Brocklehurst and St. John Rivers. Brontë clearly sides with Helen Burns, who believes that God forgives all sinners and brings all souls to glory. The reunion of Jane with Rochester at the end of the novel epitomizes this belief: Jane miraculously hears Rochester's voice at the moment he prays for a reconciliation with God. The supernatural occurrence is a sign of divine forgiveness and a sanction for love.

The effect money has on happiness is another theme that runs through the novel. Brontë seems to have had a very pragmatic attitude toward money: It cannot guarantee happiness, but without it a person suffers physical deprivation and forfeits independence. Brontë provides many instances in *Jane Eyre* that illustrate the deleterious effects of money. People like the Reeds and Ingrams think that money endows them with moral superiority. Brontë consistently exposes their moral bankruptcy.

On the other hand, poverty ties Jane against her will to the Reeds and consigns her to a kind of imprisonment at Lowood. After she flees Thornfield, lack of money brings her to the brink of starvation. Though Jane claims to make little of the inheritance that she receives at the end of the novel, it does secure for her the economic and emotional independence for which she has yearned.

The Point of View

The novel purports to be the autobiography of Jane Eyre; accordingly, the story is told from the first-person point of view of Jane herself. In the novel's last chapter, Jane claims to be writing ten years after her marriage, and her story traces her life from age ten to about age twenty. This backward-looking point of view allows the narrator to stand outside the action of the novel and comment on the experiences of her early life. In effect, the reader encounters two Janes in the novel: the mature storyteller who enjoys the wisdom that her experiences have taught her, and the often confused orphan girl who must overcome many hardships to find love and happiness.

Because Jane expresses her thoughts and feelings directly, readers very quickly begin to sympathize with her character, to take her side in her struggles against others, and to trust that what she says is true. As a narrator, Jane knows all the answers to the mysteries that confronted her as a child and young woman. Yet, like any good storyteller, she withholds information to create suspense and to make readers experience events as young Jane first experienced them. The first-person point of view, therefore, allows for a mixture of wisdom and wonder.

The Characters

The first-person point of view allows Brontë to characterize Jane fully. Readers learn about Jane not only from what others say about her and from her own speech and actions but also from what she reveals of her own thoughts and feelings. Because readers know Jane so intimately, there is little mystery about her. In contrast, Brontë portrays Mr. Rochester as a typical Byronic hero: until all is revealed in the climactic scene on his wedding day, his personality is shrouded in mysteries and contradictions. Though Mr. Rochester often expresses his innermost feelings to Jane, his motivating thoughts are kept deliberately vague. Jane often observes how he seems to be struggling against some hated thought, but it is never defined.

That these two characters are equals and perfect complements to each other is gradually revealed through the series of encounters between them. Brontë masterfully builds romantic tension as each character's passion struggles against reason. When Jane flees Thornfield after the aborted wedding, it is reason that emerges triumphant and drives her from Mr. Rochester, and she suffers because of it. Mr. Rochester suffers, too, but from a different cause: He refuses to submit his passions to the tempering influence of reason. Not until the novel's final chapters are the lovers at last joined in a harmonious balance. Their union signifies the harmony between passion and reason within their own characters as well as their integration with the novel's hierarchies of society, nature, and God.

The Setting

Brontë uses a blend of interior and exterior settings as a backdrop for her story. Though the general locale is the countryside of northern England at the beginning of the nineteenth century, Brontë is deliberately vague about geographical locations and the precise date of the events. Her purpose in describing various settings—specifically houses and their environs—is not to achieve verisimilitude but to establish dominant moods that reflect Jane's own. For example, in the opening scene at Gateshead, Jane takes refuge in a window seat behind a curtain and looks out onto a stormy November day. Her isolation from the rest of the household emphasizes her feeling of being an outcast, and the season and weather parallel the hostile turbulence raging within her.

On occasion a setting will be so suggestive as to have symbolic significance. Such is the case in the proposal scene, which occurs in an "Eden-like" garden on Midsummer Eve: The paradisiacal setting with its malevolent supernatural undertones symbolizes the disparity between Jane's innocence and Rochester's less-than-innocent intentions.

Brontë also uses settings in counterpoint, to show how Jane's character has developed. For example, at the end of Chapter 8 Jane says that she would not exchange Lowood with all its privations for Gateshead and its daily luxuries. Her realization about these two settings indicates how much Jane has grown in self-reliance and in determination to make her own way in the world.

Figurative Language and Style

Critics have noted Brontë's intentional use of poetic language in *Jane Eyre;* it permeates her prose and contributes to her distinctive style. Sensory images, imagery patterns, similes and metaphors, biblical and literary allusions, and symbolism abound. Brontë uses figurative language to make settings more vivid, to add depth to her characterizations, to give unity to seemingly disparate elements of plot, and to endow the particulars of her story with broader significance.

Readers should note especially Brontë's contrasting imagery of bondage and freedom, which colors each stage in Jane's struggle for independence and inner harmony. A typical example appears in the passage describing Rochester's attempts to lavish jewels and gowns upon his fiancée; Jane feels that Rochester is acting like a sultan toward a favorite slave.

Another recurring motif is the "elf" imagery, which is so closely associated with Jane, especially in Mr. Rochester's mind. The name "Eyre" implies a connection with sylphs and other spirits of the air, such as Ariel in Shakespeare's *Tempest*. If you are interested in the psychology of love, you might explore the ways in which Jane plays a kind of Ariel to a Prospero/Rochester.

You should note that Brontë uses names symbolically. In addition to *Eyre*, you should find significance in *Leaven*, Bessie's last name, and in *Temple, Reed, Lowood, Thornfield, Rivers*, and so on.

Brontë makes many allusions to literature, usually to add depth to characterization. Critics have made much, for example, of *Bewick's History of British Birds* and its relationship both to Jane's state of mind at the beginning of the novel and to the symbolic watercolors that she shows to Mr. Rochester. Similarly, Jane's preference for *Arabian Nights* and *Gulliver's Travels* indicates her penchant for linking the fantastic with the real.

If you are interested in the relationship of art to life, you will enjoy Rebecca Fraser's *The Brontës* (1988). There seems to be little doubt that Jane Eyre *is* Charlotte Brontë.

A motion picture of *Jane Eyre* was released in 1944, starring Joan Fontaine, Orson Welles, and Elizabeth Taylor.

Writing About the Novel

A Creative Response

1. **Using Another Point of View.** Bertha never speaks in the novel. The picture that readers get of her through Jane's **point of view** is of a woman who is more like a savage animal or vampire than a human being. That she enters only Mr. Rochester's and Jane's rooms suggests, however, that she is aware of her husband's love for the governess. What do you think is going through Bertha's mind when she sets Mr. Rochester's bed on fire and rips Jane's bridal veil? Imagine either of these scenes from Bertha's point of view. Rewrite it with Bertha as the first-person narrator. Be sure to reveal not only her actions but also her innermost thoughts and feelings. (You might read Jean Rhys's *Wide Sargasso Sea* (1982) to see how a professional novelist imagines what really happened to Mr. Rochester's first wife.)

2. **Describing a Setting.** Brontë's **settings** are memorable because she uses precise details not only to convey a vivid, realistic picture but also to suggest a distinct **atmosphere** or **mood**. In Chapter 37, for example, the description of Ferndean suggests decay and gloomy isolation and emphasizes Mr. Rochester's physical condition and state of mind. Using this or another of Brontë's descriptions of setting as a model, write a detailed description of a place so that it conveys both a vivid picture and a distinct mood.

A Critical Response

3. **Analyzing Characterization.** Brontë characterizes Jane not only in the usual ways—by revealing her thoughts and feelings, by telling us what others think of her, by showing her in action—but also by using **foils**. Some of these foils, such as the Reed sisters and Blanche Ingram, reveal Jane's character via direct contrast to their own. Others reveal Jane's character indirectly, by showing readers how Jane reacts to two contrasting characters. For example, St. John is a foil for Rochester; the different ways in which Jane reacts to them reveal contrasting sides of her personality. Write an essay analyzing Brontë's use of foils to reveal Jane's character. Cite specific examples from the novel to support your arguments and conclusions.

4. **Analyzing the Style of the Novel.** Brontë's prose **style** includes many elements that readers normally associate more closely with poetry: sensory images, imagery patterns, similes and metaphors, allusions, and symbolism. What effects does Brontë's poetic style have on the novel? Find several examples of each of the poetic elements that Brontë employs in *Jane Eyre*, and explain how she uses them to help her develop the narrative elements of **setting, character,** and **plot**. Conclude your essay by describing your own response to Brontë's style.

Lord of the Flies **by William Golding**
For a biography of William Golding, further background on the novel, further activities, and tests, see the separate study guide to this novel.

The Novel
STUDY GUIDE

Lord of the Flies by William Golding

The Elements of the Novel

The Themes

In 1964, Charles Moritz, editor of the *Current Biography Yearbook*, included these words by William Golding: "In all the books, I have suggested a shape in the universe that may, as it were, account for things. The greatest pleasure is . . . just understanding. And if you can get people to understand their own humanity—well, that's the job of the writer."

What does William Golding mean by "a shape in the universe"? Is the author referring to boundless space and constellations of stars? Or is he referring to a system of beliefs that each of us has, a way of looking at the world that helps us account for things? When you read a book, are you entering another universe—the world of another mind with its own geography? Does a book provide a map of understanding, a guide that points to the exploration of another person's thoughts? In reading, do you always like what you find, or are you sometimes shocked by revelations about human character?

Golding, examining the "beast within," spares the reader nothing in terms of exposing the defects inherent in human nature. Golding's characters are allegorical symbols of the various facets of humankind, and his story is a depiction of our continuing, and often thwarted, effort to achieve civilization. In *Lord of the Flies*, Golding asks us to think about what civilization actually is, and under which circumstances people lean toward cooperation or competition.

At first, Ralph and the boys try to model the "logical" and "respectable" system they know: they will have a leader and they will work together for the common good. As individual egos and communal fears begin to surface, however, the system rapidly malfunctions. It is replaced by a different system: a reign founded on personal gratification, intimidation, and terror.

Golding's portrayal of human defects, our isolation from others, and our barely suppressed savage tendencies, is both uncompromising and merciless. With civilization far removed and nothing but a faded memory, the boys readily lapse into barbaric thinking and behavior. Only Simon knows that the real "beast" is man's lack of integrity, his lack of ethical/moral fiber, and his lack of true self-knowledge. In the end, the rational Ralph becomes the scapegoat for the tribe. If the boys can eliminate him, not a single vestige of the old ordered, restrictive life will remain to hamper them.

LORD OF THE FLIES
WILLIAM GOLDING

OVER 10 MILLION COPIES IN PRINT

The Characters

The characters in *Lord of the Flies* are, for the most part, not presented as well-rounded, fleshed-out individuals. Rather, they serve more as allegorical symbols representing various human types. They are a microcosm of humanity, expressing the range of human reactions under extraordinary circumstances.

Ralph is elected chief of the assembly of boys and is, in the end, the one unconquered foe of Jack and his savage tribesmen. Ralph is the protagonist of the novel— he represents sense, order, rational thought, debate, and ethical behavior.

Jack Merridew resents and attempts to usurp Ralph's authority. When that fails, he breaks from the group, proclaims himself chief of those who follow him, and begins a reign of terror. Jack is Ralph's opposite—his antithesis—and his major antagonist, representing anarchy and untempered savagery.

Piggy is a stabilizing force for Ralph. Piggy helps Ralph to focus his thoughts when the pressures of responsibility overwhelm him. The second victim of the boys' disintegrating society, Piggy represents intellectual power and insight gained from observation.

Simon is the first victim of the rising anarchy. With his early statement about the beast, "Maybe it's only us," his conversation with the Lord of the Flies, and his belief that Ralph will be rescued, Simon represents intuitive insight and self-awareness.

The Biguns, the other older boys, most of whom remain relatively undeveloped characters, represent the unthinking masses who blindly follow the current established authority.

The Littluns, the younger boys, represent the innocents who are unaware of the realities of life and, consequently, are rarely affected by them. Percival Wemys Madison's concern about the beastie and his screams in the night represent a fear of the unknown, shared by both the innocents and the sophisticates.

The Setting

The story takes place on an uninhabited tropical island in the twentieth century during a fictional nuclear war. The location of the island is never specified. This island setting is significant—it is a reverse of our idea of Eden. With no authority figures and no societal restraints to influence the young boys, the conflict between civilized, conditioned behavior and man's suppressed savage tendencies becomes increasingly obvious and sinister.

To see how motion-picture director Peter Brook visualized the setting, you might enjoy the movie version of *Lord of the Flies* (released in 1963).

Irony

Golding's abundant use of irony figures significantly in the development and final outcome of the plot.

The isolated, uninhabited island is a virtual paradise, and the reader is encouraged to believe that the boys will manage quite well. After all, being stranded on a primitive island paradise is a boy's dream, fostered by the reading of such books as *The Swiss Family Robinson* and *Robinson Crusoe*. In the end, however, the island is anything but paradisiacal, for it has become the setting of Simon's murder, Piggy's death, and the tribe's efforts to kill Ralph. The very premise of the novel is thus predicated on situational irony.

Early in the novel, Jack states that the boys are "not savages." Ironically, Jack is the first to hide behind a painted face and to declare they have no need for rules. Though at first Jack's compulsion to kill centers on pigs, Simon and Piggy become human victims, killed as a result of Jack's leadership. Under Jack's direction, the tribe deliberately and willfully attempts to kill Ralph. Contrary to Jack's proclamation is the reality that, of those left at the novel's end, they are all savages except Ralph.

The boys think they will have fun while they're waiting to be rescued. Ironically, before long, the fun hampers the group's need for building shelters and for keeping the fire lit. Their fun becomes tainted with foreboding, beginning with the hunters' reenactment of their first pig kill. Eventually, they progress to killing Simon during one of their dances. Finally, Jack's tribesmen snicker outside Ralph's hiding place and cheer uproariously when they roll huge boulders off the cliff (originally an act of boyish glee and camaraderie) in an attempt to kill Ralph. The irony of the situation is driven home when the naval officer, looking at the boys, comments, "Fun and games."

The most barbed irony is the novel's final one, however. Though the boys are rescued from the island and their own savagery, they will return to a "civilized" society embroiled in a war—the very war that brought them to the island, and a face-to-face confrontation with their darkest selves, in the first place.

Symbolism

Not only do the characters themselves serve more as symbols than as individuals, but also many recurring objects in the novel serve symbolic functions. The most striking symbol in the novel is the sow's head which Jack places on the sharpened stake, a sacrifice to the beast. Ironically, as it tells Simon, the sow's head is the beast itself, and represents the inherent and often uncontrollable dark side of humankind. The sow's head chides Simon, and the absent others, for thinking that the beast they all feared was something they "could hunt and kill." It is the "Lord of the Flies," a translation of the Hebrew *Ba' alzevuv* and the Greek *Beelzebub*, both synonyms for the devil himself. Golding, however, uses the Lord of the Flies to represent the savagery, kept in check only by willful and deliberate ethical behavior, that exists in all people. This symbol gives the book its title and encapsulates Golding's theme as well.

The conch is a symbolic extension of Ralph, but it also represents order and civilization. Very early in the story, Jack tries to limit the rule of order to the beach area, proclaiming that the conch doesn't have any meaning on the mountaintop. It is the shattering of the conch, which Piggy is holding when the boulder strikes him, that symbolizes the end of all sense, order, and ethical behavior on the island.

Piggy's glasses are also used symbolically. As Piggy himself is a symbol of intellect and insight gained from observation, his glasses serve as a symbol of clearsightedness, of "seeing truly." When Piggy joins the attack on Jack, Jack hits him, knocking Piggy's glasses off and onto the rocks. One lens is shattered, symbolically indicating the increasing disintegration of sense and reason among the boys. At the end of the story, Jack still possesses the glasses with one lens undamaged. The lens is then used as a burning glass to start the holocaust intended to kill Ralph and likely to destroy the whole island. The glasses, once symbols of hope, show that in the wrong hands, what once supported civilization can also destroy it, if its purposes are perverted by those ruled by their beast sides.

The fire, which is originally controlled by the forces for civilization, at first represents hope of rescue. Later, when it is controlled by the savages, it becomes the means for destruction.

Writing About the Novel

A Creative Response

1. **Adding a Scene.** Golding deliberately does not invade Jack Merridew's thoughts. At the end of the novel, Jack, in response to the naval officer's question of who the boss is, starts to step forward and then hesitates. Write a passage that could be inserted into the novel at this point if Golding had, as he did on occasion with Ralph and Simon, revealed Jack's thoughts to the reader.

2. **Writing a Script.** There are several important scenes in the novel that Golding does not develop for the reader. For example, the reader knows that Jack interrogates one of the twins to discover Ralph's hiding place. The reader also knows that Jack then orders the tribesmen to hurl large rocks down from the Castle in an attempt to kill Ralph. Choose *one* of these two undeveloped scenes (or your choice of another that has been approved by your teacher) and write a script that dramatizes the scene.

A Critical Response

3. **Defining a Hero.** The ancient Greeks formulated the concept of a **tragic hero,** a person of great stature whose downfall is the result of some character flaw or deficiency. Using this definition, write an essay in which you discuss Ralph as a tragic hero. If you believe he qualifies, what, in your opinion, is his tragic flaw? Use incidents from the novel to support your opinions.

4. **Choosing a Setting.** Golding, for obvious reasons, specifically chooses to have the plot of his novel unfold on an uninhabited island. Consider other possible **settings** that would allow for basically the same development of the plot. Select one setting that you believe would work as well and discuss your reasoning, giving specific details to support your choice.

WRITING ABOUT LITERATURE

Writing Answers to Essay Questions

The following strategies will help you organize and write your answers to the essay questions following each selection in this book. Step-by-step instructions in the writing process may also be found in the Exercises in Critical Thinking and Writing. A list of these exercises appears in the index on page 1325.

1. Begin by reading the essay question carefully. Make sure you understand exactly what the question is asking you to do, and note how much evidence it asks you to provide.

2. Identify the key verb in the question. It will help you pinpoint your assignment. Look for these key verbs:

• **Analyze (Examine).** To *analyze* something is to take it apart and see how it works. Usually you will be asked to analyze one element of a work and explain its effect on the other elements and on the work as a whole. Sometimes you will be asked to analyze an entire poem, story, or play. In these cases, you will examine each major element in the work and describe what it contributes to the work as a whole. (See **Analyzing a Passage,** page 65; **Analyzing a Poet's Work,** page 445.)

• **Compare/Contrast.** When you *compare,* you point out similarities; when you *contrast,* you point out differences. At times, the verb *compare* implies both comparison and contrast. If the text of the question does not make this clear, ask your instructor for clarification. When you compare and contrast pieces of literature, you can take one of two main approaches: (1) In the **block method,** you will discuss all the similarities first and all the differences later. (2) In the **point-by-point method,** you will compare various elements in the pieces of literature, one element at a time. If you use this method, you will discuss differences and similarities simultaneously. The most helpful technique you can follow before you write an essay of comparison and contrast is to make a list itemizing the similarities and differences in the two pieces of literature. Here is a type of list you can use:

	Poem 1	Poem 2
Subject		
Theme or main idea		
Figures of speech		
Imagery		
Tone		
Form		

• **Describe.** To *describe* means to paint a picture in words. A description will use words that will help your reader to visualize a subject (a character, a setting), and perhaps to hear, smell, taste, and touch it as well.

• **Discuss.** To *discuss* means to comment about something in a general way. When you discuss a topic, be sure to stick to your subject; do not let your essay wander off the track.

• **Evaluate.** To *evaluate* something is to judge how good or bad, effective or noneffective, it is. Evaluation is subjective, but a good evaluation is based on objective criteria. A poor evaluation will simply state "I liked this," or "I hated this," or "This was boring." A good evaluation will develop an idea: "This story was successful because it held my interest and made me realize something I had never thought of before." A good evaluation will then go on to support the judgment with examples from the piece of literature. Before you write an essay of evaluation, be sure you know what criteria you are going to base your evaluation on. These criteria can be stated in the form of questions:

For fiction and drama:

1. Is the **plot** believable? Did it hold your interest?
2. Are the **characters** convincing? Do their actions seem credible, based on what you are told about them and on your own experience of human nature? Does their **dialogue** sound like real people are talking?
3. Is the **theme** interesting and fresh? Or is it a cliché?
4. Is the **point of view** consistent? How does it affect the story?
5. Does the story have a vivid **setting?** What is the function of the setting in the story?

For poetry:

1. Are the poem's **images** and **figures of speech** fresh and original, or are they trite and overused?
2. Do the poem's **form** and **sounds** contribute to its sense? Do the sounds ever seem forced and unnatural?
3. Is the poem's **message** fresh and original or is it trite and overused?

For nonfiction:

1. What is the writer's **purpose?**
2. Is the writer **subjective** or **objective?**
3. What is the writer's **tone?**
4. Is the writer's **message** clear? Do you agree with it?
5. Is the writing **logical?** Are the facts **accurate?**
6. Does the writer try to manipulate your feelings in any way? Does the writer use any **loaded words?**

For further help, see **Evaluating Literature in Group Discussion,** page 163.

• **Illustrate.** To *illustrate* means to provide examples to support an idea or statement. You can either quote directly from the piece of literature, or paraphrase from it.

• **Interpret.** To *interpret* something means to explain its meaning and importance. Most questions calling for interpretation ask for an interpretation of **theme** or meaning. Sometimes you will be asked to interpret the significance of some particular element in the piece of literature.

• **Respond.** To *respond* is to give your personal reaction to something. If you are asked to explain your response to a work, you should state whether you liked or disliked it, how it made you feel, and what it made you think about. Whenever possible, you should give reasons for your response.

3. **Write a thesis statement stating the main idea of your essay.** Include your thesis statement in the first para-

graph, along with any additional sentences that help you catch the reader's attention.

4. **Gather evidence to support this thesis statement.** If you can use your book, look back over the work for examples and illustrations. For a closed-book essay, make notes on all the supporting details you can remember before you start writing.

5. **Write one paragraph for each main point.** Include a topic sentence for each paragraph, and try to express your ideas as clearly and simply as you can. Don't pad your answer with unrelated details or ideas.

6. **End with a concluding paragraph.** Summarize or restate your main points, and if you wish, give your personal response to the work. Try to end your essay with a dynamic "clincher sentence."

Writing and Revising an Essay

You may be asked to choose your own topic for an essay on a specific work. Here are some suggested steps to follow.

Prewriting

1. **Choose a limited topic that you can cover adequately.** If your assignment is an essay of four paragraphs or five hundred words, you can't possibly analyze all the elements in *The Secret Sharer.* But you do have room to analyze one character or the novel's tone or the significance of its title. For ideas on the kinds of topics you can choose, review the list of key verbs on page 1237.

2. **Write a thesis statement.** Ask yourself, "What main idea about my topic do I want to discuss?" Then write one or two sentences that state this main idea. If you have trouble expressing your idea in only one or two sentences, you should consider narrowing the topic of your essay. For help with formulating a thesis statement, see **Developing and Supporting Generalizations,** page 925.

3. **List two or three main ideas that develop your thesis statement.** Jot down the ideas that come to mind when you think about your thesis statement, and choose the strongest two or three. Then go back over the work and do a close reading to come up with specific points you may have overlooked. Don't rely simply on your memory.

4. **Gather and arrange supporting evidence.** Your essay should include quotations, specific details, examples, and incidents from the literary work you are writing about—known as the **primary source.** You might also wish to refer to other works, letters, or interviews by the same writer. Finally, you can also include information from **secondary sources**—biographies, reviews, and critical essays about the work or the writer.

Before you begin writing, decide which evidence best supports your thesis statement. Then discard any weak or unrelated material. Once you've arranged your main ideas and evidence in the order that seems the most logical, you'll have an informal outline to work from.

Writing

Write a draft of your essay, following your outline and notes. Be sure to include enough evidence to support your thesis statement and the main idea of each paragraph. Structure your essay according to this plan.

> I. INTRODUCTORY PARAGRAPH
> Catches the reader's interest.
> Tells what the essay will be about.
> Begins or ends with the thesis statement.
>
> II. BODY (Paragraphs 2, 3, etc.)
> Develops the thesis statement.
> Includes a topic sentence and supporting evidence in each paragraph.
>
> III. CONCLUDING PARAGRAPH
> Tells the reader the essay is completed.
> Restates or summarizes the thesis statement and main ideas.
> Often includes a personal response.

Revising

Reread your first draft at least twice, checking once for content and once for style.

1. Content. Check to see that you've supported your thesis statement with at least two main ideas and that you've supported each main idea with sufficient evidence. If any part of your essay sounds weak or vague, go back over the work to find more convincing evidence.

2. Style. To make your essay read smoothly, you may need to combine related sentences or break up long sentences into shorter ones. Cut unnecessary or repetitive words and phrases. Make sure your ideas are clear and easy to follow, and that your wording "sounds" right.

Proofreading

The titles of poems, short stories, and essays should be enclosed in quotation marks; the titles of plays, novels, and other long works (such as epic poems) should be in italics. (However, the Bible and the individual books of the Bible are neither italicized nor in quotes.) In handwriting and typing, italics are indicated by underlining. Use the following proofreader's symbols to correct errors in spelling, punctuation, and style.

Symbol	Example	Meaning of Symbol
≡	Virginia woolf	Capitalize a lower-case letter.
/	Sir Gawaine And The Green Knight	Change a capital letter to a lower case.
∧	The Secret Sharer	Insert a word or phrase.
∧	My Odipus Complex	Insert a letter.
⊙	A. E. Housman	Insert a period.
⌄	Tears Idle Tears	Insert a comma.
⹂⹂	How do I love thee?	Insert quotation marks.
(underscore)	David Copperfield	Set in italics.
(tr) (or ⌣)	Nadine Gordmier	Change the order of the letters.
℈/	Dereck Walcott	Delete and close up space.

¶	¶In 1066, the Normans	Begin a new paragraph.
.....	~~From~~ Beowulf	Let it stand (stet).
(15) (sp)	(15)	Spell it out.
⊂	Pyg malion	Close up space.
#	Sredni Vashtar	Insert space.

A Model Essay

The following essay is an interpretation of "The Death of the Moth" by Virginia Woolf (page 1046). The essay shows the writer's revisions for a second draft.

My introductory paragraph opens with my thesis statement about the essay's main idea.
Then I tell in a general way how the essay reveals this idea.

The second paragraph begins to summarize the content of the essay and to give details to support my main idea.

"The Death of the Moth" by Virginia Woolf

The ~~Death of the Moth is an important essay because it~~ reminds us that the life of all beings is important and beautiful no matter how different ~~that life~~ *those lives* may be. Virginia Woolf ~~does this by using~~ *from our own* *uses* the moth to illustrate how *a* life may seem insignificant because it is much simpler ~~and (in a way)~~ uglier than our own. When that life is noticed, however, and carefully ~~(even for several moments)~~ studied, we can appreciate it for its own special movements within its own special space. ~~At first~~ *¶In the beginning of the essay,* Virginia Woolf describes the moth as pathetic: it is a *hybrid--a* mixture of a butterfly and a nightmoth and *it is* uglier than both. In the first paragraph ~~it is is said it~~ *Woolf says the moth* "seemed to be content with life." ~~This is meant as a complement. By comple-menting the day moth in this way, the narrator~~ *The tone in which this remark is expressed* seems to suggest that ~~her~~ *the speaker's* own life is ~~a lot~~ more important and "interesting" then *a* the day moth's and that the narrator herself is maybe even more ~~attractive.~~

¶The horses, the rooks, the plowmen, the author,

Other creatures are also compared to the moth. ~~For example~~ "the rooks, the plowmen, the horses and even, it seemed, the lean *are compared to the moth.* bare-backed ~~downs.~~ The moth's life seems dismal compared to the *around it. He* lives of other creatures. ~~It~~ flies ~~form~~ to corner of the window pane (which reminds me of all of the people *confined to small* ~~living in~~ separate *of the isolated* apartments in my apartment building or people in separate houses in the development off ~~of~~ Route 3). ~~At first the moth's life seems~~ *the day moth* ~~pitiful and dreary because~~ all ~~he~~ can do is flutter back and forth.

in the same way He can't enjoy the beautiful September day that the rooks and *can its The horses can plow and the rooks can fly into the blue sky and onto the branches of trees.* horses enjoy. Virginia Woolf points out, though, that "What he could *9* do he did." And ~~then~~ after observing the moth for a while, ~~she says~~ *Woolf* "It was as if someone had taken a tiny bread of pure life and decking it as lightly as possible with down and feathers, had set it dancing and zigzagging to show us the true nature of life." ~~At this point the~~ *Suddenly the moth is transformed, and rather than seeming unimportant to the author, he* ~~moth~~ represents life itself ~~because~~ of its simple nature ~~in addition~~ *It is interesting that the same thing that made* ~~to this realization, it helps the narrator and the reader appreciate~~ *the day moth insignificant in the beginning of the essay makes him very* ~~her own life. This is ironic, yet believable because it is truthful.~~ *important in the end. Its simplicity is inspiring -- especially when his life is* *compared to the hectic and distracting life of the speaker.*

All lives—no matter how different or simple—are important, *often* and the differences can help us appreciate our own lives. Many *others the way Woolf treats the* people ~~take apart other people and~~ treat them like ugly day moths. *The reason can be* *gender* ~~Sometimes because~~ of race or religion, ~~their sex~~ or age or social background. ~~But~~ all lives are important. ~~All beings~~ live *Everyone* *s like* and ~~as~~ *Nothing* *Nothing is* the day moth all beings die. ~~None of us~~ can escape death. ~~None of~~

The third paragraph continues the summary and the citation of supporting details,

I am adding a personal comment on what the moth reminded me of.

I'm quoting what I think is the most important passage in the essay.

The last paragraph includes a restatement of the essay's main idea and some of my responses to it.

us are that powerful. It is easy as the author points out, to think we are better than others and not to pay attention to creatures (including human beings) that seem weaker or uglier or less important than we are. But if we open our eyes we can learn a great deal from a moth or another human being or any other creature or landscape (like the downs) we may come across in our own busy and special lives.

[handwritten annotations: "As", "writer", "it is easy", "beings", "as Woolf opened hers,", "the middle of", "we may learn to appreciate the beauty and power and simplicity of life itself"]

[handwritten note in left margin: "I tried to end with a strong clincher sentence."]

Documenting Sources for a Research Paper

Find out which method of documentation your teacher prefers: parenthetical citations, footnotes, or end notes.

1. Parenthetical citations give brief information in parentheses immediately after a quotation or other reference. More detailed information about each source is given in the bibliography. This simplified method of documenting sources is recommended by the MLA (Modern Language Association).

For a quotation from a prose passage by a writer who is identified in the text (page number):

At the end of *A Secret Sharer*, Joseph Conrad describes Leggatt as "a free man . . . striking out for a new destiny" (page 946).

For a quotation by a writer whose name is not mentioned in the text (author's last name, page number):

Nothing is known of the identity of Lucy "or whether Wordsworth had any actual person in mind" (Perkins, 263).

For a quotation from a play (act and scene, and line number if a poetic drama):

The witches set the tone of the play when they say right at the outset: "Fair is foul, and foul is fair" (Act I, Scene 1, line 10).

For a quotation from a poem (line number):

In "London, 1802," Wordsworth describes England as "a fen/Of stagnant waters" (lines 2–3).

---

2. Footnotes are placed at the bottom of the page on which the reference appears. A raised number at the end of the reference within the essay indicates a footnote.[1] Footnotes are generally numbered consecutively within a work.

1. Perkins, David, *English Romantic Writers* (New York: Harcourt Brace Jovanovich, 1967).

2. Welty, Eudora, "The Radiance of Jane Austen," in *The Eye of the Story, Selected Essays and Reviews* (New York: Random House, 1977).

Check a writing handbook, or ask your teacher for the style for footnoting poems, magazine articles, interviews, and books with more than one author.

3. End notes are identical to footnotes except that they are listed on a separate page entitled "Notes" at the end of a paper. End notes are numbered consecutively.

4. A **bibliography** should be included at the end of your essay. This is an alphabetical list of all the sources you consulted in researching your essay, even if they don't appear in your footnotes. Bibliography entries are listed alphabetically by the author's last name. Here is a sample bibliography.

Bibliography

Atlas, James, "Derek Walcott: Poet of Two Worlds," *The New York Times Magazine*, May 23, 1982.

Ellman, Richard, and Robert O'Clair, *The Norton Anthology of Modern Poetry* (New York: W. W. Norton & Company, Inc., 1973).

Thomas, Jo, "For a Caribbean Poet, Inner Tension and Foreign Support," *The New York Times*, August 21, 1979.

PRETEACHING NOTE
You might use this lesson to help students focus on the use of pronouns and antecedents in their own writing. Students who speak English as a second language might wish to review problems in pronoun usage on pages 1285–1287 of **Grammar, Usage, and Mechanics: A Reference Guide** before beginning this lesson.

Memoirs of Childhood
Both English and American literature have a rich tradition of memoirs of childhood. Charles Dickens, Dylan Thomas, Virginia Woolf, Floyd Dell, Truman Capote, and Maya Angelou are among the most well-known authors who have written moving, evocative portraits of the world in which they grew up.

A key element in these memoirs is *point of view*. Although the essay is written by an adult, it takes the point of view of a child, trying to recreate the world as he or she sees it. At the same time, adult understanding informs the descriptions, word choices, and tone. The writer tries both to share his or her childhood thoughts and feelings with the reader and to reflect upon that experience now that he or she has grown up.

Literature & Language

Using Pronouns and Antecedents Correctly

Literary Model

Did you ever wonder why you remember some people and events from your childhood and forget so many others? Read the following passage by one English author to find out what he recalls from his childhood in a village in the early 1900's.

Granny Trill and Granny Wallon were traditional ancients of a kind we won't see today, the last of that dignity of grandmothers to whom age was its own embellishment. The grandmothers of those days dressed for the part in that curious but endearing uniform which is now known to us only through the music hall. And our two old neighbors, when setting forth on errands, always prepared themselves scrupulously so. They wore high-laced boots and long muslin dresses, beaded chokers and candlewick shawls, crowned by tall poke bonnets tied with trailing ribbons and smothered with inky sequins. They looked like starlings, flecked with jet, and they walked in a tinkle of darkness.

Those severe and similar old bodies enthralled me when they dressed that way. When I finally became king (I used to think) I would command a parade of grandmas, and drill them, and march them up and down—rank upon rank of hobbling boots, nodding bonnets, flying shawls, and furious, chewing faces. They would be gathered from all the towns and villages and brought to my palace in wagonloads. No more than a monarch's whim, of course, like eating cocoa or drinking jellies; but far more spectacular any day than those usual trudging guardsmen.

In spite of their formal dressing-up, the two old ladies never went very far—now and again to church for the sermon, and to the village shop once a week. Granny Wallon went for her sugar and yeast; Granny Trill for her tuppence of snuff.

Snuff was Granny T.'s one horrible vice, and she indulged it with no moderation. A fine brown dust coated all her clothes and she had nostrils like badger holes. She kept her snuff in a small round box, made of tin and worn smooth as a pebble. She was continually tapping and snapping it open, pinching a nailful, gasping *Ah!* flicking her fingers and wiping her eyes, and leaving on the air a faint dry cloud like an explosion of fungoid dust.

The snuffbox repelled and excited us boys and we opened its lid with awe. Reeking substance of the underworld, clay-brown dust of decay, of powdered flesh and crushed old bones, rust scrapings and the rubbish of graves. How sharp and stinging was this fearful spice, eddying up from its box, animating the air with tingling fumes like a secret breath of witchery. Though we clawed and sniffed it, we could not enjoy it, but neither could we leave it alone.

"You at me snuff agen, you boys? I'll skin yer bottoms, I will!"

We looked up guiltily, saw her cackling face, so took a big pinch between us. With choking tears and head-rocking convulsions we rolled across the floor. The old lady regarded us with pleasure; our paroxysms shook the house.

"That'll learn you, I reckon; you thieving mites. Here, give it to me, I'll show 'ee."

She took up the box and tapped the lid, then elegantly fed her nose. A shudder of ecstasy closed her eyes. She was borne very far away.

—from *Cider with Rosie*,
Laurie Lee

Grammar Note

Pronouns are words used in place of a noun or of several nouns. The word a pronoun replaces is called its **antecedent**. When you write, it is important to make the antecedent of each pronoun clear. In the following sentence, the pronouns are italicized. Most pronouns *follow* the noun they refer to.

I would command a parade of grandmas, and drill *them*, and march *them* up and down.

The pronoun *I* refers, of course, to the speaker. The pronoun *them* is used twice to replace the noun *grandmas*.

Skillful writers vary the order in which noun and pronoun are introduced.

In spite of *their* formal dressing-up, the two old *ladies* never went very far.

In this sentence, Lee has used the pronoun *their* first and the antecedent noun *ladies* afterward. Because this

Using Pronouns and Antecedents Correctly   1243

EXAMINING THE WRITER'S STYLE
1. *she*—Granny T.; *it*—snuff
2. *which*—uniform; *us*—the speaker and his readers
3. *we/we*—the speaker and his friends; *it/it/it*—snuff
4. *I'll*—Granny; *yer*—the speaker and his friends; *I*—Granny
5. *her*—Granny
6. *me*—the speaker; *they*—grannies
7. *We*—the speaker and his friends; *her*—Granny; *us*—the speaker and his friends
8. *She*—Granny; *her*—Granny

USING PRONOUNS AND ANTECEDENTS IN YOUR WRITING
1. Writing About a Childhood Memory. Student writing should include specific details about the subject, use the pronoun *we* to include readers, and correctly match pronouns and antecedents. Encourage students to incorporate useful suggestions from partners.
2. Creating a Fantasy. Although students are urged to pay special attention to the use of pronouns and antecedents, they should let their imaginations flow freely. Remind students that specific details will create vivid word pictures.

Literature & Language/*cont.*

sentence comes within the context of a long passage on the grandmothers, the antecedent is clear, even though it actually follows the pronoun in this sentence.

Sometimes writers use pronouns with an antecedent that is implied rather than stated.

> Granny Trill and Granny Wallon were traditional ancients of a kind *we* won't see today.

There is no antecedent for the pronoun *we* in the passage. Yet, the reader is able to understand the implied antecedent, *people* or *readers* (or even *you and I*). In this case, Lee has deliberately chosen to address his readers familiarly, to create a conversational tone and sense of intimacy between writer and reader. However, in most cases, using a pronoun without an antecedent leaves the reader confused and the meaning of a sentence ambiguous.

> The money was supposed to be used to build a ceramics plant, but it fell through. [What fell through: the money, the plant, or something unnamed?]

Examining the Writer's Style

Read the following sentences from *Cider with Rosie*. Identify the pronouns and their antecedents. You may have to go back to the selection to find the antecedents in the sentences surrounding the given sentence. (Some sentences may have more than one pronoun.)

1. Snuff was Granny T.'s one horrible vice, and she indulged it with no moderation.
2. The grandmothers of those days dressed for the part in that curious but endearing uniform which is now known to us only through the music hall.
3. Though we clawed and sniffed it, we could not enjoy it, but neither could we leave it alone.
4. "I'll skin yer bottoms, I will."
5. A shudder of ecstasy closed her eyes.
6. Those severe and similar old bodies enthralled me when they dressed that way.
7. We looked up guiltily, saw her cackling face, so took a big pinch between us.
8. She kept her snuff in a small round box, made of tin and worn smooth as a pebble.

Using Pronouns and Antecedents in Your Writing

1. **Writing About a Childhood Memory.** In two or three paragraphs, describe a person that you remember from your own childhood. Write from the first-person point of view. Try to make your narrative personal and conversational by using the pronoun *we* to include your readers, as Laurie Lee does.

   a. Before you begin writing, choose your topic and freewrite for a few minutes to record all the descriptive details that you remember. Think of details describing this person's setting, appearance, voice, and actions, and the ways other people felt about this character. Decide how you are going to introduce yourself as the first-person narrator.

   b. As you write, be particularly aware of the way you are using pronouns and their antecedents. When you have finished, exchange compositions with a partner. With a red pencil, circle your partner's pronouns and their antecedents. Are the references all clear? Has the writer used the first-person pronoun *we* to achieve the goal of conversational intimacy?

   c. Look at the way your own composition has been edited. If you don't agree with the changes, discuss them; if you think they improve your composition, incorporate them into a final version.

2. **Creating a Fantasy.** Laurie Lee had a specific wish or fantasy he wanted to fulfill if he became king. What order would you enforce if you became king or queen? Who would you like to see marching before you in orderly ranks? What persons or customs from the past would you like to revive—if only for a day? Before you write, let your mind roam freely and freewrite various wishes you would like to have come true. Then write a short narrative, telling what happens the day you are in command. When you finish, evaluate your use of pronouns. Are all the antecedents clear?

This lesson can be used in a variety of ways. It can help students understand how authors develop style through varying their sentences. It can also encourage students to vary their own sentences. The sentence is reviewed on pages 1274–1276 of **Grammar, Usage, and Mechanics: A Reference Guide.**

Boarding Schools and Public Schools

British boarding schools, which took students starting at age seven, were preparation for the British "public school" system, which took students starting at about age twelve. These exclusive *private* schools—called "public" because they were run by a "public" board of governors—served for centuries as the training ground for the British aristocracy. At these schools, boys were taught a traditional curriculum stressing the classics and ancient history, trained in a rigorous system of athletics, and inaugurated into a strictly defined hierarchy in which the younger boys learned blind obedience to teachers and to the older boys. The "public school spirit" was a given of British life and thinking.

Literature & Language

Varying Sentences

Literary Model

Winston Churchill, Prime Minister of England during World War II, was admired at home and abroad for his courage, resolution, and fighting spirit during the dark years of the war. What was such a man like as a child? This biographical excerpt shows how seven-year-old Winston met one of his earliest challenges. Jennie is young Winston's beautiful (and distant) mother. Randolph is his father.

He was seven years old and his parents decided it was time he left home. On November 3, 1882, five weeks after the start of the autumn term, he was enrolled as a boarder at St. George's School near Ascot, a place famous for its women and horses. St. George's was an expensive school—fifty-two pounds for the first month, payable in advance—which prepared boys for Eton. Winston wept when told he must go. "I had been so happy in my nursery," he wrote later; ". . . now it was to be all lessons." Precisely how he traveled there is unclear. Jennie rode with him to Paddington Station in Randolph's private hansom, but on the train platform they parted; she gave him three half crowns and sent him on alone. He lost the coins, panicked, found them, and arrived trembling. It was late afternoon, and dark. A master led him to a desk, handed him a thin, brown-green Latin grammar, told him to memorize the declension of *mensa*, and departed. When the teacher returned, Winston reeled off a perfect recitation. The man seemed satisfied, and Winston, encouraged, asked, "What does it mean, Sir?" He was told, "*Mensa* means a table." Winston pointed out that according to the book, one of the forms would then be translated as "O table." He asked why. The master explained that this was the vocative case, that "you would use that in addressing a table." Astonished, the boy blurted out: "But I never do." The master snapped: "If you are impertinent, you will be punished, and punished, let me tell you, very severely."

That was the quintessential St. George's, the school in microcosm. Churchill would remember "how I hated this school, and what a life of anxiety I lived there for more than two years. I made very little progress at my lessons, and none at all at games. I counted the days and the hours to the end of every term, when I should return home from this hateful servitude and range my soldiers in line of battle on the nursery floor." However, he did not tell his parents that. At the end of his first month there he wrote his father, "I am very happy at [s]chool. You will be very pleased to hear I spent a very happy birthday," and the same day he wrote Jennie, "I hope you are quite well. I am very happy at school." But this is unsurprising. Boarding-school boys who feel wretched and badly treated seldom mention it in letters home. They think the flaw is in them, and they hide it. He doubtless assumed that his father would have snorted had he complained, and he was probably right. Like all Victorian children of his class, he had been taught to keep a stiff upper lip, so he did. Now and then he hinted at his immense yearning to quit St. George's. In March he wrote: "30 day [sic] more and the *Holidays* will be *Here*." Then: "Only 18 more days." And then, on the eve of his next vacation: "I am coming home *In a month*." He dragged out the end of his letters, as though he could not bear to break this frail tie with his family:

    ...W...I...T...H
     love & kisses
     I
     Remain
       your
       loving
       Son
       W.L.S. Churchill
          —from *The Last Lion*,
           William Manchester

A Note on Sentence Variety

To avoid monotony in your writing, you should experiment with the lengths and structures of your sentences.

1. You can vary the lengths of your sentences. In the beginning of the first paragraph of this selection, three rather long sentences are followed by this short sentence that grabs the reader's attention:

    Winston wept when told he must go.

2. You can vary your sentences by opening some of them with a subordinate clause, with a single word modifier, or with a phrase.

EXAMINING THE WRITER'S STYLE
Answers will vary. Possible answers:
1. He was seven years old. His parents decided it was time he left home. He was enrolled as a boarder at St. George's School on November 3, 1882. That was five weeks after the start of the autumn term. St. George's School was near Ascot, etc. Students will agree that Manchester's ideas are just as clearly expressed.
2. When Winston was seven years old, his parents decided it was time he left home.
3. Winston's sentences are mostly simple and "sound" quite different from Manchester's.
4. Manchester's short sentences are dramatic and especially important.
5. Answers will vary.

VARYING SENTENCES IN YOUR WRITING
Students' responses will vary, but all paragraphs should read smoothly and use sentences of different lengths. Encourage students to add words and details—or to rephrase existing ones—to make sentences read more smoothly. If necessary, show students how to incorporate the first two or three sentences into a smoothly written paragraph.

Literature & Language/*cont.*

On November 3, 1882, five weeks after the start of the autumn term, he was enrolled as a boarder at St. George's School . . . [sentence opens with a string of prepositional phrases]

When the teacher returned, Winston reeled off a perfect recitation. [sentence opens with a subordinate clause]

Astonished, the boy blurted out . . . [sentence opens with a single-word modifier]

3. Sentences can also vary in structure. You can use **simple sentences** with one subject and one predicate; **compound sentences**, with two independent clauses; **complex sentences**, with one independent clause and at least one subordinate clause; or **compound-complex sentences** with two or more independent clauses and at least one subordinate clause. In the first paragraph of this passage, the opening sentence is compound-complex; the second is a long simple sentence with many phrases; and the third is a complex sentence. Note that by using these different sentence structures and lengths Manchester has created a pleasing rhythm.

Ideally, sentence variety should be built into the writing so that readers are not aware of the effort. Manchester, a skilled writer, most likely varied his sentences automatically. When you are reviewing your own writing, read it aloud. If the writing sounds choppy and awkward, try to vary your sentences for a more pleasing sound.

Examining the Writer's Style

The following exercises will help you examine the way Manchester has constructed his sentences to comunicate very clearly his main ideas and also to create a pleasing narrative flow.
1. Take the first four sentences of this passage and rewrite them into a series of simple sentences. Read them aloud. Do they sound choppy and awkward? Are Manchester's ideas less clearly expressed?

2. Rewrite the first sentence so that it opens with a subordinate clause.
3. Find the sentences the seven-year-old Winston uses in his sad little letters to his parents. Are they mostly simple sentences, or are they more complex? Do they "sound" different from Manchester's own sentences?
4. Find all the short simple sentences Manchester uses in his own account. What effect do these brief sentences have? (Are they dramatic? Are they especially important sentences?)
5. Take at least four consecutive sentences from this passage and rewrite them using other sentence constructions (do not change any words). Compare your versions in class. Do you find any of your revised sentences superior to Manchester's?

Varying Sentences in Your Writing

Following are ten simple statements. Put these statements into a paragraph that reads smoothly and that is clear and effective. You will have to vary your sentence constructions to avoid monotony. Add words and details as you wish.
1. Churchill was one of the great public figures of the twentieth century.
2. His firsthand accounts of the South African War gained him fame as a journalist.
3. In 1900 he was elected to Parliament.
4. He served as first lord of the Admiralty, minister of munitions, secretary of state for war and air, and colonial secretary.
5. He was out of office from 1929 to 1939.
6. He became prime minister in 1939, when Neville Chamberlain was forced to resign.
7. His stirring oratory and energy led Britain through the war years.
8. He coined the expression "Iron Curtain."
9. In 1953 he was knighted and received the Nobel Prize of literature.
10. Throughout his career Churchill strove to maintain Britain as a great power and democracy.

This lesson may be particularly useful in helping students to understand some of the pitfalls that attend the use of subordinate clauses: sentence fragments, unclear use of pronouns and antecedents, and incorrect punctuation (lack of commas before or after the clause). Once students have learned to identify subordinate clauses, they can be on the lookout for the grammatical problems that such clauses can pose. Students may wish to refer to appropriate sections of **Grammar, Usage, and Mechanics: A Reference Guide** as they study this lesson.

Margaret Atwood

Margaret Atwood (1939–   ) is a Canadian poet, novelist, and essayist whose work often focuses on the surreal. She is particularly concerned with women's issues and likes to create fantastic situations that symbolize the dilemmas facing women. Her first novel, *The Edible Woman*, for example, tells of a woman who reacts to her impending marriage by becoming unable to eat anything because she identifies too strongly with the food that is being eaten. "My Life As a Bat" uses the bat's "different" sensibilities to remind the reader of oppressed groups for whom "the mythologies are different."

See a biography of Atwood and a poem on text pages 1142–1144.

Literature & Language

Using Subordinate Clauses Correctly

Literary Model

In literature, anything is possible. Margaret Atwood imagines that in a previous life she was a bat, a possibility she likes to consider because bats "never gloat." In this part of her short story, she tells about recurring nightmares.

I have recurring nightmares.

In one of them, I am clinging to the ceiling of a summer cottage while a red-faced man in white shorts and a white V-necked T-shirt jumps up and down, hitting at me with a tennis racquet. There are cedar rafters up here, and sticky flypapers attached with tacks, dangling like toxic seaweeds. I look down at the man's face, foreshortened and sweating, the eyes bulging and blue, the mouth emitting furious noise, rising up like a marine float, sinking again, rising as if on a swell of air.

The air itself is muggy, the sun is sinking; there will be a thunderstorm. A woman is shrieking, "My hair! My hair!" and someone else is calling, "Anthea! Bring the stepladder!" All I want is to get out through the hole in the screen, but that will take some concentration and it's hard in this din of voices, they interfere with my sonar. There is a smell of dirty bathmats—it's his breath, the breath that comes out from every pore, the breath of the monster. I will be lucky to get out of this alive.

In another nightmare I am winging my way—flittering, I suppose you'd call it—through the clean-washed demilight before dawn. This is a desert. The yuccas are in bloom, and I have been gorging myself on their juices and pollen. I'm heading to my home, to my home cave, where it will be cool during the burnout of day and there will be the sound of water trickling through limestone, coating the rock with a glistening hush, with the moistness of new mushrooms, and the other bats will chirp and rustle and doze until night unfurls again and makes the hot sky tender for us.

But when I reach the entrance to the cave, it is sealed over. It's blocked in. Who can have done this?

I vibrate my wings, sniffing blind as a dazzled moth over the hard surface. In a short time the sun will rise like a balloon on fire and I will be blasted with its glare, shriveled to a few small bones.

Whoever said that light was life and darkness nothing?

For some of us, the mythologies are different.

—from "My Life as a Bat,"
Margaret Atwood

Grammar Note

A **subordinate clause** has a subject and a verb, but it does not express a complete thought and cannot stand alone as a sentence. It must always be combined with an independent clause. Here are some subordinate clauses: *When I left; After it snowed; Before the dance began; which proved nothing*. You can recognize subordinate clauses because they often begin with a word like *although, when, where, because, after, who, which, that*. Subordinate clauses are used in several ways. A subordinate clause that modifies a noun or pronoun in the independent clause is called an **adjective clause**. A subordinate clause that modifies a verb is called an **adverb clause**. A subordinate clause used in a noun position (subject, object, or complement) is called a **noun clause**. Writers also use subordinate clauses to convey the relative importance of the ideas contained in a sentence. Margaret Atwood writes ("I" is the bat):

But when I reach the entrance to the cave, it is sealed over.

The subordinate clause ("when I reach the entrance to the cave") modifies the verb *is sealed* in the independent clause. The significant point of the passage is the nightmare discovery that the cave, the refuge that the bat seeks, is sealed over. The subordinate clause tells the reader *when* the discovery was made, but that information is clearly less important. The fact that it is expressed in a subordinate clause emphasizes its lesser importance. Suppose the sentence were rewritten with two independent clauses, like this:

I reach the entrance to the cave, but it is sealed over.

EXAMINING THE WRITER'S STYLE
1. adverb clause—*clinging*
2. adjective clause—*breath*
3. adjective clause—*cave*
4. adverb clause—*chirp, rustle, doze*
5. noun clause

USING SUBORDINATE CLAUSES IN YOUR WRITING
1. Creating Subordinate Clauses. Student responses will vary. Have students check their writing carefully to make sure that their sentences contain subordinate and independent clauses rather than sentence fragments, compound sentences, or run-ons.

2. Narrating the Further Adventures of the Bat. Encourage students to include specific sensory details that reveal the bat's perceptions and feelings. Students' compositions should also work as short stories or anecdotes, each with a clear beginning, middle, and end. Be sure students use and punctuate subordinate clauses correctly.

Literature & Language/*cont.*

This version makes the information that the bat reached the cave just as important as the fact that the entrance was sealed over.

Examining the Writer's Style

Below are some subordinate clauses from the passage by Margaret Atwood. Review each one in the context of the passage. Then classify each as an adjective or an adverb or a noun clause. Identify the word or words that each adjective or adverb clause modifies.
1. while a red-faced man in white shorts and a white V-necked T-shirt jumps up and down
2. that comes out from every pore
3. where it will be cool
4. until night unfurls again
5. that light was life and darkness nothing

As a class, discuss why you think Atwood chose to use subordinate clauses in these sentences. What other options might she have chosen?

Using Subordinate Clauses in Your Writing

1. **Creating Subordinate Clauses.** For each of the following pairs of ideas, write a sentence that links the two ideas together, using one independent clause and at least one subordinate clause.
   a. the thirsty deer/the mountain stream
   b. the morning sun/the dew on flowers
   c. starched napkins/two place settings
   d. a gray kitten/a ball of yarn
   e. a hard-earned victory/the smell of sweat
   f. the factory building/black smoke
   g. gusty March winds/broken umbrellas
   h. a clear night sky/a shooting star
   Exchange sentences with a partner. Then edit your partner's work to make sure each sentence contains one independent clause and at least one subordinate clause.

2. **Narrating the Further Adventures of the Bat.** The power of Atwood's narrative arises from her ability to imagine how the bat perceives and feels. In two or three paragraphs, narrate a further adventure from the point of view of the bat. You might choose to continue the story and tell what happens after the cave is sealed, or you might recount a different experience in another time and place. After you have finished your composition, check whether you have used subordinate clauses to combine your ideas and to suggest relationships between ideas.

This lesson can help students learn to use commas correctly in their own writing. It can also give them an appreciation for the style of nineteenth-century prose that relied upon long, complicated sentences.

During this lesson, you may wish to review the rules for proper comma usage; if so, **Grammar, Usage, and Mechanics: A Reference Guide,** pages 1302–1304, will prove helpful. Be prepared to discuss with the class the effect of long, complicated sentences that rely upon commas to make their meaning clear.

The French Revolution

The subject and setting for *A Tale of Two Cities* is the French Revolution, an event that began in 1789 and altered world history profoundly. When the French Revolution overthrew a long-standing monarchy and replaced it with a democratic republic, peoples around the world saw new possibilities in their own countries for the "liberty, equality, and fraternity" promised in France.

Dickens focuses on two aspects of the revolution: the grinding poverty of the French peasants and city-dwellers, and the Revolution's bloody battles and political actions. Although some factions within the revolutionary movement believed that political change could be accomplished peacefully, other groups thought that the French monarchy and aristocracy would never relinquish power. Therefore, these groups believed, a "Reign of Terror" was necessary to consolidate power. King Louis XVI was executed, as well as his family and chief aides. Supporters of the old regime clashed in fierce battles with proponents of the new republic.

In the Literary Model, Dickens foreshadows, through the spillage of wine, the blood that shortly will be spilled in these same streets.

Literature & Language

Using Commas Correctly

Literary Model

In this famous scene from his novel set in London and Paris during the French Revolution of 1796, Charles Dickens describes the suffering of the Parisian masses and foreshadows the bloody conflicts to come.

A large cask of wine had been dropped and broken in the street. The accident had happened in getting it out of a cart; the cask had tumbled out with a run, the hoops had burst, and it lay on the stones just outside the door of the wine shop, shattered like a walnut shell.

All the people within reach had suspended their business, or their idleness, to run to the spot and drink the wine. The rough, irregular stones of the street, pointing every way and designed, one might have thought, expressly to lame all living creatures that approached them, had dammed it into little pools; these were surrounded, each by its own jostling group or crowd, according to its size. Some men knelt down, made scoops of their two hands joined, and sipped, or tried to help women, who bent over their shoulders, to sip, before the wine had all run out between their fingers. Others, men and women, dipped in the puddles with little mugs of mutilated earthenware or even with handkerchiefs from women's heads, which were squeezed dry into infants' mouths; others made small mud embankments to stem the wine as it ran; others, directed by lookers-on up at high windows, darted here and there to cut off little streams of wine that started away in new directions; others devoted themselves to the sodden and lee-dyed pieces of the cask, licking and even champing the moister wine-rotted fragments with eager relish. There was no drainage to carry off the wine, and not only did it all get taken up, but so much mud got taken up along with it that there might have been a scavenger in the street if anybody acquainted with it could have believed in such a miraculous presence.

A shrill sound of laughter and amused voices—voices of men, women, and children—resounded in the street while this wine game lasted. There was little roughness in the sport and much playfulness. There was a special companionship in it, an observable inclination on the part of everyone to join some other one, which led, especially among the luckier or lighter hearted, to frolicsome embraces, drinking of healths, shaking of hands, and even joining of hands and dancing, a dozen together. When the wine was gone, and the places where it had been most abundant were raked into a gridiron pattern by fingers, these demonstrations ceased as suddenly as they had broken out. The man who had left his saw sticking in the firewood he was cutting set it in motion again; the woman who had left on a doorstep the little pot of hot ashes, at which she had been trying to soften the pain in her own starved fingers and toes or in those of her child, returned to it; men with bare arms, matted locks, and cadaverous faces, who had emerged into the winter light from cellars, moved away to descend again; and a gloom gathered on the scene that appeared more natural to it than sunshine.

The wine was red wine and had stained the ground of the narrow street in the suburb of Saint Antoine in Paris where it was spilled. It had stained many hands, too, and many faces and many naked feet and many wooden shoes. The hands of the man who sawed the wood left red marks on the billets; and the forehead of the woman who nursed her baby was stained with the stain of the old rag she wound about her head again. Those who had been greedy with the staves of the cask, had acquired a tigerish smear about the mouth; and one tall joker so besmirched, his head more out of a long squalid bag of a nightcap than in it, scrawled upon a wall with his finger dipped in muddy wine lees—BLOOD.

The time was to come when that wine too would be spilled on the street stones and when the stain of it would be red upon many there.

—from *A Tale of Two Cities*,
Charles Dickens

Grammar Note

Dickens's style is typical of nineteenth-century prose: it is generally marked by long complicated sentences, composed of many phrases and clauses. Careful punctuation, especially the use of commas, is needed to help readers grasp the sense of these very complex constructions.

Commas have many uses, but mainly they group words that belong together, separating them or setting them off from the rest of the sentence.

EXAMINING THE WRITER'S STYLE
Student answers will vary. Following are key elements that students should be encouraged to identify in each sentence.
1. Commas help to separate items in a series; to set off a participial phrase; to separate a parenthetical comment from the rest of the sentence; and to break up a long and complicated sentence.
2. Commas separate independent clauses and set off a participial phrase from the noun (*shop*) that it modifies.
3. Commas set off items in a series and separate an adjective clause from the rest of the sentence.

USING COMMAS CORRECTLY
Student answers will vary. Here is one possible version of the edited paragraph:

When I was acting with my children and friends in Mr. Wilkie Collins's drama of *The Frozen Deep,* I first conceived the main idea of this story. A strong desire was upon me then to embody it in my own person, and I traced out in my fancy the state of mind of which it would necessitate the presentation to an observant spectator with particular care and interest.

Literature & Language/*cont.*

1. Commas are used to separate independent clauses, as in this compound sentence:

   . . . the cask had tumbled out with a run, the hoops had burst, and it lay on the stones just outside the door of the wine shop . . .

2. Commas are used to separate items of similar grammatical rank that occur in a series, such as a list of nouns, verbs, adjectives, or parallel phrases or clauses:

   . . . voices of men, women, and children [a series of nouns]

   Some men knelt down, made scoops of their two hands joined, and sipped . . . [a series of verbs]

3. Commas are used to set off words, phrases, and clauses that are not essential to the basic meaning of the sentence:

   A Tale of Two Cities, a novel written in 1859, describes a terrible period of French history.

4. Commas are used to set off certain introductory words in a sentence, often to avoid ambiguity:

   Based on facts taken from Thomas Carlyle's *History of the French Revolution*, *A Tale of Two Cities* sees the Revolution as a time of horror.

   While acting in an amateur production of a play, Dickens conceived the main idea for *A Tale of Two Cities*.

5. Sometimes commas are used to set off a word, phrase, or clause for emphasis. In the following sentence, the phrase "or their idleness" is set off for emphasis (the point is that many of them *were* idle):

   All the people within reach had suspended their business, or their idleness, to run to the spot and drink the wine.

Note that when a modifier, especially an adjective clause, is *restrictive* (that is, when the basic meaning of the sentence is changed without it), commas are *not* used to set it off. In the following sentence, the adjective clause beginning with *who* tells *which* man performed the action and is thus necessary to the meaning of the sentence.

   The man who had left his saw sticking in the firewood he was cutting set it in motion again. . . .

Here the restrictive adjective clause *who had left his saw sticking in the firewood he was cutting* tells which particular man set the saw in motion again: not *any* man, but the man who left his saw sticking in the firewood.

Examining the Writer's Style

As a class, read aloud the following passages and discuss how commas aid in clarifying meaning. Remember that commas always indicate a slight pause. All of these passages refer to the spilled wine.
1. The rough, irregular stones of the street, pointing every way and designed, one might have thought, expressly to lame all living creatures that approached them, had dammed it into little pools. . . .
2. The accident had happened in getting it out of a cart; the cask had tumbled out with a run, the hoops had burst, and it lay on the stones just outside the door of the wine shop, shattered like a walnut shell.
3. . . . men with bare arms, matted locks, and cadaverous faces, who had emerged into the winter light from cellars, moved away to descend again. . . .

Using Commas Correctly

The punctuation in the passage you have just read from *A Tale of Two Cities* has been modernized. Years ago, commas were used much more frequently than they are today. Following is another passage from *A Tale of Two Cities*, this one printed exactly the way Dickens published it.

Act as an editor and modernize its use of commas. Type the passage out on a separate piece of paper, double spaced. Indicate your editorial changes in red pencil. Compare your editing with that of your classmates. Do you all agree on the way commas should be used? Remember that your chief concern is clarity. Remember also that commas indicate pauses. Before you make a change, be sure to read the passage aloud.

   When I was acting, with my children and friends, in Mr. Wilkie Collins's drama of *The Frozen Deep,* I first conceived the main idea of this story. A strong desire was upon me then, to embody it in my own person, and I traced out in my fancy, the state of mind of which it would necessitate the presentation to an observant spectator, with particular care and interest

PRETEACHING NOTE

The material in this lesson can help students to appreciate how writers use the narrative mode; it also can give them a handle on using narration in their own writing.

Before introducing the Literary Model you may wish to have students discuss narratives that they would like to recommend. The narratives may include movies, TV programs, novels, or even songs with a strong narrative element. Encourage students to explain why they found each "story" meaningful.

Margaret Drabble

The English novelist Margaret Drabble (1939–   ) is known for her stories about women's lives. Drabble creates richly textured portraits of "ordinary" women, whose lives reveal the fabric of the middle-class society in which they live. For this reason, her work has been compared to that of the nineteenth-century novelist George Eliot. In fact, *The Waterfall*, from which the excerpt is taken, is Drabble's reworking of George Eliot's *The Mill on the Floss*, in which the heroine, Maggie, competes for a man with her cousin, Lucy, wins the man's love but eventually yields to her cousin. Drabble's novel, on the other hand, asks what would have happened if Eliot's heroine had *not* yielded. The growing rivalry between Lucy and Jane is conveyed in the selected passage.

Literature & Language

Using the Narrative Mode

Literary Model

Imagine the reunion of two young cousins who had been separated during World War II, one going to live in the United States and the other remaining in Great Britain. See if the reunion you imagine is anything like the one Margaret Drabble describes between Lucy and her cousin Jane, who is the narrator of these events.

I don't know what expectations I had formed of Lucy. I think I did not much like the idea of her, largely because during the war Aunt Bridget, suffering from the universal American fear that all the British were starving and clad in rags, kept sending us parcels of American food and clothes, which gave me a very strange idea of what American children must be like. The clothes were not at all what comparable English children would have worn, and indeed, even in those desperate days, my mother, whose taste was not of the most sensitive, considered some of them too outré to inflict on us, and put them away in a drawer with mothballs. I can't now see quite what was wrong with them, except that they were all rather coy and girlish and heavily frilled and flowered, whereas most English girls at that time were dressed in boyish garments remarkable only for their utility. Also, I think the Americans had a tendency—still current, I believe—to make pointless, useless, nonclassical mock-up inventions, such as frilly dungarees, matching shirts and trousers, odd-shaped playsuits, dresses with braces, and so forth. I did not like these things that kept arriving in these parcels, and I was relieved when I was not compelled to wear them. It took me years to realize that in some sense they must also have reflected Aunt Bridget's taste, as well as the American nation's, and she certainly was capable of greater lapses than my mother, as well as of greater felicities.

I think I had expected Lucy to stroll down the garden path wearing some embarrassing and unsuitable garment, and I was not far wrong. She was wearing an embroidered white shirt under a red pleated pinafore dress, and she looked (as my mother said, in a vain search for idiom) cute. She looked cute. Imagine the ferocious dignity and integrity of a child that could survive such a description. Because survive it she did. She stood there, in the corner of the room, and when my name was mentioned to her, in introduction, she scowled at me with such poise that I was afraid.

"This is Jane," said my mother.

"Yes, I know it is," said Lucy, not moving an inch.

She had an American accent, which I had not foreseen: it was the strangest thing of all. From time to time our mothers had made us write letters to each other, and I had always read her dull epistles out to myself in pure King's English, and it amazed me to hear her speak like the child in the only film I had ever seen—some haunting saga of hospitals and saintliness and reunited parents, I recollect.

I had always disliked writing to Lucy.

"What on earth should I write to *her* for?" I used to say, crossly, chewing my pencil, denting the soft wood angrily with my teeth.

"Because she's your cousin," my mother would say. "Because you'll see her again, when the war's over."

"What shall I *say* to her?" I would say, groaning, bored by my own boredom.

"Oh, I don't know," my mother would say, losing interest at this stage, as she always did. "Anything. Tell her what you've been doing."

And I would, under duress, compose laborious sentences, saying, I went fishing today, I caught two minnows; our cat had three kittens; it is my sister's birthday; knowing that these trivial scraps could hardly merit a transatlantic journey, knowing that she would read them with as little love as I composed them.

And suddenly, there she was, American, strange, my own cousin. I despaired, as I stared at her, of ever bridging that gap, that separation, that enforced distance of relationship, of ever making good those halting childish phrases on the blue airmail paper. She stood there, demure as her name, self-possessed, detached, whereas in myself I could feel only panic. It took me years to realize that my panic was so great that I rightly knew that I must never, never show it and that the front I presented was her own front: demure, self-possessed, detached. We looked alike. Adults, seeing us, thought we were alike. Cold, they said we were. Cold fish.

EXAMINING THE WRITER'S STYLE
Student answers will vary but may include the following.

1. The writer's use of *first-person point of view* makes the narrative seem true, as though it really happened to the writer.

2. The writer focuses on one very telling area of background information, revealing the cultural differences between Americans and the English through the differences in their clothes.

3. The writer includes many details that seem true to life, including the narrator's unwillingness to write letters and her reaction to her cousin's accent.

4. The writer gives a great deal of information about the narrator and her mother; she suggests the cousin's thoughts and feelings through key actions.

5. The writer suggests but does not state the meaning of the experience.

6. The events are arranged in an order that helps answer this question: "What was the origin of Lucy and Jane's adult relationship?"

7. The writer creates suspense about what the cousins' meeting will be like.
(Answers continue in left-hand column.)

(Continued from top.)

WRITING IN THE NARRATIVE MODE
Student narratives should unify events by means of a common, compelling theme, one that is indicated or suggested in the topic sentence. Events should unfold in an order that is easy to follow and that clarifies the theme. Although this activity emphasizes narration, other modes have a role to play: For example, characters should be vividly conveyed through telling detail or by description that differentiates them clearly.

Literature & Language /*cont.*

> From the first, we treated each other with great delicacy. Our parents flung us together, crudely, without finesse, as parents do, as we had known they would.
>
> —from *The Waterfall*,
> Margaret Drabble

A Note on the Narrative Mode

Narrative writing relates a series of events. Narratives may be fiction or nonfiction. They may be very brief and complete in themselves, such as a personal experience you relate quickly to a friend, or they may be a part of a longer work. The narrative passage extracted here is from a novel called *The Waterfall*. In this passage the writer tells of the meeting between Jane, the narrator, and her cousin Lucy.

Note that Drabble's narrative passage has a topic sentence:

I don't know what expectations I had formed of Lucy.

This sentence implies that the narrator is meeting Lucy after a long separation. The sentence also suggests the theme of the passage: the testing of expectations against reality. The topic sentence helps the reader bear in mind the purpose of the passage. The rest of the first paragraph provides necessary background for understanding the two characters and the significance of the meeting. When the narrator begins to relate the events of the meeting in the second paragraph, the reader is curious about what will happen next. In longer narrative passages, topic sentences help focus the reader's attention and prevent the narrative from degenerating into a series of meaningless events or details. A clincher statement at the end of a narrative passage sums up a writer's main points and makes the focus even clearer.

Examining the Writer's Style

You might use the following guidelines for evaluating narrative passages. With a partner, review the passage by Drabble and write a few sentences of evaluation for each guideline.

1. What point of view does the writer use? What is the effect of the point of view?
2. Has the writer included enough background information?
3. Has the writer included details that make people and events seem real?
4. Has the writer described characters' thoughts and feelings?
5. Has the writer said anything about the meaning of the experience?
6. Are the events arranged in an order that makes sense? (If flashbacks are used, do they help clarify the action?)
7. Does the writer create suspense, that quality that makes you want to keep reading?

Writing in the Narrative Mode

Writing a First-Person Narrative. Like the passage by Drabble, a narrative may be told from a first-person point of view. Write your own narrative passage (perhaps about an emotional meeting or separation), using "I" as the narrator.

1. After you have selected your subject, make a chronological list of the events your narrative will cover. Then think about the theme of your passage, or the point you want to make. How will you keep your narrative from turning into a boring series of unconnected events or details? Finally, think about the characters who will be in your narrative, including the narrator. What characteristics will each actor in your story display?
2. Begin by writing a topic sentence that will tell readers what the narrative is about. Then write the body of the passage, using the chronology you have developed. If necessary, use flashbacks to add detail or to explain motivation. Exchange your narrative with a partner. Read your partner's narrative and evaluate it in terms of the guidelines cited above.
3. Think about your partner's evaluation of your narrative, and revise it for effectiveness and clarity, as necessary. Pay special attention to your topic sentence and your clincher statement.

PRETEACHING NOTE
Once students understand the essence of expository writing, they can begin to notice its uses in the writing of others and cultivate it in their own writing. You may wish to use this lesson as an introduction to selections in this book that feature expository writing, particularly those from the eighteenth century.

Shipboard Literature
After the development of huge ocean-going luxury vessels in the 1920's and 1930's, the sea cruise became a popular activity of the rich and near-rich—and an intriguing image for writers and readers. A group of strangers, living in proximity for several weeks, possibly coming into periodic contact with exotic locales, was an attractive premise for novels of all types. Agatha Christie used the backdrop in her mystery novels; Katherine Anne Porter mined its symbolic dimensions in her novel *Ship of Fools*.

Waugh's travel books take advantage of the reader's interest in the glamorous and exotic aspects of the sea cruise; at the same time, Waugh satirizes would-be adventurers who go on cruises expecting romantic escapades.

Literature & Language

Using the Expository Aim

Literary Model

When you travel, do you write about what you see and do? Why do you think travelers write or writers travel? In the following excerpts from one of his travel books, satirist Evelyn Waugh explains his reasons. In this passage, he is talking about a journey made to Brazil in 1932. Of course, he traveled by ship.

One does not travel, any more than one falls in love, to collect material. It is simply part of one's life. For myself and many better than me, there is a fascination in distant and barbarous places, and particularly in the borderlands of conflicting cultures and states of development, where ideas, uprooted from their traditions, become oddly changed in transplantation. It is there that I find the experiences vivid enough to demand translation into literary form.

Just as a carpenter, I suppose, seeing a piece of rough timber feels an inclination to plane it and square it and put it into shape, so a writer is not really content to leave any experience in the amorphous, haphazard condition in which life presents it; and putting an experience into shape means, for a writer, putting it into communicable form.

• • •

Out on the savannah there is no twilight; the sun goes down blazing on the horizon, affording five or ten minutes of gold and crimson glory; then darkness. In the forest, night opens slowly like a yawn. The colors gradually deepened, the greens pure and intense to the point of saturation, the tree trunks and the bare earth glowing brown; the half shades, the broken and refracted fragments of light all disappeared and left only fathomless depths of pure color. Then dusk spread; distances became incalculable and obstacles detached themselves unexpectedly and came suddenly near; and while it was almost night in the trail the tops of the trees were still ablaze with sunlight, till eventually they too darkened and their flowers were lost. And all the pattering and whistling and chattering of the bush at night broke out loudly on all sides, and the tired little horse—who was doing a double journey and, being always on the move, had no instinct for home—

suddenly pricked his ears and raised his head and stepped out fresh as though his day were only just beginning.

• • •

I do not think these happier travelers are ever disappointed in anything they see. They come back to the ship from each expedition with their eyes glowing; they have been initiated into strange mysteries, and their speech is rich with the words of the travel bureau's advertising manager; their arms are full of purchases. It is quite extraordinary to see what they will buy. I suppose it is the housekeeping habit run riot after twenty years of buying electric light bulbs and tinned apricots and children's winter underwear. They become adept in bargaining and may be seen in the lounge over their evening coffee, lying prodigiously to each other, like the fishermen of comic magazines, comparing prices and passing their acquisitions from hand to hand amid a buzz of admiration and competitive anecdote. I wonder what happens to all this trash. When it reaches England and is finally unpacked in the gray light of some provincial morning, has it lost some of its glamour? Does it look at all like the other bric-a-brac displayed in the fancy goods emporium down the street? Is it distributed among relatives and friends to show that they are not forgotten during the voyage?—or is it treasured, every bit of it, hung upon walls and displayed on occasional tables, a bane to the house-parlormaid but a continual reminder of those magical evenings under a wider sky, of dance music and the handsome figures of the officers, of temple bells heard across the water, of the inscrutable half light in the bazaars. . . .

—from *When the Going Was Good*,
Evelyn Waugh

A Note on the Expository Aim

The purpose of writing with an **expository aim** is to provide information. Waugh's primary purpose in writing about his travels is to share what he has experienced and to explain why the experiences are important to him. Waugh opens with a flat explanation of his reasons for traveling:

EXAMINING THE WRITER'S TECHNIQUE
Student responses will vary but should resemble the following.
1. Waugh likes writing about foreign places because their strangeness makes them "vivid."

In typical 1930's English fashion, he considers any non-European culture "barbarous."
2. He compares writers to carpenters.

3. Sight: images of sun, darkness, colors; hearing: the "pattering," "whistling," and "chattering" of the bush.
4. Waugh feels awe and affection for the savannah and communicates it well.
5. Waugh contrasts lofty adjectives with mundane images of advertising managers and children's underwear to express his distaste. He probably thinks the items are treasured as talismans.

WRITING WITH AN EXPOSITORY AIM
Student compositions should be organized around a clear thesis statement directed to a specific audience. Information should support the thesis; word choice and style should be appropriate for the audience. Encourage students to spend ample time on the prewriting stage.

Literature & Language / cont.

One does not travel, any more than one falls in love, to collect material. It is simply part of one's life.

Sometimes Waugh wants to **describe** what he has experienced in such vivid sensory language that readers will be able to imagine themselves in the setting—seeing, hearing, and feeling what Waugh sensed.

Out on the savannah there is no twilight; the sun goes down blazing on the horizon, affording five or ten minutes of gold and crimson glory . . .

Waugh is a great satirist, so it's not surprising that he also wishes to **persuade** his readers to accept a point of view on some aspect of travel. In the last paragraph, he gives his view of tourists on cruise ships who, even back in 1932, spent most of their time buying souvenirs and talking about their purchases. Although this paragraph is also vividly descriptive, Waugh gets across his point of view by using strong comparisons and highly charged emotional language:

. . . lying prodigiously to each other, like the fishermen of comic magazines. . .

I wonder what happens to all this *trash*.

Examining the Writer's Technique

In order to examine Waugh's techniques in writing this selection, work with a partner to answer the following questions:

1. In the first paragraph, how does Waugh explain his interest in writing about foreign places? What do you think he means by describing distant places as *barbarous*?
2. What comparison does he use to explain why writers write?
3. When describing his experience of the savannah, what senses does Waugh appeal to? Give examples.
4. How would you describe Waugh's feeling for the savannah? How effective is he in sharing his feeling with the reader?
5. Give examples of how Waugh conveys his opinion of the tourist-shoppers he describes in the last paragraph. How

do you think he would answer the series of questions he poses about the souvenir "trash" when it is brought home?

Writing with an Expository Aim

Writing an Expository Composition. Select your own subject for an expository composition of three to five paragraphs. You might write about a trip you made, as Waugh does, or you might consider these topics: your favorite film; the benefits of recycling (paper, glass, aluminum, etc.); the importance of a national space program; teenage chess masters. You should pay special attention to the prewriting stage, because planning and organization are especially important to the success of an expository composition.

a. The first step is to select and limit your subject. Next you should make notes about your audience, your primary expository purpose, and any secondary writing aims you have. You should then gather the information you will use in your composition. Consider the sequence in which you will present the information. Create an outline, indicating the topic and writing aim of each paragraph. Choosing a title will help you focus on the main idea of your composition.

b. Begin by writing your thesis statement, the sentence that sums up your main idea or purpose. Then follow your outline as you write your composition. Bear in mind your methods to fulfill your aims, and let these methods guide your choice of language. Exchange your first draft with a partner. Review your partner's work. Is the topic of the composition clear? Does it convey all the information you need to understand the topic? Is the organization clear and easy to follow? Are any writing aims, such as description and persuasion, made clear by the appropriate use of sensory or evaluative language? Discuss your ideas for revisions with your partner.

c. Making use of your partner's ideas, revise your expository composition to make it more effective. Check that your thesis statement is precise and that your language is appropriate for your aim. Your title should reflect the main idea of the composition. Edit for correct spelling, punctuation, and grammar.

opinion, either as a reader or as a writer.

The Woman Question

Woolf wrote *A Room of One's Own* at a time when there was great debate about the "place" of women. *Room* was based on lectures given at Girton, a women's college, in 1928, when women's higher education was still relatively new in England. Many scholars and politicians of

the time argued that women's biology made them inherently unfit to think about serious issues or to hold positions of responsibility. In this context, Woolf's attribution of women's difficulties to *social* causes, rather than biological ones, was a radical position.

Literature & Language

Using the Persuasive Aim

Literary Model

If William Shakespeare had had an equally talented sister, what would have happened to her gift in sixteenth-century England? This is the question Virginia Woolf asks and answers in the following passage.

Here am I asking why women did not write poetry in the Elizabethan age, and I am not sure how they were educated; whether they were taught to write; whether they had sitting rooms to themselves; how many women had children before they were twenty-one; what, in short, they did from eight in the morning till eight at night. They had no money evidently; according to Professor Trevelyan they were married whether they liked it or not before they were out of the nursery, at fifteen or sixteen very likely. It would have been extremely odd, even upon this showing, had one of them suddenly written the plays of Shakespeare, I concluded, and I thought of that old gentleman, who is dead now, but was a bishop, I think, who declared that it was impossible for any woman, past, present, or to come, to have the genius of Shakespeare. He wrote to the papers about it. He also told a lady who applied to him for information that cats do not as a matter of fact go to heaven, though they have, he added, souls of a sort. How much thinking those old gentlemen used to save one! How the borders of ignorance shrank back at their approach! Cats do not go to heaven. Women cannot write the plays of Shakespeare.

    Be that as it may, I could not help thinking, as I looked at the works of Shakespeare on the shelf, that the bishop was right at least in this; it would have been impossible, completely and entirely, for any woman to have written the plays of Shakespeare in the age of Shakespeare. Let me imagine, since facts are so hard to come by, what would have happened had Shakespeare had a wonderfully gifted sister, called Judith, let us say. Shakespeare himself went, very probably—his mother was an heiress—to the grammar school, where he may have learned Latin— Ovid, Virgil, and Horace—and the elements of grammar and logic. He was, it is well known, a wild boy who poached rabbits, perhaps shot a deer, and

had, rather sooner than he should have done, to marry a woman in the neighborhood, who bore him a child rather quicker than was right. That escapade sent him to seek his fortune in London. He had, it seemed, a taste for the theater; he began by holding horses at the stage door. Very soon he got work in the theater, became a successful actor, and lived at the hub of the universe, meeting everybody, knowing everybody, practicing his art on the boards, exercising his wits in the streets, and even getting access to the palace of the queen. Meanwhile his extraordinarily gifted sister, let us suppose, remained at home. She was as adventurous, as imaginative, as agog to see the world as he was. But she was not sent to school. She had no chance of learning grammar and logic, let alone of reading Horace and Virgil. She picked up a book now and then, one of her brother's perhaps, and read a few pages. But then her parents came in and told her to mend the stockings or mind the stew and not moon about with books and papers. They would have spoken sharply but kindly, for they were substantial people who knew the conditions of life for a woman and loved their daughter—indeed, more likely than not she was the apple of her father's eye. Perhaps she scribbled some pages up in an apple loft on the sly, but was careful to hide them or set fire to them. Soon, however, before she was out of her teens, she was to be betrothed to the son of a neighboring wool stapler. She cried out that marriage was hateful to her, and for that she was severely beaten by her father. Then he ceased to scold her. He begged her instead not to hurt him, not to shame him in this matter of her marriage. He would give her a chain of beads or a fine petticoat, he said; and there were tears in his eyes. How could she disobey him? How could she break his heart? The force of her own gift alone drove her to it. She made up a small parcel of her belongings, let herself down by a rope one summer's night and took the road to London. She was not seventeen. The birds that sang in the hedge were not more musical than she was. She had the quickest fancy, a gift like her brother's, for the tune of words. Like him, she had a taste for the theater. She stood at the stage door; she wanted to act, she said. Men laughed in her face. The manager—a fat, loose-lipped

EXAMINING THE WRITER'S TECHNIQUE
1. Student answers will vary. In general, students should identify all character and physical descriptions of "Judith" as pure conjecture, all information about William Shakespeare as fact, and most elements of what happens to "Judith" as plausible argument with some basis in fact.
2. Student answers will vary. Many students may feel that it brings the reader,

after following an engrossing scenario, back to reality.

WRITING WITH A PERSUASIVE AIM
Encourage students to think through all possible aspects of the bishop's opinions based on how they can infer them from Woolf's comments. You may wish to brainstorm for a time with the entire class before having students work on their

own. Student writing should present views that plausibly reflect the bishop as Woolf depicts him.

Literature & Language /cont.

man—guffawed. He bellowed something about poodles dancing and women acting—no woman, he said, could possibly be an actress. He hinted—you can imagine what. She could get no training in her craft. Could she even seek her dinner in a tavern or roam the streets at midnight? Yet her genius was for fiction and lusted to feed abundantly upon the lives of men and women and the study of their ways. At last—for she was very young, oddly like Shakespeare the poet in her face, with the same gray eyes and rounded brows—at last Nick Green the actor-manager took pity on her; she found herself with child by that gentleman and so—who shall measure the heat and violence of the poet's heart when caught and tangled in a woman's body?—killed herself one winter's night and lies buried at some crossroads where the omnibuses now stop outside the Elephant and Castle.

That, more or less, is how the story would run, I think, if a woman in Shakespeare's day had had Shakespeare's genius.

—from *A Room of One's Own*, Virginia Woolf

A Note on the Persuasive Aim

A writer with a **persuasive aim** wants to convince readers to accept a particular point of view or to take a particular action. **Facts**, such as the number of women who were published writers before the eighteenth century, can be proven by producing evidence, such as publisher's records. **Opinions** or **interpretations of facts**, however, require argumentation. In such cases, writers have to use logical reasoning and appeals to the emotions to persuade their readers to accept a particular point of view. Skillful persuasive writers, such as Virginia Woolf, present convincing arguments using factual information, plausible logic, and subtle appeals to readers' imagination and sympathy. Note in the following passage how quickly Woolf moves from a hypothetical ("let us suppose") statement to a plausible conclusion.

Meanwhile, his extraordinarily gifted sister, let us suppose, remained at home; . . . she was not sent to school. She had no chance of learning grammar and logic. . . .

As she embellishes the portrait of Shakespeare's sister, Woolf ceases to remind her readers that she is writing about a person who never existed. The character is so vivid, the details so specific, and the outcome so tragically wasteful that, by the end of the essay, the reader is quite ready to believe that social conditions are what limit women writers. (Do you agree?)

Examining the Writer's Technique

1. Working with a partner, analyze the long paragraph in the passage that begins "Be that as it may . . ." Indicate which statements are based on verifiable facts, which are pure conjecture or imagination, and which are logical or plausible arguments with some basis in fact. Then discuss with your partner which of these statements you find most convincing.

2. As a class, discuss the effect of the sentence that concludes this passage. Does it undermine the persuasiveness of the preceding material, or does it have a different effect? Explain.

Writing with a Persuasive Aim

Writing to Persuade Readers of the Opposite Opinion. The first paragraph of the passage from *A Room of One's Own* mentions a bishop who was convinced that no woman could ever have the genius of Shakespeare. Woolf then presents her opinion: She feels that the problem in Shakespeare's day was not lack of female genius, but lack of a nurturing environment that would allow such genius to grow and express itself. In one or two paragraphs, write a rebuttal or argument against Woolf's opinion, as it might have been written by this elderly bishop. Even though you do not share the bishop's opinion, try to think of the persuasive points he would use to convince readers of his point of view. You may choose to write in direct rebuttal of Woolf's arguments, or you may simply set forth the bishop's opinion without reference to Woolf's points.

This material on word choice can be extremely helpful in all types of lessons. Students will find it helpful in work on fiction, nonfiction, and even poetry. You may also want to use it to help students appreciate a writer's technique for creating a particular tone or mood. Students might enjoy comparing a passage from the work of American writer Edgar Allan Poe to the Brontë selection, comparing and contrasting how each writer chooses words to convey a mood of horror and danger.

Emily Brontë

The Brontë family's real life had many of the elements of Emily's novel. The Brontë children—novelists Charlotte, Anne, and Emily, and their brother, Branwell—lived with their stern parson father in an isolated vicarage in Yorkshire. Their mother died early, and their father was a cold and remote figure, so the children soon developed an active fantasy life, writing detailed histories of imaginary kingdoms they called Angria and Gondal. Branwell died young, worn out by addiction to drugs and alcohol. His three sisters lived isolated lives at the parsonage, where they, too, died young. (Only Charlotte married; she died shortly thereafter from complications of pregnancy.) Before their deaths, however, the sisters each wrote one or more novels.

The novels of Charlotte Brontë and the poetry and novel of Emily Brontë rank among the finest works of English literature. The themes of loneliness, isolation, early death, and motherlessness, along with other autobiographical elements, mark the work of all three Brontës.

Literature & Language

Choosing Words to Create a Tone

Literary Model

A lonely house on an isolated, wind-swept moor in northern England is the perfect setting for one of literature's most interesting characters, the dark and brooding—and mysterious—Heathcliff.

Wuthering Heights is the name of Mr. Heathcliff's dwelling, "wuthering" being a significant provincial adjective, descriptive of the atmospheric tumult to which its station is exposed in stormy weather. Pure, bracing ventilation they must have up there at all times; indeed, one may guess the power of the north wind, blowing over the edge, by the excessive slant of a few stunted firs at the end of the house and by a range of gaunt thorns, all stretching their limbs one way, as if craving alms of the sun. Happily, the architect had foresight to build it strong: the narrow windows are deeply set in the wall, and the corners defended with large jutting stones.

Before passing the threshold, I paused to admire a quantity of grotesque carving lavished over the front, and especially about the principal door, above which, among a wilderness of crumbling griffins and shameless little boys, I detected the date "1500" and the name "Hareton Earnshaw." I would have made a few comments and requested a short history of the place from the surly owner, but his attitude at the door appeared to demand my speedy entrance, or complete departure, and I had no desire to aggravate his impatience previous to inspecting the penetralia.

One step brought us into the family sitting room, without any introductory lobby or passage; they call it here "the house" preeminently. It includes kitchen and parlor, generally; but I believe at Wuthering Heights the kitchen is forced to retreat altogether into another quarter; at least I distinguished a chatter of tongues and a clatter of culinary utensils deep within; and I observed no signs of roasting, boiling, or baking, about the huge fireplace; nor any glitter of copper saucepans and tin colanders on the walls. One end, indeed, reflected splendidly both light and heat from ranks of immense pewter dishes, interspersed with silver jugs and tankards, towering row after row in a vast oak dresser to the very roof. The latter had never been underdrawn; its entire anatomy lay bare to an inquiring eye, except where a frame of wood laden with oatcakes, and clusters of legs of beef, mutton, and ham, concealed it. Above the chimney were sundry villainous old guns and a couple of horse pistols, and, by way of ornament, three gaudily painted canisters disposed along its ledge. The floor was of smooth, white stone; the chairs, high-backed, primitive structures, painted green, one or two heavy black ones lurking in the shade. In an arch under the dresser reposed a huge, liver-colored pointer surrounded by a swarm of squealing puppies; and other dogs haunted other recesses.

The apartment and furniture would have been nothing extraordinary as belonging to a homely, northern farmer with a stubborn countenance and stalwart limbs set out to advantage in knee breeches and gaiters. Such an individual, seated in his armchair, his mug of ale frothing on the round table before him, is to be seen in any circuit of five or six miles among these hills, if you go at the right time after dinner. But Mr. Heathcliff forms a singular contrast to his abode and style of living. He is a dark-skinned gypsy in aspect, in dress and manners a gentleman, that is, as much a gentleman as many a country squire; rather slovenly, perhaps, yet not looking amiss with his negligence because he has an erect and handsome figure and rather morose. Possibly, some people might suspect him of a degree of underbred pride; I have a sympathetic chord within that tells me it is nothing of the sort. I know, by instinct, his reserve springs from an aversion to showy displays of feeling—to manifestations of mutual kindliness. He'll love and hate, equally under cover, and esteem it a species of impertinence to be loved or hated again.

—from *Wuthering Heights,* Emily Brontë

A Note on Tone

Tone is the writer's attitude or feeling toward a subject, characters, or an audience. One of the writer's most powerful tools for establishing tone is **diction,** or word choice. Emily Brontë's choice of words in the opening chapter of *Wuthering Heights* sets the darkly romantic,

**Emotionally
Charged Words**	**Definition**
tumult	chaos or disturbance
stunted	kept from reaching full growth
gaunt	thin, bare
craving	begging
jutting	thrusting
crumbling	falling apart, into crumbs
clatter	rattling sound
glitter	shine, sparkle, gleam
splendidly	magnificently
towering	reaching high, like a tower

ESTABLISHING TONE IN YOUR WRITING
1. Describing a Landscape. Student writing should include specific, vivid details that appeal to the senses.
2. Writing a Parody of *Wuthering Heights*. Student writing should follow the premise of the parody consistently, so that the informed reader will recognize what is being parodied as well as how the parody differs from it.

Literature & Language/*cont.*

even primitive, emotional tone that characterizes the entire novel.

Vivid adjectives and adverbs and strong nouns and verbs can be used with great effectiveness to convey emotion and set a tone. Brontë helps us share her feelings for a "*grotesque* carving," "*villainous* old guns," and "*gaunt* thorns." Her feelings even about the chairs are suggested in the verb "*lurking*" and her feelings about Heathcliff's dogs by the verb "*haunted*." If you doubt the power of words to convey tone, make these substitutions: *intricate* for *grotesque*; *slim* for *gaunt*; and *resting* for *lurking*.

Examining the Writer's Style

With a partner, read through the passage from *Wuthering Heights* and list words that you think contribute to its emotional tone. Choose *ten* of these words, and create a chart like the one below. Check your definition of each word in the dictionary.

Emotionally Charged Words	**Definition**
grotesque	weird or distorted

Establishing Tone in Your Writing

1. Describing a Landscape. Poet Ted Hughes (see page 1138) found in his own teaching of writing that students do better when they write about some special setting, something strange or extreme. "Deserts, steppes, the Antarctic, the moon, all come more easily than the view from their bedroom window." Here are seven subjects he suggests. Choose one, or another topic of your own, and write a paragraph describing it. Try to find words to reveal the way you feel about this topic. Be sure your details are sharp and evocative. When you have finished, review your composition and underline the emotionally charged words you find in it.

1. I am a giant octopus. A tidal wave has carried me into the wrong sea—too cold. I am trying to find my way home over the sea floor.
2. I am a hermit or castaway on an island in the far Southern Atlantic. I do nothing but search for food.
3. I am a creature from outer space. I have landed near the sea. This is my report to headquarters.
4. I am the Amazon.
5. What can you see through this telescope?
6. I am blind. Once, for just five minutes, I could see. This is what I saw.
7. I am an escaped prisoner being hunted by dogs.
   —Ted Hughes

2. Writing a Parody of *Wuthering Heights*. Generations of comic writers have found that writings that convey a strong tone are often attractive targets for parody. A **parody** treats another work in a humorous or satirical way by imitating or exaggerating some aspects of the writer's style. The enormous success of *Wuthering Heights* and other highly romantic novels prompted a number of contemporary parodies. Even Jane Austen wrote a spoof of the romantic novel in her *Northanger Abbey*. Try your hand at writing a parody of *Wuthering Heights*. Imitate the first few paragraphs, creating your own setting and leading character.

a. Begin by selecting a setting. You might want to exaggerate Brontë's setting of a mysterious, brooding house, or you might want to completely thwart expectations and describe in exaggerated romantic terminology something quite different (perhaps a luxurious seaside resort or the pretty cottage of a young couple).
b. Choose a character to place in the setting. Use overblown, highly emotional language to describe your setting and character. Keep in mind that names, such as Wuthering Heights and Heathcliff, help to establish tone. Your choice of names can also add to the comic effect. (You might create a character named Cliff Hanger who lives in Fear-of-Heights.)

A HANDBOOK OF LITERARY TERMS

ALEXANDRINE   A line of poetry made up of six iambs—that is, a line written in iambic hexameter. The following alexandrine is from Percy Bysshe Shelley's "To a Skylark":

> Our sweetest songs are those that tell of saddest thought

See page 200.

ALLEGORY   A story in which the characters, settings, and events stand for abstract or moral concepts. Allegories thus have two meanings: a literal meaning and a symbolic meaning. Allegories were a popular literary form during the Middle Ages. The best-known English allegory is John Bunyan's *Pilgrim's Progress* (Unit Four), which recounts the adventures of a character named Christian. The hero's journey to the Celestial city brings him up against many trials that stand for the pitfalls facing the Christian traveling through this world toward the spiritual world.

See page 590.

ALLITERATION   The repetition of consonant sounds in words that are close to one another. Alliteration occurs most often at the beginning of words, as in "rough and ready." But consonants within words sometimes alliterate, as in "baby blue." The echoes alliteration creates can increase a poem's rhythmic and musical effects and make its lines especially memorable. In this line from Alfred, Lord Tennyson's "The Eagle," the alliteration of harsh *k* sounds reinforces the stark image of the bird:

> He clasps the crag with crooked hands

Alliteration is an essential feature of Anglo-Saxon poetry; in most lines, two or three of the four stressed syllables alliterate.

See pages 40, 146, 1089.

ALLUSION   A reference to a statement, person, place, event, or thing that is known from literature, history, religion, myth, politics, sports, science, or pop culture. For example, the concluding lines of Wilfred Owen's poem "Dulce et Decorum Est" (Unit Seven) are *"Dulce et decorum est / Pro patria mori."* These lines allude to a line from an ode by the Latin poet Horace: "It is sweet and proper to die for one's country." The title of the English writer Barbara Pym's novel *A Glass of Blessings* is an allusion to a line from George Herbert's poem "The Pulley" (Unit Three). The title of William Faulkner's *The Sound and the Fury* is an allusion to a line from Shakespeare's *Macbeth*. The following cartoon alludes to William Butler Yeats's poem "The Second Coming" (Unit Seven).

"Basil, do you think the center is going to hold?"

Drawing by George Booth; © 1984 The New Yorker Magazine, Inc.

See pages 155, 814, 1084.

ANALOGY   A comparison of two things to show that they are alike in certain respects. Writers often make analogies to show how something unfamiliar is like something well known or widely experienced. For example, people often draw an analogy between creating a work of art and giving birth to a child.

ANTAGONIST   The character or force that opposes or blocks the protagonist in a narrative. Usually the antagonist is human, like Sir Mordred, the villainous rebel who destroys the Round Table in Malory's *Le Morte Darthur* (Unit Two). Sometimes the antagonist is supernatural, like Satan, who opposes God in Milton's *Paradise Lost* (Unit Three).

ANTITHESIS   A contrast of ideas expressed in a grammatically balanced statement. In the following line from *The Rape of the Lock,* Alexander Pope balances noun against noun and verb against verb: "And wretches hang that jurymen may dine."

See pages 528, 832.

APHORISM   A concise, sometimes witty saying that expresses a principle, truth, or observation about life. Alexander Pope's poetry contains some of the most famous aphorisms in the English language, as in this example from *An Essay on Criticism:* "To err is human, to forgive divine."

APOSTROPHE **A figure of speech in which a speaker directly addresses an absent or dead person, an abstract quality, or something nonhuman as if it were present and capable of responding.** Apostrophe was a popular device with the Romantic poets: Wordsworth apostrophizes the dead poet Milton in "London, 1802"; Shelley apostrophizes the west wind and a skylark; Keats apostrophizes a star, a nightingale, a Greek vase, and the season of autumn (all in Unit Five).

See page 700.

ASIDE **Private words that a character in a play speaks to the audience or to another character, which are not supposed to be overheard by others onstage.** Stage directions usually tell when a speech is an aside. For example, in Act I, Scene 3 of Shakespeare's *Macbeth,* Macbeth makes numerous asides to the audience as he ruminates about the possibility of becoming king.

See page 329.

ASSONANCE **The repetition of similar vowel sounds followed by different consonant sounds in words that are close together.** Assonance differs from **exact rhyme** in that it does not repeat the consonant sound following the vowel. The words *face* and *base* rhyme, while the words *face* and *fade* are assonant. Like alliteration, assonance can create musical and rhythmic effects. In this line from Alfred, Lord Tennyson's "The Lotos-Eaters," the repetition of long *o* sounds is **onomatopoetic:**

All day the wind breathes low with mellower tone

See page 1089.

ATMOSPHERE **The mood or feeling in a literary work.** Atmosphere is usually created through descriptive details and evocative language. For example, Ben Okri sets the mood of his short story "In the Shadow of War" (Unit Seven) with a dreamlike description of the wartime jungle around Lagos, Nigeria.

See pages 963, 1040.

AUTOBIOGRAPHY **An account of a person's own life.** One of the most famous autobiographies of the twentieth century is *Goodbye to All That* by Robert Graves. Dylan Thomas's "A Child's Christmas in Wales" (Unit Seven) is another well-known autobiographical account.

BALLAD **A song or songlike poem that tells a story.** Most ballads have a regular pattern of **rhythm** and **rhyme,** and they use simple language with a great deal of repetition. Ballads generally have **refrains**—lines or words that are repeated at regular intervals. They usually tell sensational stories of tragedy, adventure, betrayal, revenge, and jealousy. **Folk ballads** are composed by anonymous singers and are passed down orally from generation to generation

before they are written down (often in several different versions). "Lord Randall" (Unit Two) is an example of a folk ballad. **Literary ballads,** on the other hand, are composed and written down by known poets, usually in the style of folk ballads. Keats's "La Belle Dame Sans Merci" (Unit Five) is a famous literary ballad.

The typical **ballad stanza** is a quatrain with the rhyme scheme *abcb.* The first and third lines have four stressed syllables, and the second and fourth lines have three. The number of unstressed syllables in each line may vary, but often the meter is primarily **iambic.**

See pages 76, 83.

BIOGRAPHY **An account of a person's life written or told by another person.** *The Life of Samuel Johnson* by James Boswell (Unit Four) is one of the most famous biographies of all time.

See page 574.

BLANK VERSE **Poetry written in unrhymed iambic pentameter.** "Blank" means the poetry is unrhymed. "Iambic pentameter" means that each line contains five iambs, or metrical **feet,** each consisting of an unstressed syllable followed by a stressed syllable (‿ ′). Blank verse is the most important metrical form used in English dramatic and epic poetry. It is the verse line used in Shakespeare's plays and Milton's *Paradise Lost* (Unit Three). One of the reasons blank verse has been so popular, even among modern poets, is that it combines the naturalness of unrhymed verse with the structure of metrical verse. Except for free verse, it is the poetic form that sounds the most like natural speech. It also lends itself easily to slight variations within the basic pattern. Like most of the English Romantic poets, Wordsworth made extensive use of blank verse, as in these lines from *The Prelude:*

Oh! yet a few short years of useful life,
And all will be complete, thy race be run,
Thy monument of glory will be raised.

See pages 271, 330, 434.

CADENCE **The natural rise and fall of the voice.** Poets who write in **free verse** often try to imitate the cadences of spoken language.

See also *Rhythm.*

CAESURA **A pause or break within a line of poetry, usually dictated by the natural rhythm of language.** A mid-line, or **medial,** caesura is a characteristic element of Anglo-Saxon poetry; it divides the four-beat line in half. Later poets have used the caesura less predictably, as in the following lines from "Dulce et Decorum Est" by Wilfred Owen. (The caesuras are indicated by the symbol ‖.)

Bent double, ‖ like old beggars under sacks,
Knock-kneed, ‖ coughing like hags, ‖ we cursed
  through sludge

See pages 10, 42, 193.

CANTO **A subdivision in a long poem, corresponding to a chapter in a book.** Poems that are divided into cantos include Dante's *Divine Comedy,* Pope's *Rape of the Lock,* and Byron's *Don Juan* and *Childe Harold.* Not all major subdivisions of long poems are called cantos, however; Milton's *Paradise Lost* is divided into books and Coleridge's *Rime of the Ancient Mariner* into parts.

The word *canto* comes from a Latin word for "song," and originally designated a section of a narrative poem that a minstrel could sing in one session.

See page 684.

CARPE DIEM **A Latin phrase that literally means "seize the day"—that is, "make the most of present opportunities."** The *carpe diem* theme is quite common in sixteenth- and seventeenth-century English poetry, as in this famous line from Robert Herrick's "To the Virgins, to Make Much of Time": "Gather ye rosebuds while ye may." The theme is also forcefully expressed in Andrew Marvell's "To His Coy Mistress" (both in Unit Three).

See page 436.

CHARACTER **An individual in a story or play.** A character always has human traits, even if the character is an animal, as in *Alice's Adventures in Wonderland;* or a god, as in the Greek and Roman myths; or a monster, as in *Beowulf.* A character may also be a godlike human, like Superman. But most characters are ordinary human beings, like David Copperfield in Dickens's novel.

The process by which the writer reveals the personality of a character is called **characterization.** A writer can reveal a character in the following ways:

1. By telling us directly what the character is like: humble, ambitious, impetuous, easily manipulated, and so on
2. By describing how the character looks and dresses
3. By letting us hear the character speak
4. By revealing the character's private thoughts and feelings
5. By revealing the character's effect on other people—showing how other characters feel or behave toward the character
6. By showing the character's actions

The first method of revealing a character is called **direct characterization.** When a writer uses this method, we do not have to figure out what a character's personality is like—the writer tells us directly. The other five methods of revealing a character are known as **indirect characterization.** When a writer uses these methods, we have to

exercise our own judgment, putting clues together to figure out what a character is like—just as we do in real life when we are getting to know someone.

Characters can be classified as static or dynamic. A **static character** is one who does not change much in the course of a story. A **dynamic character,** on the other hand, changes in some important way as a result of the story's action. Characters can also be classified as flat or round. **Flat characters** have only one or two personality traits. They are one-dimensional—they can be summed up by a single phrase. In contrast, **round characters** have more dimensions to their personalities—they are complex, solid, and multi-faceted, like real people.

See pages 330, 496.

CLASSICISM **A movement in art, literature, and music that advocates imitating the principles manifested in the art and literature of ancient ("classical") Greece and Rome.** Classicism emphasizes reason, clarity, balance, harmony, restraint, order, and universal themes. Classicism is often placed in direct opposition to Romanticism, with its emphasis on unrestrained emotions and personal themes. However, this opposition should be approached with caution, as it is sometimes exaggerated for effect.

See also *Neoclassicism, Romanticism.*

CLIMAX **The point of greatest emotional intensity or suspense in a plot.** The climax usually marks the moment when the conflict is decided, one way or another. In Shakespeare's plays, the climax usually occurs in the last act, just before the final scene. Following the climax, the story is **resolved,** or closed.

Some critics talk of more than one climactic moment in a long work (though usually the greatest climax still occurs near the end of the plot). In drama, one such climactic moment is called the **turning point,** or **crisis.** In Shakespeare's plays, this moment usually occurs in the third act. The turning point is the pivotal moment when the hero's fortunes begin to decline or improve. All the action leading up to this turning point is **rising action,** and all the action following it is **falling action.** The turning point in *Macbeth* occurs during the banquet scene in Act III, Scene 4, when Macbeth sees Banquo's ghost. From that point onward, it is downhill for Macbeth—everything goes wrong, culminating in the play's climax in Act V, Scene 8. It is at this point that we finally learn for certain that Macbeth will be defeated. The witches' prophecies are borne out: Birnam wood does come to Dunsinane, and Macduff, "not born of woman," faces Macbeth. This confrontation is the climax of the play. After this point, the play moves rapidly toward its resolution, with Malcolm, Duncan's legitimate heir, assuming the throne.

See page 333.
See also *Plot.*

COMEDY **In general, a story that ends happily.** The hero or heroine of a comedy is usually an ordinary character who overcomes a series of obstacles that block what he or she wants. Often a comedy pits two young people who wish to marry against parental blocking figures who want to prevent the marriage. The wedding that concludes these comedies suggests the formation of a new society and a renewal of life. Comedy is distinct from **tragedy,** in which a great person comes to an unhappy or disastrous end, often through some lapse in judgment or character flaw. Comedies are often, but not always, intended to make us laugh. Two examples of the genre are Oscar Wilde's *The Importance of Being Earnest* (Unit Six) and George Bernard Shaw's *Pygmalion* (Unit Seven).

See pages 181, 253.

CONCEIT **A fanciful and elaborate figure of speech that makes a surprising connection between two seemingly dissimilar things.** Although a conceit may be a brief metaphor, it usually forms the framework of an entire poem. One of the most important kinds of conceits is the **metaphysical conceit,** so called because it was widely used by the seventeenth-century metaphysical poets. This type of conceit is especially startling, complex, and ingenious. Two famous examples are John Donne's comparison between separated lovers and the legs of a compass in "A Valediction: Forbidding Mourning" and George Herbert's comparison between belief in God and a pulley in "The Pulley" (both in Unit Three).

See pages 191, 366, 386.

CONFLICT **A struggle or clash between opposing characters, forces, or emotions.** In an **external conflict,** a character struggles against some outside force: another character, society as a whole, or some natural force. An **internal conflict,** on the other hand, is a struggle between opposing needs, desires, or emotions within a single character. Many works, especially longer ones, contain both internal and external conflicts. In Shakespeare's *Macbeth,* for example, Macbeth undergoes an internal conflict between his excessive ambition and his obsessive guilt. He also experiences various external conflicts with characters who attempt to block his ambition.

See pages 231, 1027.
See also *Plot.*

CONNOTATIONS **All the meanings, associations, or emotions that a word suggests.** For example, an expensive restaurant might prefer to advertise its "delicious cuisine" rather than its "delicious cooking." *Cuisine* and *cooking* have the same literal meaning—"prepared food." But *cuisine* has connotations of elegance and sophistication, while *cooking* does not. The same restaurant would certainly not describe its food as "great grub."

Notice the difference between the following pairs of words: *young/immature, ambitious/cutthroat, uninhibited/shameless, lenient/lax.* We might describe ourselves using the first word but someone else using the second. The English philosopher Bertrand Russell once gave a classic example of the different connotations of words: "I am firm. You are obstinate. He is a pig-headed fool."

See pages 524, 705.
See also *Denotation.*

CONSONANCE **The repetition of final consonant sounds after different vowel sounds.** The words *east* and *west, dig* and *dog, turn* and *torn,* and Shakespeare's famous "*struts* and *frets*" (from *Macbeth*) are examples of consonance. The term is also used sometimes to refer to repeated consonant sounds in the middle of words, as in *solemn stillness.* (Consonance, when loosely defined, can be a form of **alliteration.** Strictly speaking, however, alliteration is the repetition of initial consonant sounds.) Like assonance, consonance is one form of **approximate rhyme.**

COUPLET **Two consecutive lines of poetry that rhyme.** The couplet has been widely used since the Middle Ages, especially to provide a sense of closure. A couplet that presents a completed thought is called a **closed couplet.** Shakespeare used closed couplets to end his sonnets, as in this example from Sonnet 18:

So long as men can breathe or eyes can see,
So long lives this, and this gives life to thee.

A couplet written in **iambic pentameter** is called a **heroic couplet.** Although the heroic couplet has been used in English literature since Chaucer, it was perfected during the eighteenth century. Here is an example from Pope's *Essay on Man* (Unit Four):

Twŏ prínciplĕs ĭn húmăn nátŭrĕ reígn;
Sĕlf-lóve, tŏ úrgĕ, ănd Réasŏn, tŏ rĕstraín

See pages 85, 109.

DENOTATION **The literal, dictionary definition of a word.**

See also *Connotations.*

DÉNOUEMENT See *Plot.*

DEUS EX MACHINA **Any artificial or contrived device used at the end of a plot to resolve or untangle the complications.** The term is Latin, meaning "god out of the machine." The phrase refers to a device used in ancient Greek and Roman drama: At the conclusion of the play, a god would be lowered onto the stage by a mechanical device so that he could save the hero and end the story happily.

See page 906.

DIALECT A way of speaking that is characteristic of a particular region or group of people. A dialect may have a distinct vocabulary, pronunciation system, and grammar. Generally, one dialect becomes accepted as the standard for a country or culture. In the United States today, the dialect used in formal writing and spoken by most TV and radio announcers is known as standard English. Writers often use other dialects, however, to establish character or to create local color. For example, Robert Burns (Unit Five) wrote his poetry in Scottish dialect. This passage by V. S. Naipaul captures the dialect spoken by Trinidad's Asian Indian population. (A pundit is an Indian wise or learned man. *Sahib* means "sir" or "master.")

Another day he said, "You does read real sweet, sahib. I could just shut my eye and listen. You know what Leela tell me last night, after I close up the shop? Leela ask me, 'Pa, who was the man talking in the shop this morning? He sound just like a radio I hear in San Fernando.' I tell she, 'Girl, that wasn't a radio you was hearing. That was Ganesh Ramsumair. Pundit Ganesh Ramsumair,' I tell she."

"You making joke."

"Ah, sahib. Why I should make joke with you, eh? You want me call Leela here self, and you could ask she?"

Ganesh heard a titter behind the lace curtain. . . .

—from *The Mystic Masseur*,
V. S. Naipaul

See pages 613, 616, 1158.

DICTION A writer's or speaker's choice of words. People use different types of words depending on the audience they're addressing, the subject they're discussing, and the effect they're trying to produce. For example, slang words that would be suitable in a casual conversation with a friend ("He's a total nerd") would be unsuitable in a political debate. Similarly, the language that a nutritionist would use to describe a meal would be different from the language used by a restaurant reviewer—or a novelist.

Diction is an essential element of a writer's **style.** A writer's diction can be simple or flowery *(shop/boutique)*, modern or old-fashioned *(pharmacy/apothecary)*, general or specific *(sandwich/grilled cheese on rye)*. Notice that the **connotations** of words (rather than their strict, literal meanings, or **denotations**) are an important aspect of diction.

See pages 524, 832, 1123.

DISSONANCE A harsh, discordant combination of sounds. The opposite of **euphony,** dissonance is usually created by the repetition of harsh consonant sounds. Dissonance is also called **cacophony.**

DRAMATIC MONOLOGUE A poem in which a character addresses one or more listeners who remain silent or whose replies are not revealed. The occasion is usually a critical one in the speaker's life. Tennyson's "Ulysses" and Browning's "My Last Duchess" and "Porphyria's Lover" (all in Unit Six) are famous dramatic monologues.

See pages 800, 802.

ELEGY A poem that mourns the death of a person or laments something lost. Elegies may lament the passing of life and beauty, or they may be meditations on the nature of death. A type of **lyric,** an elegy is usually formal in language and structure, and solemn or even melancholy in tone. Much of English poetry is elegiac, from the Anglo-Saxon lyrics "The Wanderer" and "The Seafarer" (Unit One) to the great elegy of the Victorian era, Tennyson's *In Memoriam* (Unit Six).

See pages 42, 354, 573.

EPIC A long narrative poem that relates the great deeds of a larger-than-life hero who embodies the values of a particular society. Most epics include elements of myth, legend, folklore, and history. Their tone is serious and their language grand. Most epic heroes undertake quests to achieve something of tremendous value to themselves or their society. Homer's *Odyssey* and *Iliad* and Virgil's *Aeneid* are the best-known epics in the Western tradition. The two most important English epics are the Anglo-Saxon poem *Beowulf* (Unit One) and Milton's *Paradise Lost* (Unit Three).

See pages 11, 178, 420, 532.

EPIGRAM A brief, clever, and usually memorable statement. Alexander Pope's writings are epigrammatic in style. Here is an example from his *Essay on Criticism* (Unit Four):

We think our fathers fools, so wise we grow,
Our wiser sons, no doubt, will think us so.

See page 528.

EPIPHANY In a literary work, a moment of sudden insight or revelation that a character experiences. The word comes from the Greek and can be translated as "manifestation" or "showing forth." The term has religious meanings that have been transferred to literature. James Joyce gave the word its literary meaning in an early draft of *A Portrait of the Artist as a Young Man* (Unit Seven).

In Joyce's story "Araby" (Unit Seven), the narrator experiences an epiphany at the end of the story when he recognizes the cheap vulgarity of the bazaar and the emptiness of his dream.

See page 963.

EPITAPH An inscription on a tombstone, or a commemorative poem written as if for that purpose. Epitaphs range from the solemn to the comic. Here is a witty example by John Dryden:

> Here lies my wife, here let her lie:
> Now she's at rest, and so am I.

See pages 177, 377.

EPITHET An adjective or other descriptive phrase that is regularly used to characterize a person, place, or thing. Phrases such as "Peter the Great," "Richard the Lion-Hearted," and "America the Beautiful" are epithets. Homer created so many descriptive epithets in his *Iliad* and *Odyssey* that his name has been permanently associated with a type of epithet. The **Homeric epithet** consists of a compound adjective that is regularly used to modify a particular noun. Famous examples are "the wine-dark sea," "the gray-eyed goddess Athena," and the "rosy-fingered dawn."

See also *Kenning*.

ESSAY A short piece of nonfiction prose that examines a single subject from a limited point of view. There are two major types of essays. **Informal essays** (also called **personal essays**) generally reveal a great deal about the personalities and feelings of their authors. They tend to be conversational, sometimes even humorous in tone, and they are usually highly subjective. **Formal essays** (also called **traditional essays**) are usually serious and impersonal in tone. Because they are written to inform or persuade, they are expected to be factual, logical, and tightly organized.

In English literature, the essay began with Sir Francis Bacon, who published his extremely formal *Essays* (Unit Three) in 1597. The English informal essay was pioneered by Joseph Addison and Sir Richard Steele (Unit Four) in the early eighteenth century. Another outstanding informal essayist is Charles Lamb (Unit Five).

See page 740.

FABLE A very brief story in prose or verse that teaches a moral, or a practical lesson about life. The characters in most fables are animals that behave and speak like human beings. Some of the most popular fables are those attributed to Aesop, who was supposed to have been a slave in ancient Greece.

See pages 110, 467.
See also *Parable*.

FALLING ACTION See *Climax*.

FARCE A type of comedy in which ridiculous and often stereotyped characters are involved in farfetched, silly situations. The humor in farce is based on crude physical action, slapstick, and clowning. Characters may slip on banana peels, get pies thrown in their faces, and knock one another on the head with ladders. Abbott and Costello, Laurel and Hardy, and Marx Brothers movies are examples of farces.

The word *farce* comes from a Latin word for "stuffing," and in fact farces were originally used to fill in the waiting time between the acts of a serious play. Even in tragedies, farcical elements are often included to provide comic relief. Shakespeare, for example, frequently lets his "common" characters engage in farcical actions.

See pages 869, 906.

FIGURE OF SPEECH A word or phrase that describes one thing in terms of another and is not meant to be understood on a literal level. Figures of speech always involve some sort of imaginative comparison between seemingly unlike things.

Some 250 different types of figures of speech have been identified, but the most common are the **simile** ("My beloved is like a roe or a young hart"), the **metaphor** ("The Lord is my shepherd"), and **personification** ("Death, be not proud").

See also *Metaphor, Personification, Simile, Symbol*.

FLASHBACK A scene in a movie, play, short story, novel, or narrative poem that interrupts the present action of the plot to "flash backward" and tell what happened at an earlier time. "The Demon Lover" by Elizabeth Bowen (Unit Seven) includes a flashback that describes Mrs. Drover's farewell to her fiancé twenty-five years before the main action of the story takes place.

See page 999.

FOIL A character who is used as a contrast to another character. This contrast emphasizes the differences between two characters, bringing out the distinctive qualities in each. In Bernard Shaw's *Pygmalion* (Unit Seven), Colonel Pickering is a foil to Henry Higgins. The colonel is thoughtful, considerate, and courteous at all times, while Higgins is consistently inconsiderate and self-centered.

FORESHADOWING The use of clues to hint at what is going to happen later in the plot. Foreshadowing arouses the reader's curiosity and builds up **suspense**. Foreshadowing occurs in Elizabeth Bowen's "The Demon Lover" (Unit Seven) when Mrs. Drover imagines "spectral glitters in the place of" her fiancé's eyes, and when we learn that she made an "unnatural promise" to him—that she "could not have plighted a more sinister troth."

See page 1158.
See also *Suspense*.

FREE VERSE Poetry that has no regular meter or rhyme scheme. Free verse usually relies instead on the natural **rhythms** of ordinary speech. Poets writing in free verse may use **alliteration, internal rhyme, onomatopoeia,** and other musical devices to achieve their effects. They may also place great emphasis on **imagery.** "Snake" by D. H. Lawrence (Unit Seven) is written in free verse.

See pages 1101, 1117.

HYPERBOLE A figure of speech that uses exaggeration to express strong emotion or create a comic effect. While hyperbole (also known as **overstatement**) does not express the *literal* truth, it is often used in the service of truth to capture a sense of intensity or to emphasize the essential nature of something. For instance, if you claim that it was 250 degrees in the subway, you are using hyperbole to express the truth that it was miserably hot.

See pages 365, 549.

IAMBIC PENTAMETER A line of poetry made up of five iambs. An **iamb** is a metrical **foot,** or unit of measure, consisting of an unstressed syllable followed by a stressed syllable ( ). The word *suggest,* for example, is made up of one iamb. *Pentameter* derives from the Greek words *penta* ("five") and *meter* ("measure"). Here are two lines of poetry written in iambic pentameter:

> Forlorn! the very word is like a bell
>
> To toll me back from thee to my sole self!
>
> —from "Ode to a Nightingale,"
> John Keats

Iambic pentameter is by far the most common verse line in English poetry. Shakespeare's sonnets and plays, for example, are written primarily in this meter. Many modern poets, such as W. H. Auden, have continued to use iambic pentameter. Other than free verse, it is the poetic form that sounds the most like natural speech.

See pages 187, 271.

IMAGERY Language that appeals to the senses. Most images are visual—that is, they appeal to the sense of sight. But imagery can also appeal to the senses of sound, touch, taste, or smell. While imagery is an element in all types of writing, it is especially important in poetry:

> What is more gentle than a wind in summer?
> What is more soothing than the pretty hummer
> That stays one moment in an open flower,
> And buzzes cheerily from bower to bower?
> What is more tranquil than a musk-rose blowing
> In a green island, far from all men's knowing?
>
> —from "Sleep and Poetry,"
> John Keats

See pages 131, 330, 334, 718, 1083.

INCREMENTAL REPETITION A device widely used in ballads whereby a line or lines is repeated with slight variations from stanza to stanza. Each repetition advances the plot of the narrative. Incremental repetition is used in the folk ballad "Lord Randall" (Unit Two).

IN MEDIAS RES The technique of starting a story in the middle and then using a flashback to tell what happened earlier. *In medias res* is Latin for "in the middle of things." Traditional epics begin *in medias res.* For example, Milton's *Paradise Lost* (Unit Three) opens with Satan and his cohorts in Hell, after the war in Heaven and their fall, recounted later in a flashback.

IRONY A contrast or discrepancy between expectation and reality—between what is said and what is really meant, between what is expected and what really happens, or between what appears to be true and what really is true.

1. **Verbal irony** occurs when a writer or speaker says one thing but really means the opposite. If you tell your boyfriend that "you just love being kept waiting in the rain," you are using verbal irony. A classic example of verbal irony is Jonathan Swift's suggestion in "A Modest Proposal" (Unit Four) that the Irish solve their poverty and overpopulation problems by selling their babies as food to their English landlords.

2. **Situational irony** occurs when what actually happens is the opposite of what is expected or appropriate. In James Joyce's story "Araby" (Unit Seven), the boy hears about a bazaar called Araby and imagines that it will be a splendid, exotic place. Yet when he arrives, he finds that in reality Araby is cheap and commonplace.

3. **Dramatic irony** occurs when the audience or the reader knows something important that a character in a play or story does not know. Forceful dramatic irony occurs at several points in Shakespeare's *Macbeth.* One example is in Act II, Scene 4: Macduff suspects that Duncan has been murdered by his own sons, but the audience knows that Macbeth is the murderer. Dramatic irony is a powerful device in William Blake's "innocence" poem "The Chimney Sweeper" (Unit Five). The speaker is a child who believes what he has been told: that "if all do their duty, they need not fear harm." But the reader, who is not so innocent, realizes that this is not so.

See pages 517, 839, 955, 964.

KENNING In Anglo-Saxon poetry, a metaphorical phrase or compound word used to name a person, place, thing, or event indirectly. *Beowulf* includes the kennings "whale-road" for the sea and "shepherd of evil" for Grendel.

See pages 10, 40, 47.
See also *Epithet.*

LYRIC POETRY Poetry that focuses on expressing emotions or thoughts, rather than on telling a story. Most lyrics are

A Handbook of Literary Terms 1265

short, and they usually imply rather than directly state a single strong emotion. The term *lyric* comes from the Greek. In ancient Greece, lyric poems were recited to the accompaniment of a stringed instrument called the lyre. Today poets still try to make their lyrics melodious, but they rely only on the musical effects they can create with words (such as **rhyme, rhythm, alliteration,** and **onomatopoeia**). John Keats's "To Autumn" (Unit Five) and Matthew Arnold's "Dover Beach" (Unit Six) are both lyric poems.

METAPHOR   A figure of speech that makes a comparison between two seemingly unlike things without using the connective words *like, as, than,* or *resembles.* You are using a metaphor if you say you're "at the end of your rope" or describe two political candidates as "running neck and neck."

Some metaphors are **directly** stated, like Percy Bysshe Shelley's comparison "My soul is an enchanted boat." (If he had written, "My soul is *like* an enchanted boat," he would have been using a **simile.**) Other metaphors are **implied,** like John Suckling's line "Time shall molt away his wings." The words *molt* and *wings* imply a comparison between time and a bird shedding its feathers.

An **extended metaphor** is a metaphor that is extended, or developed, over several lines of writing or even throughout an entire poem. In the following stanza, the speaker develops a comparison between two lovers and two separate streams that flow into the same river. (The title and last line allude to the biblical Song of Songs.)

Even like two little bank-dividing brooks,
   That wash the pebbles with their wanton streams,
And having ranged and searched a thousand nooks,
   Meet both at length in silver-breasted Thames
Where in greater current they conjoin:
So I my Best-Beloved's am, so he is mine.

   —from "My Beloved Is Mine and I Am His,"
   Francis Quarles

A **dead metaphor** is a metaphor that has become so common that we no longer even notice that it is a figure of speech. Our everyday language is filled with dead metaphors, such as *the foot of the bed, the bone of contention,* and *the mouth of the river.*

A **mixed metaphor** is the inconsistent mixture of two or more metaphors. Mixed metaphors are usually unintentional and often conjure up ludicrous images: "If you put your money on that horse, you'll be barking up the wrong tree."

See pages 178, 334, 346.

METER   A generally regular pattern of stressed and unstressed syllables in poetry. When we want to indicate the metrical pattern of a poem, we mark the stressed syllables with the symbol ´ and the unstressed syllables with the symbol ◡ . Indicating the metrical pattern of a poem in this way is called **scanning** the poem, or **scansion.** Here is how to scan these lines from William Blake's "The Tyger":

Tyger! Tyger! Burning bright
In the forests of the night

Meter is measured in units called feet. A **foot** consists of one stressed syllable and usually one or more unstressed syllables. The standard feet used in English poetry are the **iamb** (as in convince), the **trochee** (as in borrow), the **anapest** (as in contradict), the **dactyl** (as in accurate), and the **spondee** (as in seaweed).

A metrical line is named both for the type and number of feet it contains. For example, a line of iambic pentameter consists of five iambs, while a line of trochaic tetrameter consists of four trochees.

See pages 83, 193.

METONYMY   A figure of speech in which something closely related to a thing or suggested by it is substituted for the thing itself. You are using metonymy if you call the judiciary "the bench," the king "the crown," the President (or presidential staff) "the White House," or the race track "the turf." Closely related to metonymy is **synecdoche,** a figure of speech in which a part of a thing stands for the whole, as in "lend a hand."

MOCK EPIC   A comic narrative poem that parodies the epic by treating a trivial subject in a lofty, grand manner. A mock epic uses dignified language, elaborate figures of speech, and supernatural intervention. The style of the mock epic is called **mock heroic** (and short mock epics are often called mock heroics). Alexander Pope's *Rape of the Lock* (Unit Four) is considered the supreme mock epic in the English language.

See pages 532, 541.

MOTIF   In literature, a word, character, object, image, metaphor, or idea that recurs in a work or in several works. The rose is a motif that runs through many love poems. The motif of ill-fitting clothes appears throughout Shakespeare's *Macbeth.* It starts in Act I, Scene 3, when Macbeth asks Ross: "The thane of Cawdor lives: why do you dress me / In borrowed robes?" This is soon followed by Banquo's observation: "New honors come upon him, / Like our strange garments, cleave not to their mold / But with the aid of use." The motif of ill-fitting clothes reaches its culmination in Act V, Scene 2, when Angus says of Macbeth: "Now does he feel his title / Hang loose about him, like a giant's robe / Upon a dwarfish thief." A motif almost always bears an important relationship to the theme of a work of literature.

MYTH   An anonymous traditional story, supposedly based on historical events, that usually serves to explain a belief, custom, or mysterious natural phenomenon. Most myths grew out of religious rituals, and almost all of them involve the exploits of gods and heroes. Every culture has its own mythology, but in the Western world, the most important myths have been those of ancient Greece and Rome.

See pages 315, 462.

NEOCLASSICISM   The revival of classical standards and forms during the late seventeenth and eighteenth centuries. The neoclassicists valued the classical ideals of order, reason, balance, harmony, clarity, and restraint. In particular, they studied and tried to emulate the Latin poets Horace and Virgil. Alexander Pope and John Dryden were leaders of the neoclassical movement in England.

See page 448.

NOVEL   A long fictional prose narrative, usually of more than fifty thousand words. In general, the novel uses the same basic literary elements as the short story: **plot, character, setting, theme,** and **point of view.** The novel's length usually permits these elements to be more fully developed than they are in the short story. However, this is not always true of the modern novel. Some are basically character studies, with only the barest plot structures. Others reveal little about their characters and concentrate instead on setting or **tone** or even language itself.

Some of the greatest novels in English literature are *Tom Jones* by Henry Fielding, *Pride and Prejudice* by Jane Austen, *Jane Eyre* by Charlotte Brontë, *David Copperfield* and *Great Expectations* by Charles Dickens, *Middlemarch* by George Eliot, *Jude the Obscure* by Thomas Hardy, *Lord Jim* by Joseph Conrad, *Sons and Lovers* by D. H. Lawrence, and *Ulysses* by James Joyce.

See pages 767, 917.

OCTAVE   An eight-line stanza or poem, or the first eight lines of an Italian, or Petrarchan, sonnet. The usual rhyme scheme of the octave in this type of sonnet is *abbaabba.* It is followed by a six-line **sestet** with the rhyme scheme *cdecde* or *cdcdcd.*

See pages 191, 219, 710.

ODE   A complex, generally long lyric poem on a serious subject. In English poetry there are basically two types of odes. One is highly formal and dignified in style and is generally written for ceremonial or public occasions. This type of ode derives from the choral odes of the classical Greek poet Pindar. John Dryden's "Song for St. Cecilia's Day" is an English version of the Pindaric ode. The other type of ode derives from those written by the Latin poet Horace, and it is much more personal and reflective. In English poetry it is exemplified by the intimate, meditative odes of such Romantic poets as Wordsworth, Keats, and Shelley.

See pages 456, 646, 699.

ONOMATOPOEIA   The use of a word whose sound imitates or suggests its meaning. Many familiar words, such as *clap, squish, snort,* and *whine,* are examples of onomatopoeia. In poetry, onomatopoeia can reinforce meaning while creating evocative and musical effects. The following lines contain several imitative sounds:

> The sparrow's chirrup on the roof,
>   The slow clock ticking, and the sound
> Which to the wooing wind aloof
>   The poplar made, did all confound
> Her sense. . . .

> —from "Mariana,"
> Alfred, Lord Tennyson

See pages 723, 1101.

OTTAVA RIMA   An eight-line stanza in iambic pentameter with the rhyme scheme *abababcc.* The form developed in Italy and was popularized by the fourteenth-century Italian poet Boccaccio. The most famous example of ottava rima in English poetry is Lord Byron's *Don Juan* (Unit Five). William Butler Yeats's "Sailing to Byzantium" (Unit Seven) is another notable example.

See page 684.

OXYMORON   A figure of speech that combines apparently contradictory or incongruous ideas. "Bitter sweet," "cruel kindness," and "eloquent silence" are oxymorons. The classic oxymoron "wise fool" is almost a literal translation of the term from the Greek: *oxys* means "sharp" or "keen," and *moros* means "foolish." A famous oxymoron in literature is Milton's description of Hell in *Paradise Lost:* "No light, but rather darkness visible . . ."

PARABLE   A short, allegorical story that teaches a moral or religious lesson about life. The most famous parables in Western literature are those told by Jesus in the Gospels of the Bible.

See page 409.

PARADOX   An apparent contradiction that is actually true. A paradox may be a statement or a situation; as a statement it is a figure of speech. The metaphysical and Cavalier poets of the seventeenth century made brilliant use of paradoxes, as in this famous example:

> One short sleep past, we wake eternally
> And death shall be no more: Death, thou shalt die.

> —from "Death Be Not Proud,"
> John Donne

The speaker in this cartoon doesn't understand the famous series of paradoxes that open *A Tale of Two Cities* by Charles Dickens:

"I wish you could make up your mind, Mr. Dickens. Was it the best of times or was it the worst of times? It could scarcely be both."

Drawing by J. B. Handelsman; © 1987 The New Yorker Magazine, Inc.

See pages 906, 1173.

PARALLELISM   The repetition of words, phrases, or sentences that have the same grammatical structure, or that restate a similar idea. Parallelism is used frequently in literature meant to be spoken aloud, such as poetry, drama, and speeches, because it can help make lines emotional, rhythmic, and memorable. It is also one of the most important techniques used in Biblical poetry. The parallelism in the following lines heightens their emotional effect and sharpens their meaning:

> Cruelty has a human heart
> And Jealousy a human face;
> Terror the human form divine,
> And Secrecy the human dress.
>
> —from "A Divine Image,"
> William Blake

See pages 400, 630.

PARODY   The imitation of a work of literature, art, or music for amusement or instruction. Parodies usually use exaggeration or inappropriate subject matter to make a serious style seem ridiculous. Alexander Pope's *The Rape of the Lock* (Unit Four) is a parody of a serious epic.

See pages 346, 382, 513.

PASTORAL   A type of poem that depicts rustic life in idyllic, idealized terms. The term *pastoral* comes from the Latin word for shepherd, and originally pastorals were about shepherds and nymphs. Today the term has a looser meaning and refers to any poem that portrays an idyllic rural setting or that expresses nostalgia for an age or place of lost innocence. The most famous traditional English pastoral is Christopher Marlowe's "The Passionate Shepherd to His Love," which is satirized in Sir Walter Raleigh's "The Nymph's Reply to the Shepherd" (both in Unit Three). Examples of untraditional pastorals include William Wordsworth's "Tintern Abbey" (Unit Five), William Butler Yeats's "The Lake Isle of Innisfree" (Unit Seven), and Dylan Thomas's "Fern Hill" (Unit Seven).

See pages 176, 232, 456, 573.

PERSONIFICATION   A kind of metaphor in which a nonhuman thing or quality is talked about as if it were human. In these lines the speaker describes the wind as if it were capable of feeling the human emotion of grief:

> Rough wind, that moanest loud
> Grief too sad for song
>
> —from "A Dirge,"
> Percy Bysshe Shelley

See page 196.
See also *Apostrophe, Figure of Speech, Metaphor.*

PLOT   The series of related events that make up a story or drama. The plot is the underlying structure of a story. Most plots are built on these "bare bones": A **basic situation,** or **exposition,** introduces the characters, setting, and, usually, the story's major **conflict.** Out of this basic situation, **complications** develop that intensify the conflict. **Suspense** mounts until a **climax**—the tensest or most exciting part of the plot—is reached, where something happens to determine the outcome of the conflict. Finally, all the problems or mysteries of the plot are unraveled in the **resolution,** or **dénouement.**

See page 906.
See also *Climax.*

POINT OF VIEW   The vantage point from which a writer tells a story. There are three main points of view: **omniscient, first-person,** and **limited third-person.**

1. In the **omniscient** (or "all-knowing") **point of view,** the person telling the story knows everything that's going on in the story. This omniscient narrator is outside the story, a godlike observer who can tell us what all the characters are thinking and feeling, as well as what is happening anywhere in the story. For example, in "The Rocking-Horse Winner" by D. H. Lawrence (Unit Seven), the narrator enters into the thoughts and secrets of every character, revealing both the "hard little place" in the

mother's heart and Paul's determination to "compel her attention" by being lucky.

2. In the **first-person point of view,** the narrator is a character in the story. Using the pronoun *I*, this narrator tells us his or her own experiences but cannot reveal any other character's private thoughts. When we read a story told in the first person, we hear and see only what the narrator hears and sees. We may have to interpret what this narrator says because a first-person narrator may or may not be objective, honest, or perceptive. For example, in Frank O'Connor's "My Oedipus Complex" (Unit Seven), the narrator is a young boy whose understanding and insight are limited by his age, who believes that babies are purchased.

3. In the **limited third-person point of view,** the narrator is outside the story—like an omniscient narrator—but tells the story from the vantage point of only one character. The narrator can enter the mind of this chosen character but cannot tell what any other characters are thinking except by observation. This narrator also can go only where the chosen character goes. For example, "Miss Brill" by Katherine Mansfield (Unit Seven) is told entirely from the title character's point of view. We see the park setting and the characters in it only through her eyes—and we are even told that what others "understood she didn't know."

See pages 495, 857.

PROTAGONIST   The main character in fiction, drama, or narrative poetry. The protagonist is the character we focus our attention on—the person whose conflict sets the plot in motion. (The character or force that blocks the protagonist is called the **antagonist.**) Most protagonists are **rounded, dynamic** characters who change in some important way by the end of the story. Whatever the protagonist's weaknesses, we still usually identify with his or her conflict and care about how it is resolved.

See page 1209.

PUN   A play on the multiple meanings of a word, or on two words that sound alike but have different meanings. Many jokes and riddles are based on puns. ("Why was Cleopatra so negative? Answer: Because she was queen of denial.") Shakespeare was one of the greatest punsters of all time. Some of his puns are humorous, but others are more serious and subtle word plays. A sinister pun occurs in Act II, Scene 2, after Macbeth has murdered Duncan. Lady Macbeth says:

> I'll gild the faces of the grooms withal.
> For it must seem their guilt.

See pages 627, 906.

QUATRAIN   A four-line stanza or poem, or a group of four lines unified by a rhyme scheme. The quatrain is the most common verse unit in English poetry. Here is a quatrain with the rhyme scheme *abba* (sometimes called the "envelope stanza"):

> Thy voice is on the rolling air,
>   I hear thee where the waters run;
>   Thou standest in the rising sun,
> And in the setting thou art fair.

> —from *In Memoriam,*
> Alfred, Lord Tennyson

See page 339.

REALISM   In literature and art, the attempt to depict people and things as they really are, without idealization. Realism as a movement developed during the mid-nineteenth century as a reaction against Romanticism. Realist writers believed that fiction should truthfully depict the harsh, gritty reality of everyday life without beautifying, sentimentalizing, or romanticizing it. Charles Dickens, George Eliot, Thomas Hardy, and Joseph Conrad are all considered realists.

See page 991.
See also *Romanticism.*

REFRAIN   A repeated word, phrase, line, or group of lines. While refrains are most common in poetry and songs, they are sometimes used in prose, particularly speeches. Refrains are used to create rhythm, build suspense, or emphasize important words or ideas.

See pages 76, 77, 78.

RESOLUTION   See *Plot.*

RHYME   The repetition of accented vowel sounds and all sounds following them in words that are close together in a poem. *Park* and *bark* rhyme, as do *sorrow* and *borrow*. The most common type of rhyme, **end rhyme,** occurs at the ends of lines. **Internal rhyme** occurs within lines. They are used throughout *The Rime of the Ancient Mariner* by Samuel Taylor Coleridge (Unit Five), contributing to the poem's bouncy, songlike rhythm:

> The fair breeze blew, the white foam flew,
> The furrow followed free;
> We were the first that ever burst
> Into that silent sea.

When words sound similar but do not rhyme exactly, they are called **approximate rhymes** (or **half rhymes, slant rhymes,** or **imperfect rhymes**). In the following stanza, *began/gun* and *flush/flash* rhyme by means of **consonance,** while *began/flash* and *flush/gun* rhyme (very loosely) by means of **assonance:**

That night when joy began
Our narrowest veins to flush,
We waited for the flash
Of morning's leveled gun.

—from "That Night When Joy Began,"
W. H. Auden

The pattern of rhymed lines in a poem is called its **rhyme scheme.** A rhyme scheme is indicated by giving each new rhyme a new letter of the alphabet. For example, the rhyme scheme of Coleridge's lines is *abcb.* There are two interlocking rhyme schemes in Auden's stanza. The one based on consonance is *abba;* the one based on assonance is *abab.*

See pages 76, 109, 200, 757.

RHYTHM   The alternation of stressed and unstressed syllables in language. Rhythm occurs naturally in all forms of spoken and written language. The most obvious kind of rhythm is produced by **meter,** the regular pattern of stressed and unstressed syllables found in some poetry. But writers can also create less structured rhythms by using **rhyme,** repetition, pauses, variations in line length, and by balancing long and short words or phrases. (Poetry that is written without any regular meter or rhyme scheme is called **free verse.**) The rhythm of the following lines reinforces their meaning. The words themselves seem dappled, as if a painter's brush has stippled them onto the page:

All things counter, original, spare, strange,
    Whatever is fickle, freckled (who knows how?)
    With swift, slow; sweet, sour; adazzle, dim;

—from "Pied Beauty,"
Gerard Manley Hopkins

See pages 367, 843.
See also *Free Verse, Meter.*

RISING ACTION   See *Climax.*

ROMANCE   Historically, a medieval verse narrative chronicling the adventures of a brave knight or other hero who must overcome great danger for love of a noble lady or high ideal. Today the term *romance* has come to mean any story that presents a world that is happier, more exciting, or more heroic than the real world. Characters in romances "live happily ever after" in a world where good always triumphs over evil. Many of today's most popular novels, movies, TV shows, and even cartoons are essentially romances. *Sir Gawain and the Green Knight,* Sir Thomas Malory's *Le Morte Darthur* (both in Unit Two), and Edmund Spenser's *Faerie Queene* (Unit Three) are famous English romances.

See pages 132, 147.

ROMANTICISM   A literary, artistic, and philosophical movement that developed during the late eighteenth and early ninteenth centuries as a reaction against neoclassicism. While neoclassicism (and classicism) emphasize reason, order, harmony, and restraint, Romanticism emphasizes emotion, imagination, intuition, freedom, personal experience, the beauty of nature, the primitive, the exotic, and even the grotesque. However, many critics feel that the traditional opposition between Romanticism and classicism is all too often forced and exaggerated.

In English literature, William Blake, Samuel Taylor Coleridge, William Wordsworth, Percy Bysshe Shelley, John Keats, Lord Byron, and Sir Walter Scott are the leading Romantic writers.

See Unit Five.

SATIRE   A kind of writing that ridicules human weakness, vice, or folly in order to bring about social reform. Satires often try to persuade the reader to do or believe something by showing the opposite view as absurd or—even more forcefully—vicious and inhumane. Among the most brilliant and scathing satirists in English literature are Geoffrey Chaucer, Alexander Pope, John Dryden, Jonathan Swift, Jane Austen, George Bernard Shaw, and Evelyn Waugh. Swift once defined satire as "a sort of glass wherein beholders do generally discover everyone's face but their own. . . ."

See pages 516, 549.

SCANSION   See *Meter.*

SESTET   A six-line stanza or poem, or the last six lines of an Italian, or Petrarchan, sonnet. The usual rhyme scheme of the sestet in an Italian sonnet is *cdecde* or *cdcdcd.* It follows an eight-line **octave** with the rhyme scheme *abbaabba.*

See page 191.

SETTING   The time and place of a story or play. Usually the setting is established early in a story. It may be presented immediately through descriptive details, as in Joseph Conrad's *The Secret Sharer,* or it may be revealed more gradually, as in Katherine Mansfield's "Miss Brill" (both in Unit Seven). Setting often contributes greatly to a story's emotional effect. The wild heath setting at the opening of Shakespeare's *Macbeth* produces an atmosphere of horror. Setting may also play a role in the story's conflict, as the desert island does in Daniel Defoe's *Robinson Crusoe.* Two of the most important functions of setting are to reveal character and suggest a theme, as the setting of blitzed London does in Graham Greene's "The Destructors" (Unit Seven).

See pages 300, 963.
See also *Atmosphere.*

SIMILE A figure of speech that makes a comparison between two seemingly unlike things by using a connective word such as *like, as, than,* or *resembles.* Here is a simile from "It Is a Beauteous Evening" by William Wordsworth, which makes a connection between two sound images:

> The holy time is quiet as a Nun
> Breathless with adoration. . . .

See pages 211, 366, 434.
See also *Figure of Speech, Metaphor.*

SOLILOQUY A long speech in which a character who is usually alone onstage expresses his or her private thoughts or feelings. The soliloquy is an old dramatic convention that was particularly popular in Shakespeare's day. Perhaps the most famous soliloquy is the "To be or not to be" speech in Shakespeare's play *Hamlet.* Another major soliloquy occurs toward the end of *Macbeth,* when Macbeth bewails his wife's death in his "Tomorrow, and tomorrow, and tomorrow" speech (Act V, Scene 5, lines 19–28).

See pages 226, 231, 329.

SONNET A fourteen-line lyric poem, usually written in iambic pentameter, that has one of several rhyme schemes. There are two major types of sonnets. The oldest sonnet form is the **Italian sonnet,** also called the **Petrarchan sonnet** (after the fourteenth-century Italian poet Francesco Petrarch, who popularized the form). The Petrarchan sonnet is divided into two parts: an eight-line **octave** with the rhyme scheme *abbaabba* and a six-line **sestet** with the rhyme scheme *cdecde* or *cdcdcd.* The octave usually presents a problem, poses a question, or expresses an idea, which the sestet then resolves, answers, or drives home. John Donne's sonnets (Unit Three) and John Keats's "On First Looking into Chapman's Homer" (Unit Five) are written in the Italian form.

The other major sonnet form, which was widely used by Shakespeare, is called the **Shakespearean sonnet,** or the **English sonnet.** It has three four-line units, or **quatrains,** followed by a concluding two-line unit, or **couplet.** The organization of thought in the Shakespearean sonnet usually corresponds to this structure. The three quatrains often express related ideas or examples, while the couplet sums up the poet's conclusion or message. The most common rhyme scheme for the Shakespearean sonnet is *abab cdcd efef gg.*

A third type of sonnet, the **Spenserian sonnet,** was developed by Edmund Spenser (Unit Three). Like the Shakespearean sonnet, it is divided into three quatrains and a couplet, but it uses a rhyme scheme that links the quatrains: *abab bcbc cdcd ee.*

A group of sonnets on a related theme is called a **sonnet sequence** or a **sonnet cycle.**

See pages 191, 338.

SPENSERIAN STANZA A nine-line stanza with the rhyme scheme *ababbcbcc.* The first eight lines of the stanza are in iambic pentameter, and the ninth line is an **alexandrine**—that is, a line of iambic hexameter. The form was created by Edmund Spenser for his long poem *The Faerie Queene* (Unit Three). Several English Romantic poets have used the Spenserian stanza, including John Keats, Percy Bysshe Shelley, Lord Byron, and Robert Burns.

See pages 200, 693.

STANZA A group of consecutive lines in a poem that form a single unit. A stanza in a poem is something like a paragraph in prose: It often expresses a unit of thought. A stanza may consist of only one line, or of any number of lines beyond that. The word *stanza* is an Italian word for "stopping place" or "place to rest."

See pages 200, 693.

STREAM OF CONSCIOUSNESS A writing style that tries to depict the random flow of thoughts, emotions, memories, and associations rushing through a character's mind. James Joyce and Virginia Woolf both wrote stream-of-consciousness novels.

See pages 976, 979.

SUSPENSE The uncertainty or anxiety we feel about what is going to happen next in a story. Writers often create suspense by dropping hints or clues that something—especially something bad—is going to happen. In "The Demon Lover" by Elizabeth Bowen (Unit Seven), we begin to feel suspense when Mrs. Drover receives a mysterious letter that makes her lips "go white"; our anxiety increases sharply when the flashback reveals that the letter-writer is her old fiancé; and our suspense reaches a climax when she escapes into a taxi and we discover who the driver is.

See pages 284, 316.

SYMBOL A person, place, thing, or event that stands both for itself and for something beyond itself. Many symbols have become widely recognized: A lion is a symbol of power; a dove is a symbol of peace. These established symbols are sometimes called **public symbols.** But writers often invent new, personal symbols, whose meaning is revealed in a work of poetry or prose. For example, the old house in Graham Greene's "The Destructors" (Unit Seven) is a symbol of civilization and beauty.

See pages 146, 155, 641, 718, 991.

SYMBOLISM A literary movement that began in France during the late nineteenth century and advocated the use of highly personal symbols to suggest ideas, emotions, and moods. The French Symbolists believed that emotions are fleeting, individual, and essentially inexpressible—and that therefore the poet is forced to suggest meaning rather than directly express it. Many twentieth-century writers were influenced by the Symbolists, including William Butler Yeats, T. S. Eliot, James Joyce, Virginia Woolf, and Dylan Thomas.

TERZA RIMA An interlocking, three-line stanza form with the rhyme scheme *aba bcb cdc ded* and so on. Terza rima is an Italian verse form (Dante used it in *The Divine Comedy*) that many English poets have used. Shelley's "Ode to the West Wind" (Unit Five) is one of the most famous examples of English terza rima.

See page 699.

THEME The central idea or insight of a work of literature. A theme is not the same as the subject of a work, which can usually be expressed in a word or two: old age, ambition, love. The theme is the idea the writer wishes to convey *about* that subject—the writer's view of the world or revelation about human nature. For example, one theme of James Joyce's "Araby" (Unit Seven) might be stated this way: One of the painful aspects of growing up is that some of our dreams turn out to be illusions.

A theme may also be different from a **moral,** which is a lesson or rule about how to live. The theme of "Araby" stated above, for example, would not make sense as a moral.

While some stories, poems, and plays have themes that are directly stated, most themes are implied. It is up to the reader to piece together all the clues the writer has provided about the work's total meaning. Two of the most important clues to consider are how the main character has changed and how the conflict has been resolved.

See pages 38, 231, 637, 948, 1020.

TONE The attitude a writer takes toward the reader, a subject, or a character. Tone is conveyed through the writer's choice of words and details. For example, Jonathan Swift's "A Modest Proposal" (Unit Four) is satiric in tone, while the tone of "Pied Beauty" by Gerard Manley Hopkins (Unit Six) might be described as awed.

See pages 46, 344, 549, 981.

TRAGEDY A play, novel, or other narrative depicting serious and important events, in which the main character comes to an unhappy end. In a tragedy, the main character is usually dignified, courageous, and often high ranking. This character's downfall may be caused by a **tragic flaw**—an error in judgment or character weakness—or the downfall may result from forces beyond his or her control. The tragic hero or heroine usually wins some self-knowledge and wisdom, even though he or she suffers defeat,

possibly even death. Tragedy is distinct from **comedy,** in which an ordinary character overcomes obstacles to get what he or she wants. *Beowulf*, Shakespeare's *Macbeth,* and Milton's *Paradise Lost* are all tragedies.

See pages 330, 332, 545.
See also *Comedy.*

UNDERSTATEMENT A figure of speech that consists of saying less than what is really meant, or saying something with less force than is appropriate. Understatement is the opposite of **hyperbole** and is a form of **irony.** You are using understatement if you come in from a torrential downpour and say, "It's a bit wet out there," or if you describe a Great Dane as "not exactly a small dog." Understatement can be used to create a kind of deadpan humor, but it can also function as a sustained ironic tone throughout a work, as in W. H. Auden's "The Unknown Citizen" (Unit Seven).

See pages 437, 549.

VILLANELLE A nineteen-line poem divided into five tercets (three-line stanzas), each with the rhyme scheme *aba*, and a final quatrain with the rhyme scheme *abaa.* Line 1 is repeated entirely to form lines 6, 12, and 18, while line 3 is repeated as lines 9, 15, and 19. Thus there are only two rhymes in the poem, and the two lines used as refrains (lines 1 and 3) are paired as the final couplet. The villanelle was originally used in French pastoral poetry. Dylan Thomas's "Do Not Go Gentle into That Good Night" (Unit Seven) is an example of a modern villanelle.

See page 1131.

WIT A quality of speech or writing that combines verbal cleverness with keen perception, especially of the incongruous. The definition of *wit* has undergone dramatic changes over the centuries. In the Middle Ages it meant "common sense," in the Renaissance it meant "intelligence," and in the seventeenth century it meant "originality of thought." The modern meaning of *wit* began to develop during the eighteenth century with the formulations of John Dryden and Alexander Pope. In his *Essay on Criticism* (Unit Four), Pope said:

True wit is Nature to advantage dressed:
What oft was thought, but ne'er so well expressed

Perhaps the best examples of more modern wit can be found in the works of Oscar Wilde (Unit Six) and Bernard Shaw (Unit Seven).

See pages 542, 684.

The ELEMENTS OF LITERATURE program provides three features to help you integrate language study with the study of literature. (1) The first feature is a series of exercises in the student text called **Literature and Language.** (See text pages 1243–1258.) (2) The second is a series of **Language Skills Worksheets** that are found in the Core Components Binder. (3) The third is this complete and succinct guide to grammar, usage, and mechanics.

This handbook can be used in several ways. It will be particularly useful to students for whom English is a second language. It will be a convenient reference handbook for all students who need to confirm definitions and the rules of grammar, usage, and mechanics, particularly as they need this help in their writing. The guide will also be useful to you, the teacher, when you wish to review terminology and rules.

The guide consists of the following: (1) grammatical terminology and definitions, with examples; (2) rules governing standard English usage, with examples; (3) spelling hints; and (4) occasional boxed *(Continued on next page.)*

GRAMMAR, USAGE, AND MECHANICS: A REFERENCE GUIDE

> **NOTE TO STUDENTS**
> As you write and revise formal essays and papers on topics in literature, you may want to review points of grammar, usage, capitalization, punctuation, and spelling. This reference section provides rules and examples that you will find helpful in your writing.

PARTS OF SPEECH

Nouns

1. A *noun* is a word used to name a person, place, thing, or idea.

2. A *common noun* names a class or a group of persons, places, or things. A *proper noun* names a particular person, place, or thing.

3. An *abstract noun* names a quality, a characteristic, or an idea. A *concrete noun* names an object that can be perceived by the senses.

4. A *compound noun* is a single noun made up of two or more words. Compound nouns may be common or proper.

   EXAMPLES
   scientist, city, car, honesty [common nouns]
   Dr. Salk, Houston, Buick [proper nouns]
   freedom, charity, hope [abstract nouns]
   apple, rocket, building [concrete nouns]
   passer-by, lifeguard, San Diego [compound nouns]

Pronouns

1. A *pronoun* is a word used in place of one or more than one noun. The noun the pronoun stands for is called its *antecedent*.

2. Forms of personal pronouns combined with *-self* or *-selves* may be used reflexively, to refer to the subject, or intensively, for emphasis.

3. *Relative pronouns* are used to introduce subordinate clauses.

4. *Interrogative pronouns* are used in interrogative sentences to ask questions.

5. *Demonstrative pronouns* point out a particular person or thing.

6. *Indefinite pronouns* refer to persons, places, or things but not to any specific ones.

   EXAMPLES
   Julia played **her** role very well. [The pronoun *her* refers back to its antecedent *Julia*.]
   myself, yourself, ourselves, themselves [reflexive]
   who, whom, which that, whoever [relative]
   who, whom, whose, which, what [interrogative]
   this, that, these, those [demonstrative]
   all, anybody, everybody, nobody, none [indefinite]

Adjectives

1. An *adjective* is a word used to modify a noun or a pronoun. Adjectives answer questions such as *What kind? Which one? How much?* or *How many?*

2. *A, an,* and *the* are special adjectives called *articles.*

3. A *proper adjective* is an adjective that is formed from a proper noun. Proper adjectives, like proper nouns, are always capitalized.

4. Other parts of speech, such as pronouns and nouns, may be used as adjectives.

   EXAMPLES
   red car [What kind?] **this** house [Which one?}
   a book, **an** owl, **the** farm [articles]
   French history, **Chinese** art [proper adjectives]
   The **school** library is not open. [noun as adjective]

Verbs

1. A *verb* is a word that expresses action or otherwise helps to make a sentence. An *action verb* is a word that expresses a physical or mental action.

2. A *linking verb* is a word that does not express an action. A linking verb helps to make a sentence by joining the subject with another word in the predicate.

3. A one-word verb is called a *main verb.* Sometimes a main verb is accompanied by other verbs called *helping verbs.* The main verb and the helping verb together make up a *verb phrase.*

(Continued from previous page.) "Tips for Writers." If you wish to help students improve their skills in grammar, usage, and mechanics, we refer you to the Core Components Binder. There you will find the **Language Skills Worksheets** which directly integrate the study of language and its application to specific literary selections in the text. To find these **Language Skills Worksheets,** simply read the lists of Supplementary Support Materials that precede each selection in this Annotated Teacher's Edition.

EXAMPLES
jump, run, fall [physical actions]
imagine, think, realize [mental actions]
James Stewart is an excellent **actor.** [*Is* links the subject *James Stewart* with the noun *actor* in the predicate.]
He **has acted** in many movies during his career. [The verb phrase is **has acted**. The main verb is *acted* and the helping verb is *has.*]

Adverbs

An *adverb* is a word used to modify a verb, an adjective, or another adverb. Adverbs usually answer questions such as: *Where? When? How? To what extent?* Some nouns may be used adverbially.

EXAMPLES
I saw the movie **yesterday.** [When?]
We walked **home.** [Where?]
The movie ended **happily.** [How?]
I am **completely** exhausted. [To what extent?]

Prepositions

1. A *preposition* is a word used to show the relationship of a noun or a pronoun to some other word in the sentence. Common prepositions include *about, after, around, at, before, between, by, for, from, in, into, of, since, under, with.*

2. The noun or pronoun following the preposition is called the *object of the preposition.* Words that modify the object may come between the preposition and the object. Taken together, the preposition, its object, and the modifiers of the object are called a *prepositional phrase.*

EXAMPLES
She told a story **about her vacation.** [In this sentence, the prepositional phrase is *about her vacation. About* is the preposition, *vacation* is the object of the preposition, and the word *her* modifies *vacation.*]

Conjunctions

1. A *conjunction* is a word that joins words or groups of words. *Coordinating conjunctions* join two or more words, phrases, or sentence parts of equal rank. The words *and, but, or, nor, for, so,* and *yet* are called coordinating conjunctions.

2. *Correlative conjunctions* are always found in pairs that have other words separating them: *either . . . or, neither . . . nor, both . . . and, not only . . . but also.*

3. *Subordinating conjunctions* are used to introduce subordinate clauses in complex sentences. Common subordinating conjunctions include *after, as soon as, because, if, so that, until, when,* and *while.* (See pages 1275–1276 for an exploration of complex sentences.)

EXAMPLES
Her uncle **and** my aunt are married. [coordinating conjunction]
Both you **and** I know the answer. [correlative conjunctions]
After I heard the news, I called. [subordinating conjunction]

Interjections

An *interjection* is a word that expresses emotion and that is not related grammatically to other words in the sentence.

EXAMPLES
Gosh! That exercise is very difficult.
Wow! I'm surprised at you.

THE SENTENCE
Elements of a Sentence

1. A *sentence* is a group of words expressing a complete thought. A group of words that does not express a complete thought is a *fragment.*

2. The *subject* of a sentence is the part about which something is being said. The *simple subject* is the main word in a subject. The *complete subject* is the simple subject and all the words that go with it.

3. The *predicate* of a sentence is the part that says something about the subject. The *simple predicate,* or *verb,* is the main word in a predicate. The *complete predicate* is the simple predicate and all the words that go with it.

EXAMPLES
The nervous singer. [fragment]
The nervous singer took a deep breath. [*The nervous singer* is the complete subject. *Took a deep breath* is the complete predicate. *Singer* is the simple subject, and *took* is the simple predicate.]

Phrases

1. A *phrase* is a group of related words that is used as a single part of speech and does not contain a verb and its subject. Three common types of phrases include verb phrases, noun phrases, and prepositional phrases.

2. An *adjective phrase* is a prepositional phrase that modifies a noun or a pronoun.

3. An *adverb phrase* is a prepositional phrase that modifies a verb, an adjective, or another adverb.

4. A *verbal* is a form of a verb used as another part of speech. Verbals may have modifiers and complements. There are three kinds of verbals: participles, gerunds, and infinitives.

5. A *participle* is a verb form used as an adjective. Both present participles and past participles can be used as adjectives.

6. A *participial phrase* consists of a participle and any modifiers or complements, all of which act together as an adjective.

7. A *gerund* is a verb form ending in *-ing* that is used as a noun.

8. A *gerund phrase* consists of a gerund and any complements or modifiers it may have.

9. An *infinitive* is a verb form, usually preceded by *to*, that is used as a noun, an adjective, or an adverb.

10. An *infinitive phrase* consists of an infinitive and any complements or modifiers it may have.

11. An *appositive* is a noun or pronoun that follows another noun to identify or explain it. An *appositive phrase* is made up of an appositive and its modifiers.

EXAMPLES
The car **with the blue convertible top** is mine. [adjective phrase]
The car is parked **in front of their garage.** [adverb phrase]
The **honking** horn was very annoying to everyone there. [participle]
Honking loudly, the driver annoyed everyone. [participial phrase]
Driving is very serious business. [gerund]
Driving an automobile requires a lot of attention. [gerund phrase]
Johanna likes **to drive.** [infinitive]
My brother Bob likes **to drive his old Chevy.** [infinitive phrase]
My cousin **Rachel** is an experienced race car driver. [appositive]
Paul Newman, **the well-known film actor,** is also a race car driver. [appositive phrase]

Clauses

1. A *clause* is a group of words that contains a verb and its subject and is used as part of a sentence. An *independent clause* expresses a complete thought and can stand by itself as a sentence. A *dependent* (or *subordinate*) *clause* does not express a complete thought and cannot stand alone. Subordinate clauses can be used as adjectives, nouns, or adverbs.

2. An *adjective clause* is a subordinate clause that modifies a noun or pronoun.

3. An *noun clause* is a subordinate clause that is used as a noun.

4. An *adverb clause* is a subordinate clause that is used as an adverb.

EXAMPLES
The woman **who sold me the car** is driving it here. [adjective clause]
She said **that she deposited my check.** [noun clause]
I will call you **when she gets here.** [adverb clause]

Kinds of Sentences

1. A *declarative sentence* makes a statement. It is followed by a period.

2. An *interrogative sentence* asks a question. It is followed by a question mark.

3. An *imperative sentence* gives a command or request. It is followed by a period. Strong commands are followed by exclamation points.

4. An *exclamatory sentence* shows excitement or expresses a strong feeling. It is followed by an exclamation point.

EXAMPLES
I liked the movie. [declarative]
Is there a review in today's paper? [interrogative]
Check the newspaper. Watch out! [imperative]
What a terrific film this is! [exclamatory]

Sentence Complements

1. A *complement* is a word or phrase that completes the meaning begun by the subject and verb.

2. The *direct object* receives the action expressed by the verb or names the result of the action. A direct object answers the question *What?* or *Whom?* after the action verb.

3. The *indirect object* of the verb precedes the direct object and tells *to whom* (or *what*) or *for whom* (or *what*) the action of the verb is done.

4. A *subject complement* is a word that follows a linking verb and refers to (explains or describes) the subject.

5. If the subject complement is a noun or pronoun, it is called a *predicate nominative*.

6. If the subject complement is an adjective, it is called a *predicate adjective*. A predicate adjective modifies the subject of the sentence.

7. An *objective complement* is a complement that refers to the direct object of an action verb. The objective complement may be either a noun or an adjective. Verbs that take objective complements include *make, consider, elect, appoint, name, choose,* and *render*.

EXAMPLES
Kimi sang a **song**. [direct object]
Tor wrote **me** a letter. [indirect object]
That woman is a **poet**. [predicate nominative]
Her poems are **beautiful**. [predicate adjective]
The gold medal made her very **happy**. [objective complement]

Sentence Structure
1. A *simple sentence* has one independent clause and no dependent (or subordinate) clauses. A simple sentence may have a compound subject, a compound predicate, or both.

2. A *compound sentence* has two or more independent clauses but no dependent (or subordinate) clauses.

3. A *complex sentence* has one independent clause and at least one dependent (subordinate) clause.

4. A *compound-complex sentence* has two or more independent clauses and at least one dependent (subordinate) clause.

EXAMPLES
Mark Twain wrote many humorous short stories. [simple sentence]
He worked as a riverboat pilot, and he also worked as a newspaper reporter. [compound sentence]
He worked as a riverboat pilot before he wrote *Huckleberry Finn*. [complex sentence]
Tina likes *Tom Sawyer*, but I prefer *Huckleberry Finn*, which is more satirical in its view of American society. [compound-complex sentence]

PROBLEMS OF AGREEMENT

Agreement of Subject and Verb
1. A verb should agree with its subject in number. Singular subjects take singular verbs. Plural subjects take plural verbs.

EXAMPLES
He watches movies. [The singular verb *watches* agrees with the singular subject *he*.]
They watch movies. [The plural verb *watch* agrees with the plural subject *they*.]

Like single-word verbs, verb phrases also agree with their subjects. However, in a verb phrase, only the first auxiliary (helping) verb changes its form to agree with a singular or plural subject.

EXAMPLES
The **train was arriving** late.
Two **trains were arriving** late.

2. The number of the subject is not changed by a phrase following the subject.

EXAMPLES
This **bag** of marbles **is** full. [*Bag* is the subject, not *marbles*.]
These **marbles** of glass **are** blue. [*Marbles* is the subject, not *glass*.]

3. Compound prepositions such as *together with, in addition to, as well as,* and *along with* following the subject do not affect the number of the subject.

EXAMPLE
Sarah, along with Chris, **is going** on the trip. [The subject of the sentence is singular because it names one person, *Sarah*. Therefore, the predicate of the sentence uses the singular auxiliary verb form *is*.]

4. The following indefinite pronouns are singular: *each, either, neither, one, everyone, everybody, no one, nobody, anyone, anybody, someone, somebody.*

EXAMPLES
Each of the dessert chefs **bakes** pastry. [*Each one* bakes.]
Neither of the pastries **is** an éclair. [*Neither one* is an éclair.]
Someone was eating the pastry. [*One* person was eating.]

5. The following pronouns are plural: *several, few, both, many.*

EXAMPLES
Several of these trails **are** dangerous for hikers who are inexperienced.
Few of the trails **lead** north.
Are both of these trails new?

6. The pronouns *some, all, most, any,* and *none* may be either singular or plural. These pronouns are singular when they refer to a singular word and plural when they refer to a plural word.

EXAMPLES
Some of the writing **is** scary. [*Some* refers to the singular noun *writing.*]
Some of the words **are** descriptive. [*Some* refers to the plural noun *words.*]

All of the painting **is** abstract.
All of the paintings **are** hung.

Most of the imagery **seems** strange.
Most of the images **seem** strange.

7. Compound subjects joined by the word *and* are usually plural in form and therefore take a plural verb.

A **compound subject** contains two or more nouns or pronouns that are the subject of the same verb.

EXAMPLES
Andy and **Gabe practice** their instruments. [Two persons *practice.*]
Dante, Machiavelli, and **Tasso are** great writers in the Italian language. [Three people are *writers.*]

TIPS FOR WRITERS
The words *any* and *none* may be singular even when they refer to a plural word if the speaker is thinking of each item individually. The words *any* and *none* are plural only if the speaker is thinking of several items as a group.

Any of these sports **is** good exercise. [*Any one sport is good exercise.*]
None of the sports **was** boring. [*Not one sport was boring.*]
Any of these sports **are** worth playing. [*All the sports are worth playing.*]
None of the sports **were** hard. [*No sports were hard.*]

---

8. Compound subjects that name only one person or thing take a singular verb.

EXAMPLES
My **best friend and constant companion is** Sally Gooden. [One person is my best friend and constant companion.]
Yogurt and raisins is a good snack.

9. Singular subjects joined by the words *or* or *nor* take a singular verb.

EXAMPLE
Either **Michael** or **Tony bikes** to school. [*Either* Michael *or* Tony bikes, not both.]

10. When a singular subject and a plural subject are joined by *or* or *nor,* the verb agrees with the subject nearer the verb.

ACCEPTABLE
Neither the producers nor the **director was** present at the screening.
Neither the director nor the **producers were** present at the screening.

Other Problems in Subject–Verb Agreement
11. The contractions *don't* and *doesn't* must agree with their subjects.

With the subjects *I* and *you* and with plural subjects, use the contraction *don't (do not).*

EXAMPLES
I **don't** speak.   They **don't** tell.
You **don't** read.   These **don't** fly.
We **don't** try.   Pens **don't** break.

With singular subjects, use the singular *doesn't (does not).*

EXAMPLES
He **doesn't** ride long.   One **doesn't** last.
She **doesn't** study.   This **doesn't** move.
It **doesn't** work well.   Donna **doesn't** work here.

12. Use a plural verb with a singular collective noun when you are referring to the individual parts or members of the group acting separately. Use a singular verb when you refer to the group acting together as a unit. *Collective nouns* are singular in form, but they name a group of persons or things.

EXAMPLES

army	club	fleet	jury
assembly	committee	flock	panel
audience	faculty	group	swarm
class	family	herd	team

EXAMPLES

The family **have** sat down for their dinner. [*Family* is thought of as individuals.]
The family **has** its meals mostly at home. [*Family* is thought of as a unit.]

Be sure that any pronoun referring to the collective noun has the same number as the noun (*their* in the first example above, *its* in the second).

TIPS FOR WRITERS

When the subject follows the verb, find the subject and make sure that the verb agrees with it. The most common uses of the subject-following-verb form are in sentences beginning with *here* and *there* and in questions.

Here **is** a **boat**.   Here **are** two **boats**.
There **is** my **skateboard**.   There **are** my **skateboards**.

13. **A verb agrees with its subject, not with its predicate nominative.**

STANDARD
  S   PN
Cavities are my biggest problem.
          S   PN
My biggest **problem is** cavities.

14. **Contractions such as *here's*, *where's*, *how's*, and *what's* include the verb *is*. Do not use one of these contractions unless a singular subject follows it.**

NONSTANDARD
There's some mice on the counter.

STANDARD
There **are** some **mice** on the counter.

15. **A word or a phrase stating a weight, a measurement, or an amount of money or time is usually considered one item and takes a singular verb.**

EXAMPLES
Five dollars is all I can spend.
One quarter of the grain **was** sold at the market.
Ten bushels of grain **costs** $5.00

Sometimes, however, the amount is thought of as individual pieces or parts. If so, a plural verb is used.

EXAMPLES
Ten of the pages **were** missing.
Two thirds of the apples **taste** sour.

16. **The title of a work of art, literature, or music, even when plural in form, takes a singular verb.**

EXAMPLES
Monet's ***Waterlilies* is** a well-known painting. [one work of art]
***Dubliners* contains** some of my favorite short stories. [one collection]

17. ***Every* or *many a* before a subject calls for a singular verb.**

EXAMPLES
Almost every member **was** tired.
Many a student **enjoys** poetry.

18. **A few nouns that look plural in form take singular verbs.**

EXAMPLES
The **news is** on at six and ten o'clock.
Physics was Frances' best subject.

Some nouns that end in *-s* take a plural verb even though they refer to a single item.

EXAMPLES
The **pliers are** in the toolbox.
Your **pants are** very stylish.

Agreement of Pronoun and Antecedent

1. **A pronoun should agree with its antecedent in number and gender.**

A pronoun usually refers to a noun or another pronoun that comes before it. The word that a pronoun refers to is called its **antecedent.**

A few singular personal pronouns have forms that indicate the gender of the antecedent. *He, him,* and *his* are masculine; *she, her,* and *hers* are feminine; and *it* and *its* are neuter.

EXAMPLE
Frank ran **his** last race yesterday.
Betty won **her** first tennis tournament today.

2. **When the antecedent of a personal pronoun is another kind of pronoun, look in a phrase following the antecedent to determine gender.**

EXAMPLES
Each of the **boys** reads **his** own newspaper.
One of the **girls** cooks **her** own dinner.

3. **When the antecedent may be either masculine or feminine, use both the masculine and the feminine forms.**

EXAMPLES
Every one of the passengers sat in **his or her** assigned seat.
Each **camper** should bring **his or her** own sleeping bag.

4. **Use a singular pronoun to refer to** *each, either, neither, one, everyone, everybody, no one, nobody, anyone, anybody, someone,* **or** *somebody.*

EXAMPLES
Somebody forgot **his or her** locker combination.
One of the monkeys has a banana in **its** paws.
Every boy in the bus fastened **his** seatbelt.
Each hotel room has **its** own parking space.

When the meaning of *everyone* and *everybody* is clearly plural, use the plural pronoun.

CONFUSING
Everyone talked to **his or her** parents.

CLEAR
Everyone talked to **their** parents.

5. **Two or more singular antecedents joined by** *or* or *nor* **should be referred to by a singular pronoun.**

EXAMPLES
Neither **June nor Alicia** made **herself** any cookies.
Dan or Pablo will pass **his** test tomorrow.

6. **Two or more antecedents joined by** *and* **should be referred to by a plural pronoun.**

EXAMPLES
Tia and Reg grew **their** own vegetables.
Mark and Jane won **their** relay race.

7. **The number of a relative pronoun is determined by the number of its antecedent.**

EXAMPLES
Everyone who comes to the party will have a good time. [*Who* refers to the singular pronoun *everyone* and thus takes the singular verb form *comes.*]
All who come will have a good time. [*Who* refers to the plural pronoun *all* and thus takes the plural verb form *come.*]

TIPS FOR WRITERS
Sentences with two or more singular antecedents joined by *or* or *nor* can sound awkward if the antecedents are of different genders. If a sentence sounds awkward, revise it to avoid the problem.

AWKWARD
Nelson or **Liz** will bring **his** or **her** records.

REVISED
Nelson will bring **his** records, or **Liz** will bring **hers**.

USING VERBS CORRECTLY

The Principal Parts of Verbs

1. **The four principal parts of a verb are the** *infinitive,* **the** *present participle,* **the** *past,* **and the** *past participle.*

The principal parts of the verb *come,* for example, are *come* (infinitive), *coming* (present participle), *came* (past), and *come* (past participle). These parts are used to form all of the verb tenses.

EXAMPLES
The bus **comes** every day.
The bus is **coming** now.
The bus **came** after school.
The bus has **come** on schedule.

Regular Verbs

2. **A regular verb forms its past and past participle by adding** *-d* or *-ed* **to the infinitive.**

INFINITIVE	PRESENT PARTICIPLE	PAST	PAST PARTICIPLE
bake	baking	baked	(have) baked
wish	wishing	wished	(have) wished

The present participle of most regular verbs ending in *-e* drops the *-e* before adding *-ing*.

One common error in the use of the past and the past participle forms is to leave off the *-d* or *-ed* ending.

NONSTANDARD
He use to live on that street.

STANDARD
He **used** to live on that street.

NONSTANDARD
She was suppose to walk me home.

STANDARD
She was **supposed** to walk me home.

Another error is doubling the ending.

NONSTANDARD
The waves were so rough we almost drownded.

STANDARD
The waves were so rough we almost **drowned.**

A few regular verbs have an alternate past form ending in -*t*. For example, the past form of *leap* may be written *leaped* or *leapt.*

Irregular Verbs

3. **An *irregular verb* forms its past and past participle in some other way than by adding -*d* or -*ed*.**

Irregular verbs form their past and past participle in one or more of these ways: changing a vowel, changing consonants, adding -*en,* making no change at all.

INFINITIVE	PAST	PAST PARTICIPLE
drink	drank	(have) drunk
hold	held	(have) held
drive	drove	(have) driven
hit	hit	(have) hit
take	took	(have) taken

If you are not sure about the parts of a verb, look in a dictionary, which lists the principal parts of irregular verbs. In the next column, you will find a list of frequently misused irregular verbs.

Irregular Verbs Frequently Misused

INFINITIVE	PRESENT PARTICIPLE	PAST	PAST PARTICIPLE
arise	arising	arose	(have) arisen
begin	beginning	began	(have) begun
bet	betting	bet	(have) bet
bleed	bleeding	bled	(have) bled
blow	blowing	blew	(have) blown
break	breaking	broke	(have) broken
bring	bringing	brought	(have) brought
burst	bursting	burst	(have) burst
choose	choosing	chose	(have) chosen
come	coming	came	(have) come
dig	digging	dug	(have) dug
do	doing	did	(have) done
drink	drinking	drank	(have) drunk
drive	driving	drove	(have) driven
eat	eating	ate	(have) eaten
fall	falling	fell	(have) fallen
fly	flying	flew	(have) flown
freeze	freezing	froze	(have) frozen
give	giving	gave	(have) given
go	going	went	(have) gone
grow	growing	grew	(have) grown
know	knowing	knew	(have) known
leave	leaving	left	(have) left
lend	lending	lent	(have) lent
put	putting	put	(have) put
ride	riding	rode	(have) ridden
ring	ringing	rang	(have) rung
run	running	ran	(have) run
see	seeing	saw	(have) seen
seek	seeking	sought	(have) sought
shake	shaking	shook	(have) shaken
shrink	shrinking	shrank	(have) shrunk
sink	sinking	sank	(have) sunk
speak	speaking	spoke	(have) spoken
steal	stealing	stole	(have) stolen
sting	stinging	stung	(have) stung
strike	striking	struck	(have) struck
swear	swearing	swore	(have) sworn
swim	swimming	swam	(have) swum
take	taking	took	(have) taken
tear	tearing	tore	(have) torn
throw	throwing	threw	(have) thrown
wear	wearing	wore	(have) worn
win	winning	won	(have) won
write	writing	wrote	(have) written

4. **When the present participle or the past participle is used as a main verb (simple predicate) in a sentence, it always requires a helping verb to form a verb phrase.**

MAIN VERB	+ HELPING VERB	= VERB PHRASE
taking	am	am taking
going	have been	have been going
walking	was	was walking
taken	have	have taken
gone	had	had gone
walked	has	has walked

5. The time expressed by a verb is called the *tense* of the verb. Every verb in English has six tenses: present, past, future, present perfect, past perfect, future perfect.

The following list shows six tense forms of *take*. Giving all the forms of a verb in this way is called **conjugating** the verb.

Conjugation of *Take*

Present Tense

Singular	Plural
I take	we take
you take	you take
he, she, *or* it takes	they take

Past Tense

Singular	Plural
I took	we took
you took	you took
he, she, *or* it took	they took

Future Tense

Singular	Plural
I will (shall) take	we will (shall) take
you will take	you will take
he, she, *or* it will take	they will take

Present Perfect Tense

Singular	Plural
I have taken	we have taken
you have taken	you have taken
he, she, *or* it has taken	they have taken

Past Perfect Tense

Singular	Plural
I had taken	we had taken
you had taken	you had taken
he, she, *or* it had taken	they had taken

Future Perfect Tense

Singular	Plural
I will (shall) have taken	we will (shall) have taken
you will have taken	you will have taken
he, she, *or* it will have taken	they will have taken

Each of the six tenses has an additional form called the **progressive form**, which expresses continuing action. It consists of a form of the verb *be* plus the present participle of the verb. The progressive is not a separate tense but an additional form of each of the six tenses in the conjugation.

Progressive Forms

Present Progressive: am, are, is taking

Past Progressive: was, were taking

Future Progressive: will (shall) be taking

Present Perfect Progressive: has, have been taking

Past Perfect Progressive: had been taking

Future Perfect Progressive: will (shall) have been taking

6. The present tense is used mainly to convey these ideas:

An action occurring now, at the present time. (The progressive form is used to express continuing action or action in progress.)

EXAMPLES
John **works** with a film company.
Marion **is watching** a documentary.

Customary or habitual action or state of being.

EXAMPLES
I usually **eat** lunch outside.
He often **skips** lunch altogether.

A general truth, something true at all times.

EXAMPLES
Crime never **pays**.
The product of four and six **equals** twenty-four.

The historical present is used to describe events or characters in a novel way or past events described as if they were happening now.

EXAMPLE
As the play opens, Nigel **finds** several hundred dollars.

7. The past tense is used mainly to express an action (or to help make a statement) that occurred in the past but did not continue into the present.

EXAMPLES
Last summer he **got** a tan.
The buzzer **sounded** just as I **was shooting** the basketball.

Past action can also be expressed idiomatically.

EXAMPLES
I **used to** love broccoli.
He **did like** to go swimming.

8. **The future tense is used to express an action that will occur in the future.**

EXAMPLES
We **will be traveling** through New Mexico by train.
The bus **will depart** tonight.
I **will attend** classes at the university during the fall semester.

Future action can also be expressed idiomatically using the present tense.

EXAMPLES
Next month I **vacation** in California.
I **am going to vacation** in California next month.

9. **The present perfect tense is used mainly to express an action that has been completed at some indefinite time in the past or an action begun in the past and still going on.**

EXAMPLES
He **has read** the report.
They **have been standing** in line for an hour.
I **have known** her since the third grade.

10. **The past perfect tense is used mainly to express an action that was completed in the past and preceded some other past action or event.**

EXAMPLES
Then he understood why his father **had warned** him about speeding. [The warning preceded the understanding.]
She **had taken** all the available journalism classes by the time she was a junior. [The taking preceded being a junior.]

11. **The future perfect tense is used mainly to express an action that will be completed in the future before some other future action or event takes place.**

EXAMPLES
The market **will have closed** by the time we get there.
In June I **will have had** my driver's license for one year.

Consistency of Tenses
12. **Do not change needlessly from one tense to another.**

NONSTANDARD
Janet took the class and passes it. [*Took* is past tense; *passes* is present tense.]

STANDARD
Janet **took** the class and **passed** it. [*Took* and *passed* are past tense.]

The perfect tenses are used to express completed action.

NONSTANDARD
She remembered that she made an appointment for noon. [Since the action of making was completed before the action of remembering the verb should be *had made* not *made*.]

STANDARD
She remembered that she **had made** an appointment for noon.

13. **Use the present infinitive to express an action that follows another action.**

CONFUSING
Maria wanted to have graduated by age seventeen.

CLEAR
Maria wanted **to graduate** by age seventeen.

14. **Use the perfect infinitive to express an action that occurred before another action.**

EXAMPLE
The police claimed **to have arrived** on the crime scene first. [The arriving occurred before the claim.]

TIPS FOR WRITERS
Using the correct verb tense can help make your instructions clear by showing whether an action occurs before, after, or at the same time as another action.

BEFORE / AFTER
When you have mowed the lawn, rake the clippings together in a pile.

SAME TIME
As you mow the lawn, be careful not to hurt yourself on the blades.

Active and Passive Voice

1. **A verb in the active voice expresses an action done *by* its subject. A verb in the passive voice expresses an action done *to* its subject.**

ACTIVE VOICE
The acrobat **thrilled** the audience. [The subject, *acrobat,* performs the action.]

PASSIVE VOICE
The audience **was thrilled** by the acrobat. [The subject, *the audience*, receives the action.]

In the pair of sentences above, the object of the active sentence becomes the subject of the passive one. The subject of the active sentence is now expressed in a prepositional phrase. In fact, this phrase can often be omitted from the passive sentence.

PASSIVE
The audience **was thrilled.**

In a passive sentence, the verb phrase always includes a form of *be* and the past participle of the main verb. Other helping verbs may also be included.

ACTIVE VOICE
    S   O
Someone **has borrowed** my notebook.

PASSIVE VOICE
    S
My notebook **has been borrowed.**

2. **When a verb that takes both a direct and an indirect object is changed from the active voice to the passive voice, either object may be the subject of the passive-voice sentence. The other object becomes the complement of the passive-voice verb. The object is called a *retained object*.**

ACTIVE VOICE
He gave me a pen.
I received a pen.

PASSIVE VOICE
I was given a **pen.**
A pen was given to **me.**

The following list shows the conjugation of the verb *drive* in the passive voice. Compare this conjugation with the one on page 1281.

Conjugation of *Drive* in the Passive Voice

Present Tense

Singular	Plural
I am driven	we are driven
you are driven	you are driven
he, she, *or* it is driven	they are driven

Past Tense

Singular	Plural
I was driven	we were driven
you were driven	you were driven
he, she, *or* it was driven	they were driven

Future Tense

Singular	Plural
I will be driven	we will be driven
you will be driven	you will be driven
he, she, *or* it will be driven	they will be driven

Present Perfect Tense

Singular	Plural
I have been driven	we have been driven
you have been driven	you have been driven
he, she, *or* it has been driven	they have been driven

Past Perfect Tense

Singular	Plural
I had been driven	we had been driven
you had been driven	you had been driven
he, she, *or* it had been driven	they had been driven

Future Perfect Tense

Singular	Plural
I will have been driven	we will have been driven
you will have been driven	you will have been driven
he, she, *or* it will have been driven	they will have been driven

3. **Verbs have three moods. The *indicative mood* is used to make statements of fact. The *imperative mood* is used to express a request or command. The *subjunctive mood* is used to express a condition contrary to fact or to express a wish.**

EXAMPLES
I **am** polite. (indicative)
Be polite. (imperative)
If you **were** polite, people would like you. (subjunctive)

4. **The subjunctive mood has three tenses: *present*, *past*, and *perfect*.**

Conjugation of *Be* in the Subjunctive Mood

Present Tense

Singular	Plural
I be	we be
you be	you be
he, she, *or* it be	they be

Past Tense

Singular	Plural
I were	we were
you were	you were
he, she, *or* it were	they were

Present Perfect Tense

Singular	Plural
I have been	we have been
you have been	you have been
he, she, *or* it have been	they have been

Past Perfect Tense

Singular	Plural
I had been	we had been
you had been	you had been
he, she, *or* it had been	they had been

5. **Use the present subjunctive in certain formal constructions.**

EXAMPLES
I suggest that we **forget** about that.
It is very important that you **be** there.
She **need** not attend extra classes this summer.

6. **Use the past and perfect subjunctive in contrary-to-fact statements and statements expressing a wish.**

EXAMPLES
If I **were** you, I would read both her poetry and her novels.
If she **had warned** us, we wouldn't have gone to that beach.
It was as if all the dogs in the neighborhood **were barking** at once.
I wish my grandfather **were** still alive.

Special Problems with Verbs

Using *Lie* and *Lay* Correctly
1. **The verb *lie* means "to rest" or "recline," "to remain lying in a position." *Lie* never takes an object. The verb *lay* means "to put" or "to place" (something). *Lay* usually takes an object.**

INFINITIVE	PRESENT PARTICIPLE	PAST	PAST PARTICIPLE
lie	lying	lay	(have) lain
lay	laying	laid	(have) laid

EXAMPLES
We like to **lie** on soft sheets.
The spoon **is lying** on the counter.
Those shoes **have lain** there for three days.
Ruth **lay** in bed because she was sick.
Has this message **lain** here since yesterday?

Lay that basket over here.
She **is laying** the towels out.
Martin **laid** bricks yesterday.
He **has laid** everything aside.
First **lay** your hands in your lap.

Using *Sit* and *Set* Correctly
2. **The verb *sit* means "to rest in an upright, seated position." *Sit* almost never takes an object. The verb *set* means "to put" or "to place" (something). *Set* usually takes an object. Notice that *set* does not change form in the past or past participle.**

INFINITIVE	PRESENT PARTICIPLE	PAST	PAST PARTICIPLE
sit	sitting	sat	(have) sat
set	setting	set	(have) set

Using *Rise* and *Raise* Correctly
3. **The verb *rise* means "to go in an upward direction." *Rise* never has an object. The verb *raise* means "to move something in an upward direction." *Raise* usually takes an object.**

INFINITIVE	PRESENT PARTICIPLE	PAST	PAST PARTICIPLE
rise	rising	rose	(have) risen
raise	raising	raised	(have) raised

EXAMPLES
The smoke **rose** out of the chimney.
Lucy asked Rickey to **raise** the picture slightly.

USING PRONOUNS CORRECTLY

Nominative and Objective Uses

Case

1. *Case* is the form of a noun or pronoun that shows its use in a sentence. In English, there are three cases: *nominative, objective,* and *possessive.*

Choosing the correct case form for a noun is no problem, because the form remains the same in the nominative and objective cases.

EXAMPLE
Her **mother** carpools with another **mother.**

Only in the possessive case does a noun change its form, usually by adding an apostrophe and *s.*

EXAMPLE
My **father's** workshop is cluttered with gardening tools and broken appliances.

EXAMPLE
I [nominative] forgot to mail **my** [possessive] application to **her** [objective] yesterday.

The Case Forms of Personal Pronouns

2. Here are the case forms of personal pronouns. Notice that all personal pronouns, except *you* and *it,* have different nominative and objective forms.

PERSONAL PRONOUNS

SINGULAR

Nominative Case	Objective Case	Possessive Case
I	me	my, mine
you	you	your, yours
he, she, it	him, her, it	his, her, hers, its

PLURAL

Nominative Case	Objective Case	Possessive Case
we	us	our, ours
you	you	your, yours
they	them	their, theirs

The Nominative Case

1. The subject of a verb is in the nominative case.

EXAMPLE
He was excited that **they** had come. [*He* is the subject of *was; they* is the subject of *had come.*]

TIPS FOR WRITERS

Sometimes the pronouns *we* and *they* sound awkward when used as parts of a compound subject. In such cases, it is a good idea to revise the sentence.

AWKWARD
We and they count on barbecuing on Sunday.

BETTER
We count on barbecuing with **them** on Sunday.

---

2. A *predicate nominative* is in the nominative case.

A *predicate nominative* is a noun or pronoun that follows a linking verb and explains or identifies the subject of the sentence.

A pronoun used as a predicate nominative always follows a form of the verb *be* or a verb phrase ending in *be* or *been.*

EXAMPLES
It is **he.**
That could be **she.**

The Objective Case

3. The *direct object* of a verb is in the objective case.

A *direct object* is a noun or pronoun that receives the action of the verb or shows the result of the action.

EXAMPLES
Ted asked **her** for the address. [*Ted* is the subject of the verb *asked.* Ted asked *whom?* The answer is *her.*]
Martha's skill impressed **him** and **me.**

4. The *indirect object* of the verb is in the objective case.

An *indirect object* is a noun or pronoun that tells to whom or for whom something is done. Pronouns used as indirect objects are in the objective case: *me, him, her, us, them.*

EXAMPLES
The teacher gave **him** an assignment.
The noise gave **me** a headache.

5. The *object of a preposition* is in the objective case.

A prepositional phrase begins with a preposition and ends with a noun or pronoun, which is the *object of the preposition*. A pronoun used as an object of a preposition must be in the objective case.

EXAMPLE
Jack sat in back of **us**.

Errors often occur when the object of a preposition is compound. You can usually figure out the correct pronouns by trying each one separately in the prepositional phrase.

NONSTANDARD
Mike raced ahead of him and I. [*Mike raced ahead of him* is correct. *Mike raced ahead of I* is incorrect. The correct forms of the pronouns are *him* and *me*.]

STANDARD
Mike raced ahead of **him** and **me**.

TIPS FOR WRITERS

Some mistakes in usage are more common than others. In speech, for example, people often incorrectly use the pronoun *me* for *I* in a compound subject.

INCORRECT
Faith and me built a clubhouse.

CORRECT
Faith and **I** built a clubhouse.

---

6. In an *infinitive clause*, both the subject and object of the infinitive are in the objective case.

EXAMPLE
My baby sister wanted **me to carry her**. [*Me* is the subject of *to carry*. *Her* is the object of *to carry*. The entire infinitive clause is the direct object of *wanted*.]

Many people use incorrect pronoun forms with the preposition *between*. You have probably heard phrases such as *between you and I* and *between you and he*. These phrases are incorrect. The pronouns are objects of a preposition and should be in the objective case. The correct phrases are *between you and me* and *between you and him*.

Special Pronoun Problems

Using *Who* and *Whom* Correctly

7. *Who* is used as a subject or predicate nominative, and *whom* is used as an object.

NOMINATIVE	OBJECTIVE
who	whom
whoever	whomever

In spoken English, the use of *whom* is becoming less common. In fact, when you are speaking, you may correctly begin any question with *who*, regardless of the grammar of the sentence. In written English, however, you should make a distinction between *who* and *whom*.

8. The use of *who* or *whom* in a subordinate clause depends on how the pronoun functions in the clause.

When you choose between *who(ever)* or *whom(ever)* in a subordinate clause, follow these steps:

STEP 1:   Find the subordinate clause.
STEP 2:   Decide how the pronoun is used in the clause—as subject, predicate nominative, object of the verb, or object of a preposition.
STEP 3:   Determine the case of the pronoun according to the rules of standard English.
STEP 4:   Select the correct form of the pronoun.

EXAMPLE
(*Whoever, whomever*) I choose will lead the group.
STEP 1:   The subordinate clause is (*whoever, whomever*) I choose.
STEP 2:   In this clause, the subject is *I*, the verb is *choose*, and the pronoun is the direct object of the verb *choose*; *I choose* (*whoever, whomever*).
STEP 3:   The direct object of a verb is in the objective case.
STEP 4:   The objective form is *whomever*.
ANSWER: **Whomever** I choose will lead the group.

Remember that no words outside the subordinate clause affect the case of the pronoun. In this example, the entire clause is used as the subject of *will lead*, the verb in the main clause. The pronoun *whomever* is used as the direct object (objective case) within its clause.

1286   Grammar, Usage, and Mechanics

Frequently, in subordinate clauses *whom* is omitted (understood).

EXAMPLES
The person [whom] he asked is Joyce.
The person [whom] she talked to is from the Australian outback.

9. **Pronouns used as *appositives* are in the same case as the word to which they refer.**

An *appositive* is a noun or pronoun that follows another noun or pronoun to identify or explain it.

EXAMPLES
The members, **he, she,** and **I,** each read a different part. [Since *members* is the subject of the sentence, the pronouns in apposition with it (*he, she, I*) must be in the nominative case.]

TIPS FOR WRITERS

To figure out the correct form for a pronoun used with an appositive or as an appositive, read the sentence with only the pronoun.

EXAMPLES
The teacher asked two students, Emma and (*he, him*), to wash the blackboard. [Omit the direct object, *students:* The teacher asked Emma and him to help.]
(*We, us*) swimmers decided to compete. [Omit the appositive, *swimmers:* We decided to compete.]

---

10. **Use the possessive case of a noun or pronoun before a gerund. Do not confuse the gerund form with the present participle, also an -ing form of the verb, which is used as an adjective.**

EXAMPLES
The panel applauded **my dancing.** [The gerund *dancing* is the object of the verb *applauded.* The possessive form *my* modifies the gerund.]
Can you see **me dancing** a ballet with a professional troupe? [Here the participle *dancing* modifies *me,* the object of *see.*]

The Pronoun in an Incomplete Construction

11. **After *than* and *as* introducing an incomplete construction, use the form of the pronoun that you would use if the construction were completed.**

Notice how pronouns change the meaning of sentences with incomplete constructions.

EXAMPLES
Vicky likes Paula better than **I.**
Vicky likes Paula better than **me.**

In the first sentence, the nominative case pronoun *I* is the subject of an understood verb: *Vicky likes Paula better than I* [*like Paula*]. In the second sentence, the objective case pronoun *me* is the object of the understood verb: *Vicky likes Paula better than* [*Vicky likes*] *me.*

EXAMPLES
I call you more often than **he** [calls you].
I call you more often than [I call] **him.**

Did she fool Jason as much as **I** [fooled Jason]?
Did she fool Jason as much as [she fooled] **me?**

USING MODIFIERS CORRECTLY

1. **Adjectives and adverbs are modifiers, that is, they state qualities of other parts of speech. Adjectives modify nouns and pronouns. Adverbs modify verbs, adjectives, and other adverbs.**

EXAMPLES
ripe apple   **juicy** peaches   [adjectives]
talk **softly**   jump **well**   [adverbs]

2. **Use adjectives to compare one noun with another noun that has the same quality.**

EXAMPLES
That apple is **riper** than this one.
This peach is **juicier** than that one.

3. **Use adverbs to make comparisons between verbs.**

EXAMPLE
I shoveled the snow slowly, but Phoebe shoveled even **more slowly.**

4. **There are three degrees of comparison: *positive*, *comparative*, and *superlative*.**

POSITIVE	COMPARATIVE	SUPERLATIVE
cool	cooler	coolest
wet	wetter	wettest
tasty	tastier	tastiest
helpful	more helpful	most helpful
slowly	more slowly	most slowly
good	better	best
bad	worse	worst

5. **A one-syllable modifier regularly forms its comparative and superlative degrees by adding *-er* and *-est*.**

POSITIVE	COMPARATIVE	SUPERLATIVE
tall	taller	tallest
gray	grayer	grayest
short	shorter	shortest

6. **Some two-syllable modifiers form their comparative and superlative degrees by adding *-er* and *-est*. Other two-syllable modifiers form their comparative and superlative degrees with *more* and *most*.**

POSITIVE	COMPARATIVE	SUPERLATIVE
able	abler	ablest
lively	livelier	liveliest
woeful	more woeful	most woeful
scenic	more scenic	most scenic
foolish	more foolish	most foolish

Some two-syllable modifiers may take either *-er*, *-est* or *more*, *most*: *often, oftener, oftenest* or *often, more often, most often*.

If you are unsure of how a two-syllable modifier is compared, look in an unabridged dictionary.

7. **Modifiers that have more than two syllables form their comparative and superlative degrees with *more* and *most*.**

POSITIVE	COMPARATIVE	SUPERLATIVE
popular	more popular	most popular
serious	more serious	most serious
voraciously	more voraciously	most voraciously

8. **Modifiers that indicate less of a quality use the word *less* or *least* before the modifier.**

POSITIVE	COMPARATIVE	SUPERLATIVE
neat	less neat	least neat
costly	less costly	least costly
soggy	less soggy	least soggy

Irregular Comparison
9. **Here are some commonly used modifiers which do not follow the regular methods of forming their comparative and superlative degrees.**

POSITIVE	COMPARATIVE	SUPERLATIVE
bad	worse	worst
good	better	best
well	better	best
many	more	most
much	more	most

Do not add the *-er*, *-est* or *more*, *most* forms to irregularly compared forms: *worse*, not *worser* or *more worse*.

Use of Comparative and Superlative Forms
10. **Use the comparative degree when comparing two things. Use the superlative degree when comparing more than two.**

COMPARATIVE
I think the bus is **more comfortable** than the subway.
Baking bread seems **more time-consuming** than baking cookies.
I think that Nolan Ryan is a **better** pitcher than Dwight Gooden.
The service in this restaurant could not be **worse** than in the one across the street.

SUPERLATIVE
Out of the Past is the **best** movie I've ever seen.
Golden retrievers are the **gentlest** breed of dog.
That was the **most boring** article I've ever read.

In everyday conversation, people sometimes use the superlative degree in comparing two things: *Put your best foot forward.*

11. **Include the word *other* or *else* when comparing one thing with others that belong in the same group.**

NONSTANDARD
Andy cooks better than any member of his club. [Andy is a member of his own club, and he cannot be a better cook than himself. The word *other* should be added.]

STANDARD
Andy cooks better than any **other** member of his club.

NONSTANDARD
Adele shops more than anyone. [The word *anyone* includes all people, and Adele is a person. Since she cannot shop more than herself, the word *else* should be added to clarify the meaning.]

STANDARD
Adele shops more than anyone **else**.

12. Avoid double comparisons.

A **double comparison** is incorrect because it contains both -er and *more* or -est and *most.*

NONSTANDARD
This floor is more dirtier than that one.

STANDARD
This floor is **dirtier** than that one.

NONSTANDARD
This is the most ugliest sweater you have ever worn since I've known you.

STANDARD
This is the **ugliest** sweater you have ever worn since I've known you.

13. Be sure your comparisons are clear.

UNCLEAR
The snowfall here this year was as much as the Rockies. [This sentence incorrectly compares snowfall to mountains.]

CLEAR
The snowfall here this year was as much as it was in the Rockies.

UNCLEAR
The height of the new statue is the same as my brother. [This sentence incorrectly compares the height of a statue to a brother, not the brother's height.]

CLEAR
The height of the new statue is the same as that of my brother.
or
The height of the new statue is the same as the height of my brother.

Both parts of an incomplete comparison should be stated if there is any chance of misunderstanding.

UNCLEAR
He told her less than Lisa.

CLEAR
He told her less than he told Lisa.

CLEAR
He told her less than Lisa told her.

TIPS FOR WRITERS
In writing papers about literary topics, you will often need to compare and contrast two or more literary works or specific aspects of them, such as character, plot, or setting. Comparisons, accurately expressed, can help you to make distinct points about works of literature. For example, you may wish to show that the characters in one novel are "more carefully developed" than in another or that the plot of one novel is "less complex" than that of another.

Dangling Modifiers

14. A modifying phrase or clause that does not clearly and sensibly modify a word in a sentence is a *dangling modifier.*

When a modifying phrase containing a verbal comes at the beginning of a sentence, the phrase is followed by a comma. Immediately after that comma should come the word that the phrase modifies.

UNCLEAR
Opening the door, the newspaper sailed toward me.

CLEAR
Opening the door, I saw the newspaper sailing toward me.

UNCLEAR
Trained in first aid, an ambulance transports medical technicians.

CLEAR
Trained in first aid, medical technicians are transported by an ambulance.

UNCLEAR
Stacked in a corner of the basement, Susan found a pile of old records.

CLEAR
Susan found a pile of old records stacked in a corner of the basement.

UNCLEAR
Hanging on the wall, the woman admired her new painting.

CLEAR
The woman admired her new painting hanging on the wall.

15. **To correct a dangling modifier, rearrange the words in the sentence or add words to make the meaning logical and clear.**

DANGLING
To make lemonade, lemons must be squeezed.

CORRECTED
To make lemonade, you must squeeze lemons.
or
If you want to make lemonade, you must squeeze lemons.

DANGLING
While dusting the mantel, a vase fell and broke.

CORRECTED
While dusting the mantel, I let a vase fall and break.
or
While dusting the mantel, I dropped a vase and broke it.

Misplaced Modifiers

16. **A misplaced modifier is a phrase or clause that sounds awkward because it modifies the wrong word(s). Modifying phrases should be placed as near as possible to the words they modify.**

MISPLACED
I read of the tragic fire in the newspaper.

CORRECTED
In the newspaper, I read of the tragic fire.

MISPLACED
I was awarded a scholarship after four years of study yesterday.

CORRECTED
Yesterday, I was awarded a scholarship after four years of study.

MISPLACED
I made a necklace for Tanya with colored beads.

CORRECTED
I made a necklace with colored beads for Tanya.

MISPLACED
I learned about the revolt in school.

CORRECTED
In school, I learned about the revolt.

TIPS FOR WRITERS
A sentence may appear to have a dangling modifier when *you* is the understood subject. In such cases, the modifier is not dangling; it is modifying the understood subject.

EXAMPLE
To learn how to operate a computer, (you) read the manual.

MISPLACED
Our volleyball team played a match after practicing for only two weeks last month.

CORRECTED
Last month, our volleyball team played a match, after practicing for only two weeks.

MISPLACED
My sisters fed all the animals at the petting zoo with delight.

CORRECTED
With delight, my sisters fed all the animals at the petting zoo.

Misplaced Clause Modifiers

17. **Place an adjective or adverb clause as near as possible to the word it modifies.**

MISPLACED
I carried the box from school, which weighed thirty pounds.
Mary had a long lunch in St. Louis, which took her two hours.

CORRECTED
From school, I carried the box, which weighed thirty pounds.
In St. Louis, Mary had a long lunch, which took two hours.

Always place the modifying clause as close as possible to the word it modifies.

MISPLACED
She is baking a birthday cake for a friend that has vanilla frosting.

CORRECTED
For a friend, she is baking a birthday cake that has vanilla frosting.

COMMON USAGE PROBLEMS

a, an

These *indefinite articles* refer to one of a general group. Use *a* before words beginning with a consonant sound; use *an* before words beginning with a vowel sound.

EXAMPLES
We saw **a** giraffe and **an** ostrich at the zoo.
An hour ago, we bought **a** hot dog.

In the second example above, *a* is used before *hot dog* because the *h* in *hot dog* is pronounced. *An* is used before *hour* because the *h* in *hour* is not pronounced.

accept, except

Accept is a verb that means "to receive." *Except* may be either a verb or a preposition. As a verb, it means "to leave out" or "to omit." As a preposition, *except* means "excluding."

EXAMPLES
She **accepted** the award.
No one is **excepted** from this requirement.
All of the players **except** Monica tried out for the team.

affect, effect

Affect is a verb meaning "to influence." *Effect* used as a verb means "to accomplish." Used as a noun, *effect* means "the result of some action."

EXAMPLES
Rainfall **affects** the water level.
Her speech had a powerful **effect** on the audience.
It is necessary to research the causes of a problem in order to **effect** a solution.
To **effect** change, people can vote.

ain't

Avoid the word *ain't* in speaking or writing. Use of this word is always considered to be nonstandard English.

all the farther, all the faster

This should be "as far as" and "as fast as."

DIALECT
That is all the farther I can throw.

STANDARD
That is **as far as** I can throw.

allusion, illusion

An *allusion* is an intentional reference to something. An *illusion* is a false idea or a misleading appearance.

EXAMPLES
The author made several scholarly **allusions** to other novels.
High heels create the **illusion** of height.

a lot

Do not write the expression *a lot* as one word. It should always be written as two words.

EXAMPLE
She owned **a lot** of dresses.

alumni, alumnae

Alumni is the plural of *alumnus* (a male graduate). *Alumnae* is the plural of *alumna* (a female graduate).

EXAMPLES
Several **alumni** of our college have become fathers since last year's reunion.
Many **alumnae** have gotten jobs that pay the same salaries as those of their male co-workers.

among

see **between, among.**

amount, number

Use *amount* to refer to a singular word. Use *number* to refer to a plural word.

EXAMPLES
A large **number** of telephones [plural] ring.
The **amount** of food [singular] on your plate is enough for two people.

and etc.

Etc. is an abbreviation of the Latin phrase *et cetera*, meaning "*and* other things." Thus, do not use *and* with *etc.*

EXAMPLE
My grandmother bakes cakes, pies, muffins, **etc.** [not *and etc.*]

anywheres, everywheres, nowheres, somewheres

Use these words without the final *s*.

EXAMPLE
I've met you before **somewhere.** [not *somewheres*]

as, like
　　See **like, as.**

as if
　　See **like, as if.**

at
　　Do not use *at* after *where.*

　　NONSTANDARD
　　Where do you go to school at?

　　STANDARD
　　Where do you go to school?

bad, badly
　　Bad is an adjective. *Badly* is an adverb.

　　EXAMPLES
　　Tom was very disappointed because he scored **badly** on the test.
　　His prospects for passing look **bad.**

because
　　In informal English the expression *The reason is* is often completed with a clause introduced by *because.* In formal English use the conjunction *that* to introduce the clause.

　　INFORMAL
　　The reason I called was because I missed you.

　　FORMAL
　　The reason I called **was that** I missed you.

being as, being that
　　Do not use these phrases for *since* or *because.*

　　NONSTANDARD
　　Being as I couldn't sleep, I decided to read.

　　STANDARD
　　Because I couldn't sleep, I decided to read.

beside, besides
　　Beside is a preposition that means "by the side of" someone or something. *Besides* as a preposition means "in addition to." As an adverb, *besides* means "moreover."

　　EXAMPLES
　　Leave the mail on the table **beside** the plant.
　　Besides swimming and tennis, I like volleyball.
　　You should come with us. **Besides,** you don't have anything better to do.

between, among
　　Use *between* when you are referring to two things at a time, even though they may be part of a group consisting of more than two.

　　EXAMPLES
　　He was sitting **between** Jenny and Carol.
　　I couldn't decide **between** the two puppies.

　　Use *among* when more than two things or persons are involved.

　　EXAMPLES
　　She divided the cookies **among** the three children.
　　Are you sure you want to walk **among** the animals?

bring, take
　　Bring means "to come carrying something." *Take* means "to go carrying something." Think of *bring* as related to *come, take* as related to *go.*

　　EXAMPLES
　　Bring something warm to drink.
　　Please **take** these dirty dishes to the kitchen and wash them.

bust, busted
　　Avoid using these words as verbs. Use a form of either *burst* or *break.*

　　EXAMPLES
　　The dam **burst** [not *busted*] during the flood.
　　When the vase **broke,** [not *busted*] glass was scattered all over the rug.

can't hardly, haven't scarcely
　　The words *hardly* and *scarcely* convey a negative meaning. They should never be used with another negative word.

　　EXAMPLES
　　I **can** [not *can't*] **hardly** see him.
　　We **have** [not *haven't*] **scarcely** enough rain for the crops.

can't help but
　　Avoid this expression in formal English.

　　INFORMAL
　　I can't help but notice how polite that little boy is.

FORMAL

I can't help **noticing** how polite that little boy is.
I cannot but **notice** how polite that little boy is.

could of

Do not write *of* with the helping verb *could*. Write *could have*. Also avoid *ought to of, should of, would of, might of,* and *must of.*

EXAMPLE

Karen could **have** [not *of*] been on time.

discover, invent

Discover means "to be the first to find, see, or learn about something that already exists." *Invent* means "to be the first to do or make something."

EXAMPLES

Lou **discovered** that the door was unlocked.
Edison **invented** the light bulb.

don't, doesn't

Don't is the contraction of *do not. Doesn't* is the contraction of *does not.* Use *doesn't,* not *don't,* with *he, she, it, this,* and singular nouns.

EXAMPLE

It **doesn't** [not *don't*] pay.
She **doesn't** [not *don't*] pay attention.

done

Never use *done* as the past form of *do;* the past form of *do* is *did. Done* is the past participle and requires an auxiliary verb.

NONSTANDARD

She done everything.

STANDARD

She **did** everything.
She **has done** everything.

effect

See **affect, effect.**

emigrate, immigrate

Emigrate means "to go away from a country." *Immigrate* means "to come into a country."

EXAMPLES

Jews **emigrated** from Germany during WW II.
Many people **immigrated** to the United States from Puerto Rico.

everywheres

See **anywheres,** etc.

fewer, less

Fewer refers to number; *Less* refers to quantity. *Fewer* tells "how many"; *less* tells "how much."

EXAMPLES

There are **fewer** girls than boys in our high school orchestra.
Overall, there is **less** work to be done.

good, well

Good is always an adjective. Never use *good* to modify a verb; use *well,* which is an adverb.

NONSTANDARD

The model dressed good.

STANDARD

The model dressed **well.**

Although it is usually an adverb, *well* is used as an adjective to mean "healthy."

EXAMPLE

She did not feel **well.**

Feel good and *feel well* mean different things. *Feel good* means "to feel happy or pleased." *Feel well* simply means "to feel healthy."

EXAMPLES

The massage felt **good.**
He left school early because he didn't feel **well** after he had eaten his lunch.

The use of *good* as an adverb is increasing in conversational English, but it should not be used that way in writing.

had of

See **of.**

had ought, hadn't ought

Unlike other verbs, *ought* is not used with *had.*

NONSTANDARD

You had ought to be more careful; you hadn't ought to cross the street without looking.

STANDARD

You **ought** to be more careful; you **ought not** to cross the street without looking.

haven't but, haven't only
>In these expressions *but* and *only* convey a negative idea. Avoid using them with *not* in formal writing.

>INFORMAL
>I haven't but one kitten left to give away.

>FORMAL
>I **have but** one kitten left to give away.
>I **have only** one kitten left to give away.

he, she, they
>Do not use an unnecessary pronoun after a noun. This error is called the **double subject.**

>NONSTANDARD
>My brother he bakes his own bread.

>STANDARD
>**My brother** bakes his own bread.

immigrate
>See **emigrate.**

imply, infer
>*Imply* means "to suggest something." *Infer* means "to interpret or get a certain meaning" from a remark.

>EXAMPLES
>My father **implied** that he would buy me a new bicycle.
>I **inferred** that he was proud of my good report card.

in, into
>*In* means "within." *Into* means "from the outside to the inside."

>EXAMPLES
>The cat was lying **in** the box.
>He reached **into** the car and got the keys.

kind, sort, type
>The words *this, that, these,* and *those* should always agree in number with the words *kind, sort, type.*

>EXAMPLE
>**That type** of cereal has more sugar than **these** other **types.**

lay, lie
>See page 1284.

learn, teach
>*Learn* means "to acquire knowledge." *Teach* means "to instruct" or "to show how."

>EXAMPLE
>A tutor **is teaching** me Spanish; I **am learning** to speak well.

leave, let
>*Leave* means "to go away" or "to depart from." *Let* means "to allow" or "to permit."

>NONSTANDARD
>Leave me carry your suitcase.

>STANDARD
>**Let** me carry your suitcase.

>STANDARD
>Let's **leave** this boring party.

less
>See **fewer, less.**

like, as
>*Like* is a preposition. In informal English, *like* is often used as a conjunction meaning "as." In formal English, always use *as.*

>EXAMPLES
>It is not **like** her to be rude. [The preposition *like* introduces the phrase *like her.*]
>He should listen to his mother, **as** his father requests. [*His father requests* is a clause and needs the subordinating conjunction *as* to introduce it.]

like, as if
>In formal written English, *like* should not be used for the compound conjunctions *as if* or *as though.*

>EXAMPLE
>He looks **as though** [not *like*] he has lost a great deal of weight.

might of, must of
>See **could of.**

no, none, nothing
>Do not use these words with another negative.

>NONSTANDARD
>I don't have nothing.

STANDARD
I **have nothing**.
I **don't have anything**.

NONSTANDARD
That man won't give you no job.

STANDARD
That man **won't give you** a job.
That man **will give you no** job.

NONSTANDARD
She looked for pink notebooks everywhere, but there weren't none.

STANDARD
She looked for pink notebooks everywhere, but there **weren't any**.
She looked for pink notebooks everywhere, but there **were none**.

nowheres
See **anywheres,** etc.

number, amount
See **amount, number.**

of

Do not use of with prepositions such as *inside, off,* or *outside.*

EXAMPLES
He jumped **off** [not *off of*] the trampoline and landed on a mat.
The cat lay **outside** [not *outside of*] the house.
What's **inside** [not *inside of*] your bag?

Of is also unnecessary with *had.*

EXAMPLE
If I **had** [not *had of*] gone to the carnival, I would have had fun.

or, nor
Use *or* with *either*; use *nor* with *neither.*

EXAMPLES
We can choose **either** red **or** black stripes for our baseball uniforms.
Unfortunately, **neither** Jack **nor** Juliana passed the chemistry test.

ought to of
See **could of.**

respectfully, respectively
Respectfully means "with respect" or "full of respect." *Respectively* means "each in the order indicated."

EXAMPLES
He answered the question **respectfully**.
The heights of Scott, Charlene, and April are 72, 62, and 64 inches, **respectively**.

rise, raise
See page 1284.

shall, will
Some people prefer to use *shall* with first person pronouns and *will* with second and third person pronouns in the future and future perfect tenses. Nowadays, most Americans do not make this distinction. *Will* is acceptable in the first person as well as in the other two.

sit, set
See page 1284.

slow, slowly
Slow is generally used as an adjective. *Slowly* is always used as an adverb.

EXAMPLES
The snake moved **slowly** through the grass.
He showed **slow** improvement in his ability to walk without crutches.

so
Avoid using *so* in writing whenever you can.

EXAMPLE
The town was snowed in, so the trams weren't running.
Because the town was snowed in, the trams weren't running.

some, somewhat
In writing, do not use *some* for *somewhat* as an adverb.

NONSTANDARD
Her sewing has improved some.

STANDARD
Her sewing has improved **somewhat**.

take, bring
See **bring, take.**

than, then
Do not confuse these words. *Than* is a conjunction; it is used to make comparisons. *Then* is an adverb; it tells about time.

EXAMPLES
We applied the glaze and **then** placed our clay mugs in the kiln.
This ball is bigger **than** that one.
First the ball was made. **Then** it was sold in a store.
I like vanilla ice cream much more **than** I like chocolate ice cream.

them
Them should not be used as an adjective. Use *those.*

NONSTANDARD
Have you met them folks?

STANDARD
Have you met **those** folks?

this here, that there
The words *here* and *there* are unnecessary after *this* and *that.*

EXAMPLE
Sit in **this** [not *this here*] chair instead of **that** [not *that there*] one.

this kind, sort, type
See **kind,** etc.

type, type of
Do not use *type* as an adjective before a noun. *Type* is a noun. Do not omit *of* after type.

EXAMPLES
That **type of** fruit is sweet.
That **type of** music really does get on father's and mother's nerves, you know.

way, ways
Use *way,* not *ways,* in referring to a distance.

EXAMPLES
They've come a long **way** [not *ways*] in their studies.
Our house is a long **way** [not *ways*] from here.

when, where
Do not use *when* or *where* incorrectly in writing a definition.

NONSTANDARD
A "debate" is when two or more people argue over a certain issue.

STANDARD
A "debate" is an argument over a certain issue between two or more people.

where
Do not use *where* for *that.*

EXAMPLES
I heard from your brother **that** [not *where*] you were grounded.
We learned **that** [not *where*] her nephew had been promoted to the rank of admiral.

which, that, who
The relative pronoun *who* refers to people only; *which* refers to things only; *that* refers to either people or things.

EXAMPLES
The man **who** works in the main office is my father. [person]
This chair, **which** is wooden, is an antique from France. [thing]
Her dress was one **that** seemed to flatter anyone **who** wore it. [thing]
Our principal is a person **that** works hard for our school. [person]

who, whom
See pages 1286–1287.

without, unless
Do not use the preposition *without* in place of the conjunction *unless.*

EXAMPLES
She can't read **unless** [not *without*] she puts her glasses on.
He cannot practice law **unless** [not *without*] he passes the bar exam.
She will not be allowed in the pool **unless** [not *without*] she wears a bathing cap.

would of
See **could of.**

THE RULES FOR CAPITALIZATION

First Words
1. **Capitalize the first word in every sentence.**

   EXAMPLES
   Each room of the house seemed to have its own color theme. In one room there were a host of blues—pale, slate, and midnight. In yet another we found only orange and yellow tones.

   Traditionally, the first word of a line of poetry is capitalized.

   EXAMPLES
   Water, water, everywhere,
   And all the boards did shrink;
   Water, water, everywhere,
   Nor any drop to drink.

   —from "The Rime of the Ancient Mariner,"
   Samuel Taylor Coleridge

   Some writers do not follow these practices. When you are quoting, be sure to use capital letters exactly as they are used in the source of the quotation.

Pronoun *I* and Interjection *O*
2. **Capitalize the pronoun *I* and the interjection *O*.**

   EXAMPLE
   Ralph and I always walk to school.

   Although it is rarely used, *O* is always capitalized. Generally, it is reserved for invocations and is followed by the name of the person or thing being addressed. You will more often use the interjection *oh,* which is not capitalized unless it is the first word in a sentence.

   EXAMPLES
   "Sing, **O** Muse, of the wrath of Achilles" is the opening line of Homer's *Iliad.*

   Oh, how lovely the forest is!

Proper Nouns and Proper Adjectives
3. **Capitalize proper nouns and proper adjectives.**
   A **common noun** names a class or a group of people, places, or things. A **proper noun** names a particular person, place, or thing. Proper adjectives are formed from proper nouns.

Common nouns are not capitalized unless they begin a sentence or a direct quotation or are included in a title (see pages 1297–1300, 1306). Proper nouns are always capitalized.

COMMON NOUNS
a philosopher, a country, a ruler, a writer

PROPER NOUNS
Plato, France, King Arthur, Machiavelli

PROPER ADJECTIVES
Platonic ideas, French bread, Arthurian legend, Machiavellian leader

Some proper names consist of more than one word. In these names, short prepositions (generally, fewer than five letters) and articles are not capitalized.

EXAMPLES
Joan of Arc
American Federation of Labor
Alexander the Great

Proper nouns and adjectives sometimes lose their capitals through frequent usage.

EXAMPLES
volt   quixotic

To find out whether a noun should be capitalized, check in a dictionary. The dictionary will tell you if a word should always be capitalized or if it should be capitalized only in certain uses.

Names of People
4. **Capitalize the names of people.**

   EXAMPLES
   GIVEN NAMES
   Timothy
   Beth

   SURNAMES
   Griffin
   Schwartz

Geographical Names
5. **Capitalize geographical names.**

   TOWNS, CITIES
   Los Angeles, New Orleans, Beijing, Kingston, Madrid, San Diego, Houston

COUNTIES, TOWNSHIPS
Nassau County, Township of Soweto

STATES
Missouri, Nebraska, Connecticut, Oregon, Arizona,
California

REGIONS
the North, the Northwest, the Eastern Seaboard,
Continental Divide

Words such as *north, west,* and *southeast* are not
capitalized when they indicate direction.

EXAMPLES
west of here, heading northeast

However, these words are capitalized when they
name a particular place.

EXAMPLES
colleges in the Middle West
traveling in the Southeast

COUNTRIES
the United States of America, Scotland,
Australia

CONTINENTS
North America, Europe, Australia, Antarctica

ISLANDS
Ceylon, Madagascar, Hawaii

MOUNTAINS
the Himalayas, Mount McKinley, the Urals, the
Rockies

BODIES OF WATER
Lake Pontchartrain, Atlantic Ocean, Gulf of Mexico,
Katterskill Creek

PARKS
Yellowstone National Park, Hyde Park

ROADS, HIGHWAYS, STREETS
Route 45, Interstate 80, Boston Post Road, Acorn
Lane, East Eleventh Street

In a hyphenated number, the second word begins
with a small letter.

EXAMPLE
Seventy-seventh Street

Organizations

6. **Capitalize names of organizations, businesses,
institutions, and government bodies.**

ORGANIZATIONS
American Medical Association, National Association
for the Advancement of Colored People, Mickey
Mouse Club, United Nations

The word *party* is usually written without a capital
letter when it follows a proper adjective.

EXAMPLES
Republican party, Democratic party, Independent
party

BUSINESSES
General Electric, New York Telephone, Taco Bell

INSTITUTIONS
Sloan-Kettering Hospital, Boston University,
Crossroads High School

Do not capitalize words like *hotel, theater, college,
high school,* and *post office* unless they are part of
a proper name.

EXAMPLES

Howard University	a college course
Trocadero	a hotel in Miami
Shubert Theater	a theater in New York
Seattle Post Office	a local post office
Suffolk County Courthouse	the courthouse doors

GOVERNMENT BODIES
Federal Bureau of Investigation, Congress,
Department of Agriculture

Historical Events

7. **Capitalize the names of historical events and periods,
special events, and calendar items.**

HISTORICAL EVENTS AND PERIODS
French Revolution, Battle of Gettysburg, the
Vietnam War, Middle Ages, Great Depression

SPECIAL EVENTS
Special Olympics, the U.S. Open, the Masters
Tournament

CALENDAR ITEMS
Thursday, June, Thanksgiving, Arbor Day

Nationalities and Races
8. **Capitalize the names of nationalities, races, and peoples.**

EXAMPLES
African, Greek, Bantu, Chinese, Swiss, Commanche, Korean

Brand Names
9. **Capitalize the brand names of business products.**

EXAMPLES
Nylon, Skippy, Chrysler

Do not capitalize the noun that often follows a brand name: Skippy peanut butter.

TIPS FOR WRITERS
Do not capitalize the names of seasons unless they are personified or are part of the names of special events.

EXAMPLES
"I saw old Autumn in the misty morn." [personification]
Suzanne was noted Most Likely to Succeed in the annual Spring Election. [special event]

Particular Places, Things, Events
10. **Capitalize the names of ships, planets, monuments, awards, and any other particular places, things, or events.**

SHIPS, TRAINS
the *Santa Maria*, the *U.S.S. Minnow*, the *Titanic*, the *City of New Orleans*, the *Clipper*

AIRCRAFT, SPACECRAFT, MISSILES
Apollo 7, Challenger, Patriot

PLANETS, STARS
Saturn, Betelgeuse, Orion Nebula

Sun, moon and *earth* are not capitalized unless they are listed with other heavenly bodies.

MONUMENTS, MEMORIALS
Graceland, the Lincoln Memorial

BUILDINGS
Museum of Modern Art, the Empire State Building

AWARDS
Medal of Honor, Nobel Prize, Palm d'Or

Specific Courses, Languages
11. **Do *not* capitalize names of school subjects, except for languages and for course names followed by a number.**

EXAMPLES
Chris is taking English, history and typing. I'm taking French, drama, Trigonometry II, and English literature.

Do *not* capitalize the name of a class (*freshman, sophomore, junior, senior*) unless it is used as part of a proper noun.

EXAMPLE
The sophomore class is going to win the Freshman-Sophomore game.

Titles of People
12. **Capitalize the title of a person when it comes before a name.**

EXAMPLES
President Reagan   Mr. Covello
Dr. Valdez   Ms. Welch
Professor Allen   Principal Quint

Do not capitalize a title used alone or following a person's name, especially if the title is preceded by *a* or *the*.

EXAMPLES
Our group met with the principal at lunchtime on the first Friday of every month.
We passed out flyers to elect Edward Kennedy senator for another term.
Julius Caesar wanted to be emperor of Rome.
The governor is to be present at the ground-breaking ceremony.

13. **Capitalize words showing family relationship when used with a person's name but *not* when preceded by a possessive or article.**

EXAMPLES
Ramon's grandmother visited us last year.
For Thanksgiving, we usually go to Aunt Carlene and Uncle Tom's house.
Last Sunday we visited relatives.
Does Cousin Ed like your cat?
But: My cousin Ed loves my dog.

Titles of Literary and Other Creative Works

14. **Capitalize the first and last words and all important words in titles of books, periodicals, poems, stories, historical documents, movies, television programs, works of art, and musical compositions.**

Unimportant words in a title are
articles: *a, an, the*
short prepositions (fewer than five letters): *of, to, for, from*
coordinating conjunctions: *and, but, so, nor, or, yet, for*

BOOKS
The Sound and the Fury, Do Androids Dream of Electric Sheep?, The Mayor of Casterbridge, Tess of the d'Urbervilles, Cotton Comes to Harlem

PERIODICALS
Cosmopolitan, Life, Newsweek, Field and Stream, Esquire

POEMS
"Small Eternity," "Ode to a Grecian Urn," "My Last Duchess"

STORIES
"A Good Man Is Hard to Find," "The Necklace," "The Demon Lover"

HISTORICAL DOCUMENTS
Constitution, Declaration of Independence, Magna Carta

TELEVISION PROGRAMS
Murphy Brown, Nova, Murder She Wrote, Saturday Night Live

WORKS OF ART
Odalisque, Waterlilies

MUSICAL COMPOSITIONS
Aida, "You Can't Touch This," Mozart's *Requiem, The Magic Flute*

The words *a, an,* and *the* written before a title are capitalized only when they are the first word of a title.

EXAMPLES
the *Chicago Sun Times, For Whom the Bell Tolls, The Diary of Anne Frank, An American Tragedy,* "The Eve of St. Agnes"

Before the names of magazines and newspapers, *a, an,* and *the* are usually not capitalized.

EXAMPLES
Did you see the article on hiking in the *New York Post?*
He reads the *Los Angeles Times.*
My mother buys the *Weekly World News.*
Esther subscribes to the *Wall Street Journal.*

Religions

15. **Capitalize names of religions and their followers, holy celebrations, holy writings, and specific deities.**

RELIGIONS AND FOLLOWERS
Catholicism, Quaker, Jehovah's Witness, Protestant, Jewish, Muslim, Methodist, Buddhist, Anglican, Presbyterian

HOLY DAYS AND SEASONS
Easter, Yom Kippur, Quamsa, Passover, Christmas, Ramadan

HOLY WRITINGS
the Bible, the Talmud, Koran, Psalms, Upanishads, Acts of the Apostles

SPECIFIC DEITIES
Allah, God, Brahma, Jehovah

The word *god* is not capitalized when it refers to the gods of ancient mythology.

EXAMPLES
Zeus was the father of all gods.
The goddess Athena was thought of as being all-wise.
The Greek god Hermes was the messenger of the other gods; in Roman mythology he is known as Mercury.

TIPS FOR WRITERS
In some writings, you may see pronouns that refer to the Deity capitalized. In other cases, writers capitalize such pronouns only to prevent confusion. The practice of capitalizing pronouns referring to the Deity is customary, however.

EXAMPLES
The Lord called upon Moses to lead His people into the promised land.
It is written that the Lord shall "cover thee with His feathers."
"God shed His grace on thee."

PUNCTUATION

End Marks

End marks—*periods, question marks,* and *exclamation points*—are used to indicate the purpose of a sentence.

1. Use a period to end a statement (*or* declarative sentence).

EXAMPLES
Your father is here.
The child wanted to know where the toy was.

Notice in the second example that a declarative sentence containing an indirect question is followed by a period.

2. Use a question mark to end a question (*or* interrogative sentence).

EXAMPLES
Should we buy these?
Is it time yet?
May I come over now?

A direct question may have the same word order as a declarative sentence. Since it is a question, however, it is followed by a question mark.

EXAMPLES
We can go soon?
She was a nice person?

3. Use an exclamation point to end an exclamation.

EXAMPLES
Excellent! What a great job!
Oops!
Look out!

TIPS FOR WRITERS

Be sure to distinguish between a declarative sentence that contains an indirect question and an interrogative sentence, which asks a direct question.

INDIRECT QUESTION
Al asked what road he should take to get to the beach.

DIRECT QUESTION
Al asked, "What road should I take to get to the beach?"

Sometimes declarative and imperative sentences show such strong feeling that they are more like exclamations than statements or questions. If so, an exclamation point should be used instead of a period or question mark.

EXAMPLES
The house is on fire!
Won't you leave!
Don't break that!
This is a blast!

4. Use a period or exclamation point to end an imperative sentence.

When an imperative sentence makes a request, it is generally followed by a period. Imperative sentences, particularly commands, may also show strong feeling. In such cases, an exclamation point should be used.

EXAMPLES
Please run fast.
Run faster!

Sometimes, a command or request is stated in the form of a question. Because of the purpose, however, the sentence is really an imperative sentence and is followed by a period or an exclamation point.

EXAMPLES
May I point out the statue to you.
Will you go!

5. Use a period after an abbreviation.

Personal Names: D. H. Lawrence, T. S. Eliot
Titles Used with Names: Mr., Ms., Mrs., Dr.
States: Fla., Mo., Pa., Ala.
Time of Day: A.M., P.M.
Years: B.C., A.D.
Addresses: Ave., St., Blvd.,
Organizations and Companies: Assn., Co., Corp., Inc.
Units of Measure: lb., oz., in., ft., yd., mi.

Abbreviations for government agencies and international organizations and some other frequently used abbreviations are written without periods. Abbreviations in the metric system are often written without the periods, especially in science books.

TIPS FOR WRITERS
If an abbreviation comes at the end of a statement, do not use an additional period as an end mark. However, use a question mark or an exclamation point if one is needed.

EXAMPLES
I'm going to Boca Raton, Fla.
Does she work for Rowe, Inc.?

Commas

1. **Use commas to separate two or more adjectives preceding a noun.**

    EXAMPLE
    Mom cleaned the **hot, damp, smelly attic.**

    When the last adjective in a series is thought of as part of the noun, the comma before the adjective is omitted.

    EXAMPLE
    We washed the **small, round glass windows.**

    You can use two tests to determine whether two adjectives should be separated by a comma:

    TEST 1:
    Insert the word *and* between the adjectives. If *and* fits sensibly between the adjectives, use a comma. In the first example sentence, *and* can be logically inserted: *hot and damp attic.* In the second sentence, *and* sounds logical between the first two adjectives (*small and round*) but not between the second and third (*round and glass*).

    TEST 2:
    Change the order of the adjectives. If the order of the adjectives can be reversed sensibly, use a comma. *Round, small glass windows* makes sense, but *glass, small round windows* does not.

2. **Use commas before *and, but, or, nor, for, so,* and *yet* when they join independent clauses.**

    EXAMPLES
    Howard pulled her hair, and **she screamed.**
    Maria gets up early, yet **she is always late.**

    Do not be misled by compound verbs, which often make a sentence look as though it contains two independent clauses.

COMPOUND SENTENCE
Jean cut the vegetables, and **Malcolm made the salad.**
[two independent clauses]

SIMPLE SENTENCE
Milton outlined the story and **wrote** it. [one subject with a compound verb]

In the following correctly punctuated compound sentence, notice that independent clauses appear on both sides of the coordinating conjunction.

He wrote poetry, and **he loved to act.**

3. **Use commas to set off nonessential clauses and nonessential participial phrases.**

    A *nonessential* (or *nonrestrictive*) clause or participial phrase adds information that is not necessary to the main idea in the sentence. Omitting such a clause or phrase will not change the meaning of the sentence.

    NONESSENTIAL CLAUSES
    The letter, **which is not stamped,** cannot be mailed.
    Joan, **who is my sister,** is going to Russia.
    This dress, **which I bought for twenty dollars,** is still my favorite.

    NONESSENTIAL PHRASES
    William Black, **an accomplished artist,** illustrated many of his own poems.
    Mark, **very tired after work,** played with the children.
    The fall line, **designed by Mary McFadden,** will be out in October.
    That book, **bound in red leather,** is an expensive first edition.

    When a clause or phrase is necessary to the meaning of a sentence—that is, when it tells *which ones*—the clause or phrase is *essential* (or *restrictive*), and commas are *not* used.

    Notice how the meaning of each sentence below changes when the essential clause or phrase is omitted.

    ESSENTIAL CLAUSES
    Only those students **who are taller than five feet eight inches** may try out for the basketball team.
    A story **that I wrote** was read out loud in class.

    An adjective clause beginning with *that* is usually essential.

TIPS FOR WRITERS
A comma is always used before *for, so,* and *yet* joining two independent clauses. The comma may be omitted, however, before *and, but, or,* or *nor* when the independent clauses are very short and when there is no chance of confusion.

EXAMPLES
I'd never been there before, yet I didn't go.
I saw the play and I liked it.

ESSENTIAL PHRASES
A man **without an umbrella** ran through the rain.
The most famous speech **made by Dr. Martin Luther King, Jr.,** began "I have a dream . . ."

4. **Use a comma after introductory words such as** *well, yes, no,* **and** *why* **when they begin a sentence.**

EXAMPLES
Yes, my hair is natural.
Well, it's always been this color.

5. **Use a comma after an introductory participial phrase.**

EXAMPLES
Resting in the shade of the tree, I felt cooler.
Disappointed with the results, Tia left the room.

6. **Use a comma after a series of introductory prepositional phrases.**

EXAMPLES
Toward the end of the speech, we started clapping.
From the back of the bus, we heard laughter.
By the end of the night, we were all tired.

A short introductory prepositional phrase does not require a comma unless the comma is necessary to make the meaning clear.

EXAMPLES
With my car I can get to work faster.
With my car, driving is a pleasure. [The comma is necessary to avoid reading *car driving*.]

7. **Use a comma after an introductory adverb clause.**

EXAMPLES
As the team ran onto the field, the crowd cheered.
When you get home, give me a call.
After you figure it out, tell me what to do.

8. **Use commas to set off elements that interrupt the sentence.**

EXAMPLES
He is, **in fact,** my best friend.
My brother, **of course,** scored the winning run.

If an "interrupter" comes at the beginning or at the end of a sentence, only one comma is needed.

EXAMPLES
After all, he is an expert.
There are two more days, **however.**

9. **Use commas to set off appositives and appositive phrases.**

EXAMPLES
My cat, **a Siamese,** was neutered.
His favorite player, **Darryl Strawberry,** hurt his ankle.
The Minters, **our neighbors,** were invited to the picnic.

When an appositive has no modifiers and is closely related to the word preceding it, it should not be set off by commas.

EXAMPLES
The Polish composer **Chopin** is her favorite.
We **students** took a poll.

10. **Use commas to set off words used in direct address.**

EXAMPLES
John, you need a new notebook.
I need to ask your advice, **Ms. Anders.**
That dress, **Marina,** is very flattering.

11. **Use commas to set off parenthetical expressions.**

EXAMPLES
Strictly speaking, I don't like it.
Yesterday, **I believe,** was Wednesday.
It came from Alabama, **in fact**.

A contrasting expression introduced by *not* is parenthetical and must be set off by commas.

EXAMPLE
It was my brother, **not my sister,** who borrowed my coat.
I'm sure it was Eliot, **not Pound,** who wrote *The Waste Land.*

12. Use a comma to separate items in dates and addresses.

EXAMPLES
My friend traveled to **Paris, France,** on **Sunday, July 14, 1991.**
I mailed the letter to **29 West Orange Road, Teaneck, NJ 07631,** on **May 19, 1991.**

Notice that no comma separates the month and day (May 19) or the house number and street name (29 West Orange Road) because each is considered one item. Also, the ZIP code is not separated from the name of the state by a comma: Teaneck, NJ 07631.

13. Use a comma after the salutation of a friendly letter and after the closing of any letter.

EXAMPLES
Dear Mr. Kilgannon,
Yours truly,
My dear Robert,
Sincerely,

14. Use a comma after a name followed by an abbreviation such as *Jr., Sr.,* and *M.D.*

EXAMPLES
Johnny Chin, **Sr.**
Ens. F. A. Riley, **U.S.N**.
Christopher Beatty, **M.D.**
John F. Kennedy, **Jr.**
Roseanne Ellis, **Ph.D.**

Semicolons

1. Use a semicolon between independent clauses in a sentence if they are not joined by *and, but, or, nor, for, so,* or *yet.*

Notice in the following examples that the semicolon replaces the comma and the conjunction joining the independent clauses.

EXAMPLES
First I filled the tub, **and** then I took a bath.
First I filled the tub; then I took a bath.
Jack will go to college, **but** his sister will join the Army.
Jack will go to college; his sister will join the Army.

A semicolon can be used between two closely related independent clauses.

EXAMPLE
Phoebe baked the bread. Then she set the table.
Phoebe baked the bread; then she set the table.

2. Use a semicolon between independent clauses joined by conjunctive adverbs or transitional expressions.

EXAMPLES
Gabe was tired; **however,** he couldn't fall asleep.
I made several dishes; **in addition,** several friends brought appetizers.

When conjunctive adverbs and transitional expressions appear *within* one of the clauses and not *between* clauses, they are usually punctuated as interrupters (set off by commas). The two clauses are still separated by a semicolon.

EXAMPLE
We tried to see all the Seurat paintings; the museum, **however,** closed before we could do so.

3. Use a semicolon (rather than a comma) to separate independent clauses joined by a coordinating conjunction when there are commas within the clauses.

CONFUSING
Broccoli, peppers, and mushrooms are vegetables, and nectarines, peaches, and bananas are fruits.

CLEAR
Broccoli, peppers, and mushrooms are vegetables; nectarines, peaches, and bananas are fruits.

CONFUSING
Reaching into the closet and taking out the gray sweater, Steven noticed the tatters and holes, fingering the dirty wool, but, despite his mother's pleading, he could not part with the sweater.

CLEAR
Reaching into the closet and taking out the gray sweater, Steven noticed the tatters and holes, fingering the dirty wool; but, despite his mother's pleading, he could not part with the sweater.

4. Use a semicolon between items in a series if the items contain commas.

EXAMPLES
He visited **Brussels, Belgium; Naples, Italy; Bombay, India; and Bangkok, Thailand,** on his trip.
Auditions will be held **Tuesday, July 16; Wednesday, July 17; and Thursday, July 18.**

Colons

1. **Use a colon before a list of items, especially after expressions like *the following* and *as follows*.**

   EXAMPLES
   You will visit **the following cities:** London, Athens, and Cairo.
   Other colors are **as follows:** green, yellow, brown, and white.

   If a noun is followed by a list of appositives, then the colon is used to make the meaning of the sentence clear.

   EXAMPLES
   On the menu there were three choices: French, Italian, or blue cheese dressing.
   You need to bring three things: a blanket, a pillow, and a toothbrush.

   Do *not* use a colon before a list that follows a verb or a preposition.

   INCORRECT
   Additional sports include: table tennis, badminton, croquet, and horseshoes.

   CORRECT
   Additional sports include table tennis, badminton, croquet, and horseshoes.

2. **Use a colon before a long, formal statement or quotation.**

   EXAMPLE
   Alfred North Whitehead wrote: "Intelligence is quickness to apprehend as distinct from ability, which is capacity to act wisely on the thing apprehended."

3. **Use a colon between the hour and the minute.**

   EXAMPLES
   4:08 A.M.   9:14 P.M.

4. **Use a colon between chapter and verse in referring to passages from the Bible.**

   EXAMPLES
   Psalms 110:2   Genesis 2:3

5. **Use a colon between volume and issue number or between volume and page number of a periodical.**

   EXAMPLES
   Life 58:4 [volume and issue number]
   Life 58:102 [volume and page number]

6. **Use a colon after the salutation of a business letter.**

   EXAMPLES
   Dear Dr. Adell: Dear Ms. Cahane:
   Gentlemen: To Whom It May Concern:

Italics

When writing or typing, indicate italics by underlining. If your composition were to be printed, the underlined words would be set in italics. For example, if you type:

Anton Chekhov wrote <u>The Cherry Orchard</u>.

the sentence would be printed like this:

Anton Chekhov wrote *The Cherry Orchard*.

If you use a personal computer, you can probably set words in italics yourself.

1. **Use italics (underlining) for titles of books, plays, films, newspapers, periodicals, works of art, long musical compositions, long poems, television programs, ships, aircraft, and so on.**

   BOOKS: *The Cat in the Hat, Knight's Gambit*
   PLAYS: *A Man for All Seasons, Twelve Angry Men*
   FILMS: *Casablanca, Pretty Woman*
   PERIODICALS: *Time,* the *New Statesman*
   WORKS OF ART: *Starry Night, Nightwatch*
   LONG MUSICAL COMPOSITIONS: *Aida, The 1812 Overture*
   TELEVISION SERIES: *The Brady Bunch, MacGyver*
   SHIPS: *Titanic, Andrea Doria*
   AIRCRAFT, SPACECRAFT: *Luna 7, Saturn 2, Hindenburg*

   The words *a, an,* and *the* written before a title are italicized only when they are part of the title. Before the names of newspapers and magazines, however, they are not italicized, even if they are capitalized on the front page of the newspaper or on the cover of the magazine.

   EXAMPLES
   He read ***A Bell for Adano.***
   Holst composed ***The Planets.***
   My parents read the ***Boston Phoenix*** and ***People.***

Magazine articles, chapter headings, and titles of short poems, short stories, short musical compositions, and individual episodes of TV shows, when referred to in a composition, should be placed in quotation marks, not italicized. See the following section.

2. **Use italics (underlining) for words, letters, and figures referred to as such and for foreign words.**

EXAMPLES
The word *hullabaloo* comes from Scottish.
The word *Mississippi* has four *i*'s.
The *5* on my test looks like an *8.*
When I tipped the waiter he said, *"Merci."*

Quotation Marks

1. **Use quotation marks to enclose a direct quotation—a person's exact words.**

EXAMPLES
Cynthia asked, **"How long is it?"**
"It's two hours," I answered.

2. **Begin a direct quotation with a capital letter.**

EXAMPLES
When he was finished raking the yard, Dad said, "Let's cook out."
Amy said, "**A**bout ten minutes." [Although this quotation is not a sentence, it is Amy's complete remark.]

If the direct quotation is obviously a fragment of the original quotation, it may begin with a small letter.

EXAMPLE
Please take the advice of Shakespeare's Polonius, and "neither a borrower nor a lender be." [The quotation is obviously only a phrase from Polonius's sentence.]

3. **When a quoted sentence is divided into two parts by an interrupting expression, begin the second part with a small letter.**

EXAMPLE
"Before yesterday," she said, "there were trees here."

If the second part of a quotation is a new sentence, a period (not a comma) follows the interrupting

expression; and the second part begins with a capital letter.

EXAMPLE
"The game already started," May said. **"L**et's go to the movies, instead."

An interrupting expression is not a part of a quotation and therefore should never be inside quotation marks.

INCORRECT
"If he doesn't come, he said, we won't have enough people."

CORRECT
"If he doesn't come," he said, **"we won't have enough people."**

When two or more sentences by the same speaker are quoted together, use only one set of quotation marks.

INCORRECT
Wanda said, "Yesterday seemed warmer than today." "I wonder what the temperature is?"

CORRECT
Wanda said, **"Yesterday seemed warmer than today. I wonder what the temperature is?"**

TIPS FOR WRITERS
Do not use quotation marks for *indirect quotations*.

DIRECT QUOTATIONS
Sasha said, "I already read that book."
She asked him, "Have you ever been to Memphis?"

INDIRECT QUOTATION
Sasha said that he'd already read that book.
She asked him if he'd ever been to Memphis.

4. **Set off a direct quotation from the rest of the sentence by commas or by a question mark or an exclamation point.**

EXAMPLES
Mr. Rosenfield's mother said, "Please come back and visit us soon," as she let me off in front of my house.
Grace said, "Have you been able to locate Surinam?" as she opened the oversized atlas on her desk.

5. **Place commas and periods inside closing quotation marks.**

   EXAMPLES
   "I haven't read the book," said Janine, "but I saw the movie."
   "Mushrooms," a poem by Margaret Atwood, presents vivid images.

6. **Place semicolons and colons outside closing quotation marks.**

   EXAMPLES
   Father's advice was, "Always be polite"; I wonder if his father told him that, too.
   Choose one of the following "specials of the day": pot roast, chicken, or pasta salad.

7. **If the quotation is a question or an exclamation, place question marks and exclamation points inside the closing quotation marks. Otherwise, place them outside.**

   EXAMPLES
   "Are we there yet?" I asked, hoping for the best.
   "You just asked me that!" he answered.
   What is the meaning of **"censer"**?

8. **When you write dialogue (a conversation), begin a new paragraph every time the speaker changes.**

   EXAMPLE
   "I won't go through with it," said Adam softly.
   "Well, then," Alice said, "I guess I'll have to do it alone."
   "Yes," he said. "You will."

9. **When a quoted passage consists of more than one paragraph, put quotation marks at the beginning of each paragraph and at the end of the entire passage. Do not put quotation marks after any paragraph but the last.**

   EXAMPLE
   "Today," the reporter said, "several buildings were burned to the ground in Trenton, New Jersey.
   "Police are ruling the fires accidental, and are still searching for the cause of the blaze. Eyewitnesses speculate that it may have been caused by a gas leak."

10. **Use single quotation marks to enclose a quotation within a quotation.**

    EXAMPLES
    Vernon said, "I saw Run DMC live, singing **'Rockbox.'"**
    The poem I want you to read," said Miss Walters, "is **'Small Eternity.'"**
    Michael asked, "Who said **'Go West, young man'**?"

11. **Use quotation marks to enclose titles of articles, short stories, essays, poems, songs, individual episodes of TV shows, chapters, and other parts of books or periodicals.**

    EXAMPLES
    I'm going to read Flannery O'Connor's short story **"A Good Man Is Hard to Find."**
    He likes the song **"My Way."**

    Italicize the title of a poem long enough to be published in a separate volume. Such poems are usually divided into titled or numbered sections, such as cantos, parts, or books. Long musical compositions include operas, symphonies, ballets, oratorios, and concertos.

    EXAMPLES
    When I read *Thurber's Carnival*, I wanted to read "The Scotty Who Knew Too Much," too.
    I read "Canto 6" of the *Divine Comedy* by the Italian poet Dante.

Apostrophes
With the Possessive Case

1. **Add an apostrophe and an s to form the possessive case of a singular noun. The *possessive* of a noun or pronoun shows ownership or relationship.**

   EXAMPLES
   an **editor's** opinion   a **brother's** love
   the **interviewer's** notes   **Francine's** book
   one **dollar's** worth   the **bird's** feathers

2. **Add only an apostrophe to a proper name ending in an s-sound if the name has two or more syllables or if the addition of 's would make the name awkward to pronounce.**

   EXAMPLES
   Euripides' plays
   Ms. **Rodriquez'** wallet

3. **Add only an apostrophe to form the possessive case of a plural noun ending in s.**

EXAMPLES
countries' populations
dentists' bills

Although most plural nouns end in *s*, some are irregular. To form the possessive case of a plural noun that does not end in *s*, add an apostrophe and an *s*.

EXAMPLES
children's toys   **women's** careers

Do not use an apostrophe to form the *plural* of a noun. Remember that the apostrophe shows ownership or relationship.

INCORRECT
Three runners' wore sneakers.

CORRECT
Three **runners** wore sneakers.

CORRECT
Three **runners'** sneakers were white.

4. **Do not use an apostrophe with a possessive personal pronoun.**

My, your, her, its, our, and *their* are used before a noun. *Mine, yours, hers, ours,* and *theirs,* on the other hand, are never used before a noun; they are used as subjects, complements, or objects in sentences. *His* may be used in either way.

EXAMPLES
I saw **your** jacket. I saw a jacket of **yours.**
That is **her** baby sister. That baby sister is **hers.**
Roland has **his** opinion; I have **mine.**
This is **their** house. This house is **theirs.**

The possessive form of *who* is *whose,* not *who's.* Do not write *it's* for *its,* or *they're* for *their.*

5. **Add an apostrophe and an *s* to form the possessive case of an indefinite pronoun.**

EXAMPLES
anyone**'s** guess   neither**'s** book
everyone**'s** friend   another**'s** ball

6. **For possessives of compound words, names of organizations and businesses, and words showing joint possession, make only the last word possessive in form.**

COMPOUND WORDS
someone else's problem
state legislature's decision
sister-in-law's lamp

ORGANIZATIONS
World Wildlife Conservation's plea
Greenpeace's funding

BUSINESS
Con Edison's workers

JOINT POSSESSION
Matt and Julie**'s** story had the fewest characters and the most dialogue. [The story belongs to both Matt and Julie.]

When one of the words showing joint possession is a pronoun, both words should be possessive in form.

EXAMPLES
Eddie's and my surfboards were in desperate need of wax. [not *Eddie and my surfboards*]
Alex's and my relationship has improved since we began to write to each other.

7. **When two or more persons possess something individually, make each of their names possessive in form.**

EXAMPLES
Mrs. Mackay's and **Mrs. Stone's** husbands both work in the local post office. [the husbands of two different women]
Bill's and **Leon's** backpacks have reflective strips attached to them. [individual, not joint, possession]

With Contractions
8. **Use an apostrophe to show where letters or numbers have been omitted in a contraction.**

EXAMPLES
who is . . . who's   I am . . . I'm
1991 . . . '91   you are . . . you're
is not . . . isn't   were not . . . weren't

EXCEPTIONS
will not . . . won't
shall not . . . shan't

9. **To prevent confusion, use an apostrophe and an *s* to form the plurals of lowercase letters, some uppercase**

letters, numerals, and some words referred to as words.

EXAMPLE
My daughter is learning her ABC**'s**.
Good writers dot their *i***'s** and cross their *t***'s**.
Some writers cross their 7**'s** to distinguish them from 1**'s**.

Hyphens

1. **Use a hyphen in some compound nouns.**

EXAMPLES
brand-new, great-grandmother, mother-in-law
will-o'-the-wisp

2. **Use a hyphen to divide a word at the end of a line.**

EXAMPLES
One of my favorite words is the noun **an-**
thology.
It was time to do some of our **house-**
cleaning chores.

Divide an already hyphenated word only at a hyphen.

INCORRECT
Yesterday at the fair he went on the merry-go-round.

CORRECT
Yesterday at the fair he went on the **merry-**
go-round.

Do not divide a word so that one letter stands alone.

INCORRECT
The young couple rented a new a-
partment.

CORRECT
The young couple rented a new **apart-**
ment.

3. **Use a hyphen with compound numbers from *twenty-**
***one* to *ninety-nine* and with fractions used as**
adjectives.

EXAMPLES
twenty-four degrees
one-third gallon [but *one third* of the paint]
three-fourths inch [but three fourths of the length]
sixty-second omelette

4. **Use a hyphen with the prefixes *ex-, self-, all-,* and**
with the suffix *-elect,* and with all prefixes before a
proper noun or proper adjective.

EXAMPLES
ex-governor, **mid**-September, **self**-taught, **all**-round,
President-**elect**

Dashes

Use a dash to indicate an abrupt break in thought or
speech or an unfinished statement or question.

Many words and phrases are used parenthetically: that is, they break into the main thought of a sentence. Most parenthetical elements are set off by commas or parentheses.

EXAMPLES
The general, **I believe,** is a brilliant strategist.
Radishes, **however,** do not agree with me.
The answer, **she realized,** was incorrect.
The key, **he recalled,** was in the drawer.

Sometimes these elements demand a stronger emphasis. In such instances, a dash is used.

EXAMPLES
The best scene in the play is—but you should decide that yourself.
She had only one desire—flee, flee from the dull life she led—but it was too late.
The real culprit you see—ah, but that information must remain a secret for the moment.

Parentheses

Use parentheses to enclose material that is added to a
sentence but is not considered of major importance.

EXAMPLES
During World War I **(from 1914 to 1918)**, the airplane came into prominence in military strategy.

Punctuation marks are used within parentheses when the parenthetical matter is a full sentence. However, a punctuation mark is not placed within parentheses if the mark belongs to the sentence as a whole.

EXAMPLE
Mark your answers clearly. (Do not use ink**.)**
Senator Albert Gore (Democrat, Tennessee) has made several speeches on that subject.
The graph shows the changes clearly (see Figure 3**)**.

SPELLING

TIPS FOR WRITERS

Here are five tips for improving your spelling.
1. To learn the spelling of a word, pronounce it, study it, and write it.
2. Use a dictionary.
3. Spell by syllables.
4. Proofread for careless spelling errors.
5. Keep a spelling notebook.

Words with *ie* and *ei*

1. **Write *ie* when the sound is long *e*, except after *c*.**

   EXAMPLES

achieve	niece	ceiling	reprieve	believe
conceit	thief	siege	fiend	field

2. **Write *ei* when the sound is not long *e*.**

   EXAMPLES

neighbor	weigh	freight
reign	heinous	height

   EXCEPTIONS
   friend, conscience, financier, seize

Words with *-cede*, *-ceed*, and *-sede*

3. **Only one English word ends in *-sede: supersede*; only three words end in *-ceed: exceed, proceed*, and *succeed*; all other words with this sound end in *-cede*.**

   EXAMPLES

precede	recede	secede
intercede	concede	accede

Adding Prefixes

4. **When a prefix is added to a word, the spelling of the original word itself remains the same.**

   EXAMPLES
   dis + satisfy = **dis**satisfy
   im + mature = **im**mature

Adding Suffixes

5. **When the suffix *-ness* or *-ly* is added to a word, the spelling of the original word remains the same.**

   EXAMPLES
   casual + ly = casual**ly**
   habitual + ly = habitual**ly**

   EXCEPTIONS
   Words ending in *y* usually change the *y* to *i* before *-ness* and *-ly:*

   empty—emptiness; busy—busily

   But most one-syllable adjectives ending in *y* follow rule 5: *sly—slyness; dry—dryly*
   True, due, and *whole* drop the final *e* before *-ly: truly, duly, wholly*

6. **Drop the final silent *e* before adding a suffix that begins with a vowel.**

   EXAMPLES
   care + ing = caring
   dose + age = dosage
   seize + ure = seizure
   sense + ible = sensible

   EXCEPTIONS
   1. Keep the final silent *e* in words ending in *ce* or *ge* before a suffix that begins with *a* or *o*: *manageable, courageous*
   2. To avoid confusion with other words, keep the final silent *e* in some words: *dyeing* and *dying, singeing* and *singing.*

7. **Keep the final silent *e* before adding a suffix that begins with a consonant.**

   EXAMPLES

nine + ty = ninety	definite + ly = definitely
love + ly = lovely	care + less = careless

   EXCEPTIONS
   true + ly = truly
   judge + ment = judgment

8. **When a word ends in *y* preceded by a consonant, change the *y* to *i* before any suffix except one beginning with *i*.**

   EXAMPLES
   accompany + ment = accompaniment
   plenty + ful = plentiful
   defy + ed = defied
   satisfy + ing = satisfying

   EXCEPTIONS
   1. Some one-syllable words:
      shy + ness = shyness
      sky + ward = skyward

2. *lady* and *baby* with suffixes:
ladylike   ladyship   babyhood

9. **When a word ends in *y* preceded by a vowel, simply add the suffix.**

EXAMPLES
buoy + ant = buoyant
joy + ful = joyful
display + ed = displayed
cloy + ing = cloying

EXCEPTIONS
day + ly = daily   pay + ed = paid
say + ed = said

Doubling Final Consonants

10. **When a word ends in a consonant, double the final consonant before a suffix that begins with a vowel only if the word: (1) has only one syllable or is accented on the last syllable, and (2) ends in a single consonant preceded by a single vowel.**

EXAMPLES
swim + ing = swimming
repel + ent = repellent
rob + ery = robbery
plan + ed = planned

Otherwise, simply add the suffix.

EXAMPLES
wink + ed = winked
crack + ing = cracking
insist + ence = insistence

Plurals of Nouns

11. **To form the plurals of most English nouns, add *s*.**

EXAMPLES
pack / packs   pallet / pallets   peel / peels
night / nights   violin / violins

12. **To form the plurals of other nouns, follow these rules.**

If the noun ends in *s*, *x*, *z*, *ch*, or *sh*, add *es*.

EXAMPLES
dress / dresses   fox / foxes   match / matches
waltz / waltzes   dash / dashes

If the noun ends in *y* preceded by a consonant, change the *y* to *i* and add *es*.

EXAMPLES
cry / cries   theory / theories   ruby / rubies

EXCEPTION
The plurals of proper nouns: the *Murphys*, the *Rileys*.

If the noun ends in *y* preceded by a vowel, add *s*.

EXAMPLES
monkey / monkeys   buoy / buoys
journey / journeys

For some nouns ending in *f* or *fe*, change the *f* to *v* and add *s* or *es*.

Noticing how the plural is pronounced will help you remember whether to change the *f* to *v*.

EXAMPLES
roof / roofs   safe / safes   knife / knives
kerchief / kerchiefs   elf / elves   wharf / wharves

If the noun ends in *o* preceded by a consonant, add *es*.

EXAMPLES
potato / potatoes   hero / heroes   tomato / tomatoes

If the noun ends in *o* preceded by a vowel, add *s*.

EXAMPLES
patio / patios   radio / radios   tattoo / tattoos
studio / studios

EXCEPTIONS
poncho / ponchos   zoo / zoos   tango / tangos

Nouns for musical terms that end in *o* preceded by a consonant form the plural by adding only *s*.

EXAMPLES
soprano / sopranos   solo / solos   piano / pianos
dynamo / dynamos

A number of nouns that end in *o* preceded by a consonant have two plural forms.

EXAMPLES
tornado / tornados *or* tornadoes
mango / mangos *or* mangoes
zero / zeros *or* zeroes
flamingo / flamingos *or* flamingoes

The best way to handle plurals of words ending in *o* preceded by a consonant is to check their spelling in a dictionary.

The plurals of some nouns are irregular.

EXAMPLES
tooth / teeth   man / men   mouse / mice

Some nouns have the same form in both the singular and the plural.

EXAMPLES
deer   moose   salmon   Japanese

Plurals of Compound Nouns

13. **If a compound noun is written as one word, form the plural by adding *s* or *es*.**

    EXAMPLES
    cupful / cupful**s**   leftover / leftover**s**
    eyelash / eyelash**es**   strongbox / strongbox**es**

    If a compound noun is hyphenated or written as two words, make the main noun plural. The *main noun* is the noun that is modified.

    EXAMPLES
    mother-in-law / mother**s**-in-law
    notary public / notar**ies** public

    EXCEPTIONS
    drive-in / drive-ins   lean-to / lean-tos

Plurals of Latin and Greek Loan Words

14. **Some nouns borrowed from Latin and Greek form the plural as in the original language.**

    EXAMPLES
    nucleus / nucl**ei**   crisis / cris**es**   datum / dat**a**
    vertebra / vertebr**ae**   phenomenon / phenomen**a**
    basis / bas**es**

    A few Latin and Greek loan words have two plural forms.

    EXAMPLES
    vortex / vort**ices** *or* vort**exes**
    curriculum / curricul**a** *or* curriculum**s**
    gymnasium / gymnasi**a** or gymnasium**s**

    Check a dictionary to find the preferred spelling of such plurals.

Plurals of Numbers, Letters, Symbols, and Words Used as Words

15. **To form the plurals of numerals, most capital letters, symbols, and words used as words, add an *s*.**

    EXAMPLES
    Put the **Ss** through **Vs** there.
    Change the **Us** to **Vs.**

    To prevent confusion, use an apostrophe and an *s* to form the plurals of lowercase letters, certain capital letters, and some words used as words.

    EXAMPLE
    Your **r's** look like **z's.**

    The plurals of decades and centuries may be formed by adding an *s* or an apostrophe and an *s* (*'s*).

    EXAMPLE
    During the **1900's** (*or* **1900s**) many new inventions appeared.

Spelling Numbers

16. **Always spell out a number that begins a sentence.**

    EXAMPLE
    Two thousand two hundred cows are there.

17. **Within a sentence, spell out numbers that can be written in one word or two words; use numerals for other numbers.**

    EXAMPLES
    Over the weekend we drove **sixty-two miles.**
    He has a collection of **325** different butterflies.

18. **Spell out numbers used to indicate order.**

    EXAMPLE
    I placed **third** [not 3rd] in the tournament.

    EXCEPTION
    Use numerals for dates when you include the name of the month. Always use numerals for years.

    EXAMPLES
    School ends on June **3** [not 3rd]. [Writing *the third of June* is also correct.]
    In **1945** Ricardo came from Italy to the United States.

Words Often Confused

You can prevent many spelling errors by learning the difference between the words grouped together in this section. Some of them are confusing because they are *homonyms*—that is, they're pronounced alike. Others are confusing because they're spelled the same or nearly the same.

all ready	[pronoun plus adjective] *everyone ready*
	By then we were *all ready* to board the train.
already	[adverb] *previously*
	I have *already* seen the dentist.
all right	[This is the only acceptable spelling. Although the spelling *alright* appears in some dictionaries, it has not become standard usage.]
altar	*a table or stand at which religious rites are performed*
	The *altar* was covered with lace.
alter	*to change*
	She had to *alter* my dress.
all together	*everyone in the same place*
	All together now, repeat this sentence.
altogether	*entirely*
	You are *altogether* right to go tonight.
born	*given life*
	John was *born* in 1981.
borne	*carried; endured*
	The spores are *borne* aloft by the wind.
	She has *borne* much pain.
brake	*a stopping device*
	The *brakes* on our car are fine.
break	*to shatter, sever*
	This beautiful glass figurine must not *break*.
coarse	*rough* or *crude*
	I prefer a *coarse* salt.
	The language was *coarse*.
course	*path of action or progress* or *unit of study* or *track* or *way*; also used with *of* to mean *naturally* or *certainly*
	The detours got us somewhat off *course*.
	I must take a *course* in biology.
	The golf *course* is huge.
	Of *course*, you and I didn't go.

complement	[noun] *something that completes or makes perfect*; [verb] *to complete or make perfect*
	What is the *complement* of this angle?
	That jade necklace *complements* your green eyes.
compliment	[noun] *a remark that expresses approval, praise, or admiration*; [verb] *to pay a compliment*
	He enjoyed the *compliment*.
	Let me *compliment* you on your beautiful dress.
councilor	*a member of a council*
	He was not re-elected district *councilor*.
counsel	[noun] *advice*; [verb] *to give advice*
	I sought his *counsel* about my problem.
	Did you *counsel* her to see another professor?
des´ert	[noun] *a dry region*
	What wildlife is in the *desert*?
desert´	[verb] *to leave*
	I hope you won't *desert* the puppies.
dessert	[noun] *the final course of a meal*
	Dessert was served after the show.
formally	*properly, according to strict rules*
	They were not *formally* introduced.
formerly	*previously, in the past*
	Our new dean *formerly* taught at Duke University.
its	[possessive of *it*]
	Each room has *its* own special character.
it's	[contraction of *it is*]
	It's going to rain.
later	*after some time; subsequently*
	He came *later* that day.
latter	*the second of two*
	Cookies or cupcakes will do, but I prefer the *latter*.
lead	[verb, present tense, pronounced *leed*] *to go first*
	Lead the way to the tunnel.
led	[verb, past tense of *lead*]
	The guide *led* us to the museum.
lead	[noun, pronounced *led*] *a heavy metal*; also *graphite in a pencil*
	What is the Latin word for *lead*?

loose	[adjective, rhymes with *noose*] *free* or *not close together*		The lecture occurred on a higher *plane* than the class expected.
	Are the chickens running *loose* in the road?		The craftsman smoothed the surface with his *plane*.
	We made a rather *loose* pact.		Our *plane* was overbooked.
lose	[verb, pronounced *looz*] *to suffer loss*	**principal**	[noun] *head of a school*; [adjective] *main, most important*
	Don't *lose* your umbrella.		The *principal* greeted the guest.
miner	*a worker in a mine*		The *principal* issue was the economy.
	The *miners* were weary from a day's work.	**principle**	[noun] *a rule of conduct*; also *a law* or *a main fact*
minor	*under legal age*; also, *smaller or less important* (as opposed to *major*)		The philosopher is guided by *principles*.
	Minors cannot vote.		I studied the *principles* of biology.
	The other problems I have are relatively *minor* ones.	**quiet**	*silent, still*
moral	[adjective] *having to do with good or right*; [noun] *a lesson in conduct*		I am *quiet* when he speaks.
		quite	*to a great extent or degree, completely*
	Moral issues were debated.		His muscles are *quite* developed.
	Each fable has a *moral*.		I was *quite* pleased to go.
morale	[noun] *mental condition, spirit*	**stationary**	*in a fixed position*
	The team's *morale* was high.		Are these supports *stationary*?
passed	*verb*	**stationery**	*writing paper*
	His horse *passed* hers in the race.		The new *stationery* has not arrived.
past	*noun* or *adjective* or *preposition*	**than**	[conjunction, used for comparisons]
	Grandmother's *past* (n.) was full of adventure.		I saw more bears *than* tigers.
	Past (adj.) events are sometimes pleasing to remember.	**then**	[adverb, indicating *at that time* or *next*]
	Don't forget to go *past* (prep.) the supermarket on your way home.		Were you *then* given the award?
peace	*absence of conflict*		I wrote the letter, and *then* I mailed it.
	Peace ruled the nation.	**waist**	[noun] *the middle part of the body*
piece	*a part of something*		
	Take this *piece* of cake.		These shorts are too small in the *waist*.
personal	*individual; private*	**waste**	[noun] *unused material*; [verb] *to squander*
	Her *personal* opinion is that we should sell the land.		The removal of *waste* concerned the mayor.
personnel	*a group of people employed in the same work or service; a staff*		Don't *waste* your time seeing the exhibit.
	Most of the *personnel* in this office are new employees.	**who's**	[contraction of *who is, who has*]
			I don't know *who's* over there.
plain	[adjective] *not fancy* or *clear*; [noun] *a flat area of land*		*Who's* got my book?
	I buy *plain* shoes.	**whose**	[possessive of who]
	The aim seemed quite *plain*.		*Whose* copy of the book was it?
	These *plains* were once teeming.	**your**	[possessive form of *you*]
plane	[noun] *a flat surface, a level*; also *a tool* or *an airplane*		Give me *your* scissors.
	How many geometrical *planes* are in the problem?	**you're**	contraction of *you are*
			You're the winning contestant.

GLOSSARY

The glossary that follows is an alphabetical list of words found in the selections in this book. Use this glossary just as you use a dictionary—to find out the meanings of unfamiliar words. (A few technical, foreign, or more obscure words in this book are not listed here but are defined instead for you in the footnotes that accompany each selection.)

Many words in the English language have more than one meaning. This glossary gives the meanings that apply to the words as they are used in the selections in this book. Words closely related in form and meaning are usually listed together in one entry (*brusque* and *brusquely*), and the definition is given for the first form.

The following abbreviations are used:

adj., adjective	**n.**, noun	**prep.**, preposition
adv., adverb	**pl.**, plural form	**v.**, verb

Unless a word is very simple to pronounce, its pronunciation is given in parentheses. A guide to the pronunciation symbols appears at the bottom of each right-hand glossary page.

For more information about the words in this glossary, or about words not listed here, consult a dictionary.

abasement (ə·bās′mənt) *n.* Humiliation.
abash (ə·bash′) *v.* To make ill at ease.
abate (ə·bāt′) *v.* To subside.
abhor (əb·hôr′) *v.* To hate.
abject (ab′jekt) *adj.* Miserable.
abjure (əb·joor′) *v.* To give up; renounce.
abstinence (ab′stə·nəns) *n.* The act of voluntarily doing without food, drink, or other pleasures.
adjudge (ə·juj′) *v.* To decide or declare by law.
affability (af′ə·bil′ə·tē) *n.* Friendliness and pleasantness.
affectation (af′ek·tā′shən) *n.* A pretense or mannerism intended to make an impression on others.
allay (ə·lā′) *v.* To calm; relieve.
alluring (ə·loor′iŋ) *adj.* Very attractive.
altruistic (al′trōō·is′tik) *adj.* Of or motivated by unselfish concern for others.
amiss (ə·mis′) *adj.* Wrong; improper.

animadversion (an′ə·mad·vʉr′zhən) *n.* Unfavorable criticism.
annul (ə·nul′) *v.* To end; cancel.
anoint (ə·noint′) *v.* **1.** To rub oil upon. **2.** To put oil on something in a ritual so as to make it sacred or give it a special position.
appease (ə·pēz′) *v.* To pacify or satisfy by giving in to demands.
arduous (är′joo·wəs) *adj.* Difficult; strenuous.
array (ə·rā′) *n.* Fine clothes.
assailable (ə·sāl′ə·b′l) *adj.* Open to attack.
augment (ôg·ment′) *v.* To increase; grow.
avaricious (av′ə·rish′əs) *adj.* Greedy.

beauteous (byōōt′ē·əs) *adj.* Beautiful.
beguile (bi·gīl′) *v.* **1.** To charm. **2.** To pass the time in a pleasant way.
benediction (ben′ə·dik′shən) *n.* A blessing.
bereavement (bi·rēv′mənt) *n.* Sadness caused by loss or death.
bewail (bi·wāl′) *v.* To lament; mourn.
blaspheme (blas·fēm′) *v.* To speak irreverently; to curse.
blithe (blī*th*) *adj.* Showing a cheerful, carefree disposition.
bodkin (bäd′k′n) *n.* A dagger.
bombast (bäm′bast) *n.* Language that is pompous, loud, and empty.
brandish (bran′dish) *v.* To show or wave in a challenging and proud way.
bravado (brə·vä′dō) *n.* False courage or confidence.
brindled (brin′d′ld) *adj.* Having a grayish coat spotted or streaked with a darker color.
brusque (brusk) *adj.* Rough and abrupt. —**brusquely** *adv.*
burnish (bʉr′nish) *v.* To make shiny by rubbing; polish.

cadaverous (kə·dav′ər·əs) *adj.* Like a corpse; pale and gaunt.
cajole (kə·jōl′) *v.* To coax with flattery.
calamitous (kə·lam′ə·təs) *adj.* Causing or bringing trouble or disaster.
capacious (kə·pā′shəs) *adj.* Spacious; able to contain a lot.
cavalcade (kav′′l·kād′) *n.* Procession of horses and carriages.

---

fat, āpe, cär; ten, ēven; is, bīte; gō, hôrn, tōōl, look; oil, out; up, fʉr; get; joy; yet; chin; she; thin, *th*en; zh, leisure; ŋ, ring; ə for *a* in *ago, e* in *agent, i* in *sanity, o* in *comply, u* in *focus;* ′ as in *able* (ā′b′l).

celibacy (sel′ə·bə·sē) *n.* The state of being unmarried, as when a person has vowed not to marry.

chalice (chal′is) *n.* Cup or goblet.

chaste (chāst) *adj.* Pure; virtuous; modest.

chastise (chas·tīz′) *v.* To scold or punish.

chide (chīd) *v.* To scold.

circumscribe (sʉr′kəm·skrīb′) *v.* **1.** To encompass. **2.** To set off; confine.

cistern (sis′tərn) *n.* A large receptacle for storing water.

clamorous (klam′ər·əs) *adj.* Noisy and confused.

cloister (klois′tər) *v.* To seclude or confine.

cogitation (käj′ə·tā′shən) *n.* Deep and serious thought.

combustible (kəm·bus′tə·b′l) *adj.* Flammable.

comely (kum′lē) *adj.* Attractive.

complaisant (kəm·plā′z′nt) *adj.* Willing to please; agreeable.

compliance (kəm·plī′əns) *n.* **1.** Yielding. **2.** Agreement.

compunction (kəm·puŋk′shən) *n.* Sharp guilt; remorse. —**compunctious** *adj.*

confabulation (kən·fab′yə·lā′shən) *n.* An informal talk.

congeal (kən·jēl′) *v.* To solidify or thicken by cooling or freezing.

congenital (kən·jen′ə·t′l) *adj.* Inherent. —**congenitally** *adv.*

consecrate (kän′sə·krāt′) *v.* To make or declare sacred or holy.

consummation (kän′sə·mā′shən) *n.* Completion; fulfillment.

contagion (kən·tā′jən) *n.* Disease.

contemn (kən·tem′) *v.* To treat or regard with contempt.

continence (känt′′n·əns) *n.* Moderation; self-restraint.

contrite (kən·trīt′) *adj.* Deeply sorry for having done wrong.

contrition (kən·trish′ən) *n.* A feeling of sorrow for wrongdoing.

contrivance (kən·trī′vəns) *n.* Something made up; an invention.

copious (kō′pē·əs) *adj.* Abundant; full.

corrugated (kôr′ə·gāt′əd) *adj.* Shaped into parallel ridges and grooves.

covetous (kuv′it·əs) *adj.* Greedy for something another person has.

credulous (krej′oo·ləs) *adj.* Tending to believe too easily.

crystalline (kris′tə·lin) *adj.* Clear and transparent, like crystal.

dalliance (dal′ē·əns) *n.* Flirtation.

debase (di·bās′) *v.* To cheapen.

declamation (dek′lə·mā′shən) *n.* Statement delivered in a dramatic, passionate way.

decoction (di·käk′shən) *n.* An extract made by boiling a substance down to its essence.

decussate (di·kus′āt) *v.* To cross so as to form an X.

delineate (di·lin′ē·āt′) *v.* **1.** To trace the outlines of. **2.** To draw or depict.

delirious (di·lir′ē·əs) *adj.* Wildly excited.

delusive (di·lōōs′iv) *adj.* Misleading.

demented (di·ment′əd) *adj.* Insane. —**dementedly** *adv.*

deplorable (di·plôr′ə·b′l) *adj.* Regrettable; very bad.

depraved (di·prāvd′) *adj.* Corrupt; perverted.

deprecate (dep′rə·kāt′) *v.* To belittle; to disapprove of.

deride (di·rīd′) *v.* To ridicule or scorn.

derisive (di·rī′siv) *adj.* Ridiculing.

despoil (di·spoil′) *v.* To rob or ruin.

destitute (des′tə·tōōt′) *adj.* Without the necessities of life.

devolve (di·välv′) *v.* To pass on to others.

didactic (dī·dak′tik) *adj.* Used or meant for teaching; instructive.

diffidence (dif′ə·dəns) *n.* Shyness.

diffuse (di·fyōōz′) *v.* To spread out or scatter widely.

dilapidation (di·lap′ə·dā′shən) *n.* A condition of disrepair or shabbiness.

dilate (dī′lāt) *v.* To widen or expand.

diminutive (də·min′yoo·tiv) *adj.* Very small.

direful (dīr′fəl) *adj.* Terrible.

disapprobation (dis·ap′rə·bā′shən) *n.* Disapproval.

discern (di·sʉrn′) *v.* To perceive or recognize clearly.

discomfit (dis·kum′fit) *v.* To defeat; discourage.

discomposure (dis′kəm·pō′zhər) *n.* Condition of being flustered or disturbed.

discourse (dis′kôrs) *n.* Conversation.

disjoin (dis·join′) *v.* To separate; detach.

dispirited (di·spir′it·əd) *adj.* Uncaring, discouraged. —**dispiritedly** *adv.*

disport (dis·pôrt′) *v.* To play.

disposition (dis′pə·zish′ən) *n.* Arrangement.

disquisition (dis′kwə·zish′ən) *n.* Formal discussion.

dissipation (dis′ə·pā′shən) *n.* Overindulgence in pleasure.

distemper (dis·tem′pər) *n.* Disorder or disturbance. —**distempered** *adj.*

doleful (dōl′fəl) *adj.* Mournful; melancholy.

dolorous (dō′lər·əs) *adj.* Very sad or sorrowful.

dominion (də·min′yən) *n.* **1.** The power to rule; authority. **2.** Lands subject to control of an authority.

dross (drôs) *n.* Worthless material.

duteous (dōōt′ē·əs) *adj.* Dutiful; obedient.

efface (i·fās′) *v.* To wipe out.

efficacy (ef′i·kə·sē) *n.* Effectiveness.

effluvium (e·flōō′vē·əm) *n.* A real or imagined flow of vapor or invisible particles.

egress (ē′gres) *n.* A way out.

ejaculation (i·jak′yə·lā′shən) *n.* An exclamation.

elocution (el′ə·kyōō′shən) *n.* Style or manner of public speaking.

emulate (em′yə·lāt′) **v.** To imitate.

enamored (in·am′ərd) **adj.** Full of love and desire for; captivated by.

engender (in·jen′dər) **v.** To bring about; produce.

enmity (en′mə·tē) **n.** Bitterness; hostility.

ennoble (i·nō′b′l) **v.** To dignify or give a noble quality to.

ensue (in·sōō′) **v.** To follow.

enthrall (in·thrôl′) **v.** To fascinate; hold as though in a spell.

enticing (in·tīs′iŋ) **adj.** Attractive; tempting.

entreat (in·trēt′) **v.** To ask earnestly; beg.

epitome (i·pit′ə·mē) **n.** A person or thing that is typical of the whole.

equanimity (ek′wə·nim′ə·tē) **n.** Evenness of mind or temper.

ere (er) **prep.** Before.

ethereal (i·thir′ē·əl) **adj.** Very light; delicate.

evanescent (ev′ə·nes′′nt) **adj.** Tending to vanish or fade.

exalt (ig·zôlt′) **v.** To elevate; lift up.

exasperate (ig·zas′pə·rāt′) **v.** To anger or annoy extremely.

execrable (ek′si·krə·b′l) **adj.** Detestable.

exempt (ig·zempt′) **adj.** Free from; not subject to.

exhort (ig·zôrt′) **v.** To urge or warn strongly.

exigence (ek′sə·jəns) **n.** An urgent situation.

exorbitant (ig·zôr′bə·tənt) **adj.** Excessive; extravagant.

expatiate (ik·spā′shē·āt′) **v.** To speak or write about in great detail.

expedient (ik·spē′dē·ənt) **adj.** Advantageous; convenient.

expostulate (ik·späs′chə·lāt′) **v.** To reason earnestly with someone.

expurgation (eks′pər·gā′shən) **n.** The removal of objectionable passages, as from a book.

extenuate (ik·sten′yoo·wāt′) **v.** To underrate or lessen.

facetious (fə·sē′shəs) **adj.** Joking.

fallow (fal′ō) **adj.** Uncultivated.

fastidious (fas·tid′ē·əs) **adj.** Over-refined.

feign (fān) **v.** To make up; pretend.

felicitous (fə·lis′ə·təs) **adj.** Appropriate; well-chosen.

fluctuate (fluk′choo·wāt′) **v.** To move in a changing, waving, or irregular way.

forlorn (fər·lôrn′) **adj.** Miserable.

forsake (fər·sāk′) **v.** To give up.

furbish (fur′bish) **v.** To brighten by polishing.

furtive (fur′tive) **adj.** Done in a secret or stealthy manner.

garrulous (gar′ə·ləs) **adj.** Very talkative.

gaudy (gôd′ē) **adj.** Brightly decorative, but in poor taste.

governance (guv′ər·nəns) **n.** The act or manner of government.

graven (grāv′′n) **adj.** Engraved or otherwise permanently fixed.

guileful (gīl′fəl) **adj.** Deceitful.

hallowed (hal′ōd) **adj.** Honored as holy.

hapless (hap′lis) **adj.** Unfortunate.

harangue (hə·raŋ′) **v.** To speak in a loud and scolding manner.

harbinger (här′bin·jər) **n.** A person or thing that comes before to indicate what will follow.

haughty (hôt′ē) **adj.** Having or showing great pride in oneself and contempt for others.

heinous (hā′nəs) **adj.** Outrageously evil.

hyperbolical (hī′pər·bäl′i·kəl) **adj.** Exaggerated; overstated.

idolatrous (ī·däl′ə·trəs) **adj.** Worshiping or devoted.

immaculate (i·mak′yə·lit) **adj.** Flawless.

immaterial (im′ə·tir′ē·əl) **adj.** Unimportant.

imminence (im′ə·nəns) **n.** The quality or fact of being about to happen.

impassive (im·pas′iv) **adj.** Placid; calm.

impediment (im·ped′ə·mənt) **n.** An obstruction.

imperious (im·pir′ē·əs) **adj.** Arrogant; overbearing.

imperturbable (im′pər·tur′bə·b′l) **adj.** Incapable of being disturbed or excited.

impetuous (im·pech′oo·wəs) **adj.** 1. Impulsive. 2. Forceful.

impiety (im·pī′ə·tē) **n.** Lack of reverence for God.

implacable (im·plak′ə·b′l) **adj.** Relentless.

implore (im·plôr′) **v.** To ask earnestly for.

importune (im′pôr·tōōn′) **v.** To request persistently.

impracticable (im·prak′ti·kə·b′l) **adj.** Incapable of being carried out in practice.

imprecation (im′prə·kā′shən) **n.** A curse.

impromptu (im·prämp′tōō) **adj.** Without preparation; offhand.

impunity (im·pyōō′nə·tē) **n.** Freedom from punishment.

incantation (in′kan·tā′shən) **n.** The chanting of words or formulas meant to cast a spell.

incarcerate (in·kär′sə·rāt′) **v.** To imprison.

incarnate (in·kär′nit) **adj.** In human form.

incense (in·sens′) **v.** To make very angry.

incessant (in·ses′′nt) **adj.** Endless; constant.

incipient (in·sip′ē·ənt) **adj.** Just beginning to exist.

fat, āpe, cär; ten, ēven; is, bīte; gō, hôrn, tōōl, look; oil, out; up, fur; get; joy; yet; chin; she; thin, then; zh, leisure; ŋ, ring; ə for a in ago, e in agent, i in sanity, o in comply, u in focus; ′ as in able (ā′b′l).

inconstancy (in·kän′stən·sē) *n.* The quality of being changeable or unsteady.

incorrigible (in·kôr′i·jə·b'l) *adj.* Incapable of being corrected or reformed.

incredulity (in′krə·doo′lə·tē) *n.* Unwillingness or inability to believe.

incur (in·kur′) *v.* To bring upon oneself.

indecorous (in·dek′ər·əs) *adj.* Improper; lacking in good taste.

indignation (in′dig·nā′shən) *n.* Anger resulting from ingratitude or injustice.

indiscretion (in′dis·kresh′ən) *n.* An act that shows a lack of judgment.

indissoluble (in′di·säl′yoo·b'l) *adj.* Unbreakable.

indolence (in′də·ləns) *n.* Laziness.

inducement (in·doos′mənt) *n.* Something that persuades.

ineptitude (in·ep′tə·tood′) *n.* Awkwardness; clumsiness.

insatiate (in·sā′shē·it) *adj.* Never satisfied.

inscrutable (in·skroot′ə·b'l) *adj.* Absolutely mysterious or obscure.

insipid (in·sip′id) *adj.* Uninteresting; dull.

inter (in·tur′) *v.* To bury.

intercede (in′tər·sēd′) *v.* To plead for or act in behalf of others. —**intercession** *n.*

interim (in′tər·im) *n.* The period of time between.

intermittent (in·tər·mit′'nt) *adj.* Stopping and starting at intervals.

interstice (in·tur′stis) *n. pl.* Small or narrow space between things.

intimidated (in·tim′ə·dāt′əd) *adj.* Made afraid.

intrepidity (in·trə·pid′ə·tē) *n.* Boldness; bravery.

invective (in·vek′tiv) *n.* A violent verbal attack; strong criticism and insults.

inveigh (in·vā′) *v.* To attack verbally.

inveterate (in·vet′ər·it) *adj.* Deep-rooted.

ire (īr) *n.* Anger.

irksome (urk′səm) *adj.* Tiresome; annoying.

jocularity (jäk′yə·lar′ə·tē) *n.* Humorousness.

jocund (jäk′ənd) *adj.* Cheerful.

judicious (joo·dish′əs) *adj.* Having or showing good judgment; wise.

languid (laŋ′gwid) *adj.* 1. Uninterested; indifferent. 2. Without vigor.

languish (laŋ′gwish) *v.* To lose vigor; weaken.

languor (laŋ′gər) *n.* A lack of vigor or interest.

largess (lär·jes′) *n.* Generosity.

lassitude (las′ə·tood′) *n.* Weariness.

laudable (lôd′ə·b'l) *adj.* Worthy of praise.

ligature (lig′ə·chər) *n.* Something used for tying.

lineament (lin′ē·ə·mənt) *n.* Distinctive feature.

lionize (lī′ə·nīz′) *v.* To treat as a celebrity.

litany (lit′'n·ē) *n.* The recitation of prayer.

livid (liv′id) *adj.* Inflamed.

loath (lōth) *adj.* Unwilling.

lugubrious (loo·goo′brē·əs) *adj.* Sad or mournful to an almost excessive degree.

lustrous (lus′trəs) *adj.* Brightly shining.

luxuriant (lug·zhoor′ē·ənt) *adj.* Marked by richness or extravagance.

magnanimous (mag·nan′ə·məs) *adj.* High-minded and generous.

malevolent (mə·lev′ə·lənt) *adj.* Malicious; wishing harm to others.

malignity (mə·lig′nə·tē) *n.* Persistent, intense desire to harm others.

manifold (man′ə·fōld′) *adj.* Having many and various forms or parts.

martial (mär′shəl) *adj.* 1. Having to do with war. 2. Warlike.

meek (mēk) *adj.* Mild-mannered to the point of submissiveness.

mendacity (men·das′ə·tē) *n.* 1. The quality or state of being false. 2. A lie.

mendicant (men′di·kənt) *n.* A beggar.

mirth (murth) *n.* Joyfulness; merriment.

misanthrope (mis′ən·thrōp′) *n.* A person who hates or distrusts all people.

missive (mis′iv) *n.* A letter.

mitigate (mit′ə·gāt′) *v.* To soften; moderate.

modulation (mäj′ə·lā′shən) *n.* A variation in pitch or stress in speaking.

morose (mə·rōs′) *adj.* Gloomy. —**morosely** *adv.*

mortify (môr′tə·fī) *v.* 1. To cause to feel shame. 2. To cause to decay.

mountebank (moun′tə·baŋk′) *n.* A quack.

multitudinous (mul′tə·tood′'n·əs) *adj.* Very numerous.

munificence (myoo·nif′ə·səns) *n.* Great generosity.

noisome (noi′səm) *adj.* Harmful to health.

nomenclature (nō′mən·klā′chər) *n.* A system or set of names.

nonpareil (nän′pə·rel′) *adj.* Unequaled; peerless.

noxious (näk′shəs) *adj.* Harmful to health.

obdurate (äb′door·ət) *adj.* Hardhearted.

oblique (ə·blēk′) *adj.* 1. Indirect. 2. Underhanded.

oblivious (ə·bliv′ē·əs) *adj.* Unmindful.

ocular (äk′yə·lər) *adj.* Of, for, or like the eye.

odious (ō′dē·əs) *adj.* Hateful; disgusting; offensive.

officious (ə·fish′əs) *adj.* Ready to serve.

omnipotent (äm·nip′ə·tənt) *adj.* All-powerful.

opulence (äp′yə·ləns) *n.* A quality that indicates wealth or abundance.

oracle (ôr'ə·k'l) *n.* **1.** A person believed to possess special knowledge. **2.** A statement or opinion made by such a person.

ostentatious (äs'tən·tā'shəs) *adj.* Showy, pretentious.

paean (pē'ən) *n.* A hymn or song of praise, triumph, or joy.

palpable (pal'pə·b'l) *adj.* **1.** Tangible; that can be felt. **2.** Easily perceived by the senses.

panegyric (pan'ə·jir'ik) *n.* A formal statement of praise.

parricide (par'ə·sīd') *n.* The murder of a parent.

pedantic (pi·dan'tik) *adj.* Trivial, picky, and narrow-minded.

peremptory (pə·remp'tər·ē) *adj.* **1.** Commanding; dictatorial. **2.** Final; absolute; unchangeable. —**peremptorily** *adv.*

perfidiousness (pər·fid'ē·əs·nəs) *n.* Treachery.

perfunctory (pər·fuŋk'tər·ē) *adj.* Done without care or interest. —**perfunctorily** *adv.*

perjury (pur'jər·ē) *n.* The breaking of a promise or an oath.

pernicious (pər·nish'əs) *adj.* Destructive; deadly.

perpetual (pər·pech'oo·wəl) *adj.* Lasting forever; eternal.

perturbation (pur'tər·bā'shən) *n.* Something that alarms or upsets; a disturbance.

pestiferous (pes·tif'ər·əs) *adj.* Dangerous; evil.

petulance (pech'ə·ləns) *n.* Impatience; irritability.

physiognomy (fiz'ē·äg'nə·mē) *n.* Facial features and expressions.

piebald (pī'bôld') *adj.* Patched or spotted with two colors, usually black and white.

placid (plas'id) *adj.* Tranquil; calm; quiet. —**placidly** *adv.*

plaintive (plān'tiv) *adj.* Expressing sorrow; sad.

portentous (pôr·ten'təs) *adj.* Ominous.

precipitate (pri·sip'ə·tit) *adj.* Moving or happening quickly. —**precipitately** *adv.*

prevail (pri·vāl') *v.* **1.** To master; triumph over. **2.** To succeed.

pristine (pris'tēn) *adj.* Pure; uncorrupted.

prodigal (präd'i·gəl) *adj.* Wastefully extravagant.

prodigious (prə·dij'əs) *adj.* Enormous.

profanation (präf'ə·nā'shən) *n.* A violation.

profane (prə·fān') *v.* To violate.

proffer (präf'ər) *v.* To offer.

profuse (prə·fyoos') *adj.* Poured out freely and generously.

progeny (präj'ə·nē) *n.* Children.

prognosis (präg·nō'sis) *n.* Forecast; prediction.

promiscuous (prə·mis'kyoo·wəs) *adj.* Casual; undiscriminating. —**promiscuously** *adv.*

protracted (prō·trakt'əd) *adj.* Drawn out.

protuberance (prō·too'bər·əns) *n.* A projection; bulge; swelling.

prowess (prou'is) *n.* **1.** Bravery. **2.** Skill.

pugnacious (pug·nā'shəs) *adj.* Eager to fight; quarrelsome.

pungent (pun'jənt) *adj.* Sharp-smelling.

purgative (pur'gə·tiv) *adj.* Cleansing.

querulous (kwer'ə·ləs) *adj.* Complaining.

quietude (kwī'ə·tood') *n.* Calmness; state of rest.

raiment (rā'mənt) *n.* Clothing.

ravenous (rav'ə·nəs) *adj.* Extremely hungry.

recoil (ri·koil') *v.* To draw back or stagger back.

recompense (rek'əm·pens') *n.* Repayment; compensation.

redress (ri·dres') *v.* To set right; rectify.

regress (rē'gres) *n.* **1.** A return. **2.** A movement backward.

reiterate (rē·it'ə·rāt') *v.* To repeat.

remonstrance (ri·män'strəns) *n.* A protest.

repine (ri·pīn') *v.* To feel or express unhappiness.

replenish (ri·plen'ish) *v.* To fill or complete again; restore.

replete (ri·plēt') *adj.* Well-filled or plentifully supplied.

repudiate (ri·pyoo'dē·āt') *v.* To refuse to have anything to do with.

requite (ri·kwīt') *v.* To repay.

resplendent (ri·splen'dənt) *adj.* Full of splendor.

reticulated (ri·tik'yə·lāt'id) *adj.* Having a network of veins like the threads of a net.

revel (rev''l) *n.* Festivity; celebration.

revelation (rev'ə·lā'shən) *n.* A revealing of something.

reverence (rev'ər·əns) *n.* A feeling of deep respect or love.

reverend (rev'ər·ənd) *adj.* Worthy of reverence.

rogue (rōg) *n.* A wandering beggar.

sacrilegious (sak'rə·lij'əs) *adj.* Disrespectful toward something held sacred.

sagacious (sə·gā'shəs) *adj.* Keenly perceptive.

salutary (sal'yoo·ter'ē) *adj.* Healthful.

sanctity (saŋk'tə·tē) *n.* Holiness; sacredness.

satiety (sə·tī'ə·tē) *n.* The condition of having had enough or more than enough.

scarify (skar'ə·fī') *v.* To cut or puncture.

scruple (skroo'p'l) *v.* To hesitate because of one's conscience.

---

fat, āpe, cär; ten, ēven; is, bīte; gō, hôrn, tool, look; oil, out; up, fur; get; joy; yet; chin; she; thin, then; zh, leisure; ŋ, ring; ə for *a* in *ago*, *e* in *agent*, *i* in *sanity*, *o* in *comply*, *u* in *focus*; ' as in *able* (ā'b'l).

semblance (sem′bləns) *n.* Outward appearance or form.

sepulcher (sep′′l·kər) *v.* To put in a tomb; to bury.

sequestered (si·kwes′tərd) *adj.* Secluded.

serous (sir′əs) *adj.* Thin and watery. —**serosity** *n.*

servile (sʉr′v′l) *adj.* **1.** Not free. **2.** Submissive.

slovenly (sluv′ən·lē) *adj.* Untidy; careless; dirty.

solicit (sə·lis′it) *v.* To ask or seek earnestly. —**solicitation** *n.*

solvent (säl′vənt) *adj.* That can dissolve.

sovereignty (säv′rən·tē) *n.* The state or quality of being supreme in authority, rank, or power.

squalid (skwäl′id) *adj.* **1.** Unclean; unsanitary. **2.** Wretched.

stolid (stäl′id) *adj.* Having or showing very little emotion; unexcitable. —**stolidly** *adv.*

straitened (strāt′′nd) *adj.* Difficult; wanting; distressful.

strident (strīd′′nt) *adj.* Harsh-sounding; shrill. —**stridently** *adv.*

strife (strīf) *n.* Conflict; struggle.

stupefying (st$\overline{oo}$′pə·fī′iŋ) *adj.* Making dull or lethargic.

sullen (sul′ən) *adj.* Somber; dull.

sumptuous (sump′choo·wəs) *adj.* Lavish; costly; magnificent.

sundry (sun′drē) *adj.* Various; miscellaneous.

supercilious (s$\overline{oo}$′pər·sil′ē·əs) *adj.* Disdainful; contemptuous; proud. —**superciliously** *adv.*

superfluous (soo·pʉr′floo·wəs) *adj.* Unnecessary. —**superfluously** *adv.*

surfeit (sʉr′fit) *v.* To feed or supply to excess.

surly (sʉr′lē) *adj.* Rude; hostile.

surmise (sər·mīz′) *n.* Guessing.

sustenance (sus′ti·nəns) *n.* That which sustains life; food; nourishment.

temperate (tem′pər·it) *adj.* Moderate; mild.

tempestuous (tem·pes′choo·wəs) *adj.* Like a tempest; turbulent.

tenacity (te·nas′ə·tē) *n.* Firmness; strength; persistence.

terrestrial (tə·res′trē·əl) *adj.* Of the earth.

timorous (tim′ər·əs) *adj.* Very timid and afraid.

titillating (tit′′l·āt′iŋ) *adj.* Exciting; stimulating.

torpor (tôr′pər) *n.* A state of being inactive, motionless, or insensible.

tortuous (tôr′choo·wəs) *adj.* Devious; tricky.

trammel (tram′′l) *v.* To catch, as in a net.

transgress (trans·gres′) *v.* To overstep or break (a law or commandment).

transitory (tran′sə·tôr′ē) *adj.* Impermanent; temporary; fleeting.

travail (trav′āl) *n.* Hard work.

tremulous (trem′yoo·ləs) *adj.* Trembling.

unassailable (un′ə·sāl′ə·b′l) *adj.* That cannot be successfully attacked.

undaunted (un·dôn′tid) *adj.* Undiscouraged; unafraid.

unrelenting (un·ri·len′tiŋ) *adj.* Not lessening.

unsanctified (un·saŋk′tə·fīd) *adj.* Not made holy.

unslaked (un·slākd′) *adj.* Unsatisfied; unrelieved.

unwieldy (un·wēl′dē) *adj.* Hard to handle, deal with, or manage.

urbane (ʉr·bān′) *adj.* Smooth; refined. —**urbanely** *adv.*

usurp (y$\overline{oo}$·sʉrp′) *v.* To take or assume forcefully or without right. —**usurper** *n.*

utilitarian (yoo·til′ə·ter′ē ən) *adj.* Useful.

vehement (vē′ə·mənt) *adj.* Forceful; violent.

veneration (ven′ə·rā′shən) *n.* Deep respect or reverence.

verbatim (vər·bāt′əm) *adv.* Word for word; in exactly the same words.

verdant (vʉr′d′nt) *adj.* Green.

verity (ver′ə·tē) *n.* Truth.

vindictive (vin·dik′tiv) *adj.* Revengeful in spirit.

visage (viz′ij) *n.* The face.

viscous (vis′kəs) *adj.* Having a thick, sticky fluid consistency.

vociferation (vō·sif′ə·rā′shən) *n.* Loud, forceful utterance.

voluble (väl′yoo·b′l) *adj.* Very talkative.

vouchsafe (vouch·sāf′) *v.* To condescend to give.

waggish (wag′ish) *adj.* Joking; playful.

wily (wī′lē) *adj.* Sly.

wistful (wist′fəl) *adj.* Showing or feeling vague longing.

wizened (wiz′′nd) *adj.* Shriveled, dried up.

wry (rī) *adj.* Ironic. —**wryly** *adv.*

zephyr (zef′ər) *n.* A gentle breeze.

INDEX OF SKILLS

LANGUAGE AND VOCABULARY SKILLS

Writing an essay 797, 837, 1078
Writing an explanation 581
Writing an expository composition 1254

CRITICAL THINKING SKILLS

The following list refers to the two-page Exercises in Critical Thinking and Writing that follow each unit. Additional exercises in all of the critical thinking skills, including synthesis, will be found in the Composition Skills index on the preceding pages.

PICTURE CREDITS (*continued from p. ix*)

damm Collection, The Billy Rose Theatre Collection, New York Public Library, Lincoln Center for the Performing Arts; pp. 1176, 1177: Zoe Dominic; p. 1182: Martha Swope; p. 1185: Vandamm Collection, The Billy Rose Theatre Collection, New York Public Library, Lincoln Center for the Performing Arts; p. 1188: Zoe Dominic; p. 1191: Vandamm Collection, Billy Rose Theatre Collection, New York Public Library, Lincoln Center for the Performing Arts; p. 1194: Zoe Dominic; p. 1210: Vandamm Collection: Billy Rose Theatre Collection, New York Public Library, Lincoln Center for the Performing Arts; p. 1212: Robert Harding Associates, London; p. 1213: Bridgeman Art Library/Art Resource; p. 1214: White Studio Collection, The Billy Rose Thea- tre Collection, New York Public Library, Lincoln Center for the Performing Arts; p. 1215: Julie Hamilton, The Billy Rose Theatre Collection, New York Public Library, Lincoln Center for the Performing Arts; p. 1216: Martha Swope; p. 1217: Beatriz Schiller; p. 1218: Martha Swope; p. 1219: George Karger/Pix-International, The Billy Rose Theatre Collection, New York Public Library, Lincoln Center for the Performing Arts; p. 1220: Martha Swope; p. 1221: Hank Kranzer, The Billy Rose Theatre Collection, New York Public Library, Lincoln Center for the Performing Arts; p. 1222: Robert Harding Associates, London; p. 1227: Max Polster Archive.

INDEX OF AUTHORS AND TITLES